THIRTY-FOURTH EDITION

KOVELS'
ANTIQUES
& COLLECTIBLES

PRICE LIST

FOR THE 2002 MARKET

ILLUSTRATED

THREE RIVERS PRESS

NEW YORK

Published by Three Rivers Press, New York, New York.
Member of the Crown Publishing Group.

Random House, Inc. New York, Toronto, London, Sydney, Auckland
www.randomhouse.com

THREE RIVERS PRESS is a registered trademark and the Three Rivers Press
colophon is a trademark of Random House, Inc.

Printed in the United States of America

Library of Congress Catalog Card Number: 83-643618
ISBN 0-609-80841-9 (pbk.)
10 9 8 7 6 5 4 3 2 1

Books by Ralph and Terry Kovel

American Country Furniture 1780–1875

A Directory of American Silver, Pewter, and Silver Plate

Kovels' Advertising Collectibles Price List

Kovels' American Art Pottery: The Collector's Guide to Makers,
Marks, and Factory Histories

Kovels' American Silver Marks: 1650 to the Present

Kovels' Antiques & Collectibles Fix-It Source Book

Kovels' Bid, Buy, and Sell Online

Kovels' Book of Antique Labels

Kovels' Bottles Price List

Kovels' Collector's Guide to American Art Pottery

Kovels' Collectors' Source Book

Kovels' Depression Glass & Dinnerware Price List

Kovels' Dictionary of Marks—Pottery & Porcelain

Kovels' Guide to Selling, Buying, and Fixing
Your Antiques and Collectibles

Kovels' Guide to Selling Your Antiques & Collectibles

Kovels' Illustrated Price Guide to Royal Doulton

Kovels' Know Your Antiques

Kovels' Know Your Collectibles

Kovels' New Dictionary of Marks—Pottery & Porcelain

Kovels' Organizer for Collectors

Kovels' Price Guide for Collector Plates, Figurines,
Paperweights, and Other Limited Editions

Kovels' Quick Tips—799 Helpful Hints on
How to Care for Your Collectibles

Kovels' Yellow Pages: A Collector's Directory

The Label Made Me Buy It: From Aunt Jemima to Zonkers—
The Best-Dressed Boxes, Bottles and Cans from the Past

This is the 34th year *Kovels Antiques & Collectibles Price List* has been published. And the book is still being written by the original authors, Ralph and Terry Kovel. It has changed from a book with no illustrations and typewriter-style letters to this edition with hundreds of pictures and logos, about 50,000 prices, dozens of tips about care, and a special color-picture report, "Hands Down, Feet First: A Collecting Odyssey."

READ THIS BEFORE YOU USE THIS BOOK—IT WILL HELP

This is a book for the average collector. All year we check prices, visit shops and shows, read our mail, check online computer services and the Internet, and decide what antiques and collectibles are of most interest. We concentrate on the average pieces in any category. Sometimes one or two high-priced pieces are included in a category so you will realize that some of the rarities are quite valuable. For example, this year very special collections of lunch boxes and Buddy "L" toys, including many prototypes and mint-condition pieces were sold at auction and brought exceptionally high prices. A few of these prices have been included.

Examples of furniture, silver, Tiffany, and art pottery may sell for more than $50,000; we list a few of those examples. The highest price in this book is $58,250 for an ebony cabinet-on-stand. The lowest price is $1.00 for a Temple National Bank matchbook. Most pieces we list cost less than $10,000. We even list the weird and the wonderful. This year you can find prices for a bellows used for glove and wig powder that sold for $85, a 1967 Rudi Gernreich woman's topless swimsuit for $650, and a black tole ear trumpet wrapped in black crepe, used by a person in mourning who was hearing impaired, that sold for $450. A brass doorknob shaped like a skeleton's hand was priced at $260. The smallest object is a celluloid button. The largest is a pine backbar with lighted slag glass panels.

Prices are up in some categories. Arts and Crafts and Art Pottery continue to rise in price. Especially active is Roseville pottery. A recent auction of 1,200 pieces brought $700,000. Prices for costume jewelry and Bakelite remain strong. There is continued interest in garden antiques of all kinds, from old flowerpots to large fountains. California-made pottery of the 1950s era, and Western and farm collectibles are popular in certain regions. The antiques malls that had been springing up all over of the country seem to be doing less business. Many have closed. Auctions and sales on the Internet are also influencing prices. A survey showed that for 18,000 items sold by a group of mall dealers the prices have dropped 39 percent on eBay when compared to last year. Small collectibles that are inexpensive and easy to identify sell quickly. It is said that about 40 percent of the serious buyers of antiques now use computers (and most of the new users are more than sixty years old.) This percent is increasing each year. The online market is getting larger and is international. Objects that are known in most of the world, such as pens, cigarette lighters, toys, Royal Doulton pottery, majolica, and oak furniture, are selling at the same or slightly lower prices than last year. Only the exceptional pieces are going for the extraordinary prices reported in the news media.

Each year categories are added or omitted to make it easier for you to find your antiques. A new category this year is Dirk Van Erp. We have rearranged the various pottery sections; this year we have Pottery-Art, Pottery-Contemporary, Pottery-Midcentury, and Pottery. We also have Porcelain-Contemporary, Porcelain-Midcentury, and Porcelain. Important makers like Roseville or Noritake are still listed in their own sections.

The book is kept at about 800 pages because it is written to go with you to sales. We try to have a balanced format—not too many glass, pottery, or collectible items, a variety of furniture from the 18th through the 20th centuries, not too many items that sell for over $5,000. The prices are *from* the American market *for* the American market. Few European sales are reported. We take the editorial privilege of not including any prices that seem to result from "auction fever." The computer-generated index is so complete it amazes us. Use it often. An internal alphabetical index is also included. For example, there is a category for Celluloid. Most items made of celluloid will be found there, but if there is a toy made of celluloid, it will be listed under Toy and also indexed under Celluloid. There are also cross-references in the listings and in the paragraphs. But some searching must be done. For example, Barbie dolls are found in the Doll category; there is no Barbie category. And when you look at "doll, Barbie" you will see a note that tells you that Barbie is under "doll, Mattel, Barbie" because most dolls are listed by maker. We differentiate between doll furniture made to a scale suitable for displaying dolls and dollhouse furniture made in the small scale meant for a dollhouse. All pictures and prices are new every year, except pictures that are pattern examples shown in Depression Glass and Pressed Glass. The pictures have been computer-enhanced to make them as crisp as possible. Antiques pictured are items offered for sale, not museum pieces. We hate to waste space, so whenever computer-generated spaces appear, we fill them with tips about care of collections, security, and other useful information. These tips are set in special type, so they will not be confused with the prices. Leaf through the book and learn how to wash porcelains, store textiles, guard against theft, and much more. We use new tips every year. Don't discard this book when it is time to buy a new one next year. Old Kovels' price books should be saved for future reference, and for tax and appraisal information.

The prices in this book are reports of the general antiques market. Each year, every price in the book is new. We do not estimate or "update" prices. Prices are actual asking prices, although a buyer may have negotiated a price to a lower figure. No price is an estimate. We do not ask dealers and writers to estimate prices. Experience has shown that a collector of one type of antique is prejudiced in favor of that item, so those estimated prices are usually high or low, but rarely a true report. If a price range is given, it is because at least two identical items were offered for sale at different times. The computer prints the high and low figures. Price ranges are found only in categories like Pressed Glass, where identical items can be identified. If the price listed in this book is from an auction, it includes the buyer's premium, but like all the prices, it does not include sales tax. Some prices in *Kovels' Antiques & Collectibles Price List* may seem high and some may seem low because of regional variations. But each price is one you could have paid for the object.

If you are selling your collection, do not expect to get retail value unless you are a dealer. Wholesale prices for antiques are from 20 to 50 percent less than retail. Remember, the antiques dealer must make a profit or go out of business. Internet auction prices are less predictable. Because of the international audience and "auction fever," prices often are higher or lower than retail.

THE RECORD PRICES HYPE

The media loves to report record prices, amazing auctions, high-priced discoveries, and events that really have little to do with the antiques and collectibles market familiar to the average collector. Over the past year front-page stories told of a painting found in a garage eventually attracting a bid of more than $100,000 (the painting was later found to have a questionable background); and a Tiffany poppy table lamp stored in a basement for forty years that auctioned for $123,200. Strangest was a broken Baker & Cutting Glass & Pickle jar found in four pieces in a dig, which sold at auction for $165. If it had been unbroken, it probably would have set the record for an American bottle. Great stories, but—like winning the lottery—not likely to happen to everyone. So study the auction records, but remember that these are the prices for the rarest and best.

CLOCKS & WATCHES

- **Tall-case clock:** $611,000 for a tall-case clock with a Townsend-Goddard school block-and-shell case and a dial signed by Samuel Rockwell; originally made for David Harris (1714–1797) of Smithfield and Providence, Rhode Island; 95½ inches.

FURNITURE

- **Eames prototype armchair:** $107,000 for a prototype "DCW" chair with armrests, produced at the Eames office prior to December 1945, stamped underneath "10"; 29½ x 29¾ x 21½ inches.
- **Eames "DTW-3," dowel-leg dining table:** $10,350 for a DTW-3 dining table with a wood and plywood top and dowel legs connected by cast aluminum mounts, produced by Herman Miller c.1952; 29 x 54 x 34 inches.

- **Eames "ESU-421-C" wall unit:** $70,700 for a plywood, steel and masonite "ESU-421-C" wall unit, composed of nearly 250 parts, consisting of a steel vertical frame, open shelves, drawers, and geometric primary color panels, produced by Herman Miller c.1951; 58½ x 47 x 16 inches.
- **Eames "DKR-1" dining chairs:** $10,063 for a set of six painted steel and partially upholstered "DKR-1" dining chairs, also known as the "Eiffel Tower" chairs, produced by Herman Miller c.1951; 32¾ x 19 x 21½ inches.
- **Folding stand/candlestand:** $409,500 for a Philadelphia-area cherry Chippendale candlestand with carved birdcage, molded rim, suppressed belted ball, leaf and C-scroll carving on the knees, and pad feet on cabriole legs; 1760–1780, 21-inch-diameter dished top, 28¼ inches.
- **American Gothic Revival furniture:** $233,500 for a rosewood Belmead table with a hexagonal white marble top and turreted frieze over six cluster columns; 1845–1850, 28½ x 41 x 35½ inches.
- **Shaker furniture:** $222,500 for a Shaker six-drawer sewing cabinet, of red-painted pine, cherry, and butternut, and two short drawers over four long drawers; inscribed in ink in upperlong drawer "January 7, 1846, Joseph Wilber, gave this table to Martha Johnson, May 2, 1872"; 28 x 24¾ x 36 inches.
- **Gerrit Rietveld "Steltman" chair:** $71,250 for a Gerrit Rietveld "Steltman" chair, designed by Gerard A. van de Groenekan in 1963, solid oak, branded "H.G.M./GA vd Groenekan' De bilt Nederland"; 27½ x 19¾ x 17¾ inches.
- **Mitchell & Rammelsberg hat rack:** $36,400 for an American, carved walnut hat rack by Mitchell & Rammelsberg of Cincinnati, Ohio, with a carved Rocky Mountain goat and free-flowing oak tree branches fitted with acorns, husks, and articulated oak leaves; 1857–1868, 98 x 58 x 19 inches.

GLASS

- **Imperial Glass jade slag pitcher:** $310 for a jade slag pitcher by Imperial Glass; 1 pint.
- **Early American pressed glass:** $16,500 for a clear Sandwich Vine goblet with gilt highlights on pattern, rim, and foot; 6¼ inches.
- **Bellflower spoon holder:** $7,000 for a cobalt blue Bellflower single-vine variant spoon holder, with a scallop-and-point, plain-banded rim, with forty-five rays under the foot; 5⅝ inches.
- **Historical glass:** $4,000 for a pressed glass, covered dish in the shape of a terrestial globe, with a Columbia head finial; 9½ inches.
- **Salamander paperweight:** $154,000 for a French Pantin Salamander magnum glass paperweight.
- **Masonic-Eagle flask, GIV-1:** $55,000 for a Keene Marlboro Street Glass Works Masonic-Eagle flask, GIV-1, with a sheared lip and pontiled base, deep purple shading to a lighter brilliant purple throughout the middle and returning to the deep purple color at the shoulder and neck; 1 pint.
- **Corn for the World amethyst quart flask, GVI-4:** $46,200 for a Washington Monument/Corn for the World amethyst quart flask, GVI-4, with collared mouth and smooth base, made by Baltimore Glass Works; 1 quart.
- **Double eagle flask:** $11,200 for a ½ pint, Double eagle flask, in dark amethyst, probably made by the Louisville Glass Works, Louisville, Kentucky; 1855–1860.

- **Masonic-Eagle flask, GIV-14 variant:** $15,680 for a Masonic-Eagle flask from New England, in the traditional form of the Keene, New Hampshire area, dark olive green with exaggerated and elongated neck, applied sloping collar mouth and ring pontil; 1820–1830, ½ pint.
- **Mason fruit jar:** $21,280 for a Mason fruit jar, aquamarine with profuse milk glass striations and a single olive streak through the center; 1860–1880, cylindrical quart jar embossed "Mason's/Patent/Nov. 30th/1858."

LAMPS & LIGHTING

- **Pairpoint lamp:** $145,600 for a Pairpoint Puffy "Lilac" table lamp; 14 inches.
- **Duffner & Kimberly lamp:** $95,000 for an Oriental poppy floor lamp, with a leaded shade with red poppy blossoms, variegated green and white foliage, and a purple background, on a Duffner & Kimberly bronze senior floor base; 28½-inch-diameter shade.

MISCELLANEOUS

- **Armitage Herschell carousel horse:** $11,000 for an all-wood, Armitage Herschell carousel horse, considered a traveling carnival-type, which is smaller than the park-type carousel animals; late 1800s.
- **Civil War sword:** $192,500 for a heavy gold-plated sword set with four amethysts, marked by Bailey & Co.; presented to General Rufus King in 1862.
- **Enigma machine:** $86,933 for a 10-rotor "Enigma" cipher machine from World War II, manufactured as the Secret Writer T 52A in 1935 by German "Siemens & Halske AG."
- **Remington claw-and-ball percussion gun cane:** $16,240 for a Remington claw-and-ball percussion gun cane curio, c. 1859, with an eagle's claw-and-ball handle made of molded gutta percha. The shaft unscrews 3½ inches down for insertion of powder and a 44-caliber ball, and the steel ferrule is stamped with "J.F. Thomas, patent, Feb'y 9 1858, Remington & Sons, Illion N.Y."
- **Ames sword:** $109,000 for an Ames presentation sword, belonging to Civil War Major General Jesse Reno, with a double-edged blade with etching and classic designs including armed warriors and Roman faces; 31 inches. The brass and gold-washed scabbard also has a classical theme, battle scenes in high relief, and the names of General Reno's battles engraved below the throat.
- **Edison Spectacle phonograph:** $49,500 for the rare 1880, Spectacle model, Edison phonograph, produced in a limited number, with a battery-run mechanism that had to be mixed with acid in order to generate electricity.

PAINTINGS & PRINTS

- **Miniature portrait:** $1,216,000 for a locket with a 2⅛-inch watercolor-on-ivory miniature portrait of George Washington and a lock of his hair, painted on October 3, 1789, and mounted in a gold locket for his wife, Martha; painted by John Ramage.

PAPER

- **Declaration of Independence:** $8,140,000 for a copy of the Declaration of Independence that was printed in Philadelphia by printer John Dunlap, July 4, 1776.

- **American ski poster:** $6,325 for a paper ski poster mounted on linen, "Yosemite Winter Sports," depicting a woman preparing her skis for a day on the slopes; c. 1930, 41¾ x 28⅜ inches.
- **Amazing Fantasy #15 comic book:** $40,250 for the 1962 Marvel Comic Amazing Fantasy #15, featuring the first appearance and origin of "The Amazing Spiderman," written by Stan Lee and illustrated by Steve Ditko.

PHOTOGRAPHY

- **Cabinet photograph:** $10,080 for a cabinet photograph of Pat Garrett, wearing a western-style suit and broad-brimmed hat. Beneath the image on the mount is written "Pat F. Garrett, who shot & killed Billy the Kid the most notorious desperado in New Mexico."

POTTERY & PORCELAIN

- **Adelaide Alsop Robineau covered jar:** $162,000 for a 1922 covered jar by Adelaide Alsop Robineau, with detailed carvings of hounds and grapes and framed fields of concentric lines of crystalline glaze.
- **Marblehead pottery:** $120,750 for a Marblehead pot decorated by Hannah Tutt, with carved tall stylized flowers in umber, black, and cream on a speckled matte green background; 6 inches.
- **Victorian pub jug:** $4,222 (£2,860) for a black-necked Buchanan's pub jug, with a hunting dog picture and the base marked "Frank Beardmore & Co., Fenton"; 7 inches.
- **Mochaware:** $19,250 for a 5¾-inch mug decorated with three "dipped fans" on a wide, rust-colored band, lime green bands, and brown stripes on the base and rim.

SILVER & OTHER METAL

- **Andirons:** $70,500 for a pair of brass urn-top andirons; Philadelphia, 1770–1790.
- **Doorknob:** $8,500 for a cast-bronze doggie doorknob with a ruffled border, arches and fleur-de-lis around the outer edge, featuring the "Kruzinger" design with face and paws extended outward from the center. This rare "varietal" doggie knob is neither marked nor dated and the reverse has no decoration.
- **Doorstop:** $11,000 for a Bradley & Hubbard, Whistling Jim, cast-iron doorstop; young boy wearing knickers and striped shirt with hands in pockets, whistling; 6½ inches.
- **Single piece of American silver:** $775,750 for a plain, beaker-shaped, 17th-century wine cup, initialed for Richard and Alice Brackett with a lightly pricked B above RA, punctuated by a heart with scrollwork; by John Hull and Robert Sanderson, Sr., of Boston, c. 1660.
- **Italian silver coffeepot:** $65,309 (135.125.000 lire) for an Italian silver coffeepot with the maker's mark Giuseppe Bartolotti, Rome; 1773–1775.
- **American Gold:** $732,000 for the John Jay freedom box, an American gold snuff box with the Seal of the City of New York and an inscription, along with the original parchment document signed by New York mayor James Duane, attached by a light blue ribbon to a wax impress of the city seal.

SPORTS

- **Honus Wagner card:** $1,265,000 for a Honus Wagner T206 baseball card, depicting the Hall of Fame Pittsburgh Pirates shortstop; issued in 1909 by the American Tobacco Company.
- **Joe Doyle T206 card:** $178,598 for a 1909, T206 Joe Doyle variation card, "N.Y. Nat'l." Card shows Joe Doyle with his hands above his head.
- **Connie Mack cabinet photograph:** $30,240 for a Connie Mack cabinet photograph, for Old Judge Cigarettes, by Goodwin & Co., New York. Mack is posed in his Washington uniform holding a baseball bat; copyright 1887, 6½ x 4¼ inches.
- **Feather-filled golf ball:** $42,780 for a feather-filled golf ball, stamped with the name W. Robinson and inscribed in ink "St. Andrews, 30, Made by Lang Willie"; c. 1840.

TEXTILES

- **Woolie:** $44,800 for a 19th-century English nautical Woolie, a woven wool-yarn picture depicting four different naval vessels; framed, 18¼ x 55¼ inches.
- **Antique dress:** $101,500 for an 1888 court dress made of velvet and satin by Charles Frederick Worth, with a 23-inch waist and a 10½-foot detachable train. The gown belonged to Esther Maria Lewis Chapin, the great-great-grandaughter of Elizabeth Washington Lewis, George Washington's sister.
- **Eames "Sea Things" fabric sample:** $6,900 for a fabric sample printed on one selvage "Sea Things by Ray Eames"; produced by Schiffer Prints c.1948, 37 x 25½ inches.

TOYS, DOLLS & GAMES

- **Hot Wheels:** $72,000 for a Hot Wheels, hot pink, Volkswagen Beach Bomb van with rear-loaded surfboards; a one-of-a-kind prototype.
- **Disney toy/any production toy:** $110,000 for a 1930s Mickey and Minnie Mouse on Motorcycle toy; a tin lithograph windup with the only known original box, which pictures Mickey and Minnie riding through the countryside; by Tipp and Co. of Germany, 9½ inches.
- **Mickey Mouse & Felix sparkler toy:** $22,000 for a tin lithograph Mickey and Felix toy, with Mickey and Felix lighting their cigars over a candle's flame. A hand-held sparkler activates leaning motions and candle's flame; marked "La Isla R.S.," 6 inches.
- **Dentist bank:** $33,000 for a J. & E. Stevens mechanical Dentist bank; cast iron, c. 1885, 9⅝ inches.
- **Horse-drawn cast-iron toy:** $66,300 for a Carpenter Tally-Ho cast-iron coach with a four-horse team and seven passengers; has a galloping motion when wheeled forward; c. 1885, 28 inches.
- **Jupiter robot:** $46,600 for a Yonezawa Jupiter robot, battery operated, painted and tinplate lithograph; the robot walks forward and its arms move back and forth; made in Japan c. 1955, box, 13 inches.
- **Radar robot:** $27,200 for a Nomura Radar robot, a.k.a. Topolino; battery oper-

ated, tinplate lithograph and plastic, walks, arms move back and forth, three colored gears spin in abdomen; made in Japan c. 1960, box, 11 inches.

- **Television robot:** $24,900 for a Television robot, by Kanto, Japan, keywind, tinplate lithograph, walks forward as sparks in its chest illuminate a space scene; with posable head and arms; c. 1955, box, 8 inches.
- **Space Patrol car:** $39,850 for an Ichiko & Yonezawa Space Patrol car, friction powered, tinplate lithograph, rolls forward with space sound; made in Japan c. 1955, box, 8¾ inches.
- **Buddy "L" Insurance Patrol truck:** $40,700 for a red Buddy "L" Insurance Patrol truck, with headlights, front bumper, and original box, along with the sample room I.D. tag; 27 inches.
- **Buddy "L" truck-mounted steam shovel:** $35,200 for a battery operated, 1930s Buddy "L" International truck-mounted steam shovel, red and yellow paint; original box, 25 inches.
- **Buddy "L" locomotive, tender, and caboose:** $33,000 for a Buddy "L" copper- and nickel-plated locomotive, tender, and caboose; the only known set, specially created at the factory for show and display purposes; 64 inches.
- **Buddy "L" Express truck:** $33,000 for a Buddy "L" Express truck with headlights and functional doors; 25 inches.

A NOTE TO COLLECTORS

You already know that this is a great overall price guide for all sorts of antiques and collectibles. Each entry is current, every picture is new, all prices are accurate.

But in the collecting world, things change quickly. Important sales produce new record prices. Fakes appear. Rarities are discovered. To keep up with these developments, read *Kovels on Antiques and Collectibles,* a monthly newsletter with up-to-date information on the world of collecting. It is filled with color photographs, about forty to an issue. The newsletter reports prices, trends, auction results, Internet sales, and other pertinent news for collectors *as it happens.* For a free sample of *Kovels on Antiques and Collectibles,* fill out and mail the postage-paid postcard at the back of this book. We also have a FREE informational website that gives pricing information, lists of important publications and sources for collectors, and excerpts from our newsletter. Visit www.kovels.com to learn more.

KEEP READING—HOW TO USE THIS BOOK

There are a few rules for using this book. Each listing is arranged in the following manner: CATEGORY (such as Pressed Glass or Furniture), OBJECT (such as vase), DESCRIPTION (as much information as possible about size, age, color, and pattern). Some types of glass, pottery, and silver are exceptions to this rule. These are listed CATEGORY, PATTERN,

OBJECT, DESCRIPTION. All items are presumed to be in good condition and undamaged, unless otherwise noted. If a maker's name is easily recognized, like Gustav Stickley, we try to include it near the beginning of the entry. If the maker is obscure, the name may be at the end. Because the descriptions are part of actual reports, we do not edit to make everything consistent in each entry. We try to edit enough to be sure that two items are not actually two descriptions of the same piece.

Several special categories were formed to make the most sensible listing possible. For instance, "Tool" includes special equipment because the casual collector might not know the proper name for an "adze." Many of the glass entries are in special categories: Glass-Art, Glass-Blown, Glass-Contemporary, Glass-Midcentury, and Glass-Venetian. Major glass factories are still listed under the factory names, and well-known types of glass, such as cut, pressed, Depression, Carnival, etc., can be found in their own categories. The silver listings are also a bit different. You will find silver flatware in either Silver Flatware Plated or Silver Flatware Sterling. You will also find a section for Silver Plate, which includes coffeepots, trays, and other plated pieces. Solid or sterling silver is listed by country, so look for Silver-American, Silver-English, etc. Silver jewelry is listed under jewelry. This year we are also changing the way we list pottery and porcelain. Most pottery or porcelain is listed by factory name, such as Weller, or by item, such as Calendar Plate, or in sections like Dinnerware or Kitchen, or in one of the new sections, Pottery-Art, Pottery-Contemporay, Pottery-Midcentury, etc.

Sometimes we make arbitrary decisions based on the number of entries or the amount of interest in a subject. Fishing has its own category, but hunting is part of the larger category called Sports. We have eliminated all guns except toys. It is not legal to sell weapons without a special license, so guns are not part of the general antiques market. Airguns, BB guns, rocket guns, and others are listed in the "Toy" section. Several idiosyncrasies of style appear because the book is printed by computer. Everything is listed according to the computer alphabetizing system. This means words such as "Mt." are alphabetized as "M-T," not as "M-O-U-N-T." All numerals are before all letters; thus "2" comes before "A." A quick glance will make this clear, as it is consistent throughout the book.

We made several editorial decisions. A bowl is a "bowl" and not a "dish," unless it is a special dish, such as a pickle dish. A butter dish is a "butter." A salt dish is called a "salt" to differentiate it from a saltshaker. It is always "sugar and creamer," never "creamer and sugar." Political collectors often refer to "pinbacks," the round celluloid or tin pins that are decorated with candidates' names and faces. The word "button" is sometimes used in this book instead of the word "pinback." Of course, the word "button" is also used when referring to the fasteners used on clothing. Where one dimension is given, it is the height; or if the object is round, the dimension is the diameter. The height of a picture is listed before width. Glass is clear unless a color is indicated.

Every entry is listed alphabetically, but the problem of language remains. Some antiques terms, such as "Sheffield" or "Pratt," have two meanings. Be sure to read the paragraph headings to know the meaning used. All category headings are based on the language of the average person at an average show, and we use terms like "mud figures" even if not technically correct.

This book does *not* include price listings of fine art paintings, antiquities, stamps, coins, or most types of books. *Big Little Books* and similar children's books *are* included. Comic books are *not* listed, but original comic art and cels *are* listed in their own categories.

All pictures in *Kovels' Antiques & Collectibles Price List* are listed with the prices asked by the seller. "Illus" (illustrated nearby) is part of the description if a picture is shown.

There have been misinformed comments about how this book is written. We *do* use the computer. It alphabetizes, ranges prices, sets type, and does other time-consuming jobs. Because of the computer, the book can be produced quickly. The last entries are added in June; the book is available in October. This is six months faster than would be possible any other way. But it is human help that finds prices and checks accuracy. We read everything at least three times, sometimes more. We edit from 60,000 entries to the 50,000 entries found here. We correct spelling, remove incorrect data, write category headings, and decide on new categories. We sometimes make errors. Information in the paragraphs is reviewed and updated each year. This year over fifty-two corrections and additions were made in the category headings.

Prices are reports from all parts of the United States, Canada, and Europe, translated to U.S. dollars at the rate of exchange prevalent at the time of the sale. The averate rate of exchange between June 2000 and June 2001 was $1.50 U.S. to $1 Canadian. Prices are from auctions, shops, Internet sales, and shows. Every price is checked for accuracy, but we are not responsible for errors.

We cannot answer your letters asking for specific price information. But please write if you have any requests for categories to be included in future editions or any corrections to information in the paragraphs or prices.

When you see us at the shows, stop and say hello. Don't be surprised if we ask for your suggestions for the next edition of *Kovels' Antiques & Collectibles Price List.* Or you can write us at P.O. Box 22200-K, Beachwood, Ohio 44122 or visit us at our website: www.kovels.com.

RALPH & TERRY KOVEL
July 2001

ACKNOWLEDGMENTS

Special thanks should go to those who helped us with pictures and deeds: 20th Century Art & Design; Alderfer Auction Company; Allard Auctions Inc.; Anderson Auction; Andre Ammelounx; Antiquorum Auctioneers; Auction Team Köln; Auctions Unlimited Inc.; Autopia, Inc.; Be-Hold, Larry Gottheim; Bill Bertoia Auctions; Brian Moran's; Buffalo Bay Auction Co.; C. Wesley Cowan; Cerebro; Charles E. Kirtley; Christie's; Cincinnati Art Galleries; Collectors Auction Services; Conestoga Auction Co.; Craftsman Auctions; Cyr Auction Company; David Rago Auctions, Inc.; Davies Auctions; DeFina Auctions; Fink's Off the Wall Auctions; Fontaine's Auction Gallery; Frank H. Boos Gallery; Freeman's; Garth's Auctions, Inc.; Gary Metz's Muddy River Trading Co.; Gene Harris Antique Auction Center, Inc.; Glass-Works Auctions; Green Valley Auctions, Inc.; Henry/Peirce Auctioneers; Jackson's Auctioneers & Appraisers; James D. Julia, Inc.; John Toomey Gallery; Ken Farmer Auctions; Lang's Sporting Collectibles, Inc.; Leland's Auctions; Los Angeles Modern Auctions; McMasters; Michael Ivankovich Auction Co., Inc.; Neal Auction Company; New Orleans Auction Galleries, Inc.; Noel Barrett Antiques; Norman C. Heckler & Company; Northeast Auctions; Old Barn Auction; Pacific Glass Auctions; Page Auctioneers & Appraisers; Phillips; Phillips-Selkirk; Phoenix Militaria Corporation; Pook & Pook, Inc.; R.G. Munn Auction; Randy Inman Auctions; Replacements, Ltd.; Richard Opfer Auctioneering, Inc.; Robert C. Eldred Co., Inc.; Skinner, Inc.; Sloan's Auction Galleries; Smith & Jones, Inc.; Smith House; Sotheby's; Southern Folk Pottery Collector's Society; Strawser Auctions; Theriault's; Tom Pritchard; Tony Murland; Treadway Gallery, Inc.; Vickie & Bruce Waasdorp Stoneware Auctions; W. Fagan & Co., Inc.; Waddington's; Web Wilson Auctions; William Doyle Galleries; Wm. Morford; York Town Auction Inc.

To the others in the antiques trade who knowingly or unknowingly contributed to this book, we say "thank you": A Moment in Time; A Squirrel's Nest; A Touch of Glass Ltd.; Adventures Down Memory Lane; Affordable Antiques & Collectibles; Alicia & Jorge Valino Antiques & Collectibles; All Buttoned Up; Alphanaar's Antiques & Collectibles; American Toys; Americana Resources, Inc.; Angie's Antiques & Collectibles; Angz Antiques & Collectibles, Etc.; Anna Jobson; Anticus; Antique Arts; Antique Haven; Antique Plaza; Antiques & Collectibles Store; Antiques at O'Connors; Aunt Lucy's Parlor; Aunt Nancy's Antiques; Awsum Advertising; B.M. Creskoff; Back Door Antiques & Collectibles; Balwin Collectibles; Barbara T. Hillman; BayWatch, Linda Frost; Betty Gorman Kaye; Bill Heitkotter; Bill Hermanek; Bishopric Agency; Blue & Gray Antiques; Boyd & Helen Deets; Bram Hepburn; Brass Armadillo; Butterfly and the Bear; C & K Collectibles; Calico Cats Antiques; California Collectibles Plus; Carriage House Antiques Gallery; Cats Cradle Antiques;

Chat's Collectibles; CM Murray; Collectible Restorations International Inc.; Collectibles & Such; Collector Online; Coollectibles; Copperfields Antiques; Cowait Antiques & Collectibles; Cribtoy's Closet; Cyberattic; Dale E. Rutherford; Dan Brown; Dan's Collectibles; Danese Theisen; David Smith; Days Gone By; Decades – The Nostalgia Store; Dee Boese; Delmer H. Youngen; Dennis Raleigh; Diana Turner; Dick's Antiques; Dishes Are Us; Dis-n-Dat Glass Shop; Doe's Treasure; Don Sherman; Donald Snell; Doris Stephan's Antiques & Collectibles; Doug Brown; Doug Mac Gillvary; Dover Antiques Mart; Downtown Antiques & Consignment Shop; Drawing Room & The Zsolnay Store; EAC Gallery; Eagle Ridge Collectibles; Earthly Remains; East End Galleries; eBay Inc.; Eden West Antiques, Gloria Bodell; Elegance for Hire; Emery Antiques; Essential Porcelain & Pottery Company; Estate Goodies; Evening Star Collectibles; Florence Archambault; Foley's Uniques; Forestwood; Foxden Antiques; Frozen in Time, Inc.; Gasoline Alley Antiques; Gateway Antiques Center; Gator Trading Co.; Geri Bawin; Gisela Antiques; Golden Harvest Antiques; Good Time Collectibles; Gray Menagerie; Gryphon's Nest; Gus Knapp; Gwen Daniel Antiques; Harbor Bazaar; Harlowe's Web; Hart's Old Country Store; Heartland Memories; Hellen Mueller; Heritage Harvest Antiques; Heritage Museum; Hickory Tree Antiques; Hope's Time & Again; Hourglass Antiques & Collectibles; Hyacinth House; Irene Brockmann; Jack Adamson; Jean Deibel; Jeff Siptak; Jerry's Antiques; Jewell Malone; Jim Snyder; Joan's Jewels & Collectibles; Joe Clements; John L. & Ellen Williams; Jr's Antiques; Judy Posner Collectibles; Junkyard Jeweler; Kay G. Previte of Antiques of Chester; Ken Grenz; Kentucky Sandpiper; Keystone Toy Trader; Kinzua Country Antiques; Kitschy Koo Kollectibles; Krazy Cat Collectibes; LaBelle; Lake Ontario Books; Leigh's House of Antiques & Collectibles; Leland's Auctions; Lewis & Clark Antiques; Looking Back Antiques; Lost Treasures; Lou's Antiques; LuAnna's Attic; M.S. Rau Antiques; Mad Hatter Antiques; Maine Collectible Connection; Man, With Dish Pan Hands; Mapleside Antiques; Marcia Petrella; Marion Antiques & Collectibles; Mary Hatfield; Mary Tupta Antiques; Mastro Fine Sports Auctions; Mayer & Patricia Gold; Memory Lane Vintage Jewelry & Collectibles; Memory's Antiques; Merri's House; Michael's Memories-Paper Pandemonium; Michael's Unpaper Items; Michelle's Antiques & Collectibles; Mike Bauer; Milan Village Antiques; Minnie Matilda's; Mongenas Antiques; Nancy Bumgardner; Neddon Antiques; Neeley's Antiques; Nooks & Crannies; Nostalgia Antiques; Ol' South Antiques; Old Friends; Olden Times Antiques & Collectibles; Ole Tyme; Palmer Media Enterprises; Pascoe & Company; Past Glories; Pat & Grant Windson; Pat Collins; Patriot House Antiques; Paul Efron Antiques; Peanut Gallery; Petticoat Junction Antiques & Collectibles; Pitzwick's Antiques; Playthings Past; Prairie Valley Store; Queen of Hearts; R.S. Goldberg; R.T. Capin; Really Good Things; Recollectibles

Antiques; Red Barn Gallery Antiques; Relics; Reyne Hogan Antique; Rich Weingarten; Richard Housman; Richard's Store; Robert E. Bender; Roma & Dick Taylor; Ron & Carol Harris; Ron Farley; Ruby Lane; Scintillations Antiques; Seitz & Co.; Serendipity Enterprises; Sesame Past; Shed Antiques; Shirley Jacobitz; Sidmore Antiques; Sims Creek Antique Mall; Snow Hill Antiques; South Dakota Antiques; Sovereign House Antiques of Westfield, Mass.; St. James Bay Tool Co.; Stephanie Seguin; Stuff n' Such; Susan's Antiques; Sweetened on the Vine; Team's Tiffany Treasures; Ted Kromer; Temple's Antiques; Tess's Treasure Trove; Thanks for the Memories; Things from the Past; Thomas C. Campbell; Time Travelers Antiques & Collectibles; Tin Man Antiques; Tin Signs USA; Tins n' Toys; Tom Nathan; Tom Polansky; Tom Snook; Tomlinson Antiques; Too Late Antiques & Collectibles; Toy Collector Turned Upside-Down; Trader Fred's Toys of Yore; Treasures, Trinkets & Treats; Triple Cross Antiques; Unlimited Ltd.; Victorian Angel; Vintage Memories; Violet Morway; Virtually Anything; Warwick Henderson Gallery; We Love Auctions; Well Dressed Table; Wharton Antiques; Whistle Stop Treasures; White Rose Antique; Winona F. Fletcher; Winter Brook Farm Antiques; Yankee Tools & Collectables; Yesterdays South, Inc. Special thanks to TIAS.

No one can write a price list like Kovels without help from many people. They record prices, comment, check facts, review artwork, solve computer problems, and much more. This is what makes an accurate book that's published on time every year. Pam Stinson-Bell of Crown Publishers read almost every word and every correction. She also supervised the staff who had to put the pieces together to get the color insert, cover, and main copy as perfect as possible. Chip Gibson, Linda Lowenthal, Dorothy Harris, Kathryn Henderson, Karen Minster, and John Sharp of Crown did more than their jobs. Merri Ann Morrell of Precision Graphics unraveled computer mysteries to get the information to behave and form proper printed pages. Benjamin Margalit took all the color and many of the black-and-white photographs. Our daily companions at work—Carmie Amata, Kitty Busher, Marcia Goldberg, Evelyn Hayes, Karen Kneisley, and Nancy Saada—did their usual overtime work in writing and proofing to produce another good year for the *Kovels' Antiques and Collectibles Price List.*

And this year we give special thanks to the unsung heroes of this book. All year long they record prices in the secret Kovel style to make this easy to use format a reality. It takes a special talent to go through thousands of prices and put them in the right form and location. Thank you to Debbie Bedell, Grace DeFrancisco, Katie Karrick, Liz Lillis, Eleanore Melzak, Cherrie Smrekar, Edie Smrekar, Virginia Warner, and Ann Wochner. But Gay Hunter once again was the "mother of the book." She kept us all on schedule, read copy over and over again, solved problems, ran interference between departments, and watched the details. To all, thank you. There would be no book without you.

A. WALTER made pate-de-verre glass under contract at the Daum glassworks from 1908 to 1914. He started his own firm in Nancy, France, in 1919. Pieces made before 1914 are signed *Daum, Nancy* with a cross. After 1919 the signature is *A. Walter Nancy.*

Bird, Turquoise, Henri Berge, Signed, 3 1/2 In. 977.00
Dish, Mottled Green, Frog, 4 3/8 In. 1705.00
Figurine, Reclining Maiden, 1920, 10 In. 11500.00
Vase, Dark Blue, Brown Base, Henri Berge, 1925, 8 3/4 In. 3600.00
Vase, Geometric, Blue, Yellow, Flared, Signed, 3 3/4 x 6 1/4 In. 4025.00
Vase, Green, Carved Flowers, Signed, 5 1/4 x 5 3/4 In. 2415.00

ABC plates, or children's alphabet plates, were most popular from 1780 to 1860, but are still being made. The letters on the plate were meant as teaching aids for children learning to read. The plates were made of pottery, porcelain, metal, or glass. Mugs and other items were also made with alphabet decorations.

Plate, 2 Cats In Basket, In A Soft Place 310.00
Plate, Beaded Edge, Alphabet On Rim, 7 In. 49.00
Plate, Bird In Bush, 1 Side, Alphabet, Other Side, 8 5/8 In. 55.00
Plate, Chairs To Mend, Man Carrying Chairs, Alphabet Border, 8 1/2 In. 220.00
Plate, Child, Hanging Laundry, Alphabet Border, 7 1/4 In. 60.00
Plate, Choo-Choo Train, Pearlware, Edge & Malkin Co., c.1900, 7 In. 325.00
Plate, Clock Face, Number Of Year, Number Of Weeks 80.00
Plate, Dost Thou Love Life, Not Squander Time, 7 1/8 In. 87.00
Plate, For Age & Want Save While You May, 8 In. 176.00
Plate, Franklin Proverb, Now I Have A Sheep & Cow, 1830, 8 In. 175.00
Plate, Girl Playing Piano, Staffordshire 195.00
Plate, Hunt Scene, Men & Dogs In Field, 6 In. 88.00
Plate, If You Would Know The Value Of Money, Try To Borrow Some, 6 In. 132.00
Plate, Kite Flying, He That Hath A Trade, 1870s, 6 1/2 In. 125.00
Plate, Lion & Palm Tree, Stippled Background, 6 In. 50.00
Plate, Little Boys At Marble Play On Summer Holiday, 5 In. 192.00
Plate, Nightingale, Alphabet Border, E.M. & Co., 6 1/4 In. 110.00
Plate, Robinson Crusoe Finding Footprint, 5 1/2 In. 110.00
Plate, Rugby, Blue & White, 6 3/4 In. 265.00
Plate, Village Blacksmith, 5 1/8 In. 176.00

ABINGDON POTTERY was established in 1908 by Raymond E. Bidwell as the Abingdon Sanitary Manufacturing Company. The company started making art pottery in 1934. The factory ceased production of art pottery in 1950.

Cookie Jar, Brown-Eyed Susan 135.00
Cookie Jar, Choo Choo, 12 In. 100.00
Cookie Jar, Humpty Dumpty, Sitting On Wall 427.00
Cookie Jar, Money Bag, 1947 .... 80.00
Planter, Ruffled Rim, Signed, 3 x 2 In. 45.00
Trivet, Embossed Figures Of Oriental Man Seated, Woman Kneeling, 5 In. 66.00
Vase, Bird, Matte Glaze, 1939, 7 3/4 In. 50.00
Vase, Cornucopia, Signed, 5 x 7 1/2 In. 25.00
Vase, Double Cornucopia, 1940s, 11 In. 35.00
Vase, Embossed Wreath, Square Base, Signed, 9 In. 55.00
Vase, Wedgwood Blue, Wide Base, Weeping Top, c.1950, 10 5/8 In. 75.00
Vase, Wide Base, Medium White Swirl, 1940s, 9 x 6 1/4 In. 50.00

ADAMS china was made by William Adams and Sons of Staffordshire, England. The firm was founded in 1769 and became part of the Wedgwood Group in 1966. The name "Adams" appeared on various items through 1998. All types of tablewares and useful wares were made. Other pieces of Adams will be found listed under Flow Blue and Tea Leaf Ironstone.

Berry Bowl, Singapore Bird, 5 3/4 In. 6.00
Biscuit Barrel, Continuous Fox Hunting Scene, Silver Plated Collar, 5 1/2 In. 172.00

Bowl, Cereal, Empress, White	33.00
Bowl, Cereal, Metz	17.00
Bowl, Dessert, Sharon	6.00
Bowl, Vegetable, Cover, Baltic	99.00
Bowl, Vegetable, Empress, White, Oval	87.00
Bowl, Vegetable, Oval, Ming Toi	40.00
Bowl, Vegetable, Oval, Sharon	35.00
Candlestick, Classical Style Figures, Columnar, 7 In., Pair	172.00
Coffeepot, Cover, Empress, White	315.00
Creamer, Baltic	25.00
Creamer, Florida	30.00
Creamer, Pink, Princess	16.00
Creamer, Singapore Bird	54.00
Cup & Saucer, Anita	20.00
Cup & Saucer, Azalea	22.00
Cup & Saucer, Baltic	16.00 to 22.00
Cup & Saucer, Florida	21.00
Cup & Saucer, Metz	27.00
Cup & Saucer, Persimmon	23.00
Cup & Saucer, Singapore Bird, 2 1/2 In.	15.00
Cup & Saucer, Vermont, Red	21.00
Cup Plate, Cries Of London, Green Rim, Polychrome, 3 1/4 In.	22.00
Eggcup, Empress, White	167.00
Eggcup, Singapore Bird	30.00 to 35.00
Gravy Boat, Ming Toi	40.00
Gravy Boat, Singapore Bird, 9 x 4 1/2 In.	85.00
Gravy Boat, Tokio, Blue & White, Transfer, 7 1/2 x 4 In.	58.00
Gravy Boat, Underplate, Cambodia	10.00
Marmalade Jar, Hunt Scene, Hammered National Silveroid Cover, Incised J. C., 4 In.	150.00
Plate, Bamborough Castle, Blue, 10 In.	155.00
Plate, Blenheim Castle, Oxfordshire, Blue, c.1825, 10 1/8 In.	295.00
Plate, Bread & Butter, Baltic	7.00 to 11.00
Plate, Bread & Butter, Regent, Gold, 5 7/8 In.	12.00
Plate, Dinner, Anita	26.00
Plate, Dinner, Baltic	14.00
Plate, Dinner, Florida	22.00
Plate, Dinner, Metz	28.00
Plate, Dinner, Princess, Pink	18.00
Plate, Dinner, Singapore Bird, 10 In.	20.00 to 40.00
Plate, Khayyam Bird, Bread & Butter, 5 7/8 In.	7.50
Plate, Landscape, Pagoda, Blue & White, Square, Scalloped Corners, 9 1/2 In.	13.00
Plate, Palestine, Blue, 9 1/4 In.	120.00
Plate, Salad, Ming Jade	20.00
Plate, Salad, Old Colonial	19.00
Plate, Windsor Castle, Blue, 10 In.	120.00 to 139.00
Platter, Chelsea Sprays	78.00
Platter, Deer In Park, Dark Blue Transfer, 13 1/2 In.	1100.00
Platter, Harper's Ferry, U.S., 15 1/2 In.	635.00
Ramekin, Empress, White	70.00
Soup, Dish, 2 Fishermen, On Shore, Junk On River, Blue, 10 In.	120.00
Sugar, Cover, Princess, Pink	25.00
Sugar, Cover, Singapore Bird, 5 1/2 In.	45.00 to 68.00
Teapot, Cover, Empress, White	161.00
Vase, Classical Figures, Dark Blue & White, Incised J. C., 6 3/4 In.	350.00

ADVERTISING containers and products sold in the old country store are now all collectibles. These stores, with the crackers in a barrel and a potbellied stove, are a symbol of an earlier, less hectic time. Listed here are many of the advertising items. Other similar pieces may be found under the product name, such as Planters Peanuts. We have tried to list items in the logical places, so large store fixtures will be found under the Architectural category, enameled tin dishes under Granite-ware, paper items in the Paper category, etc. Store fixtures, cases, and

other items that have no advertising as part of the decoration are listed
in the Store category.

Apron, Reddy Kilowatt, Tea Type, Plastic, 1950s	50.00
Ashtray, Breyer's Ice Cream, 90th Anniversary, 1965	30.00
Ashtray, Fireman, Metal, Advance Products, 7 x 4 1/2 In. ....*Illus*	85.00
Ashtray, Greyhound, Bronze, Greyhound Mounted On Onyx Base, 1930, 8 3/4 In.	125.00
Ashtray, Lion's Club, Bronze, 3 1/2 x 5 In.	110.00
Ashtray, Match Holder, Neuweiler's Brewing, 6 x 3 1/2 In.	35.00
Ashtray, Sealed Power Piston Rings, Figural Nude, 6 In.	33.00
Ashtray, Star Of Bethlehem Cigars, Girl With Long Blond Hair, Cast Iron, Painted	65.00
Ashtray, Statler Hotel, Pottery, Teal, Match Holder In Center, 1940s, 5 1/4 In.	25.00
Ashtray, Whirlpool, October 1954, 1 1/2 In.	10.00
Bag, Mash, Western Grain Co., Uncle Sam Picture, 50 Lb.	38.00
Bag, Moxie Soda, Paper, 1932, 11 x 9 1/4 In.	45.00
Banner, A & W Root Beer, Dennis The Menace, Canvas, 36 1/2 x 91 1/2 In.	220.00
Banner, Annapolis Zia Cigarette, Silk, Naval Academy, Song, 1913, 4 x 5 1/2 In.	38.00
Banner, Canvas, Schmidt's City Club Brewing, Gilt Frame, 28 1/2 x 39 In.	460.00
Banner, Drink Moxie, Man On Horse, Horseless Carriage, Cloth, 27 x 36 In.	1850.00
Banner, New Holiday Goods, Come In & See, Muslin, 3 x 6 Ft.	3080.00
Banner, Poor & Son Drug Store, Canvas, Sanborn, 2 Sides, 42 x 96 In. ....*Illus*	6750.00
Beer Pull, Brut Super Premium	13.00
Beer Pull, Cee Bee, 1960s	550.00
Beer Pull, Colorado Imperial, 1960s	10.00
Beer Pull, Great Lakes Beer, Lacrosse Version, 1970s	20.00
Beer Pull, Lime Lager, 12 Oz.	11.00
Billfold, Leather, Opera Bar & Club Rooms, Las Vegas, N.M., 6 x 3 1/2 In.	150.00
Bin, Coffee, W.S. Quimby Company	795.00
Bin, Johnson's Log Cabin, Tin Lithograph, Cabin Form, 28 x 24 In.	2750.00
Bin, Lorillard's Beech-Nut Chewing Tobacco, Slant Front, Countertop, 9 x 9 3/4 In.	220.00
Bin, New Process Coffee, C.A. Cross, Fitchburg, Mass, Tin Lithograph, 13 x 21 In.	160.00
Bin, Polar Bear Tobacco, 9 x 13 In.	125.00
Bin, Sterling Tobacco, Countertop, Graphics On Reverse, 7 x 8 1/4 In.	170.00
Bin, Sweet Cuba, Cardboard, Tin Base & Top, 8 In.	555.00
Bin, Van Melle's Toffee, Countertop, 10 x 9 1/2 In.	660.00
Blotter, Kellogg's Rice Krispies, Girl On Swing	15.00
Blotter, Kingham's Boiled Ham, Indianapolis, In., 1920s, 3 x 6 In.	10.00
Blotter, Lake Side Dye Works, Monthly Calendar, Photo, Jane House, Model, 1940s	7.50
Blotter, Mercury Insurance Co., Man, Crystal Ball, Unused, 1930s, 3 1/2 x 6 1/4 In.	6.00
Blotter, Peters Employment Service, Boston Map, Blue, White, Gold, Red, Yellow	5.00
Blotter, Silver Top, Pale Export Beer, 1910s	26.00
Books may be included in the Paper category.	
Booklet, Recipe, Jell-O, Illustrated By Rose O'Neill, 5 1/4 x 6 7/8 In.	50.00
Bottles are listed in their own category.	
Bottle Openers are listed in their own category.	
Bowl, Diamond Crystal Shaker Salt, Crystal, 7 1/2 In. Diam.	15.00
Bowl, H.P. Hood & Sons Milk, Porcelain, Enamel, Blue Ground, Gold Rim, 4 In.	100.00
Bowl, United Airlines, Porcelain	9.00
Box, see also Box category.	

Advertising,
Ashtray, Fireman,
Metal, Advance
Products,
7 x 4 1/2 In.

Advertising, Banner, Poor & Son Drug Store,
Canvas, Sanborn, 2 Sides, 42 x 96 In.

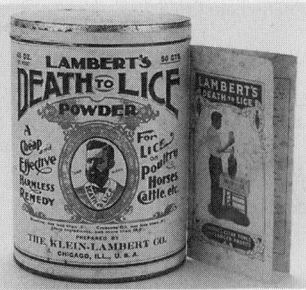

Advertising, Box, Lambert's Death To Lice,
Contents, Pamphlet, 7 In.

Any lithographed can with a
picture is of more value than a
lithographed can with just names.
Any paper-labeled can that can
be dated before 1875 is rare. Any
ad that pictures an American flag
or a Black person has added value.

Box, Aunt Lydia's Thread, Countertop, 11 1/4 x 9 In. 253.00
Box, Avon Jasmine Soap, 1940 . . . . 5.00
Box, Baker's Chocolate, Wooden, 4 x 10 x 10 In. 40.00
Box, Blue Bird Handkerchiefs, Lithograph Metal, Countertop, Hinged Top, 1920s 550.00
Box, Budweiser, Custer's Last Fight, 1950s, 3 1/2 x 2 1/2 In. 275.00
Box, Budweiser, Custer's Last Fight, Wooden Frame, 2 x 2 1/2 In. 350.00
Box, Butter, Purdue Creamery, Paper, 1 Lb. 75.00
Box, Cereal, Fairway Oats, Elves Sliding Down Banister 67.00
Box, Cereal, Harvest Queen Oats, Contents, Round, 1 Lb. 4 Oz. 155.00
Box, Cereal, Kellogg's Pep, Tom Corbett, Mask Back 465.00
Box, Cereal, Kellogg's, 1954 . . . . 1000.00
Box, Cereal, Quaker Puffed Wheat, Shirley Temple, My Cereal, c.1937, 3 1/2 Oz. 310.00
Box, Cigar, Fire Brigade, 50 Count, c.1901 . . . . 520.00
Box, Cigar, Lord Grasby Cigar, Indians Returning With Tobacco Leaves, c.1915 . . . . 45.00
Box, Cigar, Mahogany, Cedar Lined, Base Drawer, Key, England, 12 x 6 1/2 In. 850.00
Box, Cigar, Moki, Wood, 50 Count, Image Of Indian In Headdress, New York, c.1906 . . . 85.00
Box, Cigar, Sandow, Strongman, 5 Cents 250.00
Box, Cigar, Seal Of Montana, Wood, Brass Feet, 50 Count 95.00
Box, Cigar, Totem, Label On Side, c.1901 . . . . 95.00
Box, Cigar, Web Foot, Inner Label Of Indian Maiden, c.1920 . . . . 90.00
Box, Cigarette, Turkey Red, Woman Wearing Fez, 1910, 3 x 2 x 1/2 In. 500.00
Box, Dennison's Paper Fasteners, Brass, T Pins, Embossed, Round, 2 In. 15.00
Box, Display, Nylo, New Miracle Treatment, For Nylon Stockings 65.00
Box, Fli-Back Championship Tournament Yo-Yo, Countertop, 1950s 75.00
Box, Lambert's Death To Lice, Contents, Pamphlet, 7 In. . . . . *Illus* 125.00
Box, Lux Soap, Housewife Holding Soap, 1940s 15.00
Box, Police Foot Powder, Paper, Cardboard, Plastic Pour Lid, Contents, 1940s, 5 In. 88.00
Box, Purdue Creamery Ice Cream, Unused, Round, 1/2 Gal. 100.00
Box, Red Star Cleaning Powder, Cardboard, 1880s, 5 x 3 1/2 In. 360.00
Box, Shell Lubrication, Pressed Metal, 13 x 12 1/2 x 7 In. 20.00
Box, Talcum Powder, Lucky Strike, Cardboard, Madrid, Spain, c.1940, 4 5/8 In. 45.00
Box, Topsy Chocolates, Topsy, 2 Children, Pacific Coast Biscuit Co., 1890, 15 x 19 In. . . . 275.00
Box, Virginity Smoking Tobacco, Women & Factory, c.1880, 3 7/8 x 4 1/2 x 7 In. 440.00
Brochure, Eames Contract Storage, Herman Miller Furniture Co., c.1961, 8 In. 345.00
Brochure, Utica Club Ginger Ale, Color, Graphics, 1920s 15.00
Broom Holder, Climax Baking Powder 176.00
Cabinet, Belding Spool, 5 Drawers 500.00
Cabinet, Diamond Dyes, Children With Balloon, 1912, 15 x 24 x 8 In. . . . . *Illus* 977.00
Cabinet, Diamond Dyes, Evolution Of Woman, Front Tin Panel, 30 x 9 In. . . . . . . .690.00 to 1295.00
Cabinet, Diamond Dyes, Mansion, Children, 1908, 15 x 24 x 8 In. . . . . *Illus* 1150.00
Cabinet, Diamond Dyes, Maypole, It's Easy To Dye With, Tin, Embossed, 30 In. 4070.00
Cabinet, Diamond Dyes, Washer Woman, Tin Lithograph Front Panel, 30 x 21 In. 3080.00
Cabinet, Display, Ribbon, 12 Doors, 4 Drawers, Oak & Glass, 38 x 28 In. 1150.00
Cabinet, Dr. Daniels' Veterinary Medicines, Tin Panel, 19 x 27 x 7 In. . . . . *Illus* 6000.00
Cabinet, Dy-O-La Dye, Tin Lithograph, Girls Dyeing Clothes, Product, 12 x 14 In. 330.00
Cabinet, Freihofer's Cake, Tin Lithograph Sides, Tin Framed Glass, 22 x 17 In. 550.00

Advertising, Cabinet, Diamond Dyes, Children With Balloon, 1912, 15 x 24 x 8 In.
Advertising, Cabinet, Dr. Daniels' Veterinary Medicines, Tin Panel, 19 x 27 x 7 In.
Advertising, Cabinet, Diamond Dyes, Mansion, Children, 1908, 15 x 24 x 8 In.

Cabinet, J.W. Brant Co. Dye, Magic Dyes, Tin Lithograph, 37 In. 2640.00
Cabinet, Jiffy Dyes, Packages, Drummer Dyes 650.00
Cabinet, Johnson's Medicated Plasters, Tin Lithograph, 5 Drawers, 13 x 16 In. 330.00
Cabinet, Milward's Celebrated Needles, Reverse Labels On 3 Drawers, 10 1/8 In. 880.00
Cabinet, P. Lorillard & Co., Walnut, 2 Glass Doors, Drawers, 43 x 18 x 34 In. 1035.00
Cabinet, Putnam Dye, Metal, Dye Still In Back, 1940s 605.00
Cabinet, Spool, 6 Cord Merrick's Standard Soft Cotton, 5 Drawers, 16 x 30 In. 275.00
Cabinet, Spool, Chadwick's, Oak Lift Top, 6 Drawers, Gilt Fronts, 33 x 15 In. 750.00
Cabinet, Spool, Clark's, Stepback Shelves, 1950s, 23 x 10 In. 225.00
Cabinet, Spool, Clark's, Twin Drawers, Reverse Gilt Glass Labels, 22 In. 288.00
Cabinet, Spool, Clark's, Walnut Cabinet, 6 Drawers, Ruby Fronts, 29 x 22 In. 1265.00
Cabinet, Spool, Clark's, Wooden, 4 Drawers, Desk Style, Lift Top, 21 x 30 In. 195.00
Cabinet, Spool, Coats & Clark, Oak, 2 Drawers, Black Glass Fronts 215.00
Cabinet, Spool, Coff's Braid, Wooden, 2 Drawers, Desk Style, 18 x 18 In. 275.00
Cabinet, Spool, Heminway & Sons, Oak, Glass Front Drawers, 19 In. 1035.00
Cabinet, Spool, J. & P. Coats', 6 Drawers, Wooden, Advertising On Side Panel, 21 In. . . . 990.00
Cabinet, Spool, J. & P. Coats', Oak, 2 Drawers, Decals, 21 x 15 1/2 x 9 In. 345.00
Cabinet, Spool, J. & P. Coats', Oak, 2 Drawers, Desk Style, 17 x 21 In. 275.00
Cabinet, Spool, J. & P. Coats', Oak, Original Finish 325.00
Cabinet, Star Zephyr Company Germantown Yarn, Roll-Up Door, 37 In. 360.00
Cabinet, West Hair Nets, Images 3 Sides, Access Rear Door, 1921, 20 x 12 3/4 In. 2420.00
Calendars are listed in their own category.
Can, Cilux Enamel Paint, Children Riding Tricycle, Father Painting Doghouse, 3 In. 30.00
Can, Coulee Coffee, Paper Label On Cardboard, J. J. Hogan, LaCross, Wis., 1 Lb. 225.00
Can, Duck & Sea Shooting Gunpowder Can, Red, Boston, Mass., 1890, 1/4 Lb. 1265.00
Can, Hazard Smokeless Powder Can, Canada Goose On Front, Red Ground, 1 Lb. 5175.00
Can, Hazard Smokeless, A Double No Trouble, Hazard Powder Co., N.Y., 1 Lb. 2875.00
Can, Old Fashioned Malt Syrup, Family On Patio, Old German Village, 1930 . . . . 15.00
Can, Parrot & Monkey Baking Powder, Paper Label, Tin Top & Base, 2 1/2 x 5 In. 240.00
Can, Quick Shot Powder Can, King Powder Co., Cincinnati, Oh., 1890, 1/2 Lb. 6325.00
Canisters, see introductory paragraph to Tins in this category.
Cap, Oilzum Service Station, Stenciled Leather, Image On Reverse, 1 x 4 1/2 In. 55.00
Cards are listed in the Card category as card, advertising.
Carton, Wigwam Spice, Paper On Cardboard 88.00
Case, Arrow Collar Button, Curved Glass, Wooden Frame, Pat. July 10, 1910 . . . . 805.00
Case, Bar's Root Beer, 6-Bottle, Wooden 120.00
Case, Carborundum, Triangular, Wooden, Glass Front, 41 x 25 In. 715.00
Case, Castle Pencils, A.W. Faber, Drop Front, Drawer, Poplar 385.00
Case, Frank Jones Brewing Co., Snap Lock 85.00
Case, J.R. Torrey & Co., Razors & Strops, 3 Shelves, 36 x 24 1/2 In. 2013.00
Case, Pabst, Wooden, Glass Front, 1920s 24.00
Case, Spencerian Pen Nibs, Hinged Glass Lid, Square, c.1910, 14 In. 175.00
Case, Yankee Razor Blade, Patriotic Graphics, 1 x 2 1/4 In. 80.00
Case, Zeno Gum, 3 Glass Shelves, Mirror In Floor, Oak, 17 x 10 In. 535.00

Chair, Beech-Nut Spearmint Gum, Folding, Wood & Metal, 31 In. 200.00
Chair, RCA Victor Trademark, Backrest Shows Image Of Nipper, 21 1/2 In. 415.00
Change Purse, Ozark Airlines, Blue Plastic, Zipper, 3 In. 5.00
Change Receiver, see also Tip Tray in this category.
Change Receiver, Doral Cigarettes 25.00
Change Receiver, S & H Green Trading Stamps, Young Woman, 1907, 4 1/4 In. 104.00
Checkerboard, 1841 Security Insurance Co. Of New Haven, Wooden, 15 x 17 In. 109.00
Cigar Cutter, Champion Knight, Enterprise, July 25, 1871-January 20, 1885, 19 In. 38.00
Cigar Cutter, El Tino, Reverse On Glass, Key Wind, 8 1/4 x 6 3/4 In. 395.00
Cigar Cutter, Flor & DeManuel, Allen R. Crewssman & Sons, Countertop, c.1900 ...... 303.00
Cigar Cutter, Fritz Emmett, Town Crier, Mouth, Operated By Left Arm, Iron, 8 In. 980.00
Cigar Cutter, Globe Democrat Cigars, Ernie Specialty Co., Patented 1889 .... 795.00
Cigar Cutter, La Amenidad, Cast Iron, Copper Wash Base, 9 1/2 x 6 x 5 1/2 In. 748.00
Cigar Cutter, Linch Standard, Cast Iron, Black, Gold Striping, Painted, 13 In. 44.00
Cigar Cutter, Royal Dutch Cigars, One Today Beats 2 Tomorrows, Iron, 6 x 6 In. 460.00
Cigar Holder, Hoffman House Bouquet Cigar, Logo, Pot Metal, 17 In. 5500.00
Cigar Lighter, Aladdin's Lamp, Jeweled Brass, Cedar Falls, Countertop, 8 In. 450.00
Cigar Lighter, Garcia Grande, Metal Stand, Countertop 224.00
Cigar Lighter, Kerosene, Owl Cigar, N.Y. & Florida, Vaseline Glass, Countertop 2016.00
Cigarette Silk, Zia, Michigan, Ann Arbor, Mascot, Song, 1913, 4 x 5 1/2 In. 37.00
Cigarette Silk, Zia, Naval Academy, Emblem, Annapolis, 1913, 4 x 5 1/2 In. 37.00
Clamp, Celluloid, Paper Clamp, Hazen-Brown Co., Clamp, Brockton, Ma., 1 1/4 In. 5.00
Clicker, Cricket, John Deere Plow Co., Omaha, Neb., 1 1/4 In. 740.00
Clicker, John Deere Plow Co., Brown Deer Leaping Over Plow, 1 1/4 In. 742.00
Clicker, John Deere Plow Co., I Chirp For John Deere Plows 742.00
Clocks are listed in their own category.
Clothes Brush, Altes Lager, Tivoli Brewing Co., Detroit, Mich., 7 In. 60.00
Coaster, Bub's Pilsen, 1940s, 4 1/4 In. 34.00
Coaster, Daeuffer's Beer, 1930s, 4 1/4 In. 13.00
Coaster, Haberle's Light Ale, Square, 1940s, 4 1/4 In. 17.00
Coaster, Hoosier Beer, 1930s, 4 1/8 In. 39.00
Coaster, Nickle Plate Beer, 1930s, 3 1/2 In. 28.00
Coaster, Schmidts Beer & Ale, Original Wrapper, 2 Sides, 4 1/4 In. 7.00
Coaster, Tivoli Beer, 1930s, 4 In. 17.00
Compote, Lutted's Cough Drops, Glass Log Cabin, Pedestal Base, Countertop, 10 In. ... 690.00
Container, Cover, Purdue Creamery Cottage Cheese, Paper, 1 Lb. 60.00
Container, Midwest Ice Cream, Cardboard, Tin Lid & Bottom, 1950s, 1/2 Gal. 9.50
Cookie Cutter, Betty Crocker Gingerbread Mix, Gingerbread Boy, Red Plastic, 4 In. 10.50
Cookie Cutter, Heinz, Pickle Shape, Tin, Loop Handle, 5 1/2 In. 8.50
Cookie Cutter, Robin Hood Flour, Shape & Image Of Robin Hood, Red Plastic, 4 In. 8.50
Coupon, Utica Club, Try 6 Bottles Of Beer, Brewery's Risk, 2 Sides, 1900s 3.00
Crate, M. Morrison, Stenciled On 2 Sides, c.1910 .... 23.00
Crock, Clarke's Miraculous Salve, For Eruptions, England, 1 11/16 x 1 7/16 In. 55.00
Crock, Heinz Apple Butter, Black Ceramic Cover, 1906, 8 1/2 x 4 1/4 In. 51.00
Crock, Heinz Apple Butter, Cover, Handle, 1883, 6 x 4 3/4 In. 57.00
Crock, Heinz Apple Butter, Stoneware, Paper Label, Lid, 8 1/2 In. 247.00
Crock, Heinz Mincemeat, Stoneware, Paper Label, Handle, Lid, 9 In. 1320.00
Crock, Heinz Peach Butter, Handle, 1883, 5 1/2 x 4 3/4 In. .... 143.00 to 303.00
Crock, Heinz Pineapple Preserve, 1901, 7 1/2 x 4 1/2 In. 253.00
Crock, Heinz Quince Preserve, Cover, Handle, 1883, 6 x 4 1/2 In. 143.00
Crock, Heinz Raspberry Jelly, Cover, 5 x 4 3/4 In. 195.00
Crock, Heinz Strawberry, Cover, Handle, 5 3/4 x 4 3/4 In. 115.00
Crock, Holloway's Ointment, Black Lady, Serpent, England, 1 9/16 x 1 1/2 In. 55.00
Cup, Biltmore Daisy, 1 Pt. 7.00
Cup, Nestle's Coffee, Restaurant Ware, Heavy Duty, Shenango China 18.00
Cup, Zigzag, Clark's Teaberry Chewing Gum, Tin, Lithograph, 1/8 In. 75.00
Decanter, Anheuser-Busch, Ceramarte Blue Dutch, 6 Cups, Box, 1970s 990.00
Decanter, Anheuser-Busch, Ceramarte Clydesdale, 1970s 1320.00
Decanter, Hamm's Beer, Bear, Ceramarte, 1973 .... 40.00
Demitasse Set, Anheuser-Busch, White, Gold Logo, Given To Executives In 1950s 175.00
Dexterity Puzzle, Miller High Life Beer, 10 Pieces, 5 In. 20.00
Dispenser, Bowey's Hot Chocolate, Aluminum, Powder Container, Enamel, 8 1/2 In. 150.00
Dispenser, Buckeye Root Beer, Jovial Elves, Ceramic, 8 x 15 In. 2200.00

Dispenser, Cardinal Cherry Syrup, Gilt Lettering On Base, c.1910, 9 In. 4600.00
Dispenser, Cherri Ben 6325.00
Dispenser, Cherry Smash, Red Glass, Faucet, 1930s 325.00
Dispenser, Cocoa, Copper, Matthew J. Hart & Sons, Birmingham, 1890s, 22 In. 440.00
Dispenser, Dr. Swett's Root Beer, Bottle Form, 22 x 7 In. 1760.00
Dispenser, Dr. Swett's Root Beer, Boy Drinking, Grass Around Bottom, 13 In. 6600.00
Dispenser, Fowler's Cherry Smash, Gold Band, c.1920 .... 2970.00
Dispenser, Hires Root Beer, Drink Hires It Is Pure, Ceramic, c.1920, 14 In. 805.00
Dispenser, Hires Root Beer, Iron & Metal, 20 In. 675.00
Dispenser, Ice Cream Cone, Cone Dispenser Corp., Metal, Glass Dome, c.1937, 33 In. ... 575.00
Dispenser, Jersey Creme Syrup, Red & Green Letters, c.1910, 7 1/2 x 15 1/2 In. 1610.00
Dispenser, Kraft Malted Milk, Aluminum, Cobalt Cameo, Cover, 9 In. 110.00
Dispenser, Monastic Special Scotch Whisky, Ceramic, Monks, c.1900, 13 x 9 In. 770.00
Dispenser, National Dairy Malted Milk, Aluminum, Enamel Logo, Cover 135.00
Dispenser, Orange Crush, Metal Base, Glass Jar, 14 In. 360.00
Dispenser, Rochester Syrup, Barrel On Stump, 12 1/4 x 7 In. 357.00
Dispenser, Selmix, 1940s 253.00
Dispenser, Straw, Hires, Cast Iron, Drink Hires, 1911, 9 3/4 x 5 x 4 1/2 In. 2415.00
Dispenser, Ward's Lemon Crush Syrup, Ceramic Lemon, Floral Base, 13 In. 1380.00
Dispenser, Ward's Orange Crush Syrup, Orange, 14 In. 975.00
Dispenser, World's Liquid Force, Resembling Planet Earth, 1900, 13 x 9 In. 6037.00
Display, Adam Hats, Hat Of The Month, Cardboard, Countertop, 13 x 16 In. 65.00
Display, Adams Pepsin Tutti-Frutti, Oak & Glass, Mirrored Back, 17 1/2 In. 920.00
Display, Baby Ruth, Red & White, Tin Lithograph, Curtiss Candies, Rack, 10 In. 190.00
Display, Black Card Darning Cotton, Wooden, Countertop, 1840, 13 x 7 1/2 x 3 In. 100.00
Display, Buster Brown, Easel Back, Buster & Tige, Electric, Countertop, 18 x 20 In. 285.00
Display, Chesterfield Cigarettes, Martin & Lewis As Sailors, 1950s, 30 x 60 In. 275.00
Display, Falls City Beer, Balloon, Vinyl, 1970s, 24 In. 26.00
Display, Gay Comb, 6 Piece, 1950s, 8 x 10 In. 10.00
Display, Heinz Strained Foods, Wire Rack, Tin Lithograph, Baby Image, 9 x 14 In. 110.00
Display, Hibbarb Spencer, Oak, Sliding Doors, Glass Shelves, 21 x 60 x 64 In. 1210.00
Display, Ivory Soap, Die Cut, Cardboard Lithograph, Angel, Pat. 1879, 11 x 6 In. 1155.00
Display, Johnson's Nuts, Tin, Glass, Porcelain Bins, Warming Light, 24 x 14 x 15 In. 490.00
Display, Just Born Nuts, Tin Framed Glass, Brazils & Almonds, 11 x 7 x 7 In. 195.00
Display, Knickerbocker, Plastic, Cardboard, Box, 1950s, 9 x 12 In. 28.00
Display, Knox Gelatin, 4 Sides, 2 Children Holding Product, Countertop, 16 x 10 In. 760.00
Display, Kryptok Bifocal, Wall Hanging, Reverse Decal On Front, 23 1/2 x 17 In. 230.00
Display, Lighter Flints, Ronson, Cardinal, Red Crown, 1950s 25.00
Display, Mayfair Fruit Drops, Glass Case, Countertop, 7 x 12 In. 77.00
Display, Nestle's Chocolate Blocks, More For Money, Glass, Tin, 10 x 6 1/4 In. 400.00
Display, Old Dutch Cleanser, Cardboard, 25 x 36 In. 55.00
Display, Pop Store, Dog & Sides, Plaster, 7 x 5 1/4 In. 205.00
Display, R. G. Sullivan, Pipe Rack, Wooden Base, 2 Metal Pipe Rests, 9 In. 95.00
Display, Smile Soda, Waffled Bottle, Embossed, July 11, 1922, 1 Gal., 18 In. 575.00
Display, Smith & Son's, Nuts & Candies, Oak, Glass, Mirror Door, 13 x 10 x 24 In. 920.00
Display, Snow King Baking Powder, Santa's Sleigh, Cardboard, Die Cut, 17 x 29 In. 825.00
Display, Squirt, Bottle, Cardboard, Die Cut, 1960s, 8 x 17 In. 14.00
Display, Sunbeam Bread, Little Girl With Bread, Cardboard, Die Cut, 1950s, 22 x 11 In. 850.00
Display, U.S. Nut Co., Nut House, Wood, 2 Embossed Jar, Lids, Scoop, 18 x 14 x 9 In. ... 1440.00
Display, U.S. Nut Co., Nut House, Wood, 4 Embossed Jars, Lids, 17 x 24 x 8 In. 2415.00
Display, Whistle, Thirsty? Just Whistle, Cardboard, Die Cut, 1939, 13 x 27 In. 525.00
Display, Zeno Gum, Oak & Glass, Mirror Back, Marquee, 10 x 18 x 8 In. 805.00
Dolls are listed in their own category.
Door Push, 7-Up, Aluminum, 1940s, 3 1/2 x 9 In. 165.00
Door Push, 7-Up, Aluminum, Yellow Ground, Black Lettering, 1940s, 8 1/2 x 8 3/4 In. .. 165.00
Door Push, Bireley's, 1940, 9 1/2 In. 150.00
Door Push, Crescent Flour, Tin Lithograph, 9 3/4 In. 330.00
Door Push, Dr. Caldwell's Syrup Pepsin Laxative, Porcelain, 3 3/4 x 6 1/2 In. 300.00
Door Push, Dukes Mixture, Porcelain, 1930s, 3 3/4 x 6 1/2 In. 220.00
Door Push, Golden Bridge Root Beer, Embossed Tin, 11 3/4 x 3 3/4 In. 95.00
Door Push, Hires Root Beer, Tin, 1940s-1950s, 3 3/4 x 14 In. 110.00
Door Push, Hires, Bottle Cap Graphic, 4 x 29 1/2 In. 55.00
Door Push, King Cole Tea & Coffee, 31 1/2 In. 190.00

Door Push, Nachtegall & Veit Bar Room Fixtures, 10 In. 165.00
Door Push, Orange Crush, Porcelain, 1930s-1940s, 3 1/2 x 9 1/2 In. 415.00
Door Push, Ox-Heart Brand Dutch Process Cocoa, Porcelain, 6 1/2 x 4 In. 580.00
Door Push, Sunbeam Bread, Batter Whipped, Girl, Steel, 26 1/2 x 8 3/4 In. 247.00
Doorknob, Ballantine Beer, Bakelite, Enamel Insert Logo, Newark, N.J., 1940s 30.00
Doorknob, Cadillac Emblem, Enamel, Brass Lockset, 1920s, 12 In. 225.00
Dress, Paper, Campbell's Soup, Sleeveless, A-Line, Labels, Red, White, Black, 1960s 460.00
Emery Board, Nail File, Spenger Beer, 1930s, 5 In. 9.00
Envelope, Gamewell Fire Alarms, Postmark 1895 .... 60.00
Envelope, Ithaca Guns, Picture Of Rifle, 1906 Postmark 235.00
Envelope, Underwriters Fire Extinguisher, 1902 Postmark 50.00
Fans are listed in their own category.
Figure, Big Bill Best Bitters, Portly Man, Plaster, 1910, 15 1/4 In. 1650.00
Figure, Big Boy, Bobbing Head, 1950s, 7 1/2 In. 250.00
Figure, Chameleon, Sherwin Williams Paint & Varnish Makers, Cast Iron, 8 1/4 In. 250.00
Figure, Chief Watta Pop, Plaster Indian, Suckers Headdress, Countertop, 9 x 8 In. 952.00
Figure, Dutchboy Paint, Composition & Wood, Blue Hat, White Shirt, 25 In. 220.00
Figure, Falstaff Beer, 3-D, Chalk, 1940s, 10 x 17 In. 215.00
Figure, Pfeiffers, Chalk, 1940s, 7 1/2 In. 12.00
Figure, RCA Victor, Nipper, 1920, 36 In. 1500.00
Figure, RCA Victor, Nipper, Chalkware, 1950s, 14 In. 100.00
Figure, Toucan, Guinness Stout, Wiltshaw & Robinson, 1930s, 22 1/2 In. 1345.00
Figure, Wooden Shoe Beer, Chalk, 1950s, 2 x 6 In. 37.00
Foam Scraper, Berghoff Beer, Celluloid, 2 Sides, Curved, 1930s 50.00
Foam Scraper, Hupfel's Beer & Ale, 2 Sides, 1930s 113.00
Foam Scraper, Valley Forge, Rams, 2 Sides, 1940s 25.00
Foam Scraper Holder, Pabst, The Original Is Here, Bottle, 4 Patrons, Metal, 11 In. 45.00
Foam Scraper Holder, Schmidt's Of Philadelphia, Bartender, Metal, 13 In. 60.00
Furnace, Stanco, Carrying Case, Salesman's Sample, 13 In. 385.00
Game, Dominos, Warner's Safe Yeast, Warner's Safe Remedies, Wooden Box, 28 Piece .. 270.00
Glass, Braumeister Fine Beer, Red & Blue Print, 1950s, 5 1/2 In. 4.00
Glass, Brewery's Own Bottle, Gold Rim, Frosted 45.00
Glass, Bromo Seltzer, Dark Blue, 5 In. 35.00
Glass, Carnation Malted Milk, Milk Glass, Tin Cover, 8 In. 270.00
Glass, Chief Oshkosh Beer, Red & White Logo, 1950s, 5 1/2 In. 4.00
Glass, Dr Pepper, 2-Color Applied Logo, White Ground, 1960s, 9 1/2 In. 90.00
Glass, Dubois Budweiser, Red Print, 1930s, 3 3/4 In. 29.00
Glass, Eulberg Brothers, Etched, 1890s, 3 1/2 In. 398.00
Glass, Gamble's 20 Years Of Progress, 1 Oz. To 1 Cup Measure On Back, 4 3/4 In. 10.00
Glass, Gunther Beer, Red Print, 1960s, 6 3/8 In. 3.00
Glass, Holihan's Ale & Beer, Red, Blue Print, 1950s, 4 1/2 In. 4.00
Glass, Klee KO, Red Logo, 1950s, 5 In. 7.00
Glass, Maritime Association Of The Port Of New York, Schooner, 4 In., 4 Piece 20.00
Glass, Miller High Life, Red Print, 1950s, 4 1/4 In. 4.00
Glass, Narragansett, 1960s, 5 1/2 In. 4.00
Glass, National Bohemian Beer, Orange & Black Print, 1960s, 5 3/4 In. 4.00
Glass, National Bohemian Beer, Red Print, 1950s, 4 1/2 In. 13.00
Glass, Oklahoma Vinegar Co., Fort Smith, Ark., Frosted, Fluted Base, 5 1/4 In. 35.00
Glass, Old German Lager, Independent Brewing Co., Seattle, Keg Shape, Frosted 45.00
Glass, Old Reading Beer, Red, Black, Yellow Logo, 1930s, 7 3/4 In. 165.00
Glass, Pennsylvania Railroad, Tumbler, Engine No. 4902 & Passenger Cars, 4 1/4 In. 25.00
Glass, Rainier, Etched Graphics, 1890s, 3 1/2 In. 175.00
Glass, Van Merritt, Blue Print, 1930s, 8 In. 20.00
Glove Case, Red Rider Playmate, Picture Cover, Salesman's Sample 475.00
Golf Ball, Rolling Rock Beer 7.00
Gum Wrapper, Pulver's Yellow Kid Chewing Gum, Yellow, Black, 1 x 2 3/4 In. 175.00
Handkerchief, Goldilocks & 3 Bears, Kellogg's Cereal Premium, 1930s, 7 x 13 In. 175.00
Hat, Fedora, Stetson, Box, Miniature 25.00
Hat, Paper, McDonald's, Employee's, Red & Yellow, 1950s 70.00
Hat Box, Pan-American Airlines, 22 Piece, Cardboard, 11 1/2 x 14 x 6 3/4 In. 195.00
Hook, Glove, Wilbur's Cocoa, Celluloid & Metal, 2 1/2 In. 55.00
Hot Pad, Butter-Nut Bread, Hartford Bakery Premium, 6 x 6 In. 10.50
Humidor, Bagdad Tobacco, Ceramic, 5 x 6 1/2 In. 130.00

Humidor, Best Virginia Tobacco, Stoneware, Indian Maiden, 6 In. 66.00
Humidor, Cigar, Cremo, The World's Best Cigar, 16 1/2 x 28 x 18 1/2 In. 316.00
Ice Chest, Narragansett Spring Ginger Ale, Backsplash 400.00
Jar, Blue Accent, C.D. Brooks, Boston, 1870, 9 In. 110.00
Jar, Curtiss Chicos Spanish Peanuts, 5 Cents, Glass, Tin Lid & Band, 12 In. 468.00
Jar, Hale's Leader Coffee, Glass, Fox Hunt Graphics, Screw-On Lid, 1 Lb. 32.50
Jar, National Beer, Glass, Red Print, 1960s, 1/2 Gal. 25.00
Jar, Soda Mint Gum, For Your Stomach's Sake, Glass, Pedestal Base, 14 In. 1553.00
Jar, Syrup, Johnson's Cold Fudge, Chrome Pourable Lid, c.1950, 8 1/2 In. 50.00
Jigsaw Puzzle, Razor, Keen Kutter 15.00
Jigsaw Puzzle, White Sewing Machine, Woman, Bicycle, Machine, c.1910, 10 x 16 In. . . . 235.00
Jug, Heinz Vinegar, Brown Cover, 1906, 7 1/2 x 4 1/2 In., 1 Qt. 57.00
Kaleidoscope, Campbell's Vegetable Soup, Shaped Like Soup Can, Steven, 1981, 5 In. . . . 60.00
Key Fob, Duquesne, Good Luck Penny, Plated, 1940s 4.00
Kick Plate, Dr Pepper, 1970s 44.00
Kick Plate, Simbea, White Enriched Bread, On Silver Tray, 1961 . . . . 358.00
Kit, First Aid, Standard Oil Company, California, Wall Mount, Contents, 12 In. 33.00
Label, Beer, Haehnle's Temperance, Early Prohibition 22.00
Label, Beer, K & S Special Bock Brew, Prohibition 17.00
Label, Beer, Pabst Hofbrau, Pre-Prohibition, N.Y. 94.00
Label, Beer, Tivoli Brewing Co., Denver, 1950s, 3 x 3 3/4 In. 3.00
Label, Cigar, Abraham Lincoln, Outer 70.00
Label, Cigar, Admiral Fairfax, Picture, Salesman Sample 180.00
Label, Cigar, Beauty Belle, Salesman Sample 65.00
Label, Cigar, Bombay, English & Indian Soldiers, Inner 130.00
Label, Cigar, Capt. Howard, Cohn Bros., Proof 35.00
Label, Cigar, Clara Belle, Salesman Sample 60.00
Label, Cigar, Cornelius, Outer 100.00
Label, Cigar, Daniel Defoe, Picture, Inner 450.00
Label, Cigar, Duke Of Malta, Outer 45.00
Label, Cigar, Four Graces, 4 Women Picture, Salesman Picture, 1899 . . . . 55.00
Label, Cigar, Fox Terrier, Dog Picture, Inner 150.00
Label, Cigar, Gold Bug, Large Bug Picture, Salesman Sample 150.00
Label, Cigar, Golden Fruit, Proof 30.00
Label, Cigar, Grandmother, Outer 180.00
Label, Cigar, Indiana Moose, Proof 170.00
Label, Cigar, Lion Head, Silver, Outer 40.00
Label, Cigar, Pride Of Havana, Sun Lithograph, Toronto, Proof 45.00
Label, Cigar, Tuscarora Club, F. Fletcher, Ottawa, Proof 300.00
Label, Citrus, Blue Lake, Topless Indian Maid, Winter Haven 75.00
Label, Citrus, Blue Tip, Winter Garden 40.00
Label, Citrus, Clark's Select, Indian River City 25.00
Label, Citrus, Dixie Delight, Weirsdale 15.00
Label, Citrus, Four Star, Arcadia 50.00
Label, Citrus, Intrinsic, Deleson Springs 25.00
Label, Citrus, Lake Caloosa, Babson Park 100.00
Label, Citrus, Maple Leaf, Oviedo 10.00
Label, Citrus, Wabasso, Indian 125.00
Label, Food, Banner Mill Beans, Country Valley View 7.00
Label, Food, Butterfly Brand Wax Beans 7.00
Label, Food, Cobcut, Hand Cutting Corn From Ear, 1930 . . . . 10.00
Label, Food, Defender Brand Tomatoes, Sailing Ship On Ocean 5.00
Label, Food, Dellford White Potatoes, Young Boy With Basket Of Food 1.00
Label, Food, Dixie Land Watermelon, Black Man's Head, 1930s, 4 1/2 x 7 1/2 In. 6.00
Label, Food, Edmondson's Favorite Blackberries, Boy Picking Berries, Owl 20.00
Label, Food, Forest City Lima Beans, Beans In Pod 2.00
Label, Food, Jack Sprat Chili Con Carne, Man Dressed In Green Bowl Of Chili 25.00
Label, Food, Monarch Chicken Soup, Lion Head, 1922 . . . . 25.00
Label, Food, Okeanos Marrow Peas, Seahorse, Cupid Standing On Shell 15.00
Label, Food, Osseo Early Peas, 2 Prospectors, Knight On Horse 25.00
Label, Food, Oysters, Casserole, Bowl Of Oysters In Cream 5.00
Label, Food, Pee-Wee Beans, Shows Elves Working On Billboard, 4 1/2 In. 5.00
Label, Food, Peter Pan Sugar Peas, Peter Playing Flute 15.00

Label, Food, Purdue Creamery Gouda Cheese, 6 In. 30.00
Label, Food, Rose Bowl Apricots, Football Players 35.00
Label, Food, Syrup Can, Black Mammy Picture, 1930 . . . .   3.00
Label, Ginger Ale, Caddy, Prohibition Label, Neck 33.00
Label, Hotel, Alcazar, Miami, Fla., Hotel Picture, 1930s, 3 1/2 x 4 1/2 In. 17.00
Label, Hotel, Columbus, Miami's Finest Bayfront Hotel, Unused, 4 1/2 x 4 1/2 In. 15.00
Label, Hotel, Westward Ho Hotel, Phoenix, 1930s, 3 1/2 x 4 1/2 In. 35.00
Label, Powder, Vadco Talcum Powder, City Skyscraper, 1923 . . . .   30.00
Label, Travel, Glacier National Park, See America First, Goat, Logo, 1922, 5 In. 26.00
Label, Travel, McKinley Park, Hotel, Mountains, Totems, 1940s, 4 1/2 In. 25.00
Label, Whiskey, Cap'n Jack, Cincinnati Distillers, 1930s, 3 1/2 x 4 1/2 In. 6.00
Label, Whiskey, Old Anvil Brand, Louisville, Ken., 1940s, 3 1/2 x 5 In. 5.00
Lamps are listed in the Lamp category.
Letter Opener, Eastern Machine Screw Corp, H & G, New Haven, Conn., Metal, 9 In. . .   20.00
Letter Opener, Fred B. Rooney, Member Of Congress, Light Blue, Plastic, 7 1/2 In. 4.00
Letter Opener, Harrison Brewster Agency Inc., Bonds Insurance, Chicago, Brass 15.00
Letter Opener, Marseille, Sword Handle, Steel, Engraved, 6 In. 8.50
Letter Opener, Victor J. Evans & Co., Patent Attorney, Washington, DC, Brass 25.00
Letter Opener, Will & Baumer Co., The Candle Manufacturers, N.Y., 7 1/2 In. 25.00
Loving Cup, Purdue Creamery, Brown Swiss Cattle Breeders, Silver Plate, 1935 . . . .   325.00
Lunch Boxes are listed in their own category.
Magazine Page, Swifts Ham, Jack Sprat, Maxfield Parrish, 1921, 7 x 10 1/2 In. 295.00
Mannequin, First Nat'l. Bank, Black Boy, Automated, Eyes Roll, Head Nods, c.1930 . . . .   1005.00
Map, Sgt. Preston Of Yukon, Quaker Cereal, 1955 . . . .   35.00
Mask, Lone Ranger, Cutout From General Mills Cheerios Box, 6 x 10 In. 45.00
Matchbook, Manners Big Boy, Paper, Picture Of Double-Decker Hamburger, 1960 . . . . . .   10.00
Matchbook, Merry Christmas, Happy New Year, 408 Musical Bar, Baltimore, 1940s 25.00
Matchbook, Temple National Bank, 28 Matches, Unstruck, Dallas, Tex., 1970 . . . .   1.00
Memo Pad, Hanging, Lysol, Mammy, Resin Coated Composition, c.1940 . . . .   85.00
Menu Board, Ehret's Extra Beer, 1940s 10.00
Menu Board, Fitzgerald's Beer & Ale, 1930s 13.00
Menu Board, Hershey's Ice Cream, 10 Paper Flavor Inserts, Tin Litho, Embossed 204.00
Menu Board, Hires Root Beer, Embossed Tin, 29 1/4 In. 187.00
Menu Board, Hires, Cardboard, 24 x 12 In. 225.00

Advertising mirrors of all sizes are listed here. Advertising pocket mirrors range in size from 1 1/2 to 5 inches in diameter. Most of these mirrors were given away as advertising promotions and include the name
of the company in the design.

Mirror, A Saving In Furniture, Jacox Bros., Sacramento, Girl, Flood Waters, 3 1/2 In. 200.00
Mirror, Adams Bros., Sepia Portraits, Celluloid, Pocket, Iowa, 2 3/16 In. 44.00
Mirror, Bar-Keeper's Friend, George Wm. Hoffman, Nude Woman At Bar, 2 In. 525.00
Mirror, Bletzacker Furniture, Lancaster, Ohio, Woman Picture, Round, 2 In. 29.00
Mirror, Continental Cubes, Celluloid, Pocket, 2 3/4 In. 143.00
Mirror, Emblem Motorcycle Co., Image Of 2 Motorbikes, 1 1/4 x 2 1/4 In. 685.00
Mirror, Fink's Detroit Special Overalls, Celluloid, 1 3/4 x 2 3/4 In. 385.00
Mirror, Goodlow's Suits & Overcoats, Celluloid, 2 3/4 In. 37.00
Mirror, Green's August Flower, Ague Conqueror, Frame, 1910, 21 1/2 In. 105.00
Mirror, Hamm's Beer, Colors, 1980s17 1/2 x 13 1/2 In. 24.00
Mirror, Hotel Tuller, In The Heart Of Detroit, Building, Celluloid, 3 1/2 In. 275.00
Mirror, Howard Johnson, 31 1/2 x 31 1/2 In. 650.00
Mirror, J.A. Folger & Co., Steam Coffee & Spice Mills, Wooden Frame, 13 x 9 In. 55.00
Mirror, Louisiana Pilsener, Celluloid Face, 1900s, 3 1/2 In. 121.00
Mirror, Lucky Strike, American Tobacco Co., Square, Logo, 1938, 2 x 3 In. 215.00
Mirror, Old Reliable Coffee, Celluloid, 2 In. 93.00
Mirror, Overland Model 38 Double Bucket, Roadster, Celluloid, Sepia, 3 1/2 In. 600.00
Mirror, Paul Diller, Watchmaker & Jeweler, Celluloid Birthstone Type, 2 x 3 In. 25.00
Mirror, Photo Of Uniformed Man, Public Safety Service, Celluloid, 3 In. 25.00
Mirror, Rainbow Gardens, Dancing, Marion, Ohio, Woman, Multicolor, 3 1/2 In. 175.00
Mirror, Sheridan Sugar Factory, Wyoming's First Plant, Buildings, Sack, 3 1/2 In. 285.00
Mirror, Specialty Clothes For Young Men, Pocket, Football Center, 1 3/4 In. 467.00
Mirror, Stoney's Beer, Reverse Glass, 1970s, 12 x 10 In. 8.00
Mirror, Studebaker Vehicle Works, South Bend, Factory, Celluloid, 3 1/2 In. 250.00

Mirror, The Tailor Who Made New York Jealous, Red, White, Yellow, Black, 3 In. 40.00
Mirror, Vogue, Kearney, Neb., Celluloid, 2 3/4 In. 33.00
Mirror, Wilbur's Cocoa, Box Shape, Angel Stirring Cocoa, Celluloid, 1 3/4 In. 440.00
Mirror, With Thermometer, Royal Crown Cola 110.00
Money Clip, Copper, Frontier Hotel, Las Vegas, Oval, Rope Edging, 3/4 x 1 1/2 In. 50.00
Mug, Black Label, Ceramic, 1960s, 5 In. 18.00
Mug, Budman, Ceramic, 20 In. 15.00
Mug, Hires Root Beer, Ceramic, Boy With Bib, Mettlach, 5 In. 300.00
Mug, Lowenbrau, Rebers Motel, Barryville, N.Y., Ceramarte, 1970s, 5 3/4 In. 3.00
Mug, M.K. Goetz Brewing Co., St. Joseph, Mo., Cream, Brown, 1915, 6 In. 176.00
Mug, Schlitz Beer, University Of Iowa, Reunion, 1960s, 16 Oz. 9.00
Napkin Holder, RC Cola, 1940s 385.00
Packet, Seed, Carrots, Alfred Brown, Unopened, 1954 .... 3.50
Pail, American Sunrise Lard, Tin, Indians, Village, 8 x 8 1/2 In. ....148.00 to 480.00
Pail, Blue Plate Strawberry Preserves, Wooden, Handle, Cover 20.00
Pail, Campbell Brand Coffee, Wire Handles, Camels In Desert, 4 Lb. 75.00
Pail, Fast Mail Tobacco, Tin Lithograph, Gold Tone Lid, 5 x 5 1/2 In. 2447.00
Pail, Golden Ear Cookies, 8 1/2 In. 170.00
Pail, Inca Maiden Coffee, Temple Scene On Back, 7 1/2 x 7 1/2 In. 205.00
Pail, Just Suits Cut Plug, Tax Stamp, 5 x 7 3/4 In. 105.00
Pail, Lovell & Covel Candy, 3 Pigs, Handle, 3 x 2 3/4 In. 185.00
Pail, Merry Christmas & A Happy New Year Candy, Children Sledding, Tin, 4 In. 145.00
Pail, Milk, Sears Rivera Coffee, 7 1/4 In. 303.00
Pail, Nash's Coffee, c.1921, 7 1/2 x 8 In. 93.00
Pail, Niggerhair Tobacco, Handle 430.00
Pail, Pallas Peanut Butter, Bail Handle, Lithographed 60.00
Pail, Red Wolf Coffee, Tin Lithograph, Wire Handle, Wolf In Front, 6 Lb. 200.00
Pail, Riley's Rum & Butter Toffee, Children Playing, Handle, England, 4 Lb. 110.00
Pail, Sanders Candy, Wire Bail Handle, Paint Can Shape, 1950s, 5 1/4 x 5 1/2 In. 121.00
Pail, Stone's Peanut Butter, Inset Pry Lid 70.00
Pail, Winner Cut Plug, 5 x 7 1/2 In. 400.00
Pamphlet, Misty Mom, Budget Keeper, Cardboard, Brown & Bigelow, 11 1/2 x 8 In. 110.00
Pamphlet, Pulver Chewing Gum Machine, Yellow Kid, 11 x 14 In. 225.00
Paper Clip Holder, Regal Typewriter Co., Typewriter Shape, 1930, 3 1/2 x 4 In. 125.00
Paper Clip Holder, Royal Typewriter, c.1930, 3 1/2 x 4 1/2 In. 125.00
Pennant, Gilmore Lion Head Motor Oil, 2 Sides, Paper, 10 x 23 3/4 In. 300.00
Pie Plate, Dawes Black Horse Ale, Montreal, Quebec, 1930s, 13 In. 80.00
Pie Plate, Eagle Catasauqua Beer, Eagle Brewing Co., 1930s, 13 In. 135.00
Pie Plate, George Ehret's Extra, New York, N.Y., 1910s, 12 In. 275.00
Pie Plate, Glennon's Beer, Liberty Brewing Co., Pittston, Pa., 1930s, 13 In. 140.00
Pie Plate, St. Louis ABC Beers, American Brewing Co., 1900s, 12 In. 400.00
Pie Plate, Stegmaier Gold Medal Beer, Wilkes-Barre, Pa., 1930s, 13 In. 190.00
Pillow, Dr Pepper, Heart Shape, To Try It Is To Like It, Love, 1960s 30.00
Pin, Blue, Yellow, Celluloid, Big Bull Tractor, Minneapolis, 1 In. 8.00
Pin, Bond Bread, Amelia Earhart, 1 1/4 In. 20.00
Pin, Bond Bread, Mark Airplane, 1 1/4 In. 18.00
Pin, I'm On My Way To Wanamakers, Santa In Plane, 1 1/4 In. 140.00
Pin, Joe Camel, As G. Washington, Camel Party, Bigwig, Multicolor, Celluloid 10.00
Pin, Nabisco, Golden Anniversary, 1898-1948, Celluloid, Boy Picture, 1 1/2 In. 22.00
Pin, Pabst Brewing, Pinback, Ribbon, 1950s, 1 3/4 x 3 In. 8.00
Pin, Shoot Remington UMC Lesmok Cartridges, 22, Bears, Celluloid, 1 1/2 In. 150.00
Pin, Try Black Cat Stove & Shoe Polish, Black, Orange, Yellow, Celluloid, 1 In. 20.00
Pitcher, Maytag 60.00
Pitcher, Quaker Oats, Plastic, Quaker Head, 1950s 12.00
Pitcher & Mugs, Leisy Brewing Co., Desert Oasis, 5 Piece 115.00
Plaque, RCA, Radio Service & Television 160.00
Plate, Western Airlines, 7 1/2 In. 9.00
Pot Scraper, Fairmont Creamery, Tin Litho, Yellow, Black, Red Ground, 2 7/8 x 3 In. ... 305.00
Pot Scraper, Henkel's Flour, Tin Lithograph, Turquoise, Red Trim, 2 7/8 x 3 3/8 In. 240.00
Pot Scraper, Sharples Tubular Cream Separator, Woman, Pail, Cream, Red, 3 x 2 In. 305.00
Pot Scraper, Ward's, Remedies, Extracts, Lithograph, Red, Yellow Trim, 3 x 3 In. 230.00
Printed Cloth, Doll, Ice Skates, American Rice Food & Mfg. Co., 1881 .... 250.00
Rack, R.G. Sullivan's Pipe Display, 2 Pipe Rests 95.00

Ring, Casper, Tin, Post Toasties Corn Flakes, 1949, 2 1/2 In. 35.00
Ruler, Gamble Store, Authorized Dealer, Ed. Lajza, Wooden, 8 In. 5.00
Sack, Flour, Pillsbury, 1960, 3 In. 45.00
Salt & Pepper Shakers are listed in their own category.
Scales are listed in their own category.
Scorekeeper, Hires Root Beer, Soda Jerk, Celluloid 187.00
Shoehorn, Carson Pirie Scott Shoes 8.00
Sign, 7-Up Likes You, Flange, 10 x 12 In. 110.00
Sign, 7-Up, Bottle Shape, Tin, Die Cut, 1962, 13 x 45 In. 99.00
Sign, 7-Up, Fresh Up With 7-Up, Bottle & Hand, Embossed, 1949, 20 x 28 In. 550.00
Sign, 7-Up, Glass With Ice & Straw, 3-Color, Neon, Box, 13 x 28 In. 220.00
Sign, 7-Up, Revolving, Light-Up, 1950s, 14 x 12 In. 495.00
Sign, 7-Up, Tis Uncola Season, Santa Claus & Holly, 2 Sides, String Hanger, 10 In. 39.00
Sign, 7-Up, You Like It, It Likes You, Bottle Center, Dispenser, 1950s, 17 x 6 1/2 In. 468.00
Sign, 7-Up, Your Fresh Up, Kick Plate, Embossed, 1947, 11 x 31 In. 358.00
Sign, A & W Root Beer, Plastic, Wooden Frame, Cutout Barrel, 1960s, 52 x 21 In. 121.00
Sign, Acme Beer, On Tap, Reverse On Glass, Back Lighted, 5 x 13 In. 230.00
Sign, Allen's Worm Syrup, Painted, 68 In. 300.00
Sign, Ansco Photo Supplies, Films, Metal Bracket, 2 Sides, 12 x 19 In. 990.00
Sign, Arbuckles Ground Coffee, Tin, Embossed, 1920s-1930s, 11 x 26 In. 1760.00
Sign, Ask For A Crush, Tin, 3 1/4 x 26 1/2 In. 60.00
Sign, Ask For Wayne Dairy Ice Cream, Porcelain, 2 Sides, 20 x 15 In. 440.00
Sign, Atlantic White Flash, Porcelain, 13 x 17 In. 175.00
Sign, Avalon Cigarettes, Cardboard, Frame, 1930s, 10 1/4 x 15 1/4 In. 44.00
Sign, Ayer's Cathartic Pills, Die Cut, Black Doctor, Child, Frame, 1883, 7 x 12 1/2 In. . . . 865.00
Sign, B-L Tobacco, Porcelain, Square, 15 In. 132.00
Sign, Back Bar, Anheuser-Busch, Clydesdale Wagon, 36 In. 90.00
Sign, Bancroft Tennis Racquets, 9 x 6 In. 440.00
Sign, Barq's Root Beer, Bottle Image, Paper Lithograph, Frame, 12 1/2 x 30 In. 90.00
Sign, Bates, Reed & Cooley, N.Y.C., Building Inside Horseshoe, Cardboard, 10 x 13 In. . . 100.00
Sign, Berghoff, Back Bar, Pink, Neon, Box, 1950s, 8 x 3 1/2 In. 66.00
Sign, Bit-O-Honey Candy, Embossed Tin, Frame, 1930s, 9 x 20 In. 690.00
Sign, Bixby's AA Brown Shoe Color Restorer, Cardboard, Die Cut, Frame, 10 x 33 In. . . . 230.00
Sign, Black Horse, Porcelain, Bilingual, 16 1/2 x 6 In. 525.00
Sign, Blacksmith, Heart Shape Horseshoe In Horseshoe, Iron, 1890s, 23 In. 550.00
Sign, Blaney, Wine Merchants, Metal, England, 22 x 69 In. 285.00
Sign, Blatz Beer, Motion, 1950s, 18 1/2 In. 80.00
Sign, Blue Ribbon Coffee, Silk Screen On Paperboard, 19 x 26 In. 135.00
Sign, Bluff City Special, Metal, Painted, 1930s, 18 x 10 In. 30.00
Sign, Boot Trade, On Stand, White, Black Detail, Old Gilt, 25 1/2 In. 385.00
Sign, Boot, Gold Brown, Cast Zinc, Wrought Iron Bracket, 19th Century, 22 1/2 In. 1380.00
Sign, Boschee's German Syrup, Tin, Train, House Scene, 19th Century, 19 x 13 3/4 In. . . . 1150.00
Sign, Boston Brownies, Gilt, Brown, Carved Wood, 19 x 28 In. 240.00
Sign, Boston's Oceanic Pharmacy, Lighthouse, 46 1/2 In. 1677.00
Sign, Bradford & Co., Lumber & Millwork, St. Joseph, Mich., 3 1/2 x 6 In. 18.00
Sign, Breinig's Pure Linseed Oil, Line Of Hooks For Samples, 2 Sides, 51 In. 412.00
Sign, Brinly Plows, Green & Red, 1920s, 12 x 24 In. 45.00
Sign, Brown's Household Panacea, Canvas, Rolldown, 16 x 10 1/2 In. 1430.00
Sign, Brown's Jumbo Bread, Elephant & Logo, Tin, Die Cut, Frame, 15 x 13 In. 290.00
Sign, Brucks Beer-Ale, Horseshoe Form, 85 Years Of Brewing, 11 1/2 In. 125.00
Sign, Buckeye Mower, Aultman, Miller & Co., Ohio, Cloth, Rolldown, 12 x 19 In. 500.00
Sign, Buffalo Brewing Company, Tin, Self-Framed, 28 x 22 1/2 In. 460.00
Sign, Bull's Eye Beer, Porcelain, 9 1/4 In. 310.00
Sign, Burgermeister Beer, Horse, 1950s, 20 x 16 1/4 In. 30.00
Sign, Buster Brown Shoes, Neon, Eye Blinks Off & On, Frame, 55 x 54 In. 1540.00
Sign, Butter-Nut Bread, Cardboard, Die Cut, Frame, 1920s, 13 x 17 In. 39.00
Sign, Buy Your Duncan Yo-Yo Here, Arrow, Paper, Red & White, 1950s, 17 x 7 1/2 In. . . . 95.00
Sign, C.D. Kenney, Little Girl With Rabbits, Stand-Up, Folding, 18 x 20 In. 135.00
Sign, C.W.S. Soaps, Never Mind Sis, Wheatsheaf Soap Will Put It Right, 23 In. 431.00
Sign, Call Again Cigars, Paper, Frame, 1950s, 9 x 17 In. 40.00
Sign, Call For Philip Morris, Image Of Johnny, Tin, Embossed, 27 x 14 1/2 In. 165.00
Sign, Camel Pack 10 Cent 1 Side, Prince Albert On Reverse, 17 1/2 x 10 1/2 In. 1600.00
Sign, Cardboard, Cremo Ale, 1930s, 11 x 15 3/4 In. 50.00

Sign, Centlivre's Brewing Co., Victorian Couple In Dining Car, Paper Litho, 24 In. 115.00
Sign, Chancellor Cigar, Pretty Woman, Fan, 12 x 6 In. 990.00
Sign, Cherry Smash, George & Martha Washington, White House, Slave, 30 x 35 In. 575.00
Sign, Church & Company, Arm & Hammer Baking Soda, Birds Of America, 25 x 17 In. . . . 88.00
Sign, Cigar, Daniel Spangler, Red Lion, Penn., Wooden, Painted, 14 x 31 In. 805.00
Sign, Cliquot Club Kola, Boy & Bottle Left Side, Tin, 30 x 12 In. 60.00
Sign, Colgate Toothpaste, Tri-Fold, Paper Lithograph, Wooden Frame, 35 x 61 In. 740.00
Sign, Continental Fire Insurance, Revolutionary War Soldier, Porcelain, 12 x 18 In. 2070.00
Sign, Cool Soda 5 Cent Fruit Syrups, Wooden, 19 x 30 x 2 In. . . . . *Illus* 3800.00
Sign, Copenhagen Castle Beer, Tin Over Cardboard, Embossed, 1940s, 9 x 11 In. 35.00
Sign, Cremo Old Stock Ale, Cardboard, Die Cut, 1930s, 11 x 15 1/2 In. 45.00
Sign, Cresthaven Ice Cream, Take Home Enuff, Reverse On Glass, Light-Up, 14 x 4 In. . . . 220.00
Sign, Crown & Pillow Tavern, 20 3/4 In. 4730.90
Sign, Crusader Tobacco, Crusader With Banner, 14 x 8 In. 50.00
Sign, Cunard White Star, Queen Mary Ship, Paper Lithograph, Frame, 21 x 34 In. 248.00
Sign, Dad's Black Cow Root Beer, Die Cut Cardboard, Cow Image, 21 x 33 In. 190.00
Sign, Dad's Root Beer, Bottle Cap Form, 28 x 20 In. 375.00
Sign, Dairy Made Ice Cream, Little Boy With Cone, Tin, 34 x 26 In. 550.00
Sign, De Laval Cream Separators, Farm Scene, Mother & Child, 26 In. 1725.00
Sign, De Laval Cream Separators, Woman, Child, Farm, Tin Lithograph, Round, 23 In. . . . 4400.00
Sign, Devoe Paint, Indian On Ground, Using Product, Metal, 29 x 19 In. 45.00
Sign, Directional, Finger Pointed Right, Texaco Red Star Oil, Tin, 6 3/8 x 28 In. 605.00
Sign, Display, Hershey's Chocolate Soldier, Stand-Up, Cardboard, 1935, 6 In. 75.00
Sign, Dodge & Plymouth Service, Banner At Bottom, Die Cut, 1930s, 48 In. 1760.00
Sign, Dorothy Vernon Perfume, Woman On Bottle, Die Cut Cardboard, 15 x 25 In. 150.00
Sign, Dr Pepper Bottling Company, Triangular, Porcelain, 22 x 14 In., 1940s 330.00
Sign, Dr Pepper, Central Logo, Horizontal, Frame, 1940s, 30 x 48 In. 1210.00
Sign, Dr Pepper, Good For Life, Flange, 2 Sides, Sidewalk, 24 x 36 In. 1045.00
Sign, Dr Pepper, Neon, Box, 21 x 13 In. 145.00
Sign, Dr. Morse's Root Pills, Cardboard, Easel Back, 13 x 24 1/2 In. 168.00
Sign, Dr. Swett's Root Beer, Tin On Cardboard, Red, Blue, Gold, 9 1/4 x 6 1/4 In. 1725.00
Sign, Drink Dr Pepper, Good For Life, Porcelain, Embossed, 10 1/2 x 26 In. 250.00
Sign, Drink Moxie, Factory At Bottom, Cardboard, 39 x 28 In. 120.00
Sign, Drink Pop Kola, White Lettering, 1940s, 10 x 27 In. 135.00
Sign, Drink Triple XXX Root Beer, Curved, Porcelain, 13 1/2 x 17 1/2 In. 240.00
Sign, Drink Wilke's Better Buttermilk, Sample Nicolene Sign No. 6, 11 1/2 x 6 1/2 In. . . . 70.00
Sign, Drug Store, Mortar & Pestle, Sheet Zinc, 36 In. 770.00
Sign, Drug Store, Mortar & Pestle, Wooden, 19th Century, 11 x 7 1/2 In. 375.00
Sign, Drug Store, Raised Letters, Ochre Paint, Blue Asphaltum Ground, 19 x 72 In. 2300.00
Sign, Duke Of York Cigarettes, Tin Lithograph, 16 In. 580.00
Sign, Duxbak, Sheds Water Like A Duck's Back, Tin Over Cardboard, 18 x 15 In. 330.00
Sign, E.H. Smith, Bootmaker, 2 Sides, 19th Century, 39 x 34 In. 1750.00
Sign, Ebbert Wagons, Horse, Wagon, Orchard Scene, Tin, Self-Framed, 37 x 25 In. 3200.00
Sign, Egg-O-See Cereal, Boy Talking To Pet, Paper, Frame, 10 x 16 In. 32.00
Sign, Elliot Protector, Ear Plugs, Blue Ground, Celluloid, 7 1/2 x 9 1/2 In. 85.00
Sign, Emmerlings Beer, Tin, 19 1/2 x 28 In. 400.00
Sign, Enterprise Brewery, Tin, 24 x 17 In. 410.00
Sign, F & S Beer & Ale, Football Players, Flocked Foil, Cardstock, 1940s, 14 x 22 In. . . . 359.00
Sign, F & S Beer & Ale, Ice Skater, Foil, Cardstock, 1940s, 14 x 22 In. 560.00
Sign, Fairy Soap, Girl Blows Bubbles Using Fairy Soap, Lithograph, 1899, 18 x 24 In. . . . 250.00
Sign, Fatima, Turkish Blend Cigarette, Tin Lithograph, 28 5/8 x 18 In. 770.00
Sign, Ferry's Seeds, Woman Watering Her Robust Flowers, Frame, 1915, 27 In. 345.00
Sign, Fine Parker Guns, Gus Peret, World Famous Shot, Cardboard, 13 x 17 In. 500.00
Sign, Flurshutz, Black Man Holding Sign, Tin, Die Cut, 53 x 36 In. 2970.00
Sign, Franconia Inn, New Hampshire, 2 Sides, Green & White, 45 1/4 In. 805.00
Sign, Frank's Choice Cigar, Clock Indicates Closing Hour, Tin, 1887, 6 1/2 In. 210.00
Sign, Frostie Old Fashioned Root Beer, Tin, 1930s, 19 1/2 x 3 In. 80.00
Sign, Gem Overalls, Tin On Cardboard, Gold Lettering, 9 1/4 x 13 1/4 In. 128.00
Sign, Glendora Coffee, Tin, 6 1/2 x 20 In. 200.00
Sign, Gray's Horse Power Threshing Machines, Lithograph, 18 x 23 In. 800.00
Sign, Grayline Bus, Sight Seeing Everywhere, Round, Porcelain, 20 In. 145.00
Sign, Green Wheeler Shoes, Woman With Shoes, Tin On Cardboard, 11 3/4 x 14 In. 660.00
Sign, Grimaud, Cards, Exposition Universelle, Linen, France, 1900-1905, 16 x 24 In. 775.00

Sign, Gulf Diesel, Porcelain, 11 3/8 x 8 5/8 In. 198.00
Sign, Hamm's Beer, Cardboard, Die Cut, 1960s, 10 x 14 In. 9.00
Sign, Hanford's Balsam Of Myrrh, Know Your Horse, Lithograph, 1916, 18 x 22 In. 175.00
Sign, Harmonica, Hanging, Cardboard, Pipe Holes On Bottom, 7 x 24 In. 120.00
Sign, Hartshorn's Sarsaparilla & Iron, Blacksmith With Bottle, Lithograph, 20 x 27 In. . . . 600.00
Sign, Have You Tried W.H. Smith's Lung & Cough Syrup, Cardboard, 11 x 14 In. 45.00
Sign, High Ball Ginger Ale, Crown Cork & Seal, Baltimore, Tin Lithograph, 9 x 9 In. 160.00
Sign, Hires Root Beer, Bottle Shape, Embossed, Painted, 57 In. 385.00
Sign, Hires Root Beer, Bottle Shape, Tin, Die Cut, 1950s, 16 x 57 1/2 In. 315.00
Sign, Hires Root Beer, Celluloid Over Tin, c.1917, 10 x 7 In. 345.00
Sign, Hires Root Beer, Child With Glass, Bottle, Cardboard, String Hanger, c.1910 . . . . . . 2070.00
Sign, Hires Root Beer, Girl About To Take A Drink, Tin, Embossed, 11 x 29 In. 415.00
Sign, Hires Root Beer, It's High Time, Tin, Embossed, Painted, 11 1/2 x 30 In. 55.00
Sign, Hires Root Beer, R-J, Girl Holding Tray, Stand-Up, Cardboard, Die Cut, 11 In. 110.00
Sign, Hood's Ice Cream, Cow, Flange, 2 Sides, 1930s, 19 x 22 In. 3410.00
Sign, Hood's Ice Cream, Tin Lithograph, 28 x 20 In. 200.00
Sign, Horlacker Pilsener, Delivery Van, Paper, Frame, 1940s, 9 x 12 In. 29.00
Sign, Hosters Famous Bottled Beers, Cardboard, 1910s, 13 1/2 x 10 1/2 In. 255.00
Sign, Hy-Quality Coffee, Woman In Swing, Lithograph, Die Cut, 36 1/2 In. 1000.00
Sign, Hyram Sibley & Co. Flower Seeds, Girl With Flowers, Paper, 17 x 24 In. 230.00
Sign, Indian Rifle Gunpowder, Tin Lithograph, c.1890, 3 x 2 1/2 In. 660.00
Sign, Ingersoll Watches, Pocket Watch, Silver, Black, Tin, Late 1800s, 34 x 24 In. 400.00
Sign, Insurance Company Of North America, Porcelain, 18 x 12 In. 200.00
Sign, Ivory Soap, Cardboard, 2 Sides, String Hanger, 11 x 6 In. 1155.00
Sign, J. & P. Coats', Comical Fairy Tale Image, Frame, 1872, 24 x 19 In. 258.00
Sign, Jackson's Best Chewing Tobacco, Black Boy, Paper, 15 1/4 x 18 1/4 In. 320.00
Sign, John Deere, Stag Pulling Buckboard, Frame, 23 1/2 x 31 1/2 In. 1770.00
Sign, John Hohenadel, Brewer & Bottler, Phila., Colonial Scene, Lithograph, 14 x 19 In. . 300.00
Sign, Kantorowicz, Bitters Bottle Picture, Gold, Back Tab, Oval, 11 3/4 In. 85.00
Sign, Kellogg's Coffee, Tin Lithograph, Key Wind, 1 Lb. 30.00
Sign, Kellogg's Corn Flakes, Camp Fire Girl Fixing Bowl, 1920s, 28 x 23 In. 800.00
Sign, Kis-Me Gum, Vixen, The Popular Favorite, Tin, 13 3/4 x 16 3/4 In. 1725.00
Sign, Kist Beverages, She's Happy Drinking A Bottle Of Kist, 18 1/2 x 13 In. 275.00
Sign, Klondike-Cough Nuggets, 5 Cents, Cowgirl, Red Ground, Matted, Frame, 8 x 11 In. 500.00
Sign, Knox's Gelatin, Child Decorating Dessert, 1901, 25 x 17 In. 460.00
Sign, Korbel Champagne, Young Woman Holding Cluster Of Grapes, Tin, 19 In. 189.00
Sign, Ladies' Home Journal Patterns, Porcelain Flange, 2 Sides, 7 1/2 x 18 In. 385.00
Sign, Leinenkugel's Chippewa Pride, Tin, Curved Corner, 1910s, 20 1/2 x 17 In. 145.00
Sign, Leonard Eppig Brewery, Factory Scene, Horse & Wagons, Paper, 27 1 2 x 17 In. . . . 1035.00
Sign, Lipfert, Scales & Co., Red Meat, Cardboard, Hanger, 11 x 17 1/4 In. 300.00
Sign, Love Nest Candy Bar, Best Eating Candy Bar In World, 1930s, 10 x 28 In. 300.00
Sign, Lowell Fertilizer Co., Wagon, Woman, Chickens, Cardboard Lithograph, 11 x 14 In. 200.00
Sign, Lucky Strike Tobacco, Tin Lithograph, Die Cut, 2 Sides, Pipe Shape, 19 In. 2420.00
Sign, Lyon's Kathairon For Hair, Woman, Reverse Painted, Frame, 22 x 18 In. 825.00
Sign, Madison Cigar, Indian Maiden, Paper, 1906, 30 x 15 In. 1320.00
Sign, Maxine Shoes, Tin Lithograph, Die Cut, Easel Back, 13 1/4 x 19 1/2 In. 308.00
Sign, Mayo's Plug, Light & Dark, Linen, 30 x 27 3/4 In. 770.00

Advertising, Sign,
Cool Soda 5 Cent
Fruit Syrups,
Wooden,
19 x 30 x 2 In.

Advertising, Sign,
Pioneer Of
All-Tobacco
Cigarettes,
Lithograph, Frame

Sign, Meerschaum Pipe, Tin, 19 x 16 In. 345.00
Sign, Merita Bread, Lone Ranger At Full Gallop, Tin, Self-Framed, 35 3/4 x 23 3/4 In. . . . 1650.00
Sign, Midsummer Meet, Readville, Trotting Horses, Dunley, 1905, 19 x 25 In. 500.00
Sign, Minnesota Chief Thresher, Hail To The Chief, 1876, 13 x 19 In. 175.00
Sign, Moir's Chocolates, Porcelain, Curved Corner, Wooden Bracket, 6 1/2 x 30 In. 800.00
Sign, Morning Sip Coffee, Paper, Yellow & White, Red Ground, 1920s, 11 1/2 x 21 In. . . . 150.00
Sign, Moxie, Wake Up, Cardboard, Frame, Under Glass, 1910-1915, 22 x 37 In. 1430.00
Sign, Nabisco, Christmas, Santa Holding Products, Paper, 1940s, 17 x 25 1/2 In. 187.00
Sign, Napoleon Flour, Portrait, Napoleon Bonaparte, Paper, Metal Strips, 18 x 35 In. 561.00
Sign, National Music String Co., Spanish Lovers, Lithograph, 1911, 10 x 15 In. 60.00
Sign, Navajo Truck Lines, Indian, Blue Eyes, Porcelain, 17 x 23 1/2 In. 745.00
Sign, Nesbitt's Orange Soda, Metal, Weigard Mfg. Co., St. Louis, 17 1/2 x 22 1/2 In. 75.00
Sign, Nesbitt's, Embossed Bottle, Tin, 1938, 11 x 27 1/4 In. 20.00
Sign, Neuweiler Cream Ale, 1930s, 17 1/2 x 13 1/2 In. 249.00
Sign, New Perfection Stove, Woman Near Stove, Cardboard, Die Cut, 27 x 19 In. 495.00
Sign, New York Champion, Patten, Stafford & Myer, Horse & Rake, Textile, 21 x 29 In. . . 375.00
Sign, Night Storage, Painted Wood, Black Letters, Mustard Ground, 25 3/4 In. 295.00
Sign, North Danvers & Salem Coach, Frame, Picture Of Coach, 1849, 10 x 12 In. 400.00
Sign, NuGrape, Embossed, Die Cut, 17 x 5 In. 475.00
Sign, O.L. Schwencke, Cigar Box Labels, Lithograph, 1870s, 17 x 22 In. 300.00
Sign, Oceanick Pharmacy, Lighthouse, Boston, Mass., Porcelain, 34 x 46 1/2 In. 1170.00
Sign, OFC Whiskey, Cardboard Lithograph, Stecher Litho Co., 15 x 26 In. 220.00
Sign, Ogbaurn, Hill & Co., Indian Maiden Paddling A Canoe, 21 x 17 3/4 In. 175.00
Sign, Oh Boy Gum, Boy Holding 4 Packs Of Candy, Frame, 1930s, 16 x 7 1/2 In. 690.00
Sign, Old Dutch Beer, Tin Over Cardboard, 1950s, 13 x 9 In. 55.00
Sign, Old Overholt Rye Whiskey, Lithograph On Canvas, Gilt Frame, 30 x 19 In. 585.00
Sign, Old Reliable Coffee, Classic Gentleman, Tin Lithograph, 9 1/4 x 6 1/4 In. 235.00
Sign, Old Reliable Coffee, Man Smoking Cigar, Self-Framed, c.1910, 6 1/2 x 9 In. 350.00
Sign, Old Reliable Coffee, Trolley Car, Welcome As April Showers, 11 x 21 In. 225.00
Sign, Old Woolen Mills Pants, Flirting Woman Lifting Skirt, Tin, 1906, 13 x 19 In. 1150.00
Sign, Omar Cigarettes, Gentlemen Enjoying A Smoke, Cardboard, Frame, 25 In. 275.00
Sign, Optometrist, Polychrome, Cast Iron, Zinc, 2 Sides, 11 1/2 x 26 In. 4315.00
Sign, Orange Crush Soda, There's Only One, Tin, Painted, 2 Sides, 13 1/2 x 18 In. 300.00
Sign, Orange Crush, Bottle On Left, Horizontal, 1940s, 7 x 17 In. 300.00
Sign, Orange Crush, Reverse Painted Mirror, Logo, Frame, 9 1/8 x 11 1/8 In. 275.00
Sign, Orange Crush, Schoolgirl, 3-D Hand Holding Bottle, Die Cut, 1930s, 18 x 20 In. . . . 500.00
Sign, P.F. Brown & Co., Dairy, Yellow Pine, Black Paint, Gilt, 1850s, 27 1/2 x 22 In. 275.00
Sign, Pabst Ale, Glass, Reverse, 1940s, 14 x 8 3/4 In. 230.00
Sign, Pages Ice Cream, Old-Fashioned Santa, Cardboard, Embossed, Die Cut, 5 x 9 In. . . . 475.00
Sign, Papa's Best, Cigar Shape, Wooden, Painted, Red On Brown, 1880s, 37 In. 405.00
Sign, Park Brewing, Pheasant, Mallard, Park Malt Extract, 1910, 24 In. 825.00
Sign, Penn-Drake Motor Oil, Logo, Tin, Embossed, 27 7/8 x 9 11/16 In. 210.00
Sign, Pennsylvania Fire Insurance Co., Quaker & Shield, Porcelain, 20 x 14 In. 460.00
Sign, Pennzoil, Bonded For $1000, 2 Sides, Chain Hung, 13 5/8 x 10 1/2 In. 230.00
Sign, Perkiomen Valley Fire Insurance, Enamel, Painted, 2 Sides, 14 x 20 In. 260.00
Sign, Peugeot, Lion Logo, Plastic & Aluminum, 10 1/2 x 37 1/2 In. 45.00
Sign, Pexwear Clothing, Pharmacist Holds Container, Die Cut, Easel, 17 x 40 In. 65.00
Sign, Pilsener Brewing, Cleveland, Ohio, P.O.C., Plastic, 1950s, 11 1/2 In. 175.00
Sign, Pioneer Of All-Tobacco Cigarettes, Lithograph, Frame . . . . *Illus* 2420.00
Sign, Piper Heidsieck Chewing Tobacco, Cardboard & Paper, 17 x 17 In. 275.00
Sign, Popsicle 5 Cents, Frozen Drink On A Stick, Cardboard, 1932, 9 3/4 x 12 In. 175.00
Sign, Popsicle, Paper, 1950s, 13 1/4 x 5 1/4 In. 20.00
Sign, Prince Albert, Chief Joseph, Nez Pierce, Tin Lithograph, Frame, 28 x 22 In. 3745.00
Sign, Prince Albert, Gentleman Smoking Pipe, Tin Lithograph, Dish Style, 24 In. 360.00
Sign, Razors Ground, Folding Straight Razor, Black, Gray, 1800s, 14 1/2 x 31 In. 865.00
Sign, Red Goose Shoes, Porcelain, Mounted To Wooden Box, Handle, Neon, 37 In. 440.00
Sign, Red Man Tobacco, Indian Chief, Headdress, Paper Lithograph, 30 x 44 In. 385.00
Sign, Rheingold Beer, Wood, Composition, Paper Logo, 1950s, 12 x 15 In. 30.00
Sign, Rheumatism Plaster Of Absalon Patenaude, Watercolor, Frame, 19 x 25 In. 1250.00
Sign, Rialto Farm Tavern, Tavern, Tin, Painted, 12 x 39 In. 165.00
Sign, Rib Mountain Lager, Paper, 1940s, 15 1/4 x 8 1/4 In. 25.00
Sign, Rochelle Club Beverages, Cardboard, Frame, 19 x 23 In. 40.00
Sign, Rockford Watch, Wife & Daughter Meeting Father At Train, 15 x 21 In. 1035.00

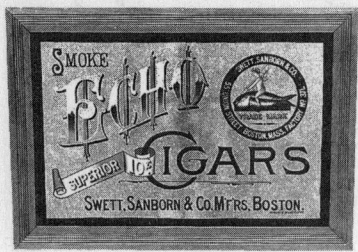

Advertising, Sign, Smoke Echo Cigars, Swett,
Sanborn, Reverse On Glass, 16 x 24 In.

Fray Check, a product found in sewing supply shops, is useful for repairing tears in cardboard signs.

You can remove stickers from most things by spraying them with a lubricant.

Sign, Royal Crown Cola, Figural Bottle, Tin, Die Cut, 1951, 58 1/2 x 16 In. 288.00
Sign, Roza De Luzon Cigars, Battle Of Chattanooga, Stone Lithograph, 21 x 28 In. 715.00
Sign, Rummy Grapefruit Mixer, Woman In Swimsuit, Cardboard, 19 x 12 In. 100.00
Sign, S & H Green Stamps, Save As You Spend, Enamel, 2 Sides, 20 x 33 1/4 In. 50.00
Sign, Sanford's Inks, Tin Lithograph, 1898, 13 1/2 x 19 1/2 In. 3360.00
Sign, Satin Skin, Cherub Whispering To Lady, Cardboard, Die Cut, c.1911, 18 x 18 In. . . . 485.00
Sign, Schell's Bock Beer, Flat, Frame, 1970s, 12 x 9 1/2 In. 21.00
Sign, Schlitz Beer, Chas. Shonk Lithograph, 13 1/2 x 19 In. 2233.00
Sign, Schmidt & Sons Brewing Co., Cherubs, Woman, Stone Lithograph, 16 x 22 In. 385.00
Sign, Schraft's Chocolates, Victorian Woman, Hanging Tray, Tin, Die Cut, 37 In. 5500.00
Sign, Shamrock Dairy, Elf & Bottle, c.1945, 22 x 66 In. 435.00
Sign, Shamrock Gasoline, Cloud Master Premium, 10 1/2 x 12 1/2 In. 175.00
Sign, Sharples Cream Separator, Milkmaid, Cows, Dog, Cardboard, Hanging, 14 x 21 In. . 250.00
Sign, Sheboygan Mineral Water, Waiters, Indian Chief, 10 1/2 x 14 1/2 In. 800.00
Sign, Silver Spring Brewery, Ltd., Fireman Staring Intently At Beer, 21 In. 70.00
Sign, Sinclair Aircraft, Airplane In Center, Porcelain, Round, 12 In. 22.00
Sign, Singer Sewing Machine, Woman At Machine, Porcelain, Red S, 36 x 24 In. 172.00
Sign, Smith's Overalls, 1930s, 2 1/2 x 7 In. 247.00
Sign, Smoke Echo Cigars, Swett, Sanborn, Reverse On Glass, 16 x 24 In. . . . . *Illus* 4500.00
Sign, Sparrow's Empress Chocolates, Showing Empress Herself, 22 3/4 In. 1035.00
Sign, Spear & Jackson, Saw Shape, 13 x 54 In. 275.00
Sign, Squeeze Orange Soda, Cardboard, Die Cut, Children Playing Baseball, 20 In. 205.00
Sign, Stanley Tools, We Are Specialists, Cardboard, England, 1970s, Countertop 33.00
Sign, Star Brilliant Dyes, The Dye That Dyes Everything, Tin, Embossed, 12 x 17 In. 135.00
Sign, Star Soap, Granddad Cuddling Grandchildren, Frame, 14 x 22 In. 200.00
Sign, Starins's Glen Island Excursions, Woman With Ticket, Lithograph, 14 1/2 x 22 In. . . 375.00
Sign, Statue Of Liberty, Loved By Millions, Jos. Schlitz, 1941, 41 x 31 In. 195.00
Sign, Sun Spot, Bottled Sunshine, Tin, Painted, 2 Sides, 15 1/2 x 17 In. 175.00
Sign, Sun-Drop Cola, Bottle Cap Shape, 33 1/2 In. 485.00
Sign, Sun-Maid Raisins, 2 Little Girls At Breakfast Table, Grandfather, 48 x 33 1/2 In. . . . 172.00
Sign, Sunbeam Bread, Energy Packed, Girl Eating Slice, 1953, 54 x 18 In. 800.00
Sign, Sunbeam Bread, Sliced, Loaf Form, 1950s, 30 x 56 In. 1210.00
Sign, Sunlight Soap, $5000 Challenge, Tin Lithograph, Die Cut, c.1900, 11 x 8 1/2 In. . . . 440.00
Sign, Sunlight Soap, Porcelain, Hand Painted, 36 x 27 In. 290.00
Sign, Sunshine Andy Gump Biscuits, Paper, Window Display, 12 x 11 In. 385.00
Sign, Sunshine Beer, Cardboard, Frame, 1960s, 34 1/4 x 27 1/4 In. 300.00
Sign, Tarrant's Cubebs & Copaiba Comp. Extract, Reverse Painted, 25 x 21 In. 1430.00
Sign, Tea, Spice, Coffee, T-Shape, Yellow, Red Ground, Wheeling, W.Va., 42 x 41 In. 3450.00
Sign, Teem, A Lemon-Lime Drink, Pepsi-Cola Co., Tin, Embossed, 12 x 32 In. 11.00
Sign, Tennent's Lager, Tin, 1930s, 8 x 12 In. 32.00
Sign, Thirsty? Just Whistle, On Ice, Tin, 6 3/4 x 9 3/4 In. 715.00
Sign, Tokio Cigarettes, The New Smoke, Frame, 25 x 33 In. 235.00
Sign, Tom Moore Cigar, Tom Moore In Tuxedo, Tin, Self-Framed, 11 1/2 x 15 1/2 In. 110.00
Sign, Tourist, Wooden, 6 Sides, Light-Up, Green Paint, 41 In. 1250.00
Sign, Uncle John's Syrup, Cardboard, Die Cut, Red & White Suit, 14 x 16 1/2 In. 80.00
Sign, Upper 10, Cardboard, Frame, 1930s, 9 1/2 x 12 In. 22.00
Sign, Utica Club Beer, X-Mas, Printers Proof, 1950s, 17 x 18 In. 40.00

Sign, Valley Forge Beer, Boxers, Vacuum Formed, 1950s, 10 x 12 In. 127.00
Sign, Van Houten's, Little Girl Preparing Her Pure Soluble Cocoa, 29 1/2 In. 345.00
Sign, Vasser Bank, New York, Wooden, 2 Sides, 20 3/4 x 32 3/4 In. 1200.00
Sign, Velvet Tobacco, Fireside Image Of Father & Son, 21 x 27 3/4 In. 400.00
Sign, Vic's Special Beer, Celluloid Over Tin On Cardboard, 11 1/2 x 5 1/4 In. 45.00
Sign, Vincent Portuondo Cigars, Tobacco Farmer, Tin, 9 1/2 x 13 1/2 In. 205.00
Sign, Walk Over Shoes, Man, Large Shoe, Tin, Flange, 2 Sides, 13 1/2 x 19 1/2 In. 1093.00
Sign, Walter's Beer, Cardboard, 1960s, 22 x 9 In. 25.00
Sign, Warner's Safe Yeast Use, Boy, Bread Loaf, Yeast, Self-Framed, 10 1/2 x 19 In. 475.00
Sign, Wedding Bouquet Cigar, Puritan Wedding Scene, Tin Lithograph, 27 1/2 In. 525.00
Sign, Weed Chains, Tin Lithograph Over Wood, Hanging, 23 2/4 x 17 1/4 In. 1540.00
Sign, Whistle Soda, 4 Elves, Tin, Embossed, 1946, 32 x 57 In. 745.00
Sign, Whistle Soda, Bottle Image, Cardboard, Frame, 9 x 31 In. 155.00
Sign, Whistle Soda, Tin, Embossed, 1930s, 14 x 20 In. 415.00
Sign, White Label Cigars, Tin, Embossed, Suspension Chain, 10 x 13 1/2 In. 290.00
Sign, White Pheasant Wine, Bottle On Table, Tin On Cardboard, 17 x 13 1/2 In. 120.00
Sign, Whitely Harvesting Machines, Paper Lithograph, 2 Sides, 14 x 28 In. 600.00
Sign, Wilson & McCallay Tobacco, Happy Thought, Paper Lithograph, 30 x 41 In. 1155.00
Sign, Winchester Arms & Ammunition, Rifle Shape, 41 1/4 In. 500.00
Sign, Wine Cooler, Bartles & James, Stand-Up, 6 Ft. 50.00
Sign, Wine French Coca, 5 Cents, Lithograph, 3 Colors, 1920, 28 x 20 In. 4125.00
Sign, Wings Cigarettes, Paper, Frame, 1950s, 25 x 15 In. 46.00
Sign, Winner Plug Tobacco, Jockeys On Horseback, 10 1/2 In. 65.00
Sign, Wright & Taylor Distillers, Louisville, Factory, Tin, Wooden Frame, 28 x 38 In. 2200.00
Sign, Wrigley's Chewing Gum, Paper Board, Steel Pedestal Frame, 2 Sides, 18 In. 80.00
Sign, Wrigley's Gum, Various Flavors, Tin Lithograph, Paper Board Back, 7 x 11 In. 440.00
Sign, Wrigley's Gum, White & Yellow Letters, Green Ground, 14 x 36 In. 920.00
Sign, Wrigley's, Spearmint & Doublemint Gum, Porcelain, 14 x 36 In. 2090.00
Sign, Yuengling Brewing, Wooden Frame, Reproduction, 22 1/2 x 18 3/4 In. 22.00
Soap, P&G, The White Naptha Soap, Proctor & Gamble 10.00
Tap Knob, Beverwyck Irish Brand Cream Ale, Bakelite, Enamel Insert, 1940s 52.00
Tap Knob, Chief Oshkosh Beer, Polyester, Enamel Insert, 1940s 45.00
Tap Knob, Cold Spring Export Beer, Plastic, Enamel Insert, 2 Sides, 1930s 130.00
Tap Knob, Dutch Club Beer, Chrome, Enamel Insert 99.00
Tap Knob, Evans Ale, Bakelite, Enamel Insert, 1930s 358.00
Tap Knob, Hamm's Beer, Chrome, Enamel Insert, 1950s 139.00
Tap Knob, India Pale Ale, Bakelite, Painted Metal Insert, 1930s 108.00
Tap Knob, Old Port Lager, Bakelite, Enamel Insert, 1940s 237.00
Tap Knob, Stroh's Pilsener, Plastic, Enamel Insert, 2 Sides, 1940s 143.00
Tap Knob, Tech Golden Pilsener Beer, Bakelite, Enamel Insert, 1940s 111.00
Tea Strainer, It Pays To Trade At Ashton's Rockford, Embossed Edge 35.00
Thermometers are listed in their own category.

Advertising tin cans or canisters were first used commercially in the
United States in 1819 and were called *tins*. The English language is
sometimes confusing. Today the word *tin* is used by most collectors to
describe many types of containers, including food tins, biscuit boxes,
roly poly tobacco containers, gunpowder cans, talcum powder sprinkle-
top cans, cigarette flat-fifty tins, and more. Beer cans are listed in their
own category. Things made of undecorated tin are listed under
Tinware.

Tin, Abbey Garden Coffee, 1 Lb. . . . . *Illus* 1815.00
Tin, Air Float Talcum, 6 In. 55.00
Tin, Beech-Nut Coffee, Key Opener Attached To Lid, c.1950, 1 Lb. 18.75
Tin, Beeman's Gum, 10 x 7 12 In. 1265.00
Tin, Big Ben, Clock, Roll Cut, Smoking Tobacco, Pocket, 4 x 2 In. 1045.00
Tin, Blanke's Cabin Tea, c.1910, 2 3/4 x 5 In. 120.00
Tin, Bluebird Shape, Biscuit, England, 9 In. 695.00
Tin, Bluhill Coffee, Milk Pail, Wire Bail Handle, Denver, Colo., 5 Lb. 214.50
Tin, Borden's Malted Milk, Cover, 8 1/4 In. 200.00
Tin, Buckingham Cut Plug, Pocket, 4 x 2 In. 77.00
Tin, Bunte Marshmallow, Canister, Blue, Boy In Sailor Suit, 12 1/2 x 9 1/2 In. 220.00
Tin, Buster Brown Cigar, Lithograph, Buster & Dog, Man Blowing Smoke, 5 x 5 In. 4400.00

Tin, Calumet Baking Powder, Red, Paper Label, 5 1/2 x 3 In. 25.00
Tin, Campus Mixture, Leavitt & Pierce, Cambridge, Mass., 4 1/4 x 3 1/4 x 2 1/4 In. 704.00
Tin, Capital Brand Peanuts, Tin, White House Dome, Pry Lid, 10 Lb., 8 x 10 In. 214.50
Tin, Captain Jack's Oyster, Lithograph Of Fisherman & Boy, 7 1/2 x 6 1/2 In. 98.00
Tin, Central Union Tobacco, Girl's Face Profile, Red Ground, 4 x 3 x 1 In. 358.00
Tin, Century Tobacco, P. Lorillard & Co., Jersey City, Red & Black, 1 1/4 x 2 x 3/8 In. 185.00
Tin, Charm Of The West Tobacco, Yellow, Woman, Horse, 2 3/8 x 3 3/4 x 5/8 In. 330.00
Tin, Charmis Talc, Plastic Cap, Contents, Colgate-Palmolive India, 1950s, 4 7/8 In. 55.00
Tin, Chase & Sanborn Coffee, 10 Cent Coupon On Lid, Stamped 93 Cents, c.1955, 1 Lb. .. 9.50
Tin, Chesterfield Cigarettes, Flat, 50s, 6 x 4 In. 25.00
Tin, Chickencock Whiskey, Factory On Back, 7 1/2 x 4 1/4 In. 110.00
Tin, Clock, Tall Case, Biscuit, England, 11 1/2 In. 1400.00
Tin, Colman's Mustard, Yellow, 3 1/8 In. 6.00
Tin, Comfort Talc, Baby Face Lithograph, Nurse On Other Side, c.1890, 3 1/2 x 2 In. 850.00
Tin, Condor Coffee, Key Wind, Lid, 1 Lb. 40.00
Tin, Country Club Coffee, Nashua, N.H., 1 Lb. 264.00
Tin, Dactylis Talc Powder, Colgate Company 55.00
Tin, Dan Patch Salve, Tin Lithograph, c.1909, 2 1/2 In. 38.00
Tin, Deep Sea Brand, Nude Bathing Woman, Oysters, 4 1/4 In. 175.00
Tin, Dixie Salted Peanuts, Black Boy Holding Peanut In Mouth, Pry Lid, 7 3/4 In. 467.00
Tin, Dr. Blumer's Baking Powder, 3 1/2 In. 48.00
Tin, Droste's Cocoa, Train Car Scene, 5 In. 175.00
Tin, Drug-Pak, Condom, Black & White, Lithograph, Nutex Corp, 1 5/8 x 2 x 1/4 In. 410.00
Tin, Duke's Mixture, Best Tobacco, Cowboy With Pistols, Ginna, 18 x 12 x 9 In. 1300.00
Tin, Egyptian Bouquet Talcum Powder, Lithographed, Sphinx Cover, 1920, 6 In. 75.00
Tin, Ensign Perfection Cut Tobacco, 3 Flags, Cream Ground, 4 x 3 x 7/8 In. 990.00
Tin, Fi-Na-St Peanut Butter, 3 x 3 In. 143.00
Tin, Forest & Stream Tobacco, 2 Men, Pocket 400.00
Tin, Forest & Stream Tobacco, Fishermen, Canoe, Red Ground, Canada, 4 x 3 x 7/8 In. .. 468.00
Tin, Fort Pitt Coffee, Lithographed, 4 1/4 x 5 1/2 In. 467.00
Tin, Gallagher's Honeydew Tobacco, Image On Inside Of Lid, 1 1/4 x 6 1/2 In. 198.00
Tin, Garden Of Allah Coffee, Slip Lid 65.00
Tin, Gibson Girl, Vertical Pocket, Germany, 3 3/4 x 3 3/4 x 3/4 In. 250.00
Tin, Glendora Coffee, Inset Lid, Key Wind 38.00
Tin, Golfing Scene, 2 Golfers, McCormick, Biscuit, 10 3/4 x 3 1/4 In. 373.00
Tin, Grand Duchess Coffee, Woman Wearing Tiara, Red Ground, Cream & Blue, 1 Lb. 990.00
Tin, Grand Union Mustard, Sliding Lid, 2 3/4 Oz. 9.50
Tin, H. & P. Waverly, Book, Biscuit 695.00
Tin, Hard A Port Cut Plug, Sailor, Ship's Wheel, Moore & Calvi, 3 1/4 x 3 1/4 In. 200.00
Tin, Heekin's Ginger Spice, Deer, Woman, Dial Dispenser 20.50
Tin, Hemstreet Company Sweet Pea Talcum Powder 145.00
Tin, Hercules Latex Prophylactic Sheaths, 3 x 1 7/8 In. ....*Illus* 935.00
Tin, Hi-Plane Tobacco, One Engine, Pocket, 4 x 2 In. 82.00
Tin, Howe's Vacuum Bass Bait 450.00
Tin, Huntley & Palmers, China Cabinet, Biscuit, c.1911, 7 x 5 3/4 In. 577.00
Tin, Iten Biscuit Co., Animal Cookies, Tin Cover, Bail Handle, 4 1/2 x 3 x 2 1/4 In. 220.00
Tin, Jack Frost Baking Powder, Embossed Lid, Paper Label, 3 x 5 1/2 In. 385.00
Tin, Jacobs Biscuits, Santa Cake, Lithograph, c.1920, 4 In. 35.00

Advertising, Tin,
Abbey Garden
Coffee, 1 Lb.

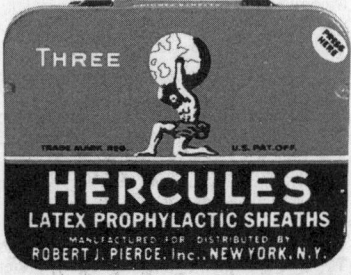

Advertising, Tin,
Hercules Latex
Prophylactic Sheaths,
3 x 1 7/8 In.

Tin, Kelly Confection Co., Peter Rabbit, Peanut Butter, 3 1/2 In. 287.00
Tin, Key West Perfectos Cigar, 25 Count, Round 55.00
Tin, King George Tobacco, Ivory & Red, Shield & Lion Center, 4 x 3 x 1 In. 468.00
Tin, Kohl's Superfine Coffee, Slip Lid, Image Also On Reverse 605.00
Tin, Land O'Lakes Powdered Milk, Indian Maiden Holding Product, c.1940, 4 In. 137.00
Tin, Lecroy Cinnamon Spice, Red, Green, White, Sliding Lid, Camden, New Jersey 8.50
Tin, Louisiana Perique, Genuine, Allen & Ginter, 1 3/4 x 3 1/2 In. 82.00
Tin, Lucky Tiger Dandruff, Factory On Back, 1 Qt. 44.00
Tin, Lucky Tiger Dandruff, Lady Hugging Tiger, 10 1/2 x 6 1/4 In. 132.00
Tin, Luzianne Coffee, Black Woman Holding Coffeepot, 1928, 3 Lb. 110.00
Tin, Mammy Salted Peanuts, 8 x 9 3/4 In. 784.00
Tin, Manhattan Coffee, Key Wind, Lid, 1 Lb. 33.00
Tin, Mazawattee Tea, Scenes Of Children Playing, 5 3/4 x 8 1/2 In. 27.00
Tin, Mennen's Sen Yang Toilet Powder, Newark, N.J. . . . . *Illus* 204.00
Tin, Mennen's Toilet Powder, Classic Baby Image, Lithograph, 1906, 4 1/2 In. 110.00
Tin, Merry Christmas From Santa, Old Lady In Shoe On Lid, Candy, 2 3/4 x 4 1/2 In. . . . 302.00
Tin, Mohican Spice, 2 Oz. 66.00
Tin, Monadnock Coffee, Screw Lid, Keene, N.H., 1 Lb. 220.00
Tin, Monarch Coffee, Key Wind 50.00
Tin, Monarch Toffees, Children At Play All Around, Key Wind, 1928 . . . . 167.00
Tin, Muhammad Ali's Champion Brand, Shoe Polish, Picture, c.1970 . . . . 25.00
Tin, Mulford's Toilet Talcum, Philadelphia, Textured, Lithograph . . . . *Illus* 127.00
Tin, Murdoch's Tropical Spice, Paper Label, 2 Oz. 33.00
Tin, Musgo Baking Powder, 4 3/4 In. 145.00
Tin, Nabor Baking Powder, Canada, 8 3/4 In. 55.00
Tin, North Star Tobacco, Woman, Cherubs, Clouds, Yellow, Brown, 2 x 4 x 5/8 In. 358.00
Tin, Nustaci's Pointer Brand Coffee, Key Wind 50.00
Tin, Old Black Joe, Grease, Bail Handle, 7 9/16 In., 5 Lb. 110.00
Tin, Old Dutch Coffee, Windmill Graphics, Key Wind, Lid 35.00
Tin, Old Glory Tobacco, Spaulding & Merrick, Eagle, Red & Black, 2 x 4 x 5/8 In. 355.00
Tin, Old Virginia Cheroots Cigar, Slant Lid, Late 1800s, 12 x 18 x 14 In. 448.00
Tin, Page Baby Talc, 4 1/2 In. 660.00
Tin, Palmy Days Tobacco, Green Ground, Red On Cream Triangle, 4 x 3 x 7/8 In. 525.00
Tin, Panter Senoritas, European Cigars, Lithograph, 1930s, 4 3/4 In. 25.00
Tin, Parke's Newport Coffee, Pry Lid, Factory Scene, 6 x 4 1/4 In. 143.00
Tin, Paul Jones Tobacco, Naval Hero, Sea Battle, Blue Ground, 4 x 3 x 7/8 In. 3190.00
Tin, Pony Brand Marshmallow, Ponies & Canadian Flags Around Sides, 12 In. 95.00
Tin, Post Office Tobacco, Denver Colorado Post Office Building, Somers, 5 x 3 1/2 In. . . . 2420.00
Tin, Postmaster Smokers Cigar, 5 x 5 1/4 In. 50.00
Tin, Powerlube Lubricant, Grease, 4 1/2 In., 1 Lb. 577.00
Tin, Prexy Tobacco, Graduate, Black & Gold Robe, Red Ground, 4 1/2 x 3 x 7/8 In. 2970.00
Tin, Prince Albert Tobacco, Dome Top, Tax Stamp, c.1909, 8 Oz. 85.00
Tin, Punch Cigar, Graphics Front & Back, 50 Count 60.00
Tin, Qboid Tobacco, Plantation & Plant, Brown To Cream Ground, 4 x 3 x 1 In. 210.00
Tin, Rawleigh's Talcum, 7 1/2 In., 14 Oz 44.00
Tin, Rayo Brand Peanut Butter, 3 x 3 In. 250.00
Tin, Red Jacket Tobacco, Jockey, Horse, Silver Circle, Red Ground, 4 x 3 x 7/8 In. 1100.00
Tin, Rich's Canton Ginger, Lithograph, 3 3/4 x 6 In. 11.00
Tin, Richmond Maid Baking Powder, Handle, 3 3/8 In. 5.00
Tin, Roly Poly, Inspector, Mayo's, Tin Lithograph, 7 x 5 1/4 In. 1595.00
Tin, Roly Poly, Mammy, Mayo's, Tin Lithograph, White & Red, 7 x 5 In 910.00
Tin, Roly Poly, Storekeeper Smoking Pipe, Mayo's Cut Plug, Blue Coat, 2 Pieces, 7 In. . . 375.00
Tin, School Boy Peanut Butter, Bail Handle 155.00
Tin, Sea Gull Baking Powder, 3 1/2 In. 85.00
Tin, Searele's Horse & Cattle Powder, Green, Black Graphics, 3 x 3 x 1 3/4 In. 495.00
Tin, Silver Tex, Condom, White, Silver, Black, Killian Mfg. Co., 1 5/8 x 2 x 1/4 In. 143.00
Tin, Sir Walter Raleigh Tobacco, Pocket, 4 x 2 In. 29.00
Tin, Snow King Baking Powder, Sample, 3 1/4 In. 85.00
Tin, Snow Sprinkles, Color Graphics, B. Heller Co., Chicago, c.1937, 10 Lb., 10 1/4 In. . . 60.00
Tin, Southern Coffee Savanilla, Norton Bros., 7 1/2 x 5 In. 262.00
Tin, Stowman Brothers, Oyster, 7 3/4 x 6 3/4 In. 44.00
Tin, Sunset Trail Cigar, Cowboy, Cowgirl, Riding Horses, Black Ground, 5 x 6 x 4 In. . . . 770.00
Tin, Sweet Girl, Girl Adorning Front, Sand Castle Images, Peanut Butter, 3 1/2 In. 402.00

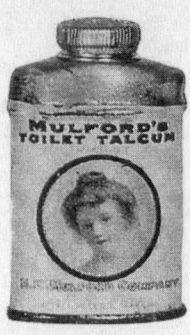

Advertising, Tin, Mennen's
Sen Yang Toilet Powder,
Newark, N.J.

Advertising, Tin, Mulford's
Toilet Talcum, Philadelphia,
Textured, Lithograph

Advertising, Tin, Williams'
Violet Talc Powder,
Glastonbury, Conn.

Tin, Swell Brand Coffee, Key Wind 100.00
Tin, Syke's Comfort Powder, 4 1/2 In. 180.00
Tin, Telfer Coffee Company, Metal, Belle Isle, Ideal Coffee, c.1910 . . . .   400.00
Tin, Tiger Chewing Tobacco, Tiger Pictured On Front, Cylindrical, 12 x 8 1/2 In. 168.00
Tin, Toyland Peanut Butter, Pail, Wire Bail Handle, Continental Can Co., 1 Lb. 335.00
Tin, Trout-Line Smoking Tobacco, Fisherman, Pocket, 3 x 2 In. 720.00
Tin, Trout-Line Tobacco, Fisherman, Green Ground, Red, Yellow, Litho, 4 x 3 x 1 In. 852.00
Tin, Uncle Sam Shoe Polish, Boy Shining Uncle Sam's Boots On Back, 3 1/2 In. 45.00
Tin, Uniform Cut Plug, Sailor, Blue Suit, Red Ground, Lithograph, 6 1/4 x 5 In. 1375.00
Tin, Universal Coffee, Knob Top 110.00
Tin, Vanity Coffee, Key Wind 55.00
Tin, Victor Coffee, The Ripe Coffee, Chariot Driver, 4 Horses, Key Wind, 1 Lb. 43.00
Tin, Virginity Tobacco, Women On Front & Lid, Factory Reverse, 1880s, 7 In. 440.00
Tin, W & R Jacob, Coronation Coach, Biscuit, 9 x 6 In. 302.00
Tin, Wagon Wheel Tobacco, 4 x 2 In. 1275.00
Tin, Wampum Coffee, Bare Breasted Indian Maiden, 9 1/4 x 5 1/2 In. 120.00
Tin, Weddles Tea, Early Automobile Graphics, Lid, 5 x 3 x 3 1/4 In. 275.00
Tin, Wharco Baking Powder, 4 In. 155.00
Tin, White Villa Spice, 4 Oz. 100.00
Tin, Wigwam Coffee, Pry Lid 187.00
Tin, Williams' Violet Talc Powder, Glastonbury, Conn. . . . .*Illus*   66.00
Tin, Wishbone Coffee, Pink & Turquoise, Key Wind, 1 Lb. 40.00
Tin, Woods Lolacapop, Mosquito Antidote, Mosquito, 3 1/4 x 1 3/4 x 3/4 In. 110.00
Tin, Yellow Bonnet Coffee, Key Wind 88.00
Tin, ZBT Baby Powder, 3 1/2 In. 14.50

Advertising tip trays are decorated metal trays less than 5 inches in
diameter. They were placed on the table or counter to hold either the
bill or the coins that were left as a tip. Change receivers could be made
of glass, plastic, or metal. They were kept on the counter near the cash
register and held the money passed back and forth by the cashier.
Related items may be listed in the Advertising category under Change
Receivers.

Tip Tray, Baker's Cocoa, Walter Baker Co., Dorchester, Mass., 6 In. 295.00
Tip Tray, Boston Fish Co., 4 1/4 In. 135.00
Tip Tray, Dawes Brewery, Black Horse, 4 In. 285.00
Tip Tray, De Laval, 4 1/4 In. 275.00
Tip Tray, El Verso Havana Cigars, Man In Recliner Smoking, 6 1/2 x 4 1/2 In. . . . . .95.00 to 100.00
Tip Tray, Goebel Brewing, 1910s, 4 3/8 In. 72.00
Tip Tray, Hetol Splits, For Health's Sake, 1904, 4 3/16 In. 175.00
Tip Tray, Hubig's Pie Co., Horse Drawn Delivery Wagon, Factory, 1906, 3 5/8 In. 265.00
Tip Tray, Kenny's Teas & Coffees, 3 Monkeys, Hear No Evil, Strauss, 4 1/4 In. 264.00
Tip Tray, Kenny's Teas & Coffees, Woman In Diaphanous Blouse, 4 1/4 In. 176.00

Tip Tray, Lemon Kola, Kaufmann Strauss, Lithograph, 4 1/4 In. 198.00
Tip Tray, Miller High Life, 1940s, 6 1/2 x 4 1/2 In. 10.00
Tip Tray, Old Reliable Coffee, Cossack Type Man Smoking Pipe, 4 1/4 In. 179.00
Tip Tray, Red Raven, Dear Old Red Raven, 4 1/4 In. 143.00
Tip Tray, Red Raven, For High Liver's Livers, 4 1/4 In. 69.00
Tip Tray, Red Raven, Little Girl Eyeing Red Raven Store Display, 4 1/4 In. 201.00
Tip Tray, Red Raven, Ravens Working On Hangover Remedy, 1904, 4 1/4 In. 57.00
Tip Tray, Ruppert's Beer, Hans Flato 45.00
Tip Tray, Tennessee Cola, Dog, Wearing Glasses, Cigar, 4 In. 450.00
Tip Tray, White Rock Lithia Water, Atlantic City Beach Scene, 4 3/8 In. 410.00
Tire Cover, City Club Beer, Screened Leather, W. Union Bottling Works, 28 In. 80.00
Tobacco Cutter, Climax, Iron, 4 x 6 x 19 In. 70.00
Tobacco Cutter, Iron, Original Paint, Embossed Star, 19 In. 375.00
Tobacco Cutter, Iron, Painted, RJR Tobacco Satisfies Blade Arch, 1886, 16 In. 1200.00
Tobacco Cutter, T.F. Reynolds, Brown Mule, Enterprise Manufacture Co. 175.00
Token, All's Tavern, Plymouth Road 1.50
Token, Front Clothiers, Norwich, Connecticut, 50 Cent Rebate On Suit Or Overcoat 25.00
Token, J. Klein, Liquor Dealer, Omaha, Hard Rubber, Yellow, Uniface 125.00
Token, Key Chain Fob, Harvard Beer, Good Luck, 1930s 24.00
Token, Potosi Brewing Co., Good For 50 Cents With Return Of Empty Keg 17.00
Token, Potteiger, Reading, Pennsylvania, Good For One 5 Cent Cigar 17.00
Token, Prima Beer, Picture Of FDR, 1930s 14.00
Token, Smith Music Store, Piano Pictured 7.50
Token, St. Louis Board Of Education Cafeteria 3.00
Token, St. Paul House Furnishing Co. 6.00
Token, Stern Brau Beer, Good For Free Bottle Of Beer, 1930s 10.00
Token, W.C. Proctor Jewelry Co, Rocky Mount, North Carolina 6.50
Trash Can, General Mills, Twinkles & His Friends, Metal, 1961 . . . . 295.00
Tray, Tip, see Tip Trays in this category.
Tray, Anheuser-Busch Brewing Co., St. Louis, Mo., 10 x 13 In. 30.00
Tray, Anheuser-Busch, Eagle, Cherubs Holding Beer, Tin, 13 1/2 x 16 1/2 In. 300.00
Tray, Arctic Cream Co. Ice Cream, Round, 12 In. 775.00
Tray, Ballantine's Ale & Beer, 1950s, 12 In. 28.00
Tray, Barmann Beer, P. Barmann Brewing Co., Round, 1930s, 12 In. 100.00
Tray, Bartholomay Rochester Beer, Pre-Prohibition, Round, 12 In. 135.00
Tray, Beer Driver's Union 132, Independent Union Beer Workers, 16 x 13 In. 265.00
Tray, Berghoff Dortmunder Style Beer, 1930s, 10 x 13 In. 105.00
Tray, Beverwyck Brewing Co., Albany, N.Y., c.1910, 17 1/4 x 12 1/4 In. 555.00
Tray, Bevo, Duquesne Brewing, Prohibition Era, 10 x 13 In. 30.00
Tray, Blatz, Round, 1960s, 13 In. 30.00
Tray, Boswell Ale & Porter, Canada, Pre-Prohibition, Round, 12 In. 70.00
Tray, Braumeister Beer, Independent, Milwaukee, Wisc., Round, 1950s, 12 In. 50.00
Tray, Braumeister Beer, Round, 1950s, 12 In. 35.00
Tray, Brilliant Ale, Porter & India Pale, Syracuse, N.Y., Round, 1930s, 12 In. 250.00
Tray, Bull Durham, Round, 1910, 24 In. 525.00
Tray, Canadian Ace Brewing, Round, 1950s, 13 In. 17.00
Tray, Crescent Ice Cream, 2 Children Eating Ice Cream, Lithograph, Round, 13 1/2 In. . . . 750.00
Tray, Dawson's Ale & Beer, New Bedford, Mass., Round, 1930s, 12 In. 76.00
Tray, Derby Cream Ale, National Brewing Co., Horse Picture, Round, 1930s, 12 In. 325.00
Tray, Edelbrew Beer, Round, 1940s, 12 In. 46.00
Tray, Ehret's Extra Beer, Round, 1930s, 13 In. 66.00
Tray, Eichler Beer, New York, N.Y., Woman Picture, Pre-Prohibition, Round, 12 In. 115.00
Tray, Esslinger's Ale, Esslinger Brewing Co., Philadelphia, Round, 1940s, 12 In. 80.00
Tray, Fort Pitt Special Beer, Round, 1950s, 13 In. 28.00
Tray, Frank's Ginger Ale, 1920s, 10 1/2 x 13 1/4 In. 45.00
Tray, Genesee, Round, 1950s, 12 In. 80.00
Tray, George Ehret's Extra, New York, N.Y., Round, 1910s, 12 In. 46.00
Tray, Goldenrod Beer, Hittleman Goldenrod, Brooklyn, N.Y., 1930s, 15 x 12 In. 75.00
Tray, Goldenrod Brewing, 1930s, 12 x 15 In. 40.00
Tray, Good Old German Lager, Independent Brewing Co., Round, 1930s, 12 In. 160.00
Tray, Graham's Ice Cream, Children, Mother, K&S Co., Lithograph, 10 1/2 x 13 In. 776.00
Tray, Grain Belt Beer, Schlitz Brewing, Round, 1950s, 13 In. 90.00
Tray, Green River Whiskey, Round, 12 In. . . . . 156.00 to 675.00

Tray, Harvard Beer, Tin, Round, 12 In. 190.00
Tray, Horse Head Beer & Ale, Lang Brewery, Round, 1940s, 12 In. 160.00
Tray, Leinenkugel's Beer, Round, 1960s, 12 In. 14.00
Tray, Logan Johnson, Fruit Syrup, Tin, 13 3/4 x 10 1/2 In. 80.00
Tray, Maxwell House Coffee, Tilted Cup Of Coffee Center, Oval, 12 1/2 x 15 In. 25.00
Tray, Monarch, Eagle Brewing Co., Utica, N.Y., Bottle Picture, Round, 12 In. 255.00
Tray, Muchener, Pilsener White Seal, St. Louis, Mo., 1900, 13 3/4 x 10 In. 330.00
Tray, Neuweiler Brewing, Round, 1950s, 13 In. 7.00
Tray, Old Timer's Lager, West Bend, Wisc., Round, 1940s, 12 In.   55.00
Tray, Pacific Beer, Tin Lithograph, Round, Pre-1919, 12 In. 45.00
Tray, Phoenix Beer, Moffats Ale, Round, 1930s, 13 In. 78.00
Tray, Pickwick Ale, Haffenreffer Brewing, Round, 1940s, 12 In. 22.00
Tray, Pie, Amsdell Albany Ale, Albany, N.Y., Porcelain, Pre-Prohibition, Round, 12 In. . . .   210.00
Tray, Pie, Black Horse Ale & Porter, Montreal, Quebec, Porcelain, Round, 1930s, 13 In. . .   100.00
Tray, Pie, Congress Beer, Haberle-Congress, Syracuse, N.Y., Round, 1930s, 13 In. 180.00
Tray, Pie, Labatt's Labatt Brewing Co., London, Canada, Porcelain, 13 In. 105.00
Tray, Pie, Pickwick Ale, Haffenreffer & Co., Boston, Mass., Round, 1930s, 12 In. 30.00
Tray, Red Raven Splits, Round, 12 In. 485.00
Tray, Rheingold Beer, Round, 1950s, 12 In. 33.00
Tray, Ruhstaller's Brewing Co., Sacramento, Calif., Pre-Prohibition, Round, 12 In. 100.00
Tray, Schlitz Brewing Co., Milwaukee, Wisc., Pre-Prohibition, Round, 12 In. 125.00
Tray, Seipp's Extra Pale Beer, Chicago, Ill., Pre-Prohibition, Round, 12 In. 195.00
Tray, Sunrise Beer, Field, Sunrise Brewing Co., Cleveland, Round, 1930s, 12 In. 185.00
Tray, Trommers Malt Beers, Brooklyn, N.Y., 1910, 15 1/2 x 12 1/2 In. 200.00
Tray, Virginia Dare, American Wines, Round, 12 In. 200.00
Tray, Zipp's Cherri-O, Bird, Soda, H. D. Beach Co., Coshocton, Ohio, Round, 12 In. 748.00
Tray Liner, Iroquois Beer & Ale, Heavy Paper, 1950s 4.00
Trophy, Bowling, Goebel Beer, Card, Chalk Trophy, Cup, Crying Towel, 1950s 15.00
Window Decal, Green's August Flower, Boschee's Syrup, Mortar & Pestle, 8 x 11 1/2 In. .   100.00
Yardstick, Strohs Beer, Folding, Wooden, 1960s 18.00

AGATA glass was made by Joseph Locke of the New England Glass
Company of Cambridge, Massachusetts, after 1885. A metallic stain
was applied to New England Peachblow and the mottled design characteristic of agata appeared.

Pitcher 2500.00
Salt & Pepper, Metal Caps, 4 In. 896.00
Sugar & Creamer, Applied Loop Handles, 3 x 6 In. 3737.00
Tumbler, 3 1/2 x 2 1/2 In. . . . . .300.00 to 940.00
Vase, 6 In. 885.00
Vase, Lily, Fluted, Label, 15 In., Pair 4000.00

AKRO AGATE glass was made in Clarksburg, West Virginia, from 1932
to 1951. Before that time, the firm made children's glass marbles,
which are listed in this book in the Marble category. Most of the glass
is marked with a crow flying through the letter *A*.

Ashtray, Marbleized, Blue, Square, 2 7/8 In. 8.00
Bowl, Cereal, Concentric Ring, Marbleized Blue, 3 3/8 In. 18.00
Creamer, Interior Panel, Marbleized Oxblood 68.00
Creamer, Interior Panel, Opaque Blue 68.00
Creamer, Interior Panel, Opaque Green 65.00
Creamer, Interior Panel, Opaque Pink 68.00
Creamer, Interior Panel, Transparent Green 65.00
Creamer, Interior Panel, Transparent Topaz 65.00
Creamer, Stacked Disc, Interior Panel, Marbleized Blue 98.00
Creamer, Stacked Disc, Interior Panel, Opaque Blue 28.00
Creamer, Stacked Disc, Interior Panel, Transparent Cobalt 49.00
Creamer, Stacked Disc, Interior Panel, Transparent Green 44.00
Cup, Chiquita, Opaque Lavender . . . . .70.00 to 75.00
Cup, Interior Panel, Marbleized Blue 48.00
Cup, Interior Panel, Marbleized Oxblood 40.00
Cup, Interior Panel, Opaque Green 14.00
Cup, Interior Panel, Opaque Pink 27.00

Cup, Interior Panel, Opaque Yellow 32.00
Cup, Interior Panel, Pumpkin 30.00
Cup, Interior Panel, Transparent Green 16.00
Cup, Interior Panel, Transparent Topaz 16.00
Cup, Raised Daisy, Opaque Green 28.00
Cup, Stacked Disc, Interior Panel, Marbelized Blue 73.00
Cup, Stacked Disc, Interior Panel, Opaque Pumpkin 32.00
Cup, Stacked Disc, Interior Panel, Transparent Cobalt 45.00
Cup, Stacked Disc, Interior Panel, Transparent Green 33.00
Cup & Saucer, Transparent Cobalt 30.00
Pitcher, Stacked Disc, Interior Panel, Transparent Green 31.00
Planter, Orange Swirls, White, Horizontal Ribs, 4 1/4 In. 18.00
Plate, Concentric Ring, Opaque Yellow, 3 1/4 In. 5.00
Plate, Interior Panel, Marbleized Green 12.00
Plate, Interior Panel, Marbleized Oxblood 22.00
Plate, Interior Panel, Opaque Blue 16.00
Plate, Interior Panel, Opaque Green 7.00
Plate, Interior Panel, Opaque Pink 12.00
Plate, Interior Panel, Opaque Yellow 12.00
Plate, Interior Panel, Transparent Green 9.00
Plate, Interior Panel, Transparent Topaz 9.00
Plate, Raised Daisy, Opaque Blue .... .21.00 to 23.00
Plate, Stacked Disc, Interior Panel, Opaque Yellow 13.00
Plate, Stacked Disc, Interior Panel, Transparent Cobalt 26.00
Plate, Stacked Disc, Interior Panel, Transparent Green 21.00
Saucer, Chiquita, Opaque Yellow 13.00
Saucer, Interior Panel, Marbleized Green 12.00
Saucer, Interior Panel, Marbleized Oxblood 18.00
Saucer, Interior Panel, Opaque Blue 16.00
Saucer, Interior Panel, Opaque Green 5.00
Saucer, Interior Panel, Opaque Pink 15.00
Saucer, Interior Panel, Opaque Yellow 17.00
Saucer, Interior Panel, Transparent Topaz .... .13.00 to 19.00
Saucer, Raised Daisy, Opaque Yellow 14.00
Saucer, Stacked Disc, Interior Panel, Marbelized Blue 32.00
Saucer, Stacked Disc, Interior Panel, Opaque Green 11.00
Saucer, Stacked Disc, Interior Panel, Transparent Cobalt 23.00
Saucer, Stacked Disc, Interior Panel, Transparent Green 18.00
Sugar, Interior Panel, Marbleized Oxblood 68.00
Sugar, Interior Panel, Opaque Blue 68.00
Sugar, Interior Panel, Opaque Green 72.00
Sugar, Interior Panel, Opaque Pink 75.00
Sugar, Interior Panel, Transparent Green 65.00
Sugar, Interior Panel, Transparent Topaz 65.00
Sugar, Stacked Disc, Interior Panel, Opaque Blue 28.00
Sugar, Stacked Disc, Interior Panel, Transparent Cobalt 49.00
Sugar, Stacked Disc, Interior Panel, Transparent Green 44.00
Teapot, Interior Panel, Opaque Green 15.00
Teapot, Interior Panel, Opaque Pink 21.00
Tumbler, Interior Panel, Transparent Green 13.00
Tumbler, Raised Daisy, Opaque Yellow 29.00
Tumbler, Stacked Disc, Interior Panel, Transparent Blue 26.00
Tumbler, Stacked Disc, Interior Panel, Transparent Green .... .13.00 to 14.00
Vase, Pumpkin, 3 1/4 In. 14.00

ALABASTER is a very soft form of gypsum, a stone that resembles marble. It was often carved into vases or statues in Victorian times. There
are alabaster carvings being made even today. Because the alabaster is
very porous, it will dissolve if kept in water, so do not use alabaster
vases for flowers.

Bookend, Owl, Signed, 5 3/4 In., Pair 30.00
Bowl, Pliny's Doves On Rim, Egg & Dart Border, Bulbous Stem, 1890s 632.00
Box, Jewelry, Dark Green, Italy, 5 x 2 In. 22.00

Box, Terrier Dog Sitting On Top, 3 1/8 x 2 1/4 In. 55.00
Bust, Abraham Lincoln, 6 1/4 In. 120.00
Bust, David & Delilah, Italy, 1930, 5 x 4 1/2 In. 300.00
Bust, Girl, Raised On Marble Pedestal, Signed, A. Cipriani, 29 1/2 In. 4800.00
Bust, Mozart, Carved, 13 1/4 x 14 In. 250.00
Bust, Napoleon, A. Plazza, Carrara, 19 In. 795.00
Bust, Neoclassical Woman, Carved Upswept Hair, Green Marble Socle, Italy, 15 In. 315.00
Bust, Peasant Woman, 11 x 11 In. 420.00
Bust, Plato, 1890, 8 In. 379.00
Bust, Serene Woman, 18 x 8 In. 1250.00
Bust, Venus De Milo, Gazing To Her Left, Matching Socle, White, Italy, 23 In. 2300.00
Bust, Woman, Dressed As Clown, Gray Marble Base, J. Aoily, 9 3/4 In. 275.00
Bust, Young Dante, Head Wreath, Tunic, Italy, 11 3/4 x 5 1/2 x 4 1/2 In. 345.00
Bust, Young Woman In Renaissance Dress, Pink Marble Bodice, Italy, 13 In. 1150.00
Bust, Young Woman, Ponytail, M. Bezzi, Roma, 1881, 23 In. 1155.00
Coffer, Quartzite, Recumbent Dog, Beaded Rim, Octagonal Cover, 7 x 6 x 8 1/2 In. 690.00
Compote, Green & Gray Striations, Square Base, Dolphins, 14 3/4 x 8 In., 2 Piece 165.00
Eggcup, Metal Stand, 2 1/2 In. 10.00
Ewer, Roaring Dragon At Lip, Bird Of Paradise Handle, 19th Century, 29 1/4 In., Pair . . . 1150.00
Figurine, Allegorical Figure Of Night, Late 19th Century, 39 1/2 In. 9000.00
Figurine, Egyptian Woman, Pietro Bazzanti, Late 19th Century, 28 In. 5775.00
Figurine, Maiden At Well, Exposed Breasts, Perched On Ledge, Italy, 15 In. 750.00
Figurine, Nude Woman, Seated Demurely On Ledge By Waterfall, 14 In. 1320.00
Figurine, Woman Water Bearer, Kneeling, Stylized Rocky Base, 16 1/2 In. 1095.00
Lamp, Electric, Balloon Shade, Center Band Of Putti, 3 Putti Supports, 27 In. 4310.00
Lamp, Electric, Bronze, Seal, Marcel-Andre Bouraine, 24 In. 4200.00
Lamp, Electric, Carved Garlands Of Flowers, Claw Feet, Maidenheads, 70 x 22 In. 5825.00
Lamp, Electric, Dish Shape, Gilt Bronze, Beaded Corona, Italy, c.1900, 24 x 21 In. 1840.00
Pedestal, Columnar Standard, Carved, Flat Leaves, Octagonal Base, 41 In. 315.00
Urn, Acanthine Rim, Scroll Handles, Square Plinth, 28 1/2 In., Pair 2760.00
Urn, Baluster Shape, Scroll Handles, Rose Bouquet, Continental, 21 In., Pair 316.00
Urn, Gray & White, Entwined Serpents, Opposed Eagles On Staff, c.1900, 25 In. 1955.00
Urn, Neoclassical, Gray, White Variegated, Italy, 1900, 25 x 13 In. 1955.00
Urn, Pedestal, Maiden's Head, Grape Clusters, Vines, c.1885, 99 x 22 In., Pair 19600.00
Urn, White, Downswept Leaves On Edge, Cylindrical Base, 1900, 15 1/4 In. 575.00
Vase, Belle Epoque, Carved, Baluster Shape, Lyre Relief, 14 In., Pair 805.00

ALUMINUM was more expensive than gold or silver until the 1850s. Chemists learned how to refine bauxite to get aluminum. Jewelry and other small objects were made of the valuable metal until 1914, when an inexpensive smelting process was invented. The aluminum collected today dates from the 1930s through the 1950s. Hand-hammered pieces are the most popular.

Ashtray, 3 Ducks In Marsh, 5 1/4 In. 10.00
Ashtray, Duck In Marsh, Marked, 4 In. 25.00
Basket, 6-In. Plate Inset, Cromwell 38.00
Basket, Chrysanthemum, Continental, 13 1/2 x 10 1/2 x 12 In. 45.00
Basket, Floral Design, Twisted Brass Handle, 11 1/2 In. 15.00
Basket, Rectangular, Continental, 10 x 6 x 3 1/2 In. 9.00
Bowl, 2 Sprays Of Flowers On Interior & Exterior, 10 In. 8.00
Bowl, Flower Clusters, Deep, Fluted, Federal, 8 In. 20.00
Bowl, Flowers, Wilson Metal Prod., Inc., Brooklyn, N.Y., 11 3/4 In. 14.00
Bowl, Grape, Everlast, 8 In. 17.00
Bowl, Grape, West Bend, 14 In. 10.00
Bowl, Low, Round, Buenilum, 9 In. 6.00
Bowl, Rose And Leaf Design, Fluted Rim, Hand Forged, 12 1/2 In. 12.00
Bowl, Wilson Specialties, 10 In. 27.00
Bowl & Tray Set, Glass Bowl, Cover, Rosebud Knob, Rodney Kent, 8 In. 42.00
Bread Basket, Handle, Rodney Kent, 12 1/2 x 8 In. 12.00
Bread Tray, Apple, Handles, Everlast 6.00
Candy Dish, Cover, Finial, Buenilum, 7 x 2 In. 9.00
Casserole, Chrome, Silver, 16 1/2 In. 45.00
Casserole, Divided, Wooden Finial, Twisted Handles, Buenilum 30.00

Casserole, Glass Insert, Daisy, Everlast 22.00
Casserole, Looped Finial Cover, Buenilum 35.00
Chafing Dish, Banded Design, With Casserole, Everlast 85.00
Coaster, Anodized, Ducks In Marsh, 1950, 3 1/4 In., Pair 10.00
Coaster, Duck, Hammered, 3 1/4 In. 3.00
Coaster Set, Flowers, Holder, Everlast 18.00
Coffeepot, Campfire, Chrome, Silver 15.00
Coffeepot, Gold Finish, Color Glo, West Bend, 8 Cup 55.00
Compote, Footed, Marked Kensington Moire, 3 7/8 In. 27.00
Drink Stirrer, Leaf Shape, Anodized, Red, Pink, Blue, 8 In., 6 Piece 30.00
Ice Bucket, Chrysanthemum, No. 705, Continental 125.00
Ice Bucket, Hammered, Aqua, Green Porcelain Liner, 1950, 12 x 8 3/4 In. 100.00
Ice Bucket, Liner, Bamboo, Everlast 20.00
Ice Bucket, Rodney Kent, 7 3/4 x 6 In. 19.00
Lazy Susan, Glass, Cromwell 10.00
Pitcher, Chrome, Silver, Regal 15.00
Pitcher, Gold, Chrome, Silver, 7 1/4 In. 8.00
Pitcher, Hammered, Chrome, Silver, Ice Stopper, 9 1/4 In. 10.00
Pitcher, Water, Cover, Black Plastic Handle, 10 In. 18.00
Plate, 3 Flying Ducks On Rim, 10 In. 5.00
Plate, Canape, Rayed Design, Kensington, 12 In. 30.00
Platter Set, Zodiac, One Symbol On Each Plate, Kensington, 18 In., 12 Piece 600.00
Sandwich Tray, Handles, Berry Design, Farberware, 12 In. 35.00
Scoop, Marked Pat. Pend. Arnold C. Eichin Inc. 9.00
Server, 3 Tiers, Wilson Specialties ....40.00 to 50.00
Server, Hot & Cold, Penguins, Wooden Handles, Round, West Bend 25.00
Server, Twisted Vine Handles, Twisted Vine Top Handle, Hammered, 1950s, 10 1/2 In. .. 15.00
Silent Butler, Apple, Everlast 24.00
Silent Butler, Bali Bamboo, Everlast 22.00
Silent Butler, Etched Rose, Hammered, Hinged Lid, 11 1/2 x 6 In. 25.00
Silent Butler, Wild Rose, Continental 30.00
Spaghetti Set, Pot With Cover, Cheese Shaker, Cane Accents, Russel Wright, 8 In. 1800.00
Tea Container, Copper, Chrome, Silver, 5 1/2 In. 4.00
Teakettle, Bail Handle, Marked, 1920s, 5 Qt. 40.00
Toothpick, Wall, Oak Leaf, Acorn Design, 4 In. 25.00
Tray, Bamboo, Handles, Everlast 32.00
Tray, Chrome, Silver, Wilcox Co., 24 x 15 1/2 In. 15.00
Tray, Daisies, Hammered, Curled Handles, Fluted Sides, 15 1/2 In. 20.00
Tray, Drink, Chrome, Silver 20.00
Tray, Flower, Vertical Ribbon Handles, Rodney Kent, 12 x 18 In. 38.00
Tray, Grape, Scalloped, Everlast, 9 x 12 In. 20.00
Tray, Grasshopper, Wendell August Forge, 5 1/2 In. 130.00
Tray, Hammered, Grape, Marked, World Hand Forged, 14 1/2 x 6 3/4 In. 14.00
Tray, Rolled Handles, Everlast, 14 x 24 In. 68.00
Tray, Serving, Round, Designed Aluminum, 18 In. 55.00
Tray, Serving, Russel Wright, 15 x 21 1/2 In. 460.00
Tray, Snack, Hammered, Pinecone Design, Curled Handle, Fluted Sides, 7 3/4 In. 12.00
Tray, Tidbit, Handle, 11 In. 20.00
Tray, Tulip, 2 Handles, Hammered, Rodney Kent, Signed, 11 1/2 x 16 In. 20.00
Tray, Tulip, Rectangular, Rolled Handles, 1950s 24.00
Tray, World Map, Rectangular, Arthur Armour 170.00
Tray, Zodiac, Arthur Armour, 14 In. 175.00
Vase, Cover, Wooden Handle, Russel Wright, 10 In. 46.00
Water Set, Bamboo, Pitcher & 6 Tumblers, Everlast 245.00

AMBER, see Jewelry category.

AMBER GLASS is the name of any glassware with the proper yellow-brown shading. It was a popular color just after the Civil War and many pressed glass pieces were made of amber glass. Depression glass of the 1930s–1950s was also made in shades of amber glass. Other pieces may be found in the Depression Glass, Pressed Glass, and other glass categories. All types are being reproduced.

Candleholder, Enameled, 1950s, Pair 10.00

Compote, 3 Panels, 10 1/2 x 4 In. 22.00
Compote, Cover, Diamond Variant Bands, 8 x 10 1/2 In. 27.00
Decanter, Crackle, Flame-Shape Hollow Stopper, Pilgrim, 22 In. 86.00
Decanter, Fish, Figural, Crackle, 7 x 15 1/4 In. 17.50
Figurine, Cat, Viking, 6 1/4 In. 40.00
Jug, Tumble-Up 61.00
Vase, Bud, Automobile, Satin, 8 In. 40.00
Vase, Gold Enameled, Floral Medallions, 20 In. 431.00
Vase, Ribbed, Flared, Square Foot, Art Deco, 4 In. 13.00
Wall Pocket, Daisy & Button, 8 1/4 x 2 1/2 In. 75.00

AMBERETTE pieces are listed in the Pressed Glass category under the pattern name Amberette.

AMBERINA is a two-toned glassware made from 1883 to about 1900. It was patented by Joseph Locke of the New England Glass Company, but was also made by other companies. The glass shades from red to amber. Similar pieces of glass may be found in the Baccarat and Plated Amberina categories. Glass shaded from blue to amber is called *Blue Amberina* or *Bluerina.*

Basket, Melon Ribbed, Amber Thorn Handle, 7 1/2 x 6 In. 345.00
Basket, Ribbed, Quatrefoil Handle, 6 3/8 x 5 In. 2817.00
Basket, Swirl, Applied Amber Edge, Thorn Handle, 6 x 6 In. 575.00
Bowl, Daisy & Button, 9 x 2 5/8 In. 488.00
Bowl, Fruit, 5 x 9 1/4 In. 1150.00
Bowl, Gilded Gold Enameled Flowers, 9 1/2 x 16 x 11 In. 2530.00
Bowl, Inverted Thumbprint, Applied Amber Reeded Handles, 4 In. 373.00
Bowl, Inverted Thumbprint, Enameled Flowers, Square, 8 1/2 x 8 1/2 In. 550.00
Bowl, Swirl, Applied Amber Wishbone Rim & Handles, Footed, 6 x 2 In. 575.00
Bowl, Swirl, Enameled Flowers, Amber Footed, 4 x 8 In. 500.00
Butter Dome, Cover, Reeded Amber Pigtail Finial, Ruffled Edge, 4 x 4 In. 2530.00
Celery Vase, Inverted Thumbprint, Scalloped Ends, Folded Sides, 8 1/2 x 6 In. 395.00
Celery Vase, Venetian Diamond, Ruffled Edge, 4 x 3 In. 230.00
Creamer, Inverted Thumbprint, Applied Amber Reeded Handle, 2 3/4 In. 450.00
Creamer, Inverted Thumbprint, Applied Pale Amber Handle, 4 1/2 In. 287.00
Creamer, Venetian Diamond, Applied Amber Handle, 4 3/8 x 3 In. 632.00
Cruet, Applied Amber Handle, Amber Faceted Stopper, 3 In. 575.00
Cruet, Inverted Thumbprint, Faceted Stopper, 6 In. 450.00
Cruet, Swirl, Applied Amber Handle, Stopper, 9 In. 235.00
Cup & Saucer, Applied Amber Ring Handle, Signed, Libbey, 4 3/4 x 2 x 2 In. 920.00
Finger Bowl, Crimped Rim, 2 1/2 x 5 In., Pair 747.00
Fish Bowl, Ribbed, Rolled Rim, 5 In. 1207.00
Goblet, Deep Amber, Red Stem, 8 1/2 In. 460.00
Ice Bucket, Inverted Thumbprint Handle, Star On Base, 6 x 5 In. 575.00
Jug, Syrup, Applied Amber Handle, Silver Plate & Cover, 5 1/2 x 3 1/2 In. 1207.00
Jug, Whiskey, Inverted Thumbprint, Applied Amber Reeded Handle, 6 In. 1092.00
Mustard, Cover, Silver Plated Rim, 3 x 2 In. 747.00
Mustard, Cover, Silver Plated Rim, 4 1/4 x 1 7/8 In. 1035.00
Nappy, Inverted Thumbprint, Heart Shape, Amber Handle, 7 In. 373.00
Nappy, Swirl, Tricorner Rim, 7 1/2 In. 395.00
Pitcher, Diamond-Quilted, Applied Amber Reeded Handle, 10 In. 143.00
Pitcher, Inverted Thumbprint, Applied Amber Double Rope Handle, 4 7/8 In. 2185.00
Pitcher, Inverted Thumbprint, Applied Amber Handle, 6 In. 345.00
Pitcher, Venetian Diamond, Applied Amber Handle, 7 In. 747.00
Pitcher, Water, Inverted Thumbprint, Deep Fuchsia, Purple, Handle, 7 x 6 In. ... 1035.00
Pitcher, Water, Optic Rib, Applied Amber Handle, 6 In. 135.00
Pitcher, Water, Optic Rib, Reeded Amber Handle, 1900-1930, 6 1/2 In. 110.00
Pitcher, Water, Venetian Diamond, Deep Amber, Applied Amber Handle, 8 In. 690.00
Punch Cup, Barrel Shape, Applied Handle, 2 3/4 x 3 3/4 In. 2242.00
Punch Cup, Inverted Thumbprint, Applied Amber Reeded Handle, 3 In. 230.00
Punch Cup, Ribbed, Applied Amber Reeded Handle, 2 1/2 In., Pair 172.00
Rose Bowl, Applied Amber Rigaree, Amber Band Center, 4 3/4 In. 632.00
Rose Bowl, Diamond-Quilted, Applied Amber Rigaree, 3 Amber Feet, 2 7/8 In. ... 172.00

Rose Bowl, Diamond-Quilted, Berry Prunts, Applied Handles, 4 3/4 In. 2242.00
Rose Bowl, Inverted Thumbprint, Applied Amber Rigaree, 3 In. 402.00
Rose Bowl, Inverted Thumbprint, Applied Flowering Vines & Rigaree, 4 1/2 x 5 In. 115.00
Rose Bowl, Venetian Diamond, Applied Amber Rigaree, 6 In. 402.00
Salt, Silver Plated Holder 175.00
Salt & Pepper, Honeycomb, Silver Plated Tops, 3 In. 379.00
Salt & Pepper, Pillar, Silver Plated Tops, 4 x 1 1/2 In. 690.00
Sugar & Creamer, Inverted Thumbprint, Applied Amber Reeded Handles, 3 x 2 In. 2012.00
Tumbler, Inverted Thumbprint, 3 7/8 In., Pair 150.00
Tumbler, Ribbed, 3 5/8 In. 86.00
Vase, Bud, Enameled Flower, Tapered Neck, 8 3/8 In., Pair 345.00
Vase, Egg Shape, 3 Amber Reeded Feet, 6 5/8 x 5 1/4 In. 1035.00
Vase, Egg Shape, Applied Berry Prunt & Amber Reeded Feet, 7 x 5 In. 1552.00
Vase, Flared Rim, 7 5/8 x 3 In. 1322.00
Vase, Inverted Diamond, Tapered Neck, 6 3/8 In. 115.00
Vase, Inverted Swirl, Cushion Base, Applied Amber Rigaree, 10 1/2 In., Pair 616.00
Vase, Jack-In-The Pulpit, Applied Apple Blossom, Signed, Libbey, 7 1/4 In. 1035.00
Vase, Lily, Deep Ruby, 11 3/4 In. 201.00
Vase, Lily, Deep Ruby, 9 In. 230.00
Vase, Lily, Honeycomb, Applied Amber Handle, 8 1/4 x 3 7/8 In. 230.00
Vase, Lily, Ribbed, 12 1/2 x 5 In. 575.00
Vase, Lily, Ribbed, Crimped Edge, 8 1/8 x 4 1/2 In. 1495.00
Vase, Ribbed, Pinched Waist, Applied Amber Rigaree, Gilt, Libbey, 8 5/6 In. 1437.00
Vase, Ruffled Edge, Signed, Libbey, 6 1/4 x 6 In. 1207.00
Vase, Signed, Libbey, 9 x 1 1/2 In. 575.00
Vase, Signed, Libbey, 11 3/4 x 1 1/2 In. . . . . .690.00 to 805.00
Vase, Swirl, 8 x 3 1/4 In. 517.00
Water Set, Pitcher, 6 Tumblers, Diamond Point, 7-In. Pitcher 616.00
Wine, Ribbed, 4 1/2 x 2 1/2 In., Pair 402.00

AMERICAN DINNERWARE, see Dinnerware.

AMERICAN ENCAUSTIC TILING COMPANY was founded in Zanesville,
Ohio, in 1875. The company planned to make a variety of tiles to com-
pete with the English tiles that were selling in the United States for use
in fireplaces and other architectural designs. The first glazed tiles were
made in 1880, embossed tiles in 1881, faience tiles in the 1920s. The
firm closed in 1935 and reopened in 1937 as the Shawnee Pottery.

Panel, Classical Woman, 10 Piece, 60 In. . . . .*Illus* 2600.00
Panel, Woman, With Birds, Brown Glaze, H. Mueller, 3 In., 20 Piece 2860.00
Paperweight, Blue Matte Glaze, 1907 . . . . 231.00
Paperweight, Blue Matte Glaze, 1911 . . . . 143.00
Paperweight, Green Matte Glaze, Signed, 1910, 2 1/8 x 4 1/4 In. 231.00
Tile, Cross With Halo, Square, 6 In. 55.00
Tile, Gold, Black, White Scrolled Design, Square, 6 In. 55.00
Tile, Medallion Center, Striped Corners, Square, 6 In. 55.00
Tile, Peacock, Matte & Iridescent Glaze, Square, 6 In. 935.00
Tile, Stylized Tulip, Aqua, Emerald, Cobalt, Yellow, 6 In. 66.00
Tile, Stylized Tulip, Cobalt, Salmon, Emerald, 6 In. 55.00
Tile, Stylized Tulip, Orange, Cobalt, Dark Brown, 6 In. 55.00

American Encaustic
Tiling Co., Panel,
Classical Woman,
10 Piece, 60 In.

AMETHYST GLASS is any of the many glasswares made in the dark purple color of the gemstone called amethyst. Included in this category are many pieces made in the nineteenth and twentieth centuries. Very dark pieces are called *black amethyst* and are listed under that heading.

Box, Enameled Gold Leaves, 1 1/2 x 2 In. 145.00
Carafe, Water, Broken Column, 8 1/2 In. 395.00
Compote, Enameled Gold & White Beading, Children Gather Wheat, Dogs, 6 In. 93.00
Creamer, Applied Handle, 3 In. ....88.00 to 90.00
Salt, Enameled Gold, Scroll Feet, 1 1/4 x 2 In. 65.00
Vase, Cut Diamond-Quilted Neck, Classical Scenes, Swan Handles, 12 In. 2415.00
Vase, Enameled Birds & Flowers, Gold Trim, 10 1/4 In., Pair 300.00
Vase, Footed, 11 In. 125.00
Vase, Garniture, Gilt Bronze Mount, Louis XVI Style, Marble Base, 11 1/2 x 4 In. 1725.00

AMPHORA pieces are listed in the Teplitz category.

ANDIRONS and related fireplace items are included in the Fireplace category.

ANIMAL TROPHIES, such as stuffed animals, rugs made of animal skins, and other similar collectibles made from animal, fish, or bird parts, are listed in this category. Collectors should be aware of the endangered species laws that make it illegal to buy and sell some of these items. Any eagle feathers, many types of pelts or rugs (such as leopard), ivory, and many forms of tortoiseshell can be confiscated by the government. Related trophies may be found in the Fishing category. Ivory items may be found in the Scrimshaw or Ivory categories.

Black Bear Head 250.00
Blue Jay & Bird Eggs, Circular Shaped Dome, 11 x 17 In. 172.00
Chicken 175.00
Finches, Oval Shaped Dome, 17 1/2 x 11 x 17 In. 230.00
Pheasant, Standing, 14 1/2 x 25 In. 89.00
Rooster 295.00
Rug, Buffalo Hide, Head & Horns 830.00
Rug, Polar Bear, 1950s 3900.00
Stag's Head, 6-Point Antlers, Oak Shield, 49 x 26 In. 230.00
Walrus Skull, Ivory Tusks, Engraved, 25 In. 847.00

ANIMATION ART collectibles include cels that are painted drawings on celluloid needed to make animated cartoons shown in movie theaters or on TV. Hundreds of cels were made, then photographed in sequence to make a cartoon showing moving figures. Early examples made by the Walt Disney Studios are popular with collectors today. Original sketches used by the artists are also listed here. Modern animated cartoons are made using computer-generated pictures. Some of these are being produced as cels to be sold to collectors. Other cartoon art is listed in Comic Art and Disneyana.

Cel, Alice In Wonderland, Alice Swings Paintbrush, Red Paint, 1951, 10 x 12 In. 1610.00
Cel, Aristocats, Amelia, Abigail & Uncle Waldo, 1 1/2 x 6 In. 377.00
Cel, Bambi, Looking Down At Thumper, 1942, 7 x 7 1/2 In. 4025.00
Cel, From Hare To Eternity, Bugs Bunny, Yosemite Sam, Frame, 1996, 20 x 17 In. 632.00
Cel, Jungle Book, Mowgli Scolding Snake Kaas, 1967, 12 1/2 x 16 In. 8050.00

ANNA POTTERY was started in Anna, Illinois, in 1859 by Cornwall and Wallace Kirkpatrick. They made many types of utilitarian wares, bricks, drain tiles, and giftware. The most collectible pieces made by the pottery are the pig-shaped bottles and jugs with special inscriptions, applied animals, and figures. The pottery closed in 1894.

Flask, Pig, Albany Slip-Type Glaze, Good Old Rye Whiskey, 6 1/2 In. 3500.00
Flask, Pig, Albany Slip-Type Glaze, Railroad & River Guide, 6 1/2 In. 5800.00
Jug, Temperance, Multiple Applied Snakes, Blue, Brown Glaze, c.1890, 10 In. 14300.00

APPLE PEELERS are listed in the Kitchen category under Peeler, Apple.

ARCHITECTURAL antiques include a variety of collectibles, usually very large, that have been removed from buildings. Hardware, backbars, doors, paneling, and even old bathtubs are now wanted by collectors. Pieces of the Victorian, Art Nouveau, and Art Deco styles are in greatest demand.

Altar, Faux Painted Marble Columns, Open Back, Quebec, 39 x 27 x 37 In.	2775.00
Backbar, Barbershop, 3 Stations, Koken	6700.00
Backbar, Pine, Lighted Slag Glass Panels, 14 Ft.	3500.00
Basin, Bathroom, Porcelain, Marble Counter, Beveled, Brass Fixtures, 20 x 31 In.	280.00
Bathtub, Copper	1250.00
Bathtub & Pedestal Sink, Claw Foot	975.00
Bracket, Carved Acanthus, Giltwood, Italy, 15 x 11 In., Pair	747.00
Bracket, Cast Iron, Scrollwork, Flowers, Black Enamel, France, 60 x 12 3/4 In.	300.00
Bracket, Giltwood, Shelf On C-Scroll Support, 8 1/2 In., Pair	1920.00
Bracket, Giltwood, Shell Form, Laurel Band Rim, Early 19th Century, Pair	575.00
Bracket, Wall, Eagle, Gilt, Beaded Trim, Oval Shelf, 1800s, 16 x 11 1/2 x 9 In.	2185.00
Bracket, Wall, Giltwood, Scalloped Shelf, Eagle, Spread Wings, 1800s, 9 x 17 In.	1760.00
Bracket, Wall, Giltwood, Serpentine Outline Shelf, Scrolled Fern Leaves, 11 In.	90.00
Bracket, Wall, Mahogany, Rosewood, Fretwork, Pillars, 1800s, 5 x 6 In.	1035.00
Bracket, Wall, Rococo, Giltwood, Serpentine Shelf, Italy, 7 1/2 In., Pair	431.00
Bracket, Wall, Rococo, Putto, Floral Spray, Germany, 7 In., Pair	230.00
Broken Pediment, Wooden, White Painted Layers, 1800s, 5 1/2 Ft.	395.00
Capital, Carved, Flowers, Leaves, Paint Traces, 12 1/2 x 12 In.	175.00
Capital, Pine, Carved, Painted, Scrolls, Acanthus Leaves, 13 x 16 x 16 In., Pair	2185.00
Capital, Walnut, Corinthian, Incurved Top, Iron Hooks, 11 x 13 In., 4 Piece	7920.00
Chimney Breast, Wooden, Grain Painted Cedar Type	6600.00
Column, Aesthetic Movement, Ebonized, Parcel Gilt, 1890s, 44 x 11 x 11 In.	460.00
Column, Ebonized, Parcel Gilt, Aesthetic Movement, Fluted, 38 1/2 In.	230.00
Column, Giltwood, Ivory, Gray Vein, Deep Brown Ground, 114 x 18 In., Pair	4600.00
Column, Stylized Corinthian Capital, Fluted Cylindrical Stem, 7 Ft. 10 In., 4 Piece	5760.00
Cornice, Giltwood, Shallow Arched Center, France, 19th Century, 48 In., Pair	4022.00
Cornice, Scroll, Leaves, White Paint, Cast Iron, 19th Century, 55 In., Pair	403.00
Door, Elevator, Waldorf Astoria, Griffins, Winged Cupids, 86 x 24 In., Pair	28000.00
Door, Leaded Glass, Arts & Crafts Frame, Female Figures, 31 x 24 In., Pair	4900.00
Door, Leaded Glass, Floral Decoration, Oak Frame, 20 x 66 In., Pair	920.00
Door, Sliding, 3 Pandanus Panels, George Nakashima, 19 x 104 x 19 In.	8050.00
Door, Swinging, Brown, Rosehead Nails, Iron Hinges, 1850s, Pair	750.00
Door, Walnut, Raised Panel Doors, Leaded Panels, c.1870, 106 x 64 In.	6720.00
Door, Wooden, Carved, Gilt Grids, Floral, Brass Hardware, Oriental, 14 x 31 In.	605.00
Door Knocker, 8 Inset Jewels, Arts & Crafts, 7 1/2 In.	412.00
Door Knocker, Eagle Shape, Iron, 19th Century, 8 3/4 In.	345.00
Door Knocker, Enraged Dragon, Heraldic Shield, Iron, Oak Plaque, 26 In.	1454.00
Door Knocker, Lion's Head, Man & Knocker In Clenched Teeth, 7 In.	55.00
Door Knocker, Messenger Boy, Iron	22750.00
Door Knocker, Parlor Maid, Iron	3300.00
Door Knocker, White Owl, Iron	605.00
Door Knocker & Letter Gate, Iron, Black, Victorian, 3 x 8 5/8 In.	80.00
Doorknob, Cobalt Blue, 19th Century	70.00
Doorknob, Glass, Dewdrop, Nashua	240.00
Doorknob, Wooden, Brass Ferrule, Atwater's, Pa., October 11, 1887, 2 1/4 In.	130.00
Doorway, Renaissance Revival, Carved Mahogany, Cherub Cornice, 116 In.	2800.00
Downspout, Sheaf Of Wheat Design, Lead, c.1794, 12 x 21 In.	195.00
Downspout, Tin, Cutout 10-Pointed Star, 1/2 Round, Funnel Shape, 13 x 9 1/2 In.	288.00
Elevator, Hand Rope System, For 3-Story House	3000.00
Finial, Copper, Pyramidal Top, Rope, Leaves, Verdigris, 1800s, 57 1/4 In.	6900.00
Finial, Fluted, Leaves, White Paint, Gilt, 19th Century, 7 1/4 In., Pair	288.00
Finial, Pineapple, Cast Iron, Dark Green, Mold Number, 20 1/2 In.	220.00
Gate, Arrow Point Finials, Iron, Stewart Iron Works, 46 x 50 1/4 In.	192.00
Gate, Carved Cross Stretcher, Iron Latch, Wood, 36 1/2 x 38 In.	1035.00
Gate, Iron, Lion & Lamb, Embossed P. Cobb, P. Holmes, 1857, 50 x 32 In.	1210.00
Gate, Leaf Scrolls, Scrolled Cresting, Lock, Iron, 47 1/2 x 38 In.	7475.00
Gate, Peak Top, Scrollwork, Iron, 73 1/2 x 38 In.	1760.00
Gate, Window, 4 Heart Center, Iron, 24 x 34 1/2 In., Pair	115.00

Half Column, Faux Marble, Marble Base, Gilt Capital, 1850s, 114 In., Pair 4600.00
Handle, Door, Bronze, Embossed Floral, 2 1/2 & 4 1/4 In., Pair 45.00
Hitching Post, Brass, Iron, Tubular Shaft, 19th Century, 38 In. 402.00
Hitching Post, Iron Ring On Dome, Granite, New England, 30 x 6 1/2 In. 920.00
Hitching Post, Jockey Form, Square Column Base, Cast Iron, 36 In. 288.00
Hitching Post, On Columnar Pedestal, Concrete Base, Cast Iron, 48 In. 518.00
Hook, Brass, Wall Mounting Plate, 1 3/4 In., Pair 67.00
Latch, Iron, Spring Movement, Decorative Cutout, Continental, 1700s, 7 x 6 In. 29.00
Mantel, Birds, Fern & Leaf Design, 83 In. 5600.00
Mantel, Classical, Oak, Columns, Bowfront, Shelf, Mirror, c.1905, 80 x 58 In. 392.00
Mantel, Dark Mahogany, Hooded Top, Gold Incised Carvings, 1875, 103 x 62 In. 7840.00
Mantel, Marble, 4 Carved Female Faces Forward, 48 x 61 In. 4025.00
Mantel, Marble, Gilt Bronze Mounted, 45 x 68 In. 7200.00
Mantel, Marble, Shelf Over Frieze, Leaf Border, Fluted Legs, 1870s, 42 1/2 In. 7223.00
Mantel, Ornate Flowers, Ornate Cast Iron Insert, 1885, 87 x 61 In. 3360.00
Mantel, Pine, Blue Paint Traces, Bucks County, Pa., 19th Century, 57 x 56 x 7 In. 230.00
Mantel, Surround, Marble, Keystone Cabochon, Victorian, 47 x 62 x 17 In. 4370.00
Mantel, Surround, Marble, Serpentine Shelf, Carved, Victorian, 43 x 62 x 12 In. 2990.00
Mantel, Surround, Oak, Carved Pediment, Fluted Jams, 66 x 66 In. 375.00
Mantel, Surround, Original Copper Patina, 37 x 25 1/2 In. 575.00
Mantel, Surround, Shelf Above Cornice, Cushion Frame, Gilt Floral, 51 1/4 In. 4800.00
Mantel, Surround, Wire Front, Brass Top, 19th Century, 12 x 26 x 12 In. 545.00
Mantel, Walnut, Block Front, Gothic Arch, Egg & Dart Molding, 62 x 96 1/2 In. 1540.00
Mantel, Walnut, Punched Design, 52 x 73 In. 690.00
Medallion, Ceiling, Plaster, Embossed, 27 In. Diam. 28.00
Model, House, 2 Story, Dormer, Shingle Roof, Fence, Clapboard, c.1900, 41 In. 575.00
Model, Staircase, Round, England, 41 1/2 In. 2300.00
Overmantel Mirror, 3 Sections, Half Columns, Capitals With Medallions, 60 x 26 In. 1020.00
Overmantel Mirror, Belle Epoque, Gilt Gesso, Beveled, Molded, c.1875, 67 x 61 In. 1150.00
Overmantel Mirror, Burl Veneer, 3 Sections, Beveled, Beaded, c.1840, 49 x 24 In. 112.00
Overmantel Mirror, Classical, Acanthus Frame, Gilt, Mid 19th Century, 26 In. 920.00
Overmantel Mirror, Gilt Urn Crest & Frame, Beveled, Decorative Arts Company 140.00
Overmantel Mirror, Giltwood, Carved Leaves, Late 19th Century, 63 1/2 x 44 1/2 In. 635.00
Overmantel Mirror, Regency Style, Giltwood, Bas Relief, Columns, 35 x 55 x 4 In. 1035.00
Overmantel Mirror, Regency, Giltwood, Garland Frieze, Swags, 53 x 35 x 9 In. 3450.00
Overmantel Mirror, Regency, Giltwood, Spherule Cornice, 34 1/2 x 2 x 4 1/4 In. 2300.00
Overmantel Mirror, Renaissance Revival, Carved Walnut, Beveled Plate, 76 In. 1035.00
Overmantel Mirror, William IV, Giltwood, Half Round Pilasters, 48 x 38 x 7 In. 2530.00
Overmantel Mirror, William IV, Giltwood, Mid 19th Century, 58 x 56 x 4 In. 4370.00
Panel, Basket Of Fruit With Bird, Flowers, Blue, Green, Pink, Italy, 82 In. 2760.00
Panel, Gilt Frame, Goth Fountains, 18th Century, 29 x 49 In. 1095.00
Panel, Giltwood, Molded Edge, Floral Swags, 112 x 36 In., 4 Piece 3910.00
Panel, Neoclassical, Green Paint, Scrolled Vines, Italy, 1900, 23 x 67 In. 2990.00
Panel, Neoclassical, Green Paint, Trailing Ribbon Vines, 41 1/2 In., Pair 2185.00
Panel, Neoclassical, Pinewood, White, Gray Fans, Italy, 11 1/2 x 42 x 2 In. 315.00
Panel, Overdoor, Louis XVI, Oak, 63 x 62 1/2 In. 1955.00
Panel, Pine, Carved Girl, Cat & Lotus Blossoms, Painted, Oriental, 26 x 68 In. 1430.00
Panel, Wallpaper, Allover Exotic Birds, Blossoming Tree Branches, 9 Ft. 8 In. 6000.00
Panel, Walnut, Carved, Dentil Crest, Mounted As Coatrack, 16 1/2 x 35 x 2 In. 635.00
Panel, Wood, Carved, Deity Figures, South Indian, 19th Century, 61 x 17 1/2 In. 345.00
Panel, Wood, Carved, Erotic Scenes, South Indian, 19th Century, 72 x 18 In. 520.00
Pedestal, Column, Corinthian, White, Cast Stone, 38 x 13 1/2 x 13 1/2 In. 196.00
Pedestal, Walnut, Column, Carved, Burl Panels, c.1880, 50 x 14 x 14 In. 670.00
Pediment, Eagle, Spread Wings, Copper, 28 1/4 x 24 In. 1725.00
Pelmet, Curtain Fixture, Napoleon III, Giltwood, Shell Crest, Pair 3220.00
Pelmet, Napoleon III, Pinewood, Tied By Bow, 6 x 9 In., 3 Piece 1495.00
Pilaster, Cypress, Polychromed, Doric Shape, Early 1900s, 88 1/2 x 9 3/4 In. 115.00
Push Plate, Silver & Silver Plate, Birds & Flowers, Relief, Gold, 9 3/4 x 3 1/2 In. 75.00
Roof Ornament, Owl, Molded, Hemispherical Form, Glass Eyes, Hinged Head, 27 In. 2875.00
Sink, Porcelain, Rectangular, Countertop, Brass Legs, Brackets, 1902, 23 x 32 In. 560.00
Strap Hinge, Bird Beak Design, Fastening Holes, 10 x 4 In., Pair 288.00
Street Light, Iron Pole, Round Glass Globe, Baltimore Street 330.00
Surround, Tile, Delft, Blue & White Soldiers, 17th Century, 24 Piece 1450.00

Teller's Screen, Bank, Iron, White Paint, Samuel Yellin, 1926, 41 x 69 In. 9200.00
Thumb Latch, Brass Inlay, Iron, Symmetrical, 28 In. 518.00
Tieback, Millefiori, Latticinio, Twists, Pewter, Screw, New England Glass, 1850 . . . . 385.00

AREQUIPA POTTERY was produced from 1911 to 1918 by the patients of the Arequipa Sanatorium in Marin County, north of San Francisco. The patients were trained by Frederick Hürten Rhead, who had worked at the Roseville Pottery.

    Vase, Bulbous, Textured Glaze, Robin's-Egg Blue, Stamped, 1912, 3 x 4 1/4 In. 430.00

ARGY-ROUSSEAU, see G. Argy-Rousseau category.

ARITA is a port in Japan. Porcelain was made there from about 1616. Many types of decorations were used, including the popular Imari designs, which are listed under Imari in this book.

    Bowl, Flowers, Leaves On Edge, Blue, White, Late 19th Century, 11 1/2 In. 201.00
    Bowl, Overall Spheres Of Brocades, Blue & White, 19th Century, 18 In. 1495.00
    Cup & Saucer, Lagoon, Pearl 20.00
    Dish, Chrysanthemums & Quail, Blue, Green, Red Enamels, c.1710, 8 In. 1080.00

ART DECO, or Art Moderne, a style started at the Paris Exposition of 1925, is characterized by linear, geometric designs. All types of furniture and decorative arts, jewelry, book bindings, and even games were designed in this style. Additional items may be found in the Furniture category or in various glass and pottery categories, etc.

    Ashtray, Glass Insert, 8 x 23 In. 374.00
    Bust, Black Woman, Pearl Necklace, Terra-Cotta, Philipps, 1930, 19 x 11 In. 675.00
    Desk Set, 7 Piece, Black Ebony, Chamois Lined Box With Faux Alligator Covering 300.00
    Figurine, Gypsy Girl, White, Cobalt, Gold Highlights, Porcelain, Moriyama, 12 x 13 In. . . 225.00
    Penholder, Gold, Jade, Onyx, Orange Enamel, Charlton & Company, 3 In. 316.00
    Plaque, Wall, Archer Design, Copper, 18 x 12 In. 337.00
    Sculpture, Kneeling Nude, Bronze Patina Finish, Manuel Carbonell, 19 x 23 In. 1800.00
    Vase, Cast Metal, Flared, Buttressed Sides, Brass Patina, 14 1/2 x 8 1/2 In. 105.00

ART GLASS, see Glass-Art category.

ART NOUVEAU is a style of design that was at its most popular from 1895 to 1905. Famous designers, including Rene Lalique and Emile Galle, produced furniture, glass, silver, metalwork, and buildings in the new style. Ladies with long flowing hair and elongated bodies were among the more easily recognized design elements. Copies of this style are being made today. Many modern pieces of jewelry can be found. Additional Art Nouveau pieces may be found in Furniture or in various glass categories.

    Basket, Cream Glass, 9 1/2 x 9 In. 1380.00
    Centerpiece, Silver, Gold Wash, Handles, Floral Spray Base, Sides, 8 In. 1610.00
    Chocolate Set, Porcelain, Gold & White, Continental, 11 1/2-In. Pitcher, 16 Piece 345.00
    Pitcher, Silver Overlay, Handle, Flowers & Lattice, Water Lilies, 8 1/4 In. 230.00

ART POTTERY, see Pottery-Art.

ARTHUR OSBORNE plaques are found in the Ivorex category.

ARTS & CRAFTS was a design style popular in American decorative arts from 1894 to 1923. In the 1970s collectors began to rediscover Mission furniture, art pottery, metalwork, linens, and light fixtures from this period. The interest has continued. Today everything from this era is collectible, including jewelry, graphics, and silverware. Additional items may be found in the Furniture category, various glass categories, etc.

    Jardiniere, Molded Leaves, Green Matte Glaze, 8 In. 245.00
    Lampshade, Prairie, Brown Leaded Glass, Domed, Giannini & Hilgart, 21 In. 3360.00
    Vase, Bell-Shaped Cover, Flower-Form Rim, Agate Finial, Frank Marshall, 8 x 5 In. 560.00

AURENE glass was made by Frederick Carder of New York about 1904. It is an iridescent gold, blue, green, or red glass, usually marked *Aurene* or *Steuben.*

AURENE

Basket, Gold, Applied Handle, 8 1/4 x 7 3/4 x 5 1/4 In.	1495.00
Bowl, Blue, 3 1/4 x 8 In.	750.00
Bowl, Gold, Calcite Interior, 10 In.	650.00
Bowl, Gold, Footed, Acid Stamp Mark, 6 x 2 1/2 In.	400.00
Bowl, Gold, Ruffled Edge, 5 1/4 In.	250.00
Bowl, Gold, Signed, 8 In.	448.00
Bowl, Red, 6 7/8 x 2 3/8 In.	990.00
Compote, Gold, Acid Stamp Mark, 8 x 6 1/4 In.	2300.00
Compote, Ribbed, Gold, 6 7/8 x 3 In.	495.00
Cordial, Gold, 2 1/4 In.	275.00
Goblet, Gold, 6 Piece	2600.00
Nut Dish, Gold, 1 1/2 In.	325.00 to 525.00
Plate, Gold, 10 In.	460.00
Shade, 10 Ribs, Gold, 5 7/8 In.	126.00 to 290.00
Shade, Gold, Melon Ribbed, Scalloped, 5 x 5 1/2 In.	130.00
Shade, Gold, Scalloped Rim, 5 7/8 In.	275.00
Vase, Blue, 2 1/2 In.	975.00
Vase, Blue, 4 1/2 x 2 1/2 In.	635.00
Vase, Blue, 7 1/2 In.	750.00
Vase, Blue, 12 In.	1350.00
Vase, Blue, Footed, 5 1/4 x 5 5/8 In.	690.00
Vase, Blue, Tree Trunk Shape, No. 2744, 6 1/2 In.	1450.00
Vase, Bud, Blue, 8 In.	895.00
Vase, Bud, Gold, 8 1/4 In.	795.00
Vase, Bulb, Gold, Dimpled, Swirled Texture, 8 In.	575.00
Vase, Gold, 2 1/2 In.	675.00
Vase, Gold, Applied Prunts, 11 3/4 In.	2200.00
Vase, Gold, Footed, 5 1/2 In.	520.00
Vase, Gold, Ribbed, 5 In.	490.00
Vase, Gold, Ruffled Edge, 8 1/4 x 8 In.	995.00
Vase, Gold, Ruffled Edge, Iridescent, 6 In.	145.00

AUSTRIA is a collecting term that covers pieces made by a wide variety of factories. They are listed in this book in categories such as Royal Dux, or Porcelain.

AUTO parts and accessories are collectors' items today. Gas pump globes and license plates are part of this specialty. Prices are determined by age, rarity, and condition. Signs and packaging related to automobiles may also be found in the Advertising category. Lalique hood ornaments will be listed in the Lalique category.

Ashtray, Michelin Man, Bakelite	125.00
Blotter, Oldfield Tires, 3 1/4 x 6 1/4 In.	100.00
Brush, Dietrich Motor Car Co., Allentown, Pa., Cadillac Emblem, Celluloid, 3 1/2 In.	135.00
Cabinet, A.C. Spark Plug, Oak Frame, Slanted Glass Front, Back Door, 34 2/3 In.	275.00
Dispenser, Soap, Shell Oil, Logo On Front, 6 1/2 In.	467.00
Gas Pump, Wayne Fire Chief, 80 x 28 x 16 In.	650.00
Gas Pump Globe, Apco Premium Gas, 13 1/2 In.	100.00
Gas Pump Globe, Barnsdall Super-Gas, Ethyl, Milk Glass, 16 1/2 x 15 1/2 In.	550.00
Gas Pump Globe, Bay Gas, Plastic, 13 1/2 In.	165.00
Gas Pump Globe, Danciger Road Runner Anti-Knock	2600.00
Gas Pump Globe, Johnson Winged 70 Gasoline	2600.00
Gas Pump Globe, Koolmoter High Test	900.00
Gas Pump Globe, Mobilgas, Flying Horse	600.00
Gas Pump Globe, Red Indian, 13 1/2 In.	687.00
Gas Pump Globe, Ryan's Jet Regular, Milk Glass, Both Sides, 16 1/2 In.	385.00
Gas Pump Globe, Shell Gasoline, Clamshell Form, Fill Nozzle, Logos, 5 Ft.	1495.00
Gas Pump Globe, Skelly, It's Better Gasoline, Red Paint, 15 In.	135.00
Gas Pump Globe, X-Tane Globe, Plastic Body, 16 1/2 x 13 1/2 In.	120.00
Gas Stick, Red Crown, Wooden	30.00

Gas Stick, Texaco, Wooden 30.00
Gasoline Can, Pep Boys Motor Oil, 2 Gal. 143.00
Glass, Esso Tiger, Put A Tiger In Your Tank, 5 1/2 In. 23.00
Hood Ornament, Bronze, Signed, F. Basin, c.1930, 8 In. 672.00
Hood Ornament, Jocko The Monkey, Gilt Bronzed, Brunswick, c.1920 .... 1300.00
Hood Ornament, Mack Bulldog, Chrome, 1950s, 4 In. 75.00
Hood Ornament, Pickup Truck, Texas, Longhorn Steer 45.00
Hubcap, Model T 45.00
Kit, First Aid, Flying Red Horse, Mobil Gas, Tin, 3 1/2 x 3 3/4 In. 33.00
License Plate, Arizona, 1959 .... 15.00
License Plate, Arkansas, 1959 .... 17.00
License Plate, Illinois, 1913, Pair 310.00
License Plate, Illinois, 1916 .... 30.00
License Plate, Illinois, 1928 .... 24.00
License Plate, Illinois, 1934 .... 25.00
License Plate, Illinois, 1935, Designated TR 17.00
License Plate, Maine, Porcelain, 1914, Pair 137.00
License Plate, Maryland, 1932 .... 20.00
License Plate, Michigan, 1926, Pair 30.00
License Plate, New Hampshire, 1978 .... 25.00
License Plate, Ohio, 1947, Embossed Farm 20.00
License Plate, Pennsylvania, 1907, Porcelain, Red, 6 1/2 x 8 1/4 In. 305.00
License Plate, Pennsylvania, 1942, Steel, Yellow, Navy, 1943 Renewal Tag 15.00
License Plate, Pennsylvania, 1958 .... 8.00
License Plate, Pennsylvania, 1964, Truck 8.00
License Plate, Tennessee, 1962, Pair 18.00
License Plate Tag, Buckeye Beer, Drive Safely, Embossed Metal, 1930s 45.00
Mirror, Jordan Auto, Southwest Motor Co., Kansas City, Mo., Tinted Sepia, 3 1/2 In. 450.00
Oil Can, Beacon Premium Motor Oil, Showing A Lighthouse, 5 1/2 x 4 In. 305.00
Oil Can, Bugatti, Horse On 1 Side, Tin, 8 3/4 x 6 1/2 x 2 3/8 In. 350.00
Oil Can, Golden Shell, Tin, 11 x 8 x 3 In. 600.00
Oil Can, Grand Champion Special Motor Oil, Race Track Scene, 5 1/2 x 4 In. 400.00
Oil Can, Husky Premium Motor Oil, Husky Dog With Starburst, Tin, 5 1/2 x 4 In. 475.00
Oil Can, Marathon Endurance, 1 Qt. 130.00
Oil Can, Marquette Motor Oil, Showing Bust Of Pere Marquette, 5 1/2 x 4 In. 210.00
Oil Can, Mohawk Chieftain Motor Oil, Mohawk Indian On Front, 5 1/2 x 4 In. 190.00
Oil Can, Motor Gold Motor Oil, High Point, N.C., Tin, 5 1/2 x 4 In. 125.00
Oil Can, National Enarco Motor Oil, Tin, 5 1/2 x 4 In. 60.00
Oil Can, Oilzum, Tin, 1 Gal. 250.00
Oil Can, Pennzoil Motor Oil, 3 Owls With Train, Tin, 5 1/2 x 4 In. 70.00
Oil Can, Pennzoil Outboard Motor Oil, Man, Motor Boat In Center, Tin, 5 1/2 x 4 In. 100.00
Oil Can, Pennzoil, Plane, United Airlines Uses Pennzoil Exclusively, Tin, 1 Qt. 90.00
Oil Can, Premier Ranger Motor Oil, Tin, 5 1/2 x 4 In. 150.00
Oil Can, Red Indian, 1 Qt. 110.00
Oil Can, Richlube Motor Oil, Blue Ground, Tin, 5 1/2 x 4 In. 110.00
Oil Can, Richlube Motor Oil, Tin, 6 1/2 x 8 x 3 In. 950.00
Oil Can, Richlube Oil & Greases, Tin, 6 x 7 x 3 In. 150.00
Oil Can, Signal Outboard Motor Oil, Factory Seal, Stop Light Logo, 1 Qt. 253.00
Oil Can, Sinclair Motor Oil, Dinosaur Image, Tin, 5 Qt. 60.50
Oil Can, Texaco Chassis Lubricant S Grease, Cover, Tin, 5 x 4 1/4 In. 40.00
Oil Can, Texaco Marine Motor Oil, Marina Scene, White Ground, 5 1/2 x 4 In. 375.00
Oil Can, Texaco Marine Motor Oil, Water & Boat Scene, Tin, 10 x 5 In. 555.00
Oil Can, Texaco Motor Cup Grease Can, Black Outline, Tin, 3 x 3 3/4 In. 70.00
Oil Can, Texaco Motor Oil, T Logo, 1 Qt. 77.00
Oil Can, Texaco Outboard Motor Oil, Dark Green Ground, Tin, 5 1/2 x 4 In. 15.00
Oil Can, Texaco Outboard Motor Oil, Tin, 7 1/4 x 4 1/4 In. 60.00
Oil Can, Thermo Antifreeze, Infamous Snowman Racing To Overheated Car, 5 x 4 In. 130.00
Oil Can, Thompson Products Aerotype Motor Oil, Tin, 5 1/2 x 4 In. 100.00
Oil Can, Valvespout Oil, Brass Spout 38.50
Oil Can, Wash R Lube Lubricant, Washing Machine On Front, 5 1/2 x 4 In. 50.00
Oil Can, Waverly Oil Works, Motor Oil, 1 Qt. 110.00
Oil Can, Wings Heavy Duty, 3 Birds, Tin, Wichita, Ks., 5 1/2 x 4 In. 100.00

Pennant, Haynes, America's First Car, Haynes Light Six, Green & White, 19 In. 65.00
Pennant, Maxwell, Automobiles, Blue, Orange, 26 In. 100.00
Rack, Display, Cities Service Oil Can Logo, Holds 18 1-Quart Tins, 36 x 17 In. 312.00
Rack, Map Holder, Texaco, Logos At Top, 9 x 4 In. 180.00
Radiator Cap, Ford, Model T, Brass 35.00
Sign, Amalie Pennsylvania Motor Oil, Porcelain, Lollipop Shape, c.1936, 32 x 54 In. 403.00
Sign, Amoco, American Gas, Courtesy Cards Accepted, 2 Sides, 24 x 15 In. 110.00
Sign, Associated Motorways, Porcelain, Flange, 2 Sides, 1930s-1940s, 23 x 18 In. 1553.00
Sign, Buick Service, Porcelain, Round, 1930s, 42 In. 468.00
Sign, C & S Axle Grease, Whittier Corbin Co., Paper Lithograph, 18 x 26 In. 220.00
Sign, Chevrolet, OK Used Cars, Authorized Dealer, Porcelain, 2 Sides, 46 x 52 In. 1210.00
Sign, Esso Touring Service, Porcelain, 2 Sides, c.1963, 19 1/2 x 19 1/2 In. 200.00
Sign, Eveready Prestone, The Perfect Anti-Freeze, Does Not Boil Off, Tin, 2 Sides, 1 Gal. 121.00
Sign, Exide Batteries, Tin, Self-Framed, 16 x 47 1/2 In. 130.00
Sign, Firestone Tires, Auto Supplies, Lollipop Shape 375.00
Sign, Fisk Tires, Cardboard, 1917, 17 x 33 In. 3410.00
Sign, Fisk Tires, Magic Shoes, Cardboard, Frame, c.1917, 17 1/2 x 33 1/4 In. 3210.00
Sign, Ford, Model T, Wooden, Max Swain & Bathing Beauties, 1901, 41 x 67 In. 275.00
Sign, Gillette Tires, Blue & Yellow, A Bear For Wear, Tin, Wooden Frame, 19 x 73 In. ... 403.00
Sign, Goodyear Tires, Porcelain, Wall Bracket, Diamond Shape, 2 Sides, 48 In. 345.00
Sign, Humble Gasoline, Porcelain, Oval, 14 x 7 In. 240.00
Sign, Humble Oil Co., Porcelain, Die Cut, Blue & Yellow Oil Drop Man, 24 x 48 In. 1100.00
Sign, Johnson Ethyl, Porcelain, Lollipop Shape, Round, 30 In. 1300.00
Sign, Kendall Motor Oil, Penzbest, Porcelain, Round, 2 Sides, 24 In. 385.00
Sign, Mobilgas Special, Pegasus, Porcelain, Die Cut, Shield Shape, c.1947, 12 x 12 In. ... 115.00
Sign, Mobilgas, Porcelain, Pump, 12 x 11 1/2 In. 450.00
Sign, Mobilgas, Red Pegasus Horse, Porcelain, Round, 12 In. 33.00
Sign, Mobiloil, Ask Here For Gargoyle Mobiloil, Lollipop Shape, 2 Sides, 24 x 64 In. ... 460.00
Sign, Mobiloil, Porcelain & Metal, White & Black, c.1920, 36 x 84 In. 900.00
Sign, Phillips 66, Shield Form, 2 Sides, 1955, 29 x 29 In. 440.00
Sign, Pro-Tex-U-Lite, Highway Safety Light, Cardboard, Die Cut, 16 1/2 x 20 1/2 In. 27.50
Sign, Pump Plate, Signal Gasoline, Stoplight Graphics, Porcelain, Round, 12 In. 33.00
Sign, Pump Plate, Texaco Sky Chief Gasoline, Porcelain, Dated 3/4/54, 12 x 18 In. 143.00
Sign, Pump Plate, Texaco, Texaco Star, Porcelain, Round, 12 In. 22.00
Sign, Speed Limits, Teams Not Faster Than A Walk, Zinc, 2 Sides, 24 x 35 In. 335.00
Sign, Standard Oil Co., Tin, 48 x 72 In. 375.00
Sign, Sunoco Motor Oil, Distilled, Porcelain, Yellow Ground, 10 x 12 In. 190.00
Sign, Texaco, Fire Chief Hat, Porcelain, 1940, 18 x 10 In. 198.00
Sign, Texaco, No Smoking, Porcelain, 4 x 23 In. 155.00
Sign, Tydol Motor Oil, Porcelain, 14 x 42 In. 475.00
Sign, Union 7600 Marine Gasoline, Porcelain, 11 1/2 In. 300.00
Sign, United Motors, Porcelain, Orange, Blue, 2 Sides, Hanging Bracket, 48 x 28 In. 1035.00
Sign, Valvoline Motor Oil, Lubester, Round, 7 In. 155.00
Spark Plug, Adko, Take-Apart, Brass Body, Patent 1910 .... 175.00
Spark Plug, Atlas, Champion, Logo, JJ8 .... 5.50
Spark Plug, Atlas, N9Y Or AC 3.00
Spark Plug, Automatic, 3/8 In. 7.50
Spark Plug, Blue Crown X-Citer, 3 Times Indy 500 Winner, Box, 1950s, 2 1/2 In. 50.00
Spark Plug, Caterpillar, Cat Logo, 18mm 5.00
Spark Plug, Champion, H12 .... 6.50
Spark Plug, Champion, J11 .... 6.50
Spark Plug, Chrome Plated, 7/8 Inch Thread 8.50
Spark Plug, Cruisemaster, Logo, No. 57 .... 4.00
Spark Plug, Dunlop, Gas Saver 8.00
Spark Plug, Firestone, White Insulator 8.00
Spark Plug, John Deere, Champion, H10 .... 5.00
Spark Plug, Mica, Insulated, Brass Sleeve Nut 25.00
Spark Plug, Motormeter, Take-Apart, Patent 12-15-25 .... 35.00
Spark Plug, Prestolite, Champion Jr. 4.25
Spark Plug, Taper Seat, Ford Type 6.50
Token, New Paris Car Wash, Good For 25 Cents 2.50
Tumbler, Phillips 66, Package, 4 Piece 32.00

AUTUMN LEAF pattern china was made for the Jewel Tea Company beginning in 1933. Hall China Company of East Liverpool, Ohio, Crooksville China Company of Crooksville, Ohio, Harker Potteries of Chester, West Virginia, and Paden City Pottery, Paden City, West Virginia, made dishes with this design. Autumn Leaf has remained popular and was made by Hall China Company until 1978. Some other pieces in the Autumn Leaf pattern are still being made. For more information, see *Kovels' Depression Glass & Dinnerware Price List*.

Baker, Fort Pitt, Oval, Individual, 12 Oz.	225.00
Baker, French, 4 1/2 In.	50.00
Bean Pot, Handle, 2 1/4 In.	950.00
Bowl, Fruit, 5 1/2 In.	10.00
Bowl, Sunshine, No. 4, 7 1/2 In.	27.00
Bowl, Vegetable, Oval, Ruffled	30.00
Butter, 1/4 Lb.	229.00
Clock, 1956	96.00
Coffeepot, Drip	350.00
Cookie Jar, Tootsie	295.00
Cup & Saucer	60.00
Gravy Boat, Underplate	51.00
Gravy Boat, Underplate, Ruffled	65.00
Jug, 2 1/2 Pt.	18.00
Jug, Ball, No. 3	60.00
Mixing Bowl, Nested, Set Of 3	110.00
Mug, Irish Coffee	100.00
Pepper Shaker, Stove Top	6.00
Pitcher	65.00
Plate, 6 In.	9.00
Plate, 9 In.	11.00
Plate, Dinner, 10 In.	18.00
Plate, Dinner, Ruffled, 10 In.	20.00
Saucer	3.00
Soup, Cream	36.00
Soup, Dish, 8 1/2 In.	18.00
Stack Set, 4 Piece	150.00
Sugar, Cover, Ruffled	32.00
Sugar & Creamer	46.00
Teapot, Aladdin	60.00
Teapot, Newport	60.00
Warmer, Oval	122.00
Warmer, Oval, Decal	245.00

AVON bottles are listed in the Bottle category under Avon.

AZALEA dinnerware was made for Larkin Company customers from 1918 to 1941. Larkin, the soap company, was in Buffalo, New York. The dishes were made by Noritake China Company of Japan. Each piece of the white china was decorated with pink azaleas.

Bowl, Oatmeal, Gold, 1930, 5 1/2 In., Pair	16.00
Bowl, Vegetable, Green Mark, 5 x 8 In.	45.00
Bowl, Vegetable, Handles, 9 1/4 In.	55.00
Butter, Cover, Gold Trim, 1 1/2 x 6 1/2 In.	65.00
Cake Plate, 9 3/4 In.	50.00
Creamer, 1932	22.00
Cup & Saucer	15.00 to 22.00
Cup & Saucer, Gold, 1930, 2 x 3 1/2 In.	12.00
Dish, Pickle	18.00
Gravy Boat, Gold Trim, 1930, 9 x 6 In.	34.00
Gravy Boat, Underplate	42.00
Plate, Bread & Butter, Gold Trim, Green Mark, 6 1/2 In., 5 Piece	38.00
Plate, Dinner, 10 In.	25.00
Plate, Gold Trim, 1930, 10 In., Pair	20.00

Plate, Gold Trim, Green Mark, 7 5/8 In. 12.00
Plate, Salad, Gold Trim, 1930, 7 5/8 In., Pair 8.00
Plate, Serving, Gold, Handle, 1920, 9 3/4 In. 28.00
Platter, Gold Handles, Green Mark, 10 In. 39.00
Platter, Gold Trim, 1930, 11 3/4 In. 44.00
Platter, Medium ....54.00 to 56.00
Platter, Small 54.00
Relish, Divided, Gold Trim, 8 1/4 In. 58.00
Salt & Pepper, Gold 25.00
Soup, Dish, Gold, 1930, 7 1/2 In., Pair 20.00
Sugar, Cover, 1932 .... 24.00
Sugar & Creamer, Cover 45.00
Sugar & Creamer, Cover, Gold, 1920 .... 36.00
Tureen, Cover, Green Mark, 3 In. 149.00

BACCARAT glass was made in France by La Compagnie des Cristalleries de Baccarat, located 150 miles from Paris. The factory was started in 1765. The firm went bankrupt and began operating again about 1822. Cane and millefiori paperweights were made during the 1860 to 1880 period. The firm is still working near Paris making paperweights and glasswares.

Bowl, Red Cut To Green, Gold Designs, Silver Rim, Cameo, 4 1/2 In. 650.00
Cordial Set, Gold, Iridescent, Blue Iridescent Handles, 11 Piece 575.00
Decanter, Art Deco Style, Cutting, Square, Silver Collar, 1925 .... 1800.00
Decanter, Hexagonal, Narrow Neck, Stopper, 8 7/8 In. 86.00
Decanter, Zipper Cut, Stopper, 10 In. 225.00
Goblet Set, Harcourt, Signed, 6 In., 12 Piece 1035.00
Inkwell, Swirl, Silver Plated Cover, Square, Large, 1900 .... 900.00
Jar, Cover, Flared, Hexagonal, 5 1/4 x 5 1/2 In. 810.00
Lamp, Gone With The Wind, Hunting Dogs, Mountain & Lake, Signed, 18 In. 1850.00
Lamp, Pinwheel, 8 3/4 In. 275.00
Paperweight, Butterfly, Multicolored Wings, Green & White Canes, 2 x 3 In. 2415.00
Paperweight, Central Yellow Flower 86.00
Paperweight, Concentric Cane Circle, Millefiori Center, Crow's Foot, 1850, 1 In. 300.00
Paperweight, Dahlia, Millefiori, Star, Cog, Arrow & Stardust Canes, 2 1/16 In. 300.00
Paperweight, Green, Yellow Snake, Blue Flowers, Mottled Ground, 1970, 3 1/8 In. 385.00
Paperweight, Pansy, Millefiori Star Cane Center, Star Cut Base, 1850, 2 5/16 In. 465.00
Paperweight, Sulphide, Eleanor Roosevelt 225.00
Pitcher, Swirl, Amberina Coloring, Swirl, Crystal Handle, 9 1/4 In. 295.00
Sculpture, Angel, Fitted Box, 7 In. 230.00
Sculpture, Rabbit, Satin, Signed, 3 In. 105.00
Sculpture, Tennis Player, Signed, 9 1/2 In. 295.00
Sculpture, Tiger, Standing, Signed, 5 3/4 x 2 1/4 In. 55.00
Toothpick, Swirl 150.00
Vase, Amber, Snake, Insect In Marsh, Satin Glass, Signed, 8 In. 730.00
Vase, Bud, Opalescent, Enameled Maiden, Gold Trim, 8 In., Pair 260.00
Vase, Star Cut Body, Swags Of Flowers, Scrolls, Tapered, 15 1/2 In. 2990.00
Vase, Trumpet, Flared, Paneled, Floral Collar, Brass Base, 12 In. 402.00
Wine Cooler, Tapered, Octagonal, 9 1/8 In. 575.00

BADGES have been used since before the Civil War. Collectors search for examples of all types, including law enforcement and company identification badges. Well-known prison or law enforcement badges are most desirable. Most are made of nickel or brass. Many recent reproductions have been made.

3rd Cavalry Reunion, Custer Bust, Crossed Swords, Guidons 650.00
Alert Affiliated League Of Emergency Radio Teams, 3 x 2 1/4 In. 25.00
American Ambulance, Kentucky 32.00
Automobile Association, Auckland, New Zealand, Mount Bracket, 3 x 3 In. 16.00
Automobile Association, Auckland, New Zealand, Yellow, c.1950 .... 30.00
California Department Of Corrections, Great Seal, Blackinton, 2 3/4 In. 85.00
Chauffeur, Arizona, Bronze, 1933, 1 3/4 In. 105.00
Chauffeur, City Of Cincinnati, 1968 .... 25.00

Chauffeur, Licensed, Illinois, 1951, 1 3/4 x 1 1/4 In. 25.00
Chauffeur, New York, Enamel On Bronze, 1917, 1 1/8 In. 24.00
Chauffeur, New York, Screw Back, Oval, 1922-1923 .... 35.00
Convention, 17th, Western Pa. Fireman's Assn., Penn. Delegate, 1910 .... 85.00
Convention, 18th, Western Pa. Fireman's Assn., Monongahela Delegate, 1911 .... 85.00
Convention, 20th, Western Pa. Fireman's Assn., Punxatawney Delegate, 1913 .... 85.00
Convention, 22nd, Western Pa. Fireman's Assn., Sharpsburg Delegate, 1915 .... 85.00
Employee, Interborough Rapid Transit Co., 2 1/4 In. 28.00
Employee, Sharpshooter's Park, 20, 2 3/8 In. 290.00
Employee, United States Postal, Shield Shape 100.00
Fishing, Metal, Dark Brown, Pennsylvania, 1 3/4 In. 22.00
Fishing, Metal, Light Beige, Pennsylvania, 1 3/4 In. 20.00
Game Warden, Wyoming Game & Fish Department, Shield Shape, Clasp Back 275.00
Game Warden, Wyoming, Game & Fish Department, 17, Brass, Deer Design 250.00
Guard, Am-Gard America's Guard Co., 3 x 2 In. 28.00
Guard, Ford, 1950s 16.00
Guard, Pitchfork Dingbats, Oval, Ticked Edge, Wire Pin, 1890s, 2 1/8 x 1 3/8 In. 135.00
Inspector, U.S. Naval Air Station, Fire Department 50.00
Junior Fire Fighting, Orange County, California 35.00
Labor, Convention, Delegate, AFL-CIO, Gold, Embossed, Washington, D.C., 1979, 3 In. . 25.00
Labor, Convention, Delegate, Amalgamated Clothing Workers, Atlantic City, 1946, 3 In. . 38.00
Labor, Convention, Delegate, Bricklayers, Masons & Plasterers, Miami, 1950, 4 In. 28.00
Labor, Convention, Delegate, United Food & Commercial Workers International Union .. 18.00
Labor, Convention, Delegate, United Steelworkers Of America, Ribbons, 1964, 4 1/4 In. . 30.00
Labor, Convention, Delegate, United Steelworkers, Embossed Figures, 1970, 4 1/4 In. ... 28.00
Letter Carrier, U.S. Post Office, Hat, 11, 2 1/2 x 2 In. 18.00
License, Hunting, Fishing, Trapping, New York, 1930, 1 3/4 In. 55.00
N.S.G.W., Suspension, Gilt, Die Cut, Bear, Enamel, Shield, 4 Scenes, Shreve, S.F. 140.00
Police, 2nd Assistant Chief, Boston, Pa., 2 3/4 x 1 7/8 In. 35.00
Police, Chief, Wire Pin, Brass, Gold Wash, Embossed Wreath, 2 3/4 x 1 1/2 In. 150.00
Police, Philadelphia Police, Scalloped Edge, Number In Center, Oval, 1920, 3 In. 90.00
Police, Stamped Chief Police In Black, Hat, 3 7/8 x 1 5/8 In. 200.00
Police, Washington, D.C., Metropolitan Asst. Chief, 2 1/4 x 2 1/8 In. 195.00
Railroad, Canadian Pacific Express, J.R. Caunt, Montreal 71.40
Reporter, Department Of Public Safety, Pittsburgh, Copper Castle Center, 1920s, 2 In. ... 50.00
Sheriff, Linn Co. Illinois, 6-Point Star, Ball Tips, Tower & Lyon, N.Y., 2 1/4 x 2 1/2 In. ... 600.00
Taxi Driver, Yellow Cab Co., Inlaid Enamel, c.1950, 2 3/4 x 2 1/4 In. 180.00
Trooper, Texas Department Of Public Safety, Retired Trooper, 1 7/8 In. 55.00
U.S. Mail, Motor Service, Truck Wheel Shape, Nickel Plated 75.00
Volunteer, U.S. Marine Corps Recruiting Agent, Nickel Plated 75.00
Water Department, Baltimore City 35.00
Workman's, Quaker State Oil Refining Corp., 1 7/8 x 1 7/8 In. 83.00
Workman's, Tennessee Valley Authority, Metal 8.00

BANKS of metal have been made since 1868. There are still banks, mechanical banks, and registering banks (those that show the total money deposited on the face of the bank). Many old iron or tin banks have been reproduced since the 1950s in iron or plastic. Some old reproductions marked Book of Knowledge or John Wright, or Capron are listed. Pottery, glass, and plastic banks are also listed here. Mickey Mouse and other Disneyana banks are listed in Disneyana. We have added the M-numbers based on *The Penny Bank Book: Collected Still Banks* by Andy and Susan Moore.

A-1 Beer, 72-73 Phoenix Roadrunners 17.00
Acorn Form, Gold Textured Cap, Redware, 4 1/2 In. 326.00
Andy Gump Thrift Bank, Tin, c.1920, M 218, 4 3/4 In. 305.00
Aunt Jemima, Mammy With Spoon, Cast Iron, A.C. Williams, 1900, M 168, 5 7/8 In. ... 115.00
Bank Building, City Bank, Cast Iron, Gold Paint, Inscribed City Bank & Pay Teller, 5 In. . 380.00
Bank Building, Cupola Bank, Cast Iron, J. & E. Stevens, 1872, M 1145, 5 In. .....340.00 to 489.00
Bank Building, Cupola Bank, Cast Iron, J. & E. Stevens, 1872, M 1146, 4 1/8 In. ..165.00 to 605.00
Bank Building, Home Savings, Cast Iron, M 1201, 10 1/2 In. 800.00
Bank Building, State Bank, Cast Iron, M 1083, 4 1/4 In. 295.00
Barrel, Dodge Saves, Detroit Area Dealer, Tin, Chein, 1920s, M 1583, 4 In. 130.00

Never repaint an old bank. It lowers the resale value.

Bank, Book, Cinderella, Tin, 5 3/4 In.   Bank, Church, Tin, 3 1/4 In.

Baseball Player, Cast Iron, A.C. Williams, 1909-1934, M 18, 5 3/4 In.	176.00 to 385.00
Beaky Buzzard, Metal, Warner Brothers, 5 In.	125.00
Bear, Sitting, Front Paws Up, Black Paint, Cast Iron, 5 1/4 In.	66.00
Bear Stealing Pig, Cast Iron, M 693, 5 1/2 In.	385.00
Bear With Honey Pot, Cast Iron, Hubley, 1936, M717, 6 1/2 In.	144.00 to 172.00
Begging Bear, Cast Iron, A.C. Williams, 1910-1925, M 715, 5 3/8 In.	253.00
Begging Rabbit, Cast Iron, A.C. Williams, 1908-1920, M 566, 5 1/8 In.	155.00
Big Boy, Figural, Vinyl, 8 In.	12.00
Billiken On Throne, Good Luck, Cast Iron, A.C. Williams, 4 1/2 In.	40.00 to 57.00
Black Boy, 2 Faces, Cast Iron, A.C. Williams, 1901-1919, M 84, 3 1/8 In.	220.00
Blackpool Tower, Brown Japanning, Cast Iron, Chamberlain & Hill, 1908, M 984, 7 In.	220.00
Boat, Battleship Maine, Cast Iron, Grey Iron Casting, 1897-1903, M 1441, 5 1/4 In.	350.00
Boat, Battleship Oregon, Cast Iron, Brown Japanning, J. & E. Stevens, M 1450, 5 In.	412.00
Book, Cinderella, Tin, 5 3/4 In.	*Illus* 33.00
Buffalo, Amherst Stoves, Cast Iron, c.1930, M 556, 8 In.	104.00
Bugs Bunny, With Barrel, Painted Aluminum, W.B. Co., 5 3/4 In.	49.00
Building, Castle, With 2 Towers, Cast Iron, England, c.1908, M 1114, 7 In.	1430.00
Building, Columbia Tower, Cast Iron, Columbia Grey Iron Casting, 1897, M 1118, 7 In.	770.00
Building, Get Rich Quick, Tin, Lithographed, Marx, c.1930, 4 x 2 1/2 In.	185.00
Building, High-Rise, Cast Iron, Kenton, M 1217, 5 1/2 In.	340.00
Building, Mosque, Cast Iron, Grey Iron Casting, 1903-1928, M 1177, 4 1/4 In.	175.00
Building, New England Church, Cast Iron, Nickel Finish, M 986, 7 1/2 In.	220.00
Building, Roof, Cast Iron, J. & E. Stevens, 1887, M 1122, 5 1/4 In.	230.00
Building, Rose Window, Cast Iron, England, M 1170, 2 1/2 In.	425.00
Building, Strauss Building, Lead, 5 In.	209.00
Building, West Side Presbyterian Church, Cast Iron, M 958, 3 1/2 In.	340.00
Building, Westminster Abbey, Cast Iron, England, c.1908, 6 1/4 In.	253.00
Building, Woolworth Building, Dark Green, Ceramic, M 1043, 5 1/4 In.	242.00
Building, World's Fair Administration Building, Cast Iron, M 1072, 6 In.	1232.00
Building, Wrigley Building, Spelter, Banthrico, 1981, M 1223, 7 1/2 In.	90.00
Calumet Baking Powder, Waxed Cardboard, Tin Top & Bottom, 4 In.	70.00
Camel, Cast Iron, Gold Paint, A.C. Williams, 1917-1920, M 767, 7 1/4 In.	257.00
Camel, Small, Cast Iron, M 768, 4 3/4 In.	204.00
Camel With Pack, Composition, Hausser, Germany, 1929, M 771, 4 In.	110.00
Car, Ford, Model T, Arcade, Cast Iron, 1923-1925, M 1484, 6 1/2 In.	1595.00
Car, Yellow Cab, Arcade, Cast Iron, 1921, M 1493, 4 1/4 In.	935.00
Car, Yellow Cab, Driver, Arcade, 1921, M 1489, 4 1/4 x 7 3/4 In.	2310.00
Cash Register, Junior, Cast Iron, J. & E. Stevens, 1920s, M 931, 5 1/4 In.	264.00
Champion Heater Safe, Cast Iron, M 1355, 4 1/8 In.	155.00
Church, Steeple, Tin, 16 In.	440.00
Church, Tin, 3 1/4 In.	*Illus* 33.00
Clock, Glass, Candy Container, M 1625, 3 3/4 In.	130.00
Cockatoo, Metal, M 656, 5 In.	85.00
Cook County Federal Savings, Spelter, 4 1/4 In.	88.00
Cottage With Side Shed, Composition, 2 7/8 In.	231.00
Cream Of Corn Soup, Tin Lithograph, Aylmer, 4 In.	20.00

Crosley Radio, Cast Iron, Kenton, 1931-1936, M 820, 4 5/16 In. 220.00
Daffy Duck At Barrel, Metal, Metal Moss Mfg., 1930s, M 285, 4 1/4 In. 60.00
Deer, Standing, Cast Iron, M 736, 6 In. 125.00
Devil, 2 Faces, Original Paint, Cast Iron, A.C. Williams, 1904-1912, M 31, 4 1/2 In. 517.00
Dick Whittington Book, Tin, 5 3/4 In. 55.00
Dog, Begging, Lead, Continental, M 384, 3 1/2 In. 800.00
Dog, Boston Bull Terrier, Paint Wear, Cast Iron, Vindex, c.1931, M 421, 5 1/4 In. 175.00
Dog, Fala, Scotty, Cast Iron, U.S., 1930s, M 430, 2 3/4 In. 365.00
Dog, Fido, Cast Iron, Hubley, 1914-1946, M 417, 5 In. 165.00
Dog, On Tub, Cast Iron, A.C. Williams, 1920-1934, M 359, 4 1/6 In. 175.00
Dog, Spaniel, Standing, Cast Iron, Hubley, 1930s, M 418, 3 3/4 In. ....110.00 to 330.00
Dolphin, Cast Iron, Grey Iron Casting, c.1900, M 33, 4 1/2 In. 440.00
Donkey, With Saddle, Cast Iron, 1913-1934, M 499, 4 1/2 In. 115.00
Donkey, With Saddle, Stirrups, Composition, Hausser, Germany, 1929, M 492, 4 1/2 In. ... 121.00
Eagle, With Shield, Old Abe, Cast Iron, U.S., c.1880, M 676, 3 7/8 In. 910.00
Eight O'Clock Coffee, Tin, Red, Gold & Black, Coffee Logo, 1940-1950 .... 50.00
Elephant, Art Deco, Cast Iron, M 449, 4 3/8 In. 220.00
Elephant, G.O.P., Cast Iron, M 450, 4 3/8 In. 523.00
Elephant, Howdah Slot, Cast Iron, A.C. Williams, 1934, M 457, 2 1/2 In. 75.00
Elephant, Howdah, Cast Iron, A.C. Williams, 1912-1934, M 459, 3 In. 160.00
Elephant, On Tub, Cast Iron, A.C. Williams, 1920s-1934, M 484, 5 1/2 In. 175.00
Elephant, On Tub, Cast Iron, A.C. Williams, c.1920s, M 483, 5 1/4 In. 125.00
Elmer Fudd, Tree Trunk, Metal, Metal Moss Mfg., 1930s, M 308, 5 1/2 In. 60.00
Empire State Building, Silvered Lead, M 1047, 7 3/4 In. 50.00
Eureka Stove, Tin, John Wright & Co., England, M 1350, 5 1/4 In. 120.00
Face, Earthenware, Pennsylvania, 19th Century, 5 1/2 In. 935.00
Felix The Cat, Vinyl, 10 In. 16.00
Fidelity Trust Vault, Lord Fauntleroy, Cast Iron, J. Barton Smith Co., M 901, 4 7/8 In. 165.00
Foxy Grandpa, Cast Iron, Wing, c.1900, M 326, 5 1/2 In. 350.00
Foxy Grandpa, Tin, Germany, 3 1/2 In. 265.00
Fred & Barney, Flintstone, Plastic, 1960-1967, 13 In., Pair 75.00
Garage, 2-Car, Cast Iron, A.C. Williams, 1927-1931, M 1010, 2 1/2 In. 230.00
Gas Station, With Cars, Tin, 2 1/4 In. 115.00
General Butler, Cast Iron, J. & E. Stevens, M 54, 6 1/2 In. 1120.00
German Helmet, Tin, Germany, M 1405, 2 5/8 In. 176.00
Give Me A Penny, Cast Iron, Hubley, 1902-1926, M 166, 5 1/2 In. ....200.00 to 550.00
Globe, Pennies First Then Dollars, Bell & Eagle, Cast Iron, Enterprise, 5 3/4 In. 230.00
Globe Furnace, Lead, 4 7/8 In. 220.00
Golliwog, Cast Aluminum, John Harper, England, 1910-1925, M 85, 6 3/16 In. ....195.00 to 420.00
Golliwog, Cast Aluminum, John Harper, England, M 86, 6 In. 150.00
Graf Zeppelin, Cast Iron, A.C. Williams, 1920-1934, M 1428, 1 3/4 x 6 5/8 In. ...150.00 to 175.00
Grenade, Cast Iron, M 1422, 4 1/4 In. 165.00
Hanger, Goodyear Zeppelin, Aluminum, Ferrosteel, 1930, M 1430, 2 5/16 In. 385.00
Help Shipwrecked Mariners, Tin, 7 In. 155.00
High Rise, Cast Iron, Gold & Silver Trim, Kenton, M 1216, 7 In. 82.00
Home Savings Building, Cast Iron, J. & E. Stevens, 1891, M 1236, 3 1/2 In. 242.00
Horse, Prancing, On Rear Legs, Cast Iron, A.C. Williams, 1920s, M 513, 5 1/8 In. 275.00
Independence Hall Tower, Brass, 9 1/8 In. 286.00
Independence Hall Tower, Cast Iron, Enterprise Mfg., 1876, M 1202, 9 1/2 In. ...176.00 to 363.00
Indian, With Tomahawk, Cast Iron, Hubley, 1915-1930s, M 228, 6 In. 357.00
Indiana Silo, Cast Iron, Gold Trim, M 1247, 3 5/8 In. 2640.00
Infantry Helmet Lead, Germany, M 1386, 3 1/8 In. 143.00
International Building Credit Union, Spelter, 2 1/4 In. 83.00
Jelly Bean King, Aluminum, Reynolds, 1981, M 456, 3 7/8 In. 70.00
Jewel Safe, Nickel Finish, J. & E. Stevens, 1907, M 896, 5 3/8 In. 104.00
John Deere, Tin Lithograph, Plow Logo, John Deere Centennial 1837-1937, 4 x 3 In. 110.00
Jumbo, Elephant, Glass, 4 1/4 In. 910.00
Keyless Safety Deposit, Cast Iron, 5 7/8 In. 195.00
Kitty, With Bow, Cast Iron, Hubley, 1930-1946, M 349, 4 3/4 In. 200.00
Liberty Bank, Silver & Gold, Original Trap, Cast Iron, 10 In. 518.00
Liberty Bell, Cast Iron, Grey Iron Casting, 1928, M 782, 3 3/4 In. 75.00
Lincoln Memorial, Metal, 6 3/16 In. 75.00
Log Cabin, Pottery, Overall Green, Orange Mottled Glaze, Pa., 3 1/4 x 5 1/2 In. 1210.00

Log Cabin, Shake Roof, Cast Iron, England, M 1024, 3 3/8 In. 525.00
Mailbox, U.S. Mail, Brown Finish, Cast Iron, Kenton, 5 1/4 In. 46.00
Mailbox, U.S. Mail, Eagle, Cast Iron, Kenton, 1932-1934, M 849, 5 1/8 In. 150.00
Mailbox, U.S. Mail, Green, Inscribed Letters & U.S. Mail, Slight Paint Wear, 3 3/4 In. ... 120.00
Mailbox, U.S. Mail, Hanging, Cast Iron, A.C. Williams, 1921-1934, M 856, 5 1/8 In. 70.00
Mailbox, U.S. Mail, On Ornate Base, Cast Iron, Hubley, 1906, M 861, 6 1/2 In. 430.00
Mailbox, U.S. Mail, Pull Down Slot, Cast Iron, Hubley, 8 In. 345.00
Mailbox, U.S. Mail, Slot & Combination Lock On Front For Rear Trap, Nickled, 7 In. ... 259.00
Main Street, Trolley With People, Cast Iron, A.C. Williams, 1920s, M 1471, 4 5/8 In. ... 242.00
Mammy, Spoon, Cast Iron, A.C. Williams, M 168, 5 7/8 In. 65.00
Mammy, With Hands On Hips, Cast Iron, Hubley, 1914-1946, M 176, 5 1/4 In. 230.00
Mary & Little Lamb, Cast Iron, U.S., 1901, M 164, 4 3/8 In. 115.00
Mascot Safe, Tin, 4 1/8 In. 105.00

Mechanical banks were first made about 1870. Any bank with moving parts is considered mechanical. The metal banks made before World War I are the most desirable. Copies and new designs of mechanical banks have been made in metal or plastic since the 1920s. The condition of the paint on the old banks is important. Worn paint can lower a price by 90%.

Mechanical, 2nd National Duck Bank, Tin, Chein 175.00
Mechanical, Acrobat, Gymnast, Cast Iron, J. & E. Stevens, 1883, 4 3/16 In. 6050.00
Mechanical, Artillery, Cast Iron, 1892, 8 In. ....1650.00 to 1955.00
Mechanical, Artillery, Coin In Cannon, Cast Iron, J. & E. Stevens, c.1900, 8 In. 1320.00
Mechanical, Atlas, Money Moves The World, Lever Slot, Figure Of Atlas, Cast Iron, 8 In. 5175.00
Mechanical, Bulldog, Coin On Nose Of Dog, Catches Coin, J. & E. Stevens, 1878, 6 In. . . 5225.00
Mechanical, Cabin, Man Stands On Head, Cast Iron, J. & E. Stevens, 3 5/8 In. 660.00
Mechanical, Calumet Baking Powder, Tin, Paper, Boy Nods Head, 3 3/16 In. 94.00
Mechanical, Chief Big Moon, Frog Jumps For Fish, Cast Iron, J. & E. Stevens, 10 In. 805.00
Mechanical, Chocolate Vendor, Cherubs, Elves, Children, Tin, Stollwerck, 5 1/4 x 10 In. . 690.00
Mechanical, Clown, Chein, 5 In. 88.00
Mechanical, Clown, Extends Tongue, Eats Coin, Tin, Chein. 100.00
Mechanical, Clown, Harlequin, Columbine, Cast Iron, 1950, 7 In. 266.00
Mechanical, Coffin, Tin, Windup, Japan, Box, 6 1/2 In. 100.00
Mechanical, Creedmoor, Shooter In The Tree, Cast Iron, J. & E. Stevens, 10 In. . . .402.00 to 661.00
Mechanical, Destination Moon Spaceship, Metal, Vacumet Company, 1950-1960 .... 300.00
Mechanical, Dinah, Yellow Dress, Raises Hand, Cast Iron, John Harper, 6 1/2 In. . .345.00 to 880.00
Mechanical, Dog Tray, Cast Iron, Kyser & Rex, 1880, 4 1/4 In. 1035.00
Mechanical, Eagle & Eaglets, Cast Iron, J. & E. Stevens, 6 3/4 In. ....518.00 to 575.00
Mechanical, Eagle & Eaglets, Chirping, Cast Iron, J. & E. Stevens, 6 3/4 In. 1265.00
Mechanical, Elephant, Man Pops Out, Bronze Paint, Wood Sculpture, Enterprise, 6 1/2 In. 575.00
Mechanical, Elephant, Tin, Chein ....*Illus* 110.00
Mechanical, Ferris Wheel, Wind Mechanism, Coin Activates Wheel, Hubley, Cast Iron ... 7150.00
Mechanical, Frog On Rock, Swallows Coin, Cast Iron, Kilgore Mfg., 4 In. 604.00
Mechanical, Frogs, One Kicks Coin Into Other's Mouth, Cast Iron, J. & E. Stevens 8500.00
Mechanical, Girl In Victorian Chair, Cast Iron, W.S. Reed Toy Co. 4750.00
Mechanical, Girl Skipping Rope, Cast Iron, J. & E. Stevens 17360.00
Mechanical, Hall's Excelsior Building, Cast Iron, J. & E. Stevens, 5 In. 830.00
Mechanical, Hall's Liliput, Teller, Cast Iron, J. & E. Stevens, 1876, 3 In. ...517.00 to 604.00
Mechanical, Hawaii, Pineapple, 50 State Commemorative, Plastic, 1960, 4 1/4 In. 172.00
Mechanical, Hen & Chick, Cast Iron, J. & E. Stevens, 1901 .... 7700.00
Mechanical, Home Savings Bank, Nickel Finish, J. & E. Stevens, 6 In. 1237.00
Mechanical, Indian & Brown Bear, Cast Iron, J. & E. Stevens, 10 1/2 In. 798.00
Mechanical, Jolly Nigger, 1882, 4 3/4 In. 345.00
Mechanical, Jolly Nigger, White Top Hat, Cast Iron, 4 3/4 In. 259.00
Mechanical, Leap Frog, Boys & Tree, Shepard Hardware, 1891, 13 1/2 In. 2495.00
Mechanical, Lion & 2 Monkeys, Single Peanut, Kyser & Rex Co., Pat. 1883 ....932.00 to 2000.00
Mechanical, Lucky Wheel Money Box, Tin, Wheel Spins, Tells Fortune, England 160.00
Mechanical, Merry-Go-Round, Attendant Gathers Coins, Cast Iron, Kyser & Rex 900.00
Mechanical, Milking Cow, Cow Kicks, Boy Falls, Cast Iron, 1930s 207.00
Mechanical, Monkey Bank, Monkey Deposits Coin, Cast Iron, Hubley, 8 7/8 In. 715.00
Mechanical, Monkey With Tray, Raises Hands, Tin, Continental 230.00

Mechanical, Monkey, Tips Hat, Tin Lithograph, J. Chein & Co. . . . .*Illus*   225.00
Mechanical, Novelty, Cast Iron, J. & E. Stevens, 6 1/2 In. 747.50
Mechanical, Novelty, Orange Paint, Cast Iron, J. & E. Stevens, 4 1/4 In. 517.00
Mechanical, Organ Bank, Cat & Dog Spin, Cast Iron, Kyser & Rex, 5 3/4 In. . . . . .748.00 to 977.00
Mechanical, Organ Grinder, Cast Iron, 9 In. 358.00
Mechanical, Owl Turns Head, Cast Iron, J. & E. Stevens, 3 7/8 In. 400.00
Mechanical, Owl, Slot In Book, Moving Eyes, Cast Iron, Kilgore, 5 3/4 In. 1035.00
Mechanical, Paddy & Pig, Kicks Coin, Cast Iron, J. & E. Stevens, 7 1/8 In. . . . .2500.00 to 4500.00
Mechanical, Pegleg Beggar, Nods Head, Cast Iron, J. & E. Stevens 2250.00
Mechanical, Reclining Chinaman, Cast Iron, J. & E. Stevens, 1882, 8 1/4 In. . . .3472.00 to 7700.00
Mechanical, Reclining Chinaman, Cast Iron, No Coin Trap, J. & E. Stevens, 8 1/4 In. 4250.00
Mechanical, Santa Claus, Drops Coin, Original Paint, Shepard Hardware, 4 1/8 In. 8000.00
Mechanical, Stump Speaker, Mouth & Hand Move, Cast Iron, Shepard Hardware 1792.00
Mechanical, Tammany, Cast Iron, Gray Trousers, J. & E. Stevens, 5 3/4 In. 1610.00
Mechanical, Teddy & The Bear, Bear Pops Up, Cast Iron, Book Of Knowledge 88.00
Mechanical, Thrifty Tom's Jigger, Figure Dancing, Clockwork, Strauss, 10 In. 2185.00
Mechanical, Toad On Stump, Mouth Opens, Cast Iron, J. & E. Stevens, 3 1/4 In. 575.00
Mechanical, Trick Dog, Cast Iron, 8 3/4 In. 345.00
Mechanical, Trick Dog, Dog Jumps Through Hoop, Cast Iron, Hubley, 8 9/16 In. . .230.00 to 345.00
Mechanical, Trick Dog, Solid Base, Cast Iron, Hubley, 1920s, 9 In. 620.00
Mechanical, Trick Pony, Coin In Trough, Cast Iron, Shepard Hardware, 7 1/16 In. 495.00
Mechanical, Uncle Remus, Door Opens, Figures Move, Cast Iron, Book Of Knowledge . .   77.00
Mechanical, Uncle Sam, Hand Drops Coin, Cast Iron, Shepard Hardware, 11 1/2 In. 748.00
Mechanical, Uncle Wiggily, Arm Holding Carrot Moves, Tin, Chein, 5 In. 265.00
Mechanical, Vending, Queen Victoria, Stollwerck, Tin 375.00
Mechanical, Watchdog, Safe, Opening Mouth, Cast Iron, J. & E. Stevens, 6 In. 460.00
Mechanical, William Tell, Coin Knocks Apple Down, Cast Iron, J. & E. Stevens 3500.00
Mechanical, Zoo, Monkey, Lion & Bear In Window, Cast Iron, Kyser & Rex, 4 1/4 In. . . .   3163.00
Merry-Go-Round, Cast Iron, Grey Iron Casting, 1925-1928, M 1614, 4 5/8 In. 340.00
Michigan State Spartans, Spelter, 7 In. 72.00
Minnesota Golden Gophers, Spelter, 6 1/8 In. 121.00
Minstrel In Hat, Tin, M 279, 5 3/4 In. 140.00
Monkey On Cage, Composition, Germany, c.1929, M 741, 5 In. 275.00
Mulligan The Cop, Cast Iron, A.C. Williams, 1905-1932, M 177, 5 3/4 In. 220.00
Multiplying, Cast Iron, J. & E. Stevens, 7 In. 3500.00
Mutt & Jeff, Cast Iron, Gold Painted, A.C. Williams, 1912-1931, M 157, 4 1/4 In. .110.00 to 225.00
New Heatrola, Red, Cast Iron, Kenton, 1927-1932, M 1354, 4 1/2 In. 100.00
Noah's Ark, Composition, Hausser, Germany, 1929, M 1465, 2 5/8 In. 308.00
North Pole Bank, Nickeled Cast Iron, Grey Iron Casting, M 1371, 1922-1928, 4 1/4 In. . . .   650.00
Notre Dame, Fighting Irish, Metal, 5 7/8 In. 170.00
Obelisk, Vinyl, Removable Coin Trap, Vial, Spain, 11 In. 45.00
Oklahoma University, Indian, Metal, 6 1/8 In. 90.00
Owl, Cast Iron, Vindex, c.1930, M 597, 4 1/4 In. 110.00
Palace, Cast Iron, Ives, 1885, M 1116, 7 1/4 In. 485.00
Patriotic Hat, Liberty Bell, Tin, M 1387, 2 In. 105.00
Pep Boys, Boys In Bank Setting, Tin Lithograph, 4 Sides, 2 1/2 x 2 1/4 In. 285.00

Bank, Mechanical,
Elephant, Tin, Chein

Bank, Mechanical,
Monkey, Tips Hat,
Tin Lithograph,
J. Chein & Co.

**Re-key all locks when
you move to a new house
or apartment or if you
lose a key.**

Pickaninny, Bust, Cast Iron, England, M 171, 5 1/8 In. 605.00
Pig, Inscribed Decker's Iowanna, Cast Iron, M 603, 2 1/2 In. 175.00
Pig, Pottery, Brown, Blue Marbleized Glaze, 3 3/4 x 4 1/2 In. 60.00
Pig, Pottery, Brown, Olive, Red, Cream Marbleized Glaze, 6 1/4 In. 93.00
Pig, Pottery, Red, Brown, Cream Marbleized, 6 1/4 In. 49.00
Pig, Pottery, Tan, Cream, Pale Green Marbleized Glaze, 6 1/2 In. 49.00
Pig, Sitting, Red Tongue, Gold Paint, Cast Iron, 3 In. 11.00
Pig, Thrifty The Wise Pig, Verse Inscription, Cast Iron, Hubley, 1930-1936, M 609, 6 In. . 195.00
Pineapple, 50th Anniversary Of Hawaii, Cast Iron, 4 1/4 In. ....121.00 to 201.00
Policeman, Cast Iron, Arcade, 1920-1934, 5 1/2 In. 90.00
Policeman, Pottery, Blue Glaze, Keystone Cop Bust, 3 1/4 In. 235.00
Poll Parrot & Star Brand Shoes, Tin, 1950, 2 x 1 1/2 In. 25.00
Porky Pig, Tree Trunk, Metal, Metal Moss Mfg., 1930s, M 263, 4 7/16 In. 85.00
Porky Pig At Barrel, Metal, Metal Moss Mfg., 1930s, M 265, 4 7/16 In. 95.00
Professor Pug Frog, A.C. Williams, 1900s, M 311, 3 1/4 In. 275.00
Radio, 3 Dials, Cast Iron, Tin, Kenton, 1927-1931, M 830, 3 1/2 In. 350.00
Radio, Large Crosley, Cast Iron, Kenton, 1931-1936, M 819, 5 1/8 In. 1870.00
Radio, Plastic, Knobs Turn, Reliable, Canada, 1950, 4 x 1 3/4 x 2 3/4 In. 75.00
Red Goose School Shoes, Cast Iron, Arcade, 1920s, M 610, 3 3/4 In. 300.00
Red Goose School Shoes, Cast Iron, Arcade, 1920s, M 628, 3 3/4 In. 275.00
Refrigerator, Kelvinator, Cast Iron, Tin, Arcade, 1932-1934, M 1338, 3 7/8 In. 430.00
Register, Bank Of America, Cash Register, Tin, Girard Model Works, 4 7/16 In. 55.00
Register, Beehive, Inscribed, H & H Registering Beehive Savings Bank & Dime, 5 In. 250.00
Register, Ben Franklin Thrift, Cash Register, Louis Marx, Tin, 4 In. 70.00
Register, Elf, Dime 145.00
Register, Horloge, Telauto Maat Clock, Dial Moves, Tin, Germany, 1920s, 5 15/16 In. ... 140.00
Register, Jackie Robinson, Painted Tin, 1950s, Dime 670.00
Register, Liberty Penny, Lincoln Portrait, Tin, Girard Model Works, 5 9/16 In. 95.00
Register, Max & Moritz, Box, Tin Lithograph, Germany, 1950s, 5 3/8 In. 33.00
Register, Trunk, Phoenix, Cast Iron, M 947, 3 3/4 In., Dime 255.00
Register, Uncle Sam's, Cash Register, Tin, 3 7/16 In., Dime ....40.00 to 50.00
Resting Swan Bank, Chalkware, 5 1/2 In. 187.00
Rooster, Beak Moves, Cast Iron, Kyser & Rex, 6 1/4 In. 288.00
Rooster, Polish, Cast Iron, U.S., M 541, 5 1/2 In. 750.00
Rooster, Silver Paint, 4 3/4 In. 195.00
Rooster On Basket, Composition, Germany, 1929, M 543, 5 1/2 In. 264.00
Royal Safe Deposit, Cast Iron, Combination Lock, 6 In. 275.00
Safe, Bank Of Industry, Nickel Finish, Kenton, 5 1/2 In. 200.00
Safe, Daisy, Cast Iron, 3 3/8 In. 75.00
Safe, Fireproof Child's Safe, Tin, Chein, 1906, M 900, 5 1/2 In. 125.00
Safe, National Safe, Cast Iron, M 862, 4 3/4 In. 155.00
Safe, Security Safe Deposit, Cast Iron, M 891, 4 In. ....165.00 to 175.00
Santa Claus, Cast Iron, Gold Finish, c.1890, M 56, 7 1/4 In. 1150.00
Santa Claus, Entering Chimney, Lead, Miller Bank Service, 1925, M 104, 3 3/4 In. 440.00
Santa Claus, Red, Gold, Green, Cast Iron, 5 3/4 In. 776.00
Save For Your Sunny Suds, Brass, Record Player, U.S., M 824, 4 1/2 In. 165.00
Sea Lion, Gold Paint, Cast Iron, Arcade, 3 1/2 In. 165.00
Sharecropper, Cast Iron, A.C. Williams, 1901, M 173, 5 7/8 In. 115.00
Sharp Shooter Book, Tin, 5 3/4 In. 185.00
Shell, Cast Iron, Ferrosteel, 1919, M 1420, 1 1/2 x 8 In. 75.00
Shell Premium Gasoline, Gas Pump, 4 5/8 x 1 1/4 In. 265.00
Singer Sewing Machine, Tin, Metal, Germany, c.1925, M 1369, 5 1/8 In. 190.00
Snowman, With Broom, Aluminum, Reynolds, M 92, 1981, 4 5/8 In. 33.00
Soldier Hat, Buddy Bank, Steel, Stronghart, c.1918, M 1399, Box, 1 7/8 In. 185.00
Speedy Alka Seltzer, Slot On Top Of Hat, Red Hair, Rubber, 8 In. 350.00
Squirt, Figural Boy, Composition, 7 1/2 In. 176.00
State Bank, Cast Iron, Kenton, c.1900, M 1078, 8 x 5 1/2 In. 632.00
State Bank, Key Opening Front Door For Coin Retrieval, Cast Iron, 6 In. 402.00
State Safe, Cast Iron, 4 In. 185.00
State Safe, Tin, Iron, 19th Century, 4 1/2 In. 61.00
Statue Of Liberty, Cast Iron, A.C. Williams, 1910-1930, M 1164, 6 1/16 In. 95.00
Statue Of Liberty, Cast Iron, M 1166, 9 5/8 In. 495.00

Steamboat, Cast Iron, A.C. Williams, c.1912-1920, M 1459, 2 7/16 In. 297.00
Stoneware, Bulbous, Cobalt Blue Decoration, Leaves, Jesse Leister, 1872, 4 3/4 In. 6600.00
Stop Sign, Cast Iron, Dent, 1920, M 1481, 5 5/8 In. 660.00
Stove, Black, Tin, Cast Iron, Cook With Cash, John Wright, 1970, M 1343, 2 1/4 In. 45.00
Stove, Gas, Save Your Money & Buy A Gas Stove, 5 1/2 In. 170.00
Television, Tin, 5 1/2 In. 50.00
The Thing, Addams Family, 1972 . . . . 10.00
Tommy's Tin Hat, England, c.1917, M 1398, 1 5/8 In. 248.00
Treasure Island Book, Tin, 5 3/4 In. 95.00
Truck, Postal Savings, Tin, Friction, SSS, Japan, Box, 7 In. 160.00
Turkey, Large, Cast Iron, A.C. Williams, 1905-1912, M 585, 4 1/4 In. 633.00
Turkey, Small, Cast Iron, A.C. Williams, c.1905-1935, M 587, 3 3/8 In. 308.00
U.S. Tank, Cast Iron, U.S., 1919, M 1438, 1 3/4 In. 100.00
Uncle Sam, Bust, Overall Brown Glazing, Pottery, Late 19th Century, 4 1/2 In. 220.00
Uncle Sam, Stoneware, 4 In. 248.00
Victorian Cottage, Porch, Stenciled Windows & Doors, Stevens & Brown, 6 In. 412.00
Washington Monument, Gold Trim, Cast Iron, A.C. Williams, 1910-1912, 6 1/8 In. 165.00
White City, Pail, Cast Iron, Nicol, 1893, M 911, 2 5/8 In. 116.00
White City Puzzle Safe, No. 12, Cast Iron, Nicol, 1893, M 910, 4 3/4 In. 155.00
Yawning Bonzo, On Pillow, Composition, 4 3/8 In. 300.00

BANKO, Korean ware, and Sumida are terms that are often confusing.
We use the names in the way most often used by antiques dealers and
collectors. Korean ware is now called *Sumida Gawa* or *Sumida* and is
listed in this book in the Sumida category. Banko is a group of rustic
Japanese wares made in the nineteenth and twentieth centuries. Some
pieces are made of mosaics of colored clay, some are fanciful teapots.
Redware and other materials were also used.

Cup & Saucer, Tapestry Interior, Demitasse, 1920s 75.00
Figurine, Akita Puppy, White With Black Spots, Bisque, 3 1/2 In. 395.00
Figurine, Crab, Red, Yellow, Black, Bisque, 5 In. 195.00
Teapot, Cover, Relief Masks On Each Side, Nose Finial & Spout, 5 1/2 In. 350.00
Teapot, Relief Flying Cranes, Flowers, Tan Ground, Circa 1910, 3 1/2 In. 250.00

BARBED WIRE was first patented in 1867. Collectors want eighteen-
inch samples.

Brinkerhoff's Saberpoint, 1879, 18 In. 4.50
Crandal's Zigzag, 1879, 18 In. 3.50
Frentress' Split Diamond, 18 In. 4.50
Glidden's 7-Strand Cable Barb, 1874, 18 In. 8.00
Haish's Parallel, 18 In. 10.50
Havenhill's Long & Narrow Arrow, 1892, 18 In. 12.50
Hodge's Spur Rowel, 1887, 18 In. 8.00
Patented By S.H. & J.M. St. John, July 2, 1878, 22 In. 36.00
Pooler-Jones' 3-Point Barbed Wire, 1876, 18 In. 14.50
Preston's Braid, 1881, 18 In. 8.00
Sunderland's Kink Single Line, 1884, 18 In. 5.50
Wilke's 2 Staple Around 2, 18 In. 15.00

BARBER collectibles range from the popular red and white striped pole
that used to be found in front of every shop to the small scissors and
tools of the trade. Barber chairs are wanted, especially the older models with elaborate iron trim.

Antiseptic Sterilizer, Decal On Door, Glass Shelf, Wood & Glass, 24 x 11 1/2 In. 209.00
Bank, Razor Blade, Policeman Holding Up Hand, Reads Old Razor Blades, Metal, 4 In. . . 85.00
Bellows, Glove & Wig Powder, Leather, Brass Nozzle, Hole In Base, 1800s, 6 1/2 In. 85.00
Chair, Hansen, Oak 3750.00
Chair, Horse Head, Small Seat, Child's, 1930s 4300.00
Chair, Horse, Wood, White Paint, Leather Seat, Porcelain Base, Child's, 48 In. 3410.00
Globe, Triangular, Milk Glass, Fired-On Barber Shop, 12 x 9 1/2 In. 825.00
Heater, Hot Water, The Superior, Milk Glass Globe, Patent August 30, 1910, 17 1/2 In. . . 253.00
Mirror, Brass, 2 Arms, Adjustable, Chair Clamp, Candle Arm, 5 7/8 x 8 1/4 In. 155.00

Pole, Cast Iron, Red, White, Blue Enamel Paint, Porcelain, 82 In. 1840.00
Pole, Iron & Glass 1540.00
Pole, Koken, Leaded Glass & Porcelain 2310.00
Pole, Red & White Candy Glass, Copper Trim, Porcelain, Leaded Glass, 34 In. 770.00
Pole, Red & White Striped, Square, Round Top, 35 1/2 In. 340.00
Pole, Sign, Silver, Red Striped Paint, Wood, 1880, 36 In. 1210.00
Shaving Vase, Frosted, Clear, Enamel & Gilt Design, 1925, 7 7/8 In. 415.00
Shaving Vase, Turquoise Opalescent, Enameled Flowers, 4 1/2 In. 330.00
Sign, 2 Sides, Red & White Stripes, Shield Shape, Porcelain, 18 x 19 In. 385.00
Sign, Carved Enamel, Mounting Bracket, 24 In. 230.00
Sign, Red, White & Blue Stripes, Porcelain, Curved, 15 x 24 In. 82.00
Sterilizer, Hot Towel, Stainless Steel, Porcelain Stand, 1924 .... 660.00

BAROMETERS are used to forecast the weather. Antique barometers with elaborate wooden cases and brass trim are the most desirable. Mercury column barometers are also popular with collectors. It is difficult to find someone to repair a broken one, so be sure your barometer is in working condition.

Aneroid, Giltwood, Circular Paper Dial, Laurel Crest, Louis XVI, 35 x 21 In. 1495.00
Banjo, A. Poncione, Mahogany, Inlay, Broken Pediment, George III, 39 In. 2300.00
Banjo, Boyce, Exmouth, Mahogany, Early 19th Century, 40 In. 990.00
Banjo, L. Negretti, Liverpool, Signed, 19th Century, 38 In. 660.00
Banjo, Lioni Tormaloico, Mahogany, London, Early 1800s, 37 1/4 In. 85.00
Banjo, Mahogany Veneer, Ivory Knob, England, 42 In. 977.00
Banjo, Mahogany, Engraved Silver Dial, Center Thermostat, 39 x 10 x 2 In. 560.00
Banjo, Mahogany, Inlay, Hygrometer, Spirit Level, Regency, c.1810, 38 1/4 In. 920.00
Banjo, P. Frigero, Mahogany, Inlaid, Conch Shells, Thermometer, c.1800, 39 In. 605.00
Banjo, Pozzi & Co., Wheel, Mahogany, Temperature Gauge, 38 3/8 In. 1610.00
Black Forest, Birds, Leafy Branches, 11 In. 672.00
Black Forest, Figural, Man With Bird, 1880, 17 x 11 x 6 In. 952.00
Black Forest, Thermometer, With Deer, Game Carvings, c.1880, 34 In. 1624.00
C. Aiano, Northgate, Canterbury, Arch Top, 19th Century, 39 In. 1150.00
Cast Iron, Enameled, Round Frame, Brass Adjustment Screws, 12 In. 165.00
F. Pastorelli, Mahogany, Satinwood Conch Shell, Signed, 19th Century 770.00
Giltwood, Celadon Paint, Ribbon Crest, Floral, Gilt, Louis XVI, 20 1/2 In. 460.00
Giltwood, Overflowing Cornucopia, Flower Filled Urn, France, Louis XVI, 45 In. 3450.00
Giltwood, Signed Dial, Glass Cover, Louis Philippe, Mid 1800s, 36 x 21 In. 3910.00
J.L. Polti, Leeds, Mahogany, Inlaid Flowers, England, 1800s, 38 In. 2530.00
Joseph Pomalvico, Rosewood, Mother-Of-Pearl Inlay, 1817 .... 605.00
National Liberty Insurance, 3 1/2 In. 160.00
Olof Ekfeldt, Figured Veneer, Paper Label, Engraved Chart, Walnut, 39 In. 660.00
Stick, Charles Wilder, Troy, New York, Bird's-Eye Maple, c.1890, 39 In. 2200.00
Stick, Faverio & Golli, Mahogany, Regency, Bull's-Eye At Base, 37 1/2 In. 1760.00
Stick, Gimbaled Mount, 36 In. 860.00
Stick, Isaiah Lukens, Federal, Cherrywood, Faceted Glass Well, 1840, 37 In. 5700.00
Stick, John Merrick & Co., Worcester, Mass., Walnut, Early 19th Century, 37 In. 825.00
Stick, Mahogany, Arch Top, Silver Face, Inlaid Case, George III, c.1780, 38 In. 1430.00
Stick, Mahogany, Field Aylesbury Plate, George III, 37 1/2 In. 1955.00
Stick, Mahogany, Inscribed Leoni Fecit, Georgian, Inlay Stringing, 39 In. 1840.00
Stick, Mahogany, Pediment Crest, Brass Face, Georgian, c.1780, 39 In. 1430.00
Stick, W. Foyne, Mahogany, Steel Dial Plate, Center Bone Disk, 37 1/2 In. 575.00
Storm King, E.C. Spooner, Walnut, 42 In. 2245.00
T.B. Winter, Newcastle, Victorian, Oak 300.00
Thermometer, 3 Temperature Scales, c.1890 .... 400.00
Thermometer, Mahogany Case, Satinwood Line Inlay, 38 1/2 In. 1495.00
Walnut, Carved Grape, Fruit, 40 In. 1400.00
Wheel, Carved, Giltwood, Ribbon Crest, Louis XVI Style, Late 1800s, 38 In. 1495.00
Wheel, F. Uago, Mahogany, Swan's-Neck Crest, Roundel Design, Signed, 38 In. 862.00
Wheel, F.H. Hester, Mahogany, Mercury Thermometer, George III, 47 In. 1730.00
Wheel, Fitted Thermometer & Hygrometer, T. Garward, 1840s, 41 1/4 In. 1265.00
Wheel, Giltwood, Tied Ribbon Crest, Bell Flowers, Thermometer, 38 In. 1495.00
Wheel, Leaves & Grape Cluster, Putti On Dial, Gray & Green Paint, 1850s, 52 In. 2530.00

Wheel, Mahogany, Brass Bezel, Alcohol Thermometer, George III, 44 In. 810.00
Wheel, Mahogany, Brass Bezel, Alcohol Thermometer, George III, 47 In. 1380.00
Wheel, Mahogany, Gabled Crest, Ormolu Bust, Calendar, Louis Philippe, 37 In. 1380.00
Wheel, Mahogany, With Vertical Thermometer, Convex Mirror, England, 39 In. 805.00

BASEBALL collectibles are in the Sports category, except for baseball cards, which
are listed under Baseball in the Card category.

BASKETS of all types are popular with collectors. American Indian,
Japanese, African, Shaker, and many other kinds of baskets can be
found. Of course, baskets are still being made, so the collector must
learn to tell the age and style of the basket to determine the value.

Bamboo, Carved Leaves, 2 Tiers, Handle, China, 13 1/2 In. 290.00
Burl, 12 In. . . . .*Illus* 175.00
Buttocks, 8 Ribs, Bentwood Handle, 7 In. 137.00
Buttocks, 26 Ribs, Bentwood Handle, 13 x 15 In. 110.00
Buttocks, 28 Ribs, Painted Exterior, Arched Bentwood Handle, 13 3/4 x 16 3/4 In. 1292.00
Buttocks, 30 Ribs, Center Band, Bentwood Handle, 6 1/2 x 7 In. 300.00
Buttocks, Splint, 12 3/4 x 19 1/2 In. 190.00
Buttocks, Splint, 14 Ribs, 2 1/2 x 3 In. 440.00
Buttocks, Splint, 34 Ribs, 7 x 14 x 12 In. 190.00
Buttocks, Splint, Eye Of God Design, Bentwood Handle, 3 In. 55.00
Cheese, Double Rim, Silver Gray, 7 x 24 In. 385.00
Coil, Cover, Early 20th Century, 15 x 14 In. 150.00
Double Gourd, Rustic Branches, Japan, Early 20th Century, 14 1/2 In. 290.00
Eel, Splint, 2 Sections, Long Island, N.Y., 31 In. 105.00
Eel, Split Oak, Late 19th Century, 48 x 8 In. 95.00
Egg, Delicate Construction, 3 x 4 1/2 In. 450.00
Egg, Rectangular, 8 Large Middle & 2 Small Side Handles, 36 x 14 x 8 In. 400.00
Feather, Splint, Swollen Shape, Diamond Motifs, Painted, 1800s, 25 1/2 x 20 1/2 In. 1380.00
Gathering, Cross Weave, Bentwood Top & Bottom, Oval, 9 x 19 3/4 In. 100.00
Gathering, Pumpkin-Color Wash, Iron Handle, 18 In. 7015.00
Gathering, Rectangular, 2 Handles, 6 x 16 In. 275.00
Gathering, Splint, Handles, Early 20th Century, 18 x 14 1/2 In. 115.00
Gathering, Splint, Notched Handles, Rounded, Square Base, 14 x 25 In. 345.00
Key, Leather, Oval, Embossed Lines, Chesterfield County, Virginia, 19th Century, 5 In. . . . 3080.00
Key, Leather, Raised Ends, Elongated Oval Base, Handle, 19th Century, 7 x 4 1/2 In. 2240.00
Laundry, Splint, Early 20th Century, 35 x 10 In. 50.00
Market, Split Oak, Open Weave Top, Early 20th Century, 16 x 18 1/2 In. 195.00
Melon, 34 Radiating Ribs, Arched Handle, 13 1/4 x 15 1/2 In. 195.00
Melon, Brown Patina, 20 Radiating Ribs, Arched Handle, 10 1/2 In. 85.00
Melon, Splint, 16 Flat Bentwood Staves, Arched Handle, 13 1/2 In. 176.00
Melon, Splint, 6 1/2 In. 300.00
Melon, Splint, Double, Early 20th Century, 19 x 11 1/2 In. 210.00
Melon, Splint, Early 20th Century, 10 x 13 In. 95.00
Melon, Splint, Eye Of God Design On Side Of Handles, 8 7/8 x 9 1/4 In. 275.00
Melon, Splint, Square Base, Round Top, Bentwood Handle, 8 3/4 In. 165.00
Nantucket, 19th Century, 5 x 8 1/2 In. 290.00
Nantucket, Bail Handle, Oval, Mitchell Ray, 10 In. 970.00
Nantucket, Brown, Swing Handle, 8 3/4 x 3 3/4 In. 1265.00
Nantucket, Cane & Splint, Swivel Handle, Wooden Bottom, 8 1/4 x 9 In. 715.00
Nantucket, Cane & Splint, Wooden Bottom, Bentwood Swing Handle, 6 x 9 1/2 In. 1485.00
Nantucket, Handles, 3 1/2 x 7 3/4 In. 920.00
Nantucket, Hinged Lid, Scrimshaw Plaque, Feet, Parnum, Oval, c.1978, 9 x 6 1/2 In. 380.00
Nantucket, Hoop Handle, 14 x 13 In. 100.00
Nantucket, Ivory Bird Carved Top, Lined, Braided Leather, 1940s, 9 x 9 x 6 In. 495.00
Nantucket, Lightship, Handles, Early 20th Century, 8 3/4 In. 440.00
Nantucket, Lightship, Signed, 5 1/2 x 3 In. 345.00
Nantucket, Lightship, Swing Handle, Early 20th Century, 5 1/4 x 9 1/2 In. 470.00
Nantucket, Stenciled Base Interior, Faceted Ear, Swing Handle, R. Folger, 4 x 7 In. 4600.00
Nantucket, Swing Handle, Ferdinand Sylvaro, Label & Address, 4 1/4 x 7 1/4 In. 1380.00
Picnic, Wicker, Automobile, Brass Hardware, Accessories, Wanamaker, 10 x 15 In. 625.00

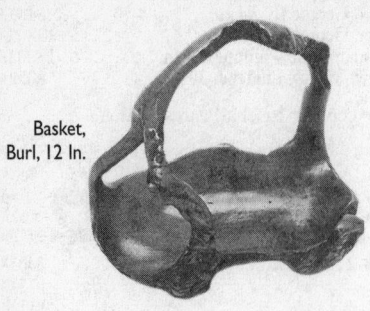

Basket,
Burl, 12 In.

Basket, Wedding,
Gold & Black
Painted Design,
Octagonal, Chinese,
14 1/2 In.

Splint, 20 Ribs, 2 Lines Along Bottom, 6 1/2 In. 85.00
Splint, Ash, 13 x 12 In. 196.00
Splint, Cutlery, Green Paint, Handle, 3 x 11 x 8 1/2 In. 5500.00
Splint, Feather, Woven, Painted Green, Cover, Baluster Shape, White Paint, 34 1/2 In. ... 1725.00
Splint, Goose Feather, Lid, 18 x 15 In. 715.00
Splint, Hanging, Modified Cone Shape, Handles, Early 20th Century, 11 x 10 In. 140.00
Splint, Kettle Shape, Bentwood Handle, 6 x 9 In. 825.00
Splint, Kettle Shape, Yellow Paint, Bentwood Handle, 8 x 13 1/2 In. 550.00
Splint, Oak, Rectangular, Wrapped Rim, 1900 .... 140.00
Splint, Oak, White, Tapered, Wrapped Rim, Handle, Franklin Co., c.1900, 10 x 9 1/2 In. . 365.00
Splint, Raised Side Handles, Painted Blue, 8 1/2 In. 2585.00
Splint, Rectangular, 37 x 22 x 13 In. 365.00
Splint, Salmon Stain, Black Weaving, Square Base, Arched Handle, 13 3/4 In. 360.00
Splint, Square Base, Bentwood Swing Handle, Looped & Pierced Ends, 4 1/2 x 4 In. 275.00
Splint, Square Base, Oval Rim, Bentwood Handle, Green Paint Over Red, 7 x 4 In. 470.00
Splint, Wooden Bottom, Handle, 8 In. 138.00
Storage, Bulbous Sides, Side Handle, Hanging, 18 1/2 In. 140.00
Straw, Coiled, 3 Rod, Splint Wrapped, Arched Handle, 13 1/2 x 16 In. 1000.00
Straw, Coiled, Applied Oak Hoop Footed, 2 Oak Side Handles, 18 In. 6750.00
Straw, Cover, Rye, 2 Carrying Handles, Pa., 19th Century, 9 x 13 In. 1870.00
Straw, Cover, Rye, Footed Base, Pa., Mid 19th Century, 20 In. 990.00
Straw, Cover, Rye, Original Wooden Handles, Wood Base, Pa., 1850, 12 x 22 In. 3410.00
Straw, Footed, Round, 9 1/2 x 13 1/4 In. 85.00
Twigs Woven Onto Sides, Bail Handle, Japan, 20th Century, 12 In. 175.00
Wall, Splint, 8 x 8 1/2 In. 80.00
Wedding, Bentwood, Brass Handle, 2 Removable Sections, Domed Cover, Japan, 23 In. ... 175.00
Wedding, Gold & Black Painted Design, Octagonal, Chinese, 14 1/2 In. ....*Illus* 85.00
Wirework, White, Center Handle, White, Scrolled Terminals, 16 In. 1035.00
Wishbone, Constructed Of Wishbones & Other Bones, Stand Of Turkey Bones, 8 In. 385.00
Wooden, Branch, Acorn, Leaves On Edges, Bear Handles, Switzerland, c.1910, 12 x 2 In. 699.00

BATCHELDER products are made from California clay. Ernest
Batchelder established a tile studio in Pasadena, California, in 1909
and expanded until 1916. Then he built a larger factory with a new
partner. The Batchelder-Wilson Company made all types of architectural tiles, garden pots, and bookends. The plant closed in 1932. In
1936 Batchelder opened Batchelder Ceramics, also in Pasadena, and
made bowls, vases, and earthenware pots. He retired in 1951 and died
in 1957. Pieces are marked *Batchelder Pasadena* or *Batchelder Los
Angeles.*

**BATCHELDER
LOS ANGELES**

Console, Green Exterior, Pink & Peach Interior, 13 In. 255.00
Tile, Bird In Grapevine, Blue, 1920-1932, 2 3/4 x 2 3/4 In., 3 Piece 180.00
Tile, Crystalline Matte Green Glaze, Raised Grapes & Vines, 9 3/4 x 5 In.. .... 140.00
Tile, Over The Plains, Tableau, Arts & Crafts, Oak Frame, 1923, 8 x 56 In. 4180.00
Tile, Recessed Scene Under Arch, Mission Building With Palm Tree 391.00
Tile, Scrolls, Matte Green, White, Blue, 5 3/4 x 4 3/8 In. 69.00
Tile, Stylized Flower, Matte Green, Blue, Yellow, White, 6 x 6 In. 133.00

BATMAN and Robin are characters from a comic strip by Bob Kane that started in 1939. In 1966, the characters became part of a popular television series. There have been radio and movie serials that featured the pair. The first full-length movie was made in 1989. The third movie was made in 1995.

Batmobile, Batman At Wheel, Tin, Friction, ASC, Japan, Box, 11 In.	1680.00
Batmobile, Die Cast, Rockets, Instructions, Corgi, Box, 5 1/2 In.	235.00
Batphone Hot Line	575.00
Boots, Unused, 1969	35.00
Button, Batman To The Rescue, Vietnam, Lithograph, 1 3/4 In.	30.00
Eyeglass Holder, 3 1/4 x 7 In.	8.00
Glass, Batgirl & Robin, Pepsi-Cola, 1977	1792.00
Lunch Box, Vinyl	25.00
Model Kit, Batman Hanging On Tree Trunk, Plastic, Unassembled, Aurora, Box, 1966	300.00
Poster, Movie, Adam West, Burt Ward, France, 1966, 60 x 40 In.	715.00
Puppet, Hand, Unopened Package, Ideal, 1965	85.00
Ring, Batwing Logo, Sterling Silver, Box	88.00
Sculpture, Riddler, Bend-A-Body, On Card, 1966	25.00
Slippers, Batgirl, 1967	95.00
Telephone, PTT, Batphone	23.00
View-Master, The Purr-Fect Crime, 3 Reels, Booklet, 1966	70.00
Wristwatch, 1989	25.00
Wristwatch, Marx, 1978	20.00
Wristwatch, Tin, Bracelet, Occupied Japan, 1953	25.00
Yo-Yo, Batman Running, Red Plastic	8.50
Yo-Yo, Yellow & Black Logo, DC Comics, Specra Star Yos, On Card, 1989	13.00

BATTERSEA enamels, which are enamels painted on copper, were made in the Battersea district of London from about 1750 to 1756. Many similar enamels are mistakenly called *Battersea.*

Box, Colonial Couple In Park, Obelisk Monument, Bridge, c.1760, 3 x 1 1/8 In.	250.00
Box, The Gift Of A Friend, Black, White Border, Cream Oval, Blue Base, 1 1/2 x 1 In.	255.00
Candlestick, Enameling On Copper, White Panels, Florals, 9 In., Pair	2530.00

BAUER pottery is a California-made ware. J.A. Bauer moved his Kentucky pottery to Los Angeles, California, in 1909. The company made art pottery after 1912 and dinnerwares marked *Bauer* after 1929. The factory went out of business in 1962.

Art Pottery, Planter, Green, Ruffled Edge, Matt Carlton, 7 1/2 In.	320.00
Art Pottery, Vase, Delft Blue, Matt Carlton, 10 In.	450.00
Art Pottery, Vase, Delft Blue, Ruffled, Matt Carlton, 12 In.	458.00
Brusche, Creamer, Burgundy	15.00
Brusche, Platter, Burgundy, 12 1/4 In.	20.00
Cal-Art, Candleholder, Tan, Pair	65.00
Chicken Of The Sea, Baker, Fish Shaped, Turquoise	43.00
Chicken Of The Sea, Plate, Fish Shaped, Yellow, 10 1/4 In.	21.00
Florist Ware, Planter, Speckled Pink, 12 1/4 In.	25.00
Florist Ware, Planter, Swirl, Burgundy, 7 1/2 In.	54.00
Florist Ware, Planter, Swirl, Chartreuse, 9 1/2 In.	51.00
Florist Ware, Vase, Elongated Lily Shape, Lavendar & Gold, 11 1/4 In.	125.00
Monterey, Cup & Saucer, Turquoise Blue	7.00
Monterey, Plate, Bread & Butter, Canary Yellow, 6 In.	5.00
Monterey, Plate, Dinner, Green, 10 In.	8.00
Monterey, Platter, Oval, Turquoise Blue, 11 In.	14.00
Moonsong, Platter, Spicy Green, 2 Sections, 13 In.	28.00
Plainware, Bean Pot, Jade Green, 4 1/2 In.	96.00
Plainware, Coffee Server, Cover, Yellow	53.00
Plainware, Pitcher, Pale Green Glaze, 8 In.	308.00
Ring, Baking Dish, Cover, Orange, Red, 4 In.	55.00
Ring, Bowl, Soup, Cover, Lug Handle, Orange, 5 1/2 In.	90.00
Ring, Casserole, Cover, Orange Red, Individual, 5 1/2 In.	200.00
Ring, Pitcher, Yellow, 3 Qt.	235.00

Ring, Sugar & Creamer, Cover, Orange 75.00
Stoneware, Bean Pot, 2 Handles, Yellow, 4 1/2 In............................. 100.00
Stoneware, Chicken Fountain, Metal Base, 8 In. 41.00
Stoneware, Dog Dish, Embossed Word Dog, Yellow 100.00
Stoneware, Jar, Dripping, Wooden Cover, Apple, Strawberries & Grapes, 5 In. 49.00
Stoneware, Pitcher, Apple, Yellow Border, 4 3/8 In. 47.00
Stoneware, Plate, Apple & Cherries, Yellow Border, Square, 6 7/8 In. 47.00
Stoneware, Trivet, Apple, Yellow Border, 8 1/4 x 6 1/2 In. 47.00

BAVARIA is a region in Europe where many types of porcelain were made. In the nineteenth century, the mark often included the word *Bavaria.* After 1871, the words *Bavaria, Germany,* were used. Listed here are pieces that include the name *Bavaria* in some form, but major porcelain makers, such as Rosenthal, are listed in their own categories.

Cake Plate, Scalloped Rim, Flowers, Green & White Ground, Footed, 15 1/4 In. 230.00
Charger, Painted, Otto Greiner, 12 1/2 In. 135.00
Compote, Reticulated Bowl, Entwined Cherubs, 1837, 9 x 6 1/2 In. 1110.00
Cup, Raised White Flowers, 3 Footed, Gold Trim, Mittertiech 10.00
Group, Sheep & Shepherd, Pastel, Gerold Porzellan, 7 x 6 1/2 In. 110.00
Hair Receiver, Lilac, Signed, 4 1/2 In. 50.00
Plate, Fruit, Signed, A. Koch, 1902, 8 1/2 In. ....55.00 to 75.00
Tray, Dresser, 2 Women On Balcony, Rose Border, 11 In. 63.00
Urn, Gold Angels Adorn Each Side, Handles, 18 x 5 x 19 In....................... 158.00

BEADED BAGS are included in the Purse category.

BEATLES collectors search for any items picturing the four members of the famous music group or any of their recordings. Because these items are so new, the condition is very important and top prices are paid only for items in mint condition. The Beatles first appeared on American network television in 1964. The group disbanded in 1971. Ringo Starr, George Harrison, and Paul McCartney are still performing. John Lennon died in 1980.

Banjo, Mastro, Beatle Faces On Skin, 22 In., 1964 .... 800.00
Bank, Register, Make A Date With The Beatles, Plastic, MC, 3 3/4 In................. 22.00
Cartoon Kit, Colorforms, 1966 .... 500.00
Costume, Paul McCartney, Ben Cooper 800.00
Doll, Bobbin' Head, 1960s, 4 Piece 750.00
Guitar, Jr., Mastro, 1960s, 15 In. 425.00

Beatles, Lunch Box,
Beatles, Metal, Aqua,
Aladdin, Thermos, 1965

Beatles, Lunch
Box, Yellow
Submarine, Metal,
King Seeley
Thermos, 1968

Beatles, Record, I Want To Hold Your
Hand, I Saw Her Standing There, Capitol

Guitar, Selcol, 1960s 550.00
Lunch Box, Beatles, Metal, Aqua, Aladdin, Thermos, 1965 ....*Illus* 1495.00
Lunch Box, Kaboodle Kit, Vinyl, Lithograph On Front, Standard Plastic, 1965 .... 975.00
Lunch Box, Let It Be, Tin, 8 5/8 x 6 3/8 In. 25.00
Lunch Box, Please, Please Me, Tin, 8 5/8 x 6 3/8 In. 25.00
Lunch Box, Portrait Below White Signatures, Air Flite 690.00
Lunch Box, Red Background, Printed Autographs, Vinyl, Air Flite 690.00
Lunch Box, Sgt. Pepper, Tin, 8 5/8 x 6 3/8 In. 25.00
Lunch Box, White Album, Tin, 8 5/8 x 6 3/8 In. 25.00
Lunch Box, Yellow Submarine, Metal, King Seeley Thermos, 1968 ....*Illus* 1093.00
Magic Slate, Merit 500.00
Paint Your Own Beatle Kit, Artistic Creations, 1960s 400.00
Photograph, John Lennon, Autographed, Black & White, Self Caricature, 1960, 10 In. ... 600.00
Record, I Want To Hold Your Hand, I Saw Her Standing There, Capitol ....*Illus* 10.00
Record, Sgt. Pepper's Lonely Hearts Club Band, Limited Edition, Capitol, 1978 .... 130.00
Ticket, Cumberland Theater, Brunswick, Maine, Sept. 1, 1964, Die Cut Busts 115.00
TWA Flight Bag, Red, Vinyl, Autographs Of 4 Beatles, 1965, 10 x 14 In. 125.00
Wallet, Vinyl, Day-Glo Pink, Facsimile Autographs, Ramat & Co. Ltd., London, 1964 ... 135.00

BEEHIVE, Austria, or Beehive, Vienna, are terms used in English-speaking countries to refer to the many types of decorated porcelain bearing a mark that looks like a beehive. The mark is actually a shield, viewed upside down. It was first used in 1744 by the Royal Porcelain Manufactory of Vienna. The firm made porcelains, called *Royal Vienna* by collectors, until it closed in 1864. Many other German, Austrian, and Japanese factories have reproduced Royal Vienna wares, complete with the original shield or *beehive* mark. This listing includes the expensive, original Royal Vienna porcelains and many other types of beehive porcelain. The Royal Vienna pieces include that name in the description.

Beaker, Classical Figured Frieze, Landscape, Royal Blue Ground, 3 Handles, 6 In. 230.00
Charger, Children At Play, Maroon, Pink, Blue, Gold Border, N.J., 14 In. 1705.00
Charger, Children At The Hunt, Maroon, Pink, Blue, Gold Border, N.J., 14 In. 1705.00
Cup & Saucer, Swan In Cup, Gold Handle, Royal Vienna Mark, Demitasse 60.00
Ewer, Classical, Children, Cattle By River, Green Ground, 10 In. 240.00
Plaque, Beautiful Woman, Florentine Gilt Frame, c.1880, 10 x 8 1/2 In. 3250.00
Plaque, Cupid & Maiden, Views Of Garden, Uhlmann, Frame, 18 1/4 In. 2415.00
Plaque, Putti & Dragon Border, Gladiator, Women & Child, 14 3/4 In. 1430.00
Plate, Cabinet, Scene Of Women In Landscape, Cobalt Border, 10 In. 80.00
Plate, Game Bird, 9 3/4 In. 36.00
Plate, Royal Vienna, Classical Figures, Artist Signed Knoiller, 9 In., 6 Piece 3360.00
Urn, 2 Griffin Form Handles, Oval, Central Portrait Medallion, Copper Luster, 17 In. 3450.00
Urn, Hand Painted Scene, Snake Handles, 18 In. 5600.00
Vase, Amorous Putto Couple, Putti In Clouds With Garlands, Handles, 7 1/4 In. 253.00
Vase, Full-Figure Woman, Long Hair, Signed 1850.00

BEER BOTTLES are listed in the Bottle category under Beer.

BEER CANS are a twentieth-century idea. Beer was sold in kegs or returnable bottles until 1934. The first patent for a can was issued to the American Can Company in September of that year; and Gotfried Kruger Brewing Company, Newark, New Jersey, was the first to use the can. The cone-top can was first made in 1935, the aluminum pop-top in 1962. Collectors should look for cans in good condition, with no dents or rust. Serious collectors prefer cans that have been opened from the bottom.

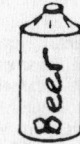

Aspen Gold, Tivoli Brewing Co. 30.00
Becker's Mellow Beer, 11 Oz. 40.00
Black Horse Ale, Cone Top, Cap & Contents 605.00
Brown Derby, Flat, 12 Oz. 11.00
Bullfrog Beer, Full, Flat, 1950s 51.00
Canadian Ace, Flat Top 50.00
James Bond's 007 Special Blend, Top Opened, 1960s 605.00
Koenig Brau, Flat 20.00

Miller High Life, Flat, Rolled, 1940s 29.00
Reading, Light Premium Beer, Bicentennial Series, Pull Tab, Reading Brewing Co. 5.00
Sunshine Premium, Pull Tab 75.00
Swinger Malt Liquor, Maier Brewing Co. 65.00
Wisconsin's Private Club Beer, Rolled, Flat, 12 Oz. 68.00

BELL collectors collect all types of bells. Favorites include glass bells,
figural bells, school bells, and cowbells. Bells have been made of
porcelain, china, or metal through the centuries.

Dinner Gong, Art Nouveau, Bronze, Mahogany, Floral Carving, 10 x 12 x 10 In. 500.00
Figures Around Sides, Jacobean Head Finial, Brass, 4 In. 110.00
Fluted Columns, Urn Finial, Carved Wooden Stand, Brass, Continental, 12 In. 173.00
Girl, Victorian Dress, Holding Arms Out, Brass, 3 3/4 In. 65.00
Mythical Creatures & Man, Angel, Brass Swivel Bracket, Chain Pull, 11 1/2 In. 105.00
Putti & Bacchanalian Figures, Bronze, Figural Handle, Germany, 16th Century, 5 In. 230.00
Rockwell, Loves Harmony, Fondly We Remember, Wooden Handle, 1977, 9 In. 35.00
Scrolled Leaves, Masks, Jewels, Stylized Lion Mask Handle, Renaissance Revival, 6 In. ... 127.00
Sleigh, 12 Bells, Brass, Leather Strap, Early 19th Century, 35 In. 110.00
Sleigh, 15 Graduated Bells, Brass, Black Leather Strap 165.00
Sleigh, 30 Bells, Leather Strap, 19th Century 550.00
Temple, Pair Of Dragons, Lotus Petals Shoulder, Bronze, 18th Century, 50 In. 7475.00
Vaseline Glass, Chartreuse, Hung By Chain, Clear Glass Clapper, 7 In. 57.00

BELLEEK china was made in Ireland, other European countries, and the
United States. The glaze is creamy yellow and appears wet. The first
Belleek was made in 1857. All pieces listed here are Irish Belleek. The
mark changed through the years. The first mark, black, dates from 1863
to 1890. The second mark, black, dates from 1891 to 1926 and includes
the words *Co. Fermanagh, Ireland*. The third mark, black, dates from
1926 to 1946 and has the words *Deanta in Eirinn*. The fourth mark,
same as the third mark but green, dates from 1946 to 1955. The fifth
mark, green, dates from 1955 to 1965 and has an R in a circle added in
the upper right. The sixth mark, green, dates after 1965 and the words
Co. Fermanagh have been omitted. The seventh mark, gold, was used
from 1980 to 1993 and omits the words *Deanta in Eirinn*. The eighth
mark, introduced in 1993, is similar to the second mark but is printed
in blue. The word *Belleek* is now used only on the pieces made in
Ireland even though earlier pieces from other countries were sometimes marked *Belleek*. These early pieces are listed by manufacturer,
such as Ceramic Art Co., Haviland, Lenox, Ott & Brewer, and Willets.

Cake Plate, Shamrock, Twig Handles, 4th Mark 100.00
Cracker Jar, Shell Design, 4th Mark, 7 In. 140.00
Cream Jug, Shell, Blue Glazed Handle, 1st Mark, Black, c.1880, 5 1/4 In. 518.00
Creamer, Yellow Ribbon, Bow Accents, 7th Mark, 3 1/2 In. 60.00
Cup & Saucer, Gilt Trimmed, Orange Peel Ground, 1st Mark, Black, c.1870, 5 3/4 In. ... 175.00
Cup & Saucer, Nautilus On Coral, Pink Tinted, 1st Mark, Black, c.1880, 8 3/4 In. 1150.00
Ewer, Applied Floral Design, Scalloped Rim, 5th Mark, Green, 9 1/4 In. 100.00
Honey Pot, 1st Mark, Black 1200.00
Salt, Fluted Diamond, 3rd Mark, Black 25.00
Sculpture, Clytie, Maiden Set In Flower, Round Socle, 3rd Mark, 12 In. 460.00
Sugar & Creamer, Lily, 3rd Mark, Black 125.00
Sugar & Creamer, Ribbon, 3rd Mark, Black 130.00
Tea Set, Neptune, 3rd Mark, Black, 21 Piece 1150.00
Toothpick, 3rd Mark, Black 75.00
Vase, Stylized Tulips, Scroll Double Handles, 5th Mark, Green, 16 In., Pair 400.00
Vase, Swan Design, 4th Mark, 6 x 7 1/2 In. 110.00

BENNINGTON ware was the product of two factories working in
Bennington, Vermont. Both the Norton Company and the Lyman
Fenton Company were out of business by 1896. The wares include
brown and yellow mottled pottery, Parian, scroddled ware, stoneware,
graniteware, yellowware, and Staffordshire-type vases. The name is

also a generic term for mottled brownware of the type made in Bennington.

Bank, Uncle Sam, Flint, 4 1/4 In. 610.00
Bottle, Book, Battle Of Bennington, Brown, Tan, Green, Mottled Glaze, 1880, 6 In. 130.00
Bottle, Book, Mottled Brown & Blue 1500.00
Bottle, Coachman's, Figure In Cloak, Holding Cup, 1849, 10 1/2 In. 880.00
Bottle, Coachmen, Lyman Fenton & Co., 1849, 10 In. 385.00
Bottle, Flask, Book, Enamel, Departed Spirits, Gold, Green, 7 3/4 x 5 3/4 In. 1670.00
Bottle, Flask, Book, Flint Enamel, Blue, Orange, 4 Qt., 10 1/2 x 8 In. 2013.00
Coffeepot, Blue & Orange Streaks, 13 3/4 In. ....*Illus* 1025.00
Crock, Brushed Plume Design, Stoneware, E. & L.P. Norton, 1880, 1 Gal. 176.00
Crock, Cake, Stylized Fitted Plume, Stoneware, E. & L.P. Norton, c.1880, 5 In. 330.00
Crock, Cobalt Blue Flowers, Applied Double Handles, Stoneware, L.P. Norton, 7 In. 300.00
Ewer, Pink & White, Footed, Experimental Type, Mid 1800s, 11 1/2 In., Pair 1600.00
Inkwell, Lion Head, Rockingham Glaze, 2 x 3 1/2 In. 862.00
Jar, Canning, Blue Flower Spray, Stoneware, J. & E. Norton, 1855, 2 Gal. 745.00
Jar, Canning, Stylized Flowers, Stoneware, E. & L.P. Norton, 1880, 2 Gal. 415.00
Jug, Bird On Front Near Spout, Wood Stopper, Stoneware, J. Norton & Co., 1861, 1 Gal. . 770.00
Jug, Bird On Front, Handle, Stoneware, J. & E. Norton, 1855, 1 Gal. 385.00
Jug, Bird On Twig, Stoneware, J. Norton & Co., 1861, 1 Gal. 470.00
Jug, Cobalt Blue Flowers, Stoneware, Julius Norton, 14 In. 330.00
Jug, Flowers, Cobalt Blue, Grayish Tan Glaze, Stoneware, L. Norton & Co., 1800s, 15 In. 495.00
Jug, Standing Deer, Stoneware, J. & E. Norton, 1855, 2 Gal. 2500.00
Jug, Stylized Flowers, Stoneware, E. & L.P. Norton, 1880, 4 Gal. 1045.00
Jug, Triple Flower Design, Stoneware, Julius Norton, 1848, 3 Gal. 165.00
Mug, Rockingham, Unmarked, 3 1/2 In. 87.00
Pitcher, Double Blue Plume, Sunburst In Middle, Stoneware, F.B. Norton, c.1870, 12 In. . 740.00
Pitcher, Eagle With Shield, Stars, Cannon & Banner, Rockingham Glaze, 9 In. 1035.00
Pitcher, Embossed Hunt Scene, Fox Handle, c.1860, 9 In. 225.00
Pitcher, Face Spout, c.1850, 9 In. 1275.00
Pitcher, Hound Handle, Rockingham Glaze, 9 In. 430.00
Pitcher, Mask Spout, Brown & Cream Glaze, Signed, 4 1/2 In. 840.00
Pitcher, Peacock, 8 1/2 In. 285.00
Pitcher & Bowl Set, Flint Enamel, Alternate Rib, Bluish Green, Mark, 14 In. 1438.00
Pitcher Set, Blue Stripes, 8 Mugs, 11 In. 250.00
Salt Box, Peacock, Round Lid, 6 In. 250.00
Sculpture, Poodle, Seated, Blue-Green Mottling, 12 x 10 x 7 In. ....*Illus* 1090.00
Sugar, Flint Enamel, Cover, Impressed Base Mark, 8 1/2 In. 800.00
Teapot, Brown Sponge Design, Yellowware Base, 5 In. 495.00
Water Cooler, Gothic Style, No Cover, 16 1/2 In. ....*Illus* 2195.00

Bennington, Coffeepot,
Blue & Orange Streaks,
13 3/4 In.

Bennington, Sculpture, Poodle,
Seated, Blue-Green Mottling,
12 x 10 x 7 In.

Bennington, Water Cooler,
Gothic Style, No Cover,
16 1/2 In.

BERLIN, a German porcelain factory, was started in 1751 by Wilhelm Kaspar Wegely. In 1763, the factory was taken over by Frederick the Great and became the Royal Berlin Porcelain Manufactory. It is still in operation today. Pieces have been marked in a variety of ways.

Basket, Fruit, Gilt Design, Applied Flowers, Branch Handles, Late 19th Century, 12 In. . . .	430.00
Bowl, Octagonal, Painted, Flared Rim, Gold Ground, White Flowers, c.1830, 10 1/8 In. . . .	9000.00
Dish, Sweetmeat, Putto, Standing In Center, Birds Raised On Base, Blue, 5 In.	360.00
Plaque, Farm Girl In Landscape, Frame, Early 20th Century, 4 x 5 3/4 In.	1610.00
Plaque, Maiden With Candle, Young Woman With Open Necked Blouse, 9 3/8 In.	2530.00
Plaque, Sistine Angels, Painted, K Impression, Gilt Frame, 14 1/4 x 9 1/4 In.	952.00
Plaque, St. Jerome, Kneeling Before Tomb, House In Background, 9 7/8 x 7 In.	520.00
Plaque, Woman With Apples, Seated, Peeling Apples, 12 3/8 x 10 In.	2300.00
Plaque, Young Victorian Bride, Wedding Gown, Frame, 12 1/2 x 7 1/2 In.	2645.00
Plate, Ornithological, Exotic Birds Perched In Tree, Insects, Gilt, Blue, 1860, 8 1/2 In. . . .	235.00
Sculpture, Lion, Recumbent, White Biscuit, Lapis Lazuli Plinth, c.1840, 6 1/2 In.	7200.00
Stein, Raised Bands Of Flowers, Pewter Lid, Signed, 19th Century, 6 1/4 In.	230.00

BESWICK started making earthenware in Staffordshire, England, in 1936. The company is now part of Royal Doulton Tableware, Ltd. Figurines of animals, especially dogs and horses, Beatrix Potter animals, and other wares are still being made.

Character Jug, Sairey Gamp, No. 371, 6 1/2 In.	150.00
Creamer, Cottage Ware	40.00
Creamer, Pecksniff, No. 1117	70.00
Figurine, Appley Dapply, No. 2333/2	40.00
Figurine, Aunt Pettitoes, No. 2276	75.00
Figurine, Benjamin Bunny, No. 1105/4	40.00
Figurine, Gryphon, Alice Series, No. 2485	295.00
Figurine, Hunca Munca Sweeping, No. 2584	85.00
Figurine, Jemima Puddleduck, Gold Scarf Clip, No. 3373	100.00
Figurine, Jemima Puddleduck, No. 3373c	95.00
Figurine, Johnny Town-Mouse, No. 1276	225.00
Figurine, King Of Hearts, Alice Series, No. 2489	125.00
Figurine, Little Black Rabbit, No. 2585	50.00
Figurine, Little Pig Robinson, No. 1104b	75.00
Figurine, Mr. Alderman Ptolemy, No. 2424	175.00
Figurine, Mr. Drake Puddleduck, No. 2628	65.00
Figurine, Mr. Jeremy Fisher, No. 1157	40.00
Figurine, Mrs. Rabbit & Bunnies, No. 2543	40.00
Figurine, Old Mr. Brown, No. 1796a	75.00
Figurine, Old Woman Lived In Shoe, No. 1545	40.00
Figurine, Peter Rabbit, 1098/2	250.00
Figurine, Peter Rabbit, Gold Buttons, No. 3356/2	100.00
Figurine, Pigling Bland, No. 1365/1	500.00
Figurine, Pigling Bland, No. 1365/2	40.00
Figurine, Squirrel Nutkin, No. 1102/2	200.00
Figurine, Strained Relations, Kitty McBride, No. 2532	125.00
Figurine, Timmy Tiptoes, No. 1101/2	45.00
Figurine, Timmy Willie, No. 1109, 2nd Mark	225.00
Figurine, Tom Kitten, No. 1100/1	195.00
Figurine, Tom Kitten, No. 1100/2, 3b Mark	90.00
Mug, Robert Burns, No. 1596	125.00
Pepper Shaker, Sairey Gamp, No. 689	45.00
Saltshaker, Mr. McCawber, No. 690	45.00

BETTY BOOP, the cartoon figure, first appeared on the screen in 1931. Her face was modeled after the famous singer Helen Kane and her body after Mae West. In 1935, a comic strip was started. Her dog was named Bimbo. Although the Betty Boop cartoons ended by 1938, there was a revival of interest in the Betty Boop image in the 1980s and new pieces are being made.

Bank, Biker Babe, Vinyl, 10 In.	17.00

Candy Box, Betty, Bimbo, Koko On Side Panels, Schutter-Johnston, c.1920, 11 In. 350.00
Cookie Jar, 1985 . . . .   350.00
Doll, Wood & Composition, Jointed, Green Dress, Decal, Fleisher, 1930s, 12 In. 1000.00
Doll, Wooden, Jointed, Jaymar 52.00
Frame, Ceramic, Paper Label, 5 7/8 x 6 1/2 In., 1985 . . . .   65.00
Jack-O'-Lantern, Betty's Head, Molded Cardboard, Germany, 5 In. 68.00
Marble 5.00
Ornament, Christmas, Betty Sitting On Candy Cane, 1940s 12.00
Ornament, Christmas, Full Skirt 34.00
Pin, Betty Boop For President, 1980 National Convention, Tin, 1 1/4 In. 8.00
String Holder, Chalkware, 1930s, 7 1/2 In. 750.00

BICYCLES were invented in 1839. The first manufactured bicycle was
made in 1861. Special ladies' bicycles were made after 1874. The modern safety bicycle was not produced until 1885. Collectors search for
all types of bicycles and tricycles. Bicycle-related items are also listed
here.

Bislyder, Bicycle-Form Sled, Steel & Wood, c.1930 . . . .   440.00
Boneshaker, 39-Inch Front Wheel, 35-Inch Rear Wheel, Wooden Pedals, c.1860 . . . .   3410.00
Boston Cycle & Sundry Co., Woman's, Cork Handles, Leather Seat, Oak Rims, c.1915 . .   225.00
Cart, 4-Wheel, Hand Propelled, Daniel Albright's Wagon Shop, Pa., c.1903, 34 x 58 In. . . .   1100.00
Columbia, 3 Star Deluxe, Girl's, Diamond Anniversary Model, 1952 . . . .   110.00
Columbia, 5 Star, Chrome Tank, Headlamp, Bookrack Seat, Keylock Steering Column . . .   645.00
Columbia, 5 Star, Woman's, Springer Truss, Headlamp, Carrier, Front Drum Brake 245.00
Columbia, Cyclone, Woman's, Skirt Guard, Drop Stand, Front Basket, Cream & Blue 80.00
Columbia, Fire Arrow, Light Tank, Horn, Carrier, Black & White, c.1960 . . . .   168.00
Columbia, Fire Arrow, Woman's, 3-Speed, Horn Tank, Carrier, Headlamp, c.1960 . . . .   55.00
Columbia, Racycle, Headlamp, Carrier, Leather Seat, Red & White 112.00
Columbia, Superb, Curved Crossbar Handlebars, Rear Carrier, c.1941 . . . .   575.00
Dayton, Twin Flex, Gray, Silver, Red, Chrome Wheels, Messenger Seat, 1939, 70 In. 1610.00
Elgin, Falcon, Twin Bar, Tool Tank, Messenger Leather Saddle, Balloon Tires, c.1937 . . . .   504.00
Elgin, Special, Siren, Truss Rods, Delta Rocket Headlamp, Carrier, Tail Lamp, c.1930 . . .   196.00
Elgin, Tool Tank, Drop Stand, Carrier, Troxel Leather Saddle 336.00
Elliot Hickory, Model C, c.1892 . . . .   6370.00
Gormully & Jefferies, High Wheeler, Leather Seat, Missing Handle, c.1880, 54 In. 1624.00
Hartford Cycle Company, Cork Handles, Leather Seat, Wooden Rims, Black, c.1910 . . . .   246.00
Haverford Bicycle Co., Black Beauty, Woman's, Chain Guard, Dual Drop Stand 56.00
Hawthorne, Flier, Tool Kit, Battery Can, Siren, Headlamp, Troxel Leather Saddle, 1920s .   364.00
Hawthorne, Woman's, Twin Headlamps, Locking Fork, Skirt Guard, Carrier, Blue 112.00
Hawthorne-Ward's, Balloon, Rear Carrier, Running Lights 198.00
High Wheel, Spoke Wheels, Iron Frame, Wooden Handlebars, c.1870, 52 In. 2860.00
High Wheel, Victor, Down-Swept Handlebars, Red Pinstriping, 54 In. 4675.00
Howe Machine Co., Huntington Leatherwork, Green Finish, Gilt, 1880, 52 In. 4025.00
Huffy, Yellow Submarine, Woman's, 3-Speed, Yellow, 1960s 2585.00
Indian, Pneumatic Safety, Girl's, 2-Speed, Messenger Seat, Logo 715.00
Iver Johnson, Pneumatic Safety, Woman's, Wooden Chain Guard, c.1897 . . . .   260.00
J.C. Higgins, Balloon, Girl's, Spring Fork, Gold Pinstriping, 1950s 165.00
J.C. Higgins, Colorflow, Delta Rocket Rack Headlamp, Carrier, Jewel Tank, c.1950 . . . . . .   78.00
Lamp, Carbide, Nickel On Brass, Faceted Side Lenses, Spring Suspension, Pink 90.00
Lamp, Carbide, Nickel Plated, Colombia, c.1900 . . . .   60.00
Lamp, Kerosene, Lucas King Of The Road Hub Light, For High Wheelers, Burner 1624.00
Lamp, Oil, Imperial, Concave Lens 82.00
March Davis, The March, Man's, Pneumatic Safety, Down-Swept Handles 962.00
Matthews, Horse Head, Saddle, White, Firestone Tires, Metal Training Wheels, 33 In. 325.00
Monarch, Silver King, Hex Tube, Springer Front Fork 290.00
Monarch, Silver King, Woman's, Aluminum Frame, Locking Steering, Stand 213.00
Monark, Super Deluxe, Steel, Rubber, 26 In. . . . . .275.00 to 350.00
Murray, Mercury, Truss Rod, Bell, Red & White 157.00
National Sewing Machine Co., Standard, Woman's, Pneumatic Safety, 19th Century 742.00
Pennant, Model 10, Man's, Pneumatic Safety, Gold Transfers, 1898 . . . .   247.00
Ranger, Aristocrat, Mead Saddle, Siren, Headlamp, Bell, Tool Tank, Wood Rims, c.1915 .   560.00
Roadmaster, Woman's, Red, White, & Blue, Full Fenders, Front Lamp, Bookrack, c.1950 .   84.00
Schwinn, Ace, Boy's, Balloon, Horn Tank, Spring Action Front 825.00

Schwinn, Autocycle, Standard, c.1937	950.00
Schwinn, B107, Silver Ray Headlight & Tank, Tool Box Door, c.1936	1870.00
Schwinn, BF Goodrich, Challenger, Deluxe, Chain Guard, 1940	522.00
Schwinn, Black, Red, Battery Headlight, Tank Horn, Spring Seat, 69 In.	287.00
Schwinn, D97XE, Boy's, Horn Tank, Light, Red & Cream, Whitewall Tires, 1939	1300.00
Schwinn, Girl's, Blue & White, Basket & Light, 1950s	250.00
Schwinn, Jaguar, 3-Speed, Horn Tank, Carrier, Headlamp, 1960s	134.00
Schwinn, Packard, Tank, Leather Seat, Toolbox, Red, White Highlights	224.00
Schwinn, Panther III, Front & Rear Carriers, Black & Chrome, 1960s	39.00
Schwinn, Phantom, Green, 1956	1550.00
Schwinn, Phantom, Green, 1957, 26 In.	1650.00
Schwinn, Starlet, Girl's, Horn Tank, Front & Rear Carrier, Purple, Chrome, c.1960	90.00
Schwinn, Stingray, 5-Speed, Lemon Peeler, Stick Shift, c.1968	440.00
Schwinn, Whizzer, Carrier, Springer Fork, Tank, Orange	224.00
Sears, Jewel, Woman's, Oak Rim, Chain Guard, Split Leather Seat, Bell, c.1890	448.00
Sears, Spyder, Girl's, Purple, Banana Seat, Butterfly Handlebars, 24 In.	185.00
Seat, Flexible No. 8, Padded Leather, Sager	62.00
Shelby, Donald Duck, Yellow, Blue, White, Handlebar, Chrome Wheels, 1951, 24 In.	3162.00
Shelby, Eagle, Girl's, Horn Button, Shelby, Ohio, 26 In.	180.00
Shelby, Flyer, Airflow, Boy's, 2-Speed, Balloon, Bendix Front Brake	1210.00
Shelby, Flyer, Chrome Spring Bike Seat, Headlight, Red, Blue, 70 In.	2415.00
Sherrell Classic, Red Dice Air Caps, Rubber Tires, 26 In.	1000.00
Sherrell Classic, Type 1, Red Paint, 1987	715.00
Siren, Acme, Nickel-Plated, Trumpet Form, England, 19th Century	82.00
Stearns, Shaft Drive, Oak Rims, Handlebar Bell, c.1890	448.00
Syracuse, Gilt Edge, Wolverine Saddle, Wooden Rims, c.1910	112.00
Tool Kit, Simplex, Model WL36, Spoke Hole, Box	17.00
Tricycle, Boneshaker, c.1860	3400.00
Tricycle, Cast Iron, Orange Paint, Leather Seat, c.1880	1017.00
Tricycle, Colson & Co., Elyria, Ohio, 1930s, 29 In.	123.00
Tricycle, Pinstripes, Fringed Fabric Seat, c.1875	1540.00
Tricycle, Pressed Steel, Spoked Wheels, Pedal Arms, 2-Toned Blue, 32 x 30 In.	316.00
Tricycle, Sulky, Pony, Leather Tack, Rubber Wheels, Metal Frame, 1930s	995.00
Tricycle, Victorian, Joystick Steering, Reupholstered Seat, Child's, c.1890	252.00
Tricycle, Wooden Seat, Wooden, c.1875	1210.00
Velocipede, Child's, 3 Wheels, Self-Propelled, Horse Head, Hand Levers, c.1840	5500.00
Velocipede, Horse & Sulky, Ponies Stenciled On Seat, Metal Wheels, 23 x 48 In.	2530.00
Velocipede, Horse Head, 3 Wheels	4750.00
Velocipede, Horse Head, c.1890	550.00
Velocipede, Horse Head, Wood, Metal, Painted, Chain Drive, France, 19th Century	440.00
Velocipede, Velvet Upholstered Seat, Fringe On Iron Frame, Patent 1884	412.00
Western Flyer, Boy's, Balloon Tires, Tank, Truss Rod, 20 In.	67.00
Western Flyer, Buzz, 1970s, 20 In.	200.00
Western Flyer, Cosmic, Red, Black & Chrome, 1960s	28.00

BING & GRONDAHL is a famous Danish factory making fine porcelains from 1853 to the present. Underglaze blue decoration was started in 1886. The annual Christmas plate series was introduced in 1895. Dinnerwares, stoneware, and figurines are still being made today. The firm has used the initials B & G and a stylized castle as part of the mark since 1898.

MADE IN
DENMARK

Plate, Christmas, 1899, Crows Enjoying Christmas, 7 In.	2247.00
Plate, Christmas, 1900, Church Bells Chiming In Christmas, 7 In.	430.00
Plate, Christmas, 1901, Three Wise Men From The East, 7 In.	230.00
Plate, Christmas, 1902, Interior Of A Gothic Church, 7 In.	172.00
Plate, Christmas, 1904, View Of Copenhagen From Frederiksberg Hill, 7 In.	85.00
Plate, Christmas, 1907, Little Match Girl, 7 In.	143.00
Plate, Christmas, 1908, St. Peter Church Of Copenhagen, 7 In.	6000.00
Plate, Christmas, 1909, Happiness Over The Yule Tree, 7 In.	104.00
Plate, Christmas, 1968, Christmas In Church, 7 In.	12.00
Plate, Christmas, 1970, Pheasants In The Snow At Christmas, 7 In.	12.00
Plate, Christmas, 1971, Christmas At Home, 7 In.	12.00
Plate, Christmas, 1974, Christmas In The Village, 7 In.	12.00

Bing & Grondahl, Vase,
Birds, Leafy Branches,
Green Mark, 16 In.

When packing a piece of pottery for shipping, look at the shape. If it has a hollow space larger than one inch across, fill the space with sponge foam or bubble wrap.

Plate, Christmas, 1975, Christmas At The Old Water Mill, 7 In. 12.00
Plate, Christmas, 1979, White Christmas, 7 In. 12.00
Plate, Mother's Day, 1987, Sheep With Lambs 83.00
Salt & Pepper, Dutch 40.00
Sculpture, Antelope, Signed, 7 In. 224.00
Sculpture, Reclining Nude Nursing 2 Children, Signed, 21 In. 1265.00
Sculpture, Young Girl Tripping On Her Skirts, Wearing Gray Frock, 6 In. 121.00
Sculpture, Young Lad, Hugging His Dog, Signed, 4 1/2 In. 157.00
Vase, Birds, Leafy Branches, Green Mark, 16 In. .... *Illus* 90.00
Vase, Farmland, House, Stables & Barns, Signed, 12 In. 252.00
Vase, Harbor Scene, Sailing Vessels, Monastery In Distance, Signed, 17 In. 1120.00
Vase, Lavender Clover, Butterfly, Ivory To Light Gray Ground, 9 1/2 In. 35.00
Vase, Water Lilies, Green, Ivory Ground, 2-Tone, Incised, 9 In. 58.00
Vase, Windmill On Barren Landscape, Signed, 11 3/4 In. 168.00

BINOCULARS of all types are wanted by collectors. Those made in the eighteenth and nineteenth centuries are favored by serious collectors. The small, attractive binoculars called *opera glasses* are listed in their own category.

Field, Protracting Lens Shields, Leather Bound, France 39.00
U.S. Navy, Leather Case, 7 x 50 In., Pair 230.00

BIRDCAGES are collected for use as homes for pet birds and as decorative objects of folk art. Elaborate wooden cages of the past centuries can still be found. The brass or wicker cages of the 1930s are popular with bird owners.

Architectural Design, Arched Portico, Domed Top, Front Pillars, 33 1/2 In. 440.00
Brass, Circular, Early 20th Century, 15 x 18 In. 115.00
Brass, Enamel Cast Iron Water Bowls, 24 1/2 x 22 x 18 In. 56.00
Gabled Roof, Steepled Facade, Attached Feeders, Elevated Spires, 19 1/2 x 22 In. 316.00
Gilt Metal, Palazzo Style House, Gothic Windows, Wooden Base, 1880s, 19 In. 1092.00
Hanging, Brass Ring, Steel Stem, Cast Iron Base, 70 In. 55.00
Mahogany, Neoclassical Temple Shape, Turreted Stand, Victorian, 79 x 28 In. 4600.00
Pine, Hinged Door, Green, Blue, Red, Turquoise Paint, 19th Century, 21 In. 1440.00
Stylized Castle, Colored Bands, Tin Glazed Earthenware, 19th Century, 9 1/4 In. 316.00
Tin, Painted, Folk Art, 13 x 12 x 9 In. 46.00
Wire, Black & Gold, Ship, Swings & Perches, Pottery Feeders, 3 Scalloped Legs 150.00
Wire, Painted, 3 Cast Iron Owls, Perches, Glass Feeders, Domed Top, 14 x 12 In. 125.00
Wood & Wire, Manor House Frame, 2 Doors, 4 Windows, Corner Towers, 50 1/2 In. 805.00
Wooden, Gabled Roof, Steepled Facade, Elevated Spires, 19 1/2 x 22 x 10 In. 316.00

BISQUE is an unglazed baked porcelain. Finished bisque has a slightly sandy texture with a dull finish. Some of it may be decorated with various colors. Bisque gained favor during the late Victorian era when thousands of bisque figurines were made. It is still being made. Additional bisque items may be listed under the factory name.

Bust, Woman, Downcast Pose, Solemn Expression, Painted Blue Eyes, 1875, 11 In. 775.00
Cake Topper, Bride & Groom, Japan, 1940s, 4 In. 28.00

Figurine, Bathing Beauty, Painted Eyes, Mohair Wig, Original Hat, 1 3/4 In. 400.00
Sculpture, Angel Kneeling, France, Late 19th Century, 22 x 15 x 11 In. 863.00
Sculpture, Cupid & His Consort, Circular Plinth, 12 x 5 In., Pair 431.00
Sculpture, Dutch Girl Seated, 6 1/2 In. 195.00
Sculpture, Girl & Boy, Carrying Monkey, Lavender, Gilt Clothes, 12 1/2 In., Pair 28.00
Sculpture, Girl, Holding Doll, Pale Yellow Hat, White, Yellow Dress, Yellow Shoes, 8 In. 325.00
Sculpture, Happifat Boy, Green Jacket, Shoes, Brown Pants, Jointed, 1914, 4 1/8 In. 126.00
Sculpture, Lady Wearing Century Dress, Floral Fabrics, 1860, 15 In. 1150.00
Sculpture, Young Boy With Goat, England, Victorian, c.1850 .... 2750.00
Statue, Classical Woman, Gray Hair, Headband, Sandals, Marbleized Base, 10 1/8 In. 135.00
Tile, Profile Of Woman With Head Bent Forward, Hair Twisted, Frame, 6 In. 198.00

BLACK memorabilia has become an important area of collecting since the 1970s. The best material dates from past centuries, but many recent items are also of interest. F & F is the mark used on plastic made by Fiedler & Fiedler Mold & Die Works, Inc. in the 1930s and 1940s. Objects that picture a black person may also be listed in this book under Advertising, Tins; Banks; Bottle Openers; Cookie Jars; Salt & Pepper; Sheet Music; Toys; etc.

Ashtray, Black Boy, Japan, 4 1/8 x 3 3/8 In. 60.00
Ashtray, Coon Chicken Inn, Black Man's Head, 1940-1951, 3 1/2 In. 20.00
Badge, Slave Tax, Charleston, 1831, No. 218 Servant, Copper, Charleston S.C., 2 In. 1725.00
Badge, Slave Tax, Charleston, 226 Mechanic, Copper, 1857, 1 1/2 x 1 In. 1150.00
Bag, Mammy Brand Potatoes, Red, Mammy In Black, Yellow, Burlap, 15 In. 25.00
Booklet, Aunt Jemima Recipe, Published By Quaker Oats, c.1932, 15 Pages 42.00
Booklet, The Negro & The National Guard, Isham G. Newton, Atlanta Univ., c.1962 .... 8.00
Box, Am I Not A Man & A Brother, Kneeling Slave, Battersea Enamel, 2 In. 3750.00
Box, Cigar, The Booker T. Washington, Perfecto 675.00
Bust, Black Man, Wearing Tuxedo, Tin Collared Shirt, Penn., Wood, 1890s, 6 1/2 In. 770.00
Card Holder, Carved Black Boy, Holding Tray, Black & Red Paint, 45 In. 1760.00
Catalog, Everything For Your Minstrel Show, T.S. Denison & Co., 1930s 110.00
Cookie Jars are listed in the Cookie Jar category.
Dancer, Folk Art, Painted Wood, Metal Knee Hinges, Wire Handle, c.1920, 12 x 19 In. 25.00
Document, Purchase Agreement, Slave, John Parry, Massachusetts Bay Colony, c.1748 .. 525.00
Doll, Cowboy, Brown Velvet, Glass Eyes, Orange Pants, Striped Shirt, 1930s, 13 1/2 In. ... 145.00
Doll, Golliwog, Velveteen Face, Hands, Feet, Crepe Pants, Shirt, Jacket, 1930, 20 In. 460.00
Doll, Napkin, Wood, Multicolored, Basket Of Fruit On Head, Movable Arms, 6 1/4 In. .. 95.00
Doll, Nut Head Mammy, With Twins, Whiskbroom Body, Dress, Organdy Outfits, 12 In. .. 633.00
Doll, Oil Cloth, Painted Head, Shoulders & Lower Arms, Bandanna, Dress, 1930s, 15 In. . 748.00
Doll, Papier-Mache, Curly Hair, Necklace, Cloth Body, Wooden Limbs, Dress, 8 In. 748.00
Doll, Patsykins, Composition Head, Molded Hair, Suit, Roller Skates, c.1930, 11 In. 1050.00
Doll, Rag, Dinah, Toy Stove, Embroidered Features, Wool Wig, Silk Dress, 1904, 22 In. ... 1035.00
Earrings, Shape Of Africa, Nelson Mandella Profile, Gold On Black Ground 15.00
Fan, Darkie Toothpaste, Cardboard, Black Man, Top Hat, Big Smile, 13 1/2 In. 220.00
Fan & Menu, Hand Held, Black Sambo Face, Smoking Joe's Restaurant 10.00
Figure, Boys Eating Watermelon, Painted Plaster, 1920s, 17 x 6 x 11 1/2 In. 154.00
Figure, Dice Player, Green Glove, Pink Hat, Down On All Fours, Brayton Laguna 60.00
Figure, Smoking Black Sambo, Counter Display, Paperboard, 16 x 8 1/2 In. 95.00
Game, The Game Of Sambo, Ring Toss, c.1921, 6 x 10 1/2 x 2 In. 61.00
Glass, Water, Coon Chicken Inn, Black Man's Head, 1940-1950 .... 30.00
Jar, Mammy, Wearing White Bandanna, 1940 .... 230.00
Letter, From Massachusetts Vigilance Committee, Anti-Fugitive Slave Act, 1854 .... 2850.00
Lobby Card, Come Back Charleston Blue, G. Cambridge, Black & White, 1972, 8 x 10 In. 8.00
Manuscript, Listing 63 Slaves For Sale, 7 Pages 220.00
Masque, Gourd, Dancing, Dan Tribe, Black, Gold, Ivory Coast 35.00
Medallion, Slave, Am I Not A Brother, Wedgwood, c.1891, 1 1/8 x 1 1/4 In. ... 635.00
Memo Holder, Mammy, Arms Hold Roll Of Paper, Wooden, 1950s 48.00
Minstrel Book, Charts, Joke, Poems, Songs, Belmont Music Company, c.1938, 28 Pages . 110.00
Nickel, Wooden, Black Sambo, 5 Piece 3.00
Nodder, Mammy, Holding Apple & Banana, Large Earrings, 6 3/4 x 3 1/2 In. 475.00
Notebook, Remember Cream Of Wheat, Chef Holding Box, Black & Tan Leather 47.00
Pencil Holder, Young Boy, Hands In Back Pockets, Green Pants, Made In Japan 42.00
Picture, Black Boys Eating Watermelon, Carved & Painted, Watermelon Shape 1760.00

Pie Bird, Mammy, Porcelain, Doubles As Spoon Holder 100.00
Pin, African Native, Silver, Signed Simba, South Africa, 2 1/2 In. 20.00
Pin, Aunt Jemima Breakfast Club, Eat A Better Breakfast, Picture, Pinback, 4 In. 18.00
Pin Bag, Mammy Clothes, 17 In. ....55.00 to 75.00
Plate, Coon Chicken Inn, Inca Ware On Reverse, 5 1/2 In. 165.00
Playbill, Uncle Tom's Cabin, Cardboard, Dancing Child, Woman, c.1890, 21 x 28 In. 285.00
Postcard, Now What, Anti-Black, Ridpath's History Of The World, John Wanamaker 250.00
Potholder Hanger, Mammy & Cook, 4 3/4 In.. 60.00
Program, Mountain Minstrels, Blackface Sketch, c.1950, 32 Pages 4.00
Puppet, Jim Dandy, Jointed, Cardboard, String Toy, Crudoform Linament, 8 1/4 In. 325.00
Receipt, Anti-Slavery, Seal Of Bought Of Anti-Slavery Society, Signed F. Wedgwood ... 490.00
Roly Poly, Bust Of Black Boy, Painted Celluloid, Weighted Base, France, c.1920, 2 In. ... 133.00
Saucer, Coon Chicken Inn, 6 In... 148.00
Shaker, Paprika, Aunt Jemima, Plastic, F & F, 1950s 52.00
Slave Tag, Porter, No. 254, Signed LaFar, Charleston, S.C., 1828 .... 4000.00
Songbook, Negro Songs For Mixed Voices, John W. Work, c.1940, 260 Pages 25.00
Spoon Rest, Mammy, Head Bandana, 1950s, 8 In............................... 135.00
Spoon Rest, Mammy, Red Dress, White Shawl & Apron 10.00
Stereoview, Black Man, Watermelon, Rooster, Jes' Dis Niggah's Fool Luck!, c.1904 .... 25.00
Stringholder, Mammy, Pottery, 7 In... 100.00
Toaster Cover, Mammy, Embroidered Face 38.00
Toy, String Climbing, Aunt Jemima's Pancake Flour, Die Cut 7590.00

BLACK AMETHYST glass appears black until it is held to the light, then
a dark purple can be seen. It has been made in many factories from
1860 to the present.

Ice Bucket, Diamond-Quilted Interior, Silver Handle, 6 x 5 In. 65.00
Tray, Center Handle, c.1925, 6 1/2 x 4 In. 35.00
Vase, Applied Clear Decoration, Hand Blown, 4 1/4 In. 55.00
Vase, Enameled Dancing Ladies In Center Heart, Open Handles, c.1925, 7 In. 75.00
Vase, Waffle Design, Ruffled Top, Art Deco Style, 6 x 4 1/2 In. 55.00

BLOWN GLASS, see Glass-Blown category.

BLUE GLASS, see Cobalt Blue category.

BLUE ONION, see Onion category.

BLUE WILLOW, see Willow category.

BOCH FRERES factory was founded in 1841 in La Louviere in eastern
Belgium. The wares resemble the work of Villeroy & Boch. The factory is still in business.

Charger, Center Portrait, Blue & White Border, Signed, 15 1/2 In. 159.00
Charger, Inner Nautical Theme, Blue & White, Signed, 13 3/4 In. 155.00
Lamp, Painted Deer, Art Deco Design, Signed, 23 In. 545.00
Pottery, Bowl, Gazelle, Incised, Painted, Blue, Black, Ivory, Keramis, 9 1/4 In. 1380.00
Vase, Baby Chicks, Leaf & Berry, Painted, Brown Matte Glaze, Keramis, 13 1/2 In. 865.00
Vase, Bat, Light Green Ground, Charles Catteau, 1929, 10 In. 3840.00
Vase, Bear, Dark Brown, Charles Catteau, 1930, 9 1/2 In. 5100.00
Vase, Birds, Painted, Brown, Blue, Yellow, Stylized, Charles Catteau, 10 1/2 In. 3105.00
Vase, Brown, White Ground, Charles Catteau, 1925, 12 1/4 In. 6600.00
Vase, Dark Brown, Light Tan Glaze, Charles Catteau, 1925, 12 1/8 In. 4800.00
Vase, Dark Green, Light Green Glaze, Charles Catteau, 1925, 11 In. 9000.00
Vase, Deer, Dark Blue, Green Grass, Charles Catteau, 13 In. 6000.00
Vase, Flowers, Light Green, Signed, Charles Catteau, 1925, 19 1/2 In. 6000.00
Vase, Gazelle, Bird, Flowers, Incised, Painted, Blue, Green, Ivory, Keramis, 9 In. 1400.00
Vase, Gazelles, Stoneware, Charles Catteau, c.1939, 12 3/4 In. 6600.00
Vase, Leaves, Flowers, Yellow, Rust, White, Black Ground, Keramis, 12 In. 460.00
Vase, Monkeys In Trees, Stoneware, Glazed, Charles Catteau, c.1925, 14 In. 21450.00
Vase, Owl, Light Tan Ground, Charles Catteau, 1925, 12 In. 5760.00
Vase, Panels, Swirl, Blue, Brown, Yellow & Ivory Ground, Keramis, 12 1/2 In. 374.00
Vase, Peacock, Branch, Orange, Pink, Green Flowers, Black, Bulbous, Keramis, 9 x 9 In. . 805.00
Vase, Penguin, Dark Brown, Charles Catteau, 1925, 11 In............................. 10200.00

Vase, Penguin, Dark Brown, Charles Catteau, 1929, 8 In. 6600.00
Vase, Roses, Pink, White, Incised, Painted, Mottled Green, Blue Ground, Keramis, 11 In. . 863.00
Vase, Stylized Birds, Gazelles, Flowers, Leaves, Blue, Green, Ivory, Black, 13 In. 2185.00
Vase, Stylized Flowers & Leaves, Geometric Borders, 1930, 7 3/4 In. 1850.00
Vase, Stylized Flowers & Leaves, Geometric Borders, Signed, 1920s, 13 In. 2690.00
Vase, Stylized Flowers, Blue, Yellow, White Crackle Ground, 8 In. 219.00
Vase, Stylized Flowers, Leaves, Pink, Blue, Yellow, Red Ground, Keramis, 11 3/4 In. 546.00
Vase, Stylized Leaves, Broad Shoulders, Ivory High Glaze, 14 1/2 In. 518.00
Vase, Stylized Leaves, Yellow, Green, Black, Ivory Ground, Tapered, Keramis, 12 In. 805.00
Vase, Stylized Organic Design, Brown, Ivory Crackle Ground, Charles Catteau, 6 1/2 In. . 863.00
Vase, Tulips, Incised, Painted, Yellow, Pink, Panels, Blue, Green, Keramis, 6 In. 489.00
Vase, White Crackled Glaze, Stylized Flowers, Brown, Blue, Marked, Keramis, 10 In. ... 58.00

BOEHM is the collector's name for the porcelains of Edward Marshall Boehm. In 1953 the Osso China Company was reorganized as Edward Marshall Boehm, Inc. The company is still working in England and New Jersey. In the early days of the factory, dishes were made, but the elaborate and lifelike bird figurines are the best-known ware. Edward Marshall Boehm, the founder, died in 1961, but the firm has continued to design and produce porcelain. Today, the firm makes both limited and unlimited editions of figurines and plates.

Bookends, Owl, Studio Mark, No. 453, 9 1/2 In. 850.00
Sculpture, Black-Topped Chickadee, In Holly Tree, Mark, No. 438, 8 In. 77.00
Sculpture, Blue Bird, Baby, On Branch, Signed, 4 1/2 x 3 1/2 In. 135.00
Sculpture, Blue Jay, Baby, On Ground, Signed, 4 1/2 x 3 1/2 In. 135.00
Sculpture, Canada Goose & Her Goslings, With Male, Oval Base, U.S.A., 7 In., Pair 368.00
Sculpture, Choirboy, With Candle, 1950s 75.00
Sculpture, Common Tern, Open Winged, Shell, Driftwood & Rock Base, 15 In. 385.00
Sculpture, Crested Flycatcher, Baby, On Branch, Mouth Open, Signed, 5 x 3 In. 148.00
Sculpture, Giant Panda Cub, 8 1/2 In. 143.00
Sculpture, Hunter, Saddled Horse, Standing, Mark, No. 203, 14 x 14 In. 1600.00
Sculpture, Kitten, White & Gray, Signed, 3 1/2 x 6 1/2 In. 90.00
Sculpture, Panda Cub, On 4 Paws, Black Eyes, Quizzical Expression On Face, 3 In. 116.00
Sculpture, Prothonotary Warbler, 6 In. 115.00
Sculpture, Rabbit, At Rest, Signed, 4 1/4 x 3 1/2 In. 196.00
Sculpture, White-Throated Sparrow, Yellow Flower, Green Leaves, Signed, 9 1/2 In. 245.00

BOHEMIAN GLASS, see Glass-Bohemian.

BONE DISHES were considered a necessary part of a table setting for the Victorian table. The crescent-shaped dish was kept at the edge of the dinner plate so the bones removed from the fish could be stored away from the uneaten food. Some bone dishes were made in more fanciful shapes and many resemble fish.

Blue, Flowers, Medallion Insert, Dado 45.00
Brown, Flowers, Medallion Insert, Dado 45.00
White, Butterflies, Herend, Hungary, 8 1/4 x 5 1/4 In. 165.00
White, Green & Gold Trim, W.H. Grindley, 3 1/2 x 7 In. 15.00

BOOKENDS have probably been used since books became inexpensive. Early libraries kept books in cupboards, not on open shelves. By the 1870s bookends appeared, especially homemade fret-carved wooden examples. Most bookends listed in this book date from the twentieth century. Bookends are also listed in other categories by manufacturer or material.

3-Masted Sailing Ships, Cast Iron, 6 3/4 In. 55.00
American Eagle, Embossed 1776, Gray Metal, Paper Label, 1970s, 6 1/4 x 5 1/2 In. 75.00
Amish Man & Woman, Sitting On Bench, Cast Iron, 4 3/4 In. 22.00
Arched Form, Arts & Crafts, Gustav Stickley, c.1910, 5 1/2 In. 670.00
Basket Of Flowers, Cast Iron, 5 1/2 In. 28.00
Bear, Cornell University, Brass, 4 In. 20.00
Bears Wrestling, Wood, Carved, Adjustable Shelf, Switzerland, c.1910, 7 x 6 In. 759.00

Buddha, Cast Iron, 5 In. 55.00
Charles Dickens Bust, Gilt Metal, Bradley & Hubbard, 5 3/4 In. 144.00
Charles Lindbergh, Aviator, Bronze, 1929, 5 1/2 x 5 In. 75.00
Chippendale Chair Back, Cast Bronze, Bradley & Hubbard 375.00
Circus Lion, Pottery, Glazed & Painted, 8 In. 50.00
Colonial Women, Metal, Japan 30.00
Columns, Cast Iron, Bronzed, Bradley & Hubbard, c.1922, 4 7/8 x 3 1/2 In. . . . . .67.00 to 75.00
Crab, Zodiac Series, Metal, Incised Fred Press Signature, 6 In. 45.00
Cross, Pointed Arch Top, Oak, Inlaid, 7 x 6 x 7 In. 52.00
Dog, Art Deco, Metal, 1920s, 5 1/2 In. 110.00
Dog, Ceramic, White, Black Ears & Spots, Gold Collar, Staffordshire Style, 1950s 65.00
Dog, Irish Setter, Landscape Background, Cast Iron, 5 1/2 In. 248.00
Dog, Scotty, Sitting, Black, Red Collar, Cast Iron, 5 In. 275.00
Dog, Setter, Bradley & Hubbard, 5 In. 155.00
Dog, Setter, Cast Iron, Painted, Hubley, 8 x 4 7/8 In. 290.00
Dog, Terrier, Impressed, 5 1/2 x 4 1/4 In. 75.00
Doorway, Garden Scenery, B & H, Cast Iron, 5 3/4 In. 193.00
Dutch Children, Boy Kissing Girl, Cast Iron, Hubley, 5 In. 176.00
Eagle, Ivory, Carved, Inlaid Pedestal, 1800s, 4 3/4 In. 75.00
Eagle, Outspread Wings, Gilt Bronze, Ivory Beaks, Verde Antico Marble, 26 In. 545.00
Eagle Head, Art Deco, Bronze, Marble Base, Signed, 5 In. 865.00
Elephant, Bronze, Wooden Brackets, A.J. Bitter, 11 In., Pair 5700.00
Elephant, Cast Iron, 5 1/4 In., Pair 145.00
Elephant, Connecticut Foundry, 5 3/4 In. 125.00
Enameled Design, Copper, Hammered, Craftsman Studios, 4 3/4 In. . . . .*Illus* 90.00
Exotic Birds, Bronze, Wooden Stands, Patina, Art Deco, 9 In. 219.00
Fireplace, With Kettle, Cast Iron, 6 x 6 1/2 In. 125.00
Fish, Cast Iron, Hubley, 5 1/4 In. 175.00
Flowers, Red Ground, Albany Foundry, No. 53, 5 3/4 x 4 3/4 In. . . . .*Illus* 95.00
Football Players, Ball Under Arm, Cast Iron, 5 1/2 In. 275.00
Geometric, Asymmetrical, Rectangular Platform, Bronze, 6 1/2 In. 143.00
Geometric Design, Copper, Hammered, Forest Craft Guild, 6 x 4 1/2 In. 575.00
Greek Reader, J. Ruhl, K&O Metal Novelties Co., 5 1/4 In. 200.00
Hepplewhite Chair Backs, Bronze, Bradley & Hubbard, 5 5/8 In. 375.00
Horse & Carriage, 2 Horses, Cast Iron, Hubley, 7 In. 60.00
Horse Head, Iron, Black 30.00
Hunter & Huntress, Afghan Hound, Wooded Landscape, Cast Metal, 5 3/4 In. 92.00
Jockey, On Pedestal, Cast Iron, Polychrome Paint, American, c.1900 . . . . 550.00
Liberty Bell, Cast Iron, 5 In. . . . .*Illus* 60.00
Lion, Gift House Inc., N.Y.C., c.1926, 5 1/2 In. 100.00
Lion In Relief, Bronze, Stamped B & H, Bradley & Hubbard, 3 3/4 x 4 5/8 In. 115.00
Lovebirds, Acorn Mark, 7 1/4 In. 185.00
Nude, Art Deco, Spelter, Gilt Patina, Onyx Base, 6 In. 138.00
Old Coaching Days, Horses, Pulling Stagecoach, Bronze Finish, 4 1/4 In. 45.00
Owl, Perched On Book, Cast Iron, 5 9/16 In. 130.00
Owls, On Branches, Mountain Forest, Pottery, 6 x 4 3/4 In. 40.00
Pan Figures, Bronze, Signed, Silvestre, Paris, 5 In. 785.00
Parrots On Books, Gray Metal, Signed K & O, c.1928, 6 In. 125.00
Pegasus, Cast Iron, Paper Label, CJO, 5 3/4 In., Pair 185.00
Pirates, Carrying Treasure Chest, Tropical Background, Cast Iron, 5 1/4 In. 39.00

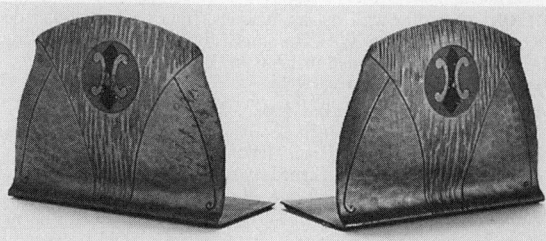

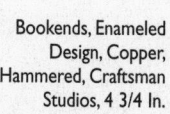

Bookends, Enameled
Design, Copper,
Hammered, Craftsman
Studios, 4 3/4 In.

Bookends, Flowers, Red Ground,
Albany Foundry, No. 53, 5 3/4 x 4 3/4 In.

Bookends, Liberty Bell,
Cast Iron, 5 In.

Sailing Ship, Arts & Crafts, 5 1/2 x 5 3/4 In.	90.00
Scholar, Man Reading Book, Metal, 5 3/4 x 6 3/4 In.	210.00
Sea Salt, Holding Large Fish, Cast Bronze	165.00
Seated Bears, Wood, Glass Eyes, Switzerland, c.1910, 5 x 3 1/2 In.	544.00
Speak No Evil, Hear No Evil, See No Evil, Bradley & Hubbard, 5 1/2 In.	125.00
Sphinx Bust, Bronze, Gilt, Signed, 8 1/4 In.	287.00
Steer Head, Bronze, C.M. Russell, 1916, 6 x 8 x 9 In.	465.00
Swashbuckler, Metal, Paul Herzi, 1940s, 7 3/4 In.	100.00
Terra-Cotta, Dark Green Matte Glaze, Art Deco, 1930, Pair	440.00
The Thinker, Nu-Art, 1928, 6 3/4 In.	200.00
Tooled & Embossed, Copper, Hammered, Elizabeth Eaton Burton, 6 In.	550.00
Washington Crossing The Delaware, Brass, Jennette & Sons Stamp, 1930, 6 In.	95.00
Woman With Tray, Cast Iron, Walter Baker, 5 3/4 In.	275.00

BOOKMARKS were originally made of parchment, cloth, or leather. Soon woven silk ribbon, thin cardboard, celluloid, wood, silver, tortoiseshell, and metals were used. Examples made before 1850 are scarce, but there are many to be found dating before 1920.

American Brake Co., Ribbon, Steam Locomotives, 1800s, 9 1/2 x 3 In.	75.00
Belly Dancer, Geometric Design, Woven, Turkey, 9 In.	10.00
Champion Sparkplug, Metal, 2 1/2 In.	15.00
Chesterfield Cigarettes, Jo Stafford, Perry Como, NBC Logo, 1947, 8 1/2 In.	18.00
Copper, Silver Cattails, 4 3/4 In.	41.00
Equestrian, Standing Horse, Red Enamel Harness, 14K Gold	345.00
Fanny Farmer Candy, Pinkie, By Sir Thomas Lawrence, 1920s, 5 1/2 In.	22.00
Heart, Sterling Silver, Tassels, 2 1/4 In.	24.00
Hupmobile, Car Of The American Family, Celluloid, Blue, White, 1920s	38.00
Liberty Bell, On Shield, Celluloid, Wm. H. Hoskins Co., Philadelphia, 2 1/4 x 2 In.	36.00
Logan College, Chiropractic, Brass, 1935, 2 In.	10.50
Lucky Strike Cigarettes, Mystery League, 7 x 2 1/2 In.	14.00
Smokey The Bear, Remember, Only You Can Prevent Forest Fires, 1968	3.25
Sterling Silver, Embossed Floral & Scroll, Corner Page, Gorham, 1 13/16 In.	31.00
Sterling Silver, Enameled Flowers, Webster, 2 1/2 In.	46.00
Sterling Silver, Scrollwork, Reed & Barton, 2 3/4 x 1 1/2 In.	7.50
Turkey, Use Bookmarks As Business Reminders, Celluloid, c.1900	87.00

BOSSONS character wall masks, plaques, figurines, and other decorative pieces are made by W.H. Bossons, Limited of Congleton, England. The company was founded in 1946 and closed in 1996.

BOSSONS

Abdhul, Head, Marked, 1960, 8 In.	165.00
Bretonne Lady, Head, Marked, 1982, 5 1/2 In.	85.00
Coolie, Head, Marked, 6 3/4 In.	68.00
Desert Hawks, Bedouin's Head, Marked, 7 1/2 In.	145.00
Himalayan, Head, Marked, Signed By Artist, 1971	55.00
Old English Manor House, Plaque, 14 1/2 In. Diam.	195.00
Pathan, Bust, Marked, 10 In.	175.00

BOSTON & SANDWICH CO. pieces may be found in the Sandwich Glass category.

BOTTLE collecting has become a major American hobby. There are several general categories of bottles, such as historic flasks, bitters, household, and figural. Pyro is the shortened form of the word *pyroglaze,* an enameled lettering used on bottles after the mid-1930s. *ABM* means the bottle was made by an automatic bottle machine after 1903. For more bottle prices, see the book *Kovels' Bottles Price List* by Ralph and Terry Kovel.

Ale, Black, Drippy Top, Pontil, 9 1/2 In.	65.00
Amethyst Swirl, Blown, 6 In.	784.00
Apothecary, Amethyst, Cylindrical, Flat Feet, Ball Stopper, 1800s, 12 1/4 In., Pair	715.00
Apothecary, Cobalt Blue, 11 5/8 In.	80.00
Apothecary, Tinct. Cinnamomi, Label Under Glass, Flared Lip, Stopper, Pontil, 6 In.	34.00

Avon started in 1886 as the California Perfume Company. It was not until 1929 that the name *Avon* was used. In 1939, it became Avon Products, Inc. Avon has made many figural bottles filled with cosmetic products. Ceramic, plastic, and glass bottles were made in limited editions.

Avon, Bay Rum, Stopper, California Perfume Co., 1896, 4 Oz.	165.00
Avon, Bright Night Toilet Water, Neck Card, 1955	8.00
Avon, Car, Dune Buggy, 1971	6.00
Avon, Car, Sterling Six, 1968	7.00
Avon, Car, Volkswagen, Blue, 1973	5.00
Avon, Decanter, Short Pony, 1968	5.00
Avon, Decanter, Wine, Cape Cod, 1977	20.00
Avon, Firefighter 1910, 1975	6.00
Avon, Goblet, Hummingbird, 1987, Pair	25.00
Avon, Leisure Hours, Clock, Bath Oil, 1970	6.00
Avon, Liberty Dollar, 1970	5.00
Avon, Little Bo Peep, Sweet Honesty Perfume, Box, 1976	6.00
Avon, Mansion Lamp, 1975	4.00
Avon, Pistol, 1850 Pepper Box, 1979	5.00
Avon, Spirit Of St. Louis, 1970	8.00
Avon, Stein, American Armed Forces, 1990	7.00
Avon, Stein, Christopher Columbus, 1992	35.00
Avon, Stein, Conquest Of Space, 1991	6.50
Avon, Stein, Ducks Of American Wilderness, 1988	35.00
Avon, Stein, Fishing, 1990	7.00
Avon, Stein, Great American Football, 1982	35.00
Avon, Stein, Great Dogs Of Outdoors, 1991	36.00
Avon, Stein, Winner's Circle, 1992	35.00
Avon, Sure Winner, Racing Car, 1972, 7 1/2 In.	10.00
Avon, Town Pump, 1968	8.00
Avon, Train, Hudson Locomotive, 1993	35.00
Avon, Western Boot, 1973	7.00
Barber, Amberina, Silver Overlay, Sheared Lip, 8 In.	1430.00
Barber, Bay Rum, Milk Glass, Enameled Horseshoe, Floral, 1920, 9 1/8 In.	210.00
Barber, Bay Rum, Milk Glass, Enameled Tulip Design, 8 5/8 In.	405.00
Barber, Blue & Cranberry, Opalescent Stripes, 7 1/2 In.	58.00
Barber, Blue Hobnail, Rolled Lip, Improved Pontil, 7 In.	100.00
Barber, Brilliantine, Bell Shape, Yellow Topaz, Tooled Mouth, 1925, 3 7/8 In.	155.00
Barber, Brilliantine, Cobalt Blue, 2 Indented Panels, 3 1/8 In.	415.00
Barber, Brilliantine, Frosted Cobalt Blue, Floral, Brass Neck Band, Cap, 3 3/4 In.	660.00
Barber, Brilliantine, Purple Amethyst, White Design, Ribbed, 3 In.	355.00
Barber, Brilliantine, Purple Amethyst, White Enameled Design, Polished Lip, 3 3/4 In.	800.00
Barber, Brilliantine, Turquoise, Enameled Flowers, Ribbed, 3 7/8 In.	690.00
Barber, Clear, Bell Shape, Fluted, Shield, Cork Stopper, 10 3/4 In.	25.00
Barber, Clear, Raised Letters, Bottle Loaned By F.W. Finch Co., Rubber Cap, 8 In.	35.00
Barber, Clear, Removable Metal Stopper Imbedded In Cork, 6 In.	15.00
Barber, Clear, Sea Foam Cut In Shoulder, Red Flashed Neck & Shoulder, 6 3/4 In.	305.00

Bottle, Barber, Log
Cabin Hair Tonic,
Rochester, N.Y.,
Root Beer Amber,
Label, 9 In.

A paper beer bottle label reacts to wet
and dry conditions like hair does. If
the label is curled, cover it with water
to wet the fibers, then dry it flat.

**Clean the inside of a bottle with
detergent powder and a Water Pik.**

Barber, Cobalt Blue Ribbed, Bell Shape, Enameled Flowers, Pontil, 1925, 7 5/8 In.	360.00
Barber, Cobalt Blue, Enameled Flowers, Pinched Waist, Ribbed, Pontil, 7 5/8 In.	275.00
Barber, Cobalt Blue, Girl With Butterfly, Mary Gregory Type, Pontil, 1885-1925, 8 In.	260.00
Barber, Cobalt Blue, Ribbed, Enameled Flowers, Pontil, 1925, 7 1/4 In.	1020.00
Barber, Cobalt, Melon Ribbed, Pewter Stopper, 8 1/2 In.	69.00
Barber, Cologne, Milk Glass, Dark Blue, Enameled Cottage, Pontil, 8 5/8 In.	465.00
Barber, Cranberry & White Splatter Design, Polished Pontil, Metal Stopper, 9 1/4 In.	275.00
Barber, Cranberry, Brass Wire Roman Building, Madeleine Underneath, 10 In.	825.00
Barber, Cranberry, Melon Shape, Reversed Thumbprint, Lady's Leg Neck, 8 In.	88.00
Barber, Enameled Girl, Offering Flowers, Milk Glass Shaker Cup, 8 1/2 In.	220.00
Barber, Fountain Of Youth Hair Restorer, Cobalt Blue, 7 1/2 In.	1045.00
Barber, George Clark Bay Rum, Milk Glass, Label, Neck Band, Stopper, 10 7/8 In.	2070.00
Barber, Green, Hobnail, Rolled Lip, Pontil, 7 In.	99.00
Barber, Hair Tonic, Milk Glass, Enameled Clover, Pontil, 9 1/2 In.	300.00
Barber, Hall's Hair Renewer, Peacock Blue, 6 3/4 In.	90.00
Barber, Hobnail, 7 In.	55.00
Barber, Lime Green, Enameled Flowers, Open Pontil, 7 3/4 In.	165.00
Barber, Log Cabin Hair Tonic, Rochester, N.Y., Root Beer Amber, Label, 9 In. *Illus*	2576.00
Barber, Melon Form, Flowers, Milk Glass Shaker Top, 7 1/2 In.	104.00
Barber, Milk Glass, Cherub, Blue & Yellow Ground, Pontil, 1925, 7 3/4 In.	305.00
Barber, Milk Glass, Cherub, Grapes, Blue & Yellow Ground, 1825, 7 5/8 In.	330.00
Barber, Milk Glass, Cherub, Yellow & Blue Ground, Pontil, 7 1/2 In.	355.00
Barber, Milk Glass, Painted 3 Cherubs On Bed Of Straw, Metal Stopper, 7 In.	415.00
Barber, Milk Glass, Pink, Floral, 1930, 7 5/8 In.	240.00
Barber, Milk Glass, Powder Blue, Petals Around Shoulder, 1925, 6 1/2 In.	440.00
Barber, Opalescent Cranberry, Hobnail, Tooled Mouth, Pontil, 1925, 8 In.	165.00
Barber, Opalescent, Cranberry Top, Blue Base, Yellow Spots, Stopper, Bakin, 1982, 7 In.	120.00
Barber, Parker's Hair Balsam, Amber, BIMAL, 7 1/2 In.	4.50
Barber, Pink Amethyst, Ribbed, Yellow & Gold Enameled Flowers, Pontil, 8 3/4 In.	305.00
Barber, Pink Satin Quilt Design Over White, Sheared Lip, Open Pontil, 7 1/2 In.	305.00
Barber, Professor Woods Hair Restorative, St. Louis, New York, Aqua, 7 In.	125.00
Barber, Purple Amethyst, Ribbed, Bell Shape, Enameled Flowers, Pontil, 8 In.	465.00
Barber, Purple Amethyst, White, Blue & Gold Flower, Ribbed, Pontil, 7 In.	180.00
Barber, Red, Clear, Blue & Green Alternating Bands, Pontil, Venice, 8 5/8 In.	385.00
Barber, Sea Foam, Opalescent, Milk Glass, Clover, Pontil, 8 3/4 In.	300.00
Barber, Silver Overlay, Floral, Polished Pontil, 7 1/2 In.	358.00
Barber, Teal Green, White Enameled Design, Pinched Waist, Ribbed, Pontil, 1925, 7 In.	230.00
Barber, Vase, Cremex Shampooing, Dark Blue, Notched Handles, Registered, 7 In.	165.00
Barber, White & Gold Strawberry, Ribbed, c.1885, 7 7/8 In.	410.00
Barber, Witch Hazel, Milk Glass, Light Blue, Multicolored Bird, 1925, 8 3/4 In.	605.00
Barber, Witch Hazel, Milk Glass, Opalescent, Enameled Poppy, Tool Lip, 8 1/2 In.	275.00
Barber, Witch Hazel, Milk Glass, Roses, Flowers, 9 1/4 In.	576.00
Barber, Witch Hazel, Opalescent, Milk Glass, Tulip, 8 5/8 In.	495.00
Barber, Yellow Green, Barrel, Enameled Flowers, Ribbed, Pontil, 1925, 7 1/2 In.	300.00
Barber, Yellow Green, White Gold Trimmed Design, Ribbed, Pontil, 6 3/4 In.	100.00

Beam bottles were made to hold Kentucky Straight Bourbon, made by the James B. Beam Distilling Company. The Beam series of ceramic bottles began in 1953.

Beam, Executive, Bowl, Italian Marble, 1986 .... 40.00
Beam, Harolds Club, Man In Barrel, No. 2, 1957 .... 520.00
Beam, Kentucky Derby, 98th, Horse & Rider In Wreath, 1972 .... 55.00
Beam, Train, Casey Jones, 1988, 5 In. 15.00
Beer, Buffalo Brewing Co., Sacramento, Ca., Red Amber, Applied Top, 1 Qt. 110.00
Beer, Drewry & Sons, Paper Label, 7 Oz. 6.50
Beer, Felsenbrau Beer, Mini Bottle, 1930s, 4 1/4 In. 18.00
Beer, Kuebler Beer, Painted Label, 1950s, 7 Oz. 23.00
Beer, Lucky Lager, Painted Label, 1950s, 7 Oz. 9.00
Beer, Nude Beer, Label, Full Bottle, 1980s, 12 Piece 19.00
Beer, Peoples Brewing Company, Hand Painted Eagle Over Logo & Shield, 11 1/2 In. ... 45.00
Beer, Peter Hand Brewing Co., Il., Label, 1950s, 12 Oz. 6.00
Beer, Rainear Brewing & Malting Co., Seattle, Wa., Green, Split Crown Top, 1/2 Pt. 132.00
Beer, Seal Rock Bottling Co., J. Kroger, San Francisco, Ca., Amber, Tooled Top, 1/2 Pt. .. 99.00
Beer, Swan Brewery Co., XXX Ale, This Bottle Never Sold, Swan, Yellow Olive 1430.00
Beer, Weiss Beer, Joseph Loder, Atlantic City, N.J., Aqua, Blob, Squat 45.00
Bininger, A.M. & Co., Barrel, Amber, 1 Qt. 240.00
Bininger, A.M. & Co., Clock, Yellow Amber, Pontil, 6 In. 795.00
Bininger, A.M. & Co., No. 19 Broad St., N.Y., Canon, Amber, 12 1/2 In. 700.00
Bininger, A.M. & Co., No. 338 Broadway, Old London Dock Gin, Yellow Olive, 9 In. ... 420.00
Bininger, A.M. & Co., No. 338 Broadway, Yellow Green 187.00
Bininger, Clock, Regulator, N.Y., Yellow Amber, Double Collar, 5 In. 615.00
Bininger, Knickerbocker, N.Y., Gold Amber, Sloping Collar Mouth, Pontil, 6 In. 2910.00
Bitters, Baker's Orange Grove, Green Citron, Roped Corners, Applied Top, 9 1/2 In. 8800.00
Bitters, Baker's Orange Grove, Topaz Puce, Roped Corners, 9 1/2 In. 910.00
Bitters, Baker's Orange Grove, Yellow Amber, Sloping Collar, Label, 9 1/2 In. 755.00
Bitters, Berkshire, Amann & Co, Cinci., Pig, Pottery, Brown Glaze, 9 In. 855.00
Bitters, Berkshire, Pig, Pottery, Medium To Dark Amber, Short Fat Variant, 9 1/2 In. 2070.00
Bitters, Big Bill Best, Medium Amber, Tooled Mouth, Foil Neck Seal, 12 1/8 In. 130.00
Bitters, Brown's Celebrated Indian Herb, Patented 1867, Chocolate, 12 1/4 In. 1540.00
Bitters, Brown's Celebrated Indian Herb, Patented Feb. 11, 1867, Crystal, 12 1/4 In. 520.00
Bitters, Brown's Celebrated Indian Herb, Patented Feb. 11, 1868, Amber, 12 1/8 In. 305.00
Bitters, Brown's, Indian Queen, Patented Feb. 11, 1867, Yellow Amber, 12 1/4 In. 695.00
Bitters, California Herb, Pittsburgh, Pa., G.W. Frazier, Amber, 9 1/2 In. 3850.00
Bitters, Coca, Hartwig Kantorowicz, Onion, Red Amber, Deep Kick-Up, 7 3/4 In. 330.00
Bitters, Doyles Hop, Amber, Sloping Double Collar, Labels, 10 In. 125.00
Bitters, Doyles Hop, Yellow Amber, Square, 9 5/8 In. ....265.00 to 305.00
Bitters, Dr. Ball's Vegetable Stomachic, Northboro, Mass., Aqua, 6 7/8 In. 245.00
Bitters, Dr. C.D. Warners, German Hop, Amber, Square, 10 In. 110.00
Bitters, Dr. C.W. Roback's Stomach, Cincinnati, O., Barrel, Amber, 9 3/8 In. 230.00
Bitters, Dr. Fischs, W.H. Ware, Pat. 1866, Fish, Amber, 11 5/8 In. 310.00
Bitters, Dr. Henley's Wild Grape Root, IXL, Aqua, Applied Square Collar, 12 1/2 In. 165.00
Bitters, Dr. J. Hostetter's Stomach, 18 Fluid Oz., ABM, Amber, 8 3/4 In. 9.00
Bitters, Dr. J. Hostetter's Stomach, Olive, Square, c.1880, 9 3/8 In. 264.00
Bitters, Dr. J. Hostetter's Stomach, W. MCG & Co., Yellow, 9 In. 935.00
Bitters, Dr. J. Hostetter's Stomach, Yellow Amber, 9 In. 45.00
Bitters, Dr. Petzold's Genuine German, Incpt. 1862, Amber, 10 1/8 In. 220.00
Bitters, Dr. Petzold's Genuine German, Incpt. 1862, Yellow Amber, 10 5/8 In. 245.00
Bitters, Dr. Soule Hop, Cabin, Gasoline Puce, 7 In. 1075.00
Bitters, Dr. Soule Hop, Cabin, Tobacco Amber, Sloping Double Collar, 1872, 9 1/2 In. 125.00
Bitters, Drake's Plantation, 4-Log, Amber, 10 1/4 In. ....95.00 to 105.00
Bitters, Drake's Plantation, 4-Log, Amber, Sloping Collar, Labels, 10 1/4 In. 200.00
Bitters, Drake's Plantation, 4-Log, Apricot Amber, 10 1/4 In. 145.00
Bitters, Drake's Plantation, 4-Log, Yellow Green, Applied Top, 10 1/4 In. 2420.00
Bitters, Drake's Plantation, 6-Log, Amber, 10 In. 95.00
Bitters, Drake's Plantation, 6-Log, Amber, Sloping Collar, 10 1/4 In. 115.00
Bitters, Drake's Plantation, 6-Log, Celery Green, 10 1/4 In. 2040.00
Bitters, Drake's Plantation, 6-Log, Cherry Puce, 10 In. 145.00
Bitters, Drake's Plantation, 6-Log, Cherry Puce, Applied Top, 10 In. 358.00

Bitters, Drake's Plantation, 6-Log, Deep Cherry Puce, Bubbles, Sloping Collar, 10 In. ... 590.00
Bitters, Drake's Plantation, 6-Log, Root Beer Amber, Corner Panels, 10 In. 355.00
Bitters, E.E. Hall, New Haven, Barrel, Yellow Amber, Disc Type Mouth, 9 1/8 In. 720.00
Bitters, E.E. Hall, New Haven, Est. 1842, Barrel, Yellow, Applied Square Collar, 9 1/8 In. 440.00
Bitters, Edw. Wilder's Stomach, Cabin, 10 1/2 In. 321.00
Bitters, Estd 1834 Telliers, Herb, Gold Amber, 9 7/8 In. 375.00
Bitters, Fish, W.H. Ware, Deep Amber, Label, 11 3/4 In. 305.00
Bitters, Fish, W.H. Ware, Pat. 1866, Amber, 11 3/4 In. 264.00
Bitters, Fish, W.H. Ware, Pat. 1866, Yellow Green, 11 3/4 In. 10360.00
Bitters, Greeley's Bourbon Whiskey, Barrel, Plum, Applied Top, 9 3/8 In. 715.00
Bitters, Greeley's Bourbon Whiskey, Barrel, Strawberry Puce, 9 1/2 In. 385.00
Bitters, Greeley's Bourbon, Barrel, Dark Puce, 9 3/8 In. 650.00
Bitters, Greeley's Bourbon, Barrel, Grape Puce, 9 3/8 In. 220.00
Bitters, Greeley's Bourbon, Barrel, Olive Green, Disc Type Mouth, 9 1/2 In. 6720.00
Bitters, Greeley's Bourbon, Barrel, Smoky Copper Puce, 9 3/8 In. 2200.00
Bitters, Herkules, Green, 1 Qt., 7 1/2 In. 1760.00
Bitters, Holtzermann's Patent Stomach, Cabin, 2-Sided, Yellow Amber, 9 1/4 In. 2350.00
Bitters, Hutchings Dyspepsia, Aqua, Rectangular, Pontil, 8 1/2 In. 220.00
Bitters, Iron Bitters, Brown Chemical Co., Amber, Square, 8 3/4 In. 55.00
Bitters, Jno Moffat Phoenix, New York, Price $1, Tobacco Amber, 5 1/2 In. 1925.00
Bitters, John Moffat, New York, Phoenix, Olive Green, Sloping Collar, Pontil, 5 3/8 In. ... 1010.00
Bitters, John Root's, Buffalo, N.Y.1867, Semi-Cabin, Amber, Labels, 9 1/2 In. 2520.00
Bitters, Johnson's Calisaya, Burlington, Vt., Red Copper, Bubbles, 10 In. 410.00
Bitters, Johnson's Calisaya, Burlington, Vt., Red Copper, Sloping Collar, 10 In. 450.00
Bitters, Kelly's Old Cabin, Patented 1863, Cabin, Amber, Applied Top, 9 5/8 In. 2200.00
Bitters, Kelly's Old Cabin, Patented 1863, Cabin, Deep Amber, Sloping Collar, 9 5/8 In. . 2465.00
Bitters, Marshall's, Best Laxative & Blood Purifier, Amber, Square, 8 5/8 In. 80.00
Bitters, Morning Inceptum, Star, Amber, Triangular, Iron Pontil, 12 7/8 In. 350.00
Bitters, National, Ear Of Corn, Patent 1867, Amber, Label, 12 1/2 In. 980.00
Bitters, National, Ear Of Corn, Patent 1867, Blue Aqua, 12 5/8 In. 5150.00
Bitters, National, Ear Of Corn, Patent 1867, Cherry Puce, 12 1/2 In. 1870.00
Bitters, National, Ear Of Corn, Patent 1867, Yellow, 12 1/2 In. 1980.00
Bitters, Roback's Stomach, Cincinnati, Oh., Barrel, Olive Green, Applied Top, 10 In. 3300.00
Bitters, Warner's Safe Nervine, London, Yellow, 1/2 Pt. 140.00
Bitters, Warner's Safe Tonic, Rochester, N.Y., Amber, Tooled Mouth, 7 1/2 In. 925.00
Black Glass, Dutch Kidney, Olive Green, Amber Tone, 6 3/4 In. 770.00
Black Glass, Dutch Onion, Olive Amber, Applied String Collar, Open Pontil, 7 3/4 In. ... 165.00
Black Glass, Dutch Onion, Olive Green, Pontil, 6 1/4 In. 330.00
Black Glass, English Mallet, Olive Amber, Pontil, 8 5/8 In. 175.00
Black Glass, English Mallet, Olive Green, 7 7/8 In. 175.00
Black Glass, Gin, Olive, Flat Lip, Open Pontil, 10 1/2 In. 110.00
Black Glass, Onion, Blue Green, Pontil, 6 3/8 In. 1650.00
Black Glass, Onion, Olive Green, Pontil, 6 In. 330.00
Black Glass, Tabac De A Delpit, Nouvelle Orleans, Yellow Olive, 1850-1880, 10 1/8 In. ... 825.00
Blown, Yellow Olive, Globular, Bubbles, Pontil, 10 1/4 In. 605.00
Coca-Cola bottles are listed in the Coca-Cola category.
Cologne, Philadelphia, Memorial Hall, 1876, Tooled Mouth, 6 1/8 In. 365.00
Cologne, Purple Amethyst, Blown Stopper, Toilet Water, Pontil, 6 1/8 In. 415.00
Cordial, L.Q.C. Wishart's Pine Tree Tar, Emerald Green, Sloping Collar, 7 1/2 In. 260.00
Cordial, L.Q.C. Wishart's Pine Tree Tar, Phila., Patent 1859, Deep Green, Bubbles, 9 In. . 360.00
Cordial, L.Q.C. Wishart's Pine Tree Tar, Phila., Patent 1859, Emerald Green, 8 In. 180.00
Cordial, L.Q.C. Wishart's Pine Tree Tar, Phila., Patent 1859, Teal Green, 9 5/8 In. 895.00
Cosmetic, Dermetics Complexion Cleanser, Pink Plastic Cap, Paper Labels, 1 Oz., 4 In. ... 8.00
Cosmetic, Evening In Paris, Talcum Powder, Cobalt Blue Glass, 5 x 2 5/8 In. 23.00
Cosmetic, Face Lotion, Green Aqua, Enameled Woman With Laundry, Dutch, 5 1/2 In. .. 55.00
Cosmetic, Fitch's Dandruff Remover, F.W. Fitch Mfg. Co., 2 5/8 Oz., 5 In. 8.00
Cosmetic, Watkins Shampoo Jelly, Medical Complaint, Winona, Minn., 3 x 2 In. 35.00
Cure, Cactus Blood, By Alva's Brazilian Specific Co., Cactus Shape, 9 1/4 In. 2860.00
Cure, Original Dr. Craig's Kidney, Rochester, N.Y., Amber, Double Collar, 9 1/2 In. 560.00
Cure, Safe Cure, Frankfurt, A/M, Green, 4 1/4 In. 4400.00
Cure, Safe Cure, London, Green, 7 1/2 In. 90.00
Cure, Warner's Diabetes, Rochester, Amber, 9 3/4 In. 130.00
Cure, Warner's Rheumatic, Rochester, Amber, 9 1/4 In. 100.00

Decanter, Blown, Olive Green, Diamond Pattern, Pontil, 8 1/4 In. 4400.00
Decanter, Crystal, Cranberry Cased, Gilt, Square, Clear Stopper, 11 1/2 In. 165.00
Decanter, Drape Style, Applied Square Collar, 11 1/2 In. 90.00
Decanter, Duck Shape, Leather Covered, Red Glass Eyes, Italy, 12 x 6 1/2 In. 125.00
Decanter, Emerald Green, Stopper, 6 1/4 In. 390.00
Decanter, Enameled Coat Of Arms, Etched Fleur-De-Lis, Gilt, 12 3/4 In. 165.00
Decanter, Green, Leather Covered, Florence, Italy, 13 In. 50.00
Decanter, Olive Amber, Blown, Funnel Mouth, Applied Ring, c.1840, 10 3/4 x 3 In. 360.00
Decanter, Rigaree, Etched Bird & Grape Around, 2 Handles, Pontil, 8 7/8 In. 155.00
Decanter, Rum, Blown, Cobalt Blue, Brass Neck Ring, Applied Handle, Pontil, 7 3/4 In. . . 120.00
Decanter, Sapphire Blue, Fluted Base & Shoulders, Applied Band, Stopper, 12 1/2 In. . . . 230.00
Decanter, Scotch, Ruby Red Cut To Clear, Heart Shape, Stopper, 1910, 1 Qt. 70.00
Decanter, Whiskey, Barrel, Ground Top, Metal Spigot, 10 In. 145.00
Demijohn, 3-Piece Mold, Black Glass, Bulbous, Open Pontil, 1840-1860, 18 In. 90.00
Demijohn, Aqua, Squat Cylinder, Iron Pontil, 1/2 Gal., 12 1/2 In. 30.00
Demijohn, Dark Amber, Whittled, Bubbles, 16 In. 120.00
Demijohn, Light Green Aqua, Applied Lip, 1 Gal., 12 1/2 In. 20.00
Demijohn, Tobacco, Amber, Pebbled, Applied Lip, 13 1/2 In. 66.00
Demijohn, Yellow Amber, Olive Tone, Sloping Collar, Pontil, Bubbles, 1855, 10 7/8 In. . . 145.00
Demijohn, Yellow Emerald, Applied Lip, 15 In. 110.00
Ezra Brooks, English Setter With Bird, Pheasant In Mouth, 1970 . . . . 65.00
Ezra Brooks, Turkey, White, 1971 . . . . 70.00
Figural, Atterbury Duck, Milk Glass, Sheared Ground Mouth, 1871-1885, 11 5/8 In. 560.00
Figural, Bear, Black Amethyst, Applied Face, 1890, 11 1/4 In. 415.00
Figural, Bear, Blue Aqua, Applied Face, 1895, 10 1/2 In. 880.00
Figural, Bear, Blue Aqua, Applied Face, A.N.T., 1890, 8 1/8 In. 825.00
Figural, Bear, Kummel, Dark Grape Amethyst, Tooled Lip, 1885-1895, 11 1/8 In. 110.00
Figural, Bear, Kummel, Dark Green, 11 In. 80.00
Figural, Bear, Ointment Pot, Black, 1860, 3 3/4 In. 275.00
Figural, Book, Coming Thro' The Rye, Stoneware, Cobalt Blue Glaze, 1910, 5 In. 450.00
Figural, Cannon, T. Gayen, Altoona, Dark Amber 1650.00
Figural, Clam, Blue Aqua, Ground Lip, Metal Screw Cap, 1890-1910, 4 3/4 In. 90.00
Figural, Clock, Clear, Stopper, Pontil, D & D, 1900, 16 1/4 In. 80.00
Figural, Coachman, Van Dunck's, Ware & Shmitz, Deep Amber, 8 5/8 In. 200.00
Figural, Ear Of Corn, Green Carnival Glass, Ground & Polished Lip, 1900-1920, 5 In. . . . 645.00
Figural, Elephant, Amber, 10 1/2 In. 30.00
Figural, Frog, Yellow Olive, Gold Warts Painted Back, Depornirt, 1925, 4 5/8 In. 175.00
Figural, Hand Holding Dagger, Turquoise, Pontil, Depose, 1910, 11 1/2 In. 3410.00
Figural, Hot Air Balloon, Ballon Captif 1878, Depose, Tooled Mouth, France, 9 1/8 In. . . . 505.00
Figural, Hot Air Balloon, Crystal, France, 1910, 9 1/4 In. 525.00
Figural, Jester, Tooled Lip, 1890-1910, 6 7/8 In. 75.00
Figural, Joan Of Arc, c.1915, 13 5/8 In. 70.00
Figural, Moses In Bulrushes, Tooled Mouth, 1890-1910, 4 3/4 In. 95.00
Figural, Old Quaker Wheat Man, Embossed, Screw Cap, 7 1/2 In. 30.00
Figural, Pig, Duffy Crescent, Rooster On Crescent Moon, Aqua, Sheared Lip, 7 5/8 In. . . . 2240.00
Figural, Policeman, Amber To Yellow Arms, Continental, 1915, 9 1/8 In. 185.00
Figural, Policeman, French, Cobalt Blue, Contents, Labels, 15 In. 295.00
Figural, Policeman, Milk Glass, Gold Paint Traces, Pontil, 1910, 9 1/2 In. 155.00
Figural, Pretzel, Pottery, 6 In. 70.00
Figural, Radio/Bank, Cobalt Blue, c.1940, 3 In. 175.00
Figural, Revolver, Yellow Amber, Ground Lip, Metal Screw Cap, 9 5/8 In. 80.00
Figural, Santa Claus, Crystal, Painted, Tooled Mouth, 1910, 7 1/2 In. 305.00
Figural, Statue Of Liberty, Milk Glass, Cast Metal, Sheared Ground Lip, 15 1/2 In. 560.00
Figural, Woman With Muff, Tooled Mouth, 1890-1910, 6 3/8 In. 80.00
Flask, Adams, Jefferson, Portrait, Light Yellow Olive, Sheared Mouth, c.1850, 1/2 Pt. 358.00
Flask, Adolph Harris & Co., Amber, Slug Plate, Pewter Cap, 1/2 Pt. 30.00
Flask, Anchor & Sheaf Of Grain, Yellow Olive With Copper Tone, 1/2 Pt. 2910.00
Flask, Bardwell's Root Beer, Stags On Rear, Wire Handle, 10 In. 546.00
Flask, Byron & Scott, Yellow Olive Amber, Tooled Mouth, Open Pontil, 1/2 Pt. 250.00
Flask, Chestnut, 20 Broken Ribs, Swirled Left, Straw Yellow, Pontil, 7 In. 5500.00
Flask, Chestnut, Emerald Green, Flattened Sides, String Lip, Pontil, Bubbles, 8 1/4 In. . . . 420.00
Flask, Chestnut, Forest Green, Applied Mouth Ring, Pontil, 1780-1830, 7 5/8 In. 415.00
Flask, Chestnut, Light Olive Yellow, Applied Mouth Ring, Pontil, 1830, 5 In. 468.00

Flask, Chestnut, Olive Green, Pontil, 8 3/8 In. 255.00
Flask, Chestnut, Orange Amber, Collared Mouth, Pontil, 1800-1830, 11 In. 330.00
Flask, Chestnut, Yellow, Olive Tone, Pontil, 5 7/8 In. 385.00
Flask, Civil War, Militaria, 8 1/4 In. 60.00
Flask, Coffin, Orange Amber, Inside Rolled Lip, Applied Ring, 1 Qt. 60.00
Flask, Cornucopia & Urn, Sapphire Blue, Sheared Lip, Bubbles, Iron Pontil, 1 Pt. 2630.00
Flask, Cornucopia, Urn, Coventry Glass Works, Yellow, Olive Tone, c.1848, 1 Pt. 385.00
Flask, Double Eagle, Apple Green Aqua, 1/2 Pt. 125.00
Flask, Double Eagle, Green, Sheared Lip, Iron Pontil, 1 Qt. 2745.00
Flask, Double Eagle, Kentucky Glass Works, Aqua, Pontil, c.1855, 1 Pt. 165.00
Flask, Eagle & Anchor, Yellow Olive Amber, Double Collar, Iron Pontil, 1 Qt. 6440.00
Flask, Eagle & Cornucopia, Blue Aqua, Tooled Mouth, Pontil, 1/2 Pt. 450.00
Flask, Eagle & Louisville, Yellow Olive Amber, Pontil, 1/2 Pt. 3250.00
Flask, Eagle & Prospector, Deep Blue Aqua, 1 Pt. 260.00
Flask, Eagle, Green Aqua, Smooth Base, Applied Mouth, 1/2 Pt. 150.00
Flask, Flora Temple, Red Puce, Handle, Sloping Double Collar, 1 Qt. 615.00
Flask, For Pike's Peak, Eagle, Applied Band, 1 Pt. 120.00
Flask, For Pike's Peak, Prospector, Hunter, Deep Yellow Amber, 1 Pt. 2185.00
Flask, For Pike's Peak, Prospector, Hunter, Ice Blue Aqua, 1/2 Pt. 200.00
Flask, General Taylor, Fell's Point Monument, Portrait, Gray Aqua, c.1850, 1 Pt. 265.00
Flask, Good Game, Stag, Willow Tree, Coffin & Hay, N.J., Aqua, c.1837, 1 Pt. 165.00
Flask, Granite Glass Co., Stoddard, N.H., Olive Amber, Pontil, c.1860, 1 Pt. 495.00
Flask, Henry Chapman & Co., Montreal, Teardrop, Straw Yellow, 6 In. 1020.00
Flask, Horse Pulling Cart & Eagle, Yellow Olive Amber, Sheared Lip, 1 Pt. 310.00
Flask, Hunter & Fisherman, Calabash, Blue Green, Open Pontil, Applied Top 330.00
Flask, Hunter & Fisherman, Calabash, Copper Puce, Sloping Collar Mouth, Iron Pontil ... 895.00
Flask, Jenny Lind & Glasshouse, Calabash, Aqua, Open Pontil, 1 Qt. 99.00
Flask, Jenny Lind & Lyre, Deep Blue Aqua, Tooled Mouth, Pontil, 1 Qt. 1010.00
Flask, Keene Eagle & Cornucopia, Yellow Olive, Sheared Lip, Pontil, 1 Pt. 195.00
Flask, Lafayette & Clinton, Light Yellow Olive, 1/2 Pt. 1035.00
Flask, Lafayette & Liberty, Yellow Olive Amber, Tooled Mouth, Pontil, 1/2 Pt. 925.00
Flask, Masonic & Eagle, Sunburst, Deep Green Aqua, Tooled Mouth, Pontil, 1 Pt. 980.00
Flask, Masonic & Eagle, Yellow Olive, Sheared Lip, Pontil, Keene Glassworks, 1 Pt. 303.00
Flask, Merry Christmas, Happy New Years, Crystal, Ribbed, Screw Cap, 1890, 7 3/8 In. .. 440.00
Flask, Milk Glass, Pocket Watch, Merry Christmas, Happy New Century, Lid, 4 In. 150.00
Flask, Murdock & Cassel, Zanesville, Bluish Green, Pontil Scar, c.1837, 1 Pt. 523.00
Flask, Our Choice, Cleveland & Stevenson, Rooster, Half Barrel, Amber, 1/2 Pt. 785.00
Flask, Picnic, Pumpkinseed, Medium Amber To Yellow Amber, Tooled Lip, 5 1/4 In. 200.00
Flask, Pig, Incised Railroad Map, Albany Glaze, Kirkpatrick Pottery, c.1870, 8 In. 1925.00
Flask, Pike's Peak, Prospector, Hunter Shooting Deer, Aqua, c.1870, 1 Pt. 303.00
Flask, Pocket, Pattern Molded, Handles, 24 Vertical Ribs, Aqua, c.1830, 5 5/8 In. 523.00
Flask, Portrait, Benjamin Franklin, Aqua, 8 1/2 In., 1 Qt. 137.00
Flask, Pretzel, Salt Pieces, Patent 1908, 5 1/2 In. 380.00
Flask, Pumpkinseed, Sunburst & Spider Web, Amber, Pt. 45.00
Flask, Pumpkinseed, Try It, Medium Amber, 4 3/4 In. 100.00
Flask, Ravenna Glass Works, Star, Lettered, Amber, Olive Tone, c.1860, 1 Pt. 1210.00
Flask, Resurgam, Phoenix, Anchor, Baltimore Glass Works, Amber, c.1870, 1 Pt. .. 220.00
Flask, Rough & Ready, Taylor, Masterson, Eagle Portrait, Light Pale Green, 1 Qt. 1430.00
Flask, Sailor, Banjo Player, Aqua, Maryland Glass Works, c.1860, 1/2 Pt. 198.00
Flask, Scroll, Corseted, John Robinson & Son, Aqua, Amber, c.1834, 1 Pt. 198.00
Flask, Scroll, Lime Green, Sheared Mouth, Pontil Mark, c.1860, 1 Qt. 880.00
Flask, Shield & Clasped Hands, Aqua, 1/2 Pint, 6 3/8 In. 105.00
Flask, Sloop & Star, Pale Apple Green, Tooled Mouth, Pontil, 1/2 Pt. 1010.00
Flask, Sporting, Leather, Pewter, England, 1920s 59.00
Flask, Sterling Silver, Napier, 3 1/2 In. 315.00
Flask, Success To The Railroad, Golden Yellow Amber, Sheared Lip, Open Pontil, 1 Pt. .. 6440.00
Flask, Success To The Railroad, Lancaster Glass Works, Aqua, c.1860, 1 Pt. 305.00
Flask, Summer & Winter, Dark Puce, Double Collar, 1 Pt. 3695.00
Flask, Summer Tree, Pictorial, Light Bluish Green, Pontil Scar, c.1860, 1 Qt. 305.00
Flask, Sunburst, Blue Green, Sheared Mouth, Pontil Scar, c.1840, 1/2 Pt. 440.00
Flask, Sunburst, Deep Blue Green, Sheared Lip, Open Pontil, 1 Pt. 2690.00
Flask, Sunburst, Green, Tooled Mouth, Pontil, 1 Pt. 1065.00
Flask, Sunburst, Medallion, Scroll, M'carty & Torreyson, Aqua, c.1850, 1 Qt. 1760.00

Flask, Traveler's Companion & Star, Aqua, Sheared Lip, Pontil, 1800s, 1/2 Pt. 264.00
Flask, Traveler's Companion, 8-Point Star, Ravenna Glass Co., Olive, c.1860, 1 Pt. 1430.00
Flask, Traveler's Companion, Ravenna, Yellow Amber, Double Collar, Iron Pontil, 1 Pt. .. 615.00
Flask, Ulysses S. Grant, Wreath, Eagle, Aqua, Applied Mouth, c.1880, 1 Pt. 110.00
Flask, Union, Clasped Hands & Cannon, Gold Amber, Whittled, Mouth, c.1870, 1 Pt. 440.00
Flask, Union, Clasped Hands & Eagle, Orange Amber, Applied Band, Qt. 523.00
Flask, Union, Clasped Hands, Pittsburgh, c.1870, Aqua, Mouth, Ring, 1 Pt. 88.00
Flask, Washington & Baltimore, Yellow Green, Sheared Lip, Pontil, 1 Pt. 335.00
Flask, Washington & Eagle, Adams & Jefferson, Pale Aqua, Tooled Mouth, Pontil, 1 Pt. .. 615.00
Flask, Washington & Jackson, Yellow Olive Amber, Tooled Mouth, Pontil, 1/2 Pt. 505.00
Flask, Washington & Sailing Ship, Albany Glass Works, Yellow Amber, Iron Pontil, 1 Pt. . 2015.00
Flask, Washington & Taylor, Never Surrenders, Grape Amethyst, Tooled Mouth, 1 Pt. 4370.00
Flask, Westford Glass Co., Olive Amber, Applied Collar Mouth, Conn., 1800s, 1/2 Pt. ... 330.00
Flask, Wheat Price & Co., Bust, Fairview Works, Portrait, Blue Amber, c.1840 .... 8800.00
Food, Beehive & Bees, Aqua, Rolled Lip, Indented Panel, Rolled Lip, 7 1/8 In. 355.00
Food, Berry, Tobacco Amber, 10 Petals Around Neck, Double Collar, Bubbles, 11 In. 1230.00
Food, Crock, Heinz Apple Butter, Cover, Labels, 1906, 8 In. 550.00
Food, H.J. Heinz Catsup, Pittsburg, Pa., 1891 .... 85.00
Food, Heinz's Pure Malt Vinegar, Salesman's Sample, Original Label, Stopper, 4 5/8 In. ... 145.00
Food, Jar, Ice Blue, Wide Mouth, Applied Lip, Red Iron Pontil, 9 1/4 In. 125.00
Food, Jelly Jar, Blue Aqua, Flared & Folded Lip, Pontil, 3 3/4 In. 110.00
Food, Lily White Corn Syrup, Jar, White Calla Lilies, Paper Label, 3 1/2 Lb. 12.50
Food, N.W. Opermann Mustard Factory, Aqua, Pontil, 4 7/8 In. 120.00
Food, R. & F. Atmore, Blue Aqua, Pontil, 11 1/2 In. 605.00
Food, Shriver's, Oyster, Ketchup, Baltimore, Emerald Green, 1865, 7 5/8 In. 1265.00
Food, T.A. Bryan & Co.'s Perfection Tomato Sauce, Amber, Whittled, 8 1/4 In. 265.00
Food, Vaughn's Vegetable Lithontriptic Mixture, Buffalo, Aqua, Smooth Base, 8 In. 175.00
Fruit Can, Spratt's Patent July 18, 1854, Tin, Glass Lid 415.00
Fruit Jar, A. Dufour & Co., Bordeaux, Barrel, Whittled, Bubbles, France, 10 1/8 In. 120.00
Fruit Jar, A. Stone & Co., Aqua, Applied Collared Mouth, Glass Lid, c.1880, 1 Pt. 110.00
Fruit Jar, A.E. Bray, 4 Leaf Clover, Gold Amber, Milk Glass Lid, c.1910, 1 Qt. 550.00
Fruit Jar, Air-Tight Fruit Jar, Ravenna Glass Works, Barrel, Aqua, Wax Sealer, Lid, 1 Pt. . 6440.00
Fruit Jar, Atlas E-Z Seal, Amber, ABM Lip, Glass Lid, Lightning Closure, 1 Qt. 28.00
Fruit Jar, B.B. Wilcox, Patd March 26th 1867, Aqua, Glass Lid, c.1880, 1 Qt. 110.00
Fruit Jar, Ball Mason, Yellow Olive, Amber Striations, Screw Lid, 1 Qt. 465.00
Fruit Jar, Ball Standard, Yellow Olive, Amber Striations, Wax Sealer, 1 Qt. 275.00
Fruit Jar, Ball, Mason, Bright Green, Amber Striations, Zinc Lid, c.1920, 1 Pt. 130.00
Fruit Jar, Beaver, Ground Mouth, Glass Lid, Zinc Band, c.1890, Midget Pt. 55.00
Fruit Jar, Bloeser Jar, Aqua, Ground Mouth, Glass Lid, Metal Clamp, c.1890, 1 Qt. 230.00
Fruit Jar, Cohansey Glass Mfg. Co., Pat Feb 12 1867, Embossed, Soldered Clamp, 48 Oz. . 176.00
Fruit Jar, Columbia, Gold Amber, Glass Lid, Wire Clamp, c.1900, 1 Pt. 1870.00
Fruit Jar, Cunningham & Co., Pittsburgh, Pa., Cornflower Blue, c.1880, 1 Qt. 3025.00
Fruit Jar, Cunningham & Co., Pittsburgh, Pa., Embossed, Aqua, c.1880, 1 Qt. 83.00
Fruit Jar, Dunningham & Co., Pittsburgh, Pa., Kelly Green, 1 Qt. 440.00
Fruit Jar, Eagle, Aqua, Applied Collared Mouth, Glass Lid, c.1880, 1 Qt. 145.00
Fruit Jar, Eureka, Patd Dec 27th 1864, Aqua, Metal Lid, c.1880, 1 Pt. 1650.00
Fruit Jar, Flaccus Bros., Steer's Head, Yellow, Amber Lid, Glass Screw Lid, c.1900, 1 Pt. 1210.00
Fruit Jar, Globe, Yellow Amber Glass Lid, Wire & Iron Clamp, c.1900, 1 Qt. 605.00
Fruit Jar, Griffen's Patent, Oct. 7 1862, Embossed, Aqua, c.1870, 1 Qt. 440.00
Fruit Jar, H & S, Aqua, Metal Clamp, Lid Closure, 1860-1870, 1 Qt. 5225.00
Fruit Jar, Haines Combination, Aqua, Glass Lid, c.1880, 1 Qt. 230.00
Fruit Jar, Hartell & Letchworth, Patent May 22 1866, Embossed, Aqua, 1 Pt. 525.00
Fruit Jar, Imperial, Hand Holding Mace, Glass Lid, Metal Clamp, c.1900, 1/2 Gal. 470.00
Fruit Jar, J.D. Willoughby & Co., Aqua, c.1880, 1 Qt. 880.00
Fruit Jar, J.P. Barstow, Sun, Aqua, Ground Lip, Glass Lid, Metal Yoke, 1 Qt. 100.00
Fruit Jar, K.Y.G.W, Yellow Green, Wax Sealer, Repro Tin Lid, 1 Qt. 355.00
Fruit Jar, Lafayette, Aqua, 3-Piece Glass & Metal Closure, 1885-1895, 1 Qt. 2520.00
Fruit Jar, Lafayette, Aqua, 3-Piece Glass & Metal Closure, 1890s, 1 Pt. 198.00
Fruit Jar, Lafayette, Aqua, Tooled Rolled Mouth, Metal, Glass Stopper, 1 Qt. 135.00
Fruit Jar, Lindell Glass Co., Embossed, Gold Amber, Applied Wax Sealer Mouth, 1 Qt. .. 120.00
Fruit Jar, M.G. Co. A, Citron, Ring Wax Sealer, 1 Qt. 330.00
Fruit Jar, Macomb Pottery Co., Jan. 24, 1899, Stoneware, Zinc Lid, 1/2 Gal. 50.00
Fruit Jar, Mason's Improved, Aqua, Glass Lid, Metal Band, H. Brooke, 1 Gal. 2530.00

Fruit Jar, Mason's Patent Nov 30th 1858, CFJ Co., Yellow Amber, 1 Qt. 1870.00
Fruit Jar, Mason's Patent Nov 30th 1858, Cross, Gold Amber, 1 Pt. 770.00
Fruit Jar, Mason's Patent Nov. 30, 1858, Amber, Zinc Lid, Midget Pt. ....2000.00 to 4125.00
Fruit Jar, Mason's Patent Nov. 30th 1858, Citron, Ground Lip, Zinc Screw Lid, 1 Pt. 420.00
Fruit Jar, Mason's Patent Nov. 30th 1858, Yellow, Amber Glass Lid, 1/2 Gal. 230.00
Fruit Jar, Mason's Patent Nov. 30th, 1858 Dupont, Aqua, Zinc Lid, 1/2 Gal. 330.00
Fruit Jar, Mason's Union, Shield, Aqua, Zinc Lid, c.1880, 1 Qt. 1650.00
Fruit Jar, Mason's, CFJ Co., Improved, Amber, Screw Lid, 1/2 Gal. 255.00
Fruit Jar, Mason's, Cross, Patent Nov. 30th, 1858, Amber, Zinc Lid, 1/2 Gal. 155.00
Fruit Jar, Mason's, Cross, Patent Nov. 30th, 1858, Yellow Amber, 1/2 Gal. 305.00
Fruit Jar, Mason, Keystone, Amber, Zinc Lid, c.1890, 1 Qt. 605.00
Fruit Jar, McCarty, Pat Mar 7 1899, Embossed, Glass Stopper, c.1900, 1 Pt. 210.00
Fruit Jar, Millville Atmospheric, Aqua, Applied Collared Mouth, Glass Lid, 1 Pt. 385.00
Fruit Jar, Millville Atmospheric, Aqua, Glass Lid, Iron Yoke Clamp, 1 Qt. 265.00
Fruit Jar, Millville W T Co. Improved, Aqua, Ground Mouth, Glass Lid, 1 Pt. 130.00
Fruit Jar, N. Osburn, Rochester, N.Y., Deep Ice Blue, Rolled Lip, 1 Qt. 700.00
Fruit Jar, National 1, Aqua, Metal Willoughby Stopple, 1860-1880, 1 Qt. 305.00
Fruit Jar, Pansy, Amber, Vertical Panels, Glass Lid, Zinc Band, 1890s, 1 Qt. 415.00
Fruit Jar, Peerless, Aqua, Glass Lid, Iron Yoke Clamp, c.1870, 1/2 Gal. 120.00
Fruit Jar, Pet, Aqua, Applied Collared Mouth, Lid, Spring Coil Clamp, c.1880, 1/2 Gal. ... 198.00
Fruit Jar, Petal, Blue Aqua, Iron Pontil, 1 Qt. 120.00
Fruit Jar, Petal, Cobalt Blue, Red Iron Pontil, 1 Qt. 7150.00
Fruit Jar, Potter & Bodine's Air-Tight Fruit Jar, Philada, Barrel, Aqua, Wax Sealer, 1 Qt. . 1625.00
Fruit Jar, Protector, Blue Aqua, Ground Lip, Metal Lid, Wire Closure, 1/2 Gal. 90.00
Fruit Jar, Protector, Blue Aqua, Metal Lid, Wire, 1 Pt. 75.00
Fruit Jar, Protector, Blue Aqua, Metal Lid, Wire, 1/2 Gal. 90.00
Fruit Jar, Put On Rubber Before Filling, Star & Crescent, Aqua, c.1900, 1 Qt. 660.00
Fruit Jar, Schaffer Jar, Rochester, N.Y., JCS, Aqua, Lid, Wire Bail, Swirl Lines, 1 Pt. 1230.00
Fruit Jar, Star Glass Co., New Albany, Indiana, 1/2 Gal. 65.00
Fruit Jar, Star, Circle Of Fruit, Aqua, Zinc Band, Tin Lid, c.1880, 1 Qt. 255.00
Fruit Jar, Swayzee's Improved Mason, Green, Metal Stopper, 1 Qt. 230.00
Fruit Jar, T. Hopkins Jr., Skipton, Md., Aqua, Pontil, c.1860, 1 Qt. 2200.00
Fruit Jar, The Leader, Gold Amber, Glass Lid, Wire Clamp, c.1900, 1 Qt. 415.00
Fruit Jar, The Pearl, Aqua, Ground Mouth, Glass Lid, Metal Screw Band, c.1890, 1 Pt. .. 305.00
Fruit Jar, Thompson & Hills Ltd., Auckland, Sun Colored Amethyst, c.1920, 1 Qt. ... 255.00
Fruit Jar, Thorne & Wilcox Co., Wellsville, NY, Pat May 10, '90, Metal Lid, 1 Gal. 305.00
Fruit Jar, Trademark Lightning Putnam, Amber, Glass Lid, 1 Pt. 145.00
Fruit Jar, Triumph No. 1, Blue Aqua, Milky Stain, Ground Lip, Wax Ring, 1 Qt. 355.00
Fruit Jar, Van Vliet Jar Of 1881, Aqua, Ground Lip, Glass Lid, Metal & Wire Yoke, 1 Qt. 925.00
Fruit Jar, Victory, Aqua, Glass Lid, Zinc Screw Band, c.1880, 1 Qt. 880.00
Fruit Jar, W.W. Lyman, Aqua, Ground Mouth, Tin Lid, c.1880, 1 Gal. 3025.00
Fruit Jar, Wax Sealer, Yellow Amber, 1 Qt. 100.00
Fruit Jar, Wheat Sheaf Design, Malted Beef, Blue, 6 In. 220.00
Fruit Jar, Wheeler, Embossed, Aqua, Ground Mouth, 6 Piece Hinged Clamp 468.00
Fruit Jar, Winslow, Aqua, Ground Mouth, Brass Clamp, c.1880, 20 Oz. 220.00
Fruit Jar, Wm. L. Haller, Aqua, Square Mouth, Willoughby Stopple, 1880s, 1 Pt. 522.00
Gemel, Gourd Shape, Pedestal, 10 In. 375.00
Gin, Booth & Sedgwick's, London, Cordial Gin, Emerald Green, Iron Pontil, 9 7/8 In. ... 495.00
Gin, Case, Daniel Visser & Zonen, Scheidam, Light Amethyst, Blue Seal, 11 In. 413.00
Gin, Case, Tapered, Deep Olive Amber, Open Pontil, Bubbles, 10 1/2 In. 235.00
Gin, Cosmopoliet, J.J. Melchers, WZ Scheidam, Olive Green, 9 1/2 In. 130.00
Gin, London Jockey Club House, Deep Olive Green, 9 3/8 In. 385.00
Gin, London Jockey Club House, Emerald Green, Jockey On Horse, 9 5/8 In. 1015.00
Gin, Olive Green, Vertical Lines, 10 1/2 In. 9.00
Ginger Beer, Brown Top, London Ginger Beer Co., Pottery, c.1880, 6 1/2 In. 150.00
Ginger Beer, Dr. Cronk's Sarsaparilla Beer, Stoneware, Red Brown, 12-Sided, 9 7/8 In. .. 60.00
Ginger Beer, Pilgrim Bros. & Company, Black Transfer Print, 1875, 7 In. 65.00
Ginger Beer, W. Bidwell, Sarsaparilla Beer, 12-Sided, Stoneware, Tan, 9 3/4 In. 325.00
Household, Ammonia, F.F.D., Gas Light Co., Aqua, Bubbles 45.00
Household, Anthony's Diamond Varnish For Single Ambrotypes, Blue, Label, 5 7/8 In. .. 810.00
Household, Beau Peep Baby Shoe Cleaner, Figural, Paper Label, 1920s-1930s, 6 1/4 In.. 50.00
Household, Blacking, Oval, Aqua, Inward Rolled Mouth, Scar, Albany, c.1860, 4 1/2 In. . 210.00
Household, Blacking, Yellow Olive Amber, Sheared Mouth, Pontil, 4 1/2 In. 155.00

Household, Gypsy Dy-Kleen, Chicago, Ill., Paper Labels, Screw Cap, 3 x 1 1/2 x 5/8 In. . 32.00
Household, Paste, Sanford's Inks & Library, Embossed, 1 Pt., 7 1/2 In. 12.00
Household, Shoe Polish, Figural, Mikado, Amber 310.00
Ink, A.B. Tallman, Pat. Apl. For, Aqua, Tooled Mouth, Domed Base, 2 5/8 In. 615.00
Ink, A.D.R., Albany, Igloo, Green Aqua, 2 1/8 In. 525.00
Ink, Bertinguiot, Olive Amber, Tooled Mouth, Pontil, 2 1/4 In. 365.00
Ink, Bertinguiot, Yellow Olive, Sheared Lip, Pontil, 2 x 3 In. 255.00
Ink, Cabin, Blue Aqua, Tooled Mouth, 2 5/8 In. 280.00
Ink, Cabin, Gray Tint, Tooled, Collared Lip, Mid 1800s, 2 1/2 In. 770.00
Ink, Carter's, Cathedral, Cobalt Blue, ABM, Hard Rubber Stopper, 1 Pt. . . . . .165.00 to 175.00
Ink, Carter's, Cathedral, Cobalt Blue, ABM, Label, 1 Qt. 145.00
Ink, Carter's, Cathedral, Cobalt Blue, Embossed, 6-Sided, Master 225.00
Ink, Carter's, Igloo, Aqua, 1 3/4 In. 660.00
Ink, Carter, Cobalt Blue, 6-Sided, ABM, 2 7/8 In. 120.00
Ink, Chas. Hardt., Philada, Blue Green, Embossed Shoulders, 3-Piece Mold, 1 Pt. 70.00
Ink, Cone, X, Backwards 200, Yellow Olive Amber, Tooled Mouth, Pontil, 2 1/8 In. 810.00
Ink, Davids, Igloo, Gold Amber, 1 3/4 In. 575.00
Ink, Davids, Igloo, Teal Blue, 1 3/4 In. 605.00
Ink, F.D.A., Domed, Blue Green, Rolled Lip, Bubbles, 2 In. 335.00
Ink, Farleys, Yellow Amber, Olive Tone, 8-Sided, c.1860, 1 3/4 x 1 7/8 In. 1210.00
Ink, G.A. Moss, Igloo, Blue Aqua, 1 5/8 In. 275.00
Ink, Geometric, Deep Olive Green, Tooled Disc Mouth, Pontil, 1 7/8 In. 190.00
Ink, Harrison's Columbian, Aqua, Rolled Lip, 8-Sided, Open Pontil, 1 3/4 In. 170.00
Ink, Harrison's Columbian, Cobalt Blue, Rolled Lip, Open Pontil, 2 1/8 In. 645.00
Ink, Harrison's Columbian, Igloo, Blue Aqua, 8-Sided, 1 7/8 In. 330.00
Ink, J. & I.E.M., Igloo, Blue Green, Sheared Lip, 1 7/8 In. 130.00
Ink, J. & I.E.M., Igloo, Cobalt Blue, 1 7/8 In. 2420.00
Ink, J. & I.E.M., Igloo, Yellow Olive, 1 7/8 In. 1100.00
Ink, Locomotive, Pat. Oct. 1874, Aqua, Ground Lip, 2 In. 1790.00
Ink, Olive Green, Spout, Iron Pontil, 12-Sided, Bubbles, 1/2 Gal., 10 In. 6440.00
Ink, Steel & Co., Philada., Pa., Blue Green, Embossed Shoulders, 3-Piece Mold, 1 Pt. . . . 70.00
Ink, Stoddard Glasshouse, N.H., Umbrella, 16-Sided, Amber, Pontil, 2 1/4 x 2 3/8 In. . . . 660.00
Ink, Stoddard Style, Deep Stoddard Amber, Sheared Top, Open Pontil, Master, 4 In. 154.00
Ink, Stoneware, Denby Pottery London England, Alkaline Glaze, 6 In. 22.00
Ink, T. Davids, N.Y., Stoneware, 1 Pt., 7 In. 95.00
Ink, Teakettle, 8-Sided, Amethyst, Spout, Brass Collar, c.1860, 2 x 3 1/8 In. 385.00
Ink, Umbrella, 8-Sided, Cobalt Blue, Rolled Lip, Pontil, 2 1/2 In. 2015.00
Ink, Umbrella, Stoddard Style, Olive, Sheared Lip, Open Pontil 220.00
Ink, Umbrella, Teal, Rolled Lip, Open Pontil 99.00
Ink, Waters, Troy, N.Y., Umbrella, Aqua, Pontil, Mid 1800s, 2 3/4 x 2 In. 935.00
Jar, Apothecary, Domed Cover, Inverted Baluster Shape, Birds, Sunflowers, 24 In. 748.00
Jar, Battle Scene, Mounted As Table Lamp, Cover, Chinese, 23 1/2 In. 69.00
Jar, Butter, Gilberts, Airtight, Ground Mouth, Smooth Base, 1880-1900, 8 1/2 x 7 In. 330.00
Jar, Confit, Ocher Glaze, Twin Handle, France, 9 3/4 In. 46.00
Jar, Confit, Ocher Glaze, Twin Handle, France, 11 In. . . . . .172.00 to 230.00
Jar, Confit, Ocher Glaze, Twin Handle, France, 12 1/2 In. 92.00
Jar, Confit, Ocher Glaze, Twin Handle, France, 13 In. 200.00
Jar, Confit, Ocher Glaze, Twin Handle, France, 14 In. 143.00
Jar, Footed, Globular, 19th Century, 14 1/4 In. 235.00
Jar, Green, Blown, 19th Century, 26 In. 70.00
Jar, Storage, Aqua, Dip Mold, Open Pontil, 1770-1820, 5 In. 29.00
Jar, Storage, Cover, Applied Blue Bands, Cylindrical, 1840-1860, 10 1/2 In. 55.00
Jar, Storage, Light Olive, Applied Top, 7 In. 155.00
Jar, Storage, Stoddard, Gold Amber, Folded Rim, Bubbles, Open Pontil, 8 1/2 In. 358.00
Jar, Storage, Strawberry Puce, Sloping Collar, Open Pontil, Bubbles, c.1810, 17 In. 980.00
Jar, Storage, Yellow Olive, Torpedo Shape, Collared Mouth, Pontil, 1830-1860, 6 In. 660.00
Jug, Cider, Aqua, 5 Gal. 165.00
Jug, Golden Hill, Toledo, Ohio, Pottery, White, 4 3/4 In. 77.00
Jug, Whiskey, Mount Hickory Special Rye, Pottery, Black Transfer, c.1885, 8 1/2 In. 100.00
Medicine, Al S. Lamb, Aspen, Colorado, Lamb Picture, 4 3/4 In. 75.00
Medicine, Apothecary, A.M. Cole, Virginia, Nev., Embossed, Square, 5 In. 60.00
Medicine, Aspirin, Bayer, Tin Cap, Paper Label, 2 1/2 In. 3.00
Medicine, Blose Drug Co., In Banner, 5 In. 30.00

Bottle, Medicine,
H.H. Warner & Co.,
Tippecanoe, Olive
Green, 9 In.

Bottle, Medicine,
Warner's Safe
Remedies Co.,
Rochester, N.Y.,
Amber, 7 1/4 In.

Trim shrubs near the house so they don't hide burglars trying to break in basement or first-floor windows. Keep basement windows locked at all times. All outside doors should be made of solid wood or metal.

Medicine, Carter's Spanish Mixture, Olive Green, Open Pontil, 8 In. 525.00
Medicine, Carter's Spanish Mixture, Olive Green, Sloping Double Collar, Label, 8 In. 1455.00
Medicine, Davis Drug Co., Rexall Store, Leadville, Colo, Amber, 12 Panels, 4 3/4 In. 80.00
Medicine, Derwent Cough Balsam, Aqua, 5 In. 8.00
Medicine, Dr. Browder's Compound Syrup Of Indian Turnip, Aqua, Contents, 7 In. 525.00
Medicine, Dr. D.C. Kellinger's Remedies, N.Y., Aqua, Recessed Panels, Whittled, 7 In. .. 275.00
Medicine, Dr. J.F. Churchill's Specific Remedy For Consumption, Blue Aqua, 9 In. 39.00
Medicine, Dr. Kennedy's Medical Discovery, Aqua, BIMAL, 8 1/2 In. 9.00
Medicine, Drug, Canfields One Horse Drug Store, Leadville, Co., 4 In. 225.00
Medicine, Drug, Herbs Of Life, Blood Purifier, Denver, Co., Aqua, 9 In. 225.00
Medicine, Drug, Owl,-Wm. Thebus Drug Co., Denver, Co., Purple, 7 1/2 In. 125.00
Medicine, Duff's Remedy, Stopper, Label Under Glass, 10 In. 358.00
Medicine, Force's Asthmania, S.B. Force M'f'g', Chemist, Amber, 8 7/8 In. 160.00
Medicine, Glovers Imperial Distemper Remedy, Citron Yellow, 5 In. 58.00
Medicine, Gun Was Chinese Remedy, Amber, 7 3/4 In. 300.00
Medicine, H. Lake's Indian Specific, Blue Aqua, Tooled Lip, Pontil, 8 1/4 In. 3135.00
Medicine, H.H. Warner & Co., Tippecanoe, Olive Green, 9 In. .... *Illus* 5800.00
Medicine, Henshaw Ward & Co., Druggists, Boston, Yellow Olive Green, Pontil, 11 In. .. 6440.00
Medicine, Hoods Pills, Cure Liver, Aqua, 1 3/4 In. 55.00
Medicine, Hunt's Liniment, C.E. Stanton, Sing Sing, NY, Green, c.1860, 4 1/2 In. 715.00
Medicine, I. Covert's, Balm Of Life, Olive Green, Open Pontil, 6 In. 2585.00
Medicine, John Hart & Co., Heart Shape, Amber, Double Collar, 6 7/8 In. 810.00
Medicine, John Wyeth Bros., Cobalt Blue, Dose Cap, 5 13/16 In. 18.00
Medicine, Kennedy's Salt Rheum, Ointment, Jar, Blue Aqua, Open Pontil, 3 1/2 In. 130.00
Medicine, Kickapoo Oil, Light To Medium Yellow Olive, Tooled Mouth, 5 3/8 In. 125.00
Medicine, L.H. White Homeopathic Pharmacy, Cleveland, Oh., Amber, Square, 4 1/2 In. .. 35.00
Medicine, Liniment, Prairie Weed, Roxbury, Mass., Embossed, Square, 8 In. 75.00
Medicine, Log Cabin Cough & Consumption Remedy, Pat. Sept. 6, 1887, Amber, 9 In. ... 365.00
Medicine, Log Cabin Extract, Rochester, N.Y., Amber, Label, Contents, Box, 8 1/4 In. ... 730.00
Medicine, Longley's Panacea, Olive Green, Sloping Double Collar, Pontil, 6 3/4 In. 4030.00
Medicine, Lydia E. Pinkham's Vegetable Compound, Aqua, 14 1/2 Oz., 8 1/8 In. 8.00
Medicine, Lydia E. Pinkham's Vegetable Compound, Green, Disc Type Mouth, 8 In. 3695.00
Medicine, Lyon's Powder, B & P, N.Y., Pink Amethyst, Rolled Lip, Open Pontil, 4 In. ... 365.00
Medicine, Manzanita Oil, Sacramento, Light Aqua, 1860s, 4 1/2 In. 440.00
Medicine, Moxie Nerve Food, Denver, Co., Root Beer Amber, Seed Bubbles 700.00
Medicine, Pepsinola, Label Under Glass, 11 In. 187.00
Medicine, Prof. I. Hubers Malvina Lotion, Toledo, Ohio, Milk Glass, Square, 4 7/8 In. .. 80.00
Medicine, Red & White Murrines, Cobalt, Aldo Nason, 11 x 6 In. 4600.00
Medicine, Rolfe's Pharmacy, Brandon, Vt., Aqua, 7 In. 200.00
Medicine, Shaker, Syrup, No. 1, Canterbury, N.Y., Aqua, Open Pontil, 5 1/2 In. 145.00
Medicine, Smith's Green Mountain Renovator, E. Georgia, Vt., Amber, 7 1/2 In. 2695.00
Medicine, Swaim's Panacea, Philada, Apple Green, Pontil, 8 In. 440.00
Medicine, Swaim's Panacea, Philada., Olive Green, Sloping Double Collar, Pontil, 8 In. .. 700.00
Medicine, Swift's Syphilitic Specific, Cobalt Blue, Disc Type Mouth, 9 In. 1345.00
Medicine, U.S.A. Hosp. Dept., Cobalt Blue, 3-Piece Mold, Tooled Mouth, 7 3/8 In. 605.00
Medicine, U.S.A. Hosp. Dept., Copper Amber, Swirls, 5 13/16 In. 1430.00
Medicine, University Of Free Medicine, 6-Sided, Aqua, Pontil, 4 7/8 In. 145.00

Medicine, Vaughn's Vegetable Lithontriptic Mixture, Buffalo, Blue Aqua, 8 In. . . . .130.00 to 150.00
Medicine, Vial, Puce Amethyst, 1855-1865, 4 In. 29.00
Medicine, Wakelee's Camelline, Cobalt Blue, 4 3/8 In. 78.00
Medicine, Wakelee's Camelline, Cobalt Blue, Applied Mouth, Whittled, 7 1/2 In. 255.00
Medicine, Warner's Safe Kidney & Liver Remedy, Rochester, N.Y., Olive Green, 5 1/2 In. 605.00
Medicine, Warner's Safe Remedies Co., Rochester, N.Y., Amber, 7 1/4 In. . . . . *Illus* 448.00
Medicine, Wormser Bros., San Francisco, Barrel, Orange Amber, 9 1/2 In. 2420.00
Medicine, Wyeth & Bro., Phosphate Of Lime & Cod Liver Oil, Blue, 8 3/4 In. 190.00
Milk, A.J. Carter Dairy, Frewsburg, N.Y., Cream, Top, ABM, 1 Qt. 120.00
Milk, Anderson Bros., Worcester, Ma., Round, Embossed, 1 Qt. 20.00
Milk, Borden's, Elsie The Cow Picture On 2 Sides, Square, 1 Gal. 80.00
Milk, Borden's, Sour Cream, Embossed, 8 Oz. 5.00
Milk, Branglebrink Farm, St. James, N.Y., Round, Embossed, 1/2 Pt. 6.00
Milk, Brookfield Dairy, Hellertown, Pa., Phone TE 8-3041, Baby Face, Paper Cap, 1/2 Pt. 73.00
Milk, Brookside Dairies, Waterbury, Ct., Embossed, Round, 1 Qt. 10.00
Milk, Burrough's Brothers, Walnut Grove Farm, Red Pyro, 1 Qt. 30.00
Milk, Carnation Fresh Milk, Carnation Co., Amber, Square, 1 Qt. 45.00
Milk, City Farm Dairies, Orange, Square, c.1957, 5 1/2 In. 13.00
Milk, Clardy's Dairy, Home Of Space Ship Crash, Roswell, N.M., Painted, 1947, 1 Qt. . . . 95.00
Milk, Cloverleaf Farms, Stockton, Calif., Cream Top, Ribbed Neck, Orange, 1 Qt. 28.00
Milk, College View Dairy, Maroon, Square, Norwich, Vt., 1 Pt. 30.00
Milk, Cortez Dairy, Colorado, Embossed, Round, 1 Pt. 45.00
Milk, Crane, Leominster, Ma., Embossed, Round, 1 Qt. 20.00
Milk, Deerfoot Farms, Southboro, Ma., Embossed, Round, 1/2 Pt. 15.00
Milk, Diamond Milk Dairy Farms, For Mothers Who Care, Orange, Tall, 1 Qt. 20.00
Milk, Dietrichs, Cream, Milk, Butter, Pyro, Square, 1/2 Pt. 25.00
Milk, Duncan's Dairy, MILK-Pioneers The Way To Health, Catskill, N.Y., 1965, 1 Qt. . . . 18.00
Milk, Elm Haven Farm, Real Guernsey Milk, Dunstable, Orange, Round, 1/2 Pt. 35.00
Milk, Elmhurst Dairy, Shrewsbury, Ma., Embossed, Round, 1 Qt. 20.00
Milk, English's Dairy, Holbrook, Embossed, Round, 1 Qt. 20.00
Milk, Fairlea Farms, Red, Square, 1960, 1 Qt. 16.00
Milk, Farmers' Co-Op Inc., Hartford, Conn., Maroon, Tall, 1 Qt. 15.00
Milk, Forest Lake Dairy, Palmer, Ma., Cream Top, Embossed, 1 Pt. 10.00
Milk, Gaffney Bros., Worcester, Ma., Embossed, Round, 1928, 1 Pt. 20.00
Milk, Gail Borden, Amber, 1 Qt. 20.00
Milk, Gail Borden, Pet, Amber, 1/2 Gal. 30.00
Milk, Gendrons Dairy, Bedford, N.H., Pyro, Round, 1/2 Pt. 35.00
Milk, Giles Dairy, Franklin, New Hampshire, Orange, Square, c.1960, 1 Qt. 16.00
Milk, Guernsey Farms, Waynesboro, Pa., Pyro, Square, 1/2 Pt. 18.00
Milk, H.P. Hood & Sons Dairy Experts, Red, Round, 1/2 Pt. 45.00
Milk, Hamden Creamery Co., Registered, ABM, Wire Closure, 1/2 Pt. 90.00
Milk, Hollywood Dairy, Durango, Colo., Cream Top, Embossed, Round, 1/2 Pt. 35.00
Milk, Hycrest Tri City Farm, Orange, Square, 1957, 1/2 Pt. 13.00
Milk, Indian Hill Farm, Charlton, Ma., Embossed, Round, 1 Qt. 20.00
Milk, Jensen's Wayside Dairy, Shrewsbury, Ma., Embossed, Round, 1 Pt. 20.00
Milk, Lantz's Dairy Pasteurized Milk, St. Clairsville, Ohio, Round, 1 Pt. 75.00
Milk, Macomber Dairy, Red, Round, 1/2 Pt. 30.00
Milk, Madden's Sunnymeade Dairy, Pyro, Round, 1/2 Pt. 30.00
Milk, Oneonta Dairy, Oneonta, N.Y., Square Cream Top, Orange, 1 Qt. 29.00
Milk, Original Plastic Carry Holder, Bonfoey's Dairy, 1960, 1/2 Gal. 15.00
Milk, Pine Ridge Farm, Lowell, Mass., Maroon, 1 Qt. 20.00
Milk, Pink Creek Farm, Barre Plains, Mass., Tin Top, Embossed, Round, 1/2 Pt. 75.00
Milk, Pittsfield Milk Exchange, Pittsfield, Ma., Cream Top, Embossed, Round, 1 Qt. 25.00
Milk, Purdue, Round, 1 Pt. 475.00
Milk, Rider Dairy, Danbury, Ct., Cream Top, Pyro, Square, 1 Qt. 5.00
Milk, Roger Jessup Farms, Red, 1 Qt. 11.00
Milk, Rogers Rogue River Ranch, Original Cap, 1950, 8 1/2 In. 150.00
Milk, Rossingaris Dairy, Waterville, Me., Orange, Round, 1/2 Pt. 35.00
Milk, Salem Dairy, Shaklefords, Va., Green, Round, Pyro, 1/2 Pt. 50.00
Milk, Seward Dairy, Seward, Alaska, 1 Qt. 143.00
Milk, Steeds Dairy Products, Logan, Utah, Pyro, Round, 1/2 Pt. 25.00
Milk, Sunrise Dairy, Gastonia, N.C., Boy Carrying Bottle, 1951, Square, 1 Qt. 16.00
Milk, Superior Dairy, Martinsburg, W.V., Pyro, Square, 1/2 Pt. 20.00

Milk, Townsend's Dairy, Methuen, Mass., Maroon, Tall, 1 Qt. 20.00
Milk, United Dairy System, Cream Top, Embossed, Round, 1/2 Pt. 10.00
Milk, Upton's Farm, Bridgewater, Mass., Babyface, Black, Embossed, Round, 1 Pt. 75.00
Milk, Van's Dairy, Hudson, N.Y., Square Cream Top, Maroon, 1 Qt. 22.00
Milk, W.H. Chamberlain, Shrewsbury, Ma., Embossed, Round, 1925, 1 Qt. 30.00
Milk, WAWA Dairy, Embossed, Flower, Cap, 1/2 Pt. 10.00
Milk, Whiting Milk Cos. Store, Boston, 1926, Embossed, Round, 1/2 Pt. 10.00
Milk, Willow Farms, Frizzellburg, Maryland, Square Cream Top, Red, 1 Qt. 25.00
Milk, Wilson-MacDonald Co., Haverhill, Mass., Orange, Tall, 1 Qt. 15.00
Mineral Water, A.W. Cudworth & Co., San Francisco, Green, Iron Pontil, 7 3/8 In. 176.00
Mineral Water, Adirondack Springs, Westport, N.Y., Blue Emerald Green, 1 Qt. 176.00
Mineral Water, Artesian Spring Co., Green, 1875, 1 Pt. 120.00
Mineral Water, Avon Spring Water, Amber, Sloping Double Collar, 1 Qt. 1735.00
Mineral Water, B & G Superior, San Francisco, Cobalt Blue, Iron Pontil, 6 5/8 In. 690.00
Mineral Water, B.R. Lippincott & Co., Stockton, Cobalt Blue, Iron Pontil, 7 1/4 In. 1100.00
Mineral Water, Beard's, F & B Boston, Blue Green, Blob Top, 6 7/8 In. 70.00
Mineral Water, C. Cleminshaw, Troy, N.Y., Sapphire Blue, c.1845, 7 In. 88.00
Mineral Water, Chase & Co., San Francisco, Ca., Green, Lug Plate, Iron Pontil, 7 3/4 In. .. 165.00
Mineral Water, Chippewa Spring Water, Aqua, Metal Closure, Stopper, 11 In. ....220.00 to 275.00
Mineral Water, Clarke & White, C, New York, Olive Green Amber, 1 Qt. 35.00
Mineral Water, Clarke & White, New York., Emerald Green 99.00
Mineral Water, Cloverdale Lithia Water, Harrisburg, Pa., Jug, Cobalt Blue, 1 Gal. 160.00
Mineral Water, Empire Spring Co., Saratoga, N.Y., Emerald Green, 1 Qt. 65.00
Mineral Water, F & B, Blue Green, c.1865, 7 In. 70.00
Mineral Water, G.W. Weston & Co., Saratoga, N.Y., Olive Green, 1 Qt. 2130.00
Mineral Water, Highrock Congress Spring, C & W, Saratoga, N.Y., Yellow Green, 1 Pt. .. 310.00
Mineral Water, Lynde & Putman, San Francisco, Cal.A, Teal Blue, Iron Pontil, 7 1/2 In. . 355.00
Mineral Water, Massena, Massena Spring, Blue Green, Sloping Collar, Ring, c.1880, 1 Pt. 265.00
Mineral Water, Middletown Healing Springs, Grays & Clark, Vt., Golden Amber, 1 Qt. .. 660.00
Mineral Water, Missiquoi A Springs, Squaw, Yellow Olive, Sloping Double Collar, 1 Qt. . 450.00
Mineral Water, Napa Soda, Natural Mineral Water, Sapphire Blue, Cleaned, 7 5/8 In. 185.00
Mineral Water, Saratoga Spring, Star, Red Amber, Bubbles, 1 Qt. 155.00
Mineral Water, Saratoga, Pacific Congress Water Springs, Running Deer, Green, 7 In. ... 1760.00
Mineral Water, Smith & Kelly's Soda & Mineral Waters, Green, Iron Pontil 230.00
Mineral Water, Tahoe Soda Springs, Natural Mineral Water, Aqua, Tooled Lip, 7 In. 185.00
Mineral Water, Young's Natural, Napa Co., Cal., Blue Aqua, 6 1/2 In. 35.00
Miniature, Jug, Arkansas Corn Straight, Uncle Sam Distilling, Stoneware, 3 3/8 In. 120.00
Miniature, Jug, C.W. Butcher & Son, Neogesha, Kansas, Pottery, 3 1/8 In. 100.00
Miniature, Jug, Hoffman House, Blended Whiskey, Pottery, 2 7/8 In. 60.00
Nursing, H.G. Paris, Scroll Design With Logo, Clear, 3 In. 135.00
Nursing, St. Of David, Mo., Clear, 2 5/8 In. 55.00
Pepper Sauce, Cathedral, 4-Sided, Blue Aqua, Applied Top, Smooth Base 66.00
Pepper Sauce, Cathedral, 6-Sided, Aqua, Double Collar, 10 3/4 In. 165.00
Pepper Sauce, Cathedral, Blue Green, Double Collar, Open Pontil, 8 5/8 In. 230.00
Pepper Sauce, Cathedral, Green, 4-Sided 55.00
Pepper Sauce, L & B, Cathedral, Aqua, Double Collar, 9 1/8 In. 525.00
Perfume bottles are listed in their own category.
Pickle, Cathedral, Blue Aqua, Rolled Lip, Pontil, 8 7/8 In. 355.00
Pickle, Cathedral, Blue Green, 4 Panels, Iron Pontil, 13 5/8 In. 1850.00
Pickle, Cathedral, Emerald Green, 8 7/8 In. 467.00
Pickle, Cathedral, Green Aqua, Rolled Lip, 11 5/8 In. 175.00
Pickle, Cathedral, Green, Clock Faces, Arches, Shells, 11 1/8 In. 3920.00
Pickle, Cathedral, Ice Blue, Crosshatch On 3 Panels, 13 1/4 In. 1400.00
Pickle, Milwaukee Pickle Co., Wauwatosa, Wis., Amber, 1/2 Gal., 9 5/8 In. 145.00
Pickle, Sanborn Parker & Co., Boston, Amber, Conical, Ground Top, 8 In. 165.00
Pickle, Skilton Foote & Co.'s Trade Bunker Hill Pickles, Yellow Amber, 7 In. 78.00
Pickle, T.B. Smith & Co., Philada., Cathedral, Blue Aqua, Pontil, 9 1/4 In. 330.00
Pickle, T.B. Smith & Co., Philada., Cathedral, Blue Green, Panels, Square, 9 In. 1540.00
Pickle, W.D. Smith, N.Y., Cathedral, Light To Medium Teal, Open Pontil, 8 1/2 In. 660.00
Pickle, W.K. Lewis & Co., Cathedral, Green, Cylindrical, Iron Pontil, 10 3/4 In. 855.00
Poison, Ammonia, Poison, Caution, Not To Be Taken, Light Aqua, Knobs, Bee Hive, 6 In. 25.00
Poison, Embossed Not To Be Taken, Cobalt Blue, 5 3/4 In. 23.00
Poison, Embossed Poison, Not To Be Taken, Cobalt Blue, 6 1/2 In. 25.00

Poison, Embossed, Skull, Cobalt Blue, Tooled Mouth, 1880-1890, 3 3/8 In. 1980.00
Poison, Lattice & Diamond, Cobalt Blue, Poison Stopper, 4 3/4 In. 115.00
Poison, Lattice & Diamond, Cobalt, Poison Stopper, 5 5/8 In. 150.00
Poison, Little Giant, Sure Death To All Kinds Of Bugs, Aqua, Tooled Lip, 8 1/2 In. 40.00
Poison, Mercury Bichloride United Drug Company, Boston, Sapphire Blue, 8 In. 1210.00
Poison, Norwich Coffin, Amber, Tooled Lip, 1890, 5 In. 935.00
Poison, Not To Be Taken, Hastings, Worcester, Mass., Yellow Green, 6 1/2 In. 775.00
Poison, Wm. Radam's Microbe Killer Co., Jug, Stoneware, Handle, 11 In. 260.00
Sarsaparilla, Dr. Guysott's Compound Extract Of Yellow Dock, Emerald Green, 9 In. 5880.00
Sarsaparilla, Dr. Townsend's, Albany, N.Y., Dot On Base, Green, 7 In. 190.00
Sarsaparilla, Dr. Townsend's, The Blood Purifier, Aqua, 4-Sided, Embossed, 7 1/2 In. . . . 95.00
Sarsaparilla, John Bull Extract Of Sarsaparilla, Louisville, Aqua, BIMAL, 9 1/2 In. 35.00
Sarsaparilla, John Bull Extract Of Sarsaparilla, Louisville, Ky., Blue Aqua, 1860, 9 In. . . . 275.00
Sarsaparilla, Old Dr. J. Townsend's, N. Y., Green, Sloping Collar, Iron Pontil, 9 1/2 In. . . 700.00
Sarsaparilla, Old Dr. Jacob Townsend's, London, Blood Purifier, Aqua, 7 1/2 In. 65.00
Sarsaparilla, Old Dr. Jacob Townsend's, London, Green Aqua, 7 1/2 In. 85.00
Scent, Garden Scene With Figures, Gilt Metal Putti, 5 1/4 In. 980.00
Scent, Seahorse Design, Blue & White Stripes, 2 3/4 In. 175.00
Scent, Sterling Silver Overlay, England, 1912 . . . . 60.00
Scent, Sterling Silver Top, Birmingham, England 135.00
Scent, Sunburst, Cobalt Blue, Pontil, 1865, 3 1/4 In. 3410.00
Scent, Sunburst, Pink Amethyst, Pontil, 1870, 2 7/8 In. 1075.00
Scent, Swirled Right, Cobalt Blue, Pontil, 3 In. 175.00
Scent, Vertical Rib, Teal Green, Pontil, 3 In. 155.00
Seal, Daniel Visser & Zonen Scheidam, Dark Amber, Cobalt Shoulder Seal, 11 In. 415.00
Seal, Dyottville Glass Works, Phila, Olive Green, Amber Tone, 11 In. 415.00
Seal, Marken Schutz Gesetz V. Bolen 1876, 6-Sided, Olive Amber, 9 1/4 In. 415.00
Seal, Redges & Butler, Tobacco Amber, 3-Piece Mold, Pontil, 8 1/2 In. 255.00
Seltzer, American Bottling, Etched 18.00
Seltzer, New York Seltzer Water Co., Siphon, Turquoise, 11 In. 95.00
Seltzer, Shamrock Saloon, Pat Gallagher, Prop., Bodie, Cal., Pewter Top 1430.00
Seltzer, Siphon, Pilgrim, Blue, Etched Eagle, On Rock, Raised, Wings, c.1890, 12 In. . . . 150.00
Snuff, Agate, 2 Male Figures In Relief, Chinese 400.00
Snuff, Agate, Carp With Carved Fins, Glass Stopper, 3 In. 375.00
Snuff, Agate, Flowers, Chinese 460.00
Snuff, Agate, Horses & Monkeys, 1 1/2 x 6 1/2 In. 260.00
Snuff, Agate, Rotund Bearded Man, Red Cover, Oriental, 2 3/4 In. 230.00
Snuff, Agate, Shield Shape, Carved Foo Lion Mask, Ring Handles, Chinese 185.00
Snuff, Agate, Silver Cover, Boy On Ox 750.00
Snuff, Amber, Birds In Tree, Dragon Head, Faux Handles, Brass Stopper, 3 In. 250.00
Snuff, Baltic Amber, Coral Stopper, 18th Century, 2 1/2 In. 1150.00
Snuff, Bamboo, Carved Jadeite Stopper, 2 In. 196.00
Snuff, Carnelian, Heart Shape, Silver Mounted Jade Stopper 1035.00
Snuff, Carnelian, Insect & Flowering Branch, 19th Century, Chinese 805.00
Snuff, Chalcedony Agate, Flowers & Vine Design, No Stopper, 2 5/8 In. 105.00
Snuff, Coral, White, Raised Leaf & Vine, Melon Shape, Green Serpentine Top, 2 1/4 In. . . 300.00
Snuff, Enamel, Woman Musician, Mother & Child, 6 Floral Reserves, 2 1/2 In. 259.00
Snuff, Flattened Shape, Medallions, Figures, Famille Rose, Chinese Export 632.00
Snuff, Glass, Bird Perched On Rockery, Flowering Prunus Tree, White, Blue Overlay 115.00
Snuff, Glass, Black, Gray Striations, Simulated Coral Stopper, 20th Century, 2 In. 50.00
Snuff, Glass, Black, Iron Red Warrior Decoration, Chinese, 4 In. 160.00
Snuff, Glass, Boys On Raft, Amber, Purple Overlay, Tortoise & Metal Stopper, 1 In. 250.00
Snuff, Glass, Cameo, Lotus On 1 Face, Rose Quartz Stopper, Black Hair, 2 1/4 In. 805.00
Snuff, Glass, Carved Dragon, Wave, Ivory Stopper, Early 19th Century, 2 1/4 In. 978.00
Snuff, Glass, Carved Fish, Sea Green Design, Rose Quartz Stopper, 19th Century, 2 In. . . . 115.00
Snuff, Glass, Children Planting A Blossom Tree, Carved Foot, 20th Century, 3 1/4 In. 230.00
Snuff, Glass, Elephant, Carved, White, Brown Overlay, 2 Elephants, Metal Stopper 340.00
Snuff, Glass, Military Scene, Red Overlay, Green Jade & Brass Stopper, 1 1/2 In. 240.00
Snuff, Hardstone, Celadon, Carved, Leaves, Fruit, Asymmetrical, Blue Stopper, 3 In. 403.00
Snuff, Hornbill, 1 Side Figures, Birds, Calligraphy On Other, Chinese 1610.00
Snuff, Hornbill, Boys Among Lotus Flowers, Leafy Tree, Birds, Chinese 230.00
Snuff, Hornbill, Cicada Design, Chinese 2300.00
Snuff, Hornbill, Flattened Oval, Shaped Cartouches, Figural Design, Chinese 635.00

Snuff, Ivory, Cafe Au Lait Tone, Melon Shape, Chinese 160.00
Snuff, Ivory, Carp In The Water, 19th Century, 2 In. 489.00
Snuff, Ivory, Cicada Design, Chinese 460.00
Snuff, Ivory, En Grisaille, Figures, Mountain Landscape, Calligraphy, Japan 175.00
Snuff, Ivory, Exotic Fruit Design, Chinese 460.00
Snuff, Ivory, Figural Medallions, Bat & Cloud Design, Chinese 161.00
Snuff, Ivory, Leaping Carp, Frog, Lotus, Patina & Ivory Stopper, Stand, c.1800, 3 1/4 In. . . 850.00
Snuff, Ivory, Lozenge Shape, Figural, Flowers, Bird, Brocade Design 258.00
Snuff, Ivory, Man & Woman Figures Seated On Elephants, Late 19th Century, Pair 373.00
Snuff, Ivory, Shield Shape, Grisaille Riverscape, Calligraphy, Chinese 173.00
Snuff, Jade, Buddha's Hand, Green 200.00
Snuff, Jade, Double Fish, Brass & Red Porcelain Stopper, 4 1/4 x 2 In. 300.00
Snuff, Jade, Flattened Vase Shape, Ivory, Lapis Lazuli, Seed Pearl Cover, 3 In. 400.00
Snuff, Jade, Vase Form, Scroll Designs, Seed Pearl Lid, 3 1/2 In. 402.00
Snuff, Jade, White Crane Standing On Rock Under Pine Tree, Children At Play 1090.00
Snuff, Jade, White To Light Gray Tones, Russet, Pebble Form, Chinese 230.00
Snuff, Jade, White, 4 Mask Ring Handles, Rose Quartz Stopper, 2 1/4 In. 290.00
Snuff, Jade, White, Mountain Landscape Scene, Black, Coral Stopper, 2 1/8 In. 1840.00
Snuff, Jade, White, Yellow Inclusion, Green Stone Stopper, 19th Century, 2 1/4 In. 345.00
Snuff, Landscape Design, Green Stone Stopper, Early 20th Century, 2 5/8 In. 230.00
Snuff, Lavender, Green, 2 Glass Cicadas, Stopper, 20th Century, 2 In. 980.00
Snuff, Malachite, Carved Musician, Flowers, Stopper, Chinese, c.1950, 3 In. 316.00
Snuff, Moss Agate, Shield Form, Cafe Au Lait & Chocolate Inclusions 258.00
Snuff, Mother-Of-Pearl, European Subjects, Chinese 115.00
Snuff, Nephrite, Lotus Pond, Green Glass Cabochon, Brass Stopper, 1 x 3/4 x 2 1/4 In. . . . 260.00
Snuff, Onyx, Black, Pear Shape, Flowers, Calligraphy, Chinese 172.00
Snuff, Pa Hua Design, Carved Dragon, Stopper, 1800, 2 3/4 In. 1035.00
Snuff, Porcelain, Actor With A Boat Paddle, No Stopper, 19th Century, 3 In. 29.00
Snuff, Porcelain, Bats, Tortoises, Carp Scene, Chinese, 19th Century 460.00
Snuff, Porcelain, Butterfly, Flowers, Ceramic Stopper, 19th Century, 2 1/4 In. 69.00
Snuff, Porcelain, Celadon, Apple Green, Cabbage Design 160.00
Snuff, Porcelain, Celadon, Figural, Fruit & Butterfly Design, Angular, Chinese 230.00
Snuff, Porcelain, Celadon, Jade, Iris On 1 Side, No Stopper, 2 3/4 In. 115.00
Snuff, Porcelain, Children At Play, Blue, White 288.00
Snuff, Porcelain, Children, Blue Border, Red Glass Stopper, Marked, 1800s, 2 x 3/4 In. . . . 475.00
Snuff, Porcelain, Erotic Graphics, Yellow, Faux Gilt, Stopper, 1800s, 1 3/4 x 2 3/4 In. 575.00
Snuff, Porcelain, Famille Rose, Boat With Figures, Chinese 290.00
Snuff, Porcelain, Famille Rose, Johan Design, 19th Century, Chinese 402.00
Snuff, Porcelain, Famille Rose, Mountainous Riverscape Scene 115.00
Snuff, Porcelain, Ivory, Bird, Flowers, Stopper, Early 20th Century, 2 1/2 In. 127.00
Snuff, Porcelain, Raised Basketry Design, Handles, 2 In. 127.00
Snuff, Porcelain, Rounded Shoulder, Concave Foot, Coral Stopper, 19th Century, 3 In. . . . 200.00
Snuff, Red Coral Flowers, Stopper, 20th Century, 2 1/2 In. 635.00
Snuff, Red, Brown Glaze, Agate, Tiger's Eye Stopper, 1900, 1 1/2 In. 80.00
Snuff, Rock Crystal, Flattened Oval, Animal & Nut, Chinese 170.00
Snuff, Rose Quartz, Birds & Flowering Branches, Rose Quartz Stopper 145.00
Snuff, Ruby Cut To White, Scrolling Archaic Dragon, Tourmaline Glass Stopper 630.00
Snuff, Silver, Repousse Foo Lion Design, Stopper, Late 19th Century, 2 1/4 In. 290.00
Snuff, Smoky Quart, Square Shoulder, Carnelian Agate Stopper, 19th Century, 2 In. 259.00
Snuff, Tortoiseshell, Faceted, Calligraphy, Green Hardstone Knob Finial, 2 1/2 In. 518.00
Snuff, Wood, Carved Burl, Foo Dog Shoulders, No Cover, 2 1/8 In. 50.00
Soaky, Mummy, 1960s 90.00
Soaky, Wolfman, Blue Pants, 1960s . . . . .40.00 to 95.00
Soda, 7-Up, Salutes The Bicentennial, Green, Red, White, Blue Printing, 1976, 16 Oz. . . . 6.00
Soda, Barr's Soda, Hardwick Bottling Works, Hardwick, Vermont, 8 Oz. 9.00
Soda, Boonville Mineral Spring, N.Y., Amber, Tooled Mouth, Hutchinson, 7 In. 785.00
Soda, Brennan & Graham, Steubenville, Aqua, Applied Top, Iron Pontil, 7 1/4 In. 198.00
Soda, California Soda Works, Eagle, Light Blue, Hutchinson, 7 In. 55.00
Soda, Cherry Smash Syrup, Reverse Label, 12 In. 1045.00
Soda, Cherry Smash, 5 Cents, Reverse Glass Label, 12 In. 176.00
Soda, Crystal Soda Water Co., Patented Nov 12 1872, Ten Pin, Sapphire Blue, 1 Pt. 110.00
Soda, Dr. Brown's Root Beer, Stoneware, Salt Glaze, Cobalt Slip, 1855-1865, 9 1/4 In. . . . 245.00
Soda, Dr. Cronk Gibbons & Co., Superior Ale, Buffalo, N.Y., Emerald Green, 1860, 6 In. . . 440.00

Soda, E. Ottenville, Nashville, Tenn., Cobalt Blue, Hutchinson 295.00
Soda, Eureka California Soda Water Co., San Francisco, Aqua, Eagle, Whittled 55.00
Soda, Gnome 20.00
Soda, Graven-Hurst, Aqua, Hutchinson, Stopper Inside, c.1890 .... 85.00
Soda, Hagerty's Glass Works, Aqua, Blob Top, 1855-1865, 6 1/4 In. 50.00
Soda, Hugh P. McFadden Bottler, S. Bethlehem, Pa., Green Aqua, Hutchinson 59.00
Soda, Italian Soda Water Manufactory, San Francisco, Green, Iron Pontil, 7 1/8 In. 465.00
Soda, Kimball & Co., Cobalt Blue, Iron Pontil, 7 In. 200.00
Soda, Lancaster XXX Glassworks, Light Green, Blob Type, Iron Pontil, 6 5/8 In. 420.00
Soda, Luke Beard, Blue Green, Sloping Collar Mouth, Tenpin, Iron Pontil, 7 In. 505.00
Soda, Owen Casey, Eagle Soda Works, Cobalt Blue, Sloping Collar Mouth, 7 In. 145.00
Soda, Owen Casey, Eagle Soda Works, Sac City, Cobalt Blue, 7 1/4 In. 100.00
Soda, Pacific Congress Water, Saratoga, Ca., Running Deer, Aqua 125.00
Soda, Pink Poodle, White, Gray & Black, La Junta, Co. 95.00
Soda, Seymour & Co., Buffalo, N.Y., Cobalt Blue, Blob Type Mouth, Iron Pontil, 7 In. ... 420.00
Soda, Smith & Kelly's Soda & Mineral Waters, Green, Applied Top, Iron Pontil 230.00
Soda, Sun Crest, Blue Label, 8 1/2 In. 4.00
Soda, Taplin & Co., New Port, I.W., Codd, 9 In. 35.00
Soda, Taylor & Co., San Francisco, Eureka, Cobalt Blue, Iron Pontil, 7 3/8 In. 440.00
Soda, Taylor & Co., Valparaiso, Chili, Green, Iron Pontil, 7 1/4 In. 200.00
Soda, W.H. Burt, San Francisco, Green, Bubbles, Iron Pontil, 7 1/4 In. 190.00
Soda, Whistle, Blue & White, 8 In. 4.00
Soda Fountain, Syrup, Swirls, Plastic Pour Spout, Cork, Rickee Label, Hazel Atlas 20.00
Spirits, Opalescent Milk Glass, Flowers, Rectangular, Beveled, 1735, 5 In. 605.00
Target Ball, Bogardus, Amber, Patd. Apr. 10, 1877, 1 3/4 In. 385.00
Target Ball, C.T.H., Composite Pitch, Sept. 19, 1879, 1880, Round, 2 3/4 In. 415.00
Target Ball, Charlottenburger Glashutten, Yellow, Diamond, 1895, 2 5/8 In. ......745.00 to 800.00
Target Ball, Cobalt Blue, 3-Piece Mold, 1890, 2 5/8 In. 120.00
Target Ball, Copper Puce, Diamond, Sheared, 1890, 2 5/8 In. 165.00
Target Ball, Deep Purple, Man Shooting On Side, 2 5/8 In. 375.00
Target Ball, Ira Paine's, Pat. Oct. 23, 1877, Yellow Amber, 2 5/8 In. 240.00
Target Ball, L. Jones Gunmaker, Blackburn, Lancashire, Blue, Diamond, 2 5/8 In. 440.00
Target Ball, Moss Green, Man Shooting, Diamond, Sheared Mouth, 2 5/8 In. 420.00
Target Ball, N.B. Glass Works Perth, Sapphire Blue, Diamond, 2 5/8 In. 130.00
Target Ball, N.B. Glass Works, Perth, Blue Aqua, Inside Feathers, 1 5/8 In. 165.00
Target Ball, Purple Amethyst, 3-Piece Mold, Sheared Mouth, 1890, 2 5/8 In. 275.00
Target Ball, Purple Amethyst, Man Shooting, Diamond, Sheared Mouth, 2 In. 395.00
Target Ball, Sapphire Blue, Small Square Pattern, 1890, 2 5/8 In. 275.00
Target Ball, Tobacco Amber, 7 Horizontal Rings, 1890, 2 5/8 In. 305.00
Target Ball, Van Cutsem, A St. Quentin, Cobalt Blue, Diamond, 2 5/8 In. ....95.00 to 120.00
Target Ball, W.W. Greener's St. Mary's Works, Cobalt Blue, Diamond, 2 5/8 In. 255.00
Target Ball, Yellow Amber, Dot Design, Horizontal Lines, 3-Piece Mold, 2 In. 1370.00
Tonic, Rohrer's Expoctoral Wild Cherry, Lancaster, Pa., Amber, Iron Pontil, 10 1/2 In. ... 355.00
Tonic, Warner's Safe, Rochester, N.Y., A. & D.H.C., Amber, 7 1/2 In. 870.00
Vinegar, Pacific & Pickle Vinegar Works, San Francisco, Amethyst, 11 In. 130.00
Water, Emerald Green, Embossed Waterfall, Original Cap, 1931 .... 85.00
Whiskey, A.K. Clark, Denver, Col., 1 Qt. 1200.00
Whiskey, A.P. Hotaling's Private Stock Bourbon, Amber, 12 In. 2970.00
Whiskey, Amber, Bell Shape, Applied Mouth & Handle, 1870, 8 1/2 In. 360.00
Whiskey, Amber, Conical, Swirled Vertical To Right, Applied Handle, c.1860, 8 In. 358.00
Whiskey, B.M. & E.A. Whitlock & Co., New York, Barrel, Aqua, 8 In. 825.00
Whiskey, Booth & Co., Sacramento, Embossed Anchor, Light Amethyst, Tooled Top 300.00
Whiskey, Buchanan's Extract Of Sugar Corn, Cannon, Amber, 8 3/4 In. 1850.00
Whiskey, C.A. Richards & Co., 99 Washington Street, Boston, Blue Aqua, 1 Pt. 75.00
Whiskey, Casper's, Made By Honest North Carolina People, Cobalt Blue, 12 In. 525.00
Whiskey, Casper's, Made By Honest North Carolina People, Cobalt Blue, 1900, 11 In. ... 605.00
Whiskey, Chesnut Grove Whiskey, C.W., Red Variant, Handle, Pontil 210.00
Whiskey, Chesnut Grove, C. Wharton, Amber, Seal, Vertical Ribs, Double Collar, 9 In. ... 1065.00
Whiskey, Chicken Cock, Pure Rye Whiskey, Embossed, Tin Cap, 7 1/2 x 4 1/2 In. 20.00
Whiskey, Coronation Scot, Duncan MacAlpine Scotch Whiskey, Jug, Pottery, 7 In. 100.00
Whiskey, Cream Of Highland Whiskies, My Queen, Jubilee Blend, Jug, Pottery, 7 In. ... 230.00
Whiskey, Cream Of Old Scotch Whiskey, Bonnie Castle, Jug, Pottery, Transfer, 8 3/4 In. . 95.00
Whiskey, Croff & Collins Wines & Liquors, Denver & Salida, Coffin, 1 Qt. .....900.00 to 1400.00

Whiskey, Dewar's Perth Whisky, Jug, Pottery, Brown, 9 3/4 In. 210.00
Whiskey, Dewar's Scotch Whisky, Jug, Pottery, Tan, 2-Sided Transfer, 6 1/4 In. 330.00
Whiskey, Duffy Malt Whiskey, Amber, 10 1/4 In. 9.00
Whiskey, Duffy Malt Whiskey, Olive Amber, 10 1/4 In. 15.00
Whiskey, E.G. Booz's Old Cabin, Cabin, Amber, Chamfered Corners, 1 Qt. 3080.00
Whiskey, E.G. Booz's Old Cabin, Cabin, Amber, Sloping Collar, 7 3/4 In. 4255.00
Whiskey, Galway Bay Export Old Irish Whiskey, Jug, Pottery, Black Transfer, 6 7/8 In. . . .   360.00
Whiskey, Glen Garry Old Highland Whisky, Jug 49.00
Whiskey, Golden Wedding Rye, Amber, Embossed, Paper Label, Metal Cap, 4 1/2 In. 8.00
Whiskey, Gottschalk Co., Baltimore, Md., Jug, Pottery, Cream, Black Transfer, 7 3/8 In. . .   685.00
Whiskey, J.F. Cutter, Extra Trademark Old Bourbon, Star, Shield, Green, 11 3/4 In. 1870.00
Whiskey, J.H. Cutter, Old Bourbon, Crown, Amber, 11 3/4 In. 1155.00
Whiskey, Jesse Moore & Co., Louisville, Gold Amber, Embossed Antlers, Top, 6 In. 210.00
Whiskey, Jesse Moore & Co., Louisville, Ky., Red, Amber Tone, 11 3/4 In. 550.00
Whiskey, John Dewer & Sons, Perth, N.B., Jug, Robert Burns, Countryside Scenes, 6 In. .   120.00
Whiskey, John Hudspeth, Merchants Bar, Flask, El Reno, O.T., Strap Side, 1/2 Pt., 6 In. . .   330.00
Whiskey, Jug, Deep Purple Amethyst, Sloping Collar, Iron Pontil, 6 1/4 In. 475.00
Whiskey, Kentucky Nectar, Label, Applied Top, Fifth 80.00
Whiskey, Klein Bros. & Hyamnn, Jug, Pottery, White, Green Transfer, 7 3/8 In. 230.00
Whiskey, Lancaster Glass Works, Lancaster, N.Y., Barrel, Yellow Olive Green, 9 1/2 In. . .   1175.00
Whiskey, Landsberg's Pure Blackberry Brandy, A. Heller & Bro., N.Y., Aqua, 11 In. 4510.00
Whiskey, Miller's Extra, E. Martin & Co., Old Bourbon Gold, Applied Top, 1 Pt. 1045.00
Whiskey, Mohawk, Pure Rye, Figural, Indian Queen, Gold Amber, Rolled Ip, 12 In. 2630.00
Whiskey, Monk's Old Bourbon, Medicinal Purposes, Yellow Olive, Iron Pontil, 8 In. 1735.00
Whiskey, My Queen, Royal Blend Whisky, Pottery, Jug, Cream, Black Transfer, 9 In. 635.00
Whiskey, Night Cap, Milk Glass, Sleeping Man's Face, Painted, Metal Screw Cap, 4 In. . . .   180.00
Whiskey, Old Gilt Edge, Wichman, Lutgen, San Francisco, Amber, 12 In. 1595.00
Whiskey, Old Man, With Robe, Figural, Here's The Poison, Bisque, Germany, 8 7/8 In. . . .   355.00
Whiskey, Phoenix Bourbon Nabor Alfs & Brune, San Francisco, Amber, Bird, 11 3/4 In. . .   185.00
Whiskey, Pig, Corn Cob In Mouth, c.1890, 6 1/4 In. 522.00
Whiskey, Pure Cognac, Amber, Seal, Handle, Pontil, 8 7/8 In. 855.00
Whiskey, R.B. Cutter Pure Bourbon, Cherry Puce, Jug, Handle, Pontil, 8 1/2 In. 495.00
Whiskey, R.B. Cutter, Louisville, Ky., Gold Yellow, Jug, Handle, 8 5/8 In. 800.00
Whiskey, Ramsay's Trade Mark Superior Scotch Malt Whisky, Jug, Pottery, 7 1/4 In. 75.00
Whiskey, Rob Roy Old Highland, Jug, Pottery, Cream, Black Transfer, 6 7/8 In. 176.00
Whiskey, Rosslyn Distillery Old Scotch Malt, Jug, Pottery, Transfer, 7 1/4 In. 165.00
Whiskey, S.B. Rothenberg & Co., Old Judge Kentucky Bourbon, Amber, 11 1/4 In. 230.00
Whiskey, Scotch Whisky Long John's Celebrated Dew Of Ben-Nevis, Jug, Pottery, 7 In. . .   230.00
Whiskey, Scotch, Vieux Paris, Floral Bouquets, Gilt Palmettes, 11 In., Pair 228.00
Whiskey, Shillaly Irish Blend Whisky, Jug, Pottery, Brown, Transfer, 7 1/4 In. 110.00
Whiskey, Special Highland Whisky Greenlees Brothers, Jug, Pottery, 7 1/8 In. 2310.00
Whiskey, Special Old Irish Whisky, Jug, Raised Letters, Design, Doulton, Lambeth, 7 In. . .   305.00
Whiskey, Udolpho Wolfe's Schiedam, Aromatic Schnapps, Olive Green, Label, 8 1/8 In. . . .   180.00
Whiskey, Voldner's Aromatic Schnapps Schiedam, Olive Amber, Pontil, 9 7/8 In. 165.00
Whiskey, Vonthofen's Aromatic Scheidam Schnapps, Green, Iron Pontil, 8 1/8 In. 185.00
Whiskey, W.C. Peacock & Co., Honolulu, Wine & Liquor Merchants, Red Amber, 11 In. .   415.00
Whiskey, West India Bay Rum, Imported, Tin Screw Cap, North Shore Dist., 9 In. 12.00
Whiskey, Wharton's, 1850, Chestnut Grove, Flask, Teardrop, Amber, Bubbles, 5 1/4 In. . .   200.00
Whiskey, Wharton's, 1850, Chestnut Grove, Whitney Glass Works, Amber, 10 In. 935.00
Wine, H.J. Woolacott Pure Wines, Los Angeles, Ca., Amber, 11 3/4 In. 176.00
Wine, Olive Green, Applied String Top, Open Pontil, 11 In. 176.00
Wine, Poire Williams, Amber, Seal Label, 19 x 13 In. 225.00
Zanesville, 24 Ribs, Swirled Left, Amber, Globular, 8 1/2 In. 495.00

BOTTLE CAPS for milk bottles are the printed cardboard caps used during the past 85 years. Unusual mottoes, graphics, and caps from dairies that are out of business bring the highest prices.

Abbeville Pasteurizing Plant, Abbeville, South Carolina, Plug Type 1.50
Hires Root Beer, Orange, White Lettering 8.00
Indian Valley Creamery, Pull Tab 3.00
Lumber Company, Breckenridge, Minnesota, See Irv Or Doug, Yellow, Plastic, 2 In. 5.00
Pearman's Dairy, Anderson, South Carolina, Plug Type 1.50
Round Oak Stove Co., Cap Lifter, Metal, 4 In. 35.00

Saint Bernard, Cork, Carved Wood, 3 1/2 In. 35.00
Silver Leaf Dairy, Greer, South Carolina 2.50
Table Cream, Pull Tab 3.00
Willkie-Bricker, Miami County, 1 3/4 In. 13.00

BOTTLE OPENERS are needed to open many bottles. As soon as the commercial bottle was invented, the opener to be used with the new types of closures became a necessity. Many types of bottle openers can be found, most dating from the twentieth century. Collectors prize advertising and comic openers.

Alligator, Black Boy, Cast Iron, 2 3/4 In. 145.00
Black Face, Cast Iron, 1940s, 4 1/4 x 3 1/2 In. ....125.00 to 155.00
Boot, Corkscrew, Inside, Sterling Silver, 4 In. 175.00
Calvert Gin, Bottle Shape 10.50
Chief Oshkosh, Special Old Lager, c.1910 .... 19.00
Clown's Head, Cast Iron, 4 1/4 x 3 3/4 In. 97.00
Cowboy With Guitar, Cast Iron, 4 3/4 In. 95.00
Dog, Black, Metal, Scott Products, 4 x 5 In. 85.00
Dog, Brown, Scott Products, 3 x 6 1/2 In. 85.00
Elephant, Gray, Cast Iron, 3 1/2 In. 58.00
Elephant, On Ashtray, Cast Iron, 3 In. 40.00
Fish, Aluminum, 7 1/4 In. ....*Illus* 18.00
Fish, Rainbow Trout, Metal, Scott Products, 4 1/2 x 2 In. 95.00
Fish, Trout, Metal, Scott Products, 5 x 2 In. 95.00
Four Eyes Man, Cast Iron, 1940s, 3 3/4 In. ....65.00 to 125.00
Fox, Metal, Scott Products, 3 x 5 In. 110.00
Goose, Metal, Scott Products, 5 1/2 x 4 1/4 In. 85.00
Horse, Hindquarters, Cast Iron, 5 1/4 In. 47.00
Horse Head, Aluminum, Brass Tone 45.00
Horse Head, Black Mane, White Streak Down Face, Rubal, 1960s, 4 1/2 In. 110.00
Jack's, Steel, Duff Norton, Pittsburgh, 4 3/4 In. 11.00
Lady's Leg, Big Boys Saloon, Royalton, Ill., Skate Key, Nickel Over Steel, 3 In. 85.00
Lobster, Red & Black, Cast Iron, 3 1/2 In. 36.00
Mallard Duck, Green Head, Yellow Bill, Red Breast, Scott Products, 5 3/4 In. .....75.00 to 110.00
Mallard Duck, Metal, 2 1/4 x 5 1/2 In. 75.00
Owl, Painted, Scott Products, 3 7/8 In. ....*Illus* 20.00
Paddy The Pledgemaster, Blue Shirt, Phi Kappa Psi On Paddle, 4 In. 225.00
Parrot, On Stand, Cast Iron, 5 1/4 In. 95.00
Pelican, On Ashtray, Orange Beak & Feet, Cast Iron, 3 1/4 In. 75.00
Pelican, On Ashtray, Orange Beak & Feet, Cast Iron, 4 3/4 In. 175.00
Pelican, White, Red, Black, Yellow Beak, Cast Iron, 3 1/2 In. 121.00
Pretzel, Brown, White Dots, Cast Iron, 3 1/2 In. 88.00
Ram's Head, Chromium Alloy, 4 1/4 In. 95.00
Rooster, Orange, Yellow, Brown & Black, Cast Iron, 3 1/4 In. 75.00
Rooster, Red, Yellow & Black, Cast Iron, 3 1/4 In. 85.00
Sea Horse, On Ashtray, Green & White, Cast Iron, 4 3/4 In. 165.00
Seal, End Of Tail Pries, Twist In Belly Opener, German, 5 1/4 In. 75.00
Signpost Drunk, Black Tuxedo, Plymouth, Mass. On Post, 4 1/4 In. 20.00
Squirrel, Gray & White, Cast Iron, 3 In. 125.00

Bottle Opener,
Owl, Painted, Scott
Products, 3 7/8 In.

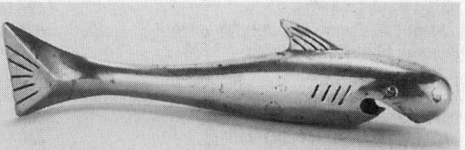

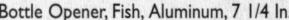

Bottle Opener, Fish, Aluminum, 7 1/4 In.

BOW is an English porcelain works started in 1744 in East London. Bow made decorated porcelains, often copies of Chinese blue and white patterns. The factory stopped working about 1776. Most items sold as Bow today were made after 1750.

Figurine, Allegorical, Four Seasons, Spring & Winter, Summer & Autumn, 9 In., Pair	2700.00
Figurine, Bunting, Perched On Tree Stump, Flowers, Leaf Scene, 1765, 3 3/4 In.	6600.00

BOXES of all kinds are collected. They were made of thin strips of inlaid wood, metal, tortoiseshell, embroidery, or other material. Additional boxes may be listed in other sections, such as Advertising, Battersea, Ivory, Shaker, Tinware, and various Porcelain categories. Tea Caddies are listed in their own category.

Ballot, Rosewood, Grain Paint, Two Compartments, 12 In.	1080.00
Ballot, Walnut, Early 19th Century, 13 In.	125.00
Band, Blue, White, Green Wallpaper, Flowers, Hannah Davis, c.1837, 14 x 19 x 14 In.	2070.00
Band, Wallpaper Covered, 3 State Buildings, Fox Hunt Scene, Yellow, c.1820, 18 In.	2200.00
Band, Wallpaper Covered, Blue, Orange Top, 1884 Lancaster Newspaper Lined, 10 In.	2200.00
Band, Wallpaper Covered, Brown, Gold, Green Flowers, American, 19th Century, 8 In. ..	1495.00
Band, Wallpaper Covered, Dome Top, 11 In.	865.00
Band, Wallpaper Covered, John F. Long, August 5, 1846, Round, 2 x 1 3/4 In.	4675.00
Band, Wallpaper Covered, Landscape Scene, Center Classical Building, 11 1/4 In.	1610.00
Band, Wallpaper Covered, Sepia Firemen, Pumper Rushing To House Fire, 15 x 22 In. ...	10450.00
Band, Wallpaper Covered, Tumbling Pattern, White, Brown, 19th Century, 9 x 12 In.	715.00
Band, Wallpaper Covered, Wood, Flowers, Lined With 1845 Newspaper, 10 In.	455.00
Band, Wallpaper Covered, Yellow & Black Flowers, Burgundy Ground, Oval, Small	3575.00
Band, Walnut, Rectangular Top, 1 Drawer, Stand, Square Legs, Georgian, 13 x 10 In.	575.00
Bible, Candle, Oak, Stylized Leaf & Stipple, Charles II, 29 x 17 x 10 In.	690.00
Bible, Hinged Lid, Fitted, Square, Scratch Initials, 17th Century, 23 x 10 x 17 In.	375.00
Bible, Oak, Fluted Carving, Slant Lid, England, c.1680, 8 1/2 x 19 In.	330.00
Bible, Oak, Hinged Slope, Carved Lunettes Base, 9 3/4 x 25 3/4 In.	920.00
Bible, Oak, Sloping, Leaf Frieze, Charles I, 23 x 9 x 19 In.	750.00
Bible, Oak, Wrought Iron Butterflies, Hasp, William & Mary, 11 x 24 In.	880.00
Bible, Pale Blue, Turned Black Feet, 22 In.	40250.00
Bible, Slide Cover, Panel Lid, Flowers, Inscribed Ana Maria M, c.1900, 6 x 14 In.	3850.00
Bible, Walnut, Rope Carved Cover, Flowering Vines, Leaves & Shells, 14 x 10 x 7 In. ...	330.00
Black Forest, Hinged Cover, Animals Around Tree Trunk, 1875, 9 x 13 x 7 In.	1000.00
Book, Wooden, Leather Cover, Gilt, Strap, Divina Commedia Title, 8 5/8 x 12 3/4 In.	220.00
Brass, Hinged Cover, Tavern Scenes & Scenes Of Daily Life, Continental, 12 x 18 In. ...	85.00
Bride's, Bentwood, Laced Seams, Flowers At Base, 12 1/4 x 18 3/4 In.	797.00
Bride's, Bentwood, Tulips At Sides, Rose On Lid, 12 x 7 3/8 In.	550.00
Bride's, Laced Seams, Courting Couple, Tulips On Side, 6 3/8 x 18 In.	1100.00
Bride's, White Pine, Landscape Scene On Top, Red Field, 5 x 18 1/2 In.	564.00
Burl, Ashwood, Divided Interior, Inlay, Northern Europe, c.1860, 10 1/4 x 6 x 13 In.	748.00
Burl, Fitted, On Stand, To E.J.W. Houchton, From Keele College, c.1890, 31 x 17 In.	1045.00
Candle, Beveled Slide Lid, Old Green Paint, White Pine, 19th Century, 5 x 6 In.	140.00
Candle, Oak, Carved, Reconstructed, 15 In.	60.00
Candle, Oak, Inlays In Sycamore, Boxwood & Mahogany, North Wales, c.1840, 18 In. ...	2400.00
Candle, Pine, Brown, Flowering Tulip, Stars, Buds, Rarkus Anna, 1869, 13 x 9 x 6 In. ...	935.00
Candle, Pine, Mustard Paint, New England, 10 In.	325.00
Candle, Pine, Red Paint, Black, Yellow-Striped Base, Yellow Interior, 12 x 4 In.	546.00
Candle, Poplar, Stenciled, Slide Lid, Lollipop Handle, Lock, Key, 20 x 7 1/2 x 6 3/8 In. ..	990.00
Candle, Salmon Paint, Flower Design On Sides, Slide Lid, 3 1/4 x 9 x 7 1/4 In.	302.00
Candle, Slide Lid, Swan & Stamp Border, Cream Ground, 13 1/2 x 8 1/4 x 3 In.	1265.00
Candle, Wall, Blue Paint, Black Trim, 7 1/4 x 13 x 4 1/2 In.	7475.00
Candle, Wall, Mahogany, Scalloped Back, Slant Lid, Drawer, c.1790, 11 x 16 In.	605.00
Candle, Wall, Mahogany, Star, Flower, Diamond, Fluted Slide Cover, c.1780, 21 x 11 In. .	358.00
Candle, Walnut, 2 Divided Interior Compartments, 18th Century, 18 1/2 In.	862.00
Candle, Walnut, Slide Lid, 17 1/2 In.	316.00
Cigar, Walnut, Slide-Out Trays, Carved Fish & Game, 1885, 11 x 7 x 8 In.	1008.00
Cigarette, Allover Leaves, White, Light Green Cloisonne, Enamel, Gilt, 3 3/4 In.	230.00
Cigarette, Green, Bakelite, Brass Trim, 3 x 1 In.	150.00
Circular, Ivory, Silver Pineapple Finial, Medium Patina, Arts & Crafts, 6 x 9 In.	562.00
Coffer, Chased, Tacked Decoration, Polychrome, Armorial, 17th Century, 27 x 44 In. ...	1430.00

Coffer, Mahogany, Brass Mounted, Porcelain Plaque, Hinged Cover, 3 1/2 x 9 x 8 In. 635.00
Coffer, Pollard Oak, Tooled Leather, Hinged Cover, Brass, George IV, 18 3/4 x 19 x 16 In.   290.00
Coffer, Satinwood, Sarcophagus Shape, Faceted Studs, Continental, 9 x 22 x 13 1/2 In. ... 1265.00
Cutlery, Floral Swags, Compartment Interior, 20th Century, 24 1/2 x 11 In. 2645.00
Cutlery, Oak, Central Handle, England, 19th Century, 11 1/2 x 6 1/4 In. 145.00
Cutlery, Softwood, Heart Cutout, 1 Drawer, Orange Paint, 13 x 8 1/2 In. 250.00
Cutlery, Sponge Design, Red, Black & Ocher 4950.00
Cutlery, Wooden, Old Yellow Paint, 5 1/2 x 10 1/2 x 9 1/2 In. 230.00
Desk, Leather Hinged Cover, Green, Dark Orange, Early 19th Century, 5 x 10 In. 1840.00
Desk, Mahogany, Reeded Ivory Finial, Banded Sides, 1780s, 5 3/4 x 6 1/2 In. 690.00
Desk, Silver Mounted, Cut, Etched Glass, Locking Cover, Continental, 4 1/2 x 5 x 4 In. .. 290.00
Desk, Slide Lid, Rows Of Porcupine Quills, Ebony With Ivory Inlay, 2 x 7 In. 145.00
Desk, Tortoiseshell, Flying Crane On Hinged Lid, 3 1/2 x 12 In. 530.00
Document, Bird's-Eye Maple, Brass Mounted, Ebonized Acorn Escutcheon, Ball Feet, 14 x 9 In. .   300.00
Document, Brass, Rosewood, 10 1/2 x 17 1/4 x 11 In. 195.00
Document, Burl Elm, Banded Lid, Storage Compartment, Edwardian, 7 x 11 x 7 In. 230.00
Document, Carved Hex Symbol Cover, Paint Traces, Hasp Lock, 16 x 10 1/2 x 7 1/2 In. .. 195.00
Document, Carved Walnut, 1 Drawer, Applied Scroll Handle To Center, 5 x 14 x 10 In. .. 255.00
Document, Cock-Beaded Glazed Door, 4 Glass Panels, Blue Paper Interior, 30 x 3 In. ... 2185.00
Document, Dome Top, Pine, Blue, Green Paint, 19th Century, 6 x 10 x 10 In. 14400.00
Document, Eagle, Black, Gold Stencil, Copper Flowers, 19th Century, 9 x 5 1/2 x 4 In. .. 575.00
Document, Flowers, Blue Base, 5 3/4 x 10 1/4 x 5 1/2 In. 110.00
Document, Grain Paint, Mid 19th Century, 5 1/2 x 14 x 8 1/2 In. 385.00
Document, Hinged Cover, 1 Drawer, Va., 1750, 14 x 18 x 9 In. 1400.00
Document, Mahogany, Brass Inlay, Recessed Handles, Fitted Interior, 10 x 19 x 12 In. ... 490.00
Document, Medallion Enclosing Pavilion Amid Pine Trees, 15 x 12 In. 3105.00
Document, Oak, Satinwood Inlay, Lift-Off Pediment, Door, Sections, Regency, c.1820 ... 2500.00
Document, Ogee-Molded Cover, Bone Eagle, Crossbanded Border, 12 1/4 In. 2415.00
Document, Painted, Flowers, Urn, Swags, Dome Top, Lock, 10 1/2 x 7 1/2 x 4 5/8 In. ... 220.00
Document, Pine, Dome Top, Smoke Decorated, Lock, 10 x 20 In. 230.00
Document, Polychrome Design, Dome Top, Hinged Lid, Eagle Pull, c.1820, 6 x 16 In. ... 1800.00
Document, Poplar, Stenciled Gold Design On Lid, Brass Lock, 1910, 19 x 8 1/2 In. 880.00
Document, Red Rose, Ivory Ground, Wallpaper Interior, 1848, 7 x 14 In. 5750.00
Document, Tin, Dome Top, Painted, Red, Green, Cream Flowers, 7 1/2 x 13 x 8 1/2 In. .. 460.00
Dome Top, Bird, Flowers, Red, Green, Orange, Dark Blue Ground, 7 3/4 In. 805.00
Dome Top, Flowers, Leaves, Blue, Red, Mustard Paint, 7 1/4 x 7 7/8 x 12 In. 2990.00
Dome Top, Hide Covered, Brass Tacks, Initials, 19th Century, 12 x 27 In. 165.00
Dome Top, Hinged Cover, Brown Painted Interior, Brass Swing Handle, 7 x 15 In. 920.00
Dome Top, Horsehair, Brass Tack Decoration, Initials, Early 19th Century, 14 x 24 In. ... 55.00
Dome Top, Lift, Romantic Couple With Trees & Hills In Distance, 7 7/8 x 7 1/4 x 13 In. . 1035.00
Dome Top, Oak, Dovetailed, Strap Hinge, Dated 1830 .... 300.00
Dome Top, Painted Birds, Tulips & Basket Of Flowers, 19th Century, 14 x 25 In. 1760.00
Dome Top, Painted, Flowers, Horse Heads, Vine, New England, 1880s, 7 1/2 x 16 In. 4180.00
Dome Top, Pine, Painted, Blue, Yellow, Tulips, Leaves, Bail Handle, 8 1/2 x 4 x 4 5/8 In. . 303.00
Dome Top, Rosewood Decoration, Pinstripe & Leaf, Maine, 21 x 11 x 8 1/2 In. 575.00
Dome Top, Stylized Fan Design, Yellow, Red, Black Ground, 12 x 23 1/2 In. 6325.00
Dresser, Basket Of Flowers On Lid, Lovebirds, Strawberry Plants, c.1815, 10 1/4 In. 2310.00
Dresser, Bent Whalebone Sides & Lid Rim, Pine Bottom, Oval, 3 5/8 x 7 In. 3080.00
Dresser, Bird's-Eye Maple, Classical Decoration, Mass., c.1810, 5 x 14 1/2 x 8 In. 3190.00
Dresser, Blue Flower Interior, Bird, Flower Exterior, 5 1/2 In. 405.00
Dresser, Brass, Porcelain Plaque, Head Of Maiden, Cover, Round, 2 1/2 In. 63.00
Dresser, Cover, Circular, Gilt Garlands, Enamel, Portrait Of Female, France, 3 In. 316.00
Dresser, Enamel, Venus At Her Toilette, Vermeil Interior, 1900, 3 1/2 In. 1150.00
Dresser, Green Striated Marble, Canted Corners, Green Lined Interior, 3 3/4 x 2 3/4 In. .. 316.00
Dresser, Hinged Cover, Woman Painted On Top, Blue, Pink Landscape, Circular, 2 1/4 In. . 633.00
Dresser, Mahogany, Spread-Winged Eagle, Banner In Beak, Herringbone Border, 10 In. .. 220.00
Dresser, Mother-Of-Pearl Inlay, Gilt, Papier-Mache, 4 x 7 1/2 x 3 1/2 In. 374.00
Dresser, Pine, Dome Top, Painted, Stenciled, Bracket-Shape Feet, 5 3/8 x 8 x 4 In. 575.00
Dresser, Rosewood Veneer, Mirror, Drawer, Fitted, Jars, 8 3/8 x 7 5/8 x 5 x 3/4 In. 880.00
Dresser, Rosewood, Maroon Velvet Lid Lining, William IV, 5 3/4 x 11 1/2 x 5 3/4 In. 605.00
Game, Hinged Lid, Black Lacquer, Serpentine, Gilt, Fitted, Chinese, 1840 .... 4500.00
Glove, Ebony, Brass Rocaille Cartouche, Tortoise, France, Mid 19th Century, 10 In. 259.00
Glove, Red, Green Poinsettias, Pyrography, 10 x 3 1/2 In. 38.00

Grain Painted, Gilt, Pincushion, Mirror Inside, Stencil, Hinged Cover, 1800s, 2 x 3 In. ... 690.00
Grain Painted, Octagonal, Divided, Top, Morning Glories, Roses, c.1830, 15 1/2 x 6 In. . 650.00
Handkerchief, Leather, Painted Wreath Design, Satin Interior, Snap Closure, c.1940, 6 In. 22.00
Hat, Bentwood, Pine, Old Finish, Steel Nails, Wooden Pegs, Cover, 14 1/4 x 11 x 10 In. ... 193.00
Hat, Bentwood, Red Paint, Figures Riding Dragon, Oriental, 14 1/2 x 11 1/4 In. 165.00
Hat, Leather Trim & Strap Handle, Tag, Vuitton Logo, 1950s, 11 x 8 In. 288.00
Hat, Tin, Oval, Marked, Dr. J.W. Hammond, 14 x 17 In. 345.00
Hinged Cover, Lacquer, 6 Gilt Cartouches Segments, Ball Finial, Chinese, 1820, 6 In. 375.00
Hinged Cover, Lacquer, Handles, Chinese, 1820, 13 x 13 x 9 1/2 In. 375.00
Ivory, Dragon, Cloud Carving, Cylindrical, Chinese, Late 19th Century, 3 1/4 In. 260.00
Jewelry, Armorial, Porcelain, Paris, 1 1/4 x 5 1/2 x 3 1/2 In. 230.00
Jewelry, Bicolored Stringing, Rays Of Exotic Woods, 5 3/4 x 11 1/8 In. 630.00
Jewelry, Black Lacquer, Mother-Of-Pearl, Brass, 3 Drawers, Cover, Asian, 14 x 10 In. ... 69.00
Jewelry, Brass Mounted, Enamel, Cupid, Landscape Scenes, France, 8 In. 1725.00
Jewelry, Brass Mounted, Porcelain, Gold Geometric, Pink Ground, Napoleon III, 9 In. ... 980.00
Jewelry, Brass, Enamel, France, 19th Century, 2 1/2 x 6 3/4 x 5 1/2 In. 220.00
Jewelry, Building Shape, Reverse Painted, Wooden, c.1800, 19 x 15 In. 2300.00
Jewelry, Carved Walnut, Bevel-Edged Mirror, Velvet Lined Interior Drawers, 13 In. 1265.00
Jewelry, Casket, Inlay, Stars, Diamonds, Crackle Varnish, 19th Century, 10 x 7 x 5 In. ... 175.00
Jewelry, Cast Iron, Claw Foot, Reclining Whippet Handle, 7 x 7 x 4 1/2 In. 896.00
Jewelry, Cover, Black Forest, Carved Birds, 12 x 14 x 9 In. 2968.00
Jewelry, Dome Top, Classical Scrolls, Bronze, Gilt, France, 2 1/4 In. 575.00
Jewelry, Ebonized, Porcelain, Cherubs, Hinged Cover, 1880s, 9 1/2 x 13 x 10 In. 1725.00
Jewelry, Ivory, Bone, Lock & Key, Belle Epoque Period, 7 1/2 x 26 1/4 x 18 1/2 In. 690.00
Jewelry, Ivory, Dome Top, Serpentine Sides, Ball Feet, 1900, 2 x 5 3/4 x 4 In. 460.00
Jewelry, Leather, Silver Mounted, Relief Woman In Medieval Dress, Pearls, Jewels, 5 In. . 345.00
Jewelry, Mahogany, Inlaid, Exotic Woods, Hinged Cover, 1850s, 7 x 12 x 8 In. 460.00
Jewelry, Maple, Roll-Top Desk Shape, Tambour Cover, 2 Swivel Drawers, 9 x 5 x 7 In. .. 440.00
Jewelry, Mother-Of-Pearl & Ivory, Canted Lid, Bun Feet, 2 x 6 In. 290.00
Jewelry, Mother-Of-Pearl, Silver, Leaf Escutcheon, William IV, 1 1/4 x 6 x 3 In. 315.00
Jewelry, Original Green, Brown Patina, 2 Seahorses On Top, E.T. Hurley, 2 x 5 In. 865.00
Jewelry, Piano Form, Mythological Figures, 1700s Nobles, Neoclassical, 6 x 13 x 5 In. ... 460.00
Jewelry, Piano Form, Mythological Figures, Gilt Metal Legs, 6 x 13 In. 460.00
Jewelry, Satinwood, Harp Shape, Inlay, Regency, 12 In. 1750.00
Jewelry, Tortoiseshell, Diamond-Quilted, Ivory Ball Feet, 1900, 1 x 6 x 3 1/4 In. 635.00
Jewelry, Tortoiseshell, Dome Top, Hinged Lid, Ivory Lined Interior, William IV, 2 x 4 In. . 489.00
Jewelry, Walnut, Parquetry, Vaulted, Geometric Patterns, Metal, Ottoman, 13 x 7 In. 127.00
Jewelry, Woman Feeding Her Child, Late 19th Century, 6 1/4 In. 160.00
Keeper's, Pine, Paint, Horse Painted On Lid 850.00
Knife, Mahogany, Carved, Hinged Lid, Cutlery Shelf, Federal, c.1820, 14 x 15 In., Pair .. 6600.00
Knife, Mahogany, Inlay, 19th Century, 9 x 9 x 15 In. 995.00
Knife, Pine, Brown Grained Design, Canted Sides, Open Handle, Square Nails, 12 x 8 In. . 248.00
Letter, Brass, Fitted Mahogany Interior, 19th Century, 4 x 9 x 6 In. 220.00
Letter, Cranberry Glass, Raised Bird, Insect Design, 19th Century, 5 x 9 1/2 x 5 In. 220.00
Letter, Hinged Cover, Allover Gilt Chinoiserie, Black Ground, Brass Handle, 8 In. 865.00
Letter, Mahogany, Inlaid Fans, Hinged Cover, 3 Compartments, 7 1/2 x 4 3/4 In. 490.00
Letter, Porcupine Quill & Tortoiseshell, Ivory Crest On Lid, c.1840, 4 1/2 x 4 1/2 In. 400.00
Letter, Rosewood, Brass Inlay, Fitted Interior Compartment, 5 x 16 x 10 In. 165.00
Letter, Walnut, Hinged Lid, Slotted Interior, 14 x 24 In. 315.00
Mahogany, Rosewood, Vertical Geometric Bands, 10 & 9 In., Pair 488.00
Offering, House Shape, Iron, Painted, Decorated, German Lettering, 7 x 5 1/2 x 8 In. 275.00
Paint, Watercolors, Mahogany, Fitted Interior, Drawer, Reeves & Inwood, 8 3/4 In. 440.00
Painted, Feather, Swag, Flowers, Mustard Yellow, Black Ground, Mass., 8 x 16 x 8 In. ... 5175.00
Painted, Octagonal, Carved Top, Flowers, Divided, c.1830, 15 1/2 x 9 1/2 x 6 1/2 In. 650.00
Painted, Wooden, Argyle Pattern, Rectangular, Sliding Lid, 19th Century, 7 x 6 x 12 In. ... 1610.00
Pantry, Allspice, Red Paint, Yellow Lettering, Bentwood, 9 1/4 In. 357.00
Patch, Enamel, Fishing Scene, No Toil Is Pain When Love's The Gain, 1 x 1 1/2 In. 489.00
Patch, Hinged Cover, Enameled Purple Violets, Pink Bow On Top, 1 1/2 In. 125.00
Patch, Round Hinged Cover, White Flowers, Orange Centers, Cobalt Blue, 1 1/2 x 2 In. ... 115.00
Pencil, Chromolithograph, Mother Goose On Lid, Worn Varnish, 7 7/8 In. 70.00
Pencil, Dixon, Typhonite Eldorado, T Master Drawing, N.J., 7 1/4 x 2 x 3/4 In. 10.00
Pencil, Kellogg's Tony The Tiger School Bus, With Pencils, 1978 .... 18.00
Pine, Embossed Brass Cover, Tin Straps & Bosses, 14 1/2 x 10 1/4 x 6 In. 135.00

Pine, Grain Painted, Hinged Life Top, Rectangular, 19th Century, 6 x 12 x 7 In. 345.00
Pine, Green & Yellow Paint, Flowers, Hinged Lid, American, 19th Century, 6 x 7 x 12 In.   460.00
Pine, Handle, Allover Design, 19th Century, 6 In. 295.00
Pine, Hearts, Half Circles, Yellow, Red, New England, 19th Century, 11 x 29 In. 825.00
Pine, Hinged Lid, Gray, Black Grain Paint, 19th Century, 8 1/2 x 9 x 19 In. 1265.00
Pine, Lift Lid, Eagle Clasping Branch In Talons, 19th Century, 10 x 14 In. 27.00
Pine, Lift Lid, Leafy Vine Design, Yellow, Dark Gray, Brown Ground, 5 1/4 x 16 In. 345.00
Pine, Oak, Rectangular Pintle Hinges, 1700, 7 3/4 x 23 3/4 In. 14950.00
Pine, Painted House & Tree, Red, Blue, Green, Black, Wooden Peg Construction, 10 In. . . . 660.00
Pine, Painted, Blue, New England, c.1820, 10 1/2 x 36 In. 770.00
Pine, Painted, Brown, Ocher Grained Surface, Dome Cover, c.1820, 4 3/4 x 7 1/2 In. 525.00
Pine, Painted, Red, Flowers, Yellow, Blue, Black, Green Pinstriping, Cover, 4 x 9 1/2 In. . 305.00
Pine, Slide Cover, Red Vinegar Graining, Painted, Chamfered Lid, 13 3/4 x 9 x 3 3/4 In. . 440.00
Pine, Slide Cover, Star & Pinwheel Design, Blue Ground, c.1800, 5 x 7 1/2 In. 605.00
Pipe, Painted Decoration, Drawer, 15 In. 315.00
Pipe, Pine, Heart Shape Backboard, Drawer, Red Paint, 1800s, 16 x 5 x 5 In. 3105.00
Pipe, Pine, Painted, Carved Scroll Backboard, Top, Drawer, Early 1800s, 20 x 6 x 4 In. . . . 4025.00
Poplar, Blue Paint, W.H. Robinson Stencil, Cover, Late 1800s, 6 1/4 x 18 3/4 In. 415.00
Poplar, Dovetailed Case, Turned Legs, Box Stretcher, Red Wash, c.1780, 28 x 43 In. 770.00
Powder, Cover, Enamel, Circular, Aqua Field, Signed, Gamet, 18th Century, 3 In. 430.00
Powder, Slip On Cover, Gold, Engine Turned Dots, Leaf Border, Paris, 1787, 2 3/8 In. 2040.00
Presentation, Folk Art, Sallie Seilhamer, 1885, 17 1/2 x 10 x 4 1/2 In. 690.00
Prisoner Of War, Napoleonic, Bone, Ivory, 4 1/2 x 7 1/2 In. 575.00
Prospector, Walnut, Shell Carved, Tulip & Rope Stems, c.1800, 9 3/4 x 11 x 8 1/4 In. . . . 110.00
Pyrography, Hinged Lid, Sailboats, Dutch Windmill, Victorian, 5 1/2 x 2 1/2 In. 19.00
Resin, Dragons On Top, Carved Ivory, 1900, 3 In. 80.00
Ring, Tortoiseshell, Tripodal, Moleskin Interior, 1896, 1 x 3 1/2 In. 489.00
Rosewood, Crossbanded Satinwood, George III, c.1790, 6 x 12 In. 920.00
Rosewood, Vertical Geometric Multicolored Bands, 11 3/4 In. 287.00
Salt, Bentwood, Stenciled Label, Table Salt, Mason City, Iron Tacks, 6 3/4 In. 220.00
Seal, Wooden, Red Leather Cover, Gilt Brass, Sections, 1740, England, 3 3/4 In. 250.00
Slippers, Pine, Slant Lid, Copper Sheet Cover, Red Leather Interior, 14 x 11 x 8 In. 220.00
Snipe Hinges, Wooden, Green, 5 3/4 x 9 1/2 In. 800.00
Stamp, Leather, 3 Wooden Pockets, Gold Color Trim, Italy, 2 x 1 1/2 x 1/2 In. 100.00
Storage, Cover, Painted Poplar, Black, Red Design, Blue Corners, Pa., 1820, 8 x 14 In. . . 2860.00
Storage, Cover, Pine, Black Paint, Red, Yellow Striping, 4 x 10 3/4 x 6 1/2 In. 980.00
Storage, Cover, Poplar, Whimsical Tree Branch, Salmon Ground, 7 1/4 x 16 In. 2530.00
Storage, Dark Green Paint, Red, Yellow, Gray Enamel Cover, 5 1/2 x 5 3/4 In. 1840.00
Storage, Diamond Grid Design On Cover, Olive Green, Black, 5 1/4 x 7 3/4 In. 4600.00
Storage, Dome Top, Pine, Brass Handle, Iron & Brass Lock, Green Paint, 6 x 12 x 6 In. . . . 1150.00
Storage, Embossed Leather, Newspaper Lined, Hand-Drawn Compass, England, c.1720 . . 85.00
Storage, Faith, Hope, Charity, Miniature 3450.00
Storage, Grain-Decorated Surface, Red & Black, New England, 19th Century, 6 x 14 In. . 660.00
Storage, Gray Blue Paint, Hinged Top, Tapered, Bracket Feet, Pine, 1800s, 46 x 22 In. . . . 3450.00
Storage, Mahogany, Hinged Cover, Bracket Base, 11 3/4 x 17 x 11 1/4 In. 220.00
Storage, Old Blue Paint, Square Nails, Hand Plane Marks, 9 1/2 x 8 5/8 x 9 1/8 In. 220.00
Storage, Pine, 6 Board, Painted, Sponged Ground, Striping, 8 1/2 x 18 x 9 In. 2645.00
Storage, Pine, Green Paint, Hinged Cover, Leather Handle, 10 3/4 x 13 In. 6325.00
Storage, Pine, Painted, Hinged, Molded Edge, Cover, 7 x 17 3/4 In. 160.00
Storage, Pine, Painted, Stencil, Bowls Of Fruit, Step Cover, c.1830, 7 3/4 x 11 1/2 In. . . . 2200.00
Storage, Poplar, Molded Lift Cover, Base, Pennsylvania, 19th Century, 9 x 17 In. 220.00
Storage, Red Paint, Black Stripes, Geometric Design, Mid 19th Century, 3 1/4 x 7 In. . . . 520.00
Storage, Rosette Cover, Green Paint, 19th Century, 3 1/4 x 5 1/2 In. 3680.00
Storage, Slant Lid, Strap Hinges, Pine, 13 1/4 x 34 1/2 In. 360.00
Storage, Tiger Maple, Brass Handle, Hinged Cover, 19th Century, 6 x 31 x 9 In. 750.00
Storage, Tiger Maple, Chamfered Edge, Hinged Cover, Rectangular, New England, 14 In. 403.00
Storage, Walnut, Carved, Leaves, Arched Panels, Continental, c.1780, 12 x 25 3/4 In. . . . 275.00
Storage, Walnut, Star & Line Inlay, Dovetailed, Virginia, c.1800, 13 1/2 x 10 x 10 In. . . . 4070.00
Strong, Metal, Engraved, Interior, Complete Lock, Continental, 18th Century, 9 In. 460.00
Strong, Stagecoach, Iron, Deep Red 375.00
Strong, Steel, Cover, Handles, England, 19th Century, 13 x 20 x 14 1/2 In. 1140.00
Tea, Mahogany, Fitted Center Mixing Bowl, Lined, 1820s, 7 x 11 In. 315.00
Tiger Maple, Pen & Ink Drawing, Hinged, Sections, 1800s, 2 1/2 x 7 x 9 In. 1495.00

Tigereye, Silver Mounted, Scrolling Feet, Continental, 5 1/2 In. 635.00
Tobacco, Book Shape, Engraved Design, Holland, 18th Century, 4 1/2 x 1 x 2 1/2 In. 200.00
Tobacco, Brass, Hip Pouch, c.1800, 3 3/4 In. 225.00
Tobacco, Cast Brass, Dancing Revelers, Reverse Side Has Heart, c.1820 . . . . 250.00
Tobacco, Engraved Brass & Copper, Holland, 18th Century, 6 1/4 In. 165.00
Tobacco, Tin, Pewter Mounts, Oval, Late 18th Century, Early 19th Century, 4 3/8 In. 58.00
Toothpick, Wooden, Slide Lid, Shell Carved, Original Horn Toothpicks, France, 1700s . . . 350.00
Travel, Banded, Brass Plaque, Cubbyholes, Paneled Jar, Tooled Leather, 5 x 10 x 7 In. . . . 315.00
Travel, Painted Leather, Slant Front, Interior Wells, Hidden Compartment, 18 1/2 In. 4680.00
Travel, Rosewood, Brass, Compartments, Gilt Tooled Leather File, 6 1/2 x 12 x 9 In. 490.00
Vanity, Burl Walnut, Gilt, Brass, Charles X, 4 1/2 x 6 1/4 x 11 In. 1035.00
Vanity, Embroidered Plants, Flowers, Silk Lining, 4 Sections, England, 1660 . . . . 2250.00
Vanity, Hinged Cover, Bronze Swag, Rectangular, 3 x 5 1/2 x 4 1/2 In. 690.00
Vanity, Mahogany, Brass Inlaid, Interior Compartments, Tray, Lift Lid, 8 3/4 x 17 1/2 In. . 358.00
Vanity, Marble, Inlaid Onyx, Lapis, East Indian Tags, 4 x 3 x 1 1/2 In. 30.00
Vanity, Pine, Painted, Early 20th Century, 6 x 12 In. 1760.00
Vanity, Shellfish & Flowers, Mirror Interior, Wood, 7 In. 170.00
Vanity, Tin, Black, Gold Chinoiserie Design, 18th Century, 7 1/2 In. 250.00
Voting, Mahogany, Saw-Grip Handle, Hinged Cover, Painted, England, 12 x 5 1/2 x 4 In. . 220.00
Wall, Lift Lid, Ocher Paint, 1 Drawer, Chamfered Edge, 11 1/2 x 8 1/2 x 8 In. 5465.00
Wall, Scalloped Sides, Yellow Paint, 8 3/4 x 4 x 11 In. 405.00
Wall, Scalloped, Molded Lid, White Porcelain Mounts, 19th Century, 11 1/4 x 5 x 11 In. . 175.00
Wall, Walnut, Scalloped Back, Early 19th Century, 9 1/2 x 10 1/4 In. 330.00
Wall, Wooden, Painted, Round Hanger, Slant-Front Compartment, 24 x 9 x 5 In. 2070.00
Wooden, Beehive, Rosebush, Compartments, Eunice Foster, 2 x 3 x 6 In. 5175.00
Wooden, Canted Hinged Cover, Compartmentalized Interior Tray, Rounded Feet, 8 In. 865.00
Wooden, Carved, Flowers, 2 Compartments, Key Lock, Fox Paw Finial, c.1910, 11 x 6 In. 1589.00
Wooden, Hinged Cover, Copper, Iron Legs, Curled Feet, Arts & Crafts, 18 x 15 In. 865.00
Wooden, Hinged Cover, Molded, Yellow Grain Paint, 28 x 15 x 16 In. 360.00
Wooden, Painted, Green, Hideaway Handles, G.L.B. & Co., 19th Century, 12 x 24 In. . . . 175.00
Wooden, Painted, Strawberry Basket, Black Ground, Putty Border, 4 3/8 x 10 x 7 In. 316.00
Wooden, Red Paint, Design, 3 Sections, Handle, Chinese Lunch Box 345.00
Wooden Cover, Landscape, Brown, Gold Trees, Mountains, Grinnell, Arts & Crafts, 7 In. . 618.00
Writing, Alligator, Hinged, Leather Lined Interior, Chrome Inkwell, 12 x 8 1/4 x 2 In. . . . 200.00
Writing, Lacquer, Gold Pine Interior, Silver Edge, 8 1/2 x 7 1/4 In. 1840.00
Writing, Mahogany, Brass, Fitted Corners, Inlaid Label, Tooled Leather, 20 x 10 x 7 In. . . 575.00
Writing, Mother-Of-Pearl Inlay, Ebonized Rosewood, Leather, 23 x 16 1/2 x 10 In. 430.00
Writing, Rosewood, Ormolu Mount, Ebonized, Louis Philippe, 14 1/2 x 12 x 7 In. 1095.00
Writing, Rosewood, Stand, Hinged Lid, Bird's-Eye Maple Reed Legs, 22 x 14 x 11 In. . . . 290.00
Writing, Slant Lid, Oak, Old Dark Finish, 2 Slotted Compartments, 11 3/4 x 8 In. 110.00
Writing, Victorian, Walnut, Burr, Gilt Bronze, Mid 1800s, 16 x 16 x 11 1/2 In. 1725.00
Writing, Walnut, Molded Top, Brass Bail, Applied Molded Base, Bracket Feet, c.1790 . . . 1250.00

BOY SCOUT collectibles include any material related to scouting,
including patches, manuals, and uniforms. The Boy Scout movement
in the United States started in 1910. The first Jamboree was held in
1937. Girl Scout items are listed under their own heading.

Badge, Merit, Saturn, Untrimmed, 1958-1960 . . . . 75.00
Bank, Cast Iron, 5 7/8 In. 105.00
Bank, Figural, 5 7/8 In. 154.00
Blanket, Military, 75 Scout Patches, 1970s 35.00
Book, 3 Boy Scouts In Africa On Safari, 1928 . . . . 15.00
Book, Boy Scouts In Alaska 12.00
Book, Boy Scouts In Camp, George Durston, Saalfield Publishing Co., 1921 . . . . 12.00
Book, Cubmaster's Packbook, New Brunswick, 1967, 345 Pages 8.00
Book, Merit Badge, Canoeing, 1966 . . . . 2.00
Book, Merit Badge, Personal Fitness, 1961 . . . . 2.00
Book, Merit Badge, Soil & Water Conservation, 1961 . . . . 2.00
Book, Merit Badge, Space Exploration, 1979 . . . . 2.00
Book, Merit Badge, Woodcarving, 1937 . . . . 3.00
Book, Sea Explorer Manual, 7th Edition, 1950, 640 Pages 12.00
Book, Webelos Scout Book, New Brunswick, 1967, 300 Pages 8.00
Book, Wolf Cub, 1952 . . . . 10.00

Bugle, 1940s, 16 3/4 In.	42.00
Camera, Folding, Olive Green, Boy Scout Logo, Kodak, 5 x 2 1/2 In.	125.00
Chaps Slide, Leather, 1948, 2 x 2 1/4 In.	19.00
Coat, Dress, Army Green, Size 46	70.00
Compass, Pathfinder, Sivla-System, Instruction Booklet, Box	10.00
Compass, Pocket, 8 Sides Case, Taylor Instruments, 2 In.	17.00
Cookstove, Tool Tender, Trays, Pot, Skillet, Coffeepot, Nuttle, Inc., Joplin, Mo.	36.00
Doll, Steve Scout, Uniform, Booklet, Sticker Badges, Kenner, 1974, 9 In.	55.00
Drum, Snare, Wooden Barrel, Ludwig, 14 3/4 x 11 1/4 In.	80.00
Drum, Tin, Chein & Co., Pat. Feb. 8, 1908, 9 x 5 1/2 In.	96.00
Handbook, For Boys, 1948	5.00
Handbook, For Boys, 5th Edition, 1949	8.00
Handbook, Scoutmaster's Handbook, Black & White Photos, 1927, 676 Pages	50.00
Handbook, Scoutmaster's, Volume One, 1944, 4 1/2 x 6 3/4 In.	21.00
Hat, Leather Band, 1920s-1930s	20.00
Knife, Acorn Shield, Bone Handles, Remington, 1920s	152.00
Match Safe, Brass, Emblem Logo	10.00
Mess Kit, Knife, Fork, Spoon, Geo. Schrade, Bridgeport, Conn., Pat. Jan. 27, 1942	30.00
Neckerchief, Slide, National Colorado Springs Jamboree	12.00
Patch, 1964 National Jamboree, Valley Forge, 6 In.	21.00
Patch, Merit Badge, Fruit & Nut Growing, Untrimmed, 1953-1960	67.00
Patch, Pocket Flap, Order Of The Arrow, Sioux Lodge 62	52.00
Plaque, Souvenir, 1950 Boy Scout Jamboree, Masonite, 5 1/2 In.	13.00
Poster, Boy Scout Troop 12, Remington Schuyler Art, 1942, 16 1/2 x 24 In.	255.00
Sash, Merit Badge, 21 Badges, c.1960, 30 In.	33.00
Sash, Merit Badge, 57 Square Badges, 1920s	3550.00
Shirt, Ouachita Valley Council Of Louisiana, Trained, American Flag, X-Large	23.00
Signal Set, Box, Boy Scouts Of America National Supply Service Division, c.1950	15.00
Telescope, Wolf Insignia, Aluminum, Retractable, Box, Extends To 9 1/2 In.	16.00
Token, 50th Anniversary, Brass, Oath On Back, 1960	14.00
Toy, Boy Scout Rider, Bucking Horse, Composition, Windup, Germany, 1950s, 4 In.	175.00
Watch, Pocket, 1 7/8 In.	410.00
Whittling Kit, Deluxe, Manual, Knives, Wood, Box, 1945	52.00
Wristwatch, Ingersoll, Box	302.00
Yearbook, 1916, McGuire & Matthews, 269 Pages	75.00

BRADLEY & HUBBARD is a name found on many metal objects. Walter Hubbard and his brother-in-law, Nathaniel Lyman Bradley, started making cast iron clocks, tables, frames, andirons, lamps, chandeliers, sconces, and sewing birds in 1854 in Meriden, Connecticut. The company became Bradley & Hubbard Manufacturing Company in 1875. Charles Parker Company bought the firm in 1940. Their lamps are especially prized by collectors.

Andirons, Iron, Hammered, Black Paint Finish	1600.00
Andirons, Owl Figures, Seated On Plinth, 1930, 14 1/2 x 19 1/2 In.	488.00
Ashtray Stand, Iron, Celtic Repousse, Liner, Match Holder, 27 x 8 1/2 In.	144.00
Basket With Bird, Silver, 11 3/4 x 7 x 9 1/2 In.	850.00
Candlestick, Flying Owl, Bumblebee, Beetle, Brass, Stamped, 8 1/2 In.	200.00
Decanter Set, Ruby Scotch & Rye, Etched, Marked	600.00
Inkwell, Hammered, Tin, 2 x 4 In.	159.00
Lamp, 4-Panel Shade, Arts & Crafts, Bronze Base, 19 In.	2420.00
Lamp, 6-Light, Slag, Bronze, Cone Shaped Shade, 19 In.	635.00
Lamp, 6-Sided Crackle Glass Shade, Copper Frame & Base, 21 In.	200.00
Lamp, 8-Panel Shade, Molded Flower, Bronzed Metal Base, 20 x 23 In.	1095.00
Lamp, 8-Panel Shade, Ribbed, Bronze Frame, Iron Base, 20 In.	1380.00
Lamp, 9-Panel Shade, Mesh, Incised Garland, Signed, 22 1/4 In.	630.00
Lamp, Aladdin, Green Glass, Geometric Amber Border, Tulip, Leaf, 6 In.	2800.00
Lamp, Arts & Crafts, Oak Base, Metal Fixture, Glass Shade, 23 In.	920.00
Lamp, Banquet, 1890, 28 1/2 In.	500.00
Lamp, Brass, Caramel & Yellow Slag Glass Shade, 19 x 11 In.	770.00
Lamp, Brass, White & Green Slag Glass Panel Shade, 22 In.	400.00
Lamp, Butterscotch Cased, White Shade, Mushroom Shaped Shade	275.00
Lamp, Desk, Caramel & White Slag Tulip Shade, 2 Inkwells Base, 14 In.	415.00

Lamp, Floral Beige, Green, Blue Shade, Signed, 14 x 22 In. 575.00
Lamp, Gilded Cast Iron, Octagonal Shade, Carmel Slag, 19 1/2 In. 440.00
Lamp, Gone With The Wind, Floral, Kerosene, 1895, 23 In. 425.00
Lamp, Gone With Wind, Blown-Out Elephants, 26 In. 4200.00
Lamp, Green & White Slag Shade, Metal Standard, Signed, 26 In. 860.00
Lamp, Kerosene, Red Roses On Milk Glass Shade, Iron Base, 17 In. 175.00
Lamp, Marble Base, Shade, Signed, 19 1/2 In. 435.00
Lamp, Oil, Green Cased Shade, Electrified, Waterloo, N.Y., 10 In. 975.00
Lamp, Oil, Hanging, Black Cast Iron, Waterloo, N.Y. 675.00
Lamp, Parlor, Brass Handles, 20 In. 375.00
Lamp, Pierced, Portrait, Flowers, Onyx, Acid Finish, Peach, Shade, 13 In. 950.00
Lamp, Pipe Cone Slag Panels, 25 In. 1450.00
Lamp, Pond Flowers, Frogs, Electrified, 19 x 15 In. 1295.00
Lamp, Reverse Painted Floral Border, 6 Sections, 23 x 15 In. 660.00
Lamp, Reverse Painted Shade, Pond Scene, Swans, Pond Lilies, 25 In. 4600.00
Lamp, Shade, Leaded Glass, 16 In. 952.00
Lamp, Slag Glass, Orange Medallions, Tree-Trunk Base, 20 In. 2800.00
Lamp, Slag Glass, Ornate Metal Trim, Floral, 23 x 18 In. 1250.00
Lamp, Slag Glass, Shade, Waterloo, N.Y., 21 x 18 1/2 In. 895.00
Lamp, Student, Brass, Double Arm, Green Glass Shades 660.00
Lamp, Student, Double, Green Ribbed Shade, Adjustable, 21 In. 825.00
Lamp, Student, Green Cased Shade, Electrified 1795.00
Lamp, Table, Oak Leaves On Bronze Base, Stylized Flowers, 26 x 18 In. 2310.00
Lamp, Table, Reverse Painted, Hexagon Dome Shade, 20 In. 865.00
Lamp, Table, Slag Glass, Ornate Metal Leaves, Berries, 1900, 18 1/4 In. 12000.00
Lamp, Wrought Iron Base, Ivory Globe, Electrified, 1880, 32 In. 425.00
Letter Holder, Brass, Cast Iron, 5 1/2 In. 135.00
Letter Holder, Brass, Signed, 12 x 10 1/2 x 4 1/2 In. 525.00
Letter Holder, Bronze, 5 1/2 x 5 In. 110.00
Letter Holder, Cast Iron, Paw Foot, Medallion Center, 12 x 4 1/2 In. 112.00
Mortar & Pestle, Brass, 8 1/2 x 6 1/4 x 4 1/2 In. 300.00
Sculpture, Bucking Bronco, Bronze, Marble Based, Signed, 9 1/2 In. 1550.00
Smoking Set, Arts & Crafts Design, 4 Piece 195.00
Smoking Set, Brass, 4 1/2 x 6 1/2 In., 4 Piece 195.00

BRASS has been used for decorative pieces and useful tablewares since
ancient times. It is an alloy of copper, zinc, and other metals. Additional brass items may be found under Bell, Candlestick, Tool, or
Trivet.

Ashtray, Geometric Design, Black Enameled Center, Chrome, Paul Evans, 2 x 8 In. 225.00
Bed Warmer, Pierced Design, Raised Stars, Wooden Handle, c.1810, 50 In. 200.00
Bed Warmer, Pierced, Engraved Cover, Flower Urn, Holland, 18th Century, 46 In. 575.00
Bed Warmer, Rosette On Lid, Scrolls & Rope Rim, Wooden Handle, 44 3/4 In. 275.00
Bin Pull, Quarter Moon & Star 80.00
Booksafe, Late 18th Century, 6 In. 295.00
Bowl, Deep Blue, Purple Iridescent, Footed, Art Nouveau, 5 1/2 In. 385.00
Box, Oval, 19th Century, 3/4 x 4 1/2 x 3 1/4 In. 110.00
Box, Studded, Leather Covered, Camphor Wood, Name Plaque, 16 1/2 x 36 1/2 In. 230.00
Brush & Mirror, Removable Brush Head, 2-Tone Brass, Pocket, c.1950 .... 45.00
Bucket, Mahogany, 3 Brass Rings, Applied Bail Handle, 19th Century, 16 In. 2588.00
Bucket, Mahogany, Lower Bottom Brass Ring, Upper Brass Band, Bail Handle, 15 In. 2645.00
Bust, George Washington, Circular Face, Wingspread Eagle, 1800, 22 x 12 In. 3000.00
Cake Stand, 3 Tiers, 1920, 34 In. 230.00
Can, Kerosene Dispenser, For Hanging Lamps 75.00
Candlesnuffer, Door Stamped Heart & Cross, Late 17th Century, 3 In. 250.00
Candlesnuffer, Wood, Conical, Tubular Wick Holder, Circular Oak Handle, 32 3/4 In. 69.00
Candlestand, Candle Sockets, Dished Stand, Scrolled Tripod Base, 54 In. 4890.00
Cane Holder, Hand, 4 x 3 In. 145.00
Carriage Step, Cast Iron, Raised On Cabriole Legs, Pierced Design, Square, 12 x 12 In. ... 196.00
Carriage Steps, Rectangular, Curved Legs, Bulbous Knees, Handle, 18 x 12 In. 375.00
Cigar Cutter, Art Deco, Figural, Erotic, Recumbent Nude, Hinged Leg, 2 x 8 1/2 In. 1035.00
Coal Bucket, 13 1/2 In. 55.00
Coat Rack, 4-Sided Post, Arts & Crafts, 67 x 24 In. 225.00

Coffee Urn, Copper, Lion Head Handles, Repousse Bands, Spigot Handle, 17 In. 220.00
Cuspidor, Archetype, Original Patina, Weighted Base, 6 x 8 In. 75.00
Cuspidor, Copper Plated, Weighted Bottom, Wire Across Opening, Manhattan Brass Co. . 95.00
Desk Set, Rosewood, Magnifying Glass, Letter Opener, 10 In. 48.00
Dish, Caviar, Cover, Hammered Handles, Arts & Crafts, Germany, 14 x 13 1/2 In. 440.00
Door Knocker, Dog Bonzo 110.00
Door Knocker, Dog, Wire Fox Terrier, Dog Collar Backplate, 2 x 4 In. 65.00
Door Knocker, Hand, 6 1/2 In. 195.00
Doorknob, Entry Type, Branford 40.00
Doorknob, Entry, Bluebird & Rosette 170.00
Doorknob, Fleur-De-Lis, R & E 220.00
Doorknob, Hedgehog 20.00
Doorknob, Saturn 40.00
Doorknob, Skeleton Hand, Bone Lever Handle 260.00
Doorknob, Sunken Center, 1875 . . . . 80.00
Eagle, Flagpole, Iron Base, 8 1/2 In. 175.00
Figurine, Continental, Bound Cupid, Seated Nude, Late 19th Century, 5 In. 345.00
Figurine, Footman, George III, Late 18th Century 250.00
Figurine, Indian Deity, Seated, Right Foot Supported By Cushion, 5 In. 315.00
Frame, Hunter Green Nephrite, Gilt, Chinese, 11 3/4 In. 1840.00
Goblet, Coconut, Carved With Trophies & Birds, Continental, 5 In. 172.00
Horn, Domed Foot Rising To Knop, Applied Cartouche, Domed Cover, 20 In. 552.00
Horn, Snake With Leather Ball, 64-In. Lens 1700.00
Incense Burner, Champleve, Diamond Ground, Pierced Lid, Dragon Handles, 6 3/4 In. . . . 28.00
Jar, Circular, Cover, 5 1/2 x 10 3/4 In. 109.00
Jardiniere, Lion Mask, Ring Handles, Heraldic Motif, Tripod Feet, Continental, 23 In. . . . 230.00
Kettle, Spirit, Caned Handle, Square Lantern-Shaped Base, 3 Glass Panels, 10 x 6 3/4 In. 35.00
Kettle, Spirit, Stand, Secessionist Style, Sterno, Signed, J. Eisenloeffel, 29 1/4 In. 747.00
Knob, Bilston, Black & White Urns, 1 5/8 In., Pair 160.00
Knob, Bilston, Enameled, Polychrome Dancing Girl, Playing Triangle, 1 7/8 In. 275.00
Knob, Bilston, Floral Bouquet, Shepherdess With Flock, 1 1/2 In. 60.00
Knob, Bilston, Village Scenes, Towers In Background, 1 3/4 In., Pair 60.00
Knob, Dancing Girls, Tambourines, Oval, 2 In., Pair 55.00
Ladle, Tapered Handle, Deep Circular Bowl, Richard Lee Jr., Vt. 1680.00
Letter Box, Hanging, Hotel, Iron, Lock, Keys, Coulter Mail Shute Co., 36 x 21 x 11 In. . . . 4760.00
Light, Signal, England, 10 In. 17.00
Lock, Door, Mounted On Wooden Board, Key, 12 x 7 In., Pair 518.00
Night-Light, Hanging Candle, Glass Holder, 9 3/4 In. 185.00
Note Holder, Hand, 7 In. 125.00
Pan, Warming, Engraved & Pierced Cover, Mahogany Handle 132.00
Pan, Warming, Engraved Cover, c.1790 . . . . 110.00
Pan, Warming, Multi-Petal Flower, Turned Handle, 39 In. 200.00
Planter, Cast Lion Heads, Ring Handle, Contemporary, 10 In., Pair 110.00
Planter, Footed, Lion Mask Form Handles, 7 1/2 x 5 In. 58.00
Plaque, Fruit Center, Satyr Masks & Mermen Around Rim, Round, 24 1/2 In. 50.00
Plaque, Men Drinking Scene, Woman With Well Ground, 16 3/4 x 21 1/2 In. 55.00
Plaque, Porcelain Woman Silhouette, Cherubs & Masks Ornate Rim, 13 In. Diam. 135.00
Plaque, William Shakespeare Bust, Muses Each Side, 37 3/4 In. 410.00
Samovar, Dovetailed Construction, 19th Century, 19 In. 28.00
Samovar, Russia, 19th Century, 16 In. 220.00
Sconce, Wall, Geometric Design, Art Deco, 9 x 16 In., Pair 1100.00
Seal, Ivory, Dragon & PhoeniX Design, 19th Century, 2 3/4 In. 126.00
Shoehorn, Lady's Leg, Engraved Shoe & Petticoat, Leaf & Flower Design, c.1800, 9 In. . . 150.00
Snuffer, Stand, England, 20th Century 55.00
Stand, Burner, Stylized Fish Handles, 19th Century, 11 x 13 In. 46.00
Stand, Kettle, Pierced Top, Engraved Beehives & Grapes, England, 25 x 8 3/4 x 7 In. . . . 135.00
Tappit, Hen Measure, Hinged Thumbpiece Lid, Scotland, 1800, 10 5/8 In. 595.00
Teacup & Saucer, 18th Century 165.00
Tieback, Curtain, Trumpet Flower, Opaline Glass, Blue, Mid 19th Century, 10 In., Pair . . . 175.00
Tieback, Curtain, Trumpet Shape, Gilt White Glass, Mid 19th Century, 9 In., Pair 115.00
Tieback, Drapery, Gryphons Shape, Scroll Plate, 7 1/4 In., Pair 200.00
Tieback, Hand, 4 In. 45.00
Tongs, Spill, England, 18th Century, 8 1/4 In. 495.00

Tray, Cloisonne Insert, Men, Animals, L. De La Cuesta, Oct. 31, 1883, 8 3/8 x 14 1/2 In. . . 275.00
Tray, On Stand, Edwardian, Mahogany, Marquetry, c.1900, 20 x 17 1/2 x 27 In. 550.00
Tray, Porcelain Fish & Parrot Picture Insert, Diamond Shape, 12 3/4 x 18 5/8 In. 715.00
Tray, Tea, Green Glaze Base, Cutout Handles, 20th Century, 20 3/8 In. 170.00
Umbrella Stand, Carolers & Violin Players Scenes, Ring Handles, 8 x 16 x 25 In. 135.00
Umbrella Stand, Tavern Scene Both Sides, Removable Tin Liner, 21 x 7 x 19 In. 165.00
Urn, Cover, Dragon Designs, High Cabriole Legs, Oriental, 19 1/2 In. 165.00
Urn, Hot Water, Ivory Spigot, Scrolled Handles, Ball Feet, 19th Century, 17 x 13 In. 110.00
Vase, Central Classical Medallion Against Black, Brown, Gray Flambe Glaze, 17 In. 485.00
Vase, Cover, Hammered, Original Patina, Arts & Crafts, 7 1/2 In. 185.00
Water Pump, Salesman's Sample, Brass Plaque, Cast Iron, J.H. Best, Pat. 1906, 20 In. . . . 1440.00
Wick Trimmer, Holder, 7 1/2 In. 1045.00

BRASTOFF, see Sascha Brastoff category.

BREAD PLATE, see various silver categories, porcelain factories, and pressed glass patterns.

BRIDE'S BASKETS OR BRIDE'S BOWLS were usually one-of-a-kind novelties made in American and European glass factories. They were especially popular about 1880 when the decorated basket was often given as a wedding gift. Cut glass baskets were popular after 1890. All bride's baskets lost favor about 1905. Bride's baskets and bride's bowls may also be found in other glass sections. Check the index at the back of the book.

BRIDE'S BASKET, Inverted Thumbprint, Amber, Griffin Handles, Footed Brass Holder 275.00
Peachblow, Diamond-Quilted, Applied Frond, Crimped Rim, 6 1/2 In. 138.00
Peachblow, Ruffled Edge, Silver Plated Holder, Twisted Rope Handle, 10 In. 288.00
Peachblow, Satin, Ormolu Holder, Victorian 2150.00
Silver Plate, Repousse Art Nouveau, Fixed Handle, 16 x 12 x 7 In. 112.00
Vaseline, Frame 195.00
BRIDE'S BOWL, Blue Cased, Enameled White Flowers, Ruffled Edge, 3 1/2 x 10 3/4 In. . . . 225.00
Enameled Flowers, Ribbed, Quadruple Silver Plated Frame, Smith, 9 1/2 In. 595.00
Enameled White & Yellow Flowers, Sprays Of Pink Buds, Bug On Back, 10 In. 275.00
Ivory, Yellow & Lavender Enameled Flowers, J. Rogers Co. Frame, 10 1/4 In. 450.00
Pink Over White, Ruffled Edge, 2 1/2 x 10 1/2 In. 225.00
White, Enameled Pink Flowers, Leaves, Ruffled Edge, 11 3/8 In. 195.00
White Over Blue, Enameled Yellow, White & Brown Flowers, 10 In. 215.00
Yellow Flowers, Leaves, Beaded Satin, Ruffled Edge, 3 x 11 In. 295.00

BRISTOL glass was made in Bristol, England, after the 1700s. The Bristol glass most often seen today is a Victorian, lightweight opaque glass that is often blue. Some of the glass was decorated with enamels.

Cruet, Original Stopper, Numbered, c.1880, 9 3/4 In., Pair 165.00
Humidor, Hunting Dog Design, 6 1/2 In. 175.00
Jar, Enameled Flowers, 10 3/4 In. 85.00
Lamp, Enameled White & Tan Flowers, Spelter Leaf Base, 26 3/4 In., Pair 110.00
Lamp, Pink & Gilt, Electrified, 15 In. 45.00
Mug, Blue Accent Bands, Handle, Iroquois Brewing Co., Buffalo, N.Y., 5 In. 185.00
Pitcher, Building On Reverse, Basket Of Flowers, Monogrammed, 1823, 8 1/2 In. 2970.00
Ring Tree, Enameled Blue & Pink Flowers, Dots Below Band, 3 1/2 In. 125.00
Urn, Dome Cover, Gold Enameled Flowers, 18 3/4 In. 149.00
Vase, Blue, Bands Of Gold, Silver Flowers, 7 In. 125.00
Vase, Enameled Birds & Branches, Gold Rim, c.1880, 17 In. 225.00
Vase, Enameled Design Of Bird & Flowers, 12 1/2 In. 150.00
Vase, Enameled Flowers & Thrush, 10 1/2 In., Pair 70.00
Vase, Enameled Flowers, Butterflies & Leaves, 13 In. 95.00
Vase, Enameled Gold & Lavender Flowers, Ruffled Edge, 1800s, 12 1/2 In. 225.00
Vase, Enameled Pink Roses, Green, Gold Band Around Rim & Base, 1880, 16 1/4 In. . . . 288.00
Vase, Enameled Portrait Of Woman, 14 In. 56.00
Vase, Ivory, Enameled Flowers, 10 1/2 In. 75.00
Vase, White Enameled Gold & Pink Roses, 7 1/2 In. 120.00

BRITANNIA, see Pewter category.

BRONZE is an alloy of copper, tin, and other metals. It is used to make figurines, lamps, and other decorative objects. Bronze lamps are listed in the Lamp category. Pieces listed here date from the eighteenth, nine-teenth, and twentieth centuries.

Armillary Sphere, Gilt, Regency Style, Tripod Dolphin Base, Step Plinth, 10 x 6 In.	865.00
Bowl, Gilt Mounting, Leaf Scroll Handles, Louis XVI Style, Glass Insert, 21 In.	1840.00
Bowl, Overall Diamonds, Reeds, Footed, Africa, 19th Century, 8 1/4 x 5 1/4 In.	115.00
Bowl, Scrolling, Rectangular, Footed, Ring Handles, Southeast Asia, 10 x 12 x 4 1/2 In. . .	85.00
Bowl, Tripod Base, Angled Loop Handles, Bulbous, 17th Century, 8 In.	490.00
Box, Cover, Rectangular Top, Heraldic Shields On Sides, Gilt, 2 1/2 x 15 In.	2280.00
Box, Dresser, Cover, Block Feet, Charles X, 7 1/4 x 10 x 5 1/4 In.	520.00
Box, Dresser, Gilt, Arches, Finials, Berry, Charles X, 5 3/4 In.	1380.00
Box, Dresser, Gilt, Bronze Patina, Block Feet, Charles X, 6 3/4 In.	3680.00
Box, Dresser, Gilt, Patinated, Footed, Charles X, 7 x 9 x 5 In.	1095.00
Box, Mother-Of-Pearl Figures, 4 In.	196.00
Box, Prairie Design, Original Patina, Jarvie, 1912, 4 1/2 x 2 In.	865.00
Bucket, Champagne, Missile Form, Removable Liner, Silvered, 1879, 28 In.	3050.00
Bust, D'Illiers, Gaston, Man On Pack Horse, Black Patina, 10 In.	635.00
Bust, Diana The Huntress, 19th Century, 12 In.	400.00
Bust, Emile Guillame, Director French Salon, 1930s, 7 3/4 x 8 1/2 x 7 3/4 In.	220.00
Bust, Louis-Philippe, Praxitelean, Patinated, Late 19th Century, 11 1/2 In.	1610.00
Bust, Man & Woman, Victorian Clothes, Roman Bronze Works, 26 In., Pair	2530.00
Bust, Rodin, Woman, Signed, 15 In.	1870.00
Bust, Socrates, Patinated, 19th Century, 8 In.	920.00
Bust, Tadolini, Giulio, Man, 2-Tone Patina, 27 1/2 In.	13200.00
Bust, Usher, Leila, Woman, 1910, 9 1/2 x 3 3/4 x 3 3/4 In.	110.00
Bust, Villani, Emmanuele, Female Warrior, With Winged Helmet, 17 In.	575.00
Bust, Woman, On Marble Base	335.00
Candleholder, Birds, Mythical Beasts Form Legs & Handles, Chinese, 8 1/2 In., Pair	135.00
Candleholder, Gilt, Patinated Shafts, Detachable Bobeches, Charles X, 10 3/4 In., Pair . . .	805.00
Candleholder, Gilt, Patinated, Faceted Cut Glass Pendants, Regency, 8 3/4 x 5 In.	1265.00
Candleholder, Gilt, Sphinx Heads, Detachable Bobeches, Louis XVI, 11 x 5 In., Pair	1725.00
Candleholder, Gilt, Tapered, Detachable Bobeches, Empire, 8 1/2 x 3 3/4 In., Pair	460.00
Candleholder, Gilt, Urn-Form Nozzle, Bobeches, Leaves, Stars, Empire, 10 x 4 In., Pair . .	1035.00
Candleholder, Marble, Beaded Nozzle, Napoleon III, 20 x 5 1/2 In.	2760.00
Candleholder, Ostrich Egg, Gilt, Plain Nozzle, Acanthus Leaf Sprig Base, 11 In.	575.00
Cardholder, 2 Children, On Marble Base, Gold Dore, 1880, 8 x 11 x 6 In.	1230.00
Cauldron, Sauce, Masked Legs, Flemish, 17th Century, 3 In.	235.00
Censer, Dragon Chasing A Flaming Pearl Between Band Of Stylized Animals, 7 In.	1610.00
Censer, Gold Spot, Lotus Petal Form, Low Base, Scroll Feet, 5 In.	1610.00
Censer, Standing Foursquare, Wavy Fur, Open Jaw With Large Fangs, 12 1/2 In.	750.00
Centerpiece, Marquetry, Circular Dish Inset, Ivory, Signed F. Duvinage, 1880	10800.00
Compote, Gilt, Petal Cut Glass, Engraved, Paw-Footed Stand, Napoleon III, 9 x 12 In. . . .	1610.00
Compote, Lotus Leaf, Frog, Flower Blossom, 4 In.	127.00
Desk Set, Galleried Base, Ormolu Mask, Swans, Butterflies Trim, Continental, 1800	9000.00
Desk Set, Preston, Jessie, Stylized Thistle, Art Nouveau, 15 1/2 x 6 1/2 In.	2025.00
Dish, Lotus Form, 2 Full Relief Frogs, 19th Century, 6 In.	69.00
Door Knocker, Raised Scroll Design, 10 1/8 x 4 3/4 In.	60.00
Door Knocker, Striker, Original Sets Of Bolts & Nuts, Mid 19th Century, 6 1/4 In.	250.00
Ewer, Scrolls, Dragon Handle, Gilt, Blue Porcelain, Louis XV, 26 1/2 In.	2760.00
Fountain, Circular, Leaf-Capped Standard, Stepped Circular Base, 95 In.	4600.00
Fountain, Winged Putto Blowing A Triton Horn, Seated On Dolphin, 37 1/2 In.	1840.00
Garniture Set, White Marble, Greek Style, 11 1/4 x 8 3/4 x 6 1/4 In.	1495.00
Incense Burner, Dragons, Pierced Lid, Foo Dog Finial & Handles, 7 7/8 In.	95.00
Incense Burner, Grotesque Mask, Golden Brown Patina, 19th Century, 2 In.	58.00
Jardiniere, Animal Faces, Monkey, Lion, Elephant, Buffalo, Deer, Tiger, 10 x 15 In.	1210.00
Jardiniere, Elephant Herd Scene, Bronze & Brown Patina, 10 x 15 In.	1725.00
Jardiniere, Wall, Patinated, Arched Frame, Copper-Lined Well, 24 x 10 x 6 In., Pair	865.00
Jug, Flemish, c.1550-1650, 4 In.	250.00
Letter Holder, Arches, Quatrefoil, Regency, 4 3/4 In., Pair	489.00
Paper Clip, Horse Head, Vienna, 1880	3000.00
Paper Clip, Hound Head, Vienna, 1880	3000.00
Picture Frame, Little Girl In Center, Arts & Crafts, 7 1/2 x 6 In.	633.00

Planter, Relief Sculpted Insects, Rectangular, Scroll Feet, Japanese, 3 x 6 In. 115.00
Plaque, Bust, George Washington Profile, Ivory, Black Ground, 11 x 8 1/2 In. 145.00
Plaque, Karkadoolia, Mythological Green Man, 1977, 9 x 11 7/8 In. 275.00
Plaque, Leach, Louis L., Charles Lindbergh, 1927, 10 1/4 x 13 1/4 In. 175.00
Plaque, Lizzie Borden, Courtroom Rail, Engraved, c.1892, 6 x 4 1/2 In. 375.00
Plaque, Perales, M., Figural, Landscape, Relief, 7 1/2 x 10 In. 127.00
Plaque, Satyrs, Chased With Bacchanalian Scene, 19th Century, 5 7/8 In. 3600.00
Plaque, Virgin & Child In Glory, Gilt, Baroque Style, c.1870, 8 x 6 In. 345.00
Sconce, Wall, Cherub, 1895, 25 In., Pair 10864.00
Sculpture, 2 Kittens On Bench, Cold Cast, Austria, 2 1/2 In. 145.00
Sculpture, 2 Monkeys At Play, 8 In. 1092.00
Sculpture, Abstract Free-Form Sculpture, 29 x 8 In. 255.00
Sculpture, Arab, Sitting On Prancing Steed, Rockwork Base, 92 In. 1495.00
Sculpture, Art Nouveau, Nude Maiden, On Conch Shell, Signed, 12 In. 2300.00
Sculpture, Bacchus & Orpheus, Leaning Against Grapevines, 14 In., Pair 3450.00
Sculpture, Barrias, Louis-Ernest, Nature Revealing Herself Before Science, 9 1/2 In. 4025.00
Sculpture, Barye, Antoine-Louis, Lion, Dark Green, Signed, 9 x 15 1/4 In. 4900.00
Sculpture, Barye, Antoine-Louis, Lion, Green Patination, 13 1/2 x 16 1/2 In. 6875.00
Sculpture, Barye, Antoine-Louis, Panther Attacking Stag, 19 In. 2040.00
Sculpture, Beach, Chester, Nude With Fish, Marble Base, Signed, 9 In. 1380.00
Sculpture, Beetz, E., Boy, Long Cape, Hood, Signed, 23 In. 2590.00
Sculpture, Bennes, J., Trotter With Jockey, 18 1/2 In. 3000.00
Sculpture, Bergman, 2 Barefoot Maidens, Playing Ring Game, 8 x 16 In. 3450.00
Sculpture, Bergman, Servant Boy With Chest Of Diamonds, 6 x 5 1/2 x 4 In. 900.00
Sculpture, Bernoud, E., The Sower, Ivory, Gilt Bronze, 1915, 15 3/4 In. 5100.00
Sculpture, Bizard, Suzanne, Peasant Girl, 10 In. 750.00
Sculpture, Bock, Arthur, Female Snake Charmer, Entwined Snake On Arms, 11 In. 1725.00
Sculpture, Bodhisattva Seated On Lion, Lotus Base, 9 In. 1035.00
Sculpture, Bodhisattva, Seated On Lotus Base, Wearing Serene Expression, 12 3/4 In. ... 517.00
Sculpture, Boy, Basket, Umbrella, Signed R.W. Lange, Vienna 500.00
Sculpture, Bregno, J.J., Boy, Wreath Crown, Drinking From Wine Bottle, 10 1/4 In. 1035.00
Sculpture, Brose, Carl, Farm Girl, Bull, 12 In. 1035.00
Sculpture, Bruchon, Emile, Neoclassical Sculpture, 13 x 6 x 4 In. 785.00
Sculpture, Buddha, Seated In Dhyanasana, Serene Expression, 9 In. 747.00
Sculpture, Buddha, Seated On Lotus Throne, Gilt Finish, 7 3/4 In. 288.00
Sculpture, Buddha, Seated On Lotus Throne, Hands In Alms Bowl, 17th Century, 10 In. .. 345.00
Sculpture, Buddha, Seated On Separate Lotus Base, Holding Cup, 15 1/2 In. 2070.00
Sculpture, Bull, Man Sitting Sideways, Reading Book, Signed, Chinese, 6 1/2 x 14 In. ... 288.00
Sculpture, Calvano, Pointer, On Base, S.C. Tarrant Co., 5 x 11 In. 650.00
Sculpture, Carrier, A., Historic Nobleman, Bronze Socle, Marble Base, 21 In. 2300.00
Sculpture, Carver, Ludwig, Herder & Cow, 18 1/2 x 16 1/2 x 7 In. 990.00
Sculpture, Centaurs, Holding Grapevines, Cornucopia, 18th Century, 5 In., Pair 6600.00
Sculpture, Children At Sundial, 1880, 6 x 7 x 3 In. 448.00
Sculpture, Children Riding Goat, Whimsical, 1885, 21 x 16 x 7 In. 2070.00
Sculpture, Chiparus, Demetre, H., Reclining Woman, Green Patina, 22 3/4 In. 4800.00
Sculpture, Choate, Nathaniel, Zumbara, c.1935, 12 In. 460.00
Sculpture, Christopher Columbus, Reclining, Formerly Lamp Base, 21 In. 575.00
Sculpture, Classical Maiden Kneeling, Restraining A Pigeon, Marble Plinth, 16 In. 1610.00
Sculpture, Cupid On Marble Pedestal, Brown Patina, Late 19th Century, 32 In. 6000.00
Sculpture, Cupid, Standing On Orb, Holding A Bow, Charles X, 7 In. 1265.00
Sculpture, Daniels, John Karl, Woman, 5 7/8 In. 259.00
Sculpture, Dasson, Henry, Putti Blowing Horn, Dark Brown Patina, 1880, 24 In. 6000.00
Sculpture, Davis, Howell, Bear, With Kill, Light Mahogany Base, 7 In. 190.00
Sculpture, De Angelis, K.G., Prancing Horse, Made For Enzo Ferrari, 1958, 40 In. ..*Illus* 6215.00
Sculpture, De Vains, H.R., Trotter & Jockey, 13 1/2 In. 7200.00
Sculpture, Debut, Jean-Didier, Arab, Standing, Drinking From Jug, 15 In. 1150.00
Sculpture, Debut, Marcel, Woman Holding Artist's Paint Board, Signed, 18 In. 1035.00
Sculpture, Dedmore, Michael, The Pipeholder, 1980, 13 x 6 x 5 In. 495.00
Sculpture, Dell, Juan, Man, On Knees, Protecting Himself, 9 1/2 x 14 x 10 In. 525.00
Sculpture, Deming, E., Polar Bear, 17 In. 1610.00
Sculpture, Denslow, Pelicans On Rocky Ledge, 16 In. 3920.00
Sculpture, DeVeel, Armand, Jules, Soldier, Holding Musket, Marble Base, 30 In. 7170.00
Sculpture, Dog, Biting Hindquarters, Onyx Base, France, 2 1/2 In. 145.00

Sculpture, Drouot, E., Eagle Attacking Mountain Goats, 29 1/2 In. 5270.00
Sculpture, Dumaige, Musician & Young Girl, 24 1/2 In. 5720.00
Sculpture, Dumont, Archer, Green, Brown Patina, 1780, 35 In. 7200.00
Sculpture, Eberle, Abestenia, Pouting Child On Step, Pre-1942, 5 In. 2240.00
Sculpture, Elephant With Ivory Tusks, 14 1/2 In. 748.00
Sculpture, Elf Playing Violin, Continental, 6 3/4 In. 345.00
Sculpture, Eros Standing, Holding Lantern, Circular Base, 77 In. 2070.00
Sculpture, Fenn, Abstract Figures On Bleachers, Signed, 23 In. 335.00
Sculpture, Feuchere, Jean-Jacques, Bagpiper, Seated On Sheaf Of Wheat, 9 3/4 In. 520.00
Sculpture, Figures Holding Lotus Vases, 30 In., Pair 2415.00
Sculpture, Foo Lion, Rectangular Plinth, Chinese, 5 1/2 In. 80.00
Sculpture, Fox, Austria, 5 In. 385.00
Sculpture, Fremiet, Emmanuel, Chariot, Horses, 24 In. . . . . *Illus* 11000.00
Sculpture, Gamucci, C., Gentleman, 19th Century, 25 1/2 In. 2880.00
Sculpture, Gardet, A., Child, 24 In. 2240.00
Sculpture, Geraud, Henri, Woman In Flowing Dress, Carrying Basket, 13 In. 400.00
Sculpture, Gilbert, A., Revelers, Ivory, Gilt Bronze, Marble Base, 22 In. 18000.00
Sculpture, Girl Riding Dolphin, Gorham Foundry, 16 In. 3080.00
Sculpture, Gregoire, Jean-Louis, 2 Women, Brown Patina, 28 In. 2760.00
Sculpture, Grevin, A., Girl With Basket, 10 1/2 In. 560.00
Sculpture, Guiraud-Riviere, M., Stella, Gilt, 24 In. 9600.00
Sculpture, Hagenauer, Head With Uplifted Hands, c.1930, 7 In. 1550.00
Sculpture, Hagenauer, Man & Woman Golfer, Original Patina, 5 In., Pair 1265.00
Sculpture, Hagenauer, Native Peoples, Original Patina, 6 In., 4 Piece 345.00
Sculpture, Hagenauer, Warrior With Bow & Arrow, Brass, 7 1/2 x 4 1/4 In. 340.00
Sculpture, Harvey, Eli, Lioness, 1904, 22 In. 4025.00
Sculpture, Haverfield, S.N., Bear Clan, 13 x 9 In. 110.00
Sculpture, Heikka, E.E., Deer, Pronghorn, 1938, 7 x 5 x 12 In. 550.00
Sculpture, Hoffmann, 2 Boxers, 12 x 17 1/2 In. 2300.00
Sculpture, Holand, C., Young Man, 19th Century, 12 x 9 In. 360.00
Sculpture, Horse, Rearing, Austria, 5 In. 445.00
Sculpture, Hyatt, Anna Vaughn, Charging Rams, Gorham Foundry 0447, 8 In. 4480.00
Sculpture, Jester, Wearing Mask, Chocolate Brown Patina, Red Marble Socle, 7 In. 4500.00
Sculpture, Jockey On Racehorse, Black, Brown Patina, 22 In. 550.00
Sculpture, Kauba, C., Indian, Wearing Headdress, Swinging Hatchet, 5 In. 345.00
Sculpture, Kirchner, Swordsmith, Standing At Anvil, Sword Aloft, Marble Base, 23 In. . . 860.00
Sculpture, Kley, 2 Nude Boys Standing On Grassy Knoll, Red Marble Base, 7 In. 395.00
Sculpture, Knox, Jim, Water Carrier, Man On Horse Pointing Downward, 1980, 19 In. . . . 415.00
Sculpture, Kowalczewski, Ludwig P., Blacksmith, Marble Socle, 20th Century 690.00
Sculpture, Kuhne, August, Woman, 1889, 43 In. 8400.00
Sculpture, Ladd, Anna Coleman, Crab, Open Claws, 9 1/2 x 12 1/2 In. 1668.00
Sculpture, Lanceray, Eugene-Alex, 2 Military Figures, 1 On Horseback, 1887, 19 1/2 In. . . 3680.00
Sculpture, Lanceray, Eugene-Alex, Shepherdess With Her Flock, 1872, 11 3/4 In. 3600.00

Be careful when cleaning bronze figurines, lamp bases, bowls, etc. Never use steel wool, stiff brushes, or chemicals. Outdoor bronze sculptures need special care. Wash with soap, water, and a little ammonia to remove oil and dirt. Then rinse, dry, and rub with a cloth dipped in olive oil or boiled linseed oil. Rub with a dry cloth to remove extra oil. Outdoor bronzes should be oiled several times a year.

Bronze, Sculpture, De Angelis, K.G., Prancing Horse, Made For Enzo Ferrari, 1958, 40 In.

Bronze, Sculpture, Fremiet, Emmanuel,
Chariot, Horses, 24 In.

Bronze, Sculpture, Moigniez, Jules,
Sheep, 11 x 16 In.

Sculpture, Lathrop, Gertrude, Bird, Preening, Standing In Rushes, 1929, 5 In. 690.00
Sculpture, Laurent, E., Fisherwoman, Signed, 25 In. 1095.00
Sculpture, Lavergne, Adolphe-Jean, Young Fisherman, Gold Brown Patina, 1900, 11 In. ... 978.00
Sculpture, LeCourtier, P., Dog, Guarding 2 Sheep, 17 x 16 In. 990.00
Sculpture, Leonard, A., Heron, Medium Brown Patina, Black Marble Plinth, 6 1/4 In. 1495.00
Sculpture, Leonard, Agathon, Woman, Raised Hand, Signed, 14 In. 7475.00
Sculpture, Linke, A., Buffalo, Standing, Stone Base, 6 1/4 In. 259.00
Sculpture, Lorenzi, J., Woman Dancer, Silver, Wood, Marble Base, 1920, 20 In. 4200.00
Sculpture, MacMonnies, Frederick, Dancing Nymph, Shield, 1894, 33 In. 8250.00
Sculpture, MacMonnies, Frederick, Pan, Roman Bronze Works, N.Y., 15 1/2 In. 16800.00
Sculpture, Male & Female Harlequins, 19 x 22 In. 500.00
Sculpture, Man Carrying Basket Of Fruit, Japan, 19 In. 920.00
Sculpture, Man Seated On Pedestal, Drinking From Glass, Honey Patina, 5 In. 175.00
Sculpture, Man With Hunting Dog, Sword, Overcoat, Cap, Dog, Brown Patina, 24 In. ... 635.00
Sculpture, Man, Standing, Holding A Book, Square Base, Russia, 1891, 14 In. 750.00
Sculpture, Martel, J., Pigeon, Stylized, Marble Base, 10 In. 1725.00
Sculpture, Mene, Pierre-Jules, 2 Horses, Dark Brown Patina, 13 x 8 In. 575.00
Sculpture, Mene, Pierre-Jules, Dog, c.1850, 6 3/4 In. 2200.00
Sculpture, Mene, Pierre-Jules, Goat, With Bell, 1845, 5 1/2 x 9 3/4 In. 3520.00
Sculpture, Mene, Pierre-Jules, Gypsy Falconer, Falcon Raised Over Rabbit, 25 In. 1870.00
Sculpture, Mene, Pierre-Jules, Spaniard On Horseback, 28 In. 8800.00
Sculpture, Mene, Pierre-Jules, Startled Retriever, Dark Brown Patina, 13 In. 1095.00
Sculpture, Moigniez, Jules, Eagle With Spread Wings, Balance On A Branch, 29 In. 2530.00
Sculpture, Moigniez, Jules, Pheasant, Marble Base, 8 1/4 x 7 In. 550.00
Sculpture, Moigniez, Jules, Sheep, 11 x 16 In. .... *Illus* 3080.00
Sculpture, Monginot, C.H., Seated Girl, Sewing, Alabaster Base, 7 1/2 In. 2860.00
Sculpture, Monkey, Hear No Evil, See No Evil, Speak No Evil, 12 In. 1035.00
Sculpture, Monkey, Seated Holding Peach, 5 1/2 In. 460.00
Sculpture, Moreau, Auguste, Cupid, Gilt Bronze Base, Marble Plinth, 26 x 30 In. 2760.00
Sculpture, Moreau, Auguste, Fairy Blowing A Kiss, 1900, 30 1/2 In. 5520.00
Sculpture, Moreau, Auguste, Girl, Carrying Bucket, Brown Patina, 10 3/8 In. 230.00
Sculpture, Moreau, M., Girl, 30 In. 7800.00
Sculpture, Moreau, M., Woman Standing With Arms Upward, Brown Patina, 26 In. 2700.00
Sculpture, Moreau, Neoclassical Woman Reading, Signed, 23 In. 2185.00
Sculpture, Napoleon I, Military Dress, Folded Arms, Square Base, 16 x 5 In. 2530.00
Sculpture, Napoleon On Horseback, Marble Base, Pedestal, 31 In. 14400.00
Sculpture, Nude Woman, Art Nouveau, Marble Base, Signed, 20th Century, 14 In. 715.00
Sculpture, Okimono, Of A Tiger, Cat Striding Forward, Burl Base, 9 1/4 In. 1610.00
Sculpture, Omerth, George, Violin Player, Carved Ivory Face, c.1900, 6 3/4 In. 635.00
Sculpture, Park, Madeleine, Doberman Pinscher, Marble Plinth, 12 x 5 In. 2840.00
Sculpture, Pautrot, 2 Thrushes Chasing Insects, 17 x 18 1/4 In. 2415.00
Sculpture, Peasant Scene, Horse & Cart, 1880, 14 x 8 x 9 In. 1345.00
Sculpture, Peiffer, Diana The Huntress, 1880, 15 In. 3360.00
Sculpture, Pheasant, Cold Painted, Austria, 3 In. 85.00
Sculpture, Pheasant, Gold Dore, Marble Base, 8 x 5 In. 670.00

Sculpture, Philippe, Bacchante, Onyx Base, 19 In. 3450.00
Sculpture, Picault, Emile, Seated Roman Soldier, Drawing Sword, Signed, 25 In. 4025.00
Sculpture, Picault, Emile-Louis, Archer, 29 x 13 x 7 1/2 In. 1980.00
Sculpture, Ple, Henri, Winged Angel, Marble Base, 1885, 19 In. 2912.00
Sculpture, Poertzel, Otto, Snake Dancer, Marble Base, 20 1/2 In. 10200.00
Sculpture, Pollet, J., Nude Female, The Night, Brown, Green, Gold Patina, 38 In. 4200.00
Sculpture, Ponsard, P., Plowman & Woman At Work, 13 x 38 In. 2970.00
Sculpture, Potter, Louis, Eskimo Hunter, 18 x 17 x 10 In. 6720.00
Sculpture, Proctor, A. Phimister, Horse, Standing, Base, 15 1/2 In. 11550.00
Sculpture, Prophet, Nathan, Robed, Stroking Head, 15 1/2 In. 1380.00
Sculpture, Prost, Maurice, Panther, 24 In. 5175.00
Sculpture, Putti, Gilt, Seated On Pedestal, Upraised Arms, Mouth Agape, 21 In., Pair 3220.00
Sculpture, Putti, Seated On Rock, Scroll Plinth, Louis XV, 13 x 8 x 5 In., Pair 3220.00
Sculpture, Remington, Frederic, Mountain Man, 28 x 14 In. 330.00
Sculpture, Representing Astronomy, Patinated, Late 1800s, 11 1/2 x 11 1/2 In. 575.00
Sculpture, Riezzy, T., Female, Kneeling, Holding Flowers, Signed, 21 In. 4480.00
Sculpture, Rossi, Eugene, Mermaid Seated, Holding Bird In Hand, 45 In. 3450.00
Sculpture, Rougelet, Benedict, Youth, 11 In. 5100.00
Sculpture, Ruff, Andreas, Farmer On Horseback, Brown Patina, Naturalistic Base, 9 In. ... 750.00
Sculpture, Russell, Charles, M., Lone Buffalo, 1920, 8 x 6 x 5 In. 300.00
Sculpture, Sala, Elia, 3 Children Playing, 19 x 12 x 14 In. 450.00
Sculpture, Samurai Standing, Dressed In Armor, Holding Fish Standard, 50 In. 1725.00
Sculpture, Shou Lao, Seated On Deer, Ming Period, 11 1/2 In. 3335.00
Sculpture, Silversmith, 24 In. 3000.00
Sculpture, Somme, Theophile, Woman In Long Dress, Ivory Face, Amber Socle, 12 In. ... 1380.00
Sculpture, Spagna, P., North African Man, Carrying Jugs, Brown, Green, 32 In. 7200.00
Sculpture, Sun King, 17th Century, 6 1/2 In. 4500.00
Sculpture, Temple Lions, Platform Base, 7 In., Pair 190.00
Sculpture, Tereszczuk, Peter, Dancer, Ivory, 22 1/2 In. 7200.00
Sculpture, Tharel, Leon, Boy Musician, Reclining With Stringed Instrument, 13 In. 920.00
Sculpture, The Dying Gaul, Semi-Nude Warrior Lying With Horn, 19 In. 980.00
Sculpture, Thomire, Pierre Phillippe, Woman, Holding Torchere, 31 1/2 x 67 In. 8800.00
Sculpture, Tiger Attacking A Monkey, Signed, Japan, 17 1/2 In. 1840.00
Sculpture, Unicorn, Tortoiseshell Back, Flame Tail, Chinese, 19th Century, 5 In. 127.00
Sculpture, Vannetti, Antonio, Napoleon On Horseback, Brown, Green, 1900, 27 In. 7800.00
Sculpture, Voulot, 2 Maidens Dancing, Long Flowing Gowns, 8 1/4 x 9 In. 1045.00
Sculpture, Wheeler, Hughlette, Sweet Briar, Marble Base, 13 1/2 In. 4840.00
Sculpture, Wild Boar, Standing, Continental, 4 1/2 x 3 In. 575.00
Sculpture, Woman, Praying, Folded Hands, Leaf Base, 32 In. 365.00
Sculpture, Woman, Standing With Shawl Draped Over Shoulder, Gilt, 10 1/2 In. 415.00
Sculpture, Woman, Standing, Drawing Up Nightgown, Gilt, Marble Base, 12 1/4 In. 4025.00
Sculpture, Young Dionysius, 1905, 22 In. 1610.00
Sculpture, Young Girl, Seated On Stepped Balustrade, Looking Down At Box, 16 In. 3000.00
Sculpture, Young Woman, Holding Urn On Her Shoulder, Continental, 17 3/4 In. 460.00
Sculpture, Young, Mahonri, Old Man Reading With Dog, Roman Bronze Works, 7 In. 4480.00
Sculpture, Zach, Bruno, Dancer, Marble Base, 1920, 14 3/4 In. 3300.00
Smoking Set, Nymph Standing On Tree Stump, Circular Base, 12 In. 860.00
Stand, Gospel, Gilt, Paste Stones, Enamel Plaque, 11 1/2 In. 560.00
Tazza, Anthemion Handles, Slate Base, France, 19th Century, 6 3/4 x 13 In. 230.00
Tazza, Cherubs & Psyche, Serpent Handles, 3 1/4 x 9 1/2 x 11 In. 545.00
Tazza, Coiled Serpents, Festooned Classical Masks, Flared Rim, 16 x 14 x 19 In. 4370.00
Tazza, Leaf Panels, Putti Scene Interior, Figural Handles, 10 x 13 In. 402.00
Tazza, Neoclassical, Gadrooned Edges, Handles, Green Marble, 9 In., Pair 460.00
Tray, Charles X, Gold Dore, Circular Mirrors Plate, 2 x 11 In. 690.00
Tray, Classical Plaque, 2 Handles, Signed, France, 1 3/4 x 7 1/4 x 17 In. 750.00
Tray, Marione, A., Berries, Leafy Branches, Signed, 18 In. 4140.00
Umbrella Stand, Female Whippet, Whip In Mouth, 30 3/4 In. 690.00
Urn, Allegory Scenes, Etruscan Style, Patinated, Sienna Marble, Cover, 21 x 11 In. 230.00
Urn, Bacchanalian Scene, Continental, 9 1/4 In. 230.00
Urn, Calligraphy, Cylindrical, Leaves, Footed, Base, Chinese, 9 1/2 x 10 1/2 In., Pair 635.00
Urn, Campana, Wheat, Pelican, Serpent, Gilt, Red, Green Marble Plinth, 10 In., Pair 635.00
Urn, Classical Relief, Silver Finish, Gilt Highlights & Handles, Red Marble Base, 9 In. .. 825.00
Urn, Classical, Cherubs On Wide Band, Removable Liner, Marble, France, 11 1/2 In. 440.00

Urn, Everted Rim, Twin Scrolled Handles, Stepped Plinth, 11 3/4 In., Pair	805.00
Urn, Flower, Leaf, Scroll Motif, Mask-Form Handles, Ebonized Wood Plinth, 10 In.	316.00
Urn, Grotesque Rams' Masks, Flared Rim, Inverted Neck, 16 In., Pair	4140.00
Urn, Laurel, Fluted Border, Domed Lid, Napoleon III, 13 1/2 x 9 x 11 1/2 In., Pair	4370.00
Urn, Marble, Napoleon III, 1820, 17 In., Pair	4300.00
Urn, Satyr's Masks, Drapery Swags, Marble, Louis XVI, 23 In., Pair	6600.00
Urn, Terrace, Campana, Continuous Band Of Running Antelope, Handle, 10 In., Pair	630.00
Urn, Terrace, Compressed Form, Lion-Mask Ring Handles, 16 x 27 In., Pair	1610.00
Urns, Mythological Relief, Handles, Marble Base, Oval, 18 In.	2875.00
Vase, Archaic Form, Pear Shape, Bow-String Marks Around Base, Chinese, 16 1/2 In.	145.00
Vase, Cloud & Stylized Dragon Design, 10 In.	105.00
Vase, Cupids, Rococo Style, Gilt, Trumpet Glass, Champleve Enamel, 15 In., Pair	2990.00
Vase, Fisherman Raising Sail, Copper, Silver Inlay, Japan, 20th Century	230.00
Vase, Gilt, Opaline Glass, Calla Lily Shape, William IV, Marked Abbott, 16 1/4 In.	518.00
Vase, Harpies, Bacchic Revel, Gilt, Vienna Enamel, Renaissance Style, 3 In.	546.00
Vase, Leaf & Ring Crown, C-Scroll Handles, Flowers, Napoleon III, 17 In., Pair	3910.00
Vase, Moreau, Auguste, Children Playing, Dragonflies, Butterflies, 18 In., Pair	2915.00
Vase, Patinated, Hand Hammered, Ring-Form Handles, Arts & Crafts, c.1900, 14 1/2 In.	633.00
Vase, Putti Cavorting, Square Plinth, Charles X, 15 In., Pair	4140.00
Vase, Riverscape, Pagoda, Globe Shape, Meiji, Japan, 7 In.	105.00
Vase, Taotieh Mask, Archaistic, Molded Handles, Inscribed, Chinese, 1958, 12 In.	115.00
Vase, Terrace, Campana, Palm Leaf Design, 14 In., Pair	520.00
Vase, Vibert, Alexandre, Flowers On Neck, 9 1/2 In.	1495.00
Watch Holder, Cherub Holding A Lyre, On Sienna Marble Base, Charles X, 7 1/4 In.	750.00

BROWNIES were first drawn in 1883 by Palmer Cox. They are characterized by large round eyes, downturned mouths, and skinny legs. Toys, books, dinnerware, and other objects were made with the Brownies as part of the design.

Advertisement, Snag-Proof Rubber Boots, Lambertville Rubber Co., N.J.	29.00
Blotter, Gold Mine Flour	68.00
Book, 16 Stories, Hubbard Publishing, 1897, 10 x 7 1/4 In.	15.00
Cup, Brownie Camera, Eastman Kodak, 2 1/2 In.	160.00
Cup & Saucer, Child's, Golf Scenes, Palmer Cox	195.00
Game, Nine Pins, Chinese Man, Policeman, P. Cox, McLoughlin Bros., c.1890	850.00
Spoon, Palmer Cox	50.00
Trade Card, Brownies Making Ice Cream, American Machine Co.	49.00
Trade Card, Domestic Sewing Machine, Brownies Climbing Tree	38.00

BRUSH Pottery was started in 1925. George Brush first worked in 1901 in Zanesville, Ohio. He started his own pottery in 1907, but it burned to the ground soon after. In 1909 he became manager of the J.W. McCoy Pottery. In 1911, Brush and J.W. McCoy formed the Brush-McCoy Pottery Co. After a series of name changes, the company became The Brush Pottery in 1925. It closed in 1982. Collectors favor the figural cookie jars made by this company. Because there was a company named Brush-McCoy, there is great confusion between Brush and Nelson McCoy pieces. See McCoy category for more information.

Cookie Jar, Cookie House, 10 3/4 In., 1962	90.00
Cookie Jar, Cow With Cat Finial, Brown, 8 1/2 In., 1950s	110.00 to 225.00
Cookie Jar, Cow With Cat Finial, Purple & White, 8 1/2 In., 1950s	1500.00
Cookie Jar, Elephant, With Ice Cream	350.00
Cookie Jar, Happy Bunny, Gray, 12 3/4 In., 1960	395.00
Cookie Jar, Hippo, Laughing, 1961, 8 x 11 In.	700.00
Cookie Jar, Hippo, Sitting, 1969, 11 In.	375.00
Cookie Jar, Pig, Formal, Green	375.00
Cookie Jar, Squirrel On Log, 10 3/4 In.	175.00
Cookie Jar, Teddy Bear, Feet Apart, Green Apron, 10 1/2 In., 1950s	295.00
Match Holder, Kolor Kraft, Striker, 1930s, 6 1/4 In.	650.00
Pedestal, Green, 17 1/2 In.	81.00
Pitcher, Bristol Glaze, Blue Flower, c.1911, 8 1/2 In.	295.00
Salt Box, Lid, 4 1/4 x 6 In.	225.00

BRUSH MCCOY, see Brush category and related pieces in McCoy category.

BUCK ROGERS was the first American science fiction comic strip. It started in 1929 and continued until 1967. Buck has also appeared in comic books, movies, and, in the 1980s, a television series. Any memorabilia connected with the character Buck Rogers is collectible.

Battle Cruiser, Box, Tootsietoy, 1937, 5 In.	650.00
Book, Big Little Book, Moons Of Saturn	15.00
Boots, Lightning Bolt, Rubber, Red, Goodyear Tires Premium, 1935	1000.00
Button, Rocket Pistol, Spaceship On Side, 1935, 1 In.	75.00
Figure Set, Buck, Wilma, Twiki, Ardella, Dr. Huer, Box, Mego, 1979, 4 In., 9 Piece	70.00
Flash Blast Attack Ship, Tootsietoy, Box, 1937	400.00
Gun, Disintegrator, Box	1300.00 to 1350.00
Gun, Rocket Pistol, 1930s	125.00
Gun, Space, Sheet Metal	225.00
Gun, Twenty-Fifth Century Laser Pistol, Daisy	144.00
Helmet, Lightning Bolt, Rubber, Red, Goodyear Premium, 1931	1000.00
Helmet, Navigation, Celluloid Shield, Cream Of Wheat Premium, Daisy, 1935	1200.00
Pencil Box, Buck Rogers In The 25th Century, Blue & Gold, U.S. Map, 1935	175.00
Pistol, Liquid Helium	785.00
Printing Set, Stamper Kraft Set, Astral Heroes, 7 Stamp Pads, c.1931	525.00
Puzzle, 3-D, XZ-35 Disintegrator Pistol, 1950, 2 1/2 In.	185.00
Ring, Ring Of Saturn, Instruction Sheet	150.00
Rocket Fighter, Pressed Steel & Wood, Wyandotte, 1936	235.00
Rocket Ship, Lithographed Tinplate, Clockwork Motor, Box, Marx, 12 In.	1495.00
Rocket Ship, Tin, Windup, Sparks, Boinging Noise, Lithograph Characters, 12 In.	2700.00
Spaceship, Rocket Police Patrol, Marx	500.00 to 700.00
Strato-Kite, Jet Propelled, Unassembled, Aero Kite, 1946, 15 x 19-In. Envelope	73.00
Thermos, Plastic, Aladdin Industries, 1979, 6 5/8 In.	35.00

BUFFALO POTTERY was made in Buffalo, New York, after 1902. The company was established by the Larkin Company, famous manufacturers of soap. The wares are marked with a picture of a buffalo and the date of manufacture. Deldare ware is the most famous pottery made at the factory. It has either a khaki-colored or green background with hand painted transfer designs.

BUFFALO POTTERY, Bowl, Cereal, Willow, 6 1/2 In.	50.00
Bowl, Vegetable, Cover, Willow, Rectangular, 1909	500.00
Bowl, Vegetable, Willow, Oval, 1916, 9 5/8 In.	140.00
Bowl, Willow, 5 1/2 In.	50.00
Bread Plate, Willow, 1908, 6 1/8 In.	25.00
Candleholder, Village Scene, Gentlemen Gathered, 6 Sides, 8 3/4 In.	275.00
Chamberstick, Village Scene, Miniature Village, 1909, 5 1/4 In.	1100.00
Compote, Roycroft, 3 3/4 x 9 1/4 In.	805.00
Creamer, Willow, 1911	100.00
Cup & Saucer, Willow, 1916, 2 1/8 In.	80.00 to 90.00
Dish, Little Boy Offering Candy To Console Little Girl, Child's, 1 3/8 x 7 In.	132.00
Gravy Boat, Willow, 1911	220.00
Pitcher, John Paul Jones, Blue Transfer, Soldier Aboard Ship, 1907, 9 In.	715.00
Pitcher, Landing Of Roger Williams, Magenta, Blue, Green, 1907, 6 In.	523.00
Pitcher, Oriental, Blue Transfer, Oriental Landscape, Handle, 5 In.	303.00
Pitcher, Oriental, Blue Transfer, Oriental Landscape, Handle, 7 In.	468.00
Pitcher, Robin Hood, 1906, 8 1/4 In.	500.00 to 795.00
Pitcher, Roosevelt Bears, Bears At Home, Bears Take Auto Ride, 1907, 8 In.	990.00
Pitcher, Sailors, Lighthouse Scene, White Glaze Ground, 1906, 9 In.	495.00
Plaque, Wall, Friday, Monks Are Gathered Around Banquet Table, 12 In.	2860.00
Plaque, Wall, Thursday, Monks Are Gathered Along Embankment, 12 In.	4125.00
Plate, Dessert, Willow, 1908, 7 In.	34.00
Plate, Dinner, Willow, 1909, 10 1/4 In.	90.00 to 100.00
Plate, Game Bird, Grouse, Scalloped Edge, Gold Trim, Ralph Stuart, 1908, 9 In.	40.00
Plate, Harvest Scene, Magenta, Yellow, Green, Brown Border, 7 In.	248.00
Plate, Hunting, The Gunner, Hunter Taking Aim Toward Wild Ducks, 9 In.	413.00

Plate, Luncheon, Willow, 1918, 9 1/4 In. 40.00
Plate, Luncheon, Willow, 9 1/4 In. 40.00
Plate, Salad, Willow, 1908, 8 3/8 In. 40.00
Plate, U.S. Capitol, Green Transfer, 10 In. 40.00
Plate, Willow, 6 3/8 In. 28.00
Plate, Willow, 9 1/4 In. 40.00
Platter, Willow, Oval, 1908, 14 1/8 In. 220.00
Platter, Willow, Oval, 8 3/4 In. ....140.00 to 150.00
Platter, Willow, Oval, 9 5/8 In. 130.00
Relish, Willow, 1911, 8 3/8 In. 80.00
Soup, Coupe, Willow, 1909, 6 1/2 In. 50.00
Sugar, Willow, Cover 140.00
Tankard, All You Have To Do Is Teach The Dutchman English, 12 1/4 In. 1100.00
Tray, Harvest Scene, Farmhouse Surrounded By Fields, Haystacks, 10 In. 77.00
Tray, Lake Scene With Sailboats, Abino, 1911, 12 In. 1100.00
Vase, Geranium, White Geraniums, Cobalt Blue Ground, Closed Mouth, 4 In. 55.00
BUFFALO POTTERY DELDARE, Bowl, Dr. Syntax Reading His Tour, Emerald, 9 In. 880.00
Bowl, Fallowfield Hunt, The Death, Hunters Cheering, 3 3/4 In. 358.00
Bowl, Fallowfield Hunt, The Death, Olive Green, 9 x 3 3/4 In. 385.00
Bowl, Fox Hunting, 5 1/2 In., 6 Piece 1210.00
Bowl, Ye Village Street, Gentleman Walking, 1908, 9 In. ....330.00 to 448.00
Candlestick, Shieldback, Village Scene, 5 1/4 In. 715.00
Candlestick, Village Scene, Group Of 3 Gentlemen, 1909, 9 In. 990.00
Creamer, Dr. Syntax With The Dairymaid, Emerald, 3 In. 605.00
Creamer, Dr. Syntax, With The Dairymaid, Emerald, 4 In. 252.00
Creamer, Fallowfield Hunt, Breaking Cover, L. Newman, 2 In. 55.00
Cup & Saucer, Dr. Syntax At Liverpool, Emerald, 2 1/8 In. 523.00
Garden Seat, Ye Lion Inn, 13 1/2 In. 3630.00
Humidor, There Was An Old Sailor, Sitting On Barrel, 7 1/2 In. 1540.00
Humidor, Ye Lion Inn, Interior Lodge Scene, 1909, 7 x 6 In. 715.00
Jardiniere, Colonial Men Talking, Signed, 6 In. 460.00
Match Holder, Fallowfield Hunt, Miniature Hunt Scene, 3 In. 1045.00
Mug, Dr. Syntax Made Free Of Cellar, Emerald, 4 1/2 In. 385.00
Mug, Fallowfield Hunt, Breaking Cover, Signed, L. Anna, 1908, 3 5/8 In. 385.00
Mug, Fallowfield Hunt, Dogs & Horses, 2 1/3 In. 550.00
Mug, Scenes Of Life In Olden Days, Embossed Handle, Child's, 2 In. 523.00
Mug, Scenes Of Life In Olden Days, Handle, 1924 .... 1320.00
Pin Tray, Dr. Syntax Received By Maid, Emerald, 1911, 6 x 3 In. 1125.00
Pitcher, Dr. Syntax Amused With Pat In The Pond, 1911, 7 x 6 In. 1100.00
Pitcher, Fallowfield Hunt, Breaking Cover, Dogs Frolicking, 9 In. 495.00
Pitcher, Fallowfield Hunt, Men On Horses, Black Lining, 6 In. 550.00
Pitcher, Great Controversy, 12 1/2 In. 990.00
Pitcher, Their Manner Of Telling Stories, 6 In. 440.00
Pitcher, This Amazed Me, Paneled, 10 In. 935.00
Pitcher, To Advise Me In A Whisper, 6 3/4 In. 440.00
Pitcher, To Spare An Old Broken Soldier, 7 7/8 In. ....303.00 to 550.00
Pitcher, Ye English Village, 11 In. 660.00
Plaque, Fallowfield Hunt, The Start, 13 In. 1430.00
Plaque, Wall, Dr. Syntax Sells Grizzle, Emerald, 13 In. 1870.00
Plate, Dr. Syntax Disputing His Bill, With Landlady, 1909, 9 1/4 In. 165.00
Plate, Dr. Syntax Loses His Wig, Emerald, Signed, Broel, 1911, 9 In. ....880.00 to 995.00
Plate, Dr. Syntax Losing His Way, 10 In. 825.00
Plate, Dr. Syntax Sells Grizzle, 10 In. 247.00
Plate, Dr. Syntax Star Gazing, 10 In. 770.00
Plate, Dr. Syntax, Taking Possession, Emerald, 10 In. 247.00
Plate, Fallowfield Hunt, Breaking Cover, Emerald, Horse, Dog, 10 In. 193.00
Plate, Fallowfield Hunt, Portraying A Rider Falling, 6 In. 220.00
Plate, Yankee Doodle, Emerald, 1911, 10 In. 2750.00
Plate, Ye Olden Days, 9 In. 270.00
Plate, Ye Olden Times, Signed W. Foster, Buffalo Logo, c.1909, 9 In. 224.00
Plate, Ye Town Crier, 8 In. 270.00
Plate, Ye Village Street, 7 In. 250.00
Teapot, Dr. Syntax Disputing His Bill, Emerald, 5 In. 523.00

Tray, Calling Card, Dr. Syntax Robbed Of His Property, 1911, 8 In.	468.00
Tray, Calling Card, Ye Lion Inn, 7 3/4 In.	247.00
Tray, Dancing Ye Minuet, B. Willon, 12 x 9 In.	385.00
Tray, Dr. Syntax Mistakes A Gentleman's House, Emerald, 13 In.	1320.00
Tray, Ye Olden Times, Trio Of Gentlemen Along Boardwalk, 12 In.	440.00
Vase, 3 Costumed Women, Man, Women On Beds, Signed, c.1908	1456.00
Vase, Ye Village Parson, Walking Along Boardwalk, 1909, 8 In.	825.00

BUNNYKINS, see Royal Doulton category.

BURMESE GLASS was developed by Frederick Shirley at the Mt. Washington Glass Works in New Bedford, Massachusetts, in 1885. It is a two-toned glass, shading from peach to yellow. Some pieces have a pattern mold design. A few Burmese pieces were decorated with pictures or applied glass flowers of colored Burmese glass. Other factories made similar glass also called *Burmese*. Related items may be listed in the Fenton category, the Gunderson category and under Webb Burmese.

Basket, Single Handle, 10 1/2 x 5 3/4 In.	285.00
Bowl, Floral, Footed, Applied Edge, 7 1/2 x 7 In. ....*Illus*	4025.00
Cruet, With Caddy, 2 Bottles	2150.00
Epergne, Enameled Flowers, 8 1/4 In.	5750.00
Ewer, Dragons & Flowers, Bulbous	2000.00
Fairy Lamp, Shade & Base, Pair	4100.00
Finger Bowl, Applied Yellow Edging, 2 x 3 1/2 In.	235.00
Ginger Jar, Cover, Enameled Egyptian Scene	3500.00
Mustard, Pewter Cover, Swing Handle, 3 1/4 In.	200.00
Pitcher, Pale Pink Petticoat Foot, White Handle, 5 1/2 In.	400.00
Rose Bowl, Circular Bulbous, 3 In.	170.00
Salt & Pepper, Silver Plated Holder	236.00
Salt & Pepper, White, Light Pink Neck, 4 In., Pair	335.00
Toothpick, Fig Mold, Crimped, 1888	750.00
Toothpick, Glossy, 1885, 2 1/4 In.	300.00
Toothpick, Parallel Greek Key	590.00
Tumbler, Egyptian Pharaoh With Bow, Chariot, Pyramids In Background, 3 In.	290.00
Tumbler, Queen's, Yellow Daisies, Green Leaves, 4 In.	1750.00
Tumbler, Satin, Acid Finish, 3 1/2 In.	275.00
Vase, Beaded, Flowers & Leaves, Bulbous, 2 1/8 x 2 9/16 In.	400.00
Vase, Enameled Conifers, Leaves & Berries, 4 1/4 In., Pair	690.00
Vase, Enameled Flowers, 7 3/4 In.	575.00
Vase, Feather, Footed, 7 x 9 In.	690.00
Vase, Gold Centered Stylized Beaded Blossoms, 10 In.	1785.00
Vase, Lily, Enameled Flowers, Egyptian Jewels, 24 In., Pair	2500.00
Vase, Satin, Applied Ribbon Trim	465.00
Vase, Trumpet Shape, Circular Base, 16 In., Pair	690.00
Water Set, 8-In. Pitcher, 5 Piece	1150.00

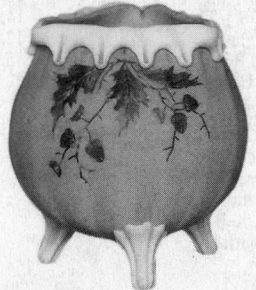

Burmese, Bowl, Floral, Footed,
Applied Edge, 7 1/2 x 7 In.

When buying antiques, beware of stickers, Magic Marker numbers, or other dealer-added labels that may damage the antique. Any type of sticky tape or label will leave marks on paper or paint finishes. Metal with an oxidized finish is damaged when ink marks are removed. Pencil or pen notations often leave indentations.

BUSTER BROWN, the comic strip, first appeared in color in 1902. Buster and his dog, Tige, remained a popular comic and soon became even more famous as the emblem for a shoe company, a textile firm, and others. The strip was discontinued in 1920, but some of the advertising is still in use.

Bank, Buster Brown & Tige, Cast Iron, 5 1/2 In.	231.00
Button, Buster Brown Hose Supporters, Celluloid, Tin, 1900, 5/8 In.	20.00
Button, Buster Brown Walking Club, Picture, Celluloid, 1 1/4 In.	53.00
Display, Buster & Tige, America's Favorite Shoe, Easel Back, Electric, 20 In.	285.00
Roly Poly, Papier-Mache, Head Wobbles When Moved, Schoenhut, 9 1/4 In.	240.00
Throw Rug, Nylon, 54 In.	315.00
Yo-Yo, Buster & Tige, Tin, Yellow, Green, Japan, 1950s	75.00

BUTTER CHIPS, or butter pats, were small individual dishes for butter. They were the height of fashion from 1880 to 1910. Earlier as well as later examples are known.

Cherry Blossoms, Pink, Embossed Leaves, 2 7/8 In.	14.50
Colonial Man & Woman, Purple Ground, Gold Rim, Limoges, Crown, 2 3/4 In.	15.00
Crown, Pink Rose Border, Gold, Black, Yellow, Green, Gold Rim, Johnson Bros., 3 In.	12.00
Dahlia, Blue, Black, White, Ironstone, 2 3/4 In.	20.00
Dogwood Flowers, Gold, White, White Edge Design, Clipped Corners, 2 1/2 In.	10.50
Flow Blue, Gold Trim, Colonial, J & G Meakin, Hanley, England, 3 In.	28.00
Flower, In Center, White, Gold, 3 1/8 In.	8.00
Flower, Leaf Design, Muted Color, Square, White, Rounded Corners	18.00
Flowers, Blue, Green Leaves, Gold Bands, Scalloped Edge, 3 1/2 In.	15.00
Flowers, Brown, Slanted Sides, Semi-Ruffled Edge, Square, Glazed	12.00
Flowers, Glazed, Pink, Rust, Yellow, Hand Painted, 3 In.	8.50
Flowers, Leaves, Blue Green, Gold, Scalloped Edge, 3 In.	25.00
Flowers, Leaves, White Bird, Multicolor, Shell Shape, c.1939	18.00
Flowers, Rounded Bottom, Green, Gold, Scalloped, J & O Meakin Hanley, 3 In.	20.00
Flowers, White Glaze, Gold Edge, Semi-Scalloped, O. & E.G., Royal Austria, 3 In.	12.00
Green, Gold, Haviland, 1896, 2 3/4 In.	30.00
Horse Drawn Car, Flowers On Edge, Lamberton China, Baltimore & Ohio, 3 3/8 In.	50.00
Moth, Multicolor, Gold, Pink, Embossed, Scalloped Trim, 2 7/8 In.	23.50
Pansy Shape, Black, White, 3 In.	18.00
Peach Cluster, Leaves, Stem, Center Design, Gold Band, Scalloped Edge, 3 1/2 In.	14.50
Pink Rose, In Center, Green Leaves, Thin Gold Band, Mark, 3 1/8 In.	12.00
Red, Gold Trim, Haviland, 1896, 2 3/4 In.	28.00
Rose, In Center, Pink, 3 Gold Bands, 3 1/8 In.	15.00
Rose, Pink, Center, Green Leaves, Gold Scalloped Edge, White Porcelain, 3 1/8 In.	18.00
Roses, Pink, Leaf Groupings, Embossed Edge Design, Haviland, 3 1/8 In.	14.00
Roses, Pink, White Glaze, Embossed, Limoges, T & V, c.1901, 3 1/8 In.	13.00
Roses, Pink, Yellow, Leaves, Semi-Scalloped Edge, Bassett Austria, Limoges, 3 In.	14.00
Roses, Teal, Gold, Mark, Alfred Meakin, England	20.00
Square, Center Flower Design, Scalloped Edge, Semi-Porcelain, 2 7/8 In.	12.50
White, 6-Petal Flower Shape, Unusual Design, Glazed, Gold Detail, 3 1/8 In.	10.00
White, Flower Design, Porcelain, 2 Outer Bands, Scalloped Edge, 3 1/2 In.	14.00
White, Gold Trim, 10 Sides, Porcelain, Johnson Bros., Crown, England, 3 In.	12.00
White, Ironstone, Rectangular, Vertical Side Lines, Mark, England Royal, 3 x 2 In.	15.00
White, Wide Gold Band, Porcelain, Knowles, Taylor & Knowles, Eagle Mark, 3 In.	12.00

BUTTER MOLDS are listed in the Kitchen category under Mold, Butter.

BUTTON collecting has been popular since the nineteenth century. Buttons have been known throughout the centuries, and there are millions of styles. Gold, silver, or precious stones were used for the best buttons, but most were made of natural materials, like bone or shell, or from inexpensive metals. Only a few types are listed for comparison.

3 Shepherds, Motiwala Transfer, Large	154.00
Amber Glass, Foil, Tingue, Rectangular Center	220.00
Bakelite, Black Cherry, Sew Through, 7/8 x 1/2 In.	22.00
Bakelite, Brass, Amber Glass, Domed, Catalin Base, 1 5/8 x 5/8 In.	23.00
Bakelite, Butterscotch, Scalloped Edge, Embedded Metal Shank, 1 In.	5.00

Bakelite, Celluloid Overlay, Green, 1 1/4 In. 8.00
Bakelite, Cylinder Shape, Orange, 1 In. 3.50
Bakelite, Daisies, Reverse Carved, Yellow Paint, 1930s, 1 1/2 In. 22.00
Bakelite, Dark Tortoiseshell, Acorn, 1 x 3/4 In. 12.00
Bakelite, Flowers In Pot, Yellow, Sew Through, 1 3/4 In. 14.00
Bakelite, Pot Metal, Green Glass, Filigree, 1 3/4 In. 30.00
Bakelite, Scotty, Black Paint, France 30.00
Brass, Flower Petal Design, Wire Border, Metal Shank, 1 3/8 In. 10.00
Brass, Leaf & Bug Design, Brass Shank, 3/4 In. 12.00
Brass, Spelter, Dragon, 1 1/2 In. 15.00
Cameo, Gilt Setting, 6 Piece 165.00
Celluloid, 3-D Eyeballs, 2 In. 5.00
Celluloid, Applied Bow, Round, 2 Hole, 1 3/4 In. 2.00
Celluloid, Carved Design, Grooved Shank, 1/2 In. 1.50
Celluloid, Gold, Pink, Plastic Deer Escutcheon, Cupped, 1 In. 5.00
Celluloid, Lady Feeding Bird, Square 250.00
Celluloid, Oriental Pheasant, Oval, Large 44.00
Celluloid, Saturn, Concentric Rings, Transparent, Yellow Base, Red Center, 1 7/16 In. ... 6.00
Celluloid, Tear Drop Design, Green, Brown, Self Shank, 7/8 In. 1.50
Celluloid, Tussy Mussy, Flowers, Leaves, Round, 1 1/8 In. 5.00
Ceramic Studio, Animal Sculpture, Enamel, 1 1/4 In. 18.00
China, Bluebirds On Branch Transfer, Large 330.00
China, Fox & Stork, Polychrome Transfer 355.00
Cloisonne, Polychromatic, 1 1/4 In. 30.00
Composition, China, Wood, Cloth, Sailboat Design 3.00
Composition, Syroco, Faux Wood, 2 Scotty Dogs, Brown, c.1940, 1 1/2 In. 20.00
Cuff, Mother-Of-Pearl, Silvertone Edge, 5/8 In. 3.50
Enamel, Blue Design, Brass Loop Shank 37.00
Enamel, Champleve, Large 44.00
Enamel, Flowers, Small 22.00
Enamel, Flowers, Steel Cut, Beaded Border, Brass Base, 1 1/4 In. 69.00
Gay Nineties, Green, 3 Piece 132.00
Gay Nineties, Lavender, 3 Piece 132.00
Glass, Beige, Leaf Design, Self Shank, 3/4 In. 3.00
Glass, Black, Gold Luster, 3-Leaf Design, Self Shank, 7/8 In. 3.50
Glass, Black, Gold Trim, Rosette Design, Shelf Shank, 7/8 In. 3.00
Glass, Black, Incised, Castle Design, Self Shank, 3/4 In. 4.00
Glass, Black, Raised Design, Silver Trim, Self Shank, 1 In. 2.50
Glass, Clear, Gold Design, Self Shank, 3/4 In. 2.50
Glass, Clear, Gold Leaf Design, Self Shank, 3/4 In. 2.00
Glass, Clipper Ship, Black, Metal Setting, Medium 88.00
Glass, Cobalt Blue, Paste Border & Center, 18th Century 110.00
Glass, Floating Gold Flake, Design, Domed, Waistcoat, 9/16 In. 8.50
Glass, Green Stone Inlay, 9/16 In. 23.00
Glass, Green, High Dome, Gold Trim, Self Shank, 7/8 In. 2.00
Glass, Molded, Red, Fruit, Yellow, Green, Blue, Painted, 1/2 In. 3.00
Glass, Red, 3 Rhinestones, Brass Border Accents, Loop Shank, 1/2 In. 8.00
Glass, Red, Painted Trim, Self Shank, 9/16 In. 1.25
Goose Girl 44.00
Greenaway, 5 Piece 88.00
Hunter & Dog 77.00
Igloo, Black & White, Small 165.00
Ivory, Woman In Swing, Large 330.00
Last Supper, Motiwala Transfer, Jewel Border, Large 413.00
Leather, Brass Heart, 3/4 In. 3.50
Leather Ground, Thumbelina, Riding Swallow, Large 110.00
Little Colonel, Large 100.00
Little Miss Patty & Mr. Paul, 4 Piece 210.00
Lucite, Carved Line, Square, 1 1/2 In. 1.50
Lucite, Clear, Applied Green Grape Bunch, 1 3/8 In. 8.00
Mercury, Head, Large 120.00
Metal, 3 Flying Birds, Flowers, Pressed, Self Shank, 1 3/8 In. 15.00
Metal, Cut Steel Middle, Loop Shank, 3 Sections, 7/16 In. 1.50

Metal, Enameled, Gold Tone, Open Work, Loop Shank, 5/8 In. 6.50
Metal, Flower Basket, Tools, Domed, Open Work Design, Loop Shank, 1 In. 12.50
Metal, Mirror, Gold, Filigree Flower Pattern, 3/4 In. 12.00
Metal, Raised Leaf Design, 2 Sections, Loop Shank, 1 1/4 In. 12.00
Molded, Flowers, Reverse Painted, Self Shank, 1 In. 7.50
Owl Family 110.00
Paperweight, Israel 16.00
Plastic, Bareback Rider, Circus Set, 3/4 In. 2.25
Plastic, Black, Rhinestones, Metal Loop Shank, 1 x 3/8 In. 3.00
Plastic, Black, White Sailor Design, Hexagon, 3/4 In. 12.00
Plastic, Bow Shape, Loop Shank, 1 In. 1.00
Plastic, Brass Shank, Art Deco, 1 In. 12.00
Plastic, Leaf Shape, Tan, 2 Holes, 5/8 In. 1.50
Plastic, Lion, Unicorn, Goldtone, Black Background, 3/4 In. 5.00
Plastic, Mica Flakes, Opaque Top, Self Shank, 1 1/4 In. 3.00
Plastic, Urn Shape, Black, 3/4 In. 2.00
Plastic, Urn Shape, Green, 3/4 In. 2.00
Queen Elizabeth, Motiwala Transfer, Large 110.00
Rhinestone, Deep Red Garnet, White Metal, Self Shank, 7/8 In. 3.50
Rooster, Ashlee 122.00
Rooster, Tortoiseshell, Etched 250.00
Silver, Lily, Marked 28.00
Silver, Man With Rooster, 2 In., 2 Piece 77.00
Steel Cut, Brass Flower Bouquet, Bead Center, Loop Shank, 1 3/8 In. 48.00
Stud, Doctor, Pair 405.00
Stud, Silver, Composition, Woman Dressing, Medium, Pair 77.00
Swallow Flying, Liverpool Transfer 285.00
Tingue, Red Barrel, Red Center 120.00
Tom Thumb, Riding Butterfly 88.00
Tortoiseshell, By Gold Disk Center, 1 In., 6 Piece 345.00
Wood, Tan Paint, 4 Hole, 7/8 In. 2.00

BUTTONHOOKS have been a popular collectible in England for many years but are now gaining the attention of American collectors. The buttonhooks were made to help fasten the many buttons of the old-fashioned high-button shoes and other items of apparel.

Bakelite, Handle, 7 In. 22.00
Celluloid, Flowrers, Etched, Black, 7 1/8 In. 13.00
Shoe, Flowers, Ornate 20.00
Shoe, Polish & Lace, 3 1/2 In. 19.00
Sterling Silver, Closes Like Pocket Knife, 2 Glove, 1 Shoe, 4 1/8 x 2 3/8 In. 65.00
Sterling Silver, Flowers, Handle, Victorian, 7 In. 25.00
Sterling Silver, Handle, Turned Design, Hallmark, 7 1/4 In. 25.00
Wooden Handle, Shoe 17.00

BYBEE POTTERY was started in 1845 and is still working. The Lexington, Kentucky, firm makes pottery that is sold at the factory. Pieces are marked with the name or with the name enclosed by the outline of the state of Kentucky.

Bowl, 10 1/2 In. 19.00
Bowl, Brown, Double Tab Handles, No. 137, 12 1/2 x 6 1/2 In. 15.00
Candleholder, Green, Finger Hold 15.00
Pan, Baker, Mark, 13 1/3 In. 23.00
Pan, Baker, Pink Splatter, Signed, 12 3/4 In. 28.00
Pitcher, Blue, 6 In. 38.00
Pitcher, Blue, Mark, 7 1/4 In. 45.00

CALENDARS made to hang on the wall or to be displayed on a desk top have been popular since the last quarter of the nineteenth century. Many were printed with advertising as part of the artwork and were given away as premiums. Calendars with guns, gunpowder, or Coca-Cola advertising are most prized.

1876, Metropolitan Printing Co., Lithograph, Allegorical Women, 14 In. 350.00

1881, Phoenix Insurance, Little Girl, Reading Catalogue, 10 1/2 x 7 In. 80.00
1882, Phoenix Insurance Co., Dog On Leash, Tugging Girl's Dress, 11 x 9 In. 86.00
1888, Hood's, Young Girl In Bonnet, Die Cut, 4 3/4 x 8 In. 182.00
1891, Gus V. Brech Butcher's Supply Co., 14 x 10 In. 1045.00
1892, Voltaic Compound, Baby Girl In Crib, Die Cut, 5 3/4 x 10 In. 171.00
1893, Hood's Sarsaparilla, Boy & Girl With Globe, 6 x 8 1/2 In. 220.00
1900, John G. Watts, Meat Market, Cardboard, 18 x 14 In. 180.00
1902, Champion Implements, Paperboard, May Through December, 6 In. 215.00
1902, Combat Cigar, Nouveau Image, 10 x 6 In. 161.00
1902, Metropolitan Life Insurance, Young Girl, Roses, Diamond Shape, 10 In. 28.00
1902, Stillings Bros., Berwick, Me., Children Making Bread, 8 x 14 In. 100.00
1903, Marguerite Cigar, Cameo Center, 12 x 15 In. 62.00
1904, Dupont, First Day Of Open Season Scene, 28 1/4 x 15 1/2 In. 3080.00
1905, Air Castles, Antique Frame, 17 1/2 x 13 1/2 In. 466.00
1906, Pabst, Indian Images Front & Back, History, 9 x 37 In. 412.00
1907, Scherling Bros., General Merchandise, Girl & Doll, 10 x 17 In. 105.00
1908, Circes Palace, Sealed In Antique Frame, 13 x 10 1/2 In. 687.00
1908, Peters Cartridge Company, Duck Hunters In Marsh, 27 x 14 In. 2070.00
1908, Roycroft, Daily Pages, On Board, 7 1/2 x 9 1/2 In. 863.00
1910, Hood's, Girl, Pink Bow In Hair, Frame, 7 x 7 1/2 In. 193.00
1911, Wrigley's Gum, Boy Holding Package, Teasing Dog, 9 1/4 x 5 In. 60.00
1912, Fox Bread, July Through December 120.00
1913, A.V. Diependerfer & Son, Orefield, Pa., Polo Scene, Die Cut, 13 In. 100.00
1913, Winchester, Hunter With Rifle Over Shoulder, 30 x 15 1/2 In. 935.00
1915, West Union Herrick Grocery, Lady Fair, Art Nouveau Lady Brush 60.00
1916, De Laval Cream Separators, Little Boy & Girl, 12 x 24 In. 230.00
1916, Geo. Weiss Thrashing & Shredding, Die Cut, Cardboard, 10 x 21 In. . . . . . . .94.00 to 210.00
1916, S.W. Kerr, Paper Lithograph, Girl In Farmyard, Frame, 13 x 17 In. 45.00
1918, Edison Mazda, Maxfield Parrish, Dawn, 17 x 13 In. 1375.00
1920, Chevrolet Motor Cars, 30 1/2 x 16 In. 302.00
1920, Young Woman, Flowers In Hair 55.00
1921, Edison Mazda, Maxfield Parrish, Primitive Man, 19 x 8 In. 2310.00
1921, Sharples, Milkmaid With Cows, Top Metal Strip, 12 x 22 In. 182.00
1922, Sunshine Biscuit, Ocheleta Mercantile Co., Ocheleta, Ok., 7 x 18 In. 40.00
1923, Edison Mazda, Lampseller Of Bagdad, 19 1/8 x 8 1/2 In. 850.00
1924, Lute Players, House Of Art, 23 x 35 In. 330.00
1924, Western Ammunition, Dog Tugging On Blanket, Frame 440.00
1924, Winchester, Duck Hunter, Frame, 13 x 26 1/2 In. 165.00
1925, Edison Mazda, Maxfield Parrish, Dreamlight . . . . .1400.00 to 2500.00
1926, Edison Mazda, Enchantment 1155.00
1927, Edison Mazda, Reveries, Maxfield Parrish, 24 x 16 In. 1600.00
1927, Nehi Beverages, Girl Sitting On Boat, Frame 275.00
1928, Remington, Man By Fireplace Holding Rifle, Henry Watson, 27 In. 660.00
1929, Edison Mazda, Golden Hours, Maxfield Parrish, 9 1/2 x 7 In. 500.00
1929, Edison Mazda, Golden Hours, Maxfield Parrish, 19 1/8 x 8 1/2 In. . . . . .850.00 to 907.00
1930, Edison Mazda, Maxfield Parrish, Ecstasy, 22 x 14 In. 2000.00
1931, Edison Mazda, Waterfall, Maxfield Parrish, 19 1/8 x 8 1/2 In. 850.00
1931, Peters Cartridge Company, Pheasants, 32 x 13 1/2 In. 402.00
1934, Edison Mazda, Moonlight 1705.00
1938, Black Horse Ale 247.00
1938, Edison Mazda, Egyptian Priestess, Maxfield Parrish, 19 x 8 In. 902.00
1939, Lucky Strike, Green Pack, Pinup Girl, Bradford Crandell, 11 x 14 In. 9.00
1940, Never Too Young To Yearn, Earl Moran, 10 x 12 In. 10.00
1940, Pinup Girls, Earl Moran, 12 Months, 10 x 12 In. 10.00
1941, Woman With New Packard, Celluloid, Orange, Black & White 125.00
1942, Clicquot Club Ginger Ale, Woman, Eskimo Child, Soda, Hanger 140.00
1942, Disney, Morrell Meats, 20 x 8 In. 275.00
1945, Great Northern Railroad, 33 In. 335.00
1945, Hercules Powder, Group Of Children On Way To School, 38 x 13 In. 28.00
1946, Esquire, Women, Different Outfits Each Month, Vargas, 8 1/2 x 12 In. 190.00
1947, Kist, Girl On Grass, Frame, 13 1/2 x 26 In. 198.00
1947, Orange Crush, Red Haired Girl With Book, 15 1/2 x 30 1/2 In. 275.00
1948, Edison Mazda, Mill Pond, Brown & Bigelow 577.00

1948, Pinup Girls, Vargas, 12 Months, 8 x 12 In. 60.00
1948, Squirt 77.00
1950, Brown & Bigelow, Sunlit Valley, Full Uncut Pad, 45 3/4 x 22 1/4 In. 687.00
1951, Dr Pepper 82.00
1951, New York Central Line, Trains At Top, 27 x 18 In. 34.00
1952, Gay Products Company, If It's Gay It's O.K., Pinup Girl 10.00
1953, Gillette, Pinup, A Shady Trick, 30 x 24 In. 44.00
1953, Greyhound Bus, Crossing Over Bridge In New York City, 19 1/2 In. 25.00
1953, Industrial Supplies, Metal Strips Top & Bottom, 33 1/2 x 16 In. 33.00
1957, Brown & Bigelow, At Close Of Day, Full Pad, 9 x 7 1/2 In. 364.00
1957, Fort Orange Radio Distributing Co., Nude Woman, 22 x 39 In. 55.00
1958, Sinclair, 16 x 11 In. 15.00
1966, Simon Pure Beer, 18 x 27 In. 13.00
1973, Buy Winston Today 55.00
1983, Engagement, Norman Rockwell 10.00

CALENDAR PLATES were very popular in the United States from 1906 to 1929. Since then, plates have been made every year. A calendar and the name of a store, a picture of flowers, a girl, or a scene were featured on the plate.

1909, Dove With Ribbon, Scalloped Edge, 8 1/4 In. 38.00
1909, O.D. Blanke & Co., Embossed, Gibson Girl 15.00
1909, Sailboat On Lake, Blue Flowers 55.00
1910, Roses & Vines, 7 3/4 In. 45.00
1910, Victorian Lady 58.00
1910, Washington's Home At Mt. Vernon, 9 1/8 In. 47.00
1911, Abraham Lincoln, 9 In. 95.00
1911, Cherries Center, Flower Border 32.00
1911, Flower Decals, Compliments Of F.W. Seidel, Bowers, Penn., 8 1/4 In. 61.00
1912, Theodore Roosevelt, 8 3/4 In. 90.00
1914, Monona, Iowa 35.00
1951, Dutch Mills & Sailboats, Scalloped Edge, 10 In. 15.00
1952, Dutch Mills & Sailboats, Plain Edge, 10 In. 15.00
1953, Jubilee, Pink, Homer Laughlin, 10 In. 15.00
1966, Sabin, Metallic Gold, Seasonal Sports, 10 In. 10.00
1969, Zodiac, Alfred Meakin, Staffordshire, 9 In. 30.00

CAMARK POTTERY started in 1924 in Camden, Arkansas. Jack Carnes founded the firm and made many types of glazes and wares. The company was bought by Mary Daniel. Production was halted in 1983.

Basket, Iris, Blue & Green, Impressed Mark, 9 1/2 In. 185.00
Ewer, Pastel Blue, Spiral Shape, Impressed Mark, 6 3/4 In. 39.00
Planter, Maroon, Moon Shape, Footed, Impressed Mark, 4 1/2 In. 45.00
Planter, Mauve & Light Green, 6 In. ....*Illus* 10.00
Strawberry Pot, White, Ribbed, Impressed Mark, 7 In. 45.00
Vase, Green, Impressed Mark, 1930s, 8 In. 165.00
Vase, Lily, Pink, Sticker, 10 In. 40.00
Vase, Rose & Blue Matte Glaze, 6 In. 88.00

For a pollution-free glass cleaner, use a mixture of white vinegar and water. Glass becomes cloudy if not kept completely dry when not in use. That is why decanters and vases often discolor.

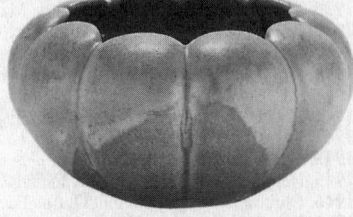

Camark, Planter, Mauve & Light Green, 6 In.

CAMBRIDGE GLASS Company was founded in 1901 in Cambridge, Ohio. The company closed in 1954, reopened briefly, and closed again in 1958. The firm made all types of glass. Their early wares included heavy pressed glass with the mark *Near Cut*. Later wares included Crown Tuscan, etched stemware, and clear and colored glass. The firm used a C in a triangle mark after 1920. Some Cambridge patterns may be included in the Depression Glass category.

Apple Blossom, Bowl, Footed, 13 In.	175.00
Apple Blossom, Bowl, Fruit, Topaz, 5 1/2 In.	125.00
Apple Blossom, Bowl, Topaz, Gold Trim, Footed, 11 In.	125.00
Apple Blossom, Cup	13.00
Apple Blossom, Finger Bowl, Topaz	95.00
Apple Blossom, Goblet, Topaz, 8 Oz.	25.00
Apple Blossom, Ice Bucket, Emerald	165.00
Apple Blossom, Jug, Martini Jug, 60 Oz.	950.00
Apple Blossom, Nut Dish, Topaz	95.00
Apple Blossom, Plate, Luncheon, 8 1/2 In.	25.00
Apple Blossom, Platter, Amber, Gold Trim, 12 In.	45.00
Apple Blossom, Sherbet, Topaz, High, 6 Oz.	28.00
Apple Blossom, Tumbler, Footed, 3 Oz.	30.00
Apple Blossom, Tumbler, Footed, 8 Oz., 5 In.	35.00
Apple Blossom, Tumbler, Juice, Footed, 5 Oz.	20.00
Apple Blossom, Tumbler, Whiskey, Emerald, Footed, 2 Oz.	85.00
Apple Blossom, Tumbler, Whiskey, Topaz, Footed, 2 Oz.	28.00 to 65.00
Apple Blossom, Vase, Topaz, 6 In.	150.00
Baroque, Bowl, Moonlight Blue, Handle, Square, 4 In.	22.00
Baroque, Cup & Saucer, Moonlight Blue	35.00
Baroque, Plate, Bread & Butter, Moonlight Blue, 6 In.	25.00
Blossom Time, Candlestick, Pair	75.00
Blossom Time, Candlestick, Prism, Pair	175.00
Blossom Time, Goblet, Cordial, 1 Oz.	65.00
Blossom Time, Hat, 6 In.	295.00
Blossom Time, Plate, Cupped, 14 In.	35.00
Blossom Time, Vase, 10 In.	150.00
Cambridge Square, Candleholder, 1 3/4 In., Pair	30.00
Caprice, Ashtray, 4 In.	10.00
Caprice, Ashtray, Moonlight Blue, 5 In.	22.00
Caprice, Ashtray, Shell, Footed, Moonlight Blue, 2 1/4 In.	20.00
Caprice, Ashtray, Triangular, Moonlight Blue, 3 In.	12.00
Caprice, Bonbon, Moonlight Blue, Oval, Footed, 6 In.	60.00
Caprice, Bonbon, Moonlight Blue, Square, 2 Handles, 6 In.	45.00
Caprice, Bonbon, Moonlight Blue, Square, Footed, 6 In.	65.00
Caprice, Bowl, Belled, 3-Footed, Moonlight Blue, 9 1/2 In.	150.00
Caprice, Bowl, Belled, 3-Footed, Moonlight Blue, 12 1/2 In.	150.00
Caprice, Bowl, Belled, 4-Footed, Moonlight Blue, 12 1/2 In.	95.00
Caprice, Bowl, Crimped, Moonlight Blue, 10 1/2 In.	175.00
Caprice, Bowl, Crimped, Moonlight Blue, Square, 8 1/2 In.	200.00
Caprice, Bowl, Fruit, Oval, 13 In.	42.00
Caprice, Bowl, Jelly, Moonlight Blue, Oval, 2 Handles, 5 In.	40.00
Caprice, Bowl, Moonlight Blue, Square, 8 1/2 In.	150.00
Caprice, Cake Plate, 3-Footed, 13 In.	38.00
Caprice, Candlestick, 2 1/2 In., Pair	35.00
Caprice, Candlestick, Alpine, Prism, Pair	125.00
Caprice, Candlestick, Moonlight Blue, 2 1/2 In., Pair	65.00 to 75.00
Caprice, Candlestick, Moonlight Blue, Alpine, Prism, 7 In.	125.00
Caprice, Candy Dish, Cover, Alpine	45.00
Caprice, Coaster, Pink, 3 1/2 In.	55.00
Caprice, Cocktail, Moonlight Blue, 3 Oz.	195.00
Caprice, Compote, Moonlight Blue, 6 In.	24.00 to 45.00
Caprice, Cordial, 1 Oz.	140.00
Caprice, Cup & Saucer, Moonlight Blue	15.00 to 50.00
Caprice, Dish, Mayonnaise, Underplate, 5 1/2-In. Bowl	35.00

Caprice, Finger Bowl, Underplate, Moonlight Blue 110.00
Caprice, Ice Bucket, Moonlight Blue 190.00
Caprice, Oil, No Stopper, 3 Oz. 25.00
Caprice, Oyster Cocktail, 4 1/2 Oz. 45.00
Caprice, Pitcher, Ball, Amber, 32 Oz. 250.00
Caprice, Pitcher, Ball, Moonlight Blue, 80 Oz. 360.00
Caprice, Plate, 4-Footed, Moonlight Blue, 11 In. 86.00
Caprice, Plate, Bread & Butter, 6 1/2 In. 24.00
Caprice, Plate, Dinner, 9 1/2 In. 40.00
Caprice, Plate, Luncheon, 8 In. 7.00
Caprice, Plate, Luncheon, Moonlight Blue, 8 1/2 In. 28.00
Caprice, Plate, Luncheon, Pink, 8 In. 35.00
Caprice, Plate, Moonlight Blue, 11 1/2 In. 89.00
Caprice, Plate, Moonlight Blue, 16 In. 110.00
Caprice, Plate, Salad, Moonlight Blue, 7 1/2 In. 24.00
Caprice, Relish, Moonlight Blue, 8 In. 35.00
Caprice, Rose Bowl, Footed, 6 In. 60.00
Caprice, Rose Bowl, Moonlight Blue, 4-Footed, 6 In. 120.00
Caprice, Rose Bowl, Moonlight Blue, 4-Footed, 8 In. 250.00
Caprice, Salt & Pepper, Moonlight Blue, Individual 150.00
Caprice, Salt & Pepper, Tray, Moonlight Blue ....125.00 to 140.00
Caprice, Saucer 3.00
Caprice, Saucer, Moonlight Blue 5.00
Caprice, Sherbet, Low, 6 Oz. ....10.00 to 15.00
Caprice, Sugar & Creamer, Alpine 50.00
Caprice, Sugar & Creamer, Moonlight Blue, Individual 35.00
Caprice, Tray, Oval, 9 In. 22.00
Caprice, Tumbler, 12 Oz. 125.00
Caprice, Tumbler, Footed, 10 Oz. 18.00
Caprice, Tumbler, Footed, Moonlight Blue, 3 Oz. 70.00
Caprice, Tumbler, Footed, Moonlight Blue, 10 Oz. 35.00
Caprice, Tumbler, Iced Tea, Amber, 12 Oz. 60.00
Caprice, Tumbler, Iced Tea, Footed, 12 Oz. ....22.00 to 43.00
Caprice, Tumbler, Iced Tea, Moonlight Blue, 12 Oz. ....55.00 to 115.00
Caprice, Tumbler, Juice, Footed, 5 Oz. ....12.00 to 18.00
Caprice, Tumbler, Juice, Footed, Moonlight Blue, 5 Oz. ....30.00 to 40.00
Caprice, Tumbler, Moonlight Blue, 9 Oz. 90.00
Caprice, Tumbler, Whiskey, Alpine, 2 Oz. 32.00
Caprice, Vase, Ritz Blue, 4 1/2 In. 140.00
Caprice, Wine, 2 1/2 Oz. 22.00
Chantilly, Bowl, Footed, 11 1/2 In. 85.00
Chantilly, Candlestick, 3-Light, 6 In., Pair 100.00
Chantilly, Candy Dish, Cover 30.00
Chantilly, Celery Dish, 12 In. 50.00
Chantilly, Cocktail Shaker, 12 Oz. 375.00
Chantilly, Cocktail, 3 Oz. 26.00
Chantilly, Ice Bucket, Chrome Handle 145.00
Chantilly, Jug, Martini, Sterling Silver Base 175.00
Chantilly, Pitcher, Sterling Silver Base 300.00
Chantilly, Sherbet, Tall, 6 Oz. 25.00
Chantilly, Sugar & Creamer 42.00
Chantilly, Vase, Bud, 10 In. 125.00
Cleo, Asparagus Server, With Sauce Indent, Cover 395.00
Cleo, Candy Dish, Willow Blue, Footed 300.00
Cleo, Pitcher, Cover, Amber, 22 Oz. 275.00
Cleo, Sandwich Server, Center Handle, Gold Trim, 12 In. 50.00
Corinth, Bowl, Topaz, 11 In. 14.00
Crown Tuscan, Bowl, Shell, 3-Footed, 10 In. 60.00
Crown Tuscan, Box, Cigarette, Cover 50.00
Crown Tuscan, Compote, Shell, 7 In. 45.00
Crown Tuscan, Plate, 7 In. 45.00
Crown Tuscan, Relish, 3 Sections, 6 1/2 In. 35.00
Crown Tuscan, Swan, 8 1/2 In. 550.00

Crown Tuscan, Torte Plate, 14 In. 125.00
Daffodil, Cocktail, 3 Oz. 50.00
Daisy, Berry Bowl, 4 1/2 In. 9.00
Daisy, Cup & Saucer 8.00
Daisy, Plate, Dinner, 9 3/8 In. 9.00
Daisy, Soup, Cream 12.00
Daisy, Tumbler, Iced Tea, 12 Oz. 40.00
Daisy, Tumbler, Water, 9 Oz. 20.00
Decagon, Bouillon, Underplate, Pink 25.00
Decagon, Bowl, Fruit, Flat Rim, Pink, 5 3/4 In. 18.00
Decagon, Compote, Moonlight Blue, 6 1/2 In. 30.00
Decagon, Creamer, Emerald, Scalloped Rim 18.00
Decagon, Creamer, Pink 15.00
Decagon, Cup & Saucer, Moonlight Blue 12.00
Decagon, Goblet, Water, Moonlight Blue, 9 Oz. 32.00
Decagon, Goblet, Water, Royal Blue, 9 Oz. 30.00
Decagon, Plate, Amber, 7 1/2 In. 15.00
Decagon, Plate, Bread & Butter, Amber, 6 1/4 In. . . . . .3.00 to 8.00
Decagon, Plate, Footed, Pink, 8 1/4 In. . . . . .20.00 to 28.00
Decagon, Sandwich Server, Center Handle, Amber, 12 In. 12.00
Decagon, Saucer 25.00
Decagon, Sherbet, Amber, High, 6 Oz. 20.00
Decagon, Sherbet, Moonlight Blue, Low, 6 Oz. 22.00
Decagon, Snack Plate, Indent, Pink, 8 1/4 In. 28.00
Decagon, Soup, Cream, Pink, 8 1/2 In. 22.00
Decagon, Soup, Cream, Underplate, Amber 32.00
Decagon, Sugar & Creamer, Tray, Ebony 40.00
Decagon, Tumbler, Juice, Royal Blue 25.00
Decagon, Wine, Pink 30.00
Diane, Bowl, 4-Footed, Square, 10 In. 75.00
Diane, Bowl, Cereal, Amber, 6 In. 12.00
Diane, Bowl, Vegetable, Amber, 9 In. 22.00
Diane, Butter, Cover 195.00
Diane, Candlestick, Pair 325.00
Diane, Cup & Saucer, Amber 10.00
Diane, Ice Bucket 150.00
Diane, Plate, Dinner, Amber, 9 1/2 In. 9.00
Diane, Sugar & Creamer, Amber 16.00
Doric, Cake Plate, Pink, Footed, 12 In. 27.00
Doric, Candlestick, Pink, Pair 100.00
Doric, Cup & Saucer, Pink 13.00
Doric, Plate, Dinner, Pink, 9 1/2 In. 18.00
Doric, Sugar, Cover, Pink 34.00
Elaine, Bottle, Bitters 295.00
Elaine, Cocktail, 3 Oz. 24.00
Elaine, Compote, 7 1/4 In. 65.00
Elaine, Decanter, Footed 450.00
Elaine, Pitcher, Doulton, 90 Oz. 350.00
Elaine, Relish, 2 Sections, 6 In. 22.00
Elaine, Relish, 3 Sections, Center Handle, 12 In. 125.00
Elaine, Relish, 5 Sections, 12 In. 250.00
Elaine, Sandwich Server, Center Handle, 12 In. 75.00
Elaine, Sherbet 20.00
Elaine, Vase, Gold, 13 1/2 x 6 3/8 In. 469.00
Elaine, Wine, 2 1/2 Oz. 30.00
Georgian, Basket, Carmen 95.00
Gloria, Cup & Saucer, After Dinner 125.00
Gloria, Goblet, 18 Oz. 125.00
Gloria, Vase, 10 In. 250.00
Imperial Hunt Scene, Claret, Peach-Blo, Gold Trim, 4 Oz., 5 1/2 In. 150.00
Imperial Hunt Scene, Decanter, Peach-Blo, Stopper, Gold Trim 950.00
Imperial Hunt Scene, Goblet, Crystal, 10 Oz. 40.00
Imperial Hunt Scene, Tumbler, 7 Oz. 75.00

Imperial Hunt Scene, Tumbler, Emerald, 8 Oz. 55.00
Martha, Sugar & Creamer, Tray, Emerald 70.00
Martha Washington, Powder Jar 70.00
Mt. Vernon, Cordial, 1 Oz. 20.00
Mt. Vernon, Cup & Saucer 14.00
Mt. Vernon, Decanter, 40 Oz. 150.00
Mt. Vernon, Goblet, Water, 10 Oz. 15.00
Mt. Vernon, Plate, Bread & Butter, 6 In. 4.00
Mt. Vernon, Sherbet, 6 1/2 Oz. 10.00
Mt. Vernon, Tumbler, Juice, 5 Oz. 12.00
Mt. Vernon, Tumbler, Juice, Footed, 3 Oz. 9.00
Mt. Vernon, Wine, 3 Oz. 25.00
Nude, Compote, Moonlight Blue 395.00
Portia, Decanter Set, Sherry, 28 Oz., 5 Piece 535.00
Portia, Decanter, Sherry, 28 Oz. 250.00
Portia, Goblet, Water, 10 Oz. 22.00
Portia, Pitcher, Doulton, 90 Oz. 350.00
Portia, Relish, 4 Sections, Center Handle, 12 In. 95.00
Portia, Sherry, 2 Oz. 40.00
Portia, Sugar 16.00
Portia, Tumbler, Footed, 10 Oz. 20.00
Regency, Goblet, Water, 10 Oz. 13.00
Regency, Sherbet, 7 Oz. 10.00
Rosalie, Candy Dish, Cover, Peach-Blo, Gold Encrusted 125.00
Rosalie, Tumbler, Iced Tea, Footed, Topaz, 12 Oz. 45.00
Rose Point, Ashtray Set, 5 Piece 385.00
Rose Point, Ashtray, 3 1/2 In. 40.00
Rose Point, Basket, 2 Handles, 6 In. 58.00
Rose Point, Bonbon, 5 1/2 In. 38.00
Rose Point, Bowl, 2 Handles, 10 In. 110.00
Rose Point, Bowl, 4-Footed, 12 In. ....95.00 to 120.00
Rose Point, Bowl, Crimped, 4-Footed, 13 In. 150.00
Rose Point, Bowl, Footed, 11 In. 135.00
Rose Point, Bowl, Fruit, 11 In. 110.00
Rose Point, Bowl, Ruffled Edge, 4-Footed, Handles, 12 1/2 In. 425.00
Rose Point, Candelabrum, Bobeche, Prisms, 7 1/2 In. 170.00
Rose Point, Candlestick, 2-Light, Gold Encrusted, Keyhole, Bobeche, Pair 450.00
Rose Point, Candy Dish, Cover 125.00
Rose Point, Celery Dish, 3 Sections, 15 In. 235.00
Rose Point, Cocktail Shaker, 32 Oz. 325.00
Rose Point, Cocktail, 3 Oz. 35.00
Rose Point, Compote, 5 3/8 In. 100.00
Rose Point, Compote, 6 In. 85.00
Rose Point, Cordial, 1 Oz. 250.00
Rose Point, Cup & Saucer 45.00
Rose Point, Decanter, 14 Oz. 775.00
Rose Point, Decanter, 28 Oz. 595.00
Rose Point, Decanter, Footed, 18 Oz. 550.00
Rose Point, Ice Bucket, Chrome Handle, Ice Tongs ....195.00 to 225.00
Rose Point, Lamp, Hurricane 260.00
Rose Point, Marmalade Jar, Cover, 8 Oz. 215.00
Rose Point, Oyster Cocktail, 4 1/2 Oz. 65.00
Rose Point, Pitcher, 20 Oz. 500.00
Rose Point, Pitcher, Ball, 80 Oz. 350.00
Rose Point, Plate, Bread & Butter, 6 In. 18.00
Rose Point, Plate, Dinner, 10 1/2 In. 210.00
Rose Point, Plate, Salad, 8 In. 29.00
Rose Point, Platter, Oval, 13 1/2 In. 175.00
Rose Point, Relish, 2 Sections, 7 In. 46.00
Rose Point, Relish, 3 Sections, 6 1/2 In. 45.00
Rose Point, Relish, 9 In. 85.00
Rose Point, Salt & Pepper, Footed 75.00

Rose Point, Sherbet, Tall, 7 Oz. 28.00
Rose Point, Sugar & Creamer 55.00
Rose Point, Tumbler, Mushroom, 12 Oz. 85.00
Rose Point, Vase, Bud, 10 In. 70.00
Rose Point, Vase, Footed, 6 In. 79.00
Rose Point, Vase, Footed, 8 1/2 In. 110.00
Rose Point, Wine, 2 1/2 In. 75.00
Roselyn, Dish, Mayonnaise, 2 Sections, 6 In. 30.00
Roselyn, Vase, Bud, 10 In. 45.00
Sports Novelty, Decanter, 3 Scottish Terriers, 10 In. 200.00
Swan, Carmen, 8 1/2 In. 350.00
Swan, Emerald, 3 1/2 In. 225.00
Swan, Gold Krystol, 8 1/2 In. 365.00
Swan, Milk Glass, 4 1/2 In. 95.00
Tally-Ho, Mug, 5 Oz. 85.00
Valencia, Bowl, Cereal, 6 In. ....35.00 to 60.00
Valencia, Bowl, Footed, Oval, 12 In. 125.00
Wildflower, Basket, 2 Handles, Gold Encrusted, 6 In. 45.00
Wildflower, Bowl, 4-Footed, 10 In. 55.00
Wildflower, Bowl, Crimped, 4-Footed, 12 In. 80.00
Wildflower, Bowl, Gold Encrusted, 4-Footed, 12 In. 95.00
Wildflower, Bowl, Scalloped, Tab Handles, 11 1/2 In. 250.00
Wildflower, Butter, Cover 195.00
Wildflower, Cake Plate, Gold Encrusted, Handles, 11 In. 65.00
Wildflower, Celery Dish, 12 In. 45.00
Wildflower, Compote, Gold Encrusted, Footed, 5 3/8 In. 65.00
Wildflower, Cup & Saucer 45.00
Wildflower, Goblet, Water, 10 Oz. ....35.00 to 45.00
Wildflower, Ice Bucket 125.00
Wildflower, Pitcher, Ball, 80 Oz. 400.00
Wildflower, Relish, 2 Sections, 8 3/4 In. 55.00
Wildflower, Relish, 3 Sections, 12 In. 25.00
Wildflower, Salt & Pepper 40.00
Wildflower, Sherbet, Low, 6 Oz. 28.00
Wildflower, Sugar & Creamer 50.00
Wildflower, Vase, 6 In. 300.00
Wildflower, Vase, Bud, 10 In. 165.00
Wildflower, Wine, 2 1/2 Oz. 50.00

CAMBRIDGE POTTERY was made in Cambridge, Ohio, from about 1895 until World War I. The factory made brown glazed decorated art wares with a variety of marks, including an acorn, the name *Cambridge*, the name *Oakwood*, or the name *Terrhea*.

Mug, Barrel Shaped, Brown, Painted Cherries & Leaves 39.00
Vase, Brown, Autumn Leaves On Side, 3 1/2 x 5 1/2 In. 180.00
Vase, Green, Brown, Yellow, Embossed Flowers, Leaves, 7 1/2 In. 89.00

CAMEO GLASS was made in much the same manner as a cameo in jewelry. Parts of the top layer of glass were cut away to reveal a different colored glass beneath. The most famous cameo glass was made during the nineteenth century. Signed cameo glass pieces are listed under the glasswork's name, such as Daum or Galle.

Vase, Amber Satin, Blue Leaves, Flower, Incised Butterfly, Darcy, 16 In. 290.00
Vase, Aubergine Tree & Lake Design, Orange Rust, Yellow, Signed, Harrach, 6 In. 632.00
Vase, Flowers & Leaves, Satin Pink, Signed, Weis, 1 5/8 In. 275.00
Vase, Flowers, Prussian Blue, England, 7 In. 2100.00
Vase, Nautilus Shell Shape, Writhing Dragons, Birds & Animals, Flowering Vines, 4 In. ... 1440.00
Vase, Palm Trees, Boat, Riders, Mountain Range, 7 In. 300.00
Vase, Pink Leaves, Thistles Design, Light Brown, Signed, Christian, 11 In. 1840.00
Vase, Trees By Mountain Lake, Purple Tone, Gus Crystal Works, 1900, 16 In. 3600.00

CAMPAIGN memorabilia is listed in the Political category.

CAMPBELL KIDS were first used as part of an advertisement for the Campbell Soup Company in 1906. The kids were created by Grace Drayton, a popular illustrator of the day. The kids were used in magazine and newspaper ads until about 1951. They were presented again in 1966; and in 1983, they were redesigned with a slimmer, more contemporary appearance.

Bank, Campbell Kids Sitting Side By Side, Cast Iron, 3 5/16 In.	330.00
Bank, Green Paint, 3 1/2 In.	137.00
Crock, Cover, Baked Beans, Monmouth, 5 In.	14.00
Doll, Girl, Plastic, Ideal, 7 1/4 In.	75.00
Doll, Scottish, Made In U.S.A., 10 1/2 In.	125.00
Doorstop, Cast Iron, Wearing Knickers, Holding Teddy Bear, 1920s, 10 x 5 In.	615.00
Lunch Box, Kids Playing Various Sports Activities, Ohio Art, 1975	290.00
Postcard, Tuck	24.00
Sign, Enameled, Porcelain, 7 3/4 x 12 1/2 In.	20.00
Spoon, Soup, Girl, 6 In.	15.00
Thimble, Girl Stirring Soup, Porcelain	15.00
Toy, Top, Wooden, Plastic Point, Red, Duncan, 1960s	95.00

CAMPHOR GLASS is a cloudy white glass that has been blown or pressed. It was made by many factories in the Midwest during the mid-nineteenth century.

Candlestick, Black Trim At Top & Bottom, 8 1/4 In., Pair	40.00
Decanter, Blue Forget-Me-Nots, 7 In.	165.00
Vase, Gold & Lavender Design, Early 1900s, 12 1/2 In.	125.00

CANDELABRUM refers to a candleholder with more than one arm to hold many candles; a candlestick is designed to hold one candle. The eccentricity of the English language makes the plural of candelabrum into candelabra.

2-Light, Altar, Pierced Trefoils, Graduated Finial, Electrified, 47 1/2 In.	635.00
2-Light, Boys Holding Light In Each Hand, 1 Hand Raised, 18 1/2 In., Pair	1035.00
2-Light, Bronze Dore, Flowers, Scrolled Branches, 12 1/2 In., Pair	1380.00
2-Light, Bronze Dore, Marble, Louis XVI Style, Bacchic, 19th Century, 13 In.	2760.00
2-Light, Bronze, Gilt, Partially Robed Classical Maiden, 8 1/2 In., Pair	690.00
2-Light, Bronze, Louis XVI, Leaves & Berries, Electrified, 11 1/4 In.	260.00
2-Light, Bronze, Scrolled Branches, Candle Nozzles, Leaf Feet, 16 In., Pair	2530.00
2-Light, C-Scrolls, Shells, Fringed Silk Shade, Bun Feet, Electrified, 13 In., Pair	315.00
2-Light, Cut & Pressed Glass, Prisms, 16 In., Pair	70.00
2-Light, Gilt Bronze, Charles X, Patinated, Cherub, Scroll Arms, 14 x 7 In.	1955.00
2-Light, Gilt Bronze, Napoleon III, Cut Glass Spear Finial, 15 x 8 x 9 In., Pair	980.00
2-Light, Gilt, Bronze, Louis XVI, Scrolled Branch, Wall Mounted, 21 In., Pair	750.00
3-Light, Brass, Bronze, Winged Female Figure, Neoclassical, 24 In., Pair	3300.00
3-Light, Brass, Cornucopia Type Arms, Applied Cherubs, Gilt, 22 In., Pair	1595.00
3-Light, Bronze Dore, Napoleon III, Chased Parrot, 21 In., Pair	5290.00
3-Light, Bronze, Louis XV, Porcelain Flowers, Drops, Electrified, 18 In., Pair	525.00
3-Light, Bronze, Louis XVI, Obelisk, With Rock Crystal Beads, 36 In., Pair	9600.00
3-Light, Bronzed Metal, Lilies Sprouting From Urns, Garland, France, 15 In., Pair	575.00
3-Light, Copper, Fluted Stem, 15 1/4 In.	770.00
3-Light, Copper, Separate, Removable Bobeche, 12 7/8 In.	660.00
3-Light, Detached At Corners To Form 1-Light Candlesticks, c.1900, 15 In.	140.00
3-Light, Gilt, Brass, Louis XVI, Scrolled Branches, 17 In., Pair	2070.00
3-Light, Gilt, Bronze, Louis XVI, Scroll Arms, Triangular Plinth, 23 In., Pair	2760.00
3-Light, Gilt, Louis XV, Rooster Surmounted By Foliate Branches, 18 In., Pair	6600.00
3-Light, Hexagonal Base, Opposed Scrolling Arms, Wax Pans, 1860s, 21 In.	520.00
3-Light, Scrolling Branches, Leaf Rings, Figural, Marble Plinth, 20 x 6 In.	805.00
3-Light, Silver Plate, Bobeche, Drip Pan, 7 1/4 In., Pair	135.00
3-Light, Silver Plate, Bobeches, Removable Arms, 18 3/4 In.	580.00
3-Light, Silver Plate, Detachable Bobeches, Sheffield, 1810, 14 3/8 In., Pair	1095.00
3-Light, Silver Plate, Gadroon, Shell Cassolette Finial, 1809, 21 In., Pair	4140.00
3-Light, Silver Plate, Swag Designs, Reeded Columns, 22 1/4 In., Pair	415.00
3-Light, Silver, 3 Candle Sockets, Gorham, 11 1/2 In., Pair	300.00
3-Light, Silver, Detachable Bobeches, Continental, 21 1/4 In., Pair	546.00

3-Light, Sterling Silver, Gadrooned Edges, 5 1/2 In., Pair 138.00
3-Light, Sterling Silver, Inverted Bell Sockets, Round Base, 6 3/8 In., Pair 90.00
3-Light, With Prisms, Gold Dore, 19th Century, 17 In. 165.00
4-Light, Altar, Bronze Painted, Scrolling Wire Arms, Continental, 27 x 14 In. 490.00
4-Light, Altar, Scrolling Wire Arms, Pierced 3-Part Base, 19th Century, 27 In. 490.00
4-Light, Bluejohn Standard, Leaves, Giltwood Plinth, 13 In. 9600.00
4-Light, Brass, Knop Standard, Hanging, 19th Century, 12 x 15 In., Pair 1495.00
4-Light, Bronze, Gilt Bronze, Empire, Figural, 20 1/2 In., Pair 2875.00
4-Light, Bronze, Man & Woman Mythological, Snakes, 23 1/2 In., Pair 2145.00
4-Light, Bronze, Shaped Circular Base, Louis XIV, Purple Prisms, 21 In., Pair 690.00
4-Light, Cast Iron, Argente, Gilt Antimony, Indian Standard, 22 1/2 x 6 In. 865.00
4-Light, Charles X, Foliate Arms, Leaf Cast Paw Feet, 3-Part Base, 19 In., Pair 1840.00
4-Light, Gilt, Patinated Bronze, Charles X, Fluted, Leaf Chasing, 21 1/2 In. 2990.00
4-Light, Louis XVI Style, Gilt Bronze, Crystal, Cage, Electrified, 26 x 13 In. 460.00
4-Light, Napoleon III, Gilt Bronze, Neoclassical Maiden, Electrified, 35 In. 1380.00
4-Light, Porcelain, Applied Flowers, Classical Figures, Birds, 20 In., Pair 980.00
4-Light, Pressed Glass, Twisted S-Shape Arms, Beaded Pendants, 23 In. 920.00
4-Light, Silver Plate, Magnum Gadroon & Flower, Mid 19th Century, 21 In. 865.00
4-Light, Silver Plate, Oriental, Tripod Base, Reclining Camels, 21 In., Pair 2070.00
4-Light, Silver Plate, Stepped Hoof Base, Ornate, 32 In., Pair 1265.00
4-Light, Silver Sterling, Knop Stem, Molded Square Base, 15 1/2 In., Pair 7130.00
4-Light, Silver, Rococo Revival, Scrolls & Flowers, Gorham, 1910, 15 In., Pair 2700.00
5-Light, Brass, Scrolled Footed, Rococo, Minerva Heads Base, 28 In. 185.00
5-Light, Bronze Dore, Louis XVI Style, Scroll Branches, 20 1/4 x 15 In. 1095.00
5-Light, Bronze Dore, Louis XVI, Pair Of Cherubs Holding Urn, 20 In., Pair 3450.00
5-Light, Bronze, Female Supporting Flower Filled Basket, 31 In., Pair 6000.00
5-Light, Bronze, Girandole, Marble Base, 13 1/2 In., Pair 1595.00
5-Light, Bronze, Louis XVI, Medallions Supporting Chains, 21 In., Pair 2185.00
5-Light, Faux Marble, Classical Maidens, Candle Cup With Bobeche, 26 In. 115.00
5-Light, Gilt Bronze, Napoleon III, Red Marble, Neogreco, 26 x 13 1/2 In. 3220.00
5-Light, Gilt Metal, Louis XVI, Floral Swag Centering Medallion, 20 In. 860.00
5-Light, Gilt, Patinated Bronze, Charles X, Urn, Leaf, Domed Base, 24 In, Pair 4830.00
5-Light, Patinated Bronze, Empire Style, Classical Maiden, 25 In., Pair 3220.00
5-Light, Pewter, Rococo, Figures Of 2 Nude Putti Cavorting, 24 x 15 In. 430.00
5-Light, Silver On Brass, Trumpet Shaped Stems, 19 In., Pair 330.00
5-Light, Silver Plate, Acanthus Leaf, Flower Branches, Oval Foot, 18 In., Pair 1380.00
5-Light, Silver Plate, Overall Scroll, Tilden-Thurber Co., 23 In., Pair 405.00
5-Light, Silver Plate, Rococo, Scrolled Footed, Fluted Column, 12 1/2 In. 95.00
5-Light, Sterling Silver, Acanthus Bone Foot, 4 S-Scroll Branches, Italy, 16 In. 2587.00
5-Light, Sterling Silver, Edward VII, 4 Scrolled Arms, England, 21 In., Pair 8740.00
6-Light, Bronze, Gilt, Louis XVI, Putti Seated On Tree Stump, 37 In., Pair 2185.00
6-Light, Bronze, Louis XVI, Cherub Holding Cornucopia, 26 In., Pair 3900.00
6-Light, Gilt, Marble, Belle Epoque, Satyr Masks, Lattice Border, 36 In., Pair 4830.00
7-Light, Brass, Angular Incised Design, Slate, Marble Base, 1870, 24 In. 290.00
7-Light, Bronze, Louis XV, Nude Maiden Draped With Flowers, 30 x 17 In. 3220.00
7-Light, Bronze, Louis XV, Putto, Seated, Pierced Rocaille Base, 28 In., Pair 4370.00
7-Light, Columnar Support, Scroll Arms, Candle Cups, 33 3/8 In. 2300.00
7-Light, Gilded Cast Brass, Black Enameled Column, Raised Leaf, 32 In. 600.00
7-Light, Gilt, Bronze, Putti, Brown Patina, France, 19th Century, 29 In., Pair 4140.00
7-Light, Sterling Silver, Chased With Classical Leaves, Italy, 26 1/2 In., Pair 7200.00
8-Light, Bronze, Gilt, William IV, 2 Tiers Of Scroll Branches, 27 In., Pair 1095.00
12-Light, Gilt Brass, Alternating Decorative Borders, Leaf Standard, 24 In. 172.00
Bronze, Goddess Holding Vase Aloft, Swag Of Flowers, 33 In., Pair 8400.00
Bronze, Gold Dore, Empire, 1870, 27 In., Pair 4480.00
Girandole, 3-Light, Brass, Glass Prisms, Man & Woman On Marble Base, 17 In. 165.00
Girandole, 5-Light, Bronze, Marble, Cornelius & Co., Dec. 5, 1848, 21 In., Pair 1595.00
Girandole, Brass, Reclining Stag, Prisms, White Marble Base, 12 1/2 In., Pair 160.00
Girandole, Bronze, American Indians, Standing, Pendant Prisms, 17 1/2 In. 230.00
Girandole, Gilt Brass, Girl, Bowl, Trees, Cut Prisms, Marble Base, 14 1/2 In., Pair 110.00
Grape & Vine Carvings, 1870, 28 In., Pair 3640.00
Porcelain, English Dogs, On Cushions, Tassels, Brownfield, 10 1/2 In., Pair 1320.00
Silver Plate, Rococo Design, 17 1/2 In., Pair 330.00
Silver Plate, Sphinxes On Tripod Base, Foliate Arms, Elkington, 1866, 24 In. 3220.00

Sterling Silver, Francis I, Scrolled Branches, Reed & Barton, 14 In., Pair 2300.00
Sterling Silver, Stepped Square Bases, Rupert Fabell, England, 1881, 20 In., Pair 7200.00

CANDLESTICKS were made of brass, pewter, glass, sterling silver, plated silver, and all types of pottery and porcelain. The earliest candlesticks, dating from the sixteenth century, held the candle on a pricket (sharp pointed spike). These lost favor because in times of strife the large church candlesticks with prickets became formidable weapons, so the socket was mandated. Candlesticks changed in style through the centuries, and designs range from classic to rococo to Art Nouveau to Art Deco.

Bell Metal, Federal, Square Base, 9 In., Pair 200.00
Bell Metal, George III, Square Bobeche, Base, 19th Century, 9 3/4 In., Pair 440.00
Bisque, Nodder, Blackamoor, Man & Woman, Yes & No, 9 1/2 In., Pair . . . . *Illus* 450.00
Brass, 6-Sided Base, England, 1725, 6 1/2 In., Pair 1450.00
Brass, Altar, Scrolling Foliage & Shells, 18th Century, 36 In., Pair 4025.00
Brass, Baluster, Push-Up, England, 19 In., Pair 90.00
Brass, Beehive, 10 1/2 In, Pair 170.00
Brass, Charles X, Border Of Playful Felines, Domed Base, 10 1/2 In., Pair 690.00
Brass, Column Form, Ringed Foot, Anthemions, 9 1/4 In., Pair 170.00
Brass, Column Form, Stepped Base, 8 1/4 In., Pair 805.00
Brass, Continental, Swirl Form, Punched Flower-Form Design, 4 3/4 In. 575.00
Brass, Copper, Thistle Design, 9 In., Pair 60.00
Brass, Cornelius & Baker, Phila., 1850s, 9 1/2 In., Pair 305.00
Brass, Domed Base, Stepped Footed, Turned Columns, 17 1/4 In., Pair 190.00
Brass, Ecclesiastical, Tripod Base, Knurled Candle Socket, 27 In., Pair 220.00
Brass, Empire, 3 Relief Panels, Cherub, Paw Feet, 26 In., Pair 495.00
Brass, Floral Enameled Posts, Minerva Head Handle, 6 x 4 5/8 In., Pair 190.00
Brass, Fluted Shafts, Square Bases, England, c.1800, 9 3/4 In., Pair 110.00
Brass, George II, Push-Up, Ruffled Cup, Corner Stepped, 9 In., Pair 4600.00
Brass, Georgian, Baluster Stem, Lobed Base, England, 7 In. 86.00
Brass, Gilt, 3-Part Base, Scrolled Lion Supports, Continental, 9 5/8 In., Pair 460.00
Brass, Louis Philippe, Bead Swirls, Waves, Diamond Base, 10 1/4 In., Pair 550.00
Brass, Malachite Adornments On Base, Arts & Crafts, 9 In. 250.00
Brass, Neoclassical, Urn Shape Nozzle, Electrified, Continental, 23 In., Pair 805.00
Brass, Octagonal Dome Foot, England, 1740, 7 In. 275.00
Brass, Patinated, Tripodal, Beaux Arts Style, Mounted As Lamp, 32 1/2 In. 690.00
Brass, Platform Base, Primitive Paw Feet, Raised Rim, Incised Rings, 9 In. 250.00
Brass, Pricket, Multilobe Base, Top Drip Pan, 5 In., Pair 230.00
Brass, Pulpit, Push Up, Ribbed Bands, Scribe Lines, England, 1800s, 20 In., Pair 980.00
Brass, Push Up, Cylindrical, Shaped Base, 7 3/4 In., Pair 460.00
Brass, Push-Up, Beehive, Hurricane Shade, England, 17 In., Pair 460.00
Brass, Push-Up, Tulip Shaped Scone, 6 7/8 In., Pair 60.00
Brass, Queen Anne Style, Central Raised Dome, Square, 18th Century, 6 In. 230.00
Brass, Queen Anne, Columnar Form, Domed Base, 8 3/4 In., Pair 2185.00
Brass, Queen Anne, Petal Base, c.1740, Pair 1210.00
Brass, Queen Anne, Scalloped Base, 7 1/2 In., Pair 1870.00
Brass, Queen Anne, Signed Geo. Grove, c.1750, Pair 1750.00
Brass, Queen Of Diamonds, Push-Up, 11 1/2 In., Pair 275.00
Brass, Regency Style, Faceted Standard, Footed, 10 3/4 x 5 In., Pair 115.00
Brass, Ring Turned Bases, Columns, 9 1/2 In., Pair 40.00
Brass, Ring Turned Column, Flared Rib Socket, Pan Base, 8 7/8 In., Pair 40.00
Brass, Ring Turned, Round Base, 10 1/8 In., Pair 80.00
Brass, Ring Turned, Stepped Base, Baluster Stem, Polished, 8 1/2 In. 250.00
Brass, Round Base, Raised Swirl Design, Reeded Baluster Stem, 9 In., Pair 190.00
Brass, Scalloped Corners, Seamed Columns, 8 1/4 In., Pair 55.00
Brass, Screw-In Base, Fleur-De-Lis, Floral, Face Carvings, 7 In., Pair 39.00
Brass, Shade, Circular Turned Form, Handle, Electrified, 18 1/2 In. 575.00
Brass, Silver, Tapered Stem, 2 Knops, Octagonal Base, 10 In., Pair 575.00
Brass, Spanish Dome, 17th Century, 7 1/2 In. 460.00
Brass, Square Cut Corner Base, 19th Century, 4 1/2 In., Pair 115.00
Brass, Stylized Eagle With Upraised Wings, Black Metal Case, 5 1/8 In., Pair 840.00
Brass, Taperstick, Seamed Construction, England, 1715, 4 In. 950.00

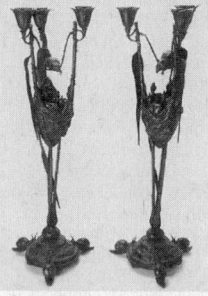

Candlestick, Bisque, Nodder,
Blackamoor, Man & Woman,
Yes & No, 9 1/2 In., Pair

Candlestick, Spelter, Black,
Baby Birds In Nest, Mother, Rat,
Art Nouveau, Cain, 20 In., Pair

Candlestick, Bronze, Rococo,
2 Putti, Open Foot,
11 1/8 In., Pair

Brass, Traveling, Saucer Base, Stamped NN25, 3 1/4 x 4 1/2 In. 66.00
Brass, Turned & Faceted Shafts, c.1890, 12 1/2 In., Pair 300.00
Brass, Twist, Spreading Foot, 19th Century, 11 1/4 In., Pair 290.00
Brass, Twist, Welled Round Base, 19th Century, 18 1/4 In., Pair 460.00
Brass, Victorian, Push-Up, Beehive, Diamond Design, 8 3/4 In., Pair 80.00
Bronze, Art Nouveau, 15 x 5 In., Pair 635.00
Bronze, Baluster Stem, Bulbous Cup, 13 In., Pair 460.00
Bronze, Cherub Form Standard, White Marble Base, Gilt, 11 In., Pair 1495.00
Bronze, Concave Sides, Acanthus Capped Claw Feet, 12 In., Pair 150.00
Bronze, Continental, Gilt, Griffin Shape, 13 1/2 In. 259.00
Bronze, Empire, Berry, Flower Design, Round Base, Acanthus Leaf, France, 11 In. 1055.00
Bronze, Figural, Satyr Figures, Holding Sconces, 3 Hairy Paw Feet, 10 5/8 In., Pair 1725.00
Bronze, Gilt, Reeded Standard, Leaf Border, Paw Feet, Louis Philippe, 12 In., Pair 575.00
Bronze, Griffin Shape, Continental, Patinated, 7 x 7 In., Pair 690.00
Bronze, Leaf-Tip Nozzle, Hipped Animal Legs, 1830s, 10 1/4 In., Pair 3600.00
Bronze, Napoleon III, Foliated Scroll Triangular Pedestal, 12 1/2 In., Pair 1840.00
Bronze, Neoclassical, Cut & Frosted Shade, Column Support, 21 In., Pair 1800.00
Bronze, Original Green, Brown Patina, Signed, E.T. Hurley, 12 In., Pair 4600.00
Bronze, Patinated, Gilt, Charles X, Hairy Paw Feet, Triangular Base, 11 In., Pair 865.00
Bronze, Preseton, Jesse, Original Patina, 12 1/2 In., Pair 2415.00
Bronze, Regency, Graduated Oblong Cut Drops, 12 1/2 In., Pair 4370.00
Bronze, Ribbon Tied Wheat Sheaf With Flowers, Black Patina, France, 4 In. 230.00
Bronze, Rococo, 2 Putti, Open Foot, 11 1/8 In., Pair . . . . *Illus* 490.00
Bronze, Seahorse Base, Concentric Ridges, E.T. Hurley, 1916, 10 3/4 In., Pair 2530.00
Bronze Dore, Regency, Sculpted Seated Classical Maiden, Prisms, 1805, Pair 9500.00
Clambroth, Opaque Blue Socket, Sand Finish, 1860, 7 1/4 In. 40.00
Copper, 4 Applied Brass Bands, Original Patina, 12 In. 1100.00
Copper, 4 Brass Bands, Vertical Dovetail Joint, Original Patina, 9 3/4 In. 360.00
Copper, 6 Sides, 9 1/8 In. 220.00
Copper, Blue, Red Flowers, Green Stems, Enameled, Art Crafts Shop, 14 In., Pair 845.00
Copper, Copper Banding Below The Rim, 14 In., Pair 1650.00
Copper, Hammered, 5 Brass Rods, 10 1/8 In., Pair 3300.00
Copper, Hammered, Applied Brass Bobeches, Stickley Brothers, 11 In., Pair 2250.00
Copper, Hammered, Karl Kipp, 6 1/2 In., Pair 2645.00
Copper, Original Patina, Jarvie, 11 In., Pair 150.00
Copper, Radial, Hammered, Original Patina, Karl Kipp, 8 In., Pair 920.00
Copper, Repousse, C-Scroll Form, Tripod Base, 1880, 29 In., Pair 1150.00
Copper, Ring Joint, Drip Guard, 9 1/2 In., 9 Piece 728.00
Copper, Triangular Base, Medium Patina, 7 1/2 In. 360.00
Cut Glass, Russian, Brilliant Cut, Teardrop Footed, 8 In., Pair 700.00
Enamel, Battersea, Transfer Print, Lozenged Foot, 9 1/2 x 5 In., Pair 575.00
Enamel, White, Flowers, Brass Sockets, 15 In., Pair 195.00
Garniture Set, Gilt Bronze, Roman Figure, Cherubs, Clock, 15 In., 3 Piece 1870.00
Gilt, William IV, Greyhound Scene, 19th Century, 6 1/2 In., Pair 800.00

Gilt Brass, Gambling Fox & Drinking Bear, Goblet Shape, 7 1/2 In., Pair 1065.00
Gilt Bronze, Charles X Style, Standing Putto Figure, 7 3/4 In., Pair 200.00
Gilt Bronze, Charles X, Columnar, Reeded Shaft, Urn Nozzle, 13 In., Pair 3910.00
Gilt Bronze, Empire, Fluted Column, Tripod Base, 1815, Pair 6750.00
Gilt Bronze, Leaf Shaft & Nozzle, Tripartite Base, 12 1/4 In., Pair 635.00
Gilt Bronze, Louis XVI Style, Shaft & Nozzle, Tripartite Base, 12 1/4 In., Pair 635.00
Gilt Metal, Animalier, Beaded Nozzle, Grapevine Shaft, 12 1/2 In., Pair 1800.00
Gilt Metal, Shell, Acanthus Shape, 3 Winged Putti Faces, 29 In. 520.00
Giltwood, Altar, Ocher Pricket, Circular Foot, Italy, 19 1/2 In. 345.00
Giltwood, Altar, On Triangular Standard, Paw Feet, 22 In., 3 Piece 2760.00
Giltwood, Altar, Pricket, Neoclassical, 19th Century, Italy, 38 In. 1955.00
Giltwood, Altar, Pricket, Polychrome, Italy, 20 In., Pair 1150.00
Giltwood, Altar, Projecting Angel Mask, Triangular Plinth, 26 In., Pair 2990.00
Giltwood, Carved, Rococo, Ram's Heads, 1910s, 28 In., Pair 860.00
Giltwood, Turned Leaves Carved Stem, Paw Feet, 21 1/2 In., Pair 1095.00
Glass, Free-Blown, Gray Tint, Flared Socket Rim, Pontil, 1800-1840, 9 1/8 In. 440.00
Glass, Leaves, Grape Design, Cobalt Etch, 15 3/4 In., Pair 315.00
Iron, Pricket, S-Scroll, Drip Pan, Flower Brass, Hook, 5 1/2 In. 27.00
Iron, Stamped Yellin, Pair 10350.00
Lead Glass, Lotus Socket, Solid Columnar Stem, 7 3/8 In., Pair 50.00
Lead Glass, Lotus Socket, Solid Columnar Stem, 8 1/4 In. 110.00
Oak, Original Copper Patina, Rohlfs, 1903, 14 1/2 In., Pair 4315.00
Parcel Gilt, Altar, Green, Black, Vase Shape, Acanthus Carving, 45 3/4 In. 430.00
Parcel Gilt, Restauration, Tole Peinte, Leaf Banding, Cowherd, Cows, 7 In., Pair 575.00
Pewter, Art Nouveau, Swirled Form, Original Patina, 11 In. 920.00
Pewter, Circular Turned, Late 18th Century, 11 In., Pair 520.00
Pewter, Original Patina, Liberty & Company, Tudric, 1902, 5 In. 400.00
Pewter, Stepped Petal Base, Paneled Baluster Stem, Scalloped Socket, 10 In. 110.00
Pewter, Stylized Raised Design, Liberty, 4 In., Pair 1840.00
Porcelain, Birds Amidst Blossoms, Blue, White, 7 3/4 In., Pair 460.00
Porcelain, Fighting Cock, 11 1/4 In., Pair 430.00
Porcelain, Figural, Putto, C-Scroll Base, Gilt, Germany, 8 In. 575.00
Pressed Glass, Boston & Sandwich, Dolphins, Opalescent Blue, 10 1/2 In, Pair 1870.00
Pressed Glass, Boston & Sandwich, Petal & Loop, Canary, c.1860, 7 In., Pair 145.00
Pressed Glass, Dolphin Shape, Hurricane Shade, 16 In., Pair 315.00
Silver, Beaded Border, Snuffer, Bobeche, George Ivory, London, 1851, 5 In. 460.00
Silver, Circular Domed Base, Grape, Leaf Design, Ball Knop, 12 In., Pair 460.00
Silver, Circular Pans, Detachable Nozzles, Handle, John Troby, 1791, 6 In., Pair 1680.00
Silver, Classical Style Columnar Stems, Square Nozzles, 1889, 6 In., Pair 920.00
Silver, Copper, Lion's Mask, Sconce, Detachable Bobeche, 11 In., 4 Piece 920.00
Silver, Flowers, Silver Trim, 4 x 4 1/4 In., Pair 35.00
Silver, Georgian Style, Sheffield, H.W. & Co., England, 1837, 9 In., Pair 460.00
Silver, Hung With Shells, Iron Rod, South America, 16 In., Pair 5100.00
Silver, Leaf Base Design, Zhytomyr, Russia, 1860, 14 In., Pair 1800.00
Silver, Neoclassical, Acanthine Carved, Italy, 13 1/2 In., Pair 800.00
Silver, Ornate Scroll & Beading, Sheffield, 1825, 7 7/8 In. 660.00
Silver, Parcel Gilt, Carved, Tapering, Fluted Standard, Round Base, 18 In., Pair 400.00
Silver, Plain Circular Foot, Knop, Royal Danish, 10 In., Pair 370.00
Silver, Ridge Pattern, Weighted, 2 1/2 In., Pair 80.00
Silver, Scalloped Shell Base, Ring Sockets, Bobeche, Sheffield, 12 3/8 In., Pair 410.00
Silver, Sea Horses At Base, E.T. Hurley, Signed & Dated, 1914, 13 In. 1210.00
Silver, Spring Load, Leaf Cut Glass Shade, Scrolled Plinth, 1850s, 26 1/4 In., Pair 1610.00
Silver, Stepped Beaded Base, Reeded Column, Bobeche, 10 1/2 In., Pair 440.00
Silver, Stylized Petal Shape, Towle, 5 In., 4 Piece 90.00
Silver, Turned Base, Hurricane Etched Eagles Shades, 12 In., Pair 55.00
Silver Gilt, Altar, Baroque Style, Carved, Urn Shape Support, 21 In. 400.00
Silver Gilt, Urn Shape, Round Base, Carved, Mounted As Lamps, 20 In., Pair 230.00
Silver Plate, Adam Style, Urn Socket, 1870, Pair 2250.00
Silver Plate, Baluster Stem, Round Base, Repousse, Marked EPN, 10 In., Pair 300.00
Silver Plate, Banquet, Sheffield, Monumental, Late 19th Century, 16 In., Pair 1495.00
Silver Plate, Louis Philippe, Columnar, Neoclassic, c.1845, 12 In., Pair 750.00
Silver Plate, Removable Bobeches, Georgian, Sheffield, c.1780, 10 In., 4 Piece 3910.00
Silver Plate, Stepped Circular Base, 19th Century, 8 3/4 In. 115.00

Silver Plate, Telescoping Columns, Bobeches Detach, Sheffield, c.1790, 10 In., Pair 750.00
Silvered, Altar, Broad Gallery, Drip Pans Above Knopped Column, 24 In., Pair 750.00
Silvered, Altar, Pricket, Reeded, Acanthine Carved, Columns, Italy, 28 1/2 In. 1035.00
Spelter, Black, Baby Birds In Nest, Mother, Rat, Art Nouveau, Cain, 20 In., Pair . . . *Illus*   1500.00
Spelter, Figural, Crane Holding Flower Blossom, On Rockery, 17 In. 115.00
Sterling Silver, Altar, Baroque, Pricket, Serpentine Base, Scroll Feet, Italy, 27 In., Pair . . .   1035.00
Sterling Silver, Beaded Edge, Bobeche, London Hallmarks, 1777, 2 1/2 In. 440.00
Sterling Silver, Dunce Cap Snuffer, John Crouch, England, 1799, 3 1/2 x 5 1/2 In. 630.00
Sterling Silver, Flared Cup, Square Plinth, Signed, Mexico, 3 1/4 In., Pair 805.00
Sterling Silver, Oval Shaped Base, Top & Bobeches, Stieff, America, 5 1/2 In., Pair 330.00
Sterling Silver, Raised Rims, Fluted Stems, Fixed Nozzles, Italy, 1831, 10 In., Pair 4200.00
Sterling Silver, Rococo Shells, Foliage, Howard & Co., 1905, 10 In., 4 Piece 3300.00
Sterling Silver, Spirally Fluted Stems, Johann J. Biller, Germany, 1761, 8 1/2 In., Pair . . .   7200.00
Sterling Silver, Table, Rustic Architectural Views, 1900, 10 In., 4 Piece 8400.00
Terra-Cotta, Classical Figures, Anthemions, 8 1/4 In., Pair 315.00
Terra-Cotta, Etruscan Style, Classical Figures, c.1875, 7 1/2 x 4 In. 460.00
Wooden, Altar, Pricket, Polychrome, Parcel Gilt, Italy, 39 In., Pair 1495.00
Wooden, Blackamoor, Carved, Polychrome, Gilt, 19th Century, 29 In. 1495.00
Wooden, Ecclesiastical, Cherub Faces, Ringed Columns, Drip Pan, 17 In., Pair 275.00
Wooden, Georgian, Columnar, Carved, c.1900, 24 In., Pair 660.00
Wooden, Lotus, Crab, Spider Design, Early 20th Century, 23 In.   115.00

CANDLEWICK items may be listed in the Imperial and Pressed Glass categories.

CANDY CONTAINERS have been popular since the late Victorian era. Collectors have long favored the glass containers, but now all types, including tin and papier-mache, are collected. Probably the earliest glass container sold commercially was the Liberty Bell made in 1876 for sale at the Centennial Exposition. Thousands of designs were made until the cost became too high in the 1960s. By the late 1970s, reproductions were being made and sold without the candy. Containers listed here are glass unless otherwise described. A Belsnickle is a nineteenth-century figure of Father Christmas.

Airplane, Army Bomber, Glass, Paper Propeller, 4 1/8 x 4 1/4 In. 30.00
Ambulance, Tin, France, 1930s 250.00
Amos & Andy, Open Air Taxi, Victory Glass Co., Tin Closure, 4 1/2 In. 700.00
Baby, Crying, Ruffled Muslin, Rose Silk Ribbons, c.1890, 6 In. 275.00
Banty Rooster, Composition, Black Body, Red Head & Comb, 5 1/2 In. 385.00
Baseball Bank, Glass, Bottom Screw Cap, 2 1/4 In. 55.00
Baseball Bank, Indian Chief, Flying Horse, Plastic Stand 45.00
Bear In Car, Purple Glass, No Closure 300.00
Belsnickle, Composition, Feather Tree, Red Robe, White Beard, 7 1/4 In. 385.00
Belsnickle, Feather Tree Sprig In Arm, 7 1/4 In. 1870.00
Belsnickle, Feather Tree, Flecked Robe, Papier-Mache, 10 In. 550.00
Belsnickle, Gold Robe, 14 In. 4600.00
Belsnickle, Robe, Mica Flecks, Black Boots, Pipe Cleaner Trim, Tree, 11 In. 825.00
Belsnickle, Silver Glitter, Red & Pink Trim, Feather Tree, Germany, 8 In. 110.00
Belsnickle, White Robe, Mica Flecks, Glitter Trim, Feather Tree, 9 1/8 In. 660.00
Belsnickle, Wide-Eyed, Pink Robe, Mica Flecks, Boots, Feather Tree, 6 In. 190.00
Belsnickle, Windup, Travels In Circles, c.1930 . . . .   360.00
Boat, Battleship On Waves, 5 1/4 In. . . . . .80.00 to 100.00
Boat, Submarine F-6, Glass & Tin, 5 1/2 In. 325.00
Bus, Victory Lines Special, No Paint, 4 7/8 In. 340.00
Camera, On Tripod, Metal Ring On Lens 385.00
Candy Shop Fountain, Red, Yellow Clips, Box 55.00
Cannon, 2-Wheel Mount No. 3, Original Wheels 1100.00
Car, Electric Coupe, Pat. 18, 1913, 2 1/2 x 1 5/8 x 3 3/8 In. 88.00
Car, Hearse No. 2, 4 3/8 In. 60.00
Car, Little Sedan, 3 In. 60.00
Car, Racing, Stutz Bearcat, Tin Closure 4050.00
Car, V.G. Co. Airflow, Yellow Repaint, Replaced Wheels, 5 In. 175.00
Carpet Sweeper, Dolly Sweeper, Painted 630.00
Cat On Pumpkin, Paper & Composition, 5 In. 145.00

Chick, Nodder 175.00
Christmas Scene, Santa With Toys, Little Girl & Deer, Cardboard, 3 1/4 In. 30.00
Christmas Tree, Ornament, Paper, 8 1/2 In. 44.00
Clock, Kiddie Clock, Dime Bank, 2 5/16 In. 60.00
Clown, Composition, Germany, 5 3/8 In. 45.00
Clown, Glass, Red Screw-On Lid, 5 In. 20.00
Coach, Parlor Car, New York Central Railroad, 5 1/8 In. 300.00
Dirigible, Los Angeles, V.G. Co., Aluminum Cap, 6 In. 310.00
Dog, Hound, Clear Glass, Black Metal Screw-On Hat, 1952, 3 5/8 In. 25.00
Dog, Hound, Paper & Metal Hat, Cobalt Blue Glass 27.00
Dog, Metal Screw-On Closure Forms Tail, c.1925 .... 1700.00
Dog, Papier-Mache, Curly Mohair, Silver Bells, c.1890, 13 In. 450.00
Dove, Pink Metal Feet, Orange Glass Eyes, 4 1/2 x 8 In. 165.00
Drum, Candy Filled Bank, Gold Paint, Slotted Closure 550.00
Duckling, Composition, Hand Painted, 4 3/4 In. 20.00
Easter Egg, Papier-Mache, Western Germany, 2 Piece 11.00
Fire Engine, 3 Dot U.S.A. 33.00
Fire Hydrant, Cover, Candy Fleer Co., Philadelphia, 3 In. 5.00
Fire Truck, V.G. Co. Little Boiler, Glass 45.00
Flapper, Glass, With Paper Mask & Belt, 10 13/16 In. 66.00
Flossie Fisher Bed, Original Cover, Geo. Borgfeldt Label, 3 3/4 In. 3520.00
Football, Tin Lithograph, 2 x 1 In. 18.00
Football Player, Painted Composition & Cloth, Dressed, 19 In. .... .6240.00 to 6270.00
French Girl, Blue Paperweight Eyes, All Original 995.00
George Washington, On Horseback, Bisque Head, Uniform, Sword, 10 1/2 In. 1870.00
George Washington, On Horseback, Removable Horse Head, 11 x 9 In. 2138.00
George Washington, Papier-Mache, Cherry Tree Canoe, 1920s, 4 x 8 In. 375.00
Gingerbread Man, Papier-Mache, Brown, Waist Separates, Germany, 8 In. 47.00
Girl, Painted Eyes, Crepe Paper Clothes, Germany 595.00
Golf Club, Marked D.R.G.M., 4 5/8 In. 60.00
Googly, Bisque Head, Row Of Teeth, 8 In. 500.00
Gun, 6-Shooter, Glass, West Bros., 8 In. 95.00
Gun, Red Plastic 55.00
Happifat, Fat Boy On Drum, No Paint, 4 3/8 In. 137.00
Hat, Irish, Cardboard Top, Shamrock, 3 1/2 In. 15.00
Heart Shape, Cupid, Dresden, 1880s 145.00
Helicopter, Two Blade, 5 In. 410.00
Hen On Nest, Basket, Milk Glass 55.00
Hen On Nest, Glass, 3 1/2 In. 15.00
Hen On Nest, Glass, 6 1/4 In. 35.00
House, Cabinet Bank, Clear 290.00
Indian Hatchet & Gun 60.00
Jackie Coogan, Blue Glass, Reproduction Closure, 5 In. 110.00
Jackie Coogan, Some Paint, 5 In. 80.00
Kiddie Kar, Horse & Wagon, 4 1/2 In. 126.00
Kiddie's Candy Pencil Box 90.00
Lantern, Beaded No. 2, Green Glass, With Bail, 3 1/4 In. 33.00
Lantern, Dec. 20, '04, 6 Vertical Ribs, With Bail, 4 1/2 In. 14.00
Lantern, Magnifying Lens, 3 In. 110.00
Lantern, Twins On Anchor, Glass & Metal Lanterns, Metal Anchor 11.00
Lawn Swing, Tin Lithograph, Glass Seat, c.1915, 1 Oz. 840.00
Liberty Bell, Centennial Exposition, Sheared Ground Lip, Screw Cap, 3 In. 245.00
Liberty Bell, With Hanger, Amethyst, Hanger, 3 3/8 In. 110.00
Little Miss Washing Machine 110.00
Locomotive, 2 Stacker No. 23, 3 13/16 In. 330.00
Locomotive, American Type No. 23, Blue Glass, 4 3/4 In. 130.00
Locomotive, PRR 666, Lithographed Tin Slide Closure, 1920-1925, 2 7/8 In. 280.00
Log Cabin, Lutted's S.P. Cough Drops, Glass, 6 1/2 x 7 x 5 In. 225.00
Monkey, Glass, Mu-Mu, South America, 1950s, 4 In. 110.00
Naked Child, Glass, 3 5/8 In. 40.00
Opera Glass, Plain Panels, Ruby Flash, Maple Beach Park, Albany, N.Y. 285.00
Parlor Car, New York Central Railroad, No Closure 40.00
PEZ, Bozo, White With Red Paint, Cutout Design On Side, Austria 81.00

PEZ, Casper, No Feet Red Insert, Cutout White Body ....185.00 to 223.00
PEZ, Charlie Brown, Chicago Cubs, 50th Anniversary 152.00
PEZ, Daffy Duck, Blue Body 15.50
PEZ, Dumbo, Red Body, Blue Head, Yellow Hat, Austria 40.00
PEZ, Green, Embossed Pez, No Character Head, Germany 157.00
PEZ, Jerry, Mouse From Tom & Jerry, Green Body 29.00
PEZ, Jiminy Cricket, Green 61.00
PEZ, Kabaya, Japan ....61.00 to 71.00
PEZ, Knight, Black Plume, Stem, Silver Helmet 768.00
PEZ, Popeye, Blue & White, Red Insert 66.00
PEZ, Pumpkin Head, Green Base, No Feet, Austria 13.00
PEZ, Red, White Textured Grips, Austria, 1960 .... 200.00
PEZ, Roadrunner, Blue Head 15.00
PEZ, Santa Claus, No Feet, Yugoslavia 11.00
PEZ, Uncle Sam, 1970s 110.00
PEZ, Zorro, 1960s 195.00
PEZ, Zorro, Cast Script Logo, Austria 73.00
Pigeon, Metal Feet, Iridescent Purple Paint, 4 1/2 x 6 In. 220.00
Policeman, Mounted 3300.00
Policeman, Pumpkin Head, 4 3/4 In. 2970.00
Pumpkin Head, Witch, Green Paint, Glass, Original Closure, 4 1/2 In. 1495.00
Pumpkin Man On Watermelon, Metal Wheels 250.00
Rabbit, Avor, U.S.A., Gold Paint, ABM Lip, Metal Screw Cap, 1920-1930, 5 In. 335.00
Rabbit, Carrying Wicker Basket, Composition, 6 1/2 In. 40.00
Rabbit, Composition, 7 3/4 In. 60.00
Rabbit, Dressed, Pressed Cardboard, Germany, c.1920, 8 In. 195.00
Rabbit, Flocked, 9 In. 80.00
Rabbit, In Egg Shell, Some Paint, 5 1/8 In. 110.00
Rabbit, Papier-Mache, Painted Eyes 90.00
Rabbit, Pushing Chick In Shell Car, Some Paint 176.00
Rabbit, Tan, Sitting & Standing, Papier-Mache, 1920, 4 1/4 In., Pair 145.00
Rabbit, Wheelbarrow 675.00
Rabbit, White Fur, Hide Feet & Ears, Pink Glass Eyes, 10 In. 125.00
Rooster, Composition, Gold Dripped Paint, 5 3/4 In. 27.00
Rooster, Composition, Polychrome, Metal Feet, Germany, 7 1/4 x 7 1/2 In. 360.00
Rooster, Nodder 90.00
Rooster, Red & Brown Paint, Metal Feet, 4 1/2 x 4 3/4 In. 230.00
Safe, Milk Glass, Painted Closure 170.00
Safe, Ruby Flash, No Panels In Rear 385.00
Sand Pail, With Shovel, Tin, U.S. Metal Toy Mfg. Co. 50.00
Santa Claus, Ball 450.00
Santa Claus, Banded Coat, Some Repaint 175.00
Santa Claus, Blue Pants, Red Coat, Rabbit Fur Beard, 1910, 16 In. 850.00
Santa Claus, Glass Body, Plastic Head, J.H. Millstein Co., 1947, 5 In. 95.00
Santa Claus, Holding Tree & Bag, Germany, 10 In. ....*Illus* 220.00
Santa Claus, In Stocking, Wool Beard, Pipe Cleaner Trim, 5 1/2 In. 95.00
Santa Claus, Leaving Chimney, 5 1/6 In. 125.00

Splint baskets should have an occasional light shower. Shake off the excess water. Dry the basket in a shady spot.

Candy Container, Santa
Claus, Holding Tree &
Bag, Germany, 10 In.

Candy Container, Santa
Claus, Red Felt Robe,
Holding Tree, Germany, 7 In.

Santa Claus, Leaving Chimney, No Paint, 5 1/6 In. 88.00
Santa Claus, On Skis, Plastic, Open Bag On Back, E. Rosen Co., c.1945, 4 In. 20.00
Santa Claus, Red Felt Robe, Holding Tree, Germany, 7 In. ....*Illus* 66.00
Santa Claus, Robe, Composition Face & Hands, Rabbit Fur Beard, 13 1/2 In. 600.00
Santa Claus, Sleigh 300.00
Santa's Boot, Cardboard, Felt Covered, Green Ribbon Trim, Japan, 2 1/2 In. 12.00
Santa's Boot, Papier-Mache, Holly Sprig, 7 1/2 In. 35.00
Sheep, Lying Down, Germany, 19 In. 220.00
Skookum, By Tree Stump, Glass 475.00
Snow Angel, Bisque Head, Papier-Mache Body & Hands, 23 In. 2100.00
Snowman, Brown Arms Extended, Germany, 1950, 6 3/4 In. 28.00
Snowman, Flocked, Spring Bobbing Head, Stovepipe Hat 49.00
Snowman, Spun Cotton, Papier-Mache, Germany 195.00
Spark Plug, Horse, King Feature, Orange, Tin Snap-On Closure, 3 In. 670.00
Stag, Brown Flocking, Metal Antlers, Glass Eyes, Marked Germany, 10 In. 465.00
Suitcase, Milk Glass, Gold Paint, Wire Handle, Tin Slide Lid, 1906-1915, 3 In. 155.00
Tank, Man In Turret 38.00
Telephone, Candlestick, Glass, Wooden Receiver With Cord, 1942, 4 1/4 In. 55.00
Telephone, Dial Type, Victory Glass Co., Red Paint 19.00
Telephone, Plastic Mouthpiece, Stough Co., 3 1/2 In. 125.00
Telephone, West Bro's. Co., 1907 .... 38.00
Three Little Pigs, Tin 82.00
Toonerville Depot Line, Some Paint, 3 5/8 x 3 x 1 5/16 In. 155.00
Top, Spinning, Wooden Winder, 3 3/4 In. 77.00
Top Hat, Shaved Fur, Sateen Lining, Pops Out To Form Sack, 3 In. 225.00
Train, Halloween, Sparkle Black, 3 Faces 135.00
Train, Loft's Candyland Express, Litho Cardboard, Wooden Wheels, 9 x 4 In. 59.00
Tricycle, Condiment Set In Back 50.00
Truck, Loft's Candies, Tin 65.00
Trumpet, Clear 95.00
Trunk, Round Top, Milk Glass, Blue Flower On Front, Gilt, Junction City 94.00
Village, English Cottage, Red Gables, Insert 187.00
W.C. Fields 40.00
Wagon, 3 3/8 x 2 1/2 x 2 1/2 In. 132.00
Wheelbarrow, Original Wheel 33.00
Witch Head, Red Crepe Paper Collar, Papier-Mache, Germany, 4 In. 345.00
Yellow Chick 42.00

CANES and walking sticks were used by every well-dressed man in the nineteenth century, but by World War I the style had changed. Today canes are used by few but the infirm. Collectors prize old canes made with special features, like hidden swords, whiskey flasks, or risqué pictures seen through peepholes. Examples with solid gold heads or made from exotic materials, such as walrus vertebrae, are among the higher priced canes.

Allover Carved, W.J. Thomas, RFD No. 5, Tazewell, Tenn., Mar. 13, 1909, 39 In. 253.00
Amber & Horn, Horn Mounted With Sterling Silver, c.1880-1900 .... 200.00
Auger Shape, Iron, Ball Handle, Tapering Shaft, Mid 19th Century, 34 In. 165.00
Bamboo, Horn, Gold Mounted, France, c.1880-1910 .... 175.00
Bamboo, Sterling Silver Top, Chester, England, 1892 .... 175.00
Bartender's, Hides Gadgets, Shot Measure, Corkscrew, 1910 .... 425.00
Bird Handle, Simmons, Pa., Late 19th Century, 33 3/4 In. 880.00
Bone, James Garfield, Bust, Thermoplastic, Brass Band, 34 In. 550.00
Bone, Snake, Coiled, Handle, L Shape, Wood, 34 1/2 In. 58.00
Brass, Grover Cleveland, Bust, Knob Handle, Wooden Shaft, 34 1/2 In. 250.00
Britannia Metal, Benjamin Harrison, Levi Morton, Silver Plated 2530.00
Britannia Metal, John F. Kennedy Bust, Copper Plated, Varnished 990.00
Britannia Metal, William Jennings Bryan, Pewter Plated, c.1908 .... 825.00
Bronze, James Blaine, Bust, Cast Metal Head, Wooden Shaft, 1884, 33 In. 600.00
Carved, William McKinley, Theodore Roosevelt 2310.00
Carved Root, Free-Form Handle Carved As Dog, 35 1/2 In. 165.00
Cast Metal, Benjamin Harrison, Top Hat, Embossed Inscription 1045.00

Celluloid, Benjamin Harrison, Bust, Brass Frame, Dome Glass, Varnished Shaft, 32 In. 360.00
Celluloid, Benjamin Harrison, Bust, Brass Frame, Grain Finish Shaft, 35 In. 715.00
Celluloid, Photo Disc, Alton B. Parker, For President, Black Wooden Frame 880.00
Celluloid, Photo Disc, Woodrow Wilson, Silver Plated Metal Frame 770.00
Celluloid, Slogan Disc, You Can't Monkey With Teddy, c.1904 ....   770.00
Celluloid, William McKinley, Bust, 5 Blue Stars, 5 Red Stars, White Ground, 36 In. 385.00
Celluloid, William McKinley, Bust, Red, White Diagonal Stripes, 6 White Stars, 36 In. 412.00
Celluloid, William McKinley, Bust, Red, White Stripes, 9 White Stars, 31 In. 880.00
Century Of Progress, Franklin D. Roosevelt, Bronze Colored Cast Metal, c.1933 ....   770.00
Deer Horn, 3-Point, Black Lacquered Shaft, Pewter Sleeve, 37 In. 155.00
Dog's Head, Silver Crook Handle, Dark Varnished Shaft, 35 1/2 In. 330.00
Dog's Head Handle, Droopy Ears, Pa., Late 19th Century, 38 1/4 In. 550.00
Eagle's Head Handle, Chip Carved, Sailor Art, 19th Century, 35 1/2 In. 402.00
Ebony, Dog's Head, Glass Eyes, Rosewood Shaft, Original Ivory Ferrule, 34 In. 137.00
Ebony, Inlaid Silver Head, England, Late 19th Century 150.00
Ebony, Sterling Silver Top, London, 1903 ....   110.00
Flag, Daniel H. Hastings, Pa. Gubernatorial Race, Dark Wooden Shaft, 1894, 36 In. 137.00
Glass, Amber, Twisted Handle, End, Zanesville, 37 1/4 In. 28.00
Glass, Grover Cleveland, Bust, Knob, Top Handle, 2 Flags, Flowers, 27 In. 660.00
Glass, Parade, Red, White, Blue Swirl Pattern, South Jersey, Mid 19th Century, 40 In. ...   110.00
Glass Top, Grover Cleveland, Photo Disc, Pewter Color Metal Frame 990.00
Gold & Mother-Of-Pearl Handle, Brass Tip, 35 In. 205.00
Gold Plate Knob, William Henry Harrison, Log Cabin Disc, Wood 935.00
Gun, Percussion, Walrus Ivory, Bamboo Carved Shaft, Continental, c.1850 ....   1430.00
Horn, Andrew Jackson, Molded, Bark Covered Shaft 330.00
Horn, Coursing Hound, Carved Sheep Horn, Glass Eyes, Hardwood Shaft, 1920, 35 In. ..   165.00
Horn, Patriotism, Protection, Prosperity, William McKinley, 1900 Campaign, Zinc 715.00
Horse & Rider, Dog, Stag, Rooster, Birds Spiraling Up Shaft, 1879, 41 In. 1870.00
Inlaid Silver Head, Ebony Wood Shaft, Late 19th Century 150.00
Ivory, Animal Head, Child's, 18th Century, Pair 395.00
Ivory, Bird Perched On Tree Trunk Fighting With Turtle, Dark Bamboo Shaft, 38 In. 330.00
Ivory, Carved Dog, Glass Eyes, Silver Collar Like Strap, Walnut Shaft, 35 In. 1200.00
Ivory, Comic Head, Vegetable, Glass Eyes, Original Ferrule, 34 1/2 In. 55.00
Ivory, Engraved Gold Band, Man's Face, Wearing Hat, Steel Tip, 32 1/2 In. 165.00
Ivory, Family, Old Woman & 2 Children, Root Burl, 1880, 35 In. 220.00
Ivory, Gold Band, Wood, 35 In. 172.00
Ivory, Horse Head, Carved Walrus, Gold Plate, Ebony Shaft, 32 1/2 In. 300.00
Ivory, Horse Head, Gold Mounts, Aurustus Oskamp, Memory Of Father, 37 In. 360.00
Ivory, Reclining Dog, Carved Walrus, Thornwood Shaft, 1890, 33 In. 165.00
Ivory, Silver Ferrule, England, Late 19th Century 240.00
Ivory, Silver Mounted With Repousse, England, Late 19th Century 240.00
Ivory, Snake, Rev. J.P. Steinluger, 1900 ....   695.00
Ivory, Walrus, Circular Knob, White Metal 1/12 In. Band, 29 In. 275.00
Ivory, Walrus, Head Shape, Phrenology Markings 1320.00
Ivory, Walrus, Sailor's, Snake Clenching Fish, Rosewood, 1860, 35 1/2 In. 550.00
Ivory, Walrus, Wood, 39 In. 170.00
Ivory, Whale, Wood, Gold Band, 35 In. 170.00
Man's Head Handle, Mustache, Beard, Pa., 34 3/4 In. 470.00
Metal, Bust, William McKinley, 33 1/2 In. 700.00
Metal, Grover Cleveland, Allen Thurman, Pewter Colored, Wood 2420.00
Metal, James A. Garfield, Bronzed Plated, Varnished 880.00
Metal, James Blaine Bust, Pewter Colored, Varnished 605.00
Metal, Ulysses Grant, Bronzed Plated, Varnished 1980.00
Metal, Woodrow Wilson, Golf Club, Wilson For President, Dark Bamboo Shaft, 36 In. ...   165.00
Mother-Of-Pearl, Cross, Birds, Animals, Black, White, Arch Burkholder, c.1900, 31 In. ..   440.00
Parade, South Jersey, White & Cranberry Swirl, 19th Century, 38 In. 275.00
Parade, Torch, McKinley, Metal, 1896, 33 In. 300.00
Parade, White & Cranberry Swirl, South Jersey, 38 In. 175.00
Pewter, Grover Cleveland, Bust, Dark Wooden Shaft, 33 In. 660.00
Pewter, Grover Cleveland, Bust, Knob Handle, Dark Varnish Shaft, 34 In. 990.00
Pewter, Skull, Rustic Shaft, 33 In. 330.00
Pewter Plate, Benjamin Harrison, Bust, Black Wooden Shaft, 33 In. 300.00

Polychrome, Carved, Bird Form Handle, Black, Gold, Simmons, Pa., 32 3/4 In. 2970.00
Polychrome, Carved, Bird Handle, Black Head, Tail, Red Wings, Simmons, Pa., 37 In. 4620.00
Polychrome, Carved, Soldier Shape Handle, Red Jacket, Brass Buttons, 34 In. 3180.00
Porcelain, Dwight D. Eisenhower, Painted, 31 In. 357.00
Porcelain Top, Rosewood Shaft, 1890 .... 175.00
Presentation, Handle, Gold Plate, Inscription, Maj. Thomas McManus, 2 x 3 In. 520.00
Presentation, Ornate Gold Band, Wooden Shaft, 34 1/2 In. 110.00
Presentation, Postal, Carved Lion's Head, Glass Eyes, Malacca Shaft, 35 1/2 In. 470.00
Presentation, Sterling Silver, From James Buchanan To James Maxfield, c.1856 .... 1100.00
Rawhide Handle, Yardstick, Alabama Presents Metcalf For President, 36 In. 55.00
Rawhide Handle, Yardstick, Page For Governor In Maine, 1936, 36 In. 55.00
Reclining Dog Handle, Extended Front Paws, Simmons, Pa., 36 In. 660.00
Republican Elephant, Green Collar On Elephant, Red Painted Shaft, 34 In. 275.00
Republican Elephant, Nickel Plate, Blond Wooden Shaft, 1930, 33 1/2 In. 140.00
Rosewood, Bakelite Head, Bone Foot, Flower Shape, England, 20th Century 130.00
Rosewood, Ivory Ball Head, Sterling Silver Mounted, Horn Foot 275.00
Shark's Spine, 19th Century, 35 In. 138.00
Silver Crook, Spelter Ferrule, Ebony Shaft, Late 19th Century, 35 1/2 In. 1250.00
Silver Crutch, Eagle On 1 Side, Malacca Shaft, Late 19th Century, 35 In. 650.00
Silver Plate, Benjamin Harrison, Bust, Black Wooden Shaft, 35 In. 880.00
Silver Plate, Benjamin Harrison, Bust, Cherry Varnished Shaft, 35 In. 600.00
Silver Plate, Benjamin Harrison, Bust, Dark Varnished Shaft, 36 In. ....275.00 to 550.00
Silver Plate, Grover Cleveland, Bust, Cast Metal Head, Wooden Shaft, 35 In. .....220.00 to 660.00
Silver Plate, James Blaine, Bust, Cast Metal Head, Bamboo Shaft, 37 In. 247.00
Silver Plate, Woodrow Wilson, Bust, Dark Varnished Shaft, 34 In. 770.00
Spiraling Snake, Black Bead Eyes, Mushroom Cap Handle, 31 1/2 In. 360.00
Star Fish, Silver Branch Coral, 15 Star Fishes Encircling Base, 35 In. 410.00
Sterling Silver Top, Bamboo Shaft, Hallmark, 1892 .... 175.00
Sterling Silver Top, James Buchanan, Bust, Dark Varnish Shaft, 37 In. 1100.00
Sterling Silver Top, London, Ebony Shaft, 1903 .... 110.00
Sterling Silver Top, William H. Taft, Initials TCW 525.00
Sword, Bamboo Sheath, Brass Ferrule Tip, Antler Handle, c.1810, 35 1/2 In. 350.00
Sword, Carved Horn, Stork's Head Handle, 32 3/4 In. 580.00
Sword, Damascus Blade 890.00
Sword, Nubby Wooden Shaft, Nickel Tip, Push Button Release, Marked Toledo, 36 In. ... 770.00
Sword, Stag Handle, Shape Of Bird's Head, Curved Bead, 36 In. 250.00
Sword, Sterling Silver Handle, Engraved Blade, Toledo, Tapered Handle, 36 In. 550.00
Walking Stick, 5 Stylized Leaves, Lady Emerging, Wooden Shaft, 34 1/2 In. 605.00
Walking Stick, Ball Form, Ivory Handle, Late 19th Century, 37 1/2 In. 160.00
Walking Stick, Bronze Knob, Dog's Head, Bronze Ferrule, Wooden Shaft, 35 3/4 In. 115.00
Walking Stick, Coin Silver Crook Handle, Flowers, Scroll Design, Walnut Shaft, 36 In. .. 360.00
Walking Stick, Coin Silver Handle, Flowers, Dark Varnish Shaft, 34 1/2 In. 360.00
Walking Stick, Elf Head, Varnished Wood Shaft, Scrolled Leaves, 36 In. 250.00
Walking Stick, Figured Tiger Maple, Incised, Bone Escutcheons, 18th Century, 36 In. 950.00
Walking Stick, Globular Goldstone Handle, Gold Collar, Exotic Wooden Shaft, 35 In. ... 370.00
Walking Stick, Gold Hexagonal Handle, Bamboo Type Shaft, 35 1/2 In. 172.00
Walking Stick, Gray Guilloche, Silver Seed Pearls, Enameled Handle, 1900, 37 In. 825.00
Walking Stick, Horn & Ivory, Humanesque Face, Exaggerated, Malacca Shaft, 34 In. 1035.00
Walking Stick, Indian Head Handle, Redman Lodge, Late 19th Century, 35 1/2 In. 138.00
Walking Stick, Ivory, Dog, Scotty Handle, Open Mouth, Bamboo Shaft, 39 In. 575.00
Walking Stick, Ivory, Knob Handle, Bulldog, Collar, Bamboo Shaft, 35 In. 520.00
Walking Stick, Ivory, Mongoose Attacking Snake, Ivory Handle, 1900, 36 In. 605.00
Walking Stick, Ivory, Turkish Knot, Knob Handle, Dark Varnish Shaft, 34 In. 550.00
Walking Stick, Naked Leg, Horn Section In Shaft, 31 In. 520.00
Walking Stick, Opera Handle, Bearded Man, Tasseled Fez, 31 In. 28.00
Walking Stick, Profile Of Maiden, Gilt Hair, Jewels, Brass Ferrule, Wooden Shaft, 33 In. .. 200.00
Walking Stick, Scenes Of North African Life, Ebony Shaft, Silver Metal Handle, 33 In. ... 165.00
Walking Stick, Silver Handle, Art Nouveau Woman Emerging From Leaves 600.00
Walking Stick, Silver, Knobbed Handle, Inset Animal Tooth, Square Shaft, 36 In. 200.00
Walking Stick, Silver, Pre-Revolutionary, Crook Handle, Rosewood Shaft, 37 In. 360.00
Walking Stick, Silver, Tortoise Shell, Art Nouveau, 21 x 3/4 In. 39.00
Walking Stick, Sterling Silver Mount, Monogram, January 6, 1908 .... 110.00

Walking Stick, Sterling Silver, Bust, Fashionable Lady, Mahogany Shaft, 35 In. 605.00
Walking Stick, Tortoiseshell, Mushroom Gilt Cap, Early 19th Century, 33 1/4 In. 980.00
Walking Stick, Whale Ivory Handle, Whalebone Shaft, 31 1/2 In. 375.00
Walking Stick, Whale Ivory Handle, Wooden Shaft, 19th Century, 56 In. 835.00
Walking Stick, Wood, Carved, Dog's Head Pommel, Glass Inset Eyes, Chinese, 35 In. ... 185.00
Walking Stick, Wood, Ivory Handle, Silver Mounted, Late 19th Century, 33 In. 430.00
Walking Stick, Wood, Wrap Around Carved, Dog Handle, Hearts 1450.00
Whale Ivory, Turned Handle, Wooden Shaft, 19th Century, 56 1/2 In. 170.00
Whalebone, Captain's, Going Ashore, Carved, Ring Wood Ferule, Hexagon Top, 37 In. ... 5290.00
Whalebone, Carved, 5 Baleen Bands, 1800s, 34 1/2 In. 1265.00
Whalebone, Ivory Handle, Hand Holding Snake, Inlaid Rings, 37 1/2 In. 1760.00
Whalebone, Ivory Knob, Black Baleen, Inlaid Dots, 35 In. 2200.00
Whalebone, Whale Ivory, Octagonal Shaft, 19th Century, 38 In. 835.00
Whalebone Shaft, Rosewood, Baleen, Walrus, 31 1/2 In. 275.00
Whalebone Shaft, Whale Ivory Handle, 31 1/2 In. 375.00
White Metal, Benjamin Harrison, Bust, Metal Top Hat, 1776, 35 In. 1045.00
Wood, Abraham Lincoln, Bust, Dark Wood Varnish Brass Band, 35 In. 1430.00
Wood, Benjamin Harrison, Bust, Plain Burl, Cast Metal, Wooden Shaft 770.00
Wood, Carved, Dog's Head Handle, Shellacked Finish, Simmons, 35 1/4 In. 660.00
Wood, Cast Aluminum, Embossed Gerald R. Ford, For President, Curved 165.00
Wood, Celluloid Crook, Fox, Wooden Shaft, 34 1/2 In. 220.00
Wood, Duck Head, Ivory Beak, Carved, Malacca Shaft, Late 19th Century, 35 3/4 In. 875.00
Wood, F.D. Roosevelt, Balance Budget, Let's Have A New Deal, Pencil Shape, 35 In. ... 825.00
Wood, Hard Rubber, Molded Bust Of Lincoln, Brass Band, Varnished 1430.00
Wood, Ivory Ball, Sterling Silver Mount, Rosewood, Horn Foot 275.00
Wood, James Garfield, Bust, Bronze Metal, Varnished Shaft, 35 In. 880.00
Wood, Parakeet's Head, Glass Eyes, White Metal Band, 33 1/2 In. 192.00
Wood, Spelter, Jockey's Head, Elongated Nose, 1890, 36 In. 110.00
Wood, Ulysses Grant, Bust, Bronze Metal Head, Varnished Shaft, 1872, 36 In. 1980.00
Wood, William Henry Harrison, Bust, Wooden Shaft, 1840, 30 1/2 In. ....440.00 to 935.00

CANTON CHINA is a blue-and-white ware made near the city of Canton, in China, from about 1785 to 1895. It is hand decorated with Chinese scenes. Canton is part of the group of porcelains known today as Chinese Export Porcelain.

Basket, Fruit, Undertray, Reticulated, Oval, 4 1/2 x 8 5/8 x 10 In. 1150.00
Bowl, 7 In. 103.00
Bowl, Fruit, Landscape Scene, Reticulated Sides, 1840, 8 3/4 In. 747.00
Bowl, Square, Scalloped Edge, 4 3/4 x 9 1/2 In. 825.00
Bowl, Tray, Central Open Blossom, Vines, Flowers, Painted Sides, 19th Century, 12 In. ... 6600.00
Bowl, Vegetable, Cover, Diamond Shape, Fruit Finial, Scalloped, 8 1/2 x 3 In. 220.00
Bowl, Vegetable, Cover, Rectangular, 19th Century, 4 1/2 x 7 1/2 x 8 3/4 In. 345.00
Bowl, Vegetable, Lozenge Shape, Pinecone Finial, Early 19th Century, 11 In. 517.00
Box, Cover, Flowers, Symbols, Diamond Trellis, 4 Sections, 19th Century, 6 3/4 In. 300.00
Canister, 6 In., 3 Piece 517.00
Censer, Domed Cover, Figural Cartouches, Flowers, Dragon Handles, 1800, 62 In. 575.00
Dish, Lozenge Shape, Early 19th Century, 11 In. 517.00
Dish, Octagonal, Sailboats, Willows, Buildings, Dash Border, c.1780, 10 In. 140.00
Dish, Pagoda & Lake Design, 1790, 9 In. 546.00
Ginger Jar, Wooden Cover, Rectangular, Mounted As Lamp, 14 1/4 In., Pair 575.00
Jug, Cider, Double Strap Handle, 4 1/2 In. 600.00
Jug, Cider, Foo Dog Finial, 19th Century, 7 In. 2185.00
Lamp, Square, Was Tea Caddy, Drilled & Electrified, 8 x 8 In. 1210.00
Mug, Cider, 5 1/2 In. 935.00
Mug, Cylindrical, Entwined Lapped Handle, 19th Century, 4 1/4 In. 520.00
Mug, Cylindrical, Fitzhugh, Ear Shape Dragon Handle, 4 In. 200.00
Plate Set, 9 1/2 In., 11 Piece 345.00
Plate Set, Rain Cloud Border, 8 1/2 In., 8 Piece 695.00
Platter, c.1829, 8 1/2 x 5 1/4 In. 325.00
Platter, Crane, Butterfly, Floral Design, Leaf Rim, 3 1/2 x 16 x 12 1/4 In. 2070.00
Platter, Cut Corner Form, 18 1/4 x 15 In. 990.00
Platter, Cut Corner Shape, 19th Century, 17 x 21 1/8 In. 1840.00

Platter, Early 19th Century 1045.00
Platter, Octagonal, 19th Century, 13 3/4 In. 750.00
Platter, Undertray, Pierced, 8 1/2 x 7 1/2 In. 860.00
Sauceboat, Scalloped Top, Loop Handle, 1 3/4 x 7 3/4 x 3 3/4 In., Pair 460.00
Strainer Insert, Pierced Holes, 10 x 13 In. 520.00
Teapot, 19th Century, 9 In. 1210.00
Teapot, Peach Finial, Interwoven Handle, 19th Century, 5 3/4 In. 625.00
Tureen, Cover, Boar's Head Handles, Early 19th Century 980.00
Tureen, Cover, Rectangular, Leaf Shape Knop, Boar's Head Handles, 1800s, 8 x 13 In. . . 1955.00
Tureen, Footed, Animal Head Handles, 8 x 12 x 10 In. 1540.00
Tureen, Underplate, Octagonal, Boar's Head Handles, Cover, 8 1/2 x 14 1/4 In. 1955.00
Umbrella Stand, 24 1/2 In. 400.00
Washbowl, Man & Woman Archer In Garden, 1800, 14 1/2 In. 410.00

CAPO-DI-MONTE porcelain was first made in Naples, Italy, from 1743 to 1759. The factory moved near Madrid, Spain, reopened in 1771, and worked to 1834. Since that time, the Doccia factory of Italy acquired the molds and is using the crown and N mark. Societe Richard Ceramica is a modern-day firm often referred to as Ginori or Capo-di-Monte. This company uses the crown and N mark.

Box, Cherubs Rollicking, Enamel, Gilt, Marked, France, 4 5/8 In. 93.00
Box, Classical Figures, Chariot On Hinged Lid, 8 1/4 In. 230.00
Box, Figural & Landscape Relief, Footed, 9 x 6 x 8 In. 80.00
Box, Hinged, Continental, Oval, Mark, Late 19th Century, 5 1/8 In. 200.00
Casket, Cherubs Supporting Garland, Hinged Lid, Paw Beet, 5 3/4 In. 345.00
Dish, Cover, Underplate, Gold & Flowers, Putti Musicians, Twig Handles 55.00
Dresser Set, 2 Lotion Bottles, Powder Bowl, Mirrored Tray, 7 Piece 800.00
Figurine, Boy With Basket Made Out Of Handkerchief, Marked, 4 5/8 In. 53.00
Figurine, Man In Tailor Shop, Girl Holding Teddy Bear, 1951, 10 x 7 In. 165.00
Figurine, Mare & Foal, 6 1/2 x 7 1/2 In. 215.00
Figurine, Old Pug Dog, Marked, 2 1/2 In. 361.00
Figurine, White Doves, On Tree Stand, 7 x 8 In. 190.00
Figurine, White Stallions, 10 x 14 In. 325.00
Figurine, Woman With Basket, 11 1/4 x 4 1/4 In. 125.00
Figurine, Woman, Basket Of Clothes, 10 In. 200.00
Figurine, Woman, Walking Dog, 12 x 7 3/4 In. 235.00
Figurine, Young Couple In Chariot, Lions & Cherubs, 12 3/4 x 10 1/2 In. 1350.00
Group, Allegorical Figure, 3 Girls Playing With Child, Oval Base, 10 In. 405.00
Group, Bacchus Riding Chariot Pulled By 2 Goats, Oval Base, 9 1/2 In. 115.00
Group, Young Couple With Boy Drinking From Pitcher, 7 In. 29.00
Lamp, Classical Figures, Brass Griffins, Brass Base, 18 In. 300.00
Plaque, Center Medallion, Woman's Head, Border Of Figures, 22 1/2 In. 935.00
Plaque, Hercules & Athena, Surround Of Other Figures, 14 1/2 In. 1725.00
Stein, Man's Face On Handle, Classical Figures, 15 1/2 In., Pair 695.00
Sugar & Creamer, Lion On Cover, Dragon Handles, Scenes All Around, 6 In. 250.00
Urn, Amphora Shape, Classical Figures, 3-Part Base, 19 1/2 In. 175.00
Urn, Cherubs Rollicking, Gilt, 12 3/8 In., Pair 110.00
Urn, Classical Figures, Low Relief, Oval Body, Mounted As Lamp, 13 In. 489.00
Vase, Lion Mask Handles, Cherubs, Mounted As Lamp, Oval, 20 In. 345.00
Vase, Mythological Figures Around Rim, 17 x 15 1/2 In. 200.00

CAPTAIN MARVEL was introduced in February 1940 in Whiz comic books. An orphan named Billy Batson met the wizard, Shazam, and whenever he said the magic word he was transformed into a superhero. A movie serial was released in 1940. The comic was discontinued in 1954. A second Captain Marvel appeared in 1966, a third in 1967. Only the original was transformed by shouting *Shazam.*

Bank, Dime Register 110.00
Toy, Car, Racing, No. 1, Key Wind, 4 In. 152.00
Toy, Car, Racing, No. 4, Key Wind, 4 In. 60.00
View-Master, Shazam, Return Of Black Adam, 3 Reels, Booklet, 1976 .... 25.00
Wristwatch, Box, 1960s 190.00

CAPTAIN MIDNIGHT began as a radio show in September 1940. The first comic book appeared in July 1941. Captain Midnight was really the aviator Captain Albright, who was to defeat the Nazis. A movie serial was made in 1942 and a comic strip was published for a short time. The comic book Captain Midnight ended his career in 1948. The radio premiums are the prized collector memorabilia today.

Airplane, Wright, Box, c.1940	285.00
Book, Captain Midnight & Secret Squadron vs. Terror Of Orient, 1942	105.00
Book, Trick & Riddle Book, Skelly, 1939	17.00 to 50.00
Cup, Ovaltine, Decal, 1950s	15.00
Decoder, Goldtone Metal Front, Plastic Back, Signaling Mirror, 1948	322.00
Medal Of Membership, Skelly Oil Co., 1940, 1 1/4 In.	14.00
Membership Kit, Decoder Insert	625.00
Pin, Decoder, 1946	50.00
Ring, Decoder, Ovaltine	25.00
Whistle, Radio Premium	225.00
Wings Patch, Cloth	150.00

CARAMEL SLAG, see Imperial Glass category.

CARDS listed here include advertising cards (often called trade cards), greeting cards, baseball cards, playing cards, and others. Color pictures were rare in the nineteenth century, so companies gave away colorful cards with pictures of children, flowers, products, or related scenes that promoted the company name. These were often collected and stored in albums. Baseball cards also date from the nineteenth century when they were used by tobacco companies as giveaways. Gum cards were started in 1933, but it was not until after World War II that the bubble gum cards favored today were produced. Today over 1,000 cards are issued each year by the gum companies. Related items may be found in the Postcard and Movie categories.

Advertising, Arbuckle Brothers, Alaska, 3 x 5 In.	9.00
Advertising, Ariosa Coffee, 2 Sailors, 1 Sitting, 1 Standing, Arbuckle Factory	10.00
Advertising, Ariosa Coffee, 2 Sailors, Factory, Train, Ship, Buggy	10.00
Advertising, Ayer's Hair Vigor, Mermaids, Sinking Ship	6.00
Advertising, Barbour's Irish Flax Thread	5.00
Advertising, Beechnut Life Savers, U.S. Playing Card Co., 1970s, 3 1/2 x 2 3/8 In.	7.50
Advertising, Blookers Dutch Cocoa, Foldover, New York	50.00
Advertising, Brooks Bank Note Co., Springfield, Mass., Engraved, 3 1/2 x 5 1/4 In.	135.00
Advertising, Brown's Dentifrice, 2 Women Hugging, 1 Woman Standing	15.00
Advertising, Capadura Cigar, Nude Woman, Major & Knapp Lith. Co., N.Y., 1883	20.00
Advertising, Capadura Cigar, Woman By River, Smoking Cigar	25.00
Advertising, Chicago Yeast Powder, Peru, Illinois, Dealer J. Cahill, 3 x 4 1/2 In.	12.00
Advertising, Chocolat Du Planteur, Woman Reading, Green Dress	20.00
Advertising, Chocolat Du Planteur, Woman, Red Coat & Muff	20.00
Advertising, Chocolate Menier, American Branch Of Menier	7.00
Advertising, Clark's Thread, Cliff House, Seal Beach, San Francisco, 1890, 5 x 7 In.	26.00
Advertising, Conqueror Washer, Woman Putting Sleeping Child In Basket	12.00
Advertising, Coupling Spring Water, 2 3/4 x 4 1/2 In.	20.00
Advertising, D. Danziger, Fancy & Staple Dry Goods, New Orleans, c.1880, 2 3/8 x 4 In.	18.00
Advertising, Diamond Sewing Machine, Cairo, Ill., Boy & Girl, Dog, 1880s, 2 3/8 x 4 In.	9.00
Advertising, Dr. Hebra's Viola Cream For Complexion & Skin Blemishes, 1880s, 6 In.	45.00
Advertising, Dr. Jayne's Sanitive Pills, Little Red Riding Hood	7.00
Advertising, Dr. Kilmer's Liver Pills, Animals Weeping Over Sick Piglet	35.00
Advertising, Duffy's Malt Whiskey, Ancient Mariner's Stellar Time Piece, 7 In.	135.00
Advertising, E. Remington & Sons, Firearms, Ilion, N.Y., Wooded Scene, Tents, Boats	150.00
Advertising, Empire Mower, Family Of Rabbits, Gies & Co., Buffalo, N.Y.	6.00
Advertising, F. C. Corsets, Woman In Corset, Surrounded By Flowers	8.00
Advertising, Flint & Walling Mfg. Co., Star Windmills, Kendallville, Ind., 1889, 6 In.	18.00
Advertising, Handsen's Danish Butter, Foldover, 6 1/2 x 5 1/2 In.	20.00
Advertising, Honey Dew Dry Powder Face Cream, Cherubs, 2 3/4 x 4 1/2 In.	20.00
Advertising, Hop Ointment, Girl With Doll, Kellogg & Buckley, Hartford, Conn., 1887	20.00
Advertising, Horsford's Acid Phosphate, J.W. Colton & Stratton, 1880s, 3 x 4 1/2 In.	16.00

Advertising, Hunt's Remedy, Kidney & Liver, Stamford, Conn., 1883, 3 1/8 x 4 1/2 In. .. 9.00
Advertising, Irving W. Allen, Job Printer, Beverly, Mass., 2 1/2 x 5 In., Pair 1900.00
Advertising, L. I. Fisk & Co., Japanese Soap, Springfield, Mass. 25.00
Advertising, LePage's Liquid Glue, Police Pulling Man Off Bench, Children Watching ... 15.00
Advertising, Libbey's Extract Of Beef, 1893-1894 Calendar, Milwaukee Lith. Co. 35.00
Advertising, Libby, McNeill, & Libby, Canned Meats 20.00
Advertising, Love Tobacco, Myers Bros. & Co., Union & Confederate Soldiers Sharing .. 100.00
Advertising, Lydia Pinkham Vegetable Compound 4.00
Advertising, Maillard's Chocolate, Girls Drinking Cocoa, Donaldson Bros., 5 Points, N.Y. 40.00
Advertising, Maillard's Chocolate, Recipes For Chocolate Milk & Hot Cocoa 45.00
Advertising, Neuhauser Brothers, Girl Walking Dog, Bird-In-Hand, Pa., c.1900 .... 10.00
Advertising, Playing, NuGrape Soda, 1926 .... 90.00
Advertising, Rising Sun Stove Polish, Foldover, Major & Knapp Lith. Co. 35.00
Advertising, Santa Holding A Simplex Typewriter In His Hands, 1920, 5 x 2 1/2 In. 40.00
Advertising, St. Louis Beef, Trading, Black Man Signing, Wemple & Co., 4 3/4 x 2 In. .. 65.00
Advertising, Standard Screw Boots, 3 Black Caricatures, 1883 Calendar On Back 40.00
Advertising, Sterling Stoves & Ranges, 2 Clowns, 1 In Barrel 20.00
Advertising, Thomas The T-Man Coffees, Spices, New Haven, Conn., 2 3/8 x 4 In. 6.00
Advertising, Toledo Brewing & Malting Co., Cleveland, Candidates Drinking, 1884 ..... 85.00
Advertising, Trick Pony Mechanical Bank, Promotional Information On Back, 5 x 3 In. .. 115.00
Baseball, Albert Bridwell & Christy Mathewson, Mecca T201, Double Folder 200.00
Baseball, Billy Martin, Topps, No. 13, 1954 .... 400.00
Baseball, Cal Ripken, Topps, 1982 .... 70.00
Baseball, Dave Winfield, Topps, No.160, 1976 .... 15.00
Baseball, Earl Gardner & Tris Speaker, Mecca T201, Double Folder, 1911 .... 80.00
Baseball, Early Wynn, Topps, No. 61, 1953 .... 625.00
Baseball, Eddie Mathews, Topps, No. 37, 1953 .... 750.00
Baseball, Frank Chance & John Evers, T201 Mecca Double Folder, Card No. 13, 1911 ... 175.00
Baseball, Kirby Puckett, Topps, No. 536, 1985 .... 7.00
Baseball, Mickey Mantle, Topps, No. 10, 1959 .... 3500.00
Baseball, Played At Our Picnic, Umpire In Cage, 1889 .... 50.00
Baseball, Rod Carew, Topps, 1968 .... 40.00
Baseball, Roger Maris, Topps, No. 47, 1958, Rookie 1000.00
Baseball, Sam Mele, Bowman, No. 118, 1949 .... 80.00
Baseball, Sandy Koufax, Topps, 1956 .... 89.00
Baseball, Tom Seaver, Topps, 1967 .... 449.00
Baseball, Tony Kubek, Topps, No. 20, 1963 .... 55.00
Baseball, Warren Spahn, Topps, 1960 .... 35.00
Baseball, Yogi Berra, Bowman, No. 60, 1949 .... 5000.00
Basketball, Larry Bird & Magic Johnson, Topps, 1980 .... 149.00
Basketball, Michael Jordan, Fleer, 1987 .... 219.00
Basketball, Scottie Pippen, Fleer, 1988 .... 25.00
Football, Dan Marino, Topps, 1984 .... 49.00
Football, Frank Gifford, Bowman, 1955 .... 149.00
Football, Norm Van Brocklin, Topps, 1957 .... 65.00
Football, Steve Largent, Topps, No. 177, 1977 .... 25.00
Greeting, Flu Epidemic, I Will Be Down, Epidemic Is Lifted, Woburn, Mass., 1918, 5 In. . 16.00
Greeting, Valentine, Cutwork, Sawtooth Border Around Tulip & Bird, c.1840, 13 In. 495.00
Greeting, Valentine, Jiggs, Be My Valentine Or The Jigg's Up, 1930s, 4 x 5 In. 14.00
Hockey, Jaromir Jagr, Score, 1990-1991, Rookie 600.00
Hockey, Wayne Getzky, O-Pee-Chee, 1984 .... 15.00
Playing, American Rover, Box, 8 1/4 x 5 1/2 In. 137.00
Playing, Bridge Set, Celluloid, Box, c.1930, 6 1/2 x 8 3/4 In. 248.00
Playing, Eagle, 16 Stars, Paperboard, Thomas Crehore, Stoughton, Mass., c.1796 ...... 2500.00
Playing, Great Northern Railroad, Full Deck 70.00
Playing, Marilyn Monroe, Unused, 1976 .... 15.00

CARDER, see Aurene and Steuben categories.

CARLSBAD is a mark found on china made by several factories in
Germany, Austria, and Bavaria. Many pieces were exported to the
United States. Most of the pieces available today were made after
1891.

Biscuit Jar, 3 Women Dancing In Field, Kauffmann, 1891-1918, 7 1/4 In. 51.00

Biscuit Jar, Bunches Of Forget-Me-Nots, Green Leaves, Brass Fittings, Signed, 7 In. 125.00
Creamer, Pink Roses, Gold Trim, 4 1/2 In. 33.00
Cup & Saucer, Portrait Of Josephine, Blue 22.00
Inkstand, 2 Wells, Roses, Pink, Green & Yellow, Gold Trim, 8 x 3 1/2 In. 91.00
Spooner, Pink Roses, Gold Trim, 3 3/4 In. 33.00
Sugar, Cover, Pink Roses, Gold Trim, 5 In. 33.00
Sugar & Creamer, Women, Cupid, Green Border, Gold Trim 117.00
Tray, Dresser, Rococo Couple Kissing, Square, 4 In. 15.00
Vase, Women, Playing Tamborine, Dancing, Cupid 2 Handles, Kauffmann, 11 1/2 In. 25.00

CARLTON WARE was made at the Carlton Works of Stoke-on-Trent, England, beginning about 1890. The firm traded as Wiltshaw & Robinson until 1957. It was renamed Carlton Ware Ltd. in 1958. The company went bankrupt in 1995, but the name is still in use.

Biscuit Box, Pink & White Flowers, Green Leaves, Signed, 9 In. 125.00
Bowl, Harebell, Bell-Like Flowers, Gold & Black Leaves, 3 1/2 x 9 In. 395.00
Bowl, Kingfisher, Gilded, Signed, 3 1/4 x 9 In. 86.00
Bowl, Lobster, With Spoon 29.00
Compote, Bird Of Paradise, Butterflies & Dragonflies, Gold Trim, 1927, 10 In. 66.00
Compote, Bird Of Paradise, Trees, Butterflies & Dragonflies, 1894, 4 x 10 In. 300.00
Eggcup, Brown Shoes, Signed, 3 x 4 In. 31.00
Ginger Jar, Cranes In Flight, Stylized Tree, Enamel, Cover, 1920s, 12 1/2 In. 5100.00
Jar, Cover, Oxblood, Gold Trim, 6 In. 20.00
Pitcher, Yellow, Floral Design, W & R, 9 In. 80.00
Tankard, Musical, Fruit Seller Wagon, Handle Of Flowers, 6 In. 145.00
Toast Rack, Poppies 91.00
Vase, Chinese Bird, Blue Luster Ground, Drilled For Lamp, 8 In. 535.00
Vase, Oriental Pagoda, Draped Figures, Leaf Borders, Double Handles, 8 1/4 In. 275.00

CARNIVAL GLASS was an inexpensive, iridescent, pressed glass made from about 1907 to about 1925. More than 1,000 different patterns are known. Carnival glass is currently being reproduced. Additional pieces may be found in the Northwood category.

Acorn Burrs, Punch Cup, Marigold 25.00
Acorn Burrs, Sugar, Amethyst, 6 3/4 In. 118.00
Acorn Burrs & Bark pattern is listed here as Acorn Burrs.
Beaded Cable, Rose Bowl, Aqua 595.00
Blackberry Bramble, Compote, Amethyst 125.00
Blossom & Palm, Bowl, Ruffled Edge, Blue Opalescent, 9 In. 55.00
Brocaded Grapes, Bowl, Blue, 12 3/4 x 2 3/4 In. 135.00
Brooklyn Bridge, Bowl, Marigold, 8 1/2 In. 225.00
Bull's Eye & Leaves, Bowl, Marigold, 3 x 2 3/4 In. 39.00
Butterfly & Cable pattern is listed here as Springtime.
Cherries & Mums pattern is listed here as Mikado.
Cherry, Bowl, Amethyst, Deep, 7 1/2 In. 150.00
Cherry, Bowl, Deep, Amethyst, Millersburg, 7 1/2 In. 150.00
Cherry Wreathed pattern is listed here as Wreathed Cherry.
Christmas Cactus pattern is listed here as Thistle.
Cosmos, Pitcher, Marigold, Enameled White Flowers, 7 In. 350.00
Dandelion, Pitcher, Amethyst, 13 1/2 In. 550.00
Embroidered Mums, Bowl, Electric Blue, Scalloped, 9 In. 485.00
Fantasy pattern is listed here as Question Marks.
Feathered Scroll pattern is listed here as Feathered Serpent.
Feathered Serpent, Bowl, Marigold, 5 In. 25.00
Fine Rib, Vase, Red, 10 1/4 In. 287.00
Good Luck, Bowl, Blue, 8 1/2 In. 475.00
Grape & Cable, Banana Boat, Amethyst 510.00
Grape & Cable, Bonbon, 2 Handles, White 195.00
Grape & Cable, Bowl, Ice Cream, White, Individual 150.00
Grape Leaves, Bowl, Green, 9 In. 95.00
Harvest Poppy, Compote, Marigold, 8 1/2 In. 20.00
Hobnail pattern is listed in this book as its own category.
Interior Of Cherries & Mums pattern is listed here as Mikado.

Labelle Rose pattern is listed here as Rose Show.
Leaf & Beads, Bowl, Amethyst, Footed, 5 1/4 In. . . . . .175.00 to 185.00
Maple Leaf, Tumbler, Amethyst 35.00
Mikado, Compote, Marigold, White Base, 7 1/2 In. 67.00
Mums & Greek Key pattern is listed here as Embroidered Mums.
Octagon, Pitcher, Water, Marigold 75.00
Orange Tree, Bowl, Marigold, Footed, 9 In. . . . . .150.00 to 295.00
Orange Tree, Hatpin Holder, Cobalt Blue 200.00
Orange Tree, Shaving Mug, Cobalt Blue, 3 1/2 In. 45.00
Orange Tree, Tumbler, Marigold 50.00
Peacock At The Fountain, Berry Bowl, Marigold 32.50
Peacock At The Fountain, Tumbler, Marigold 30.00
Peacock On The Fence, Bowl, Aqua Opalescent, Ruffled Edge, 9 In. 1500.00
Persian Medallion, Hair Receiver, Marigold, 4 1/2 In. 39.00
Princess Lace pattern is listed here as Octagon.
Question Marks, Bonbon, 2 Handles, Marigold, 4 x 6 1/2 In. 35.00
Question Marks, Compote, Amethyst 35.00
Rainbow, Compote, Amethyst, 5 1/2 In. 90.00
Raindrops, Bowl, Peach Opalescent, 9 In. 225.00
Raspberry, Pitcher, Milk, Green 375.00
Ribbon Tie, Bowl, Amethyst, 8 1/4 In. 145.00
Ribbon Tie, Bowl, Blue, 7 1/2 In. 84.00
Ripple, Vase, Fluted Top, Marigold, 11 1/2 In. 35.00
Rose Show, Plate, Marigold, 9 1/2 In. 1400.00
Rose Show, Plate, White, 9 1/2 In. 795.00
Sailboat & Windmill pattern is listed here as Sailboats.
Sailboats, Bowl, Amethyst, 6 In. 22.00
Shell & Wild Rose pattern is listed here as Wild Rose.
Singing Birds, Mug, Marigold 190.00
Springtime, Sugar, Marigold 200.00
Stag & Holly, Bowl, Footed, Marigold, 11 In. 84.00
Stippled Acorns, Candy Dish, Cover, Light Marigold 65.00
Stippled Leaf & Beads pattern is listed here as Leaf & Beads.
Sunflower pattern is listed here as Dandelion.
Swirl Hobnail, Vase, Amethyst, 10 In. 85.00
Teardrops pattern is listed here as Raindrops.
Thistle, Banana Boat, Amethyst, Footed 495.00
Tree Trunk, Vase, Marigold, 6 In. 65.00
Wild Grapes pattern is listed here as Grape Leaves.
Wild Rose, Bowl, Marigold, 7 1/2 In. 55.00
Wishbone & Spades, Plate, Black Amethyst, 6 In. 1000.00
Wreathed Cherry, Berry Set, 7 Piece 161.00
Wreathed Cherry, Water Set, Marigold, 6 Piece 810.00

CAROUSEL or merry-go-round figures were first carved in the United
States in 1867 by Gustav Dentzel. Collectors discovered the charm
of the hand-carved figures in the 1970s, and they were soon classed
as folk art. Most desirable are the figures other than horses, such
as pigs, camels, lions, or dogs. A jumper is a figure that was made
to move up and down on a pole; a stander was placed in a stationary
position.

Horse, Galloping, Cast Iron, 26 x 53 In. 227.00
Horse, Jumper, Carved, Glass Eyes, Gems, Open Mouth, Shoe Rests, Stand, 20 x 54 In. . . . 784.00
Horse, Jumper, Saddle Extends To Rump, 52 x 42 In. 1153.00
Horse, Leaping, Carved Mane, Facial Features & Saddle, 41 In. 230.00
Horse, Middle Row, Gray, Pink Over Blue Paint, Loff, c.1900, 48 x 13 x 65 In. 3737.00
Horse, Middle Row, Jumper, Dapple Gray, Spillman, 1926 . . . . 5500.00
Horse, Middle Row, Jumper, Jewels, Signed, c.1896, 86 In. 9625.00
Horse, Middle Row, Jumper, Looff 8750.00
Horse, Middle Row, Jumper, Park Paint, Looff 9625.00
Horse, Outside Row, Eagle Back Saddle, Dentzel, c.1910, 58 x 12 x 57 In. 10350.00
Horse, Outside Row, Standing, Looff 6600.00
Horse, Painted Pine, Open Jaw, Eagle Carved Saddle, Black Base, 56 In. 7200.00

Horse, Running, 2 Seats, England, 72 In. 2750.00
Horse, Second Row, Standing, Looff 7700.00
Pony, Inside Row, Standing, Looff 4400.00

CARRIAGE means several things, so this category lists baby carriages, buggies for adults, horse-drawn sleighs, and even strollers. Doll-sized carriages are listed in the Toy category.

Baby Buggy, Spoke Wheels, Spindles On Sides, Oilcloth Folding Hood, 41 1/2 In. 990.00
Baby Buggy, Wicker, Adjustable Back, Foot, 1870, 33 x 45 In. 672.00
Buckboard, 2 Seater, 1880 .... 895.00
Buggy, Davenport Buggy Co., Doors & Windows, Fringed Canopy, 1800 .... 3800.00
Donkey Cart, Rectangular Seat, Roman Warrior In Center, Red Paint, 51 In. 1610.00

CASH REGISTERS were invented in 1884 because an eye on the cash was a necessity in stores of the nineteenth century, too. John and James Ritty invented a large model that resembled a clock and kept a record of the dollars and cents exchanged in the store. John Patterson improved the cash register with a paper roll to record the money. By the early 1900s, elaborate brass registers were made. About World War I, the fancy case was exchanged for the more modern types.

Michigan, Nickel Plated, Marquee Top, 23 x 19 In. 187.00
National, Brass, Bronze, Mahogany, 4 Drawers, 35 x 21 x 29 1/2 In. 460.00
National, Model 332, 3 Dollar Tills, Register Tape On Side, 23 x 17 In. 805.00
National, Model 333, Brass Plated, Oak Base, Marble Coin Shelf, 22 x 17 In. 748.00
National, Model 542, Crank Model, 1 Drawer, Tiger Oak, Keys, 30 x 28 1/2 In. 402.00
National, Model No. 313, Brass, Marble Coin Shelf, 10 1/2 x 16 x 17 In. 690.00

CASTOR JARS for pickles are glass jars about six inches in height, held in special metal holders. They became a popular dinner table accessory about 1890. Each jar had a top that was usually silver or silver plate. The frame, also of a silver metal, had a handle that arched above the jar and a hook that held a pair of tongs. By 1900, the pickle castor was out of fashion. Many examples found today have reproduced glass jars in old holders. Additional pickle castors may be found in the various glass categories.

Pickle, Blue Enameled, Inverted Thumbprint, Meriden Frame, 12 In. 695.00
Pickle, Blue, Embossed Flowers & Leaves, Square, Toronto Frame, 12 In. 1230.00
Pickle, Cobalt, Mary Gregory-Style, Little Boy Fishing 383.00
Pickle, Cranberry, Hobnail, Meriden Quadruple Silver Plated Frame 1005.00
Pickle, Cranberry, Inverted Thumbprint, Silver Plated Frame, 11 In. 377.00
Pickle, Cranberry, Thumbprint, Pear-Shaped, Enameled Roses, Floral Frame ., ... 1375.00
Pickle, Daisy & Button, Silver Plated Holder, Lid & Tongs 289.00
Pickle, Flower And Quill, Square, Toronto Silver Plated Frame, 13 1/4 In. 450.00
Pickle, Hanging Basket, Grapevine, Flowers, Figural Bird Handle, 7 1/4 x 12 In. 140.00
Pickle, Mother-Of-Pearl, Silver Plated Holder, Lid & Tongs 1365.00
Pickle, Pink, Diamond-Quilted, Satin, 12 1/2 In. 355.00
Pickle, Pressed Glass, Square, Column Corners, Glass Cover, 6 3/4 x 10 In. 180.00
Pickle, Pressed Glass, Swirl, Poole Silver Co., Taunton, 10 In. 263.00
Pickle, Ruby Glass, Pink & White Flowers, Gold Leaves, Silver Plated Frame, 10 1/4 In. . 550.00
Pickle, Silver Plate, Cranberry Chrysanthemum Swirl Insert, Tongs, c.1880, 13 x 4 In. ... 985.00
Pickle, Silver Plate, Diamond & Buttons 200.00

CASTOR SETS holding just salt and pepper castors were used in the seventeenth century. The sugar castor, mustard pot, spice dredger, bottles for vinegar and oil, and other spice holders became popular by the eighteenth century. These sets were usually made of sterling silver. The American Victorian castor set, the type most collected today, was made of silver plated Britannia metal. Colored glass bottles were introduced after the Civil War. The sets were out of fashion by World War I. Be careful when buying sets with colored bottles; many are reproductions. Other castor sets may be listed in various porcelain and glass categories in this book.

I Bottle, 1 Cruet, Salt & Pepper, Vaseline, Hobstar Cutting, 9 In. 220.00

2 Bottles, Cut Glass, Cinquefoil Frame, Baluster Handle, Samuel Wood, 1756, 8 In.	4320.00
3 Bottles, Diamond Band, Ribbed, Salt Cellar, Salt Spoon Holder, Meridan	183.00
4 Bottles, Cut Facets, Etched, Silver Plated, Figural Frame, 9 In.	63.00
4 Bottles, Pressed Glass, Silver Plated Frame	35.00
4 Cruets, Vaseline, Daisy & Button, Pewter Frame, 11 In.	125.00
5 Bottles, Cut Glass, Tufts Silver Plated Frame	275.00
5 Bottles, Deer & Castle Scene, Stoppers, 6 x 9 In.	675.00
5 Bottles, Embossed Leaves, Faceted Stoppers, Filigree Handle On Frame, 17 In.	560.00
5 Bottles, Silver Plate, Cut Facets, Etched Leaf Design, 17 1/2 In.	86.00
5 Bottles, Silver Plated Frame, c.1900, 16 1/2 In.	115.00
5 Bottles, Thumbprint Band, Lazy-Susan Style, Triple-Plated Silver, Rogers	242.00
6 Bottles, Cranberry, Maid's Bell, 3 Griffins With Shields At Base, 22 In.	1650.00
6 Bottles, Floral Feet & Handle, Silverplated Fern-Etched Frame, 11 1/2 In.	132.00
6 Bottles, Greek Key Border, Medallion, Silver Plated Holder, 14 In.	247.00
7 Bottles, Cut Panels, Scalloped Base, Silver Plated Frame	258.00
Salt & Pepper, Maple, New England, 18th Century, 2 Piece	595.00

CATALOGS are listed in the Paper category.

CAUGHLEY porcelain was made in England from 1772 to 1814. Caughley porcelains are very similar in appearance to those made at the Worcester factory. See the Salopian category for related items.

Cup & Saucer, Fisherman, Signed, c.1785	120.00
Cup & Saucer, Interior Badge Of Duke Of York, Bell Flower Garlands, 3 In.	3300.00
Plate, Blue Transfer, Chinoiserie Design, 8 1/2 In., Pair	195.00

CAULDON Limited worked in Staffordshire, Great Britain, and went through many name changes. John Ridgway made porcelain at Cauldon Place, Hanley, until 1855. The firm of John Ridgway, Bates and Co. of Cauldon Place worked from 1856 to 1859. It became Bates, Brown-Westhead, Moore and Co. from 1859 to 1862. Brown-Westhead, Moore and Co. worked from 1862 to 1904. About 1890, this firm started using the words *Cauldon* or *Cauldon ware* as part of the mark. Cauldon Ltd. worked from 1905 to 1920, Cauldon Potteries from 1920 to 1962. Related items may be found in the Indian Tree category.

Cake Plate, Floral, Gilt Trim, Flow Blue, 10 1/2 In.	195.00
Chop Plate, Messina, Flow Blue, 13 1/4 In.	110.00
Cup & Saucer, Demitasse, High Ring Handle, c.1905	40.00
Cup & Saucer, Gilt Grapes & Vines, Trailing Vine, c.1905	40.00
Pitcher, Pewter Hinged Lid, Flow Blue, Floral, 6 In.	245.00
Teapot, Blue Flowers On White, Silver Trim, Handle, 8 In.	250.00
Teapot, Sugar & Creamer, Scattered Flowers, 7 1/2-In. Teapot	195.00
Tureen, Cover, Blue & Orange Flowers, Leaves, Off-White Ground, 19th Century, 8 In.	115.00

CELADON is the name of a velvet-textured green-gray glaze used by Chinese, Japanese, Korean, and other factories. The name refers both to the glaze and to pieces covered with the glaze. It is still being made.

Bowl, Bombe, Flared Lip, Incised, Trellis Design, 3-Footed, Ming Dynasty, 10 In.	540.00
Bowl, Cone Shape, Sandy Foot, 6 1/4 In.	86.00
Bowl, Flowers & Green Crickets, Scalloped Gilt Rim, Footed, Oval, 10 3/4 x 3 In.	165.00
Bowl, Incised Petals, Chinese, 6 1/2 In.	120.00
Bowl, Stylized Lotus Petals, Jade, Chinese, 5 In.	575.00
Charger, Continuous Leaf, Flowering Peony Scrolls, 14 In.	490.00
Charger, Leaf Decorations, Japan, c.1926, 17 In.	127.00
Dish, Green Jade, Mogul Flower Form, Late 19th Century, 3 1/2 In.	320.00
Dish, Incised Ring, Carved Floral Border, Channel Rim, Ming Dynasty, 13 7/8 In.	540.00
Dish, Mid 19th Century, 5 1/2 x 9 In., Pair	1815.00
Figurine, Cockerel, Iron Red, Cafe-Au-Lait, Chinese, 15 1/2 In.	860.00
Figurine, Foo Lion, Crouching On Its Haunches, Jade, Chinese, 2 1/2 In.	400.00
Jar, Blue Carp, Cover, 11 1/2 In.	115.00
Jar, Wooden Cover, Figural Landscape Design, Blue, Late 19th Century, 8 3/4 In.	196.00
Jar, Wooden Cover, Rich Green Glaze, 12 In.	1552.00
Jardiniere, Chinese, 14 In.	230.00

Plate, Cloud Design, Flower Shape, Blue, 19th Century, 11 1/4 In. 145.00
Plate, Flowers, Fruits, Vegetable, & Butterflies, Signed, 18th Century, 7 3/8 In., Pair 236.00
Platter, Basket Of Flowers, Apple Blossoms, Blue Underglaze, Chinese, 12 x 15 In. 165.00
Platter, Bird & Leaf Design, Scalloped, Oblong, 20th Century, 12 x 13 1/2 In. 145.00
Platter, Peacock & Chrysanthemum, Blue & White Transfer, 9 x 12 In. 100.00
Platter, Urn Of Blue & White Chrysanthemums, Branches, 12 x 15 In. 175.00
Seal, Green Jade, Foo Lion Finial, Red Skin, 1 1/2 In. 138.00
Snuff Bottle, Flattened Oval, 2 Kylin Amidst Clouds, Jade, Chinese 630.00
Snuff Bottle, Raised Panel Sides, Rose Quartz Stopper, 19th Century, 2 1/8 In. 80.00
Umbrella Stand, White Flowers, China, 22 1/2 In. 345.00
Vase, Cafe-Au-Lait, Bulbous Shape, Molded Basket Weave Design, Korea, 6 1/4 In. 29.00
Vase, Carved, Lotus, Chinese, 8 In. 2300.00
Vase, Flower Decoration, Korea, 11 1/2 In. 65.00
Vase, Mandarin Duck, Lotus Design, Pear Shape, 19th Century, 24 1/4 In. 290.00
Vase, Meiping, White Glaze, Pheasant, Butterfly, Peony Branches, 18 1/2 In. 1500.00
Vase, Oasis & Middle Eastern Design, France, 17 1/2 In., Pair 2185.00
Vase, Opaque Black Glaze, Gold Brown Crackle, 6 1/2 In. 1265.00
Vase, Phoenix Head Handles, 8 1/2 In. 345.00

CELLULOID is a trademark for a plastic developed in 1868 by John W. Hyatt. Celluloid Manufacturing Company, the Celluloid Novelty Company, Celluloid Fancy Goods Company, and American Xylonite Company all used Celluloid to make jewelry, games, sewing equipment, false teeth, and piano keys. Eventually, the Hyatt Company became the American Celluloid and Chemical Manufacturing Company, the Celanese Corporation. The name *Celluloid* was often used to identify any similar plastic. Celluloid toys are listed under Toys.

Bottle Stopper, Old German Man, Nodder Head, 7 In. 44.00
Brush, Natural Bristles, c.1920 . . . .   20.00
Button, Yellow Kid, With Tennis Racket, No. 44, 1 1/4 In. 50.00
Comb, Amber & Black, Sapphires, 1920s 75.00
Comb, Openwork, Pale Green, Green Rhinestones, 1910, 19 In. 110.00
Dresser Set, Amber Glass Inserts, Empire Lucite, Box, 10 Piece 200.00
Dresser Set, Green, Marbleized, 2 Trays, 14 Piece 65.00
Dresser Set, Pearlized, Pale Yellow & Butterscotch, Black Trim, 1930s, 11 Piece 245.00
Figurine, Indian, 5 1/2 In. 10.00
Figurine, Uncle Sam, Red, White, Blue, Standing, U.S.A., 1920, 7 In. . . . . .230.00 to 250.00
Glove Stretcher, Center Spring, 6 1/2 In. 19.00
Hair Comb, Bakelite, Black, 5 Teeth, Hinge Attachment, Beaded, Crescent Shape 72.00
Mirror, c.1930 . . . .   37.00
Mirror, Rhinestone Butterfly, Pocket 40.00
Music Box, Piano, Moving Keys 20.00
Pin, Sled Dog Championship Pin, Red, White, 1938, 1 1/4 In. 10.00
Pin, Winged Roller Skates, Pinback, 2 3/4 In. 7.00
Powder Puff, Long Handle, Painted, Swan's Down Puff, 12 In. 100.00
Rattle, Easter Duck Girl, Textured Look, Prewar Japan, 5 1/4 In. 110.00
Roly Poly, Chick Jester On Egg, 3 1/4 In. 200.00
Roly Poly, Duck In Easter Bonnet, Prewar Japan, 3 1/4 In. 139.00

CELS are listed in this book in the Animation Art category.

CERAMIC ART COMPANY of Trenton, New Jersey, was established in 1889 by J. Coxon and W. Lenox and was an early producer of American Belleek porcelain. It became Lenox, Inc. in 1906. Do not confuse this ware with the pottery made by the Ceramic Arts Studio of Madison, Wisconsin.

Bottle, Wild Roses, Henriette Wright, Signed, 1898, 12 1/2 x 6 In. 297.00
Bowl, Nouveau Style Woman, Gilded Medallion, 1904, 7 1/2 In. 340.00
Inkwell & Penholder, Pink Roses, Green Leaves, Signed, E.M.N., 9 In. 310.00
Loving Cup, 3 Monograms, Inscription At Rim, F.M.B., 1904, 8 x 6 In. 120.00
Pitcher, Grapevines, Blue Ground, Signed, 6 x 7 1/2 In. 175.00
Rose Bowl, Brown, Golden, Green Chestnuts, Off-White Ground, Belleek, 5 In. 250.00
Tankard, Nude, Posing As Bacchus, Grape Arbor, E.I. Beck, 1896, 8 In. 605.00

Tankard, Seated Monk, Artist Signed, D.L. Kemp, 14 1/2 In. 198.00
Urn, Women & Cupids, Landscape, A. Gunter, 11 x 9 In. 635.00
Vase, Nude Maiden, Holly, Dark Green & White, A.S. Thissell, 11 In. 450.00
Vase, Pink Roses, Leaves, Pale Yellow & Green Ground, Handles, 19 In. 745.00
Vase, Trumpet Flowers, Bottle Shape, Ink Stamp, 11 1/4 In. 330.00

CERAMIC ARTS STUDIO was founded about 1940 in Madison, Wisconsin, by Lawrence Rabbett and Ruben Sand. Their most popular products were expensive molded figurines. The pottery closed in 1955. Do not confuse these products with those of the Ceramic Art Co. of Trenton, New Jersey.

Bowl, Rabbit, Signed, 6 In. 500.00
Figurine, Adonis & Aphrodite, 9 In. & 7 3/4 In., Pair 430.00
Figurine, Bride, Blond, 4 3/4 In. 178.00
Figurine, Camel, 5 1/2 In. 120.00
Figurine, Carmelita, 4 1/4 In. 42.00
Figurine, Dog, Boxer Butch, Prancing, 3 x 4 In. 100.00
Figurine, Dog, Kirby, 2 In. 175.00
Figurine, Guitar Boy, 5 In. 50.00
Figurine, Miss Lucindy, Southern Belle, No. 159, Brown & Yellow, 7 In. 65.00
Figurine, Our Lady Of Fatima, 9 In. 223.00
Figurine, Pixie, Waving, 2 1/2 In. 35.00
Figurine, Skunks, Inky & Dinky, 2 1/4 In. & 2 In., Pair 60.00
Figurine, Skunks, Mr. & Mrs. Skunk, 2 7/8 In., Pair 100.00
Figurine, Winter Willie, 4 In. 26.00
Figurine, Woman, Jester Lutist, 11 1/2 In. 255.00
Figurine, Zebra, Maize, Brown, Black, 5 In. 142.00
Head Vase, Mei-Ling, 5 In. 85.00
Pitcher, Adam & Eve, 3 In. 15.00
Plaque, Zor & Zorina, 9 In., Pair 85.00
Plate, Paul Bunyan Of Wisconsin, 5 In. 205.00
Salt & Pepper, Doe & Fawn, Stylized, 4 In. & 3 1/2 In. 125.00
Salt & Pepper, Dutch Boy & Girl 14.00
Salt & Pepper, Monkey, Mother & Baby, 4 In. & 2 1/2 In. 20.00
Salt & Pepper, Mouse & Cheese, 2 In. & 3 In. 35.00
Salt & Pepper, Penguins, Mr. & Mrs. Penguin, 3 3/4 In. 30.00
Salt & Pepper, Sambo & Tiger, 3 1/4 In. & 5 In. 305.00
Salt & Pepper, Suzette Poodle & Pillow, 3 In. & 1 In. 55.00
Shelf Sitter, Boy With Dog, 4 1/4 In. 20.00
Shelf Sitter, Budgie & Pudgie, Parakeets, Metal Cage, 5 In., 13 1/2-In. Cage ... 129.00
Shelf Sitter, Kissing Girl 36.00

CHALKWARE is really plaster of Paris decorated with watercolors. One type was molded from Staffordshire and other porcelain models and painted and sold as inexpensive decorations in the nineteenth century. Figures of plaster, made from about 1910 to 1940 for use as prizes at carnivals, are also known as chalkware. Kewpie dolls made of chalkware will be found in their own category.

Ashtray, Trout, 11 x 5 3/4 In. 18.00
Bank, Cat, Green, Polychrome Body, Red Bow, Holding Mouse In Mouth, 7 x 6 In. 220.00
Bank, Molded Branches & Leaves On Base, Brown Wings & Eyes, 11 1/8 In. 330.00
Bank, Roly Poly, Man, Hands Behind Back, 8 In. 165.00
Bookends, Dutch Couple, With Basket, Red, Metro Ware, 7 1/2 x 6 1/2 In. 30.00
Doorstop, Fifi, Gray Coat, 13 In. 20.00
Figurine, Assorted Fruits, Vegetables In A Pile, Green, Yellow, Brown, 13 In. 230.00
Figurine, Basket Of Fruit, Polychrome Design, 10 1/2 In. 1840.00
Figurine, Beautiful Black Lady, Wearing Green Dress, 12 In. 195.00
Figurine, Black Woman, Wearing Violet Dress, 10 In. 145.00
Figurine, Cat, 10 1/4 In. 10350.00
Figurine, Cat, 1880s, 5 In. 1650.00
Figurine, Cat, Seated With Pipe In Its Mouth, Black Eyes, 19th Century, 10 In. ... 241.00
Figurine, Cat, Seated, Green, Red Striped Pedestal, 19th Century, 6 In. 2875.00
Figurine, Cat, Seated, Yellow, Black Stripes, Black, Red Collar, 10 In. 10350.00

Figurine, Cat, Yellow Eyes, Yellow Collar With Bell, Black Tail, 1830, 9 In. 2860.00
Figurine, Compote Of Fruit, Lovebirds, American, 19th Century, 11 1/2 In. 1840.00
Figurine, Dog, Molded Fur, Tail Curving Over Back, Yellow Eyes, 7 5/8 x 6 In. 935.00
Figurine, Dog, Seated, Free-Standing Front Legs, Dotted Collar, 6 1/8 x 4 1/8 In. 295.00
Figurine, Dog, Seated, Holding Basket In Mouth, Green Ears & Tail, 6 x 4 7/8 In. 605.00
Figurine, Girl, White Pantaloons, Yellow Dress, Matching Hat, 9 1/2 In. 1155.00
Figurine, Hula Girl, Long Hair, Arm On Head, Short Skirt, 1947, 15 In. 150.00
Figurine, Lamb, Reclining, Curly Wool, 3 3/4 x 5 In. 275.00
Figurine, Love Birds, Kissing, Yellow Bodies, Red Breasts, Green Wings, 5 1/4 In. 165.00
Figurine, Parrot, Polychrome, Decorated, Pennsylvania, Mid 19th Century, 9 1/2 In. 303.00
Figurine, Pigeon, Branch With Berries, 11 1/2 In. 155.00
Figurine, Rooster, 1958, 7 In. 10.00
Figurine, Rooster, Green, Yellow, Red Paint, Pennsylvania, 19th Century, 7 In. 3080.00
Figurine, Rooster, Yellow, Red & Green Paint, 5 1/2 In. 2970.00
Figurine, Sailor, 10 1/4 In. 25.00
Figurine, Stag, Seated, Mid 19th Century, 8 1/2 In. 1092.00
Figurine, Umpire, 6 1/2 In. 32.00
Match Holder, Jester, 5 In. 20.00
Note Holder, Fire Place Shape, Holds Pen, 6 3/4 x 6 1/4 In. 6.00
Salt & Pepper, Mammy, 2 1/4 In. 13.00
Stringholder, Cat & Ball, Wire Hanger, 7 1/4 In. 10.00
Stringholder, Dutch Girl, Red Hat, Polka Dots, 6 x 7 In. 37.00
Toothbrush Holder, Dutch Girl, Wall Plaque, Miller Studio, Ohio, Box, 6 3/4 In. 165.00
Utensil Holder, Pig, 10 In. 40.00

CHARLIE CHAPLIN, the famous comic and actor, lived from 1889 to 1977. He made his first movie in 1913. He did the movie *The Tramp* in 1915. The character of the Tramp has remained famous, and in the 1980s appeared in a series of television commercials for computers. Dolls, candy containers, and all sorts of memorabilia picture Charlie Chaplin. Pieces are being made even today.

Bank, Charlie Bust, Bubbles Inc. 36.00
Bell, Brass, 3 1/4 In. Wide 43.00
Candy Container, Figural, Glass, Borgfeldt 286.00
Condiment Set, Porcelain, Germany, 1920, 5 1/2 In. 450.00
Doll, Composition Head, Cloth Body, Louis Amberg, 1915, 14 In. 595.00
Figure, Walking, Composition Head & Arms, Cloth Cut, Windup, 1920s, 12 In. 650.00
Letter Opener, Figural, Pewter, 1930s, 8 1/2 In. 150.00
Movie Drawing Book, Rubbing Transfer, Germany, 1920, 3 x 4 In. 65.00
Pencil Box, Tin, Picture, Henry Clive, Becutebox, Canco, 7 3/4 x 2 x 3/4 In. 50.00
Pennant, Photo, Black & White, Paper, Applied Gold Lettering, 1910-1915, 8 In. 39.00
Toy, Bike Rider, Tin, String, 1925, 7 In. 468.00
Toy, Flat Tin Figure With Cane, Crank Driven, Germany, 1920s, 6 1/2 In. 750.00
Toy, Hat Tipper, String, England, 1930s, 4 In. 115.00
Toy, Little Tramp With Hat & Cane On Base, Cast Metal, Painted, 2 1/2 In. 12.00
Toy, Push Plunger, Charlie Plays Cymbals, Tin, Germany, 1920s, 5 1/2 In. 1365.00
Toy, Windup, Gunthermann 840.00
Toy, Windup, Key, Box, Schuco, 1930 .... 1220.00

CHARLIE MCCARTHY was the ventriloquist's dummy used by Edgar Bergen from the 1930s. He was famous for his work in radio, movies, and television. The act was retired in the 1970s.

Bank, Mortimer Snerd Hometown, Marx 1500.00
Book, Big Little Book, The Story Of Charlie McCarthy, 1938 .... 45.00
Car, Mortimer Snerd, Crazy, Marx 495.00
Charm, Charlie Sitting On Radio With Microphone, Brass, 1 1/2 In. 15.00
Doll, Composition Socket Head, Muslin Body, Effanbee, 1937 .... 625.00
Doorstop, Iron 1100.00
Drummer, Mortimer Snerd, Tin, Windup, Marx, 9 In. 495.00
Dummy, Cloth Tuxedo, Straw Hat, 29 In. 58.00
Dummy, Composition Head, Cloth Body, Effanbee, Box, c.1940, 16 In. 1000.00
Dummy, Composition, Cloth Body, Jaw Attached To String, Effanbee, 20 In. 300.00
Dummy, Juro, 1977, 30 In. 31.00

Charlie McCarthy, Toy, Benzine Buggy,
Windup, Marx, 1938, 8 x 7 x 3 In.

**Never bid at an auction if you have
not previewed the items.**

**Look in your hardware store for
the new glues that can fix almost
anything. Buy the proper one to
fix transparent glass, porous
pottery, or non-porous metals.
There will be one that will work.**

Game, Radio Party, Chase & Sanborn Premium, Instructions, 1938		63.00
Teaspoon, Silver Plate, Duchess, 6 In.		7.50
Toy, Benzine Buggy, Windup, Marx, 1938, 8 x 7 x 3 In.	*Illus*	356.00
Toy, Car, Charlie McCarthy & Mortimer Snerd, Heads Spin, Marx, 1939, 16 In.		1300.00
Toy, Walker, Windup, Jaw Moves When Walking, Marx, 1930, 8 1/2 In.	160.00 to	275.00

CHELSEA porcelain was made in the Chelsea area of London from
about 1745 to 1784. Some pieces made from 1770 to 1784 may include
the letter *D* for *Derby* in the mark. Ceramic designs were borrowed
from the Meissen models of the day. Pieces were made of soft paste.
The gold anchor was used as the mark but it has been copied by many
other factories. Recent copies of Chelsea have been made from the
original molds. Do not confuse Chelsea porcelain with Chelsea Grape,
a white pottery with luster grape decoration.

Basket, Interior Floral Swags, Turquoise Rim, Rope Twist Handles, c.1770, 7 In., Pair		1440.00
Cup, Bird, Leaves, Hand Painted, Gilt Anchor Mark, 18th Century, 2 1/2 In.		67.00
Cup & Saucer, White, 2 3/4-In. Cup, 5 1/2-In. Saucer		35.00
Dish, Saucer, Botanical, Large Flowering Branch, Gray, Green, Iron Red, Puce, 9 In.		4500.00
Dish, Variety Of Fruit Resting On 2 Large Green Leaves, 1760, 13 1/4 In., Pair		3120.00
Figurine, Chinese Man, Seated On Rockwork Base, Colorful Flowers, Leaves, 3 In.		2400.00
Figurine, Cupid & Pan, Putto & Satyr Entwined, Flowers, 1760, 2 In.		2700.00
Figurine, Poodle, Lying, Orange Base, Face Right & Left, 2 1/4 & 3 In., Pair		465.00
Plate, Fruit Reserve, Scalloped, Gilt Roundel, Gilt Claret Ground, 1765, 8 1/2 In., Pair		6000.00
Tea Bowl, Saucer, Bird In Flight Near Japanese Lady Standing, 1752, 1 3/4 x 5 In.		3300.00
Tea Bowl, Saucer, Harbor Scene, Castles & Sailing Vessel, Flower Sprigs, 1752, 2 In.		9600.00

CHELSEA GRAPE pattern was made before 1840. A small bunch of
grapes in a raised design, colored with purple or blue luster, is on the
border of the white plate. Most of the pieces are unmarked. The pattern is sometimes called *Aynsley* or *Grandmother*. Chelsea Sprig is
similar but has a sprig of flowers instead of the bunch of grapes.
Chelsea Thistle has a raised thistle pattern. Do not confuse these
Chelsea patterns with Chelsea Keramic Art Works, which can be found
in the Dedham category, or with Chelsea porcelain, the preceding
category.

Cup & Saucer, Raised Cartouche, c.1850	26.00
Pitcher, 5 1/2 In.	58.00
Plate, 2 Handles, Anchor In Wreath Mark, 10 In.	61.00
Platter, Bridgewood & Son, 1830-1880, 10 x 9 1/4 In.	19.50
Teapot, Domed Cover, Grape Finial, 8 Sides	175.00

CHINESE EXPORT porcelain comprises all the many kinds of porcelain
made in China for export to America and Europe in the eighteenth,
nineteenth, and twentieth centuries. Other pieces may be listed in this
book under Canton, Celadon, Nanking, and Rose Medallion.

Basin, Water, Boys At Play, Flowers, Raised Rim, Bamboo Rim, 15 In.	460.00

Bowl, Barber's, Arms Of Clayton Impaling Cunningham, c.1733, 13 1/2 In. 415.00
Bowl, Barber's, Flowers, Blue & White, Flower Border, 18th Century, 14 In. 575.00
Bowl, Buddha Symbols, Late 18th Century, 9 In. 345.00
Bowl, Butterfly & Chrysanthemum, Vine Border, Gilt, 19th Century, 11 In. 230.00
Bowl, Chased Figural Landscape, Bamboo Reserves, Dragon Handle 1035.00
Bowl, Cobalt Blue Flowers, c.1800, 10 In. 370.00
Bowl, Cockerel, Flowers, Gilt Spearhead Border, Famille Rose, c.1740, 4 3/4 In. 600.00
Bowl, Court Scene, Enamel, Raised Foot, Famille Rose, 11 In. 550.00
Bowl, Dragon, Wave Ground, Conical, Green, 11 In. 195.00
Bowl, Flower Sprigs, Birds, Butterflies, Famille Rose, 5 3/4 x 12 In. 240.00
Bowl, Flowers & Urn, Blue & White, Square, 10 x 5 In. 990.00
Bowl, Landscape Design, Early 19th Century, 9 In. 150.00
Bowl, Leaf Design, Blue Underglaze, Handles, Famille Rose, 11 1/4 In. 2760.00
Bowl, Openwork Chrysanthemum Design, Glass Liner, 1860 . . . . 3220.00
Bowl, Orange Fitzhugh, Orange Peel Glaze, 18 3/4 x 8 In. 715.00
Bowl, Pagodas & Landscape, Plum Blossom On Rim, 18th Century, 9 In. 2100.00
Bowl, Peacocks, Ships, Black & White, Gilt Chain Border, 5 x 12 In. 460.00
Box, Cover, Central Armorial Design, 5 1/4 In. 85.00
Box, Dome Cover, Enamel Bands, Flowers, Bird, Foot, Round, 2 1/4 x 3 1/4 In. 260.00
Box, Game, Hinged Cover, Courtyard Reserve, Rectangular, 1850, 2 3/4 In. 3100.00
Box, Green, Fitzhugh, 7 1/2 x 3 3/4 x 2 5/8 In. 575.00
Cachepot, Animals, Flowers, Yellow, Hexagonal, 11 In. 460.00
Cachepot, Flowers, Leaves, Scallop Rim, Globular, Famille Rose, 10 In. 490.00
Cachepot, Flowers, Yellow, Hexagonal, 12 In., Pair 430.00
Cachepot, Underplate, Hexagonal, Figure, Flower Panels, Famille Rose, 8 In. 315.00
Censer, Passion Flowers, Pink, Turquoise Lion's Heads, Famille Rose, 11 In. 750.00
Censer, Relief Bat Design, Yellow, 20th Century, 5 In. 150.00
Charger, 4 Landscape Reserves, Cell Diaper Border, Blue, White, 1730, 15 In. 5100.00
Charger, 5 Dragons Among Clouds, Yellow, 18 In. 145.00
Charger, Armorial, Center Arms & Crest Of Mackay, c.1740, 15 In. 1380.00
Charger, Armorial, Center Arms Of Hansbury, Vine Border, c.1735, 13 In. 8400.00
Charger, Armorial, Poppies, Buds, 16 1/2 In. 4840.00
Charger, Boy On Raft, Waving To Figure On Land, Famille Rose, c.1760, 15 In. 1890.00
Charger, Central Tree, Sunken Center, Polychrome, 13 1/2 In. 330.00
Charger, Diaper Border, Gilt Flowers, c.1740, 15 1/4 In. 720.00
Charger, Flowers & Landscape, Raised Rim, 1870s, 11 1/8 In., Pair 200.00
Charger, Flowers, Famille Rose, 30 In. 745.00
Charger, Flowers, Molded Cavetto Shape Rim, c.1700 . . . . 1850.00
Charger, Flowers, Red & Gold Scalloped Rim, c.1770, 15 In. 2900.00
Charger, Flowers, Scrollwork Band, c.1740, 15 1/8 In. 1320.00
Charger, Man At Table, Boy, 2 Women, Blue & White, 1700-1710, 13 1/2 In. 5400.00
Charger, Riverscape, Green, Mid 18th Century, 15 In. 575.00
Chocolate Pot, Cover, Black & White, Pistol Handle, Fruit Knob, c.1780, 8 In. 360.00
Creamer, C-Handle, Crowned Monogram Within Crest, 1860s, 5 In. 290.00
Creamer, Flower Spray Design, Helmet Shape, Porcelain, 5 In. 260.00
Creamer, Heraldic Lion, Monogram, 3 In. 145.00
Cup, Italian Comedy, Scaramouche Wooing Columbine, c.1740, 2 5/8 In. 2100.00
Cup, Libation, Blanc De Chine, Dragon, Kylin, & Tiger Relief, c.1800, 8 In. 480.00
Cup, Pheasant, Flowers, Shell & Leaf Border, 2 Handles, Famille Rose, c.1755 . . . . 480.00
Cup & Saucer, Armorial, Arms Of Bishop Impaling Campbell, 1 1/2 In. 520.00
Cup & Saucer, Lotus Pattern, Famille Rose, Chinese, 18th Century 215.00
Dish, Armorial, Reserve, Gilt Rim, 19th Century, 6 1/4 In. 345.00
Dish, Blue Dragon, Phoenix Design, Cavetto, 8 In., Pair 300.00
Dish, Children & Mother At Play, Blue, White, Scalloped Rim, 5 In. 287.00
Dish, Court Scene, Medallions Of Flowers, Famille Rose, 9 1/2 In. 345.00
Dish, Courtyard Scene, Birds, Diaperwork Border, Oval, c.1800, 10 1/4 In. 175.00
Dish, Cuckoo In House, Blue & White, Pierced Center, 1770-1790, 8 3/4 In. 540.00
Dish, Domed Cover, Landscape & Animal Scene, Gold Canted Finial, 6 In. 490.00
Dish, Figural Design, Famille Rose, Octagonal, 8 1/2 In. 230.00
Dish, Flower Border, Oval, 6 3/4 In. 185.00
Dish, Flower Scene, 4 Reserves Interior, Famille Rose, Oval, 9 x 7 1/4 In. 290.00
Dish, Flower Sprays, Pink Border, Famille Rose, Oval, Late 1700s, 12 In. 290.00
Dish, Hot Water, Blue Fitzhugh, Early 19th Century, 11 In. 520.00

Dish, Pagoda & Lake Design, Leaf Shape, White, Blue, Scalloped, 8 In. 345.00
Figurine, 2 Geese, Black, 19th Century, 9 1/2 In., Pair 1150.00
Figurine, 2 Roosters, Famille Rose, Early 20th Century, 8 1/2 In., Pair 170.00
Figurine, Bull, Recumbent, Wooden Stand, 20th Century, 13 1/2 In. 1725.00
Figurine, Foo Lions, Blue, White, Reticulated Pearl Ribbon, 16 1/2 In., Pair 1150.00
Figurine, Goat, Standing, White, Curly Horn, Black Eyes, 19th Century, 6 In. 1500.00
Figurine, Piggyback, Smiling Boy On Man's Back, c.1810, 15 1/2 In. 4890.00
Figurine, Quail, Pierced Base, Glazed Biscuit, 19th Century, 7 1/2 In. 2400.00
Figurine, Woman, Floral Jacket, Holding Peach & Hankie, c.1800, 8 In. 1800.00
Figurine, Woman, Standing, Holding Scepter, Yellow Robe, 22 In. 865.00
Fishbowl, Flowering Branches, Iron Red, Gilt Border, Famille Rose, 18 3/4 In. 185.00
Foo Dogs, Fierce Expression, Extended Tongue, Green, 7 1/2 x 7 In. 1380.00
Garden Seat, Flowers, Leaves, Geometric Design, Famille Rose, 19 In. 230.00
Garden Seat, Light Green Leaves, Pink Buds, Blue, Gilt, 1880s, 12 3/4 In. 575.00
Ginger Jar, Blue & White, 19th Century, 9 1/2 In. 385.00
Ginger Jar, Cover, Hawthorn, Allover Floral Sprig Design, Blue, White, 8 In. 290.00
Ginger Jar, Mandarin Scene, Carved Wooden Base, 15 1/2 In., Pair 770.00
Jar, Court Figure Within A Pavilion, 33 3/4 In. 460.00
Jar, Cover, Allover Landscape Design, Blue, White, 19th Century, 11 In. 835.00
Jar, Cover, Barrel, 4 Women, Gardens, Gilt Kylin Knob, 2 Gilt Handles, c.1700 ...... 9600.00
Jar, Globular, Famille Rose, Lamp Mounted, Pair 345.00
Jar, Wooden Cover, Flowers, 2 Reserves, Blue Ground 375.00
Jardiniere, Birds & Flowers, Passion Flower, Green, 16 In. 600.00
Jardiniere, Birds Perched On Flowering Branches, Famille Rose, 15 In. 1035.00
Jardiniere, Everted Rim, Landscape & Figure Roundels, 7 1/4 In. 490.00
Jardiniere, Tobacco Leaf, 14 In., Pair 230.00
Jug, Cider, Cover, Strap Handle, 11 1/4 In., Pair. 4315.00
Jug, Entwined Strap Handle, Gilt Monogram JES, 9 3/8 In. 2160.00
Lamp, 2 Foo Dogs, White Ground, Famille Rose, 1900, 19 In., Pair 1725.00
Lamp Base, Hundred Butterflies, Ivory Elephant Finial, 1890s, 26 3/4 In. 460.00
Lamp Base, Tobacco Leaf, Oval, Waisted Neck, Famille Rose, 14 In., Pair 430.00
Lamp Base, Vase Shape, Relief Flowers, Famille Rose, Oval, 12 In. 490.00
Mirror, Enamel, Hand, Rose & Blue Lappet Designs, Beveled, Canton, 7 In. 145.00
Mug, Allover Dragon & Cloud Design, Dragon Handle, 19th Century, 4 In. 920.00
Mug, Armorial, American Design, 6 In. 255.00
Mug, Armorial, Arms Of Gough, Loop Handle, c.1720, 5 5/8 In. 2300.00
Mug, Armorial, Arms Of Lamaretia, 18th Century, 4 1/4 In. 345.00
Mug, Black Floral Border, Reeded Strap Handle, Cylindrical, c.1810, 4 In. 1080.00
Mug, Blue & White Fitzhugh, Entwined Handle, 4 1/2 In. 750.00
Mug, Figural Reserves, Iron Red Ground, Braided Strap Handle, 4 In. 575.00
Mug, Floral Medallion, Butterfly & Insect, Gilt Banding, Strap Handle, 5 In. 330.00
Mug, Orange Fitzhugh, Gilt, Leaf Handle & Rim, 4 1/2 In. 220.00
Mug, Various Floral Sprays, Lobed Handle, 18th Century, 4 1/2 In. 230.00
Plaque, Figures In Landscape, Wooden Frame, Green, 11 1/4 x 8 In., Pair 200.00
Plate, Armorial, Black Design, Woman Bathing Center, 9 In., Pair 135.00
Plate, Armorial, Coat Of Arms, Gilt Lions, Stag Head Crest, c.1755, 8 1/2 In. 1080.00
Plate, Armorial, Willis Impaling Brewsyard, Hawk Crest, c.1750, 12 1/2 In. 840.00
Plate, Cape Of Good Hope, Flags Anchored At Table Bay, c.1740, 8 7/8 In. 6615.00
Plate, Central Figure, Stylized Leaf Border, Famille Rose, 9 3/4 In. 80.00
Plate, Central Reserve Of Figures, Conforming Reserves, 11 3/4 In. 50.00
Plate, Cherry Pickers, Famille Rose, c.1775, 10 In. 980.00
Plate, Deshima Island, Blue & White, 3 People, Cow, Hook Border, c.1700, 8 In. 600.00
Plate, Green Fitzhugh, c.1800, 10 In., Pair 575.00
Plate, Iron Red Floral Sprays, Puce Enamel, Famille Rose, 1775, 9 In. 105.00
Plate, Iron Red Lotus, Blue & White, 8 1/4 In. 105.00
Plate, Leaves, Garlands & Swags, Center Circle E Monogram, 10 In. 165.00
Plate, Medallion, Flowers, Lotus Form, Famille Rose, c.1730, 9 1/2 In. 635.00
Plate, Mythological Figures On Waves, Green, 9 1/2 In. 30.00
Plate, Orange Center, Green Border, Fitzhugh, c.1800, 10 In. 3105.00
Plate, Orange Fitzhugh, 10 In., Pair 518.00
Plate, Orange Fitzhugh, c.1800, 8 1/2 In., Pair 633.00
Plate, Painted Flowers, Swag, Gilt, Scalloped Rim, 1790s, 9 3/4 In. 490.00
Plate, Painted, Bird, Dog, Peony, Bamboo, Gilt, 19th Century, 13 3/4 In. 575.00

Plate, Seamstress, Embroidering Under Drapery, c.1745, 9 In. 690.00
Plate, Spread Winged Eagle, 9 1/4 In., Pair 690.00
Plate, Temple Of Hiram, Masonic Symbols, 9 In. 375.00
Plate Set, Pink & Floral, 19th Century, 9 In., 13 Piece 825.00
Plate Set, Various Birds, Butterflies, Trees, Blue, Turquoise, 9 In., 7 Piece 1150.00
Platter, Armorial, Coat Of Arms, Blue Enamel, Gilt, Oval, c.1795, 12 In. 840.00
Platter, Armorial, Crest, Edge Trim, Blue & Gilt Enamel, 18 3/4 x 16 1/4 In. 405.00
Platter, Blue & White, Octagonal, 19th Century, 19 1/4 x 15 1/2 In. 360.00
Platter, Blue & White, Shaped Edge, Fitzhugh, 13 3/4 x 10 3/4 In., Pair 1495.00
Platter, Center Basket Of Flowers, Famille Rose, c.1735, 11 1/2 In., Pair 3700.00
Platter, Center Flower, Garland Border, Polychrome Design, 13 1/2 In. 300.00
Platter, Central Figural Scene, Floral Border, Late 19th Century 110.00
Platter, Fitzhugh, Oval, 19th Century, 18 In. 865.00
Platter, Flowers, Garland, Famille Rose, Table Stand, c.1775, 15 In. 1150.00
Platter, Fruit & Vegetable Center, Geometric Border, 13 1/2 In. 440.00
Platter, Lake Scene With Pagodas, Blue, White, 1790, 14 1/4 In. 440.00
Platter, River Landscape, 2 Figures In Sampan, c.1800, 18 1/2 In., Pair 2300.00
Platter, Serving, Famille Rose, c.1830, 16 1/2 x 13 1/2 In. 660.00
Platter, Traditional Lake Scenes With Pagodas, Blue, White, 14 1/4 In. 440.00
Pot, Cover, Flower Spray Basket Weave Ground, Strap Handle, 1780s, 6 In. 3300.00
Punch Bowl, Birds, Flowers, Hardwood Stand, Famille Rose, 14 1/2 In. 1725.00
Punch Bowl, Chrysanthemums, Famille Rose, 18 1/2 In. 345.00
Punch Bowl, Flowers, Shield Design Interior Rim, Footed, 10 x 4 1/2 In. 110.00
Punch Bowl, Tiger Hunt, Figures In Landscape, Sprays, 13 1/2 In. 2400.00
Sauceboat, Armorial, Johnson Coat Of Arms, 2 Handles, Gilt Rim, c.1740, 9 In. 2400.00
Sauceboat, Flared Rim, Painted, Raised Foot, Bulbous, c.1800, 3 x 7 1/4 In. 805.00
Sauceboat, Genre Scene, Double Handle, Double Spout, 2 1/2 In. 605.00
Serving Dish, American Eagle & Shield Center 1250.00
Spill Vase, Turquoise Horse, c.1850, Pair 3900.00
Spoon Tray, Black & White, Gilt Flowers, 5 1/2 In. 316.00
Spoon Tray, Black & White, Queen In Clouds, 5 In. 316.00
Spoon Tray, Central Flowers, 1770, 4 3/4 In. 195.00
Spoon Tray, Flowers, Scalloped Gilt Rim, Diamond Shape, 5 In. 345.00
Sugar, Flowers, Iron Red Leaves, Intertwined Handles, 5 1/2 In. 285.00
Taperstick, Blanc De Chine, Buddhist Lion, Pierced Pedestal, c.1700, 11 In. 2100.00
Tea Set, Figural Medallions, Green Lattice Ground, 16 Piece 575.00
Tea Set, Thousand Butterfly Pattern, 19th Century, 5 Piece 1045.00
Teapot, Armorial, Arms Of Davison Impaling Clark, 1820s, 5 In. 2990.00
Teapot, Cone Top, Armorial, Heraldic, Flanked By 2 Lions, 7 1/2 In. 316.00
Teapot, Cover, Basket Of Flowers Body, Lobed Handle, Famille Rose, 5 1/2 In. 80.00
Teapot, Cover, Court Scenes, Bird, Flowers, Famille Rose, 4 1/2 In. 345.00
Teapot, Cover, Drum Shape, Intertwined Handle, 1770, 5 1/2 x 5 1/2 In. 633.00
Teapot, Cover, Lotus Shape, Bud Spout, Stem Handle, Floral Feet, c.1730, 5 In. 7800.00
Teapot, Creamer, Court Scenes, Flower Border, Lapped Handle, 6 1/4 x 4 In. 431.00
Teapot, Domed Lid, Blue Insect & Flowers, 4 3/4 In. 253.00
Teapot, Domed Lid, Exotic Birds, Gilt Rims, c.1760, 5 1/4 In. 3600.00
Teapot, Drum Shape, Intertwined Handles, 1770, 5 1/2 In. 632.00
Teapot, Figures In Landscape, Polychrome Panels, 7 1/2 In. 825.00
Teapot, Flower Spray, Molded Spout, Branch Handle, 1850s, 5 1/2 In. 240.00
Teapot, Lighthouse Shape, Painted Flower 2650.00
Teapot, Squatting Monkey, Blue Glaze, Lobed Handle, Serpentine Spout, 8 In. 345.00
Tray, Pair Of Deer Beneath Pine Design, Scalloped, 14 1/2 In. 833.00
Tray, Scalloped Corners, Famille Rose, 6 1/2 x 9 1/2 In. 220.00
Tureen, Blue & White, Fitzhugh, Strap Handle, Flower Finial, Oval, 10 1/2 x 14 In. 863.00
Tureen, Cover, Central Landscape Design, Blue, White, 19th Century, 13 In. 2185.00
Tureen, Cover, Central Landscape Design, Peach Shape Finial, Oval, 13 In. 2185.00
Tureen, Domed Cover, Landscape, Blue & White, Handles, 9 x 14 x 8 1/2 In. 460.00
Tureen, Domed Cover, Pinecone Knop, 2nd Warwickshire Regiment, c.1812 . . . . 840.00
Tureen, Domed Cover, Scroll Finial, Mask Handles, Octagonal, 9 1/2 x 15 In. 1035.00
Tureen, Duck, Lying Down, Molded Feathers, Yellow Bill, 9 1/4 In. 1370.00
Tureen, English Country House, Savage Mask Handles, c.1745 . . . . 6037.00
Tureen, Pressed Form Cartouche, Gilt & Flowers, Monogram, c.1900, 8 x 3 In. 132.00
Tureen, Soup, Blue Flowers, Blue Leaf Trim, Acorn Knop, Strap Handle, 11 In. 550.00

Tureen, Soup, Chinese Garden Design, Blue, White, Bovine Handles, 8 In. 288.00
Tureen, Soup, Cover, Flowers, Pale Celadon, Blue, 19th Century, 8 In. 374.00
Tureen, Soup, Gold Star Design, Shell Flared Handles, 10 In. 412.00
Tureen, Soup, Panels Of Peonies & Landscape, 1765, 12 11/16 In. 5462.00
Urn, Drapery Swags, Stiff Leaves, Bracket Handles, Iron Red, Gilt, 18 In. 3900.00
Urn, Leaf Draped Rim, Crane & Water Hydra Scene, 25 1/2 In., Pair 4140.00
Vase, 4 Medallions Of Court, Flowers, Bird Scene, Famille Rose, 18 In. 690.00
Vase, Allover Bird, Flowers, Kylin Handles, Famille Rose, 17 1/2 In., Pair 1610.00
Vase, Allover Reserve Scene, Flowers, Blue, White, 22 In., Pair 2070.00
Vase, Bird & Florals, Floral Under Rim, 19th Century, 10 1/2 In., Pair 460.00
Vase, Bird, Flowers, Yellow, 13 In., Pair 184.00
Vase, Blossoming Trees, Pheasants, Dark Green, Orange, Gold, 36 5/8 In. 880.00
Vase, Club Shape, Dragon Design, Black, 15 In., Pair 414.00
Vase, Cobalt Blue & Iron Red Flowers, Swirled Panels, Inside Rim Design, 35 In. 550.00
Vase, Court Scene Panels, Gilt, Baluster, Famille Rose, 12 In., Pair 430.00
Vase, Court Scene, Baluster Shape, Ringed Handles, Famille Rose, 14 In., Pair 920.00
Vase, Court Scene, Scalloped Rim, Lion Handles, Famille Rose, 13 In., Pair 1150.00
Vase, Court Scene, Warriors At Battle, Birds, Painted, Roses, 30 In. 58.00
Vase, Court Scenes & Battles, Dragons On Shoulder, Famille Rose, 13 1/2 In. 862.00
Vase, Cover, Court & Avian Scenes, Foo Dog Finial, 19th Century, 13 In. 130.00
Vase, Devil Work Dragon Medallions, Gourd, Famille Rose, 10 In., Pair 1035.00
Vase, Dome Cover, Lappet Reserves, Spade Shape Form Finial, 21 In., Pair 2160.00
Vase, Dome Cover, Overall Decoration, Flowers, Insects, Green, 24 In., Pair 1150.00
Vase, Famille Rose, 19th Century, 10 1/2 In. 315.00
Vase, Fantastic Rocks, Birds, Flowering Trees, Green, 14 In., Pair 430.00
Vase, Figures On Horseback With Hunting Dogs, 20th Century, 30 In. 90.00
Vase, Figures, Calligraphy, Foo Lion Handles, Square, Famille Rose, 13 In., Pair 490.00
Vase, Filled Cartouche, Flying Cranes, Turquoise Ground, Famille Rose, 23 In. 520.00
Vase, Flowers, Bird, Mustard, Fruit Handles, Famille Rose, Hexagonal, 14 In. 546.00
Vase, Flowers, Yellow, 5 3/4 In., Pair 65.00
Vase, Gilt Bronze, Baluster Shape, Handles, Famille Rose, 18 In., Pair 1725.00
Vase, Heraldic Design, Polychrome, Table Lamp, Mounted, 25 In. 224.00
Vase, Lotus Scroll, Gilt, Turquoise Ground, 11 1/2 In., Pair 460.00
Vase, Lotus, Blue & White, Beaker, Trumpet Neck, Late 17th Century, 17 In. 2400.00
Vase, Mandarin Scene, Iron Red Diaper Ground, Famille Rose, 13 In. 865.00
Vase, Palace, Yellow Passion Flower, Ring Handles, Yellow, 23 In. 23000.00
Vase, Plum Blossoms, Cracked Ice, 19th Century, Lamp, Mounted, 22 In. 980.00
Vase, Rose, Yellow, Turquoise, Gilt Handles, Famille Rose, 1800s, 24 In. 635.00
Vase, Seasonal Flowers & Birds, Blue Underglaze, Green, 19 In. 5750.00
Vase, Splayed Neck, Tapered, Footed, Rectangular, 17 1/2 x 6 In., Pair 805.00
Warming Dish, Floral Reserves, Gold Lacquer, Handles, Blue, White, 9 3/4 In. 460.00
Wig Stand, Figures In Courtyard, Cutouts, Cylindrical, Celadron, 11 In., Pair 1840.00
Wine Pot, Champleve, 19th Century, 3 1/2 In. 70.00
Wine Pot, Foo Lion Handle, Green, 1900, 8 3/4 In. 460.00
Wine Pot, Rooster & Flower Design, Handle, Famille Rose, 6 In. 175.00

CHINTZ is the name of a group of china patterns featuring an overall
design of flowers and leaves. The design became popular with English
makers about 1928. A few pieces are still being made. The best known
are designs by Royal Winton, James Kent Ltd., Crown Ducal, and
Shelley. Crown Ducal and Shelley are listed in their own sections.

Blue Tulip, Creamer, Royal Winton, Countess Shape, 3 In. 84.00
Cheadle, Cup & Saucer 84.00
Cheadle, Sugar, Royal Winton, Hastings Shape, 2 1/2 In. 67.00
Crocus, Charger, Royal Winton, Wedgwood Border, 12 In. 560.00
Delphinium, Breakfast Set, Teacup, Sugar, Creamer, Tray, Royal Winton, 8 In., 4 Piece . . 700.00
Dubarry, Vase, Bud, James Kent, Elongated Globe Shape, 5 1/2 In. 195.00
Estelle, Candy Box, Royal Winton 1000.00
Florida, Rose Bowl, With Frog, James Kent 2600.00
Hazel, Butter Pat, Royal Winton, Raised Scroll Design Along Edge, 3 1/2 In. 70.00
Hazel, Charger, Royal Winton, Wedgwood Border, Ascot Shape, 12 In. 630.00
Heather, Teapot, Lord Nelson, Globe Shape, 6 Cup, 5 1/2 In. 700.00
Joyce-Lynn, Teapot, Royal Winton 1295.00

A hair dryer set for cool can be used to blow the dust off ornate pieces of porcelain.

Chintz, Royal Albert, Cup & Saucer,
Thos. C. Wild & Sons Ltd.

Kew, Cup & Saucer, Royal Winton	135.00
Majestic, Creamer, Globe Shape, Royal Winton, 3 In.	175.00
Majestic, Pot, Hot Water, Royal Winton, 7 In.	1047.00
Majestic, Sauceboat, Underplate, Globe Shape, Royal Winton, 2 1/2 In.	350.00
Majestic, Sugar & Creamer, Ascot Shape, Royal Winton, 2 1/2 In.	370.00
Marguerite, Plate, Ascot Shape, Royal Winton, 10 In.	125.00
Marina, Cup & Saucer, Lord Nelson, Angular Hastings Shape, 3 In.	70.00
Mayfair, Salt & Pepper, Tray, Royal Winton	150.00
Nantwich, Coffee Set, Coffeepot, Sugar & Creamer, Royal Winton, 3 Piece	2300.00
Nantwich, Cup & Saucer, Royal Winton	116.00 to 245.00
Old Cottage, Cup & Saucer, Royal Winton	68.00
Old Cottage, Platter, Royal Winton	75.00
Old Cottage, Sugar, Royal Winton, Up-Ended Globe Shape, 2 In.	53.00
Old Cottage, Teapot, Royal Winton	115.00
Queen Anne, Trio, Royal Winton, 5 1/2-In. Plate	115.00
Royal Albert, Cup & Saucer, Thos. C. Wild & Sons Ltd.	*Illus* 40.00
Royalty, Celery Dish, Royal Winton, 13 x 6 1/4 In.	810.00
Royalty, Jam Pot, Metal Lid, Royal Winton, 3 1/2 In.	263.00
Royalty, Platter, Royal Winton, 9 5/8 x 5 7/8 In.	500.00
Somerset, Music Box, Royal Winton, 5 x 3 1/4 x 3 1/4 In.	6100.00
Spring, Breakfast Set, Royal Winton	950.00
Summertime, Breakfast Set, Royal Winton	3150.00
Summertime, Candy Dish, Royal Winton, 6 3/4 x 5 1/4 x 1 1/2 In.	270.00
Summertime, Casserole, Cover, Royal Winton, 9 1/2 In.	875.00
Summertime, Cup & Saucer, Demitasse, Royal Winton, Can Shape, 2 1/2 In.	116.00
Summertime, Dish, Royal Winton, 4 Sections, 11 1/2 In.	263.00
Summertime, Jug, Royal Winton, 6 In.	200.00
Summertime, Tray, Royal Winton, 4 x 8 In.	80.00
Summertime, Tray, Royal Winton, Rectangular, 8 x 5 In.	145.00
Welbeck, Breakfast Set, Royal Winton	2500.00
Welbeck, Salt & Pepper, Royal Winton	240.00

CHOCOLATE GLASS, sometimes mistakenly called caramel slag, was made by the Indiana Tumbler and Goblet Company of Greentown, Indiana, from 1900 to 1903. It was also made at other National Glass Company factories. Fenton Art Glass Co. also made chocolate glass from about 1907 to 1915. More recent pieces have been made by Imperial and others.

Aurora, Relish	175.00
Cactus, Butter, Cover	75.00
Cactus, Compote, 5 5/8 In.	77.00
Cactus, Compote, 8 In.	204.00
Cactus, Toothpick, Greentown, 2 3/4 In.	35.00
Cord Drapery, Syrup, Greentown, 5 1/2 In.	130.00
Gold Cherry Design, Cracker Jar, Westmoreland	235.00
Indoor Drinking Scene, Mug, Greentown	103.00
Leaf Bracket, Butter, Cover	100.00
Outdoor Drinking Scene, Mug, McKee, 4 3/8 In.	40.00

Racing Buck & Doe, Pitcher, 9 In.	600.00
Serenade, Mug, McKee, 4 3/4 In.	60.00
Uneeda Milk Biscuit, Tumbler, National Biscuit Company, 5 3/4 In.	70.00

CHRISTMAS collectibles include not only Christmas trees and ornaments listed below, but also Santa Claus figures, special dishes, and even games and wrapping paper. A Belsnickle is a nineteenth-century figure of Father Christmas. A kugel is an early, heavy ornament made of thick blown glass, lined with zinc or lead, and often covered with colored wax. Christmas cards are listed in this section under Greeting Card. Christmas collectibles may also be listed in the Candy Container category and. Christmas trees are listed in the section that follows.

Bag, Candy, Santa Claus Shape, 1920-1930	185.00
Bell, Angel, Red Coat, Earmuffs, Holding Basket, Napco, Paper Label, 4 In.	20.00
Belsnickle, Chalkware, Pennsylvania, 19th Century	595.00
Belsnickle, Papier-Mache, Olive Green, 10 In.	1750.00
Belsnickle, Wooden, Socket Head, Painted Features, Pa., 11 In.	300.00
Belsnickle, Yellow Coat, Gold Glitter, Base, Silver Glitter, Green Feather Tree, 13 In.	990.00
Book, Little Golden Book, Rudolph The Red Nosed Reindeer, 1958	10.00
Book, Night Before Christmas, Linen, 13 x 9 1/2 In.	55.00
Button, Santa Claus, 2 Children, May Co., Celluloid, 1 1/2 In.	162.00
Button, Santa Claus, Merry Christmas Baron's, 1 1/4 In.	12.00
Button, Santa Claus, World War I Soldier, Strawbridge Clothier, Celluloid, 1 In.	200.00
Candle Lantern, Gold, Gothic Arches, Mica Sheets, Marked D.R.G.M., 4 In, Pair	28.00
Candy Box, Bobbing, Gold, Germany, 1950	75.00
Display, Santa Claus, With Bells, Electric	145.00
Display, Santa Claus, With Lantern, Celluloid	85.00
Figure, Angel, Singing, Holding Wreath, Norcrest, Paper Label, 3 In., Pair	30.00
Figure, Elf, Playing Accordion, Plaster Face, 2 1/2 In.	8.00
Figure, Santa Claus In Sled, Reindeer, Celluloid, 3 3/4 In.	125.00
Figure, Santa Claus, Holding Tree, Mica Covered, 3 In.	5.00
Figure, Santa Claus, Hooded Robe, Feather Tree, Germany, 8 3/4 In.	137.00
House, Cardboard, Mica Covered, 3 1/2 x 3 In.	8.00
Lantern, Santa Claus Head Shape	1250.00
Lantern Set, Santa Claus & Tree	150.00
Planter, Angel, Holding Wreath, Wrapped Gift, Napco, 1950s, 7 In.	30.00
Plates that are limited editions are listed in the Collector Plate category or in the correct factory listing.	
Postcard, Purple Santa Claus	29.00
Rattle, On Ring, Christmas Stocking, Celluloid, Prewar Japan, 4 1/4 In.	190.00
Roly Poly, Santa Claus, Large	770.00
Soap, Baby Shape, Merry Christmas With Santa On Box, 1890	65.00
Talking Door Ringer, Santa's Face, Plastic, Battery Operated, Box, Japan, 1970s, 9 In. ...	35.00
Toy, Market Stall, German Village Scene, Wooden, Faux Rosewood Finish, 23 In.	4750.00
Toy, Paint Kit, Wooden Frame, Chromograph Of St. Nicholas, c.1900-1910	44.00
Toy, Roly Poly, Father Christmas, Celluloid, Continental, 3 1/2 In.	150.00
Toy, Roly Poly, Santa Claus In Egg, Celluloid, 3 1/2 In.	300.00
Toy, Roly Poly, Santa Claus On Ball, 3 3/4 In.	175.00
Toy, Roly Poly, Santa Claus, Celluloid, Prewar Japan, 1 1/2 In.	50.00
Toy, Roly Poly, Santa Claus, Composition, 8 In.	650.00
Toy, Roly Poly, Santa Claus, Tin, 4 In.	132.00
Toy, Santa Claus Christmas Eve, Windup, Tin, Celluloid, Japan, Box, Prewar, 6 In. .110.00 to 210.00	
Toy, Santa Claus On Box, Celluloid, 3 1/2 In.	165.00
Toy, Santa Claus On Reindeer, Pull Toy, Polychrome Paint, Signed, Schifferl, 14 In.	1045.00
Toy, Santa Claus, Bouncing, Rings Bell, Tin, Celluloid, Cloth, Japan, 1960s, 4 3/4 In.	86.00
Toy, Santa Claus, Celluloid Head & Arms, Plays Drum, Nods, c.1930, 11 1/2 In.	765.00
Toy, Santa Claus, Covered Cart, Reindeer, Composition Face & Hands, Germany, 10 In. ..	523.00
Toy, Santa Claus, In Sleigh, Nodding Reindeer, 1962, 37 In.	3450.00
Toy, Santa Claus, On Sled, Mechanical, Plastic, Metal, Japan, Box, Mid 1900s, 8 In.	127.00
Toy, Santa Claus, On Wheels, Moves In Circle, Head Turns, Windup, Celluloid	250.00
Toy, Santa Claus, Rings Bell, Box, Japan, 1950s, 7 In.	175.00
Toy, Santa Claus, Rings Bell, Holds Sign, Tin, Celluloid, Windup, TN, Box, Japan, 5 In. ..	89.00

Toy, Santa Claus, Sack On Back, Rings Bell, Celluloid, Windup, Occupied Japan, 5 In. 315.00
Toy, Santa Claus, Santa In Sleigh, Papier-Mache, Germany 125.00
Toy, Santa Claus, Scooter, Hard Plastic 70.00
Toy, Santa Claus, Sled, Sack, Stenciled Wood, Iron Bar Runners, c.1880, 33 1/2 In. 1052.00
Toy, Santa Claus, Sleigh, Reindeer, Celluloid, 1930s, 3 1/2 In. 125.00
Toy, Santa Claus, Walker, Tin, Windup, Japan, 1950s, 6 In. 85.00
Toy, Santa Claus, Walking, Battery Operated, Plastic, Taiwan, Box, 1970s, 10 In. 45.00
Toy, Santa Claus, Waving Celluloid Lantern, Japan, 5 1/2 In. 110.00
Toy, Santa Whirligig, Tin, Celluloid, Windup, 1950, 6 In. 225.00
Toy, Santa's Candy Express, 4 Reindeer, Sled, Plastic, Sears, Box, 1930s, 15 In. 75.00
Toy, Sled, Santa Claus, Wood, Stencil, Iron Bars, Santa, Sack Of Toys, 1880, 33 In. 1050.00

CHRISTMAS TREES made of feathers and Christmas tree decorations of
all types are popular with collectors. The first decorated Christmas tree
in America is claimed by many states, including Pennsylvania (1747),
Massachusetts (1832), Illinois (1833), Ohio (1838), and Iowa (1845).
The first glass ornaments were imported from Germany about 1860.
Dresden ornaments were made about 100 years ago of paper and tinsel. Manufacturers in the United States were making ornaments in the
early 1870s. Electric lights were first used on a Christmas tree in 1882.
Character light bulbs became popular in the 1920s, bubble lights in the
1940s, twinkle bulbs in the 1950s, plastic bulbs by 1955. In this book
a Christmas light is a holder for a candle used on the tree. Other forms
of lighting include light bulbs. Other Christmas memorabilia is listed
in the preceding section.

Aluminum, 3 1/2 Ft. 50.00
Aluminum, 5 Ft. 75.00
Color Wheel, For Aluminum Tree 25.00
Feather, Chicken, Finial, Germany, 5 Ft. 365.00
Fence, Diamond Pattern, Green, Gold, Cast Iron, 7 Sections, Gate, 84 In. 240.00
Fence, Spindle Picket, 5 1/2 x 16 1/2 In. 302.00
Garland, Glass Bead, 84 In. 6.00
Garland, Gold Glass Beads, 100 In. 20.00
Kugel Ball, Green, 7 1/2 In. 220.00
Light, Aqua, Pineapple, Sheared Rim, England, 1910, 4 1/8 In. 72.00
Light, Blue Milk Glass, Flowers & Rib, Pontil, England, 1910, 3 1/4 In. 305.00
Light, Cobalt Blue, Harlequin, Sheared & Tooled, England, 1910, 3 5/8 In. 72.00
Light, Cobalt Blue, Pineapple, Sheared Rim, England, 1910, 4 1/8 In. 150.00
Light, Cranberry Red Flash, Diamond, England, 1910, 3 3/4 In. 90.00
Light, Crystal, Allover Diamond, Depose/BS/Lyon, 1900, 2 3/4 In. 155.00
Light, Diamond, Green, VR In Shield, England, 1900, 3 3/8 In. ....*Illus* 143.00
Light, Green, 4 Panes, Gothic Sterling Frame, Germany, 1880, 3 7/8 In. 185.00

Christmas Tree, Light, Diamond,
Green, VR In Shield, England,
1900, 3 3/8 In.

Christmas Tree, Light,
Harlequin, Cobalt Blue,
England, 1900, 3 3/4 In.

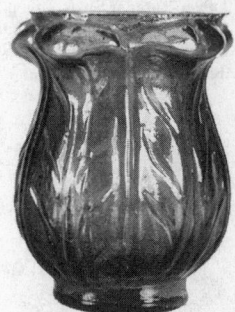

Christmas Tree, Light, Tulip,
Yellow Amber, Hearn Wright &
Co., 1900, 3 1/2 In.

Light, Green, Diamond, VR Inside Shield, England, 1890, 3 3/8 In. 145.00
Light, Harlequin, Cobalt Blue, England, 1900, 3 3/4 In. . . . . *Illus* 121.00
Light, Ruby Red, Interior Ribbed, Germany, 1915, 3 1/8 In. 185.00
Light, Straw Yellow, Orange Tone, Harlequin, England, 1910, 3 1/2 In. 160.00
Light, Tulip, Yellow Amber, Hearn Wright & Co., 1900, 3 1/2 In. . . . . *Illus* 100.00
Light, Tulip, Yellow Green, Hearn Wright & Co., 1910, 3 1/2 In. 150.00
Light Bulb, Betty Boop, Fleischer, 1931, 3 In. 265.00
Light Bulb, Dirigible 60.00
Light Bulb, Screw-In, Santa Claus Shape, Red Suit, Painted, 2 Faces, 2 In. 15.00
Ornament, Angel, Harp In Hand, Cellophane, Tinsel, 12 In. 67.00
Ornament, Angel, Pink Wax, Fur Dress, Fiber Wings, Brass Horn, 4 1/2 In. 28.00
Ornament, Bear, Seated, Blown Glass, Gold Paint, 3 In. 82.00
Ornament, Black Santa Claus, Jolly Ol' Soul 45.00
Ornament, Brass, Biedermann, 1972 . . . . 200.00
Ornament, Clown's Head, Blown Glass, Germany 46.00
Ornament, Doll's Head, Silver Bonnet, Red Trim, 2 3/4 In. 49.00
Ornament, Dresden, Hand Pressed Paper, 5 1/8 In. 38.00
Ornament, Energizer Bunny, 3-D 3.75
Ornament, Flapper Head, White Hat, Blue Brim, Blond, Blown Glass, 1920, 3 In. 300.00
Ornament, Grinning Clown Head, Cone Shaped Hat, Clip On End, 5 In. 330.00
Ornament, Hot Air Balloon, Cardboard, Passengers, Dresden, 3 In. 660.00
Ornament, Lion, Glass Eyes, Open Mouth, Teeth, Dresden, 4 3/4 In. 605.00
Ornament, Man & Woman Kissing Front, Windmill On Back, 3 1/2 In. 154.00
Ornament, Musician Donkey, Fiddler, Red Violin, Cardboard, 4 1/4 In. 55.00
Ornament, Pears & Peaches, Wire & Mica Flecks, 1 3/4 x 3 In., 6 Piece 126.00
Ornament, Sailboat, Cloth Sails, Cabin On Deck Level, Dresden, 4 1/2 In. 523.00
Ornament, Santa Claus Faces, Red Balls, Blown Glass, Germany, 13 In. 152.00
Ornament, Santa Claus, Red Silvered Glass, Green Tree, Gold On Robe, 9 1/4 In. 55.00
Ornament, Snake, Free-Blown Glass 165.00
Ornament, Treetop Angel, Poured Wax Head, Paper Wings, c.1920, 15 In. 86.00
Stand, Openwork Stars & Plumes, 2 Scenes, German Verses, Cast Iron, 10 In. 55.00
Stand, Santa Claus, Painted Cast Iron, Stump & Stairs, 9 1/2 x 9 1/2 In. 1320.00
Stand, Snowman, Metal, Red 95.00

CHROME items in the Art Deco style became popular in the 1930s.
Collectors are most interested in high-style pieces made by the
Connecticut firms of Chase Brass and Copper Company, and Manning
Bowman.

Ashtray, Swiss Air, 6 1/2-In. Wingspan 175.00
Bell, Yacht, 5 7/8 x 4 1/4 In. 45.00
Beverage Set, Bakelite Handles, Tray, Pitcher, Cover, 6 Glasses, M. Bowman, 1930 . . . . . 575.00
Canister, Tea, Art Deco Design, Red Plastic Insert, Ribbed Lid, Bakelite Knob, 5 1/4 In. . 34.00
Cocktail Shaker, Ruby Glass Leg Section, Tray & Cups, c.1937 . . . . 2835.00
Lamp, Tubular Shaft, Linen Shade, Black Lacquer Wooden Base, D. Deskey, 49 In. 3125.00
Napkin Holder, Aluminum, Silver 3.00
Sugar & Creamer, Cream, Red Bakelite Handles, Manning Bowman, 5 x 6 In. 28.00
Toothpick, Swan Shape, Catalin Head, Napier, 5 3/4 In. . . . . *Illus* 45.00

Chrome, Toothpick, Swan Shape,
Catalin Head, Napier, 5 3/4 In.

**Chrome should be cleaned with a mild chrome
cleaner, not an abrasive. If you leave salty food
on a chrome plate, it may corrode the chrome.
The only "cure" for this is replating.**

CIGAR STORE FIGURES of carved wood or cast iron were used as advertisements in front of the Victorian cigar store. The carved figures are
now collected as folk art. They range in size from counter type, about
three feet, to over eight feet high.

Indian, Black Painted Braids, Black Base, 20th Century, 21 In.	1210.00
Indian, Chief, Pine, Holding Tobacco Blocks, Cigars, Base, c.1860, 58 In.	8400.00
Indian, Princess, Headdress, Holding Tobacco Leaves, c.1860, 61 In.	4200.00
Indian, Princess, Headdress, Holding Tobacco Leaves, c.1900, 64 In.	8800.00

CINNABAR is a vermilion or red lacquer. Pieces are made with tens to
hundreds of thicknesses of the lacquer that is later carved. Most
cinnabar was made in the Orient.

Box, Cover, Red Pigskin, Red Ground, Rectangular, Chinese, 14 1/2 In.	230.00
Box, Dragon Chasing Flaming Pearl Of Wisdom, Red, Rectangular, 9 3/4 x 6 In.	103.00
Button, Flowers, Silver Setting, Medium	28.00
Cabinet, Rectangular Form, 2 Doors, Cloisonne Handles, Flowers, 22 In.	1610.00
Jardiniere, Lobed, Horizontal Gilt Rib, Vertical Columns, Lotus, c.1800, 6 In.	1920.00
Server, Sweetmeat, Cover, Foliated Rim, Central Medallion, 6 1/4 x 18 1/2 In.	978.00
Snuff Bottle, Broad Shoulders, Landscape Scene, 2 7/8 In.	345.00
Snuff Bottle, Court Scene, Chinese	230.00
Snuff Bottle, Inverted Pear Shape, Lohans & Cloud Design, Glass Stopper, 2 In.	345.00
Snuff Bottle, Landscape Design, Stopper, 20th Century, 2 7/8 In.	58.00
Snuff Bottle, Pagodas & A River, Chinese	115.00

CIVIL WAR mementos are important collectors' items. Most of the
pieces are military items used from 1861 to 1865. Be sure to avoid any
explosive munitions.

Badge, G.A.R., Bear & Seal On Pin, Soldier, 46th Nat. Encampment, 1912	34.00
Badge, G.A.R., Encampment, 46th, Los Angeles, Bear, Grosgrain Ribbon, Sept. 1912	65.00
Badge, G.A.R., Soldier, 19th Annual Encampment, Portland, Me., 1885	30.00
Belt, Leather, Black, Narrow, U.S. Belt Plate, Oval, Brass, Small, 1860s	290.00
Belt, Saber, Cavalry, Brown Buff Leather, Eagle Belt Plate	748.00
Canteen, 1 Side Flat, Convex Reverse, Red Paint, Strap Loops	495.00
Canteen, Bull's Eye, Tin, Fabric Covered, Hadden Porter & Booth	299.00
Canteen, Wooden, Carved Inscription, J.M. Reed, Co. D, 2nd Virginia	4800.00
Carpet Bag, Brass Lock, 12 x 14 In.	200.00
Cartridge Box, Leather, Belt, Buckle, Bayonet Scabbard, 15th New York Volunteers	1320.00
Cartridge Box, Navy, Anchor, c.1863	175.00
Cartridge Box, U.S. Navy, Leather, Black, Embossed USN	460.00
Case, Covered, Ivory Rule, Ebony & Brass Instruments	285.00
Case, Dispatch, W.F. Mead, MD Dart	165.00
Coat, Frock, Union, Infantry Blue, Shoulder Straps	975.00
Doll, Made By Union Soldier, Wood Carving, Glass Eyes, Uniform Fabric, 7 In.	286.00
Engraving, Stonewall Jackson, Confederate Uniform, 7 x 5 In.	135.00
Escutcheon, Surgeon M.J. McKinnon, 53rd Penn., 1861-1863, 22 x 19 In.	275.00
Fife, Ebony, Brass Caps, 17 1/8 In.	145.00
Fife, Ebony, Silver Plate Caps, Mouthpiece, Corey, 17 1/8 In.	190.00
Guard, Button Polishing, Brass	25.00
Jacket, Union, Cavalry, Dark Blue Wool, 11 Buttons, Yellow Trim, Ohio Depot	2300.00
Knapsack, Canvas, Tarred, Soft Sides, Standard Contract, Shoulder Strap	144.00
Knapsack, Militia, Box Frame, Tarred Leather Flap, Canvas	201.00
Lapel Stud, Seated Liberty Half Dollar, Bullet Indentation, Engraved Chattanooga	250.00
Medal, GAR Veteran's, Bronze, Silk Flag Ribbon, Late 19th Century, 3 1/4 In.	24.00
Mirror, Tin Frame, Wood, 7 7/8 In.	110.00
Pin, CSA Flag, Gold Wreath, DC 61-65, Daughters Of Confederacy, Inlaid Enamel	150.00
Ring, Bone, Cannon & Cannonballs, Prisoner Of War	300.00
Rope Tighteners, Tent	30.00
Roster, Guard List Of Confederate Libby Prison	285.00
Shako, Infantry, Leather, Stamped Brass Eagle, Chin Straps, Pa. Regiment, France	748.00
Shaving Cup, Copper, Tin Lining, 3 5/8 In.	126.00
Shaving Cup, Tin, 4 3/8 In.	115.00
Sign, G.A.R. Post, Black & Gold, 35 x 55 In.	770.00

Straps, Shoulder, Officer, Braid Border, Navy Blue Wool, Gold Braid, Fouled Anchor ... 460.00
Sword, Officer's, Shield & U.S., Brass Hilt, Silver Plate Handle, 37 In. 467.00
Sword, Officer's, Steel Sheath, 39 In. 247.00
Sword, Veteran's, Brass Hilt, Leather Wire Wrapped Grip, 1850, 26 1/2-In. Blade 295.00
Uniform, Badge, GAR 7500.00

CKAW, see Dedham category.

CLAMBROTH glass, popular in the Victorian era, is a grayish color and
is somewhat opaque, like clam broth. It was made by several factories
in the United States and England.

Candlestick, Fluted Column, Petal Socket, Stepped Base, 9 1/4 In. 247.00
Goblet, Swan Design 90.00
Lamp, Oil, Stepped Base, Fluted Column, Brass Collar, 12 1/2 In. 302.00
Pitcher, Pewter Cover, Pontiled Foot, Handle, Thumb Lever, April 9, 1886, 11 In. 302.00

CLARICE CLIFF was a designer who worked in several English factories
after the 1920s. She is best known for her brightly colored Art Deco
designs. She died in 1972.

Apples, Plate, Deep Green Apples, Lime Accents, Magenta, Yellow, Leaf, 6 In. 660.00
Autumn Crocus, Bizarre, Plate, Side, 1935, 7 In. 82.00
Autumn Crocus, Teapot, Bulbous, Orange, Violet, Blue, Yellow Cover, 6 In. 550.00
Biarritz, Plate, Ring Of Multicolored Flowers, Signed, 10 3/8 In. 370.00
Bizarre, Ashtray, Orange & Brown Panels, 1930s, 5 In. 403.00
Bizarre, Bowl, Stylized Flowers & Leaves, Stippled Ground, 1930s, 10 In. 875.00
Bizarre, Crocus, Butter, Cover, Ivory Ground, 4 x 2 3/4 In. 550.00
Bizarre, Plate, Stylized Horse, Brown, Black, Cream Ground, 1930s, 9 In. 540.00
Bizarre, Plate, Stylized Pink, Blue, Green Calla Lilies, Blue Edge, 1938, 10 In. 195.00
Bizarre, Salt & Pepper Pot 120.00
Bizarre, Tea Set, Sugar, Creamer, 6-In. Teapot 545.00
Bizarre, Toast Rack, Stylized Flowers & Trees, 1930s, 3 3/4 In. 369.00
Bizarre, Urn, Abstract Flowers, Polychrome, Stamped, 11 3/4 x 7 3/4 In. 920.00
Blue Crocus, Bonjour, Sifter, 1930s, 5 In. 1225.00
Broth, Plate, Orange, Bubbles, Cobwebs, 7 3/4 In. 230.00
Crocus, Honey Pot, Blue, Violet, Orange Crocus, Sun Yellow Band, 3 In. 385.00
Crocus, Sugar Shaker, Conical Form, Signed, c.1930, 5 5/8 In. 460.00
Delecia Citrus, Bowl, Greens & Brown, 4 x 8 3/4 In. 440.00
Delecia Citrus, Lotus Jug, Black, Yellow, Lime, Gray, Green, Yellow Fruit, 6 In. 660.00
Delecia Citrus, Plate, Orange, Yellow, Green Leaves Border, Honey Glaze, 8 In. 300.00
Double V, Plate, Cobalt Blue Interior, Sun Yellow Center, Green Leaves, 6 In. 248.00
Feather & Leaves, Pitcher, Bright Orange Feather, Green, Sun Yellow, 7 1/8 In. 1760.00
Gardenia, Fantasque, Plate, c.1932-1932, 8 1/2 In. 350.00
Gardenia, Pitcher, Spattered Ground, 8 Sides, 7 x 6 1/2 In. 1980.00
Geometric, Bowl, Horizontal Bands Squares, Deep Blue, Red, 3 In. 385.00
Geometric, Pitcher, Broad, Deep Violet, Orange, 7 3/4 In. 660.00
Hollyhocks, Vase, Stylized Flowers & Leaves At Base, 1930s, 9 In. 302.00
Honolulu, Bizarre, Jug, Trees, Green & Black Trunks, 11 3/4 In. 575.00
Melon, Lotus Jug, 12 x 8 1/2 In. 1760.00
Morocco, Pot, Abstract, Curved Design, Cobalt Blue, Orange, Wicker Handle, 6 In. 1320.00
Persian, Plate, 4 Broad Cobalt Blue Leaves, Speckled Brown Border, 9 In. 1540.00
Picasso Flower, Fern Pot, Blue Circles Overlapping Orange Circles, 3 x 3 In. 550.00
Pine Grove, Plaque, Stylized Pine Branches, 10 1/4 In. 605.00
Red Roofs, Lotus Jug, Red Roof Cottage, Orange Circles, Stylized Trees, 11 In. 2310.00
Rhodanthe, Daffodil Bowl, Orange, Sun Yellow Marigolds, Honey Glaze, 5 In. 385.00
Sliced Fruit, Lotus Jug, Violet, Lavender, Blue, Green, Handle, 11 3/4 x 9 In. 1980.00
Sunray, Pitcher, Stylized Purple Stars, Brown Bridge, 3 1/4 In. 825.00
Tonquin, Bone Dish, Black 12.00
Tonquin, Bone Dish, Blue & White, Signed, 6 3/4 In. 22.00

The best time to buy an antique is when you see it.

Tonquin, Candlestick, Red, Pink & White, 10 In. 71.00
Trees & House, Lotus Jug, Green Roofed House, Signed, c.1930, 12 In. 1265.00
Trees & House, Pitcher, Green Roofed Houses, Orange, Black Trees, Handle, 6 In. 660.00

CLEWELL ware was made in limited quantities by Charles Walter Clewell of Canton, Ohio, from 1902 to 1955. Pottery was covered with a thin coating of bronze, then treated to make the bronze turn different colors. Pieces covered with copper, brass, or silver were also made. Mr. Clewell's secret formula for blue patinated bronze was burned when he died in 1965.

Urn, Copper Clad, Metal, Bronze Verdigris Patina, Marked, 9 x 4 In. 1125.00
Vase, 2 Handles, Signed, 6 1/2 In. 375.00
Vase, Bronze & Verdigris Patina, Signed, 7 1/2 In. 1725.00
Vase, Bronze & Verdigris Patina, Signed, 8 1/2 In. 975.00
Vase, Brown Patina, Crusty Green Glaze, 3 3/8 In. 260.00
Vase, Copper Clad, Bronzed Finish, 7 In. 375.00
Vase, Copper Verdigris Finish, Inverted Rim, Canton, Ohio, 11 1/4 x 8 1/2 In. 2760.00
Vase, Dark Green, Brown Patina, Marked, 8 1/2 In. 440.00
Vase, Fish Under Water, 8 x 5 In. 1380.00
Vase, Flared Rim, Tapering To Bulbous Foot, Signed, 7 3/4 In. 575.00
Vase, Freeform Incised & Cut Back Design, 8 1/2 In. 412.00
Vase, Green Over Brown Patina, Signed, 8 1/2 In. 450.00
Vase, Green, Brown Patina, 4 5/8 In. 230.00
Vase, Shouldered, Bronzed & Verdigris Patina, Incised, 8 3/4 x 6 1/4 In. 635.00
Vase, Verdigris Patina, Signed, 7 1/2 In. 920.00

CLEWS pottery was made by George Clews & Co. of Brownhills Pottery, Tunstall, England, from 18906 to 1961. Additional pieces may be listed in the Flow Blue category.

Cup & Saucer, American Eagle On Urn, Blue, Handleless 300.00
Cup & Saucer, Landing Of General LaFayette, Blue, Handleless, Clews 360.00
Cup Plate, Landing Of General LaFayette, Blue, 4 3/8 In. 467.00
Pitcher, English Castle Scene, States Border, 10 1/2 In. 1150.00
Plate, Blue & White Transfer, Men Fishing Scene, Village Background, 9 In., 5 Piece. ... 715.00
Plate, Landing Of General LaFayette At Castle Garden, 1824, 9 In. 250.00
Plate, Landing Of General LaFayette, Blue, 6 1/2 In. ....305.00 to 360.00
Plate, Landing Of General LaFayette, Blue, 7 1/2 In. ....220.00 to 275.00
Plate, Landing Of General LaFayette, Blue, 10 1/2 In. 385.00
Plate, Peace & Plenty, 10 1/4 In. 450.00
Plate, Peace & Plenty, Blue, 9 In. 165.00
Plate, Wilkie Series, Valentine, Blue, 9 In. 192.00
Plate, Wilkie Series, Valentine, Blue, 10 In. 302.00
Plate, Winter View Of Pittsfield, Mass., Blue, Scalloped, 7 1/2 In. 522.00
Plate, Winter View Of Pittsfield, Mass., Blue, Scalloped, 8 In. 330.00
Plate, Winter View Of Pittsfield, Mass., Blue, Scalloped, 10 1/2 In. 468.00
Plate, Winter View Of Pittsfield, Mass., Dark Blue Transfer, 8 In. 110.00
Platter, Landing Of General Lafayette At Castle Garden, 14 1/2 x 19 In. 748.00
Platter, Landing Of General LaFayette, Blue, 9 3/4 In. 715.00
Platter, States, 3-Story Building, Blue, 9 3/4 In. 1210.00
Soup, Dish, Peace & Plenty, Blue, 10 In. 330.00

CLIFTON POTTERY was founded by William Long in Clifton, New Jersey, in 1905. He worked there until 1908 making a line called *Crystal Patina.* Clifton Pottery made art pottery. Another firm, Chesapeake Pottery, sold majolica marked *Clifton ware.*

Pitcher, Mug, Little Colorado, Arizona, Geometric, Ivory, Terra-Cotta Ground, 5 x 9 In. ... 430.00
Vase, Crystal Patina Glaze, Silver Overlay, Tapered, c.1906, 4 3/4 x 3 3/4 In. 690.00
Vase, Crystal Patina Glaze, Squat Base, Flared Rim, c.1906, 7 x 5 1/2 In. 375.00
Vase, Crystal Patina, Squat, 2 Handles, Incised, 1906, 3 x 4 1/2 In. 200.00
Vase, Incised & Painted Indian Ware, Signed, 9 1/2 In. 330.00
Vase, Indian Ware, Brown Shades, Incised, Middle Mississippi Valley, 12 1/4 In. 430.00
Vase, Indian Ware, Homolobi, Abstract Designs, Glossy Black Interior, 5 x 7 In. 580.00
Vase, Tirrube, White Chrysanthemums, Green Leaves, Terra-Cotta Ground, 11 x 5 In. 489.00

CLOCKS of all types have always been popular with collectors. The eighteenth-century tall case, or grandfather's clock, was designed to house a works with a long pendulum. In 1816, Eli Terry patented a new, smaller works for a clock, and the case became smaller. The clock could be kept on a shelf instead of on the floor. By 1840, coiled springs were used and even smaller clocks were made. Battery-powered electric clocks were made in the 1870s. A garniture set can include a clock and other objects displayed on a mantel.

Advertising, Azuki Sport Bicycles, Square, 15 In.	38.00
Advertising, Black Horse, Mellow Ale, Porcelain	1100.00
Advertising, Black Horse, Mellow Ale, Tin	440.00
Advertising, Burger Beer, Electric, Tin Lithograph Face, 14 1/2 x 18 1/2 In.	70.00 to 75.00
Advertising, Burger Bohemian Beer, Wooden Frame, Electric, 14 1/2 x 19 In.	230.00
Advertising, Byrne Chevrolet Of Granado, Texas, Neon, 21 In.	715.00
Advertising, Calvert Whiskey, Light-Up Telecon Bubble, Center Logo, Name On Face	150.00
Advertising, Canada Dry, Metal Housing, Glass Face, Light-Up, 15 1/2 In.	95.00
Advertising, Double Cola Soda, Bubble Glass, c.1950, 12 In.	197.00
Advertising, Dr Pepper	5750.00
Advertising, Drink Vernor's, Round, 19 1/2 In.	145.00
Advertising, Ever-Ready Safety Razor, Wooden, Lather Faced Man Center, 22 x 18 In.	687.00
Advertising, Gem Damaskeene Razor, Man Shaving, Baby On Lap, Pendulum, 28 In.	715.00
Advertising, GMC Trucks, Neon	1750.00
Advertising, Grand Price Beer, Plastic Cover Over Wood, Light-Up, 14 1/2 In.	265.00
Advertising, Green Neon, Display Drum, Wood, Metal, c.1940, 20 x 14 x 9 In.	334.00
Advertising, Harley-Davidson, Alarm, Soldier On Cycle, Buy War Bonds, 1940s, 4 In.	240.00
Advertising, Hastings Piston Rings, Plastic, Light-Up, 16 In.	255.00
Advertising, Hires, Plastic, Metal, 13 x 27 x 4 In.	90.00
Advertising, Kendall Motor Oil, Round	500.00
Advertising, Metz Beer, Tin Lithograph, Square, The Old Reliable, Product Bottle, 15 In.	192.00
Advertising, National Cash Register, Electric, 1953	245.00
Advertising, Nesbitt's Orange, Light-Up, 16 1/4 In.	495.00
Advertising, Neuweiler Ale & Beer, Metal Case, Plastic Dial 1940s, 12 x 10 1/2 In.	292.00
Advertising, Neuweiler Ale & Beer, Reverse Glass, Brand Name Dial, 1940s, 12 x 10 In.	290.00
Advertising, Pan-American Exposition, Tin, Frying Pan, C.F. Chouffer, 1899, 12 In.	160.00
Advertising, Pennzoil Sound Your Z Light, Metal, Red Letters, White Ground, 20 In.	150.00
Advertising, Phillips 66 Tires, Double Bubble 15 In.	740.00
Advertising, Sauer's Flavoring Extracts, Gilbert Regulator	605.00
Advertising, Schweigert, Double Bubble, 16 In.	190.00
Advertising, Seagrams, Seven Crown, Composition Board, Dancing Horses, 14 1/2 In.	45.00
Advertising, Sealtest, Gold Lettering, 13 In.	185.00
Advertising, Simonize, Cardboard Housing, Light-Up, 15 In.	195.00
Advertising, Skelly, Brown, Red Lettering, Triangular Shape, 21 1/2 In.	170.00
Advertising, Time To Repaint, Auto Repair, Neon Tubes On Face, Metal Body, 36 x 8 In.	1045.00
Advertising, Vernor's Ginger Ale, 19 1/2 In.	145.00
Advertising, Whistle, Sparkling, Orange Goodness, Light-Up, 14 1/2 In.	230.00
Alarm, Big Ben, Pat. 1908	50.00
Alarm, Black Sambo, Cardboard & Plastic Face, c.1946, 3 1/2 x 2 3/4 In.	190.00
Alarm, Terry & Andrews, Silver Door, 30-Hour, Early 19th Century, 26 x 15 1/2 In.	305.00
Ansonia, Beveled Glass Over Dial, White Metal Figures, 18 x 24 In.	1100.00
Ansonia, Brass, Painted Wood, Blue Porcelain Blue, N.Y., 19 x 9 x 8 In.	365.00
Ansonia, Carriage, Brass, Mercury Glass Pendulum, Black Roman Numerals, 9 3/4 In.	275.00
Ansonia, Carriage, Cast Brass Framework, Orange Borders, Green Ground, 8 1/4 In.	140.00
Ansonia, Chestnut, Palm Trees On Glass Door, Time & Strike, Faux Pendulum	130.00
Ansonia, Crystal, No. 3	4290.00
Ansonia, Desk, Enameled Round Face, Flower & Scroll Feet, Cast Metal, 4 1/8 In.	35.00
Ansonia, Figural, Patinated Metal, Seated Classical Maiden, Wooden Plinth, 16 In.	490.00
Ansonia, Flow Blue Borders, Pink Rose Transfer, China Case, 11 3/4 In.	605.00 to 695.00
Ansonia, Gilt, Metal, Figural, Boy & Girl Choralists Standing On Either Side, 22 In.	1150.00
Ansonia, Mahogany Veneer, Niobe, 45 x 17 x 7 In.	1825.00
Ansonia, Mahogany, Arched Pediment, Roman Numerals, 24 x 16 x 6 In.	615.00
Ansonia, Mantel, Figural, Black Marble, Cherubs, Porcelain Dial, Patent June 18, 1882	275.00
Ansonia, Mantel, Gilt Metal Scroll, Porcelain, Cherub, Time & Strike, 14 x 8 x 5 In.	415.00
Ansonia, Mantel, Tuscola, China Cased	275.00

Ansonia, Ormolu Fluted Columns At Corners, Flowers, 13 1/4 In. 835.00
Ansonia, Queen Elizabeth, Paris Exposition, Walnut Case 875.00
Ansonia, Regulator, Brass, Green Onyx, Beveled Glass, 12 x 7 1/2 In. 925.00
Ansonia, Regulator, No. 16, Walnut, Roman Numerals, 30 x 25 x 12 In. 3920.00
Ansonia, Steeple, Mahogany Veneer, Painted Tin Dial, Mirror Lower Door, 20 x 11 In. . . . 75.00
Ansonia, Swinging Arm, Mahogany, 28 In. 3690.00
Ansonia, Tuxedo, Porcelain, Green & Gilt Flowers, Time & Strike, 10 1/2 x 9 x 5 In. 145.00
Ansonia, Wall, Time Only, Day Chapters, 25 In. 290.00
Art Deco, Matching Bookends, Metal Archer, Marble, 3 Pieces, 27 x 6 x 20 In. 4025.00
Arts & Crafts, Enameled Face, Hammered Copper, Original Patina, 8 x 10 In. 1495.00
Atkins, School, Mahogany, Arched Pediment, 25 x 17 x 4 In. 1065.00
Atmos Le Coultre, Mantel, Arch Form, Ebony Leaves, 8 1/4 In. 520.00
Attentioneer, Neon, Wrinkle Finish Steel, 3-Color Neon, 6 Sides, 1930s, 22 x 24 In. 1320.00
Bailey Company, Mantel, Black Marble, Winding Key, c.1850, 12 In. 895.00
Banjo, 3 Weight, Reverse Painted Chariot, 2 Horses, Alarm, Reuben Tower, 1820, 33 In. . 8800.00
Banjo, Federal, Mahogany, Acorn Finial, White Enamel Dial, 1810, 33 In. 1880.00
Banjo, Federal, Mahogany, Gilded Door, Enamel Dial, Bucolic Scene, c.1810, 40 In. 3000.00
Banjo, Federal, Mahogany, Vine & Urn Design, Brass Bezel, Gilt Gesso, c.1820, 41 In. . . 2185.00
Banjo, Howard & Davis, No. 4, Mahogany Veneer, 32 x 13 x 4 In. 2072.00
Banjo, Howard, E., Boston, Signed, 29 x 12 x 4 In. 2240.00
Banjo, Mahogany, Eglomise Glass Panels, c.1810, 33 1/2 In. 1320.00
Banjo, New Haven, Black Case, 40 x 12 x 5 In. 870.00
Banjo, Sawin, Mahogany Veneer, Signed, 39 x 11 x 3 In. 3080.00
Banjo, Seth Thomas, Time & Strike Movement, 29 In. 115.00
Banjo, Waltham, Walnut, Signed, 41 x 10 x 3 In. 1680.00
Banjo, Willard, Aaron, Federal, White Dial, Acorn Finial, Boston, 1810, 42 x 10 In. 2700.00
Banjo, Willard, Eagle Finial, 42 In. 1265.00
Bartholomew, Eli, Mahogany, Roman Numerals, 34 x 17 x 5 In. 1680.00
Birge & Fuller, Shelf, Steeple-On-Steeple, Mahogany, Roman Numerals, 26 x 4 In. 2688.00
Black Forest, Carved Thermometer, Barometer Shape, Germany, 1890, 50 In. 2690.00
Black Forest, Figural, Cuckoo, Carved Shelf, 8-Day Spring, 1895, 29 In. 2520.00
Black Forest, Figural, Large Cuckoo, Carved Case, Germany, 1890, 30 In. 1345.00
Black Forest, Mantel, Birds, Acorns, 19th Century 1250.00
Black Forest, Mantel, Full Eagle & Eaglets In Nest, 1880, 35 x 21 In. 4780.00
Black Forest, Mantel, Large Deer & Foliage Scene, 1880, 31 x 22 In. 3080.00
Black Forest, Mantel, Spread-Winged Bird On Top With Babies, Nest Below, 21 In. 1960.00
Black Forest, Pine, Rabbit, Bird, Rifles, Allover Leaves & Branches, Stag's Head 2750.00
Black Forest, Wall, 8-Day, Striking, 1890, 24 In. 840.00
Black Forest, Wall, Carved Deer, Pheasant & Rabbit, 8-Day, 1890, 30 x 20 In. 1230.00
Black Forest, Wall, Carved Walnut, France, 34 In. 2520.00
Blinking Eye, Banjo Player, Clock In Body, Cast Iron, Bradley & Hubbard, 16 In. 6050.00
Blinking Eye, Black Woman, Figural, Clock Face Set In Skirt, Cast Iron, 17 In. 4400.00
Blinking Eye, Lion, Clock Face Set In Mane, Cast Iron, 8 1/2 In. 3630.00
Bracket, 2-Train Chiming Movement, Pull Repeater, Tin Case, Brass Pendulum, 54 In. . . 290.00
Bracket, Alberg, A., Enameled Dial, Sphinxes, Corbels, Drapery Swag, 1900, 24 In. 4230.00
Bracket, Brass Movement & Silver Dial, Bronze Feet, Late 19th Century, 17 1/2 In. 1045.00
Bracket, George II, Roman & Arabic Numerals, Green, Brass Handle, 21 1/2 In. 7200.00
Bracket, Giltwood, Carved, France, 20th Century, 23 In. 110.00
Bracket, Mahogany, Brass Inlaid Case, Finials, Ball Feet, 19th Century, 17 1/2 In. 410.00
Brewster & Ingraham, Gothic, Mahogany, Bristol, Conn., c.1850, 20 1/4 In. 220.00
Bristol, Eagle Pediment, Split Baluster Pillars, Sherman Treat, 33 x 17 In. 400.00
Brockbank, Engraved Brass Dial, Fusee Movement, Time Only, Walnut, 16 x 15 In. 2250.00
Bronze, Art Nouveau, Girl In Relief, Original Patina, 11 3/4 In. 35.00
Bronze, Winged Eagle Pediment, Gold Dore, Flowers, Ram's Head Urns, 3 Piece 2520.00
Brown, J.C., Acorn, Mahogany, 24 x 15 x 5 In. 7280.00
Brown, J.C., Ripple Front, Heart In Tablet, Beehive . . . . .1300.00 to 1925.00
Caldwell, J.E., Carriage, Brass, Chapter Ring, Alarm, 5 1/2 In. 770.00
Calendar, Double Dial, Glass Tablet, Paper Rolls, Oak 650.00
Carriage, 1-Hour Repeater Movement, Enameled Face, Leather Case, 5 In. 775.00
Carriage, Aiguilles, Alarm Mechanism, Brass Cade, 7 In. 385.00
Carriage, Alarm, Floral Panels Top & Bottom, Subsidiary Dial, 6 1/8 In. 630.00
Carriage, Beveled Convex Glass Panels, Black Roman Numeral Dial, 5 In. 460.00
Carriage, Beveled Glaze Panel, Stepped Base, Bracket Feet, Alarm, 5 In. 345.00

Carriage, Brass Case, Beveled Glass, Roman Numerals, Chapter Ring, Alarm, 5 1/2 In. . . . 770.00
Carriage, Brass Case, Corinthian Column Corners, France, 8 In. 805.00
Carriage, Brass Champleve Corner, Gilt Openwork, Faux Diamond, France, 6 In. 259.00
Carriage, Brass, 2 Enamel Faces, Fitted Leather Traveling Case, France, 7 1/2 In. 805.00
Carriage, Brass, Bands Of Granulated Scrollwork, Early 20th Century, 7 5/8 In. 545.00
Carriage, Brass, Beveled Glass, Enameled Dial, Pendulum, France, 16 In. 220.00
Carriage, Brass, Beveled Glass, Enameled Face, Travel Case, France, 4 In. 440.00
Carriage, Brass, Beveled Glass, Pendulum, France, 9 In. 550.00
Carriage, Brass, Grande Sonnerie, Leafy Scrolls, Dragons' Heads, 20th Century, 7 In. 7475.00
Carriage, Brass, Oval, Glass Panels, Exposed Works, Leather Case, France, 4 In. 345.00
Carriage, Brass, White Enamel Face, Fitted Traveling Case, 20th Century, 5 1/2 In. 175.00
Carriage, Champleve Enamel, 4 Circular Column Corners, France, 5 In. 920.00
Carriage, Champleve Enamel, 4 Corinthian Columns, Gray, White Face, France, 8 In. . . . 345.00
Carriage, Circular Enameled Dial, Gilt, Alarm, 6 1/4 In. 750.00
Carriage, Enameled Face, Brass & Beveled Glass Case, Leather Case, 4 In. 505.00
Carriage, Enameled Face, Roman Numerals, Brass, 5 In. 315.00
Carriage, Gilt Metal, Beveled Glaze Panels, Circular Enamel Dial, 6 In. 400.00
Carriage, Landscape Scene, Painted Porcelain Panels, France, 18th Century, 7 In. 1095.00
Carriage, Repeater, Porcelain Dial, Black & Blue Letters, 6 In. 690.00
Carriage, Striking, Enamel, Square, Putti, Birds, France, 1845-1880, 4 1/4 In. 5175.00
Cartel, 2-Train Chiming Movement, Enamel Dial, Gilt Bronze, 1900s, 35 x 14 In. 3150.00
Cartel, Dial In Marble Case, Suspended In Lyre, Gilt Bronze, 16 In. 1150.00
Cartel, Louis XV, Tortoiseshell, Scrolls, Enamel Dial, Roman & Arabic Numerals, 9 In. . . . 805.00
Cartel, Louis XVI, Bronze, Gilt, Scroll Band, 4 Pendant Pineapples, 32 3/4 In. 5750.00
Cartier, Desk, Onyx Base, Bronze, Signed, 3 1/2 x 4 In. 860.00
Castle, Wendell, Circular Face, Carved Ebonized Base, 1989, 14 x 24 1/2 In. 3450.00
Castle, Wendell, Ribbon Mahogany Box, Mr. Clock, Copper Legs, 1988, 24 x 6 In. 8625.00
Castle, Wendell, Table, Square Ribbon Mahogany Box, Turquoise Copper Legs, 24 In. 8625.00
Champleve, Dial Suspended In Beveled Glass Case, Bronze, 18 1/2 In. 1035.00
Chaunce Of London, Bracket, Brass Inlay, 8-Day Fusee Movement, 1820s, 21 In. 2120.00
Cincinnati Time, Recorded Clock, Pull Down Lever, 30 x 14 x 8 In. 300.00
Classic Revival, Silver Plate, France, 20 x 11 x 5 1/2 In. . . . . *Illus* 1265.00
Continental, 3 Bacchic Putti, Gilt Bronze, 27 1/2 In. 2645.00
Coultishall, Mantel, Brass, Pierced, Chapter Ring, Sam Steel, 15 In. 275.00
Cuckoo, Game Carvings & Deer Head, 1885, 52 x 30 In. 2800.00
Cuckoo, Roman Numerals, Allover Carved Leaf Design, 20th Century, 17 In. 110.00
Cyma, Glass, Chrome Metal, c.1970, 7 x 3 x 5 In. 210.00
Delft Type, Tall Case Shape, Blue, White, Flowers, Windmill, Brass Works, Austria, 11 In. 110.00
Desk, Enamel, Figures & Putti Scene, Gilt Metal, Circular Base, Austria, 6 3/4 In. 1840.00
Dome, Gilt Bronze, Zachary Taylor On Horse, 7 In. 8470.00
Downs, Ephraim, Mahogany Veneer, Black Painted Columns, Wooden Works, 28 In. 230.00
Duverdry & Bloquel, Carriage, Brass, c.1920, 4 1/2 In. 115.00
Eli Terry, Mahogany Veneer, Wooden Works, Time & Strike, Reverse Painted, 34 In. 275.00
Eli Terry, Mahogany, 30-Hour, Plymouth, Conn., c.1817-1818, 20 3/4 x 16 In. 4255.00
Eli Terry & Sons, Pillar, Scroll, Mahogany Veneer, Weights, Key, Pendulum, 32 In. 1430.00
Eli Terry Jr., Shelf, Reverse Painted Panel Of Georgian House 1006.00
Enamel, 3 Putti, Painted Porcelains, Faux Diamond, Champleve, France, 1890, 16 In. 4600.00
Enamel, Multiple Gilt Metal Putti Finials, Painted Scenes, 4 Scroll Feet, 11 In. 2990.00
Enamel, On Stand, Silver Putti Finial, Allegorical Garden Scene, Phoenix Bird, 8 In. 2530.00
Enamel Dial, Roman Numerals, Pair Of Putti, Bronze Doves, 28 1/2 In. 3740.00
European Figure On Ship, Rocaille Relief Design Base, French Design, 1850, 17 In. 690.00
Ferdinand, J., Brass, Chromed Metal, Figurines On Either Side Of Clock, 7 1/2 In. 18000.00
French Design, Bleu Celest, Cartouche With Figures, Floral Garlands, 8 1/2 In. 145.00
French Empire, Enamel, Putti Scene, Faux Diamond, 1890, 16 1/2 In. 5500.00
French Empire, Louis XVI, Neoclassical Female Figure Reclining, 16 In. 5175.00
Garland, Mantel, Napoleon III, Gilt Bronze, Marble, Eagle, Columns, 20 x 12 x 7 In. 3680.00
Garner, Gilt Metal, 4 Cobalt Columns, Rectangular Case, Gilt Frame, Signed, 17 In. 3680.00
General Electric, Desk, Brass, Electric, Enamel Face, Alarm, Easel Back, c.1935, 5 In. . . 125.00
General Electric, Faux Wood Plastic Base, 5 x 6 In. 130.00
General Electric, Kitchen, Art Deco, Sweep 2nd Hand, Ashland, Mass. 60.00
Gilbert, Mantel, Faux Marble Design, Full & One Half Hour Gong 220.00
Gilbert, Regulator, Mahogany, Roman Numerals 12320.00
Gilbert, Regulator, Oak, Short Drop Case, Octagon Top, Standard Time Stencil, 28 In. 130.00

Clock, Classic
Revival, Silver
Plate, France,
20 x 11 x 5 1/2 In.

Clock, Jerome,
Chauncey, Gothic,
2 Steeples, 8-Day, 1852,
20 x 10 In.

Gilbert, Silver Deposit Front Glass, Applied Pencil Carvings, 19 In.	130.00
Gilbert, Walnut, Bronze, Carved, Gold Stencil Glass Door, Time & Strike, 22 In.	130.00
Gilbert, Walnut, Stencil Glass Door, Time & Strike, 25 x 16 x 5 In.	355.00
Gilbert, Windmill Shape, Dutch Girl Carrying Pail, 18 x 11 x 4 In.	259.00
Gilt Bronze, Marble, Female Grecian, Porcelain Face, Regency, 1800s, 22 In.	730.00
Gilt Bronze, Scrolls & Fruiting Vine, Figures In Landscape, Paris	630.00
Gilt Bronze & Marble, Reclining Classical Female, Enamel Dial, Signed, 11 1/4 In.	575.00
Gilt Metal, 4 Cobalt Blue Columns, Ball Feet, Blue Underglaze, Austria, 14 1/2 In.	1610.00
Gilt Metal, 4 Cobalt Blue Columns, Flared Square Porcelain Plinth, Austria, 15 In.	2530.00
Gilt Metal, 4 Finial Cobalt Columns, Flattened Circular Feet, Blue Glaze, 12 1/4 In.	2070.00
Gilt Metal, 4 Painted Architectural Columns, 4 Spherical Feet, Austria, 14 In.	2530.00
Gilt Metal, 5 Gilt, Cobalt Highlighted Columns, 5 Ball Form Feet, Porcelain, 12 In.	1610.00
Gilt Metal, Allegorical Subjects Within Cobalt Blue Reserves, 4 Footed, 16 In.	3450.00
Gilt Metal, Barrel Form, 4 Pink Gilt Highlighted Columns, Austria, 19 In.	3680.00
Gilt Metal, Flowers, Leaves On Case, Porcelain, Spherical Feet, 9 1/2 In.	1380.00
Gilt Metal, Leaf Crest, Parlor Scene, Gentleman, 2 Women, France, 11 3/4 In.	3450.00
Gilt Metal, Putti Scene, Claret Square Stepped Base, Blue Underglaze, 17 1/2 In.	4025.00
Gilt Metal, Putti Scene, Cobalt Blue, Gilt Highlighted Pedestal, Blue Glaze, 19 In.	3910.00
Gilt Metal, Young Women With Putti, Metal Dolphins At Each Corner, 17 1/2 In.	4830.00
Giltwood, Copper Dial, Time & Strike, Floral Frame, Sweden, 1780s, 36 In.	5235.00
Haddon, Multicolored Face, Higgins, 11 1/2 x 11 1/2 In.	805.00
Hamann & Koch, Carriage, Enameled Porcelain Inserts, Landscape Scenes, 5 1/2 In.	880.00
Hanging, Reverse Painted White Face, Black Numerals, Brass Works, 20 x 15 1/2 In.	275.00
Herschede, Mantel, Mahogany Veneer Finish, Round Dial, Brown Enamel, 20 x 9 In.	80.00
Hill, Samuel, Wall, Mahogany, Inlaid Oak Leaves, Eagle Top, 18th Century, 46 In.	4887.00
Hoadley, Silas, Mahogany, Carved Columns, 38 x 17 x 4 In.	1680.00
Howard, E., Dark Mahogany Veneer, Roman Numerals, Boston, 34 x 11 x 5 In.	5320.00
Howard, E., Ivory, Marble, Roman Numerals, Signed, Boston, 43 x 25 x 5 In.	2520.00
Howard, E., Regulator, Walnut, Roman Numerals, Boston, 31 x 15 x 5 In.	1980.00
Howard Miller, Asterisk, Black Spikes, Original Finish, G. Nelson, 13 In.	560.00 to 920.00
Howard Miller, Atomic Ball, Brass Face, Black Wooden Markers, G. Nelson, 13 In.	790.00
Howard Miller, Concave Wooden Disk, Roman Numerals, G. Nelson, 14 In.	140.00
Howard Miller, Enameled White Hands, G. Nelson, 10 1/4 In.	395.00
Howard Miller, Hexagonal Cutout Metal, Polymer Disks, G. Nelson, 10 1/2 In.	7700.00
Howard Miller, Mosaic Face, Enameled Hands, Walnut Case, G. Nelson, 13 In.	790.00
Howard Miller, Spider Web, Enameled Metal Rays, G. Nelson, 1954, 8 x 4 In.	1035.00
Howard Miller, Starburst, White Face, Walnut Arms, G. Nelson, 18 In.	620.00
Howard Miller, Steering Wheel, Black Enameled Dial, G. Nelson, 12 In.	790.00
Howard Miller, Wall, Watermelon, Wooden, Brass Legs, G. Nelson, 1954, 8 x 4 In.	978.00
Hun Da Lee, Bracket, Mahogany, Roman Numerals, 25 x 14 x 11 In.	895.00
Ingraham, Kitchen, 8-Day Time & Strike	185.00
Ingraham, Mantel, Mahogany, Brass Handles & Feet, Roman Numerals, 14 x 11 In.	125.00
Ingraham, Pressed Oak Case, 32 x 17 x 4 In.	410.00
Ingraham, Shelf, Figure 8 Door, 8-Day, Label, 15 3/4 In.	230.00
Ingraham, Venetian, 30-Hour Time & Strike	175.00
Ithaca, Mahogany, Roman Numerals, 25 x 12 x 4 In.	1344.00
Ithaca, No. 4, Double Dial, Wooden Base	950.00

J.C. Brown & Co., Mantel, Federal, Acorn, Mahogany, Flower Glazed Door, 1805, 25 In. . . 3600.00
Japy Freres, Regulator, Brass, Onyx Crystal, 19 x 8 x 5 In. 1268.00
Jerome, C. & N., Hollow Column, 22 x 15 In. 345.00
Jerome, Chauncey, Gothic, 2 Steeples, 8-Day, 1852, 20 x 10 In. . . . . *Illus* 430.00
Jerome, Chauncey, School, Mahogany, Roman Numerals, 22 x 5 In. 2485.00
Jerome, Chauncey, Steeple, Mahogany Veneer, Stenciled Glass Door, Time & Strike 155.00
Junghans, Bracket, 3 Dials, German Fuss, Brass Face, Walnut Case, 17 x 11 1/2 In. 490.00
Keller & Guerin, Foo Dog, Signed, 1900, 15 1/8 In. 2880.00
Kerr, Travel, 8-Day, Sterling Silver, 4 x 4 1/2 In. 110.00
Kessler, John, Mantel, C-Scroll Case, 8-Day Brass Works, Brass Dial, c.1810, 24 In. 4125.00
Kitchen, Pressed Oak, Rose Model, Partial Label 225.00
KMG, Regal Figure, Bronze & Malachite, Bronze Base, 19th Century, 32 x 25 In. 5645.00
L. Ladomus & Co., Regulator, Walnut, Signed, 74 x 23 x 13 In. 4480.00
LaCoultre, Atmos, Skeleton Movement, Brass & Glass Case, 13 3/4 In. 1175.00
Lamp Post, 8-Day, Alarm, Champs Elysees Street Sign, Switzerland 170.00
Lantern, Floral Plate Behind Dial, Urn Finials, Panels Hiding Bell, 13 1/2 x 6 1/2 In. 1670.00
Le Roy, Regulator, Gilt, Bronze, Champleve Enamel Panels, Onyx, 1900, 54 In. 12000.00
LeCoultre, Mantel, Perpetual Motion, 8 x 6 x 9 1/2 In. 375.00
Liberty, Pewter, Flowers, Embossed, 4 In. 1380.00
Liberty, Tree Of Life Design, Pewter, Enamel Dial, 7 1/2 x 5 In. 5175.00
Liberty & Co., Mantel, Pewter, Hammered, Signed, Tudric, 5 1/2 x 5 In. 2300.00
Looping, Articulated Mount, 15 Jewel, 5 Functions, 7 3/4 In. 1150.00
Louis Philippe, Mantel, Gilt, Bronze, White, Black Enamel, Portico, 23 3/4 In. 5060.00
Lumley & Gudgeon, Wall, Mahogany Trunk Dial, Brass Bezel, Time Only, 26 In. 5553.00
Lux, Chrome, Crystal Face, Stepped Base, Signed, 4 1/2 x 5 In. 200.00
Mahogany, Brass Finials, Painted Floral Face, Reverse Painted Castle, 31 1/2 In. 920.00
Man With Harpoon, Sailboat On Base, Clock In Center, 30 In. 630.00
Manross, Elisha, Shelf, Steeple-On-Steeple, Mahogany, Roman Numerals, 24 x 4 In. 1345.00
Mantel, 2-Train Chiming Movement, Glass 4 Sides, Brass, Ogee Bracket Base, 11 In. . . . 490.00
Mantel, Alabaster, Gilt Brass, Beveled Glass Panel All Sides, France, 8 x 6 x 14 In. 990.00
Mantel, Art Deco, Rose Marble, Enameled Metal Impalas, c.1940, 9 x 18 In. 185.00
Mantel, Art Nouveau, Gilded Copper Case, Porcelain Dial With Flowers, 1900, 14 In. . . . 225.00
Mantel, Arts & Crafts, Quartersawn Golden Oak, Metal, 20 x 12 In. . . . . *Illus* 805.00
Mantel, Arts & Crafts, Variegated Green Matte Glaze, Roman Numerals, 14 3/4 In. 1320.00
Mantel, Black, Red Marble, Enamel Dial, Victorian, 12 3/4 x 10 1/2 x 6 1/2 In. 430.00
Mantel, Brass, Circular Clock Face, Rectangular Glass Paneled Frame, 10 3/4 In. 315.00
Mantel, Brass, Marble, Round Dial, Brass Appliqued Base, 19th Century, 19 x 14 In. 110.00
Mantel, Brass, Ornate Scrolled Case, Porcelain Face, France, Early 20th Century 275.00
Mantel, Bronze & White Marble, Musical Pieces At Sides, Doves On Plinth, 11 In. 1610.00
Mantel, Bronze Dore, Enameled Frieze Of Putti Frolicking On Blue Field, 15 In. 6325.00
Mantel, Bronze, Enamel Face, Acorn, Laurel Branches, Beaded Edge, France, 18 In. 2760.00
Mantel, Bronze, Figure Of Cupid Removing Thorn From His Foot, Cast Feet, 18 In. 1610.00
Mantel, Bronze, Gilt, Circular Dial, 2 Winged Mermen, 13 In. 3300.00
Mantel, Bronze, Gilt, Concave Pedestal, Ram's Heads, Swag Design, 14 In. 2400.00
Mantel, Bronze, Winged Griffins, 1875, 17 In. 896.00
Mantel, Carriage, Brass, Glass Octagonal Case, Mercury Pendulum, France, 11 In. 825.00
Mantel, Carved Song Birds Amid Laurel Garlands, 17 1/2 x 9 In. 1380.00
Mantel, Carved, Brass Works, Painted Dial, Victorian, c.1890 . . . . 250.00
Mantel, Cast Metal, White, Victorian, Mid 19th Century, c.1859 . . . . 330.00
Mantel, Charles X, Gilt, Patinated Bronze, Seated Cherub, 14 x 10 x 4 In. 2300.00
Mantel, Column Front, Peak Top, Brass 8-Day, Walnut, 15 In. 410.00
Mantel, Continental, Burl, Porcelain Dial, Pendulum, Late 19th Century 165.00
Mantel, Dial On Fluted Column, Gilt Bronze & Marble, Cupid Surmount, 14 1/2 In. 1090.00
Mantel, Drapery Swag Supports, Lyre Form Case, Painted Floral Swags, 22 1/2 In. 520.00
Mantel, Egyptian Revival, Bronze, Onyx, Figural, Seated Maidens, 21 1/2 In. 1035.00
Mantel, Empire, Gilt Bronze, Ebony Wood, Corinthian Column, Stepped Plinth, 19 In. . . . 1095.00
Mantel, Empire, Sphinxes By Psyche Figure, Winged Bull Flanked By Scrolls, 19 In. 4800.00
Mantel, Enamel Dial, Leafy Swag Slabs, Bronze, France, 19th Century, 17 In. 690.00
Mantel, Federal, Mahogany, Pagoda Top, White Enamel, Gilt Dial, 1815, 40 In. 7200.00
Mantel, Figure Of Armored Warrior Drawing His Sword, Bronze, 23 3/4 x 20 In. 2300.00
Mantel, Figure Of Young Man, Period Dress, Lion's-Mask Handles, Bronze, 21 1/2 In. . . . 1035.00
Mantel, French Renaissance, Gilt, Brass Dial, Roman Numerals, France, 16 In. 460.00
Mantel, Gilt Brass Trim, Black Onyx, Pendulum, Key, 15 5/8 x 6 1/2 x 9 1/2 In. 330.00

Mantel, Gilt Brass, Tree Branch Column, France, 24 1/2 In. 990.00
Mantel, Gilt Bronze, Brown Patina, White Face, Egg & Dart Border, 14 3/4 x 10 x 4 In. . . 1840.00
Mantel, Gilt Bronze, Porcelain, Urn Shape, Lion's Mask, Birds, Putti, Continental, 21 In. . 460.00
Mantel, Gilt Faced, Mercury Pendulum, 4 Floral Columns, Bronze, 13 1/2 In. 316.00
Mantel, Gilt, Mother-Of-Pearl Bouquet, White Alabaster Columns, Continental, 23 In. ... 575.00
Mantel, Gothic Revival, Carved Mahogany, Engraved Silver Dial, Blocked Base, 19 In. . . 805.00
Mantel, Inlay, Marquetry, Angled Design, Arrow, Flag, Picture Boards, 13 x 35 x 5 In. ... 1150.00
Mantel, Louis XV, Bronze, Putti Within Leafy Cast Case, Gilt, 44 In. 16800.00
Mantel, Louis XV, Tortoiseshell, White Enamel Dial, Leaf Crest, 16 x 8 In. 980.00
Mantel, Mahogany, Allover Flowers, Gilt Design, 8 x 3 1/2 x 10 In. 80.00
Mantel, Mahogany, Ogee, Reverse Painted Glass Panel, c.1845, 15 1/4 In. 140.00
Mantel, Man Holding Book, Gilt, Scroll Footed, 20 In. 1320.00
Mantel, Marble, Arizona, Grand Canyon State, Electrified, 6 In. 25.00
Mantel, Marble, Circular White Enamel Dial, Goddess Of The Sun, 18 In. 1955.00
Mantel, Marble, Classical Roman Soldier Figure, Engraved Face, 17 x 23 1/2 In. 1870.00
Mantel, Napoleon III, Gilt Bronze Mounted, Putto Holding Shell, 17 In. 920.00
Mantel, Napoleon III, Porcelain Circular Dial, Roman Numerals, Bun Feet, 17 1/2 In. ... 2760.00
Mantel, Neoclassical, Bronze, Gilt Chapter Dial, 11 1/2 In. 750.00
Mantel, Neoclassical, Gilt Bronze, Scarlet Lacquer, Pinewood, 14 1/2 x 9 1/2 x 3 In. 1610.00
Mantel, Neoclassical, Ormolu & Marble, Enamel Dial, Inscribed, France, 13 In. 5700.00
Mantel, Painted & Gilded Wood, Garden Pavilion, Enamel Dial, Side Vases, 47 In. 2875.00
Mantel, Patinated, Gilt Bronze, Putti, Hunt Finial, Continental, 22 In. 3680.00
Mantel, Regency, Double Fusee, Time & Hour Strike, Mahogany, 20 x 12 1/2 In. 1840.00
Mantel, Repeater, Mahogany, Brass Finials, 19th Century, 24 1/2 x 11 x 6 1/2 In. 3680.00
Mantel, Rococo Ormolu Floral Scroll, White Enamel Dial, Swags, 1889, 14 1/4 In. 920.00
Mantel, Rococo, Oak, Allover Flowers, Leaf Carvings, 30 x 25 x 12 In. 2465.00
Mantel, Seated Cherub, Pointing Arrow, Marble Base, Claw Feet, 12 In. 2090.00
Mantel, Seated Maidens, 1855, 22 x 22 In. 1230.00
Mantel, Walnut, Column Front & Peak Top, Round Face, 8-Day, 15 In. 355.00
Mantel, With Pair Of 5-Light Candelabra, Brass, Porcelain, France, 17 In., 3 Piece 880.00
Mappin & Webb, Carriage, Champleve Enamel Front, Handles, 20th Century, 6 In. 290.00
Marble, Bronze, Gilt Face, Circular Dial, Dragons, Masks, Gilt Bronze Base, 25 In. ... 15600.00
Marble, Bronze, Roman Numerals, Figures Of Socrates, Plato, Marble Base, 15 In. 1725.00
Marchand, J.G., Mantel, Classical Woman, Cupid Over Base, Porcelain Dial, 29 In. 1254.00
Miller, I., Regency, Kneeling Female, Under Seashell, Flowers, 1830, 21 In. 2300.00
Mitchell & Son, Bracket, Silvered Dial, Strike & Silent, 13 2/3 In. 1597.00
Mobilier, Walnut, Courting Couple, Leaf Scrolls, 18th Century, 96 3/4 In. 2300.00
Montgomery Brothers, Mahogany, Key Wind, Los Angeles, Calif., 13 x 10 x 6 In. 225.00
Natural Elegance, Desk, Green Marble, 2 1/2 x 1 1/2 In. 10.00
Nelson, G., Enameled Wood, Pyramid Base, Plexiglas Face, 13 1/2 x 14 In. 865.00
Nelson, G., Watermelon, Wooden, Brass Legs & Hands, 1954, 4 3/4 x 8 In. 978.00
New Haven, Art Nouveau, Copper Plate Over Wood, 12-Day, 5 1/2 x 13 In. ....*Illus* 173.00
New Haven, Copper Plate, Wood, Art Nouveau Style, 12 Day, 13 x 2 1/2 x 5 1/2 In. 175.00

Clock, New Haven, Art Nouveau, Copper Plate
Over Wood, 12-Day, 5 1/2 x 13 In.

Clock, Mantel, Arts & Crafts,
Quartersawn Golden Oak,
Metal, 20 x 12 In.

Clock, Tall Case, Music
Box, Deutsche Standuhr,
Symphonion No. 30 St., 1900

New Haven, Figure Eight, Walnut Case, Alarm, Time & Strike Movement, 16 1/2 In. 259.00
New Haven, Mantel, Empire, Cast Iron, Metal, Bronze, Silver Finish, 20 In. 580.00
New Haven, Ogee, Brass Works, Reverse Painted Glass, 29 x 15 1/2 In. 85.00
Norris North, Pillar & Scroll, Mahogany, 29 x 15 x 4 In. 3360.00
Numechron, Dark Mahogany Plastic Shell, 1940, 7 x 3 1/2 x 4 In. 105.00
Ogee, Eglomise Panel, Royal Coat Of Arms, American, c.1845 .... 138.00
Papier-Mache, Mother-Of-Pearl Style Insert, Iridescent, Wooden Base, 11 x 4 x 16 In. ... 375.00
Plateau, Bronze Flower Form Finials, 2-Chiming Movement, Glass Face, 1880s, 6 1/8 In. 920.00
Porcelain, Violets & Roses, Germany, 8 1/4 x 4 1/4 In. 135.00
Porcelain Mounted, Branches, Flower Heads, Chinese Woman In Base, 16 3/4 In. 2305.00
Price, Brass Lantern, London, England, Early 18th Century, 7 x 5 In. 2420.00
Regulator, Biedermeier, Mahogany Case, Enamel Dial, Roman Numerals, 38 In. 2300.00
Regulator, Bronze, Marble, Ornate Trim, 1885, 19 In. 1065.00
Regulator, Cloisonne Enamel Dial, Porcelain Pendulum, 17 3/4 In. 490.00
Regulator, Hanging, Cherry Veneer, Arched Crest, Ormolu Swag Design, 38 1/2 In. 190.00
Regulator, Jeweler's, Mahogany Veneer, Roman Numerals 4480.00
Regulator, Multi Wood, Painted Dial, Pillars, Carved Crest, Banded Inlay, 40 x 20 In. ... 1265.00
Regulator, Standing, Mahogany, Roman Numerals, Floor 2296.00
Regulator, Time & Strike, Enamel, Roman Numerals, Vienna, 19th Century, 15 x 7 1/2 In. 259.00
Regulator, Wall, Mahogany, American, Late 19th Century, 19 x 14 In. 300.00
Reverse On Glass, Portrait Of General Harris, 33 In. 8760.00
Robin, Mantel, Neoclassical, Figural, Ormolu, Enamel Dial, Inscribed, 1821, 19 x 14 In. . 6600.00
S. Marti & Cie, Mantel, Napoleon III, Bronze 660.00
Secessionists, White Metal Frame, Copper Face, Slag Glass Panel, 14 1/2 In. 140.00
Sessions, Flowers, Gold Trim, Electric, 10 1/4 x 7 1/4 In. 125.00
Sessions, Key, Mantel, Forestville, Conn. 180.00
Sessions, Mantel, Mahogany, Chimes, Pendulum, Key 95.00
Sessions, School, Regulator, Pendulum 110.00
Seth Thomas, Calendar Paper, Office, No. 7 .... 1540.00
Seth Thomas, Figural, Bronze Finish, Roman Numerals, Ogee Feet, Cast Metal, 17 In. ... 495.00
Seth Thomas, Mantel, Brass, Beveled Glass All Sides, Pendulum, Key, 9 3/4 In. 110.00
Seth Thomas, Mantel, Federal, Mahogany Veneer, Faux Paint, c.1780, 25 x 14 3/4 In. ... 140.00
Seth Thomas, Mantel, Seated Frame, Basket Of Flowers, Time & Strike, 10 x 20 In. 460.00
Seth Thomas, Mantel, Simulated Wood Veneer, Eastlake Carved Base, 18 x 7 x 11 In. ... 190.00
Seth Thomas, Original Patina, Arts & Crafts, 13 In. 1265.00
Seth Thomas, Regulator, Santa Fe Railway, Walnut Case, Pendulum & Key, 24 In. 630.00
Seth Thomas, Reverse Painted Flowers Top, Stepped Cornice, 32 1/2 x 18 In. 495.00
Seth Thomas, Rosewood Veneer, 8-Day, Painted Tin Dial, Time & Strike, 16 In. 155.00
Seth Thomas, Simulated Wood Veneer, Ionic Column Pilasters, Gold, 13 1/2 In. 130.00
Seth Thomas, Wall, Mahogany, 36 x 15 x 15 1/2 In. 690.00
Shelf, Empire, Mahogany, Dark Finish, Wood, Brass Works, 32 1/4 In. 410.00
Shelf, Mahogany, Roman Numerals, Ogee, Time & Strike, 8 3/4 x 13 1/4 In. 60.00
Shelf, Neoclassical, Mahogany, Flame Birch Veneer, Mass., 19th Century, 34 In. 6900.00
Skeleton, Brass, Pierced Metal Chapter Ring, Mahogany Base, Bun Feet, 7 1/2 x 5 In. ... 635.00
Smith & Goodrich, Ogee Type, Reverse Painting Of Horn Of Plenty 370.00
Smith & Goodrich, Ogee Type, Reverse Painting Of St. Luke's Church 300.00
Spartus, Kitchen, Plastic, Art Deco Style, Off-White, Black, Yellow 25.00
Stand, J., Regulator, Walnut, 3-Train Chiming Movement, Enameled Dial, 1880s, 52 In. .. 1265.00
Stevens, Bracket, George III, Mahogany, Stepped Cornice, Columns, 13 x 8 x 5 In. 1725.00
Tall Case, 30-Hour Rope Pulley, Alarm, Anchor Escapement, England, c.1700, 84 In. 2245.00
Tall Case, 30-Hour, Hand Painted Face, Chime On Hour, Box, England, c.1850 .... 4200.00
Tall Case, American Chime Clock Co., Chippendale, Cherry, Broken Arch Hood, 97 In. .. 1430.00
Tall Case, Arched Face, Flowers, Ogee Bracket Feet, Bucks County, c.1815, 91 In. 3850.00
Tall Case, Arched Glazed Door, Roman Numerals, Square Base, Ogee Feet, 92 In. 6325.00
Tall Case, Arts & Craft, Brass Face, Pendulum, Arched Skirt, 75 x 22 x 13 In. 1440.00
Tall Case, Bailey, J., Brass Eagle Finial, 8-Day, Moon Phase Dial, Calendar Dials, 97 In. . 4950.00
Tall Case, Bixler, Chippendale, Cherry, Swan Neck Pediment, Late 1700s, 92 1/2 In. .. 16100.00
Tall Case, Broken Arch Bonnet, Rosettes, Moon Phase Dial, Mahogany, Oak, 87 x 24 In. . 880.00
Tall Case, Budgeon, Thos., George III, Chinoiserie, Red Lacquer, 2 Weights, 92 In. 8050.00
Tall Case, Cherry, 8-Day Moon Dial, Second & Calendar Dial, Ogee Feet, 101 In. 8525.00
Tall Case, Chippendale, Mahogany, Swan Neck Bonnet Top, Animal Feet, 100 In. 2530.00
Tall Case, Chippendale, Walnut, Broken Arch Bonnet, Philadelphia, c.1785, 91 In. 10450.00
Tall Case, Cope, Jacob, 30-Hour Movement, Date Wheel, Cherry Case, c.1800, 95 In. ... 2640.00

Tall Case, Directoire Style, Oak, Enameled Face, Tapering Case, Carving, 98 x 13 In. 1725.00
Tall Case, Elliot, Oak, Heavily Carved, Signed 7000.00
Tall Case, Federal, Mahogany, Chamfered Corners, Bracket Feet, Phil., 1800, 97 In. 4890.00
Tall Case, Federal, Mahogany, Inlay, Scrolled Crest, Brass Rosettes, c.1810, 92 In. 7475.00
Tall Case, Federal, Maple Inlaid, Chinoiserie Painted Dial, French Feet, 1800, 94 In. 6325.00
Tall Case, Figural, Bronze, Oak, Winged Cherubs, Classical Figures, Flowers, 103 In. 17920.00
Tall Case, Fisher, John, Moon Phase Dial, Second Hand, Rosettes, Flame Finials, 102 In. . 5250.00
Tall Case, George III, Mahogany, Allegorical Figure By Sailing Vessel, 88 3/4 In. 2300.00
Tall Case, George III, Mahogany, Broken Arch Bonnet, 8-Day Dial, c.1790, 86 In. 4930.00
Tall Case, George III, Mahogany, Fluted Columnar Supports, Bracket Feet, 85 In. 1035.00
Tall Case, George III, Mahogany, Painted Hunting Scenes, Early 1800s, 90 3/4 In. 4025.00
Tall Case, Georgian, Mahogany, Walnut, Allegorical Figures Of Seasons On Corners 1610.00
Tall Case, Gibbs, Wm., George II, Arched Glazed Door, Chinoiserie Figures, 90 In. 10200.00
Tall Case, Gibson, Tho., George III, Mahogany, Inlay, Early 19th Century, 93 1/2 In. 4600.00
Tall Case, Gothic Revival, Mahogany, Crenellated Pediment, Bowed Front Door, 84 In. .. 1380.00
Tall Case, Green Lacquer, Woodley Kington, 2 Weights, Pendulum, 90 In. 8630.00
Tall Case, Harrison, F., Pagoda Cornice, Glazed Door, Brass Face, Moon Dial, 94 In. 3795.00
Tall Case, Herschede, Mahogany, 7 Tubes, Westminster, Canterbury Chimes, 97 In. 1570.00
Tall Case, Herschede, Mahogany, Weight, Tubular Chimes, 24 x 15 x 83 In. 4900.00
Tall Case, Hutch, Carved, Spire Finials, Dentil Molding, 19th Century, 17 x 5 x 3 In. 1265.00
Tall Case, Hutchins, L & A, Tiger Maple, Arched Bonnet, 8-Day, c.1790, 87 x 18 In. 17600.00
Tall Case, Jacques, Walnut, Roman Numerals, Signed, Signed, 80 x 26 x 16 In. 4480.00
Tall Case, Kelly, Jno, Scrolled Bonnet, Fretwork, Enameled Dial, 1760s, 92 In. 8395.00
Tall Case, Mahogany Veneer, Flowers & Butterfly Inlays, 1870, 92 x 26 x 14 In. 6720.00
Tall Case, Mahogany, 8-Day, Arch Door, Beaded Corners, Bracket Feet, Finial, 98 1/2 In. . 1210.00
Tall Case, Mahogany, 8-Day, Brass Dial, Moon Phase, Weight Driven, 90 x 20 1/2 In. 1230.00
Tall Case, Mahogany, Bonnet Top, Barley Twist Pilasters, 8-Day, c.1880, 83 In. 2100.00
Tall Case, Mahogany, Carved, Scrolled Crest, Arabic Numerals, Mid 20th Century, 86 In. . 860.00
Tall Case, Mahogany, Cotters Saturday Night Scene, Continents, 85 1/2 In. 3395.00
Tall Case, Mahogany, Inlay, Rocking Devil Over Numeral Face, Time & Strike 4000.00
Tall Case, Mahogany, Moon Dial, Conch Shell Face, England 4620.00
Tall Case, Mahogany, Moon Phase, 5 Wire Loop Chimes, Beveled Door, 101 In. 6900.00
Tall Case, Marshall, Richard, George III, Oak, Pendulum, Striking, 85 In. 6900.00
Tall Case, Mason, I. & E., Brass Spherule Finial, Enameled Dial, 1780s, 82 In. 1265.00
Tall Case, Muirhead, J., Oak, Cartouche, 8-Day, Brackets & Waist Door, Signed, 90 In. .. 3850.00
Tall Case, Mulliken, Jonathan, Brass Dial 7215.00
Tall Case, Music Box, Deutsche Standuhr, Symphonion No. 30 St., 1900 .... *Illus* 13555.00
Tall Case, Oak, Striking, Free Standing Columns, 1 Weight, Pendulum, 84 In. 4600.00
Tall Case, Painted Dial, 2 Figures, 8-Day, Dog, New Castle, London, 84 In. 3740.00
Tall Case, Painted Dial, Brass Finials, Pine Case, Warren, R.I., 90 In. 7150.00
Tall Case, Preston, Tho. Hodgson, Chippendale, Mahogany, Painted Dial, England, 84 In. . 1320.00
Tall Case, Provincial, Pine, Brass Dial, Cast Scroll, Cherub Design, 73 1/4 x 10 In. 1610.00
Tall Case, Read & Watson, Cherry, Tombstone Door, Wooden Works, 90 1/2 In. 2475.00
Tall Case, Rococo, Walnut, Arched Cornice, Brass Chapter Dial, Paw Feet, 94 In. 2990.00
Tall Case, Rudd, Joseph, Silvered Dial, Date & Seconds, Starburst Inlay, 1760s, 91 In. ... 4405.00
Tall Case, Saltcoats, M., George III, Mahogany, Inlaid, Painted Dial, c.1800, 82 In. 2415.00
Tall Case, Scott, William, Engraved Brass Dial, 8-Day, Oak, 1880s, 90 In. 5025.00
Tall Case, Smith, J., Oak, Brass Dial, Dentil Cornice, Arched Door, 82 1/4 In. 1840.00
Tall Case, Spalding, Edward, Tombstone Top Arch, Brass Works, Steel Face, 84 In. 3025.00
Tall Case, Stennes, Elmer, Maple, Eagle Finial, 68 In. 1265.00
Tall Case, Strieby, M., Walnut Case, Second Hand, Date, Moon Phase Dial, 87 In. 6050.00
Tall Case, Turner, Poplar, Scalloped Aprons, Brass Works, Painted Face, 82 1/2 In. 2530.00
Tall Case, Urn Finials, Columns Top Corners, Eagle & Shield, c.1830, 104 In. 2195.00
Tall Case, Urn Finials, Mounted Lions' Heads, Angel & Cherub, Germany, 86 In. 3025.00
Tall Case, Victorian, Mahogany, Arched Bonnet, Scrolled Acanthus Leaf, 101 In. 1150.00
Tall Case, Wallenhorst, Mahogany, 95 x 23 1/2 In. 4620.00
Tall Case, Walnut, Broken Arch Pediment, Urn Finials, Arched Door, 1830, 104 In. 1960.00
Tall Case, Walnut, Chester County, Pa., c.1740, 85 1/4 In. 7975.00
Tall Case, Waterbury, 2-Train Movement, Seconds Dial, Glass Door, 1870s, 90 1/2 In. ... 3450.00
Tall Case, Watson, L., Cherry, Inset Panel, Burl Banded Door, Floral Dial, 1809, 92 In. .. 8745.00
Tall Case, Whiting, R., Painted Dial, Seconds Register, Figure On Door, c.1810, 83 In. ... 1840.00
Tall Case, Whiting, R., Painted Face, Wooden Works, Masonic Panel, Pine Case, 91 In. ... 1650.00
Tall Case, Willard, Mahogany, Painted Floral Spandrels, Bonnet, 106 In. 2200.00

Tall Case, Wooden Works, Red Case, 2 Spindle Top, 18th Century, 87 In. 5800.00
Telechron, Electric, Refrigerator Form, Polished Metal, 3 x 4 x 5 In. 185.00
Telechron, Kitchen, Electric, Plastic, Metal, Incised Numerals, 1950s, 6 1/2 In. 48.00
Temple, Repeat Mechanism, Marquetry Fruit Inlay, Biedermeier, 1860s, 17 In. 630.00
Terry, Samuel, Pillar & Scroll Mahogany, Wooden Works, 30-Hour, c.1820, 31x 16 In. 3350.00
Thuret, J., Gilt Bronze Mounted, Engraved Movement, 1720s, 22 1/2 In. 6610.00
Tiffany clocks are listed in the Tiffany category.
Travel, Reichenberg & Co., Silver, Rectangular, George V, England, 1936, 3 1/2 x 3 In. . . 345.00
Turler, World, Table, Hexagon, Brass Case, Malachite Inlay, Bun Feet 8 In. 175.00
Unghans, Regulator, Pine, Half Turned Columns, 2 Lower Finials, Time & Strike, 25 In. . . 130.00
Unghans, Regulator, Pine, Mahogany Veneer, Time & Strike, Germany, 22 x 11 x 7 In. . . . 230.00
Wag-On-Wall, Brass Face, Overall Flowers, Thermometer, France, 19th Century, 56 In. . . 430.00
Wag-On-Wall, Painted Wooden Dial, 8-Day, 19th Century, 13 1/2 x 9 1/4 In. 28.00
Wag-On-Wall, Weight Driven, Time & Strike, Wood Face, Roman, Mahogany, 12 In. 259.00
Wall, Arts & Crafts, Fumed Oak, Brass Numbers & Hands, 8-Day, 13 x 4 1/2 x 26 In. 140.00
Wall, Brass Works, 24-Hour, Diamond Form Hour Markings, Drawer, 10 x 15 3/4 In. 4370.00
Wall, Carved Walnut, Enamel Numerals, Scrolls Sides, Fruit, 20th Century, 28 In. 460.00
Wall, Hanging, Pendulum, 18th Century, 37 In. 358.00
Wall, Louis XVI Style, Mahogany, Lyre Shape, Gilt Brass Mounts, 36 x 12 x 2 In. 345.00
Wall, Mahogany, Domed Glass Door, Half-Column, Arabic Numerals, 13 x 6 x 21 In. 80.00
Wall, Round, White Face, Occupied Japan 250.00
Wall, Tole, Enamel Face, Roman & Arabic, Circular Stepped Design, 1800s, 7 1/4 In. 201.00
Waterbury, Mahogany Veneer, White Face, Alabama, 40 x 16 x 6 In. 784.00
Waterbury, Mantel, Brass Frame, Glass Sides, Mercury Vial Pendulum, 5 1/2 x 11 In. . . . 330.00
Waterbury, Porcelain, Blue & White Floral, Gilt, Time & Strike, 11 1/2 x 13 1/2 x 5 In. . . 66.00
Waterbury, Porcelain, Peasant Woman & Child, 9 1/2 In. 69.00
Waterbury, Regulator, Crystal, Time & Strike, Arabic, Brass, 5 3/4 x 5 1/8 x 9 1/2 In. . . . 320.00
Waterbury, Regulator, Dark Mahogany, 75 x 25 x 10 In. 6720.00
Waterbury, Regulator, No. 66, Oak, Roman Numerals, 58 x 26 x 7 In. 1064.00
Welch, Cary, Mahogany, Roman Numerals, White Face, 21 x 12 x 6 In. 1736.00
Welch, Gerster, Mahogany, 18 x 12 x 6 In. 1904.00
Welch, Patti, Mahogany, Roman Numerals, 19 x 12 x 6 In. 2072.00
Welch, Shelf, 8-Day, Reverse Painting On Lower Panel 88.00
Western Clock Mfg., Dresser, Scrolled Case, Angel Face, Gilt Iron 100.00
Willard, Aaron, Brass Finials, Kidney Shaped Painted Dial, c.1810, 35 1/2 In. 8625.00
William Gilbert & Co., Mantel, Mahogany, Ogee, c.1840, 18 1/2 x 11 3/4 In. 140.00
Wise, Luke, Bracket, Ebony, Pierced Basket Top, Reading, 17th Century, 16 In. 6330.00
World War II, RCAF, Face Centered In Propeller 70.00

CLOISONNE enamel was developed during the tenth century. A glass
enamel was applied between small ribbons of metal on a metal
base. Most cloisonne is Chinese or Japanese. Pieces marked *China* are
twentieth-century examples.

Basin, Enamel, Long Tailed Bird, Branches, Butterflies, Late 19th Century, 10 In. 201.00
Biscuit Jar, Cover, Barrel, Dragons Around Body, Royal Blue, 6 1/2 In. 115.00
Bowl, Blue Flowers, Cream Ground, 20th Century, 12 x 4 1/4 In. 80.00
Bowl, Dragon & Cloud Design, Black Ground, Chinese, Early 20th Century, 8 In. 86.00
Bowl, Flower & Butterfly, Blue Ground, Chinese, 3 3/4 In. 25.00
Box, Card, Flowers, Blue Ground, 19th Century, 6 x 4 1/2 In. 28.00
Box, Cover, Blue Interior, 1920s, 3 1/2 x 5 In. 65.00
Box, Cover, Crane, Pink, Green Ground, 2 1/2 In. 1995.00
Box, Floral Cover, Copper Circles, 4 5/8 x 3 1/8 x 1 3/4 In. 60.00
Box, Insect & Peach Branches, Japan, Early 20th Century, 6 x 4 1/2 In. 259.00
Box, Peacock Standing On Rock Among Flowering Peonies, Celeste Blue, 6 In. 375.00
Box, Stamp, Scrolled Flowers, Cartouche, Hinged Lid, 3 x 2 1/4 x 1 1/4 In. 127.00
Box, White Quail, Removable Wings, 1800, 6 In. 230.00
Buckle, Butterflies & Flowers, Black Ground, 2 Piece 120.00
Candlestick, Pricket, Bell Shape Base, Blue Ground, 19th Century, 14 In. 545.00
Censer, Incense, Deer Shape, Cobalt Blue, Turquoise, Jewel Tones, Chinese, 9 In. 8000.00
Charger, 2 Birds, Blossoming Tree, Carved Ground, Brace Back Hanger, 14 1/2 In. 355.00
Charger, Fans & Flowers, Blue Ground, 12 1/4 In. 185.00
Charger, Goose & Marsh Grass, Blue Ground, 12 In. 185.00
Desk Set, Flowers, Yellow-Green Ground, 4 Sections, Foo Dog Finials, 13 x 7 In. 440.00

Dish, Fishscale, Light Blue, Flowers & Butterflies Interior, 7 1/8 In. 80.00
Figurine, Dragon, Wooden Base, 1930-1940, 19 x 14 In. 315.00
Figurine, Monkey, Hollow Metal, 1920s, 14 1/2 x 12 x 8 In. 585.00
Incense Burner, Peony Cartouches, Blue, White Leaf Ground, Enamel, 5 In. 316.00
Incense Burner, Stylized Hydrangea Flower, Blue Body, 3 Green Leaves, 4 In. 2070.00
Jar, Cover, Flowers, 2 Yellow Dragons, Black Ground, 12 1/2 In. 275.00
Jar, Cover, Flowers, Green Ground, 6 5/8 In. 49.00
Jar, Flowers, Red Ground, 8 1/2 In., Pair 60.00
Jar, White Crane, Green Ground, 3 In. 115.00
Lamp, Flowers, Red Ground, No Shade, 6 1/2 In. 110.00
Planter, Green Dragons, White Ground, Double Handles, 5 1/2 In., Pair 165.00
Plate, Bamboo Birds, Hawk & Dragon Border, Speckled Blue Ground, 12 In., Pair 82.00
Plate, Woman & Child Scene, Enamel, 11 3/4 In. 173.00
Seal Case, Passion Flower, Rectangular, 3 In. 161.00
Snuff Bottle, Fan Form Cartouches, Blue Ground, Stopper, 4 In. 104.00
Snuff Bottle, Flowering Archaic Shape Vessels, White Ground, Chinese 460.00
Snuff Bottle, Pear Shape, Flowers, Scroll Design, Chinese 207.00
Spoon, Scrolling Leaves, White Beading, Agafonov, Russia, 7 3/4 In. 670.00
Sugar, Gilded Ground, Swing Handle, Cyrillic Mark, c.1917, 5 In. 2016.00
Teapot, Butterflies, Flowers, Deep Blue, Black, 19th Century, 4 x 6 In. 88.00
Teapot, Butterflies, Flowers, Mosaic Green Foil Background, 3 x 5 1/2 In. 58.00
Tray, Bird & Flowers, 8 x 10 In. 126.00
Tray, Bird On Rose Bush, Gray Ground, Late 19th Century, 10 3/4 In. 3335.00
Vase, Autumn Leaf & Berry, Cobalt Ground, 7 1/4 In. 115.00
Vase, Bird & Flowering Tree, Blue Ground, 15 1/4 In. 58.00
Vase, Bird & Flowering Tree, Midnight Blue Ground, 9 3/4 In. 115.00
Vase, Bird & Flowers, Blue Ground, 18 1/4 In., Pair 920.00
Vase, Bird & Flowers, Green Aventurine Spotted Ground, 7 In. 345.00
Vase, Bird Design, 4 Panels, Floral Band Around Center, Green Ground, 11 3/4 In. 192.00
Vase, Bird, Flowering Branch, Blue, Sea Green, White Ground, Chinese, 12 In. 604.00
Vase, Bird, Flowers, Tree Bark, On Porcelain, 4 1/2 In. 300.00
Vase, Birds & Flowering Tree, Club Form, 19th Century, 9 In. 29.00
Vase, Blue, Lavender Wisteria Design, White Foil Ground, Signed, 6 In. 144.00
Vase, Blue, Yellow, Brown Dragon, Dark Green Band, 8 3/4 In., Pair 121.00
Vase, Blues, Golds & Reds, Japan, 1800s, 12 In., Pair 1150.00
Vase, Cabinet, Inverted Pear Shape, Green Dragon Design, White, 2 1/2 In. 63.00
Vase, Chrysanthemum, Blue Shaded Ground, 4 3/4 In. 253.00
Vase, Cockerel Among Floral Sprays, Copper, Dark Green Ground, Japan, 10 In. 431.00
Vase, Cone Shape Iris, Blue Ground, 7 1/4 In. 138.00
Vase, Deep Blue Into White, Ando Jubel, 1950s, 9 1/4 In. 495.00
Vase, Dragon Design, Black Ground, 4 7/8 In. 316.00
Vase, Flattened Baluster, Overall Flower Design, Black Ground, Chinese, 14 In. 489.00
Vase, Flowering Branch, Olive Green Ground, Ando Mark, 14 1/2 In. 2070.00
Vase, Flowers, Black Ground, 6 1/8 In. 126.00
Vase, Flowers, Bronze Rim, Foot, 20th Century, 8 1/2 In., Pair 316.00
Vase, Flowers, Chinese, Jingfa Label, 9 1/4 In. 125.00
Vase, Flowers, Red Ground, Akasuka, 7 1/4 In., Pair 545.00
Vase, Flying Bird, Branches, Flowers, Black Ground, Silver, Ando Jubel, 6 3/8 In. 450.00
Vase, Geometric Border, Daisies, Palm Trees, Blue Ground, Kyoto School, 12 1/4 In. 225.00
Vase, Green & White Leaves, White Herring, Goldstone Ground, 7 In. .... .110.00 to 125.00
Vase, Green Crane Design, Blue Ground, Enamel, 6 In. 259.00
Vase, Inverted Pear Shape, Butterfly, Hydrangea, Blue Ground, 5 In. 125.00
Vase, Inverted Pear Shape, Fan Tailed Carp, Sea Grasses, Green Ground, 9 1/4 In. 375.00
Vase, Inverted Pear Shape, Iris, Wisteria, Dragon Panels, Black Ground, 6 In. 125.00
Vase, Inverted Pear Shape, Pink Prunus, Pale Blue Ground, 5 In. 259.00
Vase, Inverted Pear Shape, Prunus, Cream Ground, 2 1/4 In. 115.00
Vase, Iris Design, Black Ground, Baluster Shape, 19th Century, 4 5/8 In., Pair 690.00
Vase, Iris Design, Midnight Blue Ground, 7 In. 230.00
Vase, Palace, Flowering Tree, Hawk, Song Bird, Blue Ground, 69 In., Pair 7360.00
Vase, Palace, Pink, White Chrysanthemum, Blue Field, 69 In. 405.00
Vase, Passion Flower, Bronze, Blue Ground, 19th Century, 6 In. 115.00
Vase, Phoenix & Dragon Lappets, Red Ground, 6 In. 1035.00
Vase, Pink & White Flowers, Birds, Bottle Form, 15 1/2 In. 110.00

Vase, Pink Prunus, Pale Blue Transparent Ground, 7 In. 69.00
Vase, Pink, White Roses, Gold, Green Leaves, Yellow Ground, 1930, 10 In. 175.00
Vase, Pink, Yellow Flowers, Powder Blue Ground, 1900, 7 1/2 In. 460.00
Vase, Red, White & Green Flowers, Blue Ground, Chinese, 9 1/4 In. 185.00
Vase, Red, Yellow Flowers, Pale Blue Ground, 4 1/2 In. 130.00
Vase, Rich Lavender Flowers, Early 20th Century, 7 1/4 In. 720.00
Vase, Roses, Red Foil Ground, Red & White Roses, Green Leaves, Silver Rim, 7 1/2 In. .   425.00
Vase, Seed Form, Flowers, 4 1/2 In. 60.00
Vase, Stylized Phoenix & Dragon Panels, Silver Wirework, Japan, 1890, 12 In. 690.00
Vase, Violet, Blue & White Iris Base, Wisteria Top, Chickadees, 47 In. 935.00
Vase, White & Yellow Flowers, Bird, Red Ground, 7 1/2 In. 295.00
Vase, White Cranes, Blue Field, Purple, Blue Peonies, Pale Blue Ground, 6 In., Pair 690.00
Vase, White Iris Design, Red Ground, 7 In. 115.00
Vase, Wide Rust Band, Small Flowers, Bird In Flight, 8 1/2 In. 210.00
Wall Pocket, Oriental, 6 3/4 In. 196.00
Water Pipe, Lift Cover, Flowers, Enamel, 10 1/2 In. 127.00

CLOTHING of all types is listed in this category. Dresses, hats, shoes, underwear, and more are found here. Other textiles are to be found in the Coverlet, Movie, Quilt, Textile, and World War I and II categories.

Apron, Flowers, Blue, Green, 18 x 18 In. 5.00
Apron, Muslin, White, Slipwork Embroidery, Flowers With Leaves, England, c.1750 . . . .   750.00
Apron, White, Pink, Turquoise, Stylized Pictures, 12 Months, 1958 . . . .   22.00
Belt, Black Karung, Butterfly Buckle, Semiprecious Stones, Judith Leiber, 1980s, 35 In. .   200.00
Belt, Gold Chain Link, 4-In. Snake Twining Buckle, Kenneth Jay Lane 127.00
Belt, Plastic, Interwoven Multicolored, France, 1960s, 4 In. Wide 29.00
Belt, Stretch Fabric, Red, White, Blue, Pair Of Doves, Metal Buckle, Peter Max, 1970 . . .   200.00
Blouse, Silk Twill, Tailored, Geometric Circles, Floral, Pink, Green, Peach, Size 10 . . . . .   345.00
Bodysuit, Black Lace Over Red Satin Leotard, Giorgio Sant'Angelo, American, 1970s . . .   748.00
Boots, Riding, Brown Leather, Wooden Forms Inside, England, 20 In. 245.00
Cape, Cashmere, Gathered Flounce, Welt Seam At Edges, Halston, 1970s 575.00
Chasuble, Priest's Robe, Silk, Gold Metallic Stripe, Hand Sewn 66.00
Chasuble, Priest's Robe, Silk, Metallic Multicolored, Gold & Silver, Mexico 130.00
Cloak, Silk Metallic, Gold, Red, Blue, & Wine Compound Weave, Mexico, c.1870 . . . . . .   110.00
Coat, Evening, Black, Silk, Sequined, Folded Collar, Trumpet Sleeves, France, Size 6 . . .   489.00
Coat, Evening, Ivory Organdy, Pleated Silk, Bill Blass, 1960s, Size 6-8 . . . .   172.00
Coat, Evening, Printed Velvet, Fur Trim, Knee Length, Pauline Trigere, 1970s, Size 6 . . . .   1495.00
Coat, Fawn Wool, Knee Length, Courreges, 1970s, Size 8-10 . . . .   405.00
Coat, Flying, Leather, Collar, Plaid Wool Lining, Button Front, 1930s, Size Large 155.00
Coat, Opera, Silk Velvet, Flared Skirt, Puffed Sleeves, Floor Length, 1940s, Size 6-8 . . . .   200.00
Coat, Red & Gray Plaid Tweed, Single Breasted, Harris, 1960s, Size 6 . . . .   230.00
Coat, Shearling, A-Line, Peacock, High Fur Collar, Oscar De La Renta, 1980s, Size 6-8 . .   345.00
Coat, Vermont Militia, Epaulets, 40 Brass Buttons, Ragged, Moth Eaten, 1830 . . . .   2420.00
Corset, Dr. Warner Coraline Health, Linen, Lace, Front Clasp, c.1881, Size 32 In. 460.00
Dalmatic, Priest's Robe, Metallic Gold Thread Strips, Floral Ground, 1850-1900 . . . .   220.00
Dalmatic, Priest's Robe, Silk, Metallic, Brown, Gold & Silver Weave 66.00
Dress, Black Wool Twill, Cap Sleeves, Courreges, 1960s, Size 2 . . . .   345.00
Dress, Brown Damask, Embroidered Leaves, Ruffled Collar, 1890s, 2 Piece 630.00
Dress, Chemise, Black Chiffon, Black & Blue Beaded, Sleeveless, 1920s, Size 10 . . . . . .   316.00
Dress, Cocktail, Black Silk Satin, Elbow Sleeves, Christian Dior, 1959, Size 8-10 . . . . . .   172.00
Dress, Cocktail, Black Silk, 3/4 Raglan Sleeves, Cummerbund Waist, Norell, 1955 . . . . . .   575.00
Dress, Cocktail, Black Silk, Polka Dots, Sleeveless, Pierre Balmain, 1970s, Size 8 . . . . . .   172.00
Dress, Cocktail, Black Tulle, Cap Sleeves, Taffeta Waistband, P. Balmain, 1950s, Size 4 . .   546.00
Dress, Cocktail, Flesh Color, Lace, Gold Sequins, Flowers, Bill Blass, 1950s, Size 4-6 . . .   517.00
Dress, Cocktail, Knit, A-Line, Knee Length, Turtleneck, Pauline Trigere, 1950s, Size 8 . . .   172.00
Dress, Cocktail, Metallic Pattern, Peasant Type, Mollie Parnis, 1970s, Size 6 . . . .   47.00
Dress, Cocktail, Peach Voile, Gold, Orange Beads, Sleeveless, Malcolm Starr, Size 6 . . . .   230.00
Dress, Cocktail, Silk, Blue, Sleeveless, Sequins, Rhinestone Buttons, 1960 . . . .   1035.00
Dress, Disco, Silver & White, A-Line, Sleeveless, Bead Fringe, Malcolm Starr, Size 6 . . .   862.00
Dress, Evening, Beaded Chiffon, Ankle Length, Paul Louis Orrier, 1980s, Size 4 . . . .   745.00
Dress, Evening, Beaded Chiffon, Floor Length, Empire, Malcolm Starr, 1960s, Size 6 . . .   460.00
Dress, Evening, Brocade, Fur Trim, A-Line Skirt, Oscar De La Renta, 1970s, Size 6-8 . . .   316.00

Dress, Evening, Satin, Sleeveless, Bloused Top, Starburst, House Of Worth, Size 6 . . . . . .   1285.00
Dress, Evening, Silk Gauze, Black Teardrop Plastic, Silk Lining, 1960s, Size 6 . . . .   575.00
Dress, Evening, Silk Jersey, Grecian Halter Top, Norman Norell, 1950s, Size 4-6 . . . .   517.00
Dress, Evening, Silk, Gold Stripes, Roses Neck, Straps, Callot Soeurs, 1930s, Size 6 . . . .   690.00
Dress, Evening, Taffeta, Velvet, Peasant Type, Yves Saint Laurent, 1976, Size 6-8 . . . .   460.00
Dress, Girl's, Red Silk Satin & Moire, Waterfall Drapery Skirt, Victorian, 1880 . . . .   750.00
Dress, Mini, Orange Beads, A-Line, Silk Lining, 1960s, Size 8-10 . . . .   230.00
Dress, Navy Silk, Allover Stars, Sailor Collar, Bow, Lord & Taylor, 1945, Size 8 . . . .   172.00
Dress, Pink, Fringed, Empire, V Neck, Long Sleeves, Emilio Pucci, 1970s, Size 4-6 . . . . .   690.00
Dress, Shirtwaist, Black Silk Faille, Front Satin Bow, Balenciaga, 1950s, Size 10 . . . .   375.00
Dress, Silk Crepe, Blue & Black, Sleeveless, Japanese Type Embroidery, 1920s 595.00
Dress, Silk, Flowers, White, Knife Pleats, Strapless, Wrapped, Christian Dior, 1950s 500.00
Dress, Tea, White Silk Net, Geometric & Floral Beaded, 1915, Size 2 . . . .   430.00
Dress, Wedding, Graduating Rows Of Chantilly Lace, Spaghetti Straps, Jacket, 1939 . . . .   490.00
Dress, White Cotton, Lace Bodice & Wide Ruffle, Long Sleeves, 1880 . . . .   165.00
Dress, Wrap, Floral Silk, V Neck, Valentino, 1980s, Size 6-8 . . . .   173.00
Girdle, White, Mold 'n Hold Zipper, Blue Metallic Tube, Playtex, 1950s, Medium 55.00
Gloves, Black Suede, Silver Bugle Beads, Sequins, Daniel Swarovski, 1980s, Size 7 . . . . .   277.00
Gloves, Leather, Brown Kidskin, Elbow Length 25.00
Gloves, Leather, White Doeskin, Pink Embroidery, England, 8 In. 15.00
Gloves, Opera, White Leather, Pearl Button Closure, 22 In. 25.00
Handkerchief, Lace Trim, 1930s, Unused 10.00
Hat, Black, Horsehair Plume, Rhinestones, Flo Raye, New York, Size 22 . . . .   35.00
Hat, Clasped Hands Shape, Satin, Nails, Ring, Cigarette Holder, Bes-Ben, 1940s 2530.00
Hat, Ponytail, Red Beaded Skullcap, Ostrich Feathers, J. Suzanne Talbot, France, 1950s . .   863.00
Hat, Sailor, Straw, Man's 15.00
Hat, Shell, Faux Pearls, Shells & Leaves, Net, Bes-Ben, 1940s 172.00
Hat, Strap On Front, Richfield Products 33.00
Hat, Sun, Barbie, Straw, Woven, Green, Teal, Gray, White, Chiffon Tie, c.1962, 14 In. . . .   83.00
Hat, Top Hat, Strap, Leather Case, Brush, 20 x 13 1/2 x 12 In. 100.00
Hat, White Flowers, Plastic Leaves, Fitted, Bes-Ben, 1940s 230.00
Hatband, Leather, Silver Coin Design, 27 In. 125.00
Jacket, Baseball, Silver Sequins, Zipper Front, Bishop Sleeves, Halston, 1980s, Size 6 . . .   230.00
Jacket, Black Velvet, Mid-Torso, Leg-Of-Mutton Sleeves, Victorian, 1890s, Size 8 . . . . . .   300.00
Jacket, Bolero, Allover Gray Sequins, Short Sleeves, 1940s, Size 6 . . . .   70.00
Jacket, Bowling, Jim's Brighton Ave. Cafe Champs 75, Bowling Pins, c.1974, Size 48 . . .   30.00
Jacket, Brown Goatskin, Side Laces, Levi Strauss, 1930s 1250.00
Jacket, Buckskin, Fringed, Patch Pocket, Stag Button, Scalloped Edge, 19th Century 518.00
Jacket, Child's, Fur, Double-Breasted, Red Satin Lining, Ben Kahn, 1960s, Size 2-3 . . . . .   92.00
Jacket, Riding, Wool, Black, Gigot Sleeves, Fitted Collar, Schreiber & Kerr, 1895 . . . . . .   210.00
Jacket, Satin, Black, Cutaway Front, Button Waist, Soutache Braid, France, c.1890 . . . . . .   316.00
Jacket, Uniform, H.P. Hood & Sons Dairy Products 175.00
Jacket, Wool Crepe, Plum, Rhinestone Buttons, Diagonal Pleats, Billie Dugan 400.00
Kimono, Child's, Brocade, Gold Threads, Dragon Design, Early 20th Century 258.00
Maniple, Church Arm Scarf, Metallic Blue, Green, Silver & Gold Weave, Mexico 33.00
Mittens, Baby's, Leather, Red, Flannel Lining, Washington Gloves, Size 2 . . . .   69.00
Mittens, Child's, Red Ryder, Includes 6 Trading Cards, Uncut, 1952 . . . .   100.00
Muff, Teddy Bear, 1920s 375.00
Nightgown, White, Late 19th Century 100.00
Overcoat, Leopard Pattern, Black Silk Trim, Knee Length, Lilli Ann, 1950s, Size 6-8 . . . .   345.00
Pants, Sports, Plaid, Wool, Green, Brown, Tan, Black, L.L. Bean, c.1898 . . . .   575.00
Petticoat, Drawers, Button Back, Embroidered, Lace Insert, Ribbon Trim, Ivory, c.1890 .   259.00
Pocket, Floral Sprig, Black Ground, Loomed Belt, Oval, Cotton, c.1840, 9 x 7 3/4 In. . . .   374.00
Raincoat, Brown Plastic, A-Line, Knee Length, Pierre Cardin, 1960s, Size 8 . . . .   635.00
Robe, Brocade, Celadon, Silk, Embroidered Flowers, Continental 104.00
Robe, Canterbury Shaker Sister's, Wool Broadcloth, The Dorothy, Hart & Shepard 1150.00
Robe, Silk Brocade, Embroidered Longevity Emblems, Birds, Flowers, 19th Century 488.00
Robe, Silk, Black Embroidered, Flower Sprays, China, 19th Century 633.00
Robe, Silk, Black Embroidered, Flowers, Peaches, Butterflies, China 805.00
Robe, Silk, Summer, Gold Threads, Pearls Amidst Dense Cloud Scrolls, Blue 1495.00
Robe, Winter, Embroidered Flowers, Fur Lined, Early 20th Century 316.00
Robe, Yellow Silk Embroidered, Flying Crane Amidst Clouds, Blue, Gold, 1900 . . . .   575.00

Scarf, Blue & Green Flowers, Silk Twill, Vera, Ladybug, 31 x 31 In. . . . . *Illus* 9.00
Scarf, Burgundy Border, Jungle Flora & Fauna, Square, Gucci, 1984, 34 In. 57.00
Scarf, Eagle With Shield & Stars, Silk Twill, Echo, 31 x 31 In. . . . . *Illus* 100.00
Scarf, Holland, Michigan, Plain Weave Silk, 28 x 28 In. . . . . *Illus* 50.00
Scarf, Lime Green Roses, Silk Crepe, Vera, Ladybug, 63 x 13 3/4 In. . . . . *Illus* 50.00
Scarf, Silk Twill, Gold Crowns, Arabesques, Navy Blue Ground, Hermes, Paris, 1960s . . . 115.00
Scarf, Silk, Circles In Square Design, Pale Blue, Blue Fringe, Vasarely, 1969 . . . . 250.00
Scarf, Silk, White, Black Border, Zodiac Design, Earth Center, Peter Max, 1970s 150.00
Scarf, Yellow Abstract Design, Pin On Cream Ground, Emilo Pucci, 1960s, 28 In. 235.00
Shawl, Multicolored, Wool, Box, Cartier, 1980s, 54 x 54 In. 115.00
Shawl, Paisley, Allover Cone Design, Red, Green, Blue, Fringed, 64 x 66 In. 345.00
Shawl, Paisley, Allover Design, 131 x 61 In. 275.00
Shawl, Paisley, Black Center, Red, Black, Blue, Ivory Arabesques, 72 x 62 In. 201.00
Shawl, Paisley, Black Center, Red, Black, Blue, White Paneled Border, Fringed, 62 In. . . . 230.00
Shawl, Paisley, Plain Center, Blue, Red Cone, Ivory Wool Ground, 122 x 58 In. 287.00
Shawl, Paisley, Woven, Allover Boteh Design, Black Ground, 68 x 68 In. 115.00
Shawl, Silk, Black, Pastel Flowers, Gold Overlay, Knotted Fringe, France, 1930s 747.50
Shoes, Baby's, Leather, c.1915-1925, 3 In. 45.00
Shoes, Baby's, Leather, Laces, c.1900, 5 1/8 In. 40.00
Shoes, Dress, Black Leather, Bow, Florsheim, Late 1950s, Size 6A, 2-In. Heels 32.00
Shoes, Dress, Oxford, 2-Tone, Oxblood Leather, Gray Linen Insert, 1950s, Size 8 . . . . 110.00
Shoes, High Heel, Rhinestone, Ankle Strap, Yves Saint Laurent, 1970, Size 7 . . . . 155.00
Shoes, High Top, Tan Wool, Black Leather Bottom, 9 Buttons, 2-In. Heel, c.1912 . . . . 375.00
Shoes, High Top, Woman's, Tan Twill, Black Patent Leather, 9 Buttons, I. Miller, 1912 . . . 325.00
Shoes, Men's, Primitive, Mass., 18th Century 650.00
Shoes, Silk, Brass Buckles, Worn By Joanna Kingsbury At Her Wedding In 1784 . . . . 1850.00
Shoes, Woman's, Embroidered Green & Red Wool, Lined, Square Toe, 1800s 950.00
Skirt, Maxi, Velveteen, A-Line, Geometric Pattern, Emilio Pucci, 1970s, Size 6 . . . . 345.00
Skirt, Silk, Green, Black Embroidered, Satin Stitch, Flowers 230.00
Skirt, Silk, Panels Of Flowers, Satin Stitch, Pink Ground 431.00
Socks, Golf, Gray Checkered, Box 18.00
Stole, Mink, 4 Pelt, 1920s 48.00
Stole, Silk Brocade, Gray, Blue, Green, Rust & White, Japan, 1778 . . . . 130.00
Suit, Black Wool, Waist Length Jacket, A-Line Skirt, Pauline Trigere, 1960s, Size 8 . . . . . 405.00
Suit, Ultrasuede, Green, Hip Length, Zip Jacket, Halston, 1970s, Size 10 . . . . 230.00
Suit, Wool Twill, Navy, Thigh Jacket, Box Pleats, Chanel, 1980s, Size 6-8 . . . . 173.00
Suit, Wool, Purple, Fitted Jacket, C Buttons, Chanel, 1980s, Size 6 . . . . 202.00
Suit, Wool, Woman's, Emilio Pucci, 1960s, 2 Piece 275.00
Surcoat, Robe, Dark Blue Embroidered, Gold Thread, Double Gourd 230.00
Swimsuit, Blue Sequins, Strapless, Heart Neck, Cole Of California, c.1940, Size 34 . . . . . 315.00
Swimsuit, Gold Lame, Fan Pleated Bust, Shirred, Elasticized, Alix Of Miami, 1950s 57.50
Swimsuit, Silver Lame Beauty Queen, Diamond Cutout, DeWeese Designs, Size 8 . . . . . . 70.00
Swimsuit, Woman's, Topless, Rudi Gernreich, 1967 . . . . 650.00

Clothing, Scarf, Blue & Green Flowers,
Silk Twill, Vera, Ladybug, 31 x 31 In.

Clothing, Scarf, Eagle With Shield & Stars,
Silk Twill, Echo, 31 x 31 In.

Clothing, Scarf, Holland,
Michigan, Plain Weave
Silk, 28 x 28 In.

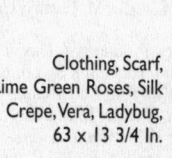

Clothing, Scarf,
Lime Green Roses, Silk
Crepe, Vera, Ladybug,
63 x 13 3/4 In.

Uniform, Royal Canadian Mounted Police, Wool Blouse, Hat, Belt, Boots, 1960s	510.00
Vest, Silk Brocade, Dragon & Cloud Design	173.00
Wallet, Barbie, Carryall, Clutch, Patent Vinyl, Light Blue, Snap Closure, c.1961, 7 In.	55.00
Wallet, Barbie, Ponytail, Patent Vinyl, Red, Snap Closure, c.1962, 3 1/2 x 4 In.	49.00
Weskit, Child's, Homespun, Brown Sawtooth, Dotted Stripe, Late 1700s	55.00

CLUTHRA glass is a two-layered glass with small air pockets that form white spots. The Steuben Glass Works of Corning, New York, made it in 1920. Kimball Glass Company of Vineland, New Jersey, made Cluthra from about 1925. Victor Durand signed some pieces with his name. Related items are listed in the Steuben category.

Vase, Black, No. 2683, 6 3/8 In.	1095.00
Vase, Blown, Lavender, Signed, Steuben, 8 In.	1568.00
Vase, Green, Urn Shape, 6 1/4 In.	920.00
Vase, Light Green, Signed, Carder, 10 1/4 In.	690.00

COALPORT ware has been made by the Coalport Porcelain Works of England from 1795 to the present time. Early pieces were unmarked. About 1810–1825 the pieces were marked with the name *Coalport* in various forms. Later pieces also had the name *John Rose* in the mark. The crown mark has been used with variations since 1881. The date 1750 is printed in some marks, but it is not the date the factory started. Some pieces are listed in Indian Tree.

BONE CHINA
COALPORT
MADE IN ENGLAND
EST. 1750

Dessert Service, Floral Sprays, Green Border, Gilt Edge Claret, 1830, 60 Piece	3600.00
Dessert Service, Gilt, Gray Border, Gilt Edged Rim, Handles, 1835, 20 Piece	1920.00
Figurine, Britomartis Inveigling Amoret, Josh. Pitts, Parian, 1851	3038.00
Plate, Scrolled Rims, Floral Cartouches, Apple Green, 9 In., 12 Piece	460.00
Plate Set, Cobalt Blue, Gilt Border, Gilt Leaf & Scrolls, 10 1/2 In., 6 Piece	150.00
Vase, Cover, Bone China, Portrait Of Rider On Horseback, 1976, 12 1/4 In.	172.00
Vase, Garniture, Gilt Bronze Mounted, 2 Handles, Signed, 13 In.	690.00

COBALT BLUE glass was made using oxide of cobalt. The characteristic bright dark blue identifies it for the collector. Most cobalt glass found today was made after the Civil War. There was renewed interest in the dark blue glass in the late 1930s and dinnerwares were made.

Goblet, Cognac, Enameled Gold Design, 5 1/2 In.	10.00
Hat, Sunburst In Square, 3-Piece Mold, Early 19th Century, 2 1/4 x 2 1/2 In.	719.00
Match Holder, Pipe Shape	60.00
Mug, Alberta Treasury Branch, Celebrating 60 Years, 3 5/8 In.	8.00
Mug, Blown, Tooled Rim, Applied Handle, Pontil, 1865, 3 5/8 In.	575.00
Salt, Footed, Pontil, 1870, 2 1/4 In.	130.00
Sugar, Blown Cover, Polished Pontil, Continental, 1880, 3 3/4 In.	305.00
Tumbler, Whiskey, Flute, Pontil, 2 1/4 In.	120.00
Tumbler, Whiskey, Souvenir, Idaho, Winter Landscape, 2 In.	10.00
Vase, Drape, Trumpet Neck, Globular, 9 3/4 In.	1380.00

COCA-COLA was first served in 1886 in Atlanta, Georgia. It was advertised through signs, newspaper ads, coupons, bottles, trays, calendars, and even lamps and clocks. Collectors want anything with the word *Coca-Cola*, including a few rare products, like gum wrappers and cigar bands. The famous trademark was patented in 1893, the *Coke* mark in 1945. Many modern items and reproductions are being made.

Bank Check, 1930s	2.25
Bank Check, Art Deco Design, 1940s	2.00
Banner, Edgar Bergen & Charlie McCarthy, Canvas, 42 x 60 In., 1950s	1210.00
Blotter, 1953, 4 x 8 In.	6.60
Blotter, 58 Million Bottles Produced A Day, 1957, 4 x 8 In.	6.60
Blotter, Drink Coca-Cola I Think It's Swell, Lithograph, 1942	18.00
Blotter, Elf Digging Bottle From Snowbank, 1952, 3 1/2 x 7 1/2 In.	15.00
Bookmark, Fishtail Logo, Plastic, In Package, 1950s, 3 In.	6.50
Bookmark, Opera Singer Hilda Clark, c.1904, 6 1/4 In.	522.00
Bottle, Cincinnati, Ohio, Amber, Tooled Crown Top, 1895-1915, 7 1/2 In.	225.00
Bottle, Display, Plastic Cap, Green Glass, 1970s	38.00
Bottle, Grand Opening Springfield, 1976	55.00
Bottle, Seltzer, Acid Etching, Superior, Wisconsin, Original Top	1045.00
Bottle, Somersworth, N.H., Christmas, 1923	80.00
Bottle, Syrup, Drink Coca-Cola, White Pyro, Tooled Mouth, Tin Cap, c.1915, 11 1/2 In.	530.00
Bottle, Wilkes-Barre, Blue Aqua, Crown Top, Stars On Shoulder, 6 Oz.	25.00
Bottle Cap, 1950s	2.00
Bottle Cap, Cork, 1920s	7.00
Bottle Rack, Wire & Metal, 3 Tiers, 1950s	320.00
Bowl, Pretzel, Aluminum, 3 Coke Bottle Legs, 1930s	100.00
Bridge Tally, Compliments Of Coca-Cola Bottling Company, LaGrange, Georgia	3.00
Bucket, Drink Coca-Cola In Bottles, Steel, 12 In.	154.00
Calendar, 1915, Woman With Hat & Parasol, Frame, 12 1/2 x 31 1/2 In.	1100.00
Calendar, 1917, World War I Girl, Sitting, Frame, 11 1/2 x 30 1/2 In.	1650.00
Calendar, 1919, Knitting Girl, Holding Bottle Of Coke, 27 1/2 x 13 In.	635.00
Calendar, 1923, Flapper Girl, Holding Bottle, 12 x 24 In.	201.00
Calendar, 1925, Girl At Party, White Fur Stole, Frame, History Page	3520.00
Calendar, 1935, Boy & His Dog, Fishing, Norman Rockwell, 12 x 25 In.	172.00
Calendar, 1937, Boy With Fishing Pole & Dog, N.C. Wyeth, Frame, 25 In.	550.00
Calendar, 1944, Flight Attendant, Holding Bottle	413.00
Calendar, 1947, Woman Holding Skis, Frame, 8 In.	190.00
Calendar, 1954, Santa With Coke	74.00
Calendar, Girl Carrying Tray & 4 Bottles	110.00
Calendar, Woman Wearing Cap, With Bottle	187.00
Can, Syrup, Designed For Cruise Ship, 1940s, 1 Gal.	275.00
Chalkboard, Embossed, Tin, 27 1/4 x 19 1/4 In.	135.00
Clock, Drink Coca-Cola, Walnut, Sidney, 69 x 28 x 10 In.	4200.00
Clock, Plastic, Metal, Light-Up, 37 1/4 x 24 x 3 1/2 In.	300.00
Clock, Regulator, Coca-Cola Delicious Drink 5 Cents Refreshing, Ornate, 38 In.	517.00
Clock, Regulator, Wooden, 31 x 15 In.	275.00
Clock, Selectoclock, Wooden Frame, Selected Devices Co., 1939, 16 x 16 In.	258.00
Cooler, 4 Tin Embossed Signs, English & French Lettering, Wooden Lids, 35 In.	495.00
Cooler, Cavalier, 1940s	400.00
Cooler, Picnic, Cavalier, Inner Tray, 1950s	303.00
Crate, 24 Full Bottles, Wooden, Masonite, 1940s	413.00
Dart Board, Drink Coca-Cola, 4 Red Circles, Milton Bradley, 1950s	75.00
Dispenser, Porcelain, 2 Sides, 1950s, 27 x 28 In.	1650.00
Display, Girl At The Fountain, The Pause That Refreshes, 3-Dimensional, 1929	12100.00
Display, No After-Lunch Drowsiness, Easel, Die Cut, 1933	3740.00
Display, Sign Of Good Taste, Cardboard, 1956, 16 x 27 In.	500.00
Door Pull, Bottle Form, Aluminum, 1940s	358.00
Door Pull, Delicious, Refreshing, Bakelite Handle, Tin, Box, 1930s-1940s, 3 x 12 In.	605.00
Door Push, Drink Coca-Cola, Be Really Refreshed, 2 Piece, Tin, 1950s, 4 x 8 In.	825.00
Door Push, Refresh Yourself, Drink Coca-Cola In Bottles, 2 Piece, Tin, 1950s, 6 In.	1100.00
Door Push, Refresh Yourself, Drink Coca-Cola, 2 Piece, Porcelain, 1950s, 4 x 8 In.	1375.00
Door Push, Thanks Call Again, Porcelain, Canada, 1950s, 4 x 11 1/2 In.	660.00
Earrings, Classic Formula, Pierced	8.00

Ice Pick, Bottle Opener, Wooden Handle, Metal Pick, 10 1/2 In. 25.00
Ice Pick, Drink Coca-Cola, Delicious & Refreshing, Wooden Handle, 1960s, 8 In. 19.50
Jar, Coca-Cola Chewing Gum, Crystal, 1903-1905 .... 1430.00
Keg, Syrup, Wooden, 1939, 10 Gal. 155.00
Kick Plate, Bottle, Arrow, 1950s 93.00
Kit, Promotion, Santa Holiday, 1950s 110.00
Lighter, Bottle Shape, Plastic, Metal Cap, 1953, 2 1/2 x 3/4 In. 25.00
Menu, Cap & Wings Each End, Tin, 1950s, 14 x 60 In. 2530.00
Menu Board, Sport Characters Adorn Sides Of Menu Board, 34 1/2 x 31 In. 25.00
Mirror, Purse, Green, Women On Beach, Delicious & Refreshing, Atlanta, 1918 .... 10.00
Pin Set, 100 Cloisonne Pins, Centennial 373.00
Poster, Circus, 49 x 32 In. 9350.00
Poster, Hello Refreshment, Woman Exiting Pool, Cardboard, c.1939, 29 x 50 In. 247.00
Poster, So Good With Food, Vertical, 1952 .... 908.00
Poster, The Best Of Taste, Vertical, 30 x 50 In. 935.00
Punchboard, Win A 6 Bottle Carton, 1940s, 4 x 5 In. 4.50
Radio, Cooler Shape, Red, White Lettering, 1950s, 12 1/2 x 8 x 9 In. ....506.00 to 600.00
Sheet Music, Coca-Cola Girl, 1927 .... 200.00
Sign, 6-Pack, Embossed Tin, 6 Bottles, Die Cut, 1960s, 36 In. 798.00
Sign, Bottle Shape, Embossed, 30 x 108 In. 1150.00
Sign, Bottle Shape, Tin, Die Cut, 1960, 20 x 72 In. 518.00
Sign, Bottle, Ice Cold, Die Cut Arrow, Hanging Bracket, Bottle, 2 Sides, 1936, 23 In. 2640.00
Sign, Bottle, Metal, 8 x 2 1/2 In. 55.00
Sign, Bottle, Tin, Embossed, Die Cut, December 25, 1923, 39 In. 467.00
Sign, Cap Shape, Tin, Silkscreen, Red Background, 24 In. Diam. 374.00
Sign, Cap, 1960s, 16 In. 251.00
Sign, Coca-Cola, Plastic Fishtail Background, Neon, Box, 28 x 15 In. 330.00
Sign, Coke Bottle, Tin, Die Cut, 1952, 72 In. 550.00
Sign, Countertop, Glass & Wood, Silver Reverse Paint On Crest, 1948, 18 x 12 In. 715.00
Sign, Enjoy Coca-Cola, Neon, Box, 27 x 15 In. 385.00
Sign, Enjoy That Refreshing, Bottle At Bottom, 1960s, 54 x 18 In. 330.00
Sign, Gas Today, Tin, 20 x 28 In. 4950.00
Sign, Lunch, Cap Sign, Box, April, 1950, 22 x 18 In. 4400.00
Sign, Lunch, Porcelain, 1950s, 28 x 26 In. 2200.00
Sign, Pause That Refreshes, Cardboard, Cutout, 1937, 14 x 34 In. 220.00
Sign, Slow School Zone, Drink Coca-Cola, Policeman, Shield, Cast Iron, 1950s 1300.00
Sign, Take Home A Carton, 8-Bottle Carton, 1960s, 20 x 28 In. 4000.00
Sign, Things Go Better With Coke, Bottle, Tin, 1960s, 54 x 18 In. 385.00
Sign, Things Go Better, Tin, Square, Square, 1960s, 24 In. 319.00
Sign, Tin, Red Background, Bottle, 11 In. 20.00
Sign, Woman Preparing Buffet On 1 Side, Family Picnic On Other, 50 x 29 In. 172.00
Stadium Vendor, 20 To 25 Bottle, 1950s 660.00
Straws, Graphics On 4 Sides, 1930s, 8 1/2 In. 638.00
Syrup Barrel, Paper Label, Ingredients State Coca Leaves, 5 Gal. 325.00
Thermometer, Bottle Shape, 7 In. 40.00
Thermometer, Bottle Shape, c.1953, 16 3/4 In. 55.00
Thermometer, Bottle Shape, Tin, Late 1950s, 17 In. 80.00
Thermometer, Cap Top, Tin, 1950s, 9 In. 413.00
Thermometer, Plastic, 1980s 35.00
Thermometer, Red Ground, Tin, 16 x 6 3/4 In. 120.00
Thermometer, Red Rock, 26 In. 125.00
Tip Tray, 1901, Hilda With Rose, Coke Glass On Table, 6 In. 1980.00
Tip Tray, 1909, Exhibition Girl, St. Louis World's Fair, 4 1/2 x 6 In. ....1208.00 to 1322.00
Tip Tray, 1910, Coca-Cola Girl, 4 1/4 x 6 In. 345.00
Tip Tray, 1913, Hamilton King Girl, 4 1/4 x 6 In. 80.00
Tip Tray, 1914, Betty, 4 1/4 x 6 In. 51.00
Tip Tray, 1916, Elaine, 4 1/4 x 6 In. 86.00
Tip Tray, 1920, Golfer Girl, 4 1/4 x 6 In. 63.00
Toy, Marble, Black, Red 6.00
Toy, Marble, White, Red 6.00
Toy, Marbles, Paper Label 55.00
Toy, Truck, Bottles, Plastic, Marx, Box, 10 In. 500.00
Toy, Truck, Cast Iron, 12 1/2 In. 375.00

Toy, Truck, Die Cast, England, 1950s, 5 1/4 In. 145.00
Toy, Truck, Yellow Plastic, Gull Wing Doors, 6 Cases, Marx, 10 3/4 In. 238.00
Toy, Yo-Yo, Kooky Kap, Crimped Like Bottle Cap, 1950s-Early 1960s 32.00
Tray, 1916, Elaine, Yellow Dress, Holding Glass Of Coke, 19 x 8 1/2 In. .... .230.00 to 522.00
Tray, 1923, Flapper Girl, Drinking Coca-Cola 237.00
Tray, 1927, Soda Jerk, American Art Works, 13 1/4 x 10 1/2 In. 345.00
Tray, 1933, Frances Dee, 13 1/4 x 10 1/2 In. 180.00
Tray, 1938, Girl In Yellow Hat, 13 1/4 x 10 1/2 In. 225.00
Tray, 1939, Springboard Girl, 13 1/4 x 10 1/2 In. 175.00
Tray, 1940, Sailor Girl, 10 1/2 x 13 1/4 In. .... .100.00 to 200.00
Tray, 1941, Skater Girl, 13 1/4 x 10 1/2 In. 175.00
Tray, 1942, 2 Girls At Car, 13 1/4 x 10 1/2 In. 605.00
Tray, 1950, Menu Girl, 13 1/4 x 10 1/2 In. 75.00
Tray, 1963, Christmas, Green, Santa Reading Child's Note, Coke Bottle, 14 x 10 In. 40.00

COFFEE GRINDERS, or coffee mills, of home size were first made about
1894. They lost favor by the 1930s. Large floor-standing or counter-
model coffee grinders were used in the nineteenth-century country
store. The renewed interest in fresh-ground coffee has produced many
modern electric and hand grinders, and reproductions of the old styles
are being made.

American Beauty, Cast Iron, Tin Cup, 12 In. 825.00
Arcade, Dovetailed Wooden Upper Bin, Sliding Window, Wall Mount, 15 In. 120.00
Beveled Base & Top, Drawer, Wooden Pull, Pewter Hopper, Iron Crank, 9 1/4 In. 137.00
Cast Iron, Ceramic Knob, Marbleized Glaze, Drawer, 5 7/8 In. 82.00
Charles Parker Co., No. 700, Double Wheel, Meriden, Conn., Pat. Mar. 9, 1897 .... 775.00
Enterprise, 2 Wheels On Base, Drawer, Oct. 21, 1873, 15 In. 672.00
Enterprise, Black Paint, Wooden Base, 12 In. 287.00
Enterprise, Countertop, Double Wheel, Eagle Finial, c.1900, 25 1/4 In. 440.00
Enterprise, Double Wheel, Decals, Porcelain Pull, Base Drawer, 24 3/4 In. 385.00
Enterprise, No. 00, 2 Wheel, Cast Iron, Original Paint & Decals, 12 x 9 In. 1595.00
Enterprise, No. 9, Cast Iron, Red Paint, Decal, 36 In. 4750.00
Enterprise, No. 16, Seal Of Award Given By Columbian Exposition Of 1893 .... 4125.00
Enterprise, Original Paint, Double Wheel, Cast Iron, Wooden Base, 7 x 12 In. 833.00
Enterprise, Red, Flower Decals, Cast Iron, Philadelphia, c.1873, 24 In. 770.00
Enterprise, Wooden Base, Dovetailed Drawer, Brass Eagle Finial, Painted, 16 In. 605.00
Favorite, No. 7, Cast Iron, Hinged Lid, Wall Mount, Late 1800s 160.00
Fruitwood, Pine, Dovetailed, Drawer, Tin Hopper, Iron Crank, 10 1/2 In. 275.00
Iron, Wall Mount, Clip-On Cup, c.1890, 8 In. 160.00
John Wright, Cast Iron, Tabletop, Painted, Red, Wrightsville, Penn., 1900s, 11 In. 230.00
Landers, Frary & Clark, No. 30 .... 1300.00
Parker, Chuck Wagon, No. 70 .... 125.00
Parker, No. 900, Cast Iron, 36 In. 1200.00
Pine, Brown Alligatored Finish, Drawer, Fluted Iron Hopper, 7 x 7 x 9 1/2 In. 165.00
Woodruff & Edwards, Cast Iron, No. 42, Decal Of Eagle Holding Banner 2130.00

Paper collectibles like sports cards, trading cards, old newspapers, prints, or books should be kept in an area that is not too wet, not too dry. Experts say 50% humidity is best, so if you live near an ocean you need a dehumidifier and if you live in a desert you need a humidifier.

Coin-Operated Machine, Gambling,
Knockout, Automated, 1930

COIN SPOT is a glass pattern that was named by the collectors for the spots resembling coins, which are part of the glass. Colored, clear, and opalescent glass was made with the spots. Many companies used the design in the 1870–1890 period. It is so popular that reproductions are still being made.

Syrup, Handle, Pewter Top, 6 1/4 In. 175.00
Vase, Satin, White, Gourd Shape, Tall Neck, 7 1/2 In. 66.00

COIN-OPERATED MACHINES of all types are collected. The vending machine is an ancient invention dating back to 200 B.C. when holy water was dispensed in a coin-operated vase. Smokers in seventeenth-century England could buy tobacco from a coin-operated box. It was not until after the Civil War that the technology made modern coin-operated games and vending machines plentiful. Slot machines, arcade games, and dispensers are all collected.

Arcade, Electricity Is Life, 1 Cent, Cast Iron, Glass Front, 13 x 19 In. 2530.00
Bowling, Gatter Ten Pin, Oak, Pays Out Cigars, c.1920, 8 x 9 In. 719.00
Candy, Stollwerck's Chocolate & Gum, Oak, 1 Cent, 32 In. 3565.00
Cigarette, Lights, Masterbilt, Copper Plated, 2 1/2 In. 85.00
Cigarette, Radio Shape, Metal, Perpetual Calendar, Pat. 1929, 5 In. 85.00
Cigarette, Woman, Turban, Push Plunger, Wood, 1920s, 6 In. 450.00
Coin Changer, McGill, 4 Coin Slots, High Speed, 1920s, 6 x 5 1/4 In. 99.00
Collar Buttons, 5 Cent, 8 Selections, c.1905, 11 x 7 In. 1668.00
Collar Buttons, Arrow, Curved Glass Case, Velvet Interior, 14 In. 805.00
Football, 1 Cent, Chester Pollard Amusement Co., 44 x 70 In. 1870.00
Gambling, Knockout, Automated, 1930 ....*Illus* 10732.00
Golf, 1 Cent, Floor Model, Chester Pollard Amusement Co., 67 In. 13750.00
Gum, Aqua, Tan, 1 & 5 Cent, Norris Mfg. Co., 1923, 8 x 16 In. 460.00
Gum, Ford, Original Red Paint, Pat. Nov. 11, 1919, 7 x 11 1/2 In. 172.00
Gum, Indian Opens Door, 1 Cent, Manikin Vendor Co., 16 In. 3680.00
Gum, Penny, Baby Grand, Oak 155.00
Gum, Pulver, Clown Figure Inside, Porcelain Cased, 21 x 9 In. 880.00
Gum, Silver King Chloramints, 2 For 5 Cents 150.00
Gum, Zeno, Oak Case, 1 Cent, 10 1/2 x 9 x 16 1/2 In. 977.00
Gumball, Glass Top, 1 Cent, 1950s 250.00
Gumball, Home Run, 1 Cent, Arcade Style, Baseball Field, 11 x 28 In. 825.00
Gumball, Lions Club Charities, Ford Gum Co., 1970s 125.00
Gumball, Marvel, Cigarette, Slot, Bakelite Knob, 3 Reels, 1 Cent 550.00
Horse Race, Rock-Ola, Key Lock, Wooden Case 1800.00
Matches, 1 Cent, Dark Green Enamel Base, 7 x 17 1/2 In. 575.00
Matches, Northwester, 2 Figural Dolphins, 1 Cent, 13 1/2 In. 1035.00
Matches, Rosebud 578.00
Movie Viewer, Mills No. 608, Wooden, Seminudes, 1900s, 1 Cent 660.00
Mutoscope, Harem Dancer Marquee, Cast Iron Base, Tin, 72 In. 805.00
Mutoscope, Indian 3000.00
Mutoscope, Iron Stand, Sheet Metal, Peep Show 2127.00
Mutoscope, U.S. Army World War I Marquee, Wood, 70 In. 345.00
Orchestrion, Various Instruments, Alvin Martin, c.1980, 72 In. 1265.00
Peep Show, 1 Cent, Drop Card, Rosenfield Mfg. Co., 18 x 73 In. 3190.00
Pinball, Fire Power, 25 Cent, 60 x 28 In. 165.00
Shock, Electricity Is Life, Floor Model 8525.00
Shooting Gallery, Saloon Scene 3000.00
Skill Test, Crane Retrieves Prize, 10 Cents, Novelty, 80 In. 2750.00
Slot, Eclipse, Upright, Oak Case, Caille Co., 25 x 67 In. 14850.00
Slot, Golden Nugget, 50 Cents, 26 In. 1045.00
Slot, Jennings, Club Chief, Light-Up Front, 10 Cent, c.1940 .... 2350.00
Slot, Jennings, Victory Chief, 5 Cent, Metal Rear Door, 28 In. 1380.00
Slot, Mills, 5 Cent, Blue, Gold Cast Aluminum Front, 12 x 18 In. 1150.00
Slot, Mills, 5 Cents, Horse Head Casting On Front, 25 In. 1760.00
Slot, Mills, Aluminum Front, 5 Cent, 16 x 15 1/2 x 25 1/2 In. 1150.00
Slot, Mills, Blue-Bell Hightop, 3 Reel, 5 Cent, Wooden Base, 16 x 26 In. 920.00
Slot, Mills, Cast Aluminum Front, 3 Reel, 27 x 16 In. 1760.00

Slot, Mills, Diamond Front, Oak Case, 10 Cent, c.1939, 26 In.	1150.00
Slot, Mills, Novelty Co., 25 Cent, Carved Oak Case, 66 x 14 In.	20720.00
Slot, Mills, Poinsettia, Oak Base, 5 Cent	500.00
Slot, Mills, Sweetheart 5 Cents, 18 1/2 In.	1650.00
Slot, Oak Case, 64 x 22 x 12 In.	7640.00
Slot, Old Reno 25 Cent, Aluminum Gunslinger, 80 In.	1092.00
Slot, Speculator, England	395.00
Stamp, 10 Cent, Floor Model, Roovers Brothers, 13 x 57 In.	4950.00
Stamp, U.S. Postage, Slot Type, Vogue Ent., 1960s, 13 x 8 x 7 In.	110.00
Strength, Punch, 1 Cent, Cast Iron, Marshfield Novelty Co., 72 In.	5500.00
Strength Tester, Cast Iron, Oak, Caille Co., 14 x 61 In.	4950.00
Target, Big Game Hunter, Embossed, Marguee, 1 Cent, 26 x 18 In.	1380.00
Trade Stimulator, Five Jacks, 1 Cent, Cast Aluminum, 16 x 19 In.	632.00
Vending, Viking Snuff, Tin, Wall Hanging, 3 1/2 x 3 x 15 In.	28.00
View-A-Scope, Movie, 1 Cent, 1940s	295.00

COLLECTOR PLATES are modern plates produced in limited editions. Some may be found listed under the factory name, such as Bing & Grondahl, Royal Copenhagen, Royal Doulton, and Wedgwood.

Charlotte, Christmas, Box, 1973	40.00
Disney, Happy Birthday Mickey	45.00
Haviland, Mother's Day, 1973	8.00
Haviland, Mother's Day, Parlon, 1977	7.00
Schmid, Mother's Day, Raggedy Andy, 1977	8.00
Schmid, Valentine, Raggedy Ann & Andy, 1978	8.00

COMIC ART, or cartoon art, is a relatively new field of collecting. Original comic strips, magazine covers, and even printed strips are collected. The first daily comic strip was printed in 1907. The paintings on celluloid used for movie cartoons are listed in this book under Animation Art.

Drawing, Charles Addams, Battling Football Players At Table, c.1937, 12 x 17 In.	4675.00
Drawing, Hirshfeld, Carol Channing, 12 7/8 x 9 5/8 In.	690.00
Drawing, The New Yorker, James Thurber, September 12, 1942, 6 3/4 x 9 1/2 In.	7150.00
Page, Sunday, Blondie, Chic Young, 1932	960.00
Page, Sunday, Jungle Book, Disney, 1967	1800.00
Page, Sunday, Mandrake, 1944, 22 x 17 1/2 In.	1920.00
Page, Sunday, Prince Valiant, Harold Foster, 1958, 34 x 23 In.	2880.00
Page, Sunday, Rescuers, Disney, 1977	960.00
Pennant, Green Hornet, Orange, Green, 1966, 28 In.	185.00
Strip, Barney Google, Daily, Billy DeBeck, 1940s, 4 1/2 x 17 1/2 In.	1080.00
Strip, Donald Duck, Daily, Al Taliaferro, 1950s, 4 Strips, 5 1/2 x 19 1/4 In.	1440.00
Strip, Li'l Abner, 1930s, 3 Strips, 5 1/2 x 22 1/2 In.	720.00
Strip, Peanuts, Charles M. Schulz, August 12, 1962, 15 1/4 x 22 1/2 In.	11000.00
Strip, Terry & Pirates, George Wunder, 1950s, 10 Strips, 5 1/2 x 16 1/4 In.	1200.00

COMMEMORATIVE items have been made to honor members of royalty and those of great national fame. World's fairs and important historical events are also remembered with commemorative pieces. Related collectibles are listed in the Coronation and World's Fair categories.

Beaker, British War Relief Society, Copeland, Spode, 4 1/2 In.	24.00
Box, Elizabeth II Silver Jubilee, 1952-1977, Wedgwood	80.00
Cup & Saucer, Queen Elizabeth & Prince Philip, Visit To Canada, June 1959	25.00
Medal, Wiley Post & Harold Gatty, 1931 World Flight, 2 Sides, Porcelain, 2 In.	110.00
Mug, Philip & Elizabeth, Shelley, 1959	85.00
Mug, Queen Elizabeth II Silver Jubilee, Wood & Sons, 1977, 5 In.	28.00
Mug, Wedding Of Prince Charles & Diana, 1981	35.00
Plate, Elizabeth II Silver Jubilee, Cottage Garden, Aynsley Plate, 10 1/2 In.	45.00
Plate, Prince Charles & Diana's Wedding, Fenton China, 1981, 3 In.	70.00
Plate, Queen Elizabeth II Silver Jubilee, Crown Fine Bone China, 1977, 4 In.	20.00
Plate, Sesquicentennial Of George Washington As Freemason, 1903	80.00
Spoon, Battleship Maine, Blown Up, Engraved, Enamel Flag	175.00
Tray, Queen Elizabeth II Silver Jubilee, Metal, 12 In.	19.00

COMPACTS hold face powder. A woman did not powder her face in public until after World War I. By 1920, the beauty parlor, permanent waves, and cosmetics had become acceptable. A few companies sold cake face powder in a box with a mirror and a pad or puff. Soon the compact was designed by jewelers and made of gold, silver, and precious materials. Cosmetic companies began to sell powder in attractive compacts of less valuable metal or plastic. Collectors today search for Art Deco designs, commemorative compacts from world's fairs or political events, and unusual examples. Many were made with companion lipsticks and other fittings.

14K Gold, Geometric Designs All Sides, Interior Mirror, Square, 2 1/2 In.	525.00
Abalone Shell, Round, 3 1/2 In.	45.00
Avon, Perfume Glace Regence, Goldtone, Embossed Pineapple, Green Marble, Pouch	9.00
Bakelite, Powder Holder, Round, Signed, 4 1/2 In.	17.00
Bloodstone, Rose Cut Diamonds, Reverse Cabochon Rubies, Interior Mirror, Chain	2960.00
Blue, White Stars, Oval, Mirror, 2 Powder Buffs, Perforated Liner, 4 In.	40.00
Brass, Enamel, Metal Mirror, Art Deco, c.1930	18.00
Brass, Yellow Cloth Cover, 2 1/2 x 3 1/4 In.	20.00
Cameo, Square, Powder Puff, Screen, 2 In.	36.00
Cara Nome, Silver, Blue Enamel, Fold-Out Compartments	75.00
Carryall, Applied Decorations, Enameled Flowers, Lipstick Holder, 2 1/2 x 3 In.	135.00
Case, Cigarette & Compact, Black Enamel, Round Single Cut Diamonds, 18K Gold	690.00
Chrome, Enamel, Pyramids, Palm Trees, Ring Chain	125.00
Deauville, R. Hudnut, Silver, Double Fold, Powder, Rouge, Patent 12-2-24, 2 In.	59.00
Dorothy Gray, Fifth Avenue, Rectangular, 2 3/4 In.	35.00
Dorset-Rex Fifth Avenue, Brocade, White Pearls, Lipstick Holder, 6 1/4 x 4 1/2 In.	55.00
Elgin, American, Cigarette Case, Flowers, Goldtone, Original Box, 4 1/2 x 7 In.	50.00
Elgin, Red, Honeycomb Silvertone Mesh, Square	25.00
Enamel Design, Art Deco, Finger Ring	85.00
Evans, Silvertone, Prong Set Stone	45.00
Evans, Square, Matching Pin, Victorian Scene, 2 1/2 x 2 1/2 In.	28.00
Gainsboro, Empire State Building, Original Puff, 1930s	45.00
Goldtone, Leather Top, Made In England, Round, 3 1/2 In.	52.00
Helena Rubinstein, Brushed Gold, Rhinestones, Brocade Holder, Rose Blush, 2 x 2 In.	15.00
Henriette, Army Hat Shape, Plastic, Puff, Strainer, Inspection Tag, Unused, 3 In.	50.00
Houbigant, Heart Shape, Puff, Refill, Original Box	70.00
Hudnut, La Soiree, Black & Ivory, Enamel, Silver Moon, Bird & Stars	135.00
Illinois, Mirror, Closed Powder Compartment, Rectangular, 2 1/4 x 3 1/2 In.	15.00
Jeweled, Flower Basket, Rhinestones, Pearls, Mirror, 2 1/2 x 2 3/4 In.	35.00
Lattice Weave, Goldtone Stripes, Mirror, Comb, Powder, Lipstick Holder, Box, 4 In.	145.00
Leather, Red, Lipstick Holder, 2 1/2 x 2 7/8 In.	40.00
Lin Bren, Black & Gold, Embroidered Flowers, Gold Trim, Mirror, Change Purse	44.00
Majestic, Powder Puff, Box	46.00
Metal, Enamel Inset, Pink, Green Flowers, Round, 3 1/4 In.	69.00
Mother-Of-Pearl, Rhinestones On Top, 3 1/2 x 1 1/2 In.	20.00
Nocida, Patent 150400, Round, c.1930, 2 1/4 In.	110.00
Revlon, White Enamel Top, Gold Leaves, Crest, Round	20.00
Rhinestone, Gold Leaves, Powder Puff, Mirror	36.00
Richard Hudnut, Blue & Silver	85.00
Silver, Gilt, Enamel Lid, 18th Century Couple, Lipstick Holder, 3 x 2 1/2 In.	355.00
Silvertone, Gold Leaf Design, c.1955, 3 x 2 1/2 In.	18.00
Silvertone, Used Screen & Powder Puff, Square, Canada Souvenir	24.00
Souvenir, Cumberland, Maryland, Square, Blue Enamel, Mother-Of-Pearl, Mirror	24.00
Sterling Silver, Blue Enamel Surrounding Couple & Shepherdess, Mirror, 3 In.	162.00
Stratton, Pat. No. 764125, Flower Power, Mod, Enamel, Gold, Scalloped Edge, 5 In.	62.00
Sweetheart, British Insignia, Original Box	40.00
Tortoiseshell, Mirror & Pad, 2 1/2 x 2 3/4 In.	15.00
Vautine, Monarch Butterfly, Mirror, Rouge, Powder, Goldtone, Celluloid, Round, 3 In.	110.00
Volupte, Art Deco, Brass, 3 x 2 1/2 In.	120.00
Volupte, Blue, Gold, Mirror, Square, 2 3/4 x 2 3/4 In.	25.00
Volupte, Lollipop Shape, Lipstick Handle, Mirror On Back	60.00
Volupte, Silvertone, Box	75.00

Vovan, Medieval Scene, Men In Armor, England 62.00
Zell, Fifth Avenue, Pocket Watch Shape, Chain Loop, Push Button, Mirror, 2 1/2 In. 38.00

CONSOLIDATED LAMP AND GLASS COMPANY of Coraopolis, Pennsyl-

vania, was founded in 1894. The company made lamps, tablewares,
and art glass. Collectors are particularly interested in the wares made
after 1925, including black satin glass, Cosmos (listed in its own category in this book), Martele (which resembled Lalique), Ruba Rombic
(1928–1932 Art Deco line), and colored glasswares. Some Consolidated pieces are very similar to those made by the Phoenix Glass
Company. The colors are sometimes different. Consolidated made
Martele glass in blue, crystal, green, pink, white, or custard glass with
added fired-on color or a satin finish. The company closed for the final
time in 1967.

Bowl, Ruba Rombic, Jungle Green, 8 1/2 In. 747.00
Compote, Martele, Orchids, Gray, 6 x 3 1/4 In. 65.00
Plate, Dancing Nudes, Satin Details, 8 1/4 In. 70.00
Vase, Chickadee, 6 1/2 In. 185.00
Vase, Dogwood, Brown, Green, Ivory Ground, 10 1/2 In. 865.00
Vase, Jonquil, Yellow, Green, Ivory Ground, 6 1/2 In. 145.00
Vase, Martele, Vines, Glossy White, 6 1/2 In. 90.00
Vase, Martele, Vines, Satin Details, 7 In. 115.00
Vase, Ruba Rombic, Silver, 20th Century, 6 3/8 In. 990.00
Vase, Ruba Rombic, Smokey Topaz, 6 1/2 x 4 3/4 In. 575.00

CONTEMPORARY GLASS, see Glass-Contemporary.

COOKBOOKS are collected for various reasons. Some are wanted for

the recipes, some for investment, and some as examples of advertising.
Cookbooks and recipe pamphlets are included in this category.

Amana 15.00
Betty Crocker, For Boys & Girls, First Edition, 1957 . . . .   55.00
Betty Crocker, World War II 5.00
Betty Crocker Picture Cooky Book, 1948, 44 Pages 11.00
Budweiser, How To Cook With Budweiser, 1950s, 40 Pages 40.00
California Magic With Cottage Cheese, California Dairy Industry, 1956 . . . .   12.00
Calumet Ovens, 32 Pages 10.00
Carlton Fredericks Cookbook For Good Nutrition, With Letter, 1960 . . . .   12.00
Cooking With Flowers, 1971 . . . .   10.00
Gold Metal Flour, 1917 . . . .   25.00
La Cuisine Creole, 1885 . . . .   125.00
Virginia Cookery Cookbook, Mary Stuart Smith, 1885 . . . .   75.00
Warner's Safe, 9th Edition, c.1887, 474 Pages 335.00

COOKIE JARS with brightly painted designs or amusing figural shapes

became popular in the mid-1930s. Many companies made them and
collectors search for cookie jars either by design or by maker's name.
Listed here are examples by the less common makers. Major factories
are listed under their own names in other categories of the book, such
as Abingdon, Brush, Hull, McCoy, Red Wing, and Shawnee. See also
the Disneyana category.

Aunt Jemima, Hard Plastic, F & F Dye Works 595.00
Aunt Jemima, Quaker Oats Premium, Soft Plastic, 1950s 395.00
Banjo, Man, Rick Wisecarver 425.00
Barney & Bam Bam, J.D. James 350.00
Basket Weave, Pink, Zeisel 50.00
Basset Hound, Enesco, 6 In. 49.00
Bear, Beating Drum, Maurice Of California 95.00
Bear, Boy, Girl, Turnabout, Ludowici Celadon, 12 In. 145.00
Benjamin Franklin, With Liberty Bell, Treasure Craft 175.00
Big Bird, On Nest, Muppet, California Originals, 13 1/2 In. 55.00
Bulldog, Glass Eyes, Unmarked 350.00
Cactus, Green, Treasure Craft, 1990, 13 In. 50.00

Canister, Brown, Monmouth, 9 In. 30.00
Canister, Olive Green, Monmouth, 8 1/2 In. 25.00
Cat, Head, Metlox, 9 In. 275.00
Chick, Wearing Beret, American Bisque, 12 In. 125.00
Clock, Cookie Time, California Originals, 13 1/2 In. 165.00
Clown, California Originals 75.00
Clown, One Foot Raised In Step, New Rose Collection 95.00
Coffee Grinder, 1960s-1970s, 10 In 55.00
Cookie House, Musical, Wicker Handle, Japan, 8 1/2 x 5 In. 22.00
Cookie Monster, California Originals, Box, 12 In. 80.00
Cookie Truck, American Bisque, 11 1/2 In. 195.00
Corn, Stanford 160.00
Cow Jumped Over Moon, Flasher, American Bisque 1550.00
Dinosaur, Gray Body, Purple Spots, Treasure Craft, 11 1/2 In. 65.00
Donkey, Milk Wagon, Pulling, American Bisque 125.00
Elf, California Originals 70.00
Elf, Sitting On Stump, Cookie In Hand, Sack On Back, Twin Winton, 14 In. 55.00
Ernie, Muppets, California Originals, 12 In. 145.00
French Chef, Cardinal 250.00
Frog, Holding Flower, Metlox 275.00
Goldilocks, Regal 330.00
Golfer, Mexico 125.00
Granny, Yellow Dress, Pink Apron, American Bisque 200.00
Hippo-Limpix, Fitz & Floyd, 1989, 10 In. 165.00
Juggler, Clown, California Originals, 13 In. 175.00
Kitten & Beehive, American Bisque, 11 3/4 In. 165.00
Lamb, American Bisque, 11 1/2 In. 75.00
Leopard Head, Mexico 150.00
Lion, Marcia California 55.00
Lion, Sitting, Metlox 350.00
Little Red Riding Hood, Open Basket, Regal 475.00
Little Red Riding Hood, Poinsettia, Closed Green Basket, Regal 1200.00
Little Red Riding Hood, Pottery Guild 225.00
Log Cabin, House Of Webster, 6 In. 46.00
Majorette, Head, Regal 425.00
Mammy, Blue Dress, White Apron, Kayes Kreations, 12 In. 45.00
Mammy, National Silver 335.00
Mammy, Stove, Rick Wisecarver 325.00
Mammy, White Dress, Yellow Polka Dot, Metlox 550.00
Mammy, Yellow Dress, Pearl China Co. 725.00
Mammy, Yellow, Mosaic Tile 495.00
Mammy With Basket, Rick Wisecarver 325.00
Monk, Holding Bible, Thou Shalt Not Get Fat, 10 1/2 In. 95.00
Monk, Thou Shalt Not Steal, Twin Winton, 12 In. 50.00
Mother Goose, Metlox, 14 In. 65.00
Nestle Toll House, Original Toll House Cookies On Front, Recipe On Back, Unmarked .. 70.00
Oscar The Grouch, Muppets, California Originals, 12 In. 155.00
Peek-A-Boo, Regal 1200.00
Pencil, Yellow, Black Tip, Eraser Side Down, M. Kamenstein 95.00
Pillsbury Best Flour Sack, Benjamin & Medwin, 1988 .... 110.00
Pillsbury Dough Boy, Benjamin & Medwin, 1988, 12 In. 35.00
Pineapple, Metlox, 12 In. 65.00
Pink Panther Car, Treasure Craft 300.00
Puppy, California Originals 95.00
Quaker Oats, Recipe On Back, Regal ....120.00 to 160.00
Raggedy Ann, Foil Label, Royal Sealy, Japan 45.00
Rocking Horse, Regal 285.00
Sailor, Jack, Robinson Ransbottom 295.00
Sailor Mouse, Twin Winton, 11 1/4 In. 45.00
Santa, Driving Rolls Royce, Fitz & Floyd, Signed, 1987 ....450.00 to 1000.00
Santa, On Motorcycle, Reindeer In Sidecar, Fitz & Floyd, 11 In. 595.00
Santa, Plastic, Carolina Enterprises, 1973, 12 In. 25.00
Santa, Standing With Presents, Made In China 65.00

Santa, With Teddy Bear, Made In China 65.00
Schoolhouse, American Bisque 100.00
Schoolhouse, Metlox 784.00
Sheriff, Bullet Hole In Hat, California Originals, 13 1/2 In. ....40.00 to 60.00
Snoopy On Doghouse, Benjamin & Medwin 40.00
Space Capsule, Decals, A Lasting Reminder Of The Space Age, 1965, 8 1/2 In. 225.00
Spaceship, Blue, Yellow, Cookies Out Of This World, American Bisque 550.00
Stack Of Oreo Cookies, Nabisco, Block China Co., 10 In. 45.00
Stagecoach, Sierra Vista 325.00
Stoneware, Brown, Scalloped Design, Marcrest, 1960s-1970s, 9 In. 65.00
Strawberry, Leaning, 10 In., 1960s-1970s 45.00
Swirl, Blue, White Cover, Handles, American Bisque, 1940s 25.00
Teddy Bear, Avon, Californina Originals 65.00
Turnip, Fitz & Floyd, 1984, 7 1/2 In. 65.00
Walrus, Doranne Of California, 10 In. 125.00
Witch, Halloween Hoedown, Fitz & Floyd 160.00
Yarn Doll, Gold Trim, American Bisque .... .200.00 to 250.00

COORS ware was made by a pottery in Golden, Colorado, owned by the Coors Beverage Company. Dishes and decorative wares were produced from the turn of the century until the pottery was destroyed by fire in the 1930s. The name *Coors* is marked on the back. The company is still in business making industrial porcelain. For more information, see *Kovels' Depression Glass & Dinnerware Price List.*

COORS
U.S.A.

Ashtray, Dark Brown, Anholt, 1940s, 6 In. 15.00
Ashtray, Green, Triangular, Raised Letters On Base 15.00
Ashtray, Orange, Triangular, Raised Letters On Base 15.00
Mug, White, Handle, Marked, 1 1/2 In. 6.00
Pitcher, Water, Rosebud, Orange, Handle, 3 Pt., 6 1/2 x 7 1/2 In. 110.00
Tray, Green, Square, 5 In. 12.00
Vase, Blue Matte, White Interior, Handles, Triangular Ink Stamp, 1930 .... 100.00
Vase, Blue, Handles, 5 1/2 In. 75.00

COPELAND pieces listed here are those that have a mark including the word Copeland used between 1847 and 1976. Marks include Copeland Spode and Copeland & Garrett. See also Copeland Spode and Royal Worcester.

Bust, Mercury, Parian, 12 In. 1202.00
Compote, Flowers, Turquoise, Gold Trim, 6 x 10 In. 230.00
Cup & Saucer, Child's, 1895 .... 35.00
Cup & Saucer, Gainsborough Pattern 25.00
Dinner Set, European Country Scenes, Leaf Border, Crown Mark, 99 Piece 1705.00
Figurine, Apollo, Parian, 10 In. 443.00
Figurine, Storm, Parian, 19th Century, 19 In. 1200.00
Lamp, Figural, Cherub, Supporting Cornucopia, Turquoise Banded Foot, 11 1/2 In. ... 185.00
Pitcher & Bowl, Elgin, Allegorical Figures, Terra-Cotta & Black, 1830s, 8 1/2 In. 290.00
Plate, Birds, Palm Trees, Flowers, Flow Blue, 9 3/8 In. 165.00
Plate, Dessert, Flying Crane, Butterfly, Palm Tree, Fluted Edge, 8 1/2 In., 8 Piece 126.00
Plate, Jeweled, Coral & Pearl, Dark Green, 1883, 8 1/4 In. 595.00
Plate, Tea, Child's, Square, 1895, 5 1/2 In. 30.00
Platter, Well & Tree, Floral Spray Design, Ocher Enamel, Stoneware, 21 In. 115.00
Serving Dish, Cover, Floral, 1894, 11 1/4 In. 325.00
Soup, Dish, Rhine Pattern, Brown, Crazed 28.00
Tazza, Elgin, Allegorical Figures, Terra-Cotta & Black, 1830s, 9 1/2 In. 316.00
Vase, Landing Of Columbus, Blue Ground, Wedgwood Type, Double Handles, 11 In. 165.00

COPELAND SPODE appears on some pieces of nineteenth-century English porcelain. Josiah Spode established a pottery at Stoke-on-Trent, England, in 1770. In 1833, the firm was purchased by William Copeland and Thomas Garrett and the mark was changed. In 1847, Copeland became the sole owner and the mark changed again. W.T. Copeland & Sons continued until a 1976 merger when it became Royal Worcester Spode. Pieces are listed in this book under the name that

COPELAND
SPODE
ENGLAND

appears in the mark. Copeland Spode, Copeland, and Royal Worcester
have separate listings.

Compote, Flowers, Scrolled Gilt, 1875-1890, 9 1/2 x 5 1/2 In. 450.00
Cup & Saucer, Cobalt Blue & Gilt, 1890s 45.00
Cup & Saucer, Green Flowers, 1940-1956, 1 1/4-In. Cup, 2 1/4-In. Saucer 115.00
Cup & Saucer, Heather Rose, Demitasse 20.00
Cup & Saucer, Paisley Star, Gilt Trim, 1 1/4-In. Cup, 2 1/4-In. Saucer 115.00
Cup & Saucer, Rosebud Chintz 38.00
Cup & Saucer, William IV, Flowers, Gilt 45.00
Jug, Ale, Blue & White, Tavern Scene, Wedgwood Style, 7 In. 115.00
Pitcher, Cobalt Blue, White Horse Scene, Pate-Sur-Pate, 4 3/4 x 5 1/2 In. 225.00
Plate, Blue & White, Runnymede Design, 1928, 9 In. 35.00
Plate, Blue Flowers, Ironstone, 10 1/2 In., 10 Piece 192.00
Plate, Dessert, Exotic Birds, Gilt Edged Rim, Signed, 8 1/4 In., 10 Piece 5700.00
Plate, Fish, 4 Swirled Design, H.C. Lea, 1891, 9 3/4 In. 175.00
Plate, Summer Flowers, Gilt Border, Felspar, 1820, 7 In., Pair 72.00
Punch Set, 1920s, 12-In. Bowl, Ladle, 14 Piece 205.00
Saucer, Claret Color, Floral, Gilt Trim, Garrett, 1835, 6 In., Pair 138.00
Soup, Cream Set, Pembrook, 2 Handles, 3 Piece 25.00
Tea Set, Blue Willow, Auld Lang Syne, Gilt Trim, Marked, 5 Piece 330.00
Tea Set, Trade Winds, Gilt Trim, 7 Piece 825.00
Teapot, Indian Tree 170.00
Tureen, Cover, White, Gold, Blue, 2 Handles, Spode New Stone, 11 x 13 In. 1470.00
Tureen, Underplate, Indian Tree 160.00

COPPER has been used to make utilitarian items, such as teakettles and
cooking pans, since the days of the early American colonists. Copper
became a popular metal with the Arts & Crafts makers of the early
1900s, and decorative pieces, like desk sets, were made. Other pieces
of copper may be found in the Arts & Crafts, Bradley & Hubbard,
Kitchen, and Roycroft categories.

Ale Warmer, Shoe Shape, Tin Lined, England, 19th Century, 18 In. 375.00
Alms Dish, Repousse, Punch Design, Nuremberg, 1650, 14 In., Pair 1500.00
Ashtray, Repousse, 4 Compartments Surrounding Circular Compartment, 16 1/2 In. 220.00
Bed Warmer, Brass, Wood, Turned Handle, Stipple Floral Spray, 19th Century, 45 In. ... 200.00
Bed Warmer, Hinged Cover, Stars & Crescent Moons, Turned Wood Handle, 12 In. 345.00
Bed Warmer, Treen Handle, 47 3/4 In. 490.00
Bowl, Hammered, 8 In. 58.00
Bowl, Hammered, Old Mission Kopperkraft, Original Patina, Signed, 8 In. 546.00
Bowl, Hammered, Original Patina, Jarvie, 8 In. 865.00
Bowl, Imperial Double Headed Eagle, Old Slavonic, Russia, c.1890, 10 3/4 In. 896.00
Bowl, Rolled Rim, Dark Patina, 2 1/4 x 5 1/8 In. 220.00
Box, Cover, Original Patina, Hammered, Harry Dixon, Lacquer Interior, 4 x 3 In. 240.00
Box, Tea, Hammered, Original Patina, Green Enamel Insets, Arts & Crafts, 1900, 8 1/2 In. 334.00
Bucket, Coal, Ring Handles, 2 Bands Encircle Body Below Rim, Arts & Crafts, 16 In. ... 1456.00
Bucket, Hammered Surface, Nailhead Trimmed Rim, Arts & Crafts, 11 1/2 In. 172.00
Bust, Gentleman, Wide Brim Hat, Dr. Burghardt In German On Plaque, 17 3/4 In. 220.00
Carafe, Hinged Cover, Hammered, Long Serpentine Handle, 5 In. 275.00
Chamberstick, Hammered, Bronze, Enameled Owl, B & W, 5 1/2 In. 250.00
Chamberstick, Handle, Hook Candlesnuffer, 6 1/2 In. 275.00
Chamberstick, Riveted Handle, 3 1/4 x 6 1/4 In. 220.00
Chamberstick, Tapered Shaft, Riveted Handle, Original Patina 660.00
Charger, Rolled Rim, 18 1/8 In. 1430.00
Charger, Rolled Rim, Center Recessed Compartment, 18 1/2 In. 1456.00
Coal Bucket, Iron Handles, Riveted Brass Foot, Hammered, 16 5/8 In. 2420.00
Coal Scuttle, Brass Rim, Overlapping Dovetail Joint On Side, 13 1/2 In. 2128.00
Desk Set, Hammered, Original Patina, Stamp Box, Gustav Stickley 1910.00
Figurine, Eagle, Outstretched Wings, Perched On Ball, 19th Century, 14 1/2 In. 1495.00
Figurine, Lobster, Copper Articulated, Signed, 15 In. 1100.00
Fry Pan, Ram's-Horn Top, Long Handled, Tin Lining, 39 In. 58.00
Humidor, Benedict, Hammered, Original Patina, 7 1/4 x 10 x 6 1/4 In. 523.00
Humidor, Hammered, Arrowhead Leaves, Circular Oak Base, Shreve, 8 1/4 x 5 In. 1462.00

Humidor, Panels Of Floating Swans, Carence Crafters, 6 3/4 x 6 In. 843.00
Inkwell, Hammered, Splayed Riveted Base, Gustav Stickley, 3 x 5 1/2 In. 920.00
Jardiniere, 2 Ring Handles, Marked, 13 1/2 In. 550.00
Jardiniere, 2 Rolled Handles, Ropelike Border, 15 1/4 In. 2750.00
Jardiniere, Applied Square Collar, Original Patina, 9 1/4 In. 600.00
Jardiniere, Blown-Out Vertical Lobes, 10 7/8 In. 840.00
Jardiniere, Brass, Pendant Ring Handless, Oval, 7 1/2 x 14 x 12 In. 230.00
Jardiniere, Copper, Stickley Brothers, Rolled Rim, Fruit & Plant, Signed, 12 1/2 In. 6325.00
Jardiniere, Embossed Flowers, Hammered, Arts & Crafts, 3-Footed, 8 1/2 In. 115.00
Jardiniere, Gustav Stickley, Hammered, Original Patina, 12 1/2 x 11 In. 4600.00
Jardiniere, Hammered, Handles, Arts & Crafts, 18 x 12 In. 431.00
Jardiniere, Hammered, Original Patina, Arts & Crafts, 13 x 12 In. 374.00
Jardiniere, Hammered, Ruffled Edge, Heinrichs, Signed, 10 In. 490.00
Jardiniere, Ring Handles, Vertical, Horizontal Lap Joints, Bun Feet, 8 3/4 In. 470.00
Jardiniere, Rolled Handles, Repousse Body Band, Stickley Brothers, 6 x 14 1/2 In. 1495.00
Jardiniere, Rolled Rim, Hammered, Original Patina, 7 In. 605.00
Jardiniere, Rolled Rim, Stylized Fruit & Plant, Signed, Stickley Brothers, 17 1/2 In. 2990.00
Jardiniere, Secessionist Design, 4 Riveted Strap Handles, 14 x 18 1/2 In. 1415.00
Jardiniere, Twin Loop Handles, Faceted Foot, 15 1/8 In. 550.00
Jug, Ale, Dovetail Construction, England, 10 In. 295.00
Jug, Hammered, Center Handle, Arts & Crafts, Original Patina 175.00
Kettle, Apple Butter, Wrought Iron Handle, Penn., 19th Century, 24 In. 300.00
Kovsh, Long Back Handle, Hand Hammered, Arts & Crafts, Russia, c.1900, 7 1/4 In. 170.00
Lamp Base, Original Acorn Pulls, Hammered, 19 In. 2330.00
Light, Ship's, 90 Degree Clear Lens, 15 In. 138.00
Lunch Pail, Dovetail Construction, Tin Lined, Bail Handle, Late 18th Century 275.00
Molds are listed in the Kitchen category.
Mug, 3 Iron Handles, Riveted To Body, 7 3/4 In. 672.00
Mug, 3 Sweeping Iron Handles, Original Crusty Patina, 7 3/4 In. 660.00
Mug, Applied Brass Trim, Handle, 4 3/4 In. 330.00
Mug, Barrel Shape, Hollow Tube Handle, 6 In. 220.00
Mug, Barrel Shape, Hollow Tube Handle, Impressed 25, Limbert, 6 In. 224.00
Mug, Barrel Shape, Rolled Tube Handle, 6 In. 275.00
Mug, Rolled Rim, Riveted Handle, Original Patina, 5 3/8 In. 275.00
Mug, Rolled Rim, Riveted Tube Handle, 6 5/8 In. 247.00
Mug, Rolled Tube Riveted Handle, 5 1/2 In. 275.00
Picture Frame, Hammered, Tooled Design, Carence Crafters, 4 x 5 1/2 In. 978.00
Pin Tray, Gustav Stickley, Hammered, Original Patina, 10 In. 1155.00
Pitcher, Children, Grapes, Brass Handle, Copper Lid Of Child, Wheat, 1 Liter 288.00
Pitcher, Hammered, Keswick School Of Industrial Art, Original Patina, 1901, 9 In. 161.00
Pitcher, Long Tapered Neck, Vertical, Horizontal Lap Joints, Dark Patina, 13 In. 1100.00
Pitcher, Rolled Rim, Loop Riveted Handle, Original Patina, 9 7/8 In. 357.00
Pitcher, Spade Shape, Raised Hemispheres, 6 7/8 In. 275.00
Pitcher, Stickley Bros., Hammered, Brass Rim, Handle, Pointed Spout, 12 In. 316.00
Pitcher, Wine, Brass Riveted Handle, Medium Patina, 15 7/8 In. 770.00
Pitcher, Wine, Stickley Bros., Hammered, 14 1/2 In. 690.00
Pitcher, Wine, Wrought Iron Handle, 14 1/2 In. 990.00
Plaque, 3 Stylized Leaves Around Border, 7 1/2 In. 385.00
Plaque, 4 Hemispheres, Original Patina, 6 3/4 In. 275.00
Plaque, Minerva & Marx Head, Brass Plating, 25 In., Pair 126.00
Plaque, Spade Shape, Rolled Rim, Medium Patina, 6 3/4 In. 275.00
Pot, Arts & Crafts, Hammered, Squat, Movable Handle, Bronze Patina, 4 x 8 In. 86.00
Pot, Cover, Soup, 11 x 11 In. 230.00
Pot, Domed Cover, Strap Handle, Brass Lugs, Oval, 19th Century, 12 1/2 x 16 1/2 In. . . . 430.00
Pot, Middle Band, Decorative Rivets, 13 x 19 3/4 In. 86.00
Pot, Soup, Rolled Edge, Bail Handle, 7 x 11 3/4 In., 2 Piece 170.00
Puff Box, Cover, Hammered, A.K., 5 1/2 In. . . . . *Illus* 50.00
Roaster, Chestnut, Pierced Lid, Engraved Tulip, Handle, 36 In. 360.00
Roaster, Peanut, Gas Fed, Glass Sides, Metal Frame, Hot On Front Side Door, 37 x 17 In. 115.00
Rush Holder, Wooden Base, Curled Handle, Brass Rivet, 10 In. 115.00
Stein, Hammered, Stickley Bros., Applied Flower, Handle, 12 1/4 In. 345.00
Tankard, Tapered, Iron Riveted Handle, 14 In. 1045.00

To hang copper molds in your kitchen, try this method: Mount a solid brass or wooden curtain rod across the top of the hanging area. Molds can then be hung by hooks and easily moved when new ones are added.

Copper, Puff Box, Cover, Hammered, A.K., 5 1/2 In.

Teakettle, Articulated Handle, Turned Brass Finial, Tinned Interior, Miniature, 1765	650.00
Teakettle, G. Tryon On Handle, 11 In.	440.00
Teakettle, Gooseneck Spout, Stamped J.H. Blondel VI	385.00
Teapot, Gooseneck Spout, Brass & Copper Fixed Handle, 8 In.	140.00
Teapot, Gooseneck Spout, Domed Lid, Acorn Finial, Maurice Cohen & Co., 12 In.	165.00
Teapot, Hammered, Cherry Blossoms, Butterflies, Bird, Gorham, 11 In.	3738.00
Tray, Benedict Studios, Hammered, 25 1/2 x 11 In.	690.00
Tray, Gustav Stickley, Embossed Dots Around Rim, New Dark Patina, 8 In. Diam.	170.00
Tray, Gustav Stickley, Hammered, Raised Design, 21 1/2 In.	4025.00
Tray, Hammered, Arts & Crafts, c.1900, 24 x 15 In.	250.00
Tray, Hammered, Brass Riveted Handles, 15 5/8 In.	330.00
Tray, Hammered, Scalloped Edge, Signed, Westside Staff, 1964, 14 In.	1095.00
Tray, Riveted Copper Handles In Scroll Form, Dark Patina, 16 3/8 In.	440.00
Tray, Rolled Rim, 2 Heavy Handles, Medium Patina, 18 In.	330.00
Tray, Rolled Rim, 4 Compartments, Central Recessed Area, Original Patina, 6 3/4 In.	210.00
Tray, Rolled Rim, Scrolled Handles, Original Patina, 19 1/2 In.	495.00
Tray, Stickley Bros., Hammered, 13 In.	1095.00
Umbrella Stand, 3 Applied Brass Bands, Applied Brass Rim, 23 5/8 In.	1100.00
Umbrella Stand, Applied Brass Rim, Rolled Foot, Arts & Crafts, 27 In.	1100.00
Umbrella Stand, Bands, Jos. Heinrichs, Die-Stamped Mark, 16 x 8 In.	80.00
Umbrella Stand, Brass Rim, Stylized Flowers, 23 5/8 In.	1120.00
Umbrella Stand, Twin Scroll Handles, Armorials & Fleur-De-Lis, 1900, 22 1/2 In.	925.00
Vase, Alternating Fingers Around Neck, 10 1/2 In.	530.00
Vase, Applied Tube Handle, 9 1/4 In.	440.00
Vase, Elephant Trunk Handles, Repousse Trim, 11 In.	660.00
Vase, Flared Rim, Marle Zimmerman, 10 x 10 In.	1725.00
Vase, Fluted Rim, 13 Flutes, 23 Fingers On Base, 21 1/8 In.	840.00
Vase, Fluted Rim, Repousse Work Around Bulbous Bottom, Dark Patina, 21 In.	825.00
Vase, Fluted Rim, Swelled Body, Original Patina, 12 3/8 In.	412.00
Vase, Gold Aventurine, Pigeon Blood Ground, France, 16 In., Pair	750.00
Vase, Hammered, 2 Sweeping Handles, Bulbous Head, 9 7/8 In.	275.00
Vase, Hammered, Baluster Shape, Original Patina, 18 1/2 In.	750.00
Vase, Hammered, Buttressed, Original Patina, 7 In.	635.00
Vase, Hammered, Flared Rim, 6 7/8 In.	385.00
Vase, Hammered, Original Patina, 4 Applied Feet, Benedict, 8 1/2 x 3 In.	375.00
Vase, Hammered, Raised Flowers, Original Patina, Arts & Crafts, 11 In.	185.00
Vase, Hammered, Raised Geometric Design, Original Copper Patina, W.M.F., 8 In.	460.00
Vase, Heavy Brass Handles, Rolled Rim, 8 1/2 In.	880.00
Vase, Horned, 2 Riveted Handles, Repousse Eyes & Mouth, 9 In.	935.00
Vase, Repousse Fingers, Original Patina, 10 1/2 In.	520.00
Vase, Repousse Neck Design, Bulbous, Original Patina, 10 3/8 In.	520.00
Vase, Stickley Bros., Hammered, Original Patina, 6 1/2 In.	605.00
Vase, Stylized Flowers, Dark Original Patina, Karl Kipp, 4 x 1 3/4 In.	5465.00
Vase, Tapered Neck, Hammered, 9 1/2 In.	715.00
Vase, Tube Handles, Tapering Sides, 9 1/4 In.	450.00

Vase, Wood Grain, 3 Buttresses, Original Patina, 8 x 3 3/4 In. 560.00
Warmer, Plate, Fixed Copper Handle, Cabriole Legs, Snake Feet, 22 1/2 In. 460.00
Warming Pan, Engraved, Turned Handle, American, 45 In. 115.00
Wine Flacon, Arts & Crafts, Hand Wrought, Stylized Iris In Relief, 11 In. 230.00

COPPER LUSTER items are listed in the Luster category.

CORALENE glass was made by firing many small colored beads on the
outside of glassware. It was made in many patterns in the United States
and Europe in the 1880s. Reproductions are made today. Coralene-
decorated Japanese pottery is listed in the Japanese Coralene category.

Vase, Amber, Flower Branch, Hand Blown, 4 1/2 In. 125.00
Vase, Amethyst, Flowers At Base, 8 In. 125.00
Vase, Flowers & Leaves, Gold Trim, 9 1/2 In. 198.00
Vase, Seaweed & Shell, Coral, White Enameled Flowers, 9 1/2 In. 155.00
Vase, Seaweed, Bright Yellow Ground, 5 x 3 1/2 In. 260.00
Vase, Seaweed, Coral, Blue, Yellow, White Ground, 6 x 5 1/4 In., Pair 375.00
Vase, Seaweed, Pink To Fuchsia, 7 1/4 In. . . . . *Illus* 288.00

CORDEY China Company was founded by Boleslaw Cybis in 1942 in
Trenton, New Jersey. The firm produced gift shop items. In 1969 it was
acquired by the Lightron Corp. and operated as the Schiller Cordey
Co., manufacturers of lamps. About 1950 Boleslaw Cybis began making Cybis porcelains, which are listed in their own category in this
book.

Figurine, Colonial Couple, Man & Woman, Pink & Yellow, 15 3/4 In. 285.00
Figurine, Colonial Couple, Man, No. 5043, Woman, No. 5081, 1940s, 11 3/4 In., Pair 390.00
Figurine, Woman, Stamped & Marked, 14 In. 275.00
Vase, Cornucopia Shape, 6 1/2 In. 175.00

CORKSCREWS have been needed since the first bottle was sealed with
a cork, probably in the seventeenth century. Today collectors search for
the early, unusual patented examples or the figural corkscrews of
recent years.

Bottle Opener, Boot, Marked Sterling, Stores In Boot, 4 In. 175.00
Brass, Traditional Form, 19th Century, 6 1/2 In. 58.00
Champagne Tap, Chrome Plated, France, Early 1900s 120.00
Eyebrow Type, WCH 40.00
Knife, American Brew Co., Phila., Brewery Buildings, Embossed Nickel 350.00
Male Figure Form, Sommelier, Mid 20th Century, Box, 8 1/4 In. 125.00
Medicine Ball, To Open Medicine Bottle, Nickel Ball Handle, c.1870 . . . . 180.00
Picnic & Cap Lifter, 1920s 110.00
Roundlet, Nickel, France 145.00
Sterling Silver & Horn, John Hasselbring, 6 In. 121.00
T Type, Turned Wood Handle, R. Jones & Son, England 135.00
T Type, Twist Shaft, Hanging Ring In Handle, England 45.00
Turned Handle With Cleaning Brush 45.00

Coralene, Vase, Seaweed,
Pink To Fuchsia, 7 1/4 In.

Coronation, Cup, Czar
Nicholas II & Alexandra
Feodoravna, Metal, 1896

CORONATION souvenirs have been made since the 1800s. Pottery, glass, tin, silver, and paper objects with a picture of the monarchs and date have been sold at many coronations. The pieces that mention King Edward VIII, the king who was never crowned, are not rare; collectors should be sure to check values before buying. Related pieces are found in the Commemorative category.

Ashtray, Elizabeth II, Crystal, Gold Trim, Square, 1953, 3 1/2 In.	15.00
Bank, Cast Iron, George V, 1911, 6 3/8 In.	85.00
Beaker, George V & Mary, Royal Winton Stoke On Trent, June 22, 1911, 4 In.	50.00
Beaker, George V & Mary, Sepia Portraits, Coronation 1911, Royal Doulton, 4 In.	.85.00 to 95.00
Beaker, George VI & Elizabeth, Cream Petal, Profile Portraits, 4 1/4 In.	55.00
Biscuit Tin, Elizabeth II & Philip, Carr's, 11 1/2 x 8 3/4 In.	50.00
Book, Paper Dolls, Coloring, Queen Elizabeth II, Family, Saalfield, 1953, 48 Pages	90.00
Bowl, Elizabeth II, Child's, Square, Kensington Ware, Gold Trim, 1953, 5 1/2 In.	24.00
Cup, Czar Nicholas II & Alexandra Feodoravna, Metal, 1896 ....Illus	1150.00
Cup, Czar Nicholas II, Crowned Imperial Cipher, Eagle, Enamel, c.1896, 4 In.	1232.00
Cup, Elizabeth II, Child's, Kensington Ware, Gold Trim, 1953, 2 1/2 In.	24.00
Cup, Elizabeth II, Handleless, British Pottery Manufacturer's Federation, 1953, 4 In.	25.00
Cup & Saucer, Queen Elizabeth II, Gold Trim, 1953	38.00
Dish, Edward VIII, Royal Coat Of Arms, Gilt Rim, Handles, 1937, 1 x 9 1/2 In.	189.00
Dish, Elizabeth II, Rosina Bone China, 1953, 3 3/4 In.	22.00
Plate, Elizabeth II, Clarice Cliff, Royal Staffordshire, 1953, 10 In.	125.00
Tea Tile, George V & Mary, Dieu Et Mon Droit, 6 1/2 In.	25.00
Tin, Jacob's Biscuits, King George VI, 1937, 8 3/4 In.	350.00
Tin, Toffee, Elizabeth II & Philip, Hinged Top, GW Horner & Co., 1953, 5 x 4 In.	45.00
Tumbler, Elizabeth II, Blue, Gold Rim, 4 3/4 In.	24.00
Tumbler, Victoria's Profile, Coat Of Arms, Landscapes, Enamel, 1837, 4 In., Pair	397.00
View-Master, Queen Elizabeth II, June 2, 3 Reels, Booklet, 1953	34.00

COSMOS is a pressed milk glass pattern with colored flowers made from 1894 to 1915 by the Consolidated Lamp and Glass Company. Tablewares and lamps were made in this pattern. A few pieces were also made of clear glass with painted decorations. Other glass patterns are listed under Consolidated Lamp and also in various glass categories. In later years, Cosmos was also made by the Westmoreland Glass Company.

Butter, Cover	150.00
Condiment Set, Salt, Pepper, Condiment Jar, Consolidated Glass Co.	310.00
Lamp, Oil, Yellow, Nutmeg Burner, 7 1/2 In.	400.00
Pickle Castor, Silver Plated Frame	650.00
Pitcher, 5 In.	161.00
Pitcher, 9 In.	431.00
Saltshaker, Pink, Blue, & Yellow Flowers, Consolidated Glass Co., 3 1/2 In.	104.00
Saltshaker, White, 3 x 2 1/2 In.	45.00
Spooner, Pink, Blue & Yellow, Pink Band, Consolidated Glass Co., 4 In.	108.00

COVERLETS were made of linen or wool during the nineteenth century. Most of the coverlets date from 1800 to the 1880s. There was a revival of hand weaving in the 1920s and new coverlets, especially geometric patterns, were made. The earliest coverlets were made on narrow looms, so two woven strips were joined together and a seam can be found. The weave structures of coverlets can include summer and winter, double weave, overshot, and others. Jacquard coverlets have elaborate pictorial patterns that are made on a special loom or with the use of a special attachment. Quilts are listed in this book in their own category.

3 Colors, Phillip Schum, Lancaster, Pa., 19th Century, 73 x 84 In.	300.00
4 Roses Medallions, Border 3 Sides, Blue, Wool, 92 x 74 In.	600.00
5 Colored Bands, Centennial, 1776-1876, Memorial Hall Center, Eagles, 77 x 80 In.	230.00
Blue, White, Red, Green Floral Rows, Carolina Hottenstein, Pa., 1800s, 84 x 92 In.	300.00
Double Weave, Blue, White, House & Tree Border, Dated 1838, 80 x 90 In.	750.00
Double Weave, Red, Blue, Mid 19th Century, Fringe 3 Sides, 65 x 75 In.	325.00
Double Weave, Red, Blue, White Ground, Pine Tree Border, 19th Century, 64 In.	155.00

Jacquard, 4 Rose Design, 2 Rows Of Flowers On Borders, E. Willse, 1831, 69 x 83 In. ...   660.00
Jacquard, 6 Medallions, Tulip Border, Red, Tan, Mid 19th Century, 76 x 90 In. 575.00
Jacquard, 9 Medallions, Flowerpot Border, Flying Pheasants In Corners, 90 In. 715.00
Jacquard, Block Pattern, House Border, Dated Ohio 1848, 72 x 83 In. 325.00
Jacquard, Blue, Light Blue, Red, White Ground, 1839, 72 1/2 x 84 In. 425.00
Jacquard, Building Borders, Trees, Eagle & 5 Stars, Urns Of Flowers, 72 x 82 In. 275.00
Jacquard, Buildings Border, Flowers, Green, Red, White, 1852, 83 In. 360.00
Jacquard, Center Medallion With 4 Eagles, Red, Fringe, Late 19th Century, 78 In. 275.00
Jacquard, Circular & Floral Medallions, Floral Borders, John Muir, 1834, 98 In. 110.00
Jacquard, Double Leaf Borders, 16 Leaf Design, 1834, 72 x 89 In. 195.00
Jacquard, Double Weave, Peacocks, Urns, Flowers, Blue, White, Fringe, Ohio, 84 In. 385.00
Jacquard, Eagle, Tree Border, Stars, 4 Medallions, M.B. Brenemen, 1838, 76 x 88 In. ...   550.00
Jacquard, Floral Arch, Davidson ....*Illus*   1600.00
Jacquard, Floral Medallions, 4 House Border, Sailboat Corners, 1841, 74 x 91 In. 2420.00
Jacquard, Floral Medallions, Eagle & Tree Border, M. Sharp, 1835, 78 x 88 In. 770.00
Jacquard, Floral Medallions, Flowering Tree Border, D.L. Myers, 1839, 72 x 96 In. 220.00
Jacquard, Flower Medallion, Urns, Columns, Blue, White, c.1852, 86 x 75 In. 175.00
Jacquard, Flower, Leaves, Medallion, Red, Blue, Green, Cream Ground, Pa., 86 In. 460.00
Jacquard, Flowers, Blue & White, Signed Lavina Voorhis, c.1840, 92 x 76 In. 415.00
Jacquard, Flowers, Red, Blue, Green, Signed, 1855, 82 x 86 In. 280.00
Jacquard, Flowers, Scrolls, Blue, White, 1843, 80 x 100 In. 290.00
Jacquard, Geometric, Pine Tree Border, Blue, White, 86 In. 110.00
Jacquard, Hemfield Railroad, Man Bust In Corner, Rust, Blue, Fringe, 19th Century 4000.00
Jacquard, Large Center Star Medallion, Eagles At Corners, 82 x 80 In. 330.00
Jacquard, Leaf & Heart Medallions, Grapevine Border, 69 x 86 In. 195.00
Jacquard, Lilies Of France, Blue Wool, Cotton, Anna Hasbrouck, N.Y., 1838, 91 x 73 In. .   935.00
Jacquard, Lilies, American Flags, Blue, White, Ira Hadsell, 1851, 92 x 78 In. 3600.00
Jacquard, Medallion, Washington Images, Eagle, Red & White, Hail 1871, 76 In. 495.00
Jacquard, Muir Family Corner Block, Floral Medallions, 1850, 74 x 80 In. 250.00
Jacquard, Multicolored, 19th Century, 80 x 86 In. 375.00
Jacquard, Pairs Of Peacocks Amidst Flowers, Navy, Tan Wool, 68 x 80 In. 315.00
Jacquard, Peacock, Urn, Flower, Blue, Green, Red, 96 x 80 In. 440.00
Jacquard, Red, Corner Block, Fringe 3 Sides, 1885, 68 x 78 In. 175.00
Jacquard, Rose & Dove Borders, 4 Center Star Medallions, Red, Blue, Green, 84 In. 425.00
Jacquard, Rose Medallions, Flower Buds, Navy Blue, Natural, 1839, 72 x 90 In. 275.00
Jacquard, Single Weave, Flowers, Star Corner Blocks, Green, Gold, Red, 1845, 96 In. 300.00
Jacquard, Snowflake, Navy, David Haring ....*Illus*   1400.00
Jacquard, Star & Rose Medallions, Eagle Border, Mt. Joy, Pa., 2 Piece, 1833, 96 In. 330.00
Jacquard, Vining Flower Border, Spread Eagle & Banner, Deer, Birds, 1857, 94 In. 715.00
Jacquard, Wool & Cotton, Flowers, Jacob C. Shriver, Hampton, 2 Piece, 1855, 86 In. 325.00
Masonic, Columns, Blue, White, Amelia Davis, 19th Century ....*Illus*   375.00
Overshot, Applied Fringe, Green, Tan, 3 Piece, Late 19th Century, 97 x 101 In. 325.00

Although coverlets and blankets should be rolled for storage, quilts can be folded. Fold the quilt in thirds and pad the folds with acid-free tissue paper so there is no sharp crease. Wrap the folded quilt and store it in a cool, dry place. Periodically refold the quilt so the folds are in a different place.

Coverlet, Jacquard,
Floral Arch, Davidson

Coverlet, Jacquard,
Snowflake, Navy,
David Haring

Coverlet, Masonic,
Columns, Blue, White,
Amelia Davis,
19th Century

Overshot, Geometric, Green, White, 92 x 108 In. 230.00
Overshot, Geometric, Linsey Woolsey, Blue, White, 19th Century, 92 x 90 1/2 In. 175.00
Overshot, Optical Pattern, Fringe 3 Sides, Navy Blue & Natural, 74 x 88 In. 110.00
Overshot, Optical Pattern, Navy Blue, Natural, 70 x 86 In. 190.00
Overshot, Red, White, Brown, Blue, 92 x 108 In. 200.00
Overshot, Snail Trail, Blue, White Cat's Track, 19th Century, 96 x 80 In. 196.00
Summer & Winter, Blue, White, Early 19th Century, 66 x 88 In. 210.00
Summer & Winter, Snowflake & Flowers, Blue, Cream, C.M. Palmer, 1838, 82 x 88 In. .. 720.00

COWAN POTTERY made art pottery and wares for florists. Guy Cowan
made pottery in Rocky River, Ohio, a suburb of Cleveland, from 1913
to 1931. A stylized mark with the word *Cowan* was used on most
pieces. A commercial, mass-produced line was marked *Lakeware*.
Collectors today search for the Art Deco pieces by Guy Cowan, Viktor
Schreckengost, Waylande Gregory, or Thelma Frazier Winter.

Ashtray, Denset, Feu Rouge, 5 1/2 In. 72.00
Ashtray, Egyptian Blue, Spherical, Original Ivory Cover, 3 1/4 In. 138.00
Ashtray, Lemon, Ivory Cover, Spherical, 3 1/4 In. 99.00
Ashtray, Shell, Apple Blossom Pink, 3 1/2 In., Pair 39.00
Bookends, Elephant, Push-Pull, Bronze, Margaret Postgate, 4 1/2 In. 1980.00
Bookends, Elephant, Semimatte Green Glaze, Stamped, 8 In. 770.00
Bookends, Girl, Standing, Figural, Katherine Barnes Jenkins, 7 In. 450.00
Bookends, Kicking Horse, Egyptian Blue, Waylande Gregory, 9 In. 2000.00
Bookends, Polar Bear, Primrose, Margaret Postgate, 6 1/4 In. 1210.00
Bookends, Pouter Pigeon, October, Elmer Novotny 1980.00
Bookends, Sunbonnet Girl, Gray Velour, 7 1/2 In. 120.00
Bookends, Unicorn, Leaves, 7 1/4 In. 190.00
Bowl, 2-Headed Pterodactyl, Ivory Ground, Green Interior, 15 In. 165.00
Bowl, Apple Blossom, 13 1/2 x 9 3/4 In. 90.00
Bowl, Console, Nasturtium, 13 1/2 x 9 3/4 In. 60.00
Bowl, Delphinium, 12 1/4 x 7 3/4 In. 55.00
Bowl, Etruscan, Leaves, 9 1/2 x 5 1/4 In. 55.00
Bowl, Larkspur, 11 3/4 x 3 3/4 In. 55.00
Bowl, Marigold, 12 In. 44.00
Bowl, Marigold, Monogram, RGC, Rolled Edge, 7 1/2 In. 35.00
Bowl, Modern, Special Ivory, 15 x 7 x 7 1/2 In. 220.00
Bowl, Oriental Red, 6 1/4 In. 385.00
Bowl, Seahorse, Hyacinth, 16 1/4 x 4 In. 66.00
Bowl, Terpsichore, April, 16 1/2 x 12 In. 55.00
Candelabrum, 2-Light, 2 Flower Grids, Special Ivory, 10 In. 66.00
Candleholder, Oriental Red, Scrolled Handles, 1 1/2 In., Pair 95.00
Candlestick, Byzantine, Turquoise, 9 In., Pair 120.00
Candlestick, Etruscan, Oriental Red, 1 3/4 In., Pair 39.00
Candlestick, Leaf Design, Feu Rouge, Waylande Gregory, 6 In., Pair 176.00
Candlestick, Marigold, 7 In., Pair 28.00

Candlestick, Nubian, Black, 4 In., Pair 120.00
Candlestick, Parchment Green, 4 In., Pair 66.00
Candlestick, Rowfant Club, Pine Green, Frank N. Wilcox, 9 1/4 In. 1210.00
Candy Box, Egyptian Blue, Raoul Josset & Jose Martin, 4 In. 550.00
Charger, Mermaid, Fish, Waves, Blue Green, Crackled Glaze, W. Gregory, 1935, 14 In. ... 3300.00
Cigarette Holder, Ashtray, Plum, Wrought Iron Handle, 2 3/4 In. 110.00
Cigarette Holder, Sea Horse, Special Ivory, 3 1/2 In. 28.00
Figurine, Awakening, Flower, Ivory, R. Guy Cowan, 9 In. ..../.................... 745.00
Figurine, Colonial Head, Ivory, Peach Crackled Glaze, Waylande Gregory, 14 x 7 In. 3656.00
Figurine, Debutante, Special Ivory, R. Guy Cowan, 10 In. 688.00
Figurine, Flower, Original Ivory, R. Guy Cowan, 8 In. 1980.00
Figurine, Head, Clear Crackle, Private Commission, James L. McCreery, 9 In. 2420.00
Figurine, Introspection, Black, A. Drexler Jacobson, 8 1/2 In. 1980.00
Figurine, La Reveuse, Black, A. Drexler Jacobson, Limited Edition, 11 1/2 In. 10000.00
Figurine, Margarita, Waylande Gregory, Clair De Lune, Label, 1989, 16 In. 7920.00
Figurine, Pavlova, Flower, Special Ivory, R. Guy Cowan & Walter Sinz, 6 In. 358.00
Figurine, Pavlova, Special Ivory, R. Guy Cowan, Walter Sinz, 6 In. 220.00
Figurine, Scarf Dancer, Flower, Original Ivory, R. Guy Cowan, 6 In. 385.00
Figurine, Scarf Dancer, Flower, Special Ivory, R. Guy Cowan, 6 In. 310.00
Figurine, Swan, Flower, Special Ivory, Waylande Gregory, 12 In. 1595.00
Figurine, Swirl Dancer, Original Ivory, R. Guy Cowan, 10 In. 1760.00
Flower Frog, 2 Dancing Girls, Clasped Hands, Wave Design, Signed, 7 3/4 In. 520.00
Flower Frog, Daffodil Yellow, 6 3/4 In. 90.00
Flower Frog, Lotus, Special Ivory, 3 1/4 In. 80.00
Flower Frog, Swirl Dancer, Ivory Glaze, Stamped, 10 3/4 x 4 In. 920.00
Jar, Strawberry, Oriental Red, Saucer, 6 1/4 In. 90.00
Lamp, Marigold, 7 3/4 In. 70.00
Match Holder, Cream, 3 1/2 In. 55.00
Paperweight, Elephant, Arabian Night, Margaret Postgate, 4 1/2 In. 385.00
Paperweight, Elephant, Cream High Glaze, Marked, 4 5/8 In. 330.00
Paperweight, Elephant, Logo On Back Of Plinth, 4 5/8 In. 636.00
Pitcher, Leaves, 9 In. 90.00
Plate, Vine Pattern, Special Ivory, Scalloped, 8 In. 30.00
Tile, Clover Design, Green, Black, Buff Clay, 4 x 4 In. 100.00
Vase, Amphora, April Green, 7 In. 39.00
Vase, Antique Green, Stilt Pulls On Base, 4 1/2 In. 100.00
Vase, April Green, 6 1/4 In. 50.00
Vase, Azure, Horizontal Rib Surface, 7 1/2 In. 155.00
Vase, Blue Luster Glaze, Marked, 9 3/4 In. 80.00
Vase, Bud, Palmetto Green, 6 In. 39.00
Vase, Delphinium, 7 1/2 In. 35.00
Vase, Diamond, Ivory, Bud, 6 In. 45.00
Vase, Fan, Flowers, Apple Blossom Pink, 8 3/4 In. 80.00
Vase, Fan, Flowers, Daffodil Yellow, 8 3/4 In. 70.00
Vase, Fan, Seahorse, Larkspur, 8 In. 80.00
Vase, Grape, Covered, Peacock, 10 In. 145.00
Vase, Green Matte Matrix, Marked, 5 In. 120.00
Vase, Lakeware, Flemish Blue, 6 1/2 In. 55.00
Vase, Lakeware, Peacock, 7 3/4 In. 55.00
Vase, Larkspur, 3 3/4 In. 20.00
Vase, Larkspur, 8 In. 55.00
Vase, Larkspur, Hexagon, 6 In. 110.00
Vase, Larkspur, Miniature, 3 1/2 In. 39.00
Vase, Logan, Sunrise, 8 In. 195.00
Vase, Mahogany Drip On Magenta, Drilled For Lamp, 11 1/2 In. 440.00
Vase, Marigold, 7 In. 28.00
Vase, Modernist, Antique Green, 8 In. 225.00
Vase, Morning Glory, Azure, 5 3/4 In. 66.00
Vase, Peacock, 8 3/4 In. 100.00
Vase, Peacock, Hexagon, 6 In. 39.00
Vase, Pillow, Antique Green, Raised Design, 6 3/4 In. 120.00
Vase, Plum Drip On Orchid, 7 In. 330.00

Vase, Plum Glaze, 9 In. 175.00
Vase, Plum, Handle, 9 1/4 In. 195.00
Vase, Russet Brown, Horizontal Rib Surface, 9 In. 176.00
Vase, Seahorse, Special Ivory, Bud, 7 1/2 In. 35.00
Vase, Special Ivory, 6 1/4 In. 35.00
Vase, Stylized Fish, Seaweed, Light Green Sgraffito, Emerald Ground, 6 x 5 1/4 In. 1070.00
Vase, Yellow Rose, 5 3/4 In. 39.00
Vase, Yellow Rose, Horizontal Rib Surface, 4 3/4 In. 35.00

CRACKER JACK, the molasses-flavored popcorn mixture, was first
made in 1896 in Chicago, Illinois. A prize was added to each box in
1912. Collectors search for the old boxes, toys, and advertising materials. Many of the toys are unmarked.

Charm, Bowling, Metal 7.50
Charm, Cowboy On Bronco, Metal 8.50
Charm, Domino, Plastic, Black 7.50
Charm, Elephant, Plastic 6.00
Charm, Goddess, Plastic, Blue On White 10.00
Postcard, Cracker Jack Bears, No. 6, With Offer, Rueckhelm Bros. & Eckstein 40.00
Prairie Whistle, Warbler Bird Call, Japan, 1950s, 1 In. 3.25
Toy, Bulldozer, Tin 45.00
Toy, Delivery Truck, 1 1/2 In. ....78.00 to 80.00
Toy, Horse & Wagon, Driver, Tin, Red, Blue & White, 1930s 50.00
Toy, Locomotive, Tin, Red, 4-6-9, 1939, 2 1/4 In. 35.00
Toy, Spinner, White & Blue 95.00
Whistle, Flat, 1 x 2 5/8 In. 110.00
Whistle, Man's Head, Large Mouth, Gold Colored Tin, 2 1/4 In. 65.00
Whistle, Tin, Metal Chain, Policeman On Card, Japan, 1950s 25.00

CRACKLE GLASS was originally made by the Venetians, but most of the
ware found today dates from the 1800s. The glass was heated, cooled,
and refired so that many small lines appeared inside the glass. It was
made in many factories in the United States and Europe.

Bowl, Pink Over Vaseline, Applied Thorn Feet, 4 x 4 In. 195.00
Cup & Saucer, Cranberry, Clear Applied Handle, 2 1/2 & 4 1/4 In. 75.00
Vase, Foo Dog Handles, Mounted As Lamp, 23 In., Pair 1300.00
Vase, Vaseline, 10 In. 65.00

CRANBERRY GLASS is an almost transparent yellow-red glass. It resembles the color of cranberry juice. The glass has been made in Europe
and America since the Civil War. It is still being made, and reproductions can fool the unwary. Related glass items may be listed in other
categories, such as Northwood, Rubena Verde, etc.

Biscuit Jar, Melon Ribbed, Silver Plated Cover, 9 In. 400.00
Bottle, Wine, White Enameled Flowers, Leaves, Clear Ball Stopper, 9 1/2 In. ....185.00 to 225.00
Bowl, 3 Clear Applied Branches Of Leaves, Crimp Edge, 6 3/4 In. 295.00
Bowl, Applied Gold Threading, Ruffled Edge, 5 In. 135.00
Compote, Cranberry Over White, Gold Trim, 13 1/4 x 9 1/4 In. 750.00
Compote, Enameled Gold Draped Sides, White, Gold, Black Flowers, 3 In. 175.00
Decanter, Enameled Gold, Cut To Clear, 9 In. 150.00
Decanter, Wine, Pinched Sides, Enameled Gold Flowers, 12 1/4 In. 245.00
Epergne, 13 1/2 In. 260.00
Finger Bowl, Reverse Swirl Pattern, Gold Trim, 8 Piece 330.00
Jewelry Box, Squiggle Design, Enameled Flowers & Gold Panels, 3 x 5 In. 275.00
Lamp, Miniature, Molded Swirl & Bead, 8 1/2 In. 250.00
Pitcher, Hobstars & Stripes 3800.00
Punch Set, Enameled Design, Bowl, Cover, Ladle, Cups, 15 In., 12 Piece 695.00
Salt, Open, Art Nouveau Sterling Holder 225.00
Tumbler, Amber Base, Enameled Gold Women, Urn, Flowers, 1850s, 5 In. 415.00
Vase, Baluster Form, Enameled Floral Gold Medallion, 14 In., Pair 920.00
Vase, Clear Overshot, Teardrops, Collared Rim, 4 1/2 In. 145.00
Vase, Enameled Gold German Buildings, 6 In. 605.00

Vase, Shading To Opalescent Rim, 6 Petal Feet, Slender, 10 In. 242.00
Vase, Trumpet, Enameled Blue & White Flowers, 6 In. 165.00

CREAMWARE, or queensware, was developed by Josiah Wedgwood about 1765. It is a cream-colored earthenware that has been copied by many factories. Similar wares may be listed under Pearlware and Wedgwood.

Basket, Flowers, Pierced Turned Out Sides, Cord Twist Handles, 7 In. 430.00
Bowl, Black Transfer, Benjamin Franklin & George Washington, c.1790, 8 In. 1150.00
Bowl, Black Transfer, Maritime Design, Motto, c.1800, 7 In. 460.00
Bowl, Brown Mottled Glaze, Green Center Interior, Staffordshire, 11 In. 1265.00
Bowl, Interior Scene Of Figures In Chinese Garden, Rose Exterior, 4 1/2 x 9 1/2 In. 1430.00
Coffeepot, Ball Finial, Acanthus Scroll Spout, Strap Handle, 11 In. 550.00
Coffeepot, Queen's Rose, c.1780, 9 1/2 In. 1500.00
Creamer, Cover, Cow, Milkmaid, Spotted Coat, Staffordshire, 1830s, 7 1/4 In., Pair 3000.00
Cup, Handles, Cottage Scene On Verso, J. Renshaw, Dated 1803, 5 1/4 In. 546.00
Mug, Frog, 2 Figures Flanked By Flags, 1825 .... 990.00
Mug, Medallion Of Captain Ordney, 1785 .... 1260.00
Persian, Jardiniere, Stylized Orchid, Angled Scrolls, c.1916, 11 1/2 In. 230.00
Plate, Grisaille Master Ship, American Flag, 14 Stars, 10 In. 230.00
Plate, Hot Water, c.1780, 9 1/2 In. 150.00
Plate, Pierced Rope-Work Edge, c.1810, 8 1/2 In. 175.00
Plate, Queen's Rose, Scalloped Edge, c.1790, 8 In. 300.00
Tankard, Farmer & Wife In Landscape, Barn, Workers, Late 18th Century, 6 In. 345.00
Tea Solitaire, Urn Shape, Maroon, Black, Octagonal Handled Tray, 1890s, 6 Piece 1840.00
Teapot, Bullet, Strap Handles, When This You See Remember Me, Cover, c.1780 .... 1500.00
Tureen, Cover, Pierced Rim, Melon Finial, Floral Sprays & Wreaths, 1780s, 8 In. 980.00
Tureen, Stand, Grisaille, Ribbon Borders, Trophies, Muses, 10 x 15 x 10 1/2 In. 345.00

CREDIT CARDS, credit tokens, metal charge plates, phone cards, and other similar collectibles that replace money are now part of the numismatic collecting hobby.

Avis-Visa, Jackie Robinson's 200.00
Bloomingdales, Metal, 1980 .... 14.00

CROWN DERBY is the name given to porcelain made in Derby, England, from the 1770s to 1935. Pieces are marked with a crown and the letter *D* or the word *Derby*. The earliest pieces were made by the original Derby factory, while later pieces were made by the King Street Partnerships (1848–1935) or the Derby Crown Porcelain Co. (1876–1890). Derby Crown Porcelain Co. became Royal Crown Derby Co. Ltd. in 1890. It is now part of Royal Doulton Tableware Ltd.

Bowl, Lions' Heads Corners, Scrolled Handles, Signed, 9 x 11 1/4 In. 440.00
Dish, Lozenge Shape, Heart, Cobalt, Gilt Rims, 11 In., 4 Piece 460.00
Dish, Oriental Pattern, Green & Gilt Flowers, Signed, 8 1/2 x 10 In. 165.00
Jar, Cover, Allover Flowers, Cream Ground, Painted Marks, 14 In. 920.00
Tureen, Cover, Chestnut, Puce Florets, Vine Handle, Insects, 8 x 9 In. 345.00
Vase, Cover, Flowers, Club Form, Ivory & Gilt Finish, 13 3/4 In. 287.00
Vase, Urn, Campana Form, Floral Reserve, Gilt Ground, 1825 .... 8000.00

CROWN DUCAL is the name used on some pieces of porcelain made by A. G. Richardson and Co., Ltd., of Tunstall and Cobridge, England. The name has been used since 1916.

Bowl, Bristol, Purple, Embossed Flower Border, 8 In. 20.00
Bowl, Rose & Peony Chintz, 8 In. 260.00
Cup & Saucer, Marigold 85.00
Hot Water Pot, Cover, Orange Tree, 6 1/2 In. 118.00
Pitcher, Leaves, White & Red, 7 1/2 In. 67.00
Plate, Bristol, Purple, Embossed Flower Border, 8 In. 31.00
Plate, Bristol, Red Transfer, Birds & Flowers 51.00
Plate, Florentine, Fruit & Flower Center, Signed, 10 1/2 In., 12 Piece 373.00
Plate, Gainsborough, 9 In. 10.50

Plate, Gainsborough, Square, 7 1/2 In.		15.50
Plate, Harmony Chintz, 9 In.		60.00
Plate, Pink Chintz Roses, Black Border, 8 Sides, 9 In.		77.00
Platter, Bristol, Blue, Transfer, Exotic Bird With Peonies, 15 3/4 In.		86.00
Salt & Pepper, Primula Chintz		91.00
Teapot, Pansy Chintz, 6 3/4 In.		400.00
Vase, Fan, Exotic Birds On Tree Peonies, Blue, 7 7/8 In.		463.00

CROWN MILANO glass was made by Frederick Shirley at the Mt. Washington Glass Works about 1890. It had a plain biscuit color with a satin finish. It was decorated with flowers and often had large gold scrolls.

Bowl, Yellow Green, Pansies, Roses, Tricornered, Crown Mark, 9 1/2 In.	1200.00
Box, Cover, Melon Ribbed, Allover Pansies, Gold Trim, Fitted, 3 1/2 x 2 1/2 In.	350.00
Bride's Bowl, Pansies, Tricornered, Grapevines, Pairpoint Holder, 11 In.	3750.00
Cracker Jar, Bail, Peach Shaded To Cream Enameled Flowers, Silver Plate	950.00
Cracker Jar, Bail, Turtle Finial, Roses, Silver Plate	1200.00
Cracker Jar, Gold Chrysanthemums & Scrolls, Signed, 9 In.	575.00
Cracker Jar, Silver Cover, Barrel Shape, Flowers, Crown Mark, 7 1/4 In.	1200.00
Cracker Jar, Silver Plate Domed Cover, Lotus Blossoms, Squat, Signed	750.00
Cracker Jar, Silver Plated Cover, Bail, Orange Leaves, 7 1/2 In.	896.00
Ewer, Colonial Couple, Egg Shape, Gold Trim, Wreath Mark, 16 In.	5775.00
Ewer, Enameled Blossoms, Gold Crosshatching, 6 1/2 In.	835.00
Ewer, Green & Gold Enameled Flowers, Squat, Serpent Handle, c.1894, 8 In.	2000.00
Ewer, Lotus Blossoms, Gold Enameled, Pale Green, Squat, 1894, 8 x 8 In.	2000.00
Jar, Cover, Roses, Tulips, Allover Gold Enameled, Squat, Footed, 9 x 5 3/4 In.	2200.00
Jar, Sweetmeat, Cover, Diamond-Quilted, Barrel Shape, Silver Plated Frame, 4 In.	1100.00
Jardiniere, Pansies, Medallions, Gold Enameled Neck, Bulbous, Signed, 9 x 7 In.	1250.00
Jardiniere, Pansies, Medallions, Pink & Gold Enameled Neck, Bulbous, 10 In.	750.00
Mustard, Gold Flowers, Silver Plated Cover, Handle, 4 In.	575.00
Perfume Bottle, Atomizer, Trumpet Vine Design, Swirled, 6 1/2 In.	595.00
Pickle Castor, Floral Crosses, Footed, Silver Plated Cover, Frame, Tongs	1100.00
Pitcher, Syrup, Silver Plated Hinged Cover, Flowers, Beaded, Cream Ground	1500.00
Plate, Multicolor & Gold Enameled Flowers & Trim, Tricornered, Signed	475.00
Rose Bowl, Allover Daisies & Roses, 3 1/2 x 4 1/2 In.	350.00
Rose Bowl, Enameled Pastel Pansies, Gold Leaves, Spherical, 5 1/8 In.	675.00
Sugar & Creamer, Enameled Violets, Label, 4 1/4 & 3 1/2 In.	1250.00
Sugar & Creamer, Silver Plated Cover, Pink Enameled, Bulbous, Handles	800.00
Sugar & Creamer, Silver Plated Cover, Scrolls & Flowers, Ribbed, 6 In.	450.00
Tumbler, Gold Enameled Garlands, Flowers, Red Crown & Wreath Mark, 4 In.	550.00
Vase, Allover Enameled Leaf, Flowers, 5 1/2 x 17 7/8 In.	860.00
Vase, Allover Gold Enameled Fern, Scrolls Around Neck, 8 3/4 In.	1200.00
Vase, Allover Gold Enameled Mums, Bulbous, Squat, 4 1/2 In.	825.00
Vase, Gold Enameled Cherubs Frolicking, Signed, 19 x 8 In.	1725.00
Vase, Gold Enameled Flowering Cacti, Squat, 7 1/4 In.	1715.00
Vase, Gold Enameled Medallions, Allover Flowers, 5 1/2 x 7 In.	1260.00
Vase, Gold Enameled Pansies, Gourd Shape, Large Neck Ring, 9 In.	950.00
Vase, Gold Enameled Peony Blossoms, Gold Outlined, 6 In.	1450.00
Vase, Gold Enameled, Applied Jewels, Tapered, Ruffled Edge, 11 1/2 In.	350.00
Vase, Gold Gingko Design, Shields, 6 1/2 x 7 1/2 In.	520.00
Vase, Grape Leaves & Vines, Sepia Wash, Footed, Bulbous, 7 1/2 In.	725.00
Vase, Jeweled, Green Highlights, 13 x 6 In.	2240.00
Vase, Ocean Wave, Gold Enameled Starfish, Footed, 10 In.	7975.00
Vase, Overlapping Fern Fronds, Tan Shadows, Bulbous, Squat, 15 In.	1500.00
Vase, Peony Blossoms, Yellow Ground, 8 In.	765.00
Vase, Persian, Jeweled Serpent, Red, Green, Flowers, 10 In.	3160.00
Vase, Persian, Wild Rose Design, 13 In.	1780.00
Vase, Pink Wild Roses, Yellow, White Ground, 9 1/2 x 4 In.	747.00
Vase, Snake, Mottled Tan Leaf Design, 9 1/2 In.	172.00
Vase, Tan Shadow Ferns, Gold Enameled, Bulbous, Squat, Footed, 5 In.	770.00
Vase, Teasel Leaves, Fall Colors, Egg Shape, Marked, 12 In.	2200.00
Vase, White Blossoms & Buds, Gold Enameled, Blue Scrolls, Baluster, 7 In.	1100.00

CROWN TUSCAN pattern is included in the Cambridge glass category.

CRUETS of glass or porcelain were made to hold vinegar, oil, and other condiments. They were especially popular during Victorian times and have been made in a variety of styles since the eighteenth century. Additional cruets may be found in the Castor Set category and also in various glass categories.

Amber Glass, Enameled White Flowers & Leaves, Applied Handle, 8 x 4 In.	145.00
Art Glass, White, Cranberry Spatter, Clear Handle, Victorian, 6 3/4 In.	100.00
Clear Glass, Enameled White Flowers, Leaves, Strawberries, Applied Blue Handle, 8 In.	175.00
Clear Glass, Enameled Yellow Dots, Flowers, Handle, 7 1/2 In.	175.00
Cranberry Glass, Diamond-Quilted, Floral, Applied Clear Handle, Cut Stopper, 9 In.	225.00
Cranberry Glass, Enameled Branches, Footed, Applied Clear Handle, Cut Stopper, 11 In.	235.00
Cranberry Glass, Inverted Thumbprint Applied Ribbed Handle, Cut Stopper, 6 7/8 In.	100.00
Olive Glass, Enameled Violets, 3-Petal Top, Applied Handle, Blown Stopper, 8 1/2 In.	165.00
Sapphire Blue Glass, Enameled Lily-Of-The-Valley, 3-Petal Top, Blown Stopper, 8 In.	175.00

CT GERMANY was first part of a mark used by a company in Altwasser, Germany, in 1845. The initials stand for C. Tielsch, a partner in the firm. The Hutschenreuther firm took over the company in 1918 and continued to use the *CT*.

Basket, Pink & White, Inscribed Hartford, Connecticut In Gold, 3 1/2 In.	27.00
Bowl, Ribbed, Robin's-Egg Blue, White Floral Spray, Ornate Open Handle, 12 In.	47.00
Cup & Saucer, Orchids, Green Ground, Artist, C. Tielsch & Co., 1875-1935	45.00
Plate, Flowers, C. Tielsch & Co., 1875-1934, 8 1/4 In.	55.00

CUP PLATES are small glass or china plates that held the cup while a diner of the mid-nineteenth century drank coffee or tea from the saucer. The most famous cup plates were made of glass at the Boston and Sandwich factory located in Sandwich, Massachusetts. There have been many new glass cup plates made in recent years for sale to gift shops or limited edition collectors. These are similar to the old plates but can be recognized as new.

Acorn, Yellow, Green, Black Leaves, Teal Caps, Spatterware, 5 In.	1870.00
Building, 3-Story, Staffordshire, 3 1/2 In.	330.00
Castle Garden, Battery At New York, Wood & Sons, Staffordshire, 3 3/4 In.	385.00
Flower Basket In Center, Scalloped Wheat Sheaf Rim, 3 11/16 In.	2400.00
Glass, Eagle, Medium Blue, Scalloped Edge, 19th Century	440.00
Glass, Sunburst, Blue	385.00
Hoboken In New Jersey, Blue, Stubbs, Staffordshire, 3 1/4 In.	300.00
King's Rose, Oyster Variation, Staffordshire, Mid 19th Century, 5 1/4 In.	275.00
Lacy, Amethyst, American, 19th Century	1100.00
Palmetto Tree, Blue, Staffordshire, 4 In.	770.00
Peafowl, Green, Blue, Red, Spatterware, 5 1/4 In.	1265.00
Pressed Glass, Bunker Hill, No. 640	10.00
Pressed Glass, Eagle, 3 1/8 In.	53.00
Pressed Glass, Heart Rim, Heart Center, 3 1/4 In.	7.50
Pressed Glass, Henry Clay, 3 1/2 In.	18.00 to 38.00
Pressed Glass, Log Cabin, Heart, No. 595	37.00
Pressed Glass, Ship, No. 619-A	16.50
Pressed Glass, Stars In Center, Around Border, Scalloped	43.00
Pressed Glass, Sunburst Center, Rings Around Border, Scalloped Edge, 3 1/2 In.	28.00
Pressed Glass, Waffle, 3 3/4 In.	10.00
Ship, Yellow Green, Scalloped Edge, Glass, American, 19th Century	468.00
Spatterware, Red & Green Parrot, 4 In.	660.00
Staffordshire, Dark Blue Transfer, Castle Garden, 3 5/8 In.	265.00
Staffordshire, Feather Edge, House Pattern, Sponged Trees, Cobalt, 4 1/4 In.	192.00
Staffordshire, Medium Blue Transfer, Scenic Cartouches, Scrollwork, 4 3/4 In.	66.00
Staffordshire, Rhone Scenery, T.J. & J. Mayer	54.00
Staffordshire, Steamer City Of Bangor, Scalloped Edge, Gold Trim, Carle & Jones	38.00
Staffordshire, Worcester Cathedral, Ralph Hall	51.00
Star, Blue, Glass, American, 19th Century	330.00

CURRIER & IVES made the famous American lithographs marked with their name from 1857 to 1907. The mark used on the print included the street address in New York City, and it is possible to date the year of the original issue from this information. Earlier prints were made by N. Currier and use that name from 1835 to 1847. Many reprints of the Currier or Currier & Ives prints have been made. Some collectors buy the insurance calendars that were based on the old prints. The words *large, small,* or *medium folio* refer to size. The original print sizes were very small (up to about 7 x 9 in.), small (8.8 x 12.8 in.), medium (9 x 14 in. to 14 x 20 in.), large (larger than 14 x 20 in.). Other sizes are probably later copies. Other prints by Currier & Ives may be listed in the Card category under Advertising and in the Sheet Music category. Currier & Ives dinnerware patterns may be found in the Adams or Dinnerware categories.

4 Seasons Of Life, Childhood, Frame, 15 1/8 x 23 1/8 In.	1955.00
American Country Life, October Afternoon, Frame, 1855, 16 1/8 x 23 In.	1495.00
American Express Train, Frances F. Palmer, Frame, 1864, 17 5/8 x 28 In.	7800.00
American Hunting Scenes, A Good Chance, Frame, 1863, 18 x 27 1/8 In.	6900.00
Battle Of Gettysburg, July 3, 1863, Bird's-Eye Maple Frame, 16 1/2 x 14 In.	250.00
Battle Of The Wilderness, Va., Frame, 1864, Large Folio	1650.00
Bombardment & Capture Of Fort Fisher, Frame, 10 x 14 In.	165.00
Bombardment Of Fort Pulaski, Frame, April 1862, 13 12 x 17 5/8 In.	220.00
Bombardment Of Fort Sumter Charleston Harbor, 11 3/4 x 19 1/8 In.	330.00
Bombardment Of Island, Frame, 13 1/2 x 17 5/8 In.	110.00
Butt Of The Jokers, Reprint, Frame, 13 1/2 x 17 3/4 In.	165.00
City Of New York, 1876, 21 x 34 In.	630.00
City Of Philadelphia, 23 x 32 In.	360.00
Clipper Ship Dreadnought Off Tuuskar Light, Frame, 16 1/4 x 24 1/8 In.	3450.00
El Capitan From Mariposa Trail, Frame, 12 1/4 x 13 3/4 In.	275.00
Fall Of Richmond, Virginia, On Night Of April 2d. 1865, 22 1/2 x 28 1/2 In.	550.00
Fiend Of The Road, 19 x 27 In.	550.00
Futurity Race At Sheepshead Bay, 1889	719.00
General Z. Taylor, Rough & Ready, 17 1/2 x 13 1/2 In.	305.00
Great St. Louis Bridge, Across The Mississippi, 9 1/4 x 15 1/4 In.	345.00
Hudson River View, From Ruggles House, Newburgh, Frame, 8 3/4 x 12 3/4 In.	290.00
James K. Polk, Frame, 16 3/4 x 12 3/4 In.	220.00
Last Shot, Louis Maurer, 1858, Frame, 17 3/8 x 25 3/8 In.	4500.00
Lookout Mountain, Tennessee, Frances F. Palmer, Frame, 1866, 15 x 21 In.	1440.00
Maiden Rock, Mississippi River Reprint, 10 x 13 1/4 In.	345.00
Maple Sugaring, Early Spring In Northern Woods, Maple Frame, 12 x 16 In.	1595.00
Mule Train On Down Grade, Clar De Track, We's A Comin, Foxing, 1881, 9 In.	275.00
New England Winter Scene, French Wash Matte, Frame, 1861, 18 x 25 In.	7200.00
Old Windmill, 10 3/4 x 14 1/8 In.	650.00
Pigeon Shooting, Playing The Decoy, 1862, 19 x 27 1/8 In.	4888.00
Pride Of The Garden, Frame, 16 5/8 x 13 1/2 In.	110.00
Pursuit, A.F. Tait, 1856, Frame, 18 x 25 1/2 In.	5400.00
Rabbit Catching, The Trap Spring, Black Frame, 10 15/16 x 14 1/2 In.	385.00
Siege Of Charleston, 11 7/8 x 15 1/4 In.	275.00
Splendid Naval Triumph On Mississippi, 1862, 27 1/2 x 35 1/2 In.	1320.00
Star Spangled Banner, Lady Liberty Holding Flag, 12 1/4 x 16 3/8 In.	165.00
Summer Scenes In New York Harbor, Frame, 1863, Large Folio	9200.00
The Storming Of Fort Donelson, Tenn., Matted, Reprint, 15 1/2 x 22 1/2 In.	170.00
To The Coney Island Jockey Club, Frame, 31 1/2 x 43 In.	1000.00
Trotting For A Great Stake, Frame, 1890, 26 x 36 1/2 In.	800.00
Valley Falls Virginia, Veneered Frame, 19th Century, Reprint, 9 1/2 x 13 In.	140.00

CUSTARD GLASS is a slightly yellow opaque glass. It was first made in England in the 1880s and was first made in the United States in the 1890s. It has been reproduced. Additional pieces may be found in the Cambridge, Fenton, Heisey, and Northwood categories. Custard glass is called Ivorina Verde by Heisey and other companies.

Argonaut Shell, Salt & Pepper	1500.00
Beaded Circle, Salt & Pepper	2400.00

Chrysanthemum Sprig, Celery Vase 950.00
Chrysanthemum Sprig, Celery Vase, Blue 2050.00
Chrysanthemum Sprig, Cruet, 7 In. ....100.00 to 263.00
Chrysanthemum Sprig, Pitcher 650.00
Chrysanthemum Sprig, Pitcher, Blue 1500.00
Chrysanthemum Sprig, Salt & Pepper 400.00
Chrysanthemum Sprig, Toothpick 275.00
Chrysanthemum Sprig, Tumbler, Blue 150.00
Harvard, Toothpick, Souvenir, Topeka, Kansas 25.00
Intaglio, Compote, Green & Gold, Footed, 3 x 4 1/2 In. 125.00
Intaglio, Pitcher, Green & Gold Trim, 8 1/2 In. 585.00
Intaglio, Water Set, Green & Gold Trim, 7 Piece 750.00
Inverted Fan & Feather, Creamer 195.00
Inverted Fan & Feather, Spooner 195.00
Louis XV, Creamer 65.00
Louis XV, Cruet, Gold Trim, Stopper 220.00
Louis XV, Table Set, 5 Piece 580.00
Maize is its own category in this book.
Maple Leaf, Creamer, Gold Trim 65.00
Maple Leaf, Spooner, Gold Trim 65.00
Maple Leaf, Table Set, 4 Piece 335.00
Maple Leaf, Toothpick, Enameled, Gold Trim 1000.00
Ribbed Drape, Toothpick 145.00
Three Fruits, Plate, Blue, 9 In. 350.00
Wild Bouquet, Cruet, Enameled, Gold Trim 850.00
Wild Bouquet, Pitcher, Enameled, Gold Trim 2950.00
Wild Bouquet, Salt & Pepper, Enameled, Gold Trim 5000.00
Wild Bouquet, Table Set, Enameled, Gold Trim, 4 Piece 5450.00
Wild Bouquet, Toothpick, Enameled, Gold Trim 2000.00

CUT GLASS has been made since ancient times, but the large majority of the pieces now for sale date from the brilliant period of glass design, 1880 to 1905. These pieces have elaborate geometric designs with a deep miter cut. Modern cut glass with a similar appearance is being made in England, Ireland, and the Czech and Slovak republics. Chips and scratches are often difficult to notice but lower the value dramatically. A signature on the glass adds significantly to the value. Other cut glass pieces are listed under factory names.

Basket, Hobstar & Pinwheel, Twist Handle, 4 3/4 x 6 1/2 In. 275.00
Basket, Oval Shape, Handle, Ruffled Edge, 7 1/2 In. 525.00
Bell, Rockport, Unger Bros., 5 1/4 In. 265.00
Bowl, 5 Jewel Center Hobstars, Clark, 2 1/2 x 9 In. 1525.00
Bowl, Amber, Cut To Crystal, 3-Footed, Scrolled, 9 1/2 In. 35.00
Bowl, Amethyst, Gilt, Bronze Mount, Sienna Marble Base, 10 x 8 In. 1150.00
Bowl, Brilliant Cut, Signed, Libbey, 9 1/4 x 4 In. 176.00
Bowl, Columbia, Blackmer, 9 In. 595.00
Bowl, Flower Spray, Low, Hawkes Gravic, 9 In. 195.00
Bowl, Flowers, Cover, Ireland, 8 1/4 In. 184.00
Bowl, Fluron, J. Hoare, 4 1/2 In. 375.00
Bowl, Grapes & Leaves Engraving, Medallions, Green & Gold Design, 7 In. 125.00
Bowl, Hobstar & Fan, Harvard Type, 8 x 3 1/2 In. 275.00
Bowl, Hobstar Base, Fluted & Scalloped Edge, 8 In. 325.00
Bowl, Hobstar, 3 3/4 x 8 In. 185.00
Bowl, Hobstar, Fan, Crosshatch, Scalloped Sawtooth Rim, Bulbous, c.1900, 11 5/8 In. ... 633.00
Bowl, Low Dome Cover, Underplate, Diamond Border, Rayed Knob Finial, 10 In. 1955.00
Bowl, Stars, Round, Signed, Hawkes, 3 1/2 x 8 In. 144.00
Bowl, Sunburst, 4 1/2 x 9 1/2 In. 155.00
Bowl, Thistle, 9 x 4 1/2 In. 165.00
Bowl, Triple Square, Dentil Edge, Clark, 4 x 10 1/2 In. 3250.00
Box, Handkerchief, Hinged Cover, Intaglio, Silver Fittings 450.00
Box, Hinged Cover, 8-Point Star, C.F. Monroe, 5 In. 345.00
Butter, Cover, Plymouth, Meriden, 5 1/2 x 8 In. 425.00

Butter Tub, Pluto, Hoare 275.00
Candlestick, 6 Sides, Paneled, Teardrop, 14 In., Pair 1200.00
Candy Dish, Hobstar, Heart Shape, 6 In. 350.00
Carafe, 8 Sides, Notched Panel Neck, 7 In. 295.00
Carafe, Victoria, Hoare, c.1890, 7 In. 140.00
Carafe Set, Diamond Facets, Panels, Swags, Gold Trim, 8 In., Pair 345.00
Celery Dish, Ruby Cut To Clear, Scalloped Base, 9 In. 185.00
Centerpiece, Everted Gilt Rim, Cobalt Ground, 9 x 12 1/2 In. 2300.00
Centerpiece, Ovals On Flared Stem, Circular, Footed, 10 1/2 x 10 In. 258.00
Cheese Dish, Domed Cover, Stars, Strawberry-Diamond, Octagonal, 9 In. 575.00
Compote, Allover Fan, 12 In., Pair 29.00
Compote, Central Beaded Star, Hobstar & Fans, Scalloped Base, 10 1/4 In. 224.00
Compote, Chains Of Hobstars, Separated By Strawberry-Diamond, 3 x 7 In., Pair 405.00
Compote, Diamond, Paneled Pedestal, Urn Shape, 5 3/4 x 8 3/4 In., Pair 440.00
Compote, Hobstars, Fans, 4-Point Stars, Teardrop Stem, 9 3/4 In. 275.00
Compote, Monarch, Scalloped Base, Teardrop Stem, Hoare, 7 x 8 In. 395.00
Compote, Paneled, Faceted Stem, Footed, Anglo-Irish, c.1850, 9 3/4 x 11 In. 374.00
Compote, Strawberry-Diamond, Sawtooth, Rays & Fans, Applied Stem, 9 In. 610.00
Compote, Twist Cut, Hobstar, Hexagonal, Controlled Air Bubble, 1900, 10 1/2 In. 345.00
Cruet, Greek Key, Silver Stopper, 5 1/4 In. 850.00
Cruet, Hobstars, 2 Neck Rings, 24-Point Star Base, 3-Notch Handle, Stopper, 7 In. 450.00
Cruet, Strawberry-Diamond & Fan, Stopper, 6 In. 95.00
Cup, Punch, Strawberry-Diamond & Fan, Applied Handles, c.1830, 3 In., 4 Piece 375.00
Decanter, Alternating Diamond & Printies, Stopper, 13 In. 143.00
Decanter, Band Of Diamonds, Band Of Flowers, Flutes, Fluted Stopper, 12 In. 103.00
Decanter, Brandy, Blue To Clear, Facade Gold Trim, Cut Steeple Stopper, 30 In. 3220.00
Decanter, Circles & Panels, Cranberry To Clear, Stopper, Silver Bourbon Tag, 11 In. 275.00
Decanter, Club Shape, Green To White, To Clear, Continental, 9 1/2 In. 150.00
Decanter, Crossed Strawberry-Diamond, Crosscut Diamond & Stars, 11 1/2 In. 185.00
Decanter, Diamond Band, Octagonal, Ball Stopper, 9 In., Pair 173.00
Decanter, Diamond, Silver Sterling Scotch & Bourbon Tags, 12 1/2 In., Pair 275.00
Decanter, Faceted, Blown Stopper, 12 x 4 In. 161.00
Decanter, Flowers, Medallions, Handle, Signed, Sinclaire, 9 x 5 In. 354.00
Decanter, Harvard, Stopper, Libbey, 15 In. 395.00
Decanter, Leafy Scroll, Sunburst Base, Mushroom Stopper, Alvin Co., 1905, 9 In. 345.00
Decanter, Ring Neck, Strawberry-Diamond & Fan, Domed Stopper, 10 In., Pair 1380.00
Decanter, Stars, Tapering To Long Petal At Neck, Stopper, 14 1/2 In. 340.00
Decanter, Whiskey, Faceted Sides, Mushroom Stopper, Silver Plated Coaster, 10 In. 115.00
Decanter Set, Tantalus, Gilt Bronze, Stopper, 12 3/4 In., 19 Piece 6600.00
Dish, Ice Cream, Hobstar & Daisy, Edenhall Type Rim, 4 Piece 140.00
Dish, Mayonnaise, Hobstar, 6 In. 65.00
Epergne, Crenellated Rolled Edge, Octagonal Star Base, 21 3/4 In. 1265.00
Finger Bowl, Russian, 2 1/2 In. 75.00
Goblet, Cranberry To Clear, Floral, Continental, 7 3/4 In., 4 Piece 115.00
Goblet, Flowers, Vine, 1900, 8 1/8 In., 12 Piece 489.00
Goblet, Garland, Geometric Gold Trim, Continental, 9 1/2 x 4 1/4 In. 259.00
Hatpin Holder, Band Of 6-Point Stars, Hobstar Center, 8 In. 875.00
Ice Pail, Diamond, Star, Crosshatch, 7 1/2 In. 201.00
Jar, Cover, Hobstars, Hobstar Base, 3 3/4 In. 335.00
Jar, Cover, Numa, Maple City, 3 1/4 In. 165.00
Knife Rest, Notched Panel, 5 In. 75.00
Knife Rest, Panels, 6 Sides, Emerald Green, Pair 80.00
Lamp, Boudoir, Hobstars, Mushroom Shade, 13 In. ....*Illus* 1200.00
Lamp, Hobstars & 3-Point Stars, Mushroom Shade, 15 x 10 In. 1120.00
Napkin Ring, Hobstar, Pair, 1 3/4 In. 175.00
Nappy, Buzz Stars, Diamond Hobnail, Handles, 6 In. 70.00
Pitcher, Champagne, Hobstars In Ovals On Sides, Cane & Hobstar Handle, 11 In. 475.00
Pitcher, Diamond With Cane, Zipper, Sterling Repousse, 12 1/2 In. 975.00
Pitcher, Flowers, Etched Flower Petals, Scalloped Rim, c.1895, 10 1/4 In. 265.00
Pitcher, Hobstar & Notched, Crosshatch, Punt Handle, 32 Point Star Base, 8 In. 360.00
Pitcher, Hobstar Base, Cut Handle, Ruffled Edge, Clark, 7 In. 400.00
Pitcher, Hobstar, Sawtooth Rim, Double Notch Applied Handle, c.1900, 11 In. 175.00

Cut Glass, Punch Bowl, Flared
Base, Harvard, 12 1/2 In., 2 Piece

Cut Glass, Lamp, Boudoir,
Hobstars, Mushroom Shade, 13 In.

Pitcher, Hobstars, Crosshatch, Diamonds, 32 Point Star Base, Ice Lip, 9 In.	675.00
Pitcher, Oriental, Cut Handle, Hobstar Base, Dorflinger, 9 1/4 In.	975.00
Pitcher, Paneled Neck, Sterling Silver Handle & Band, 8 7/8 In.	50.00
Pitcher, Star & Swirl, 7 In.	120.00
Pitcher, Viscaria, Pairpoint, 10 In.	285.00
Plate, Carnation Spray, 10 In.	195.00
Punch Bowl, Base, Engraved, Daisy, Sawtooth Rim, 10 1/2 In.	200.00
Punch Bowl, Cover, Knob Finial, Notched Collar, Crenellated Edge, 13 In.	575.00
Punch Bowl, Flared Base, Harvard, 12 1/2 In., 2 Piece ....*Illus*	784.00
Punch Bowl, Stand, Fern, Ohio Cut Glass Company, 12 1/2 x 14 In.	9500.00
Punch Cup, Hobstar, 2 1/2 In.	58.00
Punch Cup, Hobstars, Strawberry-Diamond, Cane, 2 In.	40.00
Punch Cup, Pattern No. 28, Crosshatch, Fans, Dorflinger, 2 1/8 In.	25.00
Rose Bowl, Crosscut Diamonds, Football Shape, 4 1/4 x 9 3/4 In.	490.00
Rose Bowl, Engraved, Daisy, Melon Ribbed, 7 In.	55.00
Salad Set, Russian, Clear Buttons, Rayed Star-Center Plate, Mt.Washington, 9 In.	1695.00
Sherry, Leaf & Stalk, 4 1/4 In., 12 Piece	63.00
Sugar, Hobstar, Fan & Crosshatching, Handles	40.00
Sugar & Creamer, Carnation, 3 In.	125.00
Sugar & Creamer, Double Notched Handles, Rayed Base, 4 In.	124.00
Sugar & Creamer, Hobstar, Footed, 5 1/4 In.	435.00
Sugar & Creamer, Hobstars, Crosshatch Bands, Double Notched Handles, Hoare	295.00
Sugar & Creamer, Hobstars, Crosshatch, Zipper & Fans, Notched Handle	425.00
Sugar & Creamer, Plantation, Footed	3500.00
Sugar & Creamer, Pluto, 3-Notch Handle, Hoare, 3 1/2 x 4 In.	395.00
Syrup, Hobstars, Notched Prisms & Fans, Silver Plated Cover, 5 1/2 In.	395.00
Syrup, Notched Prism, Silver Plated Cover, 3 3/4 In.	225.00
Syrup, Notched Prisms, Triple Notched Handle, Sterling Silver Cover, 5 1/4 In.	390.00
Tazza, Napoleon III, Flared Leaf Petal, Black Stepped Plinth, 15 3/4 In., Pair	3680.00
Tazza, Propeller, 24-Point Rayed Star Base, 9 x 7 1/2 In.	425.00
Toothpick, Pineapple	40.00
Tray, Hobstar, Button, Crosshatch, Fan, Leaf, Scallop Sawtooth Rim, c.1900, 12 x 8 In.	230.00
Tumbler, Daisy & Leaf, Crosshatch, 16-Point Star, Gravic Cut	35.00
Tumbler, Daisy, Gravic Cut, 3 7/8 In.	45.00
Tumbler, Hobstar & Fan, 16-Point Star, 3 3/4 In.	45.00
Tumbler, Hobstar & Fan, 24-Point Star, 4 In.	40.00
Tumbler, Hobstar Chair Bottom, Fan & Crosshatching, 16-Point Star, 4 In.	49.00
Tumbler, Hobstar Outline, Fan & Crosshatching, 24-Point Star, 3 3/4 In.	48.00
Tumbler, Juice, Venetian, Straus, 3 1/2 In.	45.00
Tumbler, Whiskey, Thistle	75.00
Vase, 6 Panels Of Hobstars, Zipper, 14 In.	1750.00
Vase, 24-Point Star, Bulbous Top, Narrow Bottom, 16 In.	850.00
Vase, Bulbous Hobstar Base, Scalloped Rim, 14 1/2 In.	975.00
Vase, Comet, Hoare, 1910, 13 1/2 In.	5500.00
Vase, Diagonal Branches, Florets, Dome Fool, Flared, 11 In., Pair	259.00
Vase, Florentine, Footed, Higgins & Seiter, 14 In.	775.00

Vase, Harvard, Seven Way Layout, 12 In.	235.00
Vase, Honeycomb, Crystal, 24-Point Hobstar, 9 3/4 x 6 1/2 In.	980.00
Vase, Ruby To Clear, Enamel & Gold Design, Ground Pontil, 11 In.	1045.00
Vase, Ruby To Clear, Flower Heads, Acanthus Leaves, Gilt Bronze, 9 1/2 x 8 1/2 In.	1265.00
Vase, Ruby To Clear, Scrollwork, Bird & Castle, Scalloped Rim, 8 In.	80.00
Vase, Scalloped, Cut Panels, Enameled Gold, Cranberry To Clear, Footed, 9 In., Pair	770.00
Vase, Violet, Hobstar Cut Foot, 7 1/2 In.	235.00
Vase, Violet, Hobstar, 2 3/4 In.	110.00
Water Set, Wheat, Hoare, Signed, 7 Piece	6450.00
Wine, Flowers, Leaves, Leaf Foot, Webb Corbett, 1930, 8 In.	3600.00

CUT VELVET is a special type of art glass, made with two layers of blown glass, which shows a raised pattern. It usually had an acid finish or a texture like velvet. It was made by many glass factories during the late Victorian years.

Rose Bowl, Mt. Washington	325.00

CYBIS porcelain is a twentieth-century product. Boleslaw Cybis came to the United States from Poland in 1939. He started making porcelains in Long Island, New York, in 1940. He moved to Trenton, New Jersey, in 1942 as one of the founders of Cordey China Co. and started his own Cybis Porcelains about 1950. The firm is still working. See also Cordey.

Figurine, Ballerina, 7 In.	126.00
Figurine, Beavers, 6 1/4 In.	95.00
Figurine, Buffalo, 4 In.	70.00
Figurine, Carousel, Pony, Sugar Plum, 12 1/2 In.	795.00
Figurine, Little Red Riding Hood, White Cape, Red Gloves, Signed, 6 1/2 In.	140.00
Figurine, Madonna, Bird On Hand, 11 In.	140.00
Figurine, Moses, Holding Tablets, No. 714, Wood Base, 19 1/2 In.	420.00
Figurine, Mr. Snowball, Bunny, 4 In.	69.00 to 135.00
Figurine, Pillar Of Families Religious Group With Animals, 11 1/2 In.	105.00
Figurine, Prince Florimund, Princess Aurora, 1973, 11 1/2 In., Pair	2750.00
Figurine, Spring Dancer, 10 In.	115.00
Figurine, Unicorn, 10 In.	1850.00
Figurine, Wendy, Girl In Nightgown Holding Doll, Signed, 6 1/2 In.	85.00 to 120.00

CZECHOSLOVAKIA is a popular term with collectors. The name, first used as a mark after the country was formed in 1918, appears on glass and porcelain and other decorative items. Although Czechoslovakia split into Slovakia and the Czech Republic on January 1, 1993, the name continues to be used in some trademarks.

CZECHOSLOVAKIA GLASS, Decanter, Art Glass, Silver Neck & Stopper, 8 1/2 In.	185.00
Vase, 6 Lobed Black Rim, Pulled Stripes, Yellow & Red, 8 In.	65.00
Vase, Blue, Purple, Pulled Stripes, Kralik, 7 1/4 In.	38.00
Vase, Fan, Orange & Blue, 8 1/2 In.	95.00
Vase, Green, Blue Pulled Stripes, 7 In.	100.00
Vase, Green, Cobalt Blue, Lavender, Yellow, Mottled, Cylindrical, 10 In.	250.00
Vase, Mottled Red & Blue, Tapered, Bulbous Top, Signed, 7 1/4 In.	40.00
Vase, Oil Spot, Gold Ground, Stamped Mark, 6 1/2 In.	185.00
Vase, Oil Spot, White Cased, Urn Shape, 8 1/2 In.	50.00
Vase, Pulled Leaf & Vine, Pink Satin, 8 1/2 In.	140.00
Vase, Purple & Gold Design, 10 1/2 In.	375.00
Vase, Red & Blue Speckled, Snake Around Neck, c.1930, 9 1/2 In.	180.00
Vase, Royal Blue, Mountain & Lake, Elongated, Cameo, 4 In.	580.00
Vase, Trumpet, Green, Black, 10 In., Pair	126.00
Vase, Yellow Pulled Drape On Blue, Footed, Applied Handles, 4 In.	28.00
CZECHOSLOVAKIA POTTERY, Bowl, Indian Tree, Zdekauer Porcelain, 1918-1939, 5 3/16 In.	25.00
Dish, Feeding, Boy & Girl Decals, 3 Sections, Red Circle Mark, 7 In.	35.00
Pitcher, Bird, 6 In.	83.00
Vase, Incised People, Handle, Impressed Mark, 8 In.	23.00
Vase, Sponged, Floral Band, 9 In.	140.00

D'ARGENTAL is a mark used in France by the Compagnie des Cristalleries de St. Louis. The firm made multilayered, acid-cut cameo glass in the late nineteenth and twentieth centuries. D'Argental is the French name for the city of Munzthal, home of the glassworks. Later they made enameled etched glass.

Box, Cover, Wild Orchids, 3 Moths, Pale Blue, Amethyst, Cameo, 4 x 6 In.	805.00
Vase, Maple Leaves, 7 Seeds, Bulbous Neck, Cameo, Signed, c.1920, 10 In.	1035.00
Vase, Orchids, Red Over Yellow, Cameo, Signed, 5 In.	975.00
Vase, Trumpet, Continuous Mountain Landscape, Cameo, 12 In.	1092.00

DANIEL BOONE, a pre-Revolutionary War folk hero, was a surveyor, trapper, and frontiersman. A television series, which ran from 1964 to 1970, was based on his life and starred Fess Parker. All types of Daniel Boone memorabilia are collected.

Bedspread, Woven, Twin, 94 x 75 In.	35.00
Billfold, Fess Parker As Daniel Boone, 1964	40.00
Book, Daniel Boone Wilderness Scout, Hardcover, Illustrated, 308 Pages, 1925	12.50
Book, Little Golden Book, No. 256, Simon & Schuster, First Edition	5.50
Book, Story Of Daniel Boone, Illustrated, Grosset & Dunlap, 1953	6.00
Cap, Coonskin, Tail, 23 In. Diam.	8.50
Card, Playing	2.50
Doll, Madame Alexander, Box, 8 In.	35.00
Game, Card, Legend On Box, Ed-U-Cards, 1965	5.00
Lunch Box, Fess Parker, Kaboodle Kit, Standard Plastic Products, 1960s	160.00
Lunch Box, Raised Panel, Aladdin Industries, 1955	66.75
Photograph, Fess Parker As Daniel Boone, Black & White, NBC, 7 x 9 In.	16.50
View-Master, Four Leaf Clover, Fess Parker, 3 Reels, Booklet, 1965	45.00

DAUM, a glassworks in Nancy, France, was started by Jean Daum in 1875. The company, now called *Cristalleries de Nancy*, is still working. The *Daum Nancy* mark has been used in many variations. The name of the city and the artist are usually both included.

Bowl, Amber Cased, Foil Inclusions, Pulled Points, Signed, 1925, 8 1/4 In.	345.00
Bowl, Applied Carved Beetles, Green, Cranberry, Beige, Signed, 1 1/2 x 5 In.	2600.00
Bowl, Gold Foil Inclusions, Wrought Iron Frame, Signed, 10 1/2 In.	2240.00
Bowl, Gold Foil Inclusions, Wrought Iron Stand, Majorelle, c.1920, 6 1/2 In.	805.00
Bowl, Green Daisy, Green Base, Gold Trim, Cameo, Signed, 2 3/4 x 5 1/2 In.	1150.00
Bowl, Landscape, Daisies & Leaves, 2 Loop Handles, Signed, 6 1/2 In.	5750.00
Bowl, Landscape, Trees, Lakefront Scene, Sunset, 2 3/4 In.	1150.00
Bowl, Red Berry, Leaf Design, Gold, White, Cameo, Signed, 3 1/2 x 7 In.	2590.00
Box, Cover, Enameled Flowers, Green, Maroon, Cameo, Signed, 2 1/4 In.	1670.00
Box, Cover, Pale Blue, Gold, Enameled, Cameo, 5 x 3 In.	1725.00
Box, Cover, Red, Purple Fuchsias, White, Purple, Cameo, Signed, 3 x 4 In.	3625.00
Ceiling Light, Hanging, Red Design, Signed, 1925, 26 In.	5400.00

Daum, Lamp, Desk, Chrysanthemums, Mauve, Purple, Gold & Pink, Cameo, 16 In.

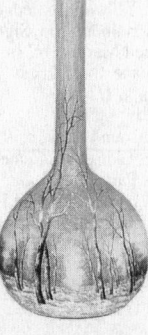

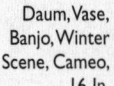

Daum, Vase, Banjo, Winter Scene, Cameo, 16 In.

Daum, Vase, Bright Red, Orange Rose Hips, Yellow, Purple, Cameo, 6 x 5 1/2 In.

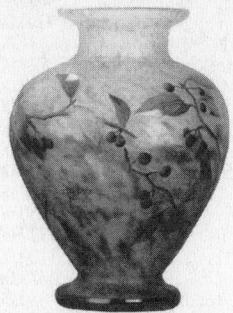

Daum, Vase, Brown Berries &
Branches, Cameo, Signed,
8 x 6 In.

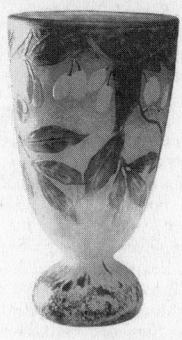

Daum, Vase, Green Leaves,
Red Berries, Footed,
Cameo, 1910, 9 In.

Daum, Vase, Mushrooms,
Yellow, Enameled, 4 Footed,
Cameo, Square, 5 1/4 In.

Centerpiece, Dutch Winter Village Scene, Windmills, Buildings, Oval, 16 x 10 In. 7475.00
Decanter, Stopper, Green, Enameled Croix De Lorraine, 13 1/4 In. 1150.00
Dish, Frog Design, Purple, Green, Yellow, Marked, 6 1/4 In. 3335.00
Figurine, Polar Bears, On Ice Flow, 17 In. 1150.00
Inkwell, Spider Web, Dark Brown, Cameo, 1900, 11 7/8 In. 10800.00
Jar, Condiment, Cover, 4 Bands Of Cut Flowers, Gold, Cameo, Signed, 5 1/4 In. 1325.00
Lamp, Desk, Chrysanthemums, Mauve, Purple, Gold & Pink, Cameo, 16 In. ......*Illus* 6050.00
Lamp Base, Leaves & Berries, Yellow, Cameo, Drilled Hole, Metal Footed, 23 In. 1000.00
Pitcher, Dutch Winter Scene, Windmill, Houses, Pale Blue, White, Cameo, 6 In. 6325.00
Pitcher, Enameled, Autumn Landscape, Applied Handle, Cameo, Signed, 6 In. 4315.00
Pitcher, Red Bleeding Hearts, Pink, White, Peach Handle, Cameo, 3 In. 2185.00
Pitcher, Water, Smoky Gray, Etched, 9 1/2 In. 145.00
Plate, Beethoven, Amethyst, Pate-De-Verre, 1970, 9 3/4 In. 109.00
Rose Bowl, Ducks, Swimming With Flowers, White Opalescent, Egg Shape, 5 1/2 In. ... 2300.00
Rose Bowl, Winter Dutch Scene, Sailboats, Windmills, People, White Opalescent, 4 In. .. 2990.00
Salt, Etched Band Of Florets, Embossed Band Of Florets, c.1900, 1 1/8 In. 375.00
Salt, Landscape, Trees, Snow Covered, Enameled, Cameo, 1 3/4 In. 1150.00
Salt, Rain Scene, Pink On Green, Enameled, 1 x 2 In. 2875.00
Salt, Winter Scene, Windmill & Boats, White, Cameo, Signed, 1 1/4 x 1 1/2 In. 690.00
Shade, Burnt Orange, Signed, 22 In. 3360.00
Shade, Light Orange, Signed, 15 In. 2800.00
Tumbler, Purple, Red Flowers, Gold Leaves, Cameo, Signed, 1 3/4 In. 1265.00
Vase, Alternating Bands Of Blossoms, Cushion Base, Signed, 4 3/8 In. 315.00
Vase, Autumn Scene, Fall Colors, Cameo, 8 In. 5500.00
Vase, Banjo, Winter Scene, Cameo, 16 In. ....*Illus* 10350.00
Vase, Blackberry Branch, Red, Purple, Yellow, Cameo, 14 In. 2070.00
Vase, Blackbirds In The Snow, In Flight & Resting, Pale Yellow Green, 5 In. 9775.00
Vase, Blossoms & Leaves, Pale Salmon, Yellow, Pale Green, Cameo, 1900, 18 In. 8280.00
Vase, Blueberries On Green Leaves, Yellow Mottled, Satin, Cameo, 14 1/2 In. 1100.00
Vase, Bright Purple Flowers, Green Leaves, White, Pale Orange, Signed, 5 In. 1610.00
Vase, Bright Red, Orange Rose Hips, Yellow, Purple, Cameo, 6 x 5 1/2 In. ....*Illus* 2185.00
Vase, Brilliant Purple Violets, Green Leaves, White, Cameo, Signed, 4 3/4 In. 1850.00
Vase, Brilliant Red Poppies, Leaves, Orange, Yellow, Cameo, Signed, 6 x 3 In. 2130.00
Vase, Broad Leaves, Vines, Signed, 13 1/2 In. 1725.00
Vase, Brown Berries & Branches, Cameo, Signed, 8 x 6 In. ....*Illus* 2587.00
Vase, Cameo, Enameled, Blue Flowers, Green, Cameo, 7 3/4 In. 3450.00
Vase, Columbines, Leaves, Yellow, Green, Cameo, Signed, 12 In. 4315.00
Vase, Deep Purple Flowers, Dark Green, Cameo, 1900, 16 1/4 In. 13200.00
Vase, Dragonflies, Gold, Enameled, Cameo, 9 3/4 In. 1725.00
Vase, Dutch Winter Scene, Snow Laden Trees, Pale Blue, Pink, 8 3/4 x 4 In. 4600.00
Vase, Etched Lilies On Stalks, Floral Medallions, Lozenge Shape, Signed, 1893, 9 In. 1380.00
Vase, Etched Magnolia, Deep Burgundy, Signed, 11 In. 5375.00

Vase, Flowers & Leaves, Red Mottled, Signed, 3 1/2 In. 3100.00
Vase, Flowers, Pale Pink, Cameo, Signed, 1900, 8 1/2 In. 6000.00
Vase, Forest Scene, Deep Green Trees, Orange, Peach Design, Cameo, 11 3/4 x 4 1/4 In. . 8337.00
Vase, Gilt Flowers, Light Blue Opalescent, Gilt, Cameo, Signed, 4 3/4 In. 520.00
Vase, Green & Black, Foil Inclusions, Wrought Iron Frame, Majorelle, 10 1/2 In. 1840.00
Vase, Green Leaves, Red Berries, Footed, Cameo, 1910, 9 In. ....*Illus* 5320.00
Vase, Green, Carved Art Deco Design, Cylindrical, Signed, 6 1/2 In. 635.00
Vase, Green, Gold, Zinnias, Signed, 3 1/2 In. 60.00
Vase, Harbor Scene, 4 Boats, Mountains On Horizon, Cameo, Signed, 5 1/2 In. 1100.00
Vase, Holly Branch, Green, Deep Red, Footed, Cameo, 5 3/4 In. 1265.00
Vase, Lake Scene, Cattails Base, Cameo, Signed, 14 1/2 In. 1650.00
Vase, Landscape Of Prominent Trees, Uneven Top Edge, Signed, 2 1/4 In. 1320.00
Vase, Landscape, 3 Trees, Branches & Leaves, Signed, 2 1/4 In. 1100.00
Vase, Landscape, Enameled Cameo, Signed, c.1905, 17 3/4 In. 4085.00
Vase, Landscape, Green Trees, Water, Mountain Range, Birds, Frosted, Yellow, 2 In. 980.00
Vase, Landscape, Mold Blown, Cameo, Signed, c.1910, 11 1/2 In. 7800.00
Vase, Landscape, Tree, Lush Leaves, Landscape, Yellow, Cameo, Signed, 3 In. 1265.00
Vase, Landscape, Trees In Background, Blown, 1910, 11 1/4 In. 7200.00
Vase, Landscape, Trees, Gold, Brown, Green, Cameo, Signed, 24 In. 10350.00
Vase, Lavender, Pink Fuchsia, White, Purple Mottled, Cameo, 4 1/2 x 3 In. 1725.00
Vase, Leaf & Berry Design, Orange, Green, Yellow Mottled, 15 In. 4025.00
Vase, Leaves & Berries, Signed, 4 In. 990.00
Vase, Leaves, Cameo, Orange, Frosted, Mottled Ground, Cylindrical, Tapered, 13 1/4 In. . 2645.00
Vase, Light Brown Deer Standing Looking Up, Etched, Signed, 1925, 14 In. 7200.00
Vase, Lily Of The Valley, Lime Green Opalescent Highlights, Cameo, Signed, 4 In. 2875.00
Vase, Lily Of The Valley, Martele, Cameo, Signed, 4 x 3 3/4 In. 5225.00
Vase, Magnolia Design, Acid Cut, Opaque Burgundy Glass, Yellow-Orange, Signed, 11 In. 300.00
Vase, Marquetry Orange Flowers, Cameo, 8 3/4 In. 4025.00
Vase, Mottled Orange & Tan, Long Narrow Neck, Signed, 7 In. 425.00
Vase, Mottled, Red, Amber, Orange, Narrow Neck, Squat Body, Signed, 12 In. 750.00
Vase, Mushrooms, Yellow, Enameled, 4 Footed, Cameo, Square, 5 1/4 In. ....*Illus* 7280.00
Vase, Orchids, Green, Black, Yellow, Green Enameled, Satin, Cameo, 3 1/2 In. 1035.00
Vase, Pillow, Purple Carnations, Pink, Blue, Signed, 1 1/2 x 2 In. 1092.00
Vase, Pillow, Sailboat Scene, Orange, Yellow, Cameo, Signed, 4 x 5 1/2 In. 2070.00
Vase, Pillow, Snow Covered Mountains, Alpine Cottage, Pale Blue, 4 1/2 In. 3450.00
Vase, Pillow, Summer Landscape, Trees, Green, Blue, Cameo, Signed, 5 In. 3450.00
Vase, Purple Ripened Grapes, Dangle From Vine, Croix De Lorraine, 19 In. 8960.00
Vase, Purple Wisteria, Green Leaves, Green, Purple, Yellow, Cameo, Signed, 7 In. 9200.00
Vase, Purple, Green Violets, Gold Enameled, Deep Violet, White, Cameo, 22 In. 7150.00
Vase, Purple, Red Flowers, Orange Leaves, White, Yellow, Cameo, Signed, 5 In. 1725.00
Vase, Snow Scene, 8 Crows Flying, Perched In Trees, Signed, 1 x 2 In. 2200.00
Vase, Speckled Blue, Green, Signed, 4 1/2 x 7 In. 840.00
Vase, Storks In Marsh Scene, Sterling Silver Overlay, Handles, Signed, 4 1/2 In. 4760.00
Vase, Summer Scene, Green, Yellow, Enameled, Cameo, Signed, 8 x 4 In. 3565.00
Vase, Summer Scene, Purple Mountains, Trees, Blue, Green, Cameo, 5 1/2 In. 1323.00
Vase, Swans, Swimming, White, Green, Black, Pale Blue, Cameo, Signed, 10 In. 6325.00
Vase, Thistle, Leaves, Pale Peach, Enameled, Cameo, Signed, 9 1/2 x 3 1/2 In. 4255.00
Vase, Trees, Sailboats, Mountain Scene, Orange, Yellow Mottled, 4 1/2 In. 1900.00
Vase, Violets, Blue, Green, Purple, White, Enameled, Cameo, 2 1/4 In. 1495.00
Vase, White Apple Blossoms, Pink, Green, Peach, Cameo, Signed, 7 1/4 In. 3680.00
Vase, Winter Scene, Snow Laden Trees, Yellow, Orange, 2 1/4 x 6 3/4 In. 3738.00
Vase, Winter Scene, Yellow, Peach, Cameo, Signed, 5 1/2 x 5 In. 2760.00
Vase, Zinnias, Scrolled Leaves, Yellow, Gold Enameled, Footed, 5 1/2 x 4 3/4 In. 9200.00

DAVENPORT pottery and porcelain were made at the Davenport factory
in Longport, Staffordshire, England, from 1793 to 1887. Earthenwares,
creamwares, porcelains, ironstone, and other ceramics were made.
Most of the pieces are marked with a form of the word *Davenport*.

DAVENPORT
LONGPORT
STAFFORDSHRE

Bowl, Sugar Cubes, Blue Leaves, Enameled Flowers, 2 3/4 In. 52.00
Cup & Saucer, Blue & Red Flowers, Transfer, Gold Enameled 43.00
Mug, Relief Scene, Huntsmen, Blue Enameled, Stoneware 53.00
Pitcher, Embossed Strawberries & Leaves, 5 1/2 In. 138.00

Plate, Amoy, Flow Blue, 8 1/4 In.	51.00
Plate, Blue Willow, 1870-1887, 7 In.	41.00
Plate, Italian Veranda, Flow Blue, 10 1/4 In.	40.00
Plate, Red Transfer, 2 Oriental Long Tailed Birds, 7 3/8 In.	39.00
Platter, Amoy, Flow Blue, 20 In.	2000.00
Platter, Dark Blue Transfer, English Scene, Boats, Children, Floral Border, 14 1/2 In.	385.00
Tureen, Lady With Lute, Pearlware, Blue & White, c.1795-1810, 15 1/2 In.	203.00

DAVY CROCKETT, the American frontiersman, was born in 1786 and died in 1836. The historical character gained new fame in 1954 when the Walt Disney television show ran a series of episodes featuring Fess Parker as Davy Crockett. Coonskin caps and buckskins became popular and hundreds of different Davy Crockett items were made.

Cookie Jar, American Bisque	315.00 to 450.00
Cookie Jar, Gold Trim, Brush	600.00
Costume, Accessories, Box, Fess Parker On Cover	120.00
Doll Outfit, For Ginny Doll, Coonskin Cap, Metal Rifle, Pin, Box, Vogue, c.1955	44.00
Flasher, From Tennessee To Alamo, Portrait, Plastic, Black & Gold	20.00
Fork, Child's, Davy On Handle, Stainless Steel, Disney Productions, 1950s, 6 In.	29.00
Lamp, Original Shade	165.00
Lasso, Display Card	75.00
Lunch Box, Thermos, Metal, Packaging, Holtkemp, 1955	230.00
Plate, Paper, Indian Fighter, c.1955, 6 1/4 In.	18.00
Playset, Davy Crockett At The Alamo, Marx, Box	334.00
Projector, Magic Picture, Gun Form, Battery Operated, Box	140.00
Record, Story Book, LP & 24-Page Book, Walt Disney Productions, 1971	29.00
Spoon, Child's, Davy On Handle, Stainless Steel, Disney Productions, 6 In.	29.00
Target Set, Metal Target, 2 Plastic Guns, Knickerbocker, Box, 1950s	75.00
Tie Clip, Metal, 1950s	18.00
Tumbler, Glass, 1955, 6 Piece	125.00
Wall Pocket, Moccasin Form, Pottery	100.00
Wallet	30.00
Wristwatch, Bradley, 1956	130.00
Wristwatch, Powder Horn Case, U.S. Time, 1954	385.00

DE MORGAN art pottery was made in England by William De Morgan from the 1860s to 1907. He is best known for his luster-glazed Moorish-inspired pieces. The pottery used a variety of marks.

Charger, Faience, Persian Style, Reptile Band, 1880s, 16 1/8 In.	18000.00
Charger, Ruby Luster, Whimsical Fish, Flower Border, 1880s, 20 1/2 In.	28350.00
Plate, Bird Center, Crimson Luster, Artist CP, Frame, 1900, 10 1/4 In.	1955.00
Plate, Faience, Stylized Birds Holding Snake, Leaf Border, c.1897, 10 3/4 In.	4800.00
Vase, Faience, Persian Style, Chrysanthemums, Leaves, c.1890, 7 1/8 In.	3300.00
Vase, Faience, Persian Style, Eagle, Leaf Bands, c.1897, 15 1/4 In.	9600.00
Vase, Faience, Persian Style, Fish, Leaves, c.1897, 15 7/8 In.	5100.00
Vase, Faience, Persian Style, Fish, Leaves, Leaf Panels, c.1890, 8 3/4 In.	3300.00
Vase, Faience, Vase Bands, Scrolling Leaves, c.1897, 12 1/2 In.	2400.00

DE VEZ was a signature used on cameo glass after 1910. E. S. Monot founded the glass company near Paris in 1851. The company changed names many times. Mt. Joye, another glass by this factory, is listed in its own category.

Lamp, Milk Glass, Blue Sailboats, Electric, Signed, 20 In.	5600.00
Lamp, Vines, Leaves & River Shade, Salmon & Peach, Shade & Base, 12 In.	2185.00
Vase, Black Forest Scene, Numerous Trees, Deep Purple, Yellow, Orange, 10 x 5 In.	1725.00
Vase, Flowering Poppy Stems, Dark Persimmon, Butterfly, Opalescent, 1855, 8 In.	2250.00
Vase, Forest Scene, Light Green To Forest Green, Pink, Light Blue Ground, Signed, 4 In.	920.00
Vase, Lakeside Castle With Raspberries, Pink, Purple, Pale Yellow, 17 In.	2070.00
Vase, Mountain, Lake Scene, Yellow, Amethyst, Orange, Signed, 13 x 6 In.	1783.00
Vase, Nature Scene, Mountains, Lake, Trees & Birds, Amber, Pink Ground, Signed, 2 In.	690.00
Vase, Navy Cut To Yellow To Pink, Satin, Ships Scene, Cameo, 7 1/4 In.	625.00
Vase, Red & Yellow Satin, Gondola In Venice, Cameo, 8 In.	750.00 to 825.00

DECOYS are carved or turned wooden copies of birds, fish, or animals. The decoy was placed in the water or propped on the shore to lure flying birds to the pond for hunters. Some decoys are handmade; some are commercial products. Today there is a group of artists making modern decoys for display, not for use in a pond.

Black Duck, A. Elmer Crowell, Mass., 6 1/2 x 17 1/2 In.	1380.00
Black Duck, Painted, Carved, 5 1/2 x 13 1/2 In., Pair	316.00
Black Duck, Preening, Crowell	3630.00
Black-Bellied Plover, Brown, Tack Eyes, George Boyd, N.H.	4315.00
Black-Bellied Plover, Carved Wings, Inserted Bill, Chincoteague, Va.	5175.00
Black-Bellied Plover, Painted Eyes, Inserted, Spined Bill, Charles Clark	1380.00
Blackhead, Elton Willis, Elmer Salter, Stacy, N.C.	225.00
Blue Goose, Field Silhouette, Ben Schmidt, 1930s, 15 x 24 In.	110.00
Blue Wing Teal Drake, Hand Carved, Painted, Bill Zack Ward, Crisfield, Md., 11 In.	146.00
Brant, Brown, William McClellan, Eureka, Ca., 1989	1150.00 to 4315.00
Brant, Dark Brown, Inserted Wooden Bill, Crossed Wing Tips, Elmer Crowell	9775.00
Brant, Swimming Position, Hollow Body, Amos Weaterfield, 1930, 19 In.	385.00
Bufflehead, Tony Watimer, Glass Eyes	105.00
Canada Goose, Canvas Covered, George Boyd	7700.00
Canada Goose, Painted White & Brown, Langan, 20th Century, 25 1/2 In.	300.00
Canada Goose, Painted, Carved, 9 1/2 x 30 In.	690.00
Canada Goose, Preening, Gray, Black & White Paint, 8 x 20 1/2 In.	250.00
Canada Goose, Preening, Iron Nail Legs, White Chest, Black Neck, Tack Eyes, 15 3/4 In.	550.00
Canada Goose, Swimmer, Dark Brown, White Body, Black Head, 31 x 11 1/2 In.	165.00
Canvasback Drake, Carved Bill Detail, Black, Tan, Gray Wing, Harry Fennimore	5750.00
Canvasback Drake, Carved, White Body, Hiram Hotze, Peoria, Illinois	8625.00
Canvasback Drake, Hollow, Carved, Charles Schoenheider, St. Louis	9200.00
Canvasback Hen, High Head, Hand Carved, Bob Mcgraw	480.00
Canvasback Hen & Drake, Signed, Charlie Joiner, 1965	685.00
Coot, Brown Eyes, Gray Beak, R.M. Mitchel, White Tail, c.1938, 12 In.	230.00
Curlew, Preening, Hand-Carved, Painted, Driftwood, Signed, Bill Sachse, 13 1/2 In.	260.00
Duck, Blue Bill, Glass Eyes, Mason, 13 3/4 In.	247.00
Duck, Carved, Black, Glass Eyes, c.1900, 10 In.	375.00
Duck, Carved, Polychrome Design, 15 1/4 In.	145.00
Dunlin Shorebird, Standing, Glass Eyes, Hand Carved, Painted, Bill Sachse, 7 In.	67.00
Eagle, Pine, Spread Wings, Giltwood, 19th Century, 17 x 40 3/4 In.	3600.00
Eider, Carved, 1976, Mass., 6 x 17 In.	865.00
Fish, On Stand, Applied Tin Fins, Incised Gills & Mouth, Signed S.W., 7 1/2 x 14 In.	55.00
Golden Plover, Light Brown, Tack Eyes, Joseph Lincoln, Early 20th Century	7475.00
Goldeneye Drake, Hollow, Black, Early 20th Century	5465.00
Goldeneye Drake, Hollow, Dark Brown, Feather Painted, Vern Cheesman, Illinois	6325.00
Goldeneye Duck, Arthur Lavoie	75.00
Goldeneye Hen, Carved Wing, White Stomach, David K. Nichol	9200.00
Goldeneye Hen, Whistler, Nova Scotia, 1930s	195.00
Goose, Glass Eyes, R. Van Wagoner, Full Size, 18 In.	195.00
Green-Winged Teal, Carved, 20th Century, 4 1/2 x 12 In., 3 Piece	1150.00
Green-Winged Teal, Carved, Glass Eyes, Amiel Garibaldi, Ca.	1265.00
Herter's Redhead Hen & Drake, Balsa Wood, 12 3/4 In.	150.00
Herter's Widgeon, Hand Carved, 15 1/2 In.	225.00
Loon, Hand Carved, Maine, 10 1/2 x 23 In.	300.00
Mallard Drake, Brown, Hollow, Mason Decoy Factory, Detroit, Mi., 1905	9775.00
Mallard Drake, Mason Challenge Grade, 1920s	520.00
Mallard Drake, Moveable Metal Wings, Rubber Flap-O-Matic, 1950s	123.00
Mallard Drake, Tack Eyes, Mason, 15 1/2 In.	250.00
Mallard Duck, Gray Body, Dark Green Head, Glass Eyes, Orange Bill, Mason, 15 1/2 In.	220.00
Mallard Duck, Preening Head, Hollow Body, Painted, Carved, Charles Moore, 16 In., Pair	520.00
Mallard Hen, Glass Eyes, Carved & Painted Pine, Ken Ingraham	330.00
Mallard Hen, Sleeper, Hank Walters, Michigan	366.00
Merganser, Swimmer, Carved Feathers & Wings, Glass Eyes, R.C. Watson, 23 In.	385.00
Merganser Drake, Painted, Carved, 5 x 16 In.	90.00
Merganser Drake, Red Breasted, A. Elmer Crowell, Mass., 5 1/2 x 19 1/2 In.	8625.00
Merganser Hen, Carved Eyes, Inlet Head, George Huey, Friendship, Me., 1910	4600.00

Merganser Hen, Mandible Carved Bill, Flowing Crest, Ira Hudson, 1930 .... 9600.00
Pintail Drake, Dark Brown, Cork Body, Inserted Wooden Tail, Lifted Head, Crowell 9200.00
Rat, Ice Spearing, Wire Wiskers, Leather Tail, Black Spinners 86.00
Redhead Drake, Glass Eyes, Comb Paint, Stevens Decoy Factory, N.Y. 6040.00
Ring-Billed Hen, Dark Brown, Carved, Warren Dettman 4900.00
Ruddy Duck, Ehn & Drake, Delbert Cigar Daisy, Chincoteague, Virginia, 10 In. 750.00
Ruddy Turnstone, Brown, Light Brown Stomach, Inset Glass Eyes, N.J. 7475.00
Ruddy Turnstone, Light Brown, Carved Eyes, Obediah Verity, Long Island, N.Y. 7475.00
Ruddy Turnstone, Light Brown, Painted Eyes, Inserted Hardwood Bill, N.J. 7765.00
Shorebird, Carved, Early 20th Century, 10 1/2 In., Pair 430.00
Shorebird, Carved, Early 20th Century, 13 x 9 In., Pair 1610.00
Shorebird, Sanderling, Inserted, Splined Hardwood Bill, Carved Wings 7475.00
Snipe, Robin, Red Knot, Painted Eyes, Inserted Hardwood Bill, Carved Wings 7475.00
Snipe, Robin, Red Knot, Painted Eyes, Inserted Hardwood Bill, Chincoteague, Va. 4310.00
Snow Goose, Painted Body, Black Sponging, White Head, Tack Eyes, 18 In. 70.00
Songbird, Carved Black, White, 19th Century, 4 1/4 x 10 1/4 In. 1610.00
Sunfish, Randall Factory, Willmar, Minn., 4 3/4 In. 155.00
White-Winged Scoter Drake, Black, Mason Decoy Factory, Detroit, Mi., 1910 .... 5175.00
Widgeon Drake, Dark Brown, Cork Body, Slightly Turned Wooden Head, Elmer Crowell 4600.00
Wisconsin Bluebill, Hand Carved, George Shrake, Tustin, Wisconsin, 1933 .... 300.00
Yellow-Throated Warbler, Crowell 2750.00
Yellowlegs, Brown, Carved Tail, Inserted Hardwood Bill, Ira Hudson 8050.00
Yellowlegs, Carved Eyes Inserted, Stylized Wing Carving, Chincoteague, Va. 5462.00
Yellowlegs, Dark Brown, Chipman, Sandwich, Mass. 6325.00
Yellowlegs, Flattie, Dark Brown, Tack Eyes, A.E. Crowell, East Harwich, Mass. 4310.00
Yellowlegs, Hollow, Light Brown, Head, Inserted Bill, Mass., Early 20th Century 4255.00
Yellowlegs, Inserted, Splined Hardwood Bill, Light Brown, Ira Hudson 6325.00
Yellowlegs, Light Brown, Tack Eyes, George Boyd, N.H., Early 20th Century 6040.00
Yellowlegs, Painted Eyes, Inserted, Splined Bill, Charles Clark, Va. 5750.00
Yellowlegs, Painted Eyes, Light Brown, Ira Hudson 8625.00
Yellowlegs, Shoebutton Tack Eyes, Joseph Lincoln 7475.00

DEDHAM Pottery was started in 1895. Chelsea Keramic Art Works was
established in 1872 in Chelsea, Massachusetts, by members of the
Robertson family. The factory closed in 1889 and was reorganized as
the Chelsea Pottery U.S. in 1891. The firm used the marks *CKAW* and
CPUS. It became the Dedham Pottery of Dedham, Massachusetts. The
factory closed in 1943. It was famous for its crackleware dishes, which
picture blue outlines of animals, flowers, and other natural motifs.

Azalea, Bacon Rasher, 9 1/2 In. 220.00
Azalea, Pitcher, 5 x 6 In. 467.00
Azalea, Tile, 5 1/2 In. 2750.00
Birds In Potted Orange Tree, Plate, 10 In. ....660.00 to 880.00
Birds In Potted Orange Tree, Plate, Doves, 6 In. 715.00
Bottle, Slate Gray, Oxblood Glaze, CKAW, 6 1/2 x 4 In. 1725.00
Butterfly, Plate, Broad Butterfly, Complex Wings In Repeat, 10 In. 825.00
Butterfly & Flower, Plate, 10 In. 770.00
Crab, Plate, 7 1/2 In. 440.00
Crab, Plate, Deep Blue, Crab Painted, Wavy Blade Of Seaweed, 8 1/2 In. 825.00
Day Lily, Plate, Painted Lily With 2 Bending Blossoms, 6 In. ....990.00 to 1310.00
Dolphin, Plate, CPUS, 10 In. 844.00
Dolphin, Plate, Inverted Waves In Center, CPUS, 10 In. 770.00
Duck, Cup & Saucer, Ducks & Water Lilies, 2 3/4 x 6 In. 358.00
Duck, Plate, Deep Blue, Ducks & Water Lilies, 9 3/4 In. ....220.00 to 275.00
Elephant, Ashtray, Deep Blue, 3 3/4 In. 2310.00
Elephant, Ashtray, Slots For Cigarettes, 3 3/4 In. 410.00
Fish, Plate, Deep Blue, Fish In Arched Position, 8 3/4 In. 6875.00
Flask, Deep Steel Blue Glaze, Honey Brown, Hollow Side Handles, CKAW, 9 x 6 In. 605.00
Flask, Pilgrim Walking Through Landscape, Teal Glossy Glaze, 6 3/4 x 4 In. 730.00
Flask, Pilgrim, Girl Feeding Geese, Blue, Green Glaze, Chelsea Keramic, Robertson, 9 In. 1840.00
Flask, Pillow, Flattened, 2 Handles, Olive Green, Brown, Chelsea Keramic, 1880, 9 In. 460.00
Grape, Plate, Deep Blue, Stylized Grape Clusters, 8 1/2 In. ....140.00 to 193.00

Grape, Plate, Signed, Maude Davenport, 6 In. 165.00
Grouse, Plate, Grouse Cavorting, Field Of Grass, 8 1/2 In. 4125.00
Horse Chestnut, Cup & Saucer, Horse Chestnut & Stylized Flower, 2 x 6 In. 220.00
Horse Chestnut, Plate, Blue Ink Stamp, 1 Impressed Rabbit, Pre-1929, 8 1/2 In. 345.00
Iris, Plate, Blue Ink Stamp, 1929-1945, 6 In. 295.00
Iris, Plate, White Iris Surrounded Solid Blue Leaves, Deep Blue, 8 1/2 In. ....145.00 to 165.00
Lobster, Plate, 8 1/4 In. 660.00
Lobster, Plate, Deep Blue, Shell Segments, Blue Glaze Ripples, 6 In. 358.00
Lobster, Plate, Signed, 9 In. 800.00
Magnolia, Plate, Blue Ink Stamp, Pre-1929, 6 In. 355.00
Magnolia, Plate, Thin Brush Strokes, Maude Davenport, 8 1/2 In. 358.00
Match Holder, Soft Steel Blue Glaze, CKAW, Chelsea Keramic, 6 In. 468.00
Medallion, Postboy Trumpeting, Green Ground, Robertson, Chelsea Keramic, 5 In. 845.00
Moth, Plate, Blue Glaze Wings, Vivid White Glaze, 6 In. 413.00
Moth, Plate, Moths, Full Moon Design, 8 1/2 In. ....825.00 to 1150.00
Mushroom, Plate, 8 1/2 In. 690.00
Mushroom, Plate, Maude Davenport, 8 1/2 In. 1540.00
Mushroom, Plate, Spotted, Striped Mushrooms, 6 1/8 In. 1980.00
Nasturtium, Plate, Hazy Blue Ground, Hugh Robertson, 8 1/2 In. 1980.00
Night & Morning, Pitcher, 5 x 5 1/4 In. 618.00
Owl, Plate, 61/8 In. 4400.00
Pineapple, Plate, 10 In. 465.00
Pineapple, Plate, Multicolored Deep Blue, Alternating Pineapple, 8 1/2 In. 715.00
Pitcher, Deep Brown Flambe Style, Green Ground, CKAW, 8 1/2 In. 605.00
Polar Bear, Plate, Deep Blue, Snowcap Background, 6 In. 523.00
Pond Lily, Plate, Deep Blue Pond Lilies, Pools Of Pond Water, 9 3/4 In. 358.00
Poppy, Bowl, Stylized Poppies In Varied Positions, Deep Blue, 3 3/4 x 9 1/4 In. 660.00
Poppy, Plate, Deep Blue, Oriental Poppy Blossom, Medium Blue, 8 1/4 In. ......230.00 to 605.00
Rabbit, Bouillon, Underplate, Blue Ink Stamp, 1929, 4 1/2-In. Cup 355.00
Rabbit, Bouillon, Underplate, Blue Ink Stamp, 2 Impressed Rabbits, 1929-1943 .... 355.00
Rabbit, Bowl, 3 1/2 x 8 In. 230.00
Rabbit, Bowl, Blue Ink Stamp, 3 x 8 In. 632.00
Rabbit, Bowl, Blue Ink Stamp, Registered, c.1929, 8 In. 535.00
Rabbit, Bowl, Deep Blue, 1 1/2 x 5 3/4 In. 193.00
Rabbit, Bowl, Deep Inverted Center, 2 1/8 x 7 1/2 In. 138.00
Rabbit, Candlestick, Blue Mark, 15 In., Pair 425.00
Rabbit, Charger, Blue Mark, 12 In. 735.00
Rabbit, Creamer, Deep Blue, Petite Circular Handle, Pinched Spout, 2 3/4 In. 495.00
Rabbit, Creamer, Deep Blue, Spout, 3 1/2 x 5 1/2 In. 220.00
Rabbit, Cup & Saucer, Blue Ink Stamp, c.1929-1943 .... 265.00
Rabbit, Jelly Jar, Blue Ink Stamp, 1931, 4 1/4 x 3 1/4 In. 750.00
Rabbit, Pitcher, Deep Blue, Angular Handle, 4 1/2 In. 385.00
Rabbit, Pitcher, Water, Floral Border, Inverted Neck, Handle, 6 1/2 In. 1980.00
Rabbit, Plate, Blue Stamp, 2 Impressed Rabbits, c.1929-1943, 9 3/4 In. ....225.00 to 248.00
Rabbit, Plate, Blue, Maude Davenport, 6 In. 248.00
Rabbit, Plate, Deep Blue, 8 1/2 In. 385.00
Rabbit, Plate, Deep Blue, CPUS, 8 3/4 In. 193.00
Rabbit, Plate, Floral Band Below Rabbits In Repeat, 7 1/2 In. 193.00
Rabbit, Plate, Signed, Pre-1932, 8 1/2 In. 86.00
Rabbit, Salt & Pepper, Blue Ink Mark, 2 3/4 In. 450.00
Rabbit, Salt & Pepper, Signed, 3 1/2 In. 303.00
Rabbit, Soup, Dish, Blue Ink Stamp, 8 1/2 In. 144.00
Rabbit, Soup, Dish, Deep Blue, Broad Band Of Rabbits In Repeat, 9 In. 193.00
Rabbit, Stein, Deep Blue, Rabbit Hiding Behind Stalk, Handle, Robertson, 5 1/8 In. 660.00
Rabbit, Sugar & Creamer, Blue Ink Mark, c.1929-1943 .... 805.00
Rabbit, Tray, Rolled Edge, 13 In. 1760.00
Rabbit, Two Ear, Bowl, Blue Ink Stamp, 2 x 5 1/2 In. 149.00
Rabbit, Two Ear, Creamer, Blue Stamp, 3 1/2 In. 196.00
Rabbit, Two Ear, Cup & Saucer, Blue Ink Stamp 100.00
Rabbit, Two Ear, Plate, Blue Ink Stamp, 8 1/2 In. 127.00
Rabbit, Two Ear, Plate, Breakfast, Blue Ink Stamp, 7 1/2 In. 230.00
Snowtree, Plate, Blue Ink Stamp, 10 In. 345.00

Snowtree, Plate, Deep Blue, Large Adult Elephants, Varying Walking Stance, 8 In. 990.00
Swan, Bacon Rasher, Swans & Cattails, 10 1/2 In. 468.00
Swan, Bowl, Cover, Deep Blue, Swan & Cattails, 2 3/4 x 4 1/2 In. 440.00
Swan, Bowl, Deep Blue, Swans & Cattails, 3 1/2 x 9 In. 1100.00
Swan, Creamer, Swans & Cattails In Repeat, 5 1/2 In. 303.00
Swan, Dish, Pickle, Swans & Cattails, 2 x 10 In. 715.00
Swan, Plate, 6 In. 495.00
Swan, Plate, Swans & Cattails, 8 1/2 In. ....440.00 to 715.00
Turkey, Bowl, Deep Blue, Turkeys Alternating Between Stalks, 2 x 5 1/2 In. 330.00
Turkey, Cup & Saucer 385.00
Turkey, Plate, Alternating Open Winged, Closed Wing Turkey, Deep Blue, 9 3/4 In. 360.00
Turtle, Plate, Pairs Of Turtles Smiling, 6 1/3 In. ....1760.00 to 3575.00
Vase, Dark Brown Drip Glaze, Hugh Robertson, 3 3/4 In. 440.00
Vase, Maroon, Dragon Blood Finish, Iridescent, CKAW, Sang De Boeuf, 7 1/4 In. 1045.00
Vase, Oxblood Glaze, Bulbous, Hugh Robertson, 7 1/2 x 4 In. 4315.00
Vase, Pillow, Flowers, Butterflies, Bees, Green Glaze, Embossed, Chelsea Keramic, 11 In. . 633.00
Vase, Sang De Boeuf, Oxblood Glaze, Flared Foot, Chelsea Keramic, 1894, 8 3/8 In. 2530.00
Vase, Squeezebag, Flowers, Deep Cobalt Blue, CKAW, 6 1/4 In. 660.00
Vase, Yellow Vellum Glaze, Chelsea Keramic, 3 1/4 In. 489.00
Wall Pocket, Micawber, Hugh Robertson, Chelsea Keramic 460.00
Wall Pocket, Swallows, Glossy Ocher, Hugh Robertson, Chelsea Keramic, 9 In. 1093.00
Wild Rose, Butter Pat, Rolled, Line Blue Glaze, 3 1/2 In. 385.00

DEGENHART is the name used by collectors for the products of the Crystal Art Glass Company of Cambridge, Ohio. John and Elizabeth Degenhart started the glassworks in 1947. Quality paperweights and other glass objects were made. John died in 1964 and his wife took over management and production ideas. Over 145 colors of glass were made. In 1978, after the death of Mrs. Degenhart, the molds were sold. The D in a heart trademark was removed, so collectors can easily recognize the true Degenhart piece.

Dish, Gypsy Pot, Lavender Blue, Marked 16.00
Dish, Hen On Nest Cover, Aqua, Satin, 5 In. 61.00
Figurine, Hand, Amberina, 4 In. 10.00
Figurine, Owl, Marbled Green, 3 1/2 In. 21.00
Figurine, Pricilla Doll, Heatherbloom, 1976-1978 .... 40.00
Figurine, Pricilla Doll, Light Amethyst, 1976-1978 .... 33.00
Jewelry Box, Heart Shaped, Apple Green, 3 1/2 In. 65.00
Paperweight, Plaque, Poco Sabo, Painted Red & Yellow Flowers, 3 1/4 In. 94.00
Salt, Bird Shaped, Lime 16.00
Slipper, Cat, Tomato Color, Marked, 6 In. 49.00
Toothpick, Elephant Head, Jade 35.00

DEGUE is a signature acid-etched on pieces of French glass made in the early 1900s. Cameo, mold blown, and smooth glass with contrasting colored rims are the types most often found.

Vase, Mottled Orange & Cobalt Blue, Signed, 14 1/4 In. 1380.00
Vase, Stylized Flowers, Signed, 15 In. 1265.00
Vase, Triangle Shapes, Orange To Clear, Internal Bubbles, Signed, 9 1/4 x 8 In. 1150.00

DELATTE glass is a French cameo glass made by Andre Delatte. It was first made in Nancy, France, in 1921. Lighting fixtures and opaque glassware in imitation of Bohemian opaline were made. There were many French cameo glass makers, so be sure to look in other appropriate categories.

Vase, 3 Egyptian Dancing Girls, Black Over Orange, Signed, 1925, 6 1/4 In. 1840.00
Vase, Black Amethyst Leaves & Stems, Fuchsia Blossoms, Signed, 13 1/2 In. 1054.00
Vase, Deep Amethyst Roses, Leaves, Pink, Signed, 6 1/4 In. 316.00
Vase, Enameled Poppy, Deep Purple, Signed, 7 In. 415.00
Vase, Morning Glories, Leaves, Brown, Lime Green, 7 In. 575.00
Vase, Mottled Pink, Purple, Pinched Bulbous Base, Signed, 10 In. 405.00

DELDARE, see Buffalo Pottery Deldare.

DELFT is a tin-glazed pottery that has been made since the seventeenth century. It is decorated with blue on white or with colored decorations. Most of the pieces sold today were made after 1891, and the name *Holland* appears with the Delft factory marks. The word *delft* also appears on pottery from other countries. Delft was made in England in the eighteenth century.

Bottle, Water, England, c.1760, 8 1/2 In.	1450.00
Bowl, Berry, White Star Pottery, c.1730, 8 1/4 In.	1400.00
Bowl, Blue, Oriental Design, Octagonal Edge, 6 1/4 In.	58.00
Bowl, Fruit, Blue Butterfly & Flower, White Ground, 18th Century, 9 In.	430.00
Bowl, Peacock Tail, Blue & White, Yellow Rim, Mid 18th Century, Hole, 7 3/4 In.	385.00
Bowl, Shaving, Pastoral Scene, England, c.1780, 9 x 11 In.	2400.00
Bust, Young Girl, Dress, Cap, 7 3/4 In.	315.00
Chamber Pot, Bug-Eyed Monsters, Late 17th Century, 3 In.	495.00
Charger, Adam & Eve, Beneath Fruiting Tree, Entwined Serpent, c.1670, 13 5/8 In.	4800.00
Charger, Adam & Eve, England, 13 1/2 In.	7475.00
Charger, Bird & Flowers, c.1750, 13 In.	1350.00
Charger, Flowers, Polychrome, England, c.1750, 13 1/4 In.	1095.00
Charger, Holland, 1760, 2 1/2 x 14 In.	140.00
Charger, Man In Boat, House In Forefront, Mid 18th Century, 13 1/2 In.	950.00
Charger, Overall Flowers, c.1750, 12 3/4 In.	660.00
Charger, Polychrome, Floral Panels, Rust, Blue, Gray Green, Signed, 13 In.	920.00
Charger, Stag Drawn Flower Cart, Blue, Stylized Design, 19th Century, 22 In.	2160.00
Charger, Tulip, Leaves Either Side, Looped Border, c.1680, 13 1/4 In.	8100.00
Cistern, Figural, Fat Mustached Man, Blue & White, Mid 18th Century, 13 1/4 In.	9600.00
Dish, Monochrome Cobalt Portrait Of King William, c.1690, 10 In.	2900.00
Dish, Monochrome Cobalt Portrait Of Queen Mary, 1688, 8 1/2 In.	2500.00
Figurine, Courting Couple, Man Playing Flute, Woman With Flower, 10 7/8 In.	995.00
Figurine, Woman & Man, 7 In., Pair	35.00
Jar, Apothecary, Blue & White Stylized Flowers, 6 1/4 In.	220.00
Jar, Cover, Oak Leaf Design, Blue & White, Mid 18th Century, Crazed, 9 1/2 In., Pair	685.00
Lamp, Boats On Base, Shade With Windmill & Boat, 6 1/2 In.	175.00
Lamp, Oil, Bulbous, Handles, Incised Panels, Pink, Green, Latin Phrase, 10 1/2 In.	520.00
Plaque, Harbor Scene, Large Building, Ships, 17 1/2 x 21 In.	690.00
Plaque, Outdoor Scene, Hunters, Farmers, Town, Frame, 17 1/2 x 21 In.	345.00
Plaque, River Scene By Windmill, Scrolling Surround, Late 19th Century, 24 3/4 In.	170.00
Plaque, William Of Orange, On Horseback Within Rolling Landscape, 15 In.	805.00
Plate, Birds & Flowers, c.1720, 8 1/4 In.	1200.00
Plate, Blue & White Vintage Design, Mid 18th Century, 8 3/4 In.	165.00
Plate, Blue Insect & Flower, Blue Ground, Early 18th Century, 10 1/2 In.	290.00
Plate, Central Medallion With Chinese Basket, Blue, White, 18th Century, 10 In.	60.00
Plate, Chinoiserie Design, Signed, 18th Century, 9 In., Pair	320.00
Plate, Floral Vase, Bamboo Background, Blue & White, Yellow Glaze, 9 In.	385.00
Plate, Oak Leaf, Blue & White, England, Mid 18th Century, 7 5/8 In.	55.00
Plate, Octagonal, Dublin, c.1760, 8 1/2 In.	800.00
Plate, Oriental Scene, Blue & White, Octagonal, England, Mid 18th Century, 7 5/8 In.	600.00
Plate, Seaside Scene, 2 Ships, 5 Floral Sprays, 19th Century, 8 1/2 In., Pair	127.00
Plate, Stylized Flower, Blue & Red, c.1730, 8 1/2 In.	1600.00
Platter, Bonnet Design, Blue & White, Octagonal, England, 11 1/2 In.	550.00
Punch Bowl, 1760, 4 1/2 x 10 1/4 In.	140.00
Punch Bowl, Blue & White, c.1720, 7 1/4 In.	1650.00
Punch Bowl, Geometric Design, England, 18th Century, 7 1/4 In.	1100.00
Punch Bowl, Interior Sprays Of Flowers, Sprays Of Flowers Exterior, 4 1/2 x 12 In.	978.00
Salt, Striped Exterior, Floral Interior, 2 In.	230.00
Shoe, Dutch, Blue & White, 3 In.	25.00
Spoon Holder, With Spoons, Dark Navy Flowers, Yellow, Burgundy, 6 Spoons, 8 In.	65.00
Tea Caddy, Red & Blue, Cover, England, 5 In.	230.00
Tile, 3 Galleon Sailing Ships Set Against Clouded Sky, Barnwood Frame, 12 1/8 x 4 In.	275.00
Tile, Adam, With Unicorn, Garden Of Eden, c.1750, 18th Century	225.00
Tile, Arts & Crafts, Deer Rearing, Broad Wooden Frame, 4 x 4 In.	288.00
Tile, Bird In Cage, 18th Century	2200.00
Tile, Dog & Cat 2 Sections Each Tile, Walnut Frame, 11 3/8 x 6 1/2 In., Pair	825.00
Tile, Dutch Landscape, Hand Painted, Frame, Signed, 11 1/2 x 17 1/4 In.	230.00

Tile, Fazackerly, Flower Bouquets, c.1760, 5 x 5 In., Pair 345.00
Tile, Fisherman Tending To His Nets, Crystalline Glaze, 4 3/4 x 4 3/4 In. 110.00
Tile, Gentleman In Full Dress, c.1630 .... 175.00
Tile, Mother & Daughter Walking On Seashore, Mother With Basket, 4 3/4 x 4 3/4 In. ... 110.00
Tile, Mother & Son, Military Planes, Crystalline, Frame, Vordsel-Vaede-Vrijheid 300.00
Tile, Mother & Young Son Waving From Ground As 2 Fighter Planes Fly By, Frame 300.00
Tile, Raised Railroad Sign, Tracks Running Around Station, 1945, 7 3/4 x 5 1/2 In. 300.00
Tile, Urn Of Flowers Center, Tulips In Corners, 17th Century, c.1650 .... 195.00
Tile, Winged Fish, Flying Above Water Surface, 1650 .... 195.00
Tile Set, Blue & White, Framed, Deity, Man In Boat, Kneeling Figure, 5 In. 115.00
Tile Set, Blue & White, Framed, Early 18th Century, Miniature, 6 Piece 230.00
Tile Set, Various Decorations, 18th Century, 5 In., 10 Piece 280.00
Tobacco Jar, St. Vincent, Two Ships Workshop, 18th Century, 8 1/2 In. 1350.00
Vase, Blue & White, Chinoiserie Scenes, Geometric Bands, 19th Century, 10 In. 375.00
Vase, Chinese Style Design, Female Figure In Courtyard, Cat Finial, 18th Century, 23 In. . 800.00
Vase, Continuous Scenes Of Oriental Figures & Landscape, 27 In., Pair 4025.00
Vase, Faience, Garniture, Polychrome Blue, Signed L.P.K., 18th Century, 11 In. 975.00
Vase, Fluted, Octagonal, Baluster Shape, Polychrome, Cover, Early 1900s, 14 In. 1680.00
Vase, Raised Rim, Panels, Heart Shape, Footed, Pastoral Scene, 9 x 9 In., Pair 375.00

DENTAL cabinets, chairs, equipment, and other related items are listed
here. Other objects may be found in the Medical category.

Cabinet, Oak, Double Roll Top, Swing Out Compartments, 45 x 58 In. 3360.00
Cabinet, Oak, Swivel Shelves, Drawers, Roller Front, Drop Front Desk, 19th Century ... 7400.00
Chisel, Blackwood Handle, 18th Century, 3 In. 665.00
Tool Kit, Rosewood Chest, Top Tray 117 Tools, Drawer, Lock, Lower Tray, Drawer 9900.00

DENVER is part of the mark on an American art pottery. William Long
of Steubenville, Ohio, founded the Lonhuda Pottery Company in 1892.
In 1900 he moved to Denver, Colorado, and organized the Denver
China and Pottery Company. This pottery, which used the mark
Denver, worked until 1905 when Long moved to New Jersey and
founded the Clifton Pottery. Long also worked for Weller Pottery,
Roseville Pottery, and American Encaustic Tiling Company.

DENVER
C T &
P Co

Vase, Violet & Leaves, Green Matte Glaze, Squat, 2 3/4 x 5 3/4 In. 2137.00

DEPRESSION GLASS was an inexpensive glass manufactured in large
quantities during the 1920s and early 1930s. It was made in many colors and patterns by dozens of factories in the United States. Most patterns were also made in clear glass, which the factories called *crystal.*
If no color is listed here, it is clear. The name *Depression glass* is
a modern one. For more descriptions, history, pictures, and prices
of Depression glass, see the book *Kovels' Depression Glass &
Dinnerware Price List.*

Adam, Ashtray, Green, 4 1/2 In. 24.00
Adam, Berry Bowl, Pink, 4 3/4 In. 24.00
Adam, Bowl, Cereal, Green, 5 3/4 In. 65.00
Adam, Bowl, Vegetable, Cover, Oval, 9 In. 47.00
Adam, Bowl, Vegetable, Cover, Pink, Oval, 9 In. ....34.00 to 80.00
Adam, Butter, Cover, Pink 95.00
Adam, Cake Plate, Footed, Pink, 10 In. ....26.00 to 30.00
Adam, Candlestick, Pink, 4 In., Pair ....100.00 to 125.00
Adam, Candy Jar, Cover, Pink, 2 1/2 In. 120.00
Adam, Creamer, Green 25.00
Adam, Cup & Saucer, Green 30.00
Adam, Cup & Saucer, Pink ....30.00 to 37.00
Adam, Grill Plate, Green 27.00
Adam, Lamp, Pink 3000.00
Adam, Pitcher, Pink, 52 Oz., 8 In. 60.00
Adam, Plate, Dinner, Pink, Square, 9 In. 39.00
Adam, Plate, Salad, Green, Square, 7 3/4 In. 18.00
Adam, Platter, Pink, 11 3/4 In. ....24.00 to 37.00
Adam, Relish, 2 Sections, Pink, 8 In. 24.00

Adam, Salt & Pepper, Footed, Pink, 4 In. ....85.00 to 100.00
Adam, Sherbet, Pink, 3 In. ....30.00 to 37.00
Adam, Sugar & Creamer, Cover, Pink 72.00
Adam, Sugar, Cover, Pink 50.00
Adam, Tumbler, Pink, 4 1/2 In. ....30.00 to 40.00
Alice, Cup & Saucer, Jade-Ite 16.00
Alice, Cup & Saucer, White, Blue Trim 14.00
Alice, Plate, Dinner, Jade-Ite, 8 1/2 In. 35.00
American Pioneer, Bowl, Cover, Pink, 8 3/4 In. 75.00
American Pioneer, Console, Pink, 10 3/8 In. 75.00
American Pioneer, Cup & Saucer 14.00
American Pioneer, Dish, Mayonnaise, Green, 4 1/4 In. 115.00
American Pioneer, Plate, Luncheon, Green, 8 In. 14.00
American Pioneer, Sherbet, Amber, 4 3/4 In. 50.00
American Pioneer, Tumbler, Green, Pilsner, 6 In. 150.00
American Pioneer, Vase, Cupped, Green, 8 In. 165.00
American Pioneer, Vase, Flared, Pink, 7 In. 115.00
American Sweetheart, Berry Bowl, Pink, 9 In. ....50.00 to 60.00
American Sweetheart, Bowl, Cereal, Monax, 6 In. 20.00
American Sweetheart, Bowl, Vegetable, Monax, Oval, 11 In. 85.00
American Sweetheart, Bowl, Vegetable, Pink, Oval, 11 In. ....65.00 to 70.00
American Sweetheart, Chop Plate, Monax, 11 In. 22.00
American Sweetheart, Console, Monax, 18 In. 650.00
American Sweetheart, Console, Red, 18 In. 1800.00
American Sweetheart, Creamer, Footed, Monax ....11.00 to 13.00
American Sweetheart, Creamer, Footed, Red 165.00
American Sweetheart, Cup & Saucer, Monax ....12.00 to 16.00
American Sweetheart, Cup & Saucer, Pink 25.00
American Sweetheart, Cup, Monax 11.00
American Sweetheart, Pitcher, Pink, 60 Oz., 7 1/2 In. ....1200.00 to 1250.00
American Sweetheart, Pitcher, Pink, 80 Oz., 8 In. 1000.00
American Sweetheart, Plate, Bread & Butter, Pink, 6 In. ....8.00 to 9.00
American Sweetheart, Plate, Dinner, Monax, 10 1/4 In. ....28.00 to 30.00
American Sweetheart, Plate, Dinner, Pink, 9 3/4 In. 44.00
American Sweetheart, Plate, Luncheon, Monax, 9 In. ....10.00 to 14.00
American Sweetheart, Plate, Salad, Monax, 8 In. 10.00
American Sweetheart, Plate, Salad, Red, 8 In. ....110.00 to 125.00
American Sweetheart, Platter, Monax, Oval, 13 In. ....65.00 to 75.00
American Sweetheart, Salt & Pepper, Pink 595.00
American Sweetheart, Salver, Monax, 12 In. 28.00
American Sweetheart, Salver, Red, 12 In. ....205.00 to 245.00
American Sweetheart, Sandwich Server, Monax, 15 1/2 In. ....275.00 to 325.00
American Sweetheart, Sandwich Server, Red, 15 1/2 In. 650.00
American Sweetheart, Sherbet, Pink, 4 1/4 In. 22.00
American Sweetheart, Soup, Cream, Monax, 4 1/2 In. ....130.00 to 135.00
American Sweetheart, Soup, Dish, Monax, 9 1/2 In. 100.00
American Sweetheart, Sugar & Creamer, Monax 19.00
American Sweetheart, Sugar, Cover, Footed, Monax ....550.00 to 600.00
American Sweetheart, Tumbler, Pink, 9 Oz., 4 1/4 In. ....89.00 to 100.00
American Sweetheart, Tumbler, Pink, 10 Oz., 4 3/4 In. 185.00
Anniversary, Butter, Cover Only 19.00
Anniversary, Compote, Iridescent, 6 In. 25.00
Anniversary, Creamer, Pink 10.00
Anniversary, Cup & Saucer 4.00
Anniversary, Dish, Pickle, 9 In. 6.00
Anniversary, Vase, Pink, 6 1/2 In. 35.00
Apple Blossom pattern is listed here as Dogwood.
Aunt Polly, Butter, Cover, Blue 230.00
Aunt Polly, Dish, Pickle, Blue, Handles, 7 1/4 In. 50.00
Aunt Polly, Nappy, Blue, 7 7/8 In. 60.00
Aunt Polly, Plate, Luncheon, Blue, 8 In. 25.00
Aunt Polly, Sherbet, Blue 15.00
Aunt Polly, Tumbler, Footed, Blue, 6 1/2 In. 40.00

Depression Glass, Adam

Depression Glass, Block Optic

Aurora, Bowl, Cereal, Pink, 5 3/8 In. . . . . .17.00 to 19.00
Aurora, Bowl, Deep, Blue, 4 1/2 In. 85.00
Aurora, Cup & Saucer, Blue . . . . .15.00 to 24.00
Aurora, Plate, Blue, 6 1/2 In. . . . . .13.00 to 15.00
Avocado, Bowl, Deep, 9 1/2 In. 52.00
Avocado, Creamer, Footed, Green . . . . .25.00 to 40.00
Avocado, Plate, Luncheon, Green, 8 1/4 In. . . . . .22.00 to 25.00
Avocado, Saucer, Pink, 6 3/8 In. 24.00
Avocado, Sherbet, Green . . . . .65.00 to 75.00
Avocado, Sugar & Creamer, Footed, Green . . . . .55.00 to 105.00
Ballerina pattern is listed here as Cameo.
Banded Rib pattern is listed here as Coronation.
Banded Rings pattern is listed here as Ring.
Basket pattern is listed here as No. 615.
Block Optic, Bowl, Cereal, Green, 5 1/4 In. 15.00
Block Optic, Butter Tub, No Cover, Green . . . . .63.00 to 85.00
Block Optic, Candlestick, Pink, 1 3/4 In., Pair 78.00
Block Optic, Candy Jar, Cover, Green, 2 1/4 In. 60.00
Block Optic, Console, Rolled Edge, Pink, 11 3/4 In. . . . . .122.00 to 140.00
Block Optic, Cup & Saucer, Green . . . . .15.00 to 20.00
Block Optic, Cup, Yellow 8.00
Block Optic, Dish, Mayonnaise, Green, 4 In. 35.00
Block Optic, Goblet, Wine, Pink, 4 1/2 In. 45.00
Block Optic, Pitcher, 54 Oz., 8 1/2 In. . . . . .40.00 to 50.00
Block Optic, Pitcher, Bulbous, Green, 54 Oz., 7 5/8 In. 82.00
Block Optic, Plate, Luncheon, Green, 8 In. . . . . .4.00 to 4.50
Block Optic, Saltshaker, Footed, Green 20.00
Block Optic, Sandwich Server, Center Handle, Pink . . . . .75.00 to 100.00
Block Optic, Sherbet, Green, 4 3/4 In. 17.00
Block Optic, Sugar & Creamer, Cone, Green 25.00
Block Optic, Sugar & Creamer, Yellow 40.00
Block Optic, Tumbler, Footed, Pink, 12 Oz., 4 7/8 In. 28.00
Block Optic, Tumbler, Pink, 12 Oz., 4 7/8 In. . . . . .28.00 to 30.00
Bouquet & Lattice pattern is listed here as Normandie.
Bowknot, Plate, Green, 7 In. 12.00
Bubble, Berry Bowl, Blue, 4 1/2 In. 15.00
Bubble, Berry Bowl, Milk White, 8 3/8 In. 8.00
Bubble, Bowl, Cereal, Blue, 5 1/4 In. . . . . .13.00 to 14.00
Bubble, Cup & Saucer, Blue . . . . .5.00 to 6.00
Bubble, Grill Plate, Blue, 9 3/8 In. 10.00
Bubble, Plate, Bread & Butter, Blue, 6 3/4 In. 4.00
Bubble, Plate, Dinner, Green, 9 3/8 In. 24.00
Bubble, Platter, Blue, Oval, 12 In. . . . . .15.00 to 16.00
Bubble, Sugar & Creamer, No Cover 15.00
Bubble, Sugar, No Cover, Blue 25.00
Bubble, Tumbler, Iced Tea, Footed, 12 Oz. 22.00

Depression Glass,
Bubble

Depression Glass,
Cherry Blossom

Depression Glass,
Circle

Bubble, Tumbler, Juice, Ruby Red, 6 Oz. ....12.00 to 16.00
Bullseye pattern is listed here as Bubble.
Butterflies & Roses pattern is listed here as Flower Garden with Butterflies.
Buttons & Bows pattern is listed here as Holiday.
Cabbage Rose pattern is listed here as Sharon.
Cameo, Berry Bowl, Green, 8 1/4 In. ....42.00 to 50.00
Cameo, Bowl, Cereal, Green, 5 1/2 In. ....35.00 to 42.00
Cameo, Bowl, Salad, Green, 7 1/4 In. ....60.00 to 90.00
Cameo, Bowl, Vegetable, Green, Oval, 10 In. ....30.00 to 35.00
Cameo, Butter, Cover, Green ....235.00 to 250.00
Cameo, Candlestick, Green, 4 In., Pair ....140.00 to 150.00
Cameo, Candy Jar, Cover, Green, 6 1/4 In. 250.00
Cameo, Cookie Jar, Cover, Green ....62.00 to 71.00
Cameo, Creamer, Green, 4 1/4 In. 30.00
Cameo, Creamer, Yellow, 3 1/4 In. 14.00
Cameo, Cup & Saucer, Green 19.00
Cameo, Decanter, Stopper, Green, 10 In. ....185.00 to 210.00
Cameo, Goblet, Water, Green, 6 In. 65.00
Cameo, Grill Plate, Yellow, 10 1/2 In. 10.00
Cameo, Pitcher, Water, Green, 56 Oz., 8 1/2 In. ....65.00 to 75.00
Cameo, Plate, Green, Square, 8 1/2 In. ....65.00 to 75.00
Cameo, Plate, Sherbet, Green, 6 In. ....4.00 to 6.00
Cameo, Platter, Closed Handles, Green, 12 In. ....20.00 to 30.00
Cameo, Relish, 3 Sections, Footed, Green, 7 1/2 In. 30.00
Cameo, Salt & Pepper, Footed, Green ....75.00 to 100.00
Cameo, Sherbet, Molded, Green, 3 1/8 In. 18.00
Cameo, Sugar & Creamer, Green, 4 1/4 In. 75.00
Cameo, Sugar, Green, 3 1/4 In. ....20.00 to 25.00
Cameo, Tumbler, Footed, Green, 11 Oz., 5 3/4 In. 50.00
Cameo, Tumbler, Green, 11 Oz., 5 In. 35.00
Cameo, Tumbler, Water, Green, 9 Oz., 4 In. ....33.00 to 35.00
Cameo, Vase, Green, 8 In. 45.00
Candlewick pattern is listed in the Imperial Glass category.
Caprice pattern is included in the Cambridge Glass category.
Charm, Bowl, Dessert, Azure-Ite, 4 3/4 In. 9.00
Charm, Bowl, Dessert, Royal Ruby, 4 3/4 In. ....5.50 to 10.00
Charm, Bowl, Salad, Forest Green, 7 3/8 In. 18.00
Charm, Creamer, Forest Green 10.00
Charm, Cup & Saucer, Forest Green ....8.00 to 9.00
Charm, Cup & Saucer, Jade-Ite 15.00
Charm, Plate, Dinner, Forest Green, 9 1/4 In. 32.00
Charm, Plate, Luncheon, Forest Green, 8 3/8 In. 7.00
Charm, Plate, Luncheon, Royal Ruby, 8 3/8 In. ....7.50 to 14.00
Charm, Platter, Jade-Ite, Oval, 11 x 8 In. 65.00
Charm, Sugar, Forest Green 10.00
Cherry Blossom, Berry Bowl, Pink, 8 1/2 In. ....55.00 to 60.00

Cherry Blossom, Bowl, Cereal, Green, 5 3/4 In. 46.00
Cherry Blossom, Bowl, Pink, 3-Footed, 10 1/2 In. 92.00
Cherry Blossom, Bowl, Pink, Handles, Oval, 9 In. .... .58.00 to 60.00
Cherry Blossom, Child's Set, Delphite, 14 Piece 350.00
Cherry Blossom, Coaster, Green 17.00
Cherry Blossom, Cup & Saucer, Pink .... .26.00 to 30.00
Cherry Blossom, Grill Plate, Green, 9 In. 30.00
Cherry Blossom, Grill Plate, Pink, 10 In. 35.00
Cherry Blossom, Mug, Green, 7 Oz. 375.00
Cherry Blossom, Pitcher, Green, 42 Oz., 8 In. .... .60.00 to 70.00
Cherry Blossom, Pitcher, Scalloped, Pink, 36 Oz., 6 3/4 In. .... .65.00 to 98.00
Cherry Blossom, Plate, Dinner, Pink, 9 In. .... .26.00 to 30.00
Cherry Blossom, Plate, Salad, Pink, 7 In. 30.00
Cherry Blossom, Platter, Green, Oval, 11 In. .... .55.00 to 60.00
Cherry Blossom, Sandwich Server, Pink, 10 1/2 In. 35.00
Cherry Blossom, Saucer, Green 8.00
Cherry Blossom, Sherbet, Pink 20.00
Cherry Blossom, Soup, Dish, Green, 7 3/4 In. 82.00
Cherry Blossom, Soup, Dish, Pink, 7 3/4 In. .... .100.00 to 125.00
Cherry Blossom, Sugar, Cover, Pink 25.00
Cherry Blossom, Tumbler, Footed, Delphite, 9 Oz., 4 1/2 In. 22.00
Cherry Blossom, Tumbler, Footed, Green, 4 Oz., 3 3/4 In. .... .16.00 to 22.00
Cherry Blossom, Tumbler, Footed, Green, 8 Oz., 4 1/2 In. 40.00
Cherry Blossom, Tumbler, Pink, 12 Oz., 5 In. 125.00
Cherry Blossom, Tumbler, Scalloped Foot, Pink, 8 Oz., 4 1/2 In. .... .35.00 to 40.00
Cherry-Berry, Tumbler, Green, 3 5/8 In. 25.00
Chinex Classic, Sandwich Server, Ivory, 11 1/2 In. 8.00
Chinex Classic, Soup, Dish, Ivory, Castle Decal, 7 3/4 In. 38.00
Christmas Candy, Cup 5.00
Christmas Candy, Plate, Luncheon, 8 1/4 In. 7.00
Christmas Candy, Saucer, Teal 15.00
Christmas Candy, Sugar, 3 1/4 In. 9.00
Circle, Cup & Saucer, Green 6.00
Circle, Goblet, Water, Green, 8 Oz., 4 In. 15.00
Circle, Plate, Luncheon, Green, 8 1/4 In. 8.00
Circle, Plate, Sherbet, Green, 6 In. 2.00
Circle, Sherbet, Green, 4 3/4 In. 4.00
Cloverleaf, Berry Bowl, Green, 4 In. .... .40.00 to 48.00
Cloverleaf, Bowl, Salad, Green, 7 In. .... .110.00 to 125.00
Cloverleaf, Cup & Saucer, Black .... .26.00 to 27.00
Cloverleaf, Cup, Black 22.00
Cloverleaf, Cup, Green 10.00
Cloverleaf, Grill Plate, Green, 10 1/4 In. .... .25.00 to 32.00
Cloverleaf, Plate, Luncheon, Pink, 8 In. 3.50
Cloverleaf, Salt & Pepper, Black 100.00
Cloverleaf, Salt & Pepper, Green .... .80.00 to 90.00
Cloverleaf, Sherbet, Green .... .10.00 to 12.00
Cloverleaf, Sugar & Creamer, Footed, Black .... .30.00 to 45.00
Cloverleaf, Tumbler, Footed, Green, 9 Oz., 4 In. 35.00
Cloverleaf, Tumbler, Green, 10 Oz., 3 3/4 In. .... .63.00 to 80.00
Colonial, Berry Bowl, Pink, 4 1/2 In. 16.00
Colonial, Bowl, Cereal, Green, 5 1/2 In. 10.00
Colonial, Butter, Cover, Green .... .55.00 to 60.00
Colonial, Creamer 17.00
Colonial, Cup, Opaque White 7.00
Colonial, Goblet, Claret, Green, 4 Oz., 5 1/4 In. 25.00
Colonial, Goblet, Cordial, Green, 1 Oz., 3 3/4 In. .... .27.00 to 30.00
Colonial, Goblet, Water, 8 1/2 Oz., 5 3/4 In. 22.00
Colonial, Grill Plate, Green, 10 In. .... .28.00 to 30.00
Colonial, Pitcher, Milk, Green, 16 Oz., 5 In. 28.00
Colonial, Pitcher, Milk, Pink, 16 Oz., 5 In. .... .60.00 to 70.00
Colonial, Pitcher, Pink, 68 Oz., 7 3/4 In. 75.00
Colonial, Plate, Dinner, Pink, 10 In. 59.00

Colonial, Plate, Luncheon, Green, 8 In.	9.00
Colonial, Plate, Sherbet, Green, 6 In.	9.00
Colonial, Platter, Oval, Pink, 12 In.	22.00
Colonial, Sherbet, 3 3/8 In.	7.00
Colonial, Sherbet, Green, 3 3/8 In.	14.00
Colonial, Soup, Dish, Pink, 7 In.	85.00
Colonial, Sugar & Creamer, Cover, Green	65.00
Colonial, Tumbler, Footed, 3 Oz., 3 1/4 In.	12.00
Colonial, Tumbler, Footed, Green, 5 Oz., 4 In.	46.00
Colonial, Tumbler, Footed, Pink, 3 Oz., 3 1/4 In.	20.00
Colonial, Tumbler, Footed, Pink, 5 Oz., 4 In.	28.00
Colonial, Tumbler, Water, Pink, 9 Oz., 4 In.	25.00
Colonial, Tumbler, Whiskey, Pink, 1 1/2 Oz., 2 1/2 In.	15.00
Colonial Block, Berry Bowl, Green, 4 In.	8.00
Colonial Block, Candy Dish, Cover, Green, 8 1/2 In.	35.00
Colonial Block, Sugar, No Cover	6.00
Colony, Tumbler, Juice, Footed, 5 Oz.	24.00
Columbia, Bowl, Cereal, 5 In.	10.00 to 22.00
Columbia, Bowl, Ruffled Edge, 10 1/2 In.	20.00
Columbia, Bread Plate, 6 In.	3.00
Columbia, Chop Plate, 11 In.	15.00
Columbia, Cup & Saucer	5.00 to 12.00
Columbia, Plate, Luncheon, 9 1/2 In.	5.50
Columbia, Tumbler, Water, 9 Oz.	25.00
Coronation, Berry Set, Royal Ruby, 5 Piece	35.00
Coronation, Berry Set, Royal Ruby, 7 Piece	48.00 to 75.00
Coronation, Nappy, Royal Ruby, 8 In.	14.00
Coronation, Plate, Luncheon, Pink, 8 1/2 In.	10.00
Coronation, Plate, Sherbet, Pink, 6 In.	2.00 to 5.00
Coronation, Saucer, Pink, 6 In.	2.00 to 4.00
Coronation, Sherbet, Pink	5.00 to 12.00
Coronation, Tumbler, Pink, Footed, 10 Oz., 5 In.	22.00 to 40.00
Cremax, Cup & Saucer, After Dinner	15.00
Cremax, Cup, Gold Rim	4.50
Cubist, Bowl, Deep, Pink, 4 1/2 In.	7.00 to 10.00
Cubist, Bowl, Salad, Pink, 6 1/2 In.	11.00
Cubist, Butter, Cover, Green	60.00
Cubist, Candy Jar, Cover, Green	25.00 to 40.00
Cubist, Coaster, Pink, 3 1/4 In.	7.00
Cubist, Creamer, Pink, 2 5/8 In.	2.00
Cubist, Plate, Luncheon, Pink, 8 In.	10.00
Cubist, Plate, Sherbet, Pink, 6 In.	4.00 to 5.00
Cubist, Salt & Pepper, Pink	35.00
Cubist, Saucer, Pink	3.00
Cubist, Sherbet, Green	7.00 to 11.00
Cubist, Sugar, Cover, Green	23.00
Cubist, Sugar, Green, 3 In.	8.00

Depression Glass,
Cloverleaf

Depression Glass,
Colonial

Depression Glass,
Dogwood

Cubist, Tumbler, Green, 9 Oz., 4 In. 75.00
Daisy pattern is listed here as No. 620.
Dancing Girl pattern is listed here as Cameo.
Diamond Arch, Nappy, Square, 5 1/2 In. 12.00
Diamond Arch, Nappy, Square, Pink, 5 1/2 In. 24.00
Diamond Pattern is listed here as Miss America.
Diana, Bowl, Salad, Pink, 9 In. ....22.00 to 32.00
Diana, Candy Jar, Cover Only, Pink 20.00
Diana, Console, Pink, 11 In. 45.00
Diana, Cup & Saucer, After Dinner 13.00
Diana, Plate, Bread & Butter, Pink, 6 In. 5.00
Diana, Plate, Dinner, 9 1/2 In. 10.00
Diana, Soup, Cream, Pink, 5 1/2 In. 45.00
Diana, Tumbler, Pink, 9 Oz., 4 1/8 In. 50.00
Dogwood, Berry Bowl, Pink, 8 1/2 In. ....62.00 to 65.00
Dogwood, Bowl, Cereal, Pink, 5 1/2 In. ....33.00 to 42.00
Dogwood, Bowl, Fruit, Green, 10 1/2 In. 300.00
Dogwood, Coaster, Pink, 4 In. 20.00
Dogwood, Creamer, Pink, Thin ....17.00 to 20.00
Dogwood, Cup & Saucer, Pink ....24.00 to 25.00
Dogwood, Grill Plate, Pink, 10 1/2 In. 25.00
Dogwood, Plate, Bread & Butter, Pink, 6 In. 9.00
Dogwood, Plate, Dinner, Pink, 9 1/4 In. ....35.00 to 43.00
Dogwood, Plate, Luncheon, Green, 8 In. 9.00
Dogwood, Platter, Oval, Pink, 12 In. 725.00
Dogwood, Sugar & Creamer, Green, Thick 120.00
Dogwood, Sugar & Creamer, Pink, Thin 60.00
Dogwood, Tidbit, 2 Tiers, Pink 100.00
Dogwood, Tidbit, 3 Tiers, Pink 150.00
Dogwood, Tumbler, Pink, 10 Oz., 4 In. ....45.00 to 50.00
Doric, Berry Bowl, Pink, 4 1/2 In. 14.00
Doric, Berry Bowl, Pink, 8 1/4 In. 35.00
Doric, Bowl, Vegetable, Oval, Pink, 9 In. 45.00
Doric, Sherbet, Delphite 18.00
Doric, Sugar, Cover, Green 35.00
Doric, Tumbler, Footed, Pink, 9 Oz., 4 1/2 In. ....80.00 to 100.00
Doric & Pansy, Butter, Cover, Ultramarine 450.00
Doric & Pansy, Child's Set, Ultramarine, 14 Piece 350.00
Doric & Pansy, Salt & Pepper, Ultramarine 415.00
Doric & Pansy, Sugar, Pink, Child's 27.00
Double Shield pattern is listed here as Mt. Pleasant.
Dutch Rose pattern is listed here as Rosemary.
Early American Rock Crystal pattern is listed here as Rock Crystal.
Fine Rib pattern is listed here as Homespun.
Fire-King, Batter Bowl, Pour Spout, Handle, Jade-Ite, 7 1/2 In. 43.00
Fire-King, Bowl, Cereal, Blue, 6 In. 23.00
Fire-King, Bowl, Footed, Jade-Ite, 10 Oz. 14.00
Fire-King, Bowl, Ivory, 5 1/2 In. 12.00
Fire-King, Bowl, White, Blue Dots, 8 1/2 In. 12.00
Fire-King, Cake Plate, Footed, Ivory, Gold Trim, 10 In. 12.00
Fire-King, Casserole, Au Gratin Cover, 1 1/2 Qt. 8.00
Fire-King, Casserole, Cover, Peach Blossom, 5 1/2 In. 15.00
Fire-King, Creamer, Ivory 6.00
Fire-King, Cup, Jade-Ite, After Dinner 49.00
Fire-King, Cup, St. Denis, White 6.00
Fire-King, Custard Cup, 6 Oz. 6.00
Fire-King, Custard Cup, Blue, 6 Oz. ....4.00 to 7.00
Fire-King, Grease Jar, Cover, Ivory, Black Dots 68.00
Fire-King, Grease Jar, Cover, Ivory, Tulip ....70.00 to 115.00
Fire-King, Mixing Bowl Set, Beaded Edge, Jade-Ite, 3 Piece 110.00
Fire-King, Mixing Bowl, Blue, Rainbow, Swirl, 2 Qt. 20.00
Fire-King, Mixing Bowl, Ivory, Red Dots, 2 Qt. 55.00
Fire-King, Mixing Bowl, Ivory, Tulip, 2 Qt. 30.00

Depression Glass,
Doric & Pansy

Depression Glass,
Fire-King

Depression Glass,
Floragold

Fire-King, Mixing Bowl, Ivory, Tulip, 4 Qt. . . . . .28.00 to 56.00
Fire-King, Mug, Ivory, 8 Oz. 7.00
Fire-King, Mug, Jade-Ite, 7 Oz. 12.00
Fire-King, Nurser, Blue, 4 Oz. 15.00
Fire-King, Pie Plate, Blue, 9 In. . . . . .8.00 to 10.00
Fire-King, Pie Plate, Juice Saver, Blue, 10 3/8 In. 180.00
Fire-King, Pitcher, Milk, Jade-Ite, 4 1/2 In. 95.00
Fire-King, Plate, Jade-Ite, 6 3/4 In. 13.00
Fire-King, Refrigerator Dish, Cover, Ivory, 4 1/8 x 4 1/8 In. 27.00
Fire-King, Roaster, Blue, 10 3/8 In. . . . . .60.00 to 95.00
Fire-King, Skillet, 1 Spout, Jade-Ite, 7 In. 150.00
Fleurette, Bowl, White, 4 5/8 In. 3.00
Fleurette, Plate, Dinner, White, 9 1/8 In. 6.00
Fleurette, Platter, White, Oval, 12 In. 12.00
Fleurette, Saucer, White, 5 3/4 In. 1.00
Floragold, Berry Bowl, Iridescent, Square, 4 1/2 In. 8.00
Floragold, Butter, Cover, Iridescent, 1/4 Lb. 25.00
Floragold, Candlestick, 2-Light, Iridescent, Pair . . . . .50.00 to 65.00
Floragold, Candy Dish, Cover, Iridescent, 6 3/4 In. 55.00
Floragold, Cup, Iridescent . . . . .5.00 to 6.00
Floragold, Pitcher, Iridescent, 64 Oz. 38.00
Floragold, Plate, Dinner, Iridescent, 8 1/2 In. . . . . .36.00 to 45.00
Floragold, Plate, Indentation, Iridescent, 13 1/2 In. . . . . .62.00 to 145.00
Floragold, Salt & Pepper, Iridescent 55.00
Floragold, Sugar & Creamer, Cover, Iridescent 27.00
Floragold, Tray, Iridescent, 13 1/2 In. 22.00
Floragold, Tumbler, Footed, Iridescent, 10 Oz. 23.00
Floral, Bowl, Vegetable, Cover, Green, 8 In. . . . . .20.00 to 40.00
Floral, Butter, Cover, Pink 105.00
Floral, Candlestick, Green, 4 In., Pair 105.00
Floral, Candy Jar, Cover, Pink 49.00
Floral, Creamer, Green . . . . .14.00 to 15.00
Floral, Cup & Saucer, Pink . . . . .24.00 to 27.00
Floral, Pitcher, Cone, Footed, Pink, 32 Oz., 8 In. 55.00
Floral, Pitcher, Lemonade, Pink, 48 Oz., 10 1/4 In. 295.00
Floral, Plate, Dinner, Pink, 9 In. 23.00
Floral, Plate, Salad, Green, 8 In. . . . . .12.00 to 20.00
Floral, Plate, Sherbet, Pink, 6 In. 10.00
Floral, Platter, Green, Oval, 10 3/4 In. . . . . .18.00 to 24.00
Floral, Salt & Pepper, Footed, Pink, 4 In. 55.00
Floral, Sherbet, Green . . . . .18.00 to 22.00
Floral, Sugar, Cover, Green 17.50
Floral, Sugar, No Cover, Green 10.00
Floral, Tumbler, Juice, Footed, Pink, 5 Oz., 4 In. 18.00
Floral, Tumbler, Lemonade, Footed, Green, 9 Oz., 5 1/4 In. .47.50 to 50.00
Floral, Tumbler, Water, Footed, Pink, 7 Oz., 4 3/4 In. . . . . .19.00 to 29.00
Floral, Tumbler, Water, Pink, 7 Oz., 4 3/4 In. 22.00

Floral & Diamond Band, Berry Bowl, Green, 4 1/2 In. 12.00
Floral & Diamond Band, Butter, Cover, Pink 150.00
Floral & Diamond Band, Creamer, Green 18.00
Floral & Diamond Band, Pitcher, Green, 42 Oz., 8 In. 125.00
Floral & Diamond Band, Sugar, Cover, Green 80.00
Florentine No. 1, Berry Bowl, 5 In. 10.00
Florentine No. 1, Berry Bowl, Pink, 5 In. 19.00
Florentine No. 1, Bowl, Vegetable, Cover, Yellow, Oval, 9 1/2 In. 60.00
Florentine No. 1, Butter, Cover, Pink 170.00
Florentine No. 1, Creamer, Green 10.00
Florentine No. 1, Cup & Saucer, Yellow 14.00
Florentine No. 1, Pitcher, Pink, 48 Oz., 7 1/2 In. 145.00
Florentine No. 1, Plate, Dinner, 10 In. 15.00
Florentine No. 1, Plate, Salad, Green, 8 1/2 In. ....15.00 to 20.00
Florentine No. 1, Platter, Yellow, Oval, 11 1/2 In. 22.00
Florentine No. 1, Salt & Pepper, Footed, Pink ....55.00 to 59.00
Florentine No. 1, Sherbet, Pink, 3 Oz. 17.00
Florentine No. 1, Sugar & Creamer, Cover, Pink ....65.00 to 69.00
Florentine No. 1, Sugar & Creamer, No Cover, Pink ....32.00 to 35.00
Florentine No. 1, Tumbler, Juice, Footed, Pink, 5 Oz., 3 3/4 In. 27.00
Florentine No. 2, Berry Bowl, 4 1/2 In. 12.00
Florentine No. 2, Berry Bowl, Yellow, 8 In. ....23.00 to 35.00
Florentine No. 2, Bowl, Cereal, Yellow, 6 In. 45.00
Florentine No. 2, Butter, Cover, Yellow ....175.00 to 185.00
Florentine No. 2, Candy Dish, Cover, Yellow 165.00
Florentine No. 2, Compote, Ruffled, 3 1/2 In. 6.00
Florentine No. 2, Creamer, Yellow 10.00
Florentine No. 2, Cup & Saucer, Green 10.00
Florentine No. 2, Cup & Saucer, Yellow ....13.00 to 25.00
Florentine No. 2, Cup, Green 7.50
Florentine No. 2, Gravy Boat, Yellow, 11 1/2-In. Underplate 135.00
Florentine No. 2, Parfait, Yellow, 6 In. 65.00
Florentine No. 2, Pitcher, Juice, 28 Oz., 7 1/2 In. 38.00
Florentine No. 2, Pitcher, Juice, Footed, Yellow, 28 Oz., 7 1/2 In. 35.00
Florentine No. 2, Pitcher, Milk, Cone, Yellow, 28 Oz., 7 1/2 In. 30.00
Florentine No. 2, Pitcher, Water, 48 Oz., 7 1/2 In. 38.00
Florentine No. 2, Plate, Dinner, Yellow, 10 In. ....14.00 to 20.00
Florentine No. 2, Plate, Salad, 8 1/2 In. 9.00
Florentine No. 2, Plate, Salad, Yellow, 8 1/2 In. ....8.00 to 14.00
Florentine No. 2, Plate, Sherbet, 6 In. 4.50
Florentine No. 2, Plate, Sherbet, Yellow, 6 In. ....5.00 to 9.00
Florentine No. 2, Platter, Green, Oval, 11 In. ....16.00 to 23.00
Florentine No. 2, Relish, 3 Sections, Yellow, 10 In. ....29.00 to 45.00
Florentine No. 2, Salt & Pepper, Yellow ....49.00 to 55.00
Florentine No. 2, Saucer, Yellow 5.00
Florentine No. 2, Sherbet, Green 10.00
Florentine No. 2, Sherbet, Yellow ....12.00 to 13.00
Florentine No. 2, Soup, Cream, 4 3/4 In. 14.00
Florentine No. 2, Soup, Cream, Green, 4 3/4 In. ....14.00 to 16.00
Florentine No. 2, Soup, Cream, Yellow, 4 3/4 In. ....22.00 to 25.00
Florentine No. 2, Sugar & Creamer, No Cover, Green 17.00
Florentine No. 2, Sugar, Cover, Yellow ....25.00 to 32.00
Florentine No. 2, Tumbler, Iced Tea, Footed, Yellow, 12 Oz., 5 In. 48.00
Florentine No. 2, Tumbler, Juice, 5 Oz., 3 3/8 In. 10.00
Florentine No. 2, Tumbler, Juice, Footed, Yellow, 5 Oz., 4 In. ....17.00 to 18.00
Florentine No. 2, Tumbler, Juice, Yellow, 5 Oz., 3 3/8 In. 23.00
Florentine No. 2, Tumbler, Water, Footed, Green, 9 Oz., 4 1/2 In. 30.00
Florentine No. 2, Tumbler, Water, Yellow, 9 Oz., 4 In. 21.00
Flower & Leaf Band pattern is listed here as Indiana Custard.
Flower Garden With Butterflies, Ashtray, Blue 294.00
Flower Garden With Butterflies, Candy Dish, Cover, Heart, Yellow 1500.00
Flower Garden With Butterflies, Dresser Set, Power Jar, Cologne, Tray, Green 925.00
Flower Rim pattern is listed here as Vitrock.

Depression Glass,
Floral

Depression Glass,
Florentine No. I

Depression Glass,
Georgian

Forest Green, Berry Bowl, Square, 4 5/8 In. 6.00
Forest Green, Bowl, Vegetable, Oval, 8 1/2 In. 34.00
Forest Green, Cup & Saucer, Square 7.00
Forest Green, Goblet, Clear Bubble Foot, 11 Oz. 10.00
Forest Green, Mixing Bowl, 6 In. 9.00
Forest Green, Punch Bowl Set, 12 Cups, 14 Piece 110.00
Forest Green, Soup, Dish, Square, 6 In. 20.00
Fortune, Tumbler, Juice, Pink, 5 Oz., 3 1/2 In. 10.00
Fruits, Cup & Saucer, Green . . . . .13.00 to 15.00
Fruits, Plate, Luncheon, Green, 8 In. 12.00
Game Bird, Ashtray, Ruffled Grouse, 5 1/4 In. 18.00
Game Bird, Berry Bowl, Canada Goose, 4 3/4 In. 5.00
Game Bird, Mug, Ruffled Grouse, 8 Oz. 8.00
Game Bird, Plate, Dinner, Mallard Duck, 9 1/8 In. 6.50
Game Bird, Plate, Salad, Ring-Necked Pheasant, 7 1/8 In. 10.00
Game Bird, Platter, Ring-Necked Pheasant, 9 x 12 In. 50.00
Game Bird, Tumbler, Iced Tea, Mallard Duck, 11 Oz. 12.00
Georgian, Berry Bowl, Green, 4 1/2 In. . . . . .9.00 to 12.00
Georgian, Butter, Cover, Green 95.00
Georgian, Creamer, Footed, Green, 3 In. 10.00
Georgian, Cup & Saucer, Green 20.00
Georgian, Plate, Dinner, Green, 9 1/4 In. 18.00
Georgian, Plate, Luncheon, Green, 8 In. 10.00
Georgian, Saucer, Green 4.00
Georgian, Sherbet, Green . . . . .12.00 to 15.00
Georgian, Sugar, Green, 3 In. 9.00
Georgian, Tumbler, Iced Tea, Green, 12 Oz., 5 1/4 In. 185.00
Hairpin pattern is listed here as Newport.
Harp, Cake Stand, 9 In. . . . . .17.00 to 50.00
Harp, Cake Stand, Blue, 9 In. 45.00
Harp, Plate, Gold Trim, 7 In. 15.00
Harp, Tray, Handles, Rectangular 35.00
Heritage, Berry Bowl, 5 In. 8.00
Heritage, Bowl, 10 1/2 In. . . . . .14.00 to 15.00
Heritage, Sugar & Creamer, Cover, Footed 35.00
Hex Optic pattern is listed here as Hexagon Optic.
Hexagon Optic, Creamer, Green, 5 In. 25.00
Hexagon Optic, Tumbler, Water, Green, 9 Oz., 3 3/4 In. 8.00
Hobnail pattern is listed in the Hobnail category.
Holiday, Candlestick, Pink, 3 In. 50.00
Holiday, Creamer, Footed, Pink . . . . .12.00 to 22.00
Holiday, Cup & Saucer, Pink 22.00
Holiday, Pitcher, Pink, 52 Oz., 6 3/4 In. 43.00
Holiday, Plate, Dinner, Pink, 9 In. . . . . .15.00 to 18.00
Holiday, Platter, Iridescent, Oval, 11 3/8 In. 13.00
Holiday, Tumbler, Juice, Footed, Iridescent, 4 In. 16.00
Homespun, Plate, Pink, Child's . . . . .13.00 to 16.00
Homespun, Platter, Closed Handles, Pink, 13 In. 20.00

Honeycomb pattern is listed here as Hexagon Optic.
Horizontal Ribbed pattern is listed here as Manhattan.
Horseshoe pattern is listed here as No. 612.
Indiana Custard, Berry Bowl, Ivory, 5 1/2 In. 14.00
Indiana Custard, Bowl, Vegetable, Ivory, Oval, 9 1/2 In. 39.00
Indiana Custard, Cup & Saucer, Ivory 20.00
Indiana Custard, Plate, Dinner, Ivory, 9 3/4 In. 34.00
Indiana Custard, Plate, Salad, Ivory, 7 1/2 In. 20.00
Indiana Custard, Sugar & Creamer, Cover, Ivory 59.00
Iris, Berry Bowl, Beaded Edge, Iridescent, 4 1/2 In. ....7.50 to 10.00
Iris, Bowl, Cereal, 5 In. ....125.00 to 145.00
Iris, Bowl, Ruffled, Iridescent, 11 In. ....20.00 to 24.00
Iris, Bowl, Salad, Ruffled, Iridescent, 9 1/2 In. ....9.00 to 13.00
Iris, Butter, Cover, Iridescent 34.00
Iris, Candlestick 18.00
Iris, Candlestick, 2-Light, Pair ....43.00 to 45.00
Iris, Creamer, Footed ....8.00 to 13.00
Iris, Cup & Saucer, Iridescent ....20.00 to 25.00
Iris, Goblet, 8 Oz., 5 1/2 In. ....14.00 to 28.00
Iris, Goblet, Cocktail, 4 Oz., 4 1/2 In. 12.00
Iris, Goblet, Wine, Iridescent, 3 Oz., 4 1/2 In. ....24.00 to 35.00
Iris, Lamp Shade, Pink, 11 1/2 In. 75.00
Iris, Pitcher, Footed, 9 1/2 In. 79.00
Iris, Plate, Dinner, 9 In. 55.00
Iris, Plate, Sherbet, Iridescent, 5 1/2 In. 14.00
Iris, Sandwich Server, Iridescent, 9 In. 53.00
Iris, Sherbet, Iridescent, 2 1/2 In. ....15.00 to 16.00
Iris, Soup, Dish, 7 1/2 In. 165.00
Iris, Sugar & Creamer, Cover, Iridescent 26.00
Iris, Tumbler, Footed, 6 1/2 In. ....30.00 to 35.00
Iris, Vase, Footed, Iridescent, 9 In. 25.00
Iris, Vase, White, 9 In. 12.00
Jadite, Ashtray, 4 1/4 In. 35.00
Jadite, Canister, Coffee, Round, 40 Oz. 320.00
Jane-Ray, Bowl, Oatmeal, Jade-Ite, 5 7/8 In. ....20.00 to 30.00
Jane-Ray, Bowl, Vegetable, Jade-Ite, 8 1/4 In. 45.00
Jane-Ray, Cup & Saucer, Jade-Ite ....7.00 to 20.00
Jane-Ray, Cup & Saucer, Jade-Ite, After Dinner 115.00
Jane-Ray, Plate, Dinner, Jade-Ite, 9 1/8 In. 11.00
Jane-Ray, Soup, Dish, Jade-Ite, 7 7/8 In. 35.00
Jubilee, Cake Plate, Handles, 11 In. 45.00
Jubilee, Creamer, Topaz 18.00
Jubilee, Cup & Saucer, Topaz 17.00
Jubilee, Goblet, Topaz, 11 Oz., 7 1/2 In. 175.00
Jubilee, Plate, 3-Footed, Topaz, 14 In. 210.00
Jubilee, Plate, Luncheon, Topaz, 8 3/4 In. ....12.00 to 17.00
Jubilee, Tumbler, Water, 10 Oz., 6 In. 50.00

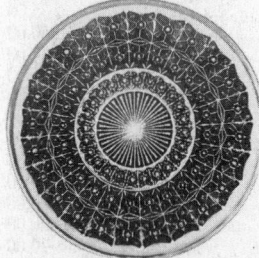

Depression Glass,
Holiday

Depression Glass,
Iris

Depression Glass,
Jadite

Knife & Fork pattern is listed here as Colonial.
Lake Como, Bowl, Cereal, 6 In. 29.00
Lake Como, Cup & Saucer 49.00
Lake Como, Sugar & Creamer, Footed 69.00
Laurel, Berry Bowl, French Ivory, 4 3/4 In. 10.00
Laurel, Bowl, Vegetable, Jade Green, 9 x 7 In. 55.00
Laurel, Bowl, White Opal, 11 In. 45.00
Laurel, Creamer, French Ivory 15.00
Laurel, Plate, Dinner, French Ivory, 9 1/8 In. . . . . .10.00 to 18.00
Laurel, Plate, French Ivory, 9 1/8 In. 18.00
Line 300 pattern is listed in the Paden City category as Peacock & Wild Rose.
Lorain pattern is listed here as No. 615.
Louisa pattern is listed here as Floragold.
Lovebirds pattern is listed here as Georgian.
Madrid, Console, Amber, 11 In. 14.00
Madrid, Cookie Jar, Cover, Amber 45.00
Madrid, Creamer, Footed, Amber 15.00
Madrid, Cup & Saucer, Pink 12.00
Madrid, Cup, Amber 6.00
Madrid, Cup, Madonna Blue 8.00
Madrid, Grill Plate, Amber, 10 1/2 In. . . . . .8.00 to 12.00
Madrid, Plate, Luncheon, Amber, 8 7/8 In. 8.00
Madrid, Plate, Luncheon, Blue, 8 7/8 In. 28.00
Madrid, Platter, Madonna Blue, Oval, 11 1/2 In. 55.00
Madrid, Salt & Pepper, Footed, Green, Metal Lids, 3 1/2 In. 125.00
Madrid, Sherbet, Green . . . . .12.00 to 15.00
Madrid, Soup, Dish, Amber, 7 In. . . . . .12.00 to 15.00
Madrid, Sugar & Creamer, Footed, Amber 15.00
Madrid, Tumbler, Amber, 9 Oz., 4 1/4 In. 15.00
Madrid, Tumbler, Amber, 12 Oz., 5 1/2 In. . . . . .24.00 to 25.00
Madrid, Tumbler, Juice, Footed, Amber, 5 Oz., 4 In. 28.00
Madrid, Tumbler, Madonna Blue, 12 Oz., 5 1/2 In. 45.00
Manhattan, Berry Bowl, Handle, 5 3/8 In. 15.00
Manhattan, Bowl, Fruit, Open Handle, Pink, 9 1/2 In. 50.00
Manhattan, Pitcher, Tilted, Pink, 80 Oz. 85.00
Manhattan, Plate, Dinner, 10 1/4 In. . . . . .20.00 to 22.00
Manhattan, Relish, 4 Sections, 14 In. 18.00
Manhattan, Salt & Pepper, Square, 2 In. . . . . .24.00 to 30.00
Manhattan, Sherbet, Pink 18.00
Manhattan, Sugar & Creamer, Oval 25.00
Manhattan, Tumbler, Footed, 10 Oz. 20.00
Many Windows pattern is listed here as Roulette.
Martha Washington pattern is included in the Cambridge Glass category.
Mayfair Federal, Plate, Dinner, Amber, 9 1/2 In. 15.00
Mayfair Federal, Sugar, Footed, Amber 13.00
Mayfair Open Rose, Bowl, Cereal, Pink, 5 1/2 In. 30.00
Mayfair Open Rose, Bowl, Deep, Scalloped, Blue, 12 In. . . . . .75.00 to 125.00
Mayfair Open Rose, Bowl, Vegetable, Cover, Blue, 10 In. 210.00
Mayfair Open Rose, Bowl, Vegetable, Cover, Pink, 7 In. 75.00
Mayfair Open Rose, Butter, Cover, Blue 330.00
Mayfair Open Rose, Cake Plate, Handles, Pink, 12 In. . . . . .35.00 to 50.00
Mayfair Open Rose, Candy Dish, Cover, Blue 285.00
Mayfair Open Rose, Cookie Jar, Cover, Pink 55.00
Mayfair Open Rose, Creamer, Footed, Pink 35.00
Mayfair Open Rose, Cup & Saucer, Blue 80.00
Mayfair Open Rose, Decanter, Stopper, Pink, 32 Oz. . . . . .215.00 to 225.00
Mayfair Open Rose, Goblet, Cocktail, Pink, 3 Oz., 4 In. 99.00
Mayfair Open Rose, Goblet, Thin, Blue, 9 Oz., 7 1/4 In. 310.00
Mayfair Open Rose, Pitcher, Blue, 80 Oz., 8 1/2 In. 260.00
Mayfair Open Rose, Pitcher, Juice, Pink, 37 Oz., 6 In. 70.00
Mayfair Open Rose, Pitcher, Pink, 60 Oz., 8 In. . . . . .69.00 to 75.00
Mayfair Open Rose, Plate, Luncheon, Pink, 8 1/2 In. . . . . .30.00 to 33.00
Mayfair Open Rose, Plate, Sherbet, Pink, 6 1/2 In. 20.00

Depression Glass,
Manhattan

Depression Glass, Mayfair Open Rose

Depression Glass,
Miss America

Mayfair Open Rose, Sandwich Server, Center Handle, Pink ....43.00 to 50.00
Mayfair Open Rose, Soup, Cream, Pink, 5 In. 60.00
Mayfair Open Rose, Sugar & Creamer, Footed, Pink 69.00
Mayfair Open Rose, Tumbler, Whiskey, Pink, 1 1/2 Oz., 2 1/4 In. 95.00
Mayfair Open Rose, Vase, Sweet Pea, Blue ....125.00 to 150.00
Miss America, Bowl, Cereal, Pink, 6 1/4 In. ....28.00 to 30.00
Miss America, Bowl, Vegetable, Pink, Oval, 10 In. 40.00
Miss America, Cake Plate, Footed, 12 In. 26.00
Miss America, Candy Jar, Cover, 11 1/2 In. ....55.00 to 59.00
Miss America, Celery Dish, Oblong, 10 1/2 In. 15.00
Miss America, Celery Dish, Pink, Oblong, 10 1/2 In. 40.00
Miss America, Coaster, Pink, 5 3/4 In. 45.00
Miss America, Compote, Pink, 5 In. 39.00
Miss America, Cup 10.00
Miss America, Cup & Saucer, Pink ....30.00 to 36.00
Miss America, Goblet, Juice, 5 Oz., 4 3/4 In. 24.00
Miss America, Goblet, Water, Pink, 10 Oz., 5 1/2 In. ....55.00 to 65.00
Miss America, Goblet, Wine, 3 Oz., 3 3/4 In. 22.00
Miss America, Grill Plate, Pink, 10 1/4 In. ....27.00 to 30.00
Miss America, Plate, Dinner, 10 1/4 In. 17.00
Miss America, Platter, Oval, 12 1/4 In. 40.00
Miss America, Relish, 4 Sections, Pink, 8 3/4 In. 25.00
Miss America, Salt & Pepper, Pink 60.00
Miss America, Sherbet, Pink 19.00
Miss America, Sugar & Creamer 19.00
Miss America, Tumbler, Water, 10 Oz., 4 1/2 In. 15.00
Miss America, Tumbler, Water, Pink, 10 Oz., 4 1/2 In. ....32.00 to 45.00
Moderntone, Berry Bowl, Cobalt Blue, 5 In. 23.00
Moderntone, Cheese Dish, Cobalt Blue, Metal, Cover 500.00
Moderntone, Creamer, Cobalt Blue ....11.00 to 16.00
Moderntone, Cup & Saucer, Amethyst ....15.00 to 16.00
Moderntone, Custard Cup, Cobalt Blue ....22.00 to 25.00
Moderntone, Plate, Dinner, Cobalt Blue, 8 7/8 In. ....15.00 to 21.00
Moderntone, Plate, Luncheon, Amethyst, 7 3/4 In. 12.00
Moderntone, Plate, Sherbet, Cobalt Blue, 5 3/4 In. ....7.00 to 11.00
Moderntone, Platter, Cobalt Blue, Oval, 11 In. 45.00
Moderntone, Salt & Pepper, Cobalt Blue ....40.00 to 45.00
Moderntone, Sherbet, Amethyst 13.00
Moderntone, Soup, Cream, Amethyst, 4 3/4 In. ....20.00 to 22.00
Moderntone, Soup, Cream, Ruffled, Cobalt Blue, 5 In. 60.00
Moderntone, Tumbler, Whiskey, Cobalt Blue, 1 1/2 Oz. ....46.00 to 50.00
Moderntone Little Hostess Party Set, Plate, Burgundy, 5 1/4 In. 9.00
Moderntone Little Hostess Party Set, Sugar, Rust 15.00
Moderntone Platonite, Bowl, Cereal, Pink, 5 In. 10.00
Moderntone Platonite, Creamer, Blue 8.00
Moderntone Platonite, Cup & Saucer, Pink 6.00
Moderntone Platonite, Cup & Saucer, Yellow 5.00

Moderntone Platonite, Plate, Dinner, Blue, 8 7/8 In. 12.00
Moderntone Platonite, Plate, Dinner, Pink, 8 7/8 In. 8.00
Moderntone Platonite, Salt & Pepper, Pink 23.00
Moderntone Platonite, Sandwich Server, Orange, 10 1/2 In. 22.00
Moderntone Platonite, Sherbet, Blue 9.00
Moderntone Platonite, Sherbet, Yellow, 3 In. 9.00
Moderntone Platonite, Soup, Cream, Yellow 7.00
Moondrops pattern is listed in the New Martinsville category.
Moonstone, Bonbon, Heart Shape 16.00
Moonstone, Bowl, Crimped, 9 1/2 In. . . . . .22.00 to 30.00
Moonstone, Candy Dish, Cover, Handles 32.00
Moonstone, Plate, Luncheon, 8 3/8 In. 16.00
Moonstone, Puff Box, Cover, 4 1/2 In. 25.00
Moonstone, Sherbet . . . . .7.00 to 8.00
Mt. Pleasant, Candlestick, Amethyst, 5 3/4 x 4 3/4 In., Pair 75.00
Mt. Pleasant, Cup & Saucer, Cobalt Blue 19.00
Mt. Pleasant, Saucer, Black 5.00
Mt. Pleasant, Tumbler, Footed, Cobalt Blue 26.00
Mt. Vernon pattern is included in the Cambridge Glass category.
New Century, Butter, Cover, Green 60.00
New Century, Cup, Green 14.00
New Century, Goblet, Wine, Green, 2 1/2 Oz. 30.00
New Century, Pitcher, Pink, 80 Oz., 8 In. 40.00
New Century, Plate, Salad, Green, 8 1/2 In. 15.00
New Century, Tumbler, Blue, 9 Oz., 4 1/2 In. 20.00
Newport, Berry Bowl, Cobalt Blue, 8 1/4 In. 35.00
Newport, Bowl, Cereal, Amethyst, 5 1/4 In. . . . . .33.00 to 35.00
Newport, Creamer, Cobalt Blue . . . . .16.00 to 20.00
Newport, Plate, Bread & Butter, Cobalt Blue, 6 In. . . . . .7.00 to 9.00
Newport, Plate, Luncheon, Amethyst, 8 1/2 In. 15.00
Newport, Plate, Sherbet, Amethyst 8.00
Newport, Platter, Cobalt Blue, Oval, 11 3/4 In. 45.00
Newport, Sandwich Server, Cobalt Blue, 11 3/4 In. 40.00
Newport, Sherbet, Cobalt Blue . . . . .15.00 to 16.00
Newport, Soup, Cream, Cobalt Blue, 4 3/4 In. . . . . .20.00 to 24.00
Newport, Sugar & Creamer, Monax 15.00
No. 601 pattern is listed here as Avocado.
No. 610, Bowl, Pink, Oval, 9 1/2 In. 60.00
No. 610, Dish, Pickle, Pink, 5 3/4 In. 60.00
No. 610, Ice Tub, Cover, Yellow 1100.00
No. 612, Berry Bowl, Green, 9 1/2 In. . . . . .54.00 to 55.00
No. 612, Bowl, Cereal, Green, 6 In. 45.00
No. 612, Creamer, Footed, Green 22.00
No. 612, Cup & Saucer, Green 17.00
No. 612, Plate, Luncheon, Yellow, 9 1/8 In. 13.00
No. 612, Relish, 3 Sections, Footed, Yellow 38.00
No. 612, Saucer, Green 5.00
No. 612, Sherbet, Yellow 13.00

Depression Glass, Moderntone   Depression Glass, No. 615   Depression Glass, No. 620

No. 612, Sugar, No Cover, Footed, Handles, Green ....16.00 to 22.00
No. 615, Creamer, Yellow 35.00
No. 615, Cup, Yellow 16.00
No. 615, Plate, Luncheon, Yellow, 8 3/8 In. 28.00
No. 615, Plate, Salad, Yellow, Square, 7 3/4 In. ....13.00 to 27.00
No. 615, Tumbler, Footed, Yellow, 9 Oz., 4 3/4 In. 38.00
No. 616, Tray, For Sugar & Creamer, Center Handle, Yellow 65.00
No. 618, Berry Bowl, 4 1/2 In. 20.00
No. 618, Bowl, Cereal, 6 In. 35.00
No. 618, Bowl, Salad, 7 In. ....2.00 to 3.00
No. 618, Cup & Saucer ....14.00 to 15.00
No. 618, Plate, Dinner, Amber, 9 3/8 In. 15.00
No. 618, Plate, Salad, Amber, 8 3/8 In. 8.00
No. 618, Platter, Closed Handles, Amber, 11 In. 18.00
No. 618, Relish, 2 Sections, 11 1/2 In. 20.00
No. 618, Sherbet ....13.00 to 20.00
No. 618, Sugar & Creamer 13.00
No. 618, Sugar & Creamer, Amber 20.00
No. 618, Tumbler, 8 Oz., 4 1/4 In. 40.00
No. 620, Berry Bowl, Green, 7 3/8 In. 9.00
No. 620, Creamer, Footed, Green 5.00
No. 620, Cup, Green 3.00
No. 620, Plate, Dinner, Amber, 9 3/8 In. 9.00
No. 620, Relish, 3 Sections, Amber 29.00
No. 620, Sandwich Server, 11 1/2 In. 7.00
No. 620, Saucer, Amber 2.00
No. 620, Sugar & Creamer, Amber 16.00
No. 620, Tumbler, Footed, Green, 12 Oz. 22.00
No. 622 pattern is listed here as Pretzel.
Normandie, Berry Bowl, Amber, 8 1/2 In. 18.00
Normandie, Berry Bowl, Iridescent, 5 In. 6.00
Normandie, Bowl, Cereal, Iridescent, 6 1/2 In. ....9.00 to 12.00
Normandie, Cup, Amber ....7.50 to 8.00
Normandie, Grill Plate, Iridescent, 11 In. 10.00
Normandie, Plate, Salad, Pink, 8 In. 9.00
Normandie, Platter, Amber, 11 3/4 In. ....22.00 to 23.00
Normandie, Sherbet, Pink ....9.00 to 12.00
Old Cafe, Candy Dish, Low, Pink, 8 In. ....7.50 to 12.00
Old Cafe, Cup, Pink 8.00
Old Cafe, Cup, Royal Ruby 10.00
Old Cafe, Relish, Handles, Pink, 6 In. 17.00
Old Cafe, Sherbet, Low, Pink 14.00
Old Colony, Bowl, Cereal, Pink, 6 1/2 In. ....22.00 to 32.00
Old Colony, Bowl, Plain, Pink, 9 1/2 In. 33.00
Old Colony, Butter, Cover, Pink ....55.00 to 75.00
Old Colony, Candlestick, Pink, Frosted, Pair ....75.00 to 95.00
Old Colony, Candy Jar, Cover, Ribbed, Pink 59.00
Old Colony, Compote, Cover, Footed, Pink, 7 In. 85.00
Old Colony, Cookie Jar, Cover, Pink 100.00
Old Colony, Cup & Saucer, Pink ....42.00 to 45.00
Old Colony, Grill Plate, Pink, 10 1/2 In. 25.00
Old Colony, Plate, Dinner, Pink, 10 1/2 In. ....35.00 to 40.00
Old Colony, Platter, 4 Sections, Pink, 13 In. 63.00
Old Colony, Platter, Pink, 12 3/4 In. ....45.00 to 50.00
Old Colony, Relish, 3 Sections, Pink, 10 1/2 In. ....25.00 to 33.00
Old Colony, Sherbet, White 19.00
Old Colony, Tumbler, Pink, 9 Oz., 4 1/2 In. 35.00
Old Florentine pattern is listed here as Florentine No. 1.
Open Rose pattern is listed here as Mayfair Open Rose.
Ovide, Creamer, Black 7.00
Oyster & Pearl, Bowl, Handles, Royal Ruby, 6 1/2 In. ....15.00 to 25.00
Oyster & Pearl, Candlestick, Royal Ruby, 3 1/2 In., Pair 50.00
Panelled Aster pattern is listed here as Primo.

Parrot pattern is listed here as Sylvan.
Patrician, Berry Bowl, Amber, 8 1/2 In. 45.00
Patrician, Bowl, Vegetable, Green, Oval, 10 In. 30.00
Patrician, Butter, Cover, Amber 90.00
Patrician, Cookie Jar, Cover 79.00
Patrician, Creamer, Amber . . . . .11.00 to 15.00
Patrician, Creamer, Footed, Amber 10.00
Patrician, Cup, Green 11.00
Patrician, Grill Plate, Amber, 10 1/2 In. 13.00
Patrician, Pitcher, Amber, 75 Oz., 8 In. 125.00
Patrician, Plate, Dinner, Amber, 10 1/2 In. . . . . .6.50 to 8.00
Patrician, Plate, Dinner, Pink, 10 1/2 In. 52.00
Patrician, Plate, Luncheon, Green, 9 In. 14.00
Patrician, Platter, Amber, Oval, 11 1/2 In. . . . . .24.00 to 30.00
Patrician, Saucer, Green 9.50
Patrician, Sherbet, Amber . . . . .10.00 to 13.50
Patrician, Soup, Cream, Amber, 4 3/4 In. . . . . .16.00 to 18.00
Patrician, Sugar, No Cover, Pink 12.00
Patrician, Tumbler, Amber, 9 Oz., 4 1/2 In. 30.00
Patrician, Tumbler, Footed, Green, 8 Oz., 5 1/2 In. 75.00
Patrician, Tumbler, Pink, 9 Oz., 4 1/2 In. 25.00
Peach Lustre, Bowl, Fruit, 4 7/8 In. 4.00
Peach Lustre, Cup & Saucer 4.50
Peach Lustre, Plate, Dinner, 9 1/8 In. 5.00
Peach Lustre, Punch Cup, 3 In. 8.00
Peach Lustre, Sandwich Server, 11 In. 14.00
Peach Lustre, Sugar & Creamer, Footed 8.00
Peacock & Wild Rose pattern is listed in the Paden City category.
Petal Swirl pattern is listed here as Swirl.
Petalware, Berry Bowl, Pink, 9 In. 35.00
Petalware, Bowl, Cereal, Pink, 5 3/4 In. . . . . .10.00 to 18.00
Petalware, Cup & Saucer, Cremax 10.00
Petalware, Plate, Dinner, Monax, 9 In. . . . . .10.00 to 15.00
Petalware, Plate, Salad, Cremax, 8 In. 8.00
Petalware, Plate, Sherbet, Cremax, 6 In. 5.00
Petalware, Salver, Florette, Monax, 11 In. 19.00
Petalware, Soup, Cream, Cremax, 4 1/2 In. 10.00
Petalware, Soup, Dish, Monax, 7 In. 90.00
Petalware, Sugar & Creamer, Cremax 22.00
Philbe, Tumbler, Iced Tea, Footed, Blue, 6 1/2 In. 305.00
Pineapple & Floral pattern is listed here as No. 618.
Pinwheel pattern is listed here as Sierra.
Poinsettia pattern is listed here as Floral.
Poppy No. 1 pattern is listed here as Florentine No. 1.
Poppy No. 2 pattern is listed here as Florentine No. 2.
Pretty Polly Party Dishes, see also the related pattern Doric & Pansy.
Pretzel, Creamer 6.00
Pretzel, Cup & Saucer 7.00
Pretzel, Plate, Bread & Butter, 6 In. 3.00
Pretzel, Plate, Dinner, 9 3/8 In. 10.00
Pretzel, Soup, Dish, 7 1/2 In. . . . . .10.00 to 12.00
Primo, Tumbler, Yellow, 9 Oz., 5 3/4 In. 30.00
Primrose, Bowl, Dessert, 4 5/8 In. 4.00
Primrose, Cake Pan, Round, 8 In. 16.00
Primrose, Casserole, Cover, Oval, 1 1/2 Qt. . . . . .17.00 to 18.00
Primrose, Plate, Dinner, 9 1/8 In. 7.00
Primrose, Plate, Salad, 7 3/8 In. 6.00
Princess, Ashtray, Green, 4 1/2 In. 100.00
Princess, Berry Bowl, Pink, 4 1/2 In. 40.00
Princess, Bowl, Cereal, Green, 5 In. . . . . .30.00 to 32.00
Princess, Bowl, Hat Shape, Pink, 9 1/2 In. . . . . .50.00 to 65.00
Princess, Bowl, Vegetable, Green, Oval, 10 In. . . . . .30.00 to 33.00
Princess, Cake Stand, Green, 10 In. . . . . .20.00 to 30.00

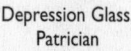
Depression Glass,
Patrician

Depression Glass,
Peach Lustre

Depression Glass,
Rock Crystal

Princess, Candy Dish, Cover, Green ....37.00 to 75.00
Princess, Cookie Jar, Cover, Green ....35.00 to 66.00
Princess, Cup & Saucer, Topaz 18.00
Princess, Grill Plate, Green, 9 1/2 In.. 14.00
Princess, Pitcher, Green, 37 Oz., 6 In...45.00 to 55.00
Princess, Pitcher, Green, 60 Oz., 8 In...59.00 to 75.00
Princess, Plate, Dinner, 9 1/2 In. 34.00
Princess, Plate, Dinner, Green, 9 1/2 In... 18.00
Princess, Plate, Salad, Green, 8 In..14.00 to 20.00
Princess, Plate, Sherbet, Green, 5 1/2 In.. 10.00
Princess, Platter, Closed Handles, Green, 12 In. ....24.00 to 40.00
Princess, Relish, 2 Sections, Green, 7 1/2 In. ....26.00 to 27.00
Princess, Salt & Pepper, Topaz, 4 1/2 In.. 92.00
Princess, Saucer, Green 10.00
Princess, Sherbet, Pink ....25.00 to 30.00
Princess, Spice Shaker, Green, 5 1/2 In., Pair 44.00
Princess, Sugar, Cover, Green ....22.00 to 38.00
Princess, Tumbler, Footed, Pink, 10 Oz., 5 1/4 In....................................... 34.00
Princess, Tumbler, Iced Tea, Green, 13 Oz., 5 1/4 In. ....30.00 to 40.00
Prismatic Line pattern is listed here as Queen Mary.
Provincial pattern is listed here as Bubble.
Pyramid pattern is listed here as No. 610.
Queen Mary, Berry Bowl, Pink, 4 1/2 In. ....6.00 to 8.00
Queen Mary, Bowl, Cereal, Pink, 6 In. ....23.00 to 27.00
Queen Mary, Candlestick, 2-Light, 4 1/4 In., Pair 29.00
Queen Mary, Candy Dish, Cover, Pink 100.00
Queen Mary, Cup, Pink, Large 10.00
Queen Mary, Plate, Dinner, Pink, 9 3/4 In. ....57.00 to 60.00
Queen Mary, Tumbler, Water, Pink, 9 Oz., 4 In.. 20.00
Ribbon, Berry Bowl, Green, 8 In... 39.00
Ribbon, Plate, Sherbet, Green, 6 1/4 In... 4.00
Ring, Berry Bowl, Green, 5 In... 6.00
Ring, Cocktail Shaker, Aluminum Cover, Green, 11 In....................................... 25.00
Ring, Pitcher, 60 Oz., 8 In... 18.00
Ring, Tumbler, Iced Tea, Footed, Silver Trim, 6 1/2 In.................................... 10.00
Ring, Tumbler, Water, Footed, 10 Oz., 4 3/4 In.. 6.50
Rock Crystal, Butter, Cover 400.00
Rock Crystal, Candlestick, 2-Light, Pair 36.00
Rock Crystal, Centerpiece, Footed, 12 1/2 In. 75.00
Rock Crystal, Compote, Red, 7 In. 95.00
Rock Crystal, Goblet, 8 Oz., 6 7/8 In..10.00 to 18.00
Rock Crystal, Goblet, Cordial, 1 Oz. 18.00
Rock Crystal, Plate, 10 1/2 In. 60.00
Rock Crystal, Plate, Red, 7 3/4 In. 20.00
Rock Crystal, Relish, 5 Sections, 12 1/2 In. 45.00
Rock Crystal, Sundae, Low, 6 Oz. 12.00

Rock Crystal, Tumbler, Old Fashioned, Red, 5 Oz. 40.00
Rose Cameo, Bowl, Cereal, Green, 5 In. 24.00
Rose Cameo, Tumbler, Footed, Green, 5 In. ....25.00 to 26.00
Rosemary, Creamer, Footed, Amber 9.00
Rosemary, Plate, Dinner, Amber, 9 1/2 In. 9.00
Rosemary, Plate, Salad, Amber, 6 3/4 In. 6.00
Rosemary, Soup, Cream, Pink, 5 In. 32.00
Rosemary, Sugar & Creamer, Footed, Amber 17.00
Rosemary, Tumbler, Green, 9 Oz., 4 1/2 In. 35.00
Roulette, Cup & Saucer, Green 8.00
Roulette, Pitcher, Green, 64 Oz., 8 In. 54.00
Roulette, Plate, Luncheon, 8 1/2 In. 5.00
Roulette, Plate, Salad, Green, 8 In. 8.00
Roulette, Sherbet, Green 8.00
Roulette, Tumbler, Water, Pink, 9 Oz., 4 1/8 In. 30.00
Roulette, Tumbler, Whiskey, Pink, 3 1/4 In. 14.00
Royal Lace, Berry Bowl, Blue, 5 In. 125.00
Royal Lace, Bowl, Footed, Pink, 10 In. 39.00
Royal Lace, Bowl, Footed, Rolled Edge, Pink, 10 In. ....150.00 to 225.00
Royal Lace, Bowl, Footed, Straight Edge, Blue, 10 In. 90.00
Royal Lace, Butter, Cover, Blue ....800.00 to 875.00
Royal Lace, Candlestick, Blue, Pair 375.00
Royal Lace, Cookie Jar, Cover, Pink 65.00
Royal Lace, Cup & Saucer, Green ....29.00 to 30.00
Royal Lace, Cup & Saucer, Pink 28.00
Royal Lace, Cup, Blue 40.00
Royal Lace, Grill Plate, Green, 9 7/8 In. 29.00
Royal Lace, Pitcher, Blue, 64 Oz., 8 In. 350.00
Royal Lace, Pitcher, Green, 64 Oz., 8 In. 135.00
Royal Lace, Plate, Dinner, 10 In. 22.00
Royal Lace, Plate, Sherbet, Green, 6 In. 12.00
Royal Lace, Platter, Pink, Oval, 13 In. 60.00
Royal Lace, Salt & Pepper, Green 135.00
Royal Lace, Sherbet, Blue ....55.00 to 65.00
Royal Lace, Soup, Cream, Blue 55.00
Royal Lace, Sugar & Creamer, Cover, Pink 125.00
Royal Lace, Sugar & Creamer, No Cover 24.00
Royal Lace, Toddy Set, Blue, 11 Piece 260.00
Royal Lace, Tumbler, 9 Oz., 4 1/8 In. ....11.00 to 15.00
Royal Lace, Tumbler, Green, 9 Oz., 4 1/8 In. 32.00
Royal Lace, Tumbler, Pink, 9 Oz., 4 1/8 In. 38.00
Royal Ruby, Ashtray, Leaf, 4 1/2 In. 5.00
Royal Ruby, Bowl, Fruit, Deep, 10 In. 35.00
Royal Ruby, Bowl, Scalloped, 5 1/4 In. 10.00
Royal Ruby, Cup & Saucer 8.00
Royal Ruby, Goblet, Wine, 5 1/4 In. ....9.00 to 13.00
Royal Ruby, Plate, Luncheon, 8 1/2 In. 7.00
Royal Ruby, Sherbet, Clear Bubble Foot, 6 Oz. 7.00
Royal Ruby, Sugar & Creamer, Cover, Footed 28.00
Royal Ruby, Tumbler, 13 Oz., 5 3/8 In. ....4.50 to 13.00
Royal Ruby, Vase, 6 1/2 In. 10.00
S Pattern, Cup & Saucer 6.00
S Pattern, Sugar, Thick 6.00
S Pattern, Tumbler, 10 Oz., 4 3/4 In. 9.00
Sail Boat pattern is listed here as Sportsman Series.
Sandwich Anchor Hocking, Bowl, Cereal, Desert Gold, 6 1/2 In. 12.00
Sandwich Anchor Hocking, Bowl, Cereal, Forest Green, 6 1/2 In. 50.00
Sandwich Anchor Hocking, Bowl, Royal Ruby, Oval, 8 1/4 In. 40.00
Sandwich Anchor Hocking, Bowl, Scalloped, 5 1/4 In. 12.00
Sandwich Anchor Hocking, Butter, Cover ....38.00 to 45.00
Sandwich Anchor Hocking, Cookie Jar, Cover, Desert Gold 32.00
Sandwich Anchor Hocking, Creamer, Forest Green 30.00
Sandwich Anchor Hocking, Cup & Saucer, Desert Gold ....5.00 to 7.00

Sandwich Anchor Hocking, Plate, Dessert, Desert Gold, 7 In. 35.00
Sandwich Anchor Hocking, Plate, Dinner, 9 In. . . . . .18.00 to 20.00
Sandwich Anchor Hocking, Punch Bowl Set, 14 Piece 50.00
Sandwich Anchor Hocking, Sherbet 8.00
Sandwich Anchor Hocking, Sherbet, Footed 8.00
Sandwich Anchor Hocking, Sugar & Creamer, No Cover 15.00
Sandwich Anchor Hocking, Tumbler, Juice, Forest Green, 5 Oz., 3 3/4 In. . . . . .8.00 to 10.00
Sandwich Anchor Hocking, Tumbler, Water, Footed, 9 Oz. . . . . .25.00 to 33.00
Sandwich Indiana, Ashtray, Spade, Teal 6.00
Sandwich Indiana, Cup, Amber 3.50
Sandwich Indiana, Goblet, Wine, Green, 4 Oz., 3 In. 6.00
Sandwich Indiana, Sherbet, 3 1/4 In. . . . . .5.00 to 9.00
Saxon pattern is listed here as Coronation.
Sharon, Berry Bowl, Amber, 5 In. . . . . .7.00 to 10.00
Sharon, Berry Bowl, Amber, 8 1/2 In. . . . . .6.00 to 8.00
Sharon, Bowl, Cereal, Green, 6 In. 25.00
Sharon, Bowl, Fruit, Pink, 10 1/2 In. . . . . .37.50 to 65.00
Sharon, Bowl, Vegetable, Amber, Oval, 9 1/2 In. 19.00
Sharon, Bowl, Vegetable, Green, Oval, 9 1/2 In. 45.00
Sharon, Butter, Cover, Pink . . . . .60.00 to 70.00
Sharon, Cake Plate, Footed, Pink, 11 1/2 In. . . . . .37.00 to 45.00
Sharon, Candy Jar, Cover, Amber . . . . .45.00 to 50.00
Sharon, Cheese Dish, Cover, Pink 2300.00
Sharon, Cup & Saucer, Amber . . . . .13.00 to 15.00
Sharon, Pitcher, Ice Lip, Amber, 80 Oz. 165.00
Sharon, Pitcher, Ice Lip, Green, 80 Oz. . . . . .395.00 to 500.00
Sharon, Plate, Bread & Butter, Amber, 6 In. 5.00
Sharon, Plate, Bread & Butter, Green, 6 In. . . . . .8.00 to 18.00
Sharon, Plate, Salad, Amber, 7 1/2 In. 15.00
Sharon, Platter, Pink, Oval, 12 1/2 In. . . . . .30.00 to 32.00
Sharon, Salt & Pepper, Amber . . . . .34.00 to 45.00
Sharon, Saucer, Pink . . . . .12.00 to 14.00
Sharon, Sherbet, Amber 13.00
Sharon, Soup, Cream, 5 In. 25.00
Sharon, Soup, Cream, Pink, 5 In. . . . . .45.00 to 51.00
Sharon, Soup, Dish, Amber, 7 3/4 In. . . . . .40.00 to 55.00
Sharon, Sugar & Creamer, Cover, Pink . . . . .42.00 to 59.00
Sharon, Tumbler, Amber, Thick, 12 Oz., 5 1/4 In. . . . . .60.00 to 65.00
Sharon, Tumbler, Iced Tea, Footed, Amber, 15 Oz., 6 1/2 In. 65.00
Sharon, Tumbler, Pink, Thin, 12 Oz., 5 1/4 In. 60.00
Sierra, Bowl, Cereal, Green, 5 1/2 In. 24.00
Sierra, Cup & Saucer, Pink 19.00
Sierra, Plate, Dinner, Pink, 9 In. . . . . .22.00 to 30.00
Sierra, Platter, Pink, Oval, 11 In. 50.00
Sierra, Salt & Pepper, Pink 58.00
Sierra, Sugar, Cover, Pink 50.00
Spiral Flutes pattern is listed in the Duncan & Miller category as Swirl.

Depression Glass,
Rosemary

Depression Glass,
S Pattern

**Do not wash or rinse gold-
decorated glass with very
hot water or strong soap.
It will remove some of the
gold. Store glass right side
up to protect the rims.**

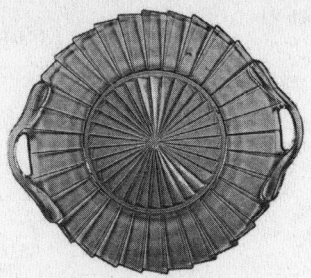

Depression Glass, Sierra   Depression Glass, Swirl

Spoke pattern is listed here as Patrician.
Sportsman Series, Cocktail Shaker, White Ship, Cobalt Blue 38.00
Sportsman Series, Pitcher, Ice Lip, White Ship, Cobalt Blue, 86 Oz. ....70.00 to 75.00
Sportsman Series, Plate, Dessert, White Ship, Cobalt Blue, 5 7/8 In. 30.00
Sportsman Series, Plate, Dinner, White Ship, Cobalt Blue, 9 In. ....28.00 to 50.00
Sportsman Series, Tumbler, Juice, 5 Oz., 3 3/4 In. 15.00
Sportsman Series, Tumbler, Old Fashioned, White Ship, Cobalt Blue, 8 Oz. 18.00
Sportsman Series, Tumbler, Roly Poly, White Ship, Cobalt Blue, 6 Oz. 11.00
Starlight, Bowl, Cereal, Closed Handles, 5 1/2 In. 7.00
Stars & Stripes, Plate, 18 In. 20.00
Stars & Stripes, Tumbler, 10 Oz., 5 In. 40.00
Stippled Rose Band pattern is listed here as S Pattern.
Strawberry, Butter, Cover, Green 220.00
Strawberry, Compote, Pink, 5 3/4 In. 28.00
Sunburst, Plate, Dinner, 9 1/2 In. 20.00
Sunflower, Cake Plate, 3-Footed, Pink, 10 In. 25.00
Sunflower, Plate, Dinner, Green, 9 In. 22.00
Swirl, Berry Bowl, Pink, 4 7/8 In. 10.00
Swirl, Bowl, Cereal, Ultramarine, 5 1/4 In. ....15.00 to 19.00
Swirl, Butter, Cover, Pink 235.00
Swirl, Candlestick, 2-Light, Ultramarine 39.00
Swirl, Candy Dish, Cover, Ultramarine 170.00
Swirl, Creamer, Footed, Ultramarine ....15.00 to 16.00
Swirl, Cup, Ultramarine ....15.00 to 18.00
Swirl, Plate, Dinner, Ultramarine, 9 1/4 In. ....20.00 to 22.00
Swirl, Plate, Sherbet, Ultramarine, 6 1/2 In. 8.00
Swirl, Salt & Pepper, Ultramarine ....45.00 to 50.00
Swirl, Sandwich Server, Ultramarine, 12 1/2 In. 38.00
Swirl, Sherbet, Low, Ultramarine ....20.00 to 25.00
Swirl, Soup, Dish, Lug Handles, Ultramarine 59.00
Swirl, Sugar & Creamer, Footed, Ultramarine 32.00
Swirl Fire-King, Bowl, Dessert, Azure-Ite, 4 3/4 In. 5.50
Swirl Fire-King, Bowl, Vegetable, Azure-Ite, 8 1/2 In. 25.00
Swirl Fire-King, Cup & Saucer, Azure-Ite 5.00
Swirl Fire-King, Plate, Dinner, Azure-Ite, 10 In. 7.00
Swirl Fire-King, Plate, Salad, Ivory, 7 1/4 In. 14.00
Swirl Fire-King, Sugar & Creamer, Azure-Ite 14.00
Sylvan, Bowl, Vegetable, Green, Oval, 10 In. ....65.00 to 70.00
Sylvan, Butter, Cover, Green 425.00
Sylvan, Cup & Saucer, Green ....65.00 to 75.00
Sylvan, Grill Plate, Amber, 10 1/2 In. 25.00
Sylvan, Plate, Salad, Amber, 7 1/2 In. 25.00
Sylvan, Plate, Salad, Green, 7 1/2 In. 38.00
Sylvan, Platter, Green, Oblong, 11 1/4 In. 65.00
Sylvan, Sherbet, Cone, Amber 20.00
Sylvan, Soup, Dish, Green, 7 In. 50.00
Sylvan, Sugar, Cover, Green 200.00

Tea Room, Candlestick, Green, Pair 100.00
Tea Room, Creamer, Footed, Pink, 4 1/2 In. 35.00
Tea Room, Dish, Banana Split, Pink, 7 1/2 In. 225.00
Tea Room, Ice Bucket, Green . . . . .75.00 to 100.00
Tea Room, Parfait, Pink 145.00
Tea Room, Pitcher, Green, 64 Oz. 200.00
Tea Room, Salt & Pepper, Green 135.00
Tea Room, Sandwich Server, Center Handle, Green 210.00
Tea Room, Sugar & Creamer, Footed, Pink 75.00
Tea Room, Sugar & Creamer, Tray, Center Handle, Green . . . . .65.00 to 75.00
Tea Room, Tumbler, Footed, Green, 8 Oz. 39.00
Tea Room, Tumbler, Green, 6 Oz. . . . . .30.00 to 50.00
Tea Room, Vase, Ruffled Edge, Pink, 6 1/2 In. 120.00
Tea Room, Vase, Straight Edge, Green, 11 In. 200.00
Turquoise Blue, Berry Bowl, 4 1/2 In. 6.00
Turquoise Blue, Cup & Saucer 5.00
Turquoise Blue, Mixing Bowl Set, 3 Piece 162.00
Twentieth Century, Child's Set 115.00
Vernon pattern is listed here as No. 616.
Vertical Ribbed pattern is listed here as Queen Mary.
Victory, Goblet, Blue, 7 Oz., 5 In. 70.00
Victory, Sandwich Server, Center Handle, Pink 30.00
Vitrock, Bowl, Fruit, White, 6 In. 5.00
Vitrock, Plate, Dinner, White 9.00
Waterford, Berry Bowl, 4 3/4 In. 8.00
Waterford, Cake Plate, Handles, 10 1/4 In. 10.00
Waterford, Goblet, 5 1/4 In. 16.00
Waterford, Plate, Dinner, 9 5/8 In. 11.00
Waterford, Saucer, Pink . . . . .5.00 to 6.00
Waterford, Sherbet, Pink . . . . .11.00 to 18.00
Waterford, Sugar & Creamer, Cover 28.00
Waterford, Tumbler, Footed, Pink, 10 Oz., 4 7/8 In. 24.00
Wexford, Pitcher, 64 Oz. 8.00
Wexford, Relish, 3 Sections, 8 1/2 In. 4.00
Wexford, Sugar & Creamer 6.00
Wheat, Bowl, Vegetable, 8 1/4 In. 12.00
Wheat, Custard Cup, 6 Oz. 4.00
Wheat, Plate, Dinner, 10 In. 6.00
Wheat, Snack Set 35.00
Wheat, Soup, Dish, 6 5/8 In. 8.00
Whirly Twirly, Tumbler, 12 Oz. 6.00
Whirly Twirly, Tumbler, Green, 9 Oz. 4.00
White Ship pattern is listed here as Sportsman Series.
Wild Rose pattern is listed here as Dogwood.
Windmill pattern is listed here as Sportsman Series.
Windsor, Berry Bowl, 4 3/4 In. 4.00
Windsor, Berry Bowl, Pink, 8 1/2 In. 20.00
Windsor, Bowl, Cereal, Pink, 5 1/8 In. 20.00
Windsor, Bowl, Pointed Edge, Pink, 5 In. 39.00
Windsor, Bowl, Vegetable, Green, Oval, 9 1/2 In. 32.00
Windsor, Butter, Cover, Pink 55.00
Windsor, Cake Plate, Footed, 10 3/4 In. 18.00
Windsor, Candleholder, 3 In., Pair 18.00
Windsor, Chop Plate, Green, 13 5/8 In. . . . . .40.00 to 45.00
Windsor, Creamer, Pink 12.00
Windsor, Cup & Saucer . . . . .7.00 to 19.00
Windsor, Pitcher, 16 Oz., 4 1/2 In. . . . . .20.00 to 25.00
Windsor, Pitcher, 52 Oz., 6 3/4 In. 60.00
Windsor, Pitcher, Pink, 52 Oz., 6 3/4 In. 35.00
Windsor, Plate, Dinner, Green, 9 In. . . . . .25.00 to 28.00
Windsor, Plate, Dinner, Pink, 9 In. 28.00
Windsor, Plate, Salad, Green, 7 In. 25.00
Windsor, Plate, Sherbet, Pink, 6 In. . . . . .4.00 to 6.00

Windsor, Platter, Green, Oval, 11 1/2 In. 22.00
Windsor, Relish, 3 Sections, 11 1/2 In. 15.00
Windsor, Salt & Pepper, Pink 50.00
Windsor, Sandwich Server, Open Handle, Green, 10 1/4 In. 20.00
Windsor, Sherbet, Footed, Green 12.00
Windsor, Sherbet, Footed, Pink 12.00
Windsor, Sugar & Creamer, Cover 34.00
Windsor, Sugar, Cover, Holiday, Pink 165.00
Windsor, Tray, Pink, 8 1/2 x 9 3/4 In. 195.00
Windsor, Tumbler, Green, 9 Oz., 4 In. 26.00
Windsor, Tumbler, Pink, 5 Oz., 3 1/4 In. 28.00
Windsor, Tumbler, Pink, 12 Oz., 5 In. 30.00

DERBY has been marked on porcelain made in the city of Derby,
England, since about 1748. The original Derby factory closed in 1848,
but others opened there and continued to produce quality porcelain.
The Crown Derby mark began appearing on Derby wares in the 1770s.

Basket, Armorial, Pierced, Arms Of Pendock Of Tollerton, Stand, c.1805, 17 1/8 In. 4500.00
Beaker, Landscape Scene, Gilt Border, Shell Handles, Pale Yellow Ground, 3 1/8 In. 1265.00
Compote, Fruiting Orange Tree Branch, Sweet Pea & Aster Boot, c.1795, 13 1/2 In. 3600.00
Cup, Chocolate, Handles, 1815 .... 75.00
Figurine, Milton, Standing, Books, 1770, 12 1/4 In. ....*Illus* 2000.00
Garniture Set, Landscape Scene, Cobalt Blue, c.1815, 3 Piece 4200.00
Ice Pail, Arms & Crest Of Tynte, Gilt Rim, c.1821, 7 1/2 In. 3600.00
Potpourri, Gilt Flowers, Cobalt Blue Ground, Paw Feet, Urn Shape, 4 1/4 In. 184.00
Stand, Sweetmeat, Yellow Bird Perched On Coral Mound, Brown, 1765, 6 In. 5400.00

DICK TRACY, the comic strip, started in 1931. Tracy was also the hero
of movies from 1937 to 1947 and again in 1990, and starred in a radio
series in the 1940s and a television series in the 1950s. Memorabilia
from all these activities are collected.

Badge, Dick Tracy Detective Club, Brass, Pinback 28.50
Badge, Junior Secret Service, Tracy Profile, 1930s 65.00
Car, Riot, Machine Gun At Front Window, Tin, Windup, 7 In. 935.00
Car, Riot, Sparking Machine Gun, Tin, Friction, Marx, 6 1/2 In. 275.00
Car Set, Willar's Chocolate, Each In Plastic Sleeve, 1930s, 56 Piece 90.00
Doll, Bonny Braids, Vinyl, Cloth, Toothbrush, Tag, Ideal, Box, 1951, 15 In. 305.00
Flashlight, Bantam-Lite, Pocket Type, Box, 1950s 45.00
Game, Crime Stopper, Board, Ideal, 19 x 13, Box, 1963 .... 70.00
Lunch Box, Metal, Thermos, Instructions, Sticker, Aladdin, 1967 ....297.00 to 316.00
Lunch Box, Plastic, Aladdin, 1989 .... 25.00
Pistol, Siren, Marx, Late 1930s, 9 1/4 In. 82.00
Puzzles, Big Little Book Box, Whitman, 8 x 10 In. 285.00
Radio, Wireless, 2-Way 175.00
Salt & Pepper, Dick Tracy & Junior, 2 3/4 In. 85.00
Script, Radio Play, Dick Tracy & The Invisible Man, Quaker Cereal Broadcast, 1939 .... 30.00
Thimble, Red & Black On White, Dick Tracy Picture, Plastic 10.00

**Recycle your unused ashtrays as drip-
catching candleholders, holders for
change on your bedroom dresser, or as
holders for imitation sweeteners.**

**Display groups of at least three of your
collectibles to get decorating impact.**

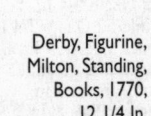

Derby, Figurine,
Milton, Standing,
Books, 1770,
12 1/4 In.

Transfer, Blue & Red, Official Member Dick Tracy Crime Stoppers, 1940, 10 x 8 In. 15.00
Water Pistol, Luger Style, 1971 .... 40.00

DICKENS WARE pieces are listed in the Royal Doulton and Weller categories.

DINNERWARE used in the United States from the 1930s through the
1950s is listed here. Most was made in potteries in southern Ohio,
West Virginia, and California. A few patterns were made in Japan,
England, and other countries. Dishes were sold in gift shops and
department stores, or were given away as premiums. Many of these
patterns are listed in this book in their own categories, such as Autumn
Leaf, Azalea, Coors, Fiesta, Franciscan, Hall, Harker, Harlequin, Red
Wing, Riviera, Russel Wright, Vernon Kilns, Watt, and Willow. For
more information, see *Kovels' Depression Glass & Dinnerware Price
List.*

Amberstone, Coffeepot, Homer Laughlin ....20.00 to 25.00
Amberstone, Sugar & Creamer, Homer Laughlin 20.00
Americana, Soup, Dish, Homer Laughlin, 8 1/4 In. 10.00
Antique Grape, Bowl, Metlox, 9 1/2 In. 15.00
Antique Grape, Plate, Metlox, 7 1/2 In. ....5.00 to 12.00
Antique Grape, Platter, Oval, Metlox, 12 1/2 In. 69.00
Apple Blossom, Plate, Homer Laughlin, 6 In. 10.00
Apple Blossom, Platter, Homer Laughlin, 11 1/4 In. 45.00
Autumn Delight, Bowl, Cereal, Square, Johnson Bros. 10.00
Autumn Delight, Platter, Johnson Bros., 12 In. 20.00
Autumn Gold, Berry Bowl, Homer Laughlin, 5 In. 6.00
Autumn Gold, Sugar, Cover, Tab Handles, Homer Laughlin 22.00
Autumn Harvest, Cup & Saucer, Taylor, Smith & Taylor ....9.00 to 19.00
Autumn Harvest, Plate, Taylor, Smith & Taylor, 6 3/4 In. 5.00
Autumn Harvest, Soup, Dish, Taylor, Smith & Taylor 18.00
Azura, Plate, Taylor, Smith & Taylor, 6 3/4 In. 14.00
Blue Bonnet, Bowl, Cereal, Taylor, Smith & Taylor 6.00
Blue Bonnet, Creamer, Taylor, Smith & Taylor 8.00
Bluebell Bouquet, Creamer, Southern Potteries 15.00
Bluebell Bouquet, Cup & Saucer, Southern Potteries 15.00
Bluebell Bouquet, Plate, Southern Potteries, 10 In. 23.00
Bonnie Green, Plate, Taylor, Smith & Taylor, 10 In. 15.00
Boutonniere, Casserole, Cover, Taylor, Smith & Taylor, 10 1/2 In. 20.00
Boutonniere, Cup & Saucer, Taylor, Smith & Taylor 7.00
Boutonniere, Gravy Boat, Taylor, Smith & Taylor 10.00
Boutonniere, Plate, Taylor, Smith & Taylor, 10 In. ....7.00 to 10.00
Brittany, Berry Bowl, Homer Laughlin, 6 In. 12.00
Brittany, Cup & Saucer, Homer Laughlin ....9.00 to 16.00
Brittany, Platter, Homer Laughlin, 13 1/2 In. 25.00
Bryn-Mawr, Teapot, Salem 48.00
Buttercup, Plate, Taylor, Smith & Taylor, 10 In. 9.00
Buttercup, Soup, Dish, Taylor, Smith & Taylor 9.00
California, Freeform, Salt & Pepper, Metlox 50.00
California Ivy, Bowl, Metlox, 9 In. 35.00
California Ivy, Butter, Cover, Metlox 60.00
California Ivy, Plate, Metlox, 9 1/4 In. 12.00
California Ivy, Sugar & Creamer, Metlox 20.00
California Peach Blossom, Bowl, Salad, Large, Metlox 75.00
California Peach Blossom, Casserole, Cover, Metlox 55.00
California Peach Blossom, Coffeepot, Metlox 50.00
California Peach Blossom, Plate, Metlox, 9 1/2 In. 10.00
California Peach Blossom, Relish, 2 Sections, Metlox 25.00
California Provincial, Creamer 43.00
California Provincial, Cup & Saucer, Metlox 27.00
California Provincial, Plate, Metlox, 10 In. 34.00
California Strawberry, Cup & Saucer, Metlox 21.00
California Strawberry, Plate, Metlox, 10 In. 26.00
California Tempo, Cup & Saucer, Metlox 12.00

California Tempo, Plate, Metlox, 10 In. . . . . .15.00 to 21.00
California Tempo, Platter, Metlox, 13 1/4 In. 25.00
Cavalier, Creamer, Homer Laughlin 20.00
Cavalier, Plate, Homer Laughlin, 7 In. 16.00
Cavalier, Platter, Homer Laughlin, 13 1/2 In. . . . . .22.00 to 55.00
Cavalier, Soup, Dish, Homer Laughlin 18.00
Cavalier, Sugar, Cover, Homer Laughlin 25.00
Classic, Bowl, Sugar, Cover, Taylor, Smith & Taylor 25.00
Classic, Creamer, Taylor, Smith & Taylor 18.00
Classic Heritage, Berry Bowl, Taylor, Smith & Taylor 8.00
Classic Heritage, Cup & Saucer, Taylor, Smith & Taylor 12.00
Classic Heritage, Plate, Taylor, Smith & Taylor, 10 In. 15.00
Colonial Homestead, Casserole, Cover, Royal China 85.00
Colonial Homestead, Gravy Boat, Underplate, Royal China 45.00
Colonial Homestead, Plate, Royal China, 6 1/2 In. 4.00
Colorstax, Cup & Saucer, Peach, Metlox 8.00
Colorstax, Plate, Peach, Metlox, 8 In. 8.00
Colorstax, Salt & Pepper, Yellow, Metlox, 2 In. 12.00
Contempora, Gravy Boat, Black & Gray, Metlox 48.00
Conversation, Server, Cover, Taylor, Smith & Taylor 45.00
Countess, Plate, Homer Laughlin, 10 In. 18.00
Countess, Soup, Dish, Rimmed, Homer Laughlin 15.00
Crinoline, Cup & Saucer, Homer Laughlin 16.00
Crinoline, Plate, Homer Laughlin, 8 3/4 In. 18.00
Crinoline, Sugar, Cover, Homer Laughlin 15.00
Currier & Ives, Bowl, Blue, Royal China, 5 1/2 In. 5.00
Currier & Ives, Butter, Cover, Blue, Oblong, Royal China 42.00
Currier & Ives, Cake Plate, Tab Handle, Blue, Royal China 18.00
Currier & Ives, Chop Plate, Blue, Royal China, 12 1/4 In. 30.00
Currier & Ives, Cup & Saucer, Blue, Royal China . . . . .3.00 to 6.00
Currier & Ives, Gravy Boat, Underplate, Blue, Royal China 47.00
Currier & Ives, Plate, Blue, Royal China, 6 In. 4.50
Currier & Ives, Plate, Blue, Royal China, 10 In. . . . . .4.00 to 7.00
Currier & Ives, Platter, Oval, Blue, Royal China, 13 In. 38.00
Currier & Ives, Salt & Pepper, Blue, Royal China 38.00
Currier & Ives, Sugar & Creamer, Blue, Royal China 24.00
Darlene, Plate, Bread & Butter, Harmony House 8.00
Darlene, Sugar, Cover, Harmony House 20.00
Della Robbia, Bowl, Metlox, 7 1/8 In. . . . . .5.00 to 19.00
Della Robbia, Cup & Saucer, Metlox . . . . .5.00 to 20.00
Della Robbia, Plate, Metlox, 10 In. . . . . .10.00 to 24.00
Diana, Cup & Saucer, Harmony House 16.00
Dogwood, Bowl, Oval, Taylor, Smith & Taylor, 9 1/8 In. 15.00
Dogwood, Plate, Taylor, Smith & Taylor, 7 In. 8.00
Dogwood, Platter, Taylor, Smith & Taylor, 11 1/4 In. 17.00
Dogwood, Sugar & Creamer, Taylor, Smith & Taylor 15.00
Echo Dell, Bowl, Cereal, Taylor, Smith & Taylor 13.00
Eggshell Georgian, Bowl, Cover, Homer Laughlin, 8 1/4 In. 30.00
Eggshell Georgian, Plate, Homer Laughlin, 6 1/4 In. 4.00
Eggshell Georgian, Platter, Homer Laughlin, 15 1/2 In. . . . . .10.00 to 25.00
Eggshell Nautilus, Creamer, Homer Laughlin 18.00
Eggshell Nautilus, Plate, Homer Laughlin, 8 1/4 In. 13.00
Eggshell Nautilus, Sugar, Cover, Homer Laughlin 25.00
Epicure, Salt & Pepper, Pink, Homer Laughlin 28.00
Gigi, Bowl, Metlox, 6 1/2 In. 19.00
Gigi, Cup & Saucer, Metlox 21.00
Golden Jubilee, Creamer, Taylor, Smith & Taylor 34.00
Golden Jubilee, Sugar, Cover, Taylor, Smith & Taylor 38.00
Hanover, Creamer, Harmony House 20.00
Hanover, Cup & Saucer, Harmony House 20.00
Hanover, Plate, Salad, Harmony House, 7 1/4 In. 16.00
Heatherton, Plate, Taylor, Smith & Taylor, 10 In. 14.00
Indian Morn, Gray Boat, Taylor, Smith & Taylor 30.00

Dinnerware, Liberty Blue, Cup & Saucer,
Old North Church

Bauer Ringware pattern can be dated from the mark. "Bauer" or "Bauer Los Angeles" were the earliest. Pieces marked "Bauer Made in USA" or "Bauer USA" were made in the mid-thirties.

Indian Morn, Ladle, Taylor, Smith & Taylor	8.00
Iona, Plate, Taylor, Smith & Taylor, 7 In.	7.00
Iona, Plate, Taylor, Smith & Taylor, 10 In.	9.00
Iona, Soup, Dish, Taylor, Smith & Taylor	10.00
Jamacia, Bowl, Cereal, Taylor, Smith & Taylor, 6 In.	12.00
Jamacia, Bowl, Taylor, Smith & Taylor, 5 In.	8.00
Jonquil, Bowl, Vegetable, Oval, Pink, Paden City	30.00
Jonquil, Cup & Saucer, Pink, Paden City	15.00
Jonquil, Plate, Dinner, Pink, Paden City	20.00
Jubilee, Casserole, Gray, Cover, Homer Laughlin	50.00
Jubilee, Plate, Pink, Homer Laughlin, 10 In.	19.00
Jubilee, Teapot, Celadon Green, Cover, Homer Laughlin	60.00
Kitchen Kraft, Creamer, Blue, Homer Laughlin	12.00 to 21.00
Kitchen Kraft, Plate, Blue, Homer Laughlin, 6 In.	6.00
La Mancha, Plate, Gold, Metlox, 6 1/2 In.	5.00
La Mancha, Plate, Gold, Metlox, 8 1/4 In.	7.00
Lazy Daisy, Plate, Taylor, Smith & Taylor, 8 In.	15.00
Lazy Daisy, Soup, Dish, Taylor, Smith & Taylor	19.00
Lazy Daisy, Sugar, Cover, Taylor, Smith & Taylor	25.00
Liberty Blue, Berry Bowl, 8 3/4 In.	55.00
Liberty Blue, Cup & Saucer, Old North Church	*Illus* 10.00
Liberty Blue, Plate, Independence Hall, 10 In.	15.00
Lu-Ray, Bowl, Vegetable, Oval, Surf Green, Taylor, Smith & Taylor	30.00
Lu-Ray, Cup & Saucer, Sharon Pink, Taylor, Smith & Taylor	14.00
Lu-Ray, Gravy Boat, Windsor Blue, Taylor, Smith & Taylor	40.00
Lu-Ray, Jug, Water, Windsor Blue	75.00
Lu-Ray, Plate, Surf Green, 10 In.	22.00
Lu-Ray, Platter, Surf Green, Taylor, Smith & Taylor, 11 1/2 In.	75.00
Lu-Ray, Salt & Pepper, Windsor Blue, Taylor, Smith & Taylor	25.00
Lu-Ray, Sauceboat, Underplate, Persian Cream, Taylor, Smith & Taylor	45.00
Magnolia, Plate, Homer Laughlin, 10 In.	13.00
Majestic, Cup & Saucer, Homer Laughlin	25.00
Majestic, Plate, Homer Laughlin, 7 In.	18.00
Majestic, Plate, Homer Laughlin, 9 In.	20.00
Marigold, Plate, Homer Laughlin, 9 In.	20.00
Mary, Plate, Harmony House, 6 In.	8.00
Mary, Plate, Harmony House, 8 In.	11.00
Mary, Sugar, Cover, Harmony House	25.00
Mayflower, Cup & Saucer, Blue Ridge	9.00
Mayflower, Plate, Blue Ridge, 9 5/8 In.	9.00
Memory Lane, Plate, Royal China, 10 1/4 In.	8.00
Mexicana, Bowl, Vegetable, Homer Laughlin, 8 1/4 In.	34.00
Mimion, Bowl, Vegetable, Cover, Green, Paden City	30.00
Mimion, Cup & Saucer, Dark Green, Paden City	15.00
Mimion, Plate, Bread & Butter, Green, Paden City	5.00
Mimion, Plate, Dinner, Green, Paden City	10.00
Mimion, Platter, Green, Paden City, Small	20.00
Moderne, Creamer, Harmony House	18.00

Moderne, Cup & Saucer, Harmony House 15.00
Moderne, Plate, Harmony House, 10 In. 15.00
Moderne, Sugar, Cover, Harmony House 25.00
Moonglow, Plate, Harmony House, 10 In. 10.00
Moulin Rouge, Creamer, Taylor, Smith & Taylor 15.00
Moulin Rouge, Plate, Taylor, Smith & Taylor, 10 In. 14.00
Mount Vernon, Plate, Harmony House, 10 In. 20.00
Nasturtium, Platter, Paden City, Medium 35.00
Old Curiosity Shop, Ashtray, Green, Royal China, 5 1/2 In. 18.00
Old Curiosity Shop, Berry Bowl, Green, Royal China, 5 1/2 In. 4.00
Old Curiosity Shop, Cake Plate, Handles, Green, Royal China, 10 1/2 In. 35.00
Old Curiosity Shop, Cup, Green, Royal China 4.00
Old Curiosity Shop, Plate, Green, Royal China, 10 In. 7.00
Orient, Bowl, Cereal, Harmony House, 5 1/2 In. 10.00
Orient, Cup & Saucer, Harmony House 12.00
Orient, Gravy Boat, Underplate, Harmony House 18.00
Peach Blossom, Creamer, W.S. George 8.00
Peach Blossom, Cup & Saucer, W.S. George ....7.00 to 8.00
Peach Blossom, Plate, W.S. George, 10 In. 10.00
Pebbleford, Plate, Pink, Taylor, Smith & Taylor, 10 In. 5.00
Pepper Tree, Cup & Saucer, Metlox 17.00
Pepper Tree, Gravy Boat, Metlox 71.00
Pepper Tree, Platter, Metlox, 11 In. 69.00
Petite Rose, Plate, Harmony House, 8 In. 8.00
Plantation Ivy, Berry Bowl, Southern Potteries, 5 1/2 In. 8.00
Plantation Ivy, Bowl, Vegetable, Southern Potteries, 8 7/8 In. 20.00
Plantation Ivy, Plate, Dinner, Southern Potteries, 10 In. 15.00
Prince Edward, Plate, Harmony House, 10 In. 4.00
Priscilla, Batter Bowl, Homer Laughlin, 10 1/4 In. 48.00
Priscilla, Cup & Saucer, Homer Laughlin 16.00
Priscilla, Gravy Boat, Homer Laughlin 20.00
Priscilla, Plate, Homer Laughlin, 10 In. 18.00
Provincial Fruit, Butter, Cover, Green, Metlox 43.00
Provincial Fruit, Plate, Metlox, 7 1/2 In. 11.00
Provincial Fruit, Plate, Metlox, 10 1/2 In. 22.00
Red Rooster, Bowl, Fruit, Metlox, 6 In. 12.00
Red Rooster, Coffeepot, Metlox 50.00
Red Rooster, Plate, Metlox, 10 In. ....13.00 to 24.00
Red Rooster, Salt & Pepper, Metlox, 4 In. 18.00
Reveille, Plate, Taylor, Smith & Taylor, 10 In. ....15.00 to 18.00
Rhythm, Cup & Saucer, Yellow, Homer Laughlin 15.00
Rhythm, Plate, Gray, Homer Laughlin, 9 In. 9.00
Rhythm, Plate, Yellow, Homer Laughlin, 7 1/4 In. 13.00
San Fernando, Bowl, Vegetable, Oval, Metlox 48.00
San Fernando, Cup & Saucer, Metlox 17.00
San Fernando, Platter, Metlox, 9 3/4 In. 47.00
Sculptured Daisy, Bowl, Vegetable, Metlox, 9 In. 10.00
Sculptured Daisy, Cup & Saucer, Metlox ....10.00 to 17.00
Sculptured Daisy, Plate, Metlox, 7 1/2 In. 12.00
Sculptured Daisy, Platter, Metlox, 11 In. 10.00
Sculptured Daisy, Sugar, Cover, Metlox 40.00
Sculptured Grape, Cup & Saucer, Metlox 20.00
Sculptured Grape, Sugar, Cover, Metlox 43.00
Sculptured Zinnia, Cup & Saucer, Metlox 21.00
Sculptured Zinnia, Platter, Metlox, 12 1/2 In. 51.00
Sculptured Zinnia, Soup, Dish, Metlox 21.00
Shakespeare Country, Creamer, Homer Laughlin 15.00
Shakespeare Country, Cup & Saucer, Homer Laughlin 10.00
Shakespeare Country, Plate, Homer Laughlin, 6 In. 6.00
Shakespeare Country, Soup, Dish, Rimmed, Homer Laughlin 12.00
Shenandoah, Bowl, Cereal, Tab Handles, White, Daffodils, Paden City, 6 1/4 In. 4.00
Skytone, Gravy Boat, Underplate, Homer Laughlin 20.00
Skytone, Plate, Blue, Homer Laughlin, 6 In. ....5.00 to 9.00

Skytone, Platter, Homer Laughlin, 11 In. 20.00
Spring Garden, Cup & Saucer, Homer Laughlin 10.00
Spring Garden, Plate, Homer Laughlin, 9 In. ....6.00 to 15.00
Sunny Glade, Creamer, Harmony House 16.00
Sunny Glade, Cup & Saucer, Harmony House 15.00
Sunny Glade, Plate, Harmony House, 8 In. 8.00
Symphony, Cup & Saucer, Chartreuse, Harmony House 13.00
Symphony, Cup & Saucer, Gray, Harmony House 20.00
Symphony, Plate, Chartreuse, Harmony House, 9 1/4 In. 20.00
Tangerine, Coffeepot, Harmony House, 10 In. 35.00
Tangerine, Creamer, Harmony House 4.00
Theme, Cup & Saucer, Homer Laughlin ....15.00 to 16.00
Theme, Plate, Homer Laughlin, 9 In. 12.00
True Blue, Coffeepot, Metlox, 8 Cup 85.00
True Blue, Cup & Saucer, Metlox 21.00
Tulip, Plate, Homer Laughlin, 6 In. 10.00
Vineyard, Bowl, Vegetable, 2 Sections, Metlox, 11 1/4 In. 69.00
Vineyard, Cup & Saucer, Metlox 20.00
Vineyard, Pitcher, Metlox, 7 1/2 In. 18.00
Vineyard, Plate, Metlox, 10 3/4 In. ....13.00 to 26.00
Vintage, Cup & Saucer, Harmony House 10.00
Virginia Rose, Bowl, Homer Laughlin, 8 In. 9.00
Virginia Rose, Plate, Homer Laughlin, 8 3/4 In. ....17.00 to 18.00
Virginia Rose, Platter, Homer Laughlin, 11 1/4 In. ....26.00 to 30.00
Vistosa, Cup & Saucer, Red, Taylor, Smith & Taylor 20.00
Vistosa, Plate, Red, Taylor, Smith & Taylor, 10 In. 25.00
Williamsburg, Creamer, E.M. Knowles 12.00
Williamsburg, Plate, E.M. Knowles, 10 In. 15.00
Williamsburg, Sugar, Cover, E.M. Knowles 25.00
Wood Rose, Cup & Saucer, Taylor, Smith & Taylor 12.00
Wood Rose, Salt & Pepper, Taylor, Smith & Taylor 12.00
Woodfield, Bowl, Salad, Gray, Steubenville, 11 In. 24.00
Woodfield, Cup & Saucer, Gray, Steubenville 11.00
Woodfield, Pitcher, Gray, Steubenville, 9 1/2 In. 75.00
Woodland Gold, Cup & Saucer, Metlox 17.00
Woodland Gold, Plate, Metlox, 10 1/4 In. 22.00
Woodland Gold, Soup, Dish, Metlox 17.00
Yellowstone, Plate, Homer Laughlin, 7 In. 6.00
Yellowstone, Platter, Homer Laughlin, 10 In. 15.00
Yellowstone, Platter, Homer Laughlin, 13 In. 30.00

DIONNE QUINTUPLETS were born in Canada on May 28, 1934. The publicity about their birth and their special status as wards of the Canadian government made them famous throughout the world. Visitors could watch the girls play; reporters interviewed the girls and the staff. Thousands of special dolls and souvenirs were made picturing the quints at different ages. Emilie died in 1954, Marie in 1970, and Yvonne in 2001. Annette and Cecile still live in Canada.

    Display, Quaker Oats, 5 Sides, Different Quint On Each Side, 60 x 30 In. 132.00
    Doll, Emilie, Composition, Sleep Eyes, Madame Alexander, Toddler, 14 In. 425.00
    Fan, Souvenir, Use Linco Gasoline Motor Oil, Sepia Tone Picture, Cardboard 30.00
    Radio, White, Images Of Girls, Green Dresses, Red Knobs, 9 1/2 In. 170.00

DIRK VAN ERP was born in 1860 and died in 1933. He opened his own studio in 1908 in Oakland, California. Van Erp made hammered copper accessories, including vases, desk sets, bookends, candlesticks, jardinieres, and trays, but he is best known for his lamps. The hammered copper lamps often had shades with mica panels.

    Basket, Wicker, Copper Mounted 7000.00
    Bookends, Sailing Ship, Square, Windmill Stamp, Copper, c.1915, 4 In. 1265.00
    Bowl, Copper, Hammered, Ring Pedestal, 5 x 17 1/2 In. 1840.00
    Box, Copper, Original Patina, 6 x 3 1/2 In. 478.00
    Box, Copper, Original Patina, Hammered, 3 1/2 x 32 1/2 In. 489.00

Dirk Van Erp, Lamp,
Copper, Hammered, Mica,
Impressed Mark, 16 In.

Disneyana, Chair, School,
Mickey Mouse Back,
Figural, Wooden,
Painted, 28 In.

Bucket, Ice, Brass, Hammered, Nickel Interior, 2 Mahogany Handles, 12 In. 3450.00
Jardiniere, Copper, Broad Form, Signed, 11 1/2 In. 2860.00
Jardiniere, Copper, Hammered, Wrought Ring Handles, 12 3/4 x 16 In. 4600.00
Lamp, Copper, Hammered, Conical Shade, 3 Mica Panels, 13 x 8 In. 9620.00
Lamp, Copper, Hammered, Mica, Impressed Mark, 16 In. . . . .*Illus* 23000.00
Stand, Drink, Copper, Hammered, Signed, 1911, 29 1/2 x 10 1/2 In. 5750.00
Vase, Copper, Hammered, Marked, 12 In. 4675.00
Vase, Copper, Hammered, Original Patina, 7 1/2 In. 2940.00
Vase, Copper, Hammered, Original Patina, 8 1/2 x 7 In. 3740.00
Vase, Copper, Hammered, Rolled Raised Rim, 1911, 6 1/2 x 7 1/2 In. 3737.00
Vase, Copper, Hammered, Warty Texture, Rolled Rim, c.1911, 6 x 7 In. 3750.00
Vase, Copper, Warty, Original Bronze Patina, Signed, 10 In. 6900.00

DISNEYANA is a collector's term. Walt Disney and his company introduced many comic characters to the world. Collectors search for examples of the work of the Disney Studios and the many commercial
products modeled after his characters, including Mickey Mouse,
Donald Duck, and recent films, like *Beauty and the Beast* and *The
Little Mermaid*.

Bag, Knitting, Mickey Mouse, Fabric, Child's, Mid 1930s, 9 In. 165.00
Bank, 3 Little Pigs Chest, Leatherette, Steel, 2 13/16 In. 115.00
Bank, Donald Duck, Nodder, Composition, Crown Toy & Novelty 275.00
Bank, Donald Duck, Tin, Moore, 3 1/2 In. 90.00
Bank, Mickey Mouse, Suitcase, Red, Handle, Tin, 2 3/4 In. 825.00
Bank, Mickey Mouse, Telephone, Tin, Cardboard, 4 1/4 In. 360.00
Bank, Pinocchio, Post Office, Tin, Moore, 5 1/8 In. 65.00
Billfold, Donald Duck & Nephews, Western Dress, Roping Calf, Plastic 88.00
Biscuit Box, Mickey Mouse & Minnie Mouse, Holland, 1931, 10 x 8 In. 950.00
Blocks, Safety, Mickey Mouse, WDE, Harlsam, Box, c.1935, 4 In. 135.00
Blotter, Mickey Mouse, Minnie, Donald, Goofy, Pluto, c.1936, 6 x 4 In. 54.00
Book, Big Little Book, Donald Duck & His (Mis)Adventures, Whitman Pub. Co., 1937 . . 25.00
Book, Big Little Book, Mickey Sails For Treasure Island, Whitman Pub. Co., 1935 . . . . . . 50.00
Book, Clarabelle Cow With Donald Duck, Mickey Mouse, Whitman Publ., 1938, 94 Pg. . 50.00
Book, Handful Of Fun, Mickey Mouse, Hand Shape, Eisendrath Glove Co., c.1935, 8 In. . 945.00
Book, Mickey Mouse, Hardcover, 1931, 8 3/4 In. 140.00
Book, Mickey Mouse, Soft Cover, 16 Pages, 1930 . . . . 935.00
Book, Pedro, Hardcover, Dust Jacket, 1943, 8 1/2 In. 125.00
Book, School Days In Disneyville, Color, Inscribed, 1939, 102 Pages, 8 1/2 x 6 In. 30.00
Bottle Cap, Donald Duck Cola, 1950 . . . . 8.00
Button, Mickey Mouse Battles Big Bad Wolf, Good Teeth, American Dental Assn. 160.00
Button, Mickey Mouse Club, Celluloid, 1 1/4 In. 54.00
Button, Mickey Mouse Head, Walt Disney World, Celluloid, 3 In. 9.00
Button, Mickey Mouse, Kay Kamen Paper, Celluloid 125.00
Calendar, 1941, Mickey & Felix, Cardboard Cover, France, 1 1/2 x 3 In. 72.00
Camera, Donald Duck, H. George Co., Box, 1950s 185.00

Candy Container, Donald Duck, Playing Drum, Plastic, 3 In. 10.00
Candy Container, Minnie Mouse, Strumming Guitar, Plastic, 3 In. 10.00
Candy Container, Pluto, With Dog Dish, Plastic, 3 In. 10.00
Car, Dipsy, Donald Duck, Tin, Windup, Linemar, Original Box, 5 1/2 In. 1250.00
Car, Parade, 4 Disney Passengers, Windup, Max 450.00
Carousel Figure, Donald Duck, With Horn, Wooden, 38 In. 358.00
Carousel Figure, Mickey Mouse, Mickey On Skis, Wooden, 38 In. 248.00
Cel, see Animation Art category.
Chair, School, Mickey Mouse Back, Figural, Wooden, Painted, 28 In. .... *Illus* 350.00
Chocolate Mold Set, Mickey, Minnie, Pluto, Donald Duck 170.00
Clock, Alarm, Mickey Mouse, W.D.P., Ingersoll, 5 In. 145.00
Clock, Alarm, Mickey Mouse, Waggling Head, Topolino, Italy, 1930s, 5 In. 380.00
Clock, Cinderella, Alarm, Bradley 70.00
Clock, Donald Duck, Blue 300.00
Clock, Donald Duck, Pink 200.00
Clock, Mickey Mouse, Alarm, France, 1930s 295.00
Clock, Mickey Mouse, Ingersoll, 1930s ....800.00 to 950.00
Clock, Mickey Mouse, Running, Red 450.00
Clothing Rack, Plywood, Minnie & Mickey On Chair Holding Rack Overhead, 42 In. 1210.00
Coin Purse, Donald Duck, Goggle Eyes, 4 x 3 In. 12.00
Colored Pencil Set, Mickey Mouse Club, Hasbro Jolly Hobby Toys, 1950s, 9 x 5 In. 35.00
Cookie Jar, 101 Dalmatians, Dalmatians In Rocking Chair, McCoy 450.00
Cookie Jar, Birthday Cake, Mickey Mouse On Top, 1978 .... 1000.00
Cookie Jar, Castle, Disneyland 40th Anniversary 145.00
Cookie Jar, Dalmatian, Treasure Craft, 13 In. 85.00
Cookie Jar, Dumbo Turnabout, Gray Glaze 495.00
Cookie Jar, Mary Poppins, Pink Dress, Parasol, Penguins On Skirt, 1964 .... 1350.00
Cookie Jar, Mickey Mouse Head, Chef Hat, Treasure Craft, 10 1/2 In. 80.00
Cookie Jar, Mickey Mouse, On Drum, California Originals, 11 3/4 In., 1977 .... 235.00
Cookie Jar, Mickey Mouse, On Toy Sack, Dressed As Santa 125.00
Cookie Jar, Mickey Mouse, Sitting, Hand On Cheek, Treasure Craft, 12 In. .... 75.00 to 95.00
Cookie Jar, Pinocchio Head, Metlox 350.00
Cookie Jar, Winnie The Pooh, California Originals 275.00
Creamer, Donald Duck, Wade Heath, c.1935, 4 1/4 In. 500.00
Creamer, Mickey Mouse, Figural 110.00
Cup, Mickey Mouse, Pluto, Wade Heath Ware, England, Box, 3 In. 450.00
Doll, Donald Duck, Socket Head, Jointed Legs, Knickerbocker, c.1935, 8 1/2 In. 550.00
Doll, Mickey Mouse, Cloth, Swivel Head, Rubber Tail, Red Shorts, Knickerbocker, 10 In. 650.00
Doll, Mickey Mouse, Pie Eyes, 4 Fingers, Pat. No. 82862, Knickerbocker, 10 In. 620.00
Doll, Minnie Mouse, Flower, Button In Ear, Steiff, 8 1/2 In. 4495.00
Doll, Pinocchio, Composition, Wooden, Jointed, Ideal, Box, 10 1/2 In. 315.00
Doll, Snow White & Seven Dwarfs, Box, Knickerbocker, 15 In., 9-In. Dwarfs 3500.00
Doll, Snow White, Composition Socket Head, Knickerbocker, 1939, 16 In. 525.00
Doll Set, Snow White & Seven Dwarfs, Cloth, 12 & 19 In., 8 Piece .... *Illus* 2200.00
Dollhouse, Mickey & Donald, Suburban Colonial, Tin Lithograph, Box, 1950 .... 1000.00
Doorstop, Pinocchio 2200.00
Figurine, Cinderella & Prince Charming, Bisque, Borgfeldt, Box, 5 1/4 In., Pair 295.00
Figurine, Donald Duck's Nephew, Reading Book, Bisque, Occupied Japan, 1940s 85.00
Figurine, Dopey, Latex, Seiberling, 1940s, 5 1/2 In. 110.00
Figurine, Gideon The Cat, Bisque, Pinocchio, 3 In. 30.00
Figurine, Mickey & Minnie Mouse, Bisque, Borgfeldt, Box, 6 In., Pair 1300.00
Figurine, Mickey & Minnie Mouse, Bisque, Disney, Japan, 4 In., Pair 225.00
Figurine, Mickey Mouse, Bisque, Name On Chest, 5 1/4 In. 230.00
Figurine, Mickey Mouse, Chalkware, 10 In. 300.00
Figurine, Mickey Mouse, Hands On Hips, Name Inscribed On Chest, Bisque, 5 1/4 In. 230.00
Figurine, Mickey Mouse, Painted Wood, Leather Ears, Fully Jointed, 1930s, 3 In. 37.00
Figurine, Mickey Mouse, Painted, Hollow Plastic, 5 3/4 In. 15.00
Figurine, Mickey Mouse, Pie-Eyed, Composition, 10 1/4 In. 295.00
Figurine, Mickey Mouse, Tuba Player, Rosenthal, 3 1/2 In. 450.00
Figurine, Mickey Mouse, With Parasol, Clockwork Motor, Celluloid, 8 In. 1437.00
Figurine, Mickey Mouse, Wooden, 1926, 5 1/2 In. 287.00
Figurine, Pluto, Howling, Brayton Leghuna, 1930s, 5 3/4 In. 185.00
Figurine, Seven Dwarfs, Plastic, Walt Disney Productions, 5 In. 70.00

Disneyana, Doll Set,
Snow White &
Seven Dwarfs,
Cloth, 12 & 19 In.,
8 Piece

Disneyana, Lunch
Box, Mickey Mouse,
Pie Tray, 1935

Figurine, Snow White & Seven Dwarfs, Bisque, Box, 9 In., 8 Piece 450.00
Figurine, Snow White & Seven Dwarfs, Bisque, Japan, Mid Size 395.00
Figurine, Snow White & Seven Dwarfs, Gardening Tools, Pottery, England, c.1939 ..... 370.00
Figurine, Snow White & Seven Dwarfs, Instruments, Japan, Prewar, 4 3/4-6 1/2 In. 525.00
Figurine, Three Little Pigs, Bisque, Borgfeldt, Japan, Box, Prewar, 3 3/4 In. 605.00
Game, Bagatelle, Mickey Mouse, 1930s, 23 1/2 In. 475.00
Game, Mickey Mouse Target Game, Marksman Baseball Game, 2 Sides, Marks Bros. 44.00
Game, Quoits, Mickey Mouse, Chad Valley, England, 1930s, 13 1/4 In. 350.00
Goldfish Bowl, Pink, Vernon Kilns, 1940 .... 275.00
Gumball Machine, Mickey & Pals Parade, Cast Iron Base, Hamilton, 1938, 16 In. 1800.00
Jam Jar, Mickey Mouse, Glass, Tin, Moore, 9 In. 70.00
Key Chain & Coin Purse, Winnie The Pooh, Hello Pooh, Zipper, 3 x 4 In. 6.00
Knife, Pocket, Mickey Mouse, World's Fair, Chicago, 1933 .... 110.00
Knife Rest, Mickey & Minnie, Continental, 1930s, 3 1/2 In. ....225.00 to 285.00
Lights, Silly Symphony, Mazda 250.00
Lime Cola, Donald Duck, 6 Bottles With Caps, Carrier 175.00
Lunch Box, Black Hole, Aladdin, Metal, 1979 .... 98.00
Lunch Box, Mickey Mouse, Pie Tray, 1935 ....*Illus* 1295.00
Lunch Box, Peter Pan, Metal, Aladdin, 1969 .... 300.00
Lunch Box, Snow White, Tin, 7 5/8 x 4 3/4 x 4 In. 375.00
Lunch Box Thermos, Wonderful World On Ice, Plastic, Aladdin, 1982 .... 10.00
Magazine, Modern Mechanix, Mickey, Donald, Pluto & Walt Disney Cover, 1937 ...... 170.00
Magazine Rack, Mickey Mouse, Art Deco, France, 1930s, 11 1/4 In. 350.00
Mold, Chocolate, Mickey Mouse, Minnie, Pluto, Long-Billed Donald Duck, 4 In., Pair ... 170.00
Mug, Mickey Mouse, Logo On Side 20.00
Music Box, Snow White, Tin Lithograph, Key Wind, Butterflies Move, Linemar, c.1940 .. 340.00
Napkin Ring, Mickey Mouse, Celluloid, Hand Painted, England, 1930s 275.00
Night-Light, Donald Duck, Cardboard Donald, Painted Mickey & Pluto, 1930s, 4 In. 360.00
Ornament, Christmas, Snow White, 1 Dwarf 40.00
Pail, Mickey Mouse, Minnie, Porky, Donald Duck, Seaside, Happynak, 1930s, 4 1/2 In. .. 251.00
Party Decorations, Ludwig Von Drake, Donald Duck, Daisy Duck, 1960s, 8 x 10 In. 25.00
Pen, Snow White, 50th Anniversary, Ballpoint, Blue Ink, c.1980, 5 1/2 In. 5.00
Pencil, Goofy, Safari Outfit, Bird's Nest, Tree Shape, Applause, 7 In. 5.00
Pencil, Mickey Mouse, Faber, Castell No. 2 .... 5.00
Pencil Box, Duck Tails, Vinyl, Side Opening, Spanish Version, 1987, 9 x 1/2 In. 5.00
Pencil Box, Fishing With Mickey, Minnie & Donald, Original Cartoon Ruler, c.1937 .... 315.00
Pencil Box, Mickey Mouse, Walt Disney Enterprises, Dixon USA, c.1933 .... 145.00
Pencil Box, Mickey Mouse, Wise Little Hen, Blue, Yellow, Dixon, 1930s, 10 x 6 In. 75.00
Pencil Box, Pinocchio, Vinyl, c.1970, 8 1/4 x 6 In. 29.00
Pencil Holder, 101 Dalmations, Cup, 3 1/4 In. 5.00
Pencil Sharpener, Jiminy Cricket, 4 1/2 In. 27.00
Pencil Sharpener, Mickey Mouse, Celluloid, 2 1/2 In. 80.00
Pencil Top Set, Minnie, Mickey Mouse, Donald Duck, On Card 5.00
Piccolo, Mickey Mouse, Tin Lithograph, Italy, 1930s, 9 3/4 In. 300.00
Pillow, Mickey Serenading Pluto, Painted, Embroidered, Vogue, 12 1/2 In. 160.00

Pin, Mickey Mouse, Celluloid, Paper Back, 3/4 In. 210.00
Pitcher, Donald Duck, Ceramic, Walt Disney, 6 In. 125.00
Pitcher, Horace Horsecollar, Marked Mickey Mouse, Bavaria, c.1933, 3 1/2 In. 260.00
Pitcher, Mickey Mouse, 1930s, 5 In. 95.00
Planter, Pluto Pulling Card, Leeds, Walt Disney 75.00
Plate, Donald Duck, Blue, Remove Donald's Head To Add Hot Water 125.00
Popcorn Popper, Mickey Mouse On Handle, Screen Over Pan, Shaking Action, 20 In. 165.00
Postcard, Goofy & Sea Turtle, 3-D, Walt Disney Productions ....*Illus* 15.00
Postcard, Mickey Mouse, Continental 45.00
Print, Thumper, Frame, Walt Disney Productions, 11 x 9 In. 28.00
Puppet, Dumbo, Vinyl, Cloth, Squeaker, Gund, Box, c.1955, 9 In. 68.00
Puzzle, 20,000 Leagues Under The Sea, Frame Tray, 1954 .... 95.00
Puzzle, Black Hole, Aladdin, Frame Tray, Whitman, 1979 .... 8.00
Radio, Emerson, Model No. 247, Snow White & 7 Dwarfs, 1939, Table Model 1035.00
Ramp Walker, Figaro, 1950s 20.00
Record, Donald Duck's Singing Lesson 15.00
Record, Mickey Mouse Club, Orange Plastic, Yellow Label, Extended Play, 45 RPM 25.00
Rocking Chair, Minnie Mouse, Walt Disney Productions, Linemar, Japan, 6 1/2 In. 995.00
Rocking Chair, Pluto Decal, White & Yellow Vinyl, Child's, 1950s 255.00
Salt & Pepper, Donald Duck, Japan, 1961, 5 In. 285.00
Salt & Pepper, Donald Duck, Leeds, 4 In. 105.00
Salt & Pepper, Ludwig Von Drake, Ceramic, Package, 1961 .... 285.00
Saucer, Mickey Playing Sax, Oswald Rabbit, Black Cat, Bavaria, c.1931, 6 In., 5 Piece .. 210.00
Scarf, Mickey Mouse, Embroidered, Dark Blue Ground, 1930s, 39 1/2 In. 250.00
Scissors, Donald Duck, Electric, WDP, 1950s, 5 3/4 In. 165.00
Scissors, Mickey Mouse, Red Handles, 1930s, 3 1/4 In. 400.00
Shoe & Coat Rack, Minnie & Mickey Mouse, Painted Plywood, 42 In. 1210.00
Snowdome, 101 Dalmations 5.00
Sparkler, Mickey Mouse, 5 1/4 In. 525.00
Sugar, Figural, Mickey Mouse 170.00
Tablecloth, Mickey Mouse, White, Light Blue Border, 1930s, 35 1/2 In. 275.00
Tea Set, Donald Teapot & Creamer, Horace Horsecollar Sugar, Mickey Cups, c.1936 .... 415.00
Tea Set, Mickey & Friends, Marx, Box 395.00
Tea Set, Mickey Mouse, Mickey Mouse Corp., Japan, Box, c.1935, 9 In. 575.00
Tea Set, Mickey Mouse, Minnie, Donald, Wade Heath, England, c.1936, 8 Piece 435.00
Tea Set, Mickey Mouse, Sugar & Creamer, 4 Cups & Saucers, Japan, c.1935 .... 553.00
Tie Rack, Mickey Mouse, Wooden, 8 3/4 In. 150.00
Tin, Candy, Mickey Mouse, Minnie, Pluto, Switzerland, c.1932, 7 1/2 In. 695.00
Tin, Peter & The Wolf, Painted, England, 1940s, 12 3/4 In. 260.00
Tin, Snow White & Seven Dwarfs Character, Belgian Biscuit, 1930s 225.00
Toothbrush Holder, Donald Duck, Figural 990.00
Toothbrush Holder, Donald Duck, Mickey Mouse & Minnie Mouse, 1930s 350.00
Toothbrush Holder, Mickey Mouse, Pat. By Walter E. Disney, Jointed, 5 In. 325.00
Toothbrush Holder, Minnie Mouse, Paper Label, Walter E. Disney, Japan, 5 In. 360.00
Towne Square, Disney, 3 Accessories, Sears, Boxes, 1988 .... 150.00
Toy, Bus, Lithographed Characters, Modern Toys, Japan, Box, 16 In. 450.00
Toy, Doc, Latex, Walt Disney, Seiberling, c.1940, 6 In. 110.00
Toy, Donald Duck & Goofy, Donald Duet, Windup, Marx, 10 1/4 In. 590.00
Toy, Donald Duck & Pluto, Car, Roadster, Sun Rubber, c.1930 .... 66.00
Toy, Donald Duck, Acrobat, Celluloid, Box, Linemar 546.00
Toy, Donald Duck, Acrobat, Linemar, Box, 5 1/4 x 6 1/2 In. 595.00
Toy, Donald Duck, Celluloid, Windup, Waddles, Borgfeldt, Box, c.1936, 5 In. 1845.00
Toy, Donald Duck, Composition, Windup, Box, France 975.00
Toy, Donald Duck, Cyclist, Celluloid, Cloth, Windup, Paradise Novelty, Japan, Box, 6 1/2 In. 3415.00
Toy, Donald Duck, Drummer, Windup, Tin, Linemar, Japan ....95.00 to 150.00
Toy, Donald Duck, Fire Engine, Plastic, Tin Bell, Windup, Modern Toys, Japan, c.1967 .. 65.00
Toy, Donald Duck, Hopping, Palm Squeeze Cable, Tin, Linemar, 9 In. 316.25
Toy, Donald Duck, In Rocket, Tin, Plastic Head, Friction, West Germany, 7 In. 300.00
Toy, Donald Duck, Mouth Opens, Metal & Plastic, Box, Schuco 450.00
Toy, Donald Duck, Plastic Feet, Fisher-Price, 8 x 6 In. 100.00
Toy, Donald Duck, Seiberling, c.1930, 6 In. 337.00
Toy, Donald Duck, Walker, Composition, Borgfeldt, 1930s, 12 In. 850.00
Toy, Donald Duck, Walker, Composition, Clockwork, Walt Disney, 11 1/2 In. 1210.00

Disneyana, Postcard, Goofy & Sea Turtle,
3-D, Walt Disney Productions

Disneyana, Toy, Mickey & Minnie Mouse,
On Elephant, Windup, Borgfeldt, 9 In.

Toy, Donald Duck, Walker, Composition, Windup, Borgfeldt, 1930s, 12 In. 850.00
Toy, Donald Duck, Xylophone Player, Pull Toy, Fisher-Price, Copyright 1938, 13 In. 345.00
Toy, Dumbo, Jumps, Flips, Tin, Windup, WDP, Marx, 1941, 4 In.   445.00
Toy, Dumbo, The Flying Elephant, Umbrella Spins, Plastic, Brazil, Box, 1960s, 6 In. 325.00
Toy, Ferdinand The Bull, Head Moves, Tail Spins, Windup, Tin, Linemar 350.00
Toy, Ferdinand The Bull, Tin, Head Moves, Tail Spins, Windup, Linemar, Box 490.00
Toy, Ferdinand The Bull, Tin, Windup, Spins Around, Rotates Tail, Marx, 4 1/2 In. 275.00
Toy, Ferdinand, Tin, Windup, B On Back, Marx, 5 In. 121.00
Toy, Ferris Wheel, Windup, Tin, Chein, 1940s 1200.00
Toy, Figaro The Cat, Tin, Windup, Walt Disney's Pinocchio, Marx, 5 In. 165.00
Toy, Happy, Latex, Seiberling, 1940s, 5 3/4 In. 110.00
Toy, Ludwig Von Drake, Go-Cart, Windup, Linemar 485.00
Toy, Ludwig Von Drake, Windup, Walking, Linemar, 5 3/4 In. 319.00
Toy, Mickey & Minnie Mouse, On Elephant, Windup, Borgfeldt, 9 In. . . . .*Illus* 6270.00
Toy, Mickey Mouse & Donald Duck, Rowboat, Celluloid, Japan, 5 3/4 In. 1750.00
Toy, Mickey Mouse & Friend, Balloon Man, Tin, Windup, 1930, 6 1/2 In. 800.00
Toy, Mickey Mouse, Acrobat, Celluloid, Battery Operated, Linemar, Japan, Box, 9 In. 525.00
Toy, Mickey Mouse, Block Set, Walt Disney Enterprises, Harlsam, Box, c.1935 . . . .   135.00
Toy, Mickey Mouse, Car, Mickey Driver, Matchbox, 1979 . . . .   45.00
Toy, Mickey Mouse, Choo Choo, Pull String, Fisher-Price, 1939, 8 1/2 In. 625.00
Toy, Mickey Mouse, Drum, Sticks, 1930s, 6 1/2 In. 195.00
Toy, Mickey Mouse, Drummer, Jazz, Squeeze Mechanism, Nifty 1250.00
Toy, Mickey Mouse, Fun-E-Flex, Wooden, Jointed, Borgfeldt, 1930s, 7 In. 500.00
Toy, Mickey Mouse, Handcar, Lionel 950.00
Toy, Mickey Mouse, Handcar, Mickey & Minnie Figures, Track, Lionel 290.00
Toy, Mickey Mouse, Jointed At Wrist, 1920s, 4 In. 203.00
Toy, Mickey Mouse, Mickey The Magician, Tin, Windup, Linemar, 6 In. 1980.00
Toy, Mickey Mouse, On Tricycle, Tin, Windup, Linemar, Box 650.00
Toy, Mickey Mouse, Playing Banjo, Bisque, Paper Label, Japan, 5 In. 345.00
Toy, Mickey Mouse, Playing Mandolin, Bisque, 1930s, 3 1/2 In.   350.00
Toy, Mickey Mouse, Playland, Box, WDP, 11 In. 4220.00
Toy, Mickey Mouse, Safety Patrol, On Motorcycle, Pull, Paper Lithograph On Wood 550.00
Toy, Mickey Mouse, Saxophone Player, Cymbals On Feet, Move Arms, 1930, 6 In. 2750.00
Toy, Mickey Mouse, Soldier Set, Marks Bros., Cork Gun, Box, 8 Piece 825.00
Toy, Mickey Mouse, Tin, Lever, Sparking Action, Geo, Borgfeldt, Box, 5 In. 2200.00
Toy, Mickey Mouse, Train, Circus, Lionel 3500.00
Toy, Mickey Mouse, Train, Meteor, Track, Marx, c.1947-1950, 35 1/4 In., 4 Piece 553.00
Toy, Mickey Mouse, Trapeze, Windup, 30 In. 385.00
Toy, Mickey Mouse, Walker, Celluloid, Windup, George Borgfeldt Corp., 7 1/2 In. 2750.00
Toy, Mickey Mouse, Walking Across Bridge, Celluloid, 1930s, 2 3/4 In. 250.00
Toy, Mickey Mouse, Whirling Tail, Windup, Linemar, Japan, 5 1/2 In. 336.00
Toy, Mickey On Pluto, Rocking, Tin, Windup, Linemar, Japan, Walt Disney Prod., 6 In. . . .   2024.00
Toy, Minnie Mouse, Minnie Knits & Rocks, Linemar, 7 In. 395.00
Toy, Minnie Mouse, Noisemaker, Tin Lithograph, Wooden Handle, 4 3/8 In. 770.00
Toy, Nautilus, 20,000 Leagues, Windup, Tin, Sutcliffe, England, Box, 10 In. 250.00
Toy, Pecos Bill, Ridin' Widowmaker, Windup, Plastic, Marx, 9 3/4 In. 450.00

Toy, Pinocchio, Walker, Eyes Move, Windup, Marx, 1939 .... 385.00
Toy, Pluto, Acrobat, Celluloid, Battery Operated, Linemar, Japan, Box, 9 In. 420.00
Toy, Pluto, Drum Major, Windup, 1950s, 6 1/2 In. 675.00
Toy, Pluto, Drum Major, Windup, Walt Disney Productions, Marx, 6 In. 450.00
Toy, Pluto, Fun-E-Flex, 6 1/2 In. 425.00
Toy, Pluto, Fun-E-Flex, Partial Sticker, 3 In. 225.00
Toy, Pluto, Fun-E-Flex, Wooden, Decal, 1930s, 4 In. 105.00
Toy, Pluto, On Tricycle, Celluloid, Tin, Windup, Bell Rings, Linemar, Japan, Box, 4 In. ... 605.00
Toy, Pluto, On Unicycle, Marx 1250.00
Toy, Pluto, Pull, Painted Wood, 1930s-1940s, 11 1/2 In. 275.00
Toy, Pluto, Pulling Mickey & Minnie Mouse In Sled 580.00
Toy, Pluto, Rollover, Tin, Windup, Marx, 8 1/2 In. 187.00
Toy, Pluto, Rolls Over, Windup, Marx, 1939 .... 460.00
Toy, Pluto, Spring Loaded, Tail Lever, Rolls Forward, Marx, 10 In. 121.00
Toy, Pluto, Windup, Linemar, 1950s, 7 In. 675.00
Toy, Score-Shot Bagatelle, Marble Shooter, Tin Lithograph, Marx 195.00
Toy, Sleepy, Latex, Seiberling, c.1940, 5 1/4 In. 110.00
Toy, Three Little Pigs, Acrobat, Celluloid, Windup, Prewar Japan, Walt Disney, 11 In. 475.00
Toy, Top, Disney Characters, Straco, Western Germany, c.1960 .... 25.00
Toy, Top, Spinning, Disney Characters, Chein, 1940s, 6 1/2 In. 165.00
Toy, Train, Casey Jr., Disneyland Express, Tin, Plastic, Windup, Marx, Box, 12 In. 235.00
Train, Meteor, Mickey Mouse, Track, Marx, c.1947-1950, 35 1/4 In., 4 Piece 553.00
Tub, Mickey Mouse, Tin, Rope Handles 700.00
Umbrella, Mickey & Minnie Mouse, Wooden Handle, Walt Disney Ent., 1930s 185.00
Umbrella, Mickey Mouse, Full Body Version, W.E. Disney, 1930s, 22 1/4 In. ..... 125.00 to 325.00
Valentine, Seven Dwarfs, Diorama, 1938 .... 20.00
View-Master, Adventureland, 3 Reels, Envelope, 1959 .... 50.00
View-Master, Aristocats, 3 Reels, Booklet, 1970 .... 30.00
View-Master, Cartoon Theater, Projector, Stage, 1950s 115.00
View-Master, Cinderella, 3 Reels, Booklet, GAF Packaging, 1965 .... 25.00
View-Master, Cinderella, 3 Reels, Booklet, Sawyers Packaging, 1965 .... 50.00
View-Master, Donald Duck, Reads Newspaper, Chip & Dale, 3 Reels, Booklet, 1969 .... 20.00
View-Master, Love Bug, 3 Reels, Booklet, Envelope, 1968 .... 45.00
View-Master, Mary Poppins, 3 Reels, Booklet, Envelope, 1964 .... 25.00 to 40.00
View-Master, Peter Pan, Peter Catches Wendy As She Walks Plank, 3 Reels, 1957 ...... 75.00
View-Master, The Shaggy D.A., 3 Reels, 1976 .... 40.00
View-Master, Winnie The Pooh & The Honey Tree, 3 Reels, Booklet, 1964 .... 32.00
Wagon, Mickey Mouse, Pulling Minnie, Dayton Toy & Specialty Co., 1930s, 24 In. 1375.00
Watch, Donald Duck, 1939, 2 In. 470.00
Watch, Lapel, Mickey Decal On Reverse, Box 2000.00
Watch, Mickey Mouse, Ingersoll, Mickey's Picture Engraved On Back, 2 In. 517.00
Watch, Mickey Mouse, Kelton, 1946, 9 In. 200.00
Watch, Pocket, Donald Duck, 1939, 2 In. 470.00
Watch, Pocket, Mickey Mouse, Ingersoll, 1930s, 2 In. 517.00
Wristwatch, Donald Duck, Birthday Series, U.S. Time Corp., Box, 1948, 4 1/4 In. 540.00
Wristwatch, Mickey Mouse, Ingersoll, Box, 1933, 6 1/4 In. .... 500.00 to 575.00
Wristwatch, Mickey Mouse, Ingersoll, Box, 1948 .... 340.00
Wristwatch, Woody Woodpecker, Ingram, 1950, 7 1/4 In. 310.00
Yo-Yo, Mickey Mouse, Skateboarding, Molded In Relief, Orange 8.50

DOCTOR, see Dental; Medical

DOLL entries are listed by marks printed or incised on the doll, if possible. If there are no marks, the doll is listed by the name of the subject or country or maker. Notice that Barbie is listed under Mattel. G.I.
Joe figures are listed in the Toy section.

A.M., 251, Bisque Head, Composition Bent-Limb Body, c.1920, 11 In. 900.00
A.M., 323, Bisque Head, Googly, Papier-Mache Body, 6 In. 850.00
A.M., 351-3k, Baby, Brown, Bisque Head, Sleep Eyes, 13 In. .... *Illus* 275.00
A.M., 353, Baby, Bisque, Sleep Eyes, Pouty, Costume, 1925, 16 In. 1200.00
A.M., 353/4, Baby, Oriental, Bisque Flange Head, Cloth Body, 15 In. .... *Illus* 760.00
A.M., 518, Baby, Bisque, Brown Sleep Eyes, Open Mouth, 2 Teeth, Dressed, Diaper, 16 In. 340.00
A.M., 991, Bisque Head, Sleep Eyes, Open Mouth, Wig, Jointed Composition, 8 1/2 In. .. 127.00

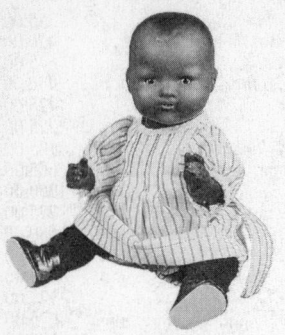

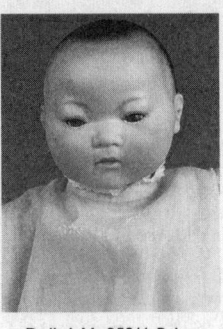

Doll, A.M., 351-3k, Baby, Brown,
Bisque Head, Sleep Eyes, 13 In.

Doll, A.M., 353/4, Baby,
Oriental, Bisque Flange
Head, Cloth Body, 15 In.

Doll, Automaton, La Bicycliste,
Leopold Lambert, France, 1890

A.M., Baby Phyllis, Flange Head, Sleep Eyes, Cloth Body, Composition Hands, 10 In. ... 120.00
A.M., Baby, Bisque Head, Brown Sleep Eyes, Open Mouth, 12 In. 184.00
A.M., Baby, Bisque Head, Gray Blue Sleep Eyes, Open Mouth, Light Brown Wig, 7 In. .. 184.00
A.M., Baby, Bisque, Blue Sleep Eyes, Open Mouth, 1920, 8 In. 92.00
A.M., Baby, Bisque, Blue Sleep Eyes, Open Mouth, Brown Wig, 15 In. 230.00
A.M., Bisque Head, Blue Glass Eyes With Lashes, Open Mouth, Jointed, 18 1/2 In. 115.00
A.M., Bisque Head, Blue Sleep Eyes, Open Mouth, Composition, 21 In. 143.00
A.M., Bisque Head, Brown Glass Sleep Eyes, Open Mouth, Blond Wig, 20 In. 172.00
A.M., Bisque Socket Head, Blue Sleep Eyes, Open Mouth, Mohair, Jointed, 33 In. 550.00
A.M., Bisque, Intaglio Eyes, Closed Mouth, Mohair Wig, c.1912, 12 In. 2800.00
A.M., Dome Head, Molded Hair, Intaglio Eyes, Open-Close Mouth, Dressed, 16 In. ... 995.00
A.M., Florodora, Bisque Head, Composition Jointed Body, 1930, 12 In. 380.00
A.M., Florodora, Bisque, Fur Eyebrows, Kid Body, Norwegian Outfit, 1920s, 24 In. 115.00
A.M., Just Me, Bisque Socket Head, Blue Glass Sleep Eyes, 1928, 11 In. 2400.00
A.M., Just Me, Bisque Socket Head, Brown Glass Sleep Eyes, Child, 1920, 9 In. 1400.00
A.M., Just Me, Bisque, Sleep Eyes, Mohair Wig, Original Dress, c.1929, 9 In. 3000.00
A.M., My Dream Baby, Bisque Head, Dark Glass Sleep Eyes, Composition, 1925, 7 In. .. 550.00
A.M., My Dream Baby, Bisque, Bent Limb Composition Body, Christening Gown, 10 In. . 288.00
Advertising, Bud Man, Rubber, Flesh Color, Red Outfit, 1960s, 18 In. 175.00
Advertising, Cream Of Wheat, Cloth, Uncut, c.1915, 17 x 28 In. 105.00
Advertising, Pillsbury Doughboy, Poppin' Fresh, Squeeze Toy, 1971, 6 1/2 In. 12.00
Advertising, Rag, Sailor, Holland American Cruises, 1950s, 11 In. 95.00
Advertising, Texaco, Station Attendant, Tin Lithograph, 13 In. 45.00
Alabama Baby, All Cloth, Painted Facial Features, Ella Smith, c.1910, 14 In. ...1300.00 to 1450.00
Alexander dolls are listed in this category under Madame Alexander.
Alt Beck & Gottschalck, 1362, Bisque Socket Head, 4 Teeth, Synthetic Wig, 21 In. 275.00
Alt Beck & Gottschalck, Bisque, Sleep Eyes, Wobble Tongue, Jointed Body, 1830s, 28 In. 230.00
Alt Beck & Gottschalck, Bisque, Woven Braid, Muslin Body, Silk Gown, c.1880, 21 In. . 950.00
American Character, Betsy McCall, Mommy's Helper Outfit, 8 In. 200.00
American Character, Betsy McCall, Schoolgirl Outfit, 1957, 8 In. 150.00
American Character, Betsy McCall, Square Dance Outfit, 1958, 8 In. 200.00
American Character, Carol Ann Beery, Composition, Sleep Eyes, c.1935, 17 In. 550.00
Armand Marseille dolls are listed in this category under A.M.
Arranbee, Littlest Angel, Sleep Eyes, Walks, Sits, Turns Head, Outfits, 1950s, 10 In. 300.00
Automaton, Abraham Lincoln, Automaton, Plaster Head Moves Side To Side, Life Size .. 1380.00
Automaton, Birdcage, Continental, 11 In. 175.00
Automaton, Bisque, Windup, Arms Go Up & Down, Bird Chirps, 18 x 23 In. 138.00
Automaton, Harpsichord, Hands Move, Key Wind, 14-In. Base 2150.00
Automaton, La Bicycliste, Leopold Lambert, France, 1890 .... *Illus* 23722.00
Automaton, Magician, Table & Wand Changes Objects, Eyes & Arms Move, 46 In. .. 2200.00
Automaton, Singing Bird, Birdcage, Wooden Base, Handle, 8 Sides, France, 1900, 22 In. 2700.00
Averill, Bonnie Babe, 2 Lower Teeth, Painted Hair & Shoes, c.1926, 6 3/4 In. 920.00
Averill, Nancy & Sluggo, Cloth Swivel Head, Cloth Body, Stitch Jointed, 13 In., Pair 825.00
Bahr & Proschild, 204, Bisque, Sleep Eyes, Closed Mouth, Jointed Body, 11 In. 27000.00

Bahr & Proschild, 208, Socket Head, Brown Glass Inset Eyes, Blond Wig, Child, 14 In. . .   1900.00
Bahr & Proschild, 261, Bisque, 4 Teeth, Composition & Wooden Body, 1890, 17 In. . . .   1200.00
Bahr & Proschild, 394, Bisque Swivel Head, Dark Blue Glass Inset Eyes, 1890, 17 In. 700.00
Bahr & Proschild, 604, Baby, Bisque, Blue Sleep Eyes, Composition, 1910s, 22 In. 370.00
Barbie dolls are listed in this category under Mattel.
Barry Toy Co., Mammy Yokum, Box, c.1957, 14 In. 375.00
Beecher, Baby, Stockinet, Painted & Needle-Sculptured Face, Yarn Hair, 20 In. 2000.00
Beetle Bailey, Original Tags, Hamilton Gifts, Long Beach, Calif.   69.00
Bergmann dolls are also in this category under S & H and Simon & Halbig.
Bergmann, Bisque Head, Blue Sleep Eyes, Open Mouth, Light Brown Wig, 1916 . . . .   345.00
Bisque, Blue Enamel Eyes, Closed Mouth, 15 In. 2700.00
Bisque, Blue Glass Eyes, Pierced Ears, Closed Mouth, Brown Wig, Kid Body, 14 In. 315.00
Bisque, Blue Stationary Eyes, Blond Mohair Wig, Jointed, Late 19th Century, 5 In. 860.00
Bisque, Blue Stationary Glass Eyes, Open Mouth, 1 Blond, 1 Brunette, 7 In., Pair 260.00
Bisque, Brown Glass Eyes, Open Mouth, Blond Mohair Wig, 1916, 28 In. 195.00
Bisque, Brown Glass Eyes, Open Mouth, Papier-Mache Body, Painted Socks, Shoes, 9 In.   70.00
Bisque, Brown Glass Stationary Eyes, Closed Mouth, Blond Mohair Wig, Jointed, 4 In. . .   260.00
Bisque, Brown Sleep Eyes, Open Mouth, Blond Frizzy Mohair Wig, 7 In. 2070.00
Bisque, Character, Bisque Socket Head, Blue Painted Eyes, Pouty Mouth, 1910, 9 In. 1500.00
Bisque, Dark Set Eyes, Mohair Wig, 5-Piece Body, 7 In. 825.00
Bisque, Lady, Bisque Shoulder Head, Cameo Face, Blond Sculpted Hair, 1870, 12 In. . . .   750.00
Bisque, Lady, Bisque Shoulder Head, Cameo Face, Blond Sculpted Hair, 1875, 9 In. 950.00
Bisque, Lady, Bisque Shoulder Head, Painted Brown Hair, Blue Eyes, 1870, 10 In. 950.00
Bisque, Pale Swivel Head, Pale Blue Glass Eyes, 1869, 14 In. 9500.00
Bisque, Shoulder Head, Swivel, Blue Paperweight Eyes, Closed Mouth, 11 1/2 In. 1725.00
Bisque, Shoulder Head, Swivel, Cobalt Blue Eyes, Blond Mohair Wig, 14 In. 1840.00
Bisque, Socket Head, Amber Brown Almond-Shaped Eyes, Closed Mouth, 1884, 12 In. . .   6500.00
Bisque, Socket Head, Brown Glass Inset Eyes, Closed Mouth, Antique Costume, 12 In. . .   1800.00
Bisque, Socket Head, Brown Stationary Eyes, Composition, Jointed, 10 In. 1380.00
Bisque, Stationary Blue Glass Eyes, Closed Mouth, Blond Mohair Wig, 3 3/4 In., Pair . . .   345.00
Bisque, Swivel Head, Smiling, Pale Blue Glass Eyes, 1873, 16 In. 5800.00
Bisque, Swivel Neck, Brown Sleep Eyes, Closed Somber Mouth, Blue Dress, 6 In. 690.00
Black dolls are included in the Black category.
Boudoir, Composition Head, Brown Mohair, Heart-Shaped Locket, c.1920, 30 In. 85.00
Bru Jne, Articulated Wooden Arms, Ball Gown, 13 In. 7500.00
Bru Jne, Bebe Bru, Bisque, Swivel Head, Pale Blue Enamel Inset Eyes, 1880, 25 In. 21500.00
Bru Jne, Bebe, Bisque Head, Swivel, Blue-Lined Paperweight Eyes, 1870, 15 In. 9775.00
Bru Jne, Bisque Shoulder Head, Swivel, Closed Smiling Mouth, 16 In. 3740.00
Bru Jne, Bisque Swivel Head, Closed Mouth, Hint Of Smile, 13 In. 2600.00
Bru Jne, Bisque, Paperweight Eyes, Kid Arms, Silk Dress, 13 In. 16500.00
Bru Jne, Bisque, Swivel Head, Bisque Forearms, Dress, Kid Body, Bonnet, 22 In. 13500.00
Bruckner, Topsy-Turvy, Printed Features, Blond Hair, Red Outfit, 12 In. 635.00
Bruno Schmidt, Baby, Bisque, Sleep Eyes, 2 Upper Teeth, Bent-Limb Body, Dress, 12 In.   230.00
Buddy Lee, Cowboy, Hard Plastic, Lee Pants & Shirt, 13 In. 220.00
Buddy Lee, Plastic, Denim Jeans, Plaid Shirt, Cowboy Hat, Boots, 1959-1962, 14 In. 900.00
Buddy Lee, Plastic, Engineer, Denim Hat, Shirt, Overalls, 13 In.   . . . . *Illus*   300.00
Bye-Lo, Bisque Head, Blue Sleep Eyes, Closed Mouth, Blue Cotton Cape, 1923, 13 In. . . .   750.00

Doll, Buddy Lee,
Plastic, Engineer,
Denim Hat, Shirt,
Overalls, 13 In.

Doll, Effanbee, Baby
Tinyette Trousseau,
Doll Suitcase, With
Clothes, 1935, 8 In.

Bye-Lo, Celluloid Hands, All Original, 16 In. 550.00
Bye-Lo, Celluloid, Tin Sleep Eyes, Cloth Body, Original Clothes, 1920s, 17 In. 145.00
Bye-Lo, Sleep Eyes, Celluloid Hands, Dress Marked F.A.O. Schwarz, 10 In. 650.00
Bye-Lo, Sleep Eyes, Painted Hair, Cloth Body, Celluloid Hands, Baby Dress, 11 In. 86.00
Cameo, Giggles, All Original, 1946, 14 In. 795.00
Celluloid, George & Martha Washington, Japan, Prewar, 7 In. 90.00
Chad Valley, Snow White, White Felt Swivel Head, Black Wig, Seven Dwarfs, 16 In. 2200.00
Chase, Martha, Blond Hair, Blue Eyes, Early 20th Century, 12 1/2 In. 260.00
China, Center Part Curls, Painted Eyes, China Arms & Legs, c.1870, 9 In. 259.00
China, Shoulder Head, Blue Eyes, Cloth Body, Brown Wool Outfit, 24 In. 345.00
China, Shoulder Head, Blue Glass Eyes, Closed Mouth, 1860, 12 In. 2990.00
China, Shoulder Head, Blue Painted Eyes, 2-Tone Mouth Paint, Brown Wig, 18 In. 1955.00
China, Shoulder Head, Blue Painted Eyes, Cloth Body, Pink Outfit, 22 In. 750.00
China, Shoulder Head, Blue Painted Eyes, Cloth Body, White Undergarments, 27 In. 375.00
China, Shoulder Head, Braided Bun In Back, Cloth Body, Kid Hands, 8 1/8 In. 345.00
China, Shoulder Head, Brown Painted Eyes, Black Molded Hair, Pink Outfit, 15 1/2 In. ... 630.00
China, Shoulder Head, Green Bows, Cloth Body, Lace Dress, 1870, 16 3/4 In. 920.00
Cloth, Baby Girl, Large Blue Eyes, Brown Yarn Braids, Blue Skirt, 1940, 19 In. 200.00
Cloth, Baby Girl, Painted Blue Eyes, Bow-Shaped Mouth, 1940, 15 In. 300.00
Cloth, Baby, Blond Hair, Painted Face, c.1910, 19 1/2 In. 69.00
Cloth, Flat Face, Blue Eyes, Light Brown Yarn Wig, Period Pink Dress, 23 In. 175.00
Cloth, Flat Face, Brown Human Hair, Cloth Body, Period Red & White Dress, 30 In. 375.00
Cloth, The Gentleman Rider, Cloth Swivel Head, Brown Side Glancing Eyes, 24 In. 2700.00
Cloth, Wax Head, Glass Eyes, Kid Arms, 19th Century, 14 In. 280.00
Darrow, Leather Shoulder Head, Black Painted Hair, Cloth Body, 1866, 16 In. 185.00
Dean, Rag, Her Dolly, Intact, Box 1600.00
Denamur, Le Baby, Bisque Socket Head, Cobalt Blue Paperweight Eyes, 15 In. 2100.00
Dennis The Menace, Vinyl, Red Jumper, Striped Shirt, Dennis Play Products, 1957, 13 In. 165.00
Dick Clark, Name On Jacket, 27 In. 525.00
Door Of Hope Mission, Bride, Wooden Head, Cloth Body, Chinese Tag, 11 In. 1350.00
Door Of Hope Mission, Mourner, Chinese, 11 1/2 In. 1425.00
Door Of Hope Mission, Widow, Chinese, 11 In. 1400.00
Dressel, Bisque, 2 Upper Teeth, Auburn Mohair Wig, Articulated Body, 1920s, 14 In. 175.00
Dressel, Bisque, Open Mouth, Fully Jointed Body, Cotton Dress, Hat, 1910s, 21 In. 201.00
Dressel, Uncle Sam, Bisque, Pointed Chin & Nose, Wooden Jointed Body, c.1900, 13 In. .. 1800.00
Dresser, Madame Pompadour, Hand Painted, Porcelain, E & R, Germany, 6 In. 40.00
Effanbee, Anne Of Green Gables, Composition, Green Sleep Eyes, Red Mohair, 16 In. 400.00
Effanbee, Anne Shirley, Composition, Brown Sleep Eyes, Human Hair, Tag, 15 In. 450.00
Effanbee, Baby Dainty, Composition, Romper, Shoes, 1926, 15 In. 125.00
Effanbee, Baby Tinyette Trousseau, Doll Suitcase, With Clothes, 1935, 8 In. ....*Illus* 1200.00
Effanbee, Baby, Black, Composition, Black Eyes, Molded Curls, Floral Romper, 11 In. ... 325.00
Effanbee, Baby, Composition Head, Blue Side-Glancing Eyes, 1930, 8 In. 225.00
Effanbee, Baby, Composition Head, Swivel Neck, Blue Flirty Eyes, Closed Mouth, 21 In. 550.00
Effanbee, Baby, Fairy Princess, Composition Head, Blue Eyes, 1935, 5 1/2 In. 425.00
Effanbee, Baby, Tinyette, Composition Head, Blue Side-Glancing Eyes, 1935, 8 In. 250.00

Doll, Effanbee, Patsy Babyette Twins, Boy & Girl,
Composition, 8 1/2 In., Pair

Doll, Effanbee,
Patsy Ruth,
Composition,
Sleep Eyes,
Cloth Body,
26 In.

Effanbee, Betty Bounce, Composition, Green Sleep Eyes, Open Mouth, 4 Teeth, 18 In. . . .   375.00
Effanbee, Dy-Dee Baby, Rubber, Basket, Blanket, Accessories, Booklet, c.1930, 15 In. . .   215.00
Effanbee, George & Martha Washington, Composition Heads, Blue Eyes, 1939, 9 In. 550.00
Effanbee, Girl, Shoulder Head, Gray Sleep Eyes, Open Mouth, 25 In. 175.00
Effanbee, Howdy Doody, Sleep Eyes, Plaid Shirt, Jeans, Cowboy Boots, 1948, 23 In. 400.00
Effanbee, Ice Queen, Composition Head, Sleep Eyes, Human Hair Wig, 15 In. 1500.00
Effanbee, Marilee, Composition, Brown Sleep Eyes, 4 Teeth, Brown Curls, 1935, 29 In. . .   500.00
Effanbee, Mickey, Composition Head & Hands, Cloth Body & Legs, 23 1/2 In. 105.00
Effanbee, Patsy & Skippy, Texas Centennial, Composition Heads, 14 & 15 In., Pair 4000.00
Effanbee, Patsy Ann, Composition, Blue Tin Sleep Eyes, Painted Hair, Bent Arm, 19 In. . .   325.00
Effanbee, Patsy Ann, Composition, Green Sleep Eyes, 5-Piece Body, Bent Arm, 19 In. . . .   500.00
Effanbee, Patsy Baby, Composition Head, Brown Side-Glancing Eyes, 14 In. 300.00
Effanbee, Patsy Baby, Composition Head, Green Sleep Eyes, Closed Mouth, 1940, 11 In. .   425.00
Effanbee, Patsy Baby, Composition, Blue Sleep Eyes, Molded Hair, Heart Bracelet, 11 In.   325.00
Effanbee, Patsy Babyette Twins, Boy & Girl, Composition, 8 1/2 In., Pair . . . . *Illus*   500.00
Effanbee, Patsy Joan, Composition Head, Green Sleep Eyes, Rosebud Mouth, 16 1/2 In. . .   425.00
Effanbee, Patsy Joan, Rabbit Fur Coat, Matching Silk-Lined Hat, 16 In. 850.00
Effanbee, Patsy Jr., Composition, Painted Brown Eyes, Molded Hair, 5-Piece Body, 11 In.   300.00
Effanbee, Patsy Ruth, Composition, Sleep Eyes, Cloth Body, 26 In. . . . . *Illus*   1150.00
Effanbee, Patsy, Chinese, 14 In. 1850.00
Effanbee, Patsy, Composition Head, Blue-Green Tin Sleep Eyes, 1920, 30 In. 3000.00
Effanbee, Patsy, Composition Head, Wig, Brown Sleep Eyes, 1930, 13 1/2 In. 375.00
Effanbee, Patsy, Right-Glancing Eyes, Original Dress, Hat, 1930, 13 In. 92.00
Effanbee, Patsyette, Composition Head, Brown Eyes, 1-Piece Romper, 9 1/2 In. 250.00
Effanbee, Patsyette, Composition Head, Wig, Brown Eyes, 1931, 9 1/2 In. 375.00
Effanbee, Patsykins, Black, Composition, Painted Eyes, Yarn Plaits, c.1932, 11 In. 850.00
Effanbee, Patsykins, Composition Head, Brown Side-Glancing Eyes, 11 1/2 In. 325.00
Effanbee, Rosemary, Composition Head, Blue-Green Tin Sleep Eyes, 1926, 24 In. 850.00
Effanbee, Skippy Aviator, Composition Head, Blue Side-Glancing Eyes, 1940, 15 In. 1250.00
Effanbee, Skippy Soldier, Composition Head, Blue Side-Glancing Eyes, 1940, 14 In. 450.00
Effanbee, Skippy Soldier, Composition Head, Blue Side-Glancing Eyes, 1943, 14 In. 400.00
Effanbee, Topsy, Composition Head, Brown Cloth Torso, Black Eyes, 12 In. 350.00
Effanbee, Wee Patsy, Brown Composition Head, Brown Eyes, 1932, 6 In. 450.00
Fashion, Bisque Socket Head, Blond Mohair, Set Eyes, Gold Dress, France, 17 In. . . . *Illus*   3000.00
Fashion, Bisque Swivel Head, Blue Spiral Eyes, Closed Mouth, France, 1872, 19 In. 5800.00
Fashion, Bisque, Blue Glass Inset Eyes, Kid Body, Antique Dress, Hat, c.1890, 19 In. 650.00
Fashion, Bisque, Blue Paperweight Eyes, Pierced Ears, Kid Body, 13 1/2 In. 1550.00
Fashion, Bisque, Painted Blue Eyes, Kid Body, Regional Clothing, France, 18 In. 1995.00
French, Bisque Socket Head, Blue Glass Sleep Eyes, Open Mouth, 1920, 10 In. 1600.00
French, Bisque Swivel Head, Gray Glass Inset Eyes, Blond Mohair Wig, 1872, 12 In. 5000.00
French, Bisque, Domed Bisque Shoulder Head, Brown Curly Hair, Barrois, 1860, 19 In. . .   2600.00
French, Bisque, Shoulder Head, Blue Paperweight Eyes, Closed Mouth, 17 In. 4025.00
French, Bisque, Shoulder Head, Swivel, Blue Paperweight Eyes, Closed Mouth, 16 In. 1495.00
French, Jester, Bisque, Blue, White Striped Jester's Hat, 1890, 2 3/4 In. 400.00
French, Polichinelle, Bisque, Blue Glass Eyes, Open Mouth, 18 In. 1500.00
French, Porcelain, Shoulder Head, Blond Mohair Wig, Cobalt Blue Eyes, 28 In. 6500.00
French, Pressed Bisque Socket Head, Amber Brown Glass Eyes, Composition, 15 In. 7500.00
French, Pressed Bisque Socket Head, Blue Glass Paperweight Eyes, 1885, 20 In. 6600.00
Frozen Charlie, China, Blue Eyes, Blond Hair, Arms Out Front, Closed Mouth, 16 In. . . .   425.00
Frozen Charlotte, China Head & Body, Pink Tint, Painted Blue Eyes, Painted Hair, 11 In.   700.00
Frozen Charlotte, China Head, Painted Blue Eyes, Molded Blond Hair, 15 1/2 In. 525.00
G.I. Joe figures are listed in the Toy category.
Gaultier, 1, Bisque Head, Paperweight Inset Eyes, Jointed Wooden Body, c.1892, 11 In. . .   3300.00
Gaultier, Bisque Swivel Head, Brown Inset Eyes, French Silk Clothes, Bebe, 1885, 29 In.   5300.00
Gaultier, Bisque, Enamel Eyes, Stuck-Out Tongue, c.1884, 10 In. 4000.00
Gaultier, Bisque, Paperweight Eyes, Wood & Composition Body, Dressed, Child, 30 In. . .   5450.00
Gebruder Heubach dolls are also in this category under Heubach.
Gebruder Heubach, 711, Girl, Bisque Socket Head, Blue Glass Sleep Eyes, 1917, 8 In. . .   1050.00
Gebruder Heubach, 6969, Character, Bisque Socket Head, Dark Blue Eyes, 1912, 16 In. .   1800.00
Gebruder Heubach, 6970, Character, Bisque Socket Head, Pink, Closed Mouth, 11 In. . . .   1050.00
Gebruder Heubach, 7622, Character, Bisque Socket Head, Pink, 1915, 14 In. 1400.00
Gebruder Heubach, 7644, Bisque Shoulder Head, Forelock Curl, Kid Body, 22 In. 1100.00
Gebruder Heubach, 7802, Character, Bisque Socket Head, Pink, Pale Blue Eyes, 20 In. . .   1000.00

Gebruder Heubach, 7911, Character, Bisque Socket Head, Closed Mouth, 1915, 11 In. .. 1050.00
Gebruder Heubach, Bisque, Sleep Eyes, Painted Features, Antique Clothing, 17 In. 1295.00
Gebruder Heubach, Character, Dome Bisque Socket Head, Blue Intaglio Eyes, 7 In. 350.00
Gebruder Heubach, Girl, Bisque Socket Head, Dark Blue Intaglio Eyes, 1910, 15 In. 6400.00
Gebruder Kuhnlenz, 41, Bisque, Set Brown Eyes, Open Mouth, 2 Teeth, Mohair, 12 In. .. 4200.00
Gebruder Kuhnlenz, Bisque Shoulder Head, Kid Body, Blue Eyes, Human Hair, 15 In. .. 425.00
Georgene Novelties, Beloved Belindy, Brown Muslin, White Button Eyes, 18 In. 3800.00
German, Baby, Porcelain Head, Pink Tint, Blond Tufted Hair, Closed Mouth, 1855, 6 In. . 2500.00
German, Bisque Dome Socket Head, Googly, 5 Piece Body, Toddler, 1915, 8 1/2 In. 6900.00
German, Bisque Head, Blue Sleep Glass Eyes, Open Mouth, Dark Blond Wig, 24 In. 230.00
German, Bisque Shoulder Head, Blue Eyes, Human Hair, Cloth & Kid Body, 13 1/2 In. .. 450.00
German, Bisque Shoulder Head, Woman, Brown Hair, Cobalt Eyes, 22 In. 1700.00
German, Bisque Socket Head, Blue Glass Sleep Eyes, Brunette Mohair Wig, Child, 13 In. 875.00
German, Bisque Socket Head, Blue Sleep Eyes, Composition, Ball Jointed, 26 In. 345.00
German, Bisque Socket Head, Brown Glass Sleep Eyes, Brunette Wig, Toddler, 4 1/2 In. . 450.00
German, Bisque Socket Head, Brown Glass Sleep Eyes, Closed Mouth, Pouty, 23 In. 7000.00
German, Bisque Socket Head, Child, Blue Sleep Eyes, 4 Teeth, Human Hair, 18 In. 500.00
German, Bisque, Lady, Sculpted Upswept Hair, Pierced Ears, Silk Gown, c.1885, 14 In. . 525.00
German, Bisque, Sculpted Hair, Closed Mouth, Leather Arms, Antique Costume, 23 In. .. 450.00
German, Bisque, Violin Player, Paperweight Eyes, Wooden Torso, Silk Dress, 13 In. 1600.00
German, Character, Baby Stuart, Bisque Socket Head, Bisque Bonnet, Floral, 1915, 13 In. 1400.00
German, China Head, Blue Painted Eyes, Closed Mouth, Cloth Body, 22 In. 180.00
German, Domed Porcelain Shoulder Head, Painted Blue Eyes, Closed Mouth, 14 In. 575.00
German, Domed Socket Head, Boy, Closed Mouth, Blond Hair, 1910, 13 In. 1600.00
German, Girl, Bisque Head, Large Brown Glass Sleep Eyes, Closed Mouth, 1925, 18 In. . 7500.00
German, Jenny Lind, China Head, Black Hair, Cloth Body, Kid Hands, 21 1/2 In. 460.00
German, Mary Had A Little Lamb, Bisque Socket Head, Blue Glass Eyes, 7 In. 3000.00
German, Parian Head, Sausage-Curl Hair, Bisque Hands, Cloth, Late 19th Century, 20 In. 115.00
German, Porcelain Head, Feet, Painted Hair, Straw Cloth Body, 12 In. 55.00
German, Porcelain Shoulder Head, Black Hair, Blue Eyes, Closed Mouth, 1865, 17 In. 950.00
German, Porcelain Shoulder Head, Cameo Face, Black Hair, Cobalt Blue Eyes, 9 In. 1100.00
German, Porcelain, Lady, Looped & Twisted Curls, Muslin Body, Silk Costume, 26 In. .. 2200.00
German, Shoulder Head, Black Hair, Blue Painted Eyes, Cloth Body, Pink, 19 In. 220.00
Greiner, Papier-Mache, Black Hair, Blue Eyes, Blue Print Cotton Dress, Greiner, 28 In. .. 460.00
Half Dolls are listed in the Pinchushion category.
Handwerck, 5, Bisque, Blue Sleep Eyes, Open Mouth, 4 Teeth, Synthetic Wig, 28 In. 475.00
Handwerck, 99, Bisque Socket Head, Open Mouth, 4 Teeth, Synthetic Wig, 23 In. 450.00
Handwerck, 99, Bisque Socket Head, Sleep Eyes, Open Mouth, 4 Teeth, c.1900, 22 In. ... 910.00
Handwerck, 109, Bisque Socket Head, Brown Sleep Eyes, 4 Teeth, Mohair, 19 In. 450.00
Handwerck, 109, Bisque Socket Head, Brown Sleep Eyes, Open Mouth, 4 Teeth, 22 In. .. 875.00
Handwerck, 109, Bisque, Blue Sleep Eyes, Open Mouth, 4 Teeth, Human Hair, 17 1/2 In. 420.00
Handwerck, Bisque Head, Blue Glass Sleep Eyes, Open Mouth, Composition, 20 In. 316.00
Handwerck, Bisque Head, Blue Glass Sleep Eyes, Open Mouth, Fully Jointed, 27 In. 373.00
Handwerck, Bisque Head, Blue Glass Sleep Eyes, Open Mouth, Jointed, 24 In. 207.00
Handwerck, Bisque Head, Brown Glass Sleep Eyes, Open Mouth, Blond Wig, 20 In. 287.00
Handwerck, Bisque Socket Head, Brown Glass Sleep Eyes, Blond Wig, Child, 31 In. 1700.00
Handwerck, Bisque Socket Head, Brown Sleep Eyes, Open Mouth, Human Hair, 18 In. .. 300.00
Handwerck, Bisque, 4 Porcelain Teeth, Wooden, Ball-Jointed, c.1900, 31 In. 1150.00
Hasbro, Raggedy Ann, 1980s, 12 In. 25.00
Hertel Schwab, 151, Baby, Bisque, Painted Hair, 5-Piece Bent-Limb Body, 20 In. 460.00
Hertel Schwab, 165, Bisque Socket Head, Gray Glass Googly Sleep Eyes, 1920, 15 In. .. 5200.00
Hertel Schwab, 172, Dome Bisque Socket Head, Gray Googly Sleep Eyes, 1920, 14 In. .. 4700.00
Hertel Schwab, Character, Bisque Socket Head, Blue Glass Eyes, 1912, 17 In. 8250.00
Hertel Schwab, Jubilee Googly, Bisque Socket Head, Brown Glass Sleep Eyes, 10 In. ... 2600.00
Hertel Schwab, Skippy Baby, Bisque Head, c.1912, 9 In. 500.00
Heubach dolls are also in this category under Gebruder Heubach.
Heubach, 300, Baby, Bisque Socket Head, Blue Sleep Eyes, 4 Teeth, Mohair, 17 In. 250.00
Heubach, 8192, Bisque, Blue Sleep Eyes, Wheat-Blond Human Hair, Braids, 15 In. 650.00
Heubach, Baby Boy, Bisque Socket Head, Blue Glass Sleep Eyes, Brunette Mohair, 9 In. . 2100.00
Heubach, Bisque Head, Blue Glass Sleep Eyes, Open Mouth, Composition, 22 In. 149.00
Heubach, Bisque Head, Brown Glass Sleep Eyes, Closed Mouth, 1920, 9 In. 230.00
Heubach, Bisque Shoulder Head, Brown Glass Eyes, Human Hair Wig, 12 In. 60.00
Heubach, Bisque, Screaming Mouth, Furrowed Brow, Overalls, Toddler, 10 1/2 In. 690.00

Doll, Fashion, Bisque Socket
Head, Blond Mohair, Set Eyes,
Gold Dress, France, 17 In.

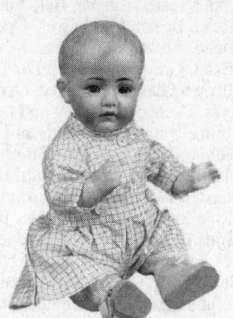

Doll, K * R, 127, Baby,
Bisque Dome Head, Sleep
Eyes, Composition, 9 1/2 In.

Doll, Lenci, Mannequin, Felt
Swivel Head, Wooden Arms,
Legs, Side-Glancing, 38 In.

Heubach Koppelsdorf, 312, Bisque, Human Hair Wig, Jointed Wood, Dress, 24 In. 220.00
Heubach Koppelsdorf, 312/SUR, Bisque, Sleep Eyes, Open Mouth, Mohair Wig, 25 In. . . 200.00
Heubach Koppelsdorf, Bisque, Ball-Jointed Body, Sleep Eyes, Open Mouth, 23 In. 115.00
Heubach Koppelsdorf, Blue Sleep Eyes, Open Mouth, Composition, 12 1/2 In. 145.00
Horsman, Bright Star, Composition Socket Head, Brown Sleep Eyes, Child's, 1938, 17 In. 1050.00
Horsman, Mary Poppins, Box, 1970s, 12 In. 125.00
Huret, Man, Gutta Percha Body, 17 In. 17500.00
Huret, Woman, Wooden Body, 17 In. 7000.00
Ideal, Baby Snooks, Composition, Posable Arms & Legs, c.1938, 12 In. 55.00
Ideal, Betsy McCall, Blue Dress, Brunette, 1952, 14 In. 225.00
Ideal, Betsy Wetsy, In Bathtub, Box, 12 In. 250.00
Ideal, Deanna Durbin, Blue-Green Sleep Eyes, Dark Brown Human Hair, 1938, 15 In. . . . 200.00
Ideal, Deanna Durbin, Composition, Brown Hair, Blue Sleep Eyes, 20 In. 410.00
Ideal, Mortimer Snerd, Composition Head, Wire Mesh Limbs, Jacket, c.1940, 12 In. 58.00
Ideal, Patti Playpal, 1959, 35 In. 57.00
Ideal, Patti Playpal, Original Dress, 36 In. 275.00
Ideal, Pinocchio, Composition Socket Head, Painted Googly Eyes, Composition, 11 In. . . 650.00
Ideal, Strawman, Pressed Ivory Face, Red Nose, Blond Hair, Cloth, 1940, 17 In. 2700.00
Ideal, Toni, Blond Nylon Hair, Blouse, Red Jumper, Shoes, 20 In. 475.00
Ideal, Toni, Plastic, Blue Sleep Eyes, Blond Nylon Wig, Tag, Box, c.1949, 14 In. . . 700.00 to 925.00
Ideal, Toni, Play-Wave Hair, Dressed, Box, 14 In. 925.00
Indian dolls are listed in the Indian category.
Jensen, Gladdie, Bisque Head, Short Brown Hair, Blue Glass Eyes, 15 In. 2400.00
Jumeau, 8, Bisque Socket Head, Paperweight Eyes, Human Hair, Pull-String Crier, 19 In. 4900.00
Jumeau, Bisque Head, Blue Paperweight Eyes, Closed Mouth, Wool Dress, 1880, 17 In. . . 575.00
Jumeau, Bisque Socket Head, Deep Blue Paperweight Eyes, 27 In. 7250.00
Jumeau, Bisque, Fashion, Glass Inset Eyes, Mohair Wig, 7 x 7 1/2 In. 4100.00
Jumeau, Bisque, Hint Of Smile, Blue Paperweight Eyes, Jumeau Shoes, 22 In. 5995.00
Jumeau, Bisque, Paperweight Eyes, Human Hair, Says Mama-Papa, Child, 1880s, 19 In. . 4900.00
Jumeau, Bisque, Swivel Head, Blue Glass Enamel Inset Eyes, Closed Mouth, 20 In. 7250.00
K * R, 58, Bisque Socket Head, Blue Sleep Eyes, Open Mouth, 4 Teeth, Mohair, 23 In. . . 450.00
K * R, 62, Bisque Socket Head, Set Brown Eyes, Synthetic Wig, 4 Teeth, 25 1/2 In. 350.00
K * R, 76, Bisque Socket Head, Blue Sleep Eyes, Open Mouth, 4 Teeth, 29 In. 600.00
K * R, 85, Bisque Socket Head, Blue Sleep Eyes, Open Mouth, 4 Teeth, Mohair, 33 In. . . . 1450.00
K * R, 100, Character, Brown Bisque Socket Head, Brown Intaglio Eyes, 1912, 11 In. . . . 550.00
K * R, 101, Bisque Socket Head, Painted Blue Eyes, Blond Mohair, Jointed, 13 1/2 In. . . . 2500.00
K * R, 112, Character, Bisque Socket Head, Blue Eyes, Closed Mouth, 1910, 18 In. 15000.00
K * R, 114, Bisque Socket Head, Dark Blue Glass Sleep Eyes, Closed Mouth, 1912, 26 In. 13000.00
K * R, 114A, Bisque, Boy, Open-Close Mouth, Sleep Eyes, Jointed Toddler Body, 16 In. . 3995.00
K * R, 115A, Phillip, Bisque Socket Head, Brown Glass Sleep Eyes, 16 In. 3600.00
K * R, 116A, Character, Bisque Socket Head, Blue Sleep Eyes, Closed Mouth, 12 In. 3600.00
K * R, 118, Character, Bisque Socket Head, Brown Glass Sleep Eyes, 1915, 14 In. 900.00
K * R, 118A, Bisque, 2 Porcelain Upper Teeth, Wooden Bent-Limb Body, 11 In. 1500.00

K * R, 122, Bisque, Sleep Eyes, Upper Teeth, Tongue, Ball-Jointed Body, c.1915, 24 In. . . 2700.00
K * R, 126, Baby, Bisque Socket Head, Brown Flirty Eyes, Open Mouth, 2 Teeth, 24 In. . 675.00
K * R, 126, Baby, Bisque Socket Head, Brown Glass Eyes, Key Wind, 24 In. 950.00
K * R, 126, Baby, Bisque Socket Head, Gray Glass Sleep Eyes, Open Mouth, 1920, 8 In. . 950.00
K * R, 126, Bisque Socket Head, Brown Glass Sleep Eyes, Open Mouth, Toddler, 23 In. . 1400.00
K * R, 126, Bisque, Flirty Sleep Eyes, Composition & Wood Body, Toddler, 1930s, 20 In. 635.00
K * R, 126, Bisque, Sleep Eyes, Spring Tongue, 5-Piece Bent-Limb Body, Toddler, 24 In. 750.00
K * R, 126, Bisque, Sleep Eyes, Wobble Tongue, Wooden Body, Dress, 20 In. 575.00
K * R, 126, Boy, Chocolate Brown Sleep Eyes, Open Mouth, Hat, 28 In. 1995.00
K * R, 127, Baby, Bisque Dome Head, Sleep Eyes, Composition, 9 1/2 In. . . . .*Illus* 245.00
K * R, 192, Bisque Socket Head, Blue Sleep Eyes, Open Mouth, 4 Teeth, 20 1/2 In. 500.00
K * R, 290, Bisque Socket Head, Blue Glass Sleep Eyes, Blond Mohair Wig, Child, 16 In. 700.00
K * R, Baby, Blue Glass Sleep Eyes, Open Mouth, Blond Wig, 13 In. 258.00
K * R, Bisque Head, Blue Glass Sleep Eyes, Open Mouth, Henna Mohair Wig, 20 In. 490.00
K * R, Bisque Socket Head, Blue Glass Sleep Eyes, Blond Human Hair, 1912, 21 In. 6200.00
K * R, Bisque Socket Head, Blue, Gray Painted Eyes, Closed Mouth, 1910, 19 In. 5000.00
K * R, Bisque Socket Head, Brown Glass Sleep Eyes, Open Mouth, 1920, 9 In. 975.00
K * R, Bisque, Pouty, Wooden Ball-Jointed Body, Embroidered Costume, 15 In. 2300.00
K * R, Bisque, Socket Head, Blue Glass Sleep Eyes, Closed Mouth, Child, 1912, 21 In. . . 4750.00
K * R, Celluloid Head, Sleep Eyes, Papier-Mache Jointed Body, Child, 32 In. 260.00
K * R, Gretchen, Bisque Socket Head, Brown Glass Sleep Eyes, 1912, 18 In. 9000.00
K * R, Gretchen, Bisque Socket Head, Gray Painted Eyes, 1910, 15 In. 3100.00
K * R, Hans, Bisque Socket Head, Blue Eyes, Brunette Mohair Wig, 16 In. 3100.00
K * R, Marie, Bisque Socket Head, Blue Eyes, Brunette Mohair, 1910, 12 In. 2100.00
K * R, Marie, Bisque Socket Head, Blue Outlined Eyes, Closed Mouth, 20 In. 5750.00
K * R, Marie, Bisque Socket Head, Gray Eyes, Closed Mouth, 1910, 15 In. 2400.00
K * R, Mein Liebling, Bisque, Sleep Eyes, Closed Mouth, Lace Costume, c.1912, 15 In. . 4300.00
K * R, Phillip, Bisque Socket Head, Blue Glass Sleep Eyes, 1910, 12 In. 2300.00
K * R, Phillip, Dome Bisque Socket Head, Brown Glass Sleep Eyes, 15 In. 4000.00
Kamkins, Boy, Cloth, Blue Eyes, Bobbed Mohair Wig, Stitch Jointed Limbs, 1930, 18 In. 900.00
Kamkins, Cloth Swivel Head, Painted Blue Eyes, Mohair, Cloth Body, 19 In. 575.00
Kamkins, Cloth, Painted Features, Mohair Wig, Undergarments, Stamped, 19 In. 1150.00
Kathe Kruse, 162738, Girl, Painted Face, Human Hair Braids, c.1935, 17 In. 1600.00
Kathe Kruse, Boy, Oil-Painted Cloth Swivel Head, Blue Eyes, Blond Wig, Tag, 20 In. . . . 950.00
Kathe Kruse, Character, All Stockinet, Painted Features, Disc-Jointed, 13 In. 5465.00
Kathe Kruse, Character, Brown Painted Hair, Brown Painted Eyes, Closed Mouth, 17 In. . 2900.00
Kathe Kruse, Character, Brown Short Hair, Amber Green Eyes, Closed Mouth, 18 In. . . . 2500.00
Kathe Kruse, Character, Cloth, Amber Green Eyes, Pouty Mouth, 1912, 17 In. 2600.00
Kathe Kruse, Character, Cloth, Brown Painted Eyes, Pouty Mouth, 1930, 14 In. 2900.00
Kathe Kruse, Character, Gray Eyes, Closed Mouth, Stitch-Jointed Arms, c.1923, 17 In. . . 3600.00
Kathe Kruse, Girl, Stationary Head, Pouty, Muslin Body, Jointed Legs, Dressed, 14 In. . . 2500.00
Kathy Kruse, Character, Pouty Lips, Disc-Jointed Legs & Arms, Linen Suit, 17 In. 2900.00
Kestner, 103, Bisque Socket Head, Ball-Jointed Composition Body, 1910, 27 In. 3000.00
Kestner, 128, Bisque Socket Head, Blue Glass Sleep Eyes, Closed Mouth, Child, 19 In. . . 3100.00
Kestner, 128, Bisque, Brown Eyes, Auburn Mohair, Jointed Composition Body, 19 In. . . . 2100.00
Kestner, 129, Bisque Socket Head, Brown Glass Sleep Eyes, Child, 1895, 23 In. 950.00
Kestner, 143, Bisque, Sleep Eyes, 2 Upper Teeth, Fully Articulated, 13 1/2 In. 635.00
Kestner, 143, Bisque, Sleep Eyes, Composition & Wooden Ball-Jointed Body, 12 In. 825.00
Kestner, 143, Bisque, Socket Head, Brown Glass Sleep Eyes, Open Mouth, 1915, 12 In. . . 1200.00
Kestner, 146, Bisque Socket Head, Brown Sleep Eyes, Open Mouth, 4 Teeth, 28 In. 500.00
Kestner, 150, Baby, Bisque, Gray Glass Sleep Eyes, Brunette Wig, 1900, 8 In. 800.00
Kestner, 160, Bisque Socket Head, Brown Sleep Eyes, 4 Teeth, Human Hair, 16 In. 750.00
Kestner, 162, Fashion, Bisque Socket Head, Brown Sleep Eyes, 1910, 19 In. 1500.00
Kestner, 164, Bisque Socket Head, Brown Sleep Eyes, Open Mouth, 4 Teeth, 30 In. 900.00
Kestner, 165, Bisque Socket Head, Googly, Mohair Wig, 5-Piece Body, Toddler, 11 In. . . 3750.00
Kestner, 167, Bisque Socket Head, Blue Glass Sleep Eyes, Open Mouth, Child, 16 In. . . . 650.00
Kestner, 167, Bisque, Socket Head, Blue Glass Sleep Eyes, Open Mouth, Child, 15 In. . . . 1700.00
Kestner, 171, Bisque Socket Head, Brown Sleep Eyes, Open Mouth, 4 Teeth, 21 1/2 In. . . 775.00
Kestner, 171, Bisque, Blue Sleep Eyes, Open Mouth, 4 Teeth, Human Hair, 28 In. 425.00
Kestner, 211, Bisque Socket Head, Blue Sleep Eyes, Blond Mohair, Toddler, 11 In. 950.00
Kestner, 213, Chinese Baby, Bisque, Upper Teeth, Antique Silk Costume, c.1910, 13 In. . . 3200.00
Kestner, 214, Azure Blue Sleep Eyes, Molded Features, Blond Wig, 19 In. 995.00
Kestner, 221, Bisque Head, Brown Glass Googly Eyes, Closed Mouth, 11 In. 6750.00

Kestner, 221, Bisque, Googly Eyes, Bobbed Wig, Jointed Body, Toddler, 11 In. 8400.00
Kestner, 247, Bisque, Composition, Blue Sleep Eyes, 2 Teeth, Wooden, Toddler, 18 In. . . 2000.00
Kestner, 260, Bisque, Sleep Eyes, Tiny Teeth, Wooden Ball-Jointed Body, c.1915, 12 In. . 650.00
Kestner, 260, Bisque, Sleep Eyes, Wooden Ball-Jointed Toddler Body, c.1915, 26 In. 1800.00
Kestner, Baby Jean, Dome Bisque Socket Head, Brown Sleep Eyes, 2 Teeth, 11 In. 675.00
Kestner, Baby, Bisque Head, Brown Glass Sleep Eyes, 9 1/2 In. 175.00
Kestner, Baby, Dome Bisque Socket Head, Brown Eyes, Open Mouth, 2 Teeth, 13 1/2 In. 325.00
Kestner, Bisque Head, Blue Glass Sleep Eyes, Blond Wig, Open Mouth, 22 In. 258.00
Kestner, Bisque Head, Blue Glass Sleep Eyes, Open Mouth, Brown Wig, 15 1/2 In. 865.00
Kestner, Bisque Head, Blue Sleep Eyes, Open Mouth, Pink Cotton Dress, 16 In. 1095.00
Kestner, Bisque Head, Brown Glass Sleep Eyes, Closed Pouty Mouth, 13 1/2 In. 2530.00
Kestner, Bisque Head, Sleeping Brown Glass Eyes, Open Mouth, Blond Wig, 15 In. 632.00
Kestner, Bisque Socket Head, Blue Glass Sleep Eyes, Open Mouth, 23 In. 4800.00
Kestner, Bisque Socket Head, Brown Glass Sleep Eyes, Open Mouth, Child, 15 In. 725.00
Kestner, Bisque Swivel Head, Brown Glass Sleep Eyes, Open Mouth, 1895, 6 In. 700.00
Kestner, Bisque, Brown Glass Sleep Eyes, Closed Mouth, Blond Mohair Wig, 4 In. 1265.00
Kestner, Bisque, Googly, Side Curls, Dimples, Military Uniform, Toddler, 14 In. 6500.00
Kestner, Bisque, Shoulder Head, Blue Glass Paperweight Eyes, Open Mouth, 17 In. 430.00
Kestner, Hilda, 2 Upper Teeth, Composition & Wooden Bent-Limb Body, 1914, 20 In. . . 3600.00
Kestner, Hilda, Bisque Socket Head, Blue Glass Sleep Eyes, Open Mouth, 1914, 21 In. . . 4000.00
Kestner, Hilda, Bisque, Brown Glass Sleep Eyes, Open Mouth, Teeth, c.1914, 17 In. 2400.00
Kestner, Hilda, Bisque, Domed Socket Head, Painted Baby Hair, 1914, 14 In. 2600.00
Kestner, Hilda, Bisque, Sleep Eyes, Open Mouth, Antique Costume, c.1915, 11 In. 2200.00
Kestner, Hilda, Blue Sleep Eyes, Open Mouth, Blond Wig, 16 In. 1265.00
Kewpie dolls are listed in the Kewpie category.
Kley & Hahn, 548, Character, Bisque Socket Head, Blue Glass Sleep Eyes, 1912, 24 In. . . 1900.00
Knickerbocker, Indian, Sleep Eyes, Leather Outfit, Leather Moccasins 450.00
Knickerbocker, Jiminy Cricket, Composition, Jointed, Cloth Clothes, 10 In. 400.00
Knickerbocker, Little Lulu, Cloth, Black Eyes, Red Dress, 17 In. 475.00
Knickerbocker, Raggedy Ann & Andy, Bean Bag, 1971, 10 In., Pair 415.00
Knickerbocker, Raggedy Ann, 1968, 48 In. 195.00
Leather, Painted Blue Eyes, Human Hair, Silk Dress & Bonnet, 21 In. 2000.00
Lenci, 109, Girl, Felt Swivel Head, Brown Side-Glancing Eyes, 1930, 23 In. 950.00
Lenci, 1005, Boxer, Cloth, Blue & Red Striped Shirt & Hat, White Shorts, 17 In. 2800.00
Lenci, 1500, Character, Felt Swivel Head, Brown Eyes, Cloth, Jointed, 1928, 19 In. 1300.00
Lenci, 1500, Character, Felt Swivel Head, Gray, Green Eyes, Closed Mouth, Cloth, 18 In. 850.00
Lenci, 300, Rodolfo, Felt Swivel Head, Painted Features, Blue Eyes, Cloth, 17 In. 2100.00
Lenci, Boy, Felt Swivel Head, Brown Side-Glancing Eyes, Brown Tie, Jacket, 17 In. 1900.00
Lenci, Boy, Felt Swivel Head, Brown Side-Glancing Eyes, Closed Mouth, 15 In. 3800.00
Lenci, Boy, Felt, Brown Painted Eyes, Light Brown Mohair Wig, 1920, 17 In. 460.00
Lenci, Child, Felt Swivel Head, Brown Side-Glancing Eyes, Closed Mouth, 1930, 17 In. . 2000.00
Lenci, Drummer Boy, Pouty, Side-Glancing Eyes, Muslin Torso, 17 1/2 In. 2500.00
Lenci, Estonian Girl, Mohair Wig, Purple Skirt, Pleated Apron, 1930s, 16 In. 460.00
Lenci, Felt Swivel Head, Brown Side-Glancing Eyes, Closed Mouth, 17 In. 1300.00
Lenci, Flora, Swivel Head, Side-Glancing Eyes, 1926, 21 In. 1600.00
Lenci, Girl, All Felt, Brown Painted Eyes, Blond Mohair Wig, 1930, 12 In. 80.00
Lenci, Girl, Bunny & Basket, Seated, Green Wicker Basket, Cloth, 1930, 11-In. Basket . . . 800.00
Lenci, Girl, Swivel Head, Fascist Youth Costume, 17 1/2 In. 4200.00
Lenci, Goose Girl, Pressed Felt Swivel Head, Felt Body, Jointed, 1940, 8 In. 800.00
Lenci, Italian Man, Swivel Head, Plump Face, Googly, Fat Stomach, c.1928, 28 In. 5000.00
Lenci, Italian Woman, Side-Glancing Eyes, Blond Ringlets, Cloth, 1926, 14 In. 800.00
Lenci, Lolita, Dance Pose, Swivel Head, Black Mohair Wig, c.1928, 26 In. 6000.00
Lenci, Mannequin, Felt Swivel Head, Wooden Arms, Legs, Side-Glancing, 38 In. . . . . *Illus* 1650.00
Lenci, Modestina, Felt Swivel Head, Painted Side-Glancing Eyes, Mohair Wig, 20 In. 1000.00
Lenci, Spanish Girl, Felt Swivel Head, Brown Side-Glancing Eyes, Cloth, 1930, 14 In. . . . 800.00
Lenci, Tennis Player, Swivel Head, Closed Mouth, Brunette Bobbed Wig, Jointed, 19 In. . 3500.00
Lenci, Winking Woman Flower Peddler, Felt Swivel Head, Auburn Hair, 12 In. 850.00
Lenci, Woman, Felt Swivel Head, Brown Side Glancing Eyes, Closed Mouth, 1930, 16 In. 1150.00
Lenci, Woman, Felt Swivel Head, Cameo Face, Brown Side Glancing Eyes, 1930, 16 In. . 1400.00
Lenci, Woman, Felt, Blue Side-Glancing Eyes, Blond Mohair Wig, Ringlets, 14 In. 800.00
Lenci-Type, Character, Black Felt, Swivel Head, White & Blue Felt Eyes, 1920, 15 In. . . . 2100.00
Lenci-Type, Character, Felt Swivel Head, Side-Glancing Eyes, Blond Wig, 1930, 21 In. . . 700.00
Lenci-Type, Character, Girl, Felt, Swivel Head, Blue Side-Glancing Eyes, 1935, 22 In. . . . 600.00

Lenci-Type, Googly Girl, Felt Face, Blond Braids, Muslin Body, Green Bonnet, 10 In. . . . 550.00
Little Lulu, Eden International, Hang Tag, Purse, 16 In. 29.00
Madame Alexander, Alexander-Kins, Sleep Eyes, Jointed Knees, Red Wig, c.1956, 7 In. . 90.00
Madame Alexander, Baby, Vinyl Head, Latex Body, Painted Blue Eyes, Tag, Box, 10 In. . 475.00
Madame Alexander, Ballerina, Coil Braided Hair, Composition Body, c.1948, 17 1/2 In. . . 690.00
Madame Alexander, Cissy, Plastic, Blue Sleep Eyes, Vinyl Arms, Taffeta Dress, 21 In. . . . 850.00
Madame Alexander, Glamour Girl, Plastic, Jointed, Walker, 1953, 18 In. 2100.00
Madame Alexander, Goldilocks, Sleep Eyes, Blue Dress, Black Vest, Box, 13 In. 60.00
Madame Alexander, Jane Withers, Composition, Socket Head, Green Eyes, 1935, 17 In. . . 1050.00
Madame Alexander, Jo, Little Women, Blue Dress, Polka-Dot Apron, Box, 8 In. 65.00
Madame Alexander, Kate Greenaway, Composition Head, Blue Sleep Eyes, 13 In. 1050.00
Madame Alexander, Little Bo-Peep, Lamb, Pink & White Dress, Floral Apron, Box, 8 In. 155.00
Madame Alexander, Little Genius, Blue Sleep Eyes, Organdy Dress, Tag, c.1949, 11 In. . . 600.00
Madame Alexander, Little Shaver, Swivel Cloth Head, Swivel, Velvet Shoes, 10 In. 160.00
Madame Alexander, Little Women, Plastic, Synthetic Wigs, Tags, 12 In., 5 Piece 750.00
Madame Alexander, Margaret O'Brien, Composition Head, Green Sleep Eyes, 21 In. 850.00
Madame Alexander, Mary Martin, South Pacific, Sailor Costume, 1950s, 18 In. 845.00
Madame Alexander, McGuffey Ana, Hard Plastic Head, Blue, Green Sleep Eyes, 18 In. . . 1050.00
Madame Alexander, Oliver Twist, Cloth, Brown Velvet Jacket, Blue Pants, 1930s 230.00
Madame Alexander, Pamela, Vinyl Head, Plastic Body, Wardrobe, Case, 1963, 12 In. 650.00
Madame Alexander, Scarlet O'Hara, Green Sleep Eyes, Closed Mouth, 1937, 17 In. 520.00
Madame Alexander, Snow White, Original Gown, Box, c.1939, 16 In. 650.00
Madame Alexander, Sonja Henie, Brown Sleep Eyes, Human Hair, Label, 1939, 18 In. . . 790.00
Madame Alexander, Wendy Bride, Walker, Sleep Eyes, Blond Wig, Tag, 1953, 18 In. 475.00
Madame Alexander, Wendy, Sleep Eyes, Blond Hair, Jointed Hips, 1950, 7 In. 60.00
Madame Alexander, Wendy, Sleep Eyes, Blond Hair, Jointed Knees, 1950, 7 In. . . . .69.00 to 103.00
Madame Alexander, Wendy, Sleep Eyes, Brown Hair, Jointed Hips, 1950s, 7 In. 80.00
Madame Alexander, Wendy-Kins, Sleep Eyes, Jointed At Knees, Red Hair, 1950, 7 1/2 In. 80.00
Marionette, Wooden, Pine, Carved, Polychrome Face, Painted Arms, Gilt Shoes, 19 In. . . 675.00
Marx, It's A Boy, Hard Plastic, Walker, Toddler, 9 In. 495.00
Mary Hoyer, Hard Plastic Head, Sleep Eyes, Caracul Wig, 5-Piece Body, c.1957, 14 In. . 700.00
Mattel, Allan, Molded Red Hair, Brown Eyes, Swim Trunks, Jacket, c.1964, 12 1/2 In. . . 130.00
Mattel, Allan, Painted Red Hair, Red Jacket, Swim Trunks, Bendable Legs, 12 1/2 In. . . . 65.00
Mattel, Allan, Painted Red Hair, Straight Legs, Gold Knit Shirt, Beige Pants, 12 1/2 In. . . 45.00
Mattel, Allan, Painted Red Hair, Striped Shirt, Tan Pants, Wire Stand, Box, 12 1/2 In. . . 95.00
Mattel, Allan, Roller Skate Date, Painted Red Hair, Knit Sweater, Brown Pants, 12 1/2 In. 25.00
Mattel, Barbie, American Girl, Ash Blond, Side Part, Stand, Tag, Box, c.1965, 11 In. 3355.00
Mattel, Barbie, American Girl, Blond, Painted Blue Eyes, Bendable Legs, c.1965, 11 In. . 880.00
Mattel, Barbie, American Girl, Titian Hair, Beige Lips, Finger Paint, Swimsuit 475.00
Mattel, Barbie, Ash Blond, Real Eyelashes, Painted Blue Eyes, Stand, Box, c.1969, 11 In. 470.00
Mattel, Barbie, Benefit Performance, Box 120.00
Mattel, Barbie, Blond, Accessories, Box, 1962 . . . . 385.00
Mattel, Barbie, Blond, Light Green Eyes, Pink Lips, Stand, Box, c.1962 . . . . 220.00
Mattel, Barbie, Blue Rhapsody, Box, 1986 . . . . 155.00
Mattel, Barbie, Brunette, Enchanted Evening Outfit, Booklet, Stand, c.1960 . . . . 3135.00
Mattel, Barbie, Bubble Cut, Black Hair, Striped Swimsuit, Pearl Earrings 95.00
Mattel, Barbie, Bubble Cut, Blond, Busy Morning Dress, Earrings 135.00
Mattel, Barbie, Bubble Cut, Blond, Painted Blue Eyes, Box, c.1962, 11 In. 495.00
Mattel, Barbie, Bubble Cut, Blond, Side Part, Blue Eyes, Bendable Legs, 1965, 11 In. . . . 685.00
Mattel, Barbie, Bubble Cut, Blond, White Lips, Straight Legs, Swimsuit 180.00
Mattel, Barbie, Bubble Cut, Brunette, Box 350.00
Mattel, Barbie, Bubble Cut, Brunette, Pearl Earrings, Striped Swimsuit, Tag, Box . . .*Illus* 375.00
Mattel, Barbie, Bubble Cut, Brunette, Turquoise Eyes, Box, c.1961, 11 In. 220.00
Mattel, Barbie, Bubble Cut, Platinum Blond, Painted Nails, c.1962 . . . . 275.00
Mattel, Barbie, Bubble Cut, Platinum Blond, Red Swimsuit, Glasses, Wire Stand, Box . . . 225.00
Mattel, Barbie, Bubble Cut, White Ginger Hair, Turquoise Eyes, Box, c.1961, 11 In. 910.00
Mattel, Barbie, Circus Star 55.00
Mattel, Barbie, Color Magic, Blond, Plaid Headband & Dress, Bendable Legs 525.00
Mattel, Barbie, Color Magic, Midnight & Ruby Red Hair, Bendable Legs, Box, c.1966 . . 2750.00
Mattel, Barbie, Crystal Rhapsody 450.00
Mattel, Barbie, Dark Red Hair, Pink Ribbon, Pink 2-Piece Swim Suit, Stand, Box 910.00
Mattel, Barbie, Eskimo, International Series, Box, 1981 . . . . .35.00 to 55.00
Mattel, Barbie, Fashion Queen, Painted Brown Hair, 3 Wigs, Box 275.00

Mattel, Barbie, Fashion Queen, Painted Hair, Brunette, Titian & Blond Wigs, Swimsuit .. 185.00
Mattel, Barbie, Flapper, 1920s 100.00
Mattel, Barbie, Goddess Of Sun, Box 130.00
Mattel, Barbie, Growin' Pretty Hair, Blond, Bendable Legs, Wrist Tag, Box, 1972 ...... 220.00
Mattel, Barbie, Growin' Pretty Hair, Blond, Extra Hair Pieces, Accessories, Box, c.1971 .. 385.00
Mattel, Barbie, Hair Happenin's, Short Titian Hair, Bendable Legs, c.1971 .... 853.00
Mattel, Barbie, Happy Holidays, Special Edition, White Gown, Fur Trim, Box, 1989 .... 85.00
Mattel, Barbie, Italian, Box 105.00
Mattel, Barbie, Live Action On Stage, Motorized Stage, Microphone, Record, c.1968 .... 275.00
Mattel, Barbie, Living, Ash Blond Hair, Box 205.00
Mattel, Barbie, Living, Brown Hair, Bendable Legs, Silver Swimsuit, Stand, Box, c.1969 . 195.00
Mattel, Barbie, Living, Light Auburn Hair, Pink Lips, Box 160.00
Mattel, Barbie, Malibu, Blond, Bendable Legs, Swimsuit, Sunglasses, Tag, In Bag 145.00
Mattel, Barbie, Malibu, Blond, Suntan, Beach Accessories, White Vinyl Case, c.1979 .... 55.00
Mattel, Barbie, No. 1, Ponytail, Black & White Swimsuit, Original Price On Box 8700.00
Mattel, Barbie, No. 1, Ponytail, Reset Blond Hair, Striped Bathing Suit, Stand, Box 4100.00
Mattel, Barbie, No. 3, Blond, Blue Eyes, c.1960 .... 800.00
Mattel, Barbie, No. 3, Blond, Blue Eyes, Circular Stand, c.1960 .... 470.00
Mattel, Barbie, No. 3, Brunette, Blue Eyes, c.1960 .... 690.00
Mattel, Barbie, No. 3, Coca-Cola Cheerleader 35.00
Mattel, Barbie, No. 6, Brunette, Painted Features, & Nails, Box, c.1962 .... 550.00
Mattel, Barbie, No. 6, Redhead, Painted Nails, Red Swimsuit, Heels, c.1962 .... 330.00
Mattel, Barbie, Peace & Love, 1970s 47.00
Mattel, Barbie, Ponytail, Brunette, Red Lips, Pearl Earrings, Swimsuit, Wire Stand, Box . 450.00
Mattel, Barbie, Ponytail, Red Jersey Swimsuit, High Heels, Pearl Earrings, 1962 .... 390.00
Mattel, Barbie, Quick Curl, Miss America, Blond, Crown, Gold Gown, Red Cape 60.00
Mattel, Barbie, Red Head, Cobalt Blue Eyes, Green Eyeliner, Stand, Box, c.1962, 11 In. . 525.00
Mattel, Barbie, Royal, International Series, Box, 1979 .... 95.00
Mattel, Barbie, Senior Prom, Brunette Ponytail, Blue Eyes, Aqua Gown, 1962, 11 In. 1300.00
Mattel, Barbie, Solo In The Spotlight, Box, 1989 .... 50.00
Mattel, Barbie, Sophisticated Lady, Box, 1990 ....65.00 to 75.00
Mattel, Barbie, Swirl Ponytail, Blond, Box, Japan, 1964-1965 .... 175.00
Mattel, Barbie, Swirl Ponytail, Blond, Red Nylon Swimsuit, Earrings 380.00
Mattel, Barbie, Swirl Ponytail, Golden Elegance, 5-Piece Body, Handkerchief, c.1964 ... 550.00
Mattel, Barbie, Twist 'n' Turn, Blond, Dayglo Bikini, Fishnet Cover-Up, c.1967 ...... 195.00
Mattel, Barbie, Twist 'n' Turn, Brunette, Bendable Legs, Tag, Plastic Stand 205.00
Mattel, Barbie, Winter Princess, Box 145.00
Mattel, Buffy & Mrs. Beasley, Blond Hair, Red & White Dress, Tag, Box 175.00
Mattel, Busy Steffie, Brunette, Rotating Wrists, Print Dress, Long, Box 135.00
Mattel, Busy Steffie, Walk Lively, Brunette Hair, Light Lips, Box 175.00
Mattel, Casey, Twist 'n' Turn, Brunette, Blue Eyes, Mod Swimsuit, Box, c.1966, 11 In. .. 385.00
Mattel, Chris, Blond, Bendable Arms, Sundress, Box 155.00
Mattel, Christie, Black Hair, Bendable Arms & Legs, Print Shirt & Pants, Fringe Trim ... 135.00
Mattel, Christie, Twist 'n' Turn, Brunette, Brown Eyes, Bendable Legs, c.1969, 11 In. 300.00
Mattel, Francie, Black, Twist 'n' Turn, Bendable Legs, Lashes, 2-Piece Swimsuit, c.1966 . 1430.00
Mattel, Francie, Blond, No Bangs, Bendable Legs, Hairband, c.1966, 10 1/2 In. 825.00
Mattel, Francie, Brunette, Painted Brown Eyes, Mod Swimsuit, Box, c.1966, 11 In. 190.00
Mattel, Francie, Hair Happenin's, Blond, Buckaroo Blues, Shoulder Purse, Boots 95.00
Mattel, Francie, Twist 'n' Turn, Blond, Brown Eyes, Box, c.1966, 11 In. 495.00
Mattel, Francie, Twist 'n' Turn, Gold Rush Outfit, c.1967, 10 1/2 In. 1400.00
Mattel, Julia, Twist 'n' Turn, Dark Hair, Bendable Legs 150.00
Mattel, Julia, Twist 'n' Turn, Oxidized Red Hair, Nurse Outfit 95.00
Mattel, Kelley, Yellowstone, Sports Set, Red Hair, Box, 1973 .... 335.00
Mattel, Ken, Blond Flocked Hair, 2-Piece Striped Pajamas 40.00
Mattel, Ken, Brunette Flocked Hair, Red Swim Trunks, Striped Jacket, Wire Stand 110.00
Mattel, Ken, Brunette, Red Swim Trunks, Jacket, Sandals, Towel, Tag, Stand, c.1961 .... 250.00
Mattel, Ken, Country Clubbin', Painted Brunette Hair, Houndstooth Jacket, Pants, Tie ... 50.00
Mattel, Ken, No. 1, Blond, Flocked Hair, Turquoise Eyes, Red Trunks, 1961, 12 In. 140.00
Mattel, Ken, No. 2, King Arthur, Brunette, Armor, Booklet, Stand, Wrist Tag, Box, c.1964 578.00
Mattel, Ken, Ski Champion, Ski Outfit, Blue Eyes, Brown Hair, 1963, 12 In. .....250.00 to 320.00
Mattel, Ken, Striped Jacket, Sandals, Box 65.00
Mattel, Midge, Ash Blond, Side Part, Blue Eyes, Tag, Stand, Box, c.1965, 11 In. 220.00
Mattel, Midge, Blond, 2-Piece Bathing Suit, Box 85.00

Mattel, Midge, Blond, Painted Eyes, 2-Piece Swimsuit, Heels, Tag, Stand, c.1962 ...... 165.00
Mattel, Midge, Brunette, Blue Eyes, Stand, Box, c.1962, 11 In. 120.00
Mattel, Midge, Let's Dance, Blond Hair, Painted Fingers & Toes, Print Dress, Wire Stand 65.00
Mattel, Midge, Titian Hair, 2-Piece Swimsuit, Wire Stand, Box 85.00
Mattel, Midge, Titian Hair, Coral Lips, Straight Legs, 2-Piece Swimsuit, Wire Stand 70.00
Mattel, P.J., Malibu, Blond, Plastic Sunglasses, Towel, Wrist Tag, 1970 .... 210.00
Mattel, P.J., Twist 'n' Turn, Fun Flakes, Blond, Bendable Legs 115.00
Mattel, Ricky, Skipper's Friend, Painted Red Hair, Swim Trunks, Striped Jacket, Box 95.00
Mattel, Skipper, Blond Hair, Swimsuit, Metal Headband 70.00
Mattel, Skipper, Pose 'n' Play, Blond, Bendable Arms 35.00
Mattel, Skipper, Titian Hair, Ship Ahoy Dress, Pleated Skirt 65.00
Mattel, Skooter, Blond, Red Hair Ribbon, Striped Knit Top, Red Nylon Swimsuit 40.00
Mattel, Skooter, Red Hair, Ribbon Ties, Riding Outfit, Tag 85.00
Mattel, Skooter, Titian, Pigtails, Brown Eyes, Red, White Bathing Suit, Box, c.1965, 9 In. 88.00
Mattel, Stacey, Twist 'n' Turn, Blond, Blue Eyes, Bendable Legs, c.1969, 11 In. 525.00
Mattel, Stacey, Twist 'n' Turn, Blond, Floral Bathing Suit, Box 450.00
Mattel, Tammy, Blond Hair, Hairpins, Cardboard Neck Insert, Box 85.00
Mattel, Todd, Red Hair, Bendable Arms & Legs, 1967, Box 135.00
Mattel, Tutti, Walking My Dolly, Blond, Bendable Arms & Legs, Baby Buggy, Box 205.00
Mattel, Twiggy, Blond Hair, Pink Lips, Painted Teeth, Knit Dress, Tag, Plastic Stand, Box 350.00
Mattel, Twiggy, Twist 'n' Turn, Blond Hair, Striped Dress, Silver Skirt 85.00
Mattel, Twiggy, Twist 'n' Turn, Booklet, Stand, Box, c.1967, 11 In. 248.00
Mego, Fonzie, Happy Days, Thumbs-Up Lever In Back, 1976, 8 In. 90.00
Mignonette, Bisque Swivel Head, Blue Glass Sleep Eyes, 5 In. 475.00
Mignonette, Bisque Swivel Head, Cobalt Blue Glass Inset Eyes, Blond Wig, 4 1/2 In. ... 400.00
Mignonette, Bisque, Blue Glass Sleep Eyes, Blond Mohair Wig, Open Mouth, 1895, 8 In. 850.00
Mignonette, Bisque, Swivel Head, Blue Enamel Inset Eyes, Closed Mouth, 5 1/4 In. 850.00
Mignonette, Bisque, Swivel Head, Blue Enamel Inset Eyes, Closed Mouth, 6 1/4 In. 1500.00
Mignonette, Bisque, Swivel Head, Brown Enamel Inset Eyes, Closed Mouth, 6 In. 1550.00
Mignonette, Bisque, Swivel Head, Cobalt Blue Enamel Inset Eyes, Closed Mouth, 4 In. .. 475.00
Mignonette, Bisque, Swivel Head, Cobalt Blue Inset Eyes, Closed Mouth, 4 1/3 In. 475.00
Mignonette, Bisque, Swivel Head, Cobalt Blue Inset Eyes, Closed Mouth, 5 1/2 In. 1500.00
Mignonette, Bisque, Swivel Head, Communion Costume, Blue Shoes, 5 In. 1150.00
Mignonette, Bisque, Swivel Head, Enamel Eyes, Jointed Body, Silk Dress, Bonnet, 4 In. . 950.00
Mignonette, Bisque, Swivel Head, Pale Blue Enamel Inset Eyes, 1880, 5 1/2 In. 1550.00
Mignonette, Brown Glass Inset Eyes, White Stockings, Blond Mohair Wig, 5 1/2 In. 1200.00
Mignonette, Cavalier, Domed Bisque Swivel Head, Blue Enamel Inset Eyes, 5 In. 1500.00
Molly'es, Raggedy Ann, Cloth, Black Round Nose, Jointed, 1935, 30 In. 5200.00
Nancy Ann Storybook, No. 160, Pretty Maid, Where Have You Been, Bisque, 5 In. 98.00
Nancy Ann Storybook, No. 185, Saturday's Child, Bisque, Box, 5 In. 105.00
Nancy Ann Storybook, Polly Put The Kettle On, Bisque, Painted Eyes, c.1941, 5 1/2 In. . 35.00
Nockler & Tittel, Character, Domed Bisque Socket Head, Closed Mouth, 1920, 13 In. ... 2000.00
Norah Wellings, Lady, Painted Eyes, Blond Hair, French Style Hat, Wire In Legs, 8 In. .. 750.00
Norah Wellings, Sailor, 8 In. 195.00
Old Cottage, Tweedledee & Tweedledum, Hanging Tags, 9 In., Pair 995.00
Paper dolls are listed in their own category.
Papier-Mache, Black Hair, Dark Eyes, Original Pink Silk Outfit, 6 In. 149.00
Papier-Mache, Boy, Shoulder Head, 4 Bamboo Teeth, Black Glass Eyes, 1840, 26 In. 430.00
Papier-Mache, Closed Mouth, Hair In Loops, Kid Body, Wooden Arms & Legs, 28 In. 4100.00
Papier-Mache, Closed Mouth, Kid Body, Wooden Lower Arms & Legs, 12 In. 600.00
Papier-Mache, Domed Head, Black Hair, Closed Mouth, 1845, 15 In. 900.00
Papier-Mache, Jester, Moustache, Whiskers, 6 Teeth, Bellows Clang Cymbals, 10 In. 316.00
Papier-Mache, Lady, Black Sculpted Hair, Dark Blue Eyes, Closed Mouth, 12 In. 850.00
Papier-Mache, Lady, Cameo Face, Dark Brown Sculpted Hair, Closed Mouth, 16 In. 1900.00
Papier-Mache, Milliner's Model, Kid Body, Wooden Arms & Legs, 13 1/2 In. 475.00
Papier-Mache, Sculpted Curly Hair, Closed Mouth, Antique Velvet Costume, 13 In. 1300.00
Papier-Mache, Shoulder Head, Black Hair, Blue Eyes, Cloth Body, 1870, 30 In. 160.00
Papier-Mache, Shoulder Head, Black Hair, Blue Eyes, Cloth Body, Cotton Dress, 28 In. .. 160.00
Papier-Mache, Shoulder Head, Black Hair, Short Curls, Brown Eyes, 22 In. 375.00
Papier-Mache, Shoulder Head, Black Molded Hair, Blue Painted Eyes, Blue Outfit, 15 In. 115.00
Papier-Mache, Shoulder Head, Black Painted Hair, Turquoise Eyes, 1850, 7 In. 400.00
Papier-Mache, Shoulder Head, Black Pupilless Eyes, Red Cotton Dress, 34 In. 750.00
Papier-Mache, Shoulder Head, Black Pupilless Glass Eyes, Brown Human Hair, 28 In. 490.00

Doll, Mattel, Barbie,
Bubble Cut, Brunette,
Pearl Earrings, Striped
Swimsuit, Tag, Box

Doll, Wax, Over
Papier-Mache, Sleep
Eyes, Cloth Body,
Organdy Dress, 25 In.

Papier-Mache, Shoulder Head, Blond Hair, Blue Painted Eyes, 36 In. 316.00
Papier-Mache, Shoulder Head, Blond Hair, Painted Blue Eyes, Closed Mouth, 21 In. 149.00
Papier-Mache, Shoulder Head, Blond Molded Hair, Blue Painted Eyes, 28 In. 258.00
Papier-Mache, Shoulder Head, Brown Painted Eyes, Cloth Body, 21 In. 750.00
Papier-Mache, Shoulder Head, Brown Painted Eyes, Cloth Body, Leather Arms, 27 In. 290.00
Papier-Mache, Shoulder Head, Bulgy Black Glass Pupilless Eyes, Cloth Body, 12 In. 290.00
Pincushion dolls are listed in their own category.
Polichinelle, Character, Mechanical, Papier-Mache Head & Hands, Painted, 1860, 11 In.   . 2700.00
Puppet, Bamm-Bamm & Pebbles, Plush, Kohner Bros., NY, 1960s, 4 In., Pair 75.00
Puppet, Colonial Man, Dandy, Satin Knickers, Velvet Coat, Embroidered Vest, Flemish . . 7500.00
Puppet, Hand, Cat In The Hat, 1970, 18 In. 45.00
Puppet, Hand, Witchepoo, Remco, Sticker On Back, 1971 . . . .   140.00
Puppet, Hand, Yoda, Box, 1980 . . . .   40.00
Queen Elizabeth, Coronation, Dynel Wig, Ginny Dolls, 1953-1954, 8 In. 900.00
Revalo, 8, Bisque Socket Head, Blue Sleep Eyes, 4 Teeth, Human Hair, 24 1/2 In. 625.00
Rollinson, Cloth Shoulder Head, Teeth, Muslin Body, Antique Costume, c.1916, 25 In. . . . 1100.00
S & H dolls are also listed here as Bergmann and Simon & Halbig.
S & H, 570, Bisque Socket Head, Brown Sleep Eyes, Open Mouth, 4 Teeth, Mohair, 23 In.   500.00
S & H, 890, All Bisque, Brown Sleep Eyes, Open Mouth, 4 Teeth, Mohair, 7 In. 525.00
S.F.B.J., 60, Bisque, Sleep Eyes, Open Mouth, Brown Hair, Composition Body, 14 In. 280.00
S.F.B.J., 233, Bisque, Open Mouth, Crying Expression, Antique Sailor Costume, 16 In. . . . 2600.00
S.F.B.J., 236, Baby, Bisque Socket Head, Blue Glass Sleep Eyes, Brunette Wig, 15 In. 1050.00
S.F.B.J., 238, Bisque, Open Mouth, Porcelain Teeth, Smiling, Blond Mohair Wig, 15 In. . . 2300.00
S.F.B.J., 252, Character, Bisque Socket Head, Bright Blue Glass Sleep Eyes, 1912, 13 In. . 4400.00
S.F.B.J., Bebe Jumeau, Bisque Socket Head, Amber Brown Paperweight Eyes, 1890, 24 In. 5000.00
S.F.B.J., Bebe Jumeau, Bisque Socket Head, Blue Sleep Eyes, Brunette Mohair Wig, 22 In. 2700.00
S.F.B.J., Bebe Jumeau, Bisque Socket Head, Brown Glass Enamel Inset Eyes, 21 In. 17000.00
S.F.B.J., Bebe Jumeau, Bisque Socket Head, Glass Eyes, Open Mouth, 1900, 27 In. . 2000.00
S.F.B.J., Bebe Jumeau, Pressed Bisque Socket Head, Blue Glass Inset Eyes, Box, 15 In. . . 10250.00
S.F.B.J., Bebe Jumeau, Pressed Bisque Socket Head, Glass Eyes, Closed Mouth, 24 In. . . . 7500.00
S.F.B.J., Bisque Socket Head, Brown Glass Sleep Eyes, Open Mouth, 16 In. 1600.00
S.F.B.J., Bisque, Painted Features, Blond Wig, 5-Piece Body, Boots, Peaked Hat, 5 In. 85.00
S.F.B.J., Bisque, Sleep Eyes, Pouty Expression, Fully Jointed, c.1912, 11 In. 4400.00
S.F.B.J., Character, Bisque Socket Head, Blue Glass Sleep Eyes, Open Mouth, 15 In. 2500.00
S.F.B.J., Character, Domed Socket Bisque Head, Blue Glass Jewel Eyes, 1912, 16 In. 1900.00
Schmitt & Fils, Bisque Head, Brown Glass Eyes, Antique Silk Gown, Bebe, 1880, 23 In. . . 15500.00
Schmitt & Fils, Bisque Socket Head, Blond, Bebe, 1880s, 9 In. 5200.00
Schmitt & Fils, Bisque, Socket Head, Dark Blue Enamel Inset Eyes, 1884, 24 In. 20000.00
Schoenhut, 300, Girl, Wooden Head, Pouty, Tacked-On Wig, Spring-Jointed Body, 17 In. . .   700.00
Schoenhut, 301, Pressed Socket Head, Brown Intaglio Eyes, Closed Mouth, 1912, 16 In. . .   750.00
Schoenhut, 308, Character, Carved Wooden Head, Blue Intaglio Eyes, 1915, 19 In. 1500.00
Schoenhut, Felix, Wooden Head & Torso, Leather Ears, Jointed, c.1922, 8 In. 200.00
Schoenhut, Girl, Carved Wooden Socket Head, Brown Intaglio Eyes, 16 In. 850.00
Schoenhut, Girl, Painted Carved Wooden Socket Head, Wooden Braids, Wood, 16 In. 2000.00
Schoenhut, Girl, Sober Face, Braids Around Head, Painted Intaglio Eyes, 1911, 16 In. 690.00
Schoenhut, Happy Hooligan, Jointed, 1924, 9 In. 925.00
Schoenhut, Maggie & Jiggs, Jointed, Jiggs With Cigar, Maggie With Rolling Pin, 9 In. . .   440.00

School Children, Bisque, Japan, Box, 3 In., 6 Piece 125.00
Shirley Temple dolls are included in the Shirley Temple category.
Simon & Halbig dolls are also listed here under S & H.
Simon & Halbig, 9 1/2, Bisque Socket Head, Sleep Eyes, Open Mouth, Teeth, 23 In. 425.00
Simon & Halbig, 49, Bisque Head, Sleep Eyes, 4 Teeth, Child, c.1900, 19 In. 1100.00
Simon & Halbig, 719, Bisque Swivel Head, 2 Square Cut Teeth, c.1890, 27 In. 1750.00
Simon & Halbig, 886, Bisque Swivel Head, Brown Glass Sleep Eyes, Open Mouth, 7 In. . 900.00
Simon & Halbig, 929, Boy, Bisque Socket Head, Brown Glass Inset Eyes, 1886, 27 In. 7250.00
Simon & Halbig, 939, Fashion, Bisque Swivel Head, Blue Glass Eyes, Blond Wig, 15 In. . 1500.00
Simon & Halbig, 949, Bisque Socket Head, Brown Glass Sleep Eyes, Child, 1890, 13 In. . 1800.00
Simon & Halbig, 1009, Brown Bisque Socket Head, Brown Sleep Eyes, Child, 16 In. 2400.00
Simon & Halbig, 1009, Brown Bisque, Brown Hair, Brown Leather Shoes, 21 In. 2400.00
Simon & Halbig, 1039, Bisque, Cloth Body, Open Mouth, 4 Teeth, Mohair, 16 In. 650.00
Simon & Halbig, 1078, Bisque Socket Head, Open Mouth, 4 Teeth, 5-Piece Body, 9 In. .. 300.00
Simon & Halbig, 1079, Bisque, Sleep Eyes, Open Mouth, Dimpled Chin, Child, 42 In. ... 3100.00
Simon & Halbig, 1079, Girl, Brown Bisque Socket Head, Brown Eyes, 1900, 15 In. 1025.00
Simon & Halbig, 1159, Fashion, Bisque Socket Head, Brown Sleep Eyes, 19 In. 2150.00
Simon & Halbig, 1428, Character, Bisque Socket Head, Blue Glass Sleep Eyes, 13 In. ... 1500.00
Simon & Halbig, 1428, Character, Bisque Socket Head, Blue Glass Sleep Eyes, 23 In. ... 3900.00
Simon & Halbig, Bisque Head, Blue Glass Sleep Eyes, Open Mouth, 18 1/2 In. 345.00
Simon & Halbig, Bisque Head, Blue Glass Sleep Eyes, Open Mouth, 22 In. 260.00
Simon & Halbig, Bisque Head, Blue Glass Sleep Eyes, Open Mouth, 29 In. 1095.00
Simon & Halbig, Bisque Head, Blue Glass Sleep Eyes, Open Mouth, Jointed, 19 In. 375.00
Simon & Halbig, Bisque Head, Blue Glass Sleep Eyes, Open Mouth, Jointed, 26 In. 316.00
Simon & Halbig, Bisque Head, Blue Sleep Eyes, Open Mouth, Brown Mohair Wig, 22 In. 287.00
Simon & Halbig, Bisque Head, Blue Sleep Eyes, Open Mouth, Brown Wig, 10 In. 290.00
Simon & Halbig, Bisque Head, Blue Stationary Eyes, Open Mouth, 14 1/2 In. 260.00
Simon & Halbig, Bisque Head, Brown Glass Paperweight Eyes, Open Mouth, 20 In. 980.00
Simon & Halbig, Bisque Head, Brown Glass Sleep Eyes, Open Mouth, 5 In. 345.00
Simon & Halbig, Bisque Swivel Head, Brown Glass Inset Eyes, Blond Mohair Wig, 6 In. . 550.00
Simon & Halbig, Bisque Swivel Head, Brown Glass Sleep Eyes, 7 1/2 In. 1550.00
Simon & Halbig, Bisque Swivel Head, Cobalt Blue Inset Eyes, Closed Mouth, 11 In. 3600.00
Simon & Halbig, Bisque, Enamel Eyes, Muslin Torso & Upper Limbs, 1885, 10 In. 2400.00
Simon & Halbig, Bisque, Human Hair Wig, Wooden Ball-Jointed Body, Dressed, 34 In. ... 1900.00
Simon & Halbig, Boy, Bisque Socket Head, Open Mouth, Blond Wig, 20 In. 920.00
Simon & Halbig, Chocolate Brown Bisque Socket Head, Brown Eyes, 1890, 21 In. 2500.00
Simon & Halbig, Girl, Bisque Socket Head, Blue Glass Sleep Eyes, Open Mouth, 6 In. 350.00
Simon & Halbig, Mignonette, Bisque Swivel Head, Dark Blue Glass Sleep Eyes, 9 In. ... 1500.00
Sonneberg, Asian Child, Bisque Head, Pouty Expression, Slippers, c.1890, 11 In. 2300.00
Sonneberg, Bisque Socket Head, Brown Glass Inset Eyes, Closed Mouth, 1885, 15 In. 2700.00
Sonneberg, Bisque, Closed Mouth, Blond Mohair Wig, Fully Jointed Body, 10 In. 2500.00
Sonneberg, Bisque, Closed Mouth, Mohair Wig, Wooden Body, Silk Dress, Child, 16 In. . 2600.00
Sonneberg, Bisque, Enamel Eyes, Wooden Body, Jointed At Shoulders, Child, 10 In. 1600.00
Sonneburg, Bisque Socket Head, Composition, Wood, Child, 1890, 15 In. 1800.00
Steiff, Character, Felt, Curly White Mohair Wig, Jointed, 1910, 11 In. 1650.00
Steiner, Baby, Bisque Head, Blue Sleep Eyes, Cloth Body, 18 In. 230.00
Steiner, Bebe, Bisque Socket Head, 1899, 18 In. 5750.00
Steiner, Bisque Shoulder Head, Cobalt Blue Glass & Enamel Eyes, Open Mouth, 14 In. .. 3400.00
Steiner, Bisque Socket Head, Blue Glass Enamel Inset Eyes, Blond Mohair Wig, 18 In. .. 12000.00
Steiner, Bisque Socket Head, Blue Glass Enamel Inset Eyes, Closed Mouth, 10 In. 5000.00
Steiner, Bisque Socket Head, Blue Glass Enamel Inset Eyes, Closed Mouth, 23 In. 8500.00
Steiner, Bisque Socket Head, Blue Glass Eyes, Closed Mouth, Composition, 14 In. 5300.00
Steiner, Bisque Socket Head, Blue Glass Paperweight Eyes, Closed Mouth, Bebe, 23 In. . 5000.00
Steiner, Bisque Socket Head, Brown Glass Inset Eyes, Closed Mouth, 1889, 8 In. 4300.00
Steiner, Bisque Socket Head, Dark Blue Inset Eyes, Closed Mouth, Bebe, 1889, 11 In. ... 5900.00
Steiner, Bisque Socket Head, Dark Brown Glass & Enamel Inset Eyes, 1889, 9 In. 4200.00
Steiner, Bisque, Brown, Row Of Tiny Teeth, Composition Jointed Body, 17 In. 3900.00
Steiner, Bisque, Closed Mouth, Blond Mohair Wig, Fully Jointed Body, 28 In. 6700.00
Steiner, Bisque, Paperweight Eyes, 17 In. 2600.00
Steiner, Bisque, Shoulder Head, Brown Glass Sleep Eyes, Open Mouth, 1900, 27 In. 170.00
Steiner, Gigoteur, Dome Bisque Head, Blue Glass Inset Eyes, 1885, 18 In. 2000.00
Steiner, Le Parisien, Bisque Socket Head, Paperweight Eyes, Human Hair, 16 1/2 In. 3400.00

Terri Lee, Dutch Girl, Hard Plastic Head, Curled Nylon Wig, c.1954, 16 In. 650.00
Terri Lee, Pouty Lips, Hard Plastic, c.1948, 16 In. 700.00
Terri Lee, Walker, 1950s, 16 In. 950.00
Thuillier, Bisque, Teeth, Human Hair Wig, Wooden Jointed Body, c.1890, 20 In. 15500.00
Tiny Town, Ballerina, Box, 4 In. 75.00
Troll, Swivel Head, Marked Thomas Dam, 1961, 7 1/2 In. 45.00
Uneeda, Ma-Ma, Composition, Cloth Body, Sleep Eyes, Brown Mohair, 1920s, 27 1/2 In. . 69.00
Ventriloquist Dummy, Jerry Mahoney, Vinyl Head & Hands, Juro, Box, 1950s, 22 In. ... 475.00
Vogue, Ginny, Blond Mohair, Painted Side-Glancing Eyes, 7 1/2 In., Pair 450.00
Vogue, Ginny, Bride, Blond, Sleep Eyes, Satin Gown, Juliet Cap, c.1950, 8 In. 1430.00
Vogue, Ginny, Bridesmaid, Brunette Wig, Sleep Eyes, Yellow Taffeta Gown, c.1952, 8 In. 660.00
Vogue, Ginny, Fun Time Series, Brown Wig, Sleep Eyes, Sunsuit, Fish Float, c.1954, 8 In. 660.00
Vogue, Ginny, Hawaiian, Brown Plastic Head, Brown Sleep Eyes, 5-Piece Body, 7 In. ... 2900.00
Vogue, Ginny, Hawaiian, Brown Wig, Sleep Eyes, Walker Body, Sarong, c.1958, 8 In. ... 385.00
Vogue, Ginny, Kindergarten, Blond Pixie Wig, Brown Sleep Eyes, 1952, 8 In. 510.00
Vogue, Ginny, Majorette, Sleep Eyes, Blond Wig, Majorette Outfit, Baton, c.1956, 8 In. .. 140.00
Vogue, Ginny, Red Wig, Sleep Eyes, Leopard Print Fur Coat, Hat, Muff, c.1952, 8 In. 715.00
Vogue, Ginny, Sweetheart, Plastic Head, Brown Sleep Eyes, 5-Piece Body, 1950, 8 In. ... 745.00
Vogue, Ginny, Valentine, Blond Wig, Painted Eyes, Red Taffeta Dress, Box, c.1949, 8 In. . 688.00
Vogue, Ginny, Walker, Bent Knee, Sleep Eyes, Brown Wig, Wrist Tag, c.1957, 8 In. 385.00
Vogue, Mistress Mary, Composition Head, Blue Eyes, 5-Piece Body, 7 In. 345.00
Vogue, Toddles, Cowboy, Composition Head, Painted Features, Brown Wig, c.1943, 8 In. . 193.00
Vogue, Toddles, Draftee, Painted Side-Glancing Eyes, Mohair, Military Uniform, 7 1/2 In. 350.00
Vogue, Toddles, Jill, Composition Head, Painted Eyes, Blond, Blue Skirt, c.1943, 7 1/2 In. 303.00
Vogue, Toddles, Red Riding Hood, Composition Head, Painted Features, 1940s, 7 1/2 In. . 413.00
Volland, Raggedy Ann & Andy, Muslin, Button Eyes, Yarn Hair, 1920s, 16 In. 2000.00
Wax, Glass Eyes, Molded Hair, Cloth Body, Original Dress, 5 1/4 In. 775.00
Wax, Over Composition, Set Blue Eyes, Mohair Wig, Cloth Body, Kid Arms, 26 In. 750.00
Wax, Over Papier-Mache, Sleep Eyes, Cloth Body, Organdy Dress, 25 In. ....Illus 625.00
Wax, Shoulder Head, Black Glass Pupilless Eyes, Red Painted Mouth, Jointed, 14 In. 230.00
Wax, Shoulder Head, Black Pupilless Eyes, Closed Mouth, Cloth Body, 1870, 14 In. 86.00
Wax, Shoulder Head, Molded Hat, Blue Painted Eyes, White Chemise, 15 In. 862.00
Wooden, Almond-Shaped Blue Enamel Eyes, Oval Shaped Face, Closed Mouth, 20 In. .. 3000.00
Wooden, Peg, Painted Black Hair, Painted Blue Eyes, Jointed, 21 In. 1150.00

DONALD DUCK items are included in the Disneyana category.

DOORSTOPS have been made in all types of designs. The vast majority of the doorstops sold today are cast iron and were made from about 1890 to 1930. Most of them are shaped like people, animals, flowers, or ships. Reproductions and newly designed examples are sold in gift shops.

3 Swans, Cast Iron, 8 In. 295.00
Basket Of Flowers, Cast Iron, 10 In. ....58.00 to 176.00
Bathing Beauties, Hubley 5250.00
Beetle, Cast Iron 80.00
Black Mammy, Cast Iron, 8 3/4 In. 405.00
Boston Terrier, Full Figure, 10 x 10 In. 65.00
Boxer, Standing, Bradley & Hubbard, Cast Iron, 2 3/4 x 5 x 5 1/4 In. 85.00
Butler, Black Waistcoat, Gold Buttons, Cast Iron, 10 In. 172.00
Caddie, Black, Holding Golf Bag & Clubs, Cast Iron, 8 1/2 In. 385.00
Caddie, Golf Clubs, Cast Iron 750.00
Cannon, Cast Iron, 16 In. 177.00
Cat, Arched Back, Green Eyes, Cast Iron, 10 5/8 In. 330.00
Cat, Arched Back, Tail Up, Black, Cast Iron, 11 In. 248.00
Cat, Green Eyes, Black Whiskers, Hubley, 10 1/4 In. 325.00
Cat, Reclining, Black Paint, White Paws, Green Bow, Cast Iron, 3 1/2 x 10 In. 1035.00
Cat, Reclining, Cast Iron, 4 5/4 x 13 1/2 In. 1265.00
Cat, Reclining, Green Eyes, Cast Iron, 3 3/4 x 7 1/2 In. 275.00
Cat, Seated, Black Paint, Copper, 19th Century, 8 1/8 x 5 3/4 In. 575.00
Cat, Sitting, White, Green Eyes, Cast Iron, 5 1/2 In. 330.00
Cat, Sleeping, Gold Paint, Cast Iron, 3 1/2 x 9 In. 86.00

Cat, White, Hubley, Cast Iron 65.00
Cat, White, Pink Ears, Green & Black Eyes, Hubley, Cast Iron, 5 3/4 x 10 1/2 In. . .325.00 to 412.00
Charleston Dancers, Couple, Art Deco, Signed Fish, Hubley 6050.00
Child, Yawning, 9 x 5 In. 275.00
Choir Boy, Cast Iron, 6 3/4 In. 340.00
Clown, Seated, 8 x 3 1/2 In. 600.00
Clown, Standing 1980.00
Coach, Horse Drawn, GR & London Royal Mail N. 17, Cast Iron, 12 In. 44.00
Colonial Woman, Cast Iron, 10 1/4 x 6 1/4 In. 110.00
Colonial Woman, Pink Flowing Gown, Holding Fan 185.00
Cottage, Flowers, Picket Fence, Cast Iron, 8 In. 11.00
Cottage, Marked 82 On Back, Cast Iron, 5 3/4 In. 175.00
Cottage, Numbered 32, Cast Iron, 5 1/4 In. 170.00
Cottage, Red Roof, Shrubbery Along Roofline, Cast Iron, 7 1/4 x 8 1/2 In. 418.00
Cow, New Holland Machine Co. 2090.00
Daisies In Bowl, Yellow & White Painted, 7 x 5 3/4 In. 82.00
Dog, Boston Terrier, 9 x 9 In. 52.00
Dog, Boston Terrier, Basket Of Flowers, 2 Frogs, Mid 20th Century, 10 In., 5 Piece 201.00
Dog, Boston Terrier, Wooden Plinth, 8 3/4 In. 57.00
Dog, Bulldog, Large 210.00
Dog, Cocker Spaniel, Hubley, Cast Iron, 6 1/2 In. 245.00
Dog, Fox Terrier, Cast Iron 245.00
Dog, French Bulldog, Hubley, Cast Iron, 7 5/8 x 6 3/4 In. 77.00
Dog, German Shepherd, Initials On Back M.G.A.F., 12 1/2 In. 135.00
Dog, Puppies In Basket, Wilton Co., Cast Iron, 6 x 8 1/2 In. 690.00
Dog, Scotty, Black, Cast Iron, 8 3/4 x 10 1/2 In. 155.00
Dog, Spaniel, Black, Cast Iron, 6 3/4 In. 145.00
Dog, Springer Spaniel, Black & White, Cast Iron, 7 x 11 In. 260.00
Dog, Terrier, Black & White, Cast Iron, 8 1/2 In. 60.00
Dog, Terrier, Brown Paint, Cast Iron, 8 1/2 x 8 In. 145.00
Dog, Yawning, Cast Iron, 7 In. 350.00
Dude With Cane, Hubley, John Held Jr. 1320.00
Dutch Children, Cast Iron 175.00
Eagle, Cast Iron, 12 In. 220.00
Elephant, Cast Iron, 8 1/4 In. ....245.00 to 360.00
Fireside Cat, Gray & White Paint, Hubley, Cast Iron 270.00
Fish Footman, Hubley 1870.00
Fisherman, Yellow Raincoat, Holding Rope & Net, Cast Iron, 11 In. 193.00
Floral, Cast Iron, 7 1/4 In. 145.00
Flower Basket, Multicolored, White Basket, 10 x 6 In. 115.00
Flower Basket, With Roses, Cast Iron, 6 3/4 In. 105.00
Flower Basket, Wood, Cast Iron, 19th Century, 9 In. 632.00
Footmen, Hubley, Large 1980.00
Fox, Sleeping, Red Paint, Wilton, 6 1/2 In. 300.00
Fraternal, Dove, 7 1/8 In. 115.00
Fruit Basket, Cast Iron, 10 x 11 1/2 In. 22.00
Geisha Girl, Cast Iron, 6 1/2 In. 320.00
General, 13 1/2 In. 365.00
Girl, Curtseying, Cast Iron 2780.00
Girl, Holding Bouquet, Blue Repaint, Albany Foundry Co., 7 5/8 x 4 3/4 In. 115.00
Girl, Holding Her Hat, Flowery Dress, Cast Iron, 8 In. 110.00
Girl, Kicking Flower 1870.00
Gnome, Enamel Over Iron, 14 1/2 In. 200.00
Gnome, Red Pants & Hat, Yellow Shirt, Cast Iron, 10 In. 77.00
Golfer, A Difficult Lie, Hubley 155.00
Guitar Player 4180.00
Harlequin, Mayfair 4180.00
Highland Lighthouse, Keepers Home On Base, 9 x 7 3/4 In. 1320.00
Horse, Booted Base, Cast Iron 120.00
Horse Shape, Steel, England, 19th Century, Pair 995.00
House, Cape Cod, Cast Iron, Albany Foundry, 5 3/4 x 8 3/4 In. 225.00
House, Cape Cod, Eastern Specialty Mfg. Co., Cast Iron, 5 3/4 x 8 1/4 In. ....245.00 to 253.00

House, Painted, Cast Iron, 4 3/4 x 8 In. 115.00
Jockey, Cast Iron, 11 In. 172.00
Koala, On Tree Stump, 7 1/4 In. 1760.00
Lady Of Victory, England 4400.00
Lighthouse, Cape Cod, Cast Iron, 7 In. 390.00
Lilacs & Roses, Marked 479, Cast Iron, 5 1/2 In. 115.00
Lion, Gold Paint, Cast Iron, 7 1/4 In. 150.00
Lobster, 12 1/2 x 6 1/2 In. 825.00
Mr. Pickwick, National Foundry 1250.00
Nichols House, Entranceway, Name On Base, 8 3/4 In. 4180.00
Parrot In Ring, 8 In. 55.00
Peacock, Cast Iron, 6 1/4 In. 175.00
Pelican, Red, Yellow, Blue, Cast Iron, 7 1/2 In. 130.00
Penguin, Painted Tuxedo, 9 3/8 x 5 In. 605.00
Penguin, With Top Hat, Hubley 660.00
Pinnochio, Cast Iron 2200.00
Police Boy, 10 5/8 x 7 1/4 In. 460.00
Poppies & Snapdragons, Wicker Style Basket, Hubley, 7 1/2 In. 220.00
Punch, Black, 12 In. 145.00
Punch, Iron, 12 1/2 In. 230.00
Punch & Judy, Polychrome, Red, Blue, Black, White, 19th Century, 12 x 8 In. 1725.00
Rabbit, Full Body, Seated, Kramer Bros., Cast Iron, 10 1/4 In. 360.00
Rabbit, Seated, Full Bodied, Cast Iron, 11 3/4 In. 300.00
Ram, White Paint, Cast Iron, 19th Century, 7 1/2 x 10 In. 490.00
Rhumba Dancer 1650.00
Santa Claus, Pulling Wooden Sleigh, Germany, 13 In. 1430.00
Sheep, Black Paint, Cast Iron, 19th Century, 7 1/2 x 10 In. 400.00
Ship, Cast Iron, 1930s, 11 3/4 In. 255.00
Southern Belle, Bonnet, Cast Iron, 5 In. 85.00
Spaniel, Pointing With Front Leg, Cast Iron, Late 19th Century, 8 1/2 x 15 In. 1265.00
Squirrel, Cast Iron, 11 1/2 In. 907.00
Stage Coach, 2 Horses, Hubley, No. 376-2, Paper Label, 5 3/4 x 11 In. 110.00
Tiger Lilies, White, Green Leaves, Hubley, 10 1/2 x 6 In. 308.00
Topsy, Hubley 550.00
Will Rogers, Cast Iron, 6 1/4 In. 295.00
Windmill, Cast Iron, 11 In. 520.00
Woman, Art Nouveau 130.00

DORCHESTER POTTERY was founded by George Henderson in 1895 in **DORCHESTER**
Dorchester, Massachusetts. At first, the firm made utilitarian **POTTERY WORKS**
stoneware, but collectors are most interested in the line of decorated **BOSTON, MASS.**
blue and white pottery that Dorchester made from 1940 until it went
out of business in 1979.

Bowl, Horizontal Striped Floral, Wavy Design, Circular Blue Band, C. Hill, 7 In. 165.00
Casserole, Blue Matte Glaze, Tab Handles, Cover, Unmarked, 5 In. 50.00
Casserole, Blueberry, Stamped, Marked, 7 x 5 In. 200.00
Charger, Blue Matte Glaze, Unmarked, 12 1/4 In. 60.00
Charger, Stylized Apples Cascading From Multi Branches, Blue, Charles Hill, 13 In. 165.00
Crock, Blue Swirl, Cover, Ear Handles, Signed, 7 1/4 In. 205.00
Crock, Rooster Painting, Joseph McCune, 7 x 9 In. 385.00
Cup & Saucer, Pinecone, Blue Swirl, Stamped & Initialed 75.00
Dish, Cobalt Blue Checkered Rim, Floral Center, Marked, 4 1/2 In. 128.00
Jar, Blue, Paper Label, 3 1/2 In. 29.00
Jar, Cover, Spouting Whale At Sea, Signed, 5 1/4 In. 70.00
Jug, Whale, Body Of Water Around Base 300.00
Mug, Thar She Blows, Whale, Circular Stamp 128.00
Perfume Bottle, Poppy Design, Carved Floral, Ceramic Stopper, 5 1/8 In. 300.00
Pitcher, Cover, Loop Handle, Plums On Branch, N. Ricci, Signed, 4 3/4 In. 85.00
Pitcher, Cover, Spout, C-Handle, N. Ricci, Mid 20th Century, 5 3/4 In. 230.00
Pitcher, Flared Top & Spout, Band Of Waves At Rim, Signed, 7 1/8 In. 70.00
Pitcher, Stylized Apples Cascading Along Midsection, Blue Glaze, C. Hill, 6 x 5 In. 300.00
Pitcher, Water, Clipper Ship, Blue, & White, Stamped & Signed, 5 1/2 In. 500.00

Plate, Colonial Lace, Sgraffito, Colonial Lace In Repeat, Blue, Charles Hill, 10 1/2 In. 140.00
Pot, Varied Floral Designs, Sgraffito, Painted Blue Bands, Blue Layers, 10 x 7 In. 415.00
Sugar, Cover, Blue & White, Hand Painted, Artist Signed, 3 x 4 1/2 In. 150.00
Sugar & Creamer, Blue Whale In Ocean, Flying Birds, Marked & Signed 410.00
Vase, Grapes & Leaves, Embossed, Cobalt Blue, 13 3/4 In. 42.00

DOULTON pottery and porcelain were made by Doulton and Co. of
Burslem, England, after 1882. The name *Royal Doulton* appeared on
their wares after 1902. Other pottery by Doulton is listed under Royal
Doulton.

Bowl, Frog, Snail, Newt Relief, Footed, Francis Pope, Lambeth, 1890s, 9 1/2 In. 840.00
Bowl, Irises On Buff Ground, Claw, Ball Feet, 1880, 11 In. 126.00
Bowl, Rose, Flow Blue, Gilt Trim, 16 x 14 x 5 In. 245.00
Butter, Cover, Tapestry, 7 x 4 In. 120.00
Candlestick, Standing Putti, Column Shape, Lambeth, c.1876, 8 1/8 In. 2700.00
Charger, Wall, Faience, Repeating Pattern, Lambeth, 1870s, 20 1/2 In. 840.00
Clock Case, Faience, Apple Blossoms, Elephant Handles, Lambeth, c.1880, 10 1/8 In. . . . 2040.00
Clock Case, Hexagonal, Flower, Leaf Bands, Mary Aitken, Lambeth, 1880s, 12 1/2 In. . . . 2400.00
Figurine, Cockneys At Brighton, Mice, Rowboat, Tinsworth, c.1886, 5 7/8 In. 6600.00
Humidor, Sgraffito Design Of Cows, Silver Banded Top & Lid, 5 1/2 In. 1015.00
Jardiniere, Red Floral Design, Gilt, Cream, Taupe Ground, Porcelain, 11 In. 287.00
Jug, Blue, Green, Brown Mottled, Lambeth, 8 1/2 In. 193.00
Jug, Commemorative, Queen Victoria, 1837 . . . . 475.00
Lamp, Oil, Metal Mouthed, Macaws, Beaded Panels, Lambeth, c.1885, 17 In. 1920.00
Loving Cup, Salt Glaze, Windmill, People, Animals, c.1840 . . . . 575.00
Match Holder, Mouse, Wheelbarrow, Silver Mounted, Lambeth, c.1893, 3 3/4 In. 3900.00
Menu Holder, Animal Group, Lost & Serve Them Right, Lambeth, 1880s, 6 In. 6600.00
Pitcher, Arts & Crafts, Copper Hammered Type, Lambeth, 7 1/8 x 5 1/2 In. 345.00
Pitcher, Raised Pictorial Design, Lambeth, 8 1/2 In. 115.00
Planter, Incised, Band Of Lions, Hannah Barlow, Lambeth, c.1884, 7 7/8 In. 3600.00
Plaque, Faience, Flowering Cactus, Florence Lewis, Lambeth, 1880s, 19 In. 1920.00
Plaque Set, Seasons, Frame, Lambeth, 1880s, 8 1/2 In., 4 Piece 8400.00
Plate, Madras, Flow Blue, 6 1/2 In. 45.00
Roundel, David Would Not Drink Of It, Frame, Lambeth, 1870s, 6 In. 1800.00
Stein, Men, Animals, Stoneware, Relief, Pewter Lid, Lambeth, No. 8795, 1/2 Liter 185.00
Vase, Bell Shape, Blue Underglaze, Deer & Fowl In Pasture, 1900, 11 1/2 In. 230.00
Vase, Birds In Tall Grass, Florence Barlow, Lambeth, 1890s, 16 1/2 In., Pair 3600.00
Vase, Birds On Branch, Classical Shape, Pate-Sur-Pate, Polychrome, c.1880, 7 In. 575.00
Vase, Eel, Flounder Relief, Wavy Ground, Harry Barnard, Lambeth, c.1800, 14 In. 6000.00
Vase, Faience, 4 Women, Billowing Dresses, Lambeth, c.1910, 16 In. 4800.00
Vase, Faience, Horses, Donkey, Hannah Barlow, c.1890, 17 1/2 In. 3300.00
Vase, Faience, Painted, Blackberry Flowers, Lambeth, 1890s, 18 3/4 In. 1200.00
Vase, Faience, Painted, White Blossoms, Leaves, Lambeth, c.1878, 10 1/4 In. 4500.00
Vase, Figural, Seated Nude Figures, Lambeth, c.1880, 12 1/2 In., Pair 4800.00
Vase, Floral, Landscape, Bulbous Form, Late 19th Century, 7 1/2 In. 1215.00
Vase, Incised, Carved, Flowers, Leaf Panels, Frank Butler, Lambeth, c.1873, 16 1/2 In. . . . 720.00
Vase, Incised, Carved, Nesting Chicks Panels, M. Marshall, Lambeth, c.1881, 16 In. 3000.00
Vase, Incised, Country Scene, Hannah Barlow, Handles, Lambeth, c.1885, 12 1/4 In. 3300.00
Vase, Incised, Deer In Landscape, Hannah Barlow, Lambeth, c.1884, 17 3/4 In. 9600.00
Vase, Incised, Faces, Animals, Leaves, Teardrop Panels, Lambeth, 1880s, 14 1/2 In. 4200.00
Vase, Incised, Field With Sheep, Hannah Barlow, Handles, Lambeth, 1880s, 14 1/2 In. 4500.00
Vase, Incised, Slip Trail, Peacocks, Butterflies, 1890s, Lambeth, 16 1/2 In., Pair 1920.00
Vase, Incised, White Flowers, Blue Ground, Mary Thomson, Lambeth, c.1880, 10 7/8 In. . . 2400.00
Vase, Leaves & Flowers, E. Simmance, B. Newbery, Lambeth, c.1900, 10 3/4 In. 1763.00
Vase, Mushroom Overlapping, Elongated Stems, Frank Butler, Lambeth, 1890s, 10 In. . . . 900.00
Vase, Narrow Neck, 2 Kimono Clad Ladies By Chrysanthemums, 1900, 13 In. 920.00
Vase, Sgraffito, 8 Deer Encircling, Blue, Black, Brown, Barlow, Lambeth, 1902, 11 In. 1456.00
Vase, Spill, Boy Riding Penny Farthing, Basket, Lambeth, 1880s, 10 In. 6600.00
Vase, Stylized Flowers, White Slip Trail, Frank Butler, Lambeth, c.1905, 12 1/2 In. 2280.00
Vase, Tall Flowering Stems, Leaves, Harry Simeon, Lambeth, 1880s, 18 In. 1560.00
Vase, The Love Vase, Cover, 3 Putti Above Knop Stem, 2 Curved Handles, 1895, 24 In. . . . 3900.00
Vase, Willow, Black Transfer Print, c.1900, 16 1/4 In. 920.00
Wall Bracket, Pierced, Budgerigar On Swag, Emma Martin, Lambeth, c.1882, 10 In. 4800.00

DRAGONWARE is a form of moriage pottery made since the late 19th century. Moriage is a type of decoration on Japanese pottery. Raised white designs are applied to the ware. White dragons are the major raised decorations on the moriage called *dragonware*. The background can be one of many different colors. It is still being made.

Ashtray, Gray, Moriage Dragon, Rectangular	10.00
Box, Cover, Blue Clouds, 2 1/2 x 5 1/2 x 4 In.	15.00
Incense Burner, Small	15.00
Keg, Elephant Cap, Cork, Wooden Spigot, 5 x 6 In.	88.00
Pitcher, 8 1/2 In.	250.00
Tea Set, Applied Design, 3 Piece	69.00
Tea Set, Satsuma Style, Black, Gray, White, Blue, 11 Piece	110.00
Vase, Gray, White, Blue, Pink, Matte Glaze, 7 1/2 In.	49.00

DRESDEN china is any china made in the town of Dresden, Germany. The most famous factory in Dresden is the Meissen factory. Figurines of eighteenth-century ladies and gentlemen, animal groups, or cherubs and other mythological subjects were popular. One special type of figurine was made with skirts of porcelain-dipped lace. Do not make the mistake of thinking that all pieces marked *Dresden* are from the Meissen factory. The Meissen pieces usually have crossed swords marks, and are listed under Meissen. Some recent porcelain from Ireland, called *Irish Dresden*, is not included in this book.

Basket, Floral Center, Cobalt & Gold Trim, 7 1/4 x 9 1/2 In.	400.00
Bowl, 4 Blown Out Portrait Panels, Late 19th Century, 5 x 7 3/4 In.	645.00
Candelabrum, 4-Light, 2 Putti Holding Flower Baskets, 11 1/2 In.	90.00
Centerpiece, Figural, Shell Shape, 4 Putti Supports, 13 1/8 In.	805.00
Chandelier, 6-Light, Hanging Floral Bouquets, Meissen Style, 23 1/2 In.	1610.00
Chocolate Pot, Flowers, Hand Painted, Silver Plated Hinged Cover, 8 1/2 In.	250.00
Chocolate Pot, Peasants Washing, Green, Flowers, Gold Handle, 1916, 9 1/2 x 4 1/2 In. ...	1210.00
Cup & Saucer, Flower Panels, Pale Yellow Ground, Empire Handle, 4 1/2 In.	120.00
Figurine, Drummer, Third Guards, Multicolor & Gold Design, 11 In.	415.00
Figurine, Gentleman, Lady, White, Blue, Gold, 13 1/2 In., Pair	660.00
Figurine, Woman, With Parrot, Wearing Wide Pannier, Dresden, 13 1/2 In.	460.00
Lamp Base, Floral Sprays, Courting Couple Scenes, Floral Borders, 21 In.	287.00
Letter Holder, White, Green Border, Flowers, 3 Pockets, Gold Trim, c.1890, 7 3/4 x 7 In.	510.00
Mirror, Rococo Cartouches, Winged Putti, Flowers & Fruit, Wall, 22 x 14 In.	635.00
Platter, 2 Deer, Transfer, R.R. Beck, Stamped, 15 1/2 In.	125.00
Platter, Mandolin Player & Seated Maiden, 5 1/4 In.	52.00
Vase, Figural, Double Serpent Handle, Lozenge Shape, Rectangular Base, 15 In.	2750.00
Vase, Portrait, Elizabeth LeBrun, Gold & Emerald Green Cartouche, 1890, 13 In.	1150.00
Vase, Portrait, Napoleon, Eagle & Crown With Festoons, 1890, 15 In.	5750.00
Wall Bracket, Cartouche Shape, Applied Floral Design, 8 In., Pair	144.00
Wall Bracket, Raised Floral, Fruit Design, Insects, 21 1/2 x 26 In.	460.00

DUNCAN & MILLER is a term used by collectors when referring to glass made by the George A. Duncan and Sons Company or the Duncan and Miller Glass Company. These companies worked from 1893 to 1955, when the use of the name *Duncan* was discontinued and the firm became part of the United States Glass Company. Early patterns may be listed under Pressed Glass.

Canterbury, Bowl, 9 In.	30.00
Canterbury, Bowl, Leaf Etch, 1930, 11 1/2 x 7 x 4 In.	45.00
Canterbury, Claret, 4 Oz., 5 In.	20.00
Canterbury, Condiment Set, 5 Piece	40.00
Canterbury, Console, Flower Frog, Pink Opalescent, 7 1/2 In.	80.00
Canterbury, Cup & Saucer	13.00
Canterbury, Goblet, Water, 10 Oz., 7 1/4 In.	17.00
Canterbury, Plate, 7 1/2 In.	10.00
Canterbury, Plate, 8 In.	8.00
Canterbury, Rose Bowl, 6 In.	23.00
Canterbury, Sandwich Server, 11 In.	24.00
Canterbury, Sherbet, 6 Oz., 4 1/2 In.	10.00

Canterbury, Sherbet, Chartreuse, 6 Oz., 4 1/2 In. 15.00
Canterbury, Sugar & Creamer 15.00
Canterbury, Torte Plate, 14 In. 25.00
Canterbury, Tumbler, Juice, 5 Oz., 4 1/4 In. . . . . .6.00 to 8.00
Canterbury, Vase, Amber, 5 In. 25.00
Canterbury, Vase, Twilight, 3 In. 15.00
Caribbean, Ashtray, 6 In. 25.00
Caribbean, Blue, Pitcher, 16 Oz. 275.00
Caribbean, Bowl, 12 In. 55.00
Caribbean, Bowl, Folded Side, 3 x 5 In. 25.00
Caribbean, Bowl, Folded Side, 5 x 7 In. 35.00
Caribbean, Bowl, Tab Handles, 9 1/2 In. 35.00
Caribbean, Cheese Dish, Blue, Footed 45.00
Caribbean, Creamer, Blue 25.00
Caribbean, Pitcher, Milk, Blue, 16 Oz., 4 3/4 In. 300.00
Caribbean, Plate, Luncheon, Blue Opalescent, 8 1/2 In. 50.00
Caribbean, Punch Bowl, 10 In. 42.00
Caribbean, Punch Cup, Clear, Amber Handles 13.00
Caribbean, Punch Set, 13 Piece 450.00
Caribbean, Relish, 4 Sections, Rectangular, 9 1/2 In. 45.00
Caribbean, Relish, 5 Sections 40.00
Caribbean, Wine, 3 Oz., 4 3/4 In. 25.00
Caribbean, Wine, Blue, 2 1/2 Oz., 3 1/2 In. . . . . .25.00 to 45.00
Chanticleer, Cocktail, 1930 . . . . 75.00
Cloverleaf, Vase, Blue Opalescent, 5 In. 50.00
Daisy & Button, Toothpick, Top Hat 60.00
Festive, Gravy Boat, Yellow, With Spoon 55.00
First Love, Bowl, Scalloped Edge, 11 In. 71.00
First Love, Candlestick, 2-Light, 6 In., Pair 180.00
First Love, Candy Dish, Cover, 3 Sections, 6 In. 75.00
First Love, Champagne, 5 Oz., 5 In. 21.00
First Love, Cocktail Shaker, 16 Oz. 145.00
First Love, Goblet, Water, 10 Oz., 5 3/4 In. 31.00
First Love, Relish, 3 Sections, Rectangular, 9 In. 45.00
First Love, Tumbler, Iced Tea, 12 Oz., 5 1/2 In. 32.00
First Love, Tumbler, Iced Tea, Footed, 14 Oz., 6 3/4 In. 28.00
First Love, Vase, 5 In. 43.00
First Love, Vase, 11 1/2 In. 155.00
Hobnail, Bowl, Blue Opalescent, 10 1/2 In. 101.00
Hobnail, Champagne, 6 Oz., 4 1/2 In. 16.00
Hobnail, Goblet, 9 Oz., 6 In. 12.00
Hobnail, Ivy Ball, Blue Opalescent, 7 1/2 In. . . . . .75.00 to 85.00
Hobnail, Plate, Bread & Butter, 6 1/8 In. 9.00
Hobnail, Plate, Salad, 7 1/4 In. 12.00
Homestead, Toothpick 75.00
Pall Mall, Ashtray, Santa Fe Railroad Etch, 3 1/2 x 5 3/4 In. 56.00
Pall Mall, Swan, Open Back, 11 3/4 In. 65.00
Pall Mall, Swan, Ruby, 13 In. . . . . .50.00 to 85.00
Sandwich, Basket, Amber, 6 In. 150.00
Sandwich, Bowl, Handle, 6 1/4 x 2 3/4 In. 50.00
Sandwich, Bowl, Salad, 10 In. 72.00
Sandwich, Cake Stand, 12 In. 75.00
Sandwich, Candlestick, 4 In. 14.00
Sandwich, Candy Dish, Cover, Green, Footed, 8 1/2 In. 75.00
Sandwich, Champagne, 5 Oz., 5 1/4 In. . . . . .15.00 to 20.00
Sandwich, Coaster, 5 In. 10.00
Sandwich, Cocktail, 3 Oz., 4 1/4 In. 30.00
Sandwich, Cup 9.00
Sandwich, Cup & Saucer 15.00
Sandwich, Dish, Almond, 1 In. 11.00
Sandwich, Egg Plate 90.00
Sandwich, Goblet, 9 Oz., 6 In. . . . . .14.00 to 18.00
Sandwich, Lazy Susan, 16 In. . . . . .72.00 to 105.00

Sandwich, Nut Dish 11.00
Sandwich, Plate, 13 In. . . . . .50.00 to 55.00
Sandwich, Saucer 4.00
Sandwich, Sherbet, 5 Oz., 4 1/4 In. 9.00
Sandwich, Sugar & Creamer 18.00
Sandwich, Sugar, 5 Oz. 7.50
Sandwich, Tray, Handles, 8 In. 18.00
Sandwich, Tumbler, Footed, 5 1/2 x 3 1/2 In. 36.00
Sandwich, Tumbler, Iced Tea, Footed 18.00
Sandwich, Tumbler, Water, Footed, 9 Oz. 12.00
Sandwich, Tumbler, Yellow, Footed, 5 3/4 x 3 3/8 In. 38.00
Sandwich, Wine, 3 Oz., 4 1/4 In. . . . . .15.00 to 17.00
Sanibel, Muffin Tray, Chartreuse, 13 In. 225.00
Star In A Square, Berry Set, Ruby Stain, Gold Trim, 7 Piece 300.00
Swirl, Bouillon, Pink, 3 3/4 In. 15.00
Swirl, Celery Dish, Amber 20.00
Swirl, Compote, Amber, 6 In. 20.00
Swirl, Plate, 7 1/2 In. 4.00
Swirl, Plate, Amber, 7 1/2 In. 4.00
Swirl, Plate, Amber, 7 In. 4.00
Swirl, Plate, Pink, 6 In. 4.00
Swirl, Plate, Salad, Green, 8 1/2 In. 15.00
Swirl, Sherbet, Green, 4 3/4 In. . . . . .15.00 to 18.00
Swirl, Swirl, Compote, Amber, 4 1/8 In. 15.00
Swirl, Tumbler, Cocktail, Footed, Amber, 2 1/2 Oz., 3 3/8 In. 7.00
Swirl, Vase, Blue Opalescent Pulled, Ruffled Edge, 3 3/4 x 5 3/4 In. 35.00
Swirl, Vase, Cornucopia, Chartreuse, 14 In. 175.00
Teardrop, Bread Plate, 6 In. 4.00
Teardrop, Butter, Metal Cover, 1 Lb. . . . . .20.00 to 24.00
Teardrop, Candlestick 10.00
Teardrop, Champagne, 5 Oz., 5 In. 10.00
Teardrop, Coaster, 3 In., 4 Piece 22.00
Teardrop, Cup 6.50
Teardrop, Cup & Saucer 7.00
Teardrop, Jam Jar, Cover 35.00
Teardrop, Marmalade, Cover 38.00
Teardrop, Nut Dish, 2 Sections, 6 In. 12.00
Teardrop, Relish, 2 Sections, Handles, 7 In. 8.00
Teardrop, Relish, 3 Sections, Applied Handle, 12 In. 24.00
Teardrop, Sherbet 6.00
Teardrop, Sugar & Creamer . . . . .15.00 to 16.00
Teardrop, Sugar, 8 Oz. 10.00

DURAND art glass was made from 1924 to 1931. The Vineland Flint
Glass Works was established by Victor Durand and Victor Durand, Jr.,
in 1897. In 1924 Martin Bach, Jr., and other artisans from the Quezal
glassworks joined them at the Vineland, New Jersey, plant to make
Durand art glass.

Compote, Gold Iridescent, 7 6/8 x 6 1/8 In. 977.00
Compote, White Interior, Emerald Green Exterior, Signed, 6 3/4 In. 345.00
Lamp, Floral, Iridescent, 10 1/2 In. 57.00
Lamp, Iridescent Gold, Spider Webbing, Gilt Metal Base & Canopy 305.00
Lamp, Iridescent Gold, Spider Webbing, Scenic Shade, Embossed Base, Bronze, 18 In. . . 1120.00
Shade, Trumpet, Crackle, Red, Orange, Iridescent White Interior, 12 In. 242.00
Sherbet, Green, Applied White Rim, Iridescent, 2 3/4 x 6 In. 115.00
Torchere, Red, White Moorish Crackle, Gold Iridescent Interior, 11 x 62 In. 2070.00
Tray, Green, Purple, Glossy, 1919, 11 1/2 In. 215.00
Vase, Blue, Gold Coil, 7 1/2 In. 805.00
Vase, Blue, White Pulled Feather, Gold Iridescent, 6 3/4 In. 1092.00
Vase, Classical Shape, Iridescent Blue, Signed, c.1918, 6 In. 748.00
Vase, Emerald Green Over Gold, Signed, 12 In. 2530.00
Vase, Gold Coil On White, 10 1/2 In. 1380.00
Vase, Gold Iridescent, Signed, 8 In. 517.00

Vase, Gold Spider Webbing, Signed, 1901, 6 1/2 In. 287.00
Vase, Gold Trailing Hearts & Vine, Blue, White, 8 In. 1380.00
Vase, Iridescent Glass, Spider Web Threading, Mounted As Lamp, c.1925, 27 1/2 In. 632.00
Vase, King Tut, Opalescent White, Gold Iridescent, Signed, c.1925, 10 1/4 In. 2530.00
Vase, Lady Gay Rose, Pink, Yellow Iridescent Interior, 6 5/8 x 3 In. 2750.00
Vase, Moorish Crackle, Red Iridescent, Signed, 8 x 7 In. 2703.00

ELFINWARE is a mark found on Dresden-like porcelain that was sold in
dime stores and gift shops. Many pieces were decorated with raised
flowers. The mark was registered by Breslauer-Underberg, Inc., of
New York City in 1947. Pieces marked *Elfinware Made in Germany*
had been sold since 1945 by this importer.

Elfinware

Figurine, Basket, Pink & Blue Forget-Me-Nots, Tall Handle, 2 3/4 x 2 3/4 In. 64.00
Figurine, Basket, Pink Rose, Forget-Me-Nots, Spinach Moss, 1 3/4 x 1 1/4 x 1 1/4 In. ... 42.00
Figurine, Shoe, Pink Roses, Spinach Moss, 4 1/2 x 2 In. 57.00
Salt, Open, Flowers, Birds, 3 x 2 In. 360.00

ELVIS PRESLEY, the well-known singer, lived from 1935 to 1977. He
became famous by 1956. Elvis appeared on television, starred in
twenty-seven movies, and performed in Las Vegas. Memorabilia from
any of the Presley shows, his records, and even memorials made after
his death are collected.

Book, Are You Lonesome Tonight?, 1st Edition, 1987 .... 20.00
Book, Softly I Must Leave You, Colored Pictures, 1976 & 1977 Tours 20.00
Marble, Yellow, 1936 .... 7.00
Pocket Calendar Set, RCA, 1966, 1977, 1978, 3 Piece 10.00
Ticket, Concert, August 22, 1977 .... 12.00
Ticket, Concert, Cumberland County Civic Center, Aug. 18, 1977, With Postcard 105.00

ENAMELS listed here are made of glass particles and other materials
heated and fused to metal. In the eighteenth and nineteenth centuries,
workmen from Russia, France, England, and other countries made
small boxes and table pieces of enamel on metal. One form of English
enamel is called *Battersea* and is listed under that name. There was a
revival of interest in enameling in the 1930s and a new style evolved.
There is now renewed interest in the artistic enameled plaques, vases,
ashtrays, and jewelry. Enamels made since the 1930s are usually on
copper or steel, although silver was often used for jewelry. Graniteware is a separate category, and enameled metal kitchen pieces may be
included in the Kitchen category.

Bowl, Copper, Russian Coin, Green Cabochon Stones, Russia, c.1900, 7 1/2 x 7 In. 560.00
Box, Champleve, Foliate Design, 18K Gold, 3 1/4 x 2 1/4 In. 1495.00
Box, Cover, Scenes Of Islands Around Body, Floral, France, 2 7/8 x 1 1/4 In. 115.00
Box, Hinged Cover, Lady In 18th Century Costume, Gilt Rim, France, 1910, 3 In. 575.00
Box, Oval, Blue Sides, White Base, Interior Mirror, Verse, 1 3/4 x 1 1/4 In. 201.00
Box, Storage, Hinged Cover, Garden Scene, Musical Scene By A River, Circular, 5 In. ... 1035.00
Card Case, Cobalt, Sterling, Sur Pat Deco Medallion Of Harvest Figure, France, 3 In. 1050.00
Card Case, Hinged Cover, Jack Of Clubs, Floral, Silver, Russia, 3 7/8 In. .... *Illus* 13440.00
Cigarette Case, Shaded, Swan, Cream Background, Leaves, Zverev, Russia, c.1908, 4 In. .. 2800.00
Copper, Plaque, Warriors At City Gate, Chinese, Late 19th Century, 20 In. 275.00
Creamer, Birds, Flowers, Scrolling Leaves, Gilt, Turquoise Beading, Russia, c.1917 ..... 2016.00
Dish, Ocean Scene, Seagull, Signed K., 8 1/2 In. .... *Illus* 54.00
Egg, Shaded Flowers, Red, Cream, Green Ground, F. Ruckert, Russia, c.1917 .... 4760.00
Ewer, Gilt Metal, Multiple Mythological Scene, 5 1/4 In. 690.00
Ewer, Musical, Playful Garden Scenes, Gilt Metal, 5 3/4 x 4 7/8 In. 1725.00
Goblet, Stylized Foliate Arches, Green, Blue Enamel, Domed Foot, 1903, 8 In. 2700.00
Kovsh, Shaded Flowers, Leaves, Gilt Ground, Turquoise Beading, Semenova, 4 3/4 In. 2464.00
Perfume Bottle, Gilt Metal, Foliate Body, Garden Scene, 5 3/4 In. 1380.00
Plaque, Portrait, Woman, Brass Frame, 6 1/2 x 5 1/4 In. 300.00
Plate, Abstract Woman, Red, Ellamarie & Jackson Woolley, 7 In. .... *Illus* 85.00
Pokal, Cover, Gilt Metal, 2 Oval Portraits Of Women In Garden Landscape, 5 In. 805.00
Stand, Watch, Garden Scene On Back, Elephant Figure Standing, 7 In. 1955.00

Enamel, Card Case, Hinged
Cover, Jack Of Clubs, Floral,
Silver, Russia, 3 7/8 In.

Enamel, Dish, Ocean Scene,
Seagull, Signed K.,
8 1/2 In.

Enamel, Plate, Abstract
Woman, Red, Ellamarie & Jackson
Woolley, 7 In.

Tray, Gilt, Metal, 3 Figures In Garden, Rococo Handle, Footed, 14 1/4 In. 1610.00
Vase, 2 Women In Garden Scene, Red Base, 5 3/4 In. 575.00

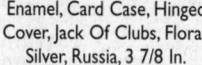

ERPHILA is a mark found on Czechoslovakian and other pottery and porcelain made after 1920. The mark was used on items imported by Ebeling & Reuss, Philadelphia, a giftware firm that is still operating in Pennsylvania. The mark is a combination of the letters *E* and *R* (Ebeling & Reuss) and the first letters of the city, Phila(delphia). Many whimsical figural pitchers and creamers, figurines, platters, and other giftwares carry this mark.

Cake Plate, Cherry Chintz, 11 1/4 In. 23.00
Cookie Jar, Poppy Design, 2 Handles, Mark, 7 In. 21.00
Creamer, Cat, Black & White, Marked Erphila, Fayence, Germany, No. 414-1, 5 In. 91.00
Creamer, Rooster, Hand Painted 58.00
Figurine, Bird, Germany, 5 In. 30.00
Figurine, Dachshund, Marked, Germany, 9 x 6 In. 41.00
Figurine, Dog, English Bulldog, Stripe On Back, Mark, Germany, 8 1/2 x 4 1/4 In. 25.00
Figurine, Dog, Fox Terrier, Sitting, White, Black Spots, Pink Tongue, 1950s, 6 x 6 In. . . . 85.00
Figurine, Pair Of Goats, Porcelain, White, Gold Trim, 4 x 5 In. 44.00
Flower Frog, Nude Woman, 8 Holes, Erphila Fayence Germany, 7 In. 51.00
Flower Frog, White Porcelain, Gold Trim, Flamingo, 3 Holes, Incised 2837 AII, Stamp . . 40.00
Pitcher, Cat, Orange, Black 2000.00
Pitcher, Orange Majolica Glaze, White Interior, Schnauzer Handle, Germany, c.1900 . . . . 60.00
Pitcher, Ram, Orange, Black 500.00
Planter, Geometric Pattern, 4 Sides, Blue & Yellow, Marked, 4 x 4 In. 12.00
Reamer, Orange, Handle, 6 In. 84.00
Salt & Pepper, Boy & Girl, Gold Foil Label, Stamps, Cork Closures, 1886, 3 1/4 In. 215.00
Sugar, Portland, Chintz 33.00
Teapot, Cat, Gray, Pink Collar, Germany, 7 1/2 In. 27.00
Teapot, Cat, Majolica, Germany 195.00
Teapot, Dog, Dachshund, Begging, Paws Spout, Tail Handle, No. 6703B, 8 In. 252.00
Teapot, Dog, Majolica, Germany, 7 1/2 In. 225.00

ES GERMANY porcelain was made at the factory of Erdmann Schlegelmilch from 1861 to 1937 in Suhl, Germany. The porcelain, marked *ES Germany* or *ES Suhl*, was sold decorated or undecorated. Other pieces were made at a factory in Saxony, Prussia, and are marked *ES Prussia*. Reinhold Schlegelmilch made the famous wares marked *RS Germany*.

Bowl, Roses, 10 In. 29.00
Cake Plate, Orange Poppies, Open Handles, 1861 Mark 20.00
Candy Dish, Stenciled River & Tree Scene, Beads, Black Rim, Scalloped, 7 In. 26.00
Cup & Saucer, Blue Flower, Brown, Handle, Erdmann Schlegelmilch, Suhl 75.00
Dresser Box, Cover, Rose Finial, Painted Roses, Round, c.1920, 7 In. 58.00

Ewer, Light Blue & Cream Ground, Gold & Silver Trim, 9 1/2 In. 67.00
Pin Tray, Pink, Lady, Gold Edge 26.00
Plate, Gibson Girl, Blue Hat, Cobalt Border, Gold Trim, Prov Saxe, 9 3/4 In. 760.00

ESKIMO artifacts of all types are collected. Carvings of whale or walrus teeth are listed under Scrimshaw. Baskets are in the Basket category. All other types of Eskimo art are listed here.

Basket, Coiled, Cover, Arrowhead Design, 6 x 8 In. 187.00
Bird, Carved, Mottled Black Stone, Inuit, 5 In. 110.00
Bowl, Basket, 1920s, 7 1/2 x 9 1/2 In. 65.00
Button, Ivory, Seal, Large 242.00
Compact, Mirrored Bottom, George Ahqupuk, Square 58.00
Cribbage Board, Bear, Walrus, Caribou, Fox, 23 1/4 In. 220.00
Cribbage Board, Ivory Tusk, Sea Eagle At Head, Birds Allover, Inuit, 21 In. 5175.00
Cribbage Board, Ivory, Hunter Confronting Bear, Walrus, Swimming Caribou, 23 In. . . . 747.00
Doll, Sealskin Parka, Mittens, Muslin Body, Inked Features, 15 In. 247.00
Dress, Inuit, Arctic Fox, Fur Hood Seal Fur On Bottom, 37 In. 1150.00
Effigy, Bear, Bone, Alaska, 4 1/2 In. 40.00
Figurine, Inuit Hunter, Parka & Snow Goggles, Soapstone, c.1965 . . . . 5750.00
Figurine, Inuit Woman, Standing, Holding Kudliq, Barnabus Arnasungaaq, Soapstone 1955.00
Game Board, Cribbage, Walrus Tusk Ivory, Scrimshaw, c.1920, 12 In. 247.00
Goggles, Carved Caribou Hoof, 2 x 5 In. 140.00
Harpoon Points, Fossil, 27 Piece 770.00
Knife, Skinning, Stamped Original Bowie, 5 3/8 In. 175.00
Moccasins, Red Felt, High Top, Beaded Toes, Alaska, Child's, 1930s 18.00
Model, Kayak, Ivory, Bone Detail, Carved Cedar Pieces, 20 In. 920.00
Model, Kayak, Sealskin, With Turret, Paddle, 1900, 27 x 4 In. 413.00
Model, Kayak, Skin Covered, Figural Bone Mounts, 25 In. 298.00
Mukluks, Fur Top, Sealskin Bottom, Puckered Toe, 11 In. 65.00
Mukluks, Sealskin, Hand Sewn, Child's, 5 3/8 In. 185.00
Necklace, Fetish, Carved, Birds, Bear, Rabbit, Wolf, 20th Century 241.00
Needle Case, Inuit, Fossil Ivory, Seal Form, 4 x 1/2 In. 275.00
Pipe, Trade, Metal Band, 11 In. 495.00
Sculpture, 2 Eskimos Skinning A Seal, Stone, 5 1/2 In. 207.00
Sled Runners, Ivory, 2 1/2 x 26 In. 330.00
Spoon, Carved Bone, Circles & Polar Bear Carved In Bottom, 5 In. 143.00
Walrus Tusk, 3 Caribou Pulling A Sled Towards An Igloo, 22 In. 3000.00
Walrus Tusk, Whale Hunt On 1 Side, Line Of Fish Traps On Other, 22 In. 3000.00

FABERGE was a firm of jewelers and goldsmiths founded in St.
Petersburg, Russia, in 1842, by Gustav Faberge. Peter Carl Faberge,
his son, was jeweler to the Russian Imperial Court from about 1870 to
1914. The rare Imperial Easter eggs, jewelry, and decorative items are
very expensive today.

ФАБЕРЖЕ

КФ

Asparagus Tongs, Shell Handle, Armorial Design, Moscow, 1890, 10 3/4 In. 2400.00
Bell Push, Greek Key, Dome Shape, Translucent Oyster, Moscow, 1900, 2 1/4 In. 9000.00
Bell Push, Translucent Pale Blue, Enameled, Leaf Design, Moscow, 1900, 2 In. 4800.00
Bowl, Copper, St. George, Dragon, Imperial Eagle, War, 1914, 4 1/4 In. 1568.00
Box, Stamp, Acanthus Medallion Flanked By Fleur-De-Lis, Gilt Interior, 3 1/2 In. 1210.00
Cigarette Case, Reeded End, Match Compartment, Gold Thumbpiece, c.1900, 5 In. 4500.00
Frame, Photograph, Translucent Apple Green, St. Petersburg, 1890, 7 1/4 In. 9000.00
Frame, Photograph, Translucent Pale Blue, Beaded Border, 1910, 4 1/2 In. 8400.00
Lighter, Cigar, Flutes, Leafage Swags, Acanthus Leaves, Scroll Handle, 1900, 7 In. 9000.00
Pendant, Maiden Clutching Jewel On Lily Pad, Moscow, 1900, 1 1/8 In. 9000.00

FAIENCE refers to tin-glazed earthenware, especially the wares made in
France, Germany, and Scandinavia. It is also correct to say that faience
is the same as majolica or Delft, although usually the term refers only
to the tin-glazed pottery of the three regions mentioned.

Bowl, Cobalt Blue Flowers, 4 Bands Rim, Tin Glaze, 1900s, 12 In. 165.00
Bust, Young Nobleman, Goldenrod Hat, Bologna, Label Carbone, 10 1/4 x 10 3/4 In. . . . 300.00
Cachepot, Belle Epoque, Baroque Style, Armorial, Late 19th Century, 4 x 4 1/2 In. 58.00
Candlestick, Peasant Man & Woman, Head Baskets, Ovington, N.Y., France, 8 In., Pair . . 410.00

Charger, Butterfly & Flowers, Cobalt Blue, 15 1/2 In. 220.00
Charger, Green Fish & Undulating Waves, Marked, Foley, 8 3/8 In. 385.00
Charger, Stylized Flowers, Leaves, France, 11 3/4 In. 115.00
Figurine, Rampant Lion, Continental, 26 In. 1093.00
Figurine, Recumbent Lion, Polychrome, France, 19th Century, 18 1/4 In. 747.00
Jardiniere, Bulls & Rustic Figure Scene, Tapered, 1900, 16 x 17 In. 575.00
Planter, Genre Scene, Horses, Carriages, Men On Horseback, 8 1/2 x 10 In. 220.00
Plate, Chinoiserie Birds & Flowers, Mid 18th Century, Pair 633.00
Plate, Cornucopia & Blackbird, Pair 632.00
Plate, Parrot, Flowers, Continental, 8 5/8 In. 173.00
Plate, Purple, Yellow, Blue Flowers, White Ground, Green Rim, 12 Piece 1380.00
Tea Set, Floral Spray Design, Handles, Early 18th Century, 27 Piece 1265.00
Tile, Qajar, Seated Ruler With Phoenix, Serpent, Polychrome, 18th Century, 21 In. 2070.00
Urinal, Blue Spots, White, France, Late 18th Century, 10 In. 950.00
Urn, Blue & White, Stylized Flowers, Leaves, Cartouche, Continental, 11 1/2 In., Pair ... 104.00
Urn, Cover, Courting Scenes, Brass Lion Heads & Wreath Handles, Ring Base, 24 In. 1595.00
Vase, Basket Of Flowers Design, Rouen, Polychrome, 8 In., Pair 316.00
Vase, Blue Matte Glaze, Marked, 6 In. 575.00
Vase, Coiled Snake Handles, Mask, Allegorical Scene, Italy, 19th Century, 18 In. 196.00
Vase, Fourmaintaux, 1877-1887, 11 1/2 In. 795.00
Vase, Green, Silver Crystalline Glaze, Buff Clay Body, 9 3/4 In. 1320.00
Vase, Heraldic Emblem, Floral, Twin Loop Handles, 7 In., Pair 259.00

FAIRINGS are small souvenir china boxes and figurines that were sold
at country fairs during the nineteenth century. Most were made in
Germany. Reproductions of fairings are being made, especially of the
famous *twelve months of marriage* series.

Box, Baby In A Covered Bassinette, White Porcelain, Gold Trim, 2 3/4 x 2 1/2 In. 68.00
Box, Cover, Boy Standing On Top, Eating, Rooster, Wants To Share Food, 4 1/2 In. 100.00
Box, Cover, Girl Feeding Her Cat & Dog, Rosettes, 3 x 2 1/2 x 1 3/4 In. 8.00
Box, Young Girl Holding Bird, Pocketbook At Her Waist, 2 x 3 1/2 In. 130.00
Figurine, Dog, King Charles Spaniel, White & Red Orange, Staffordshire 54.00
Figurine, Gentleman Doctor, 4 In. 75.00
Figurine, Ladies Of Llangollen, Wearing Traveling Coats & Top Hats, c.1890, 6 In. 61.00
Figurine, Man, Heart On His Chest, Blue Coat, Green Grass, Staffordshire, 4 In. 50.00
Figurine, Military Man, Sword, On Horse, Jumping, Staffordshire, 3 In. 40.00
Figurine, Pig, Holds Cigarettes & Matches, Ashtray, Striker, Germany, 4 1/2 In. 55.00
Figurine, Young Girl In Ribbons With Cat By Her Feet, Staffordshire, 3 In. 97.00
Trinket Box, Boy Holding Skein Of Yarn, Girl, 4 In. 55.00

FAIRYLAND LUSTER pieces are included in the Wedgwood category.

FAMILLE ROSE, see Chinese Export category.

FANS have been used for cooling since the days of the ancients. By the
eighteenth century, the fan was an accessory for the lady of fashion,
and very elaborate and expensive fans were made. Sticks were made
of ivory or wood, set with jewels or carved. The fans were made of
painted silk or paper. Inexpensive paper fans printed with advertising
were giveaways in the late nineteenth and early twentieth centuries.
Electric fans were introduced in 1882.

Advertising, Darkie Toothpaste, Die Cut Cardboard, Black Man, Top Hat, 13 1/2 In. 220.00
Advertising, Drink Moxie, Cowboy, 1922 .... 60.00
Advertising, Exchange Bar & Cafe, Denver, Woman With Drink, Shield Shape, 1910 .... 85.00
Advertising, Home Memories, Riveted, Folding, Penn Yan, N.Y. 30.00
Advertising, Moxie, Beautiful Girl, Wearing Moxie Man Necklace, 1923 .... 75.00
Advertising, Old Spice Talcum, Instructions, Proper Coquetry Of The Fan, 7 Panels 25.00
Advertising, Sultana Coffee, Puppy, Hat, Figural, Cardboard, c.1892, 13 In. 33.00
Advertising, Tums, Cardboard, c.1920, 11 In. 14.00
Beaded, Floral, Beaded Fringe 425.00
Cat's Head Shape, Red Collar, Duvelleroy, 1910 .... 1255.00
Cloth, White, Floral Design, Silver Gilt, Wooden Ribs, 9 In. 8.00
Electric, Candle, Bronze Tube, 1928, 9 1/2 In. 565.00
Electric, Century, Model S10-10, Brass Blades, 2-Speed, Oscillating, 10 In. 225.00

Electric, Cincinnati Victor Co., Cast Iron, 55 In. 345.00
Electric, Diehl Ribbonaire, Singer, Table Model, 10 In. 489.00
Electric, Emerson, Black, 4 Blades 39.95
Electric, Emerson, Chrome Blades, Oscillating, Stand, 9 x 45 In. 195.00
Electric, Emerson, Model 1010, Brass Cage, Pancake Motor, 12 In. 400.00
Electric, Emerson, Oscillating, 15 In. 35.00
Electric, Emerson, Type 73648, Brass Blades, 3-Speed, Oscillating, 12 In. 165.00
Electric, Eskimo, Model 1100J, Black & Chrome, Table Model, 11 In. 25.00
Electric, General Electric, 4-Speed, Brass Cage & Blades, 1901 .... 200.00
Electric, Houze, Black Metal, Slag Glass Base, 1920s-1930s, 12 In. 300.00
Electric, Robbins & Myers, Chrome 395.00
Electric, Westinghouse, Adjustable Fan, Metal, Cast Iron Base, Tag, Floor, 58 In. 172.00
Electric, Westinghouse, Black, Wire Cage, Table Model, 10 1/2 In. 25.00
Electric, Westinghouse, Style 803681, Table Model, 10 1/2 In. 25.00
Folding, Wire Clasp, Brass Knob Handles, Black 20.00
Hand Painted, Mounted, Gilt Display Case, Continental, 19 In., Pair 431.00
Ivory Sticks, Central Cartouche Of Figures By Bucolic Fountain, Silver, Gilt, 11 In. 345.00
Ivory Sticks, Central Marriage Scene, Floral Sprays, France, 19th Century, 11 In. 805.00
Ivory Sticks, Courting Couples In Bucolic Setting, Florals, 11 1/4 In. 920.00
Ivory Sticks, Embroidered Organza, Bird Perched On Flowering Tree 230.00
Ivory Sticks, Spangles Encircle 3 Painted Reserves, Grecian Urns, Paper, 11 In. 58.00
Lace, Mother Of Pearl, Silk Box, c.1900, 18 x 10 In. 595.00
Paper, Abalone, Gilt Silver, Courting Scene, Continental, 24 1/2 In. 172.00
Paper, Floral With Glitter Design, Hand Painted, Tassel 20.00
Paper, Folding, Painted, Ivory Handle, Tiny Mirror, 19th Century, 20 In. 230.00
Paper, Round, Multicolored, Balsa Handle, Paper Label, Occupied Japan, 1948, 6 In. 12.00
Paper, Velvet Face, Gilt Outlining Leaves, Rectangular, Ivory, 19th Century, 14 1/2 In. 46.00
Shell Sticks, Lady's, Mauve, Elegant Couples At Fete De Champetre, 12 In., Pair 373.00
Silk, Black, Mother-Of-Pearl Handle, World War II Souvenir, 10 In. 55.00
Silk, Blue, Hand Painted Bird Scene, Dark Stained Frame, Oriental, 17 x 28 In. 385.00
Wooden Slat, White, Gold, Silver, Fancy Cuts, Floral Design, Wire Hanger, Paper 17.50
Wooden Sticks, Oriental Design, Hut On Mountain Cliff, Blue Gray 14.00
Wooden Sticks, Oriental, White Cloth, Pink Flowers, Red, Green Painted Holly, 18 In. ... 20.00
Wooden Sticks, Paper, Hand Colored Flowers, Pink, Yellow, Purple, Green Leaves 5.00
Wooden Sticks, Paper, Ornate Scene, White, Red Flowers, Design, Wire Loop Handle ... 20.00

FAST FOOD COLLECTIBLES may be included in several categories, such as Advertising, Coca-Cola, Toy, etc.

FENTON Art Glass Company, founded in Martins Ferry, Ohio, by Frank L. Fenton, is now located in Williamstown, West Virginia. It is noted for early carnival glass produced between 1907 and 1920. Some of these pieces are listed in the Carnival Glass category. Many other types of glass were also made. Spanish Lace in this section refers to the pattern made by Fenton.

Bicentennial, Paperweight, Eagle, Patriot Red 30.00
Black Rose, Vase, Hand, 1953-1954, 10 1/2 In. 450.00
Burmese, Vanity Set, Enameled, 5 Piece 325.00
Burmese, Vase, Enameled, 6 1/2 In. 74.00
Burmese, Vase, Rose Decorated, Ruffled Edge, 5 In. 89.00
Burmese, Vase, Roses Decorated, 10 1/2 In. 125.00
Cactus, Compote, 8 1/4 In. 75.00
Cactus, Goblet, Topaz Opalescent 30.00
Christmas Bell, Happiness Bird, Custard, 1979 .... 50.00
Christmas Bell, Happiness Bird, Lime Sherbet, 1978 .... 48.00
Christmas Bell, Hobnail, Ruby, 1981, 5 1/2 In. 14.00
Christmas Bell, Holly, Ruby, 1982, 4 1/2 In. 15.00
Christmas Bell, Winter Chapel, 1983, 4 1/2 In. 22.00
Coin Dot, Decanter, Cranberry Opalescent 695.00
Coin Dot, Pitcher, Cranberry Opalescent 375.00
Coin Dot, Tumbler, Cranberry Opalescent, 10 Oz. 60.00
Colonial, Cake Plate, Green Opalescent 45.00
Colonial, Lamp, Boudoir, Gooseneck, Reverse Painted Butterfly, 16 In. 200.00

Elephant, Decanter, Sherry, Ball Stopper, 9 1/2 In. 250.00
Emerald Crest, Plate, 9 In. 40.00
Empress Rose, Bowl, 8 1/2 In. 29.00
Figurine, Alley Cat, Purple Slag, 10 In. 175.00
Figurine, Ballerina, Rosalene, 6 1/2 In. 110.00
Figurine, Happiness Bird, Ruby, 1981 .... 24.00
Figurine, Kissing Kids, Carnival Glass, 1981, Pair 85.00
Finecut & Block, Compote, Ruby, Sticker, 6 In. 24.00
Georgian, Sugar, Ruby 16.00
Georgian, Tumbler, Royal Blue, Footed, 9 Oz., 5 1/2 In. 18.00
Grape & Cable, Tobacco Jar, Mongolian Green, 5 1/2 x 7 In. 175.00
Hobnail, Basket, Milk Glass, 7 In. 25.00
Hobnail, Bonbon, Green Opalescent, 6 In. 25.00
Hobnail, Bottle, Oil, Cranberry Opalescent 75.00
Hobnail, Bowl, Blue Opalescent, Handles, 2 1/4 x 5 1/4 In. 52.00
Hobnail, Bowl, Fruit, Milk Glass, Ruffled Edge, 14 In. 45.00
Hobnail, Bowl, Milk Glass, Ruffled Edge, 11 7/8 In. 38.00
Hobnail, Bowl, Peachblow, 5 1/2 In. 30.00
Hobnail, Butter, Cover, Blue Opalescent 150.00
Hobnail, Candlestick, Milk Glass, Pair ....30.00 to 45.00
Hobnail, Candy Dish, Cover, Topaz Opalescent 200.00
Hobnail, Candy Dish, Cover, White, 6 1/2 In. 40.00
Hobnail, Candy Dish, Heart Shape, Milk Glass 90.00
Hobnail, Honey Pot, Milk Glass 100.00
Hobnail, Lamp, Student, Milk Glass, 19 In. 350.00
Hobnail, Plate, Milk Glass, 13 1/2 In. 95.00
Hobnail, Rose Bowl, Ruffled Edge, 3 x 4 In. 8.00
Hobnail, Sugar & Creamer, Milk Glass 9.00
Hobnail, Vanity Set, 2 Cologn Bottles, Puff Jar, French Opalescent, 3 Piece 100.00
Hobnail, Vase, Blue Opalescent, 8 In. 65.00
Hobnail, Vase, Jack-In-The-Pulpit, Blue Opalsecent, 6 3/4 In. 85.00
Hobnail, Vase, Milk Glass, 9 In. 175.00
Hobnail, Vase, White Opalescent, 6 In. 20.00
Jade Green, Jug, Cover, Black Foot, 3 Pt. 250.00
Jefferson, Compote, White Satin 150.00
Lincoln Inn, Sherbet, 4 3/4 In. 10.00
Lincoln Inn, Tumbler, Footed, 5 Oz. 15.00
Madonna, Vase, Candlelight, Blue Satin 45.00
Peach Crest, Jug, Beaded Melon, Handle, 6 In. 45.00
Peach Crest, Vase, Beaded Melon, 4 1/2 In. 25.00
Peach Crest, Vase, Pink Roses, 8 In. 55.00
Plated Amberina, Vase, Ribbed, 1961-1963, 7 In. 295.00
Plymouth, Goblet, Ruby 20.00
Plymouth, Sherbet, Ruby 13.00
Plymouth, Tumbler, Iced Tea, Ruby 20.00
Poppy, Lamp, Lime Sherbet, Gone With The Wind 240.00
Silver Crest, Banana Stand, 13 In. ....45.00 to 60.00
Silver Crest, Basket, Violets In The Snow, 1970, 5 In. 45.00
Silver Crest, Bonbon, 6 1/2 In. 12.00
Silver Crest, Bonbon, 8 In. 12.00
Silver Crest, Bowl, 10 In. 47.00
Silver Crest, Bowl, 11 In. 24.00
Silver Crest, Bowl, Footed, 8 In. ....14.00 to 18.00
Silver Crest, Candleholder, 3 1/2 In., Pair 28.00
Silver Crest, Candlestick, 6 In., Pair 70.00
Silver Crest, Compote, 4 x 6 In. 18.00
Silver Crest, Compote, 8 x 11 In. 28.00
Silver Crest, Dish, Mayonnaise, Footed 24.00
Silver Crest, Plate, 6 1/2 In. 12.00
Silver Crest, Plate, 8 1/2 In. ....20.00 to 25.00
Silver Crest, Plate, 10 In. 50.00
Silver Crest, Plate, 12 1/2 In. 50.00
Silver Crest, Rose Bowl, 4 In. 18.00

Silver Crest, Sandwich Server, Center Handle, 12 1/2 In. 40.00
Silver Crest, Saucer .... 5.00 to 7.00
Silver Crest, Tidbit, 3 Tiers, 13 In. 45.00
Silver Crest, Torte Plate, 16 In. 85.00
Silver Crest, Vase, 6 In. .... 20.00 to 35.00
Silvertone, Bowl, Tulip Shape, 11 In. 45.00
Snow Crest, Lamp, Emerald Green 50.00
Snow Crest, Vase, 8 In. 95.00
Spanish Lace, Compote, Pink 75.00
Spanish Lace, Compote, White, 7 In. .... 20.00 to 24.00
Spanish Lace, Vase, Bulbous Base, White, 8 In. 22.00
Spanish Lace, Vase, White, 4 In. 14.00
Tea Rose, Vanity Set, Tray, 4 Piece 300.00
Violets In The Snow, Candy Box, Cover, Persian Medallion 60.00
Violets In The Snow, Compote, Low 40.00
Violets In The Snow, Vase, 8 In. 48.00
Water Lily, Compote, Lavender Satin, Footed 85.00
Water Lily, Jardiniere, Blue Satin 25.00
Wisteria, Vase, Threaded, Diamond Optic, 7 In. 65.00

FIESTA, the colorful dinnerware, was introduced in 1936 by the Homer Laughlin China Co., redesigned in 1969, and withdrawn in 1973. It was reissued again in 1986 in different colors and is still being made. The simple design was characterized by a band of concentric circles, beginning at the rim. Cups had full-circle handles until 1969, when partial-circle handles were made. Harlequin and Riviera were related wares. For more information and prices of American dinnerware, see the book *Kovels' Depression Glass & Dinnerware Price List*.

Apricot, Cup & Saucer 15.00
Apricot, Plate, 10 In. .... 16.00 to 18.00
Apricot, Salt & Pepper .... 17.00 to 37.00
Apricot, Sauceboat 30.00
Black, Bowl, Vegetable, Open, Round 30.00
Black, Plate, 7 In. 12.00
Black, Plate, 10 In. 22.00
Black, Salt & Pepper 38.00
Chartreuse, Casserole, Cover 280.00
Chartreuse, Chop Plate, 13 In. .... 25.00 to 55.00
Chartreuse, Chop Plate, 15 In. 70.00
Chartreuse, Cup & Saucer, After Dinner .... 275.00 to 550.00
Chartreuse, Cup, Tea 38.00
Chartreuse, Eggcup 170.00
Chartreuse, Mug, Tom & Jerry 80.00
Chartreuse, Pitcher, Disk .... 266.00 to 295.00
Chartreuse, Plate, 6 In. 28.00
Chartreuse, Plate, 7 In. 13.00
Chartreuse, Plate, 9 In. .... 17.00 to 35.00
Chartreuse, Plate, 10 In. 65.00
Chartreuse, Platter, 12 In. 30.00
Chartreuse, Salt & Pepper 35.00
Chartreuse, Sauceboat 70.00
Cobalt Blue, Ashtray .... 40.00 to 60.00
Cobalt Blue, Bowl, 8 1/2 In. 54.00
Cobalt Blue, Bowl, Fruit, 11 3/4 In. 250.00
Cobalt Blue, Cake Server, Kitchen Kraft 120.00
Cobalt Blue, Candleholder, Bulb 75.00
Cobalt Blue, Casserole, Kitchen Kraft, 7 1/2 In. 40.00
Cobalt Blue, Casserole, Kitchen Kraft, Individual 65.00
Cobalt Blue, Chop Plate, 13 In. .... 20.00 to 40.00
Cobalt Blue, Chop Plate, 15 In. 30.00
Cobalt Blue, Coffeepot 250.00
Cobalt Blue, Creamer, Stick Handle 45.00
Cobalt Blue, Cup & Saucer, After Dinner .... 55.00 to 100.00

Cobalt Blue, Cup, Tea .... 18.00 to 35.00
Cobalt Blue, Eggcup 60.00
Cobalt Blue, Mixing Bowl, No. 1 .... 190.00
Cobalt Blue, Mixing Bowl, No. 4 .... 195.00
Cobalt Blue, Mug .... 30.00 to 55.00
Cobalt Blue, Mug, Tom & Jerry 75.00
Cobalt Blue, Nappy, 8 1/2 In. 20.00
Cobalt Blue, Plate, 6 In. 16.00
Cobalt Blue, Plate, 9 In. 24.00
Cobalt Blue, Plate, 10 In. .... 40.00 to 52.00
Cobalt Blue, Plate, Compartment, 10 1/2 In. .... 25.00 to 50.00
Cobalt Blue, Plate, Compartment, 12 In. 30.00
Cobalt Blue, Plate, Deep, 8 1/4 In. .... 25.00 to 60.00
Cobalt Blue, Salt & Pepper .... 21.00 to 36.00
Cobalt Blue, Sauceboat .... 40.00 to 65.00
Cobalt Blue, Saucer .... 13.00 to 20.00
Cobalt Blue, Spoon, Kitchen Kraft .... 90.00 to 110.00
Cobalt Blue, Stacking Unit, Kitchen Kraft 40.00
Cobalt Blue, Sugar & Creamer, Handle 15.00
Cobalt Blue, Teapot, Medium, 6 Cup .... 50.00 to 80.00
Cobalt Blue, Tray, Figure 8 .... 40.00 to 50.00
Cobalt Blue, Tumbler, Juice .... 20.00 to 40.00
Cobalt Blue, Tumbler, Water .... 90.00 to 100.00
Cobalt Blue, Vase, 8 In. .... 400.00 to 425.00
Forest Green, Bowl, Fruit, 4 3/4 In. 41.00
Forest Green, Casserole, Cover .... 70.00 to 110.00
Forest Green, Chop Plate, 14 In. 130.00
Forest Green, Coffeepot, After Dinner 795.00
Forest Green, Cup & Saucer 45.00
Forest Green, Cup & Saucer, After Dinner 300.00
Forest Green, Eggcup 110.00
Forest Green, Mixing Bowl, No. 5 .... 90.00
Forest Green, Mug, Tom & Jerry 80.00
Forest Green, Plate, 6 In. 13.00
Forest Green, Plate, 9 In. 20.00
Forest Green, Plate, 10 In. .... 35.00 to 65.00
Forest Green, Plate, Compartment, 10 1/2 In. 125.00
Forest Green, Salt & Pepper 35.00
Forest Green, Sauceboat 45.00
Forest Green, Sugar & Creamer 50.00
Forest Green, Teapot, Cover, 6 Cup 395.00
Gray, Bowl, Fruit, 4 3/4 In. 20.00
Gray, Chop Plate, 13 In. 50.00
Gray, Chop Plate, 15 In. 70.00
Gray, Creamer 19.00
Gray, Cup & Saucer, After Dinner .... 275.00 to 450.00
Gray, Eggcup 110.00
Gray, Mug, Tom & Jerry .... 73.00 to 80.00
Gray, Plate, 6 In. .... 16.00 to 28.00
Gray, Plate, 7 In. 27.00
Gray, Plate, 10 In. .... 20.00 to 30.00
Gray, Plate, Compartment, 10 1/2 In. 25.00
Gray, Plate, Deep, 8 1/4 In. 62.00
Gray, Platter, 12 1/2 In. 35.00
Gray, Teapot, Medium, 6 Cup 395.00
Gray, Tumbler, Juice 95.00
Ivory, Ashtray .... 30.00 to 55.00
Ivory, Bowl, Fruit, 11 3/4 In. 225.00
Ivory, Candleholder, Bulb 75.00
Ivory, Casserole, Cover 60.00
Ivory, Chop Plate, 13 In. 35.00
Ivory, Coffeepot 245.00
Ivory, Compote, Sweets .... 60.00 to 80.00

Ivory, Cup & Saucer ....37.00 to 50.00
Ivory, Cup & Saucer, After Dinner 98.00
Ivory, Eggcup 65.00
Ivory, Jug, 2 Pt. ....40.00 to 70.00
Ivory, Pitcher, Ice Lip, 2 Qt. 110.00
Ivory, Plate, 6 In. ....8.00 to 16.00
Ivory, Plate, 9 In. ....6.00 to 20.00
Ivory, Plate, 10 In. ....28.00 to 52.00
Ivory, Plate, Compartment, 10 1/2 In. ....30.00 to 50.00
Ivory, Plate, Compartment, 12 In. 90.00
Ivory, Platter, 12 1/2 In. ....20.00 to 30.00
Ivory, Salt & Pepper 30.00
Ivory, Sauceboat ....50.00 to 68.00
Ivory, Soup, Onion, Cover 895.00
Ivory, Sugar & Creamer 45.00
Ivory, Tumbler, Juice ....25.00 to 45.00
Ivory, Tumbler, Water ....65.00 to 81.00
Ivory, Vase, 8 In. 400.00
Ivory, Vase, 12 In. 600.00
Light Green, Ashtray ....25.00 to 45.00
Light Green, Bowl, Fruit, 11 3/4 In. 210.00
Light Green, Casserole, Cover 150.00
Light Green, Casserole, Kitchen Kraft, Individual ....70.00 to 80.00
Light Green, Chop Plate, 13 In. 35.00
Light Green, Chop Plate, 15 In. 45.00
Light Green, Compote, Sweets ....45.00 to 80.00
Light Green, Cup & Saucer, After Dinner ....25.00 to 45.00
Light Green, Jar, Cover, Kitchen Kraft ....90.00 to 175.00
Light Green, Mug ....22.00 to 30.00
Light Green, Mug, Tom & Jerry ....45.00 to 55.00
Light Green, Pitcher, Ice Lip, 2 Qt. 70.00
Light Green, Plate, 6 In. ....9.00 to 18.00
Light Green, Plate, 9 In. ....8.00 to 16.00
Light Green, Plate, 10 In. ....20.00 to 44.00
Light Green, Plate, Compartment, 12 In. ....42.00 to 55.00
Light Green, Platter, 12 1/2 In. 30.00
Light Green, Salt & Pepper 17.00
Light Green, Sauceboat ....25.00 to 55.00
Light Green, Teapot, 6 Cup ....100.00 to 150.00
Light Green, Tray, Utility ....30.00 to 40.00
Light Green, Tumbler, Water ....45.00 to 90.00
Light Green, Vase, 8 In. ....400.00 to 450.00
Light Green, Vase, 12 In. ....675.00 to 850.00
Medium Green, Ashtray ....130.00 to 200.00
Medium Green, Casserole, Cover ....450.00 to 700.00
Medium Green, Mug, Tom & Jerry ....85.00 to 100.00
Medium Green, Plate, 7 In. ....30.00 to 40.00
Medium Green, Plate, 9 In. 27.00
Medium Green, Plate, 10 In. ....95.00 to 190.00
Medium Green, Plate, Deep, 8 1/4 In. ....90.00 to 120.00
Medium Green, Plate, Salad, Individual ....35.00 to 80.00
Medium Green, Platter, 12 1/2 In. ....90.00 to 150.00
Medium Green, Salad Fork, 3 Tines, Kitchen Kraft 70.00
Medium Green, Salt & Pepper 120.00
Medium Green, Sauceboat ....130.00 to 150.00
Red, Ashtray ....35.00 to 64.00
Red, Bowl, Fruit, 11 3/4 In. 300.00
Red, Cake Lifter, Kitchen Kraft 110.00
Red, Cake Plate, Kitchen Kraft ....25.00 to 37.00
Red, Carafe, Cover 380.00
Red, Casserole, Cover ....50.00 to 125.00
Red, Casserole, Kitchen Kraft, Individual 70.00

Red, Chop Plate, 15 In. . . . . .40.00 to 71.00
Red, Coffeepot 395.00
Red, Compote, Sweets . . . . .90.00 to 110.00
Red, Creamer, Stick Handle 80.00
Red, Cup & Saucer 37.00
Red, Cup & Saucer, After Dinner 50.00
Red, Eggcup 45.00
Red, Jar, Cover, Kitchen Kraft, Medium 190.00
Red, Jug, 2 Pt. 125.00
Red, Mixing Bowl, Kitchen Kraft, 10 In. 120.00
Red, Pitcher, Disk, Large 175.00
Red, Pitcher, Ice Lip, 2 Qt. . . . . .75.00 to 120.00
Red, Plate, 6 In. . . . . .7.00 to 16.00
Red, Plate, 9 In. . . . . .16.00 to 24.00
Red, Plate, 10 In. . . . . .35.00 to 52.00
Red, Plate, Compartment, 10 In. . . . . .25.00 to 55.00
Red, Plate, Compartment, 12 In. . . . . .50.00 to 70.00
Red, Platter, 12 1/2 In. . . . . .25.00 to 55.00
Red, Sauceboat . . . . .45.00 to 70.00
Red, Spoon, Kitchen Kraft 110.00
Red, Stacking Unit, Kitchen Kraft 125.00
Red, Sugar & Creamer 40.00
Red, Teapot, 6 Cup 120.00
Red, Tumbler, Juice . . . . .40.00 to 75.00
Red, Tumbler, Water . . . . .50.00 to 90.00
Red, Vase, 10 In. 600.00
Red, Vase, 12 In. 750.00
Rose, Ashtray . . . . .40.00 to 65.00
Rose, Bowl, Fruit, 4 3/4 In. 41.00
Rose, Casserole, Cover 120.00
Rose, Chop Plate, 13 In. . . . . .55.00 to 103.00
Rose, Creamer 45.00
Rose, Cup, Tea 40.00
Rose, Jug, 2 Pt. 60.00
Rose, Pitcher, Disk, Water . . . . .125.00 to 260.00
Rose, Plate, 7 In. . . . . .14.00 to 36.00
Rose, Plate, 9 In. . . . . .15.00 to 30.00
Rose, Plate, 10 In. . . . . .20.00 to 35.00
Rose, Plate, Compartment, 10 1/2 In. 25.00
Rose, Plate, Deep, 8 1/4 In. 65.00
Rose, Platter, 12 1/2 In. . . . . .30.00 to 35.00
Rose, Salt & Pepper . . . . .30.00 to 35.00
Rose, Sauceboat . . . . .40.00 to 60.00
Rose, Sugar & Creamer 85.00
Rose, Teapot, 6 Cup 395.00
Turquoise, Ashtray . . . . .30.00 to 55.00
Turquoise, Bowl, Fruit, 11 3/4 In. 130.00
Turquoise, Casserole, Cover . . . . .75.00 to 85.00
Turquoise, Chop Plate, 13 In. . . . . .20.00 to 35.00
Turquoise, Coffeepot 255.00
Turquoise, Compote, Sweets . . . . .60.00 to 70.00
Turquoise, Creamer 24.00
Turquoise, Cup & Saucer 30.00
Turquoise, Cup, After Dinner 68.00
Turquoise, Eggcup 75.00
Turquoise, Jug, 2 Pt. . . . . .30.00 to 40.00
Turquoise, Mug 45.00
Turquoise, Mug, Tom & Jerry 55.00
Turquoise, Nappy, 5 1/2 In. 25.00
Turquoise, Nappy, 8 1/2 In. 20.00
Turquoise, Pitcher, Disk, Water 125.00
Turquoise, Pitcher, Ice Lip, 2 Qt. 80.00

Turquoise, Plate, 6 In. ....8.00 to 16.00
Turquoise, Plate, 9 In. ....8.00 to 12.00
Turquoise, Plate, 10 In. 30.00
Turquoise, Plate, Compartment, 10 1/2 In. 25.00
Turquoise, Plate, Deep, 8 1/4 In. ....28.00 to 45.00
Turquoise, Platter, 12 1/2 In. ....20.00 to 40.00
Turquoise, Salt & Pepper 17.00
Turquoise, Sauceboat ....25.00 to 50.00
Turquoise, Sugar, Cover 35.00
Turquoise, Teapot, 6 Cup 189.00
Turquoise, Tray, Figure 8 .... 210.00
Turquoise, Tumbler, Juice 52.00
Turquoise, Tumbler, Water ....50.00 to 75.00
Turquoise, Vase, 8 In. 475.00
Turquoise, Vase, 10 In. 500.00
Yellow, Ashtray ....30.00 to 45.00
Yellow, Bowl, Fruit, 11 3/4 In. ....175.00 to 210.00
Yellow, Bowl, Salad, Footed, 11 1/4 In. 410.00
Yellow, Cake Lifter, Kitchen Kraft 120.00
Yellow, Casserole, Cover ....70.00 to 90.00
Yellow, Casserole, Kitchen Kraft, 8 1/2 In. 25.00
Yellow, Casserole, Kitchen Kraft, Individual 75.00
Yellow, Chop Plate, 13 In. 60.00
Yellow, Compote, Sweets ....70.00 to 95.00
Yellow, Creamer, Individual ....30.00 to 35.00
Yellow, Cup & Saucer, After Dinner ....40.00 to 98.00
Yellow, Eggcup 65.00
Yellow, Jar, Cover, Kitchen Kraft 100.00
Yellow, Jug, 2 Pt. 87.00
Yellow, Nappy, 8 1/2 In. ....22.00 to 42.00
Yellow, Pitcher, Disk, Water 100.00
Yellow, Pitcher, Ice Lip, 2 Qt. 90.00
Yellow, Plate, 6 In. ....5.00 to 16.00
Yellow, Plate, 7 In. ....30.00 to 50.00
Yellow, Plate, 9 In. ....12.00 to 16.00
Yellow, Plate, 10 In. ....24.00 to 30.00
Yellow, Plate, Compartment, 12 In. 120.00
Yellow, Plate, Deep 90.00
Yellow, Platter, 12 1/2 In. 35.00
Yellow, Relish 375.00
Yellow, Salt & Pepper 17.00
Yellow, Sauceboat ....22.00 to 50.00
Yellow, Saucer, After Dinner ....22.00 to 30.00
Yellow, Stacking Unit, Kitchen Kraft ....25.00 to 65.00
Yellow, Tray, Utility ....30.00 to 40.00
Yellow, Tumbler, Juice ....25.00 to 40.00
Yellow, Tumbler, Water ....35.00 to 75.00
Yellow, Vase, 8 In. ....425.00 to 450.00
Yellow, Vase, 10 In. 575.00
Yellow, Vase, 12 In. ....700.00 to 850.00

FINCH, see Kay Finch category.

FINDLAY ONYX AND FLORADINE are two similar types of glass made
by Dalzell, Gilmore and Leighton Co. of Findlay, Ohio, about 1889.
Onyx is a patented yellowish white opaque glass with raised silver
daisy decorations. A few rare pieces were made of rose, amber, orange,
or purple glass. Floradine is made of cranberry-colored glass with an
opalescent white raised floral pattern and a satin finish. The same
molds were used for both types of glass.

Syrup, Metal Fittings, 6 1/2, In. 985.00
Toothpick 351.00
Tumbler, Silver Raised Flowers, 3 3/4 In. 425.00

FIREFIGHTING equipment of all types is wanted, from fire marks to uniforms to toy fire trucks. It is said that every little boy wanted to be a fireman or a train engineer 75 years ago and the collectors today reflect this interest.

Badge, 18th Century Pumper, 1876 Steam Engine	150.00
Badge, Call Man, Warwick R.I. Fire Dept.	50.00
Badge, State Fire Warden, Star, Circle, Embossed, Wire Pin, Irvine & Jachens S.F.	150.00
Blotter, Fireman's Fund, 75th Anniversary, Fireman & Child	8.50
Bucket, Leather, Bound Brook, New Jersey, With Provenance, 19th Century, 13 In.	570.00
Bucket, Leather, Franklin Fire Society, Charlestown, Washington Memorial Urn, 13 In.	7250.00
Bucket, Leather, Gilt Lettering, J. Greley, No. 14, Red Interior, 19 In.	880.00
Bucket, Leather, J. Kimmel, No. 12, Yellow On Black Ground, 13 In.	825.00
Bucket, Picture Of Burning Building, Motto, Leather, Early 19th Century, 13 In.	2530.00
Bucket, R.R.B., Green, Black Letters, Leather Handle, 12 x 8 In.	430.00
Bucket, Yellow, Green Trim, Black Ground, John Cobby, 1840, 17 x 8 In.	3335.00
Fire Mark, Eagle & Shield, Banner, Iron, Oval, Eagle Ins. Co., Cincinnati, 12 In.	575.00
Fire Mark, Eagle, Brass, Philadelphia Fireman's Hall, 20 x 16 In.	115.00
Fire Mark, Fire Association Of Philadelphia, 19th Century	242.00
Fire Mark, Hydrant, Hose, Iron, Fireman Association Of Philadelphia, 11 x 7 In.	460.00
Fire Mark, Royal Exchange, Lead, Late 18th Century	295.00
Fire Mark, Sun, Number 289744, Lead, England	395.00
Fire Mark, Union, 4 Clasped Hands, Sheet Brass, 19th Century	295.00
Grenade, C. & N.W. Ry., Clear, Cobalt Blue, Contents, 1895, 17 3/4 In.	415.00
Grenade, Harden Star Hand, Clear, Content Rings, 1 Pt., 6 1/4 In.	355.00
Grenade, Harden Star Hand, Cobalt Blue, 1 Pt., 6 3/4 In.	205.00
Grenade, Harden's Improved Hand Grenade, Cobalt Blue, Bubbles, Pt.	1790.00
Grenade, Harden, Medium Purple Blue, 1 Pt., 4 3/4 In.	415.00
Grenade, Harden, Turquoise, 1 Qt., 7 7/8 In.	200.00
Grenade, Hayward Victory, Aqua, Olive Diamond, 1880, 1 Pt., 6 1/2 In.	3190.00
Grenade, Hayward's, Smoky Ice Blue, 1 Pt., 6 1/4 In.	575.00
Grenade, Hayward, New York, Aqua, 1895, 6 1/2 In.	175.00
Grenade, Hayward, New York, Clear, Part Label, 1 Qt., 7 1/2 In.	440.00
Grenade, Hayward, New York, Clear, Tooled Mouth, Contents, 1895, 6 In.	155.00
Grenade, Hayward, New York, Cobalt Blue, 1895, 6 In.	305.00
Grenade, Hayward, New York, Yellow Amber, Olive Tone, Contents, 6 1/8 In.	230.00
Grenade, Hazelton's High Pressure Chemical Fire Keg, Amber, Barrel, 11 In.	355.00
Grenade, Healy's Hand Fire Extinguisher Co., Yellow Olive, Contents, Seal, Qt.	1175.00
Grenade, Little Giant Fire Extinguisher, Aqua, Label, Contents, Seal, 6 1/2 In.	2185.00
Grenade, Magic Fire Extinguisher, Gold Yellow Amber, Sheared Lip, 1 Pt.	700.00
Grenade, Rockford, Kalamazoo, Cobalt Blue, 11 1/4 In.	745.00
Helmet, Brass Eagle, Painted Shield, 10 LFD, Leather, 14 In.	300.00
Helmet, Edmundson, Oklahoma, Plastic, Leather Badge On Silver Metal, 1940s	125.00
Lantern, Dietz King, 19 In.	290.00
Nozzle, 2 Handles, A. J. Morse & Son, Boston, 30 In.	150.00
Shield, Helmet, Leather, Large	30.00
Sign, Painted, Eagle Fire Company Of New York, 19 1/2 x 13 1/2 In.	290.00
Trumpet, Coin Silver, Chased, Engraved, Presentation, Hoboken, N.J., 1857, 22 In.	8500.00

FIREGLOW glass is attributed to the Boston and Sandwich Glass Company. The light-tan-colored glass appears reddish brown when held to the light. Most fireglow has an acid finish and enamel decoration, although it was also made with a satin finish.

Vase, Long Neck, Enameled Flowers, 7 1/4 In.	55.00

FIREPLACES were used to cook food and to heat the American home in past centuries. Many types of tools and equipment were used. Andirons held the logs in place, firebacks reflected the heat into the room, and tongs were used to move either fuel or food. Many types of spits and roasting jacks were made and may be listed in the Kitchen category.

Andirons, Brass & Iron, Log Stop, Turned, Chippendale Style, Late 1800s, 19 In.	85.00
Andirons, Brass & Wrought Iron, Urn Form Support, Chippendale, c.1780, 17 In.	840.00

Andirons, Brass Steeple Top, Federal, Richard Whittingham, 1810, 25 In. 7200.00
Andirons, Brass, Ball & Claw Feet, Urn Top, Chippendale Style, 1890s, 26 In. 460.00
Andirons, Brass, Ball Top, High Tripod Base, Scalloped, 12 In. 192.00
Andirons, Brass, Baluster Turned, 20 x 16 In. 430.00
Andirons, Brass, Beaded, Belted, Ball & Steeple Top, 1800s, 20 x 19 In. 3220.00
Andirons, Brass, Column Shape, Reeded Ball Finial, Arched, Late 1700s, 18 1/2 In. 345.00
Andirons, Brass, Column Shape, Turned Finial, Arched Support, 20 In. 259.00
Andirons, Brass, Creeper, Turned Baluster Finial, Ball Feet, Federal, 7 x 6 In. 460.00
Andirons, Brass, Entwined Dolphins, Opposing Dolphin Feet, 1900, 26 In. 805.00
Andirons, Brass, Federal, American, c.1790, 21 In. 715.00
Andirons, Brass, Federal, American, c.1800, 15 In. 110.00
Andirons, Brass, Federal, c.1820, 21 In. 385.00
Andirons, Brass, Flame Finial, Faceted Ball, Ball & Claw Feet, 21 1/2 x 16 1/2 In. 2990.00
Andirons, Brass, George III, Octagonal Rings, Banded, Tongs, 21 x 19 In. 360.00
Andirons, Brass, Guard With Spear Finials, 1870s, 30 x 44 In. 2990.00
Andirons, Brass, Hounds, 18 In. 670.00
Andirons, Brass, Iron Knife, Brass Shield At Bottom Of Shaft, 21 x 15 In. 1380.00
Andirons, Brass, Iron Supports, Leaf, Arrow Shape, Calla Lily, Harvin, 1948, 13 1/2 In. . . 805.00
Andirons, Brass, Iron, Brass Ball Top, 11 1/2 x 4 x 33 In. 220.00
Andirons, Brass, Iron, Flame Finial, Ball & Reed Column, Scroll Feet, 32 x 12 In. 605.00
Andirons, Brass, Iron, Spurred Legs, Ball Feet, 1820, 20 In. 748.00
Andirons, Brass, Iron, Urn Top Finials, 18 1/2 In. 200.00
Andirons, Brass, Knopped Ball Top, Slipper Feet, 18 In. 1390.00
Andirons, Brass, Knopped, Fluted & Swag Pedestal, Paw Feet, Urn Finial, 14 3/4 In. 1035.00
Andirons, Brass, Leaf Scrolls, Putti, 16 In. 5250.00
Andirons, Brass, Louis XV, Comical Lady & Gentleman In Period Dress, 11 In. 690.00
Andirons, Brass, Louis XV, Gilt, Cherubs On Scrolling Base, 13 In. 1610.00
Andirons, Brass, Louis XVI, Gilt, Garland Urn Finial, 12 1/2 In. 3600.00
Andirons, Brass, Napoleon III, Strapwork, Paw & Scroll Feet, 30 x 44 x 9 In. 2990.00
Andirons, Brass, Neoclassical Style, Standard, Entwined Dolphin, 24 x 10 x 22 In. 2070.00
Andirons, Brass, Neoclassical, Fluted Column Form, Early 20th Century, 14 1/2 In. 520.00
Andirons, Brass, Ogee Footed, Ball, Scalloped Flower Design, Ring, 20 In. 330.00
Andirons, Brass, Ring Turned Shaft, Brass, Slipper Feet, 17 x 14 1/2 In. 546.00
Andirons, Brass, Ringed Top, 19th Century, 17 1/2 In. 275.00
Andirons, Brass, Seated Putto, Arm On Flaming Urn, Leaf Stalk, 22 x 10 In. 1495.00
Andirons, Brass, Shaped Handles & Crossbar, Tripod Feet, Arts & Crafts, 29 3/4 In. 230.00
Andirons, Brass, Shield On Lower Shaft, Bean Feet, 19 1/2 x 8 1/2 x 15 In. 690.00
Andirons, Brass, Splayed & Scalloped Legs, Ring Columns, Ball Tops, 11 In. 38.00
Andirons, Brass, Spool Turned Columns, Urn & Flame Finial, Cabriole Legs, 28 1/2 In. . . 145.00
Andirons, Brass, Steel, Urn Top, Brass Shield, Early 18th Century, 19 3/4 In. 805.00
Andirons, Brass, Steeple Top, Hexagon Plinths, Federal, 21 In. 978.00
Andirons, Brass, Stylized Dolphin Feet, Spiral Columns, 21 In. 330.00
Andirons, Brass, Tapered, Pyramidal Finial, Aesthetic Movement, c.1890, 26 In. 175.00
Andirons, Brass, Torch Form, Entwined Dolphin, 24 x 10 1/2 In. 2070.00
Andirons, Brass, Turned Shaft, Scrolled Legs, Ball Feet, Federal, c.1825, 19 In. 165.00
Andirons, Brass, Wrought Iron, Brass Finial, Gothic Feet, 18th Century, 30 1/2 In. 560.00
Andirons, Brass, Wrought Iron, Cabriole Legs, Ball Feet, Federal, 1800, 9 In. 5100.00
Andirons, Brass, Wrought Iron, Downswept Legs, Ball Feet, Federal, 1815, 21 In. 3600.00
Andirons, Brass, Wrought Iron, Spurred Legs, Ball Feet, Federal, 1800, 26 In. 1920.00
Andirons, Bronze, Allegorical Figures, Tripod Base, Baroque, 30 3/4 In. 4800.00
Andirons, Bronze, Louis XVI, Gilt, Fruited Floral Festoons, 29 In. 4500.00
Andirons, Bronze, Opposing Figures Of Winged Putti, With Shields, 44 In. 7188.00
Andirons, Cast Brass, Beaux Arts, Fluted Columns, Ball Final, Arched Feet, 24 In. 345.00
Andirons, Cast Iron, Arched Legs, Scrolled Finial, 20 3/4 In. 357.00
Andirons, Cast Iron, Black Paint, George Washington Maher, 1907, 23 In. 6325.00
Andirons, Cast Iron, Cat, Glass Eyes, 17 1/2 In. 1430.00
Andirons, Cast Iron, George Washington, 15 In. 220.00
Andirons, Cast Iron, George Washington, PPO Iron Works, Petersburg, Va., 15 In. 224.00
Andirons, Cast Iron, Hessian Soldier, 19th Century, 8 7/8 x 5 3/4 x 10 1/4 In. 460.00
Andirons, Cast Iron, Hessians, Some Paint, White Swords, 1775-1800, 19 7/8 In. 425.00
Andirons, Cast Iron, Marching Hessian Soldiers, 17 3/4 In. 175.00
Andirons, Cast Iron, Owl, Glass Eyes, 1900s 200.00
Andirons, Chenet, Brass, Leaf Finial, Block Feet, France, 24 x 11 x 22 In. 865.00

Andirons, Chenet, Gilt Bronze, Clothed Putti Resting On Support, Louis XVI, 14 In. 1380.00
Andirons, Chenet, Gilt Bronze, Garlands On Base, Tapered Feet, Louis XVI, 11 1/2 In. .. 980.00
Andirons, Chenet, Gilt Bronze, Lion Roaring On Back Legs, Rococo, 13 1/2 In. 1265.00
Andirons, Chenet, Gilt Bronze, Winged Putti Standing, Holding Bows, 1880, 23 In. 1495.00
Andirons, Chenet, Gilt Bronze, Woman Reclining, Holding Torch, 14 x 17 In. 3910.00
Andirons, Chenet, Italian Renaissance, Putti Resting On Columns, Italy, 47 In. 1725.00
Andirons, Chenet, Ormolu, Flame Logstops, 12 x 19 In. 1495.00
Andirons, Copper, Hammered, Inverted Heart Design, Arts & Crafts, 9 x 14 In. 575.00
Andirons, Gilt Bronze, Dolphin Standard, Regency Style, c.1900, 25 x 12 x 29 In. 2990.00
Andirons, Gilt Bronze, Lion, Rearing, Holding Cartouche, 22 In. 2090.00
Andirons, Gilt, Rococo, Early 20th Century, 14 In. 860.00
Andirons, Iron, 3 Applied Scrolled Bands, Hammered Brass Finial, Tapered, 25 In. 175.00
Andirons, Iron, Brass, Knife Blade, Urn Shape Finials, c.1780, 18 1/2 In. 2860.00
Andirons, Iron, Plinth, Sitting Whippet Top, 7 x 5 1/2 x 14 1/2 In. 220.00
Andirons, Iron, Ram's-Head Mount, Spherule Talons, Ball & Claw Feet, 1880s, 16 In. ... 1035.00
Andirons, Marble, Onyx, Ormolu Trim, Light Green, Neoclassical, 30 In. 1100.00
Andirons, Spurred Legs, Ball, Claw Feet, Chippendale, 1790, 20 In. 550.00
Andirons, Wrought Iron, Arrow Shape, 21 In. 2015.00
Andirons, Wrought Iron, Brass, Covered Urn Finial, Arched Foot, 20 3/4 In. 315.00
Andirons, Wrought Iron, Faceted Finial, Iron Legs, William & Mary, 25 In. 7200.00
Andirons, Wrought Iron, Goose Neck, 21 x 21 In. 863.00
Andirons, Wrought Iron, Gooseneck, Early 18th Century, 12 1/2 In. 1035.00
Andirons, Wrought Iron, Gooseneck, Faceted Heads, Penny Feet, 1800s, 18 In. 170.00
Andirons, Wrought Iron, Ring Top Finials, Early 19th Century, 19 1/4 In. 345.00
Bellows, Beech Fire, Painted Harbor Scene, Brass Nozzles, 22 In. 980.00
Bellows, Carved Wood, Allover Bird & Floral Design, 31 In. 50.00
Bellows, Cornucopia Of Fruit, 18 1/4 In. 200.00
Bellows, Floral, c.1840 .... 180.00
Bellows, Freehand & Stenciled Cornucopia, Fruit & Leaves, Brass Nozzle, 17 In. 1100.00
Bellows, Leather & Wood, Brass Rivets & Nozzle, 16 In. 325.00
Bellows, Leather, Brass Hardware, Spade Form, Yellow Body, 17 3/4 In. 375.00
Bellows, Leather, Cornucopia, Red Ground, Brass Finial, Tack, Early 1800s, 18 x 18 In. .. 520.00
Bellows, Pomegranate Design, c.1840 .... 180.00
Bellows, Stenciled Cornucopia, Yellow Ground, Philadelphia, Early 1800s 250.00
Bellows, Turtle Back, Bird & Berries, Brass Nozzle, 17 1/2 In. 660.00
Bellows, Wood, Leather, Ornate Painted Scene, Brush & Bellows Mfg., Phila., 1829 ..... 165.00
Box, Kindling, Brass, Hinged Sloping Cover, Brass Figural Scenes, 21 x 17 In. 80.00
Box, Kindling, Carved Horse-Head End, Painted, Rectangular, Gray Paint, 26 In. 1150.00
Box, Kindling, Sloped Hinged Lid, Fruit Gilt Borders, Brass Handle, 22 x 11 In. 690.00
Box, Kindling, Wooden, Mustard & Cream Paint 36.00
Broom, Hearth, 19th Century, 23 In. 95.00
Bucket, Peat, George III, Mahogany, 2 Bands Of Brass, Swing Handle, 17 In. 8400.00
Bucket, Peat, William IV, Brass Handle, Liner, Circular Rim, 18 1/2 x 15 In. 980.00
Bucket, Peat, William IV, Mahogany, Brass Handle, Liner, Circular Plinth, 16 In. 750.00
Bucket, Peat, William IV, Mahogany, Circular Rim, Ball Feet, 18 x 15 In. 805.00
Coal Bucket, Mahogany, Brass Bound, William IV, Liner, 13 x 16 1/2 x 12 In. 920.00
Coal Scuttle, Blue Enamel, Repousse Design, Iron Handle, Arts & Crafts, 18 In. 175.00
Coal Scuttle, Brass, Applied Swag & Leaf Medallions, Side Handles, Bun Feet, 20 In. ... 302.00
Coal Scuttle, Brass, Gilt, Embossed Flowers, Tavern Scene, c.1900, 20 3/4 x 26 In. 165.00
Coal Scuttle, Brass, Repousse Minerva & Foo Dog Heads, Pebble Lining, 16 x 20 In. ... 135.00
Coal Scuttle, Copper, Wrought Iron Handle, Gustav Stickley, 19 In. 5775.00
Coal Scuttle, Green Lift-Top, Early 19th Century 420.00
Coal Scuttle, Patinated, Hammered, Repousse Flower Heads, Arts & Crafts, 16 x 13 In. .. 489.00
Coal Scuttle, Polished Steel, Bail Handle, England, 21 1/2 In. 165.00
Coal Scuttle, Shovel, Brass, Victorian, c.1880 .... 140.00
Cricket, Turned Legs, Light Blue Paint, American, 19th Century, 6 x 6 x 12 In. 200.00
Fender, Applied Finial, Pierced Home Sweet Home, 17 1/2 x 6 x 10 3/4 In. 300.00
Fender, Brass Cap With Finials, c.1810, 54 In. 2200.00
Fender, Brass Rim, Wire, Plinth Feet, 1810, 10 x 39 1/2 In. 660.00
Fender, Brass, Cast Leaf Panel, 19th Century, 10 1/2 x 48 x 13 In. 450.00
Fender, Brass, Gilt, Low Pierced Fence, Draped Urns On Pedestals, Empire, 15 In. 1265.00
Fender, Brass, Iron, Geometric Pierced Screen, 3 Bun Feet, 28 x 9 1/2 In. 250.00
Fender, Brass, Oval Form, Vertical Wirework, Scrolls, 13 1/2 x 40 1/2 x 18 In. 2070.00

Smoke stains can be removed from a stone fireplace with an art gum eraser. Soot on the carpet in front of the fireplace can be removed with salt. Sprinkle dry salt on the soot, wait 30 minutes, then vacuum.

Don't hang an oil painting above a fireplace that is used frequently. Smoke will damage the paint.

Fireplace, Poker Holder,
Brass, Cat, England, 5 1/4 In.

Fender, Brass, Pierced, Central Reeded Bands, 3 Paw Feet, Tongs, Poker, 46 3/4 In.	375.00
Fender, Brass, Regency, Reticulated, Early 19th Century, 9 3/4 x 43 1/4 In.	575.00
Fender, Brass, Reticulated, Molded Frieze, Chinese Key Fret, c.1890, 12 x 41 In.	290.00
Fender, Brass, Scroll Design, Wirework, Early 1800s, 10 x 49 1/2 x 15 In.	2875.00
Fender, Brass, Serpentine Front, Victorian, Late 19th Century, 8 x 44 1/2 In.	185.00
Fender, Brass, Top Rail, Floral Cutout, Lattice Fretwork, 13 1/2 x 54 x 13 In.	330.00
Fender, Brass, Wire, 3 Brass Finials, Federal, c.1810, 13 1/2 x 39 In.	660.00
Fender, Bronze, Louis XVI Style, Garlands, Urns, Belle Epoque, 15 x 33 x 4 In.	1380.00
Fender, Bronze, Scalloped Center, Classical Female Masks, Garland Border, 46 In.	4140.00
Fender, Copper, 2-Tone, Mission Style, 9 x 46 1/2 x 14 1/2 In.	115.00
Fender, Gilt Bronze Mount, Verdigris Patina, Palmettes, Belle Epoque, 9 x 43 x 2 In.	1150.00
Fender, Gilt Bronze, Flame Finial, Beaded Plinth, Louis XVI, 18 x 42 x 5 In., Pair	1090.00
Fender, Gilt Bronze, Pedestal Mount, Lion, Reclining, Napoleon III, 10 x 48 In.	2070.00
Fender, Gilt Patinated Bronze, Cupids, Warming Hands, Louis XVI Style, 29 In.	1150.00
Fender, Gilt Patinated Bronze, Recumbent Lion, Reeded Shaft, Empire, 11 1/2 x 55 In.	1955.00
Fender, Gilt, Brass, Drapery, Tassels, Louis XVI, 4 x 53 1/2 x 12 1/2 In.	2070.00
Fender, Lion, Pedestal Mounted, 10 x 48 In.	2070.00
Fender, Patinated Bronze, Gilt Brass, Stallion Finials, Restauration, 9 1/2 x 38 x 3 In.	690.00
Fender, Pierced Fence, Crossed Quivers, Draped Urns On Pedestal, 15 In.	1265.00
Fender, Silvered Metal, Pierced, Engraved Mythical Beasts, 65 1/2 In.	2875.00
Fender, Wire, Brass, Ball Finials, Paw Feet, Federal, c.1840, 14 x 38 1/2 In.	880.00
Fender, Wire, Scrollwork, Brass Bail Handles, England, 19th Century, 26 x 26 x 12 In.	375.00
Fireboard, Fruit Compote, Trompe L'Oeil Surround, American, 27 x 33 In.	6900.00
Fireboard, Tree With Face, 10 Red Flowers, Animal, 42 In.	5750.00
Footman, Victorian, Brass, Cabriole Legs, Mid 19th Century, England, 12 1/4 In.	375.00
Fork, Log, Wrought Iron, Flat Handle, Signed, J.B. Stohler, 25 1/4 In.	275.00
Grill, Wrought Iron, Carrying Handle, Fat Trough, 22 1/2 In.	220.00
Grill, Wrought Iron, Heart & Scroll Design	357.50
Guard, Bronze Patina, Gilt, Volutes Joined By Chains, 12 x 44 x 3 In.	2990.00
Guard, Gilt, Bronze Patina, Leaf Design, Key Border, Louis Philippe, 11 In.	1840.00
Hood, Copper, Chimney, Golden Mile Stone	2500.00
Log Holder, Brass, Iron, Raised Sides, Curved Feet, 16 x 26 x 23 In.	575.00
Mantel is listed in the Architectural category.	
Peel, Ram's-Horn Finial, Wrought Iron, 36 1/2 In.	165.00
Poker Holder, Brass, Cat, England, 5 1/4 In. ....*Illus*	50.00
Rail, Brass, Serpentine, George II Style, Williamsburg Mark, 6 1/2 x 47 In.	85.00
Scoop, Ash, Brass, Punched Design, 19th Century, 10 1/2 x 9 3/4 In.	165.00
Screen, 3-Panel, Mesh, Louis XV, Gilt, 42 x 34 1/2 In.	287.00
Screen, 5-Panel, Children At Play In Landscape Scene, Wooden Frame, Ivory, 13 In.	175.00
Screen, Asymmetrical Form, Steel Mesh, Scrolling Foliate, 36 x 26 In.	3175.00
Screen, Beadwork Shield, 3 Splayed Cabriole Legs, 19th Century, 58 x 18 In.	920.00
Screen, Bronze, Louis XV, Gilt, Cherubs & Fire, Patinated Bronze Mount, 27 In.	1725.00
Screen, C-Scrolls, Leaves & Shells, Steel Mesh, Playful Putti, 25 1/2 In.	1610.00
Screen, Carved Oak, Full Standing Lions, 26 x 30 In.	2465.00
Screen, Classical, Rosewood Veneer, Flower Needlework, 1815, 38 x 24 x 18 In.	32200.00
Screen, Dore Mesh, Ovoid Frame, Openwork Leaves, Bronze, 29 1/2 In.	750.00

Screen, Georgian, Brass, Art Nouveau, Floral Leaded Glass Panel, 20 x 29 1/2 In. 260.00
Screen, Gilt Bronze, Cartouche Form Framing Steel Mesh, 30 1/2 x 27 In. 2115.00
Screen, Giltwood, Louis XV, Landscape Scene, Leaf Tips, Floral, 61 In. 5700.00
Screen, Giltwood, Louis XV, Molded Frame, Floral Crest, Curved Legs, 39 x 16 In. 1150.00
Screen, Kingwood, Tapestry Panel, Renaissance Woman & Man, 34 x 31 In. 2070.00
Screen, Louis XV Style, Bronze Dore, Mesh, Oval, Leafy Openwork, Feet, 30 x 29 In. ... 748.00
Screen, Louis XV Style, Gilt Bronze, Leaf Frame, Wire Mesh, Scroll Feet, 32 x 27 In. ... 1755.00
Screen, Louis XVI Style, Giltwood, Oval Print, Carved Frame, 42 x 23 1/2 In. 1035.00
Screen, Louis XVI, Bronze Dore, Pair Of Birds, Outswept Feet, 32 x 27 x 9 In. 2300.00
Screen, Pole, Federal, Mahogany, Silk Needlepoint, Flowers, c.1800, 57 1/2 In. 2090.00
Screen, Pole, Mahogany, Adjustable Needlepoint Panel, Elderly Couple, 60 In. 747.00
Screen, Pole, Mahogany, Cross-Stitch Panel, George III, England, 1700s, 60 In. 865.00
Screen, Pole, Mahogany, Oval, Floral Needlework, William IV, 62 x 16 x 16 In. 1265.00
Screen, Pole, Mahogany, Silk Floral Needlework, Ebonized Frame, Scroll Feet, 62 In. ... 1265.00
Screen, Pole, Needlepoint Panel, Still Life Of Fruit, c.1895, 56 In. 690.00
Screen, Pole, Papier-Mache & Rosewood, Needlework Floral, 1850s, 47 1/4 In. 1265.00
Screen, Pole, Queen Anne Tripod Base, 18th Century 990.00
Screen, Pole, Rosewood, Floral Needlework, Scrolled Frame, 61 x 21 x 16 In. 520.00
Screen, Pole, Theorem, Urn Finial Above Pole Shaft, Adjustable Panel, Snake Feet, 53 In. 775.00
Screen, Pole, William IV, Autumnal Landscape, Rosewood, 52 1/2 In. 633.00
Screen, Wire Mesh, Arabesques, Rolled Feet, Wrought Iron, Art Deco, 1 3/4 x 56 In. 2362.00
Screen, Wrought Iron, Art Deco, 40 1/2 x 34 In. 6900.00
Shovel, Ash, 18th Century, 9 1/2 In. 95.00
Surround, Pine, Egg & Dart Border, Painted, 72 1/4 In. 5750.00
Surround, Shelf Above Frieze, Putti, Capitals, 52 1/2 In. 9775.00
Surround, Tile, Cherubs, Cast Iron Summer Screen, Trent Tile, 6 In., 15 Piece 1650.00
Tinderbox, Steel Striker, Damper, Candle Socket In Lid, Black Paint, 3 x 3 7/8 In. 415.00
Tongs, Ember, 18th Century 1870.00
Tongs, Pipe, Wrought Iron, Ribbed Handle, Scrolled Tamper, Hand Form Tongs, 16 In. ... 550.00
Tool Set, Brass, Iron Belted, Ball Top, Early 19th Century, American, 30 In. 750.00
Tool Set, Brass, Turned Ebonized Grips, Urn Form Finial, Edwardian, c.1905 .... 210.00
Tool Set, Brass, Urn Finial, Stand, 28 In., 4 Piece 27.00
Tool Set, Marble Handles, Black Marble Base, 32 In. 250.00
Tool Set, Wrought Iron, Gothic Revival, Tool Stand, Tongs, Shovel, Late 1800s 305.00
Tool Set, Wrought Iron, Scrolled Strap Feet, Basket, Arts & Crafts, c.1880 .... 115.00

FISCHER porcelain was made in Herend, Hungary, by Moritz Fischer. The factory was founded in 1839 and continued working into the twentieth century. The wares are sometimes referred to as *Herend* porcelain.

MF

Ashtray, Hand Painted Flowers, Gilt Trim, 1 1/4 x 6 In. 60.00
Coffee Set, Cobalt Blue, Gilt Floral, Off-White, Coffeepot, Sugar, Cup & Saucer, 14 Piece 260.00
Dish, Pink & Gold Floral, Off-White, 9 1/8 In. 70.00
Figurine, Fish, Blue, Orange Gilt, Marked, 4 3/8 In. 80.00
Figurine, Sea Horse, Copper Iridescent, Orange, Yellow, Marked, 6 3/4 In. 165.00
Jar, Cover, Basket Weave Design With Birds, Insects, Marked, 4 1/4 x 4 1/2 In. 80.00
Platter, Bird, Oval, 16 1/4 In. 200.00
Tea Set, Teapot, Creamer, Sugar, Cup & Saucer, 27 Piece 750.00
Tray, Dresser, Bird, 19 1/2 In. 200.00
Tureen, Undertray, Flowers, Branch, Leaves, Brick Orange, Herend, 15 1/4 In. 920.00

FISHING reels of brass or nickel were made in the United States by 1810. Bamboo fly rods were sold by 1860, often marked with the maker's name. Lures made of metal, or metal and wood, were made in the nineteenth century. Plastic lures were made by the 1930s. All fishing material is collected today and even equipment of the past thirty years is of interest if in good condition with original box.

Box, Tackle, 10 Aluminum Cantilevered Trays, 60 Sections, 1940s, 10 1/2 x 19 In. 440.00
Box, Tackle, 500 Flies, 5 Examples, Scissors, Leader Sink 138.00
Bucket, Bait, Copper, Lift-Out Container, 8 1/4 x 10 1/2 In. 1650.00
Bucket, Minnow, Lift-Off Lid, Swing Handle, 9 1/2 In. 550.00
Button, Pinback, Junior Angler, Department Of Parks, Abraham & Straus, 1957 .... 6.00
Creel, Birchbark, Flower On Lid, Indian Made 325.00
Creel, Brown, 12 x 7 In. 517.00

Creel, Bulbous, Rattan Weave & Split Reed Bottom, Leather Trim 1980.00
Creel, George Lawrence Co., Split Willow, Leather Trim .... *Illus* 4400.00
Creel, Joseph Knockwood, Thin Strip Splint, Reed Loop, Stamp Of Indian 1320.00
Creel, Lashed Lid Rim, Rattan Hinges, Turtle Lid, Harness Loops On Back, 8 1/2 x 14 In. 3850.00
Float, Ideal, Green, Orange & White Stripes, Orange Cork Ball, 10 1/2 In. 330.00
Float, White With Red Stripe & Red Ball, Wire, Cork, 8 In. 259.00
Fly, Carrie G. Stevens, Golden Witch Streamer, Size 6 .... 385.00
Fly, Carrie G. Stevens, Green Ghost, Size 4 .... 413.00
Harpoon, Swiveling Head, 19th Century, 27-In. Shaft 83.00
Lure, Green Crackle Back 550.00
Lure, H. Comstock, Flying Helgramite, Bass, 1883 .... *Illus* 4400.00
Lure, Heddon, Glass Eyes, Wood 200.00
Lure, Heddon, Lucky 13, 3 1/2 In. 75.00
Lure, Heddon, Minnow, Underwater, Red Scale Finish, Glass Eyes, No. 150, 4 In. 175.00
Lure, Sambo, Gloom Killer, Plastic, Box, 4 1/2 In. 60.00
Meter, Zodiac, Moving Scale, 1947 Calendar On Reverse, Cardboard 5.00
Postcard, Martin Automatic Fish Reel Co., The Famous Martin 175.00
Reel, Bait Casting, No. 2 .... 1760.00
Reel, Bill Ballan, Trout, Click Reel, 3 In. 275.00
Reel, Bronson Spin King 25.00
Reel, Charles R. Orvis III, Trout, Series 229, Case 275.00
Reel, Chas. Farlow & Co., Trout, Name On Handle, Leather Half-Round Case, 2 1/2 In. .. 165.00
Reel, Chas. Farlow, Trout, Crank Handle, Click Housing, Reel, Ivory Handle, 1 3/4 In. ... 468.00
Reel, Edward Vom Hofe, Salmon, German Silver, Hard Rubber, 1926 Model, 3 1/8 In. ... 8250.00
Reel, Edward Vom Hofe, Salmon, Model 423, German Silver, Hard Rubber, 4 1/4 In. 1430.00
Reel, Edward Vom Hofe, Trout, Model 360, German Silver, Rubber, Click Switch, 3 In. .. 3850.00
Reel, Edward Vom Hofe, Trout, Silver, 1870 .... *Illus* 7810.00
Reel, Edward Vom Hofe, Trout, Silver, Hard Rubber, 1920 .... *Illus* 6820.00
Reel, Hardy's, Trout, Alnwick, England, 1896 Click, 5/8 In. 220.00
Reel, Haywood, Trout, Crank Handle, Bone Grasp, Brass Spike Mount, c.1845, 1 5/8 In. . 468.00
Reel, Hendryx, Pillar 30.00
Reel, Holden, No. 2, Stamped Genuine Bakelite, 3 1/2 In. 39.00
Reel, Julius Vom Hofe, Trout, Click Reel, Brass, 2 3/8 x 1 In. 220.00
Reel, Julius Vom Hofe, Trout, Slick Switch, Bearing Cap, Size 3 1/2, 2 1/4 x 1 In. 385.00
Reel, Leonard Mills, Trout, Model 44A, German Silver, 1920s, 2 5/8 x 3/4 In. 1320.00
Reel, Meek No. 55, Trout, Wide Click, 3 1/8 In. 140.00
Reel, Meek No. 56, Trout, Ring Line Guide, 3 3/8 In. 248.00
Reel, Morgan James, Trout, Brass, Pillbox Mount, 1860 .... *Illus* 9350.00
Reel, Shakespeare, Silent, Roseville, Calif., 3 x 2 In. 35.00
Reel, Trout, Brass Crank Handle, Rosewood Grasp, 2 1/2 x 7/8 In. 193.00
Reel, Vom Hofe, Trout, Rubber Plates, Nickel Plated, Click Switch, Box 1/4 x 1 In. 165.00
Reel, Wm. Talbot Co., Trout, German Silver, No. 2362, Click Switch, 2 1/2 In. 3740.00
Rod, Bag & Tube, Trout, 8 1/2 Ft. 1650.00
Rod, Fly, Ward's Sport King, 2 Tips, 8 Ft. 75.00
Rod, H.L. Leonard, Trout, Loose Ring Guides, 11 Ft. 230.00
Rod, Orvis, Trout, 2 Tips, Nickel Plated Tube, 6 1/2 Ft. 825.00
Rod, Trout, Model 40 DF, Maple Spacer, 8 Ft. 1870.00
Spear, Eel, 5 Tines, Brass Arrow-Tipped End, Iron, 15 1/2 In. 115.00

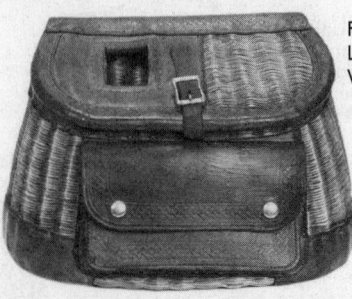

Fishing, Creel, George
Lawrence Co., Split
Willow, Leather Trim

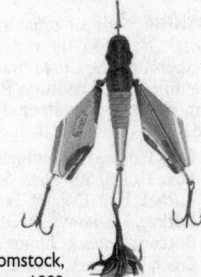

Fishing, Lure, H. Comstock,
Flying Helgramite, Bass, 1883

Fishing, Reel, Edward Vom Hofe,
Trout, Silver, 1870

Fishing, Reel, Edward Vom Hofe,
Trout, Silver, Hard Rubber, 1920

Fishing, Reel, Morgan James,
Trout, Brass, Pillbox Mount, 1860

Spear, Eel, 6 Tines, Iron, 15 In. 345.00
Spear, Eel, Iron, 22 1/2 In. 345.00
Spear, Eel, J. W. Fordham, Iron, Hand Forged, Wooden Handle, Rust, 16 In. 420.00
Spear, Fish, Hand Forged, Metal Handle, 7 Prongs, Some Rust, 17 In. 80.00
Trophy, Chub, 4 Lbs. 4 Oz., Natural Setting, W.E. Martin, 1933, Case, 27 x 14 In. 635.00
Trophy, Perch, 2 Lbs. 10 Oz., Natural Setting, R.J. Wright, 1953, Case, 20 x 12 In. 460.00
Trophy, Pike, 8 Lbs. 2 Oz., Natural Setting, Jack Lindsay, July 1910, 37 x 16 In. 978.00

FLAGS are included in the Textile category.

FLASH GORDON appeared in the Sunday comics in 1934. The daily
strip started in 1940. The hero was also in comic books from 1930 to
1970, in books from 1936, in movies from 1938, on the radio in the
1930s and 1940s, and on television from 1953 to 1954. All sorts of
memorabilia are collected, but the ray guns and rocket ships are the
most popular.

Ray Gun, Box 35.00
Rocket Fighter, Tin Lithograph, Marx, 1952, 12 In. 2100.00
Rocket Ship, Windup, Marx, 12 In. 475.00

FLORENCE CERAMICS were made in Pasadena, California, from World
War II to 1977. Florence Ward created many colorful figurines, boxes,
candleholders, and other items for the gift shop trade. Each piece was
marked with an ink stamp that included the name *Florence Ceramics
Co.* The company was sold in 1964, and although the name remained
the same the products were very different. Mugs, cups, and trays were
made.

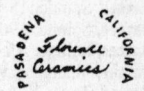

Figurine, Angel, Blond Hair, White Gown, Gold Trim, Signed, 7 3/4 In. 95.00
Figurine, Choir Boy, Brown Hair, Holding Psalm Book, Signed, 7 In. 95.00
Figurine, Christening, Woman In Blue Holding Infant In White, 8 1/2 In. 720.00
Figurine, Delia, Gray, Burgundy Trim, Blond Hair, 7 1/4 In. 165.00
Figurine, Georgette, Godey Series, 7 In. 350.00
Figurine, Kay, Brown Hair, White Dress, 7 In. 60.00
Figurine, Lillian, Rose Dress, 7 1/4 In. 120.00
Figurine, Matilda, Blue Dress, Gold Purse & Hat, 8 In. 175.00
Figurine, Matilda, Pink Dress, 8 In. 175.00
Figurine, Melanie, Gone With The Wind Series, 7 1/2 In. 135.00
Figurine, Vivian, Coral Dress, Holding Umbrella, 10 In. 275.00
Flower Holder, Girl, Dark Hair, 6 1/4 In. 65.00

FLOW BLUE was made in England and other countries about 1830 to
1900. The dishes were printed with designs using a cobalt blue coloring. The color flowed from the design to the white body so that the finished piece has a smeared blue design. The dishes were usually made
of ironstone china.

Bone Dish, Touraine, Stanley 90.00
Bowl, Vegetable, Cover, Touraine, Gold Trim, Stanley 495.00

Bowl, Vegetable, Scinde, Alcock, 11 3/4 In., Pair 345.00
Bowl, Vegetable, Touraine, Oval, Alcock, 9 1/8 In............................ 110.00
Butter Chip, Colonial 70.00
Butter Chip, Hudson 90.00
Butter Chip, Lorne, W.H. Grindley, 4 Piece 60.00
Butter Chip, Yeddo, Wilkinson 50.00
Creamer, Touraine, Stanley 325.00
Cup & Saucer, Argyle 110.00
Cup & Saucer, Auld Lang Syne, Roses Outside Cup, Center Of Saucer 165.00
Cup & Saucer, Lammore 93.00
Cup & Saucer, Scinde, Alcock 158.00
Cup & Saucer, Strawberry, Handleless, Walker 137.00
Cup & Saucer, Touraine, Alcock 35.00
Cup & Saucer, Touraine, Stanley 65.00
Jardiniere, Warwick 525.00
Pitcher, Fairy Villas, Adams, c.1891 .... 295.00
Pitcher, La Belle, Wheeling 330.00
Pitcher, Milk, Spired Building On River, 3 Figures, Burgess & Leigh, 5 1/2 In. 192.00
Pitcher, Windmill & Ship Scene, Gold Design On Edges & Handle 65.00
Pitcher & Bowl, Duchess, Wood & Sons, 19th Century 1100.00
Plate, Kin Shan, 9 In.. 110.00
Plate, La Belle, Wheeling, 10 In. 70.00
Plate, Madras, 7 1/2 In. 75.00
Plate, Manilla, Podmore, Walker, 7 1/2 In...................................... 125.00
Plate, Manilla, Podmore, Walker, 9 3/4 In...................................... 195.00
Plate, Oregon, Mayer, 8 3/4 In. 150.00
Plate, Osborne, 7 1/2 In. 75.00
Plate, Royal, Furnival, 9 In... 55.00
Plate, Royal, Furnival, 10 In.. 75.00
Plate, Scinde, Alcock, 6 In. 55.00
Plate, Shanghae 145.00
Plate, Touraine, Alcock, 8 3/4 In. ....50.00 to 80.00
Plate, Touraine, Alcock, c.1898, 7 3/4 In. 35.00
Platter, Lambrequin Border, Octagonal, 15 1/2 x 19 1/2 In.................... 345.00
Platter, Mandarin, Oval, Poultry, 11 1/4 x 8 1/4 In. 85.00
Platter, Nonpareil, 15 1/2 In.. 480.00
Platter, Nonpareil, Burgess & Leigh, 17 3/4 In................................. 374.00
Platter, Scinde, 18 x 14 In. 690.00
Platter, Scinde, 19th Century, 14 In. 288.00
Platter, Scinde, Alcock, 19th Century, 16 In.................................. 460.00
Platter, Shanghai, W.H. Grindley, 13 3/4 In.................................. 192.00
Platter, Togo, 12 x 16 In.. 55.00
Platter, Touraine, Alcock, 14 7/8 x 10 1/4 In. 175.00
Relish, Temple, Podmore, Walker 375.00
Sauceboat, Underplate, Larch, Hancock & Son, 6 1/2 x 5 1/2 In............... 145.00
Soup, Dish, Floral, 9 3/4 In... 165.00
Sugar, Cover, Touraine, Alcock 475.00
Teapot, Nankin 995.00
Teapot, Shanghae, Furnival 1095.00
Teapot, Tonquin, Adams 1095.00
Tureen, Cover, Byzantium, Brown, Westhead, Moore & Co., c.1905 .... 350.00
Tureen, Cover, Manilla, Podmore, Walker, c.1850, 12 x 10 x 7 In.............. 995.00
Tureen, Cover, Scinde, Underplate, Ladle, Alcock 8500.00
Vase, Stick, Cylinder, Bulbous, Oriental Style, Late 19th Century, 6 1/2 In. 58.00

FLYING PHOENIX, see Phoenix Bird category.

FOLK ART is also listed in many categories of this book under the actual
name of the object. See categories such as Box, Cigar Store Figure,
Paper, Weather Vane, Wooden, etc.

   Alms Box, Itinerant Figures, Peaceable Kingdom, Farmhouse, Linen Cover, 5 x 9 In. 7700.00
   Ashtray, Cigar Bands, Felt Back, 9 x 5 In...................................*Illus* 22.00
   Birdhouse, Boy's Head, Polychrome, Glass Eyes, Early 20th Century, 12 3/4 In. 3163.00

Folk Art, Ashtray, Cigar Bands, Felt Back, 9 x 5 In.

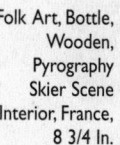

Folk Art, Bottle,
Wooden,
Pyrography
Skier Scene
Interior, France,
8 3/4 In.

Birdhouse, Pine, Painted, Shingle Roof, Cast Pot Metal Fence, 1890s, 19 1/2 x 27 In.	468.00
Book Safe, Chip Carved, England, 1690-1720, 4 In.	425.00
Bottle, Wooden, Pyrography Skier Scene Interior, France, 8 3/4 In. . . . .*Illus*	150.00
Box, Comb, Wooden, Hanging, Carved, 10 In.	80.00
Box, Storage, Lid Inset, Flower Watercolor, Scalloped Skirt, Pa., c.1900, 12 x 16 In.	880.00
Bracket, Wall, Wooden, Carved Eagle, c.1890, 12 x 9 In.	1295.00
Bust, Christopher Columbus, Mahogany, 20th Century	144.00
Candlestand, Victorian, Walnut, Mid 19th Century, 28 x 21 In.	165.00
Chair, Wooden Clothespins, 7 3/4 In. . . . .*Illus*	15.00
Chicken, Red Body, Yellow, Black, Wood, 20th Century, 31 In.	1100.00
Clam Shell, Painted, Gen. McClelan, Chickamauga, Ballou Post, R.I., 1890, 6 x 10 In. . . .	1955.00
Dog, Greyhound Type, Carved, 12 x 16 In.	374.00
Dummy Board, Flower Filled Basket, Swiveling Support, 19th Century, 28 In., Pair	4900.00
Figure, 2 Hunters Shooting Game, Birds, Dogs, Rabbits, Late 19th Century, 13 1/2 In. . . .	825.00
Figure, Flathead Catfish, Raised Eyes, Mouth & Fins, 32 1/2 In.	250.00
Figure, Indian, Decorated, Once Movable Joints, Peter Hunt, Cape Cod, 35 In.	489.00
Figure, Man, Carved, Jointed Legs & Arms	165.00
Figure, Man, Riding Horse, Twigs & Leather, 14 x 17 In.	245.00
Figure, Nude Maiden, Flowing Hair, Limestone, E. Reed, 1976.	330.00
Figure, Uncle Sam, Movable Arms, Red, White, Blue, Mounted, Moxie Box, 64 In.	635.00
Figure, Uncle Sam, Striped Pants, Red Vest, Stars On Jacket, 11 In.	5775.00
Figure, Woman, Holding Child, Classical Clothing, Sandstone, Incised E. Reed, 15 In. . . .	1155.00
Floral Arrangement, Wax, Victorian Basket, Lichen, Glass Dome, c.1875, 23 In.	431.00
Frame, Hearts, Shenandoah Valley, c.1870	1400.00
Fruit Set, Stone, 17 Piece	395.00
Golliwog, Dancing, Hand Painted	220.00
Horn, Spill Holder, Engraved Heart With M & 1834, Trailing Vines, 3 Footed	250.00
Horse, Rocking, 1870, 61 In.	1400.00
Jewelry Box, Matchstick, Stained, Varnished, 7 Drawers, Door, 1970s, 12 5/8 In. . . . . .*Illus*	40.00
Knife Box, Pine, Dovetailed, Green Paint, 15 In.	132.00
Model, House, 2 Story, Clapboard, Picket Fence, Ohio, c.1900, 41 1/2 x 28 1/2 x 35 In. . .	525.00
Model, Tugboat, Lifeboat, Wood, Flag, Gun On Roof, Painted, Black, Red, White, 51 In. .	1440.00
Model, Tugboat, Matchstick, c.1900, 28 In.	330.00
Ornament, Gate, Dog, Full-Bodied, Copper, 31 x 38 1/2 In.	6325.00
Parrot, Wood, Carved, Painted, Simmons, Berks County, Pa., 1890s, 9 7/8 In.	4400.00
Pheasant, Carved, Polychrome, Wire Legs, Wooden Base, 4 1/2 x 13 1/2 In.	175.00
Picture, Dried Floral Arrangement, Shadow Box Walnut Frame, Victorian, 25 x 22 In. . . .	240.00
Rack, Bird & Floral Design, 3 Tiers, 2 Doors & 2 Drawers, Victorian, 34 x 24 x 8 In. . . .	242.00
Retablo, Doctor & Nurse, Cardboard, Mexico, 11 x 13 3/4 In. . . . .*Illus*	100.00
Retablo, Our Lady Of Sorrows, Tin, Mexico, 1800, 10 x 14 In.	120.00
Retablo, Our Lady, Refuge Of Sinners, Tin, Glass Frame, Mexico, 1800, 15 x 19 In.	220.00
Retablo, Religious Path To Eternity & Salvation, Mural On Canvas, c.1915, 39 x 82 In. . .	280.00
Retablo, Santa Maria Concepcion, Tin, Painted Glass Frame, 1900	315.00
Sculpture, Man, With Dog & Chicken, 9 x 6 In.	65.00
Shelf, 3 Shelves, Trees, Animals, Wood, Masonite, Brown, White, c.1930, 17 x 16 1/2 In. .	410.00
Shelf, Hanging, Yellow Garlands, Leaf Designs On Side, Late 19th Century, 18 In.	2860.00
Shovel, Wood, Carved, Decorated, Scoop, Watermill Scene, Murray Mills, 33 In.	345.00
Sign, Key Shape, Red Paint, Wood, Zinc, Wrought Iron Bracket, 53 3/4 x 42 In.	862.00

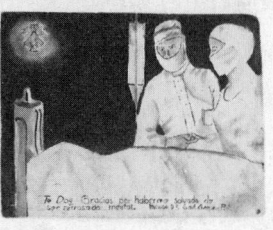

Folk Art, Jewelry Box, Matchstick,
Stained, Varnished,
7 Drawers, Door, 1970s, 12 5/8 In.

Folk Art, Chair, Wooden
Clothespins, 7 3/4 In.

Folk Art, Retablo,
Doctor & Nurse, Cardboard,
Mexico, 11 x 13 3/4 In.

Sign, Tavern, Shield Shape, Frosted Mug, Bar Service, Wood, 23 x 16 In.	1430.00
Sign, Tavern, The Volunteer, U.S. Soldier In Iron Ring, Blue, Pine, 1890s, 31 1/2 In.	1870.00
Sign, Tavern, W. Wood, 2 Sides, 37 In.	5400.00
Sign, Wooden Razor, Carved, Painted, Black, White, 19th Century, 43 1/2 In.	920.00
Song Bird, Yellow Polka Dotted Wings, Black Tail Feather, Pa., 1900, 4 3/4 x 6 In.	1980.00
Song Bird, Yellow, Black, Wire Legs, Green Carved Base, Pa., 5 3/4 In.	385.00
Spoon, Handle, Cutout Hearts, Pinwheel, Red Paint, Dot Border, Wood, 15 1/2 In.	86.00
Target, Carnival, Yellow Cat, Leather, Early 20th Century, 18 In.	1210.00
Train Model, Engine, Coal Tender, Wood, Metal, Marked LV7RR, 1890s, 47 In.	1650.00
Trowel, Memorial, Painted, Andrew L. Smith, Flag, Skyline, G.A.R., c.1893, 11 x 4 In.	1725.00
Wagon, Walnut & Pine, Wooden Disk Wheels, Windows &doors All Around, 9 1/2 In.	190.00
Walnut, Carved, Covered With Faces, 1 3/4 In.	135.00
Whirligig, Black Man With Spool Top Hat, Zinc, Pine, Green, Black Head, 22 1/2 In.	6600.00
Whirligig, Black Man, Carved, Tin Hat, Green, White, Black, 27 In.	4180.00
Whirligig, Chickens Pecking, Wood, Tin, Red, White, Blue, Black, c.1930, 11 x 11 In.	495.00
Whirligig, Fan Over 6 Pecking Chickens, Wood & Tin Polychrome, c.1930, 11 x 11 In.	495.00
Whirligig, Farmer Cutting Wood, Wood, Elmer Preston, Hadley, Mass., c.1940, 31 In.	460.00
Whirligig, Farmer Pumping Water For Cow, 18 x 25 In.	520.00
Whirligig, George Washington On His Horse, Jack, Pine, 19th Century, 20 In.	2400.00
Whirligig, Lincoln, Sawing Wood, Articulated, Painted, Pine	860.00
Whirligig, Man & Woman, Sharpening Ax, American Flag, Painted, 12 x 17 In.	770.00
Whirligig, Man At Well, Cranking Up Bucket, 18 x 20 In.	285.00
Whirligig, Man, Blue Hat, Rubber Arms, 24 1/2 In.	605.00
Whirligig, Man, Red Jacket, Green Pants, 22 In.	7150.00
Whirligig, Metal Figures On Wooden Base, Early 20th Century	2950.00
Whirligig, Mountie, Blades For Arms, 1940s, 18 In.	600.00
Whirligig, Old Tiamcim, Vermont Flood, 1939	715.00
Whirligig, Pot Bellied Man, Curled Toe Shoes, Hooked Nose, 11 3/4 In.	3300.00
Whirligig, Rooster, Spinning Wings, 18 1/2 In.	290.00
Whirligig, Sailor, Cast Iron, Coin Slot In Pocket, 19 In.	2310.00
Whirligig, Soldier, Standing, Wearing Pistol, Sword, Green, Blue, Silver, 17 In.	2400.00
Whirligig, Weather Vane, Wooden, 28 x 35 1/2 In.	75.00
Whirligig, Woman & Man, 10 1/2 In., Pair	90500.00

FOOT WARMERS solved the problem of cold feet in past generations.
Some warmers held charcoal, others held hot water. Pottery, tin, and
soapstone were the favored materials to conduct the heat. The warmer
was kept under the feet, then the legs and feet were tucked into a blanket, providing welcome warmth in a cold carriage or church.

Brass, Pull-Out Drawer For Coals, Lehman Bros., 13 3/4 In.	93.00
Punched Tin, Diamonds, Mortised, Red Frame, Wire Bail Handle, 9 In.	228.00
Punched Tin, Diamonds, Wooden Frame, Bail Handle, H-E. Brewer, 5 3/4 x 9 In.	143.00
Punched Tin, Heart, Maltese Cross On Door, Birch Frame, 7 3/4 x 8 1/2 In.	302.00
Punched Tin, Hearts, Wooden Frame, Bail Handle, Coal Pan, 8 1/2 x 7 1/2 In.	320.00
Punched Tin, Hearts, Wooden Frame, Coal Pan, Wire Bail Handle, 5 3/4 x 9 In.	275.00

Stoneware, Marked Goodwill Pat. Aug. 20, 1895 .... 275.00
Stoneware, Screw Top, Denby Bourne Derby, 11 x 4 1/4 In. 105.00

FOOTBALL collectibles may be found in the Card and the Sports categories.

FOSTORIA glass was made in Fostoria, Ohio, from 1887 to 1891. The factory was moved to Moundsville, West Virginia, and most of the glass seen in shops today is a twentieth-century product. The company was sold in 1983; new items will be easily identifiable, according to the new owner, Lancaster Colony Corporation. Additional Fostoria items may be listed in the Milk Glass category.

Alexis, Bowl, 8 1/2 In. 105.00
American, Ashtray, 3 In. 4.00
American, Ashtray, Hat, 2 1/2 In. 25.00
American, Bonbon, Handle, 6 1/4 In. 29.00
American, Bonbon, Ruby 125.00
American, Bottle, Cordial, Stopper 75.00
American, Bowl, 11 In. 66.00
American, Bowl, 2 Sections, 10 In. 25.00
American, Bowl, 3 Handles, 4 1/4 In. ....89.00 to 150.00
American, Bowl, 3-Toed, 7 In. ....13.00 to 20.00
American, Bowl, 5 In. ....15.00 to 20.00
American, Bowl, 7 In. 30.00
American, Bowl, Cupped, 9 1/2 In. 195.00
American, Bowl, Fruit, Rolled Edge, 2 3/4 x 11 1/2 In. 68.00
American, Bowl, Handle, Tricornered, 5 In. 10.00
American, Bowl, Lemon, Cover, 5 1/2 In. 45.00
American, Bowl, Square, 4 1/2 In. 20.00
American, Bowl, Tricornered, 11 In. 40.00
American, Bowl, Trophy, 2 Handles, Footed, 8 In. ....95.00 to 115.00
American, Bowl, Wedding, Cover, Small 125.00
American, Box, Glass Cover, Round, 2 7/8 In. 3200.00
American, Butter, Cover ....130.00 to 145.00
American, Cake Stand, Square, 10 In. 250.00
American, Candle Lamp, With Chimney 175.00
American, Candlestick, 2-Light, 4 1/4 In., Pair 135.00
American, Candlestick, Octagonal Foot, 6 In., Pair 30.00
American, Compote, Cover, 6 3/4 In. ....25.00 to 37.00
American, Compote, Octagonal Foot, 6 In. 50.00
American, Creamer, 4 3/4 Oz. ....16.00 to 20.00
American, Creamer, 9 1/2 Oz. 12.00
American, Cup & Saucer, Footed 20.00
American, Decanter, Gin, Stopper, Metal Frame 500.00
American, Decanter, Stopper, 24 Oz., 9 1/4 In. ....75.00 to 120.00
American, Dish, Banana Split 1200.00
American, Dish, Mayonnaise, Underplate, Spoon 40.00
American, Dish, Pickle, 8 In. 13.00
American, Goblet, 10 Oz., 6 1/8 In. ....14.00 to 18.00
American, Hat, 3 In. 25.00
American, Hat, 4 In. 50.00
American, Jar, Pickle, Pointed Cover, 6 In. 600.00
American, Marmalade, Cover, Spoon 125.00
American, Oyster Cocktail, 4 1/2 Oz. 16.00
American, Pin Tray, 5 In. ....140.00 to 150.00
American, Pitcher, 1 Qt. 28.00
American, Pitcher, No Ice Lip, 1/2 Gal. 200.00
American, Plate, 6 In. ....8.00 to 10.00
American, Plate, 8 1/2 In. ....12.00 to 18.00
American, Plate, 9 1/2 In. ....20.00 to 39.00
American, Plate, Crescent, 7 1/2 In. 13.00
American, Plate, Sauce Liner, Oval, 8 In. 25.00
American, Platter, Oval, 12 In. ....50.00 to 57.00

American, Punch Bowl, Low Base, 14 In. 250.00
American, Rose Bowl, 5 In. 25.00
American, Salt & Pepper 18.00
American, Saltshaker, 3 1/2 In. 5.00
American, Sauceboat 30.00
American, Sherbet, 5 Oz., 3 1/2 In. ....10.00 to 12.00
American, Sherbet, Tall, 5 1/2 Oz., 4 1/8 In. 14.00
American, Spooner 59.00
American, Strawholder, 12 In. ....175.00 to 300.00
American, Sugar & Creamer, Cover, 6 1/4 In. 95.00
American, Sugar & Creamer, Oval Tray 30.00
American, Sugar, Cover, 6 1/4 In. 60.00
American, Torte Plate, 20 In. 250.00
American, Torte Plate, Oval, 13 1/2 In. ....40.00 to 45.00
American, Tray, 2 Handles, 9 1/2 In. 48.00
American, Tray, Condiment, Cloverleaf Shape 250.00
American, Tumbler, Cocktail, 3 Oz., 2 7/8 In. 12.00
American, Tumbler, Footed, 9 Oz., 4 7/8 In. ....10.00 to 15.00
American, Tumbler, Iced Tea, Footed, 12 Oz., 5 1/2 In. ....12.00 to 15.00
American, Tumbler, Juice, Footed, 5 Oz. ....10.00 to 16.00
American, Vase, 6 In. ....35.00 to 40.00
American, Vase, 12 In. 275.00
American, Vase, Bud, Flared, Hexagonal Foot, 8 1/2 In. 28.00
American, Vase, Bud, Footed, 6 In. 40.00
American, Vase, Flared, 7 In. ....60.00 to 87.00
American, Vase, Flared, 9 1/2 In. ....100.00 to 250.00
American, Vase, Sweet Pea, 4 1/2 In. 75.00
American, Washbowl Set, 2 Piece 3900.00
American, Wine, Hexagonal Foot, 2 1/2 Oz., 4 3/8 In. ....12.00 to 18.00
American Lady, Cocktail, Azure 140.00
American Lady, Goblet, 9 Oz., 5 In. 14.00
American Lady, Goblet, 10 Oz. ....15.00 to 22.00
American Lady, Sherbet, Burgundy, 5 1/2 Oz. 16.00
American Lady, Sherbet, Regal Blue, 5 1/2 Oz. 60.00
American Lady, Tumbler, Iced Tea, Footed, 12 Oz. 18.00
American Lady, Tumbler, Iced Tea, Footed, Green, 12 Oz. 175.00
American Lady, Tumbler, Water, Regal Blue, 10 Oz. 110.00
Baroque, Bonbon, 3-Footed, Azure, 7 In. 95.00
Baroque, Bottle, Oil, Stopper, Topaz 295.00
Baroque, Bowl, Cupped, Azure, 8 In. 150.00
Baroque, Bowl, Flared, 12 In. 22.00
Baroque, Bowl, Handles, 4 Footed, 10 1/2 In. 85.00
Baroque, Bowl, Sauce, Azure 45.00
Baroque, Candlestick, Topaz, 5 1/2 In., Pair 45.00
Baroque, Candy Dish, Cover, Round 20.00
Baroque, Creamer, Footed, 3 3/4 In. 12.00
Baroque, Cup & Saucer 12.00
Baroque, Cup & Saucer, Azure 25.00
Baroque, Dish, Sweetmeat, Cover 75.00
Baroque, Goblet, 9 Oz., 6 3/4 In. 15.00
Baroque, Goblet, Azure, 9 Oz., 6 3/4 In. ....22.00 to 25.00
Baroque, Ice Bucket, Handle, Topaz 85.00
Baroque, Nappy, Handle, Azure, 4 In. 35.00
Baroque, Plate, 9 1/2 In. 65.00
Baroque, Plate, Topaz, 7 In. 9.50
Baroque, Plate, Topaz, 9 1/2 In. 42.50
Baroque, Relish, 3 Sections, Topaz, 10 1/2 In. 27.50
Baroque, Rose Bowl, Azure, 8 In. 260.00
Baroque, Saucer, Azure 9.50
Baroque, Soup, Cream, Underplate, Azure 325.00
Baroque, Sugar, Individual 5.00
Baroque, Torte Plate, 14 In. 15.00
Baroque, Tumbler, Cocktail, Footed, Azure, 3 Oz., 3 In. 105.00

Baroque, Tumbler, Footed, Azure, 14 Oz., 5 1/2 In. . . . . .20.00 to 30.00
Baroque, Tumbler, Old Fashioned, Azure, 6 1/2 Oz., 3 1/2 In. 85.00
Baroque, Vase, Azure, 7 In. 150.00
Baroque, Vase, Azure, 8 In. 195.00
Baroque, Vase, Cobalt Blue, 8 In. 175.00
Baroque, Vase, Cobalt Blue, 12 In. 250.00
Baroque, Vase, Footed, 7 1/2 In. 85.00
Beverly, Bouillon, Saucer, Amber 12.50
Beverly, Bouillon, Saucer, Green 16.00
Beverly, Cheese & Cracker Set, Green 85.00
Beverly, Creamer, Footed, Amber, Large 20.00
Beverly, Cup & Saucer, Amber 35.00
Beverly, Soup, Cream, Underplate, Amber 35.00
Brazilian, Toothpick 20.00
Brocade, Bowl, Footed, Oakleaf, Rose, 12 In. 115.00
Brocade, Box, Cigarette, Cover, Green, Oakleaf, Small 160.00
Brocade, Cake Plate, Handles, Oakleaf, Rose, 10 In. 70.00
Brocade, Sherbet, Oakwood, Azure, 6 Oz. 40.00
Brocade, Vase, Fan, Oakleaf, Rose, 8 1/2 In. 425.00
Brocade, Vase, Oakleaf, Rose, 8 In. 500.00
Brocade, Vase, Palm Leaf, Footed, Rose, 10 1/2 In. 425.00
Buttercup, Champagne, 6 Oz., 5 5/8in. 22.00
Buttercup, Cocktail, 3 1/2 Oz., 5 1/4 In. 20.00
Buttercup, Cup & Saucer 25.00
Buttercup, Goblet, 10 Oz., 7 7/8 In. . . . . .25.00 to 28.00
Buttercup, Tumbler, Iced Tea, Footed, 12 Oz, 6 Oz. 24.00
Buttercup, Wine, 3 1/2 Oz., 6 In. . . . . .30.00 to 32.00
Captive, Tumbler, Iced Tea, Footed, Azure 12.00
Captive, Wine, Azure 12.00
Century, Bonbon, 3-Footed . . . . .20.00 to 22.50
Century, Bottle, Oil, Stopper 45.00
Century, Bowl, 5 In. 30.00
Century, Bowl, Floral, Float, 8 In. 35.00
Century, Bowl, Footed, 11 In. 45.00
Century, Bowl, Handles, 12 In. 36.00
Century, Cake Stand 60.00
Century, Compote, Square 20.00
Century, Cup & Saucer 12.50
Century, Dish, Mayonnaise 9.50
Century, Pitcher, 16 Oz., 7 In. . . . . .58.00 to 60.00
Century, Plate, Snack, 8 1/2 In. 25.00
Century, Relish, 2 Sections, 7 3/8 In. 20.00
Century, Relish, 3 Sections, 11 1/8 In. 33.00
Century, Sherbet 11.00
Century, Sugar & Creamer 20.00
Century, Torte Plate, 14 In. 30.00
Century, Tray, Luncheon, Center Handle, 11 1/4 In. 35.00
Century, Tray, Muffin, 9 In. 30.00
Chintz, Bowl, 2 Handles, 10 1/2 In. 125.00
Chintz, Bowl, Flared, 12 In. 100.00
Chintz, Cake Plate, 2 Handles, 10 1/2 In. 47.00
Chintz, Candlestick, 2-Light, 5 1/2 In., Pair . . . . .60.00 to 85.00
Chintz, Candlestick, 3-Light, Pair . . . . .95.00 to 105.00
Chintz, Candy Dish, Cover, 3 Sections 175.00
Chintz, Cheese Dish, Footed 25.00
Chintz, Cocktail, 3 1/2 Oz., 6 In. 25.00
Chintz, Cup & Saucer . . . . .25.00 to 35.00
Chintz, Dish, Cheese & Cracker, 11 In. 115.00
Chintz, Goblet, 9 Oz., 7 5/8 In. . . . . .30.00 to 45.00
Chintz, Oyster Cocktail, 4 Oz., 3 5/8 In. 25.00
Chintz, Pitcher, Footed, 48 Oz. 725.00
Chintz, Plate, 7 1/2 In. 25.00
Chintz, Plate, 9 1/2 In. 75.00

Chintz, Relish, 3 Sections, Rectangular, 10 In. ....40.00 to 45.00
Chintz, Relish, 5 Sections, 13 1/4 In. 210.00
Chintz, Salt & Pepper 90.00
Chintz, Sauceboat 110.00
Chintz, Sherbet, 6 Oz., 4 3/8 In. 27.00
Chintz, Sherbet, Azure, 6 Oz., 4 3/8 In. 12.00
Chintz, Soup, Dish, Blue, 7 3/4 In. 42.00
Chintz, Sugar & Creamer, Footed, 3 5/8 In. 35.00
Chintz, Tumbler, Water 40.00
Chintz, Vase, Footed, 6 In. 550.00
Chintz, Wine, 3 1/4 Oz., 5 1/2 In. 45.00
Chintz, Wine, Azure, 3 1/2 Oz., 5 1/2 In. 28.00
Coin, Bowl, 8 In. 40.00
Coin, Bowl, Footed, 8 1/2 In. 65.00
Coin, Bowl, Footed, Ruby, 8 1/2 In. 70.00
Coin, Bowl, Wedding, Cover, Ruby 150.00
Coin, Bowl, Wedding, Cover, Ruby, 8 1/4 In. 75.00
Coin, Cake Stand, Amber, Satin Coins 140.00
Coin, Candy Jar, Cover, Ruby, Low 85.00
Coin, Cigarette Urn, Cover 40.00
Coin, Condiment Set, 4 Piece 150.00
Coin, Cruet, Amber 100.00
Coin, Goblet, 10 Oz., 6 5/8 In. 110.00
Coin, Lamp, Patio, Electric, Amber 150.00
Coin, Nappy, Amber, 4 1/2 In. 27.00
Coin, Pitcher, Blue, 8 In. 175.00
Coin, Salt & Pepper, Amber 35.00
Coin, Sherbet, 5 1/4 In. 80.00
Coin, Sugar, Cover, Olive 35.00
Coin, Tumbler, Iced Tea, Ruby, Satin Coins 110.00
Coin, Urn, Cover, Ruby, Satin Coins, 12 3/4 In. 110.00
Coin, Vase, Bud, Amber, 8 In. 20.00
Coin, Vase, Bud, Ruby, 8 In. 40.00
Coin, Wine, Ruby, 5 Oz., 5 1/4 In. 95.00
Colonial Dame, Sherbet, 5 Oz., 3 5/8 In. 11.50
Colonial Dame, Tumbler, Iced Tea, Footed, Green, 12 Oz., 6 In. 15.00
Colony, Bonbon, Footed, 5 In. 30.00
Colony, Bottle, Oil, Stopper 50.00
Colony, Bowl, 4 1/2 In. 32.00
Colony, Bowl, Cupped, 8 In. 51.00
Colony, Bowl, Fruit, 14 In. 85.00
Colony, Bread Plate 6.00
Colony, Butter, Cover 35.00
Colony, Cake Plate, 2 Handles, 10 In. 25.00
Colony, Candlestick, Prisms, 14 1/2 In. 100.00
Colony, Candy Jar, Cover, Black Footed 75.00
Colony, Cocktail, 3 1/2 Oz., 4 In. 12.00
Colony, Compote, Cover, 6 1/2 In. 55.00
Colony, Creamer, Individual 14.00
Colony, Cup & Saucer ....9.00 to 12.00
Colony, Dish, Pickle, 8 In. ....25.00 to 27.00
Colony, Finger Bowl, 4 3/4 In. 75.00
Colony, Goblet, 9 Oz., 5 1/4 In. ....13.00 to 16.00
Colony, Ice Bucket, Plain Edge, 6 1/4 In. 195.00
Colony, Pitcher, Ice Lip, 3 Pt., 8 1/2 In. 260.00
Colony, Plate, 8 In. 13.00
Colony, Platter, 12 In. 47.00
Colony, Punch Bowl, Footed 795.00
Colony, Punch Cup 30.00
Colony, Relish, 3 Sections, 2 Handles, Crystal, 10 1/2 In. 45.00
Colony, Sandwich Server, Center Handle 25.00
Colony, Sherbet, 5 Oz., 3 5/8 In. 10.00
Colony, Sherbet, Empire, Green, 6 1/2 Oz., 4 5/8 In. 17.50

Colony, Sugar & Creamer, Tray, Individual 27.50
Colony, Torte Plate, 15 In. ....65.00 to 75.00
Colony, Tumbler, Iced Tea, 12 Oz., 4 7/8 In. 39.00
Colony, Tumbler, Iced Tea, Footed, 12 Oz., 5 3/4 In. 18.00
Colony, Vase, Bud, Cupped, 7 In. 28.00
Colony, Vase, Bud, Flared, 6 In. 12.00
Colony, Vase, Flared, 7 1/2 In. 50.00
Colony, Wine, 3 1/4 Oz., 4 1/4 In. 24.00
Contour, Butter, Cover, 1/4 Lb. 25.00
Contour, Candlestick, 6 In., Pair 30.00
Contour, Goblet, 10 1/2 Oz. 22.00
Contour, Relish, 2 Sections 20.00
Contour, Relish, 3 Sections, 11 In. 30.00
Contour, Sugar & Creamer, Tray, Individual 25.00
Coronet, Bottle, Oil, Footed, Stopper 50.00
Corsage, Champagne 18.00
Corsage, Cocktail 22.00
Corsage, Goblet, 9 Oz. 25.00
Corsage, Sugar, Individual 17.00
Cynthia, Bonbon, 3-Toed 19.00
Cynthia, Champagne, 5 1/2 In. 17.00
Cynthia, Cocktail, 5 1/2 In. 25.00
Cynthia, Dish, Mayonnaise Set, Underplate, Spoon 45.00
Cynthia, Goblet, 7 1/2 In. 19.50
Cynthia, Plate, 7 In. 12.50
Cynthia, Relish, 3 Sections 35.00
Cynthia, Tumbler, Juice, 4 3/4 In. 15.00
Czarina, Toothpick 35.00
Dandelion, Berry Bowl, 8 In. 55.00
Diadem, Candy Jar, Cover, Black, Gold Trim 95.00
Dolly Madison, Champagne 16.00
Dolly Madison, Cocktail 15.00
Dolly Madison, Goblet, Low 16.00
Fairfax, Ashtray, Amber, 2 1/2 In. 19.00
Fairfax, Bonbon, Rose 17.00
Fairfax, Bouillon, Amber 12.00
Fairfax, Bouillon, Underplate, Rose 35.00
Fairfax, Bowl, Cornucopia, Azure, 11 In. 125.00
Fairfax, Bowl, Fruit, Amber, 5 In. 10.00
Fairfax, Bowl, Lemon, Handle, Azure, 9 In. 17.00
Fairfax, Celery Dish, Amber, 11 1/2 In. 15.00
Fairfax, Cocktail, Azure, 3 Oz., 5 1/4 In. 24.00
Fairfax, Cocktail, Rose, 3 Oz., 5 1/4 In. 35.00
Fairfax, Cup & Saucer, After Dinner, Topaz 12.00
Fairfax, Cup & Saucer, Footed, Green 12.00
Fairfax, Cup, After Dinner, Rose 20.00
Fairfax, Cup, Amber 12.00
Fairfax, Cup, Green 9.00
Fairfax, Dish, Mayonnaise, Underplate, Spoon, Rose, 7 1/2 In. 95.00
Fairfax, Dish, Pickle, Amber, 8 3/4 In. 12.00
Fairfax, Finger Bowl, Green 12.00
Fairfax, Finger Bowl, Underplate, Amber 17.00
Fairfax, Finger Bowl, Underplate, Green 14.00
Fairfax, Goblet, Azure, 10 Oz., 8 1/4 In. 28.00
Fairfax, Grapefruit, Underplate, Amber 45.00
Fairfax, Icer, Seafood, Amber 12.00
Fairfax, Icer, Seafood, Rose 30.00
Fairfax, Nut Dish, Rose ....12.00 to 20.00
Fairfax, Oyster Cocktail, Topaz 17.00
Fairfax, Plate, Lemon, Handle, Amber 17.00
Fairfax, Plate, Topaz, 7 1/2 In. 5.00
Fairfax, Plate, Whipped Cream, Handle, Amber 17.00
Fairfax, Relish, 3 Sections, Azure, 8 1/2 In. 25.00

Fairfax, Relish, 3 Sections, Topaz, 8 1/2 In. 17.00
Fairfax, Saucer, After Dinner, Topaz 22.00
Fairfax, Sherbet, Azure, 6 Oz., 4 1/4 In. 17.00
Fairfax, Sherbet, Topaz, 6 Oz., 6 In. 12.00
Fairfax, Sugar & Creamer, Azure 50.00
Fairfax, Sugar, Azure, Individual 30.00
Fairfax, Tumbler, Iced Tea, Footed, Azure, 12 Oz., 6 In. 24.00
Fairfax, Tumbler, Iced Tea, Footed, Topaz, 12 Oz., 6 In. 20.00
Fairfax, Tumbler, Juice, Footed, Topaz, 5 Oz., 4 1/2 In. 9.00
Fairfax, Tumbler, Topaz, 9 Oz., 5 1/4 In. 15.00
Fairfax, Tumbler, Whiskey, Footed, Azure, 2 1/2 Oz. 35.00
Grape, Bowl, Rolled Edge, Orchid, 11 In. 65.00
Grape, Compote, Orchid, 7 In. 75.00
Heather, Cake Plate 55.00
Heather, Cordial 40.00
Heather, Plate, 9 1/2 In. 38.00
Heather, Sugar, Individual 17.00
Heirloom, Bowl, Pilled Edge, Aqua Opalescent, c.1960, 8 1/2 x 4 1/2 In. 55.00
Heirloom, Console, Pink Opalescent, Oval, 14 1/2 In. 50.00
Heirloom, Pitcher, Pink 85.00
Heirloom, Plate, Pulled Edge, Blue Opalescent, 8 In. 20.00
Heirloom, Plate, Vaseline, Opalescent, 8 In. 100.00
Heirloom, Vase, Bud, White Opalescent 22.00
Hermitage, Oyster Cocktail 6.00
Hermitage, Sherbet, Topaz 12.00
Holly, Champagne 15.00
Holly, Cocktail 23.00
Holly, Cordial, 1 Oz. 40.00
Holly, Dish, Mayonnaise Set, Underplate, Spoon 45.00
Holly, Goblet, Low 26.00
Holly, Plate, Salad, 7 In. 12.00
Holly, Salt & Pepper, Large 45.00
Holly, Sherbet, Low 15.00
Holly, Torte Plate, 14 In. 40.00
Jamestown, Goblet, Amber, 9 1/2 Oz. 10.00
Jamestown, Goblet, Azure, 9 1/2 Oz. 20.00
Jamestown, Goblet, Green, 9 1/2 Oz. 16.00
Jamestown, Sherbet, Amber . . . . .6.00 to 7.00
Jamestown, Sherbet, Green 12.00
Jamestown, Tumbler, Iced Tea, Footed, Azure 20.00
Jamestown, Tumbler, Iced Tea, Footed, Pink 20.00
Jamestown, Tumbler, Iced Tea, Footed, Smoke 10.00
Jamestown, Tumbler, Juice, Footed, Azure 25.00
Jamestown, Tumbler, Juice, Footed, Green 21.00
Jamestown, Tumbler, Juice, Footed, Ruby 26.00
Jamestown, Wine, Green, 4 Oz. 20.00
Jamestown, Wine, Ruby, 4 Oz. 24.00
June, Berry Bowl, Topaz 28.00
June, Bonbon, Topaz 30.00
June, Bread Plate, Topaz, 6 In. 10.00
June, Candy Dish, Cover, 3 Sections, Rose 575.00
June, Candy Jar, Cover, Topaz, 1/2 Lb. 375.00
June, Celery Dish, Topaz, 11 1/2 In. 60.00
June, Centerpiece, Azure, 3-Footed 115.00
June, Centerpiece, Topaz, 12 In. 110.00
June, Cocktail, Topaz, 3 Oz., 5 1/4 In. 35.00
June, Compote, Azure, 7 In. 145.00
June, Cup & Saucer 22.00
June, Cup & Saucer, Azure 45.00
June, Cup & Saucer, Topaz, After Dinner 75.00
June, Finger Bowl, Underplate, Topaz 90.00
June, Goblet, 10 Oz., 8 1/4 In. 33.00
June, Goblet, Azure, 10 Oz., 8 1/4 In. 72.00

June, Goblet, Topaz, 10 Oz., 8 1/4 In. 60.00
June, Gravy Boat, Underplate, Topaz 325.00
June, Ice Bucket, Topaz 135.00
June, Oyster Cocktail 27.50
June, Pail, Whipped Cream, Rose 295.00
June, Pitcher, Azure 1000.00
June, Pitcher, Rose 950.00
June, Plate, 7 1/2 In. 14.00
June, Plate, Topaz, 7 1/2 In. 8.50
June, Platter, Azure, 15 In. 295.00
June, Relish, 2 Sections, Rose, 8 1/2 In. 65.00
June, Sherbet, Topaz, 6 Oz., 4 1/4 In. 20.00
June, Sherbet, Topaz, 6 Oz., 6 In. 21.00
June, Sugar & Creamer, Azure, Large 85.00
June, Sugar & Creamer, Tea, Topaz 150.00
June, Sugar, Cover, Rose 275.00
June, Sugar, Large 20.00
June, Sugar, Scalloped Edge, Large 20.00
June, Sugar, Tea, Topaz 65.00
June, Tumbler, Iced Tea, Footed, Azure, 12 Oz., 6 In. 68.00
June, Tumbler, Iced Tea, Footed, Topaz, 12 Oz., 6 In. 28.00
June, Tumbler, Juice, Footed, Topaz, 5 Oz., 4 1/2 In. 32.00
June, Tumbler, Rose, 9 Oz., 5 1/4 In. 50.00
June, Tumbler, Whiskey, Topaz, 2 1/2 Oz. 85.00
June, Vase, Rose, 8 In. 825.00
June, Vase, Topaz, 8 In. 575.00
June, Wine, 3 Oz., 5 1/2 In. 35.00
Kashmir, Plate, Azure, 10 1/4 In. 125.00
Lafayette, Champagne, Wisteria 35.00
Lafayette, Claret, Wisteria, 4 1/2 Oz., 6 1/2 In. 125.00
Lafayette, Cup & Saucer 6.00
Lafayette, Cup & Saucer, Wisteria 25.00
Lafayette, Dish, Pickle, Topaz, 6 1/2 In. 10.00
Lafayette, Goblet, Wisteria, 10 Oz., 7 1/2 In. 55.00
Lafayette, Plate, Wisteria, 7 1/2 In. 20.00
Lafayette, Plate, Wisteria, 9 1/2 In. 50.00
Lafayette, Sweetmeat, Handle, Topaz, 4 1/2 In. 9.50
Lafayette, Vase, Topaz, 7 In. 75.00
Laurel, Goblet, 9 Oz. 16.00
Lido, Claret, 4 Oz., 5 7/8 In. 35.00
Lido, Cordial, 3/4 Oz. 50.00
Lido, Plate, 5 In. 12.00
Lido, Relish, 3 Sections 35.00
Lido, Sugar, Footed 9.00
Lido, Tumbler, Juice, 5 Oz., 4 3/4 In. 16.00
Manor, Cordial, Topaz 65.00
Mayflower, Cocktail, 4 7/8 In. 25.00
Mayflower, Sherbet, 6 3/8 In. 25.00
Mayflower, Tumbler, Juice, Footed, 4 7/8 In. 25.00
Meadow Rose, Candlestick, 2-Light, Pair 650.00
Meadow Rose, Sugar & Creamer, Tray, Individual 110.00
Meadow Rose, Vase, 5 In. 68.00
Meadow Rose, Vase, 9 1/2 In. 340.00
Minuet, Vase, Topaz, 6 3/4 x 7 5/8 In. 250.00
Morning Glory, Tray 45.00
Navarre, Bowl, Flame, Oval, 12 1/2 In. 96.00
Navarre, Bowl, Handle, Footed, 10 1/2 In. 110.00
Navarre, Candlestick, 4 In., Pair 195.00
Navarre, Celery Dish, 11 In. 96.00
Navarre, Champagne, 6 Oz., 5 5/8 In. ....22.00 to 35.00
Navarre, Champagne, Azure, 6 Oz., 5 5/8 In. 75.00
Navarre, Champagne, Rose, 6 Oz., 5 5/8 In. 65.00
Navarre, Claret, Rose, 4 1/2 Oz., 6 1/2 In. 85.00

Navarre, Cocktail, 3 1/2 Oz., 6 In. 35.00
Navarre, Compote, 6 In. 87.00
Navarre, Cordial, 1 Oz., 3 7/8 In. 80.00
Navarre, Dinner Bell, Azure .... 95.00 to 125.00
Navarre, Dinner Bell, Rose 135.00
Navarre, Dish, Mayonnaise, Underplate .... 73.00 to 75.00
Navarre, Goblet, 10 Oz., 7 5/8 In. .... 35.00 to 45.00
Navarre, Gravy Boat, Underplate 275.00
Navarre, Ice Bucket, Bail Handle 275.00
Navarre, Relish, 5 Sections, 13 1/4 In. 175.00
Navarre, Salt & Pepper, Footed 116.00
Navarre, Sauceboat, Attached Plate 165.00
Navarre, Sherbet, 6 Oz., 4 3/8 In. 32.00
Navarre, Sugar & Creamer, Footed, 3 5/8 In. 75.00
Navarre, Torte Plate, 14 In. 95.00
Navarre, Tumbler, Iced Tea, Azure, 13 Oz., 5 7/8 In. 75.00
Navarre, Tumbler, Iced Tea, Footed, 13 Oz., 5 7/8 In. 45.00
Navarre, Tumbler, Juice, Footed, 5 Oz., 4 5/8 In. 42.00
Navarre, Wine, 3 1/4 Oz, 5 1/2 In. 65.00
Neo Classic, Brandy Inhaler, Burgundy, 4 In. 50.00
Neo Classic, Champagne, Burgundy, 4 3/4 In. 35.00
Neo Classic, Goblet, Burgundy, 10 Oz., 6 3/8 In. 40.00
Neo Classic, Sherbet, Burgundy, 3 1/4 In. 30.00
Neo Classic, Tumbler, Iced Tea, Footed, 13 Oz., 5 3/8 In. 40.00
Neo Classic, Tumbler, Juice, Footed, Burgundy, 5 Oz., 3 7/8 In. 35.00
Neo Classic, Wine, Burgundy, 3 1/2 Oz., 5 In. 40.00
Oriental, Box, Cigarette, Cover 170.00
Oriental, Compote, 6 In. 150.00
Pioneer, Butter, Cover, Amber 35.00
Pioneer, Cup & Saucer, Green 10.00
Raleigh, Creamer, Footed .... 8.00 to 10.00
Raleigh, Sugar, Individual 8.00
Riviera, Centerpiece, Candlesticks, Topaz, Gold Encrusted, 12-In. Bowl, 3 Piece 345.00
Romance, Candlestick, 5 1/2 In. 38.00
Romance, Sandwich Server, Center Handle 45.00
Romance, Torte Plate, 14 In. 65.00
Romance, Wine 35.00
Rose, Cup & Saucer 25.00
Rose, Goblet 18.00
Rose, Plate, 14 In. 38.00
Rose, Relish, 3 Sections, Rectangular, 10 In. 65.00
Royal, Candlestick, Amber, Pair 45.00
Royal, Compote, Azure, 7 In. 65.00
Royal, Creamer, Amber, Footed, Large 30.00
Royal, Goblet, Green, 9 Oz. 40.00
Royal, Sugar, Amber, Footed, Large 30.00
Royal, Wine, 2 3/4 Oz. 55.00
Seville, Sherbet, Amber 10.00
Shirley, Plate, 6 In. 7.00
Shirley, Plate, 7 1/2 In. 10.00
Shirley, Sugar, Individual 9.50
St. Alexis, Clock, With 5-In. Candlestick, Amber, 3 Piece 205.00
Sun Ray, Ice Bucket 50.00
Sun Ray, Sherbet, Azure 18.00
Sun Ray, Tumbler, Water, Azure 55.00
Trojan, Console Set, Candlestick, Topaz, 3 Piece 125.00
Trojan, Console, 2 Candleholder Handles, Topaz 250.00
Trojan, Ice Bucket, Topaz 125.00
Trojan, Soup, Cream, Underplate, Rose 95.00
Trojan, Tumbler, Iced Tea, Rose, 6 In. 60.00
Trojan, Vase, Topaz, 7 In. 250.00
Vernon, Plate, 7 1/2 In. 12.00
Versailles, Bowl, Azure, 6 In. 45.00

Versailles, Compote, Green, 3 In.	35.00
Versailles, Console Set, Rolled Edge, Rose, 2 Candlesticks, 12-In. Bowl, 3 Piece	115.00
Versailles, Console, Topaz, 12 In.	75.00
Versailles, Cup & Saucer, Green, After Dinner	75.00
Versailles, Vase, Azure, 10 In.	90.00
Vesper, Goblet, Water, Footed, Amber	32.00
Victoria, Relish, Boat Shape, 7 In.	65.00
Victorian, Tumbler, Iced Tea, Footed, Green, 12 Oz., 5 1/2 In.	5.00
Virginia, Tumbler, Iced Tea, Footed	55.00

FOVAL, see Fry category.

FRAMES are included in the Furniture category under Frame.

FRANCISCAN is a trademark that appears on pottery. Gladding, McBean and Company started in 1875. The company grew and acquired other potteries. They made sewer pipes, floor tiles, dinnerwares, and art pottery with a variety of trademarks. In 1934, dinnerware and art pottery were sold under the name Franciscan Ware. They made china and cream-colored, decorated earthenware. Desert Rose, Apple, El Patio, and Coronado were best-sellers. The company became Interpace Corporation and in 1979 was purchased by Josiah Wedgwood & Sons. The plant was closed in 1984 but a few of the patterns are still being made. For more information, see *Kovels' Depression Glass & Dinnerware Price List*.

Apple, Ashtray, Square	295.00
Apple, Bowl, Cereal, 6 In.	10.00
Apple, Bowl, Cereal, Footed, 6 In.	35.00
Apple, Bowl, Fruit, 5 1/4 In.	8.00
Apple, Bowl, Salad, 10 In.	105.00
Apple, Bowl, Vegetable, Oval, Divided, 10 3/4 In.	40.00 to 45.00
Apple, Butter, Cover	60.00
Apple, Casserole, Cover	125.00
Apple, Casserole, Cover, Individual	55.00
Apple, Chop Plate, 12 In.	30.00
Apple, Creamer	18.00 to 22.00
Apple, Cup & Saucer	13.00 to 15.00
Apple, Gravy Boat, Underplate	25.00
Apple, Jam Jar, Cover	145.00
Apple, Mixing Bowl, 10 In.	225.00
Apple, Pitcher, Milk, 6 1/4 In.	95.00
Apple, Plate, 6 1/4 In.	7.50 to 9.00
Apple, Plate, 8 1/2 In.	13.00
Apple, Plate, 9 1/2 In.	18.00
Apple, Plate, 10 1/2 In.	15.00 to 18.00
Apple, Platter, 12 1/2 In.	40.00 to 70.00
Apple, Platter, 14 In.	60.00 to 75.00
Apple, Platter, 19 In.	250.00
Apple, Relish, 3 Sections	65.00 to 85.00
Apple, Salt & Pepper	20.00
Apple, Sugar	30.00
Apple, Tile, Square, 6 In.	45.00
Autumn, Bowl, Vegetable, 7 1/2 In.	16.00
Autumn, Mug, 7 Oz.	10.00
Autumn, Mug, 16 Oz.	15.00
Autumn, Relish, Tab Handle, 11 7/8 In.	15.00
Cafe Royal, Bowl, Cereal	14.00
Cafe Royal, Bowl, Vegetable, 9 In.	40.00
Cafe Royal, Bowl, Vegetable, Divided, 11 In.	40.00
Cafe Royal, Canister, Tea, 5 1/2 In.	195.00
Cafe Royal, Cup & Saucer	16.00
Cafe Royal, Ginger Jar	295.00
Cafe Royal, Hurricane Lamp, Globe	295.00
Cafe Royal, Plate, 8 In.	12.00

Coronado, Ashtray, Turquoise 13.00
Coronado, Berry Bowl, Turquoise Matte, 6 In. 10.00
Coronado, Bowl, Salad, Yellow, 12 In. 65.00
Coronado, Bowl, Vegetable, Coral Matte, 8 In. 15.00
Coronado, Bowl, Yellow Matte, 6 1/2 In. 9.00
Coronado, Butter, Cover, Turquoise Matte 40.00
Coronado, Butter, Ivory 75.00
Coronado, Celery Dish, Coral Matte 20.00
Coronado, Chop Plate, Coral, 12 1/2 In. 35.00
Coronado, Chop Plate, Turquoise Matte, 11 3/4 In. 30.00
Coronado, Chop Plate, Turquoise, 11 3/4 In. 35.00
Coronado, Creamer, Coral Matte 20.00
Coronado, Creamer, Ivory Matte 20.00
Coronado, Creamer, Turquoise Matte 15.00
Coronado, Cup & Saucer, Burgundy 15.00
Coronado, Cup & Saucer, Burgundy, After Dinner 45.00
Coronado, Cup & Saucer, Coral 14.00
Coronado, Cup & Saucer, White Matte 11.00
Coronado, Cup & Saucer, White, After Dinner 45.00
Coronado, Gravy Boat, Underplate, Coral Matte 35.00
Coronado, Gravy Boat, Underplate, Turquoise 40.00
Coronado, Gravy Boat, Underplate, Turquoise Matte 35.00
Coronado, Nut Cup, Turquoise 25.00
Coronado, Pitcher, Milk, Yellow 85.00
Coronado, Pitcher, Water, Coral Matte 75.00
Coronado, Plate, Burgundy, 6 1/2 In. 8.00
Coronado, Plate, Burgundy, 9 1/4 In. 16.00
Coronado, Plate, Coral Matte, 6 1/2 In. 5.00
Coronado, Plate, Coral Matte, 8 In. 8.00
Coronado, Plate, Coral Matte, 9 1/4 In. 12.00
Coronado, Plate, Ivory Matte, 10 1/2 In. 20.00
Coronado, Plate, Turquoise Matte, 6 1/2 In. 5.00
Coronado, Plate, Turquoise, 6 1/4 In. 8.00
Coronado, Plate, Turquoise, 9 1/4 In. 18.00
Coronado, Plate, Turquoise, 10 3/8 In. 25.00
Coronado, Plate, White, 9 1/4 In. 18.00
Coronado, Plate, Yellow Gloss, 10 1/2 In. 25.00
Coronado, Plate, Yellow Matte, 8 In. 8.00
Coronado, Plate, Yellow Matte, 9 1/4 In. 12.00
Coronado, Plate, Yellow, 6 1/4 In. 8.00
Coronado, Platter, Oval, Turquoise Matte, 13 3/4 In. 30.00
Coronado, Platter, Turquoise, 13 1/8 In. 45.00
Coronado, Relish, Ivory Matte, 9 1/2 In. 20.00
Coronado, Salt & Pepper, Ivory Matte 22.00
Coronado, Sherbet, Footed, Yellow Matte 18.00
Coronado, Sugar, Cover, Turquoise Matte ....18.00 to 20.00
Coronado, Sugar, Turquoise 15.00
Coronado, Teapot, Ivory Matte 60.00
Coronado, Teapot, Turquoise 95.00
Coronado, Teapot, Turquoise Matte 45.00
Coronado, Tumbler, Ivory, 5 1/4 In. 115.00
Coronado, Tumbler, Turquoise, 5 1/4 In. 65.00
Cubist, Creamer, Green 18.00
Cubist, Plate, Sherbet, Pink 5.00
Cubist, Sherbet, Green 5.00
Daisy, Teapot 55.00
Desert Rose, Ashtray, 3 1/2 In. 20.00
Desert Rose, Ashtray, Divided, 9 In. 65.00
Desert Rose, Baking Dish, 9 5/8 In. 215.00
Desert Rose, Baking Dish, 13 5/8 In. 285.00
Desert Rose, Berry Bowl, 5 1/4 In. 6.00
Desert Rose, Bowl, Cereal, 6 In. ....12.00 to 15.00
Desert Rose, Bowl, Vegetable, 8 In. 36.00

Desert Rose, Bowl, Vegetable, 9 In. . . . . .30.00 to 42.00
Desert Rose, Bowl, Vegetable, Cover, 1 1/2 Qt. . . . . .85.00 to 90.00
Desert Rose, Bowl, Vegetable, Divided, 10 7/8 In. . . . . .45.00 to 50.00
Desert Rose, Butter, Cover . . . . .45.00 to 50.00
Desert Rose, Casserole, Cover, 2 1/2 Qt. 650.00
Desert Rose, Celery Dish 85.00
Desert Rose, Coffeepot . . . . .110.00 to 155.00
Desert Rose, Compote, 8 In. . . . . .85.00 to 100.00
Desert Rose, Creamer 18.00
Desert Rose, Cup & Saucer . . . . .8.00 to 9.00
Desert Rose, Cup & Saucer, After Dinner 50.00
Desert Rose, Cup, Oversized, 4 1/2 In. 30.00
Desert Rose, Dish, Heart Shape, 5 3/4 In. 145.00
Desert Rose, Eggcup 26.00
Desert Rose, Gravy Boat, Underplate 40.00
Desert Rose, Grill Plate, 3 Sections, 11 In. 90.00
Desert Rose, Mixing Bowl, 6 In. . . . . .125.00 to 175.00
Desert Rose, Napkin Ring 93.00
Desert Rose, Pitcher, Milk, 6 1/4 In. . . . . .35.00 to 80.00
Desert Rose, Pitcher, Syrup, 6 1/8 In. 75.00
Desert Rose, Pitcher, Water, 2 1/2 Qt. 125.00
Desert Rose, Plate, 8 In. . . . . .8.00 to 18.00
Desert Rose, Plate, 9 1/2 In. . . . . .15.00 to 22.00
Desert Rose, Plate, 10 5/8 In. . . . . .15.00 to 22.00
Desert Rose, Plate, 11 1/2 In. 22.00
Desert Rose, Platter, 11 In. 35.00
Desert Rose, Platter, 14 1/4 In. 45.00
Desert Rose, Platter, 19 In. . . . . .295.00 to 475.00
Desert Rose, Platter, Oval, 12 In. 35.00
Desert Rose, Relish, 10 1/8 In. 40.00
Desert Rose, Salt & Pepper 25.00
Desert Rose, Salt & Pepper, Tall, 6 In. 80.00
Desert Rose, Saucer 7.50
Desert Rose, Sugar & Creamer . . . . .40.00 to 70.00
Desert Rose, Sugar, Cover . . . . .20.00 to 25.00
Desert Rose, Tile, Tea, Fluted 375.00
Desert Rose, Tile, Tea, Square, 6 In. 45.00
Desert Rose, Toast Cover 225.00
Desert Rose, Tray, Square, 8 1/4 In. 245.00
Desert Rose, Tumbler, 6 Oz. 55.00
Desert Rose, Tureen, Soup, Footed, Cover 375.00
Duet, Bowl, Vegetable, Oval, 8 1/2 In. 30.00
Duet, Butter, Cover 45.00
Duet, Coffeepot 60.00
Duet, Platter, 13 In. 40.00
Duet, Relish, 3 Sections 35.00
Duet, Sugar, Cover 12.00
El Patio, Berry Bowl, Gray Satin, 5 1/4 In. 13.00
El Patio, Bowl, Cereal, Coral Satin, 6 In. 15.00
El Patio, Bowl, Vegetable, Oval, Coral Gloss, 9 In. 30.00
El Patio, Creamer, Coral Satin 13.00
El Patio, Cup & Saucer, Turquoise Gloss 18.00
El Patio, Cup, Coral Gloss 13.00
El Patio, Cup, Turquoise Satin 13.00
El Patio, Plate, Coral Satin, 6 1/4 In. 5.00
El Patio, Plate, Coral Satin, 9 1/4 In. 15.00
El Patio, Plate, Gray Satin, 8 In. 13.00
El Patio, Plate, Gray Satin, 9 1/4 In. 15.00
El Patio, Platter, Gray Satin, 11 1/2 In. 30.00
El Patio, Sugar & Creamer 55.00
El Patio, Sugar, Cover, Turquoise Satin 18.00
Forget-Me-Not, Cup 18.00
Fresh Fruit, Mug, 7 Oz. 35.00

Fresh Fruit, Napkin Ring 35.00
Fresh Fruit, Sugar, Cover 50.00
Fruit, Plate, 10 In. 155.00
Fruit, Tile, Square, 6 In. 65.00
Hacienda, Cup & Saucer, Green 20.00
Hacienda, Plate, Green, 6 3/4 In. 8.00
Hacienda, Plate, Green, 8 3/8 In. 10.00
Hacienda, Soup, Dish, Green 18.00
Ivy, Berry Bowl, 5 1/4 In. 15.00
Ivy, Bowl, Vegetable, 7 1/4 In. 50.00
Ivy, Bowl, Vegetable, 8 In. 45.00
Ivy, Butter, 1/4 Lb. 75.00
Ivy, Butter, Cover 72.00
Ivy, Casserole, Cover, Handles 95.00
Ivy, Creamer 30.00
Ivy, Cup & Saucer ....16.00 to 25.00
Ivy, Dish, Pickle, 11 In. 55.00
Ivy, Gravy Boat, Underplate 75.00
Ivy, Plate, 6 1/4 In. ....8.00 to 10.00
Ivy, Plate, 8 1/2 In. 25.00
Ivy, Plate, 9 1/2 In. 18.00
Ivy, Plate, 10 1/4 In. ....25.00 to 30.00
Ivy, Platter, 13 1/8 In. 25.00
Ivy, Platter, Oval, 11 1/4 In. 40.00
Ivy, Soup, Dish ....30.00 to 62.00
Larkspur, Bowl, 7 1/2 In. 18.00
Larkspur, Plate, 6 1/2 In. 6.00
Larkspur, Saltshaker 10.00
Larkspur, Saucer 5.00
Meadow Rose, Pitcher, Water 50.00
Meadow Rose, Teapot 195.00
Nut Tree, Bowl, Salad, 9 1/4 In. 11.00
Nut Tree, Creamer 3.00
Nut Tree, Cup & Saucer 3.00
Nut Tree, Plate, 10 1/2 In. 4.00
Nut Tree, Platter, Oval, 13 1/2 In. 13.00
Nut Tree, Sugar, Cover 4.00
Poppy, Cup & Saucer 20.00
Poppy, Gravy Boat 90.00
Poppy, Plate, 10 In. 33.00
Poppy, Platter, 13 In. 375.00
Starburst, Cup & Saucer 19.00
Starburst, Mug, 7 Oz., 3 In. 95.00
Starburst, Mustard, Cover 135.00
Starburst, Plate, 6 1/2 In. ....6.50 to 8.00
Starburst, Plate, 10 1/2 In. 16.00
Starburst, Snack Tray, Cup Rest, 12 1/2 In. 95.00
Sundance, Bowl, Vegetable, 7 3/4 In. 35.00
Sundance, Creamer 22.00
Sundance, Cup & Saucer 15.00
Sundance, Plate, 8 1/2 In. 9.00
Sundance, Soup, Dish 12.00
Sundance, Sugar 27.00
Tiempo, Berry Bowl, Chartreuse, 4 1/2 In. 13.00
Tiempo, Bowl, Vegetable, Divided, Chartreuse, 11 In. 28.00
Tiempo, Coaster, Brown, 3 In. 15.00
Tiempo, Creamer, Chartreuse 18.00
Tiempo, Creamer, Gray 23.00
Tiempo, Cup & Saucer, Chartreuse 15.00
Tiempo, Cup & Saucer, Dark Green 15.00
Tiempo, Cup & Saucer, Gray 20.00
Tiempo, Gravy Boat, Chartreuse 40.00
Tiempo, Pitcher, Water, Brown, 7 1/4 In. 75.00

Tiempo, Plate, Brown, 6 In. 8.00
Tiempo, Plate, Chartreuse, 9 3/4 In. 20.00
Tiempo, Plate, Dark Green, 6 In. 8.00
Tiempo, Plate, Dark Green, 9 3/4 In. 20.00
Tiempo, Platter, Chartreuse, 13 In. 30.00
Tiempo, Sugar, Cover, Chartreuse 23.00
Tiempo, Sugar, Cover, Dark Green 23.00
Tiempo, Teapot, Brown 75.00
Tiempo, Tray, Chartreuse, 9 1/4 x 5 In. 20.00
Tiempo, Tumbler, Chartreuse, 5 In. 25.00
Wildflower, Bowl, Vegetable, Cover 895.00
Wildflower, Tumbler, Water, 10 Oz. 175.00

FRANKART, Inc., New York, New York, mass-produced nude *dancing lady* lamps, ashtrays, and other decorative Art Deco items in the 1920s and 1930s. They were made of white lead composition and spray-painted. *Frankart Inc.* and the patent number and year were stamped on the base.

Ashtray, Elephant, White Metal, Black Amethyst, Bronze Finish, c.1920, 7 x 6 x 6 In. ... 91.00
Ashtray, Hand Holding Cigarette Pack, Notched, Gray, 7 3/8 x 5 1/2 In. 400.00
Ashtray, Young Nude Maiden Leaning Against Pole, Green Glaze, 9 1/2 In. 570.00
Bookends, Dutch, Marked, Frankart, Pat. Appld. For, Gold 40.00
Bookends, Elephant, White Metal, Bronze Finish, Marked, 5 3/4 x 3 x 4 3/4 In. 60.00
Bookends, Gray, No. B413, Marked Frankart 28 C, 9 x 4 In. 1626.00
Bookends, Posing Nudes, Gray, On Pedestal, Knees Up, Arms Back, Signed, 7 1/2 In. ... 2027.00
Candleholder, Nudes, Sitting, Arms Folded, Marked, 1928, 4 3/4 In., Pair 535.00
Lamp, Elephant, Balancing On Large Ball, Light Green Highlights, 9 1/4 In. 250.00

FRANKOMA POTTERY was originally known as The Frank Potteries when John F. Frank opened shop in 1933. The factory is now working in Sapulpa, Oklahoma. Early wares were made from a light cream-colored clay from Ada, Oklahoma, but in 1956 the company switched to a red burning clay from Sapulpa. The firm makes dinnerwares, utilitarian and decorative kitchenwares, figurines, flowerpots, and limited edition and commemorative pieces.

Baker, Cover, Mayan-Aztec 30.00
Baker, Handle, Dark Mustard, Individual, 3 1/2 x 5 1/4 In. 15.00
Bookends, Boot, Desert Gold, 7 In. 45.00
Bookends, Charger Horse 300.00
Bookends, Horse, Black, 6 In. 389.00
Bookends, Panther 271.00
Bookends, Seahorse 838.00
Bookends, Setter 177.00
Bowl, Cereal, Mayan-Aztec 10.00
Bowl, Four Leaf Clover, Prairie Green, 6 In. 10.00
Bowl, Handkerchief, White, Red Clay, 6 1/2 x 3 3/4 In. 18.00
Bowl, Leaf Shape, Low, Dusty Rose, 8 3/4 In. 13.00
Bowl, White, Oval, Marked, 10 x 3 1/4 In. 20.00
Bowl, Yellow, Marked, 9 1/2 x 3 1/4 In. 13.00
Bread Plate, Warm Bread For Your Table, Brick Red, 2 1/2 x 4 7/8 In. 40.00
Candleholder, Aladdin Lamp 132.00
Candleholder, Lazy Bones, 3-Light, Brown 85.00
Candleholder, Snail 135.00
Casserole, Cover, Horseshoe Handles, Green, Brown, 3 1/2 In. 65.00
Casserole, Cover, Mayan-Aztec, Sapulpa Clay, 10 In. 40.00
Casserole, Cover, Tab Handles, Brown Glaze, 11 In. 40.00
Charger, Mayan-Aztec, Brown, 14 1/2 In. 50.00
Chip & Dip, Plainsmen, Prairie Green, 8 1/4 In. 30.00
Chop Plate, Mayan-Aztec, 15 In. 38.50
Console, Mayan-Aztec, Yellow, 12 x 5 In. 28.00
Cookie Jar, Wagon Wheel, Horseshoe Handles, Prairie Gold 20.00
Creamer, Plainsman, Woodland Moss 14.00
Creamer, Wagon Wheel 20.00

Creamer, Wagon Wheel, Prairie Green 10.00
Cup, Plainsman, Woodland Moss 11.00
Dish, Leaf Shape, Low, Desert Gold, 12 3/4 x 6 3/4 In. 30.00
Dish, Magnolia, Light Brown 18.00
Egg Plate, Desert Gold, 11 1/2 In. 40.00
Figurine, Bucking Bronco 400.00
Figurine, Coyote Pup 1850.00
Figurine, Elephant 250.00
Figurine, Fan Dancer 455.00
Figurine, Horse Circus 167.00
Figurine, Ocelot, Walking 1991.00
Gravy Boat, Handle, Brown Glaze, 4 1/4 In. 25.00
Gravy Boat, Lazy Bones, Handle 19.00
Honey Pot, Finial, 3 3/4 x 4 3/4 In. 22.00
Honey Pot, Prairie Green ....18.00 to 20.00
Honey Pot, Woodland Moss Glaze, Cork Cover, 16 Oz. 9.50
Jardiniere, Ivy, Scalloped Edge, Desert Gold, 4 3/4 In. 16.00
Jardiniere, Light Tan, 9 x 6 1/4 In. 25.00
Jug, Dusty Rose, 24 Oz., 7 In. 25.00
Jug, Iowa Sunshine 177.00
Jug, Prairie Green, 24 Oz., 7 In. 40.00
Jug, Prairie Green, Stopper 60.00
Lemonade Set, Yellow, 4 Piece 40.00
Mask, Peter Pan 128.00
Mug, Barrel, Prairie Green, 4 In. 13.00
Mug, Boot, Prairie Green, 5 In. 15.00
Mug, Cowboy Boot, Cream, Brown, 1981, 5 In. 15.00
Mug, Donkey, Carter & Mondale, 1977 .... 45.00
Mug, Donkey, DEM, Periwinkle 20.00
Mug, Elephant, GOP, Teal 20.00
Mug, GOP, 1968 .... 40.00
Mug, Oil Rig & Tree Scene, South Side Rotary Club, Tulsa, Ok., 3 In. 10.00
Pitcher, Ice Lip, Green, Brown, 6 In. 85.00
Pitcher, Milk, Handle, Light Tan, Brown Glaze, 6 In. 22.00
Pitcher, Sunflower Yellow Glaze, Cork Cover, 24 Oz. 10.00
Pitcher, Wagon Wheel, 2 Qt. 45.00
Pitcher, Widow Maker 202.00
Planter, Duck, Gray, 10 In. 12.00
Planter, Duck, Yellow, 12 x 6 In. 42.00
Planter, Oblong, Brown, 12 1/4 x 4 1/4 In. 24.00
Planter, Oblong, Prairie Green, 12 In. 45.00
Planter, Pedestal, Blue, 5 1/2 x 6 In. 18.00
Plate, Bicentennial, White Sand Glaze, 1973 .... 30.00
Plate, Buffalo 75.00
Plate, Christmas, 1965, Good Will Towards Men 181.00
Plate, Christmas, 1969, Laid In A Manger 15.00
Plate, Christmas, 1970, King Of Kings 40.00
Plate, Christmas, 1973, The Annunication 35.00
Plate, Christmas, 1978, All Nature Rejoiced 36.00
Plate, Easter, White Sand Glaze 35.00
Plate, Mayan-Aztec, 7 In. 10.00
Plate, Ruth The Devoted, 1980 .... 32.00
Plate, Scalloped Edge, Green, Brown, 10 In. 27.00
Plate, Statue Of Liberty 10.00
Plate, White Tailed Deer 55.00
Plate, Whoooo Owl, Have A Hootin' Good Day, Marked, 6 1/4 In. 10.00
Platter, Lazy Bones, Woodland Moss, 13 In. 25.00
Salt & Pepper, Mayan-Aztec, Short 15.00
Salt & Pepper, Plainsman, Stopper, 3 In. 12.00
Salt & Pepper, Teepee, Desert Gold, 3 In. 32.00
Salt & Pepper, Wagon Wheel, Prairie Green 13.00
Saucer, Wagon Wheel, Prairie Green 8.00
Teapot, Cover, Handle, Green, Peach Glaze, 4 1/2 In. 28.00

Teapot, Handle, Brown Glaze, 6 3/4 In. 50.00
Teapot, Wagon Wheel, Prairie Green, 6 1/4 In. 45.00
Toby Mug, Baseball, 1978 .... 16.00
Toby Mug, Uncle Sam, 1976 .... 10.00
Tray, Mayan-Aztec, 8 1/2 x 14 In. 22.00
Trivet, Beige 35.00
Trivet, Eagle, 1966 .... 45.00
Trivet, Wagon Wheel 12.00
Tumbler, Black Glaze, 4 3/8 In. 8.00
Vase, Bird Handle 361.00
Vase, Boot, Brown Glaze, 4 1/2 In. 8.00
Vase, Bud, Snail, Prairie Green, 6 In. 17.50
Vase, Cactus, Marked, 7 1/2 In. 22.00
Vase, Flying Goose 38.00
Vase, Prairie Green, Signed, John Frank, 16 In. 51.00
Vase, Prairie Green, Silver Overlay 710.00
Vase, Ram's Head ....75.00 to 160.00
Vase, Thunderbird 182.00

FRATERNAL objects that are related to the many different fraternal
organizations in the United States are listed in this category. The Elks,
Masons, Odd Fellows, and others are included. Also included are service organizations, like the American Legion, Kiwanis, and Lions
Club. Furniture is listed in the Furniture category. Shaving mugs decorated with fraternal crests are included in the Shaving Mug category.

Alhambra, Fez, Tan, Cream Tassel, Rhinestone, Sequins, Carrying Case 45.00
American Legion, Certificate, Member, Golden Anniversary, Signed, 1969 .... 10.00
American Legion, License Plate, 2 1/4 x 4 In. 12.00
American Legion, Patch, Past Commander, 3 x 2 1/2 In. 7.50
American Legion, Pin, U.S.A., 1 In. 5.00
American Legion, Registration Packet, 36th National Convention, Program, 1954 .... 12.00
Eastern Star, Book, Standard Ritual Of The Order Of The Eastern Star Of N.Y., 1916 ... 10.00
Eastern Star, Cup & Saucer, Lefton, Gold Edge Paint 26.00
Eastern Star, Pin, 28th Annual Session, Grand Chapter, Ribbon, 1936, 2 1/2 In. 5.00
Eastern Star, Pin, Marked 10K, 5/8 x 3/8 In. 10.00
Elks, Whiskey Nip, Elk's Tooth, The Lotus, White China, Brown Glaze, c.1912 .... 280.00
Kiwanis, Banner, Logo, Navy Blue, White, 2 Sides, Luncheon Today, 60 x 36 In. 25.00
Kiwanis, Necktie, Peach, Textured, Logo, Atlanta, White Graphics 20.00
Knights Of Labor, Mug, Glass, Working Man, Hammer, Knight In Armor, 6 In. 60.00
Knights Of Pythias, Medal, Conn. Lodge 37, Bar Pin, Emblem 38.00
Knights Of Pythias, Program, 93rd Convention, Grand Lodge, Easton, Pa., 1960 .... 4.00
Knights Of Pythias, Sword, Brass Hilt, Scrolled Open Work, c.1865 .... 425.00
Knights Templar, Pin, Masons, White Enamel, 10K Gold 8.00
Lions International, Salt & Pepper, White, Blue Trim, Iowa, Milford Pottery, 1 3/4 In. ... 12.00
Loyal Order Of Moose, Certificate, Membership, Embossed Gold Seal, Legion 41, 1947 . 5.00
Loyal Order Of Moose, Constitution & General Laws, 1947 .... 3.50
Loyal Order Of Moose, Medallion, Moose Head, Oxidized, 3 1/2 In. 13.00
Loyal Order Of Moose, Parade Drum, Painted Loyal Order Of Moose 684, Illinois, 29 In. 395.00
Loyal Order Of Moose, Program, Dedication, Marysville Lodge No. 821, c.1951 .... 3.00
Masonic, Apron, Embroidered Silk, Frame, 12 1/4 x 14 In., 4 Piece 345.00
Masonic, Apron, White Silk, Yellow Brocade, Calipers & Eye, P. Vogler, 1885 .... 55.00
Masonic, Badge, 1939 English Masonic Stewards Festival Jewel 40.00
Masonic, Badge, 1951 English Masonic Stewards Festival Jewel 35.00
Masonic, Badge, 1954 English Masonic Stewards Festival Jewel 35.00
Masonic, Badge, Exquisite Masonic Bowls Association, Province Of Nottingham 20.00
Masonic, Bookmark, Trowel, Goldstone Handle, 3 3/4 x 3/4 In. 9.00
Masonic, Canvas Panel, Rayed Sun Face, 3 Intersecting Triangles, Oroboros, 50 x 50 In. . 920.00
Masonic, Collar Jewel, English Masonic Past Masters, Inscribed, Dated 1954 .... 45.00
Masonic, Column, Wood, Painted, Zodiac Globe Top, 19th Century, 98 In., Pair 3400.00
Masonic, Cup & Saucer, Star Logo, Multicolor, Gold Trim, Stars 25.00
Masonic, Gavel, Silver, Engraved, Walnut, Oak Handle, 11 3/4 In. 170.00
Masonic, Pin, Moonstone, Tiger's Claw, Pharaoh With A Star 490.00
Masonic, Sketch, Historical, 1733-1958, E.W. Taylor, Grand Lodge Of Mass. 30.00

Masonic, Sword, Leather Cover, Scabbard, 28 In. 325.00
Masonic, Tankard, Presentation, Gold Trim, Colneis Lodge No. 8298, England, 1975 .... 30.00
Masonic, Tankard, Presentation, Gold Trim, Gippeswyk Lodge No. 4254, England, 1975 . 30.00
Masonic, Tie Clip, Spade Shape, Emblem, Swank, Gold Tone, 1 5/8 In. 15.00
Masonic, Trivet, Horseshoe, Emblem Inside, Iron, Handle, 4 x 6 3/4 In. 20.00
Masonic, Tumbler, Cut Glass, Engraved, Moon, Sun, Tools, Symbols, 1800s, 3 3/8 In. ... 176.00
Masonic, Tumbler, Engraved, Coin Spot & Swag, 19th Century, 4 1/4 In. 143.00
Modern Woodmen Of The World, Axe, Aluminum, Wooden Handle, Twig Letterd, 35 In. 50.00
Odd Fellows, Booklet, Revised By-Laws, Kearney Lodge 247, Missouri, 1953 .... 5.00
Odd Fellows, Ceremonial Staff, Heart In Hand, 19th Century, 61 1/4 In. 1045.00
Odd Fellows, Collar, Scarlet, Sateen Lining, Silver Trim, Fringe, Silver Stars 75.00
Odd Fellows, Medallion, Chain, Bible, Round Seal, Inscription, 5 x 2 1/4 In. 25.00
Odd Fellows, Peephole, From Door, Symbols 235.00
Odd Fellows, Pin, Service, Marcasite 8.00
Odd Fellows, Postcard, Building, Kearney, Missouri, Unused, 1920s 4.00
Odd Fellows, Sword, Plymouth Encampment, Double Chains, 28 1/2 In. 375.00
Optimists International, Tie Clasp, Octagonal Shape, Gold Tone, 2 3/4 In. 15.00
Patriotic Order Sons Of America, Shaving Mug, Norman Higgins, 3 1/2 In. 145.00
Rebekahs, Certificate, Membership, Fancy Border, Wallet Size, 1912 .... 3.00
Rotary International, Pin, Plainfield Intercity Track & Field Meet, Ribbon, 1925 ...... 16.00
Shriner, Fez, Khiva, Gold Tone, Saber Tassel Clip, Tassel, Felt, Leather Liner, Size 7 3/4 . 65.00
Shriner, Name Tag, Trees, Ivory Tusks, Brass, Enamel, Seattle, July 1936, 2 x 1 1/2 In. .. 25.00
Shriner, Plate, Dinner, Murat, Syracuse China, Black, Gold Trim, 10 1/2 In. 24.00

FRY GLASS was made by the H. C. Fry Glass Company of Rochester, Pennsylvania. The company, founded in 1901, first made cut glass and other types of fine glasswares. In 1922, they patented a heat-resistant glass called *Pearl Ovenglass*. For two years, 1926–1927, the company made Fry Foval, an opal ware decorated with colored trim. Reproductions of this glass have been made. Depression glass patterns made by Fry may be listed in the Depression Glass category. Some pieces of cut glass may also be included in the Cut Glass category.

FRY, Bowl, Estelle, Sawtooth Rim, Signed, 7 In. 112.00
  Candlestick, Gold-Washed Silver Overlay Rim, 4 1/4 In. 32.00
  Candlestick, Yellow, 3 3/4 In. 50.00
  Casserole, Cover, Silver Plated Server, French Ivory Handles, Marked, 7 In. 50.00
  Cup & Saucer, Opalescent 37.00
  Custard Cup Set, Ovenglass, Wire Baking Rack, 1927, 7 Piece 55.00
  Ivy Ball, Black, Clear Swirl Connector 88.00
  Reamer, Jell-O Mold, Pink, Ruffled 230.00
  Reamer, Opalescent 40.00
  Teapot, Opalescent, 6 1/2 In. 152.00
  Tray, Elba, Hobstars, Crosshatch, Zipper, Cane, Fans, 7 3/4 x 11 1/2 In. 400.00
  Tray, Wilhelm, 12 In. 850.00
  Vase, Rosaline, Alabaster Handles, Classical Shape, 8 In. 345.00
FRY FOVAL, Champagne, Delft Blue Stem 67.00
  Cup & Saucer, Delft Blue Handle 80.00
  Eggcup, Cone Jade Foot, 3 1/4 In. 76.00
  Tumbler, Iced Tea, Amber Swirl Connector, 6 1/8 In. 21.00
  Wine, Cone Shape, Short Stem, 3 1/2 In. 131.00

FULPER Pottery Company was incorporated in 1899 in Flemington, New Jersey. They made art pottery from 1910 to 1929. The firm had been making bottles, jugs, and housewares from 1805. Doll heads were made about 1928. The firm became Stangl Pottery in 1929. Fulper art pottery is admired for its attractive glazes and simple shapes.

  Basket, Embossed Rose, Rope Handle, Blue Matte Glaze, Signed, 7 1/4 x 8 1/4 In. 130.00
  Bean Pot, Cover, Large 175.00
  Bookends, Book Shape, Crystalline Flambe Glaze, Signed, 5 x 4 3/4 In. 130.00
  Bookends, Eagles, Cucumber Crystalline Glaze, 9 x 7 1/2 In. 1068.00
  Bookends, Liberty Bell, Green Crystalline Glaze, 7 1/4 x 4 In. 690.00
  Bowl, Black Mirror Crystalline Glaze, 3 Ribbon Handles, 5 1/4 x 10 3/4 In. 100.00
  Bowl, Black Mirror Glaze, Handles, 12 1/2 In. 431.00

Bowl, Blue & Cream Flambe, Flaring Form, Signed, 10 In. 175.00
Bowl, Blue Crystalline Glaze, Flared, Footed, Paper Label, 3 1/4 x 7 1/2 In. 230.00
Bowl, Blue, Cream, Dark Olive, Ink Mark, 15 3/4 In. 750.00
Bowl, Blue, Green Crystalline Glaze, Flower Holder, 5 x 8 In. 110.00
Bowl, Blue, Green Crystalline Glaze, Marked, 4 5/8 x 9 3/4 In. 165.00
Bowl, Bulb, Closed Rim, Glossy Interior, Streaked Glaze, Signed, 9 1/4 In. 145.00
Bowl, Cat's-Eye Flambe Glaze, Scalloped Rim, 13 In. 160.00
Bowl, Chinese Blue Glaze, Marked, 3 1/2 In. 175.00
Bowl, Flower Frog Handle, Purple Glaze, Signed, 3 3/4 x 11 1/2 In. 230.00
Bowl, Glossy Brown, Green Streaked Glaze, 1920, 2 1/2 In. 60.00
Bowl, Green Crystalline Glaze, Flemington Green, Yellow Interior, 7 In. 460.00
Bowl, Green Flemington Glaze, Mustard Matte Base, 4 x 10 In. 1012.00
Bowl, Green Glossy Glaze, Inverted Rim, 1915, 3 1/4 In. 200.00
Bowl, Green Matte Glaze, Inverted Rim, 1915, 2 3/4 x 10 3/4 In. 230.00
Bowl, Green, 8 1/4 x 2 In. 140.00
Bowl, Morning Glory, For Prang, Cat's-Eye, Chinese Blue Flambe Glaze, 2 1/2 x 5 3/4 In. 345.00
Candlestick, Black Mirror Over Copper Dust Crystalline Glaze, Marked, 2 3/8 In. 110.00
Candlestick, Flattened Rim, Stepped Base, Mirror Glaze, Signed, c.1915, 3 In, Pair 145.00
Candlestick, Leopard Skin Crystalline Glaze, 9 x 5 In., Pair 1380.00
Centerpiece, Turquoise & Mustard, Crystalline Flambe Glaze, 2 Handles, Mark, 3 1/4 In. 80.00
Chamberstick, Wisteria Glaze Handle, 7 1/4 In. 176.00
Flower Frog, Blue, Gray Matte Glaze, Cafe-Au-Lait Base, 7 x 1/2 In. 200.00
Flower Frog, Canoe, Woman Seated In Beached Canoe, Signed, 3 3/4 x 7 1/2 In. 490.00
Flower Frog, Duck, Mottled Gray, Brown, Ivory Matte Glaze, Ink Mark, 3 1/2 x 3 1/4 In. . 115.00
Flower Frog, Scarab Shape, Green Over Blue Flambe Glaze, Marked, 1 3/8 x 3 In. 80.00
Flower Frog, Swan, Ivory & Chinese Blue Glaze, Signed, 6 1/2 In. 200.00
Humidor, Embossed Geometric Designs, Wisteria Matte Glaze, 4 x 5 1/2 In. 1495.00
Incense Burner, Green Crystalline Glaze, Pierced Cover, 4-Footed, 4 x 5 In. 1068.00
Jar, Cover, Chinese Blue Crystalline Flambe Glace, Ocher, Indigo, 13 x 8 1/4 In. 2300.00
Lamp, Cucumber Green Crystalline & Gunmetal Glaze, Slag Shade, Signed, 18 1/2 In. . . . 9775.00
Lamp, Daffodils, Brown Matte Mottled Glaze, Green, Blue, White, 16 1/2 In. 8625.00
Lamp, Figural, Southern Belle, Signed, 11 1/2 In. 310.00
Lamp, Mushroom Leaded Insert Shade, Glazed, Marked, 24 x 15 1/2 In. . . . .*Illus* 12100.00
Lamp, Mushroom Slag Glass Insert Shade, Glazed, Marked, 24 x 17 In. . . . .*Illus* 9350.00
Lamp, Mushroom, Cucumber Green Crystalline, Gunmetal Glaze, Slag Shade, 18 1/2 In. . 9775.00
Lamp, Perfume, Perched Parrot Shape, 10 1/4 x 6 1/4 In. 635.00
Lamp, Table, Cap Shade, Leaded Green, Yellow Slag Glass Insets, 24 x 17 In. 9560.00
Lamp, Table, Mushroom Shape, Chinese Blue, Butterscotch Flambe Glaze, 24 In. 12375.00
Lamp Base, Amber Crystalline Glaze, Mustard Matte, Marked, 11 3/4 x 8 1/2 In. 1610.00
Luminier, Parrot, Perched On 2-Part Knob Base, Signed, c.1930, 12 1/4 In. 690.00
Pipe Holder, Mahogany Glaze, Fox On Logs, 3 1/4 x 6 1/2 In. 900.00
Urn, Cat's-Eye Flambe Glaze, 15 x 8 In. 1150.00
Urn, Chinese Blue Crystalline Flambe Glaze, Bulbous, 2 Handles, Mark 643, 8 1/2 x 7 In. 400.00
Urn, Green & Brown Flambe Over Blue Glaze, Rectangular Handles, Drill Hole, 10 In. . . . 520.00
Urn, Green Mirror Glaze, Mahogany, Ivory Flambe Glaze, Handles, 12 x 7 1/2 In. 1350.00
Urn, Hammered Texture, Black Mirror Glaze, Signed, 11 x 7 1/2 In. 490.00
Urn, Mirror Black Glaze, 2 Angular Handles, Collared Rim, 9 x 9 In. 745.00
Urn, Mirror Black Glaze, 8 3/4 x 11 In. 1955.00
Urn, Turquoise & Mustard Flambe Glaze, Shoulder Handles, Racetrack Mark, 9 x 5 In. . . 260.00
Urn, Turquoise Crystalline Glaze, Ink Racetrack Mark, 7 3/4 x 6 In. 430.00
Urn, Vasekraft, Cobalt Crystalline Glaze, 2 Buttressed Handles, 11 1/4 x 5 In. 365.00
Vase, 2 Vertical Buttresses, Carmel & Blue Drip, Signed, 9 1/2 In. 550.00
Vase, 4 Raised Buttresses Above Body, Pink Matte Glaze, 8 1/4 In. 290.00
Vase, Allover Chinese Blue Mirrored Glaze, Signed, 7 x 7 1/4 In. 630.00
Vase, Art Deco, Tulips, Stylized Flowers, Amber, Blue Flambe, 3 Handles, 14 x 8 1/2 In. . 978.00
Vase, Ashes Of Rose Crystalline Glaze Over Elephant's Breath, Marked, 6 1/4 In. 410.00
Vase, Ashes Of Rose Glaze, Angular Handles, Marked, 7 3/4 In. 440.00
Vase, Black Mirror Glaze, 6 3/4 In. 490.00
Vase, Black Mirror Glaze, Blue Flambe Glaze, Bulbous, 11 1/2 x 7 1/2 In. 1840.00
Vase, Black Mirror Glaze, Incised Vertical Mark, 7 In. 431.00
Vase, Black, Brown, Blue Glaze, Handles, 7 In. 299.00
Vase, Blue & Brown Flambe, Handles, Paper Label, Signed, 8 In. 355.00
Vase, Blue Crystalline Flambe Glaze, Signed, 13 1/2 x 6 1/4 In. 750.00

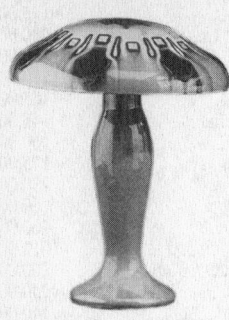

Quick cure for a leaking flower vase: Coat the outside and inside with clear silicone household glue. Coat again if it still leaks.

Small collectibles can be used as window-shade pulls.

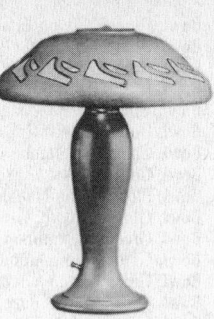

Fulper, Lamp, Mushroom Leaded Insert Shade, Glazed, Marked, 24 x 15 1/2 In.

Fulper, Lamp, Mushroom Slag Glass Insert Shade, Glaze, Marked, 24 x 17 In.

Vase, Blue Crystalline Glaze, Gourd Shape Base, Trumpet Neck, 21 x 11 1/2 In. 4900.00
Vase, Blue Flambe Glaze, Umber, Spherical, 5 1/4 x 5 1/4 In. 375.00
Vase, Blue Flambe, Green Drip, Pedestal, Signed, 7 In. 285.00
Vase, Blue Green Mirror Glaze, Classical Shape, 7 x 5 In. 490.00
Vase, Blue, Gray, Rose Glaze, Pyramid Shape, 6 1/2 x 8 1/4 In., Pair 255.00
Vase, Blue, Green Flambe Glaze, Handles, 6 In. 405.00
Vase, Blue, Purple Glaze, 10 In. 405.00
Vase, Brown Glaze, Signed, 8 In. 635.00
Vase, Brown Mirror Flambe Glaze, Chinese Blue, 17 x 8 In. 1687.00
Vase, Brown, Chinese Blue Glaze, Bulbous, 5 1/2 x 5 In. 290.00
Vase, Bud, Butterscotch Flambe Glaze, Ink Racetrack Mark, 8 1/2 In. 260.00
Vase, Bulbous, Flared Rim, Chinese Blue Flambe Glaze, Racetrack Mark, 7 x 6 In. 230.00
Vase, Butterscotch Flambe Glaze, 9 x 2 1/2 In. 310.00
Vase, Butterscotch Flambe Glaze, Baluster, 12 x 4 1/2 In. 620.00
Vase, Buttress With Squat Base, Chinese Blue Glaze, Signed, 8 1/4 In. 320.00
Vase, Caramel Glaze, Multitone, 4 1/2 In. 70.00
Vase, Cat's-Eye Flambe Glaze, Baluster, Stamped Racetrack Mark, 9 1/2 In. 360.00
Vase, Cat's-Eye Flambe Glaze, Dripping Over Mustard Matte Ground, 5 3/4 In. 320.00
Vase, Cat's-Eye Flambe Glaze, Gourd Shape, 9 x 5 In. 2960.00
Vase, Chinese Blue Crystalline Glaze, Buttressed Handles, Marked, 6 1/2 x 8 In. 460.00
Vase, Chinese Blue Flambe Glaze, 3 Angular Handles, 4 In. 259.00
Vase, Chinese Blue Flambe Glaze, Paper Label, 3 x 5 In. 115.00
Vase, Chinese Blue Flambe Glaze, Twin Handles, 3 In. 150.00
Vase, Chinese Blue Flambe, Lobed Exterior, Signed, 4 x 5 In. 625.00
Vase, Chinese Blue Glaze, Amber, Squat, Handles, Stamped, 3 x 4 In. 175.00
Vase, Chinese Blue, Flambe Glaze, Over Speckled Blue Glaze, Ink Mark, 5 x 3 1/4 In. 230.00
Vase, Closed-In Rim, Frothy Wisteria Matte Glaze, 6 x 9 In. 980.00
Vase, Copper Dust Crystalline Glaze, Signed, 10 1/2 x 10 In. 2780.00
Vase, Copper Dust Crystalline Glaze, Twin Handles, Marked, 3 In. 175.00
Vase, Copper Dust Crystalline Over Flemington Green Flambe Glaze, Signed, 9 3/4 In. . . 545.00
Vase, Crystalline Glaze, Caramel, Taupe Interior, 4 1/2 In. 315.00
Vase, Crystalline Glaze, Glossy Green & & Aqua, Scrolled Handles, Signed, 4 3/4 In. . . . 172.00
Vase, Crystalline Semigloss, Scrolled Handles, Attached Rings, Signed, c.1920, 13 In. . . . 862.00
Vase, Cucumber Green Matte Glaze, Embossed Cattails, Cylindrical, Marked, 13 In. 430.00
Vase, Drip Mirror Glaze, Signed, c.1915, 10 1/4 In. 345.00
Vase, Dripping Ivory & Blue Flame Glaze, Over Speckled Mustard, Drill Hole, 7 1/4 In. . . 750.00
Vase, Elephant's Breath Glaze, Closed-In Rim, 8 1/2 x 5 1/2 In. 920.00
Vase, Embossed Buttressed Rim, Speckled Cafe-Au-Lait Glaze, 12 3/4 In. 1265.00
Vase, Embossed Cattails, Cucumber Crystalline Matte Glaze, 13 x 4 3/4 In. 5750.00
Vase, Famille Rose Matte Glaze, Bulbous, 5 x 5 In. 175.00
Vase, Flemington Green Flambe Glaze Over Rose Matte Glaze, Marked, 8 1/4 In. 275.00
Vase, Frothy Blue Crystalline Glaze, 2 Attached Loop Handles, 13 In. 715.00
Vase, Frothy Chinese Blue Flambe Glaze, Drill Hole On Side, 15 1/2 x 7 In. 862.00
Vase, Frothy Turquoise Glaze, Blue Matte Ground, 7 x 4 1/2 In. 978.00

Vase, Frothy Wisteria Matte Glaze, Closed-In Rim, 6 x 9 In. 863.00
Vase, Geometric Designs, Embossed, Green Matte Glaze, Handles, Stamped, 9 1/4 In. 115.00
Vase, Green & Aubergine Over Rose Glaze, 2 Buttressed Handles, Stamp, 7 1/8 In. 172.00
Vase, Green Crystalline Glaze, Handles, 6 In. 374.00
Vase, Green Crystalline Matte Glaze, Handles, Marked, 8 1/2 In. 575.00
Vase, Green Luster Glaze, Bulbous, Signed, 2 1/2 x 3 In. 345.00
Vase, Green Matte Glaze, Black Highlights, Signed, 9 In. 220.00
Vase, Green, Blue, Brown High Glaze, Handles, Vertical Mark, 8 In. 690.00
Vase, Leopard Skin Crystalline Glaze, 9 1/2 x 6 In. ....490.00 to 675.00
Vase, Leopard Skin Crystalline Glaze, Collared Rim, Squat, Ink Mark, 4 x 10 In. 58.00
Vase, Leopard Skin Crystalline Glaze, Gourd Shape, 2 Buttressed Handles, 7 x 5 In. 748.00
Vase, Leopard Skin Crystalline Glaze, Vasekraft Paper Label, 2 3/4 x 4 3/4 In. 517.00
Vase, Leopard Skin Crystalline Over Cat's-Eye Flambe Glaze, Signed, 6 x 7 In. 920.00
Vase, Leopard Skin Crystalline, Ivory, Turquoise Glaze, 5 3/4 x 6 1/2 In. 920.00
Vase, Light Green Crystalline Glaze, 3 Handles, 6 1/4 x 7 3/4 In. 460.00
Vase, Mustard Over Green Crystalline Glaze, Handles, Marked, 7 3/8 In. 357.00
Vase, Olive Green Glaze, Signed, 5 x 6 In. 250.00
Vase, Olive, Autumn Green, Oatmeal Body, 5 In. 403.00
Vase, Purple-Blue Glaze, Swollen Base, Handles, Signed 460.00
Vase, Red, Green Famille Drip, 13 1/2 In. 805.00
Vase, Rose Design, Watermelon Green Flambe Glaze, Handles, 7 5/8 In. 431.00
Vase, Rose Famille Glaze, Bulbous, 6 1/4 x 3 1/4 In. 1462.00
Vase, Trumpet, Cat's-Eye, Blue Flambe Glaze, 13 x 5 1/2 In. 1955.00
Vase, Turquoise & Green Flambe Glaze, 3 Handles, Bulbous, Racetrack Mark, 6 x 8 In. ... 230.00
Vase, Turquoise & Mustard Flambe Glaze, Divided, Strap Center, Marked, 7 In. 115.00
Vase, Venetian, Frothy Turquoise, Olive Matte Glaze, 8 1/4 x 7 In., Pair 393.00
Vase, Wisteria Glaze, Twin Handles, Marked, 4 1/2 In. 175.00

FURNITURE of all types is listed in this category. Examples dating from
the seventeenth century to the 1970s are included. Prices for furniture
vary in different parts of the country. Oak furniture is most expensive
in the West; large pieces over eight feet high are sold for the most
money in the South, where high ceilings are found in the old homes.
Condition is very important when determining prices. These are NOT
average prices but rather reports of unique sales. If the description
includes the word *style*, the piece resembles the old furniture style but
was made at a later time. It is not a period piece. Garden furniture is
listed in the Garden Furnishings category. Related items may be found
in the Architectural, Brass, and Store categories.

Armchairs are listed under Chair in this category.
Armoire, 12-Paned Doors, Partially Glazed, 1870s, 86 1/2 In. 2645.00
Armoire, Art Deco, Mahogany, Marquetry, Beveled Mirror Door, 100 x 85 x 25 In. 2185.00
Armoire, Art Nouveau, Fruitwood, Carved Glass Doors, 90 x 74 1/2 x 20 1/2 In. 1725.00
Armoire, Arts & Crafts, 2 Paneled Doors, Casters, 66 x 40 x 19 In. 1780.00
Armoire, Biedermeier, Fruitwood, 2 Doors, Ebonized Columns, Tapered Feet, 79 In. 8625.00
Armoire, Burl Walnut, Arched Cornice, 2 Base Drawers, 2 Doors, 98 In. 2760.00
Armoire, Charles X, Maple, Amaranth, Molded Cornice, Turned Feet, 81 x 38 In. 2070.00
Armoire, Continental, Oak, Incised Floral Design, 61 x 20 x 82 In. 2875.00
Armoire, Directoire Style, Fruitwood, Elm, Provincial, 90 x 51 x 22 1/2 In. 2185.00
Armoire, Ecole De Nancy, Oak, Carved, Glazed Doors, Drawers, 108 x 47 x 18 1/2 In. .. 6575.00
Armoire, Empire, Mahogany, Kingwood, Gilt, Bronze Paw Feet, 108 x 47 In. 1380.00
Armoire, French Brittany, Carved Fruit & Floral, 1840-1860, 97 x 67 x 28 In. 2530.00
Armoire, French Provincial, Burl Walnut, 2 Doors, Bun Feet, 91 1/2 x 56 x 21 In. 2530.00
Armoire, French Provincial, Carved Paneled Doors, Iron Hinges, 88 x 54 In. 2875.00
Armoire, French Provincial, Elm, Molded Cornice, Cabriole Legs, 95 x 24 In. 2185.00
Armoire, French Provincial, Oak, Dentillated Cornice, Carving, 87 x 75 x 20 In. 2530.00
Armoire, French Provincial, Walnut, 1 Door, Hammered Iron Pulls, 98 x 27 In. 1610.00
Armoire, Fruitwood, Mesh Inset Door, Laurel Leaves, Carved Garden Tools, 93 In. 6000.00
Armoire, Louis Philippe, Burl Elm, Fruitwood, Ogee Cornice, 88 x 56 1/2 x 23 In. 1610.00
Armoire, Louis Philippe, Elm, Molded Cornice, Rectangular Plinth, 91 In. 1725.00
Armoire, Louis Philippe, Fruitwood, Rectangular Cornice, Doors, Plank Feet, 88 In. 1265.00
Armoire, Louis Philippe, Plum Pudding Mahogany, Panels, 84 1/2 x 64 x 27 1/2 In. 5750.00
Armoire, Louis Philippe, Walnut, Molded Cornice, Glass Panes, 80 x 63 x 23 In. 1610.00

Armoire, Louis XV, Fruitwood, Cavetto Cornice, Short Scroll Legs, 100 x 26 In. 1955.00
Armoire, Louis XV, Mahogany, Arched Bonnet, 3 Drawers, Foliate, 100 x 101 In. 1150.00
Armoire, Louis XV, Oak, 2 Door, Stile Feet, 67 x 53 x 28 1/2 In. 805.00
Armoire, Louis XV, Walnut, Carved, 2 Doors, Cavetto Molding, 84 x 61 x 18 1/2 In. 2760.00
Armoire, Louis XV, Walnut, Transitional, 2 Three-Panel Doors, 100 x 64 In. 4025.00
Armoire, Louis XVI, Fruitwood, Elm, Late 1700s, 89 x 53 x 23 In. 2300.00
Armoire, Louis XVI, Fruitwood, Serpentine Paneled Doors, Cabriole Legs, 87 In. 2300.00
Armoire, Louis XVI, Oak, 2 Doors, Rectangular Top, Three Panel Doors, 75 In. 2530.00
Armoire, Louis XVI, Oak, Provincial, Scrolled Panel Doors, 82 x 64 x 23 1/2 In. 4140.00
Armoire, Louis XVI, Walnut, Fruitwood, Shaped Apron, Bracket Feet, 84 1/2 In. 3450.00
Armoire, Mahogany, 2 Paneled Doors, Ogee Bracket Feet, 96 1/2 In. 2300.00
Armoire, Mahogany, 3 Sections, 2 Open Shelves, 2 Drop Doors, 71 x 71 In. 1955.00
Armoire, Mahogany, Dentil Cornice, Foliate Design, 2 Doors, Block Feet, 83 In. 920.00
Armoire, Mahogany, Flared Cornice, 2 Paneled Doors, Flared Feet, c.1840, 92 In. 1955.00
Armoire, Mahogany, Nickeled Bronze, Dominique, c.1930, 78 x 77 x 22 In. 4800.00
Armoire, Pine, 2 Doors, Long Drawer, Arched Cornice, 75 1/4 x 22 1/2 In. 1840.00
Armoire, Rococo, Mahogany, Beaded Cornice, 1 Drawer, 19th Century, 99 x 24 In. 6612.00
Armoire, Rococo, Rosewood, Frieze With Band Of Ribbon, 1 Door, 84 x 21 In. 230.00
Armoire, Rosewood, Single Door, 2 Base Drawers, Adjustable Shelves, c.1840, 76 In. ... 3100.00
Armoire, Walnut, Double Paneled Doors, 2 Short Drawers, 66 1/2 In. 1380.00
Armoire, Walnut, Fan & Floral Crest Top, Beveled Mirror, French Feet, 99 In. 1265.00
Banquette, Louis XVI Style, Walnut, Carved, Kidney Shape, Cane Seat, 1890, 41 In. 978.00
Banquette, Ribbon, Leaf Craved Frame, Padded Armrests, Silk Brocade, 46 In., Pair 9600.00
Bar, Wall Mounted, 2 Bronze Doors, Gold Patina, P. Evans, 71 In. 3450.00
Bed, Arts & Crafts, 10 Spindled Slats, 48 x 43 3/4 In. 230.00
Bed, Blue Paint, Telescopes 3 Sections, Child's, 22 In. To 73 In. 900.00
Bed, Brass, High Post Ball Top, Curved Footboard, Twin Size, 61 x 42 x 78 In. 280.00
Bed, Brass, Iron, Scrolled, Spoke Design, 59 In. 172.00
Bed, Camp, Mahogany & Beech, Pine Canopy, 11 Mattress Slats, 72 x 52 In. 6325.00
Bed, Cannonball, Maple, New England, c.1840, 47 x 43 x 82 In. 110.00
Bed, Canopy, Maple, Carved Bell On Posts, 69 1/2 x 55 In. 1650.00
Bed, Cherry, Cannonball, Rolled Rest Headboard, 10 Spindles, Oak Rails, 42 In. 275.00
Bed, Cherry, Pegged Construction, Carved Posts, Child's, 30 x 43 In. 2420.00
Bed, Cherry, Posts, Acanthus Leaf Carving, Pine Headboard, Rails, 62 x 50 In. 800.00
Bed, Classical, Mahogany, Carved, Reverse Scroll Ends, 1800s, 42 x 50 x 86 In. 5100.00
Bed, Eastlake, Walnut, Burl Trim, Inlaid Crests, Twin, c.1885, 70 x 39 In., Pair 2688.00
Bed, Eastlake, Walnut, Floral Carved Crest, 1880, 79 x 67 In. 3360.00
Bed, Empire, Mahogany, Rectangular Panel, Laurel Branches, 57 In. 9000.00
Bed, Federal, Maple, Birch, Reeded Posts, Arched Tester, 1800s, 61 x 53 x 75 In. 1380.00
Bed, Federal, Maple, Pine, Massive Tall Posts, Red Paint, c.1830, 84 x 76 x 50 In. 330.00
Bed, Folding, 1 Hinge Signed J.G., Original Red Paint, Early 1730s 4800.00
Bed, Four-Poster, Birch, Pine, Turned, Reeded Foot Post, New England, 1820, 74 x 54 In. 220.00
Bed, Four-Poster, Chippendale, Mahogany, Acorn Finials, Double, 57 x 61 In. 200.00
Bed, Four-Poster, Chippendale, Mahogany, Pineapple Finials, 42 1/2 x 64 In., Pair 920.00
Bed, Four-Poster, Chippendale, Mahogany, Scalloped Headboard, Fluted Posts, c.1830 ... 385.00
Bed, Four-Poster, Empire, Maple, Carved Rope, Acanthus, 74 x 83 x 55 In. 1840.00
Bed, Four-Poster, Empire, Tiger Maple, Scrolled Headboard, c.1825, 83 x 58 In. 2185.00
Bed, Four-Poster, Federal, Cherry, Scalloped Headboard, Pa., c.1810, 66 x 56 In. 880.00
Bed, Four-Poster, Federal, Maple, Arched Headboard, c.1825, 86 x 60 In. 495.00
Bed, Four-Poster, Federal, Maple, Birch, Stained, c.1815, 60 1/2 x 51 1/2 x 71 In. 1725.00
Bed, Four-Poster, Federal, Pine, Paneled Headboard, Red Paint, 1840, 78 x 52 x 74 In. ... 550.00
Bed, Four-Poster, Federal, Tester, Maple, New England, c.1805, 77 x 55 x 77 In. 825.00
Bed, Four-Poster, Mahogany, Foliate Carved, Turned Feet, 1840, 90 In. 9600.00
Bed, Four-Poster, Mahogany, Scrolled Headboard, Rope Twist Posts, 94 x 85 In. 3910.00
Bed, Four-Poster, Maple, Turned Posts, Flat Head & Footboard, Pennsylvania, 84 In. 2475.00
Bed, Frank Lloyd Wright, Mahogany, 3 Sliding Doors, 79 x 12 x 33 In. 2415.00
Bed, G. Nelson, Cane Headboard, Thin Edge, Herman Miller, 34 x 35 In. 1725.00
Bed, G. Stickley, 4 Vertical Slats To Head & Footboard, Rabbit Ear Posts, Twin 2070.00
Bed, Gothic Revival, Oak, Paneled Carved Grapes Back, 125 1/2 x 46 1/2 In. 6000.00
Bed, Half-Tester, Keystone Crest, Arched Headboard, Paneled Posts, 103 x 78 In. 3680.00
Bed, Half-Tester, Rococo, Rosewood, Canopy, 123 x 71 x 91 In. .... *Illus* 20125.00
Bed, Jean Pascaud, Sycamore, Mahogany, Galuchat, c.1932, 28 x 89 x 58 In. 16800.00
Bed, L. & J.G. Stickley, Mahogany, 5 Vertical Slats, Original Finish, 45 In. 1910.00

Furniture, Bed, Half-Tester,
Rococo, Rosewood, Canopy,
123 x 71 x 91 In.

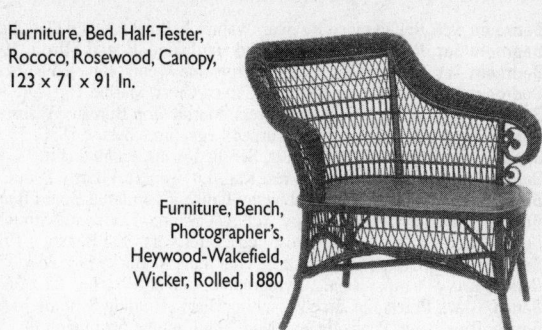

Furniture, Bench,
Photographer's,
Heywood-Wakefield,
Wicker, Rolled, 1880

Bed, Louis XVI Style, Cane, Apollo, 9 Muses, Giltwood, Foliate Design, 1900, 63 In. 1725.00
Bed, Louis XVI, Mahogany, Paneled Headboard, Footboard, Gilt, 62 In. 7200.00
Bed, Louis XVI, Walnut, Bronze Mounts, Carved Tapered Legs, 50 1/2 In. 575.00
Bed, Mahogany, Crest & Rosettes, Bead & Reel Rails, Boat Form, 79 In. 1725.00
Bed, Poplar, Peaked Headboard, Turned Posts, Blue Paint, Pa., c.1800, 50 x 76 In. 1210.00
Bed, Post, Mahogany, Tapered Octagonal Posts, 99 x 65 x 84 In. 3680.00
Bed, Renaissance Revival, Walnut, Canopy Top With Maiden Crest, 1870, 87 In. 3360.00
Bed, Robsjohn-Gibbings, Scrolling Birch Frame, Upholstered, 72 In. 1035.00
Bed, Rococo, Shell Carved Crest, Matching Footboard, 86 In. 978.00
Bed, Rohde, White Leather, 1 Drawer, Herman Miller, Twin, 32 1/2 In. 365.00
Bed, Rope, Black Mottled Design, Orange Ground, 1820, 51 x 76 In. 1430.00
Bed, Rope, Black Paint Over Red, Head & Lower Footboard, Finials, 33 x 74 In. 580.00
Bed, Rope, Cannonball, Curly Maple & Cherry, Scalloped Headboard, 76 In. 1650.00
Bed, Rope, Cherry, Poplar, Turned Posts, Tapered Feel, Urn Tops, Scrolling, 52 In. 330.00
Bed, Rope, Cherry, Turned Posts, Ball Finials, Scrolled Headboard, 76 In. 1210.00
Bed, Rope, Curly Maple, Ball Finials, Shaped Crest, 54 x 54 In. 935.00
Bed, Rope, Maple & Poplar, Turned Posts, Acorn Finials, 84 x 73 In. 1650.00
Bed, Rope, Maple, Turned Posts, Scroll Cut Head & Footboards, 69 In. 145.00
Bed, Rope, Poplar, Red & Black Grain, Mid 19th Century, 54 x 51 x 74 In. 615.00
Bed, Rope, Poplar, Ringed Turned Posts, Turned Feet, 71 x 50 x 33 In. 110.00
Bed, Rope, Red Paint, Acanthus Leaves On Footboard, Full Size, c.1820 .... 1495.00
Bed, Sheraton, Canopy, 2 Urn & Melon Posts, Red Stain, c.1810, 59 x 50 x 71 In. 2588.00
Bed, Sheraton, Cherry, Cannonball, Pennsylvania, c.1800, 58 1/2 x 45 x 77 In. 523.00
Bed, Sheraton, Pine, Cherry, Mushroom Finials, Pennsylvania, 1830, 46 x 50 x 80 In. ... 330.00
Bed, Sheraton, Poplar, Bulbous Turned Posts, Flat Canopy, c.1820, 84 x 54 In. 440.00
Bed, Sheraton, Rope, Rolling Pin Top, Acorn Finials, Carved Posts, Panel Headboard 358.00
Bed, Sleigh, Empire, Mahogany, Concave End, Scrolled Crest, Bracket Feet, 41 In. 9600.00
Bed, Sleigh, Mahogany, Carved Laurel Wreaths, 19th Century, 54 x 60 In. 5750.00
Bed, Sleigh, Mahogany, Veneer, Gothic Trim, American, 19th Century, 33 x 80 In. 625.00
Bed, Sleigh, Rococo, Rosewood, Carved Floral Sides, N.Y., 43 x 64 x 84 In. 3220.00
Bed, Spanish, Mahogany, Carved Ornate Headboard, Panther Amidst Vines 2530.00
Bed, Stickley Bros., No. 9002, Dark Mahogany, Vertical Slats, 58 x 44 In. 4900.00
Bed, Tester, Baluster Turned Posts, c.1800, 79 x 78 1/2 x 58 In. 920.00
Bed, Tester, George III, Mahogany, Arched Canopy, Reeded Posts, 79 x 81 x 44 In. 920.00
Bed, Tester, Oak, Paneled Headboard, Carved Scroll, Half Canopy, 86 x 62 x 80 In. 1065.00
Bed, Tester, Rococo, Mahogany, Canopy, Turned Posts, 97 1/4 In. 2300.00
Bed, Tole & Iron, Green Flowers, 59 x 75 In. 1320.00
Bed Steps, Mahogany, 2 Hinged Lids, Leather Inserts, 1820s, 26 1/2 In. 1725.00
Bed Steps, Mahogany, 3 Treads, Upper Storage Compartment, 25 1/2 In. 1495.00
Bedroom Set, Blond Hardwood, Round Mirror, Herman Miller, c.1933, 4 Piece 4880.00
Bedroom Set, Eastlake, Pink Marble, Rosewood Top, c.1870, 5 Piece 3500.00
Bedroom Set, Eastlake, Walnut, Burl Walnut, Swivel Mirror, Marble, 1880, 3 Piece 6700.00
Bedroom Set, Heywood Wakefield, Modern, Wheat Finish, Mirror, 1940s, 4 Piece 975.00
Bedroom Set, Mahogany, Kingwood, Carved, Armoire, 3/4 Bed, 6 Drawer Stand, France . 1680.00
Bedroom Set, Oak, Bed, L-Shape Dresser, Commode, Victorian, 3 Piece 3450.00
Bedroom Set, Pine, Twin Beds, Pseudo-Bamboo, 1890, 6 Piece 9600.00

Bedroom Set, Renaissance Revival, Walnut & Burl, Applied Carving, 1870, 3 Piece 6050.00
Bedroom Set, Rohde, Art Deco, Blond Hardwood, Round Mirror, 1933, 4 Piece 4890.00
Bedroom Set, Walnut Marble Top, Serpentine Fronts, Beveled Mirrors, 4 Piece 17920.00
Bedroom Set, Walnut, Burl Panels, Carved Crest, Marble Top, c.1870, 4 Piece 11200.00
Bedroom Set, Walnut, Carved Flowers, Marble-Top Bureau, Washstand, c.1890 .... 2530.00
Bench, 27 Spindles, Plank Seat, Turned Legs, Stretchers, c.1830, 33 1/4 x 105 In. 385.00
Bench, 3-Section Back, Plank Seat, Scrolled Arms, Painted Birds & Fruit, 73 In. 1210.00
Bench, Arts & Crafts, Curved Crest Rail, Lift Top Seat, Early 20th Century, 38 In. 400.00
Bench, Arts & Crafts, Dark Mahogany Finish, Chamfered Board Back, 60 In. 2875.00
Bench, Arts & Crafts, Mahogany, Yellow Cushion, Horizontal Stretcher, 38 x 14 In. 489.00
Bench, Arts & Crafts, Oak, 4 Post Legs, Stretchers, Slat Bench, c.1912, 28 x 17 In. 690.00
Bench, Arts & Crafts, Oak, Wide & Thin Slats At Back, 59 x 26 x 35 In. 1495.00
Bench, Arts & Crafts, Rustic, Pyrographic, Center Stretcher, 22 x 36 x 13 In. 345.00
Bench, Black Forest, 2 Carved Standing Bears, Holding Seat, 61 In. 3220.00
Bench, Blue Paint, Pennsylvania, Mid 19th Century, 56 1/2 In. 250.00
Bench, Bucket, 3 Shelves, Bootjack Ends, Early 20th Century, 35 x 38 In. 600.00
Bench, Bucket, Dovetailed Case, 3 Shelves, Bootjack Foot, 49 1/2 x 42 In. 600.00
Bench, Bucket, Green Over Mustard Paint, Maine, 19th Century 1595.00
Bench, Bucket, Oak, 3 Shelves, Bootjack Ends, Blue Paint, 1910s, 35 x 38 In. 600.00
Bench, Bucket, Pine, Bootjack Ends, 1 Shelf, Square Nail Construction, 48 In. 660.00
Bench, Bucket, Pine, Graduated Shelves, Truncated Sides, 44 x 35 2/3 In. 495.00
Bench, Bucket, Pine, Shaped Backsplash, 2 Lower Shelves, Cutout Feet, 50 1/2 In. 880.00
Bench, Bucket, Poplar, Bootjack Ends, 2 Shelves In Base, Shelves At Top, 51 1/2 In. 2200.00
Bench, Bucket, Poplar, Bootjack Ends, Center Shelf, Top Shelf, 33 1/4 In. 1160.00
Bench, Bucket, Poplar, Scrolled Backsplash, Shelf, Sides, Pa., c.1820, 46 x 43 In. 2750.00
Bench, Bucket, Yellow & Brown Paint, 2 Drawers On Top, 36 x 36 1/2 In. 6490.00
Bench, Carved Walnut, Cherubs, Horns Of Plenty, 1870, 51 x 47 x 21 In. 3640.00
Bench, Courting, Maple, Ring Turned Posts, Woven Cane Seat, Curved Arms, 32 In. 1210.00
Bench, Deacon's, 24 Turned Spindles, 8 Legs, Stenciling, 1800s, 96 In. 890.00
Bench, Deacon's, 25-Spindle Back, Yellow Paint, 16 x 96 x 34 In. 280.00
Bench, E. Wormley, Carved Walnut Plank Top, Dunbar, 60 x 19 x 12 In. 1840.00
Bench, E. Wormley, Light Mahogany, Cream, Pink Stripe Fabric, 60 x 15 In. 1840.00
Bench, E. Wormley, Walnut Veneer, Upholstered, 30 x 14 1/2 In. 560.00
Bench, E. Wormley, Walnut, No. 6948, X-Base, Upholstered Seat, c.1960, 48 In. 1093.00
Bench, Folds Flat, Stenciled Morse's Patent, 1871, 84 In. 525.00
Bench, Frankl, Light Mahogany, Maple Trim, Johnson Furniture Co., 60 x 18 In. 805.00
Bench, Frieze Carved, Greek Key, Curule Legs, 30 In. 1092.00
Bench, G. Nakashima, Walnut, Free Edge Plank Seat, Dowel Legs, 1975, 31 In. 16875.00
Bench, G. Nelson, Birch Square Top, Slat, Ebony Legs, 71 x 117 x 14 In. 575.00
Bench, G. Nelson, Mahogany, Slats, Red, Pink, Orange, Brown, 48 x 14 In. 1725.00
Bench, G. Nelson, Platform, 3-Section Base, 1946, 18 1/2 x 92 In. 733.00
Bench, G. Nelson, Primavera Top, Wooden Legs, 18 x 68 In. 1045.00
Bench, George III, Mahogany, Half Flowers, Reeded Legs, 18th Century, 16 In. 4560.00
Bench, Gothic Revival, Upholstered Seat & Side Rails, Cast Iron, Mid 1800s 300.00
Bench, H. Bertoia, Maple Finish, Black Steel Rod Base, Slatsknoll, 15 1/2 In. 978.00
Bench, Hall, Arts & Crafts, Dark Mahogany, Lift Seat, Michigan Chair Co., 47 In. 2300.00
Bench, Hall, Mahogany, Upholstered Sides & Back, Removable Cushion, 40 x 17 In. 1180.00
Bench, Hitchcock, Floral & Cornucopia Design, 98 In. 575.00
Bench, Kneeling, Green Paint, Putty Ground, 7 1/2 x 6 x 28 3/4 In. 1840.00
Bench, Kneeling, Pine, Arched Cutouts On Legs, Square Nails, 7 1/2 x 45 1/2 In. 300.00
Bench, Knoll, White Enameled Metal Frame, Slatted Wood, 15 1/4 x 66 x 19 In. 1010.00
Bench, Lifetime, Mahogany, Tapered Posts, Dark Original Finish, 38 x 18 In. 5060.00
Bench, Louis XV, Mahogany, Oblong Top, 4 Cabriole Legs, Damask, 18 x 20 In. 258.00
Bench, Mahogany, Crewel, Hinged Seat, Ball & Claw Feet, 1850s, 21 1/2 In. 920.00
Bench, Mahogany, Serpentine Back, Scroll Crest, 33 1/2 x 43 x 22 In. 520.00
Bench, Mammy's, Removable Rail To Confine Child, Green, 48 In. 2250.00
Bench, Maple, Arrow Back, Curved Splats, American, Early 1800s, 76 3/4 In. 978.00
Bench, Milo Baugman, Square Chrome Base, Wool, Thayer, 18 In. 430.00
Bench, Neoclassical, Medallions & Rosettes, Turned Legs, 16 In., Pair 2990.00
Bench, Oak, Frieze Carved, Splayed Gun-Barrel Turned Legs, England, 77 3/4 In. 2530.00
Bench, Oak, Rectangular Seat, Ring-Turned Legs, 1850s, 42 In. 3700.00
Bench, Oak, Rectangular Top, Lab Ends, 18th Century, 89 x 9 In., Pair 635.00
Bench, P. Evans, White Chrome, Black Upholstered Seat, Signed, 1973, 18 In. 635.00

Bench, Padded Seat, H-Stretcher, Pad Feet, 18 x 38 In. 1150.00
Bench, Painted Flowers On Backrest, Hinged Plank Seat, Dated 1826, 72 In. 1380.00
Bench, Photographer's, Heywood-Wakefield, Wicker, Rolled, 1880 ....*Illus* 500.00
Bench, Photographer's, Victorian, Wicker, Mahogany, c.1875 .... 840.00
Bench, Piano, Arts & Crafts, Mahogany, Octagonal Legs, 26 x 18 x 21 In. 260.00
Bench, Piano, Arts & Crafts, Mahogany, Storage Compartment, 36 x 15 x 20 In. 127.00
Bench, Pine, Blue Paint, Mortised Construction, Bootjack Legs, 10 x 11 x 18 In. 220.00
Bench, Pine, Bootjack Ends, 2-Board Top, 17 3/4 x 56 1/2 In. 140.00
Bench, Pine, Overhanging Rectangular Seat, Salmon Paint, 19 3/4 x 77 x 12 In. 2760.00
Bench, Pine, Rectangular Overhanging Seat, Old Green Paint, New England, 18 In. 400.00
Bench, Pine, Red Paint, Mortised, Scrolled Legs, Pa., c.1810, 19 x 30 In. 1100.00
Bench, Pine, Red Paint, Tilting Top Over Bench, Early 19th Century, 68 1/2 In. 715.00
Bench, Poplar, Bootjack Ends, Square Nails & Screws, 19 x 34 In. 110.00
Bench, Regency, Mahogany, Wooden Seat, Fluted Square Legs, 17 In., Pair 1495.00
Bench, Rococo, Rosewood, Serpentine Sides, Cabriole Legs, 18 1/2 In., Pair 1610.00
Bench, Trapezoid Case, Painted Scrolls & Shells, Lift Top, Early 1600s, 91 In. 2100.00
Bench, Tufted Vinyl Seat, Bright Chrome Frame, 18 x 88 x 17 1/2 In. 310.00
Bench, Upholstered Backrest, Continuing To Outward Arms, 18th Century, 58 In. 3450.00
Bench, Walnut, Bellflowers Carved At Knee, Claw & Ball Feet, 18 In. 3220.00
Bench, Walnut, Poplar, Turned Spindles & Feet, 19th Century, 31 x 73 In. 395.00
Bench, Walnut, Rectangular Paneled Back, Hinged Seat, Plinth Base, 39 In. 3165.00
Bench, William IV, Mahogany, Deep Button Upholstered, 20 x 48 x 26 1/2 In. 2760.00
Bench, William IV, Mahogany, Scrolled Apron, Tufted Leather, 15 x 44 x 17 In. 2530.00
Bench, William IV, Mahogany, Tapered Legs, Peg Feet, 52 In. 4140.00
Bench, Window, William IV, Mahogany, Rolled End Turnings, 19 1/2 x 12 In. 4150.00
Bench, Windsor, Half Spindles, Brown Over Old Green Paint, 19th Century, 35 In. 505.00
Bidet, Bench, Mahogany, Lift-Off Top, Porcelain Insert, Rectangular 385.00
Bidet, Biedermeier, Walnut, Porcelain Bowl, Cabriole Legs, 8 x 18 1/2 x 13 1/4 In. 230.00
Bookcase, Aalto, Attached Table, Dowel Leg, 4 Shelves, 100 x 59 1/2 In. 2760.00
Bookcase, Aalto, Plywood, 4 Shelves, Svenska Arteck, 100 x 59 x 34 In. 2760.00
Bookcase, Aalto, Walnut, 4 Shelves, Dowel Leg Support, 100 x 34 1/2 In. 4218.00
Bookcase, Aesthetic Revival, Walnut, Carved, 2 Glass Doors, c.1870, 104 x 72 In. 8400.00
Bookcase, Arts & Crafts, 3 Glass Doors, 3 Shelves, 56 x 61 x 13 In. 1380.00
Bookcase, Arts & Crafts, 3 Glass Paneled Doors, 8-Pane Doors, 55 x 55 x 12 In. 2015.00
Bookcase, Arts & Crafts, 3 Shelves, 2 Doors, 48 x 36 x 12 1/2 In. 1095.00
Bookcase, Arts & Crafts, Center Glass Side Paneled Doors, Shelves, 59 x 67 In. 7150.00
Bookcase, Arts & Crafts, Dark Mahogany, 8-Pane Doors, 54 1/2 x 46 x 12 In. 1460.00
Bookcase, Arts & Crafts, Mahogany, 4 Doors, Adjustable Shelves, 92 x 59 In. 6900.00
Bookcase, Arts & Crafts, Oak, 3 Shelves, Old Green Paint, c.1900, 55 x 25 1/2 In. 55.00
Bookcase, Arts & Crafts, Oak, Floral Design At Top, Leaded Glass Doors, 82 In. 575.00
Bookcase, Arts & Crafts, Oak, Upper Glass Panes, 2 Doors, 53 1/2 x 43 1/4 In. 630.00
Bookcase, Baker Furniture, Black Enamel, Brass Lattice Panel Doors, 35 x 35 In. 1375.00
Bookcase, Biedermeier, Birch, Stepped Cornice, 2 Doors, 1830s, 47 3/4 In. 2900.00
Bookcase, Biedermeier, Birchwood, Brass Grillwork, 96 x 82 x 19 In. 6040.00
Bookcase, Biedermeier, Maple, Pedimented Cornice Over Doors, 76 In., Pair 5730.00
Bookcase, Bird's-Eye Maple, Birch, Glazed & Paneled Doors, 1860s, 85 3/4 In. 7360.00
Bookcase, Carlton, Multilevel, Memphis, 1981, 72 1/2 In. ....*Illus* 14625.00
Bookcase, Cherry, Revolving, Inlaid Center, 3 Shelves, Lattice Sides, 43 In. 460.00
Bookcase, Cherry, Step Back, 4 Glass Doors, Cornice, 110 x 78 x 17 In., 2 Piece 3300.00
Bookcase, Chippendale, Robin's-Egg Blue, Black Flecks, 28 x 14 x 66 1/4 In. 550.00
Bookcase, Chippendale, Slant Front, Swan's Neck Pediment, 4 Drawers, 77 In. 402.00
Bookcase, Colonial Revival, Rectangular Top, Foliate Scrolls, 1800s, 41 1/2 In. 2185.00
Bookcase, Eastlake, 2 Framed Glass Doors, Spoon Carved Finial, 92 x 40 In. 1290.00
Bookcase, Edwardian, Mahogany, Inlay, c.1905, 60 1/4 x 66 x 15 1/2 In. 1495.00
Bookcase, Edwardian, Satinwood, Double Glazed Doors, Bracket Feet, 77 In. 1150.00
Bookcase, Empire Gothic, Mahogany, Mullioned Doors, 4 Shelves, c.1840, 83 x 52 In. ... 5700.00
Bookcase, Empire, Mahogany, 2 Glazed Doors, Shelves, c.1840, 85 x 62 In. 3900.00
Bookcase, Empire, Mahogany, Marble Top, Bronze Egyptian Stiles, 1810, 36 x 50 In. ... 3080.00
Bookcase, Federal, Mahogany, Molded Edge Top, 4 Shelves, 34 x 50 1/2 In., Pair 1440.00
Bookcase, Federal, Mahogany, Stepped Cornice, Glazed Doors, 90 x 48 In. 3630.00
Bookcase, Frank Lloyd Wright, Mahogany, 3 Gilt-Edge Shelves, 1923, 48 In. 3600.00
Bookcase, G. Stickley, 1 Door, 16 Panes, Iron V-Pull, Red Decal, 56 In. 7475.00
Bookcase, G. Stickley, 2 Doors, 12 Panes, Iron Hardware, No. 718, 56 x 54 In. 9200.00

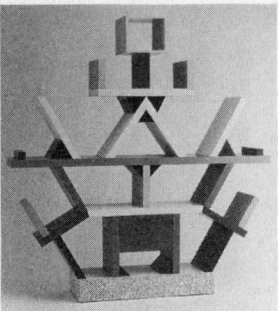

Furniture,
Bookcase,
Carlton, Multilevel,
Memphis, 1981,
72 1/2 In.

Furniture,
Bookcase,
Roycroft, I Door,
20 Panes,
46 x 16 x 71 In.

Bookcase, G. Stickley, 2 Doors, 16 Panes, Hammered Copper, 56 x 13 In. 9560.00
Bookcase, G. Stickley, 2 Doors, 16 Panes, V-Pulls, Red Decal, 56 In. 8625.00
Bookcase, G. Stickley, Mahogany, 16 Panes, Gallery Top, 55 1/2 In. 9775.00
Bookcase, G. Stickley, Mahogany, 2 Doors, 8 Panes, 56 x 43 x 13 In. 8625.00
Bookcase, G. Stickley, No. 543, Mahogany, 12 Panes, 50 x 12 x 56 In. 9520.00
Bookcase, G. Stickley, No. 715, Mahogany, 16 Panes, 36 x 56 In. 6900.00
Bookcase, G. Stickley, Overhanging Top, 3 Vertical Panes, 58 x 14 In. 10690.00
Bookcase, George II, Mahogany, Slant Front Top, 3 Drawers, Bracket Feet, 6 In. 545.00
Bookcase, George III, Mahogany, 2 Astragal Doors, Molded Cornice, 84 1/2 In. 1495.00
Bookcase, George IV, Mahogany, Gothic Arch Mullions, 90 x 45 x 22 In. 10925.00
Bookcase, Georgian, Mahogany, 2 Doors, 4 Shelves, French Feet, c.1780, 93 x 49 In. 6600.00
Bookcase, Globe-Wernicke, 4 Stack, Paper Label, 59 1/2 In. 700.00
Bookcase, Globe-Wernicke, Drop Front, Mahogany, 9 Sections, 59 x 84 x 11 In. 2910.00
Bookcase, Globe-Wernicke, Stacking, 3 Sections, 34 x 49 In. 600.00
Bookcase, Globe-Wernicke, Stacking, Leaded Glass Top Door, 34 x 47 In. 850.00
Bookcase, Gothic Revival, Mahogany, Original Glass, 83 x 52 1/4 In. 4400.00
Bookcase, Hepplewhite, Mahogany, Inlay, 2 Glass Doors, 1 Drawer, 78 In., 2 Piece 1705.00
Bookcase, Jules Leleu, Burl Walnut, c.1928, 56 1/2 x 43 x 12 1/2 In. 8400.00
Bookcase, L. & J.G. Stickley, No. 644, Open, Mortised Through Sides, Decal, 55 In. 4850.00
Bookcase, L. & J.G. Stickley, No. 645, Oak, 2 Doors, 12 Panes, 53 x 12 x 55 In. 5750.00
Bookcase, Liberty, Triple, Spade Cutouts, 3 Shelves, Leaded Glass Door, 71 In. 6900.00
Bookcase, Lifetime, 3 Doors, Gallery Top, 3 Adjustable Shelves, 56 1/4 In. 2070.00
Bookcase, Lifetime, Double Doors, Paper Label, 42 x 55 In. 3100.00
Bookcase, Lifetime, Golden Oak, 3 Doors, Glass Panels, 55 3/4 x 55 x 12 In. 2810.00
Bookcase, Lifetime, No. 7218, Mahogany, 1 Door, 10 Squares, 28 x 12 x 56 In. 1870.00
Bookcase, Louis XVI, Tulipwood, Rectangular Marble Top, Open, 46 In., Pair 3900.00
Bookcase, Mahogany Veneer, Reeded Sides, Flower Blossom In Center, 26 In. 330.00
Bookcase, Mahogany, 3 Glass Doors, Adjustable Shelves, Praying Monks, 58 1/2 In. 2530.00
Bookcase, Mahogany, 4 Doors, Wooden Panel, 121 1/2 x 89 x 19 In. 8915.00
Bookcase, Mahogany, Cherry Top, Mullioned Doors, Shelves, 92 In. 7190.00
Bookcase, Mahogany, Glass Doors, Molded Dentil, Foliate Mullions, 97 x 18 In. 7200.00
Bookcase, Mahogany, Glazed Doors, Silk Lined Shelves, Late 19th Century, 76 In. 1840.00
Bookcase, Mahogany, Grill Inset Door, Over Projecting Door, c.1835, 72 x 32 In. 2645.00
Bookcase, Mahogany, Marble Top, 1850, 55 1/2 x 56 1/2 x 16 1/4 In. 1900.00
Bookcase, Mahogany, Molded Edge, 3 Shelves, Plinth Base, 54 x 115 x 19 In. 2530.00
Bookcase, Mahogany, Molded Top Over Paneled Frieze, Tapered Legs, 70 In. 1380.00
Bookcase, Mahogany, Open, Twist Turned Columns, 3 Shelves, 64 x 72 1/4 In. 1035.00
Bookcase, Mahogany, Pierced Gallery, Glazed Bars On Doors, 1840s, 51 1/2 In. 3970.00
Bookcase, Michigan Chair Co., 2 Doors, 44 1/2 x 36 In. 3600.00
Bookcase, Oak, 3 Drawers Over 3 Glass Doors, Carved Demon Heads, 52 x 84 In. 3190.00
Bookcase, Oak, Molded Cornice, Fluted Columns, Plinth Base, 93 1/2 In. 2185.00
Bookcase, Oak, Pine, High Turned Feet, Acorn Finial, 29 1/2 x 18 x 68 In. 1045.00
Bookcase, Oak, Silver Leaf Border, Geometric Glazing On Door, c.1900, 65 1/4 In. 2530.00
Bookcase, Provincial, Louis Philippe, Oak, 3 Glazed Doors, 91 x 65 1/2 x 19 In. 2415.00
Bookcase, Regency, Celadon, Open Shelves, 3 Cupboard Doors, 64 x 20 In. 1725.00
Bookcase, Regency, Mahogany, Marble Top, 2 Open Shelves, 34 1/2 x 44 x 11 In. 2760.00

Bookcase, Renaissance Revival, Walnut, Carved Crest, Burled Side Panels, 74 In. 4370.00
Bookcase, Revolving, Edwardian, Mahogany, Inlay, 31 x 19 1/2 x 19 1/2 In. 1955.00
Bookcase, Revolving, Mahogany, 2 Shelves, 31 x 19 1/2 In. 2415.00
Bookcase, Revolving, Walnut, Square Top, Slatted Ends, England, 43 x 23 x 25 In. 1035.00
Bookcase, Rococo, Walnut, Carved Arched Pediment, Foliage, 92 x 43 In. 1095.00
Bookcase, Rohde, Burl Veneer, 1 Drop Door, 2 Lower Drawers, 27 In. 1495.00
Bookcase, Rohde, Exotic Wood, Ebonized Interior, Herman Miller, 41 3/4 In. 545.00
Bookcase, Rosewood, Marble Top, 3 Glazed Doors, c.1825, 38 In. 4310.00
Bookcase, Rosewood, Open Shelves, Term Figures, Human Feet, 48 In. 7200.00
Bookcase, Roycroft, 1 Door, 20 Panes, 46 x 16 x 71 In. . . . . *Illus* 9775.00
Bookcase, Stickley Bros., Oak, 2 Doors, 3 Small Panes, 55 x 48 x 12 In. 2510.00
Bookcase, Walnut, 2 Doors, Burl Trim, Paneled Cornice, c.1880, 93 x 60 x 15 In. 2745.00
Bookcase, Walnut, 2 Glazed Doors Over 2 Drawers, Lower Doors, 84 In. 1840.00
Bookcase, Walnut, 3 Doors, Aesthetic Floral Columns, 1875, 68 x 19 In. 3920.00
Bookcase, Walnut, Burl Columns & Panels, 2 Sections, 2 Drawers, 62 x 54 x 19 In. 950.00
Bookcase, Walnut, Gilt, Conforming Molded Frieze, Brass Plinth, 52 1/4 In. 5520.00
Bookcase, Walnut, Scroll, Shell Cornice, Arched Doors, 2 Base Drawers, 1840, 67 In. . . . 5465.00
Bookcase, Walnut, Step Back, Beveled Doors, Hold 45 Drawers, 152 x 22 x 106 In. 8960.00
Bookcase-Cabinet, George III, Mahogany, Late 1700s, 79 x 43 x 17 In. 6325.00
Bookcase-Cabinet, George III, Mahogany, Mullioned Doors, Bracket Feet, 108 In. 9000.00
Bookcase-Cabinet, Mahogany, 3 Glass Sliding Doors, Floral Panels, 86 In. 1495.00
Bookcase-Cabinet, William IV, Mahogany, Ebony Rectangular Cornice, 90 In. 6040.00
Bookrack, Applied Brass, Celluloid Leaves, Expandable, Late 1800s, 14 In. 145.00
Bookrack, Arts & Crafts, Oak, Tile Inlay, Continental, 5 x 18 x 6 In. 175.00
Bookrack, Burl Walnut, Folding, Brass Fretwork, c.1890, 25 In. Open 700.00
Bookrack, Folding, Dark, Carved Scrolls, Geometric, Continental, 17 x 7 x 12 In. 55.00
Bookrack, Rosewood, Desk, 7 Leather-Bound Books, 8 1/4 x 8 In. 1495.00
Bookrack, Roycroft, Little Journeys, Mahogany, Signed, 26 1/4 x 26 x 14 In. . . . . .546.00 to 805.00
Bookrest, Florentine, Cream Paint, Parcel Gilt, Scroll Feet, 12 x 19 x 15 In. 1150.00
Bookrest, Mottled Surface, Scroll Feet, Adjustable Stand, 12 x 19 In. 1150.00
Bookstand, George III, Mahogany, Double Action, 35 1/2 x 13 1/2 x 15 1/2 In. 920.00
Bookstand, Georgian, Backsplash, Shelf, Cabriole Legs, c.1900, 19 x 12 x 32 In. 575.00
Bookstand, Mahogany, Double Action, Hinged Top, Drawer, 1830s, 35 1/2 In. 920.00
Bookstand, Mahogany, Double, 4 Tiers, Brass Handles, Casters, 57 In. 6900.00
Bookstand, Rosewood, Open Scrollwork, Folding Shelf, Easel Support, 12 x 10 In. 115.00
Bookstand, V Trough, 2 Tenon Shelves, Triangular Cutout, 32 1/2 x 31 1/2 x 10 In. 290.00
Breakfront, Chinese Chippendale, Lacquered, 6 Drawers, 56 x 84 In. 1045.00
Breakfront, Chinoiserie, Walnut, 2 Parts, Secretary Interior, 85 x 52 x 19 In. 2300.00
Breakfront, Frank Lloyd Wright, 1 Cabinet Door Top, Shelves, 83 x 66 In. 3450.00
Breakfront, Georgian, Mahogany, Molded, Dentil Cornice, 91 x 109 x 20 In. 2760.00
Breakfront, Oriental Paint, Cream, 4 Glass Doors, 1930s, 50 x 75 In., 2 Piece 600.00
Breakfront, Regency, Mahogany, 8 Pane Doors, 87 x 68 x 19 In. 5750.00
Breakfront, Walnut, Cypress, Molded Cornice, 10 Ogee Drawers, 103 In. 6615.00
Breakfront-Bookcase, Chippendale, Walnut, 3 Paneled Door, 86 x 65 x 13 In. 2875.00
Breakfront-Bookcase, George III, Mahogany, Astragal Glaze Doors, 98 x 23 In. 9775.00
Breakfront-Bookcase, George III, Oak, Cock-Beaded Drawers, 18th Century 8400.00
Breakfront-Bookcase, Georgian, Paneled Doors, Plinth Base, 95 x 21 x 86 In. 5750.00
Breakfront-Bookcase, Glazed Doors, Medallion Each Door, Baker Co., 94 x 75 In. 4025.00
Breakfront-Bookcase, Mahogany, 4 Glazed Doors, 4 Lower Doors, 91 x 109 In. 2760.00
Breakfront-Bookcase, Regency, Mahogany, Astragal Doors, 100 x 98 x 25 In. 16625.00
Breakfront-Bookcase, Renaissance Revival, Walnut, Stepped Cornice, 108 1/2 In. 2990.00
Buffet, Classical Revival, Mahogany, 2 Convex Drawers, Tapered Feet, 1850, 54 In. 1610.00
Buffet, Classical, Bowfront, Mahogany, 3 Frieze Drawers, Paw Feet, 56 x 25 In. 750.00
Buffet, Empire, Cherry, Marble Top, 2 Doors, France, 39 1/2 x 48 x 24 In. 1725.00
Buffet, French Provincial, Cherry, 3 Frieze Drawers, Block Feet, 37 x 66 In. 2300.00
Buffet, French Provincial, Cherry, Rectangular Top, 2 Doors, Bun Feet, 38 In. 865.00
Buffet, French Provincial, Molded Cornice, 2 Doors, Molded Feet, 94 x 19 1/2 In. 2530.00
Buffet, French Provincial, Oak, Plank Top, 2 Paneled Doors, 38 x 52 x 21 In. 2990.00
Buffet, French Provincial, Oak, Scalloped Frieze, Cabriole Legs, 87 x 64 x 21 In. 4315.00
Buffet, French Provincial, Polychrome, 3 Drawers, 2 Cupboards, 44 x 50 x 20 In. 1380.00
Buffet, Louis XV, Elm, Galleried Shelves, 2 Lower Doors, 79 x 47 x 23 In. 2760.00
Buffet, Louis XV, Oak, Early 1900s, 42 x 96 1/4 x 21 1/2 In. 1725.00
Buffet, Louis XV, Oak, Molded Top, Short Cabriole Legs, 39 x 76 x 23 In. 1495.00

Buffet, Louis XVI, Fruitwood, Half Drawers, Doors, 38 1/2 x 55 x 25 In. 4140.00
Buffet, Louis XVI, Fruitwood, Rectangular Top, 2 Drawers, Incurved Legs, 42 In. 2185.00
Buffet, Louis XVI, Walnut, 2 Drawers, Molded Top, Bracket Feet, 41 x 54 In. 1610.00
Buffet, McCobb, 2 Paneled Doors, Marble Top, Tapered Legs, 34 x 72 x 29 In. 730.00
Buffet, McCobb, Walnut, 5 Narrow Drawers, Angular Brass Base, 33 In. 12375.00
Buffet, Neoclassical, Mahogany, Rectangular Fan Top, 3 Drawers, 37 1/2 In. 4025.00
Buffet, Oak, Central Geometric Door, Carved Dragon, France, 79 In. 5465.00
Buffet, P. Evans, Abstract Forms, Gold Leaf, 4 Steel Doors, 3 Block Risers, 33 In. 9000.00
Buffet, P. Evans, Brass, Steel Surface, 4 Doors, Slate Top, 38 x 77 x 21 1/2 In. 4220.00
Buffet, Robert Swanson, Eliel Saarinen, Birch Veneer, Stainless Steel, 41 In. 3040.00
Buffet, Rococo, Walnut, Geometric, Circular Crest, Marble Top, 98 In. 3680.00
Buffet, Rohde, Mahogany Veneer, 2 Flat Drawers, Flared Legs, 36 x 20 In. 520.00
Buffet, Walnut, Serpentine Crest, Foliate Carved Panels, 102 x 25 In. 1035.00
Bulletin Board, Arts & Crafts, Oak, Cross Medallion, Burlap Panel, 30 x 30 In. 290.00
Bureau, Bowfront, Mahogany Centers, Satinwood Inlay, 4 Drawers, 33 x 37 In. 1840.00
Bureau, Cottage, Child's, Pinstripe Design, c.1840, 43 1/2 In. 660.00
Bureau, Elm, Oak, 3 Parts, Serpentine Doors, Slant Front, Interior Drawers, 82 In. 8625.00
Bureau, George I, Walnut, Slant Front, Crossbanded Top, 7 Drawers, 42 x 22 In. 5750.00
Bureau, George III, Mahogany, 2 Short Over 3 Long Drawers, c.1790, 32 x 34 In. 935.00
Bureau, Hepplewhite, Cherry, Mahogany, Bowfront, Pa., c.1810, 37 x 41 In. 2310.00
Bureau, Hepplewhite, Overhang Top, 4 Drawers, Pa., c.1820, 38 x 38 3/4 In. 1430.00
Bureau, Louis XV, Cane Backrest Leaf Crest, Leather Cushion, 1900, 36 In. 1610.00
Bureau, Louis XV, Rosewood, Burl Walnut, Flowering Vines, 3 Drawers, 39 In. 2300.00
Bureau, Mahogany, Poplar, Slant Front, 3 Drawers, c.1820, 21 x 18 x 10 1/2 In. 7500.00
Bureau, Mahogany, Upper Tier With 2 Drawers, Turned Feet, c.1815, 43 x 39 In. 2530.00
Bureau, Queen Anne, Slant Front, Leather Top, Fitted Compartments, 40 In. 550.00
Bureau, Rosewood, Marble Top, 4 Drawers, Attached Mirror, 77 x 42 1/2 In. 920.00
Bureau, Sheraton, Mahogany, Veneer, 4 Drawers, Bowfront, Scroll, 46 x 42 x 21 In. 1610.00
Bureau, Victorian, Tilting Mirror, Marble Top, Stile Feet, c.1880, 72 1/2 x 40 In. 330.00
Bureau, Walnut, Fruitwood Inlay, Slant Front, Pigeonholes, 38 1/2 In. 860.00
Bureau, Walnut, Green Leather Top, 1 Drawer, Square Tapered Legs, 30 In. 3680.00
Bureau-Bookcase, Mahogany, Glazed Doors, Slant Front, Fitted Interior, 83 In. 7475.00
Bureau-Bookcase, Mahogany, Slant Front, Interior Desk, 4 Drawers, 1780s, 87 In. 5520.00
Bureau-Bookcase, Walnut, Mirror-Inset Door, Pigeonholes, 4 Drawers, 75 3/4 In. 4200.00
Cabinet, 4 Rows Of Cubbyholes, Drawers, 30 x 30 In. 9200.00
Cabinet, Apothecary, Poplar, 28 Drawers, Pa., c.1820, 50 1/2 x 39 x 10 1/2 In. 825.00
Cabinet, Art Deco, Rosewood Inlay, Carved Plank Legs, 57 1/4 x 40 x 17 1/2 In. 3940.00
Cabinet, Art Moderne, Mahogany, Plexiglas, 54 x 17 x 77 1/4 In. 4500.00
Cabinet, Arts & Crafts, Oak, Wooden Latch, Pyrographic Peasant Woman, 42 1/2 In. 980.00
Cabinet, Arts & Crafts, Single Drawer, Green Slag Glass Panel, 32 x 12 In. 900.00
Cabinet, Bar, Arts & Crafts, Oak, Copper, Ice Spot, Barrel Doors, 52 x 26 In. 1400.00
Cabinet, Bar, V. Kagan, Mahogany, Pullout Serving Shelf, Plank Legs, 48 In. 1690.00
Cabinet, Bar, Walnut, 2 Doors, Mythological Figures, 1870, 62 x 19 x 45 In. 3920.00
Cabinet, Baudouine, Gothic Revival, Rosewood, Marble Top, c.1840, 36 x 45 In. 3300.00
Cabinet, Bauhaus, Center Cupboard, 2 Side Cases, Sliding Doors, c.1927, 67 3/4 In. 1150.00
Cabinet, Bird's-Eye Maple Interior, Door Medallion, Cherubs, Dolphin, 1865, 43 In. 9500.00
Cabinet, Black Lacquer, Mother-Of-Pearl Inlay, 2 Doors, Birds, Floral Inlay, 24 In. 150.00
Cabinet, Black Lacquer, Painted Still Life, Doors, Shelf, Chinese, 1890, 31 x 26 In. 290.00
Cabinet, China, Arts & Crafts, 4 Shelves, Glass Doors, Casters, 59 x 41 x 15 In. 1610.00
Cabinet, China, E. Sottsass, Grained Wood, 2 Dark Green Paneled Doors, 84 In. 4025.00
Cabinet, China, Federal, Rectangular Molded Edge Top, Floral, Burl, 62 In. 520.00
Cabinet, China, G. Stickley, Mahogany, 2 Doors, 8 Panes, 64 1/4 x 15 In. 6325.00
Cabinet, China, G. Stickley, No. 815, Mahogany, 2 Doors, 42 x 15 x 64 In. 10640.00
Cabinet, China, G. Stickley, No. 820, Mahogany, 12 Panes, Red Decal, 36 x 63 In. 8625.00
Cabinet, China, Glass Sides, 4 Shelves, 2 Doors, Grand Rapids, 64 x 50 x 17 In. 1555.00
Cabinet, China, L. & J.G. Stickley, 2 Doors, Leaded Panels, Signed, 62 x 44 In. 9775.00
Cabinet, China, L. & J.G. Stickley, No. 761, Mahogany, Adjustable Shelves, 60 In. 8050.00
Cabinet, China, Lifetime, Mahogany, 57 x 52 x 14 In. 5175.00
Cabinet, China, Limbert, Mahogany, 3 Panes, 59 3/4 x 40 x 16 In. 7765.00
Cabinet, China, Limbert, No. 1146, 2 Doors, 8 Panes Each, Strap Hinges, 59 In. 8625.00
Cabinet, China, Mahogany, Half-Round, Late 19th Century, 69 x 52 x 15 In. 2695.00
Cabinet, China, Neoclassical, Mahogany, Beveled Glass Panels, Ormolu, 36 x 76 In. 3850.00
Cabinet, China, Oak, Bowfront, Black, Carved Floral, 4 Shelves, 37 x 17 x 68 In. 1125.00

Cabinet, China, Oak, Carved, Beveled Glass, Claw Feet, 1885, 78 x 64 x 22 In. 7840.00
Cabinet, China, Oak, Curved Glass, Figural Columns, Carved Top, 1890, 66 x 50 In. 2800.00
Cabinet, China, Oak, D-Shape Top, Early 20th Century, 39 x 15 x 63 In. 400.00
Cabinet, China, Rohde, Wood, Glass Top, 2 Doors, Herman Miller, 60 1/4 In. 1380.00
Cabinet, Chippendale, Mahogany, Greek Key Frieze, 1 Astragal Door, 23 In. 865.00
Cabinet, Circassian Walnut, Mother-Of-Pearl Inlay, 90 1/2 x 97 x 21 1/2 In. 2760.00
Cabinet, Corner, 1 Frieze Drawer, Gilt Trim, Continental, 19th Century, 47 In. 3000.00
Cabinet, Corner, American Poplar, Mullioned Doors, 80 1/2 x 47 x 23 1/2 In. 1150.00
Cabinet, Corner, Chippendale, Cherry, 2 Parts, c.1890, 93 1/4 x 43 1/2 x 32 In. 13800.00
Cabinet, Corner, Directoire, Fruitwood, Carved Panels, 75 x 31 x 16 In. 1265.00
Cabinet, Corner, Federal, Mahogany, 2 Paneled Doors, Plinth Base, 35 x 77 In. 575.00
Cabinet, Corner, George I, Chinese Figures Scene, Gold, Black, 1720, 15 In. 6600.00
Cabinet, Corner, Gilt, Gesso, Scrolling Leaves, Shelves, 34 x 22 x 12 In., Pair 2185.00
Cabinet, Corner, Mustard Over Slate Gray Paint, 1 Door, 56 1/2 x 32 x 26 In. 1035.00
Cabinet, Corner, Walnut, Game-Carved Door, Ornate Carvings, 1875, 45 x 24 In. 1400.00
Cabinet, Curio, Ebonized, Gilt Incised, Beveled Glass, N.Y., 1880, 79 x 64 x 17 In. 2800.00
Cabinet, Curio, Fruitwood, France, Early 20th Century, 40 x 28 1/4 x 11 In. 715.00
Cabinet, Curio, Hand Painted Courting Scenes, France, c.1885, 55 x 28 x 14 In. 1680.00
Cabinet, Curio, Hanging, Mirror Back, Carved Dragon, Chinese, 20 x 4 x 33 In. 170.00
Cabinet, Curio, Mahogany, Bowfront, Curved Glass Panels, Velvet Interior, 75 In. 7850.00
Cabinet, Curio, Mahogany, Hanging, Flat Front, Bow Side, Mirror, Crest, 27 x 20 In. 310.00
Cabinet, Curio, Rosewood, Bowfront, Ormolu Design, Cabriole Legs, 26 x 62 In. 715.00
Cabinet, Display, Brass Frame, Smoked Glass, 4 Shelves, Lighted, 36 x 82 1/2 In. 630.00
Cabinet, Display, George III, Scarlet Lacquer, Chinoiserie, 30 x 18 1/2 x 6 In. 1265.00
Cabinet, Display, Gold Paint, Glass Shelves, Mirror Back, 69 x 26 x 14 In. 550.00
Cabinet, Display, Hanging, Pine, Painted, Glazed Door, 3 Shelves, c.1900, 29 x 18 In. 360.00
Cabinet, Display, Louis XV, Curved Glass, Mirror Back, 1900s, 72 x 29 x 15 In. 825.00
Cabinet, Display, Louis XV, Mahogany, Glass Top, Ormolu Mounts, 1900 .... 2200.00
Cabinet, Display, Louis XV, Oak, Carved, Glazed Doors, Shelves, 54 x 20 x 82 In. 575.00
Cabinet, Display, Mahogany, Glass Lift Top & Sides, Bronze, 1920, 35 x 38 In. 1320.00
Cabinet, Display, Mahogany, Hanging, Glazed Door, Lattice Sides, 37 In. 460.00
Cabinet, Dovetailed Case, Plated Bindings, Paper Interior, 35 x 16 x 24 In. 140.00
Cabinet, Ebony & Rosewood, Bronze Panel, Mythological Scene, 1860s, 78 In. 5460.00
Cabinet, Elm, 2 Doors Over 3 Drawers, Late 19th Century, 80 x 42 x 21 In. 750.00
Cabinet, Elm, 2 Panel Doors, 2 Shelves, Rectangular Feet, Chinese, 75 In. 1840.00
Cabinet, Elm, 3 Drawers, Brass Mounts, Burgundy Lacquer, 33 x 19 In. 520.00
Cabinet, Elm, Burgundy Lacquer, 3 Drawers, Carved Bats, Kuei Dragons, 33 In. 520.00
Cabinet, Elm, Burgundy Lacquer, 4 Double Doors, 2 Drawers, 90 x 24 In. 1150.00
Cabinet, Elm, Floral & Cloud Design, 2 Doors, Lion's Claw Feet, 78 x 36 In. 3680.00
Cabinet, Elm, Red Diamond, Chinese, 19th Century, 84 1/2 x 21 x 43 In. 690.00
Cabinet, Empire, Mahogany, Marble Top, Drawer, Cupboard Doors, c.1830, 30 x 36 In. ... 4200.00
Cabinet, Federal, 2 Paneled Doors, Shelf, Bracket Foot Base, 87 1/2 x 34 1/2 In. 2590.00
Cabinet, Federal, Mahogany, Marble Top, Drawer Over 2 Doors, c.1815, 30 x 36 In. 3600.00
Cabinet, Federal, Mahogany, Swan's Neck Pediment, 3 Drawers, 45 x 79 In. 170.00
Cabinet, Filing, Oak, 3 Parts, 12 Drawers, Brass Hardware, 19 1/2 x 33 x 17 In. 225.00
Cabinet, Filing, Oak, 3 Parts, Drawers, Index File, Brass, 1910, 41 x 41 In. 700.00
Cabinet, Filing, Oak, 5 Piece Stacking, 16 Card Files, Brass, 64 x 18 x 18 In. 730.00
Cabinet, Frank Lloyd Wright, Mahogany, 2 Doors, Red Decal, Henredon, 22 x 28 In. 750.00
Cabinet, Frank Lloyd Wright, Oak, 3 Drawers, Recessed Handles, Henredon, 28 In. 460.00
Cabinet, French Provincial, Fruitwood, Floral Carved Panel, 45 x 36 x 12 1/2 In. 1150.00
Cabinet, G. Nakashima, Walnut, 2 Doors, Burl Handle, 1965, 22 In. 12365.00
Cabinet, G. Nakashima, Walnut, Dovetail Case, 4 Drawers, 1970, 32 x 20 In. 5060.00
Cabinet, G. Nelson, 4 Drawers, 2 Doors, Porcelain Pulls, 24 x 57 In. 1870.00
Cabinet, G. Nelson, 5 Drawer Front, 1 Door, Chrome Pulls, Hairpin Legs, 39 1/4 In. 1495.00
Cabinet, G. Nelson, Ash, 5 Drawers, Hairpin Legs, Herman Miller, 39 In. 1495.00
Cabinet, G. Nelson, Blond Wood, 2 Doors, Plank Legs, Herman Miller, 30 In. 505.00
Cabinet, G. Nelson, Burnt Orange Lacquer, 3 Drawers, Herman Miller, 29 In. 1840.00
Cabinet, G. Nelson, Rosewood, 4 Drawers, Aluminum Legs, 30 In. 3450.00
Cabinet, G. Nelson, Steel Frame, 1 Turquoise Laminated Drawer, 29 In. 1265.00
Cabinet, G. Nelson, Steel Frame, 3 Drawers, White Enameled Frame, 29 In. 1725.00
Cabinet, G. Nelson, Steel Frame, Glass Top, 2 Yellow Laminated Drawers, 29 In. 2185.00
Cabinet, G. Nelson, Walnut Veneer, Door, Plank Legs, Herman Miller, 29 x 24 In. 115.00
Cabinet, G. Nelson, Walnut, Black Laminated Sliding Doors, 60 x 19 x 26 In. 690.00

Cabinet, Game, Arts & Crafts, Mahogany, 2 Vertical Slats, 21 x 12 x 37 In. 1035.00
Cabinet, George III, Mahogany, Astragal Glazed Doors, On Cupboard, Late 1800s 2300.00
Cabinet, Georgian, Mahogany, Incurved Front, Doors, Fretwork, 35 x 40 In., Pair 1840.00
Cabinet, Giltwood, Hanging, Glazed Door, Interior Shelves, Floral Crest, 60 In. 1495.00
Cabinet, Gothic Style, Scrolling Leaves Cornice, 2 Doors, 94 x 56 x 16 1/2 In. 6900.00
Cabinet, Hanging, Arts & Crafts, Oak, Grueby Tile Door, Sailing Ship, 28 x 14 In. 2990.00
Cabinet, Hanging, G. Nakashima, Spindled Sliding Doors, 19 x 104 In. 8050.00
Cabinet, Hanging, G. Nakashima, Walnut, 2 Doors, Adjustable Shelf, 14 In. 1910.00
Cabinet, Hanging, G. Nakashima, Walnut, Ebonized Wood, Walnut Burl, 26 x 84 In. 3900.00
Cabinet, Hanging, P. Evans, Welded Steel Door, Sunburst, Bronze Finish, 20 In. 3450.00
Cabinet, Hanging, Phil Powell, Walnut, 8 Long Drawers, Turquoise Cabochon, 22 In. . . . 5060.00
Cabinet, Hanging, Pine, 5 Interior Drawers, 2 Hidden Drawers, Painted, 25 x 21 In. 330.00
Cabinet, Hanging, Shell, Foliate Carved Crest, Glazed Door, Red, Gold Paint, 22 In. 1035.00
Cabinet, Hardwood, Lacquered, Flowering Bushes, Chinese, 53 x 28 1/2 x 14 1/2 In. 460.00
Cabinet, Hepplewhite, Mahogany, Astragal Glazed Doors, Spade Feet, 67 In. 1955.00
Cabinet, Hepplewhite, Mahogany, Veneer, 3 Drawers, Inlay, Bracket Feet, 69 In. 1100.00
Cabinet, James I, Oak, Shell-Carved Frieze, 2 Paneled Doors, 57 x 21 In. 920.00
Cabinet, Japanese Style, Floral Carved, 2 Doors, Gold Leaf, 61 x 45 x 12 In. 6800.00
Cabinet, Jewelry, 6 Drawers, 3 False Drawers, Cityscape, Scrolls, c.1600, 20 In. 6900.00
Cabinet, Jules Leleu, Burled Amboyna, Marble Top, Ivory Inlay, c.1925, 54 1/2 In. 5750.00
Cabinet, Kimbal & Cabus, Rosewood, Ebonized, Bronze, c.1875, 51 x 51 In. 12040.00
Cabinet, Lacquer, Painted Figures & Temple, Carry Handles, Japan, 17 x 9 x 11 In. 575.00
Cabinet, Lacquer, Palace Scenes, Gardens, 2 Doors, Fitted Interior, c.1830, 13 In. 1035.00
Cabinet, Lacquered Wood, Red, Rabbit, Squirrel Motif, 2 Drawers, Chinese, 19 3/4 In. . . 290.00
Cabinet, Limbert, Mahogany, 5 Drawers, Curved Apron, Original Dark Finish, 44 In. 2475.00
Cabinet, Liquor, Mahogany, Fruit Baskets, 6 Large, 2 Small Decanters, 34 In. 5460.00
Cabinet, Liquor, Mahogany, Marquetry, Gilt Flowers, Square Tapered Legs, 34 In. 5460.00
Cabinet, Liquor, Silver Structure Over Doors, Shelves, Steel Mounted, 45 In. 520.00
Cabinet, Louis XIV, Gilt Bronze Mounted, Marble Top, Doors, 39 x 46 x 17 In. 1150.00
Cabinet, Louis XV, Bibelot, Ebonized, Curved Plexiglas Panels, 67 1/2 In. 920.00
Cabinet, Louis XV, Central Glazed Door, Gilt Gesso Floral Design, 68 1/2 In. 2415.00
Cabinet, Louis XV, Gilt Bronze Mounted, Marquetry, 63 x 30 1/2 x 16 In. 2990.00
Cabinet, Louis XV, Shaped Square Top, Cast Metal Knee Sabots, 18 x 40 In. 430.00
Cabinet, Louis XVI, Mahogany, Rosewood Marquetry, Bronze, Millet, 70 x 27 In. 8000.00
Cabinet, Mahogany, 2 Glazed Doors, Satinwood Stringing, 1740s, 38 In. 1955.00
Cabinet, Mahogany, Bibelot, Clover Form, Gilt Metal Mounts, Cabriole Legs, 37 In. 1095.00
Cabinet, Mahogany, Marble Top, Brass, Fluted Column Front, 61 x 19 x 15 In. 1344.00
Cabinet, Mahogany, Metal Galleried Top, Swags, Garlands, 2 Drawers, 64 In. 980.00
Cabinet, Mahogany, Oval, 2 Parts, Mirror, Curved Glass Doors, 57 x 32 x 107 In. 1345.00
Cabinet, Mahogany, Rectangular Marble Top, Mesh Door, Rectangular Plinth, 34 In. 980.00
Cabinet, Mahogany, Rectangular Pagoda Top, 2 Doors, Scrolled Feet, 25 x 67 In. 600.00
Cabinet, Mahogany, Upper Glazed Door, Mirrored Frame, Lower Drawer, 64 1/2 In. 1840.00
Cabinet, Majorelle, Mahogany, Burl Walnut, Mounted Poppy, c.1900, 94 x 81 In. 7200.00
Cabinet, McCobb, Open Shelves, Brass Frame, 34 x 48 x 18 In., Pair 730.00
Cabinet, Molded Top, 2 Doors, Claw, Ball Feet, Mid 19th Century, 77 1/2 In. 2185.00
Cabinet, Music, Black Lacquer, Gallery, 2 Doors Over Door & Drawer, 61 x 24 In. 440.00
Cabinet, Music, Burl Walnut, Inlaid Glazed Door, Plinth Base, Casters, 1870s, 36 In. 860.00
Cabinet, Music, Chair Shape, 1 Glazed Door, Carrying Handles, 19 x 46 x 19 In. 865.00
Cabinet, Music, Cherry, Leaded Glass Door, Claw, Ball Feet, Italy, 82 In. 800.00
Cabinet, Music, G. Stickley, Gallery Top, Copper, Hammered, 47 1/2 In. 6325.00
Cabinet, Music, Mahogany, Bowfront Top, 1 Door, Cabriole Legs, 20 x 44 1/4 In. 80.00
Cabinet, Music, Mahogany, Painted Design, Divided Interior, 2 Doors, 30 x 43 In. 375.00
Cabinet, Napoleon III, Brass Mounted, Ebonized, Glazed Doors, 39 x 19 1/2 x 10 In. 460.00
Cabinet, Neoclassical, Rosewood, Ormolu Mounts, Marble, Gilt, 37 x 42 x 19 In. 5060.00
Cabinet, Oak, Applied Scroll, Leaf Design, 2 Drawers, 16 3/4 x 37 1/2 In. 260.00
Cabinet, Oak, Figural Corbels, Lower Door, 19th Century, 66 1/2 x 34 1/2 In. 1840.00
Cabinet, Oak, Scenic Carved Panel, c.1880, 27 x 15 x 77 In. 3360.00
Cabinet, Oriental Style, 2 Blind Doors, Mirror Back, Scenes, 1920, 65 x 38 In. 465.00
Cabinet, Ornate Iron Mounts, Bootjacked Sides, 19th Century, 41 x 38 In. 1090.00
Cabinet, Otto Prutscher, Mahogany, Carved, 4 Curved Legs, 1910, 61 In. 9600.00
Cabinet, P. Evans, Bar, Disc, 2 Semicircular Bronze Doors, Gold Patina, 71 In. 3450.00
Cabinet, P. Evans, Steel Door In Sunburst Design, 20 3/4 x 42 1/2 In. 3450.00
Cabinet, Phil Powell, Walnut, 4 Floor To Ceiling Posts, 3 Sliding Doors, 94 In. 2475.00

Cabinet, Pine, 2 Glazed Doors Over 4 Drawers, Wooden Pulls, 76 1/2 x 49 In. ` 800.00
Cabinet, Portfolio, Mahogany, Applied Scalloped Design, 56 x 52 3/4 In. 935.00
Cabinet, Queen Anne, Chinoiserie, Gilt, Black Japanned Ground, Scrolled Legs, 42 In. ... 25.00
Cabinet, Red Lacquer, 2 Doors, Shelf, Carved Plinth Base, Chinese, 37 x 25 x 21 In. 750.00
Cabinet, Red Lacquer, 2 Drawers, 2 Shelves, Rectangular Legs, 72 x 20 In. 1725.00
Cabinet, Red Paint Over Blue, Door, 4 Shelves, 30 x 16 x 31 1/2 In. 350.00
Cabinet, Red Paint, 75 Small Drawers, 7 Bins, 14 Deep Drawers, Red Paint, 108 In. 16000.00
Cabinet, Regency, Japanned, Lacquered, Drawer, 2 Doors, 36 x 33 x 18 In. 6900.00
Cabinet, Regency, Mahogany, Inlaid Ebony, Rectangular Top, 35 3/4 In., Pair 6040.00
Cabinet, Regency, Rosewood, Pair Of Brass Doors, Plinth Base, 34 1/2 x 13 In. 4485.00
Cabinet, Regency, Rosewood, Scagliola Marble Top, 13 Half Drawers, 42 In. 4140.00
Cabinet, Reliquary, Giltwood, Glazed Door, Velvet Lined Interior, Italy, 29 In. 2530.00
Cabinet, Renaissance Revival, Ebonized, Gilt, Marble Top, c.1870, 50 x 60 x 16 In. 5600.00
Cabinet, Renaissance Revival, Mahogany, Pink, Gray Mottled Top, Bun Feet, 104 In. 1095.00
Cabinet, Renaissance Revival, Variegated Red Marble Top, 2 Doors, 1870, 51 In. 4715.00
Cabinet, Renaissance Revival, Walnut, 1 Long Drawer, Step Molded Base, 48 In. 2530.00
Cabinet, Renaissance Revival, Walnut, 2 Sections, Arched, Putti, 67 x 35 x 20 In. 6900.00
Cabinet, Renaissance Revival, Walnut, Carved Columns & Panels, 1875, 55 x 61 In. 6440.00
Cabinet, Rohde, 2 Doors, Ivory Leather Facing, 2 Shelves, Brass, 42 x 40 x 17 In. 2875.00
Cabinet, Rohde, Burl, Black Enameled Interior, Herman Miller, 41 3/4 In. 1093.00
Cabinet, Rohde, Mahogany, 2 Doors, 3 Drawers, Herman Miller, 33 1/4 In. 920.00
Cabinet, Rosewood, Satinwood, Olive Wood, Gilt, 1870, 46 x 58 x 18 In. 5750.00
Cabinet, Sewing, Stickley Bros., Mahogany, 3 Drawers, Wooden Knobs, 27 In. 1725.00
Cabinet, Shop-Of-The-Crafters, Monk Pouring Wine Or Beer, 67 x 19 x 15 In. 1462.00
Cabinet, Smoking, G. Stickley, No. 89, Drawer, Iron Hardware, Cabinet, 29 In. 8250.00
Cabinet, Smoking, L. & J.G. Stickley, Oak, Rectangular Top, 1 Drawer, 1907, 29 In. 4890.00
Cabinet, Smoking, Lakeside, Chamfered Board Door, Strap Hinges, 12 x 34 In. 1495.00
Cabinet, Spice, 5 Drawer, Stenciling, Frank Tea & Spice Co., Named Spices, 26 In. 1705.00
Cabinet, Spice, Black Walnut, 15 Graduated Drawers, Porcelain Pulls, 14 3/4 In. 715.00
Cabinet, Spice, Oak, 6 Drawer, Labels, Porcelain Pulls, 12 1/2 x 8 In. 300.00
Cabinet, Spice, Pine, Wire Nail Construction, 15 Drawers, Wooden Knobs, 18 In. 2200.00
Cabinet, Spice, Scratch Beaded Door, 8 Drawers, 1700s, 13 1/2 x 13 x 7 1/2 In. 1750.00
Cabinet, Steel, Marble Top, Cupboard Doors, Shelves, Neogothic Border, 37 3/4 In. 5760.00
Cabinet, Step Back, Carved Walnut, Full Men, Women Caryatids, Floral, Fruit, 58 In. 7840.00
Cabinet, Stereo, Jens Risom, Teak, White Lacquered Interior, 2 Doors, 25 In. 1495.00
Cabinet, Stereo, Wood, 2 Drawers, Herman Miller, 41 3/4 x 40 x 17 In. 690.00
Cabinet, Stickley Bros., Oak, Quaint Furniture, 1 Door, Interior Shelves, 32 In. 5375.00
Cabinet, Tulipwood, Chevron Veneered Tambour Front, Open Shelf, 40 In. 3450.00
Cabinet, Tulipwood, Floral Marquetry Door, Gilt Bronze Mounted, 1900, 67 In. 4200.00
Cabinet, Tuscan, Inlaid Mahogany, Geometric, Drawers, 31 x 27 x 13 In. 4830.00
Cabinet, Victorian, Ebony, Classical Maiden Scene, Top-Shaped Feet, 44 x 16 In. 2300.00
Cabinet, Victorian, Maple Burl, Rectangular Top, Tapered Feet, 34 1/4 In. 9600.00
Cabinet, Walnut, A. Franz, 4 Drawers, 2 Linen Spindled Doors, Plank Top, 72 In. 4900.00
Cabinet, Walnut, Banded Top, Brass Bead Molded, Ebony, 2 Doors, 39 1/2 In. 4370.00
Cabinet, Walnut, Foliate Edge, Wool Floral Needlework Panel, On Stand, 52 In. 2895.00
Cabinet, Walnut, Marble Top, 1 Inlaid Drawer, Burl Panel Door, 45 x 49 In. 4950.00
Cabinet, Walnut, Marble Top, Mirrored Doors, Mid 19th Century, 29 1/2 In. 1035.00
Cabinet, Walnut, Pair Of Turned Columns, Molded Plinth, Pad Feet, 39 In. 5100.00
Cabinet, Walnut, Reverse Breakfront Form, 2 Glazed Doors, Shelved Interior, 73 In. 520.00
Cabinet, Walnut, Star & Heart Frieze, Paneled Door Over 2 Drawers, c.1740, 84 In. 4370.00
Cabinet, Wedding, Old Red Lacquer, 2 Doors With Moon Brasses, 42 x 18 x 70 In. 330.00
Cabinet, William IV, Mahogany, Pilasters, Doors, Reeded Feet, 35 1/2 x 55 x 17 In. 4600.00
Cabinet, Writing, Mahogany, Carved Pilaster Over Double Cabinet Doors, 46 In. 1380.00
Cabinet, Writing, Mahogany, Compartments, Early 19th Century, 16 x 11 x 12 1/2 In. ... 800.00
Cabinet-On-Stand, Chinese Export, Scarlet Lacquer, Gilt, 62 x 35 x 20 In. 5750.00
Cabinet-On-Stand, Clement Mere, Ebony, Gilt Leather, c.1925, 56 x 34 In. 58250.00
Cabinet-On-Stand, Louis XVI, Mahogany, Rosewood, Marquetry, 70 x 27 x 16 In. 8000.00
Cabinet-On-Stand, Mahogany, Ivory, Tortoiseshell, 1800s, 58 3/4 x 45 x 14 In. 4025.00
Cabinet-On-Stand, Painted Wood, England, 1930, 52 3/4 x 28 x 17 1/2 In. 5400.00
Cabinet-On-Stand, Tudor Revival, Painted, 2 Doors, 1850s, 49 1/2 x 27 x 17 In. 1495.00
Candlestand, Adjustable, Socket On Spring-Loaded Bracket, Wrought Iron, 60 In. 770.00
Candlestand, Black, Scalloped Edge, Tripod Legs, Conn., Late 1700s, 27 x 14 In. 9775.00
Candlestand, Cedar, Octagonal Shaft, White Paint, 19th Century, 31 x 12 1/2 In. 1615.00

Candlestand, Cherry, Birch, 1 Drawer, Dish Top, c.1800, 24 2/4 In. 2440.00
Candlestand, Cherry, Maple, Dish Top, Baluster-Turned Shaft, 1780, 27 1/4 x 16 In. 495.00
Candlestand, Cherry, Tiger Maple, 3 Legs, Oval Top, Refinished, 24 x 17 In. 355.00
Candlestand, Cherry, Tilt Top, Spider Base, 2-Board Top, Scalloped Corners, 27 In. 360.00
Candlestand, Cherry, Turned Pedestal, 3 Splayed Legs, 29 x 17 x 17 1/2 In. 200.00
Candlestand, Cherry, Urn Shape, Octagonal Top, Spider Base, 28 In. 605.00
Candlestand, Chippendale, Cherry, Snake Feet, Urn Column, 15 x 17 x 22 In. 260.00
Candlestand, Chippendale, Cherry, Square Top, Tripod Cabriole Legs, 15 x 14 In. 2990.00
Candlestand, Chippendale, Mahogany, Tilt Top, Birdcage, 27 x 26 In. 920.00
Candlestand, Chippendale, Mahogany, Tilt Top, Birdcage, Claw & Ball Feet, 27 In. 925.00
Candlestand, Chippendale, Mahogany, Tilt Top, Birdcage, Snake Feet, c.1790, 20 In. 3740.00
Candlestand, Chippendale, Maple, Ovolo Corners, Tripod Legs, 1780, 28 x 16 x 17 In. . . 575.00
Candlestand, Federal, Cherry, Baluster Pedestal, Red Wash, c.1810, 26 1/2 x 22 In. 385.00
Candlestand, Federal, Mahogany, Baltimore, c.1800, 28 x 22 3/4 x 15 3/4 In. 2860.00
Candlestand, Federal, Mahogany, Oval Top, Ring-Turned Pedestal, 1790, 17 x 29 In. 2415.00
Candlestand, Federal, Mahogany, Reeded Octagonal Top, Block Feet, 30 In. 5100.00
Candlestand, Floor, Tin, 2-Light, Adjustable Tray, Conical Base, c.1840, 27 In. 920.00
Candlestand, George III, Mahogany, Circular Top, Cabriole Legs, 32 1/4 x 18 In. 170.00
Candlestand, Gothic Revival, Bronze, Gilt, France, c.1850, 15 In. 195.00
Candlestand, Green Paint, Tripod Cabriole Legs, Pad Feet, 26 x 17 3/4 In. 2530.00
Candlestand, Hepplewhite, Cherry, Spider Legs, 27 x 19 x 19 3/4 In. 115.00
Candlestand, Hepplewhite, Maple, Canted Corners, Urn Shaft, 23 x 15 x 29 In. 360.00
Candlestand, Hepplewhite, Round Top, Scalloped Skirt, Square Legs, 28 x 18 In. 1320.00
Candlestand, Hepplewhite, Spider Legs, Square Top, Turned Post, 30 In. 175.00
Candlestand, Hepplewhite, Walnut, Tilt Top, Urn Pedestal, Tapered Legs, 28 1/2 In. 825.00
Candlestand, Mahogany, Birdcage, Vase-Form Pedestal, Cabriole Legs, 19 x 27 In. 1760.00
Candlestand, Mahogany, Cartouche Top, 3 Scrolled Legs, 1825, 29 In. 575.00
Candlestand, Mahogany, Carved, Leaf-Carved Standard, 1815, 28 1/2 x 27 In. 2400.00
Candlestand, Mahogany, Chestnut, Round Dish Top, Tilt Top, c.1820, 28 x 20 In. 415.00
Candlestand, Mahogany, Dish Top, Ball Standard, Snake Feet, c.1770, 28 In. 2200.00
Candlestand, Mahogany, Dish Top, Tripod Base, Pennsylvania, c.1770, 30 x 18 In. 1650.00
Candlestand, Mahogany, Round Dish Top, Tilting, England, c.1780, 26 1/2 x 27 In. 880.00
Candlestand, Mahogany, Tilt Top, Snake Feet, 1-Board Top, 28 In. 550.00
Candlestand, Maple, Beech, Adjustable, Tulip Finial, Tripod Base, c.1740, 35 In. 2310.00
Candlestand, Neoclassical, Tiger Maple, Tripod Base, c.1825, 28 1/2 x 17 x 22 In. 1380.00
Candlestand, Oak, Baluster Column, Round, 3 Cabriole Legs, 1740, 17 x 26 In. 865.00
Candlestand, Pine, Drop Leaf, 4 Spider Legs, Drawer, 17 x 12 1/2 In. 2200.00
Candlestand, Pine, Oak, X-Shape Base, Square Column, 1-Board Top, 15 x 16 x 25 In. . . 55.00
Candlestand, Poplar, Round Top, Tripod Base, Stained, c.1800, 28 1/2 x 19 In. 220.00
Candlestand, Queen Anne, Dish Top, Tripod Base, Snake Feet, c.1775 . . . . 1210.00
Candlestand, Queen Anne, Mahogany, Dish Top, Cabriole Legs, 20 1/2 x 14 3/4 In. 315.00
Candlestand, Queen Anne, Mahogany, Tilt Top, Round Top, Snake Feet, 28 x 17 In. 600.00
Candlestand, Renaissance Revival, Ebonized, Hoof Feet, c.1875, 32 x 19 In. 1000.00
Candlestand, Round Top, Vase, Ring-Turned Pedestal, Cross Base, 23 1/2 x 17 In. 3740.00
Candlestand, Shaker, Cherry, Circular Top, Cabriole Legs, Narrow Snake Feet, 14 7/8 In. . 1840.00
Candlestand, Urn-Carved Shaft, Square Top, Snake Feet, 25 1/4 In. 400.00
Candlestand, Walnut, Round Top, Bamboo-Turned Legs, Pa., c.1820, 27 x 17 In. 330.00
Candlestand, Walnut, Round, Tilt Top, Baluster Support, c.1820, 28 x 20 In. 330.00
Candlestand, Walnut, Tilt Top, Dish, Pad Feet, 26 1/2 In. 2430.00
Candlestand, Walnut, Tilt Top, Inlaid Shamrock Top, Snake Feet, 1800s, 27 In. 470.00
Candlestand, Walnut, Tripod Base, Cabriole Legs, Snake Feet, c.1800, 30 x 16 In. 2860.00
Candlestand, William IV, Mahogany, Round, Dish-Shape Marble Top, 30 x 16 In. 1035.00
Candlestand, Wrought Iron, Triangular Base, Pointed Feet, 19th Century, 36 In. 310.00
Candlestand, Wrought Iron, Tripod Base, 63 x 18 In., Pair 400.00
Canterbury, Burl Walnut, 1 Drawer, Turned Legs, Casters, 18 1/2 x 15 x 19 In. 1725.00
Canterbury, Edwardian, Rosewood, Brass Inlay, Turned Legs, 20 1/2 In. 3450.00
Canterbury, Ferguson Bros., Sheraton, Mahogany, 1 Drawer, Casters, 20 x 14 In. 165.00
Canterbury, Mahogany, 3 Compartments, 20th Century, 18 x 18 In. 220.00
Canterbury, Mahogany, 3 Sections Over 1 Drawer, Turned Feet, c.1800, 17 x 18 In. 470.00
Canterbury, Regency, Brass-Inlaid Drawer, Turned Legs In Caster, 20 x 16 In. 4800.00
Canterbury, Rococo, Rosewood, Walnut, Turned Columns, 1 Drawer, 21 1/2 In. 1380.00
Canterbury, Sheraton, Mahogany, Spindles Supported By Legs, c.1790, 23 x 21 In. 1210.00
Canterbury, Victorian, Ebonized, Burl, Drawer, Casters, 21 x 19 x 14 1/2 In. 1095.00

Canterbury, Victorian, Rosewood, 2 Shelves, Lyre-Form Dividers, 1850, 39 x 23 In. 1800.00
Canterbury, Victorian, Walnut, Drawer, Carved Pulls, 27 1/2 x 17 x 17 In. 490.00
Canterbury, William IV, Rosewood, Half Spindles, Beaded Border, 23 x 25 In. 9000.00
Cart, Serving, McCobb, Light Mahogany, Brass Frame, Calvin, 40 x 29 In. 240.00
Cassone, Baroque, Walnut, Carved, Paneled, Stylized Paw Feet, 27 x 57 1/2 x 23 In. 1725.00
Cassone, Italian Renaissance, Walnut, Bombe Stiles, Paw Feet, 1600s, 25 x 65 In. 1725.00
Cellarette, Chippendale, Mahogany, Brass Handles, 1900s, 31 x 27 In., Pair 1760.00
Cellarette, Federal, Mahogany, Grape, Leaf Finial, Rectangular Top, 1830, 27 In. 4500.00
Cellarette, Federal, Mahogany, Inlay, Hinged, Bail Handles, c.1790, 10 x 13 x 11 In. 635.00
Cellarette, Georgian, Mahogany, Hexagonal Top, Inlay, C-Scroll Brackets, c.1775 ...... 1650.00
Cellarette, Hinged Octagonal Opening, Lead Lined, Stand, 1775, 27 1/2 In. 3740.00
Cellarette, Jamestown Furniture Co., Chestnut, Floriform Brace, 5 x 17 x 7 In. 1265.00
Cellarette, Lift Lid, 8-Bottle Compartment, Square Legs, 25 1/2 x 15 1/4 In. 280.00
Cellarette, Mahogany, Brass Bound, Circular Top, England, c.1790, 17 x 27 In. 2990.00
Cellarette, Mahogany, Brass, Cover, Handles, Casters, England, c.1790, 25 x 18 In. 1430.00
Cellarette, Mahogany, Carved Bunches Of Grapes, Leaves, England, 1835, 19 In. 8400.00
Cellarette, Mahogany, Copper Lined, Handles, Winged Animal Legs, 1900, 28 1/2 In. 6600.00
Cellarette, Mahogany, Sarcophagus, Stand, Hinged Top, England, c.1790, 19 In. 1725.00
Cellarette, Regency, Ebony, Inlaid Mahogany, Fitted Interior, 1800s, 29 x 36 In. 9000.00
Cellarette, Regency, Mahogany, Sarcophagus Shape, 21 x 29 x 22 In. 8050.00
Cellarette, Rosewood Veneer, Inlaid Medallion Cover, Leather, England, 13 In. 495.00
Cellarette, Stickley Bros., Interior Shelves, Glass Holder, 51 x 22 x 13 1/2 In. 1095.00
Chair, Aalto, Birch Frame, Original Black Webbing, Arms, Artek, 24 x 36 In. 575.00
Chair, Adirondack, Horseshoe, Cane Seat & Back, Arms, 1930s 475.00
Chair, Aesthetic Revival, Mahogany, Carved Panel, Gray, Black, Gold, 36 In. 1380.00
Chair, Aesthetic Revival, Mahogany, Square Legs, Late 19th Century 1840.00
Chair, Aesthetic Revival, Polychrome, Carved Crest, Galleried Arms, 33 In. 400.00
Chair, Alexander Begge, 1 Orange, 1 Yellow, Plastic, Child, 1970, 20 1/2 In., Pair 460.00
Chair, American Restauration, Rosewood, Gondola Shape, Concave Crest, 32 In., Pair ... 5060.00
Chair, Arched Crest, Arched Wings, Outscrolled Arms, c.1810, 44 In. 9775.00
Chair, Arched Slat Back, Ring-Turned Stiles, Rush Seat, c.1750, 42 1/2 x 16 In. 2070.00
Chair, Arne Jacobsen, Ant, Rosewood Veneer, Chrome Tubular Base, 30 In., Pair 480.00
Chair, Arne Jacobsen, Egg, Upholstered, Swivel Chrome Base, 41 In. 3260.00
Chair, Arne Jacobsen, Swan, Upholstered, Aluminum Base, Fritz Hansen, 33 In. 1035.00
Chair, Arne Jacobsen, Swan, Wool, Chrome Base, 29 1/2 In. 1240.00
Chair, Arts & Crafts, Barrel, Harped Back, Slats To Floor, 42 x 24 x 20 In. 460.00
Chair, Arts & Crafts, Mahogany, 2 Vertical Slats, Saddle Seat, 16 x 39 x 17 In. 185.00
Chair, Arts & Crafts, Mahogany, Floral Crest Rail, Dark Finish, 36 x 22 In. 2360.00
Chair, Arts & Crafts, Morris, Flat Arms Over 2 Slats, Upholstered Back, Seat, Child's ... 175.00
Chair, Arts & Crafts, Oak, 4 Vertical Slats, Flat Arms, 1912, 38 1/2 In. 2760.00
Chair, Arts & Crafts, Oak, Stylized Floral Design, Woven Rush Seat, 1910, 37 In. 750.00
Chair, Baker Co., Black Enamel, Gold Trim, Leather Seat & Back, Arms, Pair 550.00
Chair, Banister Back, 3 Half-Spindle Splats, Rush Seat, Sausage-Turned Legs, 1740 ..... 410.00
Chair, Banister Back, Black Paint, Bulbous Front Stretcher, 46 In. 1440.00
Chair, Banister Back, Painted, Scalloped Crest, Serpentine Arms, c.1775, 49 In. 6900.00
Chair, Banister Back, Scalloped Crest, 3 Half-Spindle Back Splats, Rush Seat, 1740 ..... 410.00
Chair, Banister Back, Turned Front Stretcher, 3 Slats, Finials, Rush Seat, 42 In. 990.00
Chair, Banister Back, Turned Posts, 3 Slats & Yoke Crest, 19th Century 165.00
Chair, Barber Brothers Chair Co., Barrel, 3-Slat Arms, Upholstered, Mich., c.1908 ...... 6900.00
Chair, Baroque, Carved Crest, Upholstered Seat, X-Form Stretcher, 57 In. 805.00
Chair, Baroque, Walnut, Carved Scroll Supports, Leather Seats, Continental, Pair 260.00
Chair, Baroque, Walnut, Rectangular Back, Carved Crest, Pad Feet, Continental 260.00
Chair, Beech, Cartouche Backrest, Scroll Arms, Cabriole Legs, 1900, 38 1/2 In. 1150.00
Chair, Beech, Cartouche Backrest, Scroll Arms, Stuffed Seat, 38 1/2 In., Pair 2185.00
Chair, Beech, Leaf-Carved Arms, Padded Seat, Carved Square Feet, 46 In. 3680.00
Chair, Belter, Rococo, Laminated Rosewood, 42 In. ....*Illus* 5520.00
Chair, Belter, Rococo, Rosewood, Rosalie With Grapes, Burgundy Ground, 43 In.4400.00 to 7200.00
Chair, Bergere, Art Deco, Oak, Padded Back, Closed Arms, France, 20th Century 460.00
Chair, Bergere, Art Deco, Walnut, Arched, Velour, Closed Arms, c.1925, Pair 4025.00
Chair, Bergere, Empire, Curved Back, Closed Arms, Incurved Legs, 41 1/2 In. 2070.00
Chair, Bergere, Empire, Green Paint, Oval Cane Backrest, Closed Arms, 44 In., Pair 5520.00
Chair, Bergere, George III, Mahogany, Cane Seat, Closed Arms, 39 In., Pair 2990.00
Chair, Bergere, Louis Philippe, Mahogany, Rectangular Back, Closed Arms, 35 In. 1265.00

Furniture, Chair, Belter,
Rococo, Laminated
Rosewood, 42 In.

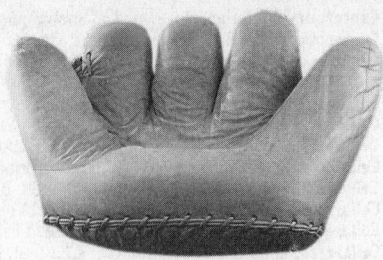

Furniture, Chair, De Pas, D'Urbins & Lomazzi,
Baseball Glove, Joe, Italy

Chair, Bergere, Louis XV, Beech, Carved, Cane Panels, Upholstered, Closed Arms 230.00
Chair, Bergere, Louis XV, Beech, Carved, Padded, Closed Arms, Pair 1840.00
Chair, Bergere, Louis XV, Beech, Serpentine Seat, Closed Arms, 25 1/2 In., Pair 4830.00
Chair, Bergere, Louis XV, Carved Flowers, Cabriolet Legs, Suede, Closed Arms, 41 In. .. 805.00
Chair, Bergere, Louis XV, Fruitwood, Barrel Back, Closed Arms, 20th Century 517.00
Chair, Bergere, Louis XV, Giltwood, Pierced Crest, Cabriole Legs, 42 In. 2990.00
Chair, Bergere, Louis XV, Ivory, Padded Back, Downcurved Closed Arms, Fluted Legs .. 546.00
Chair, Bergere, Louis XV, Mahogany, Giltwood, Carved, Muslin, Closed Arms, Pair 805.00
Chair, Bergere, Louis XV, Needlepoint, Cabriole Legs, Closed Arms, 19th Century 575.00
Chair, Bergere, Louis XV, Painted, Parcel Gilt, Carved, Cabriole Legs, Closed Arms 632.00
Chair, Bergere, Louis XV, Walnut, Scrolling Crest, Upholstered, 37 1/2 In. 2530.00
Chair, Bergere, Louis XV/Louis XVI, Ivory Paint, Closed Arms, Late 1800s 575.00
Chair, Bergere, Louis XVI, Carved Crest, Cane Back, Circular Legs, 31 In. 748.00
Chair, Bergere, Louis XVI, Fruitwood, Bouquet Center, Damask, Closed Arms 805.00
Chair, Bergere, Louis XVI, Giltwood, Beaded Crest, Closed Arms, 34 In., Pair 2530.00
Chair, Bergere, Louis XVI, Giltwood, Rectangular Back, Canvas, Closed Arms, Pair 2300.00
Chair, Bergere, Louis XVI, Walnut, Finials, Fluted Legs, Closed Arms, 40 In., Pair 2530.00
Chair, Bergere, Louis XVI, Walnut, Shield Back, Fluted Legs, Closed Arms, 36 In. 1725.00
Chair, Bergere, Louis XVI, Wood, Painted, Oval Back, Fluted Tapered Legs 345.00
Chair, Bergere, Restauration, Mahogany, Closed Arms, Cushioned Seat, 36 1/2 In. 1729.00
Chair, Biedermeier, Fruitwood, Black Inlay, Cabriole Legs, Velvet Seat, 33 In. 220.00
Chair, Biedermeier, Fruitwood, Concave Top Rail, Ebonized Splats, Arms, 33 In., Pair ... 750.00
Chair, Biedermeier, Fruitwood, Horizontal Splat, Padded Seat, Side, 1830, 36 In. 345.00
Chair, Biedermeier, Walnut, Bird's-Eye Maple Interior, 19th Century, 61 In. 1265.00
Chair, Biedermeier, Walnut, Compass Shape, Square Splayed Legs 800.00
Chair, Biedermeier, Walnut, Pierced Carved Crest, Padded Arms, c.1840 .... 690.00
Chair, Biedermeier, Walnut, Reclining, Arched Backrest, Padded Arms, 52 1/2 In. 1610.00
Chair, Birch Root, Natural Finish, Arms, Native, 1920 .... 2200.00
Chair, Black Lacquer, Pierced & Waisted Back, Cane Seat, Mother-Of-Pearl 690.00
Chair, Blue Anodized Finish, Velvet, 30 1/2 x 22 x 18 In. 1495.00
Chair, Bow Back, Bamboo-Turned Legs, Stretcher Base, Shield-Shaped Seat, 37 In. 330.00
Chair, Brass, Wrought Iron, Spiral Uprights, Legs, Arms, Italy 2300.00
Chair, Broad Crest Rail, Leather Seat, Angular Arms, Signed, 38 In., Pair 3737.00
Chair, Bruno Mathsson, Tan Webbing, Arms, 20th Century, 32 1/2 In. 375.00
Chair, C.F. Harsdorff, Giltwood, Upholstered Backrest, Padded Armrests, Pair 9600.00
Chair, Cane Backrest, Cane Seat, Padded Arms, Green Paint, 1760s 3960.00
Chair, Captain's, G. Nakashima, Walnut Dowel Legs, Woven Seat, 1955, 27 In. 1380.00
Chair, Cartouche Shaped Padded Backrest & Arms, Loose Cushion Seat, Pair 8625.00
Chair, Carved Acanthus Leaves, Cane Seat, Floral Upholstery On Arms, 45 In. 250.00
Chair, Carved, Painted, Oval Back, Cane Seat, Arms, France, 19th Century 470.00
Chair, Carved, Shallow Wings, Upholstered, Brass Tacks, Fringe, Arms, 51 x 19 In. 1095.00
Chair, Center Grotesque Mask Backrest, Paw Feet, 1880s, 42 1/4 In. 1150.00
Chair, Charles II, Beech, Leaf Carving, Arms, Early 18th Century 5000.00
Chair, Charles II, Oak, Wainscot, Tapestry Seat, Open Scrolled Arms 2190.00
Chair, Charles II, Walnut, Carved, Rectangular Back, Square Seat, Pair 9200.00
Chair, Charles Rennie McIntosh, Black Enameled Frame, Leather Seat, 59 In., Pair 675.00
Chair, Charles X, Mahogany, Acanthus Scrolled Arms, Leather Seat, 30 In. 2600.00

Chair, Charles X, Mahogany, Bronze Dore Mounted, Arms, Pair 2875.00
Chair, Chesterfield, Leather, Button Tufted, Arms, 28 In., Pair 575.00
Chair, Chesterfield, Leather, Button Tufted, Arms, 29 In., Pair 920.00
Chair, Chinese Official's, Brown, Crest, Square Legs, Shaped Arms, 44 In., Pair 550.00
Chair, Chinese Official's, Brown, Pierced Apron & Back Splat, Arms, 45 In., Pair 660.00
Chair, Chinese Official's, Red Brown, Carved Splat, Scroll Apron, Arms, 40 In., Pair 550.00
Chair, Chippendale Style, Mahogany, Upholstered, Burgundy Black, Red, Blue, 45 In. ... 275.00
Chair, Chippendale, Birch, Shaped Crest, Baluster Splat, New England, c.1790 .... 275.00
Chair, Chippendale, Carved Leaves, Pierced Back Splat, Cabriole Legs, Arms, 26 In. ... 575.00
Chair, Chippendale, Carved Shell Design, Drop-In Seat, Cabriole Legs, 38 In., Pair 3900.00
Chair, Chippendale, Cherry, Roundabout, Scrolled Arms, Rush Slip Seat, 32 x 17 In. 5175.00
Chair, Chippendale, Fireside, Upholstered, Straight Fluted Legs, 44 In. 475.00
Chair, Chippendale, Mahogany Finish, Wing-Back, Upholstered, Arms, 38 In. 225.00
Chair, Chippendale, Mahogany, Arched Crest, Gothic Splat, Beaded Legs, Pa., c.1775 ... 6325.00
Chair, Chippendale, Mahogany, Carved Crest, Pierced Splat, 38 x 18 1/2 In. 635.00
Chair, Chippendale, Mahogany, Carved Crest, Slip Seat, c.1770, 39 In., Pair 7800.00
Chair, Chippendale, Mahogany, Carved, Slip Seat, Claw & Ball Feet, c.1775, 39 In. 6600.00
Chair, Chippendale, Mahogany, Eared Crest, Floral Lattice Pierced Back, Arms 1380.00
Chair, Chippendale, Mahogany, Gothic Tracery Splat, Padded Seat, c.1875 .... 5750.00
Chair, Chippendale, Mahogany, Pierced Back Splat, Shaped Crest, 36 x 16 1/2 In. 345.00
Chair, Chippendale, Mahogany, Pierced Ribbonback, Carved Arms, Pair 385.00
Chair, Chippendale, Mahogany, Pierced Splat, Square Legs, Upholstered, 39 In., Pair 440.00
Chair, Chippendale, Mahogany, Rectangular Backrest, Side, England 1495.00
Chair, Chippendale, Mahogany, Ribbonback, Square Leg, Stretchers, 18th Century, Pair . 950.00
Chair, Chippendale, Mahogany, Ribbonback, Trapezoid Seat, Pa., c.1780, Pair 5225.00
Chair, Chippendale, Mahogany, Scroll Rail, Pierced Splat, Seat, 1800s 800.00
Chair, Chippendale, Mahogany, Serpentine Crest, Cabriole Legs, 1780, 17 In. 4800.00
Chair, Chippendale, Mahogany, Shell Crest, Claw & Ball Feet, 38 x 21 x 17 In. 1700.00
Chair, Chippendale, Mahogany, Wing, Upholstered, American, c.1770, 46 In. 3600.00
Chair, Chippendale, Pierced Splat, Square Legs, H-Stretcher, England 260.00
Chair, Chippendale, Serpentine Crest, Upholstered, Corner Bead, Arms 1100.00
Chair, Chippendale, Walnut, Carved Crest, Pierced Splat, Slip Seat, c.1770, 42 In. 9600.00
Chair, Chippendale, Walnut, Heart-Pierced Vase-Shape Splat, Pad Feet, 1780, 37 In. 1955.00
Chair, Chippendale, Walnut, Serpentine Crest, Knuckle Arms, Pierced Splat, c.1780 ..... 550.00
Chair, Chippendale, Walnut, Yoked Crest, Stiles, Virginia, 1775-1800, 37 3/4 In. 400.00
Chair, Circular Back, Blue, Red, Yellow Painted Bull's-Eye, 34 x 15 1/2 x 20 In. 140.00
Chair, Club, Art Deco, Original Cordovan Leather, Wooden Arms, 30 In. ......2810.00 to 4220.00
Chair, Club, Art Deco, Upholstered, Ebonized Wood, Short Block Feet, 1930s 690.00
Chair, Club, Art Moderne, Loose Cushion, Tan Leather, Sepia Trim, Padded Back, Arms . 1150.00
Chair, Club, Leather, Rectangular Back, Padded Overscroll Arms, Block Feet, Pair 2760.00
Chair, Club, Mahogany, Upholstered, Fabric, Dominique, c.1930 .... 9000.00
Chair, Club, William IV, Mahogany, Serpentine Seat, Uprights, Cabriole Legs, 49 In. 3680.00
Chair, Colonial Revival, Rosewood, Rolled Crest, Anthemion, Cane Seat, 34 In., Pair 5465.00
Chair, Concave Crest Rail, 4 Molded Spindles, Red, Green Paint, Arms, 1800 .... 1150.00
Chair, Corner, Arched Back Splat, Alligatored Surface, Paper Rush Seat, 30 1/4 In. 440.00
Chair, Corner, Cherry, Sloped, Sculpted Arms, Ball, Claw Feet, 33 x 27 x 24 In. 1400.00
Chair, Corner, Chippendale, Continuous Back & Arms, Drop In Seat 220.00
Chair, Corner, Chippendale, Elm, Comb Back, Pierced Splat, Scroll Crest, c.1760 .... 5975.00
Chair, Corner, Chippendale, Walnut, Cherry, Crest, Curved Arms, 32 1/2 In. 135.00
Chair, Corner, George I, Walnut, 2 Vase-Form Splats, Padded Seat, Curved Arm 2300.00
Chair, Corner, Mahogany, Carved Crest, Arms, Cabriole Legs, c.1750, 31 x 29 In. 7975.00
Chair, Corner, Mahogany, Continuous Arm, Vase-Form Splat, Pad Foot 2415.00
Chair, Corner, Maple, Painted, Pillow Back, New England, c.1780, 30 In. 345.00
Chair, Corner, Maple, Turned Stretchers & Legs, Scrolled Handrests, 31 1/2 In. 330.00
Chair, Corner, Queen Anne, Mahogany, Scrolled Arms, Mass., c.1780 .... 1925.00
Chair, Corner, Queen Anne, Mahogany, Vase Splat, Carved Armrests, 32 In. 2400.00
Chair, Corner, Sheraton, Mahogany, Old Dark Finish, Turned Legs, 17 x 30 3/4 In. 1100.00
Chair, Corner, Urn-Shaped Splats, Leather Seat, Arms, 30 In. 5060.00
Chair, Corner, Wicker, Old Burgundy Finish, Woven Cane Seat, 16 x 28 In. 250.00
Chair, Crossed Antlers Back, Arched Crest, Upholstered Seat, Splay Legs, Pair 5460.00
Chair, Curly Maple & Bird's-Eye Maple, Rolled Crest, Paper Rush Seat, 34 In., Pair 550.00
Chair, Curved Crest, Spindle Back, Arms, Chinese, 19th Century, 33 x 17 In., Pair 230.00
Chair, De Pas, D'Urbins & Lomazzi, Baseball Glove, Joe, Italy ....*Illus* 7875.00

Chair, Deck, Mahogany, Brass, Tag Reads First Class Only, Queen Elizabeth Style 250.00
Chair, Deck, Out-Turned Hook Arms, 18th Century, 34 In., Pair 4600.00
Chair, Drafting, Jorgen Rasmussen, Plywood Seat, Gray Enameled, 1973, 35 In. 80.00
Chair, Dutch Rococo, Walnut, Inlay, Vase-Form Splat, Chevron Banding 1495.00
Chair, E. Laverne, Lucite, Buttercup, Scooped Shaped Seat, Plastic Base, 1957 .... 2300.00
Chair, E. Wormley, Ash Laminated Frame, Brass Spindles, 19 x 30 1/2 In. 1035.00
Chair, Eames, Ash Veneer, Black Enameled Legs, Herman Miller, 28 In., Pair 620.00
Chair, Eames, Birch Plywood Frame, Pale Yellow Fabric, 26 In. 1840.00
Chair, Eames, Black Naugahyde, Aluminum Frame, 23 x 30 In..................... 375.00
Chair, Eames, Blue, Gray Fiberglass, Plastic Feet, 31 x 17 In., 4 .... 620.00
Chair, Eames, DCM, Molded Plywood, Herman Miller, c.1952, 29 In. 575.00
Chair, Eames, DKR, Leather, Steel Wire, Postman's Bag, Herman Miller, c.1952, 32 In. ... 1035.00
Chair, Eames, Eiffel Tower, White Fiberglass Shell, Black Base, 1960, Set Of 4 .... 1495.00
Chair, Eames, Gold Fiberglass, Shell, Black Steel Legs, Miller, 27 In. 185.00
Chair, Eames, Gray Fiberglass, Shell, Rope-Edge Shell, Zenith, 31 In. 240.00
Chair, Eames, Gray Fiberglass, Tubular Chrome Base, Herman Miller, 29 In. 500.00
Chair, Eames, La Fonda, Blue Vinyl, Herman Miller, c.1976, 30 In. 750.00
Chair, Eames, LAX, Fiberglass, Rubber, Steel, Zenith Plastics, c.1952, 26 In. 690.00
Chair, Eames, LCM, Birch Veneer, Molded Plywood, Chrome Steel Rod, Rubber, Pair ... 3910.00
Chair, Eames, Molded Birch Plywood, Original Finish, Herman Miller, 29 In., Pair 920.00
Chair, Eames, Molded Fiberglass, Tomato Red On Black, Steel Rods, 1950s 1500.00
Chair, Eames, Molded Plywood, Red, Child's, c.1945, 14 1/2 In. 7475.00
Chair, Eames, PKW, Wood, Steel, Swivel, Dowel Legs, Herman Miller, 32 3/4 In. 2645.00
Chair, Eames, Plywood Seat, Red Orange, Chrome Frame, 26 In. 920.00
Chair, Eames, Red Aniline Finish, Herman Miller, 26 1/2 x 22 x 26 In. 2300.00
Chair, Eames, SAX, Fiberglass, Rubber, Steel, Zenith Plastics, Herman Miller, 19 1/2 In. .. 490.00
Chair, Eames, Seat & Back On Chrome Tubular Frames, Pair 500.00
Chair, Eames, Tubular Chrome Frame, Herman Miller, 26 x 22 x 26 In. 500.00
Chair, Eames, Walnut Veneer, Tubular Metal Base, Herman Miller, 26 3/4 In. 340.00
Chair, Eames, Walnut, Black Enameled Legs, Herman Miller, 28 In. 365.00
Chair, Eames, White Fiberglass Shell, Black Legs, 1959, 31 In. 115.00
Chair, Eames, White Fiberglass Shell, Dowel Legs, Arms, Zenith, 29 1/4 In. 1610.00
Chair, Eames, White Laminate Shell, Black Wire Base, 26 In. 1035.00
Chair, Eames, Zenith, Elephant Gray Fiberglass, Shell, 24 x 30 In. 345.00
Chair, Easy, Beech, Upholstered Back, Padded Arms, Fluted Legs, 1780s, 37 In. 7200.00
Chair, Easy, Chrome, Black Cowhide Seat, Tilting Backrest, 25 In., Pair 635.00
Chair, Ecole De Nancy, Oak, Arched Crest, Pierced Back, Square Tapered Legs 260.00
Chair, Eero Aarnio, Tomato, Red Molded Fiberglass, Polyester, 54 x 44 x 27 In. 3105.00
Chair, Elizabethan Revival, Walnut, Needlepoint, American, 19th Century 90.00
Chair, Elm, Carved Back & Arms, Chinese, 19th Century, 37 x 19 In., Pair 400.00
Chair, Elm, Lacquer, Carved Back Splats, 45 x 20 1/2 In., Pair 805.00
Chair, Elm, Yoke Back, Carved Basket, Flowering Tree, 18th Century, Pair 2070.00
Chair, Elm, Yoke Back, Rectangular Splat, Serpentine Arms, Black, Pair 690.00
Chair, Empire, Mahogany, Black Leather, Paw Feet, Arms, 25 In., Pair 575.00
Chair, Empire, Mahogany, Black Upholstered Seat, Ball Feet, 31 1/2 In. 4900.00
Chair, Empire, Mahogany, Bowed Seat Frame, Saber Legs, Arms, 1900, 40 In. 1380.00
Chair, Empire, Mahogany, Scrolled Edge, Downswept Padded Arms, Saber Legs 2880.00
Chair, Eugene Schoen, White Linen, Laminated Wood Base, 32 In. 1350.00
Chair, Federal, Bamboo Turnings, Gilt Highlights, Painted, Black Ground, Arms, 1830 ... 440.00
Chair, Federal, Gilt Eagle Stenciled Crest, Rush Seat, 1830, Pair 720.00
Chair, Federal, Green Paint, Stenciled, New England, 1815, 34 In.................... 90.00
Chair, Federal, Mahogany, Arched Crest Rail, Lattice Splat, c.1810 .... 550.00
Chair, Federal, Mahogany, Leaf & Swag-Carved, Upholstered Seat, c.1810, 35 In. 2700.00
Chair, Federal, Maple, Leaf-Carved Splat, Cane Seat, Scrolled Arms, c.1915, 32 In. 1320.00
Chair, Figured Mahogany, Ormolu, Bowed Seat, Crest, Arms, Continental, 34 In. 465.00
Chair, Finn Juhl, Teak, Taupe Velour, Tapered Dowel Legs, 32 x 22 In., Pair 170.00
Chair, Flemish, Mahogany, Fruit Trees On Seat, Turned Ball Feet, Arms, 19 x 49 In. 1155.00
Chair, Flemish, Matte Brown, Cane Seat, Kaufmann's, Pittsburgh, 64 In. 165.00
Chair, Florence Knoll, Ivory Tweed, Bright Chrome Base, 31 x 28 1/2 x 30 In. 1460.00
Chair, Florence Knoll, Walnut Frame, Upholstered, Signed, 32 x 31 In. 1265.00
Chair, Folding, Anglo Colonial, Hardwood, Rail Over Slats, Curved Legs, 31 In. 175.00
Chair, Folding, Huntzinger, Carved Lions, Needlework Seat & Back, Arms, 35 1/2 In. ... 720.00
Chair, Frank Lloyd Wright, Aluminium, Hexagonal Seat, 1956, 33 x 27 x 24 In. 1070.00

Chair, Frank Lloyd Wright, Tufted Beige Wool, Henredon, 30 1/2 In. 550.00
Chair, French Provincial, Carved, Cabriole Legs, Upholstered, Molded Arms 385.00
Chair, French Provincial, Floral & Leaf, Carved Arms, Blue, Ivory, 34 x 22 In., Pair 900.00
Chair, French Provincial, Fruitwood, Rush Seat, Stretchers, Arms, 1880s, 36 In. 345.00
Chair, French Provincial, Fruitwood, Serpentine Rail, Rush Seat, 41 In., Pair 750.00
Chair, French Provincial, Walnut, Carved, Upholstered, Open Arms, 36 1/2 In. 935.00
Chair, Fruitwood, Crest Rail, Inlaid Bands, Spade Feet, c.1900, 42 In., Pair 1380.00
Chair, Fruitwood, Curved Arms, Cabriole Legs, Damask, Child's 2800.00
Chair, Fruitwood, Curving Tablet Crest Rail, Upholstered, Arms, 32 In. 460.00
Chair, Fruitwood, Incurved Back, Saber Front Legs, Arms, Early 20th Century 400.00
Chair, G. Nakashima, Walnut, Saddle Seat, Dowel Legs, 37 In., Pair 2645.00
Chair, G. Nelson, Coconut, Purple Woven Fabric, Tubular Legs, Miller, 33 In. 4025.00
Chair, G. Nelson, Coconut, Purple, Upholstered, Tubular Legs, 40 x 33 1/2 In. . .4000.00 to 5750.00
Chair, G. Stickley, 3 Horizontal Back Slats, Leather Seat, Child's 1840.00
Chair, G. Stickley, 5 Vertical Back Slats, Leather Cushion, Red Decal, 36 In. 2070.00
Chair, G. Stickley, Light Oak Finish, Flat Arm, Drop-In Seat, 38 x 31 x 36 In. 2310.00
Chair, G. Stickley, Mahogany, 3 Vertical Slats, Inset Rush Seat, 39 x 16 In. 4600.00
Chair, G. Stickley, Mahogany, Ladder Back, 4 Back Slats, Brown Leather, 37 In. 575.00
Chair, G. Stickley, Mahogany, Ladder Back, Cordovan Leather Seat, Arms, 37 In. 1495.00
Chair, G. Stickley, Mahogany, Leather Drop-In Seat, 45 1/2 x 17 In. 920.00
Chair, G. Stickley, No. 306, Mahogany, Ladder Back, 3 Horizontal Slats, 36 In. 430.00
Chair, G. Stickley, No. 314, Mahogany, Original Finish, Arms, 40 x 21 In. 980.00
Chair, G. Stickley, No. 318, Leather Spring Cushion, Arms, 37 In. 1725.00
Chair, G. Stickley, No. 335, Cube, 6 Vertical Slats, 26 x 28 x 29 In. 4900.00
Chair, G. Stickley, No. 342, Mahogany, Leather Seat, Child's, 13 x 23 In. 460.00
Chair, G. Stickley, No. 344, Mahogany, Original Finish, Arms, Child's 1035.00
Chair, G. Stickley, No. 354 1/2, Mahogany, 5 Vertical Slats, Leather Seat, 36 In. 1840.00
Chair, G. Stickley, No. 356, Mahogany, Leather Seat, Red Decal, 37 In. 1725.00
Chair, G. Stickley, No. 360, Mahogany, Arms, 37 x 27 x 20 1/2 In. 1150.00
Chair, G. Stickley, No. 376, Mahogany, 11-Slat Back, 9-Slat Arms, 49 In. 2910.00
Chair, G. Stickley, No. 388, Mahogany, Ladder Back, 20 x 21 x 37 In. 3450.00
Chair, G. Stickley, No. 390, Mahogany, 24 Spindles Under Each Arm, 39 In. 5465.00
Chair, G. Stickley, No. 394, Mahogany, Drop-In Seat, Red Decal, 17 x 40 In. 520.00
Chair, G. Stickley, No. 396, Mahogany, Brown Leather Seat, 32 x 46 In. 1495.00
Chair, G. Stickley, No. 2341, Mahogany, Leather Cushion, 37 In. 6900.00
Chair, G. Stickley, Oak, Concave Crest Rail, Adjustable Back, Flat Arms, 39 In. 6325.00
Chair, G. Stickley, Original Brown Finish, Drop Arm, 1914, 40 In. 9775.00
Chair, G. Stickley, Slat Back, Flat Arms, Leather Seat, 37 1/2 x 27 1/2 x 23 In. 575.00
Chair, Geometric Painted Crest Rail, Cross Splat, Cane Seat, 1820s, 34 In. 2990.00
Chair, George I, Mahogany, Floral Needlework, Cabriole Legs, 38 In., Pair 6900.00
Chair, George I, Mahogany, Waisted Rectangular Back, Over-Stuffed Seat, 1800s, Pair . . . 800.00
Chair, George I, Oak, Open Rectangular Back, Crest, Outcurved Arms, 1720, Child's 1035.00
Chair, George I, Walnut, Concave Top Rail, Cabriole Legs, Pad Feet, Pair 300.00
Chair, George I, Walnut, Scroll-Carved Top Rail, Compass Seat, Pair 3600.00
Chair, George I, Walnut, Vase-Form Splat, Drop-In Seat, Early 18th Century 375.00
Chair, George II, Mahogany, Neogothic Splat, Scrolled Crest Rail, c.1750 . . . . 980.00
Chair, George II, Mahogany, Serpentine Crest, Claw, Ball Feet, Arms, Child's, 25 In. 3300.00
Chair, George III, Beech, Cream Paint, Wheat Sheaf, Padded Seat, 35 In., Pair 2530.00
Chair, George III, Beech, Serpentine Seat, Upholstered, Arms, 1775, Pair 6000.00
Chair, George III, Black Paint, Padded Armrests, Upholstered Seat, Pair 5400.00
Chair, George III, Mahogany, Canted Backrest, Cabriole Legs, Arms, 36 In. 1840.00
Chair, George III, Mahogany, Carved Swag, Padded Seat, Spade Feet, Child's, 24 In. 490.00
Chair, George III, Mahogany, Carved, Shaped Crest, Arms, c.1770 . . . . 360.00
Chair, George III, Mahogany, Drop-In Cushion, Arms, 18th Century, 38 In. 1095.00
Chair, George III, Mahogany, Molded Top Rail, Stuffed Seats, H-Stretcher, 35 In. 630.00
Chair, George III, Mahogany, Openwork Splat, Slip Seat, Late 18th Century 345.00
Chair, George III, Mahogany, Padded Seat, Arms, 38 1/2 In., Pair 5290.00
Chair, George III, Mahogany, Ribbonback, Slip Seat, Side, Pair 400.00
Chair, George III, Mahogany, Rococo, 1 Drawer, Straight Fluted Legs, 30 In. 320.00
Chair, George III, Mahogany, Serpentine Crest, Slip Seat, 18th Century, Pair 1150.00
Chair, George III, Mahogany, Serpentine Top Rail, Ball, Claw Feet, 42 In. 520.00
Chair, George III, Mahogany, Shield-Shape Backrest, Balloon Seat, 41 1/2 In. 980.00
Chair, George III, Mahogany, Trapezoid Stuffed Seat, Canted Back, Arms, 39 In. 635.00

Chair, George III, Mahogany, Upholstered Backrest, Scrolled Arms, c.1770 . . . . 1610.00
Chair, George III, Mahogany, Upholstered Seat, Padded Armrests, Pair 6000.00
Chair, George III, Mahogany, Upholstered Seat, Pierced Brackets, 1765, Pair 7800.00
Chair, George III, Oak, Rectangular Back, Crest Rail, Dished Seat, 1800, Pair 975.00
Chair, George III, Walnut, Carved, Pierced Floral Splat, Cabriole Legs, 1890, Pair 1840.00
Chair, George IV, Beech, Stained, Pierced Splat, Scrolled Arms, 34 1/2 In. 145.00
Chair, George IV, Leaf-Carved Concave Top Rail, Tapered Reeded Legs, 1830 . . . . 9600.00
Chair, George IV, Mahogany, Cane Back, Seat, Tapered Legs, Library, 39 In., Pair 4600.00
Chair, George IV, Mahogany, Tufted Back, Brass, c.1825, 41 3/4 In. 7200.00
Chair, Georgian, Carved Crest, Pierced Splat & Arms, Cabriole Legs, Dolphin Feet 550.00
Chair, Georgian, Carved Crest, Pierced Splat, Cabriole Legs, Claw & Ball Feet 1320.00
Chair, Georgian, Mahogany, Balloon Seat, Cabriole Legs, Carved Arms, c.1740 . . . .   935.00
Chair, Georgian, Mahogany, Carved Crest, Cabriole Legs, Shell Knees, c.1760, Pair 1210.00
Chair, Georgian, Mahogany, Crest, Scroll Arms, Cabriole Legs, Slipper Feet, c.1740 . . . . . 2750.00
Chair, Georgian, Mahogany, Pierced Back Splat, 4 Legs, Padded Seat, Pair 260.00
Chair, Georgian, Mahogany, Scroll-Carved Crest, Cabriole Legs, 19th Century 460.00
Chair, Georgian, Mahogany, Serpentine Crest Rail, Pad Feet, 1860 . . . . 2760.00
Chair, Georgian, Mahogany, Shaped Crest, Serpentine Arms, Stiles, Bowed Front, 1730 . . 2640.00
Chair, Gerrit Reitveld, Zigzag, Elm, 1934 . . . . .3000.00 to 4600.00
Chair, Gerrit Rietveld, Crate, Dark Mahogany Finish, 1934, 29 x 23 x 22 In. 5175.00
Chair, Giltwood, Cane Back, Ribbon, Fluted Columns, Late 19th Century 115.00
Chair, Giltwood, Padded Back, Floral & Shell Crest, Padded Arms, 1860, 44 In., Pair 2070.00
Chair, Gothic Revival, Arched Back, Quatrefoils, Padded Seat, France, 45 In, Pair 865.00
Chair, Gothic Revival, Mahogany, Carved, Pierced Back, Solid Seat, Victorian, Pair 920.00
Chair, Gothic Revival, Mahogany, Pierced Backrest, Cane Seat, 41 In., Pair 3680.00
Chair, Gothic Revival, Oak, Decorated Backrest, Pierced, 49 In., Pair 1265.00
Chair, Gothic Revival, Rosewood, Carved Crest, Arms, Upholstered, 1860, 41 1/2 In. 3335.00
Chair, Gothic Revival, Serpentine Crest, Tapestry, Late 19th Century, Pair 360.00
Chair, Gothic Revival, Spindle Back, Original Finish, 37 x 19 In.   225.00
Chair, Gothic Revival, Walnut, Carved, Gilt, Needlepoint Back, Arms, Continental 525.00
Chair, Gothic Revival, Walnut, Turned Legs, Scalloped Apron, Seat Opens, 44 In. 220.00
Chair, Green Paint, Splint Seat, Mushroom Finials, Turned Arms, 1800, 36 In. 170.00
Chair, H. Bertoia, Black Enameled Wire, Gold, Orange, Knoll, 30 x 21 x 17 In. 140.00
Chair, H. Bertoia, Diamond, Black Enameled Wire Frame, 27 x 44 x 33 In. 460.00
Chair, H. Bertoia, Diamond, Red Fabric, White Enameled, Knoll, 30 3/4 In. 255.00
Chair, H. Bertoia, White Coated Wire, Avocado Green Seat, 21 x 30 1/2 In. 345.00
Chair, Hall Stand, Arts & Crafts, Beveled Mirror, Medium Dark Finish, 77 x 16 In. 1010.00
Chair, Harden, Mahogany, Original Finish, Leather Seat, Arms, 37 x 29 x 23 In. 800.00
Chair, Hardoy, Bonet & Kurchan, Sling, Leather, Knoll, 35 x 31 x 28 1/2 In. 290.00
Chair, Heart-Pierced Crest, Crown, Out-Splayed Arms, Gilt Leaf Design, 44 In. 4315.00
Chair, Heather Helfrich, Pine, Landscape Crest, Fox, Child's, 18 x 14 x 12 In. 130.00
Chair, Hepplewhite, Floral Carved Crest, Trapezoid Slip Seat, 1795, 38 x 19 In. 400.00
Chair, Hepplewhite, Mahogany, Carved Back, Patera & Urn Splat, c.1795, 17 1/2 In. 4600.00
Chair, Hepplewhite, Mahogany, Carved, Shieldback, Upholstered, Arms, c.1876, 37 In. . . .   115.00
Chair, Hepplewhite, Mahogany, Fruitwood Inlay, Back Splat, H-Stretcher, 34 In. 995.00
Chair, Hepplewhite, Mahogany, Shieldback, Needlepoint Seat, 37 In. 220.00
Chair, Hepplewhite, Mahogany, Shieldback, Needlepoint Seat, Stretchers, c.1800 . . . .   275.00
Chair, Hepplewhite, Satinwood, Floral Bouquet, Swags, Spade Feet, Arms, 1900 . . . . 2070.00
Chair, Heywood-Wakefield, Oak, 3-Slat Back, 38 x 19 x 16 In. 115.00
Chair, Hickory, White Paint, 7 Spindles, Splint Seat, Arms, 34 x 16 In., Pair 805.00
Chair, Horn, Walnut Frame, Western, Mid 19th Century, 49 x 36 x 32 In. 2145.00
Chair, Horn, With Headrest, Arms, 48 x 38 x 27 In. 1570.00
Chair, Irish Chippendale, Mid 19th Century, 37 1/2 In. 2990.00
Chair, J. & J.W. Meeks, Rosewood, Laminated, Hawkins, 1865, 43 x 18 In. 3360.00
Chair, J. Hovelskov, Harp, Blond Wood Frame, Strung Rope Seat, 53 x 38 In. 1725.00
Chair, J.H. Travis, Walnut, Folding, Upholstered Panel Seat & Back, 1870, 35 In. 520.00
Chair, J.M. Young, Drop-In Seat Cushions, Original Finish, 38 1/2 x 37 In. 3335.00
Chair, J.M. Young, Mahogany, 5 Vertical Back Slats, Original Cushion, Arms, 29 In. 575.00
Chair, Jacobean, Oak, Leaf-Carved Arms, Turned Stiles, Cane Seat, Spiral Legs, 1890 . . .   495.00
Chair, Jacobean, Walnut, Carved, Crouching Lion, Late 1800s 405.00
Chair, Jeliff, Walnut, Rosewood, Ornate Female Busts, 1870 . . . .   560.00
Chair, Jens Risom, Birch Frame, Tan Webbed Seat, Knoll, 1948, 29 In., Pair 450.00
Chair, Jens Risom, Scissors, Birch Frame, Upholstered Cushions, 29 In. 1045.00

Chair, John Dunnigan, Mahogany, Aluminum Inlay, 1983, 34 x 27 x 25 In. 3450.00
Chair, John Jeliff, Walnut, Female Busts, Portrait Crests, Arms, 1870, Pair 2070.00
Chair, Jorgen Rasmussen, Wool, Aluminum Base, 37 3/4 In. 840.00
Chair, Kochs, Walnut, Stork Heads, Satinwood Inlay, Bleeder, Signed, 1888 . . . . 5050.00
Chair, Koloman Moser, Beech, Plywood, Bent, Arms, c.1904 . . . . 5175.00
Chair, L. & J.G. Stickley, 3 Vertical Back Slats, Brown Leather Seat, 35 x 16 In. 535.00
Chair, L. & J.G. Stickley, Cushions, Open Arm, Handcraft Decal, 42 In. 4125.00
Chair, L. & J.G. Stickley, Mahogany, 8 Spindles, Rush Seat, 18 x 36 In. 750.00
Chair, L. & J.G. Stickley, Mahogany, Burnt Orange Cushion, Arms, 40 In. 1380.00
Chair, L. & J.G. Stickley, No. 330, 8 Spindles, Original Leather Seat, 16 x 36 In. 460.00
Chair, L. & J.G. Stickley, No. 332, Mahogany Finish, 36 1/2 x 17 x 16 In. 375.00
Chair, L. & J.G. Stickley, No. 446, Mahogany, Ladder Back, Brown Leather, 40 In. 2185.00
Chair, L. & J.G. Stickley, No. 1160, Mahogany, 6 Vertical Slats, 32 x 40 In. 1265.00
Chair, L. & J.G. Stickley, Oak, 8 Spindles, Leather Seat, 36 In. 460.00
Chair, Ladder Back, 3 Arched Slats, Raised Rings On Arms, Child's, 21 1/2 In. 190.00
Chair, Ladder Back, 3 Slats, Rush Seat, Arms, New England, c.1800 . . . . 110.00
Chair, Ladder Back, 3 Slats, Webbed Seat, Brown Paint, Child's, c.1790 . . . . 385.00
Chair, Ladder Back, 5 Graduated Slats, Rush Seat, Pa., 1770, 46 In. 3080.00
Chair, Ladder Back, Arts & Crafts, 5 Slats Each Arm, Leather Cushion, 41 1/2 In. 1150.00
Chair, Ladder Back, Cherry & Oak, 5 Slats, Ring Rear, Front Stiles, Stretchers, 1780 . . . . 110.00
Chair, Ladder Back, Sewing, Short Turned Legs, 3 Finials, 31 3/4 In. 170.00
Chair, Ladder Back, Weaver's, 2 Arched Slats, Turned Feet, Splint Seat, 38 In. 770.00
Chair, Ladder Back, Yellow Pine, Spire, Rush Seat, 1800, 46 1/2 In., Pair 1265.00
Chair, Leafy Scrolled Frame, Upholstered Back, Padded Arms, Pair 5700.00
Chair, Leather, Slope Back, Ship Wheel Each Side, Platform Frame, 35 In. 1090.00
Chair, LeCorbusier, Leather, Tubular Steel Frame, 27 1/2 In. 1380.00
Chair, Lifetime, Brown Leather Cushions, 40 x 32 1/2 x 37 1/2 In. 2645.00
Chair, Limbert, Mahogany, 3 Vertical Back Slats, Drop-In Seat, 37 x 22 1/2 In. 620.00
Chair, Limbert, Mahogany, Tapered Posts, Brown Leather Seat, 42 1/4 In. 2300.00
Chair, Limbert, No. 895, 2 Horizontal Slats, Original Tray, 18 x 37 In. 800.00
Chair, Limbert, Oak, Cutout Back, Slanted Arms, Dark Finish, 26 x 34 In. 9775.00
Chair, Lolling, Chippendale, Mahogany, Scalloped Back, Square Legs 275.00
Chair, Lolling, Elizabethan Revival, Spool Style, Yellow Damask, Baltimore, 1840 . . . . . . 1650.00
Chair, Lolling, Federal, Mahogany, Flame-Stitch Back, Seat, Tapered Legs 300.00
Chair, Lolling, Federal, Mahogany, Inland, Kittinger 990.00
Chair, Lolling, Mahogany, Carved Knees, Claw & Ball Feet 660.00
Chair, Louis Philippe, Fruitwood, Provincial, Arched Top, Woven Seat, 32 In., Pair 1035.00
Chair, Louis Philippe, Mahogany, Arched Top Rail, Scroll Arms, Padded, 36 In. 2530.00
Chair, Louis Philippe, Mahogany, Upholstered, Arms, 36 In., Pair 3410.00
Chair, Louis XIII, Ivory, Outcurved Scroll Arms, Over-Stuffed Seat 290.00
Chair, Louis XIII, Walnut, Rectangular Back, Scroll Arms, H-Stretcher 220.00
Chair, Louis XIV, Walnut, Brown, Upholstered, Arms, Paw Feet, 44 In. 2070.00
Chair, Louis XIV, Walnut, Carved Scrolled Armrests, Scrolled Legs, 46 In. 575.00
Chair, Louis XIV, Walnut, Needlework Back, Seat, Scrolled Arms, 43 1/2 In. 920.00
Chair, Louis XIV, Walnut, Rectangular Backrest, Figures Dancing, Birds, Arms, Pair 2300.00
Chair, Louis XIV, Walnut, Rectangular Padded Backrest, Padded Seat, Arms, 45 In. 3450.00
Chair, Louis XIV, Walnut, Rectangular Padded Seat, Floral Needlework, Arms, 48 In. 290.00
Chair, Louis XV Style, Beech, Arch Rail, Floral Crest, Leather, Arms, 33 1/2 In. 1840.00
Chair, Louis XV Style, Beech, Carved, Foliate Carved Crest, Upholstered, Pair 2875.00
Chair, Louis XV Style, Gilt Beech, Padded Arms, Seat, 37 1/2 In., Pair 3220.00
Chair, Louis XV Style, Mahogany, Padded Back, Seat, Scroll Arms, 39 In. 1380.00
Chair, Louis XV Style, Pickled Beech, Cabriole Legs, Arms, 36 1/2 In. 1035.00
Chair, Louis XV Style, Polychrome, Padded Back, Scrolled Arms, 38 In. 1150.00
Chair, Louis XV Style, Walnut, Balloon Back, Tufted & Pleated, Arms, 37 In. 230.00
Chair, Louis XV Style, Walnut, Beech, Leaf Crest, Serpentine Frame, 37 1/2 In. 635.00
Chair, Louis XV Style, Walnut, Carved Crest, Padded Back, Cabriole Legs, Pair 690.00
Chair, Louis XV Style, Walnut, Carved Molding, Upholstered, Victorian 240.00
Chair, Louis XV, Beech, Cane Back, Flowers, Upholstered Seat, 1740s, Pair 9000.00
Chair, Louis XV, Beech, Cartouche Padded Back, Seat, 37 x 27 x 21 In. 5060.00
Chair, Louis XV, Beech, Carved, Cartouche Back, Arms, c.1750 . . . . 2645.00
Chair, Louis XV, Beech, Crested Back, Floral Shell, Cabriole Legs, Arms, 44 In. 2300.00
Chair, Louis XV, Beech, Padded Back, Serpentine Frame, 38 1/4 In. 5290.00
Chair, Louis XV, Beech, Padded Back, Shell, Cabriole Legs, Arms, 36 1/2 In. 1495.00

Chair, Louis XV, Beech, Serpentine Seat, Cabriole Legs, 36 In., Pair 1610.00
Chair, Louis XV, Giltwood, Rectangular Back, Cabriole Legs, Flower Heads, Arms 170.00
Chair, Louis XV, Mahogany, Maiden & Cherub Harvesting Grapes, 44 In. 3450.00
Chair, Louis XV, Mahogany, Padded Back, Arms, Shell Frame, 39 1/4 In. 2760.00
Chair, Louis XV, Walnut, Beech, Outcurved Arms, Cabriole Legs, 36 In. 1265.00
Chair, Louis XV, Walnut, Cartouche Backrest, Padded Arms, 35 1/2 In. 2760.00
Chair, Louis XV, Walnut, Needlework Back, Foliate Seat Frame, Arms, 44 In. 980.00
Chair, Louis XV, Walnut, Scrolled Crest, Floral Needlework, Arms, 37 In. 400.00
Chair, Louis XV, Walnut, Serpentine Rail, Padded Seat, Cabriole Legs, Arms, 40 In. 1610.00
Chair, Louis XV, Walnut, Shell Top Rail, Cabriole Legs, Child's, 26 1/2 In. 520.00
Chair, Louis XVI Style, Beech, Padded Back, Crest, Serpentine Front, Arms, Pair 632.00
Chair, Louis XVI Style, Mahogany, Padded Back, Seat, Tapered Legs, 28 In., Pair 375.00
Chair, Louis XVI Style, Walnut, Molded Crest Rail, Padded Back, Seat, 38 1/2 In. 2990.00
Chair, Louis XVI, Beech, Bead Oval Back, Bowed Seat Frame, Arms, 37 In., Pair 1610.00
Chair, Louis XVI, Beech, Floral, Arched Top Rail, Cabriole Legs, Arms, 35 In. 980.00
Chair, Louis XVI, Beech, Molded Crest Rail, Cabriole Legs, Arms, Padded, 34 In. 750.00
Chair, Louis XVI, Beech, Padded Back, Bowed Seat Frame, 36 In., Pair 4600.00
Chair, Louis XVI, Beech, Padded Back, Leaves, Scrolled Legs, 45 In., Pair 7200.00
Chair, Louis XVI, Floral Bouquet Crest, Circular Padded Back, Arms, 37 In., Pair 2760.00
Chair, Louis XVI, Giltwood, Crest Rail, Curved Arms, Fluted Legs, Pair 3000.00
Chair, Louis XVI, Giltwood, Curved Arms, Muslin, Tapered Fluted Legs, Pair 3100.00
Chair, Louis XVI, Giltwood, Rectangular Back, Tapered, Fluted Legs, Arms 1380.00
Chair, Louis XVI, Giltwood, Turned & Fluted Feet, 2 Birds Tapestry, Pair 980.00
Chair, Louis XVI, Giltwood, Upholstered, Cabriole Legs, Arms, France, 1800s 660.00
Chair, Louis XVI, Green Paint, Oval Backrest, Circular Legs, 1790, Pair 920.00
Chair, Louis XVI, Mahogany, Padded Rectangular Back, Bun Feet, Arms, 42 In. 1725.00
Chair, Louis XVI, Ribbon Top, Oval Back, Gold & White Paint, Upholstered, Pair 1430.00
Chair, Louis XVI, Walnut, Padded Rectangular Back, Floral Scrolls, 37 3/4 In. 1495.00
Chair, Lounge, Florence Knoll, Dark Brown Leather, Chrome Frame, 28 In., Pair 1840.00
Chair, Lounge, G. Nakashima, Walnut, Hickory Spindles, 33 1/2 x 32 In. 3738.00
Chair, Lounge, G. Nakashima, Walnut, Hickory Spindles, Webbed Seat, 32 In. 4500.00
Chair, Lounge, G. Nakashima, Walnut, Slatted Back, Dowel Legs, 29 3/4 In. 20250.00
Chair, Lounge, Macassar & Sycamore, Curved Back, Zigzag Upholstered, Pair 3680.00
Chair, Lounge, Mahogany Stained Frame, Tweed Upholstered Cushions, 31 In. 980.00
Chair, Lounge, Richard Meiers, Leather, Wood Base, 28 x 73 In. 13500.00
Chair, Lounge, Richard Schultz, White Enameled Metal, Tubular Base, Knoll, 30 In. 900.00
Chair, Lounge, Robsjohn-Gibbings, Mahogany, Dark Brown Cushion, 30 In. 575.00
Chair, Lounge, Thayer-Coggin, Vinyl, Arched Legs, 28 x 26 In. 1010.00
Chair, Lounge, Tobia Scarpa, Black Leather Cushion, Rosewood Frame, Knoll, 28 In. . . . 690.00
Chair, Lounge, V. Kagan, Textural Green Striped Fabric, 27 x 31 In. 1380.00
Chair, Lounge, Vinyl Upholstered Frame, Black Cushions, 37 x 60 x 50 In. 560.00
Chair, Lounge, Walnut, Cone Shape, Brown Ultra Suede Cushion, Signed, 33 3/4 In. 4900.00
Chair, Lounge, Wegner, Orange, Upholstered, 27 x 25 In., Pair 375.00
Chair, Lounge, Wolfgang Hoffman, Red Leatherette, Chrome Studs, Howell, 36 In. 990.00
Chair, Lyre Back, Ivory, White Pinstripes, Red Ground, Pa., 17 In. 715.00
Chair, MacArthur, Tubular Aluminum Frame, Velvet, Arms, 24 x 21 In. 1495.00
Chair, Mahogany, Arched Backrest, Downswept Armrests, Drop Seat, c.1820, Pair 5760.00
Chair, Mahogany, Arched Crest, Pierced Back Rail, Slip Seat, 1820, 32 In. 420.00
Chair, Mahogany, Arched Top Rail, Padded Backrest, Scroll Arms, Bowed Seat, 36 In. . . . 2530.00
Chair, Mahogany, Balloon Back, Back Braces, Carved Fruit, Upholstered Seat 2295.00
Chair, Mahogany, Cane, Tufted Leather Seat, Saber Legs 2760.00
Chair, Mahogany, Cloth Seat, Turned Legs, Stretchers, Caribbean, 72 In. 1150.00
Chair, Mahogany, Lyre-Form Splat, Caryatid Arm Supports, Bronze Paw Feet, 1830s 2185.00
Chair, Mahogany, Metamorphic, Trapezoid Seat, Legs Joined By Shelf, 35 3/4 In. 1725.00
Chair, Mahogany, Needlework Seat & Back, Outscrolled Arms, Dated 1776 . . . . 5400.00
Chair, Mahogany, Out-Scrolled Arms, Vase & Ring Front Legs, c.1820, 18 1/2 In. 3450.00
Chair, Mahogany, Padded Back, Dolphin Arms, Padded Seat, Saber Legs, 36 In. 1265.00
Chair, Mahogany, Padded Rectangular Back, Saber Legs, Arms, 38 1/2 In., Pair 6615.00
Chair, Mahogany, Rolled Arms Continue To Crest, Upholstered, Tacks, 33 In., Pair 220.00
Chair, Mahogany, Rush Lift Seat, Square Legs, Arms, Child's, 19th Century 800.00
Chair, Mahogany, Serpentine & Looped Crest Rail, Trapezoid Seat Frame, 37 In. 2760.00
Chair, Mahogany, Serpentine Crest, Arched Wings, Loose Cushion, c.1780, 46 1/2 In. . . . 9200.00
Chair, Mahogany, Serpentine Crest, Pierced Gothic Splat, 1775, 38 In. 1870.00

Chair, Mahogany, Shaped Wings, Scrolled Arms, Shell-Carved Legs, 46 In. 980.00
Chair, Mahogany, Shieldback, Carved Foliage, Upholstered, S. Badlam, 1751, 37 In. 1700.00
Chair, Mahogany, Shieldback, Fan Inlay, Serpentine Rail, Tapered Legs, c.1800 . . . .   330.00
Chair, Mahogany, Shieldback, Inlay, Swags, Ruffles, Upholstered Seat, 39 In. 5750.00
Chair, Mahogany, Spindle, Arms, 1750, 40 3/4 x 24 x 17 1/2 In. 3360.00
Chair, Mahogany, Stylized Lyre Plate, Caryatid Arm Supports, 19th Century 2185.00
Chair, Mahogany, Tufted Loose Cushion Seat, Leather, c.1825 . . . .   2645.00
Chair, Mahogany, Turned Legs, Stretchers, Upholstered Seat & Back, 48 In. 140.00
Chair, Mahogany, Turned, Cane Seat, North Carolina, 18th Century, 42 x 14 In. 785.00
Chair, Mahogany, U-Shaped Crest, Pierced Backrest, Arms, Upholstered Seat, 1820s 5400.00
Chair, Mahogany, Upholstered Back, Seat, Gold Wreath Design, 37 In., Pair 990.00
Chair, Mahogany, Upholstered Seat & Back, Gilt Classical Designs, c.1900, 38 In. 430.00
Chair, Mahogany, Upholstered Seat, Ormolu Trim, Saber Legs, 17 1/2 x 37 In. 110.00
Chair, Mahogany, Wing, Square Beaded-Edge Legs, Late 19th Century 935.00
Chair, Maple, 4 Graduated Slats, Rush Seat, Ball Feet, Pa., 1770, 42 1/2 In. 7700.00
Chair, Maple, Ash, Slat Back, Rush Seat, Ring-Turned Arms, 23 x 7 In. 920.00
Chair, Maple, Ash, Turned, 4 Arched Slats, Mushroom Handholds, 45 In. 4600.00
Chair, Maple, Black Paint, Rush Seat, 5 Curved Slats, Delaware Valley, 1700, Pair 10500.00
Chair, Maple, Serpentine Crest, Vase-Shape Splat, Rush Seat, N.Y., c.1760, 40 In. 2990.00
Chair, Maple, Turned, Rush Seat, 1790, 39 x 20 x 13 1/2 In. 112.00
Chair, Maple, Vase-Form Splat, Trapezoid Rush Seat, Red Finish, Arms, 1770, 46 In. 33350.00
Chair, Marcel Wassily, Black Leather Seat, Tubular Steel Frame, 31 x 29 In. 320.00
Chair, Marcel Wassily, Canvas Seat, Tubular Steel Frame, Knoll, 31 x 29 In. 375.00
Chair, McCobb, Mahogany, Reupholstered Seat, Side, 18 x 17 1/2 In. 575.00
Chair, McCobb, Orange Fiberglass, Swivel, Aluminum Base, 33 1/2 In. 450.00
Chair, Ming Design, Wooden Side, Splat Back, Early 19th Century, Pair 345.00
Chair, Moravian, Heart Cutout, Yellow Paint, Continental, c.1800 . . . .   165.00
Chair, Morris, Arts & Crafts, Flat Arms Over Slats, Upholstered, 41 x 30 x 32 In. 1900.00
Chair, Morris, Back Support, Seat Springs, Reeded Legs, Pierced Sides 195.00
Chair, Morris, G. Stickley, 5 Vertical Slats, Corbels Under Arms, 38 1/2 In. 7950.00
Chair, Morris, G. Stickley, Loose Seat, Arched Arms, Red Mark, 38 In. . . . . *Illus* 47600.00
Chair, Morris, G. Stickley, Mahogany, Bow Arm, Upholstered, 38 In. 5175.00
Chair, Morris, G. Stickley, No. 336, Mahogany, Faceted Pegs, 32 x 38 In. 6900.00
Chair, Morris, G. Stickley, No. 360, 5 Slats, Drop Arm, 38 In. . . . . *Illus* 18400.00
Chair, Morris, G. Stickley, No. 2342, Oak, 5 Slats, Red Decal, 32 x 41 In. 9775.00
Chair, Morris, G. Stickley, Vertical Slats, Brown Leather Cushion, 41 In. 9200.00
Chair, Morris, J.M. Young, Arts & Crafts, Flat Arms Over 4 Slats, Tenons 2300.00
Chair, Morris, J.M. Young, Mahogany, 3 Vertical Slats, Brown Leather Seat, 42 In. 1035.00
Chair, Morris, J.M. Young, Slats Under Flat Arms, Leather Cushions, 1910, 38 In. 3740.00
Chair, Morris, L. & J.G. Stickley, Oak, Upholstered, 40 1/2 x 24 3/4 In. 2015.00
Chair, Morris, Mahogany Finish, Leather, Arms, 40 x 29 x 30 In.   2130.00
Chair, Morris, Mahogany, Winged Cupid Supports, Claw Feet, 1885, 45 In. 4480.00
Chair, Morris, Mahogany, Winged Griffin Supports, Claw Feet, 1865 . . . .   1900.00
Chair, Morris, Oak, Winged Griffin Supports, Claw Feet, 1885 . . . .   2352.00

Furniture, Chair, Morris, G. Stickley, Loose Seat,
Arched Arms, Red Mark, 38 In.

Furniture, Chair, Morris, G. Stickley,
No. 360, 5 Slats, Drop Arm, 38 In.

Chair, Morris, Stickley Bros., No. 343, Mahogany, Leather Seat, 40 x 31 x 37 In. 4540.00
Chair, N. Cherner, Plywood, Bent Seat, Bent Arms, 4 Tapered Legs, Label, Pair 1150.00
Chair, Naturalistic Carved Arms, Black Figures On Legs, Continental, 53 In. 2875.00
Chair, Neoclassical, Curved Splat, Scrolled Arms, Bow Seat Frame, 37 In., Pair 2990.00
Chair, Neoclassical, Mahogany, Arms, Arched Top Rail, Continental, 37 In. 1150.00
Chair, Neoclassical, Mahogany, Carved Top Rail, Anthemion Splat, 34 In., Pair 1035.00
Chair, Neoclassical, Mahogany, Giltwood, Leather Seat, Russia, 1810, 35 1/2 In. 4025.00
Chair, Neogrecque, Walnut, Carved Ribbon Crest, Upholstered Cushion, Arms, 39 In. 3220.00
Chair, Nutting, No. 461, Dutch Country, Arms 440.00
Chair, Nutting, No. 490, Ladder Back, 5 Slats, Arms 910.00
Chair, Oak, Angled Side Stretchers, Woven Cane Seat, Side, 17 x 37 1/2 In. 110.00
Chair, Oak, Arched Backrest, Shells & Leaves, Leather, 51 In., Pair 4800.00
Chair, Oak, Bentwood, Adjustable Back 295.00
Chair, Oak, Carved Back Panels & Crest, Sawtooth Carved Apron, England, 50 In. 440.00
Chair, Oak, D-Backrest, Seat Over Drawer, Rush & Rattan Seat 1840.00
Chair, Oak, Leather, Continuous Arms, 20th Century, 34 In. 300.00
Chair, Oak, Ornate Crest & Splat, Cane Seat, Leaf Carved Arms, 54 1/4 In., Pair 920.00
Chair, Oak, Pine, Spindle Back, Canted Legs, Stretchers, Child's, 36 x 18 x 17 In. 200.00
Chair, Oak, Steamship, Down Curved Pierced Arms, German, 1930s 632.00
Chair, Oak, Wainscot, Paneled Backrest, Carved Flower Heads & Leaves, Arms, 1890s . .   230.00
Chair, Old Hickory, 5-Spindle Back, Slatted Seat, Branded Mark, 35 x 24 x 22 In. 115.00
Chair, Ottoman, Eames, Duck Feather Cushion, Herman Miller 1955.00
Chair, Ottoman, Eames, Rosewood, Black Leather, 32 x 33 In. 2590.00
Chair, Ottoman, Eames, Tigerwood Veneer Frame, 33 x 36 In. 3040.00
Chair, Ottoman, Eero Saarinen, Grasshopper, Upholstered, 37 In.   2415.00
Chair, Ottoman, Engstrom, Bentwood, Lamb's Wool, 40 In. 1070.00
Chair, Ottoman, Foam-Filled Cushion, Brown Leather, Herman Miller 1610.00
Chair, Ottoman, Warren McArthur, Biltmore, 27 x 39 x 33 In. 6325.00
Chair, Oval Back, Cresting In Floral Urn, Padded Armrests, 1880s, 37 1/2 In., Pair 610.00
Chair, Padded Back, Carved Crest Rail, Flowers On Frame, Padded Arms, 38 In. 920.00
Chair, Padded Back, Downswept Arms, Serpentine Bottom Rail, Pair 2070.00
Chair, Painted Eagle, Ring-Turned Legs, Feather Design, 1830, 32 In., Pair 1610.00
Chair, Painted, Padded Back, Continuing Into Downswept Arms, c.1930, Pair 460.00
Chair, Painted, Upholstered Backrest & Seat, Padded Armrests, 1760s 5700.00
Chair, Panton, Cone, Red Vinyl, White Wire Frame, 31 In. 1495.00
Chair, Papier-Mache, Mother-Of-Pearl & Gilt, 1800s 150.00
Chair, Papier-Mache, Painted Floral, Pair 430.00
Chair, Parchment & Suede, Upholstered Back, Cushion Seat, Open Arms, 1930, Pair 3680.00
Chair, Paul Iribe, Black, Lacquer, D-Shape, Upholstered, Curved Arms, 1925 . . . .   800.00
Chair, Paul Kjaerholm, Chrome Flat Steel Frame, Brown Leather Seat, 1950, 29 In. 490.00
Chair, Pedro Friedeberg, Hand Shape, Laminated Wood, Pedestal Base, 34 x 19 In. 3515.00
Chair, Piano, Mahogany, Satinwood Inlaid Front, Back, Seat, 1910 . . . .   615.00
Chair, Piedmont Cigarettes, Folding, Wooden, 31 In. 160.00
Chair, Pierre Paulin, Donut, Upholstered, Round, Artifort, 25 x 34 In. 690.00
Chair, Pine, Rush Seat, Plank Arms, U-Shape Backrest, British Orkney Island 1600.00
Chair, Pine, Shaped Crest, Vase-Form Turned Splat, Straw Seat, Ball Feet, 44 In. 480.00
Chair, Pine, U-Shaped Backrest, Rush Upholstered Seat, Arms, 19th Century 1610.00
Chair, Plank Seat, Green Paint, Black, Gold Detail, Fruit, Half Spindles, 31 In. 110.00
Chair, Plate Glass Sides, Metal Supports, Rolled Foam, Red Blend Fabric, c.1960 . . . .   3500.00
Chair, Ponti, Upholstered, Flared Brass Legs, Arms, 35 1/2 x 24 In. 900.00
Chair, Potty, Hepplewhite, Upholstered Back, Arms & Seat, Arms, c.1790, 40 1/2 In. 190.00
Chair, Potty, Rocking, Walnut, Oak, Heart Cutout, Handles, Scalloped Sides, c.1770 . . . . .   405.00
Chair, Pretzel Back, Original Webbing, Pair 5300.00
Chair, Quaker Mission Craft Co., Arts & Crafts, Mahogany, Leather Cushion, 42 In. 489.00
Chair, Queen Anne, Carved Walnut, Incised Crest, Vase-Form Splat, Pad Feet, 41 In. 8400.00
Chair, Queen Anne, Elm, Over-Upholstered Seat, Cabriole Legs, 40 In. 1035.00
Chair, Queen Anne, Floral Design, Upholstered, Wing, 19 x 42 3/4 In., Pair 770.00
Chair, Queen Anne, Mahogany & Veneers, Shell-Carved Crest, Late 1800s, 41 In. 420.00
Chair, Queen Anne, Maple, Serpentine Crest & Arms, Vase Splat, c.1800, 23 In. 860.00
Chair, Queen Anne, Maple, Shaped Crest, Rush Seat, Stretchers, c.1760, Pair 415.00
Chair, Queen Anne, Painted, Yoke Crest Rail, Mass., 18th Century, 40 In. 920.00
Chair, Queen Anne, Slipper, Yoke Crest, Slip Seat, Massachusetts, c.1750, 37 In. 1200.00
Chair, Queen Anne, Walnut, Vase-Form Splat, Slip Seat, Trifid Feet, c.1740, Pair 9200.00

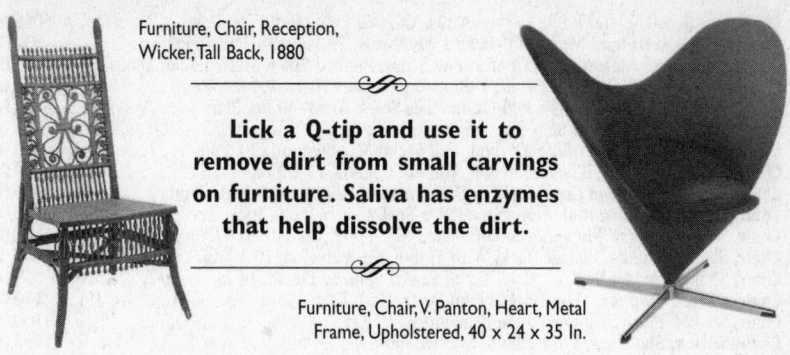

Furniture, Chair, Reception,
Wicker, Tall Back, 1880

**Lick a Q-tip and use it to
remove dirt from small carvings
on furniture. Saliva has enzymes
that help dissolve the dirt.**

Furniture, Chair, V. Panton, Heart, Metal
Frame, Upholstered, 40 x 24 x 35 In.

Chair, Rattan, Bucket, Metal, Pair	160.00
Chair, Rattan, Circular Back, Woven Center, Serpentine Arms, Splint Seat, 41 In.	55.00
Chair, Reception, Wicker, Tall Back, 1880 ....*Illus*	390.00
Chair, Red Leather, Button Tufting, Loose Cushion, Bun Feet, 29 In., Pair	920.00
Chair, Regency Style, Beech, Scroll Arms, Tapestry	1035.00
Chair, Regency Style, Mahogany, Curved Open Back, Upholstered, c.1810, Pair	750.00
Chair, Regency Style, Mahogany, Greek Key-Carved Crest, Cane, Arms, 33 In., Pair	2990.00
Chair, Regency Style, Mahogany, Key Style Carved Crest, Arms, 33 1/2 In.	2990.00
Chair, Regency Style, Mahogany, Open Back, Carved Crest, Arms, c.1825, Pair	690.00
Chair, Regency, Beech, Padded Seat, Floral Arms, Hoof Feet, 45 1/2 In.	1495.00
Chair, Regency, Foliate Carved Arms, Beaded, Splayed Legs, Arms, Pair	6037.00
Chair, Regency, Mahogany, Cane Back, Padded Seat, Circular Legs, Arms, 35 In.	1840.00
Chair, Regency, Mahogany, Cane Back, Sides, Leather Cushions, 28 In.	3220.00
Chair, Regency, Mahogany, Concave Back, Wooden Seat, Hall, 33 In., Pair	1725.00
Chair, Regency, Mahogany, Leather, Buttoned Back, Arms, Pair	7200.00
Chair, Renaissance Revival, Carving, Upholstered, Open Arms, 40 1/2 x 15 In., Pair	690.00
Chair, Renaissance Revival, Gilt, Carved Wood, Pierced Leaf Design, Figures, Arms	4025.00
Chair, Renaissance Revival, Inlaid Panel, 1870	1000.00
Chair, Renaissance Revival, Marquetry, Ebonized, Gilt Incised Rosewood, 35 In.	2185.00
Chair, Renaissance Revival, Mixed Hardwoods, H-Stretcher, Ram's-Head Arms, 48 In.	385.00
Chair, Renaissance Revival, Walnut, Ornate Crest, Arms, 1880, 46 x 26 x 31 In.	840.00
Chair, Renaissance Revival, Walnut, Padded Back Rosette, Carved Legs, 41 In.	1150.00
Chair, Renaissance Revival, Walnut, Padded Back, Arms, Seat, 1890s, 43 In.	800.00
Chair, Renaissance Revival, Walnut, Padded Back, Seat, 43 1/2 In., Pair	3220.00
Chair, Restauration Revival, Mahogany, Open Back, Leaf Capped Crest, Cabriole Legs	80.00
Chair, Risom, Walnut, Vinyl Seat & Back, Paper Label, Arms, 28 In., Pair	315.00
Chair, Robsjohn-Gibbings, Tufted Back, Rose Silk, 33 1/2 x 28 1/2 In.	500.00
Chair, Robsjohn-Gibbings, Walnut, Light Green, Arms, Widdicomb, 22 In., Pair	2070.00
Chair, Robsjohn-Gibbings, Walnut, Upholstered, Dowel Frame, 31 In.	980.00
Chair, Rocker, is listed under Rocker in this category.	
Chair, Rococo, Cream Paint, Carved Top Rail, Padded Seat, Arms, 38 x 26 In.	170.00
Chair, Rococo, Gesso, Upholstered Back, Cabriole Legs, Mid 18th Century	2300.00
Chair, Rococo, Giltwood, Padded Back, Arms, Seat, 44 In., Pair	2070.00
Chair, Rococo, Mahogany, Tufted Back, Open Carved Crest, 49 x 29 x 28 In.	5290.00
Chair, Rococo, Oak, 2 Intertwining Dolphins, Paw Feet, 31 1/2 In., Pair	2530.00
Chair, Rococo, Rosalie Without Grapes, Rosewood, Cabriole Legs, Arms, 38 In.	3450.00
Chair, Rococo, Rosewood Laminate, Rosalie Pattern, 36 1/2 In.	4830.00
Chair, Rococo, Rosewood Laminated, Pierced, Floral Carved Back, 1860, 38 In.	1000.00
Chair, Rococo, Rosewood, Carved Splat, Needlework, 41 In.	575.00
Chair, Rococo, Sedan, Giltwood, Polychrome, Leather, 76 x 31 1/2 x 36 In.	4600.00
Chair, Rococo, Upholstered Seat & Back, American, 19th Century	145.00
Chair, Rococo, Walnut, Floral Crest, 1865, 48 x 27 x 32 In.	1510.00
Chair, Rod Back, 7 Bamboo Spindles, Downward Curving Arms, c.1820, 33 In.	415.00
Chair, Rohde, Black Lacquer Openwork Frame, Club, Art Deco, 29 x 26 In.	900.00
Chair, Rohde, Brown Leather Seat, Dowel Legs, 30 1/2 x 22 x 20 In., Pair	480.00

Chair, Rosewood, Barrel Back, Carved Arms, Tapered Legs, Ball Feet, Pair 5040.00
Chair, Rosewood, Floral Mother-Of-Pearl Inlay, Arms, 20 1/4 x 38 3/4 In., Pair 330.00
Chair, Rosewood, Molded Rail, Conforming Stiles, Pierced Splat, Stuffed Seat, 1880s . . . 805.00
Chair, Rosewood, Skyscraper Backs, Upholstered Square Arms, c.1924, Pair 6900.00
Chair, Roycroft, Mahogany, Tacked-On Leather Seats, Arms, 40 In., Pair 3740.00
Chair, Rufus Merrill, Cane Seat, Painted Scene Back 440.00
Chair, Savonarola, Renaissance Revival, Gilt Metal Mounted, c.1890, Pair 690.00
Chair, Savonarola, Renaissance Revival, Walnut, Carved, 43 1/2 In. 1840.00
Chair, Scalloped Beaded Crest, Shell & Scroll Apron, Upholstered, 19th Century 1265.00
Chair, Serpentine Crest Rail, Serpentine Front Seat, Cream Paint, Italy 2530.00
Chair, Shaker, Cherry, Maple, Arched Beveled Slats, N.Y., c.1840, 41 1/2 In., Pair 2185.00
Chair, Shaker, Child's, Ladder Back, With Tilters, Mt. Lebanon, 10 3/4 In. 3450.00
Chair, Shaker, Ladder Back, 3 Slats, Taped Seat, Ebonized Finish, 14 In. 575.00
Chair, Shaker, Maple, Ladder Back, Finial Posts, Bark Seat, 1850s 170.00
Chair, Shaker, Plush Seat Over Tape Seat, Arms, c.1875 . . . . 3100.00
Chair, Shaker, Slat Back, With Tilters, Mt. Lebanon 1495.00
Chair, Shaker, Splint Seat, Low Back, Cylindrical Legs, With Tilters, Child's, 16 1/4 In. . . 980.00
Chair, Shaped Crest, Vase-Form Splat, Turned Stiles, Mass., 1700s, 44 x 17 In. 13800.00
Chair, Sheraton, Bamboo Turnings, Half-Spindle Back, Shaped Seat, Arms, 34 In. 190.00
Chair, Sheraton, Country, Rush Seats, Unpainted, Pair 138.00
Chair, Sheraton, Mahogany, Reeded Splat, Medallion, Slip Seat, England, 34 3/4 In. 85.00
Chair, Sheraton, Thumb Back, Crisscross Back, Rush Seat, Scrolled Arms, 33 In. 245.00
Chair, Slipper, Ebonized, Serpentine Backrest, Tasseled Seat, 19th Century 230.00
Chair, Slipper, Gold & Green Paint, Flowers, Cherubs, Upholstered Seat 135.00
Chair, Slipper, Walnut, Padded Needlepoint Seat & Back, Turned Front Legs, 47 In. 126.00
Chair, Slipper, Walnut, Shell On Crest, Trifid Feet, Pennsylvania 7475.00
Chair, Square Backrest, Open Arms, Over-Upholstered Seat, Saber Legs, 1840s, Pair 5750.00
Chair, Stacking, J. Columbo, Yellow Plastic, 2 Curved Leg Panels, c.1965, 28 3/4 In. 80.00
Chair, Starck, Black Leather Seat, Angular Black Tubular Steel Frame, 1980, 28 In. 750.00
Chair, Stickley & Brandt Co., Mahogany Finish, Leather Seat, Arms, 37 x 22 In. 920.00
Chair, Stickley & Brandt Co., Mahogany, Arms, 37 x 30 x 22 In. 1610.00
Chair, Stickley Bros., Mahogany, White Canvas Seat, Open Arms, 38 x 34 In. 1350.00
Chair, Stickley Bros., No. 283 1/2, Signed, 38 In. 650.00
Chair, Stickley Bros., No. 718, Mahogany, 1 Notched Slat, 16 x 39 In. 115.00
Chair, Stickley Bros., Vertical Slats, Leather Seat, 40 x 35 In. 1800.00
Chair, Tapio Wirkkala, Pressed Plywood, 1950s 7500.00
Chair, Teak, Carved Back, Cane Seat, Cabriole Legs, 37 1/2 In., Pair 690.00
Chair, Teak, Carved, Dark Finish, Pierced Seat Frame, Oriental, 38 In. 410.00
Chair, Teak, Curved Back, 2 Curved Arms, c.1955, 30 3/4 In. 145.00
Chair, Teak, Leather Seat, Tapered Legs, Pair 120.00
Chair, Tiger Maple, Arms, 37 x 21 In., Pair 2200.00
Chair, Tiger Maple, Rush Seat, Arms, Pair 220.00
Chair, Tub, Louis XVI, Green Highlights, Floral Crest, Cabriole Legs, 39 In., Pair 920.00
Chair, Tub, Oak, Spindle Back, Knurled Seat, 4 Peg Feet, Child's, 1700s, 14 In. 1095.00
Chair, Tubular Aluminum, Velvet, Arms, 31 x 24 x 21 In. 1725.00
Chair, Twig, Bent Branches, Pieced Star Pattern On Round Seat, Child's, 19 In. 165.00
Chair, Upholstered, Block & Ball Turned Arms, Continental, Late 17th Century 660.00
Chair, V. Panton, Heart, Covered In Red Wool Fabric, Steel Base, 39 In. 8050.00
Chair, V. Panton, Heart, Metal Frame, Upholstered, 40 x 24 x 35 In. . . . . *Illus* 10350.00
Chair, V. Panton, Heart, Original Velour Striped Fabric, Chrome Base, 33 1/2 In. 9562.00
Chair, Van Der Rohe, Barcelona, Chrome, Leather, Straps, Brown Velour, 28 x 29 In. 225.00
Chair, Van Der Rohe, Dark Tan Leather Cushions, Knoll, 30 In. 3100.00
Chair, Van Der Rohe, MR, Tubular Chrome, Rattan Seat, Back, 31 1/2 x 18 x 27 In. 85.00
Chair, Van Der Rohe, Tufted Brown Leather Cushions, Knoll, 29 x 30 x 27 In. 956.00
Chair, Vase Back, Black Paint, Rush Seat, Arms, 18th Century, 44 In. 575.00
Chair, Victorian, Brown Leather, Padded Arms, Club, 19th Century, 32 1/2 In. 800.00
Chair, Victorian, Mahogany, Scenic Needlepoint Seat, 1865, 35 x 17 x 16 In. 335.00
Chair, Victorian, Modified Balloon Back, Upholstered, Continuous Arms 285.00
Chair, Victorian, Mother-Of-Pearl, Inlay, Painted, Cane Seat, c.1875 . . . . 575.00
Chair, Victorian, Striped Floral Seat, 3 Vertical Slats, Child's, 23 In. 275.00
Chair, Victorian, Walnut, Balloon Back, Leaf, Fruit Carving, Crest, Needlepoint Seat 140.00
Chair, Victorian, Walnut, Carved Grapes On Crest Back, Arms, 1870 . . . . 55.00
Chair, Victorian, Walnut, Leaf-Carved Crest, Floral, Leaf, Cabriole Legs, Arms 920.00

Chair, Victorian, Walnut, Tufted Upholstered Back, Scrolled Leaf Design, Arms 920.00
Chair, Wallace Nutting, 8 Swelled Spindles, Saddle Seat, Paper Label, 38 1/4 In. 550.00
Chair, Wallace Nutting, Arched Crest, Carved Ears, 7 Spindles, Shaped Arm Rests 1730.00
Chair, Wallace Nutting, Windsor, Comb Back, 8 Spindles, 1930, 47 1/2 In. 1495.00
Chair, Walnut, Arched & Canted Backrest, Scrolled Arms, Bun Feet, 51 In. 1840.00
Chair, Walnut, Arched Back, Brass Nail Heads & Finials, Scrolled Arms, 58 In. 1840.00
Chair, Walnut, Arched Back, Foliate Carved & Pierced Splats, Arms, Pair 1150.00
Chair, Walnut, Arched Crest & Stiles, Padded Arms, Casters, c.1860, Pair 1925.00
Chair, Walnut, Arched Rail, Lyre Back Splat, Downswept Arms, Cushion, 1790s, Pair ... 4320.00
Chair, Walnut, Bird Heads, Leaves & Scrolls Seat & Back, Continental, 45 In. 1045.00
Chair, Walnut, Cabochon Flanked By Maidens Backrest, 43 1/2 In., Pair 1495.00
Chair, Walnut, Canted Back Joined By Arms, Tapestry Upholstered, 48 In. 1150.00
Chair, Walnut, Carved Backs, Cupid, Shell Crests, Arms, 46 x 27 x 22 In., Pair 1230.00
Chair, Walnut, Carved Crest, Pair Of Birds Amidst Fruit, Foliage, 53 In., 8 .... 5520.00
Chair, Walnut, Carved Crest, Raised On Twist Turned Legs, Arms, 48 x 30 In., Pair 800.00
Chair, Walnut, Carved Frame, Florals, Needlepoint, 1870s, 35 In. 800.00
Chair, Walnut, Cherry, Spindles, Va., 1790, 45 x 27 x 20 In. 1680.00
Chair, Walnut, Elm, Curved Crest Rail, Upright Splat, Outcurved Arms 2875.00
Chair, Walnut, Embroidered Leather, Fringed, Bobbin-Turned Arms, 1880s, 36 In. 1725.00
Chair, Walnut, Floral & Leaf Pediment, Shaped Backrest, Scroll Arms, Upholstered 145.00
Chair, Walnut, Folding, Armrests, Iron Hinges, Square Legs, Early 17th Century 9775.00
Chair, Walnut, Foliate-Carved Frame, Slip Seat, Scrolled Toes, 1780s, Pair 165.00
Chair, Walnut, Heavily Carved, Cherubs, Scrolls, Needlepoint Seat & Back, 48 In. 450.00
Chair, Walnut, Human Crest, Mustache & Beard, Medallion Back 200.00
Chair, Walnut, Leaf-Scrolled Arms, Upholstered Seat, Scrolled Stretcher, 51 In. 575.00
Chair, Walnut, Lions On Top Rail, Leather Covered Arms & Seat, Foot Rest, 35 In. 860.00
Chair, Walnut, Lyre Back, Carved Cherubs & Foliage, Whimsical, 19th Century, Pair 2070.00
Chair, Walnut, Ornately Carved Characters, Paw Feet, Upholstered, 42 1/2 x 27 In. 635.00
Chair, Walnut, Padded Back, Joined To Seat, Needlework, 47 In. 3450.00
Chair, Walnut, Padded Oval Panel, Griffin Crest, Arms, Continental, Late 1800s 115.00
Chair, Walnut, Scrolled, Fruited Crest, Pair Of Birds, Sgabello, Italy, 48 In. 1090.00
Chair, Walnut, Serpentine Crest, Trapezoid Slip Seat, Cabriole Legs, 1765, 37 In. 5400.00
Chair, Walnut, Spread-Winged Eagle Back, Eagle Support Seat, Continental, 47 In. 1045.00
Chair, Walnut, Upholstered, Turned Leg, Pot Casters, 1880s 160.00
Chair, Walnut, Veneer, Eastlake Carving, Crest, Velvet Upholstered, Rolled Arms 190.00
Chair, Walnut, Volute Splat, Arched Rails, Compass Slip Seat, c.1750, 34 1/2 In. 9775.00
Chair, Ward Bennet, Oiled Ash Frame, Sky Blue Upholstered Seat, Arms, 31 In., Pair 115.00
Chair, Warren McArthur, Black Lacquered Wood, 1920s ....*Illus* 3940.00
Chair, Warren McArthur, Tubular Aluminum Frame, Charcoal Gray Leather, 29 In. 1240.00
Chair, Warren McArthur, Tubular Aluminum, Arms, Hockey Puck Feet, 1930 .... 1900.00
Chair, Warren Platner, Orange Wood Fabric, Bent Wire Base, Knoll, 29 x 27 In. 255.00
Chair, Wegner, Blond Wood Frame, Tweed, 27 x 30 In., Pair 1610.00
Chair, Wegner, Dovetailed Crest Rails, Beige Fabric Seat, 30 x 20 In., Pair 505.00
Chair, Wegner, Getama, Cane Seats, Backs, Side, 32 x 20 1/2 x 17 In., Pair 115.00

Furniture, Chair, Warren McArthur, Black Lacquered Wood, 1920s
Furniture, Table, Side, Warren McArthur, Brown Lacquered Top, Tubular Legs, 21 x 14 in.
Furniture, Settee, Warren McArthur, Lacquered Wood, Drop Cushions, Mid 1920s

Chair, Wegner, Oak, Loose Seat, 1955, 26 x 30 In. 255.00
Chair, Wegner, Papa Bear, Upholstered, Arms, 38 In. 1495.00
Chair, Wegner, Rosewood, Original Upholstery, 1960, 27 x 33 In. 195.00
Chair, Wegner, Teak, Dark Brown Leather Seats, Johannes Hansen, 1949, 30 In. 505.00
Chair, Wegner, Teak, Leather Seat, 1955, 29 3/4 In. 488.00
Chair, Wegner, Teak, Steel Sling Support, Blue Tweed Seat, Getama, 25 In., Pair 900.00
Chair, Wegner, Teak, T Shape Back, Dowel Legs, Leather Seat, c.1950, 30 x 20 In. 365.00
Chair, Wegner, Teak, Wishbone, Open Back, Cord Seat, Curved Seat Rail Forms Arms ... 460.00
Chair, Wharton Esherick, Poplar, Woven Hard Leather Seat, Arms, 1959, 30 x 23 In. 2475.00
Chair, Wharton Esherick, Walnut, Leather, Arms, 1951 .... 9200.00
Chair, Wicker, Reception, 1880 .... 395.00
Chair, William & Mary Style, Walnut, Upholstered, Arms, 19th Century 440.00
Chair, William & Mary, Maple, Banister Back, Crest Rail, Downswept Arms, 47 In. 7765.00
Chair, William & Mary, Pierced Crest, Splat, Curved Arms, c.1680 .... 1100.00
Chair, William IV, Mahogany, Padded, Arms, Casters, 39 In. 3220.00
Chair, William IV, Mahogany, Padded, Reclining, Pullout Footrest, 38 1/2 In. 2185.00
Chair, William IV, Mahogany, Reclining, Scrolled Padded Back, Arms, 41 In. 6900.00
Chair, William IV, Mahogany, Wooden Seat, Top-Shaped Feet, 34 In., Pair 1495.00
Chair, William IV, Oak, Padded Back, Seat, Paneled Square Legs, 33 In., Pair 750.00
Chair, William IV, Rosewood, Upholstered, Padded Seat, 37 1/2 In. 5290.00
Chair, William IV, Walnut, Padded Circular Seat, Iron Base, Ship's, 1830, 34 In. 520.00
Chair, William Spratling, Carved Frame, Sling Leather Seat, Taxco, 18 In. 1035.00
Chair, Windsor, 5 Spindles, Bamboo, Mustard Paint Design, 18 x 34 1/2 In. 275.00
Chair, Windsor, 7 Spindles, Bamboo, Painted, Shield Seat, Arched Crest, 17 x 34 In. 195.00
Chair, Windsor, 7 Spindles, D-Shape Seat, 35 1/2 In. 220.00
Chair, Windsor, 9 Spindles, Continuous Arms, Shield Seat, Ring-Turned Legs, c.1770 .... 715.00
Chair, Windsor, 11 Spindles, Black Paint, Turned Stretchers, Splayed Legs 1150.00
Chair, Windsor, 13 Spindles, Green Paint, Continuous Arms, c.1795, 34 1/2 In. 3000.00
Chair, Windsor, Ash, Elm, Openwork Splat, Saddle Seat, Turned Legs, Arms 315.00
Chair, Windsor, Bamboo Turnings, Plank Seat, Arms, c.1830 .... 275.00
Chair, Windsor, Birdcage, Painted, Concave Crest Rail, Mass., c.1810, 35 In., Pair 3565.00
Chair, Windsor, Birdcage, Shield Seat, Bamboo Legs, 32 1/2 In. 250.00
Chair, Windsor, Bow Back, 7 Spindles, Back, Black Paint, Saddle Seat, 36 1/2 In. 310.00
Chair, Windsor, Bow Back, 7 Spindles, Flat Arms, Saddle Seat, Baluster Legs, Conn. 635.00
Chair, Windsor, Bow Back, 8 Spindles, Mixed Hardwoods, Arms, 45 3/4 In. 660.00
Chair, Windsor, Bow Back, 9 Spindles, Bamboo, Plank Seat, Turned Legs, c.1800 ...... 715.00
Chair, Windsor, Bow Back, Bamboo Turnings, Brown Paint, Pa., c.1810 .... 220.00
Chair, Windsor, Bow Back, Dark Stained Finish, Shaped Seat, 18 x 43 In. 415.00
Chair, Windsor, Bow Back, Maple, Ash, Bamboo Spindles, S.J. Tuck, 1790 .... 1095.00
Chair, Windsor, Brace Back, 7 Ringed Spindles 1495.00
Chair, Windsor, Brace Back, E.B. Tracy, Stained, Lisbon, Conn., 37 x 17 1/4 In. 4025.00
Chair, Windsor, Brace Back, Shaped Seat, Turned Decorated Legs 75.00
Chair, Windsor, Brace Back, Upholstered Seat, Arms 1380.00
Chair, Windsor, Carved Splat, Arms, England, c.1820 .... 495.00
Chair, Windsor, Comb Back, 9 Spindles, Arched Crest, Scrolled Ears, 17 x 44 In. 1045.00
Chair, Windsor, Comb Back, Oak, Ring Turned Legs, Shaped Seat, Continuous Arm 330.00
Chair, Windsor, Comb Back, Wormy Chestnut, Tapered Spindles, Arms, 1700s, 40 In. ... 575.00
Chair, Windsor, Continuous Arm, New England, c.1800 .... 525.00
Chair, Windsor, Curved Open Back, Bamboo-Turned Rods, A. Haggett, c.1825 .... 550.00
Chair, Windsor, Fanback, 7 Spindles, Blue Paint, Shaped Crest, 36 In., Pair 2000.00
Chair, Windsor, Fanback, 7 Spindles, Painted, Turned Legs, H-Stretcher, 17 x 33 In. 1980.00
Chair, Windsor, Fanback, 7 Spindles, Pennsylvania, 19th Century 550.00
Chair, Windsor, Fanback, 9 Spindles, Black Paint, Plank Seat, c.1780, 36 In. 2400.00
Chair, Windsor, Fanback, Black Paint, Serpentine Crest Rail, 1770, 35 In. 5225.00
Chair, Windsor, Fanback, Black, Red, Green Paint, 4 Turned Legs, 1790, 18 In. 4800.00
Chair, Windsor, Fanback, Comb, Arms, Saugus, Mass., Child's, 27 x 10 1/2 In. 1380.00
Chair, Windsor, Fanback, Green Paint, 1790 ....*Illus* 2090.00
Chair, Windsor, Fanback, Hardwoods, Black Paint, Stenciling, 1800s, 37 In., Pair 450.00
Chair, Windsor, Fanback, Turned Legs, Stretcher, 34 1/2 In. 1200.00
Chair, Windsor, Fanback, Vase & Ring-Turned Legs, H-Stretcher Base, 36 1/2 In. 580.00
Chair, Windsor, Fanback, Woven Rattan, Cane Seat, Brown, Tan Weave, 16 1/2 x 60 In. ... 198.00
Chair, Windsor, Green Paint, Crest, Saddle Seat, Bamboo Legs, H-Stretcher 4400.00
Chair, Windsor, Low Back, 15 Spindles, D-Shaped Seat, c.1775 .... 1760.00

Furniture, Chair, Windsor,
Fanback, Green Paint, 1790

Furniture, Chair, Windsor, Maple,
Hickory, Continuous Arm, 18th Century

Furniture, Chair, Windsor, Sack
Back, 7 Spindles, Painted, Arms

Chair, Windsor, Low Back, Flared Arms, Saddle Seat, Arrow Feet, c.1770 . . . . 3850.00
Chair, Windsor, Mahogany, Brace Back, Continuous Arms, 1780, 36 In. 3000.00
Chair, Windsor, Maple, Hickory, Continuous Arm, 18th Century . . . .*Illus* 2070.00
Chair, Windsor, Oak, Pine, Continuous Arm, Plank Seat, c.1790, 39 In., Pair 1455.00
Chair, Windsor, Oak, Turned Legs, Oval Seat, England, 36 In. 140.00
Chair, Windsor, Rod Back, 7 Spindles, Bamboo, c.1820 . . . . 360.00
Chair, Windsor, Rod Back, 7 Spindles, Painted, New England, c.1820, Pair 1210.00
Chair, Windsor, Sack Back, 5 Spindles, Painted, Paddle Arms, Youths, c.1780, 37 In. 4200.00
Chair, Windsor, Sack Back, 7 Spindles, Arms, Bamboo Legs, Pa., c.1820 . . . . 495.00
Chair, Windsor, Sack Back, 7 Spindles, Elliptical Seat, Painted, c.1780, 38 In. 715.00
Chair, Windsor, Sack Back, 7 Spindles, Elm, Ash, England, Arms 155.00
Chair, Windsor, Sack Back, 7 Spindles, Knuckle Arms, Elliptical Seat, Pa., c.1780 . . . . 715.00
Chair, Windsor, Sack Back, 7 Spindles, Maple, Ash, 1790s, 39 1/2 x 17 1/2 In. 2185.00
Chair, Windsor, Sack Back, 7 Spindles, Painted, Arms . . . .*Illus* 1840.00
Chair, Windsor, Sack Back, 9 Spindles, Green Paint, c.1770, 36 In. 3575.00
Chair, Windsor, Sack Back, Black Over Green Paint, Continuous Arm 5800.00
Chair, Windsor, Sack Back, Elm, Beech, Ash, H-Stretcher, 1840-1850 . . . . 185.00
Chair, Windsor, Sack Back, Green Over Red Paint, Arms, Child's, 28 3/4 In. 660.00
Chair, Windsor, Sack Back, Maple, Hickory Spindles, Arms, 18th Century 1600.00
Chair, Windsor, Sack Back, Saddle Seat, Swelled H-Stretcher, Continuous Arm, Pair 2875.00
Chair, Windsor, Spindles, Pierced Splat, Arms, Stretchers, 19th Century 110.00
Chair, Windsor, Spindles, Saddle Seat, Splayed Turned Legs, 19th Century 200.00
Chair, Windsor, Stepped Crest, Bamboo Turned Stiles, Legs, Red Paint, 1800s, 34 In. 4025.00
Chair, Windsor, Swivel Base, Bamboo Turnings, Late 1800s, 36 In. 170.00
Chair, Windsor, Thumb Back, Leaf-Painted Crest, Plank Seat, Arms, Child's, 21 In. 3000.00
Chair, Windsor, Yew Wood, Oak, D-Shape Seat, Bowed Arm Rail & Back, England 660.00
Chair, Wing, Cane Back, Cypress, Pine, Louisiana, c.1800, 40 1/2 x 23 x 22 In. 3220.00
Chair, Wing, Chippendale, Mahogany Base, Marlboro Legs, 1700s, 44 x 32 In. 560.00
Chair, Wing, Chippendale, Mahogany, Square Molded Legs, Late 19th Century 220.00
Chair, Wing, Chippendale, Mahogany, Upholstered, Rolled Arms, 20th Century, 39 In. 220.00
Chair, Wing, Federal Style, Mahogany, Late 19th Century 165.00
Chair, Wing, George II, Serpentine Padded Back, Outscrolled Arms, Cushion Seat 9000.00
Chair, Wing, George III Style, Parcel Gilt Beech, Green Paint, 44 1/2 In. 800.00
Chair, Wing, George III, Mahogany, Padded Backrest, Stuffed Seat, 43 In. 2300.00
Chair, Wing, Leather Upholstered Backrest, Outscrolled Armrests, Loose Cushion 8400.00
Chair, Wing, Mahogany, Padded Back, Over-Scroll Arms, Cushion Seat 400.00
Chair, Wing, Mahogany, Padded Back, Scroll Arms, Loose Cushion, c.1900, 48 1/4 In. 2970.00
Chair, Wing, Mahogany, Upholstered, Casters, Rolled Arms, 50 1/2 In. 575.00
Chair, Wing, Padded Back, Outset Arms, Cushioned Seat, Shell Carved Legs 7200.00
Chair, Wing, Queen Anne Style, Mahogany, Cabriole Legs, Curving Arms 345.00
Chair, Wing, Queen Anne Style, Mahogany, Tapered Seat, Scroll Arms, Cabriole Legs . . . 400.00
Chair, Wing, Sheraton, Mahogany, Turned Legs, New England, c.1815 . . . . 1540.00
Chair, Wing, Upholstered Crest, Out Scrolled Arms, Pad Feet, 19th Century, 33 In. 275.00

Chair, Wing, Walnut, Camelback, Raked Back Legs, Scrolled Arms, 46 1/2 In. 6600.00
Chair, Wing, Woman's, Paper Rush Seat, Upholstered Sawtooth Design, 49 In. 330.00
Chair, Wishbone, Light Gray Triangular Seat, Plywood Base, 1970, 26 In. 750.00
Chair, Writing, Maple, Sliding Drawer Under Arm, c.1770 . . . . 5200.00
Chair, Yoke Back, Hardwood, Undulating Arms, Top Rail, Foliate, 44 In., Pair 230.00
Chair, Young, J.M., Mahogany, Dark Brown Leather Cushions, 37 x 18 In., Pair 690.00
Chair, Youth, Stenciled Crest Rail, Painted Shells & Foliage, Cane Seat, 25 In. 45.00
Chair & Ottoman, Arizona Biltmore, W. MacArthur, 39 x 27 In. 6325.00
Chair & Ottoman, E. Saarinen, Grasshopper, Bentwood Frame, Upholstered, 36 In. 2415.00
Chair & Ottoman, E. Saarinen, Womb, Burnt Orange Fabric, 36 In. . . . . .1265.00 to 2250.00
Chair & Ottoman, Eames, Blond Finish, Leather, Tan, 40 In. 335.00
Chair & Ottoman, Eames, Leather, Light Wood, 38 In. 60.00
Chair & Ottoman, Eames, Mahogany, Leather, Black, 40 In. 335.00
Chair & Ottoman, Eames, Wooden Shell, Leather, 1956, 33 In. 750.00
Chair & Ottoman, G. Nakashima, Cherry, Upholstered Cushions, 1957 . . . . 4900.00
Chair & Ottoman, Rosewood, Plywood Shell, Pronged Aluminum Base, 32 x 33 In. 4025.00
Chair & Ottoman, Walnut, Bone Inlay, Pierced Back, Peacocks, Arms, Pair 1840.00
Chair Set, Aesthetic Revival, Ash, Upholstered Back, Leaf-Tip Frame, 12 . . . . 4500.00
Chair Set, Angel Wing Crest, Cutout Fiddle Back, Floral, Salmon Ground, 1840s, 6 . . . . . 4050.00
Chair Set, Arched Back, Nail-Head Trim, Molded Frame, Upholstered Seat, 41 In., 4 . . . . 750.00
Chair Set, Arts & Crafts, Mahogany, Green Leather Seat, 3/4 x 54 In., 6 . . . . 2600.00
Chair Set, Baroque, Carved Walnut, Reeded Legs, Velvet, Italy, 8 . . . . 1495.00
Chair Set, Beech, Arched & Padded Back, Overstuffed Seat, 8 . . . . 690.00
Chair Set, Berkey & Gay, Federal, Upholstered Seats, Tapered Fluted Legs, 8 . . . . 545.00
Chair Set, Biedermeier, Fruitwood, Arched Cresting In Splat, Mid 19th Century, 10 . . . . . 2415.00
Chair Set, Birdcage Back, Bamboo Turnings, 3 Side, 1 Arm, 4 . . . . 1265.00
Chair Set, Captain's, Arts & Crafts, Oak, Dark Finish, 30 1/2 In., 6 . . . . 500.00
Chair Set, Carved Scrolls & Leaves, Upholstered, 1920, 2 Armchairs, 6 . . . . 1320.00
Chair Set, Centennial, Mahogany, Carved Crest Rail, Cabriole Legs, Ball Feet, 10 . . . . . . 8625.00
Chair Set, Chinese Chippendale, Upholstered Seats, 2 Armchairs, 6 . . . . 800.00
Chair Set, Chippendale, Cherry, Pierced Slat Back, Needlework Slip Seat, 5 . . . . 1840.00
Chair Set, Chippendale, Mahogany, Claw & Ball, Slip Seat, 2 Armchairs, 12 . . . . 4400.00
Chair Set, Chippendale, Mahogany, Ladder Back, Slip Seat, 38 In., 8 . . . . 2760.00
Chair Set, Chippendale, Mahogany, Molded Edge, Ball, Claw Feet, 31 In., 6 . . . . 1265.00
Chair Set, Chippendale, Mahogany, Serpentine Crest Rail, Shell-Carved Seat, 6 . . . . 2070.00
Chair Set, Chippendale, Mahogany, Slip Seat, Cabriole Legs, Claw, Ball Feet, 8 . . . . 2990.00
Chair Set, Chippendale, Mahogany, Vase Splat, Upholstered Seat, 1920s, 6 . . . . 2530.00
Chair Set, Chippendale, Mahogany, Walnut, Needlepoint Seat, 2 Armchairs, 8 . . . . 2750.00
Chair Set, Chippendale, Serpentine Top Rail, Pierced Slats, Marlboro Legs, Arms, 8 . . . . . 2760.00
Chair Set, Classical, Concave Top Rail, Downswept Arms, Animal Feet, 34 In., 6 . . . . 4025.00
Chair Set, Classical, Mahogany, Concave Crest, Boston, c.1835, 35 x 17 In., 4 . . . . 2300.00
Chair Set, Club, Art Deco, Ribbed Caning Frame, Red Woven Fabric, 29 In., 4 . . . . 3740.00
Chair Set, Downswept Crest Rail Over Padded Velvet Back, Velvet Seat, 4 . . . . 630.00
Chair Set, E. Wormley, Cane Backs, Black Upholstered Seats, Dunbar, 38 In., 4 . . . . 920.00
Chair Set, Eames, Black Vinyl Padding, Black Wire, 32 x 19 x 20 In., 6 . . . . 1240.00
Chair Set, Eames, Black Wire, Cobalt Bikini Pads, 32 x 18 x 16 In., 4 . . . . 730.00
Chair Set, Eames, Chrome Pedestal, Upholstered, Arms, Fiberglass Shell, 28 In., 6 . . . . . . 490.00
Chair Set, Eames, DCM, Chrome, Upholstered, Plastic Feet, Herman Miller, 6 . . . . 950.00
Chair Set, Eames, DKR-1, Painted Steel Mesh, Upholstered, Herman Miller, 33 In., 6 . . . 10065.00
Chair Set, Eames, Eiffel Tower, Fiberglass, Rubber, Steel, H. Miller, 1953, 31 In., 6 . . . . . 2300.00
Chair Set, Eames, Fiberglass Shell, Orange, Swivel Mounted, Pedestal Base, 4 . . . . 1150.00
Chair Set, Eames, Fiberglass, White, Steel H-Base, Herman Miller, 31 In., 6 . . . . 175.00
Chair Set, Eames, Orange Fiberglass Shell, Swivel Pedestal Base, 31 In., 6 . . . . 1465.00
Chair Set, Eames, Tubular Black Metal Base, Herman Miller, 29 x 20 In., 4 . . . . 920.00
Chair Set, Eames, Tubular Chrome Frame, 30 x 19 1/2 x 22 In., 6 . . . . 1800.00
Chair Set, Eames, White Fiberglass, Black Eiffel Tower Base, H. Miller, 1960, 4 . . . . 1495.00
Chair Set, Eames, Yellow Fiberglass Shell, Herman Miller, 5 . . . . 1240.00
Chair Set, Eero Saarinen, Leather, Bentwood Base, 31 In., 8 . . . . 1350.00
Chair Set, Elm, Rush Seat, Turned Spindles, Raised Pad Feet, England, 5 . . . . 1150.00
Chair Set, Empire, Mahogany, Walnut, 2 Armchairs, 1860, 8 . . . . 4315.00
Chair Set, Empire, Tiger Maple, Open Back, Dipped Crest Rail, Early 1800s, 6. . . . . 1150.00
Chair Set, Empire, Tiger Maple, Rolled Back, Vase Splat, Cane Seat, 9 . . . . 3190.00
Chair Set, Federal, Mahogany, Curved Rectangular Top Rail, Tapered Legs, 4 . . . . 1265.00

Chair Set, Federal, Mahogany, Shieldback, Arched, Open Back, Upholstered Seat, 8 . . . . . 2990.00
Chair Set, Federal, Mahogany, Spiral-Reeded Backrest, Boston, 1810, 10 . . . . 10200.00
Chair Set, Fiddleback, Upholstered Seat, Woodbury, Conn., c.1790, 6 . . . . 22000.00
Chair Set, Foliate Carved Cresting, Pierced Splats, Slip Seat, 20th Century, 10 . . . . 5175.00
Chair Set, Frank Lloyd Wright, Mahogany, Dark Brown Leather Seat, 23 In., 6 . . . . 1840.00
Chair Set, Frank Lloyd Wright, Mahogany, White Cushion, Original Finish, 28 In., 4 . . . . 2415.00
Chair Set, French Provincial, Oak, Scalloped Crest, Carved, Rush Seat, 37 1/2 In., 6 . . . . 690.00
Chair Set, G. Nakashima, Walnut, Grass Seat, 26 3/4 x 23 x 19 In., 6 . . . . 4025.00
Chair Set, G. Nakashima, Walnut, Grass Seats, 1967, 27 x 18 In., 4 . . . . 2815.00
Chair Set, G. Stickley, 3 Vertical Back Slats, Green Leather, 39 In., 6 . . . . 3450.00
Chair Set, G. Stickley, Ladder Back, Original Tacked On Brown Leather Seat, 6 . . . . 4160.00
Chair Set, G. Stickley, No. 306, Ladder Back, Leather Seat, Red Decal, 36 In., 6 . . . . 2645.00
Chair Set, G. Stickley, No. 353, Mahogany, 3 Vertical Slats, Arms, 17 x 39 In., 5 . . . . 4025.00
Chair Set, G. Stickley, No. 1297, Oak, 4 Horizontal Slats, Green Finish, 38 In., 6 . . . . 7480.00
Chair Set, Gehry, Laminated Corrugated Cardboard, 32 In., 4 . . . . 2875.00
Chair Set, George I, Oak, Ladder Back, Arched Crest, Woven Rush Seat, U-Stretcher, 4 . . 460.00
Chair Set, George III, Mahogany, Leaf-Carved Crest, Ball, Claw Feet, 38 In., 8 . . . . 9200.00
Chair Set, George III, Mahogany, Rectangular Back, Upholstered, 6 . . . . 1725.00
Chair Set, George III, Mahogany, Rosettes, Serpentine, Cabriole Legs, 37 In., 8 . . . . 2530.00
Chair Set, George III, Mahogany, Serpentine Crest, Shell-Pierced Splat, 40 In., 13 . . . . . . 2990.00
Chair Set, George III, Mahogany, Serpentine Crest, Slip Seat, 4 . . . . 1265.00
Chair Set, George III, Mahogany, Serpentine Top Rail, 42 1/2 In., 10 . . . . 4830.00
Chair Set, George III, Mahogany, Shell Crest, Trailing Vines, 39 In., 10 . . . . 2990.00
Chair Set, George III, Mahogany, Yoke Crest, Pierced Splat, Cabriole Legs, 12 . . . . 6900.00
Chair Set, George III, Serpentine Top Rail, Pierced Splat, c.1900, 39 In., 8 . . . . 5060.00
Chair Set, Gilt Metal Mounted, Curved Arms, Sphinx Supports, Paw Feet, 39 In., 6 . . . . . 6040.00
Chair Set, Grain Painted, Vase Back Splat, Gold Stencil, 19 1/2 In., 6 . . . . 460.00
Chair Set, Grand Lodge Chair Co., Arts & Crafts, 36 x 17 1/2 x 16 In., 12 . . . . 1495.00
Chair Set, H. Bertoia, Red Vinyl Seat, Black Wire Frame, Child's, 16 x 24 In., 4 . . . . 635.00
Chair Set, H. Bertoia, White Coated Web, Yellow Seat Cushion, 30 In., 10 . . . . 690.00
Chair Set, Hale, 3-Slat Back, Leather Seat, 5 . . . . 690.00
Chair Set, Hans Olsen, Teak, Spade-Shaped Seat, Black Leather, Dowel Legs, 28 In., 4 . . 70.00
Chair Set, Hardwood, Scrolled Crest, Pierced Backrest, Cane Seat, 8 . . . . 9600.00
Chair Set, Hepplewhite, Mahogany, c.1900, 8 . . . . 3190.00
Chair Set, Hepplewhite, Mahogany, Sheaf-Of-Wheat Splats, c.1880, 2 Armchairs, 8 . . . . . 483.00
Chair Set, Hepplewhite, Mahogany, Shieldback, Padded Seats, 38 1/2 In, 8 . . . . 4600.00
Chair Set, Hitchcock, Curved Back, Rush Seat, 8 . . . . 880.00
Chair Set, Hitchcock, Stained Hardwood, Rush Seat, Early 1800s, 5 . . . . 375.00
Chair Set, John Mascheroni, Lounge, Dark Brown Paisley Sling Seat, 1969, 5 . . . . . .80.00 to 92.00
Chair Set, John Mascheroni, Lounge, Light Brown Paisley Sling Seat, 1969, 5 . . . . 115.00
Chair Set, Jules Bouy, Lacquered Wood, 1936, 8 . . . . 11400.00
Chair Set, L. & J.G. Stickley, Mahogany, Reupholstered Seat Cushions, 7 . . . . 3940.00
Chair Set, Ladder Back, Broad Stretcher To Front & Back, Vinyl Seat, 36 In., 4 . . . . 1725.00
Chair Set, Ladder Back, Curved, Shaped Slats, Rush Seat, 42 In., 6 . . . . 1150.00
Chair Set, Ladder Back, Old Blue Over Red Paint, Rush Seat, 6 . . . . 60.00
Chair Set, Ladder Back, Rush Seat, Turned Stretchers, Ball Feet, 47 In., 10 . . . . 1725.00
Chair Set, Leather, Bright Chrome Frame, 31 3/4 In., 6 . . . . 3260.00
Chair Set, Limbert, 3 Horizontal Slats Under 1 Wide Slat, Leather Seat, 37 In., 6 . . . . 3335.00
Chair Set, Limbert, Arts & Crafts, 2 Armchairs, 38 x 26 x 21 In., 6 . . . . 2475.00
Chair Set, Limbert, Mahogany, 3 Vertical Slats, 36 x 24 x 19 In., 5 . . . . 2360.00
Chair Set, Limbert, Vertical Back Splats, Rush Seat, 1 Arm, 5 Side, 6 . . . . 8625.00
Chair Set, Louis XV, Beech, Cartouche-Form Back, Floral Crest, Cane Panel, 6 . . . . 3220.00
Chair Set, Louis XV, Oak, Ladder Back, Woven Rush Seat, 10 . . . . 4900.00
Chair Set, Louis XV, Oak, Molded, Cane Back, Seat, Cabriole Legs, 36 In., 8 . . . . 2875.00
Chair Set, Louis XV, Upholstered Seat, Scrolled Legs, 40 In., 4 . . . . 980.00
Chair Set, Louis XV, Walnut, Carved Flower Sprays, Velvet, 6 . . . . 1095.00
Chair Set, Louis XVI Style, Ivory Paint, Cartouche Shape Back, Padded, 8 . . . . 1150.00
Chair Set, Louis XVI Style, Painted, Parcel Gilt, Upholstered, 4 . . . . 290.00
Chair Set, Louis XVI, Gilt, Carved, Arched Crest, Upholstered, Arms, 4 . . . . 1840.00
Chair Set, Louis XVI, Walnut, Padded Oval Back, Fluted Legs, Arms, 4 . . . . 345.00
Chair Set, Louis XVI, Walnut, Rectangular Backrest, Circular Turned Legs, 6 . . . . 2760.00
Chair Set, Lucite, Swivel Seats, T-Shaped Steel Pedestal Base, 33 3/4 In., 8 . . . . 1010.00
Chair Set, Mahogany, Leaf Carved Rail, Bellflower Splat, Balloon Back, 1880s, 6 . . . . . . 9490.00

Chair Set, Mahogany, Prince Of Wales Feathers, Trapezoid Slip Seat, 6 . . . . 6612.00
Chair Set, Mahogany, Racket-Form Back, Serpentine Seat, c.1900, 2 Armchairs, 6 . . . . . . 2185.00
Chair Set, Mahogany, Scroll Rail, Vase-Form Splat, Slip Seat, c.1720, 4 . . . . 5520.00
Chair Set, Mahogany, Square Back, Sphinx Arm Supports, 39 In., 6 . . . . 6037.00
Chair Set, Neoclassical, Fruitwood, Floral Crest, Slip Seat, 1800, 35 1/2 In., 4 . . . . 805.00
Chair Set, Norman Cherner, Bentwood, Arms, 31 In., 4 . . . . 960.00
Chair Set, Oak, Carved, English Figural Busts, Rich Original Patina, 12 . . . . 3360.00
Chair Set, Oak, Faux Bamboo Splat, Vertical Stays, Side, 33 In., 6 . . . . 1090.00
Chair Set, Oak, Winged Griffin Crests, 1885, 8 . . . . 3585.00
Chair Set, Old Hickory, Original Finish, 30 x 60 x 36 In., 6 . . . . 2820.00
Chair Set, Oriental, Mahogany, Upholstered, 37 In., 4 . . . . 190.00
Chair Set, Plank Bottom, Original Grain, Flower Decorated Surface, Pa., 6 . . . . 990.00
Chair Set, Queen Anne, Black Lacquer, Chinoiserie, England, 1900, 6 . . . . 2875.00
Chair Set, Queen Anne, Maple, Black Paint, Rush Seat, c.1750, 43 In., 4 . . . . 4200.00
Chair Set, Queen Anne, Walnut, Yoked Crest Rail, Padded Seat, 8 . . . . 1380.00
Chair Set, Regency, Ebonized, Rounded Crest, Padded, 8 Piece 2300.00
Chair Set, Regency, Fruitwood, Saddle Seat, Saber Legs, 1900, 3 In., 8 . . . . 4140.00
Chair Set, Regency, Griffins Flanking An Urn, England, c.1880, 5 . . . . 3680.00
Chair Set, Regency, Mahogany, Brass Rectangular Top, Reeded Saber Legs, 8 . . . . 13200.00
Chair Set, Regency, Mahogany, Overhanging Crest Rail, Scroll-Carved Splat, 6 . . . . 1610.00
Chair Set, Regency, Rosewood, Back Scroll Crest, Slip Seat, Saber Legs, 6 . . . . 4800.00
Chair Set, Renaissance Revival, Mask, Leaves & Scroll Crest, Upholstered, 10 . . . . . 2300.00
Chair Set, Richard Schultz, Mesh Seat, Outdoor, Beige Metal Frame, Knoll, 29 In., 4 . . . . 960.00
Chair Set, Robsjohn-Gibbings, Walnut, Cream Webbed Seat, 33 x 21 In., 4 . . . . 1840.00
Chair Set, Rococo, Oak, Shieldback, 19th Century, 36 x 36 1/2 In., 10 . . . . 11500.00
Chair Set, Rohde, Cloud, Mahogany Veneer, Cordovan Leather, 31 In., 4 . . . . 1265.00
Chair Set, Rose Crests, Acorns & Line Detail, 32 In., 6 . . . . 550.00
Chair Set, Sheraton, Bird's-Eye Maple, Cane Seat, 33 1/2 In., 6 . . . . 1570.00
Chair Set, Sheraton, Mahogany, Upholstered, Medallion Back, 2 Armchairs, 6 . . . . 1540.00
Chair Set, Sheraton, Saber Leg, Grain Painted, Line Design, Cane Seats, 6 . . . . 400.00
Chair Set, Stenciled Grape Crest Rail, Rush Seat, White Paint, 19th Century, 6 . . . . 3500.00
Chair Set, Stickley Bros., Mahogany, 38 x 18 x 17 In., 6 . . . . 4450.00
Chair Set, Thomas Day, Mahogany, Tobacco Leaves On Crest, Slip Seats, 6 . . . . 2400.00
Chair Set, Thumb Back, 4-Back Spindles, Ring-Turned Legs, c.1835, 4 . . . . 935.00
Chair Set, Tiger Maple, Cane Seat, Saber Legs, c.1820, 4 . . . . 220.00
Chair Set, Tubular Black Enameled Base, Woven Back, Slatted Seat, 31 In., 4 . . . . 115.00
Chair Set, Walnut, Arched Crest Rail, Cane Back, Reeded Arms & Legs, 34 In., 4 . . . . . . 4600.00
Chair Set, Walnut, Banister Back, Hump Back, Rush Seat, 1920s, 35 In., 4 . . . . 370.00
Chair Set, Walnut, Cane Seat & Back, Fluted Legs, Mid 19th Century, 4 . . . . 4315.00
Chair Set, Walnut, Leather Seat & Back, Brass Nail Heads, 36 1/2 In., 4 . . . . 1265.00
Chair Set, Walnut, Scroll Finials, Silk, Shaped Front Stretcher, 6 . . . . 3740.00
Chair Set, Warren McArthur, Green Vinyl Back, Armrests, Orange Seat, 33 In., 4 . . . . 900.00
Chair Set, Wegner, Rosewood Frame, Upholstered Seat, Denmark, 4 . . . . 980.00
Chair Set, Wegner, Teak, Wishbone, Rush Seat, Branded, 28 1/2 In., 4 . . . . 1265.00
Chair Set, White Florals & Grapes On Crests, Yellow Striping, Cane Seats, 6 . . . . 2310.00
Chair Set, William IV, Mahogany, Cornucopia Splat, Slip Seat, 34 x 19 x 16 In., 4 . . . . . . 980.00
Chair Set, William IV, Mahogany, Open Back, Slip Seat, c.1835, 6 . . . . 980.00
Chair Set, William IV, Oak, Balloon Back, Carved, Upholstered, 34 In., 6 . . . . 4830.00
Chair Set, William IV, Oak, Lion Medallion, Circular Wooden Seat, 37 In., 4 . . . . 3220.00
Chair Set, Windsor, Arrow Back, Bamboo-Turned Legs, Gold Fruit & Leaves, 1825, 6 . . . 2300.00
Chair Set, Windsor, Arrow Back, Stenciled, Massachusetts, 1815-1825, 34 In., 7 . . . . 2645.00
Chair Set, Windsor, Bow Back, 7 Spindles, 37 x 36 1/2 In., 6 . . . . 1375.00
Chair Set, Windsor, Fanback, 7 Spindles, 1800, 23 x 16 x 18 In., 6 . . . . 7280.00
Chair Set, Windsor, Sack Back, Woven Paper Rush Seat, Scrolled Arms, 4 . . . . 495.00
Chair Set, Wrought Iron, Leather Seat & Back, 33 1/2 In., 4 . . . . 4140.00
Chair-Table, Jacobean, Oak, 2 Arm Supports, Plank Seat, c.1680, 28 x 33 In. 1890.00
Chair-Table, Lipped Drawer, Red Paint, 46-In. Top 6600.00
Chair-Table, Maple, Pine, Chamfered Cleats, Block Vase Supports, 28 x 54 In. 13800.00
Chair-Table, Pine, Battened Lift Top, Scalloped Ends, Plank Seat, c.1800, 50 In. 1100.00
Chair-Table, Pine, Painted, Plank Seat, Arms, 18th Century, 27 1/2 x 54 x 49 In. 6900.00
Chair-Table, Rectangular, Breadboard Ends, Lift Seat, Arched Base, 66 x 33 In. 2933.00
Chair-Table, Richard Schultz, Rectangular Brown Top, Metal Base, Knoll, 26 In. 535.00
Chaise En Gondole, Louis Philippe, Mahogany, Swan's-Neck Uprights, 32 In. 2990.00

When regluing loose rungs or parts of chairs, remove old glue with vinegar. Drip it into any holes with a small oil can.

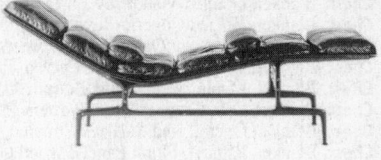

Furniture, Chaise Longue, Eames, Aluminum, Leather Cushions, 1968, 75 In.

Chaise Longue, Boudoir, French Mohair, Tassels, Fringe, Yellow Silk Cord, 26 In. 550.00
Chaise Longue, Eames, Aluminum, Leather Cushions, 1968, 75 In. ....*Illus* 7475.00
Chaise Longue, Heywood-Wakefield, Wicker, Cushion 355.00
Chaise Longue, Louis XIV Style, Oak, Pierced Splat, Needlework Seat, 48 In. 405.00
Chaise Longue, Louis XV, Cream, Down-Filled Cushion, Cabriole Legs, 33 In. 1150.00
Chaise Longue, Louis XV, Fruitwood, Brocade, 65 In. 1150.00
Chaise Longue, Louis XV, Walnut, Pierced Backrest, Shell, Cane Seat, 37 1/2 In. 1380.00
Chaise Longue, Louis XVI Style, Grissaille, Beech, Cream, 37 x 23 x 62 In............ 2070.00
Chaise Longue, Tobey, Mahogany, Square Posts, Leather Sling Seat, 34 x 45 In. 3450.00
Chaise Longue, V. Kagan, Wool, Tufted Seat, 26 x 65 In. 675.00
Chaise Longue, Wicker, Flowered Cushion, 40 1/2 x 66 In. 950.00
Chaise Longue, Wood, Rattan Sling Seat, Black Wrought Iron Frame, 36 x 38 In........ 1035.00
Chest, 2 Over 4 Drawers, Backsplash, New England, c.1800 .... 3200.00
Chest, 4 Birch Flame-Grain Drawer Fronts, Walnut Pulls, 34 3/4 In. 1320.00
Chest, 4 Drawers, Turned Legs, 19th Century, 39 x 19 x 43 In. 230.00
Chest, 4 Lipped Drawers, Pierced Brasses, Carved Ogee Feet, c.1770, 34 x 36 In....... 6600.00
Chest, 6-Board, Lidded Till, Yellow, Burnt Sienna Graining, 22 x 38 x 17 In. 10350.00
Chest, 6-Board, Painted, Olive, Red, Brown, Vt., 1835-1840, 25 1/2 x 40 1/2 x 21 In. 3450.00
Chest, 6-Board, Poplar, Painted, Stencil, Initials, 10th Century, 22 x 36 x 19 In. 3000.00
Chest, American Empire, Mahogany, Arched Swing Mirror, 68 x 45 x 21 In. 920.00
Chest, Amish, Child's, 2 Tiers, Porcelain Pull Knobs, 3 Drawers, 10 1/2 x 12 In. 165.00
Chest, Apple, Cherry, Carved, Painted, 4 Drawers, Continental, 37 x 35 x 18 In. 3400.00
Chest, Art Deco, 5 Drawers, 50 1/2 x 38 x 20 In. 805.00
Chest, Bachelor's, Chippendale, Mahogany, 2 Over 3 Graduated Drawers, 33 x 18 In. ... 1760.00
Chest, Bachelor's, Copper, Parquetry & Lattice Coconut Shell, 4 Drawers, 30 In. 1600.00
Chest, Bachelor's, Mahogany, 4 Drawers, Veneered Edges, 31 3/4 In. 3190.00
Chest, Bachelor's, Mahogany, Fitted Upper Drawer, Mirror, Dressing Slide, 31 In. 1850.00
Chest, Bachelor's, Mahogany, Veneer, 4 Drawers, Ball Pulls, Kittinger, 28 x 31 In. 715.00
Chest, Bachelor's, Yew, Slide, 4 Graduated Drawers, 28 3/4 x 25 1/4 In. 980.00
Chest, Baroque, Hinged Rectangular Top, Griffins, Putti, Flower Heads, 20 x 22 In. 1850.00
Chest, Biedermeier, Walnut, Parquetry, 4 Drawers, c.1850, 17 x 15 x 7 In. 1495.00
Chest, Birch, Reverse Serpentine, 4 Drawers, Ogee Bracket Feet, c.1780, 32 1/2 In. 9200.00
Chest, Bird's-Eye Maple, Marble Top, Frieze Drawer, 3 Drawers, 1830s, 37 1/4 In. 7200.00
Chest, Bird's-Eye Maple, Serpentine Front, Beveled Mirror, 1900, 27 In. 1400.00
Chest, Black Lacquer, Rosewood Veneer, 7 Burl Veneer Drawers, 33 x 49 In. 115.00
Chest, Blanket, 1 Drawer, Applied Bracket Front Feet, 33 x 37 1/2 x 17 In. 635.00
Chest, Blanket, 6-Board, Cutout Ends, Molding, Secret Compartment, 48 x 23 x 17 In.... 895.00
Chest, Blanket, Bird's-Eye Maple, Painted, Pennsylvania, c.1830, 23 x 41 1/2 In. 330.00
Chest, Blanket, Black Panels, Feet, Rosette, Floral, Red Ground, 24 1/2 In............. 9900.00
Chest, Blanket, Brown, Ochre Grain Painting, Pa., c.1820, 39 1/2 In. 850.00
Chest, Blanket, Burl Walnut, Interior Till, Pa., c.1790, 25 x 11 1/2 In. 470.00
Chest, Blanket, Chippendale, Cherry, Pennsylvania, c.1780, 29 x 51 In. 4400.00
Chest, Blanket, Chippendale, Pine, Bracket Base, 18th Century, 41 x 45 x 20 In........ 1230.00
Chest, Blanket, Chippendale, Walnut, Molding, 2 Drawers, Ogee Feet, 50 x 23 In. 3575.00
Chest, Blanket, Cotter Pin Hinges, Cutout Feet, New England, 24 x 13 x 15 In. 300.00
Chest, Blanket, Cotter Pin Hinges, Lidded Till, Bootjack Ends, 24 x 50 x 18 In. 345.00
Chest, Blanket, Dovetailed Case, 2 Drawers, Ball Feet, c.1770, 29 x 53 In. 1760.00
Chest, Blanket, Federal, Inlaid Walnut, Hinged Lid, c.1810, 10 x 17 x 8 In. 3600.00
Chest, Blanket, Flower & Leaf Decoration, Mustard Ground, 14 In. 27600.00
Chest, Blanket, Flower Basket Decoration, Bracket Feet, 20 x 42 x 17 In. 2015.00
Chest, Blanket, Grain Painted, Brown, Red, 2 Drawers, 39 x 41 1/2 x 18 In. 3100.00

Chest, Blanket, Grained Mahogany Burl Panels, 6-Board, 24 x 40 x 17 In. 1430.00
Chest, Blanket, Hinged Cover, Allover Blue, Red Painted Molding, 24 x 22 3/4 In. 400.00
Chest, Blanket, Jacobean, Oak, Carved Corners, 25 x 37 1/2 x 16 1/2 In. 315.00
Chest, Blanket, Lift Top, 3 Drawers, Carved, France, 18th Century, 30 x 54 x 21 In. 1080.00
Chest, Blanket, Maple, Yellow Pine Bottom & Back, 20 1/2 x 32 In. 800.00
Chest, Blanket, Oak, Grain Painted, Western Pa., Mid 19th Century, 18 x 39 In. 1100.00
Chest, Blanket, Overall Red & Black Stippled, c.1835, 24 x 41 3/4 In. 1320.00
Chest, Blanket, Painted, Floral Panels, Wood Grained, c.1850, 30 x 58 x 25 In. 430.00
Chest, Blanket, Painted, Overall Yellow & Ocher Sponging, c.1830, 27 x 49 1/2 In. 1100.00
Chest, Blanket, Painted, Tapered Feet, Molded Base, Inset Panels, 40 x 18 x 22 In. 660.00
Chest, Blanket, Pine, 3 Drawers, Cutout Feet, c.1850, 31 1/4 x 49 3/4 In. 525.50
Chest, Blanket, Pine, Black Grain, Red Ground, Susan Slanter, 1826, 22 x 43 In. 1695.00
Chest, Blanket, Pine, Brown, Molding, Dovetailed, c.1850, 38 x 17 1/2 x 23 In. 715.00
Chest, Blanket, Pine, Dovetailed Case, 2 Drawers, Pa., c.1830, 33 x 50 1/2 In. 525.00
Chest, Blanket, Pine, Dovetailed Case, Beveled Lid, 9 1/2 x 15 1/4 In. 5225.00
Chest, Blanket, Pine, Faux Figured Maple, Bracket Feet, c.1810, 20 x 35 In. 440.00
Chest, Blanket, Pine, Grain Painted, Red, Black, 2 Drawers, Pa., c.1810, 29 x 45 In. 468.00
Chest, Blanket, Pine, Hinged Lid, Apple Green Paint, 27 1/4 x 54 1/4 In. 2070.00
Chest, Blanket, Pine, Hinged Paneled Lid, Candle Till, Painted Flowers, 52 1/2 In. 860.00
Chest, Blanket, Pine, Lift Top, Pierced Bracket Feet, Early 19th Century, 23 In. 3000.00
Chest, Blanket, Pine, Orange Sponge Painted Panels, Painted Case, 29 x 49 In. 6600.00
Chest, Blanket, Pine, Painted, 3 Floral Panels, Salmon Ground, 25 1/2 x 51 x 21 In. 920.00
Chest, Blanket, Pine, Painted, Drawer, Cutout Ends, N.H., c.1770, 29 1/2 x 45 In. 2310.00
Chest, Blanket, Pine, Painted, Overall Green Vinegar Grain, c.1800, 22 x 43 In. 6710.00
Chest, Blanket, Pine, Painted, Paneled Front & Sides, Swirl Design, c.1825, 38 In. 1100.00
Chest, Blanket, Pine, Rosewood, Painted, Stenciling, Bootjack Feet, 1790, 20 x 36 In. . . . 600.00
Chest, Blanket, Pine, Salmon Paint, 1-Board Top, Ball Feet, 37 1/2 x 15 x 19 In. 330.00
Chest, Blanket, Pine, Sponge Paint, 1 Drawer, 33 1/2 x 44 x 20 In. 660.00
Chest, Blanket, Pine, Till, Lower Drawer, Incised Border, Late 19th Century, 32 In. 370.00
Chest, Blanket, Poplar, Bracket Feet, Beveled Apron, Brass Escutcheon, 37 x 21 In. 715.00
Chest, Blanket, Poplar, Figured, Bracket Feet, 6-Board, 25 x 47 x 20 In. 770.00
Chest, Blanket, Poplar, Painted, Red, Yellow Feather Grain, Pa., c.1820, 24 x 42 In. 440.00
Chest, Blanket, Poplar, Paneled, Hinged Top, Opens To Well, Bun Feet, 1730, 41 In. 5465.00
Chest, Blanket, Poplar, Pine, Painted, Panel Front, Turned Feet, 1800s, 25 x 50 In. 450.00
Chest, Blanket, Poplar, Red Washed, Dovetailed Bracket Feet, Till, I.H., 1855, 49 In. 600.00
Chest, Blanket, Poplar, Walnut, Till, Dovetailed Case, Turned Feet, 22 1/2 In. 6600.00
Chest, Blanket, Poplar, Yellow Pine, Panel & Post, Marked 1850, 32 x 18 x 20 In. 1870.00
Chest, Blanket, Queen Anne, Tiger Maple, Scalloped Skirt, c.1750, 50 1/2 x 36 In. 7700.00
Chest, Blanket, Red, Gold, Black Camphor, Scalloped Apron, 37 x 19 x 24 In. 265.00
Chest, Blanket, Shaker, Blue Paint, Dovetailed, Enfield, N.H., 17 1/2 x 37 x 18 In. 1150.00
Chest, Blanket, Snipe Hinges, Lock, Cutout Feet, 19th Century, 43 In. 650.00
Chest, Blanket, Softwood, Molded Lid, Bracket Feet, Red, Brown Paint, 23 In. 440.00
Chest, Blanket, Softwood, Scrolled Painted Design, 21 x 43 x 19 In. 250.00
Chest, Blanket, Striped Brown Over Mustard Design, Turned Feet, 27 x 43 x 20 In. 300.00
Chest, Blanket, Walnut, 2 Overlapping Drawers, Covered Till, 26 x 48 1/2 In. 1870.00
Chest, Blanket, Walnut, Bracket Feet, Drawers, Rattail Hinges, 1800, 26 x 51 x 24 In. 1765.00
Chest, Blanket, Walnut, Dovetail Construction, Bone Escutcheon, 10 x 19 In. 800.00
Chest, Blanket, Walnut, Dovetailed Case, Bun Feet, 25 x 40 In. 990.00
Chest, Blanket, Walnut, Strap Hinges, Dovetailed Case, 7 3/4 x 15 1/2 In. 1650.00
Chest, Blanket, Yellow Pine, Applied Molding, Bracket Feet, 24 x 22 x 44 1/2 In. 660.00
Chest, Blanket, Yellow Pine, Red, Yellow Feather Grain Painted, c.1830, 20 x 41 In. 300.00
Chest, Blanket, Yellow, Ocher Feather Design, Yellow Highlights, Pa., 25 3/4 In. 16500.00
Chest, Bombe, Burl Veneer, 2 Drawers, Inlaid, Italy, 30 1/2 x 40 1/2 x 16 1/2 In. 460.00
Chest, Bombe, Burl Walnut, Fruitwood, 4 Long Drawers, 33 x 22 1/2 In. 3335.00
Chest, Bowfront, 4 Drawers, Rope Twist Colonettes, Scalloped Skirt, 1820, 42 In. 2300.00
Chest, Bowfront, Cherry Veneer, 6 Drawers, Inset Center At Top, 46 x 41 In. 5225.00
Chest, Bowl Of Flowers, Rosette, Foliate, Red, Brown Ground, 1866, 48 In. 5225.00
Chest, Bride's, Wooden Peg Design, Woman On Horseback, 32 x 14 3/4 In. 440.00
Chest, Campaign, Camphorwood, 3 Short Drawers Over 3 Long Drawers, 41 In. 3000.00
Chest, Campaign, Oak, 4 Graduated Drawers, Bun Feet, 1850s, 44 x 48 In. 800.00
Chest, Campaign, Teakwood, Brass Handles, 19th Century, 37 x 30 In. 1495.00
Chest, Campaign, Teakwood, Brass Handles, Compartmented Interior, 37 In. 1495.00
Chest, Campaign, Teakwood, Brass Handles, Feet, 19th Century, 45 x 45 In. 1725.00

Chest, Campaign, Teakwood, Lift Top Storage Box, Brass Bound, 19th Century, 36 In. 1120.00
Chest, Camphor, Brass Mounts, Branch Design, Late 19th Century, 20 x 41 x 19 In. 520.00
Chest, Camphor, British Colonial, 2 Short, 3 Long Drawers, 1850s, 44 1/2 In. 3150.00
Chest, Camphor, Lift Top, Polychrome Floral Pigskin, Metal Mounts, 35 x 20 In. 633.00
Chest, Cedar, Flower, Chrysanthemum Carvings, Japan, 1913, 26 x 44 In. 1380.00
Chest, Cedar, Lane, Bottom Drawer, Waterfall 245.00
Chest, Charles II, Oak, Frieze Drawer, 3 Graduated Drawers, Bracket Feet, 36 In. 4600.00
Chest, Cherry Veneer, Oak, Scalloped Bracket Feet, 3 Drawers, 23 x 16 x 28 In. 770.00
Chest, Cherry, 4 Graduated Drawers, Bowed Skirt, Line Inlay, 40 In. 7810.00
Chest, Cherry, 4 Graduated Drawers, Bracket Feet, 40 x 35 In. 2750.00
Chest, Cherry, 6 Drawer, Scratch Beading, Brass, French Feet, 39 x 18 x 50 In. 2200.00
Chest, Cherry, 6 Drawers, Side Lock, Spindled Gallery, c.1885, 37 x 60 x 20 In. 1624.00
Chest, Cherry, Line Inlay, 4 Drawers, Inlaid Escutcheons, French Feet, 1800, 33 In. 1980.00
Chest, Cherry, Mahogany Veneer, Front Diamond Inlay, 4 Drawers, 42 1/4 In. 2750.00
Chest, Cherry, Reeded Half Columns, 43 x 40 In. 4400.00
Chest, Cherry, Side Lock, Brass Hardware, Beveled Mirror, 81 3/4 In. 2795.00
Chest, Cherry, Yellow Pine, 2 Over 3 Drawers, Bracket Feet, 1800s, 48 x 39 In. 2800.00
Chest, Chestnut, Handmade, 2 Drawers, 1800s, 9 1/4 x 6 1/8 x 8 1/8 In. 220.00
Chest, Chippendale, Cherry, 4 Drawers, Columns, Pa., c.1780, 34 x 40 x 22 1/4 In. 7700.00
Chest, Chippendale, Cherry, 4 Drawers, Poplar, White Pine, c.1860, 36 1/2 x 42 In. 2330.00
Chest, Chippendale, Cherry, Applewood, 4 Drawers, Pa., c.1780, 40 x 38 1/2 In. 3300.00
Chest, Chippendale, Cherry, Fluted Quarter Columns, Claw Feet, c.1790, 63 x 38 In. 2970.00
Chest, Chippendale, Cherry, Poplar, 10 Dovetailed Drawers, 42 1/4 x 70 In. 2100.00
Chest, Chippendale, Mahogany, 4 Drawers, 31 1/2 x 28 1/2 x 17 In. 690.00
Chest, Chippendale, Mahogany, 4 Drawers, Maryland, c.1770, 32 x 34 1/2 In. 1045.00
Chest, Chippendale, Mahogany, Block Front, 4 Graduated Drawers, 36 x 21 In. 1150.00
Chest, Chippendale, Mahogany, Carved Block, Shell Front, 1885, 80 In. 2800.00
Chest, Chippendale, Mahogany, Veneers, 5 Drawers, England, 1800s, 40 x 38 In. 645.00
Chest, Chippendale, Maple, 2 Short Over 5 Long Drawers, 1780, 58 x 36 x 16 In. 9200.00
Chest, Chippendale, Maple, Cherry, 6 Graduated Drawers, 1780, 55 In. 5400.00
Chest, Chippendale, Maple, Cock-Beaded, 4 Drawers, c.1800, 36 x 37 x 18 In. 2070.00
Chest, Chippendale, Tiger Maple, 4 Thumbmolded Drawers, c.1781, 38 1/2 In. 2990.00
Chest, Chippendale, Walnut, 2 Short Over 4 Long Drawers, Pa., c.1790, 59 x 42 In. 660.00
Chest, Chippendale, Walnut, 3 Over 2 Over 4 Drawers, Pa., c.1780, 62 1/2 x 38 In. 9900.00
Chest, Chippendale, Walnut, 4 Drawers, Bracket Feet, c.1800, 33 1/2 x 39 In. 990.00
Chest, Chippendale, Walnut, 4 Drawers, Delaware Valley, c.1790, 37 x 38 In. 1210.00
Chest, Chippendale, Walnut, 4 Graduated Drawers, Ogee Feet, c.1780, 38 x 38 In. 3630.00
Chest, Chippendale, Walnut, 8 Drawers, Late 1700s, 55 x 42 x 21 In. 5175.00
Chest, Chippendale, Walnut, 9 Drawer, Molded Cornice, Apron, 60 x 45 x 24 In. 3450.00
Chest, Chippendale, Walnut, Pennsylvania, c.1780, 87 3/4 x 38 1/2 In. 2750.00
Chest, Classical, Mahogany, Oblong Top, 4 Veneered Drawers, Turned Feet, 47 In. 4560.00
Chest, Classical, Maple, 2 Over 4 Drawers, 19th Century, 54 x 44 In. .... *Illus* 1035.00
Chest, Classical, Walnut, 3 Long Drawers, Rectangular Top, 44 x 20 In. 460.00
Chest, Cock-Beaded Drawers, Teardrop Pulls, Secret Drawer, c.1740, 18 x 27 In. 1400.00
Chest, Continental, Oak, Carved, Hinged Top, 18th Century, 22 x 38 x 23 In. 460.00
Chest, Cottage Pine, Grain Painted, 4 Drawers, Matching Mirror, 19th Century 415.00

Furniture, Chest,
Classical, Maple,
2 Over 4 Drawers,
19th Century,
54 x 44 In.

Furniture, Chest,
Federal, Mahogany,
Cherry, 4 Drawers,
1820, 41 x 44 In.

Chest, Cutlery, George III Style, Yew, Inlay, 3 Drawers, Stand, 33 x 20 x 13 1/2 In. 865.00
Chest, Dark Brown, 3 Small Drawers On Right, 3 Wide Drawers On Left, 36 In. 275.00
Chest, Dome Top, Various Bone Inlays, Morocco, 26 x 38 x 19 In. 2240.00
Chest, Domed Top, Red Paint, Wrought Iron Lock, Side Handles, 29 1/2 In. 460.00
Chest, Dower, 3 Stippled Panels, Diamond Border, Lebanon County, Pa., 24 x 51 In. 1760.00
Chest, Dower, Lift Lid, Painted, Tulips, Dovetailed, Pa., c.1785, 28 1/2 x 48 In. 9900.00
Chest, Dower, Lift Lid, Storage Compartment, Till, Anna-B.F. Machrin 1777, 24 In. 1210.00
Chest, Dower, Lift Lid, Strap Hinges, Dovetailed Case, Ogee Feet, c.1800, 48 In. 4950.00
Chest, Dower, Painted, Unicorns, Hearts, Tulips, Late 1700s, 24 x 52 In. 415.00
Chest, Dower, Pine, Geometric & Foliate Panels, 32 1/2 x 57 1/2 In. 1400.00
Chest, Dower, Pine, Lift Lid, Storage, Till, Dovetailed Case, 18th Century, 48 In. 1210.00
Chest, Dower, Poplar, Painted, Stenciled Floral, Red Ground, 1857, 25 1/2 x 42 In. 1320.00
Chest, Eliel Saarinen, 5 Drawers, Wooden & Brushed Chrome Pulls, 45 In. 750.00
Chest, Eliel Saarinen, Walnut Veneer, 4 Drawers, Johnson Furniture, 30 x 20 In. 395.00
Chest, Eliel Saarinen, Walnut, 4 Graduated Drawers, Chrome Pulls, 31 1/2 In. 450.00
Chest, Elm, 2 Suspended Drawers, Stile Lets, 33 1/2 x 36 1/2 x 24 In. 575.00
Chest, Elm, 3 Frieze Drawers, Scroll Feet, Late 19th Century, 25 1/2 In. 345.00
Chest, Elm, Lacquered, Center Doors, Provincial, Tibet, 31 1/2 x 43 1/2 In. 345.00
Chest, Elm, Rectangular Top, 2 Doors, 3 Frieze Drawers, Brass, 35 x 16 In. 635.00
Chest, Empire, Cherry, 2 Over 3 Drawers, Ring & Pineapple, 55 x 47 x 21 In. 1150.00
Chest, Empire, Cherry, 3 Graduated Drawers, Tiger Maple Columns, Gallery, 55 In. 825.00
Chest, Empire, Cherry, Poplar, 2 Short Over 4 Long Dovetailed Drawers, 44 x 52 In. 715.00
Chest, Empire, Cherry, Tiger Maple, Large Hanging Drawer Over 3, Backsplash, 51 In. . . 525.00
Chest, Empire, Mahogany Flame Veneer, 4 Drawers, Replaced Brasses, 40 x 20 In. 660.00
Chest, Empire, Mahogany, 4 Drawers, 1 Hidden, Mushroom Knobs, 44 x 42 x 18 In. 310.00
Chest, Empire, Mahogany, Hairy Paw Feet, Mid 19th Century, 60 x 31 x 20 In. 1045.00
Chest, Empire, Pine, Painted, Ochre, Yellow Grained, Child's, c.1840, 24 x 17 3/4 In. . . . 660.00
Chest, Empire, Satinwood, 4 Drawers, Ormolu Pilasters, 36 x 19 x 45 In. 1150.00
Chest, Empire, Tiger Maple, Cherry, 4 Graduated Drawers, c.1820, 45 x 44 In. 550.00
Chest, Eugene Schoen, Walnut, 4 Graduated Drawers, 34 x 42 x 21 In. 1125.00
Chest, Federal, Birch, Cherry, Mahogany Veneer, 4 Drawers, 39 x 41 x 18 1/2 In. 2070.00
Chest, Federal, Birch, Mahogany, Rectangular Top, 4 Drawers, 43 1/2 x 20 In. 2300.00
Chest, Federal, Birch, Wavy, Grained Cherry, 49 x 39 1/2 x 17 1/2 In. 1380.00
Chest, Federal, Cherry, 4 Graduated Beaded Drawers, 41 x 44 x 21 In. 2300.00
Chest, Federal, Cherry, Inlaid, Bowfront, c.1800, 37 1/2 x 44 1/2 x 21 1/2 In. 3220.00
Chest, Federal, Cherry, New England, c.1840, 45 x 40 In. 770.00
Chest, Federal, Cherry, Painted, Ocher Comb, 4 Drawers, Pa., c.1815, 46 x 42 In. 4070.00
Chest, Federal, Cherry, Tiger Maple, Applied Half Columns, c.1835, 50 x 40 In. 550.00
Chest, Federal, Mahogany, 2 Short Over 2 Long Beaded Drawers, 1820, 36 In. 2300.00
Chest, Federal, Mahogany, 3 Graduated Drawers, Shaped Skirt, 35 x 39 x 19 In. 1850.00
Chest, Federal, Mahogany, 4 Drawers, Reeded Stiles, Ball Feet, c.1815, 45 x 46 In. 5400.00
Chest, Federal, Mahogany, Bowfront, Scroll Backboard, 2 Drawers, 48 x 41 x 20 In. 1380.00
Chest, Federal, Mahogany, Cherry, 4 Drawers, 1820, 41 x 44 In. . . . . *Illus* 2300.00
Chest, Federal, Mahogany, Figured, Inlaid, 6 Drawers, Apron, 48 x 45 x 21 In. 1840.00
Chest, Federal, Mahogany, Inlay, Bowfront, c.1800, 36 3/4 x 42 1/4 x 21 1/2 In. 4025.00
Chest, Federal, Mahogany, Reeded Rectangular Top, Bracket Feet, 1810, 36 In. 3680.00
Chest, Federal, Maple, Cherry, 4 Graduated Drawers, 1810, 44 In. 11400.00
Chest, Federal, Maple, Mahogany, 4 Drawers, Mass., c.1830, 42 1/2 x 42 x 18 In. 1090.00
Chest, Federal, Pine, 6 Drawers, Scalloped Base, Pennsylvania, c.1830, 20 x 17 In. 595.00
Chest, Federal, Walnut, 4 Drawers, Chamfered Stiles, 31 1/2 x 29 x 16 1/2 In. 1095.00
Chest, French Provincial, Mahogany, 4 Drawers, Mirror Top Insert, 16 x 7 x 34 In. 880.00
Chest, G. Nakashima, Walnut, 4 Drawers, Double Plank Base, 1950, 26 In. 5750.00
Chest, G. Nakashima, Walnut, Dovetailed Case, Plank Base, 1968, 53 In. 9000.00
Chest, G. Nelson, 5 Drawers, Black Lacquered Finish, Label, 41 3/4 In. 5175.00
Chest, G. Nelson, Oak, 5 Graduated Drawers, Wire Pulls, Hairpin Legs, 30 1/2 In. 4900.00
Chest, G. Nelson, Oak, Thin Edge, 5 Drawers, Black Hairpin Legs, 40 In. 4900.00
Chest, G. Nelson, White Enamel Frame, Black Laminate Top, 34 x 29 In. 980.00
Chest, G. Stickley, Mahogany, 2 Short Drawers Over 4 Long Drawers, 53 In. 5465.00
Chest, G. Stickley, No. 909, Mahogany, 2 Drawers Over 3, 36 x 42 In. 2760.00
Chest, Galle, Domed Top, Inlaid Courting Scene, Signed, 12 x 7 x 11 In. 4200.00
Chest, Gentleman's, Mahogany, 6 Drawers, Ornate Gallery, c.1885, 57 x 34 x 22 In. 2240.00
Chest, George I, Burl Walnut, Veneered Top, 3 Graduated Drawers, 37 In. 1495.00
Chest, George I, Oak, Rectangular Top, Brass Pulls, 2 Doors, 79 x 33 x 20 In. 3680.00

Chest, George I, Walnut, Dentil Frieze, 2 Over 6 Drawers, 60 x 47 x 22 In. 3220.00
Chest, George I, Walnut, Parquetry, 3 Short Over 3 Long Drawers, 1720, 38 x 40 In. 2990.00
Chest, George I, Yew, 3 Graduated Drawers, Bracket Feet, 27 x 26 x 17 In., Pair 1095.00
Chest, George I, Yew, Brushing Slide, 4 Drawers, 29 x 25 1/4 In. 1090.00
Chest, George I, Yew, Rectangular Top, 3 Graduated Drawers, 37 In. 4800.00
Chest, George II, Mahogany, Carved, Mid 1700s, 32 1/4 x 35 1/2 x 19 In. 4600.00
Chest, George II, Mahogany, Satinwood, 4 Graduated Drawers, 32 3/4 In. 4370.00
Chest, George II, Mahogany, Serpentine, 4 Graduated Drawers, 42 x 35 In. 2880.00
Chest, George II, Walnut, Parquetry, 2 Over 3 Drawers, 50 1/2 x 40 x 21 In. 3220.00
Chest, George III Style, Mahogany, Bowfront, 4 Drawers, 32 3/4 x 27 1/2 x 18 In. 1095.00
Chest, George III, Burl Walnut, 3 Drawers, Bracket Feet, 1780s, 37 x 37 x 22 In. 2645.00
Chest, George III, Mahogany, 2 Drawers, 5 Lower Drawers, Block Feet, 57 7/8 In. 1035.00
Chest, George III, Mahogany, 2 Short, 3 Long Drawers, Splay Feet, 40 x 18 1/2 In. 2185.00
Chest, George III, Mahogany, 3 Graduated Drawers, French Bracket Feet, 46 In. 1725.00
Chest, George III, Mahogany, 3 Graduated Drawers, Rectangular Top, 32 In. 1095.00
Chest, George III, Mahogany, 4 Graduated Drawers, Bracket Feet, 27 x 26 x 15 In. 1380.00
Chest, George III, Mahogany, 5 Drawers, Bracket Feet, 38 3/4 x 45 1/2 x 21 In. 1265.00
Chest, George III, Mahogany, 5 Drawers, French Bracket Feet, 42 x 39 1/2 x 20 In. 1725.00
Chest, George III, Mahogany, 5 Drawers, Rectangular Top, Bracket Feet, 43 In. 1610.00
Chest, George III, Mahogany, Bowed Top, 3 Graduated Drawers, 39 1/2 In. 1495.00
Chest, George III, Mahogany, Bowfront, 2 Short Over 3 Long Drawers, 40 x 41 In. 2185.00
Chest, George III, Mahogany, Bowfront, 3 Drawers, 41 x 40 1/2 In. 1955.00
Chest, George III, Mahogany, Bowfront, 3 Graduated Drawers, Bracket Feet, 40 In 1955.00
Chest, George III, Mahogany, Bowfront, 4 Drawers, c.1790, 39 1/2 x 44 In. 1210.00
Chest, George III, Mahogany, Bowfront, Banded Top, 3 Graduated Drawers, 43 In. 1610.00
Chest, George III, Mahogany, Bowfront, Drawers, 41 x 40 3/4 x 20 5/8 In. 1495.00
Chest, George III, Mahogany, Bowfront, Ebony Outline, 35 x 35 x 18 1/2 In. 1610.00
Chest, George III, Mahogany, Bowfront, Late 18th Century, 45 1/2 x 46 x 24 In. 1150.00
Chest, George III, Mahogany, Bowfront, Reeded Edge, 6 Drawers, 47 x 41 x 21 In. 1955.00
Chest, George III, Mahogany, Crossbanded Rectangular Top, 33 1/4 In. 6600.00
Chest, George III, Mahogany, Fitted Case, 2 Short Over 3 Long Drawers, 35 In. 3740.00
Chest, George III, Mahogany, Inlay, 2 Short Over 3 Long Drawers, 1800, 42 x 106 In. . . . 690.00
Chest, George III, Mahogany, Molded Rectangular Top, 3 Graduated Drawers, 34 In. 1035.00
Chest, George III, Mahogany, Overhanging Top, 4 Drawers, c.1790, 40 1/2 x 32 In. 1540.00
Chest, George III, Mahogany, Rectangular Top, 2 Graduated Drawers, 34 1/2 In. 1265.00
Chest, George III, Mahogany, Rectangular Top, 2 Long Drawers, 36 1/2 In. 1840.00
Chest, George III, Mahogany, Rectangular Top, 4 Graduated Drawers, 36 x 19 In. 1265.00
Chest, George III, Mahogany, Satinwood Drawers, Bracket Feet, 53 x 41 x 21 In. 1840.00
Chest, George III, Oak, Mahogany Banding, Inlaid Ivory Star, 38 x 35 1/2 x 20 In. 2300.00
Chest, George III, Oak, Reeded-Edge Top, 4 Graduated Drawers, 40 x 35 x 19 1/2 In. . . . 345.00
Chest, George III, Rosewood, 5 Drawers, French Bracket Feet, 41 1/2 x 43 x 21 In. 3450.00
Chest, George III, Tulipwood, Bowfront, Crossbanded, 4 Drawers, 42 x 37 In. 2760.00
Chest, George III, Walnut, Oyster Veneer, Geometric Inlay, 31 1/2 x 31 x 21 In. 1035.00
Chest, Hardwood, Latticework Design, Rectangular Top, 2 Drawers, 44 In. 400.00
Chest, Hardwood, Rectangular Top, 2 Doors, Carved Spandrels, 44 1/2 In. 460.00
Chest, Hepplewhite, 4 Drawers, Fluted Columns, French Feet, c.1800, 36 x 39 In. 2970.00
Chest, Hepplewhite, 9 Drawers, French Feet, 72 x 40 x 20 In. 3920.00
Chest, Hepplewhite, Cherry, 4 Drawers, French Feet, 36 x 43 x 20 In. 1680.00
Chest, Hepplewhite, Cherry, 4 Graduated Drawers, Bracket Feet, 35 x 40 x 19 In. 2970.00
Chest, Hepplewhite, Mahogany, Birch, Bowfront, 4 Drawers, New England, 38 x 21 In. . . 2200.00
Chest, Hepplewhite, Mahogany, Bowfront, 3 Oak-Lined Drawers, Splay Feet, 41 In. 2300.00
Chest, Hepplewhite, Mahogany, Bowfront, Fan Inlay, 37 1/4 x 37 In. 770.00
Chest, Hepplewhite, Mahogany, Figured, Bowfront, Inlay, 6 Drawers, 46 x 40 In. 1210.00
Chest, Hepplewhite, Mahogany, Poplar, 4 Drawers, French Feet, 42 x 20 3/8 x 38 In. 1375.00
Chest, Hepplewhite, Maple, 5 Drawers, Butler's Drawer, 39 1/2 x 42 x 18 1/2 In. 2185.00
Chest, Hide Covered, Brass Binding, Polychrome Flowers, 13 x 30 1/2 In. 825.00
Chest, Imperial Dragons Clasping Pearl Of Serenity, 51 x 38 x 20 7/8 In. 460.00
Chest, Jewel, Satinwood, Faux Front Drawer, Fitted Interior, England, 15 1/2 In. 1095.00
Chest, Leather, Stack Of Books, Tooled, Drawers, Bun Feet, 24 1/2 x 24 1/2 x 18 In. 490.00
Chest, Leather, Stacked Luggage Form, 4 Drawers, Bracket Base, 32 x 28 In. 980.00
Chest, Lift Top, 3 Raised Panels, Red, Yellow Paint 7800.00
Chest, Lift Top, Grain Paint, Yellow, Brown Paint, Turned Feet, 25 x 19 1/2 In. 9220.00
Chest, Lift Top, Gray, Yellow, Cream Paint, New England, 15 x 42 x 15 In. 13800.00

Chest, Limbert, Mahogany, 5 Drawers, 69 x 36 x 20 In. 3335.00
Chest, Lingerie, Floral Marquetry All Sides, 52 In. 520.00
Chest, Louis Philippe, Mahogany, Semainier, Marble Top, c.1830, 57 x 33 x 18 In. 630.00
Chest, Louis XV, Beige, Green Marble Top, Leaf Border, 6 Drawers, 25 x 49 In. 200.00
Chest, Louis XV, Fruitwood, Serpentine Front, 19th Century, 14 1/2 x 11 1/4 In. 1650.00
Chest, Louis XVI, Mahogany, Marble Top, 3 Drawers, 33 x 49 x 22 In. 2645.00
Chest, Louis XVI, Semainier, Fruitwood, Marble, 7 Drawers, Inlay, 1800s, 56 In. 2860.00
Chest, Mahogany, 1 Deep Over 3 Drawers, Reeded Stiles, 42 1/2 x 45 In. 750.00
Chest, Mahogany, 2 Short Drawers, Bracket Supports, Paw Feet, Italy, 21 In. 1840.00
Chest, Mahogany, 2 Short Over 2 Long Drawers, Ogee Bracket Feet, 1790s 1600.00
Chest, Mahogany, 2 Short Over 3 Long Drawers, Bracket Feet, 1820, 43 x 43 In. 980.00
Chest, Mahogany, 2 Short Over 3 Long Drawers, Ivory Feet, c.1800, 10 1/4 x 9 In. 1100.00
Chest, Mahogany, 2 Short, 3 Graduated Drawers, Late 18th Century, 42 In. 1150.00
Chest, Mahogany, 2 Short, 3 Long Drawers, Mid 1880s, 43 x 45 x 21 In. 800.00
Chest, Mahogany, 3 Long Graduated Drawers, Rectangular Top, 1800, 31 In. 3000.00
Chest, Mahogany, 3 Short Drawers Over 4 Lower Drawers, 19th Century, 61 In. 345.00
Chest, Mahogany, 4 Long Graduated Drawers, French Feet, c.1810, 37 x 43 In. 1265.00
Chest, Mahogany, 6 Drawers, 2 Short Drawers, Bracket Feet, 1860s, 13 1/2 In. 865.00
Chest, Mahogany, Bowfront, 2 Drawers At Top, 3 Lower Drawers, 1770s, 37 In. 1985.00
Chest, Mahogany, Bowfront, 2 Short Drawers, 4 Lower Drawers, 1770, 48 In. 1610.00
Chest, Mahogany, Bowfront, 4 Graduated Drawers, Line Inlay, 36 x 39 In. 1555.00
Chest, Mahogany, Bowfront, Birch & Cherry, 4 Graduated Drawers, 1790, 42 In. 7150.00
Chest, Mahogany, Bowfront, Flared French Feet, 36 x 41 1/2 In. 2200.00
Chest, Mahogany, Classical Carved, Basket Weave Posts, Pineapples, 47 x 63 In. 1980.00
Chest, Mahogany, D-Shape Marble Top, 3 Drawers, Molded Stiles, 37 1/2 x 42 3/4 In. 605.00
Chest, Mahogany, Figured, 2 Short & 3 Long Drawers, Turned Feet, 43 x 41 x 19 In. 460.00
Chest, Mahogany, Figured, Rosewood Veneer, Inlay, Mirror, Italy, 50 x 21 x 79 In. 770.00
Chest, Mahogany, Glass Door, Brass Feet, England, 20 In. 230.00
Chest, Mahogany, Inlaid Conch Shell, 4 Long Drawers, French Feet, 1870, 14 1/2 In. 8050.00
Chest, Mahogany, Inset Burled Panel, Parquetry Bands, Fitted Case, 36 1/4 In. 1610.00
Chest, Mahogany, Marble Top, Brass-Banded Border, 6 Drawers, 1840s, 55 1/2 In. 8640.00
Chest, Mahogany, Parquetry, Rectangular Top, 5 Drawers, Square Feet, 36 1/4 In. 1610.00
Chest, Mahogany, Recessed Frieze Drawer, 5 Lower Drawers, 1820s, 63 1/4 In. 5550.00
Chest, Mahogany, Serpentine Top, 2 Ogee Drawers, 36 x 40 1/2 x 23 In. 5750.00
Chest, Maple, 4 Upper Drawers, Lower 3 Short Drawers, c.1780, 71 1/2 In. 9200.00
Chest, Maple, Mahogany Tablet, 2 Short, 3 Graduated Drawers, c.1815, 46 1/2 In. 9775.00
Chest, Maple, Poplar, Pine, Lift Top, 2 Drawers, 1790s, 37 1/2 x 36 In. 1840.00
Chest, Marble Top, Brass Medallion On Door, 20th Century, 41 1/2 x 51 x 18 In. 1650.00
Chest, McCobb, Mahogany Veneer, 8 Drawers, Travertine Top, 32 1/4 In. 1015.00
Chest, McCobb, Walnut, 8 Drawers, Travertine Top, 32 In. 1070.00
Chest, Mule, George III, Oak, Paneled Front, Hinged Top, Drawers, 37 x 57 x 22 In. 550.00
Chest, Mule, Pine, 2 Dovetailed Drawers, Mahogany Pulls, Inside Locks, 40 1/2 In. 1320.00
Chest, Mule, Pine, Bootjack Ends, 2 Bead-Edged Drawers, 42 x 40 1/4 In. 770.00
Chest, Mule, Pine, Painted, Sponge Graining, 6-Board, Cutout Feet, 17 x 38 x 43 In. 2090.00
Chest, Mule, Walnut, Poplar, Hinged Lift Top, Brass Pulls, 15 x 19 1/2 x 10 In. 2900.00
Chest, Mustard Paint, Glass Pulls, Red Trim, 11 3/4 x 13 1/4 In. 435.00
Chest, Napoleon III, Mahogany, Semainier, c.1875, 57 3/4 x 31 1/2 x 14 3/4 In. 3220.00
Chest, Oak, 2 Small Over 4 Long Drawers, Backboard, Taper Legs, 50 x 38 x 19 In. 1095.00
Chest, Oak, 4 Panels Of Scrollwork, Franco-Flemish, 16th Century, 28 3/8 In. 6325.00
Chest, Oak, Applied Scroll Molding, Bun Feet, c.1860, 10 1/2 x 14 x 7 1/2 In. 1150.00
Chest, Oak, Canted Front Corners, Pair Of Short Drawers On Sides, 38 x 20 In. 2415.00
Chest, Oak, Carved Cover, Flowers, Tambourines, 1880, 9 x 17 x 11 In. 1795.00
Chest, Oak, Cherry, Rectangular Overhanging Top, Stile Feet, 37 x 41 x 20 In. 18400.00
Chest, Oak, Mahogany, 3 Graduated Drawers, 18th Century, 34 x 35 x 22 In. 3220.00
Chest, Oak, Overhang, Quartersawn Panels, Conn., c.1720, 27 1/2 x 46 1/2 x 21 In. 4675.00
Chest, Oak, Rectangular Top, 2 Drawers, Turned, Bun Feet, 35 1/2 In. 1725.00
Chest, Oak, Reeded, Leaf Design Panels, 26 1/2 x 19 x 17 In. 660.00
Chest, Oak, Walnut Veneer, 4 Graduated Drawers, Ogee Feet, 14 1/4 x 20 x 10 In. 1075.00
Chest, Oak, Walnut, 3 Drawers, Late 19th Century, 17 x 10 1/2 In. 220.00
Chest, Oak, White Marble Top, 2 Short Drawers, Early 20th Century, 18 x 19 In. 635.00
Chest, Oysterwood, 25 Drawers, England, 51 x 30 x 19 In. 3500.00
Chest, Pigskin, Hinged Rectangular Hasp, Gilt Design, 30 x 13 x 22 In. 115.00
Chest, Pine, 1-Board Sides & Top, 2 Over 4 Drawers, Backsplash, 52 x 44 In. 1265.00

As a general rule, the drawer bottom of an 18th-century chest was made of 2 or 3 pieces of wood, the Victorian drawer bottom was made from a single piece. The Victorian bottom was often screwed in place.

Furniture, Chest, Sheraton,
Walnut, 11 Drawers, Maple
Pulls, 1700, 40 x 73 In.

Chest, Pine, 2 Drawers, Early 18th Century, 35 1/2 x 50 1/2 x 19 In. 1380.00
Chest, Pine, 3 Long Thumb-Molded Graduated Drawers, Blue Paint, 38 x 18 In. 16100.00
Chest, Pine, 4 Drawers, Bracket Base, New England, c.1830, 49 3/4 x 45 In. 525.00
Chest, Pine, 5 Blind Drawers, 3 Graduated Drawers, Bracket Feet, 51 1/2 In. 1960.00
Chest, Pine, 6-Board, Vinegar Grain Painted, Iron Handles, 12 1/4 x 29 x 16 In. 1840.00
Chest, Pine, Canted Ends, Cutout Base, Blue Gray Paint, 42 In. 4900.00
Chest, Pine, Carved Backboard, 4 Graduated Drawers, 20 x 9 1/2 x 6 In. 575.00
Chest, Pine, Dovetailed Case, Domed Lid, Iron Banding, 16 x 36 In. 110.00
Chest, Pine, Hinged Top, Red, Yellow Design, Black Feet, 20 3/4 x 33 x 16 1/2 In. 10925.00
Chest, Pine, Lift Top, Cutout Feet, Light Blue Paint, 25 x 42 x 16 1/2 In. 4900.00
Chest, Pine, Lift Top, Thumb-Molded, Light Blue Paint, 26 x 49 1/4 x 19 In. 1955.00
Chest, Pine, Molded Lift Top, Zigzag Carved Ends, Red Paint, Cutout Feet, 25 In. 1725.00
Chest, Pine, Oak, 2 Faux Drawers, Turned Stile Feet, 40 x 38 3/4 x 19 1/2 In. 9200.00
Chest, Pine, Rectangular Molded Hinged Top, Red Painted Surface, 26 1/2 In. 8050.00
Chest, Poplar, 2 Over 3 Tiger Maple Veneer Drawers, Backsplash, 44 x 39 x 20 In. 355.00
Chest, Poplar, Turned Half Columns, Turned Feet, Brown Grain Surface, 23 In. 2420.00
Chest, Queen Anne, 3 Graduated Long Drawers, Cabriole Legs, Pad Feet, 61 In. 7360.00
Chest, Queen Anne, Birch, Butternut, Red Stain, 2 Over 3 Drawers, 40 x 37 x 19 In. 2545.00
Chest, Queen Anne, Burl Walnut, Crossband, Veneer Drawers, 39 x 36 1/2 x 18 In. 3220.00
Chest, Queen Anne, Inlaid Oak, Early 18th Century, 41 x 38 1/4 x 23 1/4 In. 1840.00
Chest, Queen Anne, Walnut, Banded Top, 3 Frieze Drawers, 39 x 40 x 22 In. 2760.00
Chest, Queen Anne, Walnut, Banded Top, 3 Graduated Drawers, 35 1/2 In. 1610.00
Chest, Rectangular Molded Top, Turned Feet, Black Paint, 25 1/4 x 48 x 21 In. 4600.00
Chest, Red Paint, 4 Dovetailed Drawers, Lock Escutcheons, Rose-Head Nails, 43 In. 2860.00
Chest, Regency, 5 Graduated Drawers, Rectangular Top, England, 31 3/4 In. 550.00
Chest, Regency, Acanthus-Carved Columns, Paw Feet, 53 x 45 In. 825.00
Chest, Regency, Mahogany, 4 Graduated Drawers, Plinth Base, 41 x 50 x 25 In. 1265.00
Chest, Regency, Mahogany, Butler's, Brass Applique, 19th Century, 49 x 23 In. 2750.00
Chest, Regency, Mahogany, Inlaid Frieze, 2 Short Drawers, Ogee Feet, 47 In. 1150.00
Chest, Regency, Mahogany, Rectilinear Top, Reeded Edge, Bracket Feet, 43 In. 1035.00
Chest, Reliquary, Wood, Carved Painted Trailing Flowers, Scrolled Feet, 14 In. 640.00
Chest, Renaissance Revival, Mahogany, 7 Drawers, Side Lock, 53 x 45 x 20 In. 1265.00
Chest, Rohde, 4 Drawers, Herman Miller, 33 x 48 x 19 In. 1725.00
Chest, Rope-Twist Edge, 4 Drawers, Reeded Columns, Paw Feet, 1850s, 43 In. 695.00
Chest, Rosewood, Gilt Brass Mounted, Drop Front, 6 Drawers, 11 x 15 x 9 In. 1610.00
Chest, Roycroft, Mahogany, Hinged Top, Metal Latch, Corner Brace, Handles, 9 In. 575.00
Chest, Shaker, 6 Short Over 3 Long Drawers, Blue Paint, 48 x 37 1/2 In. 7185.00
Chest, Sheraton, 2 Drawers Over 3 Graduated Drawers, Acanthus, 1820, 41 x 42 In. 1460.00
Chest, Sheraton, Bird's-Eye Maple, 4 Drawers, Brass Handles, 37 x 42 x 19 In. 2415.00
Chest, Sheraton, Cherry, 2 Short Over 4 Long Drawers, Turned Columns, 48 In. 1695.00
Chest, Sheraton, Mahogany Veneer, Bowfront, Mass., c.1810, 42 x 42 In. 1320.00
Chest, Sheraton, Walnut, 4 Drawers, Molded Stiles, Turned Feet, 1830, 43 x 40 In. 2200.00
Chest, Sheraton, Walnut, 11 Drawers, Maple Pulls, 1700, 40 x 73 In. . . . . *Illus* 7280.00
Chest, Spanish Baroque, Walnut, Inlaid, Pierced, Engraved, 1600s, 33 x 38 x 17 In. 2645.00
Chest, Spice, Pine, Frieze Drawer, Button Pulls, Rectangular, 16 x 14 x 10 In. 200.00

Chest, Stencil Design, 3 Drawer, Porcelain Handles, 40 x 48 x 23 In. 460.00
Chest, Storage, Hinged Cloud Hasp, Chinese, 19th Century, 27 x 41 x 25 In. 400.00
Chest, Sugar, Cherry, Divided Interior, Paneled Sides, 2 Drawers, 35 x 35 1/2 In. 6050.00
Chest, Sugar, Cherry, Dovetailed Case, Slant Front, Pullout Supports, 30 x 31 In. 1870.00
Chest, Teakwood, Lift-Top Storage, Molded Frame, Brass Bound, 36 In. 1150.00
Chest, Tiger Maple, 2 Short Over 3 Long Drawers, 41 3/4 x 19 1/2 In. 860.00
Chest, Tiger Maple, Cherry, 3 Drawers Over 3 Graduated Drawers, 42 x 22 In. 1540.00
Chest, Victorian, Burl Walnut, 7 Drawers, Molded Cornice, 1875, 60 x 39 x 21 In. 1870.00
Chest, Victorian, Cherry, 4 Inset Panels, 5 Drawers, 55 1/2 x 21 x 61 In. 300.00
Chest, Victorian, Mahogany, 5 Drawers, Leaf-Carved Columns, Block Feet, 46 In. 980.00
Chest, Victorian, Mahogany, 7 Drawers, Mother-Of-Pearl Knobs, 53 x 23 In. 2530.00
Chest, Victorian, Mahogany, Inlay, Mid 19th Century, 55 x 50 1/2 x 22 1/2 In. 160.00
Chest, Victorian, Stepped, Green Paint, Striping, Strawberries, 20 x 14 x 8 In. 4400.00
Chest, Vinegar Grained, Red, Painted, Drawer, Hinged Top, 1800s, 31 x 37 x 18 In. 7475.00
Chest, Walnut, 4 Drawers, Line Inlay, Barber Pole Inlaid Edge, 42 x 37 3/4 In. 1760.00
Chest, Walnut, 4 Graduated Drawers, Reeded Edges, Flared French Feet, 1800, 37 In. ... 3025.00
Chest, Walnut, 6 Drawers, Molded Trim, Carved Pulls, 39 x 21 In. 595.00
Chest, Walnut, 6 Drawers, Side Lock, Ornate Gallery, 1880, 63 x 38 x 19 In. 2800.00
Chest, Walnut, Concave, 2 Drawers, Cabriole Legs, Handles, Anglo-Dutch, 38 x 18 In. .. 2780.00
Chest, Walnut, Front Apron, 4 Drawers, Diamond Escutcheons, 39 1/2 In. 1650.00
Chest, Walnut, Graduated Drawers, Pa., c.1800, 36 x 39 In. 2310.00
Chest, Walnut, Oak Sides, 5 Cross-Banded Drawers, 1710, 36 x 37 1/2 In. 4025.00
Chest, Walnut, Oyster Veneer, Inlaid Top, 3 Long Drawers, c.1800, 31 1/2 In. 1035.00
Chest, Walnut, Rectangular Top, 4 Drawers, Italy, 17th Century, 31 x 35 1/2 In. 2875.00
Chest, Walnut, Rectangular Top, 9 Drawers, Bracket Feet, 18th Century, 54 In. 2300.00
Chest, Walnut, White Inset Marble Top, 4 Drawers, Block Feet, 1840, 39 In. 980.00
Chest, Walnut, Yellow Pine, Large Strap Hinges, Turned Feet, 1930, 27 1/4 In. 3920.00
Chest, Wedding, 1 Drawer, High Frame, Names, Mexico, 1900s, 48 x 37 In. 1850.00
Chest, William & Mary Style, Walnut, Parquetry, 4 Drawers, 39 1/2 x 36 x 21 In. 1840.00
Chest, William & Mary, Maple, New England, c.1720, 71 x 42 In. 3190.00
Chest, William & Mary, Oak, 2 Short & 3 Long Drawers, 38 x 38 x 21 In. 2760.00
Chest, William & Mary, Walnut, Lift Top, Till, 2 Short Drawers, 1710, 52 In. 2600.00
Chest, William & Mary, Walnut, Parquetry, 2 Over 3 Drawers, 40 x 37 1/2 x 20 In. 3740.00
Chest, William IV, Mahogany, 3 Graduated Drawers, Plinth Base, 46 1/2 In. 1035.00
Chest, William IV, Mahogany, Stepped Top, Ebonized Outlined 5 Drawers, 49 In. 1955.00
Chest, Yew, 2 Short & 3 Long Graduated Drawers, Bracket Feet, 30 3/4 In. 920.00
Chest-On-Chest, Elm, Rectangular Top, 4 Small Drawers, 38 x 31 1/2 In. 800.00
Chest-On-Chest, George I, Burl Veneer, Early 18th Century, 70 1/2 x 43 1/2 In. 5500.00
Chest-On-Chest, George I, Walnut, Parquetry, 64 3/4 x 40 3/4 x 22 1/2 In. 9200.00
Chest-On-Chest, George II, Mahogany, Mid 1700s, 77 1/4 x 43 x 21 1/2 In. 9200.00
Chest-On-Chest, George II, Oak, Provincial, Mid 1700s, 66 1/4 x 41 1/4 x 22 In. 2070.00
Chest-On-Chest, George III, Mahogany, 3 Graduated Drawers, 72 x 42 x 22 In. 4370.00
Chest-On-Chest, George III, Mahogany, 8 Drawers, 73 1/2 x 44 x 21 1/2 In. 1380.00
Chest-On-Chest, George III, Mahogany, Dentil Cornice, 73 x 44 x 22 In. 2990.00
Chest-On-Chest, Hepplewhite, Cherry, Line Inlay, Pa., c.1800, 67 1/2 x 42 In. 6600.00
Chest-On-Chest, Mahogany, 2 Over 3 Drawers, 74 1/2 In. 3025.00
Chest-On-Chest, Oak, Quartersawn, 8 Drawers, 1790 .... 6500.00
Chest-On-Chest, Regency, Mahogany, Recessed Brass Pulls, c.1840, 63 x 37 x 19 In. 9800.00
Chest-On-Frame, Queen Anne, Cherry, Maple, 6 Graduated Drawers, 48 In. 15600.00
Chest-On-Frame, Queen Anne, Walnut, Pa., c.1760, 58 1/2 x 38 1/2 In. 3960.00
Chest-On-Frame, Walnut, 3 Short Drawers, 4 Graduated Drawers, c.1760, 66 1/4 In. 6050.00
Chest-On-Frame, Walnut, Trifid Feet, c.1740, 63 1/2 x 40 1/4 In. 9500.00
Chest-On-Stand, Walnut, 3 Graduated Drawers, 35 1/4 In. 5290.00
Chiffonnier, Louis XVI Style, Mahogany, c.1900, 49 1/2 x 19 1/2 x 13 1/2 In. 1725.00
Chiffonnier, Louis XVI Style, Tulipwood, Rectangular Top, Cabriole Legs, 27 In. 750.00
Chiffonnier, Marble Top, Brass Gallery, 4 Drawers, Faux Doors, c.1900, 49 1/2 In. 1725.00
Chiffonnier, Regency, Mahogany, 2 Shelves, Paneled Doors, 67 x 47 x 13 In. 2070.00
Chiffonnier, Serpentine Marble Top, 2 Doors, Interior Mirror Panels, 68 x 43 In. 490.00
Chiffonnier, Victorian, Walnut, Carved Shelves, 2 Doors, Mirror, 73 x 59 In. 3450.00
Clothes Tree, Stickley Bros., Medium Original Finish, Tapered Posts, 72 x 20 In. 690.00
Coat Rack, Art Deco, Wrought Iron, Mirror, France, c.1928, 16 x 27 1/2 In. 3000.00
Coat Rack, Arts & Crafts, Mahogany, Anchor Design, Original Finish, 25 In. 200.00
Coat Rack, Bentwood, Original Black Paint, Turned Feet, 74 In. 250.00

Coat Rack, Black Forest, Mountain Goat, Foliage, 1880, 12 x 13 In. 1000.00
Coat Rack, Elm, Carved Birds & Flowers, Floral Finial, 65 x 83 In. 290.00
Coat Rack, G. Stickley, Tapered Posts, 6 Bronze Double Hooks, 71 In. 4025.00
Coat Rack, Pine, Carved, Red Paint, Early 19th Century, 34 1/2 In. 220.00
Coat Rack, Stickley Bros., Mahogany Finish, 70 In. 400.00
Coat Rack, Wrought Iron, Late 19th Century, 71 1/2 In. 275.00
Coffer, Charles I, Oak, 4 Frieze Diamond Panel Top, 50 x 24 x 21 In. 2650.00
Coffer, Charles II, Oak, 2-Board Top, 3 Frieze Diamond Panel, 43 x 30 x 19 In. 1035.00
Coffer, Charles II, Oak, Candle Box Interior, Panels, 50 x 24 x 20 In. 2190.00
Coffer, Dark Finish, Scroll Design, Removable Lid, Chinese, 39 x 19 x 20 In. 220.00
Coffer, Elm, 2 Doors, Brass Hinges, Hasps, 37 1/4 x 18 1/2 In. 520.00
Coffer, Hinged Top, Scrolled Vine, Foliate Inlay, Floral, 1803, 28 x 53 x 25 In. 4025.00
Coffer, Jacobean Style, Inlaid Oak, Molded Edge, c.1675, 28 1/2 x 53 1/2 x 24 In. 805.00
Coffer, Louis Philippe, Burl Walnut, Rosewood Band, Bun Feet, 5 1/4 x 12 x 8 In. 175.00
Coffer, Oak, 6 Raised Front Panels, Cotter Hinges, England, 1740, 15 x 15 x 28 In. 4800.00
Coffer, Oak, Carved, Incised Geometric Designs, 30 x 16 1/4 x 20 In. 685.00
Coffer, Oak, Hinged Cover, Interlocking Diamonds, Iron Handles, 14 In. 1095.00
Coffer, Oak, Rectangular Hinged Top, Leaves, Cabriole Legs, 30 1/2 In. 1840.00
Coffer, Rosewood, Bone & Turquoise Shell Inlay, 8 Drawers, 18th Century, 20 In. 4800.00
Coffer, Victorian, Black Lacquer, Painted, Stand, Turned Supports, 23 x 13 x 9 In. 460.00
Commode, Baroque, Walnut, 2 Drawers, Carved Lions, Faces, Bun Feet, 36 In. 2185.00
Commode, Biedermeier, Marble Top, Bulbous Feet, 30 x 14 1/2 x 14 In., Pair 1035.00
Commode, Biedermeier, Rectangular Stepped Top, 3 Graduated Drawers, 32 In. 4600.00
Commode, Biedermeier, Walnut, Ebonized, 3 Recessed Drawers, 34 x 50 x 24 In. 1325.00
Commode, Birch, Biedermeier, Projecting Frieze Drawer, 2 Center Drawers, 34 In. 2910.00
Commode, Birch, Ionic Columns, 3 Paneled Drawers, Interior Shelves, 35 x 41 In. 4370.00
Commode, Bombe, Gilt, 2 Drawers, Painted Cartouches, Marble, 1800s, 40 x 34 In. 8050.00
Commode, Bombe, Polychrome, Serpentine, Venice, c.1850, 35 1/2 x 48 x 21 In. 8625.00
Commode, Bowfront, Woman Holding Bow Surrounded By Women, 43 x 34 In. 1100.00
Commode, Continental, 3 Drawers, Circular Brass Pulls, Turned Feet, 13 x 9 In. 1725.00
Commode, Crossbanded Top, Plain Compartment, 1 Drawer, 32 x 19 In. 460.00
Commode, Demilune, Veined Black Marble Top, Garden Scene, Spade Feet, 33 In. 1840.00
Commode, Directoire, Cherry, Late 1700s, 26 x 51 1/2 x 23 In. 2300.00
Commode, Empire, Fruitwood, 1 Frieze Drawer, Tapered Columns, 1825, 36 In. 5465.00
Commode, Empire, Mahogany Veneer, Half Columns, Bun Feet, 32 x 16 3/4 In. 440.00
Commode, Empire, Mahogany, Black Fossilized Marble Top, 34 x 41 x 21 In. 2090.00
Commode, Empire, Walnut, Rectangular Top, 3 Drawers, Molded Feet, 37 x 20 In. 2300.00
Commode, French Provincial, Elm, Marble Top, 28 x 15 x 13 In. 490.00
Commode, French Provincial, Oak, Overhanging Top, Cabriole Feet, 42 1/2 In. 3680.00
Commode, French Provincial, Walnut, Empire Style, Banded Top, 37 x 51 x 25 In. 2530.00
Commode, George II, Mahogany, Inlay, 2 Doors, 28 x 21 x 20 1/4 In. 1035.00
Commode, George III, Mahogany, Shaped Gallery, Skirt, Square Legs, 31 x 21 In. 2300.00
Commode, Italian Regency, Bombe, Painted, Serpentine Edges, 2 Drawers, 44 x 25 In. .. 800.00
Commode, Italian Rococo, Burl Walnut, Mid 18th Century, 35 1/2 x 45 1/2 x 20 In. 6000.00
Commode, Kingwood, Tulipwood, Royal Marble Top, Cabriole Legs, 36 In. 7475.00
Commode, Louis Philippe, Burl Elm, Marble Top, 3 Drawers, 39 x 50 x 22 1/2 In. 1610.00
Commode, Louis Philippe, Mahogany, 3 Lower Graduated Drawers, 37 In. 2760.00
Commode, Louis Philippe, Mahogany, Figured, Marble Top, 40 x 48 x 21 In. 1610.00
Commode, Louis Philippe, Rosewood, Red Marble Top, 36 x 49 1/2 x 21 1/2 In. 1265.00
Commode, Louis Philippe, Walnut, 4 Graduated Drawers, Block Feet, 38 In. 1095.00
Commode, Louis Philippe, Walnut, Drawers, Block Feet, 37 3/4 x 46 3/4 x 22 In. 1380.00
Commode, Louis Philippe, Walnut, Variegated Charcoal Marble Top, 39 1/2 In. 3450.00
Commode, Louis XIV Style, Marquetry, Marble, Inlaid, 36 x 50 x 21 3/4 In. 385.00
Commode, Louis XV Style, 3 Drawers, Marble Surface, Curved Legs, 34 x 43 In. 920.00
Commode, Louis XV Style, Bombe, Marble Top, 2 Drawers, Brass Ormolu, 49 x 21 In. .. 405.00
Commode, Louis XV Style, Walnut, Inset Marble Top, 1 Drawer, Cabriole Legs, 32 In. .. 345.00
Commode, Louis XV, Bombe, Molded Top, 2 Drawers, 34 1/2 x 48 In. 5175.00
Commode, Louis XV, Fruitwood, Bombe, 3 Drawers, Hoof Feet, 36 x 50 x 26 In. 5465.00
Commode, Louis XV, Gray Serpentine Marble Top, 2 Drawers, 52 x 34 In. 5750.00
Commode, Louis XV, Kingwood, 2 Drawers, Gilt Bronze Handles, 9 x 10 x 6 In. 1725.00
Commode, Louis XV, Oak, Molded Rectangular Top, 3 Drawers, 33 x 41 In. 3680.00
Commode, Louis XV, Oak, Molded Top, 3 Drawers, Cabriole, Legs, 50 3/4 In. 3910.00
Commode, Louis XV, Oak, Molded Top, Frieze Drawer, Cabriole Legs, 38 In., Pair 3450.00

Commode, Louis XV, Tulipwood, 3 Drawers, Serpentine Marble Top, 33 1/2 In. 1840.00
Commode, Louis XV, Walnut, 3 Drawers, Carved Foliate, 18th Century, 41 In. 9200.00
Commode, Louis XV, Walnut, Rectangular Top, 3 Drawers, Paw Feet, 36 In. 5750.00
Commode, Louis XV/XVI Style, Demilune, 2 Drawers, Cabriole Legs, 28 3/4 In. 805.00
Commode, Louis XV/XVI, Rectangular Marble Top, 3 Drawers, 32 x 16 In. 1035.00
Commode, Louis XV/XVI, Tulipwood, Fruitwood, Pastoral Scene, Foliate, 36 In. 4600.00
Commode, Louis XVI Style, Gilt Bronze Mounted, Marquetry, 34 x 39 x 17 In. 2185.00
Commode, Louis XVI Style, Kingwood, Ormolu, Parquetry, 33 x 17 x 14 In., Pair 1150.00
Commode, Louis XVI Style, Walnut, Carved, Marble Top, 32 1/2 x 16 x 14 In. . . . 230.00
Commode, Louis XVI, Bombe, Corona Marble, 2 Doors, 1800s, 54 x 35 x 26 In. 6900.00
Commode, Louis XVI, Fruitwood, Provincial, 3 Drawers, 2 Doors, 40 x 53 x 21 In. 3220.00
Commode, Louis XVI, Mahogany, Bronze, 3 Long Drawers, Top-Shaped Feet, 35 In. 4900.00
Commode, Louis XVI, Oak, Gray, White Rectangular Top, 2 Drawers, 33 1/2 In. 575.00
Commode, Louis XVI, Rectangular Fossil Marble Top, 3 Paneled Drawers, 35 In. 3450.00
Commode, Mahogany, Green-Flecked Marble Top, 2 Drawers, Block Feet, 36 In. 1265.00
Commode, Mahogany, Hinged Top, Serpentine Front Edge, Short Legs, 18 x 17 In. 175.00
Commode, Mahogany, Pierced Gallery, Pullout Drawer, 30 In. 2300.00
Commode, Mahogany, Rectangular Top, Square Tapered Legs, Floral Sprays, 29 In. 3220.00
Commode, Mahogany, Serpentine Front, England, 19 3/4 x 19 x 17 In. 110.00
Commode, Mahogany, Serpentine Top, 2 Concave & 2 Convex Drawers, 33 1/4 In. 2530.00
Commode, Mahogany, Tambour Cupboard, Lower Drawer, Marquetry, 29 In. 3220.00
Commode, Marble Top, 2 Long Drawers, 1780s, 34 1/2 x 36 3/4 In. 9000.00
Commode, Marble Top, 3 Long Drawers, Plaque Of Butterfly Chasing Putti, 34 In. 1440.00
Commode, Marble Top, 3 Veneered Drawers, Bronze Mounted, 38 x 47 In. 940.00
Commode, Neoclassical, Birch, Figured, Stepped, Columns, Bun Feet, 35 x 41 x 24 In. . . 4370.00
Commode, Neoclassical, Kingwood, Ormolu, Parquetry, Late 1700s, 33 x 50 x 22 In. 7200.00
Commode, Neoclassical, Mahogany, Stepped Rectangular Top, 34 1/2 In. 3220.00
Commode, Neoclassical, Walnut, Rectangular Top, 3 Drawers, 32 x 22 3/4 In. 4830.00
Commode, Oak, Tan Marble Top, Molded Pilasters, 38 1/2 x 45 x 17 3/4 In. 1265.00
Commode, Painted Wood, Figures In Landscape, 2 Doors, 34 2/3 In. 575.00
Commode, Regency, Mahogany, Recessed, Grillwork, 28 1/2 x 32 x 14 1/2 In. 3220.00
Commode, Rococo, Mahogany, 2 Concave, 2 Convex Drawers, Paw Feet, 33 In. 2530.00
Commode, Rococo, Painted, Landscape Scenes, 3 Drawers, 31 x 31 1/2 x 16 In. 430.00
Commode, Rococo, Walnut, 2 Short Drawers Over 2 Long Drawers, 33 In. 3680.00
Commode, Rococo, Walnut, 4 Banded Drawers, Cabriole Legs, Italy, 37 1/2 In. 2300.00
Commode, Rococo, Walnut, Bombe, Rectangular, Floral Inlaid Drawers, 24 In., Pair 2300.00
Commode, Serpentine Rectangular Surface, 1 Drawer, Greek Key Feet, 24 In. 2875.00
Commode, Shaker, Hinged Cover, Pine, Red Wash, Child's, 27 1/2 x 17 3/4 In. 345.00
Commode, Victorian, Walnut, Marble Top, Burled Panels, Casters, 30 x 32 x 17 In. 375.00
Commode, Walnut, 2 Long Drawers, Shaped Skirt, Ormolu Mounts, 33 x 43 1/2 In. 1380.00
Commode, Walnut, Bombe, Serpentine Top Over 2 Drawers, 33 x 43 In. 3680.00
Commode, Walnut, Brown & White, Beveled, Marble Top, Drawer Over 2 Doors, 31 In. . 250.00
Commode, Walnut, Marble Top, 1 Drawer Over 2 Doors, Fruit Carving, 29 1/2 In. 635.00
Commode, Walnut, Marble Top, Mirror, 3 Drawers, 1 Door, Brass, 75 x 30 x 17 In. 560.00
Commode, Walnut, Serpentine Top, 3 Drawers, Parquetry Panels, 40 x 54 x 27 In. 10060.00
Console, Art Deco, Rectangular Black Glass Top, Chrome Base, 35 1/2 x 12 In. 1800.00
Console, Charles X, Walnut, Marble Top, Scrolled Supports, 34 1/2 x 39 x 21 In. 1035.00
Console, Cherry, Marble Top, Demilune, Early 19th Century, 32 x 37 1/2 x 19 In. 2530.00
Console, Continental, Mahogany, Marble Top, Polychrome, 35 1/2 x 58 x 17 1/2 In. 2070.00
Console, Continental, Rectangular Black Marble Top, France, 1780, 33 1/4 In. 8340.00
Console, Ebonized, Bronze Mounts, Marble Top, 19th Century, 43 x 52 In. 390.00
Console, Empire, Gilt Bronze Mounting, Marble Top, 35 x 60 x 16 In. 3450.00
Console, Empire, Mahogany, Eagle Carving, c.1825, 39 1/2 x 42 x 23 1/2 In. 3105.00
Console, Empire, Mahogany, Recessed Plinth, 33 1/4 x 24 1/4 x 16 3/4 In. 2990.00
Console, Faux Bamboo, Rectangular Top Inset, Black Leather, Green, Gilt, 48 In. 400.00
Console, French Provincial, Marble Top, 2 Legs, Wall Attachment, 32 x 32 x 14 In. 460.00
Console, Gilt, 3 Graduated Serpentine Tiers, 3 Cabriole Legs, 75 In. 3220.00
Console, Gilt, Marble Top, Reeded Frieze, Spread-Winged Eagle, 31 1/2 In. 3910.00
Console, Italian Marble Top, Gilt, Middle Drawer, 51 1/4 x 34 3/4 In. 5400.00
Console, Italian Neoclassical Style, Gilt Painted, Drawer, 21 x 20 x 9 In., Pair 865.00
Console, Italian Rococo, Painted, Parcel Gilt, 31 1/2 x 37 1/2 x 14 1/2 In. 430.00
Console, Louis Philippe, Mahogany, Marble Top, Frieze Drawer, 49 x 39 x 20 In. 1725.00
Console, Louis Philippe, Rosewood, Foliated Medallion, Reeded Edge, 39 In. 7475.00

Console, Louis XV Style, Painted, Drawers, Scalloped, 30 1/2 x 49 x 17 In. 750.00
Console, Louis XV, Gilt, Cream Paint, Faux Marble Top, Floral, 32 In. 3220.00
Console, Louis XV, Gilt, Marble Top, Shell, Wreath, Floral Design, 31 In. 1725.00
Console, Louis XV, Oak, Marble Top, Hoof Feet, 27 x 26 x 16 In. 1495.00
Console, Louis XV, Walnut, Serpentine Ocher Marble Top, Cabriole Legs, 26 In. 1035.00
Console, Louis XVI, Beech, Variegated Cream Marble Top, Top-Shaped Feet, 32 In. 1840.00
Console, Louis XVI, Gilt Beech, Marble Top, Fluted, 36 1/4 x 34 x 17 In. 3680.00
Console, Louis XVI, Gilt, D-Shaped Top, Scrolled Leaf Design, 1900, 43 In. 5760.00
Console, Louis XVI, Gilt, Rouge Marble Surface, Tapered Legs, 39 x 55 1/2 In. 1610.00
Console, Louis XVI, Mahogany, Gilt, Crossbanded Edge, Turned Legs, 35 In. 460.00
Console, Louis XVI, Square Iron Legs, 27 x 30 In., Pair 750.00
Console, Mahogany, Fold Top, 4 Acanthus Carved Legs, Paw Feet, 28 x 18 In. 800.00
Console, Mahogany, Travertine Marble Top, Lion Supports, c.1835, 39 1/4 In. 9360.00
Console, Mahogany, White, Green Mottled Marble Top, Ball Feet, 37 x 31 In. 750.00
Console, Napoleon III, Mahogany, Brass Galleried White Marble Top, 36 In. 1955.00
Console, Neoclassical, Gilt Brass Rosettes, Ebony, 32 1/4 In. 3450.00
Console, Neoclassical, Gilt, Pink, Gray Rectangular Marble Top, 39 x 28 In. 8915.00
Console, Neoclassical, Marble Top, 1 Long Drawer, Allover Floral Design, 36 In. 8050.00
Console, Painted Pineapple-Shape Top, Palm Carved Support, 30 x 22 x 14 In. 980.00
Console, Painted, Marble Top, Pierced Frieze, Cabriole Legs, Pad Feet, 31 1/4 In. 5760.00
Console, Rococo, Mahogany, 2 Shelves, Bobbin-Turned Legs, 61 x 42 x 19 In. 2300.00
Console, Rococo, Molded Marble Top, Floral, Shell Form, 58 x 35 x 27 In. 4600.00
Console, Victorian, Walnut, Pink Marble Top, Wall Mount, c.1880, 22 x 37 x 16 In. 385.00
Cradle, Cherry, Heart Cutout, Pa., 18th Century 375.00
Cradle, Mahogany, Cutout Ends, Dovetailed, 19th Century 190.00
Cradle, Mustard Color, Dovetailed Boot, Original Rocker & Brace 465.00
Cradle, Pine, Poplar, Scrolled Back, Cutout Heart Handles, c.1810, 24 x 42 In. 440.00
Cradle, Poplar, Red Paint, Black Pinstripes, Initials LS, BS, c.1871, 20 x 38 3/4 In. 55.00
Cradle, Poplar, Red Paint, Finial Posts, Heart Cutouts, 1700s, 24 x 39 In. 280.00
Cradle, Shaped Rockers, Smoke Decorated, 27 x 43 In. 170.00
Cradle, Softwood, Heart Cutout, Green, Yellow Paint, 20th Century, 21 x 27 In. 110.00
Cradle, Walnut, Canted Scrolled Sides, Oak Rockers, c.1820 . . . . 140.00
Cradle, Walnut, Cheese-Cutter Rockers, Lollipop Top, Cutouts, 38 x 18 x 25 In. 440.00
Cradle, Walnut, Heart Cutouts, Scalloped Ends, Lebanon Cty., Pa., 1770, 22 x 38 In. 440.00
Cradle, Walnut, Shaped Head & Footboard, Turned Stiles, 19th Century 875.00
Credenza, Baroque, Molded Top, Scalloped Frieze, Paw Feet, 39 3/4 In. 6000.00
Credenza, Baroque, Walnut, Rectangular Top, Carved Dentil Frieze, Italy, 36 In. 3740.00
Credenza, Bowfront, Brass, Glass Top, 1970s, 56 x 16 1/2 x 28 1/2 In. 110.00
Credenza, Chippendale, Mahogany, 3 Drawers, Gadrooned Edge, 59 x 22 x 30 In. 770.00
Credenza, Florence Knoll, 4 Sliding Doors, Bright Chrome Frame, 27 1/4 In. 480.00
Credenza, Florence Knoll, 4 Sliding Doors, Locks, Chrome Frame, 71 1/4 In. 750.00
Credenza, Florence Knoll, Walnut, 4 Sliding Doors, Bright Chrome Frame, 27 In. 560.00
Credenza, Italian Renaissance Revival, Walnut, 5 Drawers, 1800s, 48 x 70 x 23 In. 2760.00
Credenza, Louis XIV Style, Boulle Case, Glazed Doors, 43 x 57 x 14 1/2 In. 2415.00
Credenza, Walnut, Carved Head, 2 Drawers Over 2 Doors, Bun Feet, 1880, 59 x 54 In. . . . 1345.00
Crib, Bentwood, Old Yellow Paint, 30 x 37 1/2 x 21 In. 70.00
Crib, Brass, Triangular Plaque, Stork & Stylized Flowers, Tubular Rails, 51 In. 400.00
Crib, Cherry, Ring-Turned Spindles, Finials, Conn., Early 1800s, 43 x 28 x 44 In. 520.00
Crib, George III, Mahogany, Removable Sides, England, c.1810 . . . . 3750.00
Crib, Scroll Head & Footboard, Vase-Shape Slats, Turned Legs, Yellow, Stenciled 950.00
Crib, Sheraton, Cherry, Bird's-Eye Maple Panel, Pa., c.1820, 40 1/2 x 26 x 46 In. 660.00
Crib, Turned Spindles, Headboard, Painted, 28 x 46 In. 40.00
Cupboard, 2 Closets, 2 Center Shelves, Marble Top, 2-Drawer Base, 93 In. 715.00
Cupboard, 2 Panel Doors, Green Paint, Narrow, 38 x 14 x 26 In. 2880.00
Cupboard, 2 Paneled Doors, 2 Short Drawers, Cutouts On Base, c.1840, 53 1/4 In. 2850.00
Cupboard, 4 Floral Painted Panels, Segmented Interior, Shelves, Hooks, 43 In. 1150.00
Cupboard, 6 Panes, 2 Dovetailed Drawers, Red, Yellow Green Paint, 82 In. 3025.00
Cupboard, Adam, Step Back, Quebec, 19th Century . . . . *Illus* 4620.00
Cupboard, Arts & Crafts, Oak, Step Back, Beveled Glass Panes, 40 x 18 x 77 In. 995.00
Cupboard, Barn Doors, Old Green Paint, Wide Boards, Large 1980.00
Cupboard, Base Door & Shelves, Pierced Fretwork, 73 1/4 In. 1430.00
Cupboard, Biedermeier, Walnut, Marble Top, Cylinder, Pedestal, 35 x 15 In., Pair 6325.00
Cupboard, Cherry, 2 Sections, 6-Pane Doors, Pa., c.1820, 86 1/2 x 54 1/2 In. 6600.00

Don't put a large lamp or a table runner or any other opaque centerpiece on a wooden table for a long time if the table is in a strong light. The wood may fade and the outline of the centerpiece will remain.

Furniture, Cupboard,
Adam, Step Back,
Quebec, 19th Century

Cupboard, Cherry, 2 Sections, Pennsylvania German, c.1800, 86 x 57 In.	11000.00
Cupboard, Cherry, Side Beading, 2-Door Base, 2-Door Top, Shelves, 78 1/2 In.	1650.00
Cupboard, Chestnut, Red Paint, 3 Shelves, 43 x 32 x 17 1/4 In.	3220.00
Cupboard, Chimney, Poplar, 2 Doors, 4 Shelves Top, 2 Shelves Below, 92 In.	1100.00
Cupboard, Chinese Wedding, Lacquer Repaint, 2 Doors, Brasses, 50 x 74 In.	330.00
Cupboard, Continental, Mahogany Veneer, Arched Doors, c.1820, 44 x 26 1/2 In.	715.00
Cupboard, Corner, 2 Drawers Over 2 Doors, Cutout Feet, 46 x 80 In.	3080.00
Cupboard, Corner, 12-Pane Top Doors, 2 Base Doors, Blue & White, Delaware	3200.00
Cupboard, Corner, Barrel Back, Open Case, Shelves, Fluted Pilasters, Door, 87 In.	2750.00
Cupboard, Corner, Center Plinth, Glass Doors, Shelves, Spoon Slots, 36 x 54 In.	1100.00
Cupboard, Corner, Cherry, 2-Part Step Back, 12-Pane Doors, 2-Door Base, 88 In.	7975.00
Cupboard, Corner, Cherry, 16-Pane Top Doors, 2 Lower Doors, 82 1/4 In.	3520.00
Cupboard, Corner, Cherry, Poplar, 12-Pane Doors, Step Back 2-Door Base, 78 In.	6920.00
Cupboard, Corner, Chippendale Style, Cherry, 2 Sections, c.1940, 88 x 39 In.	660.00
Cupboard, Corner, Chippendale, Pine, Late 1700s, 73 x 37 x 17 In.	990.00
Cupboard, Corner, Federal, Mahogany, Pediment Top, 2-Panel Doors, 47 x 86 In.	1440.00
Cupboard, Corner, Federal, Walnut, Keystone Cornice, 10-Pane Doors, 34 In.	4500.00
Cupboard, Corner, George III, Mahogany, 1 Paneled Door, Hanging, 47 x 22 In.	2070.00
Cupboard, Corner, George III, Mahogany, Curved Front, 2 Doors, c.1780, 49 x 28 In.	880.00
Cupboard, Corner, George III, Oak, Frieze, Over Doors, Plinth Base, 84 In.	6330.00
Cupboard, Corner, Hanging, Pine, Death Of General James Wolfe, Shelves, 50 3/4 In.	1210.00
Cupboard, Corner, Hanging, Pine, Geometric Mullion Door, Red Interior, 27 x 42 In.	770.00
Cupboard, Corner, Hanging, Pine, Poplar, Panel Door, c.1820, 24 x 30 x 16 1/2 In.	470.00
Cupboard, Corner, Hanging, Walnut, 1 Panel Door, 3 Shelves, c.1760, 39 1/2 In.	6050.00
Cupboard, Corner, Hudson Valley, Butterfly Shelf, Dentil Mold, 1760, 56 x 73 In.	9800.00
Cupboard, Corner, Mahogany Veneer, Arched Crest, Ogee Feet, 92 1/4 In.	4345.00
Cupboard, Corner, Mahogany, 2 Mullioned Doors, Lower Panel Doors, c.1780, 96 In.	5500.00
Cupboard, Corner, Mahogany, 2 Parts, 4 Doors, Plinth Base, c.1780, 96 x 46 In.	5500.00
Cupboard, Corner, Mahogany, 2-Tier Cornice, 2-Pane Door, Drawer, 1820, 92 In.	4950.00
Cupboard, Corner, Oak, Crown Moldings, Glass & Paneled Doors, Shelves, 98 x 43 In.	950.00
Cupboard, Corner, Pine, 2 Dovetailed Drawers, Dark Green Interior, 45 x 84 In.	2200.00
Cupboard, Corner, Pine, 2 Parts, 2 Doors Over Paneled Doors, 79 In.	1150.00
Cupboard, Corner, Pine, 2 Sections, Step Back, Lancaster, c.1780, 82 x 42 1/2 In.	2475.00
Cupboard, Corner, Pine, 2 Shelves, Pale Yellow Paint, New England, 46 x 17 In.	7475.00
Cupboard, Corner, Pine, Bold Cornice, Arched, Glazed Door, c.1830, 108 x 38 In.	1430.00
Cupboard, Corner, Pine, Recessed-Panel Upper Doors, Brown, Blue, 1900, 80 In.	1210.00
Cupboard, Corner, Poplar, 2 Base Doors, Top Door, Butterfly Shelves, 90 1/2 In.	1100.00
Cupboard, Corner, Poplar, 2-Panel Top Door, 1 Drawer, Paneled Base Doors, 78 In.	2300.00
Cupboard, Corner, Poplar, Paneled Doors, Over 2 Drawers, 95 x 50 1/2 x 25 1/2 In.	3450.00
Cupboard, Corner, Softwood, Red Paint, 9 Panes, 2 Paneled Doors, 75 x 47 In.	1540.00
Cupboard, Corner, Walnut, 2 Double-Panel Doors, Shelves, Bracket Feet, 92 In.	4510.00
Cupboard, Corner, Walnut, Poplar, 1 Door, Inset Panel, Wooden Pull, 81 x 42 In.	3025.00
Cupboard, Corner, Walnut, Step Back, 1 Lower Door, 16 Panes, 94 In.	5500.00
Cupboard, Corner, Yellow Paint, 6-Pane Glass Door, 1 Base Door, 32 x 77 In.	7150.00
Cupboard, Curly Maple, David T. Smith, Morrow, Ohio, 40 x 18 x 90 In., 2 Piece	1540.00
Cupboard, French Provincial, Walnut, Scalloped Apron, Cabriole Legs, 67 3/4 In.	990.00

Cupboard, Gothic Revival, Fluted Panels, Dark Stain, Platform, 38 x 18 x 57 In. 905.00
Cupboard, Gothic Revival, Oak, 2 Pierced Panel Doors, England, 24 x 8 x 30 In. 300.00
Cupboard, Gothic Revival, Oak, Carved, 2 Doors, Open Base, Belgium, 37 x 57 In. 1100.00
Cupboard, Green Paint, 2 Paneled Doors, Molded Edges, 64 x 38 x 16 In. 3450.00
Cupboard, Hanging, 4-Pane Door, Arched Cornice, Dutch, 1700s, 19 x 16 x 10 In. 345.00
Cupboard, Hanging, Cherry, Ash, Mustard Paint, Open Shelf, Door, 25 x 11 x 42 In. 990.00
Cupboard, Hanging, Corner, Mullion Door, Canted Case, c.1800, 40 3/4 x 28 In. 1100.00
Cupboard, Hanging, Fruitwood, 1 Door, 2 Shelves, Spain, 1800s, 30 x 30 x 13 In. 185.00
Cupboard, Hanging, Geometric Design, 20th Century, 29 x 22 x 5 In. 5060.00
Cupboard, Hanging, George III, Mahogany, 2 Inlaid Doors, c.1800, 28 1/2 x 26 In. 825.00
Cupboard, Hanging, Mahogany, Cornice, Panel Door, Shelves, 19 x 9 1/2 x 26 1/2 In. . . . 495.00
Cupboard, Hanging, Pine, 1 Raised Panel Door, 2 Shelves, Drawer, 31 x 25 In. 880.00
Cupboard, Hanging, Pine, Brown Graining On Yellow Ground, 38 In. 440.00
Cupboard, Hanging, Pine, Chestnut, Floral, 4 Inset Panels In Door, Shelves, 29 In. 3575.00
Cupboard, Hanging, Pine, Painted, Scandinavian, c.1820, 17 1/2 x 16 1/2 In. 275.00
Cupboard, Hanging, Poplar, Molded Cornice, 2 Doors, Drawers, Pa., 64 1/2 x 40 In. 2200.00
Cupboard, Hanging, Poplar, Panel Door, Rattail Hinges, c.1770, 46 1/2 x 34 In. 3410.00
Cupboard, Hanging, Softwood, Blue Paint, Molded Cornice, 36 x 28 x 13 In. 990.00
Cupboard, Hanging, Softwood, Tiger Maple, Molded Cornice, 42 x 24 In. 5500.00
Cupboard, Hanging, Victorian, Oak, Shelf Over Panel Doors, 23 x 23 In. 185.00
Cupboard, Hepplewhite, Fluted Frieze, Astragal Glazed Doors, 68 x 36 x 16 In. 1840.00
Cupboard, James II, Vine Frieze, 4 Doors, Lancashire, 1686, 65 x 69 In. 4600.00
Cupboard, Jelly, Cherry & Poplar, Flame Veneer, 2 Doors, 3 Shelves, 59 In. 1485.00
Cupboard, Jelly, Pine, 2 Drawers, Stippled Brown, Ocher Surface, Pa., 1815, 49 In. 2970.00
Cupboard, Jelly, Pine, Painted, New England, c.1830, 50 1/2 x 46 1/2 In. 1210.00
Cupboard, Jelly, Pine, Poplar, Paneled Doors, 2 Drawers, Brass Latches, 37 In. 960.00
Cupboard, Jelly, Poplar, Scalloped Front Apron, 2 Doors, Porcelain Knobs, 51 In. 1540.00
Cupboard, Jelly, Walnut, 2 Doors, 5 Interior Shelves, 55 x 39 1/2 In. 1210.00
Cupboard, Jelly, Walnut, Galleried Top, 2 Drawers, Cupboards, c.1820, 48 x 41 In. 2090.00
Cupboard, Larder, Medieval Style, Pierced Gothic Tracery, 1800s, 43 x 55 In. 1095.00
Cupboard, Mahogany, Bedside, 2 Doors, Faux Drawer, Marquetry, 1780s, 27 1/2 In. 3450.00
Cupboard, Mahogany, Bedside, Marquetry, 2 Doors, Block Feet, 27 x 18 1/4 In. 2300.00
Cupboard, Mahogany, Bedside, Rectangular Top, 2 Doors, Block Feet, 27 1/2 In. 3450.00
Cupboard, Oak, 1 Paneled Door, Iron Hinges, 20th Century, 51 In. 315.00
Cupboard, Oak, 2 Panel Doors, 2-Drawer Base, 36 x 73 x 18 In. 1320.00
Cupboard, Oak, Carved Grape, Vine, Ornate Columns, 1885, 58 x 23 x 98 In. 3080.00
Cupboard, Oak, Carved Lower Door, Heraldic Shield, Shelf, 1880s, 62 In. 2070.00
Cupboard, Oak, Old Dark Finish, 5 Dovetailed Drawers, Scalloped Feet, 53 1/2 In. 2860.00
Cupboard, Oak, Outset Top, 2 Frieze Drawers, Stile Feet, 53 1/2 x 17 1/4 In. 690.00
Cupboard, Oak, Pierced Waist, Cabinet Top, Belgium, 28 x 18 x 51 In. 715.00
Cupboard, Oak, Step Back, Carved Fruit, Game Doors, 1885, 55 x 21 x 98 In. 2240.00
Cupboard, Oak, Step Back, Carved Fruit, Nut Doors, 1885, 50 x 22 x 99 In. 3360.00
Cupboard, Open, Neoclassical, Painted, 7 Shelves, Pilasters, c.1830, 65 x 32 In. 5460.00
Cupboard, Pewter, Pine, 3 Shelves, 3 Drawers, 2 Doors, c.1820, 60 1/2 x 54 1/2 In. 2090.00
Cupboard, Pewter, Pine, Raised Panel Door In Bottom, Rosehead Nails, 79 3/4 In. 2750.00
Cupboard, Pewter, Pine, Scalloped Base, England, Refinished, 72 x 80 In., 2 Piece 1540.00
Cupboard, Pewter, Poplar, Step Back, 4 Raised Door Panels, 3 Shelves, 79 In. 3960.00
Cupboard, Pine, 2 Glazed Doors, Over 4 Drawers, 2 Paneled Doors, 1800, 84 x 51 In. 6900.00
Cupboard, Pine, 2 Sunken Panel Doors, Bracket Feet, Stepped Molding, 54 x 36 In. 770.00
Cupboard, Pine, Geometric Doors, 3 Open Shelves, 1880s, 50 x 50 1/2 In. 490.00
Cupboard, Pine, Geometric Panels, 3 Tiers, Block Feet, 50 In. 490.00
Cupboard, Pine, Yellow Paint, Red, Glazed Doors, Lancaster, c.1810, 88 x 62 In. 13200.00
Cupboard, Poplar, Closet, Shelf, Grain Paint, Cutout Feet, N.Y., 76 x 37 x 17 In. 920.00
Cupboard, Poplar, Open Top, 2 Shelves, 2 Drawers, 3 Doors, c.1820, 54 1/2 x 53 In. 2530.00
Cupboard, Poplar, Painted, 2 9-Pane Doors, Pennsylvania German, 1820, 84 x 60 In. 5500.00
Cupboard, Poplar, Pie Shelf, 3 Drawers, 2 Doors, Bracket Feet, c.1810, 88 x 57 In. 6050.00
Cupboard, Red Wash, 2 Doors, Molded Cornice, 58 x 48 In. 440.00
Cupboard, Rosewood, Oak, Central Foliate, Figure Of Ceres, Female Busts, 90 In. 5175.00
Cupboard, Shaker, 3 Shelves Over 3 Drawers, N.Y., 62 3/4 x 24 3/4 x 12 In. 2300.00
Cupboard, Shaker, Pine, Red Paint, Rectangular, Twin Doors, 6 Drawers, 83 x 18 x 49 In. . 3450.00
Cupboard, Shaker, Poplar, 2 Drawers, 2 Doors, 4 Shelves, 1850, 73 x 36 x 16 In. 2760.00
Cupboard, Shaker, Poplar, 2 Drawers, Panel Doors, Shelves, 1850, 73 x 36 In. 2760.00
Cupboard, Sheraton, Poplar, Painted, Scalloped Gallery, Pa., 1830, 42 x 37 1/4 In. 4950.00

Cupboard, Softwood, 2 Paneled Doors, Red Ground, Black Feather Paint, 85 In. 1650.00
Cupboard, Step Back, 2 Paneled Doors, Painted Interior Shelves, 74 x 44 1/2 In. 1440.00
Cupboard, Step Back, 2 Sections, 2 6-Pane Doors, Red Paint, 82 3/4 x 51 1/2 In. 6615.00
Cupboard, Step Back, 20 Drawers, Blue Paint, 64 x 48 In. 7150.00
Cupboard, Step Back, Cherry, 2 3-Pane Doors, White Paint, 72 In. 1250.00
Cupboard, Step Back, Green Paint, Child's, 41 x 35 In. 595.00
Cupboard, Step Back, Oak, Carved, Eagle, 2 Glass Doors, Blind Doors, 104 In. 1760.00
Cupboard, Step Back, Pine, 2 Blind Doors, Bracket Base, Red Paint, c.1800, 77 In. 4400.00
Cupboard, Step Back, Pine, 3 Open Shelves, Plank Door, 1780, 76 3/4 x 36 x 18 In. 3630.00
Cupboard, Step Back, Poplar, 2-Door Top, 2 Glass Panels, 81 1/2 In. 1540.00
Cupboard, Step Back, Poplar, c.1820, 38 x 41 In. 525.00
Cupboard, Step Back, Poplar, White Pine, Mustard Paint, Turned Feet, 1850, 87 In. 5600.00
Cupboard, Step Back, Poplar, White Pine, Turned Columns, 2 Door, 1850, 87 x 52 In. ... 3290.00
Cupboard, Step Back, Rectangular Top, 3 Shelves, Paneled Door, 44 x 20 In. 1150.00
Cupboard, Tiger Maple, Scroll Top, Door, 2 Drawers, Tabletop, c.1840, 34 x 16 In. 550.00
Cupboard, Tudor, Oak, Step Back, Bi-Fold Door, 2 Drawers, Carved, c.1940, 60 In. 470.00
Cupboard, Walnut, Dentil Molded Frieze, Door, Fluting, c.1780, 73 x 41 In............ 10450.00
Cupboard, Walnut, Oak, Paneled Doors, Marble Top, Upper Shelves, 83 In. 2530.00
Cupboard, Walnut, Scalloped Apron, 2 Doors, 2 Drawers, Pie Shelf, 85 1/4 x 49 In. 1925.00
Cupboard, Welsh, Pine, 2 Raised Paneled Doors, 4 Small Drawers Base, 82 x 66 In. 5170.00
Cupboard, William & Mary, Oak, Frieze, Celtic Lattice, 46 x 63 In. 3560.00
Daybed, Art Deco, Mahogany, Carved, France, c.1925, 86 In. 7200.00
Daybed, Arts & Crafts, Mahogany, Slanted Headrest, 33 x 74 x 26 In. 90.00
Daybed, Arts & Crafts, Oak, Quartersawn, Side Fan Design Handrest, 73 x 30 In. 440.00
Daybed, Biedermeier, Walnut, Matching Head & Footboards, 75 1/2 In. 1035.00
Daybed, Chippendale, Mahogany, Rolled Back, 8 Legs, Stretchers, 35 x 83 In. 605.00
Daybed, Eugene Schoen, Exotic Wood Veneer, 30 x 80 x 36 In...................... 395.00
Daybed, French Provincial, Walnut, Arched Headboard, Turned Legs, 35 x 36 x 80 In. ... 635.00
Daybed, Fruitwood, Carved Arms & Legs, Early 19th Century, 69 1/2 In. 460.00
Daybed, Fruitwood, Dolphins Ending In Circular Feet, 19th Century, 87 In. 1380.00
Daybed, G. Nelson, Birch, Hairpin Legs, Original Finish, 27 In. 1955.00
Daybed, G. Stickley, No. 220, Oak, Square Stiles, Wide Flat Slats, 1910, 35 x 84 In. 3450.00
Daybed, Knoll, Rosewood, Tufted, Tan Leather, 18 x 78 x 40 In. 5500.00
Daybed, L. & J.G. Stickley, 22 x 72 In. 1900.00
Daybed, Louis Phillipe, Mahogany, Upholstered, Lotus Feet, 32 In. 3220.00
Daybed, Lucite Base, Upholstered, Loose Back Cushion, 67 x 30 In. 805.00
Daybed, Neoclassical, Cherry, Skirt, Rolled Arms, Saber Legs, Upholstered, 25 x 73 In. ... 715.00
Daybed, R. Schultz, Pivoting Wood Frame, Cane Headrest, Platform, 29 x 78 In. 1380.00
Daybed, Serpentine End Panels, Loose Cushion Seat, 1850s, 83 In. 1380.00
Daybed, Stickley Bros., Red Leather, Slanted Head Rest, 24 x 76 x 30 In. 575.00
Daybed, Van Der Rohe, Rosewood, Leather, Steel, 78 In. ....*Illus* 5450.00
Daybed, Wegner, Teak Back, Upholstered, Getama, 30 In. 2300.00
Daybed, Windsor, 3-Section Back, Hinged, Bamboo Turned Arms, 36 x 84 x 26 In. 4025.00
Daybed, Windsor, Fold-Out, 3-Section Back, Leaf & Berry Stencil, 36 x 84 x 26 In. 4025.00
Desk, Architect's, George III, Mahogany, 3 Drawers, Bracket Feet, 33 In. 4800.00
Desk, Architect's, Pine, 2 Long Drawers, Tapered Legs, 19th Century, 53 1/2 In. 750.00
Desk, Art Deco, Plycraft, Dark Mahogany Finish, 4 Drawers Each Side, 30 x 44 In. 490.00
Desk, Arts & Crafts, Drop Front, Drawer, Cabinet Doors, 1 Pane, 44 In. 230.00
Desk, Arts & Crafts, Mahogany, Triangular Pivoting Drawer, 2-Door Cabinet, 57 In. 1840.00
Desk, Arts & Crafts, Oak, 1 Drawer, Wooden Knobs, 34 x 20 x 35 In. 460.00
Desk, Arts & Crafts, Postcard, Mahogany, 2 Drawers, Medium Finish, 36 x 23 In. 1240.00
Desk, Arts & Crafts, Slant Front, Mahogany, 1 Single Drawer, 36 x 18 x 38 In. 320.00

A paste made of instant coffee crystals and water can be used to "paint" a scratch on dark furniture.

Furniture, Daybed, Van Der Rohe, Rosewood, Leather, Steel, 78 In.

Desk, Bamboo, Mirror, 2 Top Shelves, 1800, 55 x 31 x 22 In. 9500.00
Desk, Birch, Slant Front, Dovetailed Case, 4 Drawers, Fitted Interior, 31 3/4 In. 1325.00
Desk, Bird's-Eye Maple, Spindled Cabinet Top, 1870, 54 x 30 x 23 In. 5040.00
Desk, Burl Walnut, 4 Short Drawers, 1 Frieze Drawer, Woman's, 34 In. 865.00
Desk, Burl Walnut, Yew, Kneehole, Frieze Drawer, 6 Drawers, Recessed Door, 29 In. 9600.00
Desk, Butler's, 2 6-Paned Doors, Banded Inlay, 4 Drawers Lower Case, 89 1/2 In. 2990.00
Desk, Butler's, 3 Base Drawers, 2 Paneled Doors, 94 x 43 In. 2300.00
Desk, Butler's, Mahogany Veneer, Sliding Desk Interior, River Scene, c.1840, 45 In. 4125.00
Desk, Butler's, Mahogany, Drawer As Writing Surface, 3 Drawers, 1800, 41 In. 2760.00
Desk, Butler's, Sheraton, Slant Front, Cherry, Compartments, 1830, 53 x 40 x 21 In. 1650.00
Desk, Campaign, Teakwood, 1 Top Drawer, Brass Inset, Turnip Feet, 22 x 41 x 20 In. 3795.00
Desk, Captain's, Drop Front, Oak, Griffin, Signed RJ Horner Co., c.1885, 43 x 31 In. 7840.00
Desk, Captain's, Mahogany, Fold-Out Top, Band Of Narrow Drawers, 36 x 29 In. 1150.00
Desk, Carlton House, Brass Gallery, 3 Drawers, Square Legs, 41 x 46 In. 2530.00
Desk, Carlton House, Mahogany, Flip Lid, 4 Drawers, 9 Sections, 37 x 47 In. 675.00
Desk, Chippendale, Applewood, 4 Drawers, Pigeonholes, c.1790, 41 1/2 x 39 In. 7150.00
Desk, Chippendale, Cherry, Carved, Shells, Claw & Ball Feet, 43 x 36 x 19 1/2 In. 2415.00
Desk, Chippendale, Drop Front, Cherry, 4 Drawers, Pa., c.1780, 42 1/2 x 39 In. 3300.00
Desk, Chippendale, Drop Front, Cherry, New England, c.1770, 42 x 36 In. 3575.00
Desk, Chippendale, Drop Front, Mahogany, Massachusetts, c.1775, 44 x 37 1/2 In. 8250.00
Desk, Chippendale, Drop Front, Walnut, 4 Drawers, Bracket Feet, c.1770, 46 x 39 In. 3190.00
Desk, Chippendale, Drop Front, Walnut, 4 Drawers, Delaware Valley, 1790, 45 x 41 In. .. 6050.00
Desk, Chippendale, Drop Front, Walnut, 4 Drawers, Pa., c.1770, 43 x 38 x 22 1/2 In. 3080.00
Desk, Chippendale, Drop Front, Walnut, Prospect Door, Drawers, 39 x 37 In. 660.00
Desk, Chippendale, Slant Front, Birch, 4 Drawers, Pigeonholes Interior, 39 x 42 In. 1925.00
Desk, Chippendale, Slant Front, Birch, Cherry, Scallop Bracket Feet, 40 x 19 x 40 In. 1540.00
Desk, Chippendale, Slant Front, Cherry, Fitted, 6 Drawers, 3 Open Sections, 40 x 42 In. .. 2090.00
Desk, Chippendale, Slant Front, Cherry, Inlay Lid, 4 Drawers, 1800, 43 x 41 x 21 In. 1760.00
Desk, Chippendale, Slant Front, Cherry, Ogee Bracket Base, 42 x 38 x 17 In. 2240.00
Desk, Chippendale, Slant Front, Mahogany, 4 Drawers, 45 1/2 x 44 x 22 In. 1265.00
Desk, Chippendale, Slant Front, Maple, 42 x 40 1/2 x 19 3/4 In. 1840.00
Desk, Chippendale, Slant Front, Oak, Mahogany, 10 Dovetailed Drawers, 40 In. 2200.00
Desk, Chippendale, Slant Front, Walnut, 4 Graduated Drawers, 1780, 43 In. 5400.00
Desk, Chippendale, Slant Front, Walnut, Maple, Cherry, Pa., 1780, 42 In. 7800.00
Desk, Chippendale, Walnut, Chester County, Pa., c.1780, 42 1/2 x 39 In. 3520.00
Desk, Clerk's, George II Style, Mahogany, Felt Inlay, Shelf, 46 x 41 x 29 1/2 In. 1380.00
Desk, Cylinder, Pierced 3/4 Gallery, Leather, 2 Drawers, 1970s, 40 1/2 x 33 In. 3100.00
Desk, Cylinder, Walnut, Frieze Drawers, Fitted Interior, Woman's, c.1860, 46 In. 575.00
Desk, Cypress, Hinged Sloping Top, Fitted Interior Well, 19th Century, 36 3/4, In. 750.00
Desk, Davenport, Georgian, Mahogany, Gilt Leather Insert, 22 x 23 x 32 In. 550.00
Desk, Davenport, Mahogany, Inset Leather Top, 4 Faux Drawers, England, 31 x 20 In. ... 1265.00
Desk, Davenport, Victorian, Walnut, Tooled Leather Writing Surface, 32 x 21 x 21 In. ... 1610.00
Desk, Davenport, Walnut, Lift Writing Surface, 3 Side Drawers, 1870, 35 In. 3200.00
Desk, Davenport, Walnut, Marquetry, Flip Writing Surface, 33 In. 1150.00
Desk, Davenport, Walnut, Rectangular Compartment Top, Flip Top, Bun Feet, 34 In. 2185.00
Desk, Davenport, Walnut, Slanted Leather Writing Surface, England, 33 x 22 In. 1495.00
Desk, Drop Front, Cherry, Fitted Interior, 4 Drawers, French Feet, c.1790, 42 x 40 In. 8250.00
Desk, Drop Front, Ebonized, New York, c.1880, 74 x 36 x 17 In. 1400.00
Desk, Drop Front, Maple, 4 Graduated Drawers, 43 x 36 x 18 1/2 In. 1100.00
Desk, Drop Front, Maple, Embossed Lid, Shelf, Cat, Kittens, Child's, 39 x 23 x 12 In. 225.00
Desk, Drop Front, Marquetry, Flower, Figural Inlay, Holland, 19th Century, 41 x 41 In. .. 880.00
Desk, Drop Front, Poplar, Fitted Interior, Painted, c.1830, 43 1/2 x 38 1/2 In. 7700.00
Desk, Drop Front, Walnut, Cornice Of Stacked Bands, Leaves, 42 x 56 1/4 In. 5175.00
Desk, Drop Front, Walnut, Cubby Slots, Burl Panels, 2 Lower Doors, c.1850, 53 x 40 In. . 365.00
Desk, Drop Front, Walnut, Fitted Interior, 4 Graduated Drawers, c.1775, 44 In. 7700.00
Desk, E. Wormley, Mahogany, Circular, Top, 3 Pivoting Drawers, Dunbar, 57 In. 535.00
Desk, Eames, ESU-D-20-C, Plywood, Steel, Masonite, Herman Miller, 1951, 29 x 60 In. . 9775.00
Desk, Eastlake Style, Cylinder, Burl Panels, Woman's, 59 x 30 x 23 In. 1430.00
Desk, Edwardian, Mahogany, Leather Writing Surface, 3 Drawers, 38 1/2 In. 7200.00
Desk, Eliel Saarinen, Walnut Veneer, 4 Drawers, Johnson Furniture Co., 30 In. .....450.00 to 560.00
Desk, Empire, Mahogany, 3 Short Drawers, Over 1 Drawer, Woman's, c.1840, 38 x 28 In. 470.00
Desk, Empire, Mahogany, Gilt Bronze Mounted, Drop Front, 47 x 54 x 25 In. 1840.00
Desk, Empire, Mahogany, Rectangular Top, 3 Long Drawers, 55 In. 1495.00

Desk, Federal, Mahogany Veneer, Bird's Eye, Tiger Maple, 2 Tiers, 42 x 37 x 22 In. 3100.00
Desk, Federal, Mahogany, Pine, Tambour, Inlay, Brasses, S.J. Reyoh, 42 x 47 x 21 In. . . . 880.00
Desk, Frank Lloyd Wright, Mahogany, 2 Drawers, Red Decal, Henredon, 28 x 52 In. 115.00
Desk, G. Nelson, Dark Walnut, Roll Top, Black Laminate Sides, 54 x 34 In. 1265.00
Desk, G. Nelson, White Laminate Top, Black Hairpin Leg, 1950, 48 x 29 In. 575.00
Desk, G. Stickley, Kneehole Compartment, 1 Long Drawer, 54 x 30 In. 6900.00
Desk, G. Stickley, Mahogany, 2 Half Drawers Over 1 Full Drawer, 43 In. 865.00
Desk, G. Stickley, Mahogany, 9 Drawers, 30 x 54 x 30 In. 6325.00
Desk, G. Stickley, Mahogany, Overhanging Beveled Top, 43 3/4 x 30 x 11 In. 4315.00
Desk, G. Stickley, Mahogany, Overhanging Rectangular Top, 40 x 25 In. 4600.00
Desk, G. Stickley, No. 505, Mahogany, Chalet, Dark Finish, 24 x 17 x 46 In. 5750.00
Desk, G. Stickley, No. 705, Mahogany, Arched Toe Board, Slab Sides, 52 In. 5750.00
Desk, G. Stickley, No. 708, Mahogany, Original Finish, 35 1/2 In. 2300.00
Desk, G. Stickley, No. 720, Slotted Back Organizer, 2 Drawers, 1904, 37 x 38 In. 3740.00
Desk, G. Stickley, Postcard, 2-Letter Backsplash, 1 Drawer, Copper V-Pull, 33 In. 4315.00
Desk, G. Stickley, Postcard, Gallery, Slots, Label, Harvey Ellis, 1915, 37 x 38 In. 3250.00
Desk, George I, Walnut, Parquetry, Kneehole, Center & 6 Side Drawers, 29 x 20 In. 745.00
Desk, George III, Flame Mahogany, Leather Top, 9 Drawers, 1940s, 66 x 42 In. 3775.00
Desk, George III, Mahogany, Kneehole, Crossbanded Top, 1 Drawer, 31 In. 7200.00
Desk, George III, Mahogany, Rectangular Top, Blue Leather Writing Surface, 29 In. 920.00
Desk, Georgian Style, Drop Front, Serpentine Interior Over Case, 40 x 35 1/2 In. 110.00
Desk, Georgian, Mahogany, Tooled Leather Top, 4 Drawers, 30 x 60 x 41 1/2 In. 800.00
Desk, Hepplewhite, Drop Front, Cherry, French Feet, 41 x 45 x 20 In. 2240.00
Desk, Hepplewhite, Mahogany, Flame Veneer, Woman's, 28 x 39 In. 825.00
Desk, Hepplewhite, Slant Front, Cherry, 4 Drawers, Fitted, 44 x 43 x 21 In. 1870.00
Desk, Hepplewhite, Slant Front, Cherry, 41 x 39 x 18 In. 1290.00
Desk, Jacques Adnet, Oak, Wrought Iron, c.1935, 29 x 62 1/2 x 34 In. 10800.00
Desk, John A. Wolf, Willow Twig, Twig Gallery, Book Ledge, 33 1/2 x 27 In. 920.00
Desk, Kimbal & Cabus, Flip Top, Brass Mounts, Spindles, 1875, 37 In. 6160.00
Desk, Kimbal & Cabus, Walnut, Fold-Down Lid, Kneehole Base, 1880, 36 x 19 In. 15120.00
Desk, Kingwood, Rosewood, Leather Surface, 3 Drawers, 59 In. 8400.00
Desk, Kneehole, Rectilinear Top, Frieze Drawer, Germany, 29 3/4 x 48 x 26 In. 2300.00
Desk, Kneehole, Walnut, Wooton, Original File Drawers, Ornate Gallery, 62 x 29 In. 15100.00
Desk, L. & J.G. Stickley, Drop Front, 2 Short Over 2 Long Drawers, 43 x 42 x 17 In. 1725.00
Desk, L. & J.G. Stickley, No. 374, Mahogany, Drop Front, Dark Finish, 46 x 10 In. 1150.00
Desk, L. & J.G. Stickley, No. 400, 5 Drawers, Original Copper Pulls, 42 x 29 In. 546.00
Desk, L. & J.G. Stickley, No. 500, 1 Drawer Over Kneehole, 2 Side Drawers, 30 x 26 In. . 1265.00
Desk, L. & J.G. Stickley, No. 604, Mahogany, 3 Drawers, Signed, 40 x 36 In. 1265.00
Desk, Library, Rosewood, Floral, 1 Drawer, 28 x 48 x 30 In. 1120.00
Desk, Lifetime, Mahogany, 1 Drawer, Single Vertical Slat, 27 1/2 x 38 x 26 In. 490.00
Desk, Lifetime, Mahogany, 4 Drawers, 29 x 54 x 29 3/4 In. 4315.00
Desk, Louis XV Style, Oak, Parquetry, 5 Drawers, 31 1/2 x 49 x 31 3/4 In. 1265.00
Desk, Louis XV, Burl Walnut, Slant Front, 3 Crossbanded Drawers, 37 In. 1265.00
Desk, Louis XVI Style, Leather Panel Inset, 1 Drawer Over 4, Gilt, 45 x 26 x 30 In. 115.00
Desk, Louis XVI, Pair Of Short Frieze Drawers, Woman's, 39 x 45 x 23 In. 1035.00
Desk, Mahogany, Crescent Form, Iris, Dragon Drawers, Dragon Legs, 1900, 48 x 44 In. . . 1095.00
Desk, Mahogany, Kidney, 7 Drawers, Leather Insert, 45 x 23 x 30 In. 220.00
Desk, Mahogany, Marquetry, Slant Front Over 2 Drawers, Cabriole Legs, 39 In. 900.00
Desk, Mahogany, Maze Design, Foot Rest, 4 Drawers, Square, 32 3/4 x 26 In. 635.00
Desk, Mahogany, Mechanical Sliding & Tilted Surface, 1840, 33 In. 1095.00
Desk, Michael Correy, Pedestal, Walnut, Cantilevered Plank Top, 67 In. 2415.00
Desk, Modernage, Blond Veneer, 3 Drawers, Angular Base, 28 1/4 In. 2025.00
Desk, Morgensen, Teak, Fitted Interior, 2 Drawers Over 3 Drawers, 1955, 47 1/2 . . . . 690.00
Desk, Neoclassical, Mahogany, Rectangular Stepped Cornice, 3 Drawers, 52 In. 3900.00
Desk, Oak, Adoration Of The Magi, 6 Drawers, Italy, 31 x 52 x 25 In. 1093.00
Desk, Oak, Leather Surface, Pigeonholes, 2 Drawers, Over 3 Drawers, 1780s, 43 In. 1725.00
Desk, Oak, Old Hickory, Rectangular V-Board Top, 3 Drawers, Slab Sides, 30 In. 160.00
Desk, Oak, Pedestal, Tooled Leather Surface, Fitted With Drawers, Casters, 29 x 41 In. . . . 750.00
Desk, Partners, Chippendale, Mahogany, 10 Drawers, c.1910, 30 1/2 x 51 x 32 In. 715.00
Desk, Partners, Chippendale, Mahogany, Pedestal, 30 x 84 x 44 In. 3740.00
Desk, Partners, Chippendale, Walnut, 4 Drawers Each Side, Refinished, 48 x 27 In. 385.00
Desk, Partners, Empire, Mahogany, 2 Pedestals, Carved Leaves, 2 Drawers, 54 x 29 In. . . . 1045.00
Desk, Partners, George III, Mahogany, Crossbanded Top, 1 Drawer, 29 1/2 In. 3450.00

Desk, Partners, Mahogany, Carved Corners, Felt Surface, 1 Long, 2 Short Drawers, 30 In. 460.00
Desk, Partners, Mahogany, Shell Form, Lions Form Legs, 31 x 53 x 34 In. 1840.00
Desk, Partners, Oak, Dolphin, Lion Head, Carved Skirt, c.1885, 72 x 36 x 30 In. 4760.00
Desk, Partners, Renaissance Revival, Burled Walnut, 1875, 59 x 32 x 29 In. 3080.00
Desk, Pedestal, Mahogany, 3 Frieze Drawers, Bracket Feet, 19th Century, 30 In. 1495.00
Desk, Pedestal, Mahogany, 3 Frieze Drawers, Tooled Green Leather Surface, 29 In. 2530.00
Desk, Pedestal, Mahogany, Rectangular Top, 2 Graduated Drawers, 28 1/4 In. 115.00
Desk, Pedestal, Victorian, Mahogany Inlay, Canted Corners, 3 Drawers, 25 In. 1955.00
Desk, Pedestal, W. Plattner, Brown Leather Top, Walnut Frame, 30 In. 1840.00
Desk, Pine, Painted, 16 Upper Over 5 Lower Drawers, Red, 1800s, 48 x 36 x 19 In. 5750.00
Desk, Pine, Telephone, 2 Sliding Doors, Pigeonholes, 1 Shelf Base 440.00
Desk, Plantation, Drop Front, Walnut, Fitted Interior, Lower Frieze Drawer, 50 In. 1035.00
Desk, Queen Anne, Drop Front, Maple, Child's, New England, c.1765, 27 1/2 x 24 In. . . . 2090.00
Desk, Queen Anne, Mahogany, Rectangular Surface, 4 Short Side Drawers, 65 In. 1610.00
Desk, Queen Anne, Mahogany, Rectangular Surface, 4 Side Drawers, 30 In. 520.00
Desk, Queen Anne, Maple, Red Paint, 2 Drawers, Pigeonholes, 37 x 26 In. 3600.00
Desk, Queen Anne, Slant Front, Mahogany, Figured, 4 Drawers, 1760, 44 x 22 In. 3600.00
Desk, Queen Anne, Slant Front, Maple, Pigeonholes, Child's, c.1750, 28 x 23 3/4 In. 2200.00
Desk, Queen Anne, Slant Front, Pine, 2 Drawers, Mass., 17 x 11 In. 2160.00
Desk, Queen Anne, Slant Front, Walnut, 2 Drawers, Fitted Interior, Woman's, 37 In. 835.00
Desk, Renaissance Revival, Oak, Carved Paneled Doors, Leather Top, 51 In. 1035.00
Desk, Renaissance Revival, Slant Front, Walnut, Carved Crest, Trumpet Legs, 65 In. 2760.00
Desk, Richard Neutra, 6 Drawers, 1 Blind Drawer, Beige Paint, 1957, 30 1/2 In. 790.00
Desk, Rohde, Mahogany, 6 Drawers, Kidney Top, Herman Miller, 29 In. 1690.00
Desk, Roll Top, Pigeonholes, Small Drawers, Hidden Compartments, 49 x 48 In. 575.00
Desk, Roll Top, S Curve, Oak, Late 1800s, 52 x 60 In. 6900.00
Desk, Roll Top, Victorian, Dark Mahogany, 8 Small Drawers, Pigeonholes, 49 In. 575.00
Desk, Rosewood, Bird's-Eye Maple, Galleried Shelf, c.1850, 23 x 23 x 43 In. 4800.00
Desk, Rosewood, Chrome, 3 Drawers, Tubular Chrome Frame, 66 x 30 x 29 In. 1265.00
Desk, Rosewood, Drop Leaf, Carved Panels, Full Gallery, 4 Drawers, 42 x 35 x 16 In. . . . 145.00
Desk, Rosewood, Elm, 3 Drawers, Applied Carved Cloud, Bat Design, 33 x 25 In. 460.00
Desk, Roycroft, Slant Top, 1 Drawer, Copper, Mackmurdo Feet, Woman's, 45 In. 7700.00
Desk, Satinwood, Bombe Side, Crossbanded Top, 4 Drawers, Splayed Feet, 43 In. 1840.00
Desk, School, Oak, Writing Arm 125.00
Desk, Schoolmaster's, 2 Recessed Doors, Interior Cubbyholes, 68 x 36 In. 2300.00
Desk, Schoolmaster's, Pine, Sloping Hinged Top, 2 Short Drawers, 33 In. 2530.00
Desk, Schoolmaster's, Slant Front, Poplar, Red Wash, Stretcher, 39 x 26 1/2 x 47 1/2 In. . . 660.00
Desk, Sewing, Shaker, Red Paint, 2 Drawers, Rectangular, Turned Legs, Child's, 39 In. . . 1840.00
Desk, Shaker, Deaconess, Maple, Pine, Cherry, Butternut, Hinged Lid, c.1875, 29 In. 5250.00
Desk, Sheraton, Slant Front, Cherry, 1 Drawer, Turned Legs, 1840, 33 x 37 x 24 In. 730.00
Desk, Shop Of The Crafters, Drop Front, Mahogany, 42 x 29 x 20 In. 1440.00
Desk, Slant Front, Birch, 4 Graduated Drawers, 39 In. 4900.00
Desk, Slant Front, Cherry, 4 Interior Drawers, Hidden Compartment, 35 1/2 In. 825.00
Desk, Slant Front, Curly Maple, 7 Dovetailed Interior Drawers, 40 x 37 In. 3850.00
Desk, Slant Front, Mahogany, Fitted Interior, 3 Long Drawers, Late 19th Century, 36 In. . 1955.00
Desk, Slant Front, Mahogany, Fitted Interior, 4 Drawers, French Feet, c.1810, 44 3/4 In. . . 1760.00
Desk, Slant Front, Mahogany, Scalloped Ogee Feet, 4 Drawers, Pigeonholes, 43 1/2 In. . . 2100.00
Desk, Slant Front, Mahogany, Statehouse, Pierced Brackets, c.1790, 35 x 49 In. 1760.00
Desk, Slant Front, Pine, Maple, Gallery Top, Square Legs, c.1890, 51 x 38 x 26 In. 450.00
Desk, Slant Front, Walnut, 8 Interior Drawers, Document Drawers, 37 In. 4400.00
Desk, Van Keppel-Green, 4 Drawers, White Birch Finish, 52 x 26 x 30 In. 920.00
Desk, W. Plattner, Leather Top, 2 Rosewood Drawers, Bronze Base, 84 In. 6900.00
Desk, Walnut, Carved Floral Base, Carved Nut Apron, 1880, 39 x 63 x 31 In. 6160.00
Desk, Walnut, Leather Writing Surface, Brass Corners, 19th Century, 6 In. 175.00
Desk, William & Mary, Slant Front, Pine, 6 Pigeonholes, 9 Drawers, 43 In. 5700.00
Desk, Wooton, Oak, Rotary Base, Metal Tag, 46 x 30 x 31 In. 1960.00
Desk, Wooton, Walnut, Rotary, Pullout Slide, 4 Drawers, Pigeonholes, 53 x 56 In. 4315.00
Desk Organizer, Arts & Crafts, Oak, Cutout Sides, Pen & Ink Holder, 16 x 8 x 9 In. 300.00
Desk-Bar, Glass Liner On Barside, Drawer In Desk, Vertical Dividers, Walco, 39 In. 495.00
Dinette Set, Art Deco, Fruitwood, Upholstered, 1928, 7 Piece 4800.00
Dinette Set, Beaux Arts, Walnut, 1898, 30 x 53 x 118 In., 11 Piece 8625.00
Dinette Set, Drugstore, Octagonal Glass Top, Door, 4 Seatmore Chairs, 30 x 31 In. 460.00
Dinette Set, Jacobean, 2-Pedestal Table, 2 Pullout Leaves, 6 Chairs, 7 Piece 1870.00

Dinette Set, National Chair Co., Art Deco, Trestle Table, Stencil Chair, 1938, 5 Piece . . .   345.00
Dining Set, Art Deco, Mahogany, Rosewood, Leather Seats, France, 1925, 9 Piece 8625.00
Dining Set, Art Deco, Walnut, Iron, Leather Panels, Draw Leaf, France, 1940, 9 Piece . . .   5750.00
Dining Set, Arts & Crafts, Carved Oak, c.1910, 40 x 72 x 22 In., 7 Piece 3575.00
Dining Set, Bamboo, 6 Armchairs, Glass-Top Table, 29 1/2 In., 7 Piece 375.00
Dining Set, E. Wormley, Bleached Mahogany, Dunbar, 25 x 33 In., 6 Piece 2530.00
Dining Set, E. Wormley, Modern, Hardwood, Open Armchairs, 1950s, 9 Piece 4885.00
Dining Set, Jacobean Revival, Oak, Refractory, Cupboard, Sideboard, 1920s, 9 Piece 3410.00
Dining Set, Oak, Carved, Rectangular Table, Upholstered Seats, 1920s, 9 Piece 6800.00
Dining Set, Thuya, Art Deco, Mahogany, Center Pedestal, Continental, 1938, 7 Piece 4600.00
Dining Set, Wegner, Mahogany, Drop Leaf, Table & 6 Chairs, c.1955, 7 Piece 1725.00
Dresser, Art Deco, Enameled Wood, Chrome & Wood Trestle, 9 Drawers, 30 x 59 In. 230.00
Dresser, Bamboo, Angular Backsplash, 3 Drawers, 26 x 22 x 11 In. 460.00
Dresser, E. Wormley, Light Mahogany, 4 Drawers, Dunbar, 34 x 30 In. 865.00
Dresser, E. Wormley, Walnut Case, 8 Drawers, Dunbar, 54 x 19 x 34 In. 3575.00
Dresser, G. Nakashima, Walnut, Dovetailed Case, Low, 1968, 32 x 22 In. 6200.00
Dresser, G. Nakashima, Walnut, Triple, 12 Drawers, Slab Top, 106 x 32 In. 2875.00
Dresser, G. Nelson, Blond Wood, 5 Graduated Drawers, Plank Legs, 40 In. 845.00
Dresser, G. Stickley, No. 625, Mahogany, Original Finish, 42 x 35 In. 5175.00
Dresser, G. Stickley, No. 911, 2 Full Drawers, Red Decal, 48 x 22 x 35 In. 3740.00
Dresser, L. & J.G. Stickley, Mahogany, Hat Box, 2 Doors, 3 Drawers, 49 x 28 In. 4025.00
Dresser, L. & J.G. Stickley, No. 101, Mahogany, Original Mirror, 54 x 68 In. 2875.00
Dresser, Limbert, No. 477, Mahogany, 2 Half Drawers Over 2 Full Drawers, 67 In. 1495.00
Dresser, Mahogany, Fretwork-Topped Mirror, 19th Century, 76 1/2 In. 550.00
Dresser, Oak, Geometric Paneled Drawers, Split Column, 37 1/2 x 67 x 23 In. 3450.00
Dresser, Oak, Marble Top, 3 Drawers, 4 1/2 x 20 3/4 x 26 1/2 In. 595.00
Dresser, Rococo, Arched Mirror, Floral Swags, 88 1/4 x 45 1/2 x 25 1/4 In. 5520.00
Dresser, Rococo, Rosewood, Carved Crest, Serpentine Marble Top, 86 x 44 x 23 In. 3450.00
Dresser, Rococo, Rosewood, Raised On Carved Brackets, Marble-Top Base, 87 In. 5750.00
Dresser, Rococo, Walnut, Fruit-Carved Cartouche, Serpentine Marble Top, 92 In. 4600.00
Dresser, Rococo, Walnut, Open-Carved Crest, 81 x 42 x 19 1/4 In. 172.00
Dresser, Rohde, Maple Veneer, 4 Drawers, Herman Miller, 36 x 19 In. 1265.00
Dresser, Rohde, Rosewood, Sequoia Burl, 4 Drawers, Plank Wood Base, 33 In. 1575.00
Dresser, Rohde, Rosewood, Sequoia Burl, 6 Drawers, Wooden Base, 44 In. 1725.00
Dresser, Rohde, Wood, Herman Miller, 36 x 43 x 19 In. 1265.00
Dresser, Salesman Sample, Mirror, Pitched Pediment, Marble Top, Scroll Back, c.1880 . .   3300.00
Dresser, Semanier, Mahogany, Kingwood, Marble Top, 7 Drawers, Cabriole Legs, 50 In. .   1380.00
Dresser, Victorian, Burl Walnut, Carved Floral, Beveled Edge, 69 1/2 x 59 In. 403.00
Dresser, Victorian, Rosewood, Marble Top, Serpentine Compartments, 1860, 78 In. 3360.00
Dresser, Walnut, Bowfront, 3 Drawers, Crest, Mirror, Candleholders, 82 x 42 x 21 In. . . .   450.00
Dresser, Walnut, Drop Center, 2 Candle Shelves, Mirror, Refinished, 102 x 45 In. 525.00
Dry Sink, Cherry, 4 Drawers, 2 Paneled Doors, 27 1/2 x 53 x 23 In. 1840.00
Dry Sink, Dovetailed, 2 Drawers Over 2 Doors, 35 x 35 1/2 x 17 In. 770.00
Dry Sink, Gallery Over Tin-Lined Well, Twin Pine Doors, 31 x 45 In. 2010.00
Dry Sink, High Back, Built By Ohio Amish, 48 In. 10500.00
Dry Sink, Oak, Pine, 3 Short Drawers, Open Shelf Over 2-Door Base, 55 x 39 In. 1045.00
Dry Sink, Painted, 1-Board, Scalloped Apron, 2 Doors, Drawer, 42 x 17 1/2 x 33 1/2 In. . . .   990.00
Dry Sink, Pine, 2 Paneled Doors, Cast-Iron Latches, 1 Drawer Right Side, 36 1/2 In. 1210.00
Dry Sink, Pine, Poplar, Painted, Pennsylvania, c.1820, 36 x 42 x 19 In. 660.00
Dry Sink, Pine, Red Paint, 2 Doors, Early 1800s, 30 x 42 x 17 1/2 In. 635.00
Dry Sink, Pine, Well Over Case, 2 Doors, New England, c.1840, 37 x 38 In. 305.00
Dry Sink, Poplar, Child's, Pennsylvania, Early 19th Century, 19 1/2 x 31 1/2 In. 525.00
Dry Sink, Poplar, High Back, Additional Top, Pennsylvania, c.1890, 84 1/2 x 42 In. 605.00
Dry Sink, Shaker, Maple, Pumpkin Orange Paint, Recessed Panel Door With Knob, 36 In.   10580.00
Dry Sink, Softwood, 1 Dovetailed Drawer, Orange, Yellow Sponge, 36 1/2 In. 1375.00
Dumbwaiter, Chippendale, 3 Tiers, Brass & Leather Casters, Brace 2575.00
Dumbwaiter, George III Style, Mahogany, Revolving Dish Top, 6 x 30 In. 345.00
Dumbwaiter, George III, Mahogany, 3 Tiers, 45 x 25 1/2 In. 1150.00
Dumbwaiter, George III, Mahogany, Molded Tiers, Tripod Base, Pad Feet, 44 In. 1955.00
Dumbwaiter, Mahogany, 3 Tiers, Knop, Downswept Legs, 42 1/4 In. 1495.00
Dumbwaiter, Mahogany, 3 Tiers, Vase Turned Column, Tripod, 1800s, 23 x 49 In. 635.00
Dumbwaiter, Mahogany, Circular Tray, Cabriole Legs, Dutch Feet, 43 3/4 In. 460.00
Dumbwaiter, Mahogany, Dish Top, 2nd Rotating Tier, Brass Casters, 39 1/2 In. 1380.00

Furniture, Etagere,
Rococo, Faux
Rosewood, Marble,
Mirrors, 101 x 62 In.

Crayon marks can be removed from wooden furniture with mayonnaise. Rub in the mayonnaise, let it sit for a few hours, then wipe with a damp cloth.

Dumbwaiter, Sheraton, Mahogany, Reeded Legs, 43 x 17 In.	1265.00
Easel, Book, Mahogany, Folding, 18th Century, 10 In.	165.00
Easel, Louis XV, Oak, Shell-Carved Crest, Leaf-Carved Feet, 72 x 22 In.	1380.00
Etagere, Brass, Onyx Shelves, Stone & Brass Finials, Mirror, 34 1/2 x 14 x 46 In.	715.00
Etagere, Burled Panels, Gold, Curio Top, Brass Mounts, 1875, 66 x 90 x 19 In.	8230.00
Etagere, Chrome, Glass, 5 Shelves, 30 1/2 x 14 1/2 x 74 1/2 In.	195.00
Etagere, Ebony, Boulle Work, 3 Tiers, Serpentine Shelves, c.1870, 33 In.	630.00
Etagere, George III, Mahogany, 4 Tiers, Early 19th Century, 45 3/4 x 24 x 16 In.	1265.00
Etagere, Mahogany, 2 Tiers, Drawer, c.1800, 24 3/4 In.	1840.00
Etagere, Mahogany, Oak, Dark Varnish, Base Drawer, Sahon, N.Y., 24 x 15 x 64 In.	1705.00
Etagere, Mirror Back, Stick & Ball Supports, c.1890, 65 x 33 x 12 In.	1300.00
Etagere, Napoleon III, Bird's-Eye Maple, 3 Tiers, Floral Marquetry, 1880s, 31 x 17 In.	635.00
Etagere, Neoclassical, Mahogany, Cabinet, Brass Molding, 57 x 21 x 14 1/2 In.	3810.00
Etagere, Rococo, Faux Rosewood, Marble, Mirrors, 101 x 62 In. *Illus*	10350.00
Etagere, Rosewood, 3 Tiers, Gilt Brass Gallery, 1830s, 29 In.	9000.00
Etagere, Rosewood, 3 Tiers, Supports Over Drawer, 19th Century, 47 In.	4200.00
Etagere, Rosewood, Mahogany, Marquetry, 6 Mirrors At Top, 98 In.	5175.00
Etagere, Rosewood, Mirror-Backed Shelves, Fretted Supports, 1870s, 53 In.	3220.00
Etagere, Thomas Brooks, Rococo, Rosewood, Cabinet Base, 63 x 32 x 18 In.	2530.00
Etagere, Victorian, Cast Iron, Marble, c.1870, 77 x 35 1/2 In.	385.00
Etagere, Victorian, Walnut, Graduated Shelves, Mirror Back, Base Shelf, 71 In.	935.00
Etagere, Walnut, Carved, Mirror Back, 19th Century	2860.00
Etegere, Walnut, Marble Top, Open Carved Crest, 1870, 94 x 50 In.	3920.00
Etegere, Walnut, Marble Top, Open Carvings, 1870, 85 x 38 In.	2520.00
Fainting Couch, Arts & Crafts, Oak, Slanted Headrest, Original Finish, 78 x 31 x 24 In.	750.00
Fainting Couch, Irving Chase Co., Beige Ground, Blue & Green Needlepoint Cover	350.00
Fernery, Black Forest, Matching Tree Base, Leaves, Signed, 65 In.	390.00
Fernery, Rosewood Ebonized, Bronze Head Mounts, 1875, 38 In.	675.00
Folio Rack, Mahogany, Boydell's Shakespeare, c.1840, 25 x 11 x 34 1/2 In.	850.00
Footstool, Arts & Crafts, Keyed-Through Tenons, 15 x 15 1/2 x 9 In.	400.00
Footstool, Arts & Crafts, Mahogany, Drop-In Cushion, 4 Legs, 14 x 11 x 9 In.	25.00
Footstool, Arts & Crafts, Mahogany, Rocking, Leather Top, 25 x 13 x 18 In.	375.00
Footstool, Arts & Crafts, Oak, Leather, Model 302, 4 1/2 x 12 1/4 In.	400.00
Footstool, Arts & Crafts, Split Reed Top, 14 x 16 x 16 In.	290.00
Footstool, Arts & Crafts, Square Posts, Drop-In Leather Cushion, 9 x 18 x 11 1/2 In.	460.00
Footstool, Arts & Crafts, Wood, Red Leather, 15 1/4 x 17 1/4 In.	200.00
Footstool, Biedermeier, Fruitwood, Leaf-Carved Ball Supports, 22 x 15 x 19 In.	330.00
Footstool, Brooks, Arts & Crafts, Slat Sides, Leather Padding, 16 1/2 x 27 x 14 In.	345.00
Footstool, Carved Wood, Cabriole Legs, Needlework Top, France, 1938, 19 x 13 In.	520.00
Footstool, Carved Wood, Red Brown, Twist-Carved Stretcher, Belgium, 16 x 17 In.	110.00
Footstool, E. Burke, Poplar, Yellow Paint, Black Pinstripes, c.1820, 7 x 13 In.	385.00
Footstool, Eastlake, Gilt, Floral Needlepoint, 1875, 15 x 8 In.	575.00
Footstool, Eastlake, Walnut, Burled Panels, Turned Legs, Upholstered, 16 In.	125.00
Footstool, Empire, Mahogany Flame Veneer, Cushion, 15 1/2 x 15 1/2 x 11 In.	165.00
Footstool, F.B. Eshleman, Cherry, Hand-Carved Legs, 8 1/2 x 17 In.	110.00
Footstool, F.H. Conant, Arts & Crafts, 12 x 18 1/2 x 12 1/2 In.	315.00

Footstool, Federal Style, Square Molded Legs, Stretcher, Upholstered, 24 x 20 x 18 In. . . . 35.00
Footstool, French Provincial, Cabriole Legs, Needlepoint, 15 x 11 In. 85.00
Footstool, French Provincial, Needlework Top, X-Shaped Stretcher, 17 x 13 x 16 In. 355.00
Footstool, French Provincial, Walnut, Carved, Oval Upholstered Top, 17 3/4 In. 165.00
Footstool, G. Stickley, Japanned Leather Finish, 9 x 16 x 12 In. 1070.00
Footstool, G. Stickley, No. 301, Mahogany, Rush Seat, 20 x 16 x 17 In. . . . . .230.00 to 632.00
Footstool, G. Stickley, No. 302, Dark Green Cushion, Notched Feet, 5 In. 1380.00
Footstool, G. Stickley, Tacked On Leather Seat, Original Finish, 9 x 12 In. 1015.00
Footstool, George II, Mahogany, Wool, Tassel Trim, 22 x 15 In. 460.00
Footstool, Gold & Black Stenciled Buildings, Flowers & E.H. On Top, 6 7/8 In. 770.00
Footstool, Iron, Black Repaint, Cabriole Legs, Ornate, Leopard Print, 14 x 10 In., Pair . . . 465.00
Footstool, Iron, Owls, Black Repaint, Needlepoint, 14 1/4 x 7 1/2 In. 90.00
Footstool, Jacobean, Walnut, Rope Twist Legs & Stretcher, 23 x 16 x 17 In. 220.00
Footstool, L. & J.G. Stickley, Mahogany, Brown Leather Seat, Rectangular, 15 In. 1095.00
Footstool, L. & J.G. Stickley, Mahogany, Leather, 19 In. 805.00
Footstool, Limbert, Mahogany, 1 Drawer 1725.00
Footstool, Limbert, Original Dark Mahogany Finish, 12 1/2 x 20 In. 750.00
Footstool, Louis XV, Mahogany, Rectangular Padded Surface, Foliage, 20 In. 290.00
Footstool, Louis XV, Padded Top, Floral Design, Cabriole Legs, 19th Century, 7 In. 430.00
Footstool, Mahogany, Carved Knees, 4 Hipped Legs, Leather, 28 In. 3025.00
Footstool, Mahogany, Tacked On Leather, Tapered Legs, 10 x 15 x 9 In. 1035.00
Footstool, Mahogany, Upholstered, Chamfered Legs Joined By Stretchers, 17 1/2 In. 660.00
Footstool, Rococo, Padded Top, Frieze, Top-Shaped Feet, 19 x 23 x 17 In. 1150.00
Footstool, Shaker, No. 1, Maple, Marked Mount Lebanon, N.Y., 9 1/2 x 13 x 9 1/2 In. . . . 489.00
Footstool, Shaker, Pine, Green Paint, Rectangular Top, Cut Out Feet, 7 x 21 In. 1150.00
Footstool, Sheraton, Mahogany, Reeded Saber Legs, Claw Caps, 26 x 9 1/2 In. 145.00
Footstool, Stenciled, Yellow, Salmon Pinstriping, Brown, c.1840, 5 3/4 x 15 In. 470.00
Footstool, Turned Legs, Needlework Top, France, 16 x 10 x 8 In. 245.00
Footstool, Victorian, Molded Base, Needlepoint, 12 x 18 In. 185.00
Footstool, Victorian, Walnut, Marquetry, Padded Round Top, Stringing, 11 In. 185.00
Footstool, Walnut, Carved Frame, Cabriole Legs, Flame Stitched, 9 x 7 In. 49.00
Footstool, Walnut, Needlepoint Top, Floral Design, Carved Legs, 14 x 19 x 16 In. 168.00
Frame, Arts & Crafts, Oak, Swivel Base, Free Standing, 9 x 7 1/2 In. 98.00
Frame, Crisscross, Yellow, Green Paint Design, 19 1/2 x 15 1/2 In. 275.00
Frame, Federal, Tiger Maple, Split Baluster, Rosettes, c.1835, 13 x 11 1/2 In. 385.00
Frame, Gilt Composition, Petal Molding, Shells, Scrolling Arabesque, 13 x 15 1/2 In. 290.00
Frame, Gilt Composition, Scrolling Acanthus, Shellwork, c.1850, 38 x 30 In. 635.00
Frame, Oak, Carved Cross, Print, Victorian Women, 28 x 25 In., Pair 255.00
Frame, Renaissance Revival, Gilt, 18 x 16 In., Pair 259.00
Frame, Shadowbox, Giltwood, Fuchsias, Floral Design, France, 8 3/4 x 6 In. 345.00
Frame, Victorian, Walnut, Gilt & Burl, Oval Opening, 22 1/2 x 19 1/4 In. 90.00
Frame, Walnut, Pierced Vintage Border, Greek Key Liner, Oval Opening, 23 In., Pair 440.00
Glider, Bunting Philadelphia, Metal, 1950s . . . . .225.00 to 325.00
Glider, Rohde, Tubular Bright Chrome Frame, Roll Armrests, 31 x 77 In. 4780.00
Hall Stand, Art Deco, Black Enameled Wood, Tinted Mirror, Drip Tray, 1930s, 76 In. . . . 490.00
Hall Stand, Art Deco, Chrome Aluminum, Open Frame, Mirror, France, 1935, 70 In. 800.00
Hall Stand, Art Deco, Wrought Iron, Hat Rack, Mirror, France, 1925, 71 In. 2875.00
Hall Stand, Arts & Crafts, Copper, Metal, Pierced Frame, Mirror, 1900s, 48 x 27 In. 490.00
Hall Stand, Arts & Crafts, Oak, Mirror, Stylized Floral, Drip Tray, 1900s, 80 In. 495.00
Hall Stand, Cast Iron, Leafy Branches, Oval Mirror, Trunk Pedestal, 1959, 73 In. 2875.00
Hall Stand, Cast Iron, Oval Mirror, Trunk Pedestal, Umbrella Ring, 1959, 73 In. 2875.00
Hall Stand, Cherry Stick, 5 Beveled Mirrors, Serpent Crest, 1890, 92 x 44 x 16 In. 2200.00
Hall Stand, Greenwood, Iron, Black Paint, Scrolls Around Mirror, 8 Hooks, 74 In. 1760.00
Hall Stand, Maple, Faux Bamboo, Beveled Mirror, American, c.1880, 87 x 35 x 9 In. 5040.00
Hall Stand, Mirror Flanked By Hooks, Marble Top, Drawer, Umbrella Holder, 90 In. 1210.00
Hall Stand, Oak, 4 Iron Hooks, Mirror, Lift Seat, 81 x 31 x 15 1/2 In. 520.00
Hall Stand, Oak, Beveled Mirror, Rectangular, 1885, 96 x 60 In. 10000.00
Hall Stand, Oak, Carved Lion Heads, Floral, England, 84 x 24 x 10 In. 1495.00
Hall Stand, Oak, Chair, Beveled Mirror Back, c.1900, 29 x 15 1/2 x 82 1/2 In. 635.00
Hall Stand, Oak, Drawer, Mirror, Sen. John Culver, Iowa, 1800s, 79 x 37 1/2 In. 335.00
Hall Stand, Oak, Umbrella Holder, Brass Hooks, 1900, 77 In. 610.00
Hall Stand, Walnut, Carved Mythical Figures, Seat Storage, Mirror, 102 In. 4675.00
Hall Stand, Wood, Ivory Inlay, Mirror, Inlaid Hunt Scenes, 1880s, 91 x 59 In. 1880.00

Hall Tree, Black Forest, Mountain Goat Climbing On Ledge, 91 x 22 x 26 In. 14000.00
Hall Tree, Colebrookdale, Wrought Iron, Backrest, Scrolled Hooks, 80 In. 690.00
Hall Tree, L. & J.G. Stickley, No. 89, Mahogany, Original Copper Hooks, 72 In. 1380.00
Hall Tree, Mahogany, Ormolu Bronze, Mounted Poppy, Dragonfly, c.1900, 96 x 55 In. 12000.00
Hall Tree, Oak, Figural, Floral Design, Relief Mask, 20th Century, 55 x 19 x 81 In. 1380.00
Hall Tree, Renaissance Revival, Cast Iron, Black Paint, 1800s, 82 x 33 In. 1680.00
Hall Tree, Rococo, Cast Iron, Acanthus Leaves, Removable Tray Base, 28 x 13 x 78 In. . . . 110.00
Hall Tree, Victorian, Cast Iron, Scrolling, Hooks, Umbrella Stand, c.1880, 74 In. 1210.00
Hall Tree, Walnut, Ornate Crest, Marble Top, 100 In. 5265.00
Hall Tree, Walnut, Turned Columns, Marble Top, Center Drawer, 48 x 16 In. 2420.00
Headboard, G. Nelson, Light Mahogany, Velvet, 12 x 40 In. 1380.00
Headboard, P. Evans, White Chrome, 1 Side Drawer, Signed, 86 x 84 1/2 In. 1095.00
Headboard, Rococo, Giltwood, Ornate Carving, c.1900, 55 x 78 1/2 78 1/2 In. 1840.00
High Chair, 3-Slat Back, Rush Seat, Turned Legs, Green Paint, c.1740, 39 3/4 In. 3850.00
High Chair, Bentwood Seat Guards, Arched Crest, Red Striping, 1850s, 35 3/4 In. 415.00
High Chair, Elm, Folding Tray & Base, Wheels, Relief Design Back, 1800s 175.00
High Chair, Folds Down To Carriage, Pull Handle 350.00
High Chair, Hickory, 2-Slat Back, Splint Seat, Pennsylvania, 18th Century, 32 In. 440.00
High Chair, Ladder Back, 3 Arched Slats, Turned Finial, Rush Seat, Pa., 1800, 38 In. 3100.00
High Chair, Maple, Rolled Hand-Holds, 3 Arched Slats, Paper Rush Seat, 35 In. 470.00
High Chair, Pressed Oak Foot Rest, Cane Seat, USS Maine Motif, 40 In. 460.00
High Chair, Sheraton, Black Paint, Stencil Decoration 520.00
High Chair, Stickley Bros., No. 421 1/4, 2 Back Slats, Tacked On Leather Seat 1100.00
High Chair, Straight Slat Over 3 Spindles, Plank Seat, Footrest, Arms 66.00
High Chair, Victorian, Converts To Rocker 575.00
High Chair, Windsor, Bow Back, Ashwood, Yew, 8-Rod Back, England, 1800 . . . . 2185.00
Highboy, Cherry, Flat Top, Cabriole Lets, Claw & Ball Feet, Conn., 73 x 43 In. 6500.00
Highboy, Queen Anne, 3 Base Drawers, 5 Top Drawers, 66 In. 7700.00
Highboy, Queen Anne, Burled Walnut Veneer, 2 Doors, 3 Drawers, 35 x 17 x 67 In. 1275.00
Highboy, Queen Anne, Mahogany Veneer, Broken Arch Top, 90 x 40 1/2 x 20 In. 5175.00
Highboy, Queen Anne, Mahogany Veneer, Dark Finish, Cabriole Leg, 37 x 80 In. 880.00
Highboy, Queen Anne, Maple, Molded Cornice, 73 1/2 x 38 x 19 1/2 In. 8050.00
Highboy, Roy McFadden, Aprons On Front & Sides, 9 Drawers, Fans At Center, 63 In. . . . 2530.00
Highboy, Scrolled Broken Pediment, Cabriole Legs, Claw & Ball Feet 6750.00
Highboy, William & Mary, Walnut, 5 Drawers, Trumpet Legs, Crossbanded, 54 In. 2990.00
Humidor, Black Forest, Walnut, Floral Carvings, 22 x 23 x 11 In. 5040.00
Humidor, George III, Mahogany, Zinc, Copper Interior, 35 x 17 In. 1495.00
Huntboard, Federal, Cherry, Scrolled Backboard, 2 Drawers, 49 x 40 x 20 In. 1495.00
Huntboard, Poplar, Yellow Pine, Cherry, 2 Drawers, Wood Pulls, 44 x 22 In. 3080.00
Hutch, 3 Shelves, 4 Drawers, Flowers, Hearts, White Ground, 68 x 42 x 20 1/2 In. 2645.00
Hutch, Carved Walnut, Black Paint, Tombstone Door, 10 x 6 1/2 x 3 1/2 In. 5750.00
Hutch, Pine, 3 Middle Drawers, 3 Shelves, 96 x 72 In. 880.00
Hutch, Pine, Blue Paint, 1 Glazed Door, Gray, Blue, 11 x 7 x 2 1/4 In. 3220.00
Hutch, Pine, Open Box Base, Triangular Cutouts On Sides, 26 x 41 In. 1440.00
Hutch, Pine, Shaped Crest, Square Nail & Screw Construction, 12 In. 1320.00
Hutch, Walnut, Beveled Glass Doorsarts & Crafts, 82 x 55 x 26 In. 2185.00
Hutch, Yellow Pine, 9-Pane Door, 19th Century, 79 x 44 In. 1840.00
Kas, 2 Paneled Doors, Shelf, Zoar, Alligatored Finish, 83 x 56 1/2 In. 2750.00
Kas, Gumwood, Poplar, Paneled Doors, Cornice, Platform Feet, c.1740, 78 x 55 In. 13800.00
Kas, Painted, Paneled Doors, Shaker-Style Pegs, Pennsylvania, c.1820, 86 In. 10950.00
Kas, Walnut, Ivory Inlay, Carved Putti, Foliate, 19th Century, 91 In. 5500.00
Kas, Walnut, Stepped Cornice, Panel Doors, Bun Feet, 18th Century, 77 x 71 In. 4500.00
Kneeler, Biedermeier, Cherry, Cube Parquetry, Ebonized, 35 x 20 x 28 In. 1035.00
Ladder, Library, Folding, 3-Part Hinged, Iron, Oak, 19th Century, 92 In. 3000.00
Lampstand, Regency, Mahogany, Leather Top, Carved Legs, c.1940, 28 x 20 x 16 In. . . . 56.00
Lap Desk, Burl, Mother-Of-Pearl Rosettes, Wooden Stand, 1884, 20 x 16 In. 690.00
Lap Desk, Drop Front, 3 Drawers, Brass Carrying Handles, c.1740, 13 1/4 x 20 In. 1100.00
Lap Desk, Inlaid Border, Dome Top, Fitted Interior, 5 1/4 x 11 3/4 In. 250.00
Lap Desk, Inlay Of Courting Couple, Dancing Musicians, Fabric Lining, 14 1/8 In. 150.00
Lap Desk, Mahogany, Brass Side Straps, Fitted Interior, 19th Century, 17 In. 175.00
Lap Desk, Mahogany, Brass, 1 Drawer, Gaines, London, 19th Century, 7 x 18 In. 1380.00
Lap Desk, Mahogany, Brass, Hinged Cover, Baize Lined Writing Slope, 7 x 11 In. 345.00
Lap Desk, Mahogany, Leather Surface, Upper Lid Opens To Well, 1835, 18 In. 5175.00

Lap Desk, Mahogany, Tooled Leather Interior, Compartments, 2 Wells, 1870s, 7 1/2 In. ...   460.00
Lap Desk, Oak, Marble Top, Divided Compartments, 11 7/8 x 17 5/8 x 3 1/8 In. 250.00
Lap Desk, Papier Mache, England, 10 x 13 In. 115.00
Lap Desk, Rosewood Veneer, Brass Band Inlay, 15 3/4 x 3 3/8 In. 220.00
Lap Desk, Sandalwood, Floral Reserve On Lid, Pull-Out Drawer, 3 Bottles, 15 In. 315.00
Lap Desk, Scalloped Edge, Foliate Design, England, 1870, 4 1/2 In. 865.00
Lap Desk, Tiger Maple, Tambour, Banded Inlays, c.1800, 6 1/2 x 11 In. 1600.00
Lap Desk, Victorian, Rosewood, Brass Nameplate, Velvet Writing Slope, 9 x 14 In. 140.00
Lap Desk, Victorian, Walnut, Brass Inlay, Green Leather, Inkwell, 6 x 13 1/2 x 9 In. 690.00
Lectern, Leather Bookrest, X-Form Support, Wrought Iron, 16th Century, 60 In. 6900.00
Lectern, W. Castle, Curved Top, Chiseled & Faceted Base, 92 x 48 In. 9200.00
Lectern, Walnut, Carved Tripod Base, Candleland, Adjustable, 45 x 23 x 23 In. 390.00
Library Steps, Continental, Fruitwood, Folding, Arched Top Rail, 19th Century 6600.00
Library Steps, Edwardian, Mahogany Veneer, Red Leather, Early 19th Century 880.00
Library Steps, Mahogany, 4 Treads, Shaped Supports, Folding, 54 1/2 In. 3900.00
Library Steps, Mahogany, 4 Turned Legs, Brass Casters, 20th Century, 67 In. 495.00
Library Steps, Mahogany, Leather Inserts, 3 Steps, Compartments Under 2 Steps 1800.00
Library Steps, Victorian, Pine, Folding, 9 Tiers, 68 1/4 x 15 x 33 1/2 In. 1495.00
Library Steps, Victorian, Walnut, Carved, Chair Form, Boston, c.1880, 37 x 21 In. 2300.00
Linen Press, Engraved Brass Hardware, Floral & Scroll Over Legs, 63 In. 2315.00
Linen Press, Federal, Mahogany, 2 Doors, 3 Long & 2 Short Drawers, 89 x 56 In. 7800.00
Linen Press, George III Style, Mahogany, Pierced Pediment, Urn, 76 x 42 1/2 x 20 In. ...   980.00
Linen Press, George III, Mahogany, 2 Doors Over 4 Drawers, 86 x 47 x 21 In. 2530.00
Linen Press, George III, Mahogany, 2 Graduated Drawers, Bracket Feet, 76 In. 4830.00
Linen Press, George III, Mahogany, 3 Drawers, Bracket Feet, 83 x 45 x 22 In. 2300.00
Linen Press, George III, Mahogany, Bowfront, Drop-Front Desk, 89 x 51 x 21 In. 8050.00
Linen Press, George III, Mahogany, Cornice, Paneled Doors, Drawers, 84 x 48 x 22 In. ..   5750.00
Linen Press, George III, Mahogany, Molded Cornice, 3 Drawers, 80 x 48 x 20 In. 1840.00
Linen Press, George III, Mahogany, Molded Cornice, Paneled Doors, 81 x 48 x 20 In. 2760.00
Linen Press, George III, Mahogany, Paneled Doors, 3 Graduated Drawers, 82 In. 2070.00
Linen Press, George III, Mahogany, Paneled Doors, Drawers, 89 1/2 x 45 x 21 1/2 In. 2530.00
Linen Press, George III, Mahogany, Pediment, 2 Doors, 8 Drawers, 87 x 53 x 24 In. 4140.00
Linen Press, George III, Mahogany, Swan-Neck Pediment, 2 Doors, 1800s, 88 In. 1380.00
Linen Press, George IV, Mahogany, 2 Parts, c.1825, 31 x 58 1/2 x 26 1/2 In. 5175.00
Linen Press, George IV, Mahogany, Rectangular Cornice, Paneled Doors, 83 In. 2070.00
Linen Press, Jacobean, Oak, Molded Cornice, 2 Paneled Doors, 78 x 52 x 19 In. 3750.00
Linen Press, Louis XVI, Tulipwood, Marble Top, 2 Doors, Tapered Legs, 56 x 24 In. 860.00
Linen Press, Mahogany, 2 Glass Doors, 4 Linen Trays, 84 In. 4070.00
Linen Press, Mahogany, 2 Upper Doors, Lower 3 Drawers, 1870s, 83 1/2 In. 4140.00
Linen Press, Mahogany, Butler's Desk, Fitted Interior, 81 1/4 In. 3300.00
Linen Press, Mahogany, Lower Drawers, Paneled Doors, Bracket Feet, 79 In. 4140.00
Linen Press, Mahogany, Marble Top, 2 Doors, 4 Slide Trays, 42 x 48 x 24 1/2 In. 2400.00
Linen Press, Marquetry Case, Swell Front, Garlands, 2 Drawers, 2 Doors, 54 1/2 In. 2750.00
Linen Press, Pine, Poplar, 3 Drawers, 4 Shelves, Secret Compartment, 81 3/4 In. 4400.00
Linen Press, Regency, Mahogany, Cove-Molded Cornice, 90 1/2 x 50 1/2 x 22 In. 2990.00
Linen Press, Victorian, Mahogany, Ebonized Sphinx Heads, Feet, 79 x 47 x 23 In. 2070.00
Linen Press, Victorian, Mahogany, Ogee-Mold Cornice, 79 x 53 1/2 x 21 3/4 In. 2760.00
Linen Press, William IV, Mahogany, Paneled Doors, Bun Feet, 81 1/2 x 49 x 24 In. 2760.00
Love Seat, Arne Vodder, Upholstered, Flaring Dowel Legs, c.1965, 64 1/2 In. 1035.00
Love Seat, Bruno Mathsson, Birch Plywood Frame, Original Webbing, 34 In. 1085.00
Love Seat, Thonet, Vinyl, Black Lacquer Bentwood Arms, 31 In. 500.00
Love Seat, Victorian, Mahogany, Carved, Velvet, 42 x 74 In. 9900.00
Lowboy, Chippendale, Cherry, 5 Drawers, Carved Fan, 34 x 41 x 20 In. 575.00
Lowboy, George I, Walnut, 3 Small Drawers, Shaped Skirt, Lapeted Legs, 28 x 30 In. 2530.00
Lowboy, George I, Walnut, Quarter Veneer, 1 Frieze Drawer, 30 x 27 x 12 In. 5750.00
Lowboy, George I, Walnut, Rectangular Top, 3 Short Drawers, Pad Feet, 27 In. 6000.00
Lowboy, George II, Oak, Rectangular Molded Top, Cabriole Legs, Pad Feet, 29 In. 2645.00
Lowboy, George II, Walnut, 2 Small Drawers, Cabriole Legs, Pad Feet, 28 1/2 In. 2160.00
Lowboy, George III, Mahogany, Bowfront, 3 Drawers, Brass Handles, 36 x 13 In. 355.00
Lowboy, Mahogany Veneer, 2 Drawers, Hoof Feet, Carved, England, 28 x 33 In., Pair 1540.00
Lowboy, Oak, 1 Frieze Drawer, Knopped Legs, 19th Century, 30 x 21 x 28 In. 3270.00
Lowboy, Queen Anne, Curly Maple, Cabriole Legs, 29 1/2 x 24 1/2 x 15 In. 2875.00
Lowboy, Queen Anne, Mahogany, Cabriole Legs, 2 Over 3 Drawers, 36 x 20 x 30 In. 660.00

Lowboy, Queen Anne, Walnut, 3 Drawers, Cabriole Legs, 18th Century, 30 x 18 In. 2280.00
Lowboy, Queen Anne, Walnut, Rectangular Top, 3 Drawers, 30 1/2 x 21 In............. 2185.00
Lowboy, William & Mary, Mahogany, Figured Veneer, Ball Footed, 24 x 17 In. 550.00
Lowboy, William & Mary, Walnut, Pine, Center Drawer, Side Drawers, 31 x 35 In. 770.00
Mirror, 3 Panels, Bow Top Garland Swags, Early 20th Century, 57 In................. 575.00
Mirror, Aesthetic Revival, Walnut, Small Marble Shelf, 93 x 32 In. 460.00
Mirror, Altar, Giltwood, Cartouche Form, Leaf & Shell Standard, 1760s, 23 x 9 3/4 In. 575.00
Mirror, Art Deco, Rectangular, Rounded Crest, Stylized Flowers, 50 x 30 1/2 In. 230.00
Mirror, Arts & Crafts, Cheval, Walnut, Beveled Glass, 77 1/4 x 35 In. 1690.00
Mirror, Arts & Crafts, Copper, Hammered, Reticulated Floral Design, 16 In. 4315.00
Mirror, Arts & Crafts, Wrought Iron, 2 Snails On Each Side, France, 18 1/2 In. 800.00
Mirror, Baroque, Giltwood, Cushion Frame, Acanthus Leaves, Spain, 29 x 24 In. 127.00
Mirror, Baroque, Giltwood, Cushion Frame, Latticework, Spain, 12 1/2 x 14 In. 230.00
Mirror, Baroque, Silvered Wood, Carved, Italy, 39 x 29 In. 3910.00
Mirror, Baroque, Walnut, Inlay, Part Ebonized, c.1870, 66 3/4 x 50 In. 920.00
Mirror, Beveled, Carved Strapwork On Punched Ground, Gilt Gesso, 51 In. 2300.00
Mirror, Beveled, Pink Enameled Frame, 6 1/2 x 5 In............................. 550.00
Mirror, Beveled, Rope-Molded Frame, Rods Of Twisted Glass Flowers, 23 In. 865.00
Mirror, Beveled, Upper Basket Of Fruit, Leaves & Berries, 1770s, 35 1/2 In. 6760.00
Mirror, Biedermeier, Fruitwood, Cornice, Frieze, Pilasters, 36 1/2 x 160 x 2 1/2 In...... 489.00
Mirror, Biedermeier, Walnut, 1860s, 39 3/4 x 34 1/4 In. 8400.00
Mirror, Biedermeier, Walnut, Canted Frame, Rectangular Panel, 49 x 30 In. 230.00
Mirror, Bird's-Eye Maple, Walnut, 19th Century, 37 x 20 1/2 In. 719.00
Mirror, Black Sponge Swags, Red Polka Dots, Mustard Ground, Pa., 1820, 19 In. 3960.00
Mirror, Black Walnut, Arched Plate, 18th Century, 42 x 22 1/2 In. 4200.00
Mirror, Brass, Floral & Foliate, Triangular Pediment, Repousse Mask, 1880s, 58 In. 2300.00
Mirror, Brass, Repousse, Floral, Foliate Brass Accents, 58 x 32 3/4 In. 2300.00
Mirror, Carved Shell, Ribbon Crest, Foliate Design, Beaded Trim, Italy, 41 In. 1955.00
Mirror, Cast Iron, Ripple, Red, Black Frame, Early 19th Century, 16 3/4 x 10 1/2 In. 1035.00
Mirror, Charles X, Burl Elm, Turned Columns, Stand, 1830, 70 In. 3000.00
Mirror, Charles X, Cove-Molded Frame, 1830s, 30 1/2 In. 345.00
Mirror, Charles X, Giltwood, Classical Motifs, 30 1/2 x 23 1/2 x 2 In. 345.00
Mirror, Charles X, Giltwood, Ogee-Molded Frame, Rectangular, 44 x 33 x 2 In. 1265.00
Mirror, Charles X, Maple, Rectangular Mirror Plate, Curved Legs, 78 3/4 In. 4370.00
Mirror, Cheval, Arts & Crafts, Cutout Crest Design, Casters, 80 x 28 1/2 x 27 In. 1740.00
Mirror, Cheval, Carved Walnut Frame, 19th Century, 73 1/2 x 29 In. 1155.00
Mirror, Cheval, Louis XV, Revolving Cartouche, Beveled Glass, 73 In. 1725.00
Mirror, Cheval, Mahogany, Bronze Swan's Head, 1880s, 61 1/2 In. 2300.00
Mirror, Cheval, Mahogany, Recessed Frieze, Medallions, Candle Branches, 80 3/4 In. 5250.00
Mirror, Cheval, Mahogany, Veneer, Carved Pineapple Finial, Arched Frame, 82 In. 575.00
Mirror, Cheval, Neoclassical, Walnut, Parcel Gilt, Rosewood Frame, 74 x 34 x 32 In. 2530.00
Mirror, Cheval, Regency, Mahogany, Lion-Paw Caps, Casters, c.1820, 66 x 33 In. 980.00
Mirror, Chippendale, Gilt Phoenix Top, 41 In. 3995.00
Mirror, Chippendale, Mahogany Veneer, Inlay, Giltwood, Eagle, c.1785, 47 x 22 In. 2860.00
Mirror, Chippendale, Mahogany Veneer, Pine, Scroll, Eagle, Gilding, 42 x 23 1/4 In. 880.00
Mirror, Chippendale, Mahogany, Carved Crest, Giltwood Phoenix, 1780, 35 In. 575.00
Mirror, Chippendale, Mahogany, Conch-Shell Inlay, Carved, 36 1/2 In. 1035.00
Mirror, Chippendale, Mahogany, Dark Finish, Pine, 19th Century, 40 x 18 In. 440.00
Mirror, Chippendale, Mahogany, Parcel Gilt, Fretted, Pierced Scroll Crest, 37 x 20 In. ... 635.00
Mirror, Chippendale, Mahogany, Pierced Phoenix Crest, c.1800, 25 x 13 1/4 In. 220.00
Mirror, Chippendale, Mahogany, Pierced, Scrolled Crest, 1790, 37 x 19 In. 600.00
Mirror, Chippendale, Mahogany, Scalloped Crests, Ears, Inlaid, c.1800, 28 x 12 In. 220.00
Mirror, Chippendale, Mahogany, Scroll Crest, Pendant, c.1770, 35 x 18 In. 1095.00
Mirror, Chippendale, Mahogany, Scrolled Borders & Ears, Refinished, 35 x 18 In. 110.00
Mirror, Chippendale, Mahogany, Scrolled Crest, Giltwood Liner, c.1780, 34 x 18 3/4 In. . 550.00
Mirror, Chippendale, Scroll Cut Crest, Phoenix, Giltwood, c.1790, 28 1/2 x 16 In. 165.00
Mirror, Chippendale, Tiger Maple, Parcel Gilt, Mid 1800s, 40 x 19 3/4 In. 1380.00
Mirror, Classical, Cherry, Mahogany, Foliate Scrolling, Brass, c.1850, 36 In. 315.00
Mirror, Classical, Giltwood, Plaster, Carved, Palmettes, 41 1/2 x 21 In. 750.00
Mirror, Colonial Revival, Gilt Composition, 68 3/4 x 43 1/4 In. 1095.00
Mirror, Colonial Revival, Giltwood, Scrolling Acanthus, 1800s, 30 x 26 In., Pair 635.00
Mirror, Conforming Ogee Molding, Flora & Fauna, Beaded Frame, 39 x 28 1/2 In........ 430.00
Mirror, Continental, Giltwood, 3-Light, Girandole, 38 x 17 1/2 x 10 In., Pair 2990.00

Mirror, Continental, Giltwood, Urn Crest, Trailing Laurel, 22 x 12 1/2 In. 290.00
Mirror, Convex, Eagle Finial, Rocky Pedestal, Lower Leaf Pendant, Round, 18 In. 3300.00
Mirror, Convex, Giltwood, Eagle Finial, Leaf, Scroll, Ball Design, c.1800, 23 x 46 In. . . . 4025.00
Mirror, Convex, Regency, Giltwood, Ebonized, Round, 43 x 29 /12 In. 7475.00
Mirror, Convex, Spread-Wing Eagle Finial, Leaf-Tipped Border, 1830s, 30 In. 7475.00
Mirror, Convex, Wooden, Leaf & Ball Ornaments, Candle Arms, c.1815, 40 In. 9875.00
Mirror, Courting, Box Frame, Reverse-Painted Flowers, c.1790, 17 1/2 x 12 1/2 In. 1380.00
Mirror, Courting, Box Frame, Shaped Crest, Reverse Painted, c.1790, 17 x 11 In. 3100.00
Mirror, Courting, Giltwood, Rectangular Plate, 18th Century, 7 x 12 In. 575.00
Mirror, Courting, Reverse Painting Of Rose On White Ground, 12 3/8 x 7 3/4 In. 715.00
Mirror, Courting, Shaped Crest, Reverse Painted, Etched, 1790s, 18 1/2 x 11 In. 3740.00
Mirror, Crest, Square, Beveled, Composite, 19th Century, 54 x 25 In. 635.00
Mirror, Cut, Etched, Beveled, Arching Crest, Floral Sprays, 1880s, 37 3/4 In. 2760.00
Mirror, Dark Stained Wood, Dunbar, 28 x 1/2 x 30 In. 489.00
Mirror, Directoire, Pine, Grisaille, Beaded, Ribbon Mold, 70 1/2 x 51 In. 1380.00
Mirror, Divided Plate, Pierced Undulating Crest, Cattails Corners, 59 1/2 x 26 In. 6600.00
Mirror, Dressing, Brass, Beaded Scrolled Frame, Mahogany Back, 20 x 11 In. 546.00
Mirror, Dressing, Floral, Beveled, Tripod Scroll Base, 75 x 24 In. 1035.00
Mirror, Dressing, George III, Mahogany, c.1800, 25 x 21 x 10 In. 375.00
Mirror, Dressing, George IV, Mahogany, Satinwood, Adjustable, 54 1/2 x 24 x 25 In. 980.00
Mirror, Dressing, Gilt Bronze, Oval, France, 18 x 10 In. 345.00
Mirror, Dressing, Mahogany, Ogee Cornice, 2 Drawers, Turned Feet, 33 In. 1035.00
Mirror, Dressing, Mahogany, Swinging Plate, 2 Supports, 3 Drawers, 23 1/2 In. 800.00
Mirror, Dressing, Queen Anne, Walnut, 3 Drawers, 1705, 32 x 16 In. 920.00
Mirror, Dressing, Queen Anne, Walnut, Crossbanded, 3 Drawers, c.1705, 32 x 16 In. 1600.00
Mirror, Dressing, Sheraton, Mahogany, Bowfront Case, Bracket Feet, 21 In. 345.00
Mirror, Dressing, Walnut, Carved Drape & Floral Swags, 55 1/2 x 55 In. 465.00
Mirror, Egg & Dart, Tier Of Wheat Flowers, 51 3/4 In. 2300.00
Mirror, Eglomise Panel Of Woman With Anchor, James Todd, c.1820, 27 3/4 In. 4600.00
Mirror, Empire, Amboyna, Bronze Dore, Reeded Frame, Corinthian Columns, 57 In. 1610.00
Mirror, Empire, Giltwood, Rectangular Husk Frame, Eagles, Bellflower, 28 7/8 In. 520.00
Mirror, Empire, Mahogany Veneer, Gold Frame, Ogee Middle, 2 Sections, 51 x 27 In. . . . 405.00
Mirror, Empire, Mahogany, Rosewood Veneer, Molded Frame, 24 1/2 In. 100.00
Mirror, Engraved Baptism Of Jesus, Berried Foliate Scrolls, 18th Century, 20 In. 1725.00
Mirror, Etched Glass Girandole, Divided Plate, Candle Branch, 19 1/4 In. 9000.00
Mirror, Faux Walnut, Fleur-De-Lis, 18th Century, 31 x 14 In. 310.00
Mirror, Federal Style, Convex, Eagle On Top, Early 20th Century, Round, 34 x 24 In. 460.00
Mirror, Federal Style, Gilt Composition, Ebonized, Round, Convex, 33 x 22 In. 1035.00
Mirror, Federal Style, Mahogany, Giltwood Eagle Crest, Late 19th Century, 44 x 21 In. . . 660.00
Mirror, Federal, 2 Sections, Giltwood Turned, Reverse Painted, 40 x 21 In. 770.00
Mirror, Federal, Eglomise Garden Scene, Giltwood, Frieze, Gesso, c.1815, 48 x 21 In. . . . 12650.00
Mirror, Federal, Eglomise House, Grain Painted, c.1820, 29 x 13 In. 525.00
Mirror, Federal, Eglomise Memorial Portrait Of George Washington, 32 x 17 In. 8050.00
Mirror, Federal, Giltwood, Applied Rosettes, Eglomise Panel, c.1820, 22 x 12 In. 600.00
Mirror, Federal, Giltwood, Classical Figures In Relief, c.1815, 44 1/4 x 20 1/4 In. 1210.00
Mirror, Federal, Giltwood, Reverse Painted Panel, c.1820, 36 x 16 1/2 In. 195.00
Mirror, Federal, Giltwood, Step & Ball Cornice, Eglomise Panel, c.1810, 20 x 15 1/2 In. . . 660.00
Mirror, Federal, Half Columns, Gold-Leaf Stencil, c.1830, 36 3/4 x 17 In. 495.00
Mirror, Federal, Mahogany, Parcel Gilt, Swan's-Neck Crest, 1800, 57 x 23 In. 6600.00
Mirror, Federal, Mahogany, Shield Shape, Trestle Feet, I. Richman, 21 x 14 x 9 In. 1265.00
Mirror, Federal, Mahogany, Square, Tilting, Bowfront, 1 Drawer, c.1820, 16 x 14 In. 140.00
Mirror, Federal, Panel Of Mother & Child, 24 1/2 x 11 1/2 In. 1440.00
Mirror, Florentine, Giltwood, Beaded Frieze, Leaves, 1800s, 41 x 38 In. 750.00
Mirror, Flower, Bird Decoration, Etched, England, 18th Century, 10 1/4 x 7 3/4 In. 195.00
Mirror, Foliage, Flowers Crest, Octagonal Beveled Mirror, 41 x 28 x 2 1/2 In. 1265.00
Mirror, G. Nakashima, Walnut, Beveled, Square-Pegged Sides, 39 1/4 x 39 3/4 In. 2680.00
Mirror, G. Stickley, No. 68, Mahogany Finish, Signed, 28 x 47 In. 5125.00
Mirror, G. Stickley, No. 916, Maple, Peaked Top, Red Decal, Signed, 24 x 30 In. 1760.00
Mirror, George I, Walnut, Giltwood, Scrollwork Crest, Cavetto, Line, 51 x 18 1/2 In. 1610.00
Mirror, George II Style, Pine, Silvered, Late 1800s, 37 x 16 x 3 In. 575.00
Mirror, George II, Mahogany, Giltwood Slip, Painted Ship, 1800s, 31 x 26 In. 1210.00
Mirror, George II, Walnut, Tortoiseshell Frame, Trisected, Beveled, 21 In. 2300.00
Mirror, George III, Giltwood, Convex, Round, Ebonized Liners, 4 x 46 In. 3220.00

Mirror, George III, Giltwood, Floral Spray Crest, Pierced Apron, 63 In. 7800.00
Mirror, George III, Giltwood, Urn, Drapery Crest, Pendant, Oval, c.1790, 48 x 24 In. 6600.00
Mirror, George III, Mahogany, Cheval, Splayed Legs, 62 x 23 In. 890.00
Mirror, George III, Mahogany, Gilt Slip, Fretwork Border, 32 x 18 In. 865.00
Mirror, Georgian Style, Giltwood Frame, Flowers, Scroll, Shell Decorations, 26 x 41 In. . 92.00
Mirror, Gesso, Leaf Design, Raised Foliage, 28 3/4 x 33 In. 300.00
Mirror, Gilt Finish, Beveled, Scroll Footed, No Stand, Brass, 10 x 10 3/4 In. 55.00
Mirror, Gilt Gesso, Arched, Inverted Floral Border, 20th Century, 63 In., Pair 1495.00
Mirror, Gilt Gesso, Eagle Crest, Floral Garlands, Oval, 20 In. 250.00
Mirror, Gilt Gesso, Floral Garlands, 5 Shelves, 65 In. 1980.00
Mirror, Gilt Gesso, Geometric & Floral Corners, Ornate Frame, 37 x 32 1/2 In. 60.00
Mirror, Gilt Gesso, Molded Scrolls, Pillars Each Side, 38 x 33 1/2 In. 600.00
Mirror, Gilt Gesso, Scrolled Borders, Shells, 30 1/2 x 36 In. 135.00
Mirror, Giltwood, Band Of Reeds, Carved Geometric Design, 57 x 32 In. 3450.00
Mirror, Giltwood, Beveled Glass, 20th Century, 22 1/2 x 14 5/8 In. 55.00
Mirror, Giltwood, Carved Winged Serpent, Cattails, Shells & Flowers, 48 x 30 In. 465.00
Mirror, Giltwood, Carved, Applied Metal Floral Garlands, France, 56 x 36 In. 1870.00
Mirror, Giltwood, Carved, Polychrome, Arched, Rectangular, 29 x 20 1/2 In. 800.00
Mirror, Giltwood, Circular Plate, Cove Molded Frame, Gilt Spherules, 22 1/4 In. 430.00
Mirror, Giltwood, Convex, Lattice-Carved, Ebonized Eagle, c.1790, 31 x 18 In. 3850.00
Mirror, Giltwood, Corner Blocks, Columns, Eglomise Panel, c.1820, 40 1/2 x 21 In. 195.00
Mirror, Giltwood, Eagle Clutching Sphere, Early 19th Century, 35 x 20 In. 4200.00
Mirror, Giltwood, Ebonized, Ring-Turned Columns, 58 x 31 x 5 In. 1150.00
Mirror, Giltwood, Eglomise, Spencer & Gilman, Hartford, Conn., 48 In. 4315.00
Mirror, Giltwood, Etched Trailing Bellflowers, 1930s, 81 In. 3700.00
Mirror, Giltwood, Garland & Musical Trophies On Frieze, Gilt Molding, 54 1/2 In. 2300.00
Mirror, Giltwood, Leaf-Carved Design Over Velvet Stiles, 19th Century, 77 x 78 In. 3000.00
Mirror, Giltwood, Ornate, Basket Crest, Rake & Shovel, 20th Century, 54 x 32 In. 550.00
Mirror, Giltwood, Rosettes Corners, Rectangular, 19th Century, 57 1/2 In. 400.00
Mirror, Giltwood, Scalloped, Floral Crest, 51 x 29 1/2 In. 495.00
Mirror, Giltwood, Scrolled Acanthus Frame, Beveled, 25 1/2 In., Pair 1610.00
Mirror, Giltwood, Shell Crest, Foliage, Convex Frame, Beaded Lining, 52 x 27 1/2 In. 865.00
Mirror, Giltwood, Spread-Winged Eagle Crest, Ebonized Frame, 50 x 37 In. 1398.00
Mirror, Giltwood, Spread-Winged Eagle, Chain, Pendant Apron, 43 x 24 1/2 In. 6000.00
Mirror, Giltwood, Stepped & Ball Cornice, Reverse Painted, 31 x 15 In. 550.00
Mirror, Giltwood, Stylized Shell Crest, Foliate Segmented Frame, 1910s, 30 x 20 In. 865.00
Mirror, Girandole, Carved Scrolls & Leaves, Candle Arms, Floriform Socket, 22 In. 1380.00
Mirror, Girandole, Giltwood Pine, Encircled Gilt Balls, 34 In. 6950.00
Mirror, Girandole, Giltwood, Ebonized Eagle, Candlearms, c.1790, 35 x 18 In. 6600.00
Mirror, Girandole, Regency, Gilt Gesso, Eagle, 2 Scrolling Arms, 26 1/2 x 8 1/2 In. 1265.00
Mirror, Hitchcock, Reverse Painted, Fruit Basket, Red Drapes, Frame, Black, Gold, 20 In. 60.00
Mirror, Iron, Green Paint, Openwork Base, 1830, 25 In. 360.00
Mirror, Italian Classical, Giltwood, Spread-Winged Eagle, c.1800, 19 1/2 In. 865.00
Mirror, Italian, Giltwood, Scrolled Crest, Leaves, Chinese Mask, 1800s, 88 x 56 In. 2185.00
Mirror, L. & J.G. Stickley, No. 65, Arched Top, 4 Hooks, Onondaga Shop, 29 x 44 In. 2495.00
Mirror, Leaf Encrusted, Leaf Border, Corner Brackets, 46 x 38 In. 115.00
Mirror, Limbert, No. 21, Arched Top, Vertical Slats, Signed & Dated, 26 x 35 In. 980.00
Mirror, Louis Philippe, Cream Paint, Cavetto, Rosettes, 27 x 22 In. 345.00
Mirror, Louis Philippe, Gilt Composition, Oval, c.1830, 34 x 29 In. 1035.00
Mirror, Louis Philippe, Gilt Composition, Oval, Molded Design, c.1830, 37 x 34 In. 2185.00
Mirror, Louis Philippe, Giltwood, Gesso, 56 1/4 In. 1725.00
Mirror, Louis Philippe, Giltwood, Shell Crest, Trailing Foliage, 52 In. 865.00
Mirror, Louis Philippe, Giltwood, Stiff Leaf Border, Beaded Liner, 47 1/2 In. 2185.00
Mirror, Louis XV Style, Giltwood, Carved, Birds, Pierced Foliate, Cupids, 40 x 32 In. 1955.00
Mirror, Louis XV Style, Scrolled, Giltwood Frame, 59 x 37 In. 195.00
Mirror, Louis XV, Bronze Dore, Shell Frame, Scroll Feet, 21 x 16 x 15 3/4 In. 1725.00
Mirror, Louis XV, Carved, Wood, Gesso, Giltwood, Beveled Edge, 62 x 36 In. 2300.00
Mirror, Louis XV, Gilt Gesso, Scrolled Foliage Border On Top, Acanthus, 34 3/4 In. 220.00
Mirror, Louis XV, Giltwood, Carved C-Scrolls, Flowers, Laurel Swags, 67 x 36 In. 7200.00
Mirror, Louis XV, Woman's Portrait, Flanked By Floral Design, Rectangular, 39 In. 149.00
Mirror, Louis XVI Style, Giltwood, Leaf, Berry, P. Husson, Paris, c.1900, 69 x 27 In. 1610.00
Mirror, Louis XVI Style, Giltwood, Shell-Carved Crest, c.1900, 69 1/2 x 36 x 6 In. 2070.00
Mirror, Louis XVI Style, Ivory Paint, Parcel Gilt, 118 x 35 In. 4315.00

Mirror, Louis XVI Style, Pier, Painted, Wreath Crest, Draped Garland, 64 x 31 In. 980.00
Mirror, Louis XVI, Giltwood, Armorial Within Border Of Ribbons, 100 In. 2330.00
Mirror, Louis XVI, Giltwood, Cream Paint, Floral Crest & Border, 67 1/2 In. 8338.00
Mirror, Louis XVI, Giltwood, Floral, Leaves, 30 1/2 In. 259.00
Mirror, Louis XVI, Giltwood, Molded Frame, Leaves, Floral Accents, 24 In. 230.00
Mirror, Louis XVI, Giltwood, Ribbon Carved, Wheat Husks, Oval, c.1800, 32 1/2 x 29 In. . 800.00
Mirror, Louis XVI, Trumeau, Gray Paint, Parcel Gilt, Frieze Panel, 99 x 63 In. 4025.00
Mirror, Mahogany Veneer, Reeded, Raised Blocks, 2 Parts, 30 3/4 x 15 In. 150.00
Mirror, Mahogany, 3 Owls Perched, Foliage & Acorns, 1885, 36 In. 1120.00
Mirror, Mahogany, Eagle Crest, Scrolled Frame Work, 1910s, 55 1/2 In. 1430.00
Mirror, Mahogany, Fret-Carved Crest, Line Inlay Slip Frame, c.1790, 45 x 23 3/4 In. 1880.00
Mirror, Mahogany, Giltwood, Finials, Ogee Moldings, 1840s, 25 3/4 In. 1125.00
Mirror, Mahogany, Gold Leaf, Beveled Glass, 26 1/2 x 48 1/2 In. 310.00
Mirror, Mahogany, Oak, Scalloped Scroll, 19th Century, 14 x 9 1/2 In. 170.00
Mirror, Mahogany, Parcel Gilt, Spread-Winged Phoenix Finial, Floral Fillets, 55 In. 9200.00
Mirror, Mahogany, Pierced Crest, Center Phoenix, 1770s, 40 x 19 1/2 In. 635.00
Mirror, Mahogany, Reverse-Painted House & Sailing Ship, 43 1/2 x 21 In. 855.00
Mirror, Mahogany, Rosettes, Egg & Dart Border, Eagle Finial, 1750s, 56 In. 2310.00
Mirror, Mahogany, Scalloped Crest, Scalloped Pendant, c.1800, 41 1/4 x 20 In. 1760.00
Mirror, Mahogany, Veneer, Ormolu, Pillars, 19 3/8 x 21 1/2 In., Pair 465.00
Mirror, Napoleon III, Gilt Composition, c.1875, 53 3/4 x 37 In. 1840.00
Mirror, Napoleon III, Gilt Composition, Molded, Cast Leaves, 1890s, 25 1/4 x 23 In. 400.00
Mirror, Napoleon III, Gilt Composition, Oval, c.1875, 54 x 35 1/4 In., Pair 5175.00
Mirror, Napoleon III, Giltwood, Beaded, Leaf-Carved, 28 x 25 In. 1265.00
Mirror, Napoleon III, Giltwood, Beaded, Molded, 34 3/4 x 27 x 1 1/2 In. 550.00
Mirror, Napoleon III, Giltwood, Beaded, Molded, 49 x 34 x 2 In. 1380.00
Mirror, Napoleon III, Giltwood, Beaded, Molded, Rectangular, 34 In. 690.00
Mirror, Napoleon III, Giltwood, Beaded, Ogee Frame, 46 1/2 x 32 x 2 In. 1265.00
Mirror, Napoleon III, Giltwood, Cream, Beaded Frame, 31 1/2 x 24 x 1 1/2 In. 490.00
Mirror, Napoleon III, Giltwood, Leaf, Floral, Rectangular, 42 x 32 x 2 In. 550.00
Mirror, Napoleon III, Giltwood, Molded, Flowers, 43 1/2 x 48 In. 1265.00
Mirror, Napoleon III, Giltwood, Molded, Latticework, 58 x 42 In. 2530.00
Mirror, Napoleon III, Giltwood, Shell-Carved Crest, 84 x 49 x 9 In. 2990.00
Mirror, Napoleon III, Pine, Ogee-Molded Frame, 36 1/2 x 24 1/2 In. 1840.00
Mirror, Napoleon III, Silvered Wood, Cream Accents, Floral Swag, 31 In. 460.00
Mirror, Napoleon III, Silvered, Incised Floral Accents, 19th Century, 46 In. 1265.00
Mirror, Napoleon, Giltwood, Leaf Carving, Rectangular, 54 x 25 1/2 In. 800.00
Mirror, Neoclassical, Giltwood, Bead, Lozenge Frame, 27 3/4 x 18 3/4 In. 290.00
Mirror, Neoclassical, Giltwood, Beaded Frame, Sun, Extending Rays, 26 x 20 1/2 In. 400.00
Mirror, Neoclassical, Giltwood, Draperey Border, Cream Paint, 50 In. 2760.00
Mirror, Neoclassical, Giltwood, Fan Crest, Acanthus Apron, 45 In. 1150.00
Mirror, Neoclassical, Giltwood, Green, Leafy Frame, 35 x 19 x 2 In. 1495.00
Mirror, Neoclassical, Giltwood, Rectangular Cornice, Lotus Leaves, Italy, 52 In. 6900.00
Mirror, Neoclassical, Giltwood, Rosette Border, Paw Feet, Italy, 68 1/2 In., Pair 10000.00
Mirror, Neoclassical, Giltwood, Stiff-Leaf Frame, Classical Allegory, 52 3/4 In. 2530.00
Mirror, Neoclassical, Mahogany, Ebony, Faux Wood Molded, 24 1/2 In. 4830.00
Mirror, Neoclassical, Oblong, Carved, White Paint, Giltwood, 34 x 16 In. 1955.00
Mirror, Neoclassical, Rosewood, Leaf & Dart, Corinthian Columns, 44 In. 2185.00
Mirror, Oak, Jeweled Crest, 1880, 73 x 26 In. 1345.00
Mirror, Oscar Bach, Brass-Winged Serpents At Sides, 24 x 42 In. 2415.00
Mirror, P. Evans, Gold, Copper, Pewter Shelf, Slate Top, 30 In. 750.00
Mirror, Pagoda, Birds, Carved Wood, 54 In. 750.00
Mirror, Papier-Mache, Shelf, England, 12 3/4 x 19 1/2 In. 460.00
Mirror, Pier, Beveled, Leaf Carved Border, Ribbon-Tied Garlands, 77 1/4 In. 7200.00
Mirror, Pier, Carved Rosettes In Corner Blocks, Oxidized Gilt, c.1825, 50 x 31 In. 6100.00
Mirror, Pier, Gilt Gesso, Pine, Neoclassical, Silvered, 33 x 35 x 18 In. 5520.00
Mirror, Pier, Giltwood, Beveled, Center Bow, Ribboned Cabochon, 49 1/2 In. 3680.00
Mirror, Pier, Giltwood, Ovolo Border, Continuous Meander Design, 47 1/2 In. 1090.00
Mirror, Pier, Mahogany, Rectangular Cornice, Columns, Germany, 50 1/2 x 25 x 4 In. ... 460.00
Mirror, Pier, Napoleon III, Beech, Black & White, Angel Masks, 59 x 46 1/4 x 2 3/8 In. .. 920.00
Mirror, Pier, Napoleon III, Giltwood, Arched, Molded, Beaded, 53 x 40 In. 800.00
Mirror, Pier, Napoleon III, Giltwood, Beaded, Ogee Molded, 51 x 35 x 3 In. 2300.00
Mirror, Pier, Napoleon III, Giltwood, Carved Flowers, Shells, 52 x 41 1/2 In. 800.00

Mirror, Pier, Napoleon III, Giltwood, Slightly Arched, Molded, 73 x 42 In. 2300.00
Mirror, Pier, Napoleon III, Kingwood, Ebonized, Cornice, Frieze, 60 3/4 x 25 x 2 In. 290.00
Mirror, Pier, Napoleon III, Kingwood, Tulipwood, Recessed Frieze, 57 x 26 x 3 1/4 In. . . 315.00
Mirror, Pier, Neoclassical, Black & White, Composition, Classical Allegory, 66 x 51 In. . . 3220.00
Mirror, Pier, Neoclassical, Carved, Parcel Gilt, Ebonized, 68 x 32 1/2 In. 4830.00
Mirror, Pier, Neoclassical, Giltwood, Mahogany, Demilune, Lion Mask, 48 x 21 In. 1380.00
Mirror, Pier, Neoclassical, Mahogany, Cornice, Frieze, Denmark, c.1825, 54 x 30 x 4 In. . 460.00
Mirror, Pier, Neoclassical, Mahogany, Molded, 60 1/2 x 25 x 2 In. 460.00
Mirror, Pier, Neoclassical, Mahogany, Recessed Frieze, 57 x 24 x 2 In. 460.00
Mirror, Pier, Peaked Crest, Suspended Icicles, Vines, 51 1/2 x 27 1/2 In., Pair 2530.00
Mirror, Pier, Pine, Faux Marble, Black & White, Pediment, Recessed Frieze, 59 x 49 In. . 6900.00
Mirror, Pier, Regency, Giltwood, c.1825, 73 1/2 x 32 In. 12100.00
Mirror, Pier, Renaissance Revival, Walnut, Burl Panels, Carved, 79 x 34 x 5 In. 3680.00
Mirror, Pier, Renaissance Revival, Walnut, Cartouche, Gilt Bust, 10 1/2 x 26 In. 920.00
Mirror, Pier, Victorian, Walnut, Marble Plateau, 106 x 27 In. 1430.00
Mirror, Pine, 2 Parts, Lower Beveled Edge, Scalloped Liner At Top, 44 x 17 1/2 In. 2200.00
Mirror, Pine, Cartouche Shape, Scroll, Pierced Frame, 28 x 20 In., Pair 2300.00
Mirror, Pine, Chinoiserie, Carved, Pagoda Crest, Bells, Gilt, 63 x 31 1/2 In. 3680.00
Mirror, Pine, Reeded Columns, Reverse Painted Castle, Landscape, 21 3/4 x 13 In. 220.00
Mirror, Pine, Silvered, Leaf Cresting, 41 1/2 x 32 x 4 1/2 In. 2990.00
Mirror, Pine, Tortoiseshell, Ebonized Wood, Ribbon Frame, 29 1/2 In. 750.00
Mirror, Queen Anne, Black Lacquer, 1705, 31 x 18 x 10 In. 2645.00
Mirror, Queen Anne, Gilt Gesso, Walnut, Scrolled Crest, Gilt Liner, 23 1/2 In. 2415.00
Mirror, Queen Anne, Mahogany, Scrollwork Crest, 19th Century, 14 3/8 In. 400.00
Mirror, Queen Anne, Pierced & Scrolled Crest, Crossbanded Frame, c.1720, 17 In. 660.00
Mirror, Queen Anne, Pine, Red, Black Chinoiserie Design, Molded Frame, 16 x 9 In. 600.00
Mirror, Queen Anne, Shaped Crest, Carved Leaf Design, 18th Century, 11 1/2 x 7 In. 2760.00
Mirror, Queen Anne, Walnut, 2-Part Plate, 1740s, 57 In. 8625.00
Mirror, Queen Anne, Walnut, Bird's-Head Crest, c.1735, 38 x 22 1/2 In. 770.00
Mirror, Queen Anne, Walnut, Scrolled Crest, Bracket, 18th Century, 33 x 14 In. 3105.00
Mirror, Red Tortoiseshell, Ebonized, Ribbon Molded Frame, 11 1/2 x 10 In. 400.00
Mirror, Regency Style, Convex, Patinated Cream Cavetto Frame, 23 1/2 In. 865.00
Mirror, Regency Style, Giltwood, Molded Frame, 1 1/2 x 15 3/4 In., Pair 290.00
Mirror, Regency Style, Giltwood, Molded Frame, Shells, 36 x 32 x 2 1/2 In. 2760.00
Mirror, Regency, Giltwood, Circular Glass Mirror, 18 x 1 1/2 In. 315.00
Mirror, Regency, Giltwood, Convex, 2-Light Arms, Scrolling, 41 x 39 In. 3910.00
Mirror, Regency, Giltwood, Convex, Leaves, 47 x 4 1/2 In. 6615.00
Mirror, Regency, Giltwood, Convex, Molded Frame, Scrolled Leaf Pendant, 24 In. 2990.00
Mirror, Regency, Giltwood, Ebonized, Convex Mirror, 22 In. 750.00
Mirror, Regency, Giltwood, Molded Frame, Ebonized Eagle, 53 In. 7200.00
Mirror, Renaissance Revival, Carved Open Crest, Gold Paint, Victorian, 79 x 64 In. 250.00
Mirror, Renaissance Revival, Gilt Composition, c.1890, 105 x 42 1/2 In. 805.00
Mirror, Renaissance Revival, Giltwood, Imbricate Patterns, Late 1800s, 58 x 42 1/2 In. . . 2300.00
Mirror, Renaissance Revival, Rosewood, Open Carvings Inlay, 1870, 78 x 48 In. 3300.00
Mirror, Reverse-Painted Floral Top, Stepped Crest, Turned Finials, 22 1/4 In. 605.00
Mirror, Reverse-Painted Girl, Blue & Yellow Dress, 2 Parts, 26 x 16 In. 110.00
Mirror, Rocaille, Ears Of Wheat, Courting Scene On Crest, 28 1/2 x 46 3/4 In. 575.00
Mirror, Rococo, Giltwood, Cartouche Shape, Leaf & Vine, 47 x 31 x 2 In. 1610.00
Mirror, Rococo, Giltwood, Carved, Oval, Flowers, Italy, Late 1700s, 23 In. 1265.00
Mirror, Rococo, Giltwood, Flowers, Leafy C-Scrolls, Italy, 18th Century, 72 In. 5060.00
Mirror, Rococo, Giltwood, Italy, Late 19th Century, 30 x 19 1/2 In. 750.00
Mirror, Rococo, Giltwood, Leafy C-Scrolls, Male Mask Base, Italy, 40 In., Pair 5700.00
Mirror, Rococo, Giltwood, Leafy Crest, Rectangular, Italy, 25 In. 1840.00
Mirror, Rococo, Giltwood, Prince Of Wales Feather Crest, 1800s, 38 x 31 In. 865.00
Mirror, Rope-Molded Frame, Blue Flowers, Leaves, Late 19th Century, 23 In. 865.00
Mirror, Roycroft, Oak Frame, 32 1/2 x 22 In. 850.00
Mirror, Scalloped Arch Crest, Floral Sprays, Meander, 37 1/4 In. 2760.00
Mirror, Seaside Scene At Top, Drop Pendants Over Molded Frieze, 44 x 21 In. 2420.00
Mirror, Shaving, Art Deco, Standing Women Supports, Oval Mirror, 20 x 10 In. 200.00
Mirror, Shaving, Cherry, Adjustable Plate, Shoe Feet, c.1815, 12 3/4 x 13 In. 127.00
Mirror, Shaving, Chippendale, Tiger Maple, 19th Century, 18 x 18 x 9 In. 230.00
Mirror, Shaving, Federal, Maple, 3 Drawers, Swing Frame, Pa., c.1815, 23 x 27 In. 3300.00
Mirror, Shaving, Figured Mahogany, Bun Feet, Urn Finial, 23 x 10 1/2 x 21 In. 195.00

Mirror, Shaving, G. Stickley, Mahogany, Beveled Glass, 21 1/2 x 26 In. 1800.00
Mirror, Shaving, George II, Mahogany, Tilting, Beveled, 3 Drawers, 25 x 17 3/4 In. 1210.00
Mirror, Shaving, George III, Mahogany, 3 Drawers, Turned Feet, 26 1/2 x 23 In. 495.00
Mirror, Shaving, George III, Mahogany, 3 Drawers, England, 18 x 8 x 26 In. 275.00
Mirror, Shaving, Mahogany Veneer, Bowfront, 3 Drawers, Brass Pulls, 19 1/2 In. 190.00
Mirror, Shaving, Mahogany Veneer, Refinished, Hinged 2-Board Top, 22 x 24 In. 190.00
Mirror, Shaving, Mahogany, Brass Urn Finials, Trestle Base, 19 In. 85.00
Mirror, Shaving, Mahogany, Tapered, Reeded Posts, Shoe Feet, Late 19th Century, 16 In. . 55.00
Mirror, Shaving, Queen Anne, Mahogany Veneer, Oak, 3 Drawers, 19 x 9 x 27 In. 270.00
Mirror, Shaving, Scrollwork, Pierced, Top Shelf, Half-Barrel Holders, Paint, 21 x 10 In. . . 400.00
Mirror, Silvered Wooden Frame, Carved Shell Surround, 52 x 36 In. 345.00
Mirror, Split Spindle, Upper Fruit Bowl, Rosette Corner Blocks, 27 x 13 1/2 In. 920.00
Mirror, Stickley Bros., Mahogany Frame, Rectangular, 39 x 25 In. 1035.00
Mirror, Stickley Bros., No. 111, Mahogany, Rectangular, 50 x 28 In. 1380.00
Mirror, Tortoiseshell, Ebonized, Ribbon Carved Borders, Octagonal, 27 3/4 x 24 In. 2990.00
Mirror, Travel, Triple Fold, Silver Plated Floral Inset, c.1905, 11 1/2 x 11 1/2 In. 168.00
Mirror, Trumeau, Fruit Basket, Gilt Columns, Rectangular Plate, 20 1/2 In. 144.00
Mirror, Trumeau, Neoclassical, Faux Marble, Parcel Gilt, Pine, 50 x 54 In. 1840.00
Mirror, Trumeau, Ribbon Crest, Painted Landscape, Beveled Plate, 68 In. 1380.00
Mirror, Urn Trailing Laurel Leaves Crest, Late 19th Century, 22 x 12 1/2 In. 330.00
Mirror, Vanity, Comb Box, Towel Bar, 25 x 12 In. 275.00
Mirror, Venetian Glass, Floral Rosettes, Beveled Edges, 49 x 28 1/2 In. 280.00
Mirror, Venetian, Beveled Mirror, Amber Border, 1900, 25 3/4 In. 865.00
Mirror, Venetian, Red Lacquer, Oriental Motifs, 27 1/2 x 20 3/4 In. 750.00
Mirror, Victorian, Black Lacquer, Gilt Accents, Oriental, 23 x 20 3/4 In. 920.00
Mirror, Victorian, Bowfront Base, 3 Drawers, Rectangular, Ball Feet, 27 1/2 In. 489.00
Mirror, Victorian, Giltwood, Oval, Beveled, Reeded Molding, 43 x 31 In. 2300.00
Mirror, Vines, Cornice On Spiral Columns, 1780s, 23 x 23 1/4 In. 1380.00
Mirror, Walnut, 3-Part Beveled Glass, Tortoiseshell Frame, 21 x 63 1/2 In. 2300.00
Mirror, Walnut, Gilt Leaf Moldings, Rectangular, 1700s, 21 x 34 In. 1035.00
Mirror, Walnut, Ornate, Black, Floral, Oval Center, 20 x 15 In. 190.00
Mirror, Walnut, Pierced Leaves, 2-Part Plate, Molded Frame, 1740s, 45 In. 7475.00
Mirror, Walnut, Pilasters, Centered Scales, Urns, Rectangular, 37 x 26 1/2 x 2 In. 345.00
Mirror, Walnut, Scrolled Crest, c.1740-60, 21 1/2 x 12 In. 1265.00
Mirror, Walnut, Scrolled Top Rail, Center Shell, Denmark, 18th Century, 36 x 19 1/2 In. . 4200.00
Mirror, William IV, Mahogany, Concave Plinth, Scroll Feet, 36 x 28 x 12 In. 550.00
Mirror, Wood, Beaded Surround, Foliate Dividers, 59 1/2 In. 5400.00
Mirror, Wood, Frolicking Putti Among Drapes, Ribbons, Italy, 22 In. 920.00
Mirror, Wood, Inlaid Stringing, Landscape Scene Crest, 22 x 12 In. 345.00
Ottoman, Eames, Rosewood, Dark Brown Leather, 26 x 21 x 16 In. 400.00
Ottoman, G. Nelson, Coconut, Vinyl, Chrome Frame, 16 In. 1380.00
Ottoman, Geometric Upholstery, Multicolored Twist Cord, France, 16 x 26 In. 1035.00
Ottoman, Mahogany, Trisected, Raised, Bulbous Feet On Casters, 28 x 46 In. 2760.00
Ottoman, Wegner, Teakwood, Concave Seat, Flared Dowel Legs, J. Hansen, 18 In. 675.00
Overmantel, see Architectural category.
Parlor Set, Art Nouveau, Bentwood, 2 Chairs, Table, Austria, 29 x 23 1/2 In. 2300.00
Parlor Set, Carved, Gold Leaf Finish, Silk, 58-In. Sofa, 2 Piece 330.00
Parlor Set, Charles X, Mahogany, Upholstered Back, Seat, Paw Feet, 3 Piece 3795.00
Parlor Set, Edwardian, Mahogany, Sofa, Chairs, Satinwood Inlay, Upholstered, c.1900 . . 1840.00
Parlor Set, Horn, Settee, 2 Armchairs, Leather, Settee 36 x 60 In., 3 Piece 4025.00
Parlor Set, Louis XVI, Gilt, Upholstered Seat, Fluted Legs, 5 Piece 18000.00
Parlor Set, Renaissance Revival, Burled Trim, John Jeliff, 1870, 4 Piece 3920.00
Parlor Set, Victorian, Mahogany, Carved, c.1870, 3 Piece 1320.00
Pastry Wagon, Art Deco, Calamander, Tray Top, Mirror Shelf, 31 x 33 1/2 x 20 In. 1955.00
Pedestal, Alabaster, Octagonal Top, Stop-Fluted Column, Italy, 41 1/4 In. 690.00
Pedestal, Arts & Crafts, Mahogany, Original Finish, Platform Base, 12 x 42 In. 980.00
Pedestal, Baroque Style, Iron, Marble Top, 2 Inset Shelves, Cabriole Legs, 37 In., Pair . . . 490.00
Pedestal, Beaux Arts, Gilt Bronze, Square, Late 19th Century, 7 1/4 x 15 x 15 In. 400.00
Pedestal, Beech, Grotesque Mask Amid Foliage, Square Top, 39 In. 400.00
Pedestal, Beige Variegated Marble, Turned Column, Italy, 50 1/2 In. 1725.00
Pedestal, Belle Epoque, Marble, Gilt Bronze, Peach Blossom, c.1900, 45 x 13 x 13 In. . . . 2185.00
Pedestal, Canted Plank Legs, Carved Grotesque Mask, 1890s, 38 3/4 In. 400.00
Pedestal, Egyptian Revival, Lion Heads, Claw Feet Supporting Lamp, 1875, 69 In. 4220.00

Pedestal, Empire, Gray-Veined Beige Marble Top, Gilt, 41 x 13 x 13 1/2 In. 575.00
Pedestal, Faux Marble, Square Plaster Plinth, Italy, 42 x 17 1/4 x 17 1/4 In., Pair 2760.00
Pedestal, Figural, Stork In Marshes, 1880, 37 x 16 In. 1845.00
Pedestal, Fruitwood, Stork, Lilies & Reeds Base, 1870s, 39 1/2 In. 3220.00
Pedestal, Gilt, Faux Marble, Papier-Mache, Italy, 25 3/4 In., Pair 800.00
Pedestal, Gothic Arches, Molded Circular Base, 32 x 11 In., Pair 1150.00
Pedestal, Gray & White Marble, Molded Socle, Square Base, 43 1/2 In., Pair 8400.00
Pedestal, Gray, Rust Variegated Marble Top, Guilloche Border, 36 1/2 x 17 In. 1840.00
Pedestal, Green Marble, Bronze, Patinated, Square Top, 45 1/2 x 11 x 11 In. 1380.00
Pedestal, Green, Marble Top, Brown Paint, Foliate Gilt, Late 19th Century, 36 In. 660.00
Pedestal, Louis XVI, Walnut, Fluted Columnar Shape, Foliate Swags, 43 x 16 In. 2185.00
Pedestal, Marble, Bust Of Breche D'Alep, Square Top, Block Base, Italy, 39 1/2 In. 800.00
Pedestal, Marble, Carved, Column, Fluted Shaft, 45 x 16 In. 2400.00
Pedestal, Marble, Diagonal Fluted Column, Trumpet Base, Italy, 41 In. 490.00
Pedestal, Marble, Octagonal Top, Fluted, Leaf-Band Shaft, Socle Base, 40 1/2 In. 575.00
Pedestal, Napoleon III, Bronze, Rectangular Top, Gadroon Edge Molding, 46 1/2 In. 1955.00
Pedestal, Napoleon III, Ebonized, Ormolu, 42 x 11 1/4 x 10 3/4 In. 575.00
Pedestal, Napoleon III, Walnut, Griffin Supports, Woman Heads, 45 In. 1840.00
Pedestal, Neoclassical, Mahogany, Walnut, Stepped Square Top, 46 1/2 x 15 In. 2530.00
Pedestal, Renaissance Revival, Gilt, Marquetry, Urn Top, 1870, 42 1/2 In. 1380.00
Pedestal, Renaissance Revival, Walnut, Burled Trim, Hoof Feet, 1875, 37 x 13 In. 1790.00
Pedestal, Rosewood, Carved Lotus Plant, Late 19th Century, 32 In. 750.00
Pedestal, Serpent & Horn Of Plenty, Carved, 1870, 48 x 18 In. 2400.00
Pedestal, Victorian, Gilt Incised, Ebonized, Marble Panel, Stepped Base, 36 In. 2070.00
Pedestal, Walnut, Carved Cherub Bust, Demons, Musical Instruments, 47 x 19 In. 4130.00
Pedestal, White Marble, Octagonal, Column, Plinth Base, c.1890, 39 x 9 1/2 In. 220.00
Pedestal, William IV, Mahogany, White Marble Top, 1 Door, Plinth Base, 30 In. 1265.00
Pedestal, Winged Griffin, Shell-Carved Base, 1860, 42 x 18 In. 1120.00
Pedestal, Wooden, Black Repaint, Round Base, Removable Round Top, 10 x 38 In. 300.00
Pie Safe, 6 Tin Panels, Green Repaint, Upper Drawer, Gallery 975.00
Pie Safe, Backsplash, Drawer, 2 Doors, 3 Punched Tin Tulip Panels, 49 In. 1210.00
Pie Safe, Drawer, 2 Screened Doors, 3 Shelves, New Jersey, Early 1800s, 54 x 44 In. 2645.00
Pie Safe, Geometric Tin Doors, Side Matching Tins, Lower Drawer, 71 1/2 In. 3410.00
Pie Safe, Horse-Hair Screen, Butterfly Hinges, Painted, New Jersey, c.1720 . . . . 14500.00
Pie Safe, Pierced Tin Panels On 2 Doors & Sides, Blue Paint, 57 x 54 In. 6500.00
Pie Safe, Pine, Gallery Top, 2 Drawers, 2 Doors, Punched Tin Panels, c.1860, 60 x 41 In. . .   3190.00
Pie Safe, Poplar, Drawers Over Doors, Punched Tin Cross Panels, c.1810, 55 x 42 In. 1540.00
Pie Safe, Walnut, 2 Drawers Over 2 Doors, Punched Tin Star Panels, c.1825, 51 x 43 In. . .   1760.00
Pie Safe, Walnut, 2 Upper Doors, Punched Tin Star Panels, 1 Drawer, 72 In. 990.00
Pie Safe, Walnut, Double Doors, Shelves Inside, 48 x 42 In. 575.00
Pie Safe, Walnut, Rectangular Top, 2 Short Drawers, Square Tapered Legs, 64 In. 575.00
Pipe Rack, Stickley Bros., Mahogany, 3 Bowing Musicians, 23 x 4 In. 2875.00
Planter, Arts & Crafts, Maple, Slab Sides, Reticulated Carving, 30 x 26 In. 60.00
Planter, Carved Finials, Green Paint, Yellow Outline Border, 14 x 13 In. 4600.00
Planter, Figural, Cupids, Standing, 1880, 22 In. 1588.00
Planter, Louis XV, Floral Design, Scrolled Legs, Cluster Of Wrought Flowers, 44 In. 546.00
Rack, Baker's, Pine, 5 Graduated Shelves, 22 x 16 x 70 In. 465.00
Rack, Baker's, Wrought Iron, Dome Top, Pan Hooks, 3 Shelves, 25 x 12 x 75 In. 145.00
Rack, Hanging, Art Nouveau, Brass, Woman, Outstretched Arms, 1906, 27 x 13 1/2 In. . . .   350.00
Rack, Magazine, Arts & Crafts, 2 Drawers, Arched Rails, Slatted, 41 1/2 x 24 x 12 In. 635.00
Rack, Magazine, G. Stickley, Half-Moon Cutout Handles, 3 Shelves, 40 x 14 x 10 In. 1035.00
Rack, Magazine, Iron, Tripod, Gold, Oak Base, 3 Sections, Handle, 33 In. 245.00
Rack, Magazine, Regency, Mahogany, 3 Dividers, Drawer, 28 1/2 x 15 x 15 In. 1265.00
Rack, Magazine, Teak Frame, Inset Glass, 4 Legs, Gilt Casters, 22 1/2 In. 1725.00
Rack, Magazine, Walnut, Brass, Wire, Revolving, c.1900, 13 3/4 x 9 x 32 1/4 In. 115.00
Rack, Plate, G. Stickley, Hanging, Lower Shelf, Medium Brown, 28 x 46 1/2 In. 2815.00
Rack, Plate, Hanging, Pine, Molded Top, 4 Shelves, 49 1/2 x 6 x 50 In. 490.00
Rack, Plate, L. & J.G. Stickley, 2 Drawers, Original Finish, 49 In. 5343.00
Rack, Shoe, Beaver Dam Rock Co., 6 Shelves, Metal Casters, 57 x 35 In. 190.00
Rack, Victorian, Walnut, Gadrooned Center, Reeded Legs On Casters, 44 In. 3000.00
Recamier, Beech, Brass Inlay, Upholstered, Sloping Backrest, 1850s.76 In. 4600.00
Recamier, Charles X Style, Mahogany, Bronze Dore, Late 19th Century, 73 1/2 In. 6615.00
Recamier, Classical, Mahogany, Padded Seat, Paw Feet, Casters, 1815, 89 In. 7200.00

Recamier, Empire, Mahogany, Scrolling Back, Upholstered, c.1830, 84 In., Pair 9600.00
Recamier, Federal, Carved Mahogany, Brass Mounted, c.1815, 16 x 43 x 86 In. 8400.00
Recamier, Louis XVI Style, Mahogany, Overscroll Backrest, Padded, 80 In. 1380.00
Recamier, Mahogany, Scrolled End, Inlaid Stars & Foliage, Brass Inlay, 75 In. 2760.00
Recamier, Regency, Rosewood, Brass Inlay, Saber Legs, Paw Feet, c.1820, 65 In. 2300.00
Recamier, Renaissance Revival, Walnut, Winged Griffins, 1875, 80 x 37 x 29 In. 3475.00
Recamier, Satinwood, Floral Painted Scrolled Back & Arm, Spade Feet, c.1900, 82 In. 1150.00
Rocker, 4 Vertical Back Slats, 3 Each Arm, Through-Tenon Construction, 38 In. 430.00
Rocker, Arrow Spindles, Plank Seat, Grain Painted, 1930s, 45 1/2 x 15 1/2 In. 460.00
Rocker, Arts & Crafts, 3 Horizontal Slats, Ladder Back, 25 x 27 x 33 In. 60.00
Rocker, Arts & Crafts, 5 Vertical Slats, Burgundy Leather Seat, Back, 34 x 35 In. 1240.00
Rocker, Arts & Crafts, Carved & Cutout Slats, Paper Label, Harden, 38 x 30 In. 700.00
Rocker, Arts & Crafts, Flat Arms Over 2 Slats, Slat Back, Upholstered, 39 x 28 x 23 In. . . 405.00
Rocker, Arts & Crafts, Flat Arms, Slatted Back, 40 x 28 x 25 In. 635.00
Rocker, Arts & Crafts, Leather Seat, Back, Wavy Arms, Harden, 35 x 30 x 24 In. 1610.00
Rocker, Arts & Crafts, Leather Seat, Back, Wavy Arms, Harden, 36 x 30 x 24 In. 2245.00
Rocker, Arts & Crafts, Light Walnut, Black Vinyl Seat Pad, 2 Back Slats, 34 x 30 In. 845.00
Rocker, Arts & Crafts, Mahogany, Padded Seat, Binghamton, 30 x 19 x 18 In. 110.00
Rocker, Arts & Crafts, Seat Cushion, Brooks, 36 x 31 x 22 In. 690.00
Rocker, Balloon Back, Central Vertical Wooden Splat, Pa. 175.00
Rocker, Belter, Mahogany, Pierced Back, Scrollwork, Pad Seat, Victorian 3105.00
Rocker, Birdcage, Upholstered Seat, Arms 525.00
Rocker, Boston, Black Paint, Crest Stenciling, Child's, 23 In. 60.00
Rocker, Eames, Fiberglass Shell, Rope Edge, Black Struts, Birch Runner, 26 x 25 In. 1430.00
Rocker, Eames, Ivory Fiberglass Shell, Black Tower Base, Herman Miller, 26 In. .900.00 to 1015.00
Rocker, Eames, Salmon Fiberglass Shell, Zinc Struts, Birch Runners, 27 In. 920.00
Rocker, Floral Crest, Blue, Yellow Pinstripes, Brown Ground, Child's, 27 In. 330.00
Rocker, G. Stickley, 2 Wide Backslats, Single Vertical Arm, Oil Cloth Seat, 33 In. 3300.00
Rocker, G. Stickley, Ladder Back, Brown Leather Seat, Child's, 25 x 20 In. 560.00
Rocker, G. Stickley, Mahogany, Drop-In Seat, Dark Brown Leather, 43 x 30 In. 2315.00
Rocker, G. Stickley, No. 305, Ladder Back, 3 Horizontal Slats, Child's, 30 In. 285.00
Rocker, G. Stickley, No. 311, Mahogany, 5 Vertical Slats, Red Decal, 34 In. 920.00
Rocker, G. Stickley, No. 323, Mahogany, Leather Cushion, Red Decal, 38 In. 3220.00
Rocker, G. Stickley, No. 343, 3 Back Horizontal Slats Over Seat, Decal, Child's 240.00
Rocker, G. Stickley, Slats Under Each Arm, Upholstered Cushions, 41 In. 3105.00
Rocker, G. Stickley, V Back, 5 Vertical Back Slats, Rush Seat, 33 1/2 In. 865.00
Rocker, Hickory, Twig Construction, Woven Splint Seat & Back, Curved Arms, 32 In. 525.00
Rocker, L & J.G. Stickley, No. 817, 6 Vertical Slats, Mahogany, Leather Cushion 690.00
Rocker, L & J.G. Stickley, Oak, 6 Stick Splats, Drop In Padded Seat, c.1900 . . . . 750.00
Rocker, L. & J.G. Stickley, Mahogany, Vertical Slats, Beveled Rail, 32 x 35 In. 3740.00
Rocker, L. & J.G.Stickley, 6 Vertical Back Slats, Twill Upholstered Seat, 38 In. 3740.00
Rocker, Ladder Back, 3 Shaped Slats, Turned Stiles, Splint Seat, Child's, 1800, 23 1/2 In. 935.00
Rocker, Ladder Back, 4 Graduated Back Slats, Splint Seat, Painted Red, 44 In. 220.00
Rocker, Ladder Back, 5 Back Slats, Rush Seat, Painted, Early 19th Century 4290.00
Rocker, Ladder Back, Shaped Rockers, Splint Seat, Vase-Turned Posts, Arms, 46 In. 300.00
Rocker, Limbert, No. 644, Oak, 4 Vertical Slats, Original Finish, Mich., 1907, 39 In. 1090.00
Rocker, Lollipop, Renaissance Revival, Turned Ball Column Armrests, 29 x 19 x 22 In. . . 3450.00
Rocker, Louis Cyr Style, Raspberry, c.1920 . . . . 265.00
Rocker, Lounge, Chrome Ribbon Frame, Ultra-Suede, Italy, 40 In. 1265.00
Rocker, Mahogany, Leather Cushion Seat, Arms, J.M. Young, 36 1/2 x 29 x 23 In. 3850.00
Rocker, Maple, 5 Back Slats, Splint Seat, Delaware River Valley, 1795, 43 In. 1200.00
Rocker, Maple, Ladder Back, 4 Shaped Crossbars, Scroll Arms, Rush Seat, 19th Century . 260.00
Rocker, Maple, Ladder Back, 4 Slats, Turned Posts & Arms, Splint Seat, 46 1/2 In. 195.00
Rocker, Mustard, Red, Green, Black, Flowers, Pa., 1850s, 32 x 12 1/2 In. 750.00
Rocker, Oak, 3 Back Slats, Foliate Design, Floral Upholstered Seat, 1910, 35 In. 1035.00
Rocker, Oak, Leather Inset Seat, Arms, Child's, 17 x 22 x 26 In. 190.00
Rocker, Old Hickory, Cane Seat & High Back, Curved Arms 895.00
Rocker, Rococo, Walnut, Thumb-Mold, Balloon Back, Upholstered Spring Seat, c.1860 . . 360.00
Rocker, Royal, 6 Vertical Back Slats, Sewing, Leather Seat, 34 x 30 In. 1460.00
Rocker, Roycroft, Mahogany, 5 Vertical Back Slats, Tacked On Leather Seat, 36 In. 1687.00
Rocker, Sewing, G. Stickley, Maple, 3 Vertical Slats, Rush Seat, 35 In. 375.00
Rocker, Sewing, G. Stickley, No. 337, Mahogany, 3 Vertical Slats, 16 x 33 In. 255.00
Rocker, Shaker, 5 Slats, Arched, Tape Seat, Arms, 47 In. 5400.00

Rocker, Shaker, 5 Slats, Arms, Mt. Lebanon 6210.00
Rocker, Shaker, Maple, Ladder Back, Woven Rush Seat, Arms, 1800s 405.00
Rocker, Shaker, No. 3, Maple, Acorn Finials, Crescent Arms, Mt. Lebanon, 33 In. ... 490.00
Rocker, Shaker, No. 3, Red Brown Paint, Tape Seat, Back, Mt. Lebanon, N.Y., 35 1/4 In. . 195.00
Rocker, Shaker, No. 4, Red Wool Tape Seat & Back, Mt. Lebanon, Label 895.00
Rocker, Shaker, No. 7, Ladder Back, Bowed Crest, Mushroom Handholds, 1880s 495.00
Rocker, Shaker, Shaped Pommels, Arched Splats, Painted, Arms, 1840, 45 x 14 In. 2185.00
Rocker, Shaker, Shawl Bar, Mushroom-Capped Arms 850.00
Rocker, Shaker, Woven Tape Seat, Stenciled Label, Mt. Lebanon, 37 3/4 In. 715.00
Rocker, Shop Of The Crafters, Mahogany, Original Finish, Arms, 36 x 30 x 23 In. 805.00
Rocker, Slat Back, Scrolled Arms, Salmon Red Paint, New England, 41 x 15 1/2 In. 460.00
Rocker, Stick Form, Red Paint, Child's 28.00
Rocker, Stickley & Brandt Co., Mahogany, 4 Vertical Slats, 30 x 26 x 33 In. 1265.00
Rocker, Stickley & Brandt Co., Mahogany, Vertical Slats, Tan Leather Seat, 34 x 28 In. ... 1495.00
Rocker, Stickley Bros., 7 Narrow Vertical Slats, Original Finish, 27 x 38 In. 690.00
Rocker, Stickley Bros., Flat Arms, 4 Horizontal Back Slats, 39 1/2 x 27 x 22 In. 345.00
Rocker, Stickley Bros., No. 570, Mahogany, 2 Vertical Slats, 38 In. 2875.00
Rocker, Teakwood, Curved Crest Rail, Rust Cushions, Foil Label, M. Nissan, 27 1/2 In. ... 170.00
Rocker, Thonet, Bentwood, Cane Paneled Seat & Back, 40 x 26 x 38 In. 115.00
Rocker, Thonet, Bentwood, Cane Seat & Back, Refinished, Child's, 25 In. 230.00
Rocker, Twig, Child's 175.00
Rocker, Walnut, 4 Back Slats, Rush Seat, 19th Century, 41 x 21 x 30 In. 115.00
Rocker, Walnut, Folding, Platform, Child's, c.1880, 23 x 16 In. 115.00
Rocker, Wegner, White Paint, Spindled Back, Rush Seat, 42 In. 345.00
Rocker, White Paint, Flaring Spindled Back, Rush Seat, Wegner, 42 1/2 In. 345.00
Rocker, Wicker, Rolled Back, Ornate Beaded Turnings, 1875 .... 785.00
Rocker, Wicker, Wheeled Back, Victorian, 1875 .... 390.00
Rocker, Windsor, Bamboo Turnings, 7 Spindles, Painted, L. Clark, c.1839, 15 x 34 In. 220.00
Rocker, Windsor, Bow Back, 8 Spindles, Bamboo Turnings, Early 19th Century, 32 In. 690.00
Rocker, Windsor, Comb Back, 7 Spindles, Bamboo Turnings, Refinished 300.00
Rocker, Windsor, Comb Back, 7 Spindles, Painted, New England, c.1820 .... 385.00
Rocker, Windsor, Comb Back, Bamboo Turnings, Off White, Gilt, Arms, 40 5/8 In. 230.00
Rocker, Windsor, Comb Back, Yellow Foliage, Bamboo Turnings, Scrolled Arms 770.00
Rocker, Windsor, Rosewood, Floral Stencil, Gold Banded, Scroll Arms, 42 In. 300.00
Screen, 1-Panel, Embroidered, Appliqued, School-Girl Wool, England, c.1790, 18 1/2 In. . 489.00
Screen, 3-Panel, Arts & Crafts, Painted, Stylized Landscape Scene, 69 x 72 In. 290.00
Screen, 3-Panel, Brass, Gilt, Wreath Crest, Splayed Leafy Legs, 29 x 41 In. 1150.00
Screen, 3-Panel, Continental, Carved, Polychromed, Figures, Paw Feet, 72 x 57 In. 1840.00
Screen, 3-Panel, Egyptian Revival, Seated Pharaoh, Guards, 69 In. 8400.00
Screen, 3-Panel, Eugene Schoen, Brown, Tan Laminated Wood, Art Deco, 75 1/4 In. 2925.00
Screen, 3-Panel, Figural, Ormolu Bronze Mounts, Beveled Edge, France, 73 In. 1495.00
Screen, 3-Panel, Flowers, Birds, Figures, Continental, Early 1900s, 73 x 62 1/2 In. 1115.00
Screen, 3-Panel, Landscape, Elegantly Dressed Figures, Horse Drawn Carriage, 22 In. ... 400.00
Screen, 3-Panel, Louis XV, Gilt, Bronze Mounts, France, 34 1/2 x 54 In. 1495.00
Screen, 3-Panel, Louis XVI Style, Guilloche Carved Frame, Birds, Leaf, 45 x 56 In. 1224.00
Screen, 3-Panel, Mahogany, Allover Floral, Scrolled Leaf, Legs, 18 1/2 x 33 1/2 In. 60.00
Screen, 3-Panel, Mahogany, Front & Reverse Figural Design, 68 1/2 x 84 3/4 In. 2300.00
Screen, 3-Panel, Map Of Paris, Each Panel 68 x 60 In. 375.00
Screen, 3-Panel, Mirror, Giltwood, Reverse-Painted Floral, c.1900, 54 x 57 In. 925.00
Screen, 3-Panel, Oak Frame, Painted Birds, Cascading Foliage, Pyrographic, 63 1/4 In. ... 400.00
Screen, 3-Panel, Oak, Louis XVI, Carved Gilt Frame, 65 x 45 In. 575.00
Screen, 3-Panel, Painted Couple In Garden, Figures, 1920s, 57 x 64 1/2 In. 1150.00
Screen, 3-Panel, Printed Exotic Birds, Cherry Blossoms Reverse, 1930s, 72 1/2 In. 290.00
Screen, 3-Panel, Stenciled Paper, Continuous Battle Scene, Burlap On Wood, 75 In. 430.00
Screen, 3-Panel, Wallpaper, Blue Ground, Exotic Birds, Blossoms, 72 1/2 x 58 In. 290.00
Screen, 3-Section, Castle & Building Tapestry, Continental, 99 x 106 In. 4180.00
Screen, 4-Panel, Arts & Crafts, Medieval Stories, Script, 60 x 66 In. 575.00
Screen, 4-Panel, Birds On Flowering Branches Within Carved Dragon, 57 In. 2070.00
Screen, 4-Panel, Black Lacquer, Gilt, Polychrome Landscape, 64 x 73 In. 115.00
Screen, 4-Panel, Butterfly, Pale Yellow Ground, 1955, 79 In. 4800.00
Screen, 4-Panel, Carved Chinese Scenes, Birds, Flowers, 64 x 72 In. 220.00
Screen, 4-Panel, Carved Frame, Dragons, Flowers, Cloth Inserts, 74 x 114 In. 1430.00
Screen, 4-Panel, Charles X, Muse Design, Floral Urn, 63 1/4 x 84 x 4 In. 5750.00

Screen, 4-Panel, Cloth, Oriental Figural, Landscape Scene Panels, 70 1/2 In. 920.00
Screen, 4-Panel, Continuous Harbor Scene, Leaf Painted, 78 3/4 In. 2415.00
Screen, 4-Panel, Embroidered Birds, Flowers, Reverse Landscape, Frame, 68 x 72 In. . . . 175.00
Screen, 4-Panel, Figural Scenes Of Pavilions In Garden, Birds Reverse, 70 1/2 In. 230.00
Screen, 4-Panel, Leather, Birds, Flowering Foliage, 72 In. 6000.00
Screen, 4-Panel, Louis XV, Fruitwood, Acanthine Crest, Top Shaped Feet, 56 x 82 In. . . . 635.00
Screen, 4-Panel, Louis XV, Giltwood, Floral, Putti Scene, 67 In. 4500.00
Screen, 4-Panel, Mahogany, Boxwood Stringing, Damask Panels, 37 3/4 x 48 In. 260.00
Screen, 4-Panel, Mahogany, Carved Ivory Inlays, Mandarins, Trees, 72 In. 230.00
Screen, 4-Panel, Oak, Fluted Top Attached By Domes, 66 x 80 In. 1005.00
Screen, 4-Panel, Oriental Landscape Scene, Black Ground, 71 3/4 In. 2530.00
Screen, 4-Panel, Plywood Sections, Trim Molding, 60 x 84 In. 300.00
Screen, 4-Panel, Polychromed Leather, Florals, 72 x 72 In. 1955.00
Screen, 4-Panel, Transfer Printed, Piero Fornasetti, c.1955, 54 x 56 In. 6900.00
Screen, 4-Panel, Various Birds Against Mountains & Water, 80 In. 1380.00
Screen, 4-Panel, Various Maps Of Ireland, Scotland, England, 75 1/2 In. 865.00
Screen, 4-Panel, Victorian, Yellow, Red Diamonds, Black Ground, 69 1/2 In. 1380.00
Screen, 5-Panel, Gros Point & Petit Point, Allegorical Figures, 78 x 103 In. 5750.00
Screen, 5-Panel, Lattice Work Upper Panel Over Flower Waist Panel, 92 3/4 In. 431.00
Screen, 6-Panel, Bamboo On Gold Ground, Early 20th Century, 54 x 114 In. 920.00
Screen, 6-Panel, Eames, Birch Plywood, Canvas Webbing, 1950s, 68 x 60 In. 4315.00
Screen, 6-Panel, Geometric Designs, 84 x 108 In. 1725.00
Screen, 6-Panel, Scene Of Children At Play, Mountains In Ground, 61 In. 240.00
Screen, 8-Panel, Men In Pavilion End, Woman Other End, Black Lacquer, 78 x 172 In. . . 9000.00
Screen, 8-Panel, Procession Of Soldiers, Reserves Of Flowers, 80 In. 9600.00
Screen, 12-Panel, Black Coromandel Lacquer, Fan Reserve Border, 96 In. 4025.00
Screen, Art Nouveau, Mirror Face, Brass, c.1900, 30 1/2 In. 2310.00
Screen, Arts & Crafts, Poppies, Serpent Along Winding Road Scene, 10 x 56 In. 5465.00
Screen, Brass, Ladies In A Flower Garden Near A Pagoda, 16 x 68 x 58 In. 330.00
Screen, Brass, Stained Glass, Medallion Kingfisher Painting, 32 x 18 1/2 x 11 In. 465.00
Screen, Central Tapestry, Landscape, Easel Style, Late 1800s, 31 3/4 x 70 In. 255.00
Screen, George III, Mahogany, Needlepoint, Carved, Snake Feet, 56 x 22 1/2 In. 2970.00
Screen, Gold Gilded, Rococo Carved Crest, 1880, 41 x 24 In. 616.00
Screen, Hanging Panel, Leaf Repousse Design, Scrolled End Supports, 39 In. 660.00
Screen, Leather, Hand Painted, c.1900, 60 In. 3800.00
Screen, Mahogany Frame, Mother-Of-Pearl Overlay, Scrolled Brass Handle, 43 In. 300.00
Screen, Mahogany, Mounts Shape Of Stars, Gilt Arrows, 40 1/2 x 22 In. 2070.00
Screen, Needlepoint, Ebonized Stand, Columbus & Queen Isabella, c.1860, 60 x 31 In. . . 2640.00
Screen, Needlepoint, Figures, Landscape, House, c.1780, 24 x 20 1/2 In. 880.00
Screen, Needlework Panel, Bird & Basket Of Flowers, Trestle Base, 1840s, 51 1/2 In. . . . 862.00
Screen, Oak, Painted Leather, Jacobean Revival, Baluster Supports, 39 1/2 x 27 In. 115.00
Screen, Oak, Peacocks Inlay, Liberty & Co., 36 1/2 In. 4400.00
Screen, Oak, Poppy Frieze, Red, Green, Arts & Crafts, 68 1/4 x 19 3/4 In. 1350.00
Screen, Oil On Canvas, Flower Basket, Green, Mahogany Scroll Feet, 37 x 36 In. 330.00
Screen, Panel, Elephant In Mountain Landscape, Oriental Characters, 20 In. 115.00
Screen, Peacocks, Pheasants, Sparrows, Hawks Amidst Flowering Vines, 29 In. 1140.00
Screen, Pineapple Finial, Adjustable Panel, Maple, Snake Feet, 1770s, 55 1/2 In. 3162.00
Screen, Regency, Rosewood, Gilt Metal, Child On Horseback, 1825, 57 1/2 In. 920.00
Screen, Table, Elm Spandrels, Lion Masks, Burgundy Lacquer, 28 3/4 x 26 In. 345.00
Screen, Tapestry Panel, Floral Cresting, Scrolled Toes, 39 x 22 In. 1150.00
Secretary, Bas Relief Carving, Knowledge Is Power Legend, 19th Century, 91 In. 12500.00
Secretary, Biedermeier, Drop Front, Mahogany, Base Drawer, 68 In. 2530.00
Secretary, Bronze Mounted, Marquetry, Continental, 61 1/2 x 34 x 18 1/2 In. 1725.00
Secretary, Cherry, Mahogany, Blind Doors, Drawers, 1860, 74 In. 1760.00
Secretary, Chippendale, Birch, Maple, 2 Doors, Bird's-Eye Maple Panels, 66 In. 8050.00
Secretary, Chippendale, Cherry, Blind Front, 75 x 42 1/2 x 19 In. 5465.00
Secretary, Chippendale, Mahogany Veneer, 6 Interior Drawers, 40 x 11 x 87 In. 1980.00
Secretary, Chippendale, Mahogany Veneer, Slant Front, Henredon, 36 x 18 x 82 In. 1045.00
Secretary, Chippendale, Mahogany, 4 Drawers, Pigeonholes, Bonnet, 38 x 84 In. 440.00
Secretary, Chippendale, Mahogany, Slant Front, Henredon, 34 x 18 x 81 In. 935.00
Secretary, Chippendale, Walnut, Chester County, Pa., c.1770, 93 x 41 In. 16500.00
Secretary, Classical, Drop Front, Mahogany, Marble Top, c.1820, 58 x 37 1/2 In. 3300.00
Secretary, Dovetailed Drawer, Hinged Writing Desk, c.1920, 71 In. 395.00

Secretary, Drop Front, 3 Lower Long Drawers, Veneered Sides, Woman's, 56 x 26 In. . . . 2070.00
Secretary, Drop Front, Elm, Baize Surface, 10 Short, 3 Long Drawers, 1840s, 65 In. 6915.00
Secretary, Drop Front, Empire, Bird's-Eye Fruitwood, 3 Drawers, Bun Feet, 57 In. 4313.00
Secretary, Drop Front, Fruitwood, Fitted Interior, Marquetry, 45 1/2 In. 6900.00
Secretary, Drop Front, Mahogany, Cove-Molded Cornice, Fitted Interior, 53 In. 1840.00
Secretary, Drop Front, Mahogany, Frieze Drawer, Fitted Interior, 56 In. 4315.00
Secretary, Drop Front, Mahogany, Marble Top, Leather Surface, 55 In. 6640.00
Secretary, Drop Front, Mahogany, Stepped Top, Caryatids, 3 Drawers, 56 x 39 x 21 In. . . 3165.00
Secretary, Drop Front, Marble Top, Bombe Cabinet, 3 Drawers, 57 1/2 In. 920.00
Secretary, Drop Front, Ogee Frieze Drawer, Lower Drawers, 58 1/2 In. 3540.00
Secretary, Drop Front, Walnut, Bird's-Eye Maple Interior, Block Feet, 61 1/2 In. 1265.00
Secretary, Drop Front, Walnut, Marble Top, 3 Drawers, Plain Apron, 60 3/4 In. 2530.00
Secretary, Eastlake, Walnut, Mirror . . . .*Illus* 3080.00
Secretary, Empire, Mahogany, 2 Sections, Glass Doors, Cubby Holes, 73 x 40 In. 1210.00
Secretary, Empire, Mahogany, 2 Sections, Glass Doors, Flared Feet, 58 x 40 In. 1495.00
Secretary, Empire, Mahogany, Flip Top, 75 x 41 x 22 In. 880.00
Secretary, Federal Style, Mahogany, 2 Sections, 47 x 37 x 19 In. 1840.00
Secretary, Federal, Mahogany, 2 Sections, Document Slots, Woman's, c.1810, 51 x 39 In. . 2200.00
Secretary, French Empire, Drop Front, Mahogany, Marble Top, 57 x 38 x 18 In. 3450.00
Secretary, George III, Drop Front, Mahogany, Drawers, 83 x 37 1/2 x 20 1/2 In. 4830.00
Secretary, George III, Mahogany, Broken Arch Pediment, 4 Drawers, 94 x 43 x 24 In. . . . 3910.00
Secretary, George III, Mahogany, Slant Front, Astragal Glaze Doors, 91 x 46 x 21 In. . . . 4370.00
Secretary, Georgian, Mahogany, Foldover Top, 2 Over 3 Drawers, 31 x 37 x 21 In. 865.00
Secretary, Gothic Revival, Mahogany, Bird's-Eye Maple, Glass Doors, c.1810, 80 x 40 In. . 86.00
Secretary, Jigsaw Designs, Porcelain Studs, Inscriptions, Pa., 1848, 90 x 49 In. 7150.00
Secretary, Louis Philippe, Drop Front, Mahogany, 2 Cupboard Drawers, 63 In. 1840.00
Secretary, Louis Philippe, Drop Front, Walnut, Leather Lined, 58 x 40 x 17 In. 4370.00
Secretary, Louis XV Style, Kingwood, Marquetry, Marble Top, 44 x 29 x 29 1/2 In. 1725.00
Secretary, Louis XV Style, Marquetry, Marble Top, Fold-Out Surface, 53 x 33 x 18 In. . . 575.00
Secretary, Louis XVI Style, Kingwood, Tulipwood, Frieze Drawer, 55 x 37 x 15 In. 2070.00
Secretary, Louis XVI Style, Tulipwood, Serpentine Front, 49 x 21 1/2 x 13 1/2 In. 430.00
Secretary, Mahogany Finish, Lifetime, 63 x 26 x 18 In. 1725.00
Secretary, Mahogany, Cherry Upper Case, 9-Pane Doors, Tambour Door, 1840, 95 In. . . . 4950.00
Secretary, Maple, Cherry, Poplar, 2 Sections, Hinged Front, 70 x 38 In. 635.00
Secretary, Napoleon III, Mahogany, Marble Top, c.1870, 56 1/2 x 37 1/2 In. 3300.00
Secretary, Porcelain Medallion, Side Cabinets, Mirror Inside, 57 x 48 1/2 In. 3450.00
Secretary, Red Lacquer, Fitted Interior, Slant Front, 1830s, 88 1/2 In. 7475.00
Secretary, Rohde, Walnut, 3 Drawers, Drop Front, Herman Miller, 72 In. 1915.00
Secretary, Spires, Slant Front, Plain Interior, Lower Doors, 1860s, 84 In. 4370.00
Secretary, Tulipwood, Marquetry, Marble, 48 x 25 x 14 In. 3220.00
Secretary-Bookcase, Chippendale, Mahogany, 2 Doors, 4 Drawers, c.1775, 89 x 42 In. . . . 5500.00
Secretary-Bookcase, Cylinder, Walnut, Burl, Pullout Writing Surface, 33 x 23 x 89 In. . . . 1840.00
Secretary-Bookcase, Drop Front, 3 Shelves, Pigeonholes, 92 In. 8400.00
Secretary-Bookcase, Empire Style, Mahogany, 2 Sections, 69 x 42 1/2 x 18 1/2 In. 920.00
Secretary-Bookcase, Empire, Mahogany, Cherry, 2 Parts, c.1860, 90 x 47 1/2 x 21 In. 1955.00
Secretary-Bookcase, Federal, Cherry, Inlaid, New England, c.1790, 84 x 42 x 20 In. 24150.00
Secretary-Bookcase, Federal, Mahogany, Mullioned Doors, Shelves, 1815, 86 x 56 In. . . . 9000.00
Secretary-Bookcase, Federal, Walnut, 3 Parts, 2 Doors, 6 Drawers, 94 x 45 x 19 In. 2350.00
Secretary-Bookcase, George III, Mahogany, 2 Doors, Inlay, 93 In. 6040.00
Secretary-Bookcase, George III, Mahogany, 3 Long Drawers, Splayed Legs, 78 In. 2070.00
Secretary-Bookcase, Mahogany, 2 Doors, Lower Drop-Front Drawer, 84 In. 6000.00
Secretary-Bookcase, Mahogany, 4 Upper Glazed Doors, Desk Interior, 84 In. 7475.00
Secretary-Bookcase, Mahogany, Molded Cornice, 3 Graduated Drawers, 97 In. 1035.00
Secretary-Bookcase, Mirror Doors, Slant Front, Fitted Interior, Late 1800s, 74 In. 2415.00
Secretary-Bookcase, Renaissance Revival, Walnut, Slant Writing Surface, 84 In. 1150.00
Secretary-Bookcase, Victorian, 2 Glazed Doors, Pigeonholes, 83 x 45 In. 800.00
Server, Art Nouveau, Ecole De Nancy, Oak, Mirror, Shelf, 68 1/2 x 49 x 20 1/2 In. 2645.00
Server, Arts & Crafts, Drawer, Low Backboard, Stretcher, Lifetime, 36 x 40 x 18 1/2 In. . 1035.00
Server, Arts & Crafts, Pine, 3 Over 2 Drawers, Stretcher Shelf, 30 x 46 x 19 1/2 In. 1150.00
Server, Bauhaus, Oak, Laminate Surface, Shelf, Square Legs, c.1927, 30 1/4 In. 230.00
Server, Burl, Grain Paint, Middle Door, 6 Drawers, Backsplash, 46 x 53 1/2 In. 3750.00
Server, Empire, Mahogany, Converted Piano, New York, 1840, 29 x 69 In. 880.00
Server, Federal Style, Cherry, Drop Leaves, 2 Drawers, Shelf, Casters, 18 x 36 x 33 In. . . 490.00

Server, Federal, Mahogany, Long & 2 Short Drawers, New York, c.1830, 41 x 45 In. 1100.00
Server, Flame Mahogany, 2 Dovetailed Drawers, Kittinger, 48 x 18 x 36 In. 410.00
Server, G. Stickley, 3 Drawers, Copper Oval Pulls, Lower Shelf, Decal, 48 x 39 In. 4600.00
Server, G. Stickley, No. 802, 2 Drawers Over Arched Apron, 42 x 37 In. 5465.00
Server, George III Style, Mahogany, Serpentine Front, 35 x 42 x 21 In. 805.00
Server, Hepplewhite, Marquetry & Burl Veneer, Lift Top, 29 x 36 In. 875.00
Server, L. & J.G. Stickley, No. 741, Mahogany, Open Shelf, 44 x 18 x 40 In. 5750.00
Server, Limbert, Reticulated Backsplash, 2 Drawers, Lower Shelves, 43 1/4 In. 2760.00
Server, Louis XVI Style, Walnut, Marble Top, Cane, 28 x 26 x 15 1/2 In. 575.00
Server, Mahogany, 1 Drawer Over Cabinet Doors, Original Finish, 61 In. 1495.00
Server, Mahogany, Middle Shelf, 2 Drawers, 1840, 49 x 36 In. 3900.00
Server, Mahogany, Mirror, Sandwich Glass Pulls, Bowfront, Claw Feet, 1800s, 68 x 70 In. 900.00
Server, Mahogany, Rectangular Top, 2 Shelves, Tobey Furniture Co., 42 x 36 In. 1725.00
Server, Mahogany, Serpentine Front, 8 Drawers, Mayflower Furniture, 36 x 64 x 21 In. .. 675.00
Server, Mahogany, Serpentine Front, Brass Knobs, 23 1/2 x 66 1/4 In. 4950.00
Server, Mirror Backboard, 2 Drawers Between 2 Doors, Hersee, 52 x 64 x 20 In. 520.00
Server, Oak, 8 Lion Heads, Dolphins, Horns Of Plenty, R.J. Horner, c.1880, 66 x 84 In. .. 6160.00
Server, Oak, Stylized Winged Griffins Support, 2 Drawers, Backboard, 44 x 44 In. 220.00
Server, Pine, 3 Drawers Over 2 Doors, Kneehole, 42 1/2 x 43 x 17 In. 405.00
Server, Pine, Red Paint, Drawer, Tapered Legs, c.1810, 29 1/2 x 36 In. 300.00
Server, Pine, Red Paint, Rectangular, England, c.1820, 33 1/2 x 45 In. 305.00
Server, Renaissance Style, Ebonized Wood, 2 Doors, Claw Feet, Italy, 34 1/2 In. 635.00
Server, Sheraton, Mahogany, Shell Corners, Brass Backrail, 38 x 64 In. 2875.00
Server, Stickley Bros., Mahogany, Linen Drawer, 36 x 48 x 20 In. 3325.00
Server, Walnut, 3 Tiers, Ring-Turned Supports, Ball Finials, 43 1/4 In. 2645.00
Server, Walnut, Drawer, Tapered Legs, Pa., c.1800, 30 x 36 In. 415.00
Server, Walnut, Neptune With Dolphins & Cherubs, Oval, 1920, 28 x 21 In. 672.00
Server, William IV, Mahogany, 3 Tiers, Bun Feet On Casters, 43 1/2 In. 4370.00
Settee, Acanthus Supports, Padded Armrests, 1880s 6840.00
Settee, Arched Back, Out-Scrolled Armrests, Claw & Ball Feet, 72 In. 520.00
Settee, Arne Jacobsen, Swan, Upholstered, Aluminum Base, Fritz Hansen, 31 In. 4600.00
Settee, Art Nouveau, Ecole De Nancy, Fruitwood, Double Back, Floral Marquetry, 55 In. . 2300.00
Settee, Arts & Crafts, 7 Back Slats, Leather, 39 x 44 1/2 x 20 1/2 In. 345.00
Settee, Black Lacquered Frame, Original Finish, Carlo De Carli, 28 In. 865.00
Settee, Carlo Bugati, Wood, Painted Parchment, Repousse, Copper, c.1900, 96 In. 10200.00
Settee, Chippendale, Mahogany, Triple-Chair Back, Late 1800s, 39 1/2 x 66 In. 1320.00
Settee, Double Back, Center Blossom Backrail, Cane Seat, 50 1/4 In. 460.00
Settee, Eastlake, Leaf, Cross-Carved Crest, Tufted Upholstered Seat, 54 In. 260.00
Settee, Eastlake, Upholstered Seat & Back, 19th Century, 52 In. 200.00
Settee, Edwardian, Mahogany, Inlay, Lyre-Form Splat, c.1905, 49 1/2 In. 690.00
Settee, Federal Style, Mahogany, Spindle Triple Back, Curved Arms, Cane Seat, 56 In. .. 460.00
Settee, Federal, Crest Rails, Horizontal Spindles, Rush Seat, c.1825, 33 x 76 x 19 In. 13800.00
Settee, Federal, Painted, Crests Over Spindles, Urns, Medallions, Rush Seat, 33 x 70 In. . 2070.00
Settee, Floral Yellow Swag Crest, Yellow, Red Pinstripes, Green, Child's, 24 In. 9625.00
Settee, Florence Knoll, Parallel Bar, Upholstered, Chrome Frame, 30 In. 1150.00

Furniture, Secretary,
Eastlake, Walnut, Mirror

Furniture, Settee, Neoclassical, Kingwood,
Austria, Late 18th Century

Settee, G. Stickley, Cube, Horizontal Slats, 3 Loose Cushions, 1903, 78 In. 7375.00
Settee, George II, Mahogany, Reeded Arms, Legs, c.1800, 35 x 57 1/2 In. 275.00
Settee, George III Style, Mahogany, Chair Back, Trellis Splat, Loose Cushion, 37 x 79 In. 4600.00
Settee, George III, Mahogany, Camelback, Silk Damask, c.1790, 69 x 26 x 34 In. 6800.00
Settee, George III, Mahogany, Double Chair, Ribbonback, 39 x 47 In. 5175.00
Settee, Gilt, Ornate Carved Crest Rails, Cabriole Legs, 44 In., Pair 1610.00
Settee, Half-Spindle Back, Green Paint, Yellow Pinstripes, White Floral 935.00
Settee, Heart-Shaped Double-Chair Back, Prince Of Wales Feathers 4025.00
Settee, Hepplewhite, Mahogany, Shieldback, Upholstered, England, 17 x 37 In. 880.00
Settee, Heywood Bros., Serpentine Shape, Caning, Beadwork, c.1904, 41 x 41 In. 4025.00
Settee, Horizontal Splat Over 15 Spindles, Plank Seat, Olive Green Paint, 34 In. 800.00
Settee, Ivory Paint, Back-Rolled Crest Rail, Striped Fabric, 33 3/4 In. 920.00
Settee, Jacobean, Oak, Rectangular Backrest, Plank Seat, Ring Legs, 63 In. 2415.00
Settee, L. & J.G. Stickley, Mahogany, Drop Arm, Broad Slats, 36 x 77 x 28 In. 6750.00
Settee, Limbert, Mahogany, 8 Vertical Back Slats, 37 1/2 x 46 1/2 x 24 In. 2700.00
Settee, Limbert, Mahogany, Vertical Slats, Drop In Seat, 38 3/4 x 49 x 25 In. 5625.00
Settee, Limbert, No. 653, Mahogany, 5 Wide Slats, Leather Cushion, 68 x 33 In. 3740.00
Settee, Louis XIV, Walnut, Embossed Leather, 44 1/2 x 46 1/2 In. 4140.00
Settee, Louis XV Style, Beech, Carved, Floral Aubusson, 51 1/2 In. 1380.00
Settee, Louis XV Style, Walnut, Parcel Gilt, Cupid, Flowers, Vines, 42 x 74 x 26 In. 1955.00
Settee, Louis XV, Medallion Back, Green Chinoiserie Fabric, 61 1/2 In. 345.00
Settee, Louis XV, Walnut, Scrolled Foliate Design, Velvet, 36 In. 1100.00
Settee, Louis XVI, Gilt, Rectangular Back, Muslin Upholstered Seat, 72 In. 1440.00
Settee, Louis XVI, Mahogany, Gilt, Lyre Trophy, Pendant Flowers, 49 In. 2185.00
Settee, Mahogany Veneer, Medallion Back, c.1840, 32 1/2 x 42 x 15 In. 490.00
Settee, Mahogany, Double-Chair Back, Upholstered Seat, Pad Feet, 39 x 62 In. 1150.00
Settee, Mahogany, Harp Form, Mother-Of-Pearl, Satinwood Foliate, 35 x 25 In. 430.00
Settee, Mahogany, Upholstered Back, Tapered Fluted Arms, 34 x 47 In. 1725.00
Settee, Neoclassical, Gilt, Carved Winged Lions, Paw Feet, Italy, 84 In. 12650.00
Settee, Neoclassical, Kingwood, Austria, Late 18th Century ....*Illus* 7700.00
Settee, Oak, Antlers, 3-Part Back, Cane Seat & Back, 69 In. 16100.00
Settee, Old Hickory, 9-Spindle Back, Slatted Seat, Branded Mark, 34 x 46 x 23 In. 430.00
Settee, Queen Anne, Walnut, Cabriole Legs, Corduroy, Open Arms, 62 x 21 x 42 In. 330.00
Settee, Red Paint, Floral Design, Balloon Seat, Urn-Turned Arms, Continental, 47 In. ... 220.00
Settee, Red, Brown, Grain Painted, Crest, Horizontal Splat, c.1840, 21 1/2 x 25 In. 1610.00
Settee, Regency, Beech, Green Paint, Cane Seat, 1810, 69 In. 3600.00
Settee, Regency, Gilt, Green Paint, Curved Quadruple Top, Tapered Legs, 79 In. 8400.00
Settee, Reserve Of Putti & Foliage, Cane Chair Back, Splayed Legs, c.1810, 45 1/2 In. .. 2530.00
Settee, Restauration, Mahogany, Scrolling, Leaf-Carved Crest, 30 x 68 x 23 In. 3910.00
Settee, Rococo, Rosewood, Shell-Carved Serpentine Seat Rail, Cabriole Legs, 31 In. 1380.00
Settee, Rococo, Walnut, Domed Back, Padded Seat, Cabriole Legs, Italy, 37 In. 3220.00
Settee, Rococo, Walnut, Serpentine Crest, Padded Arms, Tufted Back, Velvet, 62 In. 360.00
Settee, Rosewood Laminate Panel, Rounded & Channeled Back, Upholstered, 49 In. 920.00
Settee, Sheraton, Brown Finish, Cane Seat, 50 5/8 x 19 x 32 1/2 In. 1045.00
Settee, Sheraton, Mahogany, 2 Leaf-Carved Crests, Padded Seat, 1900, 35 In. 1610.00
Settee, Sheraton, Mahogany, Gold Design, Upholstered, 43 In., Pair 880.00
Settee, Sheraton, Triple-Chairback, Black, Stencil, Hide-Away Bed, C. Johnson 3450.00
Settee, Simulated Rosewood, Padded Back, Loose Cushion, Brass Cup Casters, 64 In. 1150.00
Settee, Steel & Iron, Arms Curve Up To Make Back Crest, Green Paint, 33 1/2 In. 690.00
Settee, Stickley & Brandt Co., Mahogany, Tan Leather Drop-In Seat, Open Arms, 36 In. . 2415.00
Settee, Stickley Bros., 3 Seats, 38 x 65 In. 1300.00
Settee, Upholstered Back, Fluted Arm Supports, Late 19th Century, 34 x 47 In. 1725.00
Settee, V. Kagan, Lucite Plank Base, Wool, 27 x 36 In. 280.00
Settee, W. Hoffmann, Chrome Frame, Leather Cushions, Hardwood Arms, 45 In. 1150.00
Settee, W. Plattner, Upholstered, Fiberglass Shell, 34 In. 865.00
Settee, Walnut, Carved Acanthus Leaves, Scalloped Apron, Crewel, 39 In. 880.00
Settee, Walnut, Carved Floral, Scroll Crest, Cabriole Legs, Upholstered, 57 In. 145.00
Settee, Walnut, Domed Back, Outscrolled Arms, Padded Seat, Scrolled Feet, 59 In. 3220.00
Settee, Walnut, Undulating Top Rail, Pierced Backrest, Parcel Gilt, 1740s, 116 In. 8640.00
Settee, Walnut, Upholstered Backrest, Outscrolled Upholstered Sides & Seat, 84 In. 4320.00
Settee, Warren McArthur, Lacquered Wood, Drop Cushions, Mid 1920s ....*Illus* 27000.00
Settee, William & Mary, Walnut, Padded Back, Arms, Baluster Legs, 1800s, 49 1/2 In. .. 2990.00
Settee, Windsor Style, Painted, Clad Seat, Downswept Arms, Box Stretcher, 70 1/4 In. .. 260.00

Settee, Windsor, Birdcage Back, Bamboo Turned Spindles, Plank Seat, 1820, 77 In. 3800.00
Settee, Windsor, Butterfly, Bamboo Spindles Over Plank Seat, 8 Bamboo Legs, 60 In. . . . 360.00
Settee, Windsor, Maple, Pine, Straight Crest Rail, Arms, c.1810, 33 x 78 In. 3220.00
Settee, Windsor, Poplar, Maple, Step-Down Spindle Back, 10 Legs, 78 x 18 In. 2530.00
Settee, Wood, Arched Crest, Carved Foliage Continuing To Scrolling Arms, 52 In. 2185.00
Settle, Arched Crest Rail, Leather, Lifetime, 36 1/2 x 29 In. 2645.00
Settle, Arts & Crafts, Floral At Back & Posts, 9 Back Slats, 3 Arm Slats, 84 In. 4675.00
Settle, Arts & Crafts, Mahogany, 20 Vertical Back Slats, Square Post Legs, 31 In. 1150.00
Settle, Arts & Crafts, Mahogany, 7 Slats, 56 x 28 x 34 In. 690.00
Settle, Arts & Crafts, Mahogany, 8 Wide Slats At Back, Original Finish, 74 x 36 In. 2990.00
Settle, Arts & Crafts, Oak, Drop Arm, 6 Vertical Slats, 3 Vertical Side Slats, 74 In. 2415.00
Settle, Arts & Crafts, Pine, Vertical Slat Back, Upholstered Seat, 35 x 76 x 28 In. 2415.00
Settle, Broad Paneled Back, Leather Seat, Lifetime, 32 1/2 x 72 x 32 In. 3660.00
Settle, Free Hand & Stenciled Angel Wings, Fruit, Plank Seat, 70 1/2 In. 1020.00
Settle, G. Stickley, 4 Vertical Slats Each Side, Square Posts, 36 x 33 In. 5625.00
Settle, G. Stickley, Broad Backrail, Vertical Slats To Sides, Leather, 78 In. 6900.00
Settle, G. Stickley, No. 207, Mahogany, 5 Vertical Slats, 70 x 39 In. 9200.00
Settle, G. Stickley, No. 219, Mahogany, Original Spring Cushion, 71 x 38 In. 2070.00
Settle, G. Stickley, No. 222, Mahogany, Black Leather Cushion, 36 In. 8625.00
Settle, G. Stickley, No. 225, Mahogany, Green Cushion Seat, 78 x 30 x 29 In. 4600.00
Settle, L. & J.G. Stickley, 5 Wide Vertical Slats, 1912, 34 x 76 x 31 In. 4600.00
Settle, L. & J.G. Stickley, No. 275, Spring Cushion, Even Arms, Handcraft Decal, 84 In. . . 8800.00
Settle, L. & J.G. Stickley, No. 281, Pyramid Posts, Upholstered Spring Seat, 76 In. 8625.00
Settle, Limbert, Mahogany, Upholstered, Cutouts, 37 x 82 x 26 In. 2760.00
Settle, Limbert, No. 558, Mahogany, 9 Slats, Leather Cushion, 85 x 34 In. 4315.00
Settle, Limbert, Oak, 3 Square Ebony Details, Spring Cushion, 74 x 28 x 39 In. 2185.00
Settle, Mahogany, 15 Vertical Slats, 3 Loose Cushions, J.M. Young, 35 x 78 x 30 In. 4025.00
Settle, Oak, 4 Shaped & Crossbanded Panels, Shaped Arms, 19th Century, 72 In. 800.00
Settle, Paneled Backrest, Scrolled Arms, Rope Seat, Late 17th Century, 75 In. 6325.00
Settle, Porch, Original Green Finish, 26 x 60 x 24 In. 2300.00
Settle, Prairie School, Mahogany, Spindled, 43 x 70 x 27 1/2 In. 2470.00
Settle, Stickley Bros., 13 Slats At Back, Original Leather Cushion, 72 x 37 In. 1380.00
Settle, Stickley Bros., Drop Arm, Paper Label, 39 x 72 In. 1550.00
Settle, Stickley Bros., Drop Arms, Original Finish, 56 x 24 In. 1150.00
Settle, Stickley Bros., No. 3717, Mahogany, Massive Drop Arms, 84 x 39 In. 2990.00
Settle, Tavern Box, Curved Sides, Paneled Back, 1700s, 61 x 53 x 16 In. 1210.00
Shaker, Rocker, No. 3, Maple, Arms, Marked Mount Lebanon, N.Y., 33 1/2 x 15 1/2 In. . . 489.00
Shelf, 3 Shelves, Green, Heart People, Flowers, Peter Hunt, 48 x 39 x 10 1/2 In. 115.00
Shelf, Art Nouveau, Ecole De Nancy, Oak, Carved Leaves, 40 x 29 1/2 x 12 In. 575.00
Shelf, Black Forest, Demilune Bracket, Carved Head, 16 x 16 x 10 1/2 In. 545.00
Shelf, Brass, 5 Glass Shelves, Serpentine Sides, Contemporary, 41 x 15 x 80 In. 220.00
Shelf, Carved Scrolling Foliage, Inverted Blossoms, 19th Century, 7 x 7 In., Pair 115.00
Shelf, Corner, Hanging, Delicate Cutwork, Red Paint, Pa., c.1870, 36 In. 1750.00
Shelf, Corner, Hanging, Walnut, Gouge & Press Carving, 18 x 9 1/2 In. 45.00
Shelf, Frankl, Skyscraper, Ivory Lacquer, 19 x 36 x 10 In. 19800.00
Shelf, Hanging, 3 Tiers, Scalloped Sides, Late 19th Century, 29 x 25 In. 1045.00
Shelf, Hanging, G. Nakashima, Walnut, Trapezoid Top, 8 x 78 x 12 1/2 In. 4220.00
Shelf, Hanging, Georgian, Mahogany Inlay, 4 Graduated Shelves, 36 In. 2070.00
Shelf, Hanging, Gilt, Cherub, Shell, Italy, 16 In., Pair 1495.00
Shelf, Hanging, Gilt, Composition, Mirrored, Arched, Beaded, 18 x 5 1/2 x 45 In. 980.00
Shelf, Hanging, Louis XV, Walnut, 4 Bombe Shelves, Acanthus Supports, 25 In. 545.00
Shelf, Hanging, Louis XVI, Mahogany Veneer, C-Scrolls, Inlay, 36 x 15 5/8 In. 460.00
Shelf, Hanging, Mahogany, Open Lattice Sides, 30 x 31 In. 185.00
Shelf, Hanging, Mahogany, Pierced Sides, 3 Shelves, Drawers, Kittinger, 39 x 36 In. 1760.00
Shelf, Hanging, Oak, Turned Supports, Tan Paint, c.1900, 19 1/2 x 16 In. 140.00
Shelf, Hanging, Rococo, Gilt, 2 Tiers, Acanthus Supports, Italy, 14 In. 345.00
Shelf, Hanging, Walnut, Figured, Pennsylvania, c.1820, 47 1/2 x 37 In. 6600.00
Shelf, Hanging, Walnut, Jigsaw Ends, 2 Shelves, Brass Screws, 29 x 7 1/2 x 15 In. 110.00
Shelf, Hanging, Walnut, Pierced Sides, 3 Tiers, Leaf & Scroll Design, 33 x 34 x 9 1/2 In. . . 200.00
Shelf, Pine, Salmon Paint, 3 Shelves, Plate Rests, Scalloped Sides, c.1820, 31 x 31 In. . . . 195.00
Shelf, Regency, Mahogany, 5 Stepped Tiers, Brass Rosettes, 36 x 28 1/2 x 7 In. 1035.00
Shelf, Scalloped, Gilt Gesso Leaf Supports, 11 1/8 In., Pair 440.00
Shelf, Silver Gilt, Carved, Cherubs, Scrolls, Italy, 8 x 15 x 6 In. 545.00

Shelf, Stylized Shell & Flowering Vines, Gilt, Italy, 20th Century, 10 In. 920.00
Sideboard, 2 Drawers, 3 Doors, 4 Turned Columns Base, Paw Feet, 42 x 49 1/2 In. 5500.00
Sideboard, Art Nouveau, Ebonized, Mirror, Doors, Drawers, Austria, 55 x 43 x 22 In. 6040.00
Sideboard, Arts & Crafts, Mahogany, 4 Drawers, 57 1/2 x 72 x 25 In. 3940.00
Sideboard, Arts & Crafts, Oak, 3 Center Drawers, Medium Brown Finish, 54 In. 1265.00
Sideboard, Arts & Crafts, Oak, Mirror Back, 2 Drawers, England, 66 x 60 In. 2415.00
Sideboard, Bowfront, Mahogany, Central Drawer, Side Drawers, 1780s, 53 In. 7475.00
Sideboard, Brown Laminate Doors, 2 Adjustable Shelves, Italy, 69 x 19 x 30 In. 800.00
Sideboard, Burl Walnut, Marble Top, Mirror, 2 Cupboard Doors, 58 1/4 In. 550.00
Sideboard, Butler's, Federal, Mahogany Veneer, Hinged Desk, 43 x 64 x 28 In. 13800.00
Sideboard, C. Rohlfs, Mahogany, 5 Drawers, 41 1/4 x 68 3/4 x 22 In. 5175.00
Sideboard, Cherry, White Pine, 3 Drawers, Stephens City, Va., 1820, 43 1/2 x 20 In. 950.00
Sideboard, Classical, 3 Drawers, 4 Doors, Backsplash, Claw Feet, 49 x 72 1/2 x 23 In. 615.00
Sideboard, Classical, Mahogany Veneer, Gallery, Wm. Palmer, 64 x 48 In. 1445.00
Sideboard, Classical, Mahogany, 2 Doors, Marble Top, c.1830, 47 x 42 x 18 In. 4315.00
Sideboard, Classical, Mahogany, 3 Recessed Doors, Drawers, c.1825, 55 x 61 x 24 In. 2185.00
Sideboard, Classical, Mahogany, Amboyna, Gallery, 3 Drawers, 1825, 53 x 72 In. 6850.00
Sideboard, Classical, Mahogany, Egyptian Pedestals, c.1825, 46 x 77 x 24 In. 5750.00
Sideboard, Classical, Mahogany, Pedestal, Egyptian Panels, 45 x 77 x 22 In. 3680.00
Sideboard, E. Wormley, Mahogany, Dark Finish, Liquor Storage, 34 In. 4600.00
Sideboard, Empire, Cherry, 2 Tiger-Maple Drawers, 4 Doors, 63 x 73 x 24 In. 2200.00
Sideboard, Empire, Cherry, Flame Front, 3 Drawers Over 4 Doors, 1830, 54 x 73 In. 1210.00
Sideboard, Empire, Mahogany, 3 Drawers Over 4 Doors, Claw Feet, 1830, 42 x 67 In. 1460.00
Sideboard, Federal Style, Mahogany, 1 Central Drawer, Berkey & Gay, 77 x 23 x 43 In. . . 520.00
Sideboard, Federal Style, Mahogany, Parquetry, Serpentine Front, 36 x 56 x 21 In. 750.00
Sideboard, Federal, Inlaid, 19th Century . . . . *Illus* 9075.00
Sideboard, Federal, Mahogany, 3 Drawers, 4 Doors, Paw Feet, c.1825, 50 x 74 1/4 In. . . . 1760.00
Sideboard, Federal, Mahogany, Bowfront, J.C. Tapp, 69 x 25 x 36 In. 635.00
Sideboard, Federal, Mahogany, c.1800, Pair 6325.00
Sideboard, Federal, Mahogany, Rectangular Top, 4 Doors, 6 Tapered Legs, 40 In. 5750.00
Sideboard, Federal, Mahogany, Serpentine, Inlay, 1 Center Drawer 2530.00
Sideboard, Federal, Mahogany, Shaped, 3 Drawers, Doors, Pa., c.1815, 51 x 61 1/2 In. . . . 2530.00
Sideboard, Federal, Mahogany, Top Overhang, Liquor Cabinet, c.1810, 62 x 23 In. 1150.00
Sideboard, Frank Lloyd Wright, Mahogany, Red Decal, Henredon, 66 x 47 In. 1725.00
Sideboard, G. Stickley, No. 800, 6 Drawers, Lower Shelf, Red Decal, 43 x 54 In. 9200.00
Sideboard, G. Stickley, No. 814 1/2, Plate Rail, Doors, 3 Drawers, Linen Drawer, 56 In. . 5750.00
Sideboard, G. Stickley, Oak, Rectangular Top, 4 Drawers, 1909, 52 x 25 In. 12650.00
Sideboard, George III Style, Mahogany, Reeded Edge, 2 Drawers & Doors, 35 x 60 In. . . 375.00
Sideboard, George III, Bowfront, Mahogany, 2 Drawers, 35 1/2 In. 4900.00
Sideboard, George III, Bowfront, Mahogany, Central Drawer, Spade Feet, 36 In. 2530.00
Sideboard, George III, Bowfront, Mahogany, Inlay, 36 3/4 x 47 3/4 x 21 1/2 In. 4600.00
Sideboard, George III, Bowfront, Mahogany, Satinwood Band, 35 x 49 1/2 x 23 In. 4830.00
Sideboard, George III, Bowfront, Mahogany, Veneer, 5 Drawers, 36 x 66 x 25 In. 5175.00
Sideboard, George III, Mahogany, Banded Top, Drawers, 35 1/2 x 47 x 25 1/4 In. 3450.00
Sideboard, George III, Mahogany, Boxwood Stringing, 73 3/4 x 27 1/2 In. 6900.00
Sideboard, George III, Mahogany, Crossbanded Top, Reeded Legs, 1800, 38 In. 7800.00
Sideboard, George III, Mahogany, Inlay, Serpentine Front, 35 x 57 1/2 x 26 In. 12650.00
Sideboard, George III, Mahogany, Serpentine Case, 3 Drawers, 4 Doors, 41 In. 1725.00

Furniture, Sideboard, Federal, Inlaid,
19th Century

Furniture, Sofa, Rococo Revival, Laminated
Rosewood, Grape Leaves, 69 In.

Sideboard, George III, Mahogany, Serpentine Top, Inlay, c.1780, 36 x 74 x 31 In. 3080.00
Sideboard, George III, Mahogany, Sheraton, Inlay, Bowed Top, 36 x 60 x 23 In. 4370.00
Sideboard, George III, Mahogany, Tambour Doors, Bellflower Inlay, 37 x 81 x 28 In. 12100.00
Sideboard, Georgian Style, Mahogany, Fluted Frieze, Late 19th Century, 35 x 60 In. 220.00
Sideboard, Georgian Style, Mahogany, Fluted Splat, Urn, Swag, 72 x 24 x 43 In. 800.00
Sideboard, Georgian Style, Serpentine Front, Chinoiserie, 60 x 22 1/2 x 35 In. 115.00
Sideboard, Hepplewhite, Mahogany Veneer, 1 Bow Drawer, Boston, 40 1/2 In. 950.00
Sideboard, Hepplewhite, Mahogany, Bowfront, 1795, 47 1/2 x 70 x 26 In. 3850.00
Sideboard, Hepplewhite, Mahogany, Inlaid, Demilune Top, 1880s, 35 x 48 In. 1760.00
Sideboard, Jacobean, Oak, Applied Carvings, Burled Veneer, 74 x 22 x 39 In. 355.00
Sideboard, L. & J.G. Stickley, 4 Drawers, 4 Doors Over Linen Drawer, 47 x 24 In. 5625.00
Sideboard, L. & J.G. Stickley, 4 Short, 1 Long Drawers, 2 Doors, 48 x 54 x 24 In. 2070.00
Sideboard, L. & J.G. Stickley, Mahogany, Original Finish, 49 x 66 x 22 In. 7245.00
Sideboard, L. & J.G. Stickley, No. 745, 2 Doors, 5 Drawers, Brass Pulls, 48 x 54 In. 1800.00
Sideboard, L. & J.G. Stickley, With Plate Rack, 3 Drawers, 44 x 48 x 20 In. 3150.00
Sideboard, Limbert, No. 425, Dark Mahogany, Heart Design, 59 x 41 In. 8625.00
Sideboard, Louis XVI Style, Burr Elm, Gilt Metal, Mirror Backboard, 82 x 72 In. 920.00
Sideboard, Mahogany, 3 Drawers, Brass Trim, Calvin, 71 1/2 x 19 x 34 In. 1840.00
Sideboard, Mahogany, 3 Drawers, John Needles, Baltimore, c.1820, 42 x 51 In. 5400.00
Sideboard, Mahogany, Brass Gallery, Knop Finials, Bottle Drawer, 70 1/2 In. 3910.00
Sideboard, Mahogany, Drop Center, Urn Inlay, Ram's Heads, 62 x 102 In. 4000.00
Sideboard, Mahogany, Open Carved Crest, Male & Female Figure, 78 x 50 x 26 In. 3910.00
Sideboard, Mahogany, Reeded Backsplash, 4 Paneled Doors, 51 x 72 x 25 In. 3220.00
Sideboard, Mahogany, Serpentine Form, Fluted Square Legs, 1 Drawer, 56 1/2 In. 4600.00
Sideboard, Mahogany, Travertine Top, Original Finish, Calvin, 71 x 34 1/2 In. 1150.00
Sideboard, Mahogany, Veneered Drawers, 4 Panel Doors, 1820, 51 x 42 In. 5400.00
Sideboard, Marble Inlaid Top, Brown, Gray, White Ground, 37 1/2 x 28 x 85 In. 1560.00
Sideboard, Marble Top, 2 Drawers Over 2 Marquetry Doors, c.1880, 44 x 52 In. 1900.00
Sideboard, McCobb, 4 Drawers, Travertine Top, Signed, Calvin, 71 x 33 In. 2530.00
Sideboard, Neoclassical, 4 Doors Base, 3 Drawers, Henredon, 67 x 19 x 31 In. 190.00
Sideboard, Oak, Serpentine Front, Ornate Carvings, c.1885, 98 x 72 x 36 In. 5040.00
Sideboard, Open Carved Crest, Winged Caryatids, Pair Of Doors, 76 x 48 x 29 In. 4370.00
Sideboard, Ormolu Mounted, Palissandre, Jules Leleu, c.1950, 38 1/2 x 120 x 11 In. 8700.00
Sideboard, Pine, 1 Drawer Over 2 Doors, Orange Paint, 18th Century 1895.00
Sideboard, Regency, Allover Black Lacquer, Bellflower, Scroll, 72 In. 635.00
Sideboard, Regency, Mahogany, Bowfront, 2 Cellarette Drawers, 1810, 44 x 66 In. 3690.00
Sideboard, Regency, Mahogany, Brass Gallery, Bowed Doors, 52 x 72 x 26 3/4 In. 3680.00
Sideboard, Regency, Mahogany, Inlaid, Bowfront, c.1810, 36 x 72 x 25 In. 5750.00
Sideboard, Regency, Mahogany, Reeded Top, Convex Door, Reeded Columns, 41 In. 1330.00
Sideboard, Rococo, Mahogany, Scroll Brackets, Ogee Drawers, 73 3/4 In. 4600.00
Sideboard, Rococo, Walnut, Marble Top, 2 Dovetailed Drawers, 54 1/2 x 20 x 88 In. ... 5170.00
Sideboard, Sheraton, Bowfront, Mahogany, Black Paint, 65 3/4 x 40 1/2 In. 3630.00
Sideboard, Sheraton, Cherry, Mahogany Veneer, New York, c.1825, 52 1/2 x 53 In. 7150.00
Sideboard, Sheraton, Mahogany, Serpentine Top, Central Drawer, 30 x 43 In. 550.00
Sideboard, Stickley Bros., Mahogany, 51 x 54 x 22 In. 2070.00
Sideboard, Teak, 2 Sliding Doors, 3 Inner Shelves, 6 Drawers, Denmark, 30 In. 2300.00
Sideboard, Teak, Mother-Of-Pearl, Chinese, 65 x 80 x 20 In. 1380.00
Sideboard, Victorian, Bird's-Eye Maple, 1 Drawer, 2 Lower Paneled Doors, 54 In. 1210.00
Sideboard, Victorian, Chestnut, Walnut, Marble Top, Fruit Carvings, 1870, 5 In. 3080.00
Sideboard, Victorian, Marble Top, 2 Drawers, 2 Inlaid Doors, 1880, 44 x 52 x 22 In. 1905.00
Sideboard, Victorian, Oak, Mirror, Columns, 3 Drawers, 2 Doors, 42 x 22 x 72 In. 1200.00
Sideboard, Walnut, Light Finish, 2 Doors, 46 x 60 x 21 In. 4500.00
Sideboard, Walnut, Marble Top, 3 Drawer Over 2 Door, Burl Panels, 37 x 53 x 21 1/2 In. . 550.00
Sideboard, Walnut, Marble Top, Oval Burl Panels, Crest, c.1875, 83 x 41 x 18 In. 2800.00
Sideboard, Walnut, Yellow Pine, 2 Panel Doors Center, Turned Feet, 52 x 19 In. 3640.00
Sideboard, William IV, Mahogany, Carved, c.1835, 46 x 78 x 24 1/2 In. 2070.00
Sideboard, William IV, Mahogany, Rectangular Top, 3 Frieze Drawers, 36 In. 4200.00
Sofa, 3 Loose Seat Cushions, Black Leather, Post Legs, Grete Jalk, 1960, 32 x 30 In. 2925.00
Sofa, Alexander Girard, Denim, Herman Miller, 25 In. 5465.00
Sofa, American Aesthetic Revival, Carved Walnut, Scroll Crest, 72 1/2 In. 1150.00
Sofa, Art Deco, Curved Form, Purple Velvet, Upholstered, 75 x 32 In., Pair 575.00
Sofa, Backswept Crest, Cream Paint, Leaf-Carved Legs, 33 3/4 x 64 In. 2530.00
Sofa, Belter, Laminated Rosewood, Carved, Upholstered, Victorian, c.1850, 84 In. 6325.00

Sofa, Belter, Rococo Revival, Laminated, Rosewood, New York, 40 x 74 x 24 In. 6325.00
Sofa, Belter, Rosalie, Rosewood, c.1855, 40 x 70 x 32 In. 3080.00
Sofa, Black Lacquer, Cane Back Continuing To Scroll Arms, 3 Cushion Seat, 67 In. 5075.00
Sofa, Button-Tufted Back, 3 Loose Cushions, Suede, 110 In. 3300.00
Sofa, Camelback, Arms Taper From Back, Upholstered, Plaid, 31 1/2 x 59 In. 385.00
Sofa, Camelback, Chippendale Style, Upholstered, 80 In. 230.00
Sofa, Camelback, Chippendale, Cherry, Maple, Reupholstered, 1920, 96 In. 770.00
Sofa, Camelback, Chippendale, Mahogany, Marlborough Feet, Arms, 70 In. 715.00
Sofa, Camelback, Chippendale, Square Molded Legs, Upholstered, 84 In. 315.00
Sofa, Camelback, Regency, Serpentine Back, Scrolled Arms, 1800, 77 In. 1380.00
Sofa, Camelback, Triple Arched, Rolled Arms, Stretchers, 1800s, 36 x 91 x 29 In. 1870.00
Sofa, Camelback, Walnut, Carved Crest, Cabriole Legs, Tufted, 39 x 78 x 29 In. 560.00
Sofa, Chesterfield, Brass Tacking, Tufted Brown Leather, 79 In. 2185.00
Sofa, Chesterfield, Button-Tufted Back & Arms, 3 Seat Cushions, 80 In. 1380.00
Sofa, Chesterfield, Leather, 80 In. 6000.00
Sofa, Chesterfield, Leather, Tufted Back & Arms, 3 Seat Cushions, 70 In. 1265.00
Sofa, Classical, Mahogany, Carved, Dolphin Feet, Upholstered, Early 1800s, 78 In. 2415.00
Sofa, Classical, Mahogany, Carved, Shaped Crest, Arms, Paw Feet, c.1830, 35 x 84 In. . . . 935.00
Sofa, Classical, Mahogany, Scroll Back, Upholstered, Rolled Arms, 1830, 86 In. 1100.00
Sofa, Classical, Mahogany, Velvet, Loose Pillows, Rolled Arms, 86 In. 1320.00
Sofa, Classical, Mahogany, Veneer, Upholstered, 1835, Rolled Arms 5300.00
Sofa, Classical, Mahogany, Winged Animal Feet, Philadelphia, c.1835, 35 x 90 In. 1100.00
Sofa, Classical, Rosewood, Gilt, Greek Stencils, 1820-1830, 22 1/4 x 79 In. 18400.00
Sofa, Directoire, Beech, Overscroll Back, Padded, 48 1/2 In. 5290.00
Sofa, Dunbar, Tufted Wool Seat, Wooden Legs, 1950s, 84 x 33 x 29 In. 2535.00
Sofa, E. Wormley, Green, Upholstered, Brass Legs, 114 In. 3740.00
Sofa, E. Wormley, Tete-A-Tete, Wool, 80 x 27 1/2 In. 7765.00
Sofa, E. Wormley, Wool, 4 Down Cushions, 92 x 28 In. 1840.00
Sofa, Eames, Slab Seat & Back, Upholstered, Aluminum Frame, 73 In. 3740.00
Sofa, Eames, Upholstered, Chrome Steel Legs, 72 x 35 In. . . . . .1495.00 to 2645.00
Sofa, Egyptian Revival, Walnut, Gilt, Bronze, Fluted Trumpet Legs, 33 x 27 1/2 In. 1380.00
Sofa, Empire, Mahogany, Gilt, Bronze, 4 Pedestal Feet, 64 In. 1725.00
Sofa, Empire, Mahogany, Scalloped Back, Rolled Arms, Paw Feet, c.1840, 60 In. 275.00
Sofa, Empire, Mahogany, Scrolled Arms, Paw Feet, 19th Century, 36 In. 660.00
Sofa, Federal, Mahogany, Turned, Reeded Arm Supports, Legs, 1800, 36 1/2 In. 3450.00
Sofa, Federal, Mahogany, Upholstered, Rolled Arms, c.1820, 33 1/2 x 61 3/4 In. 385.00
Sofa, Florence Knoll, Suede, Chrome Base, 31 3/4 In. 2250.00
Sofa, Florence Knoll, Upholstered, Walnut Frame, Signed, 31 In. . . . . .1000.00 to 2415.00
Sofa, Frank Lloyd Wright, Taliesin Design, Upholstered, Henredon, 30 1/2 In. 1265.00
Sofa, G. Nelson, Slab Seat & Back, Black Wool Fabric On Tubular Steel Legs, 48 In. 990.00
Sofa, George III, Camelback, Mahogany, Outscrolled Arms, Upholstered Seat, 82 In. 3450.00
Sofa, Georgian, Mahogany, Silk, Foliate Cabriole Legs, 82 In. 3335.00
Sofa, Hepplewhite, Mahogany, Arched Back, Serpentine Arms, c.1800, 70 In. 550.00
Sofa, Hepplewhite, Mahogany, c.1810, 78 1/2 In. 1210.00
Sofa, Jacobean, Walnut, Flame Stitched, Scalloped Back, 76 In. 825.00
Sofa, Le Corbusier, 3 Seats, Chrome Tubular Frame, Black Leather Cushions, 70 In. 3740.00
Sofa, Le Corbusier, Leather, Tubular Steel Frame, 27 x 51 In. 1840.00
Sofa, Leather, Padded Triple Chairback, Scroll Arms, 31 1/2 x 66 x 31 In. 4140.00
Sofa, Louis XIII, Walnut, Shaped Back, Scroll Sides, France, 1630, 72 In. 9780.00
Sofa, Louis XV, Medallion Back, Deeply Carved Crest, 57 x 39 In. 950.00
Sofa, Louis XV, Wooden Rail Extends From Arms, Shell Crest, Mid 1800s, 41 x 78 In. . . . 900.00
Sofa, Louis XVI, Beech, Padded Back, Elbow Rests, Bowfront, 47 In. 865.00
Sofa, Louis XVI, White Paint, Rope, Velvet, 32 In. 865.00
Sofa, Mahogany, Arched Back, Out-Scrolled Armrests, Scroll Toes, 82 In. 400.00
Sofa, Mahogany, Damask, Brass Paw Feet, 33 x 90 In. 3025.00
Sofa, Mahogany, Downcurved Arms, Tapered & Reeded Legs, 78 3/4 In. 2070.00
Sofa, Mahogany, Egg & Dart Crest Rail, Greek Key Stiles, Upholstered Arms, 92 In. 1380.00
Sofa, Mahogany, Federal, Arched Back, Rolled Arms, c.1800, 76 In. 3850.00
Sofa, Mahogany, Flame-Grained Crest Rail, Inlaid Brass Bands At Base, 89 In. 1870.00
Sofa, Mahogany, Outlined Panel Crest, Scrolled Arms, Brass Paw Feet, 34 x 87 In. 3450.00
Sofa, Mahogany, Padded Back & Arms, Lion Paw Feet, 84 1/2 In. 1035.00
Sofa, Mahogany, Padded Back, Scrolled & Reeded Armrests, Loose Cushion, 73 In. 3225.00
Sofa, Mahogany, Padded Back, Scrolled Crest Rail, Scrolled Arms, 93 In. 800.00

Sofa, Mahogany, Padded Scrolled Back & Arms, Lion Paw Feet, 61 1/2 In. 690.00
Sofa, Mahogany, Scroll Arms, Serpentine Seat Rail, 33 x 85 x 31 In. 3220.00
Sofa, Mahogany, Serpentine Padded Back, Scroll Arms, 3 Cushions, 84 In. 5750.00
Sofa, Mahogany, Tablet Back, Fruit Basket, Scroll Arms, Paw Feet, 87 1/2 In. 3910.00
Sofa, McCobb, Walnut Legs, Upholstered, Calvin, 32 In., Pair 1150.00
Sofa, Meridienne, Rosewood, Belter, Floral Laminated Back, 1850, 38 In. 5040.00
Sofa, Napoleon III, Beech, Floral Aubusson Tapestry, 41 x 26 1/2 In. 2530.00
Sofa, Neoclassical, Ebonized Fruitwood, Lyre Back, Curved Arms, 31 x 65 1/2 x 22 In. . . 2530.00
Sofa, Original Upholstery, Signed, Gufram Multipli, 86 x 31 x 33 In. 4600.00
Sofa, Palisander, Contoured Vertical Back Slats, Open Arms, 1969, 71 In. 2910.00
Sofa, Piero Fornasetti, Upholstered, Bamboo Frame, 32 In. 4025.00
Sofa, Regency, Mahogany, Cushioned Seat, Reeded Frame, Bun Feet, 36 In. 2300.00
Sofa, Renaissance Revival, Burl Walnut, Allen Bros., Phila., 1870, 75 x 48 In. 2800.00
Sofa, Rococo Revival, Gilt Rosewood, Serpentine, Carved Floral, 43 x 73 In. 715.00
Sofa, Rococo Revival, Laminated Rosewood, Grape Leaves, 69 In. . . . . *Illus* 4140.00
Sofa, Rococo Revival, Rosewood, Asymmetrical Carved Crest, 50 x 80 x 35 In. 2530.00
Sofa, Rococo, Gilt, Carved, Pierced, Foliage, Pierced Apron, 77 In. 3680.00
Sofa, Rococo, Rosewood, Floral Carving Gadroon Trim, Stanton Hall, 50 1/2 In. 5290.00
Sofa, Rococo, Walnut, Molded Rail, 3 Cushions, Italy, 1780s, 46 1/2 x 80 x 32 In. 5520.00
Sofa, Rosewood Frame, Black Leather Cushion, Tobia Scarpa, Knoll, 83 x 28 In. 1400.00
Sofa, Rosewood Veneer, Floral, Burgundy, Blue, Upholstered, 66 x 36 In. 880.00
Sofa, Rosewood, Asymmetrical Crest, Interlocking C & S Scrolls, 50 x 80 In. 2530.00
Sofa, Rosewood, Carved Floral Sprays, Swags & Foliage, c.1850, 43 x 81 In. 3450.00
Sofa, Rosewood, Triple Back, Open Carved Crest, 1870, 75 x 33 x 42 In. 1345.00
Sofa, Rosewood, Veneers, Arched Back, Balloon Ends, Carved, c.1860, 40 x 80 In. 615.00
Sofa, Sheraton, Mahogany, 8 Legs, Reeded Arms, Lunette Inlay Panels, Mass., 1800s 3450.00
Sofa, Upholstered, Alexander Girard, 25 1/2 x 72 In. 5465.00
Sofa, V. Kagan, Chevron Shape, Wool, Lucite Leg, 27 x 38 In. 280.00
Sofa, V. Kagan, Platform, Wool, 2 Tiers, Tufted Seat, 37 In. 845.00
Sofa, Victorian, Walnut, Leaf Design, Raised On Outswept Feet, 85 In. 575.00
Sofa, Walnut, Arched Back, Brass Studs, Scrolled Rams, Upholstered Seat, 73 1/2 In. 1380.00
Sofa, Walnut, C-Scroll Panels, Silk Damask, Scrolling Legs, France, 1800s, 79 In. 2650.00
Sofa, Walnut, Leather, Turned Legs On Casters, 70 In. 2185.00
Sofa, Walnut, Medallion Back, Silk, Trumpet Legs, France, 66 x 49 In. 1650.00
Sofa, Walnut, Serpentine Front, Camel Back, Ivory, Mauve, Blue, 37 x 22 x 19 In. 450.00
Sofa, Wave, Upholstered, Foam Rubber, Pierre Paulin, 63 x 23 In. 2875.00
Sofa, Wegner, 3 Horizontal Back Slats, Upholstered Arms, Loose Seat, 1955, 81 In. 1680.00
Sofa, Wegner, Oak, Open Arms, Loose Seat, Upholstered, 1955, 26 In. 225.00
Sofa, Wegner, Teak, Jointed By Steel Rods, Seat & Arm Cushions, c.1955, 82 In. 575.00
Sofa, William IV, Mahogany, Leather, 36 x 79 x 31 In. 4370.00
Sofa, William IV, Rosewood, Leafy Cornucopia, Reeded Feet, 36 In. 2530.00
Stand, Alpine, Carved Wood Top, Cherub Supporting Top, 1880, 31 1/2 In. 1035.00
Stand, Applied & Raised Molding, Ring-Turned Post, Block Feet, 26 x 9 7/8 In. 315.00
Stand, Art Deco, Ebene De Macassar, Inset Marble Top, Drawer, 22 x 19 x 12 In. 4715.00
Stand, Arts & Crafts, Marble Top, Drawer, Paneled Door, 30 x 16 x 15 In. 460.00
Stand, Birch, Maple, 1 Drawer In Case, Button Feet, c.1760, 24 In. 715.00
Stand, Chamfered Support, Green Paint, Square Top, 30 1/2 x 18 In. 1150.00
Stand, Cherry, Curly Maple, Paneled Ends, 2 Drawers, Curly Pulls, 20 1/2 In. 605.00
Stand, Cherry, Drop Leaf, 2 Burl Front Drawers, Turned Legs, 29 x 36 In. 415.00
Stand, Cherry, Mahogany Veneer, Drop Leaf, 2 Drawers, c.1820, 21 x 28 7/8 In. 1550.00
Stand, Cherry, Tray Top, 1 Drawer, Square Tapered Legs, c.1800, 29 x 19 1/2 In. 2310.00
Stand, Chippendale, Mahogany, Circular Scalloped Edge, Cabriole Legs, 16 x 22 In. 160.00
Stand, Chippendale, Mahogany, Walnut, Drawers, 26 x 18 x 14 In. 259.00
Stand, Circular Rouge Marble Top, Leaf, Foliage Design, 19th Century, 31 1/2 x 21 In. . . 635.00
Stand, Classical, Mahogany, Veneer, Basin, Cyma Curved Splash Board, 51 x 20 1/2 In. . . 1150.00
Stand, Cloverleaf Top, Carved Beveled Edge, Scrolled Legs, 20 x 28 3/4 In. 290.00
Stand, Corner, Clip, Pedestal, 35 x 13 x 13 In. 460.00
Stand, Corner, Legs Made Of Industrial Spools, 4 Shelves, Alligatored, 43 1/2 In. 325.00
Stand, Curly Maple, 2 Drawers, Cherry Drawer Fronts, Turned Pulls, 28 1/2 In. 1210.00
Stand, Curly Maple, Thistle Design, 1 Drawer, Pegged Construction, 28 x 17 In. 4290.00
Stand, Dessert, Satinwood, Brass, 3 Tiers, Continental, 33 x 16 1/2 x 13 In., Pair 2530.00
Stand, Dictionary, Double, Cast Iron 750.00
Stand, Drink, G. Stickley, Circular Overhanging Top, 25 1/2 x 20 In. 1910.00

Stand, Drink, L. & J.G. Stickley, Mahogany, Circular Top, 29 1/4 x 18 In. 1150.00
Stand, Elm, Rectangular Top, 13 x 31 3/4 In., Pair 520.00
Stand, Federal, Birch, Butternut, Drawer, Turned Legs, 1800s, 28 x 18 1/2 x 16 1/2 In. ... 920.00
Stand, Federal, Cherry, Square Top, Drawer, Turned Legs, Pa., c.1820, 30 1/4 x 22 In. ... 440.00
Stand, Federal, Cherry, Tiger Maple, 1 Convex Dovetailed Drawer, 28 1/2 In. 715.00
Stand, Federal, Mahogany, 2 Drawers, Turned Legs, c.1820, 28 3/4 x 20 1/2 In. 440.00
Stand, Federal, Mahogany, Drop Leaf, Scrolled Legs, 22 1/2 x 18 x 27 In. 175.00
Stand, Federal, Walnut, Drawer, Turned Legs, Pa., 20 x 19 In. 385.00
Stand, Federal, Walnut, Square Top, Straight Frame, Pa., c.1810, 29 1/4 x 19 3/4 In. 385.00
Stand, Federal, Wavy Birch, Overhang, Drawer, Tapered Legs, 28 x 22 x 17 1/2 In. 1610.00
Stand, Fern, Mahogany, Marble Top, 35 x 12 In. 30.00
Stand, Fern, Square Marble Top, Brass Filigree Border, 1900, 1 1/2 x 30 In. 625.00
Stand, Fern, Teak, Foo Dog Head Knees, Soapstone, Refinished, Chinese, 25 In. 410.00
Stand, Fern, Walnut, Tripod, Pedestal, Marble Insert, Brass Swags, Victorian, 36 In. 1045.00
Stand, Fern, Wirework, 2 Tiers, Outcurved Galleries, 81 3/4 x 41 1/4 In. 575.00
Stand, French Provincial, Walnut, Pierced, Shaped Gallery, c.1770, 30 1/2 x 18 In. 415.00
Stand, G. Stickley, Tree Of Life, Mahogany, 43 x 12 1/2 In. 2130.00
Stand, George I, Black Paint, Foliate, Claw, Ball Feet, 39 1/2 x 87 In. 370.00
Stand, George III Style, Mahogany, Round, Tripod, Mid 19th Century, 34 x 11 1/2 In. 980.00
Stand, Georgian Style, Mahogany, Spider Gateleg, Drop Leaf, 9 1/2 x 30 x 27 1/2 In. 375.00
Stand, Grain Decorated, Flush Drawer, Tapered Legs, Reverse Tulip Feet, 29 1/2 In. 6400.00
Stand, Hepplewhite, Cherry, Drawer, Old Finish, 28 x 17 1/2 x 17 1/2 In. 690.00
Stand, Hepplewhite, Cherry, Pegged, Drawer, 1-Board Top, 18 3/4 x 24 1/4 In. 715.00
Stand, Hepplewhite, Demilune, Mahogany Flame Veneer, 1 Drawer, Door, 20 In. 83.00
Stand, Hepplewhite, Mahogany, 2 Drawers, Square Tapered Legs, c.1800, 28 1/2 In. 660.00
Stand, Hepplewhite, Mahogany, Corner Basin, c.1790, 40 In. 660.00
Stand, Hepplewhite, Pine, Cherry, 1 Drawer, Square Tapered Legs, c.1810, 29 x 20 In. ... 385.00
Stand, Hepplewhite, Pine, Green Paint, Rectangle Top, Square Legs, Pa., 31 x 18 In. 440.00
Stand, Hepplewhite, Poplar, 1 Dovetailed Drawer, 21 x 19 x 25 5/8 In. 165.00
Stand, Heywood-Wakefield, Sculptured, Drawer, Wheat Finish, Mark, 23 x 20 In. 230.00
Stand, Lamp, Hexagon Top, Splay Base, Adirondack, 32 x 19 x 10 1/4 In. 1100.00
Stand, Lantern, Pierced Bracket Supports, 4-Part Base, 59 In., Pair 635.00
Stand, Lift Top, Flower, Swag, String Inlay, England, 19th Century, 18 x 14 3/4 x 31 In. . 2070.00
Stand, Louis XV Style, Fruitwood, Pierced Brass Gallery, 28 1/2 x 20 x 14 In., Pair 2185.00
Stand, Louis XV Style, Kingwood, Tulipwood, Marble, 30 x 11 x 13 In. 345.00
Stand, Louis XV, Kingwood, Pink Marble Top, 32 x 16 x 10 In., Pair 2875.00
Stand, Louis XVI Style, Mahogany, Ormolu Mount, Marble Top, 30 1/2 x 17 x 13 In. ... 1725.00
Stand, Louis XVI, Mahogany, Gallery, Lacquered, France, 1890, 30 x 18 x 12 In. 1870.00
Stand, Magazine, Art Deco, Spring Leaf Design, 12 x 5 x 17 In. 805.00
Stand, Magazine, Arts & Crafts, 3 Tiered Sections, Handles, 34 x 15 1/2 x 11 In. 300.00
Stand, Magazine, Arts & Crafts, 4 Shelves, 3 Slats Each Side, Arched Toe Board, 40 In. .. 1150.00
Stand, Magazine, Arts & Crafts, 5 Shelves, Original Finish, 20 x 14 x 45 In. 520.00
Stand, Magazine, Arts & Crafts, Mahogany, 4 Shelves, 1 Vertical Slat, 18 x 38 In. 345.00
Stand, Magazine, Arts & Crafts, Oak, 4 Open Shelves, 22 x 14 x 50 In. 195.00
Stand, Magazine, Arts & Crafts, Oak, Open Shelves, Lifetime Furn. Co., 16 In. 825.00
Stand, Magazine, Bamboo, Diagonal Supports, Flared Legs, 23 1/4 In. 220.00
Stand, Magazine, E. Wormley, Walnut, 3 Shelves, 31 In. 3335.00
Stand, Magazine, G. Stickley, Mahogany, 3 Shelves, Dark Brown, 41 In. 3335.00
Stand, Magazine, G. Stickley, Mahogany, 3 Shelves, Original Finish, 38 In. 2590.00
Stand, Magazine, G. Stickley, Mahogany, Beveled Top, 34 3/4 x 15 1/2 In. 3740.00
Stand, Magazine, G. Stickley, Tree Of Life, Corbels, Leather, 43 x 13 x 13 In. 1095.00
Stand, Magazine, L. & J.G. Stickley, 3 Side Slats, 4 Open Shelves, c.1916, 41 1/2 In. 575.00
Stand, Magazine, L. & J.G. Stickley, Mahogany, 4 Shelves, Onondaga Shops, 45 In. 2700.00
Stand, Magazine, L. & J.G. Stickley, Mahogany, 4 Shelves, Tapered Sides, 42 In. 1495.00
Stand, Magazine, L. & J.G. Stickley, Mahogany, Overhanging Top, 3 Shelves, 44 In. 1955.00
Stand, Magazine, L. & J.G. Stickley, No. 47, 4 Shelves, 45 x 21 In. 1725.00
Stand, Magazine, Limbert, Mahogany, Cutout Sides, 4 Shelves, 42 x 20 x 15 In. 1240.00
Stand, Magazine, Mahogany, 3 Shelves, 3 Spindles, 31 x 26 1/2 x 12 In. 1240.00
Stand, Magazine, Mahogany, Michigan Chair Co., 45 x 14 x 13 In. 635.00
Stand, Magazine, Morris & Butler, Original Dark Mahogany Finish, 45 x 12 In. 1265.00
Stand, Magazine, Stickley & Brandt Co., Tapered Sides, 4 Shelves, Decal, 41 3/4 In. 1840.00
Stand, Magazine, Stickley Bros., Mahogany, Gallery Top, 31 1/2 x 16 x 13 In. 1350.00
Stand, Magazine, Stickley Bros., Mahogany, Signed, 30 x 28 x 12 In. 1495.00

Stand, Magazine, Stickley Bros., No. 4702, 3 Shelves, 3 Spindles Each Side, 31 In. 865.00
Stand, Mahogany Veneer, Line Inlay, Brass Gallery, 30 x 16 x 29 In. 525.00
Stand, Mahogany, 2 Doors Over Drawer, England, Early 1800s, 22 x 18 x 31 In. 1035.00
Stand, Mahogany, Alligatored Finish, Tooled Brass Knobs, 2 Drawers, 29 In. 635.00
Stand, Mahogany, Concave Cupboard Door, 2 Drawers, Spade Feet, 32 In. 3450.00
Stand, Mahogany, Oval Marble Top, Pierced Frieze, 4 Carved Legs, 22 x 25 In. 805.00
Stand, Mahogany, Square Top, 14 x 14 x 27 In. 1840.00
Stand, Maple, Birch, 1 Drawer, Square Tapered Legs, c.1810, 27 1/2 x 21 1/2 In. 495.00
Stand, Maple, Drop Leaf, Dovetailed Drawers, Glass Pulls, 20 3/4 x 18 1/4 In. 605.00
Stand, Marble Top, France, 26 1/2 x 15 x 22 1/2 In., Pair 840.00
Stand, Music, Aesthetic Revival, Carved, 19th Century, 39 In. . . . . *Illus*   2700.00
Stand, Music, Arts & Crafts, Mahogany, 4 Shelves, 20 x 14 x 39 In. 1150.00
Stand, Music, Beech, Vase-Form Support, 3 Scrolled Legs, 51 In. 460.00
Stand, Music, Bronze, Figural, Patinated, Laurel Wreath, Putti, Fluted Column, 57 In. . . .   980.00
Stand, Music, Candle Sconces, c.1820 . . . .   3200.00
Stand, Music, Mahogany, 2 Sides, Lyre Design, Adjustable, c.1900, 26 x 14 x 54 In. 748.00
Stand, Music, Regency, Brass Upper Section, Downswept Legs, 1810, 48 In. 8400.00
Stand, Music, Table Top, Brass, Bracket Footed, Adjustable, 11 1/2 x 10 1/2 x 9 In. 165.00
Stand, Music, Wrought Iron, Gilt, Lyre Form, Candle Cups, 45 In. 575.00
Stand, Oak, Scalloped Front Apron, Enameled Knob, Wire Nails, Amish, 27 1/2 In. 935.00
Stand, Oak, Yellow Pine, Beaded, X-Stretchers, Splayed Legs, c.1780, 29 1/2 x 17 1/2 In.   935.00
Stand, Phone, Cushman, Attached Stool, 31 x 18 x 14 In. 375.00
Stand, Phone, Limbert, Mahogany, 30 x 18 x 15 In. 750.00
Stand, Phone, Mahogany Finish, 31 x 18 x 14 In. 460.00
Stand, Pine, Maple, 1 Drawer, Painted, Splayed Tapered Legs, c.1820, 29 x 18 x 20 In. . .   690.00
Stand, Pine, Milliner's, Dashing Gentleman With Mustache, Pa., 1880, 20 In. 7700.00
Stand, Plant, 3 Tiers, Quarter Round, Mustard Over Green Paint, 26 x 32 1/2 x 22 In. 345.00
Stand, Plant, Arts & Crafts, Oak, Diamond Cutout Designs, Shelf, 29 x 14 x 14 In. 405.00
Stand, Plant, Arts & Crafts, Pyrography, Pyramid Base, 35 In. 330.00
Stand, Plant, Burl, Column Standard, Victorian, 31 1/2 x 22 x 11 In. 2185.00
Stand, Plant, Carved Spindles, White Paint, Tripod Scrolled Base, Round, 25 1/2 In. 690.00
Stand, Plant, Carved Wood, Rouge Marble Top, Chinese, 19th Century, 36 In. . . . .145.00 to 230.00
Stand, Plant, Charles Rohlfs, 4 Carved Legs, Reticulated Shelf, 1901, 32 In. . . . .*Illus* 22400.00
Stand, Plant, G. Stickley, No. 41, Mahogany, 27 1/2 x 14 In. 1555.00
Stand, Plant, G. Stickley, No. 660, Mahogany, 4 Splayed Legs, 20 In. . . . . .1095.00 to 2990.00
Stand, Plant, Gilt Metal, Marble Top, Early 20th Century, 13 x 32 In. 105.00
Stand, Plant, Hepplewhite, Mahogany, 2 Tiers, Mid 20th Century, 38 1/2 x 11 1/2 In. 200.00
Stand, Plant, L. & J.G. Stickley, Handcraft Decal, 28 In. 1925.00
Stand, Plant, Limbert, Mahogany, Square Plant, Original Finish, 18 x 16 In. 4600.00
Stand, Plant, Louis XVI, Marble Top, Gilt Metal Mounts, 12 x 33 In. 345.00
Stand, Plant, Mahogany, Cane, Tin Insert, 20th Century, 34 x 23 3/4 In. 525.00
Stand, Plant, Mahogany, Carved, Marble Top Insert, Chinese, 19th Century, 24 x 10 In. . .   2480.00
Stand, Plant, Mahogany, Marble Top, Square, 32 x 13 In. 80.00

Furniture, Stand, Music,
Aesthetic Revival, Carved,
19th Century, 39 In.

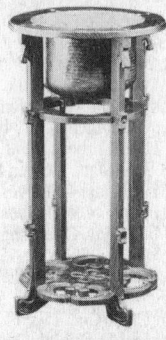

Furniture, Stand, Plant, Charles
Rohlfs, 4 Carved Legs,
Reticulated Shelf, 1901, 32 In.

Furniture, Stand,
Wicker, Lower
Shelf, 1875

Stand, Plant, Rouge Marble Top, Wood, 19th Century, 36 In. 230.00
Stand, Plant, Secessionist, Bronze, Square Raised Base, Shelf, Germany, 32 x 14 In. 635.00
Stand, Plant, Teak, Marble Top, 5 Footed, 1880, 31 In. 728.00
Stand, Plant, Teak, Worn Red Pierced Aprons, Soapstone, Oriental, 12 x 13 In. 220.00
Stand, Plant, Turned, Round Shelves, 2 Tiers, 54 In. 1665.00
Stand, Plant, Victorian, Green Paint, Scrolled Feet, 18 1/2 x 31 3/4 In. 250.00
Stand, Plant, Victorian, Walnut, Carved, Pierced Foliate Sides, 34 x 22 1/2 x 15 In. 865.00
Stand, Plant, Wire, 2 Stepped Rounded Tiers, Black Paint, 32 1/2 x 35 x 16 In. 545.00
Stand, Plant, Wire, Small Circular Tier, 6 Supports, 48 1/2 x 57 x 24 1/2 In. 575.00
Stand, Plant, Wood, Rouge Marble Top, 19th Century, 36 In. 145.00
Stand, Plant, Wrought Iron, Elephant On Base, Rectangular, 30 1/2 x 40 In. 1150.00
Stand, Poplar, 1 Drawer, Square Tapered Splayed Legs, Painted, c.1810, 27 1/4 In. 825.00
Stand, Poplar, 2 Drawers, Turned Legs, Pa., c.1830, 29 1/2 x 21 In. 220.00
Stand, Reception Card, Putto, Carved Wood, Painted, England, 19th Century, 28 In. ... 2950.00
Stand, Regency, Calling Card, Bronze, Rectangular Plinth With Leaves, 8 3/4 In. 489.00
Stand, Renaissance Revival, Walnut, Marble, Burl Panels, Drawer, 29 x 19 x 15 In. 1035.00
Stand, Rococo Revival, Mahogany, Marble Top, 30 x 18 x 17 In. 920.00
Stand, Rococo, Rosewood, Serpentine Face, White Marble Top, 31 x 17 In. 3000.00
Stand, Rosewood, 3 Tiers, Pineapple Finials, Early 19th Century, 51 x 21 In. 1380.00
Stand, Rosewood, Beaded Marble Top, Stylized Cabriole Legs, 18 x 17 In. 200.00
Stand, Rosewood, Circular Marble Top, Pink Insert, Cabriole Legs, 15 1/4 In. 290.00
Stand, Rosewood, Circular Marble Top, Pink Marble Insert, Cabriole Legs, 22 In. 260.00
Stand, Rosewood, Flush Paneled Top, Chinese, 36 x 14 In. 220.00
Stand, Rosewood, Marble Top, 19th Century, 19 x 16 1/2 In. 360.00
Stand, Shaker, Cherry, 1 Drawer, Rectangular Top, 26 3/4 x 18 x 20 1/4 In. 2300.00
Stand, Shaker, Cherry, Red, Brown, Circular Top, Cabriole Legs, 30 x 17 In. 2875.00
Stand, Shaker, Spool, Velvet Pincushion, Poplar Needle Case, Circular Turned Base, 6 In. 345.00
Stand, Shaving, Aesthetic Revival, Mahogany, Mirror, Drawer, Shelf, 62 x 18 x 13 In. ... 575.00
Stand, Shaving, Mahogany, 1 Drawer, Bun Feet, 48 x 19 x 13 In. 750.00
Stand, Shaving, Renaissance Revival, Walnut, Marble Top, 1875, 68 x 16 In. 2185.00
Stand, Shaving, Walnut, Upright Mirror, Swing-Out Top, Tripod, 59 In. 605.00
Stand, Sheraton, Birch, Drawer, Turned Legs, 29 x 22 x 20 In. 430.00
Stand, Sheraton, Bird's-Eye Maple, 2 Drawers, 28 1/2 x 17 x 15 1/4 In. 1725.00
Stand, Sheraton, Cherry, 2 Drawers, Turned Legs, Glass Pulls, 2-Board Top, 20 x 20 In. .. 605.00
Stand, Sheraton, Cherry, Drawer, Wooden Pull, Turned Legs, 19 1/2 x 20 x 28 In. 470.00
Stand, Sheraton, Mahogany, Drop Leaf, 1 Drawer, Turned Legs, 29 x 18 In. 470.00
Stand, Sheraton, Mahogany, Drop Leaf, Rope-Twist Legs, 2 Drawers, 16 x 17 x 29 In. ... 880.00
Stand, Sheraton, Maple, Birch, 1 Drawer, Signed, R.A. Shaw, 19th Century, 27 1/2 In. 385.00
Stand, Sheraton, Pine, Drawer, Shaped Top, England, c.1800, 24 1/2 x 17 3/4 In. 275.00
Stand, Sheraton, Pine, Maple, 1 Drawer, Brass Knobs, 29 1/2 x 18 1/2 In. 560.00
Stand, Sheraton, Poplar, Drawer, Pennsylvania, c.1820, 29 1/4 x 24 In. 110.00
Stand, Sheraton, Tiger Maple, 3 Graduated Drawers, Turned Legs, 28 1/4 In. 3300.00
Stand, Sheraton, Tiger Maple, Drawer, Pennsylvania, c.1830, 29 3/4 x 22 In. 770.00
Stand, Sheraton, Walnut, 2 Drawers, Octagonal Legs, Ball Feet, c.1820, 29 1/2 x 20 In. .. 550.00
Stand, Sheraton, Walnut, 2 Drawers, Pennsylvania, c.1830, 28 1/2 x 18 In. 330.00
Stand, Sheraton, Walnut, Drawer, 2 Leaves, Turned Square Legs, 29 x 24 x 15 In. 315.00
Stand, Sheraton, Walnut, Rounded Corners, Splayed Turned Legs, c.1810, 27 3/4 x 18 In. 660.00
Stand, Smoking, Art Deco, Black Enameled Metal, Chrome, Ash Holder, 21 1/2 In. 335.00
Stand, Smoking, Art Deco, Pipe, Brass Plate, Green, 27 In. 56.00
Stand, Smoking, Arts & Crafts, Humidor Below Shelf, 27 x 13 x 9 In. 115.00
Stand, Smoking, Arts & Crafts, Wrought Iron Tripod, Scroll, Copper Top, 33 In. 275.00
Stand, Smoking, Drink Holder, Black Glass Base, Aluminum, Zinc Handle, 1930 .... 375.00
Stand, Smoking, Lighter, Lights Up Top To Bottom, Chrome Tray, Akro Agate 490.00
Stand, Smoking, Louis XVI, Mahogany, Beige Marble Top, Fluted Legs, 33 In. 290.00
Stand, Smoking, McArthur, Lacquered Metal & Chrome, Steel Ashtray, 1920s, 23 In. 1455.00
Stand, Smoking, Roycroft, Copper, Hammered, Mahogany, Base, 29 x 10 In. 506.00
Stand, Smoking, Roycroft, Pine Needle, 4 Strap Shaft, Ashtray Insert, 29 In. 2415.00
Stand, Softwood, Red, Black Paint, Turned Legs, 28 x 21 In. 330.00
Stand, Stickley Bros., Mahogany, Cutouts, Signed, 26 x 19 1/2 In. 1495.00
Stand, Stickley Bros., Mahogany, Signed, 28 x 18 In. 3135.00
Stand, Teak, Cabriole Legs, Floral Apron, Quatrefoil Top, Soapstone Insert, 16 1/2 In. ... 410.00
Stand, Tiger Maple, 1 Drawer, Tiger Striping, Rebuilt Interior, 1860 .... 715.00
Stand, Tiger Maple, Square Top, Turned Legs, Pennsylvania, c.1810, 29 1/2 x 18 In. 550.00

Stand, Tooled Leather Top, Raised On Circular Base, 13 x 28 In. 345.00
Stand, Walnut, Carved Griffins, Dish Top, Victorian, 25 1/2 x 17 In., Pair 865.00
Stand, Walnut, Eastlake, Slate Top, Incised Gameboard, Central Carved Support 1980.00
Stand, Walnut, White Marble Top, 4 Scrolled Legs, Casters, 25 x 19 x 31 In. 230.00
Stand, Weaver's, T-Base, Red Paint 920.00
Stand, Wicker, Lower Shelf, 1875 . . . .*Illus* 784.00
Stand, Wood, Rouge Marble Top, 19th Century, 19 1/2 x 16 In. 175.00
Stand, Writing, Onyx, Gilt Metal, Figural, Dog Watching Bee, Early 1900s, 8 x 6 x 5 In. . 200.00
Stool, Alexander Girard, Red, Orange Fabric, Aluminum Legs, Herman Miller, 18 In. . . . 2140.00
Stool, Arts & Crafts, Circular Top, 4 Splayed Legs, 15 x 21 In. 35.00
Stool, Arts & Crafts, Mahogany, 2 Notched Slats, Upholstered Top, 16 x 18 In. 195.00
Stool, Arts & Crafts, Slatted Seat, Turned Legs, 13 x 16 In. 520.00
Stool, Bar, MacArthur, Tubular Aluminum Frame, Red Vinyl Seat, 30 In., 3 Piece 6325.00
Stool, Bar, Vinyl, Tubular Aluminum, 30 x 14 In., 3 Piece 6325.00
Stool, Beech, Upholstered Top, Concave Sides, Loose Cushion, Fluted Legs, 1780s 3600.00
Stool, Black Lacquer, Cloisonne Top, Cabriole Legs 235.00
Stool, Burl Elm, Round, Beaded Edge, Chinese, 19th Century 201.00
Stool, Chippendale, Mahogany, Slip Seat, Upholstered, H-Stretcher, 18 x 21 x 15 In. 805.00
Stool, Chippendale, Slip Seat, Molded Square Legs, 17 x 20 1/2 In. 885.00
Stool, Classical, Mahogany, Curule Base, Upholstered, 18 1/2 x 21 1/2 x 14 In. 980.00
Stool, Curved & Slatted Seat, Turned Legs, Liberty Thebes, 15 x 17 In. 1100.00
Stool, Cushion, Antique Silk Velvet, Leopard Skin, Gilt, 14 1/2 In. 3680.00
Stool, Eames, Mahogany, Bentwood, P. Evans, Child's, 8 1/2 x 14 x 11 In. 2250.00
Stool, Eames, Turned Wood, Herman Miller, c.1960, 15 x 13 In. 1610.00
Stool, Eames, Walnut, Turned, Concave Seat, Herman Miller, 15 x 13 In. . . . . .675.00 to 950.00
Stool, Egyptian Revival, Ebonized Wood, Upholstered Rectangular Seat, 1900 . . . . 9000.00
Stool, Egyptian Revival, Inlaid Wood, French Bone, Early 20th Century 2160.00
Stool, Empire, Mahogany, Octagonal Seat, 1830, 18 x 21 1/2 In. 1560.00
Stool, Empire, Mahogany, Overstuffed Top, Flowers On Black Ground, c.1825 . . . . 160.00
Stool, Empire, Rosewood, Serpentine Sides, Ogee Bracket Feet, 1830, 18 In. 1440.00
Stool, Frank Lloyd Wright, Swivel Top, Cruciform Base, 16 x 25 In. 1760.00
Stool, Fruitwood, Turned Legs, Child's, 18th Century, 12 In. 300.00
Stool, G. Nakashima, Walnut, Burl Top, 3 Dowel Legs, 22 In. 545.00
Stool, George I, Mahogany, Padded Cushion, Cabriole Legs, Padded Feet, 18 In. 575.00
Stool, George II, Mahogany, Claw & Ball Feet, Upholstered, 1800s, 19 In. 635.00
Stool, George III Style, Mahogany, Rectangular, Shell-Carved Knees, Upholstered 315.00
Stool, George III Style, Mahogany, Shell Carving, Cabriole Legs, 17 x 21 1/2 x 18 In. . . . 1150.00
Stool, George III, Mahogany, Oval, Padded, Cabriole Legs, 18 x 23 x 21 In. 1380.00
Stool, George III, Mahogany, Plain Oblong Hinged Top, Tapered Legs, 1790, 18 In. 840.00
Stool, George III, Mahogany, Rectangular Saddle Seat, Late 1700s, 17 x 14 1/2 x 20 In. . . 635.00
Stool, Georgian Style, Upholstered, 24 x 16 x 16 In. 80.00
Stool, Gilt, Upholstered Top, Flower Heads, Foliage Rails, 1780s, 16 1/2 In., Pair 9000.00
Stool, Gilt, Upholstered Top, Leaf Carved Legs, 15 1/4 x 11 In. 6600.00
Stool, Gout, G. Stickley, Original Dark Leather Cover, 4 1/2 x 12 In. 1125.00
Stool, Gout, Mahogany, Leather, Mechanical, 1800s, 21 x 18 In. 345.00
Stool, I. Noguchi, Rocking, Walnut, Chrome Steel Legs, Knoll, 16 1/2 In. 7200.00
Stool, I. Noguchi, Walnut Seat, Base, Chrome Wire Support, Knoll, Child's, 11 In. 6750.00
Stool, Jacobean, Mahogany, Carved Panel Apron, 24 In., Pair 440.00
Stool, Jacobean, Urn-Turned Legs, Kittinger Label, 20 x 12 x 22 In. 385.00
Stool, Jens Risom, Birch Frame, Original Black Webbed Seat, Knoll, 15 x 17 In. 460.00
Stool, Limbert, No. 2001/2, Dark Mahogany, Leather Cover, 18 x 7 In. 633.00
Stool, Limbert, Tacked On Leather Seat, 18 x 20 x 15 In. 1460.00
Stool, Louis XIV Style, Beech, Gilt Gesso, 19 1/2 x 19 x 23 1/2 In. 2185.00
Stool, Louis XIV Style, Stained Beech, Stuffed Seat, 12 1/2 x 15 1/2 x 17 In. 750.00
Stool, Louis XV Style, Gilt, Padded, Shell, Leaf-Carved Frieze, 16 x 20 x 15 In. 2300.00
Stool, Louis XV, Walnut, Serpentine Outline, Cabriole Legs, 1900, 19 In. 980.00
Stool, Louis XVI Style, Beech, Needlework Cover, 20 x 18 x 22 In. 315.00
Stool, Louis XVI Style, Flower Relief Design, Upholstered, 15 1/2 x 18 1/2 In. 255.00
Stool, Louis XVI, Walnut, Oval Stuffed Seat, Fluted Legs, 7 x 11 1/4 In. 145.00
Stool, Mahogany, Scrolled Handles, Palmette Saber Legs, 1830s, 24 1/2 In., Pair 3240.00
Stool, Mahogany, Serpentine Seat Rail, Dolphin-Form Legs, c.1750, 17 x 24 In. 4950.00
Stool, Molded Padded Seat Rails, Turned Toes, Giltwood, c.1775, 17 1/2 In., Pair 9775.00
Stool, Neoclassical, Painted, Parcel Gilt, Stuffed Seat, 20 x 16 1/2 x 12 1/2 In. 1095.00

Stool, Oak, Carved Frame, Splayed Legs Joined By Stretchers, 21 1/4 x 16 3/4 In. 1045.00
Stool, Oak, Curule Form, 1925, 19 7/8 x 19 x 11 1/4 In. 7800.00
Stool, Oak, Splayed Base, Keyed Stretcher, 4 Carved Medallions, 13 x 20 In. 385.00
Stool, Orator's, New Guinea, 90 In. 1100.00
Stool, Painted, Black Ground, Rope Detail, Jaunty Sailor, Mermaid, c.1940, Pair 1840.00
Stool, Painted, Scalloped Skirt, Bootjack Legs, Yellow, Green, Red, c.1830, 7 1/2 x 12 In. 250.00
Stool, Parcel Gilt, Square Upholstered Top, Tapered Legs, 18th Century, 21 In. 6000.00
Stool, Piano, Adjustable, Claw & Ball Feet, Early 20th Century 60.00
Stool, Piano, Beech, Shell Seat 1495.00
Stool, Piano, Black Forest, Kneeling Bear Cub, 20 In. 1380.00
Stool, Piano, Carved, Claw & Ball Feet, c.1880 . . . . 385.00
Stool, Piano, Classical, Mahogany, Upholstered, Tapered Pedestal, Ball Feet, 20 In. 2100.00
Stool, Piano, French Provincial, Swivel, Round, Needlework Seat, 17 x 14 In. 315.00
Stool, Piano, Mahogany, Fluted, Beaded Standard, 3 Cabriole Legs, 20 x 13 In. 920.00
Stool, Piano, Mahogany, Revolving, Overstuffed Seat, Reeded Rails, England, c.1850 . . . 140.00
Stool, Pine, Curved Aprons, Cutout Ends, Square Nails, Child's, 7 1/2 x 13 1/4 In. 220.00
Stool, Pine, Poplar, Rectangular Top, Box Stretcher, 23 1/2 x 21 In. 1320.00
Stool, Pine, Walnut, Turned Legs, Pennsylvania, 19 x 14 In. 415.00
Stool, Queen Anne, Mahogany, Drop-In Tapestry Seat, Cabriole Legs, Pad Feet 259.00
Stool, Queen Anne, Walnut, Slip Seat, Conforming Skirt, Cabriole Legs, 20 x 17 In. 315.00
Stool, Regency, Carved, Gilt, Rectangular Black Suede Seat, 19 x 18 In. 8395.00
Stool, Rococo, Mahogany, Serpentine Apron, Bracket Feet, Mid 19th Century, 17 In. 430.00
Stool, Rococo, Rosewood, Serpentine Apron, Fluted Trumpet Legs, 16 x 16 1/2 In. 1092.00
Stool, Rohde, Z Chrome Frame, Red Vinyl Seat Cover, 24 In., 4 Piece 690.00
Stool, Rosewood, Cinquefoil Top, Pierced Friezes, Incurved Legs, Pair 1125.00
Stool, Sheraton, Mahogany, Revolving, Leather Seat, Turned Legs 410.00
Stool, Teak, Bicycle Seat, 3 Flared Legs, Mogens Lassen, 20 x 18 In. 1380.00
Stool, Thebes, Cherry, Square Concave Frame, Incised, 15 x 16 1/2 x 16 1/2 In. 405.00
Stool, Turned Legs, Round Seat, Turned Stretchers, England, 20 In. 35.00
Stool, Vanity, Walnut, Carved Acanthus Leaves, Upholstered, 18 1/2 x 24 In. 110.00
Stool, Victorian, Rosewood, Square Padded Top, Cabriole Legs, 16 In. 978.00
Stool, Victorian, Rosewood, Stuffed Seat, Cabochons, C-Scrolls, 18 x 21 x 22 1/2 In. 1095.00
Stool, Walnut, Moor Arch Design, France, 18 x 17 1/4 x 17 1/4 In. 1150.00
Stool, Walnut, Multicolored Floral Needlework Seat, 19th Century, 17 In. 6000.00
Stool, Walnut, Oval Stuffed Seat, Fluted Legs, 1890s, 7 x 11 1/4 In. 145.00
Stool, Walnut, Rectangular Surface, Fringed Tapestry, 14 1/2 In. 1725.00
Stool, Walnut, Rush Seat, Turned Legs, Continental, Early 20th Century 69.00
Stool, Watchmaker's, Oak, Iron 235.00
Stool, William & Mary, Beech, Upholstered, Pierced Stretchers, 1690, 19 In. 2600.00
Stool, Windsor, Bamboo-Turned Legs, Shaped Seat, 9-Spindle Back, 1764, 13 In. 550.00
Table, 3 Antler Supports, Center Disk, Brass, 31 1/2 In. 9360.00
Table, 3 Lobed Tiers, Flowers, Inlay, Metal Scrolled Finials, 32 In. 750.00
Table, Aalto, Burl Veneer Top, Molded Beech Legs, 22 x 24 In. 165.00
Table, Aalto, Laminated Birch Legs, Rectangular Top, 22 In. 115.00
Table, Aalto, Oak Circular Top, Bentwood Legs, 24 x 28 In. 505.00
Table, Aesthetic Revival, Mahogany, Carved, Tripod Base, 28 1/2 x 23 In. 290.00
Table, Alexander Girard, Dark Green Marble Top, Aluminum Legs, 18 1/2 x 14 In. 1380.00
Table, Altar, Elm, Brown Lacquer, Everted Rims With Flowers, 34 x 98 x 11 In. 345.00
Table, Altar, Hardwood, Rectangular Top, 3 Short Drawers, 69 x 33 x 19 In. 980.00
Table, American Restauration, Mahogany, Leather Top, Drawers, 31 x 26 x 50 In. 3220.00
Table, Architect's, Chippendale, Mahogany, Raised Fitted Interior, 30 x 32 In. 2300.00
Table, Architect's, George III Style, Mahogany, Hinged, 31 1/2 x 34 x 24 In. 2875.00
Table, Architect's, Mahogany, Leather Surface, 2 Drawers, Fitted Interior, 35 1/2 In. 4800.00
Table, Architect's, Mahogany, Ratcheted, Sliding Front, Fitted Interior, 30 In. 4600.00
Table, Arne Jacobsen, Rosewood Top, Chrome Pedestal Base, Signed, 59 1/2 In. 1035.00
Table, Art Deco, Limed Oak, Flip Top, Jean-Michel Frank, c.1930, 30 x 31 1/2 In. 6000.00
Table, Art Deco, Mahogany, Inset, Wood, Mother-Of-Pearl, Flowers, 14 x 23 x 14 In. 980.00
Table, Art Nouveau, Mahogany, Bronze, Water Lily, 2 Tiers, 1900, 55 x 19 In. 7200.00
Table, Arts & Crafts, Copper Top, Slatted Sides, 28 x 30 In. 550.00
Table, Arts & Crafts, Mahogany, Dark & Light Green Tiles, 27 x 28 In. 575.00
Table, Arts & Crafts, Oak, Square Top Over Lower Shelf, 16 x 30 In. 25.00
Table, Arts & Crafts, Rectangular Top, Dark & Light Green Tiles, 21 x 28 In. 1095.00
Table, Arts & Crafts, Rectangular, Lower Shelf, Cutout Leg, 30 x 36 x 20 In. 720.00

Furniture, Table, Card, American Classical,
Mahogany, Fold, D Shape, 36 x 18 In.

Furniture, Table, Card, Dutch Rococo,
Mahogany, Serpentine, 1 Drawer, 30 x 14 In.

Table, Baker's, Iron, Brass, Scrolled Frieze, Leaf Pendants, France, 31 1/4 x 50 In. 3220.00
Table, Baroque, Maple, Gateleg, Ring-Turned Legs, 1780, 25 x 45 x 47 1/2 In. 19550.00
Table, Baroque, Oak, Rectangular Overhanging Top, Block Legs, 27 x 24 x 41 In. 9200.00
Table, Baroque, Walnut, Acanthus Base, Corners, Paw Feet, Italy, 39 x 31 In. 4600.00
Table, Baroque, Walnut, Oval Top, Frieze Drawer, Gateleg, Continental, 25 1/2 In. 920.00
Table, Basswood, Tilting Top Over Bench, Lift Lid, c.1900, 28 1/2 x 72 In. 605.00
Table, Beech, Frieze Drawer, Square Legs, 19th Century, 23 3/4 x 12 1/2 In. 865.00
Table, Beech, Oval Marble Top, Tapered Fluted Legs, 23 x 29 In. 345.00
Table, Birch, Overhanging Top, Dolphin Supports, 3 Paw Feet, Parcel Gilt, 30 In. 6480.00
Table, Bird's-Eye Maple, Mahogany, Marble Top, 3 Short Drawers, 1840s, 37 In. 7920.00
Table, Black Lacquer, Chinese Men In Costume, Landscape, Block Legs, 64 In. 2735.00
Table, Bronze, Gilt, Verde Antico Marble Top, 19th Century, 30 x 16 In. 1035.00
Table, Bronze, Seated Whippet Pedestal, Round, 34 1/2 x 15 In., Pair 1610.00
Table, Card, American Classical, Mahogany, Fold, D Shape, 36 x 18 In. ....*Illus* 2070.00
Table, Card, Chippendale, Mahogany, Folding Top, Serpentine Front, 1780, 28 x 35 In. .. 18400.00
Table, Card, Chippendale, Mahogany, Rectangular Top, 1 Drawer, 1780, 28 In. 4890.00
Table, Card, Dutch Rococo, Mahogany, Serpentine, 1 Drawer, 30 x 14 In. ....*Illus* 2990.00
Table, Card, E. Wormley, Rosewood Top, Dark Mahogany, Dunbar, 32 x 29 In. 865.00
Table, Card, Edwardian, Satinwood, Demilune, Foldover, c.1905, 28 1/4 x 30 x 15 In. 460.00
Table, Card, Federal Style, Mahogany, Inlaid, Serpentine, 1890s, 29 1/2 x 37 1/2 In. 440.00
Table, Card, Federal, Mahogany, Bird's-Eye Maple Inlay Panels, Mass., 1800 .... 4900.00
Table, Card, Federal, Mahogany, Bird's-Eye Maple, Folding Top, 30 x 36 x 20 In., Pair .. 12650.00
Table, Card, Federal, Mahogany, Folding Parquet Top, Tapered Legs, 38 x 18 x 31 In. ... 865.00
Table, Card, Federal, Mahogany, Inlay, Square, Elliptical, c.1790, 29 x 36 x 17 In. 4025.00
Table, Card, Federal, Mahogany, Reeded Edge, Ball Feet, Hinged, 29 x 36 x 17 In. 405.00
Table, Card, Federal, Mahogany, Serpentine Top, 1800, 30 x 36 x 17 1/2 In. 7765.00
Table, Card, Federal, Mahogany, Serpentine Top, Line Inlay, c.1810, 29 1/2 x 36 In. 605.00
Table, Card, George II, Mahogany, Drawer, Double Swing Leg, c.1780, 29 x 32 In. 935.00
Table, Card, George II, Mahogany, Hinged, Carved, Rope Molding, c.1760, 29 x 35 In. .. 5175.00
Table, Card, George II, Mahogany, Rectangular Hinged Top, Cabriole Legs, 29 In. 2875.00
Table, Card, George III, Mahogany, D-Shaped Top, Felt-Lined Writing Surface, 29 In. ... 750.00
Table, Card, George III, Mahogany, Hinged Top, Square Tapered Legs, 1800, 28 In. ... 977.00
Table, Card, George III, Mahogany, Rectangular Top, Felt Surface, 29 x 17 In. 1610.00
Table, Card, George III, Mahogany, Rectangular Top, Splayed Feet, 28 1/2 In. 2415.00
Table, Card, George IV, Mahogany, Hinged Rectangular Top, 28 1/2 In., Pair 10800.00
Table, Card, Hepplewhite, Birch, Cherry Stained, 3 Shape, 35 1/2 In. 2475.00
Table, Card, Hepplewhite, Cherry, Half Round, Leaf, Tapered Legs, 37 x 18 x 30 In. 1210.00
Table, Card, Hepplewhite, Mahogany, Folding Top, Felt Liner, c.1810, 28 x 36 In. 1100.00
Table, Card, Hepplewhite, Mahogany, Inlay, 1790-1810, 29 x 36 x 18 In. 625.00
Table, Card, Hepplewhite, Mahogany, Inlay, Serpentine, c.1876, 30 x 36 x 18 In. 865.00
Table, Card, Hepplewhite, Mahogany, Pine, Tapered Legs, Dovetailed Drawer, 29 In. 1985.00
Table, Card, Hepplewhite, Mahogany, Urn Cartouche, Tapered Legs, 30 x 36 In. 605.00
Table, Card, Mahogany, Accordion Action, Fabric Surface, Block Feet, 29 In. 3600.00
Table, Card, Mahogany, Accordion Action, Fabric Surface, c.1755, 30 In. 7200.00

Table, Card, Mahogany, Drawer, Square Marlborough Legs, 1775, 29 1/2 In. 1100.00
Table, Card, Mahogany, Folding, Elliptical, Line-Inlaid Frame, c.1790, 35 1/2 In. 1650.00
Table, Card, Mahogany, Hinged Top, 4 Legs, Rear Swing Leg, 36 1/2 In. 1255.00
Table, Card, Mahogany, Inlaid Apron, Reeded Saber Legs, c.1825, 29 x 38 In. 2420.00
Table, Card, Mahogany, Leather Surface, Hidden Drawer Behind Swing Leg, 1770 . . . . . . 520.00
Table, Card, Mahogany, Swivel Crossbanded Top, Foliate Carving, Paw Feet, 30 In. 2400.00
Table, Card, Regency, Mahogany, Foldover Top, Tapered Pedestal, 28 x 35 x 34 In. 1495.00
Table, Card, Regency, Rosewood, Rectilinear Foldover Top, Scroll Feet, 30 In. 2185.00
Table, Card, Renaissance Revival, Flip Top, Ornate Base, 1875, 30 x 18 x 29 In. 1230.00
Table, Card, Sheraton, Mahogany, Conforming Frame, Reeded Legs, c.1800, 29 x 33 In. . . 880.00
Table, Card, Sheraton, Mahogany, Serpentine Front & Sides, c.1785, 36 x 29 1/2 In. 3000.00
Table, Card, Walnut, Burl Veneer, 1 Drawer, Sunburst Design, 29 1/2 x 41 In. 1495.00
Table, Card, Walnut, Line-Inlaid Edge, 1 Drawer, Oval Inlay, c.1810, 29 x 35 In. 440.00
Table, Card, William IV, Mahogany, Fold Top, Felt Top, Pedestal, 36 x 18 In. . . . . *Illus* 2990.00
Table, Center, Continental, Carved Wood, Circular Beveled Glass, 30 x 54 In. 1150.00
Table, Center, Eastlake, Marble Top, Reticulated Center, 1880, 30 x 23 x 32 In. 1780.00
Table, Center, Flip Top, Mahogany, Scalloped Edge, 3 Carved Cabriole Legs, 29 In. 690.00
Table, Center, Gadroon Edge Over Apron, Fluted Legs, Top-Shaped Feet, 28 x 51 In. 6900.00
Table, Center, Gothic Revival, Mahogany, Marble Top, 29 1/2 x 42 1/4 x 28 1/4 In. 1495.00
Table, Center, Louis XVI, Giltwood, Oval Surface, Green Onyx, Fluted Legs, 30 In. 1495.00
Table, Center, Louis XVI, Mahogany, Circular Top, Leather Writing Surface, 29 In. 8400.00
Table, Center, Louis XVI, Mahogany, Tulipwood, Circular Reeded Legs, 29 x 24 In. 3900.00
Table, Center, Mahogany, Circular Top, Frieze Inlaid, Scrolled Legs, 28 3/4 In. 6040.00
Table, Center, Mahogany, Tilt Top, Acanthus Columns, 3 Feet, 1825, 29 x 47 In. 1495.00
Table, Center, Napoleon III, Tulipwood, Bronze, Circular Top, Putti Scene, 35 In. 9000.00
Table, Center, Neoclassical, Circular Green Marble Top, Padded Feet, 31 In. 4600.00
Table, Center, Neoclassical, Mahogany, White Dish-Shape Top, Scroll Feet, 29 In. 3910.00
Table, Center, Oak, Staghorn, Octagonal, Skirt Horn, 43 Placed Buttons, 30 x 33 In. 3575.00
Table, Center, Regency, Mahogany, Fluted Pedestal Base, Brass Paw Feet, 49 In. 370.00
Table, Center, Regency, Mahogany, Round Hinged Top, Saber Legs, 29 x 55 1/2 In. 4830.00
Table, Center, Renaissance Revival, Walnut, Marble, Stretchers, 32 x 38 x 22 In. 1610.00
Table, Center, Rococo Revival, Molded White Marble Top, 30 x 33 x 21 In. 980.00
Table, Center, Rococo Revival, Rosewood Laminate, Carving, 30 x 43 x 29 In. .7190.00 to 18975.00
Table, Center, Rococo Revival, Rosewood, Marble, Tortoise Shape, 29 x 36 x 25 In. 2185.00
Table, Center, Rococo Revival, Rosewood, Marble, Tortoise Shape, 30 x 31 x 21 1/2 In. . . 2530.00
Table, Center, Rococo Revival, Rosewood, Round, Column, Scroll Legs, 29 x 30 In. 4370.00
Table, Center, Rococo, Ornate Carved Tripod Legs, Italy, 30 In. 460.00
Table, Center, Rococo, Rosewood, Carved Frieze, Cabriole Legs, 28 1/2 In. 1955.00
Table, Center, Rosewood, White Marble Inset, Scroll Feet, Late 19th Century, 29 In. 520.00
Table, Center, Satinwood, Gold Carvings, Marble Top, 1875, 30 x 31 In. 8960.00
Table, Center, Walnut, Carved, Ink Graining, 4 Scrolled Supports, 37 x 26 x 30 In. 1210.00
Table, Center, Walnut, Narrow Rectangular Top, Turned Legs, 31 3/4 In. 7200.00
Table, Center, Walnut, Winged Griffins, 1890, 37 x 28 In. 3640.00
Table, Center, William IV, Mahogany, Circular Top, Concave Base, Paw Feet, 29 In. 2300.00
Table, Center, William IV, Mahogany, Oak Band, Round, Tripartite Base, 29 x 50 In. 4830.00
Table, Center, William IV, Mahogany, Round, 3-Part Base, Scrolled Toes, 28 x 49 In. 2530.00

Furniture, Table, Card, William IV, Mahogany,
Fold Top, Felt Top, Pedestal, 36 x 18 In.

**To make a new marble table top
look old, wipe it with vinegar a few
times. The dull finish of old tops
came from repeated washings.**

**To get candle wax off your antique
table, use a hair dryer set on low
heat. Melt the wax, then wipe it off.**

Table, Center, William IV, Rosewood, Figured Circular Top, Concave Base, 29 In. 2990.00
Table, Center, William IV, Rosewood, Foliate Concave Base, 30 x 47 3/4 In. 7475.00
Table, Charles II, Oak, Rule-Jointed Leaves, Box Stretcher, Oval, 46 1/2 In. 1725.00
Table, Cherry, Drawer, Tripod Cabriole-Leg Base, 29 1/2 x 19 x 19 In. 920.00
Table, Chippendale, Mahogany, 2 Tiers, Claw, Ball Feet, 30 1/2 In. 110.00
Table, Chippendale, Mahogany, Folding Leaf, Henredon, 34 x 55 In. 740.00
Table, Chippendale, Mahogany, Inlay, Scalloped Piecrust Top, 20th Century, 30 In. 55.00
Table, Chippendale, Mahogany, Rectangular Top, Gadrooned Edge, 30 1/2 In. 2875.00
Table, Chippendale, Tilt Top, Mahogany, Bellflower Pendants, Snake Feet, 27 In. 2070.00
Table, Chrome, 6 Upright Rods, Round Glass Top, 16 3/4 x 17 In. 27.00
Table, Circular Marble Top, Columnar Legs, Triangular Stretcher, 25 In. 980.00
Table, Circular, Walnut, Molded Top, Turned Legs, Mid 19th Century, 29 x 45 In. 460.00
Table, Classical, Mahogany, Duncan Phyfe, c.1820, 30 x 38 x 24 3/8 In. 7475.00
Table, Classical, Mahogany, Rectangular Top, Ogee Base, Bracket Feet, 30 In. 1780.00
Table, Classical, Mahogany, Veneer, Scrolled Foot, Leather Insert, 1900s, Pair 770.00
Table, Coffee, A. Jacobsen, Rectangular Rosewood Top, 18 1/2 x 21 1/2 In. 1035.00
Table, Coffee, Art Deco, Burl Veneer, Broad Fluted Legs, Circular, 24 x 37 In. 4780.00
Table, Coffee, Biedermeier, Black Walnut, Frieze Drawer, Pierced Trestle, 1840s, 30 In. . . . 5760.00
Table, Coffee, Black Enameled Metal Frame, Oval Glass Top, 37 1/2 x 17 In. 430.00
Table, Coffee, Black Lacquer, Pagoda By River, Peonies, 48 x 15 1/2 In. 45.00
Table, Coffee, Butterfly Inlay, Floral Design, Gold Incised Stretcher, 1920, 41 In. 1512.00
Table, Coffee, Chippendale, Mahogany, Gallery Top, England, 21 x 43 x 26 1/2 In. 165.00
Table, Coffee, Circular Thick Glass Top, Glass Column Supports, 15 x 42 In. 365.00
Table, Coffee, Contemporary Style, Glass Top, Chrome, X-Stretcher, 42 x 16 In. 316.00
Table, Coffee, Danish Rosewood Veneer, Rectangular, Shelf, Tapered Legs, 20 x 48 In. . . . 200.00
Table, Coffee, Drop Leaf, Regency, Mahogany, 2 Drawers, 19th Century, 28 In. 3740.00
Table, Coffee, E. Wormley, Burl Veneer, Brass-Capped Feet, 16 x 58 In. 1150.00
Table, Coffee, E. Wormley, Circular Plate Glass Top, Pedestal Base, 17 In. 750.00
Table, Coffee, E. Wormley, Elm Burled Top, Dark Walnut Base, 14 In., Pair 3738.00
Table, Coffee, E. Wormley, Glass Tiles, Brass Base, Trim, Mosaic Top, 16 In. 2875.00
Table, Coffee, E. Wormley, Molded Ash, Laminated, Marble Top, 15 1/2 In. 1035.00
Table, Coffee, E. Wormley, Rosewood Finish, Bronze Sheathed Ends, 16 In. 1093.00
Table, Coffee, E. Wormley, Walnut, Bentwood Hairpin Legs, 12 x 18 In. 920.00
Table, Coffee, E. Wormley, Walnut, Sectioned Burl Top, 16 x 58 In. 1150.00
Table, Coffee, Eames, Ash Top, Circular, Chrome Legs, 16 1/2 x 34 In. 575.00
Table, Coffee, Eames, Circular Ash Top, Chrome Legs, Herman Miller, 16 In. 575.00
Table, Coffee, Eames, Plywood, Steel, Black Paint, Herman Miller, 10 x 89 x 29 In. 3450.00
Table, Coffee, Eero Saarinen, Oval White Marble Top, Light Brown, Knoll, 15 In. 460.00
Table, Coffee, Fantoni, Welded Base Supports, Round Glass Top, 42 x 16 In. 490.00
Table, Coffee, Frank Lloyd Wright, Mahogany, Slab Base, Henredon, 17 x 42 In. 1150.00
Table, Coffee, French Provincial, Carved, Max Kuehne, 17 x 41 1/2 x 19 In. 4315.00
Table, Coffee, Fruitwood, 6 Tapered Legs, Oval Top, 66 x 26 1/2 x 17 1/4 In. 275.00
Table, Coffee, G. Nakashima, Rosewood, Plank Base, Flared Legs, 1953, 14 In. 8625.00
Table, Coffee, G. Nakashima, Walnut, Free Edge, Dowel Legs, 14 x 61 In. 2185.00
Table, Coffee, G. Nakashima, Walnut, Free Edge, Plank Edge, 1954, 12 1/2 In. 5060.00
Table, Coffee, H. Bertoia, Marble Inset, Black Metal Base, Knoll, 15 x 16 In. 675.00
Table, Coffee, Hohenberg, Fern Design, Green, Gold, Black, White Top, 36 x 16 3/4 In. . . . 460.00
Table, Coffee, Lacquer, Tray, Painted Floral, Mother-Of-Pearl Inlay, 21 x 31 x 18 In. 360.00
Table, Coffee, Lamm, Glass Top, Elliptical Aluminum Feet, 14 1/2 x 39 1/2 In. 2130.00
Table, Coffee, Mahogany, Satinwood, Central Leaf Patera, Lapped Border, 21 In. 635.00
Table, Coffee, Mosaic Design, Wrought Iron Base, Gilt Paw Feet, 20 1/2 In. 635.00
Table, Coffee, Mosaic Top, Abstract Blue, White, Black Design, Circular, 14 x 36 In. 115.00
Table, Coffee, Oak, Leather Rectangular Top, 15 x 54 x 26 In. 90.00
Table, Coffee, P. Evans, Copper, Bronze, Pewter Finish, Plate-Glass Top, 16 In. 690.00
Table, Coffee, P. Evans, Rosewood Veneer, Brass, Square Post Legs, 15 x 42 In. 255.00
Table, Coffee, Painted, Undulating Edges, Cabriole Legs, 18 1/2 x 41 3/4 In. 345.00
Table, Coffee, Phillip La Verne, Bronze, Creation Of Man, Bas Relief, 1962, 17 x 23 In. . . . 2760.00
Table, Coffee, Piero Fornasetti, Faux Bamboo Metal Frame, 1950, 39 x 17 1/2 In. 2875.00
Table, Coffee, Plate Glass Top, Welded Brass Base, Rectangular, 14 1/2 In. 560.00
Table, Coffee, Richard Schultz, Petal, 8 Segmented Laminated Sections, Knoll, 15 In. 505.00
Table, Coffee, Robsjohn-Gibbings, Rectangular Top, X-Shaped Base, 16 x 21 In. 560.00
Table, Coffee, Robsjohn-Gibbings, Walnut, 2 Tiers, Widdicomb, 30 x 14 In. 575.00
Table, Coffee, Robsjohn-Gibbings, Walnut, White Marble Top, Widdicomb, 17 In. 520.00

Table, Coffee, Rococo, Carved Walnut, Floral Bouquet Apron, Italy, 20 In. 520.00
Table, Coffee, Rohde, Mahogany, 2 Tiers, Curved Front, Base, 23 1/2 x 34 In. 505.00
Table, Coffee, Sottsass, Black, White Laminate Top, Metal Base, 50 x 14 In. 1095.00
Table, Coffee, Square Glass Top, Solid Wood Sections Base, 1970, 45 x 17 In. 805.00
Table, Coffee, Tapio Wirkkala, Light, Dark Wood, Birch Trim, Black Steel Legs, 16 In. . . . 2990.00
Table, Coffee, Teak, Marble Top, Curved H-Stretcher, Paw Feet, 30 x 34 x 19 In. 505.00
Table, Coffee, Tree Root, 24 x 92 In. 145.00
Table, Coffee, V. Kagan, 3 Ebonized Legs, Round Glass Top, 40 x 20 In. 805.00
Table, Coffee, Walnut Frame, Turquoise Murano Glass Mosaic Top, 24 x 60 In. 3800.00
Table, Coffee, Walnut, Marble Top, Frieze & Cabriole Legs, Metal Mounts, 39 In. 750.00
Table, Coffee, White Marble Top, Brass Circular Tapered Legs, 14 3/4 x 72 In. 170.00
Table, Conference, Berkey & Gay, Walnut, Pullout Desk, Drawers, 1900, 80 x 31 In. 4480.00
Table, Conference, George III Style, Mahogany, Leather Insert Top, 31 x 48 x 96 In. 805.00
Table, Conference, Knoll, Rectangular Walnut Veneer Top, Chrome Base, 29 x 36 In. 620.00
Table, Conference, Knoll, Teak, Elliptical, Chrome Steel Pedestal Base, 1961, 96 In. 2195.00
Table, Conference, Mahogany, Leather Top, Frieze Drawer, Spade Feet, 96 In. 805.00
Table, Conference, McHugh, Mahogany Finish, 30 x 9 x 42 In. 4025.00
Table, Console, Art Deco, Chrome, Black Enameled, 1 Drawer, T.A. Kochs, 30 In. 1460.00
Table, Console, Chippendale, Apron Drawer, Brass, 28 1/2 x 33 x 16 In. 1150.00
Table, Console, Chippendale, Mahogany, Chamfered Legs, 28 1/2 x 36 x 19 1/2 In. 345.00
Table, Console, Demilune, Mahogany, Line Inlay, 29 x 36 x 18 In. 635.00
Table, Console, Egyptian Marble Top, Serpentine Front, Carved Coquillage, 32 In. 5460.00
Table, Console, Faux Marble Top, Wrought Iron Frame, Pierced Scroll Legs 370.00
Table, Console, Gilt, Marble Top, Serpentine Front & Sides, 31 x 32 In. 1955.00
Table, Console, Italian Style, Semicircular, Painted, 34 1/2 x 58 x 22 In., Pair 2300.00
Table, Console, Marble Top, Frieze Drawer, Doric Columns, 1820s, 49 In. 3220.00
Table, Console, Regency Style, Mahogany, Marble, Plinth Base, 33 x 13 In., Pair 3220.00
Table, Continental, Burl, Marquetry, Tilt Top, Tripod Base, c.1860, 52 In. 4400.00
Table, Continental, Walnut, Rectangular Surface, Flower Heads, 2 Drawers, 31 In. 2070.00
Table, Corner, G. Nakashima, Burl Top, Original Finish, 1957, 21 1/2 In. 790.00
Table, Corner, Gilt, Scene Of Women Dancing, Flower-Head Feet, 35 In. 6000.00
Table, Corner, McCobb, Mahogany, 2 Tiers, Calvin, 32 x 22 1/2 In. 630.00
Table, Crossbanded Top, 1 Frieze Drawer, 3 Cabriole Legs, 28 x 19 In. 575.00
Table, Cube, P. Evans, Copper, Bronze, Pewter Finish, Slate Top, 19 x 13 In., Pair 920.00
Table, Cube, Tommi Parzinger, Light Walnut, 1 Drawer, 20 x 21 In. 920.00
Table, De Chevet, Louis XVI, Mahogany, Marble Top, 33 1/2 x 18 x 15 In., Pair 1150.00
Table, Demilune, Walnut, Inlaid, Diamond, Circles, c.1900, 24 x 24 In. 195.00
Table, Dinette, I. Noguchi, Black Iron Base, Chrome Wire, White Top, 29 In. 1840.00
Table, Dinette, Louis Philippe, Walnut, Foldover, Baluster-Turned Legs, 1830, 43 In. 1150.00
Table, Dining, Arts & Crafts, Oak, Round, Center Pedestal, 4 Leaves, 54 In. 1150.00
Table, Dining, Arts & Crafts, Oak, Round, Pedestal, 4 Legs, 6 Leaves, 30 x 48 In. 1150.00
Table, Dining, Barley Twist Legs, Turned Feet, 27 1/2 x 43 1/2 In. 345.00
Table, Dining, Biedermeier, Amboyna, 4 Legs, Splayed Feet, 53 In. 2015.00
Table, Dining, Birch, Red Washed, Hinged Leaf, 1800s, 29 x 42 x 17 In. . . . .*Illus* 3739.00
Table, Dining, C. Rohlfs, Mahogany, Cutout Trestle Legs, 4 Leaves, 54 In. 7475.00

Furniture, Table, Dining, Birch, Red Washed,
Hinged Leaf, 1800s, 29 x 42 x 17 In.

Don't burn red, green, black, or dark blue candles where they might drip on a wooden surface. The color may bleed into the wood. Put a dish or aluminum foil under the candleholder. Be careful of votive candles too. If burned too low, they can heat the glass holder and scorch the wood.

Table, Dining, Cherry, 2 D-Shape Sections, Ball Feet, 29 x 48 x 80 In. 1495.00
Table, Dining, Cherry, Elliptical, 4 Butterfly Joints, Trestle Base, 1950, 29 x 41 In. 8625.00
Table, Dining, Chippendale, Mahogany, 2 Leaves, Refinished, England, 21 x 78 In. 2750.00
Table, Dining, Chippendale, Mahogany, Drop Leaf, c.1770, 28 x 62 1/2 x 48 In. 980.00
Table, Dining, Chippendale, Mahogany, Molded Edge, 3 Scrolled Legs, 72 x 31 In. 1265.00
Table, Dining, Drop Leaf, Bruno Mathsson, Walnut, Gateleg, 28 1/2 In. 110.00
Table, Dining, Drop Leaf, Federal, Mahogany, Carved, c.1830, 28 1/2 x 51 x 69 In. 1100.00
Table, Dining, Drop Leaf, Federal, Tiger Maple, Early 1800s, 29 x 53 1/2 x 48 In. 1495.00
Table, Dining, Drop Leaf, George I Style, Oak, Oval, 30 1/4 x 84 1/2 x 61 In. 1840.00
Table, Dining, Drop Leaf, George I, Walnut, Oval, c.1825, 28 x 50 x 47 In. 2530.00
Table, Dining, Drop Leaf, George II, Mahogany, Plain Apron, Pad Feet, 28 x 47 In. 1725.00
Table, Dining, Drop Leaf, George III, Mahogany, 6 Legs, c.1790, 29 x 48 x 61 In. 300.00
Table, Dining, Drop Leaf, George III, Mahogany, Circular, c.1790, 28 x 48 In. 1045.00
Table, Dining, Drop Leaf, Georgian Style, Chinoiserie, 3 12-In. Leaves, 43 x 25 x 29 In. . . 115.00
Table, Dining, Drop Leaf, Hepplewhite, Mahogany, Inlaid Legs, 31 x 48 In. 345.00
Table, Dining, Drop Leaf, Mahogany, Claw & Ball Feet, c.1770, 27 3/4 In. 9200.00
Table, Dining, Drop Leaf, Mahogany, Saber Legged Pedestal, 1940s, 29 1/2 x 62 In. 260.00
Table, Dining, Drop Leaf, Queen Anne, Mahogany, Newport, c.1750, 27 x 47 In. 6900.00
Table, Dining, Drop Leaf, Queen Anne, Mahogany, Santo Domingo, 28 x 48 x 17 In. 10925.00
Table, Dining, Drop Leaf, Queen Anne, Maple, Turned Legs, Pad Feet, 1750, 27 In. 1610.00
Table, Dining, Drop Leaf, Sheraton, Turned Legs, 2 Leaves, 29 x 47 x 20 In. 460.00
Table, Dining, Drop Leaf, Walnut, 4 Leaves, Turned & Reeded Legs, 29 1/2 x 42 x 27 In. 390.00
Table, Dining, Drop Leaf, Walnut, Scalloped Skirt, Trifid Feet, c.1760, 43 1/4 In. 1650.00
Table, Dining, Drop Leaf, William & Mary Style, Mahogany, 29 x 59 1/2 x 30 1/2 In. 1840.00
Table, Dining, E. Wormley, Walnut, Tiffany Favrile Glass Tiles, 17 In. 8050.00
Table, Dining, Eames, DTW-3, Plywood, Dowel Legs, H. Miller, c.1952, 29 x 54 x 34 In. 10350.00
Table, Dining, Eero Saarinen, Oak, White Pedestal Base, Knoll, 60 x 28 1/2 In. 1380.00
Table, Dining, Federal, Cherry, Drawer, Early 1800s, 20 x 55 x 29 1/2 In. 635.00
Table, Dining, Federal, Mahogany, Rectangular Molded Edge Top, Fluted Legs, 30 In. . . . 170.00
Table, Dining, Frankl, Large Cork Top, Black Wooden Base, 96 x 40 x 30 In. 2070.00
Table, Dining, G. Nakashima, Cherry, Rosewood Butterfly Joints, 2 Leaves, 84 In. 8625.00
Table, Dining, G. Nakashima, Plank Top, Shoe Feet, Signed, 1966, 28 x 40 In. 5625.00
Table, Dining, G. Nakashima, Walnut, Rectangular Top, Dowel Legs, 28 x 36 In. 3940.00
Table, Dining, G. Nelson, Walnut, Gateleg, Herman Miller, 30 x 40 In. 900.00
Table, Dining, G. Nelson, Walnut, Rectangular Top, Extension, Herman Miller, 29 In. 790.00
Table, Dining, G. Nelson, White Laminate Top, Herman Miller, 29 x 43 In. 1125.00
Table, Dining, G. Stickley, 4 Leaves, Label, 29 x 48 In. 4310.00
Table, Dining, G. Stickley, Circular Top, 4 Original Leaves, 29 x 48 In. 4025.00
Table, Dining, G. Stickley, No. 634, Oak, 5 Leaves, Green Finish, 30 x 59 In. 4900.00
Table, Dining, G. Stickley, No. 656, Mahogany, Square Top, 48 x 29 In. 7480.00
Table, Dining, George II, Mahogany, Circular Revolving Top, Pad Feet, 28 In. 2400.00
Table, Dining, George III Style, Mahogany, 3 Pedestal, 29 x 145 1/2 x 52 In., Open 1380.00
Table, Dining, George III Style, Mahogany, Carved, 30 1/2 x 60 x 52 In., Open 1380.00
Table, Dining, George III Style, Mahogany, Inlay, 3 Pedestals, 29 x 150 x 44 1/2 In. 8050.00
Table, Dining, George III, Mahogany, 3 Pedestals, 30 x 120 x 36 1/2 In. 3450.00
Table, Dining, George III, Mahogany, Gadrooned Edge, 3 Cabriole Legs, 30 x 52 In. 630.00
Table, Dining, George III, Mahogany, Rectangular Top, Downswept Legs, 29 In. 8400.00
Table, Dining, Georgian Style, Mahogany, 2 Pedestals, Flute Standard, 28 x 88 x 48 In. . . 2185.00
Table, Dining, Gun-Barrel Columns, Downswept Legs, 2 Leaves, 29 1/4 x 108 1/2 In. . . . 1840.00
Table, Dining, Hans Bellman, Circular White Laminated Top, 26 x 48 In. 1265.00
Table, Dining, Harvey Probber, Octagonal Sandstone Top, Wooden Base, 25 x 50 In. 340.00
Table, Dining, Hepplewhite, Mahogany, Spade Feet, 6 Leaves, c.1900, 120 In. 1430.00
Table, Dining, Jules Leleu, Mahogany, Tapered Legs, Brass Feet, 2 Leaves, 47 1/4 In. 4600.00
Table, Dining, Jules Leleu, Rosewood, Marquetry, Draw Leaf, c.1935, 74 1/2 In. 6900.00
Table, Dining, Karl Springer, Marbleized Laminate, Rectangular Top, 30 x 108 In. 2250.00
Table, Dining, Lifetime, Mahogany, 2 Leaves, 29 x 54 In. 1955.00
Table, Dining, Limbert, Mahogany, Cutout Base, 2 Leaves, 29 1/2 x 48 In. 2925.00
Table, Dining, Louis Philippe, Walnut, Plank Top, 28 x 51 1/2 x 27 In. 2070.00
Table, Dining, Louis XV Style, Cherry, 30 1/4 x 99 1/4 x 40 In. 3795.00
Table, Dining, Louis XV Style, Oak, Parquetry, Draw Leaf, 29 x 85 1/2 x 39 In. 850.00
Table, Dining, Louis XV, Rectangular Surface, Scrolled Legs, 84 x 41 In. 805.00
Table, Dining, Louis XVI, Ebony Crossbands, Brass Stringing, Sabot Legs, 29 In. 5750.00
Table, Dining, Louis XVI, Mahogany, Fluted Tapered Legs, 58 x 29 In. 255.00

Table, Dining, Mahogany, Cherry, Maple Apron, Gateleg, 29 x 44 x 47 In. 2070.00
Table, Dining, Mahogany, Circular Top, Column Pedestal, 28 1/2 In. 1610.00
Table, Dining, Mahogany, Flame Veneer, Inlay, 2 Pedestals, Oval, 5 Leaves, 66 x 44 In. . .   935.00
Table, Dining, Mahogany, Flame Veneer, Pierced Geometric, 1 Leaf, Oriental, 56 In. 110.00
Table, Dining, Mahogany, Gateleg, Rectangular Top, 42 x 23 x 30 1/4 In. 170.00
Table, Dining, Mahogany, Inlaid Top, Tapered Legs, 2 Leaves, 106 In. Open 925.00
Table, Dining, Mahogany, Rectangular Top, Banded Inlaid Edge, 71 x 36 x 30 In. 630.00
Table, Dining, Mahogany, Tilt Top, Circular Hinged Top, Tripod Base, 28 In. 2300.00
Table, Dining, Oak, Carved Fruit & Floral, 1885, 27 x 50 x 44 In. 840.00
Table, Dining, Oak, Lion's-Head Fruit, Grape Supports, Floral Apron, 1880, 62 x 28 In. . .   4480.00
Table, Dining, Oak, Original Finish, 5 Legs, 2 Leaves, 28 1/4 x 54 In. 2590.00
Table, Dining, Oak, Scrolled Legs, Claw Feet, Casters, 42 x 29 3/4 In. 460.00
Table, Dining, Oak, Winged Griffin, Carved Apron, 3 Leaves, 1890, 51 In. 5600.00
Table, Dining, P. Evans, Bronze Gesso Finish, Rectangular Glass Top, 29 x 44 In. 1125.00
Table, Dining, P. Evans, Oak Veneer, 3 Leaves, 29 x 60 x 42 In. 2590.00
Table, Dining, Queen Anne, Mahogany, Swing Leg, Pad Feet, c.1750, 28 x 60 x 21 In. . . .   5265.00
Table, Dining, Queen Anne, Walnut, Oval, 29 x 100 x 42 In. Open 920.00
Table, Dining, Regency Style, Horseshoe Mahogany, Round, 5 Leaves, 30 x 62 x 88 In. . . .   3450.00
Table, Dining, Regency Style, Mahogany, 2 Parts, Reeded Saber Legs, 30 x 44 x 79 In. . .   1610.00
Table, Dining, Regency, Mahogany, Downswept Legs, Brass Paw Feet, 29 In. 7200.00
Table, Dining, Renaissance Revival, Walnut, Ornate Pedestal Base, 1870, 45 In. 2520.00
Table, Dining, Robsjohn-Gibbings, Extension, Flared Legs, 29 x 72 In. 2754.00
Table, Dining, Rococo Revival, Burl Walnut, Shaped Hinged Top, Scroll Feet, 30 In. 805.00
Table, Dining, Rohde, Wood Veneer, Plank Legs, 29 1/2 x 72 x 40 In. 1150.00
Table, Dining, Roycroft, Mahogany, Extension, 4 Legs, Shoe Feet, 29 1/2 x 60 In. 6325.00
Table, Dining, Sheraton, Mahogany, Inlay, 2 Pedestal, 3 Leaves, 1900s, 47 x 98 In. 5060.00
Table, Dining, Stickley Bros., Mahogany, Buttressed Feet, 29 3/4 x 54 In. 1800.00
Table, Dining, Stickley Bros., Mahogany, Circular Top, 30 x 54 In. 4025.00
Table, Dining, Stickley Bros., No. 2404, Mahogany, 5-Leg Base, 54 x 29 In. 3335.00
Table, Dining, Teak, Gateleg, J.O. Carlson, Sweden, 29 x 61 x 35 In. 865.00
Table, Dining, Walnut, Oval Slate Top, Phil Powell, 96 In. 3220.00
Table, Dining, Walnut, Round, Carved, Split Pedestal, 5 Leaves, c.1890, 29 x 59 In. 3190.00
Table, Dining, White Laminate Top, 4 Steel Legs, 28 1/2 x 35 1/2 In. 115.00
Table, Dining, White Laminate Top, Ebonized Popsicle Base, H. Bellman, 48 In. 1265.00
Table, Directoire, Ormolu Mounted, Tilt Top, Tripod, Late 18th Century, 31 x 22 In. 12000.00
Table, Display, Mahogany, Veneer, Carved Skirt, Victorian, 54 x 39 In., 2 Piece 1320.00
Table, Dressing, Art Deco, 5-Panel Mirror, 3 Drawers, 57 x 56 In. 290.00
Table, Dressing, Beau Brummel, Georgian, Mahogany, Easel Top, 32 1/2 x 24 x 20 1/2 In.   3220.00
Table, Dressing, Chippendale, Mahogany, 3 Drawers, c.1790, 31 x 38 1/4 In. 880.00
Table, Dressing, Chippendale, Mahogany, 5 Dovetailed Drawers, 42 x 23 x 32 In. 990.00
Table, Dressing, Classical, Backboard, Red Graining, c.1820, 32 1/2 x 19 x 14 In. 575.00
Table, Dressing, Classical, Mahogany, 6 Drawers, Medial Shelf, 1825, 39 x 37 In. 770.00
Table, Dressing, Empire, Mahogany, White Marble Top, 1840, 54 In. 5100.00
Table, Dressing, Frankl, Skyscraper, Mirror, Painted Wood, 1925, 51 In. 9000.00
Table, Dressing, G. Stickley, No. 607, Oak, 1 Drawer Over Compartment, 48 In. 2990.00
Table, Dressing, George III, Mahogany, Banded Hinged Top, Concave Frieze, 29 In. 1090.00
Table, Dressing, George III, Mahogany, Bowfront, 3 Drawers, Early 1900s, 30 x 48 In. . .   345.00
Table, Dressing, Grain Painted, Shaped Splashboard, 4 Drawers, 39 x 36 x 16 In. 920.00
Table, Dressing, Hepplewhite, Mahogany, 2 Drawers, Lift Top, Mirror, 36 x 19 x 30 In. . .   2750.00
Table, Dressing, Hepplewhite, Mahogany, Bowfront, Drawers, c.1800, 31 x 36 x 19 In. . .   8800.00
Table, Dressing, Kingwood, Center Opens To Mirror, Side Compartments, 28 1/2 In. 2645.00
Table, Dressing, Limbert, Mahogany, 56 x 36 x 24 In. 2300.00
Table, Dressing, Mahogany, Center Drawer, Step-Down Drawers, c.1810, 32 In. 1430.00
Table, Dressing, Mahogany, Inlaid Marquetry, Satinwood Inlay, c.1905, 69 x 55 In. 4600.00
Table, Dressing, Mahogany, Inlay, 6 Drawers, X-Stretcher, Mirror, 50 x 61 In. 2090.00
Table, Dressing, Mahogany, Inner Mirrored Top, Welled Interior, 29 1/4 In. 5760.00
Table, Dressing, Mahogany, Serpentine Marble Top, Central Drawer, 50 x 39 In. 1610.00
Table, Dressing, Mahogany, Triple-Divided Top, Opening Side Panels, 29 1/4 In. 3600.00
Table, Dressing, Maple & Pine, Wooden Pulls, Scrolled Backsplash, 33 x 30 In. 300.00
Table, Dressing, Marquetry, Dutch, Early 19th Century, 30 1/2 x 33 1/4 In. 990.00
Table, Dressing, Pine, Painted, Scalloped Backsplash, c.1810, 38 x 34 In. 495.00
Table, Dressing, Queen Anne, Cherry, 2 Drawers, Cabriole Legs, c.1760, 28 x 31 1/2 In. .   2420.00
Table, Dressing, Queen Anne, Mahogany, 3 Drawers, Pad Feet, c.1725, 28 x 34 In. 1045.00

Table, Dressing, Queen Anne, Mahogany, 4 Drawers, 30 1/2 x 36 In. 415.00
Table, Dressing, Queen Anne, Oak, 3 Drawers, Cabriole Legs, 35 1/2 x 22 x 28 In. 1495.00
Table, Dressing, Queen Anne, Walnut, 1 Long Over 3 Short Drawers, 1750, 34 x 17 In. . . 28750.00
Table, Dressing, Rococo, Rectangular, Feet, Continental, c.1895, 1/2 x 3 1/4 In. 200.00
Table, Dressing, Rosewood, Incised Marble Backsplash, 1880, 51 x 38 x 22 In. 2240.00
Table, Dressing, Sheraton, Cherry, Maple-Turned Legs, Marble, Bottles, 9 3/4 x 14 In. 440.00
Table, Dressing, Sheraton, Mahogany, 5 Drawers, Ring-Turned Legs, 30 x 43 1/2 In. 330.00
Table, Dressing, Sheraton, Mahogany, Mirror, J.F. Markley, c.1820, 65 x 39 1/2 In. 5225.00
Table, Dressing, Sheraton, Mirror, 2 Drawers, Rope-Turned Legs, 55 x 33 1/2 x 18 In. . . . 805.00
Table, Dressing, Silk Covered, Embroidered Strawberries, 31 x 43 In. 4500.00
Table, Dressing, Walnut, 3 Over 2 Drawers, Reeded Columns, Drake Feet, 30 1/2 In. 2195.00
Table, Dressing, William & Mary Style, Walnut, Drawer, England, 27 1/2 x 26 1/2 In. . . . 935.00
Table, Drop Leaf, Cherry, Tiger Maple, 1 Drawer, c.1830, 30 In. 770.00
Table, Drop Leaf, Chippendale, Mahogany, Oak, Marlborough Legs, 39 3/4 x 28 1/2 In. . . 600.00
Table, Drop Leaf, Chippendale, Mahogany, Square Legs, c.1775, 28 x 36 In. 410.00
Table, Drop Leaf, Empire, Mahogany, 1 Drawer, Brass Casters, 1820, 28 x 52 In. 605.00
Table, Drop Leaf, Federal, Birch, Oblong Top, Restored, 28 3/4 x 40 x 42 In. 480.00
Table, Drop Leaf, Federal, Mahogany Top, Carved Acanthus Claw Foot, 1840, 39 In. 1568.00
Table, Drop Leaf, Federal, Mahogany, Urn Base, Curving Legs, 27 1/2 x 36 x 21 In. 2530.00
Table, Drop Leaf, Federal, Maple, Pine, Drawer, Turned Legs, c.1830, 28 1/2 x 40 1/4 In. . 470.00
Table, Drop Leaf, Federal, Walnut, Early 19th Century, Child's, 36 1/4 x 23 1/4 In. 230.00
Table, Drop Leaf, Frank Lloyd Wright, Mahogany, Gateleg, 44 x 27 x 28 In. 400.00
Table, Drop Leaf, Fruitwood, Frieze Drawer, Marquetry Foliage & Birds, 28 1/2 In. 2415.00
Table, Drop Leaf, George I, Walnut, Pad Feet, 53 In. 1025.00
Table, Drop Leaf, George I, Walnut, Round Corners, 28 x 42 x 38 In. 1610.00
Table, Drop Leaf, George II, Mahogany, D-Shaped Leaves, 18th Century, 29 In. 1265.00
Table, Drop Leaf, George III, Mahogany, Rectangular Surface, Tapered Legs, 28 In. 290.00
Table, Drop Leaf, George III, Turned Legs, Padded Feet, 28 x 45 x 54 In. 2070.00
Table, Drop Leaf, Georgian, Mahogany, Cabriole Legs, Pad Feet, 28 x 42 x 21 In. 2070.00
Table, Drop Leaf, Georgian, Mahogany, Plain Chamfered Legs, 28 x 55 In. 1095.00
Table, Drop Leaf, Hepplewhite, Birch, Red Paint On Base, 28 x 42 In. 345.00
Table, Drop Leaf, Hepplewhite, Cherry, Square Tapered Legs, 2 Leaves, 29 x 48 x 18 In. . . 748.00
Table, Drop Leaf, Hepplewhite, Maple, Scrubbed Top, Stained, c.1810, 28 1/2 x 46 1/2 In. . 440.00
Table, Drop Leaf, Jacobean, Mahogany, Cane Center, Base Shelf, 27 x 10 x 28 In. 220.00
Table, Drop Leaf, Louis Philippe, Walnut, Demilune Leaves, 30 x 23 3/4 x 43 3/4 In. 1265.00
Table, Drop Leaf, Mahogany, 2 Drawers, Sandwich Glass Pulls, 30 x 20 x 17 In. 345.00
Table, Drop Leaf, Mahogany, Bird's-Eye Maple Drawer Fronts, 27 1/2 In. 1100.00
Table, Drop Leaf, Mahogany, Frieze With Drawer, Leaf-Capped Legs, 46 In. 3795.00
Table, Drop Leaf, Mahogany, Inlaid Edge, 1-Board Leaves, 41 1/2 In. 715.00
Table, Drop Leaf, Mahogany, Sticks Support Drawer & Shelf, 25 1/2 In. 300.00
Table, Drop Leaf, Pedestal, Hairy Paw Brass Feet, Boston, 48 x 60 In. 3135.00
Table, Drop Leaf, Pine, Cherry, Rear Leaf, Front Drawer, Tapered Legs, 36 In. 750.00
Table, Drop Leaf, Queen Anne, Mahogany, Cabriole Legs, Pad Feet, 42 x 14 In. 2200.00
Table, Drop Leaf, Queen Anne, Maple, Block-Turned Legs, 1760, 26 x 38 x 30 1/2 In. 6325.00
Table, Drop Leaf, Queen Anne, Pine, Cabriole Legs, Pad Feet, 26 3/4 x 10 x 28 1/2 In. 330.00
Table, Drop Leaf, Queen Anne, Walnut, Cabriole Legs, Pad Feet, c.1760, 27 3/4 x 42 In. . . 825.00
Table, Drop Leaf, Queen Anne, Walnut, Yellow Pine, Cant Legs, 29 x 14 1/2 x 43 In. 785.00
Table, Drop Leaf, Sheraton, Cherry, Rectangular Top, 1 Drawer, c.1830, 29 3/4 x 48 In. . . 275.00
Table, Drop Leaf, Sheraton, Mahogany, Bird's-Eye Maple, 28 x 22 x 42 In. 560.00
Table, Drop Leaf, Sheraton, Walnut, 1 Drawer, Turned Legs, 29 x 35 1/2 x 18 1/2 In. 330.00
Table, Drop Leaf, Sheraton, Walnut, Maple, Pa., c.1815, 29 3/4 x 38 3/4 In. 330.00
Table, Drop Leaf, Tiger Maple, 2 Drawers, 28 x 16 x 22 In. 1120.00
Table, Drop Leaf, Tiger Maple, Drawer, Square Legs, Early 19th Century, 40 x 36 1/2 In. . . 1725.00
Table, Drop Leaf, William & Mary, Oak, 1 Frieze Drawer, Spanish Feet, 28 In. 1495.00
Table, Drum, Leather Top, Inlaid, J. Arnold, New York, 29 x 32 In. Diam. 505.00
Table, Drum, Walnut, Marquetry, Floral & Butterfly Medallion, 38 x 24 In. 1210.00
Table, E. Wormley, Ash Laminated Frame, Dunbar, 53 x 23 x 24 In. 575.00
Table, E. Wormley, Grooved Plank Top, Long John, Hairpin Legs, 18 1/2 x 88 1/2 In. 920.00
Table, E. Wormley, Mahogany, Light Finish, Square, 23 x 24 In. 690.00
Table, E. Wormley, Rectangular Walnut Veneer Top, Ebony Base, 20 In. 505.00
Table, E. Wormley, Rosewood Inlay, Dark Mahogany Frame, Dunbar, 28 In. 1380.00
Table, E. Wormley, Rosewood Top, Dunbar, 15 x 19 In. 635.00
Table, E. Wormley, Sheaf-Of-Wheat, Travertine Top, Ebonized Base, 20 x 27 In. 865.00

Table, E. Wormley, Walnut, Inset Tiffany Glass Tiles, Cross Stretchers, 77 1/4 In. 8050.00
Table, Eames, Black Laminate Top, Zinc Wire Base, 15 x 10 In. 430.00
Table, Eames, DTW-2, Plywood, Steel, Herman Miller, c.1950, 28 1/2 x 34 In. 1495.00
Table, Eames, Elliptical Black Laminate Top, 89 x 29 x 10 In. 4025.00
Table, Eames, LTR, Bird's-Eye Maple Veneer, Plywood, Steel, Herman Miller, 10 x 15 In. 920.00
Table, Eames, Rectangular Black Laminate Top, 15 x 13 x 10 In. 865.00
Table, Eastlake, Marble Top, 1870, 29 x 28 1/2 x 20 In. 440.00
Table, Eastlake, Molded Skirt, Rectangular, Victorian, 29 x 29 x 20 In. 525.00
Table, Eastlake, Walnut, Burled, Marble, Quadruped Base, 30 1/2 x 28 x 20 In. 750.00
Table, Eero Saarinen, Walnut Top, White Cast Iron Base, Original Finish, 20 In. 805.00
Table, Eileen Gray, Chrome Tubular Steel, Glass Shelf, 1970, 20 x 40 In. 805.00
Table, Elm, 2-Board Top, Apron, Scalloped, 19th Century, Refinished, 91 x 20 In. 880.00
Table, Elm, Frame Over Shaped Apron, 19th Century, 18 In., Pair 1380.00
Table, Elm, Red, Black Lacquer Surface, Chinese, 18th Century, 32 x 18 x 43 In. 805.00
Table, Empire Style, Ormolu, Rectangular, Drawers, 30 x 57 x 29 1/4 In. 1840.00
Table, Empire, Mahogany, 3 Frieze Drawers, Bronze Paw Feet, 30 1/2 In. 8915.00
Table, Empire, Mahogany, Burl Veneer, 1 Drawer, Vase Pedestal, 54 x 41 In. 330.00
Table, Empire, Mahogany, Hinged Top, Anthemion & Flambeaux, Green Felt, 30 In. 2185.00
Table, Empire, Mahogany, Pedestal, Canted Scroll, c.1840, 27 3/4 x 36 In. 520.00
Table, Empire, Mahogany, Round, Gadroon Rim, Carved Pedestal, Claw Feet, 28 x 40 In. 1150.00
Table, English Oak, Recessed Drawer, Oval Stretcher, 31 1/2 x 42 x 59 In. 5520.00
Table, Extension, Rohde, Curved Top, Dark Mahogany, Miller, 1940, 30 In. 460.00
Table, Farm, Cherry, Battened Lift Off Top, Box Stretcher, Ball Feet, c.1770, 29 x 54 In. . . 1650.00
Table, Federal, Cherry, Tripod, Early 19th Century, 26 x 24 x 18 In. 405.00
Table, Federal, Mahogany Veneers, 2 Pedestals, Leaves, 65 x 44 In. 450.00
Table, Federal, Mahogany, Drawer, Turned Legs, Pa., c.1820, 28 1/2 x 36 In. 440.00
Table, Federal, Mahogany, Inlay, Late 1700s, 28 x 104 x 42 In. Open 1610.00
Table, Federal, Mahogany, Medallion, Bellflower, 20th Century, 29 In. 1230.00
Table, Federal, Mahogany, Pedestal, 3 Tapered Legs, Casters, Round Top, 29 x 36 In. 4800.00
Table, Federal, Maple, Frieze Drawer, Tripod, 28 x 18 x 17 In. 173.00
Table, Federal, Walnut, Tripod, Oval, Snake Feet, 28 x 23 x 15 In. 287.00
Table, Folding, Bruno Mathsson, Walnut, 112 1/2 x 35 x 28 1/2 In. 1265.00
Table, Folding, Eames, Walnut Veneer, Plywood, Steel, Herman Miller, 28 x 54 x 34 In. . . 1495.00
Table, Folding, Engraved Brass Inset, Carved Bird & Flower Panels, 27 x 27 In. 575.00
Table, Frank Lloyd Wright, Mahogany, 1 Lower Shelf, 1 Drawer, 21 x 27 x 23 In. 1610.00
Table, Frank Lloyd Wright, Mahogany, Hexagonal Top, Signed, 25 x 27 In. 980.00
Table, Frankl, Skyscraper, Cube Shape, Ivory, Tan, Inset Tray Top, 24 x 15 In. 1010.00
Table, French Provincial, Fruitwood, Frieze, Drawer, Tapered Legs, 28 x 38 1/2 x 27 In. . . 920.00
Table, French Provincial, Mahogany, Marble Inset, Pierced Scroll Apron, 26 x 17 x 21 In. 245.00
Table, French Provincial, Mahogany, Molded Edge, Scalloped, 26 1/2 x 23 x 14 In. 1095.00
Table, French Provincial, Oak, Planked Top, Tapered Legs, 28 1/2 In. 980.00
Table, French Provincial, Pine, Frieze Drawer, Angular Legs, 28 x 32 1/2 In. 2990.00
Table, French Provincial, Pine, Planked, Oval, Folding Top, 29 1/2 x 84 x 56 In. 1095.00
Table, French Provincial, Walnut, Flame Veneer, 1 Drawer, 24 x 14 In., Pair 770.00
Table, Fruitwood, 4 Turned & Angled Legs, Stretcher Base, 31 1/4 In. 2875.00
Table, Fruitwood, Ebony, Bone Border, 4 Rectangular Legs, 18 In., Pair 7800.00
Table, Fruitwood, Glass Top, Bronze Finished Plaque Insert, 19 x 18 x 10 1/2 In. 140.00
Table, Fruitwood, Inlaid Bouquet, Butterflies, Bone & Ebony Border, 28 1/2 In. 4610.00
Table, Fruitwood, L. Majorelle, 2 Tiers, Nancy, Signed, 1900, 30 x 22 In. 6600.00
Table, Fruitwood, Mother-Of-Pearl Birds On Leafy Branches, 1890, 28 x 34 In. 3105.00
Table, Fruitwood, Oak, Recessed Frieze, Fluted & Leaf-Clad Leg, 1820s, 29 In. 3700.00
Table, Fruitwood, Rectangular Top, Arch Frieze, Incised Geometric Motifs, 18 In. 690.00
Table, Fruitwood, Rectangular Top, Frieze Drawer, Ring-Turned Legs, 16 x 31 In. 630.00
Table, G. Nakashima, Black Walnut, Triangular, 3 Flaring Dowel Legs, 24 1/2 In. 2015.00
Table, G. Nakashima, Walnut, Free Edge Burl Top, Dowel Legs, 21 In. 2250.00
Table, G. Nakashima, Walnut, Free Edge Plank Top, Spindled Lower Shelf, 28 In. 2990.00
Table, G. Nelson, Circular White Top, Herman Miller, 21 x 18 In. 225.00
Table, G. Nelson, Walnut, Chrome Swagged Legs, 54 x 30 In. 1840.00
Table, G. Stickley, Cloud-Lift Cross Stretchers, 18 x 16 In. 1035.00
Table, G. Stickley, No. 626, Arched Cross-Stretcher Base, 30 x 40 In. 4900.00
Table, G. Stickley, No. 640, Mahogany, Child's, 18 1/2 x 28 x 20 In. 1265.00
Table, G. Stickley, No. 645, Circular Top, Faceted Central Peg, 29 In. 1725.00
Table, G. Stickley, No. 647, Mahogany Finish, 30 x 40 x 27 3/4 In. 3850.00

Table, G. Stickley, No. 667, Mahogany, Faceted Central Peg, 38 x 30 In. 1955.00
Table, G. Stickley, Walnut Leather Top, Dark Mahogany Frame, 30 x 36 In. 3740.00
Table, Galle, Bronze, Fruitwood, 2 Tiers, Signed, 1900, 32 x 36 x 26 1/2 In. 4800.00
Table, Galle, Inlaid Trees, Floral Carving, Signed, 1900, 28 x 27 x 17 In. 1980.00
Table, Galle, Quatrefoil Top, Various Inlaid Wood, Blossoming Lilies, Foliate Legs, 29 In. 1725.00
Table, Game, Arts & Crafts, Round Top, X-Tenon Stretcher, 30 x 40 In. 750.00
Table, Game, Biedermeier, Walnut, Lotus-Carved Legs, Claw & Ball Feet, 1890, 31 In. . . 1700.00
Table, Game, Chippendale, Mahogany, 4 Sunken Cups, Claw & Ball Feet 4180.00
Table, Game, Chippendale, Mahogany, Rectangular Top, Frieze Fitted, 1780, 27 In. 2040.00
Table, Game, Classical, Hinged Folding Top, Gilt Band, Tapered Feet, 30 x 19 In. 4600.00
Table, Game, Empire, Mahogany, Flip Top, Serpentine, 29 1/4 In. 520.00
Table, Game, Empire, Mahogany, Foliated Carved Frieze, 30 x 34 In. 575.00
Table, Game, Empire, Molded Front Skirt, Column On Base, 4 Scrolled Feet, 30 x 35 In. . 165.00
Table, Game, Federal, Birch, Mahogany, Serpentine Top, Peg Feet, 30 In. 7200.00
Table, Game, Federal, Mahogany, D-Shaped Crossbanded Top, 1795, 29 In. 9600.00
Table, Game, Federal, Mahogany, Rectangular Crossbanded Top, 1795, 29 In. 5700.00
Table, Game, Federal, Walnut, Flip Top, Tapered Legs, 1800, 29 1/4 In. 1265.00
Table, Game, Flip Top, Checkers & Backgammon Board, Shelf Stretcher, 28 In. 690.00
Table, Game, Flip Top, Mahogany, Carved Acanthus, Dolphin Base, 1880, 35 x 29 In. . . . 1400.00
Table, Game, Flip Top, Mahogany, Circular Felt Surface, Tapered Legs, 27 1/2 In. 1495.00
Table, Game, Flip Top, Mahogany, Hidden Drawer At Back Legs, 1900s, 30 In. 595.00
Table, Game, Flip Top, Mahogany, Pierced Gallery, Tapered Legs, 32 In. 3910.00
Table, Game, Flip Top, Mahogany, Shell-Form Apron, Cabriole Legs, 31 In. 575.00
Table, Game, George I Style, Walnut, Inlay, Square, 30 x 37 3/4 x 37 In. 1610.00
Table, Game, George II, Mahogany, Checkerboard Inlay, Drawer, 28 x 31 x 22 In. 10350.00
Table, Game, George II, Mahogany, Green Leather Circular Top, 28 x 45 In. 6000.00
Table, Game, George II, Red Walnut, Flip Top, Accordion Action, 32 x 16 In. 3795.00
Table, Game, George III, Mahogany, Hinged Rosewood Top, Square Legs, 29 In. 2990.00
Table, Game, George III, Mahogany, Inlaid, Demilune Top, Ebonized, 29 x 36 x 17 1/2 In. 1380.00
Table, Game, George III, Mahogany, Satinwood Medallions, 35 1/2 x 29 x 18 In. 2760.00
Table, Game, George IV, Mahogany, Conforming Frieze, Reeded Legs, 29 x 30 In. 2875.00
Table, Game, Georgian, Mahogany, Hinged Top, 1 Drawer, Square Legs, 30 x 17 In. 430.00
Table, Game, Georgian, Mahogany, Rectangular Folded Top, Cabriole Legs, 28 In. 1725.00
Table, Game, Hepplewhite, Demilune, Rosewood Bands On Feet, 4 Legs, 36 x 28 In. 1540.00
Table, Game, Hinged Top, Fluted Brass Borders, Baize Surface, 1820s, 30 1/2 In. 9360.00
Table, Game, Ivory Inlay, Bellflower Design, Circular Top, Italy, 29 In. 1495.00
Table, Game, Kingwood, Beige Interior, Pullout Legs, Drawer, 29 1/4 x 33 In. 1265.00
Table, Game, Louis Philippe, Mahogany, Cock-Beaded Frieze, Reeded Legs, 28 In. 1265.00
Table, Game, Louis XVI, Mahogany, Square Top, 1 Frieze Drawer, 1900, 29 In. 805.00
Table, Game, Mahogany, 1 Drawer, Brass Pulls, Swivel Top, 4 Leaves, Wells, 29 3/4 In. . . 770.00
Table, Game, Mahogany, Accordion Action, Fretwork Frieze, Felt Surface, 29 In. 2990.00
Table, Game, Mahogany, Demilune, Hinged Top, 2 Drawers, Brass Ball Feet, 32 In. 3910.00
Table, Game, Mahogany, Hinged Top, Swivels Over Frieze, c.1830, 10 1/4 x 14 In. 3740.00
Table, Game, Mahogany, Inlaid Tablet, Square Tapered Legs, c.1800, 29 1/2 In. 8625.00
Table, Game, Mahogany, Rosewood, Hinged Top, Baize Surface, 29 x 36 In. 8400.00
Table, Game, Mahogany, Scissor-Folding Top, Pedestal Legs, Claw Feet, 33 x 30 In. 475.00
Table, Game, Mahogany, White Marble Top, 4-Part Base, 30 In. 920.00
Table, Game, McHugh, Dark Mahogany, Square Posts, Circular, 30 1/2 x 44 In. 3656.00
Table, Game, Ponti, Walnut, Square Top, Tapered Legs, 29 1/4 x 30 In. 1125.00
Table, Game, Red Paint, Rectangular Breadboard Top, 27 x 18 x 21 1/2 In. 4600.00
Table, Game, Regency, Rosewood, Calamander, Lyre-Shape Supports, 29 x 36 x 18 In. . . 2300.00
Table, Game, Renaissance Revival, Molded Edge, Baize Line Interior, 30 x 18 In. 460.00
Table, Game, Renaissance Revival, Walnut, Checkerboard Top, 1870, 30 In. 19040.00
Table, Game, Rosewood, Swiveling Top, Felt Lined Interior, 30 x 34 In. 690.00
Table, Game, Sheraton, Mahogany, Flip Top, Green Baize Interior, 29 In. 1610.00
Table, Game, Walnut, Flip Top, Blind Drawer, Tapered Legs, c.1790, 29 x 16 x 33 In. 6500.00
Table, Game, Walnut, Inlaid Parquetry, Checkerboard Top, Fitted Interior, 29 x 18 In. . . . 690.00
Table, Game, Walnut, Octagonal, Lift Top, Lazy Susan, Burl Trim, 29 x 33 x 32 In. 1230.00
Table, Game, William IV, Mahogany, Rectilinear Hinged Top, Scroll Feet, 30 In. 1265.00
Table, Game, William IV, Rosewood, Baize Line Interior, Bun Feet, 29 1/4 In. 1475.00
Table, Game, William IV, Rosewood, Flip Top, Rectangular, Bun Feet, 30 In. 1495.00
Table, Game-Work, Rosewood, Sliding Panel, Inlaid Fruitwood, Chess, 28 1/4 In. 3600.00
Table, Gateleg, Drop Leaf, English Oak, Box Stretcher, c.1700, 27 x 30 In. 1265.00

Table, Gateleg, Drop Leaf, Jacobean Style, Oval Top, Carved, 30 x 60 x 77 1/2 In. 1840.00
Table, Gateleg, G. Nelson, Primavera, Herman Miller, 30 x 66 1/2 x 40 In. 920.00
Table, Gateleg, Gothic Revival, Oak, Child's, 18 3/4 x 23 1/2 In. 715.00
Table, Gateleg, Oak, Pegged Construction, 8 Legs, 36 x 11 3/4 x 30 1/2 In. 715.00
Table, Gateleg, Walnut, Butterfly Hinges, Va., 1740, 53 1/4 x 42 1/2 In. 2240.00
Table, Geometric Chrome Frame, Paola Piva Alanda, Italy, 39 1/2 x 14 In. 690.00
Table, George I Style, Mahogany, Sutherland, 29 x 32 x 28 1/2 In. 490.00
Table, George I Style, Oak, Round Center, 27 x 30 1/2 In. 690.00
Table, George I, Mahogany, Circular Scalloped Top, 4 Foliate Cabriole Legs 430.00
Table, George II, Mahogany, Circular Top, Cabriole Legs, 18th Century, 28 In. 4200.00
Table, George III Style, Mahogany, Shaped Top, Splayed Legs, 23 x 10 x 10 In. 430.00
Table, George III, Giltwood, D-Shaped Top, Circular Reeded Leaf Legs, 30 In., Pair 10200.00
Table, George III, Mahogany, 2 Frieze Drawers, Paneled Square Legs, 28 3/4 In. 545.00
Table, George III, Mahogany, Bowfront, Reeded Edge Top, 1 Drawer, 36 x 48 In. 630.00
Table, George III, Mahogany, Demilune, Hinged, Inlay, 30 x 42 x 20 In. 375.00
Table, George III, Mahogany, Fluted Frieze, Urn, Bellflower Chain, 30 x 30 x 72 1/2 In. . .   3450.00
Table, George III, Mahogany, Hinged Top, Arched Frieze, Ball, Claw Feet, 29 x 46 In. . . .   632.00
Table, George III, Mahogany, Mahogany, Crossbanded, 3 Drawers, Bowfront, 35 x 21 In. .   255.00
Table, George III, Mahogany, Rectangular Top, Pierced Bracket, 29 x 30 x 22 In. 6600.00
Table, George III, Mahogany, Satinwood, Circular, 26 1/2 In., Pair 552.00
Table, George III, Mahogany, Tilt Top, Circular Top, Slipper Feet On Casters, 28 In. 6600.00
Table, George III, Mahogany, Tripod, Dish-Shaped Top, Cabriole Legs, 27 3/4 In. 1955.00
Table, George III, Mahogany, Tripod, Hinged Top, Cabriole Legs, Dutch Feet, 29 In. 920.00
Table, George III, Mahogany, Tripod, Leaf Carved Cabriole Legs, 25 1/2 In. 805.00
Table, George III, Mahogany, Tripod, Tilt Top, Cabriole Legs, Paw, Ball Feet, 27 In. 1495.00
Table, Georgian, Mahogany, Gallery Top, 1 Drawer, Cabriole Legs, 24 x 20 In. 545.00
Table, Georgian, Mahogany, Marble Top, Cabriole Legs, Pad Feet, 36 In. 4310.00
Table, Georgian, Oak, Tilt Top, Turned Standard, Cabriole Legs, 28 x 21 In. 1955.00
Table, Georgian, Tilt Top, Figured Piecrust-Edge Top, Acanthus Base, 29 In. 1840.00
Table, Gilbert Poillerat, Iron, Glass, 1940, 20 x 21 In. 9600.00
Table, Gilt, Variegated Rouge Marble Top, Paw Feet, 24 In., Pair 2070.00
Table, Glass Top, Metal & Wire Open Abstract Base, Tubular Metal, 38 In. 1035.00
Table, Gueridon, Belle Epoque, Gilt, Marble Top, Round, France, 27 1/2 x 29 In. 1840.00
Table, Gueridon, Biedermeier, Fruitwood, Circular Black Marble Top, 29 In., Pair 1265.00
Table, Gueridon, Directoire, Black Marble Top, Animal Paw Feet, 28 In., Pair 3910.00
Table, Gueridon, Empire, Circular Veneer Top, Gilt, Animal Paw Feet, 27 1/4 x 26 In. . . .   345.00
Table, Gueridon, Empire, Mahogany, Gilt, Stylized Eagles, Paw Feet, 29 1/2 In. 6615.00
Table, Gueridon, Louis Philippe, Elm, Faded, Figured, Marble Top, Paw Feet, 30 x 39 In. .   1725.00
Table, Gueridon, Louis Philippe, Walnut, Circular Top, Sunburst Inlay, 29 1/2 x 23 In. . . .   1380.00
Table, Gueridon, Louis XVI Style, Mahogany, Marble Top, Brass Gallery, 22 x 24 In. 405.00
Table, Gueridon, Louis XVI, Gilt, Bronze, Circular Malachite Top, Paw Feet, 28 In. 5100.00
Table, Gueridon, Louis XVI, Gilt, Bronze, Circular Marble Top, Tapered Legs, 30 In. 2700.00
Table, Gueridon, Mahogany, Chrysanthemums & Bamboo Gilt, Circular Top, 31 In. 69.00
Table, Gueridon, Regency, Variegated Rouge Marble Top, Bun Feet, 28 In., Pair 2760.00
Table, Gueridon, Variegated Gray Marble Top, 3 Mounted Columnar Supports, 27 In. 4140.00
Table, Hall, Mahogany, Inlaid Medallion & Bellflower, Drawer, Square Legs 825.00
Table, Handkerchief, Gateleg, Queen Anne Style, Mahogany, Drop Leaf, 35 x 18 x 26 In. .   460.00
Table, Handkerchief, Kingwood, Frieze Drawer, Cabriole Legs, P. Sorman, 29 In. 4900.00
Table, Hardwood, Ivory, 3-Part Base, Anglo-Indian, 29 x 20 x 20 In. 1265.00
Table, Hardwood, Stylized Bird, Floral Design, Scrolled, 54 x 36 x 17 1/2 In. 405.00
Table, Harvest, 2 Dovetailed Drawers, Turned Legs, 30 x 58 1/2 x 29 In. 660.00
Table, Harvest, 2-Board Top, 2 Drawers, Baluster Turned Legs, c.1779, 28 1/2 In. 1650.00
Table, Harvest, Burl Walnut, 1 Frieze Drawer, Turned Legs, 29 x 75 In. 2070.00
Table, Harvest, Cherry, Pine, Leaves, Ring-Turned Legs, 90 In. 2640.00
Table, Harvest, Drop Leaf, Cherry, 2-Board Top, 20th Century, 29 1/2 In. 1045.00
Table, Harvest, Drop Leaf, Cherry, Painted Red, Turned Legs, Late 19th Century, 72 In. . .   1650.00
Table, Harvest, Painted Pine, Top Pinned To Frame, 2 Drawers, c.1790, 67 1/2 In. 8250.00
Table, Harvest, Poplar, 3 Board Top, Butternut Base, Turned Legs, 1800s, 30 x 35 In. 505.00
Table, Harvest, Sheraton, Walnut, Beveled End Leaves, 28 1/2 x 83 In. 1680.00
Table, Hepplewhite, Mahogany, Central Cabinet, 8 Drawers, 37 x 34 In. 495.00
Table, Hepplewhite, Mahogany, D-Shape Legs, Tapered Legs, c.1800, 29 x 84 In. 9350.00
Table, Hepplewhite, Mahogany, Drawer, Banded Leg Cuffs, Pa., 29 x 35 1/2 In. 305.00
Table, Hepplewhite, Walnut, Inlaid Legs, Swing Leg, Refinished, 28 x 52 x 44 In. 355.00

Table, Herter Style, Marquetry, Flower Spray, Urns, Gilt, Victorian, 29 x 43 x 27 In. 3740.00
Table, Heywood-Wakefield, Wicker, Oak, Stretcher, 30 x 39 x 23 In. 290.00
Table, I. Noguchi, Laminate Top, Wire Struts, Weighted Base, 20 x 24 In. 1840.00
Table, I. Noguchi, White Laminated Top, Black Wire Base, Child's, 20 In. 3335.00
Table, Ice Cream, Iron, Painted, Tripod, Shell, Acanthus, Marble Top, 22 x 27 In. 110.00
Table, Incense, Elm, Burgundy Lacquer Highlights, 1 Drawer, 31 1/4 In. 520.00
Table, Italian Renaissance, Pine, Carved Stretchers, 19th Century, 20 x 24 1/2 x 18 In. . . . 805.00
Table, Italian Renaissance, White Marble Top, Female Bust, 3 Footed, 1880, 24 In. 1085.00
Table, Jacobean Style, Mahogany, Drawers, H-Stretcher, 29 1/2 x 70 1/2 x 43 In. 2530.00
Table, Jacobean, Oak, Draw Leaf, Rectangular Top, 2 Leaves, 29 1/2 In. 2070.00
Table, Jacobean, Oak, Quartersawn, Carved Apron & Legs, Bun Feet, c.1900, 30 x 54 In. . . 1175.00
Table, John Lewis, Dark Green Top, Light Green, Blue Legs, 35 x 34 x 17 In. 5175.00
Table, Kingwood, Sevres Platter Transfer Top, Lovers In Country, Parquetry, 19 In. 290.00
Table, L. & J.G. Stickley, Mahogany, Hexagonal, 52 In. 6325.00
Table, L. & J.G. Stickley, Mahogany, Overhanging Circular Top, 28 x 30 In. 1350.00
Table, L. & J.G. Stickley, Mahogany, Split Pedestal, Original Finish, 29 x 48 In. 3937.00
Table, L. & J.G. Stickley, No. 377, Hammered Copper Hardware, 48 In. 1760.00
Table, L. & J.G. Stickley, No. 507, 2 Tiers, Handcraft Decal, 24 x 26 In. 4315.00
Table, L. & J.G. Stickley, No. 573, Mahogany, Circular Top, 18 x 29 In. 1495.00
Table, Le Corbusier, Black Enameled Base, Glass Top, 89 x 27 In. 1840.00
Table, Library, Aalto, Elm, Bentwood Legs, Bronze Feet, 1948, 108 In. 4900.00
Table, Library, Aalto, Elm, Rectangular Top, Bentwood Legs, 29 x 108 x 48 In. 6190.00
Table, Library, Aalto, Elm, Rectangular Top, Cast Bronze Feet, 30 x 48 In. 4900.00
Table, Library, Aesthetic Revival, Rectangular Top, Scrolled Legs, 30 x 22 In. 315.00
Table, Library, Arts & Crafts, 2 Drawers, Slat Stretcher, Harden, 30 x 48 x 28 In. 660.00
Table, Library, Arts & Crafts, 3 Drawers, Slat Sides, 29 x 42 x 28 In. 920.00
Table, Library, Arts & Crafts, Bookcase Sides, Center Drawer, 29 x 41 x 27 In. 290.00
Table, Library, Arts & Crafts, Oak, 1 Drawer, Hammered Copper Pulls, c.1912, 30 In. 520.00
Table, Library, Ash, Oak, 2 Drawers, 1 Drawer At Side, Casters, 31 1/2 x 36 3/4 In. 550.00
Table, Library, Baroque, Walnut, Rectangular Overhanging Top, 34 1/2 In. 7200.00
Table, Library, Carved Foliage, Pedestal, Rouge Marble Top, 19th Century, 29 In. 1610.00
Table, Library, Federal, Mahogany, 1 Frieze Drawer, Oblong Top, Phil., 1815, 29 In. 5100.00
Table, Library, G. Stickley, 3 Drawers, Oval Pulls, Red Decal, 30 1/2 x 66 In. 4025.00
Table, Library, G. Stickley, Lower Shelf, Keyed-Through Tenons, Decal, 48 In. 2070.00
Table, Library, G. Stickley, Mahogany, Overhanging Top, Lower Shelf, 30 In. 2300.00
Table, Library, G. Stickley, No. 614, Oak, 2 Drawers, c.1909, 42 In. 2200.00
Table, Library, G. Stickley, No. 616, Mahogany, Square Top, Red Decal, 30 In. 5750.00
Table, Library, G. Stickley, No. 637, Trestle, Light Original Finish, 30 x 48 In. 10125.00
Table, Library, G. Stickley, No. 653, Oak, Rectangular Top, Red Decal, 48 x 29 In. 4900.00
Table, Library, G. Stickley, No. 675, Oak, 2 Drawers, Copper Pulls, 47 1/2 In. 1840.00
Table, Library, G. Stickley, Spindles, Lower Shelf, 29 x 48 x 29 1/2 In. 4025.00
Table, Library, L. & J.G. Stickley, Double Lower Shelf, Label, 29 x 48 In. 1955.00
Table, Library, L. & J.G. Stickley, Mortised Stretcher, Decal, 29 x 48 In. 1840.00
Table, Library, L. & J.G. Stickley, No. 530, Dark Mahogany, 29 x 48 x 30 In. 920.00
Table, Library, L. & J.G. Stickley, No. 531, 1 Drawer, Original Finish, 48 x 30 In. 2300.00
Table, Library, L. & J.G. Stickley, No. 532, Mahogany, Original Finish, 30 In. 5175.00
Table, Library, L. & J.G. Stickley, No. 596, Lower Shelf Keyed Through Base, 66 In. 5175.00
Table, Library, L. & J.G. Stickley, Shelf, 2 Pairs Of Keyed-Through Tenons, Decal, 48 In. . 1725.00
Table, Library, Lifetime, Mahogany, 1 Drawer, 5 Slats, 40 x 22 x 30 In. 2530.00
Table, Library, Limbert, Dark Mahogany, Turtle Top, Original Finish, 29 x 30 In. 3655.00
Table, Library, Limbert, Drawer, Side Slat Shelves, Center Stretcher, 29 x 45 x 26 In. 635.00
Table, Library, Limbert, Mahogany, Original Finish, 29 x 48 x 30 In. 1955.00
Table, Library, Limbert, Mahogany, Single Blind Lift-Top Drawers, 29 x 27 3/4 In. 1575.00
Table, Library, Limbert, No. 106, Oak, Rectangular Top, 1 Drawer, 1907, 29 In. 1380.00
Table, Library, Mahogany, Carved Fruit & Urn Shield, Trestle, 20th Century, 61 In. 400.00
Table, Library, Mahogany, Rectangular Top, 2 Drawers, Imperial Furniture Co., 29 In. . . . 920.00
Table, Library, Oak, Cannonball Carved Legs, Fluted Returns, 29 x 12 x 36 In. 335.00
Table, Library, Oak, Scalloped Skirt, Curved Legs, Shelf, Late 19th Century, 54 In. 230.00
Table, Library, Padoukwood, Rectangular Flush Top, Frieze, Anglo-Indian, 64 x 34 In. . . . 1955.00
Table, Library, Regency Style, Inlaid Satinwood, 32 1/4 x 59 1/2 x 35 In. 2070.00
Table, Library, Regency, Rosewood, Leather Inset, Carved, 2 Drawers, 28 x 48 x 26 In. . . . 6615.00
Table, Library, Renaissance Revival, Walnut, Ornate, Gold Carvings, 48 x 29 In. 1290.00
Table, Library, Renaissance Revival, Walnut, Rectangular Top, 1870, 33 In. 3220.00

Table, Library, Roycroft, Mahogany, Straight Apron, Ebony Finish, 30 x 37 1/2 In. 7310.00
Table, Library, Shop Of The Crafters, No. 335, Mahogany, Slab Sides, 36 x 29 In. 4315.00
Table, Library, Stickley Bros., No. 2613, Mahogany, Signed, 44 x 28 x 30 In. 635.00
Table, Library, Stickley Bros., No. 2654, Mahogany, Rectangular Top, 29 In. 920.00
Table, Library, Stickley Bros., Prairie, Lower Shelf, Metal Tag, 30 x 40 In. 2640.00
Table, Library, Walnut, Foliate Banding, Carved Frieze & Stretcher, 65 In., Open 1725.00
Table, Library, Walnut, Trestle Base, Columns, Italy, 83 x 24 x 30 In. 3080.00
Table, Library, William IV, Mahogany, Leather Top, Turned Legs, 28 1/2 x 41 x 59 In. . . . 4600.00
Table, Library, William IV, Rosewood, Leather Top, Drawers, 30 x 31 x 51 1/2 In. 6900.00
Table, Library, Wolverine, 1 Drawer, 29 x 43 x 27 In. 520.00
Table, Light Mahogany, Brass Trim At Top, Leather Top, Calvin, 24 x 19 In., Pair 460.00
Table, Limbert, Mahogany, Circular Top, Cross Stretchers, 29 1/4 x 36 In. 1725.00
Table, Limbert, Mahogany, Circular Top, Stretcher Panels, 29 x 30 In. 4025.00
Table, Limbert, No. 146, Dark Mahogany Finish, Oval Top, Cutout Sides, 29 In. 1150.00
Table, Limbert, No. 1172, Oak, c.1910, 29 x 42 In. 1265.00
Table, Louis Philippe Style, Fruitwood, Plank Top, 29 1/2 x 31 x 81 In. 1380.00
Table, Louis Philippe, Fruitwood, Pine, Plank, 30 x 87 x 26 In. 3220.00
Table, Louis Philippe, Mahogany, Circular Dish-Shaped Top, Paw Feet, 29 1/2 In. 5750.00
Table, Louis Philippe, Walnut, Rectangular Top, 1 Drawer, 4 Tapered Legs, 27 In. 630.00
Table, Louis XV Style, Bronze Dore, Mounted Amaranth, Drawers, Parquetry, 31 x 73 In. 6325.00
Table, Louis XV Style, Gilt Bronze Mounted, Marquetry, 31 x 29 1/2 x 18 In. 1495.00
Table, Louis XV Style, Green Lacquer Finish, Circular Marble Top, 28 In., Pair 405.00
Table, Louis XV Style, Kidney Shape, Bronze Top, 4 Bronze Cabriole Leg, 28 x 13 In. . . . 865.00
Table, Louis XV Style, Marquetry, Round, Pierced Gallery, Frieze Drawer, 29 x 19 In. . . . 2990.00
Table, Louis XV Style, Oak, Frieze Drawer, Cabriole Legs, 28 x 19 x 14 In., Pair 1265.00
Table, Louis XV Style, Rosewood, Satinwood Floral Marquetry, Cabriole Legs, 29 In. . . . 1380.00
Table, Louis XV Style, Walnut, Circular, 1 Drawer, Brass Legs, 30 x 22 In. 405.00
Table, Louis XV, Kingwood, Leather Surface, Drawers, Bronze Dore, 30 In. 4600.00
Table, Louis XV, Tulipwood, Marquetry, 3 Drawers, France, 19th Century 6000.00
Table, Louis XVI Style, Bronze, Gilt, Circular Top, Lion Paw Feet, 26 1/2 In. 345.00
Table, Louis XVI Style, Kingwood, Marble Top, Brass Gallery, 24 x 18 1/2 x 12 1/2 In. . . . 978.00
Table, Louis XVI Style, Kingwood, Tulipwood, Marble, Inlay, Round, 29 x 24 1/2 In. . . . 2070.00
Table, Louis XVI Style, Mahogany, 2 Drawers, White Marble Top, 28 In., Pair 805.00
Table, Louis XVI Style, Mahogany, Brass Inlay, Square Tapered Legs, 30 x 17 In. 920.00
Table, Louis XVI, Fruitwood, Turned, Angled Legs, 31 x 46 x 48 1/2 In. 2875.00
Table, Louis XVI, Mahogany, Leather, Drawers, Kneehole, France, 1800s, 26 x 44 In. . . . 2645.00
Table, Louis XVI, Mahogany, Variegated Tan Marble Top, Fluted Legs, 1900, 29 In. 1955.00
Table, Louis XVI, Oak, Rectangular Top, Frieze Drawer, Ball Feet, 28 3/4 In. 1610.00
Table, Louis XVI, Walnut, Demilune, Paneled Frieze, Cabriole Legs, 31 1/4 In. 345.00
Table, Magazine, Robsjohn-Gibbings, Walnut Top, Widdicomb, 30 x 22 In. 920.00
Table, Mahogany, 2 Parts, Outswept Legs, 2 Leaves, Brass Paw Feet, 52 1/2 In. 4370.00
Table, Mahogany, 2 Tiers, Majorelle, 1902, 32 x 35 1/2 x 23 In. 7200.00
Table, Mahogany, Adjustable Book Rest, Brass Candleholders, 30 In. 9600.00
Table, Mahogany, Carved Apron, Cabriole Legs, Chinese, 19th Century, 10 1/2 In. 170.00
Table, Mahogany, Cherry Legs, Scalloped Apron, Splayed Legs, 27 In. 505.00
Table, Mahogany, Circular Top Over Frieze, Slide, Kittinger, 24 3/4 In., Pair 410.00
Table, Mahogany, Cypress Back Rail, Aiken, South Carolina, 1770, 42 x 17 In. 450.00
Table, Mahogany, Demilune, Shaped Frieze, 1780s, 30 In. 30 x 52 In. 3450.00
Table, Mahogany, Foldover, Inlaid Satinwood Panels, 29 1/4 x 34 3/4 In. 750.00
Table, Mahogany, Frieze Drawers, Squared Tapered Legs, 44 1/3 In. 425.00
Table, Mahogany, Lion's-Head Pull, 1 Drawer, Paw Feet, 29 x 38 3/4 In. 2090.00
Table, Mahogany, Marble Top, 3-Part Stretcher, Paw Feet, 1820s, 29 In. 6840.00
Table, Mahogany, Marble Top, Marble Columns, Veneered Shelf, Paw Feet, 40 In. 6050.00
Table, Mahogany, Marquetry, Carved Shells & Vine, Pedestal, 20th Century, 31 In. 1980.00
Table, Mahogany, Oak Top, Cabriole Legs, Square, Victorian, 30 x 22 In. 896.00
Table, Mahogany, Opposing Frieze Drawers, 2 Leaves, Outswept Legs, 28 1/2 In. 1725.00
Table, Mahogany, Rectangular Top, Tapered Legs, Spade Feet, 25 In. 405.00
Table, Mahogany, Reeded Edge Top, Outswept Legs, Brass Feet, 140 In. 8050.00
Table, Mahogany, Reeded Stiles, 2 Drawers, Brass Caps & Casters, c.1820, 29 1/2 In. . . . 2760.00
Table, Mahogany, Rounded Drop Leaves, Scalloped Apron, Cabriole Legs, 1765, 28 In. . . 4600.00
Table, Mahogany, Satinwood Crossbanded Top, Frieze Drawer, Casters, 27 1/2 In. 5700.00
Table, Mahogany, Tiered, 3 Squared Stiles, Sphere To Supporting Shelves, 37 In. 125.00
Table, Mahogany, Tulipwood, Marble Top, Frieze With Drawer, 1900, 28 1/2 In. 8400.00

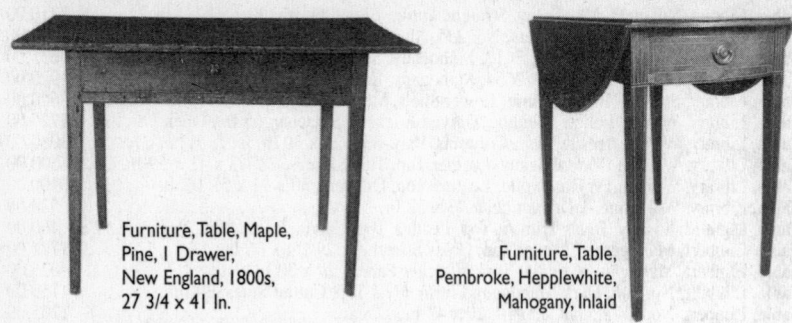

Furniture, Table, Maple,
Pine, 1 Drawer,
New England, 1800s,
27 3/4 x 41 In.

Furniture, Table,
Pembroke, Hepplewhite,
Mahogany, Inlaid

Table, Mahogany, Undulating Gallery, Shell Frieze, Leaf-Carved Feet, 27 In., Pair 270.00
Table, Mahogany, White Pine, Turned Legs, 1820, 29 x 114 x 50 In. 2800.00
Table, Mahogany, White, Gray Marble Top, Splayed Top, 29 In. 1725.00
Table, Mahogany, Wicker Top, Cabriole Legs, 30 x 27 In. 615.00
Table, Maple, Pine, 1 Drawer, New England, 1800s, 27 3/4 x 41 In. .... *Illus* 920.00
Table, Maple, Pine, Breadboard Top, Box Stretchers, Mid 1700s, 27 x 42 x 24 In. 7475.00
Table, Maple, Pine, Overhang Top, Drawer, New England, Early 1800s, 28 x 41 x 28 In. .. 920.00
Table, Marble Top, Brass Mount, Enamel Oval Plaques Base, 1960, Pair 990.00
Table, Marble Top, Square, 30 x 14 1/4 In. 60.00
Table, Marble Top, Star Design Within Marble Circle, Bronze Swan Base, 24 1/2 In. 1610.00
Table, Marble, Giltwood, Round, Geometric Inlaid Top, 26 1/2 x 20 1/4 In. 2990.00
Table, McArthur, Lacquered Metal, Steel Top & Lower Shelf, 23 1/2 x 20 In. 3640.00
Table, McCobb, Ash Veneer, Travertine Top, 2 Thin Drawers, Calvin, 24 In. 620.00
Table, Molded Plastic Top, Wood Grain, Black Metal Legs, 70 x 31 x 35 In. 980.00
Table, Nanwood, Narrow Plain Apron, Recessed Leg, Chinese, 34 In. 1840.00
Table, Napoleon III, Bronze Dore, Mounted, Ebonized, c.1875, 30 1/2 x 58 x 34 3/4 In. .. 2760.00
Table, Napoleon III, Bronze Dore, Rectangular Top, Top-Shaped Feet, 30 1/4 x 51 In. 1090.00
Table, Napoleon III, Maple, Marquetry, Carved, Leaves, Fluting, 30 x 46 x 29 1/2 In. 1610.00
Table, Napoleon III, Tulipwood, Gilt, Bronze, Leafy Scrolls, 18 1/2 x 52 x 33 In. 3900.00
Table, Neoclassical Style, Painted, Marble Top, Tapered Square Legs, 17 x 40 x 29 In. ... 2185.00
Table, Neoclassical, Painted, Ribbon-Tied Floral Garlands, Ocher Ground, 26 1/2 In. 9000.00
Table, Neoclassical, Swag Border, Reeded Legs, Early 20th Century, 32 1/2 In. 1265.00
Table, Neoclassical, Walnut, Parquetry, Octagonal, Geometric Inlay, Holland, 28 x 19 In. .. 1725.00
Table, Neoclassical, White Marble Center Top, Square Top, 29 1/2 In. 3300.00
Table, Neogrecque, Gilt Incised, Ebonized, Round, Needlework, Glass, 31 1/2 x 22 In. ... 460.00
Table, Nesting, Carved Birds & Floral, Dragons, Oriental, 4 Piece 660.00
Table, Nesting, E. Wormley, Mahogany, Cloud-Lift Apron, 24 1/2 x 22 In., 4 Piece 1265.00
Table, Nesting, E. Wormley, Mahogany, Rectangular Top, 22 In., 4 Piece 1265.00
Table, Nesting, Hardwood, Chinese, Flush Panel Top, Tallest 27 x 21 x 15 In., 4 Piece ... 430.00
Table, Nesting, Hepplewhite, Mahogany, Inlaid, 20th Century, 28 x 28 In., 4 Piece 605.00
Table, Nesting, Mahogany, Leather Tops, Top Twist Borders, 3 Piece, 24 In. 115.00
Table, Nesting, Oblong Top, Trestle Ends, Downswept Legs, 1860, 7 Ft. 2 In., 4 Piece ... 2700.00
Table, Nesting, Peche, Metal Legs, Rubber Feet, 1990, 16 In. 1150.00
Table, Nesting, Pressed Glass Enameled Top, Ebonized Tripod Base, 28 x 25 In. 365.00
Table, Nesting, Queen Anne, Mahogany, Cabriole Legs, Pad Feet, 21 In., 3 Piece 750.00
Table, Oak, 2 Hinged Leaves Stored Below Top, Bauhaus, c.1927, 115 1/2 In. 460.00
Table, Oak, 4 Leaves, Michigan Chair Co., 29 1/2 x 54 In. 1600.00
Table, Oak, Bamboo Legs, Stretcher, Oriental Style, 18 1/4 x 72 1/4 x 28 In., Pair 160.00
Table, Oak, Green Marble Top, 2 Cane Shelves, 27 1/2 In. 1380.00
Table, Oak, Large Lion Heads, Claw Feet, 5 Leaves, 1890, 60 In. 7170.00
Table, Oak, Paw Feet On 4 Pillars, 4 Self-Storing Leaves, 90 In. 1200.00
Table, Oak, Pedestal, Carved Lion Heads & Acanthus, 29 x 69 In., 126 In. Open 5230.00
Table, Oak, Rectangular Top, Vertical Sides, Old Hickory, 26 x 14 x 24 In. 430.00
Table, Oak, Split Pedestal, Claw Footed, 2 Leaves, Pre 1900, 48 In. 1900.00
Table, Oak, Square, Pedestal Base, 4 Leaves, c.1885, 54 In. 3080.00
Table, Oak, Tripod, 4-Plank Snap Top, Oval, 1740, 26 x 28 In. 805.00
Table, Oak, Walnut, Rectangular Top, Flowerheads, Turned Legs, 31 In. 1440.00

Table, Oak, Wicker, 2 Tiers, 4-Board, Quartersawn, Corner Posts, Shelf, 30 x 72 x 36 In. . 1440.00
Table, Orange, Yellow Stippled Design, 1 Drawer, Pa., 1825, 28 x 20 In. 5500.00
Table, Oval Top, Inset Mother-Of-Pearl, Foliate Designs, Papier-Mache, 28 x 26 In. 830.00
Table, P. Evans, Directional Cube, Copper, Bronze & Pewter, Slate Top, 19 x 13 In., Pair . 920.00
Table, Palissandre, 2 Tiers, Emile-Jacques Ruhlmann, c.1932, 19 3/4 x 32 In. 72625.00
Table, Panel, Red Lacquer, Riverscape Scene, Gilt, Rectangular Top, 15 1/2 In. 6000.00
Table, Papier-Mache, Gilt Floral, Inlaid Mother-Of-Pearl, 1830s, 28 x 24 In. 1450.00
Table, Pembroke, 2 Drop Leaves, 1 Drawer, Square Tapered Legs, 28 In. 880.00
Table, Pembroke, Cherry, Beaded Frieze, Heart, Diamond Stretcher, c.1780, 27 3/4 In. . . . 7475.00
Table, Pembroke, Cherry, Stretcher Base, Drawer, Taper Legs, 32 1/2 x 40 1/2 x 29 In. . . . 468.00
Table, Pembroke, Chippendale, Mahogany, Chamfered Corners, Stretcher, 32 x 35 x 29 In. 715.00
Table, Pembroke, Chippendale, Mahogany, Oak, Pine, 1 Dovetailed Drawer, 27 In. 415.00
Table, Pembroke, Chippendale, Walnut, Cross Stretchers, Pa., c.1770, 28 1/2 x 32 In. 825.00
Table, Pembroke, Drop Leaf, George I, Mahogany, Frieze Drawers, 29 x 39 3/4 In. 1265.00
Table, Pembroke, Drop Leaf, George III, Mahogany, Diamond Inlay, 27 x 20 x 34 In. 2990.00
Table, Pembroke, Drop Leaf, George III, Mahogany, Drawer, 27 1/2 x 22 x 31 In. 2185.00
Table, Pembroke, Drop Leaf, George III, Serpentine Leaves, Square Tapered Legs, 28 In. . 1440.00
Table, Pembroke, Drop Leaf, George IV, Mahogany, Early 1800s, 27 x 25 x 48 In. 1955.00
Table, Pembroke, Drop Leaf, Hepplewhite, Walnut Top, Wood Base, 29 x 36 x 45 In. 635.00
Table, Pembroke, Drop Leaf, Hepplewhite, Walnut, Drawer, c.1800, 28 x 32 In. 1100.00
Table, Pembroke, Drop Leaf, Sheraton, Cherry, 1 Drawer, 1860, 28 x 42 In. 550.00
Table, Pembroke, Drop Leaf, Walnut, Drawer, Pennsylvania, c.1800, 29 x 34 1/2 In. 360.00
Table, Pembroke, Drop Leaf, Walnut, Drawer, Spade Feet, 18 x 32 In. 2970.00
Table, Pembroke, Federal, Mahogany, Drawer, c.1820, 29 x 39 In. 1430.00
Table, Pembroke, Federal, Mahogany, Maple Inlay, Drawer, c.1800, 28 x 20 x 39 In. 5400.00
Table, Pembroke, Federal, Mahogany, Rectangular Top, 1 Drawer, 1800, 28 In. 7760.00
Table, Pembroke, Federal, Mahogany, Rectangular Top, Drop Leaf, c.1790, 29 x 30 In. . . . 1210.00
Table, Pembroke, George III, Mahogany, Inlaid, c.1790, 28 3/4 x 37 x 36 In. 3450.00
Table, Pembroke, George III, Mahogany, Plain Frieze, Square Legs, 27 1/4 In. 805.00
Table, Pembroke, George III, Mahogany, Rectangular Hinged Flaps, 26 x 19 1/2 In. 520.00
Table, Pembroke, George III, Mahogany, Rectangular Top, Frieze Drawer, 27 In. 3910.00
Table, Pembroke, George III, Satinwood, Rectangular Top, Cuffed Legs, 28 In. 7800.00
Table, Pembroke, George III, Satinwood, Rosewood, Tapered Legs, 29 In. 3000.00
Table, Pembroke, Hepplewhite, Cherry, 2 Leaves, Square Legs, c.1800, 29 x 37 3/4 In. . . . 880.00
Table, Pembroke, Hepplewhite, Mahogany, Inlaid . . . . *Illus* 6800.00
Table, Pembroke, Hepplewhite, Maple, Shaped Top, 2 Leaves, 29 x 26 1/2 x 17 In. 635.00
Table, Pembroke, Hepplewhite, Walnut, 1 Drawer, Banded Cuffs, c.1810, 29 1/2 x 36 In. . 660.00
Table, Pembroke, Mahogany, 1 Bowed Drawer, Marquetry Urn, 1790, 28 x 40 In. 5750.00
Table, Pembroke, Mahogany, Banding, String Inlaid Legs, Drawer, 28 3/4 In. 1260.00
Table, Pembroke, Mahogany, Cookie Corners, Square Legs, 27 x 19 1/2 In. 1870.00
Table, Pembroke, Mahogany, Frieze Drawer, Platform Stretcher, 28 x 22 1/2 In. 5700.00
Table, Pembroke, Mahogany, Oak, Chamfered Legs, 28 x 18 x 27 1/4 In. 440.00
Table, Pembroke, Mahogany, Rectangular Top, Foliate Carved Legs, 29 In. 635.00
Table, Pembroke, Mahogany, Walnut, White Pine, 1825, 26 3/4 x 17 x 6 1/2 In. 475.00
Table, Pembroke, Sheraton, Mahogany, Veneer, Reed Legs, 1-Board Top, 30 1/2 x 19 In. . 2090.00
Table, Pembroke, Walnut, 1 Drawer, Turned Legs, England, 29 x 37 In. 690.00
Table, Pier, Classical, Mahogany, Veneer, Black Marble, Scroll, Fan, c.1825, 34 x 38 In. . . 2760.00
Table, Pier, Empire, Mahogany, Parcel Gilt, Marble Top, c.1840, 30 x 37 In. 5400.00

**Store table leaves flat, not
on end, or they may warp.
Under the bed is a good
storage spot.**

Furniture, Table, Pine, 2-Board Top, 1 Drawer,
Painted, New England, 46 x 31 In.

Table, Pier, Walnut, Tripod, Gold Paint, Round Top, Continental, 30 x 39 In. 165.00
Table, Pine, 2-Board Top, 1 Drawer, Painted, New England, 46 x 31 In. . . . .*Illus* 3450.00
Table, Pine, Dovetailed Skirt Drawer, Turned Legs, 28 x 52 x 30 1/2 In. 550.00
Table, Pine, Maple, Overhang Base, 2 Drawers, New England, c.1760, 28 1/2 x 65 In. . . . 1650.00
Table, Pine, Painted, Demilune Overhanging Top, New England, c.1815, 29 1/2 x 32 In. . . . 550.00
Table, Pine, Painted, Galleried Top, 1 Drawer, Square Tapered Legs, 1820, 31 In. 3850.00
Table, Pine, Painted, Overhang, Serpentine Front, N.H., c.1800, 28 1/2 x 32 x 19 In. 5750.00
Table, Pine, Poplar, Pinned To Bench Base, Cutout Feet, 19th Century, 96 In. 8250.00
Table, Pine, Top Within Scrolling Leaves, Cabriole Legs, Pad Feet, 32 1/2 In. 2760.00
Table, Poplar, Pine, Sawbuck, Lower Shelf, 2-Board Top, 29 5/8 x 72 In. 440.00
Table, Prairie School, Draw Leaf, 2-Leg Base, Stretcher, Ball Feet, 30 x 48 x 78 In. 1035.00
Table, Queen Anne Style, Chinoiserie, Frieze, Pendant Shell, 28 x 32 x 22 In. 865.00
Table, Refectory, Baroque, Walnut, Ornately Carved Legs, Rectangular, 79 In. 1035.00
Table, Refectory, Mahogany, Rectangular Top, Square Tapered Legs, 30 In. 1150.00
Table, Refectory, Oak, Plank Top, Wrought Iron Braces, 29 3/4 x 36 1/2 In. 4600.00
Table, Refectory, Pine, Black, White Paint, Orange, White Panels, 77 x 30 In. 715.00
Table, Refectory, Walnut, 2-Board Top, Formal Columns, Italy, 1800s, 83 x 33 x 30 In. . . . 8050.00
Table, Refectory, Walnut, Lyre-Form Supports, 17th Century, 29 3/4 x 35 1/2 In. 5175.00
Table, Refectory, Walnut, Plank Top, Rosette, Medallion Center Stretcher, 44 In. 7200.00
Table, Refectory, Walnut, Planked Top, Block Stretchers, 33 1/4 x 80 In. 5175.00
Table, Refectory, Walnut, Rectangular Plank Top, Gadrooned Frieze, Italy, 32 In. 7200.00
Table, Refectory, Walnut, Rectangular Top, Turned Legs, Ball Feet, 34 In. 2530.00
Table, Refectory, Walnut, Thumb-Carved Skirt, 8 Baluster Legs, 17th Century, 32 In. 9350.00
Table, Refractory, Pine, Turned Legs, Red Paint, 32 x 85 x 36 In. 1650.00
Table, Regency Style, Mahogany, 2 Parts, Turned Stems, 29 1/4 x 45 In. 4830.00
Table, Regency Style, Mahogany, 3 Parts, 29 3/4 x 47 x 138 1/2 In. 4830.00
Table, Regency, 2 Tiers, Convex Lower Stretcher, France, 35 x 21 In. 2875.00
Table, Regency, D-Shaped Top, Conforming Frieze, Brass Feet, 29 1/2 In. 6615.00
Table, Regency, Mahogany, 4 Saber Legs On Brass Caps, 28 In. 3600.00
Table, Regency, Mahogany, Drawer, Turned Legs, Early 1800s, 25 x 17 3/4 In. 470.00
Table, Regency, Mahogany, Outswept Reeded Legs, Brass Paw Feet, 29 In. 4140.00
Table, Regency, Mahogany, Reeded Edge, Brass Feet, 19th Century, 29 In. 2990.00
Table, Regency, Rosewood, Frieze, Brass Rosettes, 19 1/2 x 23 1/2 x 47 1/2 In. 2990.00
Table, Regency, Rosewood, Rectangular Top, Brass Paw Feet, 28 1/2 In. 2300.00
Table, Renaissance Revival, Burl Walnut Marble Top, 1875, 28 x 26 x 22 In. 1345.00
Table, Renaissance Revival, Oval White Marble Top, Hoof Feet, 1875, 36 In. 2630.00
Table, Renaissance Revival, Walnut, Cartouche Marble Top, Cabriole Legs, 29 In. 2185.00
Table, Renaissance Revival, Walnut, Carved Skirt, Hoof Feet, 1875, 34 x 30 In. 1510.00
Table, Renaissance Revival, Walnut, Molded Top, Scrolled Plinths, 29 x 31 x 51 In. 1955.00
Table, Renaissance Revival, Walnut, Scenic, Floral Inlaid Top, 1875, 36 x 28 In. 2520.00
Table, Ribbon-Twist Border, Marquetry Band, Brass & Tortoiseshell, 36 In. 3600.00
Table, Robsjohn-Gibbings, Mahogany, Signed, Widdicomb, 29 x 19 x 22 In. 575.00
Table, Robsjohn-Gibbings, Walnut, 3 Tiers, Widdicomb, 24 In., Pair 805.00
Table, Rococo, Gilt, Carved, Pietra Dura Top, Foliate, Geometric, 33 x 44 In. 2645.00
Table, Rococo, Mahogany, Carved, Oval Marble Top, Serpentine Legs, 1860, 29 In. 4025.00
Table, Rococo, Rosewood, Turtle Top, Carved Florals, 48 x 40 x 31 In. 3415.00
Table, Rococo, Rosewood, White Turtle Top, 1865, 52 x 29 In. 3640.00
Table, Rococo, Rosewood, White Turtle Top, 1865, 52 x 31 x 29 In. 2240.00
Table, Rococo, Walnut, Gilt Brass Mounted, 1850s, 28 1/2 x 54 x 33 In. 3738.00
Table, Rococo, Walnut, Marble, Oval, Carved, 30 1/2 x 26 x 19 In. 1725.00
Table, Rococo, Walnut, Marble, Oval, Pedestal, 30 x 29 x 21 In. 1725.00
Table, Rohde, Walnut Veneer, Concave Front, Plank Base, 23 In., Pair 1010.00
Table, Rohde, Walnut, Leather Legs, Herman Miller, 23 x 27 In., Pair 1125.00
Table, Rosewood, Chinese, Pierced Frieze, Box Stretcher, 20 1/2 x 21 1/2 x 17 In. 220.00
Table, Rosewood, Ivory, Oriental Woman Holding Bird, c.1840, 28 1/4 In. 5760.00
Table, Rosewood, Marble Turtle Top, Cabriole Legs, 1860, 42 x 29 In. 1120.00
Table, Rosewood, Marquetry Flowers & Foliage, Pierced Stretcher, 1860, 48 In. 9200.00
Table, Rosewood, Molded Top, Scroll Feet, Chinese, 12 x 40 In. 345.00
Table, Rosewood, Walnut, Cartouche Inlay, Foliate Scrolls, Hoof Feet, 30 1/2 In. 8640.00
Table, Salon, Gilt, Carved, Floral Pietra Dure Top, Round, c.1890, 31 x 25 In. 3450.00
Table, Satinwood, Circular Top, Silver Leaf Edge, Fluted Legs, Side, 20 x 22 In. 1010.00
Table, Satinwood, Crossbanded D-Shaped Top, Platform Stretcher, 41 3/4 In. 6600.00
Table, Satinwood, Strung Frieze, Lower Shelf, c.1900, 27 3/4 In. 2185.00

Table, Sawbuck, Pine, Baseboards Form Well, Square Nail, 27 x 24 3/8 In. 470.00
Table, Sawbuck, Pine, Cross Legs, V Trough, Blue Green Paint, 1800s, 30 x 42 x 25 In. . . . 805.00
Table, Sawbuck, Pine, Square-Nail Construction, Beaded Edges, 25 14 x 31 3/4 In. 990.00
Table, Sawbuck, Pine, Square-Nail Construction, Removable Baseboard, 36 1/2 In. 2420.00
Table, Sewing, Bird's-Eye Maple, Tiger Maple, Cherry, 2 Drawers, c.1825, 29 In. 1610.00
Table, Sewing, Black Lacquer, Fitted Interior, Faux Bamboo Stand, 24 x 24 1/2 In. 690.00
Table, Sewing, Black Lacquer, Hinged Lid, Fitted, Frame, Anglo-Chinese, 12 x 17 In. . . . 1095.00
Table, Sewing, Black Lacquer, Landscape On Hinged Top, Ivory Implements, 34 In. 1955.00
Table, Sewing, Burl Walnut, Lift Top, 4 Interior Compartments, 3 Legs, 28 x 14 In. 1380.00
Table, Sewing, Cherry, Dovetailed Drawer, 4 Scrolled Legs, 19th Century, 28 In. 250.00
Table, Sewing, Cherry, Empire, 4 Drawers, Locking Compartment, 29 In. 280.00
Table, Sewing, Cherry, Over-Hanging Drawers, Samuel Hitchins, c.1800, 30 x 33 1/2 In. . . 4600.00
Table, Sewing, Chinese Export, Black Lacquer, Octagonal, 39 3/4 x 19 x 13 1/2 In. 575.00
Table, Sewing, Classical, Mahogany, Carved, Claw Feet, c.1830, 29 x 24 x 18 In. 1265.00
Table, Sewing, Classical, Mahogany, Hinged Leaves, 2 Drawers, 1830s, 30 x 18 x 19 In. . . 1380.00
Table, Sewing, Dome Top, Mahogany, Ornate Cabriole Legs, Victorian, 1875, 31 In. 535.00
Table, Sewing, Drop Leaf, Arts & Crafts, 2 Drawers, Tapered Legs, 29 x 18 x 18 In. 345.00
Table, Sewing, Drop Leaf, Cherry, Frieze Drawer, Ball Feet, 28 3/4 x 39 3/4 In. 230.00
Table, Sewing, Drop Leaf, Curly Maple, Drawers, Bird's-Eye Veneer, 30 1/4 In. 5060.00
Table, Sewing, Drop Leaf, Empire, Mahogany Veneer, 2 Drawers, 29 1/2 x 35 1/2 In. 248.00
Table, Sewing, Drop Leaf, Mahogany, 2 Drawers, Scroll Feet, 28 x 15 1/2 In. 310.00
Table, Sewing, Drop Leaf, Mahogany, 3 Drawers, Sewing Bag, c.1840, 28 1/2 In. 1650.00
Table, Sewing, Drop Leaf, Mahogany, Pedestal, Isaac Vose, 1825, 30 x 21 In. 2875.00
Table, Sewing, Drop Leaf, Mahogany, Tapered Legs, 29 x 19 1/4 In. 750.00
Table, Sewing, Drop Leaf, Sheraton, Mahogany, Writing Surface, 28 1/2 x 17 In. 1495.00
Table, Sewing, Drop Leaf, Sliding Work Box, 2 Drawers, 28 1/2 x 36 In. 1610.00
Table, Sewing, Eastlake, Greek Key, Mirror, Compartments, Ebonized, Gilt, 25 x 29 In. . . 840.00
Table, Sewing, Empire, Mahogany, American, c.1820, 26 1/2 x 35 1/2 In. 385.00
Table, Sewing, Federal, 2 Drawers, Square Tapered Legs, c.1800, 18 x 16 x 30 In. 805.00
Table, Sewing, Federal, Brass Inlay, 3 Drawers, Leaf Carved, Stencil, c.1815, 32 x 22 In. . 2400.00
Table, Sewing, Federal, Carved Acanthus, Interior Compartments, 30 In. 1400.00
Table, Sewing, Federal, Cherry, Tiger Maple, 3 Drawers, Carved Legs, 26 x 23 x 16 In. . . 460.00
Table, Sewing, Federal, Mahogany Veneer, 2 Drawers, Pennsylvania, 30 x 19 In. 300.00
Table, Sewing, Federal, Mahogany, 2 Drawers, Turned Columnar Legs, 29 x 19 In. 375.00
Table, Sewing, Federal, Mahogany, 2 Graduated Drawers, Mass., 1810, 17 x 19 In. 5700.00
Table, Sewing, Federal, Mahogany, Figured Maple, Crossbanded, 1820, 19 x 16 In. 1440.00
Table, Sewing, Fruitwood, Galleried Top, Arched Feet, 29 x 18 x 11 1/2 In. 805.00
Table, Sewing, Hepplewhite, Birch, Pine, Pegged, Square Nails, 42 x 27 x 29 In. 550.00
Table, Sewing, Hepplewhite, Walnut, 1 Drawer, Tapered Legs, 27 x 15 x 20 In. 410.00
Table, Sewing, Mahogany Veneer, Female Bronze Figures, 1870, 31 In. 1120.00
Table, Sewing, Mahogany Veneer, Serpentine, 1 Drawer, Tray, England, 20 x 15 In. 990.00
Table, Sewing, Mahogany, 2 Drawers, Brass Pulls, Divided Interior, 28 1/2 In. 1760.00
Table, Sewing, Mahogany, 2 Drawers, Sewing-Bag Frame, c.1810, 29 In. 880.00
Table, Sewing, Mahogany, 2 Graduated Drawers, 2 Side Doors, Baltimore, 28 1/2 In. 990.00
Table, Sewing, Mahogany, Cherry, Rectilinear Top, Spiral Reeded Legs, Ball Feet, 29 In. . 690.00
Table, Sewing, Mahogany, Flame-Veneered Drawers, Lower Shelf, 1825, 33 1/2 In. 2760.00
Table, Sewing, Mahogany, Hinged Astragal Top, Divided Interior, c.1810, 29 In. 6325.00
Table, Sewing, Mahogany, Rectilinear Lift Top, Bag Drawer, Paw Feet, 28 1/4 In. 2530.00
Table, Sewing, Mahogany, Sliding Frame For Bag, 1 Drawer, Ball Feet, 1840s, 29 In. 345.00
Table, Sewing, Martha Washington, Mahogany, 3 Drawers, End Sections, 28 x 14 In. 220.00
Table, Sewing, Mother-Of-Pearl, Painted Lift Top, Gold Trim, 1870, 31 x 13 In. 498.00
Table, Sewing, Painted, Hinged Top, Courting Scene, Wells, Beveled Mirror, 27 1/2 In. . . 230.00
Table, Sewing, Pink, Multiplank Top, 1 Plain Frieze, Turned Legs, 30 x 68 x 27 In. 1265.00
Table, Sewing, Poplar Top, Yellow Pine Base, 19th Century, 28 1/2 x 37 x 24 In. 500.00
Table, Sewing, Poplar, Maple, Square Tapered Legs, c.1790, 27 x 33 1/2 In. 880.00
Table, Sewing, Regency, Mahogany, Inlaid Top, Canted Corners, Scroll Legs, c.1810 . . . . 2530.00
Table, Sewing, Regency, Mahogany, Rectangular Top, Raised On Casters, 30 In. 1610.00
Table, Sewing, Regency, Pine, Ebonized, Penwork, Bag Drawer, 30 x 18 x 18 In. 3450.00
Table, Sewing, Rosewood, Double Lift Top, 1860, 31 x 21 x 17 In. 1456.00
Table, Sewing, Rosewood, Lift Top, Fitted Covers, Tripod Base, 29 1/2 x 10 x 16 In. 2875.00
Table, Sewing, Rosewood, Metal, Shell Inlay, Lift Top, 2 Drawers, 29 x 20 1/2 x 14 In. . . 2245.00
Table, Sewing, Rosewood, Shallow Frieze Drawer, Trestle Base, 29 3/4 x 17 1/2 In. 860.00
Table, Sewing, Sheraton, Cherry, Bird's-Eye Maple Veneer, Pa., c.1815, 29 x 22 In. 1540.00

Table, Sewing, Tiger Maple, Cherry, 2 Drawers, Tapered Legs, 28 x 28 In. 5465.00
Table, Sewing, Walnut, 1 Drawer, Storage Bag, Lower Shelf, Victorian, 29 3/4 In. 660.00
Table, Sewing, Walnut, 1 Overlapping Drawer, Removable Top, Square Feet, 26 1/2 In. .. 2090.00
Table, Sewing, Walnut, 2 Burl Veneer Drawers, Pullout Section, 30 x 31 x 16 In. 415.00
Table, Sewing, Walnut, Yarn Drawer, c.1875, 29 x 21 x 15 In. 785.00
Table, Shaker, Scrubbed Top, Red Painted Base, 29 x 84 x 37 In. 8250.00
Table, Shaker, Tailor's, Red Stain, Pine, Maple, Rectangular Top, Enfield, Ct., 28 In. 3450.00
Table, Sheraton, Cherry, Veneer, Demilune, 2 Leaves, 41 x 23 x 29 In. 2310.00
Table, Sheraton, Figured Mahogany, Ring Legs, 1 Drawer, England, 19 x 30 In. 685.00
Table, Sheraton, Mahogany, Acanthus Carved Legs, 29 x 36 1/2 x 20 In. 690.00
Table, Sheraton, Mahogany, Pine, 2 Drawers, Bowfront, 31 x 37 1/2 x 16 In. 4370.00
Table, Sheraton, Mahogany, Pine, D-Leaves, Drawer, 1820s, 21 x 41 In. 336.00
Table, Sheraton, Painted, Yellow Grain, Drawer, Pa., c.1825, 30 x 19 3/4 In. 770.00
Table, Sheraton, Pine, Overall Grain, Pinstripe Design, c.1820, 29 1/2 x 31 In. 385.00
Table, Side, Art Deco, Black Lacquered Finish, Curved Wooden Sides, 25 x 19 In., Pair .. 750.00
Table, Side, Black Enameled Shelves, Black Lacquer Top, Howell, 21 & 25 In., Pair 1265.00
Table, Side, Black Lacquer, Applied Silver Leaf Dots, Pierre LeGrain, 29 3/4 In. 2810.00
Table, Side, Charles II, Oak, Rectangular Top, Frieze Drawer, Turned Legs, 30 In. 2300.00
Table, Side, Classical, Brass, White Onyx, Incised, Acanthus Leaf Feet, 31 1/2 x 15 In. .. 500.00
Table, Side, Continental, Marquetry, Drop Leaf, 23 x 22 x 26 1/2 In. 635.00
Table, Side, Donald Deskey, Black Enameled Circular Wooden Top, 28 x 22 In. 845.00
Table, Side, E. Wormley, Sheaf Of Wheat, Circular Travertine Top, 20 x 27 In. 865.00
Table, Side, Eames, White Laminate Top, Aluminum Base, 36 In. 180.00
Table, Side, Edwardian, Mahogany, Satinwood, Turned Legs, 33 x 27 In. 230.00
Table, Side, Empire, Geometrically Veneered Tops, Paw Feet, 27 In., Pair 2070.00
Table, Side, English Oak, Frieze Drawer, Box Stretcher, 30 1/2 x 34 1/4 x 25 1/4 In. 2185.00
Table, Side, French Provincial, Beech, Marble Top, 27 1/4 x 32 x 26 3/4 In. 2185.00
Table, Side, French Provincial, Fruitwood, Banded Top, Drawer, 32 x 30 x 17 In. 430.00
Table, Side, G. Nakashima, Walnut, Free-Edge Plank Top, 21 x 28 x 25 In. 2990.00
Table, Side, G. Nakashima, Walnut, Free-Edge Top, Dowel Legs, 17 1/2 In. 460.00
Table, Side, G. Nakashima, Walnut, Triangular Free-Edge Top, 22 x 20 In. 1265.00
Table, Side, George III Style, Demilune, Fan Inlay, Fluting, 32 x 44 x 19 In. 2070.00
Table, Side, George III, Mahogany, 3/4 Gallery, 1 Door Over Drawer, 35 x 17 In. 2185.00
Table, Side, George III, Mahogany, Inlaid, Serpentine, 1 Drawer, 1790, 27 x 18 In. 3450.00
Table, Side, George III, Mahogany, Raised Gallery, 2 Doors, 28 x 23 x 19 In. 3450.00
Table, Side, George III, Mahogany, Rectangular Top, Square Tapered Legs, 36 In. 575.00
Table, Side, George IV, Mahogany, Ebony Cupboard Door, 29 x 15 In., Pair 805.00
Table, Side, George IV, Oak, Oval Top, Frieze Drawer, Top-Shaped Feet, 32 x 43 x 22 In. 1150.00
Table, Side, Jacobean Style, Oak, Frieze Drawer, H-Stretcher, 29 1/2 x 28 x 18 1/2 In. 1725.00
Table, Side, Jacobean, Oak, Plank Top, Frieze Drawers, 30 3/4 x 59 1/2 x 30 In. 690.00
Table, Side, Jacobean, Oak, Rounded Corners, Box Stretcher, 27 x 31 1/2 x 21 In. 980.00
Table, Side, Louis Philippe, Cherry, Marble Top, 29 1/2 x 16 1/2 x 14 In. 345.00
Table, Side, Louis XV, Red Lacquer, Cabriole Legs 185.00
Table, Side, Louis XV, Tulipwood, Sprays Of Flowers, Frieze Drawer, 28 In. 6600.00
Table, Side, Louis XVI, Gilt, Rectangular Marble Top, 35 1/2 In., Pair 10200.00
Table, Side, Louis XVI, Mahogany, Brass Gallery, Fluted Legs, 28 In., Pair 1380.00
Table, Side, Louis XVI, Mahogany, Gilt, Rectangular Marble Top, 28 3/8 In. 13200.00
Table, Side, Oak, Rectangular Top, Apron, Joined By Stretchers, Bun Feet, 21 In. 635.00
Table, Side, P. Evans, Rosewood Veneer, Square Legs, 24 1/2 x 29 1/2 In. 675.00
Table, Side, Rohde, Wood Veneer Top, Circular Side, Veneer Top, 27 x 30 In. 110.00
Table, Side, Warren McArthur, Brown Lacquered Top, Tubular Legs, 21 x 14 In. ....*Illus* 2760.00
Table, Side, William & Mary, Yew, Molded Frieze, 1 Drawer, 33 3/4 x 22 In. 2415.00
Table, Softwood, Rectangular Top Over Carved Apron, Chinese, 13 1/2 x 24 In. 170.00
Table, Softwood, Rectangular Top, 3 Carved Drawers, Chinese, 32 1/4 In............. 345.00
Table, Square, Lower Shelf, Open Carved Legs, Strap Hardware, 30 x 27 x 27 In. 475.00
Table, Starck, Mahogany, Round Red Top, Architectural Chrome, 20 In., Pair 920.00
Table, Stickley Bros., Mahogany, Leather Top, Hexagonal, Signed, 30 x 41 In. 1955.00
Table, Stickley Bros., No. 2894, Through-Tenon Construction, 30 x 24 In. 1955.00
Table, Stickley Bros., Rectangular, Tenon Ends, 30 x 42 x 25 1/2 In. 690.00
Table, Stickley Bros., Round Top, Shelf, Turned Legs, X-Stretcher, 29 1/2 x 36 In. 315.00
Table, Tavern, Birch, Maple, Painted, Maine, c.1780, 26 x 52 1/2 x 33 1/2 In. 440.00
Table, Tavern, Cherry, 1 Drawer, Chamfered Square Legs, c.1810, 32 In. 440.00
Table, Tavern, Cherry, 1 Drawer, Stretcher Base, 31 x 80 x 34 In. 2575.00

Table, Tavern, Cherry, Pine Top, Breadboard Ends Over Frame, 1 Drawer, c.1820, 28 In. . . 825.00
Table, Tavern, Chippendale, Pine, Painted, Southern, c.1790, 28 1/4 x 28 1/4 In. 525.00
Table, Tavern, Hardwood, Pine, 1 Drawer, Breadboard Ends, 23 3/4 x 38 In. 825.00
Table, Tavern, Hepplewhite, 2-Board Top, Square Splay Legs, 27 1/2 x 33 1/2 In. 400.00
Table, Tavern, Hepplewhite, Walnut, 3-Board Top, Pa., c.1800, 28 x 41 x 30 1/2 In. 990.00
Table, Tavern, Mahogany, Circular Top, Circular Legs, Pad Feet, 27 1/2 In. 1495.00
Table, Tavern, Maple, Birch, Dovetailed Drawer, Beaded Edge, Brass Pull, 25 In. 4675.00
Table, Tavern, Maple, Drawer, Turned Legs, Box Stretcher, 26 x 28 x 39 In. 1495.00
Table, Tavern, Maple, Overhanging Top, 4 Block Legs, Red, Brown Surface, 47 In. 19550.00
Table, Tavern, Maple, Pine Top, Oval, Square Tapered Splayed Legs, 28 x 32 x 22 In. . . . 460.00
Table, Tavern, Maple, Pine, Breadboard Ends, New England, c.1810, 27 x 38 In. 605.00
Table, Tavern, Pine Breadboard Top, Cherry Legs & Base, 1 Drawer, 29 x 41 In. 550.00
Table, Tavern, Pine, 1 Drawer Over Stretcher Base, Square Legs, 27 x 30 In. 820.00
Table, Tavern, Pine, Baluster-Turned Legs, Box Stretchers, c.1750, 26 In. 495.00
Table, Tavern, Pine, Birch, Breadboard Ends, Drawer, Stretcher, c.1770, 27 1/2 x 42 In. . . . 660.00
Table, Tavern, Pine, Breadboard Top, 1 Drawer, Turned Legs, Stretcher Base, 29 x 39 In. . 560.00
Table, Tavern, Pine, Maple, Molded Edge Aprons, 1 Drawer, Peg Pull, 27 x 39 In. 2640.00
Table, Tavern, Pine, Rounded Corners, 1 Drawer, New England, 27 x 26 x 42 In. 2800.00
Table, Tavern, Pine, Stretcher Base, Ring-Turned Legs, Ball Feet, 30 x 20 1/2 x 26 In. . . . 770.00
Table, Tavern, Pine, Walnut, Conforming Frame, Splayed & Turned Legs, 25 3/4 In. 520.00
Table, Tavern, Pine, Walnut, Red Frame, Stretchers, Pa., c.1770, 28 x 42 In. 660.00
Table, Tavern, Queen Anne Base, Maple, Curly Maple, Splayed Legs, 25 1/2 In. 1120.00
Table, Tavern, Queen Anne, Cherry, Walnut, Painted, Red, Round, c.1770, 29 x 37 In. . . . 330.00
Table, Tavern, Queen Anne, Maple, Chamfered Corners, Taper Legs, Pad Feet, 37 x 28 In. 4025.00
Table, Tavern, Queen Anne, Maple, Veneer, 1 Drawer, Breadboard Ends, 37 x 23 In. 440.00
Table, Tavern, Queen Anne, Walnut, Maple, 1 Drawer, Tapered Legs, 40 x 28 x 29 In. . . . 1320.00
Table, Tavern, Tiger Maple, 1 Drawer, Breadboard Ends, 26 1/2 x 38 In. 8050.00
Table, Tavern, Walnut, 3-Board, Box Stretcher, Button Feet, c.1790, 29 1/2 x 54 In. 1320.00
Table, Tavern, Walnut, Drawer, Baluster-Turned Legs, Box Stretcher, c.1770, 26 1/2 In. . . 1980.00
Table, Tavern, Walnut, Pin Top, 2 Drawers, Molded Skirt, Pad Feet, c.1765, 31 x 54 In. . . 7700.00
Table, Tavern, Walnut, Pine, Splayed & Turned Legs, Box Stretchers, c.1740, 26 In. 495.00
Table, Tavern, William & Mary, Rectangular Top, Breadboard Ends, 38 x 26 In. 290.00
Table, Tea, 3 Graduated Shelves, Scalloped Middle Shelf, Brass Gallery Top, 41 In. 605.00
Table, Tea, Beaded Top, Tripod Base, Kittinger, 23 In. 170.00
Table, Tea, Beech, Gilt Bronze, Drawers, Armand Albert Rateau, c.1925, 30 x 41 In. . . . 52500.00
Table, Tea, Birch, Tapered Legs, Satin Birch, 30 x 33 1/2 In. 980.00
Table, Tea, Cherry, Turned Legs, Stretcher Base, 22 x 36 x 27 In. 950.00
Table, Tea, Chippendale, Mahogany, 2 Tiers, Turned Column, 19th Century, 31 In. 660.00
Table, Tea, Chippendale, Mahogany, Carved, Molded Top, Ball Feet, 1760, 28 In. 1800.00
Table, Tea, Chippendale, Mahogany, Tray Top, Carved, Cabriole Legs, 1700s, 28 x 33 In. . 2760.00
Table, Tea, Elm, Brass Top, 1 Drawer, Cabriole Legs, 30 x 30 1/2 In. 7600.00
Table, Tea, Federal, Mahogany, Foldover, Bowfront, c.1810, 29 1/2 x 36 x 18 In. 1380.00
Table, Tea, Federal, Mahogany, Foldover, Pedestal, Early 1800s, 29 1/2 x 38 x 19 In. 2530.00
Table, Tea, Federal, Mahogany, Inlaid, Foldover, Demilune, c.1800, 29 x 36 x 18 In. 5900.00
Table, Tea, Fruitwood, Drawer, Divided By Wells, Pad Feet, 1750s, 29 3/4 In. 6910.00
Table, Tea, G. Stickley, No. 5, Thick Round Top, Splayed Legs, 24 In. . . . . *Illus* 525.00
Table, Tea, G. Stickley, No. 608, Lower Shelf, Red Decal, 26 x 24 In. 2875.00
Table, Tea, G. Stickley, No. 699, Mahogany, Circular Top, 1915, 30 x 50 In. 3375.00
Table, Tea, George II, Mahogany, Bird Cage Support, Snake Feet, c.1760, 28 x 30 In. 1320.00
Table, Tea, George II, Mahogany, Carved, Foldover, Mid 1700s, 28 1/2 x 36 x 17 3/4 In. . . 3165.00
Table, Tea, George III, Mahogany, Round Tilt Top, Spiral Pedestal, c.1780, 27 x 31 In. . . . 1210.00
Table, Tea, George III, Yew, Inlay, Oval Tray, Brass Handles, 35 x 23 In. 550.00
Table, Tea, Georgian, Mahogany, Circular Top, Tapered Legs, Padded Feet, 29 In. 315.00
Table, Tea, Hepplewhite, 4 Tapered Legs, Line & Banded Inlay, 29 x 36 In. 1580.00
Table, Tea, L. & J.G. Stickley, No. 508, Walnut, 24 x 24 In. 3450.00
Table, Tea, Mahogany, Fold Top, 1 Frieze Drawer, Chamfered Legs, 28 1/2 In. 1035.00
Table, Tea, Mahogany, Hinged Flip Top, Tapered Reeded Legs, Gateleg, 29 In. 1610.00
Table, Tea, Mahogany, Piecrust Top, Salesman Sample, 16 1/2 x 9 3/4 In. 1035.00
Table, Tea, Parquetry, Star & Geometric Inlaid Top, Baluster Standard, 30 1/2 x 29 In. . . . 605.00
Table, Tea, Queen Anne, Cherry, 1 Drawer, Cabriole Legs, Pad Feet, 30 1/2 x 35 In. 660.00
Table, Tea, Queen Anne, Eldred Wheeler, Tiger Maple, 27 1/2 x 33 x 20 In. 1440.00
Table, Tea, Queen Anne, Maple, Tray Top, Shaped Frieze, 26 x 29 1/2 x 16 1/2 In. 805.00
Table, Tea, Queen Anne, Pine, Painted, Tray Top, Drawer, Cabriole Legs, c.1760 . . . . 2750.00

Furniture, Table, Tea, G. Stickley, No. 5, Thick Round Top, Splayed Legs, 24 In.

Furniture, Table, Toilet, Pine, Serpentine, Painted, 1800, 32 x 19 In.

Table, Tea, Queen Anne, Rectangular Top, Tapered Legs, Pad Feet, 26 1/2 x 22 In. 2530.00
Table, Tea, Stickley Bros., Mahogany, Circular Top, 24 x 26 In. 1035.00
Table, Tea, Tilt Top, Cherry, Revolving Over Birdcage Support, 1730s, 28 In. 2875.00
Table, Tea, Tilt Top, Cherry, Tripod Base, Snake Feet, c.1790, 27 In. 1045.00
Table, Tea, Tilt Top, Chippendale, Mahogany, Claw & Ball Feet, Piecrust Top, 26 In. 195.00
Table, Tea, Tilt Top, Chippendale, Mahogany, Dish Top, England, 31 1/2 x 29 In. 330.00
Table, Tea, Tilt Top, Chippendale, Mahogany, Refinished, Snake Feet, Round, 31 x 27 In. 660.00
Table, Tea, Tilt Top, Chippendale, Pedestal, Cabriole Legs, Claw Feet, 27 1/2 x 35 1/4 In. 1210.00
Table, Tea, Tilt Top, Chippendale, Walnut, Tripod Base, Claw Feet, 26 x 28 In. 4000.00
Table, Tea, Tilt Top, Circular, Urn Shaft, Tripod Base, Pad Feet, c.1790, 33 In. Diam. 605.00
Table, Tea, Tilt Top, Hepplewhite, Mahogany, Banded & Line Inlay, Spider Legs, 26 In. ... 1210.00
Table, Tea, Tilt Top, Mahogany, Birdcage Support, Claw & Ball Feet, c.1750, 29 1/2 In. .. 5460.00
Table, Tea, Tilt Top, Queen Anne, Dish Top, Birdcage Support, c.1780, 28 x 32 1/2 In. ... 2860.00
Table, Tea, Tilt Top, Queen Anne, Oak, Pad Feet, Early 1800s, 27 1/2 x 23 In. 630.00
Table, Tea, Tilt Top, Santo Domingo Mahogany, Claw Feet, 27 1/2 x 33 1/2 In. 8250.00
Table, Tea, Tilt Top, Walnut, Round Dish Top, Pa., c.1780, 29 1/2 x 29 In. 470.00
Table, Tea, Walnut, Shaped Frieze, Circular Legs, Pad Feet, c.1740, 27 1/2 In. 7475.00
Table, Tea, William & Mary, Walnut, Parquetry, Foldover, 1 Drawer, 30 x 15 In. 2760.00
Table, Teakwood, 6 Shield-Shaped Components, 3 Brass Legs, Denmark, 1960, 21 In. 750.00
Table, Teakwood, Claw & Ball, Pierced Apron, Soapstone, Oriental, 25 x 18 x 20 In. 440.00
Table, Teakwood, Foo Dog Faces, Openwork Apron, Soapstone, Oriental, 21 x 32 In. 740.00
Table, Thonet, White Enameled Wood, Square Cutout Tops, Joseph Hoffman, 18 In. 675.00
Table, Tiger Maple, 2 Center Drawers, 28 x 12 x 46 In., 3-Part 275.00
Table, Tilt Top, Black Lacquer, Landscape Scene, Gilt, Pedestal, Round, 24 3/4 In. 2185.00
Table, Tilt Top, Black Lacquer, Mother-Of-Pearl Inlay, 1850s, 24 1/2 x 24 1/2 In. 290.00
Table, Tilt Top, Chippendale, Mahogany, 29 1/2 x 28 1/2 In. 575.00
Table, Tilt Top, Chippendale, Mahogany, Piecrust, Claw & Ball Feet, 28 x 29 In. 330.00
Table, Tilt Top, Chippendale, Mahogany, Tripod, Late 18th Century, 29 x 24 In. 978.00
Table, Tilt Top, Federal, Cherry, Maple, Octagonal Top, c.1790, 28 x 22 x 15 In. 4025.00
Table, Tilt Top, Federal, Mahogany, Molded, Tripod Base, Pad Feet, 27 x 17 In. 805.00
Table, Tilt Top, Mahogany, Black Painted Lacquer, Leaf-Carved Tripod Base, 30 1/2 In. ... 5750.00
Table, Tilt Top, Mahogany, Original Cane Inserts, Circular, 30 x 29 In. 2020.00
Table, Tilt Top, Mahogany, Piecrust, Birdcage, Claw & Ball Feet, 29 1/2 x 33 In. 748.00
Table, Tilt Top, Mahogany, Pointed Pad Feet, 35 1/2 x 28 In. 1495.00
Table, Tilt Top, Mahogany, Tripod, Downswept Square Section Legs, 26 3/4 In. 400.00
Table, Tilt Top, Oak, Butterfly, Step-Down Shoe Feet, 27 x 32 In. 1870.00
Table, Tilt Top, Papier-Mache, Mountain, Rivers Medallion, Scalloped, c.1860, 27 x 28 In. 385.00
Table, Tilt Top, Regency, Urn Pedestal, 3 Legs, Brass Feet, Casters, 28 x 50 x 32 1/2 In. ... 2015.00
Table, Tilt Top, Victorian, Burl Walnut, Mid 19th Century, 26 1/2 x 46 x 33 3/4 In. 2760.00
Table, Tilt Top, Victorian, Lacquered, Chinoiserie, Mother-Of-Pearl Scenes, 31 x 21 In. ... 805.00
Table, Tilt Top, Victorian, Oak, Rectangular Top, 29 In. 2185.00
Table, Tilt Top, Victorian, Papier-Mache, Mother-Of-Pearl, Gold, 28 x 25 In. 635.00
Table, Tilt Top, Walnut, Floral Marquetry, Cabriole Legs, Holland, 27 x 31 In. 1725.00
Table, Tilt Top, Walnut, Rosewood, Claw Feet, 1900, 42 x 28 In. 1065.00
Table, Tilt Top, William IV, Mahogany, Rectangular Top, 3 Cabriole Legs, 28 In. 460.00
Table, Tilt Top, William IV, Pine, Satinwood, Pliny's Doves, 28 x 18 In. 6040.00
Table, Tilt Top, William IV, Rosewood, Concave Triangular Base, 28 In. 7480.00

Table, Tobia Scarpa Andre, Smoked Glass, Tubular Steel Frame, Knoll, 92 In. 240.00
Table, Toilet, Pine, Serpentine, Painted, 1800, 32 x 19 In. . . . .*Illus*   5750.00
Table, Tray, Folding Stand, 33 In. 460.00
Table, Tray, G. Nelson, Dark Mahogany, Herman Miller, 15 x 20 In. 865.00
Table, Tray, George III, Mahogany, c.1800, 28 x 18 In. 330.00
Table, Tray, Georgian, Mahogany, Central Conch Shell Inlay, 28 In. 1200.00
Table, Tray, Mahogany, 2 Parts, Leather Tray Top, 36 x 21 x 16 In. 55.00
Table, Tray, Stand, Papier-Mache, Bamboo, Gilt Floral Branches & Butterflies, 21 1/2 In. . .   1320.00
Table, Tray, Stand, Papier-Mache, Black Lacquer, Gilt Stencil, 21 1/2 x 18 3/4 x 24 1/2 In.   980.00
Table, Tray, Stand, Papier-Mache, Black Lacquer, Gold, Scarlet, 21 1/2 x 19 1/2 x 26 In. . .   1100.00
Table, Tray, Stand, Papier-Mache, Black Lacquer, Scrollwork, 20 x 24 1/2 x 30 1/4 In. . . .   635.00
Table, Tray, Stand, Papier-Mache, Faux Bamboo, Black Ground, 20 1/2 x 16 In. 690.00
Table, Tray, Stand, Papier-Mache, Faux Bamboo, Black Ground, 21 1/2 x 25 1/2 In. 2940.00
Table, Tray, Stand, Papier-Mache, Gilt Foliage & Insects, 22 x 29 1/2 In. 1380.00
Table, Trestle, Continental, Walnut, Rectangular Top, Acanthus Scroll Feet, 32 In. 5750.00
Table, Trestle, L. & J.G. Stickley, Mahogany, Overhanging Rectangular Top, 29 In. 3450.00
Table, Trestle, L. & J.G. Stickley, No. 594, Mahogany, 29 x 72 x 44 1/2 In. 7190.00
Table, Trestle, L. & J.G. Stickley, Tenon Support, 28 1/2 x 54 x 32 In. 1610.00
Table, Trestle, Oak, Old Dark Finish, Chamfered Corners, 101 1/4 x 30 x 28 In. 3410.00
Table, Trestle, Pine, 2-Board Top, Shoe Feet, 33 x 72 In. 1320.00
Table, Trestle, Removable Sawbuck Legs, 3-Board Top, 29 x 79 1/2 In. 1210.00
Table, Trestle, Wallace Nutting, No. 609, Pine Ogee Top, 30 In. 690.00
Table, Trestle, Wallace Nutting, No. 625, Maple, Butterfly 2420.00
Table, Trestle, Walnut, Drop Leaf, Gatelegs, 19th Century, 28 x 28 3/4 x 14 In. 4310.00
Table, Tulip, Round, White Laminate, Enameled, Burke, 15 x 18 In., Pair 175.00
Table, Typewriter, Olivetti, Gray Laminate Top, Black Metal Sides, Rollers, 21 x 22 In. . .   690.00
Table, Typewriter, Oval, Drop Leaf, 2 Shelves, Maple, Art Deco, 1930, 31 x 36 x 21 In. . .   975.00
Table, V. Kagan, Snail, Molded Walnut Plywood, Square Glass Top, 14 In. 1840.00
Table, Van Der Rohe, Circular Plate Glass Top, Chrome Tubular Base, 20 In. 790.00
Table, Victorian, Burl Walnut, Turtle, Marble, 19 x 30 x 23 In. 550.00
Table, Victorian, Burl, Oval Top, Floral Marquetry, Scroll Feet, 28 x 54 x 42 In. 2760.00
Table, Victorian, Marble Top, Columns, Pedestal Base, Carved Hoof Feet, 30 x 30 In. 330.00
Table, Victorian, Marble Top, Ebonized, Mid 1800s, 30 1/2 x 40 1/2 x 16 3/4 In 575.00
Table, Victorian, Walnut Base, Turtle Top, Marble, Urn Finial, Refinished, 24 x 16 In. . . .   440.00
Table, Victorian, Walnut Veneer, Octagon, Inlaid, Triangle Wedges, 28 1/2 x 29 1/2 In. . . .   575.00
Table, Victorian, Walnut, Burl, Marble Turtle Top, Cabriole Legs, 30 x 39 x 27 In. 825.00
Table, Victorian, Walnut, Marble, Scalloped Corner Top, 29 x 26 x 18 In. 465.00
Table, Victorian, Walnut, Marble, Turtle Top, Drop Pendants, 28 1/2 x 33 x 23 In. 460.00
Table, Victorian, Walnut, White Marble Top, Carved Legs, 28 x 34 x 25 In. 660.00
Table, Victorian, Walnut, White, Oval Turtle Top, Fruit, Nut Carving, 1870, 30 x 32 In. . .   1400.00
Table, Wallace Nutting, Queen Anne, Mahogany, 2 Pedestals, Tilt Top, 28 1/2 x 47 In. . . .   1840.00
Table, Walnut, Batten Top Over Frame, 3 Drawers, Block Legs, c.1800, 30 1/2 In. 4400.00
Table, Walnut, Beaded Apron, Block Toes, Rectangular Top, Chinese, 17 3/4 In. 545.00
Table, Walnut, Canted Legs, Iron Brace, Shaped Stretcher, 30 1/2 x 27 1/2 x 52 1/2 In. . . .   2070.00
Table, Walnut, Console, Shaped Marble Top, Carved Shell & Floral Over Base, 35 In. 885.00
Table, Walnut, Exotic Animals & Palm Trees, Bear Climbing Tree Supports, 27 1/2 In. . . .   1150.00
Table, Walnut, Fruitwood, Rosette Within Border Of Tulips, Floral Marquetry, 29 In. 6050.00
Table, Walnut, Geometric & Scale On 2 Drawers, 17th Century, 32 3/4 In. 5750.00
Table, Walnut, Grapevine, Leaf Design, Peasant Scene, 1885, 18 x 14 In. 950.00
Table, Walnut, Marble Top Over Short Drawer & Cupboard Door, 1880s, 35 1/2 In. 490.00
Table, Walnut, Marble Top, Eagle & Dolphin Base, 1870, 31 x 38 x 29 In. 3360.00
Table, Walnut, Marquetry Basket Of Flowers, 1 Long Drawer, 1770s, 29 3/4 In. 8910.00
Table, Walnut, Oak, Rectangular Top, Marlboro Legs, 22 x 23 x 17 3/4 In. 310.00
Table, Walnut, Rectangular Top, Cushion Frieze Drawer, 19th Century, 29 In. 1840.00
Table, Walnut, Reeded, Painted, Carved Spandrels, Chinese, 19th Century, 33 x 78 In. 460.00
Table, Walnut, Split Pedestal, Paneled Legs, Rosettes, c.1880, 29 x 52 In. 1680.00
Table, Walnut, Turtle Top, Marble, Molded Edge, Stretcher, Finial, 28 1/2 x 34 x 25 In. . .   575.00
Table, Walnut, Veneer, Scrolled Legs, 2 Urn Supports, England, 25 x 17 In. 275.00
Table, Walnut, Yew Wood, 1-Board Top, Stretcher Base, England, 27 x 16 In. 605.00
Table, William & Mary, Oak, 1 Drawer, Block Legs, 35 x 21 5/8 x 29 In. 405.00
Table, William & Mary, Oak, Drawer, Trumpet-Turned Legs, Ball Feet, 27 x 31 In. 550.00
Table, William IV, Mahogany, 3 Sections, Paw Feet, 30 x 52 x 150 In. 7190.00
Table, William IV, Mahogany, Chalcedony, Round, Agate, Hexagon Base, 29 x 30 In. 2760.00

Table, William IV, Mahogany, Scrolled Uprights, Leaf Carved, 39 x 60 In., Pair 9000.00
Table, William IV, Rosewood, Figured Circular Top, Bun Feet, 28 In. 1380.00
Table, William IV, Rosewood, Rectangular Top, Melon Feet, 29 In. 1495.00
Table, William IV, Rosewood, Round, Plain Frieze, Faceted Stem, 29 x 52 In. 2760.00
Table, William IV, Rosewood, White Marble Top, Scrolled Feet, 30 In. 4140.00
Table, Wine Tasting, French Provincial, Fruitwood, Heart-Shape Top, 29 x 45 x 46 In. . . . 865.00
Table, Wine Tasting, French Provincial, Fruitwood, Plank Oval Top, 28 x 48 1/2 x 37 In. . 2990.00
Table, Wine Tasting, French Provincial, Pine, Fruitwood, Trestle Base, 29 x 56 x 84 In. . . 865.00
Table, Wine Tasting, George III, Mahogany, Snap Top, Tripod, Turned, 23 x 26 In. 290.00
Table, Wine Tasting, Mahogany, Beaded Apron, Round Leg, 34 x 16 x 49 In. 630.00
Table, Wine Tasting, Provincial, Pine, Oval, Hinge, Trestle Support, 28 x 36 1/2 x 43 In. . 575.00
Table, Wooden, Ebony Center, Octagonal Top, Foliate Frieze, Claw Feet, 28 In. 2400.00
Table, Writing, 3 Drawers, Leather Baize Surface, Woman's, 33 3/4 In. 1725.00
Table, Writing, Chippendale, Mahogany, Leather Writing Surface, Woman's, 29 In. 1035.00
Table, Writing, Continental, Walnut, Leather Top, 1 Drawer, 31 1/2 x 36 1/2 x 24 In. 600.00
Table, Writing, English Reform Movement, Oak, Parquetry, Ebonized, 28 x 24 x 42 In. . . 8050.00
Table, Writing, Fruitwood, Frieze Drawer, Claw & Ball Feet, Mid 18th Century, 41 In. . . . 7800.00
Table, Writing, George III, Mahogany, Frieze Drawer, Stretcher, 28 1/2 x 22 1/2 x 15 In. . 1150.00
Table, Writing, George III, Mahogany, Inlaid, Late 18th Century, 33 x 42 x 24 In. 1725.00
Table, Writing, George III, Mahogany, Inlaid, Leather Top, Kneehole, 30 x 60 In. 1610.00
Table, Writing, George III, Mahogany, Molded Rectangular Top, 29 x 30 x 19 In. 800.00
Table, Writing, George IV, Rosewood, Ring-Turned Legs, Brass Cap Casters, 28 In. 860.00
Table, Writing, Inset Leather Surface, 2 Short Drawers, Thimble Feet, 1870s, 28 1/2 In. . . 9360.00
Table, Writing, Leather Surface, 3 Drawers, Marquetry Panels, 54 1/2 In. 4800.00
Table, Writing, Louis XVI Style, Mahogany, Parquetry, Bronze Dore, 29 x 39 x 24 In. . . . 1035.00
Table, Writing, Louis XVI, Fruitwood, 2 Drawers, Tapered Legs, Top-Shaped Feet, 30 In. 980.00
Table, Writing, Mahogany, Brass Border, Leather Surface, Brass Mounted, 30 1/8 In. 5760.00
Table, Writing, Mahogany, Inset Leather, 2 Drawers, Pullout Slides, 50 1/2 In. 2530.00
Table, Writing, Mahogany, Marble Top, Drawer, Scroll Supports, c.1825, 30 x 29 In. 2185.00
Table, Writing, Oak, Kingwood Veneer, Leather, 1 Side Drawer, France, 46 x 27 In. 1100.00
Table, Writing, Queen Anne, Mahogany, Kneehole, 19th Century, 28x 34 x 19 In. 1150.00
Table, Writing, Regency, Mahogany, Rectangular Top, Leather Surface, 28 In. 1380.00
Table, Writing, Rosewood, Leather Surface, Ratchet Mechanism, c.1830, 29 1/2 In. 7920.00
Table, Wrought Iron, Bird Inset Tile Top, Scrolled Legs, Border, 24 x 13 x 20 In. 110.00
Table, Wrought Iron, Glass Top, Round, Basketweave Support, 48 x 29 In. 315.00
Table, Wrought Iron, Marble, Rectangular Inset Top, Wooden Scroll Feet, 28 In. 4370.00
Table, Wrought Iron, Scrolled Supports, Wavy Spike Finial, 62 1/2 In. 6350.00
Table Set, Nesting, Teakwood, Carved Blossoms, Oriental, 14 1/2 & 19 3/4 In., 2 Piece . . 300.00
Tabouret, Arts & Crafts, Cut Corner Top, Slab Legs, 12 x 12 x 18 In. 69.00
Tabouret, Arts & Crafts, Hexagonal Top, Original Finish, 17 x 21 In. 545.00
Tabouret, Arts & Crafts, Mahogany, Dark Finish, Round Top, 1912, 27 x 24 In. 1150.00
Tabouret, Arts & Crafts, Mahogany, Octagonal Top, Slab Legs, 17 x 19 In. 100.00
Tabouret, Arts & Crafts, Oak, 4 Canted Sides, Dark Brown Finish, 1912, 23 In. 980.00
Tabouret, Arts & Crafts, Oak, Dark Brown Finish, 1912, 19 1/2 x 16 1/2 In. 460.00
Tabouret, Arts & Crafts, Oak, Paneled Sides, Medium Brown Finish, 18 In. 230.00
Tabouret, Arts & Crafts, Octagonal Top, Splayed Legs, 16 x 21 In. 430.00
Tabouret, Arts & Crafts, Pyrography, Octagonal, Moorish Cutout, 18 x 15 x 15 In. 315.00
Tabouret, Cutout, Brooks, 27 3/4 x 18 In. 1725.00
Tabouret, G. Stickley, No. 602, Mahogany, Circular Top, Red Decal, 18 In. 1265.00
Tabouret, G. Stickley, No. 603, Dark Mahogany, Signed, 20 x 18 In. 1150.00
Tabouret, G. Stickley, Tenon Cross Stretchers, Original Finish, 18 x 16 In. 1595.00
Tabouret, George III, Mahogany, Reeded Base, Claw, Ball Feet, 9 x 16 In. 440.00
Tabouret, Georgian, Gilt, Upholstered Seat, Scalloped Apron, Pad Feet, 16 In. 1380.00
Tabouret, L. & J.G. Stickley, Mahogany, Straight Apron, Original Finish, 20 In. 1575.00
Tabouret, L. & J.G. Stickley, Original Finish, Octagonal, 17 x 15 In. 1010.00
Tabouret, Mahogany, Mayhew, Signed, 20 x 18 In. 400.00
Tabouret, Pink Scalloped Marble Top, 1900, 20 In. 375.00
Tabouret, Prairie School, Oak, 4 Cutout Rectangles, Square Top, 24 1/4 In. 500.00
Tabouret, Rococo, Walnut, Rectangular Top, Cabriole Legs, Hairy Goat Feet, 19 In. 4025.00
Tabouret, Stickley Bros., Mahogany, Mortised Cross Stretchers, 20 x 25 x 15 In. 1912.00
Tea Cart, Aesthetic Revival, Mahogany, Brass, Glass, Tray, c.1875, 32 x 41 x 21 In. 490.00
Tea Cart, Alvar Alto, Bentwood, Square Tiled Top, 1950, 23 x 25 1/2 x 36 In. 450.00
Tea Cart, Drop Leaf, Oak, With Trap, Refinish, Ferguson Bros. Label, 28 x 18 In. 440.00

Tea Cart, E. Wormley, White Laminate Top, 2 Doors, Black Surface, 30 In. 1955.00
Tea Cart, Georgian, Mahogany, Molded Lid, Bracket Feet, c.1790, 5 1/2 x 9 In. 330.00
Tea Cart, Georgian, Walnut, Canted Sides, Ball Feet, c.1800, 6 1/2 x 11 1/2 In. 250.00
Tea Cart, McCobb, Ash Veneer, Travertine Top, 2 Small Drawers, Calvin, 29 In. 560.00
Tea Cart, Old Brown Finish, Wooden Spoke Wheels, Oak Shelf At Base, 33 x 20 In. 250.00
Tea Cart, Stickley Bros., No. 2916, Dark Mahogany, Handle, 30 x 28 x 17 In. 980.00
Tea Cart, V. Kagan, Walnut, White Laminate Top, Orange, 48 x 28 In. 4025.00
Tea Cart, Wicker, Removable Tray, 2 Tiers, Shelf In Front & Rear, Heywood-Wakefield . 700.00
Tea Cart, William IV, Rosewood, Hinged Top, Fitted Interior, 2 Bowls, 30 In. 2530.00
Tea Cart, Wrought Iron, Glass, Jean Royere, 1950, 25 x 29 1/2 x 17 1/2 In. 9600.00
Tray On Stand, Papier-Mache, Chinoiserie Landscape, Stylized Floral, 28 3/4 x 21 1/2 In. . 4500.00
Trolley, William IV, Mahogany, 2 Tiers, Lobed Turned Feet, 46 1/4 In. 2070.00
Umbrella Stand, Arts & Crafts, Brass, Hammered, Original Patina, 13 x 23 In. 345.00
Umbrella Stand, Arts & Crafts, Oak, Copper Drain Pan, Sikes Co., 27 x 16 In. 195.00
Umbrella Stand, Arts & Crafts, Wood, Slats, Leather Laces, 27 In. 115.00
Umbrella Stand, Bear, Carved Walnut, Loop Holder, Black Forest, 40 In. 4620.00
Umbrella Stand, Bear, Glass Eyes, Carved Wood, Switzerland, c.1890, 38 x 21 x 18 In. . . 2900.00
Umbrella Stand, Black Forest, Carved Bear, Glass Eyes, 1880, 42 In. 5040.00
Umbrella Stand, Black Forest, Carved, Standing Bear, 32 1/2 In. 5175.00
Umbrella Stand, Black Forest, Walnut, Porcelain Liner, Germany, 48 In. 5750.00
Umbrella Stand, Classical, Draped Women, Red Applied Over Wood, 11 x 25 In. 180.00
Umbrella Stand, Elephant Hide, 20 1/4 In. 3000.00
Umbrella Stand, G. Stickley, 10 Vertical Slats, 3 Iron Rings, 24 In. 3570.00
Umbrella Stand, G. Stickley, Dark Mahogany, 4 Tapered Posts, 34 In. 575.00
Umbrella Stand, Iron, Mermaid, Floral & Shields Cast, 1880, 31 x 23 x 8 In. 525.00
Umbrella Stand, Limbert, No. 252, Original Finish, Signed, 17 x 9 x 29 In. 935.00
Umbrella Stand, Platform Base, Openwork Columns, Iron, Scrolled, 18 x 33 In. 468.00
Umbrella Stand, Sailor Shape, On Crow's Nest, Iron, Corneau Freres, 1870s 977.00
Vanity, Fruitwood, Drawers, Drop Front, Lift Top, 53 x 24 x 18 In. 140.00
Vanity, G. Stickley, No. 914, Mahogany, Original Mirror, 36 x 55 In. 2300.00
Vanity, Rohde, Black Lacquer, 6 Drawers, Curved Glass Top, Miller, 27 In. 545.00
Vanity, Rosewood, Carved, Signed, Lamb, Manchester, 1880, 54 x 22 x 69 In. 4480.00
Vitrine, Biedermeier, Fruitwood, Tabletop, Arched, Glazed, c.1850, 29 x 18 x 9 In. 345.00
Vitrine, Chest, Dutch Marquetry, 19th Century, 73 x 35 In. 7150.00
Vitrine, Dark Mahogany, Carved, 4 Curved Legs, Otto Prutscher, 1910, 92 In. 19150.00
Vitrine, Empire, Bronze, Gilt, Central Arch Door, Rectangular Base, 89 In. 9600.00
Vitrine, French Provincial, Cherry, Molded Crest, Serpentine Doors, 90 In. 1150.00
Vitrine, Kingwood, Ormolu, Marquetry Trophies, France, 1800s, 30 x 66 x 19 In. 2340.00
Vitrine, Louis XV, Mahogany, Gilt, Stand, 2 Frieze Drawers, 49 In. 9000.00
Vitrine, Louis XV, Oak, Carved, Mottled Marble Top, Carved Shell, 69 In. 2070.00
Vitrine, Louis XVI Style, Burl Walnut, Veneer, Inlay, 64 1/2 x 38 x 15 1/4 In. 2300.00
Vitrine, Louis XVI Style, Mahogany, Marble Top, 3/4 Gallery, 54 x 29 x 14 1/4 In. 1265.00
Vitrine, Louis XVI, Gilt, Half-Column Pilasters, France, 38 1/2 In. 1265.00
Vitrine, Louis XVI, Mahogany, Brass Gallery, Turned Feet, 56 x 31 x 15 In. 920.00
Vitrine, Louis XVI, Tulipwood, Marquetry, Marble Top, Glazed Door, Panels, 64 x 38 In. 1265.00
Vitrine, Mahogany, Glass Front & Sides, 4 Columns, Tapered Legs, Silk Back, 54 x 26 In. 730.00
Vitrine, Mahogany, Glass Top, Apron Drawer, Squared Legs, 31 x 18 In. 750.00
Vitrine, Napoleon III, Gilt, Bronze, Violet Marble Top, France, 1870, 51 In. 5750.00
Vitrine, Neoclassical Style, Gilt, Polychrome, c.1900, 77 1/2 x 36 x 13 In. 3450.00
Vitrine, Neoclassical, Walnut, Fruitwood, Stepped Recessed Cornice, 70 In. 3680.00
Vitrine, Renaissance Revival, Marquetry, Galleried Cornice, Scrollwork, 76 In. 1610.00
Vitrine, Victorian, Mahogany, Scrolled Bonnet, 3-Drawer Base, Bun Feet, 108 In. 1380.00
Wardrobe, Arts & Crafts, Mahogany, Carved Poppy Design Panels, 80 x 20 In. 2925.00
Wardrobe, Arts & Crafts, Yellow Pine, Painted Flowers, 80 x 45 x 23 In. 1150.00
Wardrobe, Chippendale, Burled Walnut, 1 Door, 19th Century, 17 1/2 In. 605.00
Wardrobe, Converted, Map Cabinet, 2 Doors, 21 Drawers, Carved, 73 x 54 x 45 In. 440.00
Wardrobe, Edwardian, Mahogany, 4 Drawers, Central Storage Unit, 83 In. 1840.00
Wardrobe, Federal, Mahogany, Duncan Phyfe, c.1835, 85 x 60 In. 5775.00
Wardrobe, French Provincial, Oak, Cream Paint, Arched Cornice, 85 x 70 x 24 In. 3450.00
Wardrobe, G. Stickley, 2 Paneled Doors, Medium Brown Finish, 59 x 16 In. 5625.00
Wardrobe, George II, Mahogany, Black Bust Of Demosthenes, Bracket Feet, 96 In. 4140.00
Wardrobe, George IV, Mahogany, Carved Lappets, 3 Drawers, 1820, 92 In. 4800.00
Wardrobe, Mahogany, 2 Doors, 2 Panels, 3 Linen Drawers In Side, 87 In. 1210.00

Wardrobe, Mahogany, 2 Doors, Leaf & Rose Crest, 8 Interior Drawers, 82 3/4 In. 1375.00
Wardrobe, Mahogany, Double-Door Case, Beveled Mirrors, 79 In. 865.00
Wardrobe, Mahogany, Mirror Front, Inlaid Sides, Mother-Of-Pearl, France, 60 x 46 In. ... 448.00
Wardrobe, Neoclassical, Pine, Rectangular Cornice, Cream Paint, 102 In. 12075.00
Wardrobe, Rococo, Walnut, Foliate Crest, Paneled Doors, 99 In. 980.00
Wardrobe, Shrank, Walnut, Carved Cornice, Panel Doors, Drawers, Pa., 1770, 85 x 66 In. . 8800.00
Wardrobe, Walnut, Bone Checkered Border, 1 Dovetailed Drawer, 46 x 88 1/4 In. 3410.00
Wardrobe, Walnut, Double-Domed Panels, Hanging Space Interior, 77 In. 230.00
Washstand, Chippendale, Walnut, 2 Drawers Center, Tripod Base, 19 x 32 In. 275.00
Washstand, Corner, George III, Mahogany, Backsplash Over Shelf, 44 In. 750.00
Washstand, Corner, Hepplewhite, Mahogany, Backsplash, Flared Leg, c.1820, 43 In. 935.00
Washstand, Corner, Mahogany, Arched Backboard, Corner Shelf, Drawer, 41 3/4 In. 920.00
Washstand, Corner, Victorian, White Marble Top, 1885, 59 x 45 x 30 In. 1178.00
Washstand, Curly Maple, Drawer In Base, Cutout For Bowl, Scalloped Gallery, 33 In. ... 3410.00
Washstand, Drawer, Lower Shelf, 2 Towel Rods, Child's, c.1895, 21 1/2 In. 750.00
Washstand, Elm, Carved With Lotus Pods, Shou Medallion, Chinese, 66 In. 145.00
Washstand, Empire, Mahogany, Marble Top, Corniced Backboard, 37 x 29 x 18 1/2 In. .. 805.00
Washstand, Empire, Mahogany, White Marble Top, Ogee Feet, 30 In. 1265.00
Washstand, Federal, Backsplash, Single Drawer, Sandwich Glass Knob, 28 x 21 In. 330.00
Washstand, Federal, Mahogany, 3/4 Gallery, Shelf, c.1890, 39 3/4 x 22 x 16 3/4 In. 865.00
Washstand, Federal, Mahogany, Chamfered Front, 2 Frieze Drawers, 29 x 29 x 20 In. ... 865.00
Washstand, Federal, Mahogany, S Scrolling, New England, c.1840, 30 1/2 x 18 1/4 In. .. 385.00
Washstand, Federal, Walnut, Galleried Top, Drawer, Shelf, Pa., c.1810, 32 x 23 1/4 In. .. 660.00
Washstand, G. Stickley, Slatted Backsplash, 2 Drawers, Iron Pulls, 45 x 40 In. 9200.00
Washstand, Gray Marble Top, Rectangular, Green, Yellow Tiles Over Case, 52 In. 490.00
Washstand, Hepplewhite, 1 Drawer At Base, Gallery, 28 1/2 x 16 In. 110.00
Washstand, Louis XVI Style, Mahogany, c.1850, 28 3/4 x 38 1/2 x 21 In. 1610.00
Washstand, Mahogany, 2 Drawers, Slipper Feet, 32 12 In. 1495.00
Washstand, Mahogany, 2 Triangular Frieze Drawers, Slipper Feet, 18th Century, 31 In. .. 140.00
Washstand, Painted, Stenciled, Mustard, Gold, Green, Backsplash, 38 x 17 x 14 In. 980.00
Washstand, Pine, Compartment & Drawer In Base, Button Feet, 31 In. 325.00
Washstand, Poplar, Gallery Top, Drawer, Lower Shelf, Pa., c.1830, 32 x 19 1/2 In. 300.00
Washstand, Poplar, Lower Shelf With Drawer, Turned Legs, c.1820, 36 1/4 In. 275.00
Washstand, Rococo, Rosewood, White Marble Top, 3 Serpentine Drawers, 29 In. 2185.00
Washstand, Rococo, Walnut, Serpentine White Marble Top, 47 x 33 1/2 x 21 In. 3220.00
Washstand, Shaker, Red Wash, Chrome Yellow Surface, 4 Square Legs, 34 x 23 1/2 In. .. 1955.00
Washstand, Sheraton, Cherry, Dovetail Gallery Top, 1 Drawer, Shelf, 28 x 34 x 15 In. 1750.00
Washstand, Sheraton, Cherry, Mahogany, 1 Drawer, Shelf, c.1820, 36 x 19 1/4 In. 385.00
Washstand, Sheraton, Cherry, Shelf, Drawer, Shaped Backsplash, 35 x 19 x 34 In. 330.00
Washstand, Sheraton, Cherry, Square Top, Shelf, Drawer, c.1820, 31 x 17 In. 303.00
Washstand, Sheraton, Dovetailed Gallery, Turned Legs, Shelf, Drawer, 33 x 22 In. 390.00
Washstand, Sheraton, Mahogany, Pennsylvania, c.1830, 32 x 23 In. 220.00
Washstand, Sheraton, Pine, Compartment In Base, 1 Drawer, 31 In. 385.00
Washstand, Sheraton, Pine, New England, 19th Century, 36 In. ....275.00 to 430.00
Washstand, Sheraton, Tiger Maple, Drawer, Shelf, Pa., c.1820, 37 1/4 x 22 1/2 In. 715.00
Washstand, Tiger Maple, Mahogany Shelf, 34 x 15 3/4 In. 2200.00
Washstand, Walnut, Scroll, Leaf Design, Gray Marble, Rectangular, 45 x 19 x 62 In. 430.00
Washstand, Water Jug, Hole For Bowl, 2 Drawers, Pitcher Shelf, England, 30 x 12 In. 575.00
Washstand, Yellow Pine, Flat Surface, Tapered Legs, 19th Century, 33 x 14 In. 170.00
Wastebasket, Arts & Crafts, Mahogany, Brass-Wrapped Feet, 12 x 17 In. 430.00
Wastebasket, Harden, No. 309, Mahogany, Signed, 16 x 13 1/2 In. 850.00
Wastebasket, Maple, 4 Slats Over Caned Panel, Arts & Crafts, 12 x 12 x 18 In. 300.00
Wastebasket, Roycroft, Copper, Original Patina, Mark, 13 In. 3080.00
Wastebasket, Roycroft, Mahogany, Copper Corners, 10 x 10 x 13 In. 1150.00
Wastebasket, Roycroft, Mahogany, Slatted, 16 x 13 1/2 In. 1208.00
Wastebasket, Warren McArthur, Silver, Signed, 12 x 14 In. 575.00
Welsh Dresser, Mahogany & Oak, Step Back, 6 Drawers, 2 Door, 83 x 65 x 20 In. 2915.00
Welsh Dresser, Oak, Dentil Cornice, 3 Open Shelves, Bracket Feet, 85 In. 4200.00
Whatnot Shelf, Mahogany, 5 Tiers, Lyre Supports, Base Drawers, 19th Century, 52 In. ... 1840.00
Whatnot Shelf, Regency, Mahogany, 4 Shelves, Ring-Turned Uprights, 55 x 16 x 16 In. . 1725.00
Whatnot Shelf, Regency, Painted, Gilt Balls, Concave Rattan, 15 x 58 In. 2875.00
Wheelchair, Cane Seat & Back 325.00

Wheelchair, Ladder Back, Blue Green Paint, Late 18th Century 2600.00
Window Seat, Arts & Crafts, Oak, Apron, Splayed Legs, Stretcher, 18 x 39 x 14 1/2 In. ... 750.00
Window Seat, G. Stickley, No. 152, Floral Carving Over Seat, 30 x 25 In. 1540.00
Window Seat, G. Stickley, No. 177, Mahogany, Leather Seat, 36 x 26 In. 8625.00
Window Seat, Mahogany, Shaped Frieze, Turned Legs, Handles, 49 x 12 x 17 In. 920.00
Window Seat, Oak, Scrubbed Top, Signed Kittinger, c.1920, 20 x 54 x 12 1/2 In. 475.00
Window Seat, Scrolled Arm Rests, Padded Seat, Italy, 27 x 27 In. 920.00
Window Seat, William IV, Oak, Clipped Corners, Turned Legs, 20 x 12 In. 1725.00
Wine Cooler, George III, Mahogany, Brass, Octagonal, 1770, 16 x 28 In. 1320.00
Wine Cooler, Mahogany, Brass Staves, Double Handles, England, 21 1/2 In. 1045.00
Wine Stand, George III, Mahogany, Circular Piecrust Top, Cabriole Legs, 21 In. 2130.00

G. ARGY-ROUSSEAU is the impressed mark used on a variety of objects
in the Art Deco style. Gabriel Argy-Rousseau, born in 1885, was a
French glass artist. In 1921, he formed a partnership that made pate-
de-verre and other glass. He worked until 1952 and died in 1953.

G-ARGY-
ROUSSEAU

Bowl, Birds In Flight, Pate-De-Verre, c.1930, 3 1/2 x 4 3/4 In. 6600.00
Bowl, Gourds, Pate-De-Verre, c.1922, 3 3/4 x 4 3/8 In. 4800.00
Bowl, Grapes, Pate-De-Verre, c.1930, 3 1/2 x 4 In. 6600.00
Bowl, Ivy, Pate-De-Verre, Footed, c.1919, 4 x 5 In. 6000.00
Box, Cover, Flower & Foliage, Pate-De-Verre, c.1923, 5 1/4 x 2 3/4 In. 6600.00
Box, Cover, Hydrangeas, Pate-De-Verre, c.1921, 3 7/8 x 2 5/8 In. 6000.00
Box, Roses, Purple, Blue, Green, Gray, Round, Pate-De-Verre, 3 x 3 In. 4313.00
Lamp, 3 Birds, Pate-De-Verre, Chromium Plated, c.1934, 6 1/2 x 4 In. 7800.00
Lamp, Bacchantes, Pate-De-Verre, Silvered Bronze, c.1932, 9 1/2 x 4 1/4 In. 9600.00
Lamp, Pale Purple Shade, Silver, Metal, Pate-De-Verre, 1932, 4 1/4 In. 9600.00
Night-Light, Exotic Foliage, Pate-De-Verre, Wrought Iron, c.1924, 5 5/8 In. 5400.00
Night-Light, Falling Petals, Pate-De-Verre, Wrought Iron, c.1923, 6 1/4 In. 9600.00
Night-Light, Perfume Burner, Flowered Bowl, Pate-De-Verre, c.1923, 5 1/2 In. 11400.00
Night-Light, Wood Anemones, Pate-De-Verre, Wrought Iron, c.1920, 6 1/2 In. 6000.00
Vase, Brown Matte Glaze, Pate-De-Verre, 1927, 9 3/4 In. 7600.00
Vase, Circles, Footed, Pate-De-Verre, c.1927, 9 1/2 In. 9600.00
Vase, Conifer, Pate-De-Verre, c.1924, 6 7/8 In. 4800.00
Vase, Dark Brown Patina, Pate-De-Verre, 1922, 8 3/4 In. 8400.00
Vase, Encircled Fruit, Pate-De-Verre, c.1922, 6 3/4 In. 6000.00
Vase, Fauns & Nymphs, Red, Brown, Gray, Pate-De-Verre, 8 3/4 x 5 In. 10350.00
Vase, Feathers, Pate-De-Verre, c.1922, 5 3/4 In. 6000.00
Vase, Flowered Medallions, Pate-De-Verre, c.1925, 10 In. 10800.00
Vase, Framed Roses, Pate-De-Verre, 1922, 8 3/4 In. 8400.00
Vase, Greek Frieze, Pate-De-Verre, c.1927, 8 1/2 In. 7800.00
Vase, Marigolds, Pate-De-Verre, c.1920, 6 In. 8400.00
Vase, Modern Foliage, Pate-De-Verre, c.1925, 8 5/8 In. 9600.00
Vase, Nude Female Figure Sitting, Turning Head, Pate-De-Verre, 1932, 5 In. 24900.00
Vase, Pale Lavender Glaze, Pate-De-Verre, 1920, 4 5/8 In. 9600.00
Vase, Rosettes, Leaves, Red, Black, Green, Gray, Tapered, Pate-De-Verre, 4 1/2 In. 3220.00
Vase, Snowberry, Pate-De-Verre, c.1920, 4 In. 4800.00
Vase, Spiders & Brambles, Browns, Pate-De-Verre, c.1920, 4 3/4 In. 7800.00
Vase, Spiders & Brambles, Reds, Pate-De-Verre, c.1920, 4 3/4 In. 9600.00
Vase, Thistle Leaves, Pate-De-Verre, c.1927, 9 3/4 In. 7800.00
Vase, Trees In Bloom, Pate-De-Verre, c.1925, 6 In. 9000.00
Vase, White Birds In Flight, Pate-De-Verre, 1932, 7 3/8 In. 20300.00
Veilleuse, Papillon, Pate-De-Verre, Wrought Iron, c.1924, 5 3/8 In. 11400.00

GALLE was a designer who made glass, pottery, furniture, and other Art
Nouveau items. Émile Galle founded his factory in France in 1874.
After Galle's death in 1904, the firm continued to make glass and furniture until 1931. The name *Galle* was used as a mark, but it was often
hidden in the design of the object. Galle glass is listed here. Pottery is
in the next section. His furniture is listed in the Furniture category.

Galle

Bottle, Mauve, Maroon, Chartreuse, Dragonfly, Bulbous, Mushroom Stopper, 1895, 6 In. . 1095.00
Bowl, Enameled Nasturtium Blossoms, Leafy Vines, Ruffled Edge, Signed, 5 x 9 In. 920.00
Bowl, Flowers, Glossy, Burgundy On Beige, Cameo, Signed, 2 3/4 x 4 In. 1250.00

Bowl, Oak Leaves, Windmill, Emerald, Cranberry, Cameo, Bucket Shape, Handles, 3 In. . . 3000.00
Box, Cover, Evergreens, Lavender, Bernice & Henry Blount, 4 In. 920.00
Box, Dresser, Hexagonal, Satin, Butterfly, Landscape, Cameo, Silver, Signed, 11 x 4 In. . . . 6900.00
Cordial, Amber, Enameled, Flower, Signed, 2 3/4 In., Pair 260.00
Ewer, Enameled Flowers, Blue, White, Rose, Signed, 7 x 5 In. 1208.00
Ewer, Light Brown, Applied Handle, Cameo, 1985, 9 3/4 In. 3600.00
Lamp, Flower Shape, Cameo, Bronze, Brown Patina, Signed, c.1900, 22 x 8 In. 18000.00
Lamp, Hanging Shade, Flowers, Leaves, Cut, Signed, 15 1/2 In. 7480.00
Night-Light, 3 Blue, Purple Butterflies, Amber, Cameo, Wrought Iron, 4 x 2 In. 747.00
Vase, Amethyst Flowers, Amber, Cameo, Signed, 3 3/4 In. 545.00
Vase, Amethyst Flowers, Leaves, Orange, Cameo, Signed, 5 1/4 x 2 1/4 In. 575.00
Vase, Banjo, Deep Orange Flowers, Leaves, Cameo, Signed, 5 1/2 x 4 3/4 In. 750.00
Vase, Berried Branches, White & Yellow, Signed, 15 3/4 In. 2530.00
Vase, Berries, Leaves, Red, Gray To Yellow, Satin, Applied Handles, Cameo, 3 3/4 In. . . . 865.00
Vase, Bud, Brown Jack-In-The-Pulpits, White, Cameo, Signed, 5 3/8 In. 520.00
Vase, Buds & Branches, Blue, Yellow, Cameo, 16 In. . . . .*Illus* 8050.00
Vase, Closed Flowers, Pale To Deep Amber, Cameo, 8 x 8 1/2 In. 9488.00
Vase, Crocus Blossoms, Dark Green, Leaves, Signed, 1906, 6 3/4 In. 9600.00
Vase, Crocus, Citron, Cameo, 8 1/2 In. . . . .*Illus* 6600.00
Vase, Deep Cranberry Flowers, Yellow, Cameo, Signed, 7 In. 920.00
Vase, Ferns, Dark Green, Satin, Bulbous, Long Neck, Cameo, 12 1/2 In. 1725.00
Vase, Ferns, Pale Yellow, Cameo, Signed, 3 1/2 x 10 3/4 In. 1440.00
Vase, Flowers & Leaves, Reddish Pink, Satin, Cameo, Star Signed, 7 In. 980.00
Vase, Flowers, Amber, Green, Cameo, 21 In. . . . .*Illus* 6800.00
Vase, Flowers, Branches, Buds & Leaves, Yellow, Signed, 5 1/2 In. 3575.00
Vase, Flowers, Lavender Over Yellow, Egg Shape, Signed, 3 In. 920.00
Vase, Flowers, Purple, Cameo, Signed, 1900, 14 1/4 In. 11400.00
Vase, Forest Scene, Lavender, Blue, Green, Yellow Trees, Gray Field, Signed, 15 3/4 In. . . . 2575.00
Vase, Green Thistle, Cameo, Signed, 4 In. 750.00
Vase, Green Thistles & Leaves, Dark Green Shaded To Pink, Cameo, Signed, 24 In. 3335.00
Vase, Honeycomb, Enameled Flowers & Bees, Signed, c.1890, 9 3/4 In. 4315.00
Vase, Hyacinth, Peach, Gold, Green, White Flowers, Brown Leaves, Cameo, 12 1/2 In. 9200.00
Vase, Hydrangea Blossoms, Periwinkle & Green, Signed, c.1905, 6 1/2 In. 575.00
Vase, Landscape Scene, Amber, Cameo, Signed, 4 7/8 In. 1610.00
Vase, Landscape, Blush, Gray, Cameo, Signed, Early 20th Century, 9 In. 1725.00
Vase, Landscape, Conifer In Foreground Against Mountains, Gray Glass, Signed, 8 In. . . . 4600.00
Vase, Landscape, Flowers, Pale Pink, Cameo, Signed, 17 In. 8400.00
Vase, Landscape, Lake, Boats, Brown, Gray, Yellow, Cameo, Signed, 14 1/2 In. 3450.00
Vase, Landscape, Numerous Trees, Mountain Range In Background, Signed, 13 In. 2860.00
Vase, Landscape, Trees, Mountain Range, Yellow, Cameo, Signed, 6 1/2 In. 1610.00
Vase, Large Blue Open Clematis, Vines, Amethyst, Brown, Yellow, Cameo, 5 1/2 In. 1955.00
Vase, Large Chrysanthemums, Orange, Peach, Cameo, Signed, 6 x 4 In. 690.00
Vase, Lavender Fuchsias, Yellow, Green, Lavender, Cameo, 4 1/2 In. 920.00
Vase, Lavender Over Yellow, Flowers, Egg Shape, Cameo, 5 In. 748.00
Vase, Lavender, Pink Crocus, Lilies, Cameo, Signed, 8 x 3 1/2 In. 1840.00
Vase, Leaves & Berries, Light Brown, Cameo, Signed, 10 1/2 In. 1610.00
Vase, Leaves, Berries, Browns, Satin Mustard, Cameo, Signed, 5 1/2 In. 800.00
Vase, Leaves, Berries, Deep Amethyst, Cameo, Signed, 2 1/2 In. 290.00
Vase, Leaves, Berries, Deep Burgundy, Satin, Yellow, Cameo, Signed, 15 In. 2530.00
Vase, Leaves, Deep Maroon, Orange, Cameo, Signed, 5 3/4 In. 805.00
Vase, Leaves, Flowers, Purple, Salmon, Cameo, Signed, 5 1/2 In. 690.00
Vase, Leaves, Stems, Buds, Cream, Green, Pink, Amber, Tan, Cameo, 23 1/4 In. 4025.00
Vase, Leaves, Stems, Flowers, Dark Purple, Gray, Light Blue, Cameo, 7 In. 863.00
Vase, Lily Pond, Butterfly, Yellow, Lavender, Cameo, 5 3/4 In. 862.00
Vase, Mountain Scene, Blue Mountain Range, Deep Purple Trees, Cameo, 5 x 3 In. 1955.00
Vase, Orange Flowers, Leaf, Vine, Satin, Cameo, Signed, 2 1/2 In. 520.00
Vase, Orange Flowers, Leaves, Cameo, Signed, 4 In. 290.00
Vase, Orchids, Mushrooms, Foliage, Purple, Pink, Green, Ivory, Cameo, 1900, 17 In. 4140.00
Vase, Pink Overlaid With Lavender, Cut Flowers, Flaring Oval Shape, Cameo, 4 3/4 In. . . . 690.00
Vase, Pink, Overlaid With Green, Cut Flowers, Globular Shape, Cameo, Signed, 4 In. 403.00
Vase, Pond Lilies, Deep Amethyst, Green, Lavender, Cameo, 6 1/4 In. 1100.00
Vase, Pond Scene, Blue Flowers, 5 1/2 x 5 3/4 In. 1120.00

Galle, Vase, Crocus, Citron, Cameo, 8 1/2 In.

Galle, Vase, Flowers, Amber, Green, Cameo, 21 In.

Galle, Vase, Buds & Branches, Blue, Yellow, Cameo, 16 In.

Galle, Vase, Tulip, Green, Pink, Dark Brown, Cameo, 11 In.

Vase, Purple & Green Flowers & Leaves, Peach To Gray, Cameo, 10 In. 1270.00
Vase, Purple & White Flowers, Pink To Gray, Cameo, Signed, 2 3/4 x 2 3/4 In. 440.00
Vase, Red Flowers, Yellow, Cameo, 5 In. 750.00
Vase, Seedpods, Leaves, Light Amber Citron, Deep Amber Base, Signed, 7 1/2 x 4 In. . . . 5750.00
Vase, Temptation De St. Antoine, Stylized Script, Signed, 11 In. 1725.00
Vase, Thistle Branches, Amber, Cameo, 12 3/4 In. 1725.00
Vase, Thistle, Topaz, Etched Thistles & Wildflowers, Signed, c.1885, 6 7/8 In. 690.00
Vase, Thistles, Green To Pink, Satin, Cameo, 3 3/4 In. 430.00
Vase, Thistles, Lime Green, Pink Satin, Cameo, Signed, 13 1/2 In. 1380.00
Vase, Trailing Wisteria, Vines, Foliage, Lavender, Pale Gray, Cameo, 11 3/4 In. 1495.00
Vase, Trefoil Shape, Internal Lilies, Signed, c.1905, 6 3/4 In. 1035.00
Vase, Tulip, Green, Pink, Dark Brown, Cameo, 11 In. . . . . *Illus* 5750.00
Vase, Vines & Grapes, Burgundy & Brown, Satin, Cameo, Signed, 14 3/4 In. 2840.00
Vase, Violets, Lavender, Clear, Cameo, Signed, 2 3/8 In. 316.00
Vase, Water Lilies, Dark Purple To Yellow, Narrow Neck, Cameo, Signed, 19 1/2 In. 2300.00
Vase, Yellow-Green, White, Olive Green Ferns, Cameo, Signed, 7 1/4 In. 880.00

GALLE POTTERY was made by Emile Galle, the famous French designer, after 1874. The pieces were marked with the initials *E. G.*
impressed, *Em. Galle Faïencerie de Nancy*, or a version of his signature. Galle is best known for his glass, listed above.

Figurine, Cat, Enameled Faience, Glass Eyes, c.1895, 12 3/8 In. 5700.00
Figurine, Cat, Signed, 1890, 13 In. 3600.00
Figurine, Pug Dog, Glass Eyes, Marked, 12 In. 1345.00
Plate, Praying Mantis, Blue, Black, Red, Green, Yellow Leaves, Flowers, 10 In. 2800.00
Vase, Castle, White, Blue & Brown Enameling, Textured Sand, Signed, 4 In. 575.00

GAME collectors like all types of games. Of special interest are any
board games or card games. Transogram and other company names are
included in the description when known. Other games may be found
listed under Card, Toy, or the name of the character or celebrity featured in the game.

60 Marble King, Vintage 15.00
Anchor Puzzle, Ad. Richter, Pieces, Problem Booklet, c.1915 . . . . 100.00
Authors, Milton Bradley, Card, c.1920 . . . . 35.00
Automobile Race Game, McLoughlin, c.1904 . . . . 2070.00
Backgammon, Bakelite, 2 Cups, Box 395.00
Backgammon & Checkers, Shelf, With Book, 1910, 14 3/4 In. . . . . *Illus* 110.00
Ball, Lawn Bowling, Lignum Vitae, Ivory Insert, England, 5 In. 95.00
Ball Toss, Winning Numbers, Carnival Game, 54 x 18 In. 8050.00
Baseball, Parker Brothers 125.00

Battle, Toy Soldiers, Parker Brothers 157.00
Beanbag, Chinese Man's Head, Open Mouth, Board, 3 Beanbags, 20 x 9 3/4 In. 1035.00
Big Maze, Marx, Marble, 1940s, 13 x 14 In. 45.00
Board, Blocks In Cross Design, Flower Type Pattern, Canada, 1920s 2800.00
Board, For Marbles, Arched Molding Below Corner Spandrels, Numbers, 30 x 18 In. 1325.00
Board, Parcheesi & Checkers, 2 Sides 7150.00
Board, Parcheesi & Checkers, Olive Green, Black Paint, Gilt, Mid 19th Century, 15 In. ... 2875.00
Board, Parcheesi & Checkers, Orange, Red & Yellow, Black Ground, 10 In. 9200.00
Board, Parcheesi & Chinese Checkers, 2 Sides 950.00
Board, Parcheesi, 5-Point Star Corners, Square, 20 In. 4600.00
Board, Parcheesi, Home Center Block, Black Ground, Square, 20 In. 8050.00
Board, Parcheesi, Ocher, Red, Blue, Checkerboard On Reverse, 1890s, 18 1/2 In. 1210.00
Board, Parcheesi, Red Ground, Center Cartouche With Cabin, Square, 19 In. 2875.00
Board, Parcheesi, Red, Blue, Yellow, Gray, Gilt, Off-White Ground, 18 5/8 x 18 In. 17250.00
Board, Parcheesi, Star Design, Red & Black Checkered Cross, 10 x 29 In. 635.00
Board, Parcheesi, Starflower Corners, Red, Orange, Cream & Black, Square, 19 In. 4600.00
Board, Parcheesi, White Stars & Dots, Red, Black Paint, Mid 19th Century, 17 In. 6325.00
Board, Red, Black Paint, Geometric Design, 19th Century, 13 1/4 x 15 1/4 In. 1840.00
Candid Camera, Allen Funt, Lowell, Board, 1963 .... 65.00
Carpet Ball, 1 Black, 1 Brown, 2 White, 4 Piece 150.00
Charlie's Angels, Milton Bradley, Board, 1977 ....10.00 to 20.00
Checkerboard, 24 Checkers, Quaker Oats Premium, Miniature, 6 x 3 1/2 In. 30.00
Checkerboard, Backgammon On Reverse, Inlaid 350.00
Checkerboard, Black, Yellow, Black, Spool Base, Salmon Paint 4600.00
Checkerboard, Crushed Shell & Black, Oak Frame, 20 x 20 In. 85.00
Checkerboard, Grain Painted, Allover Swirl & Sponge, 1800s, 16 x 16 In. 1955.00
Checkerboard, Iron Red, Black, Yellow Linear Design, Rectangular, 13 5/8 x 16 In. 2070.00
Checkerboard, Molded Edge, Hole For Drawer, Pine, 15 x 15 In. 635.00
Checkerboard, Painted, American Flags, 12 1/2 x 21 In. 46000.00
Checkerboard, Red & Black Squares, Yellow Border, Gallery, 14 1/4 x 14 1/2 In. 1595.00
Checkerboard, Red & Mustard, Black Border, Square, Wood, 19th Century, 15 x 15 In. .. 520.00
Checkerboard, Red, Pine, Carved, Painted, Black Squares, c.1870, 15 1/4 x 31 1/4 In. ... 385.00
Checkerboard, Scalloped-Edge Form, 19th Century, 15 In. 2400.00
Checkerboard, Scribed Checks, Black On Red, Late 19th Century, 25 1/2 x 13 1/2 In. ... 748.00
Checkerboard, Slide Lid, Compartments Each End, Wooden Checkers, Pine, 38 x 21 In. . 4400.00
Checkerboard, Walnut, Red & Black Squares, Late 19th Century, 14 1/2 In. 303.00
Checkerboard, Wood, Black & Mustard Squares, Inverse Sash, Medal, Initials, 18 x 18 In. 489.00
Checkerboard, Wood, Checkers, Square, c.1840, 17 In. 350.00
Checkerboard, Wooden, Black & Mustard, White Linear Trim, 19th Century, 18 x 18 In. . 490.00
Checkers, Shooting Stars, Board, Blue, Black, White, 19th Century 1850.00
Chess Set, Immortals & Warriors, 6 1/2-In. Figures 1150.00
Chess Set, Wood, Case, Denmark, 1950s, 14 In. 450.00
Chessboard, Red & Mustard Alternating Squares, Cutting Board Reverse, 14 x 9 In. 165.00
Chessboard, Red & Yellow Squares, Cutting Board Reverse, 14 x 9 1/2 In. 290.00
Chinese Puzzle, McLoughlin Bros., c.1860 .... 450.00
Coughing Coffins, Battery Operated 22.00
Count Down Space Game, Tom Corbett, Transogram, Board, 1960 .... 50.00
Croquet Set, Table Top 40.00

Game, Backgammon & Checkers, Shelf,
With Book, 1910, 14 3/4 In.

Game, Jigsaw Puzzle,
Dutch Children,
George E. Schwain, Box,
15 Piece, Set Of 6

Dark Tower, Milton Bradley, 1981 . . . . .165.00 to 185.00
Dating Game, Hasbro, 1967 . . . .   15.00
Dexterity Puzzle, Fish In Water, Metal Frame, Glass Front, Mirror Back, Germany, 2 In. .   40.00
Dexterity Puzzle, La Question Du Buveur, Cardboard, Wood Bottle, France, 1920s, 3 In. .   35.00
Dexterity Puzzle, Le Porte Bonheur, Wire, N.K. Atlas, Paris, 1920s, 2 1/2 x 4 In. 38.00
Dexterity Puzzle, Train, Metal Frame, Glass Front, Mirror Back, Germany, 1 5/8 In. 40.00
Down & Out, Milton Bradley, Box, 1928 . . . .   40.00
Duran Duran, Milton Bradley, Board, 1985 . . . .   75.00
Eddie Cantor's Tell It To The Judge, Board, 1930s 76.00
Famous Mill Game, Red & Black Wooden Checkers, Box, 1940s 19.00
Fibber McGee & Molly, Wistful Vista Mystery, Milton Bradley, Board, 1940 . . . . .20.00 to 30.00
Floating Satellite, Target, Battery Operated, Motor Blows Ball, Dart Gun & Darts, 1960s   185.00
Game Of Old Mrs. Goose, Milton Bradley, Spinners, Markers, Box, c.1920, 9 x 15 In. . . .   35.00
Gaming Set, Ivory, Mother-Of-Pearl, Engraved, 4 Boxes, 25 Chips, c.1750, 6 x 7 x 2 In. . 9000.00
Green Ghost, Transogram, Board, 1965 . . . .   65.00
Green Hornet, Quick Switch, Milton Bradley, Board, 1966 . . . . 3350.00
Halma, Horsman, Instructions, Box, N.Y., Pat. May 29, 1888 . . . .   35.00
Heedless Tommy, Animal Game Pieces, McLoughlin Brothers, Board, 1893 . . . .   403.00
House That Jack Built, Card, 1887 . . . .   25.00
Huggin' The Rail, Selchow & Righter, Indy Style Race Cars, Box, 1958, 10 x 19 In. 79.00
Interplanetary Race Through Space, 1953 . . . .   135.00
Jack-Pot-Game, Slot Machine Form, Coins, Instructions, Buffalo, Box 58.00
Jetsons, Transogram, Rosey The Robot, With Astro The Space Dog, Board, 1962 . . . .   95.00
Jigsaw Puzzle, Baker & Child Playing Pattycake, 8 1/2 x 10 In.   18.00
Jigsaw Puzzle, Dinner For 6, Mabel Rollins Haris, 3789 Piece, 1934 . . . .   30.00
Jigsaw Puzzle, Dutch Children, George E. Schwain, Box, 15 Piece, Set Of 6 . . . . *Illus*   75.00
Jigsaw Puzzle, Golden Galleon, Frederic Grant, 165 Piece, 1936 . . . .   15.00
Jigsaw Puzzle, Green Hornet, 4 In Box, 1966 . . . .   250.00
Jigsaw Puzzle, Howdy Doody, 1950s 60.00
Jigsaw Puzzle, Moon Map, 1970 . . . .   15.00
Jigsaw Puzzle, Ships, Die Cut Cardboard, Oxford Specialty Co., 288 Piece, 17 x 17 In. . .   30.00
Jigsaw Puzzle, Skippy, Consolidated Paper, 3 Puzzles Tell Story, Box, 1933, 7 x 10 In. . . .   120.00
Jigsaw Puzzle, Uncle Wiggily 34.00
Johnny Ringo, Transogram, Board, 1959 . . . .   200.00
Jolly Clown Spinette, Milton Bradley, Cover, Marble Top, 1932, 9 1/4 In. 39.00
Mail Express, McLoughlin, Box, Copyright 1895, 22 In. 1000.00
Marble, Board, Checkered Border, Spinning Arrow, 16 x 16 In. 2895.00
Marble, Mystery Gun Mac, Tin Lithograph, Mechanical, 1920s, 13 In. 225.00
Marble, Runs Incline, Elephant & Whirligig, Box, Germany, 1950s 350.00
Monopoly Pieces, Gold Metal, 6 Piece . . . . *Illus*   30.00
My Favorite Martian, Transogram, Bill Bixby & Ray Walston, Board, 1963 . . . .   90.00
Mystery Date, Milton Bradley, Board, 1965 . . . .   125.00
Newlywed Game, 3rd Edition, Hasbro, Board, 1969 . . . .   45.00
Old Maid, Chaffee & Selchow, Board, 1898 . . . .   150.00
Old Maid, Milton Bradley, Box, 29 Cards 65.00
Paddle Ball, Dr Pepper, Wood, Frosty Holding Bottle, 1950s, 10 In. 25.00
Parlor Football, McLoughlin, Lithographed Cover, Wooden Pieces, Board, 1890s, 20 In. . 1300.00

Game, Monopoly Pieces,
Gold Metal, 6 Piece

Peg, Mahogany, Maple Inlay, Footed, Hand Carved Pegs, Square, 1860, 8 1/4 In. 210.00
Pinball, Zoo-M-Roo Space Game, Plastic, Northwest Prod., Box, c.1930, 7 In. 79.00
Poker, Chip Holder, Bakelite, 6 Tubes, 200 Swirled Chips 220.00
Punchboard, Ace High, Deck Of Cards For Jackpot, 13 x 17 In. 90.00
Punchboard, Bars & Bells, Fruit Symbols, Deck Of Cards, 13 x 18 1/2 In. 135.00
Punchboard, Extra Bonus, Unusual Dice Tickets, 13 x 12 In. 40.00
Punchboard, Giant Win, One Dollar Board, Slot Symbols, Factory Wrapped, 14 x 16 In. .. 100.00
Punchboard, Home Run Derby, Baseball Theme With Ballpark, 10 x 12 In. 75.00
Punchboard, Huff & Puff, 2 Cents, Big Bad Wolf Puffs On Lucky Strikes, 9 x 9 In. 60.00
Punchboard, Professor Charlie, Comical Professor Overlooking Board, 10 x 12 In. 18.00
Punchboard, Tavern Maid, Win Cans Of Beer, 9 1/2 x 13 1/2 In. 55.00
Puzzle, Block, Centennial Exhibition, 1876, 6 Philadelphia Buildings, Case, 15 Piece 460.00
Puzzle, Block, Children At Play, Paper On Wood, Box, 1900s, 9 x 7 1/2 In. 127.00
Puzzle, Sliced Animals, Selchow & Richter, Construction, Box, 10 1/4 x 9 1/4 In. 88.00
Quick Draw McGraw, Private Eye, Milton Bradley, Board, 1960, 9 1/2 x 19 In. 130.00
Reward Of Virtue, Ives, 1850 .... 1200.00
Ring Toss, Ring-A-Clown, Parker, Wooden Clown, 4 Wooden Rings, Board, 1921 .... 210.00
Ring Toss, Wooden, 1930-1940, 35 3/4 x 18 In. 450.00
Rolling Ball, Marx, Skill, Box, 1949 .... 135.00
Rudolph The Red Nose Reindeer, Parker Brothers, 1948 ....175.00 to 210.00
Rummy, Felix The Cat, Card, Box 65.00
Shoot-A-Loop, Metal, Marbles, Box, 1950 .... 95.00
Shoot-A-Loop, Solitaire, Blue Peewee Marbles, 19th Century 165.00
Skee Ball, Red Metal Marble, Pressed Steel, 6 x 7 In. 15.00
Skittles, Original Paint, France, 1870, 14 1/2 In. 495.00
Snake Mountain Rescue, Mattel, Box, 1980s 35.00
Soccer, Lead Figures, Box, 1930s 110.00
Spaceman Answer, Tin Plate Body, Battery Operated, Argentina, Box, 1950s, 9 In. 2000.00
Starsky & Hutch, 1977 .... 20.00
Stratosphere, Whitman, c.1936 .... 175.00
Target, Carnival, Fox Picture Center, 16 In. Diam. 795.00
Target, Outer Space Moving Target, Marx, Shooting Range, Key Wind, 1950 .... 575.00
Target, Pim Pam Pum, Handmade, Wood, 1920s 495.00
Target, Shooting Galley, Iron, Horse Buffalo, Rooster, Bird, Bear, Squirrel, 78 In. 5500.00
Target, Soldiers Of Fortune, Marx, Rifle, Ammunition, Targets, Cork Box 253.00
Target, Wanted Dead Or Alive, Tin, Mares Laig Rifle, Marx, Box, 1959, 15 x 15 In. 315.00
Token, Casino, $10, Harrah's, Reno, Nev., Babe Ruth On Front, Silver, Gold Overlay 40.00
Toonerville Trolley, Milton Bradley, Board, Box, 1927 .... 80.00
Tootsietoy Speedway, 7 Race Cars, Paper Board, c.1930, 15 x 10 x 2 In. 1550.00
Trump Indicator, Black Cat On Wall, Wood, Pencil Holder, c.1925, 4 7/8 In. 150.00
Trump Indicator, Harp, Lacquered Brass, Celluloid Indicators, Base, c.1925, 3 1/4 In. ... 45.00
Twiggy, Milton Bradley, Board, c.1967, 19 x 9 1/2 In. 33.00
Voyage To Bottom Of Sea, Milton Bradley, 1964 .... 95.00
We Girls Can Do Anything, Barbie Career Game, Golden, 1966 .... 25.00
Wheel, Gambling, Turned Post, Mirrored Center, Cast Iron 2970.00
Whirlpool, Tin, Brinkman Engineering Co., Dayton, Ohio 50.00
Whirr, Tin Windup Top, Bowling Pins, Milton Bradley, Wooden Box, 1932, 9 In. 125.00
Who's Afraid Of The Big Bad Wolf, Parker Brothers, 1933 .... 160.00
Wild Bill Hickock, Built-Rite, Jingles, Pony Express, Board, Box, 1958, 7 x 14 In. 100.00

GAME PLATES are plates of any make decorated with pictures of birds, animals, or fish. The game plates usually came in sets consisting of twelve dishes and a serving platter. These sets were most popular during the 1880s.

2 Quails, Oblong, Johnson Brothers, England, 8 1/2 x 9 1/2 In. 21.00
2 Wild Turkeys, Oblong, Johnson Brothers, England, 8 1/2 x 9 1/2 In. 21.00
Carabou, Buffalo Pottery, 9 In. 39.00
Cartouches Of Dead Birds, Dark Blue Transfer, Separated By Cabbage Roses, 9 In. 67.00
Deer & Moose In Wild, Flow Blue, 14-In. Platter, 6 Piece 143.00
Grouse, Herman Ohme, Silesia, 1883-1900, 9 7/8 In. 43.00
Pheasant, Bavaria, Germany 40.00
Pheasant, George Borgfeldt, 1906-1920, 9 1/2 In. 178.00

Pheasant, Hand-Painted, Gold Trim, Limoges, George Borgfeldt, 10 1/8 In. 79.00
Pheasant, In Landscape, Scalloped Edge, Gold Trim, Bavaria, 10 In. 50.00
Quail In Landscape, Brown Transfer, Wedgwood, 10 In. 42.00
Rabbit, Running, Brown Transfer, Wedgwood, 10 In. 64.00

GARDEN FURNISHINGS have been popular for centuries. The stone or
metal statues, wire, iron, or rustic furniture, urns and fountains, sundi-
als, and small figurines are included in this category. Many of the
metal pieces have been made continuously for years.

Bench, Acorn, Slab Back Support & Seat, Acorn Finial, Stone, 34 x 84 In. 1150.00
Bench, Cast Concrete, Bear Form, Lomelis, 14 x 4 x 15 In. 275.00
Bench, Cast Iron, Flower & Branch, Black Paint, Snake Brackets, 1800s, 50 In., Pair 2800.00
Bench, Intertwining Branches, 52 In. 2160.00
Bench, Iron, Floral & Scroll Back, Parrot Hand Rests, Victorian, 35 x 42 In. 2310.00
Bench, Iron, Slat Back, Seat, Scrolled Supports, Wood, 31 x 56 1/4 x 24 1/2 In. 345.00
Bench, Leaves & Branches, Cast Iron, Victorian, 19th Century, 31 x 50 x 20 In., Pair 2800.00
Bench, Park, Aluminum, Wood, 31 x 39 In. 22.00
Bench, Park, Cast Iron, Wooden Slats, 31 1/2 x 49 1/2 In. 100.00
Bench, Park, Green Enameled Slats, Cast Iron, 62 In., Pair 2070.00
Bench, Polychromed, Slat Back, Rope Twist Arms, Cast Iron, 49 In., Pair 1495.00
Bench, Slab Top Marble, Carved Acanthus, Pair 4400.00
Bench, Slatted Seat & Back, Cast Iron, 19th Century, 74 In. 345.00
Bench, Twig Branch & Leaf Design, Cast Iron, 32 In. 1100.00
Birdbath, Cast Iron, White Paint, 3 Graduated Basins, 80 x 36 In. 4500.00
Birdbath, Putti Pouring Water Out Of A Jar, Clam Shell Basin, 28 x 53 In. 115.00
Birdbath, Raised On Circular Base, Cast Stone, Early 20th Century, 17 x 25 In. 92.00
Birdbath, Scalloped Shell, Figure Of Child On Edge, Cast Iron, 14 In. 230.00
Candelabra, 15-Light, Cast Stone, Sheet Iron, Putti Base, Leaf Wax Pans, 66 x 33 In. 3220.00
Chair, Hand Forged, Scroll Back & Arms, Lattice Seat, 1870, 33 x 28 x 22 In. 240.00
Chair, Renaissance, Roundel Centered Crest, Cast Iron, 35 x 20 x 16 In., Pair 430.00
Figure, Angel, Standing, Concrete, 50 In. 355.00
Figure, Bull Elephant, Standing, Trunk Up, Patinated Bronze, 67 1/2 x 60 In. 3910.00
Figure, Elf, Worn Green Paint, Contemporary, 29 1/2 In. 120.00
Figure, Foo Dogs, Carved Granite, 23 x 9 x 16 In., Pair 880.00
Figure, Gorilla, On All Fours, Glass Eyes, Cast Stone, France, 1927, 48 In. 6325.00
Figure, Mournful Angel, Wings Outspread, Hands Clasped In Prayer, Stone, 42 In. 517.00
Figure, Nude Woman With Flowers, Standing, Early 20th Century, 56 1/2 In. 115.00
Figure, Putto, Fall, Standing, Curly Tresses, Wheat Sheaves Each Arm, Stone, 36 In. 287.00
Figure, Putto, Spring, Curly Tresses, Holding Cluster Of Grapes, Stone, 36 In. 230.00
Figure, Putto, Summer, Standing, Curly Tresses, Holding Spray Of Flowers, Stone, 36 In. . . 345.00
Figure, Stag, Brown, Cast Iron, J.W. Fiske, N.Y., Late 19th Century, 62 x 47 In., Pair 6900.00
Figure, Stag, Standing, On Base, Cast Iron, J.W. Fiske, N.Y., 83 In. 5250.00
Figure, Virgin Mary, White Paint, Concrete, 36 In. 225.00
Figure Set, Cherub, 4 Seasons, Concrete, 21 x 24 In., 4 Piece 1420.00
Fountain, 2 Tiers, Mermaid & Flute Playing Putti, 3 Ducks Base, Bronze, 82 1/2 In. 7475.00
Fountain, 2 Tiers, Merman Top, Horn, Bronze, 84 In. 6325.00
Fountain, Acanthus Form Basin, Heron Pedestal, Cast Iron, 46 x 48 In. 4675.00
Fountain, Arched Panel, Lion's Head Flanked By Columns Issuing Water, Marble 6900.00
Fountain, Boy & Girl, Holding Umbrella, Cast Iron, 42 x 24 In. 5462.00
Fountain, Boy & Girl, Holding Umbrella, Cast Zinc, c.1908, 27 1/2 In. 1325.00
Fountain, Bronze Figure Of Nymph, Kneeling, Paw Feet, 30 x 26 In. 1800.00
Fountain, Cherub On Octagonal Base, Foliate Rim, Cast Iron, 19th Century 420.00
Fountain, Frog, Sitting On Lily Pad, Mouth Spout, Concrete, 6 x 7 In. 86.00
Fountain, Naked Boy, Holding Goose, 4 Goslings, Open Beaks As Fonts, Bronze, 35 In. . . 6325.00
Fountain, Swan, Painted, Cast Iron, American, Late 19th Century, 37 x 17 In., Pair 5750.00
Fountain, White Tin Glaze, Blue Floral Design, Terra-Cotta, Bjorn Winblad, 1970, 65 In. . . 2185.00
Frog, Concrete, Painted, Green, 12 In., Pair 315.00
Garden Tag, Red Pyrus Japonica & Condor Peach, Lead, 1879, Pair 160.00
Hitching Post, Black Boy, Red Shirt, White Pants, Green Base, J.W. Fiske, 48 In. 2300.00
Hitching Post, Black Jockey On Pedestal, Iron, 19th Century, 37 1/2 In. 224.00
Hitching Post, Black Man, Iron, 19th Century, 39 1/2 In. 2070.00
Hitching Post, Eagle Head, Iron, 35 In. 2800.00

Hitching Post, Horse Head, Ring, Cast Iron, Classic Style, Black Paint, 14 x 9 In. 86.00
Hitching Post, Jockey, Red, White & Black, Iron, Champion Iron Fence Co., 50 1/4 In. .. 577.00
Hitching Post, Lamp, Green, Black Boy, Holding Lantern, Iron, Slag Glass, 44 In. 880.00
Hitching Post, Lawn Jockey, Cast Iron, Electrified, 50 In. 550.00
Hitching Post, Staff Shape, Iron, c.1850, 62 In. 385.00
Hitching Post, Tree Shape, Iron, 36 In. 127.00
Jardiniere, Canted Sides, Ancient Warrior Procession, Stone, 20th Century, 15 In. 230.00
Lantern, Post, 4-Sided Glazed Body, Hinged Door, Copper & Iron, 1870s, 47 In., Pair ... 4600.00
Nozzle, Hose, Brass, Craftsman, 3 3/4 In. ....*Illus* 15.00
Nozzle, Hose, Brass, Habco, 3 1/4 In. ....*Illus* 15.00
Ornament, Rooster, Cast Iron, 19 In. 575.00
Pedestal, Serpentine Side Formed With Shell & Scroll, Stone, 19 1/2 x 20 1/2 In. 260.00
Planter, Carved Sandstone, Tree Form Base, 4 Branches, 37 x 26 In. 1540.00
Planter, Floral Garland Design, Rounded End, Lead, 6 1/2 In., Pair 430.00
Planter, On Stand, Scroll, Leaf Design, Cast Stone, Early 20th Century, 15 x 26 In., Pair . 86.00
Pot, Black Over Gray Glaze, 29 3/4 In. 1570.00
Seat, Barrel Form, Pierced Entwined Rings, Minton, 19th Century, 17 3/4 In., Pair 1095.00
Seat, Barrel Form, Rosewood, 18 1/2 In., Pair 489.00
Seat, Birds, Dragonflies, Blue Ground, Majolica, George Jones, c.1872, 17 3/4 In. 10800.00
Seat, Elephant Form, Porcelain, Chinese, 22 x 21 In. 280.00
Seat, Pair Of Peacocks, Chrysanthemums, Apple Blossoms, Green, White, 18 In. 288.00
Seat, Shaped Back, Neptune Mask, Flanked By Griffins, Terra-Cotta, 21 3/4 In., Pair 920.00
Seat, Stool, 2 Scenes Of Immortals Visiting Gardens, Chrysanthemums, Chinese, 19 In. .. 431.00
Set, Glass Top Table, 4 Wooden Open Armchairs, Leather Backs & Seats, 1960s, 48 In. .. 115.00
Settee, Renaissance, 3-Part Back, Roundel Centered Crest, Cast Iron, 36 In. 490.00
Settee, Rococo Revival, White, Floral Swags, Scroll Arms, Cast Iron, 1800s, 45 In. ... 3105.00
Settee, Scroll Design End Supports, Green Paint, Cast Iron, 20th Century, 69 In. 2645.00
Settee, Serpentine Rail, White Paint, Openwork Seat, Cast Iron, 19th Century, 46 In. 660.00
Settee, White Paint, Serpentine Crest, Pierced Back, Cast Iron, 19th Century, 43 In. 600.00
Settee Set, Cast Iron, Pierced Lyre Back, White, Scroll Arms, Victorian, 3 Piece 1200.00
Settee Set, Iron Rod & Metal, Modern, Lattice Construction, White, 1955, 6 Piece 800.00
Sprinkler, Cast Iron, Lafayette 23.00
Sprinkler, Lawn, Metal, Rain King Model H-1, Chicago Flexible Shaft Co., 11 1/2 x 8 In. 59.00
Sprinkler, Oscillating, Aluminum, Melnor, 25 1/2 In. ....*Illus* 25.00
Sprinkler, Sun-Shower, Plastic, Orange & Green, 5 1/4 x 5 3/4 In. ....*Illus* 20.00
Sundial, Brass, Engraved Numerals, Sickle, Sun & Skull, Engraved Saying, 7 3/4 In. 385.00
Sundial, Bronze, Tapered Column, Stepped Plinth Base, Early 20th Century, 43 1/2 In. ... 328.00
Sundial, Druid, Tree Trunk Supports, Putti Heads, Verse, Raised Letters, Stone, 31 1/2 In. 920.00
Sundial, Roman Numerals Around Compass, Father Time, Motto, 18th Century, 8 In. 632.00
Sundial, Slate, Iron, Incised Tulip, Heart, Pennsylvania, c.1748, 22 x 14 1/4 In. 3520.00
Table, Cast Iron, Marble Top, 18 x 19 1/2 x 9 1/2 In., Pair 336.00
Table, Potting, Lead Lined, Pine Base, c.1875, 25 1/2 x 38 In. 795.00
Topiary Frame, Iron, Latticed, Pyramidal, 89 1/4 In., Pair 1150.00
Topiary Frame, Metal, Anchor Shape, Painted, Bermuda, 78 In. 2800.00
Trellis, Oak Leaf & Acorn Design, Iron, 85 x 29 In. 950.00
Urn, Acanthus Design, Handles, Cast Iron, 19th Century, 19 In., Pair 1725.00

Garden, Nozzle, Hose, Brass,
Habco, 3 1/4 In.; Garden, Nozzle,
Hose, Brass, Craftsman, 3 3/4 In.

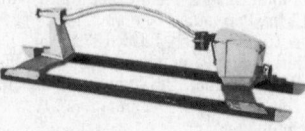

Garden, Sprinkler, Oscillating,
Aluminum, Melnor, 25 1/2 In.

Garden, Sprinkler, Sun-Shower,
Plastic, Orange & Green,
5 1/4 x 5 3/4 In.

Urn, Campana, Egg & Dart Edge, Square Plinth Base, Black Paint, 17 In., Pair 345.00
Urn, Campana, Leaf Trim On Rim, Scroll Handles, Green Paint, 39 1/2 In., Pair 1150.00
Urn, Garland Ram's Head Design, Rectangular Pedestal, 38 1/2 In., Pair 1955.00
Urn, George III, Fluted Bodies, Swag Design, Mask Handles, 24 In., Pair 2880.00
Urn, Melon Form, Turned-Out Rim, Square Base, Stone, 30 1/2 In. 460.00
Urn, Neoclassical, Composition, 58 3/4 In., Pair 4310.00
Urn, Renaissance, Foliate Casting Body, Fluted Pedestal, Cast Iron, 23 x 26 In. 920.00
Well Cover, 2 Parts, Bucket Holder, Scroll Design, Bombe Circular Base, 98 x 32 In. 3163.00

GAUDY DUTCH pottery was made in England for America from about
1810 to 1820. It is a white earthenware with Imari-style decorations of
red, blue, green, yellow, and black. Only sixteen patterns of Gaudy
Dutch were made: Butterfly, Carnation, Dahlia, Double Rose, Dove,
Grape, Leaf, Oyster, Primrose, Single Rose, Strawflower, Sunflower,
Urn, War Bonnet, Zinnia, and No Name. Other similar wares are called
Gaudy Ironstone and *Gaudy Welsh*.

Bowl, Carnation, 3 1/4 x 6 1/4 In. 302.00
Bowl, Cover, Sunflower, Shell Handles, 5 1/2 In. 770.00
Bowl, Single Rose, 3 1/8 x 6 3/8 In. 935.00
Coffeepot, Dome Cover, Oyster, 11 1/2 In. 11000.00
Creamer, Oyster, Beaded Rings, Green Mark, Allerton, 3 3/4 In.   135.00
Creamer, Primrose 4400.00
Cup & Saucer, Butterfly, Handleless 550.00
Cup & Saucer, Dahlia, 2 1/4 In. . . . . .7975.00 to 9010.00
Cup & Saucer, Double Rose, Handleless, 2 In. 575.00
Cup & Saucer, Grape, Handleless, 2 1/2 In. 495.00
Cup & Saucer, Leaf, Handleless 5500.00
Cup & Saucer, Oyster, Handless, 2 1/4 & 5 1/2 In. 467.00
Cup & Saucer, Single Rose, Handleless . . . . .522.00 to 550.00
Cup & Saucer, Urn, Handleless 605.00
Cup & Saucer, War Bonnet, Handleless 440.00
Pitcher, Carnation, 4 1/4 In. 4400.00
Plate, Butterfly, 7 1/2 In. 935.00
Plate, Carnation, 8 1/4 In. . . . . .500.00 to 935.00
Plate, Carnation, 9 7/8 In. 3850.00
Plate, Double Rose, 7 1/4 In. 385.00
Plate, Dove, 3 Leaves Form Dove, c.1780, 7 1/2 In. 500.00
Plate, Dove, 9 3/4 In. 5225.00
Plate, Grape, 8 In. 1210.00
Plate, Grape, 9 1/2 In. . . . . .440.00 to 500.00
Plate, No Name, 8 3/4 In. 17050.00
Plate, Oyster, 7 1/2 In. 575.00
Plate, Oyster, 9 3/4 In. 3025.00
Plate, Oyster, 10 In. 1540.00
Plate, Single Rose, 7 1/2 In. . . . . .495.00 to 570.00
Plate, Single Rose, 8 1/4 In. 330.00
Plate, Sunflower, 9 3/4 In. 825.00
Plate, Urn, 8 In. 915.00
Plate, Urn, 10 In. . . . . .935.00 to 1320.00
Soup, Dish, Double Rose, 9 1/2 In. 2860.00
Soup, Dish, Double Rose, 10 In. . . . . .1760.00 to 2024.00
Soup, Dish, Single Rose, 10 In. . . . . .1485.00 to 1700.00
Soup, Dish, Zinnia, 10 In. . . . . .4625.00 to 5375.00
Sugar, Sunflower, Shell Handle, 5 1/2 In. 325.00
Teabowl & Saucer, Dove, Cobalt Blue Bands, England, c.1820 . . . .   700.00
Teabowl & Saucer, Dove, Horizontal Stripe & Flower Rim Design 700.00
Teapot, Carnation 2475.00
Teapot, Cover, Oyster, 6 In. 2640.00
Teapot, Single Rose, 5 1/2 In. . . . . .1045.00 to 1200.00
Teapot, Urn, 6 1/4 In. 825.00
Teapot, War Bonnet, 7 In. 4400.00
Waste Bowl, Sunflower, 6 1/2 In. 495.00

GAUDY IRONSTONE is the collector's name for the ironstone wares with the bright patterns similar to Gaudy Dutch. It was made in England for the American market. There may be other examples found in the listing for Ironstone or under the name of the ceramic factory.

Bottle, Morning Glory, Green, Purple, White Ground, 8 3/4 In.	825.00
Bowl, Seaweed, Blue Band, Tan, Dark Brown, Blue Stripes, 4 In.	1265.00
Bowl, Strawberry, Copper Luster, Elsmore Forster, 7 5/8 In.	716.00
Coffeepot, Dome Cover, Green, 10 1/2 In.	1540.00
Cup & Saucer, Seeing Eye	155.00
Cup Plate, Floral, Blue Rim, Octagonal, 5 In.	198.00
Mug, Blue, Tan, Ivory Cat's Eye, Sprig, Dark Brown Band, 3 3/4 In.	1980.00
Mug, Brown, Tan, Ivory Tobacco Leaf, Yellow, Tan Ground, 3 In.	4070.00
Mug, Green Upper Band, Tan, Brown Bands, 2 1/2 In.	495.00
Mug, Stylized Tulips, Berries & Leaves, 4 In.	275.00
Mustard Pot, Brown, Tan, Ivory Tobacco Leaf, Tan Ground, 2 In.	3080.00
Pepper Pot, Brown, Tan, Ivory Cat's Eye, Blue Band, 4 1/2 In.	2420.00
Pitcher, Barrel Shape, Blue, Brown, Ivory Earthworm Loops, 7 In.	3410.00
Pitcher, Blackberry, Black, Yellow, Orange, Branch & Leaf Handle, 12 In.	412.00
Pitcher, Charcoal, Blue, Ivory Sprig, Cat's Eye, Handle, 8 In.	3190.00
Pitcher, Cream, White Shaped Handle, Bulbous, 5 1/2 In.	1375.00
Pitcher, Floral Border & Trim, Octagon, 5 1/2 In.	65.00
Plate, Bittersweet, Underglaze Flow Blue & Copper Luster, 8 In.	82.00
Plate, Queen's Rose, Strawberry, Vine Border, 8 1/2 In.	1265.00
Plate, Rabbits, Frogs & Trees Border, Stick Spatter Flowers, 9 3/8 In.	467.00
Plate, Running Rabbits Border, Stick Spatter Flowers, 9 3/8 In.	412.00
Plate, Seeing Eyes, 8 1/4 In.	195.00
Plate, Soup, Queen's Rose, Vine Border, Green Leaves, 10 In.	275.00
Plate, Strawberries, Pink Flowers, Underglaze Flow Blue Leaves, 10 1/4 In.	247.00
Platter, Transfer Center Of Rabbits & Frog, Flower Border, 14 1/2 In.	1100.00
Teapot, Flower Finial, Paneled, Strawberries, Domed Cover, c.1850, 9 3/4 In.	2300.00

GAUDY WELSH is an Imari-decorated earthenware with red, blue, green, and gold decorations. Most Gaudy Welsh was made in England for the American market. It was made after 1820.

Bowl, Butterfly, 7 1/4 x 5 3/4 In.	575.00
Compote, Floral, Underglaze Blue, Red & Green Luster, 8 1/4 x 4 In.	358.00
Creamer, Floral, Blue, Red & Green, 6 In.	231.00
Cup & Saucer, Tulip, Set Of 6	330.00
Jug, Cream, Handle, Ragland, 5 7/8 In.	665.00
Pitcher, Cheyenne, Handle, 7 3/4 In.	785.00
Pitcher, Handles, 8 3/8 x 6 3/8 In., Pair	445.00
Plate, 12 Sides, Dutch Rose, 9 /12 In.	99.00
Tea Set, Child's, Wagon Wheel, 11 Piece	525.00

GEISHA GIRL porcelain was made for export in the late nineteenth century in Japan. It was an inexpensive porcelain often sold in dime stores or used as free premiums. Pieces are sometimes marked with the name of a store. Japanese ladies in kimonos are pictured on the dishes. There are over 125 recorded patterns. Borders of red, blue, green, gold, brown, or several of these colors were used. Modern reproductions are being made.

Berry Bowl, Garden Bench Pattern, Gold Under Red, Set Of 4	50.00
Bowl, Boat Festival Pattern, Blue Trim, 2 x 8 1/2 In.	50.00
Bowl, Child Chasing Butterfly, Red Orange, Footed	30.00
Bowl, Garden Bench Pattern, Red Orange Trim, Footed, 3 3/4 x 6 1/2 In.	40.00
Bowl, Garden Scene, 5 1/4 In.	6.00
Celery Set, Child's, Flower Garden Pattern, Green Trim, 6 1/2-In. Master, 8 Salts	50.00
Chocolate Pot, Blue Edge, Gold, Grapes, 3 Geishas, Handle, Cover	75.00
Chocolate Set, Chocolate Pot, Cover, 6 Cups & Saucers, 14 Piece	250.00
Creamer, Hand Painted, Texture, No Mark, 3 1/2 In.	17.50
Cup & Saucer, Translucent, Stamped Wreath With M, Japan	17.50
Match Holder, Striker, Parasol Pattern, Red Orange Trim, 2 1/2 In.	25.00

Match Holder, Teahouse Pattern, Red Orange, Gold Trim, Floral Border	25.00
Nut Cup, Red Orange, Footed, 3 Piece	25.00
Nut Cup Set, White Ground, Blue & Gold Trim, Red Outlines, 4 In. & 3 In., 5 Piece	40.00
Powder Jar, Fan B Pattern, Red Orange, 2 1/2 x 4 1/4 In.	25.00
Powder Jar, Flower Gathering, Red-Orange Trim, Maple Leaf Transfer, 1 1/2 x 4 In.	30.00
Salt & Pepper, Cobalt Blue, 3 1/4 In.	25.00
Tea Set, Child's, Teapot, Cover, Cups, Saucers, Plates, 6 Piece	125.00
Tea Strainer, Red Orange, Gold Trim	40.00
Toy, Pitcher, Washbowl, Child Chasing Butterfly, Red Orange, Cover, 3 1/2 In.	30.00
Tureen, Dome Cover, Handle, 13 1/2 x 6 1/2 In.	200.00
Tureen, Rust, Cover, Handle, Pre-1960, 10 x 5 In.	140.00

GENE AUTRY was born in 1907. He began his career as the *Singing Cowboy* in 1928. His first movie appearance was in 1934, his last in 1958. His likeness and that of the Wonder Horse, Champion, were used on toys, books, lunch boxes, and advertisements.

Cap Gun, Die Cast Nickel, Butterscotch Plastic Grips, Horse Head, Leslie Henry	178.00
Cap Gun Set, 4 Guns, Holsters, Case	350.00
Doll, Plastic Head, Blue Eyes, Gold Shirt, Jeans, Boots, Terri Lee, Pat. Pending, 16 In.	1700.00
Gun Set, Double Leather Holster, Plated Studs, Diecast Guns, Plastic Handles, Marked	316.00
Record, Frosty The Snowman, When Santa Claus Gets Your Letter, Columbia, 78 RPM	25.00
Record, Here Comes Santa Claus, He's A Chubby Little Fellow, Columbia, 1950, 78 RPM	25.00
Record, Santa Claus Is Coming To Town, Up On The Housetop, Columbia, 78 RPM	25.00
Songbook, Mountain Ballads, 1932, 9 x 12 In.	25.00
Spurs, Metal, White Leather Straps, Leslie Henry, Box	150.00
Stencil Book, Gene On Champion, Western Stencils, Stencil Art, 1950, 10 x 7 In.	74.00
Wristwatch, Autry On Face, Wilane, Box, 1948, 1 1/4 In.	350.00

GIBSON GIRL black-and-blue decorated plates were made in the early 1900s. Twenty-four different 10 1/2-inch plates were made by the Royal Doulton pottery at Lambeth, England. These pictured scenes from the book *A Widow and Her Friends* by Charles Dana Gibson. Another set of twelve 9-inch plates featuring pictures of the heads of Gibson Girls had all-blue decoration. Many other items also pictured the famous Gibson Girl.

Cufflinks, Sterling Silver, c.1908, 3/4 In.	160.00
Plate, Gibson Girl, Calendar, Seasonal Designs, Steubenville China, 1910, 9 In.	78.00
Plate, Miss Babble Brings Morning Paper, Blue & White	165.00
Plate, She Finds That Exercise Does Not Improve Her Spirits, Flow Blue, 10 1/2 In.	162.50
Plate Set, Cobalt Border, Signed, Royal Doulton, c.1901, 10 1/2 In., 24 Piece	3170.00
Postcard, On Halloween There's Fun & Glee, Don't Fail To Join The Company, 1912	36.00
Print, Colliers, Black & White, Self Matted, Gibson Signed, 1908, 11 x 7 In.	11.00

GILLINDER pressed glass was first made by William T. Gillinder of Philadelphia in 1863. The company had a working factory on the grounds at the Centennial and made small, marked pieces of glass for sale as souvenirs. They made a variety of decorative glass pieces and tablewares.

GILLINDER

Candlestick, Crucifix, c.1900, 9 1/2 In., Pair	91.00
Paperweight, Turtle, 1871	125.00
Shoe, Satin Glass, Ribbed, Scalloped Edge, Hobnail & Tassel, c.1870, 4 3/8 In.	91.00

GIRL SCOUT collectors search for anything pertaining to the Girl Scouts, including uniforms, publications, and old cookie boxes. The Girl Scout movement started in 1912, two years after the Boy Scouts. It began under Juliette Gordon Low of Savannah, Georgia. The first Girl Scout cookies were sold in 1928.

Book, Leader's Nature Guide, Marie E. Goudette, 1942, 94 Pages	12.00
Doll, Effanbee, Original Scout Uniform, Hat Missing, c.1957, 8 In.	60.00
Doll, Vinyl, Walking, Original Girl Scout Uniform, 1960s, 8 In.	115.00
Handbook, 1947	10.00
Uniform, Badges, Kerchief & Braid, c.1930	58.00

GLASS-ART. Art glass means any of the many forms of glassware made during the late nineteenth or early twentieth century. These wares were expensive and production was limited. Art glass is not the typical commercial glass that was made in large quantities, and most of the art glass was produced by hand methods. Later twentieth-century glass is listed under Glass-Contemporary, Glass-Midcentury, or Glass-Venetian. Even more art glass may be found in categories such as Burmese, Cameo Glass, Tiffany, and other factory names.

Basket, Applied Clear Thorn Handle, Baby Chick, Eggs, 6 1/2 x 5 1/2 In.	450.00
Bottle, Amethyst, Deep Thistle, Floral Cutting, 6 In.	595.00
Bottle, Lime Green, Gold Flowers & Leaves, 3 Petal Top, Clear Stopper, 9 1/2 In.	135.00
Bottle, Sapphire Blue, Enameled Flowers, Amber Bubble Stopper, 9 1/4 In.	125.00
Bowl, 4 Nudes, Peacocks, Garden, Black, Multicolor Enameled, Vedar, Signed, 3 x 5 In.	230.00
Bowl, Cased Pink, Fan Shape, Footed, 8 1/2 x 13 1/2 In.	375.00
Bowl, Green, Ruffled Edge, Silver Plated Foot, 6 1/2 x 9 In.	175.00
Bowl, Molded Leaves, Light Amber Wash, Signed, France, 9 1/2 In.	175.00
Bowl, Opal, Over Pink, 3 Amber Feet, Applied Rigaree, 3 x 4 3/4 In.	299.00
Bowl, Prussian Blue, 10 Sides, 5-Petal Foot, 4 1/4 x 5 In.	175.00
Bowl, Sapphire Blue, Fan Shape, Clear Ruffled Edge, Flowers, 8 1/4 x 14 x 4 1/2 In.	365.00
Bowl, White To Pink To Clear, Flowers, Amber Vine Handles, Hobbs, Brockunier, 9 In.	165.00
Bowl, Yellow, Green & Pink Mottled, Monart, 14 1/2 In.	60.00
Box, Cover, Nude & Zodiac Emblems, 2 1/4 x 3 3/4 x 1 1/2 In.	11.00
Box, Cover, Stylized Florets, Black Enameled, White, M. Goupy, 4 1/4 In.	978.00
Car Mascot, Topaz, Draped Woman With Outstretched Arm, France, c.1927, 14 1/4 In.	1150.00
Decanter, Green, Silver Overlay, Silver Collar, Stopper, Birmingham, 1900	3000.00
Decanter, Ruby Cut To Clear, Grapes, Leaves, c.1850, 15 1/2 In.	403.00
Epergne, Amber, Sapphire Blue Rigaree, Flowers & Leaves, 14 5/8 In.	385.00
Ewer, Gold Trim, Etched, 4 1/4 In.	145.00
Goblet, Tulip Shape, Opalescent Yellow, Signed, Richardson's, 6 In., Pair	431.00
Jug, Water, Tangerine, Sandy White Texture, Handle, 7 x 5 In.	50.00
Pitcher, Pink, Flowers, Foliage, Globular, Handle, 10 1/4 In.	345.00
Shade, Clear Overshot With Cranberry Edge, Ruffled Edge, 5 1/2 x 7 1/2 In.	210.00
Shade, Pulled Feathers, White, Gold Lining, Steuben Style, 6 In.	175.00
Sugar & Creamer, Agata, Applied Loop Handles, New England ....*Illus*	3740.00
Syrup, Lime Green, Pink & White Flowers, White Dots, 6 In.	165.00
Tazza, Blue, Amethyst Oil Spots, Threading, Gold Leaf, 6 3/4 In., Pair	225.00
Tumbler, Amethyst Stripes Over Clear, Intaglio Cut, Grapes & Leaves, 5 In.	110.00
Tumbler, Red, Gold Rim, 5 In.	55.00
Tumbler, Whiskey, Enameled Flower & Gilt Base, 2 5/8 In.	135.00
Urn, Cover, Clear To Opalescent Pink, Strawberries, 15 In.	300.00
Vase, 3 Classical Medallions, Brown & Gold, White Ground, Richardson, 8 In.	175.00
Vase, Amber, Iridescent Swirl, Blue Rim, Signed, Orient & Flume, 5 1/2 In.	325.00
Vase, Applied Thorny Roses On Vines, Mushroom Shape, Signed, Honesdale, 4 1/2 In.	175.00
Vase, Cobalt Blue, Heart Shaped Rim, Gold Trim, Handles, 7 1/2 In.	125.00
Vase, Deep Green, Faceted Shape, Wiener Werkstatte, Josef Hoffmann, Signed, 7 In.	1610.00
Vase, Drape, Von Eiff, 3 1/2 In.	60.00
Vase, Enameled Tangerines, Mottled Aqua Ground, Round, M. Goupy, 5 1/2 x 5 1/2 In.	1380.00
Vase, Fan, Deep Amethyst, Floral Silver Overlay, Signed, Rockwell, 8 1/2 x 6 1/2 In.	805.00
Vase, Gold Birds In Flight, Yellow, 9 In.	110.00
Vase, Greek Goddess & Soldier, Opalescent & Gilt Glass, Richardson, 8 In.	405.00
Vase, Green Oil Spots, Iridized, Satin, Purple Threading, 7 1/2 In.	415.00
Vase, Green Pulled Feathers, Rust To Amber, Continental, 9 1/4 In., Pair	1610.00
Vase, Hibiscus Blossoms, Leaves, Iridized Body, Signed, Clement Massier, 7 3/4 In.	1035.00
Vase, Iridescent Gold, Round Geometric Design, Art Deco, 10 1/2 In., Pair	290.00
Vase, Ivory, Mottled Iridescent Design, Green Threading, 9 1/2 In.	200.00
Vase, Jade Green, Ruffled Edge, Pedestal, Richardson, 7 1/4 In.	115.00
Vase, Landscape, Enameled Trees, Snow Covered Ground, Walking Women, 8 1/2 In.	299.00
Vase, Molded Woman, Frosted Glass, Light Blue Wash, Costabella, 7 1/2 In.	80.00
Vase, Pillow, Orange & White Stripes, Floria Meydam, Label, Holland, 10 x 6 1/2 In.	805.00
Vase, Pink Over Amber, Applied Leaves, Pink, Green, 7 3/4 In.	345.00
Vase, Pulled Stripes, Yellow Iridescent, Bottle Shape, 12 In.	5520.00
Vase, Purple, Blue, Platinum Design, Gold, Double Gourd, 6 1/4 In.	200.00
Vase, Random Threaded, Gold Iridescent, Amber, Pallme Koenig, 14 In.	259.00

Don't put glass with an iridescent finish in the dishwasher. The hot water and soap will remove the finish.

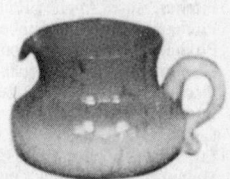

Glass-Art, Sugar & Creamer, Agata, Applied Loop Handles, New England

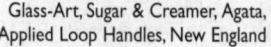

Vase, Red Iridescent, Oil Spots, Pinched Sides, 7 3/4 In.	1265.00
Vase, Red, Clear Foot & Applied Handles, 10 1/2 In.	45.00
Vase, Ruby Flashed, Applied Blue Leaves, Gold Trim, 1860s, 5 In.	45.00
Vase, Satin Stylized Floral & Art Deco Panels, A. Hunebelle, 6 1/4 In.	230.00
Vase, Stylized Flowers, Leaves, Clear & Satin, Signed, Andre Hunebelle, 4 1/2 x 6 In.	175.00
Vase, Swirled, Cranberry To Amber, Crimped Top, 5 In.	460.00
Vase, Trumpet, Coiled Snake, Satin Cerulean Blue, Gold Trim, Domed Base, 17 In.	275.00
Vase, Vaseline, Embossed, Iris Plants & Blossoms, Ruffled Edge, 10 In.	92.00
Vase, White, Opaque, Applied Flowers, Leaves, Rose, Amber, Green, Crimped, 6 In.	290.00
Washbowl & Pitcher, Amethyst, Lead Crystal, 14 3/4-In. Bowl	259.00

GLASS-BLOWN was formed by forcing air through a rod into molten glass. Early glass and some forms of art glass were hand blown. Other types of glass were molded or pressed.

Basket, Opaque White Glass, Amber Branch Handle, Pink Flowers, 9 In.	300.00
Bowl, Aqua, Flared Sides, Rolled Rim, America, Early 19th Century, 8 x 10 In.	575.00
Bowl, Cover, Starburst On Knob, Solid Stem, Flat Foot, 7 1/2 x 7 1/2 In.	55.00
Celery Vase, 3-Piece Mold, Pillar, 8 Ribs, Pontil, Pittsburgh, 10 x 10 1/4 In., Pair	525.00
Celery Vase, 3-Piece Mold, Strawberry-Diamonds, Fans, Leaf Band, 1840, 8 In.	70.00
Celery Vase, Tapered Paneled Sides, Teardrop Knop, Octagonal Foot, 10 3/4 In.	115.00
Chalice, Enameled Bird Perched In Tree, Other Bird Catching Bee, 11 In.	550.00
Champagne, Teal Green, Polished Pontil, 5 In.	160.00
Cheese Dome, Molded Base, Turned Feet, Victorian, 16 x 20 In.	316.00
Cheese Dome, Molded Base, Turned Feet, Victorian, 22 1/2 x 10 In., Pair	402.00
Compote, 3-Piece Mold, Strawberry-Diamonds, Fans, 1830, 7 In.	375.00
Compote, Cut Scalloped Rim, Wafered Pedestal, c.1850, 6 3/4 x 8 7/8 In.	330.00
Creamer, Aquamarine, White Loopings, Witch's Ball Cover, 1870, 6 1/2 In.	1760.00
Creamer, Light Aqua, Applied Handle, Crimped Foot, Jersey Type, Pontil, 3 3/4 In.	745.00
Decanter, 3-Piece Mold, Greek Key, Matching Stopper, 14 In.	49.00
Decanter, Amber, Circles, Flutes, Fruiting Grapevine, 14 In., Pair	862.00
Decanter, Amber, Student Society, Stopper, 11 1/2 In.	405.00
Decanter, Clear, 4 Bands Rigaree, Pontil, Norway, 1840, 9 In.	330.00
Decanter, Hollow Paneled Stopper, Early 19th Century, 12 1/2 In., Pair	460.00
Decanter, Plain Flutes Cut, Birds In Flight, Scrolls, Balloon Stopper, 15 In.	172.00
Decanter Set, Gold Detail, Stopper, Inlaid Box, Mahogany, 8 x 10 1/2 x 7 In.	2300.00
Dish, Sweetmeat, Cover, Ribbed, Rolled Rim, Pittsburgh, 1840, 5 x 6 3/8 In.	132.00
Figurine, Dog, Clear, Applied Ears, Feet, Medallion, Rigaree Bands, 1920, 8 In.	160.00
Finger Bowl, Cobalt Blue, Polished Pontil, 3 3/8 x 4 1/4 In.	201.00
Fly Trap, Dome, Applied Block Feet, Continental, 6 1/2 In.	85.00
Fly Trap, Dome, Knopped Stopper, Applied Block Feet, 6 3/4 In.	144.00
Goblet, Enameled Leaves, Gold Trim, Green Foot, Austria, 7 1/2 In., Pair	630.00
Goblet, Roundel, Enameled Mantle, Imperial Glass Mfg., 1900, 4 In., Pair	4200.00
Hurricane Shade, Baluster Shape, Amethyst, 22 In., Pair	3900.00
Hurricane Shade, Engraved Grapes & Leaves, Bulbous, 20 x 8 In.	230.00
Hurricane Shade, Engraved, Bulbous, Flared Rim, Base, 22 3/4 x 8 In.	748.00
Jar, Apothecary, Etched & Cut Grapes & Leaves, Rolled Rim, 19 1/4 In.	385.00
Jar, Storage, Cover, 2 Rings, Open Interior, 12 In.	55.00
Jar, Sweetmeat, Enameled Coat Of Arms, Floral Bouquets, 19th Century, 16 In.	805.00
Jar, Sweetmeat, Enameled Courtiers Hunting In A Landscape, 1860, 17 x 5 In.	1150.00
Milk Pan, Green Aqua, Cylindrical, Flared Sides, Spout, c.1860, 3 1/2 In.	990.00

Mug, Cobalt Blue, White Enameled Flowers, Gold Rim, 4 x 3 In. 90.00
Mug, Green, Continental, 10 1/2 In., 3 Piece 29.00
Pitcher, Amethyst, Pear Shape, Applied Handle, Duck Bill Spout, c.1860, 7 In. 255.00
Pitcher, Aqua, Applied Handle, Crimped End, Lily Pad Foot, 5 3/4 In. 1870.00
Pitcher, Cobalt Blue, Ribbed, Applied Handle, 3 3/4 In. 400.00
Pitcher, Crystal, White Looping, Pontil, 6 1/4 In. 180.00
Pitcher, Deep Green Aqua, Applied Lily Pad Foot, Pontil, 9 1/4 In. 165.00
Pitcher, Etched Grape & Leaf Garland, Ruby, 1840, 8 3/4 In. 314.00
Rummer, England, c.1780, 6 In. 295.00
Salt, Cobalt Blue, Pontil, 1840, 1 3/4 In. 105.00
Saltcellar, Sapphire Blue, Flat Circular Foot, Knop Stem, 3 1/2 In. 253.00
Spooner, Spiked Argus Cutting, Scalloped Rim, Footed, 7 1/4 In. 90.00
Sugar, 4 Bands, Threading, Light Blue, 5 1/2 In. 200.00
Tumbler, Flip, Cut Panel Base, Engraved Cherubs, Continental, 4 In., Pair 245.00
Tumbler, Flip, Engraved Flowers, 10 3/8 In. 200.00
Tureen, Cover, Underplate, Dark Ruby, Gold Trim, Melon Shape, 10 3/4 x 8 x 11 In. 825.00
Vase, Enameled Coat Of Arms, Floral Bouquet On Other, 15 In., Pair 1035.00
Vase, Spider-Web Design, Green, Purple Iridescent, 11 In. 115.00
Vase, Trumpet, Applied Circular Foot, Pontil, 7 3/4 & 10 3/4 In., Pair 80.00
Washbowl & Pitcher, Peach Opaline, Gilt, Chamber Pot, Tumble-Up, 6 Piece 355.00
Whimsy, Basket, 4 In. 144.00
Whimsy, Parade Ball, Long Neck, Yellow Green, White, Rose Splotches, c.1870, 6 In. 145.00
Whimsy, Turtle, Green, 6 1/2 In. 115.00
Wine, 3-Piece Mold, Strawberry-Diamonds & Fans, 1830, 4 In. 50.00
Wine Cooler, Scrolled Gold Border, Ring Handles, 8 1/2 x 9 In. 748.00
Witch's Ball, Golden Amber, Stand, Rolled Mouth, 1850-1880, 7 1/2 In. 525.00
Witch's Ball, Red, White, Blue, 5 Marbrie Loops, c.1850, 6 In. 1840.00
Witch's Ball, Sapphire Blue, 1885, 5 1/4 In. 200.00
Witch's Ball, Yellow Amber, Stand, Rolled Mouth, 1840-1860, 12 In. 550.00

GLASS-BOHEMIAN Bohemian glass is an ornate overlay or flashed glass made during the Victorian era. It has been reproduced in Bohemia, which is now a part of the Czech Republic. Glass made from 1875 to 1900 is preferred by collectors.

Beaker, Enameled Cornucopia, Trophy & Serpent, Friendship Mottoes, 4 1/2 In. 253.00
Bottle, Emerald Green Cut To Clear, Flowers, Stopper, 7 1/2 In. 202.00
Bottle, Ruby Cut To Clear, 16 In. 45.00
Bowl, Blue, Threading, Crimped Rim, Iridized, Harrach, 3 1/2 x 7 In. 58.00
Box, Dresser, Cranberry, Enameled Flowers, Ormolu Feet, 4 In. 250.00
Centerpiece, Ruby, Brown, Cut Sawtooth Edge, Footed, 7 3/4 x 11 x 6 In. 805.00
Chalice, Cover, Ruby Cut To Clear, Scalloped Base, Satin Panels, 11 1/2 In. 465.00
Compote, Ruby Cut To Clear, Clear Cut Stem, 7 1/2 In., Pair 45.00
Compote, Ruby, 19th Century, 10 In. 165.00
Decanter, Amber Cut To Clear, Etched Grapevine, Stopper, 1890 .... 1200.00
Decanter, Enameled Castle Hunting Scene, Etched, 13 In., Pair 120.00
Decanter, Ruby Cut To Clear, Stags, Doe & Fawn, Stopper, Tag, 8 1/4 In. 190.00
Decanter Set, Amber Cut To Clear, Hunt Scene, Paneled, 3 Tumblers, 9 In., 4 Piece 190.00
Ewer, Mica Flakes, Orange, Dark Green Snake Handle, 12 3/4 In. 355.00
Goblet, Amber Bowl, Clear Cut Stem, Gold Enameled, 7 1/2 In., Pair 195.00
Goblet, Trumpet Shape, Engraved Chinese Men, Asian Landscape, 5 1/4 In. 690.00
Jar, Cover, Amber Cut To Clear, Stags, Woodland Landscape, Paneled, 7 3/4 In. 170.00
Jar, Cover, Lithyalin, Mottled Brown, Green, Cut Leaves, Black Interior, 3 x 5 In. 92.00
Pitcher, Ruby Cut To Clear, Melon Ribbed, Crystal Applied Strap Handle, Pair 330.00
Plate, Enameled, Cranberry, Molded Thumbprint, 9 1/2 In. 90.00
Pokal, Cover, Ruby Cut To Clear, Hunting Scene, Cut Finial, 16 In. 990.00
Pokal, Cover, Ruby Cut To Clear, Ships, 19th Century, 24 In., Pair 3750.00
Pokal, Cut Scenes Of Dogs Chasing Deer, Cut Panels, 16 1/2 In. 715.00
Pokal, Red, Birds, Deer, Houses, Clear, Cover, 14 In., Pair 259.00
Shade, Lily, Emerald Green, Pallme-Koenig 325.00
Tumbler, Ruby Flashed, Satin, Etched German Inscription, 6 1/4 In., Pair 225.00
Vase, Amber Cut To Ruby, Josephine & Napoleon Panels, 13 In., Pair 1045.00
Vase, Amber To Clear, Grape Vine, 8 3/4 In. 184.00
Vase, Amethyst, Embossed Figural Gold Band, 8 In. 168.00

Vase, Amethyst, Rindskopf, 1900, 5 3/4 x 5 1/2 In.	750.00
Vase, Bud, Chocolate & Green, Leaf Design, Cameo, Veles, 8 1/2 In.	413.00
Vase, Cranberry, Cornucopia Shape, Clear Foot, 9 In.	215.00
Vase, Cranberry, White Enameled Flowers, Gold Trim, Applied Handles, 10 In.	336.00
Vase, Double Gourd Shape, Gold Iridescent, 10 1/2 In.	200.00
Vase, Elongated Teardrop, Gold Iridescent, 12 In.	200.00
Vase, Emerald Cut To Clear, Enameled Scroll, Panels, Meierhofen, 7 1/2 In.	56.00
Vase, Enameled Flowers, Gold Scrolling, Emerald Cut To Clear, 11 1/2 In., Pair	225.00
Vase, Gold Oil Spot, Verre De Soie, Floral, Cameo, Kralik, 7 1/2 In.	995.00
Vase, Green Random Threading Design, Pallme-Koenig, 4 In.	115.00
Vase, Green Threading, Blue, Fuchsia, Kralik, 10 1/4 In.	201.00
Vase, Green Threading, Pallme-Koenig, 8 1/2 In.	144.00
Vase, Green, Purple Iridescent, Pallme-Koenig, 14 1/2 In.	255.00
Vase, Iridescent, Pulled Stripes, Mottled Pink, Green, 7 1/2 In.	110.00
Vase, King Tut, Iridescent Purple, Green, Gold, Kralik, 6 1/4 In.	112.00
Vase, Lithyalin, Aqua To Purple, Faceted, Marbleized, Friedrich Egermann, 12 In.	3738.00
Vase, Lithyalin, Deep Green, Brown, 15 1/2 x 6 1/2 In.	1265.00
Vase, Neptune, Cranberry Iridescent, 11 1/2 In.	170.00
Vase, Neptune, Green Iridescent, 7 In.	90.00
Vase, Oil Spot, Amethyst, 3 1/4 In.	40.00
Vase, Oil Spot, Green, Ruffled Edge, 10 In.	170.00
Vase, Pulled Red, Amber Stripes Over White, Welz, 5 1/2 In.	616.00
Vase, Ruby, Grape & Windmill Panels, Rigaree, Handle, 10 In.	90.00
Vase, Tortoiseshell, Straight Neck, Pedestal Foot, Bulbous, 5 In.	35.00
Vase, White Cut To Cranberry, Enameled Floral, Gold Trim, 12 1/4 In., Pair	515.00

GLASS-CONTEMPORARY includes pieces by glass artists working after 1975. Many of these pieces are free-form, one-of-a-kind sculptures. Paperweights by contemporary artists are listed in the Paperweight category. Earlier studio glass may be found listed under Glass-Midcentury or Glass-Venetian.

Amethyst, Threads, Fused To Orange, Brown, White, M. Nourot, 9 1/4 In.	12.00
Bowl, Cobalt Blue, Clear Cased, Interior Bubbles, Labino, 5 x 3 3/4 In.	190.00
Bowl, Yellow Macchia Form, Marked, Dale Chihuly, 1982, 6 1/2 x 11 In.	6325.00
Cruet, Pale Pink To Clear, Ribbed, Handle, Stopper, Labino, 1975, 5 1/2 In.	220.00
Goblet, Iridescent Yellow, Threaded, Larcomb & Wieht, 1977, 5 In.	55.00
Sculpture, Shell, Blue & White Pieces, Del Matto, 1987, 6 5/8 In.	55.00
Vase, Black Flowers, Red, Silver Streaks, Blue Aurene, Lundberg, 4 In.	230.00
Vase, Clear Over Multicolored Swirls, Free Form, Russell, 1979, 7 7/8 In.	190.00
Vase, Clear, Opalescent Running Colors, Flared, Nourot, 7 1/8 In.	66.00
Vase, Cobalt Blue, Rainbow Iridescent, Gold Flecks, Eickholt, 6 3/4 In.	110.00
Vase, Harlequin, Swirled Stripes, Red, Orange, Black, Labino, 6 1/2 In.	220.00
Vase, Heart & Vines, Amber, Red, Signed, Charles Lotton, 1988, 7 In.	460.00
Vase, Iridized Amber Ribs, Opal Ground, Charles Lotton, 1977, 9 1/2 In.	280.00
Vase, Landscape, Signed, Mark Peiser, 1981, 5 1/4 x 4 In.	3680.00
Vase, Mottled Iridescent, Clear Threading, Douglas Becker, 5 3/4 In.	110.00
Vase, Olive Green, Controlled Air Bubbles, Labino, 1973, 4 1/4 x 4 5/8 In.	245.00
Vase, Opaque Tan & Blue Swirls, Loren Chapman, 1976, 5 1/2 In.	82.00
Vase, Opaque White, Seaweed, Labino, 1976, 4 1/4 x 3 5/8 In.	165.00
Vase, Orange Berries, Branches, Yellow Mottled, Frognet, 10 In.	490.00
Vase, Pulled Design, Pinched Waist, Signed, Lotton, 1972, 5 In.	375.00
Vase, Pulled Drape, Cypriote, Iridized Amethyst, Charles Lotton, 1981, 8 In.	252.00
Vase, Red, Black, Random Threading, Lotton, Signed, c.1975, 3 1/2 In.	405.00
Vase, Red, Translucent, Labino, 1975, 4 x 3 1/4 In.	220.00
Vase, Stylized Flowers, Berries, Leaves, Clear, Frosted, A. Henebelle, 8 In.	230.00
Vase, Swirled Opaque Brown, Red, Green & Blue, Salamandra, 5 In.	50.00
Vase, Swirled, Flower Form, Red, Signed, Lotton, 5 In.	200.00
Vase, White, Jumbled Multicolored Band, Clear Cased, Sweet, 7 3/8 In.	55.00
Vase, White, Pink Flowers, Deep Cobalt Blue Ground, Charles Lotton, 7 In.	431.00
Vessel, Dark Brown, Signed, William Morris, 1981, 8 1/4 x 4 In.	4025.00

GLASS-CUT, see Cut Glass category.

GLASS-DEPRESSION, see Depression Glass category.

GLASS-MIDCENTURY refers to art glass made from the 1950s to the 1980s. Some glass factories, such as Baccarat or Orrefors, are listed under their own categories. Earlier glass may be listed in the Glass-Art and Glass-Contemporary categories. Italian glass may be found in Glass-Venetian.

Ashtray, Embossed, Polychrome Birds, Triangular, Higgins, 14 1/2 x 12 In.	196.00
Ashtray, Green, Blue Whimsical Fish, Orange, Green Rays, Higgins, 10 x 7 In., Pair	225.00
Bird, Crystal Over Amber, 1950s, 10 In.	55.00
Bowl, Gray, Green Swirling Stripes, Shallow, Higgins, 14 1/2 In.	92.00
Bowl, White & Green Flowers, Gold Fused & Bent, 8 Sides, Higgins, 2 x 9 In.	345.00
Box, Green, Blue, Purple Geometric Cover, Wooden Base, Higgins, 4 x 7 In.	104.00
Charger, Black Ribs, Gold, Higgins, 17 In.	431.00
Cordial, Plantation, Red, Morgantown, 1 Oz.	85.00
Cup & Saucer, Flanders, Pink, Morgantown	135.00
Decanter, El Maxicano, Morgantown	175.00
Dish, Orange, Green, 3 Compartments, Rectangular, Higgins, 20 x 7 In.	112.00
Figurine, Baby Bear, Ruby, Viking, 4 1/2 In.	138.00
Figurine, Fish, Sommerso, Purple, Green, Red Details, Murano, 6 In., Pair	144.00
Figurine, Mama Bear, Ruby, Viking, 6 1/2 In.	200.00
Figurine, Mama Pig, Ebony, Dalzell Viking, 6 1/4 In.	175.00
Goblet, Water, Flanders, Pink, Morgantown, 10 Oz.	69.00
Plate, Hors D'Oeuvres, Enameled, White, Gold & Turquoise Leaves, David Douglas	15.00
Tray, Emerald Green Inclusions, Rectangular, Signed, Higgins, 14 x 6 3/4 In.	900.00
Tumble-Up, Jadite, Morgantown, 2 Piece	115.00
Tumbler, Juice, Skol, Capri Blue, 3 5/8 In.	5.00
Tumbler, Old Fashioned, Skol, Capri Blue, 5 3/8 In.	5.00
Vase, Deep Red Body, Mica Flakes, Vertical Garlands, 8 In.	4600.00
Vase, Incised Linear Design, Signed, Tapio Wirkkala, 1957, 4 In.	127.00
Vase, Sand-Blasted Blossom, Crystal, Heavy Type, Dorothy Thorpe, 6 In.	105.00

GLASS-VENETIAN. Venetian glass has been made near Venice, Italy, since the thirteenth century. Thin, colored glass with applied decoration is favored, although many other types have been made. Collectors have recently become interested in the Art Deco and 1950s designs. Glass was made on the Venetian island of Murano from 1291. The output dwindled in the late seventeenth century but began to flourish again in the 1850s. Some of the old techniques of glassmaking were revived, and firms today make traditional designs and original modern glass. Since 1981, the name *Murano* may only be used on glass made on Murano Island. Other pieces of Italian glass may be found in the Glass-Contemporary and Glass-Midcentury categories of this book.

Basket, Amber, Archimede Seguso, 1952, 6 x 6 1/2 In.	560.00
Bottle, Amethyst Murrines, Silver, Gold, Giulio Radi, 9 x 4 1/2 In.	4025.00
Bottle, Gourd Shape, Blue Merletto, Archimede Seguso, 8 x 4 In.	2760.00
Bottle, Gourd Shape, Smokey Glass, Coral Drips, Venini & Co., 12 x 6 1/2 In.	2070.00
Bottle, Olive Green, Copper, Giada Stopper, Venini & Co., 12 x 3 1/2 In.	1840.00
Bottle, Pale Blue Vertical Lines, White Opalescent, 12 1/2 In., Pair	230.00
Bottle, Soffiati, Blue, Venini & Co., 10 x 9 In.	805.00
Bottle, Sommerso, Amber, Green, 15 x 3 3/4 In.	170.00
Bottle, Sommerso, Green, Gold, Carlo Scarpa, 8 1/2 x 5 1/2 In.	4315.00
Bottle, Sommerso, Red, Blue, Cenedese, 14 x 7 In.	345.00
Bottle, Striato, Red Swirls, Barovier E. Toso, 9 1/4 x 3 3/4 In.	259.00
Bottle, Turquoise & Clear Lines, Fulvio Bianconi, 1950, 13 In.	3600.00
Bottle, Verro A Spirale, Red, Cobalt Glass, Stopper, 8 In.	375.00
Bottle, Vertically Twisted Filigree, Robin's-Egg Blue, A. Toso, 12 1/2 x 3 In.	2070.00
Bowl, Amber, Blue Trim, 1900, 4 1/2 x 10 1/2 In.	575.00
Bowl, Black, Large Murrines, Gold Foil, Giulio Radi, 3 x 8 In.	115.00
Bowl, Cenedese, Pale Green Glass, Dark Band, Tear Drop, Low, 10 x 6 In.	225.00
Bowl, Gold Opalescent Bubbles, Ercole Barovier, 3 1/2 In.	225.00
Bowl, Green, Silver, Amethyst Foot, Archimede Seguso, 1953, 4 x 10 In.	201.00
Bowl, Millefiori, Multicolored Murrines, Applied Foot & Rim, F. Toso, 8 In.	518.00
Bowl, Royal Blue, Egg Shape, Shallow, Venini, c.1950, 11 x 2 In.	900.00
Candlestick, Sunflower Shape, Amber Petals, Early 20th Century, 6 5/8 In., Pair	145.00

Chandelier, 8-Light, Leaves, Flowers, Bulbous Stem, Ribboned Bowl, 40 x 36 In. 5520.00
Chandelier, Gloriosa, Brass Ring, Glass Rods, 2 Rows Of Discs, Box, Venini 5750.00
Compote, Amber, Polychrome Relief, Applied Floral, 7 3/4 x 6 1/2 In., Pair 200.00
Compote, Figural, Shell Shape Bowl, Rose & Gold Dragon Handles, 10 In., Pair 745.00
Compote, Zanfirico & Latticinio, Blue & White, Ruffled Edge, Venini, 8 1/2 x 9 In. 460.00
Console Set, Blue & Clear, Gold Highlights, Rigaree, Ruffled Bobeches, 3 Piece 275.00
Decanter, Chartreuse Pulled Canes, Spherical Stopper, Foil Label, Murano, 18 In. 58.00
Decanter, Inciso, Dark Blue Stopper, 3 Sides, 8 x 4 1/4 In. 280.00
Decanter, Pink, Elongated Neck, Archimede Seguso, 11 1/8 In. 115.00
Decanter, Red Body, Blue Neck, Red Stopper, Gio Ponti, 1948, 11 In. 4800.00
Ewer, Volante, Red, Signed, Giorgio Ferro, 1952, 9 5/8 In. 3600.00
Figurine, Balinese Woman, Enameled Dragon & Cloud Robe, 1930s, 20 1/2 In. 570.00
Figurine, Bird, Corroso Glass, Acid Stamp, Tyra Lundgren, Murano, 1938, 7 x 7 In. 865.00
Figurine, Bird, Venini, c.1938, 7 x 7 In. 8050.00
Figurine, Man, Standing On Circular Base, Red & Aqua, c.1940, 16 1/2 In. 840.00
Figurine, Penguin, Amber To Clear, Archimede Seguso, 6 In., Pair 144.00
Figurine, Rooster, Blue, Red, Yellow, Pink Feathers, Avem, 8 1/4 x 9 In. 280.00
Figurine, Sommerso, Man, Blue, Green, Antonio Da Ros, 13 1/12 x 3 1/2 In. 920.00
Figurine, Yak, Orange Vaseline Sommerso, Orange Swirled Horns, 9 In. 690.00
Paperweight, Egg, Purple, Gold Swirls, 6 1/4 x 3 1/2 In. 140.00
Paperweight, Sommerso, Concentric Rings, Olive, Black, Vistosi, 2 x 4 In. 144.00
Paperweight, White, Smokey Topaz Swirls, 4 1/4 x 9 In. 168.00
Pitcher, Deep Purple, Green, Iridescent, Barovier E. Toso, 14 x 8 In. 2070.00
Pitcher, Mezza Filigrana, Black, White, Gold Swirls, Dino Martens, 11 x 6 In. 1380.00
Pitcher, Pink, Purple, Smoke, Blue, Gio Ponti, 12 1/2 x 4 In. 2025.00
Sconce, Figure Sitting Down In Chair, G. Cenedese, 1953, 12 x 8 In. 5175.00
Sculpture, Aquarium, Fish & Marine Life, 7 x 9 x 2 In. 290.00
Urn, Applied Swirl, Bright Green, Cenedese, 13 x 4 In. 790.00
Urn, Black, Red Handles, Fratelli Toso, 1920, 13 1/2 x 4 1/2 In. 2875.00
Urn, Carnivale, Red, Yellow, Purple, Dark Blue, Fratelli Toso, 1920, 10 In., Pair 2010.00
Urn, White, Green Inlay, Pink, Yellow Flowers, Applied Fanciful Handles, 4 In. 1840.00
Vase, Amber Glass, Applied Green Threading, Archimede Seguso, 16 x 6 In. 115.00
Vase, Amber Glass, Lug Handles, Carlo Scarpa, 9 3/4 x 7 In. 3738.00
Vase, Amber Glass, Rolled In Rim, Alfredo Barbini, 9 1/2 x 4 1/2 In. 395.00
Vase, Amethyst Pulled Feathers, Amber, Archimede Seguso, 1956, 10 x 4 1/2 In. 6325.00
Vase, Amethyst, Vertical Ribbed, Lobed Shape, Venini, 11 1/2 In. 105.00
Vase, Applied Pulled Leaf & Vine, Carlo Barovier, 1930, 11 1/2 x 8 In. 2760.00
Vase, Applied Pulled Trailings, Cobalt, Scavo, Cenedese, 19 In. 8050.00
Vase, Autunno Gemmato, Gold Mottling On Clear, Barovier, 1956, 16 x 13 In. 4365.00
Vase, Battuto, Red, Signed, Carlo Scarpa, 1940, 7 3/8 In. 13200.00
Vase, Black, Gold Latticinio, Seguso, 1940, 7 1/4 x 7 In. 845.00
Vase, Carved Aboriginal Animals, Corroso, 2 Openings, Mirco Casaril, 9 x 7 In. 6325.00
Vase, Clear Over Brown & Reds, Gold Leaf, Inclusions, 9 1/2 In. 225.00
Vase, Corroso, Sommerso, Cranberry Red, Alfredo Barbini, 5 1/4 In. 690.00
Vase, Cylindrical, Green & Blue Bands, Signed, F. Bianconi, Venini, 10 1/4 In. 345.00
Vase, Dark Turquoise, Pale Pink, Signed, Fulvio Bianconi, 1950, 6 In. 5400.00
Vase, Dark Turquoise, Red, Pale Yellow, Signed, Bianconi, 1950, 9 In. 4800.00
Vase, Deep Amber, Applied Black Horizontal Bands, Bianconi, 1950, 11 In. 4313.00
Vase, Emerald Green Corroso, Flared, Carlo Scarpa, 7 1/2 x 6 1/2 In. 3740.00
Vase, Fazzoletto, Blue, Green, White Latticinio, Fulvio Bianconi, 3 x 4 In. 110.00
Vase, Fazzoletto, Lattimo, Fulvio Bianconi, 6 x 7 In. 730.00
Vase, Fazzoletto, Opaque Turquoise, Fulvio Bianconi, 6 x 7 In. 309.00
Vase, Gold, Gray Flecked Exterior, Blue Interior, Murano, Venini, 15 In. 660.00
Vase, Green Bullicante, Gold Patches, Poli, Seguso Vetri D'Arte, 1940, 10 x 8 In. 115.00
Vase, Green Sommerso, Carlo Scarpa, 4 1/2 x 5 1/2 In. 2070.00
Vase, Green Vertical Lines, Amber Banded Rim, Archimede Seguso, 8 x 8 In. 9775.00
Vase, Hemispherical, Amethyst Casing, Antonio Da Ros, Mid 1950s, 12 In. 863.00
Vase, Incisco, Sommerso, Deep Amber, White, A. Barbini, 1962, 14 In. 5175.00
Vase, Intarsia, Green Triangles, Barovier E. Toso, 12 In. 3940.00
Vase, Mosaico Zanfirico, Slanted Rim, Turquoise, White Netting, 13 1/2 In. 7480.00
Vase, Nerox Terrazo Murrine, Lavender, Blue, Red, White, Toso, 12 x 7 In. 8050.00
Vase, Novecento, Flared Rim, Circular Foot, 1930s, 10 1/3 In. 285.00
Vase, Orange, Blue, Green Casing, Antonio Da Ros, Mid 1950s, 10 x 7 In. 3105.00

Vase, Pezzato, Apricot, White, Alfredo Barbini, 8 3/4 x 7 In. 1150.00
Vase, Pezzato, Caramel, Green Striated, Barovier E. Toso, 1958, 8 1/2 x 4 1/2 In. 3940.00
Vase, Pezzato, Purple Opalescent, Barovier E. Toso, 1958, 9 x 5 In. 3940.00
Vase, Pezzato, Smoky, Black, Amber, Cigar Shape, Bianconi, 10 In. 8050.00
Vase, Pillow, Amethyst, Gold, Archimede Seguso, 1953, 9 x 8 1/2 In. 1725.00
Vase, Pillow, Black Iridescent, Applied Handles, 1900, 6 1/2 x 8 In. 675.00
Vase, Pillow, Half-Filigrana, Aureliano Toso, 14 x 8 In. 1495.00
Vase, Red Ocher, 4 Sides, Rosa Barovier-Mentasti, 12 1/2 x 3 3/4 In. 10925.00
Vase, Red Over Opaque White, Flaring Cylinder, Signed, 11 1/4 In. 465.00
Vase, Red, Pull Swirls, Yellow, Blue & Green, Crimped, 8 In. 45.00
Vase, Sailing Ship On 1 Side, Large Anchor On Other, Gray, Barbini, 10 In. 6900.00
Vase, Sommerso, Green Lattimo Glass, 1952, 13 x 6 1/2 In. 843.00
Vase, Sommerso, Orange, Teardrop, Poli, Seguso Vetri D'Arte, 12 x 7 1/2 In. 730.00
Vase, Sommerso, Yellow, Amber Glass, Teardrop, 8 1/4 x 7 1/2 In. 1068.00
Vase, Spina, Jade, White Rectangular Patched, Barovier, 1958, 11 In. 9200.00
Vase, Turquoise, White Design, Carlo Scarpa, 1930, 11 7/8 In. 13200.00
Vase, White, Black Lines, Mezza Filigrana, Signed, Dino Martens, 11 In. 3360.00
Vase, Zanfirico, Pink, White, Fulvio Bianconi, 11 x 12 1/2 In. 1840.00
Vase, Zanfirico, Turquoise, White Netting, 1960, 14 x 3 3/4 In. 8440.00
Vase, Zanfirico, Yellow, Green, Blue, Archimede Seguso, 11 x 4 In. 1380.00
Vessel, Burgundy, Franco Deboni, 1959, 6 1/2 x 5 1/2 In. 3450.00
Vessel, Green Chimera, Barovier E. Toso, 7 x 9 1/4 In. 2875.00
Vessel, Sommerso, Light Green Swirls, Carlo Scarpa, 5 1/2 x 9 In. 11500.00

GLASSES for the eyes, or spectacles, were mentioned in a manuscript in
1289 and have been used ever since. The first eyeglasses with rigid
side pieces were made in London in 1727. Bifocals were invented by
Benjamin Franklin in 1785. Lorgnettes were popular in late Victorian
times. Opera glasses are listed in their own category.

Lorgnette, Platinum, Diamonds, Cord, Tiffany, 1890-1915 . . . . 660.00
Spectacles, Iron, Original Leather Case, c.1750 . . . . 185.00
Spectacles, Round Lenses, Gold Filled Frames, Blue Fitted Snap Case, 1940 . . . . 40.00
Sunglasses, Woman's, Orange, Lime Green & Pink, Emilo Pucci, 1960s 210.00

GOEBEL is the mark used by W. Goebel Porzellanfabrik of Oeslau,
Germany, now Rodental, Germany. Many types of figurines and dishes
have been made. The firm is still working. The pieces marked *Goebel
Hummel* are listed under Hummel in this book.

Ashtray, Friar Tuck 110.00
Cookie Jar, Friar Tuck, 1957 . . . . 800.00
Eggcup, Friar Tuck 65.00
Figurine, Bird, Seagull, 1968, 9-In. Wingspan 45.00
Figurine, Bird, Woodpecker, 3 Line Mark, 7 In. 55.00
Figurine, Buffalo, 6 In. 368.00
Figurine, Cat, Mitzi 20.00
Figurine, Dog, Cocker Spaniel, Sitting, Albert Staehle, 3 1/2 x 3 1/4 In. 275.00
Figurine, Dog, Schnauzer, Sitting, Gray, Tan Points, 3 x 4 3/4 In. 65.00
Figurine, Rabbit, Thumper, Old Mark 38.00
Figurine, Tuba Player, Musicians, No. 234 . . . . 150.00
Lamp, Figural, Girl In White Coat 265.00
Night-Light, Figural, Bambi, Eyes Light Up 550.00

GOLDSCHEIDER has made porcelains in three places. The family left
Vienna in 1938 and started factories in England and in Trenton, New
Jersey. The New Jersey factory started in 1940 as Goldscheider-U.S.A.
In 1941 it became Goldscheider-Everlast Corporation. From 1947 to
1953 it was Goldcrest Ceramics Corporation. In 1950 the Vienna plant
was returned to Mr. Goldscheider, and the company continues in busi-
ness. The Trenton, New Jersey, business, now called *Goldscheider of
Vienna,* imports all of the pieces.

Bust, Head Of Black Woman, Terra-Cotta, Black Matte, 1930, 12 In. 1350.00
Bust, Head Of Woman, Brown, Terra-Cotta, Blue, Orange, 15 In. 2485.00
Figurine, Butterfly Girl, Signed Lorenzi, 1920s, 19 1/2 In. 8395.00

Figurine, Colonial Lady, 1940s	125.00
Figurine, Easter Parade, Purple, 6 1/4 In.	798.00
Figurine, Woman's Head, Apple In Hand, Polychrome Glazes, Signed, 14 In.	1150.00
Figurine, Woman, Terra-Cotta Head, Blue, Orange, White Glaze, c.1930, 15 1/2 In.	2480.00

GOLF, see Sports category.

GONDER Ceramic Arts, Inc., was opened by Lawton Gonder in 1941 in Zanesville, Ohio. Gonder made high-grade pottery decorated with flambe, drip, gold crackle, and Chinese crackle glazes. The factory closed in 1957. From 1946 to 1954, Gonder also operated the Elgee Pottery, which made ceramic lamp bases.

Bookends, Trojan Horse Head, 7 1/2 In.	125.00
Console Set, Figural Fish, Leaping From Water, Pinks & Grays, 3 Piece	108.00
Figurine, Asian Man, Flowing Robe, Mottled Aqua & Gray, 7 1/8 In.	170.00
Figurine, Panther, Drip Brown & Drab Green, Marked, 19 In.	135.00
Lamp, Lady's Head, White Glaze, 12 In.	150.00
Sugar & Creamer, Cover, Brown & White Spattered, Drip Glaze	25.00
Vase, Black & White, Baluster, 8 1/2 In.	91.00
Vase, Cornucopia, Drip Brown & Tan, Marked, 5 x 12 In.	23.00
Vase, Figural, Polynesian Woman, Hibiscus, Water Jugs Have Openings, 13 In.	129.00
Vase, Figural, Swan, Gold Crackle, 24K Gold, 9 1/2 x 5 1/2 In.	125.00
Vase, Light Blue, Purple, Gray, Golden Brown & Pink Interior, Art Deco, 12 In.	57.00
Vase, Purple, 8 1/2 In.	50.00

GOOFUS GLASS was made from about 1900 to 1920 by many American factories. It was originally painted gold, red, green, bronze, pink, purple, or other bright colors. Many pieces are found today with flaking paint, and this lowers the value.

Bowl, Narcissus, Indiana Glass Co., 9 x 3 In.	33.00

GOSS china has been made since 1858. English potter William Henry Goss first made it at the Falcon Pottery in Stoke-on-Trent. The factory name was changed to Goss China Company in 1934 when it was taken over by Cauldon Potteries. Production ceased in 1940. Goss china resembles Irish Belleek in both body and glaze. The company also made popular souvenir china, usually marked with local crests and names.

Figurine, Manx Cottage, Chimney, W.H. Goss No. 273243, 2 1/2 x 1 3/4 In.	103.50
Mug, World War I, W.H. Goss Stamp With Eagle, 3 1/4 In.	50.00
Vase, Commemorative, Crested, 1910, 3 1/4 In.	135.00

GOUDA, Holland, has been a pottery center since the seventeenth century. Two firms, the Zenith pottery, established in the eighteenth century, and the Zuid-Hollandsche pottery made the brightly colored wares marked *Gouda* from 1880 to about 1940. Many pieces featured Art Nouveau or Art Deco designs.

Ashtray, Cigar, Victoria, Aqua, Turquoise, Abstract, Whimsical Florals, 1948, 6 1/2 In.	88.00
Basket, Sweets, Paris, Black, Orange, Yellow Abstract Forms, Ocher, White, Handle, 8 In.	220.00
Bowl, Ada, Graceful Purple Flowers, Rust Leaves, Green, Turquoise, 1920, 4 x 5 In.	300.00
Bowl, Anjer, 2 Geometric Bands, Blue, Orange, White, Handles, Green Mottled, 7 In.	80.00
Bowl, Cachina, Yellow, Rust, Orange, Cobalt Blue Leafy Shapes, 2 x 9 1/2 In.	165.00
Bowl, Delicate Lilac Flowers, Green Foliage, White, Yellow Background, 1935	360.00
Bowl, Robur, Mustard, Black, White, Orange Abstract Florals, Black, 1920, 5 In.	165.00
Bowl, Zonnebloer, Blue, Green, Vivid Orange, Yellow Sunflowers, 1925, 12 In.	880.00
Candlestick, Gold, Orange, Black, Blue Ovals, Black Border, 1925, 7 In., Pair	470.00
Candlestick, Rosario, Stylized Orange, Rust, Yellow, Black, Ocher Flowers, 4 1/2 In.	220.00
Chamberstick, Rhodian, Mint Green, Orange, Cobalt Blue, White, 1926, 3 x 5 In.	220.00
Charger, Metz, Vivid Purple, Yellow, Cobalt Blue, Burnt Orange Florals, c.1930, 10 In.	195.00
Compote, Syna, Abstract Yellow, Lilac Floral Shapes, Ocher Outline, 1923, 6 1/2 In.	250.00
Decanter, Atol, Ocher, Cobalt, Lilac, Orange, Turquoise, Black Neck Ribs, 1930, 9 1/2 In.	330.00
Ewer, Clarath, Yellow, Lila, Turquoise Ovals, Ocher Outline, Geometric Bands, 10 In.	303.00
Ewer, Danier, Mint Green, Turquoise, Ocher Geometric Band, Cobalt Dots, 1925, 8 In.	360.00

Ewer, Free-Flowing Tulips, Blue, Purple, Pink, Yellow, Warm Beige Ground, 5 In. 385.00
Ewer, Fruto, Whimsical, Yellow, Orange, Blue, Green, Tan Shapes, 1930, 8 In. 195.00
Ewer, Red Clay High Glaze, Purple, Pink, Green, Honey Flowers, A. Lansaat, 1906 ..... 413.00
Ewer, Rosario, Graceful Burnt Orange, Black, Yellow, Green Flower, Tan, 1915, 7 In. 195.00
Inkwell, Dorisa, Ocher, Burnt Orange Outline, Black Shapes, Turquoise Ground, 2 In. ... 140.00
Inkwell, Franco, Lilac Outline, Turquoise, Black, White, Plain Bands, 1925, 2 In. 248.00
Inkwell, Purple, Green Flowers, Black Border, Yellow, Blue Dots, 1920, 8 x 5 In. 605.00
Jardiniere, Purple, Pink Tulips Swirling, Green, Orange, Yellow, Gray, 1920, 7 In. 415.00
Jug, Brown Sailboats, Rust, Brown Windmill, Brown Farm, Green Trees, Muller, 7 In. ... 770.00
Lamp, Graceful Brown Boats, White, Purple, Pink, Blue, Green Florals, 17 1/2 In. 468.00
Lantern, Yellow, Orange, Blue, Ivory Foliate Design, Dark Green Ground, 10 In. 115.00
Pitcher, Stylized Rust, Green Animals, Cream Ground, C.A. Lion Cachet, 9 1/2 In. 90.00
Plaque, Chrysanthemums, Yellow, Blue, Purple, Green, Signed, 16 In. 1265.00
Pot, Rosario, Burnt Orange, Black, Yellow, Green Flower, Blue, White, 1925, 4 x 4 1/2 In. 90.00
Tazza, Nova 17, Stylized Red, Blue, Green, Brown, Gold Flowers, Turquoise Star, 6 In. .. 250.00
Tray, Ali, Abstract Feathered Shape, Orange, Green, Blue, White, Ocher Outline, 12 In. .. 275.00
Urn, Juliana, Floral Design, Purple, Lilac, Orange, Blue, Green, Black Dots, 1915, 12 In. . 330.00
Vase, Abstract Heart Shape Forms, Turquoise, Cobalt, Ocher, Burnt Orange Dots, 11 In. .. 525.00
Vase, Anjer, Burnt Orange, Rust Florals, White Ground, Ocher Random Dots, 1925, 10 In. 305.00
Vase, Asa, Cobalt Blue, Burnt Orange Border, Pink, Tan, Lilac Florals, 1927, 12 In. 275.00
Vase, Bocnara Pattern, Black, Green, Blue, Blue, Orange, Yellow, Regina, 1930s, 10 In. .. 725.00
Vase, Breetvelt, Double Gourd, Burnt Orange, Ocher, Off-White Ground, 8 1/3 In. 495.00
Vase, Cordoba, Large Rust Colored Feathers, Lilac Flowers, Blue, Green, White, 10 In. .. 525.00
Vase, Double Bulb Shape, Raised Sides Form Continuous Handle, Iris Blossoms, 13 In. .. 920.00
Vase, Exotic Blue Orchid, Sinuous Green, Yellow Black, Geometric Starbursts, 12 In. 1870.00
Vase, Exotic Flowers, Blue, Lilac, Orange, Brown, Ocher Swaying On Field, 13 In. 550.00
Vase, Floral & Abstract Design, Geometric Bands, 7 14 In. 190.00
Vase, Floral, Matte Glaze, Painted Signature, 8 In. 210.00
Vase, Handles, High Glaze, Multicolored Flowers, 6 3/4 In. 345.00
Vase, Irma, Gold, Indigo Blue Amoeba Shape, White Outline, Gray, Gold Ground, 12 In. . 605.00
Vase, Lilac, Blue, Orange, White, Green Swirls, Blue Dots, Green Mottled Borders, 12 In. 358.00
Vase, Lux, Black Designs, Dark Crimson Red Flambe High Glaze, 1920, 11 1/2 In. 358.00
Vase, Medica, 3 Large Orchids, Purple, Orange In Center, Green Foliage, 1931, 10 In. ... 1100.00
Vase, Palmet, Trumpet Shape, Abstract Feather Shapes, Brown, Black, Blue, 1925, 11 In. . 605.00
Vase, Pastel Flowers, Yellow, Gray, Green, Orange Abstract Shapes, 1910, 10 In. 360.00
Vase, Pink, Purple Lilies, Green Leaves, Dark Green Fields, Tan, 1910, 9 In. 495.00
Vase, Polychrome Geometric Design, Marked 932 Gouda, Holland, 6 x 6 In. 140.00
Vase, Rhodian, Burnt Orange Amoeba Shape, Ocher Outline, Green Mottled, 12 In. 360.00
Vase, Rhodian, Geometric, Yellow, Blue, Green, White, Burnt Orange, 1915, 11 In. 325.00
Vase, Sailing Scene, Windmills, Cottages, 1905, 17 1/2 In. 550.00
Vase, Single Lilac, Yellow Flower, Ocher Outline, Gray Field, Cobalt, Orange, 11 1/2 In. . 470.00
Vase, Stylized Pink, Purple Flowers, Green Tones, 1910, 7 In. 550.00
Vase, Swirling Foliate, Crackware Glaze, Signed, 18 In. 1955.00
Vase, Yellow, Lilac Flowers, White Ground, Green Vines, Leaves, Hargring, 1915, 12 In. . 1210.00
Wall Plate, Bird, Blue, Yellow Peacock, Full Tail Spray, On Green Branch, 1930, 8 In. ... 990.00
Wall Pocket, Central Hole, 6 Small Holes, Cobalt Blue, Yellow, 1932, 7 In. 110.00
Wall Pocket, Wooden Shoe Shape, Blue, Green, Marked, Corona, Gouda, Holland, 9 In. . 110.00

GRANITEWARE is an enameled tinware that has been used in the
kitchen from the late nineteenth century to the present. Earlier graniteware was green or turquoise blue, with white spatters. The later ware
was gray with white spatters. Reproductions are being made in all
colors.

Bowl, Salad, Red Swirl, 1950s 195.00
Bucket, Berry, Emerald 550.00
Coffeepot, Brown & Ivory Stenciled Stripes, 10 1/2 In. ....*Illus* 60.00
Coffeepot, Conical, Chrysolite 385.00
Coffeepot, Pewter Trim, Medallion Castle Scenes, 19th Century, 11 1/2 In. 525.00
Coffeepot, White, Black Handle, 12 In. 87.50
Coffeepot, Wire Bail Handle, Wooden Handle, Pouring Spout, 10 1/2 x 12 In. 95.00
Creamer, Cobalt Blue Handle, Emerald 2310.00
Creamer, Cover, Side Spout, Dark Blue Enameling, Handle, Chrysolite 440.00
Cup, Mush, Cobalt Blue Rim, Emerald, 6 1/4 In. 467.00

Graniteware, Coffeepot,
Brown & Ivory Stenciled
Stripes, 10 1/2 In.

Graniteware, Pitcher, End Of Day, 4 3/4 In.

Flowerpot, Red, Underplate, c.1930, 5 1/2 x 5 In.	59.00
Lunch Pail, Gray, Oval, Cover, 10 1/2 x 7 x 7 In.	175.00
Mold, Ring, Solid Red, Cream Inside, Black Trim	95.00
Pail, Wire Bail, Turned Wood Handle, Emerald, 9 In.	495.00
Pan, Blue & White, 2 Handles, 12 1/2 x 7 In.	73.00
Pitcher, Bulbous, Emerald, 9 In.	2420.00
Pitcher, Emerald Green, 10 In.	900.00
Pitcher, End Of Day, 4 3/4 In. ....*Illus*	80.00
Plate, Child & Begging Dog, 1930s Costume, Blue	55.00
Saucepan, Cover, Red Swirl, 1930s, 7 x 7 1/2 In.	135.00
Teapot, Yellow	30.00
Toaster, Green Swirl	925.00

GREENTOWN glass was made by the Indiana Tumbler and Goblet
Company of Greentown, Indiana, from 1894 to 1903. In 1899, the factory became part of National Glass Company. A variety of pressed
glass was made. Additional pieces may be found in other categories,
such as Chocolate Glass, Holly Amber, Milk Glass, and Pressed Glass.

Cord Drapery, Bowl, 8 In.	160.00
Cord Drapery, Cruet, Nile Green	500.00
Cord Drapery, Plate, Fluted, Cobalt Blue, 6 In.	305.00
Dustpan, 3 3/4 In.	210.00
Herringbone Buttress, Cake Stand, Nile Green	450.00
Indian Head, Creamer, 5 7/8 In.	200.00
Indian Head, Creamer, Nile Green	725.00
Indoor Drinking Scene, Mug, 5 In.	130.00
Indoor Drinking Scene, Mug, Pouring Lip, Nile Green, 5 In.	205.00
Picture Frame, Toothpick, Cobalt Blue	400.00
Pitcher, Squirrel, Water, 8 3/4 In.	200.00
Teardrop & Tassel, Butter, Cover, Cobalt Blue	200.00
Wild Rose With Bowknot, Butter, Cover	300.00

GRUEBY Faience Company of Boston, Massachusetts, was incorporated in 1897 by William H. Grueby. Garden statuary, art pottery, and
architectural tiles were made until 1920. The company developed a
matte green glaze that was so popular it was copied by many other factories making a less expensive type of pottery. This eventually led to
the financial problems of the pottery.

Bowl, Applied Carved Leaves, Ocher Matte Glaze, Wilhelmina Post, 3 x 7 1/2 In.	2300.00
Bowl, Blue Matte Glaze, 2 Paper Labels, 5 1/2 In.	935.00
Bowl, Green Matte Glaze, 1 1/2 x 6 In.	748.00
Bowl, Green Matte Glaze, Signed, 2 1/2 x 8 In.	575.00
Figurine, Scarab, Matte Green Glaze, Paper Label, Early 20th Century, 2 3/4 In.	635.00
Jar, Urn Shape, Green Matte Glaze, Cover, 6 1/2 In.	805.00
Jardiniere, Carved Leaves, Frothy Green Glaze, Wilhelmina Post, Signed, 10 1/2 In.	5225.00
Lamp, Domed Tiffany Shade, Leather Green Base, 22 x 18 In. ....*Illus*	20900.00
Lamp, Table, Lemon Leaf, Applied Buds & Leaves, Green Matte Glaze, 22 x 18 In.	21375.00

Paperweight, Scarab, Blue, Gray Matte Glaze, 4 x 2 3/4 In. 565.00
Paperweight, Scarab, Green, Brown Matte Glaze, 3 3/4 x 2 3/4 In. 730.00
Paperweight, Scarab, Mustard Matte Glaze, 4 x 2 3/4 In. 675.00
Paperweight, Scarab, Ocher Matte Glaze, 3 x 2 In. 730.00
Tile, 5-Color Galleon, 3-Masted Ship, On Water, Early 20th Century, 8 In. 690.00
Tile, Beaver, Faience, 1905, 25 x 14 In. ...._Illus_ 20500.00
Tile, Cherub With Cornucopia, Oatmeal Glaze, Early 20th Century, 6 In. 280.00
Tile, Green, 4 Pieces, 6 x 6 x 1 In. 980.00
Tile, Ivory Horses, Blue Sky, Green Ground, Frame, Marked R.E., Square, 6 In. 3220.00
Tile, Kneeling Angel, Terra-Cotta, Addison Le Boutillier, Early 20th Century, 8 1/4 In. ... 460.00
Tile, Knight, Terra-Cotta, Yellow Ground, Early 20th Century, 6 In. 550.00
Tile, Lion With Serpent, Donkey, Geese, Mountain Lions, Tree, 4 1/2 x 4 In., 6 Piece 4600.00
Tile, Rabbit In Cabbage Patch, Cuenca Ground, Yellow, Green Matte Glaze, 6 In. 3375.00
Tile, Scenic, Mountain Village, Sea, Sky, Cuerda Seca, 4 1/2 In. 980.00
Tile, St. Luke, Portrait Of 4 Evangelists, Green Matte Winged Ox, 1909, 7 3/4 In. 860.00
Tile, Stag Underneath Tree, Brown, Green, Blue, Arts & Crafts Frame, 4 In. 1070.00
Tile, Tulip Design, Light Green, Blue, Dark Green Ground, Oak Frame, 6 In. 1955.00
Tile, Turtle Design, Brown, Ivory, Green Leaves, Cuenca, Ocher Matte Ground, 6 In. 7480.00
Tile, Water Lilies, Arts & Crafts, Square, 6 In. 2420.00
Tile, White Horses Prancing, Blue, Green Ground, Cuenca, 6 1/4 In. ....2990.00 to 3450.00
Tile, Yellow Candlestick In Center, Cuenca, Arts & Crafts Frame, 6 x 4 In. 4500.00
Tile, Yellow Tulip, Green Ground, Mounted In Tiffany Frame, Flower Feet, Square, 7 In. . 5750.00
Urn, Feathered Green Matte Glaze, Applied Foliate Handles, 13 x 9 In. 1955.00
Vase, Allover Oatmeal Green, Faience Stamp, 7 In. 2415.00
Vase, Alternating Tight Yellow Buds, Oatmeal Green Matte Glaze, 4 1/2 In. 4315.00
Vase, Applied Leaves Alternating With Buds, Green Matte Glaze, 7 1/4 x 4 3/4 In. 2810.00
Vase, Applied Leaves Divided By Long Narrow Stems, Yellow Buds, 13 In. 10350.00
Vase, Applied Leaves Divided By Vertical Stems, Green Matte Glaze, 4 In. 1610.00
Vase, Applied Leaves Divided By Vertical Stems, Green, Yellow Matte Glaze, 7 In. 11500.00
Vase, Applied Leaves With Tooled Buds, Dark Green Matte Glaze, 7 In. 2990.00
Vase, Applied Overlapping Leaves, Yellow Buds, Green Matte Glaze, 11 1/2 In. ....._Illus_ 19800.00
Vase, Broad Overlapping Leaves, Green Matte Glaze, 1902, 13 3/4 In. 7475.00
Vase, Corseted, Alternating Crisp Yellow Buds, Frothy Green Matte Glaze, 9 x 4 In. 6900.00
Vase, Gourd Shape, Ocher Matte Glaze, 6 1/2 x 4 1/2 In. 1265.00
Vase, Gourd Shape, Organic Green Matte Glaze, 9 1/2 x 5 3/4 In. 5175.00
Vase, Green Matte Glaze, Applied Leaves, 6 In. 1150.00
Vase, Green Matte Glaze, Carved Vertical Panels, 7 In. 3220.00
Vase, Green Matte Glaze, Signed, 7 1/2 In. 1150.00
Vase, Green, Brown Matte Glaze, Horizontal Ribs, 6 In. 1840.00
Vase, Incised Large Leaves, Organic Green Matte Glaze, 5 1/2 x 7 In. 3240.00
Vase, Line Design, Dark Matte Green Glaze, Signed, 3 1/4 x 5 1/2 In. 1350.00
Vase, Molded Leave Exterior, Chartreuse Interior, Blue Leather Glaze, 2 In. 3450.00
Vase, Oatmeal Green Matte Glaze, Applied Leaves, Yellow, Green, 4 1/2 x 4 In. 7480.00
Vase, Oatmeal Matte Glaze, 7 x 3 In. 955.00

Grueby, Lamp, Domed Tiffany Shade,
Leather Green Base, 22 x 18 In.

Grueby, Tile, Beaver,
Faience, 1905, 25 x 14 In.

Grueby, Vase, Applied
Overlapping Leaves, Yellow Buds,
Green Matte Glaze, 11 1/2 In.

Vase, Ocher Matte Glaze, Cylindrical, 1905, 6 7/8 In. 805.00
Vase, Repeating Raised Buds On Flower Stem, Signed, Early 20th Century, 8 In. 3160.00
Vase, Rows Of Leaves, Blossoms & Buds, Leathery Glaze, Faience Mark, 13 3/4 In. 8625.00
Vase, Sculpted & Applied Leaves, Flowers On Stems, Signed, 9 In. 2310.00
Vase, Speckled Blue, Gray Matte Glaze, Collared Rim, 6 1/4 x 5 In. 900.00
Vase, Tooled Broad Leaves, Green Matte Glaze, Ellen Farmington, 7 1/4 x 4 1/2 In. 2925.00
Vase, Tooled Leaves Alternating With Buds, Oatmeal Green Glaze, Label, 7 x 5 In. 2760.00
Vase, Tooled, Applied Broad Leaves, Green Leather Matte Glaze, 8 1/4 x 5 1/2 In. 7480.00
Vase, Tooled, Applied Leaves, Ocher Matte Glaze, 5 3/4 x 8 In. 9200.00
Vase, Vertical Leaves, Carved Buds, Brown Matte Glaze, 9 In. 8625.00
Vessel, Applied Leaves, Green Matte Glaze, Wilhelmina Post, 7 1/4 x 7 3/4 In. 280.00
Wall Pocket, Applied Leaves, Oatmeal Matte Green Glaze, 8 1/2 In. 3740.00
Wall Pocket, Tooled, Applied Broad Leaves, Leather Green Matte Glaze, 7 x 5 In. 1840.00

GUNDERSON glass was made at the Gunderson-Pairpoint Glass Works of New Bedford, Massachusetts, from 1952 to 1957. Gunderson Peachblow is especially famous.

Compote, Flared, Swirled Stem, 7 1/2 In. 275.00
Paperweight, Pink Flower, Green Ground, 3 In. 143.00
Vase, Peachblow, 4 x 2 3/4 In. 132.00

GUNS that may be classed as toys, such as BB guns, air rifles, and cap guns, are listed in the Toy category.

GUSTAVSBERG ceramics factory was founded in 1827 near Stockholm, Sweden. It is best known to collectors for its twentieth-century art wares, especially a green stoneware with silver inlay called *Argenta*.

Gustafsberg

Bowl, Luster, Blue, Violet, Gold Highlights, 4 In. 56.00
Bowl, Turquoise Glaze, Inlaid Silver Flower Sprig, Signed, c.1935, 8 x 6 3/4 In. 230.00
Candleholder, Black, Gray & White, Stig Lindberg, 1960 .... 325.00
Candleholder, Faience, Blue, White & Gold, Stig Lindberg, 1960 .... 300.00
Vase, Blue Floral, 2 Tone, 8 In. 345.00
Vase, Carp Swimming Toward Rim, Silver Base, Marked, 6 3/4 In. 180.00
Vase, High Glaze, Dark Green, c.1920, 6 In. 325.00
Vase, Mermaid In Grasp Of Toothy Fish, Argenta, 10 In. 2475.00
Vase, Spherical, Blue Scroll On Turquoise Matte Ground, Ink Signed, 3 1/2 In. 92.00

GUTTA-PERCHA was one of the first plastic materials. It was made from a mixture of resins from Malaysian trees. It was molded and used for daguerreotype cases, toilet articles, and picture frames in the nineteenth century.

Button, Horse & Rider, 7/8 In. 31.00
Button, Sheaf Of Wheat, 1 1/4 In. 25.00
Case, Boy In Sailboat, Ambrotype Of Elderly Woman 127.00
Magnifying Glass Frame, Unscrews To Hold Lenses, 2 1/4 In. 60.00

HAEGER Potteries, Inc., Dundee, Illinois, started making commercial art wares in 1914. Early pieces were marked with the name *Haeger* written over an *H*. About 1938, the mark *Royal Haeger* was used. The firm is still making florist wares and lamp bases.

Ashtray, Nautilus, Green, Agate, c.1950, 11 1/3 x 10 In. 18.00
Basket, Brown, Handles, No. R988, c.1940 .... 25.00
Cookie Jar, Keebler Tree House 125.00
Figurine, Head, Old Woman, Blue Eyes, Red Lips, Gray Hair, Signed, 1950s, 8 1/2 In. ... 40.00
Lamp, TV, Gazelle, Leaping Over Waves, Ebony Cascade Glaze, 10 x 13 In. 50.00
Lamp, TV, Leaping Deer, Chestnut, Style, No. 160, Phil-Mar Corp, Cleveland, Ohio 65.00
Vase, Bud, Aqua, No. RG-68, c.1967, 7 In. 15.00
Vase, Drip Glaze, Helmut Bruchmann, 1965, 6 1/8 In. 115.00
Vase, Frond, Oxblood & White Glaze, Label, 1950s, 9 In. 15.00
Vase, Horse Head, Turquoise Glaze, c.1940 .... 85.00
Vase, Large Producing Fish Under Ivory Glaze, Light Green Ground, 10 x 12 In. 1333.00
Vase, Onion Shape, Sunset Glaze, No. R-1919, Signed, 1970s, 10 1/4 In. ....12.00 to 18.00
Vase, Peacock, Baluster Shape, No. 4030, 1960s, 12 In. 150.00

HALF-DOLL, see Pincushion Doll category.

HALL CHINA Company started in East Liverpool, Ohio, in 1903. The firm made many types of wares. Collectors search for the Hall teapots made from the 1920s to the 1950s. The dinnerwares of the same period, especially Autumn Leaf pattern, are also popular. The Hall China Company is still working. For more information, see *Kovels' Depression Glass & Dinnerware Price List*. Autumn Leaf pattern dishes are listed in their own category in this book.

Blue Blossom, Pepper, Handle	14.00
Blue Bouquet, Pepper, Handle	30.00
Blue Bouquet, Spoon	135.00
Bouquet, Percolator, Electric	135.00
Cameo Rose, Bowl, Vegetable, Oval, 10 1/2 In.	30.00
Cameo Rose, Creamer	13.00
Cameo Rose, Cup	10.00
Cameo Rose, Plate, 8 In.	10.00
Cameo Rose, Platter, Oval, 11 1/2 In.	25.00
Cameo Rose, Sugar, Cover	20.00
Caprice, Platter, 12 1/4 In.	33.00
Crocus, Bowl, 8 x 8 In.	165.00
Crocus, Bowl, Cover, Square, 7 x 3 1/2 In.	125.00
Crocus, Tureen, Soup	395.00 to 425.00
Fuji, Coffee Set, Percolator, Sugar & Creamer, 3 Piece	125.00
Fuji, Waffle Iron	95.00 to 195.00
Hercules, Pitcher, Water	110.00
Montgomery Ward, Pitcher, Water	72.00
Old Crow, Tom & Jerry Set, Bowl, Mugs, Ladle, Box, 12 Piece	235.00
Poppy, Baker, French Fluted	35.00
Poppy, Bean Pot, Handle	65.00 to 150.00
Poppy, Bowl, 10 In.	85.00
Poppy, Coffeepot, S-Lid	100.00
Poppy, Jug, Ball	150.00
Rose Parade, Bowl, Salad, 9 In.	40.00
Rose Parade, Casserole, Tab Handles	40.00
Rose Parade, Salt & Pepper	40.00
Rose Parade, Saltshaker	20.00
Rose Parade, Sugar & Creamer	30.00
Royal Rose, Pepper, Handle	16.00
Springtime, Berry Bowl, 5 1/2 In.	5.00
Springtime, Bowl, Oval	19.00
Springtime, Cake Plate	17.00
Springtime, Cup & Saucer	10.00
Springtime, Gravy Boat	19.00
Springtime, Plate, 6 In.	4.00
Springtime, Plate, 7 In.	7.00
Springtime, Plate, 9 In.	10.00
Springtime, Soup, Dish	14.00
Springtime, Sugar & Creamer, Cover	35.00
Taverne, Leftover, Cover, Square, 7 x 3 1/2 In.	125.00
Taverne, Mug	65.00
Taverne, Salt & Pepper, Banded	70.00
Taverne, Tumbler, Federal	33.00
Teapot, Aladdin, Cobalt, Gold Trim	175.00
Teapot, Aladdin, Marine, Mahogany, Gold Trim	90.00
Teapot, Automobile, Delphinium	750.00
Teapot, Birch	175.00
Teapot, Blue Blossom	395.00
Teapot, Boston, Poppy	295.00
Teapot, Crocus, Medium	50.00
Teapot, French, Cadet Daisy, Gold Label, 6 Cup	60.00
Teapot, Hollywood, Black, Gold Trim	55.00
Teapot, Lipton, Black, White Lettering, Base, 11 1/2 In.	495.00

Teapot, Lipton, Yellow 45.00
Teapot, Los Angeles, Cobalt, Gold Trim 75.00
Teapot, Los Angeles, Red 315.00
Teapot, Melody, Poppy 350.00
Teapot, Nautilus, Yellow, Gold Trim 75.00
Teapot, New York, Cobalt Blue, 2 Cup 55.00
Teapot, New York, Game Bird Decal, 2 Cup 210.00
Teapot, New York, Red Poppy ....95.00 to 125.00
Teapot, New York, Turquoise, 2 Cup 65.00
Teapot, Philadelphia, Pink, Gold Trim 59.00
Teapot, Philadelphia, Turquoise, Gold Trim 59.00
Teapot, Poppy, Boston 295.00
Teapot, Poppy, Melody 350.00
Teapot, Ronald Reagan, White ....75.00 to 125.00
Teapot, Rose Parade, Pert, 6 Cup 50.00
Teapot, Sherlock Holmes 285.00
Teapot, Streamline, Chinese Red 225.00
Teapot, Tritone, 2 Cup 325.00
Zeisel, Bowl, Caprice, 9 In. 35.00

HALLOWEEN is an ancient holiday that has changed in the last 200 years. The jack-o'-lantern, witches on broomsticks, and orange decorations seem to be twentieth-century creations. Collectors started to become serious about collecting Halloween-related items in the late 1970s. The papier-mache decorations, now replaced by plastic, and old costumes are in demand.

Apron, Crepe Paper, Witch 60.00
Black Cat Band, Die Cut, H. E. Luhrs, 9 In., 4 Piece 180.00
Candleholder, Red Cat, Ceramic 75.00
Candleholder, Witch On Moon, Handle, Metal, Painted, 7 In. 193.00
Candy Container, Cardboard, Jack O Lantern, Lollipop Lady, Germany, 7 1/2 In. 303.00
Candy Container, Cat, Devil Head 2300.00
Candy Container, Devilish Black Cat, Top Hat, Nodder, Composition, Germany, 6 In. 495.00
Candy Container, Jack-O'-Lantern, 2 Faces, Blue Glass, Tin Screw 187.00
Candy Container, Jack-O'-Lantern, Figure, Paper Lithograph 715.00
Candy Container, Jack-O'-Lantern, Glass, Painted, Metal Bail, Cover, Early 1900s 440.00
Candy Container, Jack-O'-Lantern, Man Admiral, Large 1475.00
Candy Container, Jack-O'-Lantern, Pop-Eyed, Original Bail 302.00
Candy Container, Jack-O'-Lantern, Scary Face, Bail Handle, Insert, 5 3/4 In. 275.00
Candy Container, Jumping Jack Cat Holding Jack-O'-Lantern, Tag, Rosen 79.00
Candy Container, Man, Spring Legs, Hat, Cardboard, Germany, 9 In. 770.00
Candy Container, Pumpkin Head Witch, Painted, With Bail, E & A 1210.00
Candy Container, Pumpkin, Composition, Germany, 1920s, 6 In. 578.00
Candy Container, Pumpkin, Egg Shape 400.00
Candy Container, Radish Head, Spring Neck, Arms, Cardboard, Germany, 6 1/2 In. 138.00
Candy Container, Witch On Rocket, Plastic, Pumpkin Wheels, Wrapper, 8 x 5 1/2 In. 550.00
Candy Container, Witch, Head Pulls Off, Crepe Collar, Cardboard, Germany, 6 1/4 In. ... 330.00
Candy Container, Witch, Huyler Candy Company, Composition & Wood, 6 In. 853.00
Candy Container, Witch, Plastic, Pumpkin Wheels, Cellophane, 8 x 6 In. 660.00
Centerpiece, Jack-O'-Lantern, Black Lipstick, Cardboard, Crepe Skirt, Germany, 7 In. 633.00
Costume, Archie, Ben Cooper, 1969 .... 90.00
Costume, Barbie, Navy, Pink Trim, Graphics, Rayon, Glitter, c.1963 .... 165.00
Costume, Evel Knievel, Mask, Ben Cooper, Box, 1974 .... 125.00
Costume, Little Red Riding Hood, Box, Collegeville 75.00
Costume, Mickey Mouse, Mask, Box, 1940s ....125.00 to 165.00
Costume, Popeye, Mask, Box, 1940s 125.00
Figure, Bat On Moon, Molded Cardboard, Germany, 5 In. 125.00
Figure, Black Cat Playing Trombone, Molded Cardboard, Germany, 7 1/2 In. 100.00
Figure, Black Cat's Head, Molded Cardboard, Germany, 13 In. 170.00
Figure, Black Cat's Head, Smiling, Molded Cardboard, Germany, 10 In. 209.00
Figure, Cat Boy, Cardboard, Display Stand, Germany, 19 1/2 In. 165.00
Figure, Cat With Kitten, Schuco, 14 1/2 In. 880.00
Figure, Cat, Schuco, 12 In. 500.00

Figure, Devil, Molded Cardboard, Embossed, Germany, 19 1/2 In. 150.00
Figure, Devil, Spring Wire Arms, Leather Hands, Brown Horns, 6 3/4 In. 95.00
Figure, Jack-O'-Lantern Man Playing Banjo, Cardboard, Germany, 7 1/2 In. 110.00
Figure, Owl On Branch, Orange Eyes, Molded Cardboard, Germany, 7 1/2 In. 100.00
Figure, Owl On Moon, Cardboard, Die Cut, Germany, 14 In. 235.00
Figure, Owl, Black, Die Cut, Cardboard, 2 Sides, 3 1/4 In. 60.00
Figure, Owl, Cutout Eyes, Cardboard, Germany, 11 In. 245.00
Figure, Pumpkin Man Jester, Cardboard, Germany, 7 1/2 In. 245.00
Figure, Pumpkin Man, Jointed, Die Cut, 27 1/2 In. 110.00
Figure, Pumpkin Man, With Accordion, Plastic, 5 In. 150.00
Figure, Pumpkin, Ghost, Ceramic 40.00
Figure, Skeleton, Die Cut, Posable Arms & Legs, Germany, 38 In. 75.00
Figure, Skull, Molded Cardboard, Germany, 11 In. 225.00
Figure, Walking Witch, Molded Cardboard, Die Cut, Germany, 15 1/2 In. 70.00
Figure, Witch Pulling Cat, Celluloid 830.00
Figure, Witch Scene, Embossed, 18 1/2 In. 100.00
Invitation, Envelope, Box, Dennison's 125.00
Jack-O'-Lantern, Accordion Bottom 225.00
Jack-O'-Lantern, Battery Operated, Glass, Black Metal, Box, 5 1/4 In. 190.00
Jack-O'-Lantern, Black Cat 195.00
Jack-O'-Lantern, Candleholders, Pat. July, 1903, 8 In., Pair 1265.00
Jack-O'-Lantern, Cardboard, 5 In. 225.00
Jack-O'-Lantern, Cardboard, Green Eyes, Red Cellophane Mouth, Germany, 5 In. 205.00
Jack-O'-Lantern, Cat On Pumpkin, Papier-Mache, 6 In. 29.00
Jack-O'-Lantern, Cat, Orange, Papier-Mache, 7 In. 28.00
Jack-O'-Lantern, Devil, Papier-Mache, 7 In. 30.00
Jack-O'-Lantern, Ghost 225.00
Jack-O'-Lantern, Girl With Cat, Molded Cardboard, Germany, 15 1/2 In. 185.00
Jack-O'-Lantern, Green Watermelon 250.00
Jack-O'-Lantern, Leering, Papier-Mache 26.00
Jack-O'-Lantern, Looking Down, Molded Cardboard, Germany, 9 1/2 In. 50.00
Jack-O'-Lantern, Musician With Cat, Molded Cardboard, Germany, 4 1/2 In. 270.00
Jack-O'-Lantern, Papier-Mache, 1930s, 5 1/2 x 7 In. 75.00
Jack-O'-Lantern, Papier-Mache, Orange, Green Base, 6 1/2 x 5 In. 140.00
Jack-O'-Lantern, Pressed Tin, Orange, Black Paint, 9 1/4 In. 2990.00
Jack-O'-Lantern, Skeleton, Ghost Picture, Papier-Mache, 6 In. 29.00
Jack-O'-Lantern, Solid Face, 4 3/4 In. 125.00
Jack-O'-Lantern, Standing, Full Bodied, Papier-Mache, 8 In. 55.00
Jack-O'-Lantern, Tin, Orange Paint, 7 In. 2750.00
Lantern, Black Cat Face, Cardboard, 7 3/4 In. 375.00
Lantern, Black Cat On Fence 295.00
Lantern, Black Cat, Bow Tie, Cardboard, Molded, Germany, 3 3/4 In. 798.00
Lantern, Black Cat, Paper Eyes, Wire Handle, 5 3/8 In. 1100.00
Lantern, Cardboard, Red & Black, Hand Painted, Marked DRNG, Germany, 5 In. 798.00
Lantern, Cat, Black, Flocked, Molded Nose, Germany, 4 In. 740.00
Lantern, Cat, Yellow, Metal, Eyes Glow With Candle, 6 1/4 In. 70.00
Lantern, Devil Head, Composition 800.00
Lantern, Devil Skull, Composition, Germany, 4 1/2 In. 800.00
Lantern, Devil's Head, Celluloid, Battery Operated, Japan, Box, 4 1/2 In. 370.00
Lantern, Devil, Orange, Papier-Mache, 6 1/2 In. 575.00
Lantern, Devil, Raised Nose & Ears, 2 3/4 In. 125.00
Lantern, Parade, Screw Mount, Candle Holder, Toledo Sign Company, c.1906, 10 In. 825.00
Lantern, Pumpkin Boy, Composition, Candy Dish, Head Lifts, 4 1/2 In. 770.00
Lantern, Pumpkin, Glass, Tin Base, Hong Kong, 4 1/2 In. 60.00
Lantern, Pumpkin, Metal Bail Handle, 2 3/4 In. 95.00
Lantern, Red Devil Head, Papier-Mache, American, 6 1/2 In. 400.00
Noisemaker, Black Cat, Wooden Ratchet, Germany, 10 In. 225.00
Noisemaker, Clapper, Jack-O'-Lantern, Die Cut, Embossed, Germany, 7 In. 165.00
Noisemaker, Clapper, Jack-O'-Lantern, Tin, 10 In. 225.00
Noisemaker, Crank, Wooden 90.00
Noisemaker, Horn, Witch, Exaggerated Facial Features, Papier-Mache, 8 In. 115.00
Noisemaker, Pan Slapper, Wooden, Black Face, Orange Crepe Paper Bow Tie, 6 x 2 In. ... 149.00

Noisemaker, Pumpkin Head, Cardboard, Paper Lithograph Face, 3 1/4 In. 19.00
Noisemaker, Rattle, Black Cat, Celluloid, 3 1/2 In. 450.00
Noisemaker, Witch, Paper, Litho, Cardboard, Wooden Ratchet, 2 Sides, Germany, 8 In. . . 138.00
Paperweight, Black Cat With Arched Back, Cast Iron, 3 1/4 In. 175.00
Pencil Holder, Black Cat In Top Hat, Pumpkin Body, Plastic, 3 1/4 In. 26.00
Placecard Holder, Pumpkin Woman, Cardboard, Wooden Base, Germany, 2 3/4 In. 45.00
Placecard Holder, Spider On Web, 2 In., 12 Piece 535.00
Postcard, Black Cat On Jack-O'-Lantern, 1909, 3 1/2 x 5 1/2 In. 50.00
Postcard, Bobbing For Apples 18.00
Postcard, Children, With Jack-O'-Lantern 20.00
Postcard, Jolly Halloween 18.00
Postcard, Witch On Broom 20.00
Postcard, Witches On Bats 25.00
Postcard, Witches With Moon 30.00
Poster, Movie, John Carpenter Horror Film, Jack-O'-Lantern, 1 Sheet, 27 x 41 In. 110.00
Tambourine, Black Cat, Tin 100.00
Tiara, Jack-O'-Lantern With Black Cats, Molded Cardboard, Germany, 9 1/2 In. 275.00
Toy, Cat, Holding Cane, Wobbles, Wind Up Key, Celluloid, 3 1/2 In. 688.00
Toy, Pumpkin Playing Accordion, Plastic, 5 In. 89.00
Toy, Sammy The Strolling Skeleton, Windup, Box, Japan, 1950s, 5 1/2 In. 330.00
Toy, Space Gun, Trick Or Treat, 6 3/4 In. 195.00
Toy, Train & Castle, Clowns, Devil, Black Cat, Lithograph, Box, U.S. Zone Germany 315.00
Toy, Witch, Balancing, Box, Japan, 10 In. 110.00

HAMPSHIRE pottery was made in Keene, New Hampshire, between 1871 and 1923. Hampshire developed a line of colored glazed wares as early as 1883, including a Royal Worcester-type pink, olive green, blue, and mahogany. Pieces are marked with the printed mark or the impressed name *Hampshire Pottery* or *J.S.T. & Co., Keene, N.H.* Many pieces were marked with city names and sold as souvenirs.

Bowl, Artichoke, Matte Glaze, 2 3/4 x 4 1/4 In. 220.00
Bowl, Embossed, Leaf, Mottled, Blue Glaze, 5 3/4 In. 300.00
Bowl, Embossed, Trillium, Olive Green, Marked, 9 In. 460.00
Bowl, Lily Pads, Buds, Olive Green, 3 x 10 In. 748.00
Bowl, Water Lily Bulging, Oblong Water Lily Leaves, Green Matte Glaze, 10 In. 550.00
Candelholder, Green Matte Glaze, Signed, 7 In. 230.00
Ewer, Deep Green Matte Glaze, Rolled Leaf Design, 6 3/4 In. 300.00
Ewer, Impressed Mark, 8 In. 430.00
Jardiniere, Cerulean Blue Glaze, Black, Gray, Blue, 8 1/4 x 8 In. 880.00
Jardiniere, Deep Green Matte Glaze, Dimpled Finish, Base, 9 x 7 In. 990.00
Lamp, Geometric Design, Green Matte Glaze, Leaded Shade, 17 In. 6050.00
Lamp, Green Matte Glaze, Stylized Flower, 12 x 21 1/2 In. 1870.00
Lamp Base, Embossed Leaves, Green Glaze, Metal Fixture, Signed, 12 1/2 In. 1775.00
Lamp Base, Embossed Twining Lily Pads, Olive Green Glaze, 16 x 7 In. 1012.00
Lamp Base, Inverted Trumpet Form, Stylized Tulip, 19 In. 800.00
Lamp Base, Oil, Green Matte Glaze, 11 x 11 1/2 In. 770.00
Lamp Base, Repeating Tulips, Green Matte Glaze, Keene, N.H., 1910, 11 In. 920.00
Lamp Base, Tulips, Leaves, Green Matte Glaze 1150.00
Mug, 3 Looped Handles, Green Glaze, 5 In. 165.00
Mug, Green Matte Glaze, 3 Handles, 5 x 5 1/2 In. 345.00
Toothpick, Green Glaze, Petal Shaped Mouth, 3 In. 165.00
Toothpick, Mocha Brown Matte Glaze, 3 In. 140.00
Urn, Embossed Greek Key Bands, Green Matte Glaze, Reticulated Handles, 15 In. 1910.00
Vase, Blue, Green Matte Glaze, Leaves, Signed, 7 In. 575.00
Vase, Blue-Green, Blue-Gray Matte Glaze, Bulbous, Oatmealing, 5 3/4 x 6 1/2 In. 750.00
Vase, Brown Matte Glaze, Leaves, Embossed, 3 1/2 In. 690.00
Vase, Brown, Green Matte Glaze, 6 In. 489.00
Vase, Cerulean Blue Glaze, Aqua Mottled Rim, Black Flecks, Matte, 12 In. 660.00
Vase, Cerulean Blue Glaze, Vivid Aqua, Gray, Black Body, 8 1/4 In. 660.00
Vase, Deep Cerulean Blue Glaze, Black, Gray Veining, 4 1/4 In. 358.00
Vase, Deep Cerulean Blue Glaze, Dark Black, Gray, 7 1/4 In. 660.00
Vase, Deep Olive High Gloss Glaze, Mocha Brown Ground, 6 1/4 In. 305.00

Vase, Embossed Leaves, Mottled Yellow & Green Glaze, 6 3/4 In. 672.00
Vase, Embossed Leaves, Yellow, Green Mottled Matte Glaze, Marked, 5 3/4 In. 660.00
Vase, Feathered Blue Matte Glaze, 11 3/4 x 4 3/4 In. 518.00
Vase, Frothy White Over Mocha, Elongated Flora, 7 In. 660.00
Vase, Green Matte Glaze, Bulbous, 4 In. 175.00
Vase, Green Matte Glaze, c.1909, 9 In. 975.00
Vase, Green Matte Glaze, Calla Lily Design, Floral In Repeat, 8 3/4 In. 1540.00
Vase, Green Matte Glaze, Dark Green Speckles, Pinched Neck, 5 1/4 x 5 3/4 In. 248.00
Vase, Green Matte Glaze, Elongated Buds With Closed Petals, 7 1/4 x 4 1/2 In. 1045.00
Vase, Green Matte Glaze, Floral Design, Handles, 6 1/2 In. 440.00
Vase, Green Matte Glaze, Geometric Design At Top & Bottom, Handles, 15 In. 2070.00
Vase, Green Matte Glaze, Leaves, Handle, 8 1/2 In. 748.00
Vase, Green Matte Glaze, Molded Corn, 5 1/2 In. 978.00
Vase, Green Matte Glaze, Squat, Incised Band Of Lines & Scrolls, 2 3/4 In. 690.00
Vase, Green Matte Mottled Glaze, Inverted Rim, C. Robertson, 7 In. 575.00
Vase, Leaves, Embossed, Burnt Orange, Marked, 9 1/2 In. 776.00
Vase, Lightening, Dark Green Glaze, Miniature Handles, 8 In. 1045.00
Vase, Midnight Blue Mottled Glaze, Powder White, Blue Matte Glaze, 6 1/4 In. 1100.00
Vase, Olive Green, Handles, 7 1/2 In. 575.00
Vase, Pale Cream Glaze, Dark Green Glaze Matte, 6 1/4 In. 880.00
Vase, Raised Mottled Glaze, Green Accented By Brown, 8 1/4 In. 605.00
Vase, Serpent, Green Glaze, Snake Tail Handle, 6 In. 440.00
Vase, Thick Blue & Green Glaze, Signed, 12 1/4 In. 1725.00
Vase, Variegated Brown Streaks, Mint Green Glaze, 7 In. 715.00
Vase, Vertical Leaves, Green, Blue Matte Glaze, 8 In. 1495.00
Vase, Vertical Panels, Blue Matte Glaze, Signed, Signed, 4 3/4 In. 285.00
Vase, Water Lily Scene, Salmon Pink Interior, Wallace King, 5 In. 880.00

HANDEL glass was made by Philip Handel working in Meriden, Connecticut, from 1885 and in New York City from 1893 to 1933. The firm made art glass and other types of lamps. Handel shades were made not only of leaded glass in a style reminiscent of Tiffany but also of reverse painted glass. Handel also made vases and other glass objects.

Ashtray, Owl, On Branch, Applied Leaf-Shaped Cigarette Rests, Round, 4 3/4 In. 175.00
Bookends, Arched Doorway, Bronze, Pair 560.00
Bookends, Roman Columns, Bronze 640.00
Hanging Shade, 6 Slag Glass Panels, Red Roses, Green Leaves, 11 In. 770.00
Hanging Shade, Amber Slag Shade, Landscape Overlay, Purple, Green Glass, 24 In. 5040.00
Hanging Shade, Ball Shape, Purple Parrot Amidst Tropical Foliage, 10 In. 3920.00
Hanging Shade, Birds In Flight, Woodland Scene, Ball Shade, Iridescent Ground, 10 In. . . . 4200.00
Hanging Shade, Road, Woodland Scene, Brown, Tan, 18 In. 8960.00
Humidor, Cover, 2 Squirrels On Log, Green Ground 672.00
Humidor, Cover, Buck & Doe, Brown Ground 672.00
Humidor, Cover, Dog, Signed Handelware Shield, 6 x 6 In. 1120.00
Humidor, Cover, Green Enameled Mosserine Finish 448.00
Humidor, Cover, Hinged, Female Golfer & Male Caddy, Brown Ground, Signed 2240.00
Humidor, Cover, Hinged, Grizzly Bear Design, Signed, 8 1/4 In. 1035.00
Humidor, Cover, With Horse, Brown Enamel 950.00
Humidor, Cover, With Pipe, Brown Enamel 390.00
Lamp, 2 Trees, Meadow Against Hills, Domed Shade, Signed, 18 In. 8160.00
Lamp, 2-Light, Cabin On Rocky Shore, Painted Shade, Label, 18 3/4 In. 2875.00
Lamp, 2-Light, Dark Green Mottled Shades, 21 1/4 x 7 1/4 In. 2310.00
Lamp, 2-Light, Mosaic Segments, Pink Flowers On Vine, Leaded, c.1912, 19 In. 2300.00
Lamp, 5-Light, Green-Amber Slag Glass Shade, Cone Shape, Signed, c.1907, 30 In. 9200.00
Lamp, 6 Panels, Bell Shade, Caramel Leaves, Vines Glass, Signed, 14 In. 3080.00
Lamp, 6 Panels, Metal Overlay, Palm Tree Design, Impressed Base, 9 In. 2464.00
Lamp, 8 Panels, Aquarium, Tropical Fish Swimming Among Plants, 16 In. 36400.00
Lamp, 8 Panels, Bent, Diamonds Around Lower Border, Signed, 22 In. 6720.00
Lamp, 8 Panels, Forest Scene, Green, White Opalescent Glass, Shade, Cone Shape, 25 In. . 25200.00
Lamp, 8 Panels, Frosted Field, Diamond Shaped Jewels, Signed, 25 In. 2310.00
Lamp, 8 Panels, Geometric Design, White Glass, Leaded, 65 In. 10350.00
Lamp, 8 Panels, Grape, Leaf Border, Amber Slag Glass, Signed, 23 In. 1322.00

Lamp, 8 Panels, Leaded Mica Shade, Bronze Base, 20 x 20 In. 805.00
Lamp, 8 Panels, Metal Overlay, Yellow, Red, Stylized Feathers, 18 In. 7280.00
Lamp, 8 Panels, Slag Glass, Green Paint, Signed, 21 1/2 x 18 In. 2875.00
Lamp, 8 Panels, Slag Glass, Overlay Of Roses & Leaves, Bronzed Base, Signed, 24 In. . . . 4675.00
Lamp, Allover Rose Petals & Blossoms Against Light Blue Sky, Domed Shade, 18 In. 24080.00
Lamp, Allover Stylized Wild Roses Interior, Loaf Shaped Shade, 8 In. 3360.00
Lamp, Amber Slag Glass Panels, Bell Shaped Shade, Metal Base, 17 In. 5040.00
Lamp, Bamboo, Reverse Painted, Bronzed Base, Signed, 15 x 7 In. 1840.00
Lamp, Band Of Flowers, Green Ground, 2 Handled Base, Signed, 15 1/2 In. 3910.00
Lamp, Basket Of Flowers Interior, Scalloped Shade, 18 In. 4480.00
Lamp, Birds In Flight, Clump Of Trees Ground, Gold Iridescent, Domed Shade, 18 In. . . . 7000.00
Lamp, Birds In Flight, Foliage, Cloudy Sky, Domed Shade, Painted, Signed, 16 In. 5320.00
Lamp, Border Of Rose Petals, Gray Ground, Metal Base, Signed, F.L., 8 In. 2744.00
Lamp, Brown, Light Green Shade, Bronze Patina, 9 1/2 x 12 In. 1840.00
Lamp, Canary Mottled Shade, 4 Panels, Signed, 24 In. 4675.00
Lamp, Canary-Amber Slag Glass Shade, Arts & Crafts, Signed, 24 x 18 In. 4675.00
Lamp, Cherry Blossoms, Foliage, Bronze Metal, Tree Trunk Base, Leaded, 16 In. 21280.00
Lamp, Chipped Ice Glass, Woodland Scene, Buffed Metal Base, 7 In. 715.00
Lamp, Chipped Ice Shade, Green, Bronze Base, Signed, 14 x 8 In. 1150.00
Lamp, Colorful Maple Leaves, Domed Shade, 18 In. 12320.00
Lamp, Daffodil, Green Foliage Exterior, Shade, Cone Shape, Bronze Base, 18 In. 7840.00
Lamp, Dense Forest Scene, Orange, Yellow Sky, Domed Shade, 18 In. 8960.00
Lamp, Desert Scene, Camel Caravan, Domed Shade, Bronze Base, 7 In. 3300.00
Lamp, Desert Scene, Palm Trees, Painted, Signed, 7 x 15 In. 2760.00
Lamp, Desk, Autumn Landscape, Bronze, c.1915, 12 In. 1800.00
Lamp, Desk, Sunset Palm Trees, Metal Overlay, Orange, Mauve Slag Glass, 8 In. 2240.00
Lamp, Domed Shade, Trees On Exterior, River, Rolling Hill Interior, 18 In. 14000.00
Lamp, Egyptian Scene, Camels, Yellow, Pink, Painted, 14 In. 2243.00
Lamp, Etched Geometric & Woven Design Shade, Cloth Label, 21 In. 4675.00
Lamp, Etched Pine Needles, Red Enameled Mosserine Finish, Domed Shade, 16 In. 5488.00
Lamp, Exotic Bird, Domed Shade, Metal Base, Signed 7125, 18 In. 17360.00
Lamp, Field Landscape, Bronze Base, Domed Shade, Shade & Base Signed, 18 In. 7840.00
Lamp, Flower Basket Design, Scalloped Shade, Basketweave Painted Base, 8 In. 1792.00
Lamp, Flower Border, Dogwood Blossoms, Domed Shade, Signed, 14 In. 3080.00
Lamp, Flower Form Bronze Base, River Landscape, Label, 23 In. 7474.00
Lamp, Flower Form Shade, Green Slag Glass Petals, Lily Pad Base, c.1903, 13 In. 460.00
Lamp, Flowers & Exotic Bird, Exotic Bird Border, Domed Shade, Signed, 18 In. 6720.00
Lamp, Flowers, Multicolored Rose Blossoms, Light, Domed Shade, Green Foliage, 18 In. 23520.00
Lamp, Flowers, Red Roses, Shade, Cone Shape, Shade & Base Signed, 14 In. 336.00
Lamp, Green Enameled Mosserine Finish Shade, 10 In. 1232.00
Lamp, Green Ground, Red Flower Border, Tree Trunk Shape Base, Label, 16 In. 2070.00
Lamp, Green Leaves, Shade, Cone Shape, Light Gold, Bronze Base, Signed, 18 In. 12320.00
Lamp, Green Slag Glass Shade, Bronze Verdigris Base, Acorn Finials, 22 x 17 In. 1045.00
Lamp, Green, Brown Ribbons, Purple Flowers, 14 In. 1840.00
Lamp, Green, White Leaves On Shade, Vibrant Orange Blossoms, 20 In. 5600.00
Lamp, Hanging Shade, Horizontal Metal Overlay, Signed, 21 x 7 x 23 In. 1840.00
Lamp, Hanging, Stylized Parrots On Exterior, Signed, 10 In. 2632.00
Lamp, Landscape Design, Geometric Border, Floral, Bronze Base, 24 In. 5750.00
Lamp, Landscape Scene, Domed Shade, Tree Trunk Base, 7 In. 3360.00
Lamp, Landscape Scene, Loaf Shaped Shade, 8 In. 2296.00
Lamp, Landscape Scene, Trees & Mountains In Background, Mauve Sky, 24 In. 13440.00
Lamp, Landscape Scene, Trees, Orange, Yellow Sky, Domed Shade, Signed, 10 In. 5600.00
Lamp, Landscape, House By Shore, Signed, 22 In. 1897.00
Lamp, Leafless Trees, Light Snow Covered Ground, Domed Shade, 15 In. 6160.00
Lamp, Leafy Branches, Green, Yellow Ground, Curved Shade, Tree Trunk Base, 19 In. . . . 7840.00
Lamp, Leaves, Vines, Floral Blossoms Interior, Signed, 16 In. 7840.00
Lamp, Meadow Scene, Pink Flowers, Butterflies, Brilliant Sky Blue, 14 In. 2185.00
Lamp, Metal Overlay, Red Rose Blossoms, Green Foliage, 18 In. 5040.00
Lamp, Metal Overlay, Sunset Palm Trees Against Orange Skyline, 24 In. 11200.00
Lamp, Metal Overlay, Vines, Green Leaf Ground, Amber Glass, 16 In. 4760.00
Lamp, Metal Overlay, Yellow Daffodil, Slag Glass Panels, 16 In. 3360.00
Lamp, Metal Overlays, Mushroom & Floral Slag Glass Shade, 14 In. . . . . 4313.00 to 5225.00

Lamp, Moonlit Sky, Woodland Ground, Shade, Cone Shape, 18 In. 6160.00
Lamp, Numerous Ships At Sea, Palm Tree, 23 1/2 In. 10925.00
Lamp, Opaque White Shade, Floral Design, Green Enameled Exterior, 57 1/4 In. 2310.00
Lamp, Oriental Pagoda In Wooded Landscape, Domed Shade, 18 In. 7840.00
Lamp, Oriental Pheasant, Colorful Exotic Birds In Flight, Domed Shade, 18 In. 20160.00
Lamp, Palm Tree Scene, Bell Shade, Tree Trunk Base, 6 In. 2464.00
Lamp, Palm Trees, Boats, Moon, Bronze Base, 20 In. 2990.00
Lamp, Peacock, Acid Cut, Cameo, Polychrome Tripod Base, Shade & Base Signed, 18 In. 25200.00
Lamp, Persian Design, Ball Shaped Shade, Opal, Painted, Bronze Base, 26 1/2 x 15 In. . . 1725.00
Lamp, Piano, Bronze, Caramel Slag Insert, Marked, Paper Label, 11 In. 1400.00
Lamp, Piano, Slag Glass Shade, Bronze Patina, 12 x 10 In. 843.00
Lamp, Pine Needle, Metal Overlay, Brown, Green Glass, Domed Shade, 18 In. 8120.00
Lamp, Pink Floral Blossoms, Green Leaves, Leaded Shade, Cone Shape, Signed, 24 In. . . 6720.00
Lamp, Pink Flowers, Light Green Lower Portion, Domed Shade, Signed, 12 In. 1288.00
Lamp, Pink Roses, Green Foliage, Domed Shade, Signed, F.L., 7 In. 2800.00
Lamp, Pink Tea Roses, Gray Leaves, Domed Shade, Bronze Base, 7 In. 3080.00
Lamp, Poppies, Mushroom Shaped Shade, Poppies, Bronze Metal, No. 2456, 18 3/4 In. . . 980.00
Lamp, Red Flowers, Yellow Center, Signed, 8 x 5 In. 1380.00
Lamp, Roman Ruins, Numerous Palm Trees, 24 x 18 In. . . . . *Illus* 7475.00
Lamp, Rose Blossom, Butterflies, Foliage, Domed Shade, Signed, Handel 6688R, 18 In. . 23520.00
Lamp, Rose Bouquet, Tree Trunk Base, 25 1/2 In. . . . . *Illus* 16675.00
Lamp, Rose Petals, Gray, Blue Foliage, Domed Scalloped Shade, 7 In. 2800.00
Lamp, Roses & Colorful Butterflies, Ribbed Shade, Painted, 8 In. 2578.00
Lamp, Scalloped, Yellow Flowers, Green Foliage, Domed Shade, 8 In. 3080.00
Lamp, Scenic Green Trees, Shade & Base Signed, 18 In. 8400.00
Lamp, Scenic, Colorful Trees Interior, Milky White Skies, Domed Shade, 18 In. 7280.00
Lamp, Seashore Scene Interior, Sailboat At Bay, Seagulls, Domed Shade, 18 In. 7840.00
Lamp, Shade, Glass Curved, Leafy Branches, Tree Base, Signed, 20 In. 7840.00
Lamp, Shade, Rose Border, Green Foliage, White, 12 In. 1960.00
Lamp, Slag Glass, Green, White Blossom Shade, Lily Standard Base, 13 1/2 In. 1150.00
Lamp, Snow Landscape, Bronze Replaced Base, 12 In. 1380.00
Lamp, Southwest Border Design, Scalloped, Blue Ground, Domed Shade, 18 In., Pair . . 13400.00
Lamp, Sparse Woodland On Rolling Hills, Domed Shade, Signed, 18 In. . . . . . . .4480.00 to 7640.00
Lamp, Steuben Shade, Green Iridescent Glass, 10 In. 3360.00
Lamp, Stylized Floral Design, Domed Shade, Signed, 7 In. 1344.00
Lamp, Stylized Floral, Blades Of Grass, Flaring Glass Shade, Signed, 28 In. 6325.00
Lamp, Stylized Leaves, Green, White Glass Border, Domed Shade, 24 In. 10060.00
Lamp, Stylized Leaves, Shade, Cone Shape, Bronze Base, Signed, 23 In. 4760.00
Lamp, Stylized Vines, Green Leaves, Caramel Glaze, 8 Horizontal Panels, 66 1/2 In. 7475.00
Lamp, Sunset Palm Trees, Tropical Foliage Against Orange To Red Sunset, 24 In. 11760.00
Lamp, Sunset Palm Trees, Tropical Foliage, Shade, Cone Shape, 18 In. 10640.00
Lamp, Sunset Palm, 9 Sides, Metal Overlay, Palm Tree, Green Glass, Bronze Base, 16 In. 4480.00
Lamp, Sunset Palm, Conical Shade, Palm Trees, Tropical Foliage, Red, Purple, 24 In. . . . 8680.00
Lamp, Treasure Island, Aquatic Scene, Sailing Vessels Shade, Cone Shape, 7 In. 3640.00
Lamp, Treasure Island, Sailing Vessel In Moonlit Bay, Domed Shade, Signed, 18 In. 9520.00
Lamp, Treasure Island, Sailing Vessels In Tropical Moonlit Bay, 18 In. 10640.00
Lamp, Trees, Rolling Hills, People On Path, Domed Shade, 18 In. 14000.00
Lamp, Tropical Birds, Pink & White Flowers, Signed, 23 1/2 In. 5225.00
Lamp, Tropical Sunset, Apron Of Palm Trees, Mauve, Purple Sky, Domed Shade, 20 In. . . 5600.00
Lamp, Tropical Sunset, Palm Tree, Purple, Orange Sky, Shade, Cone Shape, 20 In. 8960.00
Lamp, Tropical Sunset, Palm Trees, Tropical Foliage, Purple, Orange, Red, 20 In. 16800.00
Lamp, Venetian Harbor Scene, Domed Shade, 7 In. 3640.00
Lamp, Venetian Scene, Deep Brown Sailboats, Pale Peach Ground, 14 In. 1725.00
Lamp, Venetian Scene, Vessels, Bronze Base, 14 x 22 1/2 In. . . . . *Illus* 5175.00
Lamp, White Apple Blossoms, Yellow, Red Roses Border, Black Border, 25 In. 5750.00
Lamp, Winter Scene, Bare Trees, Tree Trunk Base, Painted, Signed, 7 In. 3360.00
Lamp, Winter Scene, Domed Shade, Tree Trunk Base, Signed, 7 In. 3640.00
Lamp, Winter Woodland Scene, Shade, Cone Shape, Brown Base, Stem, Signed, 15 In. . . 4032.00
Lamp, Wisteria, Lavender Interior, Green Leaf Exterior, Shade, Cone Shape, 15 In. 6720.00
Lamp, Woodland Hillside Scene, Shade, Cone Shape, Bronze Base, 15 In. 5600.00
Lamp, Woodland Landscape, Domed Shade, Bronze Tripod Base, 18 In. 7280.00
Lamp, Woodland Landscape, Painted, Oval, 10 In. 4480.00

Handel, Lamp, Roman Ruins,
Numerous Palm Trees,
24 x 18 In.

Handel, Lamp, Rose
Bouquet, Tree Trunk Base,
25 1/2 In.

Handel, Lamp, Venetian Scene,
Vessels, Bronze Base,
14 x 22 1/2 In.

Lamp, Woodland Scene, Birds In Flight, Domed Shade, Signed, H.B., 18 In. 6400.00
Lamp, Woodland Scene, Domed Shade, Bronze Base, 8 In. 3640.00
Lamp, Yellow Daffodils, Green, Black Ground, Domed Shade, 18 In. 22960.00
Lamp, Yellow Enameled Mosserine Finish, Vine Design, Domed Shade, 14 In. 4144.00
Lantern, Hammered Copper, Glass Shade, Original Patina, 10 x 6 In. 633.00
Night-Light, Egg Shape, Stylized Parrots, Pierced Metal Base, Shade Signed, 7 In. 1792.00
Sconce, 1-Light, Stems Supporting Floriform Shade, Signed, c.1903, 10 In. 1380.00
Shade, 8 Panels, Metal Overlay, Slag Glass, Bronze Base, 26 1/2 In. 1495.00
Shade, Amber Slag Glass Panels, Metal Overlay, Leaves & Berries, 14 1/2 x 3 5/8 In. . . . 1610.00
Shade, Apple Blossom, 5 Petal Flowers, Irregular Rim, Signed, 25 3/4 x 19 1/2 In. 4370.00
Shade, Rose, Yellow Slag Glass, Green Slag Glass Border, Tropical Trees, 20 In. 7475.00
Tray, Opalware, Pug Dog Center, Handles, Handelware Mark, 4 3/4 In. 635.00
Vase, Teroma, Mountain Scene, Broggi, 1925, 8 In. 920.00
Vase, Teroma, Scene Of Trees With Birds In Flight On Exterior, 10 1/2 In. 2352.00
Vase, Teroma, Scenic, Trees With Birds In Flight, Signed, Bedigie, 11 x 4 In. 1265.00
Vase, Teroma, Woodland & Lake Scene, Signed, 11 In. 1288.00

HARDWARE, see Architectural category.

HARKER Pottery Company was incorporated in 1890 in East Liverpool,
Ohio. The Harker family had been making pottery in the area since
1840. The company made many types of pottery but by the Civil War
was making quantities of yellowware from native clays. They also
made Rockingham-type brown-glazed pottery and whiteware. The
plant was moved to Chester, West Virginia, in 1931. Dinnerwares were
made and sold nationally. In 1971 the company was sold to Jeannette
Glass Company and all operations ceased in 1972. For more information, see *Kovels' Depression Glass & Dinnerware Price List.*

Amy, Spoon 70.00
Bouquet, Plate, Bread & Butter 12.00
Calico Tulip, Rolling Pin, Original Stopper, 14 1/2 In. 115.00
Cameoware, Bowl, Yellow, Cover 76.00
Cameoware, Casserole, Pink, White Flowers 10.00
Cameoware, Cookie Jar, Blue 75.00
Cameoware, Drip Jar, Yellow, No Lid 10.00
Cameoware, Salt & Pepper, Yellow 15.00
Cameoware, Snack Set, Child's, Blue, Duck Design, Cup, 7 1/4-In. Plate 22.00
Chesteron, Salt & Pepper 20.00
Chesteron, Sugar, Cover, Teal 18.00
Chesterton, Cake Plate, Teal, 13 In. 20.00
Chesterton, Creamer, Gray 15.00
Chesterton, Creamer, Teal 16.00

Chesterton, Cup & Saucer 11.00
Chesterton, Gravy Boat, Underplate, Gray 38.00
Chesterton, Plate, Bread & Butter 4.00
Chesterton, Plate, Dinner, Gray, 10 1/4 In. ....9.00 to 12.00
Chesterton, Plate, Dinner, Teal, 10 1/4 In. 10.00
Chesterton, Plate, Gray, 7 1/2 In. 16.00
Chesterton, Platter, Gray, 9 3/4 x 13 3/8 In. 10.00
Chesterton, Platter, Lime Green, 8 1/2 In. 16.00
Chesterton, Platter, Teal, Harker, 13 In. 25.00
Chesterton, Sugar, Cover, Gray ....10.00 to 25.00
Colonial Lady, Sugar & Creamer 45.00
Country Cousins, Tidbit Tray, Ring Handle, 10 In. 30.00
Currier & Ives, Cake Server 35.00
Deco-Dahlia, Batter Bowl, Pour Spout, White, Red & Black Floral, 4 1/2 x 9 3/4 In. 23.00
Gadroon, Cup & Saucer, Blue, Harker 11.00
Gadroon, Platter, Lime Green, Harker, Small 19.00
Golden Wheat, Cup & Saucer 11.00
Golden Wheat, Plate, 10 1/4 In. 10.00
Heritance, Sugar & Creamer, Platinum Trim 15.00
Homestead, Plate, Bread & Butter, 6 In. 6.00
Ivy Vine, Pitcher, Cover, 4 In. 41.00
Ivy Vine, Teapot 44.00
Mallow, Serving Spoon 25.00
Modern Tulip, Trivet, Octagonal, 6 1/4 In. 25.00
Persian Key, Cup & Saucer 12.00
Persian Key, Plate, 6 In. 5.00
Persian Key, Plate, 9 1/2 In. 12.00
Petit Point, Casserole, Cover, 6 1/2 In. 15.50
Petit Point, Casserole, Cover, Round, 8 1/2 In. 20.00
Petit Point, Cup 5.00
Petit Point, Gravy Boat 10.00
Petit Point Rose, Casserole, Cover, 1935, 8 1/2 In. 20.50
Petit Point Rose, Pie Plate, 1935, 10 In. 15.00
Petit Point Rose, Salt & Pepper 16.00
Red Apple II, Bowl, Vegetable 25.00
Red Apple II, Cup & Saucer 10.00
Red Apple II, Platter, 14 In. 25.00
Red Apple II, Soup, Dish 14.00
Snowleaf, Platter, Medium 35.00
Springtime, Platter, Small 33.00
Vintage, After Dinner 35.00

HARLEQUIN dinnerware was produced by the Homer Laughlin Company from 1938 to 1964, and sold without trademark by the F. W. Woolworth Co. It has a concentric ring design like Fiesta, but the rings are separated from the rim by a plain margin. Cup handles are triangular in shape. Seven different novelty animal figurines were introduced in 1939. For more information on Harlequin dinnerware, see *Kovels' Depression Glass & Dinnerware Price List.*

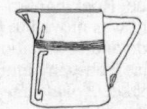

Dark Green, Bowl, 36s, 6 1/2 In. 26.00
Gray, Bowl, 36s, 6 1/2 In. 26.00
Gray, Cup & Saucer 15.00
Gray, Plate, 9 In. ....13.00 to 19.00
Gray, Salt & Pepper 12.00
Gray, Teapot 225.00
Maroon, Figurine, Cat 187.00
Maroon, Figurine, Donkey 150.00
Maroon, Figurine, Duck ....130.00 to 275.00
Maroon, Figurine, Fish 150.00
Maroon, Figurine, Lamb 90.00
Maroon, Figurine, Penguin ....110.00 to 285.00
Mauve, Bowl, 36s, 6 1/2 In. 40.00

Mauve, Figurine, Cat . . . . .110.00 to 150.00
Mauve, Figurine, Duck . . . . .198.00 to 275.00
Mauve, Figurine, Fish 170.00
Mauve, Figurine, Penguin 180.00
Mauve, Tumbler, Water, 4 1/4 In. 55.00
Medium Green, Plate, 9 In. 13.00
Orange, Bowl, 7 1/2 In. 9.00
Red, Creamer, Individual 35.00
Rose, Bowl, 36s, 6 1/2 In. 40.00
Rose, Bowl, Oatmeal, 36s, 6 1/2 In. 26.00
Rose, Casserole, Cover 160.00
Rose, Cup & Saucer, After Dinner 140.00
Rose, Jug, 22 Oz. 40.00
Rose, Plate, 6 In. 7.00
Rose, Plate, 9 In. 13.00
Rose, Salt & Pepper 12.00
Rose, Teapot 195.00
Spruce Green, Cup & Saucer 15.00
Spruce Green, Figurine, Cat 160.00
Spruce Green, Figurine, Donkey . . . . .170.00 to 325.00
Spruce Green, Figurine, Duck . . . . .180.00 to 275.00
Spruce Green, Figurine, Fish 176.00
Spruce Green, Figurine, Lamb . . . . .90.00 to 138.00
Spruce Green, Pitcher, Water 135.00
Spruce Green, Plate, 9 In. 13.00
Spruce Green, Platter, 13 In. 375.00
Turquoise, Creamer 12.00
Turquoise, Cup & Saucer 10.00
Turquoise, Plate, 9 3/8 In. 16.00
Turquoise, Spoon Rest 375.00
Turquoise, Sugar & Creamer 10.00
Yellow, Bowl, 36s, 6 1/2 In. 40.00
Yellow, Casserole, Cover 85.00
Yellow, Cup & Saucer 10.00
Yellow, Cup, After Dinner 15.00
Yellow, Eggcup, Double, 4 In. 20.00
Yellow, Figurine, Donkey . . . . .165.00 to 325.00
Yellow, Figurine, Duck 125.00
Yellow, Figurine, Fish 250.00
Yellow, Figurine, Lamb 50.00
Yellow, Figurine, Penguin 90.00
Yellow, Marmalade, Cover 50.00
Yellow, Plate, 9 In. 13.00

HATPIN collectors search for pins popular from 1860 to 1920. The long
pin, often over four inches, was used to hold the hat in place on the
hair. The tops of the pins were made of all materials, from solid gold
and real gemstones to ceramics and glass. Be careful to buy original
hatpins and not recent pieces made by altering old buttons.

Black Glass, Intricate Design, c.1905 . . . . 49.00
Celluloid, Black, Faceted, c.1910 . . . . 19.00
Coin, Egyptian Woman 125.00
Crystal, Green, Gold Tone Molding, Victorian 85.00
Edwardian, White Glass, Set In Brass 15.00
Flower, Black, Gold Highlights, Steel 85.00
Flower, Blue, Plastic, Molded 75.00
Peacock Eye, Filigree, Conical Shape, c.1900 . . . . 95.00
Rhinestone, Floral, Chaton Cut 105.00
Rhinestones, Steel 135.00
Rose, Brass, Victorian 110.00
Sequins, Black 65.00
Shell, Metal 65.00

HATPIN HOLDERS were needed when hatpins were fashionable from 1860 to 1920. The large, heavy hat required special long-shanked pins to hold it in place. The hatpin holder resembles a large saltshaker, but it often has no opening at the bottom as a shaker does. Hatpin holders were made of all types of ceramics and metal. Look for other pieces under the names of specific manufacturers.

Black Lines, Multicolored Flowers, Yellow Band At Top, 4 3/4 In.	75.00
Peacock Form, Pierced Tail Silver Leaves & Flowers, Eagle Handles, 8 1/2 In.	1150.00
Porcelain, Holds 20 Pins, RS Germany, 4 1/2 In.	295.00

HAVILAND china has been made in Limoges, France, since 1842. The factory was started by the Haviland Brothers of New York City. Pieces are marked *H & Co., Haviland & Co.,* or *Theodore Haviland.* It is possible to match existing sets of dishes through dealers who specialize in Haviland china. Other factories worked in the town of Limoges making a similar chinaware. These porcelains are listed in this book under Limoges.

HAVILAND & CO.

Bowl, Blue Garland Design, White Roses, Footed, Germany	31.00
Charger, Cupid Whispering In Psyche's Ear, Shaped Rim, Marked, 17 5/8 In.	805.00
Cup & Saucer, Pasadena, Gold Trim	10.00
Cup & Saucer, White	10.00
Dish, Blue, White, Cobalt Blue Flowers, 9 In.	37.00
Plate, Light Pink, Dark Pink Flowers, Green Branches, 9 1/2 In.	16.00
Plate, Light Pink, Dark Pink Flowers, Scalloped Edge, 7 1/2 In.	10.00
Tea Set, Rope & Anchor, Transfer Print, Hand Tinted, Blossoms, 3 Piece	80.00

HAWKES cut glass was made by T. G. Hawkes & Company of Corning, New York, founded in 1880. The firm cut glass blanks made at other glassworks until 1962. Many pieces are marked with the trademark, a trefoil ring enclosing a fleur-de-lis and two hawks. Cut glass by other manufacturers is listed under either the factory name or in the general Cut Glass category.

Basket, Marquis, Signed, 8 1/4 x 7 1/4 In.	690.00
Bowl, Gladys, 8 In., Pair	495.00
Bowl, Iris, 6 x 8 In.	2450.00
Bowl, Queen's, 4 1/4 x 10 1/2 In.	3450.00
Candy Jar, Cover, Engraved Floral & Ribbon Design, Clear, Signed, 10 In.	125.00
Compote, Iridescent, Frosty Ground, Signed, 5 x 7 1/4 In.	315.00
Compote, Iris, Fruit, Gravic, Signed	550.00
Decanter, Flute, Cut Stopper, 7 In.	350.00
Decanter, Gladys, Faceted Stopper, 11 In.	550.00
Decanter, Gold, Amber, Portrait Of Don Quixote, Eagle Padlock, Signed, 8 3/4 In.	196.00
Decanter, Ship's, Gladys, 7 x 6 1/2 In.	850.00
Decanter, Whiskey, Engraved Thistle, Metal Jigger Cap, Signed, 11 In.	456.00
Decanter, Whiskey, Golf Scene, The 19th Hole, 1900, 12 In.	335.00
Pitcher, Diamond & Fan, 8 3/4 In.	330.00
Plate, Intaglio Flowers, Basketweave Base, 8 1/2 In., Pair	3500.00
Plate, Verre De Soie, Engraved, Bow & Swag, 8 In.	115.00
Vase, 3 Mallard Ducks In Flight, Cut Bands, Puntys, Signed, 9 3/4 x 6 1/2 In.	950.00
Vase, Cut Bands, Wheel Cut Flowers, Tapering Form, 18 In.	315.00
Vase, Cylindrical, Engraved Scalloped Rim, Rose & Bud On Body, 1910s, 10 1/2 In.	345.00
Vase, Flared Top, Engraved Flowers At Base & Body, Footed, 9 3/4 In.	260.00
Vase, Prism Fans, Cane & Hobstars, Rainbow Rays, Signed, 6 1/4 x 8 In.	335.00
Vase, Queen's, 13 3/4 In.	1690.00
Vase, Queen's, Faceted Knop, Footed, 12 In.	1195.00
Vase, Teutonic Easter, Signed, 5 1/4 In.	825.00

HEAD VASES, generally showing a woman from the shoulders up, were used by florists primarily in the 1950s and 1960s. Made in a variety of sizes and often decorated with imitation jewelry and other lifelike accessories, the vases were manufactured in Japan and the U.S.A. Less elaborate examples were made as early as the 1930s. Religious themes, babies, and animals are also common subjects. Other head vases are listed under manufacturers' names and can be located through the index at the back of this book.

Baby, Blue Bonnet, Lace, Blue Bib, Ucagco, 6 In.	40.00
Baby, White Bonnet, Napco, 5 1/2 In.	55.00
Glamour Girl, Rose Colored Dress, Large Yellow Rose At Neck, 4 x 7 In.	40.00
Glamour Girl, White Trim, Gold, 1950, 4 1/2 In.	35.00
Jackie Kennedy, Inarco, 6 In.	375.00
Orange Bonnet, Bow, Napco, 5 1/4 In.	28.00
Pearl Earrings, Dangling, Necklace, Napcoware, 5 x 7 In.	125.00
Pearl Necklace, Bangs, Gold Tim, 5 1/2 In.	85.00
Teenager, Sunglasses, 7 In.	1650.00
Valerie, 6 1/4 In.	450.00

HEDI SCHOOP Art Creations, North Hollywood, California, started about 1945 and was working until 1954. Schoop made ceramic figurines, lamps, planters, and tablewares.

*Hedi Schoop
S*

Bowl, Pink & Gold, Large	30.00
Dish, White Snow Flower On Branch, Signed, Ca., 5 1/2 x 7 1/2 In.	15.00
Figurine, Cal, Dramatic Dancer, Black, Yellows, 13 1/4 In.	50.00
Figurine, Lady & Her Poodle Carrying Basket, Black Dress, 10 In.	205.00
Figurine, Marguerita, Pale Blue Skirt, Pale Purple Flower, 12 1/2 In.	80.00
Figurine, Oriental With Umbrella, Pink & Mauve, Gold Trim, 12 In.	135.00
Figurine, Oriental, White, Black, Gold, Red, Pink, 12 x 6 x 4 1/2 In.	40.00
Figurine, Peasant Girl Twirling, Dusty Rose Dress, Dark Lavender, 10 x 9 In.	56.00
Figurine, Woman With Flowing Skirt, Mauve, Brown, Green, 10 x 13 In.	120.00
Lamp, Comedy & Tragedy, White Paint, Gold	200.00
Planter, Clown Resting, Light Pink, Gold Stippling, 10 1/4 In.	150.00
Planter, Lady With Parasol, 12 In., Pair	127.00
Planter, Lady With Parasol, Green Flowers, Brown Spatter, 10 1/2 In.	50.00
Planter, Peasant Girl, Blue, White Dress, Basket On Head, 12 1/4 In.	60.00
Planter, Peasant Girl, Green Matte Dress, Matte, 13 In.	205.00
Planter, Woman Holding Vase, Purple Dress, 12 1/2 In.	150.00
Tray, Appetizer, Blue & Green Stripes, Woman Holding Up Her Arms, 13 x 10 In.	90.00
Vase, Figural, Pink, Blue Dress, Woman Holding Basket Of Flowers, 6 3/4 In.	26.00

HEINTZ ART Metal Shop made jewelry, copper, silver, and brass in Buffalo, New York, from 1906 to 1935, when a new company name was taken and the mark became *Silvercrest*. The most popular items with collectors today are the copper desk sets and vases made with applied silver designs.

Box, Cigarette, Golfer, Silver On Bronze, 3 x 3 1/2 In.	805.00
Candlestick, Branches & Berries, Copper, 10 1/2 In., Pair	315.00
Candlestick, Geometric Design, Silver On Bronze, Stamped, 11 1/2 In., Pair	505.00
Compote, Birds Perched On A Branch, Copper, 5 x 6 1/2 In.	230.00
Desk Set, Pine Bough Design, Silver On Bronze, Dark Patina	310.00
Humidor, Golfer Teeing Off, Silver On Bronze, 6 In.	360.00
Humidor, Stylized Pattern, Bronze, Patina, Stamped, 5 1/2 x 7 In.	625.00
Lamp, Boudoir, Stylized Geometric Design, Bell Shade, 10 1/4 In.	956.00
Lamp, Mushroom Shade With Leaf Design, Silver On Bronze, 15 x 14 In.	1240.00
Loving Cup, Arts & Crafts, Greek Key, Overlay, Angled Handles, 8 In.	345.00
Paper Clip, Stylized Mushrooms, Silver On Bronze, 3 1/2 x 2 In.	305.00
Plate, Pink Poppies, Bronze, Patina, 6 In.	175.00
Tray, Tulip, Scalloped Edges, Silver On Bronze, Patina, 16 1/2 x 11 In.	690.00
Trophy, Interfraternity Track Meet, Tufts College, March 27, 1926, 9 1/8 In.	110.00
Trophy Cup, Rockford Country Club, 1913, Olive, Nickel Plated Interior, 7 1/2 In.	138.00
Vase, Bouquet Of Poppies, Bronze, Patina, Stamped, 10 In.	1265.00
Vase, Daffodil, Silver On Bronze, 6 1/2 In.	286.00
Vase, Daffodils, Pinched Waist, Silver On Bronze, Stamped, 14 3/4 In.	1150.00
Vase, Daffodils, Silver On Bronze, Stamped, 12 In.	825.00
Vase, Flowering Branch, Silver On Bronze, Dark Patina, 8 x 3 1/2 In.	500.00
Vase, Flowers, Dark Brown Patina, 8 In.	345.00
Vase, Flowers, Stamped, 12 In.	440.00
Vase, Goldenrod, Silver On Bronze, Stamped, 12 1/2 In.	805.00

Vase, Landscape Scene, Windmill, Silver On Bronze, 1911, 12 x 5 In. 805.00
Vase, Peacock, Perched On A Branch, Silver On Bronze, 1912, 9 In. 316.00
Vase, Poppies, Silver On Bronze, Verdigris Patina, 12 1/4 x 5 In. 805.00
Vase, Single Rose, Copper, 5 In. 200.00
Vase, Stylized Cattails, Silver On Bronze, Stamped, 10 1/8 In. 495.00
Vase, Wild Roses, Copper, 8 1/4 In. 259.00

HEISEY glass was made from 1896 to 1957 in Newark, Ohio, by A. H. Heisey and Co., Inc. The Imperial Glass Company of Bellaire, Ohio, bought some of the molds and the rights to the trademark. Some Heisey patterns have been made by Imperial since 1960. After 1968, they stopped using the *H* trademark. Heisey used romantic names for colors, such as *Sahara*. Do not confuse color and pattern names. The Custard Glass and Ruby Glass categories may also include some Heisey pieces.

Animal, Colt, Kicking 220.00
Animal, Colt, Standing .... .95.00 to 140.00
Animal, Goose, Wings Half 95.00
Animal, Goose, Wings Up 95.00
Animal, Mallard, Wings Half 125.00
Animal, Mallard, Wings Up 145.00
Animal, Rooster, Fighting, 8 In. 145.00
Animal, Sparrow 100.00
Banded Flute, Jar, Horseradish 150.00
Banded Flute, Toothpick 115.00
Beaded Swag, Butter, Cover, Opal 225.00
Beaded Swag, Spooner, Enameled Cornflower, Opal 125.00
Beaded Swag, Sugar, Cover, Opal 175.00
Chintz, Sugar, Dolphin Footed, Sahara 50.00
Colonial, Hair Receiver 125.00
Colonial, Jar, Lavender, Footed, 4 1/2 Oz. 80.00
Colonial, Pitcher, 24 Oz. 40.00
Colonial, Sherbet, 6 Oz. 20.00
Colonial, Sherbet, Scalloped, Tall, 4 1/2 Oz. 35.00
Colonial, Spooner 75.00
Continental, Toothpick 60.00
Crystolite, Cup & Saucer 25.00
Crystolite, Goblet, 10 Oz. 35.00
Crystolite, Plate, 2 Handles, 7 In. 20.00
Crystolite, Plate, 7 In. 15.00
Crystolite, Relish, Leaf Handle, 9 In. 25.00
Crystolite, Sandwich Server, Center Handle, 11 In. 20.00
Crystolite, Sherbet, 6 Oz. 15.00
Cut Block, Sugar, Ivorina Verde Individual 85.00
Empress, Bowl, Floral, Hale, 3 1/2 In. 25.00
Empress, Ice Bucket, Handle, Club Drinking Scene Etch 230.00
Empress, Ice Tub, Moongleam Antartic Etch, Silver Plated Handle 165.00
Empress, Plate, Sahara, Square, 8 In. .... .22.00 to 35.00
Empress, Plate, Tangerine, 7 In. 165.00
Empress, Sherbet, Sahara, 6 Oz. 30.00
Empress, Vase, Ivy, Tangerine, 4 In. 275.00
Fancy Loop, Toothpick, Emerald Green 55.00
Fandango, Punch Cup 30.00
Fish, Bookends 145.00
Flat Panel, Jar, Lavender, 6 Oz. 50.00
Flat Panel, Knife Rest 60.00
Fox Chase, Cocktail, Alibi, 3 Oz. 35.00
Greek Key, Banana Split, Footed 30.00
Greek Key, Celery Dish, Oval, 12 In. 65.00
Greek Key, Punch Cup 21.00
Ipswich, Plate, Square, Sahara, 8 In. 60.00
Ipswich, Saucer 25.00

Ipswich, Sherbet, Sahara, 4 Oz. 35.00
Jamestown, Cordial, Barcelona Cutting, 1 Oz. 30.00
Lariat, Candy Dish, Cover, 7 In. 95.00
Lariat, Coaster, 4 In. 12.00
Lariat, Cup & Saucer 25.00
Lariat, Goblet, 10 Oz. 22.00
Lariat, Plate, 8 In. 22.00
Lariat, Punch Bowl, Ladle 190.00
Lariat, Punch Cup 6.00
Lariat, Relish, 3 Sections, 12 In. 28.00
Lariat, Relish, 3 Sections, 2 Handles, 11 In. ....24.00 to 36.00
Lariat, Sugar & Creamer 15.00
Locket On Chair, Cake Stand, 9 1/2 In. 210.00
Narrow Flute, Eggcup 5.00
Narrow Flute, Nut Dish 10.00
Narrow Flute, Parfait, 4 1/2 Oz. 30.00
Narrow Flute, Tumbler, Soda, Handle, 12 Oz. 40.00
New Era, Candlestick, 2-Light 100.00
New Era, Cocktail, 3 1/2 Oz. 25.00
Octagon, Ice Tub, Flamingo, Metal Handle 125.00
Octagon, Soup, Dish, Flamingo, 8 1/4 In. 9.00
Old Colony, Creamer, Dolphin Footed, Sahara 45.00
Old Colony, Cup & Saucer, Sahara, Footed 40.00
Old Colony, Sherbet, Sahara, 6 Oz. 22.00
Old Colony, Tumbler, Whiskey, Footed, Sahara, 2 Oz. 24.00
Old Dominion, Cocktail, Marigold, 3 Oz. 20.00
Old Dominion, Sherbet, Marigold, 6 Oz. 18.00
Old Glory, Goblet, Windsor Cutting, 9 Oz. 30.00
Old Sandwich, Cup & Saucer, Sahara 95.00
Old Williamsburg, Candelabrum, 3-Light, Bobeches, 15 1/2 In. 180.00
Old Williamsburg, Candelabrum, 3-Light, Sahara, 15 1/2 In., Pair 1375.00
Old Williamsburg, Sugar & Creamer, Amber Stain 20.00
Orchid Etch, Bowl, Gardenia, 9 In. 60.00
Orchid Etch, Candlestick, 2-Light, 5 In., Pair 99.00
Orchid Etch, Candlestick, Pair 60.00
Orchid Etch, Celery Dish, 12 In. 55.00
Orchid Etch, Champagne, 6 Oz., 6 In. ....25.00 to 30.00
Orchid Etch, Cocktail Shaker, 1 Pt. 275.00
Orchid Etch, Cocktail, 4 Oz. ....38.00 to 40.00
Orchid Etch, Compote 6.00
Orchid Etch, Compote, Waverly, 5 1/2 In. 90.00
Orchid Etch, Creamer, Waverly, Individual 35.00
Orchid Etch, Cup & Saucer, Waverly 55.00
Orchid Etch, Dish, Mayonnaise 56.00
Orchid Etch, Goblet, 10 Oz. 50.00
Orchid Etch, Goblet, Wine, 3 Oz., 5 1/8 In. 85.00
Orchid Etch, Relish, Waverly, 3 Sections, Oval, 11 In. 70.00
Orchid Etch, Salt & Pepper, Waverly 75.00
Orchid Etch, Sandwich Server, Center Handle, 12 In. 135.00
Orchid Etch, Sherbet, 6 Oz., 4 In. 30.00
Orchid Etch, Sugar 39.00
Orchid Etch, Sugar & Creamer 60.00
Orchid Etch, Sugar & Creamer, Individual 70.00
Orchid Etch, Sugar, Waverly, Individual 35.00
Orchid Etch, Tumbler, Iced Tea, 12 Oz., 8 1/4 In. ....50.00 to 65.00
Orchid Etch, Tumbler, Juice, Footed, 5 Oz., 5 1/2 In. ....55.00 to 58.00
Orchid Etch, Vase, Violet, 4 In. ....135.00 to 165.00
Orchid Etch, Wine, Tyrolean, 3 Oz. 50.00
Paneled Cane, Toothpick 50.00
Peerless, Saucer, 5 In. 15.00
Picket, No. 458, Basket, Engraved Flowers, 10 3/4 In. 100.00
Pied Piper, Pitcher, Footed, 13 1/2 In. 500.00

Plantation, Bottle, Oil, Stopper, 3 Oz.	80.00
Plantation, Bottle, Oil, Stopper, Etched, Stripes, 3 Oz.	175.00
Plantation, Coaster	70.00
Plantation, Goblet, 10 Oz.	80.00
Plantation, Goblet, Ivy Etch, 10 Oz.	57.00
Plantation, Plate, 8 In.	32.00
Plantation, Plate, Ivy Etch, 8 In.	38.00
Plantation, Relish, 3 Sections, 11 In.	58.00
Plantation, Salt & Pepper	85.00
Plantation, Tumbler, Iced Tea, Footed, Ivy Etch, 12 Oz.	85.00
Plantation, Tumbler, Juice, Footed, Ivy Etch, 5 Oz.	48.00
Prince Of Wales Plumes, Bowl, Oval, 12 In.	75.00
Prince Of Wales Plumes, Toothpick	100.00
Priscilla, Toothpick	20.00
Priscilla, Toothpick, Silver Overlay	65.00
Prison Stripes, Toothpick	200.00
Provincial, Tumbler, Footed, 8 Oz.	15.00
Provincial, Tumbler, Juice, Footed, 5 Oz.	11.00
Queen Ann, Bowl, Everglades, Cutting, 7 In.	100.00
Queen Ann, Toothpick	450.00
Recessed Panel, Basket, 9 In.	225.00
Ridgeleigh, Ashtray, Individual	3.00
Ridgeleigh, Creamer	30.00
Ridgeleigh, Creamer, Individual	20.00
Rose Etch, Butter, 1/4 Lb.	90.00
Rose Etch, Champagne, 6 Oz.	40.00
Rose Etch, Compote, 6 1/2 In.	55.00
Rose Etch, Compote, Cordial, 1 Oz.	175.00
Rose Etch, Compote, Oval	130.00
Rose Etch, Cordial, 1 Oz.	150.00
Rose Etch, Creamer, Individual	40.00
Rose Etch, Goblet, 9 Oz.	50.00
Rose Etch, Pitcher, 76 Oz.	695.00
Rose Etch, Plate, 7 In.	30.00
Rose Etch, Plate, 8 In.	40.00
Rose Etch, Plate, Sandwich Server, Center Handle	219.00
Rose Etch, Plate, Waverly, 8 In.	33.00
Rose Etch, Relish, 3 Sections, Oval, 11 In.	75.00
Rose Etch, Saucer Champagne, 6 Oz.	35.00
Rose Etch, Sugar & Creamer	60.00
Rose Etch, Sugar, Individual	40.00
Rose Etch, Torte Plate, 14 In.	99.00
Sawtooth Band, Nappy	10.00
Sunburst, Nappy, Tricornered	30.00
Town & Country, Plate, With Insert, Dawn, 7 1/4 In.	15.00
Town & Country, Tumbler, Iced Tea, Dawn, 13 Oz., 5 1/4 In.	40.00
Twentieth Century, Sherbet, Dawn, 6 Oz.	35.00
Twist, Console Set, Flamingo, 2-In. Candlestick, 3 Piece	165.00
Twist, Ice Bucket, Flamingo	195.00
Victorian, Goblet, 2-Ball Stem, 9 Oz.	26.00
Victorian, Sherbet, 2-Ball Stem, 9 Oz.	15.00
Waverly, Compote, 6 1/2 In.	25.00
Waverly, Cup	12.00
Waverly, Cup & Saucer	20.00
Waverly, Relish, 4 Sections, 9 In.	95.00
Whirlpool, Torte Plate, 13 1/2 In.	15.00
Whirlpool, Torte Plate, 15 In.	10.00
Williamsburg, Sherbet, 6 Oz.	20.00
Yeoman, Parfait, 5 1/2 Oz.	9.00
Yeoman, Sandwich Server, Center Handle, 10 1/2 In.	25.00
Zodiac, Bowl, Footed, 11 In.	38.00
Zodiac, Candy Dish, Cover, Footed	85.00
Zodiac, Salt & Pepper, Amber Stain, 4 In.	25.00

HEREND, see Fischer category.

HEUBACH is the collector's name for Gebruder Heubach, a firm working in Lichten, Germany, from 1840 to 1925. It is best known for bisque dolls and doll heads, their principal products. They also manufactured bisque figurines, including piano babies, beginning in the 1880s, and glazed figurines in the 1900s. Piano babies are listed in their own category. Dolls are included in the Doll category under *Gebruder Heubach* and *Heubach*. Another factory, Ernst Heubach, working in Koppelsdorf, Germany, also made porcelain and dolls. These will also be found in the Doll category under Heubach Koppelsdorf.

Figurine, Baby, Cream Nightgown, Pink Ribbon, Arms Raised Over Head, 10 1/2 In.	1025.00
Figurine, Baby, Flower Girl, Blue Bonnet, Flowered Dress, Intaglio Eyes, 7 3/4 In	975.00
Figurine, Baby, Intaglio Eyes, Beaded Enamel, Gold Trim, 12 In.	1325.00
Figurine, Girl, Reading Book, Holding Basket Of Flowers, Biscuit, 12 1/2 In.	238.00
Vase, Bulbous, Silver Overlay, Green Mark, Germany, 3 3/4 In.	515.00
Vase, Snowy Scene, Wooded Area Surrounding A Small Lake, Blue, 5 In.	101.00

HIGBEE glass was made by the J. B. Higbee Company of Bridgeville, Pennsylvania, about 1900. Tablewares were made, and it is possible to assemble a full set of dishes and goblets in some Higbee patterns. Most of the glass was clear, not colored. Additional pieces may be found in the Pressed Glass category by pattern name.

Celery Dish, Fleur-De-Lis, 2 Handles	45.00

HISTORIC BLUE, see factory names, such as Adams, Clews, Ridgway, and Staffordshire.

HOBNAIL glass is a style of glass with bumps all over. Dozens of hobnail patterns and variants have been made. Clear, colored, and opalescent hobnail have been made and are being reproduced. Other pieces of hobnail may also be listed in the Duncan & Miller and Fenton categories.

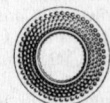

Biscuit Jar, Silver Cover, Green, England	100.00
Creamer, Vaseline, 4 In.	68.00
Cruet, Canary Yellow, Hobbs, Brockunier & Co., 7 3/4 In.	200.00
Goblet, Wine, 3 Oz.	7.00
Ivy Ball, 7 1/2 In.	35.00
Jar, Cover, Opalescent, 5 1/2 In.	43.50
Pitcher, Cranberry, Ruffled Rim, Clear Handle, Hobbs, Brockunier & Co., 4 1/4 In.	63.00
Pitcher, Milk, 18 Oz.	22.00
Pitcher, Opalescent, Footed, Hobbs, Brockunier & Co., 5 1/2 In.	51.00
Pitcher, Opalescent, Ribbed Handle, Square Mouth, 6 5/8 In.	350.00
Plate, Luncheon, 8 In.	4.00
Plate, Sherbet, 6 In.	3.00
Saltshaker, Green, Bulbous, Flat, 2 1/4 In.	64.00
Sugar, Cranberry, Ruffled Rim, Hobbs, Brockunier & Co., 2 7/8 In.	53.00
Vase, Amethyst, Swirled & Double Crimped Top, 8 In.	30.00

HOCHST, or Hoechst, porcelain was made in Germany from 1746 to 1796. It was marked with a six-spoke wheel. Be careful when buying Hochst; many other firms have used a very similar wheel-shaped mark.

Dish, Leaf Shape, Purple, Gold Flowers, Gold Trim, 7 1/2 x 6 In.	10.00
Figurine, Colonial Boy Teasing Girl, 5 1/4 In.	432.00
Figurine, Young Girl, In Floppy Hat, Pink, Rose Glaze, Dark Blue Underglaze, 5 1/2 In. . .	95.00

HOLLY AMBER, or golden agate, glass was made by the Indiana Tumbler and Goblet Company of Greentown, Indiana, from January 1, 1903, to June 13, 1903. It is a pressed glass pattern featuring holly leaves in the amber-shaded glass. The glass was made with shadings that range from creamy opalescent to brown-amber.

Vase, 6 In.	500.00

Holt-Howard,
Candle Hugger,
Snowman, Gold
Label, 3 In.

Put a small rug or drop cloth
under a piece of furniture to
move it. Pull the rug to slide the
furniture across the room. This
protects the furniture and the
wooden floor. This works well on
hard surfaces, but don't try it
over high pile carpet.

HOLT-HOWARD was an importer who started working in 1949 in Stamford, Connecticut. He sold many types of table accessories, such as condiment jars, decanters, spoon holders, and saltshakers. The figures shown on some of his pieces had a cartoon-like quality. The company was bought out by General Housewares Corporation in 1969. Holt-Howard pieces are often marked with the name and the year or *HH* and the year stamped in black. There was also a black and silver label.

Bank, Bobbing Clown, 6 1/2 In.	86.00
Candle Hugger, Snowman, Gold Label, 3 In. ....*Illus*	20.00
Candleholder, 3-Light, 3 Easter Bunnies, Each Holding Candle, 7 7/8 In.	91.00
Candlestick, Christmas Camel, 1960	15.00
Christmas Tree, Green Foil, Glass Beaded Ornaments, Gold Glitter Base, Box	51.00
Dessert Set, 2 Watermelon Bowls, 2 Canteloupe Bowls, 1959	25.00
Egg Plate, Pink Roses, Blue & Yellow Daisies, 6 Wells, 8 In.	50.00
Eggcup, Cog Rouge, Rooster	42.00
Instant Coffee Jar, Pixie Cover	250.00
Jam Jar, Pixie, Cover	80.00
Jar, Olive, Jeeves, Butler	250.00
Ketchup Jar, Pixieware, 4 1/2 In.	85.00
Mug, Cog Rouge, Rooster	11.00
Mustard Jar, Pixieware, 4 1/2 In. ....73.00 to	160.00
Napkin Doll, Sunbonnet Miss, Yellow Dress, 1958, 5 In.	95.00
Olive Jar, Pixieware, 1958 ....85.00 to	96.00
Pin Box, Kozy Kitty, Measuring Tape Tongue, 1959, 3 x 2 In.	40.00
Planter, White Bull, Black Details, Metal Nose Ring, 1960, 7 x 6 In.	23.00
Puff Box, Daisy Dorable, 2 3/4 In.	131.00
Relish Jar, Pixieware, 1959, 4 1/2 In.	225.00
Saccharin Holder, Girl, 2 3/4 In.	100.00
Salt & Pepper, Chattercoons, Noisemaker In Base, 4 3/4 In. ....*Illus*	30.00
Salt & Pepper, Kozy Kitten, 1961, 4 In.	10.50

Holt-Howard, Salt & Pepper, Chattercoons,
Noisemaker In Base, 4 3/4 In.

Holt-Howard, Salt & Pepper, Moo Cow, Noisemaker
In Base, 3 1/2 In.

Salt & Pepper, Moo Cow, Noisemaker In Base, 3 1/2 In. ....*Illus*   50.00
Salt & Pepper, Pixieware 405.00
Salt & Pepper, Santa, 1960 ....   5.00
Sugar & Creamer, Pixieware, 1958 ....   150.00
Vase, Lady Head, Dangling Christmas Ball Earrings, Sprig Of Poinsettia 75.00
Wall Pocket, Fishing Creel Basket, 5 1/4 In. 10.50
Wall Pocket, Pheasant, 1958, 6 1/4 x 4 3/4 In., Pair 56.00

HOPALONG CASSIDY was a character in a series of twenty-eight books
written by Clarence E. Milford, first published in 1907. Movies and
television shows were made based on the character. The best-known
actor playing Hopalong Cassidy was William Lawrence Boyd. His
first movie appearance was in 1919, but the first Hopalong Cassidy
film was not until 1934. Sixty-six films were made. In 1948, William
Boyd purchased the television rights to the movies, then later made
fifty-two new programs. In the 1950s, Hopalong Cassidy and his
horse, named *Topper*, were seen in comics, records, toys, and other
products. Boyd died in 1972.

Autograph Book, Horseshoe On Cover, School Days Memories 75.00
Book, America's Greatest Tuna, Chicken Of The Sea, 20 Pages, 11 x 14 In. 175.00
Button, Pinback, Hoppy Bust, Ribbon, Tin Cowboy Boot, c.1950, 1 1/4 In. 37.00
Canasta Set, Score Sheets, Plastic Saddle, Box 275.00
Chaps, 1950s 225.00
Coloring Book 100.00
Cowboy Outfit, Hat & Metal Pin, Black, White Accents 525.00
Frontier Set, 3-D Stagecoach, Buildings, Figures, Box, Milton Bradley, 1950 ....   330.00
Game, Lasso 260.00
Game, Shooting Gallery, Box 350.00
Game, Target, 2 Guns, 4 Darts, Stand, Marx, 27 In. ....175.00 to 375.00
Game, Toss 425.00
Gum Card, 5 Cent, Save 'Em Trade 'Em 40.00
Knife, Trail, With Can Opener Blade, Pocket 85.00
Label, Bread, Mary Jane 40.00
Label, Bread, Sunbeam, Hoppy's Favorite 40.00
Laundry Bag, Allover Print 450.00
Lobby Card, Diablo Anda Suelto, Mexico 24.00
Lunch Box, Aladdin, 1954 ....   145.00
Lunch Box, Metal, Thermos, Aladdin, 1950 ....   290.00
Magazine, Argosy, Hopalong Cassidy's Pal, May 2, 1925 ....   65.00
Neckerchief, Metal Slide, Steer Head 27.00
Night-Light, Bullet Form, Decal Of Hopalong Cassidy, Aladdin 475.00
Night-Light, Gun In Holster, Aladdin 205.00
Pennant, Hopalong Cassidy With Cole Bros. Circus 25.00
Pin, Mirror, Hoppy & Topper, Green, Mirror On Back, 2 In. 12.00
Plate, Hoppy Picture 125.00
Puzzle 45.00
Radio, Black, 8 1/2 In. 650.00
Radio, Silver, Black, Steel, Arvin, 8 In. 345.00
Rifle, Winchester Model 94, 30-30 ....   1800.00
Shirt, Black Corduroy, Size 12 ....   285.00
Shirt, Polo, Yellow, Hoppy Pictures 150.00
Spurs, Box 250.00
Thermos, Aladdin 50.00
Toy, View-Master, Hopalong Cassidy & Topper, 1950 ....   8.50
Toy, View-Master, Hopalong Cassidy In The Cattle Rustler, 1953 ....   13.00
Wristwatch, 100th Anniversary, Battery Operated, Box 145.00
Wristwatch, 1940 ....   150.00

HOWARD PIERCE has been working in Southern California since 1936.
In 1945, he opened a pottery in Claremont. His contemporary-looking
figurines are popular with collectors. Pieces are marked with his name.
He stopped making pottery in 1991.

Figurine, 2 Owls On Branch, Light Gray Glaze, Brown, Signed, 13 In. 75.00

Figurine, Bear, Mother, Stamped, 3 x 6 1/2 In.	50.00
Figurine, Beavers, 4 3/4 x 4 In., Pair	115.00
Figurine, Bird, Black Chest, Beak, Eyes, Gray Speckled Back, 7 In.	30.00
Figurine, Bird, Whistle, Brown Glaze, White Speckled Chest, 1950, 2 3/4 x 2 In.	80.00
Figurine, Black Native Couple, 7 1/2 In.	100.00
Figurine, Brown Bear, Mother & Cub, 3 x 6 1/2 In. & 2 3/4 x 2 In.	30.00
Figurine, Bust, African Queen, Brown Glaze, 3 1/2 x 2 3/4 In.	15.00
Figurine, Bust, Female, 1950s	480.00
Figurine, Chipmunk, Dark Brown, White Stripes, White Chest, 5 x 4 In.	70.00
Figurine, Deer, Gloss Finish, Marked, 5 1/2 In.	65.00
Figurine, Dove, Blue Glaze, Cream Color Chest, 6 1/2 x 4 1/4 In.	100.00
Figurine, Ducks, Mother & 2 Babies, Swimming, Marked, 3 Piece	90.00
Figurine, Giraffe Family, 11 1/2, 9 1/2, 5 1/2 In., 3 Piece	185.00
Figurine, Girl, With Bowls, 9 x 3 1/2 In.	65.00
Figurine, Horse, Rich Brown, Speckled Brown, Tan Mane, Tail, 8 1/2 x 7 In.	380.00
Figurine, Madonna & Child, Marked, 7 3/4 In.	50.00
Figurine, Mountain Sheep Ram On Base, Brown, Beige, White, 7 x 3 In.	230.00
Figurine, Quail Family, Mother & 2 Chicks, 5 1/4 In., 3 Piece	15.00
Figurine, Rabbits, Porcelain, 7 1/2 x 4 In., Pair	105.00
Figurine, Roadrunner, 12 In.	60.00
Figurine, Squirrel, Holding Acorn, Gray & Brown, 5 1/2 In.	80.00
Figurine, St. Francis Of Assisi, Holding Bird, Gray, Rope Belt, Marked, 12 In.	190.00
Flower Frog, 2 Owls, Small Tree, Stamped, 7 1/2 In.	90.00
Flower Frog, Owl Shape, On Rock, 5 1/4 x 4 In.	45.00

HOWDY DOODY and Buffalo Bob were the main characters in a children's series televised from 1947 to 1960. Howdy was a redheaded puppet. The series became popular with college students in the late 1970s when Buffalo Bob began to lecture on campuses.

Button, It's Howdy Doody Time, Picture, Celluloid, 1 3/4 In.	13.00
Cookie Jar, Howdy, Smiling, 9 3/4 In.	900.00
Cookie Jar, Purinton, 9 3/4 In.	650.00 to 900.00
Costume, With Mask, Box, 1950	100.00
Doll, Sleep Eyes, Effanbee, Box, 23 In.	400.00
Figure, Howdy At Microphone, Mouth Moves, Plastic, Tee Vee, Box, 1950s, 4 In.	115.00
Flashlight, Face Ring	295.00
Lithograph, Bob Smith Playing Piano, Howdy Dancing, Unique Art, 8 In.	800.00
Marionette, Box, Raye Copelan, 15 In.	80.00
Marionette, Howdy, Composition, 16 In.	152.00
Marionette, Mr. Bluster, Composition, 14 In.	322.00
Marionette, Zippy, Composition, Felt Suit, Peter Puppet Playthings, Box, 13 In.	130.00
Ornament, Christmas, Original Package, 5 In.	8.00
Periscope, 1950s	1000.00
Puzzle, Jigsaw, 1950s	985.00
Toy, Band, Windup, Unique Art	1150.00
Toy, Pumpmobile, Windup, Tin, Nylint, 9 In.	385.00
Tumbler, Howdy Shoots Apple Off Clarabell's Head With Arrow, Welch's, 1953	50.00
Window Stencil, Christmas	15.00

HULL pottery was made in Crooksville, Ohio, from 1905. Addis E. Hull bought the Acme Pottery Company and started making ceramic wares. In 1917, A. E. Hull Pottery began making art pottery as well as the commercial wares. For a short time, 1921 to 1929, the firm also sold pottery imported from Europe. The dinnerwares of the 1940s, including the Little Red Riding Hood line, the high gloss artwares of the 1950s, and the matte wares of the 1940s, are all popular with collectors. The firm officially closed in March 1986.

Bluebird, Cuspidor	225.00
Bow Knot, Wall Pocket, Basket, Blue & Green, 6 1/2 In.	100.00
Gingerbread Man, Cookie Jar	80.00 to 195.00
House 'n Garden, Bowl, 5 In.	3.00
House 'n Garden, Bowl, Fruit, 5 1/4 In.	7.00
House 'n Garden, Bowl, Oval, Divided, 11 In.	15.00

House 'n Garden, Butter, Cover, 1/4 Lb. 18.00
House 'n Garden, Casserole, Cover, Handle, Individual, 5 1/4 In. 5.00
House 'n Garden, Coffeepot 20.00
House 'n Garden, Creamer 8.00
House 'n Garden, Cup & Saucer 8.00
House 'n Garden, Gravy Boat, Underplate 30.00
House 'n Garden, Mixing Bowl, 7 In. 12.00
House 'n Garden, Mug, 3 1/2 In. 4.00
House 'n Garden, Plate, 6 1/2 In. 9.00
House 'n Garden, Platter, 11 3/4 In. 29.00
Iris, Vase, Handles, 16 In. 285.00
Little Red Riding Hood, Canister, Cereal .... 900.00 to 995.00
Little Red Riding Hood, Canister, Salt .... 900.00 to 1050.00
Little Red Riding Hood, Cookie Jar, Closed Basket 550.00
Little Red Riding Hood, Cookie Jar, Gold Stars On Apron .... 475.00 to 495.00
Little Red Riding Hood, Cookie Jar, Pin Roses, Gray Leaves 400.00
Little Red Riding Hood, Cookie Jar, Wearing Royal Blue Apron 225.00
Little Red Riding Hood, Match Holder 795.00
Little Red Riding Hood, Salt & Pepper, 5 1/2 In. 165.00
Little Red Riding Hood, Tray, Blue, Round 95.00
Magnolia, Cornucopia, Double 190.00
Magnolia, Tea Set, 3 Piece 220.00
Open Rose, Vase, 12 In. 225.00
Orchid, Vase, Pink & Ivory, Handles, 7 In. 145.00
Parchment & Pine, Basket.16 1/2 In. 120.00
Parchment & Pine, Ewer, 14 1/2 In. 185.00
Rainbow, Mug, Tangerine, Jumbo 21.00
Rainbow, Plate, Green Agate, 10 1/2 In. 5.00
Rosella, Ewer, 11 In. 125.00
Serenade, Basket, Bonbon Type, 6 3/4 In. 95.00
Water Lily, Vase, 10 1/2 In. 155.00
Wildflower, Ewer, 13 1/2 In. 350.00
Woodland, Tea Set, Teapot, Sugar & Creamer, 3 Piece 85.00
Woodland, Vase, 12 1/2 In. 395.00
Woodland, Wall Pocket, 7 1/2 In. .... 93.00 to 110.00

HUMMEL figurines, based on the drawings of the nun M.I. Hummel (Berta Hummel), are made by the W. Goebel Porzellanfabrik of Oeslau, Germany, now Rodenthal, Germany. They were first made in 1935. The *Crown* mark was used from 1935 to 1949. The company added the *bee* marks in 1950. The *full bee* with variations, was used from 1950 to 1959; *stylized bee*, 1957 to 1972; *three line mark*, 1964 to 1972; *last bee*, sometimes called *vee over gee*, 1972 to 1979. In 1979 the V bee symbol was removed from the mark. *U.S. Zone* was part of the mark from 1946 to 1948; *W. Germany*, was part of the mark from 1960 to 1990; The *Goebel, W. Germany* mark, called the *missing bee* mark, was used from 1979 to 1990; *Goebel, Germany* with the crown and WG, originally called the *new mark*, was used from 1991 through part of 1999. The newest version of the bee mark with the word *Goebel*, the *current mark* or *Goebel with full bee*, was adopted in 2000. A special *Year 2000* backstamp was also introduced. Porcelain figures inspired by Berta Hummel's drawings were introduced in 1997. These are marked BH followed by a number. They are made in the Far East, not Germany. Other decorative items and plates that feature Hummel drawings have been made by Schmid Brothers, Inc., since 1971.

Ashtray, No. 114, Let's Sing, Stylized Bee 125.00
Bell, Annual, 1978, Let's Sing .... 50.00 to 100.00
Bell, Annual, 1979, Farewell .... 40.00 to 75.00
Bell, Annual, 1980, Thoughtful 75.00
Bell, Annual, 1984, Mountaineer 125.00
Bell, Annual, 1988, Busy Student 200.00
Bell, Christmas, 1989, Ride Into Christmas 50.00

Bell, Christmas, 1991, Hear Ye, Hear Ye 65.00
Bell, Christmas, 1992, Harmony In Four Parts 75.00
Bell, Christmas, 1993, Celestial Musician 70.00
Bust, No. HU-1, Sister M.I. Hummel, White, Vee Over Gee .... .80.00 to 125.00
Candleholder, No. 24/III, Lullaby, Vee Over Gee 285.00
Candleholder, No. 37, Herald Angels, Stylized Bee 150.00
Candy Box, No. 53, Joyful, Crown Mark 275.00
Figurine, No. 2/0, Little Fiddler, Crown Mark 420.00
Figurine, No. 2/II, Little Fiddler, Full Bee 710.00
Figurine, No. 4, Little Fiddler, Stylized Bee 90.00
Figurine, No. 11/0, Merry Wanderer, Full Bee 180.00
Figurine, No. 11/0, Merry Wanderer, Stylized Bee 110.00
Figurine, No. 12/2/0, Chimney Sweep, Three Line Mark 115.00
Figurine, No. 12/2/0, Chimney Sweep, Vee Over Gee 60.00
Figurine, No. 17/0, Congratulations, New Mark 85.00
Figurine, No. 21/0, Heavenly Angel, Full Bee 207.00
Figurine, No. 23/0, Adoration, Stylized Bee 175.00
Figurine, No. 23/3, Adoration, Crown Mark 900.00
Figurine, No. 23/3, Adoration, Stylized Bee 385.00
Figurine, No. 28/II, Wayside Devotion, Full Bee 375.00
Figurine, No. 47/0, Goose Girl, Vee Over Gee 135.00
Figurine, No. 47/3/0, Goose Girl, Stylized Bee 80.00
Figurine, No. 51/2/0, Village Boy, Full Bee 75.00
Figurine, No. 70, Holy Child, Full Bee 346.00
Figurine, No. 71, Stormy Weather, Full Bee 86.00
Figurine, No. 71, Stormy Weather, Stylized Bee 350.00
Figurine, No. 71, Stormy Weather, Three Line Mark 350.00
Figurine, No. 72, Spring Cheer, Stylized Bee 85.00
Figurine, No. 80, Little Scholar, Stylized Bee 300.00
Figurine, No. 81/0, School Girl, Full Bee 180.00
Figurine, No. 82/0, School Boy, Full Bee .... .100.00 to 350.00
Figurine, No. 82/2/0, School Boy, Stylized Bee 65.00
Figurine, No. 87, For Father, New Mark 125.00
Figurine, No. 97, Trumpet Boy, Stylized Bee 70.00
Figurine, No. 99, Eventide, Stylized Bee 200.00
Figurine, No. 110/0, Let's Sing, Three Line Mark 75.00
Figurine, No. 112/I, Just Resting, Full Bee 150.00
Figurine, No. 112/I, Just Resting, Three Line Mark 163.00
Figurine, No. 119, Postman, Three Line Mark 160.00
Figurine, No. 124/0, Hello, Full Bee 375.00
Figurine, No. 127, Doctor, Stylized Bee 200.00
Figurine, No. 129, Band Leader, Vee Over Gee 105.00
Figurine, No. 129/4/0, Band Leader, Miniature, New Mark 30.00
Figurine, No. 130, Duet, New Mark 110.00
Figurine, No. 130, Duet, Stylized Bee 140.00
Figurine, No. 132, Star Gazer, Stylized Bee 175.00
Figurine, No. 136/V, Friends, Vee Over Gee 650.00
Figurine, No. 141/V, Apple Tree Girl, Vee Over Gee 625.00
Figurine, No. 142/I, Apple Tree Boy, Crown Mark 300.00
Figurine, No. 142/I, Apple Tree Boy, Full Bee 200.00
Figurine, No. 150/0, Happy Days, Full Bee 250.00
Figurine, No. 152/II, Umbrella Girl, Three Line Mark 650.00
Figurine, No. 165, Swaying Lullaby, Last Bee 260.00
Figurine, No. 171, Little Sweeper, Stylized Bee 80.00
Figurine, No. 172/0, Festival Harmony, With Mandolin, Three Line Mark 200.00
Figurine, No. 173, Festival Harmony, With Flute, Full Bee 742.00
Figurine, No. 179, Coquettes, Crown Mark 360.00
Figurine, No. 184, Latest News, Stylized Bee 380.00
Figurine, No. 195/2/0, Barnyard Hero, Stylized Bee 115.00
Figurine, No. 196/0, Telling Her Secret, Stylized Bee 330.00
Figurine, No. 197/2/0, Be Patient, Full Bee 140.00
Figurine, No. 199, Feeding Time, Full Bee 190.00
Figurine, No. 199/0, Feeding Time, Three Line Mark 105.00

Figurine, No. 199/0, Feeding Time, Vee Over Gee 175.00
Figurine, No. 203, Signs Of Spring, Crown Mark 450.00
Figurine, No. 204, Weary Wanderer, Three Line Mark 110.00
Figurine, No. 217, Boy With Toothache, Three Line Mark 105.00
Figurine, No. 218/2/0, Birthday Serenade, Vee Over Gee 78.00
Figurine, No. 226, Mail Is Here, Three Line Mark 400.00
Figurine, No. 238/C, Angel With Trumpet, Stylized Bee 55.00
Figurine, No. 255, Stitch In Time, Three Line Mark 110.00
Figurine, No. 260, Nativity Set, Stable, Vee Over Gee & New Mark, 16 Piece 3500.00
Figurine, No. 261, Angel Duet, Three Line Mark 225.00
Figurine, No. 300, Bird Watcher, Three Line Mark 170.00
Figurine, No. 307, Good Hunting, Three Line Mark 130.00
Figurine, No. 311, Kiss Me, Stylized Bee ....425.00 to 440.00
Figurine, No. 315, Mountaineer, Three Line Mark 100.00
Figurine, No. 317, Not For You, Stylized Bee 425.00
Figurine, No. 319, Doll Bath, Three Line Mark 150.00
Figurine, No. 322, Little Pharmacist, Three Line Mark 188.00
Figurine, No. 331, Crossroads, New Mark ....400.00 to 525.00
Figurine, No. 335/0, Lucky Boy, New Mark 75.00
Figurine, No. 340, Letter To Santa Claus, New Mark 370.00
Figurine, No. 346, Smart Little Sister, Stylized Bee 500.00
Figurine, No. 347, Adventure Bound, New Mark 2500.00
Figurine, No. 353/I, Spring Dance, Vee Over Gee 300.00
Figurine, No. 369, Follow The Leader, New Mark 750.00
Figurine, No. 380, Daisies Don't Tell, Three Line Mark 175.00
Figurine, No. 387, Valentine Gift, New Mark 350.00
Figurine, No. 399, Valentine Boy, Three Line Mark 160.00
Figurine, No. 406, Pleasant Journey, New Mark 1100.00
Figurine, No. 487, Let's Tell The World, New Mark 750.00
Figurine, No. 498, All Smiles, New Mark 105.00
Figurine, No. 539, Good News, New Mark 115.00
Figurine, No. 569, Free Flight, New Mark 115.00
Figurine, No. 649/0, Fascination, New Mark 80.00
Figurine, No. 698, Heart's Delight, New Mark 150.00
Figurine, No. 200/0, Little Goat Herder, Three Line Mark 130.00
Figurine, No. 200/I, Little Goat Herder, Last Bee 270.00
Figurine, No. 2003, Dearly Beloved, New Mark 315.00
Figurine, No. 2074/A, Christmas Gift, New Mark 70.00
Figurine, No. 2077/B, A Flower For You, Current Mark 68.00
Holy Water Font, No. 206, Angel Cloud, Full Bee 125.00
Lamp, No. 227, She Loves Me, She Love Me Not, Three Line Mark 173.00
Plaque, No. 92, Merry Wanderer, Vee Over Gee 100.00
Plaque, No. 93, Little Fiddler, Crown Mark 270.00
Plaque, No. 93, Little Fiddler, Vee Over Gee 100.00
Plaque, No. 139, Flitting Butterfly, Vee Over Gee 60.00
Plaque, No. 187/A, Authorized Dealer, New Mark 85.00
Plaque, No. 310, Searching Angel, Vee Over Gee 165.00
Plaque, No. 323, Merry Christmas, Vee Over Gee 165.00
Plaque, No. 690, Smiling Through, Vee Over Gee ....80.00 to 100.00
Plate, Anniversary, 1975, Stormy Weather ....100.00 to 200.00
Plate, Anniversary, 1980, Ring Around The Rosie 225.00
Plate, Anniversary, 1985, Auf Wiederschen 300.00
Plate, Annual, 1971, Heavenly Angel, Box 275.00
Plate, Annual, 1972, Hear Ye, Hear Ye 35.00
Plate, Annual, 1973, Globe Trotter, Box ....30.00 to 45.00
Plate, Annual, 1975, Ride Into Christmas, Box ....15.00 to 45.00
Plate, Annual, 1976, Apple Tree Girl 125.00
Plate, Annual, 1977, Apple Tree Boy 125.00
Plate, Annual, 1978, Happy Pastime 100.00
Plate, Annual, 1979, Singing Lesson ....45.00 to 100.00
Plate, Annual, 1980, School Girl 100.00
Plate, Annual, 1980, School Girl, Box 150.00
Plate, Annual, 1984, Little Helper 150.00

Plate, Annual, 1985, Chick Girl 150.00
Plate, Annual, 1988, Little Goat Herder 200.00

HUTSCHENREUTHER Porcelain Company of Selb, Germany, was established in 1814 and is still working. The company makes fine quality porcelain dinnerwares and figurines. The mark has changed through the years, but the name and the lion insignia appear in most versions.

Figurine, Dachshund, Standing, Tail Up, 1940s, 5 x 3 1/4 In. 225.00
Figurine, Doe, With Fawn, Whitetail, 10 In. 250.00
Figurine, Falconess, Classical Women Group, Continental, 12 In. 105.00
Figurine, Fox Terrier, Sitting, White, Tan & Black, Red Collar, Germany, 5 1/2 In. 245.00
Figurine, Kneeling Nude Female, Arms Resting On Head, K. Tutter, 20 1/2 In. 690.00
Figurine, Nude, Balancing Ball On Foot, Signed, 8 1/2 In. 825.00
Figurine, Satyr, Carrying Young Woman On His Back, 12 In. 290.00
Figurine, The Musicians, Donkey, Dog, Cat, Rooster, Forms Tower, 7 3/4 In. 200.00
Plaque, General Ulysses S. Grant, Monogram, 1868, 8 1/4 In. 2415.00
Plate, Blossoming Cherry Branch, Gilt Rim, Green, Selb, Germany, 13 In. 10.00
Plate, Flower Girl Of Provence, No. 11435/12750, Edna Hibel, 1977, 13 In. 46.00

ICONS, special, revered pictures of Jesus, Mary, or a saint, are usually Russian or Byzantine. The small icons collected today are made of wood and tin or precious metals. Many modern copies have been made in the old style and are being sold to tourists in Russia and Europe and at shops in the United States.

2 Saints, Silver Appliques, Oil On Board, Russia, 14 3/4 x 10 3/4 In. 165.00
7 Sleepers Of Ephesus, Gilt Incised Ground, c.1890, 12 1/4 x 10 1/2 In. 785.00
Anastasis With Feasts, Resurrection Of Christ, Festivals Of The Church, 15 x 12 In. 9600.00
Archangel, Angel Holding Lily Branch, Halo, Late 19th Century, 12 1/4 x 8 5/8 In. 315.00
Baptism Of Christ By John The Baptist, Carved Wood, 17 In. 1200.00
Bishop Saint, Scenes From Life Of Christ, Russia, 19th Century, 15 3/8 In. 115.00
Bogoliubskaya Mother Of God, Ruler Most Gracious, Russia, c.1800, 14 x 12 In. 1120.00
Head Of Christ, 12 Panels Of Chosen Saints, Gilt Ground, 27 1/2 x 23 In. 520.00
Holy Great Martyr Merkuriya, Painted Panel, Silver Gilt, Repousse Riza, 7 x 6 1/2 In. . . . 1120.00
Holy Mother & Child, Mother-Of-Pearl, Gilt Repousse, Early 20th Century, 8 x 6 In. 1265.00
Holy Prophet Jacob, Shaped Panel, Incised Borders, Russia, c.1890, 48 x 24 In. 1960.00
Host Of Saints, Central Row Of Male & Female Saints, Madonna Inset, 12 1/2 In. 345.00
Iveskaya Mother Of God, Enameled Halo, Russia, 8 1/4 x 7 In. 490.00
Madonna & 3 Saints, Jesus Above, Case, Glass Front, 4 3/8 x 3 5/8 In. 230.00
Madonna & Child, Hammered Brass Top Plate, 4 Evangelists Of Apocalypse, 9 In. 660.00
Madonna & Child, Silver, Brass Top Plate, On Wood, 19th Century, 7 In. 575.00
Madonna & Child, Triptych, Gilt, Russia, 19th Century, 19 1/4 x 21 In. 415.00
Madonna & Child, Wearing Crimson Cowled Robe, Gilt, On Wood, 12 In. 750.00
Mary Queen Of Heaven, Christ Child, Gilt Ground, On Wood, 7 In. 520.00
Mother Of God, Child, Gold Leaf, 19th Century, 16 1/2 x 14 1/2 In. 1440.00
Mother Of Prokov, Mother Of God, Jesus Crucified, Oil On Panel, 2 Board, 20 x 17 In. . . . 345.00
Nativity Of Christ, Inscription Borders, Yaroslav School, c.1800 . . . . 6720.00
Not Made By Hands Image Of God, Russia, 19th Century, 14 x 12 1/4 In. 800.00
Old Testament Trinity, Angels, Prophet, Faux Enameling, c.1900, 12 1/4 x 10 1/2 In. 895.00
Patriarch, Silver Brass Top Plate, 7 In. 460.00
Pentamillion, Main Saint Flanked By 2 Attendant Saints, 19th Century, 7 x 6 In. 170.00
Resurrection & Descent, Figures, Scenes, Repousse, Riza, Enamel, 1800s, 11 x 10 In. 2240.00
Resurrection With Feasts, Russia, 19th Century, 14 x 12 In. 690.00
Saint George, Guardian Angel Border, Venerable Feodosiy, Russia, 1800s, 14 x 12 In. 896.00
Saint Mary Magdalene, Silver Frame, Egg & Dart, St. Petersburg, c.1917, 3 1/2 x 3 In. . . . 1680.00
St. Baselius, Arched Bellflower Top, Corner Birds, Russia, 20 In. 430.00
St. Catherine, Santos, Glass Inset Eyes, Wire Halo, Grasping Wheel, 18th Century, 30 In. . . 460.00
St. John The Theologian, Prokhoros, Lion Symbol, Russia, 14 x 9 1/2 In. 1900.00
St. Michael, Holding Shroud Of Christ, 2 Figures On Each Side, Ural Region, 13 In. 575.00
St. Seraphim Of Sarov, Incised Ground, Borders, Russia, c.1903, 10 1/2 x 8 3/4 In. 390.00
Thangka Of White Tara, Buddhist, Frame, 18th Century, 56 x 34 In. 1150.00
Traveling, 4 Panel, Brass, Blue Enameled, Russia, Late 19th Century, 15 x 6 In. 825.00
Triptych, Gothic, Mythological Birds, Flowers, Oak, 2 Doors, 3 Panels, 1880, 21 x 16 In. . . 265.00
Triptych, Mother Of God, Joy To All Who Sorrow, Bronze, Russia, 18th Century, 6 x 7 In. . . 110.00

Triptych, Traveling, Jesus, Mary & Saint, Brass Hinged, 6 1/4 x 14 1/2 In. 520.00
Triptych, Vladimir Mother Of God, Saints, New Testament Trinity, 19 In. 7475.00
Virgin Mary & Saint John, Painted In Strong Colors, Wooden Panel, 13 x 10 In. 260.00

IMARI porcelain was made in Japan and China beginning in the 17th century. In the 18th century and later, it was copied by porcelain factories in Germany, France, England, and the United States. It was especially popular in the 19th century and is still being made. Imari is characteristically decorated with stylized bamboo, floral, and geometric designs in orange, red, green, and blue. The name comes from the Japanese port of Imari, which exported the ware made nearby in a factory at Arita. *Imari* is now a general term for any pattern of this type.

Bowl, Armorial, Figures In Cartouches, Center Coat Of Arms, Late 19th Century, 15 In. . . .   430.00
Bowl, Armorial, Flared Rim, Horsemonden Of Kent, Buildings, Flowers, c.1716, 7 3/4 In. . .   3900.00
Bowl, Blue, Landscape, Phoenix, Flowers, Orange & Gilt, Scalloped, 11 x 3 1/4 In. 440.00
Bowl, Brocade Design, 4 Petals, Chrysanthemum Shape, Gilt, Scalloped Edge, 7 In. 126.00
Bowl, Butterfly, Flowers, Late 19th Century, 9 1/4 In. 150.00
Bowl, Cover, Phoenix & Shishi, Melon Ribbed, 18th Century, 5 In. 185.00
Bowl, Cover, Polychrome, Alternating Panels, Birds, Flowering Branches, 9 1/2 In. 230.00
Bowl, Cranes Among Flowering Branches, Brocade Design, 11 In. 345.00
Bowl, Cranes In Center, Surrounded By Ginko Leaves, 19th Century, 7 1/4 In. 290.00
Bowl, Floral Brocades Around Central Landscape, Late 19th Century, 8 1/2 In. 145.00
Bowl, Floral Design, 19th Century, 9 1/4 In. 315.00
Bowl, Floral Design, 19th Century, 10 In. 125.00
Bowl, Floral Geometric Design, Orange, Blue, Gold Enamel, 19th Century, 4 In., Pair . . .   260.00
Bowl, Floral, Scalloped Rim & Sides, Footed, 11 x 4 In. 685.00
Bowl, Flower Filled Jardiniere Medallion, Flying Corners, Late 19th Century, 12 In. 750.00
Bowl, Flower Form, Butterfly Rim, Crane & Prunus Center, 6 1/2 In. 115.00
Bowl, Flowers & Animal Panels, Gilt, Ribbed, 11 In. 245.00
Bowl, Landscape Design, 19th Century, 4 1/4 In. 50.00
Bowl, Lobed, Central Medallion, Flower Jardiniere, Panels, Iron Red, Gilt, 2 x 12 In. 750.00
Bowl, Polychrome Enamel & Gilt Brocade On Underglaze, 10 In. 520.00
Bowl, Ribbed, Scalloped Edge, Triangular, 19th Century 490.00
Bowl, Shishi On Interior, Yellow, Green Maple Leaves, 18th Century, 7 In. 275.00
Bowl, Triangular, c.1879, 11 1/2 In. 1350.00
Bowl, Wave Design, Rabbit, 8 1/4 In. 130.00
Charger, Birds, Flower Design, Late 19th Century, 18 In. 196.00
Charger, Carp, Goose, Landscape, 17 1/2 In. 460.00
Charger, Center Chrysanthemum, Alternating Birds & Buildings Cartouche, 16 In. 410.00
Charger, Center Floral, Floral Border, Insect & Phoenix Scene, Polychrome, 18 In. 550.00
Charger, Center Flower Jardiniere, Flower Head Panels, Arabesques, 3 x 18 In. 1265.00
Charger, Center Quatrefoil Flower, Cartouche Of Birds In Flight, 20th Century, 21 5/8 In.   750.00
Charger, Central Jardiniere Of Flowers, Flowers Panels, Early 19th Century, 18 In. 1265.00
Charger, Central Landscape, Cranes & Foo Dogs Border, 19th Century, 16 In. 230.00
Charger, Chrysanthemum, Wide Floral & Insect Border, Phoenix, 13 In. 550.00
Charger, Figures, Floral Landscapes, Medallion, Raised Edge, Late 1800s, 3 x 5 1/2 In. . .   520.00
Charger, Floral, Paneled Border, Birds & Flowers On Reverse, 18 In. 750.00
Charger, Flower Medallion, Paneled Floral, Blue & White, Scalloped, 12 In. 165.00
Charger, Flower Shape, 2 Ships, Rolling Sea, Prowling Dragon, Enamel, Gilt, 14 1/2 In. .   400.00
Charger, Foo Lions, Brocade, 19th Century, 18 In. 1265.00
Charger, Hoteh & Karako Design, 12 1/4 In. 240.00
Charger, Landscape, Bats On Reverse, 12 In. 160.00
Charger, Panel Of 3 Friends, Brocade Border With Phoenix, Leaves, 16 In. 345.00
Charger, Phoenix, Blue Border, Floral Reserves, Late 19th Century, 14 In. 375.00
Charger, Riverscape, Dragon, Scalloped Rim, 20th Century, 15 In. 259.00
Charger, White Ground, Gilt Highlights, Early 19th Century, 16 In. 1250.00
Chop Plate, Dragon Faces & Leaves, White Panels, Gold Trim, 12 1/4 In. 110.00
Dish, Awabi Shell Form, Chidori & Waves, 6 1/2 In. 60.00
Dish, Cover, Crane & Carp Design, 8 1/2 In. 184.00
Dish, Diamond Shape, Geometric Panels, Flowers, Birds & Plants, 1910, 11 1/4 In. 200.00
Dish, Diamond Shape, Iron Red, Cobalt, Green, Gilt, Flowers, Birds, 1 1/2 x 11 x 12 In. . .   200.00
Dish, Horse & Landscape, 19th Century, 7 In., Pair 210.00
Dish, Oval, Asymmetrical Panels, Flowers, Pale Blue Scroll Ground, 2 x 13 x 11 1/2 In. . .   80.00

Dish, Oval, Palette Colors, Fluted Rim, England, 8 1/2 In. 290.00
Dish, Shaving, Lotus Sprays & Flowers, Blue, Iron Red, Gold Enamel Glaze, 11 In. 800.00
Jar, Asymmetrical Panels, Florals, Gilt Tassels, 19th Century, 13 x 11 1/2 In. 80.00
Jar, Cover, Blue, Red & Gilt Floral, Celadon Foo Dog Finial, Egg Shape, 9 1/2 In. 550.00
Jar, Cover, Bridge & Bird In Tree, Red, Blue, Gilt Trim, 13 In. ....770.00 to 885.00
Jar, Cover, Landscapes & Flowers, White Reserves, Gilt, Ribbed, 6 1/8 In. 190.00
Jar, Domed Cover, Floral Design, 19th Century, 12 In. 430.00
Jar, Domed Cover, Foo Dog Finial, Bluebirds, Roses, Butterflies, Gilt Trim, Signed, 14 In. 550.00
Jar, Domed Cover, Inverted Pear Shape, Kirin In Clouds, 24 1/2 In. 630.00
Jar, Domed Cover, Shishi Border, Floral Design, Hexagonal, 12 1/2 In. 290.00
Jar, Dragon Chasing The Flaming Pearl Of Wisdom, Octagonal, 8 In. 260.00
Jar, Flowering Tree Design, 19th Century, 6 In. 90.00
Jar, Rose, Cover, Polychrome, Panels, Late 19th Century, 10 3/4 In. 375.00
Jardiniere Base, Cobalt Blue & Orange Floral, 24 1/2 In. 440.00
Plate, Birds In Tree, Blue & White, 12 In. 165.00
Plate, Border Of Prunus Flowers Surrounding Medallion, Brick Red Ground, 12 In. 170.00
Plate, Fish & Birds, Blue & White, Scalloped, 12 In. 135.00
Plate, Floral Design, Blue Underglaze Ground, Pie Crust Edge, 11 1/4 In. 290.00
Plate, Floral Spray, Crabs, 9 1/4 In., Pair 220.00
Plate, Flower, Tendrils, Blue Underglaze, Enamel, Leaf Edges, Square, 8 1/2 In, Pair 290.00
Plate, Flowers, Bamboo, Reticulated, 8 7/8 In. 175.00
Plate, Flowers, Blue, Iron Red, Gilt Highlights, 18th Century, 12 In. 575.00
Plate, God & Goddesses, Border, Scalloped, 12 In. 115.00
Plate, Octagonal, Fan & Landscapes, Scalloped, Octagonal, 11 1/2 In. 220.00
Platter, Birds, Bridge & Flowers, Scalloped, Square, 11 1/4 x 11 1/2 In. 355.00
Platter, Gilt Birds Borders, Octagonal, 9 1/2 x 11 1/4 In. 465.00
Punch Bowl, 3 Birds, Cherry Blossom Interior, 20th Century, 11 3/8 x 6 In. 685.00
Punch Bowl, Flower Basket Center, Brocade, Shishi Ground, 12 In. 575.00
Serving Dish, Crane & Flower Design, Phoenix, Paulowinia Centers, 12 In., Pair 750.00
Serving Dish, Floral & Bird Design, Paneled Border, 11 x 13 1/2 In., Pair 715.00
Tureen, Sauce, Exhibition Piece, Signed, c.1870 .... 1395.00
Umbrella Stand, Allover Cobalt Blue & Iron Red Floral, Banding At Top, 24 In. 715.00
Vase, Allover Floral, Red, Cobalt Blue, Gilt Trim, Baluster, 18 1/2 In. 440.00
Vase, Alternating Flowers, Rustic Buildings, Ribbed, Urn Shape, 18 1/2 In. 920.00
Vase, Baluster Shape, Ribbed, Splayed Rim, Enamel, Blue, Polychrome, Footed, 10 In. .. 315.00
Vase, Baluster, Stylized Flowers, Low Neck, Iron Red, Cobalt Blue, Gilt, 10 x 6 In., Pair . 315.00
Vase, Cover, Chrysanthemum, Lotus Floral Design, Lappet Design At Base, 10 1/2 In. ... 400.00
Vase, Cover, Prunus, Chrysanthemum Design, Blue, Iron Red, Gold Enamel, 10 In. 200.00
Vase, Double Gourd, Floral Design, Early 18th Century, Japan, 12 1/2 In. 1840.00
Vase, Floral Rondels, Late 19th Century, 9 3/4 In. 170.00
Vase, Mirror, Blue Design, White Ground, Baluster, 4-Character Mark, 12 In., Pair 715.00
Vase, Pavilion, Floral & Brocade, 10 In. 200.00
Vase, Peacocks & Brocade Design, Swirled Ribbed Shape, 19th Century, 12 In. 290.00
Vase, Trumpet Form, Carp & Prunus Panels, 19th Century, 37 In. 2530.00
Vase, Various Bold Brocades, 19th Century, 8 1/4 In. 290.00

IMPERIAL GLASS Corporation was founded in Bellaire, Ohio, in 1901.
It became a subsidiary of Lenox, Inc., in 1973 and was sold to Arthur
R. Lorch in 1981. It was sold again in 1982, and went bankrupt in
1984. In 1985, the molds and some assets were sold. The Imperial
glass preferred by the collector is freehand art glass, carnival glass,
slag glass, stretch glass, and other top-quality tablewares. Tablewares
and animals are listed here. The others may be found in the appropriate sections.

Animal, Owl, Chocolate Slag 65.00
Art Glass, Bowl, Iridized Stretch, Marked, 10 In. 34.00
Art Glass, Vase, Freehand Threading, Trumpet Form, 8 1/4 In. 316.00
Art Glass, Vase, Leaves & Vines, Pale Blue, Plum Interior, 6 1/2 In. 805.00
Art Glass, Vase, Orange Luster Throat, Freehand Thread Overlay, 9 1/4 In. 115.00
Art Glass, Vase, Orange Luster, White Opal, 11 In. 224.00
Art Glass, Vase, Pulled Heart & Vine, Cobalt Blue Rim, 8 1/2 In. 1495.00
Art Glass, Vase, Pulled Heart & Vine, Flashed Orange, Ruffled Edge, 7 7/8 In. 375.00
Art Glass, Vase, Pulled Leaf, Orange Body, Tri-Handled Rim, 9 1/2 In. 518.00

Art Glass, Vase, Pulled, Heart & Trailing, Vine, Bright Orange, Deep Blue, 6 x 4 1/2 In. . . . 460.00
Beaded Block, Bowl, Blue, 6 1/2 In. 40.00
Beaded Block, Creamer, Blue 50.00
Beaded Block, Plate, Amber, Square, 7 3/4 In. 8.00
Beaded Block, Sugar & Creamer, Green, Tall 26.00
Candlewick, Ashtray, 4 In. . . . . .12.00 to 18.00
Candlewick, Ashtray, 6 In. . . . . .135.00 to 165.00
Candlewick, Ashtray, Cranberry, 6 In. 10.00
Candlewick, Ashtray, Heart Shape, 4 In. 10.00
Candlewick, Basket, 6 In. 40.00
Candlewick, Bonbon, Brass Base, 6 In. 20.00
Candlewick, Bonbon, Sterling Silver Base, 6 In. 30.00
Candlewick, Bottle, Bitters 47.00
Candlewick, Bowl, 10 In. . . . . .40.00 to 50.00
Candlewick, Bowl, 2 Handles, 10 In. 115.00
Candlewick, Bowl, 2 Sections, 6 1/2 In. . . . . .28.00 to 45.00
Candlewick, Bowl, 2 Sections, Oval, 11 In. 550.00
Candlewick, Bowl, Footed, 10 In. 175.00
Candlewick, Bowl, Heart Shape, 5 In. 25.00
Candlewick, Bowl, Ivy, Footed, 7 In. 155.00
Candlewick, Bowl, Lily, 7 1/2 In. . . . . .920.00 to 1000.00
Candlewick, Bowl, Red, 8 1/2 In. 450.00
Candlewick, Bowl, Ribbed, Footed 120.00
Candlewick, Bowl, Square, 7 In. 160.00
Candlewick, Box, Cigarette, Flat Mirrored Copper Top, Crystal Grapes 125.00
Candlewick, Butter, Cover, 5 1/2 In. . . . . .32.00 to 44.00
Candlewick, Cake Plate, Birthday, Holds 72 Candles, 14 In. 500.00
Candlewick, Cake Stand, 3-Bead Stem, 11 In. 85.00
Candlewick, Cake Stand, Sterling Silver, Base, 10 In. 65.00
Candlewick, Candleholder, Beaded Question Mark Handle 42.00
Candlewick, Candlestick, 2-Light, Floral Cutting, Pair 35.00
Candlewick, Candlestick, Silver Base, Pair 115.00
Candlewick, Candy Box, Cover, 7 In. 135.00
Candlewick, Candy Dish, Handle, 6 In. 25.00
Candlewick, Celery Dish, 2 Handles, Oval, 13 1/2 In. 25.00
Candlewick, Celery Dish, Boat Shape, Oval, 11 In. 78.00
Candlewick, Chip & Dip Set, Divided Bowl, Tray, 14 In. . . . . .455.00 to 650.00
Candlewick, Claret 55.00
Candlewick, Compote, 4-Bead Stem, 7 In. 125.00
Candlewick, Compote, Beaded, 10 In. 550.00
Candlewick, Creamer 8.00
Candlewick, Creamer, Individual . . . . .28.00 to 33.00
Candlewick, Cruet Set, Tray, 3 Piece 95.00
Candlewick, Cup & Saucer 18.00
Candlewick, Cup & Saucer, After Dinner 30.00
Candlewick, Decanter, Stopper 650.00
Candlewick, Dish, Mayonnaise, Ladle 50.00
Candlewick, Egg Plate, Center Heart Handle, 12 Wells, 11 1/2 In. 175.00
Candlewick, Epergne, 2 Piece . . . . .275.00 to 295.00
Candlewick, Fork & Spoon Set 28.00
Candlewick, Goblet, 10 Oz. . . . . .23.00 to 30.00
Candlewick, Goblet, Ruby, Clear Stem & Foot, 9 Oz., 6 In. . . . . .100.00 to 150.00
Candlewick, Goblet, Yellow, 9 Oz. 51.00
Candlewick, Gravy Boat, Underplate 190.00
Candlewick, Marmalade 100.00
Candlewick, Mirror, Standing, Round, 4 1/2 In. 110.00
Candlewick, Muffin Tray, 2 Handles, 11 1/2 In. 360.00
Candlewick, Party Set, Cup, Plate, Rose Of Sharon Etch, Gold, 2 Piece 450.00
Candlewick, Pitcher, 80 Oz. . . . . .210.00 to 320.00
Candlewick, Pitcher, Juice, 40 Oz., 9 1/2 In. 275.00
Candlewick, Plate, 6 In. . . . . .9.00 to 16.00
Candlewick, Plate, 7 In. . . . . .6.00 to 12.00
Candlewick, Plate, 10 In. 45.00

Candlewick, Plate, 14 In. . . . . .25.00 to 45.00
Candlewick, Plate, 2 Handles, 5 1/2 In. 25.00
Candlewick, Plate, 2 Handles, 12 In. 55.00
Candlewick, Plate, Caramel Slag, 12 In. 418.00
Candlewick, Platter, 16 In. 275.00
Candlewick, Punch Bowl, Cover 1395.00
Candlewick, Punch Cup 8.00
Candlewick, Relish, 2 Sections, 2 Handles, 6 1/2 In. . . . . .18.00 to 25.00
Candlewick, Relish, 3 Sections, Footed 125.00
Candlewick, Relish, 4 Sections, 4 Handles, 8 1/2 In. 30.00
Candlewick, Salt & Pepper, Bulbous, 3 In. 35.00
Candlewick, Sauceboat, Underplate, 5 1/2 In. 45.00
Candlewick, Seafood Cocktail, Icer 65.00
Candlewick, Shade, Viennese Blue, Satin, 1937, 5 1/4 x 3 5/8 In. 158.00
Candlewick, Sherbet, 6 Oz. 17.00
Candlewick, Sherbet, Ruby, Clear Stem & Foot, 6 Oz. 100.00
Candlewick, Sugar & Cream, Cranberry, Clear Handles 165.00
Candlewick, Sugar & Creamer, Individual 45.00
Candlewick, Sugar & Creamer, Lily-Of-The-Valley, Silver Overlay 75.00
Candlewick, Sugar & Creamer, Tray 25.00
Candlewick, Teacup & Saucer, 2 1/4 In. 25.00
Candlewick, Torte Plate, 14 In. 70.00
Candlewick, Tray, 2 Handles, 11 7/8 In. 25.00
Candlewick, Tray, 8 In. 45.00
Candlewick, Tray, Condiment, Kidney Shape 18.00
Candlewick, Tumbler, 5 Oz. 14.00
Candlewick, Tumbler, 10 Oz. . . . . .10.00 to 14.00
Candlewick, Tumbler, 12 Oz. 25.00
Candlewick, Vase, 6 In. 575.00
Candlewick, Vase, 8 1/2 In. 450.00
Candlewick, Vase, Crimped, Beaded Edge, 6 In. 65.00
Candlewick, Vase, Fan, Beaded Handles, Etched, 8 1/2 In. 75.00
Candlewick, Vase, Flip, 8 In. 365.00
Candlewick, Wine, 4 Oz. . . . . .22.00 to 27.00
Cape Cod, Bowl, 2 Sections, Oval, 11 In. 95.00
Cape Cod, Bowl, Spider, Handle, 6 1/2 In. 27.00
Cape Cod, Cake Stand, 11 In. 85.00
Cape Cod, Claret, 5 Oz. 15.00
Cape Cod, Coaster, 4 1/2 In. 10.00
Cape Cod, Console, 13 In. 50.00
Cape Cod, Cordial, 1 1/2 In. 10.00
Cape Cod, Creamer, Footed 15.00
Cape Cod, Cruet, 4 Oz. 20.00
Cape Cod, Cup & Saucer 7.00
Cape Cod, Decanter, Stopper, 24 Oz. 65.00
Cape Cod, Decanter, Stopper, 30 Oz. 75.00
Cape Cod, Dish, Mustard, Cover, Spoon 15.00
Cape Cod, Goblet, Verde, 9 Oz. 7.50
Cape Cod, Nut Dish, Handle, 3 In. 20.00
Cape Cod, Parfait, 6 Oz. 10.00
Cape Cod, Pepper Mill 28.00
Cape Cod, Pitcher, 2 Qt. 85.00
Cape Cod, Pitcher, Milk, 1 Pt. 45.00
Cape Cod, Plate, 8 In. 7.00
Cape Cod, Plate, 10 In. . . . . .27.00 to 38.00
Cape Cod, Plate, Cupped, 16 In. 55.00
Cape Cod, Relish, 3 Sections, 11 1/4 In. 185.00
Cape Cod, Relish, 4 Sections, 9 1/2 In. 35.00
Cape Cod, Sherbet, 6 Oz. 12.00
Cape Cod, Sherbet, Low, 6 Oz. 5.00
Cape Cod, Sherbet, Low, Verde, 6 Oz. 5.00
Cape Cod, Tumbler, Footed, 10 Oz. . . . . .9.00 to 10.00
Cape Cod, Tumbler, Footed, 12 Oz. 10.00

Cape Cod, Wine, 3 Oz.	8.00
Caramel Slag, Vase, Diamond Point, 9 1/2 In.	85.00
Diamond Quilted, Bowl, Ruffled Edge, Green, 7 In.	18.00
Diamond Quilted, Candlestick, Blue	22.00
Diamond Quilted, Creamer, Black	20.00
Diamond Quilted, Creamer, Blue	19.00
Diamond Quilted, Plate, Green, 8 In.	12.00
Diamond Quilted, Soup, Cream, Pink	25.00
Figurine, Owl, Vaseline Glass, 6 3/4 x 3 1/2 In.	86.00
Figurine, Venus Rising, Amber, 1981, 6 1/2 In.	50.00
Figurine, Venus Rising, Green, 1981, 6 1/2 In.	65.00
Grape, Decanter, Wine, Green, Stopper, 11 1/2 In.	62.00
Herringbone, Basket, Purple Slag, c.1969, 5 1/2 In.	55.00
Herringbone, Basket, Ruby, Satin, 5 1/2 In.	65.00
Laced Edge, Bowl, Ritz Blue, 8 In.	15.00
Laced Edge, Creamer	14.00
Laced Edge, Sugar	14.00
Laced Edge, Vase, Purple Slag, 6 x 4 1/2 In.	95.00
Molly, Creamer, Ruby	15.00
Molly, Cup & Saucer, Ruby	13.00
Molly, Sugar, Ruby	15.00
Peachblow, Decanter, Satin Stopper, 10 1/2 In.	375.00
Peachblow, Vase, White Interior, 4 1/2 In.	205.00
Pillar Flute, Plate Set, Rose Marie, 8 In., 6 Piece	175.00
Robin, Mug, Red	45.00
Rose Of Sharon, Sherbet	5.00
Twisted Optic, Creamer, Pink	15.00
Twisted Optic, Sherbet, Underplate, Vaseline	25.00
Twisted Optic, Sugar, Green	8.00
Windmill, Pitcher, Ruby Slag, c.1969, 1 Pt.	98.00

INDIAN art from North America has attracted the collector for many years. Each tribe has its own distinctive designs and techniques. Baskets, jewelry, pottery, and leatherwork are of greatest collector interest. Eskimo art is listed in another category in this book.

Apron, Seminole, Rainbow Colors, Blue Field, 1930, 27 x 36 In.	110.00
Ax, Plains, Iron, Brass Tacked Wooden Handle, 1870, 16 x 5 In.	330.00
Bag, Beaded, Pictorial, Road, Deer Design, Beaded Fringe, 18 x 11 1/2 In.	340.00
Bag, Blackfoot, Sinew Sewn, Maltese Cross Design, 1890, 6 In.	605.00
Bag, Cree, Hide Bag, Finger Loom Stitch, Pink, Yellow, Green, Purple, 1900, 5 x 4 In.	165.00
Bag, Cree, Hide Medicine, Beaded Geometric Designs, 1930, 6 x 3 In.	220.00
Bag, Nez Perce, Cornhusk, Geometric Forms, c.1920, 9 x 7 In.	300.00
Bag, Nez Perce, Twined Cornhusk, Buckskin Fringe, 1910, 7 x 10 In.	495.00
Bag, Nez Perce, Twined Cornhusk, Geometric Design, 1880, 22 x 15 In. .935.00 to	1210.00
Bag, Nez Perce, Twined Cornhusk, Geometric Design, 1930, 13 x 12 In.	550.00
Bag, Parfleche, Child's, 13 1/4 x 7 1/4 In.	2662.00
Bag, Quill, Beaded, Woven, Tin Cones, Leather Tassels	330.00
Bag, Sioux, Tobacco, Fringed 3 Sides, Beaded, Floral, 21 x 8 In.	630.00
Bandolier, Beaded Geometric, Red Stroud, 1870, 13 x 7 In.	1725.00
Bandolier, Chippewa, Beaded Floral, Shoulder, 1890, 44 x 14 In.	1760.00
Bandolier, Chippewa, Beaded, Floral, 1900, 79 x 14 In.	1650.00
Bandolier, Great Lakes, Contour Beads, Red Wool File Cloth, 10 x 39 In.	1650.00
Bandolier, Ojibway, Appliqued Stitched, Cloth Backing, 27 In.	1650.00
Basket, Apache, Bowl, Swastikas, Butterflies, Stars, 11 In.	2750.00
Basket, Apache, Geometric Design, c.1880, 19 1/2 In.	8000.00
Basket, Apache, Leather Fringe, Tin Cones, 10 x 11 In.	125.00
Basket, Chehalis, Twined, Line Design, Cover, 1910, 13 x 12 In.	330.00
Basket, Chippewa, Quilled Rooster On Birch Bark, 1970s, 4 x 9 1/2 In.	355.00
Basket, Hopi, Coiled, Kachina Design, 1950, 15 x 2 In.	220.00
Basket, Hopi, Coiled, Red Eagle Design, 1960, 11 x 2 In.	523.00
Basket, Hopi, Stylized Bird, Priscilla Nampeye, 11 x 12 1/2 In.	300.00
Basket, Hopi, Turtle Effigy, 1940, 9 1/2 x 1 1/2 In.	385.00
Basket, Hupa, Tobacco, Geometric, Black, Yellow, Red, 1920, 6 x 5 In.	1320.00

Basket, Hupa, Twined, Raised Geometric, 1900, 23 x 6 In. 770.00
Basket, Hupa, Winnowing, Twined, Triangles Around, 1900, 15 x 5 In. 440.00
Basket, Iroquois, Half, Green, Yellow, Tulip, Stripe, Leather Cover, 13 1/2 In. 275.00
Basket, Karok, Negative, Twined, Yellow Quill Design, Black, 1900, 4 x 2 1/2 In. 465.00
Basket, Klamath, Overlapping Quills, 1900, 5 1/2 In. 545.00
Basket, Klamath, Twined, Gold Spider Web Design, 1900, 8 x 4 1/2 In. 468.00
Basket, Klamath, Twined, Quail Top Knot Designs, 1900, 9 x 5 In. 715.00
Basket, Maine, Splint, Blue Banding, Mid 19th Century, 10 1/2 x 14 In. 275.00
Basket, Maine, Splint, Potato Stamp Decoration, Handle, Cover, 12 1/2 x 10 1/2 In. 110.00
Basket, Maine, Splint, Potato Stamp Leaf Design, Handles, 9 x 4 1/2 In. 360.00
Basket, Mission, 1 Line Rattlesnake Design, Bar & Box Design, 1920, 22 x 12 In. 1265.00
Basket, Navajo, Wedding, Coiled, Spirit Release Line, 1970, 15 x 2 1/2 In. 80.00
Basket, Nootka/Makah, Olla, Whaling Scenes, Cover, 1940, 10 In. 358.00
Basket, Ojibway, Bark, Porcupine Quills, Quilled Beaver On Top, 1975, 5 x 3 x 2 In. 250.00
Basket, Ojibway, Birch Bark, White Porcupine Quills, Floral, 1930, 5 1/2 x 2 1/2 In. 120.00
Basket, Ojibway, Fully Quilted Birch Bark & Sweetgrass, Cover, 3 x 3 In. 90.00
Basket, Paiute, Beaded Geometric, Blue, Green, Red & White, 1 1/2 x 3 1/4 In. 358.00
Basket, Paiute, Coiled, Glass Beads, Geometric, 1940, 4 x 2 In. 415.00
Basket, Paiute, Coiled, Green, Orange, Blue Seed Beads, Geometric, 1935 .... 440.00
Basket, Paiute, Horsehair, Beadwork At Top, Berry Rogers, 1980s, 4 x 6 1/2 In. 495.00
Basket, Papago, Arizona State Fair, 2nd Prize Ribbon, Cover, 8 x 9 In. 90.00
Basket, Papago, Bowl, Man-In-The Maze, 1950s, 3 x 10 In. 175.00
Basket, Papago, Bowl, Rattlesnake & Bug, 1970s, 5 1/2 x 19 In. 440.00
Basket, Papago, Coiled Olla, Human & Animal Figures Around, 1930, 13 x 18 In. 1870.00
Basket, Papago, Coiled, Black Eagle, 1950, 12 x 9 In. 275.00
Basket, Pima, Bowl, Stepped Key Design, Whipped Rim Stitch, 2 1/2 x 5 1/2 In. 190.00
Basket, Pima, Coiled, Fret & Cross Design, 1935 .... 1045.00
Basket, Pima, Geometric Design, 1935, 10 x 6 x 2 In. 248.00
Basket, Pima, Horsehair, Friendship Figures, 2 1/4 In. 90.00
Basket, Pima, Horses All Around, Padre Beads On Top, 1910, 8 x 6 In. 522.00
Basket, Pima, Olla, Coiled, Unusual Diamond & Rectangular Designs, 1930, 15 In. 1610.00
Basket, Pitt River, Parallelogram Design, 1910, 4 1/2 x 3 In. 550.00
Basket, Pomo, Tightly Woven, Feathers, 1920, 2 1/4 In. 465.00
Basket, Pomo, Woven Trinket, Quail Topknots, 1905, 4 3/4 x 2 1/2 In. 975.00
Basket, Salish, Baby Cradle, Geometric Design, 1900, 24 x 9 x 6 In. 525.00
Basket, Salish, Butterfly Design, 1910, 13 x 9 x 19 In. 990.00
Basket, Salish, Storage, Diamond Design, 1910, 18 x 12 In. 220.00
Basket, Salish, Storage, Hump Backed, 19th Century, 11 x 8 x 10 In. 385.00
Basket, Skokomish, Northwest Coast, 6 1/2 x 5 In. 270.00
Basket, Splint, Cylindrical, Woven, Painted, Stamped Decoration, Cover, 12 x 11 In. 520.00
Basket, Tlingit, 2 Repetitive Fake Embroidery Geometric Bands, 1900, 4 1/2 x 6 In. 660.00
Basket, Tlingit, Yakutat, Berry, Diamond Eye Design, Spruce Body, 4 x 4 3/4 In. 360.00
Basket, Washo, Twined, Red Line Design, Red Braided Rim, 1900, 8 x 6 In. 360.00
Basket, Yurok, Twined Acorn Mush Bowl, Geometric Design, 1910 .... 220.00
Basket, Yurok, Twined Bowl, Parallelogram Designs, 1935 .... 468.00
Basket, Yurok, Twined Woman's Hat Basket, Parallelogram Designs, 1919, 6 x 4 In. ... 305.00
Belt, Blackfoot, Slanted Multicolored Beadwork, Leather, 1 1/2 x 40 In. 120.00
Belt, Cheyenne, Beaded, Star & Cross Design, White Ground, 1930, 34 x 2 1/2 In. 130.00
Belt, Navajo, 9 Conchas, Buckle, All Set With Turquoise, Silver, 1950s, 2 3/4 In. 495.00
Belt, Navajo, 16 Conchas, Turquoise & Coral, Link, Silver Leaves, M.M., 36 In. 250.00
Belt, Navajo, Concha, All Silver Links, Butterflies, 1940, 28 x 1 In. 155.00
Belt, Navajo, Concha, Silver, Set With Turquoise, Delores Bone, 1970, 34 x 2 In. 220.00
Belt, Navajo, Concha, Silver, Turquoise, Oval Buckle, 1970, 47 In. 220.00
Belt, Navajo, Concha, Silver, Yellowhorse, 1960, 2 1/4 In. 525.00
Belt, Navajo, Oval Concha, Silver Buckle, 1935, 37 x 3 x 4 In. 5500.00
Belt, Sioux, Beaded, Loom Strings, Initialed S.D. For South Dakota, Dated 1904 .... 165.00
Blanket, Blackfoot, Boys, Cape With Fringe, 1900 .... 130.00
Blanket, Burial, Central Tree, Birds, Red, Ivory, Brown, 44 x 71 In. 840.00
Blanket, Chief, 8 Diamond Medallions, Brown, Ivory, Red, 56 x 78 In. 1065.00
Blanket, Chief, Feather & Geometric Pattern, Ivory Ground, 32 x 64 In. 504.00
Blanket, Haida, Button, Bear Center, 1900, 66 x 57 In. 1980.00
Blanket, Navajo, Banded & Geometric Design, 1910, 41 x 64 In. 690.00
Blanket, Navajo, Black, Ivory Geometric Design, Hubbell Trading Post, 60 x 77 In. 1100.00

Blanket, Navajo, Eye Dazzler, Red, Yellow Black, Ivory, Orange, 56 x 41 1/2 In. 3300.00
Blanket, Osage, Floral Crewelwork, Green Ribbon Edging, 20th Century, 66 x 52 In. 1100.00
Blanket, Saddle, 2 Gray Hills, Central Diamond, Brown, Ivory, Red, Black, 30 x 44 In. . . 615.00
Blanket, Saddle, Crow, Geometric Beadwork On Trade Cloth Trim, Canvas, 46 x 35 In. . . 550.00
Blanket, Saddle, Navajo, Chief, Stripes, Center Diamonds, 29 x 29 In. 110.00
Blanket, Saddle, Navajo, Herringbone Design, 1960s, 34 x 60 In. 220.00
Blanket, Saddle, Navajo, Sunday, Geometric Corner Design, Fringe, 1940, 26 x 32 In. . . . 770.00
Blanket, Saltillo, Plum Color, F.Z.R. In Center, 1930, 53 x 99 In. 175.00
Bolo Tie, Navajo, Braided Leather, Silver Slide, Coral & Turquoise Chip Inlay, 20 In. 300.00
Bolo Tie, Navajo, Lizard Design, Turquoise, Silver, Malachite, 1975, 2 1/2 x 2 In. 80.00
Bolo Tie, Navajo, Silver, Turquoise, Signed, Franklin Tsosie, 1970, 3 In. 110.00
Bolo Tie, Zuni, Braided Leather, Inlaid Rainbow Dancer, Silver Cone Ends, 22 In. 110.00
Bolo Tie, Zuni, Pawn Stone To Stone Knife Wing God, Matching Tips, 1950, 2 In. 155.00
Bottle, Jemez, Singing Lady Form, Cover, Estella Loretta, 13 In. 120.00
Bow, Hopi, Yarn Wrap, Cream & Purple Each End, 40 In. 385.00
Bow, Iroquois, Bear Hide Grip, Brass Tacks, Early 19th Century, 52 In. 360.00
Bowl, Acoma, Floral Design, Heartline Deer & Bear, M. Antonio, 5 3/4 x 7 3/4 In. 70.00
Bowl, Acoma, Heartline Deer, Signed R. Antonio, 9 x 11 In. 155.00
Bowl, Anasazi, 4 Mile, Geometric Design, Polychrome, 12 x 6 In. 440.00
Bowl, Anasazi, Black On White, Triangular Design, Prehistoric, 5 x 2 In. 110.00
Bowl, Apache, White Mountain Deer, Men Holding Hands, 1980s, 16 In. 440.00
Bowl, Black On White Line Design, Marie Z. Chino, 3 1/2 x 6 In. 440.00
Bowl, Hopi, Curvilinear Design, Signed, A. Taylor Palacca, Ariz., 1975, 7 x 2 In. 70.00
Bowl, Hopi, Dough, Geometric Inside Band, 1940s, 6 x 14 In. 715.00
Bowl, Hopi, Polychrome, Classic Interior, Fawn-Joy Navsic, 10 1/4 x 3 In. 465.00
Bowl, Hopi, Seed Jar, Polychrome, Signed, Tonita Nampeyo, 1990, 4 x 6 1/2 In. 385.00
Bowl, Hopi, Seed, Feather Woman, Signed, Helen Naha, 1970, 3 1/2 x 4 1/4 In. 525.00
Bowl, Mohave, Geometric Red On Buff Design, 1920s, 3 x 8 1/2 In. 350.00
Bowl, Pima, Friendship, Male & Female Figures, Hanging Wire, 1930s, 6 1/2 In. 925.00
Bowl, Pueblo, Bird On Bowl, Floral Design, 1940, 6 x 7 In. 120.00
Bowl, Santa Clara, Blackware, Signed, Carol Velarde, 1980, 3 x 2 In. 110.00
Bowl, Santa Clara, Blackware, Signed, Denise Martinez, 1980, 4 x 2 In. 65.00
Bowl, Santa Clara, Blackware, Signed, Stella Chavarria, 1980, 4 x 7 In. 468.00
Bowl, Santa Clara, Pottery, Blackware, Signed, Carol Velarde, 2 1/2 x 2 In. 155.00
Bowl, Santa Clara, Pottery, Blackware, Signed, Denise Martinez, 4 x 3 In. 99.00
Bowl, Santa Clara, Pottery, Blackware, Signed, Stella Chavarria, 6 x 4 In. 250.00
Bowl, Santo Domingo, Leaf Design, Spout, Handles, 1920, 4 x 9 In. 385.00
Bowl, Zuni, Lizard & Tadpole Design, Polychrome, 3 1/2 x 6 In. 70.00
Box, Micmac, Quillwork, Cover, Floral & Crosses, Chevron, New England, 4 x 8 In. 488.00
Box, Work, Micmac, Early 20th Century, 9 1/2 x 9 1/2 In. 5000.00
Bracelet, Comanche, Spider Web Turquoise Stone, White Buffalo, 1978, 2 3/4 x 2 In. . . . 825.00
Bracelet, Navajo, 2 Turquoise Stones, Silver Leaves, Signed L.L., 1970s, 3 x 6 In. 330.00
Bracelet, Navajo, Coin Silver, 5 Turquoise Stones, 1940, 7 1/2 x 3/4 In. 198.00
Bracelet, Navajo, Sand Cast, Silver, 3 Turquoise Stones, 1980, 8 1/2 x 2 1/2 In. 110.00
Bracelet, Navajo, Silver Inlay, 5 Turquoise Stones, 1970, 7 1/2 x 2 1/2 In. 385.00
Bracelet, Navajo, Silver Watch, Row Of Slab Stones, 1970, 8 x 1 1/2 In. 275.00
Bracelet, Navajo, Silver Wrought, Turquoise Cluster, 1970, 4 x 5 1/2 In. 90.00
Bracelet, Navajo, Silver, 1 Turquoise Stone, 2 Coral, Signed, 1980, 8 x 2 In. 55.00
Bracelet, Navajo, Silver, 3 Turquoise Stones, 1980, 8 x 1 1/2 In. 100.00
Bracelet, Navajo, Silver, Green Turquoise, 1940, 7 1/4 x 1 3/4 In. 155.00
Bracelet, Navajo, Silver, Oval Turquoise, 1960, 8 x 2 1/2 In. 90.00
Bracelet, Navajo, Silver, Triangular Turquoise Stone, 1940, 6 x 1 In. 145.00
Bracelet, Navajo, Silver, Turquoise & Coral Peyote Design, Signed, J. Nezzie, 1980 . . . . . 66.00
Bracelet, Navajo, Silver, Turquoise Cluster, 70 Turquoise Stones, 1950, 8 x 3 In. 145.00
Bracelet, Navajo, Silver, Turquoise Kachina, 1960, 3 1/2 In. 176.00
Bracelet, Navajo, Silver, Turquoise, Coral Inlay, 1975, 8 x 2 In. 100.00
Bracelet, Navajo, Silver, Turquoise, Coral, Water Bird Design, Signed, 1980, 7 x 1 In. . . . 55.00
Bracelet, Navajo, Silver, Turquoise, Signed, B. Tauchine, 1950, 8 1/4 x 1 1/4 In. 100.00
Bracelet, Navajo, Silver, Turquoise, Silver Eagle, Signed, 8 1/2 x 1 1/2 In. 145.00
Bracelet, Zuni, Cluster Of Silver, Turquoise Petit Point, 20th Century, 3 1/2 x 4 In. 165.00
Bracelet, Zuni, Silver Inlay, Flower Center, Signed, Simplicio, 1980, 2 x 8 1/2 In. 200.00
Bracelet, Zuni, Silver, 3 Bands Turquoise Stones, Needlepoint, 1970, 7 x 1 1/2 In. 120.00
Bracelet, Zuni, Silver, Turquoise Knife, Wing Dancer, Coral Shell, 1980, 7 x 2 1/2 In. . . . 120.00

Bracelet, Zuni, Silver, Turquoise Slab Inlay, 1970, 8 x 1 1/2 In. 130.00
Bracelet, Zuni, Silver, Turquoise, Cardinals & Flowers, 1980, 8 x 2 In. 200.00
Bracelet, Zuni, Turquoise Hummingbird & Flower, Bobby & Corraine 220.00
Breastplate, Plains, Bone Hair, Restrung, 19th Century, 12 x 18 In. 935.00
Bridle, Crow, Hide, Beaded Geometric Design, 1960, 120 x 15 In. 635.00
Buckle, Belt, Navajo, Bear Claw Surrounded By Silver Feathers, 3 1/2 In. 55.00
Buckle, Belt, Navajo, Silver, Turquoise, Applied Beads, Stamped CY, 3 3/8 In. 55.00
Buckle, Navajo, Silver, 2 Turquoise Stones, Oval, Jackie Many Goats, 2 x 3 In. 100.00
Buckle, Navajo, Silver, 25 Turquoise Stones, 1970, 9 x 6 1/2 In. 330.00
Buckle, Navajo, Silver, Turquoise, Coral Inlay, Signed, James Bahe, 1970, 3 x 2 In. 70.00
Buckle, Zuni, Silver, Turquoise & Coral Stones, Signed, F.C. Gasper, 3 x 2 In. 250.00
Bust, Doll, Clay, Human Hair, Leather Band, Wool Wrapped Braids, 4 In. 200.00
Bust, Plains, Chief Of The Plains, Tomahawk, Plaster Of Paris, 20 3/4 In. 240.00
Bust, Seminole, Southern Warrior, Plaster Of Paris, 1900-1920, 12 1/2 In. 155.00
Cane, Plains, Buffalo Head Handle, Wooden, 34 In. 55.00
Canteen, Acoma, Indian Head 1 Side, Deer Other, 1935, 8 x 7 In. 600.00
Canteen, Acoma, Polychrome Geometric & Parrot, Histia, 1960s, 12 1/2 x 8 1/2 In. .. 220.00
Canteen, Maricopa, Black On Red, Hanging Lugs, 1940s, 6 1/2 x 5 1/2 In. 600.00
Canteen, Navajo, 1898 Mexican Silver Coin On Front, 1940s, 4 1/2 In. 600.00
Canteen, Navajo, Tobacco, Brass, 19th Century, 2 1/2 x 3 In. 120.00
Canteen, Navajo, Tobacco, Silver, 1900, 1 1/4 x 1 1/2 In. 550.00
Canteen, Zia, Bird Design, Helen Gachupin, 1970s, 7 1/2 x 8 In. 495.00
Canteen, Zuni, Bird Effigy, D. Westika & P. Pehnetsa, 10 x 8 In. 660.00
Cap, Iroquois, Beaded, Velvet, Meandering Floral, 5 1/2 In. 860.00
Case, Awl, Apache, Hide, Geometric Beadwork, Yellow Ocher, 1920, 17 x 2 In. 990.00
Case, Awl, Sioux, Leather Wrapped, Colored Beads, Leather Hanger, Tin Cone, 9 In. ... 190.00
Case, Knife, Quilted Buckskin, Tin Cone Suspensions, 17 In. 330.00
Club, Inlay, Bottle Shape, Ball Finial, Wooden, Incised Design, 25 1/2 In. 1090.00
Club, Stone Set Into Branch Handle, Black Paint, 19 x 7 1/2 In. 310.00
Cradle, Apache, Baby, Cloth, Basketry Sunshade, Human Hair, 1900, 22 x 10 In. 250.00
Cradle, Apache, Doll's, Beaded Strips, Brass Tacks, Fringe, 1910, 22 x 9 In. 495.00
Cradle, Apache, Red, White, Blue Beaded Design, 1930, 11 x 5 In. 495.00
Cradle, Kickapoo, Carved, Painted Tacks, Sunshade & Wrap, 1920, 10 x 30 In. 495.00
Cradle, Nez Perce, Beaded, Cut Beads, Buckskin, 1900, 6 x 14 In. 1210.00
Cradle, Nez Perce, Hide, Rounded, Beaded Top, Fringe, 1920, 22 x 7 In. 1380.00
Cradle, Paiute, Basketry Sunshade, Brass Tacks, Fringe, 1910, 22 x 9 In. 495.00
Cradle, Salish, Line & Butterfly Design, 1900 .... 440.00
Cradle, Sioux, Geometric Beaded Sunshade, Red Stroud Base, 1900, 30 x 14 In. 2070.00
Cradle, Umatilla, Doll's, Beaded Sunshade, 1920, 8 x 3 In. 275.00
Cradle, Willow, Yellow Canvas, Embroidered, 1950, 30 x 13 x 13 In. 355.00
Cradleboard, Carved, Painted, 19th Century, 31 x 10 1/2 In. 6875.00
Cradleboard, Red Cloth Cover, Calico Lined, Bentwood Sunshade, 28 x 13 In. 660.00
Cradleboard, Ute, Doll's, Buckskin Cover, Beaded, Fringe, Sunshade, 1900, 20 x 9 In. ... 935.00
Cuffs, Cheyenne, Buffalo Hide, Beaded Cross & Geometric, Sinew, 1900, 7 x 6 In., Pair .. 815.00
Cup & Saucer, Pima, Basketry, Fine Weave, 1920s, 1 x 2 In. 605.00
Dance Set, Yakima, Woman's, Beaded, Crown, Bag, Fan, Leggings, 1970, 11 Piece 770.00
Dice Case, Apache, Beaded Fringe, Shell, Cross & Moon On Back, 1940s, 13 In. 880.00
Doll, Assiniboin, Buckskin, Beaded Dress & Moccasins, Missing Hair, 1910, 11 In. 440.00
Doll, Cochiti, Storyteller, Mary & Leonard Trujillo, 1900s, 7 1/2 In. 275.00
Doll, Crow, Woman, Beaded Moccasins, Belt, Pouch, 20th Century, 11 x 5 In. 250.00
Doll, Girl, Hard Plastic, Beaded Clothes & Shoes, 7 1/2 In. 28.00
Doll, Nez Perce, Corn Husk, Painted Face, 1920, 11 x 2 1/2 In. 44.00
Doll, Northwest Coast, Hunter, Shonahah, 1970s, 8 x 19 In. 550.00
Doll, Papago, Basketry, Jointed Center Of Body, 1920s, 8 In. 1430.00
Doll, Plains, Yarn Hair, Beaded Dress, Leggings & Moccasins, 11 In. 440.00
Doll, Pueblo, Wooden, No Arms, 19th Century, 8 1/2 x 2 In. 415.00
Doll, Sioux, Buckskin, Beaded Vest, Leggings & Moccasins, 1900, 12 1/2 In. 1320.00
Doll, Sioux, Buckskin, Beaded Yoke, Belt & Moccasins, Human Hair, 1900, 6 1/2 In. ... 330.00
Doll, Tlingit, With Fur Parka, Leather Mukluks, 1930, 12 x 7 In. 470.00
Doll, Zuni, Buffalo Dance Woman, 1932, 13 x 6 1/2 In. 275.00
Dress, Blackfoot, Blue Stroud, Beaded Yoke, Bead & Cowry Shell, 1900, 41 x 43 In. ... 1380.00
Dress, Crow, Girl's, Buckskin, Geometric Beaded, Fringe, 1920, 38 x 29 In. 880.00
Dress, Crow, Girl's, White Buckskin, Beaded Line Design, Fringe, 1940, 54 x 29 In. ... 770.00

HANDS DOWN, ❧ FEET FIRST: ❧ A COLLECTING ODYSSEY

A COLLECTOR WE KNOW MET HIS WIFE on a blind date at the Rabbit Run Theater. At the wedding, their friends showered them with porcelain rabbits. The couple, of course, started collecting not just rabbit figurines, but rabbit plates, rabbit-shaped candy containers, stuffed rabbits, and anything rabbit-related they could find. When they moved, they decided to keep the ten best rabbits in their collection and go on to something else. They chose hand-shaped sculptures, and at first gave each other high-quality items from antiques shops. As time went on, their house was overrun with hand-shaped dishes, cookie cutters, bottles, and glove forms. Friends added gifts of advertising signs picturing hands and jewelry with hand charms or pendants.

Hands have had special significance since the days of ancient Egypt, when the hand represented power. In the Hindu tradition, Shiva holds his hand up to say, "Do not fear," and many replicas of the hand are made to be worn as jewelry. Other traditions treat the open hand as a representation of protection, power, and strength. Linked hands mean solidarity or friendship, and the image of the handshake was used on many valentines. Clasped hands on a tombstone indicate a reunion in the afterlife.

We all understand the meaning of a hand with a pointing index finger. It tells which direction to go. The vase held by a hand is said to represent the hand of Queen Victoria or perhaps her lady-in-waiting. A heart lying on an open palm is a folk art symbol for love or friendship. The Odd Fellows use the heart-in-hand as a symbol of charity.

Feet have been less popular as collectibles, although small glass and china shoes were the rage in Victorian times. Although there are many meanings to hand symbols, there seem be few for feet. In modern times the foot usually indicates long walks and athletic ability. A winged foot represents speed. On a coat of arms a foot is a symbol of strength, stability, and speed.

Secret and Not~So~Secret Messages

Fraternal organizations use symbols as part of the moral messages in their rituals and as a means of recognition among members. The Independent Order of Odd Fellows uses a hand with a heart as a symbol of its charitable activities. This 64-inch-long late nineteenth- or early twentieth-century ceremonial staff was used in meetings. It is made of carved wood painted red and gold. It sold for $2,300 in a recent auction.

This Pottier and Stymus chair has interesting head-shaped armrests, but look at the feet— they're hoof-shaped. Sometimes motifs are brought back from faraway lands. Napoleon liked the symbols of power that were used in ancient Egyptian architecture and sculpture. Mythical beasts, regal men and women, and other ancient symbols were adapted by furniture designers. Egyptian Revival chairs like this one aren't auctioned often and sell for $50,000 to $75,000 when they are.

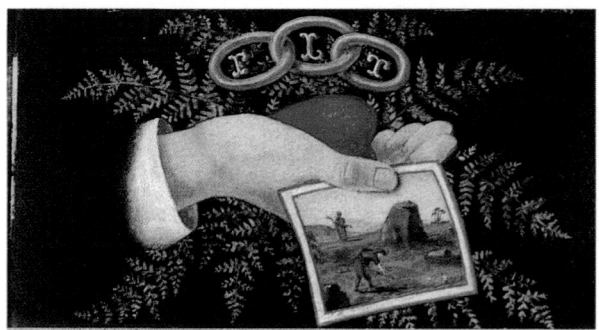

A collector paid $920 at auction for this Odd Fellows vignette. The oil-on-board painting shows several Odd Fellows symbols: a hand holding a heart and a card with an archery scene beneath three links. It measures 7 3/4 x 14 inches.

Advertising displays need to be direct to show off the product. What better way to draw attention to George's Patent Corn & Bunion Shields than with a life-sized foot with corns? The painted-plaster display is 10 inches long. Value, $250.

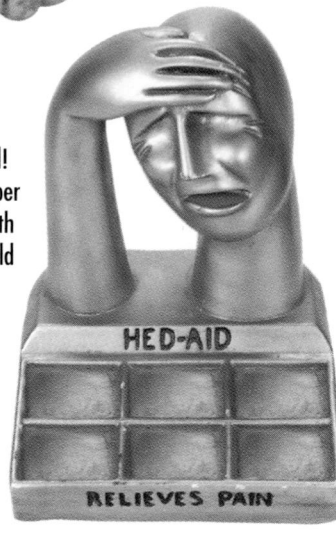

This poor person has such a bad headache that he's holding his head! Hed-Aid to the rescue—a shopkeeper could offer relief to his customer with the little tins of aspirin that were sold in this Art Deco-inspired plaster display. It measures 9 by 6 3/4 inches and would bring $200 at a flea market. It would sell for twice that much if the Hed-Aid tins were still in place.

This funeral director's sign points people in the right direction. C. L. Pinkel, of Sussex, New Jersey, would have displayed this 28-inch painted tin sign in front of the building. It brought $316 at auction.

Many shops gave customers small gifts with their purchases. This 2-inch shoe-shaped pocket knife was probably a shoestore premium. You can buy small but rare items like this for around $50.

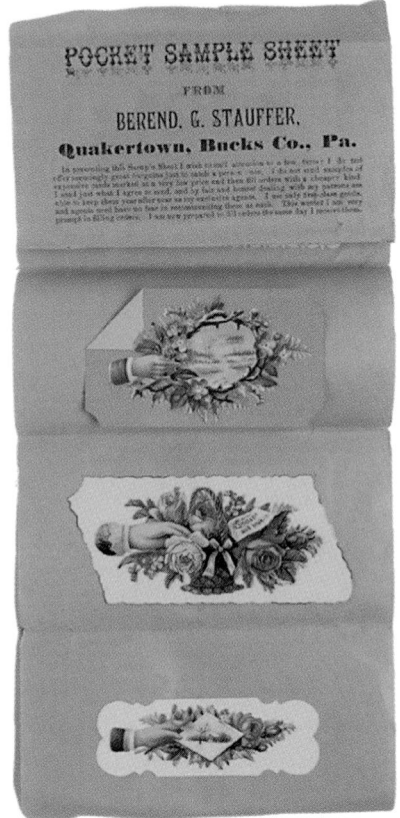

Functional Forms

A proper lady needed to leave a calling card when she visited her friends and acquaintances. This sample sheet from Berend G. Stauffer of Quakertown, Pennsylvania, shows a variety of die-cut cards with delicate hands holding flowers. The whole sheet, with seven full-color cards, sold for $3 at a dealer mall about twenty years ago.

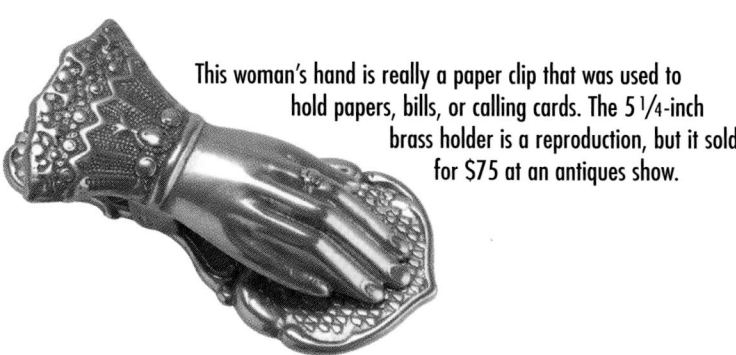

This woman's hand is really a paper clip that was used to hold papers, bills, or calling cards. The 5 1/4-inch brass holder is a reproduction, but it sold for $75 at an antiques show.

Victorian-era ladies liked to emulate the grace and femininity of the young Queen Victoria. Many decorative and functional glass, ceramic, and metal items were shaped like her hands. A realistic hand was modeled as part of a piece of glass or china. The hand design was first patented as a fruit dish in 1875. The piece was later listed in catalogs as a calling card dish and called Queen Victoria's Hands. This 5 1/2-inch example is a newer version with an enameled flower and fingernails. It was a flea market find at $25.

Ladies' hands held flowers, too. This 8-inch enameled opaline vase is supported by a hand. It was made in England about 1870. You can find one like it for around $200 to $250. Similar vases were made in porcelain.

Japanese pottery companies picked up where the Victorians left off. This 4 1/4-inch porcelain pin dish with applied rosebud is shaped like the Queen Victoria's Hands dish. The Occupied Japan mark dates it to the years following World War II. The mark gives it extra value for some collectors, who would pay $35 for it.

Some people tie strings around their fingers to remember things. This 4 1/2-inch ceramic hand will do it for you. The words "Don't Forget" are embossed on the hand, and an embossed string is tied around a finger. Remember to pick one up at a garage sale—it'll cost you $15.

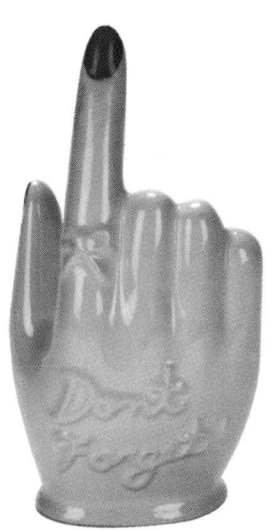

The George Zoltan Lefton Company has been in the business of importing knickknacks and giftwares since 1940. This porcelain hand-shaped dish holds rings on its fingers and pins in the dish that forms the base. It's 3 3/4 inches high and is decorated with pink rosebuds. Value, $20.

This bottle is in the shape of a hand holding a dagger. It is said to be the hand of Charlotte Corday, who killed the French revolutionary Jean Paul Marat to save her country from upheaval. Like Marie Antoinette, Corday was sent to the guillotine, and her act elevated Marat to martyr status. This 11½-inch turquoise glass bottle was made around 1890 to 1910 and is marked "Deposé," the French word for "registered." It's worth about $200.

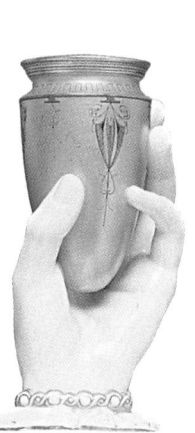

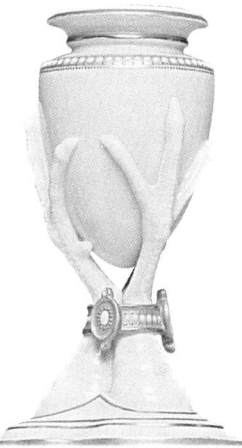

Here's a not-so-delicate variation of a hand vase held by bird's feet or claws. Three claws, bound by a jeweled band, hold an egg-shaped vase (right). If you're too squeamish for birds' feet, there is a version with human hands (left). The Royal Worcester 6¼- and 7-inch vases were made of glazed porcelain during the 1870s.

If ladies' hands are dainty, are men's feet powerful? This foot in a Roman-style sandal holds two candles. It is a nineteenth-century copy of an ancient Roman oil lamp. The bronze candlestick is 6 inches long. Value, $300.

Many parents preserve memories of their children with bronzed baby shoes. This 6 1/2-inch pair of bookends was made by Perma Plated Products in the 1950s. Don't have any tiny shoes to bronze? Don't worry—you can buy bronzed baby shoes like these at dealer malls for around $15.

Long ago, people dressed their children like adults. This 18 1/4-inch wood cane was made for a child, and has a brass finial shaped like a hand holding a monk with a cane. Small canes like this are hard to find. A collector would pay $400 for this interesting example.

For centuries, people have been interested in foretelling the future. A palm-reader-in-training might use a pottery hand like this one to decipher the lines on a person's hand. This reproduction is 7 inches high and cost $20 at a show. An old one would be worth $350.

When papers pile up on your desk, you need someone to give you a hand. Here's a midcentury modern bronze paperweight that will do the trick. It's 3 1/2 inches long and marked with an unreadable script logo and "Made in Austria." The company made a matching foot. A collector with an eye for style might find an item like this for $95.

Why would a metal camel be made with the sole of a shoe on his back? Because it's meant to hold a shoe. This 7-inch cast-iron shoe rest came from a public shoeshine bench. The intact green paint adds to its value, making it worth $125.

These wooden shoe forms look contorted. When you stand them on their toes, it's apparent that they're for women's high-heel shoes. The heels were added to the leather after the shoes were formed on these shoe lasts. The forms are marked "Como" and "7 1/4 B." The pointy toes date them to the late 1950s or early 1960s. They were purchased at a flea market for $15.

Skinner, Inc., Boston

Here's a ready-made collection of hands. These hand forms were used to make and model gloves, to show off jewelry in a store window, or as general advertising displays. Some are making gestures. Some are marked with company or store names. A few have movable fingers or wrists. The cast-iron, ceramic, wood, and composition forms, ranging in size from 4 1/2 to 23 1/4 inches, sold in a mixed auction lot for $1,725.

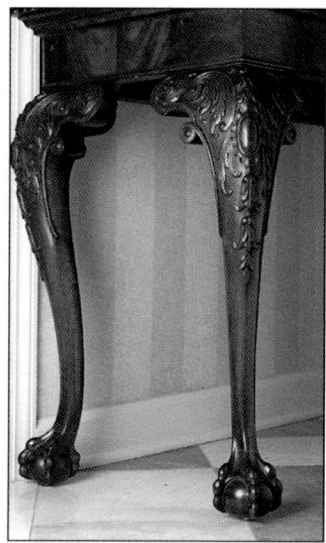

Eighteenth-century furniture often has interesting feet. This Chippendale console table has claw-and-ball feet. Tradition says a claw-and-ball foot represents a dragon claw holding a huge pearl. The idea has remained popular, and claw-and-ball feet are still used today.

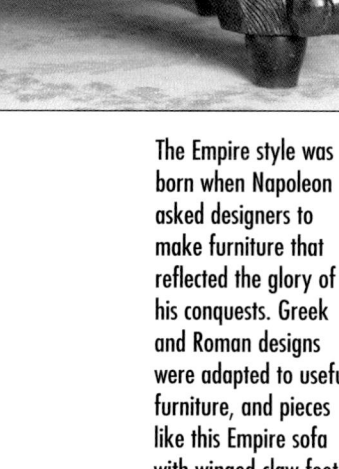

The Empire style was born when Napoleon asked designers to make furniture that reflected the glory of his conquests. Greek and Roman designs were adapted to useful furniture, and pieces like this Empire sofa with winged claw feet were made.

Designers following the Pop Art movement used unexpected forms for their furniture creations. This laminated wood "Hand" chair was designed by Pedro Friedeberg in 1962. It sold for $3,656 at a modern design auction. Similar chairs have been made ever since.

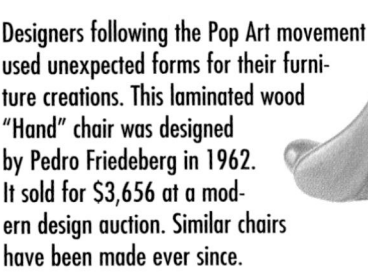

The "Joe" chair, named after Joe DiMaggio, is shaped like a baseball glove. It was made by De Pas, D'Urbino & Lomazzi of Italy in 1970. The 68-inch-wide leather chair comes in a variety of colors. A collector paid $6,900 for this one.

Who knows why this brand-new 11-inch bottle is shaped like a laced boot? To add to the mystery, it is embossed with a fort, a church, and ruins. It was made in Italy. Value, $9.

Hide and Go Seek

Now you have seen several antiques and collectibles shaped like hands and feet. But there are probably more in your collection if you look very closely.

Lady head vases are popular collectibles. The head holds the flowers, but there are many versions with other interesting details, like hands. This Napcoware lady is wearing blue gloves, pearl earrings, and daisies. The 7 3/4-inch planter sells for $28.

All figurines have feet by nature—some are more interesting than others. There are goat's feet on this 1950s Royal Copenhagen faun. The 9 1/2-inch figurine is holding a parrot. It has the crown and waves mark, and is stamped number 752. It's worth $200.

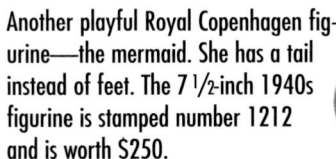

Another playful Royal Copenhagen figurine—the mermaid. She has a tail instead of feet. The 7 1/2-inch 1940s figurine is stamped number 1212 and is worth $250.

This little girl is sitting quietly under a tree, clasping her hands in contemplation. The 6 1/4-inch figurine was made by American ceramic artist Thelma Winter in the 1950s. Winter was inspired by Wiener Werkstätte designs. Pieces by this Cleveland school artist are starting to sell for higher prices in the Midwest. This figurine is worth $500.

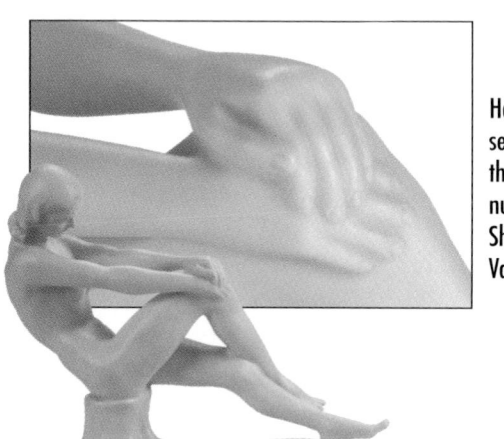

Hands and feet can be very seductive, like the ones on this 9 3/4-inch Royal Dux nude woman figurine. She is reclining on a stump. Value, $250.

You'll have to study this Japanese root deity to find his feet. The 11 1/2-inch figure is carved from a single piece of tree root and represents a mischievous forest creature. Figures like this one can be bought at upscale shows for about $600 to $800.

One foot on this Sharecropper bank is peeking out of the hole in his shoe. The 5 1/2-inch painted cast-iron bank was made by A. C. Williams of Ravenna, Ohio, and was patented in 1901. It sells for $150 to $175. A similar but less valuable bank was made showing a man without a hole in his shoe.

Children will get a kick out of the hands and feet on this Venetian glass snake charmer. It's 8 3/4 inches tall. Glass figurines are still popular souvenirs to bring home from a trip to Italy. Old ones cost $125 at shows.

Touch these nodders and their hands start to type. The 6 1/4-inch man and woman are a pair worth $250.

This sterling silver and tortoiseshell hands pendant was made by William Spratling in Mexico in the 1960s. The 5 1/4 -inch pendant with a chain is worth $7,500 to $8,500.

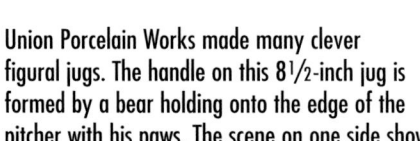

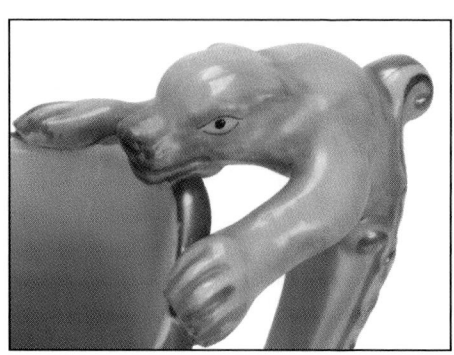

Union Porcelain Works made many clever figural jugs. The handle on this 8 1/2-inch jug is formed by a bear holding onto the edge of the pitcher with his paws. The scene on one side shows King Gambrinas, Uncle Sam, and a goat with the company's initials. The other side shows gamblers fighting. The spout is a mythical beast. Value, $2,000.

There are plenty of footed vases, but this one has four feet. This Haviland-type 7 5/8-inch vase shows a hand-painted medieval woman against a gold background. It is signed "Landry." The vase sells for $350.

Icon20.com

Dress, Crow, Red Trade Cloth, White Beadwork, 400 Elk Teeth, 1940, 52 x 45 In. 880.00
Dress, Crow, Trade Cloth, Cowrie Shell, Silk Ribbon, c.1920, 46 x 42 In. 90.00
Dress, Crow, Trade Cloth, White Beadwork, Carved Bone, 51 x 60 In. 440.00
Dress, Felt, Ribbon, Shell Beaded Yoke, 29 In. 485.00
Dress, Nez Perce, Woman's, White Buckskin, Beaded, Fringe, 1940, 57 x 49 In. 825.00
Drum, Blackfoot, Eagle Design 1 Side, Dots & Squares Other, Rawhide Covered, 14 In. . 715.00
Drum, Blackfoot, Hand Drum, Round, 1910, 20 x 2 In. 360.00
Drum, Blackfoot, Hand, Elk Hide Over Wooden Frame, 1900, 15 In. 415.00
Drum, Cheyenne, Hand, Rawhide, Buffalo & Ghost Dance Symbols, 1930, 16 x 2 In. 770.00
Drum, Plain, Hide Cover, Round Wooden Frame, 15 1/2 In. 600.00
Drum, Pueblo, With Drum Beater, 1970, 27 x 13 In. 155.00
Drum, Taos, Hollow Log, Tanned Rawhide Cover, 1950, 24 x 21 In. 220.00
Earrings, Apache, Carved Shells, Copper Loops, 5 In. 630.00
Earrings, Navajo, 7 Turquoise Stones, Applied Twisted Wire, 2 3/4 In. 315.00
Earrings, Navajo, Silver Dangle, 13 Turquoise Stones, 1940, 3 x 1 In. 66.00
Effigy, Acoma, Turkey, Jessie Garcia, Sarah Garcia, Signed, c.1870, 4 x 5 In., Pair 275.00
Effigy, Duck, Frog Design, Tara Edaakie, 7 x 10 In. 120.00
Effigy, Ivory, Canadian Goose, Shell, 6 x 3 1/4 In. 100.00
Effigy, Mohave, Frog, Polychrome, 1930s, 3 x 5 x 4 In. 525.00
Effigy, Santa Clara, Turtle, Polychrome Bug On Back, Margaret & Luther, 1970s, 8 In. 770.00
Effigy, Zuni, Owl, Pottery, 1930, 8 In. 525.00
Effigy, Zuni, Owl, Signed Initials N.B., 1950s, 7 x 8 x 7 In. 385.00
Flute, Cheyenne, Beaded Gourd Stitch, Leather Carrying Case, 1950s 248.00
Flute, Kiowa, Love Flute, Bird Shape, Red Ocher Trim, 1920, 23 x 2 In. 300.00
Fork, Navajo, Wrought Silver, Hand Stamping, 1940, 10 In. 120.00
Frontlet, Carved, Wood, Abalone Shell Inlay, Painted, Early 1900s, 6 x 4 In. 4890.00
Garters, Potawatomi, Full Loom Beaded, Geometric Designs, 3 x 29 In. 175.00
Gauntlets, Crow, Buckskin, Stylized Floral Beads, 1900, 7 x 16 In. 525.00
Gauntlets, Nez Perce, Buckskin, Floral, Beaded Cuffs, Fringe, 1930, 15 x 14 In. 300.00
Gun Case, Blackfoot, Buckskin, Beaded Geometric, Rifle Scabbard, 1890, 60 x 6 In. 3575.00
Hair Holder, Navajo, Silver Cluster, Turquoise, Signed, 3 1/2 x 2 In. 130.00
Hair Holder, Turquoise, Silver, Signed, 3 1/2 x 3 In. 198.00
Halibut Hook, Tlingit, Cotton Twine, Carved Shaman Holding Fish, 1910, 10 In. 345.00
Hatband, Navajo, 40 Sterling Silver Buttons 40.00
Jacket, Plains, Moose Hide, Fringed Top & Back Yoke, Military Buttons, 30 In. 250.00
Jar, Acoma, Bird Design, Concave Bottom, 1910, 9 x 8 In. 1045.00
Jar, Acoma, Black & White, Lucy Lewis, 1960, 4 x 4 In. 715.00
Jar, Acoma, Geometric Design, Indented Base, 1920, 9 x 8 In. 600.00
Jar, Acoma, Leaf & Bird Design, Eggshell Thin, Leno, 1970, 9 1/2 x 10 In. 715.00
Jar, Acoma, Picture, Deer, Lucy M. Lewis, 1950s, 6 1/2 In. 3300.00
Jar, Acoma, Stylized Birds, Geometric, 1940, 6 x 7 In. 165.00
Jar, Cheyenne, Storage, Beaded On Hide, 16 x 24 In. 1150.00
Jar, Cochiti, Old Style Birds, Leaf Designs, Signed, Ambrose Atencio, 5 1/2 x 6 In. 80.00
Jar, Hopi, Buff Ground, Abstract Feather Designs, 6 In. 230.00
Jar, Hopi, Feather Woman, Helen Naha, 1970, 5 1/2 x 5 1/4 In. 935.00
Jar, Hopi, Seed, Signed, Ida Sahmie, 1992, 4 x 4 In. 145.00
Jar, Hopi, Stylized Bird Design, 1960, 9 x 6 In. 660.00
Jar, Jemez, Black, Red, Signed, Geraldine Sandia, 1985, 9 x 9 In. 300.00
Jar, Laguna, Carved Eagle Dancers, Signed A. & V. Lucario, N.M., 6 x 5 In. 110.00
Jar, Maricopa, Polychrome, Signed, Barbara Johnson, 1965, 12 x 8 In. 550.00
Jar, Polychrome Birds, Signed With Bell, Sarafina Bell, 8 x 11 In. 3300.00
Jar, San Ildefonso, Polished Blackware, Maria Poveka, 3 1/2 x 5 In. 1870.00
Jar, San Juan, Seed, Flute Player & Flowers, Tan & Red, 1 1/4 x 1 1/4 In. 80.00
Jar, Santa Clara, Blackware, Carmel Romero, c.1960, 7 x 6 In. 250.00
Jar, Santa Clara, Blackware, Signed, Flora Naranjo, 1960, 5 x 5 In. 250.00
Jar, Santa Clara, Carved, Blackware, Stella Chavarria, 4 x 5 In. 145.00
Jar, Santo Domingo, Polychrome, Robert Tenorio, 1980, 5 1/2 x 6 1/2 In. 440.00
Jar, Santo Domingo, Signed, Robert Tenorio, 1975, 6 x 5 In. 550.00
Jar, Tequaeche, Seed, Indian & Horses, Signed, 1986, 12 x 4 1/2 In. 220.00
Jar, Zia, Center Cream Band, Painted Bird & Floral, Indented Base, 8 In. 1092.00
Jar, Zia, Polychrome, Ornate Design, Indented Base, 1900 .... 2750.00
Kachina, Eagle, Feathers On The Wings, 1980, 10 x 13 In. 110.00
Kachina, Hopi, Carved Cottonwood Root Crow Father, J. Noquatewa, 12 In. 70.00

Kachina, Hopi, Carved Cottonwood Root Longhair, Barry Honyouti, 12 In. 330.00
Kachina, Hopi, Carved Cottonwood Root White Buffalo, 17 In. 55.00
Kachina, Hopi, Carved Cottonwood Shalko, 9 1/2 In. 90.00
Kachina, Hopi, Carved Hummingbird, Leo Lacapa, 13 1/2 In. 120.00
Kachina, Hopi, Eagle Dancer, Legal Feather, 1930, 10 x 11 In. 200.00
Kachina, Hopi, Koshari, Clown Holding Dog, Display Case, Neil David, 1977s, 7 In. 880.00
Kachina, Hopi, Lifelike Human Figure, Mounted On Board, 15 In. 880.00
Kachina, Hopi, Signed, Egor Russell, 1980, 18 x 7 1/2 In. 165.00
Kachina, Hopi, White Bear, Watercolor Paints, Al Honanie, 1990s, 13 In. 415.00
Kachina, Hopi, Wolf, Signed, Von Masiewstewa, 1960 . . . . 55.00
Kachina, Hopi, Yellow Case Mask, Bird Tracks, c.1930, 12 3/4 In. 690.00
Kachina, Mudhead Clown, 3 Gourds On Head, 9 In. 370.00
Knife, Crow, Beaded Case, Fringe, Made From Painted Parfleche, 1890, 18 x 4 In. 1380.00
Knife, Handmade, Geometric Beaded Case, 1900s, 8 x 3 In. 430.00
Knife, Sioux, Skinning, Horn Scales, Brass Cross Guard, Late 19th Century, 14 1/2 In. . . . 470.00
Ladle, Flagstaff, Rattle Handle, 1150 AD, 12 x 5 1/2 In. 495.00
Lance, Plains, Buffalo, Hand Forged Iron Blade, Shaft Porcupine Quill, 1800s, 65 In. 3300.00
Ledger, Plains, Battle Between Indians & Soldiers, 13 3/4 x 16 1/2 In. 2640.00
Ledger, Plains, Drawing, Araposh Spirit, 13 3/4 x 16 1/2 In. 7700.00
Ledger, Plains, Drawing, Couples Embracing, Late 19th Century, 13 x 16 In. 935.00
Ledger, Plains, Drawing, Injuries Sustained During Battle, 13 x 16 In. 2190.00
Ledger, Plains, Drawing, Peace Pipe Tribal Ceremony, 13 1/2 x 16 1/2 In. 550.00
Leggings, Arapaho, Hide, Beaded Strips, Sinew Sewn, 1920 . . . . 470.00
Leggings, Arapaho, Woman's, Beaded Buckskin, 19 In. 360.00
Leggings, Blackfoot, Made From Potato Sacks, Tadpole Beaded Designs, 1890s, 36 In. . . . 275.00
Leggings, Cheyenne, Girl's, Sinew Sewn, New Tops, 1900-1972, 15 1/2 x 5 In. 990.00
Leggings, Cheyenne, Sinew Hide, White Geometric Beadwork, 1920, 22 x 8 In. 470.00
Leggings, Cheyenne, Woman's, Beaded Hide, White Field, 1890, 19 In. 800.00
Leggings, Cheyenne, Woman's, White Buckskin, Geometric Beaded, 1920, 13 x 8 In. 385.00
Leggings, Crow, Woman's, Fully Beaded, Star & Line Designs, 8 x 12 In. 190.00
Leggings, Nez Perce, Hide Trade Cloth, Beaded Panel, 11 x 32 In. 155.00
Leggings, Plains, Red, Green, Black, White Field, Late 19th Century, 12 1/2 In. 550.00
Leggings, Sioux, Woman's, Buckskin, Sinew Sewn, Geometric Beads, 1920, 14 x 6 In. . . . 880.00
Martingale, Crow, Beadwork, Triangle Design, Red Felt, c.1910, 38 In. 8625.00
Martingale, Ute, Full Beaded, Floral Design, Hawk Bell Drops, 1920, 35 x 8 In. 660.00
Mask, Kwakiutl, British Columbia, Moon, Salmon Design, 1900s, 23 In. 1100.00
Mask, Nez Perce, Corn Husk False Face, 1920, 4 1/2 In., Pair 358.00
Mask, Northwest, Tlingit Woman, Copper Labrets & Eyes, 1940, 10 x 8 In. 523.00
Medicine Bag, Sioux, Headed Animal, Trade Cloth Trim, Tin Cones, 1870, 29 x 9 In. 1980.00
Medicine Bag, Sioux, Rawhide, Painted Geometric, Long Fringe, 1920, 17 1/2 x 7 In. 465.00
Memory Cloth, Navajo, Hand Painted, Muslin, 1940, 37 x 43 In. 880.00
Mirror Case, Apache, Deerskin, Stars, Turtle, Beading, c.1890, 10 x 6 In. 880.00
Moccasins, Arapaho, Buffalo Hide, Beaded Sinew Sewn, 1890, 10 x 4 In. 1870.00
Moccasins, Arapaho, Buffalo Hide, Geometric Beaded Design, 1900, 10 x 4 In. 1760.00
Moccasins, Assiniboin, Beaded, Geometric Design, 1900, 10 x 4 In. 770.00
Moccasins, Assiniboin, Child's, Beaded, Geometric Design, 1900, 6 1/2 x 2 1/2 In. 770.00
Moccasins, Blackfoot, Buffalo Hide, Beaded Star Design Toe, Sinew, 1910, 11 x 5 In. . . . 750.00
Moccasins, Blackfoot, Buffalo Hide, Diamond Beaded Design, 4 x 10 In. 190.00
Moccasins, Blackfoot, Child's, Buffalo Hide, Beaded, 1890, 9 x 3 1/2 In. 1430.00
Moccasins, Buckskin, Beaded Geometric Design, Rawhide Soles, 1950, 10 x 4 In. 275.00
Moccasins, Cheyenne, Buffalo Hide, Sinew Sewn, Target Design, 1900, 9 1/2 x 4 In. 1210.00
Moccasins, Cheyenne, Hide, Beaded, Rawhide Soles, Sinew Sewn, 1920, 10 1/2 x 4 In. . . 880.00
Moccasins, Cree, Hide, Beaded Floral Design, Moose Hair Trim, 1900 . . . . 90.00
Moccasins, Cree, Woodland's Hide, Red Beaded Floral, 1900, 7 x 3 In. 80.00
Moccasins, Crow, Buffalo Hide, Beaded Toes, Green, Ocher, 1910, 10 x 4 In. 375.00
Moccasins, Crow, Buffalo Hide, Geometric Beadwork, 1900, 10 x 4 In. 415.00
Moccasins, Crow, Child's, Beaded Geometric, High Top, 1920, 6 x 2 1/2 x 5 In. 690.00
Moccasins, Crow, Child's, Leather, Long Tongues, Beaded Cross, c.1890 . . . . 220.00
Moccasins, Crow, Girl's, Beaded, Band Design, 1937, 7 x 3 x 5 In. 715.00
Moccasins, Crow, White Buckskin, Geometric Beaded Toes, 1930, 5 x 3 x 4 In. 330.00
Moccasins, Crow, White Buckskin, Geometric Design, 1960, 9 x 4 x 12 In. 495.00
Moccasins, Iroquois, Floral Beaded Toes, Red Cloth, Soft Sole, 1900, 11 1/2 x 4 1/2 In. . . 525.00
Moccasins, Lakota, Beaded Checkerboard Design Vamps, Hard Soles, 11 In. 375.00

Moccasins, Lakota, Toddler's, Beaded Vamp, Red Beads On White Field, c.1910, 4 1/8 In. 490.00
Moccasins, Osage, Beaded Star, Looped Edging On Cuffs & Tongue, 10 1/2 In. 600.00
Moccasins, Parfleche, Blue, Red Beads, White Ground, 1880, 11 In. 990.00
Moccasins, Plains, Beaded, Red, White, Blue, 1940s, 3 1/2 x 10 In. 525.00
Moccasins, Potawatomi, Buckskin, Geometric Beaded, Soft Sole, 1930, 9 1/2 x 3 In. 355.00
Moccasins, Seneca, Blue, Red & White Beads, Mid 19th Century 8500.00
Moccasins, Shoshone, Hide, Red, Green, Black Beaded Cross Designs, 1920, 10 x 3 In. . . . 330.00
Moccasins, Sioux, Beaded, Buffalo Hide, 1890, 10 x 4 In. 525.00
Moccasins, Sioux, Beaded, High Sides, 2 Part Tongues, 1900s, 10 1/2 In. 2750.00
Moccasins, Sioux, Green, Red Beads, White Ground, 1880, 10 1/2 In. 1100.00
Moccasins, Sioux, Quilled Inserts, Beaded Sides, Parfleche Soles, 1900s, 7 1/2 In. 440.00
Moccasins, Sioux, Sewn, Fully Beaded, Green, White, Blue, Rawhide Soles, c.1920 . . . . . 510.00
Moccasins, Southern Arapaho, Buckskin, Buffalo Soles, Beaded, Sinew, 1800s, 11 In. 1870.00
Moccasins, Tlingit, Hide, Floral Beaded Wool, Toe Design, Fur Trim, 1935, 3 x 3 In. 110.00
Model, Canoe, Northwest Coast, Haida, Natural Paint, 2 Paddles, 1910, 44 x 9 x 8 In. . . 550.00
Necklace, Bone, White Heart Beads, 19th Century Cross, 30 In. 45.00
Necklace, Fetish, Silver Cones At Clasp, 3 Strand, 28 In. 220.00
Necklace, Hopi, Silver, 1 Turquoise Stone, Signed, Thomas, 1960, 22 In. 175.00
Necklace, Hopi, Silver, Heartline Bear Pendant, 1970, 28 In. 250.00
Necklace, Navajo, 10 Fifty Cent Pieces, All Silver, 1960s, 14 1/2 In. 65.00
Necklace, Navajo, Coral Tube Heshi, 15 Strand, 20th Century, 21 In. 248.00
Necklace, Navajo, Coral, Silver Chip Inlay, Peyote Bird Squash Blossom, 1980, 35 In. . . . 145.00
Necklace, Navajo, Coral, Turquoise, Silver Beaded, 8 Strand, 1950, 30 In. 130.00
Necklace, Navajo, Cross Pendant, Chip Turquoise Inlay, 20 In. 110.00
Necklace, Navajo, Lone Mountain, Turquoise, Nugget & Silver Squash Blossom, 26 In. . . 220.00
Necklace, Navajo, Natural Coral, Silver, Handmade, 20th Century, 22 In. 80.00
Necklace, Navajo, Needlepoint Squash Blossom, Signed, Victor M. Begay, 1980, 36 In. . . 190.00
Necklace, Navajo, Silver Squash Blossom, Silver Feather On Each Blossom, 35 In. 850.00
Necklace, Navajo, Silver, 5 Turquoise Stones, Cast Pendant, Encircling Hands, 27 In. 210.00
Necklace, Navajo, Silver, Turquoise Squash Blossoms, Naja, 13 1/2 In. 290.00
Necklace, Navajo, Silver, Turquoise Stone & Turquoise Heishi, 1935, 33 In. 210.00
Necklace, Navajo, Silver, Turquoise, Coral Peyote Bird, Signed, 1970, 32 In. 210.00
Necklace, Navajo, Silver, Turquoise, Crescent Shape Pendant, Rope Twist, 23 In. 195.00
Necklace, Navajo, Squash Blossom, 2 Strand, Rope Twist, 13 Stones, 26 1/2 In. 220.00
Necklace, Navajo, Squash Blossom, Silver Beads, Petit Point, Ed Niiha, 24 In. 130.00
Necklace, Navajo, Squash Blossom, Silver, Red Coral Stones, 26 In. 330.00
Necklace, Navajo, Squash Blossom, Turquoise Stones, 1940, 26 In. 330.00
Necklace, Oxblood Coral, Bone Rondels, 26 In. 145.00
Necklace, Oxblood Coral, Turquoise, Silver Beads, 6 Strand, 30 In. 198.00
Necklace, Padre Bead, 19th Century Cross, 27 In. 30.00
Necklace, Pendant, Silver Beads, Turquoise, Rose Abeyta, 17 In. 90.00
Necklace, Pueblo, Coral, Silver Beads, 2 Coins, 10 Strand, 1950s, 16 In. 550.00
Necklace, Santa Clara, Turquoise, Graduated Nuggets, Shell At Neck, Silver Clasp, 30 In. 150.00
Necklace, Santo Domingo, Fetish, Spondulus Shell, 3 Strand, 1940, 30 In. 385.00
Necklace, Santo Domingo, Kingman Turquoise, 3 Strand, 1960, 32 In. 80.00
Necklace, Santo Domingo, Natural Turquoise Nuggets, 2 Strand, 1960, 30 In. 80.00
Necklace, Santo Domingo, Old Pawn, Turquoise Nugget, 1950, 18 In. 55.00
Necklace, Santo Domingo, Turquoise Nugget, 1950, 22 In. 1200.00
Necklace, Squash Blossom, Double Row Of Beads, Mid 1940, 24 In. 155.00
Necklace, Squash Blossom, Silver, Coin, Naja, 1970, 26 In. 150.00
Necklace, Turquoise, Beaded, 2 Jackals On Bottom, 2 Strand, 1980, 28 In. 120.00
Necklace, Zuni, Fetish, Bird, Mother-Of-Pearl, 3 Strand, 1960, 30 In. 210.00
Necklace, Zuni, Fetish, Silver, Birds, Bears, Frogs & Turtles, 28 In. 250.00
Necklace, Zuni, Shell Bird Fetish, 3 Strand, Handmade, 1940, 32 In. 110.00
Necklace, Zuni, Squash Blossom, Silver Beads, Inlaid Figures, Turquoise, Pendant, 28 In. 220.00
Necklace, Zuni, Squash Blossom, Silver, Hummingbird, Flower, 1970, 36 In. 440.00
Necklace, Zuni, Squash Blossom, Silver, Turquoise, Roger Skeet, 1935, 27 In. 715.00
Necklace & Earrings, Zuni, Silver, Turquoise, Jet, Shell & Coral Inlay, 1970 . . . . 770.00
Olla, Acoma, Deer & Parrot, Debbie Garcia Brown, 16 1/2 x 15 In. 825.00
Olla, Acoma, Geometric Polychrome, Early 20th Century, 10 1/4 In. 9350.00
Olla, Apache, Black Lightning, Horsehair Handles, 1890s, 14 In. 1650.00
Olla, Apache, Geometric Design, Interspersed Crosses, c.1910, 14 1/2 In. 3080.00
Olla, Basket, Coiled, Radiating Square & Cross Designs, 9 3/4 In. 520.00

Olla, California Mission, Woven Floral, Chickens & Birds, Dyed Juncus, 1907, 17 In. 8250.00
Olla, Cochiti, Raised Lizard & Storm Cloud Design, 1900, 13 x 13 In. 3850.00
Olla, Papago, Coiled Yellow, Black & Brown, 15 x 15 1/2 In. 880.00
Olla, Pueblo, Birds & Leaf Designs, Trios-Style, 1900, 9 x 9 In. 935.00
Olla, Salado, Black & White, Red Bottom, 10 x 14 In. 300.00
Olla, Water, Acoma, Parrot Design, 1950, 9 x 11 In. 155.00
Pants, Crow, White Buckskin, Cut Bead Floral Designs, 42 In. 300.00
Parfleche, Cheyenne, Bonnet Case, Rawhide, Geometric Painted, Round, 17 x 5 In. 495.00
Parfleche, Crow, Rawhide, Red, Green, Blue, Yellow, Geometric 1920, 23 x 10 In. 1035.00
Pendant, Zuni, Silver, Eagle & Silver Bead Chain, 1980, 27 In. 190.00
Pendant, Zuni, Silver, Turquoise & Shell Inlay, 1985, 3 x 3 1/2 In. 110.00
Pin, Navaho, Silver, Turquoise, Tear Drop Stone, J.& E. Wilson, 4 3/8 In. 80.00
Pipe, Crow, Seed Beads Wrapped, Catlinite T-Pipe, Ash Stem, 27 In. 770.00
Pipe, Plains, Buffalo Shape, Wood, Stone, c.1900 . . . . 55.00
Pipe, Plains, Catlinite Inlaid, Ash Stem, 1880, 26 In. 2090.00
Pipe, Tube, Incised, Engraved Bowl Top, Licking Co., Ohio, 3 In. 485.00
Pipe Bag, Beaded Cross 1 Side, Beaded Geometric Design Other, Quill Fringe, 40 In. . . . 715.00
Pipe Bag, Blackfoot, Geometric Beadwork, Fringe, 1890, 28 x 7 In. 1430.00
Pipe Bag, Cheyenne, Tabbed Top, Long Fringe 605.00
Pipe Bag, Crow, Woman's, Hide, Beaded Cross, Geometrics, Fringe, 6 1/2 x 2 1/2 In. 330.00
Pipe Bag, Plains, Beaded, Woven, Tassel, 1870-1880, 13 3/4 In. 635.00
Pipe Bag, Sioux, Beaded Buffalo Hide, Fringe, 1900, 28 x 7 In. 880.00
Pipe Bag, Sioux, Geometric Beaded, Quilled Panel, Fringe, 1960, 37 x 7 In. 660.00
Pipe Bag, Sioux, Quilled Panel, Fringe, Mrs. Fire Thunder, 1940 . . . . 1320.00
Pipe Tomahawk, Plains, Tacked Hardwood Haft, Steel Blade, 1900, 21 In. 300.00
Plaque, Hopi, Basketry, Woven, Tina Dallas, 1935, 9 1/2 x 1 In. 135.00
Plaque, Men Riding Horses, Women Arms Up, Dogs, 1930s, 2 x 11 In. 825.00
Plaque, Pima, Basketry, Pictorial Bugs, 1950s, 15 1/2 In. 2475.00
Plate, Acoma, Beetle Design, Polychrome, Frances, 1968, 11 1/2 x 1 In. 465.00
Plate, Black On Black, Marked, Maria & Santana, 1945, 11 x 1 3/8 In. 4400.00
Plate, Black On Black, Marked, Maria & Santana, 1945, 5 1/2 x 3/4 In. 1210.00
Plate, San Ildefonso, Matte On Black, Maria & Popovi, 5 3/4 In. 1210.00
Pot, Acoma, Allover Geometric Designs, c.1940, 6 1/2 In. 220.00
Pot, Acoma, Feathered Pattern, White Ground, c.1930, 7 In. 770.00
Pot, Pueblo, Classic Mimbres Design, 20th Century, 10 In. 100.00
Pot, Santa Clara, Black On Black, Signed, Cresencia, 1970, 5 x 4 In. 190.00
Pot, Zuni, 4 Protruding Frogs Around Top, Signed, M. Katsenin, 5 1/2 x 6 In. 145.00
Pouch, Apache, Beaded Designs, Borders, Triangles, Leather Fringe, 1890s, 8 3/4 In. 715.00
Pouch, Apache, Beadwork Both Sides, Corn Stalks, Stars, 1890s, 7 1/2 In. 715.00
Pouch, Apache, Leather, Beaded Bands, c.1880, 6 x 5 3/4 In. 410.00
Pouch, Apache, Leather, Beaded Design On Sides, Leather String Tie, 7 1/2 In. 990.00
Pouch, Beaded Red Berries, Blue Flowers, Colored Flags, c.1880, 5 3/4 In. 2710.00
Pouch, Belt, Nez Perce, Floral, Beaded, 1920, 5 1/2 x 6 In. 1100.00
Pouch, Iroquois, Black Velvet Panels, Beaded Edges, Flowers, 5 1/2 x 6 1/4 In. 55.00
Pouch, Sioux, Buffalo Hide, Sinew Sewn, 1890s, 5 1/2 x 4 1/2 In. 275.00
Purse, Nez Perce, Embroidered Geometric Design, 11 x 8 In. 495.00
Purse, Plains, Beaded Belt, Butterfly Design, Late 19th Century, 4 1/4 In. 165.00
Quirt, Crow, Elk Horn, Beaded, Tacked Strap, 1880, 23 In. 750.00
Rattle, Cheyenne, Gourd, Cut Bead Trim, Twisted Fringe, Horsehair Tip, 2 x 25 In. 250.00
Rattle, Dance, Hopi, Parfleche Top, Leather Wrapped Handle, 8 1/4 In. 110.00
Rattle, Iroquois, Turtle Shell, Head, Neck, 19th Century, 18 x 8 In. 220.00
Rattle, Medicine, Blackfoot, Buffalo Hide, Beaded Handle, Fringe, 1890, 14 x 5 In. 715.00
Rattle, Medicine, Blackfoot, Buffalo Scrotum, Red, Ocher, Cloth Handle, 1880, 6 x 5 In. . . 550.00
Rattle, Medicine, Hopi, Gourd, Painted Saguaro Spine Handle, 1900 . . . . 290.00
Retablo, Madonna & Child, Painted Tin, Wooden Nicho, 1800s, 14 x 22 In. 375.00
Retablo, San Jose, Painted Tin, Frame, 1800s, 18 x 23 In. 495.00
Retablo, Virgin & Child, Painted Tin, Tin & Glass Frame, 1800s 440.00
Ring, Navajo, Man's, Heavy, Frog On Top, Turquoise, Silver, Coral, 1980, Size 11 . . . . . . 175.00
Ring, Navajo, Man's, Heavy, Silver, 2 Turquoise Stones, 1940, Size 10 . . . . 110.00
Ring, Zuni, Silver Inlay Bird Center, Turquoise, 1980, Size 10 . . . . 55.00
Roach, Head Piece, Crow, Hair Base, Porcupine & Deer Hair, 17 x 7 x 3 In. 690.00
Robe, Crow, Sunburst, Painted Buffalo, 1940, 84 x 84 In. 2200.00
Rug, 2 Gray Hills, Geometric Design, Gray, Brown, 45 x 66 In. 2128.00

Rug, 6 Yeibeichai Dancers, Gray, Black, White, Brown, Plum, Green, 26 x 38 In. 280.00
Rug, Gallup, Triangle Center, 3 Panels, Gray Ground, Red, Black, Ivory, 50 x 81 In. 1230.00
Rug, Ganado, 3 Medallion, Gray, Brown, Orange, Black, White, 42 x 77 In. 785.00
Rug, Klagetoh, Central Diamond Medallion, Earthtones & Ivory, 42 x 67 In. 560.00
Rug, Klagetoh, Central Geometric Diamond, Ivory, Red, Browns, 41 x 62 In. 672.00
Rug, Klagetoh, Sawtooth & Diamond, Ivory, Red, Browns, 82 x 127 In. 1792.00
Rug, Navajo, 2 Central Medallions, Brown Ground, Red, Ivory, Browns, 49 x 89 In. 1230.00
Rug, Navajo, 3 Center Lozenge, Double Arrow Print, 1940, 57 x 34 In. 605.00
Rug, Navajo, 5 Central Diamonds, Gray, Brown, Black, White, Red, Stains, 53 x 92 In. . . 896.00
Rug, Navajo, Black, White Diamonds, Crosses, Red Field, c.1940, 51 x 79 1/2 In. 495.00
Rug, Navajo, Center 2 Stepped Diamonds, Feathers Throughout, 38 x 61 In. 880.00
Rug, Navajo, Diamonds, Red, Brown, Gray, White Ground, Carded Wool, 30 x 72 In. 605.00
Rug, Navajo, Double Rows Diamond Medallions, Red Field, c.1920, 64 x 93 In. 1100.00
Rug, Navajo, Expanding Diamond, Corner Blocks, Interlocking Scallops, 37 x 60 In. 330.00
Rug, Navajo, Ganado, Double Bar Cross Center, 3-Banded Border, c.1905, 42 x 69 In. . . . 385.00
Rug, Navajo, Geometric Design, St. Michaels, Esther White, 1982, 29 x 41 In. 100.00
Rug, Navajo, Geometric Gray, Ivory, Black & Red Field, 44 x 60 In. 1100.00
Rug, Navajo, Geometric, Basket Weave Pattern, Red, Brown, Tan, Fringe, 61 x 39 In. 635.00
Rug, Navajo, Geometric, Stylized Human Faces, Feather Borders, 1920, 111 x 86 In. 3200.00
Rug, Navajo, Geometric, Tan, Red, Black, Beige, Borders, Crystal, c.1920, 48 x 28 In. . . . 920.00
Rug, Navajo, Germantown, Zigzag, Diamond Design, Arrow Border, Fringe, 32 x 36 In. . . . 5900.00
Rug, Navajo, Gold & Cream Figures, Gray Ground, Zigzag Border, 41 x 58 In. 770.00
Rug, Navajo, Interlocking Diamonds, Butterfly Edges, Gray Center, 30 x 60 In. 165.00
Rug, Navajo, Ivory, Brown, Aniline Red & Purple, Teepee Border, 75 x 45 In. 2750.00
Rug, Navajo, Pine Springs Area, Multiple Line Design, 1940, 96 x 65 In. 990.00
Rug, Navajo, Serrated Bands, Geometric End Border, Hand Spun, 1920, 39 x 56 In. 1045.00
Rug, Navajo, Squares, 2 Diamonds, Center Cross, Carded Wool, 36 x 48 In. 440.00
Rug, Navajo, Storm Pattern, Wool, Brown, Tan, Gray & White, 1950, 100 x 50 In. 990.00
Rug, Navajo, Striped Western Reservation, X Design, 63 x 30 In. 200.00
Rug, Navajo, Teec Nos Pos Outline, Central Lozenge, 1940, 58 x 36 In. 440.00
Rug, Navajo, Vegetal Dye, Bernice Barber, 1985, 43 x 69 In. 360.00
Rug, Navajo, Western Reservation, Red Outline, Feather Border, 1960, 51 x 60 In. 600.00
Rug, Navajo, Wide Ruin, Vegetal Dye, Lottie Thompson, 1986, 33 x 50 In. 440.00
Rug, Navajo, Yei, Figural, Geometric, Figures Planting, Tan, Black, Red, Blue, 32 x 28 In. 490.00
Rug, Serrated Diamonds, Gray Ground, Black, White, Red, 41 x 69 In. 1232.00
Saddle Throw, Assiniboin, Canvas, Red Trade Cloth, Buffalo Hide Fringe, 1880, 30 In. . . 1100.00
Saddlebag, Nez Perce, Glass Bead, Wool, Buffalo Hide & Cotton, 25 x 14 In. 3600.00
Sally Bag, Nez Perce, Hemp Twine, Cornhusk Root, Quail, Vegetal Dye, 8 x 12 In. 1100.00
Sash, Hopi, Woven Cotton, Balls & Twisted Fringe Suspensions, 1900, 54 x 5 In. 415.00
Sash, Pueblo, Finger Woven Cotton & Wool, 4 1/2 x 54 In. 130.00
Serape, Geometric, Central Sunburst, Gray, Ivory, Red, Black, Brown, Teal, 41 x 58 In. . . 730.00
Serape, Stepped Diamond & Arrow Design, Gray Ground, 48 x 68 In. 55.00
Shawl, Pueblo, Silk, Fringe, 1935, 65 x 60 In. 80.00
Shoes, Sioux, Mary Jane Style, Beaded, 1900, 8 1/2 In. 355.00
Skirt, Seminole, Cotton, Patchwork & Appliqued, 26 In. 115.00
Snowshoes, Cree, Rawhide Lacing, Red Wool Trim, 41 In. 130.00
Snowshoes, Great Lakes, Child's, Carved, Red Wool Tufts, 10 7/8 x 29 1/4 In. 185.00
Snowshoes, Great Lakes, Leather & Wooden, 1890s 150.00
Spear Point, Yellow Jasper, Chester County, Penn. 330.00
Spoon, Ceremonial, Northwest Coast, Sheep Horn Ladle, Goat Horn Handle, 16 In. 1955.00
Spoon, Sioux, Bent Horn, Carved, Quill Covered Handle, 4 x 12 In. 155.00
Spoon, Woodlands, Tack Design, 11 In. 55.00
Storyteller, Jemez, Leader, 10 Babies, Henrietta Gauchupin, 10 1/2 In. 410.00
Tomahawk, Forged Steel Head, Rear Spike, Shaped Oak Handle, Pitted, 12 In. 140.00
Tomahawk, North American, Head, Fully Grooved, 5 1/4 In. 110.00
Tomahawk, Plains, Iron, Pewter Inlay, Brass Wooden Handle, 1880, 18 x 5 1/2 In. 980.00
Tomahawk, Plains, Pewter Mouthpiece, Silver Collar, Tin Cones, Feathers, 25 In. 7920.00
Tomahawk, War, Spontoon, Iron, Wooden Handle, 1860, 25 x 12 In. 2895.00
Totem Pole, Northwest Coast, Carved, Painted, Wooden, Early 1900s, 14 1/2 In. 805.00
Totem Pole, Tlingit, Carved & Painted Cedar, Eagle & Bear, 1920s, 20 In. 300.00
Totem Pole, Tlingit, Whale & Eagle, Painted, Ellen Neel, 1956, 24 x 13 In. 495.00
Trade Beads, Venetian, Polychrome, 19th Century, 32 In. 100.00
Tray, Apache, Basket, Animals, Splint Willow, Devil's Claw Bark, 18 In. 3000.00

Tray, Apache, Basket, Hanging Wire, 1940s, 12 1/2 In. 1155.00
Tray, Apache, Basket, Willow & Devils Claw, 3 Radiating Bands, 1900, 17 In. 3738.00
Tray, Hopi, Coiled, 4 Lobed Flowers, Analine Colors, 10 In. 110.00
Tray, Hopi, Thunderbird, 2 Colors Form Picture, 13 1/2 In. 500.00
Tray, Pima, Basketry, Coiled, 5 Stylized Lizards, 10 1/2 In. 345.00
Tray, Pima, Expanding Fret Design, Center Circle, Dark Devil's Claw, Willow, 20 1/2 In. .. 1780.00
Vase, Acoma, Wedding, Floral & Parrot, Sarah Garco, 1980s, 7 x 12 In. 230.00
Vase, Hopi, Polychrome Design, Signed With Frog, 1970s, 6 x 6 1/2 In. 580.00
Vase, Jemez, Red, Buff, Feather, Serpent Design, Signed, O. Yipa, 1985, 7 x 10 In. 385.00
Vase, Navajo, Duck Design, Pottery, Signed, William Yazzie, 1988, 8 x 5 In. 300.00
Vase, San Ildefonso, Etched Avanyu Design, Patricia Davly, 7 x 7 In. 110.00
Vase, Santa Clara, Black, Signed, Ursalita Naranjo, 1950, 6 x 5 In. 250.00
Vase, Santa Clara, Wedding, Carved Avanyu Design, Reycita Cosin, 1970s, 6 x 10 In. 220.00
Vase, Santo Domingo, Wedding, Black On Black, Rafachita Aguilar, 11 1/2 x 6 1/2 In. ... 155.00
Vase, Sioux, Pine Ridge, Lone Pine Tree, Tan, Red Brown, 3 In. 125.00
Vase, Wedding, Hopi, 4 Morning Singer Kachina Faces, Signed, 1980, 6 x 8 In. 220.00
Vest, Blackfoot, Buckskin Back, Beaded Geometric Beaded Panel, 1900, 17 x 16 In. 1320.00
Vest, Blackfoot, Geometric Beaded Panel, White Ground, 1910, 30 x 20 In. 1210.00
Vest, Plains, Beaded, Red, Yellow, Green, Sawtooth Edge, Red, Black, 1890, 22 In. 2860.00
Vest, Red, White, Blue Beaded Flags, Tanned Deer Hide, Child's, 10 In. 825.00
Vest, Seminole, Beaded Palm Trees, Butterflies, Floral, 1910, 18 x 22 In. 990.00
Vest, Sioux, Purple Quilled Bear Paws Front, White Buckskin, 20 x 44 In. 550.00
Vest & Trousers, Crow, White Buckskin, Floral Beadwork, 1930, 2 Piece 250.00
Weaving, Navajo, Colorful Geometric Design, Green Cross, 1920, 16 x 15 In. 130.00
Weaving, Navajo, Ganado Red, Winnie Yazzie, Chinle, Ariz., 1980 .... 330.00
Weaving, Navajo, Germantown, Arrow Point, Butterfly Design, 1920, 18 x 36 In. 495.00
Weaving, Navajo, Germantown, Geometric Design, 1920 .... 300.00
Weaving, Navajo, Homespun Wool, 4 Corners Area, 1950, 32 x 52 In. 220.00
Weaving, Navajo, Teec Nos Pos, Germantown, 1920 .... 385.00
Weaving, Navajo, Teec Nos Pos, Lillie B. Walker, 1980, 31 x 41 In. 468.00

INDIAN TREE is a china pattern that was popular during the last half of
the nineteenth century. It was copied from earlier Indian textile patterns that were very similar. The pattern includes the crooked branch
of a tree and a partial landscape with exotic flowers and leaves. Green,
blue, pink, and orange were the favored colors used in the design.

Bowl, Fruit, Cream, Green, Johnson Brothers 12.00
Cake Plate, Coalport, 9 In. 34.00
Creamer, Cream, Green, Johnson Brothers 25.00
Creamer, White, Johnson Brothers 26.00
Cup, Cream, Green, Johnson Brothers 14.00
Cup, White, Johnson Brothers 23.00
Cup & Saucer, Bronze, Pink, Dark Pink, Dark Blue, Coalport, Demitasse, 1920 .... 65.00
Cup & Saucer, Coalport 19.00
Cup & Saucer, Cream, Green, Johnson Brothers 16.00
Cup & Saucer, Floral Design, Handle, Coalport 35.00
Cup & Saucer, Green Glaze, Ivory Ground, Coalport, Demitasse, 1920 .... 65.00
Cup & Saucer, Johnson Brothers 10.00
Cup & Saucer, Maruta 20.00
Cup & Saucer, Royal Albert 12.00
Cup & Saucer, White, Johnson Brothers 23.00
Dish, Pickle, Cream, Green, Johnson Brothers 25.00
Gravy Boat, Underplate, Cream, Green, Johnson Brothers 25.00
Gravy Boat, Underplate, John Maddock 25.00
Gravy Ladle, Metal Bowl, Large 19.00
Plate, Burgess & Leigh, Coalport, England, 10 In. 12.00
Plate, Dinner, Cream, Green, Johnson Brothers 18.00
Plate, Dinner, Lamberton Scammell Trenton 15.00
Plate, Dinner, Maruta 24.00
Plate, Dinner, Minton, 19th Century 13.00
Plate, Dinner, White, Johnson Brothers 25.00
Plate, Gold, Green, Blue, Brown, Red, Alfred Meakin, 8 3/4 In. 25.00
Plate, Knowles, 9 In. 12.00

Plate, Salad, Cream, Green, Johnson Brothers 18.00
Plate, Salad, Gold Trim, 8 1/4 In. 90.00
Platter, Cream, Green, Johnson Brothers 45.00
Platter, Cream, Green, Johnson Brothers, Small 30.00
Platter, Maddock, 16 In. 36.00
Saucer, John Maddock 14.00
Saucer, Maruta 5.00
Soup, Cream, A. Meakin, 5 In. 15.00
Soup, Dish, Coalport 18.00
Soup, Dish, Copeland Spode 375.00
Sugar, Cover, Cream, Green, Johnson Brothers 35.00
Teapot, Spode 200.00
Vase, Ram's Head Temple, Coalport, 9 In. 199.00

INKSTANDS were made to be placed on a desk. They held some type of
container for ink, and possibly a sander, a pen tray, a pen, a holder for
pounce, and even a candle to melt the sealing wax. Inkstands date to
the eighteenth century and have been made of silver, copper, ceramics,
and glass. Additional inkstands may be found in these and other related
categories.

Brass, 2 Cut Wells, Hinged Cover, Victorian, 10 3/4 In. 190.00
Brass, Cut Glass, Jockey 's Cap Cover, Stamp Moistener, Edwardian, c.1900 .... 345.00
Brass, Ebony, Drawer, 2 Pen Rests, Crystal Wells, Handle, Napoleon III, 13 x 10 In. 2185.00
Brass, Hinged Lid, Etched Floral, 2 Tiers, Letter Holder, Signed, 3 7/8 In. 100.00
Bronze, 2 Ink Pots, Pinecones, Signed, A. Marionnet, 14 In. 2070.00
Bronze, Dome Top, Glass Well, Knop, Circular, Napoleon III, 19th Century, 6 In. 460.00
Bronze, Gilt, Dome Cover Inkwell, Front Fluted Pen Tray, Louis-Philippe, 4 x 10 In. 978.00
Bronze, Putto Reclining, Paw Feet, Charles X, 4 3/4 In. 800.00
Bronze, Sand Sifter, Palmetto Bracket Feet, Charles X, 3 In. 430.00
Copper, Camel, Gilt Trim, Pressed Glass Well, 3 1/4 x 4 1/4 In. 245.00
Copper, Cherub Riding Dolphin, Gold Repaint, Cut Glass Well, 4 1/2 x 4 1/2 In. 220.00
Gilt Brass, Goblet Shape, Birds, Dog, Farm Implements, Victorian, 12 1/2 In. 518.00
Glass, 2 Snails, Clear, Gold Painted Iron Base, American, 1870 .... 320.00
Glass, Cobalt Blue Well & Sander, Sandwich Glass Co., 3 x 7 x 4 12 In. 7500.00
Pewter, Cube, 2 Drawers, Sander In Other Drawer, Quill Holder On Top, 18th Century .. 350.00
Porcelain, Ormolu Trim, Hand Painted, Ceramic Insert Well, 4 1/4 x 5 1/2 In. 520.00
Porcelain, Scotsman, Outdoors, Figural, 2 Cloverleaf Covers, 1860 .... 300.00
Porcelain, Young Man, Stump, Woodsy Setting, Slagenveld, Germany, 1860 .... 240.00
Silver, Cut Glass Bottles, Center Bottle With Taperstick, SH, England, 1817, 8 1/8 In. 1680.00
Silver, Glass Wells, England, 1928, 9 1/4 In. 2400.00
Silver, Oval, Scrolling Rim, Glass Bottle, Edward VII, England, 11 In. 545.00
Silver Cover, Pen Trays, Leaves Flanked Shells, Paw Feet, 2 Bottles, 1823, 9 1/4 In. 3600.00
Silver Plate, Gadrooned Rim, 4 Ball Feet, James Deakin & Son, England 400.00
Toleware, Red Paint, 19th Century 375.00

INKWELLS, of course, held ink. Ready-made ink was first made about
1836 and was sold in bottles. The desk inkwell had a narrow hole so
the pen would not slip inside. Inkwells were made of many materials,
such as pottery, glass, pewter, and silver. Look in these categories for
more listings of inkwells.

Brass, Art Deco, Hinged Lid, Pen Tray, Stylized Palmettes, c.1910, 12 1/4 In. 140.00
Brass, Begging Terrier, Glass Eyes, Late 19th Century, 6 1/2 In. 935.00
Brass, Grinning Imp, Hinged Lid, 19th Century, 2 1/2 In. 90.00
Brass, Rooster Head, Late 19th Century, 4 In. 330.00
Brass, Stirrup Handle, 3 Reservoirs, Candleholder, c.1800 .... 358.00
Bronze, Barrel Of Fish, Anchor & Ropes, Marble Stand, 1880s, 5 In. 345.00
Bronze, Figural Heads, Cutout Floral Center, 13 x 6 1/2 In. 130.00
Bronze, Imp With Goatee, Shell-Form Pen Tray, Green Patina, 3 3/4 x 9 1/8 In. 105.00
Bronze, Mushroom, Elf Underneath, Grasshopper Ready To Pounce, 3 x 4 In. 475.00
Bronze, Mushroom, Grass Hopper On Top, Ready To Pounce, Cold, 3 1/4 In. 475.00
Bronze, Napoleon's Hat, Epaulets, Sword & Medal, On Marble Base, France, 1800s 750.00
Bronze, Putti, Ormolu, French Exposition, No Insert, 1867, 8 In. 355.00
Bronze, Rampant Dog On Lid, Acanthus Leaf Base, Early 19th Century, 4 1/2 In. 612.00

Bronze, Seated Scholar, Flanked By 2 Wells, Pen Drawer, Gilt Trim, 13 x 19 In. 565.00
Bronze, Woman's Bust, F. Barbidienne, 11 x 15 x 8 In. 1290.00
Copper, Crystal, Arts & Crafts, 1900, 10 In. 299.00
Cut Glass, Cover, Russian Paneled Sides, Brass Collar, 4 1/8 x 4 1/8 x 5 1/4 In. 465.00
Cut Glass, Gilt Brass Shell, Pen Rest, 4 1/2 x 6 1/2 x 5 1/4 In. 225.00
Cut Glass, Marble, 2 Faceted Hinged Lids, Prism Cut Stopper, Art Deco, 10 x 18 In. 184.00
Gilt Bronze, Porcelain, Lobed Bowl, Louis XV Style, Imari Style, 7 In. 150.00
Gilt Bronze, Sailor In Boat, Late 19th Century, 7 In. 575.00
Gilt Stenciling, Glass Insert, S. Silliman & Co., 2 1/2 x 4 1/2 In. 190.00
Hammered Copper, Gustav Stickley, 5 1/2 In. 360.00
Iron Frame, Bulldog Snail, Milk Glass Reservoir Dog's Head, 1880 . . . . 310.00
Lignum Vitae, Carved Allover, 18th Century 195.00
Marble, Art Deco, Black & Brown, Hinged Lid, Pen Tray, 7 7/8 x 2 1/2 In. 45.00
Master, Embossed Mark, T. Davids N.Y., Stoneware, 1 Pint, 7 In. 95.00
Milk Glass, Teakettle, Opalescent, Hexagon, Floral, Brass Collar, Cap, 1800s, 2 3/8 In. 410.00
Pewter, Blue Glazed Ceramic Insert, Wide Flat Base, 8 7/8 In. 120.00
Porcelain, 2 Women & Gentleman, Having Tea, Sander, 9 In. 570.00
Porcelain, Central Full-Figured Putti, Foliate, Gilt, Cobalt, Ocher, 7 x 13 In. 748.00
Porcelain, Green Glaze, Gilt Medallions, Floral Reserves, Paris, 4 In. 805.00
Porcelain, Snail, Saucer, Blue, Gold Highlights, France, 1880 . . . . .260.00 to 290.00
Pottery, Pen Rests, Brass Collar, Matching Lid, 5 x 5 5/8 In. 190.00
Satinwood, Ebony & Brass, Plinth, 1 Drawer, 13 3/4 In. 65.00
Silver, Hinged Lid Scrolling Leaves, Square Faceted Base, 3 1/2 In. 45.00
Silver Plate, Cut Glass Wells, 4 1/2 x 9 In. 170.00
Silver Plate, Lion Heads Flanked By Muses, 2 Lidded Wells, 1920s, 4 x 17 3/8 In. 490.00
Silver Plate, Queen Victoria Bust, Insert, 7 In. 535.00
Silver Plate, Stag Head, 1 Well, Hinged Lid, 5 x 6 1/2 In. 395.00
Soapstone, 5 Holes, Square, New England, 18th Century 250.00
Stoneware, Compass Rose, Cobalt Blue Glaze, Oval, Pen Rest, 1818, 2 x 6 x 4 3/8 In. 3025.00
Stoneware, Incised Bird, Leaf Design, Cobalt, 1797, Pa., 2 1/4 x 4 1/4 In. 4400.00
Tortoiseshell Veneer, Mother-Of-Pearl Florals, Silver Handles, 2 Wells, 10 In. 805.00
Wooden, Black Forest, 3 Mountain Goats, Foliage, c.1875, 10 x 13 x 8 In. 1624.00
Wooden, Carved, Glass Inserts, 12 1/4 x 8 x 11 In. 250.00

INSULATORS of glass or pottery have been made for use on telegraph or telephone poles since 1844. Thousands of different styles of insulators have been made. Most common are those of clear or aqua glass; most desirable are the threadless types made from 1850 to 1870.

American Telephone, No. 010, Light Blue Aqua 150.00
American Telephone, No. 1881, Light Blue Aqua, Embossed Base 20.00
American Telephone & Telegraph Co., Aqua, Small Bubbles 55.00
B.T. Co. Of Canada, Deep Purple, Diamond On Side 18.00
Brookfield, No. 020, Dark Green 15.00
Brookfield, No. 020, Deep Green Aqua, Amber Twist 20.00
Brookfield, No. 030, Yellow Green 20.00
Cable, No. 2, Aqua, Olive Wisps 18.00

Clean your telephone insulators with Bar Keeper's Friend. It contains oxalic acid but is safe. Mix 1/3 can and a gallon of water in a nonmetal bucket. Soak insulators in the room-temperature liquid for 12 hours. Use rubber gloves while rubbing off any remaining dirt with a nylon pad.

Insulator, Dominion, No. 42, Near Clear

Compromise Style, Dark Teal Green, Threadless, CD 729 . . . .   600.00
Dominion, No. 42, Amber 62.00
Dominion, No. 42, Near Clear . . . .*Illus*   10.00
Gould, U-683, Skytone & Black 15.00
H.G., CD 160, Milky Light Green Aqua, Smooth Base 257.00
H.G. Co., Petticoat, Ice Aqua, Amber Streak, 1893 . . . .   25.00
Hemingray, No. 9, 7-Up Green 30.00
Hemingray, No. 9/1893, Jade Green, Streaks 22.00
Hemingray, No. 19, Cobalt Blue, SDP, CD 162, 4 x 3 1/4 In. 200.00
Hemingray, No. 40, Aqua, Amber Swirls 25.00
Hemingray, No. 50, Hemingray Blue 20.00
Hemingray, No. 75, Blue 50.00
Hemingray, No. 110, Threaded Spool 8.00
Hemingray, No. D-510, Carnival Glass 50.00
L.G.T. Co., CD 131.4, Light Aqua, Threaded 100.00
Locke Victor, N.Y., Streaky Green 24.00
Lynchburg, No. 30, Light Aqua 6.00
Lynchburg, No. 38, CD 164, Yellow Green 32.00
M.T. Co., Aqua, Embossed 225.00
Maydwell, No. 16, Deep Pink 14.00
Maydwell, No. 16, Pink, SDP 22.00
McLaughlin, No. 14, Light Aqua 8.00
McLaughlin, No. 16, Yellow Lime, Small Bubbles 60.00
McLaughlin, No. 19, Yellow Apple Green, Bubbles 85.00
McLaughlin, No. 20, Emerald Green, Bubbles 18.00
McLaughlin, No. 20, Steel Aqua, Short Style 8.00
N.E.G.M. Co., Blue Aqua 8.00
New England Telegraph & Telephone, Light Aqua 8.00
New England Telephone, National, Light Blue 475.00
Pettingell Andrews, Blue, Milk In Dome 325.00
Pottery, Presentation, Leslie Durkee, Sept. 25, 1906, Pottery, Brown Glaze, 5 3/4 In. 155.00
Pyrex, No. 661 . . . .   5.00
Pyrex, No. 662, Carnival Glass, 3 In. . . . . .38.00 to 50.00
R.D. Mershon, CD 288, Single Ridge 90.00
Tillotson, No. 131, Aqua, Conical, 1860-1880, 3 1/8 x 2 3/4 In. 253.00
Tillotson, Threadless, CD 731, Yellow Green 875.00
U.S. Telephone Co., Yellow Green 30.00
Whitall Tatum, No. 1, Purple 22.00

IRISH BELLEEK, see Belleek category.

IRON is a metal that has been used by man since prehistoric times. It is
a popular metal for tools and decorative items like doorstops that need
as much weight as possible. Items are listed here or under other appropriate headings, such as Bookends, Doorstop, Kitchen, Match Holder,
or Tool. The tool that is used for ironing clothes, an iron, is listed in the
Kitchen category under Iron and Sadiron.

Aquarium, Hexagonal Tank, Red & Gold Paint, Pedestal Base, W. Adams, 50 x 26 In. . . .   3190.00
Ashtray, Antelope Shape, Enameled Black, Thomas Molesworth, 31 In. 2530.00
Ashtray, Butler, Black Man, Sheet Iron Tail Coat, 35 1/2 In. 250.00
Ashtray, Floor, Samuel Yellin 490.00
Ashtray, Griswold, No. 770, Red & White 60.00
Ashtray, Royal Host, Griswold 95.00
Ashtray, Suspended, Bucket Shape, Long Tailed Monkey On Base, Stand, 31 1/4 In. 290.00
Bed Warmer, Engraved Cover, Brass, Continental, c.1880 . . . .   220.00
Birdhouse, House Shape, Painted, Marked Miller Iron, Pedestal, 1869, 14 3/4 In. 3450.00
Bookrack, Lion, Expands To 23 In., 5 x 12 1/4 In. 165.00
Boot Scraper, Black, Scalloped Pan Base, Brushes In Brackets, Black Boy Finial, 12 In. .   250.00
Boot Scraper, Blacksmith Made, Pa., 18th Century, Pair 2100.00
Boot Scraper, Cat, Long Curved Tail, Rectangular Base, 21 In. 2200.00
Boot Scraper, Dachshund, Black Paint, 22 In. 110.00
Boot Scraper, Gothic Revival, Turreted Bridge Shape, 1880s 1760.00
Boot Scraper, Heart Cutouts, Applied Scrollwork, 19th Century, Pair 935.00
Boot Scraper, Pan Base, Flared Rim, Relief Design, Double Dolphins, 12 x 15 x 10 In. . . .   195.00

Boot Scraper, Surmounted By Mammy Figure, 15 In. 115.00
Bootjack, Naughty Nellie, Gilt Polychrome Lingerie, Late 19th Century, 11 1/2 In. 375.00
Candleholder, Bride's, Brass Rings & Candle Cups, S Foot, 4 7/8 x 4 5/16 In. 85.00
Candlesnuffer, Twisted Handle, Scrolled Finger Loops, Child Size, 4 In. 250.00
Compote, Wirework, Green Paint, Scrolls, Basket Weave, Fabre, 1889, 8 1/2 x 12 In. 5180.00
Dustpan, Blacksmith Made, New England, Late 1700s 395.00
Figure, Eagle, Outswept Wings, Yellow Beak, Eagle Roller Mill Co., No. Carolina, 10 In. . 700.00
Figure, Eagles, Cast, Outstretched Wings, Verdigris Over Gilt, 1918, 13 x 30 In., Pair 2070.00
Figure, Horse Head, Wooden Base, Gold Paint, 8 In. 140.00
Figure, Hound, Late 19th Century, 29 x 39 x 16 In. 8400.00
Figure, Kuan Yiin, 20 Character Inscriptions, 11 In. 805.00
Figure, Lion, Black, Cast, Foot On Sphere, William IV, Plinth Base, 7 x 8 1/4 In., Pair ... 978.00
Figure, Snow Eagles, Red Brown Paint, 5 In., 16 Piece 385.00
Figure, Soldier, Brim Hat, Bandanna, Saber, Blue, White Stand, 19th Century, 37 In. 1760.00
Flint Striker, Lion, Figural, 6 x 3 1/2 In. 585.00
Flower Stand, c.1900, 36 1/2 x 24 1/2 In. 895.00
Hinge Set, Door, Ram's Horn Shape, c.1800, 16 In., 4 Piece 550.00
Lectern, Eagle Bearing Arms Of Leon & Castille, Heads In Corners, Velvet, 13 In. 7475.00
Mailbox, Faux Marble Panels, Black Enamel, Carlisle Foundry, 13 x 8 1/4 x 2 In. 250.00
Mirror, Figural, Boy, Girl, Dog, 9 3/8 In. 150.00
Ornament, Ram's Head, Spiral Horns, Pitted, 13 x 15 1/2 In. 385.00
Planter, Kramer Bros. Fdy. Co., Victorian, 24 x 22 In. 175.00
Planter, Urn Shape, 33 x 23 In., 2 Piece 155.00
Planter, Urn Shape, Ornate Handles, Victorian, 33 x 31 In., 3 Piece 1295.00
Planter, Vase Shape, Handles, Lakewood, 18 x 21 In., Pair 55.00
Radiator Cover, Brass, Marble, Samuel Yellin, 1934 .... 5750.00
Rushlight Holder, Candle Socket Counterweight, Tripod Base, Twisted Stem, FM, 10 In. . 248.00
Safe, Cast Iron & Steel, Lakeside, Combination Dial, Caster Wheels, c.1910, 11 x 17 In. . 575.00
Safe, Cast Iron & Steel, The Queen, Combination Dial, Caster Wheels, 10 x 16 1/2 In. 720.00
Shoehorn, Knopped Handle, 18th Century, 15 In. 350.00
Spur, 6-Point Rowels, Question Mark Shank, Bottle Opener Style, 1 3/8 In. 225.00
Spur, Ladies Leg, Brass Trim, Stamped Initials V.O.W., Tooled Leather, 6 In. 72.00
Stove Plate, Dance Of Death, Noblemen Meeting Death, 22 x 26 In. 2090.00
Strap Hinge, Tulip Terminals, 42 & 48 In., Pair 110.00
Striker, Flint, Early 18th Century, 3 Piece 395.00
Tractor Seat, Heart Cutout, 4 x 17 1/2 In. 81.00
Warming Pan, William & Mary, Pierced, Punched Brass Cover, 17th Century, 42 In. 413.00
Warming Pan, William & Mary, Pierced, Punched Brass Cover, Late 1600s, 41 1/2 In. 193.00
Windmill Weight, Althouse-Wheeler Co., 23 1/2 Lb. 6025.00
Windmill Weight, Battleship, Maker Mfg. Company 2500.00
Windmill Weight, Bull, Brown & White Paint, 12 1/2 In. 58.00
Windmill Weight, Bull, Fairbury, Nebraska, Fairbury Windmill Co., For 10-In. Wheel ... 950.00
Windmill Weight, Bull, Red & White, Green Grass, 17 1/2 x 24 1/2 In. 1035.00
Windmill Weight, Bull, Simpson Windmill & Machine Company 2000.00
Windmill Weight, Eclipse, Crescent Moon, 10 1/2 x 7 1/2 In. 460.00
Windmill Weight, Half Moon, Cast, 10 1/4 In. 110.00
Windmill Weight, Horse, Long Tail, 15 3/4 x 16 1/2 In. 1035.00
Windmill Weight, Horse, Long Tail, Dempster Mill Mfg. Company, No. 58 .... 925.00
Windmill Weight, Horse, Painted, Dempster Mill Mfg. Co., 1970s, 6 1/2 In. 685.00
Windmill Weight, Horseshoe, Governor Weight, Holdrege Mfg. Company 2150.00
Windmill Weight, Rabbit, Sheet Iron, Silver Paint, 12 x 12 In. 242.00
Windmill Weight, Rooster, Barnacle Eye, Elgin Windmill Company 4600.00
Windmill Weight, Rooster, Elgin Wind Power & Pump Co., Ill., 18 1/2 x 19 In. 2013.00
Windmill Weight, Rooster, Elgin Windmill Co., 18 x 19 1/4 In. 2200.00
Windmill Weight, Rooster, Rainbow Tail, Black Paint, New Base, 1900 .... 2800.00
Windmill Weight, Rooster, Red, White & Green Paint, 16 x 17 In. 920.00
Windmill Weight, Rooster, White Paint, Red Comb, Rainbow Tail, Elgin Windmill Co. .. 2400.00
Windmill Weight, Squirrel, Elgin Wind Power & Pump Co., 13 3/8 x 17 1/2 In. 4900.00
Windmill Weight, Star, Flint & Walling Mfg. Company 2300.00
Windmill Weight, Star, U.S. Wind Engine & Pump Company 3400.00

IRONSTONE china was first made in 1813. It gained its greatest popularity during the mid-nineteenth century. The heavy, durable, off-white

pottery was made in white or was decorated with any of hundreds of patterns. Much flow blue pottery was made of ironstone. Some of the decorations were raised. Many pieces of ironstone are unmarked, but some English and American factories included the word *Ironstone* in their marks. Additional pieces may be listed in other categories, such as Chelsea Grape, Chelsea Sprig, Flow Blue, Gaudy Ironstone, Mason's Ironstone, Moss Rose, Staffordshire, and Tea Leaf Ironstone.

Bowl, Raised Pierced Edges, Twig-Like Handles, Underplate, 6 1/2 x 14 In.	92.00
Bowl, Vegetable, Blue & White, Cover, Late 19th Century, 7 x 11 In.	55.00
Bowl, Vegetable, Ceres Shape, Open Handles, Green Wheat, Oval, 6 x 7 In.	632.00
Coffeepot, Dome Cover, Snowflake, Blue, Spout, 10 In.	1265.00
Coffeepot, Gaudy, War Bonnet Pattern, C-Scroll Handle, 19th Century, 10 In.	220.00
Crock, Edge Field, 2 Handles, X's & O's On Handle, 1850, 3 Gal.	2900.00
Cup Plate, Snowflake, Blue, 5 1/4 In.	220.00
Dish, Shrimp, Floral, Overglaze Enamels, Gilt Trim, 19th Century, 9 1/4 In., Pair	316.00
Finger Bowl, Snowflake, Blue, 3 1/4 x 5 1/4 In.	385.00
Mug, Ceres Shape, Green Wheat, Elsmore & Forster, Signed, 4 In.	302.00
Pitcher, Bowl Set, White, Marked, J. & G. Meakin, England, 12 x 14 1/4 In.	55.00
Pitcher, Cream, Ceres Shape, Green Wheat, White Ground, Handle, 7 In.	275.00
Pitcher, Landscape Scenes, Wine Red Ground, Titled Cartouche, c.1885, 10 In.	460.00
Pitcher, The Gem, J & J Mayer, 11 In.	280.00
Pitcher, Water, Ceres Shape, Green Wheat, 10 1/2 In.	358.00
Pitcher & Bowl, Wheat	247.00
Plate, Ashworth, Imari Palette, Impressed Mark, 10 1/4 In.	230.00
Plate, Black & White Transfer, Harper's Ferry From Potomac Side, 9 In.	350.00
Plate, Enameled Tropical Bird & Floral, 19th Century, 8 3/4 In., 11 Piece	316.00
Plate, Soup, Snowflake, Blue, 9 3/8 In.	165.00
Platter, Brown Floral Design, Signed, Moore, 19 1/2 In.	38.00
Platter, Ceres Shape, Green Wheat, Signed, Elsmore & Forster, 12 x 15 In.	192.00
Platter, Octagonal, Mazarin, 19 1/2 In.	80.00
Platter, Oriental Design, Cobalt Blue Scalloped, Ashworth, 11 5/8 In.	100.00
Platter, Snowflake, Blue, Oval, 10 1/2 x 14 In.	413.00
Relish, Ceres Shape, Green Wheat, Oblong, 8 1/2 x 5 In.	192.00
Teapot, Ceres Shape	150.00
Teapot, Snowflake, Blue, 8 1/2 In.	990.00
Tureen, Cover, Vine With Leaves, Ladle, Clements & Hanley, 11 In.	110.00
Tureen, Sauce, Ceres Shape, Green Wheat, Footed, 7 1/2 In.	440.00
Tureen, Sauce, Ceres Shape, Green Wheat, Ladle, 7 1/2 In.	1100.00
Tureen, Sauce, Cover, Japanese Garden, Butterfly Handles & Finial, 5 3/4 In.	172.00
Tureen, Soup, Rambling Rose, Lily Pad Knob, 1850, 14 In.	1500.00
Tureen, Soup, Stand, Meadow Flowers, Ladle, John Maddock, c.1900, 7 x 14 In.	210.00
Turkey Set, Dark Blue Transfer Platter, Florence Bistro, England, 6 Plates, 7 Piece	400.00
Washbasin, 2 Handles, Gilt Design, 9 x 21 1/2 In.	385.00

ISPANKY figurines were designed by Laszlo Ispanky, who began his American career as a designer for Cybis Porcelains. In 1966, he established his own studio in Pennington, New Jersey; since 1976, he has worked for Goebel of North America. He works in stone, wood, or metal, as well as porcelain. The first limited edition figurines were issued in 1966.

Figurine, Susie, Signed, 1972	175.00
Figurine, Young Man With Pipe On The Road, Porcelain, 10 1/4 In.	108.00
Plate, 12 Tribes Of Israel, 24K Gold Border, West Germany	50.00

IVOREX plaques were made in England by Arthur Osborne in the beginning of the 1900s. The plaques, made of a material he called *sterine wax*, pictured buildings or room interiors modeled in three dimensions. After Osborne's death, his daughter Blanche ran the company. It was closed in 1965, then purchased by W. H. Bossons Ltd. in 1971. Production of the plaques started again in 1980 and ended in 1996 when Bossons closed.

"IVOREX"
OSBORNE-COPYRIGHT.
MADE IN ENGLAND.

Plaque, Canterbury Pilgrim, 5 3/4 x 4 In.	86.00
Plaque, Canterbury Pilgrim, Wife Of Bath, 5 3/4 x 4 In.	167.00

Plaque, City Of 3 Spires, 11 x 7 1/2 In. 108.00
Plaque, Imperial Stadium, Wembley, Soccer Match In Progress, 9 x 6 In. 365.00
Plaque, Old Curiosity Shop, 1925, 8 1/4 In. 45.00
Plaque, Oliver Twist, Oval 56.00
Plaque, Parliament Buildings, Winnipeg, 10 x 6 3/4 In. 200.00
Plaque, Rough Sea, 11 1/2 x 8 In. 193.00
Plaque, Shakespeare's Hamlet, 6 3/8 x 3 In. 77.00
Plaque, St. Mary's Church, 10 5/8 x 8 In. 305.00
Plaque, The Mayflower 56.00
Plaque, Tower Bridge, London, 11 1/2 x 7 1/2 In. 51.00
Plaque, Westminster Abbey, 1920, 4 3/4 x 4 1/4 In. 45.00

IVORY from the tusk of an elephant is thought by many to be the only true ivory. To most collectors, the term *ivory* also includes such natural materials as walrus, hippopotamus, or whale teeth or tusks, and some of the vegetable materials that are of similar texture and density. Other ivory items may be found in the Scrimshaw and Netsuke categories. Collectors should be aware of the recent laws limiting the buying and selling of elephant ivory and scrimshaw.

Box, Cover, Dragon, Swirling Motion, Mother-Of-Pearl Eyes, Round, 1 3/4 x 2 1/2 In. 144.00
Box, Cover, Foliage Scrolls, Woman In Black Dress, 4 x 2 1/4 In. 71.00
Box, Cover, Rectangular, Chamfered, Carved Lady, Flowers, Chinese, c.1790, 2 7/8 In. .. 1980.00
Box, Domed Cover, Stylized Deer & Leaves, Austria, c.1930, 3 In. 2183.00
Box, Dragon & Cloud Carving, Cylindrical, Late 19th Century, 3 1/4 In. 258.00
Box, Floral Carved, Watercolor Napoleon Portrait, M.E., Round, 2 1/2 x 1 In. 520.00
Box, Floral Sprigs, Insects, Figures & Pavilions, Rectangular, 2 1/2 In. 2160.00
Box, Fruit, Prunus Branch, Insects In Interior, Meiji Period, Japan, 3 1/2 In. 460.00
Box, Inset Woman Wedgwood Cover, Jasperware, Tortoiseshell Interior, 2 7/8 x 1 In. 440.00
Box, Miniature Portrait, Lady In Elegant Hat, Continental, Round, 2 1/2 In. 127.00
Box, Monkey, Lion, Cover, Other Head Carvings, Japan, 2 1/2 x 3 1/8 In. 230.00
Brush Pot, Carved Craftsman Scene, Forging Saber Blade, Japan, 1900 .... 550.00
Brush Pot, Flowering Branches In Mountainous Landscape, Carved Figures, 6 In. 920.00
Bust, Napoleonic Man & Woman, Ebonized Wood Plinth, 1800s, 12 1/2 In., Pair 3220.00
Calendar, Silver Clasp, Shield Plate, Sheets Of Ivory Monday To Saturday, 3 1/8 In. 220.00
Card Case, Allover Traditional Court Scene With Pavilions, Figures, 4 1/2 In. 1380.00
Card Case, Figural Landscape Design, 1830, 3 1/4 In. 149.00
Card Case, Figural Landscape On Cross Form, Chinese, Mid 19th Century, 3 In. 125.00
Card Case, Village Scene, Figures In Various Pursuits, Pavilions, China, 4 x 2 1/2 In. 598.00
Carved Female & Male Figures, Oriental Dress, Wooden Bases, 12 In., Pair 660.00
Coffer, Walrus, Stepped Top, Geometric Borders, Sea Green Mica, Russia, 11 x 7 In. 1265.00
Corpus, Carved, Inlaid Wooden Cross, 19th Century, 10 In. 2240.00
Desk Seal, Clasped Hands, Nelson & Wellington Carnelian Plaque Base, 3 3/4 In. 7920.00
Doctor's Model, Reclining, Shoes & Bracelets, Wooden Base, 6 In. 275.00
Figurine, Basket Seller, 4 1/4 In. 218.00
Figurine, Basket Seller, Child, Carved, Japan, 10 In. 1265.00
Figurine, Bearded Wise Man, Signed, Chinese, 11 In. 560.00
Figurine, Bird Dancer, Marble, Onyx Base, J. Lormier, 1920, 14 In. 5700.00
Figurine, Bodhisattva, Standing On A Lotus Throne, Wearing Long Loose Robes, 10 In. ... 980.00
Figurine, Buddha, Seated In Lotus Position, On Carved Wooden Base, 7 In. 440.00
Figurine, Carved, King Francois I, In Armor, Gothic Arcade, Marble, 19th Century, 8 In. .. 978.00
Figurine, Christ On Cross, 15 1/2 In. 750.00
Figurine, Classical Nude Fastening Her Sandal, Continental, 7 In. 920.00
Figurine, Cupid Gazing Into Mirror, 6 1/2 In. 2300.00
Figurine, Dachshund, Long-Haired, Ebonized Stand, Late 19th Century, 3 1/2 x 2 In. 175.00
Figurine, Dancer, On Point, Gilt Bronze, Octagonal Marble Base, 7 In. 1610.00
Figurine, Doctor's Lady, Reclining On A Leaf Holding An Infant, 4 7/8 In. 200.00
Figurine, Elephant, Standing On A Wooden Base, Early 20th Century, 3 1/4 In. 115.00
Figurine, Female Warrior Standing, Sword Hanging From Belt, 14 3/4 In. 605.00
Figurine, Fisherman Showing Catch To Small Child, 6 3/4 In. 290.00
Figurine, Geisha, Dancing With 2 Fans, 6 3/4 In. 150.00
Figurine, Guanyin, Attendant, Rosewood Stand, 19th Century, 8 1/4 In. 260.00
Figurine, Guanyin, Standing With Child, Held In Her Hands, 19th Century, 11 In. 345.00
Figurine, Horse, Group Of Seven, Various Positions, 2 In. 165.00

Figurine, Horse, Standing, With Turned Head, Pricked Ears, 8 1/2 In. 460.00
Figurine, Man, Looking Through Hole At Nude Woman, In Garden, Manju, 1 In. 195.00
Figurine, Nude Bather, Sitting On Stool, Arm Behind Head, Japan, 5 In. 290.00
Figurine, Okimono, Erotic, Couple Wearing Loose Robes, High Chignon, 3 In. 920.00
Figurine, Okimono, Grape Farmer Kneels On Mat, 19th Century, 2 3/4 In. 1090.00
Figurine, Okimono, Leaning Against Landscape Screen, 19th Century, 2 In. 805.00
Figurine, Okimono, Parasol Seller Kneeling Beneath His Wares, 3 In. 1265.00
Figurine, Oriental Danseuse, Marble Base, Pierre LeFaguays, 19 In. 12000.00
Figurine, Queen Elizabeth 1, Triptych With Central Court Scene, England, 7 In. 860.00
Figurine, Roman Amphitheater, Bull Baiting, Oak Shadowbox Frame, 28 x 25 In. 6900.00
Figurine, Seal, Seated With Head Held Up, Chinese, 2 1/2 In. 660.00
Figurine, Sleeping Scholar, 19th Century, 5 In. 175.00
Figurine, Snake Dancer, Marble Base, Samuel Lipchytz, 1920, 16 In. 8400.00
Figurine, St. George Slaying Dragon, Wooden Base, 6 5/8 In. 170.00
Figurine, Turbaned Man Playing Bagpipes Leaning Against Tree Stump, Stand, 7 In. 690.00
Figurine, Walrus, Inuit, 5 3/4 In. 260.00
Figurine, Woman Holding Branches Of Flowers, Silver Stand, 19 1/2 In. 2645.00
Figurine, Women, Holding Floral Sprig, Tassels, Carved Chain, 11 1/4 & 13 In. 935.00
Frame, Hinged Doors, Ivory, Figures In A Bamboo Grove, Chinese, 5 1/4 In. 210.00
Game, Ball, Cord, Turned Stem, Shallow Dish, Georgian, Mid 18th Century, 7 In. 405.00
Group, 2 Children Playing On Seesaw, 5 3/4 In. 1380.00
Group, 2 Farmers Struggling With Cart Of Vegetables, Goto, 9 In. 430.00
Group, 2 Women, 1 With Scepter & Other With Plant, 6 1/2 In., Pair 190.00
Group, 3 Walruses In Water, Inuit, 5 In. 170.00
Group, Amorous Couple In Elizabethan Dress, Woman Holding Flower, 8 In. 1093.00
Group, Birds Perched On Rockery, Flowering Branches, 11 In., Pair 1955.00
Group, Buddha, 1 With Vase, 1 With Sphere, 4 3/4 In., Pair 495.00
Group, Dragon Chasing The Pearl Of Wisdom & 3 Men, Chinese, 15 In. 490.00
Group, Equestrians, Wearing Warrior Robes Facing Sideways, 10 In., Pair 515.00
Group, Farmer With A Rake, Child With A Flower, 6 1/2 In. 130.00
Group, Man & Woman, 6 1/4 & 6 1/2 In., Pair 275.00
Group, Mountain Scene, Men, Horseback, Water Buffalo, Carved Wooden Base, 9 In. . . . 310.00
Group, Okimono, Cooper Working A Barrel With A Chisel, 2 1/6 In. 720.00
Group, Okimono, Teacher & Pupil Kneeling Across From Each Other, 2 1/2 In. 630.00
Group, Okimono, Woman & A Man Seated Wearing Traditional Robes, 9 1/2 In. 6440.00
Group, Oliphant, Spirited Stag Hunt, Hell Hounds, Late 19th Century, 35 In. 3900.00
Group, Venus, Holding Basket Of Cupids, 10 1/2 In. 6325.00
Group, Woman In Kimono, Holding A Baby, 20th Century, 6 1/2 In. 405.00
Group, Woman Making Lanterns While Rat Crawls Out Of One She Is Holding, 3 In. . . . 130.00
Group, Woman, Holding Book, Perched Owl, Wooden Base, 10 In. 3160.00
Horse, Jumping Over Waves, Demilune Base, 5 1/2 In. 310.00
Incense Burner, Dragon Chasing The Flaming Pearl Of Wisdom, China, 14 In. 575.00
Jewelry Box, Hinged Top, Ebonized Mahogany, Geometric Panels, 8 1/2 In. 2160.00
Kayak, Paddle, Harpoon, Seal, 8 1/2 In. 270.00
Koro, Serpentine, Cover, Chinese, 19 1/2 In. 1150.00
Musical Band, Different Instruments, On Treenware Barrel, 19th Century, 6 1/2 In. 2075.00
Okimono, Elephants, Crossing Bridge, Signed, 7 In. 460.00
Okimono, Father & Son, On Country Path, Basket On Back, 5 x 2 3/4 In. 575.00
Okimono, Fisherman, At Seashore, Harpoon, Crane Catching Fish, Signed, 9 In. 800.00
Okimono, Flower Seller, Holding Flower Basket, Partridge, 9 In. 575.00
Okimono, Man, Holding Ceremonial Object, Round Base, 10 x 4 3/4 In. 230.00
Okimono, Man, Holding Monkey, Peach Sprig, Signed, 10 1/2 In. 1035.00
Okimono, Man, Kneeling, Holding Peaches, Money Bag, Signed, 3 In. 290.00
Okimono, Woman, Holding Double Water Gourd, Obi, Signed Kakihan, 8 1/4 In. 750.00
Page Turner, Horse Figure, Openwork Handle, Chinese, 5 1/2 x 13 3/4 In. 230.00
Page Turner, Reed & Leaf Terminal, Swan Figure, France, 10 3/4 In. 375.00
Panel, Figures Of Deities In A Palace Garden Scene, 13 x 5 In. 1380.00
Portrait, Dutch Gentleman, Ornate Brass Frame, Signed, Miniature, 6 5/8 x 5 In. 245.00
Portrait, Gentleman, Oil, Oval, Gold Frame, Miniature, 1 3/4 In. 140.00
Portrait, John Caldwell Calhoun, U.S. V.P., Miniature, 2 1/2 x 3 1/4 In. 290.00
Portrait, Woman With Red Scarf, Signed L.R., 19th Century, Miniature, 2 x 3 In. 375.00
Puzzle Ball, Carved, Stand, Chinese, 8 In. 115.00
Skull, Allover Mouse Figures, Snake Comes From Eye Socket, Japan, 6 3/4 x 6 x 7 In. . . . 4140.00

Tusk, African Woman, Ornate Hairdo, 13 1/8 In.	110.00
Tusk, Crocodile, Relief Carving, 15 In.	58.00
Tusk, Dragon Shape, Phoenix & Tortoise, Chinese, 20th Century, 33 1/2 In., Pair	2415.00
Tusk, Dragon, Flowering Prunus Branch, Japan, 20th Century, 23 In.	1150.00
Tusk, Immortals, Chinese, 20th Century, 34 In.	1725.00
Tusk, Pagoda & Figures Amongst Pine Trees, 20th Century, China, 29 In.	138.00
Tusk, Village Scene, Wooden Plinth, Chinese, 17 1/2 In.	672.00
Vase, Cover, Figures In Palace Settings, Dragon Handles, 14 In.	1092.00
Vase, Pagoda, Figural Design, Chinese, 9 1/4 In., Pair	403.00

JACK ARMSTRONG, the all-American boy, was the hero of a radio serial from 1933 to 1951. Premiums were offered to the listeners until the mid-1940s. Jack Armstrong's best-known endorsement is for Wheaties.

Bomb Sight Kit, Unopened Box	525.00
Flashlight	20.00
Hike-O-Meter, Wheaties Premium, 1938, 2 5/8 In.	35.00
Photograph, Blackstar, Black & White, 5 x 8 In.	55.00
Sound Effects Kit, In Mailer	300.00
Telescope, Jack Armstrong Explorer, 2x Power, 1930s, 7 In. Extends To 10 In.	55.00

JACK-IN-THE-PULPIT vases, oddly shaped like trumpets, resemble the wild plant called jack-in-the-pulpit. The design originated in the late Victorian years. Vases in the jack-in-the-pulpit shape were made of ceramic or glass, and the complete list of page references can be found in the index.

Vase, Aqua Glass, Pale Green Base, Enameled Floral Spray, 6 In.	480.00
Vase, Burmese Glass, Yellow Rim, 15 x 5 1/4 In.	920.00
Vase, Cobalt Blue Glass, Vertical Ribbing, 6 1/2 x 11 1/4 In.	275.00
Vase, Pulled Feather Glass, Green Iridescent, 9 In.	201.00
Vase, Yellow, Green Glass, Light Blue Opalescent Top, 5 1/4 x 4 1/4 In.	90.00

JADE is the name for two different minerals, nephrite and jadeite. Nephrite is the mineral used for most early Oriental carvings. Jade is a very tough stone that is found in many colors from dark green to pale lavender. Jade carvings are still being made in the old styles, so collectors must be careful not to be fooled by recent pieces. Jade jewelry is found in this book under Jewelry.

Bowl, Gray, Green, White & Dark Gray Marks, Chinese, 4 In.	316.00
Box, Flowering Branch, Celadon, Qing Dynasty, Chinese, 2 3/4 In.	865.00
Brushwater, Lotus, Agate Brush Washer, Light Celadon, Chinese, 3 1/2 In.	90.00
Figurine, Bird, Spinach Jade, Chinese, 6 In., Pair	195.00
Figurine, Female Deity, Infusions Of Gray, 20th Century, 4 In.	115.00
Figurine, Kylin With A Smiling Expression, White, 2 1/8 In.	160.00
Figurine, Meiren, High Chignon, Loose Robes, Flowering Branch, Emerald, Chinese, 6 In.	375.00
Figurine, Recumbent Camel, Head Turned Back, Legs Tucked Under, Green, White, 3 In.	2645.00
Figurine, Woman With Sword, Branch In Hand, Rosewood Stand, 7 1/2 In.	170.00
Frame, Apple Green, Gilt, Brass, Chinese, 12 1/4 In.	2070.00
Frame, Green Cabochon At Center, Green, Chinese, 1900, 13 In.	2530.00
Vase, Cover, Kylin, Water Hydra On Base, Horn Handles, 12 x 5 1/4 In.	2530.00
Vase, Dragon & Cloud Scene, White, 6 In.	8050.00
Vase, Foo Lion Chasing Flaming Pearl Of Wisdom, Flat Baluster Shape, Chinese, 5 In.	980.00
Vase, Taotie Mask, Gu Shape, Chinese, Qing Dynasty, 8 3/4 In.	460.00

JAPANESE WOODBLOCK PRINTS are listed in this book in the Print category under Japanese.

JASPERWARE can be made in different ways. Some pieces are made from a solid colored clay with applied raised designs of a contrasting colored clay. Other pieces are made entirely of one color clay with raised decorations that are glazed with a contrasting color. Additional pieces of jasperware may also be listed in the Wedgwood category or under various art potteries.

Cheese Dish, Cover, Brown, White Tulips & Fern Designs, Border, 12 1/4 x 9 In.	275.00

Creamer, Slate Blue, Fox Hunt, Acanthus Leaf Spout & Handle, 3 In. 110.00
Hair Receiver, Cover, Germany, 4 In. 95.00
Jardiniere, Greek Honeysuckle, Classical Mythological Maidens, 7 3/4 x 8 In. 980.00
Planter, Blue, White Relief Figures, Trees & Cherubs, 7 x 6 7/8 In. 165.00
Urn, Cover, Blue, White, Allegorical Figures, Handles, Lamp Mounted, 11 In., Pair 1060.00
Vase, Medici Shape Urn, Egg & Dart Rim, Loop Handles, Gustafsberg, 11 x 5 In. 980.00

JEWELRY, whether made from gold and precious gems or plastic and colored glass, is popular with collectors. Values are determined by the intrinsic value of the stones and metal and by the skill of the craftsmen and designers. Victorian and older jewelry have been collected since the 1950s. More recent interests are Art Deco and Edwardian styles, Mexican and Danish silver jewelry, and beads of all kinds. Copies of almost all styles are being made. American Indian jewelry is listed in the Indian category.

Barrette, 119 Rose Cut Diamond, Edwardian, France 1150.00
Beads, Black, Lines, White Dots, Copal, Amber Annulars, Africa, 1 1/2 In. 110.00
Belt, Hinged Silver Buckle, Enameled, Blue & Yellow Stripes, Gucci, 1960s, 30 In. 750.00
Bracelet, 3 Charms, Double Ring Bracelet, 14K Yellow Gold, 7 1/2 In. 275.00
Bracelet, Alaskan Bone, Whalebone, Jade Saddle Spacers, Nome, Alaska, 1950 . . . . 690.00
Bracelet, Bakelite, Bangle, Apple Juice, Carved Floral Reverse, 1 In. 620.00
Bracelet, Bakelite, Bangle, Black, Carved, 1/2 x 3 1/4 In. 175.00
Bracelet, Bakelite, Bangle, Butterscotch & Red, Carved, 3/4 x 3 In. 275.00
Bracelet, Bakelite, Bangle, Butterscotch, Black & Red Dots, 2 In. 460.00
Bracelet, Bakelite, Bangle, Butterscotch, Carved, 1 x 3 In. . . . . .325.00 to 450.00
Bracelet, Bakelite, Bangle, Butterscotch, Red, Belle Kogan 845.00
Bracelet, Bakelite, Bangle, Butterscotch, Red, Blue Laminated, Red, Blue Dots, 1/4 In. . . 790.00
Bracelet, Bakelite, Bangle, Carved Spiked Design, Black, 3 In. 395.00
Bracelet, Bakelite, Bangle, Geometric Crosshatched Design, Apple Juice 563.00
Bracelet, Bakelite, Bangle, Green, Carved, 3/4 x 2 3/4 In. 135.00
Bracelet, Bakelite, Bangle, Laminated Zigzag Design, Blue Marbleized, Cream, 1 In. 565.00
Bracelet, Bakelite, Bangle, Olive, Red Dots, 1950, 1 x 3 In. 180.00
Bracelet, Bakelite, Bangle, Random Dots, Cream On Bright Green, 90 In. 3150.00
Bracelet, Bakelite, Bangle, Red With 4 Cream Dots, 1 5/8 In. 520.00
Bracelet, Bakelite, Bangle, Red, Carved, 1/2 x 3 In. 175.00
Bracelet, Bakelite, Bangle, Reversed Carved Floral, Cherry Red Amber, 1 In. 425.00
Bracelet, Bakelite, Bangle, Yellow, Twisted, 1/4 x 3 1/4 In. 125.00
Bracelet, Bakelite, Be-Bop, Cream With 5-Shaped Dots Record, 1 In. 635.00
Bracelet, Bakelite, Figural, 2-Tone Dice, 3/4 In. 7475.00
Bracelet, Bakelite, Green, Carved Fruit Design, 1 5/8 In. 400.00
Bracelet, Bakelite, Red, Black Plaques, Chrome Link 200.00
Bracelet, Bakelite, Stretch, Red, Hearts On Elastic, 1 In. 565.00
Bracelet, Bangle, Calibre Cut Emeralds, Art Deco 5465.00
Bracelet, Bangle, Carnelian Scarabs, 1875, 18K Gold 8625.00
Bracelet, Bangle, Granulation, Victorian, 15K Yellow Gold . . . . .115.00 to 185.00
Bracelet, Bangle, Opal & Pearl, Zircon Center, 14K Yellow Gold, c.1890 . . . . 770.00
Bracelet, Bangle, Pierced, Chased Design, Art Nouveau, 14K Gold 920.00
Bracelet, Bangle, Snake, Diamond Eyes, Ruby Cabochon, Nose, LaLaounis, 18K Gold . . 2070.00
Bracelet, Bangle, Vermeil, Onyx, Lapis Lazuli, Ribbed Body, Bands 259.00
Bracelet, Bangle, Vermeil, Onyx, Mother-Of-Pearl, Amethyst, Peridot, Ribbed 920.00
Bracelet, Baroque Style, Yellow Gold, Rubies, Sapphires, 18K, Signed GCC 1725.00
Bracelet, Basket Weave, Braided, Signed, Tiffany & Co., 14K Gold 315.00
Bracelet, Brown Leather, Oval Stone Center 8.00
Bracelet, Cameo, Pendant, White Coral, Gold Frame, c.1860, 1 3/4 x 8 In. 310.00
Bracelet, Charm, 2 Shell Cameos, 2 Black & White Onyx Cameos, Diamonds 175.00
Bracelet, Charm, 7 Photo Lockets, Gold Filled, 7 In. 84.00
Bracelet, Copper Cuff, Cut-Out Slit, Rebajes, 2 1/3 In. 225.00
Bracelet, Cuff, Coiled Copper Design, Enameled, Rebajes, 1 1/2 In. 620.00
Bracelet, Cuff, Purple, Sepia Glass Beads, Brass Base, Coppolla Toppo, 1 In. 365.00
Bracelet, Cuff, Silver, Repousse, Dragon, Phoenix, Chinese, c.1915, 2 1/2 In. 375.00
Bracelet, Cuff, Sterling Silver, Geometric Crosshatching, Miraglia, 2 1/4 In. 70.00
Bracelet, Cuff, Sterling Silver, Man From Mercury, Bjorn Weckstrom, 2 In. 2140.00
Bracelet, Cuff, Sterling Silver, Rosewood, Stepped Geometric, Spratling, 2 In. 1575.00

Bracelet, Cuff, Sterling Silver, Steig, 1 1/4 In. 115.00
Bracelet, Domed Rectangular Links, Pink, Yellow Gold, 7 1/4 In. 2070.00
Bracelet, Emeralds, Rose Cut Diamonds, Original Box, 1880 .... 2875.00
Bracelet, Gold Link, Foxtail Of Crossover, Diamonds, Van Cleef & Arpels, 1950 ...... 8750.00
Bracelet, Gold Mesh, 14K, 8 Rows, Interwoven Polished Gold Wire, 7 3/4 In. 2070.00
Bracelet, Gold Slide, Rubies, Pearls, Opals, Art Nouveau Angel, 14K, 1910 .... 2120.00
Bracelet, Gold Slide, Seed Pearls, Black Enamel, 14K 400.00
Bracelet, Gold, Chevron Design, Retro, France, 1940 .... 2500.00
Bracelet, Gold, Diamonds, Sapphire, Art Deco, 14K 1400.00
Bracelet, Gold, Enamel, Flower Link, Rose Gold Bead, 14K 520.00
Bracelet, Link, Blue, White Jasperware Plaques, 14K Gold 805.00
Bracelet, Link, Cobalt Blue Enamel Bamboo, Box, Gold Pearl, 7 5/8 In. 405.00
Bracelet, Link, Geometric, Sapphire, Art Deco, 7 1/4 In. 1150.00
Bracelet, Link, Gold Graduated Circles, Diamond Stars Center, 1920 .... 8750.00
Bracelet, Link, Hollow Yellow Gold, Oriental Style, 72 Grams, c.1950 .... 495.00
Bracelet, Link, Scrolled, Plaques, Sterling Silver, Spratling, 1940, 7 1/4 In. 920.00
Bracelet, Link, Sterling Silver, Amethyst Cabochon, Spratling, 1 In. 2025.00
Bracelet, Link, Sterling Silver, R. Rivera, Mexico 80.00
Bracelet, Link, Sterling Silver, Studded, Frame Design, Los Castillo, 1 In. 310.00
Bracelet, Locket, Gold, Enamel, Cartouche With Barn In Vale, 19th Century, 7in. 2990.00
Bracelet, Mesh, Engraved Gold, Garnet Slide, Ball Fringe Ends, Victorian, 14K 400.00
Bracelet, Open Work Coiled Links, Signed, Tiffany, 18K Yellow Gold 4025.00
Bracelet, Openwork Rectangular Plaques, Art Deco, 14K White & Yellow Gold 1300.00
Bracelet, Platinum, Pearls, Diamond, Geometric, 3 Strands, 3 Ct., Art Deco 140.00
Bracelet, Silver, Ornate, Flowers, Heavy, Mexico, Large 250.00
Bracelet, Spiral Twisted Rope, Signed, Tiffany & Co., 18K Gold 920.00
Bracelet, Sterling Silver, 18K Yellow Gold, Citrine, Bezel Cut, Stephen Dweck 290.00
Bracelet, Sterling Silver, Calla Lily Design, Signed, Georg Jensen 405.00
Bracelet, Sterling Silver, Lozenge Links, Signed, Georg Jensen, 1945, 1 x 7 In. 2645.00
Bracelet, Sterling Silver, Rosewood Geometric Inlay, Signed, 7 1/2 In. 315.00
Bracelet, Sterling Silver, Waffle Design, Signed, Greta, 1 1/4 In. 280.00
Bracelet, Textured Gold Band, Herringbone, Swiss Hallmark, Suede Box, 8 In. 490.00
Bracelet, Twisted Wire, 14K Gold, Sterling Silver, Cushion Cut Peridot, D. Yurman 865.00
Bracelet & Earrings, Sterling Silver, White Gold, Diamond, Twisted Wire, Yurman 1840.00
Bracelet Pin & Earrings Set, Aurora Borealis, Red, Lisner 76.00
Buckle, Woman, Flowing Hair, Flower Blossoms, Sterling Silver, Art Nouveau 288.00
Chatelaine, Ivory Clasp, Silk Flowers, 4 Ivory Implements 475.00
Chatelaine, Pinwheel, Thimble, Tape Measure, Scissors, Pin Container 3000.00
Chatelaine, Postage Container, Memo Pad, Match Safe, Pinwheel, Pencil 3000.00
Chatelaine, Scissors, Sheath, Needle Case, Thimble Bucket, Silver Plate, 15 1/2 In. 585.00
Chatelaine, Thimble, Shell, Mother-Of-Pearl Interior, c.1895 .... 20.00
Choker, 7 Lozenge Sections, 7 Marquise Diamonds, Diamond Borders, 13 1/2 In. 5750.00
Choker, Silver Sterling, Lozenge Links, Signed, Georg Jensen 2070.00
Cigar Case, Amber, Wood, Original Fitted Case, 5 In. 130.00
Cigar Case, Nickel Plated Brass, Leather Accordion Frame, Satin Lining, Carved, 5 In. 230.00
Cigarette Case, Geometric Design All Sides, 14K Yellow Gold, 4 x 3 1/8 In. 880.00
Cigarette Case, Gilt Metal, Striated Pattern, Marked Dunhill, 1970 .... 80.00
Clip, Aurora Borealis Trembler, Gold Leaf, Vine, Stamp, Hattie Carnegie, 1940s, 2 In. 90.00
Clip, Dog, Silver Metal, Rhinestones, Black, Red, Turquoise, Trifari, 1905, 4 In. 1210.00
Clip, Fur, Gold, Pink Stones, Large 40.00
Clip, Fur, Rhinestone, McCelland Barclay 280.00
Clip, Paisley Shape, Rhinestones, Teardrop Faux Pearl End, Chanel, 1940s 260.00
Collar Necklace, For Blouse, Rhinestones, Black Onyx, Art Deco, 1930s 2070.00
Comb, Tortoise, Faux Diamond Stones, Fan Shape, 6 In. 150.00
Cuff Links, 18K Gold, Signed, Georg Jensen, 3/4 In. 495.00
Cuff Links, Bacchus, Engraved, Collet Set, Inset Mine Cut Diamond 1725.00
Cuff Links, Bezel Set Moonstone, 15K Gold, c.1920 .... 575.00
Cuff Links, Blue Guilloche Enamel, White Border, Oval 115.00
Cuff Links, Cross Shape, Blue, Green Guilloche Enamel 115.00
Cuff Links, Diamond, Calibre Cut Emeralds, Geometric, Art Deco 2530.00
Cuff Links, Falstaff Brewing, Enameled, 1930s 28.00
Cuff Links, Mongrammed, 14K Yellow Gold, Tiffany, c.1950 .... 110.00
Cuff Links, Orange Enamel, Green, White Border 126.00

Cuff Links, Sterling Silver, Enamel, Geometric Orange, Yellow, D. Andersen, 1 In. 253.00
Cuff Links, Sterling Silver, Zeppelin Shape, Signed, Georg Jensen 345.00
Cuff Links, Turquoise, Sterling Silver, Taxco, Mexico 65.00
Earrings, 18K Gold, Faceted Teardrop, Clip-On Stamped, Dunol 316.00
Earrings, 18K Yellow Gold, Oval Cabochon Amethyst, Pear Cut Peridot, Italy 460.00
Earrings, Cameo, Shell, Portrait Of Mercury, Wire Twist & Gold Balls, Victorian 750.00
Earrings, Diamond, Abstract Snake Design, Bezel Set, Signed, Peretti, 18K Gold 630.00
Earrings, Drop, Gold, Bell Shape, Enameled, Persia 1150.00
Earrings, Fan Shape, Gold, Diamonds, Cartier, 1950 .... 3250.00
Earrings, Fan Shape, Rhinestone, Weiss 25.00
Earrings, Flower, Pansy, Enamel, Goldtone & Topaz, Nettie Rosenstein, 3/4 In. 55.00
Earrings, Gilt Metal, Turquoise & Glass, Fitted Copper Box, Early 20th Century, 6 In. 230.00
Earrings, Gold, Applied Wirework, Center Diamonds, New Clip Mount, 1870 .... 2850.00
Earrings, Gold, Domed Faceted Shape, Retro, 1940 .... 800.00
Earrings, Gold, Pearls, Mosellee 20.00
Earrings, Mabe Pearl, 18K Yellow Gold, Pair 865.00
Earrings, Micro Mosaic, Beaded Frame, Bouquet Of Flowers, c.1890 .... 575.00
Earrings, Pearl, Diamond, 18K Yellow Gold, Center Semibaroque Pearl 3320.00
Earrings, Pendant, Bezel Set Diamond, Platinum, Art Deco 2300.00
Earrings, Pendant, Cabochon Garnet, Gold, Applied Wirework, Victorian, 1860 .... 2350.00
Earrings, Pendant, Chrysoberyl, Yellow Gold Flower Heads 2530.00
Earrings, Pendant, Jade, Diamonds, White Gold Stylized Flowers, Art Deco, 2 In. 1795.00
Earrings, Pink Rhinestone, Flower Shape, Center Gemstone, Haskell, 1950s, 3/4 In. 86.00
Earrings, Round Agate Top, Suspended Triangular Agate, Gold Drops, Victorian 690.00
Earrings, Ruby, Pearl Crown, Rosen, 18K Yellow Gold 863.00
Earrings, Sapphire, 3 Collet Sapphires, Signed, Buccellati, 18K Gold 2300.00
Earrings, Seashells, Chalcedony, Cultured Pearl, 18K White Gold 4140.00
Earrings, Silver Fish Bone, Mexico, 2 1/2 In. 115.00
Earrings, Spiral Design, Signed, Tiffany & Co., 18K Gold 230.00
Earrings, Sterling Silver, 14K Yellow Gold, Door Knocker Shape, David Yurman 375.00
Earrings, Sterling Silver, Accented With Folds, Maria Fredriksen, 14K Gold 230.00
Earrings, Sterling Silver, Coiled Wing-Like Design, Bertole, 1 In. 5625.00
Earrings, Sterling Silver, Dove, Signed, Georg Jensen 259.00
Earrings, Sterling Silver, Flower, Screwback, Signed, Georg Jensen 65.00
Earrings, Sterling Silver, Hector Aguilar, 1 In. 395.00
Earrings, Stylized Bracket Design, Signed, Bulgari, 18K Gold 2185.00
Earrings, Teardrop, Gold, Diamonds, c.1880, 3/4 In. 2430.00
Earrings, Thistle, Textured Bicolor 18K Gold Leaves, Silver Wire Thistles 2300.00
Earrings, Turquoise Tops, Florets Centered By A Pearl, Victorian, 14K Gold 630.00
Earrings, Victorian Mastic, Silver, Beaded Frame, Mosaic Floral, c.1890 .... 575.00
Enhancer, 14K Yellow Gold, Crossover, Pear Shape Citrine, Brilliant Cut Diamonds 920.00
Hatpins are listed in this book in the Hatpin category.
Key Chain, Nautical, Signed, Mayor's, 14K Gold 316.00
Lavaliere, Amethyst, Openwork Scrolled Frame, Seed Pearl, 14K Gold, 15 In. 430.00
Lavaliere, Bead Set Diamonds, Silver Link Chain, Edwardian, 11 1/2 In. 2760.00
Lavaliere, Plique-A-Jour, Openwork, Blue Enamel, Blue Stones, Jugenstil 1090.00
Lavaliere, Scarab, Amethyst, Lotus Flower Mount, 14K Gold, 16 1/2 In. 1380.00
Locket, Black Enamel, Seed Pearl Design, Victorian, 14K, 1 x 3/4 In. 315.00
Locket, Child Portrait, Burmese Rubies, Half Pearls, 14K Yellow Gold, c.1810 .... 2415.00
Locket, Memorial, Born 1857, Died 1858, Gold 225.00
Locket, Monogram, 14K Yellow Gold, 23-In. Chain, 1 3/16 In. 160.00
Locket, Pearl, Blue Enamel, Victorian, 18K Gold 230.00
Locket, Seed Pearl, Black Enamel, Portrait Of Young Girl, 2 1/4 In. 60.00
Locket, Silver & Rose Gold, Owl & Palm Trees, Victorian, 1 3/4 In. 190.00
Necklace, 180 Diamonds, Pearl Dangle, 1920s, 17 In. 4950.00
Necklace, African Woman Pendant, Link, Copper, Francisco Rebajes, 1950s, 18 In. 90.00
Necklace, Bakelite & Celluloid, Bowling Ball & 10 Pins 745.00
Necklace, Bakelite, Fountain Pen, Pencil, Globe, Atlas & Inkwell On Chair, 16 In. 1840.00
Necklace, Bib, Rhinestone, Simulated Pearls, Schreiner, 1960s, 4 In. 630.00
Necklace, Cameo, 10K Yellow Gold, Chain 230.00
Necklace, Cameo, Carnelian, 14K Yellow Gold, Enamel Inlay, Engraved, 1860s 1035.00
Necklace, Cameo, Lava, Bust Of Classical Women, Metal Frames, Oval, 10K Gold 690.00
Necklace, Chain, Bakelite & Celluloid, Suspending Bananas & Leaves, 16 In. 690.00

Necklace, Chain, Gold, Pearl, France, 1880, 15 1/4 In. 975.00
Necklace, Chain, Gold, Victorian, 1870, 21 In. 975.00
Necklace, Chain, Platinum, Seed Pearls, Edwardian, 1915 . . . . 3650.00
Necklace, Chain, Rhinestone Bar & Ring Links, Green Emerald, England, 1920 . . . . 6610.00
Necklace, Chain, Spike Links, Box, Signed, Salvador Dali, 18K Gold 865.00
Necklace, Cherry Amber, Faceted Elliptical Beads, 32 In. 550.00
Necklace, Cross, Chain, Silver, Filigree, Hook Clamp, Child's 135.00
Necklace, Diamond, Pearl, 18K Yellow Gold, Tourmaline, Rosen 2530.00
Necklace, Diamonds, Lock & Key Pendant, Rubies, 18K Yellow Gold, Rosen 1265.00
Necklace, Festoon, Rose Cut Diamonds, 1860, 14K Yellow Gold 2300.00
Necklace, Festoon, Turquoise, Teardrop Shape, 14K Gold, 1900 . . . . 400.00
Necklace, Flexible, S-Shaped Links, Signed, 18K Yellow Gold, Signed, Dunol 1840.00
Necklace, Gold & Festoon, Snake Chain, Star Set Seed Pearls, Victorian, 16 In. 1495.00
Necklace, Gold Wirework, Coal, Georgian, 1830 . . . . 7250.00
Necklace, Gold, 5 Domed Rock Crystals, Star Gem Center, Pearl, Emerald, 1880 . . . . . . 8500.00
Necklace, Gold, Beaded Fringe Design, Victorian, 1880 . . . . 4800.00
Necklace, Gold, Brass Filigreed Beads, Coral Branch Accents, Miriam Haskell 109.00
Necklace, Green & Yellow Rhinestones, Goldtone Chain, H. Carnegie, 1950s, 15 In. 100.00
Necklace, Heart Links, Ruby Cabochon, Emeralds, Sapphires, Yellow Gold 1150.00
Necklace, Heart Shape Collar, 14K Yellow Gold, Red Enamel 633.00
Necklace, Lavaliere, Heart Shape, Emerald, Diamond, 18K Yellow Gold, J.B. Star 2990.00
Necklace, Medallion, Faux Rubies, Suspended Gilt Metal Angel, Josef 345.00
Necklace, Mourning, Beads Of Dark Brown Hair, Beaded Cross Pendant, 18 In. 27.00
Necklace, Mourning, Openweave Beads Of Brown Hair, 3 Dangles, 16 In. 70.00
Necklace, Pearls, 12 Fresh Water, 4 Quartz Stones, Yellow Gold, c.1890, 16 1/2 In. 770.00
Necklace, Pearls, 52 Baroque, 7.5 To 8.0 mm, Mikimoto, 14K Gold Clasp, 17 In. 3220.00
Necklace, Pearls, 67 Fresh Water, Sterling Clasp, 17 In. 115.00
Necklace, Pearls, 97 Green Cultured, Knotted, 14K Yellow Gold Clasp 170.00
Necklace, Pearls, Baroque, 2 Strands, Cream Rose, Silver, Pearl Cluster Clasp 4140.00
Necklace, Pearls, Black Onyx, Black Metal, Rhinestones, Miriam Haskell 350.00
Necklace, Pearls, Graduated Strand, Gold Navette Clasp, 1926, 21 In. 1840.00
Necklace, Pearls, Opera Length, Floral Clasp, Diamonds, Japan 2185.00
Necklace, Pearls, Single Strand, Alabaster, Japan 10.00
Necklace, Pendant, Amethyst, Gold Filled, Victorian 170.00
Necklace, Pendant, Carved Rose Quartz, Lavender Stones, Berry, Leaf, 23 1/2 In. 690.00
Necklace, Pendant, Cross, 14K Yellow Gold, Pink Foil Backed Stones, Victorian 250.00
Necklace, Pendant, Grape Cluster, Seed Pearls, Platinum Link Chain, Edwardian 690.00
Necklace, Rhinestones, Blue, Green, Pearl Bead Flowers, Gilt Metal, Chanel, Gripoix . . . 6000.00
Necklace, Rhinestones, Flower Heads, Ring, Miriam Haskell 1955.00
Necklace, Rhinestones, Pearls, Flower & Leaf Pendant, Miriam Haskell, 1940s 925.00
Necklace, Rhinestones, Rhodium Plated White Metal, Faux Sapphire, Jomaz, 20 In. 900.00
Necklace, Secessionist Style Pendant, Olive Shape, Pearls, 14K Gold 2070.00
Necklace, Shield Shaped Pendants, Trefoil, Gilt, 1890, 18 3/4 In. 375.00
Necklace, Silver, 3-Piece Links, Orange Carnelian Stones, Art Smith, 12 In. . . . . *Illus* 250.00
Necklace, Small Copper Tubes, Large Medallion Plates, 17th Century 485.00
Necklace, Snake Link, Black Opal Mosaic, Diamond, Tourmalines, Yellow Gold 1955.00
Necklace, Star, Gilt Metal, Curved Bars, Star Pendant, Chanel, 1937 . . . . 4330.00
Necklace, Sterling Silver, 3 Strands, 4 Segment Rings, Georg Jensen, 1950 . . . . 980.00
Necklace, Sterling Silver, 3 Strands, Pink, Celadon, Aqua, Wiener Werkstatte, 1920 . . . . . 4600.00
Necklace, Sterling Silver, Abstract Openwork Links, Henning Koppel, 1947, 15 In. 1150.00
Necklace, Sterling Silver, Barabarella, Bjorn Weckstrom, 3 3/4 In. 845.00
Necklace, Sterling Silver, Grapes & Leaves, Margot Of Taxco 125.00
Necklace, Sterling Silver, Moonstone, Bezel Set, 14 1/2 In. 920.00
Necklace, Sterling Silver, Opal Iridescent Inset, Lobel, 3 In. 478.00
Necklace, Sterling Silver, Oval Links, Signed, Georg Jensen, 15 In. 690.00
Necklace, Sterling Silver, Stylized Flowerhead Links, 15 In. 460.00
Necklace, Sweet 16, Brass, Oval Barbie Charm, Box, c.1974, 1/2 x 3/4 In. 55.00
Necklace, Watch Chain, Hammered Nuggets, Gold Twisted Rope, Alaska Fob 750.00
Necklace, Watch Chain, Link, Engraved End Links, 14K Gold 145.00
Necklace, Watch Chain, Rectangular Links, 14K Gold, 28 In. 230.00
Necklace, White Marble, Spring Ring Clasp, Vintage, 1935 . . . . 65.00
Necklace & Earrings, 2 Strands, Purple Glass, Miriam Haskell, 1950s, 16 In. 144.00
Necklace & Earrings, Butterfly, Faux Pearls, Rhinestone, Butterflies, M. Haskell 1610.00

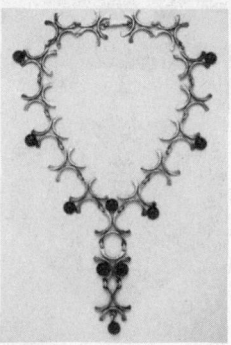

Jewelry, Necklace, Silver,
3-Piece Links, Orange Carnelian
Stones, Art Smith, 12 In.

The best care for an opal is to wear it. This helps restore the moisture to the stone. Do not oil it. If you soak an unused opal in water, use distilled water. Do not store an opal in a safe deposit box.

Necklace & Earrings, Oak Leaf, Miriam Haskell, 1950s	2185.00
Pendant, Agate, Classical Woman With Gold Laurel Leaf Frame, Victorian	290.00
Pendant, Astrological Design, Signed, Cartier, 18K Gold	345.00
Pendant, Bell Shape, Emerald, Art Deco, Pair	2875.00
Pendant, Black Enameled Plaque, Onyx, Signed, Batik	805.00
Pendant, Cameo, Gold Frame, Platinum Trim, 3 In.	850.00
Pendant, Cameo, Sterling Silver, Oval, 1900s, Large	225.00
Pendant, Cameo, Variegated Agate, Classical Warrior, Rose Cut Diamonds, 18K Gold	863.00
Pendant, Cameo, White Gold Filigree, Bows Each Corner, Square, 1910	225.00
Pendant, Cameo, Zeus & Hera, 14K Yellow Gold, 2 1/4 In., Pair	410.00
Pendant, Colombes, Doves, Opalescent Glass, Gray Patina, Marked, R. Lalique, 2 In.	402.00
Pendant, Copper Disc, Pierced For Hanging, Signed, Roycroft, 1 1/2 In.	145.00
Pendant, Cross, Enamel, Blue & Red Champleve, Gold, Moscow, c.1917, 1 3/4 In.	224.00
Pendant, Cross, Garnet, Foliate Design, Almandine Garnets, 14K Gold, 1910	345.00
Pendant, Diamond, Baroque Pearl, 1900	1840.00
Pendant, Diamond, Heart, Openwork Bracket Design, 18K Yellow Gold, Elliott	175.00
Pendant, Edelweiss Flower, Graduating Yellow To Green Leaves, 1921	1095.00
Pendant, Enameled Scarab, Black Opal, 1 1/2 In.	92.00
Pendant, Graduated Concentric Circles, Sterling Bar, Amethyst, Georg Jensen	1495.00
Pendant, Heart, Gold, Amethyst, Emeralds, Diamonds, Victorian, 1880	4650.00
Pendant, Heart, Gold, Cabochon Garnet, Initial W, Wellington's Lock Of Hair	1490.00
Pendant, Jadeite, Bird Among Leaves, 18K Yellow Gold	750.00
Pendant, Lily Flowers Against Opaque Background, Knotted Silk Cord, 1924	980.00
Pendant, Lys, Stylized Lilies, Emerald Green Glass, Green Silk Hanging Cord, Lalique	690.00
Pendant, Mosaic, Beatles & Butterflies, Openwork Coiled Frame	485.00
Pendant, Mourning, Diamond, Black Onyx, Baroque Pearl Flower, 26 1/2 In.	290.00
Pendant, Nude Dancing In Landscape, Lalique, 1924, 1 1/4 In.	345.00
Pendant, Openwork Flower, Filigree, Sapphire, Diamonds, 18K White Gold	1035.00
Pendant, Painting On Ivory, Liberty With Shield, Liberty Cap, Frame, 1800-1825, 1 In.	450.00
Pendant, Poissons, Blue Fish, Frosted Ground, Signed, Lalique, 1 5/8 In.	805.00
Pendant, Scarab, Green Garnet Eyes, Rose Diamonds Tail, 18K Gold	1610.00
Pendant, Sterling Silver, Abstract Geometric Design, Signed, Ed Wiener, 1949	2990.00
Pendant, Sterling Silver, Spoon, Signed, Georg Jensen	290.00
Pendant, Sterling Silver, Uncut Moonstone, Leather Cord, Modern, Pearson, 14 In.	145.00
Pendant, Trefles, Clover Leaves, Amber Glass, Marked, Lalique	1035.00
Pin, 5 Birds Perched On Branch, Sapphire Eye, 2 Ruby Terminates, 14K Gold	260.00
Pin, 56 Rose Cut Diamond Bow, 52 Pearl Frame, Edwardian	1610.00
Pin, Airplane, Pave Rhinestone Body, Enameled Wings & Nose, Trifari, 1940s, 1 In.	160.00
Pin, Amethyst, Pearls, Signed, Cartier, 14K Gold	805.00
Pin, Articulated Girl, Enamel Features, Gold Body, 15K Gold, 1910	980.00
Pin, Bakelite & Celluloid, 3 Convicts, Ball & Chain Strung Together, 10 In.	520.00
Pin, Bakelite & Wood, Elephant, Wearing Hat & Jacket, 3 5/8 In.	1380.00
Pin, Bakelite, Airplane, Rotating Propeller, Yellow, Brown, Red, Black, 3 3/4 In.	4600.00
Pin, Bakelite, Articulated Soldier, Brown & Yellow, Brass Rings, Buttons, 2 x 3 In.	700.00
Pin, Bakelite, Burro, Carved & Painted, Martha Sleeper, 2 3/4 In. ....*Illus*	1238.00

Jewelry, Pin, Bakelite,
Burro, Carved & Painted,
Martha Sleeper, 2 3/4 In.

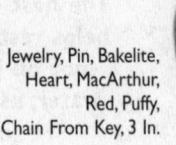

Jewelry, Pin, Bakelite,
Heart, MacArthur,
Red, Puffy,
Chain From Key, 3 In.

Pin, Bakelite, Carved Wooden Bark, 10 Cherries On Stems, Leaves, 1940s	325.00
Pin, Bakelite, Cowboy With Oversized Hat & String Whip, 3 In.	390.00
Pin, Bakelite, Crossed Swordfish, Framing A Palm Tree, Apple Juice, 3 In.	675.00
Pin, Bakelite, Drum Major, Jointed, Ivory Pants, Red Coat & Hat, Brown Head, 4 In.	610.00
Pin, Bakelite, Friday 13th, Black Cat, Crossed Knife & Fork, Ace Of Spades, 2 In.	1495.00
Pin, Bakelite, Frog Playing Guitar, Rotating Arm, Brown & Green, 3 In.	1725.00
Pin, Bakelite, Gasoline Ration, Painted Bar Suspending 2 Tires, Gasoline Can	3450.00
Pin, Bakelite, Giraffe, Rotating Neck, Yellow, Red Spots, 2 5/8 In.	1955.00
Pin, Bakelite, Googly-Eyed Clown, 2 1/2 In.	4880.00
Pin, Bakelite, Googly-Eyed Woman With Headdress, 1 1/2 In.	1725.00
Pin, Bakelite, Green, Red, Orange, Brown, Butterscotch Geometric Drops, 3 In.	565.00
Pin, Bakelite, Hat, Butterscotch, Crimped Edge, 2 1/2 In.	565.00
Pin, Bakelite, Heart, MacArthur, Red, Puffy, Chain From Key, 3 In. *Illus*	1239.00
Pin, Bakelite, Horse Head	175.00
Pin, Bakelite, Leaf Shape, 1 Orange & Other Green, 3 In., 2 Piece *Illus*	225.00
Pin, Bakelite, Pygmy, Smile, Ringed Arms, Trinkets, Bone Ornament On Head, 1920s	400.00
Pin, Bakelite, Seated Puppy, Rotating Head, Yellow, 2 1/2 In.	550.00
Pin, Bakelite, Soldier, Rotating Arm, Green Helmet, Yellow Uniform, 3 In.	1035.00
Pin, Bakelite, Squirrel, On Branch, 5 Acorns Suspended, 2 1/2 In.	750.00
Pin, Bakelite, Tiger, Leather Tail, 1950s, 4 x 1 1/2 In.	160.00
Pin, Bakelite, Violin, 3 1/2 In.	400.00
Pin, Bar, 19 European Cut Diamonds, Engraved Gallery, Platinum	1725.00
Pin, Bar, Diamond Melee, Millegrain Mount, Art Deco	690.00
Pin, Bar, Pictorial Scene With Rose Cut Diamonds, Gold Quartz	748.00
Pin, Bat Shape, Light Brown Pave Diamonds, 14K Yellow Gold	1495.00
Pin, Bird Design, Georg Jensen, Sterling	170.00
Pin, Bird Head, Pave Rhinestone, Beak Holds Branch, Mazer Bros., 1940s, 4 x 1 In.	430.00
Pin, Blue Chrysanthemum, Brass Backing, Lalique, 1 5/8 In.	604.00
Pin, Blue Marble, Silver Tone Metal, 1 5/8 In.	19.00
Pin, Butterfly, Gold Openwork Frame, Diamond, 1890	8250.00
Pin, Butterfly, Sapphire, Ruby, Diamond, Plique-A-Jour, Art Nouveau, 3-In. Wingspan	5465.00
Pin, Calla Lily, Bicolor Gold, Retro, 1940	3450.00
Pin, Cameo, 14K White Gold, Engraved	105.00

Jewelry, Pin, Bakelite, Leaf Shape, 1 Orange &
Other Green, 3 In., 2 Piece

**A diamond ring is durable but not
indestructible. Don't wear it when
using chlorine bleach that can discolor the mounting. Have a jeweler
see it once a year to check for
loose prongs or worn mountings.**

Pin, Cameo, Coral, Woman, High Relief, Yellow Gold Frame, Victorian, 2 In. 265.00
Pin, Cameo, Female Bust, Citrine, Black Enamel, 18K Gold 1840.00
Pin, Cameo, Lava, 3 Mythological Figures & Grapevine, Victorian, 14K Gold Mount 480.00
Pin, Cameo, Sardonyx, Egyptian Male, High Relief, Closed Back Frame, 14K Gold 575.00
Pin, Cameo, Shell, Classical Woman, Vermeil Roped Frame, Late 19th Century, 2 In. 115.00
Pin, Cameo, Shell, Dancing Muse, Antique Gold, Rectangular, Gold Frame 405.00
Pin, Cameo, Shell, Female Bust, Profile, Gold Filled, 1 1/2 In. 130.00
Pin, Cameo, Shell, Female Portrait, Filigree Mount, 2 In. 105.00
Pin, Cameo, Shell, Lilies Of The Valley, Gold Frame, 1 3/4 In. 140.00
Pin, Cameo, Shell, Owl & Eagle Surrounded By 2 Classical Females, 18K Gold 635.00
Pin, Cameo, Shell, Woman, Curls, Draped Clothing, Gold Filled Frame, 2 3/8 In. 88.00
Pin, Center Mine Cut Diamonds, 1.80 Ct., Platinum Topped 18K Gold 5060.00
Pin, Chased Gold Rope Twist Tassel Design, Signed, Tiffany & Co., 18K Gold 2760.00
Pin, Christmas Candle, Gold Metal, White, Green, Red Rhinestones, 1 3/8 In. . . . . . .*Illus* 35.00
Pin, Christmas Tree, Blue Rhinestones, Weiss, 2 1/2 In. 85.00
Pin, Christmas Tree, Gold Metal, Green, Blue, Clear, Red Rhinestones, 1 7/8 In. . . . .*Illus* 35.00
Pin, Christmas Tree, Gold Metal, Red, Magenta, Yellow Rhinestones, 2 1/4 In. . . . . . .*Illus* 40.00
Pin, Clusters Of Brilliant Cut Diamonds, Faceted Sapphires, 18K Gold, Platinum 3920.00
Pin, Crescent Shape, 5 Triangular Opals, Silver Topped, Yellow Gold, 1870 . . . . 805.00
Pin, Crescent Shape, Signed, Georg Jensen, 18K Gold 460.00
Pin, Crescent, 21 Mine Cut Diamonds, 1.15 Ct., Gold Mount 1610.00
Pin, Cross, Garnet, Rose Cut Stones, Silver & Gold, 1890s 242.00
Pin, Crown, Faux Sapphires, Emeralds & Rubies, Silver Vermeil, Trifari, 1940s 145.00
Pin, Devil Face, Silver, Marked Mexico, 4 In. 75.00
Pin, Diamond Center, Cabochon Amethyst, Gold Rope Twist Border, Victorian, 1870 . . . . 3500.00
Pin, Dog, Spaniel, King Charles, Gold Rope Twist Frame 865.00
Pin, Dragonfly, Silver, Pearls, Sapphires, Rubies, Diamonds, France, 1800s, 2 In. 4280.00
Pin, Eagle, Pave Rose Cut Diamonds, Guilloche Enamel 4370.00
Pin, Eagle, Plique-A-Jour, Amethyst, Green, Purple Enamel Wings 200.00
Pin, Elephants, Leather, Brass, c.1930, 2 1/2 In. 68.00
Pin, Enamel, White, Inlaid Yellow Arch, Fountain Center, Wiener Werkstatte, 1910 . . . . . . 1380.00
Pin, Fan, Bicolor Gold, Retro, 1940 . . . . 2650.00
Pin, Fish, Mother-Of-Pearl, Rubies, Diamonds, Silver, France, 19th Century, 2 3/4 In. . . . 3520.00
Pin, Floral & Leaf, Mine & Rose Cut Diamonds, Flower Heads, 14K Gold, c.1830 . . . . 6900.00
Pin, Floral Engraved Bow, Blue Enamel, Diamond, 1860, 22K Yellow Gold 4025.00
Pin, Floral, Intertwining Gold Vines, Brilliant Diamonds, 18K Yellow, White Gold 2760.00
Pin, Floral, Rhinestone, Enameled, Faux Pearl Center, Boucher, 1940s, 4 x 2 In. 185.00
Pin, Floral, Rose, Yellow, Gold, Rhinestones, Signed Trifari, Pat. No. 127043, 2 x 4 In. . . . 225.00
Pin, Floral, Sterling Silver, Amethyst, Marcarita, Mexico 45.00
Pin, Flower Blossom, 27 Rhinestones, Light Blue, 1940s, 1 3/4 In. Diam. 15.00
Pin, Flower Bouquet, Orange Enamel, Cluster Of Diamonds, 18K Yellow Gold 1380.00
Pin, Flower, Clear & Blue Rhinestones, 1940s, 2 1/2 x 4 In. 215.00
Pin, Flower, Orchid, Green Enamel Petals, Whiteside & Blank, 14K Yellow Gold 520.00
Pin, Flower, Tulip, Enamel, Light Blue & Clear Rhinestones, 1940s, 1 3/4 x 2 3/4 In. 245.00
Pin, Flowering Branch, Gold Plated, Swarovski Purple Stones, Eisenberg 1035.00
Pin, Flowerpot, Enamel, Blue Pot, Red, Yellow Flowers, Silver Trim, W. Werkstatte 1480.00
Pin, Frog, Gilt Metal, Yellow Rhinestones, Nettie Rosenstein, 1950s, 3 In. 130.00
Pin, Garland Style, Mine Cut Diamonds, 2.0 Ct., Platinum, c.1890 . . . . 2990.00

Jewelry, Pin, Christmas Tree,
Gold Metal, Red, Magenta,
Yellow Rhinestones, 2 1/4 In.

Jewelry, Pin, Christmas Candle,
Gold Metal, White, Green,
Red Rhinestones, 1 3/8 In.

Jewelry, Pin, Christmas Tree,
Gold Metal, Green, Blue, Clear,
Red Rhinestones, 1 7/8 In.

Pin, Garnet, Mine & Rose Cut Diamonds, Sapphire Drops, Victorian, Gold Mount 3565.00
Pin, Gartered Leg, Enamel, Flesh Color, Gold Heels & Garter, France 4300.00
Pin, Gold Plated Filigree, Rhinestones, Pendant, Miriam Haskell, 1950s, 2 3/4 In. 145.00
Pin, Gold Plated, Yellow Stones, Rhinestones, Eisenberg 345.00
Pin, Gold, Beads, Twisted Wire Frame, Amethyst, Victorian 517.00
Pin, Gold, Bicolor, Emerald, Diamond, Oval Openwork, Art Deco 980.00
Pin, Gold, Blue Enameled & Ball Design, Victorian, 1850 .... 1850.00
Pin, Hat, Bird Shaped, Silver Feather, Scotland, Box, c.1935 .... 100.00
Pin, Horse, Chestnut, Ruby, Diamond, Signed, Tiffany, 18K Gold 1725.00
Pin, Horseshoe Nail, Mine Cut Diamond, Pave Rose Cut Diamonds,.5 Ct., Gold Mount .. 860.00
Pin, Horseshoe, Gold Riding Crop, Horseshoe With 7 Mine Cut Diamonds, 14K Gold ... 316.00
Pin, Horseshoe, Riding Crop, Fox Head Top, Red Stone Eyes, 15K Yellow Gold 375.00
Pin, Hummingbird, Enamel, Textured Gold Feathers, 18K Gold 489.00
Pin, Inset Jewel, Hammered Brass, Forest Craft Guild, 2 1/2 In. 635.00
Pin, Jelly Belly, Cat, Sterling Silver, Pave Rhinestone Accents, 3 In. 450.00
Pin, Jelly Belly, Penguin, Sterling Silver, Red Cabochon Eye, Trifari, 2 1/2 In. 675.00
Pin, Large Octagonal Peridot, Tiffany, 1 1/4 x 1 1/8 In. 2200.00
Pin, Leaf Design, Cabochon Amethyst, Sterling Silver, D.J., Mexico 55.00
Pin, Leaf Shape, Blue Stones, Weiss, 2 1/2 In. 45.00
Pin, Light & Dark Blue Stones, Weiss, 2 1/2 In. 35.00
Pin, Mask, Gold, Diamond Eyes, France, Oval, 1940 .... 3500.00
Pin, Micromosaic, Starburst In Wheel Design, 1 1/2 In. 101.00
Pin, Moonstone, Dove, Openwork Foliate Circular Frame, Georg Jensen 545.00
Pin, Moss Agate, Oval Frames, 14K Rose Gold, Victorian 265.00
Pin, Open Textured Snake, Pink Fresh Water Pearl, 1890, 14K Yellow Gold 805.00
Pin, Openwork Scroll & Foliate, Round Cut Diamonds, Platinum, c.1910 .... 4025.00
Pin, Owl, Gold, Banded Agate Eyes, Victorian, 1880 .... 4250.00
Pin, Pendant, Diamond, Pearl, Edwardian, Open Quatrefoil Design, 1915 .... 9750.00
Pin, Pendant, Enameled Bird Design, Silver, Margot De Taxco ....*Illus* 132.00
Pin, Penguin, Sapphire Eye, 14K Yellow Gold, Marked FJG 165.00
Pin, Pink Flowers, Stone Centers, Enameled Leaves, Lucite Frame, 2 In. 75.00
Pin, Pique, 3 Acorn Dangles, Star Accents, Victoria, 1 In. 250.00
Pin, Platinum, Rose & Old European Cut Diamonds, Rectangular, Art Deco 1725.00
Pin, Portrait, Mother & Child, Hand Painted, Porcelain, Gold Frame, Victorian 850.00
Pin, Portrait, Photograph, Baby's Face, Round, 10K Gold, Victorian, 1 1/4 x 1 1/4 In. 145.00
Pin, Purple & Lavender, Faceted, Glass, Goldtone Metal, Mazer, 1 1/2 x 1 1/2 In. 49.00
Pin, Raised Mythical Deer, Leafy Fines, Georg Jensen, Signed, 1 7/8 x 2 1/8 In. 545.00
Pin, Renaissance Revival, Amethyst, Mother-Of-Pearl, Green Stones 345.00
Pin, Reverse Crystal, Birds, Gold & Pearl Frame, Victorian, 1880 .... 4950.00
Pin, Rhinestone, Blue, Pink, Layered Setting, 1950s, 2 1/2 In. 60.00
Pin, Salamander, Large Green Stone Eyes, Paste, Silver 1495.00
Pin, Sapphire, Geometric Plaque, Rectangular, Art Deco 1725.00
Pin, Scroll Filigree, Seed Pearls, 14K, Victorian, 2 x 1/2 In. 435.00
Pin, Scroll, Sailor's Knot, 14K, c.1878, 2 x 1 In. 350.00
Pin, Seed Pearl, Wire Rosette Accents, 1900 .... 315.00
Pin, Seed Pearls, Foxtail Tassel, 10K Yellow Gold, 1880 .... 149.00
Pin, Silver, Enameled, St. George Slaying Dragon, 1820 English Coin, 1 1/2 In. 110.00
Pin, Star, Garnets, Vermeil Back, Bohemia, 19th Century, 1 1/4 In., Pair 110.00
Pin, Sterling Silver Feather, Amethyst, William Spratling, 2 1/2 In. 460.00
Pin, Sterling Silver, 2 Birds, On Branches, Rhinestone, Black Wings, Coro, 1930s 115.00
Pin, Sterling Silver, Abstract Grapevine Design, Signed, Georg Jensen 550.00
Pin, Sterling Silver, Abstract Oval Foliate, Cherry Design, Box, Signed, Georg Jensen ... 375.00
Pin, Sterling Silver, Biomorphic, Archetypal Attachment, Bertoia, 2 In. 3938.00
Pin, Sterling Silver, Biomorphic, Enamel, Marked, Henning Koppel, 2 In. 900.00
Pin, Sterling Silver, Birds In Flight, Vermeil, Matching Earrings, Corocraft, 1940s 695.00
Pin, Sterling Silver, Bow, Chyrsoprase Rectangular Central Stone, Bjarne, 1 3/4 In. 169.00
Pin, Sterling Silver, Butterfly, Abalone, Mexico, JMN 25.00
Pin, Sterling Silver, Dove, Foliate Frame, Signed, Georg Jensen 315.00
Pin, Sterling Silver, Dove, Signed, Georg Jensen 345.00
Pin, Sterling Silver, Enamel, Cobalt Blue, Georg Jensen 635.00
Pin, Sterling Silver, Enameled Swirl, Margot De Taxco, 1 3/4 In. ....*Illus* 125.00
Pin, Sterling Silver, Lily, Taxco, Face Mark, 2 1/2 In. ....*Illus*   40.00

Jewelry, Pin, Pendant,
Enameled Bird Design, Silver,
Margot De Taxco

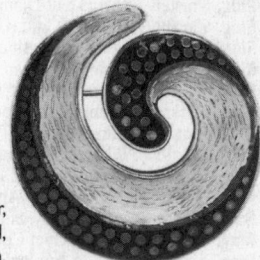

Jewelry, Pin, Sterling Silver,
Enameled Swirl,
Margot De Taxco, 1 3/4 In.

Jewelry, Pin,
Sterling Silver,
Lily, Taxco,
Face Mark,
2 1/2 In.

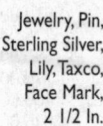

Jewelry, Pin,
Swan,
Diamonds,
Emeralds,
Rubies,
Aquamarines,
Platinum, Art
Deco

Pin, Sterling Silver, Marcasite, Marked, 2 In. 40.00
Pin, Sterling Silver, Marlin, Green & Blue Champleve, Gold Leaf, Margot De Taxco 230.00
Pin, Sterling Silver, Mexican Boy With Donkey & Cactus, Mexico, 3 In. 45.00
Pin, Sterling Silver, Owl, Amethyst Eyes, William Spratling, 2 1/4 In. 1265.00
Pin, Sterling Silver, Pearl Accents, Levin, 2 1/2 In. 310.00
Pin, Sterling Silver, Tulip With Berries, Box, Signed, Georg Jensen 230.00
Pin, Sterling Silver, Wishbone, Green Stones, Mexico, Pineda, 2 1/2 In. 140.00
Pin, Stork, Enamel, Rhinestone, Green Stone, Trifari 3450.00
Pin, Stylized Leaf, Gold, Diamond, 1950 . . . .   8250.00
Pin, Swag & Floral Design, Rose Cut Diamonds, 18K Gold 1725.00
Pin, Swan, Diamonds, Emeralds, Rubies, Aquamarines, Platinum, Art Deco . . . .*Illus* 16500.00
Pin, Terrier, Freeform Pearl Head, Gem Set Eyes, Collar, 18K Gold 115.00
Pin, Thistle, Enameled, Purple, Yellow, Red, Rhinestones, Signed Coro, 1940s, 3 In. 225.00
Pin, Tiger, Gold Stripes, Emerald Eyes, Holding Brilliant Cut Diamonds, Tiffany 1725.00
Pin, Toucan, Pave Rhinestone, Gilt, Silver, Coro, 3 1/2 In. 450.00
Pin, Woman's Face, Gold Plated, Silver & Black, Headdress, Reja 1090.00
Pin, Woodpecker Head, Gold Plated, Paint, Stones, Coco 1150.00
Pin, Zebra, Rhinestones, Hattie Carnegie 55.00
Pin & Earrings, Acorn Clusters, Oak Leaves, Metal, Joseff Of Hollywood, 4 x 2 In. 400.00
Pin & Earrings, Teardrop, Marquis, Rhinestones, Blue, Clip-On, Sarah Coventry, 3 In. 95.00
Purse Holder, Poodle, Gold, Red Rhinestone Eyes, 1950s 16.00
Ring, 3 Circular Cut Diamonds, 3.16 Ct., Reinstein, Ross, 20K Yellow Gold 5462.00
Ring, 5 Diamonds, European Cut, 14 K, Woman's 168.00
Ring, 6 French Cut Green Stones, Georg Jensen, 18K Gold 290.00
Ring, Bakelite, Geometric, Black, Cream Laminated, 4 Layers, 1 In. 425.00
Ring, Band, Pave, Tourmaline, 14K Yellow & Pink, Gold, 7 1/4 In. 230.00
Ring, Black Onyx Tablet, Flanked By 2 Diamonds, 3.2 Dwt., Man's 110.00
Ring, Bloodstone, Yellow Gold, 1907 . . . .   290.00
Ring, Calibre Cut Rubies, Diamonds, 18K Yellow Gold, Size 7 1/2 . . . .   630.00
Ring, Calibre Cut Sapphires, Diamond, 18K Gold 405.00
Ring, Cameo, Classic Female Profile, Wreath Of Pearls, Yellow Gold 518.00
Ring, Cameo, Shell, Profile Of Woman, 14K Gold Rope Frame, 1 1/4 x 3/4 In. 140.00
Ring, Cameo, Slide, Oval, 18K Gold 260.00
Ring, Class, Radford, Va., 1925, High School, Box, 14K Gold, Woman's 85.00

Ring, Cluster, 10 Mine Cut Diamonds, 85 Ct., 12 Calibre Cut Emeralds, Platinum 690.00
Ring, Cluster, 7 Garnets, Gold, Granulated Beads Around Edge, 18K, Victorian 350.00
Ring, Cocktail, Blue Aquamarine, 6 Single Cut Diamonds, Platinum 1430.00
Ring, Cocktail, Center European Cut Diamond, 6.41 mm, 12 Diamonds, Platinum 1870.00
Ring, Cocktail, Platinum, 2.31 Ct., European Cut Diamond, 10 Melee Diamonds 2310.00
Ring, Cocktail, Platinum, Diamond, Rectangular, 1.86 Ct., Art Deco 1150.00
Ring, Diamond, European Cut, Tiffany & Co., 18K, Woman's 196.00
Ring, Diamond, Filigree, Platinum, Art Deco 1840.00
Ring, Diamond, Flush Mount, Cluster, Basket Filigree, Platinum, Woman's 224.00
Ring, Dinner, Ballerina Style, Amethyst, Diamond, 14K Yellow Gold 2070.00
Ring, Dinner, Pearl, South Seas, Filigree Mounting, Platinum 1265.00
Ring, Dinner, Sapphire, Oval Cut, Tapered Baguette, Brilliant Cut, 14K Yellow Gold 1610.00
Ring, Eternity Band, 25 European Cut Diamonds, Size 5 1/4 .... 715.00
Ring, Eternity Band, Platinum Band, Channel Set Round Diamonds, Size 6 .... 413.00
Ring, Etoile, 10 Bezel Set Diamonds, 18K Gold 1380.00
Ring, Full Cut Diamond, Yellow Gold Pierced Mount, Art Deco, Size 9 .... 345.00
Ring, Garnet & Diamond, Bezel Set, European Cut, Floral Design, 14K Yellow Gold 910.00
Ring, Gold & Diamond, 14K Yellow Gold, Scalloped Edge, 29 Diamonds, Size 6 1/4 .... 275.00
Ring, Green Hornet, Seal, General Mills, 1940 .... 1650.00
Ring, Green Jadeite, 20th Century, 14K Yellow Gold 210.00
Ring, Jadeite, 3 Graduated Stones, Gold Bead Design, 22K Gold, Size 6 .... 460.00
Ring, Marquise Cut Diamonds, Platinum, Gold, Ruby, 1935 .... 2070.00
Ring, Mexican Fire Opal, Lapis Lazuli, Diamond, Signed, Amos, 18K Yellow Gold 2530.00
Ring, Oval Black Opal, 80 Diamonds, Platinum, Size 7 1/2 .... 7500.00
Ring, Oval Cabochon Cat's Eye, 2 Melee Diamonds 250.00
Ring, Oval Yellow Sapphire, 6 Round Cut Diamonds, Platinum 1840.00
Ring, Pave Diamonds, Brilliant Cut, 18K Yellow, White Gold 2530.00
Ring, Pave Diamonds, Round Cut, Flowers Of Round Cut Rubies, 18K White Gold 920.00
Ring, Peridot, Oval, 14K Yellow Gold, German Cut, Woman's 750.00
Ring, Plaque, Rubies, Diamonds, Silver, 14K Gold Band, Early 20th Century, 1/2 In. 235.00
Ring, Red Spinel, Crimped Collet, 1910, 14K Gold, Size 7 .... 1840.00
Ring, Rolling, 3 Interlocking Bands, Platinum, Cartier, Size 7 1/2 .... 750.00
Ring, Rosewood, Marked, Spratling, 1945, 18K Gold 650.00
Ring, Round Cut Diamonds, Channel Set Sapphires, 18K White Gold 1380.00
Ring, Sapphire, 8 Diamonds, Filigree, 14K White Gold, Art Deco, 1920 .... 445.00
Ring, Scarab, Aquamarine, Elizabeth Gage, 18K Yellow Gold 2300.00
Ring, Scarab, Coral, 3 Rose Cut Diamonds, Signed, Koch, 5 3/4 In. 2185.00
Ring, Scarab, Oval Cut Cabochon Jade Button, 10 Round Cut Diamonds, 25 Ct. 460.00
Ring, Snake, Diamond, Coiled 4 Times, Yellow Gold, c.1880 .... 255.00
Ring, Snake, Double Coil, Rose Cut Diamond Eyes, Gold, Size 8 .... 290.00
Ring, Star Sapphire, Leaf, Vine Design, Bezel Set, Size 7 3/4 In. 400.00
Ring, Sterling Silver, 14K Gold Bezel, 5M Square Cabochon Garnet, Ladies 69.00
Ring, Tanzanite, Diamond, 18K Yellow Gold, Ballerina Style, Oval Cut, Woman's 5060.00
Ring, Tourmaline, Cabochon Rubies, Twisted Gold Border, 18K Yellow Gold 2300.00
Ring, Unie, Stylized Leaves, Topaz Glass, Lalique, 1931 .... 1725.00
Ring, White Gold, Blue Sapphire, Diamond, 18K, Art Deco, 3.19 Ct. 1095.00
Ring & Earrings, Coral, Diamond, 14K Yellow Gold, Comma Shape Cabochon 750.00
Stickpin, Brass, Signed, Roycroft, 3 In. 230.00
Stickpin, Devil's Head, Rose-Cut Diamond Eyes, Edwardian Labradorite 430.00
Stickpin, Double Sided Sapphire, Floral & Scroll, 14K Yellow Gold Mount 460.00
Stickpin, Head Of Byzantine Woman, Polychrome Enamel, 14K Gold 550.00
Stickpin, Memorial, Grisaille Watercolor On Ivory, Be What Your Mother Was, 2 In. 260.00
Stickpin, Moonstone, Carved Moonstone Of Gentleman's Face, 14K Gold 1840.00
Stickpin, Mourning, Painting On Ivory, 5 People By Funeral Urn, 19th Century 475.00
Stickpin, President Cleveland, Whisk Broom Shape, 1888 .... 85.00
Stickpin, Sapphire, 3 Calibre Cut Sapphires, Platinum, Art Deco 518.00
Tiara, Crescent, Framed By Diamonds, Pearls, Platinum Frame, 18K Gold 3220.00
Tiara, Tortoiseshell Band, Swags Of Rose Cut Diamonds & Pearls, Victorian 2300.00
Watches are listed in their own category.
Watch Chain, Gold Filled Slide With Ruby Cabochon 55.00
Watch Chain, Jade, 12 Freshwater Pearls, Trace Link Chain, 1910, 14K Gold, Pearl 920.00
Wristwatches are listed in their own category.

JOSEF ORIGINALS ceramics were designed by Muriel Joseph George. The first pieces were made in California from 1945 to 1962. They were then manufactured in Japan. The company was sold to George Good in 1982 and he continued to make Josef Originals until 1985. The company was then sold to Southland Corporation. The name is now owned by Applause.

Cake Topper, Girl In Green Dress, Holding Umbrella, 4 In.	58.00
Figurine, Angel, Wings	5.00
Figurine, Bear Cub, 4 1/8 In.	24.00
Figurine, Birthstone Doll, January, Garnet, Pink Dress, 4 In.	15.00 to 36.00
Figurine, Birthstone Doll, July, 3 1/2 In.	25.00
Figurine, Birthstone Doll, May, Ink Mark, 4 1/2 In.	25.00
Figurine, Birthstone Doll, November, Topaz Label, Ink Signed, 4 1/2 In.	25.00
Figurine, Doll Of The Month, January, Rose Dress, Muff, 3 1/2 In.	60.00
Figurine, Doll Of The Month, June Bride, Bouquet, 3 1/2 In.	63.00
Figurine, Doll Of The Month, May, 1985	10.00
Figurine, Doll Of The Month, October, Incised Signature, 4 In.	35.00
Figurine, Duck, Label, 2 1/4 In.	15.00
Figurine, Girl With Dove, Pink Dress, Roses, White Dove, 7 In.	170.00
Figurine, Love Locket Girl, Green Dress, Butterflies, Heart Shape Locket, 8 In.	190.00
Figurine, Mouse With Drum, 3 In.	28.00
Figurine, Swedish Girl, 3 1/2 In.	65.00
Lipstick Holder, Girl	75.00
Lipstick Holder, Gold Skip On Headband, Incised, 4 In.	60.00
Music Box, Anniversary Waltz, Purple Gown, Black & Gold Label, 8 In.	85.00
Music Box, Happy Birthday, Dancing Girl, Pink Dress, 7 In.	77.00
Music Box, Music Box Dancer, Doll On Table Spins, 1985, 6 In.	80.00

JUDAICA is any memorabilia that refers to the Jews or the Jewish religion. Interests range from newspaper clippings that mention eighteenth- and nineteenth-century Jewish Americans to religious objects, such as menorahs or spice boxes. Age, condition, and the intrinsic value of the material, as well as the historic and artistic importance, determine the value.

Cup, Kiddush, Silver, Architectural View, Alternating Medallions, Russia, 2 3/4 In., Pair	140.00
Cup, Kiddush, Sterling Silver, Monogram & Star, Mexico, 4 In.	30.00
Cup, Kiddush, Wailing Wall, Scrolls Centering Cartouche, Gilt Interior, 3 In.	50.00
Cup, Scrolling Foliage, Hebrew Blessings, Hebrew Jerusalem On Foot, Silver, 6 In.	2400.00
Finials & Breastplate, 2 Rows Of Bells, Crown Top, Star Of David Finial, 14 1/4 In.	2400.00
Menorah, Brass, Stepped Base, Leaf Design, Denmark, 14 1/4 In., Pair	235.00
Mezuzah, Borders Of Fruit, Foliage, Rabbi On Gilt Interior, I. & R. Schor, Silver, 6 In.	1600.00
Seder Tray, Silver, Cartouches Flanked By Flowering Branches, Wavy Rim, 13 In.	1380.00
Spice Tower, Leafy Sides, Spire, Pendant, Square Base, Silver, Russia, 1864, 9 In.	862.00
Torah Pointer, Foliate Panels, Fitted With Chain, Silver, Continental, 7 1/4 In.	483.00

JUGTOWN Pottery refers to pottery made in North Carolina as far back as the 1750s. In 1915, Juliana and Jacques Busbee set up a training and sales organization for what they named *Jugtown Pottery*. In 1921, they built a shop at Jugtown, North Carolina, and hired Ben Owen as a potter in 1923. The Busbees moved the village store where the pottery was sold to New York City. Juliana Busbee sold the New York store in 1926 and moved into a log cabin near the Jugtown Pottery. The pottery closed in 1959. It reopened in 1960 and is still working near Seagrove, North Carolina.

Bean Pot, Orange & Brown Glaze, Early 20th Century, 7 In.	120.00
Bowl, Chinese Blue Glaze, 12 In.	1380.00
Bowl, White Matte Glaze, Ben Owen, 8 In.	210.00
Candlestick, Signed, Ben Owen	260.00
Multitone Brown High Glaze, Signed, 3 1/2 In.	120.00
Pitcher, Blue Cobalt To Interior Collar, Flower At Spout, Salt Glaze, 1940s, 3 3/4 In.	145.00
Vase, Bulbous, Flared Rim, Embossed Medallions, Chinese Blue Glaze, 7 1/2 In.	748.00
Vase, Chinese Blue Glaze, 6 In.	335.00

Vase, Chinese Blue Glaze, Tapered, 7 In.	375.00
Vase, Chinese Red Glaze, Embossed Leaf Design, Brown, Green Glaze, 6 In.	220.00
Vase, Light Green Mottled Glaze, 2 Medallions, Embossed, 7 In.	290.00
Vase, Pear Shape, Turquoise Matte Mottled Glaze, 20th Century, 6 In.	630.00
Vase, Textured Gray Semimatte Glaze, 4 Handles, Pewabic, Detroit, 5 1/2 In.	259.00

JUKEBOXES play records. The first coin-operated phonograph was demonstrated in 1889. In 1906 the *Automatic Entertainer* appeared, the first coin-operated phonograph to offer several different selections of music. The first electrically powered jukebox was introduced in 1927. Collectors search for jukeboxes of all ages, especially those with flashing lights and unusual design and graphics.

AMI, Reconditioned, 1956	2800.00
Audiophone, Seeburg, 8 Record Selections, Plays 78s, c.1929	1600.00
Evans, Reconditioned, 1952	750.00
Gabel, Reconditioned, 1935	2500.00
Rock-Ola, 1956	2800.00
Rock-Ola, Model No. 1428, Plays 78s, 60 In.	2530.00
Rock-Ola, Reconditioned, 1952	2000.00
Rock-Ola, Reconditioned, 1956	2600.00
Seeburg, 1950	2500.00
Seeburg, Coin-Operated, Golden Lounge Wall Selector, 1950s	250.00
Seeburg, Model 100 B, Select-O-Matic, 100 Records, c.1950, 54 In.	1780.00
Seeburg, Reconditioned, 1956	6500.00
Williams, 1951	1000.00
Wurlitzer, 1941	6500.00 to 8500.00
Wurlitzer, Model 61	1750.00
Wurlitzer, Model 1015, 78 RPM Records, Color Tubes, 1946 .... *Illus*	7475.00
Wurlitzer, Model 1050, 1973	6778.00
Wurlitzer, Speaker Baffle, Hand Painted Design, c.1942	6200.00

KATE GREENAWAY, who was a famous illustrator of children's books, drew pictures of children in high-waisted Empire dresses. She lived from 1846 to 1901. Her designs appear on china, glass, and other pieces. Figural napkin rings depicting the Greenaway children may also be found in the Napkin Ring category under Figural.

Button, See-Saw Jack	177.00
Figurine, Amy, No. 2958	250.00
Figurine, Anna, Purple, White, No. 2802	325.00
Figurine, Carrie, 1976, No. 2800	325.00
Figurine, Child Feeding Chickens	85.00
Figurine, Emma, 1981, No. 2834	375.00
Figurine, Lori, Yellow, Cream, No. 2801	325.00
Figurine, Sophie, Red, Green, No. 2833	325.00
Figurine, Tess, Green, 1988, No. 2865	375.00

Nineteenth-century Indian blankets are generally not restored by museums. They stabilize them, mount them on a backing fabric to keep them from further damage, and hang or frame them. There is some thought that even the dirt may be wanted in original state in the future.

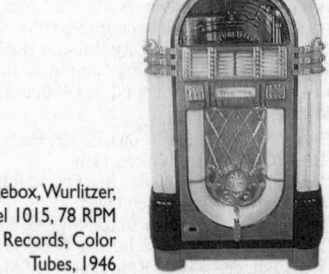

Jukebox, Wurlitzer, Model 1015, 78 RPM Records, Color Tubes, 1946

KAY FINCH Ceramics were made in Corona Del Mar, California, from 1935 to 1963. The hand-decorated pieces often depicted whimsical animals and people. Pastel colors were used.

Kay Finch
CALIFORNIA

Bank, Pig, Winkie, No. 185, 3 1/2 x 4 1/2 In.	165.00
Dish, Pink, Royal Blue Interior, Little Pink Swirls, 4 1/2 x 3 1/2 x 2 1/2 In.	89.00
Figurine, Angel, Blue Flowers In Her Hair, No. 114, 4 In.	105.00
Figurine, Cat, Jezebel, No. 179, 6 x 9 In.	325.00
Figurine, Cat, Muff, No. 182, 3 1/2 In.	75.00
Figurine, Cat, Persian, Ambrosia, Signed, No. 155, 10 3/4 In.	595.00
Figurine, Hen, Biddy, No. 176, Signed	75.00
Figurine, Man, Godey, Holding Bouquet Of Flowers, No. 122, 7 1/2 In.	85.00
Figurine, Owl, Hoot, No. 187, 5 1/2 In.	95.00
Figurine, Owl, Toot, Pink, 5 3/4 In.	105.00
Figurine, Penguin, Pee Wee, Black, White, Green Beak & Feet, No. 468, 3 1/4 In.	145.00
Figurine, Pig, Sassy, White Ears, Tail, No. 166, 3 1/2 x 4 1/2 In.	105.00
Figurine, Pig, Smiley, Signed, No. 164, 6 3/4 In.	350.00
Figurine, Swan, Pink, 3 1/2 x 3 1/2 In.	75.00
Planter, Bear, Seated, No. 4906, White Gloss, Pink Ears, Eyes & Paws, 5 3/4 In.	300.00
Planter, Cat, 7 x 6 In.	185.00

KAYSERZINN, see Pewter category.

KELVA glassware was made by the C. F. Monroe Company of Meriden, Connecticut, about 1904. It is a pale, pastel-painted glass decorated with flowers, designs, or scenes. Kelva resembles Nakara and Wave Crest, two other glasswares made by the same company.

KELVA

Box, 5 Wild Roses, Pink & Green, Hinged Cover, 4 1/2 x 3 1/2 In.	460.00
Box, Pink & White Roses, Dark Green, Hinged Cover, Signed, 4 x 3 1/2 In.	863.00
Box, Pink Flowers, Bright Blue, Hinged Cover, Signed, 4 x 3 In.	403.00
Humidor, Cigar	550.00
Vase, Dark Green, Pink Wild Rose, Signed, 14 x 4 In.	1150.00
Vase, Mottled Pink, Iris, Brass Feet, 13 1/2 In.	1890.00
Vase, Mottled Red, White Morning Glory, Silver Plated Handles & Feet, Signed, 14 In.	2310.00

KEMPLE glass was made by John Kemple of East Palestine, Ohio, and Kenova, West Virginia, from 1945 to 1970. The glass was made from old molds. Many designs and colors were made. Kemple pieces are usually marked with a *K* on the bottom. Many milk glass pieces were made with or without the mark.

Bowl, Banana Split, Milk Glass, Ivy-In-Snow, 8 1/4 In.	18.00
Bowl, Milk Glass, Ivy On The Snow, 8 1/4 In.	18.00
Compote, Milk Glass, 10 1/2 x 4 1/4 In.	17.00
Compote, Milk Glass, 1940, 6 1/2 x 5 1/2 In.	25.00
Decanter, Gold, 10 x 4 In.	40.00
Dish, Cat Cover, Split Rib Base, 5 1/2 In.	95.00
Dish, Chicken Cover, Basket Base, Amber, 6 In.	30.00
Dish, Cow Cover, Diamond Weave Basket Base	28.00
Dish, Fox Cover, Blue, Oval, 7 x 6 In.	79.00
Dish, Rabbit Cover, Split Rib Base, Amber, 5 1/2 In.	30.00
Dish, Turkey, Milk Glass	69.00
Goblet, Lace & Dewdrop, Amber, 5 7/8 x 3 1/8 In.	15.00
Goblet, Ruby Amber, Sunburst & Drape	31.00
Nappy, Snow Heart, Handle, 5 1/2 x 2 In.	11.00
Sugar & Creamer, Lace & Dewdrop, Milk Glass, Pink	40.00
Vase, Milk Glass, Wavy Top, Scalloped, 5 1/2 x 3 3/4 In.	20.00

KEW BLAS is the name used by the Union Glass Company of Somerville, Massachusetts. The name refers to an iridescent golden glass made from the 1890s to 1924. The iridescent glass was reminiscent of the Tiffany glass of the period.

KEW-BLAS

Paperweight, Signed, 1920	950.00
Vase, Pinched, Gold Iridescent, 5 x 3 In.	200.00

Vase, Pulled Feather Yellow, Gold Iridescent, 1920, 9 In. 203.00
Vase, Spherical, Gold Iridescent, Green, Pulled, Hooked Decoration, White, 5 1/2 In. 978.00

KEWPIES, designed by Rose O'Neill, were first pictured in the *Ladies'*
Home Journal. The figures, which are similar to pixies, were a success,
and Kewpie dolls and figurines started appearing in 1911. Kewpie pictures and other items soon followed. Collectors search for all items that
picture the little winged people.

Bank, Bisque, Foil Label, Lefton Exclusives, Japan, Stamped 145, 1950s, 7 1/4 In. 145.00
Bank, Chalkware, Black Carnival Kewpie, 1930s, 12 In. 195.00
Bisque, At Fountain, Out-Flung Arms, Side-Glancing, Front & Back Labels, c.1915, 5 In. 2800.00
Bisque, Black Hottentot, 5 In. 99.00
Bisque, Blue Wings, Side-Glancing Googly Eyes, Holding Black Umbrella, 4 In. 500.00
Bisque, Bride & Groom 285.00
Bisque, Jointed At Shouldered, Signed O'Neill Under Right Foot, 8 In. 316.00
Bisque, Kewpie, Holding Brown Teddy Bear, Side-Glancing Eyes, 1912, 5 In. 1050.00
Bisque, Kewpie, Standing With Gray Elephant, Germany, 1915, 3 1/4 In. 6750.00
Bisque, Kneeling, 1905, 5 In. 825.00
Bisque, On Silk Pincushion, Left-Glancing Eyes, Jacket & Hat, Paper Label, 5 1/4 In. . . . 288.00
Bisque, Playing Mandolin, Rose O'Neill, 5 In. 365.00
Bisque, Standing, Googly Eyes, Topknot, Wings, 7 In. 39.00
Blunderboo, Arms To Head, Bent Arms At Elbows, Rose O'Neill, c.1915, 3 In. 1250.00
Candy Container, Glass 99.00
Candy Container, Kewpie By Barrel, No Paint 33.00
Celluloid, Painted Hair, Googly Eyes, Feather Dress, Japan 24.95
Ceramic, Indian, Googly Eyes, Indian Leatherette Dress, Headband, Moccasins, 1940s . . . 27.00
Chalkware, Carnival Kewpie, 1930s, 12 In. 145.00
Chalkware, Carnival Kewpie, Jointed Arms, Rose O'Neill Heart Sticker, 1930s, 12 In. . . . 225.00
Chalkware, Carnival Kewpie, Marked Cast/Craft, Toledo, O, 1930s, 12 In. 155.00
Composition, Blue Wings, Heart Sticker, Copyright By Rose O'Neill, 11 In. 250.00
Composition, Cameo Doll Co., Heart Label, 12 In. 495.00
Composition, Fully Jointed, Painted Eyes, 13 In. 150.00
Display, Santa Claus, Die Cut Cardboard, Easel, Rose O'Neill, 1913, 11 1/2 x 5 5/8 In. . . . 150.00
Planter, Pink, Kewpie With Bow & Quiver, 5 1/2 In. 54.50
Plate, Sleeping Baby, Floral Design, World Wide Arts, 1973, 8 In. 30.00
Plate, Various Kewpies In Poses, Gold Trim, Royal Rudolstadt, Germany, 8 In. 150.00
Porcelain, Molded Hair, Movable Arms, Japan, 5 In. 125.00
Postcard, Bluebird Of Happiness For You, Rose O'Neill, Gibson Art, 1919 . . . . 65.00
Postcard, Christmas, Gibson Art Co., Postmarked December 1913 . . . . 25.00
Scootles, Black, Cameo Doll Co., 1915, 13 In. 995.00
Scootles, Cameo Doll Co., 9 In. 185.00
Scootles, Cameo Doll Co., 16 In. 895.00
Sign, Golden French, Special Ice Cream, Hendler's Golden Anniversary, Paper, 9 x 20 In. 45.00
Sign, Hendler's Ice Cream & Cake Wafers, 8 1/2 x 17 1/4 In. 125.00
Teapot, Rose O'Neill, Japan, 1950 . . . . 55.00
Vase, Doodle Dog, 4 1/4 In. 2600.00
Vinyl, Fully Jointed, Cameo, 15 In. 90.00
Vinyl, Jointed At Neck, Shoulder & Hips, Cameo, 12 1/2 In. 75.00
Vinyl, Jointed Neck, Shoulders & Hips, Pantaloons, Cameo, 9 In. 45.00
Vinyl, Ragsy, Googly Eyes, Topknot, 1950s 42.00
Vinyl, Red, Cameo, 10 In. 75.00

KIMBALL, see Cluthra category.

KING'S ROSE, see Soft Paste category.

KITCHEN utensils of all types, from eggbeaters to bowls, are collected
today. Handmade wooden and metal items, like ladles and apple peelers, were made in the early nineteenth century. Mass-produced pieces,
like iron apple peelers and graniteware, were made in the nineteenth
century. Other kitchen wares are listed under manufacturers' names or
under Advertising, Iron, Tool, or Wooden.

Baker's Table, 4 Drawers, Undulating Skirt, Old Paint 3950.00
Baker's Table, Double-Possum Belly, Sheet-Metal Drawers, Cutting Boards, Pine, 1880s . 575.00

Basket, Bonbon, Aluminum, Scallops, 8 x 5 1/4 In. 9.00
Batter Beater, Metal, Marked A & J, Curved To Fit Bowl, 11 1/2 In. 8.00
Batter Jug, Red, McKee 175.00
Batter Pail, 2 Brush Blue Flowers On Either Side Of Spout, Bail Handle, 1870, 2 Gal. 1210.00
Batter Pail, Bail Handle, Tin Cover, Havana, N.Y., 1860, 1/2 Gal. 360.00
Batter Pail, Blue Accents At Spout, Handle, White & Co. Binghamton, 1870, 3 Qt. 275.00
Batter Pail, Brush Bird On Front, Original Bail Handle, 1860, 3 Qt. 1020.00
Batter Pail, Slip Blue Oak Leaf Design, Original Bail Handle, Tin Cover, 1865, 9 In. 578.00
Beater, Wire, In Glass Jar, Chrome Top, Red Bakelite Handle, Speed-Dee, 5 1/4 x 5 In. .. 29.00
Bin, Dough, Poplar & Pine, Pegged Construction, Breadboard Ends, 30 x 55 In. 770.00
Bin, Flour, Sifter, Green, 27 1/4 x 12 3/4 In. 595.00
Bird Spit, Wrought Iron, Adjustable 8-Tine Frame, Tripod, Penny Feet, 27 1/2 In. 520.00
Board, Cheese, Paul Evans, Rosewood, 5 Metal Strips, Plank Base, 15 1/2 In. 790.00
Board, Cutting, Pig Form, Curly Maple, 19 1/4 In. 275.00
Board, Pie, Pine, Lollipop Handle, 19th Century, 17 x 19 In. 595.00
Bowl, Ash, Burl, Handle, Oval, c.1800, 14 x 19 In. 2970.00
Bowl, Blue, Crisscross, 6 5/8 In. 175.00
Bowl, Blue, Crisscross, 8 3/4 In. 150.00
Bowl, Blue, Crisscross, 9 5/8 In. 165.00
Bowl, Burl, Dark Finish, Shallow, Canted Sides, Raised Center Ring, 9 In. 715.00
Bowl, Burl, Elliptical, Cutout Handles, American, 18th Century, 8 x 20 In. 2760.00
Bowl, Burl, Tapered To Base, Round, American, 5 1/2 x 14 In. 978.00
Bowl, Burl, Turned, Round, Shaped Rim, Footed Form, 19th Century, 3 x 5 1/4 In. 316.00
Bowl, Chopping, Cherry, Hand Carved, Oval, Early 19th Century, 4 x 23 x 13 1/2 In. 575.00
Bowl, Chopping, Pine, 18th Century, 6 3/4 x 26 1/4 x 3 In. 215.00
Bowl, Dough, Hand Hewn, Chisel Marks, Double Handles, 20 x 21 1/4 x 7 In. 275.00
Bowl, Fruitwood, Turned, Flared, Shallow, 17th Century, 24 In. Diam. 460.00
Bowl, Maple, 3 Spoke Legs, Red Paint, C. A. Brown, Early 19th Century, 14 x 16 1/2 In. .. 460.00
Bowl, Sugar, Manganese Drip Design, Pa., Mid 19th Century, 4 In. 660.00
Bowl, Sugar, Maple, Turned, Polychrome, Cover, Footed, Lehnware, 7 x 4 In. 6600.00
Bowl, Turned Burl, Round, 19th Century, Large 2875.00
Bowl, Turned Burl, Round, Incised Linear Decoration, 19th Century, 4 x 11 1/2 In. 489.00
Bowl, Turned Wood, Gray Paint, 19th Century, 6 x 16 3/4 In. 3335.00
Bowl, Yellow, Rounded Tier Design, Betty Crocker, 8 5/8 In. 10.00
Bowl Set, Refrigerator, Stacking, Rectangular, Lids, Pyrex, 1950s, 4 Piece 55.00
Box, Pantry, Chip Carved, 1783 On Lid, 3 x 5 3/4 In. 600.00
Box, Pantry, Chip Carved, Pierced Compass, Star & Hearts, Bentwood, 9 In. 275.00
Box, Pantry, Lapped Finger, Green Paint, 7 x 16 1/2 In. 630.00
Box, Pantry, Lapped, Rosehead Nails, 1800, 6 In. 650.00
Box, Pantry, Wooden, Geometric Design, Pewter Tacks, Round, E. Hudson, 1770 .... 1350.00
Box, Pantry, Wooden, Round, Lid Branded N. Low, New England, 19th Century, 6 In. 250.00
Bread Maker, Universal, Table Clamp, Gold Medal Winner, St. Louis Exposition, 1904 .. 235.00
Broiler, Rotary, Wrought Iron, Medallion Finial On Handle, 24 1/4 In. 220.00
Broiler, Wrought Iron, Fireplace, Late 18th Century, 24 In. 195.00
Butter Chip, Carved, Chip Carved Ring, 4 Hearts, Box, 1780-1820 .... 1400.00
Butter Chip, Leaf Design, Wood, 5 In. 20.00
Butter Chip, Tulip & Leaf, Sawtooth Border, 4 3/4 In. 650.00
Butter Melter, Magnetic, Holds Butter On Toaster Top, Box ....*Illus* 18.00
Butter Mold, look under Mold, Butter in this category.
Butter Paddle, Bird's-Eye Maple, 9 1/8 In. 55.00
Butter Paddle, Burl, Wide Bowl & Handle, Circle Carved At End, 9 In. 2035.00
Butter Paddle, Heart At Top, Wooden, Early 18th Century, 13 1/2 In. 650.00
Butter Paddle, Stylized Bird Head Handle, 11 1/8 In. 715.00
Butter Stamp, Acorns, Oak Leaves, J Kozanne Houguette Name In Border, 5 1/4 In. 80.00
Butter Stamp, Carved Eagle, 3 5/8 In. 550.00
Butter Stamp, Carved Flower, Handle, Round, 3 3/4 In. 195.00
Butter Stamp, Carved Petal Flower, Handle, 4 5/16 In. 220.00
Butter Stamp, Carved Poplar, Central Sheaf Of Wheat Design, Pa., 1810, 3 1/4 x 6 In. ... 880.00
Butter Stamp, Carved Walnut, Eagle, Spread Wings, Small Star, Pa., 1820, 5 In. 550.00
Butter Stamp, Carved, Dovetailed Handle, Incised Pineapple, 19th Century, 3 1/2 In. 195.00
Butter Stamp, Carved, Incised Strawberry, Early 19th Century, 3 1/2 In. 220.00
Butter Stamp, Central Star Design, Half Moons & Squares, Pa., 1840, 3 1/4 x 6 In. 220.00
Butter Stamp, Eagle, Carved Wood, Lollipop Handle, 7 x 3 In. 1850.00

Butter Stamp, Eagle, Shield, 2 5/8 In. 220.00
Butter Stamp, Floral Carving, 1 Piece Handle, Round, 4 1/4 In. 550.00
Butter Stamp, Flower Surrounded By Leaves, 4 3/8 In. 110.00
Butter Stamp, Half Round, Carved Sheaf Of Wheat, Handle, 6 3/8 x 3 3/8 In. 525.00
Butter Stamp, Lollipop, 6 3/4 In. 175.00
Butter Stamp, Lollipop, Stylized Eagle, 7 In. 1850.00
Butter Stamp, Maple, Carved Flower, Star, Late 18th Century, 4 In. 165.00
Butter Stamp, Maple, Incised Flowers, 18th Century, 4 In. 360.00
Butter Stamp, Poplar, Large Central Tulip, Pa., 1800, 3 1/2 x 7 1/2 In. 470.00
Butter Stamp, Starflower, Jagged Edge Leaves, Initials LB, 4 7/8 In. 66.00
Butter Stamp, Stylized Eagle, Crosshatched Feathers, Stars Surround, 4 1/4 In. 770.00
Butter Stamp, Thistle, Walnut, c.1800, 3 7/8 Diam. 140.00
Cabbage Cutter, Curved Crest, Heart Cutout, Curly Maple, 19 1/2 In. 495.00
Cabbage Cutter, Heart Cutout, Chip-Carved Detail, Walnut, 20 1/2 In. 550.00
Cabbage Cutter, Indianapolis Sanitary, 3 Steel Blades, Patent April 18, 1905 . . . . 75.00
Cake Board, Carved, Dutch Woman, Rosmeulen, 18th Century, 29 x 11 In. 1095.00
Cake Board, Carved, Horse, Rider, Round, Brackets, 18th Century, 15 In. 575.00
Cake Plate, Cover, Aluminum 35.00
Canister, Ginger, Tin, Lithographed, 19th Century, 11 1/2 x 8 x 9 In. 115.00
Canister, Green, Yellow, Orange Mottled Glaze, Late 19th Century, 8 In. 715.00
Canister Set, 4 Canisters In Rack, Aqua Blue, c.1955 . . . . 50.00
Canister Set, Brushed Aluminum, Plastic Finials, AC Heller Hostess Ware, 4 Piece 40.00
Carton, Freezer, Cold Spot, Wax Coated, Blue, Red Thermometer, Sears Roebuck & Co. . 4.00
Casserole, Cover, Yellow, Pyrex, 2 1/2 Qt. 20.00
Casserole, Griswold, No. 68, Round, Red 45.00
Casserole, Griswold, No. 83, Black Iron, White Porcelain Interior 85.00
Cherry Pitter, Green Paint, 1917 . . . . 30.00
Cherry Pitter, Table Clamp, Goodell 40.00
Chopper, Cutout Heart, Steel, Brass, Wood, 18th Century, 11 In. 350.00
Chopper, Iron Blade, Double Heart Design, Wooden Handle, 18th Century, 12 In. 950.00
Chopper, Meat, Enterprise No. 12, Table Clamp 50.00
Chopping Block, Wood, Round, 1860s, 35 x 21 In. 695.00
Chuck Wagon, Scale, Spice Tins, Coffee Grinder, Flour Bin, Sifter, 32 x 18 x 37 1/2 In. . . 1460.00
Churn, 3 Scribed Accent Bands, Light Blue Slip Dragonfly Design, 1875, 4 3/8 In. 220.00
Churn, Blue Floral, Vine Design, 1860, 19 In. 800.00
Churn, Brushed Blue Puppet, Brushed Blue Cattail, 1850, 16 In. 2640.00
Churn, Dazey, 1920s, 1 Qt. 1870.00
Churn, Dazey, No. 40 . . . . 140.00
Churn, Dazey, No. 60 . . . . 175.00
Churn, Double Birch Leaves, Red Wing, 1910, 12 1/2 In. 300.00
Churn, Iron Bands, Stave Construction, Blue Paint, New England, 36 In. 460.00
Churn, Wooden, Amish, Indiana 1150.00
Clothespin, Tiger Maple, 4 1/4 In., Pair 395.00
Cocktail Set, Thermo Serv, Shaker, Glasses, Stirrer, West Bend, Box, 1960s, 4 Piece 20.00
Coffee Grinders are listed in their own category.
Coffee Mill, Canister Type, Tin, Girl Picture, Bronson-Walton Holland, Wall, 13 In. 350.00
Coffee Mill, Elgin National Coffee Mill, 30 In. 357.00
Coffee Tin, Aluminum, Chrome, Silver, West Bend, 6 1/4 In. 5.00
Coffee Tin, Scoop, Painted Word Kaffee, 26 In. 325.00
Coffeepot, Drip-O-Lator, Flora Design, Enterprise, 6 1/2 x 6 1/4 In. 65.00
Coffeepot, Glass Top, Plastic Handles, 2 Piece Bottom, 3 Piece 129.00
Colander, Metal Stand, Wooden Pestle 26.00
Colander, Yellowware, Applied Cream Bristol Glaze, 5 1/4 x 12 In. 175.00
Colander, Yellowware, Diamond Rim, White Bristol Glaze Interior, 4 x 9 1/4 In. 248.00
Confectionary Roller, Brass, Victorian . . . . .125.00 to 160.00
Cooker, Copper, 2 Doors, Conservo, Toledo Cooker Co., Pat. 1907 . . . . 220.00
Cookie Board, Dog, Sitting In Basket, 4 x 3 3/4 In. 60.00
Cookie Board, Double Sided, Man & Woman, Fancy Dress, 13 3/4 x 5 1/8 In. 300.00
Cookie Board, Heart Shape, 3 Roses, Vine Border, 7 3/4 x 6 3/4 In. 440.00
Cookie Board, Springerle, Carved, Soldiers, Religious Figures, 6 1/2 x 9 1/4 In. 220.00
Cookie Cutter, Acorn & Squirrel 715.00
Cookie Cutter, Aluminum, Stars, Heart Design, Child's, Vintage, 11 Piece 15.00
Cookie Cutter, Belsnickle 630.00

Cookie Cutter, Beulah Head 25.00
Cookie Cutter, Bird & Nest 550.00
Cookie Cutter, Bird, Heart, Tin, Pa., 8 3/4 In. 605.00
Cookie Cutter, Deer, Running 385.00
Cookie Cutter, Diamond, Club, Aluminum, Crimped Edge, Vintage, 3 1/4 x 2 In., Pair ... 6.00
Cookie Cutter, Dog, Scottie, Red Plastic, 1940s 9.00
Cookie Cutter, Dutch Man & Woman, 6 7/8 In., Pair 127.00
Cookie Cutter, Elephant, Tin, 19th Century, 5 1/4 x 8 In. 605.00
Cookie Cutter, Full Figured Man Profile, Tin, 19th Century, 10 1/4 x 4 3/4 In. 195.00
Cookie Cutter, Gingerbread Girl, Large 1650.00
Cookie Cutter, Hansel & Gretel, Witch, House, Educational Products, 1947, Set Of 6 .... 150.00
Cookie Cutter, Heart & Hand 1705.00
Cookie Cutter, Heart Shape, Green Wooden Knob, Tin 6.00
Cookie Cutter, Heart Shape, Metal Handle, 3 In. 5.00
Cookie Cutter, Heart Shape, Red Metal Handle, Aluminum, Chrome, Silver, 3 In. ....5.00 to 10.00
Cookie Cutter, Heart Shape, Sheet Iron, Pennsylvania, Early 19th Century 210.00
Cookie Cutter, Heart Shape, Tin, 19th Century, 3 1/4 In. 220.00
Cookie Cutter, Horned Stag, Square Vent Holds Square Backplate, 8 x 5 1/2 In. 2600.00
Cookie Cutter, Horse & Rider, Tin 1375.00
Cookie Cutter, Horse, Large 1485.00
Cookie Cutter, Man, Dancing, Wearing Hat, Tin, 10 In. 22.00
Cookie Cutter, Man, Hat & Waistcoat, 8 1/2 In. 110.00
Cookie Cutter, Multiple Christmas Cutouts, Santa, Angels, Deer, 7 1/2 x 11 1/4 In. 192.00
Cookie Cutter, Prancing Horse, Tin, 19th Century, 6 1/4 x 9 1/4 In. 195.00
Cookie Cutter, Rabbit Profile, Tin, 19th Century, 8 1/4 x 5 1/2 In. 165.00
Cookie Cutter, Rabbit, Running, Tin, Applied Handle, 7 1/4 In. 50.00
Cookie Cutter, Running Horse, Tin, 19th Century, 6 x 9 1/4 In. 468.00
Cookie Cutter, Santa Claus, Green Wooden Knob, Tin 10.00
Cookie Cutter, Soldier On Horseback, Plumed Helmet, 10 x 9 In. 935.00
Cookie Cutter, Soldier Profile, Tin, 19th Century, 10 1/2 x 6 In. 300.00
Cookie Cutter, Violin 220.00
Cookie Cutter, Woman, With Bonnet, On Chamber Pot, 8 x 5 In. 1500.00
Corer, Apple, Bone, Unscrews & Compacts For Traveling, c.1790 .... 165.00
Corer, Apple, Cover Unscrews To Become Handle, 18th Century 395.00
Corn Creamer, Wooden, Primitive, Handmade, 11 x 3 1/2 In. 35.00
Corn Holders, Bakelite, Yellow, Set Of 4, 3 In. 50.00
Crimper, Iron, Knob Head, Turned Shaft, Engraved Date 1840, 4 1/2 In. 2300.00
Crock Pot, Bronze, Port Dundas Glascow Pottery, 4 In. 15.00
Cup, Burled, Footed Base, Pa., 1800, 5 x 3 3/8 In. 85.00
Cutlery Box, Cherry, Canted Sides, Cutout Handle, Cherry, Pa., 1820, 5 x 14 In. 550.00
Damper, Stove, Wire Spring Handle, Diamond, Adams Co., 10 In. 40.00
Decals, Smiling Chef, Original Envelopes, Meyercord, 1940s, 8 1/4 x 8 1/2 In. 20.00
Dipper, Aluminum, Eugene, Oregon 35.00
Dipper, Chestnut, Silver & Wood, Marked M & B, 18th Century, 11 In. 700.00
Dipper, Ice Cream Sandwich, Mayer, 12 In. 145.00
Dipper, Ice Cream, Gilchrist, No. 31, 10 1/2 In. 50.00
Dipper, Ice Cream, Hamilton Beach, 9 In. 55.00
Dipper, Iron, Flared Punch & Line Handle, Initials WBKP & Date 1835, 19 In. 3000.00
Dipper, Long Handled, Round Bowl, Steel, Decorative Brass Heart Inlay, 20 1/2 In. 59.00
Dipper, With Funnel, Cylindrical, Tin, 14 3/4 In. 290.00
Dish, Aluminum, Hammered, Floral Design 3.00
Dish, Leaf Design, Aluminum, 4 In. 3.00
Dish, Loaf, 2 Large Yellow Slip Tulips, Yellow Dots, Pa., 14 x 10 1/2 In. 14850.00
Dish, Loaf, Coggled Rim, Yellow Slip Lines, Pa., Early 19th Century, 15 x 11 In. 2750.00
Dish, Refrigerator, Cover, Fruit Design, 4 x 4 5/8 In. 15.00
Dough Board, Circular, Wedge Form Handle, 20 3/4 In. 138.00
Dough Box, Cover, Carved Handle, Carrying Handles, Red Surface, Pa., 11 In. 1430.00
Dough Box, Painted, Cover, Splayed Legs, Penn., c.1790, 29 3/4 x 53 1/4 x 27 3/4 In. ... 660.00
Dough Box, Poplar, Canted Sides, Blue Paint, 19th Century, 9 x 26 1/2 In. 550.00
Dough Box, Stand, Softwood, Pegged Splay Leg, 29 1/2 x 40 1/2 In. 550.00
Dough Box, Walnut, Cover, Red Paint, Dovetailed Joints, Pa., c.1820, 10 x 35 x 16 In. 138.00
Dough Print, Wheel, Butter, Carved Walnut, 1820, Pa., 2 1/2 In. 220.00
Dough Scraper, Heart Cutout, Handle, 4 In. 200.00

Kitchen, Stringholder,
Mexican Man, Pottery,
9 x 6 3/4 In.

Kitchen, Butter Melter, Magnetic,
Holds Butter On Toaster Top, Box

Kitchen, Flatiron,
Wrought Iron,
Teardrop Shape,
Twisted Handle

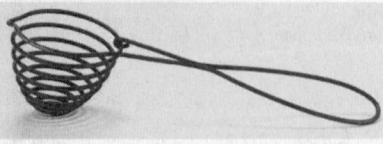

Kitchen, Egg Separator, Little Kitchen Gem,
Combination Tool, Hip-O-Lite, 8 1/2 In.

Dough Scraper, Tulip Wrigglework, Wrought Iron, 1853, 3 x 3 3/4 In. 1760.00
Dough Scraper, Wrought Iron, Heart Cutout In Blade, Round Handle, 2 x 4 In. 385.00
Dough Scraper, Wrought Iron, Rounded Handle, Signed, J. Eppinger, 4 x 4 1/4 In. 198.00
Drip Pan, 1/2 Round, Center Extension, 3 Tapered Legs, Cast Iron, 1800s, 9 x 16 In. 288.00
Dutch Oven, Griswold, No. 9, Erie, Tite-Top . . . . .60.00 to 65.00
Dutch Oven, Griswold, No. 10, Sidney, Oh., Tite-Top Chuck 125.00
Dutch Oven, Wagner, No. 9, Aluminum 35.00
Egg Cooker, With Timer, Reeves Specialty Co., USA, Oct. 1912, 14 3/4 In. 63.00
Egg Separator, Little Kitchen Gem, Combination Tool, Hip-O-Lite, 8 1/2 In. . . . .*Illus* 7.00
Egg Timer, Boy Carrying 2 Pails 75.00
Egg Timer, Colonial Woman, Bonnet, Ceramic, Germany, 3 3/4 In. 85.00
Egg Timer, Figural, Girl Skier 78.00
Egg Timer, Friar Tuck 65.00
Eggbeater, Cast Iron, Wooden Knob, Crimped Tin Blades, H-L Co., Tarrytown, N.Y., 9 In. 40.00
Eggbeater, Cyclone, Iron, Tin, Pat. 1902, 11 3/4 In. 75.00
Eggbeater, Dover, 1904 . . . . 35.00
Eggbeater, Dover, Ladd, Hi-Speed A&J, No. 34W, Ekco Products 16.00
Eggbeater, H.L. Co., Side Handle, 9 1/2 In. 395.00
Eggbeater, Jaquette No. 3, Cast Iron, 12 In. 1200.00
Eggbeater, Painted Handle, Patent Pending, Ekco Products, USA, 1940s 10.00
Eggbeater, Wire Crank Handle, Instant Whip Aluminum Beater, 1920, 10 1/2 In. 22.00
Eggbeater, Wire, Plastic Handle, Beat The High Speed Costs At Anderson & Lofgren . . . 15.00
Eggbeater, Wooden Handle, Rotary, 1916 . . . . 8.00
Flatiron, Wrought Iron, Teardrop Shape, Twisted Handle . . . .*Illus* 3106.00
Flycatcher, Domed Cover, Circular Saucer, Pat. 10/28/1890, 7 x 6 1/2 In. 1610.00
Food Chopper, 2 Wooden Handles, Rocker Style, G.G. Gusstahl 29.00
Food Chopper, Griswold, No. 2 . . . . 25.00
Food Chopper, Sargent, Clamps On Table 10.00
Food Steamer, Woven Bamboo Trunk, Chinese, 19th Century, 34 x 22 In. 230.00
Fork, Carving, 2 Tines, Wood Paneled Handle, Iron Shaft, Late 17th Century 115.00
Fork, Long Handled, Steel, Brass Inlay, Double Heart Design, 2 Tines, 27 In. 290.00
Fork, Roasting, Wrought Iron, Beveled Handle, Signed, J. Bowden, 17 1/2 In. 255.00
Fork, Roasting, Wrought Iron, Flat Handle, Signed, F.G. Farmer, 13 3/4 In. 176.00
Fork, Roasting, Wrought Iron, Flat Handle, Signed, W. Kuhn, Pa., 12 1/4 In. 467.00
Fork, Spatula Other End, Iron, Pennsylvania, 18th Century, 18 In. 225.00
Fork, Toasting, Brass, Early 18th Century, 23 In. 295.00
Fryer, Bacon, Hostess Gift, Stainless Steel 175.00

Funnel, Canning, Aluminum, Chrome, Silver	5.00
Funnel, Glass Canning, Tiny Dots On Glass, 2 3/4 x 5 In.	15.00
Grater, Flat, Metal, 2 Handles, Lorriane Metal Mfg., c.1940, 10 5/8 x 4 In.	15.00
Grater, Mouli, Metal, 7 3/4 x 3 In.	10.00
Grater, Nutmeg, Coffin Box, Metal	11.00
Grater, Nutmeg, Covered Compartment, Jacobi & Jenkins, 1900, 5 In.	900.00
Grater, Nutmeg, Edgar, 1891	135.00
Grater, Nutmeg, Snyder, Massillon, O., 3-Cap Stove Pipe Type, Pat. June 14, 1904, 5 In.	625.00
Grater, Nutmeg, Spouted Measure Cup	18.00
Griddle, Cast Iron, Hinged, Dated 1889, 14 3/4 In.	75.00
Griddle, Griswold, No. 8, Aluminum, Wooden Handle, Black Trade Mark	15.00
Griddle, Griswold, No. 110	175.00
Griddle, Iron, Heart Shape Handle	64.00
Griddle, Wagner, No. 10	65.00
Grill, Griswold, Puritan Handled	40.00
Grinder, Coffee-Nut, Wooden Knob, Zassenhaus Monk, Germany, 5 x 3 In.	35.00
Grinder, Food, Dandy, No. 25, N.S. Hdwe. Wks. Mount Joy Pa, Embossed, 6 1/4 In.	75.00
Grinder, Herb, Roller, Boat Shape, Shaped Feet, Iron, Wooden Handle, 15 1/2 In.	340.00
Grinder, Herb, Slant-Sided Trough, Disk Blade, Iron, Wooden Handles, 6 3/4 x 15 In.	920.00
Grinder, Nut, Green, Tan, Tin, 1 1/2 In.	20.00
Herb Crusher, Rolling Disk Blade, Turned Wooden Handle, Cast Iron, 3 x 18 In.	1150.00
Herb Crusher, Wood, 12 x 3 In.	350.00
Holder, Serving, Aluminum, Ornate Leaves, 7 3/4 In.	40.00
Holder, Serving, Cover, Aluminum, Handles, 12 1/2 In.	50.00
Holder, Skewer, Decorative Acorns, 5 Formed Hooked Skewers, 16 In.	316.00
Hook, Iron, 2 Prongs, 11 1/2 In.	30.00
Ice Cream Maker, Fearless Freezer, Wooden Base, Cast Iron, Child's, 7 In.	300.00
Ice Cream Maker, Pine, Plated Hoops, Peerless Iceland Freezer, 7 1/2 x 5 In.	225.00
Ice Cream Maker, Wooden Bucket, Crank Handle, White Mountain	135.00
Ice Maker, Chrome, Yellow Enamel, Ice-O-Matic	12.00
Ice Tongs, Iron, Pat. Mar. 2, 1869, 12 3/4 x 5 1/4 In.	95.00
Icebox, Lift Top, Pine	590.00
Iron, Charcoal, Dragon, Cast Iron	800.00
Iron, Child's, Lacy Double Point, Oval, Scrolls Center, 1 3/4 x 3 1/2 In.	15.00
Iron, Child's, Rope Design Handle, 2 1/4 x 4 1/4 x 3 1/4 In.	29.00
Iron, Fluter, Geneva, Il., 1866, 2 Piece	100.00
Iron, Fluter, Iron, Wooden Handle	70.00
Iron, For Lace, The Pearl, Miniature, 3 3/4 In.	40.00
Iron, Goffering, Blacksmith Made, Curl Design, Late 1600s	1350.00
Iron, Goffering, Double, Octagonal Base, Brass Barrels	1650.00
Ironing Board, Blue Painted Base, New England, Late 19th Century, 29 3/4 In.	345.00
Jar, Cone Dispensing, Countertop, Hinged Aluminum Lid, 10 In.	520.00
Jar, Cottage Cheese, Crescent Dairy, Kokomo, 2 Lb.	125.00
Juice Press, Wearever	25.00
Juicer, Aluminum, Chrome, Silver, Foley	5.00
Juicer, Cover, Juice-O-Mat, Kansas City, Mo., 1950	25.00
Juicer, Orange, Aluminum, Vintage	30.00
Knife, Mollusk, Stolff, Philadelphia, Brass, Rosewood	75.00
Knife, Pastry, Red, White Wooden Handle, 1950	8.00
Knife, Wood Tone Finish, Green Tint, Federal Bakelite Stainless Steel	4.00
Knife, Wood, Bakelite, 9 x 3/4 In.	12.00
Ladle, Crisscross Design Handle, Rolled Edge, 10 In.	55.00
Ladle, Line Scribed Handle, Iron, New England, Mid 18th Century, 23 In.	210.00
Ladle, Wood, Incised Design, Ring Around Opening, Flared Handle, 11 1/2 In.	440.00
Ladle, Wrought Iron, Brass Bowl, Replaced Copper Rivet, 10 x 11 1/2 In.	165.00
Ladle, Wrought Iron, Flat Handle, 6 1/4 In.	70.00
Laundry Stick, Wooden, Heart & F.A.T Carving	85.00
Lazy Susan, Georgian Style, Mahogany, 21 3/4 x 4 1/2 In.	150.00
Lemon Squeezer, Aluminum Insert, Arcade	55.00
Lemon Squeezer, Wood & Nickel Silver, Turned Handles, 1880s, 11 1/2 In.	70.00
Lid Lifter, Stove, Iron, Spiral Loop Wire Handle, Arctic Embossed On Handle, 7 1/2 In.	18.00

Match Holders can be found in their own category.
Match Safes can be found in their own category.

Maul, Burl, 6 5/8 x 9 1/4 In. 130.00
Measuring Cup, Aluminum, Metal Slide 95.00
Measuring Cup, Glass, Pink, Hazel Atlas, 2 Cup 80.00
Measuring Cup, Ice Cream, Aluminum, 5 3/4 x 3 3/4 In. 79.00
Measuring Cup, Kellogg's, Green, 3 Spouts, 1 Cup 35.00
Measuring Cup, Kellogg's, Pink, Embossed, Hazel Atlas 25.00
Measuring Cup, Metal Chopper, Pink Wooden Handle, Pamco 18.00
Measuring Cup, Tin, Stamped & Pieced, Wraparound Lip, Strap Handle, 1 Qt. 13.00
Meat Cutter, Tenderizer, Green Handle, Stamped Made In The USA & Pat Pending 12.00
Meat Fork, Rattail End, Twisted Shaft, Curlicue Swirls, 3 Tines, Iron, 20 1/2 x 4 In. 138.00
Meat Grinder, Rollman, No. 11, Mt. Joy, Pa., 6 1/2 In. 45.00
Meat Tenderizer, Red Wooden Handle 12.00
Melon Baller, Red Wooden Handle 10.00
Mixer, Electric, Hamilton Beach, Chrome Top, Model 33, 18 In. 140.00
Mixer, Electric, Hamilton Beach, Green Porcelain 125.00
Mixer, Herb, Whitall, Tatum 595.00
Mixer, Horlick's Malted Milk 1495.00
Mixer, Milk Shake, Hamilton Beach, Green Enamel 195.00
Mixing Bowl, Cobalt, 6 1/2 In. 35.00
Mixing Bowl, White, Red Ships, McKee Glass Co., 1930s, 7 In. 37.00
Molds may also be found in the Pewter and Tinware categories.
Mold, Butter, Acorn & Oak Leaf, Wooden 65.00
Mold, Butter, Cat, Bird, Empty Cage, 2 Sides, 19th Century, Rectangular 495.00
Mold, Butter, Cow, Round, 4 7/8 In. 187.00
Mold, Butter, Lollipop, 4 Hearts, 2 Different Designs, 9 1/2 In. ....109.00 to 172.00
Mold, Butter, Lollipop, Carved Flower, Chamfered Handle, Pennsylvania, 5 x 10 In. 770.00
Mold, Butter, Maple, 8 Floral Blocks In One Press, 19th Century 110.00
Mold, Butter, Maple, Brass, Marked, Canterbury, 6 In. 1955.00
Mold, Butter, Pine, Oval, Floral & Chestnut Design, 5 x 3 In. Diam., Pair 84.00
Mold, Butter, Pineapple, Round Case, Pat'd April 17, 1865 .... 60.00
Mold, Butter, Tulip, Carved, Half-Round, Initials J.B. On Handle 3300.00
Mold, Cake, 2 Sides, Man, Merry Christmas, Woman, Happy New Year, 7 x 4 In. 1045.00
Mold, Cake, Pine, Eagle, Spread Wings, Shield, Soldier, 19th Century, 5 3/4 x 11 1/2 In. ... 525.00
Mold, Cake, Scalloped Sides, Yellow, Manganese Slip Design, 3 1/2 In. 413.00
Mold, Candle, see Tinware category.
Mold, Cheese, Heart Form, 8 In. 990.00
Mold, Chocolate, Bonzo The Dog, Tin, 1930s ....95.00 to 150.00
Mold, Chocolate, Christmas Tree, 13 In. 77.00
Mold, Chocolate, Donkey, Standing, 1920s 5800.00
Mold, Chocolate, Easter Greetings 44.00
Mold, Chocolate, Eskimo, Metal, 4 3/4 In., 2 Piece 50.00
Mold, Chocolate, Heart, To My Valentine 105.00
Mold, Chocolate, Rabbit, 8 1/2 In., 2 Piece 100.00
Mold, Chocolate, Rabbit, Basket On Back, Standing, Hinged, 2 Piece, 10 1/2 In. 98.00
Mold, Chocolate, Rabbit, Tin, 9 1/2 In. 115.00
Mold, Chocolate, Swan Shape, 19th Century 200.00
Mold, Chocolate, Zeppelin, Tin, c.1900, 13 In. 435.00
Mold, Fish, Redware, Brown Glaze, Stahl Pottery, Signed & Dated 1939, 11 x 3 In. 165.00
Mold, Food, Pig Head, Cast Iron, 9 In. 300.00
Mold, Food, Turk's Head, Redware, Swirled Design, Brown Glaze, John W. Bell, 8 x 4 In. ... 495.00
Mold, Food, Turk's Head, Swirled Ribs, Rockingham, 3 1/2 x 10 5/8 In. 70.00
Mold, Gingerbread, Woman & Bird 1 Side, Gentleman Other, 1900s, 15 1/2 In. 650.00
Mold, Heart & Star, Griswold, No. 100 .... 900.00
Mold, Ice Cream, see Pewter category.
Mold, Ice Cube, Nude Lady, Vintage, 1 1/2 In., 8 Piece 13.00
Mold, Maple Syrup, 3 Chicks, 19th Century, 11 1/2 In. 325.00
Mold, Melon, 1 Pt. 20.00
Mold, Melon, 6 Pt. 40.00
Mold, Patty, Wagner Ware, 10 x 3 1/2 x 1 3/4 In. 25.00
Mold, Redware, Octagonal, Side Incised Arrow, Grapes & Leaf In Base, c.1880, 9 In. 295.00
Mold, Redware, Sugar Maple, Anchor Design, Dated 1820, 2 In. 150.00
Mold, Rice Cake, Handle, Carved Wood, 10 1/4 In. 27.00
Mold, Santa Claus, Casting Line Into Toy Sack, Griswold 535.00

Mold, Santa, Skillet, Griswold, No. 2 . . . . 375.00
Mold, Swirl, Rockingham, 19th Century, 9 3/4 x 3 1/2 In. 58.00
Mortar & Pestle, Burl, Maple Pestle, Wood, 6 x 3 1/4 In. 1955.00
Mortar & Pestle, Cast Iron, Bead & Cove Molding Design 110.00
Mortar & Pestle, Marble, 1/4 x 3 1/2 x 4 1/4 In. 195.00
Napkin Holder, Art Deco Lady, Green, Soft White Ground, 6 x 12 1/2 In. 130.00
Napkin Holder, Bakelite, Bird, Red, 2 1/2 In. 80.00
Napkin Holder, Bakelite, Dog, Green, Painted Eyes & Nose, 2 3/4 In. 70.00
Noodle Cutter, Hand Held, Metal, Wooden Handle, 10 Disc Blades, Germany, 7 1/2 In. . . . 22.00
Pan, Biscuit, Lodge, Wagner, No. 782, 7 Cup 50.00
Pan, Breadstick, Griswold, No. 22, Cast Iron, 1900 . . . . 50.00
Pan, Bundt, Wagner Ware . . . . .200.00 to 250.00
Pan, Casserole, Griswold, No. 83, Black Iron, White Porcelain Interior 85.00
Pan, Chicken, Cover, Griswold 70.00
Pan, Chicken, Deep, Griswold, No. 777 . . . . 95.00
Pan, Corn Stick, Griswold, No. 273, Red & Cream 100.00
Pan, Corn Stick, Griswold, No. 280, 7 Alternating Ears 500.00
Pan, Cover, Aluminum, Black Metal Handles, Strainer Inside 36.00
Pan, Griswold, No. 1, Gem 250.00
Pan, Krumb Kake, Iron, Scottsdale, Ariz., 15 x 4 In. 56.00
Pan, Milk, Blue Swag Design, Stoneware, 1860, 3 1/4 x 9 1/2 In. 275.00
Pan, Muffin, Gem, Griswold, No. 17 . . . . 130.00
Pan, Muffin, Griswold, No. 16 . . . . 1920.00
Pan, Muffin, Lodge, Cast Iron 45.00
Pan, Muffin, Wagner Ware, No. 480, Aluminum 12.00
Pan, Omelet, Wagner Ware, No. 820, Aluminum 35.00
Pan, Pie, Embossed New England Flaky Crust Pie Table Talk, 9 1/2 In. 10.00
Pan, Popover, Griswold, No. 10, Aluminum . . . . .40.00 to 55.00
Pan, Popover, Griswold, No. 18, 6 Cup 75.00
Pan, Sterilizer, Green Metal, Porcelain, 13 3/4 x 8 x 4 1/4 In. 25.00
Pan, Wagner Ware, Corn Stick, Aluminum, Senior 25.00
Pan, Wagner, No. 7, Gem, Sheppard Hardware 80.00
Pan, Wheat & Corn Stick, Griswold, No. 28 . . . . 235.00
Pan, Wheat Stick, Griswold, No. 27, Aluminum 100.00
Pan, Wheat Stick, Griswold, No. 2700 . . . . 335.00
Pastry Former, Cruciform, Brass, Ebony Handle 160.00
Patty Mold Set, Griswold, No. 3, With No. 72 Patty Bowl, Box 85.00
Peel, Tombstone, Tiger Maple, Lollipop Handle, 18th Century, New England, 56 In. 1850.00
Peel, Wrought Iron, Ram's Head Finial, 41 1/4 In. 373.00
Peeler, Apple, 1 Operation, Bonanza Model, 1890s 200.00
Peeler, Apple, 3 Sprocket Gears, Wooden Handle, Hudson, Pat'd. Jan. 24, 82 . . . . 225.00
Peeler, Apple, Cast Iron, Table Clamp, Lockley & Howland, Turntable, Pat'd. 1856 . . . . . 70.00
Peeler, Apple, Cherry, New England, c.1800, 10 1/2 In. 195.00
Peeler, Apple, Coy, Wooden 725.00
Peeler, Apple, Metal, Union, 6 In. 20.00
Peeler, Apple, Red Wooden Handle, 7 In. 12.00
Peeler, Apple, Sinclair Scott, Clamp-On, Cast Iron 90.00
Pepper Mill, Brass, Iron Turn Handle On Top, 12 1/2 In. 85.00
Percolator, Aluminum, Fire-King, 11 1/2 x 12 In. 30.00
Percolator, Red Aluminum, Cream Handle, Westbend 95.00
Pestle, Handle, Wooden 25.00
Pie Bird, Pink, Shawnee 65.00
Pie Crimper, Heart Cutout, Carved Bone, 6 1/4 In. 495.00
Pie Crimper, Ivory, Reeded Carving, 3-Tine End Cutter, 6 1/2 In. 330.00
Pie Crimper, Snake Handle, Brass & Iron, 18th Century, 6 1/2 In. 2400.00
Pie Crimper, Whalebone, Detachable Fork, 7 In. 495.00
Pie Lifter, Wood, Wire, 15 In. 65.00
Pie Plate, Bold Stylized Tulip, Yellow, Green, Manganese Slip, Pottery, 8 1/2 In. 5300.00
Pie Plate, Central Square Of Dribbled Lines, 2 Bands, Pa., 19th Century, 9 In. 3630.00
Pie Plate, Coggled Edge, Yellow Slip Circle, Yellow, Green, Manganese, Pa., 8 In. 1650.00
Pie Plate, Green, Yellow Clef Crisscross Design, Pa., 19th Century, 8 In. 2970.00
Pie Plate, Green, Yellow, Manganese Tulip, Flanked By 2 Trailing Slip Bands, 8 In. 14850.00
Pie Plate, Trailing, Yellow, Green Manganese Crisscross, Pottery, 7 3/4 In. 4950.00

Pie Plate, Yellow Slip Dotted Circle Design, Yellow Slip Border, Pa., 10 In. 2750.00
Pitcher, Syrup, Glass, Thumb Tab, Embossed Grapes On Tin Lid, 4 3/4 In. 25.00
Pitcher, Syrup, Glass, Vertical Ribs, Handle, Tin Lid, Thumb Tab, Tapered, 4 3/8 In. 28.00
Platter, Sizzling Steak, Wagner Ware, Hammered 18.00
Platter, Sizzling, Magnalite, Oak Handles, Wagner Ware 25.00
Popcorn Popper, Blue Cover, Fire-King, Electric, Aluminum Base 48.00
Pot, Cooking, Brass, Fixed Wrought Iron Handle, Cast, 7 x 13 In. 173.00
Pot, Glass Lid, Bakelite Handles, Aluminum, 3 Qt. 45.00
Pot Rack, Hanging, Provincial, Wrought, Iron, 12 Hooks, Animal Silhouettes, 31 In. 230.00
Potato Masher, Double Headed, Mushroom Shape Pestle, Turned Wood 26.00
Potato Masher, Wooden Handle, 10 1/2 In. 15.00
Potato Ricer, Red Handle, Aluminum, Chrome 10.00
Prayer Plate, Aluminum, Chrome, Silver, Little Kitchen, You're My Throne, 9 1/2 In. . . . 5.00
Press, Cider, Oak, Mortised & Pegged Construction, Wooden Shaft, 26 x 44 In. 220.00
Press, Fruit, Clamps On Table, Iron Enterprise 95.00
Rack, Display, Brown, Griswold 395.00
Rack, Hanging, Wrought Iron, 7 Hooks, Scrolled Crest, 7 x 28 1/2 In. 190.00
Raisin Seeder, Embossed, The Boss Raisin Seeder Pat. Pdg., A.C. Williams, Ravenna, O. . 175.00
Reamers are listed in their own category.
Roaster, Bird, Turned Finial, Adjustable Ball Bracket, 23 1/2 In. 396.00
Roaster, Chestnut, Brass, Pierced Handle, Openwork Hinged, 19th Century, 22 In. 375.00
Roaster, Glass Lid, Aluminum, 8 3/4 x 14 3/4 In. 70.00
Roaster, Tin, Convection, Wrought Iron Spit, 17 x 23 1/2 In. 170.00
Rolling Pin, Bird's-Eye Maple, Early 1800s, 20 In. 295.00
Rolling Pin, Blue Grass, Love & Be True, Yellow, Red, White Tall Ships, 16 In. 375.00
Rolling Pin, Cobalt 175.00
Rolling Pin, Glass, Blown, Green, Mid 19th Century, 15 1/2 In. 385.00
Rolling Pin, Maple, Carved Animals, Springerle, 18 1/2 x 3 1/2 In. 795.00
Rolling Pin, Maple, Shaped Ends, New England, Early 19th Century, 19 1/2 In. 210.00
Rolling Pin, Sapphire Blue, Multicolored Transfer Of Ship, 14 1/2 In. 110.00
Rolling Pin, Springerle, Carvings On Cylinder, Horse, Deer, Goat & Squirrel, 18 1/2 In. . . 795.00
Sadiron, Scroll Work, Iron, Wooden Handle, Chicken Catch, Repainted, AFG 3, 9 In. 88.00
Salt & Pepper Shakers are listed in their own category.
Saucepan, Mushroom Handle, Copper, Jonathan Witman, Pa., 1805, 11 x 6 In. 9600.00
Sausage Stuffer, Enterprise, No. 15, Cast Iron, Black Paint, Gilt Stencil, 17 In. 300.00
Sausage Stuffer, Wooden, Metal Funnel Tube, Hinged, 9 1/2 In. 85.00
Scoop, Aluminum, Embossed Hygia On Handle, Germany On Bottom, 5 3/4 In. 7.50
Scoop, Butter, Painted Scene, House, Bridge, Trees, 5 1/4 x 9 1/2 In. 95.00
Scoop, Double Butter Stamp Handle, Flower 1 Side, Medallion Other, 11 7/8 In. 250.00
Scoop, Dover, Toggle, No. 8, Double Lever System, 11 1/2 In. 80.00
Scoop, Flour, Plastic, Frigidaire, Crown Logo On Handle, Cream, 6 1/2 In. 7.00
Scoop, Hamilton Beach, No. 31, Wooden Handle, Original Box, 10 In. 98.00
Scoop, Hard Sugar, Level Action, Bone Handle, 10 In. 100.00
Scoop, Ice Cream, Cone Shape, Steel, Turn Ring On Top Releases Ice Cream 55.00
Scoop, Ice Cream, Dover Clipper No. 20, Pat'd. Feb. 1924, 8 In. 290.00
Scoop, Ice Cream, Dover, No. 20, Sickle Shaped Lever, Pat'd. Feb. 1924, 11 In. 230.00
Scoop, Ice Cream, Gilchrist, No. 26, Nickel Over Brass, 10 1/2 In. 45.00
Scoop, Ice Cream, Hamilton Beach, No. 31, Wooden Handle, Original Box, 10 In. 110.00
Scoop, Ice Cream, Heart, Dated 1929 . . . . 5830.00
Scoop, Ice Cream, Heart, Mahogany Handle, Pat. 1924 . . . . 7150.00
Scoop, Ice Cream, Indestructo, No. 3, 10 1/4 In. 95.00
Scoop, Ice Cream, No-Pak 31, Pat. No. 1861655, Metal, Wooden Handle, 10 In. 110.00
Scoop, Ice Cream, Stainless Steel, Shore Craft, 9 In. 39.00
Scoop, Sugar, Wagner Ware, Aluminum 20.00
Scoop, Tiger Maple, Carved Hook Handle, 19th Century, 4 1/2 x 9 In. 546.00
Scoop, Wooden, 1950, 4 x 8 & 10 x 3 In., Pair 15.00
Seeder, Cherry, Rollman No. 3, Rollman Mfg. Co., Joy, Pa. 40.00
Shaker, Milkshake, Cole's, Hand Crank Mechanism, 2 Containers, c.1910, 24 In. 4315.00
Sharpener, Knife, Red Wooden Handle, Ekco, 7 In. 10.00
Shredder, Coconut, Clamp On, Yellow Paint, Wooden Handle, Cast Iron, 7 1/2 In. 95.00
Sieve, 3 Punched Circles, Compass Stars, Tin, Ring Hanger, 13 1/2 x 14 1/2 In. 635.00
Sieve, Herb, 60-Mesh Screen, Initialed D.H., Round, 11 In. 1610.00

Sieve, Punched Lines & Holes, Strap Hanger, 3 Feet, 3 5/8 x 4 1/2 In.	300.00
Sifter, Flour, Aluminum, Chrome, 2 Cup	4.00
Sifter, Flour, Aluminum, Chrome, 3 1/2 In.	5.00
Sifter, Flour, Aluminum, Chrome, Foley	6.00
Sifter, Flour, Androck	35.00
Sifter, Flour, Sliding Trigger Grip, Tin, Embossed On Front, Sift-Chine	15.00
Sifter, Flour, Tin, Embossed 2-5 Cup Markings, Bromwells, 6 1/4 In.	15.00
Sifter, Tabletop, Double Cast Iron Gears & Cranks, Handles, J.H. Day, 23 1/4 In.	1540.00
Skillet, Breakfast, Griswold, Colonial, Red Porcelain, Cream Interior	150.00
Skillet, Cover, Favorite Piqua Ware, No. 9	115.00
Skillet, Cover, Griswold, No. 8, Self-Basting	40.00
Skillet, Favorite Piqua Ware, No. 8, The Best To Cook In	65.00
Skillet, Favorite Piqua Ware, Small Bottom	30.00
Skillet, Griswold, No. 2, Erie, Pa., Smoke Ring	525.00
Skillet, Griswold, No. 2, Smooth Bottom	375.00
Skillet, Griswold, No. 3, Block, Grooved Handle	45.00
Skillet, Griswold, No. 3, Large Block, Small Bottom, Smooth Top, High Cover	155.00
Skillet, Griswold, No. 3, Square, White Porcelain Interior	225.00
Skillet, Griswold, No. 4, Erie, Pa., Heat Ring	450.00
Skillet, Griswold, No. 6, Chrome, High Lettered	125.00
Skillet, Griswold, No. 6, Cover, Aluminum	55.00
Skillet, Griswold, No. 6, Small Bottom, Large Block	50.00
Skillet, Griswold, No. 6, Small Bottom, Small Emblem	29.00
Skillet, Griswold, No. 7, Cover, High Dome, Lettered	125.00
Skillet, Griswold, No. 7, Erie, Pa., Shield Mark	45.00
Skillet, Griswold, No. 7, Small Bottom, Small Emblem, Grooved Handle	30.00
Skillet, Griswold, No. 8, Erie	30.00
Skillet, Griswold, No. 8, Hinged, Cover, Large Logo	110.00
Skillet, Griswold, No. 8, Red & Cream Porcelain Interior	35.00
Skillet, Griswold, No. 8, Square	60.00
Skillet, Griswold, No. 9, Cover, Marked	85.00
Skillet, Griswold, No. 9, Large Emblem, Block Letters, Heat Ring, Low Cover	90.00
Skillet, Griswold, No. 15, Oval	235.00
Skillet, Griswold, No. 20, Hotel	625.00
Skillet, Griswold, No. 55, Square	45.00
Skillet, Victor, No. 9, Rib Reinforced Handle	45.00
Skillet, Wagner Ware, No. 0	55.00
Skillet, Wagner Ware, No. 2	90.00
Skillet, Wagner Ware, No. 3, Pie Logo	20.00
Skillet, Wagner Ware, No. 4, Nickel Plate	45.00
Skillet, Wagner Ware, No. 4, Smoke Ring	40.00
Skillet, Wagner Ware, No. 4, Smooth Bottom	55.00
Skillet, Wagner Ware, No. 7, Center Heat Ring	40.00
Skillet, Wagner Ware, No. 8, Heat Ring, Sidney	45.00
Skillet, Wagner Ware, No. 9, 5 Ring, Cover	40.00
Skillet, Wagner Ware, No. 9, Arc	65.00
Skillet, Wagner Ware, No. 9, Sidney	65.00
Skillet, Wagner Ware, No. 11, Raised Letter, Cover	225.00
Skillet, Wagner Ware, No. 12	55.00
Skillet, Wagner Ware, No. 13	375.00
Skimmer, Iron, Brass, Copper Rivets, Scroll Terminal Handle, 18th Century, 23 In.	125.00
Skimmer, Sieve Bottom, Tin, Round, 5 3/4 In.	17.00
Slicer, Apple, Turned Wooden Hopper, Feet, Pierced Heart Shape Handle, 5 x 17 1/4 In.	1955.00
Slicer, Bread, Slice A Slice, Chrome, Recipe & Guide Book, No Knife, Box	15.00
Slicer, Cast Iron, Enterprise Mfg. Co., Phila., Pat. June 5, 1888, 16 1/2 In.	270.00
Slicer, Cheese, Wagner Ware, Cut-Rite	75.00
Slicer, Stalk Rhubarb, Iron Fittings, Wooden, Carved 1853, Pa.	895.00
Slicer, Vegetable, Cast Iron, Table Clamp, Wooden Turn Handles, Universal	150.00
Spatula, Tin, Wooden Handle, Rumford The Wholesome Baking Powder, 13 In.	12.00
Spatula, Wrought Iron, Flat Handle, Geometric Design, 12 3/4 In.	55.00
Spatula, Wrought Iron, Flat Handle, Hanging Hook, 19 In.	60.00
Spatula, Wrought Iron, Flat Handle, Scrolled Hanging Hook, 13 3/4 In.	255.00

Spatula, Wrought Iron, Flat Handle, Signed, J.C. Carpenter, 19 3/8 In.	176.00
Spatula, Wrought, Scrolled Hanging Hook, Handle, Signed, P.E. Will, 15 1/4 In.	300.00
Spice Box, Bentwood, Round, Tin Band, Stencil Labels, 8 Containers, 9 x 3 In.	305.00
Spice Box, Butternut, 8 Drawers, Wooden Knob, Refinished, Wall	210.00
Spice Box, Fitted Interior, Walnut Drawers, c.1680, 16 1/2 x 18 In.	3250.00
Spice Box, Hanging, Labels On Drawer Fronts, Porcelain Pulls, 25 x 10 In.	495.00
Spice Box, Horn, Slide Lid, 6 Compartments, Early 19th Century	210.00
Spice Box, Oak, Recessed Panel Door, Star Inlay, 7 Drawers, c.1750, 15 3/4 In.	935.00
Spice Box, Pine, 6 Drawers Behind Door, Turned Feet, c.1800, 19 x 14 x 10 In.	3410.00
Spice Box, Scrolled Foliage, Pear Shape, Late 19th Century, 3 1/4 In.	437.00
Spice Box, Traveling, Engraved Designs, Initials & Date, 1790, 5 In.	210.00
Spice Box, Walnut, Sliding Lid, 4-Part Interior, 7 x 5 In.	825.00
Spice Box, Wooden, Carved, Slide Lid, Blue Green Paint, 1818, 3 1/4 In.	285.00
Spice Boxes, Ginger, Allspice, Cloves, Grain Painted, 11 x 9 x 14 In.	345.00
Spice Chest, Gold Lettering & Trim, 1 Drawer, Brass Ring Pulls, 15 3/4 In.	715.00
Spice Grinder, Boxwood, Carved, 19th Century	83.00
Spit, With Cage, Wrought Iron, England, c.1760	800.00
Spoon, Aluminum, Handle, 4 In.	12.00
Spoon, Cook's, Brass, Small Bowl 1 End, Larger Bowl On Other, England, 16 In.	250.00
Spoon, Cooking, Blacksmith Made, Iron, Late 18th Century, 21 1/2 In.	125.00
Spoon, Mixing, Wooden, Kellogg Incised In Handle, 13 In.	12.00
Spoon, Wagner Ware, No. 710, Aluminum	35.00
Spoon, With Pastry Wheel End, Brass, England, 1750	395.00
Spoon Rack, Pine, Spoon Slots, Scrolled Sides, Pa., 1810, 15 1/4 x 11 1/2 In.	825.00
Spoon Rack, Tulip Cutout Crest, Pine, Scrolled Base, Pa., 18th Century, 21 In.	2750.00
Sprinkler Bottle, Chinaman, White	90.00
Sprinkler Bottle, Siamese Cat, Brown	170.00
Stand, Kettle, Open Brass Top, Copper Supports, Iron Legs, 8 1/2 x 12 x 9 In.	110.00
Stand, Kettle, Steel, Black Repaint, Penny Feet, Pierced, England, 12 x 12 x 13 In.	55.00
Stand, Kettle, Wrought Iron, 3 Penny Feet, Twisted Cross Member, 12 In.	195.00
Steamer, Hot Dog, Electric Bun Warmer, Aluminum, Steamro, 1930s	570.00
Sterilizer, Towel, Sun Steam Tight & Hot, Stainless Steel, Pat. April, 1924	660.00
Strawholder, Glass, Tin Insert, 13 1/2 In.	72.00
Stringholder, Aluminum, 1900, 6 1/2 In.	65.00
Stringholder, Ceramic, German Shepherd, Royal Trico, Japan	175.00
Stringholder, Glass, Etched, Cobalt Blue Bands, Flowers, Mid 19th Century	175.00
Stringholder, Gothic Design, Cast Iron, Hexagonal Form, 5 x 5 In.	98.00
Stringholder, Mexican Man, Pottery, 9 x 6 3/4 In. ....*Illus*	50.00
Stringholder, Mouse, Ceramic	70.00
Stringholder, Red Paint, String, Tin	40.00
Sugar, Pewter Finial Cover, Classic Shape, Iron, Pa., 1780-1810	595.00
Sugar, Pewter Finial, Iron	1500.00
Sugar Nippers, Wrought Iron, Oak Base, Heart Shaped Forward Foot, 10 x 4 1/2 In.	225.00
Tea Stove, Mahogany, Drawer, Cabriole Legs, Metal Liner, Holland, c.1770	4800.00
Teabagger, Teakoe, Glass Pitcher, Metal Handle, Metal Base, Chicago, Ekco	10.00
Teakettle, Aluminum, Rooster Design On Both Sides, 12 In., 2 Qt.	15.00
Teakettle, Cover, Mushroom Handle, Gooseneck Spout, Israel Roberts, 11 1/2 In.	1800.00
Teakettle, Mushroom Handle, Copper, No. Carolina, 11 In.	3600.00
Teakettle, Mushroom Handle, Copper, Pa., 10 1/2 In.	1320.00
Teakettle, Wagner Ware, Wire Bail Handle, 10 In.	35.00
Teakettle, Wagner, No. 0, Stylized Logo	160.00
Teapot, Aluminum, With Tea Ball, Handles, c.1920	37.00
Teapot, Iron, Applied Flowers & Leaves, Silver Overlay On Handle, Signed, 8 5/8 In.	165.00
Teapot, White Ceramic, Aluminum Cozy	17.00
Thermometer, Meat, Taylor Instrument Co., Rochester, N.Y., 1934	12.00
Toaster, 2-Slice, Chrome Finish, Bakelite Handles, Toastmaster, Model 1B18, 1954	55.00
Toaster, Art Deco, Universal Toaster, 7 1/4 x 7 In.	22.00
Toaster, Automatic Pop-Up, McGraw Electric Co.	55.00
Toaster, Flip-Flop, Chrome, Energex, Patented July 28, 1914	29.00
Toaster, Plunger Type, Merit	75.00
Toaster, Pop-Up, First Home Model	80.00
Toaster, Porcelain, Wildflowers, Porcelier Mfg. Co., 7 1/2 x 10 In.	1600.00

Toaster, Revolving Rack, Black Enamel Finish, Wrought Iron, 25 1/4 In. 1290.00
Toaster, Rotating, Connected Scrolls, Feet, Formed Handle, 7 x 12 1/2 x 15 In. 200.00
Toaster, Swivel, Single Slice, 21 3/4 In. 155.00
Toaster, Torrid, Swing-Arm, Beardsley & Wolcott, Patented Nov. 15, 1920, 7 x 8 In. 49.00
Trivet, see Trivet category.
Vacuum Cleaner, Regina Pneumatic, Model A, Original Paperwork, 1910, 24 x 12 In. . . . 80.00
Wafer Iron, Incised Suns, Flowers, Birds, Hearts, Wrought Iron, Pa., 1737, 38 In. 2700.00
Wafer Iron, Krumekake, Alfred Andersen & Co. Minneapolis 2424, Cast Iron, 8 In. 120.00
Waffle Iron, 18th Century, Child's, 11 In. 250.00
Waffle Iron, Brass, Child's, c.1750, 11 1/2 In. 595.00
Waffle Iron, Crescent, No. 8, Spiral Wire Handle, Fanner Mfg. Co., Cleveland, O. 110.00
Waffle Iron, Freidag, No. 8, Spiral Wire Handles 100.00
Waffle Iron, Gasco, Floral Design, Double Press, 7 1/2 In. 50.00
Waffle Iron, Griswold, Electric, Art Deco Style 150.00
Waffle Iron, Griswold, No. 4, Square, Blue Porcelain Base, Favorite Piqua Ware, 1916-35 . . 125.00
Waffle Iron, Griswold, No. 6 . . . . 575.00
Waffle Iron, Griswold, No. 8, American, Pat'd. July 11, 1922 . . . . 50.00
Waffle Iron, Griswold, No. 8, Black Iron, Wooden Handles, 1901 . . . . 25.00
Waffle Iron, Griswold, No. 8, Finger Slot Hinge, Wooden Handles 165.00
Waffle Iron, Griswold, No. 8, Marked Selden Griswold, Web Pattern 850.00
Waffle Iron, Griswold, No. 18, Heart & Star, Wooden Handles, Cast Iron 130.00
Waffle Iron, Manning Bowman & Co., Chrome, White Bakelite Handles, 1924 . . . . 65.00
Waffle Iron, Precision Mfg., No. 80W, Chrome, Wooden Handles, Electric, N.J. 35.00
Waffle Iron, Rev-O-Noc 35.00
Waffle Iron, Round, Temperature Gauge, No. 86-5226, Montgomery Ward 15.00
Waffle Iron, Stover, No. 28, Wooden Handles, Stover Mfg. Co., Freeport, Ill., 7 In. 110.00
Waffle Iron, Wagner Ware, Sidney, O. 1408, Pat'd. Sept 15, 1925 . . . . 30.00
Waffle Iron, Wear-Ever, Aluminum, No. 340-1 . . . . 25.00
Washboard, Rockingham Ridges 950.00
Washing Machine, Motor On Top, Hamilton Beach, Copper, Pat. 1917, 23 x 27 In. 1150.00
Washing Machine, Washboard, Wringer, Lower Mfg., 15 x 15 x 4 1/2 In. 335.00
Whisk, Twisted Wire, c.1890, 8 In. 11.00

KNIFE collectors usually specialize in a single type. In the 1960s, the United States government passed a law that required knife manufacturers to mark their knives with the country of origin. This seemed to encourage the collectors, and knife collecting became an interest of a large group of people. All types of knives are collected, from top quality twentieth-century examples to old bone- or pearl-handled knives in excellent condition.

Archer, Oval Loop Guard, Transverse Bands, Iron, Gray Stained Blade, 6 1/4-In. Blade . . 200.00
Bayonet, US Marine, M6 Model, Plastic Handle, Milpar Col., 12 In. 49.00
Bowie, Counter Guard Shaped As Woman's Head, 15 In. 1400.00
Case, Brow Handle, Orange, Radford, Pa., 4 In. 200.00
Collins No. 18, Gung Ho, Scabbard 531.00
Cooper's, Champer 35.00
Dagger, Fan, Folded Fan Case, Silk Tassel, Japan, 12 1/4 In. 550.00
Dagger, Iron Spearhead, Leaf Shaped Baluster Bolster, Chocolate Patina, 7 3/4-In. Blade . 275.00

Knife, Pocket, Shoe, Plastic, 2 In.

If you spill grease on an antique tablecloth, quickly sprinkle the spot with table salt. It will absorb most of the grease. The remaining spot should wash out later.

Dagger, Waisted Leaf Shape, 7 3/4-In. Blade 425.00
Fighting, Folding, Horn, Bone & Brass Plate Grip, Scalloped Blade, Binoche, 6 1/2 In. 275.00
Folding, Antler Grips, Stone Finish Blade, Spain, 19th Century, 10-In. Blade 210.00
Folding, Hooked Blade, Sawtooth Catch, Horn Grips, 10 1/2-In. Blade 225.00
Folding, Pistol Grip Handles, Horn Panels, Brass Ferrule, 1860s 195.00
Horn Handle, Brass Ferule, Leather Sheath, 23 1/4 In. 27.00
Long, Elongate Leaf Shape, Flared Base 375.00
Long, Spearhead, Elongated Diamond Form Head 375.00
Long, Spearhead, Lineal, Welded Grain, Hexagonal Bolster, 13 1/4-In. Blade 675.00
Long, Welded Spearhead, Elongated Leaf Form, 8 3/4-In. Blade 105.00
Pen, Hart, Farnham, Staghorn Handle 42.00
Pocket, Aluminum, Manila, Dewey, Sampson & Santiago Portraits 325.00
Pocket, Ivory Snuff Spoon, 2 Picks, Horn Handle, Mid 19th Century, 2-In. Blade 75.00
Pocket, Shoe, Plastic, 2 In. .... *Illus* 50.00
Pocket, Zippo, Chas. W. Rice & Co., Inc., First In Rice Sales, Box, 1960s 55.00
Trench, German 130.00

KNOWLES, TAYLOR & KNOWLES items may be found in the KTK and Lotus Ware categories.

KOREAN WARE, see Sumida.

KOSTA, the oldest Swedish glass factory, was founded in 1742. During the 1920s through the 1950s, many pieces of original design were made at the factory. The firm is still working.

KOSTA

Bowl, Blue Fish Net Design, Purple, Signed, Warff, 5 x 4 1/2 In. 395.00
Bowl, Crosshatched Swirl, Vicke Lindstrand, 1956, 3 x 3 1/2 In. 95.00
Bowl, Smoke, Triangular, 9 1/2 x 4 In. 125.00
Candlestick, Teardrop Shape, Signed, 10 In., Pair 250.00
Figurine, Seal, Signed, 6 3/4 In. 200.00
Paperweight, Suspended Teardrop, 2 1/2 x 2 1/2 In. 115.00
Scent Bottle, Pear Shape, Signed, 5 1/8 In. 88.00
Vase, Blue Neck, Mauve, 2 x 2 1/2 In. 42.00
Vase, Blue Speckled, Amber Neck, Signed, 3 3/8 In. 42.00
Vase, Blue, Green, Amber Rainbows, Signed, 11 3/4 x 4 1/2 In. 170.00
Vase, Blue, Green, Black, Rust, White Spatter, 3 x 2 x 3 In. 75.00
Vase, Bud, Elongated Bubbles At Neck, Elongated Neck, Signed, 11 1/8 In. 230.00
Vase, Paperweight Shape, Green Horizontal Wavy Stripes, 6 In. 115.00
Vase, Sommerso, Foil Label, 13 1/2 In. 518.00
Vase, Stylized Animals & Figures, Bucket Shape, Signed, 8 1/2 In. 2300.00
Vase, Stylized Bare Trees, Leaves, Marked, 6 3/4 In. 770.00

KPM refers to Berlin porcelain, but the same initials were used alone and in combination with other symbols by several German porcelain makers. They include the Konigliche Porzellan Manufaktur of Berlin, initials used in mark, 1823–1847; Meissen, 1723–1724 only; Krister Porzellan Manufaktur in Waldenburg, after 1831; Kranichfelder Porzellan Manufaktur in Kranichfeld, after 1903; and the Kister Porzellan Manufaktur in Scheibe, after 1838.

K.P.M

Bowl, Vegetable, Cover, Krista 90.00
Charger, Daisies, Iris, Butterfly, Gilt, 1950, 14 In. 575.00
Charger, Floral Design, Gold Trim, 1891, 13 In. 525.00
Coffeepot, Cover 95.00
Cup & Saucer, Allover Floral Design, 2 1/2 x 5 3/4 In. 9.00
Cup & Saucer, Gilt, 1870, 6 1/4 x 3 In. 200.00
Cup & Saucer, Raised Floral Design, Black, Gold Trim, Handle 25.00
Cup & Saucer, Rose Design, Handles, 5 1/4 x 2 1/8 x 5 7/8 In. 55.00
Cup & Saucer, Topographical, Bavarian Mountain Scene, Castle, Paw Feet, 19th Century . 750.00
Dish, Leaf, White Beads & Bows, Aqua Ground, 9 1/4 x 7 In. 265.00
Figurine, Bear, Playful, Extended Arm, Legs Up, Toes Pointed, 4 In. 130.00
Figurine, Cat, Sleeping, Gold Trim, Orange & Blue Bow, 12 3/4 In. 135.00
Figurine, Clown, Playing Musical Instrument, Signed, 9 In. 55.00
Figurine, Colonial Couple, Birds, Fence, Blue, White, Gold, 1960s, 5 1/2 In. 95.00

KPM, Plaque, Triumphant
Of Mother Church, Frame,
15 x 12 In.

To clean an enamel or graniteware pan, fill it with water. Add the peel of an apple or some cut up fresh rhubarb. Boil the mixture for 15 minutes.

Figurine, Greek Women, Pale Peach, Gold, 6 3/4 x 2 1/2 In., Pair	1250.00
Figurine, Little Angel Holding Shield, Blue Glaze, 1887, 4 1/2 x 7 In.	550.00
Jar, Cover, Gilt & Enamel Design, Eagle Finial, 13 In.	1650.00
Lamp Base, Procession Of Frolicking Putti, Late 19th Century, 28 In.	1035.00
Lithophane, see also Lithophane category.	
Plaque, 3 Women Walking In Cityscape Scene, 6 1/2 x 9 3/8 In.	2015.00
Plaque, Beautiful Blond Haired Woman In Low Cut Blue Dress, Oval, 8 3/4 In.	4600.00
Plaque, Buffalo Bill Cody, Signed, 6 1/2 x 9 In.	1840.00
Plaque, Cloth Spinning, Giltwood Frame, Carved, Mark, 10 3/4 x 8 3/4 In.	6325.00
Plaque, Der Gratulant, Giltwood Frame Within Frame, c.1900, 9 x 6 In.	2990.00
Plaque, Expectations, c.1900, 9 x 6 In.	3450.00
Plaque, Fairy With Butterfly Near Lake, Foliate Giltwood Frame, 9 In.	5175.00
Plaque, Girl With Fruit, Giltwood Frame, Late 19th Century, 8 1/2 x 10 1/2 In.	4600.00
Plaque, Greek Maiden With Water Jug, Frame, c.1900, 15 1/2 x 10 In.	6900.00
Plaque, Gypsy Girl, Signed, Oval, 10 3/4 In.	3900.00
Plaque, Lassitude, Long-Haired Maiden, Giltwood Frame, 10 x 8 In.	7475.00
Plaque, Love Disarmed, Taking Cupid's Bow, Late 19th Century, 10 3/4 x 7 3/4 In.	6040.00
Plaque, Madonna With Infant Christ & St. John, Giltwood Frame, 13 1/2 In.	5290.00
Plaque, Maiden & 2 Cherubs, 16 3/4 x 12 1/2 In.	9487.00
Plaque, Maiden Smelling Flowers In Garden, Giltwood Frame	3450.00
Plaque, Nymphs & Cupid In Green Landscape, Rectangular, 7 7/8 In.	7480.00
Plaque, People Enjoying An Outing On Wooded Mountainside, Gilt Frame, 7 x 10 In.	3500.00
Plaque, Portrait, Woman Wearing White Dress, Veil, Oval, 17 x 13 In.	8050.00
Plaque, Rape Of Sabines, Gilt Frame, 9 x 6 In.	5500.00
Plaque, Ruth, Standing, Holding Sheaf Of Wheat, Signed, 18 1/2 x 11 In.	5750.00
Plaque, Scantily Clad Female Fairy, Sleeping Traveler, Signed, 1882, 9 1/4 x 6 1/4 In.	2530.00
Plaque, Seminude Cupid & Psyche Kneeling In Landscape Scene, 9 In.	2590.00
Plaque, Sistine Madonna, After Raphael, Marked Verso, Gilt Frame, 12 1/2 x 10 In.	6720.00
Plaque, Triumphant Of Mother Church, Frame, 15 x 12 In. ....*Illus*	9240.00
Plaque, Woman Holding Child In Front Of Oval Mirror, 9 x 7 In.	2590.00
Plaque, Woman Wearing Blue Dress, Blond Hair, Giltwood Frame, 8 In.	1440.00
Plaque, Woman With Long Flowing Hair, Oval, 10 3/4 In.	6325.00
Plaque, Woman, Feeding Pigeons At Steps, 4 1/2 x 6 1/4 In.	405.00
Plaque, Young Girl, Amid Flowers, Late 19th Century, 16 x 10 3/4 In.	7800.00
Plaque, Your Beauty, Impressed Scepter Mark, 4 1/4 x 5 1/4 In.	390.00
Plate, Berries & Leaves, 9 1/2 In.	28.00
Plate, Orange Clusters & Blossoms, Green Border, 1904, 8 3/8 In.	45.00
Plate, Pink, White Flowers, Blue Border, 10 1/2 In.	60.00
Plate, Purple Flowers, 1844, 7 In.	75.00
Plate, Purple Flowers, Hand Painted, 1844, 7 In.	75.00
Plate, Roman Scene, 7 1/8 In.	45.00
Plate, White Flowers, Gray Ground, Signed, Krister, 1903, 8 3/8 In.	65.00
Tray, Serving, Magenta Flowers, Gilt, 1905, 12 1/2 x 9 1/4 In.	250.00
Vase, Floral, Gilt Overlay, Victorian Courting Scene, 6 1/4 In.	715.00
Vase, Gilt Flowers, Swags, 1920, 13 In.	975.00
Vase, Molded Swags, Painted Flowers, Signed, 14 1/2 In., Pair	2530.00

KTK are the initials of the Knowles, Taylor & Knowles Company of East Liverpool, Ohio, founded by Isaac W. Knowles in 1853. The company made many types of utilitarian wares, hotel china, and dinnerwares. They made the fine bone china known as Lotus Ware from 1891 to 1896. The company merged with American Ceramic Corporation in 1928. It closed in 1934. Lotus Ware is listed in its own category in this book.

K.T.&K.
CHINA

Creamer, Gold Design, 1904, 5 1/4 In.	50.00
Plate, Portrait, Madame Lans-Gene, Flow Blue, 1901, 8 1/8 In.	25.00
Plate, Portrait, Marechal Lefebure, Flow Blue, Gold, 1901, 8 1/8 In.	25.00

KU KLUX KLAN items are now collected because of their historic importance. Literature, robes, and memorabilia are available. The Klan was outlawed in 1869 and reemerged in 1915. It is still in existence, so new material is found.

Book, The Clansman, Historical Romance Of The Ku Klux Klan, T. Dixon, Jr., 1905	12.00
Booklet, KKK Katechism & Song Book, Ads In Back, 1924, 72 Pages, 4 x 7 In.	65.00
Broadside, Michigan State Klororo, 1920s, 8 1/2 x 11 In.	165.00
Broadside, Plan Of Contemplated Murder Of John Campbell, Anti-Klan, 1871, 10 x 16 In.	1350.00
Broadside, Rev. E.I. Phillips Will Give Public Lecture, Bradenton, Fla., 9 x 12 In.	175.00
Calling Card Set, Hooded Klansmen Pictures, 10 Piece	5.50
Card, Ohio Will Decide Between Union Republicans Or Ku Klux Democracy, 1871	225.00
Key Tag, Frank Robins, Canaan, N.H., Mounted Klansman With Cross, Nickel Plate	75.00
Knife, Red Crosses, Celluloid	225.00
Mug, Coffee, Lettering On Back	55.00
Sheet Music, Ku Klux Kismet, Klansman On Horse, 1924	75.00
Sugar, Cover, Burning Cross & Ks All Sides	72.00
Sword, Ceremonial, Knights Head, KKK Stamped Into Grip, 36 In.	165.00

KUTANI ware is a Japanese porcelain made after the mid-seventeenth century. Most of the pieces found today are nineteenth-century. Collectors often use the term *kutani* to refer to just the later, colorful pieces decorated with red, gold, and black pictures of warriors, animals, and birds.

Box, Earthenware, Riverscape, Round, 6 In.	69.00
Charger, Center Samurai Warriors On Island, Chrysanthemum Border On Reverse, 18 In.	350.00
Charger, Figures, Birds, Showa Period, 18 In.	150.00
Charger, Foo Dog, Flowers, Showa Period, 15 3/4 In., Pair	489.00
Jar, Water, Genre & Floral, Gilt Design, Character Marks, 9 In.	355.00
Mask, Noh, Woman With Gold Eyes, Blackened Teeth, 7 1/2 In.	345.00
Platter, Fish Form, Blue, White, 16 In.	630.00
Pot, Cover, Flowers & Birds, Ice Lip Spout, Signed, 12 In.	285.00
Pot, Cover, Orange Black & Gilt, Flowers & Birds, Applied Spout, Marked, 12 In.	245.00
Saki Set, Presentation, Gourd Form, Flared Rim, Hammered, 20th Century, 1 In.	460.00
Scroll, 2 Women Viewing Cherry Blossoms, Nihonga School, Signed, Box	345.00
Scroll, Man Reading From Scroll, Signed, Shunobu, Box, 19th Century, Pair	115.00
Scroll, Warrior On Horseback, 5 Characters, Single Seal, 19th Century	85.00
Tea Service, Foliate, Geometric Design, Iron Red, Gilt, Signed, Teapot 7 1/8 In.	150.00
Vase, Band Of Beach Bloom Across Body, Blue Underglaze, Signed, 1900, 7 1/2 In.	575.00
Vase, Bird & Floral Panels, Late 19th Century, 13 In.	345.00
Vase, Comic Frogs Feasting On Butterflies, Signed, 6 1/4 In.	230.00
Vase, Peacocks In Garden Settings, Orange, Black Enamel, 13 1/2 In., Pair	805.00
Vase, Rust Red, Dragon Handles, Birds & Flowers, 14 1/2 In.	405.00
Vase, Stylized Scrolled Foliage, Blue, White, 13 1/2 In.	920.00

L.G. WRIGHT Glass Company of New Martinsville, West Virginia, started selling glassware in 1937. Founder "Si" Wright contracted with Ohio and West Virginia glass factories to reproduce popular pressed glass patterns, like Rose & Snow, Baltimore Pear, and Three Face, and opalescent patterns, like Daisy & Fern and Swirl. Collectors can tell the difference between the original glasswares and L.G. Wright reproductions because of colors and differences in production techniques. Some L.G. Wright items are marked with an underlined W in a circle.

Items that were made from old Northwood molds have an altered Northwood mark—an angled line was added to the N to make it look like a W. Collectors refer to this mark as "the wobbly W."

Cherry, Sugar & Creamer, Ruby, 4 x 5 In.	17.00
Coin Dot, Bottle, Barber, Blue	145.00
Daisy & Button, Candy Dish, Canoe, Cobalt Blue, 11 1/2 In.	10.00
Daisy & Button, Candy Dish, Canoe, Green, 11 In.	8.00
Daisy & Button, Candy Dish, Canoe, Ice Blue, 11 1/2 In.	10.00
Daisy & Fern, Tumbler, Iced Tea, Vaseline Opalescent, 6 Piece	240.00
Drapery, Vase, Jack-In-The-Pulpit, Cranberry Opalscent, 14 In.	285.00
Epergne, Blue Opalescent, Crystal Crest Horns, 17 1/4 x 12 In.	230.00
Hobnail, Fairy Lamp, Green Satin	61.00
Moon & Star, Cake Stand, Scalloped, 11 x 7 In.	85.00
Moss Rose, Cruet, Peach Blow	130.00
Pitcher, Ice Blue, 8 1/2 x 8 x 4 1/2 In.	20.00
Priscilla, Rose Bowl, Ruby, 3 1/2 In.	21.00
Purple Slag, Dish, Duck, Cover, 10 In.	25.00
S Pattern, Cruet, Ruby, 6 1/2 In.	44.00
Snowflake & Waffle, Basket, Cobalt Blue Opalescent, Handle, Ruffled, 8 x 7 In.	210.00

LACQUER is a type of varnish. Collectors are most interested in the Chinese and Japanese lacquer wares made from the Japanese varnish tree. Lacquer wares are made from wood with many coats of lacquer. Sometimes the piece is carved or decorated with ivory or metal inlay.

Bookstand, Wooden, Islamic Style, Folding A-Form	155.00
Box, Black, Gold Landscape Interior, Wood Grain Exterior, Rectangular, 4 3/4 In.	403.00
Box, Cover, Daikoku Removing Pearls From Rice Barrel, Circular, 2 3/4 In.	60.00
Box, Cover, Deep Forest Green, Signed, Jean Dunand, 1925, 1 3/4 x 5 1/8 In.	6000.00
Box, Cover, Gilt Cartouches, 6 Sections, Circular, 1820, 6 In.	375.00
Box, Cover, Red Lacquer, 14 1/4 In., Pair	460.00
Box, Document, Prunus & Pine Tree, Black, Gold Lacquer, 9 1/2 In.	490.00
Box, Eggshell, Gold Lacquer Rooster, Eggshell Ground, Square, 1 7/8 In.	11.00
Box, Fan, Black, Gold Lacquer, Rectangular, 19th Century, 12 In.	69.00
Box, Gilt Court Scene, 4 Dragon-Form Supports, 1820, 5 x 12 In.	1150.00
Box, Mother-Of-Pearl Inlay, Crane, Flowers, Leaves, Chinese, 16 1/2 In.	115.00
Box, Tea, Pewter Cover, Pavilion Scene With 3 Figures, Chinese, 5 x 10 x 7 In.	520.00
Box, Winter Troika Scene, Vishnikov Mark, Russia, c.1880, 6 3/4 x 5 1/2 x 3 In.	1120.00
Cabinet, Display, Birds & Floral Design, 19th Century, 24 x 16 1/2 In.	345.00
Charger, Black, Carved Bone, Mother-Of-Pearl, Geisha & Her Attendant In Boat, 4 In.	635.00
Cigar Caddy, Black, Domed Top, 4 Side Panels, Drawer, Chinoiserie, 14 In.	450.00
Container, Red, Black Lacquer, Rectangular Handle, China, 19 x 16 In.	160.00
Inro, Bamboo & Flowering Branch, Bone, 1 Case, 4 In.	230.00
Inro, Flowering Prunus Tree, Gold, 4 Case, 3 1/2 In.	690.00
Inro, Large Brown Ox, Gold Rope Continuing On Reverse, Gold, 4 Case, 3 In.	862.00
Inro, Mask Design, 1 Case, 2 1/2 In.	200.00
Inro, Monkey Design Amongst Clouds, Gold, 4 Case, 2 1/2 In.	1150.00
Inro, Mother-Of-Pearl, Gold, Coral Prunus, 4 Case, 3 In.	546.00
Inro, Netsuke & Ojime, Inlaid Coral, Mother-Of-Pearl Design, Japan, 5 x 4in.	4025.00
Screen, 2-Panel, Ivory Design, Birds Perched On Flowering Branches, 69 In.	978.00
Shrine, Buddha Seated On Lotus Throne, Black Lacquer, Edo Period, 6 In.	920.00
Shrine, Buddha, Foliate Designs, Gold, Black Lacquer, 3 In.	1955.00
Shrine, Buddha, Seated, Wearing Elaborate Necklace, 9 In.	316.00
Shrine, Buddha, Standing, Gilt, Japan, 23 In.	400.00
Tea Caddy, Black, Gold, Interior Fitted, Giltwood Feet, Octagonal, 5 7/8 In.	635.00
Tray, Boats, Gold Pine Trees, Silver Rim, 19th Century, 10 3/4 x 7 1/2 In.	316.00
Tray, Bouquet Of Flowers, Mother-Of-Pearl Inlay, Gilt Foliate Rim, 23 1/4 x 31 1/2 In.	170.00
Tray, Flowers, Grasses, Black, Gold, Rectangular, 13 x 12 1/2 In.	170.00
Tray, Gold, Black Figures In Landscape, Chinese Export, 19th Century, 19 x 15 In.	172.00
Tray, Village Scene, Gilt, Jade Hook Handles, Black, 15 x 22 In.	145.00
Tray-On-Stand, Black, Inlay, Oriental Landscape, 21 x 19 1/2 x 25 1/2 In.	1495.00
Tray-On-Stand, Victorian, Black, Wood, Round, Floral Decoration, 21 1/2 x 29 In.	805.00
Vase, Bird Perched On Tree, Gold, Silver, Red, Octagonal, Senpo, Japan, 8 1/4 In.	2300.00
Vase, Cormorant Fishing By Night, 3 Birds, Gold, Silver, Red, Senpo, Japan	2185.00

LADY HEAD VASE, see Head Vase.

LALIQUE glass was made by Rene Lalique in Paris, France, between the 1890s and his death in 1945. The glass was molded, pressed, and engraved in Art Nouveau and Art Deco styles. Pieces were marked with the signature *R. Lalique*. Lalique glass is still being made. Pieces made after 1945 bear the mark *Lalique*. Jewelry made by Rene Lalique is listed in the Jewelry category.

R.LALIQUE

Ashtray, Chien, Dog, Green Opalescent Glass, Marked, R. Lalique, c.1926, 3 3/4 In.	575.00
Ashtray, Cuba, Deep Amber Glass, Wheel Cut, Marked, R. Lalique, c.1928, 5 1/2 In.	977.00
Ashtray, Cygnes, Molded Frosted Swans, Signed, France, 4 In.	149.00
Ashtray, Irene, Birds, Bright Green Glass, Marked, R. Lalique, c.1929, 3 3/4 In.	1265.00
Ashtray, Lapin, Rabbit In Center Bending Over, Topaz Glass, R. Lalique, c.1929, 5 In. . . .	632.00
Blotter, Rocker, Feuilles D'Artichaut, Sepia Patina, Metal, Frosted Glass, c.1925, 6 In. . .	862.00
Bookends, Luxembourg, 3 Cupids, 8 In.	805.00
Bowl, Avallon, Birds On Branches With Fruits, Signed, 6 In.	1100.00
Bowl, Gui, Mistletoe Design, Frosted Glass, Clear Ground, 8 1/4 In.	253.00
Bowl, Nemours, Floral Wreaths, Signed, 4 x 9 1/2 In.	476.00
Bowl, Nemours, Hemispherical, Molded, Frosted Floral, Enamel Center, 1930s, 10 In. . . .	3025.00
Bowl, Pinsons, Chaffinch, Flower, Etched, 3 3/4 x 9 1/4 In.	288.00
Box, Cheveux De Venus, Flower On Cover, 1910, 2 1/2 In.	1380.00
Box, Cover, Coppelia, c.1981, 7 x 5 1/2 x 3 1/4 In.	402.00
Box, Cover, Coquilles, Shells, 1920, 1 3/4 x 2 3/4 In.	1035.00
Box, Cover, Fontainebleau, Freize Of Hares, Frosted, Marked, R. Lalique, c.1924, 3 In. . .	460.00
Box, Cover, Gabrielle, Green Glass Lid, Powder Puffs, 1919, 1 1/2 x 3 3/8 In.	1265.00
Box, Cover, Lucie, Flowers & Vines On Cover, 1924, 3 In.	230.00
Box, Cover, Trois Figurines, 3 Females On Cover, 1912, 3 3/4 In.	460.00
Box, Cover, Trois Paons, 3 Peacocks, 1919, 1 1/2 x 3 1/4 In.	920.00
Box, Fleurettes, Flowers On Lid, 1926, 2 1/4 In.	575.00
Candlestick, Soudan, Frosted, Marked, R. Lalique, c.1934, 2 x 4 1/2 In., Pair	1150.00
Ceiling Light, Dahlias, Sepia Patina, Frosted, Clear, Marked, R. Lalique	2875.00
Ceiling Light, Lierre, Hanging, Sepia Patina, Frosted, Clear, Marked, R. Lalique	3220.00
Chandelier, Eglantines, Molded, Frosted Glass, c.1926, 31 x 26 In.	14400.00
Chandelier, Hanging, Monaco, 8 Tentacle Arms, Metal Cage, 1950, 32 In.	2990.00
Chandelier, Papillons, Amber Patina, Molded, Frosted, c.1923, 16 In.	18000.00
Charger, Algues, Raised Seaweed Form Spiral, Signed, 1953, 15 3/8 In.	805.00
Clock, Deux Colombes, 2 Doves, 1926, 8 5/8 In.	6325.00
Clock, Deux Figurines, 2 Females, Molded, Frosted, c.1926, 13 x 11 In.	3300.00
Figurine, Cockatoo, 11 1/2 In.	2500.00
Figurine, Danseuse, Dancer With Arms Raised, Frosted, 1975, 9 1/2 In.	690.00
Figurine, Danseuses, Nude Females, 1980s, 9 1/4 In., Pair	672.00
Figurine, Liberte, Eagle, No. 1164, 9 1/4 In.	1125.00
Figurine, Moyenne Voilee, Draped Woman, Blue Patina, Frosted, R. Lalique, 6 In.	2875.00
Figurine, Suzanne, Molded, Frosted, Gray, c.1925, 9 1/8 In.	7800.00
Glass Set, Setubal, Molded Cherries, Frosted Amber, Signed, 4 Pieces, 4 In.	374.00
Goblet, Vigne, Sepia Patina, Marked, R. Lalique, c.1912, 7 1/4 In.	4140.00
Hood Ornament, Chrysis, Sepia Patina, Frosted, Marked, R. Lalique, c.1931, 5 3/4 In. . . .	5175.00
Hood Ornament, Coq Nain, Rooster, 1930s, 8 In.	1511.00
Hood Ornament, Saint-Christophe, Man, Holding Boy On Shoulders, Gray Patina	1150.00
Lamp, Sconce, Coquilles, Shells, Metal Fittings, Demilune Design, Frosted	2875.00
Lamp, Sconce, Lausanne, Corner, Frosted, Clear	2875.00
Letter Seal, Aigle, Eagle, Charcoal Gray Patina, Frosted, Wheel Cut	2300.00
Letter Seal, Lapin, Rabbit, Topaz Glass, Marked, R. Lalique	632.00
Letter Seal, Souris, Mouse, Mint Green Opalescent Glass, Marked, R. Lalique	632.00
Memorial Panel, Croix Aux Quatre Anges, Crouching Angel In Each Corner, 1925	7475.00
Paperweight, Chrysis, 6 1/2 x 5 In.	316.00
Paperweight, Chrysis, Fitted Box, 5 1/4 In.	138.00
Paperweight, Daim, Deer Standing, Bending Over, Frosted, 3 1/2 In.	920.00
Paperweight, Hirondelle, Swallow, 6 1/4 In.	117.00
Paperweight, Taureau, Bull, Frosted, Signed, 3 1/2 x 4 1/4 In.	193.00
Paperweight, Tete D'aigle, Eagle Head, 4 3/8 In.	575.00
Perfume Bottle, Ambre Antique, 4 Draped Maidens, Raised Stopper, 6 In.	2415.00
Perfume Bottle, Au Coeur Des Calices, 1913, 2 5/8 In.	5175.00

Perfume Bottle, Au Coeur Des Calices, Blue Glass, Frozen Stopper, Marked, Lalique ... 3795.00
Perfume Bottle, Bouquet De Faunes, Footed Rim, Frosted, Clear, 4 In. 546.00
Perfume Bottle, Calendal, Female Dancers Amid Foliage, Spherical Stopper, 4 In. 1610.00
Perfume Bottle, Coeur Joie, Heart In Center, Frosted, Clear, Stopper, 1955, 6 In. 402.00
Perfume Bottle, Fille D'Eve, Frosted, Clear, Marked, Lalique 575.00
Perfume Bottle, Fleurettes, Vertical Ribs Of Flowers, 1919, 8 In. 550.00
Perfume Bottle, Je Reviens, 1929, 2 1/2 In., Pair 230.00
Perfume Bottle, La Violette, Bouquet Of Violets, Cobalt Blue Enamel, 1925, 3 In. 3780.00
Perfume Bottle, Le Jade, Bird & Intertwined Branches, 1926, 3 1/4 In. 3400.00
Perfume Bottle, Perles, Sepia Patina, Opalescent Glass, 5 1/2 In. 1380.00
Perfume Bottle, Serpent, Gray Patina, Frosted, Clear, Marked, R. Lalique 1150.00
Perfume Bottle, Styx, Sepia Patina, Frosted, Clear, Frozen Stopper 920.00
Perfume Bottle, Tzigane, Original Magenta Silk, Black Enamel, 6 1/4 In. 517.00
Perfume Tester, La Renommee D'Orsay, Sepia Patina, Frosted, Clear 3200.00
Plaque, Menu, Raisin Muscat, Grape Leaf Design, Frosted, Marked, R. Lalique, Pair 1092.00
Plaque, Profile Of Louis Pasteur, 1922, 4 In. 975.00
Plate, Actinia, Signed, c.1933, 11 In. 550.00
Plate, Ondines, Nude Female Figures, 1921, 10 3/4 In. 1840.00
Platter, Deux Pigeons, Black Patina, Signed, 1920, 14 3/4 In. 4887.00
Platter, Serving, Coquilles, Opalescent Glass, Wheel Cut, Marked, R. Lalique 1265.00
Powder Box, Cover, Le Lys, Original Goose Down Puff, Frosted, Marked, R. Lalique ... 373.00
Powder Box, Deux Sirenes, Molded Nude Female Figures Floating On Cover 1035.00
Stemware, Cannes, 8 Goblets, 10 Wine, 10 Champagne, 1938 .... 1265.00
Tray, Glass, Ebene-De-Macassar, Ivory, Lotus, c.1929, 17 x 13 In. 7200.00
Vase, Acacia, Frosted, Clear, Marked, R. Lalique, 8 In. 805.00
Vase, Armorique, Artichoke, Allover Stylized Leaves, 1927, 8 3/4 In. 5125.00
Vase, Avallon, Birds On Branches With Fruit, 1927, 5 3/4 In. 1880.00
Vase, Bacchantes, Light Olive Green Glass, Frosted, Clear, Lalique, 1960, 9 3/4 In. 2070.00
Vase, Bagatelle, Assorted Panels Of Birds, Foliage Frame, Circular, 6 1/2 In. 1438.00
Vase, Borneo, Flared Rim, Press Molded, Black Enamel Birds, Floral, c.1930, 9 In. 2645.00
Vase, Borromee, Gray Patina, Molded, Frosted, c.1928, 8 1/4 In. 4800.00
Vase, Camaret, Opalescent, Oval Shape, Molded Fish, Signed, 5 1/2 In. 1495.00
Vase, Camargue, Frosted, Cylindrical, Molded Horses, Brown Stain, Signed, 11 In. 4025.00
Vase, Ceylan, Sepia Patina, Opalescent, Marked, R. Lalique, 10 In. 7475.00
Vase, Chevreuse, 5 Relief Hoops, Vertical Striated Bands, c.1930, 6 1/4 In. 920.00
Vase, Dahlias, Black Enamel, Frosted, Clear, Marked, R. Lalique, c.1923, 5 In. . .1495.00 to 2825.00
Vase, Dampierre, 4 7/8 In. 201.00
Vase, Davos, Simulates Sharkskin, Opalescent, Marked, R. Lalique, c.1932, 11 In. 2300.00
Vase, Domremy, Thistles, 1926, 8 1/4 In. 1840.00
Vase, Dordogne, Spiral Shells, 1927, 7 In. 1840.00
Vase, Espalion, Ferns, Blue, Gray Patina, Opalescent, Marked, R. Lalique, c.1927, 7 In. .. 1380.00
Vase, Esterel, Laurel Leaves, Blue, Green Patina, Frosted, Clear, R. Lalique, c.1923, 6 In. .. 1035.00
Vase, Faune, White Frosted, 1931, 12 In. 14400.00
Vase, Fontaines, Allover Abstract Design, 1912, 5 1/2 In. 805.00
Vase, Formose, Allover Fish, 1924, 6 3/4 In. ....1950.00 to 6900.00

Lalique, Vase, Grenade, Amber,
Overlapping Tile, Marked,
1930s, 4 3/4 In.

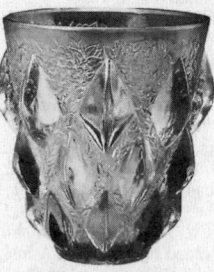

Lalique, Vase, Rampillon,
Yellow, Cabochons & Flowers,
Marked, 1927, 5 1/4 In.

Lalique, Vase, Sauterelles,
Grasshoppers, Frosted, Marked,
1932, 11 1/4 In.

Vase, Formose, Allover Fish, Gray Patina, Opalescent, R. Lalique, c.1934 .... 2875.00
Vase, Grenade, Amber, Overlapping Tile, Marked, 1930s, 4 3/4 In. ....*Illus* 2875.00
Vase, Grives, Birds On Branches, 1938, 6 3/4 In. 1150.00
Vase, Gros Scarabees, Oval, Molded Beetles, Gray Stain, Signed, c.1923, 11 In. 4025.00
Vase, Gui, Charcoal Gray Patina, Opalescent, Marked, R. Lalique, c.1920, 6 3/4 In. 1035.00
Vase, Laurier, Laurel Leaves, 1922, 7 In. 1840.00
Vase, Lievres, Blue, Gray Patina, Frosted, Clear, Marked, R. Lalique, c.1923, 6 1/2 In. ... 1495.00
Vase, Lotus, 1920, 7 3/4 In. 1380.00
Vase, Moissac, Leaf Design, Yellow Amber Glass, Marked, R. Lalique, c.1927, 5 In. 1725.00
Vase, Mossi, Allover Hemispherical Protrusions, 1933, 8 In. 1840.00
Vase, Nefliers, Flowers, Blue, Gray Patina, Frosted, Clear, R. Lalique, c.1923, 5 1/2 In. .. 517.00
Vase, Ormeaux, Charcoal Gray Glass, White Patina, Marked, R. Lalique, c.1926, 7 In. .. 3220.00
Vase, Ormeaux, Leaves, 1926, 6 3/4 In. 1840.00
Vase, Poissons, Allover Fish, 1921, 9 In. 5750.00
Vase, Poivre, Berry Design, 1921, 9 1/2 In. 2530.00
Vase, Rampillon, Blue Glass, Opalescent, Marked, R. Lalique, c.1927, 5 1/4 In. 1092.00
Vase, Rampillon, Yellow, Cabochons & Flowers, Marked, 1927, 5 1/4 In. ....*Illus* 1725.00
Vase, Ronces, Thorns, Blue, Gray Patina, Opalescent, Marked, R. Lalique, c.1921, 9 In. .. 2875.00
Vase, Ronsard, Female Figure Within Floral Wreath Handles, 1926, 8 In. 1840.00
Vase, Sauge, Leaves, Frosted, Clear, Marked, R. Lalique, 10 1/2 In. 1840.00
Vase, Sauterelles, Grasshoppers, 1912, 10 1/2 In. 6250.00
Vase, Sauterelles, Grasshoppers, Frosted, Marked, 1932, 11 1/4 In. ....*Illus* 5175.00
Vase, Sylvie, 8 1/4 In. .... .288.00 to 450.00
Vase, Tournesols, Black Enamel, Frosted, Clear, c.1927, 4 3/4 In. 862.00
Vase, Tulips, Flowers On Scrolling Stems, 1930s, 7 3/4 In. 1007.00

LAMPS of every type, from the early oil-burning Betty and Phoebe
lamps to the recent electric lamps with glass or beaded shades, interest
collectors. Fuels used in lamps changed through the years; whale oil
(1800–1840), camphene (1828), Argand (1830), lard (1833–1863), tur-
pentine and alcohol (1840s), gas (1850–1879), kerosene (1860), and
electricity (1879) are the most common. Other lamps are listed by
manufacturer or type of material.

Advertising, Charlie Tuna, Star Kist Tuna, Electric, c.1970 .... 50.00
Advertising, Gordon's Gin, Anniversary, Logo On Bottle, Shade, 1950s 85.00
Advertising, Westinghouse Mazda, Box, Miniature, 6 Piece 10.00
Aladdin, B-25, Victoria, Decorated China, Burner & Oil Fill 450.00
Aladdin, B-75, Alacite, Tall Lincoln Drape 135.00
Aladdin, B-83, Beehive, Ruby 550.00
Aladdin, B-85, Diamond Quilt, White Moonstone 350.00
Aladdin, B-91, Diamond Quilt, Pink & White 325.00
Aladdin, B-93, Vertique, White Moonstone 975.00
Aladdin, B-95, Queen, White Moonstone Bowl, Blue Flame Heater 300.00
Aladdin, B-110, Corinthian, White Moonstone Font, 1935 .... 510.00
Aladdin, B-112, Corinthian, Rose Moonstone 270.00
Aladdin, B-121, Majestic, Rose Moonstone, No Burner 380.00
Aladdin, B-425, Bronze Finish, Fluted Shade, Floor 775.00
Aladdin, EJ-200, Vogue, Tall Lincoln, Pedestal, Finial 675.00
Aladdin, G-68, Velvex, Tall Lincoln, Gray, Fluted Shade 725.00
Aladdin, G-232, Alacite, Moonsheaf Finial, Pair 300.00
Aladdin, G-292, Desk, No. 751 Shade, Anglia Finial 165.00
Aladdin, G-343, Lady With Dog, Green 600.00
Aladdin, G-379, Alacite, Tall Ribbed Urn 400.00
Alcohol, Amber, Embossed, Porter, 2 In. 56.00
Alcohol, Amber, Patd. Sep. 14th, 1880, Metal Burner, 3 1/2 In. 95.00
Argand, 1-Light, Etched Glass Shade, Gilt Bronze, c.1840, 15 x 11 In., Pair 3105.00
Argand, 2-Light, Gadrooned Collar, Fluted, Electrified, B. Gardiner, 1820, 23 1/2 In. .. 3900.00
Argand, 2-Light, Louis Veron & Co., Brass, Fitted Standard, 1815, 20 x 17 In., Pair 3900.00
Argand, 2-Light, Louis Veron, Molded Font, Reeded Arms, Scroll Bracket, 19 In., Pair ... 4500.00
Argand, 2-Light, Tripod Base, Prism Ring, Snake Handles, Glass Shade, c.1835, 18 In. .. 2875.00
Argand, Frosted Urn, Cut To Clear Shades, Winged Animal Feet, 1840, 23 In. 1150.00
Argand, Neoclassical, Cornelius & Co., Cast Brass, Candle Arm, c.1830, 22 In., Pair 3300.00
Argand, Neoclassical, Ormolu, Engraved Shade, Ribbed Font, Electrified, 17 In., Pair 2100.00

Argand, Regency, Bronze, Triangular Plinth, Gadroon, 1820, 25 In. 4800.00
Astral, Brass, Strapwork Bands, Knop Stem, Late 19th Century, 21 1/2 In., Pair 805.00
Astral, Cut Crystal Shade, Brass Font, Gilded Stem, Electrified, 23 1/2 In. 1840.00
Astral, Frosted & Cut Shade, Prisms, Square Base, Brass & Glass, 32 In. 460.00
Astral, Solar, Bronze, Gilt Lacquered, Circular Font, Crystal Spears, Electrified, 21 In. 863.00
Astral, Solar, Cornelius & Co., Corinthian Shaft, Marble Base, Font, 1855, 19 In. 750.00
Astral, Solar, Cornelius & Co., Dolphins, River God Masks, Electrified, c.1850, 14 In. 402.00
Astral, Solar, Cornelius & Co., Figure On Marble Base, Supporting Font, c.1845, 16 In. ... 690.00
Astral, Solar, Dietz Brothers & Co., Bronze, Patinated, Bulbous, Electrified, 24 x 7 In. ... 690.00
Astral, Solar, Gilt Lacquer Bronze, Star & Snowflake Pendants, Marble, Electrified, 21 In. 690.00
Astral, Solar, Gilt Lacquer, Star & Snowflake Pendants, Leaf Pedestal, Electrified, 20 In. . 750.00
Astral, Solar, Gilt Lacquered Brass, Round Shade, Marble Plinth, Electrified, 24 In. 690.00
Astral, Solar, Gilt Lacquered Bronze, Bulbous, Font, Pendants, Electrified, 25 In. 575.00
Astral, Solar, Gilt Lacquered Bronze, Pendants, Marble Plinth, Electrified, 19 In. 690.00
Astral, Solar, Gilt Lacquered, Bronze, Double Marble Plinth, Electrified, 13 x 5 In. 230.00
Astral, White Cut To Clear, Brass Font, Clear & Frosted Shade, Marble Base, 23 In. 385.00
Betty, Brass Cover, Bird Finial, Barn Beam Hook, Sliding Cover, 5 In. 230.00
Betty, Copper, Wick Pick, Stand, 12 1/4 In. 320.00
Betty, Iron, 1 Pan, Attached Beam Hook ....86.00 to 98.00
Betty, Rooster On Lid, 4 1/2 In. 525.00
Betty, Wrought Iron, Brass Swivel Plate, Handle, Brass Chain Wick Pick, 5 In. 520.00
Bouillotte, 3-Light, Brass, Gilt, Triangular Base, Upright Arms, Green Tole Shade, 29 In. 430.00
Bouillotte, 3-Light, Bronze Argente, Fluted Standard, Scrolled Branches, 27 x 12 In. 920.00
Bouillotte, 3-Light, Empire, Brass, Leaf Border, Green Tole Shade, 23 1/2 In. 575.00
Bouillotte, 3-Light, Louis XVI Style, Gilt Bronze, 30 1/2 In., Pair 2300.00
Bouillotte, 3-Light, Scroll Arms, Gilt, Metal, Circular Base, Beaded Rim, France, 25 In. . 805.00
Bouillotte, 3-Light, Tole Painted Shades, Gilt Bronze, Bird Heads, 26 In., Pair 748.00
Bradley & Hubbard lamps are included in the Bradley & Hubbard category.
Brass, Green & Yellow Glass, Square Base, Art Deco, 60 In. 196.00
Brass, Iron, & Carmel Slag Glass, Double Square Base, Art Deco, 60 In. 196.00
Camphene, Morey & Ober, Bell Shape, 5 1/2 In. 260.00
Candelabrum, 2-Light, Bronze Putto Holding Torch, Marble Pedestal, 17 In., Pair 5100.00
Candelabrum, 3-Light, Applied Bugs & Flowers, Signed, 12 In., Pair 1090.00
Candelabrum, 4-Light, Curved Candle Branches, Base Eagles, 39 In., Pair 3000.00
Candelabrum, 5-Light, Female Figures Form Shafts, Applied Floral Designs, 17 In. 170.00
Candelabrum, 5-Light, Female Holding Fruit-Filled Cornucopia, Orb, 27 In. 5760.00
Candelabrum, 5-Light, Scrolled Branches, Center Branch, Raised Orb, Bronze, 27 In. ... 5760.00
Candelabrum, 5-Light, Silver Plate, Entwined Branches Spiraling, 17 In., Pair 690.00
Candelabrum, 6-Light, Gilt Metal, Roman Woman, Holding Base, Dragon, 30 In. 240.00
Candelabrum, 7-Light, Cupid-Form Standard, Foliate Cast Arms, 20 In. 5465.00
Candelabrum, 7-Light, Opaline Glass, Removable Bobeche, Russia, 1880s, 32 In. 6940.00
Candelabrum, 9-Light, Gilt, Cherubs, 20th Century, 33 1/2 In., Pair 2090.00
Candelabrum, 10-Light, Faun Holds Bird Supporting Candle Branches, 38 In. 8400.00
Candle, Bronze, Columnar Shafts, Patinated, Charles X, Electrified, 17 x 6 In. 1150.00
Candle, Lace Maker's, Blown Glass, Hollow Stem, Round Font, 8 1/2 In. 300.00
Candle, Lace Maker's, Globular Font, Hollow Stem, Flange, Footed, 1800-1830, 9 In. ... 305.00
Ceiling Lights, Henry Dreyfuss, Chicago, Luminator Co., Art Deco, 7 3/4 In., Pair 1068.00
Chandelier, 2 Tiered Quezal Shades, Early 20th Century, 20 In. 2415.00
Chandelier, 2-Light, Cherub Holding Torch, Glass Ruffled Shades, Electrified, 18 In. 2070.00
Chandelier, 2-Light, Gilt Bronze, Flying Putto, Holding Torches, Louis XV, 23 In. 1840.00
Chandelier, 3-Light, Art Deco, Wrought Iron, Glass, Red, Yellow Shades, 34 In. 2300.00
Chandelier, 3-Light, Arts & Crafts, Oak Fixture, Green Slag Glass 460.00
Chandelier, 3-Light, Empire, Brass, Alabaster, Plumed Corona, Knop Pendant, 26 In. 980.00
Chandelier, 4-Light, Brass, Jeweled Chains, Lyre Back Plate, Louis XVI, 21 In., Pair 2990.00
Chandelier, 4-Light, Etruscan Style, Polychrome, Bronze, Wood, 36 x 15 In. 2300.00
Chandelier, 4-Light, Neoclassical, Brass, Crystal, Cobalt Blue Plate, Scrolls, 36 In. 6900.00
Chandelier, 4-Light, Regency Style, Bronze, Crystal Prisms, 3 Beaded Tiers, 33 In. 2070.00
Chandelier, 4-Light, Rococo Style, Gilt Bronze, Beads, Pendants, 36 In. 6038.00
Chandelier, 4-Light, Wrought Iron, Gilt, Medieval Style, Torches, Center Crown, 35 In. ... 518.00
Chandelier, 4-Light, Wrought Iron, Open Foliate Work, Applied Leaves, 20 In. 575.00
Chandelier, 5-Light, Arts & Crafts, Copper, Hammered, 53 x 12 In. 230.00
Chandelier, 5-Light, Bohemian Glass, White, Green Floral Design, Gilt, 18 In. 460.00
Chandelier, 5-Light, Bronze, Rondels, Bellflowers, Swags, E.F. Caldwell & Co., 23 In. ... 2400.00

Chandelier, 5-Light, Neoclassical, Gilt Bronze, Drapery, Masks, 35 x 22 In. 865.00
Chandelier, 5-Light, Regency Style, Twist Scrolled Branches, Prisms, Baluster, 36 In. . . . 575.00
Chandelier, 5-Light, Rococo Style, Gilt Bronze, Swirling Foliate Standard, 21 In. 1380.00
Chandelier, 5-Light, S-Scroll Arms, Drip Pans, Knop Pendant, 20th Century, 18 In. 290.00
Chandelier, 6-Light, Argent, Bronze, Scrolled Branches, Ribbed Bowl, 28 x 22 In. 3680.00
Chandelier, 6-Light, Baltic Neoclassical, Gilt Bronze, Cobalt Glass, 31 x 25 In. 3910.00
Chandelier, 6-Light, Brass, Cage Form, Electrified, Continental, 22 In., Pair 3220.00
Chandelier, 6-Light, Brass, Gilt, Black, Pineapple Finial, French Style, 34 In. 1870.00
Chandelier, 6-Light, Brass, Glass Fruit, Jewel Chains, 2 Tiers, Italy, 43 x 25 In. 4370.00
Chandelier, 6-Light, Bronze, Foliated Circular Corona, Gilt, Louis Philippe, 24 In. 1035.00
Chandelier, 6-Light, Bronze, Laurel Leaf Border, Laurel Band, Napoleon III, 37 In. 2530.00
Chandelier, 6-Light, Candle Arms, Central Vine Form, Green, Blue Flowers, 35 In. 2300.00
Chandelier, 6-Light, Empire Style, Gilt Bronze, Crystal, c.1900, 45 x 25 In. 2990.00
Chandelier, 6-Light, Empire, Brass, Glass Shade, Sienna Marble Plinth, 18 In., Pair 4140.00
Chandelier, 6-Light, Empire, Gilt, Flared Beaded Chains, Electrified, 36 In. 345.00
Chandelier, 6-Light, Foliate Corona, Luster Ropes To Circles, Prism, 23 In. 1380.00
Chandelier, 6-Light, Gilt Bronze, Leaf Corona, Jasperware, George III, 36 x 19 In. 3450.00
Chandelier, 6-Light, Gilt Bronze, Scrolling Arms, Napoleon III, 37 x 33 In. 3680.00
Chandelier, 6-Light, Gilt Metal, Beaded, Prisms, Cage Shape, c.1900, 28 x 25 In. 1265.00
Chandelier, 6-Light, Gilt, Brass, Swan-Form Branches, 1900, 26 x 22 In. 805.00
Chandelier, 6-Light, Gilt, Bronze, Cut Crystal, Electrified, Louis XVI, 26 In. 4600.00
Chandelier, 6-Light, Gilt, Bronze, Eagle Terminals, Empire, Electrified, 12 In. 1495.00
Chandelier, 6-Light, Gilt, Bronze, Scrolled Branches, Louis XVI, 1900, 4 x 24 In. 4600.00
Chandelier, 6-Light, Hammered Metal, Arts & Crafts, Gold Aurene Shades, Chains 1870.00
Chandelier, 6-Light, Patinated, Brass, Cage Shape, Flat Prisms, Continental, 26 In. 1380.00
Chandelier, 6-Light, Prism Drops, Lustre Ropes, 18th Century Style, 15 x 18 In. 750.00
Chandelier, 6-Light, Raised Dished Wax Pans, Black Wrought Iron, 9 x 32 In. 750.00
Chandelier, 6-Light, Rococo Revival, Giltwood, Carved, Leaf Arms, Italy, 35 x 40 In. 2070.00
Chandelier, 6-Light, Scrolling Arms, Teardrop Prisms, Pendant Drop, c.1900, 28 In. 1265.00
Chandelier, 6-Light, Tin, Round, Flat Band, Metal Rod Link Suspenders, 26 In. 1725.00
Chandelier, 6-Light, Turned Column, Smoke Design, Red, Green Lines, Crimped, 25 In. . . 338.00
Chandelier, 6-Light, Wrought Iron, Black, Openwork, Scroll Arms, Continental, 45 In. . . . 405.00
Chandelier, 6-Light, Wrought Iron, Gilt, Glass Flowers, 1900, 28 x 20 In. 2530.00
Chandelier, 6-Light, Wrought Iron, Giltwood, Cream Paint, Italy, 1900, 40 x 24 In. 5520.00
Chandelier, 7-Light, Brass, Light Brown Matte Enamel, Leaves, 39 x 38 1/2 In., Pair 440.00
Chandelier, 7-Light, Rococo, Patinated Brass, Urn Shape Support, 37 x 28 In. 315.00
Chandelier, 7-Light, Tubular Chains, Ceiling Cap, Patinated Brass, 1920s, 37 x 28 In. 315.00
Chandelier, 8-Light, Brass, Circular Corona, Leaf Petal Nozzles, 32 In. 1725.00
Chandelier, 8-Light, Brass, Garlands Of Oval Crystals, Crystal Swags, 56 x 30 In. 6040.00
Chandelier, 8-Light, Brass, Neoclassical, Pinewood, Crystal, 36 x 26 In. 2990.00
Chandelier, 8-Light, Brass, Silvered, Eagle Finial, Pendant, Scroll Arms, 22 x 28 In. 2185.00
Chandelier, 8-Light, Bronze Dore, Pierced Bowl, Scrolled Arms, France, 55 x 28 In. 6040.00
Chandelier, 8-Light, Bronze, Iron, 8 Branches Issuing Circular Drip Pans, 68 In. 2070.00
Chandelier, 8-Light, Bronze, Louis XV, Cage Form, Allover Fruits, Amethyst, 41 In. 2160.00
Chandelier, 8-Light, C-Scroll Supports, Frosted Floriform Shades, 35 x 32 In. 1840.00
Chandelier, 8-Light, Carved Giltwood, Foliated Design, Pierced Circular Tier, 37 In. 2588.00
Chandelier, 8-Light, Cut Glass, Porcelain Flower Heads & Wrought Iron, 29 In. 1225.00
Chandelier, 8-Light, Empire, Brass, Acanthus Border, Pineapple Finial, France, 13 In. . . . 1035.00
Chandelier, 8-Light, Faceted Corona Over Standard, Glass Jewels, Drip Pans, 68 In. 2070.00
Chandelier, 8-Light, Gilt Bronze, Cage Shape, C-Scrolls, Louis XV, 35 x 32 In., Pair 1840.00
Chandelier, 8-Light, Gilt Bronze, Cut Crystal, Waterfall Chains, Baltic, 42 x 38 In. 4140.00
Chandelier, 8-Light, Gilt Bronze, Foliate Chains, Draped Urn, William IV, 29 In. 7190.00
Chandelier, 8-Light, Gilt Lacquered Brass, Leaves, Flowers, Crystal Prisms, 32 In. 2530.00
Chandelier, 8-Light, Gilt, Medallions & Scenes Of Courtship, Continental, 37 In. 1380.00
Chandelier, 8-Light, Neoclassical, Agente Bronze, Round Corona, Chains, 15 x 26 In. . . . 925.00
Chandelier, 8-Light, Neoclassical, Gilt Bronze, Cased Cranberry Glass, 30 x 32 In. 3220.00
Chandelier, 8-Light, Pricket, Sheet Iron Frame, Giltwood Drops, 47 x 42 In. 4025.00
Chandelier, 8-Light, Regency Style, Argent Bronze, c.1900, 29 x 34 In. 4600.00
Chandelier, 8-Light, Rococo Style, Gilt Bronze, Harp-Shape Standard, Beads, 28 In. 2875.00
Chandelier, 8-Light, Tole Painted, Gilt Brass, Restoration Style, c.1900, 27 x 21 In. 460.00
Chandelier, 9-Light, Brass, Gilt, White Opaline Glass Bowl, 1900, 35 In. 2760.00
Chandelier, 9-Light, Flower-Filled Basket Standard, Beads, Pendants, Leaves, 26 In. 9775.00
Chandelier, 9-Light, Pink Glass Standard, Foliate Arms, White Glass Flowers, 24 In. 1610.00

Chandelier, 9-Light, Scrolled Arms Ending In Nozzles, Amber Drops, 39 In. 5400.00
Chandelier, 10-Light, Cut Crystal, Sweeping Glass Arms, Chain Of Prisms, 44 In. 5060.00
Chandelier, 10-Light, Gilt Wrought Iron, Crystal, Waterfall, 2 Tiers, Italy, 40 x 26 In. 5290.00
Chandelier, 12-Light, 6 Upturned, 6 Downturned Branches, 1850s, 42 x 36 In. 1955.00
Chandelier, 12-Light, Gilt Brass, Rococo Style, Napoleon III, 32 x 23 In. 3220.00
Chandelier, 12-Light, Gilt Metal, Prisms, Scrolling Cage Shape, c.1900, 36 In. 1095.00
Chandelier, 12-Light, Neoclassical, Early 20th Century, 24 x 46 In. 2875.00
Chandelier, 12-Light, Rococo, Gilt Metal, Scrolling Standard, Amber Beads, 45 In. 4900.00
Chandelier, 12-Light, Swedish Neoclassical, Gilt Bronze, Crystal, 46 x 23 In. 3450.00
Chandelier, 16-Light, 8 Foliate Candle Branches, Luster Ropes, 33 x 33 1/2 In. 345.00
Chandelier, 16-Light, Electric, Wrought Steel, Scrolls, Spiral, Chain, 32 x 47 In. 1430.00
Chandelier, 16-Light, Regency Style, Gilt Brass, Prism Drops, 24 1/2 x 32 3/4 In. 1093.00
Chandelier, 18-Light, Corona Draped With Jewel, Chains, Pendants, 36 In. 800.00
Chandelier, 18-Light, Gilt Metal, Crystal, Electrified, Louis XVI, 50 x 30 In. 1380.00
Chandelier, 18-Light, Neoclassical, Giltwood, Scrolled Branches, Italy, 1900, 46 In. 2990.00
Chandelier, 24-Light, 2 Tiers, Bronze Dore, Crystal, Napoleon III, Late 1800s, 41 In. 9200.00
Chandelier, 24-Light, Neoclassical, Brass, Scrolled Branches, Italy, 40 x 30 In. 4140.00
Chandelier, 28-Light, Rococo Style, Bronzed Dore, Water Leaves, Flowers, 41 x 35 In. 1840.00
Chandelier, 30-Light, Mask Relief Design, Floral, Scroll, Early 20th Century, 64 In. 1955.00
Chandelier, 33-Light, Brass, Circular Corona, Knop Pendants, 45 x 36 In. 3680.00
Chandelier, Alabaster Segments, 12 Curved Arms, c.1930, 28 1/2 In. 750.00
Chandelier, Amethyst, Spiral Ribbed Body, Electrified, 28 In. 660.00
Chandelier, Art Nouveau, Gilt Metal, Glass, Ceramic Oil Font, 17 In. 550.00
Chandelier, Arts & Crafts, Brass, Slag Glass Inserts, Original Patina, 27 In. 805.00
Chandelier, Arts & Crafts, Faceted, Slag Glass, Leaded, Black Enamel Body, 8 x 11 In. . . 345.00
Chandelier, Arts & Crafts, Leaded Geometric, 30 x 11 In. 375.00
Chandelier, Brass, Bronze, Domed Corona, Angels, Swags & Cabochons, 62 In., Pair 2185.00
Chandelier, Brass, Round Corona, Crystal Draped Jewel Chain, Knop Pendant, 45 In. . . . 3680.00
Chandelier, Bronze, Alabaster, Albert Cheuret, c.1925, 15 In. 7200.00
Chandelier, Bronze, Colored Crystal, Metal Framing, Crystal Flowers & Drops 2185.00
Chandelier, Bronze, Gilt, Glass Beads, Portrait Medallions, 46 In. 6000.00
Chandelier, Bronze, Gilt, Lattice Basket, Early 20th Century, 54 In. 5100.00
Chandelier, Floral Corona, Faceted Pendants, Electrified, 32 x 18 In. 2185.00
Chandelier, Grissaille Decorated, Mustard Tole, Antique Oil Lamp Shape, France, 16 In. . 920.00
Chandelier, Leaded Grapes & Grapevines, Art Glass, 25 x 16 In. 635.00
Chandelier, Milk & Clear Glass Lenses, Henry Dreyfuss, Signed, 1957, 8 1/2 In. 575.00
Chandelier, Rococo Style, Light Blue, Beads, Pendants, 25 In. 1610.00
Chandelier, Ropes Of Cut Glass Prisms & Beads, Floral Branches, 23 1/2 x 29 In. 7800.00
Chandelier, Silver, Bronze Beads, Emile-Jacques Ruhlmann, 1925, 22 1/4 In. 9600.00
Chandelier, Slag Glass Shade, Milk Glass Smoke Bell, Prism Drops, 30 In. 752.00
Chandelier, Slag Glass, Leaf, Floral Design, Yellow, White, Green Border, 17 x 20 In. . . . 575.00
Chandelier, Triangular Mount, 3 Link Chains, Slag Glass, 20th Century, 23 1/2 In. 630.00
Desk, Chrome, Copper, Arched Rectangular Shade, Art Deco, 10 3/4 x 7 1/2 In. 421.00
Electric, 2 Halogen Fixtures, Black Metal Shaft, Concrete Base, Arad, c.1980, 73 In. 8050.00
Electric, 4-Light, Hanging, Leaded Glass, Multicolored Floral, 24 In. 7280.00
Electric, 4-Light, Limbert, Windmills, Children, Glass Shade, Lighthouse Form, 5 In. 8635.00
Electric, 4-Light, Metal, Brass Top, Original Patina, Tommi Parzinger, 8 x 45 In. 575.00
Electric, 6-Sided Shade & Base, 6 Die Cut Peacocks, 3-Light, Copper Panels, 22 In. 7280.00
Electric, 6-Sided Shade, Copper Base, Mica Inserts, 3-Light, 21 3/4 In. 3584.00
Electric, Achille Castiglione, Spherical Bright Chrome Shade, Marble Base, 90 In. 900.00
Electric, Adjustable Aluminum Shade, Aluminum Base, Signed, Artemide, 46 x 9 In. 460.00
Electric, Adjustable Chrome Frame, Black Base, Herbert H. Schultes, Classicon, 22 In. . . 240.00
Electric, Adjustable Shade, Black Enameled Metal Base, 18 x 102 In., Pair 690.00
Electric, Adjustable Tole Shade, 3-Light, 3 C-Scroll Branches, Candle Cups, 21 3/4 In. . . 258.00
Electric, Alabaster, Variegated Gray, White, Dish Shape, Medial Tassel Ceiling, 43 In. . . . 805.00
Electric, Aluminum, Machine Age Design, Pattyn Product, 8 x 20 In. 3450.00
Electric, Armillary Sphere, Patinated Brass, Half Shade, Base, Grain Painted, 26 In. 865.00
Electric, Art Deco, Fan Shape, Bronze Mount, Alabaster, France, 1930, Pair 6000.00
Electric, Art Deco, Figural, Standing Woman, Flowing Dress & Muff, Porcelain, 31 In. . . 405.00
Electric, Art Deco, Miller Co., Brass Flared Shade, Tiered Base, Signed, 12 x 64 In. 105.00
Electric, Art Deco, Women Warriors, Rearing Horses, Alabaster Shade, 9 In. 470.00
Electric, Art Nouveau, 6-Sided Shade, Lighted Column, Flower Cutouts, 21 In. 3450.00
Electric, Art Nouveau, Bronze, Young Girl, Flowers In Hair, Circular Onyx Base, 16 In. . 3450.00

Electric, Art Nouveau, Girl With Harp Transfer, Vines On Side, Brass Base, Finial, 34 In. 55.00
Electric, Art Nouveau, Mission Oak, Umbrella Shade, Table 500.00
Electric, Art Nouveau, Nautilus Shell, Flower On Leaf-Shape Base, Brown, 16 In. 4140.00
Electric, Artichoke, Hennington 7600.00
Electric, Arts & Crafts, Copper, Hammered, Enameled, Stylized Design, 19 In. 230.00
Electric, Arts & Crafts, Leaded Geometric Border, Bronze Metal Base, 16 x 20 In. 635.00
Electric, Arts & Crafts, Mica Shade, Chicago Lamp & Frame Co., Signed, 64 In. 750.00
Electric, Arts & Crafts, Oak, Slag Glass, 22 x 14 1/2 x 14 1/2 In. 805.00
Electric, Arts & Crafts, Original Green Glass Shade, 15 x 15 x 22 In. 405.00
Electric, Benedict Studios, Copper, Hammered, Domed Shade, Mica Panels, 20 In. 3740.00
Electric, Billiard, 12 Scrolling Arms, Glass Globes, Brass, 40 x 72 In. 6600.00
Electric, Bird Design, Cast Iron, Shade, c.1920-1930, 7 3/4 In. 155.00
Electric, Bird, Vining Floral Design, Orange Ground, 12 In., Pair 400.00
Electric, Black Forest, 2 Stag Antlers, Chip-Carved Base, Boar, 6 Glass Panels, 22 In. . . . 210.00
Electric, Black Forest, Bear With Cub In Forest, 1895, 18 In. 2295.00
Electric, Black Spherical Shade, Chrome Light Reflector, Mario Fortuni, 67 In. 1800.00
Electric, Black Tubular Metal Shafts, Conical Concrete White Base, Arad, 1980, 73 In. . . 8050.00
Electric, Bohemian Glass, Cobalt Blue, Gold Floral Blossoms, 10 In. 2464.00
Electric, Boudoir, Reverse Painted, Water Lilies, Arts & Crafts, 14 In. 470.00
Electric, Brass Luster Base, White Cut To Cranberry Shade, Czechoslovakia, 27 In., Pair . 250.00
Electric, Brass, Candlestick Shape, Drip Pan, Contemporary, No Shade, 54 1/2 In. 110.00
Electric, Brass, Figural, Heron Under Flowering Plant, 64 1/2 In. 2255.00
Electric, Brass, Hammered, Parchment Shade, Wiener Werkstatte, 16 x 8 In. 9775.00
Electric, Brass, Hanging, Urn Shape, Putti Mask, Acorn, Ring Drop, 1800s, 38 In. 339.00
Electric, Brass, Maiden Posed Under Baldachin, Gilt, Porcelain, France, 15 x 6 In. 3680.00
Electric, Bronze, Allegorical Figure Against Tree, Acanthus Cast Base, 26 In., Pair 3000.00
Electric, Bronze, Art Nouveau, Oscar Bach, Dolphins, Green, Fluted Post, c.1920, 33 In. . 605.00
Electric, Bronze, Boy With Flute & Lizard, Bronze Footed Base, 20th Century, 22 In. . . . 90.00
Electric, Bronze, Bust Of Indian Maidens On Standard, Birds, Dragons, Gilt, 17 In. 2040.00
Electric, Bronze, Coiled Snake Base, Austria, 11 In. 3640.00
Electric, Bronze, Leaf Capital, Columnar Standard, Salt & Lloyd, No Shade, 1861, 21 In. 520.00
Electric, Bronze, Middle Eastern Princess Upon Chaise, 2 Servants, Chotka, 15 In. 3920.00
Electric, Bronze, Reticulated, Leaded Glass, Floral & Geometric Border, 36 In. 465.00
Electric, Bronze, Woman, Long Skirt, With Umbrella, P. Tereszczuk, No Shade, 14 In. . . . 1045.00
Electric, Call Of The Wild, Reverse Painted, Domed Shade, Moonlit Lake, 18 In. 4480.00
Electric, Cantilevered Arm, Base, Shade, Von Nessen, Brushed Steel, Adjustable, 60 In. . . 805.00
Electric, Caramel & Green Slag Glass, Metal Foliate Borders, 4 Metal Feet, 25 In. 145.00
Electric, Carcel, Brass, Columns, Pedestal Base, Leaf Border Plinth, Charles X, 35 In. . . . 1095.00
Electric, Carcel, Gilt, Classical Mount Pedestal, Leaf Border, Empire, 25 In., Pair 8625.00
Electric, Carved Clusters Of Leaves, Ebonized, Rectangular Base, 30 In., Pair 400.00
Electric, Cased Glass, Gilt Bronze, Victorian, White Cut To Ruby, 20 x 11 x 10 In. 1150.00
Electric, Chase, Ball Design, No. 6166, Alden, Table Or Wall, c.1939-1941, 15 In. 70.00
Electric, Chicago Mosaic, Cherry Tree, Glass, Domed Shade, Tree-Trunk Base, 18 In. 2240.00
Electric, Chicago Mosaic, Pink Blossoms, Green Leaves, Amber Ground, 19 In. 2185.00
Electric, Chicago Mosaic, Pink Floral Blossoms, Green Leaves, Caramel Ground, 18 In. . 2240.00
Electric, Chicago Mosaic, Pink, Pale Pink Flowers, Leaded Glass, Signed, 18 In. 3360.00
Electric, Chrome Wire Shaft, Adjustable Crane, Weighted Metal Base, Leviton, 48 In. . . . 920.00
Electric, Chrome, Aco, Sewing Arm, Spherical Shade, Marble Base, Castiglione, 91 In. . . . 1120.00
Electric, Chrome, Weighted Black Base, Pat Hoffman, 1969, 48 x 16 x 10 In. 506.00
Electric, Classical, Pressed Glass, Gilt Brass, Square Base, Diamond Design, 40 3/4 In. . . . 440.00
Electric, Classique, Dirt Road Scene, Trees, Green Meadows, 18 In. 2240.00
Electric, Cloisonne, Blue, Brass Base, Double Socket, Footed, 30 In. 450.00
Electric, Columnar, Empire, Brass Mounted, Black Faux Marble, Stepped Base, 34 In. 345.00
Electric, Columnar, Spiral Turned, Brown, Parcel Gilt, Square Plinth Base, 28 In. 145.00
Electric, Conical Mica Shade, Hammered, Metal Overlay, Arts & Crafts, 18 In. 2530.00
Electric, Copper Plate, Elongated Rectangular Shade, Faries Mfg. Co., 12 x 20 In. 265.00
Electric, Copper, Hammered, Original Patina, Arts & Crafts, 18 x 10 1/2 In. 2875.00
Electric, Cylindrical Beige Fiberglass Shade, 3 Tubular Brass Legs, 14 x 14 In. 290.00
Electric, Deer, Green Ceramic, Bulb Illuminates Behind The Deer, Art Deco, 11 x 12 In. . 59.00
Electric, Desk, Bauhaus, Brown Enameled Metal, Adjustable, Coiled Shaft, 16 x 6 In. 196.00
Electric, Desk, Black Enameled Shade, Brass Arm, 1950s, 17 x 16 In. 55.00
Electric, Desk, Dark Green Shade, Aluminum, Bakelite, Walter Teague, 1941, 12 In. 2300.00
Electric, Desk, Eagle, Green Case Shade 504.00

Electric, Desk, Emeralite, Floral Border 1570.00
Electric, Desk, G. Stickley, Oak Base, Wrought Iron Support Holding Shade, 18 1/2 In. . . 5225.00
Electric, Desk, Harp, Durand-Type Bell-Shape Shade, Blue, Green, Purple, Gold Interior . 1100.00
Electric, Desk, Metal, Wangenfeld, Chrome, Black Enameled, Cupped Shade, 17 In. 280.00
Electric, Desk, Reverse Painted, Woodland Scene, Pittsburgh Type, 14 1/2-In. Shade 310.00
Electric, Dish, Alabaster, Amber, Repousse Gilt Brass, Leaves, Rosette Ornaments, 25 In. 920.00
Electric, Domed Glass Shade, Pink Flower, Pointed Leaf Border, 25 In. 1150.00
Electric, Duffner & Kimberly, Amber Glass, Green, Domed Shade, 19 In. 4200.00
Electric, Duffner & Kimberly, Bell Shade, Pink, White Striated Blossoms, 20 In. 10640.00
Electric, Duffner & Kimberly, Berries & Green Leaves, Domed Shade, 16 In. 10080.00
Electric, Duffner & Kimberly, Greek Key Border, Geometric Brickwork, 20 In. 6160.00
Electric, Duffner & Kimberly, Lavender Floral, Geometrics, Domed Shade, 19 In. 3360.00
Electric, Duffner & Kimberly, Leaded Glass, Amber, 3-Footed Bronze Base, 18 In. 3920.00
Electric, Duffner & Kimberly, Leaded Glass, Bell Shape, Bronze Base, 18 In. 5600.00
Electric, Duffner & Kimberly, Leaded Glass, Domed Shade, Geometric, 3-Light, 19 In. . . 3640.00
Electric, Duffner & Kimberly, Scrolled Leaf Lower Border, Yellow, Orange Red, 20 In. . . 9520.00
Electric, Duffner & Kimberly, Stylized Flowers, Ribbon Border, 22 In. 6720.00
Electric, Empire, Gilt Vine, Branches With Bird Terminals, Green Paint, 1900, 21 In. . . . 690.00
Electric, Enameled Metal, Swiveling Shaft, Adjustable, Stilnovo, 18 x 15 In. 230.00
Electric, Enameled, Flowers & Dragons, Blue Ground, Brass, Black Shade, 8 In. 165.00
Electric, Farmland Scene, Metal Base, 18 In. 1175.00
Electric, Figural, Woman Holding 4-Light Lamp, Fish, Acanthus Leaf, c.1900, 50 In. 375.00
Electric, Floral Shade, Foliage, Violet, White Striated Glass Ground, Metal Base, 24 In. . . 8900.00
Electric, Floral Shade, Green Leaves, Bronze Tree-Trunk Base, 21 In. 5600.00
Electric, Floral Shade, Yellow, Orange, Green, Blue, Brass Frame, 57 In. 660.00
Electric, Flower Basket, U.S. Glass Co., Molded, 8 In. 220.00
Electric, Flower Border Shade, Leaded, 3 Panels, Slag, Bronze Base, 18 x 26 In. 575.00
Electric, Fontana Arte, Mahogany, Glass, 1955, 74 In. 8400.00
Electric, Fruitwood, Corinthian Columns, Fluted, Square Stepped Base, 35 3/4 In. 230.00
Electric, G. Stickley, Copper, Hammered, Silk-Lined Wicker Shade, 24 x 18 In. 5625.00
Electric, G. Stickley, Copper, Hammered, Split Bamboo Shade, Silk, Iron, 26 In. 8625.00
Electric, Geometric Amber Glass Shade, Bands Of Jewels Around Apron, 16 In. 2800.00
Electric, Geometric Design, Leaded Glass Shade, Oak Base, Prairie School, 21 x 30 In. . . 2415.00
Electric, Gilbert Rohde, Linen Shade, White Marble Base, Chrome Shaft, 16 x 62 In. 575.00
Electric, Gilt Lacquer, Cream Paint, Flowers, Circular Tole Shade, Louis XVI, 22 In. 1610.00
Electric, Glass Pedestal, Molded, Wheel Cut Design, 4 In., Pair 145.00
Electric, Glass, Argente Brass, Fluted Column, Ribbed Pedestal, Plinth, Paw Feet, 22 In. . 546.00
Electric, Gothic, Bronze, Trumpet Base With Fruiting Vine, 38 In., Pair 1725.00
Electric, Hall, Gilt Brass, Cage Shape, Prism Hung, Amber Teardrops, Pendant, 26 In. . . . 550.00
Electric, Hammered Copper, 3 Open Buttresses, Fringe, Stickley Brothers, 19 x 14 In. . . . 4400.00
Electric, Hanging, 5 Amber Glass Shades, Copper Patina Inset, 16 In., Pair 460.00
Electric, Hanging, 6 Panels, Bird, Flower, Butterfly Design, Early 20th Century, 16 In. . . . 100.00
Electric, Hanging, Alabaster, Patinated Bronze, Bowl Shape, Italy, c.1900, 36 x 18 In. . . . 2300.00
Electric, Hanging, Arts & Crafts, Wooden, Colored Glass, Original Finish, 10 x 12 In. 175.00
Electric, Hanging, Black Enameled, Tubular Shape, Oval Fixtures, 41 x 6 1/2 In., Pair . . . 1010.00
Electric, Hanging, Bronze, Blue Cut To Clear Glass, Link Chains, England, 56 In., Pair . . 5290.00
Electric, Hanging, Cast Metal, Slag Glass, 8 Panels, Mountain Scene, 22 x 22 x 11 In. . . . 230.00
Electric, Hanging, Duffner & Kimberly, Vine, Red, Green, White Brickwork, 28 In. 14560.00
Electric, Hanging, Floral, Burgundy, Pink Blossoms, Green, Leaves, Williamson, 24 In. . . 3920.00
Electric, Hanging, Hall, Brass, Egg Shape, Dolphins & Scrolls, 11 x 18 In. 410.00
Electric, Hanging, Horn Of Plenty, Multicolored Flowers, Amidst Leaves, 26 In. 14000.00
Electric, Hanging, Leaded Glass Shade, Grape Cluster, Leaf, Carmel, 20 1/4 In. 750.00
Electric, Hanging, Leaded Glass, Floral & Fruit, 6 Ft. Chain, 19 1/2 In. 195.00
Electric, Hanging, Leaded Glass, Floral Design, Blue & Green Ground, 24 x 12 In. 175.00
Electric, Hanging, Paul Henningsen, Chrome, White Enameled Interior, 28 x 32 In. 5625.00
Electric, Hanging, Pool Table, Bronze, Lion Heads, Floral Leaded Shades, 1910, 32 In. . . 13440.00
Electric, Hessen, Circular Parchment Shade, Leather Lacing, Brass Bases, 62 In., Pair . . . 955.00
Electric, I. Noguchi, Gray Over White, Paper Shade, Japan, 10 x 17 In. 195.00
Electric, I. Noguchi, Table, Bamboo Shaft, Black Metal Base, Silk Shade, 26 In. 730.00
Electric, Jefferson, Chipped Ice Base, Signed, 18 In. 4600.00
Electric, Jefferson, Domed, Allover Floral Design, 18 In. 4200.00
Electric, Jefferson, Nature Scene, Water, Trees, Yellow Sky, Domed Shade, 18 In. 3920.00
Electric, Jefferson, Reverse Painted, Forest Fire, Bronze Base, 18 In. 2010.00

Electric, Jefferson, Reverse Painted, House, Road, Bronzed Metal Base, 22 In. 805.00
Electric, Jefferson, Reverse Painted, Moonlight Lake, 21 x 16 In. 1650.00
Electric, Jefferson, Reverse Painted, Moonlight Red Sky, Tapestry, 21x 18 In. 1870.00
Electric, Jefferson, Woodland Scene Interior, Domed Shade, Signed, 18 In. 4030.00
Electric, Laurel Lamp Co., Brass, Angled Shade, Tubular Shaft, 18 3/4 x 12 In. 170.00
Electric, Laurel Lamp Co., Mushroom-Shaped Shades, Orange Base, 17 In., Pair 620.00
Electric, Laurel Lamp Co., Steel Base, White Glass Shade, Aluminum Holder, 66 In. 320.00
Electric, Leaded Glass, Domed Shade, Irregular Border, Shell Motif, 24 In. 6720.00
Electric, Light Green Leaded Glass, Pink Floral Border, Deep Green Leaves, 18 In. 1900.00
Electric, Light Mahogany, Birch Cone-Shape Base, Brass Trim, Calvin, 14 x 35 In., Pair . 405.00
Electric, Limbert, Arts & Crafts, Hammered Copper, Paneled Shade, Slag Glass, 28 In. . . 1095.00
Electric, Limbert, Brass, Die Cut Shade, Geese In Flight, Man Pulling Barge, 27 In. 8500.00
Electric, Limbert, Copper, Hammered, Pyramid Shade, American Eagle, 26 In. 4025.00
Electric, Limbert, Copper, Mica Die Cut Shade, 2 Loop Handles, 20 In. 7425.00
Electric, Limbert, Die Cut Shade, Geese In Flight, Man Pulling Barge, 4-Light, 25 In. . . . 8680.00
Electric, Limbert, Square Cutouts, Top Mortised Through Sides, 27 x 30 In. 4885.00
Electric, Marble, Cast Metal Figurine, Woman Holding Wreath, Socket Covers, 19 In. . . . 390.00
Electric, Marble, Urn Shape, Carved Floral Decoration, 20th Century, 15 1/2 In., Pair 195.00
Electric, Mermaid, Forming Fish Scales, Purple, Green Ground, 8 Panels, 17 In. 16240.00
Electric, Metal Shade, Bare Breasted Female In Egyptian Attire, Art Nouveau, 17 In. 1265.00
Electric, Mica Shade, Metal Overlay, Square Base, Footed, Patina, 17 x 10 x 10 1/2 In. . . 520.00
Electric, Moe-Bridges, Cone Shade, Geese In Flight Against Orange Sky, 18 In. 7840.00
Electric, Moe-Bridges, Landscape Of Lake Surrounded By Trees, 23 x 18 In. 4600.00
Electric, Moe-Bridges, Landscape Scene, Orange, Green, Reverse Painted, 15 In. 1840.00
Electric, Moe-Bridges, Reverse Painted Shade, River & Landscape, Signed, 18 In. 2185.00
Electric, Moe-Bridges, Reverse Painted, Flock Of Ducks, Bronze Base, Signed, 24 In. . . . 4125.00
Electric, Moe-Bridges, Reverse Painted, Landscape, Bronze Base, 20 1/2 In. 1650.00
Electric, Moe-Bridges, Woodland Scene Interior, Hills, Trees, Domed Shade, 18 In. 4480.00
Electric, Moe-Bridges, Woodland Scene, 16 In. 1960.00
Electric, Multicolored Flowers, Birds, Geometric, Green Glass, Domed Shade, 19 In. 4760.00
Electric, Mushroom Table Lamp, Orange Fiberglass, Nesso, Artimede, 13 x 21 In., Pair . . 390.00
Electric, Night-Light, White Owl, Glass Eyes, Contemporary, 9 In. 50.00
Electric, Nocturnal Scene, Buildings, Reverse Painted, Bronzed Base, 14 x 8 In. 460.00
Electric, Nude Supporting Globe, Cast Bronze, Amber & Fuchsia, M. Bouraine, 37 In. . . . 1495.00
Electric, Painted & Parcel, Egyptian Female, Papyrus Fronds, Tole Shade, 47 In., Pair . . . 5400.00
Electric, Panther On Tree, Planter, Swirled Chartreuse & Brown, Painted Shade, 1950s . . . 125.00
Electric, Parrot, Hand Painted, Lamp In Beak, 15 In. . . . . .320.00 to 550.00
Electric, Paul Henningson, Nickel Steel, Shade, 1933, 11 1/2 In. 5100.00
Electric, Peacock, Whimsical, Glass Beadwork Tail, Agate Column, 26 In. 2530.00
Electric, Pendant, Adjustable White Metal Rings, Verner Panton, 1960, 14 x 14 In. 546.00
Electric, Piano, Brass, J.M. Co., Pat. Sept. 25, 1906, 4 1/2 x 13 1/2 x 12 3/4 In. 55.00
Electric, Pink, Green, Caramel Slag Glass, Poppies, Copper Base, 23 In. 1840.00
Electric, Pittsburgh, Call Of The Wild, Moonlit Sky, Domed Shade, Owl Base, 18 In. 3920.00
Electric, Pittsburgh, Geometric, Dark Green Glass, Daffodils, 19 In. 670.00
Electric, Pittsburgh, Light Brown, Cream, Domed Shade, Original Base, 15 In. 1735.00
Electric, Pittsburgh, Multicolored Rose Blossoms Interior 3640.00
Electric, Pittsburgh, Opaque Body, Dahlias, Leafy Stems, Label, V. Linstrand, 13 In. 1495.00
Electric, Pittsburgh, Reverse Painted, Call Of The Wild, Teepee On Shore, 18 In. 4480.00
Electric, Pittsburgh, Reverse Painted, English Mill & Stream, Domed Shade, 20 In. 1120.00
Electric, Pittsburgh, Reverse Painted, Woodland Scene, Metal, Art Nouveau, 18 In. 495.00
Electric, Pittsburgh, Swan, Trees Exterior, Swans Swimming In Small Pond, 16 In. 3000.00
Electric, Pittsburgh, Winter Forest Scene & Sleigh Interior, 6 Panels, 16 In. 5600.00
Electric, Pittsburgh, Woodland Scene, Lake, Sun In Background, Domed Shade, 18 In. 2800.00
Electric, Pittsburgh, Yellow, White Daffodils, Floral, 16 In. 2800.00
Electric, Porcelain, Crackle, Allegorical Battle Scene, Pickled Wood, Chinese, 29 In. 230.00
Electric, Porcelain, Figural, Woman Standing, Applied Flowers On Hat & Dress, 16 In. . . 110.00
Electric, Porcelain, Portrait Of Girl, Flowers, Gilding, Cobalt Ground, 24 1/2 In. 460.00
Electric, Prairie, Leaded Glass Domed Shade, Trellis, Amber, Green, 18 1/2 x 18 In. 790.00
Electric, Reverse Painted, Lake Landscape, Rocky Shore, Brass Base, Floral, 21 In. 920.00
Electric, Reverse Painted, Landscape, Bridge, Water, Bronzed Base, 14 x 8 In. 1840.00
Electric, Reverse Painted, Water & Trees, Bronze Metal, 18 x 25 In. 410.00
Electric, Reverse Painted, Winter Landscape, Purple, Blue, Gold Painted Base, 21 In. 3850.00
Electric, Rococo Style, Bronze, Leaves, Cattails, Sea Creatures, Iridescent Shades, 31 In. . 5175.00

Electric, Sailing Vessels Scenes In Moonlit Bay, Domed Shade, Signed, Broggi, 18 In. 6400.00
Electric, Scenic, Reverse Painted, Windmill & House, Purple Sky, 18 In. 896.00
Electric, Stickley Bros., Copper & Brass, 6-Sided Pierced Shade, 21 In. 3920.00
Electric, Stickley Bros., Copper, 6-Sided Shade, Caramel Glass Inserts, 4 Sockets, 67 In. . 11110.00
Electric, Stickley Bros., Copper, Brass, 6-Sided Shade, Gold Opalescent Panels, 21 In. 7350.00
Electric, Stickley Bros., Copper, Hammered, 6 Embossed Peacock Panels, 22 In. 2530.00
Electric, Stickley Bros., Copper, Hammered, Mica Shade, Copper Overlay, 23 In. 5750.00
Electric, Stickley Bros., Copper, Hammered, Yellow, Caramel Inserts Shade, 19 In. 4900.00
Electric, Stickley Bros., Copper, Helmet, Hammered Shade, 2 Sockets, 17 3/4 In. 3410.00
Electric, Stickley Bros., Copper, Pyramid Shade, Caramel Opalescent Glass Panels, 21 In. 4180.00
Electric, Stickley Bros., Copper, Teardrop, Opalescent Caramel Glass Inserts, 21 In. 3740.00
Electric, Stickley Bros., Helmet, 2-Light, Hammered Copper Shade & Base, 17 3/4 In. 3470.00
Electric, Student, 2-Light, Emeralite, Model 8734, 19 In. 400.00
Electric, Student, 2-Light, Plume & Atwood, Scrolled Leaf, Tanks, Green Cased Shades .. 5500.00
Electric, Student, 4-Light, Nickel Over Glass, 25 In. 7150.00
Electric, Student, Brass Base & Counter Balance, Milk Glass Domed Shade, 19 x 14 In. .. 49.00
Electric, Student, Brass, Green Shade, Late 19th Century, 19 1/4 In. 305.00
Electric, Suess, Stylized Burgundy Geometric Flowers, Green Garlands, 18 In. 4480.00
Electric, Sunset Lamp Co., Brass, Chrome Plate, Flared Linen Shade, California, 62 In. .. 730.00
Electric, Swirling Floral Leaves, Green, White Striated Glass, Domed Shade, 16 In. 5600.00
Electric, Television, Lane, Afghan Hound, Bronze Tone 85.00
Electric, TV, Mallard 85.00
Electric, TV, Peacock, Standing, Colorful 115.00
Electric, TV, Planter Base, Fiberglass Shade, 14K Gold 40.00
Electric, Twin Neck Embossed, Lizard Figures, Terra-Cotta, Blue Matte, Floor, 32 In. ... 140.00
Electric, Twirling Woman Draped In Flowing Robe, Bronze, Raoul Larche, 13 In. 8050.00
Electric, Urn Shape, Fruitwood, Carved, Plinth Base, 27 1/2 In., Pair 290.00
Electric, Urn Shape, Giltwood, Ebonized, Carved, Stylized Leaves, 28 In., Pair 260.00
Electric, Vase Shape, Blue & White Sawtooth, Etched Flowers, Spelter Base 220.00
Electric, White Enameled Cone-Shaped, Black Leather Handles, Arteluce, 72 In. 3260.00
Electric, White Enameled, Adjustable Helmet-Shaped Shade, Chrome Base, 17 In. 230.00
Electric, White Opaque Glass Tiles, Leaded Shade, 6 Pink Flowers, Green Leaves, 21 In. . 575.00
Electric, White Plastic Rotating Shade, Black Enameled Hemisphere Fixture, 24 In. 315.00
Electric, Wiener Werkstatte, Brass, Stepped Geometric Design, Square Base, 8 In. 1095.00
Electric, Wilkinson, Bent Panel, Bronze, Caramel Glass, Leaf, Green Glass, 20 In. 3360.00
Electric, Wilkinson, Leaded Glass, Waterlily, 23 In. 7700.00
Electric, Wilkinson, Nasturtium Blossoms, Red, Green, Yellow, Bronze Base, 20 In. 8120.00
Electric, Wilkinson, Water Lily, Leaded Glass, Multicolored, Bronze Cattail Base, 20 In. . 7840.00
Electric, Wilkinson, Water Lily, Leaded Shade, 23 In. 7700.00
Electric, Windmill Scene With Boat In Bay, Domed Shade, 18 In. 1345.00
Electric, Woman, Standing, Clutching Her Kimono, Japan, 14 1/2 In. 230.00
Electric, Wood Laminated, Linen Parchment Shade, Phil Powell, 1956, 36 1/2 In. 1800.00
Electric, Wrought Iron, Adjustable, Linen Shade, Jean Royere, 80 x 22 In. 22600.00
Electric, Wrought Iron, Copper, Hammered, Mica Shade, Arts & Crafts, 65 x 14 In. 281.00
Fairy, Burmese Shade, Signed, Clarke, 6 1/4 x 7 1/2 In. 2015.00
Fairy, Nailsea, Blue & White, Clarke, c.1870-1895 .... 1200.00
Fairy, Pyramid Shape Clarke Base, Pink Satin Glass, 3 1/2 In. 135.00
Fairy, White Loopings, 8 Turned-Up, Turned-Down Scallops, Clarke Cup, 5 1/4 In. 1135.00
Fairy, White, Light Pink Neck, Burmese, 5 In., Pair 560.00
Fat, Brass, Heart Cutouts, 18th Century, 7 In. 395.00
Fat, Iron, Punched Design, Hanging, 18th Century, 22 In. 295.00
Figural, Standing Sage, Carved Hardstone, Chinese, 28 In. 345.00
Flared Peach Glass Shade, Chrome Dome Base, Art Deco, 13 3/4 x 11 1/2 In. 562.00
Fluid, Blown Glass Overlay, White To Clear, Gold Highlights, Brass, Marble Base, 11 In. .. 316.00
Fluid, Boston & Sandwich, Crossbar Base, Light Bulb Shape Font, c.1840, 12 In., Pair ... 470.00
Fluid, Cut To Cranberry, Florals, Electrified, Early 20th Century, 14 In., Pair 170.00
Fluid, Pressed Glass, Acanthus Leaf, Reeded Brass Stem, Square Marble Base, 11 1/2 In. . 60.00
Fluid, Pressed Glass, Argus, 6-Sided Wafer Stem, Foot, 8 1/2 In. 110.00
Fluid, Pressed Glass, Bellflower, Wafer Stem, Brass Collar, 7 1/4 In. 80.00
Fluid, Pressed Glass, Blown Conical Font, Bladed Wafer Steps, Domed Base, 6 7/8 In. 140.00
Fluid, Pressed Glass, Bull's-Eye Variant, Elongated Font, 6 Panels, 9 In. 85.00
Fluid, Pressed Glass, Bull's-Eye, Fleur-De-Lis & Heart, Square Marble Base, 9 1/2 In. 100.00
Fluid, Pressed Glass, Diamond Thumbprint, Clambroth, Blue Floral Stem, 11 In., Pair 1450.00

Fluid, Pressed Glass, Hairpin, 15 Panels, Pewter Collar, Single Tube Burner 210.00
Fluid, Pressed Glass, Hinoto Variant, Milk Glass Base, Brass Connector, Gilt, 11 In. 90.00
Fluid, Pressed Glass, Inverted Diamond & Thumbprint, Wafer Stem, 9 In. 120.00
Fluid, Pressed Glass, Lyre Pattern, Brass Standard, Marble Base, 9 In., Pair 230.00
Fluid, Pressed Glass, Prism Ring, Ornate Metal Ring, 2 x 7 x 1 7/8 In. 80.00
Fluid, Pressed Glass, Waffle & Thumbprint, 6-Sided Stem, Base, 9 7/8 In. 50.00
Fluid, Pressed Glass, Waffle & Thumbprint, Handle, Feather, Pewter Collar, 4 x 7 In. 210.00
Fluid, Pressed, Blown Glass, Etched Green Font, Amber Dolphin Pedestal, Base, 12 In. . . 430.00
Fluid, Ring Punty & Heart, Brass Connector, Square Black Glass Base, Gilt, 10 In. 160.00
Fluid, Swirled Amethyst Glass Fonts, Brass Standard, Marble Base, c.1880, 15 In., Pair . . 365.00
Gas, Brass, Caramel Slag Glass 6-Panel Shade, Electrified, 23 x 17 In. 385.00
Gas, Cherub, Holding Cornucopia, Thumbprint Shade, Portable, Electrified, 1790, 19 In. . 695.00
Gasolier, 3-Light, Gilt Lacquered, Patinated Bronze, Antimony, Glass Shades, 28 In. 3910.00
Gasolier, 6-Light, Gilt Lacquered Bronze, Glass Shades, Electrified, 48 x 34 In. 6900.00
Grease, Hanging, Continental Iron Hooks, 18th Century, Pair 125.00
Grease, Saucer Base, Long Spout, Tan Glaze, 7 In. 165.00
Handel lamps are included in the Handel category.
Jefferson, Reverse Painted Shade, Lake Landscape, Bronzed Base, 23 In. 4140.00
Kerosene, Banquet, Brass, Stepped Tripod Base, Acanthus Leaves, Electrified, 28 In. 190.00
Kerosene, Banquet, Cast Metal, Swan Finial, Relief, Rope Twist, 3 Shelf, Paw Feet, 73 In. 375.00
Kerosene, Banquet, Classical Figures In Reserve, Cobalt Ground, 17 1/2 In. 60.00
Kerosene, Banquet, English Hobnail, Satin Glass Star Shades, 26 In., Pair 385.00
Kerosene, Banquet, Hexagonal Top, Yellow Slag Panes, Sheet Brass, Urn Stem, 33 In. . . . 190.00
Kerosene, Banquet, Metal, Onyx, Blue To White Glass Globe, Flowers, Victorian, 37 In. . 375.00
Kerosene, Banquet, Pink, Brass Plated Iron Foot, Victor Burner, 18 In. 460.00
Kerosene, Bohemian Ruby Glass, Grape Leaves, Woodland Scene, Electrified, 20 x 7 In. . 575.00
Kerosene, Brass, Hanging, Pull Down, Smoke Bell, Pink Roses, Original Pulley 470.00
Kerosene, Brass, Medallion Coat Of Arms, Soldered Strap Handle, 36 In. 140.00
Kerosene, Bronze Patinated, Gilt, Sphinx Column Support, Masks, Electrified, 30 In. 345.00
Kerosene, Bronze, Thistle Leaf, Stylized Relief, Chimney, 23 In. 145.00
Kerosene, Cut Glass, Coral Pink To White To Clear, Electrified, 10 1/2 In. 385.00
Kerosene, Double Angle, Embossed Nickel Font, Hanging 295.00
Kerosene, Frosted Shade, Dome Font, Flaring Hexagonal Base, c.1820, 19 In., Pair 780.00
Kerosene, Fruit Basket, Beaded, Brass Frame, Electrified, Czechoslovakia, 10 x 8 In. 660.00
Kerosene, Gone With The Wind, Brass Font, Relief Floral, 4 Footed, c.1900, 23 1/2 In. . 259.00
Kerosene, Gone With The Wind, Cranberry Opalescent, Daisy & Fern, Satin, Brass Base . 715.00
Kerosene, Gone With The Wind, Floral Globe, Font, Cast Metal Shell Feet, 27 1/4 In. . . . 100.00
Kerosene, Gone With The Wind, Purple & Green Irises, Embossed, Electrified, 28 In. . . . 115.00
Kerosene, Gone With The Wind, Satin Finish, Chimney, Base & Globe Burmese 10000.00
Kerosene, Green Font, Brass Base, Etched Shade, Electrified, 13 1/2 In. 50.00
Kerosene, Hanging, Milk Glass Shade, Brass, Electrified, 34 In. 105.00
Kerosene, Large Flower On Stem, Silver Plate, Electrified, 25 In. 2200.00
Kerosene, Marriage, Ripley, Milk Glass Base, 2 Clambroth Fonts, 12 1/8 In. 770.00
Kerosene, Medallion Shade, Swirl, Lemon Yellow Ribbed, Nutmeg Burner, 8 1/2 In. 3105.00
Kerosene, Mother-Of-Pearl, Blue Satin Shade, Lattice Font, Spar-Brenner, 8 3/4 In. 1230.00
Kerosene, Neoclassical, Gilt, 3-Part Base, Electrified, 17 In. 980.00
Kerosene, Opaque White, Double Stem, Ribbed Onion Font, Brass Collar, 8 3/4 In. 225.00
Kerosene, Plume & Atwood, Meissen Type Floral Base, Milk Glass Shade, 8 In. 110.00
Kerosene, Pressed Glass, Acanthus Leaf, Brass Stem, Square Marble Base, 9 In., Pair 140.00
Kerosene, Pressed Glass, Applesauce, Embossed Columns, Blue, 12 In. 600.00
Kerosene, Pressed Glass, Atterbury Cottage, Burner, 11 In. 110.00
Kerosene, Pressed Glass, Cathedral, Amber Font, Blue Base, 12 1/2 In. 180.00
Kerosene, Pressed Glass, Center Medallion, 9 1/4 In. 90.00
Kerosene, Pressed Glass, Chicago, Amber, 9 7/8 In. 130.00
Kerosene, Pressed Glass, Clear Font, Black Base, Electrified, 13 In. 315.00
Kerosene, Pressed Glass, Coolidge Drape, 9 3/4 In. 75.00
Kerosene, Pressed Glass, Fishscale, 7 In. 25.00
Kerosene, Pressed Glass, Greek Key, Insert Collar, 9 1/4 In. 75.00
Kerosene, Pressed Glass, Pleat & Panel, Burner, 7 7/8 In. 45.00
Kerosene, Pressed Glass, Ripley Hollow Stem, Burner, Square Font, 9 1/2 x 4 1/2 In. 190.00
Kerosene, Pressed Glass, Ripley Hollow Stem, Square Font, 8 5/8 x 4 In. 90.00
Kerosene, Pressed Glass, Stanbury, Amber, Burner, 8 1/2 In. 150.00
Kerosene, Rayo, Banquet, Brass, Pierced Arabesque, Green Shade, Electrified, 24 In. 330.00

Kerosene, Rayo, Green Shade, Gilt Dragon, Early 20th Century, 21 In., Pair 330.00
Kerosene, Rayo, Nickel Plated, Milk Glass Shade, Pair 55.00
Kerosene, Rococo Design, Globular Shade, Red Satin Finish, 25 In. 460.00
Kerosene, Royal, Brass, Nickel Plated, Screw Adjuster, Pat'd. April 11, 1893, 12 In. 40.00
Kerosene, Sandwich Style, Metal Mantle, Square Base, 10 In. 130.00
Kerosene, Spelter, Liberty Bell Base, Floral Font, Ives Portrait Shade, 13 1/2 In. 315.00
Kerosene, Student, Adjustable Reservoir, Twin Fonts, Peach Milk Glass Shades, 11 In. . . . 415.00
Kerosene, Student, Brass, Ringed Finial Standard, Adjustable Font, 22 x 7 1/2 x 11 In. . . . 145.00
Kerosene, Student, Brass, White Shade, 7-In. Fitting, C.A. Cleemans, 21 1/2 In. 260.00
Kerosene, Student, Brass, White Shade, Electrified, 21 In. 315.00
Kerosene, Suess, Red Apple Blossoms, Pink, Electrified, 20 In. 9620.00
Kerosene, White Metal, Ewer Shape, Garlands, Handles, Marble, Electrified, 16 In., Pair . 385.00
Kerosene, Wilkinson, Leaded Glass, Electrified, 23 1/2 x 17 In. 2750.00
Lard, Tin, S.N. & H. Gufford, 6 1/2 In. 80.00
Le Verre, Cameo Glass, Purple Stylized Forms, Mottled Purple Ground, 16 In. 1980.00
Oil, 4 Putti, Supporting Porcelain Font, Scroll Base, Germany, 12 In. 750.00
Oil, Acanthus Leaves, Ribbed, Swirled, Red Satin Glass, Nutmeg Burner, 9 In. 520.00
Oil, Acanthus, Swirl, Yellow, Gold, White, End Of Day, 7 3/4 In. 750.00
Oil, Acme, Edward Miller & Co., Reflector, Glass Chimney, Nickel-Plated Bowl, 8 In. . . . 49.00
Oil, Amber Opalescent, Applied Pink Shell Feet, 8 In. 3565.00
Oil, Amberina, Applied Amber Glass Shell Leaves, Feet, Nutmeg Burner, 8 1/2 In. 3740.00
Oil, Artichoke, Amber Satin Glass, Amber Chimney, 7 3/4 In. 920.00
Oil, Arts & Crafts, Black Finish, Slag Glass, 20 x 12 x 12 In. 290.00
Oil, Banquet, Plum & Atwood, Floral, Gilt Dragons, Filigree Brass & Holder, 15 In. 420.00
Oil, Beaded Swirl, Gold, Dark Ruby, End Of Day, Hornet Burner, 8 1/4 In. 175.00
Oil, Bellflower Font, Ribbed, Fiery Opalescent Base, Brass Stem, Collar, 10 1/8 In. 165.00
Oil, Blue Cameo Glass Shade, Fern, Silver Plated Base, 9 In. 1265.00
Oil, Blue Glass Font, Brass Balusters, Milk Glass Base, American, c.1860, 13 In., Pair . . . 1450.00
Oil, Blue Overlay Cutback, Gilt Design, Ball Shade, Electrified, 23 In. 770.00
Oil, Blue, White Swirl Ruffled Shade, Silver Plated Base, 10 1/2 In. 230.00
Oil, Brass, Dish Light, Neoclassical, Gilt, 77 x 24 In., Pair 1035.00
Oil, Brass, Frosted Globe, Etched, Victorian, Tripartite Base Support, Electrified, 56 In. . . 550.00
Oil, Brass, Glass Fonts, Footed Base, Cherubs Wrapped, 20th Century, 24 In. 470.00
Oil, Brass, Griffin Base, Berry Finial, Parrot Spout, 6 In. 170.00
Oil, Brass, Horn Shape, Cherub Head Spout, Dolphin Footed & Handle, 4 3/4 In. 300.00
Oil, Brass, Oval Font, Candlestick Base, Brass Burner, 8 1/2 In. 980.00
Oil, Bronze Patinated, Gilt, Oval Font, Fluted Pilasters, Electrified, 1890s, 18 x 10 In. . . . 635.00
Oil, Bronze, Gilt, Diamond & Arch Domed Font, Paw Feet, 21 1/2 In. 2300.00
Oil, Buggy, Manhattan Lamp Works, Fixed Handles, Index Burners, 13 1/2 In., Pair 260.00
Oil, Canary, 3 Prunty Designs, Hexagonal Base, 8 1/2 In., Pair 920.00
Oil, Caramel Milk Glass, Swag & Rib Font, Aladdin Burner, Electrified 94.00
Oil, Cast Iron, Geometric Cutout, Green Slag Glass Panel Shade, Square, 19 x 11 In. 255.00
Oil, Chimney Cap, Snowflakes On Frosted Glass, 30 In. 350.00
Oil, Circle & Cross Design, Marble Base, Cobalt Cut To Clear, 10 1/2 In. 220.00
Oil, Cobalt Blue Glass, Floral Design, Cobalt Blue Chimney, 8 1/2 In. 315.00
Oil, Cone Font, Blue Satin Glass, Nutmeg Burner, 8 In. 345.00
Oil, Cone Font, Cut Fans & Diamonds, Stepped Base, 8 3/4 In. 140.00
Oil, Cornelius & Baker, Brass, Marble, Etched Glass Shade, Prisms, Mid 1800s, 21 In. . . . 360.00
Oil, Cranberry Glass, Applied Amber Berries On Shade, Base, 8 1/2 In. 2590.00
Oil, Cranberry Glass, Applied Glass Leaves, Shell Feet, 8 1/2 In. 3105.00
Oil, Cranberry Glass, Diamond, Glass Feet, Nutmeg Burner, 7 3/4 In. 865.00
Oil, Cranberry Glass, Diamond, Glass Feet, Nutmeg Burner, 8 In. 3680.00
Oil, Cranberry Glass, Gold, Orange Enamel Design, Nutmeg Burner, 8 1/2 In. 980.00
Oil, Cranberry Glass, White Opalescent Swirls, Nutmeg Burner, 8 In. 315.00
Oil, Cranberry Opalescent Swirl Satin Glass, Nutmeg Burner, 8 1/2 In. 375.00
Oil, Cranberry Optic Ribbed, 4 Crystal Feet, 9 In. 4025.00
Oil, Crusie, Candle Socket On Side, Arched Handle, Wrought Iron, 15 1/2 In. 110.00
Oil, Crusie, Spiral Beam Hook, Double Bird Cutouts, Double Pan, 8 1/2 In. 230.00
Oil, Dark Blue Satin Glass, Geometric, Embossed, 8 1/2 In. 1208.00
Oil, Dark Blue To Light Blue Satin Glass, Berry Clusters Shade, 9 In. 2875.00
Oil, Dark Cranberry Ribbed, Swirled Shade, Cone Font, 11 In. 1495.00
Oil, Dark Yellow To Cream White, Embossed, Brass Foot, 13 In. 865.00
Oil, Diamond, Floral, Blue Milk Glass, Nutmeg Burner, 7 1/2 In. 460.00

Oil, Embossed, Pink, Hornet Burner, 8 1/2 In. 575.00
Oil, Figural, American Indian Warrior, Silver Plate, Elkington Style, c.1855, 25 In. 1725.00
Oil, Figural, Greek Woman, Etched Glass Shade, Berry Pendant, 1870s, 21 1/2 x 7 In. ... 750.00
Oil, Finger, Elliptical Bull's-Eye Design, Brass Collar, 4 3/4 In. 165.00
Oil, Finger, Windows, Blue Opalescent, Hobbs, Brockunier & Co., c.1889, 8 In. 675.00
Oil, Florette, Green Glossy Glass, Nutmeg Burner, 7 1/4 In. 750.00
Oil, Gold Floral Design, Enamel, Yellow Glass, 8 In. 1380.00
Oil, Gold, White Milk Glass, Frosted Ball Shade, 12 In. 1150.00
Oil, Green Glass, Applied Leaves, Shell Feet, Nutmeg Burner, 8 1/2 In. 575.00
Oil, Hobnail, Amber Glass, Nutmeg Burner, 7 1/2 In. 259.00
Oil, Inverted Pear-Shape Font, Amethyst Glass, Marble Base, 6 1/2 In. 70.00
Oil, Kerosene, Gone With The Wind, Drapery, Cast Metal Base, Ruby Glass, 27 In., Pair . 440.00
Oil, Lace Maker's, Flint, 6 1/2 In. 95.00
Oil, Light Blue Satin Glass, Nutmeg Burner, 7 3/4 In. 635.00
Oil, Marbleized Glass, Blue, Applied Ruffling At Top, 8 5/8 In. 1555.00
Oil, Medium Blue, White Ribbed, White Cat Holding An Orange, Green Base, 13 In. 1725.00
Oil, Mica, Domed Shade, Copper, Hammered, Horizontal Mica Band, N.Y., 1912, 17 In. ... 1725.00
Oil, Milk Glass, Blue, Ribbed Panel, Nutmeg Burner, 8 In. 425.00
Oil, Milk Glass, Green, Embossed, Acorn Burner, 8 In. 500.00
Oil, Miller, Desk, 2 Caramel Slag Panels, Urn & Scroll Metal Overlay, Swivel, 13 In. 275.00
Oil, Miller, Metal, 4 Elongated Pear-Shaped Panels, 20 1/2 x 8 1/2 In. 185.00
Oil, Miller, Ornate Metal Filigree, Rainbow Glass, Shade & Base Light 1045.00
Oil, Miner's, Iron, Brass, Swivel Handle, Long Hook, Round Disk Font, Rooster, 8 1/2 In. 290.00
Oil, Moderator, Brass, Pierced Gallery, Egg Band, Verre Blancand, Electrified, 24 In. 690.00
Oil, Moderator, Brass, Spherical Shade, Key-Wind Burner, Louis Philippe, 21 x 5 In. 575.00
Oil, Moderator, Bronze, Pierced Gallery, Round Foot, Plinth, Napoleon III, 15 x 5 In. 750.00
Oil, Mother-Of-Pearl Raindrop, Blue Satin Glass, Frosted Feet, Nutmeg Burner, 8 In. 3105.00
Oil, Mother-Of-Pearl Raindrop, Green Satin Glass, Nutmeg Burner, 8 In. 2475.00
Oil, Orange, Gold Floral Design, Pink Glass, 8 In. 920.00
Oil, Ostrich Leg With Claws Base, Clear Flint Font, 19th Century 570.00
Oil, Overall Floral Design, Blue, White, Electrified, 1870, 12 1/2 x 7 In., Pair 546.00
Oil, Paneled Baluster Stem & Font, Brass Collar, 10 1/8 In. 140.00
Oil, Pewter, Fuller & Smith, New London, Conn., c.1850, 5 In. 375.00
Oil, Pink Satin Pansy Ball Shade, Melon Base, Nutmeg Burner, 7 In. 400.00
Oil, Pittsburgh, Reverse Painted, Call Of The Wild, Bronze Base, 18 x 24 In. 1840.00
Oil, Porcelain, Glazed, Gilded, Oval Font, Girl With Pitcher Handle, 9 x 4 1/2 x 10 In. ... 1150.00
Oil, Porcelain, White Flowers, Green Ground, Electrified, 17 In., Pair 460.00
Oil, Profile Medallion, Floral Swags, Gilt Brass, Late 19th Century, 15 In., Pair 210.00
Oil, Rose Petal Shade, Yellow, Square Base, Nutmeg Burner, 7 In. 635.00
Oil, Satin Glass Shade, Dark Pink To Light Pink, Brass Pedestal Base, 12 In. 1265.00
Oil, Satin Glass, Rainbow, Applied Frosted Shell Feet, 9 1/2 In. 2015.00
Oil, Sinumbra, Empire, Gilt, Patinated Bronze, Blown, Etched Shade, Cut Stars, c.1825 .. 3025.00
Oil, Sinumbra, Gilt Metal, Glass, Marble, Acid Finish, Flowers, 30 In. 750.00
Oil, Sinumbra, Patinated Bronze, Cut, Etched Blown Glass Shade, Pendants, 26 In. 1610.00
Oil, Sinumbra, Patinated Bronze, Ringed Pedestal, Square Plinth, William IV, 28 In. 2990.00
Oil, Sinumbra, Patinated Bronze, Stepped Plinth, Louis Philippe, Electrified, 25 In. 1095.00
Oil, Sinumbra, William IV, Gilt, Patinated Bronze, Gothic Arches, Spires, 23 x 6 In. 2070.00
Oil, Skeleton, White Bisque Orchid Trim, 5 1/4 In. 7475.00
Oil, Solar, Dietz Brothers, Lacquered, Patinated Bronze, Spherical, Etched, 23 In. 805.00
Oil, Stork Grasping Snake, Bronze, Patinated, Italy, 16 1/2 x 8 x 7 In. 405.00
Oil, Swirl Design, Satin Glass, Dark Pink To Light Pink, 11 1/2 In. 2358.00
Oil, Swirl Ribbed Shade, Medium Blue, Nutmeg Burner, 7 1/2 In. 200.00
Oil, Swirl, Blue, White Spatter, Nutmeg Burner, 8 In. 1495.00
Oil, Translucent Blue Glass, White, Orange Enamel Floral, 8 1/4 In. 1150.00
Oil, Triangular Pressed Glass Base, Scrolled Column & Wafers, Blown Font, 7 3/4 In. ... 360.00
Oil, White Enameled Flower, Orange Centers, Emerald Green Glass, 6 In. 690.00
Oil, White Floral, Leaf Design, Cone Shape, 8 1/2 In. 4025.00
Oil, White Owl, Yellow Eyes, Sitting, Brown, Green Base, 13 In. 690.00
Oil, Yellow Glass, Orange, Gold Enameled Flowers, Nutmeg Burner, 8 1/4 In. 1035.00
Pairpoint lamps are in the Pairpoint category.
Rush, Wrought Iron, Candleholder, Twisted Shaft, Tripod Base, Early 1700s, 12 In. 305.00
Sconce, 1-Light, Arts & Crafts, Hammered Copper, Slag Glass, 10 x 6 x 5 1/2 In. 375.00
Sconce, 1-Light, Brass, Adjustable Arm, 13 1/2 In. 49.00

Sconce, 2-Light, Brass & Bronze, Torch Shape, Plaque With Cherubs Center, 29 In. 275.00
Sconce, 2-Light, Brass, Scrolled, Old Red Paint Back, 16 3/4 x 12 1/4 In. 190.00
Sconce, 2-Light, Empire Style, Crystal, Brass, Prism Corona, 15 x 11 In., Pair 635.00
Sconce, 2-Light, Floral, Curved Square Arms, Opalescent Shades, 18 In. 2300.00
Sconce, 2-Light, Gilt Bronze, Jasperware Plaque, George III, 20 x 11 In., Pair 1265.00
Sconce, 2-Light, Gilt, Scrolled Candle Branches, Louis XVI, 20 In., Pair 3900.00
Sconce, 2-Light, Giltwood, Convex Oval Mirror Plate, S-Scroll Arms, Wax Pans, 36 In. ... 490.00
Sconce, 2-Light, Giltwood, Dolphin Design, Fish, Cattails, Electrified, c.1880, 15 In. 175.00
Sconce, 2-Light, Leaded Crystal, Cast Oval Mounting Plates, Prisms, 15 x 9 In., Pair ... 420.00
Sconce, 2-Light, Masque-Form Backplate, Scrolled Arms, 11 1/2 In., Pair 460.00
Sconce, 2-Light, Painted Scroll Backplate, Nozzles, 8 3/4 x 8 In. 3600.00
Sconce, 2-Light, Regency Style, Diana Mask Crest, Floral Cast Arms, 14 x 12 In., Pair ... 1610.00
Sconce, 2-Light, Serpentine Candle Arms, Beaded Platform, Acorn Drop, 16 In. 1840.00
Sconce, 2-Light, Spread-Wing Phoenix, Candle Arms, Faux Drapery, 1790s, 43 In. 9200.00
Sconce, 2-Light, Venetian Glass, Mirrored, Gilded, 21 1/2 x 15 In., Pair 1150.00
Sconce, 3-Light, Acanthine Accents, Italy, 32 1/2 In., Pair 860.00
Sconce, 3-Light, Argente Bronze, Turned Finial, George III, 1900, 14 In., Pair 1265.00
Sconce, 3-Light, Art Deco, Bronze, Mask Of Tragedy Standard, 13 In. 1495.00
Sconce, 3-Light, Brass, Draped Pilaster Backplate, 22 In., Pair 395.00
Sconce, 3-Light, Bronze & Crystal, Torch With 3 Scrolling Arms, Bronze, 18 In. 1035.00
Sconce, 3-Light, Cast Brass, Hanging Prisms, Late 19th Century, 18 In., Pair 165.00
Sconce, 3-Light, Empire, Gilt, Swag Ram's Head, Floral, 25 In., Pair 1265.00
Sconce, 3-Light, Foliage Backplate, Center Branch, Candle Cups, 19 3/4 In., Pair 1610.00
Sconce, 3-Light, Giltwood, Scrolled Branches, Electrified, 12 In., Pair 1955.00
Sconce, 3-Light, Gothic, Cast Iron, Crown Filigree, 38 x 12 x 6 In. 4030.00
Sconce, 3-Light, Iron, Arrow-Tip Bracket, American, 19th Century, 14 x 15 In., Pair 2530.00
Sconce, 3-Light, Lyre-Form Backplate, Laurel Leaves, Louis XVI, 72 In., Pair 4800.00
Sconce, 3-Light, Mirrored Backplate, Urn-Form Nozzles, 9 3/4 In., Pair 2530.00
Sconce, 3-Light, Regency Style, Circular Frame, Serpent Issuing Nozzles, 5 In., Pair 3680.00
Sconce, 3-Light, Regency Style, Gilt Brass, Scalloped Backplate, 22 x 14 In., Pair 3220.00
Sconce, 3-Light, Regency Style, Gilt Bronze, Floral, Mask Of Apollo, 9 x 13 In., Pair ... 2530.00
Sconce, 3-Light, Rococo Style, Patinated Bronze Backplate, 14 In. 259.00
Sconce, 3-Light, Scroll Branches, Jewel Pendants, Gilt, Metal, 30 In., Pair 7765.00
Sconce, 3-Light, Wrought Iron, Tole, Crystal, 10 x 14 x 9 1/4 In., Pair 2760.00
Sconce, 4-Light, Blown Glass, Colored Flowers, Leaves, Pendant, Venetian, 27 In., Pair . 2990.00
Sconce, 5-Light, Gilt, Bronze, Scrolled Branches, Louis XVI, Electrified, 24 In., Pair ... 1725.00
Sconce, 5-Light, Rococo Style, Gilt Wrought Iron, Crystal, Italy, 19 x 18 x 12 In. 3680.00
Sconce, Arts & Crafts, Copper, Verdigris Patina, Funnel Top, Scrolling, 20 x 10 x 5 In. ... 520.00
Sconce, Brass, Punched Flower Design, Octagonal, Holland, 18th Century 715.00
Sconce, Brass, Soldier, Lion's-Head Base, Continental, 8 x 35 In. 410.00
Sconce, Candle, Crimped Pans, Mirrored, 8 In., Pair 190.00
Sconce, Carved Wood & Gesso, Convex Mirror, Scroll Leaves, 17 3/4 x 10 In., Pair 660.00
Sconce, Gustav Stickley, Copper, Hammered, 16 1/2 x 8 In. 5750.00
Sconce, Hammered Cooper, Benedict Studio, 12 In. 385.00
Sconce, Landscape, Garden, Colorful Matte Glaze, California Art, 13 In., Pair 3105.00
Sconce, Mask, Chartreuse Highlights, Wire Features, Marked, 12 1/2 x 13 In. 545.00
Sconce, Silver Plate, Etched Hurricane Shades, 22 In. 385.00
Sconce, Tin, Corrugated Reflector, Round 1375.00
Sconce, Tin, Mirrored, Round, Dished Support, Radiating Segments, 12 x 10 1/2 In. 3740.00
Shade, Caramel Slag Glass, Bell Shape, 20 In. 1008.00
Shade, Green Slag Glass, Geometric, Beaded Trim, 26 1/2 In. 2300.00
Shade, Hanging, Leaded, 8 Panels, Arts & Crafts, 22 In. Diam. 290.00
Skater's, Brass, Glass Globe, Brass Wire Handle, 6 3/4 In. 83.00
Tiffany lamps are listed in the Tiffany category.
Torchere, 4-Light, Regency, Gilt, Bronze, Green Paint, Scroll Feet, 74 In. 2070.00
Torchere, 5-Light, Angel Figures, Gilt Bronze, Marble, Italy, c.1890, 64 In., Pair 8960.00
Torchere, Altar, Giltwood, Leaf Design, Scroll Feet, Late 19th Century, 48 In., Pair 5520.00
Torchere, Art Deco, Aluminum, Flared Trumpet Shade, Circular Chrome Base, 65 In. 300.00
Torchere, Art Deco, Black Marble Base, Bronze Trim, Amber Shade, 65 In., Pair 980.00
Torchere, Art Deco, Chrome, Hemispheric Shade, Circular Base, 72 x 14 In. 550.00
Torchere, Blackamoor, Grapes, Parcel Gilt, Tripod Base, Italy, 18th Century, 37 1/2 In. .. 1955.00
Torchere, Blackamoor, Venetian Dress, 15 1/2 In., Pair 1085.00
Torchere, Brass, Metal, Onyx Base, Durand Art Glass Shade, 67 x 8 1/4 In. 1210.00

Torchere, Bright Chrome, Flaring Trumpet Shade, 65 1/4 x 12 In. 115.00
Torchere, Cast Iron, Classical, Stylized Leaves Bowl, 3-Post Base, Gold Paint, 52 In. 925.00
Torchere, Chinoiserie, Gilt, Black Ground, Continental, 18th Century Style, 60 In. 290.00
Torchere, Chrome, Hemispheric Shade, Circular Base, Art Deco, 72 x 14 In. 618.00
Torchere, Gadrooned Edge, Fluted Standard, Swags & Medallions, 52 In., Pair 4200.00
Torchere, George III Style, Mahogany, Wheat-Stalk Standard, 52 1/2 x 20 In. 520.00
Torchere, Gilt, Bronze, Tri-Form Central Standard, Louis XVI, 80 In., Pair 12000.00
Torchere, Giltwood, Fluted, Leaf-Capped Standard, Pendant Filets, Louis XVI, 65 In. . . . 345.00
Torchere, Marble Tripod Pedestal, Silvered & Gilded, 58 In. 1380.00
Torchere, Regency Style, Black Lacquer, Pinewood, Gilt Dragons, 61 x 16 In. 430.00
Torchere, Regency, Giltwood, Swag, Acanthine Standard, Iron Paw Feet, 52 1/2 In. 1840.00
Torchere, Rococo Style, Fruitwood, Carved, Leafy Standard, Cupids, 78 In. 2300.00
Torchere, Spun Aluminum, Flared Shade, Oak Knob, Base, 66 x 12 In. 420.00
Torchere, Walnut, Raised Above Angel's Head, 19th Century, 53 3/4 In., Pair 2115.00
Torchere, Walnut, Turtle Top, Serpentine Base, Cabriole Feet, Victorian, 45 In. 345.00
Whale Oil, Blown Font, Pressed Glass Base, 19th Century, 11 In. 430.00
Whale Oil, Boston & Sandwich, 3-Mold, Tin Burner, 1825-1840, 2 1/8 x 2 1/2 In. 1870.00
Whale Oil, Boston & Sandwich, Square, Scrolled Lion & Claw Foot, c.1840, 8 In., Pair . . 990.00
Whale Oil, Boston & Sandwich, Square, Tiered, Blown, Cone-Shaped, c.1840, 5 7/8 In. . . 165.00
Whale Oil, Candlestick Base, Double Burners, 8 1/2 In. 1955.00
Whale Oil, Chamber, H. Hopper, Tooled Lines Font, Pewter, 1842, 5 In. 190.00
Whale Oil, Circular Pan Base, Single Burner, Carrying Ring, 8 1/2 In. 140.00
Whale Oil, Cut Glass, Bulbous Font, 4-Stepped Base, Carved Grape, 9 1/2 In., Pair 400.00
Whale Oil, Heart Shape, Hollow Hexagonal Base, 10 x 11 1/2 In., Pair 145.00
Whale Oil, Ornamental Design, Paw Feet, 12 1/4 In. 230.00
Whale Oil, Sandwich Style, Applied Handle, 3 1/2 In. 230.00
Whale Oil, Sparking, Free-Blown Font, Short Stem, Flat Foot, 1840s, 2 5/8 x 1 3/4 In. . . . 385.00
Whale Oil, Sparking, Light-Bulb Font, Medium Blue, Purple, Handle, Foot, 3 1/8 In. 2420.00
Whale Oil, Square Pressed Glass Base, Columnar Stem, c.1840, 10 3/4 In. 65.00
Whale Oil, Thomas Caines, Flint, Tapered Font, Pineapple Cutting On Base, 10 In. 230.00
Whale Oil, Tin, Baluster, Drop-In Font, 19th Century, 9 3/4 In., Pair 1092.00
Whale Oil, Tin, Double Burners, Cylindrical Font, Weighted & Domed Base, 6 In., Pair . . 345.00
Whale Oil, Weighted Base, Brass Mount For Hanging, 11 In. 220.00
Whale Oil, Wrought Iron, Long Iron Hook, 10 1/2 In. 275.00
Whale Oil, Yale & Curtis, Pewter, 4 1/2 In. 400.00
LAMPSHADE, 6 Panels, Green, White, Brown Wild Roses, 21 x 16 In. 1550.00
Adjustable Arching Form, Adjustable Shade, Steel, White Marble Base, 95 In. 1840.00
Allover Vines With Colorful Trumpet Blossoms, Riviere, Metal Base, 21 In. 7840.00
Chicago Mosaic, Cherry Blossoms, Green Leaves, Amber Ground, 16 In. 3360.00
Curved Caramel Panels With Tulips, Frame, Adjustable Arm, 17 x 12 In. 1345.00
Gorham, Greek Key Design Border, Medallions, 6 Sides, 19 In. 11200.00
Green Geometric Glass, Sunburst Border Design, 19 In. 895.00
Hanging, Leaded, Slag, Geometric, Flowers, Scrolls, 18 In. 460.00
Leaded Glass, Pink Floral Border, 18 In. 1455.00
Moe-Bridges, River, Trees, Cloudy Sky, Signed, 14 In. 2630.00
Pittsburgh, Cone Shape, Geometric Design, Brown Mosserine Finish, 18 In. 3920.00
Reverse Painted, Landscape Scene, Trees, Yellow, Blue, Green, Red, 20 In. 805.00
Reverse Painted, Yellow, Purple Iris, Green, Orange Ground, 22 x 17 In. 460.00
Smoky Blue, Wood Trim, Linen Shade, Signed, Martz, 26 1/2 x 9 In. 230.00
Woodland Scene, Domed, Opalescent Glass, 18 In. 1065.00

LANTERNS are a special type of lighting device. They have a light
source, usually a candle, totally hidden inside the walls of the lantern.
Light is seen through holes or glass sections.

3-Light, Hall, Suspended Scrollwork, Melon Finials, 36 x 13 In. 747.00
Barn, Tin, Glass, Square, Handle 395.00
Barn, Wood, Glass Sides, Pegged, Tin Candle Socket, Wire Handle, 9 3/4 In. 525.00
Bicycle, Kerosene, Polished Brass, 1897 . . . . 247.00
Brass, Glazed Panels, Etched Brass, Hinged Door, Pierced Dome, 1740s, 17 1/2 In. 6600.00
Brass, Oil, Ship's, Colorless Glass Lens, Semicircular, Davey & Co., c.1900, 11 In. 35.00
Brass, Scroll & Mask Design, Pierced Frame, Glass Tube Panels, 21 In. 288.00
Brass, Skater's, Kerosene, 19th Century, 9 In. 85.00
Bronze Dore & Cut Glass, Crown Corona, Faceted Globe, 1870s, 32 In. 3450.00

Bull's-Eye, Tin, Convex Lens, Hinged, Double Burner, Double Handle, Belt Clip, 7 1/2 In.   85.00
Candle, Hanging, Cranberry, Metal, Marble Base, 15 1/2 In. 325.00
Candle, Pine, Cherry Glaze, Wrought Iron Handle, Tin Reflector, Blue, Green Paint 25300.00
Candle, Tin, Cherry, Diamond-Shape Glazed Openings 25300.00
Candle, Tin, Vertical Wire Guards, Crimped Conical Top, Ring Handle, 15 1/2 In. 805.00
Carriage, 2 Beveled Panels, Red Reflector, Silvered Interior, Electrified, 1870s, 6 In. 290.00
Coach, Cut & Faceted Glass Panels, Sheffield Burner, 19th Century, 22 In., Pair 920.00
Cobalt Globe, Removable Font, Bail Handle, Punched Design, Hanging Hole, 10 In. ...   580.00
Domed Top, 2 Vents, Punched Leaf & Star, Double Sockets, Snuffer, 15 3/4 In. 360.00
G. Stickley, Heart, Arts & Crafts, Painted, Pair, 9 x 3 In. 1440.00
G. Stickley, Twin, Curved Strap Bracket, Heart Cutouts, Glass Shade, 16 x 11 In. 7375.00
Gilt, Hexagonal Form, Fretted Spire, 25 1/2 In., Pair 4460.00
Gilt Brass Mounted, Blown Glass, Biedermeier Style, Vienna, c.1900, 8 x 11 In. 375.00
Gilt Metal, Blown Glass Globe, Smoke Plate, 3 Chains, Electrified, 23 In. 1920.00
Gilt Metal & Painted, 3 Panels Of Peacocks, On Branches, Hinged Lid, 18 In. 485.00
Hall, Blown Glass, Sphere Shape, Brass Banded Neck, Knop Pendant, Chains, 15 In. 430.00
Hall, Brass, Square, Beveled Glass, Turned Finial, 19th Century, 35 In. 985.00
Hall, Hexagonal Form, Gothic Arches & Rods Joining Corona, Brass, 37 In. 4270.00
Hall, Spherical, Gilt, Brass Mounted, Blown Glass, Neoclassical, 10 1/2 x 7 In. 145.00
Hall, Wrought Iron, Foliate Corona, Arches, Glazed Panels, Victorian, 24 x 13 In. 2185.00
Hanging, Brass, Cranberry Glass, Scrolled Brackets, Victorian, 35 x 10 1/2 In. 1035.00
Hanging, Brass, Stained Glass, Arts & Crafts, 21 In. 575.00
Hanging, Bronze Dore, Cut Glass, Louis XVI Style, 32 x 12 In. 3450.00
Hanging, Etched Glass, Projecting Scrolls, Knop Pendant, 1880s, 16 x 10 1/2 In. 1840.00
Hanging, G. Stickley, Copper, Hammered, Yellow Glass Inserts, 14 1/2 x 9 In. 2362.00
Hanging, G. Stickley, Square Cutouts At Top Over Slag Glass, 33 In. 4950.00
Hanging, G. Stickley, Trellis Grid, Hammered Yellow Glass, Ceiling Plate, 10 In. 5750.00
Hanging, Gilt Bronze, Etched Glass, Globe, Projecting Scrolls, 16 x 10 1/2 In. 1840.00
Hanging, Gilt, Arched Gables, Knop Pendant, Rose Windows, 30 x 8 In. 6038.00
Hanging, Napoleon III, Gilt, Bronze, Blue, White Glass Bowl, 26 x 14 In. 1725.00
Hanging, Regency Style, Hexagonal, Patinated, Gilt Bronze, 24 x 14 In. 1840.00
Hanging, Reverse Painted Glass, Figural Panels, 20th Century, 20 x 18 In. 29.00
Hanging, Tin, Pierced, 18th Century, 15 x 6 1/2 In. Diam. 140.00
Hanging, Wire Guard, Vent Stack With Handle, Tin Font, 21 1/2 In. 290.00
Ogee Vaulted, Acanthus Capped Pendant Finial, Tole, 47 In. 290.00
Onion, Punched Tin, Glass, Burner, 11 In. 345.00
Pear Shaped Globe, Pierced Designs, Removable Font, Whale Oil Burner, 11 In. 360.00
Punched Diamond & Star, Removable Burner, Glass Shade, 18 In. 190.00
Skater's, Tin, Pressed Glove, Bail Handle, Perko Wonder Junior, 6 7/8 In. 70.00
Tin, Glass, Square, Tall Vent Stack, Handle, Chimney, Wire Guard, 21 1/2 In. 290.00
Wrought Iron, Leaded Glass, Arts & Crafts, Round 2400.00

LE VERRE FRANCAIS is one of the many types of cameo glass made in
France. The glass was made by the C. Schneider factory in Epinay-sur-
Seine from 1920 to 1933. It is a mottled glass, usually decorated with
floral designs, and bears the incised signature *Le Verre Francais*.

Bowl, Etched Trees, Ivory, Mulberry, Pink, 7 1/2 x 3 5/8 x 4 1/4 In. 355.00
Chalice, Stylized Flowers, Geometric, Orange, Red, Mottled, Cameo, 13 In. 1840.00
Shade, Spherical Shape, Cut With Butterflies, Cameo, 5 In. 1265.00
Vase, Brown Mushrooms, Yellow & Blue Ground, Cameo, 8 In. 1610.00
Vase, Flowers, Shades Of Purple, Cameo, Signed, 24 In. 2875.00
Vase, Green To Red, Beige Ground, Cameo, Signed, 3 1/2 x 3 1/4 In. 600.00
Vase, Mushrooms, Red To Brown, Mottled Yellow, Cameo, 13 In. 2185.00
Vase, Overlaid & Etched, Digitalis On Mottled Ground, Signed, 20 In. 5175.00
Vase, Ribbed, Art Deco Stylized Buds, Curled Leaves, Signed, 5 1/4 In. 560.00

LEATHER is tanned animal hide and it has been used to make decorative and useful objects for centuries. Leather objects must be carefully
preserved with proper humidity and oiling or the leather will deteriorate and crack. This damage cannot be repaired.

Bag, Shorebird Hunters, Leather Shot Flask, Interior Compartments 2760.00
Belt, Bronco, Embossed Cowboy On Horse, 3 Buckles, Billets, Mahogany Color 295.00
Box, Cartridge, Divider, Brass Corner Plates, 2 Leather Tie Straps, J.H. Crane, Toronto ... 1035.00

Canteen, Military, Brass Top, Cap Missing, Early 19th Century 165.00
Chaps, Shotgun, Patch Pockets, Fringe, Step-In Legs, 33-In. Belt, 33-In. Leg 650.00
Figurine, Horse, Rearing, Stone Eyes, English Saddle, Stand, India, 15 In. 25.00
Frame, Apple Green, Moleskin, Chinese, 13 3/4 In. 1150.00
Handbag, Hand Tooled, Bakelite Clasp, Early To Mid 20th Century, 6 In. 25.00
Holster, Colt S.A., Double Loop, Plain Skirt, Tooled, H.H. Heiser, Denver, Holds 7 In. ... 250.00
Holster, Double Loop, Embossed Rope Border, Iver Johnson Co., Marked 38 .... 175.00
Holster, Single Action, Tooled Bull Head, H.H. Heiser, Denver, Colo., Holds 5 1/2 In. 190.00
Holster, Single Action, Whip Stitch, Double Loop, R.T. Frazier, Pueblo, Colo., 5 1/2 In. ... 350.00
Holster, Slim Jim Style, Riveted Belt Loop, Chamois Lined, Colt S.A., 1800s 750.00
Pitcher, Ale, Man Form, Long Frock Coat, Tricorn Hat, Loop Handle, 1780s, 34 In. 3000.00
Saddle, Parade, Black, Tooled, Padded Seat, Covered Horn, Martingale & Bridle 975.00
Saddle, Pony, Hand Tooled, Child's 135.00
Saddle, Silver Trim, Keystone, 1900 .... 11000.00
Saddle, Western, Child's, Embossed Horse Heads 310.00
Scabbard, Buckskin Whip Stitch, H.H. Heiser, Denver, Colo., Holds 1876 Lever Action .. 325.00
Scabbard, Hand Tooled, Engraved, Sterling Buckles, Holds 1876 Winchester, 37 In. 550.00
Toiletry Case, Simulated Tortoise Implements, c.1900 .... 80.00
Wallet, Cowhide, Beaded Floral Design, Gold Stamped Design Around Edge, Daniel 12.00
Wallet, Woman's, White, Silver, Diamonds, Monogram, Tiffany, Box 220.00
Whip, Bull, Braided, Leather Wrapped Metal Handle, 10 Ft. 75.00

LEEDS pottery was made at Leeds, Yorkshire, England, from 1774 to 1878. Most Leeds ware was not marked. Early Leeds pieces had distinctive twisted handles with a greenish glaze on part of the creamy ware. Later ware often had blue borders on the creamy pottery. A Chicago company named Leeds made many Disney-inspired figurines. They are listed in the Disneyana category.

LEEDS POTTERY.

Basket, Fruit, Stand, Creamware, Molded Angel Figures, Pierced Body, 10 In. 1380.00
Bowl, Spatterware, Peafowl, Blue, Yellow, Orange, Green Highlights, 3 x 6 In. 330.00
Mustard, Blue Feather Edge, 18th Century 325.00
Plate, Bellflower Edge, Signed, 8 3/4 In., Pair 220.00
Plate, Oriental Scene, Staffordshire, 7 3/4 In. 650.00
Plate, Peafowl, Blue, Orange, Blue Border, 9 3/4 In. 715.00
Plate, Ship Design, 10 In. 430.00
Plate, Transfer Ship Design, 10 In. 430.00
Sugar, Black & White, Lines, Cover, 4 3/4 x 4 1/2 In., Pair 90.00
Sugar & Creamer, Peafowl, Knopped Lid, Yellow Banding, 4 1/2 In. 2070.00
Tureen, Sauce, Cover, Feather Edge, Blue, Soft Paste, c.1817, 6 1/2 In. 625.00

LEFTON is a mark found on pottery, porcelain, glass, and other wares imported by the Geo. Zoltan Lefton Company. The company began in 1940 and is still in business. The company mark has changed through the years; but because marks have been used for long periods of time, they are of little help in dating an object.

Lefton China
Hand Painted
MADE IN JAPAN

Bell, Cat, Black, Rhinestone Eyes & Trim, Bow 6.00

Lefton, Egg Plate, Embossed
Grapes & Leaves, Avocado
Green, 12 Wells, 9 1/2 In.

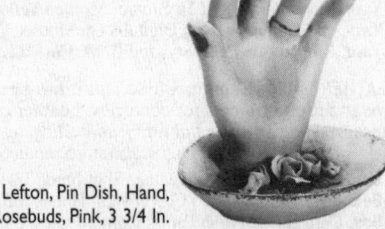

Lefton, Pin Dish, Hand,
Rosebuds, Pink, 3 3/4 In.

Cookie Jar, Bakery, Lefton, 9 1/2 In. 45.00
Decanter Set, Praying Monk, 2-In. Cups, 7 Piece 65.00
Dish, Pink, Hand With Applied Flowers On Wrist, 5 In. 40.00
Dish, Sweet, Yellow Rose, Hand Painted, 4 In. 7.50
Egg Plate, Embossed Grapes & Leaves, Avocado Green, 12 Wells, 9 1/2 In. .... *Illus* 27.00
Eggcup, Bluebird, 4 Piece 400.00
Eggcup, Dutch Girl 100.00
Ewer, Pink Roses, Gold Gilt Handle, 5 1/2 In. 8.00
Ewer, Roses, Gilt, 5 1/2 In. 10.00
Figurine, Barber, Leaning On Barber Pole, 1890s Type, 8 In. 45.00
Figurine, Colonial Woman & Man, 7 In., Pair 150.00
Figurine, Dachshund, Standing, Black & Tan, 1950s, 6 x 4 In. 45.00
Figurine, Kitten, Tabby, Orange, Marked H6364, 5 In. 25.00
Pin Dish, Hand, Rosebuds, Pink, 3 3/4 In. .... *Illus* 20.00
Pitcher, Green Heritage, 6 In. 60.00
Planter, Poodle, Paper Label 15.00
Plaque, Applied Flowers, Diamond Shape, 8 In., 4 Piece 60.00

LEGRAS was founded in 1864 by Auguste Legras at St. Denis, France. It is best known for cameo glass and enamel-decorated glass with Art Nouveau designs. Legras merged with Pantin in 1920 and became the Verreries et Cristalleries de St. Denis et de Pantin Reunies.

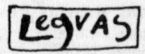

Basket, Mosaic, Cranberry Lined, Outer Gold Tone Spatter, Amber Handle, 7 1/2 In. 185.00
Vase, Amber, Carved, Etched, Art Deco Style, Signed, 25 In. 1725.00
Vase, Bottle Shape, Lavender Over White, Flowers, Cameo, 8 In. 748.00
Vase, Caramel, Green, Maroon Plants, Handles, 10 3/4 In. 805.00
Vase, Continuous Landscape, Sailboats, Signed, 7 x 6 1/2 In. 945.00
Vase, Continuous Landscape, Signed, 6 3/4 In. 1035.00
Vase, Earthtone, Colors, Woodbine Vine, Satin, Signed, 10 3/4 In. 532.00
Vase, Enameled Poppies, Mottled Orange, Yellow & Green, Signed, 9 In. 430.00
Vase, Enameled Tall Trees, Landscape, Leaves, Signed, 14 In. 660.00
Vase, Enameled Winter Scene, Signed, 8 In., Pair 575.00
Vase, Holly Berries, Leaves, Orange, Green Ground, Cameo, 23 1/2 In. 2190.00
Vase, Leaf Design, Cameo, 5 1/4 In. 575.00
Vase, Olive Green, Oval, Rolled-In Rim, Acid Etched, Gold Trim, Cameo, 1920, 8 In. 450.00
Vase, Purple Enameled Grape Leaves, Chipped Ice Ground, Signed, 11 1/2 In. 870.00
Vase, Red Flowers, Black Centers, Leaves, Enameled, Cameo, Signed, 12 In. 600.00
Vase, Seaweed, Carmel, Signed, 11 In. 315.00
Vase, Trailing Leaves, Seed Pods, Enameled, Elongated Eggshape, Signed, 1830s, 8 In. .. 460.00
Vase, Underwater Scene, 8 In. 1500.00
Vase, Winter Scene, Leafless Trees, Signed, 11 In., Pair 785.00

LENOX is the name of a porcelain maker. Walter Scott Lenox and Jonathan Cox founded the Ceramic Art Company in Trenton, New Jersey, in 1889. In 1906, Lenox left and started his own company called *Lenox*. The company makes a porcelain that is similar to Irish Belleek. The marks used by the firm have changed through the years and collectors prefer the earlier examples. Related pieces may also be listed in the Ceramic Art Co. category.

Creamer, Amethyst 105.00
Cup & Saucer, After Dinner, Lined Case, Alvin Sterling Holders 275.00
Figurine, Carousel Horse, Mounted On Wooden Base, 9 In. 100.00
Pitcher, Mask Face, 1940s 145.00
Sugar, Amethyst 115.00
Tankard, Girl, Standing, Silver Sterling, 15 In. 1870.00
Vase, Game Bird, Ring-Necked Pheasant, 12 1/4 In. 92.00

LETTER OPENERS have been used since the eighteenth century. Ivory and silver were favored by the well-to-do. In the late nineteenth century, the letter opener was popular as an advertising giveaway and many were made of metal or celluloid. Brass openers with figural handles were also popular.

General Mead Monument, Gettysburg, Pa., Combination Bookmark, 5 In. 15.00

Giraffe, Wooden, Hand Carved	45.00
Jade Handle, 14K Yellow Gold Blade, Top Ring, 7 1/2 In.	220.00
Lone Star Beer, Disk Insert On Butt Of Rifle, 8 1/2 In.	75.00
Masted Sailing Ship, Brass, 8 1/2 In.	20.00
Pewter Handle, Red & Crystal Stones, Prism Ball End	13.00
Rabbit, Stainless Steel Blade, Pewter Handle, 5 In.	8.00
Rifle, With Bayonet, Aluminum, Brass Plate, 8 In.	17.50
Scimitar, With Winged Lion, 6 1/8 In.	20.00
Writhing Dragon, Ivory, Oblong, Chinese, 9 3/4 In.	115.00

LIBBEY Glass Company has made many types of glass since 1888, including the cut glass and tablewares that are collected today. The stemwares of the 1930s and 1940s are once again in style. The Toledo, Ohio, firm was purchased by Owens-Illinois in 1935 and is still working under the name *Libbey Incorporated.* Additional pieces may be listed under Amberina, Cut Glass, and Maize.

Bowl, Controlled Bubbles, Pale Green Design, c.1930, 9 In.	130.00
Bowl, Hobstars, Deep Miters, 6-Point Rayed Star, Signed, 7 x 3 1/2 In.	165.00
Bowl, Hobstars, Russian, Crosshatch, Prisms, 11 In.	525.00
Bowl, Orange, Ellsmere, Signed, 8 1/2 In.	1175.00
Carafe, Princess, Signed, 7 1/2 In.	150.00
Compote, Ozella, 18-Point Hobstar, Scalloped Base, Signed, 5 In.	396.00
Compote, Star & Feather, 8 3/4 In., Pair	3250.00
Goblet Set, Manhattan, 4 Different Hawaiian Flowers Etchings, Signed, 4 Piece	60.00
Ice Bucket, Underplate, Hobstar & Cane	1295.00
Pitcher, Corinthian Variant, Double Row Of Half Flutes At Throat, 8 1/2 In.	335.00
Tazza, Cut Flowers, Etched, Circle Mark, 6 3/4 x 6 3/8 In.	135.00
Tray, Anita, Oval, Signed, 12 x 8 In.	525.00
Tumbler, Juice, Colonna, Signed	45.00
Tumbler, Pilsner, Seville, Pink & Black Design, Footed, 8 1/4 In., 6 Piece	70.00
Vase, Amberina, Morning Glory Rim, Ribbed, 14 In.	1345.00
Vase, Amberina, Scalloped, Signed, 7 In.	865.00
Vase, Blue Green Applied Design, Clear, Signed, 11 3/4 In.	255.00
Vase, Chintz, Green Blue, Ribbed, Tapered, Signed, 15 In.	460.00
Vase, Harvard, Trumpet, 8 In.	250.00
Vase, Hobstars & Relief Diamonds, 16-Point Hobstar Base, Signed, 7 3/4 In.	90.00

LIGHTERS for cigarettes and cigars are collectible. Cigarettes became popular in the late nineteenth century, and with the cigarette came matches and cigarette lighters. All types of lighters are collected, from solid gold to the first of the recent disposable lighters. Most examples found were made after 1940. Some lighters may be found in the Jewelry category in this book.

Aladdin, New York, Cigarette Case, Tortoiseshell, Goldtone, Art Deco, Metalfield	60.00
Bakelite, Yellow, Japan, 1 3/4 x 1 1/2 x 1 3/4 In.	75.00
Brass, Cranberry Glass, 3 1/4 In.	75.00
Cigar, Cast Iron, Black Man, Inset In Mouth & Push Button, 5 1/2 x 3 1/2 In.	90.00
Cigar, Copper Clad, Woman's Head, Hot Lips, Between Open Lips	275.00
Cigar, Gas, J.S. Clarke As Toodles, Philadelphia, 6 3/4 In.	395.00
Cigar, Gas, Metal, Man Form, 18th Century Dress, Gas, Polychromed, Dome Case, 6 In.	575.00
Cigar, Gas, Spelter, Indian Scout, Polychromed Natural Colors, c.1890, 15 In.	1120.00
Cigar, Midland, Jump Spark, Davenport, Iowa, c.1920, 15 In.	336.00
Crystal, Table, 4 Rounded Sides, 2 3/4 x 4 In.	65.00
Dunhill, Bumper, 1930s-1940s, 4 1/2 In.	495.00
Egyptian, Japan, 3 1/4 x 5 In.	22.00
Georg Jensen, Silver, Floral Finial, 5 3/4 In.	1380.00
Harley-Davidson, Slimline, Japan, Box, 2 1/8 x 1 7/8 In.	210.00
Kiwi Bird, Metal, Wooden Base, Japan, 3 1/2 In.	65.00
Leather, Green Embroidered, Japan, 3 In.	7.00
Man's Head, Metal	125.00
Pan Am Airlines, Flint, 1961	58.00
Rolex, Sinclair Gasoline, Slimline, 2 1/8 x 1 7/8 In.	82.00
Ronson, Ladylite, Varaflame, Box	30.00

Ronson, Tuxedo, Cigarette Case, Chrome, Black, White, Art Deco, Box 100.00
Sailboat, Metal, Plastic, 8 In. 90.00
Table, Ronson, Wedgwood, 1962, 2 1/2 In. 69.00
Union 76, Slimline, Delivery Truck, Blank Reverse, 2 1/8 x 1 3/4 In. 77.00
Zippo, Diagonal Lines Design, 3-Barrel Hinge, Brushed Finish, 1933 .... 500.00
Zippo, Easyriders, Chinese, 2 1/4 x 1 1/2 In. 7.50
Zippo, Mohawk Gasoline, Stitched Logo, 3 3/8 In. 230.00
Zippo, Monogrammed C.A.M., Slimline, Flints, Fluid, Marked 30.00
Zippo, NBC News, Logo, White Enamel, Polished Finish, 1979, 4 In. 210.00
Zippo, U.S.N. Insignia, Black 30.00

LIGHTNING ROD and lightning rod balls are collected. The glass balls
were at the center of the rod that was attached to the roof of a house or
barn to avoid lightning damage.

LIGHTNING ROD, Globe, Steel Tripod, 54 1/2 x 7 1/4 In. 150.00
Milk Glass, Blue, Brass, Acorn Shape, 5 1/2 x 3 1/4 In. 620.00
Milk Glass, Fluted, 3-Foot Bracket For Rooftop, Copper Ground Cable, 1900 .... 85.00
LIGHTNING ROD BALL, Cobalt Blue, Barnett 100.00
Cobalt Blue, Onion Shape, 4 x 3 1/2 In. 985.00
Cobalt Blue, Quilted, Raised 76.00
Hickock's Patent 1859, Deep Blue Green 70.00
Mercury, Original Box, 5 1/2 x 4 1/4 In. 135.00
Milk Glass, Blue, Swirl Design 105.00
Milk Glass, Diddie Blitzen 36.00
Milk Glass, Ribbed Horizontal, Circles In Center 35.00
Olive Amber, Diddie Blitzen 70.00
Red, Globe 130.00
Red Ball Flashing, W.C. Shinn, Lincoln, Neb. 280.00
Teal, Cone, Electra 50.00

LIMOGES porcelain has been made in Limoges, France, since the mid-
nineteenth century. Fine porcelains were made by many factories,
including Haviland, Ahrenfeldt, Guerin, Pouyat, Elite, and others.
Modern porcelains are being made at Limoges and the word *Limoges*
as part of the mark is not an indication of age. Haviland, one of the
Limoges factories, is listed as a separate category in this book.

Basket, Handles, Oak & Acorn Interior, c.1894, 5 1/2 In. 435.00
Bone Dish, White, Flowers 22.00
Bone Dish, White, Pink Flowers, Gold Trim 85.00
Bowl, Scattered Purple Asters, Pale Green Ground, Early 20th Century, 10 In. 149.00
Bowl, Strawberries & Strawberry Flowers & Vines, Signed, 9 3/4 In. 375.00
Bowl, White, Ornate Gold Trim, Oval, 13 In. 75.00
Box, Blown-Out Panels, Floral Sprays, Gold Trim, c.1891, 2 1/2 x 6 In. 175.00
Box, Cover, Shell Shape, Flowers, Flow Blue, White, Green & Gold, 1890s, 2 1/2 In. 200.00
Centerpiece, Molded Shell Shape, Sea Shells, Gilt, 10 1/2 In. 230.00
Charger, Gold Center Design, White, Gold Scalloped Edge, Higgins & Seiter, 13 In. 160.00
Charger, Green Scenes Center With Woman & Dog, 15 1/2 In. 520.00
Cup & Saucer, Leaf, Dark Browns 95.00
Fish Set, Fish, 23 1/2-In. Platter, 8 1/2-In. Plate, 6 Piece 300.00

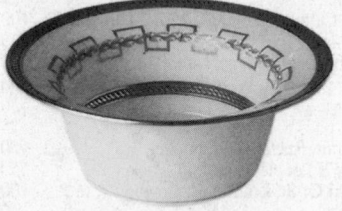

Limoges, Ramekin, Gold & Leaf Borders,
Marked, 3 1/2 In.

A vase that has been drilled for a
lamp, even if the hole for the
wiring is original, is worth 30% to
50% of the value of the same
vase without a hole.

Flask, Pilgrim, Moons, Smiling Suns, Small Red Flowers, Nichols, 1882, 6 1/4 In. 785.00
Jardiniere, Flowers, Footed, 7 In. 355.00
Jardiniere, Pink Floral Slip, White Shaded Green Ground, 4 5/8 In. 125.00
Mirror, Hand, Gold, Scalloped Design, Fan Shape Handle, Dome Back, Fragonard, 2 In. .   85.00
Mug, Grapes, Handle, 7 In. 56.00
Nut Cup, Tiny Flowers, Ivory Ground, 8 Sides, c.1890 ....   160.00
Oyster Plate, Flowers, Gilt Rim, Factory Mark, 1890, 7 1/2 In., 8 Piece 755.00
Oyster Plate, Molded Gilt Leaf Design, 7 3/8 In., 4 Piece 200.00
Pitcher, Cider, Apples, Dragon Handle, 6 x 9 1/2 In. 425.00
Pitcher, Monk, Holding Cigar, Stein, Ashtray On Table, Signed, 14 3/4 In. 550.00
Plaque, Enameled Grisaille Nativity Scene, Metal, 19th Century, Marked 155.00
Plaque, Woman's Profile, Giltwood Leaf Frame, 1900, 4 In. 400.00
Plate, Bread & Butter, Gold Trim, 1896, 6 In. 18.00
Plate, Dark Haired Woman, Gold Bands In Hair, Giltwood Frame, 9 1/4 In. 230.00
Plate, Game Birds, Pink Ground, White Underglaze, c.1900, 9 In. 125.00
Plate, Game, Flambeau, Rene, Signed, 8 1/2 In. 30.00
Plate, Game, Pheasant, Gold Trim, Scalloped Edge, Marked, 10 In. 56.00
Plate, Prince Finding Girl, Who Fits Slippers, Gold Rococo Rim, 11 1/2 In. 245.00
Plate, Purple Plums, Scalloped Gold Rim, Artist, 12 1/4 In. 225.00
Plate, Riverscapes, Gold Trim, Ruffled Edge, 9 In. 225.00
Plate Set, Different Spring Flowers, Swirled Gold Border, 1888, 7 In., 6 Piece 445.00
Plate Set, Dinner, Floral Spray Transfer, Leaf Border, Cream, T & V, 10 In., 6 Piece 205.00
Plate Set, White Center, Floral Garlands, Lyres, Scrolls, Cobalt Blue Band, 12 Piece 2845.00
Punch Bowl, Flowers, Gilt Trim, Marked, 14 In. 355.00
Punch Bowl, Stand, Fruited Branches, 14 1/2 In. 575.00
Ramekin, Gold & Leaf Borders, Marked, 3 1/2 In. ....*Illus*   10.00
Sugar & Creamer, Greek Key Border, 2 Handles, 4 In. 28.00
Sugar & Creamer, Scroll Design, Turquoise & Gold, Gold Border, c.1895, 4 In. 154.00
Tankard, Monk, Holding Cigar & Stein, Ashtray On Table, 14 3/4 In. 495.00
Tea Set, Blue & Yellow Floral Sprays, Ivory Ground, c.1891, 3 Piece 470.00
Tea Set, Branches Of Pink Flowering Wild Roses, 10-In. Bowl, 13 Piece 322.00
Tray, Central Woman Cartouche, Cupid, Gilt Border, 1900, 14 1/2 In. 1380.00
Tray, Grapes, Fluted, Round, 16 In. 220.00
Vase, Enamel On Copper, Purple, Camille Faure, 20th Century, 12 In. 3900.00
Vase, Flowers, Brown, Thiraud, 10 1/2 In. 86.00
Vase, Fox Hunt Scenes, Early 20th Century, 8 1/4 In., Pair 193.00
Vase, Gilt Flowers, Blue Glossy Finish, Iridescent, Angular Handles, 17 In. 230.00
Vase, Poppies, Leaves, Deep Cobalt Blue, Sterling Silver Overlay, Signed, 8 In. 403.00
Vase, Red, White Flowers, Green Leaves, Burgundy, Gold Ground, Signed, 2 x 3 In. 460.00
Vase, Rose Bush & Blossoming Branches, Handles, 10 7/8 In. 80.00

LINDBERGH was a national hero. In 1927, Charles Lindbergh, the aviator, became the first man to make a nonstop solo flight across the
Atlantic Ocean. In 1932, his son was kidnapped and murdered, and
Lindbergh was again the center of public interest. He died in 1974. All
types of Lindbergh memorabilia are collected.

Airplane, Lindy Prop Drive, Hubley, 10-In. Wingspan 2995.00
Airplane, Spirit Of St. Louis, Model, Tin, c.1930, 19 1/2 x 4 1/2 In. 395.00
Bank, Bust, Lead, 5 7/8 In. 125.00
Button, Lindy Photo, Celluloid, Black & White, 3 In. 100.00
Button, Lucky Lindy, Picture, Celluloid, 1 1/2 In. 27.00
Button, Lucky Lindy, Welcome, Portrait, Horseshoes, Celluloid, Blue & White, 1 In. 100.00
Button, Spirit Of St. Louis, Portrait, WE, Celluloid, 3 In. 125.00
Button, Welcome Home, Capt. Charles Lindbergh, Slim Lindy, Plane, Litho, 2 In. 125.00
Calendar, 1929, Lindbergh Circling Dome Of Our State Capitol, Wash., Celluloid 200.00
Candy Container, Spirit Of St. Louis, Green Glass, Tin 550.00
Compact, Lucky Lindy Photograph Cover 75.00
Mirror, Captain Charles Lucky Lindbergh, Plane, Portrait, Rectangular, Pocket 150.00
Mirror, Spirit Of St. Louis In Hangar, Lindy & Group Of People, Celluloid, Pocket 550.00
Pin, Lindbergh's Home Town, Little Falls, Minn., Spirit Of St. Louis, Gilt Cowboy 100.00
Pin, Spirit Of St. Louis, Spirit Of Youth Clothes, Metal 40.00
Stereo Card, Our Ambassador Of The Air, Col. Lindbergh, Plane, Keystone View Co. 12.00
Watch Fob, Lindy, Eiffel Tower, Statue Of Liberty, Brass 125.00

LITHOPHANES are porcelain pictures made by casting clay in layers of various thicknesses. When a piece is held to the light, a picture of light and shadow is seen through it. Most lithophanes date from the 1825–1875 period. A few are still being made. Many lithophanes sold today were originally panels for lampshades.

Lamp, Electric, Hanging, Square, Plaque Sides, Brass Frame, Ruby Flashed, 9 In. 1495.00
Stein, Erotic, Bonn To Munich Railroad, Pewter Lid, Germany, c.1887, 10 In. 127.00
Warmer, Plaques Of Landscape, Pierced Brass Frame, Mid 19th Century, 5 In. 285.00

LIVERPOOL, England, was the site of several pottery and porcelain factories from 1716 to 1785. Some earthenware was made with transfer decorations. Sadler and Green made print-decorated wares from 1756. Many of the pieces were made for the American market and feature patriotic emblems, such as eagles, flags, and other special-interest motifs. Liverpool pitchers are always called Liverpool jugs by collectors.

Jug, Masonic, Symbolic Picture, World Is In Pain, 11 1/2 In. 1150.00
Jug, Transfer Print 1804 Attack On Tripoli 2950.00
Jug, Transfer Ship, American Flag, Farmer Holding Scythe, c.1800, 9 1/4 In. 1725.00
Pitcher, George Washington, Esq., 10 In. 3450.00
Pitcher, Italian Transfer Design, Floral, Handle, 19th Century 430.00
Pitcher, Prosperity To United States Of America, Lower Census Chart, 7 1/2 In. 5060.00
Pitcher, Transfer, Black & White, Commodore Stephen Decator, 5 1/2 In. 2070.00
Pitcher, Washington In Glory, America In Tears 1265.00
Plate, British Ship Design, Scalloped Edge, Black, White, 9 1/4 In. 230.00
Sauceboat, Paneled Sides, Blue Floral, Oval, c.1780, 5 3/4 In. 460.00
Teapot, Prussian Scenes, 12 1/2 In. 4600.00
Tureen, Figure, 2 Monograms, Black Transfer, Cover, Oval Handle, 9 1/2 x 12 In. 1090.00
Tureen, Soup, Cover, Prussian Scenes 6325.00

LLADRO is a Spanish porcelain. Juan, Jose, and Vicente Lladro opened a ceramics workshop in Almacera in 1951. They soon began making figurines in a distinctive, elongated style. In 1958 the factory moved to Tabernes Blanques, Spain. The company makes stoneware and porcelain figurines and vases in limited and unlimited editions. Dates given are first and last years of production.

Bell, Christmas, 1987, No. 5458 . . . . 55.00
Bell, Christmas, 1988, No. 5525 . . . . 30.00
Bell, Christmas, 1989, No. 5616 . . . . 50.00
Bell, Christmas, 1990, No. 5641 . . . . .30.00 to 40.00
Figurine, Aggressive Duck, No. 1288, 1974-1995, 8 1/2 In. 207.00
Figurine, Angel Tree Topper, No. 5719, 1990, 7 In. 300.00
Figurine, Angela, No. 5211, 1984-1999, 7 In. 165.00
Figurine, Angelic Cymbalist, No. 5876, 1992, 7 1/4 In. 75.00
Figurine, Aranjuez, Little Lady, No. 4879, 1974-1976, 12 1/4 In. 350.00
Figurine, At Attention, No. 5407, 1987-1990, 12 1/2 In. 450.00
Figurine, At The Circus, No. 5052, 1979-1985, 13 In. 1300.00
Figurine, August Moon, No. 5122, 1982-1993, 8 1/2 In. 400.00
Figurine, Barrister, No. 4908, 1974-1985, 15 3/4 In. 425.00
Figurine, Basket Of Love, No. 7622, 1994-1995, 9 1/2 In. .250.00 to 425.00
Figurine, Best Friend, No. 7620, 1993-1994, 6 1/2 In. .175.00 to 350.00
Figurine, Billy Soccer Player, No. 5135, 1982-1983, 8 1/2 In. . . . . .400.00 to 615.00
Figurine, Bird Watcher, Boy, No. 4730, 1970-1985, 6 1/4 In. 380.00
Figurine, Boy With Dog, No. 4522, 1970-1997, 7 1/2 In. 130.00
Figurine, Boy, With Double Base, No. 4615, 1969-1989, 8 1/2 In. . . . . .350.00 to 475.00
Figurine, Boy, With Guitar, No. 4614, 1969-1979, 7 1/2 In. 425.00
Figurine, Bugler, No. 5406, 12 1/2 In. 450.00
Figurine, Can I Play, Collectors Club, No. 7610, 1990 . . . . 530.00
Figurine, Captain Cadet, No. 5404, 1987-1990, 12 1/2 In. 450.00
Figurine, Cat Girl, No. 5164, 1982-1985, 9 In. 600.00
Figurine, Centaur Boy, No. 1013, 1969-1989, 8 1/4 In. 500.00
Figurine, Christmas Carols, No. 1239, 1973-1981, 9 In. . . . . .373.00 to 800.00
Figurine, Christmas Seller, No. 1276, 1974-1981, 10 1/4 In. 600.00

Figurine, Chrysanthemum, No. 4990, 1978-1998, 11 1/2 In. 250.00
Figurine, Clown, No. 1027, 1969-1993, 17 3/4 In. 65.00
Figurine, Donkey In Love, No. 4524, 1969-1985, 5 In. 500.00
Figurine, Dress Rehearsal, No. 5497, 1988-1999, 7 1/2 In. 275.00
Figurine, Drummer Boy, No. 5403, 1987-1990, 12 1/2 In. 550.00
Figurine, Ducks, Flapping, No. 4759, 1971-1981, 11 3/4 In. 750.00
Figurine, Dutch Children, 1977-1981, 13 3/4 In. 287.00
Figurine, Eskimo Boy & Girl, No. 2038-3, 1971-1994, 13 In. 455.00
Figurine, Fairy Garland, No. 5860, 1992-1995, 8 1/2 In. 155.00
Figurine, Fish A Plenty, No. 5172, 1982-1994, 9 In. 500.00
Figurine, Flower Peddler, No. 5029, 1979-1985, 10 1/4 In. 1800.00
Figurine, Flowers In Pot, No. 5028, 1980-1985, 8 1/2 In. 800.00
Figurine, Flowers On The Back, No. 1286, 1974-1998, 9 In. 132.00
Figurine, Forgotten, No. 1502, 1986-1991, 3 1/2 In. 143.00
Figurine, Geese Group, No. 4549, 1969-1996, 8 1/2 In. 92.00
Figurine, Geisha, No. 4807, 1972-1993, 12 In. 86.00
Figurine, Girl & Sparrow, No. 4758, 1971-1979, 11 1/2 In. 350.00
Figurine, Girl Kissing, No. 4873, 1974-1997, 7 1/2 In. 70.00
Figurine, Girl Tennis Player, No. 4798, 1972-1981, 12 1/2 In. 450.00
Figurine, Girl Walking, No. 5040, 1979-1981, 9 1/2 In. 550.00
Figurine, Girl With Dice, No. 1176, 1971-1981, 7 3/4 In. 250.00
Figurine, Girl With Doll, No. 1083, 1969-1985, 7 In. 300.00
Figurine, Girl With Doll, No. 1211, 1972-1984, 8 1/2 In. 275.00
Figurine, Girl With Flowers, No. 1088, 1969-1989, 8 1/4 In. 645.00
Figurine, Girl With Goose & Dog, No. 4866, 1974-1993, 5 1/2 In. 161.00
Figurine, Girl With Hat, No. 1147, 1971-1985, 8 1/2 In. 350.00
Figurine, Girl With Lamb, No. 1010, 1969-1993, 8 1/2 In. 375.00
Figurine, Girl With Lamp, No. 4584, 1969-1993, 10 1/2 In. 250.00
Figurine, Girl With Lilies, Sitting, No. 4972, 1977-1997, 9 In. 190.00
Figurine, Girl With Milk Pail, No. 4682, 1970-1991, 9 1/2 In. 400.00
Figurine, Good Bear, No. 1205, 1972-1989, 4 3/4 In. 85.00
Figurine, Goya Lady, No. 5125, 1982-1990, 12 1/2 In. 350.00
Figurine, Hamlet, No. 1144, 1971-1973, 16 1/2 In. 1900.00
Figurine, Hamlet, Seated, No. 4729, 1970-1980, 15 3/4 In. 850.00
Figurine, Heavenly Harpist.No. 5830, 1991, 7 1/4 In. 80.00
Figurine, Hebrew Student, No. 4684, 1970-1985, 11 1/2 In. 800.00
Figurine, Hello, Flowers, No. 5543, 1989-1993, 7 1/2 In. 650.00
Figurine, I've Got It!, No. 5827, 1991-1995, 5 In. 200.00
Figurine, Innocence In Bloom, No. 7644, 1996-1997, 9 1/2 In. 225.00
Figurine, Jolie, No. 5210, 1984, 7 1/2 In. 165.00
Figurine, Lady At Dressing Table, No. 1242, 1973-1978, 11 3/4 In. 2000.00
Figurine, Lady Empire, No. 4719, 1970-1979, 18 In. 725.00
Figurine, Lilly, Soccer Player, No. 5134, 1982-1983, 9 In. 700.00
Figurine, Little Bird, No. 1301, 1974-1983, 4 1/2 In. 57.00
Figurine, Little Bo-Peep, No. 1312, 1974-1985, 6 1/2 In. 450.00
Figurine, Little Shepherd With Goat, No. 4817, 1972-1981, 9 3/4 In. 400.00
Figurine, Love In Bloom, No. 5292, 1985-1998, 8 1/2 In. 230.00
Figurine, Love Letter, Norman Rockwell Series, No. 1406, 1982, 7 1/2 In. 1100.00
Figurine, My Buddy, Collectors Club, No. 7609, 1989-1990, 8 In. .... 400.00 to 900.00
Figurine, My Little Pet, No. 4994, 1978-1985, 11 3/4 In. 250.00
Figurine, Nature's Bounty, No. 1417, 1982-1995, 10 1/2 In. 230.00
Figurine, New Shepherdess, No. 4576, 1969-1989, 9 1/2 In. 250.00
Figurine, Nightingale Pair, No. 1228, 1972-1981, 5 In. 86.00
Figurine, Olympic Champion, No. 5871, 1992-1994, 9 In. 300.00
Figurine, Ornament, Holy Shepherds, No. 5809, 1991, 3 1/4 In., 3 Piece 50.00
Figurine, Pekingese Sitting, No. 4641, 1969-1985, 6 In. 420.00
Figurine, Pick Of The Litter, No. 7621, 1993, 7 1/4 In. .... 320.00 to 425.00
Figurine, Picture Perfect, No. 7612, 1991, 8 1/2 In. 650.00
Figurine, Pondering, No. 5173.1982-1993, 6 1/2 In. 650.00
Figurine, Poodle, No. 1259, 1974-1985, 5 1/2 In. 450.00
Figurine, Pottery Setter, No. 5079, 1980-1985, 10 1/2 In. 800.00
Figurine, Puppy Love, No. 1127, 1971-1996, 10 1/4 In. 260.00
Figurine, School Days, No. 7604, 1988-1989, 8 1/4 In. .... 400.00 to 750.00

Figurine, Seeds Of Laughter, No. 5764, 1991-1995, 4 3/4 In. 65.00
Figurine, Seesaw, No. 1255, 1974-1978, 9 1/2 In. 475.00
Figurine, Skye Terrier, No. 4643, 1969-1985, 6 In. 350.00
Figurine, Spring Bell, No. 7613, 1991, 3 In. 50.00
Figurine, Spring Bouquets, Collectors Club, No. 7603, 1987-1988, 8 1/4 In. 1050.00
Figurine, Summer Bell, No. 7614, 1992, 3 In. 35.00
Figurine, Summer Stroll, No. 7611, 1991-1992, 9 In. 600.00
Figurine, Sweet Harvest, No. 5380, 1986-1990, 8 1/2 In. 1100.00
Figurine, Veterinarian, No. 4825, 1972-1985, 13 1/4 In. 600.00
Figurine, Violinist & Girl, No. 1039, 1969-1991, 17 3/4 In. 200.00
Figurine, Voyage Of Columbus, No. 5847, 1992-1993, 9 In. 700.00
Figurine, Walk In Versailles, No. 5004, 1978-1981, 15 3/4 In. 910.00
Figurine, Wheelbarrow, No. 1245, 1973-1981, 8 1/2 In. 338.00
Figurine, Wintry Day, No. 3513, 1978-1988, 8 3/4 In. 400.00
Figurine, Woodcutter, No. 4656, 1969-1978, 14 1/2 In. 375.00
Figurine, Yachtsman, No. 5206, 1984-1994, 13 1/4 In. 300.00
Ornament, Angels, No. 1604, 1988, 2 In., 3 Piece 250.00
Ornament, Ball, Christmas, No. 1603, 1988 .... 100.00
Ornament, Ball, Christmas, No. 5656, 1989 .... 100.00
Ornament, Christmas Morning, No. 5940, 1992, 3 1/4 In., 3 Piece 65.00
Plate, Christmas, Caroling, No. 7006, 1971, 8 In. 250.00

LOCKE ART is a trademark found on glass of the early twentieth century. Joseph Locke worked at many English and American firms. He designed and etched his own glass in Pittsburgh, Pennsylvania, starting in the 1880s. Some pieces were marked *Joe Locke*, but most were marked with the words *Locke Art*. The mark is hidden in the pattern on the glass.

Decanter, Poppy, Hollow Stopper, 11 3/4 In. 1071.00
Oyster Cocktail, Oyster Pattern, 3 3/4 In. 495.00
Sherbet, Saucer Foot 90.00

LOETZ glass was made in many varieties. Johann Loetz bought a glassworks in Austria in 1840. He died in 1848 and his widow ran the company; then in 1879, his grandson took over. Most collectors recognize the iridescent gold glass similar to Tiffany, but many other types were made. The firm closed during World War II.

Bowl, Blue, Green, Violet, On Green, 1 1/2 x 5 In. 189.00
Bowl, Electric Blue Iridescent Lower Portion, 1910, 6 3/4 In. 290.00
Bowl, Green Iridescent, Rolled Rim, Signed, 6 1/2 In. 460.00
Bowl, Green, Scalloped Edge, 13 In. 336.00
Centerpiece, Iridized Green, Stag & Foliage, Figural Base, 9 1/2 In. 364.00
Finger Bowl, Oil Spot, Blue, Green, Ruffled Edge, Signed, 2 7/8 x 6 1/2 In. 425.00
Jar, Cracker, Green, Amethyst Threading, 6 Sides, 7 x 4 3/4 In. 345.00
Lamp, Phanomen, Yellow Opaque Lava, 1913, 11 In. 1840.00
Mug, Oil Spot, Gold, Purple, Blue Over Amber, 3 Handles, 4 3/4 In. 252.00
Shade, Shell Shape, Oil Spot, 8 In. 448.00
Vase, Amber Textured, Cameo Confetti & Patches, Ear Handles, 13 In. 3360.00
Vase, Amethyst Iridescent, Pulled Design, Platinum, 3 Handles, Signed, 12 1/2 In. 6330.00
Vase, Apricot, Pink, Twisted Ribs, Dimpled Base, 1900, 10 In. 895.00
Vase, Baby Blue, Red, Mint Green, Gold Rim, 1890, 5 1/2 In. 460.00
Vase, Black, Tricornered Rim, 7 In. 850.00
Vase, Blue & Pink Iridescent, Textured Platinum Drapes, 7 In. 545.00
Vase, Blue & Purple, Iridescent, Rolled Rim, c.1902, 5 1/2 In. 460.00
Vase, Blue Diamonds, Over Frosted Ground, Cameo, Josef Hoffmann, 9 In. 9775.00
Vase, Blue Iridescent, 1900, 7 1/2 In. 1050.00
Vase, Blue Iridescent, Pulled Handles, Signed, 8 1/2 In. 4600.00
Vase, Blue, Gold, Green, Purple Iridescent, Metal Collar, 7 1/2 x 4 In. 345.00
Vase, Brown, Air Traps, Gold, Blue, White Interior, Signed, c.1888, 7 In. 1610.00
Vase, Bud, Iridescent Green, Yellow Enamel, Signed, Austria, 4 1/2 x 3 In. 265.00
Vase, Carneol Marmorierte, Red Marble, Enameled, 5 1/4 In. 224.00
Vase, Circle Design On Platinum, Green, Crimped Top, 8 1/2 In. 605.00
Vase, Cobalt Base, Green, Red, Yellow, Signed, Austria, 10 1/2 x 4 1/2 In. 225.00

Vase, Crackle Glass, Iridescent, Vertical Twisted Ribs, 12 In. 525.00
Vase, Cranberry Iridescent, Crimped, 13 In. 672.00
Vase, Cranberry, Ruffled Edge, Vertical Ribs, 9 1/4 In. 325.00
Vase, Custard, Pulled Gold Design, 1900, 8 1/2 In. 1495.00
Vase, Deep Blue Over Orange, 3 Dark Blue Handles, Cameo, Powolny, 4 In. 1725.00
Vase, Deep Orange, Brown Stripes, Cameo, Michael Powolny, 1920, 7 1/2 In. 695.00
Vase, Dimpled Sides, Oil Spot, Iridescent, 9 In. 605.00
Vase, Draped Threading, Iridescent, c.1900, 7 1/8 In. 460.00
Vase, Emerald Green, 4 Twisted Ribs, 1900, 6 In. 6500.00
Vase, Emerald Green, Iridescent Swirls, 6 In. 95.00
Vase, Flowers & Bugs, Midnight Blue, Orange Ground, Cameo, 8 In. 1350.00
Vase, Formosa, Green Iridescent, Applied Threading, 1900, 7 1/4 In. 595.00
Vase, Fuchsias, Butterfly, Burgundy, Satin Blue, Signed, 15 1/4 In. 1725.00
Vase, Gold & Green Iridescent, Ruffled Edge, Signed, 13 1/4 In. 1265.00
Vase, Gold Iridescent 3 Tendrils, Gold Iridescent Lip, 1903, 6 1/2 In. 550.00
Vase, Gold Iridescent Lip, 6 Gold Tendrils, Polished Pontil, 1903, 12 In. 1895.00
Vase, Gold Jester, Applied Threading, Tall Neck, 11 1/2 In. 1265.00
Vase, Gold Luster, 4 Pulled Iridescent Feathers, Silver Overlay Poppies, 9 5/8 In. 2530.00
Vase, Gold Oil Spot, Double Gourd, 6 1/2 In. 345.00
Vase, Green Iridescent Glass, Sterling Silver Rim, Tapered Neck, 4 3/4 In., Pair 115.00
Vase, Green Pearlized, Iridescent, 1902, 9 x 7 In. 895.00
Vase, Green Pulled Waves, On Gold, Gold Center, 6 x 3 1/2 In. 2070.00
Vase, Green Satin, Twisted Ribs, 13 1/2 In. 879.00
Vase, Green, Padded Flowers, Spotty Apple Green & Gold, Tricornered Rim, 4 In. 2128.00
Vase, Green, Silver Highlights, Polished Pontil, 3 In. 895.00
Vase, Grotesque, Blue, Green Iridescent, 6 x 3 1/4 In. 550.00
Vase, Iridescent Gold, Swirled Design, Blue & Purple Highlights, Oval, c.1902, 5 1/2 In. . . 460.00
Vase, Jack-In-The-Pulpit, Deep Amethyst Iridescent, Austria, 4 x 5 In. 975.00
Vase, King Tut, Reeded, Gold Iridescent, Applied Handles, 6 3/4 In. 287.00
Vase, Lavender, Green Iridescent, Tree Trunk Shape, 5 1/4 In. 150.00
Vase, Light Green, Applied Rigaree, 1910, 6 1/4 In. 149.00
Vase, Marmorierte, Swirled Marble, Pink Interior, Gold Enameled, c.1890, 7 3/8 In. 570.00
Vase, Mother-Of-Pearl Iridescent, White Threading, 1910, 5 In. 585.00
Vase, Muted Gold, Pulled Handles, Pinched, Tricornered Rim, c.1900, 5 In. 747.00
Vase, Oil Spot, 3 Dimpled Sides, Green Iridescent, 1900, 6 3/4 In. 650.00
Vase, Oil Spot, 4 Dimpled Sides, Gold Iridescent, 1900, 7 1/4 In. 675.00
Vase, Oil Spot, Blue, 3 Dimpled Sides, 3 3/4 x 6 1/4 In. 1195.00
Vase, Oil Spot, Blue, Light Gold Iridescent Handles, 1936, 5 x 6 1/2 In. 2250.00
Vase, Oil Spot, Crimped Edge, Green, 4 3/4 In. 230.00
Vase, Oil Spot, Deep Amethyst Iridescent Applied, Leaf, Vine, 7 1/2 In. 1850.00
Vase, Oil Spot, Deep Blue, Amethyst, 6 1/2 x 6 In. 950.00
Vase, Oil Spot, Gold Iridescent, 1900, 12 In. 495.00
Vase, Oil Spot, Green Opalescent, 1900, 3 3/4 In. 895.00
Vase, Oil Spot, Green, Pinched Top, 6 1/2 In. 285.00
Vase, Oil Spot, Green, Rolled Rim, 7 1/4 In. 115.00
Vase, Oil Spot, Lemon Yellow, Tapered, 18 1/2 x 7 1/2 In. 5465.00
Vase, Oil Spot, Stylized Foliate Base, Pewter Mounted By Liberty, 11 3/4 In. 2990.00
Vase, Paperweight, Green Pulled Feathers, Pink, Clear Cased, 6 In. 900.00
Vase, Papillon, Gold, Green, Amethyst, 4 Lobes, 8 1/2 In. 225.00
Vase, Papillon, Gold, Scrolled Handles, Rings At Mid Section, 7 1/4 In. 336.00
Vase, Peacock Eye, Green Iridescent, 7 x 3 In. 132.00
Vase, Pink, Green, Silver-Blue Oil Spots, Applied Handles, 1900, 5 In. 2500.00
Vase, Pulled Drapery, Platinum, Yellow, Blue, Squat, 8 1/2 x 6 3/4 In. 4600.00
Vase, Pulled Feather, Blue, Green, Red, White, Yellow, 8 In. 195.00
Vase, Pulled Gold, Pink Design, Twisted Body, 3 Red Tendrils, Signed, 7 In. 8050.00
Vase, Pulled Stripes, Oil Spot, Lemon Yellow, Bulbous, 5 In. 805.00
Vase, Pulled Trailed Feather Design, Gold, Red Amber Iridescent Glaze, 11 1/4 In. 690.00
Vase, Red Pulled Feathers, Iridescent, Pear Shape, 11 In. 747.00
Vase, Rosewater Sprinkler Shape, Dark Green, 1900, 11 3/4 In. 3000.00
Vase, Rusticana, Green, Pale Iridescent, c.1905, 7 x 5 1/2 In. 169.00
Vase, Salmon, Yellow, Black, Gold Swirls, Signed, 7 In. 7475.00
Vase, Silver Blue, Pulled Trails, Golden Lava, Cone Shaped, 12 In. 1065.00

Vase, Silver Pulled Feathers, Crimson, Gold, Signed, 15 1/2 In. 2300.00
Vase, Titania, Silver Overlay, Pontil, 12 1/2 x 6 1/2 In. 2300.00
Vase, White Ground, Cameo, Signed, Richard, 8 1/2 In. 675.00
Vase, White Iridescent, Pink, Blue, Signed, 4 In. 1250.00
Vase, White, Green Threading At Shoulder, 5 1/2 In. 115.00

LONE RANGER, a fictional character, was introduced on the radio in 1932. Over three thousand shows were produced before the series ended in 1954. In 1938, the first Lone Ranger movie was made. Television shows were started in 1949 and are still seen on some stations. The Lone Ranger appears on many products and was even the name of a restaurant chain for several years.

Badge Set, Masked Cowboy, Sheriff, Gun, Tin, Japan, 1960s 6.50
Coin, Lucky Horseshoe 95.00
Coloring Book, Unused, 1959 . . . . 75.00
Doll, Bond Bread Premium, Composition, Tag, 1938 . . . . 1150.00
Doll, Tonto, Accessories, Gabriel Industries, 1973 . . . . 30.00
Figure, Chalkware 40.00
Figure, Ranger, Silver, Gabriel Industries, 1973, 10 In. 75.00
Figure, Tonto, Horse, Holster, Original Clothing, Gabriel Ind. 90.00
First Aid Kit, Tin Container, Contents, 1938, 4 x 4 In. 105.00
Game, Board, Parker Brothers, Metal Horse Playing Pieces, 1938 . . . . .75.00 to 110.00
Game, Fighting Mountain Lions, Tin, 4 Balls, 3 1/2 x 5 In. 70.00
Game, Jigsaw Puzzle, Milton Bradley, Lone Ranger Legend, 250 Piece, 1980 . . . . 12.00
Game, Jigsaw Puzzle, Ranger, Silver & Tonto, By Fire, Frame Tray, 1978, 13 In. 30.00
Game, Shooting, Lone Ranger & Tonto, Box, England 110.00
Game, Target, Gun, Tin, 16 x 27 In. 300.00
Game, Target, Tin, Marx 145.00
Glass, Hi-Yo Silver, Lone Ranger On Rearing Silver, Green, 1938, 4 In., 3 Piece 175.00
Gun, Cap 295.00
Gun, Squirt, Head Of Masked Ranger, 5 1/2 In. 50.00
Handcuffs, Blister Card 50.00
Harmonica, Lone Ranger On Silver, Magnus Lone Ranger Inc., Box, 1947, 4 In. 130.00
Hike-O-Meter, Strap 95.00
Horseshoe Set, Rubber, Lone Ranger, Tonto, Gardner, TLR, Box, c.1950 . . . . 175.00
Key Chain, With Bullet 50.00
Lunch Box, Legend Of The Lone Ranger, Aladdin Industries, 1980 . . . . 36.00
Neckerchief, Red, White, Lone Ranger & Silver, 22 x 20 1/2 In. 55.00
Patch, Lone Ranger Volunteers, Victory V, 1942, 2 1/2 In. 65.00
Pencil Box, Embossed Lone Ranger, Hi-Yo Silver, TLR, 1940 . . . . 100.00
Photograph, Lone Ranger & Tonto Promoting Christmas Seals, Glossy, 10 In. 12.00
Pin, Buchan's Bread, Celluloid, Red, White, 1 In. 43.00
Plate, Hi-Yo Silver, Red Lone Rangers, White & Silver Center 85.00
Ring, Flashlight 150.00
Ring, Secret Compartment, Pictures, 1942 . . . . 650.00
Tie Tack, Lone Ranger & Silver, TV Shape, Metal, Embossed, 1 1/8 In. 18.00
Toy, Lone Ranger On Silver, Hi-Yo Silver, Windup, Tin, Marx, Box, 1939, 9 In. . . .325.00 to 500.00
Toy, Range Rider, Marx, 1940s, 10 1/2 In. 450.00
View-Master, Mystery Rustler, 3 Reels, Booklet, Envelope, 1956 . . . . .60.00 to 75.00

LONGWY Workshop of Longwy, France, first made ceramic wares in 1798. The workshop is still in business. Most of the ceramic pieces found today are glazed with many colors to resemble cloisonne or other enameled metal. Many pieces were made with stylized figures and Art Deco designs. The factory used a variety of marks.

Bowl, Stylized Flowers & Leaves Around Rim, Impressed Mark, 8 In. 550.00
Bowl, Stylized Peacock Center, Blue & Black, Stamped Mark, 14 1/2 In. 920.00
Charger, Buck, Autumn Forest Scene, Stamped Mark, 14 1/2 In. 550.00
Charger, Peacock, Gilt Branch, Flowers, Aqua To Blue Ground, 14 1/2 In. 920.00
Charger, Springtime, Firebirds, France, 14 1/2 In. 550.00
Charger, Water Birds, Pierced For Hanging, 14 1/2 In. 750.00
Plaque, Exotic Flowers, Blue Ground, Round, 14 3/4 In. 515.00
Tile, Bronze Footed Frame, 9 1/2 x 9 1/2 In. 650.00

If old magazines or books or even stuffed toys smell musty, put them in a plastic bag with some kitty litter. Be sure to get the inexpensive brands that are just clay litter with no scents or clumping additives. Leave the bag closed for at least a week. Repeat with new litter if necessary.

Low, Tile, Religieuse, Praying Nun, Yellow Brown Glaze, Arthur Osborne

Tile, Lily, Black & Ivory, Yellow Ground, 8 x 8 In.	265.00
Tray, Incised & Painted Blue Floral Cover, Impressed Mark, 8 x 2 In.	375.00
Vase, Art Deco, Black Glaze On Bottom, 7 In.	500.00
Vase, Bands Of Stylized Flowers & Leaves, Crackled Ground, 1920s, 13 3/4 In.	2686.00
Vase, Blue Stylized Woman's Face, Ivory Ground, Drilled Hole, 11 1/2 In.	235.00
Vase, Bulbous, Incised, Painted, Stylized Design, Black, Blue Ground, 11 In.	1150.00
Vase, Cylindrical, Blue Glazed Ground, Signed, 6 In.	350.00
Vase, Dark Blue Base, Carmel, Orange, Purple Ground, 12 1/2 In.	979.00
Vase, Incised, Painted, Ivory, Mauve, Gold Flowers, Blue, Ivory Panels, 9 1/2 In.	1150.00
Vase, Stylized Red Flower Panels, Lattice Design, Stamped Mark, 10 1/2 In.	805.00

LONHUDA Pottery Company of Steubenville, Ohio, was organized in 1892 by William Long, W. H. Hunter, and Alfred Day. Brown underglaze slip-decorated pottery was made. The firm closed in 1896. The company used many marks; the earliest included the letters *LPCO*.

Base, Oil Lamp, Brown, Green Floral Design, 4 3/4 x 6 1/2 In.	255.00
Vase, Blue Flower On 1 Side, 2 x 1 1/2 In.	65.00
Vase, Handles, 3 Flowers On 1 Side, 2 On The Other Side, 8 In.	379.00

LOTUS WARE was made by the Knowles, Taylor & Knowles Company of East Liverpool, Ohio, from 1890 to 1900. Lotus Ware, a thin porcelain which resembles Belleek, was sometimes decorated outside the factory. Other types of ceramics that were made by the Knowles, Taylor & Knowles Company are listed under KTK.

Bowl, Ruffled Edge, Beaded Pearl Design, Ivory, 8 In.	576.00
Dish, Shell, Leaf Shape, 4 In.	374.00
Vase, Fish Scale Border, Painted Narcissus, Footed, Frank W. Whitney, 1889, 8 In.	770.00

LOW art tiles were made by the J. and J. G. Low Art Tile Works of Chelsea, Massachusetts, from 1877 to 1902. A variety of art and other tiles were made. Some of the tiles were made by a process called *natural*, some were hand modeled, and some were made mechanically.

Tile, Boy, Riding Stork In Flight, Speckled Green Glaze, 1881, 4 5/8 x 6 1/4 In.	308.00
Tile, Brown Acanthus Leaf, Fleur-De-Lis, 4 1/4 In.	50.00
Tile, Head Of Dragon, 1881, 6 In.	160.00
Tile, Leaves, Flower, Green, 1881, 6 1/8 In.	50.00
Tile, Portrait, Benjamin Franklin, Signed, 1881, 6 In.	300.00
Tile, Portrait, Leaves On Each Side, Chelsea, Mass., 6 In.	60.00
Tile, Religieuse, Praying Nun, Yellow Brown Glaze, Arthur Osborne ....*Illus*	160.00

LUNCH BOXES and lunch pails have been used to carry lunches to school or work since the nineteenth century. Today, most collectors want either early tobacco advertising boxes or children's lunch boxes made since the 1930s. These boxes are made of metal or plastic. Boxes listed here include the original Thermos bottle inside the box unless

otherwise indicated. Movie, television, and cartoon characters may be found in their own categories. There was an important auction of lunch boxes this year and many rare, mint lunch boxes were sold. Some of these high prices are listed.

LUNCH BOX, Action Jackson, Metal, Ohio Art, 1973	173.00
Archies, Metal, Aladdin, 1969	195.00
Astronaut Space, Metal, Dome, King Seeley Thermos, 1960	345.00
Astronauts, Metal, Aladdin, 1963	125.00
Banana Splits, Vinyl, King Seeley Thermos, 1969	110.00 to 200.00
Barbie & Francie, Black, Vinyl, King Seeley Thermos, 1965	77.00
Barbie & Midge, Black, Vinyl, King Seeley Thermos, 1964	22.00 to 104.00
Barbie & Midge, Vinyl, Black, King Seeley Thermos, c.1963	110.00
Barbie & Midge, Vinyl, Dome, Black, King Seeley Thermos, 1964	220.00
Battle Star Galactica, Metal, Aladdin, 1978	58.00
Beany & Cecil, Vinyl, King Seeley Thermos, 1963	175.00 to 200.00
Beverly Hillbillies, Metal, Aladdin, 1963	140.00 to 235.00
Boating, Metal, American Thermos, 1959	201.00
Bobby Soxer, Talking On Telephone, Poodle Thermos, Aladdin	127.00
Bonanza, Brown, Metal, Aladdin, 1965	468.00
Bozo The Clown, Dome, Metal, Aladdin, 1963	161.00
Bread Loaf, Campbell Soup Thermos, Metal, Dome, Aladdin, 1968	374.00
Bullwinkle & Rocky, Boris & Natasha, Blue, Metal, Ohio Art, 1962	2300.00
Cable Car, Metal, Dome, Aladdin, 1962	45.00
Campus Queen, Metal, King Seeley Thermos, 1967	88.00
Captain Kangaroo, Vinyl, 1964	195.00
Casey Jones, Metal, Dome, Universal Industries, 1960	400.00
Casper, Vinyl, King Seeley Thermos, 1966	375.00
Close Encounters, Metal, King Seeley Thermos, 1981	55.00
Cracker Jack, Metal, Aladdin, 1979	195.00
Curiosity Shop, Metal, King Seeley Thermos, 1972	60.00
Dr. Seuss, Metal, Aladdin, 1970	345.00
Dream Boat, Vinyl, Feldco, 1960	127.00
Dudley Do-Right, Metal, Ohio Art, 1962	3335.00
Dudley Do-Right, Nell, Vinyl, Ardee, 1972	489.00
Dukes Of Hazzard, Metal, Aladdin, 1980	50.00
Fall Guy, Metal, Aladdin, 1981	40.00
Flintstones & Dino, Metal, Aladdin, 1962	345.00
Flying Nun, Metal, Aladdin, 1968	110.00
Flying Nun, Vinyl, Aladdin, 1968	225.00

Lunch Box, Jetsons, Metal, Dome, Aladdin, Thermos, 1963

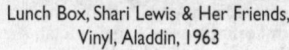

Lunch Box, Shari Lewis & Her Friends, Vinyl, Aladdin, 1963

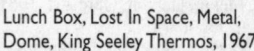

Lunch Box, Lost In Space, Metal, Dome, King Seeley Thermos, 1967

Lunch Box, Volkswagen Bus, Metal, Dome,
Omni Graphics, 1960

Lunch Box, Twiggy, Vinyl, Aladdin, 1967

G.I. Joe, Metal, King Seeley Thermos, 1967	125.00
Go Go, Vinyl, Brunch Bag, Aladdin, 1966	86.00
Gomer Pyle USMC, Metal, Aladdin, 1966	201.00
Green Hornet, Metal, King Seeley Thermos, 1967	1840.00
Grizzly Adams, Metal, Dome, Aladdin, 1977	95.00
Gunsmoke, Metal, Aladdin, 1959	200.00
Happy Days, The Fonz, American Thermos, 1978	310.00
Hogan's Heroes, Metal, Dome, Aladdin, 1966	325.00
Huckleberry Hound, Metal, Aladdin, 1961	75.00
James Bond, Metal, Aladdin, 1966	259.00 to 375.00
Jetsons, Metal, Dome, Aladdin, Thermos, 1963 *Illus*	978.00
Joe Palooka, Metal, 2 Handles, Continental Can, 1949	55.00
Junior Nurse, Vinyl, King Seeley Thermos, 1963	115.00
Knight Rider, Metal, King Seeley Thermos, 1984	65.00
Lance Link, Secret Chimp, Metal, King Seeley Thermos, 1971	275.00
Land Of The Giants, Metal, Aladdin, 1968	95.00
Linus The Lionhearted, Vinyl, Aladdin, 1965	115.00
Lost In Space, Metal, Dome, King Seeley Thermos, 1967 *Illus*	374.00
Miss America, Metal, Aladdin, 1972	316.00
Mod Tulip, Dome, Ohio Art, 1962	98.00
Munsters, Metal, King Seeley Thermos, 1965	95.00 to 550.00
Muppet Show, Metal, King Seeley Thermos, 1978	75.00
Pac-Man, Metal, Aladdin, 1980	50.00
Paladin, Metal, Aladdin, 1960	430.00
Pathfinder, Metal, Universal Industries, 1959	575.00
Pink Panther, Inspector, Vinyl, Aladdin, 1980	58.00
Ponytail, Poodle, Vinyl, King Seeley Thermos, 1960	58.00
Psychedelic, Metal, Dome, Aladdin, 1969	92.00 to 250.00
Pussycats, Vinyl, Aladdin, 1968	80.00
Rambo, Metal, King Seeley Thermos, 1985	35.00
Rat Patrol, Metal, Aladdin, 1967	187.00
Robin Hood, Archery Pose, Aladdin, 1965	240.00
Rough Rider, Metal, Aladdin, 1973	60.00
Sabrina, 2 Witches Stirring Cauldron, Vinyl, Aladdin, 1972	115.00
Shari Lewis & Her Friends, Vinyl, Aladdin, 1963 *Illus*	89.00
Skipper, Pink, Vinyl, King Seeley Thermos, c.1965	230.00
Smokey Bear, Forest Animals, Vinyl, Aladdin, 1972	230.00
Stewardess, Aladdin, 1962	290.00
Super Friends, Super Heroes, Metal, Aladdin, 1976	80.00
Super Heroes, Marvel Comics, Metal, 1976	50.00 to 63.00
Super Powers, Metal, Aladdin, 1983	75.00
Tarzan, Metal, Aladdin, 1966	145.00
Tom Corbett Space Cadet, Metal, Aladdin, 1952	175.00
Twiggy, Vinyl, Aladdin, 1967 *Illus*	175.00
U.S. Space Corps, Metal, Aladdin, Ohio Art, 1961	460.00
Underdog, Vinyl, Ardee, 1972	575.00
Volkswagen Bus, Metal, Dome, Omni Graphics, 1960 *Illus*	863.00

Wonder Woman, Blue, Vinyl, Aladdin, 1977 .... 95.00
Wonder Woman, Yellow, Vinyl, Aladdin, 1977 .... 115.00
Woody Woodpecker, Metal, Aladdin, 1972 .... 145.00
Yogi Bear, Taking Picture Of Boo Boo, Cindy & Cubs, Thermos, Aladdin 345.00
Zorro, Black Sky, Metal, Aladdin, 1958 .... 160.00
LUNCH BOX THERMOS, Back In '76, Plastic, Aladdin, 1975 .... 15.00
Barbie, Midge, Skipper, Metal, King Seeley Thermos, 1965 .... 110.00
Captain Kangaroo, Metal, 1964 .... 60.00
Fireball XL5, Metal, King Seeley Thermos, 1964 .... 60.00
H.R. Pufnstuf, Plastic, Aladdin, 1970 .... 75.00
It's A Small World, Metal, Aladdin, 1968 .... 50.00
Jonathan Seagull, Plastic, Aladdin, 1973 .... 18.00
Monkees, Metal, King Seeley Thermos, 1967 .... 75.00
Ringling Bros., Metal, King Seeley Thermos, 1970 .... 50.00
Welcome Back Kotter, Plastic, Aladdin, 1977 .... 20.00
Yosemite Sam, Metal, King Seeley Thermos, 1971 .... 60.00
LUNCH PAIL, Fashion Cut Plug Tobacco, 5 x 7 1/2 In. ....385.00 to 400.00

LUNEVILLE, a French faience factory, was established about 1730 by
Jacques Chambrette. It is best known for its fine biscuit figures and
groups and for large faience dogs and lions. The early pieces were
unmarked. The firm was acquired by Keller and Guerin and is still
working.

Bowl, Dragon Bird, Floral Design, Marked, 8 1/2 x 7 x 2 1/2 In. 24.00
Bowl, Fruit, Pink Tulips, White, 9 In. 202.00
Bowl, White, Blue, France, 1778 .... 220.00
Plate, Asparagus, France 89.00
Vase, Frosted, Mottled Cobalt Blue, Orange & Yellow, Egg Shape, 11 1/4 In. 635.00
Vase, River Landscape, Long Neck, Mustard Ground, Cameo, Signed, 10 In., Pair 1730.00

LUSTER glaze was meant to resemble copper, silver, or gold. It has
been used since the sixteenth century. Some of the luster found today
was made during the nineteenth century. The metallic glazes are
applied on pottery. The finished color depends on the combination of
the clay color and the glaze. Blue, orange, gold, and pearlized luster
decorations were used by Japanese and German firms in the early
1900s. Tea Leaf pieces have their own category.

Copper, Bowl, Central Bridge Design, Stylized Flower, Foliate Design, 15 In. 1265.00
Copper, Charger, Stylized Leaf, Vine & Shield, 16 1/2 In. 80.00
Copper, Pitcher, Blue & White Painted Flowers, 5 1/2 x 6 1/2 In. 135.00
Copper, Pitcher, Blue Band With Rose, Flared Neck, 5 1/2 In. 66.00
Copper, Pitcher, Dancing Ballerina, 6 1/2 In. 70.00
Copper, Salt, Blue Underplate, c.1915 .... 50.00
Copper, Salt, Leaves & Floral Band, Master, 1880, 2 1/4 In. 215.00
Copper, Sugar & Creamer, Old House Sketch 39.00
Copper, Vase, White Lining, Black Border, 1920s, 15 1/2 In., Pair 45.00
Fairyland luster is included in the Wedgwood category.
Pearlized, Creamer, Japan 10.00
Pearlized, Tea Set, Figural Elephant Teapot, Japan, Child's, 1930s 95.00
Pink, Bowl, Courting Couple On Terrace, 1900, 7 3/4 In. 86.00
Pink, Cup & Saucer, Pastoral Scenes, People & Animals 35.00
Pink, Pitcher, Deer In Forest, 5 1/2 In. 112.00
Pink, Pitcher, Twelve Rules Of King Charles I, 6 In. 230.00
Silver, Pitcher, Ribbed, Footed, Scroll Handle, 6 3/4 In. 35.00
Sunderland luster pieces are listed in the Sunderland category.
Tea Leaf luster pieces are listed in the Tea Leaf Ironstone category.

LUSTRE ART GLASS Company was founded in Long Island, New York,
in 1920 by Conrad Vahlsing and Paul Frank. The company made lampshades and globes that are almost indistinguishable from those made
by Quezal. Most of the shades made by the company were unmarked.

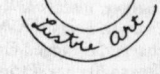

Shade, Bell Shape, 5 Pulled White Feathers, Gold, Signed, c.1920, 5 In., Pair 402.00
Shade, Floral, Ruby, 13 In., Pair 460.00

LUSTRES are mantel decorations or pedestal vases with many hanging glass prisms. The name really refers to the prisms, and it is proper to refer to a single glass prism as a lustre. Either spelling, luster or lustre, is correct.

Bristol Glass, Green, Gold & Black Bowl, Floral Medallions, Stepped Base, 12 In.	330.00
Flower Shape, Scalloped Bases, Faceted Ring, 12 Prisms, 9 1/4 In.	660.00
Opaque White Glass, Cut To Emerald, Enameled Floral, Bohemian, 17 1/4 In., Pair	1495.00
Ruby Glass, Overlay & Enameled Plaques, Cut Prisms, 12 In.	2645.00
Ruby Glass, Repeating Gothic Arches, Clear Prisms, Gold Trim, 1800s, 13 1/4 In., Pair	860.00
Trumpet Shape, Flower Shaped Base, Fan Boarder, Faceted Stem, 12 In.	175.00

MAASTRICHT, Holland, was the city where Petrus Regout established the De Sphinx pottery in 1836. The firm was noted for its transfer-printed earthenware. Many factories in Maastricht are still making ceramics.

Butter, 4 1/4 x 3 1/12 In.	10.00
Mold, White Ironstone	50.00
Plate, Black, Oriental Scene, Geisha, Man, 7 1/2 In.	10.00
Plate, Dutch Water Scene, Windmill, 12 In.	33.00
Plate, Geisha Girls & Man, Blue Luster, Canton, 1836, 8 1/2 In.	40.00
Plate, Steam Cruise Ship, Dark Orange Trim, 7 7/8 In.	16.00
Plate Set, Red & Black Card Suits, Ivory, Ink Stamp, 7 3/4 In., 6 Piece	110.00
Platter, 3 Children Playing On Ice, Royal Sphinx, Delft, 15 3/4 In.	200.00
Tea Set, Art Deco, Concentric Stripes On Cream Ground, c.1925, 18 Piece	57.00
Vase, Dutch Water Scene, Sailing Boats, Handles, 1930, 11 In.	142.00

MAIZE glass was made by W.L. Libbey & Son Company of Toledo, Ohio, after 1889. The glass resembled an ear of corn. The leaves were usually green, but some pieces were made with blue or red leaves. The kernels of corn were light yellow, white, or light green.

Celery Vase, Green Leaves, White, 6 1/4 In.	125.00
Toothpick, Yellow Husks, Gold Trim, 2 1/4 x 2 1/8 In.	363.00

MAJOLICA is a general term for any pottery glazed with an opaque tin enamel that conceals the color of the clay body. It has been made since the fourteenth century. Today's collector is most likely to find Victorian majolica. The heavy, colorful ware is rarely marked. Some famous makers include Wedgwood; Minton; Griffen, Smith and Hill (marked *Etruscan*); and Chesapeake Pottery (marked *Avalon* or *Clifton*). Majolica made by Wedgwood is listed in the Wedgwood category.

Bank, Patrie Zeppelin, Glazed, Painted, Marked FF, France, Early 20th Century, 5 In.	175.00
Basket, Begonia Leaf, Twig Hand, Turquoise, 10 In.	192.00
Basket, Bowl, Swan's Head End, Putto Other End, Mermaid Support, 26 3/4 In.	6000.00
Bowl, 2 Figural Handles, Kittens Pawing String, Minton, Oval	880.00
Bowl, Floral Leaf, Turquoise Ground, Pink Interior, 13 In.	230.00
Bowl, Grapes & Leaves, 12 x 3 In.	325.00
Bowl, Maple Leaf & Fern, c.1880, 8 3/4 In.	150.00
Bowl, Palissy Style, Frog, Snake, Butterfly, Lizard, Worms, Brown, Green, 15 1/2 In.	1840.00
Bowl, Salad, Metal Ringed Lip, Continental, 9 3/4 x 4 3/4 In.	115.00
Bowl, Scalloped Edge, Green Leaf Center, Brown Mottled Back, 9 1/4 In.	233.00
Bowl, Strawberries & Leaves, France, 7 1/2 x 1 1/4 In.	75.00
Cake Plate, Blue Basket Weave, Fringed Napkin, 8 3/4 x 4 1/4 In.	140.00
Cake Stand, Pineapple, 5 x 10 In.	360.00
Centerpiece, 2 Putti, Carrying Basket, Rope Handle, 11 In.	2200.00
Charger, Foliate Center, Foliate Banded Borders, Continental, 19th Century, 14 In.	200.00
Charger, Insects & Amphibians, War Between Serpent & Lizard, Signed, 2 x 11 In.	345.00
Charger, Insects & Reptiles, Grassy Ground, Signed, 10 In.	840.00
Charger, Scarabs & Moth, Frog & Lizard Under Grass, Signed, 2 1/4 x 12 1/4 In.	1150.00
Charger, Sprigged Grass, Serpent, Frogs & Salamander, Signed, 2 1/2 x 17 1/2 In.	1380.00
Cheese Keeper, Etruscan	4950.00
Chop Plate, Impressed Design, Farm Couple, Milk Cow, Green, Brown Glaze, 12 In.	90.00
Compote, Wheel Design, Shaded Green Ground, Eichwald, 11 x 16 1/2 In.	385.00

Console Set, Bowl, Lady Flower Frog, Candle Holders, Lavender & Pink, Eichwald 120.00
Creamer, Corn, 4 1/2 In. 225.00
Creamer, Etruscan, 4 In. 200.00
Creamer, Etruscan, 5 In. 250.00
Creamer, Figural, Owl, 4 1/8 x 3 1/2 In. 135.00
Cuspidor, Brown Floral 105.00
Cuspidor, Cobalt Sunflower, Etruscan 550.00
Dish, Aquatic Still Life, Cobalt Blue Ground, Palissy Ware, 1870s, 11 1/4 In. 978.00
Dish, Asparagus, Light Green & Brown, Austria, c.1890, 12 x 5 1/2 In. 585.00
Dish, Asparagus, White, Purple Ends, Green Leaf Footed, 6 3/4 x 9 x 3 1/2 In. 125.00
Dish, Center Still Life, Beetle, Moth, Snake, Palissy Ware, 1890s, 14 1/2 In. 2990.00
Dish, Cheese, Stilton, Cow Knop, Leaves, Pink Ground, G. Jones, 1870s, 11 3/8 In. 5100.00
Dish, Cover, Warthog, Gray & Brown, Pink Eyes, 9 1/4 x 6 In. 410.00
Dish, Fish, Eel, Shells, Pebble Border, Palissy Ware, 1870s, 12 1/2 x 18 In. 1610.00
Dish, Game, Dogs, Boars, Stag Head Handles, Cover, George Jones, 1880s, 12 1/2 In. 6600.00
Dish, Game, Rabbits, Oak Branch Handles, Cover, George Jones, 1870s, 13 1/4 In. 13200.00
Dish, Putto Standing Atop Coiled Pedestal With Blossoms, Minton, 7 3/4 In. 1725.00
Egg Holder, Chick With Eggs, Portugal, 3 1/4 In. 195.00
Figurine, 3 Putti, Holding Flower Basket, Minton, 1873, 12 In. 4675.00
Figurine, African Man, Holding Basket, Green & Yellow, 6 3/8 In. 145.00
Figurine, Merman, Supporting Shell, Minton, 7 In. 4950.00
Figurine, Rooster, Japan, 4 In. 45.00
Figurine, Woman On Shell, Austria, 12 In. 715.00
Humidor, Black Man Wearing Green Jacket, Smoking, 10 3/4 In. 605.00
Jardiniere, Gothic Revival, Acanthus Leaves Stand, Tripartite Base, Red, 43 In. 1380.00
Jardiniere, Lion Heads, Paw Feet, Cobalt Blue, Minton, 17 1/2 x 19 In. 1320.00
Jardiniere, Pedestal, 3 Sprays Of Irises, 3 Colorful Butterflies, 1900, 51 In. 12000.00
Jardiniere, Sled Form, Flower Blossoms, Seminude Figure On Rim, Signed, 9 1/2 In. 546.00
Jardiniere, Stand, Birds On Bulrushes, Water Lilies, 1870s, 13 1/2 In. 2700.00
Jardiniere, Stand, Flowering Lily Pad Form, Serpent Base, J. Dressler, 35 1/4 In. 1125.00
Jug, Face, 1902, 8 3/4 In. 330.00
Jug, Face, Fish, 11 1/2 In. 325.00
Jug, Face, Sarreguemines, France, 9 In. 395.00
Jug, Face, Utzcheneider Co., Sarreguemines, France, 5 1/2 In. ....175.00 to 250.00
Jug, Tavern, Figures, Minton, 9 1/2 In. 2310.00
Jug, Tavern, Figures, Pewter Top, Minton, 10 1/2 In. 2050.00
Match Holder, Ashtray, Frog, 3 In. 175.00
Match Holder, Black Boy Playing An Accordion, 5 In. 545.00
Match Holder, Black Boy, 4 1/2 In. 475.00
Match Holder, Black Lady With Basket Sitting By Brick Wall, 5 3/4 x 1/2 x 5 In. 595.00
Match Holder, Green, Brown, Base, Amber Border, White Striker, c.1891, 3 x 4 In. 169.00
Match Holder, Young Man, Marked, 7 3/4 In. 185.00
Mug, Floral, Lavender, Ribbon Wrapped Handle, George Jones, 4 In. 1760.00
Mustard, Cover, Pineapple, 2 1/2 In. 495.00
Oyster Plate, Blue, Cream, Brown, Green, Magenta, 6 Wells, 10 1/4 In. 620.00
Oyster Plate, Kissing Fish, Gray, Brown, Teal, Magenta, 6 Wells, 9 In. 700.00
Paperweight, Swan, Etruscan, 4 In. 1430.00
Pierced Rim, Impressed Mark, Gerbing & Stephan, 9 1/4 In. 140.00
Pitcher, Basket Weave Body, Branch Of Flowers Each Side, Yellow Rim, 4 1/2 In. 80.00
Pitcher, Bird On Branch Front & Back, Gold Bird, 6 1/2 In. 175.00
Pitcher, Birds Feeding Young In Nest, 5 In. 176.00
Pitcher, Cherries & Blossoms, 10 In. 395.00
Pitcher, Corn, 9 1/2 In. 455.00
Pitcher, Dog, 9 3/4 In. 565.00
Pitcher, Duck, 12 In. ....195.00 to 300.00
Pitcher, Duck, 13 In. 180.00
Pitcher, Duck, Marked, 10 1/4 In. 195.00
Pitcher, Figural Handle, Cobalt Blue, 10 1/2 In. 185.00
Pitcher, Fish, 6 In. 210.00
Pitcher, Fish, 9 In. 375.00
Pitcher, Fish, 10 1/2 In. ....290.00 to 295.00
Pitcher, Fish, Green, Brown Dark Teal Shades, 11 In. 85.00
Pitcher, Floral, Basket Weave, Chain & Anchor, 8 1/2 In. 295.00

Pitcher, Floral, Blue, Yellow, Pink, 7 3/4 In.	345.00
Pitcher, Frog On Gourd, 8 In.	465.00
Pitcher, Hanging Game, Fox Handle, Cranberry Glaze Interior, Belgium, 11 In.	165.00
Pitcher, Jumping Trout, 6 1/2 In.	140.00
Pitcher, Leaf On Tree Bark, 5 3/4 In.	165.00
Pitcher, Parrot, Beak Pouring Spout, 15 In.	445.00
Pitcher, Parrot, St. Clement, France, 13 In.	425.00
Pitcher, Picket Fence, Floral, 7 1/4 In.	250.00
Pitcher, Ribbon & Bow, Flowers On Picket Fence, Basket Weave Ground, 5 1/2 In.	165.00
Pitcher, Rooster, France, 11 In.	265.00
Pitcher, Rooster, Onaig, 7 In.	425.00
Pitcher, Rooster, Signed, St. Clement, France, 11 1/4 In.	395.00
Pitcher, Rooster, St. Clement, France, 13 3/4 In.	595.00
Pitcher, Shell & Seaweed, Etruscan, 4 1/2 In.	495.00
Pitcher, Shell & Seaweed, Pink Interior, Etruscan, 5 3/4 In.	220.00
Pitcher, Wheat, Cobalt Blue, George Jones, 6 1/4 In.	3300.00
Pitcher, Wild Rose, Pink, George Jones, 7 In.	3575.00
Pitcher, Yellow Flowers, Leaves, Blue Ground, Aqua Interior, Wedgwood, 7 1/4 In.	4109.00
Plaque, Red Cherries, Green Leaves, France, 12 3/8 In.	245.00
Plaque, Snake, Frog, Sea Creature, Grassy Ground, Round, 9 1/2 In.	1650.00
Plate, Asparagus, Basket Weave Border, 9 3/4 In.	110.00
Plate, Asparagus, France, 9 1/2 In.	265.00
Plate, Asparagus, Luneville, 9 In.	100.00
Plate, Begonia Leaf On Basket, 8 In.	220.00
Plate, Bird On Floral Branch, 9 1/4 In.	110.00
Plate, Birds, Berries, P.V., France, 8 1/4 In.	60.00
Plate, Game, Mallard, Frog, Birds, & Reeds, E. Boulenger & Co., c.1900, 8 1/2 In.	111.00
Plate, Green Leaf, 8 1/2 In.	145.00
Plate, Mountains, House, Rocks & Trees, West Germany, 9 In.	30.00
Plate, Pie Crust Rim, Yellow & Turquoise, Fan & Bird, 8 In.	185.00
Plate, Sprigged Grass, Lizard Eating Head Of Serpent, Signed, 12 1/4 In.	276.00
Plate, Stag & Hound, Yellow Ground, 9 1/4 In.	70.00
Plate, Tavern Keeper At Keg, Shells & Scrolls, Brown Flange, Ink Glaze, 11 In.	130.00
Platter, Artichoke & Asparagus, Luneville, 11 1/2 In.	200.00
Platter, Artichoke, France, 14 x 11 In.	535.00
Platter, Begonia Leaf On Basket, 14 In.	165.00
Platter, Cattail & Pond Lily, Minton, 24 x 15 1/2 In.	8250.00
Platter, Fish, Shells & Coral, Late 19th Century, 24 In.	980.00
Platter, Overlapping Cabbage Leaves, Green Glaze, Signed, 17 3/4 In.	240.00
Platter, Wild Rose, Cobalt Blue, 13 In.	315.00
Pot, Roses, Basket Weave, Czechoslavakia, 5 1/4 x 6 1/2 In.	100.00
Sardine Box, Fish Cover, Basket, Oval, George Jones, 15 1/2 In., 3 Piece	4125.00
Sauce, Pond Lily, 5 1/2 In.	80.00
Sconce, 2 Pheasants Hanging By Tail, 2 Branches, 16 In., Pair	750.00
Server, Chestnut, Metal Insert, Spoon, Minton	7975.00
Server, Mackerel, Pierced Silver Insert, George Jones, Tiffany, 24 In.	9350.00
Server, Strawberry, Basket, Sugar & Creamer, George Jones	6425.00
Server, Strawberry, Cobalt Blue, Handle, 2 Side Pockets, George Jones, 14 1/4 In.	4950.00
Stand, Fruit, Napkin Pattern, Morning Glories, Tree Trunk Footed, 6 x 9 1/2 In.	285.00
Stein, Dancing Scene, Relief, Dwarfs On Pewter Lid, No. 20379, 1/2 Liter	185.00
Tazza, Standing Putto, Holding Polychromed Scallop Shell, 14 1/4 x 11 In.	1035.00
Tea Set, Bird In Flight, Turquoise, 3 Piece	440.00
Tea Set, Shell & Seaweed, Turquoise Ground, 3 Piece	2475.00
Teapot, Monkey Shape, Holding Fruit, Minton, c.1878, 6 3/4 In.	5700.00
Teapot, Shell & Seaweed, Etruscan, Signed, 8 1/4 In.	625.00
Tile, Floral, Minton, Square, 7 5/8 In.	155.00
Tile, Horizontal Line, 4 Circular Depressions, Iridescent, Oak Frame, 5 7/8 In.	110.00
Tobacco Jar, Indian Chief, 8 In.	250.00
Tobacco Jar, Jester, Incised, 6 1/4 In.	170.00
Tobacco Jar, Monkey, Pipe, 6 1/2 In.	150.00
Toothpick, Picket Fence & Ivy, Turquoise Interior	30.00
Tray, Asparagus Cradle, Yellow Border, 11 1/2 In.	385.00
Tray, Trinket, Frog, George Jones, 2 1/2 In.	2310.00

Tureen, Rabbit & Bird Cover, Basket Base, Minton, 14 1/4 In. 4950.00
Umbrella Stand, Cherry Blossom Design, Knobby Aqua Ground, 22 In. 520.00
Umbrella Stand, Dragonfly, Fan Pattern, Aqua, Raspberry, Lavender Lining, 22 In. 2250.00
Urn, Open Towers, Stone Castle, Ivy & Fern On Wall, George Jones, c.1880, 11 In. 3300.00
Vase, 3-Hole, Cobalt Accent, Roses, 4 3/4 In. 440.00
Vase, 4 Deities On 1 Side, 2 Angels At Play On Other Side, Satyr Handles, 25 In. 430.00
Vase, Art Nouveau, Lavender & Pink Chrysanthemums, Lobed Body, 1910, 14 1/2 In. 405.00
Vase, Basket Weave, 3 Yellow & Pink Flower Panels, 10 1/2 In. 190.00
Vase, Bird & Floral Design, 14 1/2 In., Pair 1610.00
Vase, Green Leaves, Flower On Blue Ground, 16 1/2 In., Pair 230.00
Vase, Inverted Straw Bonnet, Leghorn Shape, 1882, 6 1/2 In. 75.00
Wall Plaque, Bacchanalian Boy, Dead Fox On Shoulder, Marked, c.1880, 15 In. 435.00
Wall Pocket, George Jones, 12 1/2 In. 2150.00

MAPS of all types have been collected for centuries. The earliest known printed maps were made in 1478. The first printed street map showed London in 1559. The first road maps for use by drivers of automobiles were made in 1901. Collectors buy maps that were pages of old books, as well as the multifolded road maps popular in this century.

Arkansas, Ornate Borders, Colton, 13 x 16 In. 105.00
Bolton, Massachusetts, Surveyed By Silas Holman, Lithograph, Frame, 1831, 20 x 26 In. .. 747.00
Cartes Des Grandes Route D'Angleterre, DeVaugondy, 1757, 18 1/2 x 22 In. 430.00
Chester County, Engraved By Yeager, 1847 .... 247.00
Cincinnati, Hand Colored, Buildings, Colton, 1855, 11 1/2 x 7 In. 65.00
Constellations, Divided Into Months, Southern Circumpolar, Frame, 1835, 19 1/8 In. 110.00
Dorchester, Milton, Mass., Surveyed By Edmund J. Baker, 1831, 33 1/2 x 26 In. 259.00
Gettysburg-Antietam, Taneytown Sheet, Topographical, 1925 .... 10.00
Globe, Celestial & Terrestrial, Mahogany Stands, Brass Meridian, 12 x 24 In., Pair 16100.00
Globe, Celestial, D. Adams, 1792, 12 In. 4310.00
Globe, Celestial, Ship Navigation, Kelvin & Hughes, c.1975, 11 x 10 1/2 x 10 1/2 In. 865.00
Globe, Charles W. Holbrook, Iron Stand, 12 In. Diam. 525.00
Globe, Mahogany Stand, Carved Paw Feet, Cast Iron Frame, 20th Century, 25 In. 825.00
Globe, Mahogany Tripod Stand, Butler, 20th Century, 43 In. 330.00
Globe, Terrestrial, Columbia Head Finial, 5 3/4 x 9 1/2 In. 4000.00
Globe, Terrestrial, Ebonized, E. Felkland Sons, 1870s, 13 1/4 In. 1840.00
Globe, Terrestrial, Glazed Paper, Walnut Stand, Philips, c.1925, 48 x 40 In. 9200.00
Globe, Terrestrial, Horizon Band, Raised On Turned Ebonized Stand, 4 Legs, 9 In., Pair .. 9000.00
Globe, Terrestrial, Hour Circle, Mahogany Stand, Johnston Mystrom, 36 x 14 In. 2070.00
Globe, Terrestrial, Mahogany Stand, S.S. Edkins, c.1825, 24 x 24 In. 5775.00
Globe, Terrestrial, Meridian, Cast Iron Stem, Footed, Wieker Costello, c.1900, 25 x 14 In. 1035.00
Globe, Terrestrial, Puzzle, 7 Sections, Tripod Support, Patinated, Cast Iron, 5 1/2 In. 978.00
Globe, Terrestrial, Rosewood & Brass Mounted, Carved Paw Feet, 35 x 15 In. 3450.00
Globe, Terrestrial, Twilight Zone, Ginn & Heath Fitz, c.1879, 15 1/2 x 13 1/2 x 13 In. ... 3910.00
Globe, Terrestrial, Walnut Stand, Flattened Ball Feet, 46 In. 5400.00
Illinois, Hand Color, Canals & Railroads, Johnson, 1863, 17 x 13 In. 125.00
Iowa, 3 Panels, Marathon Oil Co., Runner & Text, 12 x 9 In. 33.00
Italy, City States Along Border, G. Grierson, Frame, 29 x 41 In. 55.00
Japan, Insert Of Nagasaki & Yesso, Hand Colored, Johnson, 1863, 15 1/2 x 12 1/2 In. ... 200.00
Maine, Hand Colored, Colton, 1855, 12 x 16 In. 100.00
Mantua, Italy, Paper, Hand Colored, Latin, 1500s, 15 1/2 x 20 1/2 In. 140.00
Maryland, North Central States, Camping & Lake Scene, Mid 1920s, 12 x 9 In. 340.00
Middleborough, Mass., H.F. Walling, Frame, 1855, 33 x 30 In. 161.00
Minnesota, Hand Colored, Railroads, Johnson, 1865, 17 x 12 In. 125.00
Minnesota, Shell Gasoline, 3 Panels, 1929, 12 x 9 In. 190.00
Mississippi River, Delta To Memphis, U.S. Coastal Survey, 1882, 28 x 24 In. 125.00
Montreal Tramways, 1945 .... 5.00
Nashville & Vicinity, W.F. Foster, 1877, 19 3/4 x 23 3/4 In. 195.00
New Jersey, New & Accurate, c.1800, 12 3/4 x 10 1/2 In. 50.00
Ohio, Hand Colored, Johnson, 1864, 23 x 17 In. 125.00
Pennsylvania, Cartoon Style, Color, Sinclair, 1933 .... 50.00
Pennsylvania, Copper Plate, R. Baldwin, London, 1756, 7 1/4 x 9 In. 135.00
Pennsylvania, Farms, Chester County, Breou's, Set, c.1883, 16 In. 495.00
Pennsylvania, Station Graphics, Mobiloil, Early 1930s, 12 x 9 In. 225.00

Scotland, London, June 1st, 1820, Robt. Wilkinson, Matted, Frame, 22 x 19 3/4 In. 165.00
Texas, Highway, Colorful Views, 1958 .... 10.00
United States, War Department, Color, 1873, 8 x 10 In. 6.00
Virginia, North Carolina Coast, U.S. Coastal Survey, 1853, 20 x 12 1/2 In. 175.00
Washington, Oregon, Idaho, Hand Colored, Johnson, 1863, 15 1/2 x 12 1/2 In. 125.00
Washington D.C., Delaware, Maryland, Virginia, U.S. Coastal Survey, 1852, 30 x 21 In. .. 185.00
West Indies, Hand Colored, Engraved, Bowen, 1747, 13 1/2 x 16 1/2 In. 345.00
World, Double Hemisphere, Hand Colored Engraving, c.1749, 19 1/2 x 29 5/8 In. 1495.00

MARBLE collectors pay highest prices for glass and sulphide marbles.
The game of marbles has been popular since the days of the ancient
Romans. American children were able to buy marbles by the mid-
eighteenth century. Dutch glazed clay marbles were least expensive.
Glazed pottery marbles, attributed to the Bennington potteries in
Vermont, were of a better quality. Marbles made of pink marble were
also available by the 1830s. Glass marbles seem to have been made
later. By 1880, Samuel C. Dyke of South Akron, Ohio, was making
clay marbles and The National Onyx Marble Company was making
marbles of onyx. The Navarre Glass Marble Company of Navarre,
Ohio, and M. B. Mishler of Ravenna, Ohio, made the glass marbles.
Ohio remained the center of the marble industry, and the Akron-made
Akro Agate brand became nationally known. Other pieces made by
Akro Agate are listed in this book in the Akro Agate category.
Sulphides are glass marbles with frosted white figures in the center.

Bag, Ajax Agates, 4 x 1/2 x 3 In. 12.00
Bennington Type, Blue, 1800, 5 3/4 In. 35.00
Bennington Type, Brown, Black, 1800, 4 In. 30.00
Clay, Bennington, Blue, Light Brown Mottled Glaze, 1 7/8 In. 110.00
Clay, Sponge Spatter Design, Red, Blue, Green, Black Crossed Line, 2 In. 94.00
Divided Core, Yellow & White Swirl, 1 1/2 In. 90.00
Sulphide, Buffalo, Golden Amber, White Figure, 19th Century, 1 1/2 In. 1650.00
Sulphide, Elephant, 1 3/4 In. 176.00
Sulphide, Lion, White, 19th Century, 1 1/2 In. 102.00

MARBLE CARVINGS, such as large or small figurines, groups of people
or animals, and architectural decorations, have been a special art form
since the time of the ancient Greeks. Reproductions, especially of large
Victorian groups, are being made of a mixture using marble dust.
These are very difficult to detect and collectors should be careful.
Other carvings are listed under Alabaster.

Bookends, Medical, Brass, 5 In. 80.00
Bust, Augustus, Scagolia, Looking Left, Circular Support On Column, 32 In. 13200.00
Bust, Beatrice, Oval Base, Bessi, 8 x 8 In. 230.00
Bust, Boy & Girl, D.W. Stevenson, 1842, 21 In., Pair 3600.00
Bust, Euterpe, Muse Of Literature, Italy, Late 1800s, 29 1/2 In. 6038.00
Bust, Jeanne D'Arc, White, Variegated, Pedestal, France, 19th Century, 18 In. 575.00
Bust, Madame Recamier, Marble Socle, 26 In. 2300.00
Bust, Marcus Aurelius, White Marble, Curly Hair, Beard, 19th Century, 41 In. 4200.00
Bust, Modestia, G. Bessi, Rectangular Base, 15 x 15 3/4 In. 1200.00
Bust, Venus De Milo, After Antonio Canova, Socle Base, 21 In. 2760.00
Bust, Woman, Bronze Clothing, Signed, Scottino Callio, 7 1/2 x 6 x 3 In. 280.00
Bust, Woman, Flapper Style Hat, Red Veined, 10 1/2 In. 330.00
Bust, Young Girl, 1900, 24 In. 2700.00
Bust, Young Partially Draped Maiden, Carrara, Late 19th Century, 18 In. 1380.00
Cardholder, Green, Gold Golf Ball, Natural Elegance, 6 In. 20.00
Garniture, Clock, Flanked By Obelisks, Silvered Birds, c.1880, 12 3/4 In. 2760.00
Group, Children Under An Umbrella, Signed, A. Frilli, 21 In. 7200.00
Jardiniere, Everted Lip, Waisted Socle, Square Plinth, 16 x 21 In., Pair 5760.00
Obelisk, Beige, Black Variegate, Rouge Marble Plinth, Italy, 29 1/2 In., Pair 1840.00
Obelisk, Column Of Contrasting Stone, Stepped Plinth, 10 1/2 In., Pair 920.00
Obelisk, Lapis Lazuli, White Marble Base, Yellow, Red, 21 x 4 In., Pair 2760.00
Obelisk, Mottled Green & Chartreuse, Square Base, 16 1/2 In., Pair 490.00
Pedestal, Classical, Fluted Column, Dark Green, Black Mottling, 42 3/4 In. 935.00

Pedestal, Fern, Column, Rings & Stepped Round Base & Top, 37 In. 550.00
Pedestal, Marble Top, 4 Tapering Paneled Sides, Alabaster Base, 42 3/4 In. 1725.00
Pedestal, Square Top, Columnar Plinth, Stepped Base, Napoleon III, 41 In. 1150.00
Pedestal, Square Top, Volute Spiral Designs, Square Base, 42 In. 575.00
Pedestal, White, Black Striations, Stepped Rings, Octagonal Top, 39 In. 410.00
Plaque, Apostle St. James, Italy, 36 x 30 In. 2352.00
Plaque, St. John The Baptist, Italy, 36 x 30 In. 3136.00
Statue, Dolphin From Fountain Head, Open Mouth, 17th Century, 10 In. 7200.00
Statue, Eve, Signed L. Guglielmi, Roma, 55 1/2 x 26 1/2 In. 7150.00
Statue, Gypsy Girl, In Chair, Rush Seat, 19 In. 2530.00
Statue, Minerva, Allegorical, Right Hand Resting On Hip, 1700, 33 In. 4800.00
Statue, Panther, Applied Glass Eyes, White, On Wooden Base, 14 x 9 In. 355.00
Statue, Satyr Figure, Roman Legionnaire's Dress, Italy, 48 In. 3450.00
Statue, Venus, Signed, H. Batelli, 41 In. 9600.00
Statue, Virgin, Veiled Head Inclined Upwards, 18th Century, 13 In. 4800.00
Tazza, Gadrooned Body, Stepped Base, Griotte Marble, 15 In., Pair 4200.00
Urn, Nudes Carrying Musical Instruments, Mask Handle, 19 In., Pair 980.00
Urn, Ormolu, 9 In., Pair 1400.00
Urn, Ribbon, Goat Head Handles, Red, White, Brass Base, 10 x 18 In., Pair 5225.00
Urn, Women Seated 2 Sides, Light Green Striations, France, 20 3/4 In., Pair 3630.00
Vase, Elliptical, Footed, Sienna, Neoclassical, 13 x 20 1/2 x 14 In., Pair 7475.00

MARBLEHEAD Pottery was founded in 1905 by Dr. J. Hall as a rehabil-
itative program for the patients of a Marblehead, Massachusetts, sanitarium. Two years later it was separated from the sanitarium and it
continued operations until 1936. Many of the pieces were decorated
with marine motifs.

Bookends, Dark Blue, Wedge Shape, Incised Panel, 2 Sailing Ships, 1916, 6 In. 690.00
Bookends, Sailing Ships 1700.00
Bowl, Blue Matte Glaze, Broad Shape, 13 1/2 In. 265.00
Bowl, Brown Matte Glaze, Speckled, Celadon, Oxblood Interior, 8 In. 805.00
Bowl, Matte Glaze, Sky Blue Interior, Flared, Stamped Mark, 3 x 9 In. 200.00
Dish, Brown Matte Glaze, Speckled, Impressed Slip Mark, 2 1/4 In. 316.00
Humidor, Cover, Ocher, Dark Blue, Stylized Wreath Blossoms, 4 x 6 In. 1725.00
Plaque, Turquoise Glaze, Profile Portrait Of Egyptian, Signed, 7 1/2 x 4 5/8 In. 546.00
Tile, Bowl With Lavender Flowers, Providential Blank, Square, 6 In. 1540.00
Tile, Landscape, Blue, Yellow Matte Glaze, 5 3/4 In. 1910.00
Tile, Sprawling Tree Flanked By Slender Trees, Dark Green Ground, 1908, 6 In. 1380.00
Vase, Blue Gray Matte Glaze, Beaker Shape, 6 1/4 In. 259.00
Vase, Blue Matte Glaze, 5 Repeating Stylized Flowers, H. Tutt, 1912, 5 1/8 In. 1150.00
Vase, Blue Matte Glaze, 8 Repeating Stylized Flowers, H. Tuff, 1912, 4 3/8 In. 4887.00
Vase, Blue Matte Glaze, Flared Rim, Medium Blue To Light Blue Glaze, 5 1/4 In. 310.00
Vase, Blue Matte Glaze, Geese, Flying, Ocher Matte Ground, 1912, 3 3/8 In. 3220.00
Vase, Blue Matte Glaze, Speckled, Cylindrical, 4 1/2 x 5 In. 845.00
Vase, Blue Matte Glaze, Stylized Tree Design, Charcoal, Green, 8 x 7 In. 7480.00
Vase, Blue Matte Glaze, Trees With Leaves, Fruit Design, 7 In. 3740.00
Vase, Branches Of Pine Cones, Speckled Ground, Arthur Baggs, Signed, 12 In. 5175.00
Vase, Brown Matte Striated Glaze, Watermelon Rind, A. Baggs, 1904, 5 In. 2415.00
Vase, Brown, Green, Blue Floral Design, Signed, Hanna Tutt, 4 1/2 In. 5460.00
Vase, Cobalt Matte Glaze, Stylized Red Roses, Green, A. Baggs, 4 x 3 3/4 In. 1610.00
Vase, Dark Blue Matte Glaze, Speckled, 14 x 9 1/2 In. 1840.00
Vase, Dark Blue Matte Glaze, Tapered, 8 x 4 1/2 In. 980.00
Vase, Dark Gray, Rust Glaze, Incised Band Of Stylized Flowers, A. Baggs, 3 In. 690.00
Vase, Dark Green Matte Glaze, Incised 4 Stylized Foliate Panels, 1916, 5 In. 6900.00
Vase, Dark Green Matte Glaze, Mottled, 8 x 4 In. 1035.00
Vase, Dark Olive Green Glaze, Incised Stylized Floral, Geometric, 1912, 8 In. 140.00
Vase, Geese Flying In 2-Tone, Blue Gray, Speckled Gray Ground, 3 1/2 In. 1690.00
Vase, Geometric Design, Dark Brown, Green Matte Ground, Speckled, 3 x 5 In. 6725.00
Vase, Geometric Design, Dark Olive Brown, Green Ground, 1908, 3 x 4 In. 1265.00
Vase, Geometric Design, Deep Blue Matte Ground, Dark Green Border, 4 In. 2415.00
Vase, Geometric Design, Green Mottled Ground, Dark Brown, Signed, 5 In. 6325.00
Vase, Grape Vines, Blue, Green, Yellow, Brown, Gray, 3 3/4 x 4 1/4 In. 4025.00
Vase, Gray Matte Glaze, Pinched Waist, 9 x 3 1/4 In. 805.00

Vase, Gray Matte Glaze, Speckled, Rose, Cylindrical, 3 1/2 x 2 1/4 In. 316.00
Vase, Gray, Mauve Matte Glaze, Speckled, Cylindrical, 8 3/4 x 4 In. 850.00
Vase, Green Glaze, Stylized Poppies & Leaves, Ship Mark, 9 In. 10350.00
Vase, Green Matte Glaze, Incised Brown Stalk Of Flowers, 1912, 10 In. 21850.00
Vase, Green Matte Glaze, Stylized Floral, Brown, 5 1/2 In. 5750.00
Vase, Ivory, Yellow Matte Glaze, Incised Vertical Rings, A.E. Baggs, 8 1/2 In. 4025.00
Vase, Lavender Matte Glaze, Signed, 9 In. 330.00
Vase, Mauve Matte Glaze, Cylindrical, 3 1/4 x 2 1/4 In. 316.00
Vase, Mauve Matte Glaze, Tapered, 8 x 4 1/4 In. 345.00
Vase, Medium Blue Glossy Glaze, 5 In. 260.00
Vase, Mustard Glaze, Speckled Brown, Labels, 3 3/4 x 3 1/2 In. 660.00
Vase, Ocher Matte Glaze, Speckled, Spherical, 5 x 6 1/2 In. 1265.00
Vase, Olive Green Matte Glaze, 2-Tone 9 x 3 3/4 In. 9200.00
Vase, Orange Matte Glaze, Repeating Stylized Fruit Trees, Green, 1915, 7 In. 4890.00
Vase, Panels Of Blueberries, Green Leaves, Blue Berries, H. Tutt, 1912, 6 In. 12650.00
Vase, Pink Matte Glaze, Speckled, Marked, 7 1/2 x 3 In. 920.00
Vase, Smooth Green Matte Glaze, 8 3/4 x 5 In. 1150.00
Vase, Violet Gray Glaze, Glossy Interior, Marked, 2 5/8 In. 310.00
Vase, Yellow Matte Glaze, Marked, 6 3/8 In. 730.00
Wall Pocket, Brown Matte Glaze, Speckled, Ivory Interior, 6 x 7 In. 450.00
Wall Pocket, Ribbed, Blue Matte Glaze, 8 1/2 x 4 1/4 In. 175.00

MARTIN BROTHERS of Middlesex, England, made Martinware, a salt-glazed stoneware, between 1873 and 1915. Many figural jugs and vases were made by the three brothers. Of special interest are the fanciful birds, usually made with removable heads.

Martin Bro.
London

Clock Case, Mantel, Bear & Forbear, c.1881, 8 3/4 In. 4800.00
Figurine, Fish, Brown, Inscribed, c.1890, 2 3/8 x 6 3/4 In. 1680.00
Figurine, Fish, Mounted, Wooden Base, c.1890, 10 1/2 In. 5100.00
Figurine, Potter At Wheel, Relief, Inscribed, c.1873, 6 5/8 In. 5700.00
Jar, Bird, Figural, Closed Eyes, Incised, c.1887, 8 7/8 In. 16800.00
Jar, Bird, Figural, Incised, Painted Wooden Base, c.1899, 9 3/8 In. 16800.00
Jar, Bird, Figural, Painted Wooden Base, c.1913, 6 5/8 In. 12000.00
Jar, Incised, Insect In Flight, c.1905, 8 1/4 In. 4800.00
Jardiniere, Sea Creatures, Signed, 9 x 9 In. 1100.00
Jug, 2 Smiling Faces, Tan & Brown, 1903, 7 In. 3200.00
Jug, Face, 2 Sides, c.1910, 5 1/4 In. 5700.00
Jug, Incised & Painted Blossoming Branch, Buff Ground, c.1880, 7 1/4 In. 1345.00
Jug, Incised & Painted Scrolling Leaves, Floral Medallions, 1878, 7 3/4 In. 3020.00
Pitcher, Low Relief Faces, Costumed Musician, Square, c.1900, 9 3/8 In. 1920.00
Spoon Warmer, Tortoise, Open Mouth, c.1911, 3 x 5 1/4 In. 3300.00
Tobacco Jar, Grotesque, Square Marble Base, c.1890, 8 7/8 In. 6600.00
Vase, Dragons, Monsters Amid Swirling Leaves, c.1887, 15 In. 4800.00
Vase, Grotesque, Imp Holding Amphora, Wooden Stand, c.1890, 9 1/8 In. 3300.00
Vase, Incised & Painted, Pods & Leafy Vines, 9 1/4 In. 3860.00
Vase, Incised, Birds, Fruited Branches, 3 Reserves, c.1882, 21 In. 1920.00
Vase, Incised, Birds, Palm Trees, Robert Wallace Martin, c.1880, 42 In. 7200.00
Vase, Incised, Birds, Wintry Branches, c.1884, 9 3/4 In. 1320.00
Vase, Incised, Fanciful Undersea Life, Brown Slip, c.1898, 13 1/2 In. 4800.00
Vase, Incised, Insects, Colored Slip, c.1905, 9 5/8 In. 8400.00
Vase, Incised, Insects, Creatures Amid Scrolling Leaves, c.1894, 9 1/4 In. 4800.00
Vase, Incised, Parading Knights, Cover, Wooden Stand, c.1875, 25 1/4 In. 3300.00
Vase, Incised, Shore Birds Among Grasses, c.1900, 9 1/8 In. 5400.00
Vase, Incised, Winged Dragons, Monsters In Combat, c.1890, 12 3/8 In. 6000.00

MARY GREGORY is the name used for a type of glass that is easily identified. White figures were painted on clear or colored glass as the decoration. The figures chosen were usually children at play. The first glass known as Mary Gregory was made about 1870. Similar glass is made even today. The traditional story has been that the glass was made at the Sandwich Glass works in Boston by a woman named Mary Gregory. Recent research suggests that it is possible that none was made at Sandwich. In general, all-white figures were used in the

United States, tinted faces were probably used in Bohemia, France, Italy, Germany, Switzerland, and England. Children standing, not playing, were pictured after the 1950s.

Bottle, Barber, Boy, Vaseline, Ribbed, Pontil, 8 In. 240.00
Bottle, Barber, Girl, Emerald Green, Pontil, 7 1/8 In. 230.00
Bottle, Barber, Girl, Floral, Cobalt Blue, Ribbed, Pontil, 7 In. 330.00
Bottle, Scent, Girl & Tree Scene, Blue, Purple, Gold Accents, 2 1/4 x 7 1/2 In. 250.00
Cup, Boy, Swirls, Deep Green Ground, Loop Handle 125.00
Decanter, Girl Holding Bird, Green, Stopper, 11 In. 125.00
Decanter, Green, Woman, 11 1/2 x 2 In. 225.00
Dresser Set, Girl Standing In Leaves Holding Flowers, Steeple Stopper, 3 Piece 400.00
Pitcher, Boy With Bird, Handle, Gold Border, Cranberry, 11 In. 395.00
Pitcher, Boy With Birds, Enameled Dots At Top, Amber, 8 In. 245.00
Plate, Boy Fishing With His Dog, Blue Lace Trim, Signed, Miller, 1977 .... 65.00
Tumbler, Boy With Birds, Girl & Butterfly, 6 x 3 In. 139.00
Vase, Boy Fishing With Dog, Blue 45.00
Vase, Boy, Bouquet Of Roses, Gold Trim, Snail Handles, Blue, 11 3/4 In. 350.00
Vase, Boy, Fancy Outfit, Holding Flower, Sapphire Blue, 9 In. 225.00
Vase, Cherub Sitting Atop Spray Of Flowers, Black Amethyst, 11 x 4 3/4 In. 376.00
Vase, Cranberry, Diana The Huntress, Maid & Flowers, Gilt Trim, 12 1/2 In., Pair 403.00
Vase, Girl, Boy Catching Butterfly Reverse, Black Amethyst, 10 In., Pair 475.00
Vase, Woman In Landscape Holding Fan, Amethyst, 12 1/2 In. 104.00
Water Set, Boy Chasing Bird On Pitcher, Cobalt Blue, 5 Piece 295.00
Wine, Girl, Olive Green, 5 x 2 1/2 In. 32.00

MASON'S IRONSTONE was made by the English pottery of Charles J. Mason after 1813. Mason, of Lane Delph, was given a patent for this improved earthenware. He usually called it "Mason's Patent Ironstone China." It resisted chipping and breaking so it became popular for dinnerwares and other table service dishes. Vases and other decorative pieces were also made. The ironstone was decorated with orange, blue, gold, and other colors, often in Japanese inspired designs. The firm had financial difficulties but the molds and the name Mason were used by many owners through the years, including Francis Morley, Taylor Ashworth, George L. Ashworth, and John Shaw. Mason's joined the Wedgwood group in 1973 and the name is still found on dinnerwares.

Bowl, Roses, Underglaze Cobalt, Overglaze Rust, 9 1/2 In. 257.00
Cheese Plate, Cover, Regency Pattern, 7 In. 100.00
Cup & Saucer, Mandalay, Large 20.00
Gravy Boat, Fast Stand, Ladle, Country Home, Border Of Leaves, Red Transfer 105.00
Jug, Chinese Dragon, Deep Orange, Black & White, Snake Handle, 7 In. 145.00
Jug, Vista Pattern, 6 In. 72.00
Pitcher, Pagoda, Trees & Houses On River, Blue Transfer, 8 3/4 In. 204.00
Pitcher & Bowl, Bandana Pattern 440.00
Platter, Scene With Pagodas & Fishermen, Blue Transfer, 15 1/4 In. 234.00
Tureen, Castle Design, Blue & White, Handles, Cover, 13 In. 719.00
Tureen, Stand & Ladle, Blue Willow, 15 In. 430.00
Wine Cooler, Floral, Orange Luster Branch Handles, 1820, 10 In., Pair 5400.00

MASONIC, see Fraternal category.

MASSIER, a French art pottery, was made by brothers Jerome, Delphin, and Clement Massier in Vallauris and Golfe-Juan, France, in the late nineteenth and early twentieth centuries. It has an iridescent metallic luster glaze that resembles the Weller Sicardo pottery glaze. Most pieces are marked *J. Massier*.

Bowl, Grotesque Mask Handles, Streaked Green, Oval, c.1900, 18 In. 640.00
Umbrella Stand, Figural, Grotesque Mask, Delphin Massier, 28 In. 4370.00
Vase, 4 Fluted Vessels Entwined On Triform Base, Signed, c.1900, 12 3/4 In. 540.00
Vase, Clam, Seaweed Design, Metallic Glaze, Marked, 3 7/8 In. 530.00
Vase, Painted Seagulls In Flight, Burgundy Glaze, Signed, 13 1/4 In. 1255.00
Vase, Ruby Glossy Glaze, Leaves, Marked, France, 8 3/4 In. 180.00

Vase, Stylized Flowers, Luster, Metallic Glaze, Marked, 8 1/4 In. 1045.00
Vase, Stylized Flowers, Paper Label, 8 1/4 In. 1064.00

MATCH HOLDERS were made to hold the large wooden matches that were used in the nineteenth and twentieth centuries for a variety of purposes. The kitchen stove and the fireplace or furnace had to be lit regularly. One type of match holder was made to hang on the wall, another was designed to be kept on a tabletop. Of special interest today are match holders that have advertisements as part of the design.

2 Black Men With Bail Of Cotton, Metal 165.00
Aluminum, Art Deco, Leaf Design, 6 1/2 x 3 1/2 In. 22.00
Antelope Head, White Metal, Polychrome, Striker Under Lid 82.00
Ashtray, Cast Iron, Griswold, Erie, Pa. . . . . .43.00 to 45.00
At The Bryn Mawr Horse Show, Celluloid, Tin, 3 x 1 1/2 x 1/2 In. 100.00
Baby Angel Kissing On Top Of Cover, Cast Iron, 6 1/4 x 3/4 In. 32.00
Barrel, Treen, Brown, Tan Sponge Paint, American, 19th Century, 2 1/8 In. 115.00
Bearded Man Next To Tree, Stump On Malachite Base, 4 1/4 In. 282.00
Bisque, Child With Cotton Bale, Germany, 5 x 2 1/4 In. 225.00
Black, 2 Black Boys, 1 Boy Holding Watermelon, Cotton Bale, 1920, 2 In. 150.00
Black, Mammy, Black, Green, Yellow Dress, White Bandanna, 11 3/4 x 1/2 In. 55.00
Black Forest, Deer, Fawns, With Eagle Perched Above, Glass Eyes, 1875, 10 In. 672.00
Black Starr Frost, With Box Of Matches, Signed, 1 x 1 1/2 In. 18.00
Boot, Brass, 8 1/4 In. 30.00
Boy & Barrel, Cast Iron, 10 x 3 x 6 In. 15.00
Brass, Fireplace, 7 1/2 In. 15.00
Brass, Fireplace, 9 1/4 In. 15.00
Bulldog Cut Plug, Top Striker, 3 1/4 x 6 1/2 In. 148.00
Button Shoe, Cast Metal, 5 1/4 x 4 1/2 In. 45.00
Ceresota Prize Bread Flour, Boy On Barrel, Tin Lithograph, Wall . . . .*Illus*   225.00
Ceresota Prize Bread Flour, Boy, Tin Lithograph, Square, Wall . . . .*Illus*   175.00
Chew Banner Finecut, Cast Iron, 3 3/4 x 8 In. 275.00
Chicken & Egg, Victor Silver Co., 2 In. 75.00
Cigar Cutter, Ashtray, Brass, Alpine Grouse, 7 1/2 In. 224.00
Columbia Flour, Miss Liberty In American Flag, 5 1/2 x 2 1/4 In. 1455.00
Cow, Cast Iron, 9 x 7 1/2 In. 10.00
Cowboy Boots, Brass, 6 1/4 x 4 1/4 In. 32.00
Dawes Black Horse Ale & Porter, Striker, 7 x 9 3/4 In. 660.00
De Laval Separator, Wall 150.00
Devil's Head, Cast Iron, 6 In. 33.00
Dog Seated Next To Tree Stump, White Marble, 19th Century, 5 x 5 x 6 3/8 In. 259.00
Dr. King's New Discovery, 5 x 3 1/2 In. 132.00
Dutch Boy Painter, Boy Painting, Die Cut Tin Lithograph, Wall, 6 1/4 In. 660.00
Dutch Boy Painter, Tin Lithograph, Wall . . . .*Illus*   180.00
Dutch Girl, Verdigris, 8 1/4 In. 10.00
Dutch Girl Holding Buckets In Both Hands, Metal, Wall, 8 x 5 1/4 In. 50.00
Eagle, Cast Iron, Wall, 8 x 5 1/2 x 2 In. 10.00
Eagle & Deer, Cast Iron, Wall, 4 1/2 x 2 x 10 In. 10.00

Match Holder, Ceresota Prize Bread Flour, Boy On Barrel, Tin Lithograph, Wall

Match Holder, Ceresota Prize Bread Flour, Boy, Tin Lithograph, Square, Wall

Match Holder, Dutch Boy Painter, Tin Lithograph, Wall

Match Holder, Sharples Separator Co., Mother, Child, Tin Lithograph, Wall

Match Holder, Sharples Separator Co., Woman, Tin Lithograph, Wall

Old papier-mâché jack-o'-lanterns originally had a thin piece of paper in the eyes. The light from the candle showed through the paper. You can make a replacement with tracing paper and watercolor paint.

Face With Flowers, Gold, Cast Iron	115.00
Fireplace, Brown Stone House, 7 In.	6.00
Fireplace, Cast Iron, 8 x 7 x 5 1/2 In.	15.00
Fireplace, Copper, Brass, 8 1/2 In.	15.00
Fireplace, Donkey, 5 x 6 In.	15.00
Geisha Girl, Parasol, Red Orange Trim, Porcelain, 2 1/2 x 3 In.	25.00
Green Shagreen, Silver, Art Deco, Signed, Asprey, 4 1/2 x 6 In.	795.00
Hunters, Cast Iron, Wall, 9 x 6 x 1/2 In.	10.00
Iron, 2 Bins, Wall, c.1875, 6 1/2 In.	50.00
King's Crown, Small Matches, 1 3/4 x 1 1/4 In.	8.00
Leaf & Vine, Jasperware, Lavender, 5 1/2 In.	126.00
Mammy With Cotton Bale, Porcelain, 2 1/4 In.	225.00
Metal, Twist Off Top, Germany, 3 3/4 In.	20.00
Milwaukee Harvesting Machine, Basket Form, Striker At Bottom, Tin, 5 1/2 In.	285.00
Monkey, Metal, Red Nostril, Eyes, 3 In.	125.00
Mug Shape, Security Mutual Insurance, Binghampton, Milk Glass, 2 1/4 In.	75.00
Old Judson, J.G. Stevens, Kansas City, 4 7/8 x 3 3/8 In.	215.00
Pipes Mounted In Front, Old Iron, 4 x 3 In.	22.00
Pon My Soul, 5 x 2 1/2 In.	65.00
Red Peacock Bird, Cast Iron, Wall, 4 1/2 x 4 In.	35.00
Rockford Watch, L. McAyeal, Tin Lithograph	1400.00
Rooster & Roses, Red, Yellow, Green, 6 1/2 x 3 1/2 In.	75.00
Sarcophagus, 2 1/2 x 5 x 2 In.	12.00
Savage Gas Stove, Cook Getting The Matches, Wall, 4 x 2 1/2 In.	156.00
Sharples Separator Co., Mother, Child, Tin Lithograph, Wall .... *Illus*	260.00
Sharples Separator Co., Tubular Cream Separator, Tin Lithograph, Wall, 7 In. .... 325.00 to 440.00	
Sharples Separator Co., Woman, Tin Lithograph, Wall .... *Illus*	230.00
Sterling Silver, Marked, Gorham, 1 11/16 x 1 1/16 In.	15.00
Teahouse, Red, Orange, Gold Trim, Floral Border On Base, Porcelain	25.00
Tole Paint, Gold, Olive Green, 6 x 3 1/8 In.	29.00
Tree With Hands	8.00
White House Coffee, Tin Lithograph, Wall, 5 In.	375.00
Young Boy Holding Boot, 8 In.	575.00

MATCH SAFES were designed to be carried in the pocket. Early matches were made with phosphorus and could ignite unexpectedly. The matches were safely stored in the tightly closed container. Match safes were made in sterling silver, plated silver, or other metals. The English call these *vesta boxes.*

Ager Epstein, Pat. Sept. 4, 1900	25.00
American Brew Co., Salt Glaze, Blue Accents, Rochester, N.Y., 3 In.	440.00
Arbor Scene, Man In Top Hat & Woman In Bonnet Sitting On Fence, 1892, 3 In.	95.00
Art Nouveau, Sterling Silver, Hinged Cover	195.00
Cherub, Sterling Silver, Vesta, Victorian, 1 3/4 x 1 1/4 In.	185.00
Chestnut, Vesta, Late 19th Century, 1 1/2 x 2 In.	80.00
Chief Powhatan, Father Of Pocahontas, Powhatan Coal Co., Toledo, Oh., Celluloid	185.00
Cigarette, Chain, Vesta, 1 1/2 x 1 1/4 In.	70.00

Donkey & Cart, 3 1/2 x 3 In. 15.00
Elephant, Sterling Silver 68.00
Elk In Forest, Ornate Floral Border, Brass 125.00
Flowers, Sterling Silver, 1879, 2 3/8 x 1 1/2 In. 195.00
Flowers, Sterling Silver, 2 1/4 x 1 In. 175.00
Glass, Marked, Columbia, 1876, 4 In. 68.00
High Relief Design, Silver, Hinge, 7/16 x 1 9/16 In. 125.00
High Relief Design, Sterling Silver, 1910, 2 7/8 x 1 1/2 In. 175.00
High Relief Design, Sterling Silver, 1910, 5/16 x 1 3/8 In. 150.00
Hunter's Bag & Bird 80.00
Hunting Scene, Sterling Silver, c.1860, 2 3/4 In. 140.00
Ivy Leaf With Shield, Birmingham, 1900, 2 1/2 In. 225.00
Jamestown Expo, Pocahontas, Ruins Of Old Tower, Benns Church 100.00
Love Trophy, Engine Turned, Hinged Cover, 2 Interior Sections, 1783, 2 In. ... 3900.00
Match Strike, Glass, Thumb Cut, Silver Rim, Footed, Birmingham, 1901 ... 900.00
Nude Woman Surrounded By Flowers, Silver, 1910, 2 1/2 x 1 7/8 In. 150.00
Phoenix Brewery, Hinged Lid, Same Image On Back, 2 3/4 In. 270.00
Pig, Ruby Eyes, Brass, 1880, 2 In. 229.00
Pig On Top, Saber Tooth, Brass, c.1890, 2 3/4 In. 285.00
Roberts, British Flag, Tortoiseshell Design, Celluloid 125.00
Rolled Over Top, Metal, 1950 .... 30.00
Rooster, Head, Brass 300.00
Serrated Strike Plate, Silver Plate, Vesta, 1900, 2 3/4 x 1 3/4 In. 85.00
Shell Design, Sterling Silver, Vesta, Victorian, 2 3/4 In. 150.00
Skull, Brass 395.00
Slipper Shape, Silver Plated, 2 3/4 In. 250.00
Squirrel, Full Bodied, Ear Of Corn, Carved, Round Base, Ocher, Gilt, 19th Century ... 460.00
Tooled Accent Band, Blue Design, Bristol Glaze, 3 In. 121.00
Tooled Relief Design, Salt Glaze, 3 Blue Accent Bands, Syracuse, N.Y., 5 In. ... 745.00
Uncle Sam Paying France For Louisiana Purchase, Brass 200.00
Walnut, Incised Double Wall Hung, Brass Screws, Eastlake, 10 x 6 In. ... 105.00

MATSU-NO-KE was a type of applied decoration for glass patented by Frederick Carder in 1922. There is clear evidence that pieces were made before that date at the Steuben glassworks. Stevens & Williams of England also made an applied decoration by the same name.

Vase, Amber, Calcite, 6 x 1 3/4 In. 39.00
Vase, Jade Green On Alabaster, 7 x 7 3/4 In. 1500.00

MATT MORGAN, an English artist, was making pottery in Cincinnati, Ohio, by 1883. His pieces were decorated to resemble Moorish wares. Incised designs and colors were applied to raised panels on the pottery. Shiny or matte glazes were used. The company lasted less than two years.

Tile, Morning Glory, Bisque, Light Wooden Frame, 4 1/4 In. 44.00
Tile, Swirl Of Blossoms & Leaves, Bisque, Pair 121.00

MCCOY pottery was made in Roseville, Ohio. Nelson McCoy and J.W. McCoy established the Nelson McCoy Sanitary and Stoneware Company in Roseville, Ohio, in 1910. The firm made art pottery after 1926. In 1933 it became the Nelson McCoy Pottery Company. Pieces marked *McCoy* were made by the Nelson McCoy Pottery Company. Cookie jars were made from about 1940 until December 1990, when the McCoy factory closed. In 1990 the McCoy mark was put back on pottery by a firm unrelated to the original company. Because there was a company named Brush-McCoy, there is great confusion between Brush and Nelson McCoy pieces. See Brush category for more information.

Ashtray, Pheasants, Light Brown Drip Glaze, 8 x 10 In. 15.00
Basket, Hanging, Brown, Green Matte Glaze, 1926, 6 x 4 1/2 In. 34.00
Basket, Petal, 9 In. 225.00
Basket, Wicker, Yellow, Brown, 6 3/4 In. 65.00
Bookends, Lily Bud, 5 3/4 In. 300.00

Bowl, Pedestal, Green, 4 1/2 In. 45.00
Bowl, Tan, 4 1/2 x 8 In. 37.00
Bowl, Vegetable, Oval, Brown Drip 20.00
Candleholder, Starburst, White & Black, 1970, 4 3/4 In. 20.00
Candy Dish, Rustic, 8 1/2 x 2 1/2 In. 30.00
Casserole, Cover, Strawberry Country, 1980 .... 55.00
Cookie Jar, Apple, 1970, 10 In. 60.00
Cookie Jar, Bananas, 1950-1952 .... 85.00
Cookie Jar, Basket Weave, Ivory, Brown Cover, 1940s 30.00
Cookie Jar, Bear, Cookie In Vest, No Paint 40.00
Cookie Jar, Boy On Football, 1978 .... 250.00
Cookie Jar, Caboose, 1961, 7 1/2 In 250.00
Cookie Jar, Christmas Tree, 1959, 11 In. 647.00
Cookie Jar, Churn 37.50
Cookie Jar, Circus Horse, Black, 1961 .... 195.00
Cookie Jar, Clown In Barrel 125.00
Cookie Jar, Coffee Grinder, Cookies Printed On Front, 1961, 10 1/2 In. ....48.00 to 50.00
Cookie Jar, Cookie Cabin, 1956 .... 225.00
Cookie Jar, Cookie Jug, Brown & Tan, 2 Handles 30.00
Cookie Jar, Engine, Yellow, Black & Red Trim 295.00
Cookie Jar, Floral, White, 1956 .... 25.00
Cookie Jar, Goodie Goose, 1970 .... 30.00
Cookie Jar, Granny, 11 In. 125.00
Cookie Jar, Hamm's, Bear 160.00
Cookie Jar, Happy Face, Have A Happy Day, Yellow, 11 In. ....48.00 to 85.00
Cookie Jar, Harley-Davidson Hog ....188.00 to 410.00
Cookie Jar, Hot Air Balloon 65.00
Cookie Jar, Hound Dog, No Paint 20.00
Cookie Jar, Jack-O'-Lantern ....455.00 to 600.00
Cookie Jar, Keebler, Tree House 125.00
Cookie Jar, Kitten On Coal Bucket 308.00
Cookie Jar, Kookie Kettle, 8 1/2 In. 55.00
Cookie Jar, Mammy, White Dress, Red Checked Apron 325.00
Cookie Jar, Oaken Bucket, 1961-1971 .... 37.00
Cookie Jar, Owl, 1978-1979 .... 35.00
Cookie Jar, Potbelly Stove, 1967 .... 30.00
Cookie Jar, Snow Bear, White, 1965 .... 50.00
Cookie Jar, Squirrel, 1961 .... 3500.00
Cookie Jar, Strawberry, White, Green Cover, 1972 .... 35.00
Cookie Jar, Teakettle, 1963, 11 In. 55.00
Cookie Jar, Upside Down Bear, 1978-1979 .... 50.00
Cookie Jar, W.C. Fields ....145.00 to 250.00
Cookie Jar, Wishing Well, Broken Handle 90.00
Cookie Jar, Woodsy Owl, Give A Hoot, Don't Pollute, 1973-74, 12 1/2 In. 350.00
Creamer, Graystone, 1978 .... 19.00
Cup, Brown Drip, 1969 ....3.50 to 10.00
Decanter, Jupiter 60, Engine & Coal Car, McCormick Distilling Co., 1969 .... 30.00
Decanter, Mirth Is King, 9 1/2 In. 75.00
Decanter, Pierce Arrow, Model 1932 .... 65.00
Dog Feeder, Hunting, Brown Glaze, 1935, 6 In. 45.00
Flower Frog, Green, Brown, Black, White, 6 x 3 In. 16.00
Flower Holder, Angel Fish, Aqua, 3 In. 50.00
Flower Holder, Cornucopia, White, 4 x 3 1/4 In. 40.00
Flower Holder, Hands Of Friendship, Pink, 2 3/4 In. 100.00
Flower Holder, Swan, White, 3 1/4 In. 20.00
Flowerpot, Basket Weave, 5 In. 20.00
Flowerpot, Footed, Dark Brown, 4 x 4 x 3 In. 45.00
Flowerpot, Pale Yellow, Lotus Leaf On Base, 1960, 4 In. 30.00
Jardiniere, Acorn, White, 4 1/2 In. 40.00
Jardiniere, Blocks, Pink, 3 1/4 In. 33.00
Jardiniere, Pedestal, Basket Weave, Aqua, 20 In. 280.00
Jardiniere, Pedestal, Cameo, 1930s, 29 In. 300.00

Jardiniere, Sunflower, Loy-Nel Art, c.1905, 9 x 1 0 In. 650.00
Jardiniere, Swallows, Green, Brown, 4 In. 50.00
Jardiniere, White, Green, Brown Background, 1962, 7 1/2 In. 55.00
Lamp, Large Leaf, Amber, c.1950, 8 In. 23.00
Mixing Bowl, Stone Craft, Pink & Blue Stripes, 5 1/2 In. 60.00
Mug, Brown Drip, 3 1/2 x 3 1/4 In. ....3.00 to 14.00
Pitcher, Chicken, Green 75.00
Pitcher, Ducks, 1930s 110.00
Planter, Aqua, 4 x 7 x 5 In. 15.00
Planter, Bookends, Leaves & Flowers Form Bottom, 1953, 6 1/4 x 5 1/2 In. 120.00
Planter, Bowl & Pitcher, Antique Curio, Green Gloss, 1 Piece 25.00
Planter, Butterfly, Pink, 8 1/2 x 4 x 3 1/4 In. 15.00
Planter, Cowboy Hat, Cowboys On Bucking Broncos, Brown Rim, Ivory Base, 12 x 3 In. .. 130.00
Planter, Dog, Bird, 1959, 7 3/4 In. 200.00
Planter, Dogwood, Springwood, 6 x 9 1/2 x 5 In. 25.00
Planter, Double Cache Pot 50.00
Planter, Floraline, Bear, 5 x 3 1/2 In. 70.00
Planter, Flying Ducks, 1955, 10 3/4 x 8 1/2 In. 135.00
Planter, Lamb, Curly, Gray, 4 1/2 x 3 In. 50.00
Planter, Mary Ann Shoe, Holes, Pink, 5 In. 40.00
Planter, Pelican, Aqua Matte Glaze, 5 1/4 In. 85.00
Planter, Pheasant, Brown & Green, 7 1/2 x 6 In. 65.00
Planter, Pony, Stretch Animal, Aqua, 5 3/8 x 3 3/4 In. 90.00
Planter, Strawberry, White, 6 1/2 In. 45.00
Planter, Stump, Green, 4 In. 33.00
Planter, Stump, Yellow, 4 In. 33.00
Planter, Swan, Black, Orange Beak 15.00
Planter, Triple Lily, White, 6 3/4 In. 115.00
Planter, Triple Tulip, Yellow, 1950, 8 1/2 In. 33.00
Planter, Turquoise, 3 x 7 In. ....*Illus* 5.00
Planter, Village Smithy, 1953, 7 1/2 x 6 1/2 In. 55.00
Planter, Wagon Wheel, Gray, 1953, 8 In. 25.00
Plate, Dinner, Graystone, 10 In. 19.00
Platter, Brown Drip, Crimped Rim, 13 1/4 In. 12.00
Sign, The Pottery Shop, Brown, Cream Glaze, 5 1/4 x 3 15/16 In. 283.00
Soup, Dish, Canyon, Tan, Brown Slip Trim, 6 1/4 In. 5.00
Soup, Dish, Graystone, 1978 .... 17.00
Spoon Rest, Butterfly, Yellow, 7 1/2 x 4 In. 125.00
Sprinkler, Turtle, Flower, Green Glaze, Water Plants From Turtle's Mouth 50.00
Tea Set, Ivy, Branch Handle, Raised Mark, 9 x 10 In., 3 Piece 35.00
Teapot, Cover, Yellow, Individual, 4 1/2 In. 48.00
Tumbler, Tiki Leilani, 5 1/8 In., 4 Piece 45.00
Vase, Blossomtime, 6 1/2 In. ....30.00 to 40.00
Vase, Brocade, Pink & Black, 7 In. 25.00
Vase, Butterfly, Blue Gloss, Embossed, Cylinder, 6 In. 45.00
Vase, Butterfly, Lavender, 1940s 90.00
Vase, Cascade, Purple, 9 In. 50.00

Mccoy, Planter, Turquoise, 3 x 7 In.

Don't put plastic covers on
wooden furniture. The plastic may
melt onto the wood and harm the
finish. Don't even leave a plastic
tablecloth on a table for more
than a month.

Vase, Cascade, Scarlet, Bud, 6 In.	30.00
Vase, Double, Tulip, 8 In.	50.00
Vase, Hand, Moss Green Glaze, 1940, 8 1/2 In.	20.00
Vase, Leaves & Berries, White Semimatte Glaze, 2 Handles, 14 1/4 x 8 1/2 In.	230.00
Vase, Lily Bud, 10 In.	113.00
Vase, Pitcher Shape, Cobalt Blue, Rope Handle, 7 3/4 In.	40.00
Vase, Ram's Head, Chartreuse, 1953, 9 In.	350.00
Vase, Rose, Brown Leaves, Baby Breath, Cream, 8 1/2 In.	44.00
Vase, Sailboat, Aqua Matte Glaze, 9 In.	60.00
Vase, Sailing Ships, Embossed, Aqua Matte Glaze, Pedestal Base, 1930s-1940s, 9 1/4 In.	65.00
Vase, Soft Green Glaze, 1930, 3 3/4 x 4 In.	25.00
Vase, Swan, Black Glaze, 9 1/4 In.	250.00
Vase, Swan, Gold Trim, 9 In.	350.00
Vase, Swirl, White Matte Glaze, 8 In.	30.00
Vase, Triple Lily, Yellow, 8 1/2 In.	45.00
Vase, Turquoise, Double Handles, 1947, 12 In.	69.00
Vase, Yellow Glaze, 1940, 9 In.	29.00
Wall Pocket, Blossomtime, 8 In.	85.00
Wall Pocket, Butterfly, Aqua, 7 x 6 In.	169.00
Wall Pocket, Dutch Shoe, Yellow, 7 1/2 In.	30.00
Wall Pocket, Lady With Bonnet, White, Red Trim, 8 In.	40.00
Wall Pocket, Leaf Form, Blue & Pink, 7 x 5 1/2 In.	40.00
Wall Pocket, Leaves & Berries, Yellow Gloss, 7 In.	360.00
Wall Pocket, Lily Bud, 8 In.	160.00
Wall Pocket, Mail Box, 7 x 5 1/2 In.	55.00

MCKEE is a name associated with various glass enterprises in the United States since 1836, including J. & F. McKee (1850), Bryce, McKee & Co. (1850 to 1854), McKee and Brothers (1865), and National Glass Co. (1899). In 1903, the McKee Glass Company was formed in Jeannette, Pennsylvania. It became McKee Division of the Thatcher Glass Co. in 1951 and was bought out by the Jeannette Corporation in 1961. Pressed glass, kitchenwares, and tablewares were produced. Jeannette Corporation closed in the early 1980s. Additional pieces may be included in the Custard Glass category.

Bottle, Water, Custard, Cork Stopper, 5 In.	190.00
Bowl, Orange, Sunkist, Pink Footed	450.00
Butter, Cover, Jade Green	35.00
Canister, Cover, French Ivory, 48 Oz.	85.00
Canister, No Cover, French Ivory, 48 Oz.	50.00
Creamer, Tappan, Child's, 1894, 2 1/8 In.	18.00
Dish, Refrigerator, Cover, French Ivory, 8 x 5 x 2 1/2 In.	95.00
Lantern, Kerosene, Wild Rose With Festoon	400.00
Mixing Bowl, French Ivory, 8 In.	45.00
Mug, Tom & Jerry, White Opal, 3 1/2 In., Pair	35.00
Range Set, Roman Arch Side Panel, Fired-On Colors, Salt & Pepper, Flour, Sugar, 4 Piece	20.00
Tom & Jerry Set, Bowl, 5 Cups, 6 Piece	45.00
Toothpick, No. 75, Colonial, Apple Green	25.00
Tumbler, Footed, French Ivory, 5 In.	15.00

MECHANICAL BANKS are listed in the Bank category.

MEDICAL office furniture, operating tools, microscopes, thermometers, and other paraphernalia used by doctors are included in this category. Medicine bottles are listed in the Bottle category. There are related collectibles listed under Dental.

Bathtub, Baby, Alligator Shape, Plastic, Bakelite Thermometer, Germany, 26 1/2 In.	165.00
Bedpan, White Enamel, Black Trim, CESCO Hospital Ware, 14 x 12 In.	20.00
Belt, Quack, Dr. Sanden's Electric Belt, 1890, 38 In.	445.00
Bleeder, Brass, Borwick	85.00
Blood Pressure Cuff, Yacoel, 1925, 10 In.	175.00
Book, Physician's Anatomical Aid, 1890, 15 In.	675.00

**Clean dirty cloth book covers
with wads of stale bread.**

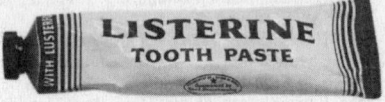

Medical, Toothpaste, Listerine,
Full Tube, 5 1/2 In.

Brace, Trepanning, Boring Tool For Skull, Charriere, Paris, 12 In. 1300.00
Breast Pump Cup, Blown Glass, Rolled Lip On Applied Siphon, 3 3/8 In. 90.00
Cabinet, Apothecary, 23 Small Dovetailed Drawers, c.1840, 57 12 x 28 1/2 In. 4950.00
Cabinet, Apothecary, 48 Drawers, Sizes & Letters, Wooden Pulls, 62 In. 4070.00
Cabinet, Apothecary, Brown Painted Surface, Rat-Tail Hinges 8900.00
Cabinet, Apothecary, Cherry, 49 Drawers, Mid 19th Century, 11 x 12 3/4 In. 2860.00
Cabinet, Apothecary, Curly Maple, Porcelain & Brass Pulls, 11 Drawers, 8 1/4 In. 770.00
Cabinet, Apothecary, Hand Painted, 16 Drawers 3080.00
Cabinet, Apothecary, Hand Painted, 24 Drawers 3025.00
Cabinet, Apothecary, Mahogany, 10 Drawers, Labels, Gold Highlights, 29 x 26 x 10 In. ... 1765.00
Cabinet, Apothecary, Pine, 23 Drawers, C.A. Butterfoss Merchandise, 1840, 57 1/2 In. 4950.00
Cabinet, Apothecary, Pine, Painted, 64 Drawers Over 3, 1800s, 39 x 43 x 14 In. 10925.00
Cabinet, Apothecary, Rectangular Top, 3 Short Drawers, 46 x 48 In. 1610.00
Case, Orthopedic Instruments, Brass Bound, Mahogany, Larkin Bros., c.1840 .... 5500.00
Chair, Doctor's, Oak & Wrought Iron, Adjustable, Matching Stool, c.1890, 38 x 14 In. 500.00
Chair, Invalid, Tireless, Tilting Seat, Adjustable Height 1295.00
Chair, Invalid, Wicker, Folding, Plank Seat, Foot Rest, 4 Wheels, 36 In. 115.00
Chest, Mahogany, Iron Mounts, China, 19th Century, 35 x 24 x 16 In. 517.00
Counter, Apothecary, 17 Drawers, 2-Door Cabinet, Shelves, c.1900, 39 x 70 In. 1600.00
Dental, Plaque Removing Kit, Mirror, Bone Handle, 5 Screw-In Tools, c.1790 .... 495.00
Ear Trumpet, Brass, Sheet Metal, Black Paint 225.00
Ear Trumpet, Mourning, Tole, Black Crepe Wrapped, 14 In. 450.00
Enema Pump, Pewter, Self-Applying, 19th Century, 13 1/2 In. 995.00
Fleam, 3 Blades, Horn Handle, Rosewood Mallet, Borwick 97.00
Hearing Aid & Sound Blocker, In Case, G. Court, 8 In. 950.00
Jar, Chemist, Stopper, Crystal, Continental, 10 1/2 x 5 1/2 In., 11 Piece 143.00
Kit, Dentist's, Tooth Color, Patient's Actual Tooth Color, Universal Dental Co., 1950 ... 20.00
Kit, Surgeon's Traveling Case, Leather, J.B. Daniel, Atlanta, Ga., 3 x 1 In. 288.00
Kit, Surgeon's Traveling Case, Rosewood, J.H. Gemeric, Philadelphia, 3 x 6 3/4 In. ... 575.00
Knife, Tenotomy, Veterinarian's 33.00
Lancet, 4 Blades, Brass Case, Ephraim & John How Cutlers, c.1730 .... 350.00
Lancet, Bone Handle, Jonathan Crookes 110.00
Lancet, Brass, 4 Steel Blades, John How Cutler, England, 18th Century 195.00
Lancet, Steel Blade Each End, Designed Shaft, England, 17th Century, 5 3/4 In. 250.00
Massager Set, Quack, Case, 7 1/2 In. 355.00
Model, Female Figure, Ivory, On Wooden Cot, Oriental, 2 1/4 x 7 1/2 x 1 7/8 In. 85.00
Model, Torso, Anatomical, Late 19th Century, 13 In. 445.00
Mortar & Pestle, 4 Figures, Dancing & Playing Instruments, Marble, 8 1/2 In. 1840.00
Mortar & Pestle, Brass, Flared Foot, Pine Hanging Holder, 5 1/2 x 3 3/8 x 17 In. 165.00
Mortar & Pestle, Maple, Old Black Paint, Late 18th Century, 4 1/2 In. 440.00
Mortar & Pestle, Pine, Early 18th Century, 8 x 5 1/2 In. 56.00
Opthalmophantome, Austria, 1880, 14 In. 2925.00
Saw, Amputating, Field, DRGM, Self-Cased, Germany, 1800s, 17 1/2 In. 495.00
Saw, Amputating, Ivory Handle, 1800, 19 1/2 In. 1275.00
Saw, Amputation, Tiemann, Civil War Era, 12 In. 385.00
Saw, Surgeon's, Aitken, 1850, 11 In. 355.00
Saw, Surgeon's, Brass, Blackwell, 8-In. Blade 190.00
Shock Machine, Cast Iron, Mills Imperial, Hoboken, New Jersey, 22 In. 7150.00
Thermometer, Rectal, Instanta, Black Plastic Case, Box, Taylor Instrument Co., c.1930 .. 15.00
Tool, Massaging, Rosewood, Bakelite, Rubber, Health Culture Co., Pat. '82, 7 1/2 In. 175.00
Toothpaste, Listerine, Full Tube, 5 1/2 In. ....*Illus* 8.00
Trumpet, Double Ear, Faux Tortoiseshell, Greek Key Design, France, 6 1/2 In. 445.00

Trumpet, Ear, Collapsing, Child's, Metal, Black Paint, 8 3/4 In. 445.00
Tweezers, Lady's Leg Shape, Stocking, Silvered Metal, 1880-1920 . . . . 50.00
Urinal & Potty, Child's, Blue Floral & Butterfly, White, England, 1840, 12 1/4 In. 1250.00

MEERSCHAUM is a soft white, gray, or cream-colored mineral named
magnesium silicate. The name comes from the German word for seafoam, because it was sometimes found floating in the Black Sea and people thought it was petrified seafoam. Pipes and other pieces of carved
meerschaum listed here date from the nineteenth century to the present.

Pipe, 6 3/4 In., 2 Piece 63.00
Pipe, Child's Head, Wreath Of Grapevines Bowl, 3 1/2 In. 55.00
Pipe, Clay Bowl, Silver Connectors, Velvet Lined Case, 15 x 2 3/4 In. 168.00
Pipe, Lion & Lioness, Fitted Case, 6 In. 115.00
Pipe, Sterling Band, Irish, 5 1/2 In. 63.00
Pipe, Turk's Head Bowl, Amber Stem, Case, Early 20th Century, 7 In. 545.00
Pipe, Victorian Lady Bust, Hand On Chin, Amber Mouthpiece, 1800s 635.00
Pipe, Woman, 7 3/4 In. 184.00

MEISSEN is a town in Germany where porcelain has been made since
1710. Any china made in the town can be called Meissen, although the
famous Meissen factory made the finest porcelains of the area. The
crossed swords mark of the great Meissen factory has been copied by
many other firms in Germany and other parts of the world. Pieces of
Meissen dinnerware in the Onion pattern are listed in their own category in this book.

Base, Snake Handle, Cobalt & Gilt, c.1880, 15 In., Pair 4620.00
Basket, Shaped Rim, 2 Putti, Tree Trunk Base, Draped, c.1770, 14 In. 720.00
Bonbon, Leaf Shape, Ivy Branch Handle, Band Of Ivy Leaves, 1 x 4 x 3 3/4 In. 80.00
Bottle, Dresser, Blue Field, Medallions With Flower Basket, 20th Century, 5 In. 336.00
Bottle Stand, Frieze Of Swans & Herons, Gilt Rim, Pale Pink, 9 In., Pair 5100.00
Bowl, 2 Putti Frolicking Among Floral Sprig Clouds, Blue Underglaze, 8 In. 460.00
Bowl, Wide Rim, Bouquet Of Garden Flowers, Blue Underglaze, 14 In. 345.00
Bust, Children Of Louis, Dauphin Of France, Pair 2875.00
Candelabra, 7-Light, Flowers, Children Playing Instruments, Signed, 22 3/4 In. 2990.00
Charger, Scalloped Edge, Peony, Yellow, Blue Flowers, c.1817, 15 1/4 In. 865.00
Clock, Mantel, Classical Female Figures & Putti, Signed, Late 19th Century, 18 In. 6040.00
Coffee Cann, Saucer, Stylized Floral Branches, Blue Underglaze, Handle 260.00
Compote, 3 Tiers, Female Flower Seller At Top, Late 19th Century, 20 3/4 In. 1380.00
Compote, Male & Female Figures, Pierced Bowl, Signed, 1880s, 22 1/2 In. 4900.00
Cup & Saucer, Small White Flowers, Yellow Vines, Red Roses, Marked, 2 1/4 x 5 In. 60.00
Dessert Service, Floral Bouquet, Gold Fluted Medallions 1955.00
Dessert Set, Pink & Blue Flowers, Gold Rim, Scalloped Edge, 8 Piece 165.00
Dish, 2 Bucolic Lovers Scene, Puce Floral Sprig Ground, Yellow Rim, 8 In. 290.00
Dish Set, Leaf Shape, Blue Onion, Handle, Graduated Sizes, Gilt Rim, 9 1/2 In., 3 Piece . 260.00
Ewer, Cupid Scene, 15 In. 900.00
Figurine, Allegorical Female, Subject On Base, Signed, 19th Century, 12 In. 8175.00
Figurine, Apollo, In Chariot, Bow & Quiver Of Arrows, Signed, 1852, 8 1/4 In. 1800.00
Figurine, Chinese Maiden, Seated, Feeding Bird, Tea From Tray, c.1971, 5 In., Pair 1320.00
Figurine, Cockatoo, On Perch, Early 20th Century, 9 In. 400.00
Figurine, Cockatoo, Perched Amid Flowers & Leaves, Signed, 1930s, 19 In. 5710.00
Figurine, Comedia Dell' Arte, Man, Masked Woman, Signed, 8 In., Pair 980.00
Figurine, Cupid, 18th Century Exotic Dress, Signed, 3 3/4 To 4 1/4 In., 7 Piece 4310.00
Figurine, Cupid, Seated On Clothed Tree Stump, Germany, 7 1/2 In. 1265.00
Figurine, Cupid, With Broken Heart, Marbleized Socle, Late 19th Century, 8 1/8 In. 1380.00
Figurine, Emblematic Of Air, Polychrome, Mark, Late 19th Century, 5 In. 1265.00
Figurine, Fall, Mark, 8 1/2 In. 1150.00
Figurine, Fecundity Woman, Classically Woman, Breast Exposed, Blue Glaze, 7 In. 560.00
Figurine, Female, Cherub, Standing, With Fan, Socle Base, Germany, 9 1/4 In. 1610.00
Figurine, Gallant & His Lady, 18th Century Couple, Floral & Chintz, 19 In., Pair 2875.00
Figurine, Gardener, Companion, Late 19th Century, 7 1/2 In, Pair 1092.00
Figurine, Gardening Children, Boy Carrying Basket With Grapes, 5 In., Pair 920.00
Figurine, Horse Tamers, 10 In., Pair 2070.00

Figurine, Lady Wearing Lace Trimmed Dress, Hat, 6 1/4 In. 1035.00
Figurine, Lady Wearing Lace Trimmed Dress, Pink Cape, Bonnet, 8 In. 690.00
Figurine, Maiden Holding Flower, Book, Muff, 8 1/4 In, Pair 860.00
Figurine, Putti Carrying Vase, Birds, Crossed Swords, 7 3/4 In. 825.00
Figurine, Putto In Cloak, Purple Flowers, Fur Lined Cloak, 5 3/8 In. 520.00
Figurine, Putto With Birdcatcher, Crossed Swords Mark, 19th Century, 4 In. 1380.00
Figurine, Sentiment, Late 19th Century, 6 In. 1840.00
Figurine, Shepherdess, Floral Painted Skirt, Sheep At Feet, Signed, 10 3/4 In. 740.00
Figurine, Sleeping Putti With Puppies, Crossed Swords Mark, 4 In. 635.00
Figurine, Swan, Black Webbed Feet, 1 Wing Outstretched, c.1750, 5 1/2 In., Pair 3000.00
Figurine, Woman Wearing Yellow Robe, Playing The Piano, 5 In. 575.00
Figurine, Woman With Duck, Man With Grapes, Mark, 5 In., Pair 805.00
Group, 3 Children Representing Science, Geography, Mathematics, 4 1/2 In. 1035.00
Group, 3 Couples At Various Pursuits Around Leafy Tree, 17 1/2 In. 2400.00
Group, Allegorical, 4 Children Representing Harvest, Autumn, 6 In. 1265.00
Group, Allegorical, Boys, Trading Goods On Rock Base, 5 In. 920.00
Group, Arab Holding Horse, Boy Wearing Green Robe, 1974, 9 1/2 In. 805.00
Group, Boy Holding Birds By Open Birdcage, Rococo Base, 5 In. 460.00
Group, Couple Blowing Bubbles, 19th Century, 5 In. 1495.00
Group, Couple With Birdcage Nest On Top, Girl Seated Making Garland, 6 In. 920.00
Group, Man, Holding Garland, Dog, Woman, Holding Post, Lamb, 9 In., Pair 2315.00
Group, Silenus, Man On Donkey, Woman With Grapes, Boy, c.1900, 8 1/2 In. 1725.00
Group, The Good Mother, Central Seated Female Figure, 3 Children, 9 In. 4600.00
Group, Young Boy & Girl With Goat, Boy Playing Recorder, 5 5/8 In. 1380.00
Group, Young Couple, Girl Playing Mandolin, 6 1/4 In. 1495.00
Group, Young Couple, Woman Carrying Basket With Grapes, 1850, 6 In. 690.00
Jug, Hot Milk, Harbor Scenes, Floral, Wishbone Handle, Blue Underglaze, 4 In. 540.00
Mirror, Applied With Leaves, Flowers, 2 Cherubs Supporting Floral Garland, 9 In. 1380.00
Mirror, Cherubs & Floral Molded Frame, Blue Crossed Swords, Round, 10 In. 495.00
Plate, Cobalt Blue, Gilt, Floral Sprays, 9 1/2 In., Pair 230.00
Plate, Fruit, Fruit & Insects, Reticulated Border, 8 In., 8 Piece 1150.00
Plate, Reserve Of Seated Maiden, Divided Paneled Border, Signed, 1880s, 9 1/4 In. 1190.00
Plate, Sprays & Sprigs, Brown Edged Rim, Signed, 9 3/8 In., 9 Piece 1140.00
Platter, Shell, Scroll Border, Pierced Handles, Blue, White, 15 7/8 x 16 In. 495.00
Salt, Figural, Girl Holding Bird, Baskets, Flowers, Scrollwork, 5 1/2 In. 405.00
Sauceboat, Undertray, Blue Cross Swords Mark, 9 1/4 In. 80.00
Saucer, Putti Amid Clouds, Vignettes Of Birds, Fruit & Flowers, 5 1/4 In., 5 Piece 600.00
Soup, Dish, Floral Sprigs, Gilt Rim, Signed, 9 1/2 In., 12 Piece 545.00
Stein, Hand Painted Gold Crest, Johann Friedrich, c.1715, 1 Liter 25400.00
Teabowl & Saucer, Floral, 19th Century, Pair 175.00
Tray, Polychrome Floral Sprigs, Cream Ground, Continuous Handles, Gilt, 11 1/2 In. 290.00
Tray, Rocaille Shells Rim, Floral Center, Square, Late 19th Century, 16 1/4 In. 1090.00
Tray, Spoon, Center Exotic Bird Within Border, Signed, c.1765, 5 5/8 In. 2700.00
Tureen, Soup, Cover, Foliate Handles, Putti Finial, Signed, 14 1/4 In. 865.00
Urn, Molded Acanthus Leaf Design, Narrow Neck, Twin Scrolled Handles, 24 In. 575.00
Utensils, Mallet, Crimper, Muddler, Treen Handle, 12 In., 3 Piece 230.00
Vase, 2 Intertwined Snake Handles, Blue Underglaze, Germany, 11 In. 115.00
Vase, Foliage Scrolling Snakes At Rim, Gilt Highlights, Cobalt Ground, 32 In., Pair 630.00
Vase, Grape Leaf Decoration, Square Plinth, Scroll Handles, 11 x 5 x 6 1/2 In., Pair 1265.00
Vase, Oval Body, Entwined Snake Handle, Cobalt Ground, 11 1/8 In., Pair 920.00
Vase, Trumpet Shape, Quatrefoil Cartouche, Flower, Cobalt Ground, 6 1/2 In. 290.00
Vase, White Enamel Cupids, Signed, 6 1/2 In., Pair 7700.00

MERCURY GLASS, or silvered glass, was first made in the 1850s. It lost
favor for a while but became popular again about 1910. It looks like a
piece of silver.

Candlestick, 6 3/4 In., Pair 210.00
Compote, Frosted Tendril Design & Band, Gold Interior, 5 1/2 In. 405.00
Goblet, Frosted Leaf & Bird Design, Gold Interior, 4 3/4 In. 86.00
Humidor, Etched Vines & Rings Cover, Frosted, Amber Diamonds, 8 In. 165.00
Pitcher, Gold Ground, Pink & Red Floral, Green Interior, 10 1/4 In. 175.00
Urn, 19th Century, 14 x 10 In. 168.00
Vase, Frosted Flowers & Leaves Design, Gold Interior, Footed, 10 In., Pair 422.00

MERRIMAC POTTERY Company was founded by Thomas Nickerson in Newburyport, Massachusetts, in 1902. The company made art pottery, garden pottery, and reproductions of Roman pottery. The pottery burned to the ground in 1908.

Bowl, Deep Green Iridescent Glaze, Crimped Edge, Ocher Interior, 2 3/4 x 7 In.	605.00
Vase, Applied Swirled Leaves, Green Matte Glaze, 7 3/4 x 4 1/2 In.	4218.00
Vase, Dark Green Matte Glaze, 4 In.	518.00
Vase, Green Matte Glaze, 10 1/2 In.	1035.00
Vase, Orange, Green Matte Glaze, 4 In.	489.00

METTLACH, Germany, is a city where the Villeroy and Boch factories worked. Steins from the firm are marked with the word *Mettlach* or the castle mark. They date from about 1842. *PUG* means painted under glaze. The steins can be dated from the marks on the bottom, which include a date-number code. Other pieces may be listed in the Villeroy & Boch category.

Beaker, No. 2327, 1/4 Liter, Cavalier Holding Staff, PUG	240.00
Beaker, No. 2327-430, 1/4 Liter, Hofbrauhaus, Munchen, PUG	185.00
Beaker, No. 2327-1191, 1/4 Liter, Fisherman On Boat, PUG	80.00
Beaker, No. 2327-1200, 1/4 Liter, Hamburg, PUG	79.00
Beaker, No. 2327-1419, 1/4 Liter, Cinderella By Fireplace, PUG	140.00
Beaker, No. 2368-1091, 1/4 Liter, Waiter Serving Wine, PUG	80.00
Beaker, No. 3327, 1/3 Liter, Man Playing Guitar	230.00
Bowl, No. 1322, Floral Design, Mosaic, 4 In.	405.00
Cake Plate, No. 3336, Art Nouveau, Etched, 9 In.	540.00
Pitcher, No. 3322, Art Deco, Green & White, Etched, 6 In.	155.00
Plaque, No. 1044-102B, Ducks Flying From Lake, PUG, 12 In.	225.00
Plaque, No. 1044-130, Schloss Heidelberg, PUG, 12 In.	275.00
Plaque, No. 1044-156, Koblenz, PUG, 14 In.	350.00
Plaque, No. 1044-411, Woman With Beer Stein, PUG, 17 In.	405.00
Plaque, No. 1044-9025, Fish & Lobster, 14 In.	250.00
Plaque, No. 1044-9033, Birds In Field, 14 In.	225.00
Plaque, No. 1108, Castle, Etched, 17 In.	725.00
Plaque, No. 1385, Warrior Scene, Signed Schultz, 1910, 14 1/2 In. ....750.00 to	775.00
Plaque, No. 1770, William Tell, Outdoor Scene, Split Apple On Ground, 15 In.	403.00
Plaque, No. 2146, Infantry Scene, Etched, 15 In.	580.00
Plaque, No. 2196, View Of Castle By River, Grape Vines, Gilt Rim, 17 1/2 In.	460.00
Plaque, No. 2322, Cavalier & Bar Maid, Etched, 15 In.	795.00
Plaque, No. 2442, Trojan Warriors, Boat, Green Ground, Cameo, Stahl, 19 In.	875.00
Plaque, No. 2443, Lady With Attendants, Green Ground, Cameo, Stahl, 19 In.	875.00
Plaque, No. 2549, Art Nouveau, Orchids Surround Woman's Head, Etched, 18 In.	660.00
Plaque, No. 2622, Man Taking Toast, 1910, Castle, Etched, 7 1/2 In.	235.00
Plaque, No. 2795, Words Of Love, Cameo, Stahl, Etched, 17 1/2 In.	1016.00
Plaque, No. 5078, Town Of Mettlach, 17 1/2 In.	2035.00
Plaque, No. 7043, 3 Ladies & Dolphin, Phanolith, Stahl, 21 In.	1450.00
Punch Bowl, Dancers Portrayed Throughout Midsection, Terra-Cotta, 15 In.	2090.00
Punch Bowl, No. 3334, Large Scene On Each Side, 14 1/2 In.	815.00
Stein, No. 783, 1/2 Liter, Children On Bock, Bierbarrel, Relief, Inlaid Lid	510.00
Stein, No. 812, 1 Liter, Hunting Scenes, Inlaid Lid	425.00
Stein, No. 1028, 2 1/3 Liter, Harvest Scene, Relief, Inlaid Lid	200.00
Stein, No. 1062, 1/2 Liter, Floral Design, Inlaid Lid	605.00
Stein, No. 1111, 3 1/2 Liter, Wheat Design, Relief, Pewter Lid	278.00
Stein, No. 1132, 1/2 Liter, Man Playing Violin, Dancing Alligator, Inlaid Lid, Etched	390.00
Stein, No. 1266, 1/2 Liter, 3 Panels Of Drinkers	110.00
Stein, No. 1288, 1/2 Liter, Leaf & Acorn Design, Mosaic, Inlaid Lid	435.00
Stein, No. 1394, 1/2 Liter, German Card, Etched, Inlaid Lid	605.00
Stein, No. 1526, 1/2 Liter, Barmaid, Pewter Lid	160.00
Stein, No. 1526, 1/2 Liter, Yale University, Relief, Pewter Lid	236.00
Stein, No. 1527, 1 Liter, Cavaliers Drinking, Etched, Inlaid Lid	865.00
Stein, No. 1641, 1 Liter, Cavalier, Pipe & Wine Jug, Tapestry Design, Pewter Lid	410.00
Stein, No. 1724, 1/2 Liter, Fireman, Inlaid Lid	1155.00
Stein, No. 1737, 2 Liter, Verse & Hops, Relief, Inlaid Lid	180.00

Stein, No. 1742, 1/2 Liter, Cartouche Of Gottingen, Swordsman Riding Crocodile 430.00
Stein, No. 1758, 1 Liter, Soldier Drinking In Window, Tapestry, Inlaid Lid 876.00
Stein, No. 1809, 1 Liter, 5 Panels, Figures In Each, Etched, Relief, Inlaid Lid 715.00
Stein, No. 1821, 3 1/5 Liter, Musician, Relief, Inlaid Lid 255.00
Stein, No. 1872, 2 Liter, Woman With Children, Inlaid Lid 544.00
Stein, No. 1892, 1/2 Liter, Floral Design, Mosaic, Pewter Lid 695.00
Stein, No. 1909, 1/2 Liter, Pilsner Export Beer, PUG, Pewter Lid 270.00
Stein, No. 1909-727, 1/2 Liter, Bowling Gnomes, PUG, Pewter Lid, Schlitt 382.00
Stein, No. 1909-1073, 1/2 Liter, Hunter, PUG, Pewter Lid, Schlitt 360.00
Stein, No. 1909-1097, 1/2 Liter, Men Thrown Out Of Bar, PUG, Pewter Lid 115.00
Stein, No. 1909-1196, 1/2 Liter, Hops, Wheat, Flowers, PUG, Pewter Lid, Art Nouveau .. 365.00
Stein, No. 1909-1280, 1/2 Liter, Fox Eating At Table, PUG, Pewter Lid, Art Nouveau 560.00
Stein, No. 1968, 1/4 Liter, Lovers, Etched, Inlaid Lid 345.00
Stein, No. 1989, 1 1/2 Liter, Floral, Etched, Glazed, Inlaid Lid 1165.00
Stein, No. 1998, 1/2 Liter, Trumpeter From Sackingen, Etched, Inlaid Lid 575.00
Stein, No. 2001A, 1/2 Liter, Law, Glazed, Hand Painted, Inlaid Lid 660.00
Stein, No. 2001B, 1/2 Liter, Physician, Glazed, Hand Painted, Inlaid Lid 430.00
Stein, No. 2001F, 1/2 Liter, Architecture, Glazed, Hand Painted, Inlaid Lid 550.00
Stein, No. 2003, 1/2 Liter, 3 Scenes Of Men, Inlaid Lid ....660.00 to 695.00
Stein, No. 2009, 1/2 Liter, Werner & Margarete Dancing, Etched, Inlaid Lid 605.00
Stein, No. 2018, 1/2 Liter, PUG, Dog, Stoneware, Inlaid Lid 1270.00
Stein, No. 2024, 1/2 Liter, Shield Of Berlin, Inlaid Lid 250.00
Stein, No. 2025, 1/3 Liter, Cherubs Carousing, Etched, Inlaid Lid 390.00
Stein, No. 2028, 1/2 Liter, Tavern Keeper Filling Steins, Inlaid Lid 315.00
Stein, No. 2030, 1/2 Liter, Soldiers Drinking, Etched, Inlaid Lid 520.00
Stein, No. 2036, 1/2 Liter, Owl, Stoneware, Inlaid Lid 1155.00
Stein, No. 2054, 1/2 Liter, Cavalier Leaning On Barrel, Inlaid Lid 170.00
Stein, No. 2054, 1/2 Liter, Seven Students Drinking, Etched, Inlaid Lid 460.00
Stein, No. 2057, 1/3 Liter, Peasants Drinking, Etched, Inlaid Lid 205.00
Stein, No. 2074, 1/2 Liter, Bird In Cage, Etched, Inlaid Lid 1385.00
Stein, No. 2082, 1/2 Liter, William Tell Shooting Apple, Etched, Inlaid Lid 1560.00
Stein, No. 2083, 1 Liter, Boar Hunting, Etched, Inlaid Lid 1815.00
Stein, No. 2083, 1/2 Liter, Boar Hunting, Etched, Inlaid Lid 1590.00
Stein, No. 2091, 1/2 Liter, St. Florian Pouring Water On Man's Head, Inlaid Lid .590.00 to 1016.00
Stein, No. 2092, 1/2 Liter, Gnome Adjusting Clock, Etched, Inlaid Lid 830.00
Stein, No. 2094, 1/2 Liter, Lady Playing Fiddle & Dancers, Etched, Inlaid Lid 400.00
Stein, No. 2121, 1/4 Liter, Children Playing, Etched, Inlaid Lid 125.00
Stein, No. 2130, 1/2 Liter, Seated Man Drinking, Etched, Inlaid Lid 145.00
Stein, No. 2230, 1/2 Liter, Man & Barmaid, Etched, Inlaid Lid 345.00
Stein, No. 2261-1012, 2 1/4 Liter, Drinking Scene, PUG, Pewter Lid, Schlitt 265.00
Stein, No. 2282, 1/2 Liter, Man Caught In Wine Cellar, Etched, Inlaid Lid 520.00
Stein, No. 2348-1022, 3 1/3 Liter, Musical, Couple Dancing, PUG, Pewter Lid . . .320.00 to 360.00
Stein, No. 2364, 3 1/2 Liter, Classical Figures, Inlaid Lid 330.00
Stein, No. 2382, 1/2 Liter, Thirsty Knight, Etched, Inlaid Lid ....750.00 to 875.00
Stein, No. 2388, 1/2 Liter, Pretzels, Pretzel Handle, Pretzel Inlaid Lid 390.00
Stein, No. 2441, 1/2 Liter, Dice Game, Etched, Inlaid Lid 690.00
Stein, No. 2531, 1/2 Liter, Monk With Jug Of Beer, Etched, Inlaid Lid 605.00
Stein, No. 2580, 1/2 Liter, Castle Tower, Etched, Inlaid Lid, Schlitt 1090.00
Stein, No. 2580, 1/2 Liter, Die Kannenburg, Knight, Castle, Etched, Inlaid Lid, Schlitt ... 575.00
Stein, No. 2582, 1/2 Liter, Drinking Scene With Jester, Etched, Inlaid Lid 495.00
Stein, No. 2583, 1 Liter, Egyptian, Man Eats & Drinks, Inlaid Lid 695.00
Stein, No. 2639, 1 Liter, Blacksmith & Cavalier, Arms Interlocked, Etched, Inlaid Lid ... 520.00
Stein, No. 2752, 1/2 Liter, Men With Tri-Cornered Hats, Etched, Inlaid Lid 580.00
Stein, No. 2776, 1/2 Liter, Keeper Of Wine Cellar, Inlaid Lid 665.00
Stein, No. 2784-6129, 2 1/5 Liter, Man Playing Mandolin, Rookwood, Pewter Lid 785.00
Stein, No. 2786-6131, 2 1/2 Liter, Man Reading Book, Rookwood, Pewter Lid 785.00
Stein, No. 2789-6145, 1/2 Liter, Bearded Man Drinking, Rookwood, Pewter Lid 360.00
Stein, No. 2917, 1 Liter, Munich Child & City Scene, Relief, Inlaid Lid 1575.00
Stein, No. 2917, 1/2 Liter, Munich Child & City Scene, Relief, Inlaid Lid 2310.00
Stein, No. 2937, 1 Liter, Night Watchman, Etched, Inlaid Lid 1330.00
Stein, No. 2951, 1/2 Liter, Prussian Eagle, Cameo, Pewter Lid 515.00
Stein, No. 3078-437, 1/2 Liter, Lover, Bavaria, Inlaid Lid 580.00

Stein, No. 3080-533, 1/2 Liter, Bavarian Girl Holding Stein, Bavaria, Inlaid Lid	600.00
Stein, No. 3085, 1/4 Liter, Postman, Tapestry, Etched, Pewter Lid	435.00
Stein, No. 3087, 1 Liter, Woman Drinking At Table, Tapestry, Pewter Lid	755.00
Stein, No. 3091, 1 Liter, Knight Drinking, Etched, Inlaid Lid, 8 1/2 In.	490.00
Stein, No. 3170, 1/2 Liter, People Walking In Falling Snow, Etched, Inlaid Lid	945.00
Stein, No. 3328, 1/2 Liter, Man Drinking, Inlaid Lid	850.00
Stein, No. 5191, 1/3 Liter, Cavalier At Table, Delft, Pewter Lid	300.00
Vase, No. 2175, Etruscan Scene, 3 Ladies, Etched, 7 In.	345.00
Vase, No. 2202, Children Dancing On Either Side, Relief, 9 1/2 In.	400.00
Vase, No. 2866, Geometric Design, Glazed, Terra-Cotta, 6 In.	160.00

MILK GLASS was named for its milky white color. It was first made in England during the 1700s. The height of its popularity in the United States was from 1870 to 1880. It is now correct to refer to some colored glass as blue milk glass, black milk glass, etc. Reproductions of milk glass are being made and sold in many stores. Related pieces may be listed in the Cosmos and Westmoreland categories.

Banana Bowl, Pedestal, Lattice Edge, 9 1/2 x 13 1/2 In.	28.00
Bottle, Enameled Flowers, Applied Pewter Collar, c.1850, 5 1/2 In.	415.00
Bowl, Blue, Ribbed, Ram's Heads, Footed, 8 1/4 x 5 1/8 In.	165.00
Box, Pig On Drum Cover, 3 In.	50.00
Compote, Goddess Of Liberty, Open, Figural Stem, 8 In.	150.00
Creamer, Hobnail, 8-Pointed Star Shape, 2 1/2 x 3 1/2 In.	15.00
Creamer, Holly With Cord & Tassel	110.00
Dish, Bird On Nest Cover, Flowers & Leaves, 6 x 6 In. . . . .*Illus*	55.00
Dish, Deer Cover, Fallen Tree Base, E. W. Flaccus Co., Wheeling, W.Va., 7 In.	455.00
Dish, Dog Lying Down Cover, Enameled Gold & Pink, 5 x 5 In.	165.00
Dish, Dresser, Blue, Embossed Scrolls Around Rim, 6 3/4 x 4 3/4 In.	35.00
Dish, Duck Cover, Glass Eyes, Atterbury, 5 x 10 1/4 In. . . . .*Illus*	154.00
Dish, Fish Cover, Red Glass Eyes, 4 1/2 x 8 3/4 In. . . . .*Illus*	330.00
Dish, Pig On Drum Cover, Blue, 3 In.	40.00
Dish, Reclining Fox Cover, Fluted Base, Pat'd August 6, 1889, 5 1/2 x 7 In. . . . .*Illus*	176.00
Dish, Reclining Lion On Lattice Cover, Pat'd 1889, 6 1/2 x 7 1/2 In. . . . .*Illus*	72.00
Goblet, Beaded Loop, 5 In.	24.00
Jar, Cover, Owl, Eagle Insert, 6 1/4 In.	110.00
Jar, Cover, Remember The Maine, 5 1/4 In.	335.00
Lamp, Acanthus Swirl, Pink & Green, 8 3/4 In.	385.00
Lamp, Swirl & Bead, Cranberry Cased, 8 3/4 In.	220.00
Salt & Pepper, Heron & Lighthouse, Original Top	110.00
Syrup, Tree Of Life, Pale Green, Copper Cover	375.00
Tumbler, Daisy, Pink, Light Green Trim, 4 In.	45.00
Vase, Bird, Yellow Roses, Blue, 8 1/2 In.	125.00
Vase, Hoover, Red Flowering Tree, Birds, Flowers, Anchor Hocking, 9 In.	20.00

Milk Glass, Dish, Bird On Nest Cover, Flowers & Leaves, 6 x 6 In.

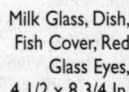

Milk Glass, Dish, Duck Cover, Glass Eyes, Atterbury, 5 x 10 1/4 In.

Milk Glass, Dish, Fish Cover, Red Glass Eyes, 4 1/2 x 8 3/4 In.

Milk Glass, Dish, Reclining Fox Cover, Fluted
Base, Pat'd August 6, 1889, 5 1/2 x 7 In.

Milk Glass, Dish, Reclining Lion On Lattice
Cover, Pat'd 1889, 6 1/2 x 7 1/2 In.

Vase, Pear Shape, Arabesque Floral Design, 8 1/4 In.	81.00
Vase, White Magnolia, 13 In.	127.00

MILLEFIORI means, literally, a thousand flowers. Many small pieces of glass resembling flowers are grouped together to form a design. It is a type of glasswork popular in paperweights and some are listed in that category.

Bowl, 4 In.	80.00
Candy Dish, 5 x 2 In.	31.00
Vase, 7 In.	154.00
Vase, Bud, Banjo, Fluted, Satin, Low Fire Murrines, 1930s, 8 In.	203.00

MINTON china has been made in the Staffordshire region of England from 1793 to the present. The firm became part of the Royal Doulton Tableware Group in 1968, but the wares continued to be marked *Minton*. Many marks have been used. The word *England* was added in 1891. Minton majolica is listed in this book in the Majolica category.

Bowl, Amherst Japan, Ironstone, c.1845, 9 1/2 In.	315.00
Dish, Berlin Biard, c.1871, 11 1/2 x 8 1/2 In.	485.00
Ewer, Chinoiserie Gilt Design, Prunus, Butterflies, Pink Ground, 11 In.	200.00
Figurine, Abysinian Slave, Parian, 1855, 10 In.	1076.00
Figurine, Atala & Chactas, Parian, July 1850, 10 In.	2278.00
Figurine, Harvester, Boy & Girl, Kneeling Beside Wooden Barrels, 7 1/2 In., Pair	1705.00
Figurine, Miranda, Parian, Seated On Rock By Ocean, Black Marble Base, 16 1/2 In.	430.00
Figurine, Nude Female Bather, Disrobing By Tree Stump, No. 267, 1867, 13 3/8 In.	546.00
Figurine, Nude Woman Reclining On Back Of Lioness, Rectangular Base, 14 In.	1725.00
Figurine, Putto, Viola On Nautilus Shell, 1873, 18 In.	6600.00
Flask, Moon, Lack Of Shakespeare, John Mayer Smith, c.1879, 6 3/4 In.	840.00
Garden Pot, Stand, Profusion Of Ferns, Foxgloves, Pink Glaze, 1869, 15 1/2 In.	9600.00
Jardiniere, Pink Interior, Dark Floral Exterior, 13 x 19 In.	2240.00
Jardiniere, Relief Plaque, Africa & America, 18 In.	5225.00
Jardiniere, Stand, Yellow, Brown Bamboo Cane, 10 1/4 In., 3 Piece	6600.00
Pitcher, Railroad & Coach Scenes, Present, Past, 2 Drivers, Label, 7 3/4 In.	60.00
Plaque, Maiden Concealing Cupid Behind Her Back, Olive Green, 1913, 11 In., Pair	14400.00
Plate, Birds, Cobalt Blue Border, Signed, 9 1/2 In., 5 Piece	2625.00
Plate, Dinner, Floral Panels, Turquoise Borders, For W.H. Plumer, 1890, 12 Piece	9500.00
Plate, Essex Bird, Late 19th Century, 9 1/2 In., 8 Piece	460.00
Plate, Florets Within Arch Frames, Center Castles, Signed, c.1910, 9 1/4 In., 12 Piece	575.00
Plate, Foliate Cartouches Band Centered By Floral Sprays, 10 1/4 In., 12 Piece	405.00
Plate, Service, Green Inner Rim & Edge, Gold, Ivory Vine Rim, 10 5/8 In., 12 Piece	1095.00
Teapot Stand, Seashell Design, Gilt Trim, Oval, Mark, c.1810, 7 In.	115.00
Tile, Boston State House, Cows On Lawn, Square, 6 In., 4 Piece	330.00
Tile, Fireplace Surround, 17 Tiles, Seasons, Late 19th Century, 43 x 37 In.	3795.00
Tile, Scenes From Idylls Of The King, By Tennyson, Square, 1875, 6 In.	190.00
Tile, Trout Under Water, Floral Inlay, Mahogany Frame, 1890	120.00
Tureen, Soup, Cover, Underplate, 19th Century, 14 In.	260.00

Vase, 5-Spout Fan Form, Fish Head Feet, Signed, c.1855, 6 1/4 In. 200.00
Vase, Cherubs Alternating With Groups Of Trophies, Green Ground, 18 In., Pair 10200.00
Vase, Cobalt Blue Top, Ram's-Head Handles, 1866, 27 1/2 In. 8250.00
Vase, Secessionist Style, Blood Red, Light Blue, Olive, Beige Ground, 10 3/4 In. 230.00

MIRRORS are listed in the Furniture category under Mirror.

MOCHA pottery is an English-made product that was sold in America during the early 1800s. It is a heavy pottery with pale coffee-and-cream coloring. Designs of blue, brown, green, orange, black, or white were added to the pottery and given fanciful names, such as *Tree, Snail Trail,* or *Moss.*

Bowl, 2 Slip Blue Accent Bands, Blue Design, Cream White, 1870, 6 In. 468.00
Bowl, Earthworm Loop, 2 Black Bands, 6 1/2 In. 660.00
Bowl, Mixing, Striping, Center Band Of Green Seaweed, White Ground, 10 1/2 In. 360.00
Bowl, Seaweed, 10 In. 575.00
Bowl, Seaweed, 19th Century, 3 x 5 3/8 In. 633.00
Bowl, Seaweed, Blue Trim, 4 1/2 x 9 3/4 In. 425.00
Bowl, Seaweed, White Stripes, Brown Band., 2 7/8 x 4 In. 360.00
Chamber Pot, Seaweed, Blue & White Band, Ribbed Handle, 5 3/4 x 9 In. 220.00
Chamber Pot, Seaweed, Blue, White Band, Applied Handle, 9 x 5 /12 In. 110.00
Chamber Pot, Seaweed, Ribbed Handle, 7 In. 330.00
Creamer, 2 Blue Stripes At Neck, Marbleized In Blue, Brown & Ocher, 4 1/4 In. 1540.00
Creamer, Black Seaweed, Beaded & Quilted Bands, Black Stripes, 4 1/2 In. 1320.00
Mug, Blue, Tan & Ivory Cat's Eye, Blue Stripes, 3 3/4 In. 1980.00
Mug, Earthworm, Blue Ground, Brown Stripes, 3 1/4 In. 440.00
Mug, Foliage Bands, Stripes, Blue & Orange Bands, Leaf Handle, 4 7/8 In. 715.00
Mug, Seaweed, Blue, Brown Stripes, White Band, 3 In. 110.00
Mug, Seaweed, Green, White Band, Blue Stripes, 2 7/8 In. 385.00
Mug, Seaweed, Pale Blue Bands, White Ground, 3 In. 220.00
Mug, Zigzag Line At Rim, Tooled, Black & White Balloon, 2 1/8 In. 1760.00
Mustard, Brown Tooled Lines, White, 3 3/4 In. 1210.00
Mustard, Tobacco Leaf On Tan Ground, Brown Bands, 2 1/2 In. 3080.00
Pepper Pot, Blue & Tan Stripes, Tooled Bands, 4 1/4 In. 1210.00
Pepper Pot, Earthworm, Tan Ground, Black Finial, Brown & Blue Stripes, 5 1/4 In. 2420.00
Pepper Pot, Light Blue & Black Stripes, 4 1/2 In. 110.00
Pepper Shaker, Seaweed, Blue & White Bands, 4 3/4 In. 1320.00
Pitcher, Black Stripes, Blue & Green Bands, Leaf Handle, 7 1/8 In. 770.00
Pitcher, Blue & Brown Stripes, 12 In. 825.00
Pitcher, Brown & White Banding, 7 1/2 In. 470.00
Pitcher, Brown Sponge Ground, Floral Decoration, White, Green Bands, 6 1/2 In. 1540.00
Pitcher, Cat's-Eye, Blue Seaweed Band, Brown Banding, Scalloped Edge, 6 3/4 In. 8250.00
Pitcher, Cat's-Eye, Brown Stripes, Ivory Ground, 7 1/4 In. 500.00
Pitcher, Cat's-Eye, Scalloped Top, Banded Blue Seaweed Over Green, 6 3/4 In. 8250.00
Pitcher, Earthworm, Black & White, Leaves On Handle, 5 1/2 In. 330.00
Pitcher, Earthworm, Leaf Handle, Green Bands, Blue Stripes, 6 3/8 In. 440.00
Pitcher, Earthworm, Tan & Brown Stripes, Leaf End Handles, 5 In. 6600.00
Pitcher, Earthworm, Tooled Green Band, Blue Ground, 6 5/8 In. 110.00
Pitcher, Orange Bands Top & Bottom, Lead On Handle & Spout, 7 7/8 In. 1320.00
Pitcher, Seaweed, Blue Bands At Top & Bottom, Tan Stripes, 6 1/4 In. 550.00
Stein, Green Bands, Pewter Lid, Engraved Laurel Wreath, 7 3/4 In. 990.00
Waste Bowl, Marbleized Band On Body, 3 x 5 5/8 In. 495.00

MONMOUTH Pottery Company started working in Monmouth, Illinois, in 1892. The pottery made a variety of utilitarian wares. It became part of Western Stoneware Company in 1906. The maple leaf mark was used until 1930. If *Co.* appears as part of the mark, the piece was made before 1906.

Ash Receiver, Duck, Mouth Open, White Stoneware, 1938, 4 In. 20.00
Batter Bowl, Handle, Light Green Glaze, Yellow Clay, 1930, 8 x 4 3/4 In. 75.00
Bean Pot, Dark Brown Glaze, 8 1/2 x 9 1/2 In. 25.00
Bowl, Brown, White Foam Edge, 4 x 8 In. 27.00
Bowl, Purple Glaze, 4 x 6 In., 2 Piece 46.00

Cookie Jar, Butter Beige, 7 x 11 In.	25.00
Jar, Canning, Early 20th Century, 8 1/2 x 5 1/2 In.	120.00
Mug, 2 Hunting Dogs In Field, Dark Brown Glaze, Handle, Pair	35.00
Urn, Light Matte Blue, Handles, 6 x 5 In.	35.00
Vase, Blue Matte Exterior, Natural Clay Finish, Western Stoneware Co., 10 In.	45.00
Vase, Brown Glaze, 9 1/4 In.	49.00
Vase, Ribbed, Beige, Handle, 8 x 7 In.	25.00
Wall Pocket, Blue Matte, 1938, 6 1/4 x 3 3/4 In.	55.00

MONT JOYE, see Mt. Joye category.

MOORCROFT pottery was first made in Burslem, England, in 1913. William Moorcroft had managed the art pottery department for James MacIntyre & Company of England from 1898 to 1913. The Moorcroft pottery continues today, although William Moorcroft died in 1945. The earlier wares are similar to the modern ones, but color and marking will help indicate the age.

Ashtray, Maroon & Blue Orchid, Green Ground, Label, 4 1/2 In.	65.00
Bell, Anemone, White, Painted Mark, 1985, 4 1/2 In.	60.00
Bell, Hibiscus, Stamped Mark, 1983, 4 1/2 In.	90.00
Biscuit Jar, Hibiscus, Impressed Mark, 6 In.	275.00
Biscuit Jar, Moonlit Blue Landscape, Metal Mounted, c.1925, 6 In.	2280.00
Bonbon, Cover, Rose Garland, Marked, 7 In.	1725.00
Bowl, African Lily, Impressed Mark, 4 1/4 In.	60.00
Bowl, Anemone, Cobalt Blue, 8 1/2 In.	675.00
Bowl, Bermuda Lily, Impressed Mark, 9 3/4 In.	290.00
Bowl, Buds & Leaves, Impressed Mark, Label, 6 1/2 In.	110.00
Bowl, Claremont, Toadstools, Impressed Mark, 8 1/4 In.	1840.00
Bowl, Clematis, Impressed Mark, 5 1/2 In.	290.00
Bowl, Columbine, Flambe, Glaze, 5 In.	140.00
Bowl, Cornflower, Flowers Exterior & Interior, Signed, c.1920, 3 In.	840.00
Bowl, Cover, Hibiscus, Flowers & Leaves, Blue Ground, Paper Label, 5 3/4 In.	570.00
Bowl, Florian Ware, Double Handle, Stamped Macintyre, 6 1/2 In.	1265.00
Bowl, Hibiscus, Cover, Impressed Mark, 6 1/2 In.	60.00
Bowl, Moonlit Blue, Landscape, 9 3/4 In.	2415.00
Bowl, Orchid, Cover, Impressed Mark, 5 1/2 In.	210.00
Bowl, Orchid, Impressed Mark, Label, 8 1/4 In.	90.00
Bowl, Pansy, Cover, Impressed Mark, 5 1/2 In.	690.00
Bowl, Pansy, Impressed Mark, 7 1/2 In.	140.00
Bowl, Pomegranate, Signed, 4 x 8 1/4 In.	575.00 to 805.00
Bowl, Poppy, Pedestal, Impressed Mark, 5 In.	140.00
Bowl, Spring Flowers, Cover, Impressed Mark, Label, 6 In.	219.00
Bowl Set, Orchid, Violets, White, Impressed Mark, 8 In., 4	550.00
Box, Clematis, Cover, Impressed Mark, 4 3/4 x 3 1/2 In.	138.00
Box, Clematis, Cover, Impressed Mark, Silver Label, 3 3/4 x 2 3/4 In.	150.00
Box, Freesia, Impressed Mark, Label, 3 1/4 x 5 1/2 In.	127.00
Box, Pansy, Impressed Mark, Label, 2 3/4 x 4 In.	220.00
Box, Poppy, Cover, Impressed Mark, 4 3/4 In.	69.00
Candleholder, Hibiscus, Impressed Mark, Label, 3 1/2 x 5 In., Pair	400.00
Candlestick, Blue Carnations, Florian Ware, 7 1/2 In., Pair	2185.00
Candlestick, Green, Stamped, Macintyre, 7 3/4 In., Pair	345.00
Candlestick, Hibiscus, Green, Impressed Mark, 3 1/2 In., Pair	230.00
Candlestick, Weeping Willow, Trees In Landscape, Signed, c.1930, 3 In., Pair	8730.00
Candy Dish, Silver Overlay, Signed, 5 x 5 In.	400.00
Center Bowl, Pansy, Stamped, Signed, 2 1/4 x 10 3/4 In.	115.00
Charger, Hot Air Balloon, Stamped, No. 45-200, 14 In.	185.00
Charger, Leaf & Fruit, Impressed Mark, 11 3/4 In.	345.00
Charger, Sailing Ship, Impressed Mark, H.M.S. Sirius, 14 In.	220.00
Coffeepot, Toadstool, Loop Handles, Signed, c.1905, 9 3/4 In.	7390.00
Compote, Hibiscus, Impressed Mark, 4 In.	115.00
Compote, Pansy, Double Handle, Impressed Mark, 6 3/4 In.	3000.00
Cracker Jar, Cover, Iris, Florian Ware, Stamped Macintyre, 5 In.	1840.00
Cup & Saucer, Claremont, Green, 2 1/4 In.	2990.00

Cup & Saucer, Clematis, Impressed Mark, 2 3/4 In. 335.00
Cup & Saucer, Garlands Of Flowers, Gilt Border, c.1908, 2 3/4 In. 1430.00
Cup & Saucer, Wisteria, Impressed Mark, 2 x 4 In. 400.00
Dish, Cover, Clematis, Cobalt Blue Ground, Green Interior, Stamped, 3 1/2 x 6 In. 115.00
Dish, Orchid, Cover, Impressed Mark, 6 1/2 In. 265.00
Dish, Sardine, Poppy, Florian Ware, Stamped Macintyre, 5 1/4 x 4 1/2 x 2 In. 1265.00
Ginger Jar, Anemone, Impressed Mark, 4 1/4 In. 90.00
Ginger Jar, Fish Swimming, Flambe, Cover, 1930s, 10 1/2 In. 1440.00
Ginger Jar, Flambe, Bats In Flight, Night Sky, Bernard Moore, Cover, c.1910, 6 1/4 In. .. 840.00
Inkstand, Moonlit Blue, Impressed Mark, 9 In. 1610.00
Inkwell, Hinged Pewter Lid, Speckled Glaze, Glass Liner, Signed, c.1914, 2 3/4 In. 369.00
Inkwell, Wisteria, Impressed Mark, 1 1/2 In. 460.00
Jam Jar, Cover, Moonlit Blue, Silver Spoon, 2 3/4 In. 1150.00
Jam Jar, Pansy, Silver, Cover, Stamped Macintyre, 3 1/2 In. 1610.00
Jam Jar, Pomegranate, Silver Cover, Handle, Impressed Mark, 2 3/4 In. 1150.00
Jar, Cover, Hibiscus, Green Ground, Ink Signed, Stamped, 7 1/4 In. 145.00
Jar, Cover, Poppy, William Moorcroft, 1920, 3 In. 840.00
Jar, Seaweed, MacIntyre, c.1902, 4 1/2 In. 3560.00
Jardiniere, Stylized Poppies, Leaves, Florian Ware, Macintyre, c.1902, 11 1/2 In. 3000.00
Lamp, Apple Blossom, Blossoms & Fruit On Tree, Silk Shade, Signed, 1918, 28 In. 7050.00
Lamp, Leaf & Flower, Dark Red, 22 1/4 In. 1750.00
Lamp, Pomegranate, Fruit & Leaves, Silk Shade, Signed, Drilled, 1928, 28 In. 2915.00
Lamp Base, Corn, Impressed Mark, Label, 11 In. 750.00
Lamp Base, Floral To Black Ground, Replaced Socket, Signed, 14 In. 550.00
Mug, Cobalt Blue, Mottled Green, Crown, Footed, Impressed Mark, 4 1/2 In. 46.00
Mug, Seascape, Sand Dunes, Palm Trees, Impressed Mark, 4 In. 430.00
Pipe Holder, Orchid, Impressed Mark, 5 1/4 In. 430.00
Pitcher, Anemone, Impressed Mark, Label, 4 3/4 In. 150.00
Pitcher, Cover, Silver, Green, Gesso Faience, Stamped Macintyre, 6 In. 265.00
Pitcher, Gesso Faience, Ivory & Green, Stamped Macintyre, 5 In. 230.00
Pitcher, Harebell & Daisy, Stamped Mark, 7 In. 160.00
Pitcher, Leaf & Fruit, Impressed Mark, 3 3/4 In. 127.00
Planter, Leaf & Fruit, Signed, c.1986, 6 3/4 In. 1259.00
Plate, Anemone, Flowers & Leaves, Blue Ground, Signed, c.1981, 10 1/4 In. 336.00
Plate, Aurelian Ware, Stamped Macintyre, 9 3/4 In. 230.00
Plate, Eventide, Center Handle, Impressed Mark, 7 3/4 In. 978.00
Plate, Hibiscus, Flowers & Leaves, Green Ground, No. 13/250, 1983, 8 3/4 In. 336.00
Plate, Magnolia, Flowers & Leaves, Cream Ground, 1980, 12 1/2 In. 36.00
Plate, Pomegranate & Berry, Glossy Cobalt Ground, Plate Hanger, Signed, 7 1/2 In. 175.00
Plate, Pomegranate & Berry, Olive Green & Cobalt Ground, Stamped, 6 1/2 In. 145.00
Plate, Tulip, Pink, Leaves, White Ground, Stamped, Signed, 8 1/2 In. 58.00
Server, Pansy, 2 Tiers, Impressed Mark, 8 1/2 In. 1495.00
Sugar, Cover, Florian Design, 3 1/4 In. 690.00
Tea Service, Stylized, Peacock Feathers, Florian Ware, Macintyre, c.1905, 6 3/4 In. 6600.00
Tea Set, Pomegranate, Green Ground, 8 x 7 1/2 In. 2990.00
Teapot, Aurelian Ware, Brown, Tan, Stamped Macintyre, 7 1/2 In. 520.00
Teapot, Aurelian Ware, Scale Panels, Flowering Foliage, Macintyre, c.1898, 5 In. 3020.00
Teapot, Claremont, 7 3/4 In. 2185.00
Teapot, Oriental, Blue & White, Stamped Macintyre, 3 1/2 x 4 x 7 In. 115.00
Toothpick Holder, Freesia, Impressed Mark, Label, 3 In. 175.00
Toothpick Holder, Hibiscus, Metal Stand, Label, Impressed Mark, 2 1/2 In. 460.00
Tray, Freesia, Impressed Mark, 4 1/2 In. 45.00
Tray, White, Impressed Mark, 8 In. 45.00
Trivet, Florian Ware, Green & Gold, Stamped Macintyre, 6 3/4 In. 489.00
Vase, Arum Lily, Impressed Mark, 4 1/2 In. 150.00
Vase, Aurelian Ware, Handles, Stamped Macintyre, 9 In. 405.00
Vase, Blue Violets, Florian Ware, Stamped, 9 1/2 In. 1380.00
Vase, Blue, Macintyre, 10 In. 920.00
Vase, Bud, Cornflower, Florian Ware, 7 1/4 In. 2185.00
Vase, Bud, Grapes & Peaches, Dark Mottled Blue Ground, 6 1/4 In. 300.00
Vase, Campanula, Impressed Mark, 6 In. 50.00
Vase, Clematis, Big Floral Pattern, Deep Amethyst, 4 In. 170.00

Vase, Clematis, Cobalt & Green Ground, Stamped, Signed, 6 1/4 In. 635.00
Vase, Corn, Blue, Green, Impressed Mark, 4 1/2 In. . . . . .635.00 to 805.00
Vase, Cornflower, 9 3/4 In. 4315.00
Vase, Cornflower, Florian Ware, 1902, 5 In. 2240.00
Vase, Daisy, Florian Ware, Stamped Macintyre, 5 1/4 In. 4025.00
Vase, Dawn, Landscape, Chevron Band, Flambe, 1930s, 3 1/2 In. 2400.00
Vase, Eventide, Encircling Landscape, Rolling Hills, Signed, c.1925, 8 In. 925.00
Vase, Eventide, Gold, Impressed Mark, 3 1/2 In. 805.00
Vase, Eventide, Squeezebag, Tall Trees, Red Flambe Glaze, 1925, 6 x 3 In. 2300.00
Vase, Fish, Impressed Mark, 8 In. 1035.00
Vase, Fish, Swimming, Aquatic Life, Blue, Green, Pink, 1930s, 9 1/2 In. 4500.00
Vase, Flambe, Red Glaze, Green Mottling, Bernard Moore, c.1912, 19 1/4 In. 7200.00
Vase, Flamminian, Pink, 7 1/2 In. 690.00
Vase, Foxglove, Impressed Mark, 7 In. 290.00
Vase, Freesia, Flambe, Label, 4 1/2 In. 400.00
Vase, Green Iridescence, Impressed Mark, 8 In. 230.00
Vase, Hibiscus, Cover, Impressed Mark, Label, 5 1/2 In. 210.00
Vase, Hibiscus, Flowers & Leaves, Blue Ground, Signed, c.1970, 7 1/2 In. 505.00
Vase, Knighthood, Printed Mark, 7 1/4 In. 240.00
Vase, Lamia, Printed Mark, 5 3/4 In. 175.00
Vase, Lattice, Stylized Geometric Floral, Signed, 1992, 10 1/4 In. 540.00
Vase, Leaf & Berry, Flambe, Impressed Mark, 3 In. 175.00
Vase, Leaf & Berry, Impressed Mark, 5 1/2 In. 375.00
Vase, Leaf & Fruit, Flambe, 1920, 7 In. 1000.00
Vase, Leaf & Fruit, Green & Cobalt Glossy Ground, Signed, Bulbous, 5 1/2 In. 230.00
Vase, Leaf & Fruit, Impressed Mark, 3 x 4 In. 276.00
Vase, Leaf & Fruit, Squeezebag, Blue Green Ground, Oval, Signed, 9 In. 1255.00
Vase, Leaf & Fruit, Squeezebag, Outline Of Fruit, Signed, c.1930, 17 In. 4900.00
Vase, Leaf & Fruit, Yellow & Green Glaze, Cobalt Blue, Impressed Mark, 9 1/2 In. 660.00
Vase, Magnolia, Impressed Mark, 8 In. 489.00
Vase, Magnolia, Tube Lined, Pink Blossoms, Branch, Baluster Form, 12 1/2 In. 980.00
Vase, Orange Luster, Impressed Moorcroft Made In England, 6 1/4 In. 140.00
Vase, Orchid, Bulbous, Green & Cobalt Ground, Signed, Stamped, 6 x 4 In. 460.00
Vase, Orchid, Glossy Cobalt Ground, Paper Label, 3 3/4 x 2 1/2 In. 230.00
Vase, Pansy, Tube Lined, Flowers, Cobalt Ground, Oval, 6 1/2 In. 345.00
Vase, Peacock, Florian Ware, Green Paint, Handles, Signed, 5 In. 1840.00
Vase, Pelicans, Ribbed Cream Ground, Signed, c.1938, 7 3/4 In. 7050.00
Vase, Persian, Impressed Mark, 9 1/2 In. 5750.00
Vase, Pineapple, Fruit & Leaves, Cream Ground, 1987, 14 1/2 In. 1090.00
Vase, Polar Bear, Arctic Landscape, Cream Ground, Signed, c.1988, 6 1/2 In. 2686.00
Vase, Pomegranate, Burslem, England, Signed, c.1915, 9 In. 1400.00
Vase, Pomegranate, Dark Red Flower, Dark Brown Ground, 3 In. 168.00
Vase, Pomegranate, Impressed Mark, 4 In. . . . . .290.00 to 335.00
Vase, Pomegranate, Impressed Mark, 5 1/2 In. 310.00
Vase, Pomegranate, Impressed Mark, 6 In. 375.00
Vase, Pomegranate, Leaf & Fruit, Leaves Band, c.1914, 16 5/8 In. 6000.00
Vase, Pomegranate, Leaf & Fruit, Signed, c.1925, 9 1/4 In. 1510.00
Vase, Pomegranate, Painted Signature, 3 In. 310.00
Vase, Pomegranate, Paper Label, Signed, 4 In. 220.00
Vase, Pomegranate, Purple Grapes, Signed, 7 1/2 In. 1000.00
Vase, Pomegranate, Silver Trim, Impressed Mark, 5 1/2 In. 255.00
Vase, Poppy, Blue-Brown Ground, Signed, c.1925, 2 3/4 In. 1763.00
Vase, Poppy, Florian Ware, Green Paint, Marked, Macintyre, 9 1/2 In. 2300.00
Vase, Poppy, Florian Ware, Stamped, 6 In. 1495.00
Vase, Poppy, Impressed Mark, 6 In. 220.00
Vase, Poppy, Impressed Mark, 7 1/4 In. 575.00
Vase, Poppy, White, Stylized Leaves, Florian Ware, Macintyre, c.1900, 11 In. 2700.00
Vase, Reeds At Sunset, Impressed Mark, 11 In. 335.00
Vase, Rose Garland, Double Handle, Stamped Macintyre, 8 In. 853.00
Vase, Rose Garland, Stamped Macintyre, 6 In. 920.00
Vase, Sea Horse, Impressed Mark, 7 In. 978.00
Vase, Spanish, Large Flowers Band, c.1915, 3 1/4 In. 1080.00
Vase, Speckled Blue, Impressed Mark, 8 In. 345.00

Vase, Toadstool, Claremont, Red, Yellow, Purple Toadstools, Blueground, 14 In. 5160.00
Vase, Trumpet Rim, Rose Blossoms, Signed, 1830s, 10 1/4 In. 2185.00
Vase, Tulip, Florian Ware, Stamped Macintyre, 7 1/2 In. 1955.00
Vase, Tulip, Stylized, Forget-Me-Nots, Handles, Florian Ware, Macintyre, c.1900, 7 In. ... 3000.00
Vase, Wisteria, Impressed Mark, 7 1/4 In. 265.00
Vase, Wisteria, Painted Blossoms, Leaves, Cream & Blue Ground, c.1920, 5 3/4 In. 2126.00
Vase, Wisteria, Red, Yellow, Dark Brown, Signed, Wm. Moorcroft, 7 In. 785.00
Vase, Yellow Irises, Leaves, Florian Ware, Macintyre, c.1900, 12 1/4 In. 4200.00
Vase, Yellow, Blue, Florian Ware, 5 In. 805.00

MORIAGE is a special type of raised decoration used on some Japanese
pottery. Sometimes pieces of clay were shaped by hand and applied to
the item; sometimes the clay was squeezed from a tube in the way we
apply cake frosting. One type of moriage is called *Dragonware* and is
listed under that name.

Compote, Tropical Seascape Design, Palm Trees, Sailing Boats, Handle, 7 3/4 In. 230.00
Cup & Saucer, Blue & Gray 45.00
Cup & Saucer, Octagonal Shaped Cup, Floral, Hand Painted 75.00
Ewer, Teal Green, Light Blue Ground, Signed, 6 x 5 3/4 In. 140.00
Hatpin Holder, Applied Gold, 4 In. 150.00
Milk Container, Cover, Purple Flowers, Aquamarine Background, 6 In. 330.00
Mustache Cup & Saucer, Turquoise, Olive, Navy Raised Dots 205.00
Mustard, Cover, Swirl & Bead Design, Blue Maple Leaf, 5 In., 3 Piece 145.00
Pitcher, 3-Dimensional Leaves, Mushrooms, Small Birds, Handle, 7 3/8 In. 330.00
Pitcher, Lemonade, Pink Roses On Light Green, Nippon, Mark No. 7, 8 1/2 In. 200.00
Salt & Pepper, Dragon, Gold Embellished, Hand Painted, 2 1/2 In. 50.00
Server, Basket Of Blue Flowers, White Fruit, Green Leaves, 4 3/4 x 10 1/4 In. 25.00
Sleeping Cat, Blue, Brown, Orange, White, Gold, 5 x 6 In. 90.00
Tea Set, Charcoal Gray, White, Pink, Gold Details, Dragonware, Fuji China, 19 Pieces ... 225.00
Urn, Pink Rose In Center, Green Wreath Mark On Bottom, Handles At Neck, 8 In. 350.00
Vase, Elephant Handles, Hand Painted, Raised Flowers, 15 In. 500.00
Vase, Floral, 4 1/2 x 5 1/4 In. 360.00
Vase, Green Lines, White Dots, Green Leaf, Hand Painted Roses, Green Trim, 6 In. 72.00
Vase, Souvenir, Niagara Falls, Canada, Dragonware, Luster, 6 In. 25.00

MOSAIC TILE COMPANY of Zanesville, Ohio, was started by Karl Lan-
gerbeck and Herman Mueller in 1894. Many types of plain and ornamental tiles were made until 1959. The company closed in 1967. The
company also made some ashtrays, bookends, and related giftwares.
Most pieces are marked with the entwined *MTC* monogram.

Dolphin Shape, Crystalline Glaze, Mouth Opens Back Of Tile, 8 x 4 1/8 In. 825.00
Light Fixture, Ceiling, White Birds, Arts & Crafts, Square, 9 x 3 1/2 In. 385.00
Paperweight, Portrait Of Abraham Lincoln, Blue, Hexagonal, 3 In. 55.00
Paperweight, Woodrow Wilson, Running Mate Marshall, 1916, Pair 88.00
Tile, Dolphin's Mouth Opens To Back Of Tile, Marked, 8 1/4 x 4 1/8 In. 825.00
Tile, Little Bo Peep, Walter Crane, Marked, 6 In. 198.00
Tile, Lotus, Olive Green, Dry Line, Square, 4 1/4 In. ....*Illus* 180.00

Do not let leather-bound books touch
a wooden shelf. Put acid-free paper
over the shelf because the acid from
the wood will harm the leather.

Mosaic Tile Co., Tile,
Lotus, Olive Green, Dry
Line, Square, 4 1/4 In.

Tile, Portrait Of Simon Bolivar, Marked 45.00
Tile, Rabbit, Standing, Raised Line, Square, 6 In. 1650.00
Tile, Small Boy On His Side, With Pet Rabbit Sitting On His Back, 2 1/2 x 3 In. 155.00
Tile, Yellow Rooster, Walking, Brown Ground, Square, 3 x 3 In. 35.00

MOSER glass is made by Ludwig Moser und Sohne, a Bohemian (Czech) glasshouse founded in 1857. Art Nouveau-type glassware and iridescent glassware were made. The most famous Moser glass is decorated with heavy enameling in gold and bright colors. The firm, Moser Glassworks, is still working in Karlsbad, West Czech Republic. Few pieces of Moser glass are marked.

Biscuit Jar, Cranberry, Silver Plated Cover, Inscribed On Base, 7 In. 476.00
Bonbon, Pink, Blue, Enameled Red, Gold Trim, Blue & Green Jewels, 6 1/4 In. 470.00
Bowl, Cranberry, Enameled, Clear Feet, 3 1/2 In. 56.00
Bowl, Enameled, Leaf Shape, Scalloped Rim, 7 In. 90.00
Centerpiece, Sapphire Blue, Enameled, Jewels, Gilt Metal Base, Angel Handles, 12 In. . . . 1120.00
Cordial, Cranberry, Acid Etched, Silver Pedestal, 6 Piece 325.00
Creamer, Gold Insects, Pulled Hearts & Trailing Vines, 3 In. 345.00
Cup & Saucer, Cranberry, Enameled, Gold Trim, 2 In. 168.00
Cup & Saucer, Emerald Green, Gold Trim, 2 1/2 In. 140.00
Decanter, Cranberry, Gold Trim, Signed, 15 In. 210.00
Decanter, Gin, Floral Engraved, Gold Word Gin, c.1910, 13 In. 715.00
Decanter, Tumbler, Irises, Dark Amethyst Cut To Clear, Signed, 11 In. 728.00
Dish, Mayonnaise, Underplate, Cranberry, Enameled Gold Scrolling, 5 In. 365.00
Pitcher, Floral Engraved, 1910, 6 In. 660.00
Pitcher, Water, Amberina, Enameled Feather & Fern, Applied Reeded Handle, 1880 . . . . . 1950.00
Sauce, Emerald Green, Applied Handle, Foot, Gold Trim Overall, 7 1/2 In. 112.00
Sugar & Creamer, Amber Cut To Clear, Gold Trim 285.00
Sugar & Creamer, Cover, Engraved Branch & Floral, Signed 289.00
Tumbler, Blue Cut To Clear, Fluted Sides, Enameled, Applied Jewels, 3 1/2 In. 202.00
Tumbler, Cranberry, Enameled Ferns, Berries, Bugs, 3 1/2 In. 280.00
Vase, Alexandrite, Cut Stepped Base, Flared, Monogram Each Side, 11 5/8 x 13 3/8 In. . . 330.00
Vase, Amethyst Cut To Clear, Flowers, 4 In. 168.00
Vase, Amethyst Shaded Top, Enameled Florals, Acid Mark, 14 3/4 In. 450.00
Vase, Birds & Butterflies, Flowers, Green, Signed, 10 In. 825.00
Vase, Blue, Enameled Flowers, Purple, Gold, Signed, 18 1/2 In. 80.00
Vase, Clear, Ruby & Gold Medallion, Allover Intaglio Cut Flowers, Handle, 11 3/4 In. . . . 715.00
Vase, Cranberry, Allover Enameled Flowers, Rigaree Handles, 4-Footed, 8 In. 728.00
Vase, Cranberry, Applied Jewels, Footed, 6 In. 310.00
Vase, Cranberry, Enameled Design, Lamp Shape, 1880s 950.00
Vase, Cranberry, Enameled, Oak Leaves, Applied Blue Acorns, Pillow Shape, 7 In. 1795.00
Vase, Cut Panel, Zipper Cut Edges, Gold Enameling, 5 In. 90.00
Vase, Enameled Bird & Branch, Lavender, Dimpled, 8 In. 394.00
Vase, Enameled Orchids, Buds & Foliage, Yellow Flowers & Pods, 10 1/2 In., Pair 420.00
Vase, Floral, Fluted Pedestal, Signed, 18 In. 605.00
Vase, Gold Enameled Flowers, Amethyst, 6 1/8 In. 170.00
Vase, Hexagonal, Amazon Women, Acid Mark, c.1925, 6 1/4 In. 150.00
Vase, Lace Curtain Ground, Enameled Mum, 4 1/2 In. 65.00
Vase, Light Amber, Undulating Neck, Footed, Marked, 11 In. 189.00
Vase, Stylized Flowers, Light Blue Cut To Green, Metallic Inclusions, Amber Foot, 10 In. 1840.00
Vase, Yellow Enameled Mums, Gold Outlined Stalks, 11 1/2 In. 280.00
Wine, Light Emerald, Gold Enameled, 3 3/4 In., Pair 100.00

MOSS ROSE china was made by many firms from 1808 to 1900. It has a typical moss rose pictured as the design. The plant is not as popular now as it was in Victorian gardens, so the fuzz-covered bud is unfamiliar to most collectors. The dishes were usually decorated with pink and green flowers.

Bowl, Winifred, Handle, 2 1/4 x 5 1/4 x 7 In. 25.00
Cup & Saucer . . . . *Illus* 25.00
Cup & Saucer, Gold Castle 11.00
Jar, Condiment, Cover, Pale Pink Rose On Cover, Gold Trim, 4 x 3 x 5 In. 29.00

Never spray liquid glass cleaner directly on the glass in a picture frame. The dripping liquid may fall behind the glass and may stain the picture. Spray the cleaning cloth, then rub the glass with the damp cloth.

Moss Rose, Cup & Saucer

Lamp, Oil, Shade, Pink Sprays On Base, Scrolls Handles, Porcelain, 10 1/4 In.	100.00
Sugar & Creamer, Footed, Bone China, England, 3 3/4 x 2 1/2 x 4 1/4 In.	21.00
Trinket Box, Cover, 3 In.	13.00

MOTHER-OF-PEARL GLASS, or pearl satin glass, was first made in the 1850s in England and in Massachusetts. It was a special type of mold-blown satin glass with air bubbles in the glass, giving it a pearlized color. It has been reproduced. Mother-of-pearl shell objects are listed under Pearl.

Bowl, Diamond-Quilted, Light Moss Green, Scalloped Rim, 4 x 6 1/2 In.	575.00
Ewer, Diamond-Quilted, Peach To Pink, Satin, Thorn Handle	275.00
Rose Bowl, Satin Blue Lattice, 4 1/2 In.	90.00
Tumbler, Diamond-Quilted, Satin, Blue, Enameled White Flowers, 4 In.	145.00
Tumbler, Diamond-Quilted, Satin, Pink, White, Signed, 4 In.	230.00
Tumbler, Diamond-Quilted, White Coralene Bellflowers, Daisies, 3 3/4 In.	230.00
Tumbler, Pink, Lattice Pattern, Victorian, 3 3/4 In.	35.00
Vase, Blue Lattice, 5 In.	70.00
Vase, Bud, Herringbone, Satin, Pink, White Lining, 8 1/2 In.	90.00
Vase, Diamond-Quilted, Blue, White, Thorn Handles, 5 3/4 In.	90.00
Vase, Diamond-Quilted, Rose, White Lining, 8 In.	105.00
Vase, Diamond-Quilted, Satin, Enameled Pink Rose, 9 1/4 x 5 In.	170.00
Vase, Herringbone, Pink, Yellow, Blue, White Lining, 7 In.	805.00
Vase, Melon Ribbed, White Lining, Fluted Top, Blue Satin, 6 3/8 In.	150.00
Vase, Petit-Point Flowers & Butterfly, 8 In.	325.00
Vase, Pink Lattice, Ruffled Edge, 4 In.	224.00
Vase, Pink, Herringbone, Satin, Flattened Oval, Handles, 11 3/4 In.	425.00
Vase, Rainbow, Satin, 4 In.	70.00
Vase, Satin, Blue, 4 3/4 x 3 3/4 In., Pair	230.00
Vase, Satin, Blue, White, Orange Coralene, Wishbone Feet, 5 In.	460.00

MOTORCYCLES and motorcycle accessories of all types are being collected today. Examples can be found that date back to the early years of the twentieth century. Toy motorcycles are listed in the Toy category.

Cap, Harley-Davidson, Eight Panels, Black Cotton, Leather Bill, Wings Logo	113.00
Gas Tank Cap, Yamaha, Embossed Logo	17.50
Helmet, Everoak, Racemaster, England, 1960s	125.00
Helmet, Rebel Flag, Glitter, c.1966, Large	115.00
Helmet, Silver, Super Magnum, Bell, 1970, Size 7	36.00
Motorcycle, BSA 650, Lightning, Painted British Flags On Side, 1969	3500.00
Patch, Honda, White Wings, Late 1960s-Early 1970s, 12 In.	25.00
Pin, Harley-Davidson, Wings Logo, Brass, 1 1/4 In.	78.00
Pin, Indian, White, Indian Head, Celluloid, 7/8 In.	75.00 to 105.00
Saddle Bags, Leather, Silver Metal Concha Closures, Harley-Davidson	160.00
Seat, Indian, Chief, Studded & Fringed Edge, 1947	283.00
Seat, Sportster, Harley-Davidson	15.00
Sign, Ducati, Electric, 1950-1960, 4 x 6 Ft.	400.00

T-Shirt, Black, Moto Guzzi Eagle Logo, Competition Cycle, Dover, N.J. 26.00
Trophy, Speedway Inc., Short Track Fast Time, Gold Tone Metal, Wooden Base, 8 In. ... 14.00
Whistle, Policeman's 22.00
Wrench, Indian, Script Logo, 7 In. 65.00

MOUNT WASHINGTON, see Mt. Washington category.

MOVIE memorabilia of all types is collected. Animation cels, games, sheet music, toys, and some celebrity items are listed in their own section. Listed here are costumes and paper collectibles. A lobby card is 11 by 14 inches. A set of lobby cards includes seven scene cards and one title card. A one sheet, the standard movie poster, is 27 by 41 inches. A three sheet is 81 by 40 inches. A half sheet is 22 by 28 inches. A window card, made of cardboard, is 14 by 22 inches. An insert is 14 by 36 inches. A herald is a promotional item handed out to patrons. A press book was sent to newspapers and magazines to promote a picture. Press books and/or press kits (with photos) were sent to the media to promote a movie.

Button, Ribbon, Marilyn Monroe, Ask Me Who The Misfits Are 275.00
Button, Zorro, Tyrone Power, Pinback 50.00
Cigarette Case, John Wayne's, Silver, Engraved John, Documentation 650.00
Cup, King Kong, 1976 .... 1.50
Lobby Card, Across The Pacific, Humphrey Bogart, Mary Astor, Warner Bros., 1942 .... 340.00
Lobby Card, Angles With Dirty Faces, Cagney, O'Brien, Bogart, 1938 .... 1650.00
Lobby Card, Leona LaMar, Girl With 1000 Eyes 1320.00
Lobby Card, River Of No Return, Marilyn Monroe, Robert Mitchum, 1954 .... 290.00
Lobby Card Set, Rear Window, Alfred Hitchcock, 1954, 8 Piece 5100.00
Pencil Kit, Lost In Space, Box, 3 Pencils, 3 Erasers, Robot, Space Ships 16.00
Photograph, Deanna Durbin, Color, 1940s, 8 x 10 In. 10.00
Photograph, Midsummer Night's Dream, Max Reinhart & Cast, 1935 .... 1100.00
Photograph, Public Enemy, James Cagney, Signed, 1931 .... 2070.00
Poster, Angels With Dirty Faces, James Cagney, 1938, One Sheet 7475.00
Poster, Breakfast At Tiffany's, Audrey Hepburn, 1961, One Sheet 10800.00
Poster, Cabin In The Sky, Lena Horne, Al Hirschfeld, 1943, One Sheet 10200.00
Poster, Casablanca, Humphrey Bogart, Ingrid Bergman, Paul Henreid, Half Sheet 82.00
Poster, Flesh & Fury, Tony Curtis, Jan Sterling, 1952, Half Sheet 15.00
Poster, Goldfinger, Sean Connery, Honor Blackman, 1964, Half Sheet 3000.00
Poster, Gone With The Wind, Clark Gable, Vivien Leigh, Metro Goldwyn Mayer, 1939 .. 19150.00
Poster, Incredible Shrinking Man, 1957, One Sheet 550.00
Poster, Key Largo, Bogart, Robinson, Bacall, 1948, Three Sheet 3900.00
Poster, Lawrence Of Arabia, Road Show, 1962, One Sheet 14400.00
Poster, Night Of The Hunter, Robert Mitchum, Shelly Winters, 1955, Three Sheet 3300.00
Poster, Ocean's 11, Frank Sinatra, Dean Martin, Sammy Davis, 1960, Three Sheet 4500.00
Poster, Postman Always Rings Twice, Lana Turner, John Garfield, 1946, One Sheet 1300.00
Poster, Royal Scandal, Tallulah Bankhead, Charles Coburn, 1945, 17 1/2 x 13 1/2 In. 22.00
Poster, Some Like It Hot, Marilyn Monroe, Tony Curtis, Jack Lemon, 1959, Half Sheet .. 1150.00
Poster, Strange Cargo, Clark Gable, Joan Crawford, Linen, 1940, Three Sheet 2880.00
Poster, The Virginian, Gary Cooper, Walter Huston, 1929, One Sheet 1320.00
Program, Metropolis, UFA, England, 1927, 36 Pages 2040.00
Prop, Lunch Box, Incredible Shrinking Woman, Multicolor, Abstract, Plastic, 30 In. 605.00
Stage Background, Cloth, Painted, House, Clothed Animals, Landscape, 77 x 225 In. 58.00
Ticket Booth, 1920s 3200.00
Window Card, Gone With The Wind, Clark Gable, Vivien Leigh, 1939 .... 910.00

MT. JOYE is an enameled cameo glass made in the late nineteenth and twentieth centuries by Saint-Hilaire Touvier de Varraux and Co. of Pantin, France. This same company made De Vez glass. Pieces were usually decorated with enameling. Most pieces are not marked.

Pitcher, Iris, Silver Plated Spout & Handle, 9 In. 315.00
Vase, Cameo, Gold Flowers, Green Ground, Stamped Mark, 6 In. 299.00
Vase, Enameled Dragonflies, Cameo, Marked, 10 In., Pair 1725.00
Vase, Floral Design, Gold Enameled, Cameo, 15 1/2 In. 1725.00
Vase, Gold, Red Decorations, 16 In. 1400.00

Mt. Washington,
Vase, Mother-
Of-Pearl,
Satin, Stripes,
Ruffled Edge,
7 x 3 1/2 In.

Small lacquered pieces should be displayed in a cabinet near a small open dish of water to keep the humidity level at 55 percent.

Mt. Washington,
Vase, Verona, Gold
Enameled Flowers,
Vines, Gold
Cavalier, 16 1/4 In.

MT. WASHINGTON Glass Works started in 1837 in South Boston, Massachusetts. In 1870 the company moved to New Bedford, Massachusetts. Many types of art glass were made there until 1894, when the company merged with Pairpoint Manufacturing Co. Amberina, Burmese, Crown Milano, Cut Glass, Peachblow, and Royal Flemish are each listed in their own category.

Basket, Satin, Pink, Yellow Swirl Stripes, Twisted Rope Handle, 6 In.	230.00
Biscuit Jar, Enameled Lilacs, Vanbergh Silver Plated, Bail, Cover, 9 In.	450.00
Bowl, Band Of Flowers, Pink, Yellow, White, Ruffled Edge, 4 x 9 In.	748.00
Bowl, Chrysanthemums, Maroon Border, Cherub On Stand, 16 1/2 In.	4600.00
Box, Hinged Cover, Gold Gingko Leaves, Green, 6 1/2 In.	748.00
Cracker Jar, Cover, Enameled Flowers & Leaves, White, 9 1/2 x 5 1/2 In.	230.00
Cracker Jar, Cover, Oriental Poppies, Pink, White, Orange, 6 1/2 x 6 In.	575.00
Cracker Jar, Cover, Wild Roses, Square, 7 x 5 In.	2470.00
Cracker Jar, Enameled Flowers, Silver Plated Mouth, Late 19th Century, 8 In.	200.00
Cracker Jar, Pink Chrysanthemums, Leaves & Buds, 10 In.	632.00
Cracker Jar, White Flowers, Yellow, Green, 9 x 5 In.	400.00
Ewer, Farmyard Scene, Spring Colors, 10 1/2 x 8 1/2 In.	4600.00
Lamp, Oil, White & Pink, Cameo	2500.00
Mustard, Barrel Shape, Silver Plated Cover, Collar, Bail, 4 1/2 In.	375.00
Mustard, Cover, Deep Fuchsia Red, Amber, 4 1/4 In.	575.00
Mustard, Silver Plated Cover, Spike Finial, 3 1/4 In.	385.00
Salt Set, Cockleshell, Original Holder	3300.00
Toothpick, Enameled, Fig Shape	440.00
Toothpick, Melon Ribbed, Enameled Blue Flowers, Leaves, Dots At Top, 2 1/4 In.	165.00
Vase, Colonial Ware, Pink, White Poppies, Leaf Handle, Signed, 9 1/2 x 8 In.	920.00
Vase, Jack-In-The-Pulpit, White, Crimped Rim, 8 1/4 x 3 1/2 In., Pair	375.00
Vase, Mother-Of-Pearl, Satin, Stripes, Ruffled Edge, 7 x 3 1/2 In. ....*Illus*	805.00
Vase, Pink, Enameled Green Azaleas, Opalescent, 7 x 9 In.	115.00
Vase, Venetian Sailing Ship In Harbor, White, 10 1/2 x 8 In.	5750.00
Vase, Verona, Gold Enameled Flowers, Vines, Gold Cavalier, 16 1/4 In. ....*Illus*	2760.00

MUD FIGURES are small Chinese pottery figures made in the twentieth century. The figures usually represent workers, scholars, farmers, or merchants. Other pieces are trees, houses, and similar parts of the landscape. The figures have unglazed faces and hands but glazed clothing. They were originally made for fish tanks or planters. Mud figures were of little interest and brought low prices until the 1980s. When the prices rose, reproductions appeared.

Man, Angry, Mustard Yellow, Blue, 3 3/4 In.	25.00
Man, Blue Robe, Green, 3 5/8 In.	28.00
Man, Blue, 3 3/4 In.	30.00
Man, Green, 4 1/8 In.	35.00
Man, Holding Oil Lamp, 4 In.	35.00
Man, With Fish In One Hand, Yellow, Green, Blue, China, 3 3/4 In.	65.00

MULBERRY ware was made in the Staffordshire district of England from about 1850 to 1860. The dishes were decorated with a reddish brown transfer design, now called *mulberry*. Many of the patterns are similar to those used for flow blue and other Staffordshire transfer wares.

Compote, Summer Flowers Pattern, Gold Handles, Circa 1840, 12 In.	122.00
Plate, Transfer, Ironstone	65.00
Platter, Madras Pattern, Depicts Ruins, Brownfield & Sons, 1850-1870, 14 In.	105.00
Platter, Peru, 10 1/2 x 8 In.	80.00
Salt, Master, Madras Pattern, Brownfield & Sons, 1850-1870, 4 3/4 In.	30.00
Sugar, Domed Cover, Figural Finial, Flora Pattern, 8 Sides, Handles, Walker	215.00

MULLER FRERES, French for Muller Brothers, made cameo and other glass from about 1895 to 1933. Their factory was first located in Luneville, then in nearby Croismare, France. Pieces were usually marked with the company name.

Bowl, Gray, Interior Cobalt Blue, Green & Pink Mottling, Low, 7 3/4 In.	475.00
Bowl, Silver Foil, Pink To Purple, Cobalt Blue Foot, Signed, 7 3/4 x 2 1/2 In.	575.00
Ewer, Owl On Branch, Amber, Brown, Olive Green, Cameo, 1900, 10 5/8 In.	11500.00
Lamp, Domed Shade, Leaves & Berries, Satin Gray, Pale Amber, 1925, 15 In.	2300.00
Lamp, Hanging Shade, Landscape, Evergreen, Rocks, Water, Cameo, 16 In.	4313.00
Lamp, Trees By Water, Cameo, Hammered Iron Base, Signed, 15 1/2 In.	3910.00
Lamp Base, Mottled Iron Red & Brown Matte, Signed, 9 1/6 In.	207.00
Shade, Orange & Blue, Signed	370.00
Vase, Aqua Fish, Blue Bubble Band, Clear Irregular Rim, Cameo, 7 x 8 1/2 In.	4070.00
Vase, Green, Blue, Amber, Paperweight Finish, Signed, 13 1/2 In.	925.00
Vase, Mottled Blue, Red, Green, Satin, Signed Muller Luneville, 5 3/4 In.	392.00
Vase, Mottled Cobalt Blue, Columnar Ridges, Layered Teardrop Forms, 12 In.	336.00
Vase, Purple & Green, Blossoms & Vines, Disk Foot, Cameo, 10 In.	2130.00
Vase, Red, Yellow, Acid Cut Rose Blooms, Peach, Blue Foot, Signed, 8 In.	3248.00
Vase, Roses, Long Stems, Orange To Yellow, Flared, Cameo, 1925, 17 In.	8485.00
Vase, Stylized Blossoms, Silver Inclusions, Turquoise, Cameo, 1925, 11 In.	3450.00
Vase, Stylized Hunting Scene, Peach, Satin Ground, Signed, 9 1/2 In.	2070.00
Vase, Translucent Amethyst Interior, Raised Neck, Signed, 8 3/4 In.	860.00
Vase, Trees, Water, Purple, Blue, Salmon Ground, Cameo, 2 1/4 In.	1380.00

MUNCIE Clay Products Company was established by Charles Benham in Muncie, Indiana, in 1922. The company made pottery for the florist and giftshop trade. The company closed by 1939. Pieces are marked with the name *Muncie* or just with a system of numbers and letters, like *1A*.

Lamp, Light Blue, Dark Blue Overspray, 6 In.	145.00
Lamp, Peachskin Glaze, Marked, 4-D, 8 3/4 In.	165.00
Vase, Arts & Crafts, Gray-Yellow Glaze, Marked 2-D, 8 1/4 In.	145.00
Vase, Blue Over Green Glaze, Arts & Crafts, 7 In.	145.00
Vase, Gunmetal Glaze, Cylindrical, Marked IA, 5 1/2 In.	100.00
Vase, White Over Blue Glaze, Ruba Rombic, 4 1/8 In.	467.00
Vase, White Over Dark Rose, Mottled, Large Handles, Marked, 7 1/2 In.	245.00

MURANO, see Glass-Venetian category.

MUSIC boxes and musical instruments are listed here. Phonograph records, jukeboxes, phonographs, and sheet music are listed in other categories in this book.

Accordion, Busson, c.1850	2000.00
Banjo, Tenor, Gibson, Little Wonder, Four-String, Case, 1960	160.00
Banjo, Tenor, National, Triple Resonator, Chrome, Mahogany Neck, 1920s, 36 In.	590.00
Banjo, Tenor, Vega Co., 30-Bracket Rim, Maple Neck, Ebony Fingerboard, 11 1/2 In.	400.00
Banjo, Weymann & Sons, Maple Rim, Ebony Fingerboard, Pearl, Inlaid, 11 3/8 In.	170.00
Baton, Conductor's, Gold Filled Head, Flowers, Ebonized Shaft, Late 1800s, 16 In.	50.00
Bow, Viola, August Lenoble, Ivory Frog, Ivory & Silver Adjuster	2300.00
Bow, Viola, Eric Grandchamp, Ebony Frog, Parisian Eye, Silver & Ebony Adjuster	2990.00
Bow, Viola, K. Werner Uebel, Ebony Frog, Parisian Eye, Gold Mounted	1610.00

Music, Box,
Coin-Operated,
Mando Liszt, 1890

Music, Box,
Frati & Co.,
Berlin, 1890

Bow, Violin, Doff, Nickel Mounted, Nickel & Ebony Adjuster, Ebony Frog, Pearl Eye ... 290.00
Bow, Violin, Ebony Frog, Pearl Eye, Silver Adjuster 260.00
Bow, Violo Cello, Albert Schuster, Silver Mounted, Parisian Eye 1150.00
Bow, Violo Cello, Beare & Son, Octagonal Stick, Silver & Ebony Adjuster 1955.00
Box, Barbie, Piano, White Plastic, Gold, Bench, I Love You Truly, c.1964, 8 x 7 In. 120.00
Box, Coin-Operated, Einwurf Pfenn, Vertical Disc, Wooden Case, 42 x 14 1/2 In. 2750.00
Box, Coin-Operated, Mando Liszt, 1890 .... *Illus* 9037.00
Box, Cover, Swiss, Black Over Red Painted Design, 10 Tunes, 17 x 7 1/2 x 5 1/2 In. 385.00
Box, Criterion, Oak, Carved, Single Comb, 15 1/2 In. 2800.00
Box, Criterion, Oak, Single Comb, 14 Discs, c.1908, 21 1/4 In. 2185.00
Box, Cylinder, 12 Tunes, Swiss, 2 In. 2500.00
Box, Cylinder, Burled Wood, Fitted Case, Mother-Of-Pearl, 13 In. 3105.00
Box, Cylinder, Carved Case, Swiss, Late 19th Century, 11 1/4 In. 3300.00
Box, Cylinder, Inlaid Flowers, Musical Notes Decoration, Late 1800s, 15 x 9 x 6 In. 690.00
Box, Floral Marquetry On Side, 8 Tunes, 12 1/2-In. Cylinder, 10 1/2 In. 1610.00
Box, Frati & Co., Berlin, 1890 .... *Illus* 17509.00
Box, Imperial Symphonion, 6 Children Singing & Playing Music, 20 1/2 x 24 In. 2090.00
Box, Jacot & Son, Oak Case, 3 Cylinders, c.1890, 34 In. 5060.00
Box, Mermod Freres, Cylinder, Outside Crank, 1881, 8 Opera Tunes 2150.00
Box, Mermod Freres, Interchangeable, 15-In. Cylinder, 4 Tunes 8500.00
Box, Mira, 2 Combs, Table, 15 1/2-In. Disc 4900.00
Box, Nichole Freres, Inlay, Key Wind, 13-In. Cylinder, 8 Tunes 4750.00
Box, Nicole Freres, Lever Wind, 3 Levers, 13-In. Cylinder 4200.00
Box, Oak Case, 12 Tunes, Swiss, c.1890, 8 x 26 x 10 1/2 In. 2576.00
Box, Obo, Sweeping Up, Signed, Emmett Kelly, Jr., 1982 .... 1000.00
Box, Obo, Thinker, Signed, Emmett Kelly, Jr., 1982 .... 1000.00
Box, Obo, Why Me, Signed, Emmett Kelly, Jr., 1982 .... 450.00
Box, Olympia, Mahogany, Double Comb, Discs, 15-In. Discs, 12 Tunes 5040.00
Box, Orchestra, Bells, Drum, Musical Motifs On Cover, 8 Cylinders, 9 x 19 In. 2415.00
Box, Orpheus, Ludwig & Wild, Walnut Case, Square Disc Drive Holes, c.1899 .... 3750.00
Box, Paillard, Table, Interchangeable Cylinders, 6 Tunes 9800.00
Box, Paillard, Walnut Case, Oval Floral Medallion On Cover, 10 Tunes, 8 1/4 x 6 In. 2760.00
Box, Painted Musical Instruments, Foliage, 6 Songs, 5 x 4 In. 1150.00
Box, Pillard Twelve Tune, Walnut Case, 12 Tunes, 6 x 22 3/4 x 8 1/4 In. 440.00
Box, Polyphon, Disc, 6 Bells, 9 1/2 In. 2850.00
Box, Polyphon, Walnut Case, 12 Discs, 1870, 78 x 48 In. 6160.00
Box, Polyphon, Walnut, 15 1/2 In. 3100.00
Box, Regina, Coin-Operated, Mahogany, Double Comb, 20 15 1/2-In. Discs 4450.00
Box, Regina, Coin-Operated, Musical Automation, 27 Discs, Oak Case, 33 x 73 In. 12650.00
Box, Regina, Mahogany Case, Double Comb, 34 Discs, 13 x 22 In. 5175.00
Box, Regina, Mahogany, Carved, Leaf Molding, Double Comb, 16 Discs, 22 x 20 In. 4600.00
Box, Regina, Mahogany, Double Comb, Serpentine All Sides, 12 15-In. Discs, 34 In. 4950.00
Box, Regina, Model 37604, Shelf, Cabinet Door, Disc Storage, 34 x 34 In. 4125.00
Box, Regina, No. 39, Mahogany, Serpentine Case, Table, 20 3/4-In. Discs 8500.00
Box, Regina, Peripheral Drive Movement, Case, 11-In. Disc 5290.00
Box, Regina, Walnut Case, Line Inlay, 13 x 19 1/4 In. 4410.00

Box, Regina, Wooden Case, Claw Feet, Musical Mechanism, 12 1/4-In. Disk, 86 In. 2200.00
Box, Renaissance Revival, Walnut, Floral Inlay Design, 1875, 30 x 53 In. 5040.00
Box, Repeater, Marquetry Design, Crank Handle, 8 Tunes, Swiss, c.1900, 25 x 12 x 9 In. . 2615.00
Box, Rosewood Case, 6 Interchangeable Cylinders, Swiss, 4 1/2 In. 715.00
Box, Singing Bird, Cage, 11 In. 360.00
Box, Singing Bird, Cage, 20 In. 2090.00
Box, Singing Bird, Cage, Birds Move & Sing, Embossed Brass, France, 21 In. 1800.00
Box, Singing Bird, Cage, Brass, Mechanical, France, 11 In. 275.00
Box, Singing Bird, Cage, Windup Mechanism In Base, Germany, 12 In. 550.00
Box, Singing Bird, Enamel, Leaf Design Engraving, Swiss, 4 1/2 In. 1150.00
Box, Singing Bird, Gilt, Metal, Applied Floral Sprays, Continental 690.00
Box, Singing Bird, Sarcophagus Form, Engraved Vines & Scrolls, 1 Drawer, 4 In. 2310.00
Box, Singing Bird, Silver & Cobalt Blue Enamel Case, 4 x 2 1/2 In. 1265.00
Box, Stella, Mahogany, 1895, 17-In. Discs 6720.00
Box, Stella, Model 4907, Oak Leaf Branches & Acorns, Lower Drawer, 22 x 29 In. 1760.00
Box, Symphonion, Sublime Harmony, 2 Combs, Decals, 9 1/2-In. Disc 1500.00
Box, Symphoniun, Oak Case, 22 x 20 In. 935.00
Box, Troubadour, B. Grosz & Co., Disc, Walnut Case, 8 Bells 3500.00
Box, Walnut, Satinwood Inlays, 1870, 41 x 23 x 13 In. 1230.00
Box, With Table, Mahogany, Victorian, Scalloped Top, 3 Drawers, 29 x 28 x 24 In. ... 430.00
Calliope, 44 Keys, Brass Whistles, Powered By Gas Or Electric Motor, c.1960, 5 x 3 Ft. . 3500.00
Case, Violin, Renaissance Revival, Mahogany, Fitted Interior, 1875, 32 x 14 x 32 In. 1345.00
Clarinet, Dark Red Finish, Case, France 105.00
Clarinet, J. Grandjon, Nickel-Plated Keys, Boxwood, 27 In. 375.00
Drum, Parade, Snare, Brass Body, C.W. Lindsay, Canada, Painted Bands, 14 1/2 x 15 In. . 110.00
Drum, Snare, Military, Maple Body, Lacquered, Painted, Tacks, 1860s, 17 x 13 In. 489.00
Drum, Snare, Military, Maple Body, Unpainted, A.W. White Mfr., Boston, 1860s 805.00
Drum, Snare, Military, Maple Body, Unpainted, Increase Blake, Drum Mfr., Maine, 1860s 1035.00
Fife, Boxwood, 5 Brass Keys, Ivory Fittings, 11 3/4 In. 315.00
Fife, Revolutionary War, Tiger Maple, 6 Hole, Brass Ferrules, 17 In. 1100.00
Flugelhorn, Al Hirt's, Leblane, Case 1915.00
Flute, Bamboo, Pierced Carved Holes, 16 1/2 In. 60.00
Flute, Heinrich C. Eisenbrandt, Ivory & Silver, Silver Fittings, 23 3/4 In. 6325.00
Flute, Transverse, Blackwood, Nickel Keys & Fittings, 26 In. 200.00
Flute, Transverse, Boxwood, Ivory Fittings & Keys, 19th Century, 23 1/2 In. 520.00
Flute, Transverse, GX Astor & Co., 1 Brass Key, Ivory Fittings, 19th Century, 24 In. 575.00
Flute, Transverse, Wm. A. Pond, 1 Brass Key, Ivory Fittings, Boxwood, 23 1/2 In. 510.00
Gramophone, Pigmyphone, Tin Plate, Horn, Simulated Wooden Case 175.00
Guitar, Gibson, Boulle Style, 48 x 62 In. 4025.00
Guitar, Gibson, Pearl Inlaid Face Plate, Rosewood Finger Board, Pearl Inlay, 19 7/8 In. ... 1035.00
Guitar, Martin D-18, Spruce Top, Mahogany Body, 1955 .... 2508.00
Guitar, Martin, Flat Top, Acoustic, Mahogany Body, Original Tuning Pegs, Case, 1940 .. 1035.00
Guitar, Martin, Mahogany Body, Spruce Top, 1955 .... 2240.00
Harmonica, Hohner Tango II, Carrying Case, Early 20th Century 85.00
Harmonica, Hohner, Carmer, No. 85280, Patent 1931, Case 95.00
Harp, Grand, R. & L. Lewis, Gothic, Allover Gilt Design, Green, Animal Feet, 68 In. 1610.00
Harp, J.F. Brown & Co., Gothic Revival, Gilt, Green, Blue Ground, 68 1/2 In. 2300.00
Harp, Lyon & Healy, Blond Wood, Pedal, Gilded Greek Revival Design, Case 6000.00
Harp, Old Red Finish, Gesso Leaf Design, 55 In. 880.00
Harp, Sebastian Erard, Pedal, No. 3689, c.1875 .... 4600.00
Harp, Sebastian Erard, Regency, Giltwood, Brass, Cherub, Angels, Lyres, 67 x 17 x 35 In. 6325.00
Harp, Sebastian Roard, Giltwood, Brass Tuning Plate, 1810s, 67 In. 11240.00
Harp, Wurlitzer, Giltwood, Satinwood, Fluted Pillar, Leaf Capital, Brass, 73 x 39 In. 8910.00
Mandolin, Gibson, Maple Back & Sides, Spruce Top, Binding, 13 5/8 In. 690.00
Mandolin, J.T.C. Carlo Ricordo, Rosewood, Napoli, 1890, 26 In. 2650.00
Mandolin, Rex, Professional, Floral Inlay, Case 450.00
Melodeon, Divided Swell, Rosewood Veneer, Late 19th Century, 29 x 30 x 17 In. 370.00
Melodeon, Rosewood, Carhart Heedham & Co. 800.00
Nickelodeon, Griffin Legs, 1918 .... 5900.00
Nickelodeon, Lyon & Healy 8000.00
Nickelodeon, Nelson-Wiggin, Coin-Operated, Xylophone, Mahogany Case, 58 x 38 In. .. 3450.00
Oboe, Golde, Boxwood, Brass Keys, Ivory Fittings, 19th Century, 21 7/8 In. 4600.00
Oboe, H. Schuck, Maple, 2 Silver Keys, Square Covers, c.1900, 22 In. 575.00

Orchestrion, KT, Seeburg, Art Glass Panel, Eagle, Oak, Brass Trim, Restored, 45 x 62 In. 15250.00
Organ, Band, Military, Wooden, Painted, British Officer, Late 19th Century, 31 In. 5750.00
Organ, Barrel, 33 Keys, Double Celestine Reeds 2000.00
Organ, Hammond 3000, Double Keyboard, Electric, 1940 .... 1995.00
Organ, Roller, Chautauqua, Walnut Case, Glass Lift-Up Door, Wooden Cob, 25 Pins 750.00
Organ, Roller, Concert, Paper, Winding Mechanism, Oak Case, 12 1/2 x 17 x 15 In. 830.00
Organ, Roller, Gem, Winding Mechanism, Oak Case, 6 1/2-In. Cob, 17 1/2 In. 460.00
Organ, Seeburg, Mortuary, Converted To Orchestrion, O Rolls 8000.00
Organola, Hohner, Chromonica 65.00
Piano, Baby Grand, Hallet & Davis, Walnut, Stool, 38 1/2 x 55 1/2 In. 1035.00
Piano, Baby Grand, Hamilton, Hepplewhite, Mahogany 1725.00
Piano, Baby Grand, Knabe Bros., Walnut 4150.00
Piano, Baby Grand, Kranich & Bach, Bench 3190.00
Piano, Baby Grand, Reproducing, Weber, Mahogany, Duo-Art, 38 1/2 x 56 In. 4950.00
Piano, Baby Grand, Sohmer & Co., Needlepoint Bench 3025.00
Piano, Baldwin, Mahogany, Molded Panels, Carved Bell Flower Legs, 44 x 58 In. 1610.00
Piano, Federal, Hiskey, Mahogany, Lyre-Form Supports, c.1820, 37 x 72 In. 7200.00
Piano, Grand, A. Guillot, Tulipwood, Bronze, Gilt, Octagonal Legs, Paris, 6 Ft. 4 In. 21450.00
Piano, Grand, Chickering, Rosewood, Square, 1850-1860 .... 440.00
Piano, Grand, Collard & Collard, Burl Walnut, Victorian, Volutes, 37 x 53 x 78 In. 5060.00
Piano, Grand, Collard & Collard, Rosewood, Paneled Legs With Casters, 38 In. 4600.00
Piano, Grand, John Broadwood & Sons, Mahogany, Massive Turned Legs, 5 Ft. 2185.00
Piano, Grand, John Broadwood & Sons, Victorian, Rosewood, 39 x 78 x 61 In. 1840.00
Piano, Grand, John Broadwood, Model 218, Brass Casters, Gilt Gadrooning, 54 In. 4830.00
Piano, Grand, Reproducing, Chickering, Ampico A, 1921, 64 In. 1200.00
Piano, Grand, Stieff, Rosewood, Square 2900.00
Piano, Grand, Victorian, Burl Walnut, Gilt Acanthine Carving, 37 1/2 x 52 x 82 In. 3910.00
Piano, Knabe, Walnut, Louis XVI, Cabinet, Ampico A, 6 Ft. 4 In. 9500.00
Piano, Orchestrion, Seeburg, Coin-Operated, Style E, No. 56714, Art Glass Panel 2530.00
Piano, Player, Aeolian, Mahogany, Electric Or Foot Pump, 30 Rolls 3200.00
Piano, Player, Mahogany, John Broadwood, Hinged Cover, Center Music Stand, 74 In. 1092.00
Piano, Player, Waltham, New Keys, Ornate Pedals, 1921 .... 3995.00
Piano, Reproducing, Knabe, Mahogany, Ampico B, Ampicron, 54 In. 8500.00
Piano, Reproducing, Steinway Duo-Art, 88 Notes, Temponamic Style 1500.00
Piano, Upright, G. Challenger & Co., Burled Walnut, 52 x 26 In. 862.00
Pitch Pipe, Brass, 18th Century 350.00
Saxophone, Alto, Nickel Plated Body, Double Octave Key, Mouthpiece, Case, c.1920 ... 1495.00
Saxophone, Baritone, Buescher, USA On Bell, Music Stand, Case 920.00
Trumpet, H.N. White Co., Brass, Nickel Plate, Case, Cleveland, Ohio, 1920 .... 115.00
Ukulele, C.F. Martin, Mahogany Back & Sides, Rosewood Fingerboard, 9 3/8 In. 862.00
Viola, Mittenwald, Irregular Curl Back, c.1880, 15 1/2 In. 2070.00
Viola, Santinao LaVazsa, Poplar Back, Wide Grain, Golden Brown, 15 1/4 In. 2300.00
Violin, Andrea Bang, Gold, Brown, 1980, 14 1/8 In. 1898.00
Violin, Carlo Antonio Testore, 1-Piece Back, 1721, 14 In. 7950.00
Violin, Gottard Ebner, Original Scroll Neck, Brown, 1900, 14 In. 415.00
Violin, Jacdous Stainer, Medium Grain Top, Mahogany, 1705, 14 In. 690.00
Violin, Joannes Crucis Finnanzza, Medium Grain Top, Gold, Brown, 14 In. 5980.00
Violin, Johann Glass Leipzig, Spruce, Yellow, Brown, 1930, 14 1/8 In. 4600.00
Violin, Tiger Maple, Carved Whale Bone, Patriotic Symbols, Case, 23 1/4 x 30 1/4 In. 2070.00
Violoncello, Paul Lorange, Narrow Curl Back, Wide Grain Top, 29 11/16 In. 8625.00
Xylophone, Western Electric, Oak Cabinet, Glazed Door, Palladian Windows 13225.00
Zither, Mahogany, Nail Construction, Clover-Shaped Ends, 37 x 15 x 4 In. 55.00

MUSTACHE CUPS were popular from 1850 to 1900 when the large, flowing mustache was in style. A ledge of china or silver held the hair out of the liquid in the cup. This kept the mustache tidy and also kept the mustache wax from melting. Left-handed mustache cups are rare but are being reproduced.

2 Men Drinking Out Of Beer Steins, Stag Running, Handle, 4 1/2 In. 15.00
Applied Ornate Flower, Pink Luster, 1 Gold Flower, 1 Green Leaf, Saucer 35.00
Band Of Roses, Green, Gilt, Saucer, 1910 .... 115.00
Blue, Burgundy, Green Design, Gold Trim, Handle 45.00
Castle Scene, Pale Pink Roses, Ornate Gold Trim, Saucer 45.00

Cobalt, Gold Floral, Saucer, 3 x 4 1/4 In.	55.00
Colorful Ducks Flight, Gilt Trim, Saucer, 1952	60.00
Dark Blue, Pink, White, Gold Trim, Handle	75.00
Fireman's Ax, Helmet, Trumpet, Handle, Marked Royal Crown	20.00
Fireman's Trumpet, Signed, W. Becker, 1879	35.00
Floral, Bamboo Handle, Saucer, 1886	60.00
Floral Design, Pale Yellow, Gilt, Saucer, Germany, 1910	75.00
Floral Design With Dragonfly, 2 Leaves, Gold, Twig Handle, Saucer, 4 In.	85.00
Floral Spray, Handle	75.00
Flowers, Green, Brown Tone, Handle	36.00
Forget-Me-Not, Calla Lily, Gold	35.00
Forget-Me-Not, Floral, Beads, Gold Rim, Handle, Saucer, Germany, 1920	75.00
Forget-Me-Not, Gold Floral Design, Pale Green Luster, Saucer, 1910	45.00
Forget-Me-Not, Gold Trim, Handle	38.00
Forget-Me-Not, White, Gold Trim, Handle, Germany	45.00
Frolicking Lovers, Porcelain, 3 1/4 x 4 In.	36.00
Gilt, Rope Handle, Saucer, Germany, 1910	57.00
Gilt Daisies On Rim, Water Lilies, Saucer, Leuchtemburg, Germany, 1935	75.00
Green Luster, Marked, Present, Saucer, Germany	45.00
Multicolored Floral Branch, White, 3 1/4 x 4 In.	20.00
Orange, Maroon Flowers, Saucer, Gaudy Welsh, 1850	75.00
Orange, White Flowers, Leaves, Gold Trim, Handle	35.00
Orchids, Lavender, Rose, Green, Gold Trim, Handle	75.00
Pink Luster, Floral Sprigs, Beads, Saucer, Germany	65.00
Pink Luster, Marked, A Present, Saucer, Germany, 1910 . . . . .60.00 to 75.00
Pink Luster Flowers, Gold, Footed, Saucer, 3 x 4 1/4 In.	55.00
Purple Flowers, White, Design, Handle	35.00
Raised Fruit, Large Green Leaf, Saucer, Germany, 7/8 x 6 In.	85.00
Remember Me, Hand Painted Flowers, Saucer, Germany, 1890	80.00
Ring Handle, Saucer, Shelley Wileman, 1892, 4 1/2 x 3 1/2 In.	245.00
Skating Pond, Handle, 4 In.	12.00
Swirl, Green, Burgundy, Saucer, Saucer, Germany	68.00
White, Gilt, Ring Handle, Saucer, Germany, 1910	60.00
Young Gentleman, Gold Trim, Handle, 4 1/2 In.	10.00

NAILSEA glass was made in the Bristol district in England from 1788 to 1873. It was made by many different factories, not just the Nailsea Glass House. Many pieces were made with loopings of either white or colored glass as decoration.

Bell, Whimsy, Gray, White Loopings, Plaster Of Paris, 1870, 12 In.	190.00
Bellows, Whimsy, Clear, Cranberry & White Loopings, Handles, 1890, 13 3/4 In.	660.00
Bellows, Whimsy, Cranberry, White Loopings, Knopped Stem, 1840-1870, 8 3/4 In.	413.00
Flask, Clear & White Loopings, Pontil, 1870, 7 3/8 In.	95.00
Flask, Opaque White & Clear Loopings, 7 3/8 In.	192.00
Flask, Pocket, Black & White Loopings, Flattened Shape, c.1850, 4 3/4 In.	220.00
Flask, Red & White Loopings, Outward Rolled Lip, Pontil, 6 5/8 In.	355.00
Flask, Red, White & Blue Loopings, 7 3/4 In.	275.00
Nurser, Blue, Pink & White Loopings, Flattened Flask Shape, c.1870, 5 1/2 In.	110.00
Rolling Pin, White & Robin's-Egg Blue Loopings, 1860s, 16 In.	375.00
Vase, Green Loopings, Frosted Ruffled Base & Edge, Footed, 19th Century	285.00

NAKARA is a trade name for a white glassware made about 1900 by the C. F. Monroe Company of Meriden, Connecticut. It was decorated in pastel colors. The glass was very similar to another glass made by the company called *Wave Crest*. The company closed in 1916. Boxes for use on a dressing table are the most commonly found Nakara pieces. The mark is not found on every piece.

NAKARA

Box, Cover, Heart Shape, Gold Ginko Leaves, Green Ground, 3 x 6 1/2 In.	748.00
Box, Cover, Hinged, Single Large Pink Rose, Lavender, Pink Ground, 4 1/2 In.	633.00
Box, Enameled Design, Top Design, 6 In.	777.00
Box, Floral, Blue, C.F. Monroe, 4 1/2 x 2 1/2 In.	425.00
Box, Gray Daisies, Pink Ground, Footed, Satin Lining, 4 x 6 In. . . . .*Illus*	460.00
Box, Hinged Cover, Portrait Of Queen Louisa, Pink Floral, Marked, 7 In.	2100.00

Nakara, Box, Gray Daisies, Pink Ground,
Footed, Satin Lining, 4 x 6 In.

Never put a stringed instrument
near a window, a heat duct, or an
air conditioning outlet.
Temperature changes and sunlight
dry out the wood and can warp or
crack the instrument.

Worcestershire sauce is a good
brass polish.

Box, Hinged, Portrait, Medallion, Man & Woman, Peach, Pink Ground, Marked, 6 In.	1035.00
Box, Hinged, Portrait, Pastel Blue, Victorian Maid, White Ground, Marked, 2 x 4 In.	520.00
Box, Portrait Of 2 Cherubs, Pink & Yellow, Marked, 5 In.	920.00
Box, Portrait, Cupid Flying, Pink Flowers, Satin Lining, Marked, 4 x 3 In.	403.00
Box, Portrait, Pale Peach, 3 Kate Greenaway Figures Having Picnic, Sky Blue, 6 In.	980.00
Box, White, Gray Daisies, Bright Pink Ground, Marked, 4 x 6 In.	460.00
Dish, Trinket, Blue, White Daisies, 3 In.	200.00
Hair Receiver, Pink Floral, Brass Top, Marked, 5 1/2 In.	265.00
Humidor, American Indian Chief Wearing Full Headdress, Brown, 8 x 6 In.	1725.00
Humidor, Cigar, Pink Daisies, Bright Blue, Cream Ground, 7 x 6 In.	1610.00
Humidor, Tobacco, Pink, White Rose Design, Green, Pink Ground, 7 1/2 In.	1610.00
Jewelry Box, Hinged Cover, Portrait Of Woman, Marked, 4 In.	550.00
Jewelry Box, Hinged Cover, Sailboat Scenes, Marked, 6 In.	2520.00
Mayonnaise Set, Gold Gilt Holder, Pink, Blue Floral, Marked, 5 In.	210.00
Planter, Leaf, High Gloss, Marked, 6 1/2 In.	185.00
Vase, Portrait, Young Woman Riding On A Butterfly, Gold, Marked, 12 x 5 In.	2300.00

NANKING is a type of blue-and-white porcelain made in Canton, China, since the late eighteenth century. It is very similar to Canton, which is listed under its own name in this book. Both Nanking and Canton are part of a larger group now called *Chinese Export* porcelain. Nanking has a spear-and-post border and may have gold decoration.

Dish, Flower Center, Borders, Leaf Shape, Scalloped Rim, Flush Foot, 5 7/8 x 8 In.	345.00
Platter, Orange Peel, Oval, 14 1/2 x 12 In.	140.00
Platter, Peafowl, Flowers, Blue & White, 18th Century, 13 3/8 x 16 In.	575.00
Platter, Roast, Oval Inset, Gilt Monogram, 15 1/4 In.	2127.00
Salt, Blue Border, Bird & Tree Interior, c.1740, 3 1/8 In.	350.00
Salt, Blue, Trencher Form, 1720s, 2 3/4 x 3 1/2 In.	350.00
Soup, Dish, 10th Century, 9 1/2 In., Pair	200.00
Teapot, Drum Shape, Braided Strap Handle, c.1800, 6 In.	184.00
Teapot Stand, Blue & White, Riverscape, c.1770, 5 1/2 In.	403.00

NAPKIN RINGS were in fashion from 1869 to about 1900. They were made of silver, porcelain, wood, and other materials. They are still being made today. The most popular rings with collectors are the silver plated figural examples. Small, realistic figures were made to hold the ring. Good and poor reproductions of the more expensive rings are now being made and collectors must be very careful.

Angelfish, Blue, Bakelite, 1940	68.00
Art Nouveau, Band Of Flowers, Monogrammed, Gorham, 1 1/2 In., Pair	460.00
Bird, Orange, Black, Bakelite, 3 1/8 x 2 5/8 x 9/16 In.	52.00
Brass, India, 1 3/4 In.	2.00
Bunny, Orange, Bakelite, 2 3/4 x 2 5/16 In.	52.00
Egg, Gold, Crowned Cipher, Alexander II Photo, Porcelain, 2 1/2 x 2 1/4 In.	627.00
Elephant, Navy Blue, Bakelite, 1940	65.00
Elephant, Olive Green, Bakelite, 2 x 3 x 1/2 In.	52.00

Elephant, Orange, Yellow, Bakelite, 2 x 3 In.	30.00
Figural, Angel Atop Holder, Reins To Dog, Tufts, 3 1/2 In.	750.00
Figural, Angel Blows Horn, Flowers, Simpson, Hall, Miller & Co., 1880s, 4 x 3 In.	700.00
Figural, Angel On Heart Base, Best Wishes On Top, Rogers & Bro., 2 In.	500.00
Figural, Baby Hercules, Pushing Square Holder, Tufts, 3 1/4 In.	750.00
Figural, Baseball Player, Silver Plate	3200.00
Figural, Baseball Player, Silver Plate, Pairpoint, 1890s	3190.00
Figural, Bird, Bakelite, Red, 2 1/2 In.	80.00
Figural, Birds With Basket, Silver Plate, Pairpoint, 1880	95.00
Figural, Boy At Fence, Silver Plate	395.00
Figural, Boy Pulling Holder On Sled, Wilcox, 2 1/2 In.	850.00
Figural, Branch With Berries, Silver Plate, Flowers On Leaf Base	95.00
Figural, Bulldog, Silver Plate, 1 3/4 In.	420.00
Figural, Bunny, Silver Plate, Pairpoint, No. 69, 2 In.	470.00
Figural, Cat & Bird Heads, Silver Plate, Meriden, No. 361, 4 In.	425.00
Figural, Cherub Holding Bud Vase, Reed & Barton, 1880s, 5 x 3 In.	900.00
Figural, Cherub Rides Turtle, Carrying Sword, Middletown Plate Co., 2 1/4 x 3 In.	850.00
Figural, Cherubs On Either Side, 4 3/4 In.	100.00
Figural, Cherubs, Silver Plate	118.00
Figural, Crossed Rifles, Silver Plate, c.1880, 3 3/4 x 2 1/2 In.	750.00
Figural, Eagle, Silver Plate, Forbes, 1880, 4 In.	575.00
Figural, Eagle, Silver, 2 In.	125.00
Figural, Fireman's Hat, Silver Plate	3500.00
Figural, Giraffe Under Palm Tree, Silver Plate, Rockford Silver Co.	1800.00
Figural, Girl Standing At Fence, Silver Plate	395.00
Figural, Girl With Rifle, Kate Greenaway	800.00
Figural, Goat Pulling Holder On Wheels, Meriden Britannia, 1880s, 2 x 4 In.	700.00
Figural, Grape Leaf, Oak Leafs, Silver Plate, Meriden Silver	125.00
Figural, Horse, 1910	78.00
Figural, Horse, Pulling Holder On Wheels, Rogers, Smith & Co., 2 3/4 In.	695.00
Figural, Lady With Parasol, Pewter, 4 In.	64.00
Figural, Men Kneeling On Pedestals, 4 x 2 1/4 In.	207.00
Figural, Peacock Atop Ring, Rogers, 3 3/4 In.	600.00
Figural, Stag, Ring On Back, Meriden	800.00
Figural, Turtle, Pewter, 2 1/2 In.	28.00
Figural, Wheelbarrow, Silver Plate, Tufts, 2 1/2 x 3 1/3 In.	450.00
Figural, Woman, Well Dressed, Silver Plate, Derby Silver Co.	1300.00
Holder, Wood, 5 Piece	10.00
Rabbit, Yellow Bakelite	75.00
Renaissance, Cerulean Blue, Fitz & Floyd	18.00
Renaissance, Cinnabar	11.00
Rooster, Bakelite, 2 3/4 In.	75.00
Silver, 1 5/8 In.	85.00
Silver, 1 x 2 3/8 In.	59.00
Silver, 3/4 x 2 1/4 In.	35.00
Silver, Bakelite Liner, Center Medallion, England, 1 1/4 In.	95.00
Silver, Brown Bakelite Liner, Center Medallion, England, 1 1/4 In.	95.00
Silver, Central Medallion, 1939, 2 1/2 x 1 In.	30.00
Silver, Central Medallion, Hexagonal, England, 1957	30.00
Silver, Enameled Design, Red., White & Greens, Russia, 1 3/4 In.	140.00
Silver, Rectangular, Marked Susie Gymer, 3/4 In.	49.00

NASH glass was made in Corona, New York, from about 1928 to 1931. A. Douglas Nash bought the Corona glassworks from Louis C. Tiffany in 1928 and founded the A. Douglas Nash Corporation with support from his father, Arthur J. Nash. Arthur had worked at the Webb factory in England and for the Tiffany Glassworks in Corona.

NASH

Bowl, Drapery Iridescent, Signed, 2 x 8 In.	575.00
Bowl, Pink, Green Chintz, Signed, 3 1/2 x 11 1/2 In.	230.00
Bowl, Yellow & Orange Chintz, Flared, Signed, 2 1/2 x 7 3/4 In.	175.00
Vase, Blue Iridescent, Mold Blown, Signed, 4 3/4 In.	460.00
Vase, Flaring Shape, Ruffled Rim, Gold Iridescence, Signed, 6 In.	1610.00
Vase, Pulled Zipper, Textured Ground, Pink & Purple Highlights, Signed, 7 In.	825.00

Vase, Red Stripes, Clear Ground, Airtaps, Signed, 5 3/4 x 8 In. 200.00
Vase, Trumpet Shape, Silver Chintz On Red, Clear Knop, Signed, 12 In. 1495.00

NAUTICAL antiques are listed in this category. Any of the many objects that were made or used by the seafaring trade, including ship parts, models, and tools, are included. Other pieces may be found listed under Scrimshaw.

Anchor, Double Fluke, Cast Iron, 5 Ft. 10 In. 488.00
Anchor, Double Fluke, Iron, White Paint, 4 Ft. 6 In. 115.00
Artificial Horizon, For Shore Latitude, Mahogany Case, Mercury In Jar, 7 1/2 x 6 In. 600.00
Binnacle, Brass Hood, Wooden Stand, 20th Century, 51 x 40 In. 575.00
Binocular, U.S. Navy, Leather Case, 7 x 50 In., Pair 230.00
Boat, Model 162, Pond, Flying Cloud, 42 In. 695.00
Box, 3 Moving Handles To Set Course, 5 x 14 x 5 In. 200.00
Box, Document, Inlaid Woods, 6-Point Star Within Star, 12 3/4 x 8 x 5 1/4 In. 460.00
Box, Lift Inlaid Top, Joseph Tinkham, First Mate Out Of N.Y., 7 x 19 x 11 In. 431.00
Box, Mahogany, Star Inlay, Key, Dated 1861, 4 1/4 x 14 In. 144.00
Box, Shell, Lift Inlaid Top, First Mate Out Of N.Y., Mid 19th Century, 7 x 19 x 11 In. . . . 431.00
Bulletin Board, Ship's Case, Coronia, Mahogany Frame, 35 1/2 x 23 1/2 In. 69.00
Button, Battleship Maine Picture, 1 1/4 In. 20.00
Canoe, Canvas Covered, 1930s, 10 Ft. 2200.00
Canoe, Chestnut, Early 20th Century 394.00
Canoe, Green Body, Silver Lettering, Paddles, Kennebec Boat & Canoe, Me., 63 In. 7015.00
Chronometer, Bliss & Creighton 3300.00
Chronometer, Model 22, Mahogany Case, Brass Instrument, Pa., 7 1/2 In. 920.00
Clock, J.E. Caldwell, Ship's Wheel, Walnut Stand, 4 3/4 In. 506.00
Clock, Ship's Bell, 8-Day Movement, Strikes Watch Bells, Brass Case, Germany, 7 In. . . . 395.00
Clock, Ship's, Bell, Brass Rim, Black Plastic Case, 7 1/2 In. 143.00
Clock, Ship's, Brass, 7 x 5 1/4 In. 287.00
Clock, Ship's, Chelsea, Bell, Brass, Bronze, 14 In. 1150.00
Clock, Ship's, Chelsea, Brass, 5 1/4 In. 287.00
Clock, Ship's, Chelsea, Wheel, Walnut Stand, 4 3/4 In. 440.00
Clock, Ship's, George Walker, Boston, Mass., Brass, 10 x 12 1/2 In. 3105.00
Clock, Ship's, Riggs & Brothers, Philadelphia, Round, 5 1/2 In. 495.00
Clock, Ship's, Seth Thomas, Brass Bell, 10 x 6 In. 517.00
Clock, Ship's, Seth Thomas, Hanging, Strike, Brass 425.00
Clock, Ship's, Smith's Astral, Brass, 8 In. 287.00
Clock, Ship's, Waterbury, Brass, Porcelain Dial, Time & Strike, 8 x 6 1/2 In. 385.00
Clock & Barometer, Brass Cased, Quartz Clock, Beveled Glass Lenses, 11 x 20 In. 450.00
Compass, Ship's, E.S. Ritchie & Sons, Pembroke, Mass., Late 1800s, 5 x 4 In. 100.00
Diorama, Sailing Sloop, Full Sail, White, Flag, Ocean, Lighthouse, 28 x 30 x 7 In. 4888.00
Ditty Box, Chip Carved Lid, Round, New England, 19th Century, 9 1/2 In. 550.00
Document, Insurance Policy, Sloop Parrot, December 17, 1791, 17 1/2 x 12 1/2 In. 95.00
Fid, Rope Making Tool, Whalebone, 16 In. 920.00
Figurehead, Woman, Floral Head Wreath, Crown, Germany, 1800s, 26 1/2 x 11 In. 5175.00
Fog Horn, Ship's, Wooden Bellows, Brass Horn, 31 In. 345.00
Gauge, Brass, Sun Shipbuilding & Drydock Co., Chester, Pa., 10 In. 45.00
Gauge, Rosewood, Whale Ivory Heart Shape Mount, 23 In. 145.00
Half-Model, Deck, Defender, Mahogany Backboard, 8 x 28 In. 200.00
Half-Model, Enterprise, Full Deck, Mahogany Backboard, 8 x 28 In. 2300.00
Half-Model, Fishing Schooner, Nimbus, Thomas Conlon, Mass., 9 1/2 x 38 In. 661.00
Half-Model, Pilot Boat, Hesper, Thomas Conlon, Mass., 9 x 33 1/2 In. 600.00
Half-Model, Schooner, America, Thomas Conlon, Mass., 8 x 34 1/2 In. 546.00
Half-Model, Schooner, Bluenose, Thomas Conlon, Mass., 13 1/2 x 65 In. 1440.00
Half-Model, Schooner, Nimbus, Thomas Conlon, Mass., 9 1/2 x 38 In. 660.00
Half-Model, Ship, Carved Pine, Painted Black Stripe, 20th Century, 34 In. 300.00
Half-Model, Ship, Carved Pine, White, Blue, Sea Green Broad, 33 1/2 In. 690.00
Half-Model, Ship, Carved, Painted, White, Green, Mounted, 6 1/2 x 29 In. 2875.00
Half-Model, Sloop, Friendship, Thomas Conlon, Mass., 8 x 34 In. 375.00
Half-Model, Yacht, Schooner, Bluenose, Case, 21 x 9 x 18 In. 520.00
Helmet, Diving, Early 20th Century 5500.00
Hourglass, Pewter, 9 In. 290.00
Hourglass, Tartan Plaid Design, Turned Wood, 6 1/2 In. 345.00

Hourglass, Turned Wood, 3 1/2 In.	35.00
Hourglass, Turned Wood, 6 In.	375.00
Hourglass, Turned Wood, 8 In.	316.00
Lantern, Brass, Perkins Marine Lamp Corporation, Brooklyn, 17 1/2 In., Pair	635.00
Lantern, Copper, Electrified, 24 In.	245.00
Light, Ship's, Brass, 360-Degree Clear Lens, 10 In.	115.00
Light, Ship's, Brass, 360-Degree Lens, Marked, 19 In.	170.00
Light, Ship's, Brass, Copper, 360 Degree Clear Lens, 12 In.	185.00
Light, Ship's, Brass, Flashing Green, 10 In.	195.00
Light, Signal, Brass, England, 10 In.	17.00
Log Timing Glass, 5 In.	315.00
Log Timing Glass, Brass, France, 3 1/2 In.	145.00
Model, 2-Masted, Schooner, 9 Brass Cannon, 20th Century, 16 In.	520.00
Model, 3-Masted Schooner, Charles W. Morgan, Last Surviving Clipper, 29 x 35 x 12 In.	1456.00
Model, 3-Masted Schooner, Inside Olive Glass Ball, 20th Century, 5 In.	310.00
Model, 3-Masted, Aurora, Rigging, Black Painted, Gilt Trim, 15 1/4 x 23 In.	1265.00
Model, 3-Masted, Black Hull, Wooden Stand, Maine, 25 x 34 1/2 In.	635.00
Model, 3-Masted, Coastal Schooner, James Goodrich, 11 Stitched Sails, 34 In.	1150.00
Model, 3-Masted, Prisoner-Of-War Ship, Brass Cannons, Cased, 16 x 7 x 16 In.	8050.00
Model, 3-Masted, Sailing Ship, Rigging, Display Case, 19th Century, 28 x 38 In.	2640.00
Model, 3-Masted, The Josephine May, Carved, Painted, Display Case, 12 x 22 In.	1900.00
Model, 4-Masted, Athena Of N.Y., Bark, 26 In.	430.00
Model, America's Cup Yacht, Rainbow, White, Gold, Planked Deck, 70 x 48 x 7 In.	2070.00
Model, American Ship, In Ship's Wheel Frame, 13 In.	862.00
Model, Armed Brig, Hannah Of Boston, 38 x 16 1/2 In.	1610.00
Model, Bark, Bone, Glass Dome, 19th Century, 6 In.	750.00
Model, Brigantine, Newsboy, Solid Hull, Capt. Elisha Brown, Maine, 31 In.	575.00
Model, Britain Royal Yacht, Britannia, Mahogany Backboard, 8 x 28 In.	170.00
Model, Clipper Ship, Cutty Sark, Plank On Frame Hull, England, 31 In.	1150.00
Model, Clipper Ship, Sea Witch, Mahogany Case, 32 x 13 x 19 In.	460.00
Model, Clipper Ship, Wizard, Mahogany Case, 32 x 13 x 29 In.	520.00
Model, Frigate Espanola, Wood & Canvas, 24 x 33 In.	90.00
Model, Full-Rigged, Clipper Ship, Cutty Sark, Plank Frame, 31 x 48 In.	1150.00
Model, Full-Rigged, Fishing Schooner, Bluenose, Planked Basswood Deck, 31 In.	2185.00
Model, Half-Moon, With Sails, Henry Hudson, Case, 34 x 36 x 40 x 41 In.	1265.00
Model, Ocean Tugboat, Forever Yesterday, British, Steam Engine, 1930	4000.00
Model, Pilot Boat, Liberty, N.Y., Harbor, Mahogany Case, 29 x 12 x 22 1/2 In.	575.00
Model, Pilot Boat, Swift, Wood, 21 In.	144.00
Model, Runabout, Early 20th Century, 9 In.	345.00
Model, Runabout, Lake Winnepesaukee, Radio Control, Motor, 60 In., c.1945	4800.00
Model, Schooner, Bluenose, Cased, 21 x 9 x 18 In.	520.00
Model, Schooner, Smuggler, Glass Case, 20th Century, 30 1/2 x 36 1/2 In.	1380.00
Model, Ship, American Brig, Topaz, 6 Cannon Deck, Brass Cover, 17 x 20 x 7 In.	520.00
Model, Ship, Brig, Hannah Of Boston, 35 x 38 x 16 1/2 In.	1610.00
Model, Ship, Fishing Schooner, Bluenose, Planked Basswood Deck, Dories, 31 In.	2185.00
Model, Ship, Full-Rigged, Solid Hull, 19th Century, 26 In.	430.00
Model, Single Mast, Concordia Yawl, Mahogany, Plexiglas Case, 28 x 20 In.	1120.00
Model, Spanish Galleon, Painted, Crosses On Canvas Sails, 41 x 36 In.	245.00
Model, Submarine, USS Squalus, Steel, 1939, 7 In.	115.00

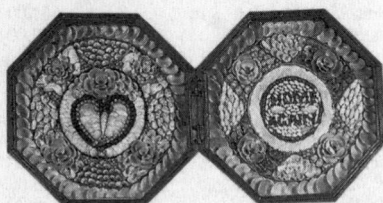

Nautical, Sailor's Valentine, Shellwork Hearts,
Flowers, Hinged Wood, 8 1/2 In.

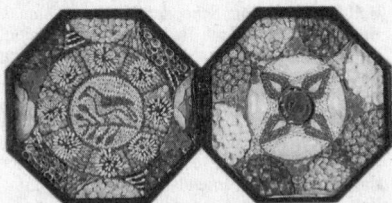

Nautical, Sailor's Valentine, Shellwork,
Floral & Bird, Hinged Wood, 10 1/2 In.

Model, U.S. Cup Defender, Columbia, Planked Deck, 30 x 24 1/2 x 6 1/2 In. 1610.00
Model, USS Constitution, Inlaid Wooden Base, Glass Case, Brass, 34 x 36 x 17 In. 2300.00
Model, Yacht, Malabar X, Full Suite Of Sails, Sonny Hodgdon, Maine, 38 x 36 In. 2070.00
Octant, J. Ford, London, Ivory, Brass, Mahogany Case 545.00
Pond Yacht, Moss Rose, Red, Black, Hull, Yellow Name, Brass, Linen, 37 x 38 x 21 In. ... 3105.00
Porthole, Brass, 14 In., Pair 575.00
Print, Spanish War, U.S. Navy, Flotilla, Sepia, 1898, 4 x 3 In. 375.00
Quadrant, Frye & Shaw, Brass, Ebony, Ivory Scales, Marked, N.Y., 19th Century 776.00
Quadrant, H. Duran, G.W. Blunt, Brass, Ebony, Marked, Ivory Scales, N.Y., 19th Century 980.00
Sailor's Valentine, Shellwork Hearts, Flowers, Hinged Wood, 8 1/2 In. ....*Illus* 3565.00
Sailor's Valentine, Shellwork, Floral & Bird, Hinged Wood, 10 1/2 In. ....*Illus* 8915.00
Sea Chest, Dovetailed, Dark Stain Finish, Lid, 15 1/2 x 43 1/2 x 19 In. 58.00
Sextant, No. 27, Cased, Metal Cover, London, 19th Century, 3 1/4 In. 400.00
Sextant, Spencer Browning & Co., Brass, Mahogany Case 805.00
Ship In Bottle, Normandie, Turk's Head Over Cork, Stand, 1944, 6 1/2 x 20 x 5 1/2 In. .. 390.00
Ship Model, see Nautical, Model.
Spool Holder, Pine, Ivory, Grain Painted, 1 Drawer, 2 Tiers, Mid 19th Century 1975.00
Sternboard, Mary Elizabeth, New London, 19th Century, 9 Ft. 5 In. x 5 1/2 In. 1265.00
Sternboard, William West, Gilt, Black Ground, Essex Mass., 1869, 8 Ft. 7 In. x 15 In. 1725.00
Sundial, Brass, Pilkington & Gibbs, Inscribed To Commander Peary USN, 1910, 9 In. 6750.00
Telegraph, Ship's, Tornborg Lundbergh, Brass, Iron, 18 In. 430.00
Telephone, Ship's, Brass, Marked, Navy Dept. Bureau Of Ships 69.00
Telephone, Ship's, Marked, Cook Room 69.00
Telescope, Carved Agate, Gold Cage Work, Diagonal Mirror, Right Angles, 1760, 2 In. .. 7800.00
Thermometer, Deep Sea, Negretti & Zambra, Metal, 3 Blades, England, 14 3/4 In. 760.00
Wheel, Ship's, Iron, Brass Hub, 66 1/2 In. 1610.00
Wheel House Ship's Bell Clock & Weather Barometer, 7 x 3 3/4 In. 675.00
Whistle, Ship's, Brass, Chain 42.00

NETSUKES are small ivory, wood, metal, or porcelain pieces used as
toggles on the end of the cord that held a Japanese money pouch. The
earliest date from the sixteenth century. Many are miniature, carved
works of art. This category also includes the ojime, the slide or string
fastener that was used on the inro cord.

Bone, Coiled Dragon, Cloud Form, 19th Century 196.00
Bone, Sennin Carrying Double Gourd Bottle On Tree Branch, 19th Century 240.00
Coral, Horse, Resting, 20th Century 375.00
Gold & Silver, Cicada & Ant, Decaying Tree Stump, Early 20th Century 8675.00
Horn, Horse, Grazing 130.00
Inro, Poetess Murasaki Shibiki, Lacquer, Gold, 5 Case 4600.00
Inro, Rooster, Wooden Frog, Ivory 55.00
Ivory, 2 Frogs On Pad 200.00
Ivory, 2 Goats, Signed, 20th Century 185.00
Ivory, 2 Melons & Frog, Signed 1500.00
Ivory, 2 Men Wrestling At Tug Of War, 19th Century 250.00
Ivory, 2 Mice On Vegetable 175.00
Ivory, 2 Monkeys With Melon, Signed, 1 1/2 In. 800.00
Ivory, 3 Figures In Tea Cup, Signed, Minko, 19th Century 115.00
Ivory, 3 Monkeys On Leaf, Shuzan 860.00
Ivory, Baby Toads, Mother 170.00
Ivory, Barking Foo Dog 315.00
Ivory, Benten Holding Biwa In Her Hand, Signed 230.00
Ivory, Bird Under Flowering Branches, 1 1/2 In. 490.00
Ivory, Bishamon Seated With Temple In His Left Hand, Signed, Tamayuki 69.00
Ivory, Boy Sleeping On Reclining Buffalo, 18th Century 630.00
Ivory, Carved Kimono & Fan, Rotating Faces, Character Marks On Base, 2 1/2 In. 275.00
Ivory, Carved, Turtles, Lily Pad 126.00
Ivory, Cicada On Roof Tile, Signed 115.00
Ivory, Coiled Serpent, Signed, 1 1/4 x 2 x 1 1/2 In. 450.00
Ivory, Courtier Discovering Demon Hiding As Servant, 18th Century 1725.00
Ivory, Daikoku Carrying His Treasure Sack On His Back, Signed, 20th Century 265.00
Ivory, Daruma Waking From His Meditations, Signed, Tomokazu, 20th Century 520.00
Ivory, Demon Mask, Signed, 20th Century 230.00

Ivory, European With Trumpet & Small Child, Inlaid Eyes, 19th Century 690.00
Ivory, Farmer With Hoe Carrying A Large Mushroom On His Back 115.00
Ivory, Farmer, Holding Rabbit, Axe, Signed, 1 1/2 In. 290.00
Ivory, Figure, Kimono & Fan, Rotating Face, Character Marks, 2 1/2 In. 275.00
Ivory, Fisherman Holding Net And Weights, Flowering Branch Coming Out Of Net 800.00
Ivory, Fisherman With Basket Of Clams, 19th Century 170.00
Ivory, Fujin Standing On Cloud With His Bag Of Thunder On His Back 195.00
Ivory, Fukurokuju Holding Double Gourd Bottle On His Back, 20th Century 230.00
Ivory, Fukurokuju Seated With Crane On His Lap, 19th Century 230.00
Ivory, Fukurokuju, Large Peach, Movable Head, Signed, Tomokazu, 19th Century 200.00
Ivory, Gama Sennin, Deep Amber, 19th Century 170.00
Ivory, Grapes & Vine On Bamboo Support, 1 1/2 x 1 5/8 x 1/2 In. 336.00
Ivory, Hare, Seated With His Ears Pulled Back, 19th Century, 1 1/2 In. 750.00
Ivory, Hippopotamus 22.00
Ivory, Horse, Standing With His Head Turned, 2 In. 184.00
Ivory, Hotei With His Bag Of Wealth, 19th Century 400.00
Ivory, Hotei, Grinning, Standing With His Treasure Sack On His Back 259.00
Ivory, Humpback Horse 90.00
Ivory, Jurojin Seated Holding Tortoise & Bottle Of Sake, 20th Century 65.00
Ivory, Karako Attempting To Bridle & Ride Large Tortoise, Late 19th Century 805.00
Ivory, Karako Holding Daruma Doll, Signed, Ikko, 20th Century 127.00
Ivory, Karako Seated By Incense Burner, 20th Century 115.00
Ivory, Lion Dancer Holding Scroll, Revolving Head, Signed, 20th Century 60.00
Ivory, Loosely Carved Chick In Egg, Signed, Mitsuhiro, 20th Century 180.00
Ivory, Maggot Eating Squash 218.00
Ivory, Man & Woman Scene 120.00
Ivory, Man Holding Rock Above His Head, Signed, 2 1/2 In. 258.00
Ivory, Man Resting, Eating Piece Of Fruit, Signed, Shunko 290.00
Ivory, Man With Scroll In His Hands, Signed 185.00
Ivory, Man, Standing With His Head Turned Over His Right Shoulder, 3 In. 630.00
Ivory, Marine, Kapa Carving Large Cucumber, 19th Century 290.00
Ivory, Marine, Man & Frog, 1 1/2 In. 258.00
Ivory, Mask, Depicting Okame, 1900 .... 158.00
Ivory, Mask, Shuichi Depicting Face Of Angry Man, Early 20th Century 90.00
Ivory, Monkey Group, 1 1/4 In. 230.00
Ivory, Monkey With Fish, Signed, 1 x 1 3/4 x 1 1/4 In. 336.00
Ivory, Monkey, Holding Gourd, 18th Century 517.00
Ivory, Mouse Grooming, Signed, 1 x 1 5/8 x 1 3/8 In. 450.00
Ivory, Noh Actor With Biwa, Revolving Head, Signed, 20th Century 60.00
Ivory, Ojime, Flying Crane, Mixed Metal, Japan, Meiji Period, 1 3/4 In. 80.00
Ivory, Owl 200.00
Ivory, Performer, Holding Parasol, Polychrome Stain, Signed, 2 In. 230.00
Ivory, Persimmon Form, Misuhiro, 19th Century 375.00
Ivory, Rat Chewing Tail 22.00
Ivory, Sage Holding Scroll Painting, Signed, Gyokusen, 1900 .... 185.00
Ivory, Sarumawashi Entertainer Form, With His Monkey & Attendant 115.00
Ivory, Sennin & Dragon, 19th Century 4600.00
Ivory, Sennin, Holding Jewel, 3 Himetoshi, 18th Century 1380.00
Ivory, Sennin, In Mugwort Cape, Signed, 18th Century 860.00
Ivory, Sennin, Scratching His Back, 19th Century 460.00
Ivory, Sennin, With Double Gourd, Inlaid Eyes 400.00
Ivory, Sennin, With Staff, 19th Century 546.00
Ivory, Shoki With Demon, 19th Century 1090.00
Ivory, Skull, Snake Coming From Eye Socket, Signed 175.00
Ivory, Swan 260.00
Ivory, Tiger Playing With Its Cub, Inlaid Eyes, 20th Century 430.00
Ivory, Traveler With Paper Lantern, Signed, 20th Century 115.00
Ivory, Walrus, Man & Dragon Perched On Rocks, Signed, 1 1/2 In. 290.00
Ivory, Woman With Movable Head Holding Lotus Blossom, 1900 .... 130.00
Lacquer, Dancer, 1 1/2 In. 260.00
Ojime, Golden Metal, Shoki, Holding Sword 5275.00
Ojime, Mixed Metal, Shojo, Emerging From Snake Pot, 3/4 In. 7245.00

Peach Pit, Hawk Flying Over A Castle, Signed, Tomokazu, 19th Century 375.00
Porcelain, Bearded Sage Seated On Brown Rock, 19th Century 345.00
Silver, 2 Warriors, On Horseback, Other Lying On Ground, Signed 230.00
Staghorn, Crab Lying Among Pile Of Sea Shells, Late 19th Century 210.00
Staghorn, Octopus & Fish, 3 1/2 In. 230.00
Turquoise, Frog On Bamboo Shoot 140.00
Wood, Bearded Warrior Holding Halberd, Inlaid Eyes, 1820 . . . . 290.00
Wood, Carved, 2 Samurai, 1 1/2 In. 260.00
Wood, Chestnut Form, Carved Ivory Worm Sliding In & Out Of Hole 150.00
Wood, Child Playing With Ball, Signed, 19th Century 200.00
Wood, Lion Dancer Wearing Fierce Mask, Signed, Komin 1610.00
Wood, Man, Massaging Back Of Outraged Shoki 5250.00
Wood, Man, Seated Holding Daruma Doll, 20th Century 60.00
Wood, Manzai Dancer With Mokugyo Bell, 19th Century 255.00
Wood, Peasant Dancing, Signed, Tomochika, Large 1265.00
Wood, Puppy Playing With Sandal, 19th Century 90.00
Wood, Sennin, With Staff, 19th Century 860.00
Wood, Shishi Head 400.00
Wood, Shishi Holding Temple Bell In Front Paws, 19th Century 250.00
Wood, Shusai In Chestnut Form, Signed, 20th Century 115.00
Wood, Wolf & Skull, 1 1/2 In. 258.00

NEW HALL Porcelain Manufactory was started at Newhall, Shelton,
Staffordshire, England, in 1782. Simple decorated wares were made.
Between 1810 and 1825, the factory made a glassy bone porcelain
sometimes marked with the factory name. Do not confuse New Hall   *New Hall*
porcelain with the pieces made by the New Hall Pottery Company,
Ltd., a twentieth-century firm.

Cup & Saucer, Wispy Gold Leaves, Cobalt Blue Border, Swirled, Ribbed, 1795 . . . . 103.00
Dish, Dessert, Basket Weave, Pink Roses In Cartouches, Open Handles 170.00
Teapot, Cover, Deep Pink Flower & Green Leaves, Blue & Deep Pink Bands 133.00
Tureen, Sauce, Cover, Allover Flowers, Cobalt Blue Ground, 7 1/4 In., Pair 575.00

NEW MARTINSVILLE Glass Manufacturing Company was established
in 1901 in New Martinsville, West Virginia. It was bought and
renamed the Viking Glass Company in 1944. In 1987 Kenneth Dalzell,
former president of Fostoria Glass Company, purchased the factory
and renamed it Dalzell-Viking. Production ceased in 1998.

Figurine, Greyhound, Black 450.00
Figurine, Mama Pig, Attached Suckling Pigs 1500.00
Janice, Basket, Light Blue, 11 In. 295.00
Janice, Bowl, Swan, 11 In. 75.00
Janice, Cake Plate, 40th Anniversary, 2 Handles, Ruby, Silver Overlay 45.00
Janice, Cup & Saucer, Light Blue 22.00
Janice, Cup & Saucer, Ruby 30.00
Janice, Platter, Light Blue, 11 In. 50.00
Janice, Sherbet, Light Blue 18.00
Janice, Swan, 6 1/2 In. 10.00
Janice, Tumbler, Footed, Ruby, 10 Oz. 35.00
Janice, Tumbler, Light Blue, Footed, 10 Oz. 20.00
Janice, Tumbler, Water, Light Blue, Footed, 10 Oz. 35.00
Janice, Vase, Ivy, Light Blue, 3 1/2 In. 25.00
Meadow Wreath, Cake Stand, Light Blue 125.00
Moondrops, Ashtray, Ruby 29.00
Moondrops, Bowl, Footed, Ruby, 8 1/4 In. 45.00
Moondrops, Bowl, Ruffled, Footed, Ruby, 9 1/2 In. 85.00
Moondrops, Butter, Cover, Amber 275.00
Moondrops, Butter, Cover, Ruby . . . . .475.00 to 550.00
Moondrops, Cordial, Cobalt Blue, 2 7/8 In. 50.00
Moondrops, Creamer, Individual 18.00
Moondrops, Creamer, Ruby 15.00
Moondrops, Cup & Saucer, Cobalt Blue 29.00

Moondrops, Cup & Saucer, Ruby 24.00
Moondrops, Cup, Amber 10.00
Moondrops, Decanter, Ruby, 9 In. 80.00
Moondrops, Goblet, Water, Metal Stem, Ruby, 6 1/4 In. 35.00
Moondrops, Goblet, Wine, Metal Stem, 3 Oz., 5 1/2 In. 15.00
Moondrops, Goblet, Wine, Ruby, 4 Oz., 4 In. 25.00
Moondrops, Plate, Canape, Ruby, 6 In. 20.00
Moondrops, Sherbet, Amber, 2 5/8 In. 11.00
Moondrops, Sugar & Creamer, Amber, 3 1/2 In. 20.00
Moondrops, Sugar & Creamer, Footed, Ruby, 2 3/4 In. 45.00
Moondrops, Sugar & Creamer, Ruby, 2 3/4 In. 33.00
Moondrops, Sugar, Ruby, 2 3/4 In. ....14.00 to 15.00
Moondrops, Tumbler, Juice, Footed, Cobalt Blue, 3 Oz., 3 1/4 In. ....20.00 to 22.00
Moondrops, Tumbler, Ruby, 5 Oz., 3 5/8 In. 16.00
Moondrops, Tumbler, Ruby, 9 Oz., 4 7/8 In. 20.00
Moondrops, Tumbler, Whiskey, Handle, Cobalt Blue, 2 Oz., 2 3/4 In. 20.00
Moondrops, Tumbler, Whiskey, Handle, Ruby, 2 Oz., 2 3/4 In. ....18.00 to 22.00
Moondrops, Wine, Ruby, 4 Oz., 4 In. 22.00
Prelude, Relish, 5 Sections, 13 In. 44.00
Queen Anne, Powder Jar, Amethyst 15.00
Radiance, Basket, Ruby, Metal Handle, 8 In. 85.00
Radiance, Cordial, Ruby, Silver Trim 38.00
Radiance, Creamer, Ruby 33.00
Radiance, Cup & Saucer, Ruby 24.00
Radiance, Dish, Mayonnaise, Underplate 32.00
Radiance, Muffin Plate, Silver Overlay, 7 In. 32.00
Radiance, Punch Cup, Amber 5.00
Radiance, Punch Ladle, Amber 85.00
Radiance, Relish, 3 Sections, Ice Blue, 8 In. 50.00
Radiance, Relish, Silver Overlay, 11 In. 32.00
Radiance, Tumbler, Amber, 9 Oz. 15.00
Radiance, Tumbler, Ruby, 10 Oz. 40.00

NEWCOMB Pottery was founded by Ellsworth and William Woodward at Sophie Newcomb College, New Orleans, Louisiana, in 1895. The work continued through the 1940s. Pieces of this art pottery are marked with the printed letters *NC* and often have the incised initials of the artist as well. Most pieces have a matte glaze and incised decoration.

Bowl, Band Of Pink Buds, Sadie Irvine, 1927, 2 1/2 x 4 1/2 In. 1240.00
Bowl, Carved Band Of Flowers, M.W. Summey, 7 1/2 In. 3220.00
Bowl, Flowers & Leaves, Carved, Henrietta Bailey, 6 In. 1380.00
Charger, 3 Crabs, Blue Ground, Sabrina Wells, 1904, 13 In. ....*Illus* 28000.00
Coaster Set, Vellum Glaze, Round, c.1913, 4 In., 4 Piece 1265.00
Cup, Incised White Flowers At Rim, Blue Glaze, Marie De Hoa LeBlanc, 1905, 5 In. 4600.00
Mailbox, Pierced Brass, Juanita M. Mauras, c.1935, 11 5/8 In. 520.00
Mailbox, Pierced Brass, Stylized S In Circle, 11 x 9 In. 600.00
Mug, Abstract Floral, Blue Against Green-Blue Ground, Artist Signed, 7 In. 4950.00
Pitcher, Cream Satin Glaze, Daisy Blooms, c.1911, 2 1/2 x 3 1/2 In. 980.00
Pitcher, Plyanthus On Blue-Green Ground, Sadie Irvine, 1909, 7 1/2 In. 4400.00
Plate, Incised Painted Daisies, Leaves, Blue, Olive Green High Glaze, 8 3/4 In. 1150.00
Teapot, Band Of Wild Roses, Alma Mason, 1911, 4 1/4 x 5 1/2 In. 3375.00
Teapot, Band Of Wild Roses, Light Pink, Yellow On Dark Blue, Mason, 1911, 5 In. 3375.00
Tile, Narcissus, Purple Ground, Mahogany Frame, J. Meyer, 12 x 5 In. 8525.00
Tile, Spanish Galleon, Whimsical Dolphins, Persian Blue Glaze, 5 1/4 In. 805.00
Trivet, Art Nouveau, Ivory Ground, Speckled Cobalt Blue Glaze, J. Meyer, 1910, 6 In. 1650.00
Trivet, Moss Covered Oak Tree, Blue, Green, Henrietta Bailey, 1923, 4 In. 1870.00
Vase, 2 Buttresses, Green Matte Glaze, 3 In. 805.00
Vase, Abstract Floral At Rim, Corinne Marie Chalaron, c.1921, 8 In. 520.00
Vase, Abstract Organic Design, Blue, Green, Ground, Roberta Kennon, 6 1/2 In. 4315.00
Vase, Band Of Carved & Painted Flowers, Green, Cynthia Littlejohn, 1917, 6 In. 3080.00
Vase, Band Of Painted Flowers At Shoulder, C.P. Littlejohn, 1917, 5 3/4 In. 3136.00
Vase, Band Of Stylized Flowers, Glossy Washed Glaze, c.1903, 5 3/4 In. 4600.00

Vase, Band Of Wild Roses, White, Green Leaves, Pale Blue, Bailey, 1922, 4 In. 1955.00
Vase, Bell Shaped Flowers, Leaves, Cobalt Ground, Henrietta Bailey, 1929, 3 3/4 In. 1465.00
Vase, Blooming Cactus With Rose Flowers, Pale Blue Stems, Handles, 8 x 6 In. 6900.00
Vase, Bulbous, Ribbed, Burnt Orange Matte Glaze, Stamped NC/JM, 4 1/2 In. 375.00
Vase, Carved & Painted Jonquils, Yellow Centers, Leaves, A.F. Simpson, 6 1/2 In. 4400.00
Vase, Carved & Painted Landscape, Sadie Irvine, 4 In. 1650.00
Vase, Carved Blue Flowers, Yellow Centers, Anna Francis Simpson, 6 In. 2875.00
Vase, Carved Budding Iris Stalks, Sadie Irvine, 1902, 6 1/2 In. 2185.00
Vase, Carved Cypress & Pines, Medium Blue, Green, 1907, 11 x 4 1/2 In. 8625.00
Vase, Carved White Lilies, Yellow Stamen, Blue, Green Leaves, Roman, 1904, 6 In. 4600.00
Vase, Carved White, Yellow Trillium, Light Blue, Green Ground, Irvine, 1917, 3 In. 1380.00
Vase, Carved, Painted Eucalyptus, Light Pink Seed Pods, Blue Ground, 10 In. 4485.00
Vase, Closed-In Rim, Oaks Under Full Moon, Henrietta Bailey, 1933, 5 1/4 In. 2990.00
Vase, Corn Stalks, Cobalt Blue Ground, Roberta Kennon, 1902, 9 3/4 In. 4400.00
Vase, Crisply Carved Spanish Moss Live Oaks, Dark Blue, Green, 1928, 11 In. 9775.00
Vase, Double Gourd, Green Dripping Over Cobalt Blue Ground, J. Meyers, 6 1/2 In. 2200.00
Vase, Flower, Panels, Amelia Roman, 12 In. . . . . *Illus* 54600.00
Vase, Flowers, Yellow Centers, A.F. Simpson, Signed, 7 1/2 In. 3080.00
Vase, Forest Green Dripping Over Cobalt Glaze, Signed, 3 3/4 In. 430.00
Vase, Full Moon Peering Through Moss Off Single Tree, Irvine, 6 3/4 In. 3140.00
Vase, Incised Floral Design, Rose, Purple Glaze, Sadie Irvine, 3 3/4 In. 1380.00
Vase, Incised Swirling Leaves, Sadie Irvine, 3 1/2 In. 1265.00
Vase, Indigo, Buff Grape Leaves, Soft Olive Ground, Marie Ross, 1896, 7 x 4 In. 8625.00
Vase, Iris Design, Light Blue Matte Glaze, Leona Nicholson, 5 1/2 In. 253.00
Vase, Ivory & Green Stylized Flowers & Leaves, Signed, 6 1/2 In. 2875.00
Vase, Ivory, Yellow Flowers, Leaves, Leone Nicholson, 5 In. 4900.00
Vase, Landscape, Moss Covered Oak Trees, Pale Yellow Moon, A.F. Simpson, 5 In. 3220.00
Vase, Landscape, Pine Trees, Harriet Joor, 1902, 12 1/4 x 7 1/2 In. 21375.00
Vase, Large Blue Tulips, Light Blue, Blue Glaze Ground, Marie Delavigne, 6 In. 5175.00
Vase, Leaves, Flowers, Squat, Henrietta Bailey, 5 In. 1380.00
Vase, Light Blue Flora Magnolias, Green Foliage, L. Nicholson, 1904, 7 In. 9775.00
Vase, Light Rose Pinecones, Green Branches, Blue Ground, Henrietta Bailey, 6 In. 3740.00
Vase, Linear Decor, Mottled Glaze, Leona Nicholson, c.1910, 4 1/4 x 5 In. 345.00
Vase, Live Oak, Spanish Moss, Full Moon, Anna F. Simpson, 1927, 11 x 5 In. 14625.00
Vase, Live Oak, Spanish Moss, Full Moon, Anna Frances Simpson, 1922, 8 1/4 In. 9350.00
Vase, Live Oak, Spanish Moss, Pink Sky, Anna Simpson, 1929, 5 x 3 In. 5463.00
Vase, Live Oaks, Spanish Moss, Full Moon, Sadie Irvine, 1929, 6 In. 4125.00
Vase, Live Oaks, Spanish Moss, Moon, Raised Neck, Oval, Blue & Green, 1910, 5 1/2 In. . 2185.00
Vase, Live Oaks, Spanish Moss, Pink Sky, Anna Frances Simpson, 1922, 4 In. 3240.00
Vase, Moonlit, Spanish Moss, Blue, Green, Sadie Irvine, 1932, 5 1/8 In. 3960.00
Vase, Morning Glories, Leon Nicholson, Paper Label, c.1907, 16 In. 86250.00
Vase, Mottled Green Glaze, Dripping Over Red Clay Body, Stamp Mark, 3 In. 290.00
Vase, Royal Blue, Carved, Anna Frances Simpson, 8 In. 3105.00
Vase, Spanish Moss, Full Moon, Sadie Irvine, 1933, 4 1/8 In. 1980.00
Vase, Stylized Floral, Anna Frances Simpson, Joseph Meyer, 3 5/8 x 5 In. 1430.00
Vase, Stylized Pomegranate, Green Highlights, E. DeHoa LeBlanc, 1902, 9 In. 11550.00
Vase, Stylized Primrose, Tall Stems, Blue Ground, Mazie T. Ryan, 1904, 7 1/4 In. 8440.00

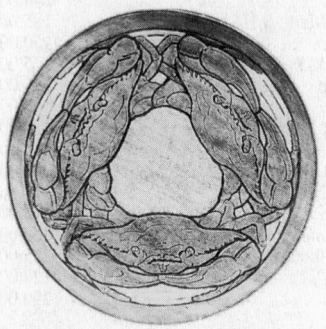

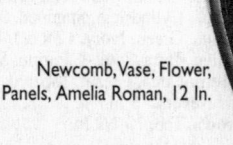

Newcomb, Charger,
3 Crabs, Blue Ground,
Sabrina Wells, 1904, 13 In.

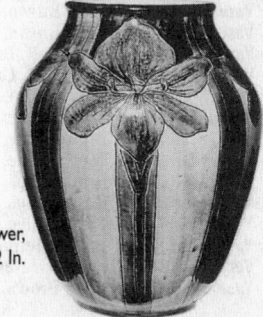

Newcomb, Vase, Flower,
Panels, Amelia Roman, 12 In.

Vase, Stylized Strawberries, Dark Blue On Pale Blue, Elliott, 1902, 3 In. 9000.00
Vase, Stylized Strawberries, Esther Elliott, 1902, 3 1/4 In. 9000.00
Vase, Stylized White Narcissus, Blue Ground, Irene Borden Keep, 1903, 10 3/4 In. 4950.00
Vase, Stylized White Narcissus, Leaves, Anna Frances Simpson, 1914, 9 In. 4125.00
Vase, Swans On Water, Tree In The Distance, Blue Glaze, 1900, 9 3/4 x 11 In. 19550.00
Vase, Tall Pines, Washed Blue Ground, Sadie Irvine, 1917, 5 1/4 In. 3450.00
Vase, Transitional, Moonlit Landscape Of Tall Pines, 1916, 8 1/2 x 3 3/4 In. 2750.00
Vase, Trumpet Creeper Flowers, Vines, Rose Ground, Simpson, 1919, 7 1/2 In. 615.00
Vase, Wisteria Blossoms, Periwinkle Blue, Cobalt, Celadon, Robinson, 1904, 9 In. 13500.00
Vessel, Stylized Floral Design, Olive Green, May Dunn, 5 In. 2990.00
Wall Pocket, Conical, 3 Large Stylized Lotus Blossoms, Blue, Wood, 1901, 12 In. 5175.00

NILOAK Pottery (Kaolin spelled backward) was made at the Hyten
Brothers Pottery in Benton, Arkansas, between 1909 and 1947.
Although the factory did make cast and molded wares, collectors are
most interested in the marbleized art pottery line made of colored   𝒩𝐼𝐿𝒪𝒜𝒦
swirls of clay. It was called *Mission Ware*. By 1931 the company made
castware, and many of these pieces were marked with the name
Hywood.

Ashtray, Marbleized, Curved Sides, Swirled Tan & Cream Colors, 3 1/2 In. 90.00
Bowl, Flower, Marbleized, Squatty, Center Opening, Brown, Cream & Orange, 3 In. 195.00
Bowl, Ozark Dawn Glaze, Impressed Mark, 3 3/8 In. 40.00
Bowl, Powder, Marbleized, Gray, Tan & Cream, Footed, 6 In. 525.00
Bowl, Speckled Glossy Interior, 5 In. 78.00
Candlestick, Marbleized, Brown, Blue, Terra-Cotta & Sand, Funnel Base, 5 In. 330.00
Canoe, Brown, Tan Green, Label, 1940s, 8 x 2 1/2 In. 60.00
Chocolate Set, Dogwood Blossom 185.00
Compote, Open, Marbleized, Gray, Tan, Orange & Cream, Flared Foot, 5 In. 825.00
Ewer, Lime Green, Original Label, 6 3/4 In. 96.00
Humidor, Cover, Marbleized, Cream, Tan & Light Brown, 6 1/2 In. 1210.00
Jardiniere, Marbleized, Brown, Blue, Ivory, Marked, 11 1/4 x 12 1/2 In. 2250.00
Jardiniere, Marbleized, Brown, Bulbous, Ovoid, 10 In. 1210.00
Mug, Marbleized, Cylindrical, C-Form Handle, 5 In. 255.00
Planter, Deer, Blue Matte Glaze, 4 1/2 In. 42.00
Planter, Duck, Green, 4 3/4 x 3 1/2 x 2 1/2 In. 30.00
Planter, Dutch Shoe, Mold Mark 55.00
Planter, Elephant, Pink 30.00
Planter, Green, Fan Appearance, Marked With N, 4 1/4 x 3 3/4 In., Pair 49.00
Planter, Squirrel, 6 In. 35.00
Planter, Swan, Blue Matte Glaze, 7 1/2 In. 65.00
Planter, Wishing Well, Light Green, Brown Matte Accent, Part Label, 8 x 4 1/2 In. 38.00
Punch Bowl, Marbleized, Cream, Tan & Brown, Pedestal, Footed, 13 In. 2640.00
Tile, Marbleized, Clay, Square, 4 In. 132.00
Vase, Bud, Ozark Dawn Glaze, 7 1/4 In. 65.00
Vase, Cornucopia, Pink, 3 1/2 In. 35.00
Vase, Green Matte Glaze, Partial Label, 3 3/4 In 65.00
Vase, Lavender, Double Handed, 6 1/2 In. 40.00
Vase, Marbleized, Blue & White Label, 5 1/4 In. 245.00
Vase, Marbleized, Blue, Brown, Cream, Urn Form, 1st Art Mark, 6 1/4 In. 185.00
Vase, Marbleized, Blue, Brown, Green, Red, 10 1/2 In. 1150.00
Vase, Marbleized, Blue, Buff, Brown, Baluster, 1st Art Mark, Paper Label, 5 1/4 In. 125.00
Vase, Marbleized, Blue, Buff, Cream, 1st Art Mark, 4 3/4 In. 135.00
Vase, Marbleized, Blue, Cream, Brown, 6 1/4 In. 145.00
Vase, Marbleized, Brown, Blue, Cream, Cylindrical, 1st Art Mark, 6 In. 170.00
Vase, Marbleized, Brown, Blue, Cream, Red Clay, 20 In. 2070.00
Vase, Marbleized, Brown, Blue, Cream, Urn Form, Marked, 6 1/2 In. . . . . .190.00 to 265.00
Vase, Marbleized, Brown, Blue, Cylindrical, Stamped, 9 1/2 In. 374.00
Vase, Marbleized, Brown, Blue, Green, Ivory, 12 x 5 1/4 In. 675.00
Vase, Marbleized, Brown, Blue, Terra-Cotta & Purple, Strumpet Neck, Footed, 9 In. 360.00
Vase, Marbleized, Brown, Terra-Cotta, Cream, Tapered, Bulbous Top, 1st Art Mark, 6 In. . . 215.00
Vase, Marbleized, Earthtone Reverse, 6 In. 123.00
Vase, Marbleized, Light Brown, Tan, 10 1/2 In. 299.00

Vase, Marbleized, Pinched Waist, Mark, 6 1/2 In. 265.00
Vase, Mauve, 6 1/2 In. 230.00
Vase, Ozark Dawn Glaze, 1930s, 8 3/4 In. 250.00
Vase, Strawberry, Pink, Gray-Green, Glaze, Turkey Feather Openings, Paper Label 65.00
Vase, Twist, Pink Gloss, Partial Label, 6 1/2 In. 40.00

NIPPON porcelain was made in Japan from 1891 to 1921. *Nippon* is the Japanese word for *Japan*. A few firms continued to use the word *Nippon* on ceramics after 1921 as a part of the company name more than as an identification of the country of origin. More pieces marked Nippon will be found in the Dragonware, Moriage, and Noritake categories.

Basket, Tapestry, Moon Shape, 9 In. 1870.00
Berry Bowl, Underplate 120.00
Bowl, Enameled Flowers, Green Leaves, Boats Sailing At Sunset Center, 8 1/2 In. 220.00
Bowl, Pink Apple Blossoms, Gold Trim On Feet, Signed, 3 3/4 x 7 1/2 In. 135.00
Candy Dish, 3 Geisha Girls, Flowers, Scalloped Edge, 3-Footed, 6 1/4 In. 15.50
Loving Cup, Wedgwood Style, 2 Handles, 5 1/2 In. 305.00
Match Holder, Blue, White Floral Design, Japan, 4 1/2 In. 125.00
Mustard Pot, Attached Underplate, Flower Sprays, Handles, Rising Sun 40.00
Nut Cup, Earthtone, Nuts & Leaves 17.00
Plate, Deer, Signed M With Wreath, Hand Painted, 8 1/2 In. 138.00
Plate, Snack, Phoenix Bird, 6 In. 25.00
Salt Set, Floral, Footed, 6 Piece 35.00
Salt Tub, Scene, Gold Handles, M In Green Wreath 25.00
Sugar & Creamer, Purple Violets, Loop Handles, Pre-1900, 5 In. 125.00
Tea Strainer, Hexagonal, Gold Trim, Enamel Berries, Handle, Ivory Center, 1 3/4 In. 150.00
Toothpick Holder, Duck, Japan, 2 1/2 In. 24.00
Urn, Orange Poppies, Blues Ground, Oriental Bands, Marked, 11 1/2 In. 259.00
Urn, Trees, Lake Scene, Six Sides, Gilt On Handles, Rim, Base, Marked, 14 3/4 In. 375.00
Vase, Bulbous, Gilt On Handles, Inside Rim, 8 1/4 In. 405.00
Vase, Floral, Outlined In Gold, 12 In. 195.00
Vase, Lake & Mountain Scene, Man On Path, Gold Handles, Gold Trim, 6 x 8 1/2 In. 715.00
Vase, Strawberries, 5 1/2 In. 112.00

NODDERS, also called nodding figures or pagods, are figures with heads and hands that are attached to wires. Any slight movement causes the parts to move up and down. They were made in many countries during the eighteenth, nineteenth, and twentieth centuries. A few Art Deco designs are also known. Copies are being made. A more recent type of nodder is made of papier-mache or plastic. These often represent sports figures or comic characters. Sports nodders are listed in the Sports category.

A Little Dab'll Do Ya, Hair Creme, Man & Girl, Kissing, Lego, 5 1/4 In., Pair 170.00
Andy Gump, Bisque, Germany, 1920s 195.00
Ashtray, Chinese Figure, Painted Petal 185.00
Big Boy, Bobbin' Head 16.00
Black Girl, Pink Socks, Yellow Hat, On Stump, Flower Insert On Back, Bisque, 2 In. 165.00
Dog, Bulldog 1705.00
Happy Hooligan, Riding Cart, Pulled By Mule, Rubber Neck, Cast Iron, Hubley 550.00
Icey, Ice Capades Mascot, 1960s 210.00
Lamb, White Wool Coat, Felt Saddle, Tin Wheels, 5 In. 1100.00
Monkey, Holding Tail, Weighted Head, Biscuit Porcelain, Continental, 5 In. 525.00
Mr. Wicker, Bisque, Germany 375.00
Priest, Black Robe & Hat, Nods At Waist & Head, Redware, Circular Mark, 9 3/8 In. ... 85.00
Salt & Pepper shakers are listed in the Salt & Pepper category.
Santa Claus, Lead Pendulum, Windup, 7 In. 550.00
Seated Geisha, Porcelain, Early 20th Century, 3 1/2 In. 35.00
Skeezix, Bisque, Germany 175.00
Turtle, Brown, Tan Spots, Paper Label, Empress, Japan, 1950s, 5 1/2 x 4 In. 65.00
Uncle Walt, Bisque, Germany 175.00
With Mule Cart, Marked, 6 In. 290.00

If you have a very ornate pair of metal candlesticks, coat them generously with the proper metal cleaner. Let dry. Rinse with a wet sponge and rub hard enough to remove the cleaner from any crevices. The chemical action of the metal cleaner will remove the tarnish.

Noritake, Candy Dish, Gold Flowers, Handle,
M In Wreath Mark, 5 1/2 In.

NORITAKE porcelain was made in Japan after 1904 by Nippon Toki Kaisha. The best-known Noritake pieces are marked with the M in a wreath for the Morimura Brothers, a New York City distributing company. This mark was used until 1941. There may be some helpful price information in the Nippon category, since prices are comparable. Noritake Azalea is listed in the Azalea category in this book.

Bowl, Oblong, White, Green, Orange, Gold Trim, 2 Gold Handles, 10 x 4 1/4 x 1 3/4 In. .	80.00
Bowl, Olive, White, Gold, Raised Green & Peach Beads On Rim, Handles, 10 x 4 1/4 In. .	79.00
Bowl, Shrimp, Tree In The Meadow	225.00
Candy Dish, Gold Flowers, Handle, M In Wreath Mark, 5 1/2 In. . . . .*Illus*	75.00
Coffeepot, Tree In The Meadow, 6 1/2 In.	350.00
Dinner Set, Plate, Cups & Saucers, Country Diary Of Edwardian Lady, Individual	30.00
Dish, Serving, Cover, Handle, Phoenix Bird, 10 x 5 1/4 In.	100.00
Gravy Boat, Phoenix Bird	19.00
Howo Bird, Blue, White	22.00
Jar, Cigarette, Art Deco, Man & Woman Smoking Scene	380.00
Napkin Ring, Adagio	40.00
Napkin Ring, Affection	63.00
Napkin Ring, Gold, Platinum	15.00
Platter, Phoenix Bird, 8 1/4 x 12 3/8 In.	61.00
Salt & Pepper, Phoenix Bird	117.00
Sauceboat, Leaf Shape, Phoenix Bird, 6 x 4 1/4 x 2 1/2 In.	127.00
Sugar & Creamer, 6 Sides, Art Deco Floral, Red Wreath Mark	35.00
Sugar & Creamer, Peacock Eye	65.00
Sugar & Creamer, Scene, Tall	80.00
Sugar & Creamer, White, Pink Flowers, Gold Trim, 2 Piece	35.00
Toothpick, Ping-Pong Bat, 1980	38.00
Tree In The Meadow, Bowl, Shrimp	225.00
Tree In The Meadow, Coffeepot, 6 1/2 In.	350.00
Tureen, High Handle, Phoenix Bird, Oval, 5 3/4 x 8 x 4 In.	160.00
Vase, Fern & Floral, Allover Gold, 6 1/2 In.	75.00
Vase, Lake Scene With Swan, 2 Gold Handles, 3-Footed, 4 1/2 In., Pair	171.00

NORTH DAKOTA SCHOOL OF MINES was established in 1892 at the University of North Dakota. A ceramic course was included and pieces were made from the clays found in the region. Students at the university made pieces from 1909 to 1949. Although very early pieces were marked *U.N.D.*, most pieces were stamped with the full name of the university.

Box, Cover, Head Of Indian Chief On Umber Ground, 2 x 5 In.	690.00
Charger, Stylized Floral Design, Cuerda Seca, 1949, 9 In.	535.00
Pitcher, Birds & Flowers, Red, Yellow, White, 1952, 5 1/4 In.	110.00
Rose Bowl, Light & Dark Green Bands, 1947, 4 1/2 x 7 In.	785.00
Vase, 2-Tone Blue High Glaze, Signed, Huck, 7 1/2 In.	330.00
Vase, Applied Circles, Green Matte Glaze, 2 5/8 In.	175.00

Vase, Band Of Pink Prairie Roses, Green Leaves, 4 x 5 In. 790.00
Vase, Blue High Glaze, 5 1/2 In. 55.00
Vase, Blue, 3 In. 263.00
Vase, Brown, Purple Matte Glaze, 7 In. 173.00
Vase, Bulbous, Incised Tulips, Matte Glaze, Signed M. Cable 805.00
Vase, Cone Shape, Stylized Geometric Design, Green, 3 x 5 In. 290.00
Vase, Cowboy & Lasso, Light Periwinkle Blue Glaze, 5 x 2 In. 420.00
Vase, Deeply Incised Vertical Lines, Yellow, Brown, 8 In. 240.00
Vase, Geometric Band, Crackled Ground, Signed, 5 x 6 In. 690.00
Vase, Green & Brown Matte Glaze, Signed, J. Mattson, 9 In. 385.00
Vase, Green Matte Glaze, 5 1/2 In. 345.00
Vase, Green, Blue High Glaze, 5 1/2 In. 175.00
Vase, Incised Design, Brown Matte Glaze, 2 Buttresses, 5 In. 196.00
Vase, Incised Floral Design, Brown Matte Glaze, 6 In. 635.00
Vase, Incised Floral, Brown Matte Glaze, 3 1/2 In. 196.00
Vase, Multicolored Green Matte Glaze, 4 In. 196.00
Vase, North Dakota Wheat, Brown, Squat, 4 3/4 x 7 In. 1350.00
Vase, Prairie Dogs, Signed, 3 1/2 x 4 In. 236.00
Vase, Stylized Figures, Brown, Green, Blue, 3 1/2 In. 320.00
Vase, Stylized Flowers, Caramel Matte Glaze, 4 x 6 In. 506.00
Vase, Stylized Flowers, Celadon Glaze, 3 3/4 x 3 In. 560.00
Vase, Stylized Flowers, Green Microcrystalline Glaze, 4 In. 506.00

NORTHWOOD Glass Company was founded by Harry Northwood, a glassmaker who worked for Hobbs, Brockunier and Company, La Belle Glass Company, and Buckeye Glass Company before founding his own firm. He opened one factory in Indiana, Pennsylvania, in 1896, and another in Wheeling, West Virginia, in 1902. Northwood closed when Mr. Northwood died in 1923. Many types of glass were made, including carnival, custard, goofus, and pressed. The underlined N mark was used on some pieces.

Beads & Bark, Vase, Mosaic, Purple Slag, 6 In. 56.00
Cherry & Cable, Table Set, Ruby Stain, Gold Trim, 5 Piece 350.00
Flute, Berry Bowl, 5 In. 29.00
Flute, Vase, 16 1/4 In. 85.00
Hobstar & Pinwheel, Lamp, Cut Glass, 26 In. 1400.00
Intaglio, Tumbler, c.1899, 4 Piece 175.00
Inverted Fan & Feather, Berry Bowl, Pink Slag, Master 800.00
Inverted Fan & Feather, Berry Set, Emerald, Gold Trim, 7 Piece 600.00
Inverted Fan & Feather, Compote, Pink Slag 2200.00
Inverted Fan & Feather, Cruet, Pink Slag 2500.00
Leaf Mold, Sugar Shaker, Yellowine, White, Pink, Vaseline, Spatter, 2 1/2 In., Pair 146.00
Quilted Phlox, Toothpick, Rose Du Barry, Pink Cased, 1903 .... 275.00
Royal Ivy, Cruet, Rubina 395.00
Royal Ivy, Pitcher, Cased Rainbow, Spatter, 4 1/2 In. 50.00
Royal Ivy, Rose Bowl, Rubina, 4 In. 64.00
Royal Ivy, Sugar, Rubina 45.00
Three Fruits, Plate, Ivory, Iridescent, 7 In. 95.00

NU-ART see Imperial category.

NUTCRACKERS of many types have been used through the centuries. At first the nutcracker was probably strong teeth or a hammer. But by the nineteenth century, many elaborate and ingenious types were made. Levers, screws, and hammer adaptations were the most popular. Because nutcrackers are still useful, they are still being made, some in the old styles.

Bear, Black Forest, Walnut, Carved, Tail Lever Opens Mouth, 8 x 4 1/2 In. 165.00
Bear, Wooden, Glass Eyes, Switzerland, c.1910, 6 1/4 In. 254.00
Cast Iron, Perfection Nutcracker Co., 4 1/2 x 5 1/2 In. 90.00
Dog, Brass 70.00
Dog, Cast Iron 100.09
Dog, Irish Setter, Bronze, 20th Century, 13 1/2 In. 350.00

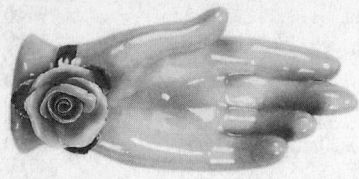

Occupied Japan, Pin Dish, Hand, Rosebud,
Pink, Porcelain, 4 1/4 In.

Office,
Arithmometer,
Graber, 1902

Eagle Head, Feather Handle, Cast Iron, 10 1/4 In.	137.00
Gendarme, Wooden, Paris, 6 In.	36.00
Hand Holding Nut Shape, Hand Is Screw, Wooden, 19th Century	495.00
Monkey, Carved Wood, Glass Eyes, 8 In.	550.00
Press, Porcelain, Brass Fittings, 19th Century	650.00
Rabbit, Cast Iron, 9 In.	20.00
Squirrel, Aluminum, 11 1/4 In.	60.00
Squirrel, Wood & Copper, Copyright 1916, 8 In.	445.00

NYMPHENBURG, see Royal Nymphenburg.

OCCUPIED JAPAN was printed on pottery, porcelain, toys, and other goods made during the American occupation of Japan after World War II, from 1945 to 1952. Collectors now search for these pieces. The items were made for export. Ceramic items are listed here.

Cracker Jar, Tomato, Handle	55.00
Cup & Saucer, Blue & White	20.00
Dish, Double Lotus Leaf, Pink Flower, Green, 3 1/2 In.	11.00
Dish, Kentucky Shape, Porcelain	15.00
Figurine, 7 Gods Of Good Luck, 6 In.	125.00
Figurine, Angel Playing Drum, 6 In.	30.00
Figurine, Angel Playing Guitar, 5 1/2 In.	30.00
Figurine, Boy, On Fence, Hummel Type, 4 In.	8.00
Figurine, Boy, With Dog, 4 1/4 In.	10.00
Figurine, Cat, With Kittens, 3 1/2 x 2 1/2 In.	10.00
Figurine, Clown Sitting On Pig, Marked Ardalt, 5 x 4 1/2 In.	100.00
Figurine, Dog, Porcelain, Marked, 1940s, 4 1/2 x 3 In.	35.00
Figurine, Dutch Boy, 4 1/4 In.	8.00
Figurine, Ethnic Woman, Winding Turban On Head, 6 In.	45.00
Figurine, Fish Bowl, Hanging Cat, White With Brown Stripes	110.00
Figurine, Hiker, Hummel Type 4 In.	10.00
Figurine, Lion Pride, 4 1/8 In.	55.00
Figurine, Madonna, 7 In.	45.00
Figurine, Man & Woman, 5 In., Pair	15.00
Figurine, Oriental Boy, Light Green Coat, 5 1/2 In.	10.00
Pin Dish, Hand, Rosebud, Pink, Porcelain, 4 1/4 In. ....*Illus*	12.00
Pitcher, Face, 3 x 4 In.	45.00
Planter, Madonna	45.00
Salt & Pepper, 2 Geisha Girls, 4 1/4 In.	17.50
Saucer, Lavender, Rust Flowers, Child's, 4 1/2 In.	5.00
Tea Set, Hand Painted Flowers, Cabaret, With Tray	85.00
Whisk Broom, Figural	35.00

Try to keep your paper collectibles out of light. If you frame and display some pieces, keep them on the dark side of the room, away from sunlight and direct lamp light.

OFFICE TECHNOLOGY includes office equipment and related products, such as adding machines, calculators, and check-writing machines. Typewriters are in their own category in this book.

Adding Machine, Spalding		3000.00
Arithmometer, Graber, 1902	*Illus*	18094.00

OHR pottery was made in Biloxi, Mississippi, from 1883 to 1906 by George E. Ohr, a true eccentric. The pottery was made of very thin clay that was twisted, folded, and dented into odd, graceful shapes. Some pieces were lifelike models of hats, animal heads, or even a potato. Others were decorated with folded clay *snakes*. Reproductions and reworked pieces are appearing on the market. These have been reglazed, or snakes and other embellishments have been added.

Bank, Green Mottled Glaze, Signed, 2 x 8 1/2 In.	6325.00
Bottle, Green, Red, Teal Matte Glaze, Closed-In Rim, 7 x 4 In.	8437.00
Bowl, Bisque, Dimpled, Script Signed, 8 In.	5175.00
Bowl, Closed-In Rim, Crenellated Base, 3 1/2 x 5 1/2 In.	863.00
Bowl, Dimpled, Cobalt Blue Exterior, Ocher Matte Glaze Interior, 3 3/4 x 5 In.	2185.00
Bowl, Rolled Rim, Bisque, 2 3/4 x 6 In.	220.00
Chamberstick, Bisque, 5 x 4 3/4 In.	1380.00
Cup, Ear Shaped Handle, Gunmetal Over Mottled & Speckled Green Glaze, 6 3/4 In.	4305.00
Hat, Red, Green, Blue Glossy Glaze, 4 x 4 1/2 In.	4313.00
Inkwell, Mule Head, Tree Under Green, Brown, Gunmetal Glaze, 4 x 7 1/4 x 4 3/4 In.	4500.00
Jug, Whiskey, Folded & Pinched Shoulder, Mottled Glaze, Signed, 6 1/2 x 6 In.	4888.00
Mug, Puzzle, Metallic Glaze, Ropelike Handle, 3 1/2 In.	1045.00
Mug, Puzzle, Mottled Brown Glaze, Embossed Rope Handle, Signed, 3 1/2 x 4 3/4 In.	345.00
Mug, Puzzle, Olive Green High Glaze, Gunmetal Black, Handle, 3 1/2 x 5 In.	990.00
Pitcher, Angular Handle, Violet Matte Glaze Exterior, Speckled Interior, 5 x 3 1/4 In.	1495.00
Pitcher, Bisque, Squat Base, Dimpled Rim, 3 3/4 x 6 In.	920.00
Pitcher, Dimpled Rim, Random Gunmetal Accents, Cutout Handles, Signed, 5 1/4 In.	3450.00
Pitcher, Light Mauve Glaze Exterior, Chartreuse Green Interior, Pinched Side, 2 x 5 In.	2250.00
Pitcher, Umber Glaze, Gunmetal, Ear Shaped Handle, 3 x 6 In.	2185.00
Teapot, Snake Spout, Cobalt Glossy Glaze, Marked, 4 x 8 3/4 In.	11250.00
Teapot, Wrinkled Fold, c.1895	7425.00
Vase, 1 Pinched Side, 1 Dimpled Side, Sponged Maroon Circles, 5 1/4 x 5 In.	8250.00
Vase, Amber Speckled Glaze, Marked, 4 3/4 x 4 1/2 In.	3656.00
Vase, Beaker Shape, Red, Green Cobalt Matte Glaze, 3 3/4 x 3 In.	2645.00
Vase, Black Drip Glaze, Sun, Buttercup Yellow, Honey Caramel Ground, 4 x 3 1/2 In.	2860.00
Vase, Black Gunmetal Glaze, Mahogany Glaze Interior, Cupped Rim, 3 1/2 x 3 1/4 In.	2185.00
Vase, Cadmium Yellow, Lavender, Green, Pink Volcanic Glaze, Marked, 4 x 3 3/4 In.	3040.00
Vase, Crenelated Rim, Black, Green, Blue Luster Glaze, 5 1/2 x 4 1/2 In.	2990.00
Vase, Dark Brown, Handles, Script Signature, 8 5/8 In.	9200.00
Vase, Dark Olive Green Speckled Glaze, Folded Rim, 4 1/2 x 2 1/2 In.	2587.00
Vase, Deep Cucumber Green, Brown Flambe Glaze, Gunmetal Streaks, 4 x 2 1/4 In.	440.00
Vase, Dimpled Body, Bisque, 5 x 5 In.	2760.00
Vase, Dimpled Neck, Mirror Cobalt, Gunmetal Glaze, 9 1/2 x 5 In.	9560.00
Vase, Dimpled Sides & Corners, Beige Bisque Clay, Signed, 3 3/4 x 5 3/4 In.	3740.00
Vase, Double Gourd, Bisque Finish, 5 x 5 In.	1540.00
Vase, Folded Rim, Exterior Blue Glaze, Interior Terra-Cotta, Signed, 5 3/4 In.	3105.00
Vase, Folded Rim, Green, Brown & Gunmetal Glaze, Signed, 4 3/4 In.	3335.00
Vase, Folded Rim, Mirrored Gunmetal Glaze, Signed, 4 x 3 1/2 In.	3335.00
Vase, Gunmetal Black Glaze, Marked, 2 x 3 In.	865.00
Vase, Gunmetal Crystalline Glaze, Spiked Rim, Marked, 3 1/4 x 3 In.	2070.00
Vase, Gunmetal, Brown Design, Multicolored Green Ground, 3 1/2 In.	2070.00
Vase, Hunter Green Accents, Caramel Brown, Sandy Tan High Glaze, 4 1/4 x 4 In.	2420.00
Vase, Ocher Glaze, Green Speckles, 3 x 3 1/4 In.	1495.00
Vase, Oval, Green Flambe Glaze, Cupped Rim, 5 1/2 x 4 1/4 In.	690.00
Vase, Randomly Ruffled Rim, Dimpled Body, Speckled Glaze, Signed, 4 1/2 In.	1725.00
Vase, Red Clay Bisque Finish, Charcoal Base, 4 3/4 x 3 3/4 In.	1650.00
Vase, Snake, Brown, Handles, Script Signature, 4 5/8 In.	4887.00
Vase, Speckled Amber, Gunmetal Glaze, Collapsed Side, 4 1/2 x 4 1/2 In.	6187.00
Vase, Spherical, Collapsed & Folded Rim, Speckled Glossy Glaze, Signed, 4 3/4 In.	7475.00

Vase, Squat, Shoulders, Speckled Brown Semimatte Glaze, Stamped, 2 1/2 x 4 In. 920.00
Vase, Stovepipe Neck, Mottled Glossy Glaze, Red Flashes, Signed, 8 1/4 In. 2760.00

OLD IVORY china was made by the Ohme Porcelain Works in Silesia, Germany, a factory working from 1882 to 1928. The china had an ivory matte background and was usually decorated with flowers or fruit. Dinner sets, fish sets, mustache cups, and souvenir pieces were also made. Pieces were marked with a crown, the cipher OH, and the word *Silesia*. Some pieces are also marked with the words *Old Ivory*. The pattern numbers appear on the base of many pieces.

Biscuit Jar	995.00
Butter, Cover	1175.00
Plate, No. 82, Yellow Tea Rose Center, Old Ivory Border, 8 In.	175.00

OLD PARIS, see Paris category.

OLD SLEEPY EYE, see Sleepy Eye category.

OLYMPIC, see Souvenir category.

ONION PATTERN, originally named *bulb pattern*, is a white ware decorated with cobalt blue or pink. Although it is commonly associated with Meissen, other companies made the pattern in the late nineteenth and the twentieth centuries. A rare type is called *red bud* because there are added red accents on the blue-and-white dishes.

Bowl, Scalloped, Meissen, Crossed Swords Mark, 9 In. 125.00
Cake Plate, Blue, Scalloped Rim, Footed, Mark, Meissen, 10 5/8 In. 81.00
Cake Stand, Blue, 2 Tiers, Child Shape Knop, Meissen, 14 In. 2530.00
Candy Dish, Leaf Shape, Meissen, Crossed Swords Mark, 6 3/4 In. 31.00
Cheese Dish, Cover, Attached Underplate, Meissen, 8 1/2 In. 250.00
Coffeepot, Blue 125.00
Compote, Blue, Reticulated, Footed, C. Teichert, Meissen, c.1900, 8 1/2 In. 196.00
Cruet, Vinegar, Germany, 9 In. 100.00
Cup, Trembleuse, Blue, Reticulated, Cover, Blue Cross Swords, Meissen, 1 1/4 In. 130.00
Dish, Blue, Stylized Flowers, Foliage, Blue Underglaze, Meissen, 10 In. 138.00
Dish, Sweetmeat, Blue, Maiden Holding Goose, Shells, Meissen, 9 1/2 In. 800.00
Dish, Sweetmeat, Blue, Meissen, 19th Century, 5 In., Pair 1150.00
Inkwell, Blue, Stylized Flowers, Blue Underglaze, Meissen, 2 1/2 x 8 1/2 x 5 In. 370.00
Nutcracker, Porcelain & Metal, Meissen 560.00
Plate, Reticulated, Meissen, 8 1/4 In. 178.00
Plate, Stoneware, Blue, Continental, Impress M, Meissen, 11 1/2 In., Pair 60.00
Platter, Blue, Impressed, Blue Mark, Meissen, 17 1/2 x 11 In. 230.00
Platter, Blue, Round, Meissen, 12 1/4 In. 210.00
Salt, Double, Meissen, c.1865 ..... 125.00
Spice Cabinet, Porcelain Oval Plaque, 12 Drawers, Wooden, 24 1/2 In. 281.00
Sugar, Meissen 76.00
Syrup Pitcher, Applied Rose On Cover, Meissen, 4 1/2 In. 511.00
Tea Canister, Cover, Meissen, 7 1/2 In. 70.00
Tray, Blue, Rococo Motifs, Cobalt Blue, Gilt Highlights, Meissen, 17 1/4 In. 920.00
Tureen, Gold Trim, Meissen, Crossed Swords Mark, 10 3/4 In. 450.00

OPALESCENT GLASS is translucent glass that has the tones of the opal gemstone. It originated in England in the 1870s and is often found in pressed glassware made in Victorian times. Opalescent glass was first made in America in 1897 at the Northwood glassworks in Indiana, Pennsylvania. Some dealers use the terms *opaline* and *opalescent* for any of these translucent wares. More opalescent pieces may be listed in Hobnail, Northwood, Pressed Glass, and other glass categories.

Alaska, Berry, Footed, Vaseline, 9 1/2 In. 89.00
Alaska, Celery Dish, Vaseline 250.00
Alaska, Creamer, Blue ..... .65.00 to 75.00
Alaska, Sauce, Vaseline 45.00
Alaska, Sauce, White 25.00

Beaded Fleur-De-Lis, Rose Bowl, 3-Petal Foot, Blue, 8 In. 90.00
Beatty Honeycomb, Creamer, Blue 60.00
Daisy & Fern, Pitcher, White, Applied Handle, 5 1/2 In. 100.00
Daisy & Fern, Rose Bowl, White, Ruffled Edge, 4 In. 78.00
Daisy & Fern, Syrup, Cranberry 200.00
Drapery, Tumbler, Blue 30.00
Fluted Bars & Beads, Vase, Green, Applied Light Green Ruffled Rim 60.00
Hilltop Vines, Compote, White 25.00
Iris, Water Set, White, 5 Piece 175.00
Pearls & Scales, Compote, Blue, 7 In. 75.00
Poinsettia, Bowl, Cranberry 250.00
Spanish Lace, Sugar Shaker, Vaseline, 4 1/2 In. 117.00
Swirl, Compote, Blue, Brass Fittings, Handle, 8 1/4 In. 225.00
Target, Vase, Peach, 11 1/2 In. ....55.00 to 65.00
Toothpicks are listed in the Toothpick category.
Victor, Berry Bowl, White 55.00
Victor, Creamer, Green, Opalescent 95.00
Waterlily & Cattails, Tumbler, Blue 25.00

OPALINE, or opal glass, was made in white, green, and other colors.
The glass had a matte surface and a lack of transparency. It was often
gilded or painted. It was a popular mid-nineteenth-century European
glassware.

Compote, Allover Gold Dome Cover & Stem, 1830s, 11 x 11 5/8 In. 635.00
Decanter, Lozenge Shape, Thin Cylindrical Neck, Stopper, 12 1/4 In. 140.00
Urn, Pale Blue, Round Dome Base, Rolled Rim, 11 1/2 In., Pair 3000.00
Vase, Blue, Enameled Daisies, France, 1880s, 18 x 7 In. 230.00
Vase, Etched Floral Sprays, Gold Enamel, Late 19th Century, 11 In., Pair 860.00

OPERA GLASSES are needed because the stage is a long way from some
of the seats at a play or an opera. Mother-of-pearl was a popular decoration on many French glasses.

Abalone, Marked LeMaire, Paris, France, 2 3/4 x 4 1/2 In. 95.00
Brass, France, 19th Century 77.00
Brass, Silver Plate & Pewter, Engraved, c.1900, 4 1/4 x 2 3/8 x 1 3/4 In. 132.00
Chevalier, Mother-Of-Pearl, Telescoping Handle, Paris 125.00
Chrome, Green Leather Case, Marked, Japan 8.00
Etched Dogs' Heads In Horseshoes, Jockeys On Horses, Gorham, 20th Century 4600.00
Howard, Enamel, France, Case 672.00
Lorgnette, Geometric Openwork Handle, Hinged Lenses, Trace Link Chain, 24 In. 375.00
Lorgnette, Rectangular Lenses, Geometric, Diamond Set Handle, Art Deco 1150.00
Lorgnette, Sterling Silver, Repousse Iris Flower Handle, Art Nouveau 345.00
Mother-Of-Pearl, c.1930, 4 x 2 1/4 x 1 1/2 In. 127.00
Mother-Of-Pearl, Continental, 4 3/4 In. 173.00
Mother-Of-Pearl, Enamel, Gilt Metal, Austria 460.00
Mother-Of-Pearl, Enamel, Red Ground, Putti Handle, France 460.00
Mother-Of-Pearl, Magenta, Gilt Metal Trim, Detachable Handle, France 460.00
Mother-Of-Pearl, Velvet Bag 165.00
Verres, Mother-Of-Pearl, Leather Case, France, 4 x 2 3/4 In. 130.00

ORPHAN ANNIE first appeared in the comics in 1924. The redheaded
girl and her friends have been on the radio and are still on the comic
pages. A Broadway musical show and a movie in the 1980s made
Annie popular again and many toys, dishes, and other memorabilia are
being made.

Book, Radio Orphan Annie's Secret Society, 1937 .... 65.00
Decoder, Brass, Silver Rim, Radio Premium, 1935 .... 72.00
Display, Annie & Sandy, Plaster, ESCO, New York News, c.1973, 14 3/4 In. 145.00
Doll, Annie, Cloth, 18 1/2 In. 20.00
Doll, Annie, Knickerbocker, 24 In. 50.00
Doll, Annie, Remco 95.00
Figure, Bisque, 3 1/4 In. 75.00

Figure Set, Annie, Sandy, Harold Teen & Lilums, Bisque, Box, 4 Piece 875.00
Game, Rummy, 35 Cards, Directions, Whitman Publishing Co., 1935 . . . . .60.00 to 65.00
Game, Treasure Hunt, Radio Premium, Wander, 1933 . . . .   50.00
Glass, Drinking, Libby, 5 3/4 In. 16.99
Jack Set, Cardboard, Display Card, Harold Gray Autograph, 1937, 5 x 7 In. 38.00
Mug, Ovaltine Shake-Up, Decal, 1935 . . . .   95.00
Mug, Ovaltine, Homer Laughlin 85.00
Pastry Set, Rollers, Pan, Breadboard, Book, Box, Transogram, 1930s, 7 x 9 In. 95.00
Planter, Annie & Sandy, Japan, 5 x 3 In. 50.00
Plate, Annie & Sandy, Collector Series, Pre-1983, 8 1/2 In. 38.00
Salt & Pepper, Orphan Annie & Sandy, 3 In. 85.00
Tea Set, 5 Plates, 4 Cup & Saucers, Casserole, Sugar & Creamer, 19 Piece 125.00
Toothbrush Holder, Bisque, Japan, 4 In. 145.00
Toy, Marbles 41.00
Toy, Sandy, Orphan Annie's Dog, Tin, Windup, With Repro Suitcase 345.00
Toy, Stove, Pressed Steel, 7 1/8 x 8 In. 70.00
Toy, Stove, Red Painted Sheet Metal, Lithograph Panel 40.00

ORREFORS Glassworks, located in the Swedish province of Smaaland,
was established in 1898. The company is still making glass for use on
the table or as decorations. There is renewed interest in the glass made
in the modern styles of the 1940s and 1950s. Most vases and decorative pieces are signed with the etched name.

Orrefors

Bowl, Engraved Female Muse, Palmquist, 7 3/4 In. 86.00
Bowl, Shaped Paneled Sides, 5 1/2 x 7 1/2 In. 105.00
Vase, Ariel, Woman Profile, Dove, Brown, Aqua, Edvin Ohrstrom 1680.00
Vase, Bird In Flight, Dark Blue, Black, White, Signed, Edvin Ohrstrom, 1937, 7 In. 8400.00
Vase, Crosshatched Panels, Flared, Oval, Ingeborg Lundin, c.1960, 15 3/4 In. 880.00
Vase, Crystal, Nude Woman, Sitting Holding Baby, Signed, Vicke Lindstrand, 10 In. 5400.00
Vase, Fish Graal, Deep Amethyst Seahorses, Seaweed, 1937, 7 In. 5465.00
Vase, Horse, Purple, Yellow, Orange, Black Ground, Signed, Jan Johansson, 7 In. 5465.00
Vase, Light Turquoise Glass, Signed, Ingeborg Lundin, 1960, 7 In. 3300.00
Vase, Serpentine Panels On Ends & Corners, Signed, 1930, 3 3/4 In. 145.00
Vase, Shark Killer, Pale Yellow, Signed, Vicke Lindstrand, 1937, 12 1/2 In. 13800.00
Vase, Slip Graal, Signed, 1940, 8 1/8 In. 3900.00
Vase, Spherical, Fish Swimming In Seaweed, Edvard Hald, c.1962, 4 3/4 In. 2250.00

OTT & BREWER Company operated the Etruria Pottery at Trenton,
New Jersey, from 1863 to 1893. They started making belleek in 1882.
The firm used a variety of marks that incorporated the initials *O & B*.

Bowl, Scalloped & Curled Rim, Flowering Stalks, Belleek, 4 1/4 In. 109.00
Cup & Saucer, Bouillon, Eggshell China, Pink Interior, 2 1/2 x 6 In. 132.00
Jar, Parrot Tulips, Brown On Cream Ground, 2 Handles, 7 1/4 x 5 1/2 In. 35.00
Pitcher, Gold Leaves, White Ground, Twig Handle, 6 3/8 In. 165.00
Pitcher, Thistle Design, Gold Finish, Handle, 5 1/2 In. 210.00

OVERBECK pottery was made by four sisters named Overbeck at a pottery in Cambridge City, Indiana. They started in 1911. They made all
types of vases, each one-of-a-kind. Small, hand-modeled figurines are
the most popular pieces with today's collectors. The factory continued
until 1955, when the last of the four sisters died.

Chalice, Camels & Mountains, Yellow, Gunmetal Glaze, Raspberry Ground, 3 In. 1687.00
Figurine, Colonial Woman, Pink & Blue Striped Dress, Signed, 5 In. 310.00
Figurine, Entire Orchestra, Yellow, Pink, Green, White Glaze, 4 1/2 In., 7 Piece 2360.00
Figurine, Fisherman, 5 1/8 In. 1450.00
Figurine, Gentleman Teeing Off, Signed, 4 In. 1430.00
Figurine, Southern Belle, Long Dress, Hat, Signed, 4 1/2 In. 190.00
Figurine, Tortoise, Barney Google, 1 1/2 x 3 3/4 & 3 1/4 x 3 In., 2 Piece 395.00
Tea Set, Stylized Lily Of The Valley, Cuerda Seca, Celadon Matte Ground, 5 x 9 In. 2475.00
Tumbler, Green Crickets, Beige Ground, 3 3/4 x 3 In., 4 Piece 1460.00
Vase, Aqua Green High Gloss Glaze, 10 In. 1100.00
Vase, Multitoned Brown Ground, Initials, E.F., 4 In. 1760.00
Vase, Purple, Brown Paneled Design, Floral Design, Slate Gray, Signed, 7 1/2 In. 5465.00

OWENS Pottery was made in Zanesville, Ohio, from 1891 to 1928. The first art pottery was made after 1896. Utopian Ware, Cyrano, Navarre, Feroza, and Henri Deux were made. Pieces were usually marked with a form of the name *Owens*. About 1907, the firm began to make tile and discontinued the art pottery wares.

Bowl, Feroza, Embossed, Lustered Gold Glaze, Squat, Handles, 7 1/2 x 13 1/2 In.	520.00
Jug, Utopian, 5 1/2 In.	225.00
Mug, Cherries & Leaves, Matte Finish, 5 In.	55.00
Pitcher, 3 Tulips, Yellow, Rust, Green, Zanesville, Ohio, 12 1/4 In.	345.00
Tile, 3-Leaf Design, Green Matte Glaze	330.00
Tile, Gold Tulip, Crown Design, Green Matte Glaze, Square, 6 In.	330.00
Tile, Landscape Scene, Trees, Cuenca, Green, Brown, Blue, Wooden Frame, 11 In.	1380.00
Vase, Amber Wild Rose, 13 x 6 1/2 In.	320.00
Vase, Bottle Shape, Leaves, Brown Bisque Ground, Impressed 1010, 10 1/2 In.	230.00
Vase, Bulbous Bottle Shape, Riblike Panels, Green Matte Glaze, Stamped, 4 1/2 In.	320.00
Vase, English Ivy, Harry Larzelere, 3 In.	90.00
Vase, Henri Deux, Orange, Blue Irises, Dark Brown Ground, 10 3/4 x 5 3/4 In.	230.00
Vase, Utopian, Bottle Shape, Spaniel Portrait, Blue, Gray Ground, 16 1/4 x 6 1/2 In.	1265.00
Vase, Utopian, Ivy Design, Black Ground, 3 In.	88.00
Vase, Yellow Wild Roses, Green, Brown Leaves, 12 1/2 x 4 In.	345.00

OYSTER PLATES were popular from the 1880s. Each course at dinner was served in a special dish. The oyster plate had indentations shaped like oysters. Usually six oysters were held on a plate. There is no greater value to a plate with more oysters, although that myth continues to haunt antiques dealers. There are other plates for shellfish, including cockle plates and whelk plates. The appropriately shaped indentations are part of the design of these dishes.

5 Seawater Wells, Gold Edging, Starfish Century, 1919, 8 In.	265.00
5 Wells, Blue Feather Scroll Rims, Yellow Centers	135.00
5 Wells, Seaweed Design, Limoges, 8 1/2 In.	395.00
5 Wells, Water Lily, Holdcroft	2420.00
6 Wells, Center Aqua Well, Late 19th Century, 9 In., 12 Piece	630.00
6 Wells, Gold Design, White Porcelain, Vienna Mark	145.00
6 Wells, Majolica, Sarreguemines, 9 1/4 In.	155.00
6 Wells, Sauce Center, Oyster, Clam & Seaweed., Majolica, 9 1/2 In.	517.00
6 Wells, Scalloped Rim, Rose To White, 8 In.	135.00
24 Wells, Quimper, 16 1/2 In.	405.00
Basket Weave, Pink, Blue, Porcelain, 1900, 9 1/4 In.	100.00
Faux Shells Surrounding Sauce Well, c.1880, 10 Piece	1380.00
Fish Heads, Brown Back, Majolica, 10 In.	195.00
Lemon Wedge Center, Majolica, Mid Twentieth Century, 10 In., 8 Piece	895.00
Pink Roses, White Ground, 1940, 5 In.	45.00
Raised Floral Design, Zigzag, Orange Peel Ground, Wedgwood, 1866, 9 In.	1495.00
Seawater Green Wells, Leaf Sprays, Haviland, 9 In.	345.00

PADEN CITY Glass Manufacturing Company was established in 1916 at Paden City, West Virginia. The company made more than seventy different colors of glass. The firm closed in 1951. Paden City Pottery is not listed here.

American Rose, Bowl, Fruit	11.00
American Rose, Cup & Saucer	8.00 to 15.00
American Rose, Plate, Dinner, 9 1/4 In.	16.00
Ardith, Cake Plate, Pink, Footed, 9 In.	125.00 to 135.00
Ardith, Candlestick, Black, 5 3/4 In.	95.00
Ardith, Candlestick, Green, 5 3/4 In.	95.00
Ardith, Candy Dish, Cover, Square, Green	150.00
Ardith, Creamer, Black	65.00
Ardith, Cup, Yellow	35.00
Ardith, Vase, Black, Cupped, 5 In.	150.00
Ardith, Vase, Pink, 8 In.	250.00
Black Forest, Bowl, Black, 11 In.	170.00
Black Forest, Bowl, Green, 13 In.	250.00

Black Forest, Candlestick, Pink, Pair	125.00
Black Forest, Compote, Green, Diadem Stem, 5 1/4 In.	40.00
Black Forest, Console, Black, 11 In.	170.00
Black Forest, Console, Green, 13 In.	250.00
Black Forest, Vase, Black, Squat, 6 1/2 In.	175.00
Black Forest, Vase, Green, 10 In.	300.00
Crow's Foot, Bowl, 2 Handles, Red, Square, 8 1/2 In.	50.00
Crow's Foot, Bowl, Oval, Red, 11 In.	40.00
Crow's Foot, Compote, 6 1/2 In.	25.00
Crow's Foot, Cup & Saucer, Red	19.00
Crow's Foot, Sugar & Creamer, Red	35.00
Cupid, Bowl, Rolled Rim, Pink, 10 1/2 In.	350.00
Cupid, Cake Stand, Green	245.00
Cupid, Creamer, Footed, Pink, 5 In.	175.00
Cupid, Ice Tub, Green, 4 3/4 In.	295.00
Figurine, Barnyard Rooster, Dark Blue, 8 1/4 In.	550.00
Figurine, Chinese Pheasant, 13 1/2 In.	260.00
Figurine, Pony, 11 1/2 In.	225.00
Figurine, Rearing Horse, 8 1/4 In.	200.00
Gazebo, Candlestick, 2-Light	65.00
Gothic Garden, Console, Footed, Yellow, 9 In.	125.00
Largo, Bowl, Red, Flared, Footed, 12 In.	175.00
Lela Bird, Cake Plate, Green, 10 In.	125.00
Nora Bird, Candlestick, Pink, Pair	125.00
Peacock & Wild Rose, Berry Bowl, Green, 8 1/2 In.	300.00
Peacock & Wild Rose, Candlestick, Green, 5 In., Pair	100.00
Peacock & Wild Rose, Compote, Pink, 3 1/4 In.	175.00
Peacock & Wild Rose, Dish, Mayonnaise, Underplate, Ladle, Green	250.00
Peacock & Wild Rose, Sugar & Creamer	125.00
Peacock & Wild Rose, Vase, Elliptical, Pink, 8 1/4 In.	550.00
Penny, Tumbler, Iced Tea, Red, 12 Oz.	23.00
Utopia, Vase, 10 In.	150.00
Utopia, Vase, Black, 10 In.	195.00

PAINTINGS listed in this book are not works by major artists but rather decorative paintings on ivory, board, or glass that would be of interest to the average collector. Watercolors on paper are listed under Picture. To learn the value of an oil painting by a listed artist you must contact an expert in that area.

Oil On Board, Boathouse On Belle Isle, Edgar Yaeger, 1961, 12 7/8 x 16 5/8 In.	200.00
Oil On Board, Castle On Island, William Trost Richards, 1896, 5 1/2 x 8 3/4 In.	3850.00
Oil On Board, Chrysanthemums In Vase, W. Noyeri, 15 3/8 x 12 1/2 In.	170.00
Oil On Board, European Tavern Scene, Gilt Frame, 8 1/2 x 10 1/4 In.	70.00
Oil On Board, Gloucester Shipyard Scene, Henrietta Sanderson, 19 3/4 x 15 3/4 In.	1980.00
Oil On Board, Great Egg Harbor Shores, Franklin Dullin Brisco, 1900, 7 1/4 x 13 1/2 In.	2530.00
Oil On Board, Harbor At Sunset, Man & Woman, Continental, Frame, 17 x 18 In.	190.00
Oil On Board, Landscape, Beach Scene, Peter Jamison, 20th Century, 29 x 45 In.	550.00
Oil On Board, Landscape, City Scene, Pearl Tussing, Frame, 1957, 28 3/4 x 22 1/2 In.	110.00
Oil On Board, Landscape, New England, Bridge, Frame, 15 3/4 x 21 3/4 In.	70.00
Oil On Board, Mediterranean Courtyard, A. Kinsey, Frame, 16 7/8 x 13 3/4 In.	1100.00
Oil On Board, Rocky Cliffs, William Trost Richards, Signed, c.1900, 5 1/2 x 8 3/4 In.	4400.00
Oil On Board, Saint George, Slaying Dragon, Russia, 34 1/2 x 24 1/2 In.	330.00
Oil On Board, Sotter House From Rear Garden, Charles Hargens, 1968, 12 x 16 In.	2090.00
Oil On Board, Still Life, Flowers, Frame, 13 1/2 x 8 1/4 In.	55.00
Oil On Board, Still Life, Fruit Basket, Wilhelmige Loes, Late Frame, 12 3/4 x 20 In.	330.00
Oil On Board, W. Manayunk Winter Scene, Antonio P. Martino, 7 1/4 x 11 1/4 In.	1650.00
Oil On Board, Winter Landscape, Karl Larsen, Signed, 24 x 26 In.	290.00
Oil On Board, Woman, Black Dress, Ruffled Collar, Frame, 21 1/2 x 14 1/2 In.	660.00
Oil On Board, Woman, Dark Eyes, Ruffled Bonnet, Frame, 1840, 14 x 11 In.	3600.00
Oil On Board, Wooded Landscape, Anne Barber Seither, 13 1/2 x 9 1/2 In.	275.00
Oil On Canvas, 3 Kittens, Playing, Schebelae, Gold Frame, 16 3/4 x 11 In.	240.00
Oil On Canvas, 3 White Sheep, Barn, Chickens, W. Michal, Gilt Frame, 20 1/2 x 8 1/4 In.	630.00
Oil On Canvas, Apple Tree Study, Signed L.M. Wiles, Frame, 22 x 16 In.	7975.00

Oil On Canvas, Barnyard Scene, J.M. Barnsley, Canada, 9 x 12 1/4 In. 770.00
Oil On Canvas, Bearded Man, White Hood, Ornate Frame, 20 x 16 In. 220.00
Oil On Canvas, Bluebonnets Blooming In Texas, I. Shipley, Frame, 21 1/2 x 28 1/2 In. ... 190.00
Oil On Canvas, Cattle With Goat In Meadow, Merle, 19 1/8 x 25 3/8 In. 920.00
Oil On Canvas, Child, Red After Play, Mary Spencer Nay, 1940, Frame, 44 1/4 x 34 12 In. 192.00
Oil On Canvas, Classical Pastoral Scene, Gilt Frame, 18 1/4 x 24 In. 880.00
Oil On Canvas, Country Scene, River, Marbleized Frame, 20 x 30 In. 300.00
Oil On Canvas, Cows Watering At Mountain Lake, J.M. Hart, 9 x 16 In. 5600.00
Oil On Canvas, European Scene, Woman Walking, Frame, C. Kustech, 12 x 24 In. 190.00
Oil On Canvas, Fishing Boat In Harbor, L. De Bury, Frame, 5 1/2 x 8 12 In. 260.00
Oil On Canvas, Fishing Boats, Choppy Sea, French Flag, Frame, 25 3/4 x 30 In. 1210.00
Oil On Canvas, Landscape, Jacques Cordier, 13 x 18 In. 140.00
Oil On Canvas, Landscape, John M. Strange, Frame, 1930, 31 3/4 x 39 1/2 In. 325.00
Oil On Canvas, Landscape, Lake, Mountain, Cabin & Trees, Frame, 32 x 46 In. 135.00
Oil On Canvas, Landscape, Virginia Lee Kiser, Frame, 25 1/2 x 20 1/2 In. 220.00
Oil On Canvas, Maison Sur La Cote, Remy E. Landeau, 24 x 19 3/4 In. 1725.00
Oil On Canvas, Man Herding Sheep & Cows, Gilt Frame, Gesso Liner, 42 x 27 In. 800.00
Oil On Canvas, Man, Overcoat, Top Hat, Inside Shop, Frame, 20 x 16 In. 1015.00
Oil On Canvas, Mediterranean Harbor, Men, Nets, J. Bowman, Frame, 9 x 16 In. 410.00
Oil On Canvas, Merchant, John Wainwright Of Liverpool, Frame, 30 x 25 In. 990.00
Oil On Canvas, Niagara Falls, Primitive, 1900, 12 5/8 x 10 1/8 In. 130.00
Oil On Canvas, Old Beau, Man, Coat, Floral Vest, K. Peake, Frame, 30 x 23 In. 495.00
Oil On Canvas, Picking Flowers, Jean Beauduin, 28 3/4 x 21 1/2 In. 8625.00
Oil On Canvas, Portrait, Boy, Large White Collar, Oval, Walnut Frame, 19 3/4 x 16 In. ... 355.00
Oil On Canvas, Roman Forum, Marc Chapaud, Signed, 29 x 36 In. 170.00
Oil On Canvas, Sailboat In Cover, Tindale, Frame, 12 x 18 In. 375.00
Oil On Canvas, Seated Young Woman Holding Book, A. Hanan, c.1810, 29 1/2 x 23 In. .. 3080.00
Oil On Canvas, Sheep Being Herded Toward Barn, Frame, 11 1/4 x 17 1/2 In. 10.00
Oil On Canvas, Still Life With Vase Of Flowers, Moses Boyer, Frame, 16 x 30 In. 3500.00
Oil On Canvas, Still Life, Fruit, Bread, Wine, H. Strauser, Oak Frame, 20 x 24 In. 220.00
Oil On Canvas, Still Life, Fruit, Carnations, Goblet, Frame, 10 x 13 1/4 In. 190.00
Oil On Canvas, Still Life, Peaches, Falling From Basket, Gessoed Frame, 21 x 17 In. 110.00
Oil On Canvas, Still Life, Pitcher & Tumbler, A. Volton, Frame, 22 x 18 3/8 In. 1056.00
Oil On Canvas, Still Life, Seashells, Black Beads, Frame, 8 x 16 In. 300.00
Oil On Canvas, Sunset, Horse, Wagon, Christopher Shearer, 14 1/2 x 24 1/2 In. 1540.00
Oil On Canvas, Winter Scene, Birch Trees, Brook, C. Gordon Harris, 25 x 30 In. 1220.00
Oil On Canvas, Woman Portrait, Black Mourning Pin, Envelope, 30 x 24 1/2 In. 550.00
Oil On Canvas, Young Woman, Blond, Carl Kabler, Frame, 15 1/2 x 11 1/2 In. 355.00
Oil On Cardboard, Rustic Cabin, Thatched Roof, Lake, Frame, 8 5/8 x 19 3/8 In. 27.00
Oil On Masonite, Cows In Fields, William Watson, 15 1/2 x 19 1/4 In. 385.00
Oil On Masonite, Dancers, In Garden Landscape, Richard A. Chase, Frame, 12 x 16 In. .. 165.00
Oil On Muslin, Mother, Child & Lamb, France, 1700s, 36 x 25 In. 1200.00
Oil On Panel, Man, Green Coat, Feathered Hat, Frame, Germany, 7 1/8 x 5 3/8 In. 85.00
Oil On Panel, Man, Woman, Soldiers, With Candle, Frame, 11 x 8 7/8 In. 1100.00
Oil On Panel, Margaret Countess Of Cumberland, Zuccaro, Frame, 23 x 16 In. 3575.00
Oil On Panel, Physician Examining Woman, Holland, Painted Frame, 12 1/8 x 10 In. 2750.00
Oil On Panel, Still Life, Roses In Bowl, Signed, Ann Elizabeth Hardy, 8 x 10 In. 1650.00
Oil On Panel, Still Life, Strawberries & Radishes, Revarnished, Gilt Frame, 8 x 12 In. ... 575.00
Oil On Panel, Woman, Blond, Pearls In Hair, Gilt Frame, 13 x 10 1/2 In. 440.00
Oil On Tin, Dentist, Pulling Boy's Tooth, Dutch Scene, Frame, 9 7/8 x 8 1/4 In. 1265.00
On Ivory, 2 Sisters Holding Bouquet Of Roses & Bird, Gilt Metal Frame, 2 1/2 In. 170.00
On Ivory, 6 Children In Wagon, Shadowbox Frame, 4 1/4 x 4 1/4 In. 770.00
On Ivory, Abraham Lincoln, Cosway Black, Frame, 5 1/4 x 4 1/4 In. 1200.00
On Ivory, Andrew Jackson, Military Uniform, Wood Frame, 8 x 2 1/4 In. 315.00
On Ivory, Anne Nichole Of Courtison, Francois, 2 1/2 x 3 1/2 In. 60.00
On Ivory, Christ, Crowned With Thorns, Image Of Saint Verso, Silver Frame, 1 3/4 In. ... 155.00
On Ivory, Elegant Woman, Basket Of Fruit, Hair Compartment, 1 1/2 In. 145.00
On Ivory, Elegant Woman, Gold Armlet, Paisley Shawl, Mid 19th Century, 4 1/8 In. 460.00
On Ivory, Gainsborough's Blue Boy, Sterling Silver Frame, 2 1/2 x 3 1/2 In. 70.00
On Ivory, Gentleman, Black Coat, Neckerchief, Gilt Frame, Early 19th Century, 5 5/8 In. .. 345.00
On Ivory, Gentleman, Frock Coat, Brass Frame, 2 3/4 x 2 1/8 In. 550.00
On Ivory, Gentleman, White Hair, Blue Jacket, 4 7/8 x 4 1/4 In. 330.00
On Ivory, George & Martha Washington, Mother-Of-Pearl Frame, 5 1/2 x 5 In. 210.00

On Ivory, George Washington, Ivory Frame, 4 1/4 x 5 In. 120.00
On Ivory, George Washington, Lacquer Frame, Acorn Hanger, 5 3/4 x 5 In. 1200.00
On Ivory, Harvest Scene, Hay Wagon Drawn By Horses, Workers Relaxing, 3 x 5 In. 190.00
On Ivory, Lord Nelson, 4 1/2 x 5 1/2 In. 155.00
On Ivory, Margaret Scott, White Cape, Rose Gold Surround, Hair Receptacle, 3 1/4 In. . . 3740.00
On Ivory, Naval Officer, Military Dress, Oval, First Half 19th Century, 3 1/4 x 2 3/4 In. . . 2875.00
On Ivory, Officer, Blue Coat, Ed Lapes, Gold Epaulettes, Lacquered Frame, 5 1/2 In. 825.00
On Ivory, Taj Mahal, 3 1/2 x 5 1/4 In. 345.00
On Ivory, Woman In Profile, Head Wrap & Shawl, Beaded Frame, 2 3/4 x 2 1/4 In. 460.00
On Ivory, Woman, Black Cap, Black Dress, Late 19th Century, 2 5/8 x 2 In. 290.00
On Ivory, Woman, Elegant Dress, Choker, Pulled Back Hair, Bronze Frame, 6 1/4 In. 260.00
On Ivory, Woman, Inlaid Ivory Frame, 1 1/2 x 2 In. 125.00
On Ivory, Woman, Jewelry, Mother-Of-Pearl Frame, Oval, Daffinger, 3 x 2 1/2 In. 250.00
On Ivory, Woman, On Recamier, Watercolor, Brass Frame, 5 3/4 x 6 7/8 In. 330.00
On Ivory, Young Girl Knitting, Braided Hair, Red & Gilt Jewelry, Brass Liner, 4 5/8 In. . . 1210.00
On Ivory, Young Man, Blue Coat, White Waistcoat, Wood Frame, 2 5/8 In. 460.00
On Ivory, Young Man, Frock Coat, Waistcoat, Lacquered Frame, 5 1/2 x 4 3/8 In. 2310.00
On Ivory, Young Man, White Ruffled Collar, Lacquered Frame, 4 3/4 x 4 In. 385.00
On Ivory, Young Woman, Dark Blue Dress, Landscape, Mid 19th Century, 3 3/8 In. 520.00
On Paper, Rustam In Combat With Demon, Frame, Persian, 11 x 6 1/2 In. 200.00
On Porcelain, Michelangelo's Winged Angel, Gilt Frame, Oval, 2 3/4 x 3 1/4 In. 60.00
On Porcelain, Woman, F. Micklewright, 4 1/2 x 6 1/4 In. 115.00
On Porcelain, Woman, Hartense, Bronze Frame, Marked, 3 1/2 x 3 In. 130.00
On Porcelain, Young Woman, White Shawl, 8 x 5 1/2 In. 2750.00
On Tin, Young Girl, Holding Flowers, Locket, Behind Curved Glass, 6 1/4 x 4 1/8 In. . . . 470.00
On Velvet, Landscape, Round, Classical Motifs, Giltwood Frame, 2 1/2 x 17 x 20 In. 518.00
On Velvet, People Animals On Steps To Water, Art Deco, 34 x 54 In. 175.00
Reverse On Glass, 2 Women, Basket Of Flowers, Chinese Export Porcelain, 17 1/2 In. 2185.00
Reverse On Glass, Cherubs Blowing Bubbles, 9 1/2 x 8 In. 535.00
Reverse On Glass, Children, Frame, Beaded Liner, Chinese, 14 x 9 1/2 In., Pair 220.00
Reverse On Glass, Drugstore Urn, Lid, Gold Mortar & Pestle Design, 26 In. 3960.00
Reverse On Glass, Harding, Flags In Background, Frame, 9 1/2 x 11 1/2 In. 350.00
Reverse On Glass, Hunting Scene, Silhouette, Black, Frame, 14 x 20 In., Pair 905.00
Reverse On Glass, Panels, Bust Of Woman, Tracery Border, 18 1/2 x 15 1/2 In. 490.00
Reverse On Glass, Silhouette, Revelers In Horse Drawn Carriage, Maple Frame, 7 3/4 In. . 440.00
Reverse On Glass, Washington, Seated, Full Uniform, Sword, Frame, 12 x 9 3/8 In. 1265.00
Reverse On Glass, Woman, Holds Flowers, July, Act Of Parliament, Frame, 18 x 10 In. . . 220.00

PAIRPOINT Manufacturing Company started in 1880 in New Bedford, Massachusetts. It soon joined with the glassworks nearby and made glass, silver-plated pieces, and lamps. Reverse-painted glass shades and molded shades known as *puffies* were part of the production until the 1930s. The company reorganized and changed its name several times but is still working today. Items listed here are glass or glass and metal. Silver-plated pieces are listed under Silver Plate.

Biscuit Jar, Gold Poppy & Leaves, Beige, 9 x 8 In. 460.00
Biscuit Jar, Landscape, Cherubs Wrestling, Barrel Shape, Signed, 7 1/2 In. 345.00
Biscuit Jar, Purple, Pink Chrysanthemums, Yellow, Signed, 9 In. 1035.00
Bowl, Swan, 10 1/2 In. 115.00
Bowl, Swan, Deep Rosaria, 12 x 12 1/2 In. 230.00
Box, Dresser, Pearl, 3 x 7 In. 480.00
Candlestick, Engraved Flowers & Leaves, Cobalt Blue Base, 16 In., Pair 1900.00
Candlestick, Putti, Holding Candlecup, 16 In. 605.00
Carafe, Adonis, 7 In. 155.00
Compote, Engraved Bouquet Of Flowers, Signed, 8 x 5 In. 230.00
Compote, Engraved Swags Of Flowers, Leaves, Cobalt Blue Stem, 9 1/2 x 8 3/4 In. 575.00
Console Set, Engraved Bouquet Of 3 Flowers, 12-In. Bowl, 3 Piece 575.00
Decanter, Nevada, Stopper, 12 1/2 In. 385.00
Decanter, Ruby, Bubble Ball Stopper, Sterling Silver Overlay, 10 In. 1265.00
Epergne, Engraved Garland With Roses 675.00
Hat, White Brim, Enameled Daisies & Flowers, Signed Also, 3 x 4 1/2 In. 150.00
Jewelry Box, Murillo, Silver Plated Cover, 8 1/4 x 4 In. 710.00
Lamp, Berkely Shade, Pineapple Base, Signed, 21 1/2 In. 1207.00

Lamp, Berkely Shade, River Scene, Men Canoeing, Trees, Full Moon, 16 In. 4200.00
Lamp, Berkely Shade, Rose Blossoms, Black Ground, 20 In. 6720.00
Lamp, Candle, Puffy, Red, Yellow Roses, Windsor, 16 1/2 In., Pair 5750.00
Lamp, Carlisle Shade, Garden Of Allah, Arabs & Camels, Sandy Desert, Village, 22 In. .. 4095.00
Lamp, Carlisle Shade, Jungle Bird, 2 Parrots Perched On Branch, 18 In. 4760.00
Lamp, Copley Shade, Sea Gull, Matching Glass Base, 26 In. 6900.00
Lamp, Exeter Shade, Exotic Birds, Floral Blossoms, 20 In. 6160.00
Lamp, Exeter Shade, Panels Representing 4 Seasons, 16 In. 4480.00
Lamp, Garden Of Allah, Arabs & Camels, Sandy Desert, Village, 16 In. 13440.00
Lamp, Lansdowne Shade, House & Fields, 15 In. 3380.00
Lamp, Palermo Shade, Purple, Lavender, Lilac, Green Leaves, Signed, 23 In. 7475.00
Lamp, Puffy, Azalea, Pink, Red Blooms, Deep Green, Variegated Leaves, 10 In. 38640.00
Lamp, Puffy, Azalea, Red Blooms Amidst Green Leaves, Dark Green Ground, 10 In. 22400.00
Lamp, Puffy, Begonia Blossoms, 16 In. ....*Illus* 67200.00
Lamp, Puffy, Bonnett Shade, Four Color Rose, Signed, 5 In. 8960.00
Lamp, Puffy, Bouquet, Pink, Red, White Rose Blossoms, Deep Green, Signed, 10 In. 21280.00
Lamp, Puffy, Hummingbird & Purple Roses, Mauve, Black Ground, 14 In. 11760.00
Lamp, Puffy, Hummingbird & Roses, Puffy, c.1910, 21 1/2 In. 9775.00
Lamp, Puffy, Lilac, Butterflies, Turquoise Border, Tree Trunk Base, Signed, 5 In. 16240.00
Lamp, Puffy, Lilac, Multicolored, Tree Trunk Base, 8 In. 39200.00
Lamp, Puffy, Lilac, Multicolored, Yellow Butterfly, Tree Trunk Base, 5 In. 24080.00
Lamp, Puffy, Lotus Blossoms, Pink Highlights, Deep Green Ground, 10 In. 11760.00
Lamp, Puffy, Multicolored Poppy Blossoms, Orange Red, Yellow, 12 In. 30800.00
Lamp, Puffy, Pansy, Multicolored, Green, Signed Base, 5 In. 16800.00
Lamp, Puffy, Papillion Butterfly & Roses Shade, Closed Top, Signed, 21 In. 10725.00
Lamp, Puffy, Papillion Butterfly & Roses Shade, Multicolored Blossoms, 8 In. . .3360.00 to 8400.00
Lamp, Puffy, Pink, Red Blossoms, Green Leafage, 9 In. 9520.00
Lamp, Puffy, Portsmouth Shade, Floral Blossoms, Green, 8 In. 4200.00
Lamp, Puffy, Red Poppy, Base Signed, 7 In. 2800.00
Lamp, Puffy, Reverse Painted, Floral Garlands, Brass Base, 21 In. 7360.00
Lamp, Puffy, Reverse Painted, Multicolored Roses, Signed, 10 In. 3360.00
Lamp, Puffy, Roses, Black Glass Base, 9 In. 355.00
Lamp, Puffy, Stratford Shade, Floral, Black Ground, 9 In. 3920.00
Lamp, Puffy, Stratford Shade, Roses, Hummingbirds, Signed, 14 In. 7280.00
Lamp, Puffy, Stratford Shade, Roses, Mums, Lattice Border, 14 In. 2070.00
Lamp, Puffy, White Grapes, Silver Plated Grape Base, 12 In. 17920.00
Lamp, Puffy, White, Purple Dogwood, Green, Turquoise Leaves, Ambero, Signed, 16 In. .. 3165.00
Lamp, Puffy, Yellow, Red Roses, Variegated Green, White Leaves, 10 In. 24192.00
Lamp, Reverse Painted Shade, Colorful Leaves, Dome Shape, Green, 10 In. 2240.00
Lamp, Reverse Painted, Fall Harvest Scene, Signed, 18 In. 3630.00
Lamp, Reverse Painted, Farm Scene, Signed, 22 In. 2300.00
Lamp, Reverse Painted, Garden Of Allah, Pyramid Scene, Camel & Arab, Pink, 18 In. ... 4480.00
Lamp, Reverse Painted, Italian Landscape, Urn Form, Signed, c.1915, 26 In. 1840.00
Lamp, Reverse Painted, Leaves, Orange Ground, 10 In. 3192.00
Lamp, Reverse Painted, New England Farm Scene, Hay Stacks, 17 In. 2875.00
Lamp, Reverse Painted, New England Scene, Signed, c.1900, 22 1/2 In. 3025.00
Lamp, Reverse Painted, Summer Landscape, Trees, Signed, 23 In. 4255.00

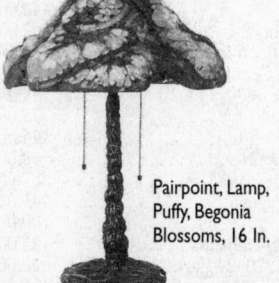

Pairpoint, Lamp,
Puffy, Begonia
Blossoms, 16 In.

Your string of pearls just broke and the pearls are bouncing on the floor. Try this method of finding them. Take the head from the end of the vacuum cleaner hose and slip one leg of a panty hose over the hose. Turn on the vacuum. The air will suck the beads into the vacuum hose but the stocking will prevent them from going into the dust bag.

Lamp, Reverse Painted, Tropical Birds & Floral Ground, Bronzed Base, 22 In.	3575.00
Lamp, Reverse Painted, Venetian Harbor Scene, Sailing Boats, 21 In.	2645.00 to 8625.00
Lamp, Reverse Painted, Winter Landscape, Signed, 8 1/2 In.	980.00
Lamp, Reverse Painted, Women In 18th Century Attire, Signed, 24 In.	1380.00
Lamp, Slag Glass, Filigree, Square Bronze Base, Signed, 22 1/2 In.	1045.00
Lamp, Venice, Floral, Stylized Tulips, Metal Base, Shade & Base Signed, 12 In.	7840.00
Paperweight, 5 Ice Pick Bubbles, Blue, White, Cranberry, 5 1/2 x 3 In.	345.00
Paperweight, 5 Ice Pick Bubbles, Pedestal, 5 1/2 x 3 1/2 In.	517.00
Paperweight, Red Spiral Swirl, Controlled Bubble Design, 2 1/2 In.	48.00
Pitcher, Burmese, Applied Handle, Ribbed, 2 1/2 In.	125.00
Punch Bowl Base, 20 Point Hobstar, 14 1/2 x 12 1/2 In.	920.00
Shade, Puffy, 4 Different Colored Tulips, Variegated Red, Rose, Yellow, 15 3/4 In.	9430.00
Shade, Puffy, Hummingbird & Roses, Yellow, White Lattice, Yellow Top, 23 In.	6900.00
Shade, Puffy, Papillion Butterfly & Roses, White, Red, 22 x 14 In.	4887.00
Shade, Puffy, Rose Tree Shade, Yellow, Pink Roses, Yellow, Blue Butterflies, 10 In.	5175.00
Shade, Puffy, Stratford Shade, Blue, Rose Apple Blossoms, Roses, Signed, 15 In.	3738.00
Shade, Roma, Landing Of The Pilgrims Scene, Floral, Signed, 15 x 26 3/4 In.	6900.00
Sugar & Creamer, Lucania Pattern	135.00
Toothpick, Burmese, Hand Painted, Signed, 2 In.	150.00
Tureen, Cover, Soup, Stand, Lilies, Leaves, Curling Tendrils, c.1900, 18 3/4 In.	2015.00
Vase, Amethyst Swirls, 10 1/2 In.	168.00
Vase, Clear Bubble Stem, Polished Pontil, Engraved Vintage On Bowl, 11 In., Pair	635.00
Vase, Garden Of Allah Design, 2 Camels, 2 Arabs, Ivory Ground, Handles, 15 In.	575.00

PALMER COX, BROWNIES, see Brownies category.

PAPER collectibles, including almanacs, catalogs, children's books, some greeting cards, stock certificates, and other paper ephemera, are listed here. Paper calendars are listed separately in the Calendar category. Paper items may be found in many other sections, such as Christmas and Movie.

Almanac, Boston, Hand Colored Folding Map, 1852, 168 Pages	45.00
Bank Note, $100, Ohio River Bank, Marietta, Ohio, 1880s	185.00
Banner, Louisiana, The Pelican State, Red & White, 1939, 3 x 7 1/2 In.	7.00
Baptismal Certificate, Flickenger Family, Hand Colored, Praying Child, 1810, 16 x 13 In.	715.00
Book, Autograph, Barbie, Snips 'n Scrapes, Black, Vinyl, c.1962, 13 1/2 x 11 In.	88.00
Book, Big Little Book, Kay & Moon Mullins	50.00
Book, Big Little Book, Story Of Skippy, Phillips Dental Magnesia Giveaway, 1929	45.00
Book, Big Little Book, The Lone Ranger & His Horse Silver, Whitman, 1935	45.00
Book, Little Golden Book, Smokey Bear & The Campers, No. 423, 1971	10.00
Book, Little Golden Book, The Three Bears, Feodor Rojankovsky, 2nd Cover, 1948	10.00
Book, Pop-Up, Minnie Mouse, Walt Disney, 1933	355.00
Book, Pop-Up, Puss-In-Boots, Blue Ribbon Press, 1934, 10 Pages	88.00
Booklet, Faultless Starch Co., Sallie Short & Lillie Long, Illustrated, 15 Pages	6.00
Booklet, Faultless Starch Co., The House That Jack Built, Illustrated, 15 Pages	6.00
Booklet, Faultless Starch Co., The Indians, Illustrated, 15 Pages	6.00
Booklet, Faultless Starch Co., The Starch Ghosts, Illustrated, 15 Pages	6.00
Bookplate, Engraved, Black & White, Curlews, 22 x 15 3/4 In.	35.00
Bookplate, Frederich Fricker, Dated—The Day Of May Anno D. 1829, 8 In.	330.00
Bookplate, Peter Rogdan, Dated 1823, 6 1/2 x 4 In.	440.00
Bookplate, Script In Brown Border, Schwenkfelder, 1812, 4 1/2 In.	302.00
Broadside, City Scavengers New Year's Address, Frame, 1836, 10 x 6 In.	259.00
Broadside, Poem, The Lamplighter, Sabine & Son, London, 19th Century, 19 x 14 In.	460.00
Calligraphy, Eagle, Penmanship By Thomas Eahniser, Peacocks, c.1870, 11 x 10 3/4 In.	138.00
Card, Admission, Mardi Gras, Rex Krewe, 1931, 3 1/2 x 6 In.	75.00
Card, Admission, Mardi Gras, Rex Krewe, Color 1 Side, 1891, 4 x 5 In.	125.00
Catalog, Barbie & Her Friends Wardrobe Booklet, Blue Cover, 1962	8.00
Catalog, Buck & Hickman, General Catalogue Of Tools & Supplies, 1935	87.00
Catalog, C.M. Mossman & Brother Horse Owners, c.1890, 304 Pages	145.00
Catalog, F.A.O. Schwartz, 1927, Christmas	100.00
Catalog, Fred Gretsch Mfg. Co., Brooklyn, 1912-1913, Musical Instruments	125.00
Catalog, Liberty & Company, Decoration, Fabrics & Fashion, c.1920, 24 Pages	20.00
Catalog, Mohr's, 1928, Toys For Boys & Girls, 16 Pages	175.00

Catalog, Montgomery Ward, 1920, Fall & Winter, 938 Pages 155.00
Catalog, S.C. Johnson & Son Wax, 1921; 32 Pages 10.00
Catalog, Schoenhut, 1918, Dolls, Games, Pianos, Accessories, 48 Pages 225.00
Catalog, Sears Roebuck, 1927, Fall & Winter 120.00
Coloring Book, Happy Days, Fonzie Cover, 1976 .... 10.00
Document, Signature, Abraham Lincoln, Ship's Passport, April 1865, Presidential Seal ... 9500.00
Family Record, Decost Family, Ink & Watercolor, Flowers, Frame, 13 x 16 In. 2300.00
Family Record, Phebe Wilson, Verse, Blue & White Chevron Border, Frame, 1803 ...... 145.00
Family Register, Stevens, Smith Family, Watercolor, Dover, N.H., 1823-1829, 13 x 16 In. 1610.00
Fraktur, Baptismal, Berks County, Martin Brechall, 1815, 11 x 16 1/2 In. 1375.00
Fraktur, Baptismal, Praying Children, Butterflies, Flowers, 1810, 16 x 13 In. 715.00
Fraktur, Bird Perched On Tulip, Blue Wing, Brown Body, Pa., 3 3/4 In. 525.00
Fraktur, Birth & Baptism, Peter Kaufmann, Ohio, 1833, 19 x 15 In. 605.00
Fraktur, Birth Announcement, Eliza Morrison, Born September 20, 1805, Frame 1650.00
Fraktur, Birth Certificate, Maria Vogel, 1821, Red, Yellow Tulip Border, 7 1/2 x 11 3/4 In. 880.00
Fraktur, Birth Of Jacob Miller, November 17, 1799, Maple Frame, 19 1/2 x 16 1/2 In. 110.00
Fraktur, Book, Sampler, Various Drawings, Signatures, Pa., 1764, 6 x 8 In., 24 Pages 385.00
Fraktur, Bookplate, Hoor Weber, 2 Birds, Dated 1844, 6 1/4 In. 4675.00
Fraktur, Bookplate, Ink & Watercolor On Woven Paper, Tulips, 5 1/8 In. 715.00
Fraktur, Central Printed Heart, Trailing Tulip Vines, Flowers, Pa., 1802, 12 1/2 x 15 In. .. 1650.00
Fraktur, Checkerboard Bird Perched On Branch, Blue, Red Flowers, 1845, 7 1/4 In. 1100.00
Fraktur, Flowers & Birds Tending Nest, Daniel Peterman, 1823, 13 x 15 In. 5100.00
Fraktur, Heart On Plinth, Women Standing In Clouds, 1800s, 10 x 8 In. 990.00
Fraktur, Hen, Rooster, White Bodies, Red, Yellow, Black Dots, Pa., 1858, 3 1/4 x 4 In. .. 770.00
Fraktur, History Of Frey Family, Red, Green, Blue, Yellow Swirled Vines, 1799, 15 In. .. 1540.00
Fraktur, Human Figures, Clock, Symbols, Sawtooth Border, Verse, 7 1/4 x 9 1/4 In. 770.00
Fraktur, Marriage, Georg Konrath & Margret Spack, 8 Children, Frame, 1857, 20 1/2 In. . 770.00
Fraktur, Mennonite, Hymn Script, Red, Blue, Green, Susanna Gehman, Penn., 1857 ..... 550.00
Fraktur, Orange, Green Flowering Branches, Pa., 1858, 7 3/4 x 6 In. 770.00
Fraktur, Printed, Hand Colored, Stylized Flowers, Johann Schuller, Penn., c.1812 .... 1540.00
Fraktur, Red, Black Striped Birds Perched, On Tulip Tree, Red, Yellow, Black, 1800, 7 In. 1650.00
Fraktur, Red, Yellow Bird Perched In Tulip Tree, Pa., 1825, 6 1/4 x 3 3/4 In. 1760.00
Fraktur, Songbook Plate, Central Black, Red, Yellow, Blue Flowers, Pa., 1825, 6 1/4 In. . 880.00
Fraktur, Stylized Red, Yellow, Black Tulip Tree, Black, Red Spotted Border, 1812, 6 In. . 605.00
Fraktur, Trailing Vines, Flowers, Bold Blue, Red, Yellow, Pa., 1786, 8 x 13 In. 2310.00
Fraktur, Trailing Vines, Flowers, Ribbon Border, Red Dots, 1829, 8 x 12 In. 825.00
Fraktur, Watercolor & Ink, Isaac Becker, December 15, 1860, 13 x 15 1/2 In. 110.00
Fraktur, Watercolor, Bible Verse, Maria Heiser-Skippack, Frame, 1843, 8 x 3 In. 302.00
Fraktur, Watercolor, Double Headed Bird, Blue Beaks, Green, 1812, 7 3/4 x 6 3/4 In. ... 3850.00
Fraktur & Baptismal, Catherine Bucher, Born 1826, Printed In English, Frame, 12 In. ... 1540.00
Fraktur & Baptismal, Frank Wishard, Born 1826, Barber Pole Border, 8 x 11 In. 550.00
House Blessing, Johannes Bertol, 1830, 13 1/4 x 12 In. 4950.00
House Blessing, Oil, Ink On Paper, Cartouche, Rose Wreath, Leaves, c.1870, 15 x 18 In. . 358.00
Invitation, Ball, Mardi Gras, Comus Krewe, Fold-Out, Feb. 11, 1901, 5 1/2 x 6 3/4 In. ... 200.00
Invitation, Ball, Mardi Gras, Knights Of Momus Krewe, Oval, Feb. 5, 1880, 6 x 7 In. 425.00
Label, Glacier National Park, See America First, Goat On Mountain, 1922, 4 3/4 In. 26.00
Land Document, Signed By Governor George Clinton, State Seal, 1789 .... 55.00
License, Saloon, Walkerville, Silver Bow County, Montana, 1894, 7 1/2 x 6 In. 150.00
License, Tobacco, Patriotic Woman, American Eagle, 1879, 7 x 14 In. 12.00
Magazine, Gleason's Pictorial, Navy, N.Y. Police, January 22, 1852 .... 12.00
Magazine, Life, April 26, 1937, White Leghorn Rooster 12.00
Magazine, Life, August 8, 1969, On The Moon 10.00
Magazine, Life, December 9, 1940, Ginger Rogers 15.00
Magazine, Life, February 8, 1943, Plane Spotter 10.00
Magazine, Life, September 11, 1939, Benito Mussolini 18.00
Magazine, Look, October 31, 1944, Bob Hope 8.00
Magazine, Newsweek, Duke & Duchess Of Windsor, Aug. 12, 1940 .... 6.00
Magazine, Police Gazette, April 1940, Carol Landis On Cover 10.00
Magazine, Popular Science, June, 1940, Future Automobiles 8.00
Magazine, Saturday Evening Post, December 6, 1943, Christmas 1943 .... 12.00
Magazine, Saturday Evening Post, January 2, 1926, New Year's Baby, J.C. Leyendecker .. 44.00
Magazine, Woman's Day, February 1944, Wartime Cooking 8.00
Magazine, Woman's Day, January 1943, Neighbors On The Home Front 8.00

Magazine, Woman's Day, November 1938, Child, Dog & Roast Turkey 7.00
Menu, Blum's, San Francisco, 1940s, 10 x 13 In., 8 Pages 30.00
Menu, Hotel Sir Francis Drake, United Airlines Plane, Feb. 27, 1941, 11 In., 4 Pages 21.00
Menu, Howard Johnson, Mineola, N.Y., April 26, 1940, 4 Pages, 8 1/2 x 11 In. 18.00
Menu, Lido Cafe, San Francisco, Art Deco Design, 1949 . . . . 28.00
Menu, Pfeiffer's Restaurant & Marine Grill, Buffalo, N.Y., 1941, 8 x 11 In., 4 Pages 55.00
Metamorphoses, Trifold, Whimsical Drawings, Verses, 18th Century, 6 1/2 x 16 1/2 In. . . . 4312.00
Pamphlet, Mother Goose, Punch-Out Pages, Unused, 10 x 14 1/2 In., 6 Pages 200.00
Program, Baseball, Old Timer's Game, Cleveland, Ohio, August 9, 1975 . . . . 11.00
Program, Buffalo Bill Wild West Show, Sen-Sen Chewing Gum Ad, 9 1/2 x 7 In. 718.00
Program, Folies Bergere, 1st Performance, California Auditorium, San Francisco, 1939 . . 95.00
Program, San Francisco 49ers V. Chicago Rockets, Mascot On Cover, Sept. 1, 1946 . . . . . 210.00
School Tablet, Gabby Hayes, Unused 65.00
Stock Certificate, American Tobacco Company, 1960s 5.00
Stock Certificate, Mining, Bullfrog Mining Co., Nevada, 1906, 100 Shares 895.00
Stock Certificate, Pyramid Oil Co., Oil Rig & Trains Picture, 1910 . . . . 2.50

PAPER DOLLS were probably inspired by the pantins, or jumping jacks, made in eighteenth-century Europe. By the 1880s, sheets of printed paper dolls and clothes were being made. The first paper doll books were made in the 1920s. Collectors prefer uncut sheets or books or boxed sets of paper dolls. Prices are about half as much if the pages have been cut.

Barbie, Twist 'n Turn, 2 Dolls, Punch-Out Fashions, 10 x 13 In., c.1967 . . . . 11.00
Bewitched, Samantha, Magic Wand, 1965 . . . . 100.00
Brady Bunch, Box, 1972 . . . . 45.00
Charlie's Angel, Box, 1977, Uncut 135.00
Eskimo Twins, Ladies Home Journal, April 1922, Uncut 15.00
Fanny Brice As Baby Snooks, Turn's, Die Cut, 1950, 16 In. 55.00
Hayley Mills, Summer Magic, 1963, Uncut 30.00
June Allyson, 1950, Uncut 90.00
Malibu Francie, Blue Plastic Stand, 21 Piece Wardrobe, Box, c.1976 . . . . 33.00
Twiggy, Cut Clothes, Mini Photo Album, Plastic Stand, Whitman, c.1967 . . . . 44.00
Twiggy, Punch-Out Clothes, Accessories, Plastilon Dress, c.1967, 10 x 13 In. 55.00
Twiggy, With Carry Pocket, Whitman, 1967, Uncut 95.00

PAPERWEIGHTS must have first appeared along with paper in ancient Egypt. Today's collectors search for every type, from the very expensive French weights of the nineteenth century to the modern artist weights or advertising pieces. The glass tops of the paperweights sometimes have been nicked or scratched, and this type of damage can be removed by polishing. Some serious collectors think this type of repair is an alteration and will not buy a repolished weight; others think it is an acceptable technique of restoration that does not change the value. Baccarat paperweights are listed separately under Baccarat.

Advertising, Absecon Lighthouse, Atlantic City, N.J., Photograph, c.1910 . . . . 20.00
Advertising, Aikin, Lambert & Company, 2 1/2 x 4 In. 106.00
Advertising, Burlington Venetian Blind Co., Image Of Venetian Blind, 4 In. 71.00
Advertising, Dutch Boy Paint, Lead, Phoenix Metal, 3 1/2 In. Diam. 80.00
Advertising, Globe, Uncalibrated 1/2 Meridian, Copper, Rand McNally, c.1900, 5 In. 460.00
Advertising, Gold Standard Coals, Mirrored 18.00
Advertising, Henry C. Werner Co., Boots & Shoes, Columbus, Oh., 1896, 2 x 4 In. 143.00
Advertising, Murdock Parlor Grate Co., Trent, 2 7/8 x 4 1/4 In. 165.00
Advertising, None Such Mince Meat, Image Of Housewife In Apron, 2 1/2 x 4 In. 64.00
Advertising, R. Petzold, Pharmacist, Baltimore, Md., Mortar & Pestle, Glass, 3 1/4 In. . . . 250.00
Advertising, Shackamaxon Worsted Co., Factory Building 3 1/2 x 2 In. 46.00
Advertising, Valvoline Gasoline, Reverse On Glass, 1920s, 4 x 2 5/8 In. 120.00
Advertising, White Eagle Refining Co., Figural, Plaster, 1924, 6 1/8 In. 210.00
Art Deco, 3 Professors, Standing, With 1 Large Book, Painted, Metal 75.00
Baccarat, Dogrose, Red, White Stardust Stamen, Green Stem, 2 1/2 In. 633.00
Black Cat, Arched Back, Iron, Painted, Yellow Eyes, Red Mouth, 3 1/2 In. 175.00
Blenko, Swirl, Amber Interior, Glass, 20th Century, 4 3/8 x 2 3/8 In. 61.00
Castelford, Silver Petaled Flowers, Bullet Shape, Green, 1800s, 5 x 2 3/4 In. 165.00

Cat, Iron, Hubley 75.00
Clichy, Concentric Circle, White Canes, Mid 1800s, 2 3/4 In. 385.00
Clichy, Green Rose, Concentric Circle Complex, Clear, 1850, 2 1/4 In. 523.00
Clichy, Millefiori, Pink, Green Rose Cane, Trefoil Garland, 3 1/4 In. 978.00
Concentric, Faceted, Star Cut Base, Opalescent, Signed, 2 1/4 In. 220.00
Controlled Bubbles, Flower Center 121.00
Cristal, D'Albret, John F. Kennedy, Jackie Kennedy Together, Sulphide 135.00
Eagle, Holding Olympic Rings, Marble, Bronze, Olympic Games, 1936, Berlin, 5 x 4 In. . . 392.00
Figural, Cupid Sitting On Glass Ball, 3 3/8 In. 86.00
Figural, Dozing Pig On Book, Enameled, 7 x 2 3/4 In. 140.00
Frog, Sapphire Blue Glass, 1890, 2 5/8 In. 975.00
Garland, Blue, Green, Red & Pink, Cane On Clear Base, France, 2 5/16 In. 415.00
Gettysburg, Shrapnel, Bullets, Eagle Center, Culp's Hill, 19th Century, 5 3/4 In. 303.00
Glass, Grover Cleveland, Wagner & Zimmerman, 2 3/4 In. 80.00
Griswold, Pup, Aluminum, Marked 225.00
Kaziun, Gunderson Stopper, Clusters Of Blossoms, Blue Ground, Label, 11 In. 1265.00
Kaziun, Morning Glory, Striped Blossom & Bud, White Trellis, Signed, 2 1/4 In. 1035.00
Kaziun, Pink Lily, Green Ground, 2 1/4 In. 345.00
Kaziun, Pink Rose, Black Ground, 2 1/4 In. 287.00
Kaziun, Rose, 3 Striped Leaves, Colorless Bottle, 4 3/4 In. 345.00
Kaziun, Spider Lily, Cobalt & Aventurine Ground, Gold K Under Lily, 3 In. 747.00
Kaziun, White, Blue Lily, Red Ground, 2 1/4 In. 230.00
Kaziun, Yellow Lily, Cobalt Blue Ground, 2 1/4 In. 287.00
Kaziun, Yellow Lily, Pink Ground, 2 1/4 In. 230.00
Kaziun, Yellow Lily, Red Ground, 2 1/4 In. 310.00
Millefiori, Concentric Circle, Latticinio Base, New England, 2 1/4 In. 240.00
Millefiori, Red, Yellow, Blue Rings, White Center Cane, Signed, 1971, 2 3/4 In. 165.00
Millefiori, Ribbon Scramble, New England, Mid 1800s, 2 In. 88.00
Moretti, 5-Petaled Flower, 4 Facets, Center Bubble, 1973 . . . . 230.00
Moretti, 5-Petaled Flower, Green & Amethyst Thread Surround Stem 143.00
Moretti, Ruby & White Spiraling Threads, 3 1/2 In. 160.00
Perthshire, Multicolored Canes, Millefiori, 1972, 2 1/2 In. 193.00
Photograph, Oliver Wendell Holmes, Round, 3 In. 40.00
Red Rose, Green Leaves, Pedestal, 6 1/8 In. 165.00
Sandwich, Pincushion, Blue Over White Bubble, Diamond Quilt, 2 5/8 In. 66.00
Sandwich, Pincushion, Lavender, Over White, Bubbles, Diamond Quilt, 2 1/2 In. 130.00
Sandwich, Weed Flower, Pontil, 1850, 2 5/8 In. 770.00
Snowdome, Big Boy, 4 1/2 In. 10.00
Snowdome, N.Y. Police Building, Gold Die Cut, Black Plastic, Gold Plaque, Skyline 90.00
St. Louis, Carpet Ground, White, Blue Fluted Canes, White Cross, 1972, 2 3/4 In. 275.00
St. Louis, Concentric Circle, Edelweiss Canes Around, Clear, 1850, 1 9/16 In. 297.00
St. Louis, Jasper Ground, Pink, Yellow, White Composite Star Can, 2 3/8 In. 633.00
St. Louis, Millefiori Scramble, Mid 1800s, 2 In. 145.00
Stankard, Bouquet, 1978, 2 7/8 In. 5255.00
Sulphide, Madonna & Child, Ruby Ground 46.00
Ysart, Floral Bouquet, Deep Blue, White, Millefiori, 2 7/8 In. 743.00
Ysart, Millefiori Canes, 5 3/4 x 4 In. 1380.00

PAPIER-MACHE is made from paper mixed with glue, chalk, and other ingredients, then molded and baked. It becomes very hard and can be painted. Boxes, trays, and furniture were made of papier-mache. Some of the nineteenth-century pieces were decorated with mother-of-pearl. Furniture made of papier-mache is listed in the Furniture category.

Box, Allegorical Scene, Women, Nude, Reading, Disc Shape, Russia, 3 1/8 In. 92.00
Card Case, Girl Carrying Water Pails, Forest Path, Lukutin Factory, 1870, 4 In. 1008.00
Coffer, Victorian, Mountainous Landscape Lid, Black Lacquer, 3 1/2 In. 345.00
Inkwell, Black, 19th Century, 2 1/4 x 6 In. 90.00
Jewelry Box, Inset Figure Of Peacock In Garden On Lid, 19th Century, 8 In. 630.00
Mask, Goliath, Horsehair Beard & Moustache, For Odd Fellows Lodge, 1900 . . . . 225.00
Tray, Seated Couple Before Pagoda, Floral, Bird & Insect, Red Rim, 31 1/2 In. 1035.00
Tray, Serpentine Edge, Mother-Of-Pearl Inlay, Gilt Flowers, England, c.1820, 25 In. 250.00
Tray, Serpentine Shape, Flower Vase, Gilt Arabesques, 10 1/2 x 14 1/2 x 1 3/4 In. 259.00
Tray, Serving, Abalone Shell Inlay, Green Leaves, Gilt Trim, 24 3/4 x 19 x 20 In. 690.00

Tray, Stand, Flowers & Butterflies, Victorian, 20 1/2 In. 4800.00
Tray, Stand, Regency, Black Lacquer, Gilt, Faux Bamboo, 22 x 31 In. 1380.00
Tray, Stenciled, Aurora Crossing The Heavens, c.1830, 20 x 15 In. 720.00
Tray, Wine, Serpentine, Victorian, Jennens & Bettridge, 15 x 28 In. 1725.00
Tray, Wine, Victorian, Cavetto Edges, Abalone, 14 1/2 x 28 1/2 In. 980.00
Urn, Cover, Allover Trailing Flowers, Temples & Pagodas Scene, 18 In., Pair 10200.00

PARASOL, see Umbrella category.

PARIAN is a fine-grained, hard-paste porcelain named for the marble it resembles. It was first made in England in 1846 and gained in favor in the United States about 1860. Figures, tea sets, vases, and other items were made of Parian at many English and American factories.

Bust, Clytie, Art Union Of London, 1855 .... 696.00
Bust, Shakespeare, P. & L., 12 In. 55.00
Figurine, Daniel Webster, Thomas Ball, G.W. Nichols, Boston, 26 In. 4250.00
Figurine, Knight & His Lady, 12 In. 759.00
Figurine, Morning Dew, Evening Dew, Pair 3291.00
Figurine, Night, 10 In. 5570.00
Figurine, Rebecca At Well, 8 In. 330.00
Figurine, Ruth In Cornfield, 8 In. 475.00
Figurine, Venus & Cupid, Robinson & Leadbeater, 10 In. 3924.00
Pitcher, Flat Leaf Design, Registry Mark, 10 In. 70.00
Plaque, Nymph & Putti In Forest, After Jacques Callot, c.1900, 6 In. 230.00

PARIS, Vieux Paris, or Old Paris, is porcelain ware that is known to have been made in Paris in the eighteenth or early nineteenth century. These porcelains have no identifying mark but can be recognized by the whiteness of the porcelain and the lines and decorations. Gold decoration is often used.

Basket, Pierced Bowl, Raised On Spreading Stem, Gilt, 1820s, 8 x 5 1/2 In. 1122.00
Basket, Wickerwork, Loop Handles, Reserve Of Lilacs, 1840s, 10 1/4 In. 1090.00
Bottle, Figural, Liqueur, George Washington Holding An Eagle, 1840, 11 x 11 In., Pair .. 460.00
Bowl, Basket Shape, Blue, Gilt Design, 1850, 10 x 12 In. 1095.00
Bowl, Basket Shape, Navette, Wickerwork, Gilded, Matte Blue, 8 x 6 1/2 x 11 1/2 In. .. 1495.00
Bowl, Basket Shape, Wickerwork, Central Guilloche Border, Square Plinth, 8 1/2 In. 920.00
Bowl, Basket Shape, Wickerwork, Gilt Band, Anthemion Border, Gilt Paw Feet, 9 1/4 In. . 1265.00
Bowl, Jacob Petit Style, Round Facet Shape, Celeste Blue, Gilt, Relief, 4 1/4 x 7 3/4 In. ... 431.00
Bowl, Roman Figures, Lions, Greek Key Border, Hard Paste, 14 In. 1430.00
Bowl, Turned Out Rim, Red Underside, Floral Border, Gilt Medallion, 2 1/2 In., Pair 575.00
Bowl, Undertray, Round, Dome Cover, Rose Border, Gilt Band, Footed, 6 1/2 x 8 In. 230.00
Cabinet Plate, Round, Flowers, Classical Figures, Insects, Early 1800s, 9 1/4 In. 1725.00
Cabinet Plate, Round, Gold Bellflowers, Stripe Border, Romantic Couple, 9 1/4 In. 173.00
Cabinet Plate, Tooled Gold Bellflowers, Anthemia, Mulberry Ground, 9 1/4 In., Pair 690.00
Candlestick, Continuous Band Of Garden Blossoms, Pale Yellow, 6 3/8 In. 488.00
Charger, Coat-Of-Arms Of Grand Duke Of Baden, Green, Gilt Band, 11 1/2 In., Pair 460.00
Coffee & Tea Set, Bird's Head Spouts, Gilt Bands & Medallions, 1820s, 20 Piece 1454.00
Coffee Cann, Saucer, Castle Landscape, Pedestrians & Dog, Gilt Handle, 1800, 5 In. 400.00
Coffee Cann, Saucer, Child, Blond Boy Playing Imaginary Game 116.00
Compote, Cherubs, Gilt Trim, Bisque, Raised Floral Rim, Leaves, 13 1/2 In. 935.00
Compote, Reticulated, Basket, Everted Rim, Kneeling Cherub, Gilded, Paw Feet, 10 In. ... 1610.00
Cup & Saucer, Loop Handle, Gilded Rim Over Foliate Border, 1820s, 3 1/2 In. 47.00
Cup & Saucer, Medallions Of Flowers 95.00
Cup & Saucer, Shepherd & His Flock, Gold Band, Sepia Border, 3 In. 345.00
Dessert Server, Concentric Design, Green Floral Reserves, Ring Handle, 17 1/2 In. 230.00
Dinner Service, Compote, Sauceboat, Gold Outline, Scroll Feet, 11 3/4 In., Pair 1265.00
Dinner Service, Gold Outline, Late 19th Century, 266 Piece 4370.00
Dish, Center En Grisaille, Sibyl Burning An Offering, 19th Century, 8 1/4 In. 115.00
Figurine, Classical Maiden Standing & Looking Pensively Downward, 14 In. 400.00
Figurine, Lion, Open Mouth, Curled Tail, Blue Cross Arrow Mark, 7 x 9 In. 230.00
Figurine, Turkish Woman, Gentleman, 13 In., Pair 980.00
Figurine, Water Sellers, Late 19th Century, 19 In., Pair 690.00
Flower Tub, Gilded Flowers, Leaves, 2 Floral Reserves, 8 1/4 In. 1495.00

Font, Holy Water, Winged Angel In Gothic Frame, Shell Form, 1850s, 15 x 5 In. 765.00
Gravy Boat, Hand Painted 375.00
Inkstand, Mother & Child Grieving Over Dead Bird, Painted Flowers, 1850, 8 3/4 In. . . . 1265.00
Inkstand, Raised Gold, Floral Reserves, Scroll Feet, 6 In. 3220.00
Jar, Tea, Royal Blue, Gilt Scrolls, Floral Reserves, Rectangular Stopper, 5 x 3 3/4 In. 375.00
Jardiniere, Gold Lion Masks, Central Floral Border, Peach Ground, 6 In., Pair 800.00
Jardiniere, Mask Handles, Cobalt Blue Ground, Flowers, 7 x 5 1/2 x 6 1/2 In., Pair 1620.00
Jardiniere, Trumpet, Gilt Everted Rim, Continuous Landscape Scene, 8 1/2 In., Pair 5290.00
Jardiniere, Undertray, Floral Spray Decoration, Blue Border, Gilt Rim, 8 x 7 x 8 In., Pair . 2185.00
Jug, Cream, Band Of Medallions, Gold Loop Handle, Circular Foot, 6 3/4 In. 70.00
Lamp, Painted Reserves Of 18th Century Figures Or Flowers, Electrified, 26 In., Pair 2990.00
Plate, Cabinet, Cobalt Blue Border, Gilt Vermiculation, Floral Reserve, 9 In., 3 Piece 345.00
Plate, Gilt Rim, Vine Border, Reserve Of Fruit, 1830s, 8 In., 12 Piece 4830.00
Plate, Putti Adorning Each Other With Garland, Gold, Gilt Border, 9 3/8 In. 290.00
Plate, Scalloped, Hand Painted 275.00
Plate, St. Paul's Cathedral With Fruiting Grapevine, Gilt Border, 9 1/4 In. 230.00
Plate Set, Gilt Rim, Vine Border, Magenta Ground, Centered Fruit, 8 In., 12 Piece 4830.00
Platter, Fish, Hand Painted 575.00
Pot, Pierced Cover, Applied Flowers, Gold, Foliated Plinth, 8 3/4 In. 1610.00
Potpourri, Green, Gilt Flowers, Pierced Domed Cover, Gilt Paw Feet, 9 1/2 x 6 x 6 In. . . 9500.00
Punch Bowl, Burgundy Rim, Clusters In Gilt Cartouches, Late 19th Century, 15 1/4 In. . . 175.00
Sauceboat, Flower, Scroll Handles, Domed Cover, Gilt, 6 1/2 x 5 1/2 x 9 In., Pair 490.00
Saucer, Pair Of Cherubs With Foliate Bodies Holding Coat Of Arms Of Grand Duke, 6 In. 345.00
Stand, Sweetmeat, 4 Tiers, 5 Section Trays, c.1830, 15 1/2 In. 7200.00
Tazza, Lavender Border, Gilt Bands, Tooled Gold Band, 5 1/2 x 8 In. 2070.00
Tea & Coffee Service, Coffeepot, Cover, 1820, 5 Piece 2300.00
Tea & Coffee Service, Rustic Landscape Scene, Gilt Band, 19th Century, 12 Piece 575.00
Tea & Coffee Set, Exotic Birds, 1870, 12 Piece 4800.00
Tea Container, Oriental Flowers, Black, Orange, 6 1/2 x 3 3/4 x 4 In. 1095.00
Tea Service, Dutch Landscapes, Of Amsterdam, With Street Scene, Gilt, 1807, 28 Piece . . 16100.00
Tea Service, Gilt Foliate Scrolls, Floral Panels, Teapot, Emile Bourgeois, 15 Piece 1265.00
Tea Service, Gold Band, Butterflies, Leopard, Bird Head Spouts, Early 1800s, 10 Piece . . 545.00
Tea Set, Classical Allegories, Gold, Cobalt Blue Ground, 6 3/4 In. 7475.00
Teapot, Egyptian Finial, Sphinx Head Terminal, Bird's Head Spout, 10 1/2 In. 975.00
Tray, Paul & Virginie Depiction, Sepia, Winged Eagles, Gilded, Square, 2 x 12 x 12 In. . . 7763.00
Tray, Serpentine Outlined Form, Gilt Banding, Cornflowers, Vines, 10 x 12 1/4 In. 920.00
Urn, Colorful Landscape Reserve, Handles, Gilded Ground, 9 In., Pair 1920.00
Urn, Garniture, Rococo, Bucolic Landscape, Rural Scenes, Blue Ground, 16 1/2 In., Pair . 1092.00
Urn, Soldier On Horse, Soldier With Musket, 2 Handles, Gilt, 12 In. 465.00
Urn, Sprays Of Flowers, Flower Handles, 16 In., 2 Piece 920.00
Urn, Step & Knop Foot, Mask Capped Handles, Mounted As Lamp, 13 In., Pair 747.00
Vase, Biscuit Garland, Blue Matte Ground Body, Gilt Turned Out Rim, 11 1/2 In., Pair . . . 5060.00
Vase, Bunches Of Grapes & Leaves, Scenic Medallion Center, 8 1/2 In. 135.00
Vase, Cherub In Shield, Scroll Handles, Pink Ground, Gold, 9 3/4 In., Pair . . . . *Illus* 2530.00
Vase, Cobalt Blue, Landscape, Gallant & Consort, Domed Cover, 21 x 7 x 5 In., Pair 1840.00
Vase, Colorful Flowers, Tooled Gold Reserves, Gilt Turned Out Rim, 12 In., Pair 4370.00
Vase, Cornucopia Shape, Salmon, Magenta, Gilt Vines, Flower, 9 x 7 x 4 1/2 In., Pair 748.00
Vase, Figural, Peasant Attire, Tree Trunk Form, 1840s, 8 1/2 In., Pair 1092.00
Vase, Floral Bouquet, Courting Couple, Swan Neck Handles, 17 3/4 In., Pair 3450.00
Vase, Foliate Molded Body, Gilt Trim, Enamel Floral Bouquet Panels, 20 In., Pair 1380.00
Vase, Garniture, 2 Handles, Troubadour Style, Bright Gilding, Signed, 13 1/4 x 7 In. 518.00
Vase, Garniture, Ruffled Gilt Edge, Garden Bouquet, 13 x 10 x 7 In., Pair 977.00
Vase, Garniture, Stylized Foliate Handles, Rose Swags, 4 x 6 In., Pair 23.00
Vase, Gilt Everted Rim, Inverted Neck, Grape Vines, 13 x 5 x 7 1/2 In., Pair 4600.00
Vase, Glacier, Urn Shape, Angled Handles, Dutertre Freres, 10 x 10 1/2 x 8 In., Pair 4370.00
Vase, Gold Everted Rim, Swan Handles, Lavender Ground Body, 14 x 6 1/2 In., Pair 3680.00
Vase, Landscape, Blue, Magenta Body, Scrolled Handles, 16 1/2 x 10 1/2 x 6 In., Pair 2300.00
Vase, Landscape, Cattle, Tooled Gold, Scroll Handles, Female Masks, 18 x 7 1/2 x 6 In. . . 2530.00
Vase, Maiden Comforting Her Friend, Pierced Rim, Colorful Flowers, 14 In., Pair 2300.00
Vase, Matte Blue Ground, Classical, Tooled Gold, Scroll Handles, 10 3/4 x 4 x 6 In. 2990.00
Vase, Medici, Rustic Landscape Scene, Gilt Everted Rim, Loop Handles, 9 1/2 In., Pair . . 747.00
Vase, Molded Handles, Fluted Lip, Garlands, Birds & Cornucopia, c.1845, 19 1/2 In. 4025.00
Vase, Oval, Glazed, Rose Pompadour, Everted Gold Rim, Handles, Painted, 11 1/2 x 7 In. . 863.00

Paris, Vase, Cherub In Shield, Scroll
Handles, Pink Ground, Gold, 9 3/4 In., Pair

**Moths will attack ivory and bone and
make small "pinholes" when the
larvae hatch. Don't wash ivory. To kill
the moth larvae, put the ivory in the
freezer for a few hours.**

Vase, Oval, Scalloped Gilt Rim, Scrolled Handles, Everted Neck, 10 x 6 1/2 x 4 In., Pair .	1150.00
Vase, Playful Youth Scene, Royal Blue, Magenta, Gold Outline, 11 1/2 x 5 In., Pair	977.00
Vase, Playful Youth, Floriform, Gold Outlined, 11 1/2 In., Pair	977.00
Vase, Raised Gilt Scrolls, Blue Ground, Masks, Gilt, Footed, 9 1/2 x 6 x 5 In., Pair	1840.00
Vase, Roses, Cartouches, Oval, Everted Rim, Inverted Neck, Swan Handles, 9 3/4, Pair ..	863.00
Vase, Rustic Landscape Scene, Inverted Neck, Tooled Gold Border, 11 In.	460.00
Vase, Scenic Decoration, Urn Shape, Swan Shape Handles, 10 In.	207.00
Vase, Scroll Handles, Egyptian Masks, Stylized Peacock, Gilded, Early 1900s, 12 In.	2070.00
Vase, Soldier, Woman, Weary Traveler, Pedestal Base, 15 x 11 x 6 1/2 In., Pair	2760.00
Vase, Stand, Oval, Scrolls, Shells, Cabochons, Apple Green Ground, Gold, 10 x 6 1/2 In. .	1035.00
Vase, Swan Form Cornucopia Base, Scroll Feet, Mid 19th Century, 9 x 8 In.	1210.00
Vase, Trumpet, Banded With Garlands Enclosing Fruit Filled Compotes, 8 1/2 In., Pair ..	517.00
Vase, Trumpet, Everted Rim, Classical Borders, Gold, Royal Blue Ground, 7 1/2 In.	1840.00

PATE-DE-VERRE is an ancient technique in which glass is made by
blending and refining powdered glass of different colors into molds.
The process was revived by French glassmakers, especially Galle,
around the end of the nineteenth century.

Plaque, Mask, Smiling Grotesque Male, Art Nouveau, Raised, Square Base, 12 In.	6900.00
Vase, Flowering Vine Around Mouth, Yellow Blooms, Pale Gray, Orange, 4 In.	2990.00
Vase, Portrait Of Man, Deep Purple, Burnt Orange Ground, 1921, 4 3/8 In.	19150.00
Vase, Purple, Pale Lavender Ground, 1920, 10 1/4 In.	12000.00

PATE-SUR-PATE means paste on paste. The design was made by painting layers of slip on the ceramic piece until a relief decoration was
formed. The method was developed at the Sevres factory in France
about 1850. It became even more famous at the English Minton factory about 1870. It has since been used by many potters to make both
pottery and porcelain wares.

Vase, White Painted Female Figure Blowing Bubbles, Pale Mauve, 5 In.	290.00

PAUL REVERE POTTERY was made at several locations in and around
Boston, Massachusetts, between 1906 and 1942. The pottery was operated as a settlement house program for teenage girls. Many pieces were
signed *S.E.G.* for Saturday Evening Girls. The artists concentrated on
children's dishes and tiles. Decorations were outlined in black and
filled with color.

Bowl, 3 Whimsical Rabbits, White On Blue, Incised Rim, 3 x 5 In.	805.00
Bowl, Pairs Of Rabbits Facing One Another In Cabbage, Goldstein, 5 In.	3080.00
Bowl, Rabbits, White Glaze, 3 Blue Bands, 1918, 5 In.	2310.00
Bowl, Squirrels, Sun Yellow Oblong Bands, Black Lining, Ivory, 5 In.	1100.00
Bowl, Stylized White Tulips, Pale Blue Rim, Galner, 1919, 6 In.	1760.00
Bowl, White Trefoils On Buff Ground, Signed, 3 1/4 x 7 1/4 In.	1610.00
Bowl, Windmill Design, Blue Glaze, R. Bacchini, 1909, 3 1/8 x 4 1/4 In.	1650.00
Candlestick, Coiled Handle, Lotus Florals, Bloom, 1926, 2 1/2 In.	550.00
Cup, Landscape, Teal Green Tree, White Sky, Brown, 3 In.	770.00

Cup & Saucer, Deep Cobalt Blue Lotus, Abstract Yellow Band, 1912, 5 In. 935.00
Eggcup, Rabbit & Cabbage, Eva Geneco, 1912, 1 1/2 In. 660.00
Inkwell, Tree, Landscape, Green Line, Brown Glaze, Navy Blue Sky, 3 In. 1760.00
Jar, Midnight Blue Wild Iris, Sage Green Leaves, Sarah Galner, 1914, 4 In. 1870.00
Loving Cup, Greek Key Design, 3 1/8 x 4 1/2 In. 302.00
Paperweight, White Sail, Brown Ship, Fannie Levine, 1914, 2 1/2 In. 467.00
Pitcher, Blue Accents, Bark Handle, 6 3/4 In. 248.00
Pitcher, Blue-Gray Matte Glaze, White Glaze Rim, Stamped, 4 1/2 In. 92.00
Pitcher, Border Of Lotus Florals, Teal Green Ground, 1926, 10 In. 1045.00
Pitcher, Buttercup Yellow Tall Tulips, Light Sage Green Leaves, 1926, 7 In. 990.00
Pitcher, Lotus Floral, Blue Glaze, Brown, 1926, 7 1/8 In. 825.00
Plaque, Sailing Ship, Enameled Mark, Round, 5 1/2 In. 245.00
Plate, Buttercup Yellow Glaze, Ivory Ground, 1914, 6 1/4 In. 1430.00
Plate, Chick Looking Upwards, White Glaze, Galner, 6 In. 1430.00
Plate, Dinner, White, Give Us This Day Our Daily Bread, 9 3/4 In. 618.00
Plate, Greek Key Design, Chicory Blue, Light Brown, Sage Green, 7 In. 495.00
Plate, Miniature White Rosettes, Steel Blue Ground, Deep Blue, 10 In. 385.00
Plate, Rabbits, Sage Green Hillside, White, Blue, 1919, 6 In. 770.00
Plate, Trio Of Yellow Chicks Peering Upwards, 1934, 6 1/4 In. 2420.00
Plate, White Rabbit, Pale Green Hillside, Chicory Blue Sky, F. Levine, 7 In. 935.00
Plate, White, Black Triple Goose, Sun Yellow Band, Levine, 7 In. 1430.00
Tea Set, Blue, Gray Glaze, Handles, 1927, 3 Piece 288.00
Teacup, Stylized Flower Band, Blue Matte Ground, 1911, 2 1/2 In. 225.00
Tile, Brown, Blue Border, Sage Green Center, White Border, Block, 5 1/4 In. 440.00
Tile, Landscape, Tree Top, Alvina Mangini, 1910, 5 1/2 In. 2860.00
Tile, Paul Revere Midnight Ride, Brown, Tan, Sage Green, 3 x 8 In. 990.00
Tray, Stylized Tulip, Yellow Buttercup, Sage Green Leaves, 14 In. 990.00
Vase, Antique Green, Silver Satin Finish, Cylindrical, 6 3/4 In. 275.00
Vase, Band Of Lotus, Blue Gray Ground, 1914, 4 1/2 x 3 3/4 In. 1237.00
Vase, Band Of Yellow Tulips, Green Matte Ground, 5 3/4 x 4 1/2 In. 1237.00
Vase, Blue Glaze, Signed, 5 1/2 In. 144.00
Vase, Blue High Glaze, Signed, 4 In. 150.00
Vase, Blue Over Rose Glaze, 3 1/4 In. 175.00
Vase, Green Matte Glaze, Signed, 8 In. 110.00
Vase, Green, Blue Glaze, 4 In. 184.00
Vase, Matte Drip Glaze, Flared Rim, Early 20th Century, 6 In. 358.00
Vase, Mustard Gloss Glaze, Marked, 4 In. 146.00
Vase, Steel Blue Glaze, White Speckling, I. Goldstein, 1916, 9 3/4 In. 467.00
Vase, Stylized Petals At Rim, Signed, Early 20th Century, 8 1/2 In. 920.00
Vase, Stylized Tulip Design, Buttercup Yellow, Brown Panel, 1926, 4 x 5 1/4 In. 1100.00
Vase, White Lotus Flowers, Steel Blue Glaze, Sarah Galner, 1917, 6 In. 1320.00
Vase, White Petals, Maroon, Yellow Glaze, Teal, Blue Green, 4 In. 1210.00
Vase, White, Teal Green, Cobalt Blue, Steel Blue Ground, 1929, 5 x 4 1/2 In. 440.00
Vase, Yellow Tulips, Green Leaves, Blue Ground, 6 1/2 x 5 In. 1462.00

PEACHBLOW glass was made by several factories beginning in the 1880s. New England peachblow is a one-layer glass shading from red to white. Mt. Washington peachblow shades from pink to bluish-white. Hobbs, Brockunier and Company of Wheeling, West Virginia, made coral glass that they marketed as Peach Blow. It shades from yellow to peach and is lined with white glass. Reproductions of all types of peachblow have been made. Related pieces may be listed under Gunderson and Webb Peachblow.

Creamer, Square Mouth, Applied Handle, Wheeling, 4 1/8 In. 575.00
Cruet, Crimped Spout, Handle, Satin, Wheeling, 7 1/2 In. 172.00
Cruet, Petticoat Shape, White Handle & Stopper, New England, 6 3/4 In. 1950.00
Cruet Set, Quadruple Plated Carrier, 5-In. Bottle, 3 Piece 575.00
Cup & Saucer, White Handle, 1960, 3 1/4 In. 115.00
Decanter, Claret, Amber Rigaree Band, Reeded Handle, Wheeling, 9 3/4 In. 7475.00
Fairy Lamp, Opaque Base, Scalloped Edges 896.00
Jug, Pilgrim, Amber Twisted Rope Handle, Wheeling, 9 x 5 1/2 In. 2587.00
Lamp, Relief Shell Columns, Blue, White, Gold, Red, Brass Base, 30 In. 275.00
Pitcher, Amber Handle, Wheeling, 4 In. 490.00

Peachblow, Pitcher,
Claret, Pinched Waist,
Wheeling, 9 3/4 In.

Clean a clock face as seldom as possible. The brass trim may be coated with colored lacquer and brass polish will remove the color.

Peachblow, Sugar, Cover,
Wheeling Drape, 6 1/4 In.

Pitcher, Champagne, Deep Amber Reeded Handle, Wheeling, 11 In.	1725.00
Pitcher, Claret, Pinched Waist, Wheeling, 9 3/4 In. ....*Illus*	7475.00
Pitcher, Tankard, Wheeling, 9 In.	5000.00
Pitcher, Water, Amber Handle, Straight, Wheeling, 7 x 6 In.	1955.00
Pitcher, Water, Square Top, Bulbous, Wheeling	1400.00
Pitcher, Wheeling Drape, Applied Amber Reeded Handle, 6 1/2 In.	460.00
Pitcher, Wheeling Drape, Crystal Reeded Handle, 4 1/2 x 5 In.	345.00
Punch Cup, Wild Rose, Reeded Handle	385.00
Rose Bowl, Strawberry Prunt, Scalloped Rim, 5 In.	165.00
Salt & Pepper, Metal Cover, Wheeling, 2 3/4 x 2 In.	520.00
Salt & Pepper, Silver Plated Cover, Wheeling, 3 x 3 In. ....825.00 to	1035.00
Sugar, Cover, Wheeling Drape, 6 1/4 In. ....*Illus*	2300.00
Toothpick	1265.00
Tumbler, 3 1/2 In.	130.00
Tumbler, New England, 3 3/4 In. ....170.00 to	260.00
Tumbler, Wheeling, 3 5/8 x 2 3/4 In. ....259.00 to	345.00
Vase, Double, Gourd Shape, Satin, 8 1/2 In.	1900.00
Vase, Enameled Flowers, Gold Trim, 4 3/4 In.	250.00
Vase, Fern Leaves, 5 In.	285.00
Vase, Gold Flowers, Stems & Leaves, Signed, 8 In.	695.00
Vase, Gourd Shape, Wheeling, 7 1/8 x 4 1/2 In.	3160.00
Vase, Lily, 8 In.	315.00
Vase, Lily, Tricornered, 15 x 5 5/8 In.	1955.00
Vase, Lily, Wild Rose, 18 3/4 x 7 In.	1150.00
Vase, Morgan, Griffin Stand, Wheeling, 10 In. ....2700.00 to	3162.00
Vase, Satin, Gold Trim, 4 3/4 In.	250.00
Vase, Stick, Wheeling, 8 1/2 In.	635.00
Vase, Wheeling Drape, Hobbs, Brockunier, 11 In.	1400.00
Vase, Wheeling, 11 In.	920.00
Vase, Wild Rose, New England, 10 1/2 In.	1250.00

PEANUTS is the title of a comic strip created by cartoonist Charles M. Schulz (1922-2000). The strip, drawn by Schulz from 1950 to 2000, features a group of children, including Charlie Brown and his sister Sally, Lucy Van Pelt and her brother Linus, Peppermint Patty, and Pig Pen, and an imaginative and independent beagle named Snoopy. The Peanuts gang has also been featured in books, television shows, and a Broadway musical.

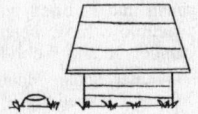

Bank, Snoopy On Doghouse	20.00
Bank, Snoopy Sailor, Chalkware, 1965	90.00
Bicycle Pedals, Snoopy, With Hardware, 3 1/2 In.	7.50
Box, Stationery, Snoopy	5.00
Button, The In Crowd, All Characters, Celluloid, 3 In.	22.00
Candle, Charlie Brown, Figural	15.00
Christmas Light Set, Snoopy World War I Flying Ace, 10 Lights, Woodstock, 5 Lights ..	8.00

Is it cut or pressed glass? Feel
the edges of the design of the
glass. Cut glass has sharp edges;
pressed-glass designs are molded
into the glass.

Peanuts, Lunch Box, Vinyl, King Seeley
Thermos, 1967

Christmas Ornament Set, Charlie Brown, Snoopy & Lucy, 3 1/4 To 4 In., 3 Piece	8.00
Cookbook, Lunchbox, 1st Edition, Signed	80.00
Figurine, Snoopy, Wearing Aviator Goggles, Vinyl	25.00
Lamp, Snoopy With Phone In Hand	370.00
Lunch Box, Metal, Snoopy & Gang Under Tree, Linus Band, King Seeley Thermos, 1973	50.00
Lunch Box, Vinyl, King Seeley Thermos, 1967 ....*Illus*	230.00
Napkin, Beverage, Good Grief Peanuts, Box, 1960s	20.00
Plate, Peanuts, 30th Anniversary, Schulz	50.00
Plate, Valentine, Box, 1978	20.00
Thermos, Lunch Box, Linus Lionhearted	60.00
Toy, Plane, Snoopy, Red Baron, 1965	90.00
Toy, Snoopy, Jack-In-The-Box, Knickerbocker, 1979, 30 In.	75.00
Truck, Snoopy Fire Dept., Aviva Toy Co., 1965, 5 In.	35.00
View-Master, Lucy With Bat Knocking Down Charlie Brown's House Of Cards, 1966	30.00
View-Master, Snoopy & The Red Baron, 3 Reels, Booklet, 1969	23.00
Yo-Yo, Snoopy Dancing, White Plastic, United Features Syndicate	35.00

PEARL items listed here are made of the natural mother-of-pearl from
shells. Such natural pearl has been used to decorate furniture and small
utilitarian objects for centuries. The glassware known as mother-of-
pearl is listed by that name. Opera glasses made with natural pearl
shell are listed under Opera Glasses.

Box, Inlaid Wood, 4 1/2 x 1 x 2 In.	46.00
Card Case, Continental, Veneer, 3 3/4 In.	63.00
Fish Service, Silver Plate, Fitted Case, 12 Piece	345.00
Pendant, Triptych, St. Nicholas Svyatogorskiy, Silver, Moscow, 3 1/4 x 4 1/4 In.	1120.00
Snuff Bottle, Flattened Double Gourd, Raised Flowers, Chinese	259.00
Thimble, Gold Trim, 3/4 In.	525.00

PEARLWARE is an earthenware made by Josiah Wedgwood in 1779. It
was copied by other potters in England. Pearlware is only slightly different in color from creamware and for many years collectors have
confused the terms. Wedgwood pieces are listed in the Wedgwood category in this book.

Pearl

Charger, Painted Pagoda, Shell Edge, 13 In.	770.00
Creamer, Blue Flowers, 3 In.	220.00
Creamer, Embossed Grapes, Leaves & Fish Scales, Gray Bands	467.00
Creamer, Impressed Leaf Ends, 3 5/8 In.	110.00
Cup, Cartouche On Front Reads Present For George, Child's, 2 In.	577.00
Cup & Saucer, Handless, Purple Floral Transfer, Green & Blue	35.00
Cup & Saucer, Polychrome, Floral & Acorn	742.00
Mug, Farm Scene, People, Buildings & Animals, c.1790, 6 1/4 In.	1750.00
Mug, Polychrome, Cow, Tree, Brown, Green, Early 19th Century, 3 1/4 In.	1955.00
Pepper Pot, Spread-Winged Eagle & Shield, 4 1/2 In.	1980.00
Pitcher, Molded Vintage, Green Glaze & Red, White Ground, Rope Rim, 5 3/4 In.	190.00
Plate, Barn Scene, Berry Border, 8 In.	1650.00

Plate, Basket Weave, Rim, Floral Center, 6 1/2 In., 7 Piece 230.00
Plate, Orange Flowers, Blue Container, c.1820, 8 In. 450.00
Plate, Syntax Taking His Tour, 6 1/2 In. 385.00
Platter, Gaudy Blue & White, Scalloped Border, Fish Scale & Feather Design, 13 In. 1540.00
Salt, Footed, Polychrome, c.1785 .... 450.00
Salt, Master, White, Blue, Late 18th Century 395.00
Soup, Dish, Blue Central Flower, 9 7/8 In. 495.00
Sugar, Cover, Green & Yellow Flowers, Blue Stripes, Beehive Finial, 5 In. 110.00
Teapot, Brown Stars & Stripes, White Ground, 7 1/4 In. 330.00
Teapot, J. & G. Meakin, 11 In. 110.00
Teapot, Pale Magenta, Daisy, Red Orange Rose, Handle 675.00
Teapot, Strawberry Leaf 302.00
Tureen, Pigeon Resting On Nest, Early 19th Century, 7 In. 2415.00
Vase, 3-Finger, Floral, Polychrome, c.1785, 6 3/4 In. 1195.00
Vase, Tulip, Blue Feather Edges, Hand Painted, 6 3/4 x 7 In. 495.00

PEKING GLASS is a Chinese cameo glass first made popular in the eighteenth century. The Chinese have continued to make this layered glass in the old manner, and many new pieces are now available that could confuse the average buyer.

Bowl, Bird, Prunus Design, Black, On Milk White, Bell Shape, 4 In. 115.00
Bowl, Squirrels & Grapes, Green On White, 19th Century, 6 1/4 In. 172.00
Jar, Cobalt Blue, Carved Fitted Rosewood Cover, 14 In., Pair 5750.00
Jar, Cover, Archaic Dragon, Garnet Red, On White, Globular, 5 3/4 In. 805.00
Snuff Bottle, Carved Dragon, Phoenix, Pale Blue, Stopper, 20th Century, 4 In. 58.00
Snuff Bottle, Red, Orange, Black, Overlay, Foot Ring, Agate Stopper, c.1880, 3 In. 345.00
Snuff Bottle, Splayed Neck, Green On White, 2 7/8 In. 288.00
Snuff Bottle, Vines, Birds, Pale Blue, Green, Flattened Shape, 3 In. 403.00
Vase, 3 Carved Carp, Wave & Cloud, Qing Dynasty, 13 In. 1955.00
Vase, Carved With Birds & Flowering Branch, Mustard Yellow, 11 In., Pair 230.00
Vase, Carved With Lotus Petals Around Body, Lotus Plants & Birds, 9 In. 1380.00
Vase, Dark Plum, Brown, Flared Rim, 14 x 6 In., Pair 1150.00
Vase, Lemon Yellow, Birds On Flowering Branches, 19th Century, 7 In. 805.00
Vase, Pear Shape, Ruby Glass Cut To Snowflake Ground, Palace Garden, 7 In. 260.00
Vase, Ruby Red, Carved In Relief, 9 In. 750.00
Vase, Stylized Foo Dogs, White, 2 Reserves Of Flowering Branches, 5 In. 145.00

PELOTON glass is a European glass with small threads of colored glass rolled onto the surface of clear or colored glass. It is sometimes called spaghetti, or shredded coconut, glass. Most pieces found today were made in the nineteenth century.

Pitcher, Crackle, Handle, 1850, 4 1/2 In. 350.00
Pitcher, Enameled Flowers, Gold, Neck Handle, 5 1/4 x 4 1/4 In. 375.00
Vase, Lavender, Ball Shape, Ruffled Edge, Applied Coconut Strings, 3 1/2 x 3 In. 195.00
Vase, Pigeon Blood, Multicolored Strings, 7 In. 145.00
Vase, Vertical Ribbing, Crimped, 1800, 6 1/2 In. 175.00

PENS replaced hand-cut quills as writing instruments in 1780 when the first steel pen point was made in England. But it was 100 years before the commercial pen was a common item. The fountain pen was invented in the 1830s but was not made in quantity until the 1880s. All types of old pens are collected.

PEN, Ballpoint, We Shall Overcome, M.L. King Picture 15.00
Billow's, Blue, Penguin, Memorable Beach, Barnson Co., Bensia 8.00
Black, Brown Rings, Initial On Clip, 5 In. 6.00
Christmas, Red, Silver, Christmas Tree On Clip 6.00
Cross, Black, Leaf Design Around Center 12.00
Cross, Silver, Engraved Band Of Seashells 10.00
Elvis Presley, Black, WriTek, Presley Signature, 5 1/2 In. 8.00
Feather, White, Heart Shape Holder, 10-In. Feather, 5 1/4-In. Pen 15.00
Federal Express, Changing Window Message, 5 1/2 In. 4.00
Float About, 2 Playing Cards Float Over Players 4.50
Float About, 7 Female Symbols Pulled Toward Magnet, White Script 4.00

Float About, 9-Man Marching Band, Passes Windsor Castle	3.50
Float About, Alligator Swims Out Of Grasses, Towards Alligator On Shore	3.25
Float About, Clown Holds Pez Dispenser, Collector Visits Booth, Buys Dispensers	3.50
Float About, Labrador Puppy, Jumps Past Mother Nursing Pup & Other Dogs	3.75
Float About, Scorpion Scurries Across Forest Floor	3.50
Fountain, Esterbrook, Silver Barrel, Felt Bottom Holder	18.00
Fountain, Maroon, Gold Band, Velvet Tip, 4 In.	50.00
Fountain, Parker, Yellow, Green, Orange, Purple, Black, White, Checks, Polkadots, 5 In.	15.00
Fountain, Safety, Ornate Design, Columbia	275.00
Fountain, Sheaffer, Brown, 14 Kt. Gold Tip, Goldtone Cap, Wood Block Holder, 5 In.	25.00
Garland, Westinghouse Emblem, Maroon, Silver	8.00
McDonald's, Green Character, c.1988, 5 3/4 In.	5.00
Parker, Insignia, Black, Gold Accents	25.00
Phillip Morris, Chrome, Smokers Have Rights Too, U.S.A.	10.00
Quill, Black, Gold Trim, Initial H	8.00
Sanford, Black, Soft Rubber Grip, Trademark, Japan, 5 1/2 In.	8.00
Sanford, Success Is A Journey Not A Destination, Soft Rubber Grip, 5 1/2 In.	5.00
Sheaffer, Ballpoint, 14K Gold	100.00
Silver, Black Rubber Grip, Japan	8.00
Waterman, Ideal, Fountain, 14K Gold, Lever Filling Action, Stamped, 5 1/2 In.	52.00
Waterman, Ideal, Lever Filling Action, 14K Gold	58.00
Waterman, Openwork, Sterling Silver	975.00
PEN & PENCIL, Fugazzi College, Engraved, Emblem, Gold	20.00
Indian, Red, Black, White & Green, Nickel Plated, 1933	90.00
Mechanical, Rhinestone Accented Case, 1950s, 3 1/8 In.	15.00
Parker, Safety Award, Bechtel Company, 5 In.	12.00
Rhinestone Case, 1950s, 3 5/8 In.	6.00

PENCILS were invented, so it is said, in 1565. The eraser was not added to the pencil until 1858. The automatic pencil was invented in 1863. Collectors today want advertising pencils or automatic pencils of unusual design. Boxes and sharpeners for pencils are also collected. Advertising pencils are listed in the Advertising category.

PENCIL, Bullet, DeLaval Milkers, Celluloid, Rueben D. Leibensperger	20.00
Hartford Fire Insurance Co., 12K Yellow Gold, Initials, 1810-1910, 3 In.	195.00
Marathon Gasoline, Lubricants, Best In The Long Run	5.00
Mechanical, General Electric Lamps, Maroon, Tan, Silver Clip, Scripto, 5 In.	6.00
Mechanical, Parrish Bakeries, Eat Diamond Pie, Calendar, Bakelite	25.00
Mechanical, Pittsburgh Auto Equipment Co., Yellow, Black, Pocket Clip, 5 In.	10.00
Chatelaine Ring, Gold Plated, Woman's, c.1900, 5 1/2 In.	15.00
Electric Cafe, Detroit, Michigan, Clip, Wearever	6.00
Eversharp, Green & Yellow	30.00
Holder, Raggedy Ann & Andy, 6 1/2 In.	20.00
Mechanical, Cannon Shape, Gold Plated, 2 In.	125.00
Mechanical, Miko, Alloy II, Clip, Blue	5.00
Mechanical, Monogrammed, 14K Yellow Gold, Late 19th Century, 3 1/8 In.	52.00
Mechanical, Pendant, Gold Filled, Woman's, 3 In.	20.00
Mechanical, Sheaffer, Marble Coloring, Hallmark, Pat'd 78-77	24.00
Mechanical, Sterling Silver, 1920s, 3 In.	10.00
Mechanical, Wearever, Read, Pearlized, Gold Clip	4.00
Mechanical, Zippo, Black, Gold Trim	10.00
Pendant, Cat, Turquoise, Gold Enamel, Blue Rhinestone Eyes, Nose, 4 x 1 1/2 In.	20.00
Propelling, Egyptian Pharaoh Form, Late 19th Century, 5 1/2 In.	475.00
Sterling Silver, Chain Holder, Fyne Poynte, Mabie Todd & Co., 3 5/8 In.	45.00
Sterling Silver, Twist Barrel, c.1900, 3 In.	22.00
Sunbeam Bread, Premium, Majer's	6.00
Supreme Court, Liberty, Justice For All, Gavel Shape	1.00
Virginia Department Of Alcoholic Beverage Control, VABC, 7 1/2 In.	2.00
PENCIL SHARPENER, Army Tank, Bronzed Metal, Turret Moves, Hong Kong, 3 In.	6.00
Bakelite, Clock, 1 In.	75.00
Coffee Grinder, Double Wheel, Metal, Red Paint, Hong Kong, 3 In.	7.50
Looney Tunes, Wile E. Coyote, Poly Bag, Header, Graphics	3.25
Puppy Dog, Red Ink, Japan, 3 3/4 In.	9.00

Rolls-Royce, Japan	15.00
Ronald McDonald, Happy Meal, August, 1984	4.00
Sailboat, 4 Sails, All Turn, Bronzed Metal, 3 1/2 x 3 1/4 In.	5.00
Sewing Machine, Moving Wheel & Needle, Plastic, Germany, 1970s, 2 x 2 In.	19.00
Stage Coach, Wheels Turn, Metal, Made In Hong Kong, 2 1/2 In.	5.00
Volkswagen Beetle, Bronzed Metal, 3 1/2 In.	7.50
Well Pump, Cast Iron Base, 11 x 10 In.	1208.00

PENNSBURY Pottery worked in Morrisville, Pennsylvania, from 1950 to 1971. Full sets of dinnerware as well as many decorative items were made. Pieces are marked with the name of the factory.

Pennsbury Pottery

Amish, Cake Plate, Harvest Scene, 4 1/2 x 11 In.	65.00
Amish, Jug, Couple, 6 1/4 In.	35.00
Black Rooster, Butter Dish, Pottery, Square	30.00
Black Rooster, Oil, Vinegar Set, 6 1/2 In.	62.00
Black Rooster, Snack Set, 3 3/8 x 2 1/2 In., 2 Piece	25.00
Dutch Talk, Bowl, 9 In.	44.00
Figurine, Bird, Barn Swallow, White High Gloss, Blue Glaze, 6 In.	53.00
Figurine, Bird, Chickadee, Signed, 3 In.	110.00
Figurine, Bird, Magnolia Warbler, Signed	229.00
Figurine, Bird, Nuthatch, Gloss Glaze, 3 1/4 In.	46.00
Figurine, Bird, Nuthatch, Signed, 3 1/4 In.	104.00
Harvest Scene, Cookie Jar, Turkey, Pumpkin	100.00
Hex, Cup & Saucer	7.00
Hex, Gravy Boat	27.00
Red Rooster, Butter Dish	21.00
Red Rooster, Pitcher, 5 In.	11.00
Red Rooster, Plate, 10 In.	37.00
Rooster, Desk Caddy	35.00
Rooster, Platter, Round, 14 In.	42.00
Wheat, Bread Plate, Give Us This Day, Green & Brown, 7 3/4 In.	35.00

PEPSI-COLA, the drink and the name, was invented in 1898 but was not trademarked until 1903. The logo was changed from an elaborate script to the modern block letters on the 1970 Pepsi label. Several different logos have been used. Until 1951, the words *Pepsi* and *Cola* were separated by 2 dashes. These bottles are called *double dash*. In 1951 the modern logo with a single hyphen was introduced. All types of advertising memorabilia are collected, and reproductions are being made.

PEPSI-COLA

Bank, Ford Model T, Cast Metal, Box, 1912	25.00
Bottle Cap, Green, White Lettering, 1910	50.00
Bottle Carton, Your Personal Carton For Pepsi-Cola, Wood, 9 1/4 x 8 1/2 In.	175.00
Bottle Opener, Church Key	6.00
Bottle Opener, Starr X, 2 3/4 x 23 1/2 In.	22.00
Button, Bottle Cap Type, Red, White & Blue, Celluloid, 1 In.	40.00
Calendar, 1911, Girl, I Love Its Flavor, Frame, Under Glass, 10 x 20 In.	3520.00
Carrier, 6 Bottles, Aluminum	62.00
Carrier, 6 Bottles, Red Lettering, 11 x 6 x 9 In.	155.00
Carrier, 6 Bottles, Wooden, 1940	150.00
Case, Display, Wooden, Varnished, 1950s	40.00
Clock, Say Pepsi Please, Light-Up	175.00
Crate, Wooden, Vintage, 18 x 5 x 12 In.	48.00
Cup, Red, White, Blue Lily Tulip, 4 Piece	10.00
Display, Monkey, Electric, Plastic, Metal, 37 x 26 In.	1100.00
Doll, Elf, Plush, 34 In.	155.00 to 167.00
Door Push, Bigger-Better, 12 x 2 3/4 In.	550.00
Fan, Rattan, 2 Sides, 1910-1915, 9 x 14 In.	1210.00
Glass, Betty Picture, 1977	805.00
Glass, Hits The Spot, Syrup & Fill Lines, Anchor Hocking, 1930s, 7 Oz., 4 1/4 In.	40.00
Glass, Raised Lettering, Tapered, 4 1/2 In.	6.00
Glass, Sylvester & Friends	5.00
Glass, Tweety Bird	5.00

Glass, White Tole 5.00
Golf Club, Putter, 35 In. 260.00
Hat, Driver's, One Size Fits All 25.00
Kaleidoscope, Catch The Spirit, Soda Can Shape, Steven, 1981, 5 In. 60.00
Key Chain, Bottle Cap Logo, Gold, 1950s 45.00
Menu Board, 49 x 20 In. 70.00
Menu Board, Self-Framed Tin, Bottle Cap Logo, 30 x 19 1/2 In. 120.00
Salt & Pepper, Drink Pepsi-Cola, 4 1/4 In. 22.00
Sign, Arrow, Tin, 27 x 9 In. 15.00
Sign, Beach Lady, Enameled, Porcelain, 11 1/2 x 8 3/4 In. 20.00
Sign, Bottle Cap, Celluloid, 1940s, 9 In. 247.00
Sign, Bottle Cap, Drink More Bounce To The Ounce, Tin, 11 3/4 In. 10.00
Sign, Bottle Cap, Enameled, Porcelain, 8 In. 20.00
Sign, Bottle Cap, Metal, Die Cut, Double Dot, Embossed, 1940s-1950s, 13 In. 249.00
Sign, Bottle Cap, Neon, Aqua, 17 x 6 In. 100.00
Sign, Bottle Cap, Neon, White, Tin Face, Black, 17 x 6 In. 90.00
Sign, Bottle Cap, Porcelain Embossed Tin, Vitracier Neuhaus, c.1950, 18 In. 374.00
Sign, Bottle, Diecut, Tin, 13 1/4 In. 160.00
Sign, Bottle, Diecut, Tin, 1930s, 30 In. 264.00
Sign, Bottle, Tin, Diecut, Embossed, Painted, 44 1/2 In. 200.00
Sign, Candle Sconce, Wood, 24 x 9 1/2 x 6 1/2 In. 149.00
Sign, Cap, Embossed, Tin, 27 x 7 In. 40.00
Sign, Embossed Script, Dark Green, White, Red, Tin, 1910, 10 In. 595.00
Sign, Ice Cold Pepsi, Porcelain, 11 x 9 In. 20.00
Sign, Marker, Metal, 36 x 4 1/2 In. 32.00
Sign, More Bounce To The Ounce, Tin, 1950s, 48 x 18 In. 577.00
Sign, Pepsi & Pete, Porcelain, 8 3/4 x 11 1/4 In. 20.00
Sign, Pepsi Thunderbirds, Porcelain, 8 5/8 x 11 5/8 In. 20.00
Sign, Pepsi, Good, Tin, 13 x 11 In. 10.00
Sign, Pepsi, More Bounce To The Ounce, Porcelain, 18 x 7 In. 20.00
Sign, Pub Clock, Wooden, 22 x 16 In. 149.00
Sign, Santa, Tin, 9 3/4 x 16 In. 10.00
Sign, Sold Here, Pepsi-Cola, Flange, 13 1/2 x 18 In. 30.00
Sign, Street, Embossed, Tin, 5 x 24 In. 10.00
Sign, Thermometer, Say Pepsi Please, 1965, 7 x 28 In. 7.00
Thermometer, 1940, 16 In. 125.00
Thermometer, Bottle Shape, 1940s, 15 1/2 In. 120.00
Thermometer, Double Dash, 27 x 7 1/8 In. 365.00
Thermometer, Gibson Girl Holding Pepsi In Glass, Wooden, 22 In. 29.00
Thermometer, Wood, 24 x 9 1/2 In. 100.00
Thimble, Drink Pepsi-Cola, 5 Cent, Gold Band Base 9.00
Toy, Tractor & Trailer, Buddy L, Red, Metal, Japan, 10 1/2 x 2 3/4 x 2 1/4 In. 25.00
Tray, Serving, Enjoy Pepsi-Cola Hits The Spot, 13 3/4 x 10 3/8 x 1/2 In. 175.00
Tray, Wooden, 24 x 16 In. 100.00
Truck, No. 4 .... 69.00
Whistle, 2 Bottles 150.00
Yo-Yo, Wooden, White, Red Double Dash Logo, Late 1930s 250.00

PERFUME BOTTLES are made of cut glass, pressed glass, art glass, silver, metal, enamel, and even plastic or porcelain. Although the small bottle to hold perfume was first made before the time of ancient Egypt, it is the nineteenth- and twentieth-century examples that interest today's collector. DeVilbiss Company has made atomizers of all types since 1888 but no longer makes the perfume bottle tops so popular with collectors. These were made from 1920 to 1968. The glass bottle may be by any of many manufacturers even if the atomizer is marked *DeVilbiss*. The word *factice*, which often appears in ads, refers to store display bottles. Glass or porcelain examples may be found under the appropriate name such as Lalique, Czechoslovakia, Glass-Bohemian, etc.

After Jacob Petit, Green, Raised Gilt Bands, Knopped Stopper, Paris, 7 x 5 In. 800.00
Amberina, Amber, Blown Stopper, 6 1/2 x 3 In. 690.00
Amberina, Stopper, 7 1/2 x 2 1/2 In. 1150.00
Amethyst, Melon Ribbed, Applied Leaves, Steuben, 6 1/2 In. 402.00

Amethyst Glass, Enameled Gold Metal Jeweled Frame, Stopper, Czechoslovakia 90.00
Ann Haviland, Lily Of The Valley Toilet Water, Triangular, 1940s 22.00
Art Glass, Bleeding Heart Flowers & Vine, Midnight Blue, Loetz, 9 1/4 In. 805.00
Art Glass, Green Jade, Clambroth, Stopper, Steuben, 5 1/4 In. 275.00
Art Glass, Rosaline, Clambroth, Stopper, Steuben, 7 In. 350.00
Art Glass, Vaseline, Green Enamel, Greek Goddesses, Musicians, Hoffman, 5 In. 2200.00
Atomizer, Adam & Eve, Apple, Malachite Green, Hexagonal, Moser, 6 1/4 In. 430.00
Atomizer, Amethyst Over Orange, 9 1/2 In. 1650.00
Atomizer, Burgundy On Peach, Signed, Galle, 7 1/4 In. 1500.00
Atomizer, Cameo Glass, Seascape, Sailboat, Olive Green To Ocher Ground, 9 In. 127.00
Atomizer, Cameo, Landscape, Green, Amber, Geese In Flight, D'Argental, 4 1/2 In. 489.00
Atomizer, Crystal, Etched, Trumpet Form, Chrome Mounts, Black Bulb, 4 In. 165.00
Atomizer, Deep Amethyst Blackberries, Blue, Richard, Loetz, 12 In. 489.00
Atomizer, Floral, Amethyst Over, Blue, Cameo, Richard, Loetz, 8 1/2 In. 950.00
Atomizer, Glass, Pink Stem, Gold, Czechoslovakia, 7 In. 125.00
Atomizer, Glass, Yellow & Red, Clear Case, Brass Top, Czechoslovakia, 5 In. 50.00
Atomizer, Leaves, Stems, Buds, Cranberry, Loetz, 9 In. 975.00
Atomizer, Moser, Cobalt Blue, Gilt Leaves, 6 1/2 In. 196.00
Atomizer, Purple Bleeding Hearts, Satin, Signed, Galle, 7 3/4 In. 920.00
Aurene, Blue Iridescent, Ground Pontil, Stopper, 6 In. 504.00
Babs Creations, Yesteryear, Figural, Woman, Blue, White Ribbons, Screw Cap 17.50
Balenciaga, Quadrille, Atomizer, Box, France 20.00
Belgium, White Flower, Pink Lavender Colored Perfume, Goldtone Cap, 3 1/4 In. 10.00
Bird Of Paradise, Stopper, Pairpoint, 11 1/4 x 3 In. 402.00
Blue Swirl, Threading On Stopper, 4 In. 425.00
Bohemian Glass, Green Cut To Clear, Stopper, Flowers, Leaves, 6 1/2 In. 374.00
Bristol Glass, Blue, Allover Enameled Flowers & Leaves, 3 1/4 In. 110.00
Bristol Glass, Turquoise Band Of Flowers, Dots & Gold Base, 6 1/2 In. 135.00
Bunker Hill Monument, Milk Glass, 12 In. 165.00
California Perfume Co., Roses, Triangular, Labels, New York, 1880-1900, 3 In. 79.00
Cameo Glass, Asters, Chased Silver Cap & Base, Daum, c.1895, 5 In. 800.00
Celeste Blue, Melon Ribbed, Celeste Blue Stopper, Steuben, 4 1/2 In. 290.00
Celeste Blue, Stopper, Steuben, 6 1/2 In. 450.00
Ceramic Overlay Aventurine Glass, 3 Portraits, Brass Cover, Chain, 2 3/8 In. 550.00
Christian Dior, Diorissimo, Atomizer, Box, 7/16 Oz., 3 1/2 In.   24.00
Cologne, Bourjois, Evening In Paris, Clear, Blue Speckled Cap, 4 Oz. 15.00
Cologne, Cobalt Blue, 12 Sides, Rolled Lip, 6 1/2 In. 120.00
Cologne, Cranberry Glass, Daisy Flowers, Gold Leaves & Trim, 7 1/4 In. 175.00
Cologne, Cranberry Glass, Ribbed, Clear Wafer Foot, Cut Stopper, 7 1/4 In. 135.00
Cologne, Cut Glass, Allover Design, 7 In. 135.00
Cologne, Dorothy Gray, Floral Fantasy, Ribbed, Turquoise Plastic Cap, 1940s 22.00
Cologne, Green, Gold Enameled, 19th Century, 7 1/2 In. 430.00
Cologne, Khus Khus, Bell Hop Sculpture, Painted, 1940s 45.00
Cologne, Lander, Apple Blossom, Toilet Water, Red Metal Cap, 3 Oz., 4 1/2 In. 14.00

Perfume Bottle, Cut
Glass, Aqua, Flowers,
Stopper, Ingrid,
Czechoslovakia,
6 9/16 In.

Perfume Bottle, Cut Glass,
Intaglio, Amber, Marked,
Czechoslovakia, 4 1/2 In.

Perfume Bottle, Cut Glass,
Intaglio, Floral, Jeweled,
Czechoslovakia, 5 1/2 In.

Cologne, Madame Rochas, 8 Sides, White Plastic Screw Cap, 2 5/8 In. 14.00
Cologne, Milk Glass, 8 Sides, 4 1/4 In. 165.00
Cologne, Mulhems, 4711, Embossed, Paper Label, Red Cap, 4 3/4 In. 10.00
Cologne, Pale Ice Blue, Herringbone, 1820, 6 1/4 In. 550.00
Cologne, Paperweight, Walled, Internal Silver Flecks, Steuben, c.1930, 7 1/4 In. 4600.00
Cologne, Peacock Blue, Corset Waist, 8 Sides, 4 3/4 In. 745.00
Cologne, Pink Amethyst, 12 Sides, Rolled Lip, 6 1/4 In. 100.00
Cologne, Pink Amethyst, 12 Sides, Sloped Shoulders, 6 1/8 In. 155.00
Cologne, Purple Amethyst, 12 Sides, Sloped Shoulders, Pontil, 1880, 4 In. 260.00
Cologne, Sapphire Blue, Rolled Lip, Pontil, 5 5/8 In. 1595.00
Cologne, Teal Green, 12 Sides, Tooled Lip, 6 3/8 In. 110.00
Cologne, Trapped Bubbles Over Crosshatch Design, Signed, Steuben, c.1925, 7 In. 632.00
Coty, L'Or, Crystal, Teardrop, Oval Facets, Yellow, White Fabric Box, 1959, 6 1/3 In. 5500.00
Coty, Sachet, Blue Satin Bag, Cord Tie, York Paris, 2 Oz. 13.00
Cranberry Glass, Diapered Finish, Stopper, 4 3/4 In. 115.00
Cut Glass, Aqua, Flowers, Stopper, Ingrid, Czechoslovakia, 6 9/16 In. ....*Illus* 1430.00
Cut Glass, Cobalt To Clear, Metal Mounts, Sandwich, 7 In. 230.00
Cut Glass, Hobstar, Stopper, 6 1/2 In. 295.00
Cut Glass, Intaglio Flowers, Hobstar Band, Stopper, Signed, Hawkes, 5 In. 350.00
Cut Glass, Intaglio, Amber, Marked, Czechoslovakia, 4 1/2 In. ....*Illus* 286.00
Cut Glass, Intaglio, Floral, Jeweled, Czechoslovakia, 5 1/2 In. ....*Illus* 550.00
Cut Glass, Intaglio, Stopper, Czechoslovakia, 5 1/2 In. ....*Illus* 297.00
Cut Glass, Intaglio, Violet, Clear, Marked, Czechoslovakia, 5 In. ....*Illus* 550.00
Cut Glass, Jewel, Stopper, Clark, 6 1/2 In. 285.00
Cut Glass, Manhattan Club, Stopper, Home Glass Co., 8 In. 345.00
Cut Glass, Navarre, Stopper, Engraved Silver Rim, Gorham, Signed, Hawkes, 6 In. 985.00
Cut Panels, Royal Blue To Clear, Steeple Stopper, 5 1/4 In. 135.00
Deep Burgundy Berries & Leaves, Green, Cameo, Galle, 4 1/4 In. 1725.00
DeVilbiss, Black, Oval, Gilt Vertical Stripes, Pedestal, c.1920, 9 In. 300.00
DeVilbiss, Cranberry, Bohemian, Acid Textured Finish, Gilt, 6 1/4 In. 123.00
DeVilbiss, Orange Fold Heart & Vine, Gilt Metal Atomizer, 10 In. 1495.00
DeVilbiss, Pink Satin Glass, Brass Mounts, Glass Applicator, Signed Base, 6 In. 138.00
Ellipse Pattern, Apple Green, Gilt Trim, Hexagonal, Stopper, 1870, 8 In. 275.00
Emerald, Glass Stopper, Steuben, 7 In. 450.00
Faberge, Brass Over Glass, Fancy Openwork, Screw Cap, Purse Size, 3 1/4 In. 39.00
Faberge, Straw Hat, Glass, Goldtone Case, Purse Size, 3 In. 10.00
Figural, Oriental Dancer, Lobed Plinth, Paris, 8 x 5 1/2 x 2 1/2 In. 1495.00
Fish Graal, Deep Amethyst Starfish, Seaweed, Stopper, Hald, Orrefors, 1938 .... 2415.00
Floral Design, Cameo, Signed, Richard, 5 1/2 In. 890.00
Floral Reserves, Green Border, Raised Gold, Paris, 10 1/2 In., Pair 1035.00
Flowers, Celeste Blue Stopper, Signed, Steuben, Peggy Hoyt, 3 1/2 In. 475.00
Formia Murano, Burgundy, Green Inside, Suspended Bubbles, 9 1/2 In. 90.00
Gold Outline, Floral Reserve, Leaf Finial Stopper, Paris, 11 In. 144.00
Green Jade, Verre De Soie Stopper, Steuben, 4 3/4 In. 425.00
Green Paint, Pink, Gold Floral Sprays, Paris, 8 1/2 In., Pair 460.00
Guerlain, Baccarat Urn, Fan Form Light Blue Glass Stopper, 5 5/8 In. 86.00
Heffront-Tanner Co., Deep Teal, Fancy Design, Square, No Stopper, 3 1/4 In. 78.00
Houbigant, Chantilly, Eau De Toilette, 2 Oz., Pink Ribbon, Plastic Cap, 4 3/4 In. 10.00
Ice Blue, Bohemian, Enameled, 3 In., Pair 28.00
Leon Applebaum, Purple, Bubble Twists & Ring, Clear Stopper, 3 x 3 3/4 In. 55.00
Louis D'Or, Joey, Mold Mark, France, Full, Miniature 8.00
Melon Ribbed, Amber, Teardrop Stopper, Steuben, 4 1/2 In. ....259.00 to 475.00
Melon Shape, Blue Aurene, Steuben 1500.00
Milk Glass, Stopper, 6 1/2 In. 40.00
Nina Ricci, Lalique Urn, Octagonal Stopper, 2 3/8 In. 46.00
Norelle, Glass, Gold Screw Top, Purse Size, Box 28.00
Paperweight, Swan Finial, Pairpoint, 1930, 5 3/4 x 2 1/4 In. 50.00
Peacock Blue, Purple Iridescent, Stopper, Signed, Steuben, 6 x 3 In. 1150.00
Perpetually Yours, Gold, Rolex, Pocket Watch Form, Glass Cover, 3 1/4 In. 600.00
Petal Cut Base, Scene Of Antelope On Savannah, Stopper, 6 1/2 In. 69.00
Pink Crackle, Flower Top Plunger, I. Rice & Co., Inc., Label, Japan, 3 1/2 In. 45.00
Plein Coeur, Heart Shape, Lay Down, Mini, Silver, Red Box, White Cap, 1 5/8 In. 18.00
Purse, Petit Point, Rose, Leaves, Buds, Frame, 2 1/2 In. 15.00

Perfume Bottle, Cut Glass,
Intaglio, Stopper,
Czechoslovakia, 5 1/2 In.

Perfume Bottle, Cut Glass,
Intaglio, Violet, Clear, Marked,
Czechoslovakia, 5 In.

Perfume Bottle, Scent, Man & Woman Shape,
J. Petit Type, Paris, 1850, 11 3/4 In., Pair

Santa Claus, Painted Glass, Plastic Base, 1940s, 4 1/2 In. 11.00
Scent, Gold Shell Outline, Scroll Feet, Paris, 19th Century, 6 3/4 In., Pair 315.00
Scent, Highland Lad, Wearing Gilt Floral Kilt, Paris, Late 19th Century, 7 1/2 In. 230.00
Scent, Man & Woman Shape, J. Petit Type, Paris, 1850, 11 3/4 In., Pair . . . .*Illus* 1265.00
Schiaparelli, Torso, Signed On Base, Miniature 20.00
Silver Floral Overlay, Pinched Glass, 4 1/2 In. 135.00
Silver Overlay On Clear Glass, Pear Shape, Ball Stopper, 3 In. 86.00
Solon Palmer, Perfumer, N.Y., Label Under Glass, Stopper, 7 7/8 In. 635.00
Superior, Cologne, Amethyst, Flowers, Birds, Cherub, Sandwich Glass, 1888, 8 3/4 In. . . 770.00
Swan's Head Shape, Silver Hinged Cap, Webb, c.1883, 4 In. 1265.00
Vaseline Glass, Green Enamel, Greek Goddess, Musicians, Hoffman, 5 In. 2200.00
Verre De Soie, Celeste Blue Stopper, Steuben, 3 1/2 In. 475.00
Verre De Soie, Green Jade, Stopper, Steuben, 3 1/2 In. 425.00
Verre De Soie, Melon Ribbed, Celeste Blue Stopper, 4 3/4 In. 425.00
Verre De Soie, Stopper, Steuben, 7 In. 450.00
Vert Vert, Blamain, Square, Brown Label, Screw Cap, Miniature, 1 5/16 In. 19.00
W. & H. Walker Perfumers, Lavender Salts, Pittsburg, USA, Teal, 3 1/4 In. 78.00
Wheel Cut, Crystal, Red Overlay, Etched Diamond Pattern, Stopper, 8 3/4 In. 165.00
Wheel Cut, Crystal, Red Overlay, Grapevine Design, 8 Sides, Stopper, 6 In. 155.00
Worth, Je Reviens, Diamond Shape Label, Screw Cap, Box, 1/20 Fl. Oz., 1 5/16 In. 22.00
Worth, Je Reviens, Round Silver Label, Red Lettering, Gold Cap, Box, Mini 22.00

PETERS & REED Pottery Company of Zanesville, Ohio, was founded
by John D. Peters and Adam Reed in 1897. Chromal, Landsun,
Montene, Pereco, and Persian are some of the art lines that were made.
The company, which became Zane Pottery in 1920 and Gonder Pottery
in 1941, closed in 1957. Peters & Reed pottery was unmarked.

Base, Cream, Yellow & Green Accents, 8 In. 100.00
Bowl, Zane, 2 Blue, 1 Brown, 8 In., 3 Piece 74.00
Ewer, Cherry Sprig, Cherries & Leaves On Front, 10 In. 145.00
Figurine, Frog, Marbleized, 4 7/8 In. 224.00
Floor Vase, Embossed Flowers, Blue Matte Glaze, 18 In. 546.00
Flower Frog, Dark Green, Marbleized, 4 7/8 In. 220.00
Jar, Cover, Landsun, Dark Green, 4 In. 330.00
Jardiniere, Chromal Ware, 7 1/2 x 9 1/4 In. 575.00
Jardiniere, Moss Aztec, c.1925, 9 x 9 1/2 In. 200.00
Jug, 3 Bunches Of Flowers On Front, 1 Handle, 6 x 5 In. 85.00
Jug, Marbleized Glaze, 19 In. 1095.00
Planter, Moss Aztec, Classical Scene, Signed Ferrell, 5 1/4 x 12 1/4 In. 230.00
Vase, Art Pottery, Floral & Leaf Embossed, Hole Drilled Base, 22 In. 100.00
Vase, Chromal Ware, 10 x 4 In. 345.00
Vase, Chromal, Dark Blue, Brown, Tan, 7 3/4 In. 220.00
Vase, Embossed Leaf & Flowers, Green Matte Glaze, 4 x 5 1/2 In. 115.00

Vase, Landsun, Multicolored Drip Glaze, Green, Light Green Ground, 11 In.	385.00
Vase, Marbleized Glaze, 16 In.	550.00
Vase, Moss Agate, Corseted, Stylized Flowers, Leaves, 10 1/2 x 4 1/4 In.	230.00
Vase, Moss Aztec, Blackberries, Embossed, 7 7/8 In.	88.00
Vase, Pinecone, 9 1/2 In.	85.00
Vase, Pinecone, Terra-Cotta, 10 In.	230.00
Vase, Shadow Ware, Green, Black Flambe Glaze, 12 x 6 1/2 In.	315.00
Vase, Shadow Ware, Yellow Glaze, 8 3/4 x 5 In.	230.00

PETRUS REGOUT, see Maastricht category.

PEWABIC POTTERY was founded by Mary Chase Perry Stratton in 1903 in Detroit, Michigan. The company made many types of art pottery, including pieces with matte green glaze and an iridescent crystalline glaze. The company continued working until the death of Mary Stratton in 1961. It was reactivated by Michigan State University in 1968.

Bowl, Blue Metallic Glaze, 5 1/2 In.	240.00
Bowl, Dove Gray Luster, Turquoise Interior, 1 3/4 x 3 3/4 In.	259.00
Bowl, Flowing Brown Matte Glaze Exterior, Lavender, Turquoise Interior, 4 x 7 In.	805.00
Bowl, Hemispherical, Drip Turquoise, Gunmetal Luster Glaze, 3 3/4 x 6 3/4 In.	2025.00
Jar, Cover, Eggplant Shape, Dark Purple Matte Glaze, 6 3/4 x 4 1/4 In.	2070.00
Jardiniere, Cobalt Luster Glaze, 8 x 9 In.	2475.00
Mug, Green Matte Flambe Glaze, 2 3/4 x 5 3/4 In.	460.00
Tile, Black Owl Resting On Perch, Crystalline Glaze, 3 x 3 In.	200.00
Tile, Bowl, Black, Crystalline Glaze, Square, 3 In.	200.00
Vase, Abstract Tree Design, Cobalt, White Ground, Marked, 4 x 3 1/2 In.	2760.00
Vase, Blue, Turquoise, Mottled Glaze, Bulbous, 7 3/4 x 5 1/2 In.	1350.00
Vase, Brilliant Green Metallic Glaze, Red Platinum, 11 In.	3740.00
Vase, Brown Semimatte Glaze, 11 3/4 x 6 1/2 In.	1495.00
Vase, Celadon & Dripping Turquoise Glaze, Signed, 8 1/4 In.	1610.00
Vase, Celadon Drip, Purple Glaze, Pear Shape, 6 x 4 1/4 In.	845.00
Vase, Celadon, Gold Luster Glaze, 10 1/2 x 5 In.	2362.00
Vase, Cobalt, Green Luster Glaze, 3 3/4 x 3 3/4 In.	730.00
Vase, Cobalt, Turquoise Luster Glaze, 9 3/4 x 6 1/2 In.	5625.00
Vase, Cream Drip Glaze Over Mottled Luster, Sloped Shoulder, Signed, 4 1/2 In.	200.00
Vase, Flowing Green Matte Glaze, Bulbous, 8 x 7 In.	2530.00
Vase, Green, Purple Iridescent Glaze, Sloping Shoulder, 5 x 5 In.	450.00
Vase, Large Leaves, Green Matte Glaze, 10 x 5 3/4 In.	4600.00
Vase, Luster Copper & Gold Glaze, Signed, 7 1/2 In.	2530.00
Vase, Luster Red & Green Glaze, Bulbous, Paper Label, 3 1/2 x 3 1/4 In.	375.00
Vase, Luster Umber Rim, White Semimatte Glaze, Signed, 3 1/2 In.	575.00
Vase, Metallic Purple Luster, Green & Rose Highlights, Signed, 4 In.	1100.00
Vase, Mustard Matte Drip Glaze, Caramel Ground, Marked, 11 x 8 1/2 In.	11250.00
Vase, Orange, Gray, Green Matte Luster Glaze, Handles, 10 x 9 In.	2990.00
Vase, Pink Drip Crackled Glaze, Blue Luster Base, 2 1/2 x 2 1/4 In.	280.00
Vase, Plaque & Sheer Crackled Dripping Glaze, Signed, 7 In.	805.00
Vase, Red, Platinum, Green Matte, Metallic Glaze, Bulbous, 10 In.	2645.00
Vase, Teal, Green, Gunmetal Glaze, 2 3/4 x 3 3/4 In.	460.00
Vase, Turquoise Drip Glaze, Gold Luster Glaze, 3 1/2 x 2 1/4 In.	200.00
Vase, Turquoise Volcanic Glaze, Bulbous, 4 3/4 x 4 In.	690.00
Vase, Yellow Matte, Brown Flambe Glaze, Stamped, Paper Label, 3 1/4 x 4 1/2 In.	489.00
Vase, Yellow, Brown, Green Flowing Matte Crystalline Glaze, 10 1/4 x 4 3/4 In.	1955.00
Vase, Yellow, Turquoise, Lavender Flowing Luster Glaze, 3 1/2 x 4 In.	518.00
Vase, Yellow, Turquoise, Purple Matte Luster Glaze, 3 1/2 x 4 In.	633.00

PEWTER is a metal alloy of tin and lead. Some of the pewter made after 1840 has a slightly different composition and is called *Britannia metal*. This later type of pewter was worked by machine; the earlier pieces were made by hand. In the 1920s pewter came back into fashion and pieces were often marked *Genuine Pewter*. Eighteenth-, nineteenth-, and twentieth-century examples are listed here.

Ale Jug, Solid Thumbpiece, Dome Top Lid, England, c.1825, 8 1/4 In.	345.00

Basin, Amos Treadwar Jr., 9 In. 1265.00
Basin, Eagle Mark, American, c.1790, 7 3/4 In. 175.00
Basin, Gershom Jones, Eagle Touch Mark, No.178, 7 3/4 In. 220.00
Basin, Richard Lee, Raised Rim, 2 x 8 3/4 In. 580.00
Basin, Samuel Pierce, 13 1/4 In. 220.00
Basin, T.D., Incised Ring, Flared Rim, Eagle Touchmark, c.1800, 12 In. 1155.00
Bowl, Baptismal, Roswell Gleason, 1822, 5 x 8 1/8 In. 1265.00
Bowl, Liberty, Hammered, Original Patina, Signed, 2 x 6 1/2 In. 145.00
Bowl, Sylvester Griswold, 13 In. 470.00
Candlestick, Baluster Stem, Round Base, B & P Touchmark, 11 1/4 In., Pair 140.00
Candlestick, R. Dunham, 6 In. 165.00
Candlestick, Round Turned Form, Ejectors, 10 In. 98.00
Charger, Jacob Whitmore, Tooled Lines At Rim & Interior Base, 13 1/8 In. 415.00
Charger, Single Reeded, England, c.1750, 18 3/8 In. 405.00
Coffeepot, A Griswold, Tooled Ring Base, Band Around Body, Scrolled Handle, 10 In. .. 580.00
Coffeepot, Archibald Knox, Short Spout, Scroll Handle, 8 3/4 In. 5035.00
Coffeepot, Calder, 8 1/4 In. 170.00
Coffeepot, Dixon & Son, Scalloped Spout, Wooden Wafer & Handle, 11 In. 105.00
Coffeepot, E. Smith, Lighthouse, Engraved Shield Panels, Beverly, Mass., 1800s, 12 In. .. 470.00
Coffeepot, Eben Smith, Lighthouse, Beverly, Mass., c.1856, 12 x 6 3/4 In. 1380.00
Coffeepot, Hall, Boardman & Co., Lighthouse, 10 3/4 In. 495.00
Coffeepot, Israel Trask, Lighthouse, Engraved Bands, 11 3/4 In. 1035.00
Coffeepot, J.B. Woodbury, Black Finial, 11 In. 110.00
Coffeepot, Lighthouse, Rings On Body, Beehive Finial, 10 3/8 In. 165.00
Coffeepot, R. Dunham, 19th Century, 10 1/2 In. 825.00
Coffeepot, Richardson, Double, Bulbous, 11 In. 230.00
Coffeepot, Tooled Lines At Base & Below Spout, Scrolled Handle, Finial, 11 1/4 In. 360.00
Coffeepot, William Calder, Lighthouse, Hinged Domed Lid, Tapered Body 1150.00
Coffeepot, Wooden Handle, Dated 1798 .... 325.00
Communion Set, 2 Cups, Flagon, American, c.1830 .... 1200.00
Cup, Footed, Surrey Verification Stamp, England, 1/2 Pt., 4 In. 58.00
Decanter, Wine, Light Amber Glass, 15 x 4 1/2 In. 245.00
Desk Set, 2 Hinged Lids, Opening To Wells, Sand Shaker, Sectioned Interior, 8 In. 185.00
Dish, Armorial, Octagonal, Monogram, Germany, 18th Century, 11 1/2 In. 290.00
Dish, Crowned Royal Cipher Of King George IV, Used At Coronation, 1820, 12 In. 395.00
Dish, Deep, Ellis Samuel, c.1760, 14 1/2 In. 200.00
Dish, Deep, Plain Rim, England, 16 3/8 In. 65.00
Dish, Peter Young, N.Y., 13 3/4 In. 480.00
Dish, Thomas Danforth II, Single Reeded, American, 12 1/4 In. 460.00
Flagon, Boardman, Rampant Lion, 11 1/2 In. 440.00
Flagon, Communion, Reed & Barton, 11 1/4 In. 220.00
Flagon, Reed & Barton, Tooled Rings On Body, Scrolled Handle, Pierced Lever, 9 5/8 In. .. 440.00
Flagon, Smith & Feltman, Flaring Form, Scrolled Handle, Domed Lid, c.1850, 10 In. 170.00
Flagon, Wine, Dutch, Late 18th Century, 10 In. 250.00
Flask, Encased Glass, Open Rib Around Body, Pewter Cap 195.00
Flask, HRT 1864, In God Is Our Trust, Florida, Camp Scene, No Cap, 1800s, 6 In. 250.00
Inkwell, Victorian, Round, Cover, England, 4 3/4 In. 58.00
Ladle, Punch, Dark Patina, England, Mid 19th Century, 13 In. 95.00
Lamp, Finger, Capen & Molineux, Scrolled Ear Handle, 4 1/2 In. 110.00
Measure, Double Volute, William Fasson, London, Verification Stamp, c.1800, 3 1/2 In. ... 230.00
Mold, Ice Cream, George & Martha Washington, 5 1/2 In., Pair 80.00
Mold, Ice Cream, Santa Claus, Hinged, 4 3/8 In. 176.00
Mug, Brass Rim, Loftus Of London, 19th Century, 6 In. 290.00
Mug, Concave, Scotland, Mark, Wood & Sons, Glascow, 1 Qt., 6 1/2 In. 115.00
Mug, Straight-Sided, England, c.1850, 6 In. 29.00
Mug, Tavern, Preston Edgar, Bristol, 1780, 1 Qt. 495.00
Mug, Tavern, Richard Mister Of London, Imperial WR Crowned Excise Mark, 1 Qt. 225.00
Pitcher, Pouring Spout, Head Of Maiden On Loop Handle, 1820s, 10 1/2 In., Pair 575.00
Plate, David Melville, Mark, Newport, Rhode Island, 8 3/16 In. 345.00
Plate, Frederick Bassett, No. 24 & No. 25, 8 1/2 In. 825.00
Plate, Frederick Bassett, Touchmark, 8 3/8 In. 550.00
Plate, Roswell Gleason, 9 1/4 In. 275.00
Plate, S. Kilbourn, c.1820, 7 3/4 In. 275.00

Plate, Samuel Hamlin & Son, Early 1800s, 11 1/2 In. 365.00
Plate, Thomas Danforth II, John Danforth, Reeded, Middletown, Conn., 7 7/8 In. 29.00
Plate, William Billings, c.1800, 8 3/8 In. 440.00
Plate, William Calder, 11 3/8 In. 360.00
Plate, William Will, Hammered Bouge, Phila., 1798, 8 In. 1200.00
Porringer, Crown Handle, Reverse Cast Initials, Triangular Bracket, c.1850, 4 1/4 In. 290.00
Porringer, Crown Handle, Signed EG, 4 1/4 In. 90.00
Porringer, Flower Handle, Booge & Gutter Bowl, Linen Mark, c.1820, 5 3/8 In. 290.00
Porringer, Pieced Handle, Crown Design, Samuel Green, 5 3/4 In. 460.00
Porringer, R.G., Roswell Gleason, Crown Handle, Stamped, Mass., 1822-1871, 2 In. 470.00
Porringer, Samuel Hamlin, Pierced Handle, 4 3/4 In. 488.00
Porringer, Thomas Danforth & Sherman Boardman, Pierced Floral Handle, 5 1/4 In. 660.00
Porringer, William Billings, Pierced Floral Handle, Early 1800s, 5 1/8 In. 550.00
Porringer, William Calder, Pierced Floral Handle, 5 In. 660.00
Porringer Set, Crown Handle, Triangular Brackets, Linen Mark, c.1825, 6 Piece 2300.00
Pot, Roswell Gleason 410.00
Sconce, 2-Light, Triple Arch Backplate, Pair 175.00
Stein, Barrel Form, Dated 1821 .... 210.00
Syrup, Mushroom Finial, 6 1/4 In. 1275.00
Tankard, Domed Lid, Ring Turned Base, Scrolled Handle, England, 10 In. 75.00
Tankard, Liberty & Co., Raised Stylized Fruiting Branch, Handle, 1930s, 5 3/8 In. 200.00
Tankard, Rings At Base, Center & Top, Domed Lid, Pierced Thumb Lever, 6 7/8 In. 1705.00
Tankard, Tulip Shape, Domed, Double Curve Handle, Open Back, c.1820, 1 Qt., 9 In. ... 1150.00
Tazza, W & Co., Griffin Handles, Hammered Surface, Hand Beaten, 10 x 11 In. 170.00
Tea Set, Kayserzinn, Arts & Crafts Floral, 19 1/2-In. Tray 1045.00
Tea Set, Tudric, Arts & Crafts, Aladdin Shape Pot, Signed, 4 Piece 175.00
Teapot, Allen Porter, Westbrook, Maine, 11 3/4 In. 1100.00
Teapot, B & V, Queen Anne, Wooden Wafer On Finial, Irish, Crowned X, 6 In. 495.00
Teapot, Boardman & Co., Eagle Touchmark, 1825, 7 1/2 In. 140.00
Teapot, Boardman & Co., Scrolled Handle, Flared Neck, Wooden Wafer Finial, 7 1/8 In. . 220.00
Teapot, Domed Cover, Pelton, Conn., c.1850, 7 1/4 In. 58.00
Teapot, Drum Shape, Tulip Finial, Dutch, 1780, 1 Cup, 2 3/4 In. 495.00
Teapot, Eben Smith, Tooled Lines, Stepped Conical Finial, 7 7/8 In. 250.00
Teapot, H. Putnam, Tooled Lines, Petal Wafer Finial, Scrolled Handle, 7 1/2 In. 330.00
Teapot, Hale, Pear Shape, Wooden Handle, c.1790, 6 In. 2300.00
Teapot, I. Trask, Queen Anne, Pear Shape 715.00
Teapot, Ivory Finial, Pear Shape, Paneled Spout, 8 In. 880.00
Teapot, J.B. Woodbury, Stepped Dome Top, c.1820, 7 1/4 In. 165.00
Teapot, J.D. Locke, 9 In. 410.00
Teapot, J.W. Cahill & Co., Tooled Lines, Black Handle & Finial, 1830s, 7 In. 360.00
Teapot, James H. Putnam, Tooled Lines, Petal Wafer On Finial, 8 3/4 In. 190.00
Teapot, Morey & Ober, Lighthouse, Gooseneck Spout, Boston, 1855, 7 In. 275.00
Teapot, Rufus Dunham, Flared Neck, Scrolled Handle, Tooled Lines, 6 1/2 In. 250.00
Teapot, Sellew & Co., Gooseneck Spout, Ear Handle, Cincinnati, c.1850, 7 1/2 In. 300.00
Teapot, Smith & Co., 6 3/4 In. 300.00
Teapot, W. Humston, Scrolled Handle, Tooled Lines On Body & Lid, 7 3/4 In. 275.00
Teapot, Wilks & C., Flattened Oval Shape, Marked, Sheffield, 19th Century, 5 In. 29.00
Tinderbox, Etched, Striker, Candle, Flint & Starter, Box, 1 1/4 x 3 1/8 In. 310.00
Vase, 5 Fish, 2 Handles, Signed, 6 1/2 In. 330.00
Vase, Liberty & Company Tudric, 1902, 5 1/2 In. 575.00
Vase, Raised & Tooled Arts & Crafts Design, 9 In. 110.00
Vase, Tudric, Trumpet Form, Raised Branches Bearing Fruit, Signed, 1930s, Pair 230.00
Whistle, Policeman's, Victorian 25.00
Wine, Poole, Taunton, Mass., 4 1/2 In. 25.00

PHOENIX BIRD, or Flying Phoenix, is the name given to a blue-and-
white kitchenware popular between 1900 and World War II. A variant
is known as Flying Turkey. Most of this dinnerware was made in Japan
for sale in the dime stores in America. It is still being made.

Casserole, 7 3/4 In. 75.00
Cup & Saucer, Demitasse 20.00
Eggcup, 3 In. 10.00
Platter, 12 5/8 In. 103.00

Platter, Oval, 14 1/2 In.	93.00
Tureen, Cover, 7 In.	200.00

PHOENIX GLASS Company was founded in 1880 in Pennsylvania. The firm made commercial products, such as lampshades, bottles, and glassware. Collectors today are interested in the "Sculptured Artware" made by the company from the 1930s until the mid-1950s. Some pieces of Phoenix glass are very similar to those made by the Consolidated Lamp and Glass Company. Phoenix made Reuben Blue, lavender, and yellow pieces. These colors were not used by Consolidated. In 1970 Phoenix became a division of Anchor Hocking, then was sold to the Newell Group in 1987. The company is still working.

Bowl, Diving Girl, Green, Yellow Highlights, Satin, Oval, 14 In.	175.00
Vase, Blackberry, Clear & Satin, 18 1/2 In.	490.00
Vase, Blackberry, Lavender On Clear, 18 In.	430.00
Vase, Blackberry, Lavender On Clear, 18 x 9 In.	750.00
Vase, Fern, Clear Satin, 7 In. ....*Illus*	77.00
Vase, Katydid, Clear Satin, 8 In.	130.00
Vase, Poppies, Tan On Clear, Drilled For Lamp, 13 In.	80.00
Vase, Poppy, Green On Clear, 10 In. ....*Illus*	165.00
Vase, White Ground, Brown Geese In Flight, 9 In., Pair	460.00
Vase, Wild Geese, Blue Iridescent On White, 9 1/2 In.	220.00
Vase, Wild Rose, Blue On Clear Satin, 10 1/2 In.	175.00

PHONOGRAPHS, invented by Thomas Edison in 1877, have been made by many firms. This category also includes other items associated with the phonograph. Jukeboxes and records are listed in their own categories.

Coin-Operated, Regina, Hexaphone, Oak Case	7100.00
Columbia Grafonola Deluxe, Carved Lion's Heads, 59 Regina Discs, 1915	5175.00
Dancer, Tango, Magnetic, Pair	75.00
Edison, Amberola, Diamond C Reproducer, Oak Case	430.00
Edison, Diamond Disc, Adapter To Play 78s, 45 In.	900.00
Edison, Home Model, Glory Horn, Oak, 160 Cylinders, 35 x 23 x 20 In.	1320.00
Edison, Oak, Tin Horn, 12 Cylinders	495.00
Gem, Edison, Key Wind	775.00
Graphophone, Columbia, Morning Glory Horn	1430.00
Home Kinetoscope, Edison	2100.00
Horn, Flower Shape, Germany, c.1910, 21 In.	575.00
Horn, Oak, Flower Shape, Germany, c.1910, 21 In.	575.00
Pocket, Mikiphone, Metal Case, Key Wind, Marked System Vadasz, Switzerland, 6 In.	675.00
Polyphon, Coin-Operated, Walnut Case, 13 Disc, 43 x 23 x 12 In.	4480.00
Regina, Hexaphone, Coin-Operated, Oak, 4 Disks, Late 19th Century, 10 x 21 In.	1456.00
Reginaphone, Mahogany, Double Comb, 1899, 15 3/4-In. Disc	9315.00
Standard, Model A, Patent 1901	517.00
Thorens, Bird's-Eye Veneer Case, 3 Tunes	55.00
Victor, Front Doors Over Oak Grill, Table Top, Oak Case	210.00
Victrola, Victor Talking Machine Co., Crank, VV-IV-271195e, 8 x 4 In.	120.00

Phoenix Glass, Vase,
Fern, Clear Satin, 7 In.

Phoenix Glass, Vase, Poppy,
Green On Clear, 10 In.

PHONOGRAPH NEEDLE CASES of tin are collected today by music and phonograph enthusiasts and advertising addicts. The tins are very small, about 2 inches across, and often have attractive graphic designs lithographed on the top and sides.

Chanteciep, Picture Of Rooster, Navy Background, 1 5/8 x 1 1/4 In.	48.00
Cover, 200 Needles, England	61.00
Dog & Angel	13.00
Dog & Puppy, 200 Pure Steel Needles	10.00
Edison, 100 Edison Bell Electric, Dark Blue	12.00
Everplay, Pack	9.00
Goldentone	20.00
Gramophone, 200 Needles, Orange, Brass, 1 3/4 x 1 1/4 In.	13.00
Gramophone, Chicken	4.00
Gramophone, Winnipeg Piano, Co., 1 5/8 x 1 1/4 x 1/2 In.	36.00
Hartney, Fox Hunt Scene	18.00
Winged Lady, Forte Brand	10.00
Wizard	11.00

PHOTOGRAPHY items are listed here. The first photograph was a view from a window in France taken in 1826. The commercially successful photograph started with the daguerreotype introduced in 1839. Today all sorts of photographs and photographic equipment are collected. Albums were popular in Victorian times. Cartes de visite, popular after 1854, were mounted on 2 1/2-by-4-inch cardboard. Cabinet cards were introduced in 1866. These were mounted on 4 1/4-by-6 1/2-inch cards. Stereo views are listed under Stereo Card. The cases for daguerreotypes are listed in the Gutta-Percha category. Stereoscopes are listed in their own section.

Album, Velvet Cover, Brass, Silver, Stand, Boothbay Harbor Family, 16 x 12 In.	224.00
Albumen, Canadian Family, E. Stanton, 1865	165.00
Albumen, Horse Drawn Wagons, Supply Wagons, F.J. Haynes, 8 7/8 x 6 3/8 In.	110.00
Albumen, Indian Agent's House, Fence, F.J. Haynes, 1883, 8 7/8 x 6 3/8 In.	55.00
Albumen, Ship Building At Port Blakely, Puget Sound, 8 3/8 x 12 1/4 In.	4400.00
Ambrotype, 2 Children, Floral Dress, Boy With Bowtie, Jacket, 1/2 Case, 5 1/2 In.	220.00
Ambrotype, Civil War Soldier & Wife, Gutta Percha Case	145.00
Ambrotype, Civil War Soldier, Arm On Table, Tunic, Kepi, Case, 1/6 Plate	143.00
Ambrotype, Confederate Soldier, Brown Gutta-Percha Case, 2 x 2 1/2 In.	550.00
Ambrotype, Confederate Soldier, Embossed Leather Case, Gilt Liner, 4 x 3 In.	770.00
Ambrotype, Confederate Soldier, S. Whitfield, Tenn., Leather Case, 3 x 3 In.	715.00
Ambrotype, Confederate Soldier, Slouch Hat, Embossed Liner, Leather Case	660.00
Ambrotype, Friendly Fight, Scalloped Mat, 1/4 Plate	1485.00
Ambrotype, Gentleman, Seated, Large Bowtie, Vest, Case, 1/4 x 3 3/4 In.	220.00
Ambrotype, Miner/Frontiersman, Standing, Hat, Jacket, Leatherette 1/2 Case	77.00
Ambrotype, Young Frances Nash, In Arms Of Nanny, 1859	1870.00
Ambrotype, Young Girl, Victorian Dress, Wearing Jewelry, Gutta-Percha Case	165.00
Ambrotype, Young Naval Office, With Sword, Thermoplastic Case	495.00
Cabinet Card, Anna Dickinson, Suffragette, Sarony, NYC	175.00
Cabinet Card, Apache Bill, Posed In Crotch Of Tree	115.00
Cabinet Card, Canadian Watch Maker, Tools Of Trade On Table	65.00
Cabinet Card, Girl, Arms On Chair, F.W. Legg, Woburn, Mass., 1880s, 4 1/2 x 6 1/2 In.	12.00
Cabinet Card, Hannah & Alfred Jackson, Servants Of Andrew Jackson, Pair	715.00
Cabinet Card, Hartlely's Studio, Building, Chicago, Ill., Dated May 13, 1889	15.00
Cabinet Card, Henry Ward Beecher & Harriet Beecher Stowe, Gurney	275.00
Cabinet Card, Issuing Cattle To Indians On Reservation, 8 1/2 x 5 1/4 In.	395.00
Cabinet Card, Phoenix Arizona Bank, Hotel, Liquor Store, Bicycle Store, 1903	75.00
Cabinet Card, Schoolgirl's Gymnastic Class	65.00
Cabinet Card, Snake Charmer, Miss Fatima, Snake On Frame, 1894	380.00
Cabinet Card, Usysses S. Grant & Family, J. Gilman, Imperial Type, 4 1/2 x 8 In.	105.00
Cabinet Card, Vulcan, Austrian Strong Man Petri	165.00
Cabinet Card, Young Boy, Long White Dress, O.F. Flatten Advertising Back, 1880s	20.00
Camera, Box, Pegon Emil Baumann, 1:9 F480mm Lens, 64 x 62 x 30 In.	345.00
Camera, Charlie Tuna, Plastic, Aqua, Flash, Cartridge Type Film, 1971, 10 In.	75.00

Photography, Camera,
Leica Dial-Compur, 1927

Photography, Camera,
Kinegraphe, Twin-Lens Reflex,
France, 1887

Photography, Camera, Movie,
Mitchell, 35 mm, 1935

Camera, Graflex, Master Studio, c.1915, 51 x 36 In.	896.00
Camera, Kinegraphe, Twin-Lens Reflex, France, 1887 ....*Illus*	5648.00
Camera, Kodak Instamatic	5.00
Camera, Kodak, Brownie, Bakelite, 1950s, 3 1/2 x 3 In. ....45.00 to	60.00
Camera, Kodak, Brownie, No. 3, Folding, Leather Carrying Case	69.00
Camera, Kodak, Vest Pocket, 1913	35.00
Camera, Leica Dial-Compur, 1927 ....*Illus*	9602.00
Camera, Movie, Mitchell, 35 mm, 1935 ....*Illus*	7342.00
Camera, Nikon, N5005, Tokina Telephoto Lens, Accessories, 35mm	374.00
Camera, Ricoh Flex, 35 mm, Leather Case, 1950s	20.00
Camera, Rochester Optical Company, 1880s	675.00
Camera, Rolleiflex 4 x 4, Baby Rollei, 1931-1938	350.00
Camera, Twin Lens Reflex Camera, E. Francais, 1887	5648.00
Camera, Wollensak, Queen City, Junior, Walnut Case, Leather Bellows, 2 Plates, Film	58.00
Camero, Agfa Memo, Slide-Lens, Leather Carrying Case, Binghamton, N.Y., 5 x 3 In. ...	39.00
Carte De Visite, 2 Northern Plains Women, Tined, Huffman, 1800s, 4 x 6 3/4 In.	55.00
Carte De Visite, Abraham Lincoln, Alex Gardner	385.00
Carte De Visite, Abraham Lincoln, Eagle & Shield Over Wreath, Flag	50.00
Carte De Visite, Alf Young, King Of Wire, Tightrope Walker	110.00
Carte De Visite, Andrew Johnson, Gardner	350.00
Carte De Visite, Black Servant	80.00
Carte De Visite, Boy, In White Dress, John Sigmond Back Advertising, 1880s	8.00
Carte De Visite, Clark's Photographic Rooms, Richmond, Ill., 1870s	7.00
Carte De Visite, Girl Holding Doll, Full Length, 1860s	20.00
Carte De Visite, Indian, Wolf Voice, Gros Ventre, Tinted, Huffman, 4 x 6 3/4 In.	165.00
Carte De Visite, Lincoln Posed With Tad, First Lady's Nephew, 1861	2200.00
Carte De Visite, Lincoln's Funeral Hearse, c.1860	120.00
Carte De Visite, Mrs. Edna Cheney, Suffragette, Warren, Boston	175.00
Carte De Visite, Princess Dull Knife, Indian, Huffman, 1870s, 4 1/4 x 6 1/2 In.	260.00
Carte De Visite, Wm. Lloyd Garrison With Daughter, Seaver, Boston	285.00
Carte De Visite, Young Girl, Bustle Type Dress, C.H. Levi, Abilene, Kans., 1880	15.00
Case, Cover, Mother-Of-Pearl, Gilt, Papier-Mache, England, 1850, 7 1/2 x 6 In.	173.00
Daguerreotype, Boy Beside Table, Full Case, 1/6 Plate	205.00
Daguerreotype, Distinguished Englishman, Full Hinged Case, 1/4 Plate	425.00
Daguerreotype, Dr. Lovell, Hand On Pile Of Books, Full Case, 1/6 Plate	300.00
Daguerreotype, Family, Double, Union Case, 3 3/4 x 3 1/2 In.	225.00
Daguerreotype, Gentleman, Seated, Knees Up, Root Gallery, Case, 1850s, 1/6 Plate	100.00
Daguerreotype, Girl, Seated, Chair, Root Gallery, Case, 1850s, 1/4 Plate	495.00
Daguerreotype, Girl, Seated, Holding Porcelain Doll, 1850s, 1/6 Plate	440.00
Daguerreotype, Man, Union Case, Rose Velvet, 2 1/2 x 1 3/4 In.	175.00
Daguerreotype, Portrait, Daniel Webster, Gilt Metal Frame, 1 3/8 x 1 In.	1093.00
Daguerreotype, Post Mortem Girl, In Bed, Leatherette Case, 1840s, 1/2 Plate	435.00
Daguerreotype, Seated Woman, Knees Up, Tinted, c.1850, 1/4 Plate	220.00
Daguerreotype, Seated Young Girl, Full Length, Root Gallery, Leather Case, 1850s	495.00

Daguerreotype, Seated, Knees Up, Colonton, Phila., Case, 1850s, 1/6 Plate 50.00
Daguerreotype, Woman, Baby On Lap, Leatherette Case, 1850s, 1/6 Plate 75.00
Daguerreotype, Woman, Seated, Bonnet, Leatherette Case, 1/2 Plate 90.00
Daguerreotype, Woman, Wearing Bonnet, Leatherette Case, 1850s, 1/6 Plate 110.00
Daguerreotype, Young Boy, Standing, Plaid Jacket, Wm. Stroud, 1850s, 1/6 Plate 105.00
Daguerreotype, Young Girl, Holding Doll, Leatherette Case, c.1850, 1/6 Plate 440.00
Ferrotype, Gen. George McClellan, Frame, 3/4 x 1 In. 325.00
Photograph, Albumen, Comenha, Daughter Of Dull Knife, 7 x 4 1/4 In. 1430.00
Photograph, Autopsy 270.00
Photograph, Blackfoot Indian Group, Tepees, Glacier Park, Mt., 1900, 19 In. 545.00
Photograph, Catalina Fishing, Baker Photograph Company, 6 x 8 In. 550.00
Photograph, George V, Heart Shape, Tortoiseshell Frame, England, 1900, 3 In. 288.00
Photograph, Guillon, French Athlete, Nude Pose, 10 x 8 In. 165.00
Photograph, Indian Congress, Geronimo & General Miles, 1901, 9 x 7 1/2 In. 1150.00
Photograph, Indian Man, E.S. Curtis, 1910, 8 x 5 1/4 In. 120.00
Photograph, Indian Women, 4th July Parade, Nespelam, Wa., 1900, 16 x 20 In. 260.00
Photograph, John Grimal, Masculine Perfection, 9 1/2 x 7 1/4 In. 790.00
Photograph, Men, Horse, Florida Building, Boger, 4 x 6 In., Pair 20.00
Photograph, Pacific Electric Railroad, Passengers, Mt. Lowe, Calif., 1910, 6 1/2 In. 25.00
Photograph, Pawnee Bill & Wife, Anniversary Invitation, 1936, 6 x 4 1/2 In. 260.00
Photograph, Pawnee Bill, Inscription, Princess White Buffalo, 1900, 5 1/2 In. 345.00
Photograph, Signal To Mountain, Indian Warrior, Curtis, Frame, 16 x 11 3/4 In. 4315.00
Photograph, South Plains Indian Group, Tepee, 1920, 9 1/2 x 7 3/4 In. 260.00
Photograph, V. Pres. With South Plains Indians Group, Curtis, 1920, 9 x 7 In. 230.00
Photograph, Young Men, Round Oak Barrel Frame, Spigot, c.1920, 4 1/2 x 11 In. 67.00
Photogravure, A Heavy Load, Sioux, Sepia Tone, Vellum, E.S. Curtis, 15 In. 1910.00
Photogravure, Cowichan, Spearing Salmon, Sepia Tone, E.S. Curtis, 15 In. 450.00
Photogravure, Jicarilla Women, Sepia Tone, Vellum, E.S. Curtis, 11 x 14 In. 520.00
Photogravure, Kutenai Duck Hunter, Sepia Tone, Vellum, E.S. Curtis, 15 In. 1070.00
Projector, Cameragraph, Large Screen, Early 1900s 700.00
Projector, Kodak, Brownie 300, 8 mm Movie, Box, 1950s-1960s 25.00
Rhode Island Wheelmen's Club, Oak Frame, Gold Velvet Lining, c.1897, 38 x 44 In. 952.00
Ruby Ambrotype, Civil War Soldier, Faux Tortoise Painted Case, 1/9 Plate 275.00
Ruby Ambrotype, Zouave, Tunic & Fez, Tinted, Leatherette Case, 1/6 Plate 275.00
Slide, Glass, Landscape, Flowers, 5 1/2 x 12 In. 365.00
Tintype, Black Man, Leather Case, 9th Plate 35.00
Tintype, Bricklayer, Seated, Trowel In Right Hand, Brick In Other, 1/6 Plate 300.00
Tintype, Civil War Soldier, Tinted, Blue Coat & Pants, High Boots, 4 x 4 7/8 In. 385.00
Tintype, Civil War, Confederate Soldier, With Musket, 1/6 Plate 1600.00
Tintype, Civil War, Negro Soldier, Standing, Leather Case, Split Hinge, 1/6 Plate 600.00
Tintype, Civil War, Portrait Of Gentleman In Uniform, 3 1/8 x 2 5/8 In. 90.00
Tintype, Gentleman In Horse Drawn Milk Wagon, 1/4 Plate 60.00
Tintype, Girl With Umbrella, Full Plate 3190.00
Tintype, Hunter With Dog, Seated, Gun Front Of Fence, 1/6 Plate 85.00
Tintype, Jefferson Davis & Alex Stephens, 1/16 Plate, Pair 1950.00
Tintype, Knitting Circle, Full Plate 440.00
Tintype, Man & Woman, Union Case, Purple Velvet, 3 3/4 x 3 1/4 In. 175.00
Tintype, Man Holding Boy On Bicycle Handlebars, 1850s, 4 3/4 x 3 1/4 In. 50.00
Tintype, Policeman, Seated, Bowler, Badge, Nightstick, 2 1/4 x 3 3/8 In. 224.00
Tintype, Proud Of His Chess Board, Uncased 285.00
Tintype, Sherman, Pendant Mount, Woven Hair Under Glass On Reverse, 3 In. 675.00
Tintype, Snowy Owl, Perched, On Table, Prescott, Boston, 1870s 22.00
Tintype, Sonora Band, Horns & Drum, Horse Drawn Wagon, 3 3/4 x 2 1/2 In. 55.00
Tintype, Ulysses Simpson Grant, George Ayer, Portland, 1 1/2 x 2 In. 700.00

PIANO BABY is a collector's term. About 1880, the well-decorated
home had a shawl on the piano. Bisque figures of babies were designed
to help hold the shawl in place. They range in size from 6 to 18 inches.
Most of the figures were made in Germany. Reproductions are being
made. Other piano babies may be listed under manufacturers' names.

Girl, Large Bonnet, Gebruder Heubach, 6 In. 600.00
Sitting, Gebruder Heubach, 10 In. ....550.00 to 880.00
Sitting, In Shoe, Gebruder Heubach, 11 3/4 In. 1900.00

PICKARD China Company was started in 1898 by Wilder Pickard. Hand-painted designs were used on china purchased from other sources. In the 1930s, the company began to make its own china wares in Chicago, Illinois. The company now makes many types of porcelains, including a successful line of limited edition collector plates.

Ashtray, Allover Embossed Gold Surface, Signed, 3 x 5 In.	38.00
Bowl, Fruit, Gold Leaf, Artist Signed, c.1905, 7 In.	607.00
Bowl, Fruit, Gold Leaf, Artist Signed, Marked, c.1905-1916, 7 In.	607.00
Bowl, Lattice Panels & Roses Exterior, Silver Overlay, 1920, 9 1/2 x 12 3/4 In.	575.00
Bowl, Sugar, Cover, Garland	58.00
Candy Dish, Footed, Artist Signed Reury, Gold Mark, J & C Malmaico, c.1903-1910, 7 In.	615.00
Candy Dish, Green, Signed Reury, c.1903, 7 In.	615.00
Coffeepot, Floral, Swan Neck Lip, C-Scroll Handle, Gold Band, Signed, 1903, 8 3/4 In.	330.00
Creamer, Garland	45.00
Creamer, Poppies, Artist Signed, Marked T & V Limoges, France, 4 1/4 In.	195.00
Cup, Barcelona	30.00
Cup & Saucer, Band Of Gold On Cup, Hand Painted Flowers, 1895	95.00
Dish, Poppy, Artist Signed, Marked In Gold, 6 In.	121.00
Pitcher, Gold Floral Scroll, Signed, 1922, 5 In.	318.00
Pitcher, Grape, Gold, Matte Green, Signed Coufall, c.1905-1919, 6 In.	805.00
Pitcher, Grape, Signed Coufall, c.1919, 5 In.	220.00
Plate, 2 Flying Mallards, James L. Lockhart, 1971, 10 1/2 In.	170.00
Plate, Chrysanthemums, Gold Whiplash, Octagonal, Stamped Design Pat. Feb. 14, 1905	350.00
Plate, Gold Baroque, 11 In.	100.00
Plate, Gold Circles On Gold Maple Leaf, Vellum, E. Challinor, 1912, 8 1/4 In.	335.00
Plate, Gold, Henrich & Company, Bavaria, Germany, 11 In.	300.00
Plate, Gooseberry, Green, Yellow, Amber, Scalloped Rim, Challinor, c.1905, 8 1/4 In.	135.00
Plate, Purple Band, Lemons, Mother-Of-Pearl Iridescence, Schroner, 8 1/2 In.	350.00
Plate, Service, Gold Trim, Signed, 8 Piece	300.00
Plate, Violets, Gold, Green Trim, Signed Wagner, A & K France, 8 3/4 In.	295.00
Platter, Cornflower Blue, Small	85.00
Punch Bowl, Large Band Of Fruit, Crawling Fruit Vines, Gilt, Vokral, 14 1/2 In.	1334.00
Relish, Divided, Embossed Flowers, Gold Plated	95.00
Salt & Pepper, Gold, Marked In Gold, Bavaria, 3 1/4 In.	90.00
Salt & Pepper, Rounded, Holes In Tops Form S & P, Marked, Gold Leaf, 3 In.	125.00
Sugar, Cover, Gold Flowers, Handles, 4 x 5 In.	38.00
Sugar & Creamer, Violets, Artist Signed, Marked T & V Limoges, France, 4 1/4 In.	450.00
Teapot, Morning Glory, Allover Gold, 4 1/2 x 8 1/2 In.	120.00
Toothpick, Hand Painted, 2 Handles, 1895	200.00
Tray, Classical Transfer Center, Gold Interior Edge, Signed, 8 3/4 In.	116.00
Vase, Green Glaze Lining, 7 In.	90.00
Vase, Poinsettias, Red & Black, Cream, Gold, Squatty, Loh, c.1905, 3 1/2 x 18 1/2 In.	295.00
Vase, Signed Vobor, Marked In Gold, 5 In.	220.00
Vase, Spring Landscape, E. Challiner, 12 In.	750.00

PICTURE FRAMES are listed in this book in the Furniture category under Frame.

PICTURES, silhouettes, and other small decorative objects framed to hang on the wall are listed here. Sandpaper pictures are black and white charcoal drawings done on a special sanded paper. Some other types of pictures are listed in the Print and Painting categories.

Calligraphy, Dove, God Bless Our Home, Scroll, Colored Ink, Framed, 6 x 10 1/2 In.	52.00
Calligraphy, Eagle & Flags, E. Pluribus Unum, March 12, 1861, 7 x 10 In.	865.00
Charcoal, New England Village Scene, Emile A. Gruppe, 7 x 13 In.	1092.00
Diorama, Butcher's Shop, 3 Figures Standing In Front Of Facade, 1840, 23 In.	11400.00
Engraving, 10 Jumping Horses, Worcester, 1856, Grand Stand, England, 22 x 27 In.	110.00
Engraving, Boys Swimming, Alonzo Schoff, 1882, 19 x 13 In.	71.00
Engraving, General Ulysses S. Grant, 1868, 21 x 16 In.	275.00
Engraving, Greek Allegorical Scene, G.T. Doo, 1848, 11 x 15 In.	5.00
Engraving, Larder, Earlom, 1775, 16 x 22 In.	110.00
Engraving, Man-Of-War Cutter Of 10 Guns, Frame, England, 1840, 18 3/4 x 21 3/4 In.	110.00
Engraving, Men, Around Billiards Table, E.F. Lambert, Frame, 19 x 24 In.	220.00
Engraving, Returning To Kennel, 3 Men On Horseback, England, Frame, 20 x 29 In.	250.00

Picture, Needlework, Embroidered
Photograph, Couple, Felicidades,
String Frame, 9 x 7 In.

Picture, Needlework, Motto, Love
One Another, 1870s, 8 1/2 x 12 In.

Picture, Motto, Happy Birthday
Wishes, Minstrel, Gibson,
Frame, 7 5/8 x 5 5/8 In.

Etching, Fair Model, Embossed Windmill Stamp, Signed, Icart, c.1937, 18 x 11 In. 2800.00
Etching, Polo Players, Molded Frame, Liner, Fransisque Rehour, 22 x 31 In., Pair 330.00
Featherwork Wreath, Peacock, Shadowbox, Walnut, Gilt, c.1875, 37 1/2 x 33 x 26 In. . . .   403.00
Gouache, Abstract Composition, Ramstonev, 9 x 11 1/2 In. 468.00
Gouache, Centennial Theme, Flags, Waving, Declaration Of Independence, 30 x 30 In. . . .   575.00
Graphite, Residence Of Col. Russell, President Of Staunton Military Academy, 14 In. . . .   84.00
Graphite, The Alamo, Oldest Hampton Sydney College Bldg., Frame, 15 3/4 x 12 In. 84.00
Graphite, The College Chapel, Hampton Sydney, Frame, 9 3/4 x 14 1/2 In. 112.00
Graphite, The Little Theatre, Hollins College, Hollins, Va., Frame, 19 1/4 x 14 3/4 In. . .   56.00
Graphite On Paper, Portrait, Nude Woman, Earl Horter, Phila., Pa., 9 3/4 x 9 3/4 In. 192.00
Micro-Mosaic, Dog & Couple, Drinking Wine, Cassio, Frame, 20 x 23 In. 8250.00
Motto, Happy Birthday Wishes, Minstrel, Gibson, Frame, 7 5/8 x 5 5/8 In. . . . . *Illus*   10.00
Needlepoint, Bishop, Crosier, St. Peter, Velvet Back, France, 1800, 39 x 31 In. 1200.00
Needlepoint, Noah & Wife, Seated, Animals In Landscape, Frame, 20 1/8 x 17 1/4 In. . . .   3450.00
Needlepoint, Peacock, Perched On Flowering Branch, Rosewood Frame, 41 1/2 x 36 In. .   805.00
Needlepoint, Petit Point, 2 Children, Dog, In Garden, 24 x 25 In.   165.00
Needlework, Apple Tree, Adam & Eve, Isabella Patterson, 1802, 20 x 17 In. 1438.00
Needlework, Cornucopia, Flowers, Butterflies, Flower Border, 1792, 21 x 17 In. 690.00
Needlework, Crewel, Panel, Birds, Trees & Flowers, 18th Century, 35 x 73 In. 375.00
Needlework, Crewel, Panel, Wool, Birds, Vines, Linen, 18th Century, 20 x 7 In. 275.00
Needlework, Embroidered Photograph, Couple, Felicidades, String Frame, 9 x 7 In. . . *Illus*   25.00
Needlework, Embroidered, Girls & Boy, Butterfly & Flowers, Silk, Frame, 17 1/2 x 15 In.   6600.00
Needlework, Embroidered, Peonies, Butterflies, Lacquered Frame, Round, 12 1/2 In., Pair   55.00
Needlework, English Towns, Ships, Acorns, Margaret Brown, 1787, Frame, 26 x 22 In. . .   825.00
Needlework, Family Register, Alphabet, Harriet A. Newell, Aged 11, 1833, 17 x 18 In. . . .   2760.00
Needlework, Family Register, Flowers, Geometric, Betsey J. Brown, 1826, 17 x 17 In. . . .   2415.00
Needlework, Farm Scene, Frame, 18th Century, 18 x 18 1/2 In. 2500.00
Needlework, Memoriam, Monument, Willow Tree, Boston, c.1830, 20 1/2 x 20 1/2 In. . . .   4370.00
Needlework, Motto, Love One Another, 1870s, 8 1/2 x 12 In. . . . . *Illus*   135.00
Needlework, Motto, Old Oaken Bucket, 1870s, 8 1/2 x 12 In. . . . . *Illus*   240.00
Needlework, Motto, What Is Home Without Mother, 1870s, 8 1/2 x 12 In. . . . . *Illus*   125.00
Needlework, Mourning, Maiden Beside Tomb, 16 1/2 x 14 1/4 In. 920.00
Needlework, Mythology, Shakespeare, Oval Mat, Frame, England, 1800s, 11 x 9 1/2 In. . . .   690.00
Needlework, On Velvet, Fruit & Floral Still Life In Vase, 21 x 17 1/2 In. 1050.00
Needlework, Parrot On Flowery Branch, Scroll Border, Framed, 17 x 16 In. 259.00
Needlework, Petit Point, Biblical Naomi & Ruth, Ornate Frame, 36 3/4 x 33 3/4 In. 825.00
Needlework, Petit Point, Wool, Botanical Still Life, Oak Frame, 19 x 23 In. 93.00
Needlework, Portraits, Children, Landscape, Mat, Frame, England, 1800s, 14 x 10 In. . . .   1610.00
Needlework, Sailing Ship, American Flag, Lighthouse, Frame, 22 x 35 In. 935.00
Needlework, Silk On Silk, Elegantly Dressed Lady, Walking Hound, 14 x 11 In. 128.00
Needlework, Silk On Silk, Farmer In Field, Barn, Landscape, England, 7 x 9 In. .   275.00
Needlework, Silk On Silk, Figures In Landscape, Lucy Beal, c.1795, 8 x 8 12 In. 522.00
Needlework, Silk, Belville & Rosina, Lad, Slumbering Behind Tree, 15 x 18 In. 17250.00
Needlework, Silk, Idyllic Scene, Tan, Brown, Blue, Green, Rose, 21 x 27 In. 21850.00

Picture, Needlework, Motto, Old Oaken
Bucket, 1870s, 8 1/2 x 12 In.

Picture, Needlework, Motto, What Is Home
Without Mother, 1870s, 8 1/2 x 12 In.

Needlework, Silk, Straw Marquetry, Man Serenading Woman, Frame, 1700s, 13 x 11 In. . . 3000.00
Needlework, Silk, Woman Gathering Roses, Landscape, Mat, Frame, 9 1/4 x 6 1/4 In. 403.00
Needlework, Silk, Young Woman, Dog, Landscape, Eglomise Mat, 9 1/2 x 11 1/2 In. 546.00
Needlework, Village, Vines, Anna Margaret Houghtaling, 1835, 16 1/2 x 16 1/2 In. 2875.00
Needlework, Woman Playing Mandolin, Dancing Man, Mary Palmer, 1778, 28 1/4 In. 3600.00
Needlework, Woman Under Tree, M.A. Arthur, May 2, 1865, Floral Border, Frame, 26 In. . 220.00
Needlework, Wool & Silk, Male Figures, Landscape, Keep In Distance, Frame, 13 3/8 In. . 2990.00
Needlework, Wool On Linen, Traveler On Foot, Barking Dog, Village, 10 x 10 In. 575.00
Needlework, Wool, Biblical Scene, Figures In Front Of A House, Framed, 27 x 20 In. . . . 173.00
Needlework, Wool, Moses In The Basket, Near-Eastern Landscape, Framed, 20 In. 1955.00
Needlework, Wool, View Of A Port With Shipping & Factory Buildings, 21 x 27 In. 3300.00
Needlework & Watercolor, Chenille, Women, Angel, Landscape, Frame, 23 x 28 In. 1668.00
Pastel, Manayunk Scene With View Of River, Antonio P. Martino, 18 1/2 x 21 1/2 In. . . . 4950.00
Pastel, Watercolor, Portrait, Hannah Chew Clement, 18th Century, 16 1/2 x 21 1/4 In. . . . 2310.00
Pastel & Charcoal On Paper, Girl In White Holding Nest With Birds, 20 x 15 In. 2185.00
Petit Point, Dog, Walnut Frame, 10 1/2 x 13 In. 95.00
Petit Point, Roses, Daisies & Morning Glories, Panel, Frame, 13 1/2 x 16 1/2 In. 275.00
Punched Paper, Needlework, Eagle, Banner, United We Stand, 1776-1876, 13 5/8 x 26 In. 193.00
Ribbon, Girl, Human Hair, Lace Dress, Bonnet, Frame, Hilda Peterson, 1931, 6 1/2 In. . . . 45.00
Ribbon, Girl, Lace Sunbonnet, Green Dress, 6 In. 35.00
Silhouette, Anthony Lispenary Bleeker, Mary Noel, Married 1763, c.1780, 2 3/4 x 2 In. . . 360.00
Silhouette, Ink Portrait Of Young Girl, Wavy Hair, Frame, 5 x 4 In. 55.00
Silhouette, Man & Woman, Inked Hair & Scarf, Round Frames, 5 1/8 In., Pair 110.00
Silhouette, Profile Bust Of Woman, Feathers In Hat, Fur Muff, Coat, 12 1/8 x 10 1/2 In. . 137.00
Silhouette, Woman With Book, Watercolor, Hollow Cut, 3 3/4 x 2 1/8 In. 1380.00
Silhouette, Woman, Black Hair, Advertising Wm. M.S. Doiyle, Gilt Frame, 5 3/8 x 4 In. . 410.00
Silhouette, Woman, Bonnet, Hair Comb, Floral Scrolls, Maple Frame, 6 x 4 3/4 In. 1127.00
Silhouette, Woman, Hoop Dress, Holding Handkerchief, Frame, 12 1/3 x 8 1/3 In. 185.00
Silhouette, Young Girl Holding Doll & Parasol, Pamela Stokes, 6 x 3 1/4 In. 1980.00
Silhouette, Young Woman, Cut With Common Scissors By Mr. Seville, 1825, 4 5/8 In. . . 605.00
Silhouette, Young Woman, Hollow Cut, Walnut Frame, 6 x 4 3/4 In. 165.00
Theorem, Basket Of Fruit, Green Marble Slab, G.B. French, 24 x 18 In. 465.00
Theorem, Basket Of Fruit, Wm. Rand, Red Grained Frame, 17 1/4 x 19 1/2 In. 440.00
Theorem, Canton, Bowl Of Fruit Overturned, Table, Frame, 18 1/2 x 22 1/2 In. 2860.00
Theorem, Classical Urn, Floral Growth, Square Plinth, Frame, 1840s, 21 1/2 x 15 1/2 In. . 3240.00
Theorem, Fruit Basket, Signed, F.G. Bernet, 20th Century, 17 1/2 x 23 1/2 In. 805.00
Theorem, On Paper, Bird, Nest, Cherries, Watercolor, Signed L. Lewis, Frame, 8 x 9 In. . . 358.00
Theorem, On Paper, Fruit In Dish, Watercolor, Frame, 15 1/2 x 11 1/2 In. 1265.00
Theorem, On Paper, Fruit, Watercolor, Frame, Lurana White, 1800s, 7 1/2 x 12 In. 1035.00
Theorem, On Paper, Rose, Pink, Buds, Green Leaves, Watercolor, Gilt Frame, 9 x 7 In. . . 375.00
Theorem, On Velvet, Basket Of Flowers & Foliage, c.1840, 15 x 15 In. 2420.00
Theorem, On Velvet, Basket Of Fruit, Bird, Bill Rank, 20th Century, 17 1/2 x 19 1/2 In. . . 715.00
Theorem, On Velvet, Basket Of Fruit, Watercolor, 24 1/2 x 21 In. 12650.00
Theorem, On Velvet, Basket Of Fruit, Yellow, Brown, Ear Handles, Frame, 17 3/4 x 20 In. 2090.00
Theorem, On Velvet, Bouquet Of Flowers, Watercolor, 19th Century, Frame, 19 x 14 In. . 460.00
Theorem, On Velvet, Fruit, Frame, Early 19th Century, 7 x 9 1/2 In. 920.00
Theorem, On Velvet, Grouping Of Flowers, Beige Ground, Frame, 15 1/2 x 14 1/4 In. . . . 330.00
Theorem, Strawberry Tree, W. Rank, Molded Frame, 14 x 11 1/2 In. 300.00
Theorem, Vase Of Flowers, Gilt Frame, 22 1/2 x 17 3/4 In. 1650.00
Theorem, Vase Of Flowers, Pink, Yellow, Blue, Watercolor, 19th Century, 18 x 15 In. 1725.00

Theorem, Wildlife, Bright Colors, Frame, Walnut Veneer, 21 1/8 x 22 1/4 In. 1760.00
Wallpaper Panel, The Hunt At The Chateau, Blocked, France, c.1825, 67 1/2 x 63 In. . . . 6038.00
Watercolor, Basket Of Flowers, D.Y. Ellinger, Frame, 8 1/2 x 9 1/2 In. 4250.00
Watercolor, Bay At Fundy, Sailboat, Rocky Coast, Ennis, Frame, 22 x 20 In. 110.00
Watercolor, Birch Trees, River, Gold Frame, 16 x 8 In. 27.00
Watercolor, Bird & Babies, Nest, Cherry Tree, Frame, G.B. French, 14 1/2 x 10 1/2 In. . . 55.00
Watercolor, Flowering Vines, Mirror Center, Corner Frame, G.B. French, 12 x 16 In. 130.00
Watercolor, Fox In Open Field, Lionel Edwards, 12 1/2 x 10 1/2 In. 2200.00
Watercolor, Girl, Blue Dress, England, Shagreen Case, 1750, Miniature 295.00
Watercolor, Gloucester, Mass., Seascape, Figures On Rocks, Hayley Lever, 17 x 21 In. . . 935.00
Watercolor, Horse Race Scene, W.V. Longe, c.1900, Signed, 11 x 16 In. 165.00
Watercolor, Hunt Scene, F.A. Stewart, 1877-1945, Signed, 11 x 17 In. 1650.00
Watercolor, Indian Landscape, Cecil L. Burns, 9 x 13 1/4 In. 403.00
Watercolor, King Charles The Second, 1662, Pendant Type, 1 1/2 In. 1500.00
Watercolor, Labrador Retriever & English Setter, Fenced Field, Gilt Frame, 25 x 16 In. . . 100.00
Watercolor, Landscape, John Varley, England, 19th Century, 14 1/2 x 10 1/2 In. 70.00
Watercolor, Mallard Hen & Drake, Oriental Characters, Frame, 18 x 23 In., Pair 28.00
Watercolor, Mt. Mansfield, Vermont, Walton Blodgett, Frame, 22 x 16 In. 3575.00
Watercolor, Peacock, Standing, Flowers, Tulips, Frame, G.B. French, 10 1/4 x 13 1/2 In. . 100.00
Watercolor, Pied Piper, Girl, With Puppy, Marshall, Frame, 14 3/8 x 10 15/16 In. 28.00
Watercolor, Potted Plants, Vine, Border, Mirror Center, G.B. French, 13 x 16 In. 100.00
Watercolor, Seascape, E.H. Flavelle, Frame, 1880-1920, 32 x 21 In. 2495.00
Watercolor & Ink, Robed Man, August Riedel, Dated August 1938, 8 x 6 1/2 In. 27.00
Watercolor On Paper, Bird On Branch, Brown, Yellow, Red, Frame, 12 x 10 In. 330.00
Watercolor On Paper, Country Sale, Amish Buggy, Hattie K. Brunner, Frame, 14 x 18 In. 4400.00
Watercolor On Paper, Folky Rooster, Red, Green, Yellow, 1812, Frame, 11 In. 1760.00
Watercolor On Silk, Girl In Garden, Flower Basket, Black Glass, Oval, 8 1/2 x 6 1/2 In. . . 805.00

PIERCE, see Howard Pierce category.

PIGEON FORGE Pottery was started in Pigeon Forge, Tennessee, in 1946. Red clay found near the pottery was used to make the pieces. Molded or thrown pottery with matte glaze and slip decoration was made. The pottery closed in 2000.

Figurine, Black Bear, 5 3/4 In., Pair 25.00
Mug, Incised Tree Design, Green Matte Ground, 4 1/2 In. 297.00
Pitcher, Dogwood, Blue Interior, Marked, 1 Qt. . . . . *Illus* 10.00
Teapot, Black Blaze 84.00

PILKINGTON Tile and Pottery Company was established in 1892 in England. The company made small pottery wares, like buttons and hat-pins, but soon started decorating vases purchased from other potteries. By 1903, the company had discovered an opalescent glaze that became popular on the Lancastrian pottery line. The manufacture of pottery ended in 1937. Pilkington's Tiles Ltd. has worked from 1938 to the present.

Vase, Apollo, Chariot, Lyre, Bronze Luster, Royal Lancastrian, c.1909, 20 1/2 In. 7800.00

Don't use tape or glue to mount photos. Don't store newspaper clippings and photographs together. The newsprint can stain the picture. The same rule applies for scrapbooks and albums. Be sure newspaper clippings are not positioned where they may touch a photograph.

Pigeon Forge, Pitcher, Dogwood, Blue Interior, Marked, 1 Qt.

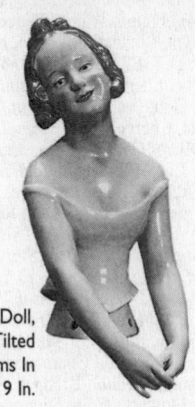

Pincushion Doll, Lady With
Mirror, Flapper, Peach
Cloche, 1925, 5 In.

Pincushion Doll,
Woman, Head Tilted
To Side, Arms In
Front, 1910, 9 In.

Pincushion Doll, Young Girl,
Blue Bodice, Head Tilted,
1910, 7 In.

Vase, Blue & Silver Luster, Frieze Of Galleons, Richard Joyce, c.1920, 6 In. 2519.00
Vase, Fish, Plants, Cover, Royal Lancastrian, c.1915, 7 3/4 In. 1920.00
Vase, Fish, Plants, Luster, Royal Lancastrian, c.1912, 7 1/2 In. 1200.00
Vase, Lions, Bronze Luster, Blue Ground, Royal Lancastrian, c.1913, 12 In. 2700.00
Vase, Rampant Lions, Silver & Copper Luster, G. Forsyth, c.1911, 9 3/4 In. 3358.00

PINCUSHION DOLLS are not really dolls and often were not even pin-
cushions. Some collectors use the term *half-doll.* The top half of each
doll was made of porcelain. The edge of the half-doll was made with
several small holes for thread, and the doll was stitched to a fabric
body with a voluminous skirt. The finished figure was used to cover a
hot pot of tea, powder box, pincushion, whisk broom, or lamp. They
were made in sizes from less than an inch to over 9 inches high. Most
date from the early 1900s to the 1950s. Collectors often find just the
porcelain doll without the fabric skirt.

Braided Coronet, Posed Fingers, Gold Metallic Skirt, German, 9 In. 600.00
Holding Flowers, Swan's Down Powder Puff, Germany, 2 1/2 In. 35.00
Lady With Mirror, Flapper, Peach Cloche, 1925, 5 In. . . . .*Illus* 500.00
Nude Woman, Flowing Curls, Right Arm Holds Flower, Dressel & Kister, 6 In. 300.00
Spanish Dancer, Fan In Hand & Hair, Silver Metallic Gown, German, 10 In. 700.00
Woman, Head Tilted To Side, Arms In Front, 1910, 9 In. . . . .*Illus* 3100.00
Young Girl, Blue Bodice, Head Tilted, 1910, 7 In. . . . .*Illus* 1100.00

PINK SLAG pieces are listed in this book in the Slag Glass category.

PIPES have been popular since tobacco was introduced to Europe by
Sir Walter Raleigh. Carved wooden, porcelain, ivory, and glass pipes
may be listed here. Meerschaum pipes are listed under Meerschaum.

Bearded Black Man, Silver Ferrule, Amber Mouthpiece, Leather Case, Austria, 1800s . . . 1265.00
Black Baby In Tub, White Baby On Stem, Carved, Amber Stem, Case, Austria, 1800s . . . 690.00
Boy Treed By Wild Boars, Cheroot, Insert, Amber Stem, Case, 19th Century 460.00
Cherub, Silver Bowl Cover, Floral Design, Wooden Stem, Case, Mid 1800s 690.00
Clay, Long Type, Dutch, 17th Century 195.00
Elderly Man Reading Paper, Metal Housefly, Case, Meerschaum Insert, 19th Century . . . 1150.00
Head Of Bacchus, Horn Ferrule, Amber Stem, Case, Austria, 19th Century 3450.00
Nude Female Playing Lyre, Cheroot, Curved Stem, Leather Case, c.1900 . . . . 290.00
Opium, Damper Holder In Form Of Fist & Mouthpiece, Ivory, Red Lacquer Shaft, 16 In. . 430.00
Opium, Hardstone, Silver Mounts, Dragon Decoration, Vietnam, 23 1/2 In. 185.00
Opium, Ivory, Red & Green Paint, Silver Mount, Early 1800s, 1 3/8 x 4 7/8 In. 145.00
Poplar & Chestnut, Box, Scalloped Back, Scrolled Top, 1 Drawer, c.1770, 17 1/2 In. 1925.00
Porcelain, Student Society, Gaudeamus Igitur, Transfer, Enameled 240.00
Silver Mounted, Silver Lid, Dragon Design, Mural Crown, England, 1807 . . . . 230.00
Striped Honey Tone, 3 Gold Bands, Agate, 18K Gold Mounts, Scotland, 1800s, 3 1/4 In. . 173.00
Wooden Frame, China Bowl, Tavern Scene, B.H. Wasmanning 55.00

PIRKENHAMMER is a porcelain manufactory started in 1802 by Friedrich Holke and J.G. Lilst. It was located in Bohemia, now Brezova, Czechoslovakia. The company made tablewares usually decorated with views and flowers. Lithophanes were also made. The mark of the crossed hammers is easy to remember as the Pirkenhammer symbol.

Bowl, Vegetable, Oval, Pastel Flowers, Epiag, Czechoslovakia, 9 3/4 In.	15.00
Platter, Oval, Pastel Flowers, Epiag, Czechoslovakia, 13 1/2 In.	20.00

PISGAH FOREST pottery was made in North Carolina beginning in 1926. The pottery was started by Walter R. Stephen in 1914, and after his death in 1961, the pottery continued in operation. The most famous kinds of Pisgah Forest ware are the cameo type with designs made of raised glaze and the turquoise crackle glaze wares.

Bowl, Musicians & Square Dancing Couples, W.B. Stephen, 9 3/4 In.	3850.00
Vase, Blue, Pearl Crystals, Ivory Glaze, 1946, 12 1/4 x 8 In.	787.00
Vase, Bulbous, White, Blue, Yellow Crystalline Glaze, 6 1/4 x 4 3/4 In.	460.00
Vase, Classical Shape, White, Gold, Blue Crystalline Glaze, c.1948, 8 x 4 3/4 In.	375.00
Vase, Covered Wagon & Riders On Horseback, White, Blue, 1953, 5 1/2 In.	305.00
Vase, Crystalline, 1943, 6 1/2 In.	395.00
Vase, Indian Scene, Yellow Glossy Glaze, Horse Tied To Base, 6 3/4 In.	1265.00
Vase, Medieval Scene, Carrying Boars, Stephen, c.1933, 6 In.	1320.00
Vase, Tan, Brown Crystalline Glaze, 7 In.	920.00
Vase, Thick Amethyst Crackled Glaze, Turquoise Body, 8 In.	225.00
Vase, Wagon Pulled By Oxen, 4 1/2 In.	175.00
Vase, Wagon Pulled By Oxen, Man With Rifle & Dog, Cameo, 1941, 7 1/2 In.	242.00
Vase, White Glass Interior, Stamp On Base, 5 In.	85.00
Vase, White, Blue Crystalline Glaze, Green, Brown Ground, 1947, 7 In.	805.00

PLANTERS PEANUTS memorabilia is collected. Planters Nut and Chocolate Company was started in Wilkes-Barre, Pennsylvania, in 1906. The Mr. Peanut figure was adopted as a trademark in 1916. National advertising for Planters Peanuts started in 1918. The company was acquired by Standard Brands, Inc., in 1961. Standard Brands merged with Nabisco in 1981. Some of the Mr. Peanut jars and other memorabilia have been reproduced and, of course, new items are being made.

Bag, Marbles, Mr. Peanut Picture, Contents, 1950s	7.00
Bag, Mr. Peanut, 8 1/2 x 3 1/2 In.	18.00
Bank, Mr. Peanut, Cast Iron	85.00
Bank, Mr. Peanut, Cast Iron, 1970s	120.00
Bank, Mr. Peanut, Turn Hat To Open, 1950s, 8 1/2 x 3 1/2 In.	50.00 to 55.00
Bank, Penny Operated, Clear Plastic Hat, 7 3/4 In.	302.00
Beach Ball, Mr. Peanut, Inflatable, Premium Mail-A-Way, 1980, 7 In.	22.00
Blotter, Mr. Peanut & Truck, 1930	10.00
Book, Mr. Peanut, Complete World Of Planter's Mr. Peanut, 8 1/2 x 11 In.	28.00
Box, Spanish Peanuts, Cardboard, Blue, World War I Plane, 1944, 9 x 6 In.	415.00
Button, Carter As Mr. Peanut, I Dig Peanuts In '76, Celluloid, 2 1/2 In.	13.00
Calendar, 1979-1980, Mr. Peanut, Display, Plastic, 3 x 6 In.	5.00
Calendar, 1983-1984, Mr. Peanut, Plastic, 3 x 6 In.	5.00
Cloth Patch, Mr. Peanut, 1970, 2 1/2 In.	8.00
Coloring Book, Mr. Peanut, 50 States, 1970	15.00
Coloring Book, Mr. Peanut, Iron On Transfer, 1970, 9 In.	7.00
Coloring Book, Mr. Peanut, Presidents, Washington To Eisenhower, 1953	29.00
Cookie Cutter, Mr. Peanut, Plastic, 5 In.	15.00
Cookie Jar, Mr. Peanut, Nabisco, Block China Corp.	110.00
Golf Set, Mr. Peanut, Metal Divot Fixer, Wooden Golf Tee, 3 Piece	15.00
Jar, Blown-Out Peanut Each Corner, Large	250.00
Jar, Glass, Paper Label, Girl With Planters Peanuts, No Lid, 9 In.	176.00
Jar, Mr. Peanut, Pennant 5 Cent Salted Peanuts, Handle On Lid, 12 1/2 In.	450.00
Jar, Mr. Peanut, Please Keep Jar Always Covered, Thanks!, 1940, 8 x 7 In.	155.00
Jar, Peanut Finial, Embossed, 13 In.	121.00
Jar, Planters Peanut, Lid, 8 x 5 In.	90.00
Knife, Peanut Butter Spreader, Plastic, 1950s	10.00
Lighter, Mr. Peanut, Bic, 1970	15.00

Plastic, Tray, Inlaid Wood,
Herb Design, Aluminum,
Mosaic, Courac Of
Monterey, 13 3/8 In.

Planters Peanuts,
Tin, Planters Salted
Peanuts, Pennant,
2 1/2 x 2 3/8 In.

Money Clip & Pocket Knife, Mr. Peanut Image, Cloisonne, 1960s	275.00
Olympic Coin, Mr. Peanut, 1980	14.00
Pen, Ballpoint, Mr. Peanut, Planter's Snacks, Metal, 1970	22.00
Pencil, Mechanical, Mr. Peanut On Top, Blue, Yellow, c.1970	12.00
Pencil, Mechanical, Mr. Peanut, 1950	28.00
Pencil, Mechanical, Mr. Peanut, Eraser	28.00
Pin, Mr. Peanut, 75th Anniversary, Enamel, 1981	22.00
Plate, Mr. Peanut, Pewter, Wilton, 1981, 6 In.	59.00
Puppet, Hand, Mr. Peanut, 6 In.	1500.00
Recipe Book, Mr. Peanut, Soup To Nuts, 1970	12.00
Salt & Pepper, Mr. Peanut, Benjamin Medwin, 1990, 5 1/4 In.	59.00
Salt & Pepper, Mr. Peanut, Plastic, 1950, 5 1/4 In.	28.00
Salt & Pepper, Mr. Peanut, Plastic, 3 1/8 In.	25.00
Spoon, Mr. Peanut On Handle, Brass	38.00
Spoon, Serving, Mr. Peanut, Red, Plastic	13.00
Spoon, Silver Plate, Carlton, 5 1/8 In.	18.00
Straw, Mr. Peanut, Figural, Plastic, 1970, 8 In.	10.00
Tankard, Mr. Peanut, Pewter, Wilton, 5 In.	35.00
Tin, Green Panel, Red Ground, 9 3/4 x 8 1/4 In., 10 Lb.	440.00
Tin, Mr. Peanut, 3 x 3 3/8 In.	45.00
Tin, Mr. Peanut, Cashew Nut, Planters Nut & Chocolate Co., 1944, 3 In.	39.00
Tin, Mr. Peanut, Peanut Crunch, E.G. Whitman & Co., 4 3/8 x 4 In.	38.00
Tin, Mr. Peanut, Planters Old Fashioned Peanut Candy, Key Wind, 4 In.	95.00
Tin, Mr. Peanut, Salted, Planters Nut & Chocolate Co., Va., 3 x 2 In.	30.00
Tin, Peanut Butter, Mr. Peanut, Handle, Planter's Nut & Choc., Va., 4 In.	1950.00
Tin, Planters Salted Peanuts, Pennant, 2 1/2 x 2 3/8 In. ....*Illus*	8580.00
Tote Bag, Mr. Peanut, Canvas, 1970, 12 x 19 In.	35.00
Tray, Mr. Peanut, Roasted Peanuts, 15 5/8 x 11 1/8 In.	18.00
Trivet, Mr. Peanut, Roasted Peanuts, 8 3/8 x 6 1/2 In.	18.00
Trophy, Winning Route Salesman, Gold, Plastic, 1960, 6 x 3 1/2 In.	685.00
Umbrella, Mr. Peanut, Gold Color, 1980, 37 In.	36.00
Whistle, Mr. Peanut, Blue, Plastic, 1970	5.00

PLASTIC objects of all types are being collected. Some pieces are listed
in other categories; gutta-percha cases are listed in photography, celluloid in its own category.

Bowl, Vegetable, 2 Handles, Turquoise Blue, Boontonware, Melmac, 8 1/4 In.	8.50
Box, Green Swirls, Embossed Dragons, Shields, Rooster Handle, Black Base, 8 x 5 In.	30.00
Cuticle Remover, Amber, 4 In.	17.00
Cuticle Remover, Bakelite, 4 In.	12.00
Cuticle Remover, Ivory, Pyralin, 5 In.	9.00
Dinner Set, Shenandoah, Royalon, Melmac, 25 Piece	28.00
Dish, Sunset, Florence, Prolon, Melmac, Rectangular, 10 In.	11.00
Drink Stirrers, Zulu Lulu, Card, Nos. 15, 20, 25, 30, 35, 40, On Card, 1940s	25.00
Flatware Set, Stainless Steel, Red Bakelite Handle, Marbleized, Knives, Forks, 12 Piece	65.00
Hostess Set, Plates With Well, Cups, Lenoxware, Melmac, Box, 8 Piece	20.00
Mirror, Magnifying, Bakelite Handle, Brass Back, Plastic Cover, Art Deco	75.00
Mixing Bowl, Speckled Green, Brookpark, Melmac, 11 1/2 In.	18.00

Mug, Yogi Bear, Hanna-Barbera, c.1964, 6 1/2 In. 9.00
Pencil Case, Barbie, Blue, Patent Vinyl, Zipper, Barbie, Midge, Ken, 8 x 4 1/2 In. 55.00
Pencil Case, Barbie, Red, Pastel, Patent Vinyl, Zipper, c.1961, 7 3/4 x 3 1/2 In. 66.00
Pitcher Set, Nesting, Country Craft, 1950s, 1 Qt., 1 1/2 Qt. & 2 Qt., 3 Piece 25.00
Place Setting, Butterscotch & Red, Bakelite, 8 Piece 200.00
Plate, Bread & Butter, Blue & Purple Violets, Royalon, Melmac, 6 1/2 In. 2.00
Plate, Frosty Pink, Talk Of The Town, Harmony House, Melmac, 10 In. 4.00
Platter, Black, Modern Design, Brookpark, Melmac, 9 1/4 In. 15.00
Platter, Light Blue, Winter Scene, Trees, Birds In Flight, Lucent, Melmac, 15 x 12 In. 15.00
Sugar & Creamer, Avocado, Mallo-Ware, Melmac 5.00
Sugar & Creamer, Dusty Rose, Texas Ware 8.50
Sugar & Creamer, Pink, Harmony House, Melmac 9.00
Tea Set, Barbie, Purple, Worcester Toy Company, Box, c.1961, 18 x 15 In., 27 Piece 143.00
Toothpick, Totem Pole, Carved, Hand Painted, 3 1/2 In. 3.00
Tray, Inlaid Wood, Herb Design, Aluminum, Mosaic, Courac Of Monterey, 13 3/8 In. *Illus* 35.00
Tumbler Set, Juice, Mixed Colors, Color-Flyte, Melmac, 3 1/2 In., 8 Piece 54.00

PLATED AMBERINA was patented June 15, 1886, by Joseph Locke and made by the New England Glass Company. It is similar in color to amberina, but is characterized by a cream colored or chartreuse lining (never white) and small ridges or ribs on the outside.

Bowl, 3 1/2 In. 5250.00
Creamer, Applied Amber Handle, ...*Illus* 9200.00
Pitcher, 8 3/4 In. ....*Illus* 16675.00
Pitcher, Applied Amber Handle, 7 In. 10350.00
Sugar, Applied Amber Handles ....*Illus* 16100.00
Vase, Lily, Gold Enameled, Signed, 8 In. 7000.00

PLIQUE-A-JOUR is an enameling process. The enamel is laid between thin raised metal lines and heated. The finished piece has transparent enamel held between the thin metal wires. It is different from cloisonne because it is translucent.

Bowl, 2 Parrots, Diaper Design Ground, Box, Wooden Stand, 1 7/8 In. 350.00
Bowl, Birds, Flowers, 6 In. 224.00
Box, Cover, Filigree Rim, Flower Finial, 1 x 1 3/4 In. 402.00
Box, Moss Agate, Green, Yellow Foliate Design, Gilt, Silver Interior, 3 x 2 In. 518.00
Teaglass Holder, Geometric, Leaves, Russia, c.1908, 2 1/2 In., Pair 3360.00
Vase, Inverted Pear Shape, Floral Design, 2 1/2 In. 230.00
Vase, Phoenix, Imperial Yellow Ground, Silver Rim, 3 1/4 In. 400.00

POLITICAL memorabilia of all types, from buttons to banners, is collected. Items related to presidential candidates are the most popular, but collectors also search for material related to state and local offices. Memorabilia related to social causes, minor political parties, and protest movements are also included here. Many reproductions have been made. A jugate is a button with photographs of both the presidential and vice presidential candidates. In this list a button is round, usually with a straight pin or metal tab to secure it to a shirt. A pin is brass, often figural, sometimes attached to a ribbon.

Ashtray, Boot Shape, Jam Your Cigarette Butts On This Heel, Tojo Inset, 4 In. 58.00

Plated Amberina, Pitcher, 8 3/4 In.
Plated Amberina, Creamer, Applied Amber Handle
Plated Amberina, Sugar, Applied Amber Handles

Badge, 1939, New York, Jefferson Dem. Assn., Berks County Democratic Day, Ribbon .. 100.00
Badge, Alternate, Republican National Convention, Chicago, Lincoln Portrait, 1912 ..... 115.00
Badge, Democratic National Convention, Chicago, Doorkeeper, 1952, 1 x 5 In. 45.00
Badge, Funeral, Lincoln, Albumen Photo, Black Ribbon, 4 1/2 In. 600.00
Badge, Garfield For President, Ferrotype, Eagle Pin, c.1880, 1 3/4 x 2 In. 1278.00
Badge, Grover Cleveland, Double Portrait, Eagle Pin, Brass Shell, c.1888 .... 180.00
Badge, Hoover, Inauguration, Celluloid, Sepia, Ribbon, 1929, 2 1/2 In. 450.00
Badge, Inaugural Committee, Kennedy, Johnson, Inaugural Seal, Ribbon, 1961, 6 1/2 In. . 70.00
Badge, Inaugural, LBJ Official Party, Capitol Dome, Numbered, 1965, 3 1/2 In. 30.00
Badge, Republican National Convention, Chicago, 1920 .... 60.00
Ballot, Samuel J. Tilden, Cream, Black, 1876, 7 1/4 In. 42.00
Bandanna, Grover Cleveland, Allen Thurman, Dated 1888, Square, 19 In. 300.00
Bandanna, Protection vs. Free Trade, U.S. Flag, Red, White & Blue, Dated 1888 .... 150.00
Bandanna, Repeal Taft-Hartley Law, Worker At Factory, Silk, 34 x 36 In. 250.00
Bandanna, Wilson & Prosperity, Portrait, Eagle, Flags, Silk, 16 In. 150.00
Bank, Donkey, McGovern, Shriver, Cast Iron, Moore, 5 3/8 In. 220.00
Bank, F.D. Roosevelt, New Deal, Nickel Plated Iron, 5 In. ....175.00 to 200.00
Bank, Reagan, On Elephant, Cast Iron, Moore, Reynolds, 6 1/4 In. 60.00
Banner, 2nd New Hampshire Volunteer Militia, Frame, 22 x 32 In. 2475.00
Banner, Votes For Women, Padded Silk, Embroidered, Hanging Cord, 13 x 16 In. 1500.00
Baseball, President Richard Nixon Autograph 510.00
Blotter, Harrison, Morton & Wives, Celluloid, 3 x 8 In. 200.00
Book, Campaign Speeches Of Vice President Nixon, 1960 .... 15.00
Book, Life Of R.B. Hayes, R. Conwell, Hardcover, 1876, 330 Pages 75.00
Book, The Fighting President, FDR, 1934, 153 Pages 50.00
Booklet, Ballad Of Gene Debs, Sarah N. Cleghorn, 1928, 8 Pages 150.00
Booklet, Eleventh National Woman's Rights Convention, New York, 1866, 80 Pages 185.00
Booklet, General Franklin Pierce, Biographical Sketch, King, By Hermitage, 96 Pages ... 135.00
Booklet, Whig Almanac 1849, Zachary Taylor, 64 Pages 150.00
Bookmark, FDR, Side Bust Profile, Aluminum, 2 In. 35.00
Bookmark, Kennedy, Ask Not What Your, 1962 Calendar, Silk, Capitol Label Co. 102.00
Bookmark, Oscar E. Thomson, For State Senator, Celluloid, Whitehead & Hoag, 2 1/2 In. 43.00
Bookplate, Anna Howard Shaw, Cherub In Front Of House, Votes For Women Pennant .. 650.00
Bottle Cap, I Like Ike, He's Tops, Plastic, Red & White 8.00
Box, Cigar, Abraham Lincoln, Rail Splitter, Inside Label 75.00
Box, Cigar, Judge Taft, A Universal Favorite, 4 1/2 x 5 x 1 1/2 In. 125.00
Broadside, President Tyler's Address To The People Of The U.S., Portrait, 13 x 16 In. 1650.00
Broadside, Republican, Yankee Vote, Irish Vote, Republican Vote, 1871 .... 250.00
Bug, Mechanical, William Jennings Bryan, Silver 16 To 1, Picture, Brass 136.00
Bumper Sticker, Another Veteran For Kennedy, Johnson, 1960 Campaign 16.00
Bumper Sticker, Cowboy Hat, LBJ, 1968 .... 4.00
Bumper Sticker, Gene McCarthy For President, Autographed 20.00
Bust, Washington, Sandstone, Relief, Late 18th Century, 15 In. 358.00
Button, Adlai E. Stevenson For Governor, Photo, Black, Cream, Celluloid, 7/8 In. 48.00
Button, Adlai For Me, Blue, Yellow, Celluloid, 1 1/4 In. 70.00
Button, Al Smith For President, Happy Warrior, Black, White, 1924, 7/8 In. 276.00
Button, Al Smith, Joe Robinson, Celluloid, 1928, 7/8 In. 248.00
Button, All The Way With Adlai, Red, White, Blue, 1952, 1 1/4 In. 6.00
Button, America Needs LBJ-HHH, Jugate, 1964, 3 1/2 .... 20.00
Button, Anderson For President, Lithograph, 1980, 1 5/8 In. 2.00
Button, Arizonans For Ducactus, Desert Background, Cactus Scene, Celluloid, 2 In. 300.00
Button, Athletes For Reagan, Bush, Celluloid, 1984, 2 1/4 In. 3.00
Button, AuH2O, Our Next President, Goldwater, Celluloid, 1964, 3 1/2 In. 8.00
Button, Better A Third Termer Than A Third Rater, FDR, Orange, White, 1 1/4 In. 14.00
Button, Better Red Than Dead, Anti-Vietnam War, Printed, 1 1/2 In. 6.00
Button, Bob LaFollette, I Am For Bob For Governor, Sepia Photo, c.1924, 7/8 In. 66.00
Button, Bomb Hanoi, Black, White, Celluloid, c.1970, 1 1/2 In. 41.00
Button, Boston Peace March, Commemorate Kent & Jackson SMC, c.1970, 1 3/4 In. 232.00
Button, Bryan, Stevenson, Celluloid, 1896, 1 1/4 In. 35.00
Button, Bush Whacker, Dukakis Picture, Celluloid, 1 3/4 In. 28.00
Button, California, Reagan Delegation, Celluloid, In Cowboy Hat, 1980, 4 In. 1863.00
Button, Calvin Coolidge, Red, Cream, Blue, Black, Celluloid, 1 3/4 In. 263.00
Button, Campaign, ABC News Political Spirit 76, Primaries, Plastic, Insert Card, 1976 .. 10.00

Button, Cape Ann For McGovern, Stars, Stripes, Red, White, Celluloid, N.J., 1 1/2 In. . . .   173.00
Button, Carter, Holtzman For America And N.Y., 1980, 1 3/4 In. 3.00
Button, Charles Evans Hughes, For President, Portrait, Cream, Black, c.1916, 1 1/4 In. . .   531.00
Button, CIO-PAC For Stevenson, Cream, Blue, Celluloid, 2 1/2 In. 484.00
Button, Clothing, George Washington's 1789 Inauguration, Initials G.W., Oval 1210.00
Button, Clothing, George Washington, Long Live The President, Brown Patina 1450.00
Button, Columbia Citizens Committee For Eisenhower & Nixon, Celluloid, 2 1/4 In. 296.00
Button, Columbiana County For Mondale, Ferraro, Red, White, Blue, Celluloid, 2 In. . . .   165.00
Button, Dan Quayle Is My Senator, Indiana, Celluloid, 1 1/4 In. 11.00
Button, Democrat For Goldwater, Celluloid, 1 In. 5.00
Button, Dewey Victory Special Press, Brown, White, Celluloid, 1948, 2 1/2 In. 508.00
Button, Dewey Victory Special Staff, Orange, White, Celluloid, 2 1/2 In. 506.00
Button, Dick & Spiro In 1968, Picture, Black, White, 1 In. 5.00
Button, Dukakis For President, American Flag, Celluloid, Square, 1988, 2 In. 2.50
Button, Dukakis, A Nice Guy In 88, Red, Black, White, Celluloid, 2 1/2 In. 28.00
Button, Dukakis, Bentsen, New Leadership In '88, 3 In. . . . .*Illus*   10.00
Button, Egg, Mechanical, Rooster Pops Out Of Egg, I Crow For Harrison 1580.00
Button, Eisenhower For President, Black, White, Celluloid, 1 1/4 In. 21.00
Button, Eisenhower, Nixon, Jugate, Celluloid, Vote For Better Future, 2 In. 44.00
Button, Elephant Ears, Taft, Sherman, 1908, 1 1/4 In. 3500.00
Button, Eugene Debs, For President, Convict No. 9653, Photo, Red, White, Black, 7/8 In.   847.00
Button, F. Roosevelt, Cactus Jack Garner, Jugate, Black, White, Celluloid, 7/8 In. 169.00
Button, Father Coughlin, Roosevelt Or Ruin, Blue, White, Celluloid, c.1932, 1 1/4 In. . . .   1509.00
Button, FDR Carry On, Red, White & Blue, 1 In. 8.50
Button, FDR, Bring Back Beer & Business, Liberty, Safety, Celluloid, c.1932, 1 1/2 In. . . .   1876.00
Button, Flasher, Goldwater, Picture, 1964, 3 In. 6.00
Button, Flasher, LBJ For The USA, U.S. Outline, Plastic, Blue, Ribbon, Calif., 2 1/2 In. .   20.00
Button, Ford, Dole, Wives, Pictures, Eagle, Celluloid, 1976, 3 1/2 In. 14.00
Button, Garfield, Arthur Ferrotype, Presidential Campaign, 1 1/2 x 1 1/2 In. 1650.00
Button, George Washington, Kindred Spirits In Cause Of Liberty, Celluloid, 1 1/4 In. . . .   889.00
Button, Go, Go, Goldwater In '64, Elephant, Celluloid, 3 1/2 In. 6.00
Button, Goldwater In '64, Picture, 7/8 In. 3.00
Button, Goldwater, Convention Speech, Picture, Celluloid, 2 1/2 In. 80.00
Button, Goldwater, Miller, Stars, 1964, 1 1/4 In. 3.00
Button, Goldwater, The Best Man For The Job, Celluloid, 1965, 3 1/2 In. 10.00
Button, GOP Convention, McKinley, Eagle Crest, Bell With Picture, 1900, 2 1/4 In. 40.00
Button, Greeks For Goldwater, English & Greek, Black, White, Celluloid, 1 1/2 In. 45.00
Button, Harding, Coolidge, Black & White Lithograph, 7/8 In. 13.00
Button, Harding, Coolidge, Jugate, Gray, White, Celluloid, c.1920, 7/8 In. 820.00
Button, Harding, On Side Of Elephant, Black, Tan, White, Gold, Celluloid, 1 1/4 In. 3801.00
Button, Have Faith In God & Hoover, Sky Blue, Gold, Celluloid, 7/8 In. 508.00
Button, Heaven Help Humanity, Celluloid, 1968, 1 1/2 In. 3.00
Button, HHH, Humphrey, Capitol City, St. Paul, 1988, 2 1/2 In. 128.00
Button, Hoover, Curtis, Jugate, Black, White, Lithograph, 7/8 In. 121.00
Button, Hoover, Curtis, My Country Tis Of Thee, Red, White, Blue, Celluloid, 1 1/4 In. .   5940.00
Button, Hoover, Curtis, Red, White & Blue, Celluloid, 7/8 In.   53.00
Button, Hoover, GOP, Elephant, Enameled, 1 In. 20.00
Button, Hoover, Picture, Black & White, 1 1/4 In. 45.00

Political, Button, Our
Nation Needs, Nixon,
Lodge, 3 1/4 In.

Political, Button, Dukakis,
Bentsen, New Leadership
In '88, 3 In.

**Never store celluloid with
metal. The celluloid gives off
a gas that will attack metal.
Don't put celluloid in the
sun. It is highly flammable
and may burn.**

Button, Hubert H. Humphrey For President, Celluloid Over Tin, c.1960, 3 1/2 In. 25.00
Button, Hubert H. Humphrey For President, Face, Celluloid, 1968, 1 3/4 In. 4.00
Button, Hughes, Red, White & Blue Around Edge, Celluloid, 7/8 In. 57.00
Button, Hughes, Sepia Shell, Gold Frame, Eagle Crest, 1 1/4 In. 194.00
Button, I Like Dick, Celluloid, 1 In. 7.00
Button, I Like Ike, Ike Likes Me, Celluloid, 1 1/4 In. 201.00
Button, I'm For King's Way, Martin Luther King Picture, 1 1/2 In. 266.00
Button, If I Were 21 I'd Vote For Barry, 1964, 3 1/2 In. 5.00
Button, If I Were 21 I'd Vote For Humphrey, 3/4 In. 7.00
Button, If I Were 21 I'd Vote For Kennedy, 1968, 4 In. 5.00
Button, Ike You Like, Dick You'll Get, Cream, Blue, c.1956, 2 1/2 In. 496.00
Button, Ike, In Morse Code, Black, White, Celluloid, 1 1/4 In. 21.00
Button, It Seems To Me It's Kennedy, Black, White, Celluloid, 1960, 1 1/2 In. 4290.00
Button, James Cox, Ohio, Red, White, Blue, Celluloid, 1920, 1/2 In. 424.00
Button, Jesse Jackson For President In '88, 2 1/2 In. 2.00
Button, JFK, Donkey Shape, 1 1/4 In. 15.00
Button, JFK, My Ambassador Kennedy, Blue, White, Celluloid, 7/8 In. 57.00
Button, Jimmy Carter For President 1980, Picture, Celluloid, 3 In. 3.00
Button, Joe Louis For Willkie, Celluloid, 1940, 1 1/2 In. 704.00
Button, John Glenn For President, Soar To New Heights, Celluloid, c.1984, 1 1/2 In. 12.00
Button, John L. Lewis, Picture, Black & White, 1 1/4 In. 25.00
Button, Johnson, Humphrey, Jugate, Lithograph, 1964, 3 In. 6.00
Button, Kennedy & Peace, 1968, RFK Photo, Red, White, Blue, Celluloid, 1 In. 13.00
Button, Kennedy Is Best For Me, Celluloid, Small Picture, 2 In. 14.00
Button, Lady Bird Special, Locomotive, 1964, 3 1/2 In. 30.00
Button, Landon Knox Out Roosevelt, Celluloid, 1936, 1 In. 5450.00
Button, Landon, Knox, Elephant, Enameled, 1 In. 35.00
Button, Landon, Knox, Jugate, Brass Eagle, 1 1/4 In. 30.00
Button, Landon, Sunflower Chain Club, Blue, Yellow, Celluloid, 1930s, 7/8 In. 215.00
Button, Landon, Yellow Oilcloth Flower, Red, White, Blue, Celluloid, c.1936, 2 1/2 In. ... 46.00
Button, LBJ, Brown, Yellow, 1 In. 4.00
Button, LBJ, Light Bulb Johnson, Turn Him Out In November, Celluloid, 2 1/2 In. 9.00
Button, Let Freedom Democracy Reign, Washington, Lincoln, FDR, Celluloid, 7/8 In. 198.00
Button, Let's Back Ike & Dick, Pictures, Lithograph, 1 1/8 In. 165.00
Button, Liberal Kennedy Row C, Green, Black, White, Celluloid, 1 In. 22.00
Button, Life Begins In '40, Win With Willkie, GOP Elephant, Celluloid, 1 3/4 In. 125.00
Button, MacArthur For President, Photo, Red, Blue, Black, Celluloid, c.1952, 1 1/4 In. ... 24.00
Button, Make Love Not War, Peace Sign, Vietnam Protest, Red, White, Black, 7/8 In. ... 23.00
Button, Martin Luther King, Civil Rights, Picture, Celluloid, 1 1/4 In. 17.00
Button, McGovern, Eagleton, Come Home America, Celluloid, 1972, 1 1/2 In. 5.00
Button, McGovern, Shriver, 2 Great Reformers, Red, White & Blue, Celluloid, 1 1/4 In. .. 17.00
Button, McGovern, Shriver, Give Peace A Chance, Jugate, 1 1/4 In. 50.00
Button, McGovern, Shriver, Jugate, Red, White & Blue, Celluloid, 1 1/4 In. 12.00
Button, McGovern, Staff, Blue, White, Keystone, Celluloid, Penn., c.1972, 1 1/2 In. 772.00
Button, McKinley, Commercial Traveler For McKinley, Celluloid, 1 1/4 In. 504.00
Button, McKinley, Hobart For President, Gold Flag, Opens To Photos, 1896, 1 1/2 In. 400.00
Button, McKinley, T. Roosevelt, Celluloid, Red, White & Blue, Flags, 1900, 1 1/4 In. ... 120.00
Button, McKinley, T. Roosevelt, Republican Club, Celluloid, 1900, 1 3/4 In. 1669.00
Button, McKinley, Tanner, John, Black, White Celluloid, 1900, 1 1/2 In. 668.00
Button, Mondale, '84, Jobs, Peace, Opportunity, 3 In. 3.00
Button, Mondale, Ferraro, Jugate, Celluloid, 1984, 3 In. 4.00
Button, Mondale, Ferraro, We Are A Mirror Of America, Black, White, Blue, 1984, 3 In. .. 191.00
Button, Mondale, Hart, Jugate, Capitol Building, Celluloid, 1984, 3 In. 3.00
Button, My First Vote Is For Reagan, Picture, 1980, 1 1/4 In. 3.00
Button, National Wheelmen's Club For McKinley, Celluloid, c.1896, 1 1/4 In. 879.00
Button, Nebraskans For Kennedy, Photograph, Red, Black, White, c.1960, 7/8 In. 391.00
Button, Need Nixon Now, 1972, 1 1/2 In. 5.00
Button, Nixon In '88, 3 In. 4.00
Button, Nixon Now, Celluloid, 1968, 2 1/4 In. 3.00
Button, Nixon, Agnew, Jugate, Now More Than Ever, Celluloid, 1972, 3 1/2 In. 5.50
Button, Nixon, U.S. Shape, Metal, 1 In. 7.00
Button, No Third Term, Willkie, Black, White, Celluloid, 1 1/4 In. 10.00
Button, Not Too Late In '68 H.H.H., 1 1/4 In. 6.00

Button, Now More Than Ever, Nixon, Agnew, Jugate, 1972, 3 1/2 In. 6.00
Button, Ohio For Carter, Picture, Soil Ground, 1 3/4 In. 2.00
Button, Oscar W. Underwood, For President, Photo, Black, Cream, c.1912, 2 1/2 In. 79.00
Button, Our Friend, William Randolph Hearst, Sepia, 1 1/4 In. 100.00
Button, Our Nation Needs, Nixon, Lodge, 3 1/4 In. . . . .*Illus* 17.00
Button, Out Of The Dog House Into The White House, Blue, White, Celluloid, 1 In. 484.00
Button, Parker, Davis, 1904 Democratic Candidates, 4-Leaf Clover, Celluloid, 2 In. 3960.00
Button, Pat For First Lady, 2 1/8 In. . . . .*Illus* 2.50
Button, Pinback, National Council Of Negro Women Inc., Black & White, 2 1/4 In. 12.50
Button, Progressive Caucus For Mondale, Ferraro, Celluloid, 2 1/2 In. 143.00
Button, Re-Elect Hoover, Blue, Light Brown, White, Celluloid, 1932, 1 1/4 In. 545.00
Button, Reagan Wearing Cowboy Hat, Picture, Celluloid, 1980, 3 1/2 In. 5.00
Button, Reagan, America, Proud, Strong, & Free, Picture, 1984, 3 In. 5.00
Button, Reagan, Bring Back The Gipper In '96, Celluloid, 1 3/4 In. 9.00
Button, Reagan, Bush, 50th Inaugural, Jugate, Celluloid, 1985, 3 1/2 In. 5.00
Button, Reagan, Bush, Inauguration Day 1985, Jugate, Capitol Dome, 2 1/4 In. 5.00
Button, Reagan, Do Not Draft Women, Green, White, Celluloid, 1 1/4 In. 10.00
Button, Reagan, End Of An Error, Celluloid, 1984, 1 1/2 In. 13.00
Button, Reagan, John Wayne, Jugate, Celluloid, 1 1/4 In. 33.00
Button, Reagan, Let's Start Our Third Century Right, 1980, 1 3/4 In. 5.00
Button, Rebus, I Work For, Picture Of Peanuts, Jimmy Carter, Celluloid, 2 1/2 In. 205.00
Button, Rebus, Teddy Roosevelt, Portrait, Red Rose, Velt On Banner, 1 1/4 In. 182.00
Button, Republican Integrity, Reagan, Lincoln, Roosevelt, Eisenhower, 1985, 2 1/8 In. 5.00
Button, Ribbon, First Woman's Vote, Harding, Yellow, Black, 1920, 4 1/2 In. 440.00
Button, Richard M. Nixon For President, Picture, 6 In. 22.50
Button, Roosevelt, Fairbanks, At Sagamore Hill, Oyster Bay, N.Y., Celluloid, 1 1/4 In. . . . 485.00
Button, Roosevelt, Fairbanks, Jugate, Celluloid, 1904, 1 1/4 In. 1375.00
Button, Roosevelt, Flathead County Young Men's Republican Club, c.1904, 1 1/4 In. 1513.00
Button, Roosevelt, Labor's Choice, Red, White, Blue, Celluloid, 1 3/4 In. 334.00
Button, Roosevelt, Labor's Friend, Red, White & Blue, Celluloid, 1 1/4 In. 40.00
Button, Roosevelt, Stewart, For Repeal, 1 In. 20.00
Button, Roosevelt, Truman, Brown Shades, 1944, 1 In. 278.00
Button, Roosevelt, Truman, Jugate, Brown, Tan, Celluloid, c.1944, 7/8 In. 240.00
Button, Rosalyn Carter For First Lady 1980, Picture, Celluloid, 3 In. 3.00
Button, Save The Country, Impeach Nixon, Celluloid, 2 1/4 In. 103.00
Button, See One Nuclear War You've Seen Them All, Red, Gray, c.1970, 1 1/2 In. 11.00
Button, Senior Power Supports Metzenbaum, Carter, Mondale, Ohio, Celluloid, 2 In. 120.00
Button, Silent Cal Coolidge & Hell & Maria Dawes, Lithograph, 1924, 7/8 In. 363.00
Button, Skinny Cat For McGovern, Celluloid, Yellow, Cat Picture, 2 1/2 In. 140.00
Button, Smiley Face, Humphrey, Yellow, Black, Celluloid, c.1972, 2 1/4 In. 88.00
Button, Smith, Robinson, Red, White & Blue, Celluloid, 7/8 In. 13.00
Button, SNCC, Civil Rights, Black Hand Clasped White Hand, 7/8 In. 15.00
Button, Staff, Bandwagon Staff, Nixon, 1960 Campaign Tour, Celluloid, 2 3/4 In. 680.00
Button, Start Packing Harry, The Deweys Are Coming, Blue & White, Celluloid, 1 1/4 In. 65.00
Button, Stevenson For President, Red, White & Blue, Celluloid, 1 In. 15.00
Button, Stevenson, Humphrey, Freeman, Blatnik, Minnesota, c.1956, 2 1/4 In. 1162.00
Button, Students For Mondale, Ferraro, Celluloid, 1 3/4 In. 6.00
Button, Support The Coolidge Administration, Picture, Celluloid, 1 3/4 In. 950.00

**Bakelite jewelry can be
cleaned with a soft damp
cloth and a mild abrasive
cleaner such as a car-body
polish. After cleaning, rub on
beeswax polish.**

Political, Button, Pat For
First Lady, 2 1/8 In.

Political, Noisemaker, Click
With Dick, 2 1/4 In.

Button, Syrians For Taft, White, Red, Blue, Ohio, Celluloid, c.1998, 2 In. 23.00
Button, T. Roosevelt, American Bankers Assoc., Celluloid, c.1905, 2 1/8 In. 525.00
Button, Taft, Black & White, Celluloid, 7/8 In. 13.00
Button, Taft, Jugate, Red, White, Blue, Black, Green, Gold, 7/8 In. 76.00
Button, Tammany, Bryan, Sewall, Red, White, Blue, Star, c.1896, 7/8 In. 88.00
Button, Teddy Roosevelt, Red, White & Blue, Eagle Ground, Celluloid, 1 1/4 In. 110.00
Button, The Nation Of Nixon, Connecticut Volunteers, Celluloid, 1 3/4 In. 75.00
Button, Theodore Roosevelt, Bull Moose, Multicolored, Celluloid, 1912, 2 1/4 In. 842.00
Button, Theodore Roosevelt, Gold Ground, Zion City Mercantile, Celluloid, 1 1/4 In. . . . 362.00
Button, Theodore Roosevelt, My Only Scuttle Policy, Coal Bucket, Celluloid, 7/8 In. 66.00
Button, Theodore Roosevelt, Prosperity, Advancement, c.1904, 1 1/4 In. 1718.00
Button, Time For Change, Baby, I Like Ike On Diaper, Blue, White, Celluloid, 1 1/4 In. . 240.00
Button, Trade In Your Ford, Gerald Ford's Head As Hood Ornament On Edsel, 2 1/2 In. . 190.00
Button, Truman, Phooey On Dewey, Black, White, 1 1/4 In. 30.00
Button, Vegetarian Party, Maxwell, Gould, Green, White, Celluloid, c.1948, 7/8 In. 51.00
Button, Vietnam Protest, Draft Beer, Not Students, Green, Celluloid, c.1968, 1 1/4 In. . . . 19.00
Button, Volunteer, I'm On The Team, Dewey, Warren, Celluloid, 2 In. 33.00
Button, Vote The Kennedy Ticket, Red, White, Celluloid, c.1960, 4 1/8 In. 1663.00
Button, Votes For Women, Blue & Gold, Celluloid, 1915, 1/2 In. 150.00
Button, Wallace For President, Stand Up For America, Face, Lithograph, 1968, 3 In. 4.00
Button, Walter Mondale For Vice President In 1980, Picture, 3 In. 4.00
Button, Warren Harding, Blackstone Hotel Meeting, Red, White, Blue, Brown, 7/8 In. . . . 1562.00
Button, Watch Willkie Wilt, Blue, White, Celluloid, c.1940, 7/8 In. 13.00
Button, We Cannot Afford A Lesser Man, Stevenson, c.1960, 1 1/4 In. 258.00
Button, We Don't Want Eleanor Either, Willkie, Blue, White, Celluloid, 1 1/4 In. 20.00
Button, We Love Mondale Labor, Red, White, Blue, Celluloid, 2 In. 97.00
Button, We Want Willkie For President, Red, White & Blue, Celluloid, 2 1/4 In. 185.00
Button, We Want Willkie, Red, White, Blue, Black, Celluloid, 1940, 1 3/4 In. 557.00
Button, Who Me Worry? Heck No, I Work For Nixon, Goofy Face, Celluloid, 1 3/4 In. . . . 13.00
Button, William Howard Taft, God Knows, Blue, White, Celluloid, 1 1/4 In. 1650.00
Button, William Howard Taft, James Sherman, In Elephant Ears, Red, 1 1/4 In. 2236.00
Button, William Howard Taft, Trumpeter, Celluloid, 1 3/4 In. 1551.00
Button, William J. Bryan, Bunch Of Corn, 2 Essentials, Celluloid, 1 1/2 x 2 1/4 In. 648.00
Button, William Jennings Bryan, Brown Jacket, Bowtie, Celluloid, 3 1/2 In. 1597.00
Button, William Jennings Bryan, Cross Of Gold, Silver Clock, Celluloid, 1 3/4 In. 2739.00
Button, William Jennings Bryan, First, Last & All The Time, Celluloid, 1908, 3 1/2 In. . . . 4095.00
Button, William Jennings Bryan, No Cross Of Gold, Celluloid, c.1896, 7/8 In. 110.00
Button, Willkie Or Bust, Blue, White, Celluloid, 1 1/4 In. 9.00
Button, Willkie, McNary, Elephant, Celluloid, 1 1/4 In. 10.00
Button, Willkie, Red, White & Blue Shield Ground, A.G. Trimble, 7/8 In. 40.00
Button, Wilson, Pershing, Black Jack, American Army In World War I, 1 1/2 In. 218.00
Button, Wilson, Picture, Black, White, Celluloid, 7/8 In. 18.00
Button, Winsted Committee Of 1000 For Ike, Red, Blue, Silver, Celluloid, 1 1/4 In. 116.00
Button, Woodrow Wilson's Wisdom Wins, Red, Cream, Blue, Celluloid, 7/8 In. 30.00
Button, Woodrow Wilson, Duckworth Club, 1880, 2 1/2 In. 563.00
Button, Woodrow Wilson, Man Of The 8 Hour Day, Safety First, 7/8 In. 66.00
Button, Woodrow Wilson, Preparedness For War, Black, White Celluloid, 1 1/4 In. 7150.00
Calendar, Theodore Roosevelt Calendar, Quotes From Speeches, Box, 1920, 5 x 8 In. . . . 100.00
Card, Inauguration Of Governor Theodore Roosevelt, Albany, N.Y., Jan. 2, 1899, 4 x 5 In. 450.00
Card, Taft, Hughes, Fairbanks, Cannon, Republican Convention, Bromo-Seltzer, 1908 . . . 120.00
Cartoon, My Policy In 1868, Johnson & Seward As Incompetent Firemen, 13 x 17 In. . . . 450.00
Cent, Elongated, Huey Long, U.S. Senator, 1893-1935 . . . . 350.00
Charm, Harris, Shield Shape, Glass 53.00
Charm, JFK, 3/4 In. 7.00
Charm, Souvenir, JFK, LBJ Inaugural Ball, Pewter, 1961 . . . . 25.00
Charm, Vest, Taft, Sherman, Tinted Sepia 200.00
Christmas Card, White House From Lafayette Square, Nixon, Envelope, 1973 . . . . 30.00
Cigar, Bubble Gum, H. Humphrey 12.00
Cigar Case, Decoupage, Taft & Sherman Pictures, 25 Presidents, 1908 . . . . 450.00
Cigarette Pack, Eisenhower, I Like Ike, Unopened 27.00
Compact, Zachary Taylor, Glass Cover, Forget-Me-Not, Matchbox, 1 7/8 x 2 7/8 In. 1330.00
Cup, Votes For Women, Drink To Success, Empire State Campaign, Paper, 1915, 4 1/2 In. 200.00
Dollar, In God We Trust For The Other 47 Cents, Bryan Caricature, Aluminum, 1896 . . . . 100.00

Emery Board, Goldwater, Miller, Liberty Bell, Plastic, 1964 .... 1.00
Fan, I'm A Fan Of Grayson Pat Williamson, Red, White, Blue, Stars, Stripes, Wood, 8 In. . 4.50
Fan, I'm A Fan Of Paul Snooky Smith, Re-Elect Magistrate, Stars & Stripes 3.50
Ferrotype, Grant, USG, Brass Shell, 1868 ....132.00 to 224.00
Ferrotype, Harrison, Morton 500.00
Ferrotype, Hayes, RBH, Brass Shell, 1876 .... 806.00
Ferrotype, Seymour, Brass Shell, 1868 .... 822.00
Ferrotype, Tilden Hake, Brass Shell 807.00
Figurine, Donkey, Wm. J. Bryan For President, Cast Iron, 6 In. 995.00
Figurine, Elephant, Celluloid Insert, GOP, Cast Iron, 5 x 7 In. 875.00
Figurine, Kitten, Votes For Women, Brown, 3 1/4 In. 2000.00
Flag, 38 Stars, Harrison & Morton Campaign, Paper, 9 x 5 In. 133.00
Flag, Wm. Taft, Welcome, Eagle, Glazed Muslin, 22 x 34 In. 1950.00
Flasher, Picture Of LBJ, U.S. Map, Johnson For President, Metal Frame, 2 1/2 In. .. 3.50
Flask, In McKinley We Trust, Gold Standard, In Bryan We Trust, Aqua, 6 In., Pair .. 1550.00
Glass, Willkie, Acceptance Speech, Elwood, Ind., Red, White, Blue, c.1940, 4 1/2 In. 24.00
Gloves, I'm Working For Nixon & Lodge, Cotton, Yellow, Black Lettering, 1960 .... 25.00
Handkerchief, Harding, Capitol, Silk, Frame, 10 In. 135.00
Hat Band, Nixon, 1968 .... 3.00
Invitation, Inauguration, Reagan, Bush, Gold Embossed Seal, Envelope, 1981 .... 11.00
Invitation, James K. Polk, 11th Presidents' Inaugural Ball, 8 x 5 1/2 In. 3300.00
Kerchief, Harrison, Morton, Bald Eagle Over Eaglets, Slogan, Frame, 27 x 25 In. 546.00
Knife, President Inset, Watergate See, Hear, Speak No Evil, Plastic, Pocket, 1974 .... 30.00
Lamp, Garfield Portrayed On 1 Side, Mother Campaigning Other, 17 In. 6590.00
Lantern, Garfield Campaign, Color Portraits Of Grant & Wilson, 10 In. 1931.00
License Plate, George Wallace, Steel, 4 x 12 In. 88.00
License Plate, Goldwater, AuH2O, 1964 .... 20.00
License Plate, I Like Ike, Blue & White, 12 x 4 1/2 In. 72.00
License Plate, Jimmy Carter, 1977, Inaugural, Metal, Red, Tan & Blue, 12 x 6 In. . .95.00 to 110.00
License Plate, Reagan, Bush, Victory In 1984, Red, White & Blue, 12 x 6 In. 66.00
License Plate, Roosevelt, Orange, Blue, Silver, Reflector Bumps 135.00
License Plate, Stevenson, Blue & White 175.00
License Plate Attachment, Willkie, Bricker, Burton, Shield Shape, Ohio 150.00
Matchbook, Betty For First Lady '76 .... 3.00
Matchbook, LBJ For The USA, Pictures, 1964 .... 3.00
Matchbook, Support Those Who Support Kennedy, Picture, Red, White & Blue 25.00
Mirror, FDR Picture, Souvenir Of Detroit, Celluloid, Pocket 125.00
Mirror, FDR Picture, Surrounded By Other Presidents, Black & White, Celluloid, Pocket . 300.00
Mug, Match Holder, McKinley, Match Striker On Base 150.00
Mug, Teddy Roosevelt, Ceramic, 2 1/4 In. 225.00
Music Box, John F. Kennedy, Rocking Chair, Happy Days Are Here Again, Kamar, 1963 . 375.00
Napkin, Votes For Women, Paper, Purple Letters, 7 In. 125.00
Necktie, Repeal Taft Hartley Law, Worker & Factory, Blue & Yellow 125.00
Noisemaker, Click With Dick, 2 1/4 In. ....*Illus* 25.00
Oyster Plate, Presidential, Rutherford B. Hayes, Haviland, c.1880, 8 3/4 In., Pair 1955.00
Paperweight, Nixon & Agnew Cartoons, Red, White & Blue, Glass, 3 In., Pair 60.00
Parasol, Bryan, Stevenson, Cloth & Wood 2355.00
Pen, Humphrey, Ballpoint, Register & Vote, 1968 .... 6.00
Pen, L.B. Johnson, Presidential Seal, 1964 .... 15.00
Pen, L.B. Johnson, Used For Signing, Felt Tip, Silver Top, 1965 .... 75.00
Pencil, Wendell Willkie Is My Man For President, Red, White & Blue 25.00
Pennant, Garfield, Arthur, Red, White & Blue, Oilcloth, Original Stick, 26 In. 850.00
Pennant, Swallowtail, Hayes, Wheeler, Muslin, 20 x 34 In. 7425.00
Pennant, Thomas Dewey, Our 33rd President, Multichromatic, Felt, 25 In. 28.00
Pennant, Votes For Women, Felt, Black & Yellow, 20 In. 450.00
Photo Album, McKinley, Celluloid, 9 x 10 In. 135.00
Picture, Calhoun, Calligraphy, Pen & Ink, 19 x 25 In. 375.00
Picture, Teddy Roosevelt, Lithograph, Howard Chandler Christy, Frame, 12 x 18 In. 275.00
Pin, Brown Derby, Smith, Sepia Photograph Inset, c.1928, 1 7/8 In. 243.00
Pin, Elephant, Hoover, Curtis, Red, Gold Enamel, 7/8 In. 16.00
Pin, Elephant, On Ball With GOP Inside, Hoover, Gold Enameled, 7/8 In. 17.00
Pin, Elephant, Wearing Glasses, Goldwater, Gold, Clutch Back, 1 1/4 In. 12.00
Pin, Glasses, Teddy Roosevelt, Fairbanks, Brass, 1 1/4 In. 129.00

Pin, Gold Bug, McKinley, 1 In. 75.00
Pin, Rebus, Winfield Scott Hancock, Rooster Inside Hand, c.1880, 1 In. 1584.00
Pin, U.S. Map, Willkie, Enamel, Red, White, Blue, Gold, 7/8 In. 20.00
Pin, Wendell Willkie, Photograph, 1 1/4 In. 95.00
Pitcher, Jefferson, Portrait 1 Side, Poem Other, Liverpool, 7 In. 5693.00
Placecard Holder, Elephant, Marching To Prosperity With Willkie, Wooden, 5 In. 75.00
Plaque, Franklin Delano Roosevelt, Metal, 1933, 8 1/4 x 12 1/4 In. 120.00
Platter, Blaine, Logan Portraits, Pressed Glass, Frosted Center, 8 1/2 x 11 In. 385.00
Popgun, Cox, Roosevelt, Popping Away, Jugate Portraits 4950.00
Postcard, Leadership For The 60s, Strength For Peace, JFK, LBJ Portraits 85.00
Postcard, Nixon & Family, Polls Don't Vote, People Do 4.00
Postcard, Nixon Get Out The Vote, Nixon Family Faces, 1972, 5 x 7 In. 5.00
Postcard, Robert F. Kennedy, Photograph On Front, 7 x 9 In. 3.00
Postcard, Special Today, Possum Eating Roast Teddy Bear For Dinner, Taft, TR 50.00
Postcard, Teddy Roosevelt On Front, Man Of The Hour, 1910 .... 78.00
Postcard, William Jennings Bryan, Profile, Signature 24.00
Postcard, Wm. H. Taft, Photo Of Taft, American Flag Background, 1908 .... 25.00
Poster, Carter, Mondale, Pictures, 1976, 11 x 17 1/2 In. 7.50
Poster, Franklin D. Roosevelt, In Memoriam, 1882-1945, 98 x 10 In. 29.00
Poster, George McGovern, For President, 3 Doves, 1972, 14 x 22 In. 53.00
Poster, Humphrey, Muskie Campaign, Pictures, 35 x 23 In. 88.00
Poster, Johnson For Vice-President, Color, 1960, 27 x 43 In. 20.00
Poster, Johnson, Humphrey For The USA, Pictures, 1964, 20 x 28 In. 20.00
Poster, Reagan, Students For Reagan, 28 x 22 In. 38.00
Poster, Robert F. Kennedy, 1968, 11 x 14 In. 13.00
Poster, Roosevelt, Pictures Of FDR, Wallace, Paper Over Linen, 10 x 27 In. 375.00
Poster, Voice Of The People, James Gulick To Run, 23 x 24 In. 230.00
Poster, Wallace, Patriot Image, A Second Call To Freedom, 1968, 11 x 14 In. 5.00
Poster, We Like Ike, Picture, Shield, Red, White & Blue, Cardboard, 11 x 14 In. 50.00
Program, N.J. Democratic State Committee Annual Dinner, 1964 .... 5.00
Purse, Willkiette, Felt, Red, White & Blue, Cutout Letters, 10 In. 100.00
Puzzle, Block, Blaine Is In, How Can Harrison Get Him Out, Wood Box, 4 In. 150.00
Puzzle, Put Roosevelt On Backs Of Both Donkeys, Cardboard 175.00
Razor, In Memoriam, Pres. Garfield, Died Sept. 19, 1881, Etched Portrait 250.00
Razor, Old Tippecanoe Impressed On Blade, Greaves, 1840s 400.00
Ribbon, Abraham Lincoln, Andrew Johnson, Lincoln's Picture, Green Silk 3650.00
Ribbon, Benjamin Harrison, 70th Indiana, Photo, White, Fringe, Pin, 10 In. 120.00
Ribbon, Benjamin Harrison, Photo, Young Men's Republican Club, Purple, Gold, 7 In. 117.00
Ribbon, Blaine Club, RWB, Gold, Cream, 9 1/4 In. 72.00
Ribbon, Coolidge, Dawes, The Whole Republican Ticket, Blue, Cream, Gold, 4 In. 2197.00
Ribbon, Coolidge, Dawes, Vote The Whole Republican Ticket, 1 3/4 In. 2197.00
Ribbon, Delegate To Territorial Democratic Convention, Prescott, Arizona, Silk, 1898 ... 185.00
Ribbon, Dewey, God Bless America, Lithograph, Elephant Hanging, 1 1/4 In. 25.00
Ribbon, F.D. Roosevelt, God Bless America, Red, White, Blue Silk, Celluloid, 1 1/4 In. ... 224.00
Ribbon, FDR, Active Press, Cardboard, Gold, Red, White, Blue, c.1944, 4 In. 50.00
Ribbon, General McClelland, Brass Frame, Red, White & Blue, 1 1/4 x 3/4 In. 245.00
Ribbon, Grover Cleveland, Black, Gold, 1885, 8 In. 267.00
Ribbon, Harrison, National Republican Club, Cream, Brown, 1892, 6 3/4 In. 85.00
Ribbon, Harry S. Truman Inauguration, Celluloid Button Picture, 2 1/2 In. 73.00
Ribbon, Hat, Clay, Frelinghuysen, Floral Weave, White Silk, 1 x 17 In. 185.00
Ribbon, Hat, Military Officer Bust Portrait, United States, Floral Weave, 1 1/2 x 25 In. 55.00
Ribbon, Henry Clay, Bust Picture, Indian Maiden, White Silk, 9 x 3 1/2 In. 75.00
Ribbon, Horatio Seymour, Frank P. Blair, Pictures, 1868, 8 In. 715.00
Ribbon, James Cox, Governor, Inaugural Ball, Floor Committee Pin, c.1913, 8 1/2 In. 2376.00
Ribbon, Jugate Button, Roosevelt, Johnson, Celluloid, 1912, 1 1/4 In. 5445.00
Ribbon, Lincoln In Center Circle, Black, Gold, 8 In. 240.00
Ribbon, Lincoln, Gold, Black, Cream, 9 1/4 In. 581.00
Ribbon, McKinley, Roosevelt, Union League, Nov. 6, 1900, U.S. Flag Bow, 7 x 2 In. 110.00
Ribbon, McKinley, Roosevelt, Union League, White Silk, Nov. 6, 1900, 6 1/2 x 2 In. 80.00
Ribbon, Mourning, Abraham Lincoln, Fallen Chief, Black Silk, 7 x 1 1/2 In. 355.00
Ribbon, Mourning, Death Of Andrew Jackson, Black On White Silk, Portrait, 8 x 3 In. 358.00
Ribbon, Mourning, General Zachary Taylor, White Silk, Printed, 7 1/2 x 2 1/2 In. 520.00
Ribbon, Mourning, William H. Seward, State Of New York, 7 x 3 1/2 In. 165.00

Ribbon, Mourning, Y.M.R.C. Garfield Memorial, White Silk, 1881, 6 3/4 x 2 1/4 In. 110.00
Ribbon, Pres. Grover Cleveland, Hendricks, Bust Portrait, 4 Colors, 5 1/4 x 3 In. 110.00
Ribbon, Shell Man's Picture, Sepia, Gold Frame, Red, White & Blue Ribbon, 2 1/4 In. ... 275.00
Ribbon, W.H. Harrison, Our Country's Hope, Silk, Black, 6 In. 277.00
Ribbon, Washington Monument, October 19th, 1847, White Silk, 7 1/2 x 3 1/2 In. 110.00
Ribbon, William Howard Taft, Celluloid, Minnesota Member, 2 1/4 In. 40.00
Ribbon, Wm. H. Harrison, Ft. Meigs Celebration, Black, Silk, c.1841, 6 1/2 In. 274.00
Ribbon, Young Men's Clay Club Of Brooklyn, Portrait, White Silk, 6 1/2 x 3 1/4 In. 275.00
Salt & Pepper, Dwight Eisenhower, Smiling, China, 1962, 2 In. 48.00
Sash, Garfield, Arthur, Black & Yellow, Silk, 5 x 30 In. 300.00
Sheet Music, Douglas Funeral March, Hewitt 100.00
Sheet Music, Hold That Line For F.D.R., FDR, Wallace Pictures, Red, White & Blue 150.00
Sheet Music, Let's Land Landon In The White House 60.00
Sheet Music, Solid Men To The Front, Quickstep, Dedicated To Boss Tweed, 1870 ...... 185.00
Sheet Music, Thomas E. Dewey March, 1952 .... 14.00
Sheet Music, Woodrow Wilson, Be Good To California, 1916, 10 1/2 x 13 3/4 In. 56.00
Sign, Minefield Warning, Vietnam War, Metal, 6 x 11 In. 10.00
Sign, Open Air Suffrage Meeting, Cardboard, 1915, 11 x 14 In. 475.00
Sign, Standup, Which, Woman On Chair, FDR, Hoover, Paper Lithograph On Wood, 9 In. 385.00
Smock, Nixon Campaign, White Cotton, Self-Tie Neck, Blue Trim, Printed Nixon, 1968 . 90.00
Soap, Teddy Roosevelt Bust, Eureka Soap, Cincinnati, 4 In. 185.00
Soap Baby, My Papa Will Vote For McKinley, Box, c.1896, 4 1/2 In. 72.00
Spoon, Serving, Grover Cleveland Portrait, Sterling Silver, 8 1/4 In. 250.00
Spoon, Teddy Roosevelt Bust, Eagle & Shield, Sterling Silver 125.00
Statue, Thomas Dewey, Republican Presidential, Painted, 7 In. 328.00
Sticker, Window, Goldwater, 1964 .... 2.00
Stickpin, Bryan, Red White & Blue Enamel 70.00
Stickpin, Harrison, Reid, Silk, Blue & Silver 65.00
Stickpin, Hatchet, Carry A. Nation, 1 In. 35.00
Stickpin, McClellan, Cardboard Picture 275.00
Stickpin, Teapot, Harding Admin., Don't Forget The Dome, Silver, 1924, 7/8 In. 565.00
Stovepipe Cover, Cleveland & V.P. Pictures, Grand Old Party Standard Bearers, 10 In. 275.00
Stud, Al Smith, Brown Derby Shape, Al On Side, 1928, 7/8 In. 27.00
Stud, Cleveland, Stevenson, Tariff Reform, Government Economy, Celluloid 125.00
Stud, Cox, Rooster Shape, Embossed, 7/8 In. 17.00
Stud, For President, S.M. Cullom, Picture, Black & White, Blue Ground, Celluloid 75.00
Stud, Grover Cleveland, Enamel, Scalloped Edges 33.00
Stud, McKinley As Wrestler On Throne, Pinning Bryan, Brass, 7/8 In. 220.00
Stud, McKinley, Hobart, Red, White & Blue, Celluloid, 1896, 7/8 In. 22.00
Stud, Teddy Roosevelt, Riding Elephant, Pewter, 7/8 In. 132.00
Stud, Thurman, Glass Sepia 51.00
Tag, String, 1961 Inauguration Ceremonies, General Admittance, Blue, 2 1/4 In. 75.00
Ticket, Andrew Johnson, Impeachment Trial, May 13, 1868 .... 644.00
Ticket, Texas Welcome Dinner For JFK, Municipal Auditorium, Austin, Nov. 22, 1963 ... 300.00
Tie, I Like Ike, Blue Ground, Yellow Letters, Washington Pictures, 1950 .... 45.00
Tie, Roosevelt, Fairbanks, Black & White, Embroidered 250.00
Tie Bar, LBJ, Presidential Seal, Silver Color, 1964 .... 40.00
Tile, Teddy Roosevelt, Stoke-On-Trent, Frame, 1916, 6 x 9 In. 300.00
Tile, Woodrow Wilson, Stoke-On-Trent, Frame, 1916, 6 x 9 In. 275.00
Tip Tray, Grand Old Party, Sherman Presidential Bid, 1908, 4 1/4 In. 325.00
Tip Tray, Grand Old Party, William Taft, James Sherman, 1908, 4 3/16 In. 175.00
Tip Tray, William Taft, James Sherman, 1908 Campaign, 4 In. 117.00
Top, Spinner, Reagan Is Tops For 1980, Blue & White, 2 In. 20.00
Torch, Campaign, Gimbal Holder, Turned Ash Handle, Brass, 30 In. 55.00
Torch, Parade, Standing Eagle, Lincoln, 1860, 49 In. 9260.00
Trolley Card, Abraham Lincoln Endorsed Woman Suffrage, Vote Yes, 11 x 21 In. 1700.00
Trolley Card, Winning The Peace Is A Lonely Battle, Support U.S.O., 1961, 11 x 28 In. .. 200.00
Umbrella, Red, White, Blue, Pictures, Teddy Roosevelt, Charles Fairbanks, 1904, 35 In. .. 339.00
Vase, William McKinley Picture, Purple Shades, 4 1/2 In. 90.00
Viewer, Stanhope, Lincoln, Pictures, Ivory 450.00
Viewer, Stanhope, McKinley, Picture, Pig Shape 225.00
Voting Machine, Stand-Up Easel, Handle, New York Candidates For 1924, 12 In. 475.00
Watch Fob, Bryan, Kern, 1908, 3/4 In. 30.00

Watch Fob, Bryan, Sepia Picture, 1 3/4 In.	40.00
Watch Fob, Cox, Roosevelt, Silver, Filled Back, 1 3/4 In.	68.00
Watch Fob, Harding, Coolidge, Gold, Filled Back, 1 3/4 In.	60.00
Watch Fob, McKinley, 1 1/4 In.	27.00
Watch Fob, Smith, Robinson, 1928, Nickel Plated	115.00
Watch Fob, Taft Picture, Converts To Bottle Opener, Celluloid Insert	475.00
Watch Fob, Taft, Multicolor Picture, Pewter Frame, 1 1/4 In.	59.00
Watch Fob, Wilson, Picture, Celluloid, Brown, White, 1 3/4 In.	85.00
Watch Fob, Wm. H. Taft, Red, White & Blue, Gold, Celluloid, 1 1/4 In.	65.00
Wedding Announcement, Woodrow Wilson, Edith Galt, 1915, 5 x 8 1/2 In.	300.00
Wristwatch, Lester Maddox, On Bicycle, 3rd Party, Display Stand, c.1972	88.00

POMONA glass is a clear glass with a soft amber border decorated with pale blue or rose-colored flowers and leaves. The colors are very, very pale. The background of the glass is covered with a network of fine lines. It was made from 1885 to 1888 by the New England Glass Company. First grind was made from April 1885 to June 1886. It was made by cutting a wax surface on the glass, then dipping it in acid. Second grind was a less expensive method of acid etching that was developed later.

Lemonade, Cornflower, 1st Grind, 5 1/4 In.	115.00
Pitcher, Cornflower, 7 In.	488.00
Sugar & Creamer, Ruffled Edge, 3 In.	138.00
Tumbler, Cornflower & Fern, Diamond-Quilted, 3 5/8 In., 6 Piece	480.00
Tumbler, Inverted Diamond-Quilted, Amber Border, 2nd Grind, 3 5/8 In.	55.00

PONTYPOOL, see Tole category.

POPEYE was introduced to the Thimble Theatre comic strip in 1929. The character became a favorite of readers. In 1932, an animated cartoon featuring Popeye was made by Paramount Studios. The cartoon series continued and became even more popular when it was shown on television starting in the 1950s. The full-length movie with Robin Williams as Popeye was made in 1980.

Bank, Dime Register, 1929	110.00
Bank, Metal, White, King Features Syndicate, 1929, 7 In.	85.00
Bank, Popeye Knockout, Tin, Moore, 1 3/8 In.	195.00
Book, Big Little Book, Popeye & The Jeep, Whitman Pub. Co., King Features, 1937	45.00
Book, Big Little Book, Popeye Sees The Sea, Whitman Pub. Co., King Features, 1936	45.00
Chalk, 2 White Pieces Of Chalk, Original Box, American Crayon Co., Sandusky, Oh.	29.00
Charm, Popeye & Wimpy, Celluloid, 1930, 1 1/4 x 1 In.	30.00
Charm, Popeye, Plastic, Japan, 1 1/4 In.	19.00 to 25.00
Clock, Alarm, Popeye & Swee' Pea, Animated, England	250.00
Cup, Olive Oyl & Popeye, Pair	75.00
Doll, Cloth, Cork Stuffed, Corncob Pipe, c.1940, 18 In.	35.00
Doll, Cloth, Wooden Pipe, Paper Shoes, Japan, Prewar, 10 In.	370.00
Doll, Composition, Jointed, Wooden, Hand Painted, 1935, 14 In.	431.00
Doll, Popeye The Sailor Man, Box, King Features Syndicate, Inc., Uneeda, 1970	32.00
Doll, Rubs Head, Stuffed Body, 10 1/2 In.	125.00
Doll, Wooden, Composition Socket Head, Googly Eyes, King Features, 1923, 11 In.	1500.00
Doorstop, Hubley	1045.00
Figure, Holding Pipe, Celluloid, Continental, 1930s, 3 3/4 In.	145.00
Figure, Popeye & Olive Oyl, Music Box, Schmid Bros.	325.00
Figure, Popeye Smoking Pipe, No. 480, Wade, 4 3/4 In.	70.00
Game, Card, Popeye & His Friends, Instructions, KFS Whitman, 1937	55.00 to 63.00
Harmonica, Popsicle Premium, Box, 1929, 4 In.	315.00
Marble, Popeye The Sailor Man	6.00
Marble Set, No. 116, Popeye, King Features Syndicate, Box, 1929, 15 Piece	770.00
Music Box, Popeye Pops Up, Graphics, Metal, No Pipe, 1960s	110.00
Napkin Ring, Bakelite	150.00
Pencil Box, 3 Sections, Eagle Pencil Co., 1/2 x 8 1/2 In.	79.00
Pencil Case, 1930s	115.00
Pencil Sharpener, Bakelite, Green, Decal, 1929, 1 3/4 In.	75.00

Pencil Sharpener, Bakelite, Orange, Decal, 1 3/4 In. 95.00
Pencil Sharpener, Bluto, Bakelite, Figural, 1940s 50.00
Pencil Sharpener, Popeye, Orange, Decal, 1 3/4 In. 95.00
Pin, Post Corn Flakes, Tin, 1949 .... 30.00
Pinback, Jeep, Enamel Paint, 1930s, 1 1/4 In. 385.00
Puppet, Hand, Gund, 9 In. 45.00
Puzzle, Picture, Vintage, Box, 18 x 13 In. 15.00
Refrigerator Magnet, Olive Oyl & Popeye 13.00
Soap, Figure, 1930, 4 In. 29.00
Sparkler, Squeeze Mechanism, Chein, 1959 .... 250.00
Thimble Theatre, Mystery Playhouse, King Features, Harding Products, 1939 .... 3300.00
Tin, Popeye Yellow Popcorn, Dixon, Ill., 1943, 4 3/4 In. 199.00
Toothbrush Holder, Movable Arm, Japan, 1930s, 4 1/2 In. 585.00
Toy, Bifbat, Wooden Paddle, Original Elastic, Ball, KFS, 1929, 11 In. 84.00
Toy, Handcar, Windup, Max, 1936 .... 550.00
Toy, Jigger, Dancing, Olive Oyl Playing Accordion, Marx, 9 1/2 In. 862.00
Toy, Olive Oyl Mechanical Tricycle, Box, Linemar 460.00
Toy, Olive Oyl Stretchy Hand Car, Pull String, Box, Linemar 1265.00
Toy, Olive Oyl, Squeaker, Push Down, Pop-Up, Umbrella, Wire Body, Linemar, 7 In. 1100.00
Toy, Olive Oyl, Swee'pea, Fun On Wheels, Empire Hong Kong, Box, 1950s, 1 3/4 In. 210.00
Toy, Paddle-Wagon, Corgi Juniors, 2 1/2 x 2 In. 65.00
Toy, Patrol Motorcycle, Movable Arms, Cast Iron, Hubley 300.00
Toy, Pilot, Windup, Popeye Flying Plane, Marx 1095.00
Toy, Pirate Pistol, Click-Clack Sound, Box, Marx, 10 In. 863.00
Toy, Popeye & Mean Man Fighters, Box, Linemar 2530.00
Toy, Popeye & Olive Oyl, Pull Toy, Linemar, 7 In. 975.00
Toy, Popeye & Olive Oyl, Rooftop Jiggers, Box, Marx ....1380.00 to 2295.00
Toy, Popeye Express, Windup, Popeye Wheels Trunk With Parrot, Marx, c.1935 ...275.00 to 795.00
Toy, Popeye In Barrel, Box, Chein, 7 In. ....575.00 to 635.00
Toy, Popeye Pushing Wheelbarrow, Clockwork, Tin Lithograph 255.00
Toy, Popeye Spinach, Motorcycle, Removable Figure, Wagon, Hubley, 1930s, 5 3/8 In. 715.00
Toy, Popeye Sports Car Driver, Plastic, Empire Hong Kong, Box, 1950s, 1 5/8 In. 315.00
Toy, Popeye, Dippy Dumper, Box, Marx 690.00
Toy, Popeye, On Patrol, Motorcycle, Movable Arms, Hubley 4200.00
Toy, Popeye, Pilot, Airplane, Tin, 7 x 6 In. 1000.00
Toy, Popeye, Roller Skater Mechanical, Box, Linemar ....862.00 to 975.00
Toy, Puncher, Windup, Tin, Celluloid Punch Bag, Chein, 1932, 9 1/2 In. ....1100.00 to 4000.00
Toy, Slinky Pull Toy, With Olive Oyl, Linemar, 7 In. 978.00
Toy, Smoking Popeye, Box, Linemar 1495.00
Toy, Sparking, Squeeze Mechanism, Box, Chein, 1959 .... 375.00
Toy, Tumbling, Rotating Arms, Windup, Linemar, 4 1/2 In. ....690.00 to 920.00
Toy, Turnover Tank, Box, Linemar 373.00
Toy, TV Set, Color, Has TV Viewer, 1957 .... 40.00
Toy, Walker, Windup, Chein, 1932, 6 In. ....440.00 to 725.00
Toy, Wimpy On Tricycle, Spinning Bell, Celluloid Arms, Linemar, 3 1/2 In. ....750.00 to 1150.00
Toy, Wimpy, Head Moves Up & Down, Windup, Occupied Japan, 5 1/2 In. 650.00
Toy, Wimpy, On Tricycle, Tin Lithograph, Ringing Bell, Linemar, 3 3/4 In. 2090.00
View-Master Reel, 3 Reels, 10 Page Book, Connect The Dots, 1959 .... 22.00
Whistle Pipe, St. Louis 70.00
Wristwatch, 1940s 950.00

PORCELAIN factories that are well known are listed in this book under
the factory name. This category and the two following list pieces made
by the less well-known factories. Porcelain-Contemporary lists pieces
made by artists working after 1975. Porcelain-Midcentury includes
pieces made from the 1950s to the 1980s.

Ashtray, Geisha Girl, Bottom Shows Naked Butt, Hand Painted 30.00
Basket, Flowers, Cobalt Rim, England, 4 In. 152.00
Bird, Perched On Flowering Branch, J.T. Jones, Crown Staffordshire, 6 In. 34.00
Birdfeeder, Nine Dragon Design, Blue & White, 1 3/4 In. 115.00
Bone Dish, Hand Painted Fish, Kidney Shape, 7 x 3 3/4 In. ....*Illus* 40.00
Bowl, Altar, Peach Form, Leaf, Branch Handle, 7 1/4 In. 58.00
Bowl, Barber's, Blue Glaze, Gilt Floral Design, Chinese, 12 5/8 In. 840.00

Porcelain, Bone Dish, Hand Painted Fish,
Kidney Shape, 7 x 3 3/4 In.

Porcelain, Ramekin, Blue, Gold Scrolls,
Scalloped Edge, Royal Austria, 3 1/2 In.

Bowl, Cabbage & Butterfly, Chinese, 10 1/2 In.	230.00
Bowl, Cover, Floral, Blue Ribbon, Gilt, Ribbon Handles, Germany, 5 3/4 In.	300.00
Bowl, Floral Interior & Exterior, Gilt, Reticulated, Blue Crown, Crossed Swords, 16 In.	275.00
Bowl, Foo Lion, Flame Design, Blue & White, 1900, 11 3/4 In.	184.00
Bowl, Fruit, Iridescent, Grape Design, Artist MGH, c.1915, 12 In.	308.00
Bowl, Gardner Alex Neusky Service, Medallion, Red Ribbon, Russia, c.1780, 9 In.	369.00
Bowl, Gilt Shou Medallions, Faux Cinnabar, Gilt Ground, 19th Century, 4 3/4 In.	200.00
Bowl, Grape, Flower Decoration, Germany, Late 19th Century, 14 In.	193.00
Bowl, Lobster Footed, Molded Lobster Claw Handle, Mustershutz, 2 Piece	55.00
Bowl, Roses & Floral Sprays, Purple, Aubergine, Green, Iron Red Enamel, 7 In.	316.00
Bowl, Waterfall Landscape, Blue, White, 11 3/4 In.	173.00
Box, Bombe Shape, 18th Century Couple, Cobalt Blue Ground, Gilt, Cover, 6 3/4 In.	316.00
Box, Capo-Di-Monte Style, Oval, Classical Scenes, Garlands, Continental, 11 In.	150.00
Box, Capo-Di-Monte Style, Oval, Hinged, Bacchanalian Scenes, 5 1/8 In.	201.00
Box, Glove, Courting Scene, Cobalt Blue Ground, Continental, 10 1/2 In.	460.00
Brush Washer, Dearform, Polychrome, Chinese, 6 3/4 In.	126.00
Brushpot, Bamboo Shape, Blue, White Floral, 19th Century, 4 1/2 In.	58.00
Brushpot, Mythological Figural Design, Blue & White, 4 3/4 In.	207.00
Cachepot, Blue & White, Foo Lion, Clouds, Chinese, 7 1/2 In.	52.00
Cachepot, Reticulated, Flowers, Leaves, Germany, 6 3/4 In., Pair	288.00
Charger, Courting Couple, Renaissance Clothes, E.E. Welhnachten, 1887, 12 In.	55.00
Charger, Doe, With 2 Fawns, Butterflies, Floral Scrolls, Border, 12 1/2 In.	138.00
Charger, Lotus, Blue, White, 1750, 11 In.	316.00
Charger, Red Flowers, Scrolling Leaves, Blue & White, c.1690, 15 1/2 In.	748.00
Cider Jug, Blue & White, Chinese, 9 1/2 In.	460.00
Coffeepot, Hinged Dome Cover, Cluster Of Violets, France, 10 1/2 In.	518.00
Compact, Lipstick Holder, Girl, Standing, Bouquet, Gold Trim, Holes	55.00
Compote, Gilt, Pink & Blue, Germany, 1850-1870, 11 x 11 In.	485.00
Compote, Herend, Reticulated, 3 Tiers, Flowers, Butterfly, Bird Finial, 10 1/4 In.	1955.00
Creamer, Spaniel Shape, England, 5 In.	58.00
Cup, Orange Blossoms, Blue & Yellow, Signed CKI, France, 1900, 2 3/4 In., Pair	100.00
Cup & Saucer, Floral Enameling, Gilt, Cobalt Blue, White Reserves, Blue Underglaze	275.00
Cup & Saucer, Swan Shape, Gilt, Puce Ground, Continental, 19th Century	402.00
Dessert Set, Scalloped Rim, Gilt Banding, Landscape Centers, 21 Piece	690.00
Dish, 2 Children In Sun Bonnets, Black Crossed Swords, 5 1/2 In.	110.00
Dish, Cover, Riverscape, Blue & White, Oval, 4 In.	172.00
Dish, Painted Medallions Enclosing Flowers, Brocade Design, 8 In.	345.00
Figurine, 2 Elegantly Dressed Ladies, 1 Holding Fan, 1 With Feathers In Hair, Pair	575.00
Figurine, Boy, Father's Hat, Shoes, Umbrella, Papa Base, Germany, 7 1/2 In. .....119.00 to	145.00
Figurine, Cellist, Man Seated In Chair, Germany, Late 19th Century, 9 In.	173.00
Figurine, Colonial Man Helping Woman Out Of Coach, Germany, 6 3/4 In.	295.00
Figurine, Country Gentleman, Blue Suit, Blouse, Top Hat, 19th Century, 5 3/4 In.	517.00
Figurine, Courting Couple, Sheep, Flowers, Sitzendorf, Continental, 9 1/2 In.	259.00
Figurine, Dog, Boxer, Sitting, Brown, Black Face, 8 1/2 In.	12.00
Figurine, Duck, Dark Turquoise, 19th Century, Chinese, 8 In.	165.00
Figurine, Figure, Carrying Different Object, Asian, 10 In., 8 Piece	990.00

Figurine, Foo Lions, Turquoise Glaze, 19th Century, 17 1/2 In., Pair 690.00
Figurine, Fox Terrier, Sitting, Royal Doulton Copy, Japan, 3 1/2 x 3 3/4 In. 35.00
Figurine, Girl On Swing, After L'Escarpolette Painting, Continental, 11 3/4 In. 403.00
Figurine, Girl, Fruit Filled Apron, Marked With Black Crown, Cross Above It, Germany . 20.00
Figurine, Girl, Peasant Dress, Flower Basket, Germany, 6 In. 126.00
Figurine, Hunters Dressing Elk, Frankenthal, Germany, c.1800, 6 In. 224.00
Figurine, Monkey Band, Scheibe-Alsbach, 4 3/4 To 6 3/4 In., 6 Piece 635.00
Figurine, Monkey, Enamel, Chinese, 20th Century, 7 1/2 In., Pair 630.00
Figurine, Poseidon, Standing By Cask Of Water, Flanked By Putto, 7 3/4 In. 230.00
Figurine, Quan Yin, Seated On Rock, Early 19th Century, 5 5/8 In. 81.00
Figurine, Shepherdess, Holding Flowers, Lamb, Frankenthal, 6 1/4 In. 460.00
Figurine, Vagabond, Resting On Knoll, Continental, 6 In. 345.00
Figurine, Woman, Preening, Pair Of Russian Wolfhounds, Germany, c.1890, 10 In. 1450.00
Ginger Jar, Character & Scroll Design, Floral, Egg Shape, Asian, 8 1/2 In., Pair 550.00
Ginger Jar, Chinoiserie, Hexagon, Seafoam Green Ground, Continental, 31 In. 518.00
Ginger Jar, Girl, With Horse, People & Banners, Teak Stand, Asian, 14 In., Pair 520.00
Ginger Jar, Thousand Flowers Design, Late 19th Century, 12 In. 104.00
Ginger Jar, Tree In Landscape, Blue & White, Chinese, 20 1/2 In., Pair 374.00
Ginger Jar, Wooden Cover, Children In Courtyard, Early 19th Century, 9 1/4 In. 184.00
Glass, Ale, Gold Band, Tapered Cylindrical, France, 6 x 3 In., 12 Piece 230.00
Group, 4 Children Huddled Over A Fire, Enameled, Gilt, Beehive Mark, 5 1/8 In. 82.00
Group, Biscuit, Children, Birds, Rock Work Base, Continental, 14 1/2 In. 288.00
Group, Gentleman Reading To 2 Ladies, Empire Style Salon, 7 In. 316.00
Group Set, Putti Playing Musical Instruments, Late 19th Century, 5 3/4 In. 403.00
Humidor, Burly Face Smoking Cigar, 19th Century 248.00
Invalid Feeder, White, W. T. & Co., 1900, 8 In. 55.00
Jar, Blue & White, Baluster Form, Medallion, Birds, Leaves, Mounted As Lamps, 14 In. . 489.00
Jar, Blue & White, Oval, Cartouche, Flying Birds, Branches, Chinese, 11 In. 546.00
Jar, Cover, Cobalt Scene, House On Water, 19th Century, 6 3/4 x 6 1/4 In. 115.00
Jar, Cover, Imperial Yellow, Baluster, Electrified, Chinese, 14 In. 172.00
Jar, Cover, Molded Cloth & String Ties Top, Brown, Gilt Flowers, Asian, 8 3/8 In. 355.00
Jar, Hand Painted Flowers, Ruin Medallions, Blue Scalloped, 5 5/8 In. 385.00
Jar, Inverted Pear Shape, Phoenix, Peony Design, 5 1/5 In. 115.00
Jar, Square, Tondo Reserve, Blue & White, Round Cover, Chinese, 14 x 9 x 9 In., Pair ... 1150.00
Jar, Thousand Flowers Design, 1900, 15 3/4 In. 431.00
Jar, Traditional Decoration, Bulbous, Mandarin, Chinese, 18th Century, 4 1/2 x 10 In. 75.00
Jardiniere, Black Glaze, Gilt Wreath, France, 19th Century, 8 1/2 In. 575.00
Jardiniere, Cartouches On Coral Floral Ground, 1900, 10 In. 201.00
Jardiniere, Flying Birds, Trees, Flowers, Egg Shape, Asian, 10 In. 150.00
Jardiniere, On Stand, Pedestal Supports, Scalloped Rim, Rose Swags, 32 In. 402.00
Lamp Base, Baluster Jar, Flowers, Scrolling Leaves, Blue & White, Cover, 12 In., Pair ... 460.00
Mug, Child's, Teddy Scouts, Decal, Early 20th Century, Germany, 2 In. 125.00
Nodder, Male & Female Seated, Articulated Hands, Head & Tongue, 4 3/4 In., Pair 862.00
Obelisk, Gilt, Leaf Medallions, Beaded Stepped Bronze Base, 28 In., Pair 3300.00
Pen Tray, Cherub & Flowers, Paw Feet, Brass Frame, 8 1/2 In. 165.00
Pitcher, Circular Shape, Flared Spout, Raised Handle, Charles Cartlidge & Co., 10 In. ... 143.00
Pitcher, Fantastic Flowering Trees Against Brown Mottled, Crown Devon, 9 In. 247.00
Pitcher, Figural, King Gambrinus, Red, Blue, Pink, Green Enamel, Stopper, 12 In. 220.00
Plaque, Capo-Di-Monte Style, Goddess, Putti, C-Scroll Border, Mark, 15 In. 175.00
Plaque, Victorian Woman, Signed, M. Girard, 19th Century, 5 1/2 x 4 In. 1320.00
Plaque, Young Lady, White Blouse, Gold Necklace, Wooden Frame, 7 2/3 In. 373.00
Plaque, Young Woman Seated, Giltwood Frame, 6 1/4 x 4 5/8 In. 690.00
Plate, 5-Claw Dragon Design, Blue, Yellow Underglaze, Chinese, 19th Century, 10 In. ... 920.00
Plate, Different Transfer Scenes, Light Green Rim, 10 3/4 In., 12 Piece 990.00
Plate, Flower Spray, Leaves, Gilt Detail, Dihl Et Guerhard, Early 1800s, 9 3/4 In., 6 Piece 259.00
Plate, Flowers, White Reserves, Blue Rim, Gilt, Marked, Couderc, Paris, 9 3/8 In. 27.00
Plate, Girl Holding Artist's Brush & Palette, 9 7/8 In. 82.00
Plate, Orange Poppies, Green, J. Lycett, St. Louis, Odean, 1915, 8 3/4 In. 50.00
Plate, Peasant Maidens At Well, Cobalt Blue Ground, 9 1/2 In. 161.00
Plate, Raised Foot & Hydrangea Design, Blue, White, 9 In. 288.00
Plate, Roses, Gilt Border, Marked Archangelski, 1896, 9 In. 825.00
Platter, Cottage By A Lake, England, 13 In. 80.00
Posy Holder, White, Embossed, 4 3/4 In. 175.00

Ramekin, Blue, Gold Scrolls, Scalloped Edge, Royal Austria, 3 1/2 In. . . . . *Illus*	10.00
Room Scenter, Figural, Moses & Rebecca, Jacob Petit, 14 In., Pair	1840.00
Serving Dish, Flowers, Leaves, Enamel, England, 19th Century, 10 3/8 In.	230.00
Sugar, Greek Key & Acanthus Leaf Design, 1805, 5 1/2 In.	300.00
Tankard, Exotic Birds In Garden, 6 1/4 In.	345.00
Tankard, Flowers & Blackberry, Artist Signed, Austria, Dated 1913, 14 1/2 In.	725.00
Tazza, Scenes Of Musical Putti, Flowers In Garland Border, 6 1/2 In., Pair	978.00
Teapot, Figural, Woman Holding Fan & Rose With Dog, Gilt, 14 In.	220.00
Temple Jar, Cover, Blue Peony Design, White, 17 In.	975.00
Tray, Dresser, Flowers, Soldiers On Horseback, 2 Wells, Crossed Swords, 6 x 9 In.	55.00
Tray, Opaque, Blue & White Transfer, Gilt Trim, Handles, WAA & Co., 20 x 15 In.	145.00
Tureen, Flower Decoration, Scroll Handles, Dome Lid, Undertray, 13 x 11 x 12 In.	230.00
Urn, Moorish, Cobalt Ground, Gold Trim, Early 20th Century, 6 1/4 In.	270.00
Urn, Pink Flowers, Silver, Scrolled Handles, Blue Ground, Signed, 2 In.	100.00
Urn, Women With Angel In Garden, Handles, Signed, 13 In., Pair	3174.00
Urn, Yellow, Red, Green Flowers, Gilt, Handles, 14 In.	220.00
Vase, Baluster Shape, Brocade Ground, Figural, Bird Designs, Japan, 12 In.	865.00
Vase, Blanc-De-Chine, Baluster Form, Applied Flowers, Leaves, Chinese, 5 1/4 In.	90.00
Vase, Blossoms, Birds, Butterflies Body, Lion Mask Handles, 23 x 8 1/2 In.	287.00
Vase, Blue & White, Tao-Kuang, Sleeve Form, Boys With Vase, 7 1/2 x 3 1/2 In.	80.00
Vase, Blue, Tan Crystalline Glaze, 3 Stepped Handles, Signed, Belgium, 8 3/4 In.	175.00
Vase, Brocade Ground, Figural & Avian Reserves, Signed, Late 19th Century, 12 In.	860.00
Vase, Brown Flambe Glaze, 2 Handles, Copper, Marked, Belgium 61, 13 In.	177.00
Vase, Bud, Portrait Of A Lady, Floral, Brass Frame, 19th Century, 8 1/4 In.	290.00
Vase, Cavorting Peasants, Lion's Head Handles, Paw Footed, 10 In.	220.00
Vase, Clair-De-Lune, Wide Foot, Chinese, 12 In.	630.00
Vase, Classical Harvest Scene, Tapestry Finish, Signed Pompadour, France, 8 In.	269.00
Vase, Club Form, Phoenix, Peony Design, Blue, White Crackle, 11 1/4 In.	29.00
Vase, Country Estate Scene, Black On White, Furstenberg Porcelain, c.1922, 6 1/4 In. . . .	75.00
Vase, Couple, Landscape Scene, Making Way Across Stream, 5 In.	345.00
Vase, Couple, Terraced Garden, Signed, Gamet, 6 In.	690.00
Vase, Court, Military Scene, Flared Lobed Rim, Lion Handles, 13 1/2 In.	175.00
Vase, Crane & Marsh Scene, Sky Blue, 7 3/4 In.	69.00
Vase, Dark Cobalt, 3 Handles, Marked, Rudolf Ditmar, 12 1/4 In.	465.00
Vase, Figural Landscape Design, Blue, White, 9 In., Pair	29.00
Vase, Flowers, Bird Design, Blue, White, Wing Handle, 17 1/4 In.	110.00
Vase, Flowers, Blue, White, 1800, 10 1/2 In., Pair	920.00
Vase, Flowers, Butterflies, Handles At Rim, Marked, Crown Devon, 5 1/2 In.	165.00
Vase, Flowers, Gold Trim, Elongated Oval, Signed Sidney T. Calloway, 11 1/4 In.	200.00
Vase, Flowers, Marked Ernst Wahliss Pergamon, 6 7/8 In.	330.00
Vase, Full-Length Portrait Of Gentleman, Gilt, Copper, 7 3/4 In., Pair	865.00
Vase, Full-Length Portrait Of Man & Woman, Red Floral Base, 4 In., Pair	635.00
Vase, Garden Landscape Scene, Couple Playing Music, Dark Green, 9 In.	1610.00
Vase, Garden Party Scene, Multiple Figured, Red Ground Base, 10 1/2 In.	1265.00
Vase, Garden Scene, Harlequin With Instrument, Signed, France, 3 In.	748.00
Vase, Landscape Scene, Couple Walking, Red Ground Neck, Gilt, 5 1/2 In.	460.00
Vase, Landscape, Man On 1 Side, Woman On Other Side, Blue, 7 In., Pair	345.00
Vase, Man & Woman In Landscape Scene, Leaf Base, 5 In., Pair	865.00
Vase, Man Wearing Yellow Coat, Garden Landscape, Red Base, 9 In.	460.00
Vase, Man, Peasant Attire, Tree Trunk Shape, Jacob Petit, 8 1/2 x 4 x 3 In., Pair	1092.00
Vase, Morning Glory Decoration, Blue Ground, Japanese Studio, Signed, 11 In.	316.00
Vase, Napoleon III, Gilt Bronze, Enamel, Lilies Of The Valley, Blue Ground, 12 1/2 In. . .	690.00
Vase, Neoclassical, Gilt Highlights, Scroll Handles, Germany, 18 In.	690.00
Vase, Orchids, Marked, Ernst Wahliss, Pergamon, 8 1/2 In.	415.00
Vase, Peacock, Gold, Marked, Forrester Phoenix Ware, 12 In.	465.00
Vase, Pearl White Matte Glaze, Cobalt Blue, Indigo Blue Accents, Cabat, 4 In.	413.00
Vase, Persian Style, Blue & White, Bohemian, 15 In., Pair	115.00
Vase, Profile Decorated, Young Woman, Colorful Costume, Oval, Frame, 10 1/2 In.	115.00
Vase, Putti In Landscape Scene, Loving Couple, Gilt, 7 3/4 In.	805.00
Vase, Quail, Pheasants, Other Colorful Birds, Yellow Scrolls, Green Ground, 14 In.	137.00
Vase, Shell, Scroll Foot, Rose Design, Open Handles, 11 3/8 In., Pair	138.00
Vase, Sunset Landscape Scene, Leaves & Berries, Gilt, France, 5 1/2 In.	400.00

Vase, Temple, Exotic Bird, Peonies, Foo Lion Handles, Blue, White, 24 In. 115.00
Vase, Temple, Phoenix & Peonies, Pink Passion Flower, Handles, 1900, 18 In. 80.00
Vase, Victorian Lady In Garden Scene, 19th Century, 3 3/4 In. 330.00
Vase, Wisteria Design, Butterflies, Small Ear Handles, Marked, Crown Devon, 5 In. 165.00
Vase, Woman In Blue & White Dress, Red Cape, Artist Signed, 4 In. 168.00
Vase, Woman Wearing Blue Dress In Garden, 5 1/2 In. 345.00
Vase, Woman Wearing Blue Dress, Wooded Landscape, 6 In. 345.00
Vase, Woman Wearing Lilac Dress Near Pond, Signed, 5 3/4 In. 460.00
Vase, Woman Wearing Long Dress, Picking Roses, Walking, 6 In. 520.00
Vase, Woman Wearing Pink Dress, Carrying Basket Of Roses, 6 3/4 In. 575.00
Vase, Woman With Blond Hair, Surrounded With Roses, 5 3/4 In. 748.00
Vase, Woman With Doves, Seated By River, Signed, Garnet, 6 In. 690.00
Wall Pocket, Cornucopia Shape, Flower Decoration, Germany, 13 1/2 In., Pair 1095.00

PORCELAIN-CONTEMPORARY lists pieces made by artists working after 1975.

Figurine, Awakening, Laszlo Ispanky, 1979, 7 1/2 In. 100.00
Figurine, New Jersey, League Of Municipalities, Laszlo Ispanky, 5 x 6 In. 45.00

PORCELAIN-MIDCENTURY includes pieces made from the 1950s to the 1980s.

Bottle, Spiral Glaze, Pitted, Dame Lucie Rie, c.1977, 9 1/4 In. 7800.00
Figurine, Cowboy On Horseback, Barsato, Italy, 18 1/2 In. 330.00
Figurine, Dog, Beagle, Sitting, Morton Studio, 1940s 65.00
Figurine, Dog, Boston Terrier, Standing, Morton Studio, 1940s, 6 x 6 In. 125.00
Figurine, Dog, Chihuahua, Black, Tan, Morton Studio, 1940s, 5 x 6 In. 150.00
Figurine, Dog, German Shepherd, Morton Studio, 1940s, 7 x 8 1/2 In. 85.00

POSTCARDS were first legally permitted in Austria on October 1, 1869. The United States passed postal regulations allowing the card in 1872. Most of the picture postcards collected today date after 1910. The amount of postage can help to date a card. The rates are: 1872 (1 cent), 1917 (2 cents), 1919 (1 cent), 1925 (2 cents), 1928 (1 cent), 1952 (2 cents), 1959 (3 cents), 1963 (4 cents), 1968 (5 cents), 1973 (8 cents), 1975 (7 cents), 1976 (9 cents), 1978 (10 cents), 1981 (12 cents), 1981 (13 cents), 1985 (14 cents), 1988 (15 cents), 1991 (19 cents), 1995 (20 cents).

3-D, 3 Little Pigs, Brick House, Big Bad Wolf, W.C. Jones Publishing Co., 1966 . . . . 25.00
African Hunt, Teddy Roosevelt, 40 Piece 150.00
All Good Wishes, Ripley Believe It Or Not, Robert Ripley Autograph, 1930 . . . . 35.00
Arizona, Folder, 18 Views, Canyon & Indians, 1940s 12.00
Birthday Greeting, Girl, Dials For Day & Month, 3 1/2 x 5 In. . . . .*Illus* 5.00
Bridgeport Yacht Club, Bridgeport, Conn., 1911 . . . . 5.00
Camelback Inn, Phoenix, Winter Resort Scene, Linen, 1952 . . . . 5.00
Chautauqua Camping Scene 3.00
Coney Island, Wakes, Piels Banner Over Street 3.30
Days Of The Week, Mama & Baby Bear Doing Chores, Wm. Heal, NY, c.1907, 7 Piece . . 125.00
Duquesne Brewing, Factory, Interior Views, 1930s 8.80

Postcard, Birthday Greeting, Girl,
Dials For Day & Month, 3 1/2 x 5 In.

Postcard, Easter, Dutch
Girl With Hyacinths,
Gold Ground,
Postmarked 1919

Easter, Dutch Girl With Hyacinths, Gold Ground, Postmarked 1919 . . . .*Illus*   15.00
Florence, California, Views Of 5 Churches, Linen 4.00
Frankfort High School, Linen, Frankfort, Kentucky 5.00
Glacier National Park, Folder, 18 Views, Color, 1930s 12.00
Goldwaters Department Store, Chrome, 1950s 5.00
Grand Canyon, View From Lipan Point, Fred Harvey, Photograph 15.00
Halloween, Black Cat On Jack-O'-Lantern, 1909, 3 1/2 x 5 1/2 In. 50.00
Halloween, Child In Clown Suit, Schmucker 330.00
Hawaiian Fish, Island Curio Co., Back Foxing 9.00
Hearty Thanksgiving Greetings, Woman In Apron & Dust Cap 3.50
Hold-To-Light, St. Louis World's Fair, 1904 . . . .   130.00
Hot Springs, Arkansas, St. Joseph's Infirmary, Building In Wooded Setting 5.00
Hotel Colfax Mineral Springs & Baths, Colfax, Iowa, 1909 . . . .   6.00
I Am Having A Strong Pull Here, Dental, 1908 . . . .   10.00
Kentucky Lake State Park, Bath Houses, 1952 . . . .   6.00
Labor Day, Reading, Pennsylvania, People On Street Scene, Photo, 1907 . . . .   50.00
Little Rock, Arkansas, All Arkansas Governors, Oval Portraits 11.00
Masonic Cemetery, Virginia City, Nevada, Linen, 1930s 10.00
Rhode Island, Little Rhody, Fabric Art Co., 1907 . . . .   20.00
Rockingham Memorial Hospital, Harrisonburg, Va, Colored Linen, c.1940 . . . .   4.00
Salter's Dental Floss, Our New Counter Display 85.00
Seelbach Hotel, Sepia Tones, 1910 . . . .   6.00
Sequined Writing, Sutherland, Iowa, Catholic Church, c.1930 . . . .   10.00
Thanksgiving, Cherub Holding Ear Of Corn, Ribbon, Postmarked 1909 . . . .   5.00
Thanksgiving, In Silver On Sign In Turkey's Beak, Postmarked 1910 . . . .   5.00
Thanksgiving, Woman In Pumpkin Patch, Gold Frame, Embossed, S. Schmucker 120.00
Titanic, Black & White 100.00
Trinity Church, Silver Alter Service, Chrome, 1960s 4.00
Troy Normal School, California, Front View, Color 4.00
Valentine's Day, Man In Tuxedo, Woman Holding Heart, Verse, Postmarked 1910 . . . . . .   6.00
Valentine's Day, Woman Holding Candlestick Phone In Red Heart Design, Verse 4.50
Will Rogers, Panama Canal Exposition, 1915 . . . .   15.00
Wilson's Pharmacy, 4 Men In Front, Photograph, Bernie, Mo., Postmarked 1915 . . . .   35.00
Wooden, This Piece Of Wood Genuine Florida Cypress-Florida Flame Vine, 1940 . . . . . .   12.00

POSTERS have informed the public about news and entertainment
events since ancient times. Nineteenth-century advertising or theatrical
posters and twentieth-century movie and war posters are of special
interest today. The price is determined by the artist, the condition, and
the rarity. Other posters may be listed under Movie, Political, and
World War I and II.

All That Is Beautiful, Manhattan Skyline, Black, Gray Ground, Ben Shahn, 24 1/2 In. . . .   168.00
American Powdermills, Dead Shot, Duck Falling From Sky, Frame, 12 1/2 x 19 1/2 In. . .   495.00
Arms Of Law & Order, Colt's, 33 1/4 x 19 3/4 In. 4850.00
Barnum & Bailey Circus, Acrobatic Acts Under Big Tent, 1894, 28 1/2 x 75 In. 3220.00
Barnum & Bailey Circus, Bear Acts, Bear On Bike, Playing Instruments, 36 x 25 In. 55.00
Book Lover, Parrish Oils, 1960s, 24 1/4 x 15 3/4 In. 275.00
Charles Eames, House Of Cards, Evening With Charles Eames, 1967, 44 x 25 In. 280.00
Colt Firearms, Image Of Tex & Patches, 1925, 30 x 19 1/2 In. 460.00
Daisy Air Rifle, Boy & Girl Walking, 1908, 15 1/2 x 22 3/4 In. 4600.00
Emsheimer Furniture, Berlin, Lithograph, Erno Barta, Frame, c.1900, 26 1/2 x 18 1/2 In.   805.00
Exhibition At Kennedy Gallery, Ben Shahn, 1968, 30 x 21 In. 450.00
French Circus, Black Groom & White Bride, Framed Paper, 49 1/2 x 35 In. 250.00
Hair, The Musical, Shrink Wrapped, 1968, 38 1/2 x 27 1/2 In. 58.00
Kar-Mi Magic, Magician In Multiple Vignette Showing Magic Act, 27 x 40 In. 400.00
Mother Goose In Prose, Frank Baum, Parrish Illustrated, Frame, 1897, 24 x 21 1/4 In. . .   7700.00
Pinup Woman As Red Riding Hood, Wolf, Color, 1929, 20 x 30 In. 15.00
Portrait Of Artist Wearing Bowler's Hat, Peter Max, 36 x 24 In. 393.00
Red Riding Hood Show, Color Lithograph, 1929, 20 x 30 In. 18.00
Remington Arms Co., Hunting Lodge Scene, Hunter & Retriever, c.1928, 17 x 22 In. 201.00
Western-Winchester Ammo, Red Squirrel In Foreground, Hunter, 1955, 42 In. 115.00
Winchester Rifles, Teddy Roosevelt Riding Horseback, 1907, 29 x 15 1/2 In. 575.00

POTLIDS are just that, lids for pots. Transfer-printed potlids had their heyday from the 1840s to the early 1900s. The English Staffordshire potteries made ceramic containers with decorative lids for bear's grease, shrimp or meat paste, cold cream, and toothpaste. Printed advertising and pictures of historical events, portraits of famous people, or scenic views were designed in black and white or color. Reproductions have been made.

Burdell's Tooth Powder, Black, Olive & Yellow Transfer, 3 In.	577.00
Cold Cream Of Roses, Red Transfer, 2 1/2 In.	165.00
Dr. Boutmars Celebrated Aromatic Tooth Paste, 3 1/4 In.	2090.00
Genuine Bear's Grease, Black, Green, Blue & Yellow Transfer, 3 In.	770.00
Genuine Bear's Grease For Hair, Standing Bear, Black Transfer, 3 1/3 In.	825.00
Genuine Beef Marrow, Standing Cow, Black Transfer, 3 In.	265.00
Jules Hauel & Co., Perfumers, Girl With Grapes, 4 7/8 In.	1760.00
Liston's Extract Of Beer, Trademark Of 2 Cows, 3 3/4 In.	137.00
Victorian Courting Couples, Holland, 4 1/4 In.	120.00
Wright's Gold Medal Saponaceous Shaving Compound, Black Transfer, 4 1/4 In.	715.00

POTTERY and porcelain are different. Pottery is opaque; you can't see through it. Porcelain is translucent. If you hold a porcelain dish in front of a strong light, you will see the light through the dish. Porcelain is colder to the touch. Pottery is softer and easier to break and will stain more easily because it is porous. Porcelain is thinner, lighter, and more durable. Majolica, faience, and stoneware are all pottery. Additional pieces of pottery are listed in this book in the categories Pottery-Art, Pottery-Contemporary, Pottery-Midcentury, and under the factory name. For information about pottery makers and marks, see *Kovels' Dictionary of Marks—Pottery & Porcelain: 1650–1850* and *Kovels' New Dictionary of Marks—Pottery & Porcelain: 1850 to the Present.*

Barrel, Shenandoah, Earthenware, Side Nozzle, Mottled Glaze, c.1850, 6 1/2 In.	467.50
Basin, Sgrafitto, Yellow, Green Manganese, Hatch & Bow Design Rim, 1796, 5 In.	6600.00
Bowl, Apple, Sgrafitto, Birds Perched On Trailing Vines, Pa., 1820, 4 1/2 x 11 In.	27500.00
Bowl, Black Glaze At Rim, Gold Brown Glazed Body, E. & M. Scheier, c.1965, 4 In.	290.00
Bowl, Custard, Blue, Oxfordware, 2 3/4 x 4 1/4 In.	19.00
Bowl, Dripped Glaze Of Matte Yellow & Green, Signed, T. Takaezu, 5 In.	670.00
Bowl, Green & Rust Circular Sponged, Left Handed, Russel Henry, 7 In.	210.00
Bowl, Greenware, Embossed Design, 9 3/4 In.	225.00
Bowl, Lustered Coral, Lavender & Purple Flambe Glaze, Signed, Natzler, 8 1/2 In.	3025.00
Bowl, Mottled Cobalt Blue Semimatte Glaze, Signed, Natzler, 8 3/4 In.	2350.00
Bowl, Off-Center Opening, Textured Brown Glaze, Gunnar Nylund, 1970s, 7 1/8 In.	115.00
Bowl, Painted Bird On Limb, White Ground, Picasso Incised, 6 In.	375.00
Bowl, Sky Blue, Rich Lavender Glaze, 6 3/4 In.	230.00
Bowl, Smooth Teal Semimatte Glaze, Signed, Natzler, 7 3/4 In.	3136.00
Bowl, Stylized Human, Fish & Animals On Body, E. & M. Scheier, c.1965, 4 3/8 In.	575.00
Bowl, White Glaze Alternating With Blue, Green, Harrison McIntosh, 2 x 8 In.	956.00
Bowl, Wide Mouth, Blue Glaze Interior, E. & M. Scheier, c.1965, 5 1/4 In.	172.00
Bowl, Zigzag Design, Tan & Brown Glaze, Edwin & Mary Scheier, c.1965, 5 In.	230.00
Bust, Buddha, Ivory Glaze, Green Glaze Hair & Crown, 8 3/4 In.	55.00
Candleholder, Foo Lion, Green Glaze, Rectangular Pedestal, 8 1/4 In.	115.00
Chalice, Beige, Black Matte Glaze, Ribbed Body, Harrison McIntosh, 5 3/4 x 4 In.	421.00
Compote, Reverse Yellow Slipware, Dark Brown Glaze, EB Initials, 1819, 9 1/2 In.	795.00
Creamer, Awata Ware, Flying Crane, Conch Shell Shape, Japan, 5 1/4 In.	46.00
Crock, Blue Flowers, C.E. Pharis & Company, Geddes, N.Y., 3 Gal., 16 In.	80.00
Cruet Set, Yellow, Cornishware, T.G. Green, England, c.1930, 3 In.	275.00
Dish, Chicken On Nest, Green & Red On White, Gold Accents, 7 1/2 x 8 1/4 In.	168.00
Dish, Chicken On Nest, Polychrome Brown & Yellow, 6 3/4 x 7 1/2 In.	280.00
Dish, Hen On Nest Cover, Green, California Pottery, 11 x 8 1/2 In.	40.00
Dish, Moravian Slip Decoration, Yellow, Green, White Glazing, c.1819, 8 3/4 In.	523.00
Dish, Sgrafitto, Red, Yellow Trailing Slip Design, 2 Green Birds, Pa., 1820, 12 In.	4070.00
Ewer, Etruscan Style, Pinched Spout, Loop Handle, Mythology Figures, 14 x 8 In.	144.00
Figurine, Bedtime, Brayton Laguna, 1943, 8 3/4 In.	150.00
Figurine, Dancer, Nubian Prince, Nude Torso, Wiener Werkstatte, 18 1/2 In.	865.00

Figurine, Dog, Seated, White Clay, Mottled Green Glaze, Hollow Molded, 6 In. 28.00
Figurine, Dog, Spaniel, Seated, Light Brown Glaze, White, 8 3/4 In. 440.00
Figurine, Dog, Visla, Standing, Red Collar, Hungary, 6 1/2 x 7 1/2 In. 125.00
Figurine, Elk, Black Stippling, White Gesso Surface, John Reber, 1900, 11 1/4 In. 9900.00
Figurine, Foo Dogs, Applied Design, Yellow & Brown Glaze, Stand, Chinese, 8 In., Pair . 185.00
Figurine, Tomb, Attendant Standing With Folded Hands, 10 1/4 In. 405.00
Figurine, Woman, Flowing Robes, Holding Leaf Dish, Austria, 19th Century, 26 In. 196.00
Flask, Pretzel, Ceramic, Patent Applied For 1908, 5 1/2 x 3 1/2 In. 330.00
Game Dish, Underplate, Basket Weave Pattern, 3 Chicks In Straw On Lid, 7 1/2 x 11 In. . 476.00
Jar, Cover, Blue Glaze, California Faience, 5 1/4 In. 115.00
Jar, Cover, Leaf & Berry Design, Metallic Glaze, Paul Dachsel, 1910, 7 1/8 In. 1232.00
Jar, Cream Drip Glaze, Dark Brown Body, 11 1/2 In. 374.00
Jar, Inverted Pear Shape, Black Glaze Dripping, Thin White Slip, 12 1/4 In. 460.00
Jar, Sgrafitto, Incised Swag, Line Of Darts, Green Glaze, Yellow Ground, 21 In. 2200.00
Jar, Storage, Ear Handles, Edgefield, 1836, 14 1/2 In. 6500.00
Jug, Acorn Distillery Tipperary Co., Black Transfer, c.1910, 7 5/8 In. 385.00
Jug, Cover, Mottled Moss Green Glaze, Flower On Handle, Stahl, 1939, 6 In. 110.00
Jug, Face, Relief Molded Features, B.B. Craig On Base, Double Handles, 19 In. 660.00
Jug, Grotesque Face, Double Ear Handles, Green Ash Glaze, Craig, 11 1/4 In. 440.00
Jug, Red Clay, Turquoise Over Black Glaze, BMP, Canada, 10 x 6 1/2 In. 45.00
Jug, Storage, Alkaline Glaze, Tooled Neck & Handle, James Franklin Seagle, 11 3/4 In. ... 1210.00
Jug, Storage, Tan, Salt Glazed, Oval, Loop Handles, France, Late 1800s, 19 x 12 In. 144.00
Jug, Wine, Green & Blue Running Glazed, Brown Oriental Characters, 13 1/2 In. 165.00
Match Holder, Acorn Shape, Brown Ground, Yellow & Green Accents, 4 In. 2750.00
Mug, Floral, 19th Century, 3 In. 70.00
Mug, White Egret On Front, Coat Of Arms On Back, Yellow, Wheeling Pottery, 4 In. 23.00
Pie Plate, Incised Tulip Design, Brown, Yellow Mottled Glaze, Pa., 10 1/4 In. 3630.00
Pie Plate, Slip Decorated, Earthenware, Pennsylvania, Early 19th Century, 10 3/4 In. 605.00
Pitcher, Milk, Hand Painted, Portugal, 4 3/4 x 5 1/2 In. 20.00
Pitcher, Pinched Spout, Green, Red Stripe, Yellow Band, Acadia, 9 In. 135.00
Pitcher, Relief, Hunting Scene, Serpent Neck, Dome Cover, c.1860, 10 x 7 1/2 x 12 In. .. 316.00
Pitcher, Squat, Textured, Turquoise Glaze, 7 1/2 x 8 1/4 In. 144.00
Pitcher, Stag Pattern, Blue & White, 9 In. 700.00
Pitcher, Streaked Manganese Design, John Bell, Va., Late 19th Century, 6 1/2 In. 4675.00
Pitcher, Windy City, Blue & White, 8 1/2 In. 300.00
Pitcher, Yellow, Green, Manganese Mottled Glaze, 5 3/4 In. 2090.00
Pitcher, Yellow, White Cat, Black Spots, Handle, 6 1/4 In. 80.00
Planter, Greenware, Strawberry, 6 3/4 In. 100.00
Plaque, 3 Figures In A Landscape, Persia, 19th Century, 13 1/2 x 19 1/4 In. 460.00
Plate, Bluebirds, Good Morning On The Bottom, Good Night On Top, Cardinal Co., 5 In. . 25.00
Plate, Purple Flowers, Burslem England, c.1903, 7 1/4 In. 195.00
Plate, Sgraffito, Birds, Flower, Pennsylvania, 12 1/2 In. 4070.00
Plate, Slip Decorated, Pennsylvania, c.1830, 10 1/4 In. 330.00
Plate, Stylized Raised Tulip, Yellow Trailing Slip Design, Pa., 5 1/4 In. 17600.00
Platter, Palissyware, Overlapping 5 Fish, Eel, Over Bed Of Leaves, Ocher, 1880, 19 In. ... 13200.00
Puzzle Jug, Sgraffito, Inscribed William Day, March 12, 1809, Flowers, 8 In. 1210.00
Puzzle Jug, Verse, Tulips, Green, Cream Glazing, England, 1796, 8 1/4 In. 1100.00
Rice Jar, Cornishware, T.G. Green, England, c.1930, 5 1/2 In. 250.00
Rundlet, Square Cover, Green, Orange Slip Design, 8 In. 303.00
Salt Box, Cornishware, T.G. Green, England, c.1930, 4 1/4 In. 345.00
Standish, Flowers, Manganese Glaze Surface, 3 1/2 x 9 In. 385.00
Tea Bowl, Hare's Fur Glaze, 3 3/4 In. 160.00
Tea Bowl, Lavender Interior, Metal Rim, 4 In. 115.00
Teapot, Robin's-Egg Blue Glaze, 19th Century, 6 1/4 In. 230.00
Toothbrush Holder, Bear, Legs In Air, Holes In Feet For Toothbrushes, Germany, 3 In. .. 195.00
Toothbrush Holder, Bellboy, Marked 5412 Germany, 5 1/4 In. 195.00
Toothbrush Holder, Boy & Girl, Holds Paste, Marked G. B. Corp., Japan, 5 3/4 In. 85.00
Toothbrush Holder, Boy Playing Flute, Japan, 2 1/2 x 4 1/4 In. 75.00
Toothbrush Holder, Boy Riding Elephant, Holds Paste, Made In Japan, 6 In. 125.00
Toothbrush Holder, Boy With Dog, Holds Paste, 6 In. 90.00
Toothbrush Holder, Bulldog, Holds Paste, Made In Japan, 3 1/2 In. 135.00
Toothbrush Holder, Candlestick Maker, Holds Paste, Marked Gold Castle, Japan, 5 In. .. 95.00
Toothbrush Holder, Clown, Right Hand Holds Brush, Left Holds Toothpaste, 5 In. 95.00

Toothbrush Holder, Cowboy, Base Tube Holder, Made In Japan, 6 1/4 In. 125.00
Toothbrush Holder, Cowboy, Holster, Paste Holder, Japan, 2 1/2 x 4 1/2 In. 75.00
Toothbrush Holder, Duck, Large Bill, Base Tube Holder, Made In Japan, 4 1/4 In. 125.00
Toothbrush Holder, Duck, Marked Hand Painted Trico Nagoya-Japan, 4 1/2 In. 125.00
Toothbrush Holder, Dutch Boy & Girl Kissing, 3 Holes, Hanging, Japan, 3 1/2 x 5 1/2 In. 85.00
Toothbrush Holder, Dutch Girl, Big Feet, Feet Hold Toothpaste Tube, 5 1/2 In. 145.00
Toothbrush Holder, Elf Girl, Holding Flowers, Paste Holder, Made In Japan, 3 1/2 In. . . . 100.00
Toothbrush Holder, Flute Player, Striped Pants, Japan, 2 1/2 x 4 1/4 In. 75.00
Toothbrush Holder, Frog Playing Banjo, Paste Holder, Marked Gold Castle, Japan, 6 In. . 115.00
Toothbrush Holder, Girl With Dog, 1 Brush Hole, Paste Holder, Japan, 2 x 5 In. 65.00
Toothbrush Holder, Mailman, Postal Box, Japan, 2 1/2 x 4 1/4 In. 65.00
Toothbrush Holder, Swami, Splayed Legs, Turban, Jewel, Made In Germany, 3 3/4 In. . . 150.00
Urn, Cover, Coggled Design, Manganese Splash Design, Pa., 9 1/2 In. 4675.00
Vase, 2 Carved Buttresses, Woman & Leaves, Renee Buthard, 14 1/2 In. 3575.00
Vase, Arts & Crafts, Incised Roses, Burnt Orange, Ribbed Neck, 11 In. 58.00
Vase, Black Matte Glaze, Gold Horizontal Line, Broad Shoulders, Luxemburg, 12 1/2 In. . 80.00
Vase, Blue, White Glaze, Persia, 10 1/4 In. 25.00
Vase, Brown Matte Glaze, Oval, W.J. Gordy, Ga., 1935, 9 1/2 In. 431.00
Vase, Brown, Green Leaves Against Pink Mottled Ground, Marc Bellaire, 13 3/4 In. 150.00
Vase, Charles Catteau, Flowers, 3 Panels, Boch & Catteau, 8 In. 520.00
Vase, Cone Shape, Olive Green Over Turquoise Blue, Freeman-McFarlan, 1962, 4 In. . . . 15.00
Vase, Cornucopia, Horse, Cream, Gold Accents, 8 1/4 x 12 x 4 3/8 In. 45.00
Vase, Dark Green Glaze, Yellow, Art Nouveau, Rudolf Ditmar, Germany, 10 3/4 In. 550.00
Vase, Figural, Flower Shape, Nymph, Water Sprite, Vergnano, 28 In. 575.00
Vase, Flowers, Reticulated Rim, Blue Mark, 5 1/4 In. 165.00
Vase, Green Matte Glaze, Mountainside Pottery Co., 7 In. 150.00
Vase, Green, Blue Multicolored Glaze, A.R. Cole, 10 1/2 In., Pair 460.00
Vase, Hollyhock, Glazed Flowers, Green Ground, Signed, W.F. Woodard, 12 1/8 In. 430.00
Vase, Horizontal Simulated Stone, Earthtone Colors, Anton Lang, 5 1/4 In. 168.00
Vase, Mardi Gras, Dancing Figures, Signed, Marc Bellaire, 11 x 10 In. 245.00
Vase, Multicolored Flowers, Iridescent, Charlotte Rhead, Signed, 6 In. 35.00
Vase, Portrait Of Classical Style Man Wearing A Helmet, Footed, Oval, 14 In. 201.00
Vase, Smokey Glass, Etched, Bayel, 6 x 4 1/2 In. 144.00
Vase, Squeezebag Shape, Yellow Flowers, Blue Ground, Max Lauger, 8 1/2 In. 196.00
Vase, Studio, Double Band Of Abstract Circles, Mocha Glaze, G. Williams, 5 x 6 In. 193.00
Vase, Stylized Male, Female & Fish, E. & M. Scheier, 7 3/8 In. 345.00
Vase, Thick Volcanic Turquoise, Umber Glaze, James Lovera, 9 3/4 x 8 In. 863.00
Vase, Volcanic Cobalt Blue Glaze, Flared, James Lovera, 9 3/4 x 8 1/2 In. 863.00
Vase, White & Yellow Flowers, White Glaze, Brown Shades, 6 1/2 x 3 1/2 In. 55.00
Vessel, White, Black Matte Glaze, Ribbed Side, Harrison McIntosh, 6 x 7 1/2 In. 1350.00
Wall Pocket, Dragon, Carp Design, Late 19th Century, 8 In. 58.00
Wall Pocket, Lobster Form, Red Glaze, 1900, 11 1/2 In. 242.00
Wall Pocket, Single Bird & Flowers, Brown, Green Slip Design, Va., 7 1/4 In. 7150.00
Whistle, Bird, Mottled Black & Specks Glaze, 2 1/2 x 3 1/4 In. 385.00
Wine Pot, Inverted Pear Shape, Dragon Handle, Deep Chestnut Glaze, 4 In. 288.00

POTTERY-ART Art pottery was first made in America in Cincinnati, Ohio, during the 1870s. The pieces were hand thrown and hand decorated. The art pottery tradition continued until the 1920s when studio potters began making the more artistic wares. American, English, and Continental art pottery by less well-known makers is listed here. Most makers listed in Kovels' American Art Pottery, such as Arequipa, Ohr, Rookwood, Roseville, and Weller, are listed in their own categories in this book. More recent pottery is listed under the name of the maker or in the Pottery category.

Ashtray, Smoker, Holes In Head, Drip Glaze, Brannan, England, 3 1/4 In. . . . .*Illus* 250.00
Bowl, 3 Nude Children, Outstretched Arms, Annette Johnson, 8 5/8 In. 2750.00
Bowl, Banded Geometric Verdigris Design, Bronze Glaze, Norse, 4 In. 173.00
Bowl, Flower Interior, Marked, Kahler, 1 1/4 x 5 3/4 In. 88.00
Bowl, Incised & Painted Gazelle, Keramis, Impressed Mark, 9 1/4 In. 1380.00
Bowl, Lotus Blossoms, Embossed, Applied Turtle, Leaves, 2 1/2 In. 250.00
Bowl, Persian Blue Crackled Glaze, Flared, Durant Kilns, c.1915, 5 1/2 x 13 1/2 In. 405.00
Charger, Brown, Mint Green Swirl Glaze, Harrison McIntosh, 13 1/2 In. 1237.00

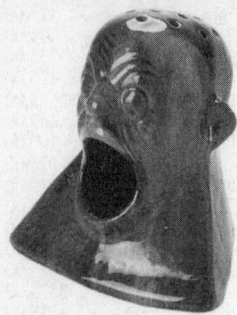

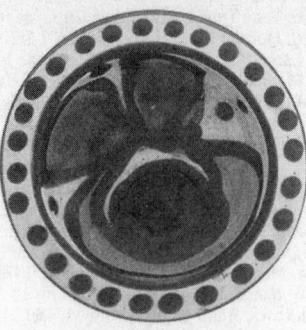

Pottery-Art, Ashtray, Smoker,
Holes In Head, Drip Glaze,
Brannan, England, 3 1/4 In.

Pottery-Art, Dish,
Green & Blue Circles, Herman Kahler,
Denmark, 4 In.

Pottery-Art, Vase,
3 Incised Men, Yellow,
Drip Glaze, 17 1/2 In.

Compote, Ribbed Oak Pedestal Base, Hagenauer, 5 1/2 x 10 1/2 In. 450.00
Dish, Green & Blue Circles, Herman Kahler, Denmark, 4 In. . . . . *Illus* 95.00
Jardiniere, Flowers & Trees, Band Of Irises On Bottom, Frederick Rhead, 1903, 8 In. . . . 1650.00
Jardiniere, Pedestal, Hunt Scene, Flambe Teal, White, Midnight Blue Glaze, 30 1/2 In. . . . 616.00
Jardiniere, Stand, Peacocks, Leaves, Burmantofts, c.1900, 40 3/4 In. 12000.00
Jug, Stylized Flowers & Leaves, Cream Ground, Charlotte Rhead, 1930s, 9 1/3 In. 907.00
Jug, Stylized Roses, Blue & Cream Ground, Frederick Rhead, c.1915, 7 In. 269.00
Pitcher, Arabesque, Hydrangea Flowers, Charlotte Rhead, 8 1/2 x 7 In. 220.00
Pitcher, Blue Tulips, Cream Ground, Avon Wheeling Pottery, 1920 . . . . 50.00
Pitcher, Orange Flowers, Squeezebag Lining, Charlotte Rhead, 8 1/4 x 7 In. 220.00
Plaque, Orange Flowers & Petals, Squeezebag Painting, Charlotte Rhead, 12 1/2 In. 275.00
Plaque, Wall, Abstract Brilliant Orange, Copper Iridescent, C. Rhead, 12 1/2 In. 248.00
Plaque, Wall, Blue Flowers, Cobalt Blue Leaves, Leaf & Berry Border, C. Rhead, 17 In. . 248.00
Plaque, Wall, Flowers, Diamond Stamen, Ivory, Orange Petals, C. Rhead, 14 1/2 In. 248.00
Plate, Joan Of Arc, Wearing Helmet, Keller & Guerin, 20th Century, 11 In. 172.00
Teapot, Circular Body, Buttressed Handle, V. Schreckengost, 12 x 7 In. 7280.00
Vase, 3 Incised Men, Yellow, Drip Glaze, 17 1/2 In. . . . . *Illus* 450.00
Vase, 5 White Swans, Swimming, Blue Sky & Water, Continental, 12 In. 125.00
Vase, Applied Geometric Design, 2 Amusing Animals, Wiener Werkstatte, 10 In. 2415.00
Vase, Applied Yellow Flower, White Brushed Glaze, 11 1/2 In. 50.00
Vase, Band Of Fruit, Leaves, Mottled Brown Ground, Charlotte Rhead, 1930s, 7 1/4 In. . . 269.00
Vase, Blue Flowers, Marked, Kahler, 10 1/2 In. 125.00
Vase, Brouwer, Copper Luster, Flame Painted, Amber & Ivory Glaze, Marked, 4 In. 430.00
Vase, Brown To Dark Green, Daffodils, Louwelsa Type, Quatrefoil, 11 5/8 In. 110.00
Vase, Brown, Gold Matte Glaze, Tapered, W.J. Walley, 7 1/4 x 3 1/4 In. 1350.00
Vase, Burgundy Swirl, 6 1/2 In. 144.00
Vase, Carved Basket, Weave Design, 4 Buttressed Handles, Denbac, 6 3/4 In. 303.00
Vase, Celadon Glaze, Fred Robertson, 7 1/2 x 4 3/4 In. 3656.00
Vase, Cylindrical Form, Abstract Faces, Blue & Purple Glaze, 10 1/4 In. 200.00
Vase, Flowers & Leaves, Aqua & Ivory Matte, Keramis, 11 In. 690.00
Vase, Gray Matte Glaze, Green Gloss Interior, Banded, White, Incised Denver/DW, 1920 . 130.00
Vase, Green Glaze, Angular Handles, Bretby Pottery Co., 1920, 4 1/2 In. 95.00
Vase, Green Glaze, Marked, Norwetta, 10 1/8 In. 165.00
Vase, Green, Tobacco Matte Glaze, Molded Vertical Leaves, 5 1/2 In. 460.00
Vase, Hammered Panels, Copper, Black, Arts & Crafts, Continental, 10 In. 140.00
Vase, Incised Nasturtium Design, Gold, Pauline, 11 1/8 In. 357.00
Vase, Incised Trees, Frederick Hurten Rhead, 1903, 4 1/8 In. 935.00
Vase, Ivory High Glaze Drip, Over Tan Matte, Keramis, 9 1/2 In. 310.00
Vase, Landscape, Mountain, Lake, Iridescent, Lessell, 5 3/4 In. 12.00
Vase, Manchu, Elongated Dragon, Gold Mane, Charlotte Rhead, 6 3/4 In. 330.00
Vase, Moss Green, Blue Azure Glaze, Pure White Interior, Footed, 1912, 4 In. 80.00
Vase, Mottled Blue Green Glaze, Palshus Denmark On Base, 8 1/4 In. 460.00

Vase, Mottled Semi-Green Glaze, William J. Walley, 16 1/2 In. 4315.00
Vase, Multicolored Flowers, Charlotte Rhead, 7 In. 80.00
Vase, Multicolored Flowers, Iridescent, Charlotte Rhead, Signed, 6 In. 345.00
Vase, Overlapping Leaves, Brown, Yellow, Green Matte Glaze, 6 In. 120.00
Vase, Painted Flowers, Charlotte Rhead, 8 1/2 In. 240.00
Vase, Painted Flowers, Slight Iridescent, Charlotte Rhead, 5 1/2 In. 335.00
Vase, Painted Landscape, 2 Handles, Wardle, 10 In. 60.00
Vase, Painted, Incised Panels, Stylized, Blue, Yellow, Tan, Keramis La Maitrise, 13 In. 489.00
Vase, Peacock, On Branch, Black Ground, Bulbous, Keramis, 9 x 9 In. 920.00
Vase, Pillow, 2 Elephant-Head Handles, Bisque Red Clay, A. Robertson, 6 x 7 In. 3940.00
Vase, Robin's-Egg Blue Glaze, 8 3/4 In. 52.00
Vase, Stylized Black Egret, Ivory Glaze Ground, 4 Sides, S. Larrieu, 13 1/2 In. 750.00
Vase, Stylized Flowers, Geometric Top, Brown Panels, Keramis, 13 3/4 In. 805.00
Vase, Stylized Leaves, Flowers, Slip Trailing, Avon, 5 3/4 In. 522.00
Vase, Stylized Panels, Script Mark, Keramis La Maitrise, 13 1/4 In. 546.00
Vase, Stylized Sun & Rays Panels, Brown, Ivory Ground, Keramis, 13 In. 1035.00
Vase, Teardrop Shape, Flame Painted, Green, Brown, Brouwer, 5 x 5 1/4 In. 489.00
Vase, Yellow Crackled Iridescent Glaze, Flared Rim, 11 3/4 In. 345.00

POTTERY-CONTEMPORARY lists pieces made by artists working after 1975.
Figurine, Easter Girls, 1 Holding Bunny, 1 Holding Chick, Napco, Japan, Pair 30.00
Mug, Cockeyed Charley, Jessop, Pfaltzgraff 45.00
Mug, Handsome German, Pfaltzgraff 45.00
Vase, Feelies, Blue, Gray Gunmetal Crystalline Glaze, Cabat, 4 1/2 x 4 In. 690.00
Vase, Feelies, Cobalt, Green Flambe Glaze, Cabat, 3 x 4 1/4 In., Pair 635.00
Vase, Yellow, Brown Matte, Signed, Rose Cabat, 2 1/2 In. 489.00

POTTERY-MIDCENTURY includes pieces made from the 1950s to the 1980s.
Bottle, Sgraffito, Dark Brown Mottled Ground, Abstract Faces, Scheier, 9 In. 562.00
Bowl, 4 Horses, Red, Blue, Purple, Mauve Ground, Polia Pillin, 1966, 7 In. 412.00
Bowl, Aqua Drip Glaze, Brown Feathers, Gray Ground, Scheier, 4 x 7 In. 193.00
Bowl, Blue, Green Hare's Fur Glaze, Footed, Natzler, 3 x 6 In. 1495.00
Bowl, Cobalt Blue Swirls, White Glaze, Deep Olive Green, Scheier, 4 x 6 In. 195.00
Bowl, Flared, Blue, Sea Green Glaze, Scheier, Marked, 7 In. 259.00
Bowl, Frothy Sky Blue Semimatte Glaze, Natzler, 3 x 5 In. 1575.00
Bowl, Lavender Matte Glaze, Flared, Natzler, 2 x 7 In. 1462.00
Bowl, Low, Turquoise Matrix Glaze, No. 22, Signature, Glidden, 11 x 9 In. 25.00
Bowl, Mermaid, Dolphins, Sea Gulls, Paul Bogatay, 1942, 4 x 5 In. 2530.00
Bowl, Midnight Blue, Signed, Natzler, 3 1/2 x 5 3/4 In. 3450.00
Bowl, Prancing Colts, Ochery Clay, Paul Bogatay, 1941, 3 x 11 1/2 In. 2415.00
Bowl, Purple Crystalline Glaze, Flared, Natzler, 1956, 7 3/4 In. 4888.00
Bowl, Sgraffito, Scroll, Figure Design, Taupe Glaze, Scheier, Signature, 6 In. 863.00
Bowl, Tigereye Glaze, Flared, Natzler, 1965, 6 1/2 In. 3450.00
Bowl, White, Brown Volcanic Glaze, Natzler, 1 1/2 x 6 1/2 In. 292.00
Bowl, Woman, Bird, Brown Glaze, Speckled Ground, Winblad, 2 1/2 x 7 1/2 In. 104.00

Pottery-Midcentury, Figurine, Girl, In Front
Of Tree, Clasping Hands, Thelma Winter

Pottery-Midcentury, Plate, Incised Zebra,
Unglazed Back, Square, Glidden, 5 1/2 In.

Box, Ming Tree, Burro Mark, No. 955, Weil, 5 x 5 In. 50.00
Charger, 2 Figures Dancing, White Glaze, Mounted, Picasso, Madoura, 7 In. 731.00
Charger, Sgraffito, Abstract Fish Faces, White, Green, Indigo Ground, Scheier 2362.00
Dish, Blue, Green, Taupe Mottled Glaze, Natzler, 6 In. 675.00
Dish, Gold Brown, Brass Handle, 3 Sections, Maurice Of California, 12 x 3 In. 20.00
Dish, Mask, Wax Resist, Mottled, Sheer White Glaze, Incised Scheier, 6 In. 144.00
Dish, Rim, Faces In Sgraffito, Blue Semimatte Glaze, Scheier, Signed, 7 1/2 In. 175.00
Dish, Sgraffito, Abstract Bird Design, Scheier, 8 1/2 In. 314.00
Figurine, Girl, Hand On Hip, Carrying Blue Basket, Sticker, Weil, 6 1/2 In. 35.00
Figurine, Girl, In Front Of Tree, Clasping Hands, Thelma Winter ....*Illus* 500.00
Figurine, Girl, Yellow Dress, Blue Flowers, Yellow Hat, Sticker, Weil, 7 1/2 In. 65.00
Figurine, Gold Gilt, Brown Matte Glaze, Signed, Waylande Gregory, 19 In., Pair 242.00
Figurine, Hippopotamus, Gray, Brayton Laguna, 7 1/2 x 8 In. 100.00
Pitcher, Orange, Hour-Glass Shape, California Pottery, 8 1/2 x 6 1/2 In. 20.00
Planter, Bride, Holding Bouquet, Weil, 6 1/2 In. 30.00
Planter, Dog, Spaniels, Brown & White, Napco 25.00
Planter, Girl Kneeling, Green Dress, Sticker, Weil, 7 1/2 In. 65.00
Planter, Girl, Blue Apron, No. 1665, Weil, 8 In. 50.00
Planter, Girl, Green Apron, Holding Yellow Blanket, Weil, 8 In. 50.00
Planter, Girl, Standing, Dark Hair, Bows On Dress, Weil, 6 In. 32.00
Planter, Lady In Blue, Sitting, 2 Pot Holes, Marked 4026, Weil, 9 In. 75.00
Planter, Lady In Pink Dress, Marked 4027, Weil, 10 3/4 In. 85.00
Planter, Peasant Woman Holding Basket, Basket Is Planter, Brayton Laguna 70.00
Planter, Turquoise Matrix Glaze, Rectangular, Incised Glidden Signature 18.00
Plate, Incised Zebra, Unglazed Back, Square, Glidden, 5 1/2 In. ....*Illus* 10.00
Plate, Sgraffito, Polychrome Fruit, Paul Bogatay, 1934, 10 1/2 In. 805.00
Plate, Sgraffito, Woman & 2 Colts, Paul Bogatay, 1934, 10 1/2 In. 315.00
Pot, Bright Yellow Glaze, Straight Walls, Natzler, 4 x 5 1/2 In. 1265.00
Sculpture, Jazz Singer, Woman, Animals On Dress, Flowers, P. Bogatay, 15 In. 2875.00
Tray, Signed, Square, Marc Bellaire, 13 1/4 In. 150.00
Vase, 2 Pretty Woman, 2 Strutting Roosters, Green Ground, Pillin, 6 7/8 In. 495.00
Vase, Black, Blue, Green Matte, Rose Cabat, Signed, 2 1/2 In. 245.00
Vase, Blue, Green Umber Crystalline Glaze, Natzler, 6 1/4 x 3 1/2 In. 2250.00
Vase, Coupe-Shape, Turquoise, Blue Semimatte Glaze, Scheier, Signed, 9 1/2 In. 518.00
Vase, Peach Blossom Glaze, Green, Blue, Red, Natzler, 1961, 6 1/2 In. 6325.00
Vase, Portrait, Studio Potter, Polia Pillin In Center, Black Ground, 11 In. 1650.00
Vase, Rolled Rim, Turquoise Matrix Glaze, Alfred N.Y., Glidden Parker, 7 1/2 In. 45.00
Vase, Sgraffito, Fish Shape, Ocher High Glaze, Mahogany, Scheier, 9 3/4 In. 770.00
Vase, Woman & Birth With Child In Womb, Tan Bisque Glaze, Scheier, 7 In. 770.00
Vase, Woman, Horse, Goose, Brown Ground, Spherical, Pillin, 6 1/4 x 5 In. 478.00
Vase, Yellow Flower, Brown Design, Ivory Ground, Ruffled, Blue Ridge, 5 In. 75.00

POWDER FLASKS AND POWDER HORNS were made to hold the gunpowder used in antique firearms. The early examples were made of horn or wood; later ones were of copper or brass.

POWDER FLASK, Brass, Suspension Cord Carrying Bullion Tassels, 17th Century, 3 1/2 In. . 2400.00
POWDER HORN, Carved, Military Ship With American Flag Of 1777, Initials, 18th Century . 395.00
  Hunter Taking Aim Behind Tree, Building, Quaint Inscription, 1813, 13 1/2 In. 660.00
  Silver Chased Ends, Coral & Turquoise Nuggets, Silver Plug, 10 In. 110.00
  Stag Horn, Pots Of Tulips, Ukraine, 5 1/4 In. 110.00
  Wood, Carved, Engraved, Raised Nipple End, Metal Patina, 20 x 2 1/2 In. 250.00

PRATT ware means two different things. It was an early Staffordshire pottery, cream-colored with colored decorations, made by Felix Pratt during the late eighteenth century. There was also Pratt ware made with transfer designs during the mid-nineteenth century in Fenton, England. Reproductions of the transfer-printed Pratt are being made.

PRATT
FENTON

Bud Vase, Blue & Yellow Flowers, Footed, Early 19th Century, 8 In. 770.00
Creamer, Scenes Of Children In Hearts, Goldenrod & Green Enamel, 4 7/8 In. 275.00
Figurine, Flora, Sponge Design Base, 19th Century, 9 In. 405.00
Figurine, Young Boy, Flowers, Leaves, 5 1/2 In. 230.00
Jug, Men & Women Scenes, Raised, 7 In. 125.00
Jug, Raised Vine & Grape Cluster, 5 1/2 In. 345.00

Plaque, Adam & Eve & Cherub, Raised, Oval, 8 3/4 In. 230.00
Plate, 2 Women In Mountain Village, Winged Cherubs, c.1817, 10 1/4 In. 395.00

PRESSED GLASS was first made in the United States in the 1820s after the invention of glass pressing machines. Hundreds of patterns of pressed glass were made in complete table settings. Although the Boston and Sandwich Works was the most famous of the pressed glass factories, there were about sixteen other factories making pressed glass from 1830 to 1850, and still more from 1850 to 1900, when pressed glass reached its greatest popularity. It is now being widely reproduced. The pattern names used in this listing are based on the information in the book *Pressed Glass in America* by John and Elizabeth Welker. There may be pieces of pressed glass listed in this book in other categories, such as Lamp, Ruby, Sandwich, and Souvenir.

1000-Eye pattern is listed here as Thousand Eye.
6 Panel, Finecut, Compote, 7 In. 35.00
Acorn, Creamer, Child's, 3 1/2 In. 150.00
Actress, Cheese Dish, 2 Dromios, 6 1/2 x 8 In. 240.00
Actress, Goblet .... .45.00 to 75.00
Actress, Marmalade, 6 1/2 x 3 1/2 In. 80.00
Alabama, Cruet, Stopper 60.00
Alabama, Toothpick, Crystal, Oak Leaf Etch 28.00
Alaska, Sauce, Emerald 40.00
Amberette, Bowl, Vegetable, Oval, 9 In. 60.00
Amberette, Cruet, 5 1/4 In. 25.00
Amberette, Spooner 110.00
Apple, Wine, Green 25.00
Arched Leaf, Goblet 160.00
Argus, Champagne, 5 1/4 In. 59.00
Ashburton, Claret, Flint, 5 1/2 In. 62.00
Ashburton, Cordial, 4 1/2 In. 20.00
Ashburton, Goblet .... .30.00 to 45.00
Ashburton, Goblet, Flared Rim 30.00
Ashburton, Sugar 40.00
Atlas, Champagne, 5 1/2 In. 20.00
Atlas, Cordial, 4 1/4 In. 20.00
Atlas, Goblet 20.00
Austrian, Plate, Square, 7 In. 32.00
Baby Face, Goblet 175.00
Baby Thumbprint pattern is listed here as Dakota.
Balder pattern is listed here as Pennsylvania.
Balky Mule pattern is listed here as Currier & Ives.
Banded Portland, Goblet, Maiden's Blush 55.00
Banded Portland, Water Set, Gold Trim, 6 Piece 90.00
Barberry, Plate, 6 In. 17.00
Basket Weave, Wine 35.00
Beaded Band, Relish 10.00

Pressed Glass,
Austrian

Pressed Glass,
Barberry

Pressed Glass,
Beaded Grape Medallion

Beaded Bull's-Eye & Drape pattern is listed here as Alabama.
Beaded Dewdrop pattern is listed here as Wisconsin.
Beaded Grape, Pitcher, Water, 10 3/8 In. 80.00
Beaded Grape Medallion, Celery Vase 55.00
Beaded Grape Medallion, Spooner . . . . .30.00 to 45.00
Beaded Mirror, Goblet, Grape & Fern Etch, 5 3/4 In. 110.00
Beaded Oval & Scroll, Creamer 26.00
Beaded Shell, Water Set, Vaseline Glass, 6 Piece 145.00
Bellflower, Bowl, Center Oval, 6 x 9 1/4 In. 275.00
Bellflower, Cake Stand, Domed Foot, 8 3/4 In. 5600.00
Bellflower, Cologne Bottle, Green Trim, Clambroth Stopper, 5 5/8 In. 350.00
Bellflower, Compote, Domed Foot, 4 1/2 In. 120.00
Bellflower, Compote, Domed Foot, 9 In. 300.00
Bellflower, Decanter, 3 Rows Of Cut Ovals On Neck, Stopper, 11 1/2 In. 850.00
Bellflower, Eggcup, Opalescent, Band Rim, 3 7/8 In. 1500.00
Bellflower, Goblet, Plain Foot 35.00
Bellflower, Goblet, Rayed Foot 40.00
Bellflower, Jug, Molasses, Flared Circular Foot, 4 1/2 x 4 In. 1700.00
Bellflower, Jug, Molasses, Opalescent, 5 1/2 In. 3500.00
Bellflower, Nappy, Cover, Beaded Rim, Acorn Finial, 5 3/4 In. 100.00
Bellflower, Pitcher, Milk, 7 5/8 In. 2000.00
Bellflower, Pitcher, Water, 8 1/4 In. 500.00
Bellflower, Spooner, Cobalt Blue, 5 5/8 In. 7000.00
Bellflower, Spooner, Cobalt Blue, Banded Rim, 5 5/8 In. 100.00
Bellflower, Tumbler, Water, 3 1/2 In. 50.00
Bellflower With Loops, Goblet, Flared Rim, 5 5/8 In. 300.00
Bent Buckle pattern is listed here as New Hampshire.
Bird & Strawberry, Bowl, Flared, 10 1/2 In. 65.00
Bird & Strawberry, Butter, Cover Only 60.00
Bird & Strawberry, Compote, Cover, Low, 6 In. 85.00
Bird & Strawberry, Compote, Ruffled Edge 65.00
Bird & Strawberry, Punch Cup 22.00
Bird & Strawberry, Tumbler 35.00
Bird & Strawberry, Wine 27.00
Bleeding Heart, Eggcup 65.00
Bleeding Heart, Goblet 45.00
Bleeding Heart, Honey 25.00
Bluebird pattern is listed here as Bird & Strawberry.
Bosworth, Wine 24.00
Bowtie, Bowl, Fruit, 5 1/2 In. 45.00
Bradford Blackberry, Goblet 70.00
Bradford Grape pattern is listed here as Bradford Blackberry.
Bridle Rosettes, Wine 25.00
Brilliant, Goblet 30.00
Broken Column, Cruet, Stopper 80.00
Broken Column, Syrup, Cover 25.00
Bryce pattern is listed here as Ribbon Candy.
Buckle, Pitcher, Green . . . . .40.00 to 50.00
Buckle & Star, Creamer 29.00
Bull's-Eye, Finger Lamp, Green, 3 1/4 In. 120.00
Bull's-Eye, Goblet 100.00
Bull's-Eye & Diamond Point, Goblet 180.00
Bull's-Eye & Fleur-De-Lis, Ale, 6 1/4 In. 650.00
Bull's-Eye & Fleur-De-Lis, Goblet 220.00
Bull's-Eye With Diamond Point, Goblet 180.00
Butterfly, Compote, Jelly 25.00
Button Arches, Creamer, Clambroth, Gold Trim, Child's 18.00
Cable, Eggcup, Clambroth, 3 3/4 In. 374.00
Cable, Goblet 75.00
Cable, Goblet, 6 1/4 x 6 1/2 In. 75.00
Cable, Wine, 4 1/8 In. 300.00
California pattern is listed here as Beaded Grape.
Canadian, Celery Vase, 7 3/4 In. 60.00

Pressed Glass,   Pressed Glass,   Pressed Glass,
Bellflower   Bird & Strawberry   Columbian Coin

Candlewick as a pressed glass pattern is properly named *Banded Raindrop*. There is also a pattern called *Candlewick*, which has been made by Imperial Glass Corporation since 1936. It is listed in this book in the Imperial Glass category.

Candy Ribbon pattern is listed here as Ribbon Candy.

Cane, Butter, Cover, Ruby Stain	195.00
Cane, Pitcher, Ruby Stain	175.00
Cane, Sugar & Creamer, Ruby Stain	95.00
Carolina, Relish	14.00
Cat Up A Tree With Dog, Pitcher, Water	350.00

Centennial, see also the related patterns Liberty Bell and Philadelphia Centennial.

Ceres pattern is listed here as Profile & Sprig.

Chain, Straw Holder, Metal Lid, 12 1/2 In.	230.00
Cherry, Salt, Master, Vaseline Glass, 3 1/4 In.	19.00
Chippendale, Compote, Vaseline Glass	225.00

Church Windows pattern is listed here as Columbia.

Classic, Celery Vase, 8 x 4 In.	60.00
Classic, Pitcher, Water, Log Feet, 10 In.	200.00

Coin Spot pattern is listed in this book in its own category.

Colorado, Creamer, Individual	40.00
Colorado, Platter, This Day Our Daily Bread, Oval	45.00
Colorado, Spooner	70.00
Colorado, Sugar, Cover, Gold Trim	60.00
Columbia, Creamer	32.00
Columbian Coin, Wine, 5 In.	100.00
Comet, Goblet	140.00 to 160.00

Compact pattern is listed here as Snail.

Cord & Tassel, Creamer	28.00
Cord & Tassel, Syrup, Tin Cover	90.00
Cord & Tassel, Tumbler	60.00

Cosmos pattern is listed in this book as its own category.

Crane pattern is listed here as Stork.

Croesus, Butter, Cover, Vaseline Glass, 7 3/4 x 5 3/4 In.	59.00
Croesus, Compote, Jelly, Emerald, Gold Trim	165.00
Croesus, Spoon, Emerald, Gold Trim	65.00
Croesus, Water Set, Amethyst, Gold Trim, 7 Piece	725.00
Crystal Wedding, Banana Stand, 9 1/2 x 12 1/2 In.	100.00

Cupid & Psyche pattern is listed here as Psyche & Cupid.

Cupid & Venus, Compote, Cover, High	80.00
Cupid & Venus, Compote, Cover, Low	40.00
Cupid & Venus, Creamer	50.00
Cupid & Venus, Cruet, Stopper, 8 In.	35.00
Currier & Ives, Cake Stand, Blue, 9 1/2 In.	90.00 to 110.00
Currier & Ives, Tumbler, Iced Tea	16.00
Currier & Ives, Tumbler, Water	14.00 to 16.00
Currier & Ives, Wine, 4 In.	10.00
Cut Log, Compote, Cover, 8 x 5 1/4 In., Pair	60.00
Cut Log, Compote, Cover, 9 x 6 3/8 In.	90.00

Pressed Glass,
Dakota

Pressed Glass,
Deer & Dog

Pressed Glass,
Dewdrop with Star

Cut Log, Cruet, Stopper, 6 1/2 In., Pair 210.00
Cut Log, Pitcher, Water, 11 3/4 In. 70.00
Cut Log, Sugar & Creamer 80.00
Dahlia pattern is listed here as Square Fuchsia.
Daisy & Button, Compote, High 140.00
Dakota, Cake Stand, Fern & Berry Etch, 9 1/2 x 6 1/2 In. 50.00
Dakota, Compote, Cover, Fern & Berry Etch, 5 x 8 1/2 In. 60.00
Dakota, Compote, Cover, Fern & Berry Etch, 8 x 12 In. 70.00
Dakota, Compote, Cover, Fern & Berry Etch, High, 13 In. 120.00
Dakota, Goblet, Etched 18.00
Dakota, Spooner 24.00
Dakota, Tray, Water, Fern & Berry Etch 160.00
Dakota, Waste Bowl, Fern & Berry Etch, 3 x 4 In. 130.00
Dakota, Wine, 4 In. 10.00
Deer & Dog, Goblet, 6 1/4 In. ....75.00 to 100.00
Deer & Pine Tree, Compote, Cover, High, 12 In. 100.00
Deer & Pine Tree, Goblet 65.00
Deer & Pine Tree, Pitcher, Milk, 7 3/4 In. 150.00
Delaware, Banana Bowl, Emerald, Gold Trim 135.00
Delaware, Lemonade Set, Gold Trim, 7 Piece 250.00
Delaware, Spooner, Emerald, Gold Trim 55.00
Dewdrop With Star, Sugar, Cover 60.00
Dewey, Pitcher, 4 In. 100.00
Diamond, Berry Bowl, Handle, Amethyst, 4 1/2 x 3 3/8 In. 52.00
Diamond & Bull's-Eye Band, Banana Boat, 11 3/4 In. 60.00
Diamond & Bull's-Eye Band, Bowl, Ruffled Edge, 10 1/4 In. 25.00
Diamond & Bull's-Eye Band, Cake Stand, 10 In. 80.00
Diamond & Bull's-Eye Band, Compote, 8 In. 90.00
Diamond & Bull's-Eye Band, Goblet 50.00
Diamond Point, Celery Vase, 9 In. 60.00
Diamond Point, Decanter, Stopper, 11 1/4 In. 170.00
Diamond Point, Eggcup, Clambroth, 3 3/4 In. ....80.00 to 100.00
Diamond Point, Eggcup, Pale Blue Opalescent, 3 3/4 In. 950.00
Diamond Point, Pitcher, Water, Applied Crimped Handle, 9 1/4 In. 50.00
Diamond Point, Tumbler, Whiskey, Handle, 3 1/4 In. 120.00
Diamond Point Band, Creamer 59.00
Diamond Point With Panels, Compote, 9 In. 82.00
Diamond Quilted, Wine, Blue 29.00
Diamond Spearhead, Compote, Vaseline Glass 595.00
Diamond Thumbprint, Celery Vase, 9 1/2 & 10 In., Pair 180.00
Diamond Thumbprint, Sugar, Cover, 7 1/4 In. 180.00
Dog With Rabbit In Hole, Pitcher, Water, 2 Palm Trees On Either Side Of Dog 200.00
Dolphin, Compote, Rayed Base, 9 1/4 In. 375.00
Doric pattern is listed here as Feather.
Double Loop pattern is listed here as Ribbon Candy.
Double Spear, Eggcup 21.00
Double Wedding Ring pattern is listed here as Wedding Ring.

E Pluribus Unum pattern is listed here as Emblem.

Egyptian, Bread Plate, Cleopatra, 13 1/2 x 8 3/4 In.	45.00
Egyptian, Creamer	50.00
Elaine, Plate, 9 In.	50.00
Emblem, Mug, 5 In., Pair	130.00
Empress, Spoon Tray, Amethyst, 9 In.	30.00
Empress, Tumbler, Ruby Stain, Footed, 6 3/4 In.	45.00

English Hobnail Cross pattern is listed here as Amberette.

Esther, Butter, Cover, Emerald	90.00
Esther, Cake Stand, 6 x 10 1/2 In.	80.00
Esther, Compote, Cover, 13 In.	30.00 to 170.00
Esther, Cruet, Emerald, Gold Trim, No Stopper	45.00
Esther, Pitcher, Water	100.00
Esther, Sugar, Cover, Emerald, Gold Trim	35.00
Esther, Toothpick, Emerald, Gold Trim	80.00

Etched Dakota pattern is listed here as Dakota.

Eugenie, Goblet	35.00
Excelsior Variant, Goblet	30.00
Eyewinker, Banana Boat	95.00
Eyewinker, Saltshaker	65.00

Fan With Diamond pattern is listed here as Shell.

Feather, Pitcher, Water	40.00
Feeding Swan, Compote, Cover, Swirled Edge, 12 1/2 In.	40.00

Fine Cut & Feather pattern is listed here as Feather.

Fine Rib, Celery Vase, Flared Rim, 8 1/2 In.	350.00
Flamingo Habitat, Compote, Cover, 11 In.	70.00
Flamingo Habitat, Wine	38.00
Flat Diamond, Creamer	50.00
Fleur-De-Lis & Thistle, Bowl, 83 Stippled Scalloped Rim, 9 x 1 3/4 In.	150.00
Florida Palm, Relish	10.00
Flower Band, Frosted, Sugar, Cover, Love Birds Finial, 9 In.	110.00

Flower Flange pattern is listed here as Dewey.

Flower Medallion, Goblet	70.00
Flute, Tumbler, Taster, 8 Panels, Sapphire Blue, 2 x 1 3/4 In.	50.00
Flying Birds, Goblet	90.00 to 120.00

Flying Robin pattern is listed here as Hummingbird.

Frog & Spider, Goblet	300.00

Frosted patterns may also be listed under name of main pattern.

Frosted Eagle, Compote, Cover, 10 3/4 In.	35.00

Frosted Flower Band pattern is listed here as Flower Band, Frosted.

Frosted Leaf, Celery Vase, 9 x 4 1/2 In.	90.00
Frosted Leaf, Goblet	80.00 to 90.00

Garden Of Eden, see the related pattern Lotus & Serpent.

Geneva, Bowl, Emerald, Gold Trim, Oval, 8 1/2 In.	35.00
Georgian, Finger Bowl, Blue	260.00
Giant Sawtooth, Goblet	40.00
Girl With Fan, Goblet	40.00 to 152.00

Good Luck pattern is listed here as Horseshoe.

Gooseberry, Creamer	34.00
Gothic, Goblet	30.00 to 40.00
Grant, U.S., Plate, Let Us Have Peace, Blue, 10 1/4 In.	15.00

Grape, see also the related patterns Beaded Grape, Beaded Grape Medallion, and Paneled Grape Band.

Grape & Cable pattern is listed in this book in the Northwood category.

Grape & Festoon With Small American Shield, Goblet	35.00
Green Herringbone, Cake Stand, Emerald, 6 1/2 x 9 3/4 In.	60.00
Halley's Comet, Wine	68.00
Hamilton, Champagne, 4 3/4 In.	160.00
Hamilton, Compote, Ribbed Stem, Domed Foot, 5 1/2 x 7 7/8 In.	25.00
Hamilton, Tumbler, Whiskey, 3 x 2 1/2 In., 8 Piece	70.00
Hamilton With Frosted Leaf, Goblet	100.00
Hand, Marmalade, 5 7/8 In.	30.00
Hand, Pitcher, Water, 9 3/4 In.	110.00

Pressed Glass,
Honeycomb

Pressed Glass,
Inverted Thumbprint

Pressed Glass,
Jacobean

Hanging Basket, Pitcher, Water	210.00
Harp, Nappy, Cover, 10-Sided Base, 48 Rays, 6 x 4 3/4 In.	80.00
Hawaiian Pineapple, Goblet	160.00
Heart, Goblet	15.00
Heart & Lyre, Bowl, 64 Even Scalloped Rim, 9 1/8 x 1 1/2 In.	260.00
Heart & Pinwheel, Tray, Oval, 8 x 5 1/2 In.	45.00
Heart With Thumbprint, Berry Bowl, Master, Gold Trim	35.00
Heart With Thumbprint, Bowl, Flared Rim, 3 x 8 1/4 In.	80.00
Heart With Thumbprint, Goblet	65.00
Heart With Thumbprint, Goblet, Green, Gold Trim	325.00
Heart With Thumbprint, Rose Bowl, 3 1/2 x 4 3/4 In.	110.00
Heart With Thumbprint, Spooner, 4 In.	110.00
Heart With Thumbprint, Syrup, Pewter Cover, 5 1/2 In.	120.00
Herringbone, Compote, Jelly, Emerald	24.00
Hexagon Block, Tankard, Floral Etch	110.00
Hinoto pattern is listed here as Diamond Point with Panels.	
Hobnail pattern is in this book as its own category.	
Hobnail In Square, Creamer, Opalescent	45.00
Holly, Compote, Open, Faceted Stem, 7 x 8 1/2 In.	100.00
Holly, Goblet	150.00
Holly, Tumbler, Water, 3 5/8 In.	180.00
Holly, Wine, 3 5/8 In.	190.00
Holly With Cord & Tassel, Butter, Cover, Opalescent, 6 x 4 3/4 In.	275.00
Honeycomb, see also the related pattern Vernon Honeycomb.	
Honeycomb, Pitcher, 8 5/8 In. . . . . .110.00 to 120.00	
Horn Of Plenty, Butter, Cover, Washington Head, 5 In.	610.00
Horn Of Plenty, Compote, 7 In.	155.00
Horn Of Plenty, Compote, 8 1/2 x 10 1/4 In.	140.00
Horn Of Plenty, Creamer, Applied Handle, 6 3/4 In.	50.00
Horn Of Plenty, Decanter, Diamond Point Stopper, 8 1/2 x 12 In.	110.00
Horn Of Plenty, Goblet . . . . .70.00 to 100.00	
Horn Of Plenty, Plate, 6 1/2 In.	30.00
Horn Of Plenty, Sugar	45.00
Horn Of Plenty, Sugar, Pagoda Cover, 7 1/4 x 4 1/4 In.	20.00
Horn Of Plenty, Tumbler, Whiskey, 3 In.	60.00
Horseshoe, Cake Stand	170.00
Horseshoe, Creamer	45.00
Horseshoe, Goblet, Knopped Stem . . . . .40.00 to 55.00	
Horseshoe, Pitcher, Water	200.00
Hummingbird, Goblet, Amber	30.00
Hummingbird, Pitcher, Water, 9 1/4 In.	120.00
Illinois, Toothpick	24.00
Indiana Swirl pattern is listed here as Feather.	
Individual Brickwork, Creamer	14.00
Industry, Bowl, 2 Farmers With Horses, Sailing Ship, Factory In Border, 6 In.	110.00
Inverted Thumbprint, Celery Vase, Cranberry, Scalloped Rim, 7 1/4 In.	120.00
Inverted Thumbprint, Wine, Amber	18.00

Jacob's Ladder, Creamer 45.00
Jacob's Ladder, Pitcher, Water, Crimped Handle, 10 In. 140.00
Jacob's Ladder, Syrup, Tin Cover, Molded Handle, 7 3/8 In. 90.00
Jacobean, Cruet, Ruby Stain, Footed, 8 5/8 In. 95.00
Jeweled Moon & Star pattern is listed here as Moon & Star.
Kamoni pattern is listed here as Pennsylvania.
Kentucky, Saucer, Cobalt Blue 25.00
King's Crown, see also the related pattern Ruby Thumbprint.
King's Crown, Goblet, Amber Stain 6.00
King's Crown, Plate, Luncheon, Amber Stain 25.00
King's Crown, Sherbet, Ruby Stain 10.00
King's Crown, Sugar & Creamer, Green 12.00
Klondike pattern is listed here as Amberette.
Lacy Dewdrop, Goblet, Opalescent 30.00
Lattice, Wine 35.00
Liberty Bell, Butter, Cover 125.00
Liberty Bell, Creamer, Applied Handle 125.00
Liberty Bell, Plate, 10 1/4 In. 90.00
Liberty Bell, Relish 50.00
Liberty Bell, Sugar, Cover, 3 1/2 x 2 1/2 In. 30.00
Lily-Of-The-Valley, Goblet ....110.00 to 130.00
Lincoln Drape, Goblet 190.00
Lion, Frosted, Bowl, Cover, Crouching Lion Finial, Oval, 8 3/4 In. 210.00
Lion, Frosted, Compote, Rampant Lion Finial, 6 In. 675.00
Lion, Frosted, Eggcup, 3 1/2 x 2 3/4 In. 80.00
Lion, Frosted, Goblet 55.00
Lion, Frosted, Marmalade, Crouching Lion Finial, 6 3/4 x 3 1/2 In. 50.00
Lion, Plate, Motto, Handle, 10 1/2 In. 90.00
Lion's Leg pattern is listed here as Alaska.
Lippman pattern is listed here as Flat Diamond.
Log Cabin, Compote, 12 x 8 x 6 In., Pair 425.00
Log Cabin, Pitcher, Water, 8 3/8 In. 625.00
Log Cabin, Spooner, Cobalt Blue 295.00
Loop, see also the related pattern Seneca Loop.
Loop, Jug, Molasses, Hinged Cover, Blue, Applied Handle, 6 In. 1700.00
Loop & Dart, Eggcup, Round Ornaments 21.00
Loops & Drops pattern is listed here as New Jersey.
Lotus & Serpent, Creamer 48.00
Lotus & Serpent, Goblet 190.00
Maine, Wine, 4 1/2 In. 30.00
Maryland, Platter 25.00
Massachusetts, Jug, Rum, 6 In. 110.00
Memphis, Pitcher, Emerald, Gold Trim 125.00
Memphis, Tumbler, Oriental Poppy, Emerald, Gold Trim 40.00
Michigan, Cruet, Maiden Blush, Blue & Gold Trim 120.00
Michigan, Pitcher, Milk, Maiden Blush, Blue & Gold Trim, 8 In. 225.00
Michigan, Toothpick Holder, Amber, Enameled Flowers, 2 1/2 In. 40.00

Pressed Glass,
Liberty Bell

Pressed Glass,
Moon & Star

Pressed Glass,
Pleat & Panel

Michigan, Water Set, Maiden Blush, 7 3/4 In., 6 Piece 425.00
Millard, Pitcher, Water, Ruby Stain, 8 1/4 In. 150.00
Minerva, Bread Plate, 13 x 9 In. 30.00
Minerva, Cake Stand, 7 1/4 x 10 1/2 In. 45.00
Minerva, Compote 50.00
Minerva, Marmalade, 6 x 3 5/8 In. 60.00
Minerva, Spooner 35.00
Moon & Star, Candy Dish, Cover, Vaseline Glass 40.00
Moon & Star, Spooner, 5 1/8 x 3 1/2 In. 110.00
Moon & Star, Spooner, Spill, 6 Sides, Plain Circular Foot, 3 x 4 3/4 In. 50.00
Moon & Stork pattern is listed here as Ostrich Looking At The Moon.
Morning Glory, Compote, 8 In. 475.00
Morning Glory, Sugar, 4 x 5 In. 160.00
Nail, Cake Stand, 7 x 9 1/2 In. 60.00
Nail, Pitcher, Water, Blossom Etch, 9 In. 80.00
Nailhead, Plate, 9 1/4 In. 12.00
New England, Salt, Floral Bouquet, Star Bottom, Footed, Fiery Opalescent 100.00
New England Pineapple, Compote, 4 x 7 In. 80.00
New England Pineapple, Pitcher, Water, Solid Handle, 8 In. 1050.00
New England Pineapple, Tumbler, Water, 3 3/4 In. 120.00
New Hampshire, Goblet, Maiden Blush 50.00
New Jersey, Goblet, Gold Trim 40.00
New Jersey, Water Set, Gold Trim, 5 Piece 90.00
Oak Leaf, Bowl, Beaded Rim, 10 1/4 x 2 In. 650.00
Old Abe pattern is listed here as Frosted Eagle.
One-Thousand Eye pattern is listed here as Thousand Eye.
Ostrich Looking At The Moon, Goblet 130.00
Oval Miter, Compote, Open, Hexagonal Stem, Circular Foot, 7 3/4 x 10 In. 70.00
Owl pattern is listed here as Bull's-Eye with Diamond Point.
Owl & Possum, Goblet 90.00
Paneled Fern, Goblet 45.00
Paneled Finetooth, Goblet 120.00
Paneled Grape Band, Creamer 60.00
Paneled Holly, Tumbler, Blue Opalescent 145.00
Paneled Sagebrush, Goblet 50.00
Paneled Smocking, Wine 20.00
Parrot & Fan, Goblet 22.00
Pavonia, Butter, Cover, Oak Leaf Etch 55.00
Peacock Feathers, Bowl, Shallow, 9 1/2 In. 50.00
Peacock Feathers, Mustard, Cover . . . . .70.00 to 130.00
Peacock's Eye pattern is listed here as Peacock Feathers.
Pennsylvania, see also the related pattern Hand.
Pennsylvania, Toothpick 29.00
Pheasant, Frosted, Dish, Cover, 8 1/2 x 7 1/2 In. 60.00
Philadelphia Centennial, Goblet 20.00
Pillar, Celery Vase, Scalloped Rim, 12 In. 358.00
Pillar, Custard Cup, Handle, 8 Ribs, Footed, 2 7/8 x 2 5/8 In. 70.00
Pinafore pattern is listed here as Actress.
Pineapple & Gothic Arch, Dish, Rectangular, 1 1/2 x 9 In. 90.00
Pittsburgh Centennial, Goblet 85.00
Pleat & Panel, Compote, Cover, 8 In. 40.00
Polar Bear, Goblet . . . . .100.00 to 130.00
Polka Dot, Cheese Dish, Cover, Amber, 6 7/8 x 5 5/8 x 4 3/4 In. 100.00
Portland, Wine 20.00
Portland With Diamond Point Band pattern is listed here as Banded Portland.
Powder & Shot, Eggcup 75.00
Powder & Shot, Goblet 50.00
Prayer Rug pattern is listed here as Horseshoe.
Princess Feather Medallion, Bowl, 2 x 7 1/4 In. 10.00
Prism, Salt, Cover, Master, 4 1/2 x 2 3/4 In. 110.00
Prism & Crescent, Goblet 130.00
Profile & Sprig, Mug, Blue Opalescent, Child's, 3 1/4 x 3 1/8 In. 20.00
Psyche & Cupid, Bowl, Cover, 10 x 5 In. 40.00

Pressed Glass,
Ribbon Candy

Pressed Glass,
Rose in Snow

Pressed Glass,
Sandwich Vine

Psyche & Cupid, Butter Dish, 8 x 6 1/2 In. 45.00
Psyche & Cupid, Creamer 50.00
Reverse Torpedo pattern is listed here as Diamond & Bull's-Eye Band.
Rhode Island, Goblet, 5 3/4 In. 350.00
Rhode Island, Goblet, 6 1/4 In. 600.00
Ribbed Grape, Butter, Cover, Acorn Finial, 6 x 5 In. 150.00
Ribbed Ivy, Compote, Domed Foot, 5 1/8 x 8 In. 70.00
Ribbed Ivy, Pitcher, Water, 9 In. 275.00
Ribbon Candy, Pitcher, Milk 20.00
Ribbon Candy, Relish 14.00
Rising Sun, Wine 25.00
Rock Of Ages, Bread Plate, Milk Glass Insert, 9 x 13 In. 160.00
Roman Key, Bowl, 9 In. 50.00
Rose In Snow, Creamer 40.00
Rose In Snow, Goblet, Blue 25.00
Rose In Snow, Relish 20.00
Rose Sprig, Celery Vase, Vaseline, 8 In. 160.00
Rose Sprig, Pitcher, Vaseline, 8 In. 160.00
Ruby Thumbprint, see also the related pattern King's Crown.
Ruby Thumbprint, Berry Set, Boat Shape, 5 Piece 175.00
Sandwich Ivy, Celery Vase, 8 1/2 x 4 1/2 In. 90.00
Sandwich Star, Oil Lamp, Pair 604.00
Sandwich Vine, Goblet, Gold Trim, Footed, 6 1/4 In. 16500.00
Sawtooth, Compote, 6 Panels, 8 x 6 In. 100.00
Scroll With Flowers, Pitcher 75.00
Seneca Loop, Decanter, Stopper, 12 3/4 In., 1 Qt. 50.00
Sheaf & Diamond, Compote, Vaseline Glass 165.00
Shell, Creamer 55.00
Shell & Tassel, Creamer 50.00
Shield & Anchor, Goblet 60.00
Snail, Bowl, Cover, 8 x 7 7/8 In. 70.00
Snail, Cake Stand, 4 3/4 x 10 In. 120.00
Snail, Compote, Cover, 11 1/2 x 7 In. 90.00
Snail, Goblet 150.00
Spanish Coin pattern is listed here as Columbian Coin.
Spooner, Moon & Star, Vaseline Glass 59.00
Square Fuchsia, Mug, Handle 30.00
Squirrel, Goblet 725.00
Star & Punty pattern is listed here as Moon & Star.
Star Band pattern is listed here as Bosworth.
Stars & Bars, Cruet, Stopper 35.00
Stippled Chain, Creamer 32.00
Stippled Dahlia pattern is listed here as Square Fuchsia.
Stippled Forget-Me-Not, Pitcher 49.00
Stippled Paneled Flower pattern is listed here as Maine.
Stork, Goblet, Etched 30.00
Stork Looking At The Moon pattern is listed here as Ostrich Looking At The Moon.

Strawberry & Cable, Goblet 45.00
Strawberry & Currant, Mug, Child's, 3 7/8 x 3 1/2 In. 45.00
Sunk Daisy, Wine 23.00
Sunrise pattern is listed here as Rising Sun.
Swan, Goblet, Amber 50.00
Swan, Goblet, Blue 110.00
Swan, Mug, Ring Handle, Amber Opalescent, Child's, 3 1/2 In. 110.00
Swimming Swan, Amber Opalescent, Child's, 3 5/8 x 3 3/8 In. 130.00
Tackle Block, Goblet 40.00
Teardrop pattern is listed here as Teardrop & Thumbprint.
Teardrop & Tassel, Pitcher, Water, Cobalt Blue, 8 3/4 In. 100.00
Teardrop & Thumbprint, Creamer 50.00
Tennessee, Compote, 6 x 7 1/2 In. 20.00
Texas, Cake Stand, 6 x 9 In. 100.00
Texas, Cruet, Stopper 120.00
Texas, Wine, 4 1/8 In. 100.00
Thousand Eye, Spooner, Amber 35.00
Thousand Eye, Spooner, Blue, Knopped Stem 45.00
Three Face, Champagne, 5 1/2 x 2 3/4 In. 60.00
Three Face, Salt, Vaseline Glass, 1 5/8 x 1/2 In., Pair 25.00
Three Graces, see the related pattern Three Face.
Three Panel, Creamer, Blue 40.00
Three Panel, Sugar, Cover, Vaseline 45.00
Three Printie, Vase, Hexagonal Knop Stem, Footed, 9 In. 80.00
Three Sisters pattern is listed here as Three Face.
Thrush & Apple Blossom, Goblet 170.00
Thrush & Apple Blossom, Tumbler, Water, Blue-Green 70.00
Thumbprint, Cake Stand, 7 3/4 In. 170.00
Thumbprint, Celery Vase, Paneled Stepped Stem, 10 1/4 In. 150.00
Thumbprint, Decanter, 11 In. 70.00
Thumbprint, Tumbler, Footed, 5 x 3 In. 50.00
Thumbprint, Tumbler, Footed, Handle, 3 1/2 x 3 In. 40.00
Thumbprint Block, Celery Vase, Vaseline Glass, 9 1/2 In. 374.00
Tiny Finecut, Wine 23.00
Torpedo, Cake Stand, 6 1/4 x 9 1/4 In. 80.00
Torpedo, Pitcher, Milk, 8 1/4 In. 30.00
Torpedo, Syrup, Tin Cover 100.00
Tree Of Life, Compote, 4 3/4 x 9 In., Pair 140.00
Two Panel, Platter 29.00
U.S. Coin, Bread Tray, 10 x 7 In. 190.00
Vernon Honeycomb, Celery Vase, 10 In. 50.00
Victoria, Bowl, Footed, Domed Foot, 7 1/4 x 10 1/4 In. 40.00
Waffle, Creamer, Applied Crimped Handle, 6 3/4 In. 60.00
Waffle & Thumbprint, Claret, 4 1/2 In. 150.00
Waffle & Thumbprint, Compote, Hexagonal Stem, 8 1/2 x 9 In. 60.00
Wedding Ring, Champagne, 5 1/4 In. 160.00
Westward Ho, Compote, Cover, 4 3/4 x 10 1/2 In. 60.00
Westward Ho, Compote, Cover, 6 x 9 1/2 In. 110.00

Pressed Glass,
Thumbprint

Pressed Glass,
Tree of Life

Pressed Glass,
Westward Ho

Westward Ho, Compote, Cover, 7 x 4 1/2 x 10 In.	175.00
Westward Ho, Compote, Cover, 7 x 7 1/4 x 12 1/2 In.	350.00
Westward Ho, Compote, Cover, 9 x 9 1/4 In.	1350.00
Westward Ho, Compote, Cover, Oval, 5 1/2 x 8 3/4 x 11 1/2 In.	175.00
Westward Ho, Dish, Pickle, Deer In Center, Deer Handles, 5 x 10 In.	150.00
Westward Ho, Goblet	90.00
Westward Ho, Marmalade, Cover, 3 1/2 x 7 1/2 In.	650.00
Westward Ho, Pitcher, Milk, 7 5/8 x 4 1/8 In.	750.00
Westward Ho, Pitcher, Water, 9 1/2 In.	200.00
Wild Rose With Bowknot, Butter, Cover, Green	170.00
Wildflower, Cordial, Amber	45.00
Willow Oak, Creamer	20.00
Wisconsin, Cake Stand, 5 x 8 1/2 In.	80.00
Wreath & Shell, Spooner, Vaseline Opalescent	85.00
Wyoming, Cake Stand, 4 x 9 In.	80.00
Wyoming, Pitcher, Water, 9 1/2 In.	120.00
Wyoming, Wine, 4 In.	150.00
Zippered Diamond Star, Wine	22.00

PRINT, in this listing, means any of many printed images produced on paper by one of the more common methods, such as lithography. The prints listed here are of interest primarily to the antiques collector, not the fine arts collector. Many of these prints were originally part of books. Other prints will be found in the Advertising, Currier & Ives, Movie, and Poster categories.

Ackroyd, Norman, Cawdrey Old Hall, Signed, 1985, 23 1/2 x 34 7/8 In.	138.00
Aldin, Cecil, Drawn Blank, Hunters On Horseback Pass The Fox & Hounds Inn, 40 In.	1760.00
Aldin, Cecil, Fallowfield Hunt, Death, Large Gathering Of Hunters, Signed, 26 In.	275.00
Aldin, Cecil, Whimsical Characters, Animals Dressed In Tennis Attire, Signed, 20 1/4 In.	660.00

Audubon bird prints were originally issued as part of books printed from 1826 to 1854. They were issued in two sizes, 26 1/2 inches by 39 1/2 inches and 11 inches by 7 inches. The quadrupeds were issued in 28-by-22-inch prints. Later editions of the Audubon books were done in many sizes, and reprints of the books in the original size were also made. The bird pictures have been so popular they have been copied in myriad sizes by both old and new printing methods. This list includes originals and later copies because Audubon prints of all ages are sold in antiques shops.

J.W.Audubon

Audubon, American Coot, Hand Colored, Frame, 1830, 16 1/2 x 25 In.	6037.00
Audubon, American Goldfinch, R. Havell, 1830, 38 x 25 7/8 In.	7800.00
Audubon, Arctic Yager, Frame, R. Havell, 1835, 38 5/8 x 25 1/8 In.	4800.00
Audubon, Arkansas Flycatcher, Swallow-Tailed Flycatcher, R. Havell, 1837, 38 In.	3300.00
Audubon, Belted Kingfisher, J. Bien, 1860, 39 1/8 x 24 5/8 In.	1800.00
Audubon, Black Vulture, R. Havell, 1831, 25 5/8 x 37 1/2 In.	3600.00
Audubon, Black-Backed Gull, R. Havell, 1835, 37 3/4 x 24 3/4 In.	3300.00
Audubon, Black-Bellied Plover, Frame, 1830, 17 1/2 x 23 In.	4890.00
Audubon, Black-Winged Hawk, No. 71, 1837, 38 x 25 In.	1870.00
Audubon, Blue-Winged Teal, Frame, R. Havell, 1836, 18 3/4 x 23 5/8 In.	6600.00
Audubon, Booby Gannet, On Branch, R. Havell, 1834, 37 3/8 x 25 3/8 In.	5700.00
Audubon, Dusky Albatross, R. Havell, 1838, 25 5/8 x 38 In.	1680.00
Audubon, Gold-Winged Woodpecker, Frame, R. Havell, 1828, 38 5/8 x 26 In.	7800.00
Audubon, Goshawk, On Branches, R. Havell, 1836, 37 5/8 x 25 3/8 In.	7800.00
Audubon, Great Footed Hawk, Frame, R. Havell, 1832, 25 x 37 In.	5400.00
Audubon, Hooded Merganser, Male & Female, Hand Colored, Frame, 1830, 22 x 28 In.	8900.00
Audubon, Kildeer Plover, R. Havell, 1834, 25 1/2 x 38 1/8 In.	1800.00
Audubon, Labrador Falcon, Frame, R. Havell, 1834, 38 1/4 x 25 1/8 In.	2400.00
Audubon, Purple Gallinule, Male, Spring Plumage, Frame, 1830, 16 x 24 1/2 In.	4300.00
Audubon, Red Texan Wolf, J.T. Bowen, 1845, 21 7/8 x 27 7/8 In.	3600.00
Audubon, Sanderling, R. Havell, 1834, 25 5/8 x 38 1/8 In.	960.00
Audubon, Tell-Tale Godwit, Frame, 1830, 18 x 24 In.	3740.00
Audubon, Yellow-Billed Magpie, Stellar Jay, Frame, R. Havell, 1837, 38 x 25 In.	5100.00
Boilly, Louis Leopold, Osages, France, Signed, 1827, 13 5/8 x 10 In.	230.00

If you want to preserve a poster, have it framed under glass with acid-free mounting, or roll and tie it loosely for safe storage. Plexiglas sheets filter out ultraviolet light and may be substituted for glass in a frame.

Print, Guttman, Lorelei,
Matted, Frame, 18 x 14 In.

Booth, J., Portuguese, Alcantara, Spanish Heavy Horse, Frame, 25 x 19 In., Pair 355.00
Burr, George Elbert, Home Of The Winds, Estes Park, Col., Signed, 5 x 6 7/8 In., 3 Piece 287.00
Butterfly, Hand Colored, Walnut Frame, Liner, Matte, 10 5/8 x 8 1/4 In., 6 Piece 220.00
Castex, Collection D'Antiques, Thebes, Karnak, 23 1/2 x 17 In. & 17 x 23 In., Pair 345.00
Chinese School, Study Of Persimmon, 13 1/2 x 17 3/4 In. 800.00
Chinese School, Two Butterflies On Pineapple Plant, 15 1/8 x 11 7/8 In. 1955.00
Currier, American Country Life Pleasures Of Winter, 20 x 26 In. 2015.00
Currier, Declaration, Ogee Frame, 13 x 9 In. 70.00
Currier, James Buchanan, 13 x 9 In. 45.00
Currier, Marriage Morning, Marriage Evening, Walnut Frame, 22 3/4 x 18 1/2 In., Pair .. 300.00
Currier, U.S. Frigate Cumberland, 54 Guns, Frame, 15 1/4 x 19 In. 275.00
Dawson, Montague, The Smoke Of Battle, Pirates Cave, Sea Witch, 24 x 30 In., 3 Piece .. 520.00
Ehret, Georg Dionysius, Hyacinthus XXIII, 13 1/16 x 9 In. 520.00
Endicott & Co., Pub., Gettysburg Battle-Field, Lithograph, 20 7/8 x 36 1/8 In. 575.00
Equestrian Dressage, Le Grand, Le Sincere, Colored, Frame, 10 1/4 x 13 3/8 In., Pair ... 220.00
Erte, Russian Fantasy, Signed, Numbered, 18 x 13 1/8 In. 345.00
Fox, R. Atkinson, Glories Of Autumn 100.00
Fox, R. Atkinson, Nature's Grandeur, 14 x 22 In. 116.00
Fox, R. Atkinson, Russet Gems, 9 x 2 In. 145.00
Fox, R. Atkinson, Shower Of Daisies 195.00
Fox, R. Atkinson, Sunset Dreams 120.00
Ginzburg, Yankel, Lovers, Signed, America, 26 3/4 x 21 1/8 In. 210.00
Gruber, Franz Xavier, White Hyacinth, 14 5/8 x 10 1/8 In. 575.00
Gutmann, Bessie Pease, Christmas Eve 525.00
Gutmann, Bessie Pease, Lantern Bearers 550.00
Guttman, Lorelei, Matted, Frame, 18 x 14 In. ....*Illus* 1320.00
H. Passiers, Arts & Crafts, Dutch Women Carrying Pail Yokes, Frame, 14 1/2 x 17 In. ... 259.00
Hartung, Hans, Signed, 1953, 9 3/8 x 11 3/4 In. 126.00
Heap, George, East Prospect Of The City Of Philadelphia, 19 1/2 x 37 In. 1210.00
Hoover, Joseph, President Lincoln & His Family, 1866, 18 1/8 x 24 1/2 In. 195.00

Icart prints were made by Louis Icart, who worked in Paris from 1907 as an employee of a postcard company. He then started printing magazines and fashion brochures. About 1910 he created a series of etchings of fashionably dressed women and he continued to make similar etchings until he died in 1950. He is well known as a printmaker, painter, and illustrator. Original etchings are much more expensive than the latter photographic copies.

Icart, Awakening, Signed, Numbered, 1925, 15 5/8 x 15 5/8 In. 630.00
Icart, Beautiful Woman With Doves, Signed, Matte, Frame, 1930, 24 x 17 In. 1725.00
Icart, Colombe Blessee, Signed, 1929, 25 1/2 x 18 3/8 In. 520.00
Icart, Duo, Signed, 1929, 29 1/2 x 20 1/2 In. 680.00
Icart, Lady Of The Camelias, Signed, 1927, 17 x 21 1/4 In. ....860.00 to 920.00
Icart, Manon, Signed, Windmill Blindstamp, 1927, 21 1/4 x 14 In. 800.00
Icart, Retiring, Signed, Number, 1925, 15 5/8 x 15 5/8 In. 690.00
Icart, Sappho, Signed, Frame, 25 1/4 x 29 1/4 In. 1840.00
Icart, Sleeping Beauty, 1927, 15 1/2 x 19 3/8 In. 800.00
Icart, Souvenir Pour Madeline Pratt, Signed, 20 1/4 x 13 3/8 In. 615.00

Icart, Tosca, Signed, 1928, 26 x 17 1/4 In. 890.00
Indian School, Hibiscus With Bird, 14 3/4 x 9 1/2 In. 1325.00
Jacoulet, Chinese Jade, 1940, 15 1/2 x 11 7/8 In. 375.00
Jacoulet, Pearls, Mandchoukuo, Peach Seal, Woodcut, 1950, 15 1/2 x 11 7/8 In. 546.00

Japanese woodblock prints are listed as follows: Print, Japanese, name
of artist, title or description, type, and size. Dealers use the following
terms: Tate-e is a vertical composition. Yoko-e is a horizontal composition. The words Aiban (13 by 9 inches), Chuban (10 by 7 1/2 inches),
Hosoban (13 by 6 inches), Oban (15 by 10 inches), and Koban (7 by 4
inches) denote size. Modern versions of some of these prints have been
made.

Japanese, Hiroshi, Yoshida, Sarusaw Pond, Temple, Signed, Frame, 15 1/4 x 10 1/4 In. . . 460.00
Japanese, Hiroshige, 2 Lake Scenes, 14 1/2 x 9 3/4 & 14 x 10 In., Pair 800.00
Japanese, Hiroshige, 2 Lake Scenes, Shokoku, 14 1/2 x 9 3/4 & 14 x 10 In., Pair 800.00
Japanese, Hiroshige, 2 Stations - Coastal Scenes, 14 1/4 x 9 1/2 x 10 In. 345.00
Japanese, Hiroshige, Shono, Travelers Climb A Hill In The Rain, 1832 . . . . 402.00
Japanese, Hiroshige, Station 16 - Night Snow, 10 1/4 x 15 1/4 In. 69.00
Japanese, Hiroshige, Station 47 - Clear Weather After A Snow, 10 x 15 In. 69.00
Japanese, Hiroshige, Sudden Shower, At Shin-Ohashi Bridge, Atake, 14 x 10 In. 69.00
Japanese, Kiyoshi, Saito, Winter In Aizu, Color, Pencil, Signed, 10 1/4 x 15 3/8 In. 805.00 to 862.00
Japanese, Oiran Utagawa Kunisada, Yoshiwara Geisha & Young Girls, 14 1/2 x 10 1/8 In. 550.00
Japanese, Toyamagahara, Winter Moon, Oban, Signed, Japan, 14 1/4 x 9 1/2 In. 230.00
Japanese, Toyokuni, Interior, Figures, Oban, Triptych, Signed, 14 1/2 x 9 1/2 In. 259.00
Japanese, Utagawa Kuniyoshi, An Artist & His Inspiration, 14 3/8 x 9 7/8 In. 90.00
Japanese, Utagawa Kuniyoshi, Kamata Matahachi Mushae, 15 x 10 1/2 In. 920.00
Japanese, Utagawa, Kunisada, Autumn Moon, 14 x 9 1/2 In. 90.00
Japanese, Utagawa, Kunisada, Kabuki Actor Holding A Suzuri Bako, 14 x 10 In. 69.00
Japanese, Utagawa, Kunisada, Kabuki Actor Playing Role Of Demura Shinbei, 14 In. . . . 145.00
Japanese, Utagawa, Kuniyoshi, Tales Of The Genji, 14 x 9 3/4 In. 170.00
Judge Magazine, Knight & Dragon, April 14, 1929, 10 x 13 1/2 In. 14300.00
Kasimir, Luigi, Oestrich Rhineland, Austria, Signed, 11 3/4 x 10 5/8 In. 290.00
Kasimir, Luigi, West Point, Signed, 14 1/8 x 17 5/8 In. 430.00
Kasimir, Robert, Montmartre, Paris, Signed, 17 1/4 x 13 1/8 In. 290.00
Kasimir-Hoernes, Tanna, Hirschhorn, Austria, Signed, 9 3/8 x 12 In. 260.00
Kelly, Thomas, American Farmyard Winter, 19th Century, 21 1/4 x 27 1/4 In. 115.00
Koning, Elizabeth Johanna, Bromelia Iridifolia, 18 5/8 x 14 1/8 In. 4240.00
Martin, Mrs. G., Clematis, 14 x 11 1/4 In. 1552.00
Martin, Mrs. G., Rhododendron, 9 5/8 x 7 1/8 In. 833.00
Midsummer Meet Readville, Sweet Marie, Tiverton March, 19 1/2 x 25 1/2 In. 260.00
Munman, Morning Glories, Arts & Crafts, Signed, Mat, Frame, 15 1/2 x 11 1/2 In. 85.00

Nutting prints are now popular with collectors. Wallace Nutting is
known for his pictures, furniture, and books. Nutting *prints* are actually hand-colored photographs issued from 1900 to 1941. There are   *Wallace Nutting*
over 10,000 different titles. Wallace Nutting furniture is listed in the
Furniture category.

Nutting, Bethel Birches, Label, 9 x 11 In. 100.00
Nutting, Breakfast Hour, Grazing Sheep & Lambs, 9 x 14 In. 310.00
Nutting, Call For More, Young Girl Eating, Mother In Chair Sewing, 16 x 20 In. 375.00
Nutting, Clustered Roses, Irish Thatched Roof Cottage, 16 x 20 In. 520.00
Nutting, Come Into The Garden, 16 x 20 In. 380.00
Nutting, Dog-On-It, 8 Puppies, Frame . . . . *Illus* 3960.00
Nutting, Down On The Cape, Cape Cod Scene, Rail Fence, 12 x 15 In. 900.00
Nutting, Fleur-De-Lis & Spirea, In Glass Vase, 15 x 12 In. 1100.00
Nutting, Grandmother's Sheffield, Birch Lined Roadway, 1917, 3 7/8 & 3 1/8 In., Pair . . . 200.00
Nutting, Memory Of Childhood, Signed, 4 1/8 x 6 1/8 In. 140.00
Nutting, Oak & Resurrection Fern, 13 x 16 In. 80.00
Nutting, Penzance . . . . *Illus* 1485.00
Nutting, Restless Deep, Waves Crashing Rocks On Maine Shoreline, 9 x 15 In. 250.00
Nutting, Rheinstein, Stone Castle On Mountain, 12 x 15 In. 2850.00
Nutting, Royal Worcester Vase, Bouquet Of Flowers, 13 x 16 In. 220.00
Nutting, Theater At Athens, Greek Scene, Hillside Ruins, 16 x 20 In. 1550.00

Print, Nutting, Dog-On-It, 8 Puppies, Frame

Print, Nutting, Penzance

Nutting, Way It Begins, Woman Playing Piano, Man, 11 x 14 In. 230.00
Nutting, Yard Of Dutchmen, 14 Figures, Around Automobile, 11 x 14 In. 2300.00

Parrish prints are wanted by collectors. Maxfield Frederick Parrish was an illustrator who lived from 1870 to 1966. He is best known as a designer of magazine covers, posters, calendars, and advertisements.

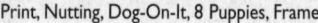

Parrish, Air Castles, 1904, 12 x 16 In. 600.00
Parrish, Cadmus Sowing The Dragon's Teeth, 1909, 11 x 13 In. 600.00
Parrish, Canyon, 1924, 11 x 14 In. 600.00
Parrish, Cleopatra, Frame, 28 x 32 In. 3080.00
Parrish, Contentment, 1928, 7 x 10 In. 500.00
Parrish, Dawn, 1918, 13 1/4 x 16 3/4 In. 3000.00
Parrish, Daybreak, 1922, 12 x 20 In. 300.00
Parrish, Daybreak, Hunt Farm, 23 x 35 In. 1815.00
Parrish, Dreaming, 1928, 18 x 30 In. 3000.00
Parrish, Enchantment, 1926, 14 x 22 In. 2000.00
Parrish, Evening Shadows, 1940, 13 3/4 x 17 1/2 In. 600.00
Parrish, Fly Away Horse, 1904, 7 x 9 In. 200.00
Parrish, Garden Of Allah, 18 x 22 In. 300.00
Parrish, Garden Of Allah, Carved Corner Frame, 15 x 30 In. 770.00
Parrish, Girl On A Surfboard, 1930, 12 x 16 1/2 In. 150.00
Parrish, Golden Hours, 1929, 24 x 16 In. 2000.00
Parrish, King & The Chancellor, 1925, 11 3/4 x 9 1/2 In. 200.00
Parrish, Knave Of Hearts, 1925, 11 x 12 1/2 In. 150.00
Parrish, Lute Players, 23 x 35 In. 3420.00
Parrish, Romance, Frame, 14 x 22 In. 1000.00
Parrish, Search For The Singing Tree, 1906 .... 250.00
Parrish, Showers Of Fragrance, 1912, 11 x 8 1/2 In. 350.00
Parrish, The Page, 1925, 10 1/2 x 13 In. 300.00
Parrish, Twilight Landscape, Figures, Photomechanical, 18 x 29 In. 288.00
Parrish, Wild Geese, 1924, 16 1/2 x 12 In. 365.00
Redoute, Pierre Joseph, Calville Blanc, 10 3/4 x 8 1/2 In. 750.00
Redoute, Pierre Joseph, Narcissus, 10 13/16 x 8 1/2 In. 750.00
Redoute, Pierre Joseph, Oreilles D'ours, 11 x 8 1/2 In. 980.00
Redoute, Pierre Joseph, Picridium Ligulatium, 21 5/16 x 14 In. 230.00
Redoute, Pierre Joseph, Prune Royale, 10 3/4 x 8 1/2 In. 345.00
Redoute, Pierre Joseph, Tulipa Gesneriana, 20 3/16 x 13 3/8 In. 3450.00
Rios, Susan, After Breakfast, Signed, 27 x 21 1/4 In. 105.00
Soper, Eileen Alice, The Hurt Paw, Signed, 4 7/8 x 7 7/8 In. 126.00
Stewart, English Hunting Scene, Mat, Red Frame, Liner, 17 x 32 In. 95.00
Taylor, Prentiss, Plant Study, Signed, 17 x 10 1/4 In. 60.00
Thebes, Karnak, France, 19th Century, Signed, 21 x 41 1/4 In. 195.00
Thornton, Dr. Robert J., Cerces & Cupid Honoring Bust Of Linnaeus, 20 1/4 x 14 3/4 In. 1610.00
Thornton, Dr. Robert J., Flora Dispensing Her Favors On Earth, 20 1/4 x 14 3/4 In. 600.00
Todo, Francisco Garcia, Spain, Signed, 13 x 23 1/3 In. 35.00
Turpin, Pierre-Jean-Francois, Fucus Denticulatus, 16 1/2 x 10 7/8 In. 800.00
Vertes, Marcel, Peasant & Mule, Signed, 38 1/8 x 58 1/4 In. 230.00
Wale, Samuel, Mary Queen Of Scots & Queen Anne, 1786, 11 3/4 & 8 In., Pair 69.00

Woodblock prints that are not in the Japanese tradition are listed here. Most were made in England and the United States during the Arts and Crafts period.

Woodblock, 2 Birds On Branch, Beaded Edge Frame, 12 1/4 x 8 1/8 In.	660.00
Woodblock, Arts & Crafts, Birds Flying Over Wooded Stream, Frame, 8 x 6 1/2 In.	175.00
Woodblock, Bartlett, Charles, Street Scene Of Kobe, Frame, Japan, 1916, 10 x 15 In.	1380.00
Woodblock, Baumann, Gustave, Hillside Woods, Mat, Frame, 9 1/2 x 10 1/2 In.	3450.00
Woodblock, Blake, Leo, Toward Evening, Ship Anchored, Purple Mountains, 9 In.	400.00
Woodblock, Dow, Arthur Wesley, 2 Houses On Shoreline, Oak Frame, 6 x 8 In.	800.00
Woodblock, Dow, Arthur Wesley, Colorful Array Of Clover, Mat, Frame, 6 x 5 In.	635.00
Woodblock, Dow, Arthur Wesley, Day Lily, Signed, Mat, Arts & Crafts Oak Frame, 5 In.	1955.00
Woodblock, Dow, Arthur Wesley, Houses Along Shoreline, Oak Frame, 6 x 4 In.	2415.00
Woodblock, Dow, Arthur Wesley, Rust Colored Flowers, Mat, Frame, 2 x 5 1/2 In.	800.00
Woodblock, Dow, Arthur Wesley, Stylized Landscapes, Orange On Beige, 1905, 3 x 3 In.	340.00
Woodblock, Dow, Arthur Wesley, Tree Design, Green Ground, Mat, Frame, 2 x 5 In.	345.00
Woodblock, Escher, M.C., Frog Scene, Mahogany, 4 x 3 1/2 In.	490.00
Woodblock, Frigate Constitution, 7 x 7 1/4 In.	400.00
Woodblock, Gearhart, Francis, Heart Of The Canyon, Mat, Frame, Signed, 10 x 11 In.	2990.00
Woodblock, Hall, Thorpe, Nasturtiums In Center, Black Ground, Signed, 9 x 12 In.	750.00
Woodblock, Harris, Sam Hyde, Landscape, White Trees, Orange Leaves, Oak Frame, 8 In.	460.00
Woodblock, Hyde, Helen, 2 Children, Either Side Of Dragon, 1914, 7 x 6 In.	430.00
Woodblock, Hyde, Helen, 3 Asian Girls, Signed, Mat, Frame, 1914, 5 x 13 In.	750.00
Woodblock, Hyde, Helen, A Rainy Night, 2 Asian Women Walking In Rain, 5 x 11 In.	575.00
Woodblock, Hyde, Helen, Child Presenting Vase To Woman, 1912, 8 1/2 x 19 In.	1210.00
Woodblock, Hyde, Helen, Young Girl Examining Flowers, Signed, 6 1/2 x 11 In.	800.00
Woodblock, Kirkpatrick, Ethel, Sea Scene, Several Boats At Sea, Signed, 4 1/2 x 6 In.	335.00
Woodblock, Kollwitz, Kathe, Gesenkter Frauenkopf, Germany, Signed, 15 x 12 1/2 In.	460.00
Woodblock, Lindenmuth, Tod, Moonlight On Cape Cod, White House, Tree, 9 x 7 In.	800.00
Woodblock, Lord, Elyse, 2 Asian Women Along River's Edge, Signed, 8 3/4 In.	230.00
Woodblock, Lord, Elyse, Asian Female With Flowering Trees, Matted, Frame, 9 x 17 In.	575.00
Woodblock, Lum, Bertha, 5 Asian Women, 2 Gentlemen, Butterflies, Frame, 10 x 15 In.	1320.00
Woodblock, Lum, Bertha, Lotus Goddesses, Signed, 36 x 19 In.	2090.00
Woodblock, Lum, Bertha, Several Birds Amidst Foliage, Signed, 1920, 10 x 16 In.	1090.00
Woodblock, Miller, Lillian, Asian Image On Umbrella, Signed, 1928, 14 x 9 1/2 In.	3740.00
Woodblock, Murphy, Gladys W., Lighthouse Scene, Signed, 5 x 6 In.	520.00
Woodblock, Norton, Elizabeth, Winding Road, Trees Scene, Signed, 9 x 7 In.	800.00
Woodblock, Ocean, Mountain Scenes, Mat, Signed, Arts & Crafts Frame, 9 x 11 In., Pair	400.00
Woodblock, Patterson, Margaret, City Scene, Arts & Crafts Oak Frame, Signed, 11 In.	290.00
Woodblock, Pittman, Hobsen, The Sideboard, Compote & Fruit, Signed, 10 1/2 x 8 1/4 In.	220.00
Woodblock, Rotky, Carl, Landscape, Mountain Range, Signed, Oak Frame, 8 x 11 In.	600.00
Woodblock, Sadahide, Oye Mountains With His Ueva Kings, 14 1/4 x 10 In.	402.00
Woodblock, Sandzen, Birger, A Mountain Lake, Trees Along Body Of Water, 5 x 6 In.	400.00
Woodblock, Thompson, H.E., Treetop Hillside With Birds Soaring, Signed, 5 x 4 In.	490.00
Woodblock, Toyonari, Parrot, Mother-Of-Pearl Ground, c.1920, 15 x 10 In.	1650.00
Woodblock, Whittemore, Margaret, Arts & Crafts Style, Tree, Matted, Frame	315.00
Woodcut, Feininger, Lyonel Charles, Virtuoso, Matted, Frame, 6 1/2 x 8 1/8 In.	2071.00
Woodcut, Leighton, Clare, Landing, Signed, 9 x 12 3/4 In.	1520.00
Wunderlich, Paul, Elles, Signed, Germany, 25 3/4 x 19 3/4 In.	230.00
Yard Long, Puppies & Kittens, Tug Of War, Frame	280.00

PURINTON POTTERY COMPANY was incorporated in Wellsville, Ohio, in 1936. The company moved to Shippenville, Pennsylvania, in 1941 and made a variety of hand-painted ceramic wares. By the 1950s Purinton was making dinnerware, souvenirs, cookie jars, and florist wares. The pottery closed in 1959.

Apple, Candy Dish, Ring Handle	90.00
Apple, Chop Plate, Scalloped Border, 12 In.	58.00
Apple, Cookie Jar, Wood Cover, Square, 9 1/2 In.	150.00
Apple, Cruet, Oil	80.00
Apple, Jug, Dutch, 2 Pt.	30.00
Apple, Jug, Kent, 1 Pt., 4 1/2 In.	45.00
Apple, Plate, Seaform, 6 3/4 In.	110.00
Apple, Relish, 3 Sections	40.00

Apple, Sugar, Cover, 5 In. . . . . .38.00 to 55.00
Apple, Teapot, 2 Cup 1000.00
Apple, Wall Pocket, 3 1/2 In. . . . . .80.00 to 120.00
Blue Pansy, Basket, Planter, 6 1/4 In. 50.00
Chartreuse, Cookie Jar, Oval 105.00
Chartreuse, Sugar, Individual 45.00
Crescent, Jug, Dutch, 2 Pt. . . . . .50.00 to 75.00
Crescent, Teapot, 2 Cup 90.00
Daisy, Canister, Coffee, Cobalt Blue Trim 160.00
Daisy, Canister, Flour, Cobalt Blue Trim 160.00
Daisy, Canister, Tea, Cobalt Blue Trim 60.00
Fruit, Bean Pot, 5 3/4 In. 56.00
Fruit, Canister Set, Round, 4 Piece 115.00
Fruit, Creamer, 3 In. 15.00
Fruit, Jug, Dutch, 2 Pt. 70.00
Harmony, Salt & Pepper, Jug 230.00
Heather Plaid, Bowl, Vegetable, 8 1/2 In. 10.00
Heather Plaid, Relish, 3 Sections 40.00
Intaglio, Bowl, Salad, Oval, Brown, 11 1/4 In. 20.00
Intaglio, Bowl, Vegetable, 8 x 2 In. 17.00
Intaglio, Cruet Set, 2 Piece 36.00
Intaglio, Cup, Brown 10.00
Intaglio, Gravy Boat, Brown 40.00
Intaglio, Jug, Honey, Coral, 6 1/4 In. 135.00
Intaglio, Jug, Honey, Green, 6 1/4 In. 125.00
Intaglio, Plate, Brown, 9 3/4 In. 18.00
Intaglio, Plate, Tea & Toast, Brown 15.00
Intaglio, Platter, Oval, Brown, 12 In. 22.00
Intaglio, Salt & Pepper, Range, Brown 30.00
Intaglio, Sugar, Cover, Brown 20.00
Intaglio, Tumbler, Juice, Turquoise 35.00
Maywood, Bowl, Cereal, 5 1/4 In. 3.50
Maywood, Bowl, Dessert, 4 In. 9.00
Maywood, Bowl, Vegetable, Cover, 9 In. 52.00
Maywood, Chop Plate, 12 In. 65.00
Ming Tree, Plate, 6 3/4 In. 26.00
Mountain Rose, Jug, Dutch, 2 Pt. 220.00
Mountain Rose, Planter, Basket, 6 1/4 In. 80.00
Mountain Rose, Teapot, 2 Cup 75.00
Normandy Plaid, Bowl, Vegetable, Cover, 9 In. 25.00
Normandy Plaid, Tumbler, 12 Oz. 20.00
Normandy Plaid, Wall Pocket, 3 1/2 In. 52.00
Oriental, Teapot, 2 Cup, 4 In. 35.00
Palm Tree, Salt & Pepper, Shake & Pour 76.00
Pennsylvania Dutch, Bowl, Vegetable, 8 1/2 In. 75.00
Pennsylvania Dutch, Chop Plate, 12 In. . . . . ' 160.00
Pennsylvania Dutch, Cookie Jar, Wood Cover, Square 350.00
Pennsylvania Dutch, Salt & Pepper, Jug 130.00
Pennsylvania Dutch, Sandwich Server 180.00
Petals, Chop Plate, 12 In. 215.00
Pitcher, Beverage, 6 1/4 In. 55.00
Provincial Fruit, Baking Dish, 7 In. 26.00
Provincial Fruit, Chop Plate, 12 In. 27.00
Provincial Fruit, Mug, Jug 48.00
Red Ivy, Coffeepot, 6 Cup 50.00
Red Ivy, Jug, Kent 20.00
Red Ivy, Teapot, 6 Cup 80.00
Rooster, Cookie Jar 495.00
Saraband, Bowl, Dessert, 4 In. 19.00
Saraband, Bowl, Vegetable, 8 1/2 In. 15.00
Saraband, Platter, 12 In. 35.00
Tulip & Vine, Tureen, Cover 79.00

PURSES have been recognizable since the eighteenth century, when leather and needlework purses were preferred. Beaded purses became popular in the nineteenth century, went out of style, but are again in use. Mesh purses date from the 1880s and are still being made. How to carry a handkerchief and lipstick is a problem today for every woman, including the Queen of England.

Alligator, 3 Inner Sections, Leather Lining, Hermes, 1960s, 10 1/2 x 8 1/4 In.	1840.00
Alligator, Black, Gold Plated Hardware, Leather Lining, Hermes, 1960, 10 x 8 In.	1800.00
Alligator, Box, Gold Chain, Clasp, Mayer, New York, 8 1/2 x 4 In.	64.00
Alligator, Brown Cord Edging, Cuba, 7 1/4 x 3 1/4 In.	35.00
Alligator, Brown, Ark Shape, Flap, 2 Sections, 12 x 7 In.	172.00
Alligator, Gold Plated Double Chain Handle, Saks Fifth Avenue, France, 7 1/2 x 5 In.	345.00
Alligator, Handle, Mark, Cuba, Child's, 4 1/2 x 4 1/2 In.	65.00
Alligator, Imitation, Black, c.1950, 11 x 8 In.	44.00
Alligator, Leather Lining, Brass Clasp, 14 In. Handle, c.1900, 6 x 6 In.	325.00
Armadillo, Includes Toenails, Brown Glass Eyes, 11 x 9 In.	110.00
Bamboo, Red Detail, WWII, Philippines, 1945, 9 x 13 1/2 In.	40.00
Basket, Key, Sharkskin, Leather Lined, Geometric Stitch, S.S. Cottrell, Va., 7 x 8 In.	2520.00
Basket, Nantucket, Cover, Oval, Cherry Plaque, Base, C.F. Sayle, 5 3/4 x 9 1/2 x 6 In.	575.00
Basket, Nantucket, Ivory Whale On Top	345.00
Basket Form, Nantucket, Bamboo Handle, Silver Metal, Fish Shaped Clasp, 1940s, 10 In.	57.00
Beaded, Beaded Handle, Ivory Satin Lining, Coin Purse, Mirror, Marked, Magid	120.00
Beaded, Beveled Beads, Black, White, Tan, 20 x 12 In.	45.00
Beaded, Black, Chocolate Brown Crochet, Black Beads, Tassel, Lined, 9 x 10 3/4 In.	95.00
Beaded, Black, Glass Beads, Czechoslovakia, 7 1/2 x 4 1/2 In.	45.00
Beaded, Black, Peacocks, Multicolored Jewels, Handles, 17 x 14 In.	65.00
Beaded, Blue, Gold Metal Trim, Clip Closure, Lining, Du Bonnette, c.1950, 6 x 8 1/2 In.	85.00
Beaded, Blue, Green, Black, Purple, Amber, Gold, Black Cloth Lining, 7 x 6 In.	28.00
Beaded, Box Shape, Pink, Green Flowers, Mirror, Fuji, 1940s, 4 1/2 x 4 1/2 In.	195.00
Beaded, Clutch, Oval, Off White Glass, White Satin Lining, Josef, 9 1/2 x 6 In.	78.00
Beaded, Clutch, Pastel, Ivory Moire Taffeta Lining, Josef, France, 1950s, 9 x 6 In.	70.00
Beaded, Clutch, White, Beige, Made In Japan, 1960s, 8 x 4 In.	30.00
Beaded, Cottage Scene, Leather Lining, Germany, 1920s	194.00
Beaded, Crochet, Blue, Drawstring, Lining, 10 In.	100.00
Beaded, Daffodil, Natural Wood Handle, Snap Top Clasp, Black Lining	14.00
Beaded, Deer Design, Embossed Silver Frame & Clasp, Fringe, 11 In.	365.00
Beaded, Donkey Decoration, Glass Seed Beads, Rhinestone, 13 1/2 x 16 1/2 In.	65.00
Beaded, Egyptian Design, Black, Blue, Pink, Ivory Beads, Bakelite Frame, Art Deco	495.00
Beaded, Evening, Red & Ecru Steel, Gold Beads, Tassel, Button Close, Lining, 5 x 4 In.	121.00
Beaded, Filigree Frame, White Gold Seed Beads, Sequins, Coral Pink Lining, 1930s	95.00
Beaded, Floral Pattern, Bead Fringe, Clasp, Taffeta Lining, Chain Handle, 8 x 5 In.	395.00
Beaded, Glass Seed Beads, Red, Blue, Green, Amber, Black, Neiman Marcus, 6 x 4 In.	45.00
Beaded, Glass Seed Beads, White, Taupe, Custard, Metal Zipper, Chain, 3 1/2 x 5 1/2 In.	19.00
Beaded, Gray, White, Gold Flower Design, Satin Lining, Saks Fifth Ave., 7 1/2 x 5 1/2 In.	135.00
Beaded, Jet, Metal, Drawstring, France, c.1920, 4 x 5 In.	85.00
Beaded, Little Lulu, Cartoon Figure, Square, 16 In.	20.00
Beaded, Miser's Bag, Silver Steel, Navy Blue, Looped & Braided Fringe, 2 Metal Rings	211.00
Beaded, Multicolored, Bag, Silver Frame, Link Strap, Coin Purse, 1846, 13 x 9 x 7 In.	110.00
Beaded, Navy Blue, Black Beads, Satin Lining, Drawstring, c.1900, 7 1/2 x 12 1/2 In.	135.00
Beaded, Red, Fan Shape, Red Taffeta Lining, Inside Pocket, Zipper, 1930s, 10 5/8 x 5 In.	35.00
Beaded, Rose Design, Black, Green, Red, Pink, Burgundy, White, Fringe, 6 x 9 In.	495.00
Beaded, Roses, Iris, Leaves, Vines, Brass Clasp, Display Frame, 7 x 7 In.	95.00
Beaded, Sequin, Pearl White, La Regale Ltd, Made In Hong Kong, 7 x 10 1/2 In.	100.00
Beaded, Sequin, Pink, Green, Peach, Yellow, Off-White Satin, La Regale, 8 1/2 x 4 3/4 In.	45.00
Beaded, Shoe Shape, White, Zipped, 1950s, 5 In.	45.00
Beaded, Silver Frame, Embossed Flowers, Blue, Purple, Black, c.1920, 5 1/2 x 8 x 5 In.	375.00
Beaded, Silver, White Beads, Chain, Mirror, 3 1/2 x 5 In.	54.00
Beaded, Steel, Alternating Panels Of Red & Ecru Beads, Gold Beads, Clutch, 5 x 4 In.	121.00
Beaded, Steel, Pink & Blue Beads, France, 1920s	173.00
Beaded, Tiny Love Beads, Plastic Closure, Mirror, K&G, Charlett, Paris, 6 x 4 In.	35.00
Beaded, White, Faceted, Fine Twisted Cord, Open Frame Handle, 9 1/2 x 8 1/2 In.	40.00
Beaded, White, Handmade, White Satin Lining, France	35.00

Beaded, White, Ungar, 1930s 59.00
Bicolored 18K Gold, Clutch, Front Row Of Diamonds Interior, Mirror, 7 /14 In. 1025.00
Brocade, Wooden Handles, 14 x 22 In. 25.00
Carpet, Black Ground, Multicolored, Chenille, Butterscotch Lucite Handles 45.00
Cloth, Clutch, Navy Blue, Metallic Threading, Satin Lining, 8 x 5 1/4 In. 34.00
Coin, Beaded, 2 Clowns Sitting On Box, Fringe, Silk Crochet Top, 2 1/4 x 5 In. 45.00
Coin, Beaded, Glass, Beige Satin, Gray, Clear, Pearl Accents, 5 x 4 In. 29.00
Coin, Burgundy Crepe, 4 x 3 In. 28.00
Coin, Chatelaine Chain Ring, Silver, Germany, 2 x 1 1/8 In. 135.00
Coin, Mesh, Gold, Marked, Whiting & Davis, 3 x 4 1/4 In. 65.00
Coin, Mushroom Shape, Yellow, Red, Beaded, Silver, Black, 4 x 3 1/2 In. 20.00
Coin, Plastic, Faux Pearls, Dot Decoration, Lined, Key Ring, 1950s, 3 1/2 x 4 In. 4.50
Coin, Tortoiseshell, Silver Inlaid, Hinged Cover, Rose Moire Lining, 1 x 3 x 2 1/4 In. 403.00
Crepe, Clutch, Confetti, Bobbie Jerome, 12 1/2 x 5 1/2 In. 25.00
Crochet, Beaded, Drawstring, Cranberry Glass Beads, Fringe, Flapper, 4 1/2 x 5 In. 95.00
Crochet, Black, Silver Beading, Beaded Tassel, Drawstring, Paris, 1930s 75.00
Crochet, Drawstring, Beaded Tassel, Tan, Burgundy, Gray, Mustard, Olive, 9 x 7 In. 30.00
Crochet, Flower Design, Drawstring Handle, 3 1/2 In. 35.00
Crochet, Lucite Handles, Tortoiseshell Pattern, Lining, 1940s, 16 x 12 In. 26.00
Crocodile, Box, Black, 3 Section Interior, 4 Inner Pockets, Rosenstein, 1950s, 9 1/2 In. . . . 920.00
Crocodile, Foldover Flaps, Roll Top Handle, Rope Twist Gilt Metal Clasp, Hermes, 1950s 1035.00
Crocodile, Front Flap, Goldstone Closures, Leather Interior, Lederer, 1950s, 10 1/2 In. . . . 375.00
Crocodile, Suitcase Shape, Goldtone Corners, Chain, Leather Lining, Leiber, 1990, 8 In. . 420.00
Crushed Velvet, Black, Gold Chain, 22 x 8 1/2 In. 25.00
Decoupage, Strawberries, Twisted Lucite Handle, c.1971, 11 1/2 x 9 In. 50.00
Embroidered, Beige, Black, Red, Navy Blue Top, Handle, Plastic Top, 10 x 6 1/2 In. 28.00
Embroidered, Canvas, Wool, Bargello Stitch, Diamond, 4 1/4 x 7 1/4 In. 517.00
Embroidered, Canvas, Wool, Diamond Design, Irish Stitch, 1759, 3 x 6 1/2 In. 1955.00
Embroidered, Canvas, Wool, Geometric Design, Irish Stitch, 1786, 4 x 6 In. 1380.00
Embroidered, Disco, Abstract Design, Metallic Thread, Belt Loop, 5 x 5 In. 16.00
Embroidered, Flamestitch, Wool Pin Flaps, New England, 18th Century 1250.00
Embroidered, Flower Design, Arts & Crafts, 7 x 13 In. 40.00
Epi Leather, Satchel, Outside Pocket, Padlocked Zipper, Suede Interior, L. Vuitton, 13 In. 230.00
Epi Leather, Suede Interior, Stamped Hardware, Wallet, L. Vuitton, 1990s, 12 x 11 1/2 In. 258.00
Faille, Black, Rhinestones, Metal Frame, Smocking, Guild Creations 39.00
Gold, 4 Gold Beads, 2 Compartments, Woven, 18K Yellow Gold 747.00
Gold Lame, Bow Shape Snap Clasp, Rhinestones, Satin Lining, Alier Fliere 17.00
Gold Lame, Goldtone Clasp, Cream Satin Lining, Attached Change Purse, Mirror, 1950s . 18.00
Gold Lame, Whiting & Davis, 5 x 8 x 5 In. 135.00
Inro, Ivory, 3 Sections, Foo Dog On Side, Bird & Floral On Reverse, Cord, 2 x 1 In. 112.00
Inro, Oval, Imperial Design On Nashiji Ground, Meiji Period, 4 In. 805.00
Knit, Clutch, Lucite Pull, Black, Cable Knit, Zipper Pull, Pocket, 13 1/2 In. 42.00
Knit, Cotton, Fringe, Drawstring, Rooster, Red, Black Ground, c.1970, 14 x 15 In. 35.00
Leather, Arts & Crafts Style, Clutch Coin Compartment, Geometric Design, Slide Handle 125.00
Leather, Black Pleated, Pouch, Shoulder, 3 Sections, Judith Leiber, 1970s, 12 x 8 x 4 In. . 98.00
Leather, Black, Enamel, Gilt Frame, Satin Lining, Mirror, Anton Moritz, 8 x 7 x 3 In. . . . 235.00
Leather, Brown, Short Leather Handle, Goldtone Hardware, Leather Lining, 1966, 10 In. . 230.00
Leather, Clutch, Silver, Retractable Handle, Saks Fifth Avenue, 8 x 4 1/2 In. 40.00
Leather, Design, Man, Woman, Dancing, Pyramid, Cactus, Strap, Mexico, 1950s 35.00
Leather, Hand Painted, Flowers, Butterfly 28.00
Leather, Oriental, 4 Sections, Multistrand Chain, Ivory Button, Brass Dragon, 3 x 5 In. . . 140.00
Leather, Postcard, Red Drawstring, Fringe, Coney Island, N.Y., c.1907 . . . . 40.00
Leather, Red & Navy, Shoulder Bag, Double C Logo Front, Chanel, 1980s, 6 x 5 x 2 In. . 200.00
Leather, Silver, Bell Shape, Beading, Fringe, Leaf Design, c.1900, 5 x 8 In. 225.00
Leather, Tooled, Flowers, Leaves, Strap, c.1960, 7 1/2 x 9 x 2 1/2 In. 50.00
Leather, White, Rhinestones, Buckle, Shoulder Strap, Seven Handbags, Dimitri, 12 In. . . . 55.00
Lizard, Ivory, Floral Crystal Stripe, White, Embroidered, Judith Leiber, 5 1/2 x 8 In. 2300.00
Lizard & Leather, Amethyst Clasp, Grosgrain Lining, Change Purse, Leiber, 13 In. 115.00
Lucite, Basketweave, Off White, Gold Stars, Design, 8 1/2 x 3 1/2 In. 125.00
Lucite, Carmel Brown, 9 x 4 In. 75.00
Lucite, Clear, Pearlescent, Handle, 1940s 25.00
Lucite, Clutch, Gold Glitter, Confetti, Rialto, 7 x 4 1/2 In. 195.00
Lucite, Cylinder, Confetti Decoration, Metal Feet, Vinyl Liner 110.00

Lucite, Gold, Amber, Gold Mesh Metal, 7 x 3 1/2 In. 35.00
Lucite, Hat Box Shape, Mirrored Top, Wilardy, 1950s, 8 1/2 x 9 1/2 In. 345.00
Lucite, Mother-Of-Pearl, Basketweave, Plastic Beads, Handle, 12 x 9 In. 55.00
Lucite, Pearl White, Embossed City Names, Gold, Gold Plate, 9 1/2 x 6 In. 175.00
Lucite, Pearl White, Gold Mesh Handle, Oval, 7 1/2 x 4 In. 125.00
Lucite, White, Iridescent Rhinestones, Wilardy Label, 10 x 7 1/2 x 5 1/2 In 399.00
Macrame, Burgundy Taffeta Drawstring, Bow, Red Satin, Red Ribbon, 14 In. 55.00
Mesh, 14K Gold, Cutout Floral Frame, Brocade Lining, 1900-1925, 4 1/2 x 4 In. 825.00
Mesh, 14K Gold, Floral, Geometric Design, Cabochon Blue Stone Clasp, 1920 . . . . 690.00
Mesh, 15K Yellow Gold, V Shape, Cross Over Sapphire Catch, Open Link Chain, 1908 . . 1265.00
Mesh, Blue Accents, Whiting Davis, 1920s 188.00
Mesh, Blue Design, Black Stones, Metal Frame, Chain, Germany, 5 1/2 x 4 1/4 In. 65.00
Mesh, Cream, Dark Gray, Chain Handle, Art Deco, 6 1/2 x 4 In. 100.00
Mesh, Double Face Mirror, Whiting & Davis, 7 1/2 x 5 In. 65.00
Mesh, Drawstring, Black Cord, Tassel, 18K Gold 820.00
Mesh, Enameled, Jewel Frame & Clasp, Big-Van 145.00
Mesh, Gate Top, Ivory Satin Lining, Vanity Mirror, Whiting & Davis 125.00
Mesh, German Silver, Drawstring, Link Chain, Ball Fringe Top & Bottom, 8 x 6 In. 115.00
Mesh, German Silver, Intricate Frame, Germany, c.1920, 12 1/4 x 5 In. 155.00
Mesh, Gold Tassel, Front Faceted Emeralds, Emerald Push Piece, 14K Yellow Gold 1495.00
Mesh, Gold, Mother-Of-Pearl Inlay On Frame, Whiting & Davis, Satin Coin Purse 110.00
Mesh, Gold, Rhinestones, Peach Satin Lining, Cloth, Compact, 1940s 185.00
Mesh, Goldtone, Envelope, Clasp, Fabric Lining, Pocket, Mirror, Whiting & Davis 20.00
Mesh, Harlequin, Ruby, Diamond, Acorn Terminals, 18K Gold 2645.00
Mesh, Ivory, Hot Pink & Lime Green, Silver Frame, Whiting & Davis, 7 x 4 In. 220.00
Mesh, Mandalian, Turquoise, Gold Metal, Fringe, 5 1/2 x 3 In. 175.00
Mesh, Scroll, Bellflower Design, Trace Link Chain Handle, 14K Gold 860.00
Mesh, Silver Tone, Chain Handle, Taffeta Lining, Rhinestone Clasp, Whiting & Davis . . . 95.00
Mesh, Silver, Chain, Hallmark, London, 1916, 4 1/4 x 5 1/4 x 15 1/4 In. 102.00
Mesh, Silver, Drawstring, Link Chain, Ball Fringe, Germany, Early 1900s, 8 x 6 In. 115.00
Mesh, Silver, Open Links, Engraved Frame, Chain Handle, Germany, c.1910, 6 x 3 1/2 In. 145.00
Mesh, Silver, Rhinestone Teardrop Clasp, Ivory Lining, 4 x 4 In. 35.00
Mesh, Sterling Silver, Fringe, Chain Handle, 4 x 5 In. 85.00
Mesh, Taffeta Lining, Knob Clasp, Snake Handle, Whiting & Davis, 8 x 6 1/4 In. 110.00
Mother-Of-Pearl, Carved, Leather Trimmed, Silk Lining, c.1820 . . . . 595.00
Mother-Of-Pearl, Engraved Silver Decoration, Silk Lining, c.1840 . . . . 475.00
Nylon, Basket Weave, Navy Blue, White, Zipper, Rope Strap, Gabriella, 12 x 10 In. 46.00
Obi Silk, Jadeite, Glass Clasp, Asia, 1930s 280.00
Patent Leather, Black, Gold Shoulder Chain, Colored Stones, Judith Leiber, 7 x 2 In. . . . 345.00
Patent Leather, Red, Silver Closure & Hardware, Leather Lining, Gucci, 1990s, 9 3/4 In. . 230.00
Patent Leather, Yellow, Cylinder, Steel Rings, Suede Lining, Ronay, 1960s, 8 x 5 In. 65.00
Plastic, Clear, Rhinestones In Diagonal Pattern, 8 1/2 x 8 In. 50.00
Plastic, Poodle, White, Glitzy Fifi, Child's 30.00
Plastic, Rhinestones, Rectangular, Attached Molded Handle, 4 3/4 x 7 3/4 In. 50.00
Plastic, Square, Pearlescent Sand Color Lining, Brass Cutouts, 4 x 4 x 2 In. 64.00
Satin, Black, Gold Tone Clasp, Chain Handle, 13 x 5 1/2 In. 24.00
Satin, Emerald Green, Gold Stain Lining, Coin Purse, Morris Moskowitz 35.00
Silk, Crewelwork, Butterflies, Strawberries, Cornucopia, c.1800, 5 x 4 1/2 In. 193.00
Silk, Embroidered, Clutch, Evening, George Jensen, 1950s, 10 x 5 1/4 In. 87.00
Silk Moire, Flowers, Compartments, Lined, Chain Link Handle, Art Nouveau 345.00
Snakeskin, Black, Pouch, Shoulder, Optional Chain, Judith Leiber, 1980s, 10 x 8 x 2 In. . . 316.00
Snakeskin, Camel, Brown Piping, Shoulder Bag, Judith Leiber, 1970s, 15 x 14 1/2 In. 460.00
Sterling Silver, Engraved Crest, Leather Lining, Birmingham, c.1916, 3 x 2 1/2 In. 85.00
Straw, Clutch, Beige, White, Bakelite Frame, 10 x 7 In. . . . . .28.00 to 35.00
Straw, Flowers, Peach, Orange, Vinyl Handle, 1970s, 12 3/4 x 9 1/2 In. 30.00
Suede, Black, Attached Coin Purse, Koret, 10 x 7 1/2 In. 25.00
Suede, Black, Leather Trim, Shoulder Bag, Gucci, 1980s, 12 x 11 1/2 x 4 In. 288.00
Suede, Leather, Black, Goldtone, Shoulder Strap, Trian, New York, 9 x 9 In. 45.00
Suede, Painted, Bluebird, Handle, 9 x 9 In. 60.00
Tapestry, Black, Floral, Pink, Blue, Yellow, Gold Metal Strap, Satin Lining, 7 1/2 x 5 In. . 95.00
Tapestry, Goldtone Embossed Closure, Flowers, West Germany, 6 x 5 In. 50.00
Tapestry, Mirror, Drawstring, France, 1940s, 8 1/2 x 3 3/4 In. 72.00
Tapestry, Multicolored, Lucite Top, 9 x 11 In. 45.00

Telephone, White Leather, Goldtone Frame, Anne-Marie, Paris, 1940s, 6 x 8 x 5 In. 2415.00
Velvet, Black, Embroidered, Metallic Thread, Satin Lining, Accordion Bottom, 4 x 7 In. . . 20.00
Velvet, Black, Zipper, Decorative Zipper Pull, Lining, 5 1/4 In. 15.00
Velvet, Clutch, Brown, Jeweled Buckle, Clasp, Satin Lining, Attached Coin Purse 35.00
Velvet, Red, Satin Muff, Bow, Hand Strap, 11 1/2 In. 75.00
Velveteen, Black, Bell Shape, Taffeta Bow, Rhinestone Accents, 15 x 10 1/2 In. 50.00
Velveteen, Printed, Brown Leather Shoulder Strap, Pucci, 8 x 6 In. 545.00
Vinyl, Clutch, Lucite Pull, Woven, Chocolate Brown, 8 3/4 x 15 In. 49.00
Vinyl, Little America, Cowboy, Bronco, Zipper Pouch, 1960s, 5 1/2 x 3 In. 6.00
Wallet, Embroidered Bargello, Blue Silk Lining, 17th Century, 8 x 5 3/4 In. 2500.00
Wicker, Golf Figures, Stuffed, Annie Laurie, Palm Beach, 11 x 9 3/4 In. 85.00
Wicker, Seashell Decoration, Made In Japan, 10 1/2 x 8 In. 15.00
Wood, Box, Basket Weave, Decoupage Buildings, Lucite Handle, Paper Lining, 7 x 5 In. . 16.00
Wood, Ornate Detail, Royal London Ltd, Handle, Red Lining, c.1968, 8 x 8 1/2 In. 45.00
Woven Cording, Chocolate Brown, Twisted Lucite Handles, 12 x 12 In. 45.00

QUEZAL glass was made from 1901 to 1924 by Martin Bach, Sr., in Queens, New York. Other glassware, such as Loetz, Steuben, and Tiffany, resembles this gold-colored iridescent glass. Martin Bach died in 1921. His son-in-law, Conrad Vahlsing, Jr., went to work at the Lustre Art Company about 1920 and his son, Martin Bach, Jr., worked at the Durand Art Glass division of the Vineland Flint Glass Works after 1924.

Quezal

Candlestick, King Tut, Blue Iridescent, Signed, 7 In. 1035.00
Chandelier, 5-Light, Gold, Blue, Green Leaves, Cream On White Ground, Brass, 23 In. . . 2990.00
Chandelier, 5-Light, Iridescent, Gold Threading, Lower Center Light . . . . .1400.00 to 2240.00
Compote, Blue, Gold Stem, Signed, 6 1/2 In. 1265.00
Cup & Saucer, Gold, Purple Highlights, Signed, 2 1/2 In. 950.00
Lamp, Figural, Man With Outstretched Arms Holding Candles, Bronze, 19 In. 1120.00
Lamp, Gold, Green, Pulled Feathers, Opalescent, Globular, Signed, 14 5/8 In. 345.00
Lamp, White Pulled Feathers, Bronze Base, 15 In., Pair 3360.00
Salt, Pink Iridescent, Ruffled Edge, Signed, 1 1/4 x 1 1/2 In. 260.00
Shade, 10 Ribs, Pink Iridescent, 6 In., Pair 410.00
Shade, 16 Ribs, Gold Iridescent, 5 1/4 In. 330.00
Shade, Blue Pulled Feather On White Iridescent, Gold Lining, Signed, 6 In. 276.00
Shade, Diamond-Quilted, Scalloped Rim, 5 1/2 In. 190.00
Shade, Pulled Feathers, Green, Signed, 4 In. 345.00
Shade, Pulled Feathers, Green, White Iridescent, Gold Interior, Gold Trim, 5 In. 250.00
Shade, Ribbed, Gold Iridescent, Signed, 5 x 2 1/4 In., Pair 375.00
Shade, Trumpet Shape, Gold Iridescent, 5 1/8 In. 110.00
Vase, 3 Large Flowers With Vines, Vertical Ribbed, Watermelon Green, Signed, 12 In. . . . 6325.00
Vase, Allover Purple Iridescent, Tapered, Signed, 1 1/4 In. 575.00
Vase, Blue Iridescent, Baluster, Signed, 7 In. 805.00
Vase, Blue Iridescent, Bulbous, Engraved Mark, 5 1/2 In. 635.00
Vase, Blue Iridescent, Ruffled Edge, Footed, Signed, 10 In. 2185.00
Vase, Butterfly, Blue Iridescent, Signed, 6 3/4 x 3 1/2 In. 805.00
Vase, Flower Shape, Pulled Feathers, Green, Stretched Gold Interior, 5 1/4 x 5 3/4 In. 1380.00
Vase, Gold Iridescent, Classical Shape, 7 In. 750.00
Vase, Gold Iridescent, Metal Holder, Signed, 13 In. 980.00
Vase, Gold Iridescent, Silver Highlighted Shoulder, Silver On Pontil, Signed, 8 3/4 In. . . . 730.00
Vase, Gold, Purple Iridescent, Cylinder, 5 1/2 x 10 In. 345.00
Vase, Green Leaves, Gold Threading, White, Gold Interior, Scalloped, Signed, 3 3/4 In. . . 345.00
Vase, Ivory, Green Feathers, Gold Iridescent Interior, 11 3/4 In. 5225.00
Vase, Jack-In-The-Pulpit, Gold, Blue, Green, Purple Red Iridescent, 10 In. 2875.00
Vase, Pulled Feathers, Green, Gold Iridescent, Signed, 5 In. 1380.00
Vase, Pulled Feathers, Green, Gold Outline, Gold Interior, 5 1/2 In. 1035.00
Vase, Pulled Feathers, Green, White, Gold Interior, 10 In. 3335.00
Vase, Rainbow, Blue, Purple Highlights, Red, Purple, Signed, 9 x 3 1/4 In. 1610.00
Vase, Stick, Rainbow Design, Gold Iridescent, Signed, 14 3/4 In. 2530.00
Vase, Sweet Pea, Gold Iridescent Lily, Ruffled Rim, Signed, 5 In. 1006.00
Vase, Sweet Pea, Green Hooked Feathers, Gold Iridescent Interior, Signed, 6 3/4 In. 2530.00
Vase, Trumpet, Green, Gold Pulled Feather Design, White Ground, 8 In. 2530.00

QUILTS have been made since the seventeenth century. Early textiles were very precious and every scrap was saved to be reused. A quilt is a combination of fabrics joined to a filler and a backing by small stitched designs known as quilting. An appliqued quilt has pieces stitched to the top of a large piece of background fabric. A patchwork, or pieced, quilt is made of many small pieces stitched together. Embroidery can be added to either type.

Album, Red, Maroon, Green, Blue Squares, Orange Floral, Pa., 90 x 90 In.	9350.00
Amish, Bar, Maroon, Slate Blue, Stitched Feather, White Cotton, Pa., 76 x 84 In.	3900.00
Amish, Chinese Coins, Old Quilt Interior, 1930s, 65 x 80 In.	900.00
Amish, Contained Crazy, 1800-1900, 68 x 70 In.	425.00
Amish, Patchwork, Double Irish Chain, Running Feather Border, 82 x 83 In.	660.00
Amish, Patchwork, Drunkard's Path, Pa., Early, 83 x 68 In.	330.00
Amish, Patchwork, Log Cabin, Pineapple, Triple Border, 80 x 81 In.	687.00
Amish, Star, Diamonds, Purples, Black & Blues, 65 x 82 In.	375.00
Amish, Sunshine & Shadows, Green, Light Green, 84 x 84 In.	600.00
Amish, Trip Around The World, Lancaster County, Pa., 1930, 80 x 80 1/2 In.	425.00
Appliqued, 2 Large Trees, Biblical Quotation, Signed, c.1877, 91 x 93 In.	8050.00
Appliqued, 4 Star Center, Surrounded By Stars, White Ground, 1928, 80 x 81 In.	1210.00
Appliqued, 6-Feather Pinwheels, Red Hearts, Green Leaves, Vine Border, 62 x 79 In.	385.00
Appliqued, 9 Floral Medallions, Tulips, Stylized Flowers, Sawtooth Border, 93 x 93 In.	1760.00
Appliqued, 9 Tulip Medallions, Floral Scrolls, Red Border & Binding, 78 x 80 In.	880.00
Appliqued, 16 Center Tulips, Sawtooth Outer Border, Feathers Inner Border, 92 x 92 In.	1540.00
Appliqued, 48 U.S. Star Flag, Red, White & Blue, Marie Miller, 1920, 60 x 78 In.	1100.00
Appliqued, Album, Baltimore, Flowers, Birds, M.R. Horn, c.1893, 106 x 102 In.	24200.00
Appliqued, Basket, Pink, White, Diamond, Heart, Triangle Border, Calico, 85 x 90 In.	468.00
Appliqued, Bridal, 16 Diamond Blocks, Red, Green, Yellow, 1878, 80 x 84 In.	299.00
Appliqued, Double Wedding Ring, Red, White & Blue, 1940, 72 x 96 In.	1800.00
Appliqued, Eagle & Star Center, Swag Border, 73 x 92 In.	899.00
Appliqued, Feather, White Ground, Sawtooth Border, 84 x 80 In.	550.00
Appliqued, Floral Center, Vine Border, Glazed Cotton, c.1825, 87 x 70 In.	2900.00
Appliqued, Floral Wreath, Vine Borders, Blue, White, Chain Stitched, 1930, 77 x 90 In.	250.00
Appliqued, Floral, Red & Green, N.J. 1875, 77 x 90 In.	1500.00
Appliqued, Floral, Red & Green, White Ground, Red Border, 1920, 72 x 80 In.	475.00
Appliqued, Flowers & Animals, Embroidered, Crib	100.00
Appliqued, Grandmother's Flower Garden, Multicolored, 1930, 88 x 99 In.	275.00
Appliqued, Green, Red, Puffed Grapes, Vine Border, Red Binding, 92 x 94 In.	2310.00
Appliqued, Hawaiian Royal Flag Aloha, Red, White & Blue, 1895, 73 x 74 In.	1900.00
Appliqued, Hawaiian, Red, White & Blue Stripes, Union Jacks, Crown, Leaf, 73 x 74 In.	2090.00
Appliqued, Lady Of The Lake, Tester Bedpost Cut, 1848, 69 x 77 In.	450.00
Appliqued, Log Cabin, Pineapple, 65 x 77 In.	485.00
Appliqued, Lone Star, 4 Small Star Corners, 78 x 93 In. *Illus*	350.00
Appliqued, Lone Star, Red & Green, White Ground, Pa., 1910-1920, 80 x 88 In.	225.00
Appliqued, Mariner's Compass, 1880, 74 x 87 In.	175.00
Appliqued, Mariner's Compass, 4-Poster Bed Cut, 1860, 80 x 87 In.	750.00
Appliqued, Oak Leaf *Illus*	1300.00

Quilt, Appliqued, Lone Star, 4 Small Star Corners, 78 x 93 In.

Quilt, Appliqued, Oak Leaf

Appliqued, Oak Leaf, Chain Stitched, 1930, 75 x 90 In. 250.00
Appliqued, Peonies, Green Calico, White Blocks, Grid, Cotton, 74 x 89 In. 460.00
Appliqued, Poinsettia, 30 Squares, Embroidered Stems & Leaves, Red, Green, 82 x 96 In. 500.00
Appliqued, Red, White, Blue, Stars, White Ground, Pa., Late 19th Century, 72 x 90 In. ... 660.00
Appliqued, Star Of Bethlehem, Red, Green, Yellow Star, White Ground, 1930s, Crib 425.00
Appliqued, Stylized Baskets, Red, Green, Mustard, White, 78 x 72 In. 288.00
Appliqued, Stylized Polka Dot Medallions, White Ground, Red Binding, 72 x 88 In. 385.00
Appliqued, Sunflower Medallions, Swag & Heart Border, 76 x 88 In. 467.00
Appliqued, Tulips In Pinwheel, Flowering Tulip Border 72 x 86 In. 880.00
Appliqued, Tulips, Late 19th Century, 88 x 86 In. 935.00
Appliqued, Washington, By Horse, Harrison, Floral Backing, 1889, 73 x 81 In. 7500.00
Cover, Copper Plate Print, Rural Life, Red, Natural Ground, c.1790, 98 x 67 In. 715.00
Crazy, Blue, Purple, Red, Brown, Velvet, Corduroy, Felt, Stitched Date 1923, 72 x 82 In. . 248.00
Crazy, Embroidered Blizzard Effect Over Floral, Frogs, Satin, Velvet, 80 x 80 In. 1650.00
Crazy, Satin & Silk, Red Satin Border, Signatures, 78 x 78 In. 110.00
Crazy, Satin, Silk, Velvet, Applied Rose Wreath, Lace Border, Burgundy, 72 x 72 In. ... 990.00
Crazy, Silk, Velvet, Nelson Hose Cooperstown, N.Y., 19th Century, 77 x 69 In. 430.00
Embroidered, Cortland Village & Lady's Fancy, Blue, White, Names 1838, 82 x 88 In. .. 700.00
Embroidered, Flowers, Vines, Wool, 94 x 82 In. 4600.00
Embroidered, Potted Tree Medallion, Scallop Inside Border, New York, 64 In. 7500.00
Patchwork, 9 Block, Pink, Green & Red, 20th Century, 75 x 73 In. 440.00
Patchwork, 9 Panel Floral Sprays, Sawtooth & Bar Border, 84 x 88 In. 1000.00
Patchwork, 9 Patch, Irish Chain, Red Printed, White, 3 Borders, Mid 1800s, 74 x 87 In. .. 345.00
Patchwork, 25 Trees, Medallions, Green & White, Meandering Borders, 80 x 80 In. 1705.00
Patchwork, Album, 25 Squares, Calico, Corner Florals, Palinda W. Rupp, 90 x 90 In. 9350.00
Patchwork, Album, Embroidered Florals, Cornucopia, Pheasant, Vine Border, 82 x 90 In. 1980.00
Patchwork, Around The World, Calico, Pa., 1900, 78 x 78 In. 1320.00
Patchwork, Around The World, Pumpkin, Purple, Maroon, Blue, Crib, 40 x 40 In. 1430.00
Patchwork, Bars & Blocks, Blue Border, Frame, 41 x 49 In. 2585.00
Patchwork, Basket, Green Stylized Basket, Red Calico Border, 1890, Crib, 51 x 39 In. 880.00
Patchwork, Baskets Of Flowers, Colors Repeat In Border, 64 x 80 In. 190.00
Patchwork, Blue Stars, Squares, White Backing, Floral Binding, 64 x 84 In. 220.00
Patchwork, Blue, White Print, White Ground, Crib, 33 1/2 x 52 In. 192.00
Patchwork, Bow Tie, 1880s, 60 x 80 In. 500.00
Patchwork, Calico, Pink, Yellow Square Design, 19th Century, 72 x 59 In. 81.00
Patchwork, Chintz, Meandering Vine, Green Dot & White, Feather, Scroll, 102 x 96 In. ... 2070.00
Patchwork, Declaration Of Independence, Calico, Cotton, 1863, 88 x 92 In. 5400.00
Patchwork, Diamond, Blue, White, Diamond Quilting, 69 x 85 In. 468.00
Patchwork, Double Irish Chain, Polychrome Patches, Serrated Border, 82 x 92 In. 495.00
Patchwork, Double Irish Chain, Red & Mustard Chains, 83 x 86 1/2 In. 247.00
Patchwork, Embroidered, Sunburst, Blue, White, Cotton, 93 x 78 In. 1093.00
Patchwork, Fan, Striped, Checked, Floral, Maroon, Gray, Green, 67 1/4 x 68 In. 220.00
Patchwork, Feathered Star, Red & White, 69 x 70 In. 165.00
Patchwork, Flying Geese, Red, Glazed Chintz Bands, Cotton, 100 x 104 In. 1430.00
Patchwork, Flying Geese, Red, Yellow, Green, Pa., 1900, 78 x 84 In. 248.00
Patchwork, Friendship, Geese In Flight, White, Cotton, Pa., 19th Century, 85 1/2 x 83 In. 168.00
Patchwork, Friendship, Sunflowers, White Field, Sawtooth Border, 77 x 78 In. 495.00
Patchwork, Friendship, Tan, & Blue Baskets, Green Border, c.1930, 84 x 55 In. 725.00
Patchwork, Geometric, Rust, White, Sawtooth Border, Calico, E.C.R., 1867, 90 x 90 In. . 1840.00
Patchwork, Irish Chain Variant, Flowers & Leaves, Stars In Medallion, 92 x 93 In. 880.00
Patchwork, Irish Chain, White Ground, Blue Border, 98 x 96 In. 357.00
Patchwork, Log Cabin, Assorted Fabrics, Wool Scalloped Border, 71 x 80 In. 935.00
Patchwork, Log Cabin, Barn Raising, Green Outer Border, 78 x 79 In. 275.00
Patchwork, Log Cabin, c.1860, 72 x 82 In. 595.00
Patchwork, Log Cabin, Red, Black, Green Chimneys, 19th Century, 105 x 77 In. 1540.00
Patchwork, Log Cabin, Sunshine & Shadow, Chevron Border, Plaid Backing, 80 x 82 In. . 1485.00
Patchwork, Log Cabin, Sunshine & Shadow, Chintz Backing, 88 x 90 In. 715.00
Patchwork, Lone Star, Multicolored Star, 77 x 77 In. 1045.00
Patchwork, Lone Star, Red & White Star, Blue Ground, 1920s, 74 x 86 In. 165.00
Patchwork, Mariner's Compass Blocks, Brown, White, Cotton, 77 x 76 In. 546.00
Patchwork, Mariner's Compass, 32 Point Star, Green, Red, Pink, Gold, 82 x 78 In. 865.00
Patchwork, Monkey Wrench, Blue Calico, White Squares, Polka Dot Border, 68 x 80 In. . 467.00
Patchwork, Multicolored Square, Interlocking Diamonds, 19th Century, 74 x 80 In. 385.00

Quilt, Patchwork & Appliqued, Hawaiian

Quilt, Patchwork, Top Only, Hexagon

Patchwork, Paisley & Chintz, Blue & Brown, 88 x 76 In. 375.00
Patchwork, Pink Calico Stars, White Squares, Brown Calico Binding, 66 x 78 In. 550.00
Patchwork, Rising Star, 19th Century, 76 x 78 In. 610.00
Patchwork, Schoolhouse, 20 Blocks, 9 Patch Corner Blocks, 66 x 84 In. 575.00
Patchwork, Schoolhouse, Ribbon Patches, Calico, Dark Blue Cotton, 74 x 75 In. 3600.00
Patchwork, Schoolhouse, Scalloped Border, 71 x 72 In. 1430.00
Patchwork, Snowflake, Red Border, 75 x 78 In. 385.00
Patchwork, Stained Glass Window, Solid, Print Fabrics, Border, Pa., c.1885, 70 x 71 In. . . 345.00
Patchwork, Star & Bar Variant, Red, Blue & Orange, 78 x 78 In. 715.00
Patchwork, Star Medallions, Red, Feather, Spiral, Border, Flower Quilting, 70 x 86 In. . . 660.00
Patchwork, Star Of Bethlehem Center, 104 x 104 In. 5500.00
Patchwork, Stars, Red & Green, 80 x 80 In. 185.00
Patchwork, Stylized Green & Yellow Calico Tulips, Maroon Ground, 90 x 77 In. 1100.00
Patchwork, Top Only, Hexagon . . . .*Illus* 1200.00
Patchwork, Triple Irish Chain, White On White Fern Quilting, J.S. Boggs, 84 x 84 In. . . . 880.00
Patchwork, Tulip & Wreath, Pink, Green, Cotton, 19th Century, 81 x 73 In. 179.00
Patchwork, United We Stand, Divided We Fall, Blue, White, 1844, 78 x 84 In. 460.00
Patchwork, Wild Goose Chase, Monogrammed WBF, 1878, 67 x 84 In. 3165.00
Patchwork & Appliqued, 9 Blocks, Stylized Blossoms, Vine Border, 87 x 92 In. 1380.00
Patchwork & Appliqued, 16 Squares, Pine Tree In Each, Green Border, 89 x 90 In. 1265.00
Patchwork & Appliqued, 35 Blocks, Multicolored, 70 x 90 In. 575.00
Patchwork & Appliqued, Courthouse, Signed Jennie Griffin, Dated 1872, 75 x 93 In. 410.00
Patchwork & Appliqued, Floral On Lattice Work, 88 x 101 In. 2600.00
Patchwork & Appliqued, Flowers & Feather, 6 Blocks, Annie Sanford, 77 x 92 In. 1135.00
Patchwork & Appliqued, Hawaiian . . . .*Illus* 1900.00
Patchwork & Appliqued, Maker's Name, Mrs. M.E. Mohortor, 1877, 91 x 93 In. 8050.00
Patchwork & Appliqued, Schoolhouse, Blue & White, Border, 56 x 72 In. 1840.00
Patchwork & Appliqued, Thanksgiving, Floral & Cornucopia, 92 x 80 In. 2300.00
Patchwork & Appliqued, Washington's March, Vining Berries Border, 81 x 84 In. 2035.00
Patchwork & Appliqued, Wreaths & Leaves, Red & Green, Trapunto, 45 x 45 In. 2880.00

QUIMPER pottery has a long history. Tin-glazed, hand-painted pottery
has been made in Quimper, France, since the late seventeenth century.
The earliest firm, founded in 1685 by Jean Baptiste Bousquet, was
known as HB Quimper. Another firm, founded in 1772 by Francois
Eloury, was known as Porquier. The third firm, founded by Guillaume
Dumaine in 1778, was known as HR or Henriot Quimper. All three
firms made similar pottery decorated with designs of Breton peasants
and sea and flower motifs. The Eloury (Porquier) and Dumaine
(Henriot) firms merged in 1913. Bousquet (HB) merged with the oth-
ers in 1968. The group was sold to a United States family in 1984. The
American holding company is Quimper Faience Inc., located in
Stonington, Connecticut. The French firm has been called Societe
Nouvelle des Faienceries de Quimper HB Henriot since March 1984.

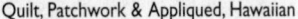

Ashtray, Orange Zigzag, Green Dots, Brown Sides, Triangular, 6 1/2 x 1 7/8 In. 40.00

Basket, Man With Cane & Pipe, HB Quimper, 6 In. 255.00
Bookends, Man & Woman, Seated, Tin-Ar-Gall, HB Quimper, 6 1/8 In., Pair 625.00
Bowl, Cream Glazed Ground, Pigeon, Borders, Striping, 10 In. 345.00
Bowl, Fruit, Scalloped Edge, Signed, 11 In. 160.00
Bowl, Man & Woman With Bird, HB Quimper, 9 3/4 In. 340.00
Bowl, Serving, Figures, Leaf Spray, Faience, 11 In. 58.00
Butter, Cover, Man On Cover, Henriot Quimper, 7 In. 300.00
Casserole, Figures, Faience, Oval, 18 In. 345.00
Cruet Set, Oil & Vinegar, Rooster, Signed, 1920s, 7 In. 250.00
Dish, Clover Shape, 3 Shell Sections, Figures, Flowers, Swan Handle, Faience, 11 In. 375.00
Dish, Cover, Woman Holding Flowers On Cover, HR Quimper, c.1930, 6 1/2 In. 335.00
Figurine, Ste. Anne, HB Quimper, 10 1/4 In. 175.00
Jug, Puzzle, Buvez Le Veux Bien, Mais, Sachez Placer Votre Main, c.1920, 4 In. 165.00
Plate, 2 Men Playing Instruments, Henriot Quimper, 9 1/2 In. 350.00
Plate, Dinner, Rooster, Faience, 10 In., Pair 200.00
Plate, Man & Woman With Basket, Henriot Quimper, 9 1/2 In. 350.00
Plate, Man's Profile, Ruffled, Henriot Quimper, c.1950, 10 1/4 In. 175.00
Plate, Peasant Man & Woman, Standing, Floral Borders, Faience, 10 1/4 In., Pair 430.00
Plate, Revolution, HB Quimper, 9 In. 195.00
Plate, Woman Holding Jug, HB Quimper, 9 1/2 In. 195.00
Plate, Woman In Profile, HB Quimper, 6 1/4 In. 75.00
Plate Set, Botanical, Bird & Branch, 9 1/2 In., 6 Piece 2300.00
Plate Set, Botanical, Leaf & Flower, 9 1/2 In., 6 Piece 2420.00
Platter, Woman Sitting, Oval, 11 3/4 In. 150.00
Server, Cover, Man Playing Instrument, Seated, Henriot Quimper, 6 In. 285.00
Sugar, Cover, Man With Cane & Pipe, Flowers, HB Quimper, 5 1/2 In. 170.00
Tureen, Red Glaze, Round, Cover, Faience, 7 1/2 In. 105.00
Tureen, Soup, Man On 1 Side, Woman On Other, Henriot Quimper, c.1930, 13 1/2 In. 465.00
Vase, 2 Men With Instruments, Crest With Lions, HR Quimper, 14 In. 1500.00
Vase, Fan, Man & Woman On 1 Side, Flowers On Other, Henriot Quimper, 8 In. 825.00
Vase, Woman With Basket, Seated, Henriot Quimper, 3 3/4 In. 215.00

RADFORD pottery was made by Alfred Radford in Broadway, Virginia,
Tiffin and Zanesville, Ohio, and Clarksburg, West Virginia, from 1891
until 1912. Jasperware, Ruko, Thera, Radura, and Velvety Art Ware
were made. The jasperware resembles the famous Wedgwood ware of   *RADURA.*
the same name. Another pottery named Radford worked in England
and is not included here.

Box, Cover, Green, White Design, Marked, 5 1/2 In. 110.00
Candleholder, Dusky Pink Flowers, Handle, 6 x 2 In. 110.00
Candlestick, 3/4 x 3 3/4 In. 65.00
Jardiniere, Ruffled Rim, Wild Roses, Shaded Ground, Impressed RUKO, 10 x 11 In. 115.00
Jardiniere, Yellow Tulip Design, Green Leaves, Black Ground, 9 1/4 In. 143.00
Jug, Blue, Green Mottled Interior, Purple Exterior, Handle, 3 x 5 In. 80.00
Jug, Pink, Green, Yellow Violets, Deep Yellow Sponge Ground, 1930 .... 111.00
Mug, Tavern Ware, 3 1/4 In. 65.00
Rose Bowl, Cream, Purple Mirror Flowers, Blue Bands On Top & Bottom, 5 x 3 In. 75.00
Vase, 10 x 5 In. 110.00
Vase, 2 Loop Handles, Green Matte Glaze, 1903, 14 1/2 In. 68.00
Vase, Blue Mottled Glaze, Mauve, Pink Flowers, 4 In. 75.00
Vase, Flower Design, 2 Handles, Marked, 6 In. 345.00
Vase, Mauve, Pink Mottled Glaze, Pale Yellow Ground, 4 1/2 x 4 1/2 In. 90.00

RADIO broadcast receiving sets were first sold in New York City in
1910. They were used to pick up the experimental broadcasts of the
day. The first commercial radios were made by Westinghouse
Company for listeners of the experimental shows on KDKA Pittsburgh
in 1920. Collectors today are interested in all early radios, especially
those made of Bakelite plastic or decorated with blue mirrors. Figural
advertising radios and transistor radios are also collected.

A-C Dayton, Model XL-25, Battery Operated, 5 Tubes, Wooden Case, 1926 .... 125.00
Addison, Model A2A, Right Front Dial, Plastic, 2 Knobs, 1940 .... 475.00
Admiral, Clock, Model 5J21, Plastic, Black, AC/DC, Table Model 20.00

Atwater Kent, Model 10, Breadboard, 5 Tubes, 3 Dials, Battery Operated, 1923 . . . .   950.00
Atwater Kent, Model 30, 1 Dial Front, Lift Top, Wooden, Battery Operated, 1926 . . . . . .   100.00
Bulova, Transistor, Model 620, Plastic, Ivory, Horizontal, Dial Knob, 1957 . . . .   80.00
Crosley, Model 9-119, 2 Knobs, Plastic, 1948, Table Model 210.00
Crosley, Playmate, Walnut Case, Double Door, 1930, Console 460.00
Ecko, Lighted Peripheral Dial, Jet Engine Design, A22, 14 x 8 x 15 In. 3450.00
Emerson, Model 375, Five One, Catalin, Blue Plastic, 1940, Table Model 7700.00
Emerson, Model 400, Patriot, Catalin, Brown, Yellow, Grill, Handle, 1940, Table Model .   400.00
Emerson, Model 400, Patriot, Catalin, Green, Yellow, 1940, Table Model 575.00
Emerson, Model 400, Patriot, Catalin, Red, White, Blue Plastic, 1940, Table Model 750.00
Emerson, Model 811, Ivory, Plastic, Small Case, 5 Tube, 1955, Table Model 30.00
Emerson, Model BM258, Catalin, 1937, Table Model 1400.00
Fada, Catalin, Green Marble Body, White Plastic Handle, Knobs, 1946, 10 x 6 x 7 In. 805.00
Fada, Catalin, Model 659, Maroon, Yellow Trim, Shortwave Band . . . . .300.00 to 690.00
Garod, Catalin, Model 1450, Peak Top, Yellow, Red Trim, 1939 . . . .   4675.00
Garod, Catalin, Model 1B55L, Drop Handle, Yellow, 1939 . . . .   4125.00
General Electric, Model P746B, Transistor, White, Turquoise, Dial Knob, 1959 . . . .   20.00
Hitachi, Transistor, Model TH-848, Black & Beige, Leather Case, 1964 . . . .   20.00
Motorola, Catalin, Model 50XC, Red, Yellow Trim, 1940, Table Model 7700.00
Philco, Model 87, Double Doors, Speaker Covered In Paisley, 1930s, 47 In. 255.00
Philco, Model B578, Transitone Multiwave, Green, Plastic, 1954, Table Model 25.00
Philmore, Model 2001, Crystal . . . . .70.00 to 100.00
RCA, Little Nipper, Marbled Yellow, Red Dial & Knob, No. 9TX, 1939, 4 In. 1760.00
RCA Victor, Model X-551, Bakelite, Black, 1950, Table Model 30.00
RCA Victor, Portable, Model 8-BX-5, Plastic, Green, 1948 . . . .   25.00
RCA Victor, Portable, Model B-411, Plastic, Dial Knob, 1951 . . . .   30.00
Realistic 10, Model 1283K, Transistor, Front Dial, Side Thumbwheel, Leather 20.00
Stewart Werner, Catalin, Model 62T36, Yellow, 1946, Table Model 715.00
True-Tone, Model D-910-B, Wood, Bakelite Knobs, 1939, Table Model 65.00
Viscount, Portable, Model 503, Ivory 30.00
Zenith, Royal 16, Transistor, Billfold Style, Plastic, 1966 . . . .   40.00

RAILROAD enthusiasts collect any train memorabilia. Everything is wanted, from oilcans to whole train cars. The Chessie system has a store that sells many reproductions of their old dinnerware and uniforms.

Badge, Boston & Maine, Hallmark 295.00
Badge, CRI & PRY, 6-Point Star, Ball Tips, Wire Pin, 1 3/4 x 2 In. 290.00
Badge, KCTRY Co., Police Kansas City, Mo., Allen Stamp & Seal Co., 1917, 2 1/4 In. . . .   290.00
Bank, B & O Queen City Station, Metal, Moore, 2 7/8 In. 145.00
Banner, V & T Railway, Nevada State Capitol, Carson City, Paper, 1939, 3 1/2 x 8 In. . . .   7.00
Bell, Bronze, Custom-Made Stand, c.1900, 10 x 12 In. 480.00
Bill Clip, Celluloid, Bull, Northern RR, World's Fair Route, St. Louis 1904, 1 3/4 In. 150.00
Doorknob, Brass, B & O Railroad, Ornate Plate, Turn Lock, 6 In.   220.00
Engine Plate, B & O, Bronze, Relief Casting, Capitol Building, Spire, Letters, 16 In. 560.00
Helmet, K-56, Signal-Audio-Communicator, Kuzan, Box, 1960s 60.00
Label, Cigar, Fast Mail, Train Picture, Inner Type 120.00
Label, Cigar, Railroad Hose Special, Train Picture, Outer 90.00
Lantern, Conductor's, 1923 . . . .   95.00
Lantern, Conductor's, Nickel Plated, Kerosene, Flower Wreath, Patent '64, 10 In. 460.00
Lantern, Dietz No. 40, Traffic Guard, Red 40.00
Lantern, Dietz, Kerosene, Bright Yellow Paint, Handle, No. 8 Air Pilot, 17 x 7 3/4 In. . . .   39.00
Lantern, Matching Glove, Rayo, No. 39 . . . .   140.00
Lantern, Pennsylvania Railroad, Yellow, Dressel & Arlington, N.J. 90.00
Platter, B & O Railroad Shenango, Cumberland Narrow 154.00
Platter, Union Pacific, Harriman Blue, China, Oval, 7 1/4 In. 70.00
Postcard, Boston Train Station Mass., Scene, Early 1900s 4.00
Postcard, Chrome, Pueblo Union Station 3.00
Postcard, First Engine Operated Over Central Pacific RR, Sacramento, Calif. 4.50
Postcard, Linen, John Bull Engine, Nation Museum, Smithsonian 5.00
Poster Stamp, Northern Pacific Railroad, Glacier National Park, 1922, 2 1/4 In. 15.00
Sign, Southern Railway, Gold Letters, Black Glass, 4 x 32 In. 85.00
Sign, St. Paul Minneapolis Manitoba Railway, Lithograph, Frame, 1880, 22 In. 375.00

Timetable, Penn Central, Laminated, Dated 1973 .... 6.00
Tool, Raising Windows, Wooden, Hinged Padded Rest 100.00

RAZORS were used in ancient Egypt and subsequently wherever shaving was in fashion. The metal razor used in America until about 1870 was made in Sheffield, England. After 1870, machine-made hollow-ground razors were made in Germany or America. Plastic or bone handles were popular. The razor was often sold in a set of seven, one for each day of the week. The set was often kept by the barber who shaved the well-to-do man each day in the shop.

Clauss, Straight, Ivory Handle, Ornately Carved 326.00
Crown & Sword, Straight, Sword On Handle, Germany, 1820 .... 80.00
Double Body, 4 Parallel Gold Stripes, Silver Razor, Matching Blade Holder 5060.00
Durham, Duplex, Celluloid Handle, Blade Guard, Leather Case, 1907 .... 24.00
Folding, California Chinese, Primitive 48.00
Frederich Reynolds, Horn Handle, Oversize Blade, Sheffield 75.00
Geneva Cutlery, Celluloid Handles, Eagle On Blade 95.00
Geneva Cutlery, Straight, Plastic Handle, Geneva, NY, 1903 .... 28.00
H. Boker, Straight, Black Bakelite Handle, Red Injun No. 101, Germany, Case 69.00
Imperial Razor Co., Straight, Bone Handle, Germany, c.1890 .... 35.00
J.R. Torrey Razor Co., Straight, Our Beauty, Green Plastic Handle, Case 198.00
Kriss Kross, Blade Sharpener 50.00
Rattler Cutlery Co., Celluloid Handles, Meat Chopper Blade, Etched Battleship 150.00
Straight, Celluloid Handles, Bird, Tang Grip, Bone Covering 85.00
Straight, Custom Made By Sheffield, King Of Diamonds, Wooden Box 100.00
Straight, Windmill Design, The Rattler, Germany, 1930 .... 75.00
W.H. Morley & Sons, Straight, Hunter Shooting Boar On Handle, Germany, 6 In. 120.00
W.H. Morley & Sons, Straight, Ivory Scrimshaw Handle, Germany 375.00
Wade & Butcher, Black Horn Handles, Hollow Ground, Sheffield 85.00
Wade & Butcher, Straight, Wooden Handle 48.00
Wm. Elliott & Co., Straight, Windmill & Boat On Handle, Germany 80.00
Worcester Razor Co., Straight, Marbled Bakelite Handle, Gladiator, Germany 25.00
Worcester Razor Co., Straight, The Magnetic, Ivory Handle, Case 295.00

REAMERS, or juice squeezers, have been known since 1767, although most of those collected today date from the twentieth century. Figural reamers are among the most prized.

Anchor Hocking, Green, Loop Handle 24.00
Cambridge, Green 200.00
Ceramic, Clown's Head 65.00
Ceramic, Windmill 125.00
Clear, Federal, 9 In. 14.00
Crisscross, Cobalt 350.00
Crisscross, Green 20.00
Crisscross, Lemon Pink 325.00
Crisscross, Orange 250.00
Fenton, Black, 2 Piece 1600.00
Fleur-De-Lis, Red 750.00
Fleur-De-Lis, Yellow, Orange 650.00
Fry, Amber 325.00
Fry, Amber, Cone 445.00
Fry, Orange 445.00
Fry, Pink 95.00
Fry, Rose 275.00
Hazel Atlas, Cobalt, 2 Piece 300.00
Hazel Atlas, Crystal, Tab Handle, 6 In. 9.00
Hazel Atlas, Green, Tab Handle 22.00
Jadite, Grapefruit 400.00
Jeannette, Blue 125.00
Jennyware, Pink 175.00
Jennyware, Ultramarine 150.00
Lemon, Wooden, Dark Brown Patina, 18th Century 275.00
Porcelain, Fruit Pattern, 2 Sections 55.00

Sunkist, Black	350.00 to 800.00
Sunkist, Blocked, Milk Glass, Cone	115.00
Sunkist, Carmel	375.00
Sunkist, Crown Tuscan	375.00
Sunkist, Custard	65.00 to 95.00
Sunkist, Jadite, Opalescent	750.00
Sunkist, Jadite, Opalescent, Fry	300.00
Sunkist, Milk Glass	25.00
Sunkist, Seville, Yellow	95.00
Sunkist, Transparent Green	95.00
Sunkist, Vaseline	105.00
U.S. Glass, Grapefruit, Green	575.00

RECORDS have changed size and shape through the years. The cylinder-shaped phonograph record for use with the early Edison models was made about 1889. Disc records were first made by 1894, the double-sided disc by 1904. High-fidelity records were first issued in 1944, the first vinyl disc in 1946, the first stereo record in 1958. The 78 RPM became the standard in 1926 but was discontinued in 1957. In 1932, the first 33 1/3 RPM was made but was not sold commercially until 1948. In 1949, the 45 RPM was introduced. Compact discs became available in the U.S. in 1982 and many companies began phasing out the production of phonograph records.

Album, Little Black Sambo, 78 RPM, 2 Records	65.00
Alvin & The Chipmunks, Witch Doctor, 45 RPM	15.00
Andy Griffith, What It Was, Was Football, Capitol Records, 45 RPM, 1950s	65.00
Arthur Godfrey, 'Twas The Night Before Christmas, Jingle Bells, Columbia, 45 RPM	25.00
Fran Allison, Songs For Fun, Peter Cottontail, RCA Victor, Little Nipper, 78 RPM	25.00
Johnny Mathis, Right From The Heart, Columbia, 45 RPM, 1985	4.00
Moxie Song, Moxie Fox Trot, 1921	75.00
Puff 'n Toot, Golden	12.00
Rosemary Clooney, Winter Wonderland, C-h-r-i-s-t-m-a-s, Columbia, 78 RPM	25.00
Space Cadet, Song & March, Tom Corbett, Rockhill Productions, 78 RPM, 1952	55.00
Who's Afraid Of The Big Bad Wolf, Golden	10.00

RED WING Pottery of Red Wing, Minnesota, was a firm started in 1878. The company first made utilitarian pottery. In the 1920s art pottery was made. Many dinner sets and vases were made before the company closed in 1967. Rumrill pottery was made for George Rumrill by the Red Wing Pottery and other firms. It was sold in the 1930s. For more information, see *Kovels' Depression Glass & Dinnerware Price List.*

Advertising, Mug, Gluek Brewing Co., Stoneware, Barrel Shape, 6-Pointed Star	180.00
Art Pottery, Ashtray, Red Wing Potteries 75th Anniversary, Wing Shaped, Red, 7 In.	150.00
Art Pottery, Figurine, Horse, Luster Ivory, No. 919, 6 In.	625.00
Art Pottery, Figurine, Lion, Tahitian Gold Glaze, No. 917	475.00
Art Pottery, Figurine, The Muse, Bronze, DeLuxe Line, 7 1/4 x 13 3/4 In.	70.00
Art Pottery, Jardiniere, No. 105, Embossed Flowers & Leaves, Green, Marked	270.00
Art Pottery, Lamp, Cattail With Flowers	250.00
Art Pottery, Lamp, No. 887, Yellow Glaze	400.00
Art Pottery, Pitcher, No. 207, Nokomis, Bottom Marked	200.00
Art Pottery, Planter, Elephant, Yellow, 5 In.	575.00
Art Pottery, Planter, Giraffe, No. 896, 7 In.	325.00
Art Pottery, Urn, No. 717, Garden Ware, Cobalt Blue Glaze, 24 In.	2000.00
Art Pottery, Vase, M-1436, Rooster, Ivory With Mint Green, Bottom Marked	225.00
Art Pottery, Vase, No. 20, Nudes, Glossy Green Glaze, Bottom Marked	230.00
Art Pottery, Vase, No. 174, Georgia Rose, Ivory With Pink, 5 In.	110.00
Art Pottery, Vase, No. 249, Rumrill Athenian Group, 2 Nudes, Yellow Glaze, 11 In.	2100.00
Art Pottery, Vase, No. 571, Rumrill Athenian Group, 2 Nudes, White, Mint Green	450.00
Art Pottery, Vase, No. 1175, Gray Engobe With Solid Turquoise, 10 1/2 In.	350.00
Art Pottery, Vase, No. 1183, Eggshell Ivory Antiqued, Brown, Bottom Marked, 6 In.	70.00
Art Pottery, Wall Planter, M-1484, Black Violin, With Sticker, 13 In.	50.00
Blossom Time, Plate, 6 1/2 In.	20.00

Bob White, Bowl, Vegetable, Oval .... 30.00 to 65.00
Bob White, Casserole, Cover, 2 Qt. .... 55.00 to 70.00
Bob White, Cookie Jar 135.00
Bob White, Creamer 18.00
Bob White, Cup 7.00
Bob White, Cup & Saucer 25.00
Bob White, Gravy Boat, Cover 70.00
Bob White, Hors D'Oeuvre, Bird 65.00
Bob White, Pitcher, Water, 60 Oz. .... 37.00 to 62.00
Bob White, Plate, Salad, 7 1/2 In. .... 19.00 to 25.00
Bob White, Salt & Pepper, Small 45.00
Bob White, Soup, Dish 16.00
Cherry Band, Pitcher, Compliments Of Olsen & Son, Frederick & Lewis ... 475.00
Churn, Birchleaf, Oval, 5 Gal. 325.00
Churn No. 3, 1890-1915 .... 250.00
Clock, Black, Mammy, 10 In. .... 336.00 to 450.00
Cookie Jar, Cabbage, Blue, Cover, Marked, 8 1/2 In. 950.00
Cookie Jar, Chef, 11 In. 325.00
Cookie Jar, Friar Tuck, Blue, 10 1/2 In. 97.00
Cookie Jar, RoundUp, Cover 425.00
Crock, Wooden Handle, Pottery, 8 x 8 In. 300.00
Damask, Bowl, Cereal 7.00
Damask, Bowl, Vegetable, Oval 20.00
Damask, Bowl, Vegetable, Square 35.00
Damask, Butter, Cover 20.00
Damask, Coffeepot, Cover 45.00
Damask, Creamer 25.00
Damask, Cup & Saucer .... 8.00 to 12.00
Damask, Gravy Boat, Underplate 25.00
Damask, Plate, 7 In. .... 8.00 to 9.00
Damask, Plate, 10 In. .... 12.00 to 14.00
Damask, Platter, Large 35.00
Damask, Salt & Pepper 25.00
Damask, Sugar, Cover .... 25.00 to 35.00
Damask, Tray, 3 Tiers 45.00
Foot Warmer 90.00
Gray Line, Bowl, Stoneware, Marked, 10 In. Diam. 100.00
Gray Line, Casserole, Cover, 8 In. 345.00
Gray Line, Reamer, 4 x 6 3/4 In. 440.00
Jar, Beater, Hartman's Store 145.00
Jar, Pantry, Pitts Bros., Alexandria Va., Stoneware, Cover 475.00
Lexington Rose, Plate, 6 1/2 In. 5.00
Lexington Rose, Plate, 10 1/2 In. 20.00
Lexington Rose, Salt & Pepper 25.00
Lotus, Bowl, Fruit 10.00
Lotus, Cup & Saucer 10.00
Lotus, Plate, 10 1/2 In. .... 14.00 to 25.00
Lotus, Plate, Salad, 8 1/2 In. 15.00
Lute Song, Bowl, Vegetable, Round, 8 1/2 In. 35.00
Lute Song, Plate, 10 1/2 In. 17.00
Lute Song, Platter, Oval, 13 In. 50.00
Magnolia, Cup & Saucer 16.00
Magnolia, Plate, 7 1/2 In. 9.00
Magnolia, Plate, 10 1/2 In. 14.00
Magnolia, Salt & Pepper 200.00
Magnolia, Sugar, Cover 35.00
Merrileaf, Bowl, 5 In. 4.00
Merrileaf, Bowl, Divided, 11 3/4 In. 25.00
Merrileaf, Casserole, Cover, 9 In. 45.00
Merrileaf, Gravy Boat, Cover, Handle, 4 1/4 In. 35.00
Merrileaf, Platter, 13 In. 19.00
Merrileaf, Soup, Dish, 6 1/2 In. 8.00
Merrileaf, Sugar & Creamer 20.00

Ovenware, Bowl, Fluted Accents, 7 In. 132.00
Random Harvest, Bowl, Serving, 9 In. ....20.00 to 35.00
Random Harvest, Bowl, Vegetable, Divided, 10 In. 45.00
Random Harvest, Gravy Boat, Underplate 40.00
Random Harvest, Platter, 13 In. 30.00
Random Harvest, Salad Bowl & Plate Set, 9 Piece 140.00
Salt & Pepper, Sponge Band, 4 1/2 In. 765.00
Stoneware, Bed Warmer, Designed By Rehder, Pat. 1901 .... 175.00
Stoneware, Bowl, Paneled, Sponged Design, 10 In. Diam. 175.00
Stoneware, Bowl, Saffron, Marked 140.00
Stoneware, Butter Jar, Gray Line, Cover, 5 Lb. 550.00
Stoneware, Churn, Butterfly Design, Salt Glazed, 5 Gal. 500.00
Stoneware, Crock, Butterfly, Salt Glazed, Back Stamped M-1, 20 Gal. 2850.00
Stoneware, Crock, Cobalt Leaf & Minnesota Owl, 8 Gal. 2000.00
Stoneware, Crock, Wing & Oval Beehive, 3 Gal. 500.00
Stoneware, Cuspidor, Albany Slip Design, Marked Minn. Stoneware 450.00
Stoneware, Cuspidor, German, Salt Glazed, Repaired 1050.00
Stoneware, Custard Cups, Gray Line, Marked, 6 Oz., 4 Piece 850.00
Stoneware, Fruit Jar, Stone Mason, 1/2 Gal. 230.00
Stoneware, Fruit Jar, Stone Mason, Black, 1/2 Gal. 275.00
Stoneware, Fruit Jar, Stone Mason, Blue, No Cover, 1 Gal. 650.00
Stoneware, Funnel, Acid Proof Measure, Union Stoneware Co., Red Wing Minn. ... 1200.00
Stoneware, Hot Water Bottle, Brown Leaf Design 225.00
Stoneware, Jug, Beehive, Stylized, Cobalt Leaf, 3 Gal. 1210.00
Stoneware, Jug, Brown, White Base, Dr's Clark & Clark, Canistota, S.D., 1 Gal. 400.00
Stoneware, Milk Pan, White, Marked, 15 1/2 Diam. 100.00
Stoneware, Pitcher, Iris, Blue, Marked, 1 Qt. 675.00
Stoneware, Salt Box, Gray Line, Cover 1350.00
Stoneware, Water Cooler, Wing & Oval, Hand Turned, 4 Gal. 675.00
Stoneware, Water Cooler, Wing & Oval, Hand Turned, Cover, 2 Gal. 4500.00
Tampico, Creamer 24.00
Tampico, Plate, 8 1/2 In. 15.00
Tampico, Plate, 10 1/2 In. ....15.00 to 22.00
Town & Country, Saltshaker, 4 Holes, Schmoo, Zeisel 55.00
Tweed Tex, Cup & Saucer 25.00
Vase, Bronze Finish, Red Wing Union Stoneware Co., 22 In. 330.00
Vase, Castle, Pink Fleck, Murphy Design, 10 3/4 In. 125.00
Vase, Dark Green, Handle, 1920s, 12 1/2 In. 150.00
Vase, Embossed Lions, Mottled Drip Glaze, Green Over Beige, Stamped, 7 1/2 In. 115.00
Vase, Nokomos, Green Variegated Glaze, 7 In. 157.00
Vase, Rooster, Green & Yellow, 9 1/2 In. 110.00
Vase, White, Green Interior, Sticker, 12 In. 45.00

REDWARE is a hard, red stoneware that originated in the late 1600s and
continues to be made. The term is also used to describe any common
clay pottery that is reddish in color.

Bank, Acorn Shape, Brown Painted, Gold Textured Cap, 4 1/2 In. 265.00
Bank, Basket Form, Bird Top, Lift Lid, 1970s 415.00
Bank, Manganese Splash Design, Pa., 1877, 6 In. 1760.00
Bean Pot, Black Manganese Splash, 6 In. 470.00
Bird Whistle, Large Bird On Perch Flanked By 2 Small Birds, Yellow, 9 3/8 In. 400.00
Bottle, Yellow Splotch Slip Design, Green, Black Glaze, Red, Brown Ground, 6 In. 16100.00
Bowl, Cover, Sponged Manganese Design, Rope Twist Handles, Pa., 7 x 7 In. 2530.00
Bowl, Manganese Glaze, Pouring Edge, 19th Century, 5 3/4 x 20 3/4 In. 385.00
Bowl, Manganese, 6 Incised Gothic Panels, Center Medallion, Star Overlay, 13 In. ... 1925.00
Bowl, Milk, Floral Interior, 2 3/4 x 8 1/2 In. 190.00
Bowl, Milk, Pie Crust Edge, 12 x 3 1/4 In. 110.00
Bowl, Mottled Green Slip, 7 x 15 1/2 In. 495.00
Bowl, Shallow, Double Wavy Crossed Lines, Scooped Bottom, 9 x 1 7/8 In. 495.00
Bowl, Shaving, Stylized Leaves, c.1790, 9 1/2 In. 995.00
Bowl, Slip, Round, 3-Line Yellow Slip Squiggles, 19th Century, 11 1/2 In. 2645.00
Bowl, Trailing Yellow Slip, Pennsylvania, 19th Century, 8 1/4 In. 415.00
Chamber Pot, Applied Strap Handle, Incised Lines, 1800s, 5 1/2 In. 690.00

Charger, Crimped Edge, 3-Line Slip, 11 In. 495.00
Charger, Crimped Edge, Allover Triple S Design, 12 In. 358.00
Charger, Slip Design, Marked 12400 In Center, Pa., 16 In. 840.00
Crock, Manganese Splotching, John Bell, 6 1/4 x 5 1/2 In. 360.00
Dish, Coggled Rim, Central Yellow Slip Design, Pa., 1830, 12 1/2 In. 4400.00
Dish, Orange Ground, 1830, 9 1/2 In. 630.00
Dish, Sgraffito, Yellow, Green Slip Glaze, Peacock Holding Tulip, 9 In. 1610.00
Dish, Stylized Windmill, Green, Ocher, Mustard Ground, Pa., 1 x 3 In. 430.00
Figurine, Dog Seated, Holding Basket In Its Mouth, 4 In. 6050.00
Figurine, Dog, Red, Black Mottled Glazing, Late 19th Century, 3 In. 110.00
Figurine, Dog, Seated, Coleslaw Coat On Head & Shoulders, Olive Glaze, 6 1/4 In. 80.00
Figurine, Dog, Shenandoah Valley, 19th Century, 3 In. 110.00
Figurine, Hippopotamus, Black Glaze, Pa., 2 1/8 x 4 1/2 In. 140.00
Figurine, Reclining, Head On Paws, Forlorn Expression, 3 1/8 x 8 7/8 In. 110.00
Figurine, Spaniel, 6 1/8 In. 275.00
Flask, Manganese Splash, Pa., 1830, 7 3/4 In. 275.00
Flask, Pumpkin Glaze, Tree, Green Ground, 4 Sides, 5 1/2 In. 5750.00
Flowerpot, Attached Underplate, 19th Century, 7 In. 715.00
Flowerpot, Attached Undertray, Workshop Of John Bell, 4 1/2 In. 250.00
Flowerpot, Brown Streak Glaze, Green Glaze Slip Design, 5 7/8 x 5 1/4 In. 2530.00
Flowerpot, Cobalt Blue Lines, Stylized Vines, White Ground, 8 x 10 1/4 In., Pair 250.00
Flowerpot, Coggled, Ruffled Rim, Manganese Splash Design, Pa., 4 3/4 x 5 1/4 In. 220.00
Flowerpot, Inscribed I.S. Stahl, Feb. 13, 1940, Penn., 5 In. 300.00
Flowerpot, Manganese Splash Design, Scalloped Trim, Pa., 4 1/2 x 7 5/8 In. 415.00
Flowerpot, Ruffled Rim, Separate Saucer, 4 1/4 In. 132.00
Flowerpot, Yellow, Green & Brown Design, Coggled Rim, 5 In. 3300.00
Jar, 2 Handles, Brown Glaze, Mottled Interior, 9 In. 150.00
Jar, Black Splotches, Tooled Lines At Shoulder, 10 5/8 In. 385.00
Jar, Brown Running Glaze, Shoulder Handles, Egg Shape, 10 1/2 In. 495.00
Jar, Canning, Green & Orange Glaze, Spots, 7 3/4 In. 580.00
Jar, Dark Reddish Brown Glaze, Raised Ring At Shoulder, Flared Rim, 6 1/2 In. 55.00
Jar, Manganese Glaze, Signed John Bell, Waynesboro, Penn., c.1860, 5 x 5 In. 300.00
Jar, Manganese Splash, Handles, 19th Century, 10 x 7 1/4 In. 880.00
Jar, Mottled Brown Glaze, Tooled Lines, Flared Rim, Handles, 4 5/8 x 5 1/8 In. 330.00
Jar, Yellow Stylized Leaves, Green Mottled, Brown Ground, 7 7/8 In. 3335.00
Jar, Yellow, Green Sponge Slip Design, Incised Rows, Early 19th Century, 6 1/2 In. 1840.00
Jar, Yellow, Slip Flower, Reddish Brown Ground, Textured Band, 8 7/8 In. 5175.00
Jug, Dark Brown Splotches, Maine, 19th Century, 7 1/2 In. 635.00
Jug, Face, Pinched Features, Applied Teeth, 8 In. 2860.00
Jug, Green, Brown Splotches, Oval, Handle, New England, Early 1800s, 9 1/2 In. 1495.00
Jug, Green, Orange Glaze, Early 19th Century, 10 1/2 In. 1090.00
Jug, Green, Orange, Glaze, 8 1/2 In. 58.00
Jug, Green, Orange, Manganese Slip, Pa., 1840, 8 1/2 In. 440.00
Jug, Incised Flower, Green Glaze, 5 1/2 In. 510.00
Jug, Incised Flower, Green Glaze, Braided Handle, Stahl, 5 1/2 In. 495.00
Jug, Ivory Glaze, Sgraffito, Man With Top Hat, 1816, 7 1/8 In. 3850.00
Jug, Oily Rockingham Glaze, John Bell, Waynesboro, 12 1/4 In. 4125.00
Jug, Pear Shape, Green, Dark Brown Glaze, Handle, 7 3/4 In. 4600.00
Jug, Red Mottled, Bulbous, Applied Handle, No. 20 On Base, 11 1/2 In. 1650.00
Jug, Tapered, Oval Shape, Brown Glaze, Handles, 1800s, 8 1/2 x 8 3/4 In., Pair 290.00
Jug, Tricornered Spout, Green Glaze, Green Design, Dated 1888, 13 In. 165.00
Loaf Pan, 3-Line Slip Clef & Sprig Decoration, Penn., c.1820, 11 3/4 x 17 In. 2860.00
Loaf Pan, Slip Design, Serrated Edge, 17 In. 3200.00
Pan, Milk, Brown Slip Glaze, Yellow Band Design, 12 7/8 In. 575.00
Pan, Pudding, Slip Design, 11 In. 950.00
Pie Dish, Orange-Olive Spotting, Ben Owen, 1930s, 2 1/8 x 10 In. 110.00
Pie Plate, Manganese & White Slip Swirl, 8 In. 2970.00
Pie Plate, Pumpkin Glaze, Slip 3 Tulips, 9 In. 4000.00
Pie Plate, Slip Crisscross Design, 7 1/4 In. 6325.00
Pie Plate, Yellow Double Wavy Line, 7 1/2 x 1 1/2 In. 470.00
Pie Plate, Yellow Slip Decoration, 9 x 1 7/8 In. 330.00
Pie Plate, Yellow Slip, Sgraffito Strawberry Pot, Breiniger, Penn., 1990, 10 1/4 In. 80.00
Pitcher, Brown Running Glaze, Strap Handle, 7 1/8 In. 385.00

Pitcher, Coggle Wheel Decoration, Glaze, Manganese Splash, c.1900, 7 1/2 In.	935.00
Pitcher, Coggle Wheel Decoration, Glaze, Manganese Splash, c.1900, 11 1/2 In.	2530.00
Pitcher, Cover, Brown Sponged Lines, Handle, 5 3/4 In.	660.00
Pitcher, Dark Brown Splotches, Flared Rim, Handle, 9 1/4 In.	880.00
Pitcher, Dog, Mastiff, Name Tip On Collar, c.1880, 9 In.	650.00
Pitcher, Eagle, Spread Wings, Orange, Manganese Splash, Medinger, c.1900, 7 In.	1870.00
Pitcher, Ice Lip, Late 19th Century, 8 1/2 x 7 In.	185.00
Pitcher, Milk, Green & Yellow Slip, Tooled Lines, Strap Handle, 4 1/4 In.	495.00
Pitcher, New Hampshire, Beehive Form, Handle, Yellow Green Glaze, c.1800, 6 In.	690.00
Pitcher, Pear Shape, Green, Orange Mottled Glaze, Early 19th Century, 11 In.	2645.00
Pitcher, Silvery Glaze, Made For Betty & Grace, Made By T. Stahl, 1936, 7 In.	55.00
Plaque, Woman, Reclining On Carpet, Unglazed Face, 19th Century, 12 x 7 x 3 In.	55.00
Plate, 3-Line Slip, Pennsylvania, c.1830, 6 1/8 In.	110.00
Plate, Coggled Rim, Tulip, Yellow Slip Design, Late, 19th Century, 5 1/4 In.	1100.00
Plate, Crimped Edge, 3 Bands Of Triple Wavy Lines, 9 In.	470.00
Plate, Polychrome Floral Design, 9 1/4 In., Set Of 8	260.00
Plate, Round, Yellow Slip, Coggled Rim, Initials, American, 19th Century, 9 1/4 In.	460.00
Plate, Sgraffito, 2 Headed Bird, Flowers, German Verse, 12 In.	55.00
Plate, Sgrafitto, Central Tulip Design, Jacob Medinger, Pa., 11 In.	935.00
Plate, Sgrafitto, Woman On Horse, Jacob Medinger, Pa., 11 In.	195.00
Plate, Shallow, Rolled Under Rim, Orange Glaze, 9 1/4 In.	165.00
Plate, Slip Design, Circular Manganese Design, Pa., Early 19th Century, 6 3/8 In.	1320.00
Plate, Slip Sprig & Squiggle Line, Coggled Rim, 10 3/4 In.	1430.00
Plate, Yellow Slip Design, Early 19th Century, 9 x 9 3/4 In., Pair	1265.00
Plate, Yellow Slip Design, Edward, c.1860, 8 In.	610.00
Plate, Yellow Twist Slip, Red Brown Ground, Textured Rim, Round, 1 1/2 x 9 In.	805.00
Pot, Bulb, Saucer, Flared Rim, 5 Holes In Shoulder, Yellow Glaze, 10 In.	330.00
Tart Plate, Coggled Rim, Yellow, Brown Floral Slip Design, Pa., 5 In.	6875.00
Tart Plate, Slip Design, Simon Singer, 19th Century, Pa., 5 In.	1430.00
Vase, Coggled Rim, Green, Orange, Manganese Slip Design, Pa., 1900, 11 In.	1980.00
Vase, Orange, Green Mottled Slip Design, Pa., 1900, 11 1/2 In.	770.00
Washboard, Dark Sponge Accents, Alkaline Glaze, Wooden Frame, 1870, 24 In.	605.00
Whistle, Chicken Shape, Pennsylvania, 19th Century	415.00

REGOUT, see Maastricht category.

RICHARD was the mark used on acid-etched cameo glass vases, bowls, night-lights, and lamps made by the Austrian company Loetz after 1918. The pieces were very similar to the other French cameo glasswares made by Daum, Galle, and others.

Bowl, Amethyst, Cameo, Signed, Loetz, 6 x 3 1/3 x 3 In.	625.00
Vase, Amethyst Over, Light Blue, Cameo, Signed, 6 1/2 In.	850.00
Vase, Clover, Cameo, Signed, 8 In.	460.00
Vase, Leaves, Cameo, 6 In.	575.00
Vase, Rose Hips, Leaf Decoration, Enameled, Cameo, 6 1/2 In.	800.00

RIDGWAY pottery has been made in the Staffordshire district in England since 1808 by a series of companies with the name Ridgway. The transfer-design dinner sets are the most widely known product. They are still being made. Other pieces of Ridgway are listed under Flow Blue.

Butter, Cover, c.1912	140.00
Butter, Cover, Marked England, c.1912	140.00
Dessert Service, Colorful Flowers, Ripe Fruit On Marble Ledge, 1850, 11 Piece	6000.00
Egg Cup, Osborne, Flow Blue, 3 1/2 x 2 3/8 In.	85.00
Pitcher, Blue & White Oriental Design, 7 In.	155.00
Pitcher, Center Satyr Masks, Neck Of Grape Vine, Male Term Handle, 9 1/2 In.	170.00
Pitcher, Salt Glaze, Jousting Knights, White, Marked, 1840, 7 5/8 In.	80.00
Pitcher, Salt Glaze, Light Green, People On Horseback Scene, Cherub Handle, 10 In. . . .	465.00
Plate, Beauties Of America, Capitol Washington, 2 x 11 In.	5500.00
Plate, Beauties Of America, Library, Philadelphia, Blue, 8 1/4 In.	415.00
Plate, City Hall, New York, Blue, 9 3/4 In.	195.00
Plate, Fairmount Garden, Blue Transfer, 9 In.	70.00
Platter, India Temple, Blue, White Transfer, 21 1/4 In.	495.00

Sauceboat, Boston State House, Blue, 7 1/2 In. 440.00
Tureen, Cover, Underplate, c.1820 .... 475.00

RIFLES that are firearms are not listed in this book. BB guns and air rifles are listed in the Toy category.

RIVIERA dinnerware was made by the Homer Laughlin Co. of Newell, West Virginia, from 1938 to 1950. The pattern was similar in coloring and in mood to Fiesta and Harlequin. The Riviera plates and cup handles were square. For more information, see *Kovels' Depression Glass & Dinnerware Price List*.

Green, Plate, 6 In. 8.00
Green, Plate, Square, 9 In. 22.00
Ivory, Plate, 9 In. 15.00
Mauve, Berry Bowl, 5 1/2 In. 10.00
Mauve, Casserole, Cover ....55.00 to 110.00
Mauve, Cup 7.00
Mauve, Saucer 7.00
Mauve, Sugar 6.00
Mauve, Tumbler, Handle 85.00
Red, Bowl, 5 1/2 In. 8.00
Red, Butter, 1/2 Lb. 100.00
Red, Cup & Saucer 30.00
Red, Tumbler, Handle 85.00
Yellow, Butter, 1/2 Lb. ....22.00 to 60.00
Yellow, Casserole, Cover 110.00
Yellow, Cup & Saucer 25.00
Yellow, Pitcher, Juice 195.00
Yellow, Plate, Square, 9 In. 20.00
Yellow, Platter, 11 1/4 In. 20.00
Yellow, Saucer 7.00

ROBLIN Art Pottery was founded in 1898 by Alexander W. Robertson and Linna Irelan in San Francisco, California. The pottery closed in 1906. The firm made faience with green, tan, dull blue, or gray glazes. Decorations were usually animal shapes. Some red clay pieces were made.

Mug, Handle, Bisque, Handle, Signed, 3 1/2 In. 385.00

ROCKINGHAM, in the United States, is a pottery with a brown glaze that resembles tortoiseshell. It was made from 1840 to 1900 by many American potteries. Mottled brown Rockingham wares were first made in England at the Rockingham factory. Other types of ceramics were also made by the English firm. Related pieces may be listed in the Bennington category.

Bank, Ram, 3 x 5 In. 129.00
Bedpan, Glazed, Yellow Stoneware, 17 x 12 x 5 In. 76.00
Bottle, Spirit, Jim Crow, American Indian, Full Figure On Keg, 9 1/8 In. 450.00
Bowl, Flat Bottom, 11 1/2 x 3 1/2 In. 300.00
Canister, Cover, Scalloped Design On Lid, 8 1/2 x 6 1/2 In. 50.00
Creamer, Cow, Cover, 5 1/2 In. 220.00
Cuspidor, Brown, Marked, L.J. Underwood, Barberton, Ohio, 1909, 4 1/2 In. 95.00
Cuspidor, Medallions Around Side, Verse At Top, 4 1/2 x 8 In. 440.00
Cuspidor, Shell Design, Cocoa, Yellowware 195.00
Figurine, Dog, Free Standing Front Legs, 10 3/4 In. 300.00
Figurine, Dog, Spaniel, Seated, 19th Century, 10 1/2 In. 495.00
Figurine, Poodle, Free Standing Front Legs, Scalloped Base, 10 1/2 In. 495.00
Figurine, Spaniel, Glaze, Base, 10 1/4 In. 345.00
Flask, Boot, Flint Enamel Glaze, Bennington Companion C On Spine, 7 3/4 In. 935.00
Flask, Boot, Lace Up One Side, 6 1/2 x 7 1/4 In. 165.00
Flask, Dismounted Horseman Each Side, Scalloped Neck, 7 1/4 In. 385.00
Flask, Laced Side, 6 1/4 x 8 3/4 In. 410.00
Flask, Scalloped Neck, Eagle With Banner 1 Side, Flowers Other, 7 1/4 In. 190.00

Hot Plate, Eagle Center, Ridged Edge, 3 Footed, 7 3/8 In. 550.00
Inkwell, Boy Asleep, Holding His Hat, 4 x 5 1/2 In. 330.00
Inkwell, Shoe Form, Mottled Brown Glazing, 5 In., Pair 660.00
Inkwell, Yellowware, Spaniels, Female, Puppy, 4 3/4 In. 225.00
Mixing Bowl, 8 x 4 In. 85.00
Mixing Bowl, 10 1/2 x 5 In. 95.00
Pie Plate, Glaze, 10 In. 105.00
Pie Plate, Mottled, Glazed, Brown, Yellow, 9 1/2 In. 165.00
Pitcher, Embossed Medallion, Man With Beard, Hat, Handle, 8 1/2 x 24 In. 295.00
Pitcher, Hound Handle, Star & Eagle On Sides, 9 3/4 In. 220.00
Pitcher, Lion, Tail Handle, 11 1/2 In. 220.00
Pitcher, Stag & Eagle Design, Hound Handle, 9 3/4 In. 192.50
Platter, Octagonal, Signed, 9 3/8 x 12 1/2 In. 715.00
Salt Crock, Turkey, Cover 186.00
Tureen, Sauce, Floral Panels, Thistle Finial, Pair 805.00
Vase, Central Bouquets, Gilt Foliage & Trim, Pierced Rim, c.1835, 11 In. 288.00

ROOKWOOD pottery was made in Cincinnati, Ohio, from 1880 to 1960.
All of this art pottery is marked, most with the famous flame mark. The
R is reversed and placed back to back with the letter P. Flames surround the letters. After 1900, a Roman numeral was added to the mark
to indicate the year. The name and some of the molds were purchased
in 1984. A few new pieces were made, but these were glazed in colors
not used by the original company.

Ashtray, Advertising, 75th Anniversary, Huenefeld Co., 1872-1947, 5 3/4 In. 100.00
Ashtray, Clown, White Matte Glaze, Light Lime Green Ground, Toohey, 1929, 4 In. 385.00
Ashtray, Fox, Yellow Glaze, 1942, 7 In. 220.00
Ashtray, Owl On Tray, White 158.00
Ashtray, Owl, Green High Glaze, 1950, 4 1/4 In. 137.00
Ashtray, Owl, Maroon Matte Glaze, 1922, 5 3/4 In. 88.00
Ashtray, Playing Card, Crystalline Blue Matte Glaze, Sallie Toohey, 1928, 10 In. 143.00
Ashtray, Rose Glaze, c.1921 . . . . 240.00
Bookends, 2 Braying Donkeys, Speckled Brown Over Yellow Glaze, 4 1/2 In. 935.00
Bookends, Beagle, Glossy Brown Glaze, c.1948, 5 x 6 In. 345.00
Bookends, Cactus Flower, Gray Over Pink Matte Glaze, 1927, 3 3/4 In. 209.00
Bookends, Dutch Boy & Girl, Tulips, Ivory Glaze, Sallie Toohey, 1933, 5 1/2 In. 467.00
Bookends, Eagle, Speckled Blue Over Tan Glaze, Louise Abel, 1934, 5 1/4 In. 392.00
Bookends, Elephant, Blue, Caramel Crystalline Matte Glaze, c.1922, 5 x 5 3/4 In. 144.00
Bookends, Elephant, Bronze Tone Matte Glaze, 1919, 4 7/8 In. 825.00
Bookends, Elephant, Brown Over Green Matte Glaze, Bronze, McDonald, 7 In. 1100.00
Bookends, Elephant, Ivory Matte Glaze, 1937, 7 In. 550.00
Bookends, Elephant, Trunk Up, Wine Matte Glaze, 1949, 7 1/4 In. 420.00
Bookends, Gold Elizabethan Ladies Design, 1919, 5 1/2 In. 220.00
Bookends, Gold Kingfisher, William McDonald, 1931, 5 1/2 In. 550.00
Bookends, Honey Bear, Nubian Black Glaze, Louise Abel, 4 3/8 In. . . . . *Illus* 2860.00
Bookends, Kneeling Angel, White Ground, Signed, 1945, 7 1/4 In. 460.00
Bookends, Lion, Ivory Matte Glaze, Louise Abel, 1929, 6 1/2 In. 495.00
Bookends, Owl, On Book, 1952, 5 7/8 In. 258.00
Bookends, Owl, On Book, Logo, 1945, 4 x 3 In. 357.00
Bookends, Owls, Ivory Glaze, Signed, 1946, 5 1/2 In. 385.00
Bookends, Panther, Black Matte Glaze, William McDonald, 5 1/2 In. 1430.00
Bookends, Rook, Brown High Glaze, William McDonald, 1946, 5 1/4 In. 220.00
Bookends, Rook, Cherry Tree, Ivory Matte Glaze, c.1933, 5 1/4 x 5 1/2 In. 259.00
Bookends, Rook, Cream, 5 1/4 In. . . . . .380.00 to 440.00
Bookends, Rook, Green & Brown Glaze, William McDonald, 1937, 5 1/2 In. 412.00
Bookends, Rook, On Flowering Branches, Brown & Amber Glaze, 1937, 6 1/8 In. 575.00
Bookends, Scarlett With Fan, Aqua Matte Glaze, 1932, 6 1/2 In. 300.00
Bookends, Seated Girl, Reading Book, Pink, Green Matte Glaze, 6 In. 290.00
Bookends, Sphinx, Brown Mottled Matte Glaze, 1920, 7 In. 1344.00
Bookends, Tree, Green Crystalline Matte Glaze, Wm. McDonald, 1929, 5 In. 550.00
Bottle, Double Gourd, Ear Of Corn, Grapevines, Stopper, c.1890, 8 1/2 In. 2300.00
Bottle, Flowers, Purple, Green, Gray Butterfat, Epply, 1927, 7 1/2 In. 1495.00
Bowl, 3 Handles, Green & Brown Glaze, Signed, 1921, 5 In. 198.00

Rookwood, Bookends, Honey Bear,
Nubian Black Glaze, Louise Abel, 4 3/8 In.

Don't display pewter on a wooden shelf. Paint and wood give off gases that damage pewter. Don't store pewter near cardboard or vinegar. The fumes will cause damage. To clean pewter, rub it with cabbage leaves.

Bowl, Abstract Wild Red Roses, Turquoise Matte Glaze, Tischler, 1925, 3 x 7 In.	500.00
Bowl, Brown & Maroon Matte Glaze, Arts & Crafts Style, 1912, 4 In.	275.00
Bowl, Cobalt Blue Matte Glaze, Brown, Tan Crystalline Glaze, 1915, 4 1/4 In.	476.00
Bowl, Flared, Pink, Green Interior, Signed, 1922, 4 x 8 In.	170.00
Bowl, Green Matte Glaze, Pink Matte Interior, Curved Handles, 1929, 4 1/2 In.	168.00
Bowl, Loop Handles, Flowers, Mauve Ground, Sara Sax, 1928, 11 In.	1064.00
Bowl, Mistletoe, Standard Glaze, Laura Lindeman, 1904, 2 5/8 In.	450.00
Bowl, Polychrome Flowers, Ivory Mottled Ground, Elizabeth Lincoln, 1930, 4 In.	420.00
Bowl, Salamander, Green Matte Glaze, 1908, 3 1/4 x 8 In.	642.00
Bowl, Steel Blue Glaze, Light Luster Finish, 1920, 3 x 5 3/4 In.	138.00
Bowl, Uncle Remus, Possum Looking Down Hole, E. Cranch, 1885, 6 1/2 In.	950.00
Box, Butterfly, 6 Sides, Elizabeth Lincoln, 5 In.	2520.00
Candlestick, Cameo Ware, White Flowers, Blue Gray Ground, Gilt Details, 10 In.	690.00
Candlestick, Double Handle, Blue Glaze, 1923, 7 1/2 In., Pair	265.00
Candlestick, Egyptian Woman, 1946, 13 7/8 In., Pair	616.00
Candlestick, Open Flower, Stem & Leaves Under Blue Glaze, 1919, 6 1/2 In., Pair	165.00
Candlestick, Pale Green Matte Glaze, Pink Rim, 1929, 5 1/8 In.	168.00
Candlestick, Seahorse, White Matte Glaze, Sallie Toohey, 1928, 3 7/8 In., Pair	385.00
Candlestick, Yellow Matte Glaze, 1920, 6 5/8 In., Pair	390.00
Chamberstick, Cherry Blossom Bough, Standard Glaze, c.1893, 3 x 5 1/2 In.	375.00
Coffeepot, Cover, Bird On Branch, Ear-Shaped Handle, Green Glaze, 1884, 9 In.	460.00
Creamer, 3 Little Pansies, Russet, Teal Ground, Emma Foertmeyer, 1890	385.00
Creamer, Apple Blossom, Orange Ground, Elizabeth Lincoln, 1892, 3 In.	920.00
Creamer, Wild Rose, Butterfly Handles, White Clay, E. Foertmeyer, 3 In.	280.00
Ewer, Apple Blossoms, Standard Glaze, Flame Mark, Toohey, 1894, 8 In.	489.00
Ewer, Branch Of Wild White Roses, Diaphanous, Matthew Daly, 1887, 12 In.	805.00
Ewer, Brown-Eyed Susan, Standard Glaze, H. Wilcox, 1894, 8 x 5 1/2 In.	730.00
Ewer, Cherry Blossoms, Standard Glaze, Yellow, Pink, Brown Ground, 7 x 4 In.	489.00
Ewer, Holly, Standard Glaze, Lindeman, 1890, 6 1/2 In.	374.00
Ewer, Incised Geometric Design, Green Matte Glaze, 1931, 9 1/2 In.	546.00
Ewer, Leaf & Berry Design, Standard Glaze, Howard Altman, 1901, 6 7/8 In.	420.00
Ewer, Star Design, Standard Glaze, Virginia Demarest, 1900, 6 In.	345.00
Ewer, Swallow, Tree Scene, Gold, 1882, 11 1/8 In.	336.00
Ewer, Yellow Roses On Leafy Branches, Standard Glaze, 1895, 11 1/4 In.	860.00
Figurine, Egret, Caramel Glaze, Signed, 1954, 9 In.	230.00
Figurine, Infant Jesus Of Prague, Clotilda Zanetta, 1946, 11 5/8 In.	252.00
Figurine, Monkey, White Glaze, 1907, 3 1/2 In.	165.00
Figurine, St. Francis, Wine Madder Glaze, Clotilda Zanetta, 1946, 11 1/8 In.	213.00
Figurine, Virgin Mary, Gilt Blue Glaze, Signed, 1950, 12 In.	330.00
Flask, Pilgrim, Limoges Style, Daisies, Foliage, Mottled Ground, c.1881, 11 1/2 x 10 In. .	690.00
Flower Frog, Nude, Glossy Rose Glaze, 6 1/2 In.	345.00
Goblet, Green Matte Glaze, Flowers, Wm. McDonald, 1906, 5 3/4 In.	560.00
Humidor, Clump Of Yellow & Red Trumpet Flowers, Standard Glaze, 5 1/2 In.	390.00
Humidor, Dogwood Design, White Clay, Standard Glaze, 1889, 6 3/4 In.	950.00
Humidor, Pipe, Matches, Cigars & Berries, Carrie Steinle, 1903, 5 1/4 In.	785.00
Inkwell, Autumn Leaf, Standard Glaze, Carrie Steinle, 1900, 2 3/8 In.	5225.00
Inkwell, Rook On Lily Pad, Matte Mustard Glaze, Signed, 9 x 11 In.	990.00
Jar, Cover, Chinese Figures Riding Horseback, White, 1921, 9 3/4 In.	4032.00

Jar, Cover, Ribbed Body, Green Glaze, 1934, 3 1/2 In. 165.00
Jar, Flowers, Maroon, Pink, Aqua Stamen, Green Leaves, Barrett, 1925, 3 In. 525.00
Jar, Potpourri, Oval, Yellow, Raised Floral Band, Pierced Cover, 1931, 4 In. 315.00
Jar, Water, 2 Swallows Swooping Through Clumps Of Tall Grasses, 1886, 8 In. 1344.00
Jardiniere, Acorns, Standard Glaze, Bulbous, A.M. Valentien, c.1891, 6 x 8 In. 750.00
Jardiniere, Disks, Flowers, Green, Brown Ground, Matthew Daly, c.1887, 12 In. 1035.00
Jardiniere, Yellow Roses, Standard Glaze, Van Briggle, Spherical, 1889, 6 x 8 In. 345.00
Jug, Beagle Portrait, Standard Glaze, E.T. Hurley, 1900, 7 3/4 x 5 In. 1495.00
Jug, Floor, Brown Glossy Glaze, Spouted Bottom, 1884, 28 x 16 In. 1068.00
Jug, Portrait Of Actor Joseph Jefferson As Rip Van Winkle, Handle, 9 3/4 In. 1725.00
Jug, Presentation, Apple Blossoms, Heavy Slip Glaze, L. Fry, 1883, 4 In. 785.00
Jug, Single Orange Butterfly, Wispy Grasses, Horton, 1883, 4 3/4 In. 476.00
Jug, Swallows, Bamboo, Limoges Style, Martin Rettig, c.1882, 5 x 3 1/4 In. 405.00
Jug, Whiskey, Bittersweet Design, Standard Glaze, Sprague, 1893, 6 In. 550.00
Lamp, Lily Design, Brown Heavy Slip Glaze, Kay Ley, 1948, 13 In. 560.00
Lamp Base, 2 Handles, Yellow Blossoms, Standard Glaze, Footed, 9 In. 200.00
Lamp Base, Green Leaves, Brown, Teal Glaze, L. Holtkamp, 1950, 13 In. 1870.00
Loving Cup, Carved, Galleons, Clouds, Matte Green Ground, 8 1/2 x 8 In. 805.00
Loving Cup, Leaf, Berry Design, Standard Glaze, Carrie Steinle, 1898, 4 1/8 In. 550.00
Match Holder, Flowers, Carrie Steinle, 1901, 3 In. 205.00
Mug, Chief Mountain, Blackfeet Tribe, Sturgis Laurence, 1899, 5 In. 2350.00
Mug, Conquering Deer, Indian Chief, 1901, 5 x 5 In. 2415.00
Mug, Flemish Woman's Head, Standard Glaze, Grace Young, c.1897, 4 x 5 In. 635.00
Mug, Incised Red Flowers, Green Leaves, Stylized, 3 Handles, 1907, 5 In. 1064.00
Mug, Man & Woman Frolicking In A Grape Arbor, White Finish, 1882, 7 In. 303.00
Mug, Portrait Of Chief Owns A Dog, Flora King, c.1945, 4 3/4 In. 224.00
Mug, Scattered Mushrooms, Carmel Exterior Glaze, Brown Handle, 1900, 5 In. 275.00
Mug, Stylized Oak Leaves, Butterfat Green Acorns, Brown, 1905, 7 x 4 1/4 In. 478.00
Paperweight, Black Panther, Black Glaze, 1921, 2 5/8 In. 728.00
Paperweight, Deer, Brown Over Tan Glaze, 1936, 4 7/8 In. 420.00
Paperweight, Elephant, Yellow Matte Glaze, McDonald, 1926, 3 In. 385.00
Paperweight, Gazelle, White Matte Glaze, Louise Abel, 1931, 5 3/8 In. 440.00
Paperweight, Geese, Ivory Matte Glaze, c.1928, 4 1/2 x 5 In. 316.00
Paperweight, Monkey On A Book, Speckled Brown Crystalline Glaze, 1923, 4 In. 530.00
Paperweight, Pelican, White Matte Glaze, 1932, 2 1/8 x 4 1/2 In. 176.00
Paperweight, Rooster, Polychrome Glaze, McDonald, 1946, 5 1/8 In. 605.00
Paperweight, Rooster, Yellow, Green High Glaze, McDonald, 1946, 5 In. 715.00
Pitcher, 2 Pterodactyls With Large Beaks Open Flying, Sea Green, Handle, 10 In. 8250.00
Pitcher, Bamboo Bushes, Gold, Black Swallows, Gilded Accents, c.1882, 8 x 8 In. 405.00
Pitcher, Brownie Type Figure, Arms Folded, Green Glaze, H. Wilcox, 1898, 10 In. 8400.00
Pitcher, Carp Swimming, Green, Gray, Blue, Matt Daly, 1885, 8 x 9 In. 1575.00
Pitcher, Corn, Green Leaves, Shirayamadani, 1899, 14 3/8 In. 4370.00
Pitcher, Corn, Standard Glaze, Shirayamadani, 1900, 14 3/8 In. 4290.00
Pitcher, Dark Blue Irises, Standard Glaze, Carl Schmidt, 1900, 4 1/4 In. 1100.00
Pitcher, Flock Of 20 Swallows, Some Perched On Tree Limb, 1882, 7 In. 1320.00
Pitcher, Gooseberry Leaves, Amber, Green, Standard Glaze, 1891, 12 In. 1800.00
Pitcher, Green & Blue Violets, Constance A. Baker, 1902, 3 1/2 In. 385.00
Pitcher, Maple Leaves, Standard Glaze, Bulbous, Caroline Steinle, c.1897, 4 In. 489.00
Pitcher, Memorial, President James Garfield Portrait, Eagle & Shield, 1885, 10 In. 545.00
Pitcher, Metal Roses, Robin's-Egg Blue Glaze, White Metal, 1895, 7 1/4 In. 1230.00
Pitcher, Mums, Amber Ground, Standard Glaze, Pinched Waist, c.1888, 4 1/2 x 5 In. 259.00
Pitcher, Nasturtiums, Standard Glaze, Flame Mark, E. Lincoln, 1898, 8 In. 230.00
Pitcher, Pink Poppies, Cameo Glaze, White Clay, Anna Valentien, 1890, 7 In. 895.00
Pitcher, Swirly Leaves, Light Blue Interior, Jens Jensen, 1949, 7 In. 935.00
Plaque, 3 Geese Along Road, House, Oak Frame, Sallie Toohey, 4 1/2 x 9 In. 3575.00
Plaque, Autumn Landscape Scene With Waterfall, Vellum, Diers, 1921, 7 x 6 In. 3220.00
Plaque, Body Of Water, Trees & Brush On Sides, Fred Rothenbusch, 1915, 9 In. 4125.00
Plaque, Distant Medieval Village, Faience, Albert Pons, 1906, 9 In. 2090.00
Plaque, Early Morning, Vellum, Original Frame, Edward Diers, 1917, 8 x 10 In. 4900.00
Plaque, Misty Landscape, Birch Trees, Purple Mountains, Vellum, 1929, 8 In. 3960.00
Plaque, Misty Landscape, Hills Across Lake With Tall Trees, Epply, 1919, 12 In. 3740.00
Plaque, Misty Morn, Birch Trees By Lake, E.T. Hurley, 1926, 6 x 8 In. 4025.00
Plaque, Mountain & Lake Scene, Frame, Ed Diers, 1912, 16 1/2 x 11 1/4 In. 4312.00

Plaque, Mountain Lake Scene, Tall Trees, Pastel Sky, Vellum, 11 x 10 In. 4313.00
Plaque, Ocean View, On Bluffs, Frame, Sara Sax, 1916, 10 3/4 x 8 1/2 In. 8050.00
Plaque, River Landscape Scene At Dusk, Vellum, Lorinda Epply, 1920, 5 x 9 In. 3450.00
Plaque, Stand Of Trees Divided By Stream, Lorinda Epply, 1917, 11 x 9 In. 6600.00
Plaque, Summer Woodland Scene With Flowers, Rothenbusch, 1917, 10 In. 7700.00
Plaque, Trees Overlooking Lake, Distant Mountains, Ed Diers, 1919, 11 1/2 In. 9200.00
Plaque, Trees, Distant Hills, Oak Frame, Edward Hurley, 9 x 11 In. 4400.00
Plaque, Woodland Scene, Twilight, Sky Ablaze, Vellum, 1921, 9 x 14 In. 8800.00
Plate, Blue Ship, 10 In., 4 Piece 450.00
Sign, Rookwood, Cincinnati, Ivory Glaze, 1890, 14 In. 330.00
Stein, Frolicking Cherubs, Olive High Glaze, Tan Interior, 1963, 7 3/4 In. 138.00
Tea Set, Teapot, Cover, Sugar & Creamer, 3 1/4-In. Teapot, 1923, 4 Piece 225.00
Tile, 4 Acorns Meeting At Their Points, Circled By Wreath Of Leaves, 4 In. 250.00
Tile, Cat, Soft Gray Shades, Tan Matte Ground, 5 3/4 In. 1100.00
Tile, Celtic Cross, Dark Brown, Green, 1971, 8 x 8 In. 300.00
Tile, Cornflower-Blue Tulip Shapes, 4-Lobed Geometric Design, Brown, 1952 . . . . 255.00
Tile, Dutch Sailing Ship Heading Out To Sea, 1910, 6 In. 550.00
Tile, Elephant With Rider, Brown, Tan, Yellow, Lime Green, 1949, 6 x 6 In. 275.00
Tile, Fish Scene, Faience, Mosaic, New Frame, W. Hentschel, 6 In., 12 Piece 5500.00
Tile, Flowers, Vines, Celadon Green Glaze, 1957, 7 1/4 In. 168.00
Tile, Frog With A Crown, 1920, 4 x 4 In. 385.00
Tile, Grapes & Leaves, Matte Green, Purple, Faience, 6 In., 4 Piece 1045.00
Tile, Greek Key Design, Lavender, Gray, Green, Square, 3 In. . . . . .110.00 to 230.00
Tile, Intertwining Lilies, Stylized, Brown Matte Ground, Square, 12 In. 1210.00
Tile, Lamp Of Knowledge, Gold, Blue Ground, 8 1/2 x 8 1/2 In. 357.00
Tile, Man & Woman, Colonial Clothes, Faience, W. Hentschel, 1935, 50 x 41 In. 4950.00
Tile, Oak Leaves, Green Matte Glaze, 6 x 6 In. 450.00
Tile, Sea Gulls In Flight, Turquoise Glaze, 1951, 5 3/4 In. 165.00
Tile, Ship, Sails, Faience, Hanger Back, Round, 12 In. 3190.00
Tile, Steamship Against Setting Sun, 3 3/4 x 5 In. 360.00
Tray, Carved Lily Under Green Glaze, 1904, 9 1/2 In. 770.00
Tray, Incised Geometric Design, Peacock Feather, Yellow Matte Glaze, 1924, 6 In. 430.00
Tray, Rook, Purple Glaze, 1915, 4 In. 145.00
Trivet, 4 Stylized Yellow Tulips, Pinwheel Design, Green Border, 1922, 5 3/4 In. 308.00
Trivet, Embossed Bird, Yellow & White Glaze, 1927, 6 In. 220.00
Trivet, Flowers, Yellow, Green Leaves, Signed, 1921, 6 In. 255.00
Trivet, Grapes, Red, Vellum, Oak Frame, 1929, 5 3/4 In. 500.00
Trivet, Parrot, Polychrome Matte Glaze, 1930, 5 3/4 In. 187.00
Trivet, Rose, Ivory Matte Glaze, 1921, 5 3/4 In. 230.00
Trivet, Sea Gulls, 1943, 5 7/8 In. 360.00
Trivet, Swirling 4-Section Tulip, Pink, Green, Blue, 1921, 5 5/8 In. 385.00
Trivet, Swirling Geometric Design, Cornflower Blue, Sea Green, 1922, 5 3/4 In. 190.00
Tumbler, Maroon, Green, Black, Silver, Metallic Glaze, Maria L. Storer, 1897, 6 In. 450.00
Tumbler, Metallic Glaze, Black Slip Base, Maria Longworth Storer, 1896, 4 7/8 In. 728.00
Urn, Baluster, Hibiscus, Glazed, Flame Mark, Edith Felten, c.1898, 5 x 3 1/2 In. 405.00
Urn, Greek Key Design, Rose, Chartreuse Butterfat Glaze, 1912, 18 x 14 In. 1910.00
Urn, Jewel, Green, Orange Cherry Blossom Branches, Shirayamadani, 1925, 8 In. 1725.00
Vase, Abstract Berries, Leaves, Flowers, Green, Orange, Turquoise, 7 x 3 1/2 In. 1068.00
Vase, American Indian, Brown Glaze, Matt Daly, 1900, 20 In. . . . .*Illus* 13200.00
Vase, Apple Blossoms, Golden, Standard Blaze, Ruffled Rim, c.1891, 4 1/4 x 7 In. 430.00
Vase, Apple Blossoms, Pink, Ivory Butterfat Ground, Shirayamadani, 1937, 5 In. 1125.00
Vase, Arrowhead Blossoms, White, Teal Leaves, Pink, Shirayamadani, 8 In. 3375.00
Vase, Art Deco Roses Rim Band, Vellum, Oval, c.1915, 7 3/4 x 3 1/4 In. 978.00
Vase, Autumn Scene, Ocher, Blue, Vellum, Ed Diers, 1930, 9 x 4 1/2 In. 2070.00
Vase, Azalea Blossoms, Standard Glaze, Round, Flame Mark, J. Zettel, 1893, 5 In. 490.00
Vase, Azure Blue Hillside, Brown, Tan Trees, Gray Ground, 1921, 8 In. 1420.00
Vase, Bachelor's Buttons, Blue, Red Ground, Catherine Covalenco, 1925, 8 x 3 In. 1350.00
Vase, Bachelor's Buttons, Red, Purple, Ivory Ground, Bulbous, c.1945, 4 x 4 In. 316.00
Vase, Band Of Cherry Blossom Branches, Rosy Pink, Blue, E.T. Hurley, 1920, 5 In. 1120.00
Vase, Band Of Ocher Dogwood Blossoms, Orange Ground, Wilcox, 1906, 12 In. 4218.00
Vase, Band Of Red & Green Crocuses, Brown Matte Glaze, Hentschel, 1914, 5 In. 1265.00
Vase, Band Of Red Cherry Blossoms, Black Branches, Vellum, Hurley, 6 x 9 In. 1910.00
Vase, Band Of Sea Gulls In Flight Over Rocky Coast, Mint Green, 1905, 12 In. 4315.00

Vase, Banded Geometric Design, Tan, Green, Wilhelmine Rehm, 1944, 7 1/8 In. 715.00
Vase, Bands Of Flowers, Concentric Circles On Base, Elizabeth Barrett, 1928, 5 In. 275.00
Vase, Berried Branches, Sea Green, Sallie Coyne, 1901, 7 In. 2415.00
Vase, Berries & Leaves Under Mustard Matte Glaze, 1929, 4 1/2 In. 165.00
Vase, Berries, Red, Green Leaves, Dark Blue Ground, Vellum, 1917, 6 In. 935.00
Vase, Birch Tree Landscape At Dusk, Vellum Glaze, Hurley, 1912, 16 x 6 In. 4310.00
Vase, Birch Trees By Lake, Pastel Sky, Vellum, Fred Rothenbusch, 1920, 7 x 3 In. 1910.00
Vase, Birds & Leaves, Textured Peach & Yellow, Limoges Glaze, Daly, 1885, 11 In. 635.00
Vase, Bisque, Branches, Blossoms, Bulbous, Harriet Wilcox, c.1882, 11 x 6 In. 546.00
Vase, Black Opal, Boughs Of Flowers, Cobalt Ground, Sara Sax, 1927, 9 In. 2070.00
Vase, Blackberries, Leaves, Green Interior, Fred Rothenbusch, 1928, 8 1/8 In. 1792.00
Vase, Blackberries, Leaves, Standard Glaze, Josephine Zettel, 1898, 5 5/8 In. 5225.00
Vase, Blossoms, Blue, Mottled, Pink Matte, Bulbous, c.1936, 4 1/2 x 4 3/4 In. 635.00
Vase, Blossoms, Mauve, Buff Ground, Arthur Conant, 1916, 7 1/4 x 4 1/4 In. 1380.00
Vase, Blossoms, White & Pink, Fred Rothenbusch, 1905, 7 In. 1380.00
Vase, Blossoms, White, Yellow Stamen, Gray, Vellum, McDermott, 6 In. 600.00
Vase, Blue Butterfat Glaze, Stylized Flowers, Oval, Flared Rim, c.1922, 6 1/2 In. 805.00
Vase, Blue Wisteria, Mauve Background, Vellum, Shirayamadani, 11 5/8 In. 2970.00
Vase, Blue Wisteria, Vellum Glaze, E.T. Hurley, 1944, 12 7/8 In. 1980.00
Vase, Blue, Cream, Brown, Silver, Maria Longworth Storer, 1896, 8 3/4 In. 280.00
Vase, Blueberries & Leaves, Lorinda Epply, 1924, 6 In. 2430.00
Vase, Blueberries, Black Ground, Standard Glaze, E. Bertha Cranch, 1894, 6 In. 440.00
Vase, Blueberries, Maroon Leaves, Pink Ground, Elizabeth Barrett, 1925, 7 In. 825.00
Vase, Branches Of Blueberries, Green Ground, Lenore Asbury, 1929, 7 1/2 In. 2300.00
Vase, Branches Of Leaves, Berries, Olga G. Reed, 1906, 4 1/4 In. 1495.00
Vase, Branches Of Peaches, Standard Glaze, Matt Daly, 1890, 10 x 9 In. 1800.00
Vase, Buckeyes, Playing Cards, Wm. McDonald, 1897, 7 1/2 In. 1495.00
Vase, Butterflies, Juniper Tree, Bisque, Matthew Daly, 1886, 19 1/2 x 7 In. 2415.00
Vase, Cactus Flowers, Stylized, Heavy Slip, High Glaze, Holtkamp, 1952, 13 In. 420.00
Vase, Calla Lilies, Dark Green Matte Glaze, S. Toohey, 1905, 14 x 5 In. 5750.00
Vase, Calla Lilies, Brown Glaze, Albert Pons, 1907, 8 1/2 x 3 1/2 In. 955.00
Vase, Canada Geese Flying Over Large Body Of Water, 1909, 8 In. 19800.00
Vase, Carnations, Standard Glaze, Handles, Harriet Wilcox, 1892, 7 5/8 In. 410.00
Vase, Carnations, White, Blue Ground, Ed Diers, 1907, 10 3/8 In. 785.00
Vase, Cavalier, Standard Glaze, Bulbous, Bruce Horsfall, c.1896, 8 x 4 In. 575.00
Vase, Chartreuse, Red Ground, Sara Sax, 1905, 7 x 3 In. 1800.00
Vase, Cherry Blossom Band, Vellum, Green Semimatte Glaze, c.1918, 6 x 3 In. 750.00
Vase, Cherry Blossom Bough, Tiger Eye, Slip Painted, Handles, c.1886, 10 x 4 In. 690.00
Vase, Cherry Blossoms, Birds, Pink Glaze, Lorinda Epply, 1922, 10 1/2 x 4 In. 2070.00
Vase, Cherry Blossoms, Blue, Orange Flowers, Sara Sax, 1920, 7 1/2 In. 9350.00
Vase, Cherry Blossoms, Blue, Pink, Vellum, E.T. Hurley, 1938, 6 1/8 In. 990.00
Vase, Cherry Blossoms, Bright Red, Elizabeth Lincoln, 1926, 5 3/8 In. 990.00
Vase, Cherry Blossoms, Maroon, Deep Green, Blue Rim, 1923, 5 1/2 In. 605.00
Vase, Cherry Blossoms, Mauve, Cobalt Blue Petals, S. Coyne, 1918, 6 In. 660.00
Vase, Cherry Blossoms, Oxblood Glaze, Sara Sax, 1920, 4 x 4 In. 1800.00
Vase, Cherry Blossoms, Sara Sax, 1920, 7 1/2 In. 9520.00
Vase, Cherry Blossoms, White, Midnight Blue Ground, McLaughlin, 1915, 9 In. 1682.00
Vase, Cherry Blossoms, White, Pink, Mint Green Ground, Coyne, 1910, 8 1/2 In. 1840.00
Vase, Cherry Branch, Clara Lindeman, 1902, 6 In. 840.00
Vase, Cicadas On Branch, Coffee Ground, Vellum Glaze, Diers, 1905, 9 x 3 In. 4780.00
Vase, Clover, White, Brown Ground, Fred Rothenbusch, 1902, 5 7/8 In. 840.00
Vase, Cluster Of Delicate Spring Hyacinths, Iris Glaze, Olga Reed, 1902, 11 In. 6325.00
Vase, Cluster Of Grapes, Handles, C. Todd, 1912, 6 7/8 In. 505.00
Vase, Colorful Flowers, Leaves In Wide Band, Feathered, Conant, 1917, 7 In. 1790.00
Vase, Conquering Bear, Sioux, A. Sehon, 1901, 9 In. 7700.00
Vase, Crisp Hydrangea, Gold, Green, Standard Glaze, Valentien, 1891, 12 x 12 In. 3150.00
Vase, Daffodils, Standard Glaze, Lena Hanscom, 1903, 8 1/8 In. 550.00
Vase, Daffodils, Yellow, Green Leaves, Standard Glaze, Rothenbusch, 1897, 7 In. 770.00
Vase, Daisies, Light Blue Ground, Vellum, M.H. McDonald, 1913, 8 In. 1350.00
Vase, Daisies, Sea Green, Brown, Ocher, Teal Ground, S. Coyne, 1902, 6 x 2 In. 2645.00
Vase, Daisies, White, Mint Green, Pink, Vellum, Elizabeth Lincoln, 1912, 8 x 4 In. 1350.00
Vase, Daisies, White, Salmon, Gray Ground, White Iris Glaze, S. Sax, 1903, 11 In. 7700.00
Vase, Daisies, White, Yellow, Green, Black Iris Glaze, Sallie Toohey, 1900, 9 In. 4290.00

Vase, Daisies, Yellow, Green Ground, Lenore Asbury, 1903, 9 7/8 In. 1540.00
Vase, Dandelions, Bright Yellow, White Iris Glaze, Fred Rothenbusch, 1903, 9 In. 1650.00
Vase, Dark Brown, Blue, Celadon Glaze, C. Todd, 1912, 7 x 8 In. 1840.00
Vase, Dark Green To Mauve Top, Pale Green Highlights, Art Deco, 1913, 5 3/4 In. 360.00
Vase, Day Lilies, Gold, Blue, Yellow Ground, K. Shirayamadani, 1943, 7 1/2 x 5 In. 865.00
Vase, Deep Purple Speckles, Apple Green, Handles, Herman Moos, 1925, 10 In. 1045.00
Vase, Deer & Flowers, Beige, Cobalt Ground, Jens Jensen, 1933, 7 x 4 In. 236.00
Vase, Deer, Leaves, Ivory Glaze, Bulbous, 7 3/4 x 5 1/2 In. 200.00
Vase, Deer, White, Exotic Flowers, Dark Gray, Rust Ground, J. Jensen, 1931, 8 In. 5170.00
Vase, Diamonds & Flowers, Aqua Matte Glaze, 1926, 6 3/4 In. 220.00
Vase, Dirt Road Winding Through Dense Forest, Vellum, 1927, 15 In. 9075.00
Vase, Dogwood Blossoms Under Olive, Purple, Shirayamadani, 1925, 6 In. 2925.00
Vase, Dogwood Branch Circling Body, Green, Blue, Janet Harris, 1930, 8 In. 920.00
Vase, Dogwood Flowers, Green Leaves, White Iris, Lenore Asbury, 1910, 8 In. 2090.00
Vase, Dogwood, Pink, Vellum Glaze, Catherine Van Horne, 1910, 7 1/2 In. 920.00
Vase, Egg Design, Yellow Flowers, Butterfly Handles, Reed, 1892, 6 1/4 In. 250.00
Vase, Embossed Grapevines, Pink Matte Glaze, Pale Green, 1934, 6 1/4 In. 190.00
Vase, Embossed Lion's Heads, Red, Black, Blue, Tan Metallic Glaze, 1896, 6 In. 450.00
Vase, Embossed Rooks Atop 5 Vertical Panels, Pink Matte Glaze, 1917, 7 In. 475.00
Vase, Eucalyptus Trees, Vellum, Rothenbusch, 1916, 11 1/4 In. 2070.00
Vase, Exotic Antelopes, Foliage, High Glaze, Jens Jensen, 1944, 8 5/8 In. 3360.00
Vase, Exotic Birds Amid Trees, Jet Black Interior, E.T. Hurley, 1931, 18 1/2 In. 8120.00
Vase, Exotic Flowers, Stylized, Blue, Violet Mauve, Brown, Epply, 1928, 8 In. 2750.00
Vase, Floating Lotus Blossoms, Sallie Coyne, 1930, 7 1/8 In. 1870.00
Vase, Flowers & Leaves, Ivory Matte Glaze, 1937, 5 In. 175.00
Vase, Flowers, 6 Panels, Sara Sax, 1927, 4 3/8 In. 2016.00
Vase, Flowers, Blue, Stylized, Green Leaves, Turquoise Ground, Epply, 1920, 9 In. 1035.00
Vase, Flowers, Brown Matte Glaze, 1929, 6 In. 230.00
Vase, Flowers, Copper Patina, Twin Handles, C.S. Todd, 1914, 6 1/8 In. 410.00
Vase, Flowers, Dark Blue, Light Blue, Green, Pink, Shirayamadani, 1925, 8 In. 3520.00
Vase, Flowers, Elizabeth Barrett, 1946, 5 In. 489.00
Vase, Flowers, Interspersed With Fish, Birds, Horses, Deer, Jensen, 1931, 12 In. 2240.00
Vase, Flowers, Leaves, Green, Yellow, Blue, Rose Fechheimer, 1903, 7 In. 545.00
Vase, Flowers, Pink, Blue Ground, Handle, Kay Ley, 1946, 10 In. 240.00
Vase, Flowers, Pink, Charcoal Ground, O.G. Reed, 1911, 8 x 4 In. 1460.00
Vase, Flowers, Pink, White, Deep Blue Ground, Hentschel, 1925, 17 In. 8525.00
Vase, Flowers, Purple, With Golden Centers, Black Vines, Epply, 1923, 10 1/2 In. 7975.00
Vase, Flowers, Purple, Yellow, Red, Blue Ground, Carved, Matte, c.1919, 6 x 3 In. 805.00
Vase, Flowers, Red, Orange, Yellow Ground, K. Shirayamadani, 1925, 8 x 4 In. 4315.00
Vase, Flowers, Red, Yellow, Blue, Green Orange Ground, Moos, 1925, 5 1/4 In. 840.00
Vase, Flowers, Sara Sax, 1924, 4 In. 865.00
Vase, Flowers, White, Brown, Navy Ground, Vellum, Vera Tischler, 1921, 6 3/8 In. 605.00
Vase, Flowers, Yellow Matte Glaze, 1937, 5 5/8 In. 135.00
Vase, Flowers, Yellow, Leaves, Silver Overlay, Amelia Sprague, 1892, 9 In. 2420.00
Vase, Flowers, Yellow, Turquoise Ground, Jens Jensen, 1934, 6 1/4 x 4 In. 1265.00
Vase, Fuchsia, Red, Stylized, Dark Green Matte Glaze, Sara Sax, 1922, 5 1/8 In. 7150.00
Vase, Garland Of Pink Flowers, Blue Blossoms, Lorinda Epply, 1919, 7 1/4 In. 1380.00
Vase, Geese, Blue Scene, Green Ground, Vellum, S. Coyne, 1908, 7 x 4 In. 1150.00
Vase, Geometric Design, Green Matte Glaze, 1904, 4 x 5 In. 374.00
Vase, Geometric Design, Molded, Blue Matte Glaze, 1945, 6 In. 207.00
Vase, Gold, Gray Matte Ground, Harriet Wenderoth, 1882, 11 1/2 In. 430.00
Vase, Goldenrod, Light Brown Ground, Harriet Wilcox, 1896, 7 3/8 In. 825.00
Vase, Gooseberries, Purple, Pink Foliage, Rothenbusch, 1913, 7 x 5 In. 1150.00
Vase, Grapes, Light Green, White Iris Glaze, Lenore Asbury, 1909, 8 3/4 In. 1540.00
Vase, Gray Blue, Kataro Shirayamadani, 8 In. 3400.00
Vase, Gray Hillside Background, Trees, Vivid Aqua, Tan, Gray Sky, Vellum, 10 In. 1540.00
Vase, Gray Sailboats, Sea Green Ground, Iris Glaze, Sallie Coyne, 1910, 8 x 4 In. 2760.00
Vase, Greek Key Design, Blue Matte Glaze, 1920, 5 3/4 In. 225.00
Vase, Green Ribbons On Top, Copper Dragon On Bottom, Sea Green, 1900, 17 In. 15960.00
Vase, Green, Brown High Glaze, Crimped, 1887, 4 1/2 In. 325.00
Vase, Harbor Scene, Venice, Light Green, Frame, Carl Schmidt, 1922, 10 In. 2200.00
Vase, Harbor Scene, Venice, Sailboats, Vellum Glaze, 1925, 10 x 4 In. 7310.00
Vase, Harbor Scene, Venice, Several Ships At Sail, 1916, 11 In. 4730.00

Vase, Hawthorn Branches, Vellum, Light Green, Lorinda Epply, 1907, 6 1/4 In. 385.00
Vase, Holly Berries, Leaves, Under Silver Overlay, Josephine Zettel, 1892, 5 In. 3080.00
Vase, Holly Branches, Charles Todd, 1901, 6 1/2 In. 1265.00
Vase, Hollyhocks, Lenore Asbury, 1925, 14 1/8 In. 5040.00
Vase, Hollyhocks, Turquoise, Maroon, 1915, 8 3/4 In. 275.00
Vase, Hydrangea, Purple, Green Ground, Iris Glaze, Rothenbusch, 1904, 12 In. 2760.00
Vase, Hydrangea, White, Leaves, Frederick Rothenbusch, 1902.9 In. 2185.00
Vase, Incised Geometric Design, Brown Matte Glaze, Yellow, Green, 1925, 5 In. 460.00
Vase, Incised Geometric Design, Purple, Brown Matte Glaze, 1915, 6 1/2 In. 405.00
Vase, Incised Peacock Feathers, Brown, Green, Blue, Vellum, S. Sax, 1911, 8 In. 4315.00
Vase, Incised Stylized Flowers, Brown Crystalline Matte, C. Todd, 1917, 12 In. 4400.00
Vase, Incised Stylized Iris Blossoms, Signed, C.S. Todd, 1920, 10 3/4 In. 980.00
Vase, Incised, Painted Daisies, Brown, Black Rim, Shirayamadani, 1899, 7 In. 1345.00
Vase, Incised, Painted Flowers, Blue Ground, Elizabeth Lincoln, 1922, 24 3/4 In. 4590.00
Vase, Indigo Violets, Charcoal Ground, Iris Glaze, C.A. Baker, 1896, 6 x 3 In. 1840.00
Vase, Iris Glaze, Allover Nasturtium Design, Mary Nourse, 1904, 8 In. 1068.00
Vase, Iris Glaze, White Poppies, Fred Rothenbusch, 1903, 9 12 x 5 1/4 In. 2415.00
Vase, Iris, Black, 2 Peacock Feathers, Black, Metal Mount, Matt Daly, 1900, 10 In. 10605.00
Vase, Irises, Purple, Blue Green Ground, Fred Rothenbusch, 1908, 11 1/4 In. 1265.00
Vase, Irises, Yellow, Shaded Ground, Flame Mark, Elizabeth Lincoln, 1903, 10 In. 375.00
Vase, Irises, Yellow, Various Stages Of Bloom, Standard Glaze, 1897, 9 x 11 In. 9075.00
Vase, Lake Landscape, Vellum, Ed Diers, 1918, 8 x 3 1/2 In. 1800.00
Vase, Landscape Of Trees, Houses, Fred Rothenbusch, Signed, 1931, 8 3/4 In. 1610.00
Vase, Landscape Scene With Hillsides, Light, Dark Gray, S. Coyne, 7 1/2 In. 1320.00
Vase, Landscape Scene, Vellum Glaze, E.T. Hurley, 1920, 11 In. 2760.00
Vase, Landscape, Birch Trees By Lake, Ed Diers, 1931, 10 1/2 x 5 1/2 In. 5060.00
Vase, Landscape, Trees Reflecting Lake At Sunset, Hurley, 1909, 10 1/2 x 4 In. 900.00
Vase, Leaves With Berries, Unglazed White Clay, 1882, 9 5/8 In. 250.00
Vase, Leaves, Brown, Soft Brown, Sky Blue, Black Lining, Barrett, 1944, 4 In. 605.00
Vase, Leaves, Maroon, Blue Berries, Pink Ground, Elizabeth Barrett, 1925, 6 In. 840.00
Vase, Leaves, Rust, Bright Yellow Ground, Jensen, 1930, 10 1/4 In. 2016.00
Vase, Leaves, Wax Matte, Flared, Flame Mark, 11 x 6 1/2 In. 1035.00
Vase, Life-Size Poppies, Standard Glaze, Amelia Sprague, 1899, 12 1/4 In. 2800.00
Vase, Lilies & Leaves, Black Opal Glaze, Harriet E. Wilcox, 1928, 13 In. . . . . *Illus* 605.00
Vase, Lily Of The Valley, Iris Glaze, Irene Bishop, 1907, 7 1/2 x 3 1/4 In. 1725.00
Vase, Lily Of The Valley, Silver Overlay, White Clay, J. Zettel, 1893, 8 1/2 In. 2688.00
Vase, Lily Of The Valley, Stylized, Blue Matte Glaze, 1913, 4 3/8 In. 250.00
Vase, Live Oaks, Distant Blue Mountains, Rothenbusch, 1920, 7 1/2 In. 1380.00
Vase, Lotus Blossoms, Leaves, Black Slip, Elizabeth Lincoln, 1929, 6 5/8 In. 758.00
Vase, Lotus Blossoms, Leaves, Blue Slip Glaze, Louise Abel, 1927, 6 1/2 In. 785.00
Vase, Magnolia Blossoms, White, Blue, Vellum, Shirayamadani, 1925, 10 In. 13750.00
Vase, Magnolia Blossoms, White, Iris Glaze, Irene Bishop, 1903, 6 1/2 x 4 In. 790.00
Vase, Magnolias, Ivory, Ocher, Teal Ground, Jens Jensen, 1944, 6 x 5 1/2 In. 1460.00
Vase, Maple Leaves, Standard Glaze, 2 Handles, C.F. Bonsall, c.1903, 7 x 4 1/2 In. 575.00
Vase, Mauve Speckled Glaze, Mold 2729, Footed, 1923, 7 In. 145.00
Vase, Misty Landscape Scene, Tall Trees, Lake, Vellum Glaze, Hurley, 1920, 11 In. 4256.00

Rookwood, Vase,
American Indian,
Brown Glaze, Matt
Daly, 1900, 20 In.

Rookwood, Vase, Lilies
& Leaves, Black Opal
Glaze, Harriet E.
Wilcox, 1928, 13 In.

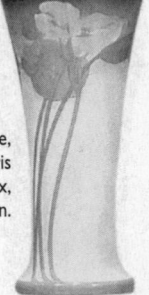

Rookwood, Vase,
Nasturtiums, Iris
Glaze, Sara Sax,
1908, 8 3/8 In.

Vase, Misty Woodland Scene, Green Glaze, Fred Rothenbusch, 1916, 12 1/8 In. 1870.00
Vase, Molded Flowers, Blue, Tan Crystalline Glaze, 1924, 5 In. 290.00
Vase, Monkeys, Stylized, Blue, Green Crystalline Glaze, 1937, 10 1/2 In. 920.00
Vase, Morning Glory, Stylized, Interior Black Glaze, Lorinda Epply, 1923, 10 In. 8120.00
Vase, Mother & Child Amid Crashing Waves, Aerial Blue, 1895, 13 x 3 In. 12375.00
Vase, Multicolored Rose Hip Design, Mocha Glaze, Vellum, 1931, 5 7/8 In. 896.00
Vase, Mushrooms, Pastel Ground, Vellum Glaze, Schmidt, 1905, 10 x 3 In. 12375.00
Vase, Nasturtium Blossoms, Brown Ground, W. Klemm, 1901, 6 7/8 In. 637.00
Vase, Nasturtium Blossoms, Leaves, Green, Cream, Standard Glaze, 1901, 7 In. 630.00
Vase, Nasturtiums, Cluster Of Flowers, Leaves, Mary Nourse, 1898, 9 In. 1904.00
Vase, Nasturtiums, Iris Glaze, Sara Sax, 1908, 8 3/8 In. . . . . *Illus* 4400.00
Vase, Nasturtiums, Red, Standard Glaze, Lenore Asbury, 1902, 6 1/8 In. 550.00
Vase, Nasturtiums, Salmon, Iris Glaze, Gray, Fred Rothenbusch, 1903, 7 In. 1462.00
Vase, Oak Leaves, Deep Violet Glaze Rim, Maroon, Black Lining, 1930, 6 x 5 In. 1650.00
Vase, Oranges & Orange Leaves, Black Outline, Arthur Conant, 1921, 7 1/4 In. 3080.00
Vase, Orchids, Crisp Blue, Amber, Standard Glaze, Valentien, 1898, 13 x 5 In. 1460.00
Vase, Owls, Brown, On Tree Branch, Sara Toohey, 1930, 8 1/2 In. 2860.00
Vase, Oxblood Red Glaze, Blue, Black Slip Base, Storer, 1895, 5 1/2 In. 840.00
Vase, Painted Daisies, Cobalt Ground, Sallie Toohey, 1900, 8 3/8 In. 4368.00
Vase, Painted Irises, Iris Glaze, Carrie Steinle, 1906, 6 1/2 In. 1840.00
Vase, Painting Of 4 Geese In Flight, Matt Daly, 1898, 5 In. 4125.00
Vase, Pale Pink, Blue, Green Ground, Vellum, 1921, 11 3/4 In. 4600.00
Vase, Palm Fronds, Standard Glaze, Caroline Bonsall, 1903, 7 In. 385.00
Vase, Pansies, Vellum Glaze, Ed Diers, 1930, 5 1/2 In. 1095.00
Vase, Pansies, Yellow & Green, Mary Perkins, 1893, 6 1/2 In. 550.00
Vase, Pansies, Yellow, Ivory Ground, Iris Glaze, Sara Sax, 1901, 6 1/2 x 4 In. 790.00
Vase, Pastel Landscape, Spring Green, Vellum, Sallie Coyne, 1917, 10 In. 1575.00
Vase, Peacock Feathers, Stylized, Green Vellum, Sara Sax, 1910, 7 1/2 x 3 1/2 In. 2700.00
Vase, Peacocks Sitting In Flowering Trees, Lush High Glaze, Hurley, 1922, 10 In. 5775.00
Vase, Peonies, White Flowers, Sara Sax, 1926, 14 In. 23100.00
Vase, Pillow, Daisies, Yellow, Brown Glaze, Grace Young, c.1886, 3 3/4 In. 259.00
Vase, Pine Boughs, Green, Tan Ground, Elizabeth Lincoln, 1923, 7 1/4 In. 1210.00
Vase, Pinecones & Needles, Green, Pink, Reticulated, 1909, 3 x 7 In. 900.00
Vase, Pink & Green Matte, 2 Handles, No. 354, 1928, 3 1/2 In. 125.00
Vase, Pink & Green Mottled Glaze, 1926, 5 In. 165.00
Vase, Poppies, Pale Yellow, Pink, White, Vellum, Sara Sax, 1905, 1 1/2 x 6 In. 450.00
Vase, Poppies, Pink, White Daisies, Blue Ground, Ed Diers, 1931, 6 x 5 In. 1495.00
Vase, Poppies, Red, Standard Glaze, 2 Strap Handles, Daniel Cook, 1894, 7 In. 1210.00
Vase, Poppies, Red, Wheat Stalks, Blue, Shirayamadani, 10 3/8 In. 20900.00
Vase, Poppies, Standard Glaze, Elizabeth Lincoln, 1899, 5 x 7 In. 450.00
Vase, Poppies, Standard Glaze, Lenore Asbury, 1902, 8 x 4 1/2 In. 1125.00
Vase, Poppies, Stems Wrap Body, Black Iris Glaze, Sallie Coyne, 1910, 8 In. 2860.00
Vase, Poppies, White, Gray, Pink & Ivory Ground, Clara Lindeman, 1908, 8 In. 2415.00
Vase, Poppies, White, Iris Glaze, Sara Sax, 1902, 9 In. . . . . *Illus* 9095.00
Vase, Portrait Of American Indian, Standard Glaze, E.T. Hurley, 1899, 8 In. 4590.00
Vase, Portrait Of Bearded Flemish Gentleman, Dark Brown, Young, 1902, 10 In. 1265.00

Rookwood, Vase,
Poppies, White,
Iris Glaze, Sara
Sax, 1902, 9 In.

Rookwood, Vase,
Stylized Poppies,
Wheat Stalks,
Shirayamadani,
1929, 10 3/8 In.

Rookwood, Vase,
Tulips, Iris Glaze,
Sara Sax, 1902,
8 3/4 In.

Vase, Queen Anne's Lace, White, Iris Glaze, Gray, Pink Ground, S. Sax, 1906, 9 In. 2700.00
Vase, Red Clay, Green, Red, Brown, Black, Tan, Storer, 1896, 5 3/8 In. 1568.00
Vase, Red Clover, Standard Glaze, Twin Handles, Ed Abel, 1891, 4 5/8 In. 450.00
Vase, Ribbed, Bamboo, Matt Daly, 1885, 21 In. 1760.00
Vase, Rook On Pine Bough, Full Moon, Iris Glaze, Lindeman, 8 In. 8625.00
Vase, Rook Perched In Tree, Sea Green Glaze, H.E. Wilcox, 1898, 5 1/4 In. 1380.00
Vase, Rooks On Bottom Of Panel, Sarah Toohey, 1944, 4 3/4 In. 275.00
Vase, Roosters, Red, Tiger Eye Glaze, Matt Daly, 1894, 7 In. 2310.00
Vase, Roses, Vellum Glaze, Ed Diers, 1905, 7 In. 635.00
Vase, Roses, Yellow, Gray Ground, Iris Glaze, Ed Diers, 1903, 8 1/2 x 4 1/2 In. 2140.00
Vase, Roses, Yellow, Green Ground, Iris Glaze, C. Lindeman, 1909, 7 x 4 In. 1265.00
Vase, Sea Horse, Squid Design, Brown, Black, Gray Metallic Glaze, 1895, 8 In. 2128.00
Vase, Sea Horse, Turtle Design, Gray, Cream Metallic Glaze, 1896, 8 3/8 In. 2350.00
Vase, Several Small Fish Swimming Through Seaweed, E.T. Hurley, 1915, 5 In. 4590.00
Vase, Single Red Flower, Green Leaves, Burgundy Glaze, Olga Reed, 1902, 6 In. 1380.00
Vase, Sitting Bull, Sturgis Laurence, 1900, 11 In. 6050.00
Vase, Snow Scene, Pine Trees At Dusk Against Sky, Vellum, Hurley, 1915, 9 In. 935.00
Vase, Snowdrops, Pearl Gray, Pale Yellow, Orange, Iris Glaze, 1900, 6 In. 1495.00
Vase, Snowdrops, White, Pink, Blue Ground, Iris Glaze, Lincoln, 1910, 7 x 3 In. 1840.00
Vase, Snowdrops, White, Yellow Glaze, Wax Matte, c.1935, 6 1/4 x 2 3/4 In. 978.00
Vase, Solitary Rook Perched On Pine Boughs, Harriet Wilcox, 1921, 9 1/8 In. 20350.00
Vase, Spider Monkeys, Soft Dove Ground, Sara Sax, 1900, 6 1/4 In. 1760.00
Vase, Squeezebag, Allover Triangles & Circles, Brown, Blue, Green, 8 x 4 In. 1910.00
Vase, Squeezebag, Green Matte Glaze, Flowers, Geometric, c.1934, 4 1/2 x 4 In. 750.00
Vase, Squeezebag, Stylized Umber Flowers, Turquoise, Blue Ground, 1929, 14 In. 3730.00
Vase, Stylized Poppies, Wheat Stalks, Shirayamadani, 1929, 10 3/8 In. . . . . *Illus* 20900.00
Vase, Sunset Landscape Of Silhouetted Trees, Pink Ground, Vellum, 12 x 5 In. 13500.00
Vase, Tall Dandelions, White, Green Matte Ground, R. Fechheimer, 1905, 12 In. 1495.00
Vase, Tan, Flowers, Green, 6 Panels, Sara Sax, 1927, 4 3/8 In. 990.00
Vase, Teal Semimatte Glaze, Textured, 3 Handles, 7 1/2 x 3 1/4 In. 489.00
Vase, Thistles, Kataro Shirayamadani, 1904, 15 In. 7700.00
Vase, Thistles, Purple, Green Leaves, Iris Glaze, Yellow, Gray, Sara Sax, 1906, 9 In. 2025.00
Vase, Thistles, Red, Yellow, Variegated Green Leaves, Olga Geneva Reed, 8 1/2 In. 7975.00
Vase, Thru Leaves, Protruding Flower In Repeat, Soft Brown, 1923, 6 1/4 In. 195.00
Vase, Trailing Cherry Blossoms, Vellum, E.T. Hurley, 1948, 7 1/4 In. 952.00
Vase, Trailing Flowers, Russet, Peach, Amelia Sprague, 1888, 4 1/4 In. 476.00
Vase, Tree-Lined Lake, Purple Hills, Fred Rothenbusch, 1920, 9 1/2 In. . . . . . . .2860.00 to 2910.00
Vase, Trillium, Rosy Pink, Light Blue, Medium Blue Ground, C. Covalenco, 1925, 7 In. . . . 896.00
Vase, Trumpet Flowers, White, Blue Ground, Margaret McDonald, 1938, 6 In. 920.00
Vase, Tulips, Iris Glaze, Sara Sax, 1902, 8 3/4 In. . . . . *Illus* 5060.00
Vase, Tulips, Red, Green Leaves, Leona Van Briggle, 1904, 6 1/2 In. 715.00
Vase, Tulips, Red, Green Leaves, Sky Blue Butterfat, Pullman, 1930, 9 x 5 In. 1840.00
Vase, Tulips, Red, Standard Glaze, Elizabeth Lincoln, 1904, 8 5/8 In. 1650.00
Vase, Tulips, Red, Yellow, Brown Mottled Glaze Interior, Sara Sax, 1926, 12 In. 1456.00
Vase, Tulips, Standard Glaze, Mary Nourse, 1903, 9 3/4 x 3 3/4 In. 1125.00
Vase, Tulips, White, Lilac Ground, Iris Glaze, Lenore Asbury, 1904, 7 In. 2465.00
Vase, Tulips, Yellow, Dark Green Ground, Iris Glaze, Sara Sax, 1902, 8 3/4 In. 5150.00
Vase, Vellum, Brown Birch Trees, Sky, Ed Diers, c.1922, 9 1/2 x 4 In. 978.00
Vase, Village Scene, Cezanne, Loretta Holtkamp, 1940, 7 x 5 In. 675.00
Vase, Violet, Flambe Blue Mouth, Blue Lining, E. Lincoln, 1927, 7 3/4 In. 935.00
Vase, Water Lilies, Reeds, Shirayamadani, Pre-1921, 9 In. 4145.00
Vase, Water Lilies, White, Yellow Centers, Vellum, Shirayamadani, 1907, 9 In. 4070.00
Vase, Water Lilies, Yellow Leaves, Dark Brown Glaze, Signed, 1906, 5 3/4 In. 407.00
Vase, Water Lilies, Yellow, Among Leaves, Dark Brown Standard Glaze, 1906, 6 In. 400.00
Vase, Wheat Stalks, Stylized, Nubian Black Glaze, 1921, 6 1/8 In. 390.00
Vase, Wild Roses Winding Around Shoulder, F. Rothenbusch, 1925, 6 In. 1345.00
Vase, Wild Roses, Bright Red, Standard Glaze, Leona Van Briggle, 1903, 7 1/8 In. 785.00
Vase, Wild Roses, Iris Glaze, Rothenbusch, 1904, 11 1/2 x 4 In. 1955.00
Vase, Wild Roses, Red, Yellow, Green Leaves, Dark Gray Ground, Olga Reed, 6 In. 1430.00
Wall Pocket, Green Over Rose Matte Glaze, 1926, 6 3/8 In. 179.00
Wall Pocket, Protruding Leaves, Persian Blue Over Taupe Glaze, 1913, 8 1/2 In. 550.00

RORSTRAND was established near Stockholm, Sweden, in 1726. By the nineteenth century they were making English-style earthenware, bone china, porcelain, ironstone china, and majolica. The company is still working. The three crown mark has been used since 1884.

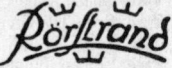

Bowl, Gray, Blue Glaze, Pottery, Gunnar Nylund, 3 1/2 x 4 1/2 In.	143.00
Bowl, Turquoise, Cobalt Blue Bands, 2 x 8 In.	45.00
Bowl, White Abstract Design On Cobalt Blue, Signed, 5 5/8 x 1 3/4 In.	52.00
Cup & Saucer, Diamant	16.00
Cup & Saucer, Gron Anna	25.00
Cup & Saucer, Louise, Demitasse	27.00
Group, Southern Woman With Nanny & Child, c.1900, 8 In.	200.00
Plate, Dinner, Gron Anna	26.00
Plate, Dinner, Louise	28.00
Plate, Salad, Diamant	9.00
Plate, Salad, Gron Anna	18.00
Plate, Salad, Louise	20.00
Thimble, Light Blue, Gold Trim	16.00
Vase, Beige, Dark Stripes, White Top, Marked, 20 In.	147.00
Vase, Ocher Speckled Matte Glaze, Collared Rim, 8 3/4 In.	562.00
Vase, Ribbed, Blue High Glaze, Impressed Mark, 9 In.	253.00
Vase, White Lilies, Black Ground, Marked, 1920, 9 1/2 x 5 In.	430.00

ROSALINE, see Steuben category.

ROSE BOWLS were popular during the 1880s. Rose petals were kept in the open bowl to add fragrance to a room, a popular idea in a time of limited personal hygiene. The glass bowls were made with crimped tops, which kept the petals inside. Many types of Victorian art glass were made into rose bowls.

Caramel To White Opalescent, Diamond Quilted, 7 x 4 1/2 In.	145.00
Cranberry To White, Crimped, Footed, 2 7/8 x 2 1/2 In.	140.00
Cream Color, Crimped Rim, Hand Blown, 4 1/2 In.	45.00
Yellow, Crimped Rim, Cased With White, Hand Blown, 4 In.	65.00

ROSE CANTON china is similar to Rose Medallion, except no people or birds are pictured in the decoration. It was made in China during the nineteenth and twentieth centuries in greens, pinks, and other colors.

Creamer, Gray, Black, Rose Floral	60.00
Cup & Saucer, Orange, Red Butterflies, Birds, Flowers, Gold Outline, Demitasse	125.00
Cuspidor, Allover Flowers, Butterflies, 19th Century, 6 In.	375.00
Jug, Cream, Hog Spout, Interior Floral Rim, 19th Century, 3 1/2 In.	260.00
Pitcher, Bamboo Handle, 5 3/4 In.	85.00
Serving Dish, Wire Handles, 1895, 9 x 5 In.	475.00
Sugar, Cover, Bamboo Handle, Gold, 6 In.	85.00
Sugar, Cover, Gray, Black, Rose Floral	75.00
Tray, Lobed, Raised Gilt Trimmed Gallery, Polychrome, 2 x 18 1/2 x 15 1/2 In.	1380.00

ROSE MANDARIN china is similar to Rose Medallion. If the panels in the design picture only people and not birds, it is called Rose Mandarin.

Bough Pot, c.1770, Pair	5200.00
Bowl, Court Scene, Ormolu Mounted, 19th Century, 10 1/2 In.	860.00
Bowl, Cut Corners, 10 In.	1900.00
Coffeepot, Lighthouse Shape, c.1820, 10 In.	2420.00
Jar, Cover, Chinese, 13 1/2 In.	80.00
Mug, 5 In.	1495.00
Mug, Palette, Floral Design, Colors, 3 1/4 In.	100.00
Punch Bowl, c.1770, 15 3/4 In.	1760.00
Punch Bowl, Chinese, 14 1/2 In.	1610.00
Punch Bowl, Figures, Landscape, Celadon Ground, Chinese, 1800s, 15 In.	3740.00
Shrimp Dish, Chinese, 19th Century, 10 1/2 In.	805.00
Teapot, Court Figures Panels, Early 19th Century, 10 1/2 In.	1320.00
Vase, Baluster Shape, 15 1/2 In., Pair	2760.00

Vase, Bottle Shape, 15 1/2 In. 1095.00
Vase, c.1829, 16 In., Pair 3800.00
Vase, Floral, Nobles, Flowers, Insects, Foo Dogs At Neck, 1850s, 15 In., Pair 4140.00
Vase, Gilded Foo Dog Handles, Lizards, 19th Century, Pair 2045.00

ROSE MEDALLION china was made in China during the nineteenth and
twentieth centuries. It is a distinctive design with four or more panels
of decoration around a central medallion that includes a bird or a
peony. The panels show birds and people. The background is a design
of tree peonies and leaves. Pieces are colored in greens, pinks, and
other colors. It is similar to Rose Canton.

Basin, 19th Century, 5 3/4 x 18 3/4 In. 805.00
Basin, Flowers & Figural Panels, 16 In. 315.00
Basket, Undertray, Fenestrated, Oval, 11 1/2 In. 545.00
Basket, Undertray, Fenestrated, Oval, Marked China, 15 In. 630.00
Bowl, 19th Century, 5 x 10 3/4 In. 440.00
Bowl, Cavetto Rim, Raised Foot, 3 1/2 x 9 1/4 In. 345.00
Bowl, Early 20th Century, 4 1/2 In. 80.00
Bowl, Mid 19th Century, 3 3/4 x 9 1/8 In. 375.00
Bowl, Mid 19th Century, 4 1/2 x 10 In. 430.00
Bowl, Nobles In Pavilions, Floral Panels, c.1900, 5 x 11 1/2 In. 750.00
Bowl, Vegetable, Cover, Double Twist Handles, Orange Peel Glaze, 7 x 6 In. 550.00
Bowl, Vegetable, Cover, Mandarin Scenes, Diamond Shape, Scalloped, 9 In. 185.00
Bowl, Vegetable, Cover, Oval, 12 x 3 In. 245.00
Bowl, Vegetable, Cover, Rectangular, Mid 19th Century, 5 x 6 1/2 x 8 In. 375.00
Bowl, Vegetable, Cover, Scalloped Rim, 19th Century, 4 x 10 In., Pair 605.00
Bowl, Vegetable, Domed Cover, Octagonal, 5 1/4 x 9 1/2 x 8 1/2 In. 690.00
Cachepot, Undertray, Hexagonal, 5 1/2 In., Pair 2070.00
Charger, Figures, Flower Panels, 19th Century, 2 x 15 In. 345.00
Charger, Mandarin Scenes, Gold Highlighted Hair, 11 1/2 x 2 In. 275.00
Cup, Cover, Birds & Flowers, Braided Strap Handles, 4 1/2 In. 60.00
Dish, Alternating Panels, 1840, 9 1/2 In. 65.00
Dish, Flowers, Bird Scene Border, 19th Century, 16 In. 1150.00
Garden Seat, Hexagonal, 1860, 19 In., Pair 9775.00
Garden Seat, Pierced, Interlocking Cash Medallions, 1890s, 18 In. 2185.00
Jar, Cover, Fruit Finial, 2 Handles, 4 x 5 3/4 In. 250.00
Jar, Cover, Mandarin Scene Reserves, Orange Peel Glaze, 3 3/4 x 4 1/8 In. 195.00
Jar, Domed Cover, Flower Bud Finial, Leaf Branch Handles, Oval, 14 1/2 In. 1495.00
Pitcher, Basin, Chinese, 19th Century, 12 1/4 x 14 7/8 In. 489.00
Planter, Alternating Mandarin Scenes, Bird & Butterfly Panels, 11 x 14 In. 385.00
Plate, Square, c.1880, 9 1/2 x 9 1/2 In., Pair 1380.00
Platter, Alternating Panels, Bird & Roses, Figures & Leaves, 14 1/2 x 18 In. 110.00
Platter, Mandarin Scenes, Orange Peel Glaze, Worn Gilt, Oval, 9 1/2 x 12 In. 330.00
Platter, Meat, 19 In. 760.00
Platter, Oval, 13 1/2 In. .... 345.00 to 375.00
Platter, Oval, 1840, 15 In. 632.00
Punch Bowl, 14 1/2 In. 750.00
Punch Bowl, 19th Century, 13 1/2 In. 1840.00
Punch Bowl, Alternating Panels Of Flowers, Court Figures, 19 1/4 In. 1725.00
Punch Bowl, Alternating Panels, Figures, Birds, Butterflies, 14 1/2 In. 2015.00
Punch Bowl, Bird Panels Interior & Exterior, Gilt, 15 x 5 1/2 In. 1320.00
Punch Bowl, Birds, Butterflies, Panels, Gilded Rim, 19th Century, 7 x 16 In. 2750.00
Punch Bowl, c.1840, 18 1/2 x 7 In. 5500.00
Punch Bowl, Gilt Bronze Mounts, Louis XVI Style, 13 x 13 1/4 In. 2760.00
Punch Bowl, Gold Trim Rim, 1890, 11 1/2 In. 400.00
Punch Bowl, Interior & External Panels Of Court Figures, 13 1/2 In. 1150.00
Sauceboat, Undertray, Mid 19th Century, 6 1/2 x 8 In. 660.00
Soap Dish, Rectangular, Drainer, Cover, 19th Century, 2 1/2 x 5 x 6 In. 430.00
Teapot, Birds, Flowers, Court Scenes, 19th Century, 5 In. 110.00
Teapot, Cover, 1840, 6 In. 400.00
Teapot, Mandarin Scenes, Gilt On Spout & Handle, 7 3/8 In. 250.00
Teapot, Mandarin Scenes, Raffia Wire Handles, 5 1/2 In. .... 72.00 to 82.00
Teapot, Overall Floral Spray, Birds, Gilt Knob Finial, Round, c.1900, 4 In. 175.00

Teapot, Wire Handle, Cylindrical 143.00
Tray, Mandarin Scenes, Orange Peel Glaze, Reticulated Rainbow Rim, 9 In. 330.00
Urn, Animal Appliques, Birds, People, 19th Century, 17 1/2 In. 825.00
Vase, 4 Figural Panels, 1840, 13 1/2 In. 1006.00
Vase, Baluster Shape, Court, Nature Scenes, Foo Dog Handles, Footed, 10 In. 345.00
Vase, Baluster Shape, Foo Dog Handle, Footed, 10 1/4 In. 345.00
Vase, Birds, Roses, Figural Lizard Handles, 12 1/4 In. 330.00
Vase, Chinese, 19th Century, 13 1/2 In. 110.00
Vase, Domed Cover, Gilt Animal Head Handles, 11 x 5 In., Pair 920.00
Vase, Dragons At Shoulder, Foo Lion Handles, Wooden Stand, 52 In. 460.00
Vase, Dragons, Mandarin Scenes, Gilt Foo Dogs Base, Handles, 11 5/8 In. 495.00
Vase, Figural & Floral Panels, Cylindrical, 1840, 8 1/2 In. 316.00
Vase, Figures In Interiors, Floral, Butterflies, Gilt Foo Lion Handles, 18 In. 2700.00
Vase, Foo Lion Handles, 1840, 10 In. 345.00
Vase, Mandarin Scene Reserves, Orange Peel Glaze, 4 1/2 x 10 7/8 In. 440.00
Vase, Mandarin Scenes, Gilt Dragons, Foo Dogs, Orange Peel Glaze, 17 In. 550.00
Vase, Peony Blossom Design, Dragon Handle, 9 1/2 In. 547.00
Vase, Tapered Body, Corseted Neck, Foo Dog Handles, Finial, 19 x 9 1/2 In. 748.00
Vase, Traditional Scene, 4 Figural Reserves, 1840, 13 1/2 In. 1006.00

ROSE O'NEILL, see Kewpie category.

ROSE TAPESTRY porcelain was made by the Royal Bayreuth factory of
Tettau, Germany, during the late nineteenth century. The surface of the
porcelain was pressed against a coarse fabric while it was still damp,
and the impressions remained on the finished porcelain. It looks and
feels like a textured cloth. Very skillful reproductions are being made
that even include a variation of the Royal Bayreuth mark, so be careful when buying.

Bowl, 3 Gold Feet, 3 3/4 In. 55.00
Bowl, Square, Scalloped, Scrolled Corners, 10 1/4 In. 473.00
Hair Receiver 295.00
Plate, 1902-1919, 6 In. 105.00
Plate, 7 1/2 In. 295.00

ROSEMEADE Pottery of Wahpeton, North Dakota, worked from 1940 to
1961. The pottery was operated by Laura A. Taylor and her husband,
R.I. Hughes. The company was also known as the Wahpeton Pottery
Company. Art pottery and commercial wares were made.

Bookends, Bison, Marked, N.D.A.C. 2200.00
Figurine, Alligator Hors D'Oeuvre 200.00
Salt & Pepper, Badger, 1 x 2 3/4 In. 1850.00
Salt & Pepper, Mallard, Paper Label, 1 x 1 3/4 In. 65.00
Sugar, Horse, Incised On Side, 2 In. 53.00
Sugar & Creamer, Turkey, 4 1/2 In. 175.00
Vase, Dickota Maroon, Plum, 8 In. 350.00
Vase, Egyptian, 8 In. 320.00
Vase, Violet Design, Hand Painted, 5 In. 350.00

ROSENTHAL porcelain was made at the factory established in Selb,
Bavaria, in 1880. The factory is still making fine-quality tablewares
and figurines. A series of Christmas plates was made from 1910. Other
limited edition plates have been made since 1971.

Decanter, Floral Design, Signed MG Hayes, 1912, 12 In. 308.00
Dessert Service, Duchess, Plates, Saucers, Cups, 8 In., 30 Piece 115.00
Figurine, Bear, Brown, Early 20th Century, 4 1/2 x 7 1/2 In. 525.00
Figurine, Dachshund, Brown, No. 6061 . . . . 170.00
Figurine, Dachshund, Sitting, Brown, Black Points, 3 3/4 x 4 1/4 In. 225.00
Figurine, Dancer, Coiled Snake At Her Feet, 11 In. 316.00
Figurine, Female, Nude, Riding Ostrich, 22 x 18 In. 2185.00
Figurine, Fox Terrier, Standing, White, Black & Tan Markings, 6 1/2 x 6 In. 275.00
Figurine, Fox Terrier, Standing, White, Dark Brown Mask, 4 1/2 x 3 3/4 In. 450.00
Figurine, Satyr, With Flute, Alligator At Feet, 14 1/2 In. 520.00
Figurine, Scottish Terrier, Sitting, White, Black, Tan & White, 5 1/2 x 8 1/2 In. 325.00

Figurine, Wire Fox Terrier, Standing, White, Dark Brown Mask, 3 1/2 x 3 1/2 In. 450.00
Gravy Boat, Pompadour, Handle, 5 In. 80.00
Plaque, Man & Woman Drinking, Signed, K. Muller, 10 x 14 In. 2750.00
Platter, Moss Rose, Pompadour, 13 In. 75.00
Teapot, Cover, Pompadour 225.00
Tray, Birds, Hand Painted, 15 In. 325.00
Vase, Baluster Form, Maiden Embracing Cupid, Gilt Leaf Border, 6 1/8 In. 145.00
Vase, Branches, Leaves, Berries, Mother-Of-Pearl Glaze, Decorator Initials, 10 In. 286.00
Vase, Putto, Seated, Rose Bouquet, Gilt Band, Baluster Shape, 10 In. 175.00
Vase, Red & Gilt Design, Vasiform, Ivory, 8 5/8 In. 70.00

ROSEVILLE Pottery Company was organized in Roseville, Ohio, in
1890. Another plant was opened in Zanesville, Ohio, in 1898. Many
types of pottery were made until 1954. Early wares include Sgraffito,
Olympic, and Rozane. Later lines were often made with molded decorations, especially flowers and fruit. Most pieces are marked *Roseville*.
Many reproductions made in China have been offered for sale the past
few years.

Roseville
U.S.A.

Apple Blossom, Basket, Hanging, Blue, 8 In. 230.00
Apple Blossom, Candlestick, Pink, Signed, 2 In., Pair 67.00
Apple Blossom, Jardiniere, Green, Pedestal, 16 In. 805.00
Apple Blossom, Planter, Pink, 2 Handles, 6 In. 70.00
Apple Blossom, Teapot, Green 134.00
Apple Blossom, Vase, Blue Ground, White Blossom, 2 Twig Handles, 16 In. 675.00
Apple Blossom, Wall Pocket, White Floral, Twig Handle, 8 1/2 In. . . . . .288.00 to 302.00
Baneda, Jardiniere, Green, 6 x 6 1/2 In. 518.00
Baneda, Jardiniere, Green, Tapered, 4 1/2 x 5 1/2 In. 400.00
Baneda, Rose Bowl, Green, Burnt Orange Floral, Green Leaves, Cobalt Blue, 4 In. 440.00
Baneda, Rose Bowl, Green, Burnt Orange Floral, Green Leaves, Cobalt Blue, 5 1/4 In. . .   495.00
Baneda, Vase, Bulbous, Pink, Black Foil Label, 10 1/2 x 7 3/4 In. 1265.00
Baneda, Vase, Burnt Orange Floral, Pink, Blue Band, 6 3/4 In. 660.00
Baneda, Vase, Burnt Orange Floral, Pink, Green Leaves, Blue Band, 10 In. 1210.00
Baneda, Vase, Green, Burnt Orange Floral, 2 Looped Handles, Blue, 6 In. 385.00
Baneda, Vase, Green, Burnt Orange Floral, 2 Side Handles, Blue Drip Glaze, 9 In. 990.00
Baneda, Vase, Green, Burnt Orange Floral, Green Leaves, Yellow Glaze, 9 1/4 In. 1210.00
Baneda, Vase, Green, Burnt Orange Floral, Incised Petals, Yellow Glaze, 8 In. 1100.00
Baneda, Vase, Pink, 2 Handles, 7 1/4 In. 336.00
Baneda, Vase, Pink, Flared, Foil Label, 7 1/2 x 4 1/4 In. 635.00
Baneda, Wall Pocket, Green, 8 In. 2645.00
Bank, Buffalo, Flecks On Ears & Tail, Burst Bubbles, 3 x 6 In. 460.00
Bank, Pig, Blue & Brown Dripping Glaze, 3 x 6 In. 46.00
Bittersweet, Basket, Yellow, Red Berries, 2 Brown Handles, 5 In., Pair 210.00
Bittersweet, Flowerpot, Gray, Dark Rose, 5 1/2 In. 67.00
Bittersweet, Wall Pocket, Gray, 7 In. 316.00
Blackberry, Basket, Hanging, 5 In. 1008.00
Blackberry, Jardiniere, 5 1/4 x 5 In. 518.00
Blackberry, Jardiniere, 8 x 10 3/4 In. 1095.00
Blackberry, Jardiniere, Green, Ocher Leaves, 10 1/2 x 1 In. 1320.00
Blackberry, Vase, 2 Handles, 6 1/8 In. 420.00
Blackberry, Vase, 4 1/2 In. 160.00
Blackberry, Vase, Handles, 8 x 5 In. 825.00
Blackberry, Vase, Incised Leaves, Black Blackberries, 4 In. 495.00
Blackberry, Wall Pocket, 8 In. 750.00
Bleeding Heart, Basket, Green, 10 In. 405.00
Bleeding Heart, Cornucopia, Green, 6 In. 134.00
Bleeding Heart, Cornucopia, Pink, 6 In. 56.00
Bleeding Heart, Jardiniere, Green, 3 In., Pair 168.00
Bleeding Heart, Wall Pocket, Green, 8 In. 633.00
Bottle, Monkey, Top Hat, Seated, Just Thinking, Green Glaze, 5 1/2 In. 250.00
Burmese, Bookends, Black, 6 1/2 In. . . . . .168.00 to 260.00
Bushberry, Basket, Ivory Glaze, Ivory Center Handle, 6 1/2 In. 112.00
Bushberry, Bookends, Green, 9 In. 335.00
Bushberry, Flower Frog, Blue 179.00

Bushberry, Jardiniere, Brown, 5 In. 105.00
Bushberry, Jardiniere, Pedestal, Orange, 25 In. 950.00
Bushberry, Tea Set, Orange, 3 Piece 280.00
Bushberry, Wall Pocket, Orange, 8 In. 259.00
Capri, Basket, Green, Center Green Handle, 8 In. 22.00
Carnelian I, Bowl, Signed, 4 x 10 In. 200.00
Carnelian I, Vase, 2 Handles, Pink & Gray Glaze, 8 In. 336.00
Carnelian I, Vase, Angled Scrolled Handles, Mauve Drip Glaze, 1915, 8 1/4 In. 546.00
Carnelian I, Vase, Deep Violet Drip Glaze, Deep Rose, Magenta, Caramel, Blue, 7 In. 248.00
Carnelian I, Wall Pocket, Violet, 9 1/2 In. 201.00
Carnelian II, Urn, Mottled Red Glaze, 8 In. 1098.00
Carnelian II, Vase, Gourd Shape, Deep Magenta, Lavender, Tan, Black Glaze, 7 In. 248.00
Carnelian II, Vase, Magenta, Lavender, Violet, Teal Ground, 2 Handles, 8 1/4 In. 605.00
Carnelian II, Vase, Purple, Rose Glaze, 9 x 5 1/2 In. 374.00
Cherry Blossom, Basket, Hanging, Brown, 5 In. 420.00
Cherry Blossom, Basket, Hanging, Brown, 7 1/2 In. 545.00
Cherry Blossom, Brown, Tan, White Flowers, 2 Handles, 7 1/8 In. 390.00
Cherry Blossom, Jardiniere, Brown, 4 In. 325.00
Cherry Blossom, Jardiniere, Turquoise & Coral, 4 In. 365.00
Cherry Blossom, Vase, Brown, White Cherry Blossoms, Yellow Stamen, 7 In. 385.00
Cherry Blossom, Vase, Light Pink, Turquoise, 2 Handles, 3 1/2 In. 390.00
Cherry Blossom, Wall Pocket, Brown, 8 In. 865.00
Chloron, Vase, Embossed Arabesques, Green Matte Glaze, 2 Handles, 8 In. 690.00
Chloron, Vase, Gourd Shape, Embossed Berry, Leaf Design, 2 Loop Handles, 6 In. 1100.00
Clematis, Basket, Blue, Impressed Mark, 7 1/2 x 6 1/2 In. ....Illus 35.00
Clematis, Basket, Raised Floral, Yellow, Handle, 10 x 12 In. 166.00
Columbine, Basket, Pink & Green, Marked Roseville U.S.A. 368-12, 12 In. 450.00
Columbine, Candlestick, Brown, 4 1/2 x 4 7/8 In., Pair 224.00
Columbine, Candlestick, Tan, 2 1/2 In., Pair 70.00
Columbine, Vase, Blue, Dainty Green Leaves, 2 Angular Handles, 9 In. 165.00
Columbine, Vase, Brown, 2 Handles, 6 1/8 In. 170.00
Columbine, Wall Pocket, Brown, 8 In. 520.00
Corinthian, Basket, Hanging, 8 3/4 In. 175.00
Cosmos, Basket, Blue, 12 In. 260.00
Cosmos, Basket, Hanging, Brown, 8 In. 255.00
Cosmos, Flower Frog, Tan, 3 1/4 In. 125.00
Cosmos, Wall Pocket, Brown, 6 In. 250.00
Cosmos, Wall Pocket, Brown, 7 In. 345.00
Creamware, Juvenile, Chamber Pot, Rabbit 300.00
Creamware, Juvenile, Creamer, Sunbonnet Girl, 5 In. 22.00
Creamware, Juvenile, Mug, 2 Puppies Sitting, Gray Band, 2 3/4 In. 212.00
Creamware, Juvenile, Mug, 2 Yellow Chicks, Green Band, 3 1/2 In. 201.00
Creamware, Juvenile, Pitcher, Yellow Chicks, 3 5/8 In. 179.00
Creamware, Juvenile, Plate, 4 Rabbits, Standing, Green Band, 8 x 1 1/2 In. 67.00
Creamware, Juvenile, Plate, Dressed-Up Piggy, With Chick, 9 1/2 In. 168.00
Creamware, Landscape, Jardiniere, Pedestal, Birds In Flight, Trees, 43 In. 5225.00
Creamware, Persian, Basket, Hanging, 7 1/2 In. 259.00
Creamware, Persian, Basket, Hanging, 10 In. 374.00
Creamware, Persian, Basket, Hanging, Stylized Vine, 3 1/2 In. 250.00
Cremona, Bowl, Green Over Cream, Embossed Floral Design, 8 In. 89.00
Cremona, Console, Pink, Oval, 2 1/4 x 11 In. 90.00
Dahlrose, Basket, Hanging, 7 In. 175.00
Dahlrose, Bowl, Oval, 2 Angular Handles, 8 In. 110.00
Dahlrose, Jardiniere, 2 Handles, 13 In. 202.00
Dahlrose, Jardiniere, Textured, 8 1/2 In. 265.00
Dahlrose, Vase, Bulbous, Black Paper Label, 8 1/4 x 5 In. 290.00
Dahlrose, Vase, Green, Light Brown, 6 1/8 In. 190.00
Dahlrose, Wall Pocket, 10 1/4 In. 316.00
Dahlrose, Wall Pocket, Handle, 9 1/2 In. 145.00
Della Robbia, Vase, Carved Floral, 14 In. ....Illus 7700.00
Della Robbia, Vase, Stylized Trees, Green, Brown, Arts & Crafts Style, 9 1/4 In. 4600.00
Dogwood, Vase, Experimental, Pillsbury, 15 In. ....Illus 2860.00
Dogwood I, Basket, Handle, 8 x 8 In. 105.00

Roseville, Clematis, Basket, Blue,
Impressed Mark, 7 1/2 x 6 1/2 In.

Roseville, Dogwood II, Jardiniere,
White Flowers, Brown Branches,
Dark Green, 8 In.

Roseville, Della Robbia,
Vase, Carved Floral, 14 In.

Dogwood I, Basket, Hanging, 7 1/2 In. 115.00
Dogwood I, Vase, Raised Blossoms, Textured Ground, Signed, 8 1/2 In. 255.00
Dogwood I, Vase, White Flowers, Olive Green Ground, 6 In. 170.00
Dogwood II, Basket, Brown Branches, Dark Green, 4 In. 123.00
Dogwood II, Basket, Hanging, 6 3/4 In. 81.00
Dogwood II, Basket, White Flowers, Green, White Handle, 8 In. 67.00
Dogwood II, Jardiniere, White Flowers, Brown Branches, Dark Green, 8 In. .... *Illus* 123.00
Dogwood II, Planter, White Flowers, Dark Green, Handles, 4 1/8 In. 44.00
Dogwood II, Wall Pocket, 9 In. ....259.00 to 288.00
Donatello, Basket, Hanging, 6 In. 201.00
Donatello, Basket, Hanging, 7 1/2 In. 69.00
Donatello, Basket, Hanging, Gray, Blue, 7 In. 190.00
Donatello, Planter, Cherubs Scene, Light Green Rim, 7 1/2 In. 56.00
Donatello, Vase, Double Bud, 9 In. 235.00
Donatello, Wall Pocket, 11 In. 201.00
Earlham, Vase, Green, Bulbous, 5 1/2 x 6 3/4 In. 290.00
Earlham, Vase, Pillow, Mottled Pink, Orange, Purple Glaze, 6 1/4 x 10 1/4 In. 375.00
Egypto, Vase, Reticulated Edge, Matte Glaze, 5 1/2 In. 523.00
Egypto, Wall Pocket, 14 In. 1840.00
Falline, Vase, Blue, Flared, 8 1/4 x 6 In. 1840.00
Falline, Vase, Brown, 2 Green Handles, Gold Foil Label, 6 1/8 In. 392.00
Falline, Vase, Brown, 2 Handles, 6 1/8 In. 280.00
Falline, Vase, Brown, Green Pea Pod, Ocher Ground, 2 Handles, 6 In. 440.00
Falline, Vase, Pea Pod, 2 Looped Handles, 14 In. 2310.00
Ferella, Bowl, Red Mottled Glaze, Pink Stems, Floral, Green Glaze At Rim, 5 x 8 In. 825.00
Ferella, Bowl, Red, 5 x 8 1/2 In. 489.00
Ferella, Wall Pocket, Red Mottled Glaze, 6 1/2 In. 2300.00
Florane, Wall Pocket, Tan Matte Glaze, 9 1/2 In. 92.00
Florentine, Lamp, Factory, Brown, Original Shade, 6 1/4 x 3 1/4 In. 115.00
Florentine, Sand Jar, Brown, 14 x 11 In. 316.00
Florentine, Sand Jar, Footed, Green, 17 x 15 In. 460.00
Florentine, Umbrella Stand, 2 Ivory Handles, Ocher Glaze, 20 In. 184.00
Florentine, Wall Pocket, Brown, 12 1/2 In. 201.00
Foxglove, Basket, Green Handle, 8 In. 204.00
Foxglove, Basket, Hanging, Blue, 10 In. 200.00
Foxglove, Vase, Blue, 8 1/8 In. 135.00
Foxglove, Wall Pocket, Blue, 8 In. 345.00
Freesia, Basket, Blue, Handle, 8 1/2 In. 130.00
Freesia, Basket, Hanging, Green, 8 In. 105.00
Freesia, Bookends, Tangerine, 5 In. 100.00
Freesia, Cookie Jar, Green, 8 In. 390.00
Freesia, Ewer, Tangerine, 6 In. 135.00
Freesia, Jardiniere, Cream Blossoms, Green Leaves, Delft Blue, 1945, 25 In. 805.00
Freesia, Jardiniere, Tangerine, 6 In. 78.00
Freesia, Teapot, Green, White, Lavender Floral, Dark Green Handle, 7 In. 193.00
Freesia, Vase, Blue, 2 Handles, 9 1/2 In. 112.00

Freesia, Vase, Pedestal, Brown, Marked, 16 3/4 x 11 In.	173.00
Freesia, Wall Pocket, Green, 8 1/4 In.	175.00
Fuchsia, Basket, Hanging, Brown, 7 In.	200.00
Fuchsia, Bowl, Green, 12 In.	430.00
Fuchsia, Bowl, Green, 2 Handles, 2 5/8 In.	100.00
Fuchsia, Jardiniere, Pedestal, Brown, 8 In.	690.00
Fuchsia, Pitcher, Blue, Ice Lip, 8 1/4 In.	420.00
Fuchsia, Vase, Blue, Pink Flowers, 2 Looped Handles, 10 In.	525.00
Fuchsia, Vase, Brown, Footed, 2 Handles, 9 1/4 In.	179.00
Fuchsia, Vase, Green, 18 In.	748.00
Fuchsia, Wall Pocket, Blue, 8 In.	575.00
Futura, Bowl, Flower Frog, Geometric Design, 3 1/2 x 8 3/4 In.	545.00
Futura, Bowl, Flower Frog, Mottled Green, Flaring, Orange Glaze, 3 3/4 x 12 In.	489.00
Futura, Bowl, Tan, 3 1/2 x 8 1/2 In.	245.00
Futura, Jardiniere, Green, Stylized Flowers, Leaves, 9 x 13 1/2 In.	430.00
Futura, Planter, Blue, Sunray, 5 1/4 In.	335.00
Futura, Vase, Ball Bottle, Blue Matte Glaze, Dark Blue, Green, 8 x 5 1/2 In.	1495.00
Futura, Vase, Blue, Green Matte Glaze, Orange, 8 1/4 x 3 3/4 In.	865.00
Futura, Vase, Brown, Embossed, Yellow Flowers, 6 1/4 x 5 3/4 In.	575.00
Futura, Vase, Clover, Embossed, Burgundy Matte Glaze, 8 x 5 3/4 In.	430.00
Futura, Vase, Conical, Footed, Blue, Green & Orange Matte Glazes, 8 x 5 In.	545.00
Futura, Vase, Double V, Teal Green Glaze, Deep Rose, 7 1/4 In.	605.00
Futura, Vase, Football Urn, Green, Light Brown, 2 Handles, 9 1/8 In.	1010.00
Futura, Vase, Gourd Shape, 4 Buttressed Feet, Blue Matte Glaze, 8 x 5 In.	920.00
Futura, Vase, Green, Brown, Light Orange, 9 3/4 x 8 1/4 In.	1495.00
Futura, Vase, Mauve & Tan Matte Glaze, Square Rim, Footed, 1928, 9 In.	625.00
Futura, Vase, Pillow, 2 Buttressed Handles, Geometric Embossing, 8 x 6 In.	865.00
Futura, Vase, Pink, Green Glaze, 8 1/4 x 4 1/2 In.	460.00
Futura, Vase, Stylized Sea Gull, 10 In. . . . . *Illus*	2090.00
Futura, Vase, Twist, Geometric Triangular, Shades Of Green, Pale Green, Blue, 8 In.	660.00
Gardenia, Planter, Hanging, Ocher, Embossed White Flowers, Green Petals, 6 In.	193.00
Gardenia, Wall Pocket, Green, 8 In.	175.00
Gardenia, Wall Pocket, Tan, 8 In.	250.00
Hexagon, Vase, Green, Flaring Rim, RV Ink Mark, 5 1/2 x 3 1/2 In.	460.00
Imperial I, Basket, Green, White Center Handle, 8 7/8 In. . . . . .115.00 to 212.00
Imperial I, Wall Pocket, 3 1/2 In.	145.00
Imperial I, Wall Pocket, 10 In.	316.00
Imperial II, Vase, Blue, Pink Mottled Glaze, 5 x 6 In.	173.00
Imperial II, Vase, Cylindrical, Blue Gray & Turquoise Semigloss Glaze, 8 In.	865.00
Imperial II, Vase, Gourd Shape, Pale Green, Ocher, 5 1/8 In.	616.00
Imperial II, Vase, Lavender, Turquoise Matte Glaze, 5 1/4 x 3 3/4 In.	374.00
Imperial II, Vase, Lavender, Yellow, Red Glaze, 6 1/4 x 6 In.	633.00
Imperial II, Wall Pocket, Pink, 6 1/2 In.	575.00
Iris, Basket, Hanging, Brown, 8 1/2 In.	255.00
Iris, Basket, Pink, Handle, 8 1/2 In.	112.00
Iris, Candlestick, Pink, 4 3/4 In.	179.00
Iris, Jardiniere, Pink, Footed, 4 5/8 In.	67.00
Iris, Wall Pocket, Blue, 8 In.	201.00
Ivory, Jardiniere, Scarab Design, 8 In.	476.00
Ixia, Vase, Green, Bulbous, Buttress Handles, Incised Mark, 9 In.	200.00
Ixia, Vase, Pink & Green, 15 In.	865.00
Jonquil, Bowl, White Flowers, Green Leaves, 2 Handles, 5 1/2 In.	67.00
Jonquil, Jardiniere, 5 1/2 x 7 In. . . . . .105.00 to 173.00
Jonquil, Jardiniere, White Flowers, Green Leaves, 2 Handles, 5 In.	112.00
Jonquil, Vase, 2 Handles, 7 x 7 3/4 In.	316.00
Jonquil, Vase, Brown, White Flowers, 2 Handles, 4 In.	67.00
Jonquil, Vase, Brown, White Flowers, 6 1/8 In.	252.00
Jonquil, Vase, Bulbous, Silver Foil Label, 4 1/2 x 6 1/4 In.	345.00
Juvenile, see Roseville, Creamware	
La Rose, Wall Pocket, 7 3/4 In.	335.00
La Rose, Wall Pocket, 13 In.	230.00
Laurel, Vase, Green, No. 670-7, c.1934	675.00
Laurel, Vase, Orange, 7 In.	330.00

Lombardy, Basket, Hanging, Dark Green, 7 3/4 In.	175.00
Lombardy, Basket, Hanging, Green, Blue, 7 1/2 In.	105.00
Lombardy, Wall Pocket, Blue, Gray Matte Glaze, 9 In.	230.00
Lombardy, Wall Pocket, Gray, Blue Matte Glaze, 9 1/2 In.	259.00
Lotus, Wall Pocket, Green, 7 In.	575.00
Lotus, Wall Pocket, Yellow & Brown, 7 In.	190.00
Luffa, Vase, Brown, 6 1/2 In.	200.00
Luffa, Vase, Green, Brown, Gold, Label, 6 1/2 In.	225.00
Magnolia, Basket, Hanging, Green, 8 In.	145.00
Magnolia, Bowl, Green, 3 1/2 x 14 In.	105.00
Magnolia, Creamer	120.00
Magnolia, Jardiniere, Brown, 17 x 9 In.	144.00
Magnolia, Pitcher, Ice-Lip	445.00
Magnolia, Teapot, Brown	168.00
Magnolia, Vase, Brown, 7 In.	195.00
Magnolia, Vase, Green, Narrow Neck, Bulbous Base, 2 Center Handles, 1940s, 7 In.	85.00
Magnolia, Vase, Green, White Magnolia Floral, Green, 4 3/4 In.	89.00
Magnolia, Wall Pocket, Brown, Handle, 8 1/2 In.	115.00
Magnolia, Wall Pocket, White Magnolia Floral, Lavender, Handle, 8 1/2 In.	138.00
Mayfair, Teapot, Dark Green	95.00
Ming Tree, Basket, Hanging, Green, 8 In.	175.00
Ming Tree, Candlestick, Garlic Form, White, 2 In., Pair	50.00
Ming Tree, Wall Pocket, Handle, Green, 8 In.	60.00
Mock Orange, Basket, Green, 10 In.	135.00 to 180.00
Mock Orange, Basket, Hanging, Pink, 7 In.	259.00
Mock Orange, Cornucopia, Green, 8 In.	110.00
Mock Orange, Ewer, Pink, 6 In.	90.00
Mock Orange, Ewer, Pink, 16 In.	310.00
Mock Orange, Planter, Pink, 8 In.	70.00
Mock Orange, Vase, Green, Handle, 8 In.	110.00
Moderne, Candlestick, 3-Light, Ivory, Incised Mark, 6 1/4 x 5 1/4 In.	375.00
Moderne, Candlestick, Turquoise, 5 1/2 In.	200.00
Moderne, Chalice, Blue, 6 In.	345.00
Moderne, Chalice, Pink, 6 In.	175.00
Moderne, Compote, Pink, 5 1/4 x 5 1/2 In.	200.00
Moderne, Console, Pink, 10 In.	230.00 to 259.00
Moderne, Console, Turquoise, 10 In.	259.00
Moderne, Vase, Blue, Spherical, Footed, 6 1/2 x 7 1/2 In.	175.00
Moderne, Vase, Bud, Blue, 8 In.	460.00
Moderne, Vase, Turquoise, 7 3/8 In.	390.00
Moderne, Vase, Turquoise, 8 In.	316.00
Mongol, Pitcher, Orange Crystalline Glaze, Marked, 6 x 4 1/4 In.	863.00
Monticello, Vase, Blue, Abstract White Designs, Ocher, 5 In.	305.00
Monticello, Vase, Floral, Light Green, 2 Angular Handles, 5 1/2 In., Pair	575.00
Monticello, Vase, Light Green, 2 Handles, 4 In.	335.00

Roseville, Dogwood, Vase,
Experimental, Pillsbury, 15 In.

Roseville, Raymor, Platter,
Oval, 12 In.

Roseville, Futura, Vase,
Stylized Sea Gull, 10 In.

Morning Glory, Basket, Green, Handle, 8 3/4 x 6 3/4 In. 520.00
Morning Glory, Basket, White, 10 In. 476.00
Morning Glory, Vase, Green, 12 In. 615.00
Morning Glory, Vase, Green, Flaring, Pillow, Label, 7 1/2 x 4 1/4 In. 690.00
Morning Glory, Vase, Green, Pink Flowers, Pale Yellow, 2 Handles, 6 3/4 In. 336.00
Morning Glory, Wall Pocket, White, 8 1/2 In. 460.00
Moss, Bowl, Pink, Green, No. 291, Marked, 7 7/8 In. 200.00
Moss, Urn, Blue, Bulbous, Buttressed Base, Incised Mark, 10 In. 200.00
Moss, Wall Pocket, Blue, 8 In. 430.00
Moss, Wall Pocket, Pink, 11 1/4 In. 430.00
Mostique, Bowl, Tan, 7 x 9 In., Pair 345.00
Mostique, Jardiniere, Gray, 9 x 12 In. 400.00
Mostique, Jardiniere, Tan, 10 1/4 x 13 In. 173.00
Mostique, Jardiniere, Tan, Floral Design, 8 1/2 x 10 In. 375.00
Mostique, Vase, 2 Handles, Tan, 8 1/2 In. 431.00
Mostique, Vase, Gray, 10 In. ....168.00 to 392.00
Mostique, Vase, Tan, Light Yellow, 8 In. 242.00
Mostique, Wall Pocket, Tan, 13 In. 259.00
Normandy, Basket, Hanging, 7 In. 259.00
Olympic, Vase, Euryclea Discovers Ulysses, 11 In. 2200.00
Orion, Vase, Turquoise, Tan, 2 Handles, 6 In. 250.00
Panel, Fan, Brown, 6 1/4 x 5 1/4 In. 545.00
Panel, Wall Pocket, Brown Sunflower Design, 9 1/4 In. 375.00
Panel, Wall Pocket, Green, 10 In. 300.00
Peony, Ewer, Blossoms, Flower Buds, Coral, Pale Pink Handle, 10 In. 110.00
Peony, Jardiniere, Pink, 8 In. 748.00
Peony, Jardiniere, Yellow, 8 In. 460.00
Peony, Wall Pocket, Brown, 8 In. 259.00
Pine Cone, Basket, Blue Twig Handle, Flower Frog, 8 In. 950.00
Pine Cone, Basket, Gray, 10 In. 200.00
Pine Cone, Basket, Green, 8 In. 200.00
Pine Cone, Basket, Hanging, Blue, 8 In. 635.00
Pine Cone, Bookends, Brown Sweeping Pine Needles, 5 1/2 In. 305.00
Pine Cone, Bowl, Brown, 15 In. 489.00
Pine Cone, Bowl, Brown, 2 Twig Handles, 3 5/8 In. 112.00
Pine Cone, Cigarette Holder, Brown, 2 3/4 In. 112.00
Pine Cone, Jardiniere, Blue Branch Handles, Signed, 8 1/4 In. 546.00
Pine Cone, Jardiniere, Brown, 2 Handles, 3 1/8 In. 112.00
Pine Cone, Pitcher, Blue, Ivory Field, 9 In. 1100.00
Pine Cone, Vase, Basket, Brown, Brown Branch Handle, 11 In. 525.00
Pine Cone, Vase, Blue, 2 Brown Branch Handles, 10 In. 990.00
Pine Cone, Vase, Blue, Branch Handle, 4 In. 250.00
Pine Cone, Vase, Blue, Brown Branch Handle, 6 In. 220.00
Pine Cone, Vase, Blue, Dark Brown Handles, Ivory, 9 1/2 In. 385.00
Pine Cone, Vase, Blue, Trumpet Shape, 2 Brown Branch Handles, 6 In. 300.00
Pine Cone, Vase, Blue, Trumpet Shape, 8 1/2 In. 410.00
Pine Cone, Vase, Blue, Trumpet Shape, 10 1/2 x 6 3/4 In. 705.00
Pine Cone, Vase, Brown, 7 In. 405.00
Pine Cone, Vase, Brown, Tapered, 10 1/2 x 7 3/4 In. 288.00
Pine Cone, Vase, Brown, Trumpet Shape, 2 Brown Branch Handles, 10 3/4 x 6 In. 385.00
Pine Cone, Vase, Brown, Trumpet Shape, Spherical Base, 8 In. 300.00
Pine Cone, Vase, Green, 2 Brown Branch Handles, Ivory, 13 In. 300.00
Pine Cone, Vase, Green, Pillow, 8 In. 325.00
Pine Cone, Vase, Green, Trumpet Shape, Dark Brown Branch Handles, Ivory, 8 In. 165.00
Pine Cone, Wall Pocket, Green, 8 In. 375.00
Poppy, Console, Pink, 5 3/4 x 16 1/4 In. 115.00
Poppy, Wall Pocket, Green, 8 1/2 In. 748.00
Primrose, Jardiniere, Light Blue, Angular Handles, 4 In. 78.00
Primrose, Vase, 6 In. 100.00
Primrose, Wall Pocket, Blue, 8 In. 863.00
Raymor, Casserole, Cover, Terra-Cotta, No. 156, Individual, 6 1/2 x 2 1/4 In. 28.00
Raymor, Cruet, Terra-Cotta Glaze, 5 1/2 In. 150.00
Raymor, Platter, Oval, 12 In. ....*Illus*   50.00

Raymor, Trivet, Beach Gray, 4-Footed, Round, 6 In. 40.00
Raymor, Vase, Bright Green, Purple Glaze, 12 x 11 In. 140.00
Raymor, Vase, Bright Yellow Crackled Glaze, 13 x 8 In. 1012.00
Raymor, Vase, Yellow, Brown Ribbed Body, 11 1/2 x 10 In. 168.00
Rosecraft, Wall Pocket, Black, 9 1/2 In. 400.00
Rosecraft, Wall Pocket, Brown, 10 1/2 In. 80.00
Rosecraft, Wall Pocket, Yellow, 10 In. 145.00
Rosecraft Panel, Bowl, Brown, Orange Floral, 8 x 2 3/8 In. 140.00
Rosecraft Panel, Vase, Brown, Orange Floral, Baluster, 9 In. 250.00
Rosecraft Panel, Window Box, Freesia Blossoms, 11 1/2 In. 190.00
Rosecraft Vintage, Vase, Brown, 10 1/2 x 7 In. 518.00
Rosecraft Vintage, Vase, Brown, 10 1/8 In. 335.00
Rosecraft Vintage, Vase, Dark Brown, 5 1/8 In. 170.00
Rosecraft Vintage, Wall Pocket, Brown, 10 In. 259.00
Rozane, Vase, Blue Flambe Glaze, 2 Handles, 6 In. 123.00
Rozane, Vase, Brown Glaze, Bull, 14 In. 2530.00
Rozane, Vase, Classical Shape, Sailboat, Brown, Walter Myers, 6 x 3 1/4 In. 805.00
Rozane, Vase, Orange Flowers, 6 x 2 1/2 In. 104.00
Rozane, Vase, Squeezebag, Stylized Cobalt, Green, Ocher Flowers, 10 x 3 3/4 In. 2925.00
Rozane, Vase, Woodland Scene, Brown, Ocher, Green Iris, 19 x 8 1/2 In. 9562.00
Rozane Royal, Vase, 4 In. 100.00
Rozane Royal, Vase, Brown, 6 In. 180.00
Rozane Royal, Vase, Brown, Woman's Profile, Oriental Style, 13 x 6 In. 1955.00
Rozane Royal, Vase, Ruffled Rim, Hunting Dog, 9 In. 896.00
Russco, Vase, Gold Glaze, Handles, 10 1/4 In. 168.00
Russco, Vase, Green, Yellow, Brown, 2 Handles At Base, 1934, 8 In. 495.00
Russco, Vase, White Morning Glory, Blue, 8 In. 100.00
Savona, Wall Pocket, Salmon, 9 In. 978.00
Silhouette, Basket, Red Flowers & Leaves, 6 In. 316.00
Silhouette, Candlestick, Tan, 3 In., Pair 58.00
Silhouette, Vase, 2 Nudes In Panel, Blue & Green, 7 1/2 In. 290.00
Silhouette, Vase, 2 Nudes In Panel, Red, 9 In. 345.00
Silhouette, Vase, Fan, Brown, 7 In. 460.00
Silhouette, Vase, Female Nudes, Footed, 6 In. 450.00
Silhouette, Vase, Foliage, Red, 7 1/4 In. 78.00
Silhouette, Vase, White, Nude Seated Under Tree, 10 3/8 In. 168.00
Silhouette, Wall Pocket, Leaves, Brown, 8 In. 431.00
Snowberry, Ashtray, Green, 5 1/4 In. 89.00
Snowberry, Basket, Blue, 7 In. 160.00
Snowberry, Basket, Pink, 12 In. 110.00
Snowberry, Candlestick, Pink, 2 In., Pair 80.00
Snowberry, Vase, Blue, 18 In. 545.00
Snowberry, Wall Pocket, Green, 8 In. 144.00
Sunflower, Basket, Hanging, 7 In. 748.00
Sunflower, Bowl, Green, Yellow Flowers, 2 Handles, 3 5/8 In. 784.00
Sunflower, Jardiniere, Yellow Blossoms, Curving Stems, 7 1/2 x 9 1/4 In. 1045.00
Sunflower, Jardiniere, Yellow Flowers, Green Leaves, Label, 7 1/2 In., Pair 2645.00
Sunflower, Vase, 5 In. 430.00
Sunflower, Vase, Bulbous, 6 3/4 x 7 In. 1150.00
Sunflower, Vase, Green, 2 Handles, 4 In. 616.00
Sunflower, Vase, Green, Yellow Flowers, 2 Handles, 5 In. ....420.00 to 560.00
Sunflower, Vase, Green, Yellow, Gold Flowers, Deep Ocher Glaze, 6 In. 1210.00
Sunflower, Vase, Green, Yellow, Gold Flowers, Looped Handles, 9 In. 1345.00
Sunflower, Vase, Pale Yellow Flowers, 2 Angular Handles, 6 1/8 In. ....430.00 to 504.00
Sunflower, Wall Pocket, 8 1/4 In. 1725.00
Sunflower, Wall Pocket, Green, 7 3/8 In. 1456.00
Thorn Apple, Basket, Hanging, Blue, 7 1/2 In. 290.00
Thorn Apple, Bowl, Brown, Green Stem, Handles, 5 7/8 In. 80.00
Thorn Apple, Centerpiece, Attached Candlesticks, Blue, 4 1/2 In. ....*Illus* 135.00
Thorn Apple, Flower Frog 125.00
Thorn Apple, Wall Pocket, Brown, 8 In. 489.00
Topeo, Bowl, Blue, 8 1/4 x 3 In. 175.00
Topeo, Bowl, Blue, 9 x 3 In. 80.00

Topeo, Console, Blue, 13 x 4 In. 200.00
Topeo, Flower Frog, Red, 9 x 3 In. 145.00
Topeo, Jardiniere, Blue, 6 1/4 x 7 In. 316.00
Topeo, Vase, Blue, 6 x 3 1/2 In. 200.00
Topeo, Vase, Blue, 8 1/4 x 6 In. ....345.00 to 635.00
Topeo, Vase, Blue, 10 1/2 x 4 1/4 In. 175.00
Topeo, Vase, Blue, Footed, 8 x 6 1/4 In. 490.00
Topeo, Vase, Blue, Gold Label, 7 1/4 x 4 1/2 In. 405.00
Topeo, Vase, Red, 6 x 3 1/2 In. 145.00
Topeo, Vase, Red, 7 1/2 x 4 1/2 In. 200.00
Tourmaline, Bowl, Blue Mottled, Glossy Yellow, 7 In. 56.00
Tourmaline, Candlestick, Blue, Yellow Gloss, 4 In. 35.00
Tourmaline, Vase, Blue Mottled Glaze, Glossy Yellow, 2 Handles, 6 In. ... 70.00
Tourmaline, Vase, Pink, Blue Glaze, 10 1/4 x 7 1/2 In. 690.00
Tuscany, Urn, Pink, 2 Handles, 10 1/2 x 9 1/4 In. 200.00
Tuscany, Vase, Pink, 7 In. 156.00
Tuscany, Wall Pocket, Gray, 9 1/2 In. 290.00
Velmoss, Vase, Broad Leaves, Green, Tan Matte Glaze, 5 3/4 x 5 1/2 In. ....345.00 to 375.00
Velmoss, Vase, Broad Leaves, Yellow, Green Matte Glaze, 11 3/4 x 5 1/4 In. 489.00
Velmoss, Vase, Footed, Blue, Gold Foil Label, 14 1/2 In. 616.00
Velmoss, Vase, Green, Signed, 6 In. 300.00
Velmoss, Wall Pocket, Rose, 11 1/2 In. 230.00
Vista, Basket, 2 Handles, 9 In. 985.00
Vista, Vase, Floral Trees Overlapping, Pale Blue, 18 x 8 In. 1210.00
Vista, Wall Pocket, 9 1/4 In. 546.00
Water Lily, Basket, Hanging, Handle, 8 3/4 In. 115.00
Water Lily, Candlestick, Brown, 2 In., Pair 56.00
Water Lily, Conch Shell, Blue, 8 In. 123.00
Water Lily, Flowerpot, Brown, 5 In. 100.00
Water Lily, Vase, 2 Handles, 8 1/4 In. 200.00
White Rose, Basket, Blue, 10 In. 200.00
White Rose, Cornucopia, Brown, Green Base, 8 1/2 In. 89.00
White Rose, Wall Pocket, Blue, 6 In. 345.00
White Rose, Wall Pocket, Pink, 8 In. 345.00
Wincraft, Ashtray, Turquoise, Yellow Flower On 2 Branch Handles, 4 1/2 In. 67.00
Wincraft, Basket, Hanging, Bulbous, 6 In. 230.00
Wincraft, Basket, Purple Grapes, Yellow, 12 In. 81.00
Wincraft, Bowl, Flower, Vine Design, Peach, Yellow, 14 In. 173.00
Wincraft, Vase, Blue Flowers, Leaves, 10 1/2 x 6 In. 230.00
Windsor, Vase, Blue, 6 1/4 x 6 In. 200.00
Windsor, Vase, Deep Magenta, Incised Green Geometric Design, 6 1/2 In. 413.00
Windsor, Vase, Magenta, Bulbous, Incised Geometric Design, Deep Violet, 6 In. 468.00
Wisteria, Vase, Blue, Brown Neck, 2 Handles, Silver Foil Label, 6 1/8 In. 530.00
Wisteria, Vase, Blue, Bulbous, Foil Label, 6 x 9 In. 1265.00
Wisteria, Vase, Blue, Deep Lavender Wisteria, Green Leaves, Ocher, 8 In. 1100.00
Wisteria, Vase, Blue, Ear Handles, 5 1/8 In. 560.00
Wisteria, Vase, Blue, Green, Pink, Gold Foil Label, 1980, 8 1/4 In. 950.00
Wisteria, Vase, Blue, Lavender Wisteria, Green Leaves, 2 Looped Handles, 6 In. 715.00
Wisteria, Vase, Brown, 5 1/2 x 7 In. 430.00
Wisteria, Vase, Brown, Squat, 4 1/4 x 6 In. 20.00

Roseville, Thorn Apple,
Centerpiece, Attached
Candlesticks, Blue, 4 1/2 In.

Wisteria, Vase, Lavender Floral, Green Leaves, 2 Looped Handles, 5 In. 660.00
Wisteria, Vase, Olive Green, Leaves, 2 Handles, 7 1/8 In. 448.00
Zephyr Lily, Basket, Blue, 10 In. 185.00
Zephyr Lily, Basket, Brown, Raised Mark, 7 In. 35.00
Zephyr Lily, Basket, Hanging, Green, 5 In. 156.00
Zephyr Lily, Bookends, Brown, Green & White Floral 145.00
Zephyr Lily, Jardiniere, Brown, Handle, 8 In. 259.00
Zephyr Lily, Vase, Green, Brown, 2 Handles, 7 In. 90.00
Zephyr Lily, Vase, Reverse Bell Shape, Green Glaze, Pink, Yellow Lilies, 8 In., Pair 200.00
Zephyr Lily, Wall Pocket, Brown, 8 In. 115.00

ROWLAND & MARSELLUS Company is part of a mark that appears on historical Staffordshire dating from the late nineteenth and early twentieth centuries. Rowland & Marsellus is the mark used by an American importing company in New York City. The company worked from 1893 to about 1937. Some of the pieces may have been made by the British Anchor Pottery Co. of Longton, England, for export to a New York firm. Many American views were made. Of special interest to collectors are the plates with rolled edges, usually blue and white.

Plate, Alaska, Seattle, Yukon, 10 In. 63.00
Plate, Albany, N.Y., 10 In. 36.00
Plate, Grand Rapids, Michigan, 10 In. 40.00
Plate, Mohawk Trail Through Berkshires, Piecrust Edge, 9 In. 46.00
Plate, Nelmes Tower, Sir George Somers & Gibbs, 1846, 10 In. 76.00
Plate, Oliver Twist Arrives, London, 10 In. 38.00
Plate, Panama Pacific Exposition, Horticulture Building, 1915, 10 In. 340.00
Plate, Souvenir, Alaska, Pacific Exposition 1909, 9 In. 55.00
Plate, Toronto, Canada, 10 In. 71.00
Plate, Valley Forge, Washington Headquarters In Center, 1778, 10 In. 126.00

ROY ROGERS was born in 1911 in Cincinnati, Ohio. In the 1930s, he made a living as a singer; in 1935, his group started work at a Los Angeles radio station. He appeared in his first movie in 1937. From 1952 to 1957, he made 101 television shows. The other stars in the show were his wife, Dale Evans, his horse, Trigger, and his dog, Bullet. Roy Rogers memorabilia is collected, including items from the Roy Rogers restaurants.

Bank, Saving, Tin, Plastic, Moore, 7 7/8 In. 205.00
Binoculars, Metal & Plastic, Rogers & Trigger Picture, Strap, Box, 5 In. 160.00
Book, Gopher Creek Gunman, Bringing The Gopher To Justice, 1945 . . . . 35.00
Book, Roy Rogers Cowboy Annual, World Distributors, 93 Pages, 7 1/4 x 10 In. 45.00
Book, Roy Rogers King Of The Cowboys, Tight Spine, 282 Pages, 1956, 5 1/2 In. 25.00
Branding Iron, White Cap, Gold, Horse On 1 Side 245.00
Button, Dale Evans, Raisin Bran, Tin, Pin Back, 1953 . . . . 30.00
Button, Trigger, Raisin Bran 20.00
Camera, Herbert George Co., 3 x 3 1/2 x 8 7/8 In. 132.00
Coloring Book, Trigger & Bullet, 10 Cents, 1956, 9 1/2 x 13 In. 45.00
Comic Book, No. 3, 1948 . . . . 20.00
Comic Book, No. 79, 1954 . . . . 20.00
Flashlight, Siren, Original Box 300.00
Game, Horseshoe, Wooden Peg, Hard Rubber Horseshoes . . . . .125.00 to 192.00
Guitar, Jefferson, Instructions 200.00
Gun, Cap, Trigger, Die Cast, Scrollwork, Stevens, 8 1/2 In. 210.00
Gun, Stag Grip, Tan Leather Holster, Wooden Bullets, G. Schmidt, 1950-1960 . . . . 310.00
Hat, Felt, Roy Rogers & Trigger On Bandanna, 1950s 79.00
Holster Set, Double, 3-Tone Leather, Relief Bust Of Roy In Center Panel 370.00
Lantern, Handle, Ohio Art Co., 8 In. 77.00
Lunch Box, Roy & Dale Chow Wagon, Dome Top, American Thermos, 1955 . . . . 450.00
Lunch Box, Thermos, Cream, Vinyl, 1960 . . . . .115.00 to 230.00
Lunch Box, Trigger, Metal, Thermos, 1957 . . . . 575.00
Marble, Red Lettering, White 6.00
Mug, Cream, Blue, Red, Roy Roger The King Of Cowboys, 4 1/2 In. 48.00
Picture Frame Clock, Box 750.00

Play Set, Swinging Door To The Saloon, 27 x 6 x 9 1/2 In. 108.00
Postcard, Western Heroes 12.00
Puzzle, Roy Rogers & Trigger, Whitman, 1953 .... 55.00
Rifle, Cap, Winchester, Silver Plastic & Metal, Marx, 1950s 69.00
Ring, Brass Band 3.00
School Bag, Roy On Trigger, Ranch In Background, Plastic, 1950s, 10 x 14 In. 110.00
Shooting Iron, Blistercard 400.00
Toy, Trailer & Jeep, Box, Ideal 395.00
View-Master, Dale Evans, Queen Of The West, 1955, 3 Piece 39.00
View-Master, Roy Rogers In The Hold-Up, 1953 .... 15.00
Watch, Metal Bracelet Band, Box 450.00
Wristwatch, Dale Evans, Pop-Up Box 525.00
Wristwatch, On Trigger, Lithographed Leather Band, 1950s 60.00
Yo-Yo, Blue For Boys, Pink For Girls 52.00
Yo-Yo, Brown Plastic, All Western Plastic, Inc. 38.00
Yo-Yo, Roy Rogers Picture, 1950s 13.00

ROYAL BAYREUTH is the name of a factory that was founded in Tettau, Bavaria, in 1794. It has continued to modern times. The marks have changed through the years. A stylized crest, the name *Royal Bayreuth*, and the word *Bavaria* appear in slightly different forms from 1870 to about 1919. Later dishes may include the words *U.S. Zone*, the year of the issue, or the word *Germany* instead of *Bavaria*. Related pieces may be found listed in the Rose Tapestry, Snow Babies, and Sunbonnet Babies categories.

Ashtray, Nautilus Shell, 5 In. 108.00
Basket, Tapestry, Floral Rose, Signed, 5 In. 390.00
Biscuit Jar, Cover, Goose Girl, 8 In. 295.00
Box, Cover, Tapestry, Colonial Curtsy, 4 1/2 In. 260.00
Charger, Goose Girl, 13 In. 250.00
Chocolate Pot, Poppy, 8 1/2 In. 1300.00
Creamer, Devil, Cards, 3 3/4 In. ....310.00 to 550.00
Creamer, Eagle, 3 3/4 In. 325.00
Creamer, Grape, White Satin, Signed, 3 3/4 In. 195.00
Creamer, Highland Sheep, Handle, 3 3/4 In. 225.00
Creamer, Orange, Signed, 4 In. 325.00
Creamer, Parakeet, 3 1/2 In. 425.00
Creamer, Red Poppy, Signed, 3 3/4 In. 235.00
Creamer, Robin, 3 3/4 In. 3395.00
Creamer, Strawberry, 3 3/4 In. 345.00
Cup & Saucer, Fisherman Scene 158.00
Hair Receiver, Tapestry, Colonial Curtsy, 4 1/2 In. 290.00
Hatpin Holder, Frog, Maroon 1200.00
Humidor, 2 Elk Heads, Blue Mark, 5 1/2 In. 180.00
Mustard Pot, Red Poppy, Cover, Signed, 3 1/4 In. 200.00
Pin Box, Cover, Tapestry, Colonial Curtsy, 3 1/2 In. 195.00
Pitcher, Apple, Water, Blue Stamp, 6 In. 795.00
Pitcher, Elk, Milk, Head, Horns, Signed, Blue Stamp, 5 In. 355.00
Pitcher, Grapes, White Satin Finish, Lavender Flowers 595.00
Pitcher, Hunter Scene, 4 In. 95.00
Pitcher, Milk, Skiff With Sail, 5 In. 200.00
Sugar, Cover, Strawberry, Handle, Gold Finial 195.00
Sugar, Rooster, Boat Shape 500.00
Sugar & Creamer, Cover, Grapes, Purple 250.00
Toothpick, Goats, 1900 .... 200.00
Tray, Tapestry, Country Curtsy, 9 3/4 In. 258.00
Vase, Brittany Woman, Boats, Silver Rim, Signed, 3 In. 85.00
Vase, Castle By The Lake, 4 In. 375.00
Vase, Cavalier, 2 Gold Trimmed Handles, Signed, 8 1/2 In. 150.00
Vase, Children & Dog, Handle, Silver Rim, 3 3/4 In. 75.00
Vase, Tapestry, 2 Cows, 4 1/2 In. 65.00
Vase, Tapestry, Cavalier Musician, Gold Rim, 6 1/4 x 4 In. 725.00

Vase, Tapestry, Cows, 4 x 5 In. 145.00
Vase, Woman With Horse, 3 Dogs, 2 x 3 1/4 In. 55.00

ROYAL BONN is the nineteenth- and twentieth-century trade name for the Bonn China Manufactory. It was established in 1755 in Bonn, Germany. A general line of porcelain was made. Many marks were used, most including the name *Bonn*, the initials *FM*, and a crown.

Charger, Dutch Peasant By The Seashore, 13 3/4 In. 185.00
Clock, Mantel, Ansonia, Flowers, Gilt Trim, 14 3/4 In. 715.00
Clock, Shelf, La Plata, Ansonia Clock Company, 12 3/4 In. 798.00
Plate, Courting Couple Transfer, Beehive Mark, 10 3/4 In. 55.00
Vase, Bluebird In Flight Above Pink, Gilt Flowering Branches, Handles, 9 In. 253.00
Vase, Cover, Flowering Vines, Large Purple Blossoms, Ivory Ground, 16 In. 185.00
Vase, Figural, Women In Period Dress In Center, Germany, 11 1/2 In. 168.00
Vase, Flowers, Gold, Handles, 13 In., Pair 420.00
Vase, Portrait, Young Woman, Bare Shoulders, Cobalt Blue, Signed, Bode, 7 In. 785.00
Vase, Roses Decoration, Signed, 5 1/4 In. 78.00

ROYAL COPENHAGEN porcelain and pottery have been made in Denmark since 1772. The Christmas plate series started in 1908. The figurines with pale blue and gray glazes have remained popular in this century and are still being made. Many other old and new style porcelains are made today.

Bowl, Center, Alternating Cobalt Blue & Gray Crackle Glaze, 8 In. 138.00
Bust, Head Of A Woman, Wearing Polychrome Kerchief, Kedegaard, 13 In. 225.00
Figurine, Bird, 3 1/8 In. 34.00
Figurine, Dog, Pointer, No. 269, White, Gray, 6 x 8 In. 265.00
Figurine, Farm Boy Struggling With A Cow, Gray, Blue, 6 1/2 In. 185.00
Figurine, Girl Putting On Shoes, No. 4642, 6 1/4 In. 285.00
Figurine, Greenland, Native Greenlander, Dog At Side, Signed, 13 In. 645.00
Figurine, Hans Christian Andersen, No. 4216, 11 In. 60.00
Figurine, Hedebo, Peasant Woman, Plaid Apron, Signed, 13 In. 430.00
Figurine, West Highland Terrier, White, Playing With Slipper, 3 x 5 In. 85.00
Group, Bust, Seminude Weeping Woman, 20th Century, 7 3/8 In. 230.00
Plaque, 2 Winged Maidens, 1 In Flowing Robe, 11 3/4 In. 632.00
Plate, Christmas, 1952, Frederiksborg Castle 150.00
Plate, Christmas, 1954, Fano Girl 170.00
Plate, Christmas, 1956, Good Shepherd 190.00
Plate, Christmas, 1958, Christmas Night 135.00
Plate, Christmas, 1960, Training Ship 125.00
Plate, Christmas, 1962, Hojsager Mill 250.00
Plate, Christmas, 1963, Fetching The Christmas Tree 45.00
Plate, Christmas, 1968, Last Umiak 15.00
Plate, Dessert, Flora Danica, Botanical, Painted, 9 In., 9 Piece 9600.00
Platter, Flora Danica, Botanical, Painted, 20 In. 3900.00
Vase, Goldfish, Swimming, Jenny Meyer, 1920, 20 1/2 In. . . . .*Illus* 3024.00
Vase, Light, Dark Green Crystalline Matte Glaze, 3 1/4 In. 575.00

Rotate your dining room chairs and turn the table once a year to keep the finish an even color. The sun will fade it. Put the leaves in a sunny window for a while to help them fade to the color of the table, or just keep a cloth on the table during the day.

Royal Copenhagen, Vase, Goldfish,
Swimming, Jenny Meyer, 1920, 20 1/2 In.

Vase, Morning Glories, Pink, Signed, 5 3/4 x 5 3/4 In.	12.00
Vase, Panoramic Coastal Scene, 2 Geese Calling To Flock, Signed, 12 In.	168.00
Vase, Panoramic Seascape, 2 Sailing Vessels, Signed, 9 1/2 In.	134.00
Vase, Poppy, Ivory To Light Blue Ground, Stamped Mark, 10 In.	60.00
Vase, Red, Gilt, Crackled Iron, 5 3/4 In.	29.00
Vase, Ship, Green Waters, Sky Ground, Stamped Mark, 7 In.	70.00
Vase, White Flowers, Leaves, Blue To Ivory Shaded, Stamped, 8 1/2 In.	35.00
Vase, White Irises, Watery Cobalt Ground, Jen Meyer, Signed, 17 1/2 In.	2016.00
Vase, White Orchid, Blue To Gray Ground, Stamped Mark, 12 In.	80.00
Vase, White Orchid, Spotted Leaves, Signed, 12 1/2 In.	252.00
Vase, White Orchids, Ivory To Light Blue Ground, Tapered, 7 1/2 In.	127.00
Vase, White Poppy, Green Leaves, Gray Ground, 10 In.	80.00
Wine Cooler, Flowering Specimens, Double Twig Handles, 6 In., Pair	7800.00

ROYAL COPLEY china was made by the Spaulding China Company of Sebring, Ohio, from 1939 to 1960. The figural planters and the small figurines, especially those with Art Deco designs, are of great collector interest.

Bank, Pig, For My Mink Written On His Belly	65.00
Figurine, Bird, Bunting, 5 In.	25.00
Figurine, Bird, Cockatoo, 8 1/2 In.	32.00
Figurine, Bird, Lark, Green Wing, Brown Breast, Red Crown, 6 1/2 In.	32.00
Figurine, Bird, Nuthatch, 4 1/2 In.	14.00
Figurine, Bird, Red Finch, On Stump, Yellow Breast, 4 1/4 In.	30.00
Figurine, Bird, Swallow, Brown, Teal, 8 In.	35.00
Figurine, Bird, Thrush, Orange & White, Black Tail, 6 3/8 In.	30.00
Figurine, Bird, Vireo, 4 1/2 In.	12.00
Figurine, Double Parakeets, Teal, Pink, Blue, Tan, 7 1/2 In.	55.00
Figurine, Duck, Mallard	45.00
Figurine, Horse Head, Gray, Long Yellow Mane	35.00
Planter, Deer & Fawn, 9 3/4 In.	28.00
Vase, Stem & Leaf, Black & White, Oval, 8 1/2 In.	10.00
Wall Pocket, Pigtail Girl, Brown Hair, Closed Eyes, Bonnet, Marked, 7 In.	45.00 to 75.00

ROYAL CROWN DERBY Company, Ltd., was established in England in 1890. There is a complex family tree that includes the Derby, Crown Derby, and Royal Crown Derby porcelains. The Royal Crown Derby mark includes the name and a crown. The words *Made in England* were used after 1921. The company is now a part of Royal Doulton Tableware Ltd.

Cup & Saucer, 1910	85.00
Plate Set, Dessert, Imari, Floral & Geometric, Gilt, 8 3/8 In., 12 Piece	805.00
Tea Service, Flowers, Gilt, Canary Yellow, 5 In., 3 Piece	373.00
Tea Service, Partial, Gilt Accents, Late 19th Century, 32 Piece	1150.00
Vase, Flowers, Gilt, 5 In.	46.00

ROYAL DOULTON is the name used on Doulton and Company pottery made from 1902 to the present. Doulton and Company of England was founded in 1853. Pieces made before 1902 are listed in this book under Doulton. Royal Doulton collectors search for the out-of-production figurines, character jugs, vases, and series wares. Some vases and animal figurines were made with a special red glaze called flambe. Sung and Chang glazed pieces are rare. The multicolored glaze is very thick and looks as if it were dropped on the clay.

Animal, Dog, Airedale Terrier, HN 1024, 4 In.	350.00
Animal, Dog, Alsatian, HN 1116, 6 In.	1100.00
Animal, Dog, Bull Terrier, HN 1100, 4 In.	425.00
Animal, Dog, Bulldog, Puppy, K 2, 2 In.	100.00
Animal, Dog, Bulldog, Standing, HN 1043, 4 3/4 In.	750.00
Animal, Dog, Bulldog, Standing, HN 1044, 3 1/4 In.	300.00 to 350.00
Animal, Dog, Bulldog, Union Jack, HN 5913c, 2 1/4 In.	250.00 to 350.00
Animal, Dog, Character, Red Ball, HN 1103, 5 x 2 1/2 In.	95.00
Animal, Dog, Cocker Spaniel, HN 1002, 6 1/2 In.	450.00

Animal, Dog, Cocker Spaniel, HN 1037, 3 1/2 In. 140.00
Animal, Dog, Cocker Spaniel, Lucky Star, HN 1000, 6 1/2 In. 675.00
Animal, Dog, Cocker Spaniel, With Pheasant, HN 1029, 3 1/2 In. ....*Illus* 275.00
Animal, Dog, Collie, Ashtead Applause, HN 1059, 3 1/2 In. 300.00
Animal, Dog, Fox Terrier, Seated, K 8, 2 1/2 In. 135.00
Animal, Dog, Foxhound, Seated, K 7, 2 1/2 In. 150.00
Animal, Dog, Greyhound, 1960, HN 1067, 4 1/2 In. 775.00
Animal, Dog, Irish Setter, HN 1056, 4 In. 300.00
Animal, Dog, Pekinese, Seated, K 6, 2 In. 75.00
Animal, Dog, Terrier Puppies In Basket, HN 2588, 3 In. 155.00
Animal, Dog, Terrier, Sitting In Basket, White, Brown, HN 2587, 3 In. 125.00
Animal, Dog, Terrier, Smooth Haired, Don Of Notts, HN 2513, 6 In. 1200.00
Animal, Dog, Welsh Corgi, K 16, 2 1/2 In. 100.00
Animal, Dragon, Veined, Flambe, HN 2085 .... 1375.00
Animal, Elephant, Trunk In Salute, Flambe, 5 1/4 In. 180.00
Animal, Fox, Seated, Flambe, HN 130, 9 1/4 In. 600.00
Animal, Guinea Fowl, Flambe, HN 125, 5 1/4 In. 400.00
Animal, Peruvian Penguin On Rock, Flambe, 5 In. 800.00
Animal, Polar Bear & Cub On Base, Flambe, Sung, 12 1/2 In. 6600.00
Ash Pot, Old Charley, D 5925 .... 200.00
Ashtray, Old Charley, D 5599 .... 200.00
Biscuit Jar, Coaching Series, c.1906, 6 1/4 In. 950.00
Bowl, White, Green Glaze, Mauve, Metal Mounted, Chang, 1920s, 3 3/8 In. .. 540.00
Candleholder, Walton Ware, Battle Of Hastings, Cream Ground, c.1910, 6 In. .. 288.00

Royal Doulton character jugs depict the head and shoulders of the subject. They are made in four sizes: large, 5 1/4 to 7 inches; small, 3 1/4 to 4 inches; miniature, 2 1/4 to 2 1/2 inches; and tiny, 1 1/4 inches. Toby jugs portray a seated, full figure.

Character Jug, 'Arriet, Large 140.00
Character Jug, 'Arriet, Tiny 225.00
Character Jug, 'Arry, Large 140.00
Character Jug, Aladdin's Genie, Large 259.00
Character Jug, Anne Boleyn, Miniature 125.00
Character Jug, Anne Of Cleaves, Large 300.00
Character Jug, Antique Dealer, Large 175.00
Character Jug, Antony & Cleopatra, Large 175.00
Character Jug, Apothecary, Small 100.00
Character Jug, Aramis, Miniature 80.00
Character Jug, Athos, Large 125.00
Character Jug, Auld Mac, Small 45.00
Character Jug, Auld Mac, Tiny 235.00
Character Jug, Bacchus, Large 75.00
Character Jug, Bahamas Policeman, Large 127.00
Character Jug, Baseball Player, Toronto Blue Jays, Small 95.00
Character Jug, Beefeater, Small 125.00
Character Jug, Benjamin Franklin, Small 135.00
Character Jug, Bootmaker, Williamsburg Collection, Miniature 85.00
Character Jug, Busker, Large 75.00
Character Jug, Buzfuz, Small 135.00
Character Jug, Cabinet Maker, Williamsburg Collection, Large 69.00
Character Jug, Captain Ahab, Small 45.00
Character Jug, Captain Henry Morgan, Large 75.00
Character Jug, Captain Henry Morgan, Miniature 75.00
Character Jug, Cardinal, Large 125.00
Character Jug, Cardinal, Tiny 275.00
Character Jug, Catharine Of Aragon, Miniature 175.00
Character Jug, Cavalier, Large 75.00
Character Jug, Chopin, Large 260.00
Character Jug, Cook & Cheshire Cat, 6 3/4 In. 115.00
Character Jug, Cricketeer 75.00
Character Jug, Cyrano De Bergerac, Large 200.00
Character Jug, Davy Crockett, Antonio Lopez De Santa Anna, 2 Faces, Large 85.00

Character Jug, Dick Turpin, Horse Head Handle, Large 105.00
Character Jug, Dick Turpin, Pistol Handle, Large 125.00
Character Jug, Dick Whittington, London Signpost Handle, Large 295.00
Character Jug, Dick Whittington, Stick & Handkerchief Handle, Large 550.00
Character Jug, Drake, Rope Handle, Large 140.00
Character Jug, Drake, Rope Handle, Small 100.00
Character Jug, Fagin, Tiny 85.00
Character Jug, Fat Boy, Small 175.00
Character Jug, Fireman, Large 69.00
Character Jug, Fireman, Small 125.00
Character Jug, Fortune Teller, Tarot Card Handle, Large 81.00
Character Jug, Friar Tuck, Large .... .201.00 to 550.00
Character Jug, General Patton, Large 375.00
Character Jug, Genie, Large 115.00
Character Jug, George Harrison, 5 1/2 In. 165.00
Character Jug, George III & George Washington, 2 Faces, Large 125.00
Character Jug, Gladiator, Large 345.00
Character Jug, Glenn Miller, Large 69.00
Character Jug, Gondolier, Large 550.00
Character Jug, Granny, One Tooth Showing, Large .... .55.00 to 105.00
Character Jug, Henry VIII, Large 75.00
Character Jug, Jester, Small 85.00
Character Jug, Jockey, Large 115.00
Character Jug, John Doulton, Small 45.00
Character Jug, John Lennon, 5 1/2 In. 165.00
Character Jug, John Peel, Large 125.00
Character Jug, Johnny Appleseed, Large 104.00
Character Jug, Juggler, Large 58.00
Character Jug, Lawyer, Large 75.00
Character Jug, Lobsterman, Large 75.00
Character Jug, Lord Nelson, Large .... .247.00 to 390.00
Character Jug, Louis Armstrong, Large .... .140.00 to 201.00
Character Jug, Mad Hatter, Large 195.00
Character Jug, March Hare, Large 92.00
Character Jug, Mikado, Large 550.00
Character Jug, Mr. Micawber, Miniature 85.00
Character Jug, Mr. Quaker, Large 431.00
Character Jug, Neptune, Large 69.00
Character Jug, Old Charley, Large .... .75.00 to 350.00
Character Jug, Old Charley, Miniature 30.00
Character Jug, Old Charley, Small .... .50.00 to 250.00
Character Jug, Old Charley, Tiny 90.00
Character Jug, Old King Cole, Brown Crown, Large 295.00
Character Jug, Old King Cole, Brown Crown, Tiny 175.00
Character Jug, Old Salt, Mermaid, Blue Tail Handle, Large 165.00
Character Jug, Oliver Cromwell, Large 350.00
Character Jug, Oliver Twist, Tiny 50.00
Character Jug, Paddy, Small 75.00
Character Jug, Parson Brown, Large .... .72.00 to 125.00
Character Jug, Paul McCartney, 5 1/2 In. 165.00
Character Jug, Pearly King, Large 200.00
Character Jug, Pendle Witch, Large 69.00
Character Jug, Pied Piper, Small 95.00
Character Jug, Poacher, Small 2175.00
Character Jug, Porthos, Large 135.00
Character Jug, Punch & Judy, 2 Faces, Large .... .374.00 to 450.00
Character Jug, Punch & Judy, Miniature 600.00
Character Jug, Queen Victoria, Large .... .58.00 to 69.00
Character Jug, Red Queen, Large 200.00
Character Jug, Red Queen, Miniature 125.00
Character Jug, Regency Beau, Large 604.00
Character Jug, Ringo Starr, 5 1/2 In. 165.00
Character Jug, Rip Van Winkle, Miniature 65.00

Character Jug, Robin Hood, Plain Handle, Large 200.00
Character Jug, Ronald Reagan, Large 403.00
Character Jug, Sairey Gamp, Large 75.00
Character Jug, Sairey Gamp, Miniature 75.00
Character Jug, Sairey Gamp, Small 45.00
Character Jug, Sairey Gamp, Tiny 90.00
Character Jug, Sam Johnson, Large 46.00
Character Jug, Sam Weller, Tiny 110.00
Character Jug, Samson & Delilah, Large 200.00
Character Jug, Sancho Panca, Large 115.00
Character Jug, Sancho Panca, Small 75.00
Character Jug, Santa Claus, Candy Cane Handle, Large 230.00
Character Jug, Santa Claus, Christmas Parcel Handle, Tiny 55.00
Character Jug, Santa Claus, Doll On Drum, Handle, Large 138.00
Character Jug, Santa Claus, Holly Wreath Handle, Large 230.00
Character Jug, Santa Claus, Miniature 125.00
Character Jug, Santa Claus, Reindeer Handle, Large ....219.00 to 350.00
Character Jug, Santa Claus, Stuffed Stocking Handle, Large 173.00
Character Jug, Santa Claus, Teddy Bear Handle, Tiny 55.00
Character Jug, Santa Claus, Wreath Handle, Miniature 100.00
Character Jug, Scrooge, Tiny 60.00
Character Jug, Shakespeare, Small 115.00
Character Jug, Simon The Cellarer, Small 75.00
Character Jug, Simple Simon, Large 490.00
Character Jug, Sir Henry & Michael Doulton, 2 Faces, Small 100.00
Character Jug, Sir Thomas More, Large 275.00
Character Jug, Smuggler, Large ....105.00 to 225.00
Character Jug, Snake Charmer, Large 144.00
Character Jug, St. George, Large ....200.00 to 400.00
Character Jug, Tam O'Shanter, Small 120.00
Character Jug, Toby Philpots, Miniature 65.00
Character Jug, Tony Weller, Miniature 85.00
Character Jug, Tony Weller, Small 45.00
Character Jug, Touchstone, Large ....58.00 to 195.00
Character Jug, Town Crier, Large 195.00
Character Jug, Uncle Tom Cobbleigh, Large ....109.00 to 295.00
Character Jug, Veteran Motorist, Large 105.00
Character Jug, Viking, Small 110.00
Character Jug, Walrus & Carpenter, Large ....46.00 to 195.00
Character Jug, Winston Churchill, Large 400.00
Character Jug, Witch, Large 173.00
Character Jug, Wizard, Small 65.00
Character Jug, Yachtsman, Large ....115.00 to 200.00
Creamer, Brown & Tan, Cream Medallions, 2 In. 68.00
Figurine, Adrienne, HN 2152 .... 135.00
Figurine, Afternoon Tea, HN 1747 .... 650.00
Figurine, Alice, HN 2158 .... 225.00
Figurine, Amy, HN 3316 .... 950.00
Figurine, Annabella, HN 1872 .... 1400.00
Figurine, Antoinette, HN 1850 .... 1500.00
Figurine, As Good As New, HN 2971 .... 200.00
Figurine, Ascot, Woman, HN 2356 .... 250.00
Figurine, Autumn Breezes, HN 1911 .... 300.00
Figurine, Autumn Breezes, HN 3736 .... 250.00
Figurine, Autumn, HN 2087 .... 700.00
Figurine, Babie, HN 1679 .... 125.00
Figurine, Babie, HN 1842 .... 450.00
Figurine, Baby Bunting, HN 2108 .... 350.00
Figurine, Bachelor, Man, HN 2319 .... 450.00
Figurine, Ballerina, HN 2116 .... 450.00
Figurine, Balloon Man, HN 1954 ....100.00 to 176.00
Figurine, Barbara, HN 2962 .... 192.00
Figurine, Beachcomber, HN 2487 .... 275.00

Figurine, Bedtime, HN 1978 .... 106.00
Figurine, Belle O' The Ball, HN 1997 .... 355.00
Figurine, Bess, HN 2002 .... 450.00
Figurine, Bess, HN 2003 .... 900.00
Figurine, Biddy, HN 1513 .... 325.00
Figurine, Blacksmith, HN 2782 .... 275.00
Figurine, Blithe Morning, HN 2021 .... 800.00
Figurine, Bluebeard, HN 2105 .... 725.00
Figurine, Bo-Peep, HN 1811 .... 175.00
Figurine, Boatman, HN 2147 .... 144.00
Figurine, Bon Appetit, HN 2444 .... 275.00
Figurine, Bonnie Lassie, HN 1626 ....220.00 to 800.00
Figurine, Breton Dancer, HN 2383 .... 1000.00
Figurine, Bride, HN 2166 .... 275.00
Figurine, Bridesmaid, HN 2196 .... 165.00
Figurine, Bridesmaid, HN 2874 .... 100.00
Figurine, Bridget, HN 2070 .... 475.00
Figurine, Broken Lance, HN 2041 ....390.00 to 725.00
Figurine, Brother & Sister, HN 3460 .... 106.00
Figurine, Bunny, HN 2214 .... 250.00
Figurine, Bunnykins, Astro Bunnykins, DB 20 .... 200.00
Figurine, Bunnykins, Aussie Surfer Bunnykin, DB 133 .... 150.00
Figurine, Bunnykins, Boy Skater, DB 152 .... 50.00
Figurine, Bunnykins, Buntie Bunnykins Helping Mother, DB 2 .... 85.00
Figurine, Bunnykins, Busy Needles, DB 10 .... 59.00
Figurine, Bunnykins, Daisie Bunnykins Spring Time, DB 7 .... 350.00
Figurine, Bunnykins, Dollie Bunnykins Playtime, DB 8 .... 75.00
Figurine, Bunnykins, Family Photograph Bunnykins, DB 1 .... 165.00
Figurine, Bunnykins, Fisherman, DB 170 .... 55.00
Figurine, Bunnykins, Freefall, DB 41 .... 375.00
Figurine, Bunnykins, Gardner, DB 156 ....25.00 to 50.00
Figurine, Bunnykins, Halloween Bunnykins, DB 132 .... 55.00
Figurine, Bunnykins, Home Run Bunnykins, DB 43 .... 125.00
Figurine, Bunnykins, Jogging Bunnykins, DB 22 .... 150.00
Figurine, Bunnykins, Mother's Day Bunnykins, DB 155 .... 55.00
Figurine, Bunnykins, Mr. Bunnykins, Autumn Days, DB 5 .... 475.00
Figurine, Bunnykins, Mrs. Bunnykins At Easter Parade, DB 19 .... 100.00
Figurine, Bunnykins, Partners In Collecting, DB 151 .... 175.00
Figurine, Bunnykins, Reginald Ratley, Up To No Good, DBR 3/3530 .... 20.00
Figurine, Bunnykins, Rise & Shine, DB 11 .... 59.00
Figurine, Bunnykins, Sailor Bunnykins, DB 166 .... 50.00
Figurine, Bunnykins, Seaside, DB 177 .... 45.00
Figurine, Bunnykins, Sleepytime Bunnykins, DB 15 .... 85.00
Figurine, Bunnykins, Tom Bunnykins, DB 72 .... 100.00
Figurine, Bunnykins, Tourist Bunnykins, DB 190 .... 40.00
Figurine, Bunnykins, William Bunnykins, DB 69 .... 20.00
Figurine, Buttercup, HN 2309 .... 268.00
Figurine, Calumet, HN 2068 .... 1100.00
Figurine, Camellia, HN 2222 .... 350.00
Figurine, Camellia, HN 3701 .... 350.00
Figurine, Camille, HN 1586 .... 1750.00
Figurine, Captain Cuttle, M 77 .... 125.00
Figurine, Carolyn, HN 2974 .... 250.00
Figurine, Celeste, HN 2237 .... 325.00
Figurine, Cellist, Formal, HN 2226 .... 650.00
Figurine, Cello, HN 2331 .... 2100.00
Figurine, Centurion, HN 2726 .... 140.00
Figurine, Charles Dickens, HN 3448 .... 40.00
Figurine, Charlotte, HN 2421 .... 275.00
Figurine, Cherie, HN 2341 .... 200.00
Figurine, Cheryl, HN 3253 .... 425.00
Figurine, Chief, HN 2892 .... 250.00
Figurine, Child From Williamsburg, HN 2154 .... 275.00

Figurine, Chinese Dancer, HN 2840 . . . . 1150.00
Figurine, Chitarrone, HN 2700 . . . . 1000.00
Figurine, Chloe, HN 1479 . . . . 1100.00
Figurine, Christine, HN 1840 . . . . .1600.00 to 1900.00
Figurine, Christine, HN 3172 . . . . 325.00
Figurine, Christmas Morn, HN 1992 . . . . 269.00
Figurine, Christmas Parcels, HN 2851 . . . . 350.00
Figurine, Christmas Time, HN 2110 . . . . .510.00 to 625.00
Figurine, Cissie, HN 1809 . . . . .100.00 to 185.00
Figurine, Clare, HN 2793 . . . . 300.00
Figurine, Clarissa, Green, HN 2345 . . . . 225.00
Figurine, Clown, HN 2890 . . . . 200.00
Figurine, Cobbler, HN 1706 . . . . .225.00 to 400.00
Figurine, Collinette, HN 1998 . . . . 1000.00
Figurine, Collinette, HN 1999 . . . . 900.00
Figurine, Coppelia, HN 2115 . . . . 875.00
Figurine, Coralie, HN 2307 . . . . 220.00
Figurine, Country Lass, HN 1991 . . . . 250.00
Figurine, Cymbals, HN 2699 . . . . 1500.00
Figurine, Daddy's Girl, Vanity Fair, HN 3435 . . . . 82.00
Figurine, Dancing Years, HN 2235 . . . . 500.00
Figurine, Danielle, HN 3001 . . . . 200.00
Figurine, Darby, HN 2024 . . . . 300.00
Figurine, Darling, HN 1319 . . . . 275.00
Figurine, Darling, HN 1985 . . . . 107.00
Figurine, David Copperfield, M 88 . . . . 100.00
Figurine, Daydreams, HN 1731 . . . . 350.00
Figurine, Debbie, HN 2385 . . . . 175.00
Figurine, Debbie, HN 2400 . . . . 165.00
Figurine, Deborah, HN 3644 . . . . 350.00
Figurine, Diana, HN 1966 . . . . 250.00
Figurine, Diane, HN 3604 . . . . 275.00
Figurine, Dick Turpin, HN 3272 . . . . 425.00
Figurine, Dinky Doo, Lavender, Child's, HN 1678 . . . . 144.00
Figurine, Doctor, HN 2858 . . . . 350.00
Figurine, Dorcas, HN 1558 . . . . 450.00
Figurine, Dulcimer, HN 2798 . . . . 1200.00
Figurine, Elaine, HN 2791 . . . . 300.00
Figurine, Elegance, HN 2264 . . . . 250.00
Figurine, Eliza Farren, Countess Of Derby, HN 3442 . . . . 335.00
Figurine, Eliza, HN 2543 . . . . 295.00
Figurine, Elyse, HN 2429 . . . . 275.00
Figurine, Embroidering, HN 2855 . . . . 325.00
Figurine, Emily, HN 3806 . . . . 75.00
Figurine, Enchantment, HN 2178 . . . . 275.00
Figurine, Eventide, HN 2814 . . . . 325.00
Figurine, Fagin, HN 3752 . . . . 275.00
Figurine, Fagin, M 49 . . . . 125.00
Figurine, Fair Lady, HN 2193 . . . . 269.00
Figurine, Fair Lady, HN 2832 . . . . 270.00
Figurine, Fair Maiden, HN 2211 . . . . 185.00
Figurine, Faith, HN 3082 . . . . 275.00
Figurine, Falstaff, HN 2054 . . . . .115.00 to 250.00
Figurine, Family Album, HN 2321 . . . . 550.00
Figurine, Favorite, HN 2249 . . . . 275.00
Figurine, Fiona, HN 1925 . . . . 1900.00
Figurine, Fiona, HN 2694 . . . . 250.00
Figurine, Fleur, HN 2368 . . . . 275.00
Figurine, Flora, HN 2349 . . . . 475.00
Figurine, Florence Nightingale, HN 3144 . . . . 1050.00
Figurine, Flowers For Mother, HN 3454 . . . . 110.00
Figurine, Flute, HN 2483 . . . . 1400.00
Figurine, Foaming Quart, HN 2162 . . . . .200.00 to 250.00

Figurine, Forty Winks, HN 1974	375.00
Figurine, Four O'Clock, HN 1760	2200.00
Figurine, Francine, HN 2422	175.00
Figurine, French Horn, HN 2795	1200.00
Figurine, Gay Morning, HN 2135	475.00
Figurine, Genevieve, HN 1962	450.00
Figurine, Genie, HN 2989	275.00
Figurine, George Washington At Prayer, HN 2861	4000.00
Figurine, Good Catch, HN 2258	285.00
Figurine, Good King Wenceslas, HN 2118	550.00
Figurine, Goody Two Shoes, Pink, Red, Child's, HN 1905	250.00
Figurine, Grace, HN 2318	121.00
Figurine, Grandma, HN 2052A	600.00
Figurine, Gulliver, HN 3750	325.00
Figurine, Gwynneth, HN 1980	525.00
Figurine, Gypsy Dance, HN 2157	1400.00
Figurine, Gypsy Dance, HN 2230	475.00
Figurine, Hannah, HN 3655	250.00
Figurine, Harlequin, HN 2186	350.00
Figurine, Harmony, HN 2824	190.00 to 275.00
Figurine, Harp, HN 2482	2300.00
Figurine, Heidi, HN 2975	200.00
Figurine, Henrietta Maria, HN 2005	850.00
Figurine, Her Ladyship, HN 1977	230.00
Figurine, Hilary, HN 2335	225.00
Figurine, Hinged Parasol, HN 1578	1650.00
Figurine, HM Queen Elizabeth II, HN 3440	500.00
Figurine, Homecoming, HN 3295	225.00
Figurine, Hometime, HN 3685	150.00
Figurine, Hurdy Gurdy, HN 2796	1500.00
Figurine, Innocence, HN 2842	200.00
Figurine, Invitation, HN 2170	250.00
Figurine, Ireland, HN 3628	325.00
Figurine, Isadora, HN 2938	250.00
Figurine, Jack, HN 2060	250.00
Figurine, Jacqueline, HN 2001	800.00
Figurine, Janet, HN 4042	220.00
Figurine, Janet, M 69	535.00
Figurine, Janice, HN 2022	700.00
Figurine, Janine, HN 2461	275.00
Figurine, Jasmine, HN 1862	1500.00
Figurine, Jean, HN 1877	950.00
Figurine, Jean, HN 2032	550.00
Figurine, Jester, HN 2016	185.00 to 493.00
Figurine, Jill, HN 2061	250.00
Figurine, Joan, HN 1422	500.00
Figurine, John F. Kennedy, HN 2893	9500.00
Figurine, Jovial Monk, HN 2144	300.00
Figurine, Judge, HN 2443	175.00 to 275.00
Figurine, Judge, HN 2443A	210.00
Figurine, Julie, HN 2705	240.00
Figurine, June, HN 1690	1200.00
Figurine, June, HN 1691	1200.00
Figurine, Kate Hardcastle, HN 1719	1300.00
Figurine, Katrina, HN 2327	475.00
Figurine, King Charles, HN 3459	1010.00
Figurine, La Sylphide, HN 2138	600.00
Figurine, Lady Betty, HN 1967	650.00
Figurine, Lady Charmian, HN 1948	290.00 to 350.00
Figurine, Laird, HN 2361	200.00 to 400.00
Figurine, Lambing Time, HN 1890	325.00
Figurine, Laurianne, HN 2719	250.00
Figurine, Lavinia, HN 1955	175.00

Figurine, Lawyer, HN 3041 .... 200.00
Figurine, Leading Lady, HN 2269 ....138.00 to 300.00
Figurine, Lights Out, HN 2262 .... 350.00
Figurine, Lilac Time, HN 2137 ....355.00 to 600.00
Figurine, Lily, HN 1798 .... 200.00
Figurine, Linda, HN 2106 .... 250.00
Figurine, Lisa, HN 2310 .... 225.00
Figurine, Little Boy Blue, HN 2062 .... 225.00
Figurine, Little Bridesmaid, HN 1434 .... 500.00
Figurine, Little Nell, M 51 .... 125.00
Figurine, Lizzie, HN 2749 .... 225.00
Figurine, Lobsterman, HN 2317 .... 275.00
Figurine, Lorraine, HN 3118 .... 300.00
Figurine, Lute, HN 2431 .... 1500.00
Figurine, Lydia, HN 1908 .... 175.00
Figurine, Margaret, HN 1989 .... 575.00
Figurine, Marie, HN 1370 .... 150.00
Figurine, Marietta, HN 1341 .... 1300.00
Figurine, Mariquita, HN 1837 .... 1900.00
Figurine, Mary Had A Little Lamb, HN 2048 .... 200.00
Figurine, Mary, HN 2374 .... 400.00
Figurine, Mary, Mary, Watering Flowers, Pink, Child's, HN 2044 .... 300.00
Figurine, Mask Seller, HN 2103 .... 275.00
Figurine, Master Sweep, HN 2205 .... 1000.00
Figurine, Master, HN 2325 .... 325.00
Figurine, Maureen, HN 1770 .... 500.00
Figurine, May, HN 2711 .... 69.00
Figurine, Meg, HN 2743 .... 225.00
Figurine, Mendicant, HN 1365 .... 350.00
Figurine, Meriel, HN 1931 .... 3000.00
Figurine, Minuet, HN 2019 .... 450.00
Figurine, Miss Demure, HN 1402 .... 97.00
Figurine, Miss Muffet, HN 1936 .... 250.00
Figurine, Monica, HN 1467 .... 175.00
Figurine, Mr. Pickwick, HN 1894 .... 420.00
Figurine, Mr. Pickwick, M 41 .... 125.00
Figurine, Mrs. Bardell, M 086 .... 100.00
Figurine, My Pet, Girl, HN 2238 .... 265.00
Figurine, Nanny, HN 2221 .... 325.00
Figurine, Newsvendor, HN 2891 ....200.00 to 275.00
Figurine, Nicole, HN 3421 .... 170.00
Figurine, Ninette, HN 2379 ....290.00 to 450.00
Figurine, Off To School, HN 3768 .... 210.00
Figurine, Old Balloon Seller, HN 1315 .... 154.00
Figurine, Old Mother Hubbard, HN 2314 .... 500.00
Figurine, Omar Khayyam, HN 2247 .... 250.00
Figurine, One That Got Away, HN 2153 .... 700.00
Figurine, Orange Lady, HN 1759 .... 400.00
Figurine, Orange Vendor, HN 1966 .... 1600.00
Figurine, Paisley Shawl, HN 1987 .... 475.00
Figurine, Patchwork Quilt, HN 1984 .... 475.00
Figurine, Pearly Boy, HN 2767A 250.00
Figurine, Pearly Girl, HN 2036 .... 250.00
Figurine, Pearly Girl, HN 2769A 250.00
Figurine, Pecksniff, HN 2098 .... 360.00
Figurine, Peggy, HN 2038 .... 170.00
Figurine, Penny, HN 2338 .... 110.00
Figurine, Philippine Dancer, HN 2439 .... 1000.00
Figurine, Pied Piper, HN 2102 .... 400.00
Figurine, Poacher, HN 2043 .... 425.00
Figurine, Polly, HN 3178 .... 150.00
Figurine, Potter, HN 1493 .... 600.00
Figurine, Pride & Joy, HN 2945 .... 350.00

Royal Doulton, Animal, Dog,
Cocker Spaniel, With Pheasant,
HN 1029, 3 1/2 In..

Royal Doulton, Figurine, Viola
D'Amore, HN 2797

Royal Doulton, Vase,
Flambe, Sung, Drip Glaze,
Noke & F. Allen, 5 In.

Figurine, Prince Of Wales, HN 2884	950.00
Figurine, Printemps, HN 3066	1000.00
Figurine, Prized Possession, HN 2942	750.00
Figurine, Professor, HN 2281	230.00 to 275.00
Figurine, Prue, HN 1996	300.00
Figurine, Queen Anne, HN 3141	575.00
Figurine, Queen Of Sheba, HN 2328	1750.00
Figurine, Rag Doll, HN 2142	165.00 to 185.00
Figurine, Regal Lady, HN 2709	275.00
Figurine, Ritz Bellboy, HN 2772	250.00
Figurine, River Boy, HN 2128	325.00
Figurine, Romany Sue, HN 1757	3385.00
Figurine, Rosalind, HN 2393	300.00
Figurine, Rose, HN 2123	115.00
Figurine, Samantha, HN 2954	225.00
Figurine, Scottish Highland Dancer, HN 2436	1750.00
Figurine, Sharon, White, HN 3047	175.00
Figurine, She Loves Me Not, Blue, Child's, HN 2045	325.00
Figurine, Silks & Ribbons, HN 2017	295.00
Figurine, Silversmith Of Williamsburg, HN 2208	250.00
Figurine, Simone, HN 2378	130.00
Figurine, Sir Henry Doulton, HN 3891	450.00
Figurine, Sir Walter Raleigh, HN 2015	1100.00
Figurine, Solitude, HN 2810	200.00 to 375.00
Figurine, Sophie, HN 3257	200.00
Figurine, Southern Belle, HN 2229	210.00
Figurine, Spanish Flamenco Dancer, HN 2831	2000.00
Figurine, Special Friend, HN 3607	110.00
Figurine, Special Treat, HN 3663	135.00
Figurine, Spring Flowers, HN 1807	375.00
Figurine, Spring Morning, HN 1922	315.00
Figurine, St. George, HN 2051	675.00
Figurine, Statesman, HN 2859	175.00
Figurine, Stiggins, M 50	125.00
Figurine, Stitch In Time, HN 2352	300.00
Figurine, Stop Press, HN 2683	200.00
Figurine, Summer Rose, HN 3309	245.00
Figurine, Sunday Best, HN 2698	225.00
Figurine, Sweet & Twenty, HN 1360	1100.00
Figurine, Sweet Dreams, HN 2380	145.00
Figurine, Sweet Seventeen, HN 1734	300.00
Figurine, Taking Things Easy, HN 2677	240.00
Figurine, Tall Story, HN 2248	375.00

Figurine, Teatime, HN 2255 .... 300.00
Figurine, This Little Pig, HN 1793 .... 61.00
Figurine, Time For Bed, HN 3762 .... 145.00
Figurine, Tinkle Bell, HN 1677 .... 135.00
Figurine, Toinette, HN 1940 .... 2600.00
Figurine, Town Crier, Standing With Bell, Red Coat, HN 2119 .... 400.00
Figurine, Toymaker, HN 2250 .... 325.00
Figurine, Uriah Heep, HN 2101 .... 500.00
Figurine, Valerie, Red, Pink, White, Child's, HN 2107 .... 175.00
Figurine, Vanity, Red, Child's, HN 2475 .... 175.00
Figurine, Veronica, HN 3205 .... 250.00
Figurine, Victorian Lady, HN 1728 .... 700.00
Figurine, Viola D'Amore, HN 2797 ...._Illus_ 1200.00
Figurine, Violin, HN 2432 .... 1400.00
Figurine, Virginals, HN 2427 .... 2100.00
Figurine, Wayfarer, HN 2362 .... 300.00
Figurine, Wedding Vows, HN 2750 .... 275.00
Figurine, Welcome, HN 3764 .... 80.00
Figurine, Wistful, HN 2472 .... 350.00
Figurine, Wizard, HN 2877 .... 575.00
Figurine, Young Master, HN 2872 .... 375.00
Flask, Watchman, Kingsware, Dewar's Whisky, Cork Stopper, 7 In. 1210.00
Inkwell, Votes For Women, Mean Looking Woman With Arms Crossed, 3 In. .. 3400.00
Jug, Charles Dickens, Limited Edition, 1936, 10 1/2 In. 1600.00
Jug, Incised & Painted Sheep In Pasture, Handle, 1905, 9 1/2 In. 2183.00
Jug, Mackinlays Very Old Scotch Whisky, Mottled Blue Green, 8 x 5 1/2 In. ... 225.00
Jug, Musical, Old Charley, D 5858 .... 1200.00
Jug, Pied Piper, Limited Edition, 1934, 10 In. 1800.00
Jug, Sir Francis Drake, Limited Edition, 1933, 10 1/4 In. 1950.00
Jug, Treasure Island, Limited Edition, 1934, 7 1/2 In. 1500.00
Jug, William Shakespeare, Limited Edition, 1933, 10 1/2 In. 1600.00
Lighter, Lawyer, D 6504, 3 1/2 In. 225.00
Lighter, Long John Silver, D 6386, 3 1/2 In. 200.00
Lighter, Old Charley, D 5227, 3 1/2 In. ....150.00 to 300.00
Liquor Container, Captain Hook, Small 125.00
Liquor Container, Falstaff, Small 150.00
Liquor Container, Mr. Micawber, Small 275.00
Liquor Container, Mr. Pickwick & Sam Weller, 2 Faces, Small 175.00
Liquor Container, Mr. Pickwick, Small 100.00
Liquor Container, Poacher, Small 150.00
Liquor Container, Town Crier, Of Eatanswill, Small 150.00
Loving Cup, Apothecary, Limited Edition, 1934, 6 In. 1400.00
Loving Cup, Geoffrey Chaucer, 2 Handles, Large 316.00
Loving Cup, King George V & Queen Mary, 1910 .... 305.00
Loving Cup, Robin Hood, Limited Edition, 1938, 8 1/2 In. 1400.00
Loving Cup, Shakespeare, 2 Handles, Large 425.00
Loving Cup, Three Musketeers, Limited Edition, 1936, 10 In. 1500.00
Plaque, Pink & Yellow Roses, H. Pipe, Frame, 16 1/2 x 13 In. 460.00
Plate, Bunnykins, Game Of Golf, Baby, HW 11 .... 250.00
Plate, Bunnykins, Postman Delivering Letters, HW 19 .... 75.00
Plate, Doctor, Black Transfer, 10 1/2 In. 60.00
Plate, Monks Series, 10 In. 125.00
Plate, Sam Weller, Dickens Ware, 10 In. 66.00
Sugar, Old Charley, D 6012, 2 1/2 In. 800.00
Tea Set, Walton Ware, Battle Of Hastings, Cream Ground, c.1910, 4 Piece ... 316.00
Teapot, Old Charley, D 6017, 7 In. 1800.00
Tobacco Jar, Old Charley, D 5844, 5 1/2 In. 1725.00
Toby Jug, Old Charley, D 6030, Large 350.00
Toby Jug, Old Charley, D 6069, Small 300.00
Toothpick, Old Charley, D 6152 .... 1650.00
Vase, Art Nouveau, Poppies, Leaves, Marshall, c.1905, 27 In. 7200.00
Vase, Blue Flowers, Salmon Ground, 8 1/4 In., Pair 373.00

Vase, Blue Persian Chintz, 6 Sides, 1900s, 7 3/4 In. 500.00
Vase, Chang, Viscous Glaze, Multicolor, 1930s, 7 3/4 In. 4500.00
Vase, Flambe, Horse & Rider Landscape, Marked, 12 In. 460.00
Vase, Flambe, Overlaid Silver Strapwork, Gorham, c.1905, 11 3/4 In. 6380.00
Vase, Flambe, Pixies Behind Toadstools, 1920s, 6 3/8 In. 2700.00
Vase, Flambe, Stags Amid Leaves, Red, Cream Ground, c.1910, 9 7/8 In. 3600.00
Vase, Flambe, Sung, Drip Glaze, Noke & F. Allen, 5 In. . . . .*Illus* 350.00
Vase, Flowers, Leaf Panels, Black Slip Tail, Marshall, c.1907, 13 In., Pair 840.00
Vase, Incised, Art Nouveau Buds, Leaves, Marshall, c.1908, 10 In. 1320.00
Vase, Incised, Painted, Open Flowers, Simmance, c.1907, 25 1/2 In. 2700.00
Vase, Oval, Deep Red, Blue, Gold, Turquoise Glaze, Marked, 8 1/2 In. 1265.00
Vase, Painted Poppies, Signed, 8 In. 385.00
Vase, Raised Flowers, Signed, 10 1/2 In. 865.00
Vase, Raised Flowers, Signed, 12 1/2 In. 690.00
Vase, Slip Trail, Incised, Art Nouveau, Tulip, Blue Ground, c.1909, 26 3/4 In. 1440.00
Vase, Small Cottage Amidst Trees & Flowers, Marked, 6 7/8 In. 357.00
Vase, Stylized Berries, Leaves, Frank Butler, c.1905, 7 7/8 In., Pair 1320.00
Vase, Stylized Flowers, Leaf Band, Francis Pope, c.1905, 11 1/2 In. 840.00
Vase, Stylized Flowers, Marked, 2 1/2 In. 209.00
Vase, Stylized Leaves, George Tinworth, Stoneware, c.1907, 11 In. 3000.00
Vase, Sung, Flambe, Flowers & Leaves, Red, Ocher, A. & C.H. Noke, 1930, 4 In. 2183.00
Vase, White Stork Flying Over Flowering Irises, 6 In. 550.00
Wall Pocket, Old Charley, D 6110 . . . . 2300.00

ROYAL DUX is the more common name for the Duxer Porzellan-
manufaktur, which was founded by E. Eichler in Dux, Bohemia (now
Duchcov, Czech Republic), in 1860. By the turn of the century, the
firm specialized in porcelain statuary and busts of Art Nouveau–style
maidens, large porcelain figures, and ornate vases with three-dimensional figures climbing on the sides. The firm is still in business.

Bust, Cosmopolitan Female, Pink Patch Mark, Signed, Elly Strobach, 6 x 3 In. 350.00
Bust, Girl Wearing Pale Pink, Green, Yellow Costume, 21 3/4 In. 1800.00
Bust, Water Nymph Emerging From Foaming Blue Waves, Pink Orchids, 21 In. 4800.00
Figurine, 2 Deer, Base, Stamped, Original Tag, 8 In. 89.00
Figurine, 3 Figures On Centerpiece, 24 x 18 x 11 In. 3696.00
Figurine, Ballerina Dancing, 6 1/2 x 4 1/2 In. 95.00
Figurine, Black Peacock, Pink Patch Mark, 10 1/2 x 7 In. 85.00
Figurine, Bohemia Bird, Pink Patch Mark, 7 1/4 In. 45.00
Figurine, Bohemia Lion, On The Prowl, Pink Patch Mark, Box, 10 In. 45.00
Figurine, Bohemia Mockingbird, Pink Patch Mark, 6 1/2 In. 45.00
Figurine, Bohemia Shepherd Dog, Pink Patch Mark, Box, 8 1/4 x 11 In. 45.00
Figurine, Boxer Dog, Pink Patch Mark, 1860, 6 1/2 In. 85.00
Figurine, Bulldog, 5 In. 55.00
Figurine, Cockatoo Perched On Branch, 1970, 15 In. 195.00
Figurine, Colonial Couple, Gold Highlights, 8 3/8 x 3/4 In., Pair 558.00
Figurine, Dancer, Topless, Cobalt Pantaloons, Gold Slippers, 17 x 13 x 6 In. 2000.00
Figurine, Doe, Brown, Base, Pink Triangle, 11 x 8 In. 125.00
Figurine, Dog, On Point, Pink Patch Mark, 16 x 8 In., Pair 225.00
Figurine, Dog, Setter With Pheasant In His Mouth, 1970, 14 In. 250.00
Figurine, Dolphin, Patch Mark, 14 In. 175.00
Figurine, Eagle Standing On Small Base, Brown, Blue, Beige, White, 7 x 2 In. 145.00
Figurine, Elephant, Trunk Raised, 6 x 20 In. 130.00
Figurine, Elephant, White, 10 In. 245.00
Figurine, Female Water Bearer, Seated, 2 Large Urns, 1920s, 16 In. 431.00
Figurine, Fisherman, Water Carrier, 20 In., Pair 1265.00
Figurine, Flamenco Dancers, Bisque Skin, Cobalt, White Glaze, Gold Trim, 15 In. 1250.00
Figurine, Folk Dancers, Native Costume, Pink Patch Mark, 9 x 5 In. 300.00
Figurine, Horse, Beige Highlights, 14 3/4 x 9 In. 575.00
Figurine, Horse, Rearing, Pink Patch Mark, 12 In. 85.00
Figurine, Lady, Seated Looking In Her Mirror, Dainty Flowers, 6 In. 75.00
Figurine, Lady, Sitting, Cobalt Blue, White, 6 1/4 In. 125.00
Figurine, Man Driving Chariot, 16 x 6 1/2 x 11 In. 173.00
Figurine, Mastiff, Honey, White Glaze, 6 3/4 x 8 In. 125.00

Figurine, Nude, Seated On Small Draped Table, Hands Folded, 19 x 10 x 8 In. 3000.00
Figurine, Peacock, Crown Headdress, Gray, Pink Plumage, 1970, 19 x 13 In. 195.00
Figurine, Seal, 8 1/2 In. 55.00
Figurine, Snake Charmer With Cobra, 9 1/2 In. 85.00
Figurine, Spaniel, 5 1/2 In. 55.00
Figurine, Station Master, Pink Raised Triangle, Blue Underglaze, 8 In. 79.00
Figurine, Tiger, 1970, 12 In. 95.00
Figurine, Water Bird, Green, White, Pink, 13 In. 185.00
Figurine, Woman, Bow In Hair, Signed, 22 In. 460.00
Figurine, Woman, Holding Ball, White, 1940, 7 1/2 In. 160.00
Figurine, Woman, Nude With Ponytail, 9 In. 185.00
Figurine, Young Lady In Blue Dress, Pink Patch Mark, Blue Mark, 9 3/4 In. 105.00
Group, Elegant Gentleman On Horseback, Peasant Holding Jug, 15 1/2 In. 460.00
Group, Pastoral Scene Of Farmer & Wife Thanking God For Their Harvest, 18 In. 650.00
Mirror, Dresser, 2 Cupids Holding Beveled Mirror, 25 x 14 In. 1680.00
Urn, Man With Lute, Other Girl With Bananas, Gold Trim, Marked, 37 In., Pair 1210.00
Vase, Blue Flowers, Cobalt Blue, White, Gold, 7 In. 125.00
Vase, Cobalt, Pale Blue, Pink Patch Mark, 5 1/2 In. 125.00
Vase, Flowers, 15 In., Pair 1120.00
Vase, Gold, Cream, White Embossed Flowers, Shell Shape, Art Nouveau, 5 1/2 In. 100.00
Vase, Grape, Vine, Moss Green, Gold Highlights, Bone Ground, 20 x 10 In. 850.00
Vase, Pastel, Pink, Green, Gold Lines, Ivory Ground, 10 1/4 x 4 In. 75.00
Vase, Woman With Flowing Hair Inside Of A Lily, Blue, White Ground, 13 1/2 In. 747.00

ROYAL FLEMISH glass was made during the late 1880s in New Bedford, Massachusetts, by the Mt. Washington Glass Works. It is a colored satin glass decorated with dark colors and raised gold designs. The glass was patented in 1894. It was supposed to resemble stained glass windows.

Vase, 3 Large White Geese In Flight, Light Violet, Blue, Green, 14 1/2 In. 6900.00
Vase, Brown, Tan, Flowers, Gilt Enamel, Globe Shape, Footed, Handles, 16 In. 6325.00
Vase, Gold Enamel Floral, Tan, Bottle Shape, Gilt Floral, 16 In. 6325.00
Vase, Gold Peacock, Pale Blue, Jeweled, 13 1/4 x 7 In. ....*Illus* 14950.00
Vase, Jack-In-The-Pulpit, Napoli, Signed, 4 1/2 In. 885.00
Vase, Raised Gold Lines, 12 In. 7500.00
Vase, Stick, Squat, 4 1/2 In. 1850.00

ROYAL HAEGER, see Haeger category.

ROYAL IVY, see Northwood, Royal Ivy

ROYAL NYMPHENBURG is the modern name for the Nymphenburg porcelain factory, which was established at Neudeck-ob-der-Au, Germany, in 1753 and moved to Nymphenburg in 1761. The company is still in existence. Marks include a checkered shield topped by a crown, a crowned *CT* with the year, and a contemporary shield mark on reproductions of eighteenth-century porcelain.

Cachepot, Cylinder, Multicolored Flowers, Gilt, Leaf Handles, 9 x 7 In. 259.00

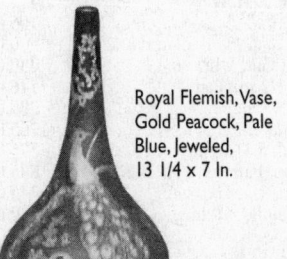

Royal Flemish, Vase,
Gold Peacock, Pale
Blue, Jeweled,
13 1/4 x 7 In.

A good way to remove rings and stains from a white marble top is to mix TSP (trisodiumphosphate, found in paint stores), water, and scouring powder. Rub on the spots. Too much rubbing may remove some of the polish, so be careful.

Figurine, 3 Children With Dog, 20th Century, 4 1/2 In. 230.00
Figurine, Woman, 18th Century Style Dress, Gilt Highlights, 7 1/2 In. 1495.00
Plate, Gilt, Blue Bands, Beaded Rim, Late 19th Century, 8 In., 11 Piece 2070.00
Tea Service, Green Enamel Floral Sprays, 1900, 12 In., 45 Piece 172.00

ROYAL OAK pieces are listed in the Pressed Glass category by that pattern name.

ROYAL RUDOLSTADT, see Rudolstadt category.

ROYAL VIENNA, see Beehive category.

ROYAL WORCESTER is a name used by collectors. Worcester porcelains were made in Worcester, England, from about 1751. The firm went through many different periods and name changes. It became the Worcester Royal Porcelain Company, Ltd., in 1862. Today collectors call the porcelains made after 1862 *Royal Worcester*. In 1976, the firm merged with W. T. Copeland to become Royal Worcester Spode. Some early products of the factory are listed under Worcester.

Biscuit Jar, Cover, Ivory Ground, Enamel Floral, Late 19th Century, 6 5/8 In. 230.00
Biscuit Jar, Red Mark, c.1905, 5 1/2 In. 1150.00
Bowl, Applied Leaf, Peach & Ivory, Gold Trim, 2 Leaf Handles, c.1895, 2 In. 95.00
Candelabra, 3-Light, Rococo Style, Scrolling Foliate Arms, 14 1/2 In., Pair 460.00
Compote, Church & Lock, The Old Bridge, 6 1/4 x 11 In., Pair 575.00
Creamer, Floral, Gilt Trim, Ribbed Handle, 5 In. 35.00
Dessert Service, Arrangement Of Fruit, Gilt Rim, 1925, 17 Piece 8400.00
Dish, Dessert, Best Queen, c.1862, 8 In., Pair 1000.00
Ewer, Blackberry Design, Butterflies, 1 Bumblebee, Dragon Handle, 11 In. 880.00
Ewer, Classical Form, Scrolled Handle, Swans In Flight, 1900, 10 In. 1540.00
Ewer, Gilt, Cylindrical Neck, Serpent Handle, Yellow Ground, 12 In., Pair 546.00
Ewer, Gold Floral & Geometric Designs, Green & Rose Ground, 16 In. 490.00
Figurine, Grandmother's Dress, Girl In Yellow Dress, 6 1/2 In. 30.00
Figurine, Le Panier, Bread Seller, Basket Of Bread, 12 In. 200.00
Figurine, Mallard In Flight, No. 72, Wooden Stand, 12 1/4 In. 460.00
Figurine, Shell, Miniature, 3 3/4 In. 275.00
Figurine, Shoe, c.1888, 6 In. 595.00
Figurine, Young Boy Frolicking With 2 Squirrels, Black, 7 1/2 In. 250.00
Figurine, Young Girl Dressed In Pinafore, Finger In Her Mouth, Blue, 6 In. 165.00
Figurine, Young Girl, Supporting Basket Of Tulips, 5 1/2 In. 178.00
Nut Dish, Applied Peach & Ivory Leaves, Gold Trim, c.1895, 2 1/2 x 2 In. 85.00
Pitcher, Floral & Leaf, Yellow, Bulbous Base, Gold Handle, c.1887, 8 In. 425.00
Pitcher, Hand Painted Bird, c.1905, 3 In. 95.00
Pitcher, Polychrome Flowers, Cream Ground, Hand Painted, Ink Stamp, 6 In. 115.00
Pitcher, Yellow Ground, Flowers & Leaves, Gold Handle, c.1887, 8 In. 380.00
Plaque, Scissor-Tailed Flycatchers, Doughty, 20th Century, 24 In. 400.00
Plate, Fish, Undersea Flora, Fish, Signed, 9 12 In., 12 Piece 750.00
Plate, Floral Spray, Maroon Border, Signed, 8 In., 12 Piece 920.00
Plate, Floral Sprays & Garlands, Maroon Border, Signed, 10 In., 12 Piece 460.00
Plate, Floral Swags, Pink Border, Signed, 9 In., 12 Piece 1495.00
Plate, Frolicking Fish Center, Gilt Edge, Signed, 9 In., 12 Piece 575.00
Plate, Gilt Arabesques, Cream Ground, 1900, 3 1/4 In., 8 Piece 375.00
Platter, Fish, Underwater Scene, Brown Transfer, 24 In. 105.00
Tazza, Floral Spray, Light Blue, Gilt Rim, 9 1/4 x 2 In. 50.00
Tea Service, Sterling Banded, Silver Bamboo & Crane Design, Gilt, 5 In. 430.00
Vase, Bud, Bamboo Clusters, Gilt Branches, c.1882, 3 x 5 x 2 1/2 In., Pair 546.00
Vase, Cornucopia Form, Backs Of Swans, 6 1/8 In., Pair 200.00
Vase, Figural, Swan, Mark, 7 In., Pair 1265.00
Vase, Gilt Decorated, Baluster Shape, Handles, Footed, Marked, 5 1/2, Pair 575.00
Vase, Green, Orange Reserves, Twin Handles, 10 3/4 x 3 1/2 In., Pair 835.00
Vase, Oval, Flowers, Gilt Highlights, 9 1/2 In., Pair 345.00
Vase, Painted, Bird Scenes, Celeste Blue Ground, Acanthus Handles, 10 In. 460.00
Vase, Sabrina Ware, Koi Fish & Seaweed, 1909, 4 1/4 In. 345.00
Vase, Silver & Gilt Japonesque Floral Sprays, Butterfly, c.1949, 13 In. 315.00
Vase, White Nautilus Shell On Coral Branch, 7 In. 190.00
Wall Bracket, Figural, Maiden Seated In Rocky Niche, Wheat, 9 In., Pair 1380.00

ROYCROFT products were made by the Roycrofter community of East Aurora, New York, in the late nineteenth and early twentieth centuries. The community was founded by Elbert Hubbard, famous philosopher, writer, and artist. The workshops owned by the community made furniture, metalware, leatherwork, embroidery, and jewelry. A printshop produced many signs, books, and the magazines that promoted the sayings of Elbert Hubbard. Furniture by the Roycroft community is listed in the Furniture category.

Ashtray, Copper, Hammered, Leather Strap, Tooled Ends, 13 3/4 x 2 1/4 In.	1012.00
Bell, Dinner, Copper, Hammered, Brass-Washed, Orb & Cross Mark, 3 x 1 3/4 In.	345.00
Book, Walt Whitman, Hand Colored, Leather Cover	120.00
Bookends, Bronze, Original Patina, Signed, 4 1/2 In.	400.00
Bookends, Copper, Hammered, 2 1/2 x 3 3/4 x 2 3/4 In.	345.00
Bookends, Copper, Hammered, Brass Wash, Tooled Leather Insets, Signed, 4 1/2 In.	805.00
Bookends, Copper, Hammered, Embossed Large Poppy, 5 1/4 x 5 In.	805.00 to 956.00
Bookends, Copper, Hammered, Embossed Owl, Rectangular, 4 x 6 1/2 In.	534.00
Bookends, Copper, Hammered, Ivy, 2 1/2 x 3 3/4 x 2 3/4 In.	560.00
Bookends, Copper, Hammered, Lotus Design, Tooled Leather, Signed, 6 x 5 In.	825.00
Bookends, Copper, Hammered, Open Design, Arch, 6 1/2 In.	495.00
Bookends, Copper, Hammered, Original Patina, 5 1/4 x 4 3/4 In.	345.00
Bookends, Copper, Hammered, Peacock, Panel Of Green, Signed, 4 x 6 In.	220.00
Bookends, Copper, Hammered, Raised & Tooled Disk, Impressed Mark, 5 In.	850.00
Bookends, Copper, Hammered, Rectangular Tooled Design, 8 1/2 In.	187.00
Bookends, Copper, Hammered, Riveted Strap Hinge, Original Patina, 5 x 4 In.	506.00
Bookends, Copper, Hammered, Stylized Owl Design, 4 In.	403.00
Bookends, Copper, Hammered, Stylized Owl Design, Riveted Corners, 5 x 5 1/2 In.	450.00
Bookends, Copper, Hammered, Tooled Floral Design, Signed, 5 In.	80.00
Bookends, Copper, Hammered, Trefoil Design, Original Dark Patina, 5 x 3 3/4 In.	281.00
Bookends, Copper, Hammered, Trillium Design, Signed, 5 x 3 1/2 In.	345.00
Bookmark, Leather, Stamped Motto, Build Strong, Elbert Hubbard, 11 In.	27.00
Bookmark, Leather, Tooled Design Of Elbert Hubbard, 11 In.	45.00
Bowl, Copper, Hammered, 3-Footed, 3 3/4 x 10 In.	478.00
Bowl, Copper, Hammered, Brass Wash, Original Patina, 4 x 5 In.	230.00
Bowl, Copper, Hammered, Brass Wash, Stamp, 4 1/8 x 2 1/4 In.	240.00
Bowl, Copper, Hammered, Closed-In Rim, 7 x 19 In.	8625.00
Bowl, Copper, Hammered, Dark Patina Exterior, Verdigris Interior, Signed, 10 In.	1035.00
Bowl, Copper, Hammered, Helmet Shape, Signed, 3 x 6 3/4 In.	575.00
Bowl, Copper, Hammered, New Patina, Low, 5 1/2 In., 3 Piece	1333.00
Bowl, Copper, Hammered, Original Patina, 6 1/2 In.	374.00
Bowl, Copper, Hammered, Signed, 2 x 5 1/2 In.	460.00
Box, Cover, Hinged, Copper, Hammered, Rectangular, Original Patina, 2 x 7 x 3 In.	912.00
Candlestick, Copper, Hammered, Original Patina, 8 In.	633.00
Candlestick, Copper, Hammered, Ring Top & Round Base, Twist Column, 13 In., Pair	880.00
Chamberstick, Copper, Hammered, 3 1/2 In.	345.00
Clock, Copper, Hammered, Brass Wash, Signed, 5 In.	715.00
Compote, Copper, Hammered, Flowers, Heavy Gauge, 2 3/4 x 8 3/4 In.	675.00

Roycroft, Lamp, Copper, Hammered,
Leaded Glass Shade, D. Hunter, 23 In.

When unscrewing a glass door or drawer knob, protect the glass part. Get a piece of thin rubber, like part of an old inner tube, and wrap it around the metal base of the glass knob. It will provide a better grip for your pliers when you try to turn the knob and will also protect the glass and metal from scratches.

Fernery, Copper, Hammered, 4 Buttresses, German Silver Squares, 7 7/8 In. 5175.00
Frame, Leather, Tooled, Rose & Leaf, Signed, 7 1/2 In. 862.00
Humidor, Copper, Hammered, Riveted Band, Original Liner, Tab Handles, 6 x In. 2300.00
Humidor, Copper, Hammered, Trillium Floral Middle & Top, Signed, 5 1/2 In. 660.00
Humidor, Cover, Copper, Hammered, Riveted Handle, Original Patina, 3 3/4 x 4 In. 534.00
Inkwell, Copper, Hammered, Geometric, Hinged Top, Signed, Square, 2 1/2 x 3 In. 630.00
Inkwell, Copper, Hammered, Original Patina, 5 In. 299.00
Inkwell, Copper, Hammered, Original Patina, Signed, 2 1/2 x 3 In. 144.00
Jardiniere, Riveted Band At Rim & Base, Signed, 11 x 10 In. 9000.00
Lamp, Copper, Hammered Frosted Glass Shade, Signed, 18 1/2 In. 2200.00
Lamp, Copper, Hammered, 11 In. 1265.00
Lamp, Copper, Hammered, Helmet Shade, 14 x 6 In. 2070.00
Lamp, Copper, Hammered, Leaded Glass Shade, D. Hunter, 23 In. ....*Illus* 33750.00
Lamp, Copper, Hammered, Signed, 13 In. 865.00
Letter Rack, Original Mahogany Patina, Signed, 4 x 5 x 2 1/2 In. 375.00
Nut Bowl, Copper, Hammered, 3-Footed, 4 x 10 1/2 In. 2140.00
Penholder, Copper, Hammered, Cleaned Patina, Signed, 3 x 9 In. 175.00
Picture Frame, Copper, Hammered, Nickel Plate, Original Patina, 8 x 10 In. 750.00
Picture Frame, Copper, Hammered, Original Patina, 4 1/2 x 6 1/2 In. 460.00
Picture Frame, Leather, Tooled Flowers, 6 1/2 x 9 In. 575.00
Pin Tray, Leather, Tooled Flowers, 10 In. 80.00
Pitcher, White, Handle, Signed, 5 1/2 In. 635.00
Plaque, Embossed Young Child, Signed Winsche, 7 In. 1100.00
Poker Chip Rack, Copper, Hammered, Signed, 7 x 4 1/2 In. 920.00
Punch Set, Bowl & 13 Cups, Brown Glaze, 5 x 10 In. 285.00
Purse, Change, Leather, Tooled Flowers, 3 1/2 x 3 In. 240.00
Purse, Leather, Butterflies & Flower Tooled Design, 6 1/2 x 6 In. 405.00
Purse, Leather, Butterflies & Poppy Tooled Design, 10 x 4 1/2 In. 290.00
Purse, Leather, Butterflies Tooled Design, 9 1/2 x 6 1/2 In. 405.00
Purse, Leather, Tooled Hummingbird Design, 12 x 7 In. 460.00
Purse, Leather, Tooled Oak Leaf & Acorn Design, 14 1/2 x 7 In. 430.00
Salt & Pepper, Hunter Green Band, Brown Squares, Ivory Ground, 3 1/8 In. 605.00
Scissor Guard, Leather, Tooled Flowers, 4 In. 130.00
Sconce, Copper, Hammered, Brass Wash, 12 1/2 In. 770.00
Tile, Motto, Copper, Hammered, Frame, Square, 6 In. 175.00
Tray, Brass Wash, 2 Handles, 12 In. 440.00
Tray, Copper, Hammered, Brass Wash, Original Patina, 15 In. 460.00
Tray, Copper, Hammered, Embossed Trillium, Bent Rim, 10 In. 112.00
Tray, Copper, Hammered, Leaf Shape Prongs, Green Steuben Liner, 6 x 3 3/4 In. 281.00
Tray, Copper, Hammered, Stylized Design, Medium Patina, 9 1/2 x 22 1/4 In. 253.00
Tray, Copper, Hammered, Tooled Design, Original Patina, 7 1/2 In. 288.00
Tray, Copper, Hammered, Tooled Design, Original Patina, 22 In. 633.00
Vase, Copper, Hammered, American Beauty, Original Dark Patina, 7 x 3 1/2 In. 2812.00
Vase, Copper, Hammered, American Beauty, Original Patina, 21 x 8 1/2 In. 6750.00
Vase, Copper, Hammered, American Beauty, Red Patina, Signed, 21 In. ....2185.00 to 3450.00
Vase, Copper, Hammered, Brass Wash, 4 1/2 x 6 1/2 In. 690.00
Vase, Copper, Hammered, Broad Leaves Around Base, Signed, 3 1/4 x 4 In. 977.00
Vase, Copper, Hammered, Broad Shoulder, Narrow Neck, Signed, 4 1/2 x 4 1/2 In. 977.00
Vase, Copper, Hammered, Glasgow Design, Cleaned Patina, 6 x 3 In. 2760.00
Vase, Copper, Hammered, Ruffled Rim, Original Patina, Signed, 9 3/4 In. 1380.00
Vase, Copper, Hammered, Silver Wash, 5 x 2 1/2 In. 633.00
Vase, Copper, Hammered, Silver Wash, Original Patina, 6 1/4 In. 1380.00
Vase, Copper, Hammered, Steuben Glass Insert, Original Patina, 6 In. 748.00
Vase, Copper, Hammered, Tooled Floral Rim, Trailing Geometrics, Signed, 10 In. 1090.00
Vase, Copper, Hammered, Tooled Flowers, Original Brass Patina, 9 1/2 In. 288.00
Vase, Copper, Hammered, Tooled Poppy Design, 10 x 3 In. 2530.00

ROZANE, see Roseville category.

RRP is the mark used by the firm of Robinson-Ransbottom. It is not a mark of the more famous Roseville Pottery. The Ransbottom brothers started a pottery in 1900 in Ironspot, Ohio. In 1920, they merged with the Robinson Clay Product Company of Akron, Ohio, to become Robinson-Ransbottom. The factory is still working.

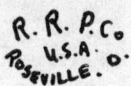

Cookie Jar, Apples & Leaves, 8 1/2 In. 76.00

Cookie Jar, Hootie Owl 90.00
Cookie Jar, Peter Peter Pumpkin Eater, 8 In. 230.00
Jardiniere, Green & Brown Swirl, Embossed Flowers, 2 Piece 120.00
Jardiniere, Green With Brown, 7 In. 18.50
Mixing Bowl, Nesting, Embossed Viking Ships, Aqua, White, Powder Blue 66.00
Mixing Bowl, Yellow Girl With Watering Can, 6 1/2 In. 50.00
Mixing Bowl, Yellowware, 3 Brown Bands, 14 In. 47.00
Planter, 2 Flowers, Yellow, 5 In. 8.50
Planter, Gray, Pink Interior, Unglazed Bottom, 10 In. 26.00
Urn, Oil Jar Shape, Robin's-Egg Blue, 2 Handles, Rope Twist Border, 18 In. 93.00

RS GERMANY is part of the wording in marks used by the Tillowitz, Germany, factory of Reinhold Schlegelmilch from 1914 until about 1945. The porcelain was sold decorated and undecorated. The Schlegelmilch families made porcelains marked in many ways. See also ES Germany, RS Poland, RS Prussia, RS Silesia, RS Suhl, and RS Tillowitz.

Ashtray, Blue Flower, Cream Ground, Triangular, Individual, Mark, 3 1/2 In. 25.00
Basket, Flowers, Classical Scene, White Ground, Silver Scrolled Handle, 4 x 8 In. 150.00
Basket, Purple Violets, Gold Rim, Molded, Scalloped, Mark, 4 1/2 x 5 3/4 In. 200.00
Berry Bowl, Dainty Daises, 16 1/2 In. 7.00
Berry Bowl, Roses Center, Shadow Flowers, Ferns, 10 1/2 x 3 In. 250.00
Bowl, 2 Women Bathing, 11 In. 315.00
Bowl, Flower Baskets, Blue Ground, Square, 6 3/4 In. 25.00
Bowl, Flower Shape, 7 1/2 x 7 1/4 In. 35.00
Bowl, Girl & Oxen, Houses, Gold Rim, Wreath Mark, 2 1/2 x 9 In. 200.00
Bowl, Pink Carnations, Yellow, Brown, 7 In. 50.00
Bread Tray, Roses, Pink, White, Wreath & Star Mark, 11 x 7 In. 100.00
Cake Plate, Fruit, Purple Border, Mother Of Pearl, Pierced Handles, 10 In. 60.00
Cake Plate, Roses, Pink, Yellow, Lily Mold, 9 3/4 In. 100.00
Cake Plate, Roses, White & Dark Green, Steeple Mark, 11 1/2 In. 65.00
Candleholder, Yellow, Iridescent, Open Wreath Mark, 3 x 4 3/8 In., Pair 50.00
Candy Dish, Chrysanthemums, Leaves, Gold Border, Pierced Handles, 7 1/2 In. 75.00
Candy Dish, Dogwood, Cream Ground, Gold Rim, 9 1/4 In. 65.00
Candy Dish, Molded Leaves, Buds, Poppies, Green Border, Handle, c.1905, 5 1/2 In. 200.00
Cheese & Cracker Set, Peacocks, Floral Border, 2 Tiers, 9 In. 165.00
Cracker Jar, Poppies, Art Deco, Blue, Yellow, Tan 200.00
Creamer, Roses, Green Ground, 8 Bun Footed, 3 1/2 In. 75.00
Cup, Gold Grape Design 35.00
Cup & Saucer, King George, Pink, Rippled, 2 3/4 x 6 1/8 In. 35.00
Dish, Golden Pheasant, Trees, Muted Green Ground, Pierced Handles, 7 1/2 In. 250.00
Dresser Set, Lilies, White & Green Tones, Hair Receiver, Powder Jar, Tray, 3 Piece 60.00
Fernery, Pink Roses, Peach, Green Leaves, 1917, 4 x 8 In. 40.00
Hair Receiver, Cover, Buckeyes Transfer, Blue Underglaze Mark 90.00
Hair Receiver & Powder Jar, Flowers Around Top, Light Blue, Artist 48.00
Hatpin Holder, Acorns, Early 1900s, 4 3/4 In. 185.00
Hatpin Holder, Flowers, 4 3/4 In. 225.00
Hatpin Holder, Flowers, Early 1900s, 4 1/2 In. 150.00
Mustard, Gold Bird Stencil, Pink, White, Melon Mold, Spoon, 3 In. 48.00
Mustard, Pink Roses, Handles, Mark 50.00
Mustard, Poppies, Green, Gold Trim, Spoon 45.00
Mustard, White Iridescent, Handles, Tillowitz Mark 15.00
Mustard, White, Gold Trim, 4 In. 30.00
Nut Dish, Roses, Clover At Top, 5 In. 45.00
Plate, Dinner, Candy Cane Mold, 9 In. 48.00
Plate, Dogwood, Leaf Design, Heavy Gold Rim, Mark, 8 1/2 In. 60.00
Plate, Parrots, Brightly Colored, Perched On Branch, Yellow, Mark, 8 In. 425.00
Plate, Poppies, Red, White, Pink, Cream, Pierced Handle, Wreath Mark, 7 In. 75.00
Plate, Roses, Pink, Green Leaves, Muted Green Ground, Gold Trim, 8 1/2 In. 30.00
Plate, Sunset Lake Scene, Brown, Yellow, Purple, 6 In. 25.00
Relish, Anemones, Lavender, Tan Ground, Marked, 8 In. 48.00
Relish, Mock Orange Flowers, Beige Ground, Wreath & Star Mark, 8 In. 35.00
Relish, Stylized Butterfly Center, Flowers, Wavy Brown Border, 9 1/4 In. 60.00

Relish, Yellow Center, Flower Border, Pierced Handles, Wreath Mark, 8 In. 25.00
Sandwich Server, Tropical Scene, Brown, Raised Center Handle, 8 1/5 In. 35.00
Shaving Mug, Mirror, Stippled Flowers Mold, Turquoise Ground 59.00
Sugar & Creamer, Gold Mark Line, c.1925 .... 115.00
Sugar & Creamer, Pink Roses, Green Luster Finish, Mold 541 .... 245.00
Sugar & Creamer, Roses, Leaves, Muted Ground, Matte Finish 225.00
Syrup Set, Poppies, Gold Trim, Blue Underglaze Mark, 3 Piece 125.00
Tea Set, Art Deco, Green & Tan, Clematis Flower, 3 Piece 75.00
Toothpick, Art Deco, Poppies, 3 Handles, Red Mark 125.00
Toothpick, Violets, Gold Handles 64.00
Tray, Pine Green, Handles, Wreath & Star Mark, 11 x 7 In. 35.00
Tray, Roses, Divided, Cloverleaf Shape, Handle, Blue Mark 45.00

RS POLAND (German) is a mark used by the Reinhold Schlegelmilch factory at Tillowitz from about 1946 to 1956. After 1956, the factory made porcelain marked PT Poland. This is one of many of the RS marks used. See also ES Germany, RS Germany, RS Prussia, RS Silesia, RS Suhl, and RS Tillowitz.

Dish, Pink Roses, Oyster Shell Shape, 8 3/4 In. 45.00
Sugar & Creamer, White & Gold Flowers, Gray Leaves, Gold Rim, 2 x 3 1/2 In. 125.00

RS PRUSSIA appears in several marks used on porcelain before 1917. Reinhold Schlegelmilch started his porcelain works in Suhl, Germany, in 1869. See also ES Germany, RS Germany, RS Poland, RS Silesia, RS Suhl, and RS Tillowitz.

Ashtray, Souvenir 150.00
Berry Set, Poppies, Light Green, Fleur-De-Lis Mold, 7 Piece 325.00
Berry Set, Surreal Flowers, Wreath & Star Mark, 10 1/2-In. Bowl, 7 Piece 195.00
Biscuit Jar, Cover, Carnation Flowers, Gold Trim 225.00
Biscuit Jar, Pink Roses, Barrel 485.00
Biscuit Jar, Sunflower, 6 1/4 x 6 1/4 In. 625.00
Bowl, Gilt Flowers, Round, 10 1/4 x 3 In. 80.00
Bowl, Leaves, Green, Yellow, Red, Daisy Mold, 10 1/2 In. 233.00
Bowl, Pink Rose, Light Green, Jeweled, 9 In. 147.00
Bowl, Pink Roses Center, Green Ground, Scalloped, Fluted Ridges 375.00
Bowl, Poppies, Pink, Tan, White Band, Crimped Edge, 10 1/2 In. 233.00
Bowl, Poppies, Red, Gray, Yellow, Iris Mold, 10 1/2 In. 270.00
Bowl, Roses, Light Blue Ground, Molded Flower Design, 10 1/2 In. 233.00
Cake Plate, Iris, Multicolor Poppy, 11 In. 158.00
Cake Plate, Lily, Carnation Mold, 10 In. 158.00
Cake Plate, Thistle, Luster Finish, 11 1/2 In. 80.00
Celery Dish, Pink & White Mums, Signed, 12 In. 345.00
Coffeepot, Miniature Iris, Lavender, Gold Stencil, 4-Footed 465.00
Cup & Saucer, Carnation Flowers, Art Deco Mold 75.00
Cup & Saucer, Deep Red, Gold Accents, Rococo Style 45.00
Fernery, Cabbage, Pink Roses, Green & Cream 53.00
Mustard, Lily Pad, 3 1/4 In. 103.00
Pitcher, Gold Stencil, Pink, Art Nouveau Handle, 10 In. 175.00
Pitcher, Pink, White & Pale Yellow Roses, White Ground, Handle, 13 In. 896.00
Plate, Flowers, Burgundy, Pink, Light Green, 8 In. 35.00
Plate, Gibson Girl Portrait, 8 1/2 In. 500.00
Plate Set, Bird Of Paradise, 8 In., 4 Piece 1400.00
Powder Jar, Melon Eater On Cover, Shadow Flowers, 4 x 3 In. 350.00
Relish, Yellow, Green, Footed, 13 In. 65.00
Salt Set, Open-Handled Plate, 2 Salts, 6 1/2-In. Plate, 3 Piece 75.00
Sugar & Creamer, Easter Lilies, Gold Trim, Red Mark, Large 225.00
Tankard, Canterbury Bells, Fleur-De-Lis Mold, 10 In. 795.00
Tankard, Roses & Snowball, Opal & Ribbon Mold, Red Mark, 9 1/2 In. 795.00
Teapot, Pink Roses, Green Leaves, Gold Trim, Signed, 6 1/2 In. 235.00
Toothpick, China Star, Marked 60.00
Tray, Dresser, Roses, Gold Trim 85.00
Vase, Parrot, Bird On Branch, Celadon Border, Handles, 7 In. 275.00

RS SILESIA appears on porcelain made at the Reinhold Schlegelmilch factory in Tillowitz, Germany, from the 1920s to the 1940s. The Schlegelmilch families made porcelains marked in many ways. See also ES Germany, RS Germany, RS Poland, RS Prussia, RS Suhl, and RS Tillowitz.

Bonbon, Flowers, Gold Trim, Open Handles, 9 In.	10.00
Tray, Dresser, Zinnia Flowers	85.00

RS SUHL is a mark used by the Erdmann Schlegelmilch factory in Suhl, Germany, between 1900 and 1917. The Schlegelmilch families made porcelains in many places. See also ES Germany, RS Germany, RS Poland, RS Prussia, RS Silesia, and RS Tillowitz.

Creamer, Rembrandt's Night Watch Scene	51.00
Cup & Saucer, Souvenir, Rathaus Hamburg City Hall, Demitasse	35.00

RS TILLOWITZ was marked on porcelain by the Reinhold Schlegelmilch factory at Tillowitz from the 1920s to the 1940s. Table services and ornamental pieces were made. See also ES Germany, RS Germany, RS Poland, RS Prussia, RS Silesia, and RS Suhl.

Bowl, Blue Glaze Base, Footed, Handles, 8 x 6 x 2 1/2 In.	85.00
Bowl, White Flowers, Purple, White Finish, Handle, 5 x 2 In.	43.00
Cake Plate, Blue Violets, Iris, Gold Leaf Trim, Handles	60.00
Cake Plate, White Wild Roses, 8 1/2 In.	65.00
Creamer, White Flowers, Gold Trim, Signed, 3 In.	85.00
Plate, Owl, Signed, 5 x 9 1/2 In.	250.00
Sugar, Cover, Dark Green To Light Green, Gold Trim, c.1904, 5 7/8 In.	55.00
Sugar & Creamer, White Flowers, Gold Trim, Signed, 3 In.	25.00

RUBENA is a glassware that shades from red to clear. It was first made by George Duncan and Sons of Pittsburgh, Pennsylvania, about 1885. This coloring was used on many types of glassware. The pressed glass patterns of Royal Ivy and Royal Oak are listed under Pressed Glass.

Basket, Diamond-Quilted, Applied Vaseline Thorn Handle, 9 In.	325.00
Condiment Set, 4 Bottles, Silver Plated, Twisted Wire Frame	330.00
Decanter Set, 2 Silver Cups, Silver Plated Half Moon Tray, 7 In., 4 Piece	175.00
Pitcher, Enameled Pink Tulips, Gold Trim, 13 In.	295.00
Rose Bowl, Embossed Swirls, 8 Crimped Top, 3 1/4 In.	95.00
Tumbler, Prism, 3 1/2 In.	60.00
Vase, Jack-In-The-Pulpit, Clear Stem & Foot, 8 3/4 In.	145.00
Vase, Overshot, Line Design, Sandwich, 1890	130.00

RUBENA VERDE is a Victorian glassware that was shaded from red to green. It was first made by Hobbs, Brockunier and Company of Wheeling, West Virginia, about 1890.

Pitcher, Fuchsia, Applied White Reeded Handle, Hobbs, 5 x 4 1/2 In.	287.00
Vase, Enameled Garland Of Flowers, Large Blue Bow, 8 1/2 In., Pair	450.00
Vase, Neptune, Bohemia, 10 1/2 In.	230.00
Vase, Thorn Feet, Applied Green Leaves, 12 1/4 In.	345.00

RUBY GLASS is the dark red color of the precious gemstone known as a *ruby*. It was a popular Victorian color that never went completely out of style. The glass was shaped by many different processes to make many different types of ruby glass. There was a revival of interest in the 1940s when modern-shaped ruby table glassware became fashionable. Sometimes the red color is added to clear glass by a process called flashing or staining. Flashed glass is clear glass dipped in a colored glass, then pressed or cut. Stained glass has color painted on a clear glass. Then it is refired so the stain fuses with the glass. Pieces of glass colored in this way are indicated by the word *stained* in the description. Related items may be found in other categories, such as Cranberry Glass, Pressed Glass, and Souvenir.

Bowl, Scalloped, Gold Trim, 19th Century, 5 1/2 x 11 In.	220.00

Compote, Applied Clear Berries, Engraved Square Foot, 10 In. 165.00
Dessert Stand, Downturned Ruffled Edge, 5 Sides, 10 x 14 In. 460.00
Goblet, Paneled, Enameled Gold Flowers, Hunter & Hounds, 3 3/4 x 6 In. 165.00
Punch Bowl, Scalloped, Paneled, Footed, 8 1/4 x 9 1/4 In. 145.00
Vase, Hyacinth, Handles, Applied Rigaree, 6 1/2 In. 125.00

RUDOLSTADT was a faience factory in the Thuringia region of
Germany from 1720 to about 1791. In 1854, Ernst Bohne began working in the area. From about 1887 to 1918, the New York and Rudolstadt Pottery made decorated porcelain marked with the RW and
crown familiar to collectors. This porcelain was imported by Lewis
Straus and Sons of New York, which later became Nathan Straus and
Sons. The word *Royal* was included in their import mark. Collectors
often call it *Royal Rudolstadt*. Most pieces found today were made in
the late nineteenth or early twentieth century. Additional pieces may be
listed in the Kewpie category.

Bust, Classical Female In Armor, With An Eagle, Garland In Her Hair, 9 In. 115.00
Group, 2 Classical Figures, Embracing, Gilt Highlights, Bisque, 16 1/2 In. 240.00
Group, Classical Maiden With Winged Eros Perched On Her Shoulder, 16 In. 230.00
Mug, Felix The Cat, 4 Leaping Poses, 2 1/2 In. 50.00
Plate, Ulysses Simpson Grant, Black & White, Gold Rim, c.1890, 8 1/2 In. 90.00
Vase, Spiraling Acanthus Leaf Handles, Star On Bottom, 15 In. 86.00

RUGS have been used in the American home since the seventeenth century. The oriental rug of that time was often used on a table, not on the
floor. Rag rugs, hooked rugs, and braided rugs were made by house-
wives from scraps of material.

Afghan Bokhara, Red & Black, c.1950, 4 Ft. 11 In. x 7 Ft. 2 In. 616.00
Agra, Central Medallion, Olive Green Field, 13 Ft. 11 In. x 10 Ft. 3 In. 2070.00
Anatolian, 7 Medallions, Navy Field, Multiple Borders, Runner, 14 Ft. 10 In. x 3 Ft. 2 In. 825.00
Aubusson, Black Medallion & Borders, 9 Ft. 6 In. x 13 Ft. 2 In. 550.00
Bagshaish, Blue & Gold Medallion, Red Field, 7 Ft. 5 In. x 11 Ft. 9 In. 1898.00
Bakhtiari, Floral Medallion, Blooming Vine Border, 10 Ft. 8 In. x 12 Ft. 7 In. 1035.00
Bakhtiari, Repeating Floral, Ivory Ground, Turtle Border, 3 Ft. 2 In. x 4 Ft. 6 In. 605.00
Bakhtiari, Stylized Trees & Floral, 9 Ft. 7 In. x 12 Ft. 1 In. 1265.00
Baku, 3 Radiating Octagons, Midnight Blue Field, 6 Ft. 3 In. x 4 Ft. 4 In. 1495.00
Baku, Allover Serrated Guls Row, Midnight Blue Ground, 1900, 5 Ft. 3 In. x 4 Ft. 1 In. .. 360.00
Bidjar, Runner, Burgundy Border, Dark Blue Ground, Contemporary, 2 Ft. 7 In. x 11 In. .. 220.00
Bokhara, 13 Medallions, Blue Field, Geometric Border, Pakistan, 25 1/2 x 61 In. 196.00
Bokhara, Allover Geometric, Deep Red Field, Black Borders, 8 Ft. 1 In. x 11 Ft. 3 In. ... 460.00
Bokhara, Cinnamon Field, 10 Ft. 3 In. x 8 Ft. 3 In. 690.00
Bokhara, Multiple Borders, 3 Oval Rows, Orange, Red, Ivory, 4 Ft. 3 In. x 3 Ft. 6 In. 175.00
Bokhara, Wine, Black, Pumpkin, Ivory Geometrics, c.1950, 3 Ft. 1 In. x 5 Ft. 1 In. 530.00
Caucasian, 6 Latch Hooks, Blue Ground, 1900, 3 Ft. 6 In. x 8 Ft. 5 In. 440.00
Caucasian, 7 Medallions, Indigo Field, Multiple Borders, 3 Ft. 5 In. x 13 Ft. 1045.00
Caucasian, Allover Geometric Design, Blue Field, Red Border, 3 Ft. 1 In. x 6 Ft. 2 In. ... 165.00
Caucasian, Dark Rust Ground, Multiple Borders, Contemporary, 6 Ft. x 6 Ft. 4 In. 565.00
Caucasian, Geometric Flowers, Red, Blue, Brown, Green, Blue, 3 Ft. 10 In. x 5 Ft. 1 In. . 460.00
Caucasian, Hexagonal Medallions, Narrow Border, Late 1800s, 12 Ft. 6 In. x 3 Ft. 6 In. .. 635.00
Caucasian, Ivory, Tan, Rust Ground, Blue & Rust Borders, 5 Ft. 8 In. x 6 Ft. 8 In. 330.00
Caucasian, Red, Camel Medallions, Navy, Ivory Border, c.1890, 3 Ft. 6 In. x 5 Ft. 6 In. .. 825.00
Chinese, Art Deco, Flowers & Birds, Lavender, Green, Rose, 5 Ft. 8 In. x 8 Ft. 10 In. 144.00
Chinese, Art Deco, Flowers, Blue Ground, Gold Border, Nichols, 6 Ft. x 8 Ft. 11 In. .*Illus* 1210.00
Chinese, Blue, Ocher & Tan, 19th Century, 7 Ft. 11 1/2 In. x 9 Ft. 6 In. 252.00
Chinese, Floral Medallion, Floral, Beige Ground, 9 Ft. 11 In. x 13 Ft. 9 In. 9900.00
Chinese, Flowers, Medallions, Birds, Butterflies, Blue Ground, 10 Ft. 6 In. x 13 Ft. 6 In. . 880.00
Chinese, Oval, Buff Field, Trees, Nichols, c.1925, 7 Ft. 8 In. x 5 Ft. 288.00
Chinese, Rosette Lattice, Flowerhead, Pale Yellow, 1910, 12 Ft. 2 In. x 9 Ft. 5 In. 9600.00
Drugget, Geometric, Tan, Brown, Bound Edges, 7 Ft. 6 In. x 5 Ft. 9 In. 403.00
Embroidered, Black Wool, Appliqued, Leaf Border, Stretcher Hanger, 25 1/2 x 40 In. ... 525.00
Feraghan, Flowers, Trees, 21 Ft. 1 In. x 10 Ft. 2 In. 6037.00
Fereghan-Sarouk, Center Medallion, Midnight Blue Ground, 14 Ft. 10 In. x 23 In. 9350.00

Rugs or tapestries can be hung as wall decorations with strips of Velcro. Sew one strip to the rug, attach another to a strip on the wall. Be sure to use a strip that is exactly the width of the hanging.

Rug, Chinese, Art Deco, Flowers, Blue Ground, Gold Border, Nichols, 6 Ft. x 8 Ft. 11 In.

Grenfell, Eskimos, Sled Dogs, Ice Floe At Sunset, c.1935, 2 Ft. 10 In. x 3 Ft. 10 In. 715.00
Grenfell, Pictorial Map Newfoundland & Labrador, Frame, 1920s 2800.00
Hamadan, Allover Crimson, Ocher, Indigo Field, 4 Ft. 2 In. x 5 Ft. 10 In. 620.00
Hamadan, Allover Floral, Navy Ground, Red Border, 20th Century, 12 Ft. x 4 Ft. 6 In. ... 550.00
Hamadan, Allover Herati Design, Tree Of Life Border, Ivory, Rose, 4 Ft. x 5 Ft. 10 In. .. 560.00
Hamadan, Beige Field, Figures, Medallion, Ivory Border, Runner, 13 Ft. 5 In. x 2 Ft. 5 In. 835.00
Hamadan, Blue Medallions, Rust Field, Ivory Border, 9 Ft. 10 In. x 12 Ft. 1100.00
Hamadan, Center Curvilinear Medallion, Red Ground, 1960, 11 Ft. 5 In. x 17 Ft. 9 In. ... 1045.00
Hamadan, Dusty Pink Ground, Blue Border, 3 Ft. 4 In. x 5 Ft. 7 In. 110.00
Hamadan, Floral Allover, Blue Field, Red Border, c.1930, 12 Ft. x 8 Ft. 6 In. 4950.00
Hamadan, Floral Motif, Blue Ground, Red Border, Mid 20th Century, 9 Ft. x 4 Ft. 8 In. .. 4400.00
Hamadan, Medallion, Geometric, Blue, Brown, Red Field, 4 Ft. 6 In. x 6 Ft. 8 In. 405.00
Hamadan, Medallion, Ivory Ground, With Floral Sprays, 1960, 9 Ft. x 11 Ft. 8 In. 605.00
Hamadan, Midnight Blue Ground, Red Border, Contemporary, 4 Ft. 3 In. x 7 Ft. 6 In. 275.00
Hamadan, Overall Boteh, Geometric, Flower Borders, Red, Blue, 3 Ft. 7 In. x 10 Ft. 9 In. 748.00
Hamadan, Red Ground, Ivory Border, Runner, 3 Ft. 4 In. x 13 Ft. 3 In. 145.00
Hamadan, Repeating Herati Motif, Navy Blue Ground, 2 Ft. 3 In. x 13 Ft. 1 In. 405.00
Hamadan, Rosette Medallion, Midnight Blue, Red Field, 7 Ft. 2 In. x 4 Ft. 8 In. 490.00
Hearth, Needlework, Wool, Linen, 32 x 64 In. 1540.00
Heriz, 3 Latch Hook Medallions, Salmon, Camel Hair Border, c.1920, 2 Ft. 6 In. x 7 Ft. ... 1100.00
Heriz, Allover Flowers, Red Field, Geometric Borders, Blues, Greens, Red, 6 x 9 Ft. ... 518.00
Heriz, Allover Stylized Rosettes, Diamond, Rust Ground, 8 Ft. 2 In. x 12 Ft. 3 In. 1430.00
Heriz, Central Medallion, Ivory, Navy Borders, Mid 1900s, 7 Ft. 10 In. x 6 Ft. 1 In. 275.00
Heriz, Central Medallion, Red Ground, Multiple Borders, c.1930, 6 Ft. 7 In. x 4 Ft. 7 In. . 360.00
Heriz, Central Medallion, Turtle Border, 8 Ft. x 11 Ft. 2 In. 2070.00
Heriz, Charcoal Medallion, Red Field, White Spandrels, Border, 10 x 13 Ft. 2185.00
Heriz, Curvilinear Medallion, Rust To Red Ground, 1960, 12 Ft. x 8 Ft. 8 In. 550.00
Heriz, Floral, Terra-Cotta, Blue, Red, Ivory, Gold, Navy Border, 9 Ft. 2 In. x 7 Ft. 7 In. .. 2300.00
Heriz, Geometric Medallion, Salmon Ground, 1900, 9 Ft. 4 In. x 12 Ft. 4 In. 4400.00
Heriz, Geometric, Flowers, Red Field, Red, Blue, Green, Rust, Border, 8 Ft. x 8 Ft. 9 In. . 4140.00
Heriz, Geometric, Red Ground, Blue Corners, Red Geometric Border, 8 x 10 Ft. 690.00
Heriz, Geometrics, Red Ground, Deep Blue Border, 8 Ft. 11 In. x 11 Ft. 10 In. 1980.00
Heriz, Ivory Spandrels, Black Ground, Red Border, 6 x 9 Ft. 515.00
Heriz, Ivory Spandrels, Blue Ground, Burgundy Border, Contemporary, 6 x 9 Ft. 330.00
Heriz, Medallion, Flowers, Red, Ivory Spandrels, Blue Border, 18 Ft. 8 In. x 9 Ft. 10 In. . 7475.00
Heriz, Medallion, Red, Sky Blue Field, Navy Border, c.1930, 8 Ft. 3 In. x 11 Ft. 9 In. 1540.00
Hooked, 2 Central Tulips, Flanked By Yellow Tulips, Corner Tulips, c.1930, 29 x 57 In. ... 1210.00
Hooked, 2 Deer, 36 x 60 In. 330.00
Hooked, 3 Dancing White Rabbits, Maroon Border, 22 x 34 In. 4315.00
Hooked, 3 Stars, Abstract Flowers & Animals, Sawtooth Border, 34 x 78 In. 6900.00
Hooked, 4 Horse Coach, Riders, Houses, Birds, & People, On Linen, 33 x 65 In. 4480.00
Hooked, Allover Floral, Central Floral Medallion, Stylized Vine Border, 9 x 12 Ft. 2012.00
Hooked, Baby & Dog, Multicolored, 1800s, 35 x 44 1/2 In. ....*Illus* 2530.00
Hooked, Bars With Stripes, Multicolored, Black Border, 1920, 38 x 22 In. 10.00
Hooked, Bears, Carrying Bowls Of Porridge, 22 1/4 x 34 1/2 In. 55.00
Hooked, Bird Gathering Berries, Chain Link Border, Brown, Red, Tan, 19 x 33 In. 2185.00

Hooked, Black Dog, Brown & Gray Ground, 1910, 36 x 36 In. 1650.00
Hooked, Black Dog, Brown Ears, Multicolor Ground, Border, Stretcher, 42 x 46 In. 6900.00
Hooked, Black Stallion, Brown Saddle, Leaf Border, Early 20th Century, 31 x 69 In. 990.00
Hooked, Black Touring Car, Red Spoked Tires, Pa., Early 20th Century, 49 x 28 In. 660.00
Hooked, Brown Horse, Green Grass, Red Tail, Red, Black Border, 25 x 35 In. 1610.00
Hooked, Butcher, Penny Rug Circles, Oval Frame, 40 x 20 In. 5745.00
Hooked, Center Floral, Red & Green Leaves, Early 20th Century, 38 1/2 x 69 In. 330.00
Hooked, Center Floral, Surrounded By Wave Border, 22 x 49 1/2 In. 360.00
Hooked, Central Medallion, Brown Variegated Ground, 25 x 37 In. 545.00
Hooked, Central Medallion, Surrounding Flowers, Tan, 20th Century, 12 Ft. x 8 Ft. 10 In. 303.00
Hooked, Central Stylized Flowers, Blue, Green, Red, Tan Waves, 49 x 39 In. 1430.00
Hooked, Cherry Pickers, 2 Girls, Dog, Among Flowers & Cherries, 24 x 38 In. 4600.00
Hooked, Child With Jacket, Boots Standing In Curtained Doorway, Pa., 24 x 15 In. 495.00
Hooked, Couple Flanking Horse, Blue Birds, Grapevine, Black Sawtooth Border, 26 In. ... 1780.00
Hooked, Couple In Open Red Sleigh Drawn By 2 Prancing Horses, 23 x 37 In. 165.00
Hooked, Crested Birds, Leaf, Floral, Green, Yellow, Orange, Blue, Pink, Pa., 44 x 21 In. . 1320.00
Hooked, Deer Leaping Over A Fallen Tree, Brown, Green, 1900, 29 x 33 In. 410.00
Hooked, Dog, Black, Gray & Cream Markings, Shadow Border, 31 x 36 In. 3160.00
Hooked, Dog, Double Border, Brown & Grays, Frame, 1910, 36 x 36 In. 1500.00
Hooked, Dog, Leaves In Corners, 32 x 42 In. 2875.00
Hooked, Dog, Quatrefoil, Cornucopia, Flowers, Ocher, Brown Ground, 26 x 39 1/2 In. 400.00
Hooked, Dog, Rolling, Tan Ground, Late 19th Century, 23 x 47 In. 880.00
Hooked, Dog, White Markings, Brown Ears, 42 x 46 In. 6900.00
Hooked, Farm Village, Boy & Dog, 22 x 41 In. 70.00
Hooked, Figural, Calico Kittens, Pink, Blue Birds, Black Ground, 1800s, 28 x 36 1/2 In. . 860.00
Hooked, Floral, Berries, Green Border, 1920, 28 x 19 In. 75.00
Hooked, Flower Basket, Floral Border, Priscilla Kepner January, 1850, 25 x 57 In. 1925.00
Hooked, Flower Baskets, Floral Border, Green, Brown, c.1900, 2 Ft. 9 In. x 5 Ft. 9 In. ... 490.00
Hooked, Flowering Tree, 2 Red Leaping Stags, Black, Horses, Geometric, 41 x 48 In. *Illus* 5460.00
Hooked, Flowers On Central Moss Ground, Brown & Black Border, Oval, 32 1/2 x 42 In. .. 80.00
Hooked, Flowers On Tan Field, Brown Border, 75 x 35 In. 115.00
Hooked, Flowers, Multicolored, Brown Border, 32 x 59 In. 275.00
Hooked, Flowers, Scroll Handle Vase, 27 x 38 1/2 In. 1840.00
Hooked, Geometric Pendant, American Indian Good Luck Border, 33 x 60 In. 172.00
Hooked, Geometric, Leafy Tile, Variegated Red, 32 x 99 In. 1035.00
Hooked, Geometric, Red Floral, Green Diamond, Dark Green, Gray, 36 x 59 In. 460.00
Hooked, Geometric, Red, Black, Green, Gray, 22 1/2 x 66 1/2 In. 1150.00
Hooked, Graphic, Bold Colors, 1930s, 39 x 53 In. 950.00
Hooked, Growler & Prowler, Dog & Cat, 25 x 38 In. 8910.00
Hooked, Hand Held Bouquet Of Flowers, 22 1/4 x 37 1/2 In. 1725.00
Hooked, Horse Drawn Carriage, 26 x 47 In. 1650.00
Hooked, House, Surround Flower Heads, Braided Border, 37 x 48 In. 2590.00
Hooked, Houses & Stream, On Frame, 1950, 9 x 23 In. 55.00
Hooked, Hunter With Gun In Forest, Rabbits Running Between Trees, c.1900, 18 x 36 In. . 325.00
Hooked, Indian Brave, Headdress, Holding Walking Stick, 36 x 18 In. 9780.00
Hooked, King Of Beasts, Jungle, Brown, Green, Red, Multicolor Border, 30 1/2 x 61 In. . 690.00

Rug, Hooked, Baby & Dog, Multicolored,
1800s, 35 x 44 1/2 In.

Rug, Hooked, Flowering Tree, 2 Red Leaping Stags,
Black, Horses, Geometric, 41 x 48 In.

Hooked, Large Brown Dog, Oak Leaves, Tan Ground, 32 x 42 In. 2875.00
Hooked, Leaves, Green, Brown Variegated, Late 19th Century, 14 x 28 1/2 In. 230.00
Hooked, Lion, Jungle Flowers, Border, 30 1/2 x 61 In. . . . . *Illus* 690.00
Hooked, Magenta Vase With Multicolored Flowers, Gray, Black, 27 x 38 1/2 In. 1840.00
Hooked, Multicolored Bands In An Opposing Angle, Stripes, 26 1/4 x 47 In. 1955.00
Hooked, Multicolored Interlocking Diamonds, Plum, Red, Tan, 36 x 58 In. 2300.00
Hooked, Multicolored, Parrots Perched, Basket Of Flowers, Butterflies, 33 x 51 In. 825.00
Hooked, Oak Leaf & Flower, Pale Colors, 9 x 12 Ft. 220.00
Hooked, Overlapping Shell Motifs, Red, Pink, Purple, Black Outlines, 27 x 46 1/4 In. . . . 200.00
Hooked, Owl & Moon, Everyone Is In Slumberland But You & Me, c.1930, 36 x 53 In. . . 550.00
Hooked, Pictorial, Cottage Amid Birch Trees, Black Border, 9 x 12 Ft. 6900.00
Hooked, Pictorial, Mill Building, Paddlewheel, Landscape, 1890s, 22 x 36 In. 920.00
Hooked, Pinwheel & Clam Shell, Pink, Red, Green, 25 1/2 x 37 1/2 In. 460.00
Hooked, Prancing Horse, Colored Border, 52 x 35 1/2 In. 605.00
Hooked, Princess Secret Garden, Multicolored, 1920, 52 x 93 In. 625.00
Hooked, Rag, Bow Ties & Checkerboard, Stripes, 26 x 36 In. 330.00
Hooked, Rag, Multicolored Stripes, Black Diamond Ground, 23 x 68 In. 247.00
Hooked, Recumbent Lion, Red Ground, Vines, Brown Ground, c.1900, 32 x 55 In. 605.00
Hooked, Red Frame House Within Border, Early 20th Century, 36 x 26 In. 880.00
Hooked, Red Horse & Cow, Leafy Branches, Fringed, Stretcher, 25 x 39 In. 1610.00
Hooked, Red Roses, Slate Blue Ground, 50 x 85 In. 6330.00
Hooked, Rooster, Blue Ground, Multicolored Checkered Ends, Early 1900s, 18 x 39 In. . . 303.00
Hooked, Sleigh Riding In New England Village, Church, Houses, Trees, 60 x 56 In. 4600.00
Hooked, Stair Cover, Various Scenes, Animals, 13 Piece 660.00
Hooked, Talk To Me, Facing Rooster, Trellis & Vine Border, Gray Ground, 32 x 44 In. . . 5750.00
Hooked, Truck & Steam Shovel, Billowing Sky, 18 x 27 1/2 In. 675.00
Hooked, Waldoboro, Basket Of Flowers, Vine Border, Blue Ground, 62 x 30 In. 4600.00
Hooked, Welcome, Tan Ground, Flowers, Semicircle, Early 20th Century, 29 x 42 In. 523.00
Hooked, Whimsical Cat, Semicircle Borders, 22 x 39 1/2 In. 5750.00
Hooked, White Dog, Brown Ground, 17 x 39 In. 2300.00
Hooked, Winter Scene Of Northampton, Massachusetts, 60 x 56 In. 4600.00
Hooked, Yellow Puppy On Green Mat, Red, Green Exotic Flowers At Ends, 31 x 61 In. . . 431.00
Indo-Persian, Floral & Geometric, Floral Border, Red, Blue, Green, 5 Ft. x 8 Ft. 2 In. . . . 316.00
Isparta, Stylized Arabesque Leaves, Floral, Burgundy Ground, 1920, 6 Ft. x 8 Ft. 11 In. . 330.00
Karabagh, Hexagonal Medallions, Cloudband, Rust Field, Blue, Ivory, 7 Ft. 8 In. x 4 Ft. . 748.00
Karabagh, Wool, Gold Border, c.1890, 3 Ft. 11 In. x 8 Ft. 2 In. 4200.00
Karaja, 7 Medallions, Red Ground, Runner, Contemporary, 2 Ft. 7 In. x 8 Ft. 10 In. 220.00
Karaja, 7 Medallions, Salmon Ground, 1960, 2 Ft. 5 In. x 8 Ft. 11 In. 255.00
Karaja, Repeating Palmettes, Rust Ground, 1920, Runner, 1 Ft. 11 In. x 8 Ft. 11 In. 715.00
Karassashli, Medallions, Rosettes, Blue Field, Ivory Border, 1903, 5 Ft. 9 In. x 3 Ft. 6 In. 1150.00
Kashan, Buff, Floral Sprays, Vase, Midnight Blue Border, 16 Ft. 10 In. x 10 Ft. 4 In. 2300.00
Kashan, Burgundy Ground, Gold Border, 11 Ft. x 22 Ft. 3 In. 5390.00
Kashan, Center Medallion, Salmon Ground, Navy Border, Early 1900s, 5 Ft. x 3 Ft. 5 In. . 550.00
Kashan, Central Persia, Mid 20th Century, 4 Ft. 7 In. x 6 Ft. 10 In. 560.00
Kashan, Floral, 5 Borders, Red, Gold, Blue, Green, 11 Ft. 8 In. x 8 Ft. 7 In. 1898.00
Kashan, Multicolored Floral, Wind Ground, Blue Floral Band Border, 8 Ft. 1 In. x 7 Ft. . . 2190.00
Kazak, 3 Geometric Medallions, Blue & Rust Border, 94 x 50 In. 1870.00
Kazak, 4 Medallions, Blue Field, Ivory Borders, c.1880, 4 Ft. 1 In. x 8 Ft. 2 In. 2970.00
Kazak, 5 Medallions, Blue, Crimson, Tan Border, 4 Ft. 2 In. x 8 Ft. 4 In. 1125.00
Kazak, Blue, Green Borders, Red Ground, 5 Ft. 2 In. x 6 Ft. 4 In. 330.00
Kazak, Boteh Allover, Indigo Field, Multiple Borders, Mat, c.1900, 5 Ft. 5 In. x 6 Ft. 6 In. 1210.00
Kazak, Figural, Ivory Border, Red Ground, 4 Ft. 1 In. x 6 Ft. 1 In. 248.00
Kazak, Prayer Mat, 1895, 3 Ft. 5 In. x 4 Ft. 8 In. 1232.00
Kazak, Russian, Persian Motifs, Navy Field, Cubic Border, 5 Ft. 3 In. x 7 Ft. 10 In. 1265.00
Kerman, Allover Floral, Blue Ground, Ivory Border, 20th Century, 20 x 12 Ft. 275.00
Kerman, Blue Ground, Urn & Floral, c.1920, 10 Ft. 6 In. x 17 Ft. 9 In. 4620.00
Kerman, Central Floral Medallion, Ivory Field, Blue Border, 14 Ft. 4 In. x 11 Ft. 4 In. . . . 2990.00
Kerman, Central Medallion, Overall Flowers, Tan, c.1950, 10 Ft. 3 In. x 7 Ft. 10 In. 2860.00
Kerman, Central Medallion, Tan Ground, Floral Motif, Early 1900s, 7 Ft. 2 In. x 4 Ft. 4 In. 440.00
Kerman, Floral Field, Navy Ground, Cypress Trees, Arabic Script, 9 Ft. 6 In. x 18 Ft. 3 In. 4600.00
Kerman, Floral Motif, Wine Ground, Mid 20th Century, 11 x 16 Ft. 1760.00
Kerman, Floral Sprays, Ivory Ground, 1940, 2 Ft. 11 In. x 14 Ft. 5 In. 1650.00
Kerman, Floral, Mauve Ground, Blue & Ivory Borders, 8 Ft. 10 In. x 11 Ft. 9 In. 385.00

Rug, Hooked, Lion,
Jungle Flowers, Border,
30 1/2 x 61 In.

Rug, Rag,
Mennonite,
Mosaic, 1930

Kerman, Medallion & Pendants, Burgundy Ground, 1940, 8 Ft. 9 In. x 12 Ft. 4 In. 990.00
Kerman, Pictorial, Tan, Light Blue, Fringed, 20th Century, 12 Ft. 2 In. x 8 Ft. 6 In. 9600.00
Kerman, Rosette Medallion, Vines, Blue, Ivory Ground, 1890, 9 Ft. 2 In. x 12 Ft. 7 In. 825.00
Kerman, Stylized Medallion, Vines & Floral Burgundy Ground, 8 Ft. 9 In. x 12 Ft. 6 In. . .   550.00
Kuba, Geometric, Navy Ground, Blue, Tan Border, c.1890, 5 Ft. 5 In. x 3 Ft. 10 In. 495.00
Kuba, Red Ground, Gold Border, 3 Ft. 1 In. x 5 Ft. 2 In. 415.00
Kurd, Central Diamonds, Black, Ivory Border, Blue, Red, Gold, 11 Ft. 2 In. x 3 Ft. 2 In. . . .   980.00
Kurd, Multicolor Diagonal Stripes, Flowers, Northwest Persia, 8 Ft. 9 In. x 4 Ft. 1035.00
Lillihan, Dark Pink Ground, Tan & Blue Border, 5 Ft. 5 In. x 6 Ft. 1 In. 825.00
Lillihan, Floral Sprays, Burgundy Ground, 6 Ft. 9 In. x 2 Ft. 11 In.` 770.00
Mahajarin Sarouk, Stylized Flower Vase, Blue Ground, 1910, 4 Ft. 3 In. x 6 Ft. 8 In. 4400.00
Mahal, Floral, Salmon Ground, Navy Border, 20th Century, 13 x 9 Ft. 1650.00
Mahal, Gold Field, Green Turtle Border, 11 Ft. 8 In. x 9 Ft. 5 In.   1725.00
Mahal, Multicolored Floral, Dark Blue, Floral Rust Border, 7 Ft. 10 In. x 10 Ft. 8 In. 3110.00
Mahal, Repeat Blossoms, Arabesques, Rust Field, Gold Border, 10 Ft. 4 In. x 13 Ft. 8 In. . .   2645.00
Malayer, Expanded Herati, Ivory, Turtle Border, 1920, 10 Ft. 6 In. x 13 Ft. 11 In. 6600.00
Mashad, Medallion, Vines, Magenta Ground, Cut Down, 11 Ft. 9 In. x 16 Ft. 10 In. 4125.00
Needlepoint, Overall Trellis Cartouches, Bouquets, Vinery Border, 20 Ft. x 12 Ft. 6 In. . .   6000.00
Needlework, Continental, 20th Century, 5 Ft. 2 In. x 8 Ft. 10 In.   170.00
Oushak, Blue Medallion, Red Ground, Blue Border, 12 Ft. 10 In. x 12 Ft. 2475.00
Penny, 3 Flowers, Wool Felt, White Ground, Burlap Fringe, 22 x 36 In. 125.00
Penny, Amish Plush Wool Table Type, 29 x 52 In. 375.00
Penny, Brown & Pink Felt Flowers, Green Silk Ground, 25 x 35 In. 225.00
Penny, Flowers, Yellow Ground, Wool Suiting & Felt, 23 1/2 x 50 In. 125.00
Penny, Wool, On Felt, Ticking Ground, Tongue Border, 26 1/2 x 42 In. 250.00
Persian, Abrash, Burgundy Border, Dark Green Ground, 8 Ft. 1 In. x 10 Ft. 6 In. 1045.00
Persian, Allover Flowers, Blue Field, Boteh Borders, Red, Blue, Sand, 4 Ft. 2 In. x 7 Ft. . .   575.00
Persian, Allover Flowers, Salmon Ground, Ivory Border, Early 1900s, 6 Ft. x 4 Ft. 8 In. . .   935.00
Persian, Center Panel, 3 Scenes, Crimson, Brown, Indigo, Green, 6 Ft. 10 In. x 4 Ft. 4 In.   1495.00
Persian, Stylized Floral, Ivory, Rose, Neutral Ground, 4 Ft. 6 In. x 7 Ft. 512.00
Phulkari, Silk On Cotton Ground, Bagh, East Punjabi, 20th Century, 7 Ft. 4 In. x 4 Ft. 460.00
Prayer, Akstafa, Ivory Mihrab & Spandrels, Ivory, 1880, 5 Ft. 11 In. x 3 Ft. 5 In. 1320.00
Prayer, Turkish, Red Mihrab, Rust Ground, Tan Border, 5 Ft. x 3 Ft. 1 In. 193.00
Rag, Mennonite, Mosaic, 1930 . . . .*Illus*   900.00
Rag, Stripes Of Colored Fabric, 100 x 156 In. 1320.00
Runner, Kurdish, Geometric Design, Red Field, Border, Red, Blue, Brown, 43 x 104 In. . . .   460.00
Runner, Porch, Cotton, Green, White, Yellow, c.1920, 38 x 147 In. 56.00
Sarouk, Allover Floral Sprays, Black Border, 1930s, 17 Ft. x 9 Ft. 4 In. 2645.00
Sarouk, Allover Flowers, Red Ground, Ivory Border, 23 Ft. 4 In. x 12 Ft. 5225.00
Sarouk, Allover Vases Of Flowers, Blossoming Shrubs, Blue Border, 11 Ft. 8 In. x 9 Ft. . . .   5175.00
Sarouk, Blue Medallion, Red Vines & Floral, 4 Borders, 3 Ft. 5 In. x 5 Ft. 1 In. 470.00
Sarouk, Burgundy Floral, 8 Ft. 9 In. x 12 Ft. 3080.00
Sarouk, Center Stylized Floral Medallion, Rose Ground, Fringe, 3 Ft. 2 In. x 4 Ft. 10 In. .   440.00
Sarouk, Detached Floral Sprays, Burgundy Ground, 1950, 2 Ft. 2 In. x 11 Ft. 11 In. 880.00
Sarouk, Floral Medallion, Burgundy Ground, Fake Fringe, 1930, 3 Ft. 5 In. x 5 Ft. 660.00
Sarouk, Floral Sprays, Burgundy Ground, 1950, 6 Ft. 8 In. x 3 Ft. 5 In. 440.00
Sarouk, Floral Sprays, Burgundy Ground, 1950, 7 Ft. 10 In. x 10 Ft. 2 In. 3300.00

Sarouk, Floral, Ivory Ground, Red Floral Band Border, 6 Ft. 6 In. x 8 Ft. 690.00
Sarouk, Garden, Ivory Floral & Insects, Blue Floral Border, 12 Ft. 6 In. x 9 Ft. 1 In. 8525.00
Sarouk, Multicolored Floral, Wine Ground, Deep Blue Floral Border, 9 x 12 Ft. 4140.00
Sarouk, Red Field, Center Flower Medallion, Blue Palmette, 9 Ft. 1 In. x 6 Ft. 1 In. 1840.00
Sarouk, Red Ground With Floral Design, Blue Border, c.1940, 13 Ft. 9 In. x 10 Ft. 3 In. . . 3575.00
Sarouk, West Persia, c.1900, 4 Ft. 11 In. x 7 Ft. 670.00
Seraband, Repeating Botehs Rows, Rust Ground, 1920, 7 Ft. 6 In. x 10 Ft. 5 In. 275.00
Seraband, Staggered, Rows Of Small Boteh, 20th Century, 15 Ft. 6 In. x 10 Ft. 4 In. 1725.00
Serapi, Center Diamond, Borders, 9 Ft. 9 In. x 15 Ft. 9 In. 12210.00
Shiraz, Burgundy Ground, Medallion Borders, Blue Spandrels, 3 Ft. 11 In. x 6 Ft. 8 In. . . 165.00
Shirred, Centered Flowers In Urn, Multicolor Concentric Bands, Oval, 42 In. 25300.00
Shirred, Urn, Flowers, New England, c.1844, 32 x 65 In. 31000.00
Shirvan, Animals, Navy Field, Ivory Border, c.1880, 3 Ft. 2 In. x 5 Ft. 7 In. 825.00
Shirvan, Lesghi Star, 3 Medallions On Brown, c.1890, 3 Ft. 3 In. x 5 Ft. 4 In. 495.00
Shirvan, Lesghi Star, 4 Medallions On Blue, Ivory Border, c.1890, 4 Ft. x 6 Ft. 4 In. 2310.00
Shirvan, Wine, Allover Floral & Vine, Blue Border, c.1940, 15 Ft. 6 In. x 11 Ft. 10 In. . . . 400.00
Tabriz, Center Medallions, Tan Ground, Red Corners, Borders, 15 Ft. 4 In. x 9 Ft. 11 In. . 1870.00
Tabriz, Hexagonal Medallion, Ivory, Meandering Vines, Geometric, Border, 7 x 10 Ft. . . . 2070.00
Tabriz, Ivory Medallion, Red, Vine, Palmette, Blossom, Navy Border, 8 Ft. 6 In. x 11 Ft. . 2415.00
Talish, Prayer, Late 19th Century, 4 Ft. 7 In. x 2 Ft. 10 In. 460.00
Tekke, Engsi, Quartered Garden Field, Rust, Blue, Red, Floral, 4 Ft. 7 In. x 3 Ft. 10 In. . . 489.00
Tekke, Hanging, Guls On Red Field, Multiple Borders, c.1910, 3 Ft. x 4 Ft. 5 In. 275.00
Tekke, Red Ground, Multiple Borders, 3 Ft. 4 In. x 5 Ft. 4 In. 300.00
Tekke Hatchli, Multiple Panels, Geometric, c.1890, 5 Ft. 9 In. x 4 Ft. 4 In. 990.00
Turkish, 2 Medallions, Stylized Flower & Leaf, Polychrome Colors, Borders, 7 x 4 Ft. . . . 545.00
Turkish, 3 Medallions, Red, Blue, Ivory, Red, Multiple Borders, 8 Ft. 10 In. x 6 Ft. 3 In. . 385.00
Turkish, Center Panel, Tree Of Life, Multiple Borders, Red, Beige, 6 Ft. x 3 Ft. 8 In. 750.00
Turkish, Geometric Medallions, Black, Indigo, Tan, Brown, 5 Ft. 10 In. x 4 Ft. 575.00
Yomud, Blue, Rust, 5 Ft. x 3 Ft. 8 In. 230.00

RUMRILL Pottery was designed by George Rumrill of Little Rock, Arkansas. From 1933 to 1938, it was produced by the Red Wing Pottery of Red Wing, Minnesota. In January 1938, production was transferred to the Shawnee Pottery in Zanesville, Ohio. It was moved again in December of 1938 to Florence Pottery Company in Mt. Gilead, Ohio, where Rumrill ware continued to be manufactured until the pottery burned in 1941. It was then produced by Gouda Ceramic Arts in South Zanesville until early 1943.

RumRill

Bowl, Apple Blossom, Indian, Green Over Rose Glaze, 4-Leaf Clover, 1930, 4 x 6 In. . . . 45.00
Bowl, Bulb, Chartreuse Exterior, Olive Green Interior, 9 In. 40.00
Console Set, Ivory Glaze, 1938, 6 1/2 x 3 In. 105.00
Jug, Tilt, Handle, Yellow, 1900, 5 1/2 x 9 In. 125.00
Urn, Off-White, Pink Speckled, 5 1/2 x 9 In. 148.00
Vase, Antique White, Purple Mauve Interior, Neoclassical, 7 1/2 In. 95.00
Vase, Cream, Yellow, Turquoise, Blue Interior, 6 1/4 x 8 In. 110.00
Vase, Double Handle, Blue, Red Wing Pottery, 8 1/2 In. 85.00
Vase, Flower, Leaf Design, White Matte Glaze, 1942, 13 In. 55.00
Vase, Grecian, Double Handle, Red Wing Pottery Co., 7 1/4 In. 75.00
Vase, Green Opalescent, Red Wing Pottery, 7 1/2 In. 60.00
Vase, Green, 4 1/4 In. 110.00

RUSKIN is a British art pottery of the twentieth century. The Ruskin Pottery was started by William Howson Taylor, and his name was used as the mark until about 1899. The factory, at West Smethwick, Birmingham, England, stopped making new pieces in 1933 but continued to glaze and sell the remaining wares until 1935. The art pottery is noted for its exceptional glazes.

RUSKIN POTTERY WEST SMETHWICK

Ginger Jar, Wooden Cover, Red Glaze, 3 1/2 In. 150.00
Pin, Pewter Set With Blue, Purple Mottled Pottery, 1930 . . . . 45.00
Pot, Purple Luster, 1921, 1 1/4 x 2 1/4 In. 76.00
Vase, Blue, Green, Red, High Glaze, Impressed Mark, c.1910, 7 In. 1725.00
Vase, Compressed Body, Purple, Mauve Ground, Speckled Green, c.1905, 8 3/4 In. 3300.00
Vase, Gourd Shape, Rust, Orange, 1921, 7 x 5 In. 78.00

RUSSEL WRIGHT designed dinnerwares in modern shapes for many companies. Iroquois China Company, Harker China Company, Steubenville Pottery, and Justin Tharaud and Sons made dishes marked *Russel Wright*. The Steubenville wares, first made in 1938, are the most common today. Wright was a designer of domestic and industrial wares, including furniture, aluminum, radios, interiors, and glassware. Dinnerwares and other pieces by Wright are listed here. For more information, see *Kovels' Depression Glass & Dinnerware Price List*.

American Modern, Bowl, Fruit, Lug, Chartreuse	15.00
American Modern, Bowl, Fruit, Lug, Coral	15.00
American Modern, Bowl, Fruit, Lug, Granite Gray	15.00
American Modern, Bowl, Salad, Granite Gray	95.00
American Modern, Bowl, Vegetable, Black Chutney	55.00
American Modern, Bowl, Vegetable, Cover, Tab Handles, Coral	75.00
American Modern, Casserole, Cover, Stick Handle, Chartreuse	45.00 to 55.00
American Modern, Casserole, Stick Handle, Coral	50.00
American Modern, Celery Tray, Coral, 13 In.	22.00
American Modern, Chop Plate, Chartreuse, 13 In.	25.00
American Modern, Cocktail, Chartreuse, Glass, 3 Oz.	25.00
American Modern, Cocktail, Seafoam Green, Glass, 3 Oz.	35.00
American Modern, Coffeepot, After Dinner, Coral	125.00
American Modern, Creamer, Coral	15.00
American Modern, Creamer, Granite Gray	15.00
American Modern, Creamer, Seafoam Green	20.00
American Modern, Creamer, White	30.00
American Modern, Cup & Saucer, Coral	13.00
American Modern, Cup & Saucer, Granite Gray	13.00
American Modern, Cup & Saucer, Seafoam Green	15.00
American Modern, Cup, Bean Brown	23.00
American Modern, Goblet, Chartreuse, Glass, 10 1/2 Oz.	40.00
American Modern, Gravy Boat, Coral	30.00
American Modern, Gravy Boat, Seafoam Green	55.00
American Modern, Gravy Boat, White	75.00
American Modern, Mug, Chartreuse	75.00
American Modern, Pitcher, Water, Coral	100.00
American Modern, Plate, Bean Brown, 8 In.	28.00
American Modern, Plate, Black Chutney, 6 In.	10.00
American Modern, Plate, Black Chutney, 10 In.	20.00
American Modern, Plate, Coral, 10 In.	13.00
American Modern, Plate, Granite Gray, 8 In.	15.00
American Modern, Plate, Seafoam Green, 10 In.	15.00
American Modern, Platter, Coral, 13 1/4 In.	45.00
American Modern, Platter, Seafoam Green, 13 1/4 In.	75.00
American Modern, Salt & Pepper, Granite Gray	20.00
American Modern, Sherbet, Seafoam Green, Glass, 5 Oz.	45.00
American Modern, Soup, Dish, Lug, Coral	20.00
American Modern, Sugar, Cover, Coral	20.00
American Modern, Sugar, Cover, Granite Gray	20.00
American Modern, Sugar, Open, Seafoam Green	10.00
American Modern, Sugar, Open, White	20.00
American Modern, Tea Set, Child's, Ideal, Teapot, Sugar, Creamer, Cover, 3 Piece	75.00
American Modern, Tumbler, Iced Tea, Coral, Glass, 13 Oz.	35.00
American Modern, Wine, Coral, Glass, 4 1/2 Oz.	30.00
Iroquois, Bowl, Cereal, Nutmeg Brown, 5 1/2 In.	15.00
Iroquois, Creamer, Ice Blue	20.00
Iroquois, Creamer, Nutmeg Brown	20.00
Iroquois, Creamer, Pink Sherbet	20.00
Iroquois, Cup & Saucer, Ice Blue	16.00
Iroquois, Cup & Saucer, Nutmeg Brown	18.00
Iroquois, Pitcher, Cover, Parsley Green, 6 1/2 In.	475.00
Iroquois, Plate, Bread & Butter, Pink Sherbet	7.00
Iroquois, Plate, Bread & Butter, Ripe Apricot	7.00
Iroquois, Plate, Dinner, Nutmeg Brown	18.00

Iroquois, Plate, Dinner, Pink Sherbet, 10 In. ....10.00 to 13.00
Iroquois, Plate, Luncheon, Dark Parsley Green, 9 In. 24.00
Iroquois, Plate, Salad, Pink Sherbet, 7 In. 8.00
Iroquois, Salt & Pepper, Nutmeg Brown 30.00
Iroquois, Sugar & Creamer, White 20.00
Iroquois, Sugar, Cover, Ice Blue 30.00
Iroquois, Sugar, Cover, Nutmeg Brown 30.00
Queen Anne's Lace, Bowl, Fruit, Footed, White 13.00
Queen Anne's Lace, Plate, Dinner, White, 10 1/4 In. 15.00
Residential, Bowl, Vegetable, Pink, Plastic, Melmac, 9 In. 20.00
Residential, Platter, Salmon, Plastic, Melmac, 14 1/2 In. 25.00
Residential, Soup, Dish, Lug Blue, Plastic, Melmac 15.00
Residential, Tumbler, Pink, Plastic, Melmac, 10 Oz., 3 1/4 In. 23.00
Sterling, Bowl, Bouillon, Ivy Green, 5 3/4 In. 32.00
Sterling, Plate, Salad, Shell Pink, 7 1/2 In. 35.00
Sterling, Plate, Shell Pink, Deco Decal, 7 1/2 In. 7.00

SABINO glass was made in the 1920s and 1930s in Paris, France. Founded by Marius-Ernest Sabino (1878–1961), the firm was noted for Art Deco lamps, vases, figurines, and animals in clear, colored, and opalescent glass. Production stopped during World War II but resumed in the 1960s with the manufacture of nude figurines and small opalescent glass animals. The new pieces are a slightly different color and can be recognized.

Sabino
France

Bottle, Bathing Scene, 4 Women, Swans, Satin, Stopper, Signed, 7 1/4 In. 400.00
Bowl, Crystal, Opalescent, Molded, Fish, 11 3/4 In. 345.00
Figurine, Dog, Signed, 2 In. 55.00
Vase, Blue, White Highlights, Thistle Design, 7 3/4 In. 805.00

SALOPIAN ware was made by the Caughley factory of England during the eighteenth century. The early pieces were blue and white with some colored decorations. Another ware referred to as *Salopian* is a late nineteenth-century tableware decorated with color transfers.

Salopian

Cup & Saucer, Boating Scene, Bridge, Cottage, Castle, Handleless 165.00
Cup & Saucer, Boy, Cow Reclining, Handleless 275.00
Cup & Saucer, Shell, Seaweed, Handleless 190.00
Pitcher, Cream, Castle Scenery, 4 1/2 In. 385.00
Plate, Indian Temple Scene, Elephant, Octagonal, 8 1/4 In. 425.00
Plate, Oriental Garden, Scroll, Grape Border, 7 1/2 In. 247.00
Tea Set, Temple River, Fisherman, 6 Handleless Cups & Saucer 2350.00
Teapot, Chintz, Oval, Cover, 5 1/2 In. 385.00

SALT AND PEPPER SHAKERS in matched sets were first used in the nineteenth century. Collectors are primarily interested in figural examples made after World War I. *Huggers* are pairs of shakers that appear to embrace each other. Many salt and pepper shakers are listed in other categories and can be located through the index at the back of this book.

Aunt Jemima, Wearing White Apron, Plastic, F & F, 5 1/2 In. 75.00
Aunt Jemima & Uncle Mose, 5 In. ....50.00 to 85.00
Bear & Beehive, Plastic Stopper 11.00
Beetle Bailey 12.00
Begging Puppies, In Package 10.00
Bird, Original Cork, Japan, 3 1/4 x 2 In. 15.00
Black Children In Yellow Basket, Center Handle, Japan 145.00
Black Cook & Maid, 3 1/4 In. 40.00
Black Plaid Mammy & Butler, 4 3/4 In. 100.00
Blue Birds, Carrying A Flower In Their Hands, Cork Stoppers, Enesco, 4 x 2 In. 25.00
Blue Jays, Perched On Branch, Black Outlines, Enesco, 3 3/4 x 2 1/2 In. 15.00
Boots, Cowboy, Brown & Tan, Spurs, Glazed Ceramic, 3 1/2 In. 15.00
Born To Shop, Woman & Credit Card, Glaze, Ceramic, 4 1/2 In. 12.00
Building Shape, Blue Luster, Porcelain, 3 1/2 In. 8.00
Captain Ahab & Moby Dick, Ceramic, 6 In. 22.50
Chef, Hollywood, California, 3 1/2 In. 20.00

Chrome, Chase, Russel Wright Design, 1930s, 1 3/4 x 1 1/2 In. 80.00
Cool Cat & Jukebox, Blue Pants, Black Jacket, Glazed Ceramic, 4 1/2 In. 15.00
Cows, Black & White, Holstein, Black & White Pedestal, Ceramic, 5 In. 18.00
Dutch Boy & Girl, Van Tellingen 55.00
Dutch People, Plastic, Pair 8.00
Falstaff Beer, Red & White Label, 1950s, 3 1/2 In. 6.00
Frontier Wagon, People Sitting On Them, Yellow, Gold Trim, Japan, 2 1/8 x 2 In. 8.00
Girl & Boy, 2 3/4 In. 35.00
Golfer & Golf Cart, Painted, Ceramic, 4 1/2 In. 15.00
Golliwog, 1970, 3 1/2 In. 225.00
Hanging Squirrels 18.00
Head, Japan, 2 3/8 x 1 1/2 In. 25.00
Humpty Dumpty, Regal 100.00
I Dream Of Jeannie 18.00
Indian Braves, One Feather, Ceramic, Marked Japan, 4 In. 20.00
John Deere 10.00
Ken-L-Ration, Dog & Cat, Plastic, F & F, 1950s 45.00
M&M's, Blue & Green, White M On Front, Ceramic, 3 5/8 In. 20.00
Mammy & Chef, Wearing White Outfits, 5 In. 110.00
Maroon Drip Glaze, Cork Stopper, 3 1/4 x 1 7/8 In. 15.00
Moon Mullins & Kayo, 2 3/4 In. 85.00
Old Coors, 4 1/4 In. 32.00
Paul Bunyan & Babe, Ceramic, Japan, 6 In. 22.50
Plastic, Red, Lustro-Ware, 1940s 16.50
Poppin' Fresh & Poppie, Plastic, 1974 . . . . 28.00
Prayer Lady, Enesco 20.00
Red Riding Hood & Wolf, 3 1/4 In. 85.00
Scottie Dog, White With Black Spots, Red Nose, Porcelain, 2 1/2 In. 4.00
Smokey The Bear, 2 Different Poses, 3 3/4 In. 75.00
Snuffy Smith & Barney Google, 2 3/4 In. 85.00
Squirt, Green Bottle, Yellow & Red Painted Labels, Metal Screw Caps, 6 In. 50.00
Terrier Dogs Quilted, White, Blue Trimmed Ears, Blue Bow, Mouth, Japan, 2 In. 15.00
Tiger, Cork Stoppers, 2 1/2 x 2 1/4 In. 20.00
Tole, Cork Stopper, Metal, 2 In. 25.00
Train & Track, 1986 . . . . 11.00
Washington Monument & U.S. Capitol, Gold Trim, Ceramic, 4 In. 16.00
Westinghouse Twins, Laundromat & Dryer, 1950s 25.00
Willie & Millie, Kool Cigarettes, Plastic Penguins, F&F, 3 1/2 In. 20.00
Yellow Candle, 5 3/4 x 2 3/8 In. 15.00

SALT GLAZE has a grayish white surface with a texture like an orange peel. It is a method of decoration that has been used since the eighteenth century. Salt-glazed pieces are still being made.

Bank, House, 7 In. 395.00
Batter Pail, Oak Leaf, Vine Design, 8 1/2 In. 330.00
Bean Pot, Original Cover, Blue Accents, Boston Baked Beans, Handle, 9 1/2 In. 440.00
Crock, Blue Eagle, Arrow Over Twin Swans, Gardner, 19th Century, 15 1/2 In. 375.00
Crock, Butter, Cover, Peacock Design, Palm Tree, Blue, White, 4 3/4 In. 495.00
Crock, Honey Colored Lateral Band, Dark Brown Body, Boston, 14 In. 322.00
Ewer, Applied Fern, Vintage Design, Blue Stippled Ground, 6 3/4 In. 27.00
Jar, Lid, Angled Rim, J.D. Craven, 9 1/2 In. 155.00
Jar, Storage, Iron Wash Interior, Goodwin & Webster, 13 3/4 x 36 1/4 In. 605.00
Jug, Storage, 2 Coggle Wheel Lines At Shoulder, E.S. Craven, c.1830, 14 In. 990.00
Match Safe, American Brew Co., Eagle Inside Logo Design, 3 In. 198.00
Mug, 2 Women Filling Jug, Handle, Blue Accents, Crystal Spring Co., N.Y., 5 In. 275.00
Mug, Blue Accents, Diamond, Handle, Bayle's St. Louis, Pretzels Are Best, 4 In. 578.00
Mug, Blue Accents, Handle, Jos. Schlitz Brewing Co., Milwaukee, 5 In. 198.00
Pitcher, Basket Weave, White Body, Brown Top, Silver Plated Rim, England, 9 In. 115.00
Pitcher, Grazing Cows Scene, Blue, White, Handle, 8 In. 176.00
Pitcher, Tan, Hound Handle, J.D. Bagster, 7 1/2 In. 495.00
Pitcher, Tan, Vintage Design, Figures Around Center, Signed, England, 11 3/4 In. 55.00
Pitcher, White, Washington Bust, Flags On Reverse, 6 1/4 In. 50.00
Tea Canister, England, 1750 . . . . 2800.00

SAMPLERS were made in America from the early 1700s. The best examples were made from 1790 to 1840. Long, narrow samplers are usually older than square ones. Early samplers just had stitching or alphabets. The later examples had numerals, borders, and pictorial decorations. Those with mottoes are mid-Victorian. A revival of interest in the 1930s produced simpler samplers, usually with mottoes.

ABCDE

ABC, Floral, Mary Appleyard, Aged 8 Years, 1845, Frame, 1800s, 15 1/2 x 16 1/2 In.	300.00
ABC, House, Birds & Trees, Catharine W., Cross-Stitch, Frame, 15 1/4 x 12 1/4 In.	1045.00
Adam & Eve, Agnes Parkenson's Work, Silk On Linen, c.1800, 21 1/2 In.	1980.00
Adam & Eve, Alphabet Top, Verse, Urns Of Flowers, Red House, Frame, 18 1/8 x 13 In. . .	1045.00
Adam & Eve, Crucifix, Couple With Pets, Vines, Alphabet, 35 1/2 x 9 3/4 In.	2300.00
Adam & Eve, Serpent, House, Elizabeth, Silk On Linen, Frame, 19 1/4 In.	2310.00
Agnes Mowlrey, House, Trees, Fence, Bird, Floral, Silk On Linen, 1831, 17 x 12 In.	880.00
Alphabet, Amelia Gross, Aged 14, 1882, Rosewood Veneer Frame, 19 3/4 x 12 In.	385.00
Alphabet, Assorted Floral Sprigs, Blue, Green, Beige, Black, 1814, 18 x 20 In.	1900.00
Alphabet, Birds, House, 19th Century, 11 1/2 x 12 In.	225.00
Alphabet, Double Sawtooth Border, Cynthia Phelps, Aged 13, 1819, 9 3/4 x 16 In.	1265.00
Alphabet, Ellen Bardon, 13 Years, New York, October 26, 1847, 11 1/2 x 9 1/2 In.	175.00
Alphabet, Geometric, Catherine Walton, Inspiration Verse, 1700s, 21 x 21 1/2 In.	460.00
Alphabet, House, Flowers, Vine Border, Albina Thornton, Frame, 1834, 17 x 17 In.	2415.00
Alphabet, Leaf Vine Border, Eliza Matthews, May 1859, Frame, 8 x 4 1/8 In.	375.00
Alphabet, Man & Woman, Animals, Red Frame, 17 1/2 x 32 In.	220.00
Alphabet, Pious Verse, Ann Apps, Aged 12, 1805, Frame, 10 1/2 x 9 3/8 In.	865.00
Alphabet, Pious Verse, Berry, Vine Border, Rebecca Charlesworth, 1829, 10 x 8 In.	575.00
Alphabet, Pious Verse, Hannah Weaver, 9th Year Of Age, 11 1/4 x 9 In.	920.00
Alphabet, Urns, Flowers, Mary Cassidy, Sisters Of Notre Dame, 16 1/4 x 21 In.	770.00
Alphabet, Verse, Bird Cage, Flowers, Dogs, Ann Nichols, Frame, 1817, 12 1/2 x 12 In. . .	290.00
Alphabet, Verse, Floral Border, Waterford Township School, 1809, 17 x 16 1/4 In.	2990.00
Alphabet, Verse, Flower Border, Sarah Sutton, Aged 9, 1811, 15 1/2 x 19 1/2 In.	345.00
Alphabet, Verse, Flowers, Seminary, Vine Border, Mary Turner, 1834, 16 x 13 In.	1265.00
Alphabet, Verse, Parrot, Flower Urns, Flowers, Sarah Starrs, 1789, 17 x 14 In.	1150.00
Alphabet, Verse, Pots Of Flowers, Martha Jane Sterret, Frame, 21 x 20 3/4 In.	1540.00
Alphabet, Verse, Wreath, Flowers, Martha Mary Miller Newport, 1823, 17 x 17 In.	1955.00
Alphabet, Vine Border, House, Baskets, Trees, Birds, Dog, Frame, 11 5/8 x 11 1/8 In. . . .	550.00
Alphabet & Numbers, Lydia Symonds, Aged 10 Years, 1791, 12 x 17 In.	5465.00
Alphabet & Verses, Martha Mary Miller, Newport, August 25, 1823, 17 x 17 In.	1955.00
Alphabet Panel, Vine Border, Agnes Sunley Aged 10 Years, 12 x 12 In.	355.00
Alphabets, 5 Alphabets In Various Stitches, Pa., 1813, 11 3/4 x 16 In.	5225.00
Alphabets, Annie Campbell, Red, Green, Lavender, Blue, Pink, 15 x 12 In.	250.00
Alphabets, Annie Lee, Stitched Border, Red, Beige, Blue, Green, Orange, 1851, 9 x 7 In. . .	336.00
Alphabets, Flowers, Crowns, Religious Symbols, England, 1760, 14 x 14 In.	575.00
Alphabets, Ivory, Green, Betsy Younglove, AD 1795, Cross-Stitch, Frame, 12 x 8 In.	770.00
Alphabets, Lacy M. Oetzmann, Red, Beige, Period Frame, 19th Century, 9 1/2 In.	196.00
Alphabets, Mary J Bradley, Age 8, Oct. 8th 1830, Cross-Stitch, Linen, 16 3/8 x 18 In. . . .	400.00
Alphabets, Numbers, Verses, Rebeckah Pilgrim, Age 12, October, 1815, 11 3/4 x 16 In. . .	518.00
Alphabets, Verse, Thompson Clark 1844, Wool On Cotton, Frame, 21 3/4 x 19 1/2 In. . . .	7150.00
Alphabets, White, Green, Blue, 5 Trees, Small Birds, Cotton, 1805, 16 x 11 In.	345.00
Angler's Delight, Oval Flower & Leaf Border, 19th Century, Frame, 13 x 15 1/2 In.	2875.00
Animals, Flowers, Ann Brown, 1833, Cross-Stitch On Linen, 13 1/2 x 12 1/2 In.	440.00
Ann Bells Sampler Wrought In The 11th Year Of Her Age, 1838, Linen, 17 x 15 In.	2050.00
Building, Trees, Verse, Elizabeth Abrey, 1841, Frame, Gilt Liner, 19 3/8 x 15 In.	2420.00
Bunch Of Summer Flowers, Pink, Yellow, Blue, Pa., 1837, 17 In.	7800.00
Central Poem, Tree & Floral, Ann Roney, October 14, 1826, 17 x 16 1/2 In.	495.00
Corner Verses, Vine & Leaf Border, Homespun Linen, Frame, 13 3/8 x 9 3/8 In.	460.00
Cross, Knotted Stitches, Blue, Green, Brown, Frame, 1846, 17 x 8 In.	460.00

**Store needlework, samplers, and small fabric pieces flat in a drawer.
Line the drawer with acid-free tissue paper from an art supplies store.**

Don't store fabrics in plastic bags. Use a well-washed white pillowcase. Plastic holds moisture, and the fabrics should "breathe." Do not store potpourri or other sachets with fabrics. The oil can harm fabric.

Sampler, Verse, Indian & Child,
Anne Summerfield, 1830, 8 x 11 In.

Dutch Style House, Windmill, Peacocks, Caged Birds, Elizabeth Poth, Frame, 21 In.	575.00
Eliza Cox, Brick House, Adam & Eve, Flowers, Trees, Angels, Birds, 16 x 19 3/4 In.	3000.00
Elizabeth Beardmore, Aged 8 Years, 1822, God Is A Rock, Never Will Decay, Frame	2200.00
Elizabeth Edwards, Stylized Strawberry Border, Verse, c.1800, 15 x 13 In.	1100.00
Elizabeth Fuller, 1806, Walnut Frame, 11 3/4 x 7 3/4 In.	627.00
Euphemia Woodger Riddell, Verse, House, Dated 1844, Frame, 12 1/4 x 13 In.	2300.00
Family Register, Bacheller-Taply Family, Verse, Cornucopia, 1779-1851, 19 x 16 In.	5175.00
Family Register, Kimball Family, Verse, Geometric Border, 1775-1821, 20 x 17 In.	489.00
Farmhouse, Figures, Flower Basket, Rachel C. Van Wort, Oct. 19th 1820, 16 x 21 In.	2475.00
Floral & Verse, Birds, Vine Border, Martha Ingleson Aged 9, 1808, 16 1/2 x 12 In.	1380.00
Flowers, Alphabet, Mary Augusta Russell, Born 1815, c.1827, Frame, 7 1/2 x 11 1/2 In.	403.00
Fruit Tree Center, Mary Elizabeth Pearson Toddington, Frame, 9 1/4 x 12 3/4 In.	385.00
Hannah Amelia Lyons, Birds In Trees, Sheep, Silk On Gauze, 19 1/2 x 23 1/2 In.	1650.00
House, Tree, Picket Fence, Floral Border, Agnes Mowlrey, 1831, 17 1/4 x 12 1/2 In.	880.00
Jannetta Harris, House, Squirrels, Deer, Dogs, 10 1/2 x 10 1/2 In.	1350.00
Lydia Freed, Her Work In Year 1826, Homespun, Frame, 13 x 15 In.	495.00
Map, England & Wales, Ann Hunter Year 1804, Gilt Frame, 24 1/2 x 22 In.	935.00
Map, England, Wales, Betsey Scott, 1793, Silk, Linen Ground, 24 1/2 x 10 1/2 In.	1725.00
Memorial, Isabella, Wife John Dixon, Verse, 1857, Frame, 22 x 19 In.	375.00
Memorial, Strawberry Border, W.H. Keely, Born 1818, Frame, 21 1/4 x 18 1/4 In.	2750.00
Mourning, Verse, Inspirational Verse, Dying Infant To His Mother, 1775, 12 x 17 In.	690.00
Numbers & Verse, Mary Orsbom, 13th Year, Linen Homespun, 18 1/4 x 11 1/8 In.	220.00
Rebecca Jeffries, With Hymn Book, Flowers, Philadelphia, c.1840, 13 1/2 x 18 In.	1150.00
Red House, Trees & Birds, Strawberry Border, Family History, Welsh, 16 3/4 x 18 In.	1210.00
Rows Of Alphabets & Numbers, Jane McCane, In Year 18---, Frame, 17 3/4 x 15 In.	192.00
Spread Wing Bird, Banner, Poem, Signed Hannah Beazel, 1815, 16 x 14 In.	5570.00
Spread Wing Bird, Poem, Hannah Beazel, Wrought In 1815, 16 1/2 x 14 3/4 In.	5750.00
Strawberry Border, Trees, Sarah Hunt, 12 Years, 1837, Frame, 15 1/4 x 12 In.	1430.00
Verse, 10 Commandments, Dianna & John Field Married June 1799, Linen, 17 x 6 In.	795.00
Verse, Assorted Flowers, Birds, Geometric Floral Vine, 1830, 18 1/2 x 17 1/2 In.	9487.00
Verse, Green & Pink, Ann Wilkinson, 8th Year, 1717, Linen, Frame, 7 1/2 x 5 1/2 In.	1080.00
Verse, House, Animals, Helen Hunter, Centralia, Pa., 1842, 22 x 18 1/2 In.	1375.00
Verse, Indian & Child, Anne Summerfield, 1830, 8 x 11 In. *Illus*	1200.00
Verse, Margaret Hughes Excudit, 11th Year Of Age, Floral Border, 1820, 16 x 19 In.	1400.00
Verse, Solomon's Temple, Hannah Johnson, 19th Century, 13 x 15 1/4 In.	550.00
Verse, Vine Border, Jane Thomas, July 25, 1828, Aged 14, 14 1/2 x 12 1/2 In.	748.00
Verse, White Floral, Green Vine Border, Ann M. Kemmerer, 1833, 17 1/2 x 17 1/2 In.	2530.00
Vine Border, Proverb Verse, Ann M. Kemmerer, April 31, 1833, 17 1/2 x 17 1/2 In.	506.00

SAMSON and Company, a French firm specializing in the reproduction of collectible wares of many countries and periods, was founded in Paris in the early nineteenth century. Chelsea, Meissen, Famille Verte, and Chinese Export porcelain are some of the wares that have been reproduced by the company. The firm uses a variety of marks on the reproductions. It is still in operation.

Bowl, Scene Of Sword Fight, Open Work Band, 2 1/2 x 9 In.	57.00

Figurine, Cockerels, Plumed & Feathered Crest, Flower Strewn Base, 10 x 10 1/2 In., Pair 920.00
Lamp, Porcelain, Famille Rose Style, Brass Base, Shade, 28 1/2 In., Pair 748.00
Urn, Medici, Painted, Heraldic Device, Floral Ground, Loop Handles, 13 x 8 1/2 In., Pair . 2760.00
Urn, Overall Floral & Gilt, 20 In., Pair 1955.00
Vase, Cover, Chinese Style, Coat Of Arms Front, Baluster, 6 In. 70.00
Vase, Wall, Chinese Type, 5 In., Pair 290.00

SANDWICH GLASS is any of the myriad types of glass made by the
Boston and Sandwich Glass Works in Sandwich, Massachusetts,
between 1825 and 1888. It is often very difficult to be sure whether a
piece was really made at the Sandwich factory because so many types
were made there and similar pieces were made at other glass factories.
Additional pieces may be listed under Pressed Glass and in related
categories.

Bell, Hobnail, Cranberry, Applied Band Ring, Ruffled Edge, 1880, 5 In. 550.00
Bottle, Emerald Green, 8 Sides, Pewter Cap, 3 1/8 x 1 1/8 x 3/4 In. 90.00
Bowl, Gothic Arch, Covered, 1840-1850, 4 3/4 x 5 In. 225.00
Bowl, Gothic Arch, Covered, Round Foot, 1840-1850, 4 3/4 x 5 In. 30.00
Bowl, Gothic Leaf, Rectangular, 7 x 5 1/4 In. 400.00
Candlestick, Canary, 7 1/2 In. 155.00
Candlestick, Clambroth, Dolphin Shape, 10 In., Pair 550.00
Candlestick, Clambroth, Dolphin, 1870, 10 x 10 3/8 In., Pair 900.00
Candlestick, Clambroth, Dolphin, 1870, 7 x 4 In., Pair 250.00
Candlestick, Clambroth, Hexagonal Base, 1860, 7 1/4 In. 90.00
Candlestick, Clambroth, Petal & Loop, 1860, 7 In., Pair 110.00
Candlestick, Clambroth, Petal & Loop, 7 In. 69.00
Candlestick, Clambroth, Sand Finish, Columnar, 1865, 9 In. 60.00
Candlestick, Petal & Loop, Yellow, Green, 1860, 6 3/4 In. 140.00
Candlestick, Petal Socket, Canary, Columnar, 1865, 9 1/4 In. 180.00
Candlestick, Wide Hexagonal Base & Socket, 1840-1860, 7 3/8 In. 83.00
Creamer, Heart & Scale, 1838-1845, 4 1/2 In. 35.00
Creamer, Heart & Scale, 4 1/2 In. 135.00
Cup & Saucer, Lacy, Child's, 1 1/4 In. 200.00
Decanter, Brandy, 3-Piece Mold, 1820-1840, Stopper, 1 Qt. 413.00
Decanter, Shell & Ribbing, 1825-1835, 7 1/4 In. 70.00
Dish, Lacy, Cobalt Bue, Oval, 1835-1850, Child's, 1 3/4 In. 1300.00
Dish, Lacy, Light Amber, 56 Even Scallops, Oval, Child's, 1 3/4 In. 250.00
Font For Bird Cage, 3-Piece Mold, Rooster On Top, c.1840, 5 1/4 In. 415.00
Heart & Scale, Creamer, Fiery Opalescent, 1838-1845, 4 1/2 In. 425.00
Lamp, Blackberry, Clear Font, Brass Connector, 10 In. 75.00
Lamp, Bull's-Eye, Fleur-De-Lis, Square Marble Base, 9 3/4 In. 85.00
Lamp, Fine Rib, Clear Font, Blue Opaque Square Base, 8 In. 400.00
Lamp, Flattened Sawtooth, 6-Sided Wafer Stem, 9 3/4 In. 160.00
Lamp, Ring Punty, Square Black Glass Base, 9 1/2 In. 120.00
Lamp, Star & Punty, Font, Hexagonal Stem, Foot, 8 3/4 In. 180.00
Lamp, Star & Punty, Wafer, Hexagonal Stem, Base, 10 x 3 1/4 x 2 3/4 In. 190.00
Lamp, White Overlay Font, Leaves, Berries, Punty Design, Gilt, 11 x 5 In. 47.00
Plate, Feather, 16 Curved Feathers, Stippled Panels, Zigzag Border, 9 3/4 In. 60.00
Salt, Boat Shape, Diamond Point Border, Deep Fiery Opalescent 600.00
Salt, Boat Shape, Lafayette, Opaque, Purple, Blue 1000.00
Salt, Chariot, Footed, Silver Opaque Blue 1050.00
Salt, Diamond Diaper, Master, 3 1/4 In. 75.00
Salt, Vertical Ribs, Applied Foot, 3-Piece Mold, c.1830, 5 1/4 In. 143.00
Spooner, Hexagonal, Electric Blue, Child's, 1850-1870, 1 3/4 x 1 In. 220.00
Spooner, Inverted Diamond & Thumbprint, Canary 800.00
Spooner, Ribbed Grape, Blue 7750.00
Sugar, Translucent Clambroth, Petaled Rim, Cover, 1830-1860, 4 3/8 In. 495.00
Toothpick, Covered Basket, 4 x 2 1/4 In. 100.00
Tray, Butterfly, 4 Pinwheel Border, Beading, 8 1/4 x 5 1/2 In. 50.00
Tumbler, Enameled Cottage, Trees, Snow Covered Hill, 4 In. 265.00
Tumbler, Fine Rib With Band, Cobalt Blue, Child's, 1850-1870, 1 3/4 In. 200.00
Tumbler, Paneled, Canary, 1845-1870, 1 5/8 In. 90.00
Tumbler, Paneled, Deep Cobalt Blue, Child's, 1845-1870, 1 1/2 In. 70.00

Vase, Blue Heron, Opalescent, 5 3/8 x 2 1/4 x 3 1/2 In. 200.00
Vase, Loop, Emerald Green, 9 1/4 In. 2645.00

SARREGUEMINES is the name of a French town that is used as part of a china mark. Utzschneider and Company, a porcelain factory, made ceramics in Sarreguemines, Lorraine, France, from about 1775. Transfer-printed wares and majolica were made in the nineteenth century. The nineteenth-century pieces, most often found today, usually have colorful transfer-printed decorations showing peasants in local costumes.

Cup & Saucer, Demitasse, 1920 . . . . 40.00
Cup & Saucer, Divided Leaf Handle, Flowers, Gilt, 1895 . . . . 95.00
Jardiniere, Fluted Pedestal, Turquoise Interior, Cobalt Blue Glaze, 48 In. 550.00
Jardiniere, Painted & Gilt Lilies, Tendrils & Leaves, Brown Ground, c.1900, 13 In. 640.00
Pitcher, Brown Party Characters, France, 1890, 8 1/2 In. 400.00
Pitcher, Figural, Man's Head, Majolica, Green, 7 3/4 In. 220.00
Plate, Abundant Fruit Border, 8 1/2 In. 22.00
Plate, Floral, 7 3/4 In. 55.00
Platter, Fish, Dark Green, 21 In. 60.00
Stein, Munich Child, Hops & Wheat, Pewter Lid, 1/2 Liter 847.00

SASCHA BRASTOFF made decorative accessories, ceramics, enamels on copper, and plastics of his own design. He headed a factory, Sascha Brastoff of California, Inc., in West Los Angeles, from 1953 until about 1973. He died in 1993. Pieces signed with the signature *Sascha Brastoff* were his work and are the most expensive. Other pieces marked *Sascha B.* or with a stamped mark were made by others in his company. Pieces made by Matt Adams after he left the factory are listed here with his name.

Ashtray, Abstract, 5 In. 39.00
Ashtray, Alaska, Hooded, Eskimo Face, 5 In. . . . . .65.00 to 85.00
Ashtray, Alaska, Hooded, Ram, 8 1/2 x 6 In. 75.00
Ashtray, Brown, Eggshell, White, Blue, Gold, Signed, 1950, 5 In. 21.00
Ashtray, Flat Flack Glaze Interior, Crescents, Wheels, Gold Swirl, 5 1/2 In. 61.00
Ashtray, Gold, Silver Aztec-Mayan Design, 6 x 3 1/4 In. 23.00
Ashtray, Green Flowers, Signed, 5 1/4 In. 35.00
Ashtray, Houses, Trees, Vegetation, Gold Highlights, 1950s, 8 1/2 In. 65.00
Ashtray, Igloo Design, Gold, Smoke Hole, 3-Footed, 4 1/2 x 6 In. 55.00
Ashtray, Orange Daisies, Enamel, 7 1/2 x 4 5/8 In. 21.00
Ashtray, Orange, Gold, Green Design, Gold Ground, 8 In. 59.00
Ashtray, Pink, Blue, Black, White Horse, Blue, Green Ground, 6 x 7 In. 25.00
Ashtray, Raised Jewels In The Center Of Flowers, Gold Ground, 10 In. 28.00
Ashtray, Rooftops, 1958, 13 1/2 x 5 In., 3 Piece 150.00
Ashtray, Rooster Head, 4 1/4 x 3 In. 32.00
Ashtray, Slant, Peacock, Jeweled, Signed In Gold, 5 In. 25.00
Ashtray, Star Steed, Teal Blue, Signed, 8 1/2 x 3 3/4 In. 26.00
Ashtray, Teepee Shape, Turquoise & Gold, 5 In. 30.00
Bowl, Lion, Blue, Green, Lion's Head, 5 1/2 x 7 x 2 In. 73.00
Bowl, Mosaic, 4 x 2 1/2 In. 35.00
Bowl, Mosaic, Gold Highlights, 1950s, 5 1/2 In. 50.00
Bowl, Rooftops, Glossy Finish, Pottery, 13 In. 350.00
Bowl, Star Steed, Sunfish Shape, 3-Footed, Signed, 8 1/2 x 9 3/4 x 2 1/2 In. 110.00
Bowl, Surf Ballet, 3 Nubbed Feet, Marked, 2 3/4 x 5 1/2 In. 36.00
Box, Aztec, Signed, 9 x 6 In. 95.00
Box, Bird Cover, Black, White, Gray, Metallic Gold, 7 1/2 x 4 3/4 In. 95.00
Box, Cigarette, Rooftops, 4 x 5 1/4 In. 20.00
Box, Cover, Fruit & Leaf Design, Brown High Glaze, 5 In. 59.00
Box, Cover, Orange, Gold, Enamel, Copper, Signed, 5 x 4 x 2 In. 45.00
Box, Dress, Abstract, Pottery, 5 1/4 x 4 In. 145.00
Box, Dress, Persian, Pottery, 5 1/4 x 4 In. 165.00
Box, Minos Design, 9 In. 95.00
Cachepot, Fins Outcroppings, Brown, Orange, Green Trim, Signed, 2 1/2 In. 85.00

Cachepot, Light, Dark Green, Pink, Mauve, White, Black Trim, Ruffled Edge, 2 1/2 In. . . . 65.00
Charger, Colorful Fruit Design, Lime Green, Black, 14 In. 145.00
Chocolate Pot, Cover, Jewel Bird, Gray, Black, White Bird, Gold, 15 In. 300.00
Cigarette Holder, Alaska, Eskimo, Gold Accents 69.00
Cigarette Lighter, Aztec, Flowers, Signed, 4 1/2 x 1 1/4 In. 45.00
Compote, Abstract, Pottery, 6 In. 75.00
Compote, Swirls Of Copper, Dark Brown Ground, Dark Blue Enamel, 8 In. 22.00
Dish, Alaska Shell, Signed, 11 1/2 In. 85.00
Dish, Aztec, Gold Bird Design, Signed, 7 In. 49.00
Dish, Aztec, Signed, 5 1/2 In. 38.00
Dish, Cover, Bluebird, 8 1/2 x 1 1/2 In. 31.00
Dish, Gold Enameled Leaf Shape, Blue, Green, Yellow Flowers, 5 1/2 In. 25.00
Dish, Jewel Bird, Signed, 10 In. 85.00
Dish, Rooftops, 13 x 6 In. 95.00
Dish, Star Steed, Signed, 7 1/2 In. 65.00
Dish, Vanity, Pink, Blue, Burnt Orange Flower, Black Ground, 9 x 5 In. 125.00
Figurine, Cat Mosaic, Turquoise, White, Brown, Gold, Signed, 17 1/4 x 8 In. 280.00
Figurine, Dove, Gold Stylized Design, Swirling, Raised Dots, 3 1/2 x 3 In. 76.00
Figurine, Horses, Standing, Blue, Silver Trim, Signed, 10 In., Pair 660.00
Figurine, Merbaby, Holding A Shell Above Her Head, Gold, 13 x 11 In. 750.00
Figurine, Pelican Resin, Light Yellow, Lime Green, Dark Winter Green, 11 In. 250.00
Figurine, Pink, Purple, Gold Horses, Signed, 10 In. 345.00
Figurine, Polar Bear, American Bisque, 9 In. 195.00
Jug, Figural, Female, Hands Folded In Front, Handle, Signed, 13 x 6 In. 261.00
Lamp, Stylized Floral & Leaf Design, Dark Green, Black, Signed, 6 1/2 In. 190.00
Pipe, Abstract, Pottery, 4 1/2 In. 48.00
Plate, Chichi Bird, Signed, 8 1/2 In. . . . . .100.00 to 195.00
Plate, Pussy Willow, Brown Drip Glaze, Pussy Willow Branches, 10 In. 100.00
Platter, Alaska, Blue Sky, Gray, Taupe, White Ice Ground, Matt Adams, 13 In. 130.00
Platter, Surf Ballet, Teal, Light Blue Ground, 13 3/4 x 10 1/2 In. 16.00
Salt & Pepper, Alaska, Walrus, 6 1/2 x 2 1/2 In., Pair 230.00
Tea Caddy, Persian, Pottery, 7 3/4 In. 250.00
Tea Set, Purple, Gold, Silver, White Porcelain, Teapot 8 x 12 In., 3 Piece 100.00
Teapot, Surf Ballet, Swirling Pink & Gold, 7 3/4 x 11 1/2 In. 75.00
Tile, Horse, Green, Gray, Blue, White, Wormwood Frame, 7 x 8 1/4 x 10 In. 76.00
Tobacco Jar, Steel Cover, 6 1/2 In. 65.00
Tray, Dancer Wearing Plume Like Feathers Holding Plume Like Fan, 7 In. 65.00
Tray, Multicolored Houses Flanked By Autumnal Colored Trees, 1950, 8 In. 45.00
Tray, Pale Oil Foam, Black Base, Gold Trim, 1950 . . . . 45.00
Tray, Tidbit, Surf Ballet, Pink, Silver Over White Glaze 40.00
Vase, Alaska, Bud, 6 1/2 x 3 In. 59.00
Vase, Alaska, Eskimo Face, Signed, 5 1/2 x 8 In. 110.00
Vase, Alaska, Gold, 5 5/8 In. 22.00
Vase, Alaska, Totem Pole With Mountains In Background, 8 1/2 x 3 3/4 In. 85.00
Vase, Aqua, Signed, 8 In. 75.00
Vase, Aztec, Gold Horse Design, 8 1/2 x 5 1/2 In. 125.00
Vase, Chichi Bird, 5 1/2 In. 95.00
Vase, Elk, Signed, 8 In. 75.00
Vase, Eskimo Totem Pole, Signed, 8 In. 75.00
Vase, Gold Leaves, White, Yellow Speckled Ground, 9 1/4 In., Pair 265.00
Vase, Gold, Pastel Stripes On White, 15 x 10 1/2 In. 90.00
Vase, Gold, White Rings Around Body, Gold, White Trim, 12 In. 125.00
Vase, Mosaic Bird, Gold Front, Gold Rooster On Bottom, 8 x 7 In. 75.00
Vase, Mosaic, Face In Mosaic Design On The Front, 5 1/2 In. 55.00
Vase, Orange, Gold, Signed, 12 In. 155.00
Vase, Persian, Pottery, 5 x 7 In. 175.00
Vase, Persian, Pottery, 9 In. 200.00
Vase, Pink, Blue Buildings On Side, 5 x 4 In. 45.00
Vase, Rooftops, 5 In. 95.00
Vase, Rooftops, Cylinder, Signed, 8 1/2 In. 115.00
Vase, Star Steed, Signed, 6 x 9 In. 125.00
Vase, Vanity Fair, 10 x 5 In. 155.00
Vase, Walrus, Brown, Gray, 8 In. 75.00

Vase, Whimsical, 8 In.	85.00
Wall Plaque, Colorful Fruits, Plants, Gold, Signed, 5 1/2 In., Pair	95.00
Wall Pocket, Provincial Rooster, Signed, 4 x 5 In.	95.00

SATIN GLASS is a late nineteenth-century art glass. It has a dull finish that is caused by hydrofluoric acid vapor treatment. Satin glass was made in many colors and sometimes has applied decorations. Satin glass is also listed by factory name, such as Webb, or in the Mother-of-Pearl category in this book.

Cracker Jar, Shell & Seaweed, Enameled Flowers, Rose To Pink, 10 In.	290.00
Ewer, Shaded Pink, Thorn Handle, 3 Petal Top, 9 3/4 In.	135.00
Figure, Madonna & Child, Monogram, S.A. Viterwall, c.1930, 9 1/2 In.	56.00
Rose Bowl, Pink, Jack-In-The-Pulpit, Victorian, 5 3/4 In.	157.00
Rose Bowl, Rust Butterfly, Pansies, Buds On Branch, Square Crimp Top, 5 1/8 In.	165.00
Rose Bowl, Shell & Seaweed, White Lining, Crimped Top, 3 1/4 In.	75.00
Tumbler, Pink, Zigzag, Enameled Flowers, 3 3/4 In.	104.00
Vase, Applied Coral, 3 1/4 x 6 7/8 In.	258.00
Vase, Blue & Cream Flowers, Gray & White Branches, Butterfly, 7 1/2 In.	135.00
Vase, Blue To White, Sawtooth Design, Egg Shape, Ruffled Edge, 10 In.	135.00
Vase, Diamond-Quilted, Cylinder, 4 1/4 x 8 1/8 In.	85.00
Vase, Double Gourd, Diamond-Quilted, Melon Ribbed, Yellow To White, 1800s	250.00
Vase, Enameled Flowers, Gold Stipple, Cased Apricot, 15 1/2 In.	525.00
Vase, Pink To White, Crimped, Victorian, 11 In.	120.00
Vase, Purple Top Shading To White, Victorian, 9 1/2 In.	90.00
Vase, White To Pink, 2 Camphor Handles, White Lining, 4 1/2 In.	175.00
Vase, Yellow, Green, Early 20th Century, 8 1/2 In.	1035.00

SATSUMA is a Japanese pottery with a distinctive creamy beige crackled glaze. Most of the pieces were decorated with blue, red, green, orange, or gold. Almost all Satsuma found today was made after 1860. During World War I, Americans could not buy undecorated European porcelains. Women who liked to make hand painted porcelains at home began to decorate plain Satsuma. These pieces are known today as *American Satsuma*.

Bowl, 6 Scholars Interior, 2 x 5 1/4 In.	220.00
Bowl, Bird, Wisteria Design, 4 1/4 In.	115.00
Bowl, Buddhist Divinities, Gosu Blue Robes, Dragon Border, 10 In.	630.00
Bowl, Calligraphy Scrolls & Immortals, Scalloped, Oriental Mark, 11 3/4 x 4 In.	880.00
Bowl, Duck & Avian, Floral, 3 x 5 In.	2760.00
Bowl, Gilt Net & Butterflies, Signed, Nichimitsu, 19th Century, 6 1/2 In.	230.00
Bowl, Lakeside Landscape Exterior, Butter & Net Design Interior, 6 In.	259.00
Bowl, One Thousand Flowers, Flower Shape Rim, Oriental Mark, 6 1/2 x 2 1/2 In.	220.00
Bowl, Royal Procession With An Official Or Emperor In Cart, Gilt, Cobalt Blue, 6 In.	69.00
Box, Cover, Butterflies & Flowers On Side, 2 In.	240.00
Box, Cover, Scene On 8 Sides, Foo Dog Finial, Head Handles, 6 1/2 In.	55.00
Buckle, Ladies With Fans, 2 Piece	880.00
Dish, Applied Gilt Curled Kirin On 1 Side, Chrysanthemums, Birds, 8 1/2 In.	69.00
Dish, Winter Landscape Design, Shrine, Village At Sunset Scene, 10 1/4 In.	518.00
Incense Burner, Cover, Figural Design, Handles, 4 1/2 In.	40.00
Incense Burner, Domed Cover, Lohans Design, 3-Footed, Handles, 12 3/4 In.	920.00
Incense Burner, Figural Design, Pottery, 4 1/2 In.	40.00
Incense Burner, Gold Decorated, 6 In.	1680.00
Jar, Temple, Enamel, c.1900, 45 In.	1760.00
Plate, Wisteria Design, 8 1/4 In.	150.00
Rice Bowl, One Thousand Butterflies Interior, Chrysanthemums Exterior, 2 x 4 In.	1430.00
Teapot, Gilt Flowers, 2 Panels Of Women & Children In Palace Scene	400.00
Tobacco Jar, Drawstring Pouch Shape, Figural Finial, Cover, 6 3/4 In.	230.00
Urn, Moriage, 2 Handles, Converted To Lamp, 13 In.	45.00
Urn, Moriage, Polychrome Enamel Design, Reticulated, 2 Handles, 20 In.	192.50
Urn, Moriage, Reticulated, 2 Handles, 20 In.	190.00
Vase, 17 Rakan In Gilt Robes, Elephant Handles, Flared Lip, 6 In.	58.00
Vase, 2 Reserves, Woman, Warrior, Signed, 20th Century, 8 1/2 In.	345.00
Vase, 4 Scholars In A Garden, Rust, Gilt, Handles, 19th Century, 15 In.	173.00

Vase, Allover Chrysanthemums, Everted Rim, Spherical, Signed, 5 1/4 In. 138.00
Vase, Courtiers & Warrior, Multicolored, Gilt, Early 20th Century, 24 In. 1150.00
Vase, Cranes, Gilt Beaded Foliage, Cream Ground, 18 In. 247.00
Vase, Dragon, Crackled White & Burgundy, Green Ground, 12 1/2 In. 83.00
Vase, Fable Scenes, Geometric Design, Blue, Iron Red, Cream, 10 1/4 In. 138.00
Vase, Figural Landscape, Midnight Blue Ground, 8 1/4 In. 518.00
Vase, Figures Of Taoist Immortals, Stylized Leaf Borders, 17 1/2 In. 288.00
Vase, Japanese Landscape, Children, Cobalt Blue Border, Gilt, Baluster, 6 In. 330.00
Vase, Moriage, Decorated Panels, Cobalt Blue, Japan, 19th Century, 6 1/2 x 8 1/2 In. 140.00
Vase, Mountainous Riverscape, 2 Large Cartouches, Cobalt Blue, 9 In. 920.00
Vase, Nishikide Diaper, Floral, Dragon King, 2 Dancing Goddesses, Cobalt Blue, 12 In. . . . 5462.00
Vase, Pagoda, Male Figure, Mountain, 7 1/2 In. 495.00
Vase, Parrot, Basket Of Flowers, Brocade Borders, Signed, Late 19th Century, 20 In. 1150.00
Vase, Samurai & Geisha, Ring & Tassel Handles, 19th Century, 26 In. 495.00
Vase, Scenes, Samurai, Pierced Half Rosette Handles, Raised Gilt, 7 1/2 In. 495.00
Vase, Women & Children At Riverbank, Views From Terrace, Medallions, 18 1/2 In. 1150.00
Vase, Women & Children, Gilt, Late 19th Century, 12 In. 230.00

SATURDAY EVENING GIRLS, see Paul Revere Pottery category.

SCALES have been made to weigh everything from babies to gold.
Collectors search for all types. Most popular are small gold dust scales
and special grocery scales.

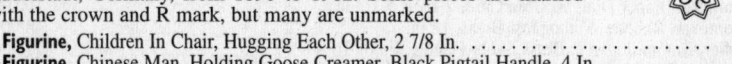

Balance, 2 Brass Trays, Mahogany Base, 19th Century, 23 1/2 In. 302.00
Balance, Aluminum, Chrome, Silver, Excelsior Spring 5.00
Balance, Birmingham, Cast Iron, Gold Painted Design, 1 Large & Small Pan, 29 1/2 In. . . . 385.00
Balance, Brass Pans, Tin Arm, Pine Glazed Case, 1 Drawer, 1800s, 18 x 12 1/2 In. 1265.00
Balance, Brass, 2 Blue Jasperware Wedgwood Insert, 5 Weights, 8 3/8 In. 465.00
Balance, Degrave Short & Fanner, 2 Brass Pans, Brass, Iron, Black, Gold, Signed, 20 In. . . 345.00
Balance, E. & T. Fairbanks, Brass & Iron 77.00
Balance, Geo. Salter & Co., Sylvester Patentee, Quadrant, Weighs To 110 Lbs. 75.00
Balance, Henry Troemner, Apothecary, Countertop 100.00
Candy, Jacobs Brothers, Pennsylvania Model, Shield, 11 x 10 In. 920.00
Computing, Dayton, Countertop, Electric Cylinder, Weight Register, 29 x 16 In. 520.00
Doctor's, Buffalo Scale Co., Brass Weight Bars & Weights, 56 In. 575.00
Egg, Germany, Green 50.00
Gold, Freeman, Wrought Iron & Brass, 9 Weights, Mahogany Case, 6 In. 660.00
Gold, Henry Troemner, Phila., Balance, Brass, Walnut Base, Drawer, 10 x 5 x 12 In. 500.00
Lollipop, Free-Weight, Black Enamel Paint, Red Pinstripe, Coin-Operated, 78 In. 1265.00
Micrometer, Marble Base, Nickel Plated Mechanism, 1903, 12 x 13 In. 635.00
Milk, Purina, Cow Chow Makes More Milk, Brass, 11 x 4 1/2 In. 130.00
Novelty, National, Floor, Brass Plated, Gold In Stripe, Early 1900s 2590.00
Pocket, Gold, Punched Wooden Case, Fitted Interior, 18th Century, 6 x 2 1/2 In. 220.00
Postage, Fairbanks, Cast Iron, Brass, 5 In. 50.00
Store, Detecto, 2 Trays, 20 x 24 In. 160.00
Table, Brass, Walnut, 19th Century, 23 1/2 x 20 x 10 1/2 In. 275.00
Weighing, Delft, Scene Of Sailing Ships, Metal Bowl, 17 In. 260.00
Weighing, Mills Standard, Paper Face, Cast Iron Bezel, Cast Iron, 67 x 15 In. 800.00
Weighing, Mills, 1 Cent, Porcelain Face, Brass & Nickel Trim, 69 x 15 In. 2015.00
Weighing, Watling, Fortune Teller Box, 1 Cent, 73 x 21 In. 175.00
Weighing, Watling, Fortune, Lollipop 1400.00
Weighing, Watling, Horoscope, Floor Model, 63 x 17 In. 275.00
Weighing, Watling, Porcelain Top Marquee, Aluminum Foot Plate, 66 In. 115.00
Weighing, Watling, Senator, Lollipop, Chicago Exposition, 1915 . . . . 1495.00
Weighing, Watling, Style One, Blue Porcelain & Cast Iron, c.1930 . . . . 2000.00
Weighing, Watling, Yur Wate, Porcelain Lollipop Face, 72 In. 115.00

SCHAFER & VATER, makers of small ceramic items, are best known for
their amusing figurals. The factory was located in Volkstedt-
Rudolstadt, Germany, from 1890 to 1962. Some pieces are marked
with the crown and R mark, but many are unmarked.

Figurine, Children In Chair, Hugging Each Other, 2 7/8 In. 135.00
Figurine, Chinese Man, Holding Goose Creamer, Black Pigtail Handle, 4 In. 135.00

Figurine, Grizzly Bear, Cowboy Dancing With Woman, No. 9870, 6 In. 310.00
Figurine, Swinger, Blue & White Dress, Apron, Cap, Body Swings, 4 5/6 In. 195.00

SCHNEIDER Glassworks was founded in 1913 at Epinay-sur-Seine, France, by Charles and Ernest Schneider. Art glass was made between 1913 and 1930. The company still produces clear crystal glass.

Bowl, Purple Mottled Glass, Signed, 1922, 13 In. 4800.00
Bowl, Stylized Bowl Of Fruit, 2 Geometric Handles, Signed, c.1925, 5 1/4 In. 750.00
Compote, Blown Into Wrought Iron Framework, Signed, 14 1/2 x 14 In. 2090.00
Ewer, Mottled Orange & Cranberry, Flaring Spout, 14 In. 1725.00
Ewer, Purple, Handle, Spout Pointing Upward, 1925, 12 1/2 In. 4800.00
Ewer, Silver Foil Inclusions, Signed, c.1930, 15 In. 12000.00
Vase, Amber, Art Deco Etch, Signed, 7 1/2 In. 375.00
Vase, Art Deco, Ice Ground, Amethyst Feet, Acid Stamped, 6 1/4 In. 550.00
Vase, Blown Into Iron Framework, 10 1/2 In. 2815.00
Vase, Blown Into Iron Framework, Removable Stand, Etched Interior, 17 In. 2530.00
Vase, Crocuses, Green Jade Flower, Deep Amethyst Foot, Signed, 14 1/2 In. 2185.00
Vase, Dark Burnt Orange, 1925, 17 3/8 In. 4800.00
Vase, Geometric Cutting, Amethyst, Signed, 19 In. . . . . .865.00 to 1540.00
Vase, Green, Brown, Orange Pussy Willows, Mottled Amber, Cameo, 17 1/2 In. 4025.00
Vase, Guirlande, Smoky Brown, Carved Frieze, Cabochons, Berries, Leaves, 7 1/2 In. . . .   1380.00
Vase, Jade, Green & Yellow To Lavender & Cobalt, Signed, 14 In. 2250.00
Vase, Jade, Orange, Blue, 12 In. 460.00
Vase, Mottled Orange, Yellow, Purple Foot, Flared, 10 In. 2300.00
Vase, Mottled Yellow, Purple Foot, Flared, 9 In. 1495.00
Vase, Orange Squares, Purple Lines, Air Bubbles, Signed, c.1925, 13 x 9 1/4 In. .3150.00 to 5750.00
Vase, Red & Yellow, Purple Foot, Signed, 8 In. 990.00
Vase, Trumpet, Mottled Yellow To Orange, Purple Stem, Iron Stand, 11 In. 1840.00
Vase, Violet Flowers, Yellow Centers, Soft Pink Ground, 9 In. 1090.00

SCIENTIFIC INSTRUMENTS of all kinds are included in this category. Other categories such as Barometer, Binoculars, Dental, Nautical, Medical, and Thermometer may also price scientific apparatus.

Adding Machine, Webb, Brass & Wood, Box, Pat'd. March 10, 1868, 6 3/4 In. 1300.00
Altimeter, From Downed German Aircraft 545.00
Binocular Microscope, Achromatic, J.B. Dancer, 1855 . . . .*Illus*   9037.00
Calculator, T.J. Marshall & Co., England, For Compound Addition, Case, 5 In. 400.00
Chronometer, Brass, Mahogany Case, Brass Binding, Battery Operated 230.00
Chronometer, Zenith, Grand Prix Paris 1900, Swiss Made, 4 1/2 x 5 3/4 In. 1160.00
Compass, Brass Case, France, 22 1/2 In. 57.00
Compass, C.C. Hutchinson, 6 x 6 x 4 In. 126.00
Compass, Dave Cook Sporting Goods, Celluloid, 1 1/2 In. 66.00
Compass, Dolphins Either Side, Tails Support Frame, Brass, 13 1/2 In. 500.00
Compass, Dry, Wooden Case, Lionel, No. 712, 1942 . . . .   495.00
Compass, Electro-Meter, Wooden Base, 3 1/2 In. 125.00
Compass, F.W. Lincoln, Jr. & Co., Boston, Mass., 19th Century, 7 In. 440.00
Compass, H.W. Hunt, Washington, D.C., Brass, Wooden Case, 9 In. 430.00
Compass, Surveyor's, Boston, Early 18th Century, 12 1/4 x 5 1/2 In. 1035.00
Compass, Surveyor's, Brass, Attributed Buff & Berger, Boston, 1800s, 11 In. 415.00
Compass, Surveyor's, Brass, Wooden Case, 19th Century 4600.00
Compass, Surveyor's, Loring & Churchill, Boston, Brass, 12 1/4 In. 1850.00
Compass, Surveyor's, Patent 1878, Wooden Case, Tripod 2970.00
Flowmeter, Ellis Pattern, Buff & Buff, Copper Pipe, Cast Iron Base, 18 In. 220.00
Galvanometer, Tangent Form, Brass, Wood, 16 1/4 In. 395.00
Gyroscope, Bohnberger's, Knott App. Co., Boston, c.1915, 16 In. 590.00
Hydrometer, Sikes, Marked, London, Brass, Box, 7 3/4 x 3 1/2 x 2 1/4 In. 155.00
Hydrometer, Sikes, Wickenden & Sons, England, Brass, Box, 1800s, 8 x 4 In. 188.00
Inclinometer, Brass, 17 In. 90.00
Inclinometer, Mahogany, Brass, 19th Century, 30 In. 680.00
Inclinometer, Paper Dial, Wooden Case, 7 1/2 x 5 1/2 In. 100.00
Inclinometer, Rabone, Mahogany, Brass, 12 In. 485.00
Magnifier, Entomologist's, Brass, Ivory Handle, Folds To 5/8 x 2 In. 210.00
Microscope, Bausch & Lomb, Dissecting, Lock, Wooden Case, 1800s, 8 1/4 In. 530.00

Microscope, Beck, Traversing, Brass, Cast Iron Base, Box, 9 x 14 1/2 In. 440.00
Microscope, Cary Type, England, Portable, Brass, c.1820, 11 1/4 In. 980.00
Microscope, Cuff Type, England, 1780 ....*Illus* 2598.00
Microscope, England, Miniature, Original Wooden Case, 4 1/2 In. 750.00
Microscope, Ernst Leitz, Brass, Cast Iron Stand, Wooden Case, 14 In. 275.00
Microscope, France, Brass, Box With Pullout Drawer, c.1830-1850, 12 In. 800.00
Microscope, France, Student, Brass, Box Of Slides, Box, 19th Century, 8 1/2 In. 335.00
Microscope, Hartnack, Paris, Brass, Box, Attachments, c.1885, 12 1/2 In. 800.00
Microscope, I.L. Lyons Co., La., Original Carrying Case, 12 In. 490.00
Microscope, Murray & Heath, London, c.1870, 9 In. 530.00
Microscope, Nachet Et Fils, Paris, Brass, Box, c.1890, 13 In. 350.00
Model, Cram, Globe, Physical, 39 In. 1550.00
Model, Venus, Square Plinth, Iron, 20th Century, 19 1/2 In. 92.00
Octant, J. Ford, England, Ivory, Brass, Ebony, Case 550.00
Octant, S. Thaxter & Son, Boston, Brown, Ivory, Case, Paper Labels 750.00
Planetarium, Tellurium, Table, c.1910, 14 x 24 x 7 1/2 In. 1610.00
Prism, Paris, Double, Liquid, 3 Adjustable Feet, 1880, 4 1/4 x 4 3/4 In. 445.00
Protractor, Calculating, G.H. Whitescarver, Metal, 13 3/4 In. 700.00
Protractor, Charting, J.W. Strange, Patent June 13, 1876, 15 3/4 In. 310.00
Quadrant, Frye & Shaw, N.Y., Brass, Ivory Scales, Ebony Case 775.00
Ruler, Smith Beck & Beck Corhill, London, Rolling, Ivory, Ebony, Brass, 15 In. 1100.00
Sextant, Brass Swing Arm, Floral Engraving, Brass & Ivory, Case 858.00
Sextant, C.C. Hutchinson, Boston, Ivory Inlay, Mahogany Box, 11 1/2 In. 748.00
Sextant, No. 27, London, Metal Cover, 19th Century, 3 1/4 In. 400.00
Sextant, W.C. Mann, Gloucester, Brass Case 315.00
Sundial, Portable, Brass, Minute Hand, 18th Century, 4 1/4 In. 1345.00
Sundial, T. Waddell, For Lat. 40 1/2 Deg., Slate, Wooden Frame, 8 x 5 1/2 In. 595.00
Telescope, 3 Draw, Brass, Mahogany Case, 30 In. 520.00
Telescope, 3 Draw, Brass, Spencer & Co., London, 26 In. 144.00
Telescope, 3 Draw, Brass, Sunshade, 20 x 1 1/2 In. 165.00
Telescope, 3 Draw, Brass, Textured Hand Grip, 17 1/2 In. 165.00
Telescope, 3 Draw, Mahogany, Brass, 12 1/4 In. 85.00
Telescope, 3 Draw, Wooden Rod, Brass Tripod Stand, 1830, 44 In. 4800.00
Telescope, 4 Draw, Brass, Leather Barrel, 38 In. 345.00
Telescope, 4 Draw, Marked Made In France, E. Vion Paris, Metal, 35 1/4 In. 310.00
Telescope, Arnold & Son, 2 Draw, Brass, Wooden Barrel, 36 In. 195.00
Telescope, Brass, Leather Covered Barrel, Lens Cover, 38 In. 345.00
Telescope, Brass, Wooden Barrel, 19th Century, 36 In. 520.00
Telescope, Brass, Wooden Barrel, England, 36 In. 195.00
Telescope, C. Zeiss, Brass Case, 12 1/2 In. 200.00
Telescope, Lord Bury, N.Y., 3 Draw, 30 In. 260.00
Telescope, Single Draw, Brass, 40 In. ....125.00 to 126.00
Telescope, T.T. Messer, Brass, Leather Wrapped Barrel, 36 In. 145.00
Telescope, Walnut Case, Mahogany, Brass Mounted, 40 In. 1840.00
Transit, Astronomical, U.S.A., Brass, c.1870, 9 1/2 In. 990.00
Transit, Builder's, Up & Down, Side To Side Movement, Brass Base 340.00
Transit, Surveyor's, Brass, Wood Base, Leather Strap Handle, Box, 11 1/2 In. 2350.00
Transit, Surveyor's, Buff & Berger Co., Boston, Mass., 1900, 10 x 9 x 14 In. 360.00

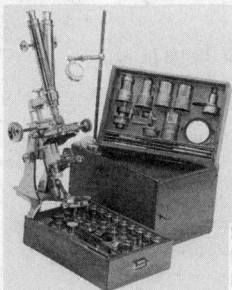

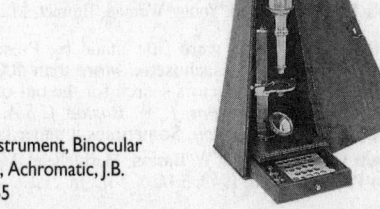

Scientific Instrument,
Microscope,
Cuff Type, England, 1780

Scientific Instrument, Binocular
Microscope, Achromatic, J.B.
Dancer, 1855

Transit, Surveyor's, Scales, Compass, 3 Fluid Levels, Case, 11 x 9 In. 795.00
Transit, Surveyor's, Theodolite, W&LE Gurley, Brass, Lacquer, 1929, 13 In. 1000.00
Traversing, R. & J. Beck Ltd., London, Brass, Cast Iron Base, Box, 9 x 14 1/2 In. 400.00
Waywiser, Tool Used To Measure Distance, Mahogany, George II, c.1740 . . . .   8750.00

SCRIMSHAW is bone or ivory or whale's teeth carved by sailors and
others for entertainment during the sailing-ship days. Some scrimshaw
was carved as early as 1800. There are modern scrimshanders making
pieces today on bone, ivory, or plastic. Other pieces may be found in
the Ivory and Nautical categories.

Basket, Whalebone, Carved Coconut Shell, Domed Pedestal Base, 6 1/2 In. 2645.00
Bone, Dogsled Team Meeting Walrus, Russia, 10 In. 115.00
Box, Ditty, Baleen, 3-Finger, Pierced With Diamonds, Hearts, Mass., 1866, 7 In. 1955.00
Box, Ditty, Mahogany Cover, Whalebone Band, Mahogany Base, 6 x 10 In. 4945.00
Busk, Baleen, Hearts, Trees, Buildings, Mid 19th Century, 13 1/4 In. 1150.00
Busk, Whalebone, 4 Panels, Woman, Hat, Man & Woman Embracing, 13 1/2 In. 920.00
Busk, Whalebone, 5 Panels, Spread Eagle, Ship, Signed, 12 1/2 In. 1265.00
Busk, Whalebone, Engraved, Various Scenes, Diamond Border, 1800s, 13 1/4 In. 3335.00
Busk, Whalebone, Flowers, Tree, Hex Design, Signed, L. Smith, 13 1/2 In. 1670.00
Cup, Horn, Engraved, Hunting Scene, England, c.1800, 4 x 2 1/2 In. 195.00
Dipper, Whalebone, Carved Coconut Shell, Gourd, 17 1/2 In. 1380.00
Dish, Whalebone, Mahogany, Oyster Shell, 20th Century, 6 In.   1150.00
Horn, Map, New York, Heraldic Crest, Lion, Unicorn, c.1760, 15 1/2 In. 860.00
Horn, Water Buffalo, Depicting Hut & Palm Tree, Southeast Asia, 35 In., Pair 69.00
Ivory, Caribou In Mountains, G. Vukson, 22 1/2 In. 750.00
Ivory, Walrus Tusk, Whale Engraving, 20 1/4 In. 310.00
Knife, Bone Sheath, Leather, Allover Sailfish Decoration, West Indies, 7 5/8 In. 105.00
Pie Crimper, Whalebone, Heart Design, Baleen Handle, 8 3/4 In. 8625.00
Pie Crimper, Whalebone, Ivory, Pierced Star Wheel, Whalebone Handle, 8 In. 3795.00
Pie Crimper, Whalebone, Star Wheel, Diamond Handle, 9 1/2 In. 2185.00
Rolling Pin, Whalebone, Baleen Cuffs, Mid 19th Century, 16 In. 750.00
Stand, Sewing, Whalebone, Ivory Inlaid, Bun Feet, Mid 19th Century, 17 In. 5405.00
Swift, Bone, Cherrywood, Ivory Standard, Ball Feet, New England, 18 In. 1080.00
Swift, Whalebone, Red, Black Linear Design, 19th Century, 25 In. 10925.00
Tooth, Whale, 3-Masted Warship, Floral Wreath, Eagle, 1801, 5 1/2 In. 2070.00
Tooth, Whale, 3-Masted Whaling Vessel, 19th Century, 6 In. 1095.00
Tooth, Whale, Boat, Billowed Sail, On Sea, Harpoon, 5 In. 200.00
Tooth, Whale, Cane Handle, Turk's Head 2000.00
Tooth, Whale, Clock Tower, Woman & Guitar, Multicolored, 4 5/8 In. 920.00
Tooth, Whale, Eagle & Shield, People On Horseback, Pedestal, 5 1/8 In. 750.00
Tooth, Whale, Engraved, Colored, Robert Spring 3800.00
Tooth, Whale, Queen Of The Sea, United States Secret Service, 1800s, 6 In. 2415.00
Tooth, Whale, Sailing Ships, 7 In., Pair 5175.00
Tooth, Whale, Sea & Island Scene, Multicolored, 8 In. 2300.00
Tooth, Whale, Sperm Whale, Whaling Scenes, Brass Mounts, 6 x 4 3/4 In. 3450.00
Tooth, Whale, The Constitution, The Union, We Live In Hopes, 4 3/4 In. 2415.00
Tooth, Whale, Whaling Scene, Signed, R. Spring, 71 x 5 In. 260.00
Tusk, Walrus, 3-Masted Sailing Ship, American Eagle, 19th Century, 19 In. 4715.00
Tusk, Walrus, Eagle, Liberty, Dancing Couple, Sailor, American, c.1850, 15 In. 220.00
Tusk, Walrus, Ivory, Copper Band, 6 7/8 In. 316.00
Tusk, Walrus, Uncarved, 16 1/2 In. 241.00
Tusk, Woman In Dress 1 Side, Girl With Flower & Mermaid Other, 18 1/8 In. 770.00
Whale's Tooth, Engraved, British Ship, Calliope, 19th Century, 5 3/4 In. 3450.00
Whale's Tooth, Engraved, Young Woman, Bonnet, Mid 19th Century, 6 In. 920.00

SEBASTIAN MINIATURES were first made by Prescott W. Baston in
1938 in Marblehead, Massachusetts. More than 400 different designs
have been made, and collectors search for the out-of-production models. The mark may say *Copr. P. W. Baston U.S.A.*, or *P. W. Baston,
U.S.A.*, or *Prescott W. Baston*. Sometimes a paper label was used.

Abraham Lincoln, Prescott W. Baston, Marblehead, Mass., 4 In.   16.00
Boston Public Garden, 1949, 5 1/2 x 2 1/2 In. 41.00

Charles Dickens, 1952, 2 7/8 In.	43.00
Clown, Emmett Kelley, 1949, 3 x 1 3/4 In.	25.00
Corner Drug Store, 1949, 3 x 3 1/8 x 1 3/4 In.	14.00
First Teddy Bear, Signed, Woody Baston, 1984, 2 1/2 x 1 3/4 In.	17.00
Hanging The Stockings, Gray Sticker, 1983, 3 x 4 In.	16.00
Holiday Sleigh Ride, Orange Sticker, 1986, 2 x 4 In.	18.00
Manger Nativity Scene, 1961, 4 x 2 x 3 1/2 In.	22.00
Manger Scene, Mary, Joseph & Baby Jesus, 3 7/8 In.	16.00
Oliver Twist & The Beadle, Original Box, 2 7/8 In.	25.00
Piano Player, 1951, 2 1/2 In.	14.00
Scrooge, Prescott W. Baston, Marblehead, Mass., 3 1/4 In.	56.00
Toll House, 1947, 3 1/2 In.	76.00

SEG, see Paul Revere Pottery category.

SEVRES porcelain has been made in Sevres, France, since 1769. Many copies of the famous ware have been made. The name originally referred to the works of the Royal Porcelain factory. The name now includes any of the wares made in the town of Sevres, France. The entwined lines with a center letter used as the mark is one of the most forged marks in antiques. Be very careful to identify Sevres by quality, not just by mark.

Bonbon, Architectural Views & Landscape, Domed Lid, Underplate, 1880s, 8 In.	805.00
Bottle Cooler, Border Of Roses, Gilt Garland, Floral Sprays, 5 x 6 1/4 In., Pair	373.00
Bowl, Decagon, Turquoise Green, Bird Design, c.1800, 9 3/4 In.	3300.00
Box, Cover, Panel Of Cherubs, Gilt, Deep Blue Ground, 16 In.	3900.00
Box, Cover, Princess Lamballe In Bath With Ribbons, Floral Garlands, Pink, 2 5/8 In.	345.00
Butter Tub, Attached Stand, Cover, Hoop Knop, 3 Floral Panels On Rim Of Stand, 8 In.	1200.00
Cachepot, Putti & French Court Women, Gilt Scroll Around Decal, Square, 8 1/4 In.	770.00
Casket, Courting Couple, Floral Side Reserves, Floral Interior, Rolli, 4 1/4 In.	1265.00
Casket, Hinged Cover, Applied Central Design, Berry Laurel, Scrolled Acanthus, 5 In.	860.00
Casket, Jewel, Gilt, Brass, Lapis Form, Leaf Mount, 3 3/4 In.	690.00
Chocolate Pot, Floral Garlands, Blue Ribbons, Gilt, Side Spout, 7 1/4 In.	520.00
Cooler, Wine, Flower Spray, Fruit, Shell & Scroll Handles, c.1771, 7 1/4 In.	6000.00
Cup, 2 Handles, Cover, Stand, Garlands, Laurel, Berries, Gilt Edge, c.1765, 7 1/4 In.	7200.00
Cup, Chocolate, Cover, Berry & Leaf Finial, 5 3/4 In.	935.00
Dresser Set, Floral Bouquet, Gilt Design, Late 19th Century, 4 Piece	230.00
Inkstand, Gilt Enamel Design, Floral Cartouches, Ball Feet, Green Ground, 3 1/4 In.	170.00
Jardiniere, Bronze, Scrolled Handles, Roses, Plum Ground, 4 3/4 x 6 x 4 In.	860.00
Jardiniere, Light Blue Bands, Gilt Highlights, Flowers, Handles, 5 1/4 In.	230.00
Paperweight, Central Colorless Entwined Spirals, 4 1/4 In.	34.00
Pedestal, Allegorical Figures, Musical Trophies, Circular, Bronze, 44 In.	4800.00
Pedestal, Figural Panels, Cobalt Ground, Gilt, Signed, L. Ferlern, 1900, 43 In.	10800.00
Plate, Dessert, Square, Medallion, Palmettes, Arrows, Mauve, Blue, c.1790, 8 1/8 In., Pair	5400.00
Plate, Portrait, Mme. De Recamier, Green Border, N In Wreath, 9 1/2 In.	165.00
Plate, Portrait, Of Madame De Lambale With Floral Garland, Ribbon In Hair, 9 1/8 In.	230.00
Plate, Women Profiles, Irises & Forget-Me-Not Border, Blue Ground, 10 In., Pair	490.00
Teakettle, Gilt Dolphin Mouth, Garland Of Flowers On Shoulder, Wooden Handle, 7 In.	3300.00
Tray, Bronze Holder, Rectangular	896.00
Urn, 2 Full Figures, Cartouches, 19th Century, 24 In.	1150.00
Urn, Courting Scenes, Hand Painted, Bronze Mounts, 23 In., Pair	3920.00
Urn, Napoleon On Horseback, Laurel Branches, Cobalt Ground, 35 1/2 In., Pair	12000.00
Vase, Allegorical Figures Within Landscape Scene, Gilt, Bronze, 37 In., Pair	14400.00
Vase, Bronze Mount, Couple, Flowers, Ram's-Head Handles, 25 In.	2300.00
Vase, Bronze Mount, Handles, Battle Scenes, Cobalt Blue Ground, 19 In.	3680.00
Vase, Continuous Scene Of Gentleman In Landscape Holding Bird, 10 In.	287.00
Vase, Drapery Swags Rising To Berry Laurel Border, Courting Couple Scene, 29 In.	6325.00
Vase, Figural Panel, Landscape Panel, Bleu Celeste Ground, 32 In., Pair	18000.00
Vase, Hand Painted Scene Of Woman, Ormolu Mount, 6 1/4 In.	196.00
Vase, Landscape Scene, Figural Panel, Yellow Ground, Handles, Bronze, Gilt, 38 In.	6600.00
Vase, Leaves, Clear Glass Ground, Frilled Foot, Signed, 8 3/4 In.	1495.00
Vase, Panel Of Courting Couple, Gilt Border, Cobalt Blue Ground, 19 In., Pair	2160.00
Vase, Portrait, Young Woman, Signed, 5 In.	448.00

SEWER TILE figures were made by workers at the sewer tile and pipe factories in the Ohio area during the late nineteenth and early twentieth centuries. Figurines, small vases, and cemetery vases were favored. Often the finished vase was a piece of the original pipe with added decorations and markings. All types of sewer tile work are now considered folk art by collectors.

Bank, Dog, Seated, Lock Collar, Slot In Back Of Head, 10 1/2 In.	220.00
Bust, Abe Lincoln, Shiny Glaze, Flowing Black On Jacket, Eyes, 7 1/8 In.	110.00
Feeder, Chicken, Incised Tree Trunk, Handle On Top, 10 1/2 In.	220.00
Figurine, Alligator, Ohio, 15 In.	440.00
Figurine, Cat, Seated, Copper Speckles, 7 In.	330.00
Figurine, Crow, On Stump, Glazed, Initials E.J.E., 9 x 14 In.	990.00
Figurine, Dog, Chas. Domino, 7 In.	195.00
Figurine, Dog, Spaniel, Incised Details, Collar & Chain, Jack Adamson, 8 1/4 In.	2275.00
Figurine, Dog, Spaniel, Incised Eyes, Nose, Mouth & Paws, 10 1/2 In.	330.00
Figurine, Dog, Spaniel, Seated, Punched Collar, Lock, 11 1/2 In.	165.00
Figurine, Lion, Red Clay, Rectangular Base, Incised, Wadsworth, O., 8 x 4 In.	275.00
Figurine, Owl, Incised Line On Trunk Base & Head, 12 3/4 In.	550.00
Figurine, Owl, On Log, 20th Century, 8 1/2 In.	165.00
Figurine, Umbrella Stand, Incised Tree Trunk, Roses, 25 1/2 In.	330.00
Pitcher, Indian Head With Headdress Form, c.1860	1210.00
Planter, Incised Made By Donald Milby, 1958, 9 1/2 x 10 In.	82.00
Planter, Lions' Heads, Leaves, Triangular Base, 23 In.	193.00
Planter, Stump, 4 Branches, Tooled Bark, 17 x 10 In.	330.00
Planter, Stump, Tooled Bark, Margaret H. Dryden, Born 1890, Died 1942, 24 1/2 In.	250.00
Planter, Tooled Bark, 5 Ducks, Impersonating Woodpecker, 19 In.	470.00
Planter, Tree Trunk Form, J.B. Leshner, Born 1888, 39 x 20 In.	385.00
Plaque, Fish, Ohio, 10 1/2 In.	358.00

SEWING equipment of all types is collected, from sewing birds that held the cloth to tape measures, needle books, and old wooden spools. Sewing machines are included here. Needlework pictures are listed in the Picture category.

Basket, Cover, Mahogany, Signed, Heywood-Wakefield, c.1880	336.00
Basket, Painted Frame, Chintz	750.00
Basket, Reed Lined, Handle Over Hinged Lid, 7 In.	89.00
Basket, Splint, Loop Handles, Compartmental Interior, 16 x 9 1/2 x 6 1/2 In.	635.00
Basket, Wicker, Wooden Beads, Round, 6 1/2 In.	19.00
Bird, Rosewood, Herringbone Inlay, Velvet Pincushion, Mirror, c.1800, 5 In.	715.00
Bird, Velvet Pincushion, Wrought Iron	550.00
Bobbin Clamp, Lacemaker's, Rosewood, England, c.1790	675.00
Box, Birch, Lift Lid, Harbor Scene, Early 19th Century, 4 3/4 x 11 1/2 In.	6600.00
Box, Canted & Scalloped Sides, Flowers, c.1800, 3 1/2 x 8 1/4 In.	6600.00
Box, Chinese Figures, Floral Sprays, Dragon's-Head Feet, Drawer, 19th Century, 6 3/4 In.	690.00
Box, Cover, Mother-Of-Pearl, Brass Inlay, Flowers, Continental, 4 1/4 In.	260.00
Box, Decorated, Mustard Paint, Stenciled Flowers, Fruit, Lift-Out Tray, 5 1/2 x 8 In.	1150.00
Box, Hinged Cover, Walnut, Black Lined Interior, Blue Fabric, Italy, 7 1/4 x 8 In.	1150.00
Box, Inlaid Star On Lid, Fitted Interior	3740.00
Box, Lithographed Image On Lid, Marbleized Paper Interior, Sectioned, 1830, 10 In.	260.00
Box, Mahogany Inlay, Philadelphia, 19th Century, 10 x 8 1/2 x 4 In.	975.00
Box, Mahogany, Lithographed, Rectangular, Marbleized, Compartments, 1830, 10 x 7 In.	220.00
Box, Neoclassical, Mahogany, Chamfered Hinged Lid, Hand Painted, 4 3/4 x 7 x 10 In.	1093.00
Box, Pincushion Top, Lined Drawer, Remember Me 1905, Bracket Feet, 6 7/8 x 5 1/2 In.	170.00
Box, Pine, Building & Trees Design, Green Pincushion Top, c.1820, 2 1/2 x 4 1/4 In.	605.00
Box, Pine, Silver & Gold Stars, Flower & Leaf Sliding Lid, 4 1/4 x 9 In.	5225.00
Box, Rosewood, Regency, Sarcophagus Shape, Velvet Pincushion, 8 x 9 x 5 In.	431.00
Box, Stencil Design, Silver & Gold Stars, Smoke Ground, Sliding Lid, 1808, 5 x 9 In.	5200.00
Box, Thread, Tartonware, 4 Bone Pegs, Clark & Co., 10 x 3 1/2 In.	1200.00
Box, Wavy Birch Inlay, Hearts, Diamonds, Interior Sections, 6 x 11 3/4 x 8 1/2 In.	1150.00
Cabinet, Metal, 18 Shuttles, 73 Tubes With Needles, 46 Bobbins, Boye Needle Co., 1906 .	370.00
Cabinet, Spool, see Advertising category under Cabinet, Spool.	
Caddy, Cherry, Ivory Lined Thread Holes, 1 Drawer In Bottom, Pincushion Top, 6 In.	220.00
Caddy, Pincushion Top, Tabs Hold Thread, Scissors In Bottom, Tin	48.00

Caddy, Thimble Drawer, Scissor Holder Back Of Chair, Plywood, 8 1/2 In. 32.00
Caddy, Thread, 3 Tiers, Wire Pins, Wooden, 10 1/4 In. 247.00
Chalk, Tailors' & Dressmakers', Tailor Box, 3 1/4 x 2 In. 10.00
Clamp, Hemming, Bronze, Fabric, Hand Clutching Hook, 3 3/4 In. 575.00
Clamp, Ivory, Carved, Leaf & Tulip Motifs, Close-Fisted Hand Screw, 5 1/4 In. 1840.00
Clamp, Spool, Cutter, Ivory, Abalone, Diamond Shape Inlay, 3 1/2 In. 633.00
Clamp, Wrought Iron, Spool Holder, Pincushion, Thumbscrew, 1800s, 7 In. 230.00
Darner Egg, Wood, Brass, 1 3/4 x 18 1/2 In. 57.50
Kit, 2 Women On Terrace On Lid, Velvet Lined, Silver Handled Tools, Lacquered, 6 In. . . . 373.00
Machine, American No. 1, Portable, Wooden Box, 1875 . . . . 595.00
Machine, Elliptic, Treadle 500.00
Machine, Gold Medal, Chain Stitch, 1870 . . . . 595.00
Machine, Grover & Baker, Plain Treadle Base, 1869 . . . . 364.00
Machine, Grover & Baker, Treadle 500.00
Machine, Ideal, Chain Stitch, Nickel Plate, Box, England, 1920 . . . . 198.00
Machine, Junior Miss Singer, Battery Operated, Instructions 25.00
Machine, National Sewing Machine Co., 1910 . . . . 106.00
Machine, Pleating, Red Wash, Shoe Feet, George R. Houghton, Pat. Aug. 8, 1869, 16 In. . 288.00
Machine, Sewhandy Model No. 20, Box, 1960 . . . . 106.00
Machine, Shaw & Clark, Chain Stitch, Biddeford, Me., 1864 . . . . 7270.00
Machine, Singer, Featherweight Model 221, Carrying Case 345.00
Machine, Singer, Featherweight, Enclosed Tray, Tools, Model 221 . . . . 300.00
Machine, Singer, Featherweight, Portable, Electric, Original Case, 1940 . . . . 152.00
Machine, Singer, Model 66, Portable, Inscribed Great Britain, 1930s 95.00
Machine, Singer, New Family, 1872 . . . . 99.00
Machine, Westinghouse, Crop Cabinet, Attachments 165.00
Machine, Willcox & Gibbs, Chain Stitch, 1885 . . . . 198.00
Machine, Willcox & Gibbs, Electric, 1930 . . . . 198.00
Machine, Willcox & Gibbs, Several Patent Dates, 1882 . . . . 195.00
Machine, Winchester Electric, Wooden Cabinet Cover, 20 1/4 In. 600.00
Mirror, Seamstress, Oak, Triple Style 1750.00
Needle Case, 1 Drawer, Porcelain Knobs, Divided Interior, Crowley's, 14 In. 220.00
Needle Case, Brass, Gilded, c.1700 . . . . 595.00
Needle Case, Butterfly Casket, Avery, 2 3/4 In. 230.00
Needle Case, Engraved Brass, Pearl Panels, France, c.1720, 3 1/4 In. 595.00
Needle Case, Floral, Avery, 1 3/4 In. 210.00
Needle Case, Geometric, Figural Design, 18K Gold 316.00
Needle Case, Golden Casket, Avery, 2 3/4 In. 225.00
Needle Case, Horseshoe, Avery 335.00
Needle Case, Linsey-Woolsey, 25 Needles, New England 55.00
Needle Case, Tole, Red, Yellow, Green, 16 Needles, Mid 19th Century, 9 1/4 In. 28.00
Pincushion, Ceramic, 3 In. 12.00
Pincushion, Embroidered, 8 x 8 In. 17.00
Pincushion, Jester, Ruffled Collar, Yellow Hat, 2 1/2 x 4 1/4 In. 125.00
Pincushion, Red, Green, Brown, Blue, Yellow, Wool Top, Pa., 1870, 5 3/4 x 4 In. 660.00
Pincushion, Scissors Holder, Poodle, Spaghetti Fur, Japan, 7 1/2 In. . . . . *Illus* 30.00
Pincushion, Silk Thread, Velvet, 3 In. 8.00
Pincushion, Silk, Straight Pin Design, Welcome Little Stranger, Rectangular, 1847 . . . . . . 650.00
Pincushion, Souvenir, Wyoming 14.00
Pincushion, Strawberry Form, Green Leaves, Pa., Mid 19th Century, 6 3/4 In. 710.00
Pincushion, Tufted Strawberry, 12 Strawberries, Pa., 8 1/4 In. 1430.00
Pincushion & Tape Measure, Figural Hen, Ceramic, Nesco Imports 35.00
Pincushion Dolls are listed in their own category.
Scissors, Buttonhole 25.00
Scissors, Dainty, 5 In. 14.00
Shears, Tailor's, Brass Handle, Wilkinson 165.00
Spool Cabinets are in the Advertising category under Cabinet, Spool.
Spool Holder, 2 Tiers For Spools, 1 Base Drawer, Ivory Pull, 11 1/2 In. 275.00
Spool Holder, Cherry, Metal Posts, Pincushion Top, J.C. Brown, 1954, 7 In. 165.00
Spool Holder, Maple, Red Paint, New England, 18th Century 495.00
Spool Holder, Merry-Go-Round Form, Tiered, Animals, 16 1/2 In. 575.00
Spool Holder, Walnut, Round, 19th Century, 8 1/2 In. 303.00
Spool Winder, Ivory, Carved, Triple Spool, Heart Shape Thumbscrew, 6 1/2 In. 805.00

When washing old fabrics, try to
use distilled water for the final
rinse. Don't use chlorine bleach on
old linens. Yellowed fabrics can
sometimes be whitened with
denture-cleaning tablets.

Sewing, Pincushion,
Scissors Holder,
Poodle, Spaghetti Fur,
Japan, 7 1/2 In.

Stand, Knitting, Maple, Open Center Section, Thread At Top, Late 19th Century, 30 In.	165.00
Stand, Mahogany, Swivel Base, 4 Drawers, Inlaid Design, 26 1/2 In.	5500.00
Swift, Brass Pin Cup, Steel, Red Silk Ribbons, 22 1/2 x 25 1/2 In.	5980.00
Swift, Carved Bone, Rosewood Base, 1 Drawer	9900.00
Swift, Double, Star, Flower, Moon Wax Inlay, Wooden, Durham & Dyer, 31 1/2 x 19 In.	2070.00
Swift, Ivory, Bone, Wood, Barrel Clamp, American, 19th Century, 17 x 16 In.	690.00
Tape Loom, Heart Cutout In Crest, Initials & Date, 1817, 14 1/2 In.	2870.00
Tape Measure, 2 Dogs In Basket, Celluloid, Japan, 2 1/4 In.	135.00
Tape Measure, Acorn, Ivory & Vegetable Ivory, Carved & Pierced, c.1875	163.00
Tape Measure, Balloon	1250.00
Tape Measure, Basket Of Fruit, Celluloid, 1 3/4 In.	95.00
Tape Measure, Basket Of Fruit, Celluloid, 2 In.	130.00 to 165.00
Tape Measure, Basket Of Fruit, Ladybug Shape Handle, 2 In.	110.00
Tape Measure, Bear, Celluloid, 1950s, 2 1/2 In.	75.00
Tape Measure, Chalet, White 1 Side, Gold Lettering On Back	155.00
Tape Measure, Donkey, On Stand, Japan, 2 1/4 In.	170.00
Tape Measure, Elephant, Celluloid, 2 In.	125.00
Tape Measure, Elephant, Cloth, Japan, 3 1/4 In.	35.00
Tape Measure, Flower Basket, Ladybug Handle, Celluloid, 1 1/2 In.	85.00
Tape Measure, Flower Girl, Celluloid, Germany, 1920s, 2 1/8 In.	90.00
Tape Measure, Flower, Celluloid, Germany, 1 3/4 In.	110.00
Tape Measure, Flowerpot, Celluloid, Japan, 2 1/4 In.	85.00
Tape Measure, Fly Pull, Original Box, Tin	16.00
Tape Measure, General Electric Monitor Refrigerator	50.00
Tape Measure, Hat, c.1860	235.00
Tape Measure, Hoover, Canister Vacuum Shape	27.50
Tape Measure, Indian Head, With Cigar, Celluloid, Japan, 1 1/2 In.	175.00 to 210.00
Tape Measure, Kangaroo With Joey, 2 3/4 In.	100.00
Tape Measure, Lady With Muff, Germany, 2 In.	155.00
Tape Measure, Lamb, Celluloid, Germany, 1900-1920, 3 In.	166.00
Tape Measure, Liberty Bell, Benson's Wild Animal Farm, Germany, 2 In.	110.00
Tape Measure, Lucky Joy Germ, Celluloid, 1920s, 2 1/4 In.	75.00
Tape Measure, Orange Crush, Celluloid, 1930s, 1 1/4 In.	132.00
Tape Measure, Pennsylvania Salt, Lewis Lye	45.00
Tape Measure, Pig In Boot, Celluloid, Japan, 2 1/4 In.	95.00
Tape Measure, Pig In Shoe	80.00
Tape Measure, Pig, Aqua, Celluloid, Occupied Japan	45.00
Tape Measure, Pig, Blue, Celluloid, Japan	45.00
Tape Measure, Pig, Celluloid, 2 1/2 In.	40.00
Tape Measure, Pig, Hat, Little Piggie Comes From Texas, Japan, 2 3/4 In.	39.00
Tape Measure, Pig, Pink, Plastic	35.00
Tape Measure, Snipe, Germany, 2 1/2 In.	280.00
Tape Measure, Terrier & Puppy, Japan, 2 In.	155.00
Tape Measure, Turtle, Pull My Head But Not My Leg, Metal, 3 In.	250.00
Tape Measure, Union Pacific, Logo	15.00
Thimble, Beethoven, Profile On Front	7.50
Thimble, Birthstone, November, Topaz, Bone China	9.00
Thimble, Bust Of Paul II, Bone China	34.00

Thimble, Chased Design, Leatherette Case, 14K Yellow Gold	120.00
Thimble, Climbing Frog, Pewter, Climbing To Top	26.00
Thimble, Cupid With Banner, Sterling Silver, 3/4 In.	355.00
Thimble, Gold Rim, Mother-Of-Pearl, 3/4 In.	525.00
Thimble, Levi's, Bone China, Gold Band Around Base	9.00
Thimble, Mermaid, Sitting On Top	10.00
Thimble, Merry-Go-Round, 6 Sides, 3 Horses Going Around, Bone China	12.00
Thimble, Owl, Sitting On Branch, Sterling Silver & Pewter, Gold Rim, 2 In.	24.00
Thimble, Rocking Horse, White Face, Brown Rockers	24.00
Thimble, Scalloped Rim, Sterling Silver	38.00
Thimble, Stitch In Time, Sterling Silver, 3/4 In.	535.00
Thimble, Winston Churchill's Face, Cigar In Mouth, Wearing Hat	21.00
Thimble Holder, Queen Victoria Centennial	195.00
Thimble Holder, Sterling Silver, Peg Inside, Victorian	135.00
Thimble Holder, Sweet Grass, With Dorcas Sterling Thimble	85.00
Thimble Holder, Vegetable Ivory, With Simon Sterling Thimble	95.00
Thread & Thimble Holder, Meriden Silver Plate, 5 3/4 In.	225.00

SHAKER items are characterized by simplicity, functionalism, and orderliness. There were many Shaker communities in America from the eighteenth century to the present day. The religious order made furniture, small wooden pieces, and packaged medicines, herbs, and jellies to sell to *outsiders*. Other useful objects were made for use by members of the community. Shaker furniture is listed in this book in the Furniture category.

Basket, Gathering, Wood, Black Band At Base, Rim, 25 1/2 x 14 In.	805.00
Basket, Splint, Cover, New England, 18 1/2 x 12 In.	978.00
Basket, Splint, Twin Inset Side Handles, Double Wrap Rim, Rectangular, 13 x 29 In.	405.00
Basket, Splint, Twin Raised Side Handles, Square Base, 9 x 4 1/2 In.	578.00
Basket, Splint, Twin Side Handles, Circular, Canterbury, 16 1/2 In.	575.00
Bed, Turned Pine, Maple, Arched Removable Headboard, Alfred, 35 x 76 In.	805.00
Bonnet, Woman's, Poplar Splint, Ribbon, Paper Lining, Stenciled 7	195.00
Bottle, Anodyne Dye, Enfield, 1870s	165.00
Box, 1-Finger, Lid, Mustard Paint, Copper Tacks, 6 1/4 In.	220.00
Box, 3-Finger, Lid, Oval, 1 5/8 x 1 1/2 In.	805.00
Box, 3-Finger, Lid, Oval, 1 3/4 x 4 1/2 In.	1150.00
Box, 3-Finger, Lid, Oval, 1 3/4 x 4 5/8 In.	460.00
Box, 3-Finger, Lid, Pumpkin Orange Paint, 5 x 8 x 11 In.	1035.00
Box, 3-Finger, Oval, Blue Green, 5 1/4 In.	4830.00
Box, 3-Finger, Painted, Pumpkin Orange, Lid, 11 x 8 x 5 In.	1035.00
Box, 4-Finger, Lid, Oval, 11 1/2 In.	805.00
Box, 4-Finger, Lid, Unpainted, 13 1/2 x 9 1/4 x 6 In.	1265.00
Box, 4-Finger, Oval, Yellow Wash, Signed H.C. Blinn, Mary Cochran Label, 9 3/8 In.	15525.00
Box, 5-Finger, Lid, Oval, 13 x 8 In.	1035.00
Box, 5-Finger, Lid, Oval, 5 5/8 x 13 5/8 In.	2300.00
Box, 5-Finger, Oval, Red Brown Paint, 13 1/2 In.	1725.00
Box, 6-Finger, Lid, Bird's Eye Maple, Handle, 13 x 15 In.	5060.00
Box, Canterbury, Butternut, Dovetailed, Swing Handle, 5 1/2 In.	1150.00
Box, Dovetail, Pumpkin Orange, Swing Handle, 18 x 6 In.	7015.00
Box, Hinged Cover, Red Wash, Gilt, Leaves & Heart Design, New England, 10 In.	255.00
Box, Oval, Lid, Blue, 1800s, 5 x 8 5/8 x 11 5/8 In.	2185.00
Box, Presentation, Inscription, Delmer C. Wilson	1725.00
Box, Seed, Divided Interior, Fruit Labels On Front, Mt. Lebanon, 3 1/2 x 23 1/2 In.	190.00
Box, Sewing, Birch, Maple, 2 Tiers, Velvet Pincushion, Late 19th Century, 7 x 7 In.	193.00
Bucket, Cover, Wooden, Bail Handle	185.00
Bucket, Painted Red	495.00
Butter Stamp, Canterbury, 6 In.	1610.00
Caddy, Sewing, Mahogany, 9 Spools, 4 3/8 x 7 1/2 In.	100.00
Candlestick, Tapered Drip Pan, Push-Up, 4 1/2 x 9 In.	400.00
Carrier, 4-Finger, Oval, Swing Handle, 8 1/2 x 11 In.	400.00
Carrier, Sewing, Dovetailed, Silk Lining, Swing Handle, 6 In.	1150.00
Cloak, Cobalt Broadcloth, Purple Taffeta Tie, Lined Hood, Canterbury	1150.00
Dipper, Side Spout, Turned Wooden Handle, Tin, Canterbury, 18 In.	290.00

Dipper, Turned Elongated Handle, 10 In. 1265.00
Dust Mop, Leaf Form Fan, Canterbury, 14 In. 115.00
Dustpan, Tapered Handle, Canterbury, Tin, 11 In. 1840.00
Hot Water Container, Tin, Curved, Handle, 10 3/4 x 6 3/8 x 1 1/2 In. 185.00
Lapboard, With Yardstick Measure, 37 1/2 In. 115.00
Machine, Pleating, Mahogany, Rectangular Frame, Pat. Aug. 8, 1869, 16 In. 290.00
Mesh Screen, Herb Sieve, Circular, Banded Base, 11 In. 1610.00
Oxen Muzzle, Splint Basket, Woven, New England, Mid 1800s, 14 1/2 x 14 In., Pair 2875.00
Peg Rail, Mustard Paint, 6 Pegs, 69 In. 690.00
Peg Rail, Mustard Paint, 8 Pegs, 75 1/2 In. 863.00
Pincushion, Turned Wood, Table Top Attachment, 9 In. 403.00
Sieve, Herb, 60 Mesh Screen 1610.00
Spool, 5 String, Turned Maple, 1 1/2 x 1 1/8 In. 1495.00
Spool, Yellow Maple, 1 3/4 In. 1725.00
Tray, Cutlery, Divided, Pierced Heart-Shaped Handle, Blue Gray Paint, 6 x 12 1/2 In. 632.00
Warming Cover, Flatiron, Goose, Tin, 15 In. 173.00
Wheel, Flax, Hardwood, Sabbathday Lake, Alfred, Me. 403.00
Windowpane, Blue, White Check In Blanket, Wool, 12 x 83 In. 403.00
Yarn Winder, Hardwood, Splayed Tripod Base, New England 175.00

SHAVING MUGS were popular from 1860 to 1900. Many types were made, including occupational mugs featuring pictures of men's jobs. There were scuttle mugs, silver-plated mugs, glass-lined mugs, and others.

Advertising, Koken's Lustre Shampoo 75.00
Couple Silhouette, My Mind Rebels At Stagnation, W.B. Irwin, 3 3/4 In. 385.00
E. Kloner, Patriotic Eagle, Shield, Crossed American Flags, 1927, 3 3/4 In. 355.00
E.E. Burlingame, Frog Smoking Pipe, Fishing, 1925, 3 3/8 In. 495.00
Fraternal, Bread & Cake Bakery, Delivery Wagon, J.M. Deldner, 4 In. 355.00
Fraternal, Brotherhood Of Railroad Trainmen 125.00
Fraternal, Elk Head, Gold Floral Design, Germany 60.00
Fraternal, L.F.E. No. 318, Locomotive & Tender, B.F. Devlin, 3 5/8 In. 275.00
Fraternal, Odd Fellows, B.F. Smith, 1860-1920, 3 3/4 In. 79.00
Fraternal, Order Of Elks 150.00
Fraternal, Order Of United Auto Mechanics, Wm. C. Bougher, 1925, 3 3/4 In. 150.00
Hanging Flower Basket, T. Williams, T. & V., Limoges, 3 5/8 In. 105.00
J.D. Hahn, Owl On Branch, Moon, 1925, 3 5/8 In. 415.00
Monkeys Shaving, Black Ground, 19th Century, 3 3/4 In. 105.00
Occupational, Anton J. Nielson, Studio Camera, 4 In. 1710.00
Occupational, Artist, A. Derould, Gilt, 3 1/2 In. 350.00
Occupational, Baker 400.00
Occupational, Baker, Horse Drawn Delivery Wagon, J. Barone, 3 3/4 In. 915.00
Occupational, Bell In Frame, Fred, 1925, C.F.H., 3 3/4 In. 410.00
Occupational, Blacksmith, Gold, Porcelain, Bavaria, 3 3/4 In. 440.00
Occupational, Butcher Tools & Steer Head, Henry F. Frain, 1860-1920, 3 3/4 In. 250.00
Occupational, Butcher, D. & C., France, 3 3/4 In. 225.00
Occupational, Butcher, Gilt, T. & V., Limoges, France, 3 1/2 In. 130.00
Occupational, Butcher, Hand Painted, Gold, Porcelain, 3 1/2 In. 470.00
Occupational, Cabinetmaker, D.A. Marble, Gilt, France, 3 3/4 In. 945.00
Occupational, Carpenter, J.S. Roshon, Gilt, E. Berninghaus, Cincinnati, O., 3 1/2 In. 445.00
Occupational, Carpenter, Planing Board, Floral Sprigs On Sides, 3 3/4 In. 260.00
Occupational, Coal Miner, Leaving Shaft In Mule Drawn Cart 3520.00
Occupational, Dentist, Raised Gold Tooth, Limoges, 1925, 3 3/4 In. 50.00
Occupational, East St. Louis Barbers Supply Co., J.W. Wiegand, 4 In. 1375.00
Occupational, Electrician, Wiring Electrical Box, T & V Limoges, 3 5/8 In. 2750.00
Occupational, Farmer, Plowing Field, Wilbert C. Newkirk, 3 1/2 x 3 5/8 In. 1540.00
Occupational, Fine Groceries, Delivery Wagon, F. Mellin, 1925, 3 5/8 In. 385.00
Occupational, Fireman, Horse Drawn Hook & Ladder, 3 3/4 In. 1540.00
Occupational, Frank Kukal, Steer's Head, Crossed Butcher's Tools, 3 5/8 In. 200.00
Occupational, Grinder, Image Of Hand Crank Operator, 3 5/8 In. 580.00
Occupational, Grocery Wagon Driver, Gold, Porcelain, 3 3/4 In. 550.00
Occupational, Hardware Store, Waiting On Customers, 4 x 3 3/4 In. 1070.00
Occupational, J.W. Kessler, Locomotive, Tender, B & O, Limoges, 3 7/8 In. 578.00

Occupational, Lineman	1200.00
Occupational, Livery Stable, William Linsey	70.00
Occupational, Man, Driving Motorcar, C. Weinhard, 1925, 3 7/8 In.	1540.00
Occupational, Man, Driving Motorcar, Charles Mannett, 1925, 3 3/4 In.	1595.00
Occupational, Man, Photograph, Koken Barber Supply Co., 1925, 4 In.	2365.00
Occupational, Oil Rig, Porcelain, 3 3/4 In.	495.00
Occupational, P.S.L. Co., Dress Shirt, With Tie, T. & V., France, 1925, 3 5/8 In.	85.00
Occupational, Patriotic, Irish Flag	200.00
Occupational, Pharmacist, 4 In.	85.00
Occupational, Pharmacist, Floral Both Sides	82.00
Occupational, Pharmacist, Mortar & Pestle, Geo. W. Rhodes, PD, Late 1800s	415.00
Occupational, Photographer, Portrait Studio, H.S. Brehman, Gold Lettering	1320.00
Occupational, Policeman, On Street Corner With Nightstick, 20th Century, 3 3/4 In.	85.00
Occupational, Pretzel Maker, Baker's Uniform, 3 5/8 In.	880.00
Occupational, Produce Wagon, R. Burke, J.P.L., France, 1885-1925, 3 1/2 In.	240.00
Occupational, Railroad Handcar, 2 Men, Hand Painted, A.N. Nelson, 3 5/8 In.	715.00
Occupational, Railroad Handcar, J. Freeze, 1925, 3 5/8 In.	1760.00
Occupational, Railroad, F.S. Gaines, Gilt, T. & V., Limoges, France, 3 1/2 In.	375.00
Occupational, Running Bull, W.K. Baird, 1925, 3 5/8 In.	465.00
Occupational, S.S. Admiral Schley, Blue Green Transfer, KTK, 3 5/8 In.	72.00
Occupational, Scholar, 1888, Gilt, 4 In.	405.00
Occupational, Seltzer Bottle, M. Goldberg 1916, 1925, 3 7/8 In.	465.00
Occupational, Shoemaker, F.F. Rodemann, Gilt, T. & V., France, 3 1/2 In.	585.00
Occupational, Square Ruler & Scissors, Henry Swarz, 1925, T. & V., 3 5/8 In.	120.00
Occupational, Steer, T.Z., Koken Barber Supply Co., 1925, 4 In.	825.00
Occupational, Telegraph Key, C.H.M. 1925, 3 7/8 In.	550.00
Occupational, Tinsmith, H.J. Douple	77.00
Occupational, W.M. Barkey, Dry Goods Store Scene, 4 1/8 In.	575.00
Occupational, Wheel, Pointed Blades, Otto C. Laabs, 1925, 3 5/8 In.	165.00
Ross R. Seaman, Floral All Around, D & Co. France, 1925, 4 In.	205.00
Sportsman's, 2 Fishermen, 1 Man In Canoe, J.E. Petry, 1925, 4 In.	145.00

SHAWNEE POTTERY was started in Zanesville, Ohio, in 1937. The company made vases, novelty ware, flowerpots, planters, lamps, and cookie jars. Three dinnerware lines were made: Corn, Lobster Ware, and Valencia (a solid color line). White Corn pattern utility pieces were made in 1945. Corn King was made from 1946 to 1954; Corn Queen, with darker green leaves and lighter colored corn, from 1954 to 1961. Shawnee produced pottery for George Rumrill during the late 1930s. The company closed in 1961.

Basket	60.00
Bookends, Flying Mallards, Signed, 6 In.	115.00
Bowl, Vegetable, Corn King, Oval, 9 In.	85.00
Butter, Cover, Corn King, Green Husks, 4 1/4 x 7 1/4 In. ....*Illus*	60.00
Casserole, Fruits, Cover, Signed, 7 1/4 In.	110.00
Casserole, Sundial	25.00
Cookie Jar, Corn King, 10 1/2 In. ....235.00 to	295.00
Cookie Jar, Dutch Boy	195.00
Cookie Jar, Muggsy, Flower, Gold, 11 1/2 In.	600.00

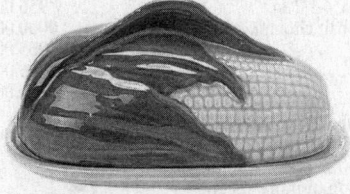

Shawnee, Butter, Cover, Corn King,
Green Husks, 4 1/4 x 7 1/4 In.

When looking at scrimshaw, check
the large hole in the base of the
tooth. Reproductions are brown,
dyed to look old. Real teeth have
clean root cavities.

Cookie Jar, Puss 'n Boots, 1945 . . . .   225.00
Cookie Jar, Puss 'n Boots, Tail Over Foot, 10 1/4 In. 295.00
Cookie Jar, Smiley Pig, Blue Neckerchief 345.00
Cookie Jar, Winking Owl . . . . .108.00 to 175.00
Cookie Jar, Winnie Pig, Shamrock 797.00
Creamer, Elephant 25.00
Creamer, Puss 'n Boots 60.00
Creamer, Smiley Pig, Clover Blossom, Red Trim 185.00
Creamer, Smiley Pig, Peach Flower 110.00
Darner Doll, 5 In. 125.00
Figurine, Cat, Sitting On Shoe, Black & White, No. 512 . . . .   60.00
Jar, Utility, Cover, Fruits, Signed, 5 1/2 In. 48.00
Pitcher, Bo Peep, Wide Eyed Girl, 8 In. . . . . .95.00 to 125.00
Pitcher, Fruits, Tilted Ball, Signed, 6 3/4 In. 115.00
Pitcher, Water, Smiley Pig, Floral, Signed 145.00
Planter, Clock, Double, Signed, Yellow, Signed, 4 1/2 In. 30.00
Planter, Dutch Girl 15.00
Planter, Elephant, Pink & Blue, Basket 11.00
Planter, Girl At Gate, 4 In. 25.00
Salt & Pepper, Boy Blue & Bo Peep 30.00
Salt & Pepper, Chef, 3 1/4 In. 43.00
Salt & Pepper, Dutch Boy & Girl, 5 In. 45.00
Salt & Pepper, Flowerpot 26.00
Salt & Pepper, Fruit, 5 In. 40.00
Salt & Pepper, Muggsy, 3 1/4 In. . . . . .50.00 to 95.00
Salt & Pepper, Muggsy, 5 In. 200.00
Salt & Pepper, Owl 25.00
Spoon Holder, Flowerpot 55.00
Sugar, Cover, Corn King, No. 78 . . . .   50.00
Teapot, Corn King 95.00
Teapot, Corn King, 6 3/4 In. 115.00
Teapot, Granny Ann, Peach Apron, Signed, 8 1/2 In. 145.00
Wall Pocket, Scotty Head 80.00

SHEARWATER pottery is a family business started by Mr. and Mrs. G.
W. Anderson, Sr., and their three sons. The local Ocean Springs,
Mississippi, clays were used to make the wares in the 1930s. The com-
pany is still in business.

Bowl, Stylized Bird, Band Of Waves, Black, White, Beige Ground, 1 1/2 x 5 In. 1125.00
Candleholder, Brown, Blue, 4 3/4 x 1 3/4 In., Pair 50.00
Candlestick, Brown, Pale Pink Curved Lines, Off-White Ground, Signed, 7 1/2 In. 150.00
Figurine, Pirate, Green, Yellow Clothing, 7 x 6 In. 36.00
Figurine, Sea Gull, Painted Blue & Teal, 5 1/2 x 10 1/2 In. 1495.00
Pitcher, Blue, Dark Blue Drip Glaze, Walter Anderson, 5 1/4 In. 109.00
Vase, Brown, Green, Blue, 1929, 6 1/4 x 3 1/4 In. 60.00
Vase, Double Gourd Shape, Turquoise, Celadon, Gunmetal Glaze, 7 x 5 In. 956.00
Vase, Earth, Air, Sea Creatures, Walter Anderson, Signed, c.1935, 12 In. 978.00
Vase, Embossed Mayan Design, Sheer Blue, Amber Flambe Glaze, 7 In. 1068.00
Vase, Embossed Primrose, Sheer Blue, Pink Matte Glaze, 5 1/4 x 6 In. 2362.00
Vase, Plantation, Embossed Dancing Figures Over Animals, Celadon, 12 In. 805.00
Vase, Red, Brown Satin Glaze, 3 3/4 In. 75.00
Vase, Stylized Carp, Sheer Blue, Purple Matte Glaze, 9 x 4 1/2 In. 956.00
Vase, Stylized Fish & Sea Plants, Sgraffito, Brushed Cobalt Ground, 10 x 6 In. 9000.00
Vase, Tennis Players, Green, Gunmetal Glaze, 9 1/2 In. 1265.00
Vase, Turquoise Blue Glaze, 1928, 4 x 3 1/2 In. 86.00
Vase, Turquoise High Glaze, 9 1/2 x 7 1/2 In. 830.00

SHEET MUSIC from the past centuries is now collected. The favorites
are examples with covers featuring artistic or historic pictures. Early
sheet music covers were lithographed, but by the 1900s photographic
reproductions were used. The early music was larger than more recent
sheets, and you must watch out for examples that were trimmed to fit
in a twentieth-century piano bench.

30-Mile Beach, March Militaire, Galveston, Louis Francis Haaren, 1895, 14 x 10 In. 21.00

An Affair To Remember, Cary Grant & Deborah Kerr	12.50
At Coonstown's Picnic, Cake Walk, Hans S. Line, c.1899	40.00
Bambi, Love Is A Song	38.00
Barney Google	10.00
Battle Of Nations, c.1915	48.00
Be A Clown, From The Movie The Pirate, Judy Garland On Cover, 1948	35.00
Blue Monday, From The Movie A Girl Can't Help It, Jayne Mansfield, Tom Ewell	30.00
Bowery Buck Rag Time Two-Step, Tom Turpin, c.1899	26.00
Cavalier Rusticana Rag, Williams & Van Alstyne, c.1910	8.00
Charge Of Light Brigade, c.1896	16.00
Chicken Rag, Mames Brockman, c.1911	26.00
Circus Parade, E.T. Paull, c.1904	60.00
Crazy Bone Rag, Charles L. Johnson, c.1911	16.00
Delores, Emil Waldteufel, 1947	2.00
Ephraim's Delight, Charles Miller, c.1898	22.00
Frosty The Snowman, 1950	9.00
God Bless America, Irving Berlin Inc. Music Pub., New York, N.Y., 1939	6.00
Goody Goody, Frankie Lymon, 1957, 6 Pages	23.00
Have Yourself A Merry Little Christmas, Judy Garland On Cover, 1944	35.00
I Never Felt This Way Before, From The Movie Bundle Of Joy, Debbie Reynolds, 1956	15.00
I Walk The Line, Johnny Cash, Hill & Range Songs, 1956	39.00
Love's Old Sweet Song, J.L. Molloy, 1911, 13 3/4 x 10 3/4 In.	25.00
Lucky Lindy, L. Wolfe Gilbert & Abel Baer, Pictures Airplane, 1927	42.00
Mammy's Little Coal Black Rose, R. Egan & Richard Whiting, c.1916	18.00
Man On Flying Trapeze, 1930s	5.00
Mellow Yellow, Donovan, 1966	9.50
Midnight Flyer, E.T. Paull, c.1903	40.00
My Ideal, Leo Robin, Newell Chase, Richard A. Whiting, 1940	7.00
North To Alaska, John Wayne, Capucine, Johnny Horton Pictured, 1960	10.00
Over The Rainbow, E.Y. Harburg & Harold Arlen, 1939	16.00
Pat Boone, Song Book, Hymns We Love, 1959, 9 x 12 In.	15.00
Plantation Melodies, Southern Airs, c.1905	8.00
Poison Ivy, Rolling Stones, 1964	104.00
Ragging The Scale, Ed Claypoole, 1915	48.00
Robin Hood, Carl Sigman, 1955 Television Series	25.00
Rudolph The Red-Nosed Reindeer, St. Nicholas Music, 1949	15.00
Semper Fidelis, Arr. For Piano Solo, J. Philip Sousa, Boston Music Co., 1928	6.00
Shall We Dance, Fred Astaire & Ginger Rogers, Gershwin & Gershwin	5.00
Silver Sleigh Bells, E.T. Paull, c.1906	20.00
Stein Song, Rudy Vallee	44.00
The King And I, Selections, Rodgers & Hammerstein, 1951, 15 Pages	15.00
Uncle Tom's Cabin Rag, Topsy Dancing, Uncle Tom Playing Banjo, 1911	9.00
When You're A Long Long Way From Home, Lewis & Meyer, 1914	10.00
Wreck Of The Titanic, Jeanette Forrest, 1912	40.00
Yellow Rose Of Texas, 1936	12.00

SHEFFIELD items are listed in the Silver Plate and Silver-English categories.

SHELLEY first appeared on English ceramics about 1912. The Foley China Works started in England in 1860. Joseph Ball Shelley joined the company in 1862 and became a partner in 1872. Percy Shelley joined the firm in 1881. The company went through a series of name changes, and in 1910 the then Foley China Company became Shelley China. In 1929 it became Shelley Potteries. The company was acquired in 1966 by Allied English Potteries, then merged with the Doulton group in 1971. The name *Shelley* was put into use again in 1980. A trio is the name for a cup, saucer, and cake plate set.

Coffee-Teapot, Crochet	225.00
Coffeepot, Blue, Dainty, 8 In.	595.00
Cup & Saucer, Blue Rock	48.00
Cup & Saucer, Crochet	80.00
Cup & Saucer, Orange & White, Gold Snowflakes	105.00
Pitcher, Harmony	38.00

Plate, Begonia, Snack Set, Scalloped Rim	125.00
Plate, Blue Rock, 8 In.	32.00
Plate, Blue, Dainty, 6 In.	450.00
Plate, Bridal Rose, 10 1/2 In.	95.00
Plate, Jacobean, 8 3/4 In.	55.00
Plate, White, Dainty, Ascot, Square, 6 In.	25.00
Platter, Blue Rock, 14 3/4 In.	185.00
Soup, Cream, Underplate, Blue Rock	70.00
Soup, Cream, Underplate, Blue, Dainty	125.00
Sugar & Creamer, Blue, Dainty	125.00
Teapot, Blue, Dainty, 7 In.	450.00
Trio, Festoons & Fruit	125.00
Trio, Green, Daisy, Cambridge	220.00
Vase, Christmas, Luster, 10 In.	195.00
Vase, Kingfisher, 10 In.	140.00

SHIRLEY TEMPLE, the famous movie star, was born in 1928. She made her first movie in 1932. Thousands of items picturing Shirley have been and still are being made. Shirley Temple dolls were first made in 1934 by Ideal Toy Company. Millions of Shirley Temple cobalt blue glass dishes were made by Hazel Atlas Glass Company and U.S. Glass Company from 1934 to 1942. They were given away as premiums for Wheaties and Bisquick. A bowl, mug, and pitcher were made as a breakfast set. Some pieces were decorated with the picture of a very young Shirley, others used a picture of Shirley in her 1936 *Captain January* costume. Although collectors refer to a cobalt creamer, it is actually the 4 1/2-inch-high milk pitcher from the breakfast set. Many of these items are being reproduced today.

Buggy, Cameo Image Both Sides, Wooden Body, 30 x 29 In.	785.00
Button, Shirley Temple, Pinback, Ideal	75.00
Chalk Figure, Sailor Cap, Turtleneck Sweater, Bell Bottoms, 7 In.	45.00
Chalk Figure, Yellow & White Dress, Stand, 5 In.	85.00
Doll, Composition, Pink Taffeta Dress, Roller Skates, Pin, 20 In.	112.00
Doll, Ideal, c.1935, 18 In.	185.00
Doll, Ideal, Captain January, Wearing Sailor Suit, Green Sleep Eyes, 1936, 22 In.	1050.00
Doll, Ideal, Composition Socket Head, Green Sleep Eyes, Blond Wig, 1939, 13 In.	900.00 to 1400.00
Doll, Ideal, Composition Socket Head, Green Sleep Eyes, Open Mouth, 20 In.	1000.00
Doll, Ideal, Composition, Sleep Eyes, Red Short Dress, White Shoes, Pin, 18 1/2 In.	168.00
Doll, Ideal, Poor Little Rich Girl, Composition Socket Head, Green Eyes, 20 In.	850.00
Doll, Ideal, Poor Little Rich Girl, Composition Socket Head, Green Eyes, 22 In.	950.00
Doll, Ideal, Sleep Eyes, Open Mouth, Jointed Composition Body, Dress, 11 In.	750.00
Doll, Ideal, Sleeping, Flirty Eyes, Yellow Curly Mohair Wig, 1930, 24 In.	230.00
Doll, Ideal, Texas Ranger, Sleep Eyes, Open Mouth, 1936, 17 In. *Illus*	1600.00
Doll, Ideal, Vinyl, Sleep Eyes, Open-Close Smiling Mouth, c.1957, 12 In.	200.00
Doll, Ideal, Wearing Dark Blue Sailor Dress, Blond Mohair Wig, 1936, 18 In.	900.00
Doll, Pin, Ideal, 25 In.	3105.00
Doll, Plastic, Red & White Polka-Dot Dress, Marked, Ideal, 16 In.	90.00
Doll, Sleep Eyes, Open Mouth, Vinyl Body, Ideal, 14 1/2 In.	115.00

When cleaning silver, use plastic or cotton gloves, not rubber. Rubber makes silver tarnish faster.

Don't have old Sheffield silver replated. You can replate wares that were originally electroplated.

Shirley Temple, Doll, Ideal,
Texas Ranger, Sleep Eyes,
Open Mouth, 1936, 17 In.

Doll Carriage, Wicker, Adjustable Sunshade, Wood Handle, Images Of Shirley, 1935 .... 2200.00
Doll Clothes, Raincoat, Hat, Purse, Fits 1957 12-In. Doll 65.00
Mug, Blue Glass, 3 3/4 In. 60.00
Paper Doll, 30 Outfits, 1934 .... 125.00
Paper Dolls, 4 Dolls, 49 Outfits 65.00
Pitcher, Blue Glass ....50.00 to 60.00
Tea Set, Pink, Plastic, 1950s, 8 Piece 100.00

SHRINER, see Fraternal category.

SILVER DEPOSIT glass was first made during the late nineteenth century. Solid sterling silver is applied to the glass by a chemical method so that a cutout design of silver metal appears against a clear or colored glass. It is sometimes called silver overlay.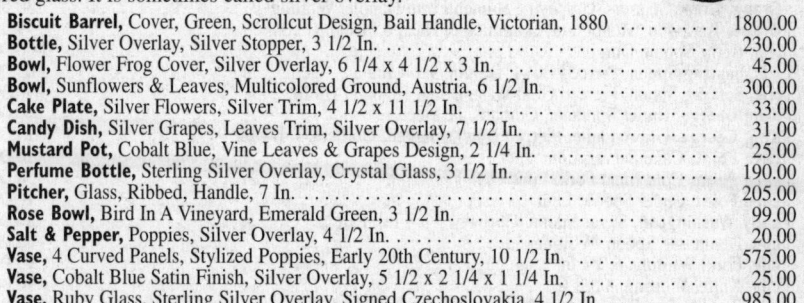

Biscuit Barrel, Cover, Green, Scrollcut Design, Bail Handle, Victorian, 1880 .... 1800.00
Bottle, Silver Overlay, Silver Stopper, 3 1/2 In. 230.00
Bowl, Flower Frog Cover, Silver Overlay, 6 1/4 x 4 1/2 x 3 In. 45.00
Bowl, Sunflowers & Leaves, Multicolored Ground, Austria, 6 1/2 In. 300.00
Cake Plate, Silver Flowers, Silver Trim, 4 1/2 x 11 1/2 In. 33.00
Candy Dish, Silver Grapes, Leaves Trim, Silver Overlay, 7 1/2 In. 31.00
Mustard Pot, Cobalt Blue, Vine Leaves & Grapes Design, 2 1/4 In. 25.00
Perfume Bottle, Sterling Silver Overlay, Crystal Glass, 3 1/2 In. 190.00
Pitcher, Glass, Ribbed, Handle, 7 In. 205.00
Rose Bowl, Bird In A Vineyard, Emerald Green, 3 1/2 In. 99.00
Salt & Pepper, Poppies, Silver Overlay, 4 1/2 In. 20.00
Vase, 4 Curved Panels, Stylized Poppies, Early 20th Century, 10 1/2 In. 575.00
Vase, Cobalt Blue Satin Finish, Silver Overlay, 5 1/2 x 2 1/4 x 1 1/4 In. 25.00
Vase, Ruby Glass, Sterling Silver Overlay, Signed Czechoslovakia, 4 1/2 In. 985.00

SILVER FLATWARE includes many of the current and out-of-production silver and silver-plated flatware patterns made in the past eighty years. Other silver is listed under Silver-American, Silver-English, etc. Most silver flatware sets that are missing a few pieces can be completed through the help of one of the many silver matching services that advertise in many of the national publications.

SILVER FLATWARE PLATED, Fish Serving Set, Ivory, Silk Lined Case, 1900, 12 In., 2 Piece . 230.00
Fish Serving Set, Staghorn, Reticulated Rim, 1895, 13 1/2 In., 2 Piece 374.00
Fruit Knife Set, Hammered Handle, Cast Fruit Finial, Silk Lined Box, EPNS, 6 Piece ... 60.00
Fruit Knife Set, Rogers, 6 Piece 30.00
Grapefruit Set, Gold Wash, 6 Spoons, 1 Knife, Box, Mappin & Webb, 7 x 9 In. 150.00
Rose, Sugar Shell, Monogram, Rockford S. P. Co. 20.00
Victorian Rose, Gravy Ladle, Wm. Rogers, 6 In. 10.00
Salem, Ice Cream Fork, Rogers 25.00
SILVER FLATWARE STERLING, Acorn, Fish Slice, Georg Jensen, 2 Piece 460.00
Acorn, Salad Servers, Georg Jensen, 2 Piece 405.00
Afterglow, Teaspoon, Oneida 12.00
American Classic, Luncheon Fork, Easterling 17.00
American Classic, Teaspoon, Easterling 9.00
Ashmont, Tablespoon, Pierced, Reed & Barton 60.00
Blithe Spirit, Salad Fork, Easterling 22.00
Blossom, Salad Servers, Georg Jensen, 2 Piece 1035.00
Buttercup, Infant Feeding Spoon, Gorham 21.00
Buttercup, Luncheon Fork, Gorham 25.00
Cambridge, Jelly Knife, Gorham 150.00
Chantilly, Dinner Set, Knives, Forks, Spoons, Gorham, 118 Piece 1955.00
Chapel Bells, Luncheon Fork, Alvin 20.00
Chapel Bells, Teaspoon, Alvin 8.00
Chased Romantique, Salad Fork, Alvin 22.00
Chased Romantique, Teaspoon, Alvin 9.00
Chateau Rose, Butter Spreader, Alvin, Individual 10.00
Contessina, Cold Meat Fork, Towle 42.00
Contessina, Tablespoon, Pierced, Towle 45.00
Cordova, Carving Knife & Fork, Towle 55.00

Damask Rose, Butter Spreader, Individual, Oneida 13.00
Danish Baroque, Tomato Server, Towle 50.00
Debussy, Cheese Cleaver, Towle 18.00
Dorothy Manners, Tomato Server, Towle 36.00
Duncan Phyfe, Serving Fork & Spoon, Whiting, 9 In. 115.00
Eloquence, Cracker Scoop, Lunt 195.00
Fairfax, Mustard Ladle, Alvin 95.00
Fairfax, Tea Infuser 210.00
First Frost, Teaspoon, Oneida 14.00
Francis I, Knife Service, 1907, 56 Piece 2300.00
Francis I, Serving Spoon, Vegetable, Reed & Barton, 1907, 9 1/2 In. 316.00
Frontenac, Spoon, International, 9 In. 138.00
Gainsborough, Teaspoon, Alvin 11.00
Grape, Grape Scissors, Grapevine Branch Form Handle, Whiting 230.00
Grape, Teaspoon, Monogram, Dominick & Haff, 6 Piece 99.00
Iris, Berry Spoon, Durgin 400.00
Iris, Serving Spoon, Pierced Bowl, Durgin, 9 1/4 In. 805.00
Isis, Serving Spoon, Pierced Gold Wash Bowl, 1870s, 8 1/8 In. 690.00
King George, Butter Spreader, Gorham, 12 Piece 300.00
King George, Gravy Ladle, Pierced Bowl, Marked, Gorham, 7 1/4 In. 325.00
Lace Point, Cake Server, Lunt 25.00
Lace Point, Cold Meat Fork, Lunt 50.00
Lace Point, Sugar Spoon, Lunt 16.00
Lady Washington, Sugar Spoon, Gorham, 5 3/4 In., Pair 80.00
Lily, Demitasse Spoon, Whiting 50.00
Lily, Fork, Whiting, 6 3/4 In. 95.00
Lily, Knife, Whiting, 8 5/8 In. 90.00
Lily, Serving Set, Fork, Fluted Tine Bowl, Serving Spoon, Whiting, 11 In. .. 805.00
Lily, Tablespoon, Whiting, 8 1/4 In. 160.00
Lily, Teaspoon, Monogram, Whiting, 5 7/8 In. 47.00
Lily Of The Valley, Berry Spoon, Monogram, Whiting, 8 1/2 In. 700.00
Lily Of The Valley, Dessert Fork, Monogram, Whiting, 6 1/4 In. 140.00
Lily Of The Valley, Fork, Monogram, Whiting, 6 7/8 In. ....97.00 to 100.00
Lily Of The Valley, Knife, Hollow, Monogram, Whiting, 9 1/4 In. 90.00
Lily Of The Valley, Soup Spoon, Monogram, Oval, Whiting, 7 In. 120.00
Lily Of The Valley, Spoon, Monogram, Whiting, After Dinner 60.00
Lily Of The Valley, Tablespoon, Whiting, 8 1/4 In. 160.00
Lily Of The Valley, Teaspoon, Monogram, Whiting, 5 7/8 In. 45.00
Louis XV, Berry Spoon, Durgin 185.00
Love Disarmed, Fish Set, Reed & Barton, 2 Piece 775.00
Love Disarmed, Salad Servers, Parcel Gilt, Reed & Barton, 2 Piece 1310.00
Madame Royale, Cold Meat Fork, Durgin, 9 1/8 In. 90.00
Madeira, Teaspoon, Towle 10.00
Madrigal, Gravy Ladle, Lunt 55.00
Madrigal, Sugar Spoon, Lunt 11.00
Majestic, Bouillon Spoon, Alvin, 6 Piece 240.00
Margaret Rose, Butter Knife, Master, National 11.00
Margaret Rose, Teaspoon, National 10.00
Marie Louise, Sugar Spoon, Blackington 33.00
Marie Louise, Tablespoon, Blackington 43.00
Martha Washington, Service For 8, Watson, 38 Piece 275.00
Medallion, Ladle, Classical Woman, Gilded Interior, Gorham, 1875s, 12 In. . 690.00
Mignonette, Butter Knife, Master, Lunt 18.00
Miss Alvin, Butter Knife, Master, Alvin 11.00
Modern Victorian, Coffee Spoon, Lunt 18.00
Newcastle, Cracker Scoop, Gorham 195.00
Old Lace, Teaspoon, Towle 10.00
Old Maryland, Cold Meat Fork, Kirk 110.00
Old Master, Teaspoon, Towle 14.00
Old Newbury, Butter Spreader, Flat Handle, Towle 25.00
Old Newbury, Cake Slice, Wedding, Stainless Blade, Towle 41.00
Old Newbury, Casserole Spoon, Shell Bowl, Towle 45.00
Old Newbury, Cheese Cleaver, Towle, 6 7/8 In. 42.00

Old Newbury, Cold Meat Fork, Towle 45.00
Old Newbury, Fork, Towle, 6 1/2 In. 44.00
Old Newbury, Fork, Towle, 7 1/2 In. ....35.00 to 50.00
Old Newbury, Gravy Ladle, Hollow, Towle, 7 7/8 In. 41.00
Old Newbury, Gravy Ladle, Towle 90.00
Old Newbury, Ice Cream Fork, Pierced, Towle, 5 5/8 In. 37.00
Old Newbury, Ice Cream Scoop, Stainless Bowl, Towle, 8 In. 45.00
Old Newbury, Ice Cream Scoop, Towle, 8 In. 42.00
Old Newbury, Knife, Hollow, Towle, 8 7/8 In. 32.00
Old Newbury, Knife, Hollow, Towle, 9 3/4 In. 40.00
Old Newbury, Lasagna Server, Towle, 9 5/8 In. 42.00
Old Newbury, Orange Knife, Towle, 7 3/8 In. 38.00
Old Newbury, Pasta Server, Stainless Bowl, Towle, 10 1/2 In. 40.00
Old Newbury, Salad Fork, Stainless Bowl, Towle, 11 1/8 In. 41.00
Old Newbury, Salad Spoon, Stainless Bowl, Towle 45.00
Old Newbury, Soup Ladle, Stainless Bowl, Towle, 10 5/8 In. ......42.00 to 60.00
Old Newbury, Steak Knife, Towle, Individual 32.00
Old Newbury, Stuffing Spoon, Stainless Bowl, Towle, 11 1/8 In. 45.00
Old Newbury, Tablespoon, Towle 70.00
Old Newbury, Teaspoon, Towle 20.00
Olympian, Sauce Ladle, Tiffany & Co., c.1878, 6 1/2 In. 345.00
Overture, Cream Soup Spoon, National 11.00
Overture, Sugar Spoon, National 10.00
Pointed Antique, Demitasse Spoon, Dominick & Haff 90.00
Princess Ingrid, Carving Fork, Frank Whiting, 10 7/8 In. 80.00
Princess Ingrid, Carving Knife, Whiting 46.00
Princess Ingrid, Iced Tea Spoon, Whiting 36.00
Princess Ingrid, Knife, Frank Whiting, Hollow, 9 In. 35.00
Princess Ingrid, Pie Server, Whiting 57.00
Princess Ingrid, Poultry Shears, Frank Whiting, 11 1/2 In. ....120.00 to 160.00
Princess Ingrid, Soup Spoon, Round Bowl, Frank Whiting, 6 1/8 In. 26.00
Quintessence, Fish Serving Fork, Lunt 40.00
Quintessence, Teaspoon, Lunt 14.00
Raphael, Soup Ladle, Gorham, c.1875, 13 1/2 In. 550.00
Repousse, Butter Knife, S. Kirk & Sons, 12 Piece. 176.00
Repousse, Carving Set, S. Kirk & Sons 135.00
Repousse, Iced Tea Spoon, S. Kirk & Sons, 4 Piece 220.00
Rondelay, Teaspoon, Lunt 18.00
Rose Spray, Teaspoon, Easterling 16.00
Shannon, Butter Spreader, Dominick & Haff, Individual 15.00
Shannon, Gumbo Soup Spoon, Dominick & Haff 16.00
Southern Charm, Butter Spreader, Alvin, Individual 10.00
Southwind Gold, Place Setting, Towle, 4 Piece 64.00
Spanish Provincial, Place Setting, Towle, 4 Piece 104.00
Strasbourg, Knife Set, Gorham, Monogram, 10 .... 195.00
Symphony Chased, Place Setting, Towle, 4 Piece 52.00
Trajan, Berry Spoon, Gold Wash Bowl, Reed & Barton, 9 3/4 In. 210.00
Violet, Seafood Fork, Wallace 30.00
Violet, Teaspoon, Monogram, Wallace, 1904, 6 Piece 33.00
Virginia, Punch Ladle, Single Monogram, Alvin Silver Co., 12 1/2 In. 145.00
William & Mary, Coffee Spoon, Lunt 8.00
Winterset, Cocktail Fork, Buccellati 18.00
Winterset, Iced Tea Spoon, Buccellati 19.00
Yankee Clipper, Serving Set, Dessert, 3 Piece 55.00
Zodiac, Food Pusher, Gorham 95.00

SILVER PLATE is not solid silver. It is a ware made of a metal, such as
nickel or copper, that is covered with a thin coating of silver. The letters *EPNS* are often found on American and English silver-plated
wares. Sheffield is a term with two meanings. Sometimes it refers to
sterling silver made in the town of Sheffield, England. In this section,
Sheffield refers to a type of silver plate, usually English.

Basket, Applied Bird, Flowers, Simpson, Hall, Miller, 8 1/2 x 7 In. 595.00

Basket, Boat Form, Band Of Piercing, Swing Handle, 19th Century, 13 1/4 In. 375.00
Basket, Fruit, Pierced Wire Body, Swing Handle, 13 x 10 In. 290.00
Biscuit Box, 2 Bowls, Pierced Scroll Liner, Leaf & Acorn Handle, Folding, 11 In. 575.00
Bowl, Fruit, Monteith Rim, Tiffany & Co., 5 1/2 In. 288.00
Bowl, Fruit, Old Sheffield Style, Scallop Shell Handles, Oval, Footed, c.1940, 14 x 9 In. . 115.00
Bowl, On Copper, Monteith, Handles, F. Valenti, Italy, c.1920, 4 1/4 x 8 x 12 1/2 In., Pair . 978.00
Bowl, Vegetable, Oval, Reed & Barton, 10 1/4 x 8 In. 16.00
Box, Cigarette, Neoclassical, Relief Landscape, Musical Design, 7 1/2 x 4 In. 86.00
Box, Rectangular, Blue Enamel, Courting Couple, Scrolled Leaves, Gilt, 3 x 2 In. 127.00
Box, Rectangular, Seed Pearls, Synthetic Sapphires, 1 3/4 x 1 1/2 In. 230.00
Box, Sardine, Engraved Leaf & Fish, Attached Underplate, Sheffield 85.00
Box, Sugar, On Copper, Oval, Fluted, Hinged Lid, Sheffield, 6 1/4 In. 259.00
Bucket, Champagne, Reeded Column, Domed Base, 27 In. 165.00
Bucket, Ice, Handles, Floral Finial, Gadrooned Border & Foot, Glass Liner, 9 1/4 In. 460.00
Bucket, Wine, Scroll & Leaf Design, Ribbed Body, 20th Century, 10 In. 440.00
Butter Dish, Egg Shape, Leaf Chase, Cast Putto, Open Frame, Feet, 12 1/2 In. 635.00
Cake Basket, 3 Mythical God Heads, Pierced Bail Handle, Hartford Silver Co., 9 In. 95.00
Cake Basket, Pierced Greek Key, Rogers Smith & Co., 9 1/4 In. 125.00
Candelabrum is listed in its own category.
Candlesticks are listed in their own category.
Card Case, Bifold, Foliate Scroll Pattern Overall, Italy, 3 1/2 x 2 3/8 In. 173.00
Castor, Sugar, Bands Of Classical Designs, 1870, 7 x 3 1/2 In. 230.00
Celery Dish, Leaf Design, Smith Bros., 12 1/2 In. 15.00
Chafing Dish, Rococo Base, Late 19th Century, 10 x 14 In. 330.00
Chalice, Edwardian, Garland Lip, Tam Masques, 1910, 10 3/4 x 5 1/2 In. 920.00
Chalice, Engraved, Leaf & Twig Strapwork, c.1870, 9 x 4 In. 115.00
Chalice, Leaf Engraved Panels, Beaded Borders, c.1870, 7 1/2 x 2 1/2 In. 920.00
Chalice, Magnum, Flowers, James Richards & Sons, Sheffield, 1900, 11 In. 345.00
Chalice, Prince's Plate, Mappin & Webb, 1885, 8 5/8 x 3 3/4 In. 460.00
Chocolate Pot, Leaves & Berries, Leaf & Berry Finial, A.C. Tirbour, 10 In. 750.00
Cigar Caddy, Engraved, Floral Panels, Pull Handle, Satin Lined, c.1900, 8 In. 515.00
Cigar Holder, Champagne Shape, Chased Leaf Design, 1921, 10 In. 255.00
Cocktail Shaker, Lighthouse Shape, Built-In Strainer, Meriden, 1927, 12 1/2 In. 715.00
Cocktail Shaker, Penguin, Hinged Beak Spout, Signed, 20th Century, 12 1/2 In. 575.00
Coffee Urn, Dome Lid, Platform Base, Ball Feet, Bone Handles, England, 11 In. 275.00
Coffee Urn, Domed Cover, Double Handles, Rococo, Reed & Barton, 14 In. 135.00
Coffee Urn, Floral, Footed, Ring Burner, Handles, Wilcox Silver Plate Co., 16 In. 190.00
Coffee Urn, Neoclassical, Minerva Head Medallion, 17 3/4 In. 385.00
Compote, Squirrel On Rim, Eating Acorn On Side, 9 x 6 In. 345.00
Cooler, Wine, Grape Leaves, Glass Liner, Signed, EPNS 140.00
Corkscrew, Magnum, Antler, Meriden Britannia Company, c.1910, 5 1/4 In. 345.00
Cornucopia, On Base, Horn, 1870 .... 1250.00
Cruet Stand, 7 Engraved Glass Bottles, Lapidary Cut Stoppers, 18 In., 8 Piece 920.00
Decanter, Reticulated Frame, Openwork Handle, 15 In., Pair. 415.00
Decanter, Vintage, Cobalt Blue Glass, Double Pouring Spout, c.1855, 14 In., Pair 575.00
Desk Set, 2 Cut Glass Wells, Silver Lids, Armorial Etched, England, 8 1/2 x 5 In. 270.00
Dish, Cover, Beaded Edge, Leaf, Shield Design, Handle, 1890, 7 1/2 In. 935.00
Dish, Cover, Rococo Leaf Border, Floral, 1875, 6 1/2 x 10 1/2 x 14 In. 460.00
Dish, Scroll & Leaf, Lift-Out Interior Dish, Pierced Strainer Base, 7 1/2 x 9 In. 287.00
Epergne, Edwardian Style, 3-Part, Neoclassical, 1 1/2 x 18 1/2 x 55 In. 1725.00
Epergne, Edwardian, Cut Glass Fruit Bowl, 1910, 13 x 26 1/2 In., 4 Piece 2300.00
Epergne, Edwardian, Old Sheffield Style, Round, c.1900, Engraved, 27 1/4 x 18 1/2 In. .. 2760.00
Epergne, Stand, Victorian, Palm Trees, Rocaille Plinth, 1890, 21 x 15 In. 345.00
Epergne, Trumpet, Oriental, Tripod Base, Reclining Camels, 21 1/2 x 8 /12 In. 1955.00
Flagon, Medieval Style, Heraldic Lion Cover Finial, P. Atkinson, c.1880, 9 In. 201.00
Goblet Set, Ice Water, Royal Metal Mfg. Co., c.1930, 6 1/2 x 3 1/4 In., 12 .... 1150.00
Gravy Warmer, Argyll, Domed Cover, Wooden Ear Handle, England, 19th Century, 5 In. . 200.00
Ice Bucket, Hinged Lion Masks, Loose Rings, Glass Liner & Cover, 9 1/2 In. 110.00
Ice Pail, Spoon & Ice Pick Sides, Art Deco, 1930 .... 900.00
Kettle, Water, George II, Floral, Leaf Scroll Repousse Design, 15 1/2 In. 489.00
Lamp, Bouillotte, 2 Female Terms Rising To Central Standard, 16 In. 635.00
Letter Opener, W.M. Rogers & Son, Stainless Steel Blade, 9 3/8 In. 6.50
Mirror, Toilet, Neoclassical, Oval, Swing, Candle Branches, On Copper, 26 In. 546.00

Muffineer, Folding, Reticulated, Twig Frame, 1900, 10 x 8 In. 1380.00
Mug, Floral Sprays & C Scrolls, Top Reeded Band, J.E. Caldwell, 1850s, 3 1/2 In. 230.00
Napkin Rings are listed in their own category.
Pitcher, Aesthetic Style, Free-Form Scrolls, Hinged Lid, Meriden, c.1868, 11 1/2 In. 230.00
Pitcher, Bauhaus, Handle, 7 x 7 In. 175.00
Pitcher, Cocktail, Art Deco, Ribbed Rim & Foot, Dunhill, 1920 . . . . 900.00
Pitcher, Insulated, Hinged Top, Ornate Handle & Spout, Stimpson, 1854 . . . . 89.00
Planter, Over Copper, Repousse Rococo, Children Playing, Cross, 6 x 14 In., Pair 245.00
Plate, Openwork Grapevine Border, Footed, 10 1/2 In. 155.00
Platter, Gadroon, Rose Spray, Cover, Leaf Scroll, Walker & Hall, 9 x 12 x 16 In. 865.00
Platter, Meat, Gadrooned Rim, Coat Of Arms, Oval, 12 1/2 In. 145.00
Platter, Raised Rococo Design Around Rim, Oval, 21 1/2 x 17 1/4 In. 60.00
Platter, Shell & Scroll, Armorial, Domed Cover, Sheffield, Oval, 10 x 13 1/2 x 17 In. . . . 635.00
Platter, Well & Tree, Shell, Leaf, Gadroon Border, Reeded Handles, Crest, 25 In. 230.00
Posy Holder, Filigree, Flowers, Victorian, 1870, 5 1/2 In. 350.00
Posy Holder, Floral & Leaf, c.1870, 5 1/2 In. 345.00
Punch Bowl, Ladle, Justis & Armiger, Arms Of Pennsylvania, Maryland, 15 3/4 In. 7700.00
Relish, Spring Flower, Crystal Divided Insert, William Rogers & Sons, 10 1/4 In. 20.00
Saltcellar, Lion Head, Glass Insert, 2 1/2 In., Pair 100.00
Salver, Leaf & Scroll, Devil's Head Medallions, E. Barker, 1880s 690.00
Sauceboat, Cover, Flared Scalloped Beaded Rim, 4 Paw Feet, 5 3/4 In. 260.00
Sauceboat, Nautilus Shell, Hinged Lid, England, 1870s, 5 3/4 In. 175.00
Serving Dish, Egg, 6 Eggcups, Reticulated Bands, Central Handle, 4 Ball Feet, 6 In. 230.00
Spoon, Souvenir, see Souvenir category.
Stand, Art Nouveau, Tripod Shape, Pierced Leaf, Christofle, 23 In. 1840.00
Stand, Cut Glass Bowl, Oriental, Tripod Base, Reclining Camels, 9 x 7 In., Pair 1840.00
Tankard, Root Beer, Murdock & Freeman Company 275.00
Tea & Coffee Set, George III, Pierced Design, Ball Feet, 5 Piece 635.00
Tea & Coffee Set, New Beverly Manor, Wilcox, 24 x 15 In., 5 Piece 345.00
Tea Caddy, Navette Form, Cover, Carved Ivory Finial, Sheffield, c.1790, 6 1/2 In. 635.00
Tea Set, Melon Form, Footed, Teapot, Hot Water Pot, Sugar, Creamer, Rogers 110.00
Tea Set, Repousse & Chased Acanthus Leaf, Medallions, Gold Wash Interior, 3 Piece 165.00
Tea Set, Scalloped Ribs, Prince Of Wales Feather Crest, 8 1/2 In., 3 Piece 220.00
Tea Urn, Medallion, 2 Handles, Redfield & Rice, 1870 . . . . 385.00
Tea Urn, Regency, Lion Masks Suspending Rings, Reeded Legs, Paw Feet, 12 In. 520.00
Teakettle, On Stand, Georgian, 1890, 14 x 10 x 5 1/2 In. 230.00
Teapot, Acorn Finial, Scroll Spout, Wooden Handle, Sheffield, 11 In. 800.00
Teapot, Embossed Acanthus Scrolls, On Copper, Monogram, Sheffield, 9 3/4 In. 120.00
Teapot, Embossed Floral, Shell Spout, Black Painted Handle, 8 3/4 In. 165.00
Teapot, Fluted Body, Floral, Ivory Finial, England, 6 1/2 In. 85.00
Toast Rack, 10 Vertical Posts, T-Bar Handle, Christopher Dresser, c.1880, 4 1/4 In. 2070.00
Toothpick, 2 Handles, Meriden Britannia Co., 1890 . . . . 95.00
Toothpick, Floral, Simpson, Hall, Miller & Co., 1890 . . . . 75.00
Toothpick, Lady With Basket 75.00
Tray, 2 Handles, Engraved, Applied Border, Birmingham Silver Co., Footed, 26 x 15 In. . . 56.00
Tray, Acanthus Leaf Center, 3 Shell Feet, Wallace Silver Plate, 17 1/2 In. 110.00
Tray, Beaded Loop Handles, Foliate, Scroll Cartouche, 25 1/4 In. 316.00
Tray, Floral & Scroll, Rococo Border, Handles, Footed, 18 1/2 x 24 1/2 In. 220.00
Tray, Gallery, Central Etched Design, English, 18 In. 345.00
Tray, Gallery, Leaf Design Handles, Central Armorial, 13 1/4 x 28 In. 430.00
Tray, Gallery, Pierced, Geometric Design, Handles, Gadroon Rim, 24 1/2 In. 375.00
Tray, Leaves Enclosed Within Roped Rim, Leafy Handles, E.P. Benetfink 310.00
Tray, Made In Sheffield, England, 24 In. 495.00
Tray, Meat, Dome Cover, Engraved Coat Of Arms, Rampant Lion, 19 1/2 In. 605.00
Tray, Oval Form, Ribbed Border, Elkington, 1800s, 11 x 17 3/4 In. 145.00
Tray, Pierced Sides, Engraved Scroll & Floral, Monogram, Wilcox, 20 x 9 In. 150.00
Tray, Reticulated Gallery, Acanthus Leaf & Ball & Claw Feet, Oval, 17 x 22 In. 495.00
Tray, Reticulated Gallery, Cutout Handles, Leaf Feet, Sheffield, 14 x 21 In. 355.00
Tray, Rococo, Reticulated, Grape Vines, Leaf Handles, Sheffield, 13 x 18 In. 190.00
Tray, Serving, Rococo Trim, Handles, 26 x 14 1/4 In. 470.00
Trophy Cup, Beaded Round Base, 2 Handles, Floral Garlands, 11 In. 385.00
Tureen, Cover, Gorham, c.1900, 10 x 13 In. 385.00
Tureen, Revolving, Floral & Scroll, Beaded Border, Handles, Cabriole Legs, H&H, 14 In. . 290.00

Tureen, Soup, Egg Shaped Bowl, Cover Revolves, Handles, Alex Clark, 13 x 9 In. 220.00
Tureen, Soup, Leafy Shell, Footed, Cover, c.1830, 12 x 16 1/2 x 10 1/2 In. 2760.00
Urn, Presentation, Corn Design, 3 Horns, Quadruple Plate, 16 In. 4200.00
Waiter, Old Sheffield Style, 2 Handles, Ellis Barker, c.1940, 17 1/2 x 30 In. 1150.00
Waiter, Scroll & Flower, Engraved Leafy Scroll, Birks Of Canada, 15 x 26 In. 490.00
Wall Pocket, Scrolls, Leaves, Crest, Oval, 12 In., Pair 230.00
Warmer, Cover, Armorials On Side, Well & Tree, 1880, 18 x 29 x 22 In. 5750.00
Warmer, Spoon, Reeded Rim, Ivory Finial, Engraved Crest, 4 Ball Feet, 5 1/4 In. 185.00
Wine Coaster, Flared Banded Rim, England, 19th Century, 5 In., Pair 230.00
Wine Coaster, Openwork Sides, Floral Medallions, Treen Interior, 5 1/2 In., Pair 290.00
Wine Cooler, Banded Rims, Ring Handles, 20th Century, 7 x 6 In., Pair 490.00
Wine Cooler, Urn Form, S-Scroll Handles, Floral Terminals, 1920s, 10 1/4 In., Pair 1495.00

SILVER, SHEFFIELD, see Silver Plate; Silver-English categories.

SILVER-AMERICAN. American silver is listed here. Coin and sterling silver are included. Most of the sterling silver listed in this book is subdivided by country. There are also other pieces of silver and silver plate listed under special categories, such as Candelabrum, Napkin Ring, Silver Flatware, Silver Plate, Silver-Sterling, and Tiffany Silver. For information about makers and marks, see *Kovels' American Silver Marks: 1650 to the Present.*

SILVER-AMERICAN, Asparagus Server, Foliate Terminal, 4 Oz., 8 In. 196.00
Basket, Pierced Border, Monogram, Cobalt Blue Liner, Gorham, 4 In. 259.00
Basket, Sugar, Footed, Swing Handle, Ball, Black & Co., 6 1/2 In. 725.00
Basket, Swing Handle, Robert W. Wilson, Signed, c.1825, 9 x 9 3/4 In. 1645.00
Bowl, Applied Iris Design, Footed, Wm. Kerr & Co., 3 1/4 x 6 3/4 In. 750.00
Bowl, Arts & Crafts, Footed, Gorham, 24 Troy Oz., 3 x 8 3/4 In. 750.00
Bowl, Banded Rim, Openwork Sides, Shreve, Crump & Low, Boston, 10 In. 430.00
Bowl, Broad Repousse Border, Flowers, Leaves, Gorham, 1919, 7 1/2 In. 149.00
Bowl, Centerpiece, Flared Rim, Circular, Gorham, 1954, 10 1/4 In. 200.00
Bowl, Chased With Swirling Waves, 3 Cast Dolphins, 1860, 9 3/4 In. 9600.00
Bowl, Chased, Round, Ringed Ram's Head Handles, Tuttle, c.1900, 3 1/4 x 8 In. 750.00
Bowl, Crimped Edge, 3 Panels Of Exotic Fish, Whiting, 1889, 8 In., Pair 3900.00
Bowl, Cupids & Leaves, Reticulated Border, Black, Starr & Frost, 12 In. 980.00
Bowl, Elongated Rim, Scrolled Edge, Gorham, 1910, 14 In. 1840.00
Bowl, Floral Repousse Rim, Ribbed, Shreve, Crump & Low Co., 10 x 1 5/8 In. 190.00
Bowl, Flowers & Leaves, Pierced Border, Redlich, 6 x 6 In. 185.00
Bowl, Flying Bird, Wheat Ears, Gorham, 1879, 11 3/4 In. 4900.00
Bowl, Footed, Gorham, 1917, 4 x 8 3/4 In. 375.00
Bowl, Footed, Relief, Chased Flowers, c.1900, 10 In. Diam. 8050.00
Bowl, Francis I, Reed & Barton, 21 Oz., 11 1/2 In. 405.00
Bowl, Fruit, Architectural Repousse, Footed, Kirk & Son, c.1923, 8 1/2 In. 865.00
Bowl, Fruit, Circular, Whiting Mfg. Co., 1910, 4 1/4 x 10 1/2 In. 805.00
Bowl, Fruit, Francis I, Flared Rim, Embossed Scrolls, Fruit, Reed & Barton, 11 1/2 In. ... 550.00
Bowl, Fruit, Lobed Quadrangular Form, Flared Rim, Reed & Barton, 11 In. 550.00
Bowl, Hibiscus, Footed, Whiting Mfg. Co., 1910, 3 1/2 In. 230.00
Bowl, Molded Rim, Hammered, Floral, Circular, Wallace, 10 1/2 In. 260.00
Bowl, Paneled, Circular Sides, Inscription, Hayes & McFarland, 1885, 10 In. 175.00
Bowl, Paul Revere, Lunt, 5 x 10 In. 170.00
Bowl, Quatrefoil Rolled Rim, Lobed, Shallow, Hammered, Mark, Kalo, c.1915, 9 In. 865.00
Bowl, Renaissance, Spaulding & Company, 1920, 2 3/4 x 9 7/8 In. 200.00
Bowl, Repousse Bull's-Eyes, Bellflowers, Floral, Gorham, 10 1/4 x 2 1/4 In. 165.00
Bowl, Reticulated Sides, Scrolled Rococo Rim, Gorham, Oval, 12 x 9 x 2 In. 250.00
Bowl, Serving, Reeded Scroll Design, Reticulated Sides, Herschede, 11 In. 1495.00
Bowl, Spring Glory, Pierced At Intervals With Flowers, International, 12 1/2 In. 97.00
Bowl & Plate, Child's, Gorham, 1910, 5 1/2 In., 2 Piece ....*Illus* 520.00
Box, Cover, Arts & Crafts, Hammered, 4 1/4 x 3 In. 431.00
Bread Basket, Cinderella, Leaf Border & Rim, Gorham, Monogram, 12 3/4 In. 90.00
Bread Tray, Whiting Mfg. Co., 1905, 12 x 8 1/2 In., 2 Piece 290.00
Brush & Mirror, Pocket, Reed & Barton 75.00
Butter, Canoe Shape, Gorham, 1890, 9 1/2 In. 1800.00
Candelabrum is listed in its own category.

Candlesticks are listed in their own category.

Candy Dish, Floral Repousse Rims, Stippled Ground, S. Kirk & Son, 6 1/4 x 3 In.	355.00
Candy Dish, Flowers & Leaves, Monogram, Gorham, c.1905, 7 In., Pair	2990.00
Cann, Double Scroll Handle, Spreading Molded Foot, Phil., 1760, 5 In.	6600.00
Cann, Leaf Capped Double Scroll Handle, 1780, 5 1/2 In.	6600.00
Card Case, Flange Interior, Coin, 1870, 3 1/2 In.	230.00
Card Case, Trinity Church, c.1850, Coin, 3 1/2 In.	700.00
Carving Set, Reed & Barton, 1907, 13 1/2 In., 2 Piece	375.00
Casket, Jewelry, Engraved Leaves, Lock, Reed & Barton, 4 1/4 x 8 3/4 In.	430.00
Chocolate Pot, Building, Bridge & Fence Reverse, Foliate Spout, Kirk, 11 In. . . .1512.00 to	1695.00
Cocktail Shaker, Art Deco, Boardman & Co., Large, 1930	1800.00
Coffee & Tea Set, Fluted Form, Scroll Handles, Durgin Co., 6 Piece	1380.00
Coffee & Tea Set, Shell & Leaf Design, Whiting, 6 Piece	5175.00
Coffee & Tea Set, Shield Shaped Body, Reed & Barton, 4 Piece	860.00
Coffee Set, Medallion, Cream Pitcher, Footed, Gorham, 1864, 64 Oz.	1610.00
Coffee Set, Medallion, Gorham, 4 Piece	1610.00
Coffee Set, Rose Repousse, Gilt Interior, Gorham, 1900, 3 Piece	430.00
Coffeepot, Carved Ivory Finial, Reed & Barton, 1951, 11 3/4 In.	860.00
Coffeepot, Domed Cover, Baluster Finial, McAuliffe & Hadley, 6 1/4 In.	200.00
Coffeepot, Floral Finial, Ram's Head On Handle, A.E. Warner, 8 In.	3600.00
Coffeepot, Shaped Dome, Fishing Scene, Obadiah Rich, Boston, 10 In.	1725.00
Coffeepot, Vase Form, Urn Finial, Swan Neck Spout, Joel Sayre, c.1805, 13 In.	5175.00
Compote, Embossed Beaded Leaf Band, Gorham, 1874, 8 x 5 3/4 In.	546.00
Compote, Flared Rim, Graff, Washbourne & Dunn, 10 In., Pair	1725.00
Compote, Gilt Interior, Lion Mask Handles, Kidney, Cann & Johnson, 4 1/2 In.	316.00
Compote, Leaf Molded Rim, Circular, Bigelow & Kennard, 8 3/4 In.	345.00
Compote, Raised Reticulated Rim, Leaf Center, Dominick & Haff, 8 In.	170.00
Creamer, 6 Panels, Floral Scenes, S Handle, S. Kirk & Son, c.1855, 5 In.	750.00
Creamer, Allover Floral Repousse Design, C Handle, Kirk, c.1855, 2 1/2 In.	325.00
Creamer, Coin, Banding, Geradus Boyce, NY, c.1857, 6 1/2 x 8 In.	460.00
Cup, Christening, Branches, Ferns, Monogram, R. Wallace & Son, 3 x 2 1/2 In.	340.00
Cup, Christening, Inscribed, 8 Sides, Gale, Wood & Hughes, c.1840, 3 1/4 In.	550.00
Cup, Regency, Handles, Howard & Company, N.Y., 1910, 17 x 14 1/2 In.	1955.00
Dessert Spoon, Fiddle, Anthony Rasch, c.1820 . . . . .460.00 to	690.00
Dish, Allover Flowers & Leaves, 2 Vacant Cartouches, Gorham, 13 1/4 In.	2300.00
Dish, Leaf Form, 3 Sections, Shreve & Company, 14 Oz.	100.00
Ewer, Chased With Rococo Scrolls, Floral Sprays, Scroll Handle, 17 In.	5400.00
Ewer, National Capital Horse Show Scene, Dominick & Haff, 1921, 19 In.	3680.00
Fish Slice, Engraved Foliate Design, Crosby, Morse & Foss, 1875, 12 In.	230.00
Flask, Monk In Wine Cellar, Hinged Lid, Locking Collar, R. Wallace, 5 1/2 In.	690.00
Goblet, Engraved, Monogram, Stieff, 6 1/2 In., 6 Piece	520.00
Goblet, Repousse Leaves, Flowers, Round Foot, S. Kirk & Son, 10 Oz., 6 In., Pair	748.00
Goblet, Tulip Form, Wallace, 6 Piece	300.00
Grater, Nutmeg, Storage Section Over Grater, Dominick & Haff, 5 In.	1210.00
Ice Tongs, Francis I, Claw Terminals, Reed & Barton, 6 3/4 In., Pair	540.00
Jar, Dresser, Chased Work, Monogram, Reed & Barton, 3 1/4 x 3 3/4 In.	375.00
Jar, Dresser, Hinged Silver Cover, Embossed Leaves, Glass Stopper, 5 In.	430.00
Jewelry Box, Cover, Cream Velvet Lined Interior, Spaulding Gorham, 1955	405.00
Jug, Beaded Bands, Scrolled Handle, Coin, Jones, Ball & Co., c.1854, 7 1/4 In.	315.00
Jug, Beaded Foot, Loop Handle, Engraved Name, Harding & Co., 8 1/4 In.	520.00
Jug, Domed Cover, Cast Swan Finial, Ear Shaped Handle, 1860, 8 3/4 In.	520.00

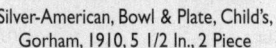

Silver-American, Bowl & Plate, Child's,
Gorham, 1910, 5 1/2 In., 2 Piece

Silver-American, Sugar & Creamer,
Hammered, Fessenden & Co., Late 1800s

Jug, Milk, Medallion, 4 Medallions, Gorham, 1895 .... 200.00
Julep Cup, Horsehead On Front, Webster Co., 1920, 3 3/4 In., 12 Piece 1915.00
Ladle, Fiddle Pattern, Monogram, Mitchell & Tyler, Richmond, Mid 1800s, 13 1/2 In. 460.00
Ladle, Monogram, Coin, S. Kirk & Son, Baltimore, 1846-1861, 13 In. 520.00
Ladle, Moreau Sarrazin, Charleston, S.C., c.1750 .... 6000.00
Ladle, Signed, Abraham Dubois, Philadelphia & New York, Late 1700s, 5 1/2 Oz. 305.00
Ladle, Signed, Thomas Shields, Philadelphia, c.1790 .... 525.00
Ladle, Twisted Handle, Double Pouring Spout, Shreve, Crump & Lowe, 16 In. 405.00
Letter Opener, Brocade, Towle 20.00
Loving Cup, 2 Handles, Whiting, c.1900, 12 In. 4025.00
Loving Cup, Morris & Essex Kennel Club Logo, Black, Starr & Frost, 11 1/4 In. 460.00
Mug, Beaded Rim, Scrolled Flowers, Foliage, Coin, W.D. Whiting, 4 1/4 In. 315.00
Mug, Gold Wash Interior, Engraved Inscription, Gorham, 3 1/2 In. 165.00
Mug, Pear Shape, Banded Rim, Handle, James Woolley, Boston, 5 1/4 In. 546.00
Mug, Presentation, Coin, Albert Henry Minot From Grandmother 1851, 4 In. 175.00
Mug, Vacant Cartouche, Angular Handle, 4 Oz., 3 1/4 In. 230.00
Mustard & Spoon, Dominick & Haff, c.1920 .... 200.00
Napkin Rings are listed in their own category.
Nut Dish, Leaf Form, Gorham-Durgin Co., 1915, 10 Oz. 460.00
Nut Serving Set, Heart Form, Reed & Barton, 1895, 6 Piece 400.00
Nut Serving Set, Water Lily, Richard Wallace & Son, 1905, 7 Piece 375.00
Pie Server, Coin, Ball, Black & Co., New York, c.1851-1864, 10 In. 375.00
Pie Server, Coin, Scrolling, Leaf Openwork, J.E. Caldwell & Co., 10 1/4 In. 160.00
Pitcher, 4 Bowknotted Wreaths At Shoulder, Floral Festoon, c.1920, 10 1/2 In. 690.00
Pitcher, Beverage, Ice Lip, Footed, Coin, Peter L. Krider, 1850, 12 In. 1495.00
Pitcher, Cream, Mark, Garrett Eoff, c.1795, 5 1/2 In. 1495.00
Pitcher, Flowers, Monogram, Rectangle, Canted Corners, Square Handle, 8 In. 578.00
Pitcher, Iced Tea, Repousse, Cooper & Fisher, c.1855, 10 In. 920.00
Pitcher, Overall Floral & Leaf, Gorham, c.1900, 7 In. 1320.00
Pitcher, Paul Revere Reproduction, Reed & Barton, 21 Oz., 8 In. 315.00
Pitcher, Plain Baluster, Flowers, Leaves On Handle, Dominick & Haff, 8 3/4 In. 489.00
Pitcher, Poppy Plants, Handle, Gorham Mfg. Co., 1905, 9 5/8 In. 9000.00
Pitcher, Water, Adam, J.E. Caldwell & Co., 1925, 10 3/4 In. 805.00
Pitcher, Water, Aquatic Plants, Fish, Swimming, N.Y., 1880, 9 1/8 In. 9000.00
Pitcher, Water, Bulbous, Scroll Handles, Footed, Mark, International, 4 1/2 Pt. 520.00
Pitcher, Water, Fluted, Gadrooned Rim, Scroll Handle, 1832, 10 In., Pair 2160.00
Pitcher, Water, Rectangular, Canted Corner, Handle, Wallace, 24 Oz., 9 1/4 In. 750.00
Pitcher, Water, Spiraled Gadroons, Bolt Handle, Gorham Mfg. Co., 11 In. 3600.00
Pitcher, Water, Waisted Cylinder, Plain Ear Handle, Shreve, Crump & Low, 7 In. 690.00
Pitcher, Water, Waisted Neck, Repousse, Chased Birds, Coin, 8 In. 2760.00
Plate, Black, Starr & Frost, c.1900, 7 Piece 2310.00
Plate, Repousse Floral Border, Engraved, Hammered, S. Kirk & Son, 10 In. 220.00
Platter, Chased With Cartouches, Flowers, Oval, Gorham, 1905, 17 In. 5400.00
Platter, Meat, Gadrooned, Bud Rim, Horse Crest, 1820, 15 In., Pair 14400.00
Platter, Meat, Oval, Gorham, 1925, 16 x 12 1/4 In. 258.00
Platter, Monogram, Arthur J. Stone, c.1915, 16 x 12 In. 575.00
Platter, Scrolling Rim, Monogram On Back, Whiting, Oval, 16 In. 315.00
Platter, Well-And-Tree, Elliptical, Gorham, 1913, 13 x 19 In. 630.00
Porringer, Double Arched Handle, John Edwards, Boston, 1740, 5 In. 4200.00
Porringer, Geometric Pierced Handle, Johannis Nys, c.1715, 5 1/8 In. 9200.00
Porringer, Jonathan Clarke, Newport, R.I., 1740, 4 3/4 In. 3300.00
Porringer, Samuel Vernon, Newport, R.I., c.1710, 7 1/4 In. 1610.00
Punch Bowl, Bombe, Pierced Seed Pod Rim, Gorham, 1905, 15 In. 3900.00
Punch Bowl, Embossed Flowers On Upper Body, Gorham, 1880, 11 In. 2875.00
Punch Bowl, Repousse, Engraved, Footed, Kirk & Son, c.1924, 8 1/2 x 11 1/4 In. 2185.00
Punch Ladle, Elliptical Bowl, Fiddle Handle, Coin, Davis, Palmer & Co., c.1846, 12 In. ... 230.00
Punch Ladle, Elliptical Bowl, Fiddle Handle, Coin, Taylor & Hinsdale, N.Y., c.1817 .... 260.00
Punch Ladle, Ivy, Leaves, Flowers, Flared Rim, Gorham, 13 1/4 In. 287.00
Punch Ladle, Monogram, Coin, Henry Longley, c.1810, New York, 12 1/2 In. 345.00
Punch Ladle, Nathan L. Hazen, 13 1/8 In. 775.00
Punch Ladle, Upturned Fiddle Handle, J. Einstein, Philadelphia, 13 In. 230.00
Purse, Change, Folding, Bigelow, Kennard, Monogram 160.00
Salver, Ball & Claw Feet, S. Kirk & Son, c.1850, 11 Oz., 9 3/8 In. 850.00

Salver, Chased With Sloping Flutes, Phil., 1760, 14 1/4 In. 3300.00
Salver, Flower, Scroll Feet, Monogram, F. Marquand, 1830, 11 3/4 In., Pair 4600.00
Sandwich Server, Hammered, William C. Finck, N.J., 1910, 6 1/4 In. 170.00
Sandwich Tray, Floral, Circular, Bigelow, Kennard & Co., 1915, 15 In. 1150.00
Sandwich Tray, Handles, Circular, Woodside Sterling Co., N.Y., 12 In. 345.00
Sauce, Scalloped Foot Footed, 2 Ladles, Reed & Barton, 4 5/8 In., Pair 135.00
Sauce Ladle, Figural Mount, Ball, Black & Co. 605.00
Scoop, Strawberry, Albert Cole, c.1845, 9 1/2 In. 175.00
Scoop, Strawberry, Repousse, Gilt, Coin, Albert Coles, N.Y., 1860, 9 1/2 In. 170.00
Serving Fork, Leaf Decoration On Tines, Crosby & Brown, American, 9 In. 160.00
Serving Spoon, Reverse Scalloped Edge Handle, John Cook, N.Y., 1795, 9 3/4 In. 180.00
Shoehorn, Hammered Surface, Monogram, Kalo, 4 3/4 In. 546.00
Sifter, Powder, Cartouche Reading, Scrollwork, Mt. Vernon Co., 1910 . . . . 200.00
Soup Ladle, Edward & David Kinsey, 13 3/4 In. 750.00
Soup Ladle, Fiddle Handle, Arthur Stone 290.00
Soup Ladle, Plain Fiddle Terminal, Inscribed, Wood & Hughes, 12 1/2 In. 170.00
Soup Tureen, Rococo Style, 2 Handles, Gorham, c.1897, 9 1/2 x 15 In. 1495.00
Spoon, Bright Cut, Engraved Monogram, J. Shoemaker, 5 7/8 In., 4 Piece 140.00
Spoon, Engraved Monogram, Willard, 7 Piece 50.00
Spoon, John McMullin, c.1790, 5 Piece 110.00
Spoon, Mark Of Joseph & Nathaniel Richardson, Philadelphia, Monogram SW 80.00
Spoon, Shell Shape, Gorham, c.1900-1915, 6 In. 45.00
Stuffing Spoon, 1867, 13 In. 374.00
Sugar, Butterfly Handles, Aesthetic Movement, Kirk, c.1915, 4 x 6 In. 1350.00
Sugar & Creamer, Cover, Vertical Fluting, Ear Handles, Gorham, 1894 . . . . 375.00
Sugar & Creamer, Hammered, Fessenden & Co., Late 1800s . . . . *Illus* 135.00
Sugar & Creamer, Hammered, Floral Repousse Work, Barbour 145.00
Sugar & Creamer, Medallion Design, Swing Handle, Coin, 1870 . . . . 690.00
Sugar Nips, Charles Heisler, 4 In. 30.00
Sugar Shaker, Peacock Sides & Finial, Tail Spread, Durgin, 1928, 7 In. 1495.00
Sugar Spoon, Shell Shape, Gorham, 1900-1915, 6 In. 45.00
Sugar Tongs, Monogram, Bennett & Caldwell, c.1843-1848, 6 1/4 In. 69.00
Sugar Tongs, Plain Scalloped, 19th Century, 11 1/2 In. 172.00
Tablespoon, Fiddle Tipped, Wood & Hughes, Monogram, c.1850, 5 Piece 145.00
Tablespoon, John Potter, c.1821, 7 1/4 In. 680.00
Tablespoon, R.W. Wilson 137.00
Tablespoon, Wood & Hughes, c.1850, 5 Piece 258.00
Tablespoon, Ziba Ferris & Son, 4 Piece 132.00
Tankard, High Domed Cover, Scroll Handle, George Hanners, 1740, 9 In. 3600.00
Tankard, Stepped Domed Cover, Shaped Peak, Scroll Handle, 1750, 8 In. 4800.00
Tazza, Marsh Scene With Heron Devouring A Frog, Gorham, 1880, 12 In. 3300.00
Tea & Coffee Set, Art Nouveau Monogram, Black, Starr & Frost, 7 Piece 660.00
Tea & Coffee Set, Chased With Naturalistic Flowers, 1884, 6 Piece 6600.00
Tea & Coffee Set, Fluted Bodies, Scrollwork Frame, c.1905, 6 Piece 6900.00
Tea & Coffee Set, Gorham, 1930, 5 Piece 2875.00
Tea & Coffee Set, Hammered, Engraved, Tray, Baltimore Silver Co., 6 Piece 4500.00
Tea & Coffee Set, Monogram, Urn Finials, Gorham, 8 Piece 5695.00
Tea & Coffee Set, Repousse, Flowers, Acanthus, S. Kirk & Son., 11 In., 5 Piece 5175.00
Tea & Coffee Set, Sagamore Pattern, Reed & Barton, 6 Piece 2875.00
Tea & Coffee Set, Scrolled Reserved Crest, Samuel Kirk, 1846, 6 Piece 5400.00
Tea Set, Bachelor, Reeded Lids, Gorham Mfg. Co., 1898, 9 1/2 x 7 1/4 In. 750.00
Tea Set, Colfax, Chased With Panels, Gorham, Providence, R.I., 5 Piece 4800.00
Tea Set, Domed Cover, Reeded Urn Finials, Gorham, R.I., 1950, 9 In. 690.00
Tea Set, Engraved Flowers, Monogram, Rand & Crane, 7 Piece 2760.00
Tea Set, Floral Repousse, Kirk & Son, 3 Piece 660.00
Tea Set, Lobed Dome Cover, Bulbous Body, N. Taylor & Co., 1825, 4 Piece 1725.00
Tea Set, Oval Body, Strap Handles, Swags, N. Harding & Co., c.1820, 6 In., 3 Piece 1610.00
Tea Set, Oval, Set With Bird, Starr & Marcus, Teapot, 4 In., 6 Piece 1035.00
Tea Set, Paul Revere Reproduction, Harris & Schafer, 5 Piece 1725.00
Tea Set, Plymouth Pattern, Gorham, 4 Piece 1320.00
Tea Set, Queen Anne Style, Gorham, 5 Piece 1150.00
Tea Set, Scrolled Leaves, Palmette Bands, N.Y., 1840, 4 Piece 3900.00
Tea Set, Swing Handle Teapot, Raised On Oval Foot, Gorham, 11 In., 3 Piece 483.00

Teakettle, Domed Cover, Stand, Molded Chrysanthemums, 14 In. 8050.00
Teapot, Winterberry, Enameled Gilt, R. Blackinton & Co., 3 1/2 In. 690.00
Teaspoon, Chaudron & Rasch, c.1812, 4 Piece . . . . .530.00 to 632.00
Toddy Ladle, Hammered, Chased With Flowers, Flutes, 1770, 12 In. 2400.00
Tongs, Marked, Wm Gale & Son, Patented 1860, 6 1/2 In. 325.00
Tongs, Serving, Wood & Hughes, c.1880, 9 In. 550.00
Tray, Arthur J. Stone, C Mark, Monogram, 15 1/2 x 11 In. 978.00
Tray, Beaded Rim, Leaves, Coin, Haddock, Lincoln & Foss, 1860, 6 In. 690.00
Tray, Canapes, Shell Form, Gorham, 9 1/4 x 9 1/4 In. 230.00
Tray, Chippendale, Reed & Barton, 13 3/4 In. 230.00
Tray, Embossed Leaves, Castles, Matte, Loring Andrews Co., 9 In. 490.00
Tray, Floral Border, Hoop Handles, Gorham Mfg. Co., 1881, 28 In. 5100.00
Tray, Floral, Foliate Repousse, Serpentine Rim, Gorham, 1924, 14 In. 400.00
Tray, Gadrooned Border, Oval, Coin, Gorham & Co., c.1865, 8 3/4 x 12 In. 375.00
Tray, Hirsch & Oppenheimer, Chicago, 1927, 13 3/4 In. 750.00
Tray, Pierced & Chased Border, Monogram, Dominick & Haff, 12 In. 230.00
Tray, Presentation, Cricket Players, Cricket Bat, Whiting, c.1884, 6 1/2 In. 230.00
Tray, Presentation, Floral Rim, Laurel Wreath Border, Kirk, 1921 . . . . 1035.00
Tray, Rococo Cartouche Border, Floral, Marshall Field & Co., 22 In., Pair 3600.00
Tray, Scroll & Shell Border, Mark, No. 376, Round, Frank Whiting Co., 16 In. 345.00
Tray, Serpentine Rim, Floral Repousse, Marked Gorham For Grogan, 1924, 14 In. 400.00
Tray, Sweetmeat, Grape Leaf Shape, Reed & Barton, 1936, 8 3/4 x 9 1/4 In. 145.00
Trophy, Scroll Handles, Circular Foot, Leaves, Meriden Britannia Co., 13 In. 690.00
Trophy, Scroll Handles, Mermaid Figures, Meriden Britannia Co., 24 In. 3450.00
Tureen, Soup, Cover, Boat Form, Cow & A Calf On A Lakeshore, 1865, 18 In. 6000.00
Tureen, Soup, Cover, Floral Swags, Lion, Ring Handles, 1905, 14 1/2 In. 4500.00
Urn, Domed Cover, Allover Embossed Leaves, Doomed Foot, 16 1/2 In. 1725.00
Urn, Reeded Shaped Cover, Leaf Sprays, Abner Reeder, Pa., 1790, 10 In. 1440.00
Vase, American Rococo Style, Reed & Barton, Footed, c.1904, 8 x 6 1/2 In. 575.00
Vase, Circular Foot, Monogram, Reed & Barton, 8 1/2 In. 80.00
Vase, Circular Foot, Weighted, Durgin, 12 In. 230.00
Vase, Repousse Frieze, Acanthus Leaf Design Base, Gorham, 10 1/8 In. 980.00
Vase, Trumpet Shape, Grotesque Fish, Gorham, 11 In. 4600.00
Waiter, 4 Fluted Triangular Feet, William Ball, Jr., c.1790, 7 1/2 In. 3450.00
SILVER-AUSTRIAN, Bell, Dinner, Elongated Stem, Ivory Knop, Josef Hoffmann, 1930, 8 In. . . 7200.00
Bowl, Fruit, Flared Lip & Handles, Reticulated, Bachrach, c.1905, 9 x 14 1/2 In. 690.00
Centerpiece, Chased With Scaly Sea Monster, Early 20th Century, 14 In. 5400.00
Cigarette Case, Enamel, Roadster, F. Zwicki, 4 In. 750.00
Cornucopia, Allegorical Scene, St. George Slaying The Dragon, 1885, 9 In. 4800.00
Ewer, Scroll Handle, Reeded Girdle, 1831, 10 3/8 In. 2400.00
Ewer, Stand, Allegorical Scene, Exotic Animal Head, Enamel, 1885, 9 In. 6000.00
Salt, Eagle, Spread Wings, Gilt Interior, Mayerhoffer & Klinkosch, 1865, 4 In. 7200.00
Spice Tower, Scrolled Leafy Filigree Sides, 4 Twisted Legs, 1865, 7 1/2 In. 460.00
Wine Jug, Chased With Scroll, Floral Band, Beaded Rims, 1797, 10 In. 1095.00
SILVER-CANADIAN, Compote, Tendril Border, Buds At Corners, P. Peterson, c.1953, 12 In. 1679.00
SILVER-CHINESE, Mug, Allover Scene Of Villages, Dragon Handle, 19th Century, 4 1/2 In. . . . 690.00
Punch Bowl, Flowerhead Design, 1910, 5 1/2 x 11 1/2 In. 400.00
Teapot, Melon Shape, 1900, 5 3/4 In., Pair 747.00
SILVER-CONTINENTAL, Beaker, Blank Fruit Wreath, Footed, 1860, 4 1/4 In. 105.00
Bowl, Flared Silver Rim, Repousse Scrolls, Circular, 4 x 2 1/2 In. 170.00
Bowl, Molded Scroll Design, Loop Handle, Angular Foot, 2 1/4 In. 260.00
Box, Cigar, Hinged Cover, Handles, Late 19th Century, 1 1/2 x 4 1/4 In. 635.00
Box, Filigree, Leaves, Acorn Finial, Late 19th Century, 4 1/2 In. 200.00
Cake Basket, Swing Handle, c.1865, 12 x 10 In. 400.00
Card Case, Gilt, Filigree, Hallmark, R. Palson, c.1870, 4 x 2 3/4 In. 315.00
Chalice, Bunch Of Grapes, Classical Warrior Standing On Dome, 12 In. 980.00
Cigarette Case, Cover, Gentleman In Evening Dress, 4 1/4 In. 1680.00
Cigarette Case, Scene Of Nude & Youth, Hand Painted, 1900, 4 In. 400.00
Dresser Set, 2 Jars, 2 Brushes, Mirror, Dog On Each Piece, c.1927 . . . . 4030.00
Fork, Engraved Band Handle, Holland, 1749, 7 In. 260.00
Fork, Serving, Pierced, 10 1/4 In. 750.00
Goblet, Flared Rim, Acanthus Band Leaves, Domed Foot, 7 In. 540.00
Ladle, Brandy, Gilt, Rosewood, Ivory, 1800, 11 1/4 In. 200.00

Lipstick Holder, Built-In Mirror, Chased, 3 x 2 1/2 In. 75.00
Marrow Scoop, Double End, Giller, c.1840, 9 1/2 In. 175.00
Mustard Pot, Repousse, Footed, 1865, 4 In. 90.00
Salt & Pepper, Louis XVI, 1900, 6 1/4 In., Pair 865.00
Sauceboat, Scroll Design Rim, Cast Ear Handle, Germany, 6 1/4 In. 1265.00
Spice Tower, Scrolled Filigree Sides, Tapered Shaft, 8 1/4 In. 485.00
Spoon, Silver, 14 1/4 In. 195.00
Stand, Sweetmeat, Cut & Parcel, White Opaline Glass, Footed, 8 In. 345.00
Sugar, Cover, Repousse Flowers, Leaf Capped Feet, Handles, 4 In. 46.00
Sugar Nips, Scissor Form, c.1800, 5 1/2 In., Pair 430.00
Sugar Nips, Scissors Shape, Gilding, c.1810, 5 1/2 In. 430.00
Sugar Tongs, With Claws, 5 1/2 In. 200.00
Tankard, Landscape Scene, Courting & Dancing Couples, 5 In. 748.00
Tea Set, Embossed Leaves, Scroll Design, 4 Foliate Feet, 4 1/2 In. 517.00
Toothpick, With Ear Scoop, 17th Century, 4 In. 395.00
Tray, Putti Within Leaves, Scrolls, Cast Scroll Handles, Germany, 17 In. 488.00
Urn, Dancing Bacchantes Above Classical Foliage, 20 In., Pair 8400.00
Vase, 7 Bands Chased Design, Engraved Leaves, Handle, 6 3/4 In. 258.00
Wedding Crown, Scroll, Shell Design, Star Shaped Top, Ball Finial, 10 In. 460.00
SILVER-DANISH, Beaker, Presentation, Leaf Lip, Cover, Georg Jensen, 1930, 10 In. 5175.00
Bowl, Centerpiece, Openwork Leaf & Berry Stem, Georg Jensen, 1945, 8 In. 2640.00
Bowl, Centerpiece, Oval, Shallow, Georg Jensen Silversmithy, 17 3/4 In. 8400.00
Bowl, Pendant Grape Clusters, Oval, Signed, Georg Jensen, 16 In. 1150.00
Box, Cover, Georg Jensen Silversmithy, Copenhagen, c.1927, 5 In. 8400.00
Cake Plate, Applied Leafy Handles, 13 In. 184.00
Compote, Grapevine Stems, Footed, Etruscan Revival Style, Georg Jensen, Pair 7650.00
Crumber, Acorn, Ball Feet, Georg Jensen, c.1933, 8 3/4 In. 3022.00
Demitasse Set, Bombe Shape, Georg Jensen, Copenhagen, c.1915, 3 Piece 4500.00
Ladle, Denmark Pattern, Georg Jensen, 7 1/2 In. 485.00
Pitcher, Rolled Rim, Hammered, Stepped Base, Georg Jensen, 1925, 11 1/2 In. 4315.00
Plate, Beaded Rim, C.C. Hermann, 20th Century, 10 1/4 In., 12 Piece 4315.00
Sauceboat, Bifurcated Scroll Handle, Georg Jensen, 1926, 5 In. 2185.00
Tankard, 78 Coins & Medals, Lion Thumbpiece, Martin Luther Finial, 11 1/4 In. ... 6000.00
Tazza, Grapevine, Georg Jensen, 1945, 7 1/2 In. 3600.00
Tea Set, Georg Jensen Silversmithy, Copenhagen, c.1929, 4 Piece 5700.00
SILVER-DUTCH, Box, Flowers, Cartouches, Putti At Play, Ball Finial, Hinged, 3 1/2 In. 230.00
Box, Tobacco, Oval, Natural Cowrie Shell, c.1802, 1 3/4 In. 518.00
Inkstand, Gadrooned Border, Central Standard, Ball Feet, 1828, 5 1/4 In. 575.00
Teapot, Domed Lid, Beaded Openwork Rim, Upright Cast Handle, 6 3/4 In. 460.00

SILVER-ENGLISH. English sterling silver is marked with a series of four
or five small hallmarks. The standing lion mark is the most commonly
seen sterling quality mark. The other marks indicate the city of origin,
the maker, and the year of manufacture. These dates can be verified in
many good books on silver.

SILVER-ENGLISH, Basket, Boat Form, Hester Bateman, 1784, 13 1/2 In. 3600.00
Basket, Dessert, Shell Form, Mermaid Handle, 3 Dolphin Supports, 1902, 10 In. ... 3000.00
Basket, Gilt Interior, Reticulated, Belle Epoque, 1910, 11 1/2 In. 1265.00
Basket, Gilt, Twin Tailed Mermaid Handles, G. Lambert, 1892, 12 In., Pair 7200.00
Basket, Sweetmeat, Swing Handle, James Dixon & Sons, 1865, 8 1/2 In. 575.00
Basket, Swing Handle, Oval, Footed, Sheffield, George V, 1925, 7 x 10 In. 145.00
Biscuit Basket, Gold Wash Interior, Scrolled Feet, 2 Folding Shells, 10 1/2 In. 467.00
Bottle, Domed Cover, Band Of Birds, Leaves, Anthony Nelme, 1707, 8 In. 6600.00
Bowl, Chased With Flowers, Leafy Scrolls, Bombe Shape, 1892, 11 In. 1920.00
Bowl, Hemispherical Shape, Harp Handles, Wakely & Wheeler, 1902, 18 In. 2880.00
Bowl, Leaf Design, Birmingham, GN-RH, 1876, 3 1/4 In. 470.00
Bowl, On Stand, Pierced With Interlaced Arches, Handles, 1779, 17 In. 8700.00
Bowl, Scalloped Rim, Footed, 1943, 1 3/4 x 8 1/4 In. 330.00
Bowl, Straight Gadroons, Chased With Ribbon Swags, 1888, 11 In. 2700.00
Bowl, Sweetmeat, Edwardian, Leaves, Scrolls, Sheffield, 1904, 3 x 10 1/2 In. ... 1035.00
Box, Repousse Allover With Birds & Leaves, Monogram, 1895, 3 1/4 In. 85.00
Box, Round, Phipps & Robinson, Engraved, Armorial, George III, 1 x 3 3/4 In. ... 1150.00
Box, Tobacco, Engraved Arms, Calligraphic Inscription, N. Locke, 1715, 3 3/4 In. 5400.00

Silver-English, Cake Basket, Swing Handle,
Hennell, 1799, 8 1/2 x 12 3/4 In.

It is said you can clean silver with a banana peel mashed in a blender.

If you break the handle on an old silver coffeepot, have it resoldered. That repair detracts little from the resale value, but a new handle lowers the value by 50%.

Bread Basket, Applied Scroll Rim, Trailing Flowers, Swing Handle, 15 In.	8400.00
Bread Basket, Embossed Beading, Corded Rim, Wm. Plummer, 1768, 13 In.	2040.00
Butter, Cut Card Work, Cover, Mappin & Webb, Sheffield, c.1927, 3 Piece	865.00
Caddy Shovel, Engraved, Taylor & Perry, Birmingham, 1844, 3 1/2 x 1 1/4 In.	325.00
Caddy Spoon, Arts & Crafts Style, Wood Handle, Birmingham, 1903, 4 In.	225.00
Caddy Spoon, Bright Cut, London, 1802, 3 1/4 In.	225.00
Caddy Spoon, Bright Cut, T.S., London, 1876, 3 3/4 In.	110.00
Caddy Spoon, Charles Boynton, London, 1841, 3 3/4 x 1 3/4 In.	210.00
Caddy Spoon, Shovel Type, Joseph Taylor, Birmingham, 1818, 3 1/4 In.	275.00
Caddy Spoon, Tavern Scene, 1910, 3 1/4 In.	70.00
Cake Basket, Applied Shell, Scrollwork Rim, Edward Aldridge, 1753, 15 In.	7200.00
Cake Basket, Flowers, Swing Handle, Robinson, Edkins & Aston, 1842, 12 1/4 In.	3480.00
Cake Basket, Oval, Latticework Band, Paul Storr, London, George III, 1800, 14 3/4 In.	4315.00
Cake Basket, Swing Handle, Hennell, 1799, 8 1/2 x 12 3/4 In. ....*Illus*	1610.00
Cake Basket, Swing Handle, Twisted Wire Foot, W. Plummer, 1766, 13 In.	2070.00
Candelabrum is listed in its own category.	
Candlesticks are listed in their own category.	
Castor, Salt & Pepper, George W. Adams, 1889, 3 1/2 In., Pair	140.00
Castor, Salt & Pepper, Trellis, Scroll Panels, George II, c.1734, 5 1/2 x 2 1/4 In.	1150.00
Castor Set, With Frame, Central Ring Handle, Edward Terry, 1835, 12 In.	7200.00
Caudle Cup, Gadrooned Decoration, Scrolls, Leaves, George III, 1763, 3 3/4 In.	980.00
Chalice, Edwardian, Gilded Interior, Atkin Brothers, 1902, 9 In.	489.00
Chalice, Edwardian, Henley & Co., 1915, 7 3/4 In.	1035.00
Chalice, Gilt, Inverted Pear Shape Stem, 1767, 8 7/8 In.	4500.00
Chocolate Pot, Woman With Parasol, Openmouthed Lion Spout, T. Heming, 1750	9600.00
Cigar Case, Engraved Scrollwork & Florals, Birmingham Hallmarks	175.00
Cigarette Case, Birmingham, 1934, 3 1/2 x 2 1/2 In.	65.00
Coffee Urn, Acanthus Leaf Finial, Egg & Dart Rim, Sheffield, 21 1/2 In.	1760.00
Coffee Urn, Acorn Ivory Finial, Swags, Cherub Face Handles, E & Co. Ltd.	3300.00
Coffeepot, Acorn Finial, Coat Of Arms On Side, John Emes, 1799, 11 1/2 In.	1380.00
Coffeepot, Bud Finial On Lid, Spiral Reeding On Body, Coat Of Arms, 12 1/4 In.	1610.00
Coffeepot, Domed Cover, Faceted Spout, George II, 1728, 10 1/4 In.	1920.00
Coffeepot, Domed Cover, Swan Neck Spout, Gabriel Sleath, 1714, 9 In.	2160.00
Coffeepot, Domed Cover, Swan Neck Spout, Handle, R. Raine, 1713, 10 In.	5400.00
Coffeepot, Floral Repousse, Ivory Handle, 1870s, 9 1/2 In.	690.00
Coffeepot, Fruitwood Handle, James Young, George III, 1786, 13 1/2 In.	1495.00
Coffeepot, Gadroon Rim, Urn Finial, John Payne, 1769, 10 In.	1920.00
Coffeepot, Georgian, Rococo Style, Robert Garrard, Ivory Insulator, 10 In.	489.00
Coffeepot, Individual, Melon Rib Design, 7 In.	200.00
Cooler, Medici, Vintage, Bottle Sleeve, Collar, 1820-1825, 12 x 9 In.	3680.00
Creamer, Bulbous, Pedestal, Scroll Handle, Flowers, London, George III, 1780, 4 5/8 In.	140.00
Creamer, Canted Corners, Cut Design Below Rim, 1799, 4 1/2 In.	460.00
Creamer, Chased Floral, Presentation Monogram, 1855, 3 1/8 In.	110.00
Creamer, Chester, 1903, 3 x 5 In.	85.00
Cruet Set, Reeded Rim, Cut Glass, Footed, J.E. & W. Frisbee, George III, 1791, 8 1/2 In.	1380.00
Cruet Stand, 6 Cut Glass Bottles, Castor, Round, Central Handle, 8 1/2 x 8 In.	375.00

Cup, Beaded Rim, Border, Gilt Interior, John Denzilow, 1778, 5 1/2 In., Pair 2520.00
Cup, Cover, Alternate Portrait Medallion, Scroll Handles, George II, 11 In. 4140.00
Cup, Cover, Leaf-Capped Double Scroll Handles, Francis Nelme, 1731, 11 In. 6600.00
Cup, Engraved Leaves Rising To Knopped Stem, 2 Vacant Cartouches, 10 In. 290.00
Cup, Gilt Interior, 1754, 2 5/8 In., Pair 2700.00
Cup, Leaves & Flowers In Cartouche, Leaf Capped Handle, E. & J. Barnard, 3 1n. 345.00
Dish, Cross, Cover, Pear Shape Crest, S. Herbert & Co., 1766, 13 3/4 In. 1680.00
Dish, Entree, Gadroon, Leaf Rim, Handles, Paw Feet, On Copper, Sheffield, 16 In. 489.00
Dish, Meat, Gadrooned Rim, George III, Andrew Fogelberg, 1779, 13 In., Pair 2640.00
Dresser Set, 2 Jars, 2 Brushes, Mirror, W. Highland Terriers, Blue, Continental, c.1927 . . 4000.00
Epergne, 3 Compartment, Shell Shape, Walker & Hall, 1910, 14 x 11 In. 315.00
Epergne, 4 Branches, Glass Baskets, Central Cut Basket, 14 1/2 x 11 3/4 In. 1725.00
Epergne, Gadrooned Rim, 4 Reeded Column Legs, Matthew Boulton, 12 In. 1840.00
Fish Server, Fiddle Handle, William Bateman, London, 1817, 11 3/4 In. 375.00
Fish Server, Monogram, London, 12 In. 355.00
Flask, Pocket, Engraved Armorial, Hinged Dome Cap, Edward VII, 6 3/4 x 4 In. 230.00
Frame, Allover Geometric Repousse, Crown Cartouche, 5 x 7 In. 90.00
Frame, Double, Bow & Garland Design, 8 1/2 x 7 In. 140.00
Frame, Enamel Design, Liberty, 4 x 4 In. 1455.00
Frame, Overall Repousse, Birds, Diapers, Rectangular Border, 11 x 8 In. 170.00
Frame, Repousse Floral Trim, Rectangular, 8 x 10 In. 140.00
Goblet, Bell Shape, Leaf Ciphers, Duncan Urquhart & Hart, 1796, 6 In., Pair 3000.00
Grater, Nutmeg, T. Phipps & E. Robinson, c.1809, 2 1/2 In. 800.00
Jug, Beer, Leaf Capped Scroll Handle, George III, 1774, 8 3/4 In. 8700.00
Jug, Beer, Spout, Leaf Capped Scroll Handle, Robert A. Cox, 1769, 8 In. 5100.00
Jug, Cream, Chester, England, 1903, 3 x 5 x 3 In. 85.00
Jug, Cream, Robert Piercy, London, 1794, 4 1/4 In. 250.00
Jug, Hot Water, Vase Form, Ball Finial, Peter & Ann Bateman, 1793, 14 In. 1680.00
Jug, Wine, Repousse, Face Of A Satyr, James B. Hennell, 1884, 11 1/2 In., Pair 5400.00
Jug, Wine, Rococo Grapevine, Bacchic Mask Handle, J. Payne, 1754, 9 In. 6600.00
Kettle, Flower & Leaf Design, Bees On 1 Side, Harris & Sons, 1905, 13 In. 2160.00
Kettle, Lampstand, Flowers, Berried Leaves, Chinese Figurines, 16 3/4 In. 6000.00
Kettle, On Stand, Melon Shape, Georgian Style, William Mann, c.1857, 11 1/2 In. 1095.00
Ladle, Shell Bowl, HB Monogram, Hester Bateman, c.1776, 13 In. 1800.00
Loving Cup, Tooled Bands Around Body, Foot, Double Handles, 6 1/4 In. 715.00
Manicure Set, Fitted Leather Case, Satin Lining, Birmingham, 1921, 9 Piece 495.00
Marrow Scoop, George III, George Smith & William Fearn, 1796, 8 1/4 In. 230.00
Marrow Spoon, George III, London, c.1762, 9 1/2 In. 315.00
Mirror, Flirt, Cherub Design, 1916, 2 3/4 In. 175.00
Muffineer, Pierced, Stepped Foot, Cylindrical, 1900, 6 5/8 In. 190.00
Mug, Cover, Molded Rim, Baroque Cartouche, Scroll Handle, R. Copper, 1710 . . . . 6000.00
Mustard, Strap Handle, Scrolled Thumb Rest, Glass Insert, S.W. Smith, 1902 . . . . 170.00
Napkin Rings are listed in their own category.
Pepper Castor, Elizabeth Goodwin, 1730, 3 1/2 In. 395.00
Pepperette, Chester, England, 1912, 3 In. 85.00
Pepperette, Sheffield, 1919, 4 In. 85.00
Picture Frame, Hammered, William Hutton, 4 x 5 In. 1955.00
Pitcher, Water, Spiral Reeded Body, Mermaid Shape, 9 1/2 In. 860.00

Silver-English, Platter, Meat, George II,
Molded Rim, F. Kandler, 1756, 15 x 23 In.

Silver-English, Punch Bowl,
Wm. Burwash & R. Sibley, England, George IV

Plate, Campana Form, Gadroon Borders, Reeded, Leafy Handles, 1810, 9 In. 3120.00
Plate, Gadroon Rim, Garrard, London, 1892, 12 Piece 7800.00
Plate, Scrolled Rims, Reeded Hoop Handles, Sheffield, 1790, 13 In. 6000.00
Platter, Meat, George II, Molded Rim, F. Kandler, 1756, 15 x 23 In. . . . . *Illus* 3335.00
Platter, Meat, Shells, Leaves & Flowers, Arms On Border, W.K. Reid, 1827, 13 In. 2500.00
Platter, Molded Gadrooned Rim, Oval, London, 1832, 15 5/8 In. 920.00
Porringer, Fredrick Bassett, 7 In. 600.00
Punch Bowl, Gold Wash Interior, Footed, 14 3/4 x 8 3/4 In. 2090.00
Punch Bowl, Village Revelry, Gold Wash Interior, P Storr, 1827, 12 1/1 In. 8050.00
Punch Bowl, Wm. Burwash & R. Sibley, England, George IV . . . . *Illus* 8800.00
Punch Ladle, Twisted Handle, Scalloped Bowl, John Younge & Sons, 13 1/2 In. 145.00
Salt, Bulbous, Flowers, Scrolls, Shell Feet, Flared Rim, George II, 1759, 3 In., Pair 316.00
Salt, Cut Glass Liner, Floral Festoon, 1808, Thomas Howell, 3 1/4 x 2 In. 345.00
Salt, Flower Girl & Boy, Pastoral Dress, Garrard, 1982, 6 1/2 In., Pair 3600.00
Salt, Footed, Edward Wood Minor, 1744 . . . . 195.00
Salt, Gadroon & Shell, Rebecca Emes, E. Barnard, George IV, 1823, 1 3/4 In. 1840.00
Salt, Round, Footed, Gilt Interior, London, George II, c.1738, 1 1/2 x 3 In. 865.00
Salt Spoon, Thomas Bradbury, Sheffield, 1918, 2 1/4 In. 30.00
Saltcellar, Beaded Rim, Shell Knees Over Hoof Feet, Mappin Brothers, 1850 . . . . 86.00
Saltcellar, London, George III, 1769, 2 1/2 In. 325.00
Salver, Applied Flowers, Shells, Leaves, Young & Co., 1824, 21 1/4 In. 4800.00
Salver, Applied Grapevine, Scroll, Fruit Rim, John Edington, 1836, 23 In. 4800.00
Salver, Beaded Rim, Thomas Daniel, 1785, 16 1/8 In. 6300.00
Salver, Beaded Rim, Thomas Hannam, John Crouch, 1799, 17 In. 9000.00
Salver, Chippendale Flowers, Scroll, George III, London, c.1775, 6 In. 405.00
Salver, Chippendale Rim, 3 Hoof Feet, Carrington & Co., 1923, 24 In. 3000.00
Salver, Coat Of Arms, Motto, Scroll Feet, Edward Jay, 1781, 12 1/4 In. 1150.00
Salver, Engraved Center Coat Of Arms, Edward Jay, George III, 1781, 12 1/4 In. 2645.00
Salver, Flared Ogee Rim, Chased Leaves, Scroll Feet, 1838, 11 In. 630.00
Salver, Gilt, Grapevine Border, Strapwork Rim, Robert Fox, 1920, 18 1/2 In. 4560.00
Salver, Incurved Angles, Bracket Feet, Augustine Courtauld, 1721, 10 In. 5700.00
Salver, Oval, Richard Rugg, 1775, 8 1/2 In. 440.00
Salver, Presentation, Scroll Design, 4 Scroll Feet, Walker & Hall, 11 In. 460.00
Sauceboat, Figural, Swan, Open Back, Glass Insert, 1897, 6 In., Pair 2070.00
Sauceboat, Georgian, Tripod, Maker's Mark, London, c.1811, 3 1/4 x 6 In. 748.00
Sauceboat, Shell Feet, London, George II, c.1750, 4 1/4 x 60 1/2 In. 315.00
Scent Bottle, Leafy Repousse Cover, England, 19th Century, 4 In. 345.00
Scent Bottle, Trellis, Teardrop Shape, 1900, 9 1/2 In. 460.00
Scoop, Stilton, Ivory Handle, Harrison Brothers & Howson, 1865, 11 In. 189.00
Serving Dish, Gadrooned Rim, Frederick Kandler, 1756, 13 1/2 In. 5700.00
Serving Dish, Scrolled, Shell Rim, Oblong, London, 1833, 12 7/8 In. 805.00
Serving Spoon, Stephen Adams, 1804, 8 1/4 In. 90.00
Skillet, Bulbous Circular Body, Turned Wooden Handle, J. Ruslen, 1705, 4 In. 3300.00
Snuffbox, Gilt Interior, Coat Of Arms, Phipps & Robinson, 1794, 5 3/4 In. 4500.00
Soup Ladle, Scalloped Rim, Thomas Chawner, George III, 1774, 13 1/4 In. 460.00
Spoon, Apostle, Hammered, Case, Henry Atkins, Sheffield, 1908, Pair 58.00
Spoon, Apostle, Molded Lamb Handle, Victorian, London, 1856, 9 In. 115.00
Spoon, Bright Cut, Thomas Watson, New Castle, England, 1806, 5 1/4 In., Pair 70.00
Spoon, Hester Bateman, 1781 . . . . 475.00
Spoon, James Barber & Co., York, 1821, 5 1/4 In. 45.00
Spoon, Tapered Cylindrical Shape, William III, 3 1/8 In. 3300.00
Spoon, Thomas Watson, New Castle, 1806, 5 1/4 In., Pair 70.00
Spoon, William Welch, Large 475.00
Stand, Decanter, Cross Shaped, 4 Panel Feet, Reeded Rims, Hennell, 1791, 9 In. 1680.00
Standish, Cut Glass, Footed Tray, Henry Greensay, George III, 1792, 4 Piece 1610.00
Standish, Oval, Footed, B. Davenport, George III, c.1773, 2 1/4 x 3 x 4 1/2 In. 690.00
Stuffing Spoon, Bateman, London, 1789, 12 In. 450.00
Stuffing Spoon, Dragon Coat Of Arms, George III, 1795, 13 1/2 In., Pair 315.00
Stuffing Spoon, Fiddle, George III, Engraved, T. Beezley, 1793, 12 In. 375.00
Stuffing Spoon, King Pattern, Engraved Crest, William Eaton, 1828 . . . . 315.00
Stuffing Spoon, Mark, Peter & William Bateman, Georgian, 1806, 11 3/8 In. 280.00
Stuffing Spoon, William Bateman, London, England, 1789, 12 In. 450.00
Sugar, Ebonized Wooden Finial, Sheffield, 3 1/2 x 4 1/2 In. 95.00

Sugar Castor, Repousse Leafy Design, Acanthus Leaves, 1851, 5 1/4 In. 200.00
Sugar Tongs, Cast Scroll Handles, London, 1903, 4 1/2 In. 85.00
Sugar Tongs, J. W. & Co., Exeter, England, 1877, 5 In. 80.00
Sugar Tongs, Robert Makepeace, c.1750 . . . . 225.00
Tankard, Domed Cover, Loop Thumbpiece, ID, 1773, 8 In. 3300.00
Tankard, Girdle, Engraved Cartouche, Serpentine Handle, Thomas Tearle, 1725 . . . . 3220.00
Tankard, Silver Plate, Child's, 1880, 4 In. 46.00
Tazza, Lobed Ornaments, Figure Of Neptune, George Fox, 1875, 13 In. 3600.00
Tea & Coffee Set, Drapery Swags, Paw Feet, Walker & Hall, 1900, 5 Piece 7200.00
Tea & Coffee Set, Square, Banded Rims, Flower Finials, J. & J. Angel, 1835, 4 Pc. 1380.00
Tea & Coffee Set, Urns Gushing Water, Joseph Angell, 1853, 4 Piece 1560.00
Tea & Coffee Set, Winged Sphinx Caryatids, Mappin & Webb, 1912, 15 In. 3900.00
Tea Caddy, Engraved Heraldic Crest, Hinged Lid, Thomas Robins, 4 3/4 In. 1495.00
Tea Set, Paddlewheel Ships, Hallmark, John James Keith, London, 4 Piece 2750.00
Tea Set, Rococo, Eagle Head Spout, Bird Finial, James Dixon & Son, 4 Piece 410.00
Tea Set, Scottish Thistle Finials, Family Crest, W. Thomason, c.1815, 3 Piece 4750.00
Tea Set, Shell & Acanthus Repousse, Thomas Baker, c.1822, 5 Piece 1980.00
Tea Set, Wicker Handles, Ebonized Finials, Asprey, 6 Piece 800.00
Tea Urn, Chased With Floral Pendants, Claw, Ball Feet, 1764, 20 1/4 In. 4500.00
Tea Urn, Presentation Inscription, Rod Holder, H. Chawner, 1791, 21 3/4 In. 4800.00
Teapot, A & G Burrows, London, 1812, 10 1/4 In. 630.00
Teapot, Engraved Leaves, Floral Vine, Mushroom Finial, Jas. Dixon, 6 In. 585.00
Teapot, Floral Repousse, Squat, Lobed, Leaf, Berry Handle, George IV, 1827, 6 In. 520.00
Teapot, Green Finial & Handle, 2 Vacant Cartouches, J. Stoyte, 1792, 7 1/4 In. 1725.00
Teapot, Hinged Lid, Ear Shaped Handle, George II Coin Inset, c.1790, 6 In. 750.00
Teapot, Neoclassical, Cherrywood Handle, Finial, George III, 1803, 6 x 12 In. 200.00
Teapot, Panels Of Interlaced Leaves, Walter Tweedie, 1771, 5 3/8 In. 5700.00
Teapot, Reeded Dome Lid, Bud Finial, Francis Crump, 1764, 7 1/4 In. 920.00
Teapot, Stand, Bright Cut Bands, Ivory Pineapple Finial, A. Peterson, 6 In. 1920.00
Teapot, Straight Tapered Spout, Strapwork Leaves, Wm. Spackman, 1726 . . . . 6000.00
Toast Rack, London, 1897, 8 x 3 x 5 1/2 In. 315.00
Tray, 4 Grotesque Masks Border, Mappin & Webb, 1925, 29 1/2 In. 4800.00
Tray, Beaded & Leafy Rim, Arabesque Strapwork, Barnard Bros., 1860, 31 1/4 In. 7200.00
Tray, Border Of Leaves, Paisley Cartouche Center, Barnard Bros., 1873, 18 1/4 In. 3000.00
Tray, Cartouche Center, Filigree Rim, 3-Footed, Martin & Hall, 1894 . . . . 495.00
Tray, Cavetto Design, Alternating Leafy Cartouches, Sheffield, 2 x 12 In. 345.00
Tray, Gadrooned Leaf & Scroll Rim, J. Craddock & W. Reid, 16 1/2 x 12 1/2 In. 1035.00
Tray, Knife, Shells & Leaves Rim, Engraved Arms, Paul Storr, 1811, 15 1/8 In. 5100.00
Tray, Openwork Rim, Swag, Rosette Band, Leaves, Elkington & Co., 1855 . . . . 20125.00
Tray, Oval Reeded, Engraved Foliate Band, Center Armorials, 1796, 22 1/2 In. 5750.00
Tray, Scalloped Rim, January 30, 1933 On Reverse, R. Comyns, 27 1/2 In. 6600.00
Trophy, Speedboat, Globe Form, Figure Of Victory On Boat, 23 5/8 In. 7200.00
Tureen, Sauce, Beaded Edge, Loop Handles, John Schofield, 1784, 10 3/8 In. 1265.00
Tureen, Soup, Cover, Floral Rim, Bombe Oval Shape, Sheffield, 1825, 15 In. 2880.00
Tureen, Soup, Cover, Gadrooned Border, 4 Scroll Feet, Heming, 1767, 11 In. 5400.00
Urn, Scrolled Ribbons, Reeded Borders, Ball Feet, John Emes, 1799, 18 In. 4500.00
Vanity Set, Engine Turned, Asprey Case, Beige Leather Interior, 1946, 9 In. 975.00
Vase, Beaker Form, London, 1896, 10 In. 1035.00
Vinaigrette, Flower, Vacant Cartouche, Pierced Grill, J. Willmore, 1848, 1 x 1 In. 375.00
Waiter, Beaded Rim, Repousse Swag Band, R. Rugg, George III, 1773, 7 In. 690.00
Waiter, Circular, 3 Scrolled Legs, Robert Abercromby, George II, 1740, 7 In. 690.00
Wine Coaster, Flared Gadrooned Rim, Wooden Base, Sheffield, 6 In., Pair 230.00
Wine Cooler, Floral Acanthus Handles, Removable Liner, 19th Century 690.00
Wine Pitcher, Flower, Mask & Animal Repousse, Dragon Finial, 1885, 15 1/2 In. 2300.00
SILVER-FRENCH, Basin, Beaded Rim, Festoons, Husks, Fluted, J. Sacher, 1779, 20 In. . . . 4800.00
Beaker, Central Cartouche, Leafy Sprays, 19th Century, 3 In. 175.00
Beaker, Tulip Shape, Coat Of Arms, Lobed Pedestal Foot, 1750, 3 1/2 In. 2160.00
Bell, Table, Baluster Handle, Coat Of Arms Viscount, N. Outrebon, 1745, 4 In. 5100.00
Bowl, Chased With Festoons, Strawberry Plant Finial, 1788, 6 1/4 In. 3000.00
Box, Sweetmeat, Cover, Napoleon III, Gild Interior, 1870, 3 3/4 In. 259.00
Centerpiece, 4 Cast Dolphins On Pedestal, Repousse Rocaille Border, 13 In. 4025.00
Chalice, Band Of Leaves Base, Flowerhead Knop, J.A. Marsal, 1680, 8 1/4 In. 1800.00
Chocolate Pot, Fluted Spout, Hinged Flap, Head Of Camel Finial, 1777, 12 In. 2280.00

Coffeepot, Gilt Leaves, Flowers, Ivory Ear Handle, 9 3/4 In. 1495.00
Coffeepot, Hinged Dome Cover, Duck Spout, Wooden Loop Handle, 9 In. 865.00
Compote, Flared Rim, Repousse Leaves, 4 Scrolled Legs, 7 x 5 In., Pair 1840.00
Ewer, Cover, Chased With Urns Of Flowers, 1911, 25 In. 7800.00
Jug, Claret, Pear Shape, Scroll Handle, Late 19th Century, 12 1/4 In., Pair 5700.00
Jug, Lemonade, Flutes & Leaves, Bud Finial, Removable Chamber, 11 3/8 In., Pair 6000.00
Jug, Traveling, Cover, Straight Turned Wood Handle, Paris, 1818, 5 In. 175.00
Mirror, Toilet, Truncated Column Base, Flowerhead Frame, 1890, 17 In. 2700.00
Pitcher, Ribbon, Laurel Swags, Acanthus, Handle, 11 3/8 In., Pair 7200.00
Plate, Asparagus, Twisted Vine Border, 2 Center Wells, 19th Century, 13 In. 977.00
Punch Ladle, Molded Acanthus Leaves, Twisted Handle, 17 1/4 In. 175.00
Salt Spoon, 19th Century, 2 3/4 In. 30.00
Sauceboat, Chased Wreath & Swag, 18th Century 315.00
Sauceboat, Liner, Stand, Hoop Handles, Berried Laurel Border, 1896, 11 In., Pair 2280.00
Sundial & Compass, Pocket, Hinged Bird Gnomon, Butterfield, 1750, 3 In. 2160.00
Tray, Beaded Molded Rim, Face With Bands, Mid 19th Century, 14 In. 550.00
Vase, Sphinx, Rosette Holders, Swag Design, Green Marble Base, 5 In., Pair 2280.00
SILVER-GERMAN, Basket, Fruit, Reserve Of Bacchic Putti & Goat, c.1895, 9 1/4 x 12 1/4 In. 575.00
Basket, Relief Reserve, 4 Frolicking Putti, Reticulated, 5 x 12 In. 1150.00
Beaker, 3 Rows Of Coins, Leafy Strapwork, 1750, 4 5/8 In. 4800.00
Beaker, Cylindrical, Floral Rim, 3 Ball Feet, 1735, 3 3/4 In., Pair 4200.00
Bottle, Reticulated Silver Dome Base, Scroll, Leaf, Grape Design, 11 In. 635.00
Bowl, Centerpiece, Oval, Pierced, Blue Glass Liner, c.1910, 21 1/4 In. 5100.00
Box, Overall Figural Landscape Design, Velvet Interior, 3 3/4 x 2 3/4 In. 280.00
Castor, Salt & Pepper, Pheasant Form, c.1915, 3 x 4 3/4 In. 230.00
Centerpiece, Oval, 18th Century Style, Bombe Body, Early 20th Century, 21 1/4 In. 3600.00
Coffeepot, Eagle Finial, Bird Spout, c.1915, 8 In. 402.00
Cup, Cover, Vertical Flutes, Pear Finial, 8 3/4 In. 6000.00
Cup, Nautilus, Serpents, Animals, Birds, 10 1/2 In. 750.00
Cup, Wedding, Woman, Hoopskirt Base, Interior Gilt, 2 3/4 In. 490.00
Figurine, Knight, In Armor, Ivory Face, 1890, 9 x 2 3/4 In. 1320.00
Fish Set, Engraved Vermeil, Cased, 19th Century, 24 Piece 2395.00
Fish Set, Stylized Leaves, Flowering Branches, 14 Piece 575.00
Goblet, Floral, Pierced, 24 Piece 1840.00
Jug, Chased With Whiplash Curves, Grape Clusters, Leaves, 13 In., Pair 7200.00
Jug, Claret, 1910, 8 1/2 In. 345.00
Ladle, Rococo Scroll Shape, Turned Ivory Handle, 1750, 14 In. 690.00
Mirror, Table, Floral Swags, Scroll & Shell Feet, Center Cast Figure, 20 3/4 In. 1495.00
Nef, Chased, Boat-Shaped Decoration, Poseidon & Amphitrite, 1890, 13 1/2 In. 4200.00
Sauceboat, Cannon Form, Wheels Turn, G. Piddington, 1901, 10 In., Pair 8400.00
Shears, Game, Sterling Handle, Kings Pattern, Pair 356.00
Sugar Basin, Cobalt Blue Glass Liner, c.1895, 3 x 3 1/2 In. 85.00
Tankard, Overall Floral Sprays, Bird, Knop Finial, Scroll Handle, 6 In. 1610.00
Tea Caddy, Hinged Lid, Gilt Interior, c.1890, 4 1/4 In. 975.00
Tray, 1915, 7 1/2 x 12 1/2 In. 345.00
Tureen, Cover, A.T. Schientsony, c.1915, 13 x 12 1/2 In. 1265.00
SILVER-GREEK, Reliquary, Constantine, Saints, Hinge, Swivel Lid, Repousse, 3 3/4 x 3 In. . 560.00
SILVER-HUNGARIAN, Compote, Putti On Domed Base, Foliate Design, 13 In. 978.00
SILVER-INDIAN, Teapot, Bombe, Lobed Body, Leaves, Ebonized Wooden Handle, 7 1/2 In. . 748.00
SILVER-IRISH, Beaker, Flared Rims, Ribbon Bows, Sprays, Gustavus Byrne, 1795, 3 3/8 In. . 5700.00
   Cup, Bell Shape Bowl, Harp Handles, John Daly, 1729, 6 5/8 In., Pair 5100.00
   Dish, Cover, Shell & Leaf Rim, Coat Of Arms, Eagle Finial, James Scott, 1814, 12 In. 3600.00

Silver-Irish, Tea Set,
Repousse Leaf,
Samuel Beere,
George IV, 3 Piece

Dish, Strawberry, Fluted, Scalloped Rim, Wm. Nowlan, 1818, 8 5/8 In. 4560.00
Dish Ring, Pierced, Chased Floral, Vintage Design, Lion, Phoenix, 1801, 3 3/8 In. 2585.00
Funnel, Wine, Dublin, George III, 1793, 4 5/8 In. 460.00
Jug, Claret, Chased Leaves, Leaf Scroll Handle, Dublin, 1860, 11 3/4 In. 3300.00
Mug, Leaf Capped Handle, Engraved Myrtle, Andrew Goodwin, c.1740, 4 In., Pair 5700.00
Sauceboat, Lion Mask Topped Legs, Scroll Handles, 4 In., Pair 1650.00
Soup Ladle, Engraved Crest, Leaves, Dublin, 1766, 14 1/8 In. 1092.00
Stuffing Spoon, Maker SN, 1799 . . . . 120.00
Tablespoon, Horse Engraving, 6 Piece 385.00
Tea & Coffee Set, Scalloped Finials, Coat Of Arms One Side, 1839, 4 Piece, 10 1/4 In. . . . 5175.00
Tea Set, Repousse Leaf, Samuel Beere, George IV, 3 Piece . . . .*Illus* 1495.00
Tureen, Sauce, Cover, Urn Finials, Monogram, Robert Breading, 9 3/8 In., Pair 3000.00
SILVER-ITALIAN, Box, Molded As Snail, 9 In. 1610.00
Centerpiece, Clam Shell Base, Shell Design, 20th Century, 13 In. 9600.00
Centerpiece, Grape Cluster, Twig Handle, Buccellati, 20th Century, 15 x 16 3/4 In. 5175.00
Coffeepot, Pear Form, Wooden Handle, Acorn Finial, Venice, c.1780, 8 In. 9600.00
Pin Tray, Buccellati, Footed, Shell Form, Crimped Edge, 5 1/2 In. 290.00
Tureen, Soup, Cover, Bombe Form, Handles, 20th Century, 17 In. 4200.00
SILVER-JAPANESE, Cigarette Case, Peacocks 1 Side, Chrysanthemums Other, 6 In. 92.00
Fan, Flowers On Gold Ground, Rice Paper, 11 1/4 In. 75.00
Tazza, Enameled Peacock Perched On Flowering Tree, 1900, 12 In. 3000.00
Vase, Bud, Repousse, Pierced Flower, Fluted Holder, Figural Base, Cranes, 8 1/4 In. 140.00
SILVER-MEXICAN, Ashtray, 3 Holders, Ball Feet, William Spratling, 2 1/2 In. 374.00
Ashtray, Original Finish, Wood, William Spratling, 3 1/2 In. 403.00
Bell, William Spratling, 3 1/4 In. 770.00
Bowl, Floral Handles, 4 Shell & Scroll Feet, Stamped, 14 x 7 In. 115.00
Bowl, Handles, William Spratling, 11 1/2 In. 6600.00
Box, Tortoiseshell, Marked, William Spratling, 4 x 2 1/2 In. 4315.00
Butter & Knife Set, Teakwood, William Spratling, 9 1/2 In. 850.00
Coffeepot, Angular Teakwood Handle, Sanborn's, 11 1/2 x 8 In. 255.00
Coffeepot, Horizontal Wood Handle, 4 Sides, Los Castillo, Taxco, 8 1/2 x 9 In. 560.00
Demitasse Spoon, Hand Wrought, Spratling, 8 Piece 5040.00
Dish, Vegetable, Removable Cover, 2-Part Interior, 4 Splayed Feet, 11 In. 345.00
Flask, Bombe Rectangular Shape, Sterling, 6 x 3 3/4 In. 90.00
Punch Bowl, Lobed, Hand Wrought, c.1930, 5 3/4 x 12 1/2 In. 690.00
Punch Bowl, Lobed, Hand Wrought, Videl Serna, c.1935, 6 x 12 1/2 In. 690.00
Spoon, William Spratling, Wood, 7 In. 184.00
Tea Set, Tray, Melon Fluted Form, Scroll Handles, Scroll Rim, 4 Piece 800.00
Tray, Serving, Marked, 20th Century, 16 x 27 In. 336.00
SILVER-NORWEGIAN, Beaker, Contemporary Arms On 1 Side, J. Reimers, 1700, 3 1/4 In. . . 9600.00
Tray, Shaded Flowers, Turquoise Beading, Hellstrom 83QS, 1906, 8 1/2 In. 560.00
SILVER-ORIENTAL, Bowl, Dragon Designs, c.1900, 8 1/2 In. 535.00
SILVER-PERSIAN, Box, Floral, Scroll Design, Polo Game In Courtyard Scene, 7 x 1 1/2 In. . . 259.00
Cup, Allover Birds On Body, Central Cartouche, Serpent Handle, 4 1/4 In. 230.00
SILVER-PERUVIAN, Punch Bowl, Trophy, Winged Figures Of Victory, 20th Century, 21 1/2 In. 4600.00
Waiter, Leafy Borders, c.1910, 37 1/2 x 20 1/2 In. 480.00
SILVER-PORTUGUESE, Bowl, Cover, Openwork, Insert, 20th Century, 11 3/8 x 8 In. 200.00
Centerpiece, Swan, Hinged Wings, Opens To Cavity, 20th Century, 19 In. 6000.00
Creamer, Cover, Ball Feet, J.T.A., 1814, 5 1/2 In. 170.00
Ewer, Basin, Eagle Head Handle, Gadroon Border, 1860, 10 In. 4500.00
Tureen, Cover, Duck Shape, Crossed Feather Handle On Cover, 14 In. 4200.00

SILVER-RUSSIAN. Russian silver is marked with the Cyrillic, or
Russian, alphabet. The numbers 84, 88, or 91 indicate the silver con-
tent. Russian silver may be higher or lower than sterling standard.
Other marks indicate maker, assayer, or city of manufacture. Many
pieces of silver made in Russia are decorated with enamel. Faberge
pieces are listed in their own category.

SILVER-RUSSIAN, Beaker, Landscape Medallions, Geometric Ground, 1864, 2 1/2 In., Pair . . 290.00
Beaker, Stylized Leaves, Geometric Border, Enamel, 1883, 6 1/8 In. 2400.00
Beaker, Stylized Rocaille, Eagles On Pediments, Floral Swags, 19th Century, 6 In. 800.00
Belt, Niello, Stylized Leaves, 35 Links, c.1900, 32 In. 1680.00
Belt Buckle, Kinjal, Dagger-Shape Closure, Filigree, 1899-1908, 3 1/4 In. 115.00

Bowl, Anthemion Rim, Loop Handles, 4 Claw & Ball Feet, 1820, 13 1/2 In. 4200.00
Bowl, Cover, Sheaf Of Wheat, Eagle Handles, St. Petersburg, 1820, 5 1/4 In. 7800.00
Bowl, Dip, Chased With 5 Medallions Of Musicians, Floral Band, 1840, 6 In. 230.00
Box, Cigar, Wood Grain, Gilded Tax Bands, Rectangular, 1900, 7 5/8 In. 6600.00
Box, Lacquer, Summer Troika Scene, Lukitin Factory, 9 1/2 x 5 1/2 x 4 In. 2915.00
Bread Basket, Ribbon Tied Branches, Geometric Border, c.1899, 11 1/2 In. 450.00
Chalice, Engraved, Christ Pantocrator, Geometric, Repousse, 1887, 8 5/8 In. 2465.00
Charger, Stylized Scrolled Leaves, Geometric Border, Moscow, 1890, 22 In. 8400.00
Cigarette Case, Birds In Leaves, Blue Beaded Border, Moscow, 4 In. 1800.00
Cigarette Case, Cover, Richly Clad Boyarina, Leaves, Moscow, 1910, 4 In. 3600.00
Cigarette Case, Faux Ruby Button, Gilt Interior, Early 20th Century, 4 1/8 In. 145.00
Cigarette Case, Flowering Leaves, Gold Charms, Moscow, 1900, 4 1/4 In. 3360.00
Cigarette Case, Repousse, Scrolling Leaves, Monogram, VK Mark, 1920s, 4 3/4 In. 195.00
Cigarette Case, Stylized Leaves, Bears, Plumed Exotic Bird, 1910, 4 1/8 In. 1920.00
Coffee Set, Geometric Design, Rooster Head Handles, Moscow, 1910, 3 Piece 9000.00
Cross, Trefoil, Repousse, Mary, Apostle John, God The Father, 1783, 14 x 8 In. 2415.00
Egg, Folding, Easter, St. Seraphim Seravskiy, 3 Sections, c.1905, 2 1/2 x 5 In. 2130.00
Kovsh, Enamel, Leaf Design, Cream, Deep Green, Pink, Gray, 1910, 5 In. 2400.00
Match Case, Strawberry Translucent Red, St. Petersburg, 1900, 1 3/4 In. 4800.00
Mug, Tree Trunk, Branch Shape Handle, Late 19th Century, 4 In. 800.00
Pendant, Cross, Niello, Marked, c.1890, 3 In. 225.00
Pendant, Reliquary Cross, Repousse, Christ, 18th Century, 5 1/2 x 4 3/4 In. 1960.00
Pitcher, Vertical Reeds, Cast Scroll Handle, Fluted Base, 8 1/2 In. 1150.00
Plaque, Pendant, Niello Saint, Monastery, Moscow, 1855, 3 In. 2160.00
Salt, Red, Green, Blue, Geometric Borders, 3-Footed, Enamel, Gilt, 1884, 2 1/2 In. 370.00
Samovar, Openwork Spigot, Geometric Border, Handles, 19 In. 145.00
Spoon, Enameled Flowers, Geometric Design, Crown Terminal, 8 In. 2530.00
Spoon, Niello Design On Reverse Of Bowl, c.1816, 7 1/4 In. 170.00
Spoon Set, Enamel, Cloisonne, Gilt Ground, Lingert, c.1899, 4 1/4 In., 6 Piece 415.00
Sugar Shovel, Scrolling Leaves, Cloisonne, Beading, Pre 1896, 4 5/8 In. 505.00
Tazza, Egg & Dart Rim, Acanthus, Fluted, Dome Base, 2nd Artel, 1908, 5 3/4 In. 615.00
Tea Glass Holder, Chased, Pierced, Flowers, Shaped Handle, Art Nouveau, 5 In. 225.00
Tea Glass Holder, Peasants & Cattle Rural Scene, Angular Handle, 1892, 4 In. 1680.00
Tea Set, Kettle, On Stand, Teapot, Creamer, Sugar, Cover, Bowl, Lobed Sides 4600.00
Triptych, Vision Of Alexander Skirskiy, 19th Century, 4 1/4 x 10 1/2 In. 785.00
SILVER-SCOTTISH, Ladle, Marked AC, 6 1/2 In, Pair 302.00
Sugar Tongs, Fiddle, George Thompson, Glasgow, Scotland, 1828, 6 1/4 In. 70.00
Sugar Tongs, P. & A., Glasgow, Scotland, 1823, 6 In. 110.00
Sugar Tongs, Scottish Queens, J. & D., Glasgow, 1858, 6 1/4 In. 110.00
Sugar Tongs, Sterling Silver, 1800, 2 Piece 185.00
Teapot, Mushroom Shape, Wooden Ear Handle, George III, 1817, 4 1/2 In. 690.00

SILVER-STERLING. Sterling silver is made with 925 parts silver out of
1,000 parts of metal. The word *sterling* is a quality guarantee used in
the United States after about 1860. The word was used much earlier in
England and Ireland. Pieces listed here are not identified by country.
Other pieces of sterling quality silver are listed under Silver-American,
Silver-English, etc.

SILVER-STERLING, Basket, Flowers, Birds, Openwork, Swing Handle, 12 1/2 x 10 In. 345.00
Basket, Flowers, Leaves, Pierced Swing Handle, Glass Liner, Art Nouveau, 9 1/4 In. 800.00
Bowl, Applied Relief Border Of Floral Festoons, Belle Epoque, 1915, 4 In. 1495.00
Bowl, Fruit, Hammered, Footed, 1916, 9 In. 170.00
Bowl, Fruit, Lily, Reticulated Flared Lip, 1904, 2 3/4 x 12 In. 630.00
Bowl, Grape Leaf Design, Applied Grapes At One End, Camusso, 8 In. 69.00
Bowl, Shell & Acanthus Leaf, I.S. Co., 10 1/2 x 2 1/2 In. 110.00
Box, Biedermeier, Gilt, Round, Allegorical Relief Of Night, c.1840, 5 1/4 In. 750.00
Box, Cigar, Hinged Cover, Crest Over Coat Of Arms, Leather Case, 1902, 8 In. 1200.00
Box, Hinged Cover, Ruby, Blue Enamel, Vermeil Interior, 1900, 3 In. 575.00
Box, Mythological Figures, 7 1/4 x 5 In. 375.00
Box, Neoclassical Design, Footed, 3 1/2 x 2 1/2 In. 110.00
Box, Sweetmeat, Tortoiseshell, Engraved, Flowers, Wreath, c.1785, 2 In. 1495.00
Box, Table, Animals In The Jungle, Octagonal, Relief, Thai, c.1930, 3 1/2 x 1 5/8 In. 145.00
Bread Basket, Oval, Lobed Sides, 12 In. 230.00

Brush, Clothes, Leaf Design On Back, 1960 .... 10.00
Brush, Clothes, Lily Pads On Top, Victorian, 1890 .... 28.00
Brush, Ornate 32.00
Butter, Flowers, Leaves, Stippled Ground, Pierced, Repousse, 6 In. 259.00
Cake Basket, Continental, Swing Handle, Lobed, Oval, Footed, 12 x 10 x 12 In. 400.00
Candelabrum is listed in its own category.
Candlesticks are listed in their own category.
Casket, Jewelry, Engraved Leaves, Lock, Reed & Barton, 4 1/4 x 8 3/4 In. 430.00
Chalice, Flared Shape, 5 Flamingos, Marble Base, Art Deco, 8 1/2 In. 805.00
Cocktail Shaker, Art Deco, 13 1/2 In. 690.00
Coffee & Tea Set, Lobed Globular Form, Flower Feet, 5 Piece 690.00
Coffee & Tea Set, Rococo Scroll Design, Angular Handles, 6 Piece 1150.00
Coffeepot, Cover, Ebony Handle, Ribbed Design, 8 5/8 In. 275.00
Coffeepot, Floral Garland Design, Ivory Spacer, Early 20th Century, 9 In. 198.00
Corncob Picks, Maize, 1960, 12 Piece 315.00
Curling Iron, Mustache 65.00
Decanter, Victorian, 1894 .... 290.00
Desk Set, Nib Pen, Letter Opener, Mistletoe Design, Box 300.00
Dish, Repousse, 1895, 1 1/2 x 6 x 5 1/4 In. 160.00
Dish, Rococo Rims, Pierced Shoulder, Monogram, 4 x 7 1/4 In. 275.00
Dish, Sweetmeat, Scale Pattern, Elizabeth II, Round, Footed, c.1963, 1 1/2 x 5 In. 316.00
Figurine, Frog, Tourmaline Eyes Set In Gold, Onyx Foot, 4 7/8 In. 690.00
Figurine, Pheasant, Gilt, One With Wings Open, 20th Century, 17 In., Pair 4800.00
Finger Bowl, Gilded Interior, c.1895, 2 1/4 x 4 1/4 In., 9 Piece 345.00
Hot Water Urn, Alcohol Lamp, 1825, 17 1/4 In. 670.00
Humidor, Cigarette, Ruby Glass, Striker Blow, Cedar Lining, 1906, 6 In. 800.00
Jug, Claret, Hinged Cover, Grape, Leaves Around Shoulder, 1837, 14 In. 2530.00
Jug, Claret, Neo-Grecque, 1875, 11 x 7 3/4 In. 430.00
Matchbox, Mailbox & Letter Form 175.00
Napkin Rings are listed in their own category.
Pie Server, Danish Modern Pattern, F.R. Gast, c.1955, 8 1/2 In. 90.00
Pie Server, Greek Key, Engraved Flower Basket, c.1870, 10 1/2 In. 345.00
Pincushion, Egg On Stand, 1910, 3 1/2 In. 115.00
Placecard Holders, Neoclassical, Tortoiseshell, 1910, 4 Piece 430.00
Platter, Shaped Edge, Webster, 13 1/2 In. 115.00
Porringer, Stylized Lion, Chased Leaf Band Around Neck, 3 1/2 In. 690.00
Punch Bowl, 12 Cups, Engraved Leaves, Repousse, 12 In. 3163.00
Punch Ladle, Repousse Pattern, 20th Century, 14 1/2 In. 345.00
Salad Servers, King's Shell, Spoon, 3 Tine Fork, c.1940, 13 1/2 In. 95.00
Sandwich Tongs, Pierced, Applied Flowers, Putti, Cartouche, 11 1/4 In. 460.00
Serving Fork, Belle Epoque, 5 Tines, Pierced, c.1900, 10 1/4 In. 742.00
Spoon, Souvenir, see Souvenir category.
Sugar Basin, Blown Cobalt Glass Interior, Handles, Belle Epoque, 1910, 5 In. 3220.00
Tea & Coffee Set, Baluster Shape, Fluted Corners, Treen Handle, 8 In., 4 Piece 430.00
Tea Caddy, Octagonal, Engraved, Marked DV&C, No. 13, 5 7/8 In. 258.00
Tea Caddy Spoon, Shovel, Hollow Handle, 3 3/4 In. 165.00
Tea Service, Floral Repousse, Flowerhead Finial, Footed, John Roth, c.1857 .... 865.00
Teapot, Cherrywood Handle & Finial, Robert Gaze, 6 1/2 In. 200.00
Teapot, Tapered Neck, Goose Neck Spout, 6 In. 110.00
Urn, Flowers, Black Marble Base, Footed, 16 1/2 In., Pair 1150.00
Vase, Belle Epoque, Louis XVI, Tripod Base, Floral, c.1910, 5 1/2 In. 863.00
Vase, Shell Shape, Aquatic & Ivy Leaves, Lilies, Footed, c.1870, 6 1/4 In. 1380.00
Vase, Trumpet, 10 In. 190.00
SILVER-SWEDISH, Coffeepot, Barrel Shape, Scrolled Wooden Handle, 1824, 9 1/4 In. 1920.00
Inkstand, Lion Mask, Engraved Cartouche, Oval Base, 1881, 12 1/4 In. 3600.00

**Never use an all-purpose metal polish on silver.
It is too abrasive. Use silver polish.**

Spoon, Cactus, Original Leather Case, 20th Century, 3 1/2 In. 230.00
Sugar Box, Curled Hound Finial, Swing Handle, A. Zelthelius, 1821, 7 5/8 In. 4200.00

SINCLAIRE cut glass was made by H.P. Sinclaire and Company of Corning, New York, between 1905 and 1929. He cut glass made at other factories until 1920. Pieces were made of crystal as well as amber, blue, green, or ruby glass. Only a small percentage of Sinclaire glass is marked with the S in a wreath.

Bowl, Blown Blue Glass, Raised Foot, Signed, c.1905, 16 1/4 In. 490.00
Bowl, Stratford, 6 Sides, Signed 410.00
Letter Holder, Miter Cut, Engraved Floral, Signed, 3 1/2 x 6 1/4 In. 375.00
Tea Set, Engraved Scrolled Floral Vines, Beaded Swags, Logo, Signed, 6 Piece 2130.00
Vase, Black, White Rim, Slender, Signed, 13 1/2 In. 195.00

SKIING, see Sports category.

SLAG GLASS resembles a marble cake. It can be streaked with different colors. There were many types made from about 1880. Caramel slag is the incorrect name for Chocolate glass. Pink slag was an American Victorian product made by Harry Barstow and Thomas E.A. Dugan at Indiana, Pennsylvania. Purple and blue slag were made in American and English factories. Red slag is a very late Victorian and twentieth-century glass. Other colors are known but are of less importance to the collector. New versions of chocolate glass and colored slag glass are being made.

Caramel slag is listed in the Chocolate Glass category.
Green, Creamer, L.G. Wright, 4 In. 36.00
Green, Sugar, L.G. Wright, 4 In. 39.00
Purple, Compote, Ruffled Edge, 5 1/2 x 4 1/2 In. 95.00
Purple, Creamer, L.G. Wright, 4 In. 36.00
Purple, Dish, Eagle On Nest Cover, Westmoreland, 6 x 6 In. 95.00
Purple, Dish, Horse Cover, 5 1/2 x 4 1/2 In. 95.00
Purple, Dish, Swan On Basket Cover, 3 1/2 x 4 1/2 In. 88.00
Purple, Spooner, 3 3/4 x 4 1/2 In. 69.00
Purple, Spooner, Tree Bark Design, 4 x 4 1/2 In. 89.00
Purple, Sugar, L.G. Wright, 4 In. 39.00
Ruby, Candleholder, Moon & Stars, Satin Finish, 6 3/4 x 5 1/2 In. 65.00
Ruby, Candlestick, Westmoreland, 4 1/2 In. 29.00
Ruby, Compote, Imperial, 6 1/2 In. 65.00

SLEEPY EYE collectors look for anything bearing the image of the nine-teenth-century Indian chief with the drooping eyelid. The Sleepy Eye Milling Co., Sleepy Eye, Minnesota, used his portrait in advertising from 1883 to 1921. It offered many premiums, including stoneware and pottery steins, crocks, bowls, mugs, and pitchers, all decorated with the famous profile of the Indian. The popular pottery was made by Western Stoneware, Weir Pottery Company, and other companies long after the flour mill went out of business in 1921. Reproductions of the pitchers are being made today. The original pitchers came in only five sizes: 4 inches, 5 1/4 inches, 6 1/2 inches, 8 inches, and 9 inches. The Sleepy Eye image was also used by companies unrelated to the flour mill.

Advertisement, Magazine 50.00
Card, Trade .... .130.00 to 300.00
Cookbook, Loaf Of Bread .... .65.00 to 110.00
Crock, Butter, Stoneware .... .370.00 to 725.00
Fan, Indian Chief, Die Cut .... .100.00 to 225.00
Jar, Vinegar, White, Brown Indian Head 800.00
Label, 1905 .... 80.00
Label, Cream Barrel 110.00
Label, Food, Sleepy Eye Milling Co., Indian Chief, Gray White Ground, 16 In. Diam. ... 220.00
Letterhead 175.00
Mug, 1952 .... .160.00 to 175.00

Mug, 1976 .... 80.00
Mug, 1977 .... 55.00
Mug, 1979 .... 30.00
Mug, 1980 .... 38.00
Mug, 1981 .... 42.00
Mug, All White, 4 1/4 In. 2200.00
Mug, Blue & Gray, 4 1/4 In. 500.00
Mug, Blue & White, 4 1/2 In. .... .100.00 to 160.00
Mug, Blue & White, 4 3/4 In. .... .180.00 to 250.00
Paperweight, Bronze .... .210.00 to 450.00
Pie Plate, Hummer Flour 75.00
Pillow Top, Monroe 500.00
Pillow Top, Trademark 260.00
Pitcher, Black Diamond Design, Monmouth, Ill., 4 In. 121.00
Pitcher, No. 1, Blue & Gray, 1/2 Pt., 4 In. .... .180.00 to 350.00
Pitcher, No. 1, Blue & White, 1/2 Pt., 4 In. .... .60.00 to 440.00
Pitcher, No. 1, Small, Odd Glaze 700.00
Pitcher, No. 2, Blue & Gray, 1 Pt., 5 1/4 In. .... .220.00 to 240.00
Pitcher, No. 2, Blue & White, 1 Pt., 5 1/4 In. .... .90.00 to 300.00
Pitcher, No. 3, Blue & Gray, 1 Qt., 6 1/2 In. 150.00
Pitcher, No. 3, Blue & White, 1 Qt., 6 1/2 In. .... .110.00 to 225.00
Pitcher, No. 4, 4 Colors, 1/2 Gal., 8 In. 1650.00
Pitcher, No. 4, Blue & Gray, 1/2 Gal., 8 In. 520.00
Pitcher, No. 4, Blue & White, 1/2 Gal., 8 In. .... .125.00 to 900.00
Pitcher, No. 4, Brown & White, 1/2 Gal., 8 In. 1225.00
Pitcher, No. 4, Indian Profile, Trees, Teepees On Reverse, Mask Head On Handle, 3 In. . . . 385.00
Pitcher, No. 5, Blue & Gray, 1 Gal., 9 In. 440.00
Pitcher, No. 5, Blue & White, 1 Gal., 9 In. .... .150.00 to 475.00
Pitcher, No. 5, Blue Rim, 1 Gal., 9 In. .... .100.00 to 600.00
Pitcher, No. 5, Unfired Glaze, 1 Gal., 9 In. 1100.00
Plaque, Macomb, 1979 .... .28.00 to 30.00
Sack, Flour, Faded Cream 70.00
Salt Bowl, Stoneware .... .330.00 to 400.00
Sign, That Sleepy Eye Flour, Tin .... .250.00 to 400.00
Spoon .... .65.00 to 90.00
Spoon, Demitasse 130.00
Stein, 1952 .... 200.00
Stein, Blue & White .... .370.00 to 725.00
Stein, Blue & White, Koehler & Hinrich Advertising ... .475.00 to 500.00
Stein, Blue & White, Odd Glaze 775.00
Stein, Brown & White 900.00
Stein, Brown & Yellow .... .600.00 to 775.00
Stein, Dark Green & White 2900.00
Sugar, 1991 .... .90.00 to 100.00
Sugar, Blue & White 350.00
Vase, Cattail, Blue & White 725.00
Vase, Cattail, Brown & Yellow 1250.00
Vase, Cattail, Chocolate Brown 1900.00
Vase, Cattail, Green Matte Glaze .... .950.00 to 1000.00
Vase, Profile Of Indian On 1 Side, Cattails On Other, Blue, Gray, 8 1/2 In. 275.00
Vase, Stoneware .... .150.00 to 325.00

SLOT MACHINES are included in the Coin-Operated Machine category.

SMITH BROTHERS glass was made after 1878. Alfred and Harry Smith had worked for the Mt. Washington Glass Company in New Bedford, Massachusetts, for seven years before going into their own shop. They made many pieces with enamel decoration.

Smith Bros. Co.

Biscuit Jar, Cover, Gourd Form, Raised Gilt Highlights, Swing Handle, 6 In. 400.00
Biscuit Jar, Gold Branch, Silver Plate Lid & Bail, 7 In. 580.00
Biscuit Jar, Melon Form, Brown Floral, Silver Plate Lid & Bail, 7 In. 630.00
Biscuit Jar, Raised Gold Flora, Silhouette Of Young Girl, 8 x 7 In. 660.00
Biscuit Jar, Stalks Of Wheat, Raised Gold, Signed, 6 1/2 In. 575.00

Rose Bowl, Floral Leaf, Vine Design, Cream Exterior, Gold Gilt, 2 x 4 In. 175.00
Salt, Purple Pansies 138.00
Sugar & Creamer, Young Woman In The Breeze, Gold, 3 1/2 In., Pair 200.00
Sweetmeat Jar, Melon Ribbed, Enameled Water Lily, Gold Trim, Satin, 5 1/2 In. 423.00
Vase, Green, Brown Fern Design, Soft Beige Ground, Signed, 4 3/4 x 4 In. 170.00
Vase, Pale Pink Flowers, Purple Enameled Leaves, 5 In. 290.00
Vase, Verona Enamel, Ribbed Interior, Enameled Iris, 1880s, 8 In. 230.00

SNOW BABIES, made from bisque and spattered with glitter sand, were first manufactured in 1864 by Hertwig and Company of Thuringia. Other German and Japanese companies copied the Hertwig designs. Originally, Snow Babies were made of candy and used as Christmas decorations. There are also Snow Babies tablewares made by Royal Bayreuth. Copies of the small Snow Babies figurines are being made today and can easily confuse the collector.

Cup, Children Sledding, 2 Handles, 2 3/4 In. 185.00
Dish, Babies Sledding With Dog, Ruffled Edge, 3-Footed, Royal Bayreuth, 5 1/4 In. 125.00
Figurine, 3 Babies Sitting On Sled, Germany, c.1910, 3 In. 310.00
Figurine, Boy & Girl On Sled, No. 2236, Germany, 1 5/8 In. 150.00
Figurine, Boy & Girl, Germany, 1 In., Pair 100.00
Postcard, Boy & Girl On Sled, Signed, Ellen H. Clappsaddle, 3 1/2 x 5 1/2 In. 45.00

SNUFF BOTTLES are listed in the Bottle category.

SNUFFBOXES held snuff. Taking snuff was popular long before cigarettes became available. The gentleman or lady would take a small pinch of the ground tobacco or snuff in the fingers, then sniff it and sneeze. Snuffboxes were made of many materials, including gold, silver, enameled metal, and wood. Most snuffboxes date from the late eighteenth or early nineteenth centuries.

Brass, Engraved Flowers, Medallion On Bottom, Richard Sawyer, Dublin, c.1806, 2 In. . . . 195.00
Brass, Relief, Incised Flower Form, Continental, Oval, 4 1/2 x 3 1/2 x 1 1/2 In. 127.00
Enamel, Cover, Alpine Lake Scene, Flowerhead Border, Deep Blue, 1820, 3 1/2 In. 9600.00
Enamel, Cover, Hinged, Cupid With Border Of Pearls, Deep Blue Translucent, 1810, 3 In. 2880.00
Enamel, Floral Thumbpiece, Scene Of Deer & Pheasants On Lid, 1824, 4 In. 2160.00
Enamel, White Body, Green Swags, Verse, Round, 1 x 1 1/4 In. 316.00
English Silver, Ribbed, Floral Medallion On Front, Nathaniel Mills, 1825, 2 3/4 In. 165.00
Gold, Cover, Chased, Cupid At Altar Of Love, 1770, 2 7/8 In. 3600.00
Gold, Cover, Cupid Riding On Back Of Lion, 1820, 3 3/4 In. 3600.00
Gold, Cover, Facets, Flutes Body, Gold Mount, 1770, 2 1/2 In. 2880.00
Gold, Cover, Hinged, Portrait Of Young Lady, Cameo, 1840, 2 3/4 In. 2880.00
Gold, Cover, Leaf Border, Rectangular, 1803, 3 5/8 In. 2280.00
Gold, Cover, Leaves, Flowerhead Design, Rectangular, 19th Century, 3 1/4 In. 7200.00
Gold, Enamel, Cover, 3 Putti Holding Open Book Amongst Clouds, 1820, 4 In. 9600.00
Gold, Enameled Egyptian Scene On Lid, Pharaoh, Slave, 3 5/8 x 2 In. 4255.00
Gutta-Percha, Ivory Portrait Of Maiden Under Glass On Lid, c.1795 . . . . 375.00
Horn, Compass Star & Sunburst On Lid, Brass Hinges, 3 5/8 In. 330.00
Horn, Fleur-De-Lis, Carved W.P./A.G. 28/1779, 3 x 2 1/4 In. 465.00
Lacquer, Hinged Lid, 2 In. 30.00
Leather, Ivory Plaque, Hunter In 18th Century Attire, Watching Pheasant, 4 1/2 In. 305.00
Mother-Of-Pearl Lid, Silver Mounted Sides, Figural Scene, 1840s 525.00
Papier-Mache, Double Cover, Hunter, Dog, Erotic Couple, 1800s, 7/8 x 3 3/8 In. 175.00
Papier-Mache, Women & Suitors, In Garden, Floral Underside, Man Interior Lid, 3 In. . . . 225.00
Porcelain, Courtship Scene On Lid, Side Figures, Pug Dogs On Bottom, 3 1/2 x 2 1/4 In. . 460.00
Porcelain, Cover, Floral, Shell Rim, Huntsman Mounting Quarry, William IV, 1834, 4 In. . 7800.00
Porcelain, Different Scenes, Cherubs On Top, Holding Globe & Telescope, 3/4 x 2 In. . . . 230.00
Pressed Burl, Les Montagnes Francais Jardins Beaujon, 3 3/8 In. 1000.00
Pressed Burl, Napoleonic Monument 1750.00
Pressed Horn, Robert Burns, Plough, Book & Lyre On Reverse, Thistle Frame 1750.00
Rosewood, Silver Inlay Of Deer & Forest Scene, 2 3/4 x 1 1/4 In. 298.00
Silver, Center Medallion, Stamped Rosettes, Circle & Dot Border, 3 1/16 In. 470.00
Silver, Enamel, Cloisonne, Flower, Cobalt Borders, Oval, Moscow, 1895 . . . . 280.00
Silver, Gadroon Molded Shoulders, John Shaw, Birmingham, 1817, 2 5/8 In. 220.00

Tortoiseshell, Gilt, Brass, Agate, Louis XVI, 3 1/2 In. 230.00
Tortoiseshell, Inlaid Silver Bouquet, 18th Century, 2 3/4 In. 405.00
Tortoiseshell, Mother-Of-Pearl Floral, 3 3/4 In. 200.00
Tortoiseshell & Horn, Hinged Lid, Stylized Floral Spray, 4 In. 175.00
Varicolored Gold, Chased Foliage On Lid, Urn Within Roundel, Leather Case, c.1775 . . . 4200.00

SOAPSTONE is a mineral that was used for foot warmers or griddles because of its heat-retaining properties. Soapstone was carved into figurines and bowls in many countries in the nineteenth and twentieth centuries. Most of the soapstone seen today is from China or Japan. It is still being carved in the old styles.

Carving, Young Boy, Girl, Exaggerated Produce, Chinese, 6 In., Pair 90.00
Figurine, Chickens, Rooster & Chicks, Artist Signed Chinese Characters, 10 In. 385.00
Figurine, Doctor's Lady, Reclining Position With Head Resting, 4 3/4 In. 1208.00
Figurine, Foo Lion Resting On Platform, 19th Century, 5 In. 80.00
Figurine, Maiden Seated With Lute, Pair Of Shoes, 3 3/4 In. 4.00
Figurine, Meijin, Seated On Rock, Holding Lotus, 6 In. 35.00
Figurine, Mother, Kneeling, Holding Her Child, Sarah Nastapoke, c.1960 . . . . 5460.00
Figurine, Seal, Carved Dragon, Phoenix, Clouds, 19th Century, 8 In., Pair 196.00
Figurine, Seal, Foo Lion Finials, Pair 2185.00
Figurine, Shou Lao, Standing While Holding Tree Branch, 19th Century, 20 In. 920.00
Figurine, Sow With Piglets, 3 1/2 In. 75.00
Figurine, Storks, Feeding By River, Dark Brown, Artist, 10 x 4 3/4 In. 300.00
Figurine, Sun Hou-Tzu, Seated On Rock Reading From Book, 1900, 8 In. 127.00
Sculpture, Carved, Green Flowers, Red Footed Base, Oriental, 12 In. 80.00
Vase, Carved Bird, Peonies, Red, Black Ground, 11 3/8 In. 115.00
Vase, Carved Foo Lion, Hawk, Pearl, Late 19th Century, 9 3/4 In. 65.00
Vase, Carved Squirrels, Grapes, Late 19th Century, 10 1/2 In., Pair 311.00
Vase, Stylized Birds, Phoenix Nesting In A Spray Of Chrysanthemums, 9 In. 160.00

SOFT PASTE is a name for a type of pottery. Although it looks very much like porcelain, it is a chemically different material. Most of the soft-paste wares were made in the early nineteenth century. Other pieces may be listed under Gaudy Dutch or Leeds.

Bowl, Fruit, Sprig, Leaf Design, 4 1/4 In. 275.00
Charger, Blue Pagoda Design, Blue Feather, Scalloped Edge, 13 In. 770.00
Charger, Trailing Floral Border, Pagoda Design, Scalloped Edge, 13 In. 2310.00
Coffeepot, Dome Lid, King's Rose, Pink Luster Bands 600.00
Coffeepot, Dome Lid, Queen's Rose, 10 3/4 In. 2310.00
Coffeepot, King's Rose, Oyster & Chrysanthemum Variation, 11 In. 2750.00
Coffeepot, King's Rose, Swan's Neck Spout, Domed Cover, Painted, c.1780 . . . . 1500.00
Coffeepot, King's Rose, Swan's Neck Spout, Strap Handle, Flower Finial, c.1780 . . . . 750.00
Creamer, Verse, Iridescent Rim, Health To Sick, Honour To Brave, 3 1/8 In. 140.00
Cup, Presentation, Sarah White, Floral, Pink Luster Bands, 1824, 3 In. 410.00
Cup & Saucer, Blue Flowers, Tan Buds, Green Leaves, Handleless, Child's 525.00
Cup & Saucer, Brown, Tan Flower, Tan, Blue Leaves, Handleless 85.00
Cup & Saucer, Floral, Acorn, Foliate, Handleless 740.00
Cup & Saucer, Red, Black, Yellow Feather, Handleless 275.00
Cup & Saucer, Tan, Green Strawberry Design, Handleless 220.00
Pepper Pot, Spread Wing Eagle, Shield Design, Blue Band, 4 1/2 In. 1980.00
Pitcher, Cream, Blue, Green, Tan Grape, Leaf, Fish Scale, Embossed, 5 In. 468.00
Pitcher, Cream, Flowers, Leaves, Bud, 3 In. 220.00
Pitcher, Relief Diamond Design, Gold Floral, Scroll Handle, Staffordshire, 6 In. 55.00
Pitcher, Sailor's Farewell, Forget-Me-Not, Verse, Apricot Luster, 6 3/4 In. 495.00
Plate, Blue Feather Edge, Flowers, Leaves, Acorn, Stubbs & Kent, Longport, 8 In. 660.00
Plate, Decorated Barn Scene, Berry Border, 8 In. 1650.00
Plate, King's Rose, Green Border, 9 In., Pair 230.00
Plate, King's Rose, Luster Border, 7 1/2 In. 190.00
Plate, King's Rose, Mid 19th Century, Staffordshire, 8 1/4 In., 4 Piece 330.00
Plate, Pink Queen's Rose, Scalloped Rim, 10 In. 165.00
Plate, Soup, Blue Onion, Mustard Highlights, Trailing Vine Border, 10 In. 578.00
Sauceboat, Spread Wing Eagle, Blue Feather Edge, 4 x 6 In. 2200.00
Sugar, King's Rose, Oyster Variation, 19th Century, 5 In. 495.00

Teapot, King's Rose, Claw Spout, Bullet Shape, England, c.1770	2200.00
Teapot, Strawberry, Leaf Design, 6 In.	303.00
Waste Bowl, Bird & Flower, Flow Blue, 6 1/2 In.	45.00

SOUVENIRS of a trip—what could be more fun? Our ancestors enjoyed
the same thing and souvenirs were made for almost every location.
Most of the souvenir pottery and porcelain pieces of the nineteenth
century were made in England or Germany, even if the picture showed
a North American scene. In the twentieth century, the souvenir china
business seems to have gone to the manufacturers in Japan, Taiwan,
Hong Kong, England, and America. Another popular souvenir item is
the souvenir spoon, made of sterling or silver plate. These are usually
made in the country pictured on the spoon. Related pieces may be
found in the Coronation and World's Fair categories.

Bank, Olympic, 1976, Montreal, Amik The Beaver, Plastic, 13 1/2 x 5 1/4 In.	115.00
Banner, Grand Canyon National Park, 6 Views, Paper, 1939, 3 1/2 x 7 1/2 In.	6.00
Bowl, Kaiser Bicentennial Bowl, Porcelain, 10 1/2 In. ....*Illus*	600.00
Bracelet, Olympic, 1976, Innsbruck, Snowflake, Logo, Silvered	75.00
Buckle, Olympic, 1988, USA Olympics, Brass	6.00
Button, Charles Lindbergh, Hero Of 1927, Spirit Of St. Louis, Celluloid, 1 1/4 In.	95.00
Cane, 1852, Panama Pacific International Exposition, Hardwood, 35 In.	192.00
Cigarette Dispenser, Donkey, Tin, Mechanical, Plymouth, Mass., 10 In.	225.00
Clamshell, Carved, Painted, 1890 Ballou Post No. 3, Central Falls, R.I., 6 x 10 In.	1955.00
Figurine, Black Wooden Musicians, Florida, Japan, 4 In. ....*Illus*	55.00
Figurine, Shoe, Red, On Crystal, 1930s	27.00
Key Chain, Olympic, 1976, Innsbruck, Mascot, Snowman, Plastic, Red, White, Blue	69.00
Lighter, Olympic, 1936, Berlin, Coat Of Arms, Blue & Gold, Olympic Rings, KW Maker	311.00
Medal, Olympic, 1936, Berlin, Pin Back, Porcelain Enameled, Dresden, 1 3/4 In.	36.00
Memo Holder, Miami Beach, Florida, Wood, 1950	75.00
Mirror, 1907, Jamestown Tercentenary, Expo, View From Pier, Reeded Edge	15.00
Pen, Float, Moving Bus, Eiffel Tour, Arc De Triomphe, Denmark On Clip, Plastic	14.00
Pennant, Boulder Dam, Burgundy Ground, Orange & Yellow Trim, 28 1/2 In.	20.00
Pennant, Norris Dam, Tenn., Maroon Felt, Torn Ties, 17 In. ....*Illus*	15.00
Pennant, Olympic, 1932, Lake Placid, Ski Jumper, Orange Felt, 29 x 11 In.	345.00
Picture, English Equestrian Circus Act, Gilt Brass Frame, Ducrow, 26 x 33 In.	1295.00
Pillow Cover, Fort Knox, Ky., Pictures, Poem About Mother, Pink Satin, Fringe, 1950s ...	15.00
Pin, Olympic, 1960, Squaw Valley, Ski & Pole, Enameled Logo, Silvered, 2 x 1 1/2 In. ..	190.00
Pin, Temperance Ax, Mother-Of-Pearl Blade, Gold Handle, 2 1/4 In.	100.00
Pin Dish, Fan Shape, Plankinton, S.D.	35.00
Plate, Battle Of Germantown, Judge Chew's House, Dark Blue, White, 1777, 10 In.	60.00
Plate, General Society Of Mechanics & Tradesmen Guilds, 1785-1910, 125 Years	350.00
Plate, Olympic, 1928, Salute To Games, Porcelain, Amsterdam Coat Of Arms, 21 In.	1150.00
Plate, Remember The Maine, BPCo., 8 5/8 In. ....*Illus*	55.00
Plate, Society Of Mechanics & Tradesmen, Anniversary, 1910	350.00
Poster, Olympic, 1940, Flight To Helsinki, Finnish Air Traffic Co., 27 x 40 In.	3450.00
Program, Olympic, 1952, Oslo, Closing Ceremony, February 25, 1952	242.00
Radio, Olympic, 1980, Lake Placid, Transistor, White, Plastic, Handle, Logo	45.00
Ribbon, Completion Of Croton Aqueduct, White Silk, Oct. 14, 1842, 7 1/2 x 3 In.	165.00
Ribbon, Hubert Davis, Troop M., 7th U.S. Cav., Yellow Silk, 2 x 7 In.	55.00
Ribbon, Washington Benevolent Society, White Silk, 19th Century, 9 1/2 In., Pair	110.00
Scarf, Olympic, 1956 Melbourne, XVI Summer Games, Hand Rolled, Made In Japan	145.00
Shoe, Manchester, Iowa	45.00
Spoon, Olympic, 1936, Berlin, Coffee, Silvered, View Of Olympic Stadium At Top, 4 In. ..	276.00
Spoon, Portrait Of Admiral Dewey Within American Flag, Silver Plate, Demitasse	35.00
Spoon, Sterling Silver, University Of Iowa	75.00
Stein, New York City, Scenic, Molded Relief, c.1955, 6 1/4 In.	15.00
Teapot, Torquay, Don't Be Afraid Of Anything, Provincetown, Mass., 4 3/4 In.	250.00
Ticket, Olympic, 1972, Sapporo, Men's Slalom, Mt. Teine, 9 In.	217.00
Torch, Olympic, 1976, Montreal, Aluminum, 30 In.	2013.00
Towel, Kitchen, Florida, State Attractions, Beige Ground, Pink Border, 16 x 27 In.	25.00
Toy, Olympic, 1968, Grenoble, Mascot, Smiling Shuss, Terrycloth, 5 In.	575.00
Toy, Olympic, 1972, Munich, Mascot, Waldi The Dachshund, Velvet, 8 In.	201.00
Toy, Olympic, 1976, Innsbruck, Mascot, Snowman, White Felt, Carrot Nose, 7 1/2 In.	575.00

Souvenir, Bowl, Kaiser
Bicentennial Bowl,
Porcelain, 10 1/2 In.

Souvenir, Plate, Remember
The Maine, BPCo., 8 5/8 In.

Souvenir, Pennant,
Norris Dam, Tenn.,
Maroon Felt,
Torn Ties, 17 In.

Souvenir, Figurine, Black Wooden
Musicians, Florida, Japan, 4 In.

Toy, Olympic, 1976, Montreal, Mascot, Amik The Beaver, Black Plush, 17 In. 633.00
Toy, Olympic, 1980, Moscow, Mascot, Vigri The Seal, Tallin Yachting, Plush, 8 In. 316.00
Toy, Olympic, 1984, Sarajevo, Mascot, Voochko, Orange Tie, Logo, 24 1/2 In. 345.00
Wall Hanging, Olympic, 1932, Los Angeles, Bamboo, Los Angeles City Hall, 14 x 20 In. . . 196.00

SPANGLE GLASS is multicolored glass made from odds and ends of colored glass rods. It includes metallic flakes of mica covered with gold,
silver, nickel, or copper. Spangle glass is usually cased with a thin
layer of clear glass over the multicolored layer. Similar glass is listed
in the Vasa Murrhina category.

Basket, Cranberry, Gold Flakes, Cherries, Applied Twisted Amber Handle, 5 In. 363.00
Vase, Brown, Red Shades, Gold Leaf, Cased With Clear, 9 1/2 In. 225.00

SPATTER GLASS is a multicolored glass made from many small pieces
of different colored glass. It is sometimes called *End-of-Day* glass. It
is still being made.

Basket, Yellow, White Spatter At Top, Thorn Handle, 6 x 5 1/2 In. 165.00
Bowl, Red & White, Gold Enameled, Signed, Numbered Base, 10 In. 475.00
Celery Vase, Cranberry, White, Satin, Rigaree, Hobbs, Bruckunier & Co., 6 1/2 In. 75.00
Flask, Lady's High Button Shoe Shape, Multicolored, American, 19th Century 1975.00
Tumbler, Burgundy, White, Blue, Enameled Forget-Me-Not, 3 3/4 In. 75.00
Vase, Waffle Pattern, Clear Over Amber & Pink, Applied Decoration, 8 1/2 In. 52.00

SPATTERWARE is the creamware or soft paste dinnerware decorated
with colored spatter designs. The earliest pieces were made in the late
eighteenth century, but most of the spatterware found today was made
from about 1800 to 1850, or it is a form of kitchen crockery with added
spatter designs, made in the late nineteenth and twentieth centuries.
The early spatterware was made in the Staffordshire district of
England for sale in America. The later kitchen type is an American
product.

Bowl, Cover, Green, Brown, Rainbow, Handles, 7 1/2 In. 7975.00
Bowl, Leaves, Red, Green, Embossed Beaded Edge, 2 1/2 x 11 1/4 In. 4510.00
Bowl, Peafowl, Red, Blue, Green Border, 7 x 10 In. 22000.00
Bowl, Tulip, Blue, Yellow, Red Buds, Green Leaves, 5 1/2 In. 325.00
Bowl, Tulip, Red & Green, Yellow Border, 4 3/4 In. 2310.00
Coffeepot, Thistle, Blue Border 1921.00
Creamer, Blue, Shaped Handle, 4 1/2 In. 190.00
Creamer, Clock, Tall Case, Red, Green, Yellow Border, 4 3/4 In. 550.00
Creamer, Peafowl, Blue, Red & Yellow, 4 In. 825.00
Creamer, Plaid, Vertical & Horizontal Bands, 3 1/2 In. 1595.00
Creamer, Purple & Blue, Rainbow, 4 In. 1430.00

Creamer, Rose Red & Green, Yellow, Paneled Sides, 19th Century, 4 3/4 In. 4675.00
Cup, Floral, Blue Border 150.00
Cup, Fort, Blue & Green 175.00
Cup, Purple, 2 Men On Raft 55.00
Cup & Saucer, 6-Star, Red & Blue, Red Striped Border 330.00
Cup & Saucer, Acorn 1580.00
Cup & Saucer, American Eagle, R. Hammersley, Handleless, 1868 . . . . 165.00
Cup & Saucer, Black, Yellow, Handleless 3850.00
Cup & Saucer, Bleeding Heart, Yellow, Red Floral Border, Handleless 4950.00
Cup & Saucer, Blue Flower, Red Outlined 5225.00
Cup & Saucer, Christmas Balls, Green Border, Handleless 4950.00
Cup & Saucer, Cranberry Flowers, Pale Blue Border 330.00
Cup & Saucer, Deer, Red Border, 1840 . . . . 110.00
Cup & Saucer, Dove, Purple Border, Handleless 4125.00
Cup & Saucer, Drape, Red, Blue, Green Ball, Handleless 2310.00
Cup & Saucer, Festoon, Red, Green, Handleless, Child's 2640.00
Cup & Saucer, Floral, Red, Blue, Green, Berry, Leaf, Handleless, Child's 770.00
Cup & Saucer, Fort, Gray, Red, Brown, Green Border, Handleless 385.00
Cup & Saucer, Morning Glory, Yellow, Blue Flower, Black Border, Handleless 3025.00
Cup & Saucer, Peafowl, Blue, Yellow, Red Border 190.00
Cup & Saucer, Peafowl, Green, Blue, Red Border, Handleless 665.00
Cup & Saucer, Peafowl, Green, Blue, Yellow, Red Border, Handleless, 1 1/4 In. 330.00
Cup & Saucer, Peafowl, Purple, Blue, Red, Yellow Border, Handleless 495.00
Cup & Saucer, Peafowl, Red Border . . . . .522.00 to 675.00
Cup & Saucer, Peafowl, Red Border, Child's 140.00
Cup & Saucer, Peafowl, Red, Blue, Yellow Border, Handleless 250.00
Cup & Saucer, Pink & Green 625.00
Cup & Saucer, Purple, Black, Rainbow, Handleless, Child's 440.00
Cup & Saucer, Red, Blue, Handleless 302.00
Cup & Saucer, Red, Green, Rainbow 2475.00
Cup & Saucer, Rooster, Blue Border, Handleless 330.00
Cup & Saucer, Rose, Red Border 440.00
Cup & Saucer, Rose, Red, Green Border, Handleless 1320.00
Cup & Saucer, Rose, Yellow, Green Border 4950.00
Cup & Saucer, School House, Red Border 880.00
Cup & Saucer, Thistle, Blue Border, Handleless 4950.00
Cup & Saucer, Thistle, Red & Green, Yellow Border, 19th Century 2200.00
Cup & Saucer, Thistle, Yellow Border 1810.00
Cup & Saucer, Tulip, Red & Blue, Blue Border, Handleless 470.00
Cup & Saucer, Yellow, Handleless, Double Bulbous 715.00
Mug, Blue, Green, Ear Handle, 2 3/4 In. 190.00
Mug, Brown, Blue Vertical Stripes, 4 In. 520.00
Mug, Red, Green, Straight Sided, Flared Base, 2 3/4 In. 140.00
Pitcher, Clover, Blue, 6 In. 3025.00
Pitcher, Rose, Blue, Cream, Red, Green Leaves, 4 1/2 In. 550.00
Pitcher, Rose, Red & Green, Rainbow, Red, Blue, 4 In. 1100.00
Pitcher, Scalloped Dark Blue Border, White Dots, 9 3/4 In. 110.00
Pitcher, School House, Red & Blue, Blue & Cream Border, 5 In. 1760.00
Pitcher, White, Blue, Red, Black, Rainbow, Scroll Handle, 8 1/2 In. 8250.00
Plate, Acorn, Purple Border 6050.00
Plate, Blue & Purple, Rainbow 5775.00
Plate, Bull's-Eye, Black & Purple, Rainbow 1245.00
Plate, Bull's-Eye, Green & Red, Rainbow, 9 1/2 In. 1320.00
Plate, Carnation, Red, Blue, Green, Blue Paneled, 8 1/4 In. 600.00
Plate, Dahlia, Red Border 1375.00
Plate, Floral Transfer, Green, Blue Border, 8 In. 175.00
Plate, Fort, Blue, Trees, 8 1/2 In. 410.00
Plate, Holly Berry, Purple Border, Paneled, 8 1/2 In. 440.00
Plate, Peafowl & Tree, Tan, Blue, Green, Brown Border, 9 1/8 In. 1045.00
Plate, Peafowl, Blue Border, 8 1/4 In. 410.00
Plate, Peafowl, Blue Border, 8 3/4 In. 770.00
Plate, Peafowl, Blue, Red, Green, Blue Border, 8 3/4 In. 440.00

Plate, Peafowl, Blue, Yellow, Red Border, 10 1/2 In. 1705.00
Plate, Peafowl, Green & Black, Red Border 275.00
Plate, Peafowl, Green Border 2260.00
Plate, Peafowl, Red & Blue, Yellow, Green Border, 6 1/4 In. 470.00
Plate, Rabbits Playing Cricket Medallion, 9 1/4 In. ....440.00 to 695.00
Plate, Red, Green, Brown, 8 1/2 In. 120.00
Plate, Rose, Red & Green, Green & Blue Border, 8 3/4 In. 798.00
Plate, Rose, Red, Blue Buds, Green, Black Leaves, Red, Blue, Rainbow, 9 1/2 In. 3520.00
Plate, School House, Red, Blue Border 6050.00
Plate, School House, Yellow & Green, Blue, Red, Black Border, 6 In. 3850.00
Plate, Star, Blue, 9 1/2 In. 1760.00
Plate, Star, Green, Red, Yellow, 8 1/4 In. 2420.00
Plate, Thistle, Red, Green Leaves, 6 1/2 In. 742.00
Plate, Thistle, Yellow, Red, Green, 6 1/4 In. 1760.00
Plate, Tulip, Blue, Red, Green, 9 1/4 In. 1650.00
Plate, Tulip, Green, Red, 9 In. 3850.00
Plate, Zigzag, Red, Blue, Green Border, 8 1/2 In. 3025.00
Platter, Peafowl, Blue, Green, Red Border, 15 1/2 x 12 In. 2070.00
Platter, Peafowl, Red, Blue, Brown Border, 12 1/4 x 16 In. 7700.00
Platter, Thistle, Red Tulip, Yellow, Green Leaves, Feather Edge, 10 1/4 x 13 In. 17050.00
Saucer, Peafowl, Blue, Green & Red, Green & Red Border, 1850s, 5 In. 415.00
Saucer, Peafowl, Green, Blue 485.00
Saucer, Peafowl, Red Border, 4 1/8 In. 110.00
Soup, Dish, Dahlia, Red, Blue, Green, 10 1/2 In. 1540.00
Soup, Dish, Rainbow, 7 1/2 In. 8250.00
Sugar, Adam's Rose, Pink & Green, Scalloped Handles, 8 3/4 In. 495.00
Sugar, Cover, Adam's Rose, Both Sides, Rose Finial, 4 1/4 In. 55.00
Sugar, Cover, Adam's Rose, Red & Green 3503.00
Sugar, Cover, School House, 4 1/2 In. 2845.00
Sugar, Peafowl, Green Border, 4 x 4 7/8 In. 440.00
Sugar, Rose, Blue, 5 1/4 In. 605.00
Sugar, Star, Purple, Blue, 5 In. 1045.00
Sugar, Tulip, Blue Border, 5 1/2 In. 495.00
Teabowl & Saucer, Blue Bands, c.1800 .... 290.00
Teapot, Blue, Paneled, 9 In. 330.00
Teapot, Cover, Peafowl, Blue, Red, Teal, 8 1/4 In. 3190.00
Teapot, Flowers Transfer, Red, On Spout & Handle, Paneled, 10 1/8 In. 660.00
Teapot, Peafowl, Blue, Red & Yellow, Tree On Other Side, 10 In. 740.00
Teapot, Peafowl, Blue, Red, Yellow, Green Border, 3 1/2 In. 275.00
Teapot, Purple & Blue, 5 1/4 In. 200.00
Teapot, Thistle, Red & Black Border 3300.00
Teapot, Thumbprint, Black, On Spout, 7 1/2 In. 3300.00
Waste Bowl, School House, Red, Yellow & Green, Brown Border 7700.00
Waste Bowl, Tulip, Blue, Yellow, Red, Green, 4 x 6 In. 1100.00

SPELTER is a synonym for a zinc alloy. Figurines, candlesticks, and
other pieces were made of spelter and given a bronze or painted finish.
The metal has been used since about the 1860s to make statues, tablewares, and lamps that resemble bronze. Spelter is soft and breaks easily. To test for spelter, scratch the base of the piece. Bronze is solid;
spelter will show a silvery scratch.

Bookends, Squirrel, LeVerrier 850.00
Centerpiece, Figural, 2 Figures Of Putti With Onyx Socle Supports, Amethyst, 12 In. 75.00
Clock, Woman & 2 Dogs, Black Marble, Blot & Drouard, 25 x 19 x 6 3/4 In. 525.00
Figurine, Arabian Dancers, Male With Drum, Female With Lyre, 32 1/4 In. 3220.00
Figurine, Cavalier With Sword & Sheath, Marble Base 75.00
Figurine, Hamlet & Ophelia, Gold & Black Paint, 33 & 21 In., Pair 275.00
Figurine, Nymph, Flowing Dress, Bronze Flesh Tones, J. Causse, 23 1/2 In. 715.00
Figurine, Roman Soldier, Knife, Light Gray Finish, Ornate Base, 22 In. 100.00
Figurine, Woman Seated In Classical Dress Contemplating Dead Sparrow, 19 In. 200.00
Figurine, Young Girl Feeding Bird, 12 In. 86.00
Lamp, 3-Light, Conquistador, Art Nouveau Newel Post, 30 In. 220.00

Lamp, Geisha Girl, Holding Lamp, Gilt, Bisque, Alonzo Style, 1880, 19 In. 575.00
Urn, Cover, Cherubs, Nautical Design, Italian Classical, 15 In., Pair 1035.00

SPINNING WHEELS in the corner have been symbols of earlier times for the past 100 years. Although spinning wheels date back to medieval days, the ones found today are rarely more than 200 years old. Because the style of the spinning wheel changed very little, it is often impossible to place an exact date on a wheel.

Black, Gold Stripes, Black, Red Legs, Fish Design, Pa., 1800 . . . . 660.00
Freegift Wells 1095.00
Nathaniel Draper 518.00
Oak, Chipped Carved Date Of 1822, 35 In. 220.00
Oak, Pennsylvania, c.1810 . . . . 470.00
Pennsylvania, Signed P. Hoffman, c.1810 . . . . 250.00
Samuel Ring 690.00
Yarn Winder, Yellow Pine 9500.00

SPODE pottery, porcelain, and bone china were made by the Stoke-on-Trent factory of England founded by Josiah Spode about 1770. The firm became Copeland and Garrett from 1833 to 1847, then W.T. Copeland or W.T. Copeland and Sons until 1976. It then became Royal Worcester Spode Ltd. The word *Spode* appears on many pieces made by the factories. Most collectors include all the wares under the more familiar name of Spode. Porcelains are listed in this book by the name that appears on the piece. Related pieces are listed under Copeland and Copeland Spode.

Stone-China

Basket, Potpourri, Cover, Band Of Flowers On Side, Twig Handle, 1820 . . . . 1550.00
Bowl, Florence, Square, 9 1/2 In. 71.00
Bowl, Orange, Rust, 9 1/4 In. 68.00
Butter, Cover, Buttercup 82.00
Cabaret Service, Chamfered Rectangular Tray, Shell Handles, 1844, 8 Piece 1200.00
Cup & Saucer, Wicker Dale, Demitasse 26.00
Dish, Cover, Fan Border, Blue, Iron Red, Gold Underglaze, 1815, 11 7/8 In. 2400.00
Gravy Boat, Attached Underplate, Florence 150.00
Plate, Buttercup, Dinner, 10 1/2 In. 18.00
Plate, Chinoiserie Floral Center, Pierced Edge, Pearlware, Plate, 9 1/2 In., Pair 747.00
Plate, Cream Center, Tilt Wave Scroll, Feathered Edge, 10 1/2 In., 17 Piece 2300.00
Plate, Dessert, Mallard, Woodland Series, England, 7 3/4 In. 22.00
Plate, Dessert, Pheasant, Woodland Series, England, 7 3/4 In. 25.00
Plate, Dinner, Indian Tree, Orange, Rust, Scalloped 40.00
Plate, Exotic Bird Center, Gilt Ground, Signed, 10 1/2 In., 12 Piece 1265.00
Plate, Purple, Willow, Marked Spode Blue Room, 10 1/4 In. 20.00
Plate Set, Turquoise Bordered, Cream Center, Tilt Wave Scroll, 10 1/2 In., 17 Piece 2300.00
Salt & Pepper, Buttercup 78.00
Sugar & Creamer, Cover, Buttercup 48.00
Sugar & Creamer, Florence 30.00
Teapot, Florence 100.00
Vase, Flowering Peony, Bamboo In Fenced Garden, 1815, Pair 8400.00

SPONGEWARE is very similar to spatterware in appearance. The designs were applied to the ceramics by daubing the color on with a sponge or cloth. Many collectors do not differentiate between spongeware and spatterware and use the names interchangeably. Modern pottery is being made to resemble the old spongeware, but careful examination will show it is new.

Baking Dish, Blue, White, 3 1/2 x 10 1/2 In. 155.00
Baking Dish, Dark Blue, Oval, 1900, 11 & 8 In., 3 Piece 200.00
Bank, House, Blue, 4 In. 395.00
Batter Bowl, 2 Pouring Spouts, Bail Handle, Tan & Green Swirl 145.00
Bowl, Blue, White, 5 1/4 x 11 In. 35.00
Bowl, Blue, White, Ribbed Exterior, 4 1/2 x 11 In. 80.00
Bowl, Heart Panels, Interior Stone Glaze, Blue, 4 3/4 x 10 In. 140.00
Chamber Pot, Handle, Blue, White, 5 1/2 x 10 In. 121.00

Cooler, Sponged Cover, Brass Spigot, Blue, White, 3 Gal. 110.00
Crock, Butter, Cover, Navy Blue Chicken-Wire Design, Blue, White, 3 3/4 In. 248.00
Cup, Blue, White, 2 3/4 In. 44.00
Cuspidor, White, Blue Accent Bands, 3 x 5 In. 66.00
Dish, Scalloped Edge, White, Deep Blue Diffusion, 1 1/2 x 9 In. 154.00
Honey Pot, Original Cover, Blue, White, Deep Navy, 4 1/2 In. 248.00
Jug, Blue, 2 Dark Blue Bands, 4 1/2 In. 880.00
Nappy, Blue, White, 3 1/4 x 10 In. 248.00
Pitcher, Blue, Gray, Dark Blue Accent Bands, 9 3/4 In. 633.00
Pitcher, Blue, Square Handle, 7 In. 150.00
Pitcher, Blue, White, 3 1/2 x 8 3/4 In. 154.00
Pitcher, Blue, White, 9 In. ....385.00 to 522.00
Pitcher, Blue, White, Wide Blue Rose Design, 9 In. 440.00
Pitcher, Bowl, Blue, White, Late 19th Century, 8 x 4 x 9 1/2 In., 2 Piece 196.00
Pitcher, Daisy, Vine Design, Blue, White, Gold Accents, 9 1/2 In. 165.00
Pitcher, Dark Cobalt Blue, Pure White, 1900, 6 3/4 In., 2 Piece 162.00
Pitcher, Swell In Base, c.1860, 9 In. 575.00
Plate, Soup, Blue, White, Scalloped Rim, 9 1/4 In. 110.00
Vase, Ribbon Design, Blue, White, 7 1/2 In. 110.00

SPORTS equipment, sporting goods, brochures, and related items are listed here. Items are listed by sport. Other categories of interest are Bicycle, Card, Fishing, Sword, Toy, and Trap.

Auto Racing, Suit, Mario Andretti, Full Body, Fire-Retardant, Tag Date 4-85 .... 4365.00
Baseball, Album Page, Autographed, Eddie Collins, Centennial Logo, 1939, 4 1/2 x 6 In. .. 275.00
Baseball, Album Page, Autographed, Joe Tinker, Chicago Cubs, Framed, 8 1/2 x 10 1/2 In. . 400.00
Baseball, Ashtray, Minnesota Twins, 1965 World Series, Red Wing Pottery 150.00
Baseball, Autographed, Lou Gehrig On Sweet Spot, New York Yankees Team 2000.00
Baseball, Ball, Autographed, Babe Ruth ....3025.00 to 5500.00
Baseball, Ball, Autographed, Babe Ruth, To Albert From Babe Ruth, 1930s 2500.00
Baseball, Ball, Autographed, Casey Stengel 675.00
Baseball, Ball, Autographed, Lou Gehrig & Joe DiMaggio, c.1937 .... 1250.00
Baseball, Ball, Autographed, Lou Gehrig & Joe DiMaggio, American League 1665.00
Baseball, Ball, Autographed, Oakland A's, 1989, With Mark McGwire 636.00
Baseball, Bat, Autographed, Ted Williams, Hillerich & Bradsby Louisville Slugger 750.00
Baseball, Button, Babe Ruth Baseball Club, Stitching, Photo, Celluloid, 1 In. 98.00
Baseball, Button, Buffalo Baseball Club Team Picture, 1897, 1 1/4 In. 323.00
Baseball, Button, Don Drysdale, Dodgers, Celluloid, Sky Blue Ground, 3 1/2 In. 100.00
Baseball, Button, Mike Higgins, Red Sox, Celluloid, Black & White, 1 3/4 In. 40.00
Baseball, Button, Washington Senators, Capitol, Bat, Black, White, Celluloid, 1950s, 3 In. 28.00
Baseball, Check, Honus Wagner, Signed John H. Wagner, Cancelled, 1921 .... 750.00
Baseball, Check, Walter Johnson, Payable To Wife Barbara Johnson, Dated March 7, 1946 950.00
Baseball, Cigar Box, Honus Wagner Pictured Inside Top 8525.00
Baseball, Contract, Nolan Ryan, 2-Year Player's Contract With California Angels, 1975 .. 1250.00
Baseball, Cuff Links, 1967 All Star Game, Angels, Anaheim Stadium, Enamel 85.00
Baseball, Figure, Cleveland Indians, Indian, Rubber, Rempel Mfg., Inc., Akron 65.00
Baseball, Glove, Willie Puddin' Head Jones Model, Rawlings, 1940s 45.00
Baseball, Golf Bag, Autographed, Joe DiMaggio, Belding Sports, Leather 1250.00
Baseball, Jacket, Al Kaline, Detroit Tigers, Souvenir, Autographed, Rawlings, Size 46 ... 250.00
Baseball, Jersey, Catfish Hunter, New York Yankees, No. 29, Size 44, Game Used, 1977 . 1250.00
Baseball, Jersey, Derek Jeter, N.Y. Yankees, Game Used 1063.00
Baseball, Jersey, Roger Clemens, Souvenir, Certification, Steiner Sports 275.00
Baseball, Jersey, Tommy John, California Angels, No. 25, Size 46, Game Used, c.1982 .. 375.00
Baseball, Magazine, Life, DiMaggio Picture, Signed Joe, Blue Sharpie, Aug. 1, 1949 .... 80.00
Baseball, Megaphone, N.Y. Yankees, Popcorn Box, 1960, 10 In. 8.00
Baseball, Nodder, Cincinnati Reds, Red Square Base, 1961 .... 195.00
Baseball, Nodder, Mickey Mantle ....850.00 to 875.00
Baseball, Pencil Set, Mickey Mantle, Photo, Attached To Original Card 95.00
Baseball, Photograph, Babe Ruth, Autographed 2723.00
Baseball, Photograph, Chicago Cubs Team, Yard Long, 1910 .... 1045.00
Baseball, Photograph, Ted Williams, Autographed, Black & White, 1st Home Run, 1939 . 175.00
Baseball, Program, Yankees vs. Royals, 1976 .... 15.00

Sports, Baseball, Uniform,
Roger Maris, New York Yankees,
Game Used, 1961, 2 Piece

Pennant collections can be ruined by moths. Store your pennants in moth-proof containers.

Baseball, Seat, Arlington Stadium, Nolan Ryan Autograph, Plastic Seat, Aluminum 450.00
Baseball, Seat, Crosley Field, Wooden, Cast Iron, Plaque, Cincinnati, 1935 . . . . 1000.00
Baseball, Seat, Milwaukee County Stadium, Green, Refinished 650.00
Baseball, Sheet Music, Babe Ruth! We Know What You Can Do, J.W. Spencer, 1928 . . . . 225.00
Baseball, Sunglasses, Willie Mays, Giants 2465.00
Baseball, Tray, Baseball Lithograph, Round, 16 5/8 In. 950.00
Baseball, Tray, Tin Lithographed, Baseball Scene, Oval, 12 In. 825.00
Baseball, Uniform, Roger Maris, New York Yankees, Game Used, 1961, 2 Piece . . . . *Illus* 58752.00
Baseball, Wristwatch, Dizzy Dean, 1933 . . . . 1075.00
Baseball, Yo-Yo, Baseball Shape, Chicago Cubs, Ace Novelty, On Card, 1993 . . . . 18.00
Basketball, Ball, Autographed, Wilt Chamberlain & Bill Russell, Official Game Ball 600.00
Basketball, Photograph, Boston Celtics, Team Autographed, 1960-1961, 20 x 24 In. 250.00
Billiards, Rack Set, Autographed, Willie Mosconi 600.00
Boxing, Button, Joe Louis, Picture, Celluloid, 1 3/4 In. 50.00
Boxing, Gloves, Autographed, Muhammad Ali 250.00
Boxing, Matchbook, Joe Louis vs. Max Schmeling, NBC, Buick, 1936, 4 1/4 x 3 3/8 In. . . 50.00
Boxing, Press Badge, Louis vs. Sharkey, Aug. 18, 1936, Cardboard 400.00
Boxing, Program, Joe Louis Funeral, April 12, 1981 . . . . 57.00
Football, Book, Bear, Bear Bryant To Tom Moon, Autographed, Dec. 16, 1975, 3rd Ed. . . 125.00
Football, Bookends, Knute Rockne Bust, Bronze, Green, 7 In., Pair 150.00
Football, Jersey, Efren Herrera, Dallas Cowboys, No. 1, Game Used, c.1976 . . . . 110.00
Football, Program, Eagles, Packers, Championship Game, Dec. 26, 1960 . . . . 525.00
Football, Program, Super Bowl XXVIII, Atlanta 10.00
Football, Program, University Of Illinois vs. Iowa, Homecoming, 1951 . . . . 40.00
Football, Ticket Stub, Championship, Cleveland Stadium, Browns, Colts, Dec. 27, 1964 . . 265.00
Football, Ticket, Unused, AFL Championship Game, Jets & Oakland, Dec. 26, 1968 . . . . . 245.00
Golf, Ball, Zippo, Minster Die-Namic Process, Box 20.00
Golf, Club Head, Pewter, Wriggled Design, 17th Century 175.00
Golf, Driver, Oak Shaft 95.00
Golf, Iron, Oak Shaft 65.00
Golf, Trophy, Bronze, Sterling, Weston, 5 3/4 In. 132.00
Hockey, Growth Chart, Wayne Gretzky Life Size, L.A. Kings Uniform, Coca-Cola 12.00
Hockey, Nodder, Boston Bruin, 1960s, 5 1/2 In. 95.00
Hockey, Ring, Jim Craig, 1980 Winter Olympics, U.S. Team Goalie 1171.00
Hockey, Stick, Jim Craig, Goalie, Miracle On Ice Game, 1980 Olympics, Northland 4230.00
Horse Racing, Glass, Kentucky Derby, 1953 . . . . 125.00
Horse Racing, Glass, Shot, 1987 . . . . 725.00
Pool, Cue Rack, Wooden, Wall Mount, Mirror, Ray Kerns, Saginaw, Mich., 60 x 46 In. . . 715.00
Pool, Table, Oak, Turned Legs, Ball, Cue Rack, 1885, 59 x 111 In. 8180.00
Pool, Table, Rosewood, Satinwood Inlay, Brunswick, 1880, 110 x 60 x 34 In. 11720.00
Skating, Ice Skates, Wooden, Bucks County, Pa., Early 19th Century, 10 In. 60.00
Skating, Ice Skates, Wooden, Screw-On, Leather Straps, Brass Plates, Steel Blades, 10 In. . 59.00
Skating, Roller Skates, Roller Derby, Disco, Orange Suede, Yellow Nylon, Box, 1977 . . . 25.00
Skating, Roller Skates, Wooden, Leather, Vineyard, Pat. 1880-1882, Size 10 1/2 . . . . 235.00
Skiing, Snow Skis, Wooden, Scottsdale, Ariz., 5 x 78 In. 295.00
Snowshoes, Leather, Lace-Up Boot Bindings, Walter Tubbs, Burlington, Vt., 45 In. 125.00
Tennis, Racket, Wooden, Wright & Ditson, Boston, Mass., Pat. 01/03/1905 . . . . 125.00

STAFFORDSHIRE, England, has been a district making pottery and porcelain since the 1700s. Hundreds of kilns are still working in the area. Thousands of types of pottery and porcelain have been made in the many factories that worked and still work in the area. Some of the most famous factories have been listed separately, such as Adams, Davenport, Ridgway, Rowland & Marsellus, Royal Doulton, Royal Worcester, Spode, Wedgwood, and others. Some Staffordshire pieces are listed under categories like Fairing, Flow Blue, Mulberry, Shaving Mug, etc.

Bank, Cottage, Coleslaw Trim Roof, 5 3/4 In.	110.00
Bidet, Charleton Exchange & Bank Exterior, Washington Capitol Interior, 18 In.	990.00
Bowl, Capitol At Washington, Dark Blue, Round	1725.00
Bowl, Fairmount Near Philadelphia, Dark Blue, Round	1380.00
Bowl, Floral, c.1820, 12 3/4 In.	495.00
Bowl, LaFayette At Franklin's Tomb, Blue, Splayed Edge, 4 x 9 In.	1320.00
Bowl, Pastoral Scene, 10 In.	220.00
Bowl, Upper Ferry Bridge Over The River Schuylkill, 10 x 12 1/2 In.	1870.00
Bowl, Vegetable, Cover, Fox & Bear, Blue Transfer, c.1830, 6 x 10 In.	880.00
Bowl, Village Church, Blue, Rogers, c.1817, 9 1/2 In.	175.00
Bowl, Windsor Castle, Men Fishing, Dark Blue Transfer, 10 1/4 x 12 1/2 In.	415.00
Box, Duck On Egg Shape, Blue Head	1265.00
Bust, Reverend John Wesley, Wood & Sons, Early 19th Century, 10 1/2 In.	470.00
Coffeepot, Lafayette At Franklin's Tomb, Blue, 19th Century, 8 1/2 In.	825.00
Coffeepot, Lafayette At Franklin's Tomb, Dark Blue Transfer, 13 In.	220.00
Crucifix, With Font, White, c.1880, 11 1/2 In.	850.00
Cup & Saucer, Floral, Dark Blue, Handleless, Wood & Sons	165.00
Cup & Saucer, Lafayette At Franklin's Tomb, Handleless	440.00 to 470.00
Cup & Saucer, Nursery Rhyme, Child's	15.00
Cup & Saucer, Railroad, Blue, Handleless	825.00
Cup & Saucer, Woman & Deer Scene, Purple Transfer, Handleless	120.00
Dish, Hen On Nest Cover, 19th Century	980.00
Dish, Hen On Nest Cover, 6 3/4 x 7 1/4 In.	385.00
Dish, Polar Bears, Blue Transfer, Enoch Wood, 11 5/8 In.	990.00
Figurine, Abandoned Child, Early 19th Century, 7 1/4 In.	145.00
Figurine, Bantam Chicken, With Chicks, Brown & White, 7 In.	715.00
Figurine, Bocage, Countryside, Landscape, Walton, 1820-1840	495.00
Figurine, Boxers, One Yellow Pants, Other Pink Pants, 9 1/4 In.	440.00
Figurine, Boy On Tree Stump, With Dog, Brown Base, Gold Trim, c.1840, 6 1/2 In.	405.00
Figurine, Cat On Pillow, Black & White, Green Pillow, c.1885, 4 In., Pair	315.00
Figurine, Cat, Black, Lustered Star On Breast, Jackfield, c.1880, 7 1/2 In., Pair	1330.00
Figurine, Cat, Black, Stars On Breast, Jackfield, c.1880, 7 1/2 In., Pair	330.00
Figurine, Cat, Seated Blue Pillows, Right & Left, Yellow & Black, 7 1/2 In., Pair	600.00
Figurine, Cat, Seated, c.1860, 8 In., Pair	400.00
Figurine, Cat, Seated, Cobalt Blue Pillow, 7 1/2 In., Pair	520.00
Figurine, Cat, Sitting, Pink & Green Cushions, Black & White, 7 1/4 In., Pair	700.00
Figurine, Cat, White, Black, Cobalt Blue Pillow, Gilt Bows, Trim, 4 In., Pair	55.00
Figurine, Cottage, 1860	175.00
Figurine, Cottage, Cobalt Blue Roof, Swans, Center Door, 6 In.	55.00
Figurine, Couple, Bagpiper & Woman, Above Clock Face, c.1850, 14 In.	800.00
Figurine, Dick Turpin, On Horse, c.1870, 6 x 9 1/4 In.	425.00
Figurine, Dog, Black & White, 1860, 15 In.	1595.00
Figurine, Dog, Comforter, White, Seated, Painted Muzzle, Eyes, Late 1800s, 13 In., Pair	400.00
Figurine, Dog, Copper Luster, Lavender & Green Highlights, 7 1/2 In., Pair	300.00
Figurine, Dog, Dalmatian, Gold Chain, Green Base, 5 In., Pair	368.00 to 495.00
Figurine, Dog, Opposing Hounds, Seated With Their Prey, Black, Iron Red, 4 In., Pair	138.00
Figurine, Dog, Opposing Poodles, Sprigged Curled Heads, Peach, 3 3/4 In., Pair	105.00
Figurine, Dog, Poodle, Black Muzzle, Yellow Eyes, Lock On Collar, 4 5/8 In., Pair	415.00
Figurine, Dog, Poodle, c.1880, 4 1/4 In.	225.00
Figurine, Dog, Poodle, Footed Pedestal, Pink & Green, Right & Left, 4 In., Pair	645.00
Figurine, Dog, Poodle, Porcelain, Cream Colored, c.1840, 2 1/4 In.	135.00
Figurine, Dog, Poodle, Seated, Cream Colored, Sanded Half Body, 6 3/4 In.	500.00
Figurine, Dog, Poodle, Seated, Cream, Sanded Half Body & Tail, 7 In.	500.00

Figurine, Dog, Poodle, Standing, Cream, c.1840, 2 1/4 In. 160.00
Figurine, Dog, Seated, Copper Luster, Open Front Legs, 9 1/2 In., Pair 410.00
Figurine, Dog, Seated, Looking Right & Left, Rust Design, 9 In., Pair 660.00
Figurine, Dog, Spaniel, Apricot Color, Glass Eyes, c.1870, 12 1/2 In., Pair 1070.00
Figurine, Dog, Spaniel, Apricot Slip Cast, c.1880, 6 1/2 In., Pair 335.00
Figurine, Dog, Spaniel, Black Glaze, Jackfield, 1860, 13 In., Pair 450.00
Figurine, Dog, Spaniel, Black, Gilt, c.1880, 10 In., Pair 750.00
Figurine, Dog, Spaniel, c.1900, 9 1/2 In., Pair 430.00
Figurine, Dog, Spaniel, Chunky, Black, Jackfield, c.1880, 7 In., Pair 715.00
Figurine, Dog, Spaniel, Chunky, c.1850, 10 In. 425.00
Figurine, Dog, Spaniel, Cream, Peach Muzzle, Blue Underglaze, c.1850, 12 In., Pair 1350.00
Figurine, Dog, Spaniel, Early 20th Century, 10 In., Pair 165.00
Figurine, Dog, Spaniel, Gold Trim, c.1895, 5 1/2 In., Pair 315.00
Figurine, Dog, Spaniel, Gray & Black Muzzle, Yellow Eyes, 7 3/8 In., Pair 385.00
Figurine, Dog, Spaniel, King Charles, 19th Century, 12 1/2 In., Pair 1795.00
Figurine, Dog, Spaniel, King Charles, 26 In., Pair 345.00
Figurine, Dog, Spaniel, King Charles, Seated, Mid 19th Century, 7 In. 420.00
Figurine, Dog, Spaniel, Luster & White, c.1850, 10 In. ....625.00 to 635.00
Figurine, Dog, Spaniel, Peach Colored Muzzle, c.1850, 12 In., Pair 1350.00
Figurine, Dog, Spaniel, Red & White, c.1850, 3 In. 185.00
Figurine, Dog, Spaniel, Red & White, Green Collar, c.1880, 3 1/2 In. 195.00
Figurine, Dog, Spaniel, Reticulated Front Legs, Spotted, Copper Luster, 1880s, 9 In., Pair 620.00
Figurine, Dog, Spaniel, Seated, Copper Luster Trim, Mid 1800s, 9 1/2 In. 405.00
Figurine, Dog, Spaniel, Seated, Separated Legs, Cobalt Blue Base, 1850s, Pair 4400.00
Figurine, Dog, Spaniel, Seated, White, Green Markings, Free Front Leg, 5 In. 210.00
Figurine, Dog, Spaniel, White Ground, Rust Trim, Late 19th Century, 6 In., Pair 330.00
Figurine, Dog, Spaniel, White, Gilt, c.1920, 5 In., Pair 225.00
Figurine, Dog, Spaniel, White, Reddish Orange & Black, 5 3/4 In., Pair 225.00
Figurine, Dog, Spaniel, White, Reticulated Front Legs, Late 19th Century, 6 1/2 In. 85.00
Figurine, Dog, St. Bernard, Black & White, Standing, 5 In. 520.00
Figurine, Dog, Whippet, Cobalt Blue Base, Reticulated Front Legs, c.1875, 5 1/4 In., Pair 250.00
Figurine, Dog, Whippet, Holding Rabbit In Mouth, Green Base, Mid 1800s, 11 1/4 In. ... 275.00
Figurine, Dog, Whippet, Lying On Grass, 4 In., Pair 385.00
Figurine, Dog, Whippet, Standing, With Game, White, Black Collar, Ink Stamp, 6 3/4 In. . 195.00
Figurine, Dog, White, Black Spot & Muzzle, Silver Luster Collar, 5 In., Pair 55.00
Figurine, Dog, White, Brown Spots, Gilt Collar & Chain, 4 3/4 x 3 1/2 In., Pair 385.00
Figurine, Dog, With 2 Puppies, Oval Base, 6 In., Pair 160.00
Figurine, Girl With Parrot & Rabbit, Applied Bocage On Hutch, c.1850, 6 1/4 In. 410.00
Figurine, Girl, On Goat, 6 In. ....275.00 to 315.00
Figurine, Guardian Angel, Royal Children, Cobalt Blue, Gilt Trim, 8 1/4 In. 275.00
Figurine, Happy Boy With Dog, Gilt Base, William Kent, c.1900, 5 x 6 In. 200.00
Figurine, Happy Couple, Carrying Wood & Jug, c.1860, 12 1/4 In. 330.00
Figurine, Hunter, With Gun, c.1865, 5 1/4 In. 100.00
Figurine, Huntsman On Horseback, Stag Across Horse's Withers, c.1900, 15 In. 290.00
Figurine, Jenny Lind, Freckles, c.1880, 4 In. 79.00
Figurine, Jockey Sitting Astride A Buff Colored Mount, 9 In. 70.00
Figurine, Lion, Bocage Center 2250.00
Figurine, Little Red Riding Hood, Cape, Carrying Basket, Dog By Side, 9 In. 395.00
Figurine, Man & Woman, On Horseback, Dogs, 19th Century, 7 1/2 In., Pair 850.00
Figurine, Man On Horse, Basket Of Fruit, 9 1/2 In. 300.00
Figurine, Man, Autumn, 6 1/2 In. 3730.00
Figurine, Man, Standing, Wearing Dark Green Jacket, Black Hat, 8 1/2 In. 140.00
Figurine, Scotsman, Rifle, Leaning Against Wall, 7 3/8 In. 275.00
Figurine, Scotsman, Tree & Sheep, Coleslaw Design, 14 In. 75.00
Figurine, Scottish Lad & Lassie At Clock Tower, 9 In. 175.00
Figurine, Snowy Owl, Linley Adams, c.1930, 5 1/4 In. ....140.00 to 200.00
Figurine, Stallion, Rearing, Copper Luster, c.1917, 12 1/2 In., Pair 605.00
Figurine, T. Smith & W. Collier, Fighting, c.1860, 12 3/4 In. 760.00
Figurine, Uncle Tom, Black Man, Girl On Knee, 10 1/4 In. 770.00
Figurine, Vicar & Moors, 9 1/2 In. 145.00
Figurine, Windmill, Flanked By 2 Children, Mid 19th Century, 9 3/4 In. 413.00
Figurine, Woman, Holding Flower To Breast, Nest Of Eggs, Mid 19th Century, 12 1/2 In. 250.00

Figurine, Woman, Horseback, Attendants, Gilt, Flat Back, 13 In., Pair 234.00
Figurine, Woman, With Posies, 9 In. 305.00
Figurine, Zebra, 5 In. 137.00
Figurine, Zebra, Seated On Grassy Base, Right & Left, 4 1/2 In., Pair 335.00
Figurine, Zebra, Seated, Looking Right & Left, 4 1/2 In., Pair 465.00
Font, Madonna & Baby Jesus, Off-White, c.1880, 10 1/4 In. 520.00
Group, Death Of Nelson, c.1840, 7 x 9 In. 705.00
Group, Musicians, Seated, One Holds Tambourine, c.1860, 8 3/4 In. 530.00
Inkwell, Swan, White, Purple & Sea Green Highlights, Gilt Accents, 3 1/2 In. 200.00
Jug, 2 Lovers Behind Wheat Stack, Farmer Peering From Fence, Black Transfer 2715.00
Jug, Commedia Dell'Arte Transfer, Orange Luster, Ellsmore & Forster, 9 In. 1295.00
Jug, Milk, Success To United States Of America, Transfer, Canary, 4 3/4 In. 115.00
Jug, United States Seal, 16 Stars Below 3995.00
Jug, United States Seal, 16 Stars, Brown Transfer, Yellow Glaze 3995.00
Loving Cup, Setter, Pheasant, Frog Inside, Mid 19th Century, 5 1/4 In. 385.00
Mug, Girl Carrying Chair Transfer, Canary Yellow, Child's, 2 1/2 In. 920.00
Mug, Great Seal Of America, 3 Prints, 1790 . . . . 1020.00
Mug, Landing Of General Lafayette, Scalloped Edge, Blue, White Handle, 3 In. 385.00
Mug, Willie Brewed A Peck O Malt, 5 1/4 x 5 In. 225.00
Pen Holder, Black & White Dogs, On Cobalt Blue Pillow, 3 3/4 x 5 In., Pair 224.00
Pitcher, Adam's Rose, Allover Leaf & Floral, White Ground, 19th Century, 9 1/2 In. 400.00
Pitcher, Almshouse, Boston, Handle, Blue, 9 In. 880.00
Pitcher, Lafayette At Franklin's Tomb, Blue, Bulbous, 7 1/2 In. 1760.00
Pitcher & Bowl, Byzantium, Persian Scene, 11 x 13 In. 258.00
Planter, Herb, Salt Glaze, Late 19th Century, Pair 7800.00
Plaque, Bearded Man, Banner Salisbury, 12 1/4 In. 55.00
Plate, Baltimore & Ohio Railroad, Blue, Wood & Sons, 9 1/4 In. 825.00
Plate, Battery At New York, Green Transfer, Scalloped & Beaded Edge, 7 3/4 In. 275.00
Plate, Boston State House, Blue, Rogers, 7 3/8 In. 195.00
Plate, Building, 3 People, Swans, Floral Border, Dark Blue Transfer, 9 7/8 In. 195.00
Plate, Columbia College, New York, 6 1/2 In. 165.00
Plate, Commodore MacDonnough's Victory, Blue, Wood & Sons, 8 1/2 In. 550.00
Plate, Commodore MacDonnough's Victory, Dark Blue Transfer, 8 3/8 In. 360.00
Plate, Don Quixote, Transfer, 10 In., 8 Piece 950.00
Plate, Erie Canal, Inscription, DeWitt Clinton Eulogy, Dark Blue, 10 1/2 In. 920.00
Plate, Fairmount Near Philadelphia, Blue, 10 1/4 In. 330.00
Plate, Floral, Leaf Design, Chain Border, Red Center Design, 10 In. 275.00
Plate, Geometric Panels, Scalloped Edge, Diamond Piercing, 10 In. 305.00
Plate, Harvard College, Acorn & Oak Leaf Border, Scalloped Rim, 10 1/8 In. 275.00
Plate, Italian Scenery, St. Peter's, Rome, 10 In. 155.00
Plate, LaGrange, Marquis Lafayette Residence, Dark Blue Transfer, Woods, 9 1/2 In. 360.00
Plate, Landing Of The Fathers At Plymouth, Blue, Wood & Sons, 10 In. 610.00
Plate, Nahant Hotel, Near Boston, Blue, 8 1/2 In. 440.00
Plate, Oriental Scene, Dark Blue Transfer, 10 1 1/2 In. 95.00
Plate, Pains Hill Surrey, Fruit & Flowers Border, Blue, R. Hall, 10 In. 110.00
Plate, Park Theatre, New York, Blue, Scalloped, 6 In. 220.00
Plate, Peace & Plenty, Man In Toga, Dark Blue Transfer, 10 1/4 In. 330.00
Plate, Pine Orchard House, Catskill Mountain, Blue, Wood & Sons, 10 In. 605.00
Plate, Sancho & Priest & Barber, Floral Border, Dark Blue Transfer, 7 5/8 In. 140.00
Plate, States, 2 Story Building, Blue, Scalloped, 7 3/4 In. 330.00
Plate, States, 3 Story Building & Observatory, Scalloped, Blue, 10 In. 385.00
Plate, Transylvania University, Lexington, Dark Blue Transfer, 9 1/8 In. 300.00
Plate, Turkey Inn State Park, Indiana, 10 In. 165.00
Plate, Union Line, Blue, Wood & Sons, 10 1/4 In. 935.00
Plate, Upper Ferry Bridge, Over The River Schuylkill, Blue, Stubbs, 9 In. 385.00
Plate, View Of Liverpool, Blue, Wood & Son, 10 In. 650.00
Plate, View Of Trenton Falls, Blue, Wood, 6 1/2 In. 330.00
Platter, America, Eagle With Shield On Breast, Dark Blue Transfer, 10 x 13 1/2 In. 302.00
Platter, Beauties Of America, Capitol, Washington, Well & Tree, Blue, 20 In. 5280.00
Platter, Blue, Cape Coast Castle On The Gold Coast Of Africa, 16 1/2 x 13 In. 4025.00
Platter, Boston State House, Blue, Rogers, 10 3/16 x 8 In. 990.00
Platter, Columbus, Ohio, Dark Blue, Neff Wanton & Co., 14 1/2 In. 1620.00

Platter, Fruit & Flowers, Flower & Leaf Border, Dark Blue Transfer, 14 3/4 In. 770.00
Platter, Man Herding Cattle, Flower Border, Dark Blue Transfer, 17 1/2 x 15 In. 990.00
Platter, Napoleon, Battle Of Marengo, Panoramic Scene, 18 In. 405.00
Platter, Niagara Falls, From The American Side, Wood & Sons, 11 3/4 x 15 In. 2200.00
Platter, Oriental Design, Green & White, Ironstone, 18 x 14 1/4 In. 115.00
Platter, Palestine, Harbor Scene, Blue Transfer, R. Stevenson, 15 1/4 x 19 1/4 In. 522.00
Platter, Scenic Center Medallion, Blue & White, 19 In. 963.00
Platter, Strawberry, c.1820, 16 3/4 x 20 3/4 In. 3520.00
Platter, Transfer Quatrefoil & Dagger Rim, 24 In. 415.00
Platter, Vegetable, Doctor Syntax, The Advertisement For A Wife, 12 x 9 x 2 In. 695.00
Platter, Windsor Castle, Floral Border, Oblong, 18 1/2 In. 1035.00
Pot, Pomade, Landing The Fare, Pegwell Bay, 1850s, 4 1/4 In. 105.00
Sauceboat, Landing Of General Lafayette, Blue, Handle, 5 In. 825.00
Server, Poached Eggs, Lion Finial, Pierced Tray, 5 Holes, Rogers, 8 1/2 In. 2090.00
Soup, Dish, Romantic, Picturesque View, Blue, 10 In. 275.00
Soup, Dish, Vue De Chateau De Coucy, Dark Blue Transfer, Wood & Son 165.00
Spill Holder, Elephant, c.1865 . . . . 1250.00
Spill Holder, Zebra, c.1850 . . . . 1400.00
Spill Vase, Stag & Dog, Grassy Base, 8 In. 330.00
Sugar, Cover, Boston State House, Rogers, 3 3/4 x 6 1/2 In. 1100.00
Tea Set, Girl Sitting In Doorway, Teal Blue Transfer, Child's, 5 1/2 In., 4 Piece 165.00
Tea Set, Green & Red Sprig Decoration, Late 19th Century, Miniature 165.00
Tea Set, Mother & Child Transfer, Canary, Waste Bowl & 2 Cup & Saucer, Child's 460.00
Tea Set, Strawberry & Grape, Rope Borders, 4 Piece 1100.00
Tea Set, Tete-A-Tete, Green, Brown, Teapot With Cover, c.1840, Child's 395.00
Teapot, Blue & White, Transfer, Mid 19th Century, 7 1/4 x 11 3/4 In. 305.00
Teapot, Cauliflower, c.1770, 6 1/2 In. 3500.00
Teapot, Floral Medallions On Shaped Sides, Swan Finial, c.1795 . . . . 1450.00
Teapot, Nest Pattern, Blue & White, Transfer, R. Hall, c.1840, 7 x 12 In. 550.00
Teapot, Oriental Buildings, Acanthus Leaf Spout, Dark Blue Transfer, 10 1/2 In. 275.00
Tobacco Jar, Barrel, Man's Hat, Match Holder, 6 In. 308.00
Tobacco Jar, Seated Man, Smoking Pipe, 8 1/2 In. 340.00
Toby Jugs are listed in their own category.
Toothbrush Holder, Daizy Bell, On Bicycle, 2 Holes, England, 5 3/4 x 5 1/2 In. 55.00
Tray, Albany, Scalloped, 19th Century, 20 1/4 In. 1150.00
Tureen, Cover, Almshouse, Boston, Dark Blue 4310.00
Tureen, Cover, Dix Cove On The Gold Coast, Africa, 1846, 11 x 15 In. 4887.00
Tureen, Cover, Fairmount, Dark Blue 6037.00
Tureen, Cover, Landing Of General Lafayette, Ladle, 1824, 10 x 16 In. 5175.00
Tureen, Cover, Strawberry Ladle, Early 19th Century, 9 1/2 x 13 In. 1650.00
Tureen, Girl With Basket, 2 Goats, Handles, 12 1/4 x 5 3/4 In. 775.00
Tureen, Gravy, Cover, Fort Ticonderoga, New York, Tray & Ladle 600.00
Tureen, Pigeon On Nest, Gilt, 8 1/2 In. 125.00
Tureen, Sauce, Cover, Marine Views, Handle, Ladle, 6 1/2 In. 1760.00
Tureen, Soup, Cover, Belleville On Passaic River, Enoch Wood, 11 1/2 x 15 In. 6875.00
Vase, Building, 2 Towers, 5 1/2 In. 110.00
Vase, Exotic Birds & Flowering Trees, Wilkinson, England, 7 7/8 In. 220.00
Vase, Figural, 1 Ram, Other Ewe, Standing On Grassy Mound, 4 3/4 In., Pair 330.00
Vase, Figural, 2 Grenadiers, Tree Trunk, Spaniel, Mid 1800s, 12 In. 220.00
Vase, Leaping Deer, Chased By Hounds, Green Ground, c.1890, 11 1/2 x 9 In. 625.00
Vase, Spill, Figural, Birds, Tree Trunk, Horse, Cow, Mid 19th Century, 10 1/2 In. 165.00
Vase, Spill, Leaping Deer, With Hound, Green Ground, c.1890, 11 1/2 In., Pair 625.00
Vase, Spill, Stag & Dog, Grassy Base, 8 In. 330.00
Warming Dish, Medium Blue Transfer, c.1800, 9 1/4 In. 335.00
Washbowl, Cottage, Rose Border, Blue Transfer, 13 In. 920.00
Watch Holder, 3 Women, 9 1/2 In. 173.00
Watch Holder, 3 Women, Round Pocket Watch Cutout, Mid 1800s, 10 3/4 In. 413.00
Watch Holder, Boy Seated Top, Boy & Girl Either Side Base, 11 1/2 In. 700.00
Watch Holder, Cherubs 595.00
Watch Holder, Clock Tower Shape, Holder Center, 14 1/2 In. 520.00
Watch Holder, Man & Woman On Side, Wearing Hats, With Peacocks, 11 In. 330.00

STANGL Pottery traces its history back to the Fulper Pottery of New Jersey. In 1910, Johann Martin Stangl started working at Fulper. He left to work at Haeger Pottery from 1915 to 1920. Stangl returned to Fulper Pottery in 1920, became president in 1926, and changed the company name to Stangl Pottery in 1929. Stangl acquired the firm in 1930. The pottery is known for dinnerware and a line of bird figurines. Martin Stangl died in 1972, and the pottery was sold to Frank Wheaton, Jr., of Wheaton Industries. Production continued until 1978, when Pfaltzgraff Pottery purchased the right to the Stangl trademark, and the remaining inventory was liquidated. A single bird figurine is identified by a number. Figurines made up of two birds are identified by a number followed by the letter "D" indicating "Double."

Basket, Blue, Twisted Handle, 11 In.	125.00
Bird, Audubon Warblers, Double, No. 3756D	375.00
Bird, Bluebird, No. 3276	125.00
Bird, Bluebirds, Double, No. 3276	250.00
Bird, Cardinal, No. 3444	125.00
Bird, Cliff Swallow, No. 3852	125.00
Bird, Hen Pheasant, No. 3491	225.00
Bird, Parakeets, Double, Green, No. 3582D	250.00
Bird, Parakeets, Double, No. 3582D	325.00
Bird, Parula Warbler, No. 3583	40.00
Bird, Passenger Pigeon, No. 3450	250.00
Bird, Rooster, Yellow, No. 3445	250.00
Bird, Scissor-Tailed Flycatcher, No. 3757	895.00
Bird, Western Tanagers, Double, No. 3750D	525.00
Bird, Wren, No. 3401	75.00
Carnival, Pitcher, 3 1/2 In.	18.00
Colonial, Cup & Saucer, Silver Green	15.00
Colonial, Cup & Saucer, Tangerine	15.00
Colonial, Plate, Silver Green, 10 In.	15.00
Colonial, Plate, Tangerine, 7 In.	10.00
Colonial, Plate, Tangerine, 10 In.	15.00
Country Life, Plate, Rooster, 10 In.	65.00
Thistle, Bowl, Salad, 10 In.	90.00
Thistle, Bowl, Vegetable, 8 In.	65.00
Town & Country, Pitcher & Bowl, Brown, Large	120.00
Tulip, Flowerpot, Satin White, 5 1/2 In.	65.00

STAR TREK AND STAR WARS collectibles are included here. The television series *Star Trek* ran from 1966 through 1969. The TV show *Next Generation,* a sequel, ran from 1987 to 1994. The first Star Trek movie was released in 1979 and 8 others followed, the most recent in 1999. The movie *Star Wars* opened in 1977 and sequels and prequels were released in 1980, 1983, and 1999. Other science fiction and fantasy collectibles can be found under Batman, Buck Rogers, Captain Marvel, Flash Gordon, Movie, Superman, and Toy.

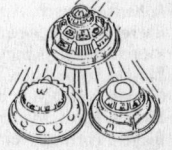

STAR TREK, Book, Activity, Punch Out & Play Album, Saalfield, 1975, 10 1/2 x 12 1/2 In.	90.00
Colorforms, Booklet, Box, 1970s	80.00
Costume, Mr. Spock, Box, Ben Cooper, Child's, 1975	70.00
Decanter, Liquor, Mr. Spock, Ceramic, Grenadier, Box, 1979	80.00
Doll, Captain Kirk, Spock, Lt. Uhura, Mr. Scott, Klingon, 1974, 8 In., 5 Piece	610.00
Figure, Ferengi, The Next Generation, On Card, Galoob, 1988, 3 3/4 In.	100.00
Figure, Lieutenant Tasha Yar, The Next Generation, On Card, Galoob, 1988, 3 3/4 In.	25.00
Figure, Lieutenant Worf, The Next Generation, On Card, Galoob, 1988, 3 3/4 In.	14.00
Figure, Mr. Spock, The Motion Picture, On Card, Mego, 1979, 3 3/4 In.	35.00
Figure, Odo, With Trading Card, Deep Space Nine, On Card, Playmates, 1993, 5 In.	15.00
Figure, Q, The Next Generation, On Card, Galoob, 1988, 3 3/4 In.	95.00
Gun, Phaser Launcher, 3 Saucers, On Card, AHI, 1976	125.00
Lunch Box, Dome Top, Thermos, Metal, Aladdin, 1968	920.00
Lunch Box, Next Generation, Plastic, King Seeley Thermos	250.00
Lunch Box Thermos, Captain Kirk, Metal, Aladdin, 1968	50.00
Ship, Klingon Battle Cruiser, Die Cast Metal, Box, Dinky, England, 1977, 9 In.	90.00

Toy, Interspace Communicator, Plastic, Capt. Kirk & Spock On Box, Lone Star, 1974 .... 80.00
View-Master, Omega Glory, 3 Reels, 1968 .... 45.00
Yo-Yo, Lt. Commander Data, Next Generation, Spectra Star Yo-Yos, On Card, 1993 ..... 13.00
STAR WARS, Binder, 3-Ring, C-3PO & R2-D2, Mead, 1977, 12 x 10 In. 20.00
  Book, C-3PO's Book About Robots, Joanne Ryder, Random House, 1983, 34 Pages 9.00
  Book, Return Of The Jedi, Storybook Based On Movie, 1983, 8 x 11 In. 10.00
  Button, Return Of The Jedi, Celluloid, On Card, Adam Joseph Industries, 1983, 2 1/4 In. . 8.00
  Card, Trading, Wonder Bread, With Bread Wrapper, Hostess, 1978, Set 65.00
  Carry Case, C-3PO, Kenner, Box 90.00
  Carry Case, Return Of The Jedi, Kenner 225.00
  Clock, Alarm, Talking, R2-D2 & C-3PO, Bradley, Box, 1980 .... 175.00
  Display Box, Figures, Black Cardboard, Photos From Movie 695.00
  Figure, Chewbacca, Kenner, Box, 1970s, 15 In. 145.00
  Figure, Darth Vader, Kenner, 1970s, 15 In. 95.00
  Figure, Han Solo In Carbonite, Power Of The Force, On Card, Kenner, 1984 .... 275.00
  Figure, IG-88, Bounty Hunter Robot, Accessories, Kenner, 1980, 15 In. 350.00
  Figure, Jawa, Vinyl Cape, On Card, Kenner, 1977 .... 3800.00
  Figure, Luke Skywalker, Kenner, Box, 1978, 12 In. 395.00
  Figure, Princess Leia Organa, Combat Poncho, On ROTJ 77-Back Card, Kenner, 1983 ... 50.00
  Figure, Princess Leia, Kenner, Box, 1978, 12 In. 225.00
  Figure, R2-D2, Pop-Up Light Saber, Power Of The Force, On Card, Kenner, 1985 ...... 225.00
  Figure, Storm Trooper, On 20-Back Card, Kenner, 1978, 3 3/4 In. 150.00
  Figure, Teebo, On ROTJ 77-Back Card, Kenner, 1983 .... 40.00
  Figure, Yoda, With Brown Snake, Empire Strikes Back, On Card, Kenner, 1980s 225.00
  Laser Pistol, Biker Scout, Return Of The Jedi, Kenner, Box, 1983 .... 125.00
  Lunch Box, Metal, King Seeley Thermos, 1977 .... 40.00
  Lunch Box, Stars On Band, Metal, King Seeley Thermos, 1978 .... 145.00
  Pen & Pencil, Luke, Darth Vader, Han Solo, C-3PO, Storm Trooper 5.00
  Phone, Darth Vader Speaker Phone, Box 125.00
  Toy, Millenium Falcon, Die Cast Metal, Kenner, Box, 1970s 150.00

STEINS have been used by beer and ale drinkers for over 500 years. They have been made of ivory, porcelain, stoneware, faience, silver, pewter, wood, or glass in sizes up to nine gallons. Although some were made by Mettlach, Meissen, Capo-di-Monte, and other famous factories, most were made by less important German potteries. The words *Geschutz* or *Musterschutz* on a stein are the German words for *patented* or *registered design*, not company names. Steins are still being made in the old styles. Lithophane steins may be found in the Lithophane category.

Anheuser-Busch, Animals Of Prairie, Wild Mustang 35.00
Barrel Man, Stoneware, Inlaid Lid, 1/2 Liter 485.00
Bicycle Form, 3 Bicycle Scenes, Relief, Pottery, Pewter Lid, No. 1308, 3 Liter 310.00
Bicycle Form, High Wheeler, Porcelain, Lithophane, Inlaid Lid, Schierholz, 1/2 Liter 465.00
Bicycle Form, Man Riding Standard Bicycle Near Lake, Porcelain, 1/2 Liter 385.00
Bicycle Form, Man Riding Standard Bicycle, Porcelain, Pewter Lid, 1/2 Liter 300.00
Bicycle Form, Several People Riding Standard Bicycles, Pottery, Pewter Lid, 1/2 Liter ... 810.00
Bicycle Form, Transfer, Enamel, Pottery, Pewter Lid, Inscription Dated 1900, 1 Liter 545.00
Birch Tree & Stag, Tan, Green, Figural Lid, Hunter, No. 1636, 2 1/2 Liter 70.00
Budweiser, Bevo Mill 550.00
Budweiser, Birds Of Prey, Peregrine Falcon 65.00
Budweiser, Bud Man 355.00
Budweiser, Clock Tower 375.00
Budweiser, Faust 90.00
Character, Bearded Man, Stoneware, Dumler & Brieden, Inlaid Lid, 1/2 Liter 485.00
Character, Christopher Columbus, Ship, Globe, Reinhold Hanke, Inlaid Lid, 1/2 Liter ... 528.00
Character, Hobo, Pottery, Inlaid Lid, ECS No. 222, 1/2 Liter 290.00
Character, Iron Maiden, Stoneware, Inlaid Lid, Marked T.W., 1/2 Liter 445.00
Character, Nuremberg Tower, Pewter Lid, 1/2 Liter 305.00
Character, Singing Pig, Porcelain, Inlaid Lid, Schierholz, 1/2 Liter 412.61
Character, Sleeping Hunter, Porcelain, Porcelain Lid, Bauer, 1/2 Liter 605.00
Character, Smoking Pig, Porcelain, Inlaid Lid, Schierholz, 1/2 Liter 525.14
Character, Terra-Cotta, Dwarf In Apron, Champagne Bottles, JM673, 10 1/2 In. 605.00

City Of Nuremberg, Enameled, Pottery, Pewter Lid, 1/2 Liter 170.00
Couple Reading Newspaper, Stoneware, Relief, Pewter Lid, White's, New York, 1 Liter . 375.00
Crest, Engraved, Coin, Marked Stockholm, Sweden, Pewter Lid, 3 Berry Feet, 8 1/2 In. . . 120.00
Crest, Painted, Pottery, Pewter Lid, 2 Liter 200.00
Devil & Skull Heads, Porcelain, Inlaid Lid, E. Bohne & Sohne, 1/4 Liter 290.00
Drinkers & Opium Smokers, Pewter, Relief, Pewter Lid, Monk & Devil, 1/2 Liter 315.00
Drinking Scene, German Verse On Opposite, Salt Glaze, Pewter Lid, 7 In. 198.00
Dutch Man, Uniform, Standing Next To Barrel, Blue Glaze, Pewter Lid, 9 1/4 In. 55.00
Dwarfs Drinking, Women Walking, Relief, Inscription, Pewter, 1908, 1/2 Liter 110.00
Dwarfs Sitting On Tree Stump, Pottery, Etched, Pewter Lid, 1/2 Liter 210.00
Eagle, Pewter, Relief, Pewter Lid With Spout Is Eagle's Head, 2 Liter 235.00
Fireman, Stoneware, Inlaid Lid, 1/2 Liter 485.00
Firemen, Tan, Brown, Green, Pottery, Pewter Lid, 1/2 Liter 49.00
Fox Hunt, Pottery, Etched, Pewter Lid, Hauber & Reuther, 1 Liter 380.00
Germans Meeting Romans, No. 1269, Etched, Pewter Lid, Pottery 190.00
Glass, Amber, Pewter Lid, 1/2 Liter 220.00
Glass, Blown, Ribbed, Pewter Base, Center Ring, Handle, Lid, Dwarf Thumblift, 1/4 Liter 180.00
Glass, Blue Prunts, Amber, Gold Trim, 1/2 Liter 290.00
Glass, Cavaliers Eating & Drinking, Amber, Ribbed, Enameled, Inlaid Lid, 1/2 Liter 390.00
Glass, Crystal, Blown, Applied Glass Circles, Cut Flowers, Pewter Lid, 1/2 Liter 105.00
Glass, Enameled Barmaid, Pewter Lid, 1/3 Liter 320.00
Glass, Green, Coralene, Enameled Flowers, Hinged Ram's Head Lid, 13 3/4 In. 495.00
Glass, Green, Ribbed, Pewter Base Ring, Lid, 1/2 Liter 305.00
Glass, Leaping Stag, Flowers, Painted, Pewter Base Ring, Lid, Coin, c.1750, 9 In., 1 Liter 3025.00
Glass, Red Stain, White Enamel Overlay, Cut, Engraved, Inlaid Lid, c.1860, 1/2 Liter 455.00
Hunter On Mountain Top With Target, Pewter Lid, Stoneware, 1/2 Liter 290.00
Iron Cross, Artillery Shell, Inscription, Copper, Brass Lid, 1914-1917 . . . . 540.00
Ivory, Hunters, Woman, Satyr, Carved, Silver Mounts, Silver Lid, Satyr Finial, 1850 . . . . . 4830.00
Jockey & Horse, Stoneware, Relief, Pewter Lid, Marked Gerz No. 1035A, 2 Liter 665.00
Knight, Suit Of Armor, Stoneware, 1/2 Liter 970.00
Knight On Horseback, Stoneware, Pewter Lid, Ludwig Hohlwein, No. 2176, 1/2 Liter . . . 1780.00
Kreussen, Apostles, Pewter Base, Lid, c.1900, 1 Liter 665.00
Lignum Vitae, c.1670, 1/2 Liter, 7 1/2 In. 9900.00
Linked Circles, Stoneware, Relief, Pewter Lid, Paul Wynand, No. 2112, c.1910, 1 Liter . . 650.00
Man, Seminude Woman, Faience, Pewter Base Ring & Lid, 1 Liter 1380.00
Man & Woman, Tan, Brown, Green, Pottery, Pewter Lid, 1 Liter 125.00
Man With Pipe, Toasting, Salt Glaze, Pewter Lid & Thumbpiece, 10 3/4 In. 220.00
Men Toasting, German Verse On Opposite, Pewter Lid, Bristol Glaze, 9 1/2 In. 125.00
Mettlach steins are listed in the Mettlach category.
Military, Red Cross, Bavarian Crest, Stoneware, Transfer, Enamel, Pewter Lid, 1/2 Liter . . 130.00
Military, Three Kaisers, Pottery, Pewter Lid, Relief, No. 193, 1/2 Liter 138.00
Monk, Pewter, Inscription On Underside Dated 1899, Pewter Lid, 1/2 Liter 240.00
Monk, Stoneware, Inlaid Lid, Marked Lowenbrau-Munchen, No-Tip Metal Base, 1/2 Liter 285.00
Monk, Stoneware, No. 61, Blue & Purple Salt Glaze, Inlaid Lid, 1/2 Liter 169.00
Monkey, Vest, Sea Serpent Handle, Ceramic, Pewter Thumbpiece, Germany, 9 1/2 In. 440.00
Munich Child, Pottery, Tan, Inlaid Lid, Marked J. Reinemann, Munchen, 1/4 Liter 145.00
Munich Child In Red Robe, Porcelain, Inlaid Lid, 1/2 Liter 115.00
North Wind Spout, Man Toasting, Child On Reverse, Bardwell, Bristol Glaze, 12 In. . . . 440.00
Nun, Stoneware, Deep Blue Glaze, Inlaid Lid, Pewter Base, 1/2 Liter 270.00
Occupational, Hat Maker, Crest, Lion, Pewter Lid, Pewter Lid, 1895, 1/2 Liter 770.00
Occupational, Locksmith, Transfer, Enamel, Lithophane, Pewter Lid, Karl Krahl, 1/2 Liter 575.00
Occupational, Milk Wagon Driver, Porcelain, Pewter Lid, 1/2 Liter 770.00
Occupational, Night Watchman, Pewter Lid, Porcelain, 1/2 Liter 1070.00
Occupational, Paper Manufacturer, Large Scene, Pewter Lid, Porcelain, 1/2 Liter 1155.00
Oktoberfest, Transfer, Enamel, Pewter Lid, Artist P. Neu, 1 Liter 725.00
Old Woman, Pottery, No. 429, Hat Is Lid, 1/2 Liter 415.00
Rabbits, Purple, Blue, Green Salt Glaze, Pewter Lid, Stoneware, 1/2 Liter 350.00
Regimental, 2 Chevauleger Dillingen 1906-09, Horse Head Thumblift, 1/2 Liter 485.00
Regimental, 2-Sided Scene, Boot S. 86, Porcelain, Eagle Thumblift, 1/2 Liter 2425.00
Regimental, 2-Sided Scene, Eagle Thumblift, Porcelain, 1/2 Liter . . . . .440.00 to 935.00
Regimental, 2-Sided Scene, Eagle Thumblift, Pottery, 1913, 1 Liter 2640.00
Regimental, 2-Sided Scene, Eagle Thumblift, Pottery, 1916, 1/2 Liter 1100.00
Regimental, 2-Sided Scene, Fallen Soldier, Red Cross, Schutzen Thumblift, 1/2 Liter 1130.00

Regimental, 2-Sided Scene, Inf. Leib, Rgt. 8 Camp, Stoneware, Lion Thumblift, 1/2 Liter   580.00
Regimental, 2-Sided Scene, Inf. Rgt. No. 14, Pottery, Eagle Thumblift, 1/2 Liter 720.00
Regimental, 2-Sided Scene, Rgt. No. 14, Porcelain, Eagle Thumblift, 1/2 Liter 698.00
Regimental, 2-Sided Scene, Sachsen Thumblift, Porcelain, 1/2 Liter 910.00
Regimental, 3-Sided Scene, Feldart, Rft. Nr. 42, Porcelain, Barbarosa Thumblift, 1/2 Liter   580.00
Regimental, 4-Sided Scene, Batt. 4 Wurtt Feld-Artill, 1912, 1/2 Liter 570.00
Regimental, 4-Sided Scene, Bayr. Inf. Reg., Porcelain, Lion Thumblift, 1/2 Liter 856.00
Regimental, 4-Sided Scene, Eagle Thumblift, Miter Lid, Porcelain, 1/2 Liter . . .1017.00 to 1375.00
Regimental, 4-Sided Scene, Inf. Reft. 11 Komp, Porcelain, Lion Thumblift, 1/2 Liter 799.00
Regimental, 4-Sided Scene, Inf. Reg. 7 Comp, Porcelain, Lion Thumblift, 1/2 Liter 720.00
Regimental, 4-Sided Scene, Lion Thumblift, Porcelain, 1/2 Liter . . . . .660.00 to 850.00
Regimental, 4-Sided Scene, Porcelain, Sachsen Thumblift, 1/2 Liter 770.00
Regimental, 4-Sided Scene, Portrait Of A Woman, Griffin Thumblift, 1/2 Liter 660.00
Regimental, 4-Sided Scene, Roster, Machine Guns, Eagle Thumblift, 1/2 Liter 2475.00
Regimental, Tree Trunk, Eagle Thumblift, 1/2 Liter 786.00
Revelers, Medallion Of Bust Of Maiden, Stoneware, Pewter Lid, German, 10 3/4 In. 230.00
Royal Vienna, Musical Design, Painted, Gold Plated Lid, Beehive Mark, 1/2 Liter 740.00
Royal Vienna Style, 3 Women, Cupid, Porcelain, Blue Beehive Mark, 1/2 Liter 3049.00
Saturday Evening Post, Do Unto Others 35.00
Shierholz, Character, Barmaid, 5 Liter 3300.00
Shoemaker, Pewter Lid, 1/2 Liter 390.00
Shooting Festival, Enameled, Stoneware, 1/2 Liter 250.00
Shooting Festival, Flowers On Sides, Enameled, Porcelain, 1/2 Liter 350.00
Shooting Festival, Glass, Transfer, Enamel, Relief Pewter Lid, Eagle Thumblift, 1 Liter . .   725.00
Silver, Repose Design, Man Figure Finial, Marked Kinceian 900, 1 Liter 1150.00
Smoking Pig, Porcelain, Inlaid Lid, Schierholz, 1/2 Liter 369.00
Tankard, Queen Anne, Figure Of Queen, Flowers, Ball Thumblift, 1762, 1 Liter 525.00
Tower, Relief, Pottery Lid, 1/2 Liter 190.00
Trumpeter Of Sackingen, Porcelain, Transfer, Enamel, Lithophane, Pewter Lid, 1/2 Liter .   186.00
Uncle Sam, Porcelain, 1/2 Liter 100.00
Verse, Porcelain, Threading, Color, Pewter Lid, Hauber & Reuther, No. 150, 1/2 Liter . . .   169.00
Wheat & Hops, Relief Pewter Lid, Monkey Thumblift, Art Nouveau, 1/2 Liter 295.00
White Glaze, Boy On The Bottom, Pewter Domed Lid, 1850, 9 3/4 In. 86.00
Whites, Stoneware, Woman Blowing Tuba, Blue, Brown Glaze, Pewter Lid, New York . .   795.00

STEREO CARDS that were made for stereoscope viewers became popular after 1840. Two almost identical pictures were mounted on a stiff cardboard backing so that, when viewed through a stereoscope, a three-dimensional picture could be seen. Value is determined by maker and by subject. These cards were made in quantity through the 1930s.

A Thousand Boys In Blue, Griffith & Griffith, 1899 . . . .   14.00
American Troops Parading In Paris, W.E. Troutman, Inc., World War I 8.00
Army Hospital, Manila, P.I., James M. Davis, B.W. Kilburn, 1900 . . . .   14.00
Back From A Successful Trip Across The German Lines, W.E. Troutman, World War I . . .   15.00
Battleship Missouri, Polychrome, 1907 . . . .   8.00
Camp On Road To Manassas 445.00
Chronicle, Call & Mutual Savings Bank, Earthquake, San Francisco, J.B. Davis, 1906 . . .   20.00
Deck Of U.S. Battleship Pennsylvania, Keystone View Co. 10.00
Dedication Of Grant's Tomb, USS Maine, Griffith & Griffith 14.00
Dr. Anna Howard Shaw, Suffrage Leader 200.00
Election Scene, Nov. 3, 1868, Grant-Colfax Banner, J.N. Wilson, Savannah, GA 1200.00
Horseguard At Entrance To Whitehall, London, England, Stereo-Travel Co., 1908 . . . . .   12.00
In Belleau Wood Where Our Boys Fought & Won, Keystone View Co. 8.00
Japanese Soldier On His Way For Water, Polychrome Stereo View, T.W. Ingersoll, 1905 .   7.00
Johnstown Calamity, General View Of Wrecked City, Underwood & Underwood, 1889 . .   12.00
London Bridge, London, England, Underwood & Underwood, 1901 . . . .   12.00
Marriage Ceremony Staged At The Front, W.E. Troutman, World War I 9.00
McClellan Hospital Ward 13, M.S. Hagaman 540.00
Merry Bathers, At Old Orchard Me., J.O. Durgan, August 15, '76 . . . .   40.00
No Man's Land, Sea Of Barbed Wire Near Bulgarian Lines, Underwood & Underwood . .   8.00
On The Lookout For An Attack At Picket Station 330.00
President & Mrs. McKinley, Keystone View Co. 10.00
Russian Cathedral At Dalny, Polychrome Stereo View, T.W. Ingersoll, 1905 . . . .   7.00

Sarajevo From Porch Of New Town Hall, Scene Of Murder, Keystone View Co. 8.00
Stereoview, New Orleans Wharf, Black Loading Steamer With Cotton, 1900 . . . .   16.00
Taking Away The Wounded In Ambulance, Somme, Keystone View Co., World War I . . .   8.00
They Shall Not Pass, Entrance To Verdun, W.E. Troutman, Inc. 8.00
USS Brooklyn, Griffith & Griffith, c.1905 . . . .   10.00
USS Monitor Mi-An-Ti-No-Mah, Bell & Brothers 445.00
Vancouver Island, Muybridge 385.00
Victory Day Celebration, July 14, 1919, Arch Of Triumph, Paris, Keystone View Co. . . .   8.00

STEREOSCOPES were used for viewing stereo cards. The hand viewer
was invented by Oliver Wendell Holmes, although more complicated
table models were used before his was produced in 1859. Do not confuse the stereoscope with the stereopticon, a magic lantern that used
glass slides.

Abrams, 2 Or 4 Power, Model CB-1 . . . .   106.00
H.C. White, Flower & Leaf Design, 152 Cards Pat'd July 28, 1903 . . . .   166.00
H.C. White, Perfectscope, 8 Cards, 1900 Exposition Universelle Internationale 188.00
Keystone View Company, Engraved Design, 33 Cards, Pat'd Apr 12, 1904 . . . .   225.00
Monarch, 13 In. 123.00
Underwood & Underwood, Wood & Tin, 40 Cards, Patented 1901 . . . .   100.00
Unis Paris, France, 1930s, 5 In. 220.00
Walnut, 25 Ferrier, Soulier & Levy Cards, 15 In. 484.00

STERLING SILVER, see Silver-Sterling category.

STEUBEN glass was made at the Steuben Glass Works of Corning, New
York. The factory, founded by Frederick Carder and T.G. Hawkes, Sr.,
was purchased by the Corning Glass Company. They continued to
make glass called *Steuben*. Many types of art glass were made at
Steuben. The firm is still making exceptional quality glass but it is
clear, modern-style glass. Additional pieces may be found in the
Aurene, Cluthra, and perfume bottle categories.

Bar Set, Teardrop, Cocktail Shaker, 6 Hourglass Tumblers, 1949, 7 Piece 545.00
Bonbon, Light Jade Blue, 1 x 4 3/4 In. 95.00
Bowl, Blue Aurene, Floral, Leaf Design, Signed, 3 x 9 1/2 In. 2245.00
Bowl, Calcite, Blue Aurene Interior, Flared Rim, Calcite, 12 1/2 In. 520.00
Bowl, Calcite, Gold Aurene Interior, 2 3/4 x 9 5/8 In. 230.00
Bowl, Calcite, Gold Aurene Underplate, 3 1/2 x 6 1/4 In. 299.00
Bowl, Clear, Spiral Scrolled Handle, 4 3/4 x 3 1/2 In. 150.00
Bowl, Diamond Optic, Blue Threading, Fluted, Signed, c.1920, 5 3/8 In. 230.00
Bowl, Floret, Donald Pollard, No. 8059, 1954, 7 3/4 x 3 1/4 In.   115.00
Bowl, Green Jade, c.1925, 4 x 8 In. 400.00
Bowl, Green Jade, Flat Rim, Signed, 4 x 11 1/4 In. 517.00
Bowl, Green Jade, Scalloped Free Form, Oval, 5 x 8 x 5 1/4 In.   460.00
Bowl, Ivrene, 8 Vertical Ribs, Iridescent, Signed, 17 x 2 1/4 In.   288.00
Bowl, Large Sunflower, Eric Hilton, No. 8530, Signed, 1986, 10 In. 480.00
Bowl, Plum Jade, Etched Water Lilies, Scrolled Ground, c.1925, 6 7/8 In. 4312.00
Candlestick, Amethyst, Ribbed, 11 3/4 In., Pair 2850.00
Candlestick, Green Jade 1500.00
Candlestick, Rosaline, Alabaster, 10 1/4 In. 402.00
Candy Dish, Cover, Ram's Head Finial, Irene Benton, No. 7936, 1943, 6 3/4 In 345.00
Centerpiece, Swirled, Pomona Green, Rosa, Acid Stamp Mark, 3 1/4 x 11 In. 345.00
Charger, Celeste Blue, Dark Blue Rim, 14 1/4 In. 55.00
Compote, Calcite, Gold Aurene Interior, 3 1/4 x 7 1/4 In. 345.00
Compote, Calcite, Gold Aurene, Flower & Leaf Design, 3 1/4 x 9 3/4 In. 1265.00
Compote, Celeste Blue, Acid Stamp Mark, 7 1/2 x 8 In. 650.00
Compote, Celeste Blue, Swirl, Rosa Mica Fleck Stem, 6 1/2 x 8 In. 804.00
Compote, Ivory, Applied Foot, Scalloped Rim, 6 1/2 In. 330.00
Decanter, Ruby Cerise, Applied Handle, Cut Ruby Stopper, 8 5/8 In. 300.00
Figurine, Deer, Orange, Brown Metallic, 15 In. 12.00
Figurine, Elephant, Trumpeting, Signed, 8 In. 460.00
Figurine, Hatching Penguin, Robert Cassetti, 3 3/4 In. 108.00
Figurine, Kitten, Lloyd Atkins, 1955, 4 1/4 In. 200.00
Figurine, Mouse & Cheese, James Houston, 1975, 4 In. 4370.00

Figurine, Mouse, Lloyd Atkins, 4 In. 240.00
Figurine, Owl, Signed, 5 In. 259.00
Figurine, Partridge In A Pear Tree, Lloyd Atkins, 5 3/4 In. 3910.00
Figurine, Porpoise, Lloyd Atkins, 9 1/4 In. 402.00
Figurine, Rabbit, Rosaline Body, Alabaster Ears, Feet, 4 1/4 In. 316.00
Figurine, Shore Bird, 1975 .... 230.00
Figurine, Swan, Lloyd Atkins, 1984, 7 1/2 In. 258.00
Figurine, Thistle Rock, James Houston, 8 In. 1840.00
Figurine, Trout & Fly, James Houston, 8 3/4 In. 1955.00
Flower Frog, Diver, Nude Woman, Rock Form, 14 1/2 In. 1095.00
Goblet, Cintra, Venetian Style, Green, Yellow, Etched Fruit, Yellow, Red, Green, 7 1/4 In. 325.00
Goblet, Eagle, Stars, Teardrop Stem, Circular Base, Red Fitted Case, 8 In. 115.00
Goblet, Rose DuBarry, Alabaster Stem, Foot, 7 1/2 In., Pair 230.00
Goblet, Spanish Green, Inverted Bell Shape, Signed, 8 1/2 In., 9 Piece 980.00
Lamp, Chandelier, 5 Steuben Shades, Gold Aurene Interiors, Signed, 39 In. 1265.00
Lamp, King Tut, White, Gold Iridescent Shade, Brass Base, 14 In. 420.00
Lamp, Molded Glass, Bronze, Wrought Iron, Oscar Bach, c.1910, 68 In. 24900.00
Lamp, Sculptured & Etched, Chrysanthemums, c.1925, 32 1/2 In. 920.00
Lamp Base, Calcite, Gold Aurene Pulled Feathers, 8 x 5 In. 520.00
Pitcher, Alabaster, Applied Black Jade Handle, 9 1/2 In. ....475.00 to 690.00
Plate, Rosaline, Signed, Carder, 8 1/2 In. .... .71.00 to 115.00
Plate, Selenium Ruby, Mark, Fleur-De-Lis, 6 1/8 In. 60.00
Powder Box, Alabaster Cover, Plum Jade, 5 1/2 x 5 1/4 In. 325.00
Powder Box, Cover, Plum Jade, Alabaster Foot, Knob, 4 1/2 In. 200.00
Powder Box, Rosaline Cover, 4 1/4 x 4 In. 295.00
Shade, Calcite, Gold Aurene Interior, Signed, 8 In. 308.00
Shade, Ivrene, 5 In. 86.00
Sugar & Creamer, Light Blue, Wisteria 350.00
Sugar & Creamer, Topaz, Amber, 2 1/2 In. 200.00
Tazza, Calcite, Gold Aurene, Molded Ribs, Paper Label, 8 In. 500.00
Tumbler, Rose DuBarry, Alabaster Base, 4 In., 4 Piece 185.00
Urn, Cover, Rolled Edge, Bristol Yellow & Green, 9 In. 260.00
Vase, Amber, Swirl, Signed, 6 3/4 In. 345.00
Vase, Blue Jade, Cylindrical, Ribbed, 8 1/2 x 5 In. 2750.00
Vase, Calcite, Gold Aurene Heart & Trailing Vines, 6 1/4 In. 545.00
Vase, Calcite, Gold Aurene Interior, Ruffled Edge, 5 1/4 In. 290.00
Vase, Celeste Blue, Footed, 6 3/4 In. 140.00
Vase, Celeste Blue, Swirl, 6 3/4 In. 165.00
Vase, Clear, Cerise Ruby Threading, Signed, 9 1/2 In. 60.00
Vase, Clear, Free-Form Top, Signed, 10 In. 115.00
Vase, Clear, Free-Form, Tooled Rim, George Thompson, 1957, 10 In. 140.00
Vase, Clear, Trumpet, Embossed Ivy, 8 In. 95.00
Vase, Conical, Selenium Ruby, Engraved Grapevine Below Rim, Acid Stamp Mark, 12 In. 750.00
Vase, Cover, Green Jade, 5 In. 545.00
Vase, Cut Stars, Circles, Cylindrical, Footed, Acid Stamp Mark, 12 In. 35.00
Vase, Diamond-Quilted, Bristol Yellow, Black Threaded, Signed, 9 1/4 x 6 In. 575.00
Vase, Fan, Green Jade, Alabaster, Ribbed, Disc Foot, Knop Stem, c.1920, 6 In. 800.00
Vase, Fan, Light Purple, Swirl, 8 1/4 x 6 1/2 In. 635.00
Vase, Fan, Topaz, Pomona Green Stem, Footed, 8 1/4 x 7 In. 230.00
Vase, Flower Form, Crystal, 10 1/2 In. 98.00
Vase, Green Jade, 8 x 6 1/4 In. 546.00
Vase, Grotesque, Cranberry, Signed, 9 In. 600.00
Vase, Iridescent, Black, Urn Shape, Signed, Frederick Carder, c.1930, 9 1/4 In. 8400.00
Vase, Ivory, Aurene Interior, Flared, Signed, 8 1/2 In. 440.00
Vase, Ivory, Iridescent, Footed, Oval, 6 1/4 In. 545.00
Vase, Ivory, Ribbed, 9 x 6 In. ....175.00 to 425.00
Vase, Ivory, Rolled & Flared Rim, Cushion Foot, 10 1/4 In. 690.00
Vase, Ivrene, Flared, 8 1/4 In. 140.00
Vase, Ivrene, Flared, Rippled Texture, Signed, 5 x 5 In. 345.00
Vase, Ivrene, Scalloped, Flared, 9 3/4 x 7 3/4 In. 250.00
Vase, Ivrene, Signed, 6 x 4 1/2 In. 690.00
Vase, Pomona Green, 9 x 6 In. 395.00
Vase, Pomona Green, Ribbed, 9 x 5 3/4 In. 201.00

Vase, Rosaline, Alabaster, Cone, Acid Stamp Mark, 6 3/4 In. 175.00
Vase, Scalloped Rim, Gold Iridescence, No. 723, Early 20th Century, 9 In. 750.00
Vase, Topaz, Paneled, 5 In. 115.00
Vase, Trumpet, Calcite, 6 In. 515.00

STEVENGRAPHS are woven pictures made like fancy ribbons. They were manufactured by Thomas Stevens of Coventry, England, and became popular in 1862. Most are marked *Woven in silk by Thomas Stevens* or were mounted on a cardboard that tells the story of the Stevengraph. Other similar ribbon pictures have been made in England and Germany.

Bookmark, 90th Pennsylvania Infantry, Gettysburg, 3 Colors, 1888, 7 x 2 1/4 In. 245.00
Bookmark, Balloon Above Poem, Many Happy Returns Of Day, Frame, 11 In. 69.00
Bookmark, Forget Me Not Verse, Forget-Me-Nots, Vase, Banner, 9 1/4 x 2 In. 25.00
Bookmark, I Wish You A Merry Christmas, Boy, Donkey & Cart, Yellow Tassels, 7 In. ... 280.00
Picture, Centennial Of Patterson, New Jersey, Bust Of Alexander Hamilton, 9 3/4 In. 94.00
Picture, George Washington, Eagle, Centennial Exposition, Phila., 1876, 11 x 8 In. 82.00
Picture, Sanitary Fair, Philadelphia, George Washington Bust, 1864, 10 x 4 1/2 In. .385.00 to 442.00
Picture, W.H. Horstmann & Sons, Exterior Of Factory, 10 1/2 In. 125.00
Picture, W.H. Horstmann & Sons, Phila., N.Y. & Paris, 1 Color, 7 x 3 3/4 In. 110.00
Picture, Washington, Eagle, Flags, Centennial Exposition, Phila., 1876, 10 1/2 x 6 In. ... 330.00

STEVENS & WILLIAMS of Stourbridge, England, made many types of glass, including layered, etched, cameo, and art glass, between the 1830s and 1930s. Some pieces are signed *S & W*. Many pieces are decorated with flowers, leaves, and other designs based on nature.

Basket, Amethyst, Soft Opal, Black Twisted Handle, 1930, 7 In. 325.00
Basket, Blue Cased, Cranberry Oak Leaf, Ruffled Edge, Loop Handle, 10 In. 165.00
Bottle, Green Amber, Tree Shape, Peacock Stopper, Footed, 5 x 11 In. 500.00
Bowl, Amethyst & Light Violet, Vaseline Lining, Bulbous Base, 7 In. 2200.00
Bowl, Blue To Clear, Amber Rigaree, Ribbed, 4 1/4 In. 165.00
Cracker Jar, Cover, Cranberry, Allover Arboresque, Handle, 8 In. 250.00
Pitcher, Peachblow, Applied Clear Vine, Leaf At Center, 8 In. 895.00
Plate, Floral, Beehive, Blue Transfer, 10 In. 100.00
Rose Bowl, Blue, Allover White Crackle, Crimped, 3 1/2 x 3 In. 135.00
Tumbler, Vertical Stripes, Opaque White & Green, Silver Rim, Flared, 3 In. 125.00
Tumbler, White & Chartreuse Alternating Stripes, Band, 4 7/8 In. 100.00
Vase, Applied Clear Flowers, Red Shading To White, Cased, 13 In. 280.00
Vase, Applied Flower & Leaf, Triple Cased Peachblow, 6 In. 225.00
Vase, Applied Fruit, Pink & White Cased, Ruffled Edge, Footed, 10 In. 290.00
Vase, Applied Irregular Trails Of Pink, Signed, 1930s, 6 5/8 In. 168.00
Vase, Cranberry & Amber Leaves Around Sides, Rose Interior, 7 1/2 In. 225.00
Vase, Dark Lavender, Mother-Of-Pearl Satin Swirl, Bulbous, 7 1/2 In. 855.00
Vase, Grotesque, Applied Green Lobes, Pontil, 9 1/2 x 4 1/2 In. 170.00
Vase, Ivory, Applied Flowers, Satin Cased, 4 1/2 In. 140.00
Vase, Leaf & Blossom Vine, Blue Satin Cased, White, Cylindrical, 4 7/8 In. 690.00
Vase, Silver Mica, White Lining, Clear Exterior, 5 In. 195.00
Vase, Yellow, Applied Moss Green Acorn & Leaf, 4 1/2 In. 145.00

STIEGEL TYPE glass is listed here. It is almost impossible to be sure a piece was actually made by Stiegel, so the knowing collector refers to this glass as *Stiegel type*. Henry William Stiegel, a colorful immigrant to the colonies, started his first factory in Pennsylvania in 1763. He remained in business until 1774. Glassware was made in a style popular in Europe at that time and was similar to the glass of many other makers. It was made of clear or colored glass and was decorated with enamel colors, mold blown designs, or etching.

Bottle, Amethyst, 20 Pointed Arches Over Flutes, Pontil, 1780, 6 In. 1320.00
Bottle, Amethyst, Diamond & Daisy, Pocket 6890.00
Bottle, Amethyst, Pocket 6895.00
Bottle, Deep Amethyst, Diamond & Daisy, Pocket 6780.00
Tumbler, Engraved, Birds, Leaves, Sheared Rim, Pontil, 1750-1800, 5 1/8 In. 231.00
Tumbler, Engraved, Swag, Sheared Rim, Pontil, 1750-1800, 2 1/8 In. 110.00

STONEWARE is a coarse, glazed, and fired potter's ceramic that is used to make crocks, jugs, bowls, etc. It is often decorated with cobalt blue decorations. In the nineteenth and early twentieth centuries, potters often decorated crocks with blue numbers indicating the size of the container. A "2" meant 2 gallons. Stoneware is still being made.

Batter Jar, Cobalt Blue Flower, E.W. Farrington & Co., Elmira, N.Y., c.1890, 6 Qt.	468.00
Batter Jar, Cover, Eagle	350.00
Batter Jar, Flowers, Cobalt Blue, Oval, Applied Handle, Lyons, 19th Century, 10 1/4 In. .	358.00
Batter Jar, Gray, Blue Flowers, Cowden & Wilcox, 1870, 11 In.	1210.00
Batter Jar, Running Bird, Bail Handle, c.1865, 8 1/2 In.	715.00
Batter Jar, Running Bird, c.1865, 6 Qt.	522.00
Bean Pot, Lid, Lug Handles, Indented Collar Under Knob, Albany Slip, 7 1/2 In.	132.00
Bean Pot, Lid, Rounded Top, Rounded Lug Handles, Alkaline Glaze, 5 1/2 In.	248.00
Bean Pot, Spirit Of 76, Bunker Hill, Handle, Lid, 7 1/2 In.	247.00
Bird Feeder, Blue Decoration, Miniature, 5 1/2 In.	440.00
Bottle, Blue Accents, J.P. Plummer, 1853, 9 1/4 In.	165.00
Bottle, Mustard Glaze, Newton & Co., California Beer, Pat. Oct. 29, 1872, 10 In.	165.00
Bowl, Cover, Blue, White, Wire Handles, 19th Century, 7 x 11 In.	196.00
Bowl, Milk, Stylized Dotted Flower, Jordan, c.1850, 2 Gal.	302.00
Butter Churn, Brushed Puppet Design, c.1850, 4 Gal.	2640.00
Cachepot, Mettlach, Handles, Campana Shape, Figures, Putto, Grapes, 9 1/4 In.	219.00
Cake Crock, Cobalt Blue Design, c.1850, 10 x 5 1/2 In.	330.00
Canister, Cover, Cobalt Floral, Leaf Design, 1846, 5 In.	5650.00
Canteen, Bail Handle, Polar Bear, Bristol Glaze, 11 In.	907.00
Canteen, Doughnut Shape, Ocher Glaze, Robert F. Falkner, 1860, 10 3/8 In.	253.00
Canteen, Dragonfly, Deer, Wooden Bail Handle, Bardwell's Root Beer, 1800s, 11 x 10 In. .	468.00
Chamber Pot, Blue Design, 2, Lyons Cooperative Co., 14 In.	190.00
Churn, Basket Of Flowers, White's, Utica, c.1865, 15 In.	2750.00
Churn, Cobalt Blue With Flowers, Wooden Cover, 12 1/2 In.	412.00
Churn, Cobalt Roses & 5 Within Wreath, Flared Rim, 17 In.	192.00
Churn, Cover, Dasher, Indian Head, Blue, 4 Gal.	200.00
Churn, Peafowl On Branch, Flowers, Number 5, New York, 17 1/2 In.	5175.00
Churn, Stylized Floral, New York Stoneware Co., c.1880, 15 1/2 In.	440.00
Churn, Tapered Loop Handle, Lug Handle Top, Lanier Meaders, 8 In.	415.00
Churn, Top To Bottom Flowers, White's, Utica, c.1860, 18 1/2 In.	1760.00
Cream Pot, Dotted Horse Head, White's, Utica, 1875, 1 Gal.	5060.00
Crock, 2 Handles, Oval, T.O. Goodwin, c.1845, 9 x 7 1/2 In.	115.00
Crock, Animated Floral, Harrington & Burger, c.1853, 11 In.	250.00
Crock, Applied Rose, Inscribed MTG, American, 8 In.	275.00
Crock, Bird & Floral, Dots, Squiggles On Bird, W.H. Farrar & Co., 1850, 10 In.	1925.00
Crock, Blue & Gray, RJ Miller & Co., Wholesale, King St., Alexandria Va., 9 1/2 In.	290.00
Crock, Blue & White, Nichols & Co., Williamsport, Pa., 8 1/2 In.	290.00
Crock, Blue Accents, Arrow On Lower Sections, Tode Bros., N.Y., 1860, 4 In.	305.00
Crock, Blue Bird On Plant, 6, Double Handles, West Troy Pottery, 13 1/4 In.	330.00
Crock, Blue Double Flower, Name At Ears, N. Clark, c.1850, 11 1/2 In.	440.00
Crock, Blue Flowers, Applied Handles, Mid 19th Century, 13 3/4 In.	550.00
Crock, Blue Flowers, Butter Churn Lid, Cortland, 11 1/2 In.	250.00
Crock, Blue Flowers, Incised Line, Raised Rim, Double Handles, 13 3/4 In.	110.00
Crock, Blue Flowers, Smith & Day, 7 3/4 In.	80.00
Crock, Blue Flowers, Stars & 22, Double Handles, Cortland, 10 1/2 In.	192.00
Crock, Blue Flowers, Strap Handles, Impressed D.P. Shenfelder, Reading, Pa., 6 Gal.	2090.00
Crock, Blue Flowers, W Impression, 6 Gal., 17 In.	440.00
Crock, Blue Flowers, W.H. Farrar & Co., 12 1/2 In.	330.00
Crock, Blue Leaf Design, Cowden & Wilcox, Harrisburg, Pa., 9 1/4 x 10 1/2 In.	660.00
Crock, Blue Ribbed Flower, Blue 6, J. Burger, Rochester, N.Y., 1885, 6 Gal.	385.00
Crock, Blue Rooster, White's, Utica, Kiln Mark, 1 Gal., 7 1/2 In.	3960.00
Crock, Blue Singing Bird Design, 1870, 7 1/4 In.	525.00
Crock, Blue Slip Bird On Branch, Flaufersweiler, 1800s, 2 Gal.	805.00
Crock, Blue Slip Flowers, 19th Century, 17 In.	80.00
Crock, Blue Trailing Flowers, Applied Strap Handles, Pa., Mid 19th Century, 17 In.	2090.00
Crock, Blue Tulip Design, M.W. Dooruff & Co., 17 1/4 In.	385.00
Crock, Brushed Airy Dotted Floral, C.W. Braun, Buffalo, N.Y., 1870, 11 In.	413.00

Crock, Brushed Cobalt 2, Rings On Shoulder, Hormell & Smyth, 11 x 8 In. 550.00
Crock, Butter, Blue Leaf Design, 2 Eared Handles, 4 1/2 x 9 In. 78.00
Crock, Cake, Brushed Branch, Edmands Factory, c.1870, 10 In. 275.00
Crock, Cake, Cobalt Blue Flowers & Line, Impressed 2, Large 410.00
Crock, Cobalt Bird On Stump, Number 2, Rim Handles, Riedinger & Caire, 9 1/4 In. 580.00
Crock, Cobalt Bird, Double Handles, Ottman Bro's. & Co., 2, 9 In. 300.00
Crock, Cobalt Bird, Double Handles, Ottman Bros., Fort Edward, 3, 13 1/4 In. 495.00
Crock, Cobalt Bird, Long Tail Feathers, Double Handles, Reidinger & Caire, 12 In. 410.00
Crock, Cobalt Blue Bird, Eared Handles, Impressed 3, 19th Century, 10 x 11 1/2 In. 196.00
Crock, Cobalt Blue Brushed Design, Applied Shoulder Handles, 17 1/4 In. 2400.00
Crock, Cobalt Blue Brushed Flowers, Dots On Handles, Penn Yan Pottery, 8 In. 385.00
Crock, Cobalt Blue Brushed Label, N.G. Humill, 9 1/2 In. 440.00
Crock, Cobalt Blue Decoration, Ballard, Burlington, Vt., 2 Gal. 200.00
Crock, Cobalt Blue Design, Flower Basket, Somerset Pottery, 2 Gal. 290.00
Crock, Cobalt Blue Design, Leaves, 1 Gal., 8 1/2 In. 150.00
Crock, Cobalt Blue Design, Selby & Co., Hudson, N.Y., 2 Gal., 12 In. 290.00
Crock, Cobalt Blue Flower, Salt Glaze, Whites, Utica, NY, 2 Gal., 10 x 10 3/8 In. 175.00
Crock, Cobalt Blue Flowering Plant, White's, Binghampton, 4, 13 1/2 In. 110.00
Crock, Cobalt Blue Flowers & Leaves, C. Hart & Son, 2, 9 In. 275.00
Crock, Cobalt Blue Flowers, N.H., 2 Gal., 12 In. 460.00
Crock, Cobalt Blue Label, Salt Glaze, Handles, Neff Bros., 12 3/4 In. 165.00
Crock, Cobalt Blue Lines, Stenciled Label, Casper & Bros., No. 7, 9 7/8 In. 110.00
Crock, Cobalt Blue Parrot, S.L. Pewtress, Fairhaven, Conn., c.1880, 11 In. 1870.00
Crock, Cobalt Blue Pecking Chicken Decoration, c.1840 .... 775.00
Crock, Cobalt Blue Quill Bird, Applied Handles, Impressed Edmonds & Co. 2, 12 In. 440.00
Crock, Cobalt Blue Singing Bird, Haxstun & Co., Fort Edward, N.Y., c.1870, 2 Gal. 690.00
Crock, Cobalt Blue Slip Bird, New York Stoneware Co., Fort Edward, N.Y., 2 Gal. 550.00
Crock, Cobalt Blue Slip Over Gray, Double Handles, D. Goodale, Hartford, 9 3/4 In. 230.00
Crock, Cobalt Blue Tulip, Double Handles, T.A. Packer, 12 1/2 In. 300.00
Crock, Cobalt Blue Tulip, Double Shoulder Handles, Higgins, 12 1/4 In. 440.00
Crock, Cobalt Blue Tulip, Geometric, Double Ear Handles, White's, Utica, 10 1/4 In. 360.00
Crock, Cobalt Blue With Flowers, Handles, 14 In. 105.00
Crock, Cobalt Blue Wreath, Billard & Scott, Mass., 1878, 11 1/2 In. 715.00
Crock, Cobalt Blue, Ear Handles, Cluster Of Grapes, Cowden & Wilcox, 3 Gal. 2310.00
Crock, Cobalt Blue, Harris Bros., Brownsville, Ohio, 18 1/2 In. 49.00
Crock, Cobalt Detail, Double Handles, I.M. Mead & Co., 3, 12 1/2 In. 165.00
Crock, Cover, Bird, Fort Edward, Ear Handles 500.00
Crock, Cover, Cobalt Blue Sprigs, Richard C. Remmey, 1 Gal. 1000.00
Crock, Double Tulip Design, Lug Handles, Brown Brothers, 1890, 9 In. 165.00
Crock, Gray Green Ash Glaze, Double Handles, 12 In. 110.00
Crock, Hugh Chicken Pecking Corn, 1870, 10 1/2 In. ....825.00 to 1265.00
Crock, Large Cobalt Tulip On Front, Smaller Tulip On Back, Stamped R. Gast, 14 In. ... 770.00
Crock, Overall Blue Flowers, Western Penn., Mid 19th Century, 3 Gal., 9 In. 2530.00
Crock, Overlapping Bluebirds, Ear Handles, N.Y., Mid 19th Century, 4 Gal., 11 In. 1760.00
Crock, Pecking Chicken, Handles, Poughkeepsie, N.Y., Adam Caire, 10 1/2 In. 605.00
Crock, Rooster, Egg Shape, White's, Utica, 1 Gal. 3960.00
Crock, Running Bird Design, Whites, Utica, 1865, 1 Gal. 965.00
Crock, Running Deer, Cobalt Blue, 5 Gal. 7800.00
Crock, Salt Glaze, Cobalt Blue Slip Of Leaves, Remmey, 5 3/4 x 9 1/2 In. 570.00
Crock, Single Dotted Bird Design, S. Hart Fulton, 1875, 9 In. 154.00
Crock, Slip Blue Tulip Design, J. Burger, Rochester, N.Y., 1885, 2 Gal. 77.00
Crock, Stenciled & Freehand Design, Double Handles, T.F. Reppert, 14 3/4 In. 297.00
Crock, Stenciled Cobalt At Angle, J.E. Enelx, New Geneva, 7 1/8 x 8 1/4 In. 250.00
Crock, Stenciled Design, Folded Over Lip, Impressed, Jas. Benjamin, 2, 10 In. 80.00
Crock, Stenciled Label, H.C. Ward, Wholesale Stoneware Depot 55.00
Crock, Stylized Blue Cobalt Flower, C.W. Braun, Buffalo, N.Y., 1870, 9 1/2 In. 330.00
Crock, Stylized Leaves, Cobalt Blue Slip, 11 1/2 In. 440.00
Crock, Swag, Dotted Design, Blue Accents, N.Y., 1830, 4 In. 1870.00
Crock, Top To Bottom Peacock, On Leafy Branch, John Burger, c.1865, 14 1/2 In. 2750.00
Crock, Trailing Flowers, Strap Handles, D.P. Shenfelder, 17 In. 2090.00
Crock, Westhafer & Lambright 6, 1 Side, 2 Names Other, Flower Other, 19 1/2 In. 935.00
Crock, Whimsical Cobalt Design On Front, Albany Glaze, 5 Gal. 55.00
Crock, Wreath & Star, Stenciled 4 In. Wreath, Double Handles, 11 1/2 In. 110.00

Crock, Wreath On Front, Burger & Co., Rochester, N.Y., 1877, 3 Gal. 415.00
Cuspidor, Blue Bowtie, Cowden & Wilcox, c.1870, 4 1/2 x 7 1/2 In. 275.00
Cuspidor, Cobalt Blue Accents, Gilt, John H. Herre, 1850, 2 x 3 1/4 In. 880.00
Cuspidor, Flower Accents All Around, c.1850, 4 1/2 x 9 1/2 In. 155.00
Cuspidor, Red, Green, Black Manganese Design, Pa., 19th Century, 8 In. 210.00
Doorstop, Mermaid Shape, Virginia, c.1850 . . . . 935.00
Ewer, Continuous Battle Scene, Blue & Gray, 21 In. 140.00
Figurine, Pig, Mottled Brown Glaze, 19th Century, 10 1/2 x 15 1/2 In. 1870.00
Figurine, Rooster, Incised Wings, Tail Feathers, Randolph County, 4 3/4 In. 1100.00
Grease Lamp, Green Gray Salt Glaze, Saucer Base, Open Font, Spout, 4 3/4 In. 470.00
Jar, Blue Brushed Rim & Base, Stripes, James Hamilton & Co., 8 1/4 In. 110.00
Jar, Blue Decoration, Incised, A.W. Boughner, c.1863, 14 1/2 In. 1550.00
Jar, Blue Design, Egg Shape, 2 Handles, N. Clark & Company, Mt. Morris, N.Y., 2 Gal. . . . 300.00
Jar, Blue Eagle Decoration, c.1876, 13 In., 3 Gal. 1450.00
Jar, Blue Flowers, Double Handles, Lyons, 9 In. 190.00
Jar, Blue Tulip, T.A. Packer, 13 1/2 In. 1100.00
Jar, Brushed Blue Flowers, S. Hart Fulton, 1875, 2 Gal. 176.00
Jar, Brushed Flowers, Stenciled Label, John Borgundshal, No. 5, 16 1/2 In. 495.00
Jar, Bulbous Ears, Band Of Tulips, H. Yers, 13 1/2 In., 2 Gal. 240.00
Jar, Butter, Buttercup Dairy Co., Brown Cover, Cream, Black Transfer, 3 Lb. 355.00
Jar, Canning, 3 Brush Blue Highlights, 1850, 6 In. 358.00
Jar, Canning, 7 Cobalt Blue Stripes, 1850, 1/2 Gal. 550.00
Jar, Canning, Black, Green Alkaline Glaze, Mid 19th Century, 11 1/4 In. 44.00
Jar, Canning, Blue, Long Stemmed Flower, D. Mooney, c.1862, 11 In. 580.00
Jar, Canning, Brushed & Stenciled Label, James Hamilton, 9 3/4 In. 220.00
Jar, Canning, Cobalt Blue Brushed & Stenciled Label, Hamilton & Jones, 10 In. 165.00
Jar, Canning, Cobalt Blue Stencil, A.P. Donaghho, Parkersburg, W.Va., 8 1/2 In. 80.00
Jar, Canning, Cobalt Blue Stencil, J. Hamilton & Co., Greensboro Pa., 10 1/4 In. 85.00
Jar, Canning, Cobalt Blue Stencil, Williams & Reppert, Greensboro, Pa., 10 In. 138.00
Jar, Canning, Cobalt Blue, Drooping Flowers, 1860, 1 Gal. 275.00
Jar, Canning, Cobalt Blue, Flowers, Flared Lip, 10 1/8 In. 190.00
Jar, Canning, Large Compote Of Blue Flowers, Lug Handles, 1855, 3 Gal. 880.00
Jar, Canning, Lid, Dotted & Filled Leaf, J. McBrunery, c.1852, 10 1/2 In. 550.00
Jar, Canning, Name & Town At Shoulder, P. Mugler & Co., c.1850, 9 1/2 In. 165.00
Jar, Canning, Star Of David, 1882, 6 3/4 In. 1870.00
Jar, Cobalt Blue Eagle, Wavy Lines, Salt Glaze, Ohio, 19th Century, 10 3/8 In. 980.00
Jar, Cobalt Design & Label, Hamilton & Jones, Flared Lip, 8 In. 165.00
Jar, Cover, Christopher Gustin, Signed, 1981, 16 x 17 In. 2300.00
Jar, H.C. Smith, 7 1/2 In., 1/2 Gal. 895.00
Jar, Harmon, Tenn., 10 1/2 x 9 1/2 In. 250.00
Jar, Impressed 3, Stenciled & Freehand Label, I. Hewitt, Excelsior Works, 14 In. 660.00
Jar, Large Leaf Design, White's, Utica, N.Y., 1865, 2 Gal. 330.00
Jar, Reverse Impressed 5 From McDonald & Benjamin, 16 In. 330.00
Jar, Running Bird Design, White's, Utica, N.Y., 1865, 3 Gal. 250.00
Jar, Starburst Design, Jordan, 1850, 10 3/4 In. 1650.00
Jar, Stencil, Freehand Flower, Hamilton & Jones, Greensboro, Pa., 14 In., 3 Gal. 525.00
Jar, Stenciled Design & Label, Shoulder Handles, Jas. Hamilton & Co., 18 1/2 In. 585.00
Jar, Stenciled Name, A.P. Donagho, 5 3/4 In. 230.00
Jar, Storage, A.W. Boughner, 1862, 14 In. 1550.00
Jar, Storage, Blue Stencil, Wm. Kinner & Co., Lynchburg, Va., 1 1/2 Gal. 250.00
Jar, Storage, Star Pottery, Hamilton & Jones, c.1875, 16 1/2 In. 1150.00
Jardiniere, Cobalt Blue Flower & Vine, H.C. Smith, 1825, 2 Gal. 855.00
Jardiniere, Vines & Flowers, J. Hamilton, c.1850, 14 1/2 In. 1430.00
Jug, 3, Cobalt Flower, Strap Handle, Impressed P.H. Smith, 17 In. 357.00
Jug, Batter, 2 Openings, Variegated Brown Glaze, Natural Clay Base, Bail Handle, 1882 . . 80.00
Jug, Batter, Blue Flowers, Bail Handle, Pour Spout, 10 1/4 In. 80.00
Jug, Batter, Bulbous Shape, Cobalt Blue Flowers, Bail Handle, c.1850, 9 In. 468.00
Jug, Batter, Cover, Freehand Design Of Flowers, Cowden & Wilcox, 9 In. 960.00
Jug, Bird Sitting On A Branch, Incised Blue Design, 9 1/2 In. 4400.00
Jug, Bird, Cobalt Leaves, New York Stoneware Co., 16 In., 1 Gal. 165.00
Jug, Bird, Cortland, N.Y., 2 Gal. 1450.00
Jug, Blue Cobalt Handle, John H. Lalor Wholesale Liquor, Utica, N.Y., 1880, 2 Gal. 300.00
Jug, Blue Decoration, Cowden & Wilcox, Pennsylvania, c.1860 . . . . 440.00

Jug, Blue Design, No. 2, Strap Handle, Fort Edward Stoneware Co., 13 1/2 In. 302.00
Jug, Blue Dotted Caterpillar Design, Howard, 1860, 14 In. 825.00
Jug, Blue Flowers, Piercing Eye Design, Dots, Squiggles, 1855, 15 In. 605.00
Jug, Blue Flowers, Trailing Vine, Stylized Eagle Holding Banner, 16 1/2 In., 3 Gal. 1760.00
Jug, Blue Glaze, Fort Edward Stoneware Co., Fort Edward, N.Y., 2 Gal. 220.00
Jug, Blue Goat, West Troy Pottery, c.1850, 14 In. 9900.00
Jug, Blue Leaf, Cowden & Wilcox, c.1850, 15 1/2 In. 440.00
Jug, Blue Stencil, John H. Sheehan, Cohoes, N.Y., 1870, 9 1/2 In. 275.00
Jug, Blue, Green, Cream Design, John Bell, Pa., 11 In. 1210.00
Jug, Brushed Blue Accent, J.B. Caire & Co., N.Y., 1850, 9 In. 176.00
Jug, Brushed Blue Tulip Design, G. Apley & Co., Ithaca, N.Y., 1860, 1 Gal. 468.00
Jug, Brushed Floral Vine Design, S. Hart & Son, Fulton, 1877, 2 Gal. 165.00
Jug, Brushed Flower, Oval, I. Seymour, Troy, c.1825, 3 Gal. 360.00
Jug, Brushed Plume Design, Handle, S. Hart, 1875, 1 Gal. 110.00
Jug, Brushed Plume, Lyons, c.1850, 1 Gal. 100.00
Jug, Brushed Slip Bold Flowers, W.A. Lewis, Galesville, N.Y., 13 In. 745.00
Jug, Cobalt Blue Apple, Leaves, Jordan, 1853, 14 1/2 In. 11275.00
Jug, Cobalt Blue Bird, W.H. Farrar & Co., Geddes, N.Y., c.1850, 2 Gal. 1705.00
Jug, Cobalt Blue Brushed Flower, Oval, Clark & Fox, Athens, N.Y., c.1830, 1 Gal. 550.00
Jug, Cobalt Blue Design, Flowers, Oval, Early 19th Century, 15 In. 140.00
Jug, Cobalt Blue Design, Flowers, Sherburne, N.Y., 2 Gal., 14 In. 200.00
Jug, Cobalt Blue Design, Oval, Trenton Wine & Liquor, N.J., Early 1800s, 3 Gal. 430.00
Jug, Cobalt Blue Double Tulip, Strap Handle, A. & J.H. Rhoads, 11 1/4 In. 1290.00
Jug, Cobalt Blue Flower Design, Poughkeepsie, N.Y., 19th Century, 11 In. 170.00
Jug, Cobalt Blue Label, No. 2, Strap Handle, C.W. Weaver, 13 1/2 In. 110.00
Jug, Cobalt Blue Pecking Chicken, Tan Glaze, Stamped Albany, NY, 1800s, 14 1/4 In. ... 1045.00
Jug, Cobalt Blue Script, Zucker & Stein, Passaic, N.J., c.1870, 8 1/2 In. 275.00
Jug, Cobalt Blue Stencil, Strap Handle, Jas. Hamilton & Co. Greensboro, Pa., 15 In. 165.00
Jug, Cobalt Blue, Salt Glaze, 2 Lug Handles, 11 1/4 In. 6900.00
Jug, Cobalt Blue, Salt Glaze, Incised Tulip Blossom, 16 In. 6900.00
Jug, Cobalt Flower, Harrisburg, Pa., Mid 19th Century, 17 In. 2310.00
Jug, Cobalt Flowers, Cowden & Wilcox, 3 Gal. 635.00
Jug, Cobalt Leaves, E.A. Buck & Co., 11 1/4 In., 1 Gal. 190.00
Jug, Cobalt Parrot On Flowering Branch, White's, Utica 2, 15 1/2 In. 770.00
Jug, Cobalt Tulip & 2, Strap Handle, I.M. Mead, 14 1/2 In. 935.00
Jug, Double Flower, G. Apley, c.1860, 1 Gal. 470.00
Jug, Flowers, Cobalt Blue, Tan Glaze, J.J. Lawlor, Albany, 19th Century, 14 3/4 In. 90.00
Jug, Hand Brushed Decoration, Blue, Applied Strap Handle, P. Cushman, 14 1/4 In. 220.00
Jug, Impressed 2, Cobalt At Ends Of Handle, I.M. Mead & Co., 8 5/8 In. 247.00
Jug, Incised Cobalt Bands On Neck, Cobalt Slip Flowers, Germany, 12 In. 280.00
Jug, Incised Script Label, Eli G. Thomas, Albany Slip, 10 In. 192.00
Jug, L. Brooks, Groceries, Fruits, Handle, Albany, 1 Gal. 165.00
Jug, Large Bird Perched On Flowered Branch, Cobalt, W.H. Farrar & Co., N.Y., 1850 .... 1705.00
Jug, Levy & Glosking Distillers Of Pure Rye Whiskey, Dover, Del., 12 In. 385.00
Jug, Lines On Shoulder Top, Squared Rim, Fly Ash Drip, 2, J.M. Hays, 14 1/2 In. 770.00
Jug, Liquor, Compliments Of J. Deuerling, Brown & White Lettering, 2 3/4 In. 175.00
Jug, Liquor, Welsh's Rye, Square Body, Compliments Of C.E. Welsh, 4 1/4 In. 198.00
Jug, Ribbed Orchid Design, White's, Utica, N.Y., 1865, 5 Gal. 1925.00
Jug, S. Purdy, Impressed 3, Ovoid, Strap Handle, 15 In. 550.00
Jug, S. Purdy, Splashed With Blue, Strap Handle, 11 1/2 In. 632.00
Jug, Salt Glaze, Incised Bird Design, Handle, 12 1/4 In. 1495.00
Jug, Signed J.F. Weiler, Allentown, Pa., c.1840 .... 165.00
Jug, Slip Blue Tornado Design, W.H. Farrar & Co., Geddes, N.Y., 1860, 2 Gal. 660.00
Jug, Spray Of Flowers Below Stamp, Cowden & Wilcox, 1 Gal. 230.00
Jug, Stenciled Cobalt Leaf, Hamilton & Jones, No. 2, 14 1/2 In. 137.00
Jug, Stylized Blue Dotted Design, W.J. Seymour Troy Factory, 1852, 13 In. 330.00
Jug, Stylized Cobalt Leaf, 3, New York, Stoneware Co., 16 In. 165.00
Jug, Syrup, Blue Bird, Ottman Bros. & Company, Fort Edwards, 13 1/2 In. 1430.00
Jug, Syrup, Double Flower & 1880, Dated Frame, N. Clark Jr., c.1880, 14 In. 385.00
Jug, Tulips, Cortland, N.Y., 2 Gal. 1495.00
Jug, Webers' Grocery, Wine & Liquors, Baltimore, 9 In. 184.00
Jug, Wide Thumb Grooved Handle, Salt Glaze, Last Half 19th Century, 9 7/8 In. 300.00
Jug, Wm. E. Warner's, West Troy, c.1885, 11 1/4 In. 70.00

Jug, Wreath, Dot Design, Jordan, 1850, 14 In., 2 Gal. 660.00
Match Safe, Tree Stump, C.W. Moores, c.1880, 2 1/2 In. 176.00
Mug, Panels Of Spider On Web, Newt, Owl & Gremlin, Verse, 1896, 4 1/2 In. 2860.00
Pitcher, Albany Glaze, c.1860, 9 1/2 In. 65.00
Pitcher, Blue Decoration, Pennsylvania, c.1840, 10 3/4 In. 138.00
Pitcher, Blue Swags All Around Rim, c.1850, 8 1/2 In. 550.00
Pitcher, Butterfly Pattern, Blue & White, 8 1/2 In. 440.00
Pitcher, Cobalt Blue Slip Flowers, Bulbous, Handle, 1 1/2 Gal. 1320.00
Pitcher, Commemorative, Flowers, Remmey, George Koeler, 1903, 10 1/4 In. 385.00
Pitcher, Freehand Label, No. 2, Williams & Reppert, 13 In. 935.00
Pitcher, Girl & Her Dog, Light Tan, Brown Alkaline Glaze, 8 3/4 In. 100.00
Pitcher, Ice Keeper At Spout, Oval, Stylized Handle, Floyd Hamilton, 8 3/4 In. 660.00
Pitcher, Indian, War Bonnet, Pale Blue, 8 1/2 In. 250.00
Pitcher, Ribbed Dots & Lines, c.1860, 11 In. 187.00
Pitcher, Tanware, c.1880, 8 In. 632.00
Pitcher, Wild Rose On Vine, Pale Blues, 9 In. 235.00
Plate, Shoji Hamada, 1949, 10 5/8 In., 3 Piece 3450.00
Pot, Blue & Gray, Relief Design, Boy & Girl At Table, Handle, 7 In. 115.00
Pot, Blue, Cream, Pinwheel, Floral, W.H. Farrar & Co., N.Y., 1850 .... 1540.00
Pot, Cream, Thick Blue Dotted Design, Horse Head, 1865, 8 In. 5060.00
Sieve, Albany Slip, Handle, 11 In. 165.00
Tenderizer, Wooden Handle, Pat'd. Dec. 25, 1877, 10 In. 209.00
Tureen, Polychrome, Bombe Body, Domed Cover, Flowers, Birds, 19th Century, 14 In. ... 546.00
Umbrella Holder, Cobalt Blue Design, White's, Utica, 20 1/2 In. 825.00
Vase, Cobalt Design, Stylized Blue Flowers, Pa., 19th Century, 18 x 11 In. 11400.00
Vase, Elaborate Flowers, Pink, Brown, Blue, Etched, England, 7 3/4 In. 185.00
Vase, Face, Nose & Ears, Sgraffito, Mottled Green Glaze, Baluster, 8 In. 275.00
Water Cooler, Blue Design, Wooden Top, Allen Germ Proof Filter, 14 x 12 In. 960.00
Water Cooler, Cobalt Blue, Flowers, Satterlee & Morry, Ft. Edward, N.Y., 1800s, 19 In. . 275.00
Water Cooler, Cover, Stenciled Leaf, Bail Handle, Monmouth, Il, 1920, 9 In. 385.00
Water Cooler, Double Flower, John Burger, c.1860, 12 In. 5170.00
Water Cooler, Double Flowers On Reverse, A. Lambright, 21 In. 1980.00
Water Cooler, Fitted Spigot, Embossed Flowers, Blue, 16 In. 2750.00
Water Cooler, Top To Bottom Flower & Vine, P. Hermann, c.1860, 14 1/2 In. 470.00
Water Cooler, Water, Wooden Spigot, Cobalt Blue Floral & Banded, Handles, 14 In. 1650.00

STORE fixtures, cases, cutters, and other items that have no advertising
as part of the decoration are listed here. Most items found in an old
store are listed in the Advertising category in this book.

Cabinet, Display, Countertop, Pine, Mahogany, Glass, c.1900, 34 x 24 x 18 In. 168.00
Cabinet, Display, Jeweler's, Brass, Glass, Mahogany, 2 Locking Doors, 59 x 42 x 17 In. . 560.00
Cabinet, Display, Knife, Wooden Slanted Front, $1 Knife, Titusville, Pa., 12 x 20 In. 412.00
Cabinet, Oak, 2 Sections, 2 Glass Doors With Side Panels Over 4 Drawers, 96 x 96 In. ... 1150.00
Cabinet, Oak, 8 Doors, Raised Panels, 118 x 34 x 22 In. 1725.00
Cabinet, Spool, 4 Drawers, c.1880, 22 1/2 x 27 In. 415.00
Cash Box, Mahogany, G.H. Gledhill & Sons, 19th Century, 7 x 19 1/2 In. 300.00
Coffee Grinders are listed in their own category.
Dispenser, Fountain, 3 Spigots, Oak Base, c.1900, 17 x 30 In. 2243.00
Dispenser, Hot Peanuts, John A. Henry, Charcoal Fuel Tray, 1900s, 22 x 18 In. 1600.00
Dispenser, Hot Water, Back Bar, Chrome, Glass Dome Reservoir, 1 Spigot, 17 1/2 In. 176.00
Display, Mahogany, Glass, Queen Anne Legs, 10 Drawers, Countertop, 1930s, 34 In. 1232.00
Display Case, Beveled Glass Panels, Hinged Cover, Tufted Satin Lining, 6 x 8 1/2 In. 195.00
Display Case, Brass, Glass, Mahogany, 2 Doors, Lighted, 59 x 42 x 17 In. 896.00
Display Case, Oak, 2 Sections, Glass Top, Wainscot Base, 47 1/2 x 26 1/2 x 11 1/2 In. ... 616.00
Display Case, Oak, Glass Panels, 3 Lockable Hinged Doors, 78 1/2 x 18 x 42 In. 460.00
Display Case, Pine, Grain Decorated, Glass Door, Scales, Mid 19th Century, 18 1/2 In. ... 110.00
Display Case, Pine, Painted, 18-Pane Cover, Countertop, c.1840, 6 x 46 1/2 x 31 In. 360.00
Display Case, Sloped Cover, Glass, Tin, Scrollwork, 9 1/2 x 7 x 4 In. 330.00
Display Case, Walnut, Double Steeple, German Silver, Quincy, Ill., 96 x 26 1/2 x 38 In. ... 6325.00
Lighter, Bradley & Hubbard, Cigar, Brass Urn, Countertop, Early 20th Century, 12 In. ... 310.00
Lighter, Cigar, Airedale Dog, Stump, Metal, Austria, Countertop, 7 3/4 x 4 In. 250.00
Lighter, Cigar, Eldred Wizard, Chicago, Countertop, 1893, 20 In. 900.00
Lighter, Cigar, Electric, Seated Monkey, Metal, Germany, Countertop, 5 1/2 In. 170.00

Lighter, Cigar, Kerosene, Sword Cutter, Heron, Opaque, Countertop, Early 1900s, 10 In. . . 590.00
Lighter, Cigar, Silver Plate, Brass Lion, Countertop, Late 1800s, 5 In. 336.00
Lighter, Cigar, Vaseline Glass, Cast Iron Base, Countertop 2016.00
Mannequin, Head, Wax, Boy, Blond, Glass Eyes, Open Mouth, Wax Teeth, 8 1/2 In. 173.00
Meal Bin, Pine, Dovetailed, 52 x 32 x 19 In. 1100.00
Shoeshine Stand, Wire, Arms 190.00
Shoeshine Stand, Wooden, Painted, Bench Seat, Mid 1900s, 5 Ft. 1950.00
Strawholder, Cranberry Glass 1090.00
Tobacco Cutter, Wooden Bellows, Cutout Horse On Blade, 13 1/2 In. 660.00

STOVES have been used in America for heating since the eighteenth
century and for cooking since the nineteenth century. Most types of
wood, coal, gas, kerosene, and even some electric stoves are collected.

Cook, 2 Side Shelves, Opening Door, Cast Iron, Crescent, 11 In. 230.00
Cook, Buck's Junior 4, Cast Iron, Accessories, Salesman's Sample, 22 In. 1980.00
Cook, Buck's, Cast Iron Doors, Legs & Stove Pipe, 15 1/2 x 22 In. 2185.00
Cook, Home Stove & Foundry Co., Chicago, Porcelain, Gas, 4 Burners, 1900s 1500.00
Cook, Ornate Design, 2 Side Shelves, Opening Door, Crescent, Cast Iron, 11 In. 115.00
Cook, Ornate Design, Interior Grate Sliding Vents, Cast Iron, 14 In. 115.00
Cook, Ornate Design, Lids, Shelves, Cast Iron, Acme, 11 In. 460.00
Cook, Ornate Design, Side Shelves, Covers, Cast Iron, Crescent, 8 In. 170.00
Cook, Ornate Design, Wood, Adam's Peckover, Pat. 1857, Cast Iron, 8 1/2 In. 290.00
Cook, Tappan, Gas Range, 1930 . . . . 425.00
Heating, Franklin, Cast Iron & Brass, Medallions, Engraved Finials, 1800s, 33 x 36 In. . . 112.00
Heating, Parlor, Co-Operative Stove Co., Iron, Architectural, 42 x 26 x 24 In. . . . . . *Illus* 5600.00
Heating, Parlor, Enameled Iron, 4 Hinged Panels, Cherubs Medallions, 36 x 14 x 33 In. . . 1015.00
Heating, Parlor, Winged Griffins & Cupid Riding Winged Demon, Cast Iron, 1860, 32 In. 2185.00
Heating, Regulir-Fullofen, Coal, Cast Iron, Corrugated Tin, Cylinder, 13 5/8 x 55 In. 440.00
Heating, Wood Burning, Stewart Fuller Warren Company, Milwaukee, 1920s 5000.00
Heating, Wood Burning, Union Airtight, Cast Iron, Patented 1851, 33 In. 165.00

STRETCH GLASS is named for the strange stretch marks in the glass. It
was made by many glass companies in the United States from about
1900 to the 1920s. It is iridescent. Most American stretch glass is
molded; most European pieces are blown and may have a pontil mark.

Bowl, Blue, Gray Smoke Iridescent, 2 x 6 1/2 x 4 In. 19.00
Bowl, Red Amberina, 6 In. 105.00
Bowl, Violet Wisteria, Curled Lip, 1920s, 12 1/2 In. 135.00
Butter, Cover, Knob Handle, Green, 4 3/4 In. 46.00
Candlestick, Tangerine Opalescent, 3 1/2 In. 50.00
Candy Dish, Cover, Blue, 6 x 5 1/4 In. 26.00
Rose Bowl, Apple Green, 3 x 6 In. 25.00
Vase, Fan, Enameled Butterfly & Pale Pink Lilacs, Vaseline, 8 1/2 x 6 3/4 In. 50.00

**Date business cards and other adver-
tising from telephone numbers.
Numbers were first used in 1878. The
seven digit number was in use by the
1940s, fewer than seven digits dates
the card from 1878 to the 1940s.**

Stove, Heating, Parlor,
Co-Operative Stove Co., Iron,
Architectural, 42 x 26 x 24 In.

SULPHIDES are cameos of unglazed white porcelain encased in transparent glass. The technique was patented in 1819 in France and has been used ever since for paperweights, decanters, tumblers, marbles, and other type of glassware. Paperweights and marbles are listed in their own categories.

Bowl, 2 Standing Figures, Allover Geometric Cutting, 3 1/4 x 2 1/4 In.	58.00
Plaque, Man's Profile, Star Shape, 19th Century, 3 1/2 In.	69.00

SUMIDA, or Sumida Gawa, is a Japanese pottery. The pieces collected by that name today were made about 1895 to 1970. There has been much confusion about the name of this ware, and it is often called *Korean Pottery.* Most pieces have a very heavy orange-red, blue, or green glaze, with raised three-dimensional figures as decorations.

Jar, Cover, 2 Men, Seated & Holding Staff, Child, Red, Blue, Green, 8 In.	550.00
Jar, Cover, Green Glazed Top Rim, Older Man, Seated, Child Crawling On Rock, 8 In.	630.00
Jar, Scrolled Feet, Raised Design, Double Phoenix Bird Handles, 12 1/4 In.	192.00
Mug, Elephant & Rocks, Red Ground, Glazed Trim & Handle, Signed, 5 1/4 In.	135.00 to 157.00
Vase, Children At Play On Black Ground, Signed, Japan, 13 In.	460.00

SUNBONNET BABIES were first introduced in 1900 in the book *The Sunbonnet Babies.* The stories were by Eulalie Osgood Grover, illustrated by Bertha Corbett. The children's faces were completely hidden by the sunbonnets. The children had been pictured in black and white before this time, but the color pictures in the book were immediately successful. The Royal Bayreuth China Company made a full line of children's dishes decorated with the Sunbonnet Babies. Some Sunbonnet Babies plates have been reproduced, but are clearly marked.

Ashtray, Cleaning	275.00
Bell, Sewing	400.00
Candlestick, Washing, 5 x 1 3/4 In.	250.00
Creamer, Ironing, 3 In.	250.00
Cup & Saucer, Washing	350.00
Mug, Washing	350.00
Pitcher, Washing, 4 1/4 In.	325.00
Plate, Washing, 6 In.	250.00
Saucer, Fishing	75.00
Sugar & Creamer, Fishing On Sugar, Cleaning On Creamer	500.00
Sugar & Creamer, Sewing	475.00
Toothpick, Ironing	420.00
Toothpick, Mending	450.00
Vase, Fishing, 3 In.	235.00

SUNDERLAND luster is a name given to a special type of pink luster made by Leeds, Newcastle, and other English firms during the nineteenth century. The luster glaze is metallic and glossy and appears to have bubbles in it. Other pieces of luster are listed in the Luster category.

Creamer, Motto, Incised Mark, Staffordshire, 3 In.	165.00
Mug, East Indies Ship, Figures Of Peace & Plenty, 1802	900.00
Pitcher, Pink Luster, 2 Verses, To A Friend, West View Of Iron Bridge, 7 3/8 In.	220.00 to 495.00
Pitcher, Pink, Bulbous Body, Nautical Scenes, Floral Border, c.1840, 7 1/4 In.	635.00
Pitcher, Pink, Bulbous, Mariner's Arms, Ship, Sailors, Verse, c.1840, 7 1/4 In.	635.00

SUPERMAN was created by two seventeen-year-olds in 1938. The first issue of *Action* comics had the strip. Superman remains popular and became the hero of a radio show in 1940, cartoons in the 1940s, a television series, and several major movies.

Buckle, Belt, Magnetic, 1977	225.00
Comic Book, No. 36, September-October 1943, Lois Lane & Superman On Cover	95.00
Costume, Pants, Cape & Top, Ben Cooper, Box, 1940s	300.00
Doll, World's Greatest Super Hero	105.00
Krypto Ray Gun, Steel Projector, Daisy Mfg. Co., 4 Film Strips, 1940, 6 1/2 In.	1650.00
Lunch Box, Superman, Flying, Thermos, Metal, 1967	805.00

Lunch Box, Thermos, Adco, Box, 1938 ....*Illus*	11500.00
Stickers, 1965	35.00
Thermos, Metal, Canada, 1967, 8 In.	95.00
Toy, Push Button, Superman Bends, Punches, Plastic, Kohner, 1966, 4 1/4 In.	130.00
Toy, Turnover Tank, Windup, Linemar, 1950s ....500.00 to	650.00
Toy, Turnover Tank, Windup, Tin, Marx, 1940s, 4 In. ....340.00 to	375.00
Wallet, Vinyl, 1966	45.00

SUSIE COOPER began as a designer in 1925 working for the English firm A.E. Gray & Company. In 1932 she formed Susie Cooper Pottery, Ltd. In 1950 it became Susie Cooper China, Ltd., and the company made china and earthenware. In 1966 it was acquired by Josiah Wedgwood & Sons, Ltd. The name Susie Cooper appears with the company names on many pieces of ceramics.

Bowl, Gloria, Orange Sections, Yellow, Black & Green Luster, 1923, 10 1/2 In.	107.00
Coffee Set, Patricia Rose, Kestrel Shape, Pink, After Dinner, 7 Piece	910.00
Cup & Saucer, Dresden Spray, Mint Green	52.00
Honey Pot, Cover, Nosegay, Yellow Wash, Kestrel Shape, 1935	108.00
Platter, Patricia Rose, 1938-1960, 9 1/4 x 12 In.	104.00
Sugar & Creamer, Patricia Rose, 1938-1960	316.00
Tankard, Orange, Blue, Yellow, Green Wide Stripes, 1932, 5 In.	103.00
Tea Set, Cubist, Tea For Two, Blue, Orange, Yellow, & Mauve, Teapot, 2 Cups, 2 Saucers	1500.00
Teapot, Patricia Rose, 5 1/2 In.	252.00
Teapot, Tiger Lily, Kestral Shape	153.00

SWANKYSWIGS are small drinking glasses. In 1933, the Kraft Food Company began to market cheese spreads in these decorated, reusable glass tumblers. They were discontinued from 1941 to 1946, then made again from 1947 to 1958. Then plain glasses were used for most of the cheese, although a few special decorated Swankyswigs have been made since that time. A complete list of prices can be found in *Kovels' Depression Glass & Dinnerware Price List*.

Antique No. 1, Brown, 3 1/2 In.	5.00
Band, Red, Black, 3 3/8 In.	4.00
Band, Red, Black, 4 3/4 In.	5.00
Bustlin' Betsy, Brown, 3 3/4 In.	5.00
Bustlin' Betsy, Orange, 3 3/4 In.	7.00
Daisy, Red, White, Green, 3 3/4 In.	4.00
Daisy, Red, White, Green, 4 3/4 In.	15.00
Forget-Me-Not, Blue, 3 1/2 In.	3.00
Kiddie Kup, Green & Yellow, Miss Muffett, Frosted, 4 1/2 In.	15.00
Kiddie Kup, Red Bicycle, Children, Animals, Plastic Lid, 4 1/2 In.	10.00
Posy Cornflower No. 1, Light Blue, 3 1/2 In.	4.50
Posy Cornflower No. 2, Dark Blue, 3 1/2 In. ....*Illus*	7.00
Posy Cornflower No. 2, Light Blue, 3 1/2 In.	4.00
Posy Cornflower No. 2, Red, 3 1/2 In.	4.00
Posy Jonquil, 3 1/2 In.	5.00
Posy Tulip No. 1, Black, 3 1/4 In.	4.50

Superman, Lunch Box, Thermos, Adco, Box, 1938

Swankyswig,
Posy Cornflower
No. 2, Dark Blue,
3 1/2 In.

Posy Tulip No. I, Red, 3 1/2 In.	4.00
Posy Violet, Purple, 3 1/2 In.	6.00
Sailboat No. I, Blue, 3 1/2 In.	10.00
Sailboat No. I, Green, 3 1/2 In.	12.00

SWORDS of all types that are of interest to collectors are listed here. The military dress sword with elaborate handle is probably the most wanted. Be sure to display swords in a safe way, out of reach of children.

Artillery, England, Sharkskin Grip, Foliate, Royal Artillery, Cannon	475.00
Bayonet, Enfield, Brass Ends, Leather Scabbard, Triangular Shape, Locking Ring, 26 In.	60.00
Bayonet, Enfield, Original Bright Finish, Blue Socket, 21 1/2-In. Blade	110.00
Bayonet, Enfield, Stamped Crown, Locking Rings, Leather Scabbard, 21 1/2 In., Pair	300.00
Bayonet, France, Ribbed Brass Handle, Steel Barrel Ring, 27 1/2 In.	27.00
Bayonet, Musket, Chocolate Brown Patina, 1816, 15 1/4-In. Triangular Blade	30.00
Cavalry, Diced Contoured Grip, 1908, 35-In. Blade	395.00
Cavalry, England, Diced Contoured Grip, 1908, 35 In.	325.00
Cavalry, Germany, Foliate Armor, Gold Overlay, Gray Stained Blade, 32 1/2-In. Blade	650.00
Cavalry, Sharkskin Grip, Iron Hilt, Heavy Iron Scabbard, 1829, 34-In. Blade	775.00
Cavalry, Spain, Contoured Diced Scale Grips, Brown Patina, 1880, 32 In.	245.00
Cavalry, Wire Wrapped Leather Grip, Iron Hilt, 1820, 32 3/4-In. Blade	450.00
Cavalry, Wrapped Leather Grip, Iron Semi Bowl Guard, Frog Base, 31 1/4-In. Blade	30.00
Dagger, Black Horn Grip, Silver Embossed Pommel, Iron Steel Blade, 7 1/4-In. Blade	275.00
Dagger, Bone Grip, Eagle Pommel, Early 19th Century	595.00
Dagger, Bone Grip, Horn Pommel, Cloth Scabbard, 7 In.	145.00
Dagger, Bone Hilt, Curved Blade, Black Finish, 6 1/2 In.	135.00
Dagger, Crocodile Skin Scabbard, 3 Segments, 11 1/2 In.	175.00
Dagger, Curved Blade, Snakeskin Scabbard, 7 1/2 In.	135.00
Dagger, Gnarled Black Buckhorn Grip, Gray Finish, 6 1/2 In.	115.00
Dagger, Horn Grip, Silver Tip Mount, 13 Transverse Silver Bands, Silver Bolster, 8 In.	400.00
Dagger, Iron Hilt, Heavy Iron Grip, Scalloped Edge, Gray Stained Blade, 7 In.	225.00
Dagger, Swagger, Leather Grip, Leather Knot At Divider, Gray Stained Blade, 12 1/2 In.	175.00
Dagger, Tortoiseshell Handle & Scabbard, 10 1/2 In.	430.00
Dagger, Vendetta, Black Horn Scale Grips, 8 In.	475.00
Dagger, Wood Grain Grip, Lobed Shape, Wooden Scabbard, 5-In. Blade	375.00
Dagger, Wooden Cross Guard, Applied Brass Bar, Scabbard, 5 1/2-In. Blade	335.00
Dayak, Indonesia, Scroll Carved Handle, Horsehair Trim, Scabbard With Bells, 38 In.	255.00
Decorative, Wire Wrapped Handle, Basket Hilt, Etched Blades, 20th Century, 37 In.	25.00
Executioner's, Germany, Wooden Grip, Brass Hilt, Double Edged Blade, 1700, 31 In.	4800.00
Grenadier's, Brass, Steel, Leather Scabbard, France, 1767, 32 1/2-In. Blade	675.00
Infantry, England, Ribbed Grip, Brass Hilt, Brass Locket, 1820, 22 1/2-In. Blade	425.00
Infantry, Germany, Brass Grip & Hilt, Plain Wedge Blade, Gray Patina, 23 1/2-In. Blade	325.00
Japanese, Carved With San Character, Gold Frogs, Centipedes, Spider, Snake, 8 In.	3737.00
Japanese, Characters On The Tang, Ferule, Gold Overlay, Enameled Scabbard, 28 In.	550.00
Japanese, Double Edge Blade, Suga Hamon & Mokume Grain, 9 3/4 In.	630.00
Japanese, Entwined Dragon, Copper Snakes, Toads, Slugs, Wooden Case, 19 x 9 1/4 In.	2280.00
Japanese, Shark & Cloth Wrapped Handle, Patinated Metal Mounts, 25 1/2 In	450.00
Japanese, Silver, Gold Sun & Moon, Menuki Of Birds, Arrows, Tsuba, Signed, 25 In.	6325.00
Kaskara, Brass Cross Guard, Pommel Cap, Gray Stained Blade, Scabbard, 25 In.	300.00
Lodge, Ivory Handle, Scrimshaw Cross, Red Enamel Scabbard, 36 In.	55.00
Military, Court, Fluted Sharkskin Grip, Straight Cross Guard, 25 7/8-In. Blade	550.00
Military, Cutlass, Brass Ferrule, Original Gray Patina, Leather Scabbard, 1840, 23 In.	525.00
Military, England, Steel Hilt, Starburst Border, Blue, Gray, Brown Finish, 31 In.	595.00
Military, England, Tudor Rose Ribbed Grip, Brass Hilt, Stirrup Guard, 27-In. Blade	475.00
Military, Faceted Grip, Stylized Urn Pommel, Gray Patina Blade, 1800, 31 3/4-In. Blade	650.00
Military, France, Iron Hilt, Gold, Shell Guards, Splays Of Flags, 1770, 31 1/4-In. Blade	2950.00
Military, France, Silver Gilt Grip, Iron Hilt, Stylized Leaf Design, 1730, 30 1/4-In. Blade	2950.00
Military, Germany, Leather Wrapped Grip, Plated Hilt, Brown Patina, Scabbard, 1880	155.00
Military, Iron Hilt, Large Spherical Pommel, 1770, 32 1/4-In. Blade	1650.00
Military, U.S. Naval, Brass Hilt, Glossy Brown Patina, 28 1/2-In. Blade	1250.00
Noncommissioned Officer's, Brass Hilt, Stirrup Guard, 1790, 26 1/4-In. Blade	85.00
Noncommissioned Officer's, France, Brass Hilt, Double Shell Guards, 1860, 31 In.	295.00
Noncommissioned Officer's, Germany, 1880, 33 1/4-In. Blade	375.00

Noncommissioned Officer's, U.S., Faceted Wooden Grip, Gray Stained Blade, 26 In. 475.00
Officer's, Artillery, England, Leather Wire Wrapped Grip, Foliate Curved Blade, 34 In. . . . 375.00
Officer's, Artillery, Iron Hilt, Ornate Lattice Blade, Gray Patina 475.00
Officer's, Black Japanned Grip, Plated Hilt, Scabbard, 1902, 34 1/2-In. Blade 285.00
Officer's, Civil War, Shagreen & Wire Grip, Gilt Brass Hilt, Locket 3080.00
Officer's, England, Silver Wire Wrapped Grip, Silver Hilt, 1790, 31 3/4-In. Blade 975.00
Officer's, England, Silver Wire Wrapped Sharkskin Grip, Iron Hilt, 32 1/4-In. Blade 410.00
Officer's, England, Wire Wrapped Grip, Spherical Pommel, 33 3/4-In. Blade 425.00
Officer's, Foot, Brass Hilt, Carved Brass Scabbard, U.S., 1840, 32 1/2-In. Blade 3600.00
Officer's, Germany, Gilt Brass Hilt, Iron Scabbard, 1900, 31 1/4-In. Blade 50.00
Officer's, Gilt Wire Wrapped Grip, Brass Hilt, Shell Guard, Gray Patina, 33 In. 450.00
Officer's, Infantry, England, Sharkskin Grip, Foliate Guard, 1897, 33 In. 350.00
Officer's, Infantry, England, Sharkskin Grip, Pierced Foliate Hilt, Leather Scabbard, 1897 . 495.00
Officer's, Ivory Grip, Cruciform Hilt, Helmet Pommel, 27 1/2-In. Blade 375.00
Officer's, Military, Gilt Brass Hilt, Foliate Pommel, U.S., 1860, 31 1/8-In. Blade 3600.00
Presentation, Union, Eagle & US Cast, Etched, W. Chelmsford, Mass., 1800s, 32 In. 2240.00
Processional, Spherical Pommel, Waved Edge, Early 17th Century, 47 3/8 In. 3900.00
Rapier, Barrel Pommel, Diamond Section Blade, 17th Century, 45-In. Blade 4800.00
Rapier, Germany, Wire Grip, Iron Hilt On Each Side, Ring Guard, 17th Century, 39 In. . . 6600.00
Rapier, Iron Hilt, Leaves With Eagle, 17th Century, 34 3/4-In. Blade 2700.00
Saber, Bone Grip, Brass Hilt, Eagle Head Pommel, 36 In. 346.00
Saber, Cavalry, Leather & Wire Wrapped Grip, 41 In. 4125.00
Saber, Cavalry, Spiral Wooden Grip, Brass Hilt, 1790, 26 5/8-In. Blade 5100.00
Saber, Cavalry, Spiral Wooden Grip, Pierced Brass Hilt, 1785, 35 3/4 In. 7800.00
Saber, England, Light Dragoon, Leather Grip, Original Iron Scabbard, 31 1/2-In. Blade . . 650.00
Saber, France, Cavalry, Napoleonic, 2-Ring Scabbard, 1813, 46 In. 345.00
Saber, German, Cavalry, Leather Grip, Iron Hilt, Knuckle Bow, Scabbard, 32 In. 525.00
Saber, Leather Cover Fluted Grip, Brass Hilt, 1830, 23 In. 195.00
Saber, Officer's, Ivory Grip, Silver Hilt, Single Edge Blade, 1805, 32 1/4-In. Blade 8400.00
Saber, Wooden Handle, Iron Single Branch Hilt, 41 1/2 In. 165.00
Staff Officer's, Brass Hilt, Plated Scabbard, Late 19th Century, 36 3/4 In. 137.00
Tsuba, Iron, Brass Rosettes, Scrolled Leaves, 3 In. 431.00
Tsuba, Iron, Hoeti, Seated At A Table, Gold, Copper, Edo Period, 3 1/2 In. 431.00
Tsuba, Iron, Monkeys & A Tree, Edo Period, Signed, 2 1/2 In. 517.00
Union, Presentation, Ornate Guard, Eagle, Etched Blade, Scabbard, Ma., 32-In. Blade . . . 2240.00
War Of 1812, Etched, Presented To Private Joe B. McCrary, 1862 CSA, 30 1/2 In. 280.00

SYRACUSE is a trademark used by the Onondaga Pottery of Syracuse,
New York. The company was established in 1871. It is still working.
The name became the Syracuse China Company in 1966. It is known
for fine dinnerware and restaurant china.

SYRACUSE China

Arcadia, Cup & Saucer 41.00
Arcadia, Plate, Dinner, 10 In. 41.00
Arcadia, Plate, Salad, 7 1/2 In. 20.00
Bowl, Cereal, Made For Santa Fe Railway, 6 1/2 In. 160.00
Bracelet, Creamer 68.00
Bracelet, Cup & Saucer 50.00
Bracelet, Gravy Boat 135.00
Bracelet, Plate, Dinner, 10 In. 54.00
Bracelet, Plate, Salad, 7 1/2 In. 34.00
Bracelet, Platter, Medium 95.00
Bracelet, Platter, Small 70.00
Cadet, Cup, Coffee, Restaurant China 3.00
Cathay, Plate, Old Ivory Ground, 8 In. 8.00
Cathay, Plate, Old Ivory Ground, 9 3/4 In. 14.00
Coralbel, Bowl, Vegetable, Smooth Edge 45.00
Coralbel, Creamer 55.00
Coralbel, Cup & Saucer . . . . .22.00 to 37.00
Coralbel, Gravy Boat 28.00
Coralbel, Gravy Boat, Attached Liner, Sculptured Handles 65.00
Coralbel, Plate, Dinner, 10 In. . . . . .12.00 to 40.00
Coralbel, Plate, Salad, 7 1/2 In. . . . . .12.00 to 27.00
Coralbel, Platter, Sculptured Handles, 12 In. 40.00

Coralbel, Platter, Sculptured Handles, 14 In.	55.00
Coralbel, Platter, Small	75.00
Coralbel, Soup, Dish	15.00
Dogwood, Creamer, Individual	13.00
Dogwood, Relish, 8 In.	25.00
Jefferson, Chop Plate	115.00
Jefferson, Gravy Boat	95.00
Jefferson, Plate, Dinner, 10 In.	42.00
Jefferson, Plate, Salad, 7 1/2 In.	27.00
Jefferson, Platter	90.00
Lyric, Cup & Saucer	40.00
Lyric, Plate, Dinner, 10 In.	40.00
Lyric, Plate, Salad, 7 1/2 In.	27.00
Mayflower, Cup & Saucer, Maroon & White Flowers	12.00
Serene, Vegetable, Divided, 10 In.	10.00
Stansbury, Cup & Saucer, Gold Trim	12.00
Stansbury, Plate, Salad, Gold Trim, 7 1/2 In.	8.50
Stansbury, Platter, Gold Trim, Flowers, Oval	22.00
Stansbury, Sugar & Creamer, Cover, Gold Trim	23.00

TAPESTRY, PORCELAIN, see Rose Tapestry category.

TEA CADDY is the name for a small box made to hold tea leaves. In the eighteenth century, tea was very expensive and it was stored under lock and key. The first tea caddies were made with locks. By the nineteenth century, tea was more plentiful and the tea caddy was larger. Often there were two sections, one for green tea, one for black tea.

Applewood, Hinged Lid, Silver Foil Interior	2530.00
Black Lacquer, Chinoiserie, Stepped Lid, Lacquered Interior, 2 Canisters, 8 1/2 In.	990.00
Brass, Cover, Octagonal, Marked, W. Howe, 1850, 4 1/2 In.	489.00
Burl, Coffin Shape, Gilt Handle, England, 6 1/2 x 13 In.	2415.00
Burl, Inlaid Tree, Oval, 19th Century, 5 x 7 x 4 In.	360.00
Burl, Regency, String Inlay	1095.00
Burl Mahogany, Coffin Shape, Concave Sides, 15 x 8 1/2 x 8 1/2 In.	2185.00
Burl Walnut, Dome Top, Fitted Interior, 19th Century, 5 1/4 x 8 1/4 x 4 3/4 In.	275.00
Cherry, Inlaid, Geometric, Lift Cover, Stylized Tulips, Scalloped, Pa., 6 x 11 In.	165.00
Chinoiserie, Gilt Sterling, c.1900, 5 1/2 In.	1850.00
Chippendale, Mahogany, Inside Compartments, 8 3/4 x 5 x 5 1/2 In.	400.00
Fruitwood, Apple Form, England, 18th Century, 4 1/2 In.	4600.00
Fruitwood, Apple Form, George III, Ivory Escutcheon, Foil Lined Interior, 6 x 4 In.	315.00
Fruitwood, Apple Form, George III, Upright Stem, Hinged Lid, 4 3/4 In.	1265.00
Fruitwood, Apple Form, Hinged Lid, Ebonized Stem, Foil Lined Interior, 1880s, 5 In.	2530.00
Fruitwood, Apple Form, Ivory Framed Escutcheon, 5 3/4 In.	920.00
Fruitwood, Melon Form, George III, Segmented Body, Ring Handle, c.1800	7800.00
Fruitwood, Pear Form, George III, Grass Stem, Iron Lock, c.1800, 7 1/4 In.	2645.00
Fruitwood, Pear Form, George III, Stem On Top, c.1800, 6 In.	5100.00
Fruitwood, Pear Shape, England, 18th Century, 6 1/2 In.	2415.00
Fruitwood, Shell Inlays Front, Sawtooth Band, Divided Interior, Bone Pulls, 4 1/2 In.	520.00
Inlaid Satinwood, Marquetry Conch Shell On Lid & Front, c.1790, 4 7/10 In.	1610.00
Ivory, Tortoiseshell & Mother-Of-Pearl, Faceted Sides, Lid, Foil Lined, 4 1/2 In.	2760.00
Ivory, Tortoiseshell, Octagonal, 5 1/4 In.	1090.00
Lacquer, Cover, Canted Corners, Figures Before Pavilions, Leaf Sprigs, 6 In.	275.00
Lacquer, Figural Landscape, Rectangular, 1840, 4 x 8 1/2 x 5 3/4 In.	750.00
Mahogany, Bands Of Marquetry, Key Escutcheon, England, 18th Century	495.00
Mahogany, Chippendale, Molded Tapered Top, Tin Lined Compartment, 10 In.	587.00
Mahogany, Compartments, Brass Ball Feet, Cover, c.1820, 6 x 10 3/4 In.	248.00
Mahogany, Crossbanded, Rectangular Form, Ring Pendant Handles, 9 In.	575.00
Mahogany, Crossbanded, Tunbridgeware, Block Feet, 19th Century, 5 1/4 x 9 In.	375.00
Mahogany, Edge Stringing, 2 Lidded Jars, Mixing Bowl, 9 1/2 In.	805.00
Mahogany, Fitted Interior, Ivory Escutcheon, 5 x 9 In.	400.00
Mahogany, George III, Hinged Cover, 4 Compartments, 10 x 6 x 6 In.	635.00
Mahogany, Inlay, 3 Brass, Tin Interior Containers, England, 7 1/4 In.	290.00
Mahogany, Marquetry Shells On Lid, Line Inlay, 7 1/2 In.	1150.00

Mahogany, Octagonal, Butterfly, Prince Of Wales Inlay, 5 x 5 In. 460.00
Mahogany, Regency, Sarcophagus Shape, Lion's Head Handles, 6 1/2 x 4 3/4 x 8 In. 520.00
Mahogany, Rose Velvet Lining, 3 Interior Compartments, 10 x 5 In. 475.00
Mahogany, Rosewood Banded, Hipped Lid, 2 Interior Sections, 6 1/4 x 8 1/2 In. 230.00
Mahogany, Sarcophagus Form, Brass Lined Cover, 2 Compartments, 9 x 6 x 6 In. 515.00
Mahogany, Sarcophagus Form, Fitted Interior, 12 In. 196.00
Mahogany, Satinwood, Hinged Cover, 3 Hinged Compartments, 5 1/2 x 9 In. 470.00
Mahogany, Slope Sided Lid, Foliate Brass Escutcheon, Fitted Interior, 8 x 5 In. 690.00
Mahogany, Zigzag Marquetry Design, Rectangular Case, England, 5 1/2 In. 160.00
Mahogany Veneer, 2 Lid Sections, Ivory Finial, 8 7/8 x 4 3/4 x 4 7/8 In. 440.00
Mahogany Veneer, Ebony Stringing, Brass Handles, Ivory Knobs, 1810, 12 In. 450.00
Mahogany Veneer, Inlay Diamond, 2 Interior Sections, England, 7 3/8 x 6 3/8 In. 360.00
Mahogany Veneer, Inlay Ovals & Escutcheon, Replaced Foil, 4 1/4 x 4 x 4 In. 550.00
Maple, Foil Lining, Pear Shape, 6 1/2 In. 300.00
Mother-Of-Pearl, Regency, Diamond Pattern Inlay, Dome Cover, 4 1/2 x 6 x 3 In. 315.00
Mother-Of-Pearl, Serpentine, Parcel Gilt Cover, Flowers, 2 Sections, 5 x 7 x 4 In. 865.00
Mother-Of-Pearl, William IV, Black Lacquer, Swag, Floral Sprays, Gold, 6 1/2 In. 978.00
Papier-Mache, Black, Floral Decorated, Victorian, 6 x 8 x 5 1/2 In. 865.00
Pewter, Gilt Scenes Of Dragons, Paw Feet, Key, Chinese 2185.00
Porcelain, Cobalt Blue, Gilt, Monogrammed Cartouche, Rectangular, 4 x 5 1/2 In. 690.00
Porcelain, Mandarin Design, Floral Spray, 1775, 5 3/4 In. 345.00
Rosewood, Burl, Marquetry, 3 Paris Bottles, 6 1/2 x 5 x 1 In. 575.00
Rosewood, Original Porcelain Containers, Scenes Of France, c.1820 . . . . 4490.00
Rosewood, Regency, 2 Lidded Foil Lined Compartments, 1820s, 6 x 7 1/2 In. 960.00
Rosewood, Sarcophagus Form, 2 Lidded Compartments, 4 Ball Feet, 7 1/2 In. 290.00
Rosewood, Sarcophagus Form, Regency, 7 x 11 In. 660.00
Rosewood, Sarcophagus Lid, 2 Interior Lidded Canister, Ball Feet, 8 1/4 In. 220.00
Rosewood Borders, Ivory Escutcheon, 2 Mahogany Inserts, Ivory Knobs, 7 In. 805.00
Satinwood, Georgian, Rayed, Ivory Knob Finial, 5 x 5 1/2 x 4 In.   550.00
Satinwood, Regency, Tapered Case, Ball Handles, 6 x 11 x 6 1/4 In. 230.00
Satinwood Lined, Hinged Dome Lids, Cutwork Brasses On Lid, c.1860, 7 x 10 In. 1300.00
Silver, Domed Cover, Swag Design, Charles Aldridge, Henry Green, 1783, 5 In. 5400.00
Silver, Festoon Design, Ribbon Border, Wm. Plummer, 1783, 4 3/8 In. 7200.00
Silver, Flush Hinged Cover, Serpentine Sides, Gilt Interior, Paul Storr, 1837, 5 In. 8400.00
Silver, Ginger Jar Form, Floral, Gorham, 1887, 4 1/2 In. 700.00
Silver, Gold Wash Interior, Early 19th Century, 5 In. 715.00
Silver, Hinged Domed Cover, Swags Of Flowers, Thomas Daniel, 1786, 6 In. 8400.00
Silver, Molded Borders, Serpents' Heads, John Lingard, 1719, 4 5/8 In. 3000.00
Silver, Repousse Cover, Band Of Genre Scenes, Early 20th Century, 5 In. 345.00
Silver, Waisted Cylinder, Allover Niello Design, Early 20th Century, 4 x 5 In. 1150.00
Silver Plate, Engraved Medallion, Flowers, Mask & Ring Handles, 1880s 275.00
Silver Plate, Musician Scene, Copper On Cover, Sheffield, 4 5/8 In. 95.00
Silver Top, 19th Century, Chinese, 5 3/4 In. 468.00
Tole, Ring Cover, Black, Red, Yellow & Blue Buds & Flowers, 19th Century, 5 In. 9350.00
Tortoiseshell, Bowed Cover, Pewter, 2 Sections, Ivory, Regency, 5 1/4 x 8 x 5 In. 2530.00
Tortoiseshell, Cover, Serpentine Front, Back, Concave Sides, 3 3/4 x 6 1/2 In. 2990.00
Tortoiseshell, Domed Cover, Plain Square Escutcheon, 2 Lidded Wells, 4 1/2 In. 2185.00
Tortoiseshell, Domed Lid, Canted Sides, Brass Ball Feet, Regency, 7 x 4 1/4 In. 1725.00
Tortoiseshell, Domed Lid, Exotic Birds & Foliage Design, Mother-Of-Pearl, 6 In. 4140.00
Tortoiseshell, Fitted Interior, Double Hinged Compartments, 5 x 8 In. 1780.00
Tortoiseshell, George III, Angled Lid, Ivory Spherule, 6 x 4 1/2 x 3 1/2 In. 1090.00
Tortoiseshell, George III, Domed Lid, Twin Lidded Compartments, Ball Feet, 5 In. 3680.00
Tortoiseshell, George III, Silver Plaque Lid, Ivory, 4 x 4 1/4 x 2 7/8 In. 1092.00
Tortoiseshell, Hinged Cover, Silver Cartouche, Bands Of Ivory Veneer, 4 1/4 In. 2530.00
Tortoiseshell, Mother-Of-Pearl, Serpentine, Flange Base, Ivory Feet, 5 1/2 x 9 x 5 In. 2185.00
Tortoiseshell, Octagonal, Ivory, Silvered Plaque, George III, 5 x 4 1/2 x 3 1/2 In. 1610.00
Tortoiseshell, Regency, Canted Cover, Inlaid Ivory, 6 1/2 x 6 x 3 3/4 In. 3450.00
Tortoiseshell, Regency, Inlaid Ivory, Silver Escutcheon, 3 1/2 x 4 1/4 x 3 In. 1495.00
Tortoiseshell, Regency, Silver Escutcheon, Ivory Finial, 5 3/4 In. 1725.00
Tortoiseshell, Serpentine Front, Wooden Ball Feet, 7 3/4 In. 1840.00
Walnut, Apple Form, Stem Finial, 3 1/8 x 3 1/2 In. 5750.00
Wood, Domed Hinged Lid, 3 Compartments, Brass Lids, Bands Of Satinwood, 4 3/4 In. . .   860.00
Wood, George III, Parquetry Design, Gilt Handle, Key, 18th Century, 4 1/2 x 8 In. 1265.00

Wood, Marquetry Shell On Lid, Nautilus & Mollusk Emerging From Shell, 3 1/2 In. 920.00
Wood, Regency, 2 Interior Boxes, Ivory Knobs, Ivory Escutcheon, 4 3/4 x 8 In. 230.00

TEA LEAF IRONSTONE dishes are named for their decorations. There was a superstition that it was lucky if a whole tea leaf unfolded at the bottom of your cup. This idea was translated into the pattern of dishes known as *tea leaf*. By 1850, at least twelve English factories were making this pattern, and by the 1870s, it was a popular pattern in many countries. The tea leaf was always a luster glaze on early wares, although now some pieces are made with a brown tea leaf.

Basin, Shaw	130.00
Bowl, Cereal, Copper Trim, Adams, 6 5/8 In.	19.00
Bowl, Fruit, Copper Trim, 5 1/8 In.	24.00
Bowl, Vegetable, Cover, Copper Trim, Oval, Adams	130.00
Bowl, Vegetable, Cover, Meakin	190.00
Bowl, Vegetable, Oval, Copper Trim, Adams, 9 3/8 In.	55.00
Bread Plate, Copper Trim, Adams, 6 1/4 In.	14.00
Bread Plate, Copper Trim, Meakin, 6 3/4 In.	25.00
Bread Plate, Wedgwood, 6 3/4 In.	25.00
Brush Box, Clementson	1400.00
Brush Holder, Grindley	50.00
Brush Holder, Shaw	225.00
Butter, Meakin, 2 Piece	65.00
Butter Chip, Copper Trim, Meakin, 3 In.	30.00
Cake Plate, Meakin	35.00
Casserole, Cover, Gold Leaf Center, Red Cliff, 7 3/4 In.	260.00
Chamber Pot, Silencer, Meakin	975.00
Coffeepot, Copper Trim, Meakin, 7 Cup	250.00
Coffeepot, Cover, Copper Center, Meakin, 6 Cup	250.00
Coffeepot, Wedgwood	80.00
Compote, Meakin, 10 In.	150.00
Compote, Shaw, 10 In.	200.00
Cover For Sugar, Copper Trim	20.00
Cover For Teapot, Copper Trim, Adams	26.00
Cover For Tureen, Copper Trim, Adams	130.00
Creamer, Flintridge	48.00
Creamer, Gold Leaf Center, Red Cliff	65.00
Creamer, Meakin	195.00
Creamer, White Flowers On Branch, Flintridge	46.00
Cup & Saucer, Copper Trim, Adams, 2 1/2 In.	30.00
Cup & Saucer, Copper Trim, Meakin	90.00
Cup Plate, Meakin, 4 Piece	120.00
Dish, Pickle, Wedgwood	40.00
Ewer, Davenport	550.00
Gravy Boat, Attached Plate, White Flowers On Branch, Flintridge	150.00
Gravy Boat, Stand, Meakin	35.00
Gravy Boat, Underplate, Copper Trim, Adams	150.00
Gravy Boat, Underplate, Flintridge	150.00
Nappy, Copper Trim, Wedgwood, 4 In.	40.00
Nappy, Wedgwood, 4 In.	35.00
Pitcher, E & F, 8 In.	600.00
Pitcher, Meakin, 9 In.	250.00
Pitcher, Milk, Grindley	165.00
Pitcher, Red Cliff	90.00
Pitcher, Walley, 9 In.	90.00
Plate, Bread & Butter, Copper Trim, Adams, 6 1/4 In.	13.00
Plate, Bread & Butter, Meakin, 6 3/4 In.	25.00
Plate, Burgess, 8 In.	20.00
Plate, Cumbow, 10 In.	36.00
Plate, Dinner, Copper Trim, 10 In.	35.00
Plate, Dinner, Copper Trim, Adams, 10 1/8 In.	38.00
Plate, Dinner, Copper Trim, Meakin, 10 In.	90.00

Plate, Dinner, Copper Trim, Wedgwood, 9 7/8 In. 65.00
Plate, Gold Leaf Center, Red Cliff, 6 1/2 In. 15.00
Plate, Gold Leaf Center, Red Cliff, 8 3/8 In. 20.00
Plate, Gold Leaf Center, Red Cliff, 10 In. 45.00
Plate, Luncheon, Copper Trim, Adams, 8 7/8 In. 29.00
Plate, Luncheon, Meakin, 8 3/4 In. 39.99
Plate, Salad, Copper Trim, Wedgwood, 7 3/4 In. 36.00
Platter, Copper Trim, Meakin, Rectangular, 12 In. 130.00
Platter, Copper Trim, Meakin, Rectangular, 15 7/8 In. 190.00
Platter, Copper Trim, Rectangular, Wedgwood, 12 1/4 In. 200.00
Platter, Oval, Copper Trim, Adams, 11 1/2 In. 100.00
Platter, Oval, Meakin, 16 3/4 In. 200.00
Platter, Oval, Wedgwood, 16 3/8 In. 240.00
Platter, Rectangular, Meakin, 12 3/4 In. ....110.00 to 140.00
Platter, Rectangular, Meakin, 15 7/8 In. 200.00
Platter, Wilkinson, 10 x 13 1/2 In. 35.00
Posset Cup, Shaw 350.00
Reamer, Child's, Clementson 525.00
Relish, Meakin 130.00
Saltshaker, White Flowers On Branch, Flintridge 24.00
Saucer, Meakin 23.00
Shaving Mug, Meakin 100.00
Soup, Dish, Copper Trim, Adams, 8 In. 34.00
Soup, Dish, Copper Trim, Wedgwood, 8 5/8 In. 60.00
Soup, Dish, Flintridge, 8 1/2 In. 40.00
Sugar, Child's, Shaw 180.00
Sugar, Cover, Gold Leaf Center, Red Cliff 80.00
Sugar & Creamer, Child's, Hughes 425.00
Sugar & Creamer, Wedgwood 100.00
Tea Set, L & P, 19 Piece 115.00
Tureen, Sauce, T. Furnival, 2 Piece 80.00
Tureen, Soup, Bridgwood, 4 Piece 525.00
Tureen, Soup, Powell Bishop, 12 In. 25.00
Tureen, Soup, Red Cliff, 4 Piece 275.00
Tureen, Stand, Walley 275.00

TECO is the mark used on the art pottery line made by the American
Terra Cotta and Ceramic Company of Terra Cotta and Chicago,
Illinois. The company was an offshoot of the firm founded by William
D. Gates in 1881. The Teco line was first made in 1885 but was not
sold commercially until 1902. It continued in production until 1922.
Over 500 designs were made in a variety of colors, shapes, and glazes.
The company closed in 1930.

```
Teco
```

Bottle, Aventurine Glaze, 5 x 3 1/4 In. 690.00
Bowl, Green Matte Glaze, 3 3/4 In. 330.00
Bowl, Medium Green Matte Glaze Exterior, White Interior, 6 x 12 In. 1725.00
Box, Cover, Green Matte Glaze, Charcoaling, 2 1/4 x 3 1/2 x 2 1/2 In. 790.00
Chamberstick, Ivory Matte Glaze, Paper Label, 5 In. 520.00
Chamberstick, Stylized Flowers, Leaves, Green Matte Glaze, 10 3/4 x 5 In. 900.00
Flask, Aventurine Glaze, 4 1/2 x 3 1/4 In. 550.00
Pitcher, Green Matte Glaze, Sinewy Handle, 8 1/2 x 5 In. 845.00
Vase, 4 Open Handles, 12 Cutouts, Fritz Albert, 6 1/2 In. 3850.00
Vase, Bullet Form, Swirling Leaves, 18 1/2 In. 42550.00
Vase, Buttressed Base, Medium Green Matte Glaze, 8 3/4 x 4 In. 4220.00
Vase, Charcoal, Green Matte Glaze, 2 Buttressed Handles, 6 3/4 x 4 In. 1840.00
Vase, Charcoal, Smooth Green Matte Glaze, 9 1/2 In. 2070.00
Vase, Double Gourd Form, Leathery Green Glaze, 4 Buttressed Handles, Signed, 7 In. ... 2990.00
Vase, Embossed Blossoms, Leaves, Bronze Aventurine Glaze, 8 1/2 x 4 In. 715.00
Vase, Embossed Tulips, Green Matte Glaze, Oval, Paper Label, 8 1/4 x 4 In. ... 105.00
Vase, Faceted, Charcoal Green Glaze, Signed, 12 1/2 In. 2415.00
Vase, Green Matte Glaze, 2 Buttressed Handles At Rim, 3 x 1 1/4 In. 960.00
Vase, Green Matte Glaze, 2 Buttressed Handles, Bottle Form, Signed, 11 1/4 In. 5175.00

Vase, Green Matte Glaze, 2 Open Buttressed Handles, W.B. Mundie, 11 1/2 In. 4315.00
Vase, Green Matte Glaze, 4 Buttressed Lobes, Flared Base, Stamped, 8 3/4 x 4 In. 1840.00
Vase, Green Matte Glaze, 4 Indentations, No. 356, 4 In. 605.00
Vase, Green Matte Glaze, 4 Open Handles, Fritz Albert, 9 In. 3450.00
Vase, Green Matte Glaze, Double Buttressed Handles, 8 1/2 In. 1320.00
Vase, Green Matte Glaze, Heavy Charcoaling, 11 3/4 In. 5465.00
Vase, Green Matte Glaze, Impressed Mark, 4 3/4 In. 385.00
Vase, Green Matte Glaze, Molded Flowers, W. Jenny, 10 In. 4600.00
Vase, Green Matte Glaze, Molded Leaves, 10 In. 9200.00
Vase, Green Matte Glaze, Ribbed Body, 3 Handles, 6 1/4 x 6 1/2 In. 1237.00
Vase, Green Matte Glaze, Squat Base, 16 1/2 x 8 In. 1690.00
Vase, Leathery Green Matte Glaze, Signed, 20 In. 4310.00
Vase, Light Green Matte Glaze, Cutout Design, Fritz Albert, 9 In. 1610.00
Vase, Smooth Brown Glaze, 4 Buttressed Handles, Signed, 7 1/2 In. 3450.00
Vase, Smooth Green Glaze, Bottle Shape, 2 Angular Handles, 9 1/2 In. 1265.00
Vase, Smooth Green Glaze, Signed, 9 x 9 In. 4600.00
Vase, Tall Leaves Under Crystalline Green Matte Glaze, 22 x 8 1/2 In. 6190.00
Vase, Tulip, Overlapping Leaf Blades & Blossoms, W.J. Dodd, No. 151, 11 In. 7475.00
Vase, Yellow Matte Glaze, Cylindrical, 4 Buttressed Handles, Marked, 6 1/2 x 2 1/4 In. . . 1045.00
Wall Pocket, Long Narrow Leaves, Smooth Green Glaze, Signed, 14 x 6 3/4 In. 1265.00

TEDDY BEARS were named for a president of the United States. The first
teddy bear was a cuddly toy said to be inspired by a hunting trip made
by Teddy Roosevelt in 1902. Morris and Rose Michtom started selling
their stuffed bears as *teddy bears* and the name stayed. The Michtoms
founded the Ideal Novelty and Toy Company. The German version of
the teddy bear was made about the same time by the Steiff Company.
There are many types of teddy bears and all are collected. The old ones
are being reproduced. Other bears are listed in the Toy section.

Berlin Bear, Brown Velvet Plush Fur, Swivel Head, Jointed, 1960, 3 In. 200.00
Cramer, Growler, Mohair, White, Humped Back, Swivel Neck, Box, 1906, 19 In. 5500.00
Fully Jointed, Excelsior Stuffed, Saffron Rayon, 1920s, 13 1/2 In. 115.00
Humpback, Long Nose, Shoebutton Eyes, Fully Jointed, 1920s, 19 In. 865.00
Ideal, Mohair, Blond, Fully Jointed, Glass Eyes, Excelsior Stuffing, Romper, 1920, 17 In. . 350.00
Ideal, Mohair, Cream, Black Shoebutton Eyes, 1915, 13 In. 230.00
Ideal, Mohair, Yellow, Glass Eyes, Fully Jointed, 1920, 17 In. 230.00
Knickerbocker, Mohair, Long Silky, Gold Eyes, Articulated Limbs, 1940s, 21 In. 520.00
Knickerbocker, Mohair, White, Tin Nose, Swivel Neck, 1930s, 19 In. 190.00
Mohair, Blond, Articulated Limbs & Head, Glass Eyes, 14 In. 125.00
Mohair, Brown, Black Bead Eyes, Jointed, Humpback, 11 In. 30.00
Mohair, Cinnamon, Black Embroidered Nose, Mouth, 1925, 15 In. 875.00
Mohair, Tan, Articulated, Seated, Glass Eyes, Voice Box, 20 In. 220.00
Panda, Mohair, Amber, Glass Eyes, Jointed Limbs, 1938, 15 In. 1485.00
Petz, Mohair, Orange, Jointed Limbs, Chest Button, 1930s, 13 In. 400.00
Petz, Polar Bear, Mohair, White, Standing, Swivel Neck, 1960s, 6 1/4 In. 135.00
Pintel Fils, Mohair, Gold, Black Embroidered Mouth, Amber Glass Eyes, 16 In. 1300.00
Pintel Fils, Mohair, White, Swivel Head, Amber Glass Eyes, 1920, 9 In. 1050.00
R. John Wright, Winnie The Pooh, Wool, Caramel, Black Glass Eyes, 8 In. 525.00
Schuco, Embroidered Nose, Mouth, Steel Bead Eyes, Tan Nose, 1920, 2 1/2 In. 145.00
Schuco, Mohair, Champagne, Pale, Amber Glass Eyes, Felt Paws, Germany, 17 In. 3400.00
Schuco, Mohair, Gold, Champagne, Pale Amber Eyes, Germany, 1930, 13 In. 2500.00
Schuco, Mohair, Golden, Bellhop, Yes/No, Tail Moves Head, 1920s, 9 In. . . . . .650.00 to 880.00
Schuco, Mohair, Light Brown, Black Nose, Amber Glass Eyes, 1953, 13 In. 850.00
Schuco, Mohair, Rose, Swivel Head, Black Mouth, Germany, 1930, 5 In. 900.00
Schuco, Perfume, Golden Mohair, Steel Eyes, 1920s, 3 3/8 In. 145.00
Steiff, Bead Eyes, Jointed Limbs, Partially Movable Neck, 1908, 3 1/2 In. 605.00
Steiff, Black Steel Eyes, Black Embroidered Nose, 1905, 7 1/4 In. 520.00
Steiff, Light Apricot, Fully Jointed, c.1905.12 1/2 In. 1610.00
Steiff, Mohair, Articulated, Straw Stuffing, Button Eyes, c.1906, 12 In. 2950.00
Steiff, Mohair, Beige, Black Steel Eyes, Fully Jointed, 1910, 5 1/4 In. 860.00
Steiff, Mohair, Blond, Articulated Limbs, Swivel Neck, c.1910, 10 In. 1650.00
Steiff, Mohair, Blond, Fully Jointed, Working Rattle, c.1910, 5 In. 405.00

Steiff, Mohair, Blond, Glass Eyes, Ear Button, Excelsior Stuffed, 13 In. 145.00
Steiff, Mohair, Blond, Script Ear Button, Excelsior Stuffed, Jointed, 30 In. 1955.00
Steiff, Mohair, Brown, Velvet Paw Pads, Black Bead Eyes, Ear Button, 9 In. 165.00
Steiff, Mohair, Champagne, Amber Glass Eyes, Jointed, Felt Paws, 1950, 15 In. 700.00
Steiff, Mohair, Ginger, Embroidered Nose, Mouth, Glass Eyes, 1910, 5 1/4 In. 375.00
Steiff, Mohair, Gold, Amber Glass Bead Eyes, Black Nose, Mouth, 1940, 5 1/2 In. 700.00
Steiff, Mohair, Golden Swivel Head, Black Bead Eyes, Jointed, 1920, 3 1/2 In. 1200.00
Steiff, Mohair, Light Gold, Amber Glass Bead Eyes, Brown Nose, Mouth, 1920, 5 In. ... 1200.00
Steiff, Mohair, Light Golden, Swivel Head, Black Nose, Mouth, 14 In. 700.00
Steiff, Mohair, Light Yellow, Black Shoebutton Eyes, 1915, 16 In. 1090.00
Steiff, Mohair, White, Glass Eyes, Articulated Limbs, Ear Batten, 1950s, 12 In. 440.00
Steiff, Mohair, White, Jointed Limbs, Swivel Neck, c.1910, 14 In. 935.00
Steiff, Mohair, White, Shaved Muzzle, Articulated Limbs, c.1908, 13 In. 6270.00
Steiff, Mohair, White, Shoebutton Eyes, Swivel Neck, c.1906, 12 In. 2090.00
Steiff, Mohair, Yellow, Black Metal Eyes, Peach Felt Pads, 1907, 25 In. 3795.00
Steiff, Mohair, Yellow, Black Steel Eyes, Black Nose, Mouth, 1905, 5 In. 1092.00
Steiff, Mohair, Yellow, Jointed Limbs, Squeaker Box, c.1933, 10 In. 5775.00
Steiff, Mr. Cinnamon, Button & Tag In Ear, 13 In. 55.00
Steiff, Panda, Mohair, Black & White, Glass Eyes, Stitched Nose, Felt Pads, 1950s, 9 In. . 750.00
Steiff, Panda, Mohair, Swivel Neck, Ear Button, 1950s, 9 In. 935.00
Steiff, Polar Bear, Mohair, White, On All Fours, Jointed Limbs, 5 x 9 In. 3300.00
Steiff, Rose, Tag Reads Teddy Rose, Box 170.00
Steiff, Tag Reads Brummbar, 12 In. 57.00
Steiff, Zotty, Mohair, Curly Beige, Apricot Chest, Button, Fully Jointed, 21 In. 175.00
Steiff, Zotty, Mohair, Glass Eyes, Jointed, Embroidered Nose, 1950, 11 In. 170.00
Wool, Golden, Swivel Head, Upturned Nose, Amber Glass Eyes, 1930, 17 In. 200.00

TELEPHONES are wanted by collectors if the phones are old enough or unusual enough. The first telephone may have been made in Havana, Cuba, in 1849, but it was not patented. The first publicly demonstrated phone was used in Frankfurt, Germany, in 1860. The phone made by Alexander Graham Bell was shown at the Centennial Exhibition in Philadelphia in 1876, but it was not until 1877 that the first private phones were installed. Collectors today want all types of old phones, phone parts, and advertising. Even recent figural phones are popular.

American Bell Telephone Co., Oak, Wall, 20 In. 290.00
American Bell Telephone Co., Wall, Oak, Intercom, Pat. March 2, 1901, 17 In. 170.00
American Bell Telephone Co. Hygiene, Candlestick, Crystal Mouthpiece 1840.00
B-R & Electric Telephone & Mfg. Co., Candlestick 460.00
Booth, Wooden, Glass, 1940s 1100.00
Brass, Rotary Dial, Black Plastic Ear, Mouthpiece & Handle, Continental, 8 1/2 In. 55.00
Brass, Ship, Navy Department Bureau Of Ships 70.00
Canada Dry Ginger Ale, Can, With Canister, Tectel Inc., 1980, 6 1/2 In. 50.00
Clark Automatic Switchboard, 74 Line 275.00
Ericsson, Eiffel Tower 690.00
Ericsson, Fiddleback, Wall 145.00
Federal, Princess, Cradle 145.00
Federal, Telegraph Key 105.00
Grammont, Candlestick, Wooden, 3 Sides, Paris 2530.00
Gray Telephone Pay Station, 5 Slot, Silver Dollar Slot, Wall 4890.00
Gray Telephone Pay Station, Candlestick, 3 Slot 920.00
Gray Telephone Pay Station, Shield, Coin Box 1610.00
Hide-A-Phone, Globe 745.00
Kellogg, Cradle, Black 90.00
Kellogg, Cradle, Red Bar 45.00
Kellogg, Wall, Oak, Rochester, N.Y., 9 x 13 x 19 In. 225.00
L.M. Ericsson, Stockholm, 1892 ....*Illus* 6780.00
L.M. Ericsson, Stockholm, Wall, 1897 ....*Illus* 9600.00
Lantern, Bell System, Pair 115.00
Leich Electric Co., Candlestick 115.00
Manhattan, Candlestick, Tapered Shaft 2015.00
Northern Electric, Candlestick 290.00

Telephone, L.M. Ericsson, Stockholm, 1892

Telephone, L.M. Ericsson, Stockholm, Wall, 1897

To clean the stem and bowl of a collectible briar pipe, dip a pipe cleaner in vodka. Push the pipe cleaner through the stem. Use a dry pipe cleaner for any pipe but a briar pipe.

PacMan, 1980s, 2 x 4 1/2 In.	12.00
Paperweight, New York Telephone, Cobalt Blue	92.00
Sears & Roebuck, 1 Box, Wall	145.00
Shade, Bell System, Blue Glass, Bell Shape	1840.00
Sign, Bell System, Public Telephone, Porcelain, 2 Sides, 18 x 18 In.	110.00
Sign, From Telephone Booth, Reverse Glass, Blue & White, 1940s, 25 1/2 x 5 1/2 In.	50.00
Sign, Indian Telephone Corp, Bracket, Blue & White, Enamel, 18 x 18 In.	345.00
Sign, Local & Long Distance Telephone, Bell Shape, 7 1/2 x 6 1/2 In.	370.00
Sign, Public Telephone Pay Station, Orange, Blue Ground, 2 Sides, 8 x 18 In.	175.00
Sign, Public Telephone, Bell System, Blue & White, 2 Sides, Bracket, 18 x 20 In.	45.00
Sign, Roseville Independent Telephone Co., Blue & White, Oval, 12 In.	375.00
Sign, Telephone Payments, NET & AT&T, Blue & White, 2 Sides, 20 x 14 In.	290.00
Sign, Telephone, Bell Shape, Plastic, Lighted, 24 In.	45.00
Sign, Tell Telephone Co. Of Pa., Blue & White, Enamel, 20 x 20 In.	290.00
Sign, Western Union, Blue & White, Arrow, 2 Sides, 18 x 30 In.	115.00
Stromberg Carlson, 2-Box, Wall	115.00
Stromberg Carlson, Cradle, Black	60.00
Toy, Truck, Bell, Cast Iron, Green, Rubber Tires, Shovel, Pick & Hoe, Hubley, 10 In.	488.00
Toy, Truck, Bell, Cast Iron, White Rubber Tires, Accessories, Hubley, 10 In.	935.00
Toy, Truck, Bell, Pole, Wagon & Wench, Hubley, 10 In.	650.00
Toy, Truck, Bell, White Rubber Tires, Hubley, 10 In.	385.00
Utica Fire Alarm, 1 Box, Wall	375.00
Victor Railroad, Candlestick	1610.00
Vollautomat, Cradle, Line Indicator	25.00
Vought Berger, Wall	175.00
Western Electric, No. 202, White	145.00
Western Electric, Vanity, Folding	1265.00
Western Electric, Wall, Oak, Table Top Handset, Pat. Sept. 16, 1924, 9 1/2 In.	85.00
Westinghouse, C & O RR, Wall	175.00

TELEVISION sets are twentieth-century collectibles. Although the first television transmission took place in England in 1925, collectors find few sets which pre-date 1946. The first sets had only five channels, but by 1949 the additional UHF channels were included. The first color television set became available in 1951.

Arvin, Model 4080, Metal Case, 1950, 10 x 16 In.	352.00
Beamsscope, Enlarger Attachment, Japan, Box, 1950, 9 x 12 In.	26.00
Capehart-Farnsworth Co., Model 16C216BD-4, Blond Cabinet, 19 In.	39.00
Coronado, Model TV3-9397C, Portable, 14 1/2 In.	20.00
General Electric, 1950s	82.00
General Electric, Plastic Body, White Trim, No. 5B5, 8 In.	7150.00
Motorola, Model 7VT5R, Suitcase Style	96.00
Philco, Predicta, Futuristic Design, Mahogany Cabinet, 24 x 20 x 45 In.	632.00
Philco, Predicta, Teak Stand	450.00
RCA, Portable, Retractable Handle 1950s, 7 1/2 x 8 3/4 In.	41.00

TEPLITZ refers to art pottery manufactured by a number of companies in the Teplitz-Turn area of Bohemia during the late nineteenth and early twentieth centuries. The Amphora Porcelain Works and the Alexandra Works were two of these companies.

Bust, Girl With Floral Bouquets, Signed, Amphora, 16 x 15 x 10 In.	2912.00
Bust, Woman With Hat, Floral Accents, Signed E.W. Turn, Wien, Amphora, 15 In.	1792.00
Bust, Young Girl, Lacey Bonnet, Collar, Marked Turn Teplitz, Bohemia, 7 In.	235.00
Ewer, Incised Egyptian Design, Egg Shape, Signed, 1920s, 14 3/4 In.	604.00
Figurine, Gladiator With Sword, Riessner, Amphora, 18 In.	510.00
Figurine, Victorian Woman, Browns, Greens, Gold, Pink, Ernst Wahliss, 24 In.	700.00
Jardiniere, Mermaid, Turtle & Seaweed, Schwarz, 10 1/2 x 11 In.	2400.00
Vase, Applied Grapes & Leaves, Cobalt Ground, Amphora, 10 x 10 5/8 In.	280.00
Vase, Birch Trees, Cylindrical, Printed Mark, 6 In.	460.00
Vase, Blue Mums, Fired On Gold, Paul Dachsel, 6 1/8 In.	110.00
Vase, Bud, Hand Painted, c.1900, 6 1/2 In.	385.00
Vase, Colored & Gilt Roses & Leaves, Gilt Ground, Signed, c.1900, 9 In.	932.00
Vase, Dragon, Figural, Amphora, 22 In.	4500.00
Vase, English Roses, Stylized, Flowers, Impressed Mark, Label, 8 1/2 In.	58.00
Vase, Floral, Pink, Green, Marked, 6 In.	143.00
Vase, Frieze Of Owls Amid Leaves, Signed, 1920s, 13 3/4 In.	302.00
Vase, Geometric Design, Open Handle At Top, Signed, 13 In.	330.00
Vase, Globular Shape, Jewels, Crouching Lioness, Gold Trim, Marked, 11 1/2 In.	1840.00
Vase, Gold, Opalescent Blue & Red Jewels, Hammered Metal Texture, Handles, 6 In.	1075.00
Vase, High Relief Flowers, Gilt Details, Handles, Oval, Marks, Amphora, 15 1/2 In.	2300.00
Vase, Incised Spider Mums, Gold Trim, Riessner & Kessel, Amphora, 10 1/2 In.	240.00
Vase, Landscape, Embossed Collar & Bottom Rim, Jewels In Top Collar, Signed, 9 1/2 In.	297.00
Vase, Numerous Trees In Ground, Painted Mushroom At Base, Paul Dachsel, 15 In.	2415.00
Vase, Pastoral Scene, Goat, Lower Scallops, Signed, Early 20th Century, 10 3/4 In.	920.00
Vase, Poppies, Iridescent Glaze, Handles, Stamped, Amphora, 6 In.	1150.00
Vase, Snake & Leaves Covered In Green & Brown Matte Glaze, 7 1/2 In.	385.00
Vase, Spider Webs, Butterflies, Jewels, Oval, Incised Mark, 8 In.	1955.00
Vase, Tan & Yellow, 2 Large Octopi, 2 Exotic Fish, Scallop Shell Opening, Stellmacher	1250.00
Vase, Woman's Portrait, Medieval Costume, Teardrop Shape, Incised Mark, 5 1/2 In.	3738.00

TERRA-COTTA is a special type of pottery. It ranges from pale orange to dark reddish-brown in color. The color comes from the clay, which is fired but not always glazed in the finished piece.

Bust, Man, Yellow Vest, Bowtie, J.W. Ketterer, 1951, 10 In.	806.00
Bust, Young Boy, 16 In.	980.00
Ewer, Etruscan Style, Pinched Spout, Loop Handle, 20 x 6 x 7 In., Pair	3450.00
Figurine, Chinese Equestrian, In Peaked Hat, Black Painted Base, 32 x 13 1/2 In.	90.00
Figurine, Classical Maiden, Flowing Wreath, Rocky Base, Vito Sabalilli, 35 1/2 In.	6480.00
Figurine, Virgin & Child, Supporting Naked Child In Her Arms, 1740, 11 1/2 In.	9000.00
Figurine, Wizard Child With Cat Leaning On Barrel, Marked BB556, 9 1/2 In.	415.00
Figurine Set, Virgin & Child, St. Joseph, Cow, Mule, 2 Shepherds, c.1900, 8 1/2 In.	1200.00
Jar, Storage, Mediterranean, Bulbous Shape, Molded Concentric Bands, 32 x 22 In.	635.00
Jardiniere, Majolica Glazed, Green Wash, Brown Glaze, France, 21 1/2 x 19 In., Pair	489.00
Plaque, Man & Monk In Wine Cellar, Relief, Brass Frame, Marked JM5232, 13 In.	145.00
Tile, Elephant, Square, 4 1/4 In.	90.00
Urn, Black Glaze, Etruscan Style, Loop Handles, Allegorical Scenes, 10 x 8 x 6 In.	920.00
Urn, Campana Form, Everted Egg & Dart Rim, Loop Handles, Signed, 29 In., Pair	7200.00
Vase, Wall, Winged Putto Head, Glazed, 8 In.	160.00

TEXTILES listed here include many types of printed fabrics and table and household linens. Some other textiles will be found under Clothing, Coverlet, Quilt, Rug, etc.

Bed Cover, Allover Diapered Ground, Leaves & Flowers, Silk Thread, 88 x 82 In.	5750.00
Bed Cover, Allover Quatrefoil Ground, Scrolling Leaves & Flowers, 1920s, 119 x 94 In.	1840.00
Bed Cover, Floral & Scroll, Knotted Bride's Form Grid, Bobbin-Lace, 1920s, 90 x 84 In.	975.00
Bed Cover, White, Yellow Border, Embroidered Yellow Flower, Cotton, 87 x 73 In.	196.00
Bed Hanging, For Corner Bed, Needlework, Blue, 4 Curtains, 2 Valances, 1900s	3200.00
Bedspread, Crocheted, 1930s, Full Size	150.00

Below: Textile, Towel, Hot Pink & Bright Green Abstract Floral, Linen, Vera, 27 In.

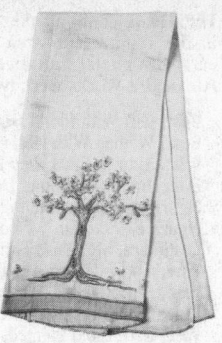

Textile, Tablecloth, Round, Cutwork, Embroidered, Scalloped, White Linen, 24 In. Diam.

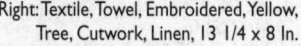

Right: Textile, Towel, Embroidered, Yellow, Tree, Cutwork, Linen, 13 1/4 x 8 In.

Bedspread, Crocheted, Fringed Border, 88 x 80 In. 70.00
Bell Pull, Needlepoint, White Flowers, Black Ground, Brass Repousse, 67 In. 330.00
Bell Pull, Woven Wool, Embossed Brass Finial, Cut White Overlay Handle, 79 In. 137.00
Blanket, Crewelwork Flowers In Vases, Blue, Green, Mustard, 81 x 73 In. 8050.00
Blanket, Hand Woven, 2 Panels, Orange & Blue Checkerboard, Wool, 1850, 85 x 81 In. ... 110.00
Blanket, Red, Blue, White, Wool, Early 19th Century, 68 x 83 1/2 In. 258.00
Blanket, Twill Design, Salmon, Indigo, Tan, Wool, 69 x 89 1/2 In., Pair 1035.00
Bunting, Flag, 48 Stars, Uncut, 12 Yards 225.00
Bunting, Stars, Red, White & Blue, 8 1/2 Ft. 55.00
Counterpane, Crewelwork, Flowers, Beige Homespun Ground, 102 x 116 In. 190.00
Feed Sack, Colorful Pattern, Opened Up For Seamstress 14.00
Flag, 31 Stars In Star Shape, California's Entry To Union, Silk, Frame, 1850 .... 13500.00
Flag, 48 Lopsided Stars, Red, White & Blue, Marie Miller, 1920 .... 1210.00
Flag, American, 34 Stars, 1861-1863, Frame 6500.00
Flag, American, 34 Stars, Blue Canton, Wool Bunting, Civil War, 4 x 6 In. 1093.00
Flag, American, 42 Stars, Silk, 18 x 26 1/2 In. 1100.00
Flag, American, 45 Stars, Leather Flag Bearer's Pole Insert, 6 x 10 In. 275.00
Flag, Civil War, Signal, Army, Red & White, Woven Cotton, 16 x 14 In. 265.00
Flag, Confederate, Battle Of Petersburg, VA 11550.00
Handkerchief, 39 Stars, United States Flag, Silkscreened, Silk, 1890, 19 x 18 In. 105.00
Handkerchief, Napoleon Center, Symbols Of Battle Border, Silk, 33 1/2 x 31 1/2 In. 650.00
Handkerchief, Washington On Deathbed, Wife, Cotton, Brown On White, 19 x 20 1/2 In. .. 1100.00
Holder, Whiskbroom, Cloth, Butterfly Shape 60.00
Obi, Allover Floral, Celadon Ground, Woven Silk, 12 x 148 In. 115.00
Panel, Embroidered, Flowers, Silk, Framed, Chinese, 40 1/8 x 20 1/2 In. 132.00
Panel, Gilt, Copper, Silver Thread, Embroidered, Indian, 49 x 46 In. 546.00
Panel, Jacquard, Pink, Blue, Gold Flowers, Vine, Ivory Ground, 93 x 41 In. 92.00
Piano Shawl, Embroidered, Silk, Flowers, Cream Ground, Victorian, Fringe, 64 In. 345.00
Pillow, Embroidered, Exotic Bird On Flowering Branch, Arts & Crafts, 14 x 16 In., Pair .. 115.00
Pillow, Needlepoint, Aubusson, Gold, Cream, Tan, Brown Fringe, Silver Silk, 15 In., Pair . 374.00
Pillow, Needlepoint, Aubusson, Parrot & Floral, Gold, Gold Tassel Fringe, 16 x 16 In. ... 259.00
Pillow, Needlepoint, Corded, Victorian, 19 1/2 x 16 1/2 In., Pair 2070.00
Pillow Case, Crewelwork, Deer, Parrot, Flowers, 23 x 29 In. 325.00
Pillow Cover, Embroidered, Brown, Green, 18 x 22 In. 288.00
Pouch, Embroidered, Flowers, Yellow, Red, Green, Drawstring, Arts & Crafts, 10 x 8 In. . 115.00
Spread, Embroidered, Candlewick, White, Central Cartouche, N.Y., 1829, 108 x 112 In. .. 1840.00
Tablecloth, Allegorical Figures, Handmade, 60 x 180 In. 224.00
Tablecloth, Blue, Red Overshot, Lace Border, Linen, 1891, 91 1/2 x 57 In. 56.00
Tablecloth, Madeira, Appliqued, Hydrangea, Cream Organdy, Beige Floral, Border, 1960s . 925.00
Tablecloth, Round, Cutwork, Embroidered, Scalloped, White Linen, 24 In. Diam. . . .*Illus* 65.00
Tablecloth, Round, Embroidered, Heart Shape Edging, Red, 30 In. 58.00
Tablecloth, Round, Embroidered, Poppies, Arts & Crafts, 31 In. 403.00
Tablecloth, Round, Flowers, Lace Edge, Arts & Crafts, 42 In. 230.00
Tablecloth, Round, Pink, Blue & Yellow Embroidered Flowers, Ivory Ground, 14 In. 38.00
Tapestry, 18th Century Outdoor Theater Scene, Machine Made, Frame, 33 x 49 1/2 In. .. 230.00

Tapestry, Allegorical Man & Woman, Birds, 19th Century, 195 x 46 In. 100.00
Tapestry, Aubusson, Chinoiserie, Bird Tree, Trompe Loeil Frame Border, 100 1/2 x 80 In. 8625.00
Tapestry, Aubusson, Floral, Foliate Garlands, Ivory Field, 137 x 192 In. 6900.00
Tapestry, Brown, Border, Mohair, Arts & Crafts, 64 x 54 In. 230.00
Tapestry, Couple Fishing, Girl Watching, Hand Woven, Iron Rod, 54 x 56 In. 1045.00
Tapestry, Ivory, Pink, White, Red Rose Border, 92 x 114 In. 412.00
Tapestry, Landscape, Parrot In Tree, Eagle Attacking Dog, 17th Century, 100 x 90 In. . . . 9200.00
Tapestry, Landscape, Parrot, Trees & Lake, Floral Border, Hand Woven, Rod, 75 x 96 In. 1430.00
Tapestry, Mediterranean Scene, Belgian, 19 x 58 In. 120.00
Tapestry, Milkmaids & Herder, Wooded Landscape, Birds, Swans, 1730s, 180 x 108 In. . . 4775.00
Tapestry, Needlework, Allover Floral, Medallions, Hunter Green Ground, 48 x 72 In. 220.00
Tapestry, Soldier Holding Urn Before Woman, Flemish, 17th Century, 82 1/2 x 39 In. . . . 9200.00
Tapestry, Woven, Repeating Bird Design, Gold Silk Thread, 40 x 76 In. 110.00
Throw, Chain Stitch, Ivory Ground, Blue Border, Cloth Backing, 3 x 5 Ft. 110.00
Towel, Embroidered, Yellow, Tree, Cutwork, Linen, 13 1/4 x 8 In. . . . . *Illus* 15.00
Towel, Hot Pink & Bright Green Abstract Floral, Linen, Vera, 27 In. . . . . *Illus* 17.00
Towel, Trees, Flowers, Potted Tulip, Birds, Drawnwork, Crewelwork, Linen, c.1824 . . . . . 935.00
Wall Hanging, Embroidered, Pierced, Floral, Cotton Backed, 51 x 72 1/2 In. 495.00

THERMOMETER is a name that comes from the Greek word for heat.
The thermometer was invented in 1731 to measure the temperature of
either water or air. All kinds of thermometers are collected, but those
with advertising messages are the most popular.

7-Up, 15 x 6 In. 147.00
Atlas Anti-Freeze 170.00
Baby Bath, Bakelite Insert, Brown Plastic, 6 1/2 In. 165.00
Barq's, 1950 Bottle, Pictures, 26 In. 95.00
Bird, Peering Through An Oak Branch, Signed, Pairpoint Mfg. Co. 402.00
Bireley's, Bottle & Orange Image, 15 3/4 x 4 1/2 In. 220.00
Bireley's, c.1950, 15 3/4 In. 170.00
Casite, Metal Housing, Glass Front, 12 In. 90.00
Deep Sea, Negretti & Zambra, London, 14 3/4 In. 760.00
Dominion Royal Tires, Porcelain, 30 x 10 In. 495.00
Dr Pepper, Friendly Pepper Upper, Box, 16 x 6 1/2 In. 250.00
Dr Pepper, Hot Or Cold, Round, 1960s, 12 In. 220.00
Dr. Townsend's Sarsaparilla, Wood, Metal, Glass, 1840, 24 x 5 7/8 In. 120.00
Dwight's Cow Brand Soda, 36 In. 920.00
Ex-Lax, Metal, Tube, 38 1/2 x 8 1/4 In. 155.00
Ex-Lax, Sign, Enameled, 36 In. 58.00
Ex-Lax The Chocolate Laxative, Porcelain, 8 x 36 In. 132.00
Fleetwing Petroleum Products, Tin, Box, 6 3/8 x 2 In. 45.00
Genuine Portuondo Cigars, 21 In. 360.00
Havoline, World's Fair, 1939, Cast Metal, 4 5/8 In. 30.00
Hires Root Beer, Tin, 7 5/8 x 28 1/2 In. 125.00
Images Of Indians, Instructions For Selling, Self Framed, c.1935, 9 In. 330.00
Kern's Bread, Tin Lithograph, 13 1/2 In. 120.00
Ma's Root Beer, Logo Bottle, 27 1/2 x 7 In. 85.00
Mail Pouch Tobacco, Black Ground, Porcelain, Wooden Frame, 18 x 72 In. 300.00
Mail Pouch Tobacco, Treat Yourself To The Best, Porcelain, 1930s-1940s, 60 x 14 In. 470.00
Mary Kania Bar, Southern Woman, Tinsel, Frame, 9 1/2 x 7 3/4 In. . . . . *Illus* 50.00
Mercury, Brass Frame, Leaf Scrollwork, Urn Top, 15 1/2 In. 220.00
Moxie, Metal, Man In White Jacket, Drink Moxie In White, 1930s, 26 x 9 3/4 In. 250.00
Moxie, Tin Lithograph, 38 1/4 x 12 In. . . . . *Illus* 6930.00
NuGrape, With Girl 75.00
Ortlieb's Beer, Tin Over Cardboard, 1950s, 9 In. 54.00
Prestone Anti-Freeze, Wooden, 1930s, 39 1/2 In. 302.00
Raybestos Brake Linings, Painted, Tin, 10 x 31 In. 187.00
RCA, Victor Radio, Porcelain, Dark Blue, 39 In. 825.00
Red Goose Shoes, Porcelain, 27 x 7 In. 260.00
Red Seal, Porcelain, Ca., 1915, 27 x 7 In. 250.00
Red Seal Batteries, 27 1/4 In. 187.00
Rolling Rock, Extra Pale, Painted Metal, Glass Tube, 1992, 27 x 8 1/4 In. 55.00
Texaco, Tin, 6 x 2 1/2 In. 135.00

Thermometer,
Mary Kania Bar,
Southern Woman,
Tinsel, Frame,
9 1/2 x 7 3/4 In.

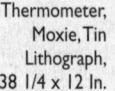

Thermometer,
Moxie, Tin
Lithograph,
38 1/4 x 12 In.

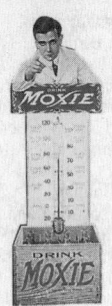

Marble will scorch. A marble statue very close to the heat of a 100-watt light bulb may be damaged.

Valvoline Motor Oil, Metal Housing, 12 In. 200.00
Veedol Motor Oil, Pressboard, Painted, 5 x 20 In. 165.00
Wall, Louis XVI, Giltwood, Cherub & Dove Scene, Sepia Paint, 31 x 12 In. 3220.00
Wayne Feed, Die Cut Tin Lithograph, Chicken & Feed Sack, 6 1/4 In. 345.00
Winston Cigarettes, Package Form 75.00
Wolfe Dairies, Milk Carton Shape, Cardboard, 6 In. 10.00
Zodiac, Gold Dore Patina, Signed, 4 1/2 x 8 In. 748.00

TIFFANY is a name that appears on items made by Louis Comfort Tiffany, the American glass designer who worked from about 1879 to 1933. His work included iridescent glass, Art Nouveau styles of design, and original contemporary styles. He was also noted for stained glass windows, unusual lamps, bronze work, pottery, and silver. Other types of Tiffany are listed under Tiffany Glass, Tiffany Gold, Tiffany Pottery, or Tiffany Silver. The famous Tiffany lamps are listed in this section. Tiffany jewelry is listed in the jewelry and wristwatch categories. Reproductions of some types of Tiffany are being made.

Louis C. Tiffany

Ashtray, Bronze, Gold Dore, Handle At Each End, Round, Signed, 4 In. 135.00
Ashtray, Bronze, Gold Dore, Pedestal, Removable Insert, 3 1/2 x 3 1/4 In. 400.00
Ashtray, Match Safe, Heraldic, Green Enamel, Hobnail Edge, 5 x 4 In. 450.00
Ashtray, Match Safe, Venetian, Sculptured Minks, Bronze, Gold Dore, 5 x 3 1/2 In. 450.00
Ashtray, Zodiac, Bronze, Gold Dore, 2 3/4 x 6 3/4 In. 2300.00
Ashtray Set, Bronze, Gold Dore, Raised Ruffled Rim, Signed, 2 3/4 To 4 1/2 In., 4 Piece . 350.00
Bill File, Bookmark, Bronze, Gold Dore, Signed, 3 3/4 x 6 1/2 In. 650.00
Bill File, Zodiac, 8 Sides, Curved Spindle, Bronze, Dark Patina, 3 1/2 x 7 3/4 In. 750.00
Blotter, Hand, Graduate, Bronze, Gold Dore, Signed, 6 x 3 In. 135.00
Blotter, Hand, Heraldic, Green Enamel, Hobnail Pattern, 5 1/2 x 2 3/4 In. 300.00
Blotter, Hand, Venetian, 5 1/4 x 2 3/4 In. 250.00
Blotter Ends, Adam, Signed, 12 1/4 x 2 1/4 In., Pair 200.00
Blotter Ends, Adam, Signed, 19 1/4 In., Pair 200.00
Blotter Ends, American Indian, Bronze, Gold Dore, Signed, 12 x 2 In., Pair 300.00
Blotter Ends, Grapevine, Bronze, Dark Patina, 4 Corners, 5 3/4 x 5 3/4 x 8 In. 550.00
Blotter Ends, Grapevine, Signed, 19 1/4 x 2 1/4 In., Pair 450.00
Blotter Ends, Heraldic, Green Enamel, Framed Dagger Pattern, 19 3/4 x 2 1/4 In. 350.00
Blotter Ends, Nautical, Signed, 19 x 2 1/2 In., Pair 750.00
Blotter Ends, Zodiac, Signed, 12 x 2 In., Pair 225.00
Bonbon, Bronze, Gold Dore, Scalloped Rim, Pedestal, Signed, 4 1/2 In. 150.00
Bookends, Abalone, Original Bronze Dore Patina, Signed, 5 1/2 In. 1955.00
Bookends, Border Line & Curved Line To Center, Bronze, Gold Dore, 5 x 5 3/4 In. 750.00
Bookends, Buddha, Raised Base, Bronze, Gold Dore, Signed, 6 x 5 In. 750.00
Bookends, Grapevine, Amber Slag Glass, Bronze, Gold Dore, 5 1/2 In. 1500.00
Bookends, Venetian, Bronze, Enameled, Red, Blue, & Green, Signed, 6 1/4 x 4 3/4 In. . . . 920.00
Bookends, Venetian, Bronze, Gold Dore, Signed, 5 x 6 In. 1200.00
Bookends, Zodiac, Bronze, Gold Dore, Signed, 6 x 6 In. 800.00
Bookrack, Grapevine, Green Slag Glass, Bronze, Dark Patina, Signed, 6 In. 2000.00
Bowl, Bronze, Gold Dore Patina, Impressed Mark, 9 In. 160.00
Bowl, Gilt Metal Base, Signed, Favrile, 5 x 12 1/2 In. 935.00

Box, Card, Hinged Cover, Ninth Century, Blue, Green Jewels, Signed, 4 x 1 1/2 In. 1200.00
Box, Card, Hinged Cover, Pine Needle, Green Slag Glass, Bronze, Signed, 3 x 2 x 4 In. ... 1500.00
Box, Copper Cover, Enameled, Marked, c.1913, 2 1/4 x 3 In. 8400.00
Box, Cover, Bookmark, Cedar Lining, Signed, 2 x 6 In. 1200.00
Box, Cover, Grapevine, Beaded Edge, 2 Sections, Green Slag Glass, Bronze, 9 x 7 In. ... 3500.00
Box, Glove, Grapevine, Green Slag Glass, Bronze, Marked, 13 1/4 x 4 1/4 In. 2700.00
Box, Graduate, Hinged Cover, Bronze, Gold Dore, Marked, 5 1/2 x 3 1/2 x 1 In. 450.00
Box, Grapevine, Amber Slag Glass, Bronze, Gold Dore, Marked, 1 1/2 x 4 1/4 In. 490.00
Box, Grapevine, Bronze, Gold Dore, Marked, 4 1/4 x 3 1/4 x 1 3/4 In. 460.00
Box, Handkerchief, Grapevine, Beaded Edge, Slag Glass, Bronze, 1928, 7 In. 1265.00
Box, Hinged Cover, Adam, Bronze, 5 x 2 In. 750.00
Box, Hinged Cover, American Indian, Signed, Bronze, Gold Dore, 2 x 5 In. 610.00
Box, Hinged Cover, Beaded Edge, Red, Green, Blue Enamel, 4 Ball Feet, 6 x 2 In. 900.00
Box, Hinged Cover, Grapevine, Amber Slag Glass, Bronze, Gold Dore, 6 1/2 x 4 x 3 In. .. 1500.00
Box, Hinged Cover, Spanish Pattern, Bronze, Gold Dore, 5 x 3 x 2 In. 900.00
Box, Jewel, Abalone, Bronze, Gold Dore, Velvet Tray, Signed, 4 1/2 x 2 1/2 In. 1500.00
Box, Jewel, Cover, Grapevine, Beaded Edge, Green Slag Glass, Bronze, 3 In. 3500.00
Box, Jewel, Hinged Cover, Grapevine, Bronze, 4 Ball Feet, Amber Velvet Lining, 6 In. 1500.00
Box, Jewel, Pine Needle, Green Slag Glass, April 21st 1905, 9 x 6 3/4 In. 3105.00
Box, Medallion, Bronze, Arabesque Curlicue Border, Signed, 5 5/8 In. 373.00
Box, Medallion, Bronze, Enameled, 4 1/2 x 3 1/2 x 2 In. 750.00
Box, Pine Needle, Amber Slag Glass, Bronze, Signed, 4 1/4 In. 460.00
Box, Stamp, Grapevine, Beaded Edge, Green Slag Glass, 4 x 1 1/2 In. 550.00
Box, Stamp, Grapevine, Green Slag Glass, Bronze, Brown Patina, Signed, 1 1/4 x 4 In. .. 460.00
Box, Stamp, Hinged Cover, Abalone, Bronze, 3-Section Tray, 4 x 2 x 1 1/4 In. 550.00
Box, Stamp, Hinged Cover, Zodiac, Entwined Lines, 3 Sections, 3 3/4 x 2 1/4 x 1 In. 500.00
Box, Twine, Bookmark, Bronze, Gold Dore, 6 Sides, 3 x 4 In. 1500.00
Box, Zodiac, Bronze, Gold Dore, Stamped, Tiffany Studios, 3 7/8 x 5 1/2 In. 161.00
Calendar, Abalone, Bronze, Gold Dore, Perpetual, Easel, Signed, 6 1/2 x 6 In. 950.00
Calendar, Heraldic, Silver Hobnail, Perpetual, Easel, 5 3/4 x 6 In. 750.00
Calendar Frame, Venetian, Easel Style, Bronze, Gold Dore, Polychrome, 6 1/2 x 6 In. ... 900.00
Candelabrum, 4-Light, Bronze, Green Glass Inserts, Snuffer, 15 x 14 In. 4025.00
Candle Lamp, Adjustable, Bronze Jeweled, 3 Arm, 16 3/4 In. 9600.00
Candle Lamp, Bamboo, Bronze, Glass, Ridged Shade, 15 1/4 In., Pair 9200.00
Candle Lamp, Bright Blue Iridescent, Peacock, Diamond Quilted Shade, Favrile, 14 In. ... 6000.00
Candle Lamp, Bronze, Ruffled, Pulled Feather, Glass Shades, 1928, 16 In. 4485.00
Candle Lamp, Damascene, Bronze, Favrile, c.1920, 12 1/4 In. 7200.00
Candle Lamp, Reticulated, Bronze, Green Glass, Favrile, 11 x 4 In. 4760.00
Candle Lamp, Twisted, Bronze, Gold Dore, Ruffled Shade, Favrile, 12 In., Pair 3500.00
Candlestick, Bamboo, Bronze, Spreading Tree Trunk Base, Bobeche, 10 1/2 In. 2000.00
Candlestick, Bookmark, Bronze, Gold Dore, Bobeche, 10 In., Pair 2500.00
Candlestick, Bookmark, Green Glass Blown Into Bronze, 13 In. 2000.00
Candlestick, Bookmark, Tree, Line, Scroll, Bronze, Gold Dore, 9 1/4 x 5 In. 950.00
Candlestick, Bronze, Original Green, Brown Patina, 6 x 7 In. 3335.00
Candlestick, Bronze, Patina, 3 Prong Feet, Bulbous Cup, Stamped, 16 In. 978.00
Candlestick, Enameled, Bronze, Gold Dore, Purple Disc Base, 3 1/2 In., Pair 1500.00
Candlestick, Green Glass Blown Into Bronze, Stick, 20 1/2 In. 2000.00
Candlestick, Queen Anne's Lace, Bronze, Patina, Signed, N.Y., 23 1/2 In. 5175.00
Candlestick, Queen Anne's Lace, Bronze, Signed, 1920s, 17 3/4 In., Pair 4600.00
Candlestick, Swirled Base, 3 Prong Feet, Bronze, 16 3/4 In., Pair 1955.00
Candlestick, Textured Dore Surface, Metal, Signed, Early 20th Century, 16 1/4 In. 2530.00
Canister, Cover, Bronze, Dark Patina, Signed, 3 1/2 x 3 In. 225.00
Card Case, Pencil, Ivory, Champleve Enameled Flowers, Gilt Metal, c.1880, 4 x 2 3/4 In. .. 275.00
Card Tray, Card, Opalescent Center, Bronze Rim, Signed, 8 In. 2500.00
Chandelier, 3 Fleur-De-Lis Ornaments, 3 Flower-Form Shades, 6 In. 3737.00
Chandelier, Glass Jewel Segments, Twisted & Coiled Bronze, 38 x 10 In. 7480.00
Chandelier, October Night, Bronze, Mottled Green & Brown Patina, 8 3/4 In. 9100.00
Chest, Cover, Raised Leaf & Floral Design, Pink, Blue, Rectangle Border, 3 1/2 In. 1800.00
Clock, Bhinexe Pattern, Bronze, Signed, 5 In. 2800.00
Clock, Desk, Adam, Octagon, Windup, Bronze, Gold Dore, 4 x 4 1/4 x 2 In. 1800.00
Clock, Mantel, Pink Marble Temple Form Case, Plinth Base, 13 1/8 In. 290.00
Clock, Zodiac, Bronze, Signed, 5 1/2 x 4 1/4 In. 1800.00
Cooler, Wine, Bacchanal Scene, Lion's Paw Feet, Late 1800s 9000.00

Desk Set, Abalone, Bronze, Gold Dore, 5 Piece 3190.00
Desk Set, Grapevine, Bronze, 5 Piece 1960.00
Desk Set, Heraldic, Bronze, Gold Dore, 4 Piece 2015.00
Desk Set, Pine Needle, Letter Holder, Blotter, Rocker, Inkwell, Bronze, Amber Slag Glass 1725.00
Desk Set, Pine Needle, Letter Rack, Blotter Corners, Bronze, 5 Piece 1380.00
Desk Set, Zodiac, Bronze, 6 Piece ....956.00 to 2475.00
Dish, Braided Rim, Bronze, Signed, 8 In. 85.00
Dish, Bronze, Bright Red, Royal Blue, Green Enamel, Gold Dore, Signed, 1 1/2 In. 1500.00
Dish, Bronze, Enameled Border, Gold Dore, Signed, 8 x 1 In. 1500.00
Dish, Narrow Geometric Lines, Floret Border, Bronze, Red Enamel, Gold Dore, 8 In. 550.00
Flower Frog, Gold Favrile Glass, Signed L.C.T., Favrile, 3 In. 255.00
Frame, Abalone, Bronze, Gold Dore, Oval Opening, Signed, 7 1/4 x 10 1/4 In. 2800.00
Frame, Adam, Swag, Oval, Bronze, 9 x 12 In. 1800.00
Frame, Bronze, Grapevine, Gold Dore, Signed, 9 x 7 In. 2128.00
Frame, Chinese Pattern, Bronze, Dark Patina, Easel, 8 3/4 x 7 1/4 In. 950.00
Frame, Etched Metal, Spider Web, Bronze, Green & Brown Patina, 7 x 6 In. 1380.00
Frame, Etched Metal, Spider Web, Bronze, Green & Brown Patina, 8 x 9 1/2 In. 2990.00
Frame, Graduate, Bronze, Gold Dore, Easel, Signed, 6 1/2 x 6 3/4 In. 650.00
Frame, Grapevine, Bronze, Green & Brown Patina, Signed, 6 x 7 In. 2530.00
Frame, Grapevine, Green Slag Glass, Bronze, Dark Patina, 12 x 14 In. 3500.00
Frame, Grapevine, Signed, 6 1/2 x 7 In. 770.00
Frame, Heraldic, Arms & Armor, Bronze, Gold Dore, Easel, 10 x 12 In. 1500.00
Frame, Nautical, Bronze, Rope Design, Sailboat, 7 x 6 1/4 In. 2500.00
Frame, Ninth Century, Bronze, Gold Dore, Jewels, Signed, 7 x 8 1/2 In. 1800.00
Frame, Pine Needle, Amber Slag Glass, Bronze, Signed, 9 1/2 In. 1265.00
Frame, Scroll Design, Bronze, Gold Dore, 6 x 5 1/2 x 4 1/2 In. 2200.00
Frame, Zodiac, Bronze, Patina, Signed, 8 1/2 x 8 In. 1955.00
Humidor, Cedar Lining, With Dehumidifying Unit, 1960, 2 1/2 x 6 In. 980.00
Humidor, Cover, Pine Needle, Green Slag Glass, Bronze, Signed, 6 1/2 In. 3200.00
Inkwell, American Indian, Raised Indian Masks, Glass Insert, Signed, 5 1/2 In. 650.00
Inkwell, Bell Shape, Dome Cover, 3-Leaf Finial, Bronze, Insert, Favrile, 4 1/2 In. 2000.00
Inkwell, Bronze Cover, 8-Sided Gourd, Paper Label, Late 19th Century, 5 1/2 In. 8050.00
Inkwell, Cover, Glass Blown Into Bronze, Glass Insert, Signed, 7 In. 2000.00
Inkwell, Flowing Tray, Raised Swirls, Bronze, Gold Dore, 2 1/2 x 8 x 6 In. 1500.00
Inkwell, Grapevine, Amber Slag, Glass, Bronze, Patina, 6 3/4 In. 980.00
Inkwell, Grapevine, Square, Ball Feet, Green Slag Glass, Bronze, Dark Patina, 4 x 3 In. .. 800.00
Inkwell, Hinged Cover, Abalone, Line, Leaf Design, Bronzed, Gold Dore, 3 1/2 x 3 In. .. 750.00
Inkwell, Hinged Cover, American Indian, Bronze, Signed, 3 1/2 x 5 1/2 In. 650.00
Inkwell, Hinged Cover, Bookmark, Bronze, 8 Sides, Gold Dore, 4 1/2 In. ....500.00 to 750.00
Inkwell, Hinged Cover, Graduate, Bronze, Gold Dore, Square, 4 x 2 In. 450.00
Inkwell, Hinged Cover, Grapevine, 3 1/4 In. 730.00
Inkwell, Hinged Cover, Grapevine, Bronze, Dark Patina, 7 x 3 In. 1800.00
Inkwell, Hinged Cover, Heraldic, Round, Green Enamel, Silver Shield, 3 1/2 x 3 In. 750.00
Inkwell, Hinged Cover, Nautical, Bronze, Dolphin Corners, Signed, 5 1/4 x 3 1/2 In. 1800.00
Inkwell, Hinged Cover, Sunburst, Ribbed, Floral, Signed, 4 x 3 x 2 1/2 In. 550.00
Inkwell, Pine Needle, Green Slag Glass, Bronze, Ball Feet, Signed, 4 x 3 In. .....575.00 to 800.00
Inkwell, Venetian, Bronze, Gold Dore, 3 x 3 x 2 1/2 In. 650.00
Inkwell, Zodiac, Crab Cover, Bronze, Green Patina, Glass Insert, 4 x 4 x 2 In. 385.00
Inkwell, Zodiac, Line Design, Bronze, Gold Dore, 10 3/4 In. 1200.00
Lamp, 3-Light, Lily, Adjustable, Bronze, Marked, 22 1/2 In. 2760.00
Lamp, 3-Light, Lily, Intaglio Finish, Marked L.C.T., 22 In. 4800.00
Lamp, 3-Light, Lily, Marked L.C.T., 1899, 8 1/2 In. 5100.00
Lamp, 7-Light, Lily, Favrile, Bronze, Gold Dore, c.1920, 19 In. 12600.00
Lamp, Abalone, Amber Slag Glass, Bronze, Gold Dore, Signed, 9 In. 4000.00
Lamp, Abalone, Etched Amber Slag Glass, Curved Arm, Bronze, Gold Dore, 9 In. 4000.00
Lamp, Acorn, Amber Slag Glass, Bronze Beveled Column Base, 1900, 21 In. 12320.00
Lamp, Acorn, Bronze, Brown & Green Patina, Favrile, c.1920, 27 x 16 In. 11400.00
Lamp, Acorn, Green Slag Glass, White, Gold Acorns, Signed, 16 In. 14560.00
Lamp, Banded Dogwood, Domed Shade, White, Green, 16 In. 26300.00
Lamp, Banded Dogwood, White Blossoms, Geometric Green Glass, 16 In. 4480.00
Lamp, Base, Glass Blown Into Bronze, Brown Patina, Favrile, c.1920, 25 x 13 In. 29500.00
Lamp, Beehive Shape, Pulled Feathers, Gold Iridescent, Rich Brown Patina, 13 In. 12320.00
Lamp, Bell Shade, Grapevine, Green Slag Glass, 13 1/2 In. 4000.00

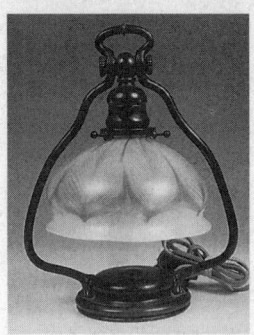

Tiffany, Lamp, Pulled
Green Feather Shade,
Bronze, Harp
Support, 12 In.

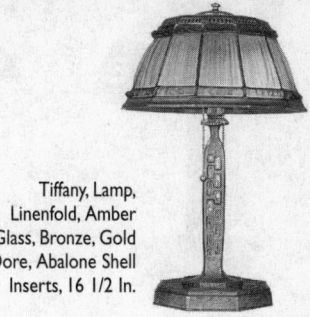

Tiffany, Lamp,
Linenfold, Amber
Glass, Bronze, Gold
Dore, Abalone Shell
Inserts, 16 1/2 In.

Lamp, Bronze, Adjustable, 5 Spade Feet, Patina, 55 In. 1410.00
Lamp, Bronze, Favrile Green Shade, Signed, 5 In. 2415.00
Lamp, Bronze, Gold Dore, Harp Support, Green Favrile Shade, Signed, 7 3/4 In. 6500.00
Lamp, Chinese Pattern, Amber Slag Glass, 8-Sided Shade, 17 In. 6000.00
Lamp, Conical Geometric Shade, White, Green Opalescent, 20 In. 15120.00
Lamp, Conical Shade, Blue, Pale Purple Blossoms, Leaves, Yellow Centers, 18 In. 3600.00
Lamp, Conical Shade, Green Slag Glass, Geometric Design, 20 In. 16800.00
Lamp, Conical Shade, White, Enameled, Bronze, Base, Signed, 14 In. 3080.00
Lamp, Crocus, Bronze, Brown Patina, Finial, Favrile, c.1920, 23 1/2 x 16 In. 12600.00
Lamp, Cut Jonquils, Leaves, Favrile, 14 1/4 x 7 In. 5750.00
Lamp, Daffodil, Studio Sample, Favrile, 11 3/4 x 10 1/4 In. 7200.00
Lamp, Damascene, Adjustable, Bronze, Gold Dore, Favrile, 23 x 8 1/4 In. 4025.00
Lamp, Damascene, Bronze, 3 Arms, Favrile, 15 In. 7500.00
Lamp, Damascene, Bronze, Finial, Mottled Patina, 17 3/4 In. 7800.00
Lamp, Damascene, Gold, Green, Favrile, Bronze, 13 In. 4025.00
Lamp, Damascene, Green, Gold, Bronze, Favrile, 55 1/2 In. 7475.00
Lamp, Damascene, Green, Platinum, Blue Highlights, Favrile, 23 x 10 In. 9200.00
Lamp, Damascene, Green, Zodiac Bronze Base, Signed, 13 x 7 In. 6325.00
Lamp, Damascene, Ribbed Shade, Favrile, Connected Lotus Buds Base, Signed, 55 x 10 In. 9800.00
Lamp, Domed Shade, Favrile Glass Prisms, Gilt Bronze Base, 16 1/4 In. 2876.00
Lamp, Domed Shade, Geometric Border, Bronze, Green Patina, Spade Feet, 54 In. 2530.00
Lamp, Domed Shade, Green Geometric Glass, Floral Turtleback Tiles, 16 In. 16576.00
Lamp, Domed Shade, Green Slag Glass, Geometric Design, 16 In. 7840.00
Lamp, Fabrique, Bronze, Gold Dore, Harp Support, Green Panels, 19 1/2 In. 6000.00
Lamp, Geometric Border, Bronze, Gold Dore, Harp Support, Signed, 17 1/2 In. 4025.00
Lamp, Gold Iridescent Glass Base, Swirling Ribs, Rippled Shade, 13 In. 3740.00
Lamp, Gold Iridescent Swirls, Bronze Base, 10 x 15 In. 3850.00
Lamp, Gold Iridescent Zipper, Favrile, Arabian Style, 15 In. 5000.00
Lamp, Intaglio Finish, Bronze Twisted Water Lily Base, Signed, 16 In. 3600.00
Lamp, Intaglio, Bronze, Gold Dore, 29 In. 7475.00
Lamp, Leaf, Vine, Mottled Yellow, White, Green, Leaded, 16 x 22 In. 8625.00
Lamp, Lily, Gold Glass, Adjustable, Bronze, Signed, 20 In. 9200.00
Lamp, Linenfold, 10 Panels, Amber Glass, Signed, 1947, 15 In. 8960.00
Lamp, Linenfold, Amber Glass, Bronze, Gold Dore, Abalone Shell Inserts, 16 1/2 In. *Illus* 9200.00
Lamp, Mosque, Green Pulled Feathers, Blue, Gold Iridescent, Signed, 8 1/2 In. 2800.00
Lamp, Oak Leaf Border, Domed Shade, Favrile, Bronze, 1920, 24 1/2 x 18 3/4 In. 6720.00
Lamp, Pine Needle, Green Bent Glass Panels, Signed, 12 In. 12720.00
Lamp, Pine Needle, Green Slag Glass, Bronze, Harp Support, Signed, 18 In. 4000.00
Lamp, Poinsettia, 21 In. ....*Illus* 36800.00
Lamp, Pomegranate, Domed Shade, Gold Fruit, Geometric Band, 16 In. 16800.00
Lamp, Pulled Feathers, Bell Shape, Gold Iridescent, Bronze, Gold Dore, Signed, 14 In. ... 3920.00
Lamp, Pulled Green & Gold Feathers, 1920s, 13 In. 5750.00
Lamp, Pulled Green Feather Shade, Bronze, Harp Support, 12 In. ....*Illus* 4760.00
Lamp, Queen Anne's Lace, Bronze, Favrile Glass, 15 1/2 In. ....* 6900.00
Lamp, Spider Web, 15 1/2 In. ....*Illus* 34500.00
Lamp, Swing, Bronze, Art Glass, Patinated, Iridescent Gold Shade, 6 1/2 In. 1725.00
Lamp, Tyler Scroll Design, 27 In. ....*Illus* 13800.00

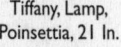

Tiffany, Lamp,
Poinsettia, 21 In.

Tiffany, Lamp,
Spider Web, 15 1/2 In.

Tiffany, Lamp,
Tyler Scroll Design, 27 In.

Lamp, Weight-Balance Base, Bronze, Patina, Favrile Glass Shade, 7 x 16 In. 5313.00
Lamp, Weight-Balance, Adjustable Arm, 5 Spade Feet, Signed, 54 1/2 In. 3740.00
Lamp, Weight-Balance, Bronze, Abalone Inserts, Signed, 9 In. 4000.00
Lamp, Weight-Balance, Damascene, Green Glass, Bronze, 7 In. 9620.00
Lamp, Weight-Balance, Domed Shade, Amber Pulled Feathers, Spade Feet, 55 In. 8625.00
Lamp, Weight-Balance, Gold Iridescent, Bronze, Gold Dore, Signed, 7 In. 5040.00
Lamp, Weight-Balance, Intaglio, Favrile, Bronze, c.1920, 52 1/2 x 9 3/4 In. 7800.00
Lamp, Weight-Balance, Leaf Design, Bronze, Signed, 15 In. 6000.00
Lamp, Weight-Balance, Metal Shade, Geometric Border, Bronze, 1930s, 17 1/4 In. 5750.00
Lamp Base, 3-Light, Shell, Vine Scroll Design, Bronze, 25 x 9 In. 2310.00
Lamp Base, Green, Brown, Red, Yellow Luster, Original Brass Font, 13 1/2 x 8 In. 1240.00
Lamp Base, Red Glass, Signed L.C.T., Favrile, 11 In. 3640.00
Letter Holder, Graduate, Bronze, Gold Dore, Ball Feet, 6 1/4 x 5 In. 500.00
Letter Holder, Ninth Century, Bronze, Blue, Green Jewels, Signed, 4 1/2 x 2 1/2 In. 950.00
Letter Holder, Zodiac, Bronze, Gold Dore, 4 1/2 x 1 1/2 In. 750.00
Letter Opener, Adam, Bronze, Gold Dore, Curved Handle, Signed, 10 In. . . . . . . .250.00 to 350.00
Letter Opener, Chinese Pattern, Bronze, Gold Dore, Signed, 11 In. 250.00
Letter Opener, Grapevine, Amber Slag Glass, Bronze, Gold Dore, Signed, 9 1/4 In. 550.00
Letter Opener, Pine Needle, Bronze, Gold Dore, Signed, 7 In. 550.00
Letter Opener, Pine Needle, Green Slag Glass, Beaded, Signed, 9 1/4 In. 550.00
Letter Opener, Scissors, Bronze, Dark Patina, Signed, 10 3/4 In. 2300.00
Letter Opener, Zodiac, Bronze, Gold Dore, Signed, 10 1/2 In. 250.00
Letter Rack, Adam, Bronze, Gold Dore, 6 In. 700.00
Letter Rack, American Indian, 2 Sections, Allover Pattern, Signed, 11 In. 900.00
Letter Rack, Bookmark, Bronze, Gold Dore, 2 Sections, 9 1/4 x 1 1/4 x 5 1/2 In. 950.00
Letter Rack, Grapevine, Green Slag Glass, Bronze, Dark Patina, 8 1/2 x 3 1/2 In. 1800.00
Letter Rack, Spanish Pattern, Bronze, Gold Dore, Signed, 3 1/3 In. 1500.00
Letter Rack, Venetian, Line & Scroll, Divided, Bronze, Gold Dore, 10 x 3 x 6 In. 950.00
Letter Scale, Bookmark, Leaf & Branch, Blue Enamel, Bronze, Gold Dore 1500.00
Letter Scale, Pine Needle, Amber Slag Glass, Bronze, Signed, 3 1/2 In. 1200.00
Letter Scale, Pine Needle, Green Slag Glass, Bronze, Dark Patina, Signed, 3 In. 1500.00
Lighter, Cigar, Aladdin's Lamp Shape, Bronze, Snuffer On Chain, Signed 1500.00
Magnifying Glass, Bookmark, Bronze, Gold Dore, 4 x 8 3/4 In. 1500.00
Magnifying Glass, Venetian, Bronze, Gold Dore, 4 x 9 In. 1500.00
Magnifying Glass, Zodiac, Beaded Edge Handle, 8 3/4 In. 1500.00
Match Safe, Grapevine, Amber Slag Glass, Bronze, Gold Dore, Signed, 4 x 5 In. 632.00
Memoranda Pad, Bookmark, Bronze, Gold Dore, Signed, 4 1/2 x 8 1/2 In. 550.00
Memoranda Pad, Hinged Cover, Bookmark, Bronze, Gold Dore, 4 x 8 1/4 In. 550.00
Memoranda Pad, Spanish, Bronze, Gold Dore, Signed, 4 1/2 x 7 1/2 In. 650.00
Memoranda Pad, Venetian, Bronze, Gold Dore, Signed, 6 x 5 x 4 In. 1200.00
Mirror, Table, Pinecone, Green Slag Glass, Bronze, 9 x 7 In. 173.00
Paper Clip, Abalone, Bronze, Gold Dore, Signed, 2 x 2 3/4 In. 550.00
Paper Clip, Adam, Sunburst, Floral Wreath, Ribbed, Bronze, Gold Dore, 2 1/2 x 4 In. . . . 350.00
Paper Clip, American Indian, Raised Mask, Geometric, Bronze, Gold Dore, 2 3/4 x 4 In. . . 350.00
Paper Clip, Grapevine, Amber Slag Glass, Bronze, Gold Dore, 2 1/2 x 3 3/4 In. 450.00

Paper Clip, Pine Needle, Green Slag Glass, Bronze, 2 1/2 x 3 3/4 In. 450.00
Paperweight, Graduate, With Bill File, Bronze, Gold Dore, 8 Sides, Signed 450.00
Paperweight, Lioness, Recumbent, Bronze, Signed, 5 In. 700.00
Paperweight, Owl, Bronze, Signed, 3 In. 850.00
Paperweight, Pine Needle, Green Slag Glass, Bronze, Knob Top, Signed, 3 1/2 In. 345.00 to 450.00
Paperweight, Pine Needle, With Bill File, Green Slag Glass, Bronze, 7 1/2 In. 750.00
Paperweight, Zodiac, Bronze, Dark Patina, Signed 500.00
Pen Brush, Ninth Century, Blue, Green Jewels, Signed, 3 In. 550.00
Pen Brush, Venetian, Bronze, Gold Dore, 8 Sides, Signed 450.00
Pen Tray, Adam, 3 Sections, 9 1/4 x 2 3/4 In. 250.00
Pen Tray, Grapevine, Green Slag Glass, Bronze Ball Feet, 9 1/2 x 2 3/4 In. 450.00
Pen Tray, Ninth Century, Bronze, Gold Dore, Raised Edge, 3 1/4 x 9 3/4 In. 450.00
Pen Tray, Pine Needle, Bronze, Gold Dore, 9 3/4 In. 405.00
Pen Tray, Shell Shape, Bronze, Signed, 9 1/2 x 2 3/4 In. 750.00
Pen Tray, Zodiac, Bronze, Gold Dore, Signed, 9 3/4 x 3 In. . . . . .172.00 to 200.00
Penholder, Adam, Pale Blue, Pink, Bronze, Gold Dore, 7 x 4 1/2 x 1 In. 650.00
Planter, Grapevine, Amber Slag Glass, Bronze, Gold Dore, Signed, 10 1/2 x 8 In. 2500.00
Plate, Bronze, Geometric Rim, 9 3/4 x 1 In. 385.00
Platter, Bronze, Gold Dore Finish, Signed, 8 In. 195.00
Scissors, Line Design, Bronze, Gold Dore, Signed, Numbered, 9 In. 750.00
Sconce, Amber Glass, Red Prisms, Favrile, Bronze, Beaded D Shape Standard, 10 In. 4025.00
Sconce, Gold Iridescent Glass, Teardrop Clusters, Bronze, Patina, 22 In. 2875.00
Shade, Pine Needle, Bronze, Gold Dore, Silk Liner, Signed, 3 1/4 x 5 1/4 In. 230.00
Smoking Stand, Overlapping Leaves, Bronze, Gold Dore, Green Enamel, 25 In. 1800.00
Tea Screen, Pine Needle, Green Slag Glass, 3 Sections, Bronze, Ball Feet, 12 x 7 In. 1500.00
Thermometer, Grapevine, Bronze, Green Slag Glass, Signed, 8 1/4 x 3 3/4 In. 1800.00
Tray, Art Nouveau Design, Bronze, Gold Dore, Round, Signed, 10 In. 250.00
Tray, Bronze, Bookmark, Bronze, Gold Dore, Signed, 13 3/4 x 8 In. 1200.00
Tray, Bronze, Gold Dore, Blue Enamel, Geometric Lines, 5 Button Feet, 10 In. 550.00
Tray, Bronze, Gold Dore, Enameled Pink Flowers, Signed, Round, 8 1/4 In. 550.00
Tray, Bronze, Gold Dore, Round, Stamped, 6 3/4 In. 115.00
Tray, Raised Leaf & Line Border, Bronze, Gold Dore, Abalone Inserts, 14 In. 800.00
Trivet, Cypriote, Teal, Purple, Bronze Mount, 4 Ball Feet, Square, 6 In. . . . . . . .1495.00 to 2500.00
Vase, Bronze, Dark Gold Dore, Thin Diagonal Ribs, 3 1/2 x 1 3/4 x 1 In. 225.00
Vase, Flower-Form, Amber Iridescent, Amber Dome Foot, 1918, 14 1/2 In. 1500.00
Vase, Sterling Silver Collar, Intaglio Cut, 12 7/8 In. 5500.00
TIFFANY GLASS, Bonbon, Gold Iridescent, Lily Pads, Gold Threading, Blue Green, 4 x 2 In. 400.00
Bowl, Amber Iridescent, Ribbed Disc Base, Signed, 2 1/4 In. 460.00
Bowl, Blue, Pinched Sides, Signed, Favrile, 4 5/8 x 2 3/8 In. 635.00
Bowl, Bright Gold, Blue Highlights, Favrile, Signed, 3 1/2 x 10 In. 690.00
Bowl, Domed Shape, Blue Iridescent, Circular Base, Signed, 1 1/2 x 4 In. 520.00
Bowl, Flared Rim, Diamond Quilted, Blue, Signed, 10 1/8 In. 520.00
Bowl, Flower Frog, Green Leaves, Vines, Blue, Favrile, 4 1/2 x 12 1/2 In. 2300.00
Bowl, Flower Frog, Peacock Blue Iridescent, 2 Tiers, 12 In. 3500.00
Bowl, Gold Iridescent, Flared, Ribbed, Favrile, 3 1/4 x 4 1/2 In. 950.00
Bowl, Gold Iridescent, Green Lily Pads, Signed, 2 1/2 x 11 In. 1380.00
Bowl, Gold Iridescent, Ruffled Edge, Gold, Steel Blue, Favrile, 4 x 2 In. 400.00
Bowl, Gold Iridescent, Signed, Favrile, 2 1/2 x 6 In. 920.00
Bowl, Gold Iridescent, Signed, Favrile, 2 x 4 3/4 In. 345.00
Bowl, Gold, 10 Ribs, Favrile, 7 1/2 x 2 7/8 In. 660.00
Bowl, Gold, Favrile, Signed, 14 1/2 In. 980.00
Bowl, Gold, Lobed, Favrile, Signed, L.C.T., 5 1/2 In. 460.00
Bowl, Gold, Pink, Blue Highlights, Tooled Lip, Favrile, 3 7/8 x 1 3/4 In. 440.00
Bowl, Gold, Platinum Iridescent, Favrile, 5 1/2 In. 490.00
Bowl, Grape Leaves & Vine, Butterfly In Flight, Signed, 3 1/2 x 8 In. 1955.00
Bowl, Green, Intaglio Trailing Vine, Flowers, Iridescent Blue, Favrile, 10 x 3 1/2 In. 1200.00
Bowl, Laurel Leaves, Opalescent Optic, Electric Blue, 6 1/4 In. 950.00
Bowl, Peacock Blue, 10 Vertical Swirl Ribs, Blue Iridescent, 3 1/2 x 10 3/4 In. 3450.00
Bowl, Pulled Green Stripes, Gold To Clear, Ruffled Edge, 5 1/2 In. 805.00
Bowl, Stretched Cobalt Blue, Feather Ribbed, Signed, 8 1/2 In. 400.00
Bowl, Victoria, Blue, Purple Highlights, Gold Iridescent, Signed, 3 x 6 In. 1095.00
Cake Plate, Shell Shape, Scalloped, Ruffled Edge, N.Y., 5 3/4 x 12 1/2 In. 2185.00
Candlestick, Gold, Favrile, Signed, 1817, 4 In., Pair 1150.00

Candlestick, Green Reticulated Glass, Bronze, 3 Feet, 10 In., Pair 3640.00
Centerpiece, Blue Butterfly, Green Lily Pads, Favrile, 5 1/2 x 13 In. 3565.00
Claret, Favrile, Gold, Blue Ground, Signed, 7 1/4 In. 316.00
Compote, Amber, Gold Iridescent, Ribbed, 1920s, 6 1/4 In. 1035.00
Compote, Blue, Iridescent, Pedestal, Favrile, 8 In. 1500.00
Compote, Double Gourd, Ribbed, Scalloped Rim, 3 3/4 In. 750.00
Compote, Geometric, Beaded, Pedestal, Gold, Etched, 10 In. 275.00
Compote, Gold Iridescent, Intaglio Leaf & Vine, Pedestal, Favrile, 4 x 4 1/2 In. 1200.00
Compote, Gold, Ribs, Expanded Diamonds, Favrile, Marked, 1726, 6 1/4 x 5 7/8 In. 1045.00
Compote, Intaglio Grape, Vine Interior, Gold, Favrile, 3 1/2 In. 575.00
Compote, Iridescent Yellow, Diamond Optic, Favrile, 6 1/4 x 2 In. 900.00
Compote, Peacock Eyes & Trailing, Gold Iridescent, Signed, 8 x 4 In. 550.00
Compote, Pulled Feathers, Green Opalescent Foot, Signed, 1884, 6 x 6 1/4 In. 980.00
Compote, Scalloped Edge, Gold, Favrile, Signed, 4 x 7 3/4 In. 862.00
Cordial, Green, Purple Highlights, Favrile, 4 1/2 x 1 1/2 In. 400.00
Cup, Gold Iridescent, 3 Applied Handles, Favrile, 4 3/8 In. 276.00
Cup, White, Gold Zigzag, Fuchsia Interior, Gold Scroll Handle, Favrile, 2 In. 460.00
Decanter, Twisted, Prunts, Gold, Favrile, 10 1/2 In. 2070.00
Finger Bowl, Gold Iridescent, Signed, 2 1/4 x 6 1/2 In. 460.00
Finger Bowl, Prunts, Twisted, Gold, Favrile, 2 1/2 x 5 3/4 In. 460.00
Finger Bowl, Underplate, Gold Iridescent, Purple, Blue, Favrile, 6 1/2 In., Pair 840.00
Finger Bowl, Underplate, Green, Signed, 6 3/4 In. 575.00
Goblet, Favrile, Tapered Knop Stem, Signed, 6 1/2 In. 345.00
Goblet, Gold Opalescent, Diagonal Rib Stem, Iridescent, 7 1/2 In., Pair 1500.00
Goblet, Light Green, Favrile, Signed, L.C. Tiffany, 6 1/8 In. 775.00
Goblet, Purple, White Opalescent Leaves, Pastel Colors, Signed, 8 1/2 x 4 In. 1150.00
Liqueur Set, Pulled Design, Amber, Signed, 2 In., 6 Piece 975.00
Nut Dish, Gold, Favrile, 1 1/4 x 4 In. 325.00
Pitcher, Grapes & Vines, Gold, Signed, 4 In. 1380.00
Punch Cup, Gold Iridescent, Pods & Trailing Vines, Handle, Favrile, 2 x 3 In. 750.00
Rose Bowl, Platinum & Gold Iridescent, Intaglio Leaves, Vines, Signed, 8 1/2 In. 1150.00
Salt, Amber Iridescent, Ruffled Edge, Signed, 3 In. 230.00
Salt, Elephant, Gold Iridescent, Violet, Blue, Diagonal Ribs, Favrile, 1 1/2 x 2 1/2 In. 1200.00
Salt, Gold Iridescent, Ribbed, Pedestal, Favrile, 1 1/2 x 2 1/4 In. 350.00
Salt, Gold Iridescent, Standing Twists, Favrile, 1 1/4 x 2 In. 350.00
Salt, Gold Iridescent, Trailing Vines, Signed, 1 1/4 x 2 1/4 In. 550.00
Salt, Tapered, 4 Scroll Legs, 8 Sides, Favrile, Signed L.C.T., 2 1/8 x 1 1/2 In., Pair 215.00
Salt, Twisted, Prunt, Gold, Favrile, Signed, 1 x 1 3/4 In. 316.00
Scarab, Red Iridescent, Favrile, Signed, 3/4 In. 150.00
Shade, Blue Iridescent, Green Highlights, Onionskin Edge, Signed L.C.T. 1064.00
Shade, Geometric, Green Slag Glass, Leaded, 5 x 12 In. 5760.00
Shade, Orange Dragonfly, Favrile, 10 x 8 In. 4480.00
Shade, Pulled Feathers, Swirl, Globe Shape, Bronze Frame, Favrile, 6 x 13 In. 2800.00
Sherbet, Favrile, Gold, Pink Highlights, 3 3/8 In. 250.00
Sherbet, Gold, Iridescent, Sample, A.J. Nash, Favrile, 3 1/2 x 3 3/4 In. 405.00
Tile, Blue Iridescent, 2 3/4 x 5 1/4 In. 230.00
Tile, Iridescent Swirls, Blue, Purple, 4 In. 400.00
Toothpick, Iridescent Gold, Flared Rim, Pinched Sides, 3 In. 290.00
Tumbler, Whiskey, Gold Iridescent, Blue, Silver Accents, Pinched, Favrile, 2 In., Pair ... 235.00
Tumbler, Whiskey, Gold Iridescent, Raised Pigtails, Violet Highlights, 1 3/4 In. 250.00
Vase, 2 Pulled Handles, Favrile, Signed, 6 1/2 x 2 1/2 In. 920.00
Vase, Agate, Brown, Tan Neck, Stripes, Signed, Favrile, 9 In. 10640.00
Vase, Amber, Pulled Prunts On Border, Gold Luster, Signed, 1930s, 3 1/4 In. 375.00
Vase, Band Of Turquoise, Green Design, Zigzag, Deep Honey Amber Glass, 9 x 5 In. 3680.00
Vase, Blue, Gold Iridescent, Favrile, 6 1/2 In. 1495.00
Vase, Blue, Purple Butterfly Highlights Iridescent, Favrile, 2 1/2 x 3 In. 748.00
Vase, Bright Peacock Blue Iridescent, Green Lily Pads, Favrile, 12 x 2 In. 3500.00
Vase, Bud, Gold Iridescent, Enameled, Favrile, 1920 .... 1400.00
Vase, Corona, Silver Pulled Feathers, Green, Gold Throat, 8 3/4 In. 2090.00
Vase, Cypriote, Brilliant Blue Interior, Handles, Agate Base, Signed, 3 In. 3100.00
Vase, Flower-Form, Blue Highlights, Gold, Favrile, Signed, 12 3/4 In. 1955.00
Vase, Flower-Form, Gold Iridescent Interior, Signed, LCT, Favrile, 15 In. 1680.00
Vase, Flower-Form, Gold Iridescent, 5-Fold Flare, Pedestal Base, Favrile, 4 x 5 1/2 In. 1800.00

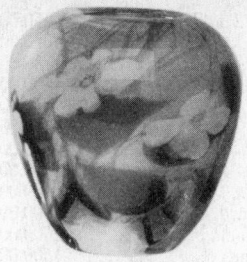

**Never cut a matchbook
or paste the matchbook
into a scrapbook. It
destroys the value.
Remove the staple and
the matches.**

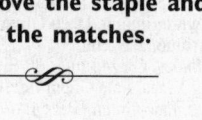

Tiffany Glass, Vase, Paperweight,
Flowers, Deep Green &
Amber Iridescent, 5 In.

Tiffany Glass, Vase,
Peacock Feather,
15 In.

Vase, Flower-Form, Gold Iridescent, Signed, 12 1/2 In.	1725.00
Vase, Flower-Form, Pale Yellow, Signed, 16 In.	4480.00
Vase, Gold Iridescent Pulled Feathers, White Ground, Gold Foot, Signed, 12 1/2 In.	1725.00
Vase, Gold Iridescent, 6-Sided Opening, Ribbed, Violet, Blue, 6 3/4 x 2 3/4 In.	800.00
Vase, Gold Iridescent, 6-Sided Top, Favrile, 6 3/4 In.	800.00
Vase, Gold Iridescent, Bulbous, Prunts Around, Signed, 7 x 3 1/2 In.	1500.00
Vase, Gold Iridescent, Chain Link Pattern Center, Prunts, Favrile, 7 x 3 1/2 In.	1500.00
Vase, Gold Iridescent, Green Leaf & Vines, Bulbous, Favrile, 6 1/2 In.	1800.00
Vase, Gold Iridescent, Green Leaves & Vines, Narrow Neck, Favrile, 5 3/4 In.	1800.00
Vase, Gold Iridescent, Pinched, Favrile, 3 x 4 In.	920.00
Vase, Gold Iridescent, Pulled Green Leaves, Trailing Vine, Favrile, 6 In.	1800.00
Vase, Gold Iridescent, Red, Orange, Green Pulled Design, 5 In.	3920.00
Vase, Gold Iridescent, Rounded Ribbed Body, Blue, Violet, Flared Top, 4 x 2 1/2 In.	750.00
Vase, Gold, Deep Pink Highlights, Favrile, 5 1/2 In.	550.00
Vase, Gold, Flared Neck, 3 Pointed Openings, 11 In.	1800.00
Vase, Gold, Green Hooked Stripes, Favrile, 2 1/2 In.	1100.00
Vase, Gold, Iidescent, Ribbed, Pedestal Foot, Favrile, 11 1/2 In.	1725.00
Vase, Gold, Lavender, Favrile, 7 1/2 In.	290.00
Vase, Gold, Pinched Waist, Firing Line Base, Favrile, 10 1/2 In.	520.00
Vase, Gold, Platinum, Pulled Top, 3 Panels Base, Favrile, 2 3/4 In.	635.00
Vase, Green Millefiori, Blossoms, Silver Blue Iridescent, Favrile, 7 x 4 In.	4000.00
Vase, Green, Brown, Vertical Bands, Bulbous To Narrow Top, Favrile, 2 1/4 In.	2500.00
Vase, Green, White Millefiori Insets, Silver Inclusions, Signed, 3 1/2 In.	5750.00
Vase, Jack-In-The-Pulpit, Ribbed Onion Form, Favrile, 10 In.	7800.00
Vase, Jack-In-The-Pulpit, Vase, Rainbow Iridescent, Signed, 17 1/2 x 9 1/2 In.	4265.00
Vase, Paperweight, Flowers, Deep Green & Amber Iridescent, 5 In. .....*Illus*	3575.00
Vase, Paperweight, St. Louis Universal Exposition, 1904, 4 3/4 In.	8337.00
Vase, Peacock Blue Base, Gold Iridescent At Top, Favrile, 11 x 2 In.	1800.00
Vase, Peacock Blue, Favrile, 1 3/4 x 1/4 In.	1200.00
Vase, Peacock Blue, Flared Flattened Top, Pedestal, Favrile, 6 3/4 x 6 In.	2800.00
Vase, Peacock Blue, Leaf & Vine, Green, Purple, Flower Frog, Favrile, 4 x 6 In.	2500.00
Vase, Peacock Feather, 15 In. .....*Illus*	18700.00
Vase, Pulled Green Feathers, Ivory Ground, Bronze Foot, 12 1/2 In.	2645.00
Vase, Pulled Green, Gold Feathers, Green, Ivory Ground, Pinched, Signed, 12 In.	8050.00
Vase, Pulled Green, Smoky & Iridescent Ground, Pinched, 5 1/2 In.	1725.00
Vase, Pulled Hearts & Trailing Vines, Gold Iridescent, Rolled Rim, Favrile, 12 In.	5060.00
Vase, Pulled Hearts & Trailing Vines, Green, Orange Ground, 8 1/2 In.	2800.00
Vase, Tapering Cylindrical Form, 2 Loop Handles, Favrile, Label, 4 In.	402.00
Vase, Trumpet, Gold Iridescent, Signed, 10 In.	2300.00
Vase, Trumpet, Iridescent Gold, Intaglio, Inlay, Favrile, 12 In.	5750.00
Vase, Trumpet, White, Green Pulled Feathers, Signed, 8 In.	1275.00
Window, Lotus, Bamboo, Favrile, c.1920, 60 x 20 In.	7800.00
TIFFANY GOLD, Flask, Pocket, 1920, 6 1/4 x 4 1/4 x 10 In.	260.00
Spoon, Coffee, Floral, Foliate Handles, 1910, 18K, 12 Piece	1800.00
TIFFANY POTTERY, Bottle, Green Matte Crystalline Glaze, 11 x 5 In.	750.00
Bowl, Raised Fish, Shell, Black, Green, Brown Glaze, 3 In.	2000.00

Dish, Gold Iridescent, Blue Glaze, Raised, Ruffled Edge, Favrile, 2 x 2 3/4 In. 450.00
Vase, Artichoke Form, Bronze, 11 In. 8050.00
Vase, Bisque, Cherry Blossoms, Reticulated, 5 1/2 In. 1725.00
Vase, Black Over Purple Textured Glaze, Small Opening, 4 1/2 x 2 In. 1500.00
Vase, Blue & Green Mottled Glaze, Signed, 4 3/4 In. 2070.00
Vase, Embossed Branches Of Berries, Signed, 8 1/4 In. 747.00
Vase, Embossed Flowers, Blue, Green Mottled Glaze, 7 In. 2300.00
Vase, Green Raised Leaf, Yellow & Brown Ground, Ruffled, Signed, 4 1/4 In. 3600.00
Vase, Green Spatters, Olive Green, Signed, 6 x 3 In. 1500.00
Vase, Green Spatters, Red, Brown Dripping, Deep Olive Ground, Signed, 6 In. 1500.00
Vase, Leaves, Green Interior, Bisque, 7 1/2 In. 2000.00
Vase, Purple, Green & Black Shades, Glazed Interior, Signed, 4 1/2 In. 1500.00
Vase, Raised Blossoms, Trailing Vines, Pale Green Interior, Signed, 13 1/4 In. 1800.00
Vase, Raised Carved Leaf Collar, Pale Green Glaze Exterior & Interior, 4 In. 950.00
Vase, Raised Flowers, Yellow Glaze Interior, Bisque, 5 1/2 x 10 In. 2900.00
Vase, Raised Tufted Floral Design, Light Green Leaves, Ivory Glaze, 1906, 7 1/8 In. 1610.00
Vase, Scalloped Rim, Pale Green Crackle, Pale Yellow Tendrils, 10 In. 3500.00
Vase, Tan Rim, Blue, Green, Blue, Purple Interior, 4 3/4 x 4 1/2 In. 2000.00
TIFFANY SILVER, Asparagus Fork, Colonial Pattern, Monogram, Marked, Pat. 1885, 9 1/2 In. 875.00
Asparagus Tongs, Engraved Stag Crest, 7 1/2 In. 950.00
Beaker, Leather Travel Case, 1930, 2 Piece 230.00
Berry Spoon, Blackberry, Shaped Bowl, c.1891, 9 1/2 In. 1200.00
Berry Spoon, Florentine Pattern, Monogram, Marked, 9 1/2 In. 775.00
Berry Spoon, Strawberry Pattern, Marked, 9 1/2 In. 850.00
Bowl, Centerpiece, Repousse Morning Glory, Leaf, 8 1/2 x 10 In. 1430.00
Bowl, Chrysanthemums, Turned-Out Rim, 12 In. 1380.00
Bowl, Clover Edge, Monogram, c.1895, 10 1/2 In. 1250.00
Bowl, Enameled, Squares & Stylized Flowers Interior, c.1925, 9 In. 690.00
Bowl, Fruit, Presentation, Circular, 1933, 9 1/2 In. 490.00
Bowl, Fruit, Reticulated Edge, Octagonal, 1920, 4 1/2 In. 400.00
Bowl, Gilded Interior, Handles, 1929, 10 In. 490.00
Bowl, Melon Form, Ivy Handles, 4 Ball Feet, Signed, 5 1/4 x 9 3/4 In. 290.00
Box, Cigar, Horizontal Gold Stripes, Wood Lined, 9 1/2 x 6 In. 630.00
Bread Tray, Oval, Georgian Style, Reticulated, Tiffany & Co., c.1910, 2 x 10 1/2 In. 200.00
Cake Tray, Engraved Border, Flowers, Leaves, 10 1/4 In. 690.00
Candelabrum, 2-Light, Stylized Leaves, Flowers, Art Deco, 14 1/2 In., Pair 6600.00
Candlestick, Turned-Out Raised Rim, Trumpet Stem, 1907, Pair 460.00
Casket, Tray With Sections, Rectangular, 3 1/2 x 6 In. 630.00
Chocolate Pot, Urn Shape, Painted Handle, Monogram, 8 1/2 In. 410.00
Cocktail Tray, Art Deco, Oblong, Handles, 1930, 9 1/2 x 24 1/2 In. 2990.00
Coffee Set, Demitasse, Shield Shape, 9 1/2 In., 4 Piece 1725.00
Coffeepot, Treen Handle, Hinged Cover, Baluster Shape, 10 1/2 In. 430.00
Creamer, Applied Vines Spreading, Twig Handle, 1878, 4 In. 3240.00
Cruet Stand, Claw Feet, 7 Bottles, Dated 1881, 14 In. 1610.00
Cup, Trophy, Chased With Dense Scrolling, Fruiting Vine, 1902, 9 In. 3900.00
Cup & Saucer, Trailing Gourd Vine, Handle, 1880, 4 In. 7800.00
Dish, Fan Shape, Scroll & Foliate Rim, Fleur-De-Lis Handle, 1891, 15 1/2 In. 275.00
Dish, Leaf Design, Beaded Rim, 1900, 1 x 4 x 2 In., 6 Piece 635.00
Dish, Scalloped Shell, 2 Pad Feet, Signed, 5 x 5 1/4 In., Pair 210.00
Egg Spoon, Monogram, 12 Piece 480.00
Fork, Renaissance, 1905 .... 375.00
Gravy Ladle, St. Dunstan Pattern, Monogram, Marked, 1909, 7 1/2 In. 325.00
Ice Cream Server, Chrysanthemum, Gilt Blade, Monogram, 1907, 11 3/8 In. 920.00
Loving Cup, Scrolled Feet, 3 Scroll Handles, Lobed Base, 9 In. 4200.00
Pastry Stand, Floral Repousse, Footed, 1910, 9 1/2 In. 1035.00
Pie Server, Reeded & Pierced Handle, Embossed Strawberries, 1880s, 11 1/4 In. 977.00
Pincushion, Bowl, Marked, Tiffany & Co., 3 x 4 1/4 In. 525.00
Pitcher, Chrysanthemum Pattern, Cylindrical, Engraved Flowers, 1880, 10 In. 4025.00
Pitcher, Chrysanthemum, Repousse Body, Handle, N.Y., 1880, 9 1/4 In. 4025.00
Pitcher, Water, Vertical Acanthus Leaves, 1885, 7 In. 5040.00
Porridge Bowl, Hammered, Raised Ducks, Cattail, Inscribed, 1933 .... 865.00
Punch Ladle, Beaded & Banded, Gilt Bowl, Embossed Flowers, 1870s, 15 In. 3220.00
Punch Ladle, Double Lipped Bowl, Honeycomb Lobes, c.1880, 14 1/2 In. 2990.00

Ring Holder, Flower Design, Molded, Signed, 3 1/2 In. 130.00
Salt, Ram's Head, Applied Heart Band, Footed, Monogram, c.1868, 1 x 3 In., Pair 695.00
Salver, Arch & Leaves Ground, Ivy Leaf & Berry, Swags Of Fruit, 1854, 10 In. 805.00
Serving Dish, Grapevine, Vine & Grape Bunch, 1875, 11 3/4 In. 690.00
Serving Dish, Strawberry, Reeded Pierced Handle, Obverse/Reverse, N.Y., 9 5/8 In. 460.00
Serving Spoon, Strawberries Pattern, Oval Bowl, Ribbed, c.1915, 9 1/4 In. 690.00
Soup Ladle, Monogram, Henry Hebbard, 12 In. 875.00
Spoon Set, Zodiac, Each Spoon Has Different Sign, 1926, 12 Piece 830.00
Sugar, Reticulated Band, Glass Insert, 3 3/4 x 4 1/2 In. 135.00
Sugar & Creamer, Scroll Handles, 3 Paw Feet, N.Y., 1902, 4 In. 315.00
Sugar Tongs, Palm Design, Oval Terminals, Sterling, c.1871, 4 In. 90.00
Tablespoon, Chrysanthemum, Late 19th Century, 8 1/2 In., 9 Piece 1265.00
Tankard, Flowers, Leaves, Acanthus, Laurel Wreath, 1885, 9 In. 3600.00
Tazza, Flared, Waved Openwork Rims, Molded Foliate Bands, 1902, 8 In., Pair 2645.00
Tea & Coffee Set, Flowers & Ferns, Leaf Tips, 1885, 7 Piece 6600.00
Tea & Coffee Set, Incurved Corners, Molded Borders, Urn Finials, 6 Piece 6900.00
Tea Caddy, Scrolling Leaves Band, Flower Heads, Gold Washed Interior, 4 1/2 In. 4900.00
Teapot, On Stand, Early 20th Century, 10 In., 2 Pt. 220.00
Teapot, Spherical, Swing Handle, Upturned Spout, Lotus Bud Finial, Signed, 6 In. 2200.00
Tray, Pierced Border, Monogram, Sterling, 10 3/4 In. 196.00
Tureen, Soup, Cover, Chrysanthemum, Ladle, 1885, 17 5/8 In. 21450.00
Vase, Shield Shape, Floral Rim Band, Handles, Sterling, 11 In. 865.00
Vase, Waisted, Beaded Neck, Leaf Bands, Circular Base, N.Y., 1947, 10 1/2 In. 1265.00

TIFFIN Glass Company of Tiffin, Ohio, was a subsidiary of the United
States Glass Co. of Pittsburgh, Pennsylvania, in 1892. The U.S. Glass
Co. went bankrupt in 1963, and the Tiffin plant employees purchased
the building and the inventory. They continued running it from 1963 to
1966, when it was sold to Continental Can Company. In 1969, it was
sold to Interpace, and in 1980, it was closed. The black satin glass,
made from 1923 to 1926, and the stemware of the last twenty years are
the best-known products.

Byzantine, Champagne ....12.00 to 17.00
Byzantine, Cocktail, Yellow, 3 1/2 Oz. 15.00
Byzantine, Goblet, Water ....22.00 to 35.00
Byzantine, Plate, Yellow, 7 1/2 In. 15.00
Byzantine, Tumbler, Juice, Footed 18.00
Cadena, Decanter, Yellow 395.00
Cerice, Champagne 20.00
Cerice, Plate, 8 In. 12.00
Cherokee Rose, Champagne 24.00
Cherokee Rose, Claret 50.00
Cherokee Rose, Goblet, Water, 9 Oz. ....28.00 to 32.00
Cherokee Rose, Sherbet, 5 1/2 Oz. ....20.00 to 22.00
Cherokee Rose, Sherry, 2 Oz. 40.00
Classic, Claret, Pink 115.00
Classic, Cocktail 40.00
Classic, Decanter, 9 1/2 In. 650.00
Classic, Goblet, Water, 9 Oz. 30.00
Classic, Pitcher ....225.00 to 275.00
Classic, Vase, Bud, 10 1/2 In. 65.00
Classic, Vase, Dahlia 450.00
Cordella, Cocktail, 3 1/2 Oz. 10.00
Cordella, Sherbet, 5 Oz., 3 3/4 In. 8.00
Dakota, Candy Jar, Slip Fit Cover, Cylindrical, 1950s, 24 In. 575.00
Drape, Tumbler, Water, Green, 7 In. 15.00
Figurine, Fawn, On Floating Garden, 10 In. 25.00
Flanders, Bowl, Rolled, Pink, 13 In. 250.00
Flanders, Celery Dish, Pink, 10 1/2 In. 140.00
Flanders, Claret 185.00
Flanders, Claret, Pink 150.00
Flanders, Cocktail, Pink, 4 3/4 In. 45.00
Flanders, Cordial, 1 Oz. 145.00

Flanders, Cordial, Pink, 5 1/8 In. 150.00
Flanders, Creamer, Pink 230.00
Flanders, Decanter, Pink 645.00
Flanders, Decanter, Yellow 475.00
Flanders, Finger Bowl, Underplate, Pink 200.00
Flanders, Goblet, Water, 9 Oz. ....60.00 to 65.00
Flanders, Goblet, Water, Pink, 9 Oz. ....65.00 to 70.00
Flanders, Parfait, Pink, 5 5/8 In. 175.00
Flanders, Plate, Dinner, 10 1/4 In. 180.00
Flanders, Plate, Dinner, Pink, 10 1/4 In. 145.00
Flanders, Plate, Pink, 8 1/4 In. 22.00
Flanders, Sandwich Server, Center Handle 295.00
Flanders, Sherbet, Pink 35.00
Flanders, Tumbler, Iced Tea, Footed, 12 Oz., 5 7/8 In. 70.00
Flanders, Tumbler, Iced Tea, Footed, Pink, 12 Oz., 5 7/8 In. 75.00
Flanders, Wine, Pink, 3 1/2 Oz. 87.00
Fuchsia, Cordial, 1 Oz. ....35.00 to 80.00
Fuchsia, Goblet, Water, 9 Oz., 7 1/2 In. ....27.00 to 29.00
Fuchsia, Sherbet, 4 1/8 In. ....14.00 to 15.00
Fuchsia, Tumbler, Iced Tea, Footed, 12 Oz., 6 5/16 In. 40.00
Fuchsia, Tumbler, Juice, Footed, 4 5/16 In. 25.00
Fuchsia, Tumbler, Water, 7 1/2 In. 40.00
Fuchsia, Vase, 10 1/2 In. 60.00
June Night, Cocktail, 3 1/2 Oz. 18.00
June Night, Cordial, 1 Oz. 35.00
June Night, Goblet, Water, 9 Oz. 25.00
June Night, Plate, 8 In. 19.00
June Night, Plate, 9 In. 11.00
June Night, Relish, 3 Sections, 6 1/2 In. 25.00
June Night, Relish, 3 Sections, 12 1/2 In. 50.00
June Night, Sherbet, 5 1/2 Oz. 18.00
June Night, Sherry, 2 Oz. 39.00
June Night, Sugar 28.00
June Night, Sugar & Creamer 55.00
June Night, Tumbler, Iced Tea, Footed 38.00
June Night, Vase, Bud, 6 1/2 In. 38.00
Jungle Assortment, Tray, Dresser, Enameled, Rectangular, 1920s 135.00
Killarney, Champagne, Green 35.00
King's Crown, Ashtray, Amber Stain, 5 1/2 In. 45.00
King's Crown, Bowl, Footed, Ruby Stain, 9 3/4 In. 120.00
King's Crown, Bowl, Ruby Stain, Footed, 5 1/2 x 8 In. 45.00
King's Crown, Bowl, Wedding, Footed, Ruby Stain, 10 1/2 In. ....155.00 to 195.00
King's Crown, Cake Stand, Ruby Stain, 12 In. 125.00
King's Crown, Compote, Ruby Border, 7 In. 50.00
King's Crown, Pitcher, Ruby Stain 185.00
King's Crown, Plate, Dinner, Ruby Stain, 10 In. 65.00
King's Crown, Plate, Indent, Ruby Stain, 10 1/2 In. 18.00
King's Crown, Plate, Ruby Stain, 8 In. 16.00
King's Crown, Sugar, Ruby Stain 22.00
La Fleur, Vase, Yellow, Squat 450.00
Modern, Compote, Twilight, Low, 6 In. 125.00
Modern, Rose Bowl, 4 Lily Pad Feet, Blue, 6 1/4 In. 98.00
Modern, Rose Bowl, 4 Lily Pad Feet, Chartreuse, 6 1/4 In. 95.00
Needle Etch, Sherbet 38.00
Needle Etch, Tumbler, Water, Footed 38.00
Nymph, Tumbler, Iced Tea, Nile Green, 6 In. 100.00
Persian Pheasant, Cordial 45.00
Persian Pheasant, Goblet, Optic, 8 In. 35.00
Persian Pheasant, Sherbet, 7 In. 22.00
Psyche, Goblet, Champagne 55.00
Queen Astrid, Tumbler, Water, 9 Oz. 25.00
Special Minton, Goblet 20.00

Vintage, Tumbler, Water, Green, 7 1/2 In.	30.00
Wistaria, Cocktail	35.00
Wistaria, Cordial	65.00
Wistaria, Sherbet	50.00

TILES have been used in most countries of the world as a sturdy building material for floors, roofs, fireplace surrounds, and surface top-
pings. Many of the American tiles are listed in this book under the
factory name.

Abraham Lincoln, Portrait, Feb. 12, 1909, Frame, 9 x 6 In.	605.00
Ancient Sailing Vessel, Against Full Moon, Crystalline Glaze, 4 3/8 In.	143.00
Bird, Chasing A Moth, Hamilton Tile Co., 6 x 6 In.	165.00
Bird, In Tree, Raised Line Design, Frame, Wheeling, 6 In.	121.00
Bird, On Limb, Incised, Floral Border, Continental, 8 x 8 In.	260.00
Birds On Branch, Mantel Facing, U.S. Encaustic Tile, 6 In., 5 Piece	465.00
Brown, Blue Matte Glaze, Arts & Crafts Oak Frame, Claycraft, 3 1/2 x 14 In., 4 Piece	920.00
Cherubs, Catching Fish, W.W. Gallimore, Trent Tile, 9 x 18 In.	2970.00
Cherubs, Playing Beneath Trees, Herman Mueller, Square, 6 In.	132.00
Children, Red, Yellow Glaze, Intaglio, Signed, Frenzel, 6 In., Pair	440.00
Colorful Flowers, Embossed, California Faience, 5 1/2 In.	185.00
Cowboy, Chasing Buffalo, Green, Purple Ground, 6 In.	303.00
Cowboy, On Horse, Chasing Buffalo, San Jose Pottery, 6 In.	300.00
Cyclamen Flowers, 3 Concentric Raised Circles, Maroon, Frame, 7 7/8 In., Pair	154.00
Desert Scene, With Adobe House, Palm Tree, Mountain In Background, Muresque, 6 In.	357.00
Dolphin, Hole In Mouth For Fountain, Maroon Glaze, Arts & Crafts, 7 7/8 In.	402.00
Dutch Scene, Green Matte Glaze, California Art Tile Co., Richmond, Ca., 5 5/8 In.	330.00
Flower Design, Molded, Arts & Crafts Oak Frame, 5 1/2 In.	299.00
Flowers, Overlapping, In Bloom Beneath Arcing Bud, Hamilton Tile Co., 4 1/4 In.	49.00
Geese, At Each Corner, Tan, Cream, Yellow Glaze, Green Matte Glaze, 1905, 9 In.	5750.00
Geometic, Black, Clay, Oak Arts & Crafts Frame, Square, 6 In.	220.00
Green Matte Glaze, 6 x 6 In.	20.00
Human Figures, Red Clay, Green Ground, Pablo Picasso, 1955, 6 3/8 x 4 In.	825.00
Knight & Castle, Marked, California Art Tile Co., Richmond, Ca., 5 5/8 In.	230.00
Landscape, Colored, Arts & Crafts Oak Frame, 7 x 4 In.	1650.00
Landscape, Green, Blue, Brown Matte Glaze, Arts & Crafts, 4 3/4 In.	546.00
Landscape, Mission In Background, Embossed, Multicolored, Claycraft, 7 x 4 In., Pair	690.00
Landscape, Multicolored Tone Matte Glaze, Embossed, Claycraft, 15 1/2 x 4 In., Pair	805.00
Landscape, Trees, Green Matte Glaze, Mahogany Frame, 3 7/8 x 3 7/8 In.	240.00
Landscape, Waterfall, Multicolored Brown Matte Glaze, Claycraft, 16 x 8 In.	865.00
Lion, Otto Metzner, Hamilton Tile Co., 6 In.	220.00
Lionesses, Facing Each Other, Purple Matte Glaze, 6 x 12 In.	360.00
Man, Laughing, Comical, Blue Matte Glaze, Square, 4 1/2 In.	165.00
Mediterranean City Scene, Panel, Original Walnut Board, Harris Strong, 48 In.	310.00
Mermen, Sea Creatures Holding Club, Conch Shell, Frame, c.1700, 5 x 5 In., 4 Piece	800.00
Mill Scene, With Human Figures, Frame, Square, Signed, Frenzel, 6 In.	275.00
Monks, Enjoying A Sip Of Beer, Square, National Tile Co., Sepia, Gold Frame, 6 In.	143.00
Mountain Peak, 4 Geese, Aqua Ground, Incised, Painted, 8 x 8 In.	245.00
Panel, Landscape With Owls, House, Full Moon, Hartford Faience, 8 x 35 In.	5062.00
Peacock, Blue Matte Glaze, 12 x 6 In.	410.00
Peacock, Iridescent, Arts & Crafts, 6 In.	935.00
Pinecone, Dark Green Ground, Trent, 6 In.	575.00
Portrait, Abraham Lincoln, 100th Anniversary Celebration, Wooden Frame, 9 x 6 In.	605.00
Portrait, Man & Woman, Red, Brown Glaze, 6 In., Pair	190.00
Portrait, Neoclassical Soldiers, 1 Officer, 1 Foot Soldier, Green Glaze, 6 In., Pair	240.00
Portrait, Soldier, 4 3/8 In.	66.00
Portrait, Teddy Roosevelt, Wooden Frame, Marked, 9 x 6 In.	360.00
Portrait, Thomas Wildey, Zanesville, Ohio, 4 5/8 In.	65.00
Portrait, Woman, Marie Antoinette Era Dress, Beaded Frame, 12 1/8 x 6 In.	176.00
Roman Hunter, With Bear, Rectangular, 4 1/4 x 7 1/4 In.	190.00
Roof, Mythical Fish, Ming Dynasty, c.1500	1650.00
Rose, Burnt Yellow Glaze, 1890, 6 x 6 In.	55.00
Sea Gull, In Flight, Clouds, Oak Frame, Arts & Crafts, Round, 4 In.	28.00

Seascape, Ship At Sea, Embossed, Square, California Faience, 5 1/2 In. 130.00
Seaside Scene, With A Windmill, Masted Sailing Ship, Square, Wheeling, 4 1/4 In., Pair . 30.00
Ship At Sea, Arts & Crafts Oak Frame, Square, 8 In. 633.00
Stag, Blue Matte Glaze, Square, 4 1/2 In. 230.00
Steamboat Design, Green Matte Glaze, Pink Ground, California Art Tile Co., 5 5/8 In. . . 210.00
Stove, 2 Different Women, Marked, Beaver Falls, 2 1/8 In., Pair 242.00
Stove, Grecian Woman, Trent, 4 1/8 In. 132.00
Stove, Rose In Bloom, 3 1/8 In. 121.00
Stove, Woman In Lace Cap, High Fluted Collar, Trent, 4 1/8 In. 70.00
Stove, Woman, Long Hair, Against Vertical Geometric Ground, Profile, 3 1/4 In. 71.00
Stove, Woman, Wearing Headband, Profile, Light Wooden Frame, 2 1/2 In. 90.00
Stove, Young Woman, With Flowers In Her Hair, Trent, 4 1/8 In. 165.00
Swan, On A Lake, Barnwood Frame, 5 7/8 In. 80.00
Water Lilies, Arts & Crafts, 6 In. 2420.00
Windmill, Against A Clouded Sky, Square, 4 1/4 In. 45.00
Woman, Arts Of Music, Painting & Poetry, Panel, Beaver Falls, 18 x 6 In., 3 Piece 1760.00
Woman, In A Flowing Lace Veil, Square, Trent, 3 In. 90.00
Woman, In Dustcap Surrounded By Acanthus Leaves, Barnwood Frame, Trent, 3 x 6 In. . 110.00
Woman, Profile, Flowing Hair, Beaded Headband, Frame, 6 In. 90.00
Woman, Profile, In A Bonnet Surrounded By Curlicue Design, 4 1/4 In. 45.00
Women, Beneath A Tree, Brown Glaze, Frame, 8 x 6 In. 220.00
Young Girl, Profile, Wearing A Bonnet, Square, 6 In. 99.00

TINWARE containers for household use have been made in America
since the seventeenth century. The first tin utensils were brought from
Europe, but by 1798, tin plate was imported and local tinsmiths made
the wares. Painted tin is called tole and is listed separately. Some tin
kitchen items may be found listed under Kitchen. The lithographed tin
containers used to hold food and tobacco are listed in the Advertising
category under Tin.

Bucket, Oval, Boat Shape, Bail Handle, Covered In Jacquard Fabric, 15 1/4 In. 23.00
Coffeepot, Domed Cover, Tapered, Gooseneck Spout, 10 1/2 In. 28.00
Coffeepot, Punched, Tulips, Flowers, Goose Neck Spout, Uebele Mark, 1850, 11 1/2 In. . . 6270.00
Foot Warmer, Punched, Wood, Red Paint, 18th Century, 6 x 9 x 8 In. 195.00
Horn, Red, White & Blue 35.00
Lunch Pail, Cup, Bail Handle, Embossed, Cream City, 9 1/2 In. 55.00
Lunch Pail, Wire & Black Wooden Handle, Cover, Signed, 9 1/2 In. 95.00
Mold, Candle, 12 Tube, Ear Handles, 11 1/2 x 9 In. 550.00
Mold, Candle, 12 Tube, Folded Rim Handle, 6 x 6 In. 1430.00
Nursing Bottle, Nipple, Strap Handle, Pennsylvania, c.1820, 4 1/2 In. 305.00
Pail, Green, Stencil, Linwood Park, Embossed Battleship, Remember The Maine, 6 x 4 In. 116.00
Tobacco Plate, Woman Holding Jug, Marked Havana Post, Feb. 21, 1905 . . . . 150.00
Tray, Painted, Village Scene, Concord, 1839, Copper Painted Rim, Flower, 15 x 18 1/2 In. 195.00
Vase, Fruiting Vine Meanders, Green, Blue, Ocher, Yellow, Handle, Cantagalli, 27 In. 2160.00

TOBACCO CUTTERS may be listed in either the Advertising or Store categories.

TOBACCO JAR collectors search for those made in odd shapes and colors. Because tobacco needs special conditions of humidity and air, it
has been stored in special containers since the eighteenth century.

Arab Boy's Head, Cream Turban & Scarf, Gold Earrings, 5 In. . . . . .165.00 to 175.00
Bear Attacking Man, Tree Stump, Branches, Leaves, Switzerland, c.1900, 7 In. 1050.00
Black Man, Top Hat, Smoking Pipe, In Barrel, Porcelain, c.1900, 8 1/4 In. 255.00
Black Man's Head, Smoking Pipe, Glass Eyes, Wood, 6 1/4 In. 560.00
Black Woman's Head, Majolica 150.00
Cat, Playing With Boot On Basket, Terra-Cotta, 7 3/4 In. 580.00
Dog, Sitting In Barrel, Terra-Cotta, 7 1/4 In. 350.00
Dog, Smoking Pipe. Wearing Fez, Terra-Cotta, 8 In. 420.00
Dog's Head, Blue Hat, Smoking Pipe, Glazed Terra-Cotta, 6 1/4 In. 170.00
Dwarf, Standing By Tree Stump, Terra-Cotta, Marked W & C, Cover, 12 1/2 In. 195.00
Flowers & Scrolling Leaves, Peacock Feather Border, 5 3/4 In. 3360.00
Indian Chief, Majolica, 8 In. 250.00
Landscape, Game Bird Scene, England, 1940, 5 1/4 In. 110.00

Man In Barrel, Terra-Cotta, 8 1/2 In. ....140.00 to 270.00
Man On Top Of Cigars, Terra-Cotta, 9 1/4 In. 270.00
Man's Head, Upturned White Collar, Terra-Cotta, Incised 8149, 8 x 6 1/2 In. 250.00
Monk, Match Holder Head, Humidor Opens At Waist, Cast White Metal, 9 1/4 In. 310.00
Scottish Man, Terra-Cotta, 5 3/4 In. 290.00
Scotty Dog, Pipe & Fez, Terra-Cotta, 6 In. 195.00
Sea Captain, Terra-Cotta, BB 8148, Bernard Block, 7 1/4 In. 225.00
Sherlock Holmes, Ceramic 110.00
Velvet, Ceramic, Enameled Pipe & Text, 6 1/2 x 5 1/2 In. 210.00

TOBY JUG is the name of a very special form of pitcher. It is shaped like the full figure of a man or woman. A pitcher that shows just the top half of a person is not correctly called a toby. More examples of toby jugs can be found under Royal Doulton and other factory names.

Cavalier, Sitting In Chair, Staffordshire, 10 In. 100.00
Colonial Man, Tricorner Hat, Erotic Shape, Glared, Rockingham, 9 1/2 In. 69.00
Hearty Good Fellow, Man Holding Pipe & Stein, Staffordshire, 11 In. 345.00
Man, Cobalt Blue Coat, Green Wig, Breeches, Copper Luster Trim, Staffordshire, 5 5/8 In. 55.00
Man, Holding Glass & Flask, Prattware Style, 1700s, 11 3/4 In. 780.00
Man, Seated, Legs Crossed, Hands On Stein, Staffordshire, 9 In., Pair 400.00
Man, Sitting On Keg, Schwelsig, Faience, Blue & White, c.1760, 7 In. 400.00
Man, With Snuffbox, Staffordshire, Miniature, 5 1/2 In. 145.00

TOLE is painted tin. It is sometimes called *japanned ware*, *pontypool*, or *toleware*. Most nineteenth-century tole is painted with an orange-red or black background and multicolored decorations. Many recent versions of toleware are made and sold. Related items may be listed in the Tinware category.

Box, Basket Of Fruit Stencil, 6 1/2 x 9 1/4 In. 770.00
Box, Document, Dome Top, Line & Leaf, White Band, Leaf Fruit & Swag, 6 x 9 1/4 In. ... 800.00
Box, Document, Dome Top, Stenciled Fruit & Floral, Brass Bail, 9 x 4 x 5 3/4 In. 385.00
Box, Document, Dome Top, Wire Bail, 3 1/4 x 6 1/2 In. 55.00
Box, Document, Painted Drape, Floral & Leaf, Black, Bail Handle, 1900 .... 7260.00
Box, Document, Yellow Leaf Design, Green, Yellow, Ring Handles, 5 1/2 In. 1320.00
Box, Dome Top, Gold Japanned Swags On Lid, 2 3/4 x 4 In. 200.00
Box, Fruit & Flowers, c.1800, 6 1/2 x 9 3/4 In. 140.00
Box, Scalloped Cover, Pink Flowers, Red Highlights, 3 1/2 x 2 1/4 x 3 In. 495.00
Bread Tray, Fruit, Leaves, Gilt Highlight, Black Ground, 3 1/2 x 7 x 14 In. 275.00
Bread Tray, Yellow Pomegranate, Chain Design, Fruit, Leaves, 2 3/4 x 13 In. 6050.00
Chandelier, 3-Light, Gilt Leaves, Gilt, Brass Corona, 19th Century, 36 x 20 In. 9775.00
Coffeepot, Allover Flowers, Leaves, Black Ground, Early 19th Century, 11 In. 605.00
Coffeepot, Bird, Flowers & Leaves, 19th Century, 9 In. 500.00
Coffeepot, Black Ground, Gooseneck Spout, Brass Button Finial, 10 3/4 In. 7975.00
Coffeepot, Domed Cover, Gooseneck Spout, Fruit, Foliate Design, Yellow, Handle, 11 In. 7975.00
Coffeepot, Flowers On Green Panels, Within Circle, Base Leaves, Brass Finial, 11 In. ... 1210.00
Coffeepot, Gooseneck Spout, Strap Handle, Painted Flowers, c.1830, 10 1/2 In. 1500.00
Coffeepot, Hinged Domed Cover, Flared, Fruit, Leaves, Black Ground, 10 1/4 In. 865.00
Coffeepot, Japanned Ground, Mustard, Red, Green, Flowers, 8 1/2 In. 2070.00
Jardiniere, Grape Leaf, Vine Design, Black, Gilt, Splayed Feet, 1920, 4 1/2 x 13 1/2 In. .. 250.00
Lamp, 3-Light, Black Equestrian Stencils Shade, Ocher Ground, 24 In. 750.00
Lamp, Black Ground, Gold Stenciling, Oval Landscape, Castle, 28 In. 315.00
Lamp Filler, Flowers, Leaves, Gilt Highlights, Bail Handle, Black Ground, 9 In. 110.00
Lantern, Green Glass Panels, Pierced Dome, 24 x 12 In. 345.00
Lantern, Hanging, Glass Panes, Victorian, 30 x 20 In. 1955.00
Mug, Red, Yellow, Green Fruit, Foliate, Brown Handle, Brown Ground, 6 In. 6325.00
Pepper Pot, White, Red, Green Floral Design, Handle, Pa., 19th Century, 2 3/4 In. 1980.00
Pitcher, Apples & Pears, Red Ground, Tin, 14 1/2 In. 190.00
Pitcher, Syrup, Red, Yellow, Green Flowers, Pa., Early 19th Century, 3 1/2 In. 605.00
Planter, Gilt Scrolls, Applied Scrolled Handles, Metal Liner, 23 x 18 In. 1725.00
Sugar, Sprays Of Foliage Around Sides & Lid, 3 x 4 1/2 In. 125.00
Table, Tray, Floral Chains, Rectangular Top, Ocher Ground, Outswept Legs, 21 x 35 In. .. 1092.00
Tea Caddy, Black, Yellow Stripes, Flowers, 7 In. 193.00
Tea Canister, Victorian, Oval, Oriental, Mounted As Lamp, 17 1/2 x 10 x 7 In. 460.00

Teapot, Red Flower, Yellow Ground, Straight Spout, Miniature 5060.00
Tray, Allegorical Figures, 18th Century Bath House, Faux Bamboo Stand, 24 3/4 In. 2530.00
Tray, Allover Gilt Oriental Figural Landscape, 1820s, 29 3/4 In. 860.00
Tray, Basket Of Pink Roses, Trellis Design Rim, 25 In. 1150.00
Tray, Black Paint, Gilt Honeysuckle Border, Pontypool, Empire, 10 1/4 In. 2185.00
Tray, Canted Corners, Yellow Fruit & Leaf Design, 6 x 8 3/4 In. 165.00
Tray, Charles X, Chicken, Rooster, Peacock Scene, Scarlet, Gilt Border, 21 In. 6325.00
Tray, Children & Women Scene, Man, Seated, Rectangular Top, 31 x 21 1/2 In. 6600.00
Tray, Faux Bamboo Stand, Birds & Flowers, Cream, Gold, Victorian, 21 x 17 3/4 x 22 In. 290.00
Tray, Faux Bamboo Stand, Black, Oriental Birds Within Wooded Marsh, 21 x 29 In. 980.00
Tray, Faux Bamboo Stand, Cattle & Sheep Grazing, Gilt Leaves, 1820s, 21 x 18 In. 1330.00
Tray, Faux Bamboo Stand, Chinoiserie Design, 1850s, 21 x 22 1/2 In. 1495.00
Tray, Faux Bamboo Stand, Chinoiserie, Gilt, Vermilion Ground, 22 1/2 x 17 1/2 In. 1495.00
Tray, Faux Bamboo Stand, Ebonized, Raised Grapevine Design, 21 1/2 x 19 In. 750.00
Tray, Faux Bamboo Stand, Gilt Stenciled, Penned, Oriental Vistas, 21 x 27 x 21 1/2 In. .. 1495.00
Tray, Faux Bamboo Stand, Landscape Scene, Vintage Border, 21 In. 3450.00
Tray, Faux Bamboo Stand, Leaf Border, Scarlet Ground, 1840s, 21 x 28 1/4 In. 1150.00
Tray, Faux Bamboo Stand, Maidens & Peacock Scene, Classical Landscape, 31 x 23 In. .. 1265.00
Tray, Faux Bamboo Stand, Nesting Eagles, Scarlet Lacquer, Dated 1963, 24 x 28 1/2 In. .. 490.00
Tray, Faux Bamboo Stand, Oriental Vistas, 1830s, 21 x 27 In. 1495.00
Tray, Faux Bamboo Stand, Regency, Floral Sprays, Gilt, 21 x 26 x 20 In. 1035.00
Tray, Floral Bouquet, Gilt Scalloped Rim, 26 1/2 x 21 In. 315.00
Tray, Flowers, Gilt Decoration, 26 1/2 x 19 In. 290.00
Tray, Flowers, Red, Blue, Yellow, Black, Copper Ground, Oblong, 8 Sides, 9 x 12 3/4 In. . 115.00
Tray, Fruit & Flower, 12 x 8 In., Pair 1045.00
Tray, George IV, Foliage Broad Border, Fruit, Pierced Handles, 1830, 36 x 26 In., Pair ... 1800.00
Tray, Gilt Vine Border, White Bell Flowers, Oval, England, 28 In. 85.00
Tray, Grazing Cattle, Figures At Stream, Castle On Rockery, 24 In. 490.00
Tray, Japanned Ground, Yellow Stripe, Red & Green Daubs, Red & Green Fruit, 8 x 14 In. 385.00
Tray, Parrots, Gilt Floral, Black Ground, 24 x 31 3/4 In. 950.00
Tray, Regency, Central Floral Spray, Canted Corners, Faux Bamboo Stand, 21 In. 2185.00
Tray, Regency, Floral Vine Design, Maroon Ground, 26 x 19 1/2 In. 690.00
Tray, Regency, Oriental Figural Scene, Canted Corners, 24 1/4 x 18 In. 1150.00
Tray, Scattered Floral Sprays, Raised Rim, Cutout Handles, 23 In. 4890.00
Tray, Scrolling Gilt Accents, Central Floral Spray, Late 1900s, 29 x 23 In. 1035.00
Tray, Stand, Black Lacquer, Polychromed Flowers, 21 x 17 1/2 x 21 In. 400.00
Tray, Stand, Charles X, Oval, Pastoral Vista, Grapes, Leaves, 21 x 19 1/2 x 15 In. 1265.00
Tray, Stand, Flowers, Black Ground, American, 30 In. 405.00
Tray, Stand, Polychrome, Flowers, Oval, Pierced Gallery, 22 x 18 x 24 In. 690.00
Tray, Stand, Scarlet Lacquer, Nesting Eagles, Victorian, Late 1800s, 24 x 28 1/2 x 21 In. . 490.00
Tray, Stand, Standing Woman, Flowers In Hand, Floral Border, c.1800, 29 3/4 x 23 In. ... 5400.00
Tray, Stand, Victorian, Black Lacquer, Flowers, Oval, 21 x 24 x 29 In. 1035.00
Tray, Stenciled Woman Picking Flowers, Cottage Background, Black, 26 1/4 x 18 3/4 In. . 300.00
Tray, Train At Center, People With Dog, Cutout Handles, 25 1/2 In. 55.00
Urn, Chestnut, Black, Oval, Gilt Leaf Scrolls, Acorn Finial, Empire Style, 13 x 5 x 7 In. .. 920.00

TOM MIX was born in 1880 and died in 1940. He was the hero of over
100 silent movies from 1910 to 1929, and 25 sound films from 1929
to 1935. There was a Ralston Tom Mix radio show from 1933 to 1950,
but the original Tom Mix was not in the show. Tom Mix comics were
published from 1942 to 1953.

Branding Iron 200.00
Button, Tom Mix Sells Floto Circus, Picture 125.00
Compass, Glow-In-The-Dark, Arrowhead, Instructions 275.00
Glow Gun, Arrowhead Whistle, Papers 225.00
Magic Spinner 200.00
Ring, Magnet 300.00
Rocket Parachute, Mailer, 1936 .... 145.00
Sheriff Of Dobie County, Siren Badge .... .60.00 to 85.00
Shooting Gallery, Cardboard Target, Peg, Wooden Stand, Parker, Box, 1930s, 12 In. 250.00
Telephone, Tin Can Type 100.00
Telescope, Metal, Ralston, 1930s 50.00
Wristwatch, 100th Anniversary, 1983 .... .275.00 to 325.00

TOOLS of all sorts are listed here, but most are related to industry. Other tools may be found listed under Iron, Kitchen, Tinware, and Wooden.

Adze, Bowl, Steel, LAM, France, 1890, 4 In.	140.00
Adze, Joiner's, Ward, No. 1, Oak Handle	40.00
Anvil, France, 1781, 31 In.	865.00
Anvil, Jeweler's, Gunmetal Base, 3 3/4 In.	110.00
Auger, Tenon, Adjustable	60.00
Ax, Boarding, Naval	545.00
Ax, Hewing, Fayette Plum, 15 In.	75.00
Ax, Logging, Walters Axe Co., Canada	70.00
Ax, Mortising, I.H. Sorby, Sheep Mark, 14 x 3 3/8-In. Head	103.00
Ax, Sabotier's, Smith's Stamp, Forged Design, France, 18th Century	117.00
Ax, Side, Cooper's, Dupont Le Pertre, 5-In. Edge	435.00
Bed Smoother, White Oak, New England, Inscribed A.T.F. 25, 1780, 24 In.	425.00
Bench Press, Helical Action, Boxwood Knob, France, 6 In.	50.00
Bevel, Eagle, Steel, 12 In.	42.00
Bevel, St. Johnsbury Tool Co., Rosewood & Steel, Pat. June 14, 1870, 15 In.	900.00
Bit, Wooden, Irwin, No. 21, Adjustable, Adjusts To 3-In. Swing	32.00
Block, Stanley, No. 60 1/2, 1930s-1940s	27.00
Bolt Cabinet, 72 Drawers, Stenciling On Swivel Base	935.00
Book Press, Cast Iron, Leaf Molded Base, Ball Finial Lever Sides, 19 x 12 x 16 In.	245.00
Book Press, Maple, Birch, Bracket Feet, Early 19th Century, 14 x 14 In.	415.00
Box, Carpenter's, Compartmentalized Interior, Conforming Case, Oak, 20 3/4 In.	195.00
Box, Clockmaker's, Lathe Accessories, 1 Drawer, 1900s, 4 1/2 x 9 x 7 1/2 In.	525.00
Box, Pine, Tongue & Groove, Bead Board, Brass Hardware, Lock & Key, 24 1/2 In.	60.00
Brace, Mathieson, Beech	100.00
Brace, Pianomaker's, Beech, France	160.00
Brace, Revolving Wooden Hand Grip, Chuck-Type Head, c.1860	125.00
Butteris, Horse Shoer's, Forged Steel Shaft, Oak Stock, 17 In.	95.00
Caddy, Softwood, Blue Paint, 2 Sections, Chisel Box, 25 1/2 x 15 1/2 In.	620.00
Caliper, Ballet Master, Holtzapffel & Co., London, 6 In.	65.00
Caliper, Cask, Cooper's, Rabone, Boxwood, Mahogany	415.00
Caliper, Dancing Master, Iron, 4 1/2 In.	50.00
Caliper, Tempered Steel, Spring Bar, Turn Screw, Wm. Johnson, Inc., Newark, N.J., 24 In.	45.00
Caliper, Thewlis & Griffiths, 20 In.	60.00
Candlesnuffer, Hobday & Co., Steel, 6 3/4 In.	245.00
Chest, Hammacher-Schlemmer, No. 55, Oak, 2 Panel Doors	500.00
Chest, Watchmaker's, Mahogany, 3 Drawers, With Pocket Watch Mainsprings, Parts	250.00
Chisel, Lock Mortise, 8 In.	90.00
Chisel, Sash Pocket, Marples, 1 3/4 In.	70.00
Chisel, Sash Scribing, Marsden Bros.	50.00
Chisel Set, Socket, Buck Bros., 5/8 x 3/4 In., 2 Piece	75.00
Chisel Set, Socket, Witherby, Box, 9 In., 4 Piece	95.00
Clamp, Boxwood, Late 18th-Early 19th Century, 18 In.	90.00
Clamp, Mahogany, Wooden Screw Handles, 19 In.	29.00
Cobbler's Bench, Original Blue Paint, c.1850	550.00
Cobbler's Bench, Pine, Low Galleries, Padded Seat, Twig Legs, 18 1/2 x 41 3/4 In.	80.00
Corn Sheller, Cast Iron, Little Giant, 12 x 12 In.	40.00
Cranberry Scoop, F.I. Buckingham Mfg., Plymouth, Mass., E.E.E., Jr., Cape Cod	605.00
Cranberry Scoop, Wooden, Cape Cod, 19th Century	430.00
Curry Comb, Iron & Brass, Wooden Handle, Heart Cutout	185.00
Curry Comb, Wrought Iron, Heart Design, Wooden Handle, 18th Century, 8 x 4 In.	880.00
Cutter, Barrel Head, Michels, May 31, 1870	250.00
Detonator, Blasting, New York Blasting Machine Co., Electrical, Wooden, 13 In.	250.00
Divider, W. & C. Wynn, Heart Shape Wing Nut, 18th Century, 9 In.	70.00
Drill, Archimedian, Mahogany, Brass	25.00
Drill, Bow, Pianomaker's, Rosewood, Brass, Original Bow	325.00
Drill, Hand, Stanley, No. 610	93.00
Drill Chuck, Jacobs, Stainless Steel, 3/8-In. Shank, 1/4 In.	25.00
File, Hand Cut, 18th Century, 21 In.	117.00
Firkin, Old Brown Paint, Cover, 7 1/2 In.	1035.00
Firkin, Pine, Painted, Swing Handle, Early 19th Century, 14 3/4 In.	440.00

Flashlight, Military, Bright Star, MX-991/U 25.00
Flashlight, Motorist's Safety, Red Plastic Head, Usalite, 7 1/2 In. 25.00
Flashlight, Silver & Black, Ribbed, Ring Handle, Apex, 6 1/2 In. 22.00
Float, Barrel, Gunmaker's, Rosewood Handle 42.00
Float, Planemaker's, Rattail 70.00
Gauge, Cutting, J. Frost, Norwich, Rosewood, Brass 40.00
Gauge, Mortise, Adjustable, Rosewood, Brass 70.00
Gauge, Mortise, Ebony, Brass 85.00
Gauge, Sun Shipbuilding & Drydock Co., Chester, Pa., Brass, 10 In. 46.00
Ginger Rasp, Iron, Case, England, 1730 .... 395.00
Grain Bin, Pine, Overhanging Lift Top, Blue Paint, Cutout Feet, 30 1/2 x 31 x 21 In. 975.00
Hammer, Planishing, Boxwood Handle 95.00
Hammer, Upholsterer's, Stanley, No. 602 .... 20.00
Hay Fork, Wooden 135.00
Hoof Shaving, Crooked Neck, Long Shaft, Wooden Handle 42.00
Jack, Stanley, No. 5 .... 35.00
Jack, Wagon, Military, Oak, Forged Iron, 6 x 2 3/8 x 17 5/8 In. 215.00
Jack, Wagon, Wood & Iron, 30 1/2 In. 60.00
Knife, Chamfer, Cooper's, Marked 35.00
Knife, Draw, H.D. Smith, Perfect Handle 80.00
Knurling Tool, Rosewood Handle, 19th Century 90.00
Level, Bench, L.L. Davis, Iron, Pedestal Type, Grooved Base For Attaching Square 350.00
Level, Brassbound, Hardwood, Owner Stamped W. Pye, Handmade Brass Case, 14 In. 130.00
Level, H.C. Son Co., Pine Meadow, Ct., Brass Ends, 26 In. 30.00
Level, Mathieson, Waisted Rosewood, Brass, 11 In. 740.00
Level, Spirit, Mathieson, Rosewood, Brass Top, 19th Century 70.00
Level, Stanley, Carpenter's, 1896 .... 40.00
Level, Stanley, No. 06, Brass Tip, 30 In. 40.00
Level, Stanley, No. 36, Cast Iron, c.1900 .... 50.00
Level, Stanley, Wood, Stamped, New Britain, Conn., Patd. 40.00
Level, Surveyor's, W. Marples & Sons, Rosewood, Brass, Plumb, Field Sight 135.00
Level, Torpedo, Rabone 40.00
Level, Wooden, Carved, Painted, Brass Plumb Bob, Mid 19th Century, 31 1/2 x 54 In. 1725.00
Level, Wooden, Disston & Morss, No. 1, 12 In. 45.00
Loom, Rag Rug, Early 19th Century, 30 In. 395.00
Mallet, Burl, Square Head, Carved Handle, 13 In. 12.00
Mallet, Carver's, Lignum, Beech, 19th Century 35.00
Measure, Wooden Handles, Painted, Yellow, Early 19th Century, 11 1/4 x 6 In. 29.00
Miter, Metal, Bronze Rabbet, J. Popping 5750.00
Miter, Metal, L. Brandt 3250.00
Miter Hook, Ebony, Brass, 10 In. 158.00
Miter Jack, Wooden, Early 19th Century 183.00
Mold, Stetson Hat 210.00
Niddy Noddy, Walnut, Chip Carved, Initialed O.P., Dated 1798, 14 1/4 x 17 1/2 In. 400.00
Pipe Block, Masterench, Heller Bros. Co., Box, 8 In. 15.00
Plane, 7 Jointer, Stanley, No. 8, Erik Anton Blade 85.00
Plane, Bed Rock, Stanley, No. 602, 1910 .... 650.00
Plane, Block, Craftsman, No. 187 .... 12.00
Plane, Block, Stanley, No. 15 .... 67.00
Plane, Block, Stanley, No. 61, Low Angle 215.00
Plane, Block, Stanley, No. 130, Double End 35.00
Plane, Block, Stanley, No. 518, Steel 83.00
Plane, Block, Stanley, No. A-18, Aluminum 275.00
Plane, Bull-Nose, Record, No. 1366, Rosewood Wedge 200.00
Plane, Chamfer, Walnut, Brass Adjustment Fittings, 3 1/4 x 1 3/4 In. 42.00
Plane, Chariot, Gunmetal, Rosewood Infill, Wedge, 5 In. 155.00
Plane, Circular, Evans, Patent March 22, 1864, By R.H. Mitchell & Co, Hudson, N.Y. 275.00
Plane, Circular, Stanley, No. 20, Victor, 1930 .... 250.00
Plane, Corrugated Gage, Stanley, No. GJ-4c 230.00
Plane, Dado, Stanley, No. 39 3/8 In. 130.00
Plane, Dado, Stanley, No. 39, 5/8 In. 300.00
Plane, Fluting, Compassed, Austria, 1834 .... 215.00
Plane, Hook Joint, Routledge 108.00

Plane, Jack, Stanley Bailey, No. 5 1/4, Type 16, 1940 .... 53.00
Plane, Jack, Transitional, Union, No. 26 .... 55.00
Plane, Jointer, Stanley, No. 7C 100.00
Plane, Miter, Cabinetmaker's, Stanley, No. 9 .... 665.00
Plane, Miter, Cabinetmaker's, Stanley, No. 9, Hot Dog Handle 1665.00
Plane, Miter, Mathieson, Dovetailed, Rosewood Infill, 8 1/2 In. 850.00
Plane, Molding, Cabinetmaker's, Stewart, Linenfold, Cabinet Pitch 75.00
Plane, Molding, Mathieson, Triple Iron, 2 1/4 In. 400.00
Plane, Molding, Robert Wooding, Complex, 10 1/2 In. 1165.00
Plane, Molding, Turner, Sheffield, Twin Iron, 2 3/4 In. 265.00
Plane, Panel Raising, Mathieson 75.00
Plane, Panel, Norris, No. A1, Dovetailed, Rosewood Infill, Pre-World War II, 17 1/2 In. ... 3410.00
Plane, Plow, Mathieson, No. 8B, Handle, Beech 140.00
Plane, Plow, Screwstem, Malloch, Perth, Boxwood Arms & Nuts 235.00
Plane, Rabbet, Stanley, No. 191, Pat. 6/7/10 .... 80.00
Plane, Scraper, Stanley, No. 85, Original Blade 615.00
Plane, Shoulder, Gunmetal, Steel Sole, Rosewood Infill ....200.00 to 310.00
Plane, Shoulder, Norris, No. 7, Steel, Rosewood Infill, Dovetailed 308.00
Plane, Side Rabbet, Stanley, No. 98/99 .... 190.00
Plane, Smoothing, Bailey Tool Co. 335.00
Plane, Smoothing, Beech, 3 1/4 In. 50.00
Plane, Smoothing, Cast Iron, Brass, Cove Front, Overstuffed Walnut Infill, Scotland 290.00
Plane, Smoothing, G. Berry, Rosewood, 5 In. 210.00
Plane, Smoothing, Spiers, Coffin Shape, Rosewood Infill, Dovetailed, Original Iron 705.00
Plane, Smoothing, Stanley Bailey, No. 3, Type 16, 1936 .... 30.00
Plane, Smoothing, Stanley, No. 2, 1936 .... 225.00
Plane, Smoothing, Stanley, No. H1204, Handyman 20.00
Plane, Stanley, No. 24, Wooden Base 45.00
Plane, Stanley, No. 26 .... 30.00
Plane, Tongue & Groove, Stanley, No. 48 .... 65.00
Plane, Toothing, Marples, Beech 50.00
Plane, Tower & Lyons, Wooden Base, 10 In. 165.00
Plane, Violinmaker's, Preston, Brass, 1 1/2 In. 175.00
Plane, Weather-Stripping, Alumo, No. 1-A 65.00
Plumb Bob, Brass, 19th Century, 3 In. 35.00
Plumb Bob, Brass, Steel Tip, 19th Century, 6 In. 185.00
Plumb Bob, Brass, Steel Tip, 5 3/4 In. 75.00
Plumb Bob, Gunmetal, Steel Tip, 5 In. 240.00
Pricker, Leatherworker's, Rosewood, Brass, 7 Wheels, France 185.00
Protractor, Elliott, 268 High Holborn, London, 360 Degrees, Silver, 6 In. 100.00
Rabbet & Filletster, Stanley, No. 78, Duplex, Box 60.00
Rake, Curd Cheese Purdue Creamery, Wooden 150.00
Rope Gauge, Rabone, Boxwood, Brass, 7 In. 85.00
Router, Fruitwood, Carved, Figured Rosewood Wedge, Continental, 18th Century 85.00
Router, Oak, Rosewood Wedge, Caved-In Shape Of 3 Turrets, 18th Century, 7 In. 800.00
Router, Pistol, Coachmaker's, Gabriel, 18th Century 185.00
Router, Record, No. 722, Box 40.00
Rule, Brass, Boxwood, 2-Fold, Hand Cut Numbering, 18th Century, 18 In. 210.00
Rule, Caliper, Carpenter's, Stanley, No. 32 .... 50.00
Rule, Caliper, Lufkin, No. 372R, England 20.00
Rule, Carpenter's, Sliding, Stanley, No. 12, 2-Fold, 24 In. 225.00
Rule, Carpenter's, Stanley, No. 18, 2-Fold, 24 In. 30.00
Rule, Carpenter's, Stanley, No. 52, 4-Fold, 24 In. 70.00
Rule, Carpenter's, Stanley, No. 61, 4-Fold, 24 In. 33.00
Rule, Draughtman's, Rolling, Centimeters, Louison Chateauneuf & Cie, St. Etienne, 12 In. 230.00
Rule, Folding, Hayes Improved Practical Mechanics Rule, Brass, Boxwood, 4-Fold, 36 In. 160.00
Rule, Folding, John Rabone & Son, Ivory, Brass Fittings, 2-Fold, 12 In. 108.00
Rule, Folding, Rabone & Son, Boxwood, 4-Fold 135.00
Rule, Folding, Vara, Ivory, Brass Fittings, Square Section, 4-Fold, 13 In. 117.00
Rule, Ironmonger's, Rabone, Boxwood, Brass 160.00
Rule, Scale, Troughton & Sims, Ivory, 4 In. 67.00
Sash Fillister, Mathieson, No. 9, Handle, Partly Boxed Sole 200.00
Saw, Band, Foot Powered, Cast Iron & Wood, Barnes & Co., Rockford, Ill., Late 1800s .. 140.00

Saw, Bow, Boxwood, Decorative Stretcher, 19th Century, 14 In.	210.00
Saw, Bow, Mathieson, Beech	125.00
Saw, Dovetail, I. Sorby, Brass Back, Pistol Grip Handle, 7 In.	110.00
Saw, Howel, London, Brass Back, 18th Century, 18 In.	110.00
Saw, Tenon, Disston, Philadelphia, 10 In.	150.00
Saw, Tenon, Mathieson, Liverpool, Brass Back, 14 In.	58.00
Scissors, Bonsai Trimming, 19th Century	58.00
Scissors, Drapers, Brass, Steel, T. Wilkinson & Co., 1820, 13 In.	58.00
Scissors, Hand Forged, Concave Blades, 11 5/8 In.	165.00
Scraper, Starrett, No. 131, Handle	45.00
Scraper, Veneer, Stanley, No. 12 1/2	400.00
Screwbox, Mathieson, Beech, Boxwood, 3/4 In.	120.00
Screwdriver, Cabinetmaker's, Marples, Boxwood Handle, 10 In.	25.00
Screwdriver, Howarth, Rosewood Handle, 7 In.	50.00
Screwdriver, Spiral, Yankee, No. 130A	50.00
Seed Planter, Wooden, Painted, Pulled By Animal Or Man, Small, New England, 1850 . .	295.00
Shoeshine Kit, Walnut, Turned Legs, Fitted Interior, 15 x 15 1/2 x 18 In.	168.00
Shovel, Potato, Forged, R. Crawford, 47 In.	100.00
Slick, Shipwright's, Witherby, 3 1/2 In.	175.00
Spirit Level, Preston, No. 98, Mahogany, Brass, Fitted Box	390.00
Splitter & Drawing Plate, Basketmaker's, Iron, 18th Century	160.00
Spokeshave, Chamfer, Preston, Adjustable	108.00
Spokeshave, Cooper's, Stanley, No. 56	125.00
Spokeshave, Marples, Boxwood, Brass Faced, 7 1/2 In.	50.00
Spokeshave, Preston, Nickel Plated, 6 1/2 In.	70.00
Spokeshave, Stanley, No. 151	15.00
Spokeshave, Travisher, Preston	40.00
Square, Coachmaker's, Swiveling, Brass Stock	185.00
Square, Folding, Brass, Butterfield Of Paris, 18th Century	695.00
Square, Marples, Rosewood, Brass Bound, 12 In.	75.00
Square, Take Down, Keen Kutter	165.00
Tape Measure, Stanley, No. 7506	20.00
Template, Miter, Preston, Brass	75.00
Tether, Cast Iron, Green Paint, Bell Shape	90.00
Tightener, Rope, Wooden, For Rope Beds	93.00
Tongs, Ember, Steel Spring, Formed Hands As Grabber, Curved Handle, 16 In.	431.00
Trammels, Brass, Steel Tips, Knurled Steel Locking Nuts, 19th Century, 7 1/2 In., Pair . . .	160.00
Trammels, Brass, Steel Tips, Pencil Holder, 5 1/2 In., Pair	150.00
Trowel, Planting, Blacksmith Made, Iron, Wooden Handle, 18th Century, 10 1/2 In.	185.00
Turnscrew, Rosewood Handle, Early 19th Century, 21 In.	42.00
V-Blocks, Starrett, No. 178	60.00
Vise, Blacksmith	75.00
Vise, Bookbinder's, Iron, Japanned, Gilt Stenciling, Early 19th Century, 20 x 12 In.	450.00
Vise, Fruitwood, 8 In.	215.00
Vise, Hand, Fenn, 3 In.	60.00
Wheelbarrow, Wooden, Red, Gold Paint, Iron Wheels, Cape Cod, Early 1900s	315.00
Wrench, Bosch, Adjustable, 3 In.	50.00
Wrench, Cromna, Adjustable, France	42.00
Wrench, Geared Plier, Eifel, Attachment, Pouch	20.00
Wrench, Klein Linesman, 13 In.	25.00

TOOTHPICK HOLDERS are sometimes called *toothpicks* by collectors. The variously shaped containers used to hold small wooden toothpicks are made of glass, china, or metal. Most of the toothpick holders are Victorian. Additional items may be found in other categories, such as Bisque, Silver Plate, Slag Glass, etc.

Amberina, Crimped Rim, 4 1/4 x 3 7/8 In.	747.00
Arched Ovals, Ruby Stain	25.00
Bulging Loops, Blue	25.00
Bulging Loops, Pink	50.00
Button Arches, Opalescent	50.00
Button Arches, Ruby Stain	15.00
Cat, Tufts	115.00

Chutes & Ladders	150.00
Colorado, Blue, Gold Trim	70.00
Colorado, Green, Gold Trim	20.00
Colorado, Ruby Stain	45.00
Croesus, Green, Gold Trim	85.00
Cut Glass, Harvard, 1900	110.00
Daisy & Button, Amberina, Hobbs, Brockunier & Co., 1885	275.00
Daisy & Button, Barrel, Amber, Metal Rim	20.00
Diamond Spearhead, Green Opalescent ....35.00 to 45.00
Diamond With Peg, Ruby Stain	25.00
Double Dahlia With Lens, Flowers ....40.00 to 75.00
Figurine, Gold, Red, Yellow, Blue, White, Ceramic, Japan, 4 x 3 In.	28.00
Heart Band, Ruby Stain	50.00
Heart Band, Ruby Stain, Souvenir, Chicago, 1905	55.00
Jefferson Colonial, Toothpick, Green, Gold Trim	40.00
Kentucky, Green	90.00
Klondike, Amberette, 1898 ....375.00 to 475.00
Minnesota, Gold Trim	25.00
Paddlewheel	35.00
Pennsylvania	45.00
Porcelain, Tulip Shape	40.00
Portland	20.00
Punty Band, Souvenir, Oxford, N.Y.	18.00
Quartered Block	35.00
Shell & Seaweed, Green	50.00
Tennessee	90.00
Texas Star	35.00
Thumbprint, Gold Trim	70.00
Thumbprint, Ruby	75.00
Victoria, Ruby Stain, 1895	365.00
Wedding Bells, Maiden's Blush	85.00

TORQUAY is the name given to ceramics by several potteries working near Torquay, England, from 1870 until 1962. Until about 1900, the potteries used local red clay to make classical-style art pottery vases and figurines. Then they turned to making souvenir wares. Items were dipped in colored slip and decorated with painted slip and sgraffito designs. They often had mottoes or proverbs, and scenes of cottages, ships, birds, or flowers. The *Scandy* design was a symmetrical arrangement of brushstrokes and spots done in colored slips. Potteries included Watcombe Pottery (1870–1962); Torquay Terra-Cotta Company (1875–1905); Aller Vale (1881–1924); Torquay Pottery (1908–1940); and Longpark (1883–1957).

TORQUAY

Butter, Cover, Motto Ware, Help Yourself, Don't Be Shy	595.00
Pitcher, Motto Ware, Cottage, Stratford On Avon Front, 5 1/4 In.	95.00
Sugar, Glossy, Motto Ware, Be Aisy With Tha Sugar	125.00
Syrup, Squat, Motto Ware	450.00
Tobacco Jar, Motto Ware	450.00

TORTOISESHELL is the shell of the tortoise. It has been used as inlay and to make small decorative objects since the seventeenth century. Some species of tortoise are now on the endangered species list, and old and new objects made from these shells cannot be sold legally.

Box, Cover, Heart Shape, Ruffled Silver Rim, England, 1895, 3 3/4 x 3 In.	977.00
Box, Domed Hinged Cover, Rectangular, 1 x 2 7/8 x 1 7/8 In.	288.00
Box, Sewing, Ivory, Pincushion, Knife, Measuring Tape, Scissors, 1 x 6 1/2 x 4 1/2 In.	460.00
Box, Sterling Silver Mount, Oval, Sandalwood Interior, c.1899, 3 1/2 x 5 x 3 In.	690.00
Box, Trinket, Serpentine Domed Cover, Bun Feet, Victorian, 2 x 7 x 4 1/2 In.	863.00
Card Case, Hinged Cover, Ivory, Rectangular, 19th Century, 3 x 4 In.	316.00
Card Case, Mother-Of-Pearl Plaque, Landscape, Birds, Late 1800s, 3 1/8 x 4 1/8 In.	201.00
Casket, Ivory, Rectangular Form, Boxwood Lined Interior, Regency Style, 1900, 3 In.	690.00
Casket, Jewelry, Bone Bands, Oblong, Satin Lining, Edwardian, 3 1/2 x 10 1/4 x 7 In.	2760.00
Casket, Jewelry, Ivory, Regency Style, England, 19th Century, 7 x 13 1/2 x 10 In.	2185.00

Casket, William IV, Pewter, Ivory, Fabric Lined Interior, 3 x 11 x 8 1/2 In. 2760.00
Casket, William IV, Rectangular Domed Lid, 19th Century, 1 x 5 x 3 1/2 In. 316.00
Comb, Folding, Carved, Indian, Feathered Headdress, Jamaica, 1700s, 6 1/2 In. 3575.00
Cricket Cage, Cover, Ivory Ring Rim, Pagoda & Pine Tree Design, 5 In. 431.00
Dish, Silver Mounted, Shell Shape, Acanthus Scrolled Handle, 5 x 5 In. 863.00
Frame, Fluted, Ebonized, Ancient Ruin Scene, 12 x 14 In. 3910.00
Knife, Paddle Shape, Silver Handle, England, 1888, 16 1/2 In. 495.00
Mirror, Mother-Of-Pearl, Beveled, 20 1/24 In. 2300.00
Snuffbox, Silver Mounted, Man, Woman, Animals, Birds, Floral, 1700s, 3 x 2 In. 850.00
Snuffbox, Walnut, Disk Form, Concave, Walnut, Ebonized Edges, 3 3/8 In. 460.00

TOY collectors have special clubs, magazines, and shows. Toys are designed to entice children, and today they have attracted new interest among adults who are still children at heart. All types of toys are collected. Tin toys, iron toys, battery operated toys, and many others are collected by specialists. Dolls, Games, Teddy Bears, and Bicycles are listed in their own categories. Other toys may be found under company or celebrity names.

Acrobat, Clown, Tin Lithograph, Windup, 1920s, 7 In. 160.00
Acrobat, Windup, Korea, Box 15.00
Airplane, Air France, 3 Engines, Tin, Windup, Jep, France, Prewar, 16 In. 420.00
Airplane, Airmail, Tri-Prop, Keystone, 24-In. Wingspan 935.00
Airplane, American, Prop, Lockheed 375.00
Airplane, Balanced On Circus Elephant, Unique Art 740.00
Airplane, Big Parade, Drive String, Tin, Windup, Marx, Box, 24 x 9 In. 995.00
Airplane, Biplane, TWA Mail, 4 Engines, Red, White, 1929 . . . . 1995.00
Airplane, Clockwork, Marx, 1940s, 7 1/2-In. Wingspan 90.00
Airplane, Coast Guard Sea Plane, Ohio Art, Box 210.00
Airplane, Float, Sea Patrol, Windup, Ohio Art, 1945-1958, 9 3/4-In. Wingspan 115.00
Airplane, Ford Tri-Motor, Box, 15-In. Wingspan 695.00
Airplane, Gullwing, Painted, Cast Iron, Kilgore, 4 3/4 In. 300.00
Airplane, Gyro Copter, Twin Engine, 1940s, 12 1/2-In. Wingspan 320.00
Airplane, Hanger, Penny Toy, Germany, 4 x 5 In. 195.00
Airplane, Jet Fighter, Sabre, U.S. Air Force, Friction, Tin, ASC, Japan, Box, 9 In. 235.00
Airplane, Jet, Navy Panther, 6 Rockets, Working Compass, Tin, Plastic, Japan, 12 In. 300.00
Airplane, Jubilee Spitfire, Dinky Toys 225.00
Airplane, Little Jim, J.C. Penney, Single Wing, Steelcraft, 1930s, 22 1/2 In. 385.00
Airplane, Looping, Advances & Performs Flip, Leather Helmet, Tin, Windup, 7 1/2 In. . . . 350.00
Airplane, Monoplane, Hanger, Tin Lithograph, 1 Cent, Germany, 3 1/4 In. 195.00
Airplane, Monoplane, High Wing, Aluminized, Windup, CK, Japan, Box, 8-In. Wingspan . 685.00
Airplane, Mustang P-51, Gas, Wen-Mac, c.1950, 26 In. 40.00
Airplane, Orange Wings, Black Fuselage, Wyandotte, 1930s, 10-In. Wingspan 126.00
Airplane, Orange Wings, Black Fuselage, Wyandotte, 1930s, 18-In. Wingspan 138.00
Airplane, Pan American Airways, 4 Props, Pressed Steel, 27-In. Wingspan 165.00
Airplane, Pan American Airways, 747 Model, Battery Operated, Pedestal, 14 In.. . . . . 25.00
Airplane, Pan American Clipper Sky Chief, Friction, WS Hudson, Japan, 14 In. 195.00
Airplane, Passenger, Propellers Spin When Plane Moves, Roix Du Sud, 23-In. Wingspan . 1950.00
Airplane, Rescue, USAF, 10 3/4 x 16 In. 45.00
Airplane, Ride 'Em Fighter, Red Wings, Propeller & Seat, Pressed Steel, Keystone, 25 In. . 518.00
Airplane, Roller, Pilot, Tinplate Body, Friction Motor, Schuco, 4 In. 115.00
Airplane, Sikorsky Amphibian, U.S. Coast Guard, Red & Silver, Tootsietoy 125.00
Airplane, Single Engine, High Wing, Black & Orange, Large 350.00
Airplane, Space Race, Clockwork, Tin Lithograph, Germany 350.00
Airplane, Spirit Of Columbia, 555, Windup, American Flyer, 18-In. Wingspan 695.00
Airplane, Stratoliner Skycruiser, 4 Propellers, Tin, Friction, Marx, Box, 19-In. Wingspan . 370.00
Airplane, Transport, Logo Both Sides, 4 Engines, 1940s, 19 1/2 In. 350.00
Airplane, United Mainliner, Friction, Tin Lithograph Seats, 1950s, 19-In. Wingspan. 390.00
Airport Tower, Sky Hawk, Windup, Planes On Rods Spin, Tin Lithograph, Marx, 8 In. . . . 220.00
Airship, Tin, Clockwork, Mueller & Kadeder, 9 In. 2420.00
Ali & The Flying Carpet, Windup, KO, Japan, 1950s, 5 3/4 In. 367.00
Ambulance, Buick, Friction, White, Red Crosses, Japan, 1961, 16 In. 395.00
Ambulance, Daimler Army, Olive Green, Dinky Toys, England, 3 3/4 In. 138.00
Ambulance, Gray, Kingsbury, 7 In. 650.00

Ambulance, Kenton, 1910, 7 In. 950.00
Ambulance, Rambler, Bandai, 12 In. 375.00
Ark, Lithographed Windows, 14 Animals, 18 x 5 x 7 1/2 In. 895.00
Army Figure, Push Top, Press Helmet Down Figure Rolls, 1960s, 6 In. 75.00
Astronaut, Aqua, Mustard, Silver, Red, Tinplate, 1955, 6 1/2 In. 600.00
Astronaut, Blue, Brown, Silver, Orange, Carrying Space Gun, 1955, 6 1/2 In. 1080.00
Astronaut, Clear Plastic Dome, Blue, Rifle, Daiyai, 14 In. 290.00
Astronaut, Clear Plastic Dome, Red, Silver, Yellow, Rifle, Cragstan, 14 In. 750.00
Astronaut, Domed Helmet, Rifle, Metallic Blue, Lights, Sound, Movement, Daiya, 14 In. 1095.00
Astronaut, Great, Red, Black Arms & Feet, Cragstan, 14 In. 1095.00
Attache Case, James Bond, Play Money, Instructions 745.00
Baby, Crawling, Papier-Mache Head, Windup, Clockwork Mechanism, Clay, 11 In. 1800.00
Baby, Crawling, Windup, Celluloid, TN, Occupied Japan, Box, 5 In. 53.00
Baby Bath, Working Drain, Spigot, Wooden Stand, Tin, Germany, Maerklin, 1900, 12 In. . 875.00
Baby In Carriage, Mother Pushing, Tin, Windup, Japan, 6 1/2 In. 295.00
Band, Bombo The Monkey, Clockwork Motor, Tin, Box, Unique Art 170.00
Bandwagon, Circus, Horse Drawn, 2 Horses, Red, Gold, Yellow Wagon, Cast Iron, 15 In. 520.00
Banjo, Riverboat, Plastic & Celluloid, 22 In. 70.00
Barbie & Ken Little Theatre, Cardboard, Nylon Curtain, Play Scripts 375.00
Barney Google, Rides Sparkplug, Windup, Tin, 1920s 975.00
Barney Google, Wooden, Cloth, Jointed, King Features Sticker, Schoenhut, c.1922 ...... 260.00
Baseball Player, Mr. Baseball Jr., Batting, Battery Operated, Mfg. By K, Japan, c.1950 .. 1200.00
Battleship, Rover, Wood, Paper Clad, Torpedo, 41-Star Flag, c.1900, 22 In. 630.00
Bear, Blacksmith Teddy, With Anvil, Hammer, Windup, Plush, Tin, TN, Japan, Box, 6 In. . 210.00
Bear, Circus, Acrobatic Moves On Chair, Guntherman, 1900 .... 475.00
Bear, Dentist, Baby Bear In Chair, Battery Operated, Box 360.00
Bear, Golfer, Windup, Box, 1950s 325.00
Bear, On Wheels, Long Snout, Glass Eyes, Rubber Tires, Metal Frame, Steiff, 17 In. 470.00
Bear, Popcorn Vendor, Pushes Cart, Battery Operated, Tin, Plush, S & E, Japan, Box, 7 In. 510.00
Bear, Teddy The Artist, Draws Animals, Battery Operated, Templates, Japan, Box, 9 In. .. 540.00
Bear, Tumbling, Mohair, Tan, Arms On Rod, Clockwork Mechanism, Steiff, c.1913, 12 In. 2640.00
Bear, With Bottle, Tin, String, Germany, 1920s, 3 1/4 In. 275.00
Bear, Yellow Tag, White, Rubber Wheels, Tan Muzzle, Button In Ear, Steiff, 18 In. 390.00
Bears are also listed in the Teddy Bear category.
Bed, Doll's, 3-Spindle Headboard, Mushroom Finials, Spring, Casters, 18 x 28 1/2 In. ... 425.00
Bed, Doll's, Murphy Style, Wooden, Feather Mattress, Black, Gold Oriental Design, 26 In. 525.00
Bed, Doll's, Oak, Pressed Headboard & Footboard, Floral Design, 17 x 21 1/2 x 13 In. ... 75.00
Bed, Doll's, Renaissance Revival, Ticking Mattress, Late 19th Century, 24 1/2 x 35 In. ... 145.00
Bed, Doll's, Rope, Spool Turned Posts, Peaked Headboard, Linen Bedclothes, 15 x 14 In. 80.00
Bell Ringer, Harold Lloyd, Plunger, Eyes & Mouth Move, Bell Rings, Germany, 6 1/2 In. 520.00
Bellhop Express, Clockwork, Composition, Pushing Tin Suitcase, Gescha, 3 1/2 In. 100.00
Betsy The Hungry Bug, Windup, Eats Plastic Crumbs, Frankonia Japan, Box, 1960s 75.00
Bicycles that are large enough to ride are listed in their own category.
Bicyclist, Gay 90s, Victorian Man On Bicycle, Windup, Tin, Box, T.P.S., Japan, Box, 7 In. 370.00
Bird, Pheasant, Windup, Walks Back & Forth, Tin, GNK, West Germany, Box, 6 1/2 In. .. 145.00
Bird & Birdhouse, Tin Wire Cage, Penny Toy, 3 In. 70.00
Bison, Cream Mohair, Short Muzzle, Felt Horns, Steiff, 1960s, 11 x 15 In. 220.00
Black Boy, Stealing Chicken, Dog Chasing, Pull Toy, Wooden, 1930s, 13 1/2 In. 570.00
Blocks, Alphabet & Animal, Titelox 185.00
Blocks, Alphabet, Exotic Animals, Nesting Sizes, Largest Is 6 3/4 x 9 1/4 In. 650.00
Blocks, Alphabet, Wood, Paper Lithograph, Child, Animal, Schoenhut, c.1900, 2 x 5 In. .. 225.00
Blocks, American Logs, Halsam, Box, Early 1900s, 20 x 16 3/4 In. 115.00
Blocks, Clown Shape, Wooden, Instruction Booklet, Bill Ding, Box, 4 1/2 & 3 1/4 In. ... 70.00
Blocks, Graduated, ABC's, Children Scenes, Wood Lithograph, Germany, 8 Piece 176.00
Boat, Aircraft Carrier, Windup, Wyandotte, 1960s, 13 x 3 1/2 x 1 1/2 In. 125.00
Boat, Battleship, 1 Lifeboat, Flag, Windup, Tin, Orobr, 11 1/2 In. 1125.00
Boat, Battleship, Rolled Waves, Dayton Friction Toy Works 880.00
Boat, Battleship, Tin, Windup, Deck Guns, Lifeboats, Airplanes, Wolverine, 14 In. 200.00
Boat, Cabin Cruiser, Clockwork, Pressed Steel, Orkin, 31 In. 1760.00
Boat, Cabin Cruiser, Mercury Outboard Motor, All Metal, Linemar, Box, 14 In. 495.00
Boat, Conqueror, Paper Lithograph On Wood, Crow's Nest, Cannons, Bliss, 1900s, 20 In. 1350.00
Boat, Ferry, Sunny Andy, Windup, Bell Rings, Tin Lithograph, Wolverine, 13 1/2 In. 290.00
Boat, Flywheel, Tin, Germany, 7 In. 175.00

Boat, Gun, Cap Firing Mechanism, Clockwork, Box, Bing, 1915 . . . . 1786.00
Boat, Little Skipper Toy Boat Fleet, 4 Wooden Boats, Transogram, Box, 8 x 13 In. 215.00
Boat, Navy Aircraft Carrier, Tin Lithograph, Friction, Plastic Propellers, Japan, 1950s . . . 175.00
Boat, New Orleans Steamboat, Pull Toy, Painted, 10 In. 425.00
Boat, Ocean Liner, Queen Elizabeth, Clockwork, Tin, Modern Toys, Japan, 19 In. 330.00
Boat, Ocean Liner, Tin Lithograph, Windup, U.S. Zone Germany, 14 In. 155.00
Boat, Ocean Liner, Twin Funnels, Black & Red Hull, Clockwork Motor, Arnold, 13 In. . . 460.00
Boat, Paddle Wheel, Nickeled Cast Iron, Wilkins 165.00
Boat, Pilot Electro Boat, Seat, Controls, Battery Operated, Tin, Japan, Box, 11 In. 235.00
Boat, Plastic, Green, Orange Seat, Wheels, Titian Midge, Allan, c.1964, 21 x 6 In. 275.00
Boat, Polly-Wog, Outboard, Tin, Wood, Red Paint, Steam Powered, Boucher, 22 1/2 In. . . 635.00
Boat, Pond, 2-Masted Sailboat, Movable Rudder, 29 1/2 In. 140.00
Boat, Pond, Planked, Gaff Rigged, Sails, 67 x 60 In. 2070.00
Boat, Propeller, Red & Green Lights, Battery Operated, Wooden, Japan, 1950s, 16 1/4 In. 170.00
Boat, Racing, Tin Lithograph, Japan, 12 In. 95.00
Boat, Sabena, Twin Engine Airliner, Germany, 16 1/2 In. 335.00
Boat, Sea Babe, Wooden, Battery Operated, Fleet/Line, Box, 13 In. 375.00
Boat, Shootingstar, Friction, Japan, 10 In. 325.00
Boat, Speedboat, Battery Operated, Wooden, Metal, Painted Dragon, Japan, 1950s, 18 In. 295.00
Boat, Speedboat, Speed Queen, Windup, Tin 85.00
Boat, Steam Propelled, Tin, Movable Rack, Early 1900s 1315.00
Boat, Submarine, Tin, Painted, Marklin, 10 1/2 In. 60.00
Boat, Torpedo Boat, Battery Operated, Remote Control, Linemar, Box, 11 In. 285.00
Boat, Tugboat, Battery Operated, Japan, Box, 12 1/2 In. 295.00
Boat, Tugboat, Radio Controlled, 1956 . . . . 4850.00
Boat, Tugboat, Texaco Fire Chief, Display Stand, 9 1/2 In. 30.00
Boat, USS Ocean Liner, Battery Operated, Linemar, 1950s, 14 In. 395.00
Boat, Warship, Sparking, Box, Marx, 15 In. 325.00
Boat, Wilmington Ocean Liner, Early 1920s, 17 In. 805.00
Boat, Zoom Prop, Blue, Red, Tin, Rudder, Windup, Box, TET, 14 In. 230.00
Bonzo, Tin, Windup, Guntherman, 1920s, 9 1/2 In. 3000.00
Bop Bag, Joe Palooka, Instructions, Pump 175.00
Boxer, In Training, Celluloid, Pre-World War II, Japan, 7 3/4 In. 4500.00
Boxer, Slugger Champions, Mechanical, Tin Lithograph, Box, Germany, 3 1/2 In. 180.00
Boxing Ring, Slugger Champions, Tin, Windup, Biller, U.S. Zone Germany, 3 1/2 In. 315.00
Boy, Black, Being Bitten On Seat By Dog, Windup, Celluloid, Japan 750.00
Boy, Express, Bell Boy Pushes Trunk, Legs Move, Tin, Gescha, 3 1/2 In. 155.00
Boy, On Scooter, Clockwork, V B & C Paris, 8 1/2 In. 2800.00
Boy Fishing, Tin, Windup, Linemar, Japan, Box, 6 In. 200.00
Bracelet Set, Faux Pearl, For Ginny & Her Mother, Doll & Child, Vogue, c.1958 . . . . 90.00
Buckboard, Buck Saw, Log Sawing Stand, Spoke Wheels, c.1900, 22 x 31 x 24 In. 950.00
Buckboard, City Express, Spoke Wheels, Brass Nameplate Gary, 18 x 36 In. 1230.00
Buckboard, Doll's, Red Painted Wood, Yellow Striped Body, Seat, 32 In. 315.00
Bucking Bronco, Cowboy Rider, Tin, Windup, Platform, Lehmann, 7 In. 415.00
Bucking Bronco, Wild West, Tin Lithograph, Windup, Box, Lehmann 1100.00
Bull, Tinplate, Clockwork Motor, Moving Head, 7 In. 105.00
Bulldozer, Caterpillar, Matchbox, Lesney, Box 120.00
Bulldozer, Lunar, Bump & Go, Battery Operated, Tin, Plastic, TN, Japan, Box, 9 1/2 In. . . 395.00
Bus, 15 Window, Dual Wheel, Driver, Fageol Safety Coach, Cast Iron, 12 In. 290.00
Bus, Century Of Progress, Cast Iron, Arcade, 1933, 12 In. 320.00
Bus, Century Of Progress, Greyhound Lines, Chicago, 1933, Arcade, 10 3/4 In. 80.00
Bus, Century Of Progress, Greyhound Lines, Cream, Blue, Cast Iron, Arcade, 7 In. 260.00
Bus, Clockwork Motor, Open Top, With Rear Stairs, Tinplate, Germany, 4 1/2 In. 230.00
Bus, Coast-To-Coast, Gray, Orange Wheels, Driver, Dent, 15 In. 1265.00
Bus, Double-Decker, Chicago Motor Coach, Arcade, Green, 13 In. 3500.00
Bus, Double-Decker, Friction, Tin, Japan, 7 1/2 In. 175.00
Bus, Double-Decker, Interstate, Clockwork, Strauss, 1926 . . . . 105.00
Bus, Double-Decker, No. 776, Schuco 195.00
Bus, Double-Decker, Railed Roof Top Seating, Clockwork, Lehmann, 7 In. 2035.00
Bus, Double-Decker, Tan Over Red, Metal Hubs, Dinky Toys 46.00
Bus, Double-Decker, Windup, Lehmann, No. 590 . . . . 3100.00
Bus, Excursion Car, Box, Prewar Japan, 8 1/2 In. 525.00
Bus, Fageol, Driver, Nickel Grille, Arcade, 12 In. 265.00

Bus, Fageol, Greyhound Lines, Blue & White Paint, Cast Iron, Arcade, 12 In. 635.00
Bus, Green Paint, Cast Iron, Kenton, 11 In. 395.00
Bus, New York World's Fair, Greyhound Lines, Arcade, 10 1/2 In. 330.00
Bus, Oh Boy, 2-Tone, 19 In. 975.00
Bus, Packard, Coast To Coast, Keystone 8250.00
Bus, Passenger Coach, Type II Belt Line, 22 Seats, Buddy L, 1927-1932, 29 1/4 In. 5720.00
Bus, Red With Gold Stripe, Cast Iron, Arcade, 13 In. 460.00
Busy Bridge, Tin, Windup, Marx, 24 In. 625.00
Busy Lizzy, Girl Sweeping Floor, Tin, Windup, Stamped, Germany, 1920s, 8 1/2 In. 695.00
Butcher, In Cart, Pulled By Pig, Windup, Stocke 650.00
Butterfly, Tin Lithograph, Penny, Wings Flutter, Penny Toy, 2 In. 38.00
Buzzy Bee, Plastic Wings, Fisher-Price, 6 x 5 1/2 In. 40.00
Calliope, Overland Circus, 2 Horses, Musician, Driver, 2 Outriders, Kenton, 14 In. 175.00
Calliope, Royal Circus, 2 Horses, Driver, Parade Headgear, Toy, Hubley, 16 In. 2640.00
Camel, Ivory Wool, Velvet Legs & Face, Brown Eyes, Steiff, 13 In. 110.00
Camel, Pull Toy, Double Humps, Cast Iron Wheels In Feet, Silk Tassels, 14 In. 425.00
Camera, Pathe, Tin, Crank Action, Marx, 1930s, 6 In. 210.00
Cannon, Artillery, Remember The Maine, Cast Iron, Kenton, c.1905 . . . . 2000.00
Cannon, Field, Painted, Cleated Wheels, Brown & Green, World War I, Marklin 350.00
Cap Gun, 45 Automatic, Metal, Hubley, On Display Card, 7 In. 80.00
Cap Gun, Bang-O, Box, J & E Stevens, 1940 . . . . 160.00
Cap Gun, Circle K, 6 Shooter, Trooper, Hubley 45.00
Cap Gun, Cisco Kid, Brown Grips, Box 375.00
Cap Gun, Colt 45, Hubley, Metal Holsters, Leather Belt 250.00
Cap Gun, Deputy, Display Card, Kilgore . . . . .75.00 to 150.00
Cap Gun, Deputy, Hubley 70.00
Cap Gun, Dragnet Special, 5 1/2 In. 275.00
Cap Gun, Fanner 50, Cartridge Loading Bullets, Instructions, 11 In. 300.00
Cap Gun, Hawkeye, USMC Holster 38.00
Cap Gun, Lightning Express, Cast Iron, Kenton 450.00
Cap Gun, Metal, Plastic Inset Grips, Box, 12 In. 240.00
Cap Gun, Mountie, Metal, Hubley, On Display Card, 7 In. 210.00
Cap Gun, Pirate Pistol, Double Barrel, Metal, Hubley, Box, 9 1/2 In. 325.00
Cap Gun, Pistol, Automatic Repeating, Pressed Steel, Instructions, Acme, 4 1/2 In., Pair . . 50.00
Cap Gun, Ranger, Kilgore, On Card 110.00
Cap Gun, Repeater, Pearl Grips, Plastic, Marx, 1950s, 12 In. 225.00
Cap Gun, Revolving Cylinder, Mattel 125.00
Cap Gun, Swivelshot, Trick Holster, Smoking, Box 500.00
Cap Gun, Texan With Star, Hubley, 1940, 10 In. 210.00
Cap Gun, Tophand 250, Metal, Plastic Inset Grips, Nichols, On Display Card, 10 In. 160.00
Cap Gun, Trooper, Hubley, Box, 6 1/2 In., Pair 210.00
Cap Gun, Unexcelled Automatic, Box 80.00
Cap Gun, Wagon Train, Revolving Cylinder . . . . .100.00 to 120.00
Cap Gun, Wyatt Earp, Buntline Special, Leather Holster, Pair 275.00
Cap Gun, Young Buffalo Bill, Hubley 20.00
Cap Gun Set, Al Capone, Plastic Handle, Die Cast, 1960, 3 1/2 x 6 1/4 In. 25.00
Captain America, Super Hero, Windup, Marvel, Box, 5 1/2 In. 150.00
Car, Airflow, Coupe, Red, Wyandotte, 1936, 6 In. 150.00
Car, Airflow, Tin, 1930s, 4 In. 34.00
Car, Airflow, White Rubber Wheels, Arcade, 6 1/4 In. 303.00
Car, Alfa Romeo, Instructions, Remote Control, Schuco 1690.00
Car, Ambulance, Mechanical, Tin Lithograph, Drivers, Wounded On Stretchers, Tipp, 9 In. 400.00
Car, Army Command, MP Soldier, Tin, Friction, Light, Marx, Box, c.1950, 20 In. 550.00
Car, Aston Martin, James Bond Figures, Tire Slashers, Corgi 95.00
Car, Aston Martin, James Bond, Ejector Seat, Working Roof Hatch, Corgi, Box 325.00
Car, Barbie, Austin Healy, Peach, Turquoise Interior, Irwin 90.00
Car, Barbie, Convertible, Plastic, Orange & Teal, Lucite Windshield, Wire Wheels, c.1962 165.00
Car, Barney Rubble, Rubble's Wreck, Flintstones, Tin, Friction, Marx, 1960s, 7 1/2 In. . . . 330.00
Car, Batmobile, Battery Operated, Gold & Black, Box, Taiwan, 1970s, 12 In. 450.00
Car, Buick Riviera Future, Japan, 1960, 15 In. 195.00
Car, Bump & Go, Tin, Clockwork, Gunthermann, Germany, 9 In. 1375.00
Car, Cadillac Coupe, Side Wheel On Passenger Side, White Top 150.00
Car, Cadillac, Convertible, Baby Blue, Box, Alps, 11 In. 2200.00

Toy, Dollhouse Furniture, Dining Set,
1 x 2 3/4 In., 3 Piece

Toy, Car, Coupe, Citroen B14, 1929

Car, Carrier, Pressed Steel, Marx, 21 1/2 In. 60.00
Car, Cast Iron, Red Paint, Dent, 5 In. 90.00
Car, Chevrolet, 1955 Model, Friction, Doors Open, Tin, Marusan, Japan, 1950s, 10 1/2 In.   1265.00
Car, Chevrolet, Police, Friction, Japan, Box, 1963, 17 In. 395.00
Car, Citroen DS19, Plastic Steering Wheel & Windshield, Tin, 8 In. 500.00
Car, Convertible, Cadillac Old Timer 1933, Tin, Friction, Bandai, Box, 8 In. 235.00
Car, Coupe, Citroen B14, 1929 . . . . *Illus*   2090.00
Car, Coupe, Silver Arrow, Tires, 7 In. 149.00
Car, Couple, Pressed Steel, Wyandotte, 1930s, 6 In. 195.00
Car, Crash, Driver, Cast Iron, Hubley, 4 1/2 In. 60.00
Car, Dodge, Coupe, Hubley, 9 1/4 In. 1250.00
Car, Dora Dipsy, Windup, Tin, Plastic Head, Marx, Box, 5 1/2 In. 215.00
Car, Dream, Friction, Retractable Top, Box, 1950, 8 1/2 In. 675.00
Car, Falcon, Art Deco Styling, Friction, Tin Lithograph, Plastic Top, Yellow, Marx, 29 In. .   310.00
Car, Fire Chief, Hudson, Bell Ringer, Marx, 1930s 475.00
Car, Fire Chief, Siren, Red Pressed Steel, Clockwork Motor, Electric Lights, Marx, 14 In.   460.00
Car, Flintstone Flivver, Vinyl Head, Linemar, 1960s, 6 7/8 In. 276.00
Car, Ford, Model A, Arcade, 6 1/2 In. 1400.00
Car, Ford, Model T, Coupe, Arcade, 6 1/2 In. 55.00
Car, Ford, Model T, Limousine, Tin, Windup, Woman Driver, Bing, Germany, 6 1/4 In. . . 576.00
Car, Ford, Model T, Sedan, Woman Driver, Bing, 6 1/4 In. 220.00
Car, Ford, Thunderbird, Convertible, Tin Lithograph, Rubber Wheels, Friction, 8 In. 155.00
Car, Ford, Thunderbird, Friction, Tin, Plastic Roof, TN, Japan, 8 In. 240.00
Car, Funny Flivver, Box, 7 In. 650.00
Car, Graham, Green, Prewar, 11 1/2 In. 2500.00
Car, Hill Climber Roadster, Pressed Steel, Ohio Art, 1930s, 10 1/2 x 4 3/4 x 3 1/4 In. 225.00
Car, Hill Climber Touring, Woman Passenger, Friction, Dayton 800.00
Car, Hot Rod, Barbie, Ken, Midge, Turquoise, Plastic, White Seats, c.1963, 17 x 7 1/2 In. . 195.00
Car, Hudson, Electric Headlights, Wyandotte, All Metal Products Co., 1930s 960.00
Car, Jaguar, XX-120, Doepke, 1955, 16 In. 595.00
Car, Kingsbury Airflow, 1915 . . . . 725.00
Car, Leapin' Lena, Windup, Strauss 475.00
Car, Limousine, 6 Cylinders, Balloon Tires, Tin, Windup, Moko, Germany, 9 1/2 In. 1075.00
Car, Limousine, Green & Black, Fisher, 5 In. 575.00
Car, Limousine, Tin Lithograph, Painted Roof & Driver, Penny Toy, 4 In. 115.00
Car, Lincoln, Driver, Black, Friction, 14 In. 795.00
Car, Mercedes Sedan, Friction, Tin Lithograph, Japan, 12 In. 110.00
Car, Milton Berle, Tin, Windup, Crazy Action, Head Spins, Marx, Box, 6 In. 525.00
Car, Mini, Box, Anguplas, 1 3/4 In. 130.00
Car, Moon Rocket, Battery Operated, Flashing Light, Spinning Antenna, 1950s, 9 1/2 In. . 285.00
Car, Mr. Magoo, Vinyl Head, Cloth Roof, Battery Operated, Metal, Hubley, Box, 9 1/4 In.   610.00
Car, Nickel Plated Driver, Wheel, Green, Cast Iron, Arcade, 7 In. 400.00
Car, Old Jalopy, Tin Lithograph, Friction, Plastic Driver, Linemar, 1955, 4 3/4 In. 135.00
Car, Oldsmobile, Friction, Siren, Nickel Plated Trim, Rubber Tires, Box, 10 In. 460.00
Car, Oldsmobile, Green & Silver, Die Cast, Rubber Wheels, Tootsietoy, 5 1/2 In. 25.00
Car, Phaeton, Canopy, Chauffeur, Passenger, Dent, Cast Iron, Dent, 9 In. 1450.00
Car, Phaeton, Gold, Wilkins, 10 In. 900.00
Car, Pierce Arrow Estate Wagon, Cast Iron, Simulated Wooden Panel, Hubley, 6 In. 200.00
Car, Police Department, Friction, Tin, Japan, 1950s, 8 1/2 In. 300.00

Car, Police Squad, Friction, Tin, Siren Noise, Lupor, Box, c.1950, 10 1/2 In. 265.00
Car, Police, 260 Metropolis, Buick, Blue & White, Corgi, Box 55.00
Car, Police, Chevrolet Impala, Israeli Police, Blue & White, Die Cast, Sabra, No. 8115/1 . 40.00
Car, Police, Citroen, 1200 Kg Van, Die Cast, C.I.J., No. 3/89 . . . . 150.00
Car, Police, Comic, Swiveling Siren On Hood, Battery Operated, Tin Lithograph, 9 1/4 In. 385.00
Car, Police, Renault, 4 CV, Die Cast, C.I.J., No. 3/49 . . . . 110.00
Car, Police, Royal Canadian Mounted Police, Blue, Corgi, No. 45, Box 110.00
Car, Police, Simca 1000, Die Cast, C.I.J., No. 3/8 . . . . 120.00
Car, Racing, Auburn Super Racer, Vinyl, Auburn Rubber, Box, 10 In. 160.00
Car, Racing, Bouncing Benny, Pull Toy, Large Tires, Marx, Box, 1930s, 7 1/2 In. 695.00
Car, Racing, Cast Iron, Nickel Plated Driver, White Rubber Tires, Champion, 9 In. 250.00
Car, Racing, Don Prudhomme Mongoose Fuel Dragster, White Paint, Hot Wheels, 1971 . . 180.00
Car, Racing, Driver, Windup, Tin, Leather Helmet, Memo, 1930s, 6 In. 160.00
Car, Racing, Giant King, Windup, Blue, Marx, Box, 1920s 800.00
Car, Racing, Golden Arrow Racer Classic, Celluloid Windshield & Driver, 1927, 21 In. . . 625.00
Car, Racing, Grandstand, 3 Stock Cars, Tin, Push Levers, Linemar, Japan, Box 235.00
Car, Racing, Green, Clockwork Motor, Box, Tin, Schuco, 5 1/2 In. 115.00
Car, Racing, Indianapolis 500, Tin, Friction Drive, Japan, 1960s, 15 In. 715.00
Car, Racing, Indy Style, No. 5, Cast Iron, Hubley, 10 In. 635.00
Car, Racing, Mario Andretti, No. 9, Old Mr. Boston, Yellow 55.00
Car, Racing, Mercedes, Metal, Battery Operated, Japan, 1950s 345.00
Car, Racing, Paya, Tin, Windup, Copy Of 1930s Bugatti, Original Box, 19 In. 275.00
Car, Racing, Penny, Red & White, Germany, 1920s, 2 1/2 In. 95.00
Car, Racing, Pinky, Monkey Driver, Tin, Windup, AAA, Japan, Box, 5 1/2 In. 135.00
Car, Racing, Piston Racer, Hubley, 11 In. 2500.00
Car, Racing, Red, Cream, Friction Motor, Driver, Hessmobile, 7 1/2 In. 575.00
Car, Racing, Rocket 7, Tin, Japan, 6 1/2 In. 40.00
Car, Racing, Sprite Soda, Gas Powered, Testors, Box, Instructions 250.00
Car, Racing, Thimble Drome Prop-Rod, Plastic, Metal, Gas, Cox MFG, Partial Box, 12 In. 225.00
Car, Roadster, Flywheel Drive, Schieble, 1920s, 17 1/4 In. 490.00
Car, Roadster, Lever Action, Blue, 1960s, 6 3/4 In. 60.00
Car, Roadster, Lever Action, Friction, Red, Loud Motor Sound, Japan, 1960s, 6 3/4 In. . . . 75.00
Car, Roadster, Tin Lithograph, Spare On Trunk, Windup, Chein, 1920s, 6 1/2 In. 1100.00
Car, Rumble Seat, Reo, Arcade, 9 In. 2500.00
Car, Runs On Round Platform, Arrested By Cop On Motorcycle, Windup, Marx, 1930s . . 575.00
Car, Sabre, Yellow Plastic, Driver, Rubber Tires, Original Box, c.1953 . . . . 495.00
Car, Salesman, Sliding Cargo Doors, Wood, Cast Brass, Hebert's Automatic Brake, 26 In. 4025.00
Car, Sedan, 1925 Model, Tin, Windup, Blue, White, Stand Fast Easel Co., 8 1/2 In. 195.00
Car, Sedan, Clockwork Mechanism, Gunthermann, 10 In. 1595.00
Car, Sedan, Ford, Tin, Friction, Ono, Japan, Box, 8 1/2 In. 115.00
Car, Sedan, Lilliput Auto, Tin, Windup, Distler, U.S. Zone Germany, Box, 2 1/2 In. 90.00
Car, Sedan, Mercury Style, Pulling Skipper Boat On Trailer, Tin, Friction, Box, 12 In. . . . 315.00
Car, Sedan, Take A Part, Nickel Plated Grill, Wooden Wheels, A.C. Williams, 1930s, 7 In. 480.00
Car, Sportster, Metal, Plastic Windshield, Rubber Tires, Friction, Marx, 1950s, 20 In. 280.00
Car, Sportster, Skipper, Green, Plastic, Red Seats, Packaging, c.1963, 17 x 6 In. 220.00
Car, Studebaker, Cast Iron, Red Paint, Silver Frame, Headlights, Hubley, 4 7/8 In. 180.00
Car, Tin Lizzy, Windup, Marx, 7 In. 115.00
Car, Touring, Driver, Nickel Plated Wheels, Green, Cast Iron, Arcade, 6 1/2 In. 345.00
Car, Touring, Ford, Model T, Black, Gold, White Painted Wheels, Cast Iron, Arcade, 6 In. 230.00
Car, Touring, Tin, Windup, Doors Open, Tin Driver, Moko, Germany, 1930s, 9 1/2 In. . . . 940.00
Car, Town & Country, Convertible, Retractable Roof, Wooden, Buddy L, 18 1/2 In. 550.00
Car, Volkswagen, Space Patrol, Battery Operated, Tin, Lights, Astronaut, Japan, 12 In. . . . 6500.00
Car, Volvo 444, Black, 1960s, 7 1/2 In. 495.00
Car, Willie, Walking On Car Tires, Tin, Remote Control, Y, Japan, Box, 8 In. 90.00
Carousel, 3 Riders, Windup, Germany 595.00
Carousel, Clockwork, 4 Tin Boats, Propellers, Mueller & Kadeder, Germany, 12 In. 1155.00
Carousel, Windup, Tin, 2 Cats, 2 Dogs, Box, 9 In. 355.00
Carousel, Windup, Unique Art, 1950s 375.00
Carriage, Doll's, Blue Paint, Mustard Lines, Wooden Spokes, Oilcloth Top, 32 x 35 In. . . 385.00
Carriage, Doll's, Enameled Tinplate, Marklin, 9 In. 1980.00
Carriage, Doll's, Leather Top, Wooden Spoke Wheels, Hand Stenciled, 36 In. 400.00
Carriage, Doll's, Pink Wicker, Green Satin Lined, Sidelights, All Wood 80.00
Carriage, Doll's, Wicker, Scroll & Fiddlehead, Parasol, Liner, Steel Wheels, 36 In. 690.00

Carriage, Doll's, Wicker, Steel Wheels, Rubber Tires, 30 x 27 In. 127.00
Carriage, Doll's, Wood & Metal, Folding Sun Screen, Wooden Spoke Wheels, 34 x 36 In. 330.00
Carriage, Horseless, Green, Blue, Clockwork Motor, Lehmann, 4 In. 375.00
Carriage, Horseless, White, Blue, No Driver, Lehmann, 5 In. 210.00
Carriage, Pushed By Black Mammy, Mechanical 825.00
Carriage, Surrey, White Horses, Red Velvet Seats, Red Fringe, Pair 395.00
Carrying Case, Barbie & Midge, Duet, Vinyl, Red, Handle, c.1963, 17 1/2 x 13 1/3 In. ... 55.00
Cart, Black Porter Pushing, Clockwork Motor, Strauss, 6 In. 195.00
Cart, Cairo Express Elephant Cart, Cast Iron, 10 In. 375.00
Cart, Coal, Green & Yellow, Single Horse, Black Driver, Cast Iron, Lenton, 12 In. 259.00
Cart, Coal, Pulled By Mule, Cast Iron, Dent, 1900s, 13 1/2 In. 1250.00
Cart, Doll's, Wooden, Red Painted Wicker, Late 19th Century, 15 x 28 In. 480.00
Cart, Dump, Black Horse, Red Steel Cart, Wilkins, 12 1/2 In. 115.00
Cart, Dump, Mule, Tip Bed, Black Driver, Cast Iron, 10 1/2 In. 170.00
Cart, Goat, Driver, Harris, 1900s, 9 1/2 In. 1395.00
Cart, Happy Easter, Rabbit Pulls Cart, Tin, Wyandotte, 7 1/2 In. 110.00
Cart, Horse Pull, Painted, 7 x 21 x 7 1/2 In. 168.00
Cart, Ice Cream, Windup, Courtland, 6 1/2 In. 190.00
Cart, Postal Delivery, 2 Wooden Spoke Wheels, Dome Top, Pull Toy, c.1900, 17 x 17 In. . 1065.00
Cart, Red, Spoke Wheel, Marked Teddy, 6 x 37 x 8 In. 140.00
Cart, Sheffield Farmers Dairy, Horse Drawn, Wood 1495.00
Case, Train, Barbie, Vinyl, Zipper, Mirror Lid, Standard Plastic Products, 1962, 10 x 6 In. 65.00
Casey The Cop, Walker, Windup, Unique Art, 1930s, 9 In. 650.00
Cash Register, Fisher-Price, 1960 .... 45.00
Casper The Friendly Ghost, Tin, Windup, Linemar, 5 In. 240.00
Cat, Black, Arched Back, Raised Tail, Tag In Ear, Steiff, 8 In. 66.00
Cat, Black, Straw Stuffed, Humpback, Glass Eyes, Stitched Nose & Mouth, 10 In. 200.00
Cat, Cream, Light Brown, Red, Tail, Wagging, Windup, Germany, 8 x 4 1/2 In. 315.00
Cat, Felix, On Scooter, Windup, 7 1/2 In. 750.00
Cat, Felix, Pull Toy, Germany, 1920s 845.00
Cat, Felix, Straw Stuffed, Felt, Glass Eyes, Stitched Mouth, 13 In. 145.00
Cat, Felix, Wood Jointed, 5 In. 60.00
Cat, Felix, Wooden, Leather Ears, Jointed, Schoenhut, Copyright 1922, 8 In. 200.00
Cat, Hungry Cat, Battery Operated, Tin, Box, Linemar 520.00
Cat, Knitting, Battery Operated, Japan, Box 175.00
Cat, Nina The Cat, Chases Mouse, Windup, Lehmann 2250.00
Cat, On Wheels, Black Wool Pile, Green Glass Eyes, Carved Wooden Legs, 6 In. 115.00
Cat, Tabby, Gray Striped, Green Glass Eyes, Bell, Pull Toy, Steiff, 10 x 6 1/2 In. 1210.00
Cat, With Ball, Marx, 6 1/2 In. 60.00
Cat & Mouse, Cat Rolls Forward Chasing Circling Mouse In Cage, Doll Co., 11 In. 1925.00
Chair, Doll's, Plank Seat, 4 Spindle Back, Green Paint, Strawberries, Leaves, 9 1/4 In. ... 605.00
Chariot, Woman Driver, Hubley, 1902, 10 1/2 In. 1600.00
Charley Chimp, Hula Expert, Windup, Plastic, Cloth, G.B.C., Japan, Box, 1960s, 8 3/4 In. 85.00
Cheery Cook, Holds Plate, Waddles, Windup, Celluloid, SNK, Occupied Japan, Box, 5 In. 125.00
Chest, Doll's, Mirror, Walnut, 3 Drawers, Porcelain Knobs, 23 x 12 x 5 1/2 In. 115.00
Chimpanzee, Brown Mohair, White Chin, Felt Face, Jointed, Seated, Steiff, 10 In. 165.00
Chinese Men, Carrying Emperor, Tin, Windup, Lehmann, 6 In. 1540.00
Chinese Men, Carrying Tea Chest, Windup, Lehmann, 1913 .... 850.00
Circus, Ring-A-Ling, Clockwork Motor, Green Base, Ringmaster, Spinning, Marx 750.00
Circus, Ring-A-Ling, Lithograph, Pink & Plum Base, Marx, 1920s, 7 1/2 In. 1210.00
Circus Wagon, Band, Gold Trim, 6 Musicians, Driver, White Horses, Kenton, 15 In. 825.00
Circus Wagon, Band, Open Carriage, Pressed Steel Body, 4 Blue Wheels, Hubley, 30 In. . 7800.00
Circus Wagon, Band, Overland Circus, Horses, Musicians, Driver, Kenton, 14 1/2 In. 860.00
Circus Wagon, Bear, 2 White Horses, Gold, Hubley, Cast Iron, 13 In. 290.00
Circus Wagon, Elephant, Yellow Carrier, Yellow Wheels, Gold Trim, Hubley, 1920, 16 In. 1080.00
Circus Wagon, Giraffe, Baby, 4 Pressed Steel Body, Yellow Wheels, Hubley, 1920, 16 In. . 5100.00
Circus Wagon, Gray Lion, Red Carriage, Red Wheels, 2 Gray Horses, 1920, 16 In. 3000.00
Circus Wagon, Pulled By 2 Iron Horses, Iron Wheels 300.00
Circus Wagon, Rhino, Steel Cage, Yellow Carrier, Yellow Wheels, Hubley, 1920, 16 In. .. 2700.00
Circus Wagon, Tiger, Gold Trim, 2 Horses, Driver, 2 Lions In Cage, Hubley, 16 In. 468.00
Circus Wagon, Tiger, Green Pressed Steel Cage, Yellow Wheels, Cast Iron, 1920, 16 In. .. 1920.00
Circus Wagon, Tin Body & Wheels, Cardboard Animals, Rocks Back & Forth, Dayton ... 190.00
Clothes Rack, Doll's, Drying, For Doll Clothes, Wooden, Folding, 8 Rods, 13 1/2 In. 75.00

Clown, Balances Whirligig On Nose, Windup, Germany, 1920s 350.00
Clown, Car, Erratic, Multicolored, Clockwork, Tin, Unique Art, 8 In. 85.00
Clown, Clockwork, Musical, Gunthermann, Early 1900s 3200.00
Clown, Handstand, Tin Lithograph, 1940s, 4 3/4 In. 90.00
Clown, Handstand, Windup, Tin, Chein, 1940s, 6 In. 110.00
Clown, Happy The Violinist, Cloth Suit, Japan, 9 In. 160.00
Clown, Juggler, Windup, Revolving Plates On Sticks 340.00
Clown, Juggling Apples, Box, Linemar, 1956 .... 795.00
Clown, Lifts Arm, He Nods, Clockwork, Germany, 5 1/2 In. 650.00
Clown, On Motorcycle, Circles Hoop, Tin Lithograph, Windup 275.00
Clown, On Motorcycle, Sidecar, Tin, Windup, England, 3 1/4 In. 685.00
Clown, On Roller Skates, Windup, Box, T.P.S. 425.00
Clown, On Tightrope, Balancing, Box 25.00
Clown, Roly Poly, Schoenhut, 5 1/2 In. 445.00
Clown, Roly Poly, Schoenhut, Early 20th Century, 12 In. 660.00
Clown, Roly Poly, Tin Lithograph, Yellow Suit, Chein, 1928, 6 1/4 In. ....195.00 to 265.00
Clown, Trombonist, Tin Lithograph, Cloth Suit, 9 In. 250.00
Clown, Tumbling, Celluloid Head & Arms, Windup, Japan, c.1950, 7 In. 65.00
Clown, Violinist, Cloth Dressed, Red Hat, Tin Figure, 4 In. 410.00
Clown, Violinist, Dressed Tin Figure, Clockwork, 4 In. 35.00
Clown, Violinist, Windup, Schuco 135.00
Clown, Walking On Hands, Celluloid, Windup, Occupied Japan 245.00
Clown, Walking On Hands, Tin, Windup, England, Box, 5 In. 290.00
Clown & Mule, Pull Toy, String Tail, Mule Kicks, Clown Swivels On Back, Tin, 10 In. 320.00
Clown With Frog, Windup, Celluloid, Tin, Prewar, 5 1/2 In. 58.00
Coach, Passenger Windows, Driver On High Mount Seat, Horse Drawn, Arcade, 11 In. 385.00
Cow, Brown, White Hide, Brown Glass Eyes, Faux Leather Harness, 1890, 7 In. 650.00
Cow, On Wheels, Glass Eyes, Fur Tip Of Tail, Wooden Hooves, Early 20th Century, 11 In. .. 230.00
Cradle, Doll's, Curved Sides, Headboard, Orange Paint, 1800s, 11 1/4 x 14 x 18 In. 345.00
Cradle, Doll's, Pine, Green & Black, Rocker Arms, 10 1/2 x 25 x 10 In. 168.00
Cradle, Doll's, Pine, Hooded, Mahogany Grain Painted, Pennsylvania 1020.00
Cradle, Doll's, Pine, Old Blue Paint, Hooded, 19 In. 127.00
Cradle, Doll's, Poplar, Red Finish, Gold Stripe, 10 3/4 x 13 5/8 In. 110.00
Cradle, Doll's, Red, Black Grain Paint, Hooded, 9 1/2 x 17 1/2 In. 175.00
Cradle, Doll's, Rocking, 14 x 25 In. 55.00
Cradle, Doll's, Scalloped Detail, Old Red Paint, American, c.1850 .... 575.00
Cradle, Doll's, Tole, Tin, Yellow Paint, Black Ground, Mid 19th Century, 8 1/2 x 19 In. ... 110.00
Crane, Driver, Die Cast, Yellow Paint, Dinky Toys, Box, 6 1/4 In. 145.00
Crane, Magnetic, No. 182, Remote Control, Lionel, Box 258.00
Crane, Power, Coles, No. 775, Hand Cranks, Schuco 230.00
Crane, Vertical, Battery Operated, Bandai, 15 In. 245.00
Crap Shooter, Waves Money, Throws Dice, Battery Operated, Cragstan, Japan, Box, 9 In. 190.00
Crime Buster Gift Set, Corgi, 1966 .... 1050.00
Crocodile, Clockwork, Walk & Jaw Moves, Lehmann, 9 1/2 In. 385.00
Cupboard, Doll's, Step Back, Open Upper Section, Lower Drawers, 29 1/2 x 19 In. 690.00
Cyclist, Boy On Tricycle, Windup, UW, Japan, Prewar, 5 1/2 In. 140.00
Cyclist, Girl, Balancing, Tin Lithograph, Pre-World War I, 6 In. 75.00
Cyclist, Kiddy, Multicolored, Clockwork, Tin, Unique Art, 9 In. ....195.00 to 300.00
Cyclist, Skippy, Trick, Tin, Windup, T.P.S., Japan, 1955, 5 1/2 x 3 1/4 In. 250.00
Cymbalist, Seated, Pull Toy, Wood & Composition, Late 19th Century, 6 In. 185.00
Dancer, Jackie, Hornpipe Dance, On Boat, Windup, Strauss, 1920s 485.00
Dancer, Strutting Sam, On Tub, Battery Operated 375.00
Dancing Couple, Celluloid, Windup, Asahitoy, Occupied Japan, Box, 5 In. 165.00
Dancing Doll, Celluloid & Tin, Windup, Box 110.00
Dancing Dude, Crank Wind, Song Plays, Lead & Plastic Man Dances, Mattel, 9 3/4 In. .. 145.00
Dancing Hawaiian, Windup, Celluloid, Tin, Occupied Japan, Box, 6 1/2 In. 140.00
Daniel Boone, Rifle, Dog, Ramp Walker, Plastic, 1960s 230.00
Dapper Dan, Coon Jigger, Marx 850.00
Deep Sea Diver, Celluloid, Air Hose, CK, Tokyo, Japan, Prewar, Box, 4 1/2 In. 210.00
Deer, Mohair, Steiff, c.1950 .... 1250.00
Dinosaur, Dino, Win, Windup, 6 In. 525.00
Dirigible, Los Angeles, Nickeled Wheels, Observation Deck, Dent, 10 3/4 In. 605.00
Doctor Kit, Medical Bag, Dr. Kildare 20.00

Doe, Mohair, Glass Eyes, Cast Iron Spoke Wheels, Ear Button, Steiff, 1913, 9 In. 260.00
Dog, Boxer, Sitting, Shoebutton Eyes, Cream Mohair, Steiff, 1913, 8 In. 345.00
Dog, Bulldog, Pull Toy, Growler, Papier-Mache, Hinged Jaw, c.1890, 17 In. 2100.00
Dog, Cocker Spaniel, Black, White With Freckles, Novelty Glass Eyes, Steiff, 1930, 12 In. 175.00
Dog, Cocker Spaniel, Composition, Jointed Legs, Pull Toy, 10 In. 75.00
Dog, Collie, Pulls Woman In Kimono, Tin, Windup, Lehmann, 1913, 7 In. 2500.00
Dog, Dachshund, Pull Toy, Papier-Mache, Spoke Wheels, Silver Bell, c.1890, 10 In. 900.00
Dog, Molly, Mohair, White & Brown, Straw, Jointed Head, Pewter Button, Steiff, 5 In. . . . 185.00
Dog, Poodle, Mimi, With Bone, Battery Operated, Barks, Eyes Light, Rosko, Box, 1950s . 58.00
Dog, Rummer, Celluloid & Tin, Japan, Box 695.00
Dog, Scotty, Shakes Shoe, Windup, Celluloid, Tin, KT, Japan, Prewar, 5 3/4 In. 345.00
Dolls are listed in their own category.
Doll Case, Betsy McCall, Pretty Pac, Round, Contents, Amsco 75.00
Doll Case, Ginny Doll, Pink Metal, Tapered, Brass Lock & Edge Guards, Vogue, c.1955 . . 190.00
Dollhouse, 2 Story, Bay Window, Porch Swing, Carpets, Curtains, c.1900, 35 x 27 In. . . . 660.00
Dollhouse, 4 Rooms, Plastic Furniture, Ohio Art, 1949-1952, 8 1/4 x 5 1/4 In. 98.00
Dollhouse, 4 Rooms, Textured Exterior, Gold Paint, 22 x 33 In. 1150.00
Dollhouse, 6 Large Interior Rooms, 10 Windows, Wooden, M. Gottschalk, 39 In. 8000.00
Dollhouse, Barbie, Dream House, Cardboard, Accessories, Fold Up, c.1964, 21 x 15 In. . . . 440.00
Dollhouse, Barbie, Vinyl, Plastic Roof, 3 Rooms, Mod Furnishings, Side Latch, c.1969 . . 55.00
Dollhouse, Colonial, Paper, Punch-Out, Tabs, Furniture, Accessories, 1940s, 28 x 15 In. . . 175.00
Dollhouse, Dentist's Surgery, Chair, Water Tank, Patient, Spring Drill, 7 3/4 x 14 1/4 In. . . 715.00
Dollhouse, Francie, Cardboard, Vinyl, Molded Plastic Furniture, c.1967, 18 x 13 x 7 In. . . 80.00
Dollhouse, Ginny, White, Blue, Cardboard, Painted Trees, Doghouse, No. 6926, c.1956 . . 1870.00
Dollhouse, Paper On Pine, Center Hall, Electric Fixtures, Late 19th Century, 24 x 30 In. . . 495.00
Dollhouse, Quilt, Log Cabin, 4 Pieced Squares, Brown Border, Square, 12 In. 143.00
Dollhouse, Wooden Gambrel Roof, Pasteboard, Rear Roof Door, 32 1/2 x 28 1/4 In. 920.00
Dollhouse Furniture, Barbie, Deluxe Bream Kitchen, 4 Appliances, Table Chairs, c.1963 . 415.00
Dollhouse Furniture, Barbie, Mountain Ski Cabin, Colored Vinyl, c.1972, 13 x 13 In. 22.00
Dollhouse Furniture, Bath Set, China, 3 Piece 95.00
Dollhouse Furniture, Bed, Silver Filigree, Blue Cotton Sateen Canopy, 1890, 6 In. 400.00
Dollhouse Furniture, Chair, Cast Iron, Stevens, 1870s, 3 Piece 200.00
Dollhouse Furniture, Chair, Spindle Back, Rose Silk Fringe Upholstery, Wooden, 9 In. . . 150.00
Dollhouse Furniture, Chair, Spindle Back, Wooden, Gold Leaf Patina, 1880, 14 In. 700.00
Dollhouse Furniture, China Cabinet, Oak, Glass Doors, 3 Shelves, 1930s, 20 x 12 In. 170.00
Dollhouse Furniture, Crib, Bakelite, 4 1/2 In. 60.00
Dollhouse Furniture, Dining Set, 1 x 2 3/4 In., 3 Piece . . . . *Illus* 40.00
Dollhouse Furniture, Dressing Table With Accessories, Tripod Base, 1880, 14 In. 900.00
Dollhouse Furniture, Kitchen, Stove, Utensils, Wooden Framed Room, 39 In. 1100.00
Dollhouse Furniture, Milliner's Shop, Mahogany Box, 1920, 23 x 22 In. 7500.00
Dollhouse Furniture, Mirror, Piano, Wooden, White Finish, Gold Paper Trim, 1885, 6 In. 400.00
Dollhouse Furniture, Refrigerator, Stove & Sink, Wolverine 115.00
Dollhouse Furniture, Salon Chair, Wooden Frame, Rubbed Cream Finish, 1870, 10 In. . . 1000.00
Dollhouse Furniture, Stove, Little Eva, Side Oven Doors, 4 Lids, N.S. Cates, c.1847 . . . . 750.00
Dollhouse Furniture, Table & 2 Chairs, Cast Iron, Stevens, 1870s 250.00
Dollhouse Furniture, Wardrobe, Susy Goose Ken, Plastic, Box, c.1963, 7 x 13 In. 66.00
Donkey, Coal Cart, Orange Cart, Green Wheels, Black Driver, Cast Iron, 13 In. 290.00
Donkey, Nodder, Pip-Squeak, Pull Toy, Felt, Glass Eyes, Metal Wheels, 8 x 9 1/2 In. . . . 360.00
Donkey, Pull Toy, Woman Riding Side Saddle, Cast Iron, Late 19th Century, 6 1/2 x 6 In. . 450.00
Dresser Set, Barbie, Pretty Up Time, Pink, Plastic, Mirror, Comb, Brush, c.1964 . . . . 220.00
Drinking Captain, Lamppost, Battery Operated, 12 1/2 In. 50.00
Drum, Bentwood Hoops, Woven String & Leather, American Flags & Stars, 6 7/8 In. 340.00
Drum Major, Windup, Tin Lithograph, Wolverine, 14 In. 225.00
Drummer, Let The Drummer Boy Play, Windup, Walks, Beats Drum, Marx, 1930s 790.00
Duck, Cycling Quacky, On Tricycle, Tin, Windup, Japan, Box, 6 In. 185.00
Duck, Mother & 2 Ducklings, Windup, Tin Lithograph, Wyandotte, 1940s 46.00
Duck, Pull Toy, 4 Wooden Ducks, Mother Clucks & Waddles, Fisher-Price, 1950s, 13 In. . 48.00
Duck, Quack-Quack, Tin, Windup, Duck & Chicks, Lithograph, Lehmann 140.00
Duck, With Ducklings, Ramp Walker, U.S.A., c.1950, 3 3/4 In. 15.00
Duck The Mailman, Windup, Turn & Go, Tin Lithograph, T.P.S., Japan, 1950s 260.00
Dudley Do Right, Movable Arms & Legs, 1976, 7 In. 52.50
Durable Scale, Battery Operated, Lights Up, 8 In. 200.00
Dutch Milkmaid, Tin Face, Cotton Costume, Tin, Prewar, Germany, Schuco, 5 In. 1335.00

Easter Rabbit, Holding Egg, On Wheeled Stand, Tin, Friction, West Germany, 8 In. 210.00
Easter Rabbit, With Cart, Plastic, Marx, 1950s, 7 In. 40.00
Elephant, Cart, Red Wagon, Gold Wheels, Native Driver, Cast Iron, Kenton, 7 1/2 In. ... 230.00
Elephant, Circus, On Wheels, Felt Blanket, Glass Eyes, Steiff, Model 1335, 13 In. 290.00
Elephant, Leather Ears, Tucks, Rubber Trunk, Schoenhut, 1903, 10 1/2 In. 60.00
Elephant, Mohair, Gray, Pointed Limbs, Swivel Neck, Steiff, 1908, 9 In. 1100.00
Elephant, Pull Toy, Musical, Fisher-Price, 8 In. 35.00
Embroidery Set, Barbie Fashion, Flannel, Standard Toykraft Inc., c.1962, 10 x 15 In. 110.00
Erector Set, A.C. Gilbert, Builds Ferris Wheel, No. 8 1/2, 1950s 255.00
Erector Set, Builds Parachute Jump, Box, 9 1/2 In. 225.00
Erector Set, Rocket Launcher No. 10053, Metal Carrying Case, Plastic Rocket, 1959 .... 210.00
Erector Set, Skipper Toy Co., Instructions, Box, 1935, 9 x 10 In. 80.00
Fan, Electric, Whizzer, Box, c.1940, 8 In. 105.00
Farm Woman Feeding Chickens, Papier-Mache, Germany, 1860, 2 1/2 In. 1000.00
Ferris Wheel, 4 Gondolas, Composition Riders, Doll & Co., 13 In. 480.00
Ferris Wheel, Giant Ride, Lithograph, Ohio Art, 17 In. 250.00
Ferris Wheel, Hercules, Windup, Chein 325.00
Ferris Wheel, Tin, Composition Figures, 3 Flag Top, 20 1/2 In. 8250.00
Fire Patrol Wagon, White Horse, Driver, 4 Riders, Cast Iron, 19 In. 460.00
Fire Pumper, 2 Black Horses, Gold, Black, Red Wagon, Cast Iron, 18 In. 345.00
Fire Pumper, 2 Firemen, Hubley, 8 In. 550.00
Fire Pumper, 2 Horses, Cast Iron, Dent, 1905, 19 1/2 In. 1200.00
Fire Pumper, 2 Horses, Driver On Bench Seat, Clockwork, Ives, 14 In. 935.00
Fire Pumper, 2 Horses, Eagle Finial, Seated Driver, Open Bench Seat, Ives, 19 In. 1320.00
Fire Pumper, 3 Horses, Driver, Cream Body, Pratt & Letchworth, 15 In. 345.00
Fire Pumper, 3 Horses, Gold Boiler, Integral Driver, Cast Iron, 17 In. 635.00
Fire Pumper, 3 Horses, Red, Gold Trimmed Boiler, Cast Iron, Kenton, 13 In. 110.00
Fire Pumper, Dayton, Iron, Metal, Wood, Tin Driver, Scheible, Early 1900s, 14 In. 365.00
Fire Pumper, Electric Headlights, Rubber Tires, Hubley, 10 1/4 In. 95.00
Fire Pumper, Embossed Gauges On Boiler, Driver, Headlight On Hood, Hubley, 11 In. .. 420.00
Fire Pumper, Red, Gold Trimmed Boiler, Kenton, 8 In. 165.00
Fire Pumper, Yellow, Gold, Silver, Maroon, Steam Powdered, Windup, Tin, 11 In. 200.00
Fire Station, Fire Chief Car, Marx, 1950s 310.00
Fire Truck, Aerial Extension Ladders, American LaFrance, Doepke, 28 In. 165.00
Fire Truck, Aerial Ladder, Buddy L, 1970s, 27 1/2 In. 350.00
Fire Truck, Ahren's Fox, Pale Green & Red, Turner Toys 605.00
Fire Truck, Extension Ladder, Pressed Steel, White Ladder, Buddy L, 29 In. 145.00
Fire Truck, Hook & Ladder, 2 Horses, 2 Drivers, Bell, Pratt & Letchworth, 24 In. 1210.00
Fire Truck, Hook & Ladder, 3 Horses, 2 Firemen, Cast Iron, Wilkins, 25 In. 545.00
Fire Truck, Hook & Ladder, 3 Horses, 2 Riders, 2 Ladders 1050.00
Fire Truck, Hook & Ladder, 3 Ladders, 2 Firemen, Pratt & Letchworth, 1880s, 23 In. 2495.00
Fire Truck, Hook & Ladder, 3 Ladders, Firemen, Wilkins, 1905, 23 In. 1495.00
Fire Truck, Hook & Ladder, Packard, Pressed Steel, Extending Ladder, Keystone, 30 In. .. 545.00
Fire Truck, Hook & Ladder, Pressed Steel, Kelmet, 1920s, 27 In. 1375.00
Fire Truck, Hose & Ladder, Red, Repainted, Cast Iron, Arcade, 9 1/2 In. 355.00
Fire Truck, Ladder, 3 Galloping Horses, Black, White, Cast Iron, 29 In. 575.00
Fire Truck, Ladder, 3 Horses, 2 Drivers, Black & Nickel, 22 In. 460.00
Fire Truck, Ladder, 3 Ladders, Rubber Tires, Spoke Wheels, Hubley, 18 In. 345.00
Fire Truck, Ladder, Front Bumper Hits Object & Ladder Extends, Kingsbury, 24 In. 230.00
Fire Truck, Ladder, Lomack Red, Smith Miller, 35 1/2 In. 550.00
Fire Truck, Mack Cab, Rose Reel & Ladder Supports, Arcade, 17 3/4 In. 550.00
Fire Truck, Pressed Steel, Keystone, 19 In. 60.00
Fire Truck, Red & Silver, No. 709, Rubber Wheels, Die Cast, Manoil, 4 1/2 In. 29.00
Fire Truck, Suburban, White, Tonka 150.00
Fire Wagon, 2 Horses, Seated Figure, Hose Reel, Rear Platform Step, Hubley, 19 1/2 In. .. 415.00
Fire Wagon, Chemical, Nickled Tank, Ladders, Fireman On Rear Platform, Wilkins, 21 In. 1870.00
Fire Wagon, Ladder, 5 Galloping Horses, White, Black, Cast Iron, 20 In. 290.00
Fire Wagon, Ladder, Horses, Seated Driver, White, Gold Trim, Wilkins, 30 In. 1045.00
Fire Wagon, Patrol, Horses, Seated Driver, Open Bed, Moving Parts, 19 In. 660.00
Fireman, Climbing, Ferrand Martin, Windup, 1904 .... 1600.00
Fireman, Climbing, Tin Base & Ladder, Marx, 8-In. Plastic Fireman 66.00
Flying Saucer, Jet Smoke, Exhaust Pipes, Stop & Go Action, Battery Operated, Japan 950.00
Flying Saucer, Spaceman, Instructions, 7 In. 95.00

Football, Peppy, Rubber, Blow Up, Occupied Japan, 1946, 6 In. 85.00
Fox, Carrying Goose In Tin Basket, Original Key, Schuco, Prewar 1250.00
Frankenstein, Walker, 8 Actions, Battery Operated, Tin, Marx, c.1958 . . . . 1100.00
Frankenstein, Windup, Walks Forward, Moving Arms, Marx, 193, 8 1/2 In. 4500.00
Fred Flintstone, On Dino, Battery Operated, Original Box, Marx, 15 1/2 In. 985.00
Fred Flintstone, On Dino, Fred In Tin Cage, Battery Operated, Marx, 13 In. 176.00
Frog, Swimmer Action, Windup, Tin, Issmayer, 19th Century, 7 In. 230.00
Frog, Tuxedo, Squeeze, Rubber, Rempel Mfg., 9 1/2 In. 60.00
Frog, Velveteen, Stuffed, Dream Pets, Dakin, 7 In. . . . . *Illus* 15.00
G.I. Joe, Action Man Luftwaffe 425.00
G.I. Joe, Action Man SAS Underwater Attack 425.00
G.I. Joe, Action Marine, Hat, Uniform, Boots, Dog Tag, Insignia, Field Manual, Box, 1964 280.00
G.I. Joe, Action Team, Police Motorcyclist 425.00
G.I. Joe, Adventure Team Commander, Black, Talking, Hasbro, 1974, 12 In. 250.00
G.I. Joe, Airborne, Helicopter Assault Trooper, 1983 . . . . 75.00
G.I. Joe, Australian Jungle Fighter, Complete 495.00
G.I. Joe, Australian Jungle Fighter, Equipment, Hasbro, 1966 . . . . 2500.00
G.I. Joe, Black Action Soldier, Accessories 895.00
G.I. Joe, Breaker, Communication Officer, 1982 . . . . 75.00
G.I. Joe, Canadian Mountie 495.00
G.I. Joe, Crash Crew, Fire Fighter, Accessories 475.00
G.I. Joe, Fighter Pilot, All Accessories 895.00
G.I. Joe, Jouncing Jeep, Tin, Windup, Unique Art Co., 1944 . . . . 375.00
G.I. Joe, Jungle Survival, Complete 375.00
G.I. Joe, K-9 Pups, Tin, Windup, Unique Art 225.00
G.I. Joe, Landing Signal Officer, Accessories 475.00
G.I. Joe, Man Of Action, Box 180.00
G.I. Joe, Marine Jungle Fighter, Accessories 995.00
G.I. Joe, Police State Trooper, All Accessories 1495.00
G.I. Joe, Scarlet, Counter Intelligence, 1982 . . . . 175.00
G.I. Joe, Sea Adventurer, Box 180.00
G.I. Joe, Talking Action Pilot 695.00
G.I. Joe, Tank Commander, Accessories 895.00
G.I. Joe, Underwater Explorer 425.00
Games are listed in their own category.
Garage, 2 Plastic Cars, Accessories, Keystone, 18 In. 330.00
Garage, Esso, Sign, Pumps, Metal, Die Cast, Lesney 70.00
Garage, Self Opening, Tin, 6-In. Plastic Friction Car, Tool Lithos, Mettoy, 5 x 8 In. 210.00
Gas Pump, Play Gas On Globe, Tin, Mohawk, 8 In. 110.00
Gas Pump, U.S. Gas Pump, Crank The Handle & Signs Says Full, 7 1/4 x 2 1/2 In. 333.00
Gentleman Frog, Smoking Cigarette, Celluloid, Windup, Occupied Japan, Box, 4 In. 295.00
Giraffe, Leather, Wood, Glass Eyes, Black Painted Features, 8 In. 30.00
Girl, In Flower, Tin, String, Germany, 1920s, 2 1/2 In. 250.00
Girl, On Tricycle, Celluloid, Clockwork, Pre-World War II, Japan, 8 In. 950.00
Girl, With Ball & Bells, On Tinplate Base, Windup, Vichy, 11 In. 4000.00
Goat, Carved Mouth, Inset Glass Eyes, Black Wooden Feet, Papier-Mache, 1885, 18 In. . . 1700.00
Goat, Pull Toy, Gray Fur Cover, Applied Ears, Horns, Green Glass Eyes, 1890, 16 In. . . . 2700.00
Godzilla, Rubber Fins, Tin, Battery Operated, Bullmark, 12 In. 750.00
Golden Goose, Tin, Windup, Lays Golden Egg, Marx, c.1930, 9 In. 105.00
Gorilla, Mechanical, Growls, Marx, Box, 7 1/2 In. 395.00
Graf Zeppelin, Silver, Steelcraft, 1929, 28 In. 735.00
Grandpa Frog, Plastic Feet, Fisher-Price, 5 1/2 x 6 In. 50.00
Grasshopper, Tin, Windup, TN, Japan, Box, 6 In. 140.00
Great Garloo, Battery Operated, Instructions, 1960s, 24 In. . . . . .745.00 to 975.00
Grocer's Shop, Varnished Wooden Cabinets, Red Painted Floor, Germany, 1900, 22 In. . . . 1600.00
Gun, Air Pistol, Schimel,.22 Caliber Luger Style 150.00
Gun, Air Rifle, Daisy, Model B, 1000 Shot 250.00
Gun, Air Rifle, Daisy, No. 11, Model 29, Loop Lever, 350 Shot 200.00
Gun, Air Rifle, Daisy, Red Ryder No. 111-40, Copper Band, Iron Lever, Reblued 215.00
Gun, Air Rifle, Golden Eagle, No. 50, Copper Anniversary 250.00
Gun, Atomic Ray, Hiller, 1930s 485.00
Gun, Atomic Ray, Tom Corbett Space Cadet, Flashlight, Batteries, Marx, 1952 . . . . 2750.00
Gun, Atomic Rifle, Tom Corbett, Marx, Box, 1952, 24 In. 1500.00

Gun, Atomic, Friction, Shoots Sparks, 4 In. 95.00
Gun, Automatic Repeater, Pressed Steel, Box Of Paper Rolls, Marx, c.1930, 7 In. 170.00
Gun, BB, Anics No. 101, Semi-Auto, 15 Shot 52.00
Gun, Border Patrol, Cast Iron, Nickel Plated, Kilgore, Box, 4 1/2 In. 68.00
Gun, Clicker, Me & My Buddy, Cowboy Pushes Arm In & Out, Wyandotte, c.1935 ..... 190.00
Gun, Cork, Markham Air Rifle Co., Plymouth, Mich. 90.00
Gun, Fast Draw Holster Set, Plastic, Simulated Leather, Studs, Kilgore, Box, 10 In. 84.00
Gun, Flintlock, Chrome, Plastic Grip, Hubley, 1950s, 9 1/2 In. 75.00
Gun, Flying Saucer, Plastic, 3 Saucers, Park Plastics, Display Box, 1950s, 5 In. 160.00
Gun, G-Man, Sparking, Steel, Windup, Marx, 1930s, 4 1/2 In. 255.00
Gun, Range, Tim Holt Rodeo, Target, Dart Fun, Darts, American Toy, 1949, 15 x 12 In. .. 225.00
Gun, Signal Pistol, Plastic, Makes Siren Noise, Marx, Box, 6 1/2 In. 84.00
Gun, Space Control, Space Scenes Loaded, Japan, Box, 1950s, 4 In. 85.00
Gun, Space Patrol, Cosmic Smoke, 1952, 4 1/2 In. 350.00
Gypsy, Cranks Organ, Monkey Dances On Top, Pete & Monk, Windup, Distler, 1920s ... 1100.00
Ham & Sam, Musician, Windup, Strauss, 1921 .... 750.00
Hand Pump, Water, Iron Nickel Plated, Adjustable Arm, 11 In. 862.00
Hansom Cab, Driver, Horse, Pratt & Letchworth, 1892, 13 In. 1950.00
Hansom Cab, Woman, Begging Dog, Driver, Tin Lithograph, Clockwork, Lehmann, 5 In. . 1870.00
Happy Bunny, Driving Car, Friction Power, Japan, 1957, 5 In. 80.00
Happy Dan, Eccentric Milkman, Carries Bottles, Tin, Windup, England, Box, 1950s, 4 In. 225.00
Happy Hooligan, In Donkey Cart, Ingap 875.00
Happy Hooligan, Wagon, Police Patrol, Kenton, 1900s, 17 In. 3995.00
Happy Meal, French Fry Guy, Fun With Food, McDonald's, 1989 .... 12.00
Happy Naughty Chimp, Battery Operated, Daishin, Japan, Box, 1960s 110.00
Harold Lloyd, Vibrates, Expressions Change, Hands Move, Tin, Windup, 7 In. 475.00
Harold Lloyd, Walker, Marx, 10 1/2 In. 140.00
Harold Lloyd, Working, Marx, 11 In. 800.00
Hat Box, Barbie, Vinyl, Zipper, Handle, Standard Plastic Products, 1961, 12 x 10 In. 66.00
Helicopter, Flies Around Satellite On Base, Brussels World's Fair, Windup, Box 95.00
Helicopter, No.2, Occupied Germany, Windup 225.00
Helicopter, Piasecki, U.S. Air Force, Tin, Friction, TN, Japan, Box, 10 In. 90.00
Helicopter, Police, Bell, Blue & Orange, Dinky Toys, No. 732, Box 35.00
Helicopter, Shadow Crime Fighter, Battery Operated, Box 200.00
Helmet, Space, Flexible Plastic, Box, Orbit Productions, c.1950, 12 In. 605.00
Helmet, Whizzer Space Pilot, Wind Powered Space Beanie, Box, Tarco, 1951, 9 In. 450.00
Helmet & Gun, Lost In Space, Remco, 1967 .... 800.00
Hen, Pip-Squeak, Animated Wings, Wood, Leather, Papier-Mache, 3 In. 300.00
Henry, Eating Ice Cream, Tin, Windup, Felt Tongue, Linemar Japan, 5 1/2 In. 510.00
Henry, Motoring, Win, Windup, Celluloid Figures, Pre-World War II, 5 1/4 In. 2200.00
Henry, On Elephant, White Type, Windup, Pre-World War II, 8 In. 1495.00
High Chair, Doll's, Padded Heart-Form Backrest 155.00
High Chair, Doll's, Wooden, Movable Tray, 26 1/2 In. 58.00

Toy, Frog, Velveteen,
Stuffed, Dream Pets,
Dakin, 7 In.

To clean terminals on batteries, use a standard pencil eraser.

If you plan to use an old crib or to place old painted furniture and toys near very young children, check the paint. The use of lead paint was discontinued in the United States in 1978.

Toy, Jazzbo Jim, Tin
Lithograph, Dances On
Roof, Unique Art, 1921

Hobbyhorse, Tin, Wood, Paper Lithograph, Gibbs, 1912-1918, 9 x 6 In. 155.00
Holster, Double, Fanner 50, Leather, 5 Plastic Bullets, Mattel 23.00
Holster, Wild Bill Hickok, Turquoise Jewels, Box 100.00
Honeymoon Cottage, Windup, Marx, 1950s, 7 In. 138.00
Hoop, Wooden, Multicolored Paint, Flat Profile, 30 1/2 In. Diam. 728.00
Horn, Tin Lithograph, Clown Shaped Into Horn, Germany, 7 1/2 In. 1045.00
Horse, Black Beauty, Pull Toy, Leather Harness, 14 x 14 In. 230.00
Horse, Hide Covered, Leather Saddle, Glass Eyes, Kellich Berlin, Pull Toy, 32 x 33 In. .. 220.00
Horse, Hide Covered, On Wheels, 19th Century, 29 x 27 In. 970.00
Horse, On Metal Wheels, Pull Ring, Ear Button, Steiff, 1930s, 17 x 21 In. 200.00
Horse, Rocking, Burlap, Wooden Base, Germany, Restored 440.00
Horse, Rocking, Dapple Painted, Black Mane & Tail, Saddle, Converse, 40 x 40 In. 575.00
Horse, Rocking, Hide Covered, Horsehair Mane, Glass Eyes, 25 x 31 In. 275.00
Horse, Rocking, Platform Base, Original Saddle & Reins, 33 1/2 x 44 In. 550.00
Horse, Rocking, Pony Hide, Trestle Base, Victorian, 33 x 31 In. 205.00
Horse, Running, Mare & Foal, Tin, Pull Toy, Worn Paint, Metal Wheels, 8 1/2 x 6 1/2 In. . 440.00
Horse, Thunderbolt, Western Range Horse, Johnny West's Horse, Marx, Box, 1962 ..... 175.00
Horse & SS Troop Rider, Tin, Windup, Germany, Pre-World War II 4500.00
Horse & Wagon, 2 Black Horses, Open Bed, Spoke Wheels, McCormick Deering, 12 In. . 468.00
Horse & Wagon, 2 Horses, Gold, Silver, Green Wagon, Red, Cast Iron, Kenton, 14 In. ... 258.00
Horse & Wagon, Bakery, 2 Horses, Cast Iron, 13 3/4 In. 138.00
Horse & Wagon, Beer, 2 Horses, Driver, Original Paint, 15 In. 415.00
Horse & Wagon, Beer, 2 Horses, Green Wagon, Kenton, Cast Iron, 14 In. 290.00
Horse & Wagon, Coal, 1 Horse, Driver, Hubley, 1906 .... 1095.00
Horse & Wagon, Dark Brown Oxen, Red Highlights, Cast Iron, 10 1/2 In. 170.00
Horse & Wagon, Driver, Nickel Metal, Friction, Alps, 1950s, 5 In. 95.00
Horse & Wagon, Fine Groceries, Tinplate, Chein, 12 In. 290.00
Horse & Wagon, Fire Patrol, 3 Galloping Horses, 5 Firemen, Kenton, 12 1/2 In. 450.00
Horse & Wagon, Fireman's, 3 Horses, Cast Iron, Polychrome, 29 In. 495.00
Horse & Wagon, Giraffe's Neck Out At Top, 2 Parade Horses, Driver, Hubley, 16 In. 5500.00
Horse & Wagon, Ladder, 4 Figures, Cast Iron, 14 In. 575.00
Horse & Wagon, Police Patrol, 2 Horses, Railing Leads To Side Steps, Kenton, 18 In. ... 4400.00
Horse & Wagon, Sand & Gravel, 2 Horses, Driver, Green, Cast Iron, Kenton, 14 In. 260.00
Horse & Wagon, Sand & Gravel, 2 Horses, Kenton, 15 In. 165.00
Horse & Wagon, Stake, 2 Horses, Driver, Cast Iron, Arcade, 12 In. 170.00
Horse & Wagon, Stake, 2 White, Black Horses, Green, Red Wagon, Cast Iron, 14 In. 170.00
House, Pop-Out-Pup, Tin, USA, 1930s 145.00
Humphrey Mobile, Comic Character Rolling Forward On Tricycle, Tin, Wyandotte, 7 In. . 400.00
Humpty Dumpty, Pull Toy, Rolling & Rocking Action, Fisher-Price, Box, 1971, 7 x 5 In. 45.00
Hydroplane, Racing, Gas Powered, 27 In. 700.00
Indoor Skeet Shoot, Daisy, Rodgers, Ark., Box 400.00
Iron, Ober, No. 1, Flat 150.00
Iron, Wapak, No. 2, Flat 85.00
Jack-In-The-Box, Blippy, Friendly Spaceman, Mattel, 1968 .... 50.00
Jack-In-The-Box, Casper The Friendly Ghost, Box 485.00
Jazzbo Jim, Tin Lithograph, Dances On Roof, Unique Art, 1921 ....*Illus* 975.00
Jeep, Combat, TV Screen, Plastic & Tin, Kuang, 1970s 100.00
Jeep, Jumping, Soldiers With Machine Guns, Windup, Tin, Marx, Box, 6 In. 310.00
Jeep, Police Patrol, 1 Steers, Other Answers Phone, Battery Operated, 1960s, 11 In. 385.00
Jeep, Rat Patrol, 2 Figures, Marx, 1960s 390.00
Jeep, Surrey, Plastic Fringe, Pink, Tonka, 10 In. 20.00
Jeep & Trailer, Army, Tonka 125.00
Jeep & Trailer, Metal, Friction, Japan, 1950s, 8 1/2 In. 75.00
Jeep & Trailer, Willy's, Red Jeep, Blue Trailer, Marx, 1950s, 22 In. 65.00
Jigger, Be-Bop, Jointed Plastic Black Man, Windup Drum, 9 1/2 In. 250.00
Jigger, Oh-My Alabama Coon, Tinplate, Clockwork Motor, 10 In. 460.00
Joe Penner, Carrying Ducks, Tin, Windup, Tipping Hat, Smoking Cigar, Marx, 8 In. 250.00
Joe Penner, Duck, Walker, Cage, Rising Hat, Marx, 8 In. 195.00
Jolly Jumper, Plastic Feet, Fisher-Price, 4 1/2 x 6 In. 60.00
Junior Mechanic Construction, Box, Mechanicraft, 1940 .... 95.00
Junior Swing Carousel, Tin, Brass, Gravity, Buffalo Toy & Tool, Box, 1924, 5 1/2 In. ... 875.00
Kaleidoscope, Battlestar Galactica Spectral Viewer, CW, Hong Kong, 1978, 8 In. 40.00
Kaleidoscope, Blue Naugahyde, Removable Lens Holder, 5 Discs, Galt Toys, 9 1/4 In. 20.00

Kaleidoscope, Butterflies, Christmas Toys, China, 4 1/2 In. 18.00
Kaleidoscope, Cowboy & Cowgirl On Mule, Japan, Early 1950s, 3 1/4 In. 25.00
Kaleidoscope, Dog Playing Guitar For Girlfriend, Occupied Japan, 8 In. 60.00
Kaleidoscope, Frosted Lens, Glass Shards, 12-Sectioned Optics, Pre-1930s, 11 In. 225.00
Kaleidoscope, Millions Of Designs, Rotator Cuff, Steven, St. Louis, Mo., 1950s, 8 3/4 In.   40.00
Kaleidoscope, Millions Of Designs, Triangular, Steven Mfg. Co., St. Louis, Mo., 7 1/2 In.   195.00
Kaleidoscope, Snowflake Designs, Red Foiled Ground, Steven's Pixie Toys, 9 In. 30.00
Kaleidoscope, Tom & Jerry, Outer Space, Rotator Cuff, Green Monk, England, 1973, 9 In.   75.00
Kaleidoscope, Travelscope, Modes Of Transportation, Green Monk, England, 1969 . . . . .   30.00
Kaleidoscope, Wonder Wheel, Rectangular, Steven, 1975, 10 1/2 In. 25.00
Kangaroo, Mama, Baby, Jumps In & Out Of Pouch, Windup, Tin, T.P.S., Japan, Box, 6 In.   305.00
Kid Flyer, Tin Lithograph, V & R 66.00
Kitchen, Copperware, Iron, Copper Exterior, Carafe With Hinged Lid, 1885, 15 Piece . . .   650.00
Kitchen, Oven & Water Pump, With Accessories, Tin, 9 x 14 In. 675.00
Kitchen, Refrigerator, Stove, Dishes, Silverware, Play Food, Deluxe Reading Corp., 1963   415.00
Knock-Out Prize Fighters, Wooden Mat & Poles, Strauss, Early 1920s, 5 1/2 x 4 In. 805.00
Krazy Kar, Clown Driver, Back & Forth Motion, Tin Lithograph, Kids, Unique Art, 8 In. .   400.00
Lady Acrobat, Bisque Head, Schoenhut, 8 In. 375.00
Lamb, Pull Toy, Mary's Lamb, Box, Hubley, 5 In. 45.00
Lamb, Pull Toy, Papier-Mache & Lamb's Wool, Wooden Legs, Platform, c.1885, 18 In. . .   650.00
Lamb, Wool, On Wheels, White Felt Face, Black Bead Eyes, Steiff, 1918, 6 1/2 In. 1035.00
Landau, White Horse, Coachman, Green Body, Yellow Wheels, Hubley, 15 In. 865.00
Launcher, Satellite, Count Down 325.00
Li'l Abner Dogpatch Band, Windup, Tin, Unique Art, Instruction Sheet, Box, 9 In. 1165.00
Lincoln Tunnel, Vehicles, Windup, Box, Unique Art, 24 In. 259.00
Lion, Mohair, Tan, Brown Mane & Tail, Embroidered Nose, Steiff, 15 In. 220.00
Lion, Reclining, Tan Mohair, Long Mane, Steiff, 1950s, 13 x 27 In. 465.00
Lion & Elephant, Bell Ringer, Tin, Base, James Fallows, 7 1/2 In. 1870.00
Lion & Lioness, Glass Eyes, Raspberry Red Nose, Black Mouth, Steiff, 1925, 12 In. 285.00
Lioness, Mohair, Gold, Jointed Legs, Swivel Neck, Steiff, 1930s, 8 x 6 In. 355.00
Little Garloo, Lizard Man, Walks, Tin, Plastic, Vinyl, Windup, Japan, 6 In. 140.00
Little King, Pull String Mechanism, Wooden, Box, 1939, 3 In. . . . . .115.00 to 135.00
Little Miss Automatic Ironer, Tin, Windup, MT, Japan, Box, 1950s, 4 In. 170.00
Little Snoopy, Pull Toy, Fisher-Price, c.1969 . . . .   25.00
Lizard, Lizzy, Velveteen, Black Dot Eyes, Felt Feet, Steiff, c.1959, 8 In. 165.00
Lizzy, Sweeps Floor, Windup, German, 1920s 650.00
Lobster, Mohair, Beige, Plastic Eyes, Elastic Antennae, Steiff, c.1963, 12 In. 355.00
Loom, Weaving, Metal, Adjustable, Pressman Toy Corp., 1963, 11 1/4 x 11 1/4 In. 225.00
Loom, Weaving, Metal, Barbie On Lid, Adjustable, Pressman Toy Corp., 1963, 11 x 11 In.   225.00
Looping Plane, Copper Finish, Marx, Box, 1941, 5 In. 600.00
Lorry, Army, Searchlight, 3 Soldiers, Windup, Box, Wells Of London, 1940 . . . .   125.00
Lucky Sledge, Boy On Sled, Windup, Celluloid, Tin, Occupied Japan, Box, 5 In. 315.00
Main Street Terminal, Windup, Tin Lithograph, Box, Marx 580.00
Mammy, Dancing, Windup, Box, Lindstrom, 8 In. 357.00
Mammy, Pushing Buggy, Pull Toy, Plaster Mammy, Composition Buggy, Tin Wheels 170.00
Man, On The Flying Trapeze, Windup, Tin, Wyandotte, Box, 9 In. 265.00
Man, Scissors Grinder, Steam, Arnold, c.1905 . . . .   375.00
Man, With Whirligig, Tin Lithograph, Clockwork, 7 1/2 In. 115.00
Manure Spreader, John Deere, Spoke Wheels, Cast Iron, Windex, 14 In. 2500.00
Marbles, Buddy, Box, 1920s, 1 x 3 x 4 In. 10.00
Mary & Her Lamb, Celluloid, Tin Platform, Windup, Japan, Prewar, Box, 4 In. 235.00
Mary Had A Little Lamb, Plastic, Windup, Wells, England, Box, 4 1/2 In. 130.00
Medical Bag, Little Country Doctor, Transogram, 1948, Unused 500.00
Merry-Go-Round, Musical, Zoo Animals, Tin, Plastic, Crank Action, Mattel, Box, 7 In. . .   140.00
Merry-Go-Round, Sail Away, Boats, Tin Men, Windup, Unique Art, 1950s, 9 In. 245.00
Merry-Go-Round, Sleighs & Reindeer, Tin, Painted, 28 1/2 In. 1000.00
Merrymakers Band, 4 Mice & Piano, Windup, Tin Lithograph, Marx, 9 In. . . . . . .605.00 to 715.00
Microscope, All Components, Instructions, Gilbert, 1930s 150.00
Milk Can Set, For Milk Truck, 2 1/2 In., 6 Piece 200.00
Milk Carrier, Metal, Lithograph, Box, Tootsietoy, 13 1/2 In. 410.00
Milk Wagon, American Milk Co., Red, Yellow Wheels, Tin Pails, 24 In. 230.00
Milk Wagon, Borden, Tin Lithograph, Wooden, Rich Toys, Clinton, Iowa, 1930s, 18 In. . .   160.00
Milk Wagon, Sealtest, Tin Lithograph, Wooden, Glass Bottles, Rich Toys, 20 In. 195.00

Minstrel Man, Banjo, Wooden Neck, Pressed Paper Body, Jefferson Mfg. Co., Box 82.00
Miss Cat, Windup, Celluloid, MT, Occupied Japan, Box, 4 1/2 In. 240.00
Model Kit, Green Beret, Box 250.00
Model Kit, Phantom Of The Opera, Aurora, Box 200.00
Model Kit, The Witch, Aurora, Box 375.00
Model Kit, Yacht, Flintstones, Motorized, Remco, Unused, 18 x 10 In. 235.00
Monkey, Banana Vendor, Windup, Tin, Yone, Japan, Box, 8 1/2 In. 85.00
Monkey, Banjo Playing, Windup, Japan, 1950s 225.00
Monkey, Blows Bubbles, Bubble Dish, Alps, Box 70.00
Monkey, Circus, Peddles Tricycle, Wheels Turn, Arnold, U.S. Zone, 4 1/2 In. 175.00
Monkey, Climbing, Jog-O, Original Package, Tot-Tested Toys, Ltd. 80.00
Monkey, Climbing, Tin Lithograph, Lehmann 30.00
Monkey, Climbing, Zippo, Marx, 10 In. 175.00
Monkey, Combs Hair, Holds Mirror, Twirls Tail, Key, Windup, Schuco, 1920s 220.00
Monkey, Cyclist, Tin, Lever Action, Marx, Box, 1930s, 6 In. 235.00
Monkey, Frankie The Roller Skating Monkey, Cloth Outfit, Battery Operated, Box 105.00
Monkey, Hits Log With Coconut, Bell Ringer, Cast Iron, 1900 . . . . 650.00
Monkey, Jocko, Glass Eyes, Clown Hat, Button In Ear, 11 In. 145.00
Monkey, On Motorcycle, Parasol, Japan 395.00
Monkey, Playing Trumpet, Battery Operated, Alps, Box, 1950s, 9 In. 105.00
Monkey, Playing Violin, Tin, Clockwork, Schuco, Box 115.00
Monkey, Trumpet Playing, Battery Operated, Germany 275.00
Monkey, Weight Lifting, Plush & Tin, Windup, Japan, 6 In. 75.00
Monorail, Rocket Express Trellises, Rails, Metallic Gray, Battery Operated, Linemar, Box 260.00
Moon Mullins & Kayo, Handcar, Tin, Windup, Box, Marx, 7 In. 1200.00
Motorcycle, 3 Wheels, Patrol Auto-Tricycle, Tin, Battery Operated, TN, Japan, Box, 9 In. 710.00
Motorcycle, Army, Tin Lithograph, Rubber Tires, Friction, TN, Japan, c.1955, 7 1/2 In. . . 230.00
Motorcycle, Blue, Gold Accents, Cast Iron, Harley, 6 In. 170.00
Motorcycle, Cab Side, France, 9 In. 2750.00
Motorcycle, Easter Rabbit, With Sidecar, Tin, Balloon Tires, Wyandotte, 9 In. 255.00
Motorcycle, Harley-Davidson, Electric, Child's 3750.00
Motorcycle, Harley-Davidson, Friction, Twin Engine, Japan, 9 In. 225.00
Motorcycle, Harley-Davidson, Policeman, Hubley, 8 3/4 In. 550.00
Motorcycle, Harley-Davidson, Sidecar, Hubley, 5 In. 475.00
Motorcycle, Harley-Davidson, Solo Driver, Movable Head, Headlights, Hubley, 7 In. 550.00
Motorcycle, Harley-Davidson, Tin, Windup, Japan 5720.00
Motorcycle, Highway Patrol, Tin Lithograph, Battery Operated, Box, Modern Toys, 11 In. 880.00
Motorcycle, Motodrill 1006, Windup, Tin, Schuco, U.S. Zone Germany, Box, 5 In. 420.00
Motorcycle, Parcel Post, Removable Driver, Sidecar, Hubley, 9 1/4 In. 3080.00
Motorcycle, Parcel Post, Separate Uniformed Driver, Harley-Davidson, Hubley, 9 In. 2200.00
Motorcycle, Patrol, Green, White Rubber Tires, Cast Iron, 6 1/2 In. 115.00
Motorcycle, Pilot, Gray Suit, Gray, Tin Lithograph, Clockwork, Lehmann, 8 1/2 In. 4950.00
Motorcycle, Policeman, Aluminum Handle Bars, Pressed Tin, Windup, Marx, 8 1/2 In. . . . 170.00
Motorcycle, Policeman, Nickeled Wheels, Cast Iron, Harley-Davidson, Hubley, 5 1/2 In. . 175.00
Motorcycle, Policeman, Red, Cast Iron, 4 In. 75.00
Motorcycle, Policeman, Sidecar, Cast Iron, 4 In. 145.00
Motorcycle, Policeman, Sidecar, Nickel Plated Wheels, Hubley, 5 In. 385.00
Motorcycle, Sidecar, Saalheimer & Strauss 505.00
Motorcycle, Sidecar, Tin, Yellow Paint, Japan 7700.00
Motorcycle, Tin, Battery Operated, Japan, 11 In. 275.00
Motorcycle, Velocette, Penny Toy, San Juan, Spain, c.1925, 4 In. 506.00
Mouse, Felt Covered, Bead Eyes, Metal Nose, Red Shorts, Windup, Schuco, 4 In. 200.00
Mule, Brown, Pulling High Wheel Sulkie, Black Jockey, J.E. Stevens, 8 3/4 In. 489.00
Music Boy, Humpty Dumpty, Windup, 6 1/2 In. 65.00
Musician, Plays Tin Xylophone, Windup, Celluloid, Box, Japan 275.00
Musician, Saxophonist, Windup, Tin, Early 1900s 2000.00
My Merry Dolly's Hostess Closet, Holds Party Items, Cardboard Box, 1958, 7 x 10 In. . . . 90.00
Mystery Station, Shell Gas, Windup Car, Key, Technofix, W. Germany, 1960s, 20 x 9 In. . 235.00
Noah's Ark, Carved, Painted Figures, 200 Piece 28750.00
Nutty Maid, Indian, Windup, Marx, 7 In. 145.00
Okapi, Mohair, Cream Color, Brush Mane, Steiff, 15 x 13 In. 220.00
Old Salt, Walker, Mechanical, Tin Lithograph, 7 In. 250.00
Orangutan, Mohair, Cinnamon Red Silky Plush, Dark Brown Eyes, Schuco, 1950, 9 In. . . 600.00

Orangutan, Mohair, Cinnamon Red Silky Plush, Swivel Head, Schuco, 1950, 18 In. 900.00
Organ, Roller, Painted Wood, On Cart, 6 Tunes, Spain 330.00
Ostrich, Skating, Windup, Original Key, Box, Occupied Japan 195.00
Paddle, Pressed Cardboard, Child, Each Side, Clap Sound, Germany 12.00
Paddy & Pig, Windup, Sways Back & Forth, Lehmann, 1903, 6 In. 440.00
Pail, Children At Beach, With Shovel, Ohio Art 115.00
Pail, Children On Carnival Rides, Tin, Chein, 4 1/4 In. 70.00
Pail, Maggie & Jiggs, With Lunch Pail, Original Felt Outfit, Silver, 1924, 7 x 8 In. 400.00
Painting Set, New Adventures Of Gilligan, Dip Dots, Kenner, 1975 . . . .   1200.00
Pan, Muffin, Wagner Ware, Little Gem, Open Frame, Aluminum, 12 Cup 110.00
Paratrooper, Happy Landing, Oilcloth, Parachute, E. Kalep Borgfeldt, Box, 14 In. 80.00
Pastry Set, Box Shows Children Cooking, Pressman, 1930s, 9 x 14 In. 90.00
Peacock, Windup, Walks, Fans Tail, Alps, Japan, 1950s, 5 1/2 In. 145.00
Pedal Car, Airplane, Lone Eagle, American National 1500.00
Pedal Car, Airplane, Prop Driven Fighter, Steelcraft, 48 In. 1955.00
Pedal Car, Buick, Green & Black, Aircraft Hood Ornament 9200.00
Pedal Car, Buick, Windshield, License Plates, Hood Ornament, Gendron, 37 In. 1650.00
Pedal Car, City Fire Department, Mack Front, Steelcraft, 40 In.   430.00
Pedal Car, Duesenberg, Gilmore Racing, Wire Wheels, Chrome Accents, 65 In. 1610.00
Pedal Car, Fire Chief's, Hood Mounted Bell, Gendron 4400.00
Pedal Car, Ford, 1939 Model, Skippy 1500.00
Pedal Car, Ford, Mustang, Pressed Steel, Plastic Trim, 1964, 39 In. 750.00
Pedal Car, Little Jim, Light Green, License Plate, Steelcraft, Oakland, 33 In. 1430.00
Pedal Car, Mack Dump Truck, Hand Control For Dumping, 52 In. 690.00
Pedal Car, Packard, Wire Wheels, Gendron, 1932 . . . .   4500.00
Pedal Car, Packard, Wooden Frame, Flip-Up Seat, Makes Clicking Noise, 45 In. 3385.00
Pedal Car, Pink Cadillac, Fins, Murray, 1957 . . . .   750.00
Pedal Car, Pontiac, Steelcraft 950.00
Pedal Car, Rolls-Royce, Vinyl Interior, Rubber Tires, Metal Hubs, 24 x 60 x 22 In. 3600.00
Pedal Car, Star Racer, No. 12, Red & Yellow, Spoke Wheels, Gendron, 32 In. 3080.00
Pelican, Tin, Windup, Chein, 5 In. 185.00
Penguin, Perky, Pull, Waddles, Squawks, Fisher-Price, Box, 1973, 5 1/2 x 7 3/4 In. 40.00
Penguin, Walker, Wooden, Painted Eyes, 5 In. 60.00
Pep Rally Gift Set, Barbie, Majorette, Cheerleader, Major Uniforms, Booklet, Box, 1964 .   633.00
Phone Set, 2 Way, Tom Corbett, 50 Feet Of Wire, Clips On Belt, Box, Rockhill, c.1950 . .   125.00
Phonograph, Pigmy, Red Riding Hood, 7 Dwarfs & Jazzbo Jim, 2 Records 192.00
Piano, Baby Grand, Celluloid Keys, Chickering, Miniature 1430.00
Piano, Baby Grand, Schoenhut . . . . .110.00 to 135.00
Piano, Chromolithograph Front, Bliss, 9 1/2 In. 115.00
Piano, Famus, Box 25.00
Piano, Player, Electric, Chein 325.00
Piano, Schoenhut 135.00
Pig, Plush Mohair, Felt Lining, Swivel Neck, Felt Clothing, Label, 1930s, 15 In. 245.00
Pig, Puller, Windup, Celluloid, Japan, 7 In. 165.00
Pig & Truck, Papier-Mache, Pork Pies Printed On Truck, Zinc Roof, c.1880 . . . .   6500.00
Pile-Driver, Corrugated Roof, Winch, Buddy L, 19 In. 4870.00
Play Set, 6 Vehicles, Comic Character Figures, Tootsietoy, Box, 9 1/2 x 15 In. 3850.00
Play Set, Captain America, Shield, Mask, Handcuffs, Dart Gun, Box, 1980s 65.00
Play Set, Family Hospital, Fisher-Price, 1960s 130.00
Play Set, Marine Beachhead, Plastic Island, Accessories, Marx, Box 205.00
Play Set, Newlywed's Kitchen, Furniture, Marx, Box, 5 x 2 1/2 x 3 1/8 In. 215.00
Play Set, Newlywed's Parlor, Furniture, Tin Lithograph, Marx, Box 215.00
Play Set, Operation Moon Base, Marx 395.00
Play Set, Presidents, Hard Plastic, Marx, Box, 1950s, 34 Piece 50.00
Play-A-Sax, Hand Crank, Metal, 7 Tunes, Q.R.S. DeVry Corp., Chicago, 1930s, 11 In. . . .   270.00
Plow, McCormick-Deering, Decal Label, 7 In. 220.00
Plow, Rubber Tires, Red Metal, Tru-Scale, 1960s 45.00
Polar Bear, Mohair, White, On All Four Wheels, 1920s, 19 x 27 In. 2970.00
Police Outfit, Plastic, Trooper, Pistol, Billy Club, Whistle, Holster, Carnell Mfg., c.1950 .   165.00
Policeman, Komikal Kop, Dog On Running Board, Tin, Windup, Marx, 8 In. 440.00
Pony, Push Toy, Metal Frame, Handle, Rubber Tires, Label, 1930s 350.00
Pony, Riding, Wheels, Plastic Harness, Steel Wheels, Expert Toys, 20 In. 80.00
Pony, Shetland, White, Brown Spots, Yellow Mane, Button, Steiff, 9 1/2 x 10 3/4 In. 190.00

Porky Pig, Cowpuncher, Tin, Windup, Revolving Lariat, Marx, 8 1/2 In. 360.00
Porky Pig, With Umbrella, Tin, Windup, Leon Schlesinger, Marx, 1939, 8 In. . . . . .230.00 to 425.00
Porter, Adam, Lithographed Pants, Pushing Cart With Trunk, Lehmann, 8 x 7 In. 1210.00
Porter, Black, Carries 2 Trunks, Head Moves, Windup, Japan 350.00
Porter, Pushing Cart, Tin, Windup, Lehman, 6 In. 145.00
Porter, Red Cap, Pushing Long Baggage Cart, Windup, Tin, Strauss, 5 1/2 In. 375.00
Printing Press, Alphabet Type & Pictures, Superior Ace, No. 8405, Box 60.00
Push Wheel, Child's, Wood, 2 Bells, Red & Green Paint, Hand Grip, 21-In. Wheel 1230.00
Puzzle Car, Tin, Windup, Kosege, Occupied Japan, Box, 6 In. 84.00
Rabbit, Carrying Carrot Basket, Celluloid, Prewar Japan, 3 1/2 In. 125.00
Rabbit, Cloth, Squeaker, Coil Spring Middle, Cotton Outfit, Papier-Mache, 1920, 8 In. . . . 230.00
Rabbit, Cyclist, Peddles Tricycle, Bell Rings, Tin, Windup, 1950s, 5 In. 300.00
Rabbit, Male, Fancy Clothes, Celluloid, Prewar Japan, 4 1/2 In. 125.00
Rabbit, Nikili, Stitched Nose, Glass Eyes, Button In Ear, Steiff, 10 In. 170.00
Rabbit, Reading, Flips Pages Of Book, Plush, Tin, Alps, Japan, 7 In. 185.00
Rabbit & Pup, Black Shoebutton Eyes, Pink Velveteen Inner Ears, Steiff, 1920, 4 x 7 In. . . 520.00
Ram, Mohair, White & Black, Felt Horns & Ears, Glass Eyes, Steiff, 8 1/4 x 9 In. 220.00
Rattle, Swimming Children, Celluloid 200.00
Record Tote, Barbie, Cream, Matte Vinyl, 10 Pockets, 45 RPM, c.1961, 7 1/2 x 9 In. 66.00
Rhino, Velvet Cover, Felt Ears & Horn, Ear Button, Named Nosy, Steiff, 13 In. 105.00
Rider, Bareback, Circus, Schoenhut, 8 1/2 In. 250.00
Ridum Cowboy, Mechanical, Occupied Japan, Box, 35 In. 50.00
Rifle, Tin, Wooden Stock, Indian Shooting Rifle, Japan, Box, 23 In. 70.00
Ring, Barbie, 9 Rhinestones, Gold Ponytail Profile Relief, Adjustable, Plastic Box, c.1962 195.00
Road Grader, Adams, Yellow, Doepke, No. 2006, 1948, 26 In. 150.00
Road Roller, Ride-Em, Decals, Steelcraft, 1935 . . . . 175.00
Roadside Rest Service Station, 2 Pumps, Bar, 2 Men & Stools, Marx, Box, 1930s 1750.00
Roaring Lion, Plush Over Tin, Windup, Alps, Occupied Japan, Box, 7 In. 78.00
Robot, Action Planet, Box, Yoshiya 45.00
Robot, Answer Game, Battery Operated, Japan 900.00
Robot, Atom, Silver, Friction Motor, Yonezawa, 6 1/2 In. 105.00
Robot, Atomic Man, Gray, Green Body, Open Eyes, Red Feet, Box, 5 In. 575.00
Robot, Attacking Martian, Tin, Battery Operated, Japan, 1960s 145.00
Robot, Bulldozer, Moves Forward & Reverse, Clock Eyes, Battery Operated, 7 In. 1025.00
Robot, Bump & Go, Lighted Turning Head, Battery Operated, Japan 800.00
Robot, Change Man, Green, Red, Yellow Plastic Arms, Remote Control, Horikawa, 13 In. 1610.00
Robot, Conehead, Sparking Eyes, Walking Movement, Metallic Blue, Yonezawa, 8 1/2 In. 3335.00
Robot, Engine, Green, Torso Gears, Horikawa, 11 In. 30.00
Robot, Gears In Chest, Shoulder Antennae, Tin, Battery Operated, Japan, Box, 11 1/2 In. . 760.00
Robot, Giant Sonic, Lit Face, Turning Movement, Sound, Box, Masaduya, 15 In. 11500.00
Robot, High Wheel, Metallic Blue, Remote Control, Box, Yoshiya, 8 In. 520.00
Robot, Interplanetary Space Captain, Naito Shoten, 8 In. 7475.00
Robot, Krome Dome, Red, Blue, Yellow Plastic, Metal Head, Box, Yonezawa, 10 In. 230.00
Robot, Lilliput, Orange, Tin, Windup, First Robot Made, Japan, 1930s, 6 In. 4675.00
Robot, Lost In Space, Battery Operated, Black & Red, Remco, Box, 1960s 685.00
Robot, Lost In Space, Plastic, Box, Ahi, 10 In. 125.00
Robot, Lost In Space, Red, Blue Plastic Arms, Remco, 12 In. 115.00
Robot, Man From Mars, Red Molded Plastic, Clear Helmet, Irwin, 11 In. 45.00
Robot, Man From Mars, Windup, Irwin, Box, 1950s 690.00
Robot, Mechanical, Walking, Sparking, Box, 7 In. 695.00
Robot, Moon Explorer, Blue, Japan 1000.00
Robot, Moon, Walking Forward As Ribbons In Helmet Rotate, Japan, 1955, 10 1/2 In. . . 3600.00
Robot, Moves Directional, Silver, Blue, Red, Yellow, Blue, Battery Operated, 1955, 11 In. 960.00
Robot, Piston Action, Walks As Pistons Light, Rubber Hands, 12 In. 1550.00
Robot, Planet, Metallic Blue, Red Feet, Remote Control, Yoshiya, 9 In. 375.00
Robot, Pug Robby, Gold, Blue, Remote Control, Battery Operated, Japan, 1955, 8 In. 1800.00
Robot, R-35, Silver, Blue Head, Light-Up Eyes, Red Claws, Box, Linemar, 7 1/2 In. 690.00
Robot, Radar, Gunmetal, Silver, Light-Up Eyes, Remote Control, Nomura, 9 In. 920.00
Robot, Radical, Metallic Blue, Red Arms, Green Plastic Chest, Cragstan, 12 In. 2590.00
Robot, Radicon, Antenna Spins, Light In Chest, Remote Control, Masaduya, 14 1/2 In. . . 8050.00
Robot, Revolving Head, Arm Swinging, Chest Door Reveals Mechanisms, Alps, 9 1/2 In. 2500.00
Robot, Robby Planet, Battery Operated, Lights Up, Japan, Box, 1950s, 9 1/2 In. 1100.00
Robot, Robert, Silver Plastic, Red Arms, Cable Control, Ideal, 14 In. 60.00

Robot, Secret Weapon Space Scout, Battery Operated, 6 Actions, SH, Japan, c.1962, 9 In.   700.00
Robot, Space Conqueror, Man Of Tomorrow, Blue, Yellow, Red Gun, Daiyai, 11 In. 345.00
Robot, Space Explorer, Battery Operated, Japan, 1967 .... 200.00
Robot, Space Explorer, Box 3340.00
Robot, Space Explorer, Gunmetal, Rising To Become Robot, Yoshiya, 11 1/2 In. 750.00
Robot, Space Flying Saucer, Battery Operated 165.00
Robot, Space Patrol, Green Drive, Red Mercedes-Benz, Blue Gun, Asahi, 8 1/2 In. 575.00
Robot, Space, Evil, Tinplate Body, Walks Forward, Guns, Sound, 11 In. 185.00
Robot, Spaceman, Fighting, Gray, Moving Gun, Horikawa, 11 1/2 In. 200.00
Robot, Sparking Ratchet, Metallic Blue, Black, Chest Spark Window, Box, Nomura, 8 In. 1495.00
Robot, Sparky, Moves Forward While Sparking Mechanism, Japan, 1955, 8 1/2 In. 2400.00
Robot, Sparky, Walks With Engine Noise, Claw Hands, Tin, Windup, 8 In. 305.00
Robot, Speaks Japanese, Hard Vinyl Body, Box, Masudaya, 12 In. 1100.00
Robot, Stop & Go Action, Turning Head, Lights, Metallic Blue, Box, Yonezawa, 11 In. .. 1495.00
Robot, Television Spaceman, Metallic Gray, Box, Alps, 14 In. 430.00
Robot, Thunder, Metallic Brown, Red Feet, Light-Up Eyes, Asakusa, Box, 11 In. 4600.00
Robot, Video, Blue, Plastic Limbs, Box, Horikawa 86.00
Robot, Walking Spaceman, Clockwork Mechanism, 1960s, 7 1/2 In. 365.00
Robot, Wheel-A-Gear, Black, Red, Belt Driven Gears, Taiya, Box, 14 1/4 In. 1610.00
Robot, X-70, Tulip Head, Lilac, Silver, Orange Plastic Arms, Nomura, Box, 12 In. 1840.00
Robot, Yoshiya, Action Planet, Sparking Chest & Mouth, Rubber Claws, 1958 .... 1200.00
Robot, Zoomer, Box, Nomura 400.00
Rocket Mobile, Battery Operated, Chein 510.00
Rocket Ride, Battery Operated, Spinning Toy, Lights, Siren, Japan, 13 In. 1525.00
Rocket Ship, Fireball, Figures & Accessories, Instructions, Stickers, Box 1270.00
Rocket Ship, Moon, Tin Lithograph, Friction, Standing Action, Japan, 13 1/2 In. 235.00
Rocket Ship, Ride A Rocket Circus Ride Toy, Chein, No. 260, 1950s, 18 1/2 In. 530.00
Rocket Ship, Space Rocket, Friction, Siren Noise, Tin, Automatic Toy, Box, c.1950, 9 In. .. 185.00
Rocket Ship, Tom Corbett, Windup, Tin Lithograph, Marx 625.00
Roller Coaster, No. 275, Chein, 1960s 225.00
Roller Coaster, Tin, Windup, Original Cars, Chein 550.00
Roller Skates, Steel, Ball Bearing Wheels, Key, Sealed In Paper, Marx, 1950, 10 In. 105.00
Roly Poly, Black Clown, Papier-Mache, White Outfit, Red Trim, Felt Hat, 8 In. 770.00
Roly Poly, Butcher, Chein 40.00
Roly Poly, Chinese Man, Papier-Mache, Blue Suit, 9 In. 1540.00
Roly Poly, Chinese Man, Papier-Mache, Head Turns, Schoenhut, 9 In. 695.00
Roly Poly, Clown On Ball, Papier-Mache, Orange Suit, Red Hat, 9 1/2 In. 890.00
Roly Poly, Clown, Germany, 13 1/2 In. 2640.00
Roly Poly, Clown, Glass Eyes, Button In Ear 115.00
Roly Poly, Clown, Papier-Mache, Internal Chimes Sound When Moved, 11 3/4 In. 310.00
Roly Poly, Clown, Tin, Moore, 6 In. 405.00
Roly Poly, Happy Hooligan, 1920s, 4 3/4 In. 275.00
Roly Poly, Happy Hooligan, Papier-Mache, Red Cap, Germany, 9 1/4 In. 530.00
Roly Poly, Monkey, Red Jacket, Weighted Base, 5 1/8 In. 240.00
Roly Poly, Rabbit, Tin, Moore, 6 1/8 In. 405.00
Roly Poly, Sailor Girl, Papier-Mache, Head Wobbles When Moved, Schoenhut, 7 5/8 In. . 530.00
Rooster, Katy Kackler, No. 140, Wooden, Fisher-Price, c.1958 .... 100.00
Rooster, Squeak, Papier-Mache, Spring Legs, 6 1/2 In. 90.00
Rooster, Tin, Battery Operated, Mikuni, Japan, Box, 7 In. 65.00
Rooster & Chicken, Pip-Squeak, In Coop, Felt Covered Birds, Wooden, 5 3/4 x 4 1/4 In. . 110.00
Roundhouse, Pressed Steel, Houses, 4 Sections Of Track, 24 In. 2090.00
Sailboat, Named Henry Ford, Wooden Case, 42 x 38 In. 105.00
Sailor, Playing Accordion, Tin Lithograph, Squeeze, George Levy, 1910, 6 In. 450.00
Sambo The Minstrel Man, Monkey With Guitar, Celluloid, Windup, Alps, Box, 8 In. 135.00
Scooter, Metal, Rubber Tires, Bell On Handle Bars, Schwinn, 27 1/2 x 48 In. 185.00
Scooter, Snow, Go Dink Printed On Top, 28 In. 45.00
Scooter, The Chief, Pressed Steel, Rubber Tires, 33 x 5 x 39 In. 50.00
Seal, Circus Queen, Windup, Celluloid Ball, Box, Alps, c.1946 .... 400.00
Seal, Sparky, Balances Styrofoam Ball, Battery Operated, Box, MT, 6 In. 69.00
Seal, Swiveling Ball, Battery Operated, Box, Japan, 1950s 455.00
Seal, Tail & Flippers Move, Windup, Box 550.00
Seesaw, Never Stop, Children Seesaw Top To Bottom, Tin, Gibbs, 1912-1931, 15 In. 90.00
Service Station, Roadside Rest, Marx 1375.00

Service Station, Shell Gas, 2 Pumps, 2 Cars, Wyandotte, All Metal Products Co., Box ... 3300.00
Service Station, Tin Station, Wooden Pumps, Gibbs, 7 In. 580.00
Service Station, Washing, Lubrication & Parking 180.00
Service Station Set, Tootsietoy, Box 695.00
Sewing Machine, 1 Cent, Trundle, Hand Crank Pedal, Tin, Meier, 1910, 3 In. 110.00
Sewing Machine, Betsy Ross, Electric, Case .... .65.00 to 100.00
Sewing Machine, Casige Eagle, Metal, Crank Operated, British Zone Germany, 7 1/2 In. . 100.00
Sewing Machine, Casige, Miniature, 4 In. 150.00
Sewing Machine, F.W. Muller, Germany, 6 In. 150.00
Sewing Machine, Germany, c.1920 .... 100.00
Sewing Machine, Green Top, Tin, Sin Rival, 4 1/4 In. 170.00
Sewing Machine, Jet Sew-O-Matic, Metal, Plastic, Crank Operated, England, 9 x 7 x 4 In. 75.00
Sewing Machine, Junior Miss, Blue 145.00
Sewing Machine, Little Red Riding Hood, Germany, 7 1/2 In. 350.00
Sewing Machine, Sew Master, Berlin, Box 95.00
Sewing Machine, Singer, Cast Iron & Metal, Crank Operated, Great Britain, 8 x 6 x 4 In. . 100.00
Sewing Machine, Singer, Cast Iron, Black, Nickel Trim, Box, 7 x 6 1/2 In. 190.00
Sewing Machine, Singer, Instructions, Clamp, No. 20, Cast Iron 200.00
Sewing Machine, Singer, Maker's Box 110.00
Sewing Machine, Stitchwell, Cast Iron, 7 x 6 In. 295.00
Sewing Machine, Stitchwell, Wooden, Box 1500.00
Sheriff Garrett, Best Of The West, Action Figure, Marx, Box 80.00
Shooting Gallery, Knock Down, Gun, Marx, Box, 25 x 29 In. 145.00
Shooting Gallery, Mechanical, Moving Targets, Spring Bound, Ohio Art 100.00
Silver Mine Express, Tin, Windup, Car, Box, 1950s, 23 x 6 In. 225.00
Singing Bird, Tin, Windup, Wing & Tail Move, 1950s, 7 1/2 In. 195.00
Singing Birds, Squeak, Tin Lithograph, Germany, 5 In. 65.00
Skeleton, Sam The Strolling, Windup, Tin, Mikuni, Japan, 1950s, 6 In. 285.00
Skipper Electric Drawing Set, Lights, Traces Outfits, Lakeside Toys, 1964, 9 x 14 In. 85.00
Skunk, Stinky, Windup, Box, Japan 125.00
Skybird Flyer, Lighthouse, Airplane & Zeppelin On Rod, Tin, Windup, Marx, Box, c.1930 815.00
Skycycle, Evel Knievel, Die Cast, Box 125.00
Sled, 1 Board Seat, Cutout, Wrought Iron Runners 95.00
Sled, American Shield On Top, Dexter On Sides, 33 In. 4900.00
Sled, Bentwood Runners, Cast Gooseneck Finials, 36 In. 275.00
Sled, Cast Iron Runners, Sprays Of Roses, Flora Temple, 1877, 55 In. 1955.00
Sled, Chester On Seat, Beveled Runners, 34 1/2 In. 605.00
Sled, Curved Wooden Runners, Shaped Top, Red Paint, 29 In. 330.00
Sled, Flexible Flyer, No. 2E, 1940s 135.00
Sled, Lettered Crusoe, 30 In. 550.00
Sled, Painted, Hudson River School Landscape Scene, 8 x 40 x 12 In. 635.00
Sled, Painted, Iron, Wood, Signed E. Hughes, American, Late 19th Century 550.00
Sled, Red Paint, Black, Yellow Stripes, Swan Head Runners, 34 In. 330.00
Sled, Red Paint, Curved Iron Bracing, 18 In. 625.00
Sled, Red, Gold Striped, Multicolored Floral 950.00
Sled, Scenery Cameo, Scene Of Lake & Trees, Metal Braces & Runners, c.1910, 39 In. .. 615.00
Sled, Scrolled End Runners, Green Diamond & Scrolls, 37 1/2 In. 385.00
Sled, Stenciled Horse, Painted, Blue & Black, Metal Runners, Handholds, 30 x 9 1/2 In. ... 460.00
Sled, Stenciled Stag, Iron Rods Under Runners, c.1900 .... 700.00
Sled, Stenciled Yellow Flowers, Head Of Indian Chief, Metal Runners, 26 In. 410.00
Sled, Wood, Cast Iron Runners, Red, Sprays Of Roses, Flora Temple, American, 1877 ... 1955.00
Sled, Wood, Cast Iron, Seat With Footrest, Push Handle, c.1900, 40 x 16 x 32 In. 250.00
Sled, Wood, Metal, Airline Flexible Flyer, Salesman Sample, Label, 9 x 23 In. 750.00
Sleigh, Horse Drawn, Prancing Black, Gold Horse, Ornate Green, Cast Iron, 14 1/2 In. ... 290.00
Sleigh, Painted Red & Black, New Upholstery, Victorian, 35 x 17 x 24 In. 1625.00
Sleigh, Reindeer Drawn, Cast Iron, Hubley 1760.00
Sleigh, Skating, Blue With Black Borders, Gold Finials, Iron & Wood Handle, 54 In. 1100.00
Slinky, Elephant, Pull Toy, Box 265.00
Smiling Sam, Carnival Man, Tin, Windup, Alps, Box, 1950s, 9 In. 325.00
Snail, Tin Lithograph, Friction, Germany, 2 1/4 In. 20.00
Snail, Velveteen Body, Long Vinyl Antennae, Steiff, 6 In. 220.00
Snowball Target, Mechanical, Moving Arm Rings Bell, Metal, c.1900 .... 4800.00
Soapbox Derby Racer, Painted Robin's-Egg Blue, Clive Alcorn, Barnard, Vt., c.1947 .... 895.00

Soldier, Arabs Of Desert, Britains, Box, 4 Piece 595.00
Soldier, Band Of Coldstream Guards, Britains, 20 Piece 130.00
Soldier, Clockwork, Roller Mechanism Under Feet, Tin, Celluloid, 9 In. 170.00
Soldier, Crescent, Box, 1950s 50.00
Soldier, Iroquois, Firing Gun, George Borgfeldt, Box, 2 1/2 In., 8 Piece 69.00
Soldier, Lancers, Mounted At Halt, Officer Turned In Saddle, Britains, c.1945, 5 Piece ... 475.00
Soldier, On Horseback, Mechanical, Tinplate Base, Papier-Mache, c.1850, 7 In. 2500.00
Soldier, Royal Canadian Mounted Police, Cast Metal, 6 Soldiers, 1 Horse, Box, c.1950 .. 100.00
Soldier, Royal Company Of Archers, Britains, 1953, 13 Piece 790.00
Soldier, Royal Horse Guards, Mounted, Britains, Box, 5 Piece 120.00
Soldier Set, Civil War, Rebel, Caisso, Cannons, Horse, Marx, Early 1960s 145.00
Space Capsule, NASA, Battery Operated 235.00
Space Car, Battery Operated, Box 575.00
Space Car, Stop & Go Action, Antenna, Satellite, Red, Silver, Plastic Fittings, 13 In. 175.00
Space Commando, White Helmet, Antenna, Remote Control, Sonsco, 7 1/2 In. 4600.00
Space Patrol Car, Red Astronaut, Firing Cannon, Battery Operated, Nomura 920.00
Space Satellite Station, Rocket Ships, Saucers, Workers, Carts, Tin, Marx, 9 x 12 In. ... 210.00
Space Station, 4 Rooms, Radar, Tin, Box, Battery Operated, S.H. 980.00
Spaceman, Green Body, Pink Feet, Windup, Japan, 1960s, 5 1/2 In. 195.00
Spaceship, Apollo, Nr. 562, Tin, Friction, West Germany, c.1955, 4 1/4 In. 65.00
Spaceship, Battery Operated, Round, Box, 1960s, 8 x 8 In. 175.00
Spaceship, Sparking, Push Plunger, Props Spin, Sparks Fly, Plastic, 1950s, 8 In. 105.00
Spaceship, Tom Corbett, Polaris, Marx, 1952 .... 785.00
Spaceship, X-7 Space Explorer, Blue, Clear Dome, Astronaut, Box, Masudaya, 7 In. 125.00
Spaceship, X-12, Painted Plastic, 1950s, 2 3/4 In. 20.00
Spaceship, X-15, Round, Battery Operated, Tin Lithograph, 1960s, Japan, 8 In. 175.00
Spaceship, X-36, Sparking Space Ranger, Tin, Friction, Japan, Box, 6 1/2 In. 720.00
Spark Plug, Wooden, Cloth, Partial King Features Sticker, Schoenhut 405.00
Spider, Spidy, Mohair, Beige, Glass Bead Eyes, Steiff, c.1960, 5 In. 220.00
Spin-A-Hoop, Girl With Hula-Hoop, Windup, Tin, Vinyl Head, Box, 1950s, 9 In. 160.00
Sprinkling Can, Mexican Children, Ohio Art 75.00
Spy Detecto Writer, Sky King, 1949 .... 95.00
Squirrel, Mohair, Ivory, Embroidered Nose & Paws, Glass Eyes, Button, Steiff, 7 1/2 In. .. 140.00
Stable, Wooden, Green Paper Roof, Cream Paint, Removable Hay Loft, 1900, 35 x 15 In. 2800.00
Stable, Wooden, Open Topped, Natural Wood Finish, France, 1890, 22 x 18 In. 3800.00
Stagecoach, Pull, Wooden, Paper Lithograph, 2 Mailbags, Fisher-Price 425.00
Stamper, Captain America, PVC, 1986 .... 12.00
Station, Space Tracking, Battery Operated 435.00
Station, Union, Tin Lithograph, Windup, Automatic Toy Co., 20 In. 165.00
Steam Engine, Chrome, Cast Iron, Tin, Instructions & Tools, Wilesco, 8 x 10 In. 345.00
Steam Engine, Upright Boiler, Flywheel, Electric, 10 In. 126.00
Steam Roller, Army Green, Gold Highlights, Cast Iron, Hubley, 7 1/2 In. 515.00
Steam Roller, Wooden Roller, Galion Master, Cast Iron, Kenton, 6 1/2 In. 165.00
Steam Shovel, Big Boy, Claw Shovel, Buddy L, 20 x 7 x 13 In. 100.00
Steam Shovel, Claw Shovel & Scoop, Buddy L, 17 In. 170.00
Steam Shovel, Pressed Steel, Claw Shovel, Scoop, Buddy L, 17 In. 170.00
Steam Shovel, Pressed Steel, Red, Tan, Black, Turner Decal, 1940s, 14 In. 285.00
Steve Scout, Giving Scout Salute With Left Hand, Box, 1975 .... 85.00
Stove, 2 Ovens, 2 Graduated Range Tops, Brass Rail, Paw Feet, Cast Iron, 9 1/2 In. 375.00
Stove, 2 Ovens, Range Tops, 2 Pots, Claw Feet, Tin, Germany, 11 In. 175.00
Stove, Cast Iron & Faience, Brass Framed Doors, Rack, c.1880, 17 x 24 In. 6000.00
Stove, Cast Iron, Removable Hot Plates, Crown, 11 In. 90.00
Stove, Cook, Pots, Pans, Lid, Little Eva, Cast Iron, 8 x 13 In. 575.00
Stove, Gem, Cast Iron, Arcade, 3 1/2 In. 70.00
Stove, Novelty Co., Cast Iron, Early 20th Century, 12 In. 80.00
Stove, Queen, Cast Iron, 3 1/2 In. 50.00
Stove, Rival, Cast Iron, J. & E. Stevens, 1895, 15 1/2 x 7 1/2 In. 935.00
Stove, Tin, Cast Iron Feet, 4 Doors, Pots, Pans, Germany, Late 1800s, 10 1/4 x 7 x 11 In. . 270.00
Stove, With Copper Cookware, Metal Oven Doors, Brass Top, Tole, France, 15 In. 1600.00
String Climber, Aunt Jemima, Cardboard, Embossed Die Cut, c.1905, 13 1/4 x 6 In. 3145.00
Submarine, 4 Horizontal Rudders, Painted, Windup, Germany, 16 In. 920.00
Submarine, S.S.N.7, Crank Windup, Tin Lithograph, SAN, Japan, 1950s, 7 3/4 In. 50.00
Submarine, Wolverine, Windup, 1940s, 13 In. 140.00

Toy, Taxi, Fresh Air, Amos 'n' Andy, Windup,
Tin Lithograph, Marx, 8 In.

Molded plastic parts of toys will become brittle and deteriorate when exposed to ultraviolet light. Although there are products that may improve the appearance of discolored plastic, it is best to keep plastic away from strong lights and pollution.

Surrey, 1 Horse, Driver, Removable Seats, Cast Iron, Dent, 1910, 11 1/2 In.	795.00
Swimmer, Clockwork Motor, Tin Arms, Celluloid, 6 1/2 In.	85.00
Table, Presentation, Bebe Triste, Wooden Frame, 20 In.	3000.00
Tango Dancers, Tin, Clockwork Mechanism In Woman's Dress, Guntherman, 8 In.	3850.00
Tank, Doughboy, Windup, Soldier Popping Up From Turret, Marx, 1930s, 10 In.	190.00 to 250.00
Tank, M-48 Army, Bump & Go, Gun Fires, Battery Operated, Tin, TN, Box, Japan, 8 In.	95.00
Tank, Midget, Climbing, Fighting, Tin Lithograph, Plastic Wheels, Marx, Box, 1941, 5 In.	145.00
Tank, Midget, Climbing, Fighting, Tin, Windup, Marx, Box, 1930s, 5 In.	310.00
Tank, Military, Camouflage, Marklin, 1930s, 7 1/2 In.	225.00
Tank, Orbit Explorer, Windup, Ball Blowing, Spaceman, Camera Under Dome, 1950s	390.00
Tank, Pop-Up Soldier, Windup, Marx, 10 In.	365.00
Tank, Revolving Turret, Firing Gun, Structo, 1922, 12 In.	385.00
Tank, Sparking Doughboy, Advances, Soldier Pops Out Of Hatch, Marx, 10 In.	420.00
Tank, Turnover, Casper Underneath, Linemar, 4 In.	450.00
Tank, Whirlybird, 25 Man Attack Force, Remco, Box, 1960s	175.00
Taxi, Austin, Cast Driver, White Tires, Dinky, 3 In.	470.00
Taxi, Delivery, Town, Original Gray Paint, Cast Iron, Kilgore, 6 In.	170.00
Taxi, Driver, Dark Mustard Yellow, Cast Iron, 4 Door, 6 In.	170.00
Taxi, Fresh Air, Amos 'n' Andy, Windup, Tin Lithograph, Marx, 8 In. ....*Illus*	750.00
Taxi, Yellow Cab, Cast Iron, Arcade, 8 In.	230.00
Taxi, Yellow Cab, Cast Iron, Gottschalk	625.00
Taxi, Yellow Cab, Radiator Screen, Cast Iron, Arcade, 9 In.	1090.00
Taxi Set, 4 Sedans, Tow Truck, Box, Tootsietoy, 6 1/2 x 10 In.	1430.00
Tea Set, Blue Willow, Tin, Ohio Art Co., 1950s, 22 Piece	125.00
Tea Set, Humpty Dumpty, Ohio Art, Box, 1930s	160.00
Tea Set, Little Red Riding Hood, Tin, 13 Piece	35.00
Tea Set, Tin, Fiesta Colors, Ohio Art, 1930s, 29 Piece	220.00
Teakettle, Griswold, Marked Use Erie Ware The Best	475.00
Teddy Bears are also listed in the Teddy Bear category.	
Telephone, Barbie, Mattel-O-Phone, Plastic, 5 Discs, Battery Operated, c.1968	415.00
Telephone, Calling Dr. Kildare, Plastic, Renzi Toys, 1960s	45.00
Telephone, Strawberry Shortcake, Kenner	55.00
Thresher, McCormick-Deering, Cast Iron, Arcade, c.1927, 12 In.	500.00
Thresher, McCormick-Deering, Decal Label, 7 In.	275.00
Tiger, Mohair, Tan, Glass Eyes, Plastic Whiskers, Jointed Limbs, Schuco, 1960s, 3 In.	120.00
Tiger, Walks & Growls, Windup, Box, Marx	185.00
Timmy Turtle, Musical, Plastic Red Shell, Fisher-Price, 6 1/2 x 12 1/2 In.	45.00
Tinko-Go-Round, Tin Lithograph, Celluloid, Clockwork, Box, Japan, 7 In.	46.00
Toddling Baby, Bottle In Hand, Windup, Celluloid, Occupied Japan, Box, 4 1/2 In.	165.00
Toiletry Set, Gold Edge, Paper Lining, Hand Mirror, Wooden Box, 1890, 12 In.	1300.00
Top, Astronauts, Spaceships, Tin, Spring Loaded Winder, SSK, Japan, c.1960, 3 1/2 In.	75.00
Top, Circus Scene, Plunger Top, Chein, 1930s, 6 1/2 In.	80.00
Top, Fish On Sides, Tin, Square, Spring-Loaded Winder, 2 1/4 x 2 1/2 In.	65.00
Top, Fortune Telling, What The Stars Say, Girard Model Works, Tin Lithograph, 5 In.	55.00
Top, Gambling, Tin Lithograph, Box, 5 1/4 In.	145.00
Top, Mobil Gas, Wooden, Red, White Top	40.00
Top, Plastic, Translucent Purple, White Cap Inset, Metal Tip, Hong Kong, 1 1/2 In.	8.50

Top, Sir Duncan, Plastic, Orange & White, Flambeau, Heraldic Shield, On Card, 1970s .. 29.00
Top, Space, Tin Lithograph, Wooden Handle, Ohio Art, 1950s, 5 In. 35.00
Top, Wooden, Painted, Orange, Yellow Stripe, 1940s, 2 3/4 In. 18.00
Top, Wooden, Painted, Round Steel Tip, 1930s, 2 In. 10.00
Tortoise, Tin, Windup, MT, Box, 5 In. 58.00
Tower, Airport, Sky Hawk, Marx 275.00
Tractor, Caterpillar, Rubber Treads, Tin Lithograph, Courtland, 1950s 25.00
Tractor, Dump Wagon, Arcade, 15 1/4 In. 220.00
Tractor, Fordson, Cast Iron, Nickel Plated Wheels, Williams, 5 1/4 In. 470.00
Tractor, Fordson, White Rear Tires, Silver & Black Front Tires, Arcade, 4 1/2 In. 150.00
Tractor, Golf Course, Tonka, 1961 .... 150.00
Tractor, McCormick-Deering, Cast Iron, Arcade, 1927 .... 525.00
Tractor, Plastic, Battery Operated, Sounds, Japan, 1950s, 7 In. 120.00
Tractor, Sparking, Driver, Marx, 1950s 85.00
Tractor, Steam, Display Model, Smith & Hunter 3850.00
Tractor, Trailer, Windup, Tin Lithograph, Driver, 1950s, 11 1/2 In. 185.00
Tractor Set, Airlines Luggage, Tonka, 2 Carts 195.00
Trailer, Sioux Freight Carriers, Tin, Friction, Linemar, Box, Japan, 8 In. 105.00
Trailer, Vacationer's, Teardrop Shape, Red Sedan, Tin, Friction, MT, Box, Japan 9 1/2 In. . 315.00
Train, American Flyer, Bunker Hill, Pullman, Observation Car, 1927 .... 920.00
Train, American Flyer, Locomotive, 3 Passenger Cars, O Gauge, 1932 .... 510.00
Train, Bo-Bo, Electric Locomotive, Marklin 1840.00
Train, Buddy L, Engine & Tender, 44 In. 2530.00
Train, Buddy L, No. 1006, Flatcar, 1921-1931 .... 932.00
Train, Buddy L, Zephyr Streamlined, 3 Piece 4400.00
Train, Freight, Union Pacific, Big Boy Engine, Rivarossi 92.00
Train, Ives, Locomotive, Clockwork, 1990s 1650.00
Train, Lionel, Engine, No. 2018, Whistle Tender, No. 6026, O Gauge 40.00
Train, Lionel, Engine, No. 2025, Whistle Tender, O Gauge 69.00
Train, Lionel, Standard Gauge, No. 408E 3520.00
Train, Lionel, Steam Locomotive & Tender, Instructions, Boxes, O Gauge, No. 6020W ... 316.00
Train, Marx, Freight, Mechanical, Miniature, Box, 1940s 285.00
Train, Marx, Mercury, Passenger, Red, O Gauge, 1938, 4 Piece 265.00
Train, Ranger, Locomotive, Coal Car, 2 Passenger Cars, Tin, Windup, Box, 14 In. 100.00
Train, Tin, Battery Operated, Whistle, Modern Toys, Japan, c.1930, 9 1/4 x 4 In. 125.00
Train, Windup, Black, Gold Paint, Cast Iron, 3 1/4 x 6 1/2 In. 110.00
Train Accessory, Lionel, Power Station, No. 840 .... 1210.00
Train Accessory, Lionel, Signal, No. 80, Semaphore 46.00
Train Accessory, Lionel, Station, O Gauge, No. 127 .... 70.00
Train Accessory, Marklin, Station, Railway, Clock Tower 2350.00
Train Accessory, Z Transformer, 275 Watts 190.00
Train Set, American Flyer, Borden's Milk Car, Lumber Car, Tank, 1935, 75 In., 8 Piece .. 465.00
Train Set, American Flyer, Hiawatha, Windup, 1936, 48 In., 5 Piece 595.00
Train Set, American Flyer, No. 4687, Annapolis, West Point, President's Special, 1927 ... 7150.00
Train Set, American Flyer, Passenger Set, Electric Locomotive, Observation Car, Box ... 490.00
Train Set, Hafner, Windup Engine, Boxcar, Phillips 66 Tank Car, Red Caboose, Tinplate . 135.00
Train Set, Lionel, Locomotive, Tender, Car, Cattle Car & Caboose, 5 Piece 795.00
Train Set, Marx, Windup Plastic Engine, 4 Tin Cars, Track 175.00
Train Set, North Hampton, O Gauge, Steam Engine & Tender, Labels, Box 560.00
Train Set, Penny, Dark Green, Black, Germany, 1920s, 12 In., 4 Piece 295.00
Train Set, Tokyo, Locomotive, 5 Cars, Tin, Box, Japan, Prewar, 13 In. 345.00
Trapeze Man, Circus, Pressed Steel Van, Yellow Carrier, Brown Plumed Horses, 16 In. ... 3000.00
Trapeze Man, Mr. Silly, Push Button, Plastic, Roger Hargreaves, 1979, 5 1/2 In. 45.00
Trick Seal, Balances Spinning Ball, Celluloid, Windup, Alps, Occupied Japan, Box, 6 In. . 130.00
Tricycle, 2 Figures, Cast Iron, Fisch 2750.00
Tricycle, Barney Rubble, Rides Tricycle, Windup, Box, Linemar ....575.00 to 650.00
Tricycle, Black & Red, BF Goodrich, 1930s, 20 In. 3600.00
Trolley, Clockwork, With Track, Trestle Bridge Sides, Tin Lithograph, Japan, 12 In. 90.00
Trolley, Shawa, Wood, Tin & Cardboard, Blue & Brown, Prewar Japan, 14 In. 1495.00
Trolley, Tin Lithograph, Penny Toy, 3 In. 412.00
Trolley, Toonerville, Cast Iron, Dent Co., Box 950.00
Trolley, Windup, Prewar, Germany, 9 In. 295.00
Trolley Car, Dayton, Tin, Painted, Friction Power, Late 1800s, 14 3/4 In. 415.00

Trolley Car, Lever Action, Tin, Box, Japan, 6 5/8 In. 45.00
Trolley Car, Windup, Black, Yellow, Pava, Box, 12 1/2 In. 240.00
Truck, 1-Wheel Cab, Friction, Mitsubishi, 10 1/2 In. 465.00
Truck, 205 Oh-Boy! American Express, Metal, 1927, 22 x 10 In. 1500.00
Truck, Aerial Ladder, Kingsbury Manufacturing Co., Wooden Crate, 1927, 34 In. 9900.00
Truck, Allied Van Lines, Friction, Box, Japan, 13 In. 275.00
Truck, Allied Van Lines, Strombeck-Becker Dollhouse Furniture Load, Buddy L, 29 In. .. 9350.00
Truck, Allstate Emergency Service, Rubber Tires, Tin, Louis Marx, Japan, 2 3/4 x 5 In. .. 100.00
Truck, American Railway Express, Model No. 2, Side Screen, Sturditoys 2970.00
Truck, Arctic Ice Cream, Red, Blue, Cast Iron, 8 In. 450.00
Truck, Army, Cast Iron, Britains, 5 1/2 In. 110.00
Truck, Army, Covered Tender, Original Box, Doors Open, Britains, 5 1/2 In. 11.00
Truck, Army, U.S. Troop Carrier, Khaki Color, Canvas Canopy, Sturditoy, 1920s, 26 In. ... 2250.00
Truck, Auto Derrick, Maroon, Kingsbury, 15 In. 1350.00
Truck, Auto Express, Black Driver, c.1915, 9 1/2 In. 1250.00
Truck, Auto Haulaway, With Cadillac & Pickup Truck, Yellow, Structo, 1953, 21 In. 145.00
Truck, Automobile Carrier, 2 Cars, 1960s, 8 1/2 In. 125.00
Truck, Barrel, Wilkins, Blue, 15 In. 650.00
Truck, Buckeye Ditcher, Kenton Toys, 5 In. 250.00
Truck, Car Carrier, 4 Art Deco Style Cars, Marx, 1940s, 21 In. 630.00
Truck, Car Carrier, 4 Cars, 11 1/4 In. 275.00
Truck, Car Carrier, A-2-A1, Matchbox 65.00
Truck, Cement Mixer, Ford, Model 1959, Tonka, 14 In. 195.00
Truck, Cement Mixer, Jaeger, Hubley, 7 1/2 In. ....275.00 to 400.00
Truck, Cement Mixer, Pressed Steel, Buddy L, 18 In. 440.00
Truck, City, 2 Mule Team, Stenciled Cast Iron, Kenton, 15 In. 1265.00
Truck, Coal, Enclosed Cab, Buddy L, 26 In. 11550.00
Truck, Coast To Coast, Tin, Removable Top, Tootsietoy, Box, 9 In. 115.00
Truck, Consolidated Freight, Tandem, Friction, Japan 250.00
Truck, Consolidated Freightways, Double 10-Wheeler, Die Cast, Box, 1990s, 16 In. 85.00
Truck, Corn Picker, Wagon, Front-End Loader, Hay Bailer, John Deere 1200.00
Truck, Crane, Kelmet, 25 In. 5500.00
Truck, Delivery, Uniform Driver, Yellow Spoke Tin Wheels, Lehmann Co., 1907, 7 In. 800.00
Truck, Deluxe Delivery, Plastic Cab, Tin Bed, Tires, Marx, Box, 12 In. 195.00
Truck, Dump, 10 Tires, Hydraulic Action, Decals, Schuco, 21 In. 260.00
Truck, Dump, A-Frame, Buddy L, Box, 1920s, 25 In. 3300.00
Truck, Dump, Bulldog Mack, 1928, 60 In. 595.00
Truck, Dump, Coal, Driver, Hubley, 1905, 10 In. 1195.00
Truck, Dump, Euclid, Dinky Toys 225.00
Truck, Dump, Ford, 1964 Model, c.1968, 16 In. 165.00
Truck, Dump, Hydraulic, Black, Cream, Pressed Steel, Marx, 15 In. 70.00
Truck, Dump, Hydraulic, Decals, 10 Tires, Structo, 21 In. 259.00
Truck, Dump, Hydraulic, Plastic, Red, Yellow, Gama, 1968, 17 In. 95.00
Truck, Dump, International Harvester, Driver, Decals, Cast Iron, 10 1/2 In. 518.00
Truck, Dump, Junior, Opening Doors, Headlights, Bumper, Buddy L, 1920s, 24 In. 770.00
Truck, Dump, Pressed Steel, Structo, 1930s, 20 In. 50.00
Truck, Dump, Pressed Steel, Wyandotte, 1930s, 15 In. 295.00
Truck, Dump, Sand & Gravel, 1920s, 8 1/2 In. 295.00
Truck, Dump, Sand & Gravel, Tin Lithograph, Marx, 1956, 13 1/2 In. ....170.00 to 200.00
Truck, Dump, Spring Released, Dual Rear Wooden Wheels, Wyandotte, 1931, 9 5/8 In. ... 195.00
Truck, Excavator & Steam Shovel, Crank Handle, Buddy L, 1941, 27 1/2 In. 1250.00
Truck, Express Line Delivery, Pressed Steel, Front Steering, Rear Doors, Buddy L, 24 In. .. 750.00
Truck, Express, Green, Cast Iron, Arcade, 7 In. 175.00
Truck, Express, Original Driver & Steering Wheel, Jones & Bixler, 15 1/2 In. 1025.00
Truck, Express, Red, Green, Pressed Steel, Rubber Wheels, Wyandotte, 1950s, 17 In. 225.00
Truck, Express, Stake Bed Body, Cast Iron, Arcade, 9 In. 400.00
Truck, Farm, Hay, Tonka, 1960s, 13 3/4 In. 125.00
Truck, Ford, Pickup, Bandai, 1968, 7 1/2 In. 250.00
Truck, Heinz 57, Electric Lights, Metalcraft, 1934, 12 In. ....475.00 to 660.00
Truck, Heinz Pickle, National Recovery Act Sticker, Metalcraft, 1930s, 12 In. ....415.00 to 450.00
Truck, Heinz Pickle, Pressed Steel, Metalcraft, 1930s, 10 In. 450.00
Truck, Highway Maintenance, Ford, Pressed Steel, Buddy L, 1960s, 13 1/2 In. 225.00
Truck, Horse, Texas Ranger, Heads Move Up & Down, Friction 195.00

Truck, Huckster's, Leiter Brothers, Red Paint, Gold Striping 825.00
Truck, Ice, 3 Blocks Of Ice, Arcade, 6 3/4 In. 425.00
Truck, Ice, Mack, 6 Blocks Of Glass Ice, 8 1/2 In. 195.00
Truck, Ice, Red, Yellow Wooden Wheels, Wyandotte, 1950s, 11 In. 175.00
Truck, Ice, With 2 Blocks Of Glass Ice, Cast Aluminum, 6 1/2 In. 80.00
Truck, International Railway Express, Wrigley's Spearmint Gum, Buddy L, 1937, 25 In. ... 715.00
Truck, Junior Dairy, Opening Doors, Headlights, Firestone Rubber Tires, Buddy L, 25 In. .. 1265.00
Truck, Kroger Food Express, Sheet Steel, 11 In. 95.00
Truck, Ladder, Aerial, Extendable Ladder, Bell, Buddy L, 39 In. 375.00
Truck, Livestock Carrier, Friction, Japan, 9 In. 50.00
Truck, Livestock, Cast Iron, Iron Wheels, Stake Bed, Kilgore, 8 In. 825.00
Truck, Log, 6 Logs, Tootsietoy, Box, 9 In. 140.00
Truck, Log, Logs & Driver, Windup, Strauss 450.00
Truck, Log, Trailer, Mack, Pressed Steel, Smitty Toys, 33 In. 550.00
Truck, Milk, Tin, Friction, Milk Tray Carrier, Yamaichi, Japan, 6 1/2 In. 315.00
Truck, Motor Express, Plastic, Hubley, Box, c.1950, 6 1/2 In. 130.00
Truck, Moving Van, Allied, Pull-N-Ride Handle, Box, Buddy L, 29 1/2 In. 3500.00
Truck, Moving Van, Lammert's Furniture & Draperies, Cast Iron, Arcade, 1928 .... 2310.00
Truck, Moving Van, North American Van Lines, Tin, Plastic Windshield, Japan, 13 In. 160.00
Truck, Neuweiler Brewing, Original Artwork, Truck, 1950s, 11 1/2 x 5 1/2 In. 31.00
Truck, Open Bed, Toolboxes, Tin, 10 1/2 In. 45.00
Truck, Packard, Keystone Police City Patrol, 1923 .... 1100.00
Truck, Police Patrol, Decal, Sonny, c.1928, 27 3/4 In. 3000.00
Truck, Police, Chevrolet Pickup, Die Cast, Sabra, No. 8122 .... 30.00
Truck, Police, Renault, Colorale Pickup, Chariot De Police, Die Cast, C.I.J., No. 3/65 .... 150.00
Truck, Pure Oil, Art Deco Style, Electric Headlights, Metalcraft, 15 In. 1650.00
Truck, R.E.A. Express, Rubber Men, Accessories, Marx, 19 1/2 In. 600.00
Truck, Railway Express, Buddy L, 24 In. 805.00
Truck, Railway Express, Green, Advertising Milk On Side, Buddy L, Box, 1950s, 24 In. . 3410.00
Truck, Robotoy, Electric, Buddy L, 21 5/8 In. 1980.00
Truck, Sanitation, Battery Operated, Jack Education Product Group, Box, Japan 75.00
Truck, Scraper, Wire Windshield, Allis Chalmers, Lionel, 1950s 500.00
Truck, Sprinkler, Tank Line, Buddy L, 1920s, 26 1/4 In. 1380.00
Truck, Stake, 2-Mule Team, Yellow Wagon, City Truck, Red Wheels, Cast Iron, 15 In. 630.00
Truck, Stake, 5 Ton, Driver, Hubley, 17 In. 960.00
Truck, Steam Shovel, Cart, Pressed Steel, Headlights, Structo, 1930s, 27 In. 230.00
Truck, Studebaker, Flat Front, Wooden Wheels, Marx, 16 In. 195.00
Truck, Tanker, Gasoline & Oil, Plastic, Hubley, Box, c.1950, 6 1/2 In. 130.00
Truck, Tanker, Gasoline One Side, Fuel Oils Other, Hess, 14 1/2 In. 65.00
Truck, Tanker, Gasoline, Motor Oils, Trailer, Windup, Courtland, Box 375.00
Truck, Tanker, Gasoline, Nickel Finish Wheels, 7 1/8 In. 55.00
Truck, Tanker, Gasoline, Shell, Ford, King, 25 In. 895.00
Truck, Tanker, Gasoline, Sinclair, Tin Lithograph, Linemar, Japan, 13 In. 240.00
Truck, Tanker, Gasoline, Studebaker, Model 1948, Tin, Friction, Japan, 10 1/2 In. 175.00
Truck, Tanker, Mack, Bulldog, White Rubber Tires, Cast Iron, Champion, 8 In. 190.00
Truck, Tanker, Oil, Cast Iron, Blue, Nickel Plated Wheels, 1920s, 3 3/4 In. 85.00
Truck, Tanker, Oil, Tootsietoy, Box, 9 In. 115.00
Truck, Tanker, Texaco, Pressed Steel, Buddy L, 23 1/2 In. 210.00
Truck, Tow, Champion, 9 1/4 In. 110.00
Truck, Tow, Pressed Steel, Marx, 1940s, 11 In. 120.00
Truck, Tow, Pressed Steel, Structo, 1950s, 11 1/2 In. 95.00
Truck, Tow, Red Trucking Company, Sturditoys 4950.00
Truck, Tow, Tonka, 1960 .... 95.00
Truck, Tow, White, Tonka, 1963, 13 1/2 In. 135.00
Truck, Tow, Working Boom, Rubber Tires, Wooden Seat, Buddy L, 31 In. 1485.00
Truck, Trailer, Cattle Hauler, Plastic, Hubley 165.00
Truck, Trailer, Dextra, Crescent, Box, 11 In. 145.00
Truck, Trailer, Sears, Tin, Rubber Tires, Friction, Linemar, Box, Japan, 1950s, 13 In. 420.00
Truck, U.S. Mail, Original Box, Buddy L, 24 In. 2420.00
Truck, Water Tower, Keystone Packard, 30 In. 2640.00
Truck Set, 2 Cabs, 3 Trailers, Tootsietoy, Box, 1940s, 8 In. 310.00
Trunk, Doll's, Burlap Exterior, Paper Interior, Clothes, Blankets, Accessories, 9 x 16 In. ... 56.00
Tunnel, Lincoln, Orange Body, Windup, 24 In. 285.00

Turkey, Tucky, Steiff, c.1961, 4 In. 395.00
Turtle, Mohair, Tan, Felt Claws, Rubber Shell, Glass Eyes, Named Slo, Steiff, 7 1/4 In. .. 55.00
Turtle, Ridden By Native, Grass Skirt, Tin, Chein 400.00
Typewriter, Capital & Small Letters, Berwin 100.00
Typewriter, Junior Dial, Marx Toys 85.00
Typewriter, Junior Dial, Tin Lithograph, Marx, Box, 1930s, 10 1/2 In. 150.00
Typewriter, Tom Thumb, Model 449E, Box 125.00
Typist, Miss Friday, Rubber Head & Arms, Battery Operated, Box, 8 In. 70.00
Umbrella, Paper, Bamboo, Burgundy Ribs & Handle, Brass Tag, Occupied Japan 15.00
Velocipede, Girl Passenger, Clockwork, 12 In. 3850.00
View-Master, Alice In Wonderland, 3 Reels, Book, 1952 .... 45.00
View-Master, Apollo Moon Landing, July 20th, 1969, 10:56 PM, 3 Reels, Booklet 42.00
View-Master, Banff National Park, Alberta, Canada, 3 Reels 15.00
View-Master, Bugs Bunny & Elmer Fudd In The Hunter, 1951 .... 3.00
View-Master, Casper The Friendly Ghost, 3 Reels, Booklet, 1970s 30.00
View-Master, Charles Dickens' A Christmas Carol, Classical Tales Series, 3 Reels, 1970s . 25.00
View-Master, Colorado, Centennial State, Vacationland Series, 3 Reels, Booklet, 1956 ... 25.00
View-Master, Hawaiian Hula Dancers, Honolulu, Hawaii, U.S.A., 3 Reels, 1956 .... 40.00
View-Master, Heidi, Johanna Spryi, 3 Reels, Booklet, 1958 .... 40.00
View-Master, Henson's Muppet Movie Scenes, Showtime Series, 3 Reels, Booklet, 1979 . 20.00
View-Master, Inauguration Of President Eisenhower, 1953 .... 15.00
View-Master, Riders Of The Desert, American Indian Series, Envelope, 1957, 3 Reels ... 50.00
View-Master, Rin Tin Tin, 1955, 3 Reels 18.00
View-Master, Rowan & Martin's Laugh-In, Envelope, 1968, 3 Reels 25.00
View-Master, Rudolph The Red-Nosed Reindeer, 3 Reels, Booklet, 1955 .... 40.00
View-Master, Salt Lake City, Vacationland Series, 3 Reels, 1956 .... 20.00
View-Master, San Diego Zoo, Packet No. 1, Animals Of Africa & South America, 3 Reels 25.00
View-Master, Talking, Barbie, Trip Around The World, 3 Reels, Booklet, GAF, c.1965 ... 80.00
View-Master, Viewer, Model C, Black Bakelite, Metal Knob, Sawyer, Box, 1951 .... 40.00
View-Master, Volcanic Eruption, Puna Hawaii, February-March 1955 .... 12.00
View-Master, Yosemite National Park, 3 Reels, 1950s 22.00
Viewer, The Virginian Movie Viewer, 2 Filmstrips, Chemtoy, 1966 .... 40.00
Wagon, Blue Paint, c.1870 .... 1295.00
Wagon, Covered, Lesney, 4 7/8 In., 2 Piece 100.00
Wagon, Delivery, Wooden, Abraham & Strauss, 22 In. 1450.00
Wagon, Deluxe Auto Wheel Coaster, Green, Yellow Lettering 66.00
Wagon, Dray, Cast Iron, Pratt & Letchworth, 1890s, 13 1/2 In. 1895.00
Wagon, Dray, Open Seat Driver, Harris Co., 13 In. 860.00
Wagon, Dump, Sand & Gravel, Driver, 2 Horses, Cast Iron, Kenton, 1950s, 15 In. 190.00
Wagon, Eclipse, Roller Bearing, Metal 45.00
Wagon, Express Stenciled On Sides, Wooden Dowel Spoke Wheels, 13 1/2 In. 250.00
Wagon, Express, Dark Green, Cream Paint, Handle, Mills Novelty Co., Chicago, 17 In. .. 260.00
Wagon, Express, Wooden Spoke Wheels, Shaft Handle, Removable Side, 29 x 37 In. 1780.00
Wagon, Farm, Driver, 2 Horses, 2 Wooden Kegs, Arcade, 11 In. 360.00
Wagon, Farm, McCormick-Deering, 2 Horses, Decal Label, Arcade, 12 1/2 In. 250.00
Wagon, Fire Chief, Painted, Kenton, 1911, 12 In. 1395.00
Wagon, Green Paint, Gold Lettering, 4 Iron Wheels, Carver Wagon Co., 40 x 17 In. 7700.00
Wagon, Hay, Tin Lithograph, 4 1/2 In. 70.00
Wagon, Ice, Ice Tongs, Cast Iron, Dent, 1905, 14 In. 1695.00
Wagon, Mirrored Sides, Humpty Dumpty Clown, 2 Horses, Hubley, 16 In. 4950.00
Wagon, Pulled By 2 Turkeys, Birdsell 40.00
Wagon, Studebaker Jr., Stake Body, Spoke Wheels, Pin Stripes, c.1900, 27 x 36 x 25 In. ... 3135.00
Wagon, The Boss, Wooden, 6-Spoke Wheels, c.1915, 21 x 14 1/2 x 10 In. 305.00
Walking Bear, Plush Over Tin, Windup, Occupied Japan, Box, 5 In. 53.00
Walrus, Paddy, Spotted Mohair, Glass Eyes, Rubber Tusks, Steiff, 5 In. 55.00
Washing Machine, Clothes Line, Steel, Wolverine, Box 145.00
Washing Machine, Fairy, Wood, Galvanized Metal, Red, Yellow, Gibson Mfg. Co., 14 In. . 1035.00
Wheelbarrow, Horse Form Sides, Tail Handles, Front Wheel, Painted 3300.00
Whistle, Airplane, Tin Lithograph, 2 1/4 In. 40.00
Whoopee Car, Cowboy Driver, Cows On Wheels, Marx, 1920s 315.00
Whoopee Car, Sheriff Sam's, Plastic & Tin, Marx 285.00
Woman, In Auto Tricycle, Clockwork Motor, Tinplate, 4 1/2 In. 3755.00
Wrestlers, Sumo, Celluloid, Squeeze Pump Action, Ring, Prewar Japan, 4 1/2 x 4 1/2 In. . 230.00

Xylophone, Pinky Lee, Music Stand, Songbook, Display Box, 9 x 15 In. 200.00
Xylophone, Tin, Battery Operated Vibrating Mallet, Songbook, Box, Japan, 9 In. 26.00
Yakity Yak Talking Teeth, Windup, H.F. & Co., Box, 1949 . . . . 15.00
Yo-Yo, Baseball Player With Bat, Baseball Diamond Behind Him, Translucent Red Plastic 15.00
Yo-Yo, Battlestar Galactica, Gray Vinyl Plastic, Larami, Hong Kong, On Card, 1978 . . . . . 45.00
Yo-Yo, Beaver With Canada Pennant, Tin, Yellow, In Bag, Hong Kong, Late 1960s 40.00
Yo-Yo, Beginner's, Genuine, Wooden, Red, Black, Duncan, 2 1/4 In. 40.00
Yo-Yo, Big Zapper, Wooden, Red, Gold Stripe, Festival, On Card, Early 1970s 85.00
Yo-Yo, Bo-Yo, Bowling Ball Shape, Duncan 65.00
Yo-Yo, Boxwood, Finger Lock Piece, England, c.1900, 2 1/2 In. 395.00
Yo-Yo, Butterfly, Translucent Green Plastic, Black Logo, Duncan 10.00
Yo-Yo, Fanta, Laughing Man Logo, Transparent Orange, Russell, Mexico 30.00
Yo-Yo, Fred Flintstone, Sleeper Action, Plastic, Hanna-Barbera, Justen, On Card, 1976 . . . 45.00
Yo-Yo, Georgia-Pacific Lumber Company, Pink Plastic, Black Logo 7.00
Yo-Yo, Golden Glider, No. 604, Plastic, Glitter, All American Yo-Yo Corp., On Card, 1971 40.00
Yo-Yo, Hi-Tech, Gold Transparent Plastic, Imperial 12.00
Yo-Yo, Levi Strauss & Co., S.F., Cal., Black Plastic, Light Gold Letters 19.00
Yo-Yo, Neo, Orange Plastic, Black Logo, Duncan 6.50
Yo-Yo, Olympic, Canada Games, Sweden, Wooden, Black, Gold Torch Logo 30.00
Yo-Yo, Orbit, Wooden, Blue, Red, Space Capsule, Stars, Mid 1960s 95.00
Yo-Yo, Plastic, 1 Side Blue, Other Side Marbelized Light Brown Swirl, Late 1940s 75.00
Yo-Yo, Tastee-Freez Ice Cream, Wooden, Red, Gold Embossed Logo 45.00
Yo-Yo, Weatherbird Shoes, Rooster On Weathervane, Wooden, Blue, Silver 65.00
Yo-Yo, Wooden, Red, Incised Letters, Genuine Yo-Yo Duncan, 1 1/8 In. 50.00
Zeppelin, Army Air Corps Insignia, Wheels, Side Propellers Rotate, Marx, 1920s, 27 In. . . 1380.00
Zeppelin, Climbing, Pull String, Green, Red Propeller, Germany, 6 In. 575.00
Zeppelin, Tin, Windup, Celluloid Propellers, Lehmann, 7 1/2 In. 275.00
Zeppelin, Windup, Lehmann, Germany, 9 1/4 In. 316.00
Zigzag, Black & White Figures Battling For Control Of Vehicle, Lehmann, 1907, 5 In. . . . 2010.00

TRAMP ART is a form of folk art made since the Civil War. It is usually
made from chip-carved cigar boxes. Examples range from small boxes
and picture frames to full-sized pieces of furniture.

Box, 2 Drawers, Drop Down From Panel, 2 Drawers Interior, 11 x 12 In. 475.00
Box, 2 Tiers, Full-Width Drawer, Lithograph Cigar Box Label In Drawer, 6 1/2 x 11 In. . . 145.00
Box, Brown Stain, Red Paint, Round Base, c.1900, 17 1/2 x 13 3/4 In. 850.00
Box, Cushioned Top, 1892, 14 x 10 x 7 In. 400.00
Box, Hinged Lid, Wooden, 30 x 14 x 14 In. 175.00
Box, Pedestal, Dark Brown Stain, Red Paint, Circular Base, c.1900, 17 1/2 x 13 3/4 In. . . . 850.00
Box, Stepped Lid, Zigzag Thistle, Carved Cigar Boxes, Painted Red, c.1880, 4 3/4 In. 520.00
Cabinet, Medicine, Mirror On Door, Drawer, Glass Knobs, Chip Carved, 24 In. 220.00
Cabinet, Mirror Door, Fall Front, Razor & Comb Holder, Pincushion, Hex Signs, 45 In. . . 825.00
Clock, Mantel, Crown Of Thorns, 24 x 23 In. 3300.00
Clock, Mantel, Crown Of Thorns, Conn. 2900.00
Dresser Box, Raised Diamonds, Decoupage, Divided Tray, c.1893, 10 x 6 1/2 x 6 In. 358.00
Frame, 8-Point Star Corner Blocks, Inscribed JK, 1933, 22 x 19 In. 4320.00
Frame, Carved & Painted, 3 Oval Openings, 24 x 13 In. 3250.00
Frame, Carved Interlocking Sections, Stars Either Side, 44 x 28 In. 440.00
Frame, Center Felt Cat, Button Eyes, Heart Corners, 9 1/2 x 7 3/4 In. 135.00
Frame, Chip Carved Stepped Designs, Oval, 27 x 21 1/2 In. 410.00
Frame, Eagle In Flight, Tulip Corners, Bunting Under Glass, 1875, 38 x 29 1/2 In. 6325.00
Frame, Gold & Silver Inner Liner, Chipped Stacked Wood, 23 x 21 In. 495.00
Frame, Pyramid, 7 Layers, 1916, 16 x 20 In. 300.00
Frame, Stepped Sawtooth Border & Liner, Mirror Center, 15 x 17 1/2 In. 275.00
Frame, Tulip Corners, Diamond Carved Crossbar, 1885, 46 x 22 In. 6900.00
Frame, Wooden, Carved, Deep Hearts, Curved Crossed Ends, 22 x 27 In. 1150.00
Mantel, Fireplace, E. Miller, Morristown, N.J., 1890, 45 x 52 In. 4000.00
Match Safe, Chip Carved Box, Hinged Lid, 3 In. 110.00
Mirror, Chip Carved, Crest, Alternating Diamonds & Starflowers, 26 In. 2010.00
Mirror, Star Form, 9 Layers, c.1890, 19 In. 675.00
Tower, Oak, Clock Inset, Chip Carved Lower Section, 3 Base Drawers, 1930s, 32 In. 1425.00
Wall Pocket, 2 Pockets, Red Paint, 17 In. 120.00

Trench Art, Butter Knife,
Shell Casing, Castle On
Handle, Brass, 6 1/4 In.

TRAPS for animals may be handmade. One of the most unusual is the
mousetrap made so that when the mouse entered the trap, it was hit on
the head with a mallet. Other traps were commercially manufactured
and often are marked with the name of the manufacturer. Many traps
were designed to be as humane as possible, and they would trap the
live animal so it could be released in the woods.

Flytrap, Glass, Pale Apple Green, 20 Ribs, Swirled Right, 3-Footed, 1910, 6 3/4 In. 355.00
Wigginton's Mouse Eliminator, Wire Stand, Pat. 1915 . . . .   35.00

TREEN, see Wooden category.

TRENCH ART is a form of folk art made by soldiers. Metal casings from
bullets and mortar shells were cut and decorated to form useful objects,
such as vases.

Belt Buckle, Made Of Metal From Spanish Cruiser Cristobal Colon, Nickel Plated, 1899 .   375.00
Butter Knife, Shell Casing, Castle On Handle, Brass, 6 1/4 In. . . . .*Illus*   25.00

TRIVETS are now used to hold hot dishes. Most trivets of the late nineteenth and early twentieth centuries were made to hold hot irons. Iron
or brass reproductions are being made of many of the old styles.

3 Sunflowers, Yellow & Green, Raised Hobnail Centers, 11 x 6 In. 25.00
Brass, Hanging, For Fire Rail, Pierced Brass Sliding Shelf 77.00
Brass, Iron, Wooden Handle, High Base, 11 1/2 x 14 1/2 In. 175.00
Brass, Pierced, 3 Wrought Iron Legs, Wooden Handle, 8 1/2 In. 290.00
Brass, Treen Mortar & Pestle, England, 13 1/4 In. 115.00
Brass, Wrought Iron, Turned Wooden Handle, Pierced Horseshoe Shape, 16 3/4 x 9 1/4 In.   138.00
Cast Iron, Round, 3-Footed, Early 18th Century, 9 1/2 x 8 In. Diam. 56.00
Cast Iron, Sadiron, Urn, Handles, 5 3/4 x 4 1/2 In. 20.00
Embossed Lettering, E In Center, Enterprise Mfg. Co., Phila USA 33.00
Iron, 2 Hearts Entwined Center, Oval, 2 1/4 x 5 In. 25.00
Iron, 5-Point Star In Circle, Handle, 5 1/4 x 7 3/4 In. 30.00
Iron, Brass Ring Rest, Cabriole Tripod Legs, Spade Feet, 9 3/4 x 10 1/2 In. 287.00
Iron, Canadian Daisy, Round Petal Design Center, Border, 1 3/4 x 2 5/16 In. 22.00
Iron, Cathedral, Large Scrollwork Center, 3 3/4 x 8 1/2 In. 18.00
Iron, Cathedral, Scroll, Handle, 1894, 3 3/4 x 9 In. 25.00
Iron, Cathedral, Scrollwork Center, Handle, 2 x 5 7/8 In. 20.00
Iron, Colebrookdale Crown & Maltese Cross, Pottstown, Pa., Embossed Panel, 4 x 6 In. . .   25.00
Iron, Consolidated Gas Iron Co., N.Y., Impressed Panel, 4 3/4 x 8 1/4 In. 25.00
Iron, E. Ketcham & Co., N.Y., 4 Pave Legs, Circle Border, Round, 5 3/8 In. 30.00
Iron, Embossed Best On Earth, Filigree, 7 x 4 In. 25.00
Iron, Embossed, Double Point IWANTU Comfort Iron, Strause Gas Iron, Pa. 40.00
Iron, Geometric, Circles Within Larger Circle, Handle, 3 1/4 x 4 1/2 In. 20.00
Iron, Good Luck To All Who Use This Stand, Horseshoe Shape, Handle, 4 1/2 x 7 3/4 In.   25.00
Iron, Hearth, Carved Wooden Handle, Tripod Support, 7 5/8 In. 316.00
Iron, Howell H., Geneva, Ill, Embossed In Panel, Spade Shape 10.00
Iron, Large B Center, Spade Shape, 4 1/4 x 6 In. 10.00
Iron, Laurel Gas, Open Center, Art Stove Co., Detroit, 4 x 7 In. 30.00
Iron, M In Center, Handle, Oval, 2 x 5 1/2 In. 40.00
Iron, Mrs. Potts Crown Iron, Phila., Pa., Cutout Lettering 35.00
Iron, O.M. Co., Logo Center, Square Grid Border, 4 1/4 x 4 1/4 In. 15.00
Iron, Oval, Half Rail, 2 1/4 x 4 3/4 In. 16.00
Iron, Sensible Cut Center, 6 Holes In Curves, Hanging Hole, 4 x 5 In. 25.00
Iron, Small A In Large S, Spade Shape, 4 x 6 3/4 In. 15.00
Iron, Spider Web, 4 x 6 In. 10.00
Iron, Splayed Tripod, Penny Feet, Round Pan Rest, 2 Grate Hooks, Handle, 21 x 11 In. . .   165.00
Iron, Trafford Foundry Family Day 1953, Westinghouse, Foundry Logo 30.00
Iron, Tulip, Handle, J. Sellers Brass Inlaid, 19th Century 7000.00

Iron, Vertical Bar Center, 14 Holes In Side Panels, 4 x 6 In. 10.00
Iron, Waffle, Crisscrossed Lines, Plain Panel, 4 x 6 In. 10.00
Iron & Brass, Tripod Base, Bird On Wooden Handle, Brass Insert, 19 1/2 In. 660.00
Pottery, Basket Of Flowers, Cuenca, Blue Ground, William Whitford, 5 1/2 In. 225.00
Pottery, Clusters Of Grapes, 4 Swirled Feet, John Bell, Late 19th Century, 8 1/4 In. 2200.00
Pottery, Galleon Ship Sailing, Yellow, Ocher Glaze, Square, California Faience, 5 1/2 In. . 385.00

TRUNKS of many types were made. The nineteenth-century sea chest
was often handmade of unpainted wood. Brass-fitted camphorwood
chests were brought back from the Orient. Leather-covered trunks
were popular from the late eighteenth to mid-nineteenth centuries. By
1895, trunks were covered with canvas or decorated sheet metal.
Embossed metal coverings were used from 1870 to 1910. By 1925,
trunks were covered with vulcanized fiber or undecorated metal.

Camphorwood, Chinese, 19th Century, 23 x 16 1/2 x 36 1/2 In. 230.00
Camphorwood, Leather, Brass Frame & Tacks, Wallpaper Lined, Handles, 19 x 41 In. 1035.00
Canvas, Wooden Bound, 12 1/2 x 39 In. 345.00
Dome Top, Charles I, Iron Lock & Handles, Initials, 1630, 36 x 18 x 17 In. 920.00
Dome Top, Leather, 19th Century, 17 x 17 x 19 1/2 In. 1198.00
Dome Top, Painted, Grain Painting Simulates Inlaid Stringing, 11 x 26 3/4 x 13 1/2 In. 1150.00
Dome Top, Pine, Slate Blue, Red, Yellow Black Flowers, 9 1/2 In. 4800.00
Dome Top, Polychrome Design, Metal Mounts, Continental, 18 x 27 In. 575.00
Dome Top, Stand, Landscape Scenes Exterior, Ball Feet, 18th Century, 33 x 22 In. 2070.00
Dome Top, Vinegar Design, Black Border, Basswood, 12 3/8 x 30 1/4 In. 1650.00
Gucci, Train Case, Printed Logo, Leather Lining, Navy Trim, 1980s, 12 1/2 x 8 x 9 In. ... 490.00
Gucci, Travel Case, Navy & White, Leather Trim, Red Stripe, Label, 17 x 9 x 10 1/2 In. ... 630.00
Leather, Brass Tacks, American Flag, Carrying Handles, Early 19th Century, 24 3/4 In. .. 660.00
Louis Vuitton, Suitcase, Brass Corners, Leather Handle, 20th Century, 25 3/4 In. 690.00
Louis Vuitton, Suitcase, Brass Corners, Leather Handle, Early 20th Century, 19 3/4 In. ... 862.00
Louis Vuitton, Suitcase, Brass Corners, Leather Handle, Early 20th Century, 32 x 8 In. ... 460.00
Louis Vuitton, Suitcase, Leather, Brass Nailhead Trim, 8 1/2 x 25 1/2 In. 635.00
Louis Vuitton, Tote Bag, Allover LV Logo, Short Brown Handles, 1980s, 15 x 19 In. 175.00
Louis Vuitton, Wardrobe, Rectangular, Leather Hands On Ends, Wood, 40 1/2 In. 1092.00
Oak, Carved, Painting, Floral Designs, Side Panels, Brass Handles, 14 x 24 1/2 x 12 In. .. 604.00
Oriental, Carved, Dovetailed Case, Moon Brass, Dragons & Foliage, 28 x 11 In. 220.00
Painted Leather, Tooled, Foliage, Binds, Wrought Iron, 15 x 35 1/2 x 19 In. 1092.00
Pine, Wood Grained, Lidded Candle Till, Bail Handles, Continental, 27 1/2 x 39 x 23 In. . 431.00
Pucci, Travel Bag, Velveteen, Leather Trim, 1970s, 18 1/2 x 12 x 9 In. 1495.00
Rosewood, Lid & Fold Front, Alligatored Varnish, Brass Handles, 14 x 11 x 10 In. 275.00
Stagecoach, Lift Top, Green Paint, 19th Century, 8 5/8 x 24 1/2 In. 2990.00
Suitcase, Canvas Covered, Leather & Iron Straps, Oshkosh Label, 43 x 25 1/2 In. 287.00
Suitcase, Lido, Blue Leather, Brass Locks, Voile Interior, Compartments, Key, 14 x 9 In. . 30.00
Suitcase, Varnished Canvas, Leather Trim, White, 15 1/2 x 26 In. ....*Illus* 30.00
Vanity Case, Etched Mirror, Coin Purse, Brush, Rouge, Powder, 1920s 200.00

TYPEWRITER collectors divide typewriters into two main classifica-
tions: the index machine, which has a pointer and a dial for letter selec-
tion, and the keyboard machine, most commonly seen today. The first
successful typewriter was made by Sholes and Glidden in 1874.

Corona, Folding, No. 3, Black, New Ribbon Feed Design, 1914 .... 55.00

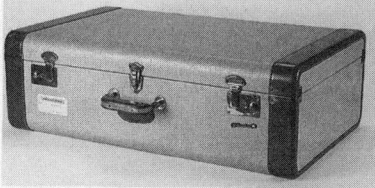

Trunk, Suitcase, Varnished Canvas, Leather Trim,
White, 15 1/2 x 26 In.

Typewriter,
North's
Typewriter Mfg.
Co., London, 1892

Hermes Rocket, Portable, Gray Metal, Lift Top Lid, Instructions, 11 1/4 x 11 1/4 In. 57.00
L.C. Smith, Standard, 1920 .... 65.00
New Century Caligraph No. 6, American Writing Machine Co., New York, 1900 .... 595.00
North's Typewriter Mfg. Co., London, 1892 .... *Illus* 7907.00
Simplex, Special Demonstration Model C, Original Box 95.00

TYPEWRITER TINS are now being collected. The lithographed tin containers have been used since the 1870s. Most popular with collectors are tins with pictorial graphics.

Burroughs, Round 18.00
Hallmark, Cameron Mfg. Co., Inc., Dallas Texas, Round 20.00
Madame Butterfly, Typewriter Ribbon 10.00
Old Hickory Ribbon, Image Of Black Man Under Tree, 2 1/2 x 2 1/2 In. 187.00
Old Town Hermetic Inked Ribbon, 2 1/2 In. 7.00
Regal Ribbon, Square 25.00
Silver Brand, Black Record Special, KeeLox Mfg. Co., 2 1/2 x 3/4 In. 10.00
Silver Brand, Square 16.00
Thorobred, Underwood Corporation, Burlington, N.J. 25.00

UHL pottery was made in Evansville, Indiana, in 1854. The pottery moved to Huntingburg, Indiana, in 1908. Stoneware and glazed pottery were made until the mid-1940s.

Crock, Corn Wares, Huntingburg, Ind., No. 6 .... 125.00
Crock, Wire & Wooden Handles, No. 10, 17 1/2 x 15 In. 200.00
Jar, Orange Blossom, Pink, No. 118 .... 70.00
Mug, Light Brown 12.00
Wine Keg Set, Wooden Stand, 6 Glasses, 8 x 10 x 8 1/2 In. 60.00

UMBRELLA collectors like rain or shine. The first known umbrella was owned by King Louis XIII of France in 1637. The earliest umbrellas were sunshades, not designed to be used in the rain. The umbrella was embellished and redesigned many times. In 1852, the fluted steel rib style was developed, and it has remained the most useful style.

Ivory Handle, 12 In. 84.00
Parasol, Bisque Headed Doll Top, Wooden Handle, Sateen Cover, 1874, 20 In. 1100.00
Parasol, Cloth, Wooden Finial, Abstract Patterns, Troy Sunshade Co., c.1928 .... 200.00
Parasol, Paper, Red, White & Blue 55.00

UNION PORCELAIN WORKS was established at Greenpoint, New York, in 1848 by Charles Cartlidge. The company went through a series of ownership changes and finally closed in the early 1900s. The company made a fine quality white porcelain that was often decorated in clear, bright colors.

Creamer, White, Eagle-Head Handle, Serpent Spout, Marked, 3 5/8 In. 50.00
Cup & Saucer, White, Gold Trim, Monogram AA 51.00

UNIVERSITY OF NORTH DAKOTA, see North Dakota School of Mines category.

VAL ST. LAMBERT Cristalleries of Belgium was founded by Messieurs Kemlin and Lelievre in 1825. The company is still in operation. All types of table glassware and decorative glassware have been made. Pieces are often decorated with cut designs.

Box, Cylindrical, Cameo, Lavender Etched Wisteria, Faceted Knob, 1920, 3 x 6 In. 865.00
Vase, Elongated Neck, Red Powder Pulled Design, Blue Ground, Signed, 11 In. 575.00
Vase, Enameled Floral, Etched, 5 1/2 In. 70.00
Vase, Enameled Red Flowers, Green Ground, Cameo, Partial Signed, 6 In. 115.00
Vase, Engraved Dragonfly Over Poppies, Signed, c.1906, 10 In. 3105.00

Early plates often have no rim on the bottom.

Vase, Engraved Fan On Martele Ground, Cobalt Blue, c.1920, 8 In. 345.00
Vase, Flared Mouth Tapering To Neck, Red Layered Glass, Signed, 6 1/2 In. 575.00
Vase, Floral, Marked, 3 1/2 In. 290.00

VAN BRIGGLE pottery was made by Artus Van Briggle in Colorado Springs, Colorado, after 1901. Van Briggle had been a decorator at Rookwood Pottery of Cincinnati, Ohio. He died in 1904. His wares usually had modeled relief decorations and a soft, dull glaze. The pottery is still working and still making some of the original designs.

Bookends, Owls Standing With Wings Outstretched, Blue, 5 In. 224.00
Bowl, Blue Matte Glaze, Rust Interior, 1916, 6 1/4 In. 160.00
Bowl, Blue, Charcoal Glaze, c.1905, 3 1/4 x 4 1/2 In. 690.00
Bowl, Green Matte Glaze, Mottled, Marked, c.1910, 2 x 6 In. 385.00
Bowl, Green Matte Glaze, Yellow Overspray, Low Closed Form, 1907, 2 x 6 In. 595.00
Bowl, Lady Of The Lake, Kneeling Woman Looking In Pool, 1930, 10 In. . . . . . . .375.00 to 575.00
Candlestick, Mulberry Lavender Glaze, Arts & Crafts, Marked, 1915, 4 In. 325.00
Candlestick-Vase, Tan, Green, 9 In., Pair . . . . *Illus* 500.00
Cup, Mermaid, Purple, Olive Green, Signed, 10 1/2 In. 5325.00
Ewer, Deep Blue Matte Glaze, Signed, 12 In. 58.00
Paperweight, Donkey, Mulberry Glaze, 3 3/4 In. 130.00
Pitcher, Oval, Persian Rose Glaze, Conforming Handle, 8 3/4 In. 172.00
Sconce, Owl, Green Matte Glaze, Incised Mark, c.1916, 6 x 3 In. 430.00
Sconce, Owl, Persian Rose Glaze, Incised Mark, 9 1/2 x 3 3/4 In. 400.00
Tile, Flowers, Quatrefoil Design, Green, Rose, Yellow, Mark, Oak Frame, 10 In. 365.00
Tile, Woodpecker, Mahogany Frame, Square, 6 In. 4600.00
Vase, 3-Headed Indian, Dark Cobalt, Brown Base, 10 7/8 In. 660.00
Vase, 4 Shallow Buttresses, Blue, Gray Matte Glaze, 5 x 4 In. 430.00
Vase, 5 Black-Eyed Susans, Blue, 11 3/4 In. 170.00
Vase, Blossoms, Chartreuse Glaze, Trumpet Shape, 1905, 7 x 3 In. 2990.00
Vase, Blue Green Matte Glaze, 1920, 7 1/2 In. 374.00
Vase, Blue Green Matte Glaze, 1927, 8 3/4 In. 750.00
Vase, Brown Glaze, Signed, 1907, 4 1/2 In. 920.00
Vase, Butterflies, Embossed, Blue, Turquoise Matte Glaze, 1916, 7 x 6 1/2 In. 560.00
Vase, Butterflies, Embossed, Matte Brown Glaze, 3 3/4 x 3 1/2 In. 230.00
Vase, Crocus, Embossed, Green, Pink Matte Glaze, 1910, 5 1/4 x 3 1/2 In. 505.00
Vase, Daffodils, Embossed, Blue, Green Matte Glaze, Pinched Waist, 1920, 9 x 4 In. 618.00
Vase, Daffodils, Embossed, Mulberry Glaze, Blue, 9 3/4 In. 310.00
Vase, Dandelions, Wide Leaves, Mulberry Glaze, Marked, 1925, 7 5/8 In. 560.00
Vase, Dragonflies, Blue, Red Matte Glaze, Signed, 7 In. 320.00
Vase, Feathered, Ocher Matte Glaze, 1903, 6 x 4 3/4 In. 575.00
Vase, Flamingos, Embossed, Persian Rose Glaze, Red Glaze, 1932, 21 x 8 In. 1840.00
Vase, Floral, Stylized, Turquoise Matte Glaze, 1920, 5 3/4 In. 115.00
Vase, Floral, Stylized, Turquoise Matte Glaze, 2 Handles, 1919, 8 1/4 In. 575.00
Vase, Flowers, 5 Petals, Chartreuse Glaze, Signed, 1903, 6 In. 2415.00
Vase, Flowers, Embossed, Purple, Gray & Green Matte Glaze, c.1907, 4 In. 715.00
Vase, Flowers, Leaves, Embossed, Mulberry Glaze, 8 3/8 In. 440.00
Vase, Flowers, Stylized, Embossed, Purple Matte Glaze, 1905, 7 1/4 x 4 In. 3150.00
Vase, Flowers, Stylized, Embossed, Teal Glaze, Gourd Shape, 1912, 7 3/4 x 5 In. 730.00

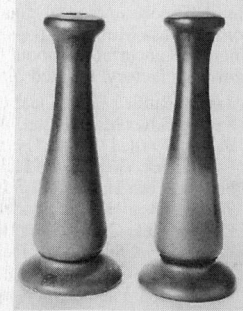

Van Briggle,
Candlestick-Vase,
Tan, Green,
9 In., Pair

Vase, Flowers, Stylized, Rows Of Leaves, Bottle Form, Signed, 1908, 6 1/2 In. 1035.00
Vase, Flowers, Stylized, Turquoise Glaze, Signed, 1908, 8 1/4 In. 1840.00
Vase, Flowers, Stylized, Turquoise Matte Glaze, Signed, 1920, 5 3/4 In. 115.00
Vase, Gingko Leaves, 1907, 7 1/2 In. 448.00
Vase, Gingko Leaves, Green, Blue Matte Glaze, 1912, 7 1/2 In. . . . . .448.00 to 990.00
Vase, Green Matte Glaze, 1904, 7 1/2 x 4 In. 1495.00
Vase, Green Matte Glaze, Blue Overspray, Tapered Top & Bottom, 1905, 3 1/2 In. 445.00
Vase, Green, Dark Purple Matte Glaze, 1905, 10 In. 3220.00
Vase, Interlocking Circles & Lines Border, Blue Matte Glaze, 1920, 3 3/8 In. 467.00
Vase, Jonquils, Mulberry Glaze, 3-Footed, c.1918, 9 3/4 In. . . . . .715.00 to 728.00
Vase, Lady Of The Lily, Brown, Green Matte Glaze, 1930, 11 x 9 1/2 In. 2137.00
Vase, Leaves, Berries, Embossed, Green, Brown Mottled Ground, 1903, 8 x 6 In. 5465.00
Vase, Leaves, Blade-Like, Vertical, Mulberry Glaze, Marked, 4 3/8 In. 112.00
Vase, Leaves, Broad, Embossed, Green, Brown Speckled Glaze, c.1920, 5 x 7 In. 489.00
Vase, Leaves, Embossed, Blue, Green Glaze, Signed, 1907, 9 In. 1035.00
Vase, Leaves, Embossed, Pinched Waist, Blue Matte Glaze, c.1918, 7 1/2 x 4 In. 520.00
Vase, Leaves, Persian Rose Glaze, Squat, c.1920, 9 In. 575.00
Vase, Leaves, Stems, Embossed, Brown Matte Glaze, Marked, 1916, 5 x 7 In. 920.00
Vase, Leaves, Stems, Embossed, Multicolored Green, Blue Matte Glaze, 5 In. 575.00
Vase, Leaves, Stylized, Embossed, Oatmeal, Yellow Green Glaze, 1903, 5 x 3 In. 4315.00
Vase, Leaves, Stylized, Mottled, Green Glaze, Signed, 1905, 7 1/4 In. 2875.00
Vase, Leaves, Swirling Stems, Embossed, Green, Brown Matte Glaze, 10 In. 4900.00
Vase, Lorelei, Blue Matte Glaze, Multitoned, Late 1940s, 11 In. 290.00
Vase, Lorelei, Persian Rose Glaze, c.1920, 9 1/2 x 4 1/4 In. 865.00
Vase, Lorelei, Persian Rose Glaze, Incised, 11 3/4 x 4 1/2 In. . . . . .230.00 to 265.00
Vase, Mountain Craig Brown, Green Overspray, Tapered, 1920s, 4 x 5 In. 250.00
Vase, Mulberry Glaze, 7 1/8 In. 560.00
Vase, Mulberry Glaze, Blue Overspray, Arts & Crafts, Marked, 5 1/4 In. 215.00
Vase, Mustard Matte Glaze, Trumpet Shape, 1911, 5 3/4 x 3 3/4 In. 535.00
Vase, Peacock Feather, Embossed, Turquoise Matte Glaze, 16 x 8 In. 7480.00
Vase, Persian Rose Glaze, Floral Rim, Incised Mark, 9 1/2 x 7 1/4 In. 460.00
Vase, Persian Rose Glaze, Squat Base, Incised Mark, Bulbous, c.1920, 7 1/2 In. 230.00
Vase, Poppy Pods, Embossed, Purple Matte Glaze, 1915, 7 1/4 x 3 1/2 In. 1125.00
Vase, Poppy Pods, Leaves, Embossed, Dark Green Matte Glaze, 14 x 9 In. 5175.00
Vase, Red, Green Feathered Matte Glaze, 1906, 6 x 5 1/2 In. 2415.00
Vase, Rose Matte Glaze, Sprinkled Green, Marked, 1905, 4 In. 695.00
Vase, Trillium, Embossed, Light Blue Matte Glaze, 7 1/2 x 3 1/2 In. 2070.00
Vase, Trillium, Stylized, Olive Green Matte Glaze, 1904, 11 3/4 In. 5460.00
Vase, Tulips & Leaves, Embossed, Blue Matte Glaze, c.1915, 7 1/2 In. 520.00
Vase, Turquoise Matte Glaze, 1903, 3 3/4 x 4 1/2 In. 900.00
Vase, Wheat Sheaves, Green Glaze, Trumpet Shape, 6 x 4 In. 2140.00
Wall Pocket, Brown, Green, 5 7/8 In. 305.00
Wall Pocket, Daisy, Mountain Craig Brown, Embossed, 7 5/8 In. 310.00

VASA MURRHINA is the name of a glassware made by the Vasa
Murrhina Art Glass Company of Sandwich, Massachusetts, about
1884. The glassware was transparent and was embedded with small
pieces of colored glass and metallic flakes. The mica flakes were
coated with silver, gold, copper, or nickel. Some of the pieces were
cased. The same type of glass was made in England. Collectors often
confuse Vasa Murrhina glass with aventurine, spatter, or spangle glass.
There is uncertainty about what actually was made by the Vasa
Murrhina factory. Related pieces may be listed under Spangle Glass.

Basket, Ruffled Edge, Clear Handle, Silver Mica Flakes, Blue Overlay, 8 3/4 In. 175.00
Basket, Silver Mica, Pastel, White Interior, Stevens & Williams, 5 x 8 In. 325.00
Basket, Twisted Crystal Thorn Handle, 5 1/2 x 6 In. 225.00
Candlestick, Green Glass Flakes, White Interior, 8 3/4 In. 125.00
Pitcher, Clear Handle, 8 1/8 In. 575.00
Pitcher, Clear Handle, Swirled Ribs, Scalloped Rim, 19th Century, 8 1/8 In. 575.00
Pitcher, Pink, Cased, Clear Handle, Silver Flecks, 8 1/2 In. 67.00
Vase, Allover Silver Mica Flakes, White Interior, 6 1/2 In. 110.00
Vase, Jack-In-The-Pulpit, Gold Spangles, Pink Interior, Ruffled, 5 In. 115.00
Vase, Melon, Pink, Silver Spangles, White Interior, 4 3/4 In. 85.00

Vase, Pink Overlay, Clear Rigaree, 6 1/2 x 4 1/2 In. 110.00
Vase, Silver Mica, Thorn Type Handles, 8 3/4 In. 250.00

VASART is the signature used on a late type of art glass made by the Streathearn Glass Company of Scotland. Pieces are marked with an engraved signature on the bottom. Most of the glass is mottled or shaded.

Vasart

Basket, Pulled Sides, Opaque Opalescent Lavender, 3 1/4 In. 65.00
Bowl, 6 Irregular Sides, Yellow Center, Multicolored Inclusions, 6 In. 60.00
Bowl, Cluthra Style, Blue 90.00
Bowl, Pale Teal To Powder Blue, Controlled Bubbles, Marked, 6 In. 31.00
Vase, Thistle, Pink & Millefiori, 3 1/2 In. 71.00

VASELINE GLASS is a greenish-yellow glassware resembling petroleum jelly. Some vaseline glass is still being made in old and new styles. Pressed glass of the 1870s was often made of vaseline-colored glass. Additional pieces of vaseline glass may also be listed under Pressed Glass in this book.

Basket, War Of Roses, Opalescent, 4 x 6 In. 110.00
Candlestick, Scalloped Edge, 8 1/4 In. 93.00
Compote, 3-Piece Mold, 19th Century 165.00
Compote, Magic Glass, Yellow, Green, 7 1/2 x 4 3/4 x 8 1/2 In. 59.00
Cruet, Art Glass, Gold Stone 95.00
Cup, Child's, Nest & Bird Design, Peek-A-Boo Cat At Bottom, 3 1/2 In. 66.00
Curtain Tieback, Pair 35.00
Mug, Singing Birds 1510.00
Pitcher, Applied Handle 100.00
Pitcher, Grape 45.00
Rose Bowl, Shell 45.00
Shoe ....15.00 to 45.00
Vase, Yellow Glass, Pontil, 6 3/4 x 1 1/2 In. 60.00
Water Set, Child's, Satin, 5 Piece 75.00

VENETIAN GLASS, see Glass-Venetian category.

VERLYS glass was made in France after 1931. It was made in the United States from 1935 to 1951. The glass is either blown or molded. The American glass is signed with a diamond-point-scratched name, but the French pieces are marked with a molded signature. The designs resemble those used by Lalique.

Verlys

Ashtray, Swallow, Crystal, 4 3/4 x 3 5/8 In. 20.00
Bowl, Water Lily, Signed, 13 1/2 In. 57.00
Vase, Thistle, Signed, 9 3/4 In. 403.00

VERNON KILNS was the name used after 1958 by Vernon Potteries, Ltd. The company, which started in 1931 in Vernon, California, made dinnerware and figurines until it went out of business in 1958. The molds were bought by Metlox and they continued to make some patterns. Collectors search for the brightly colored dinnerware and the pieces designed by Rockwell Kent, Walt Disney, and Don Blanding. For more information, see *Kovels' Depression Glass & Dinnerware Price List.*

Anytime, Creamer, 4 In. 22.00
Bits Of Old South, Chop Plate, Down On The Levee, 14 In. 210.00
Blossoms, Teacup 11.00
Brown-Eyed Susan, Cup & Saucer 18.00
Brown-Eyed Susan, Plate, 6 1/2 In. 10.00
Brown-Eyed Susan, Sauceboat 32.00
California Originals, Chip & Dip Set, Redwood Brown, Label 25.00
California Originals, Tumbler, Redwood Brown, 14 Oz. 18.00
Casa California, Plate, 7 1/2 In. 9.00
Casual California, Pitcher, Mocha Brown, 1/4 Pt. 22.00
Casual California, Tumbler, Dawn Pink, 14 Oz. 18.00
Coronado, Cup, Turquoise 8.00

Coronado, Plate, Turquoise, 6 1/2 In. 7.00
Coronado, Plate, Yellow, 6 1/2 In. 7.00
Early California, Chop Plate, Pink, 12 In. 32.00
Early California, Creamer, Pink, Round, 3 In. 15.00
Early California, Cup & Saucer, Brown 12.00
Gingham, Bowl, Vegetable, 2 Sections, 11 1/2 In. 20.00
Gingham, Creamer 10.00
Gingham, Cup & Saucer 21.00
Gingham, Plate, 6 In. 3.50
Gingham, Plate, 9 3/4 In. ....11.00 to 13.00
Gingham, Platter, 14 In. 20.00
Gingham, Salt & Pepper 43.00
Gingham, Sugar, Cover, 4 1/4 In. 10.00
Heavenly Days, Gravy Boat 20.00
Heavenly Days, Pitcher, 1 Qt. 28.00
Heavenly Days, Plate, Bread & Butter, 6 In. 8.00
Heavenly Days, Platter, 11 In. 18.00
Homespun, Chop Plate, 12 In. 36.00
Homespun, Cup & Saucer 13.00
Homespun, Cup, 4 In. 11.00
Homespun, Eggcup, Double 25.00
Homespun, Mug, 9 Oz. 28.00
Homespun, Plate, Bread & Butter, 6 1/2 In. 8.00
Homespun, Platter, 12 In. 47.00
Imperial, Bowl, Round, 9 In. 25.00
Lollipop Tree, Cup 10.00
Lollipop Tree, Plate, 6 In. 11.00
Lollipop Tree, Platter, 13 1/2 In. 55.00
May Flower, Bowl, Oval, 10 In. 33.00
May Flower, Cup 18.00
May Flower, Plate, 6 1/2 In. 8.00
May Flower, Plate, 7 1/2 In. 11.00
May Flower, Platter, Oval, 14 In. 43.00
May Flower, Sugar, Cover, Short 25.00
Moby Dick, Chop Plate, 12 In. 165.00
Moby Dick, Teapot 375.00
Organdie, Bowl, Vegetable, 9 In. 20.00
Organdie, Chop Plate, 12 In. 24.00
Organdie, Cup & Saucer 13.00
Organdie, Eggcup, Double 30.00
Organdie, Plate, 7 1/2 In. 7.50
Organdie, Plate, 9 3/4 In. 10.00
Organdie, Plate, 10 1/2 In. 15.00
Organdie, Platter, Oval, 10 In. 15.00
Organdie, Salt & Pepper 10.00
Organdie, Soup, Dish, Rim, 8 1/2 In. 15.00
Organdie, Tumbler, Water 35.00
Plate, Arkansaw Traveler, Blue, 10 1/2 In. 35.00
Plate, Colorful San Francisco, 10 1/2 In. 20.00
Plate, Song Of Iowa, Blue 27.00
Raffia, Bowl, Vegetable, Divided, 10 In. 18.00
Raffia, Sauceboat 12.00
Santa Maria, Chop Plate, 12 In. 65.00
Shadow Leaf, Cup 8.00
Tam O'Shanter, Bowl, 7 In. 6.00
Tam O'Shanter, Bowl, 8 1/2 In. 8.00
Tam O'Shanter, Bowl, Salad, Individual, 5 In. 5.00
Tam O'Shanter, Casserole, Cover, Stick Handle, 4 In. 27.00
Tam O'Shanter, Cup & Saucer 13.00
Tam O'Shanter, Mug 8.00
Tam O'Shanter, Pitcher, Juice, Streamline, 1 Qt. 55.00
Tam O'Shanter, Plate, 10 1/2 In. 5.00
Tam O'Shanter, Platter, Oval, 12 In. 20.00

Tam O'Shanter, Soup, Dish, Rim, 8 1/2 In.	15.00
Tickled Pink, Creamer	10.00
Tickled Pink, Pitcher, 1 Pt.	18.00
Tickled Pink, Pitcher, 1 Qt.	35.00
Tickled Pink, Salt & Pepper	45.00
Vernon Rose, Cup & Saucer	21.00

VERRE DE SOIE glass was first made by Frederick Carder at the Steuben Glass Works from about 1905 to 1930. It is an iridescent glass of soft white or very, very pale green. The name means *glass of silk*, and it does resemble silk. Other factories have made verre de soie, and some of the English examples were made of different colors. Verre de soie is an art glass and is not related to the iridescent, pressed, white carnival glass mistakenly called by its name. Related pieces may be found in the Steuben category.

Bowl, Applied Blue Edge, 3 1/2 x 10 In.	345.00
Box, Cover, Venetian Style, Green, Yellow, 5 1/4 x 6 In.	633.00
Compote, Celeste Blue Rim, 7 1/8 In.	110.00
Compote, Twisted Stem, 6 1/4 In.	345.00
Finger Bowl, Pair	250.00
Goblet, Flowers, 6 1/8 In.	55.00
Perfume Bottle, Black Jade, Steuben, 3 1/2 In.	425.00
Plate, Sherbet, Deep, Steuben, 1903-1933, 6 In.	125.00
Shade, 16 Ribs, 3 x 5 In.	80.00
Shade, Lily, Ruffled Edge, 5 1/4 In., 3 Piece	115.00
Vase, Pulled & Swirled Band, Signed, Carder, Marked Steuben, 11 1/2 In.	2185.00
Vase, Reeded, Diamond Optic, Signed, Fleur-De-Lis Mark, 6 In.	425.00
Vase, Ruffled Edge, 8 1/4 In.	190.00

VIENNA, see Beehive category.

VIENNA ART plates are round metal serving trays produced at the turn of the century. The designs, copied from Royal Vienna porcelain plates, usually featured a portrait of a woman encircled by a wide, ornate border. Many were used as advertising or promotional items and were produced in Coshocton, Ohio, by J.F. Meeks Tuscarora Advertising Co. and H.D. Beach's Standard Advertising Co.

Plate, George Schott Saloon, Philadelphia, Tin, 10 In.	200.00
Plate, Harvard Brewing, Flower Coifed Maiden, Calendar Month Rim, 1907, 10 In.	143.00

VILLEROY & BOCH Pottery of Mettlach was founded in 1836. The firm made many types of wares, including the famous Mettlach steins. Collectors can be confused because although Villeroy & Boch made most of its pieces in the city of Mettlach, Germany, they also had factories in other locations. The dating code impressed on the bottom of most pieces makes it possible to determine the age of the piece. Additional items, including steins and earthenware pieces marked with the famous castle mark or the word *Mettlach,* may be found in the Mettlach category.

Coffeepot, Acapulco Pattern	175.00
Plaque, Center Panel Of Figures In Forest, Signed, c.1910, 16 In.	1259.00
Plaque, Maiden, Strolling, Gilt Flowers, Oval, 11 1/2 x 6 3/4 In.	86.00
Plaque, Wall, Young Girl Wearing Flowing White Dress, 1906, 17 In.	1800.00
Seat, Mushroom, Frog & Snake In Moss Base, Signed, c.1890, 19 1/2 In., Pair	6000.00
Tray, Woman Serving Bird To Cherub, Wooden Frame, 12 1/2 x 19 In.	375.00

VOLKMAR pottery was made by Charles Volkmar of New York from 1879 to about 1911. He was associated with several firms, including the Volkmar Ceramic Company, Volkmar and Cory, and Charles Volkmar and Son. Volkmar had been a painter, and his designs often look like oil paintings drawn on pottery.

VOLKMAR
Corona N.y

Lamp, Green, Brown Hi Glaze, Roses, Leaves, Impressed Mark, 25 1/2 In.	1380.00
Mug, Flying Duck, Gray, Blue, Pinch Waist, Barbotine, 6 x 5 1/2 In.	92.00

Tile, Stylized Leaves, Hunter, Pale Green, Brown Branches, Soft Yellow Florals, 5 In. 55.00
Vase, Hammered Texture, Purple & Blue Glaze, Spherical, Incised, 1940, 5 1/2 In. 115.00

VOLKSTEDT was a soft-paste porcelain factory started in 1760 by Georg Heinrich Macheleid at Volkstedt, Thuringia. Volkstedt-Rudolstadt was a porcelain factory started at Volkstedt-Rudolstadt by Beyer and Bock in 1890. Most pieces seen in shops today are from the later factory.

Figurine, Ballerina, Pink Bodice & Slippers, Dresden Lace, Applied Flowers, 3 1/2 In. 50.00
Figurine, Classical Woman, Draped Dress, Red Sash, Pen & Scroll, Marked, 9 1/2 In. 357.00
Figurine, Woman, Gold & Cream Short Dress, Draped Scarf, Bisque, Marked, 11 In. 75.00
Figurine, Woman, Wearing White Floral Dress, Purple Top, Volkstedt, 8 In. 115.00
Nodder, Seated Chinoiserie Male, Nodding Head & Hands, 5 In. 1265.00

WADE pottery is made by the Wade Group of Potteries started in 1810 near Burslem, England. Several potteries merged to become George Wade & Son, Ltd. early in the twentieth century, and other potteries have been added through the years. The best-known Wade pieces are the small figurines given away with Red Rose Tea and other promotional items. The Disney figures are listed in this book in the Disneyana category.

Figurine, Aunt Polly, Light Blue Label, 2 3/4 In. 18.00
Figurine, Bally-Whim House, No. 8, 2 x 3 1/8 In. 38.00
Figurine, Bloodshot Hall, Whimsey-On-Why, 2 x 3 In. 26.00
Figurine, Building Days Boy, Blue Label 35.00
Figurine, Coffee House 29.00
Figurine, Colonial Carriage, Figure At The Horse's Head 20.00
Figurine, Dog In Basket 22.00
Figurine, Ezra, Yellow Label, No. 8054 ....   30.00
Figurine, House, Painted Lady, Victorian Homes Of San Francisco .... .55.00 to 77.00
Figurine, I've A Bear Behind, Boy In Blue Pajamas With Teddy Bear, 2 3/4 In. 103.00
Figurine, Little Red Riding Hood, 1 3/4 In. 10.00
Figurine, Mickey Mulligan, Irish Song, 6 In. 173.00
Figurine, Morgan Chemist House, Streetlamp, Garbage Pail, 1 3/4 x 1 1/2 In. 16.00
Figurine, Paddy Reilly, Irish Man In Cape With Walking Stick, Dog, 4 In. 49.00
Figurine, Pioneer Couple, Blue Label, Ornate Base 25.00
Figurine, Sailing Days Girl, Red Label, No. 4 ....   35.00
Figurine, Schoolteacher's House, No. 33 ....   80.00
Figurine, Snow Days Boy, Yellow Label, No. 6262 ....   35.00
Figurine, Snow Days Girl, Box, No. 6263 ....   35.00
Figurine, Southern Belle, Bisque, 6 In. 75.00
Figurine, Yankee Sea Captain, Tilted, No. 132 ....   30.00
Pitcher, Festival, Copper Luster, 6 1/2 In. 65.00
Plaque, New England Town Crier 20.00

WAHPETON POTTERY, see Rosemeade category.

WALLACE NUTTING photographs are listed under Print, Nutting. His reproduction furniture is listed under Furniture.

WALRATH was a potter who worked in New York City; Rochester, New York; and at the Newcomb Pottery in New Orleans, Louisiana. Frederick Walrath died in 1920. Pieces listed here are from his Rochester period.

Bowl, Brown Matte Glaze, Incised Mark, 8 In. 358.00
Cider Set, Flowers, Leaves, Brown, Green Matte Ground, 4 x 9 In., 7 Piece 4888.00
Figurine, Scarab, Green Matte Glaze, 3 1/2 x 2 1/4 In. 394.00
Paperweight, Scarab, Gray, Brown Matte Glaze, 3 3/4 x 2 1/2 In. 400.00
Pitcher, Stylized Yellow Lemons, Light Green Leaves, Dark Green, 4 3/4 x 7 In. 2990.00

WALT DISNEY, see Disneyana category.

WALTER, see A. Walter category.

WARWICK china was made in Wheeling, West Virginia, in a pottery working from 1887 to 1951. Many pieces were made with hand painted or decal decorations. The most familiar Warwick has a shaded brown background. The name *Warwick* is part of the mark and sometimes the mysterious word *IOGA* is also included.

Baker, Pink Rose Sprays, Gold Trim, Scalloped, 1930-1940, 9 1/2 In.	18.00
Cup & Saucer, Floral, Demitasse, 1 3/4-In. Cup	18.00
Cup & Saucer, Pink Rose Sprays, Scalloped, Metallic Gold Trim, 1930-1940	12.00
Pitcher, Gold Trim, IOGA, 9 1/2 In.	125.00
Pitcher, Green, White, 7 In.	133.00
Pitcher, Monk, 7 1/2 In.	200.00
Plate, Bread & Butter, Pink Rose Sprays, Scalloped, 1930-1940, 6 In.	6.00
Plate, Salad, Pink Rose Sprays, Gold Trim, Scalloped, 1930-1940, 9 In.	12.00
Platter, Pink Rose Sprays, Gold Trim, Scalloped, Handles, 1940, 13 In.	30.00
Saucer, Indian Tree, 1950, 6 In.	6.00
Saucer, Pink Rose Sprays, Metallic Gold Trim, Scalloped, 1930-1940	4.00
Soup, Coupe, Pink Rose Sprays, Gold Trim, Scalloped, 1930-1940, 7 3/4 In.	8.00
Vase, Bronze Patina, Circular Pedestal, Plinth, Italy, 10 1/4 In., Pair	2990.00
Vase, Hand Painted Leaves & Branches, Brown To Tan, Tall Neck, 4 In.	50.00
Vase, Rose, Marked, 9 In.	70.00
Vase, Turned Out Rim, Classical Masks Flanked By Vine Handles, France, 20 In.	3450.00
Vase, Victorian Woman Portrait, 1900-1915	250.00

WATCH pockets held the pocket watch that was important in Victorian times because it was not until World War I that the wristwatch was used. All types of watches are collected: silver, gold, or plated. Watches are arranged by company name or by style. Pocket watches are listed here; wristwatches are a separate category.

Bronzed Case, Black Enamel Dial, Gilt Bronze Holder, 20th Century, 4 3/4 In.	140.00
Bulova, Open Face, Pink & Gold Tone Dial, Gold Filled Chain, Pocket Knife	50.00
Character, Barbie, Pendant, Goldtone, Blue Dial, Ponytail, Bradley, Elgin, c.1964 .230.00 to 305.00
Character, Big Bad Wolf, Fob, Box	2800.00
Character, Goofy, Backwards, Box, Helbros, 1972	1400.00
Concord, Sterling Silver Case, Bailey, Banks & Biddle	55.09
Edouard Perregaus, Open Face, Porcelain Dial, Seconds Dial, Size 16	375.00
Elgin, 14K Gold, Engraved Design	660.00
Elgin, Hunting Case, Gold Filled, Stem Wind, 20 Year, Engraved Bird, Floral, 15 Jewel . .	275.00
Elgin, Hunting Case, Gold, Stem Wind, 15 Jewel, Engraved Jacob Ott, Case, 1887	1265.00
Elgin, Open Face, 17 Jewels, Gold Filled Chain	121.00
Elgin, Open Face, Crusade Model, 17 Jewel, 14K White Gold, 1 3/4 In.	200.00
F.A. Copper, Hunting Case, Silver, Engraved Building & Scroll, London, Key Wind	155.00
Hamilton, Open Face, Monogram, Presentation To C.R. Orndorff, 21 Jewel	154.00
Hampden, General Stark, Stem Wind, Scroll, Floral & Butterfly Engraved, Gold Chain . .	209.00
Hampden, Open Face, Coin Silver, Key Wind, Seconds Dial, Size 18	120.00
Henry Sandoz, Hunting Case, Chronograph, 35 Jewel, 18K Gold, 1890	4080.00
Howard, Open Face, Enamel Dial, Sweep Section	120.00
Howard & Co., Open Face, Silveroid Case, Enameled Dial, Seconds Dial	120.00
Hunting Case, Vacheron & Constantin, White Enamel Dial, 18K Gold, Pocket	345.00
Hunting Case, White Enamel Dial, Black Roman Numerals, 18K Gold, Pocket	978.00
Hunting Case, White Porcelain Dial, Black Arabic Numerals, 14K Gold, Pocket	259.00
Illinois, Hunting Case, Patent Pinion, Gilt Dial, Engraved Jan. 27, 1900, T-Bar Chain	275.00
Longines, Open Face, White Enamel Dial, Gilt Hands, Gold Chain, Gold Acorn Fob	132.00
Miss Jaccard, Woman's, Hunting Case, 14K Rose Gold, Scrolled Hands, 15-In. Chain . . .	248.00
Movado, Silvertone Dial, Leather Case, Alarm, 18K Gold	375.00
Ollendorf, Woman's, 14K Yellow Gold, Hinged Dial Cover, Gold Mesh Band, 17 Jewel . .	165.00
Open Face, Lapel, Bow Form, Diamonds, Rubies	690.00
Open Face, White Enamel Dial, Black Arabic Numerals, 18K Gold, Pocket	805.00
Orator Watch Co., Pendant, 15 Jewel, Enamel Dial, Silver Chain	132.00
Patek Philippe, Open Face, 18K Gold, White Enamel Dial, Roman Numerals, 1908	5100.00
Patek Philippe, Open Face, Silver Matte Dial, Arabic Numerals, 1928	1560.00
Pavel Buhre, Presentation, Imperial, Gold, White Enamel, Face, Eagle, c.1900, 2 1/8 In. . .	3025.00

Reuge, Automaton Musical, Erotic Scene Under Back Lid 2950.00
Rolex, Woman's, Oyster, Perpetual Date, Yellow Gold, 18K, Diamond, Sapphire Bezel . . . 7475.00
Seth Thomas, Railroad, Second Dial, Silveroid Case, 15 Jewel 152.00
Silver, Hallmarked Case, Bull's-Eye Crystal, Key Wind, Early 19th Century, 1 7/8 In. 110.00
Touchon, 18K Gold, Long Link Chain, Tiffany, 1911 . . . . 925.00
Touchon, Open Face, 18K Gold, Octagonal Case, 41 Simulated Diamonds, 1880 . . . . 7800.00
Waltham, Hunting Case, 14K Gold, Enamel Dial, Roman Numerals, Pocket, 1898 . . . . . . 575.00
Waltham, Hunting Case, Gold, Key Wind, Engraved Design 320.00
Waltham, Woman's, Stem Wind, 15 Jewel, Tri-Gold Hunting Case, Floral 130.00
White Face Dial, Case, Applied Rosettes, Tin, Pocket, 23 In. 1870.00
Woman's, Hunting Case, 14K Gold, Shield & Stars, Diamond 14K Chain 385.00
Woman's, Lapel, Cream Porcelain Dial, Roman Numerals, Cobalt Blue, 18K Gold 430.00

WATCH FOBS were worn on watch chains. They were popular during
Victorian times and after. Many styles, especially advertising designs,
are still made today.

Anheuser Busch, Leather Strap, c.1910 . . . . 77.00
Brunswick-Balke-Collender, Man Bowling, Nickel 100.00
Bucyrus Erie Equipment 25.00
Dog, Trace Link Chains, 1900, 14K Gold 575.00
Eagle With Banner Above Canal, Panama-Pacific, 1915 . . . . 13.00
Green River Whiskey, Logo Image On Front, 1 1/2 In. 95.00
Horse Design, Horseshoe, Baits, Crop, Head Termination, Gold Filled 187.00
Ingersoll Rand, Metal, 1930s, 1 3/4 In. 10.00
Japanese Woman On Bridge, American Flag, In Memory Of U.S. Occupation Of Japan . . 200.00
John Deere, Black Enamel, Deer Leaping Over Steel Plow 880.00
Laflin & Rand Smokeless Powders, Rifle, Shotgun, Revolver, Copper 250.00
Pancho Villa, Mexican Border Service, Battle Dates 135.00
Peru Beer Co., Brass, Enamel 110.00
RCA, Sterling Silver, Multicolored Cloisonne, Nipper, His Master's Voice, 2 x 2 In. 1155.00
Shell, Gold, Monogram, Victorian 75.00
Trap Shooting, California State Championship, 5th Prize, Copper Plated, 1 3/4 In. 143.00
Tudor Brand Tea & Coffee, Scorekeepers On Reverse, 2 In. 440.00
Tudor Tea, Coffee & Cocoa, 2 Sides, Celluloid, Leather Strap, 2 x 1 3/4 In. 440.00
Vin Fiz, Celluloid & Metal, Image Of Trademark Woman, 2 1/8 In. 770.00
Washburn's Ice Cream, Health Food, Porcelain Front, Advertising Back, 1 1/4 In. 187.00
Yellow Gold, 14K, Cameo, Spinner Locket, Onyx, Sard, Oval Link, Swivel Clip, 2 In. . . . 633.00

WATERFORD type glass resembles the famous glass made from 1783 to
1851 in the Waterford Glass Works in Ireland. It is a clear glass that
was often decorated by cutting. Modern glass is being made again in
Waterford, Ireland, and is marketed under the name *Waterford.*

Biscuit Barrel, 8 In. 250.00
Chandelier, 6-Light, Cut Glass Prisms, Bobeches, Finial, 24 1/2 In. 1035.00
Compote, Rings & Diamond Band, Ray Base, 10 1/2 x 7 3/4 In. 425.00
Decanter, Kylemore Pattern, 10 1/4 In. 92.00
Glass, Champagne, Galway, 4 3/4 In., 7 Piece 115.00
Goblet, Sherry, Maeve, 4 1/2 In. 23.00
Lamp, Cut Glass Dome Shade, Pedestal Base, Diamond Cut Base, 18 In. 248.00
Sherry, Sheila, 1920, 5 1/2 In., 9 Piece 475.00
Vase, Bud, Flared Neck, Diamond & Leaf Design, Crystal, 3 x 5 1/2 In. 126.00

WATT family members bought the Globe pottery of Crooksville, Ohio,
in 1922. They made pottery mixing bowls and tableware of the type
made by Globe. In 1935 they changed the production and made the
pieces with the freehand decorations that are popular with collectors
today. Apple, Starflower, Rooster, Tulip, and Autumn Foliage are the
best-known patterns. Pansy, also called Rio Rose, was the earliest pattern. Apple, the most popular pattern, can be dated from the leaves.
Originally, the apples had three leaves; after 1958 two leaves were
used. The plant closed in 1965. For more information, see *Kovels'
Depression Glass & Dinnerware Price List.*

Apple, Baker, Cover, No. 110 . . . . 300.00

Apple, Baker, Cover, No. 601 .... 150.00
Apple, Baker, No. 96 .... 34.00
Apple, Bowl, Salad, No. 73 .... 60.00
Apple, Bowl, Spaghetti, No. 39 .... 150.00
Apple, Bowl, Sugar, No. 98 .... 204.00
Apple, Creamer, No. 62 ....105.00 to 125.00
Apple, Dutch Oven, Cover, No. 70 .... 60.00
Apple, Mixing Bowl, 3-Leaf, No. 6 .... 44.00
Apple, Mixing Bowl, No. 6 .... 24.00
Apple, Mixing Bowl, No. 8 .... 53.00
Apple, Mixing Bowl, No. 63 ....34.00 to 41.00
Apple, Mixing Bowl, No. 64 .... 42.00
Apple, Nappy, No. 05 .... 70.00
Apple, Pie Plate, No. 33 .... 113.00
Apple, Pitcher, No. 15 .... 110.00
Autumn Foliage, Bowl, Spaghetti, No. 39 .... 68.00
Cherry, Bowl, Spaghetti, No. 39 .... 50.00
Cookie Jar, Policeman, Cover, 10 1/2 In. 1100.00
Double Apple, Baker, Cover, No. 96 .... 100.00
Dutch Tulip, Baker, Cover, No. 67 .... 200.00
Dutch Tulip, Casserole, Cover, French Handle, No. 18 .... 325.00
Kitch-N-Queen, Mixing Bowl, No. 8 .... 20.00
Kitch-N-Queen, Mixing Bowl, No. 14 .... 51.00
Moon & Stars, Casserole, Green, 8 In. 51.00
Orchard Ware, Spattered, Pink, Baker, Cover, No. 54 .... 125.00
Orchard Ware, Spattered, Pink, Ice Bucket, No. 59 .... 195.00
Pansy, Bowl, Handle, 7 1/2 x 5 1/2 x 3 1/2 In. 50.00
Pansy, Bowl, Spaghetti, Lip, No. 39 .... 90.00
Pansy, Platter, Sandwich, 15 In. 50.00
Rooster, Bowl, Cover, No. 67 .... 76.00
Starflower, Bowl, Casserole, No. 54 .... 103.00
Starflower, Bowl, No. 73 .... 15.00
Swirl, Mixing Bowl, Pink, Mauve, No. 7 .... 16.00
Swirl, Mixing Bowl, Yellow, No. 9 .... 11.00
Tear Drop, Baker, Square, No. 84 .... 800.00
Tear Drop, Mixing Bowl, No. 6 .... 32.00
Tear Drop, Salt & Pepper, Barrel, No. 45 & No. 46 .... 300.00
Tulip, Bowl, Salad, No. 73 .... 61.00
Tulip, Creamer, No. 62 .... 175.00
Tulip, Pitcher, No. 16 .... 185.00

WAVE CREST glass is an opaque white glassware manufactured by the
Pairpoint Manufacturing Company of New Bedford, Massachusetts,
and some French factories. It was decorated by the C.F. Monroe
Company of Meriden, Connecticut. The glass was painted in pastel
colors and decorated with flowers. The name *Wave Crest* was used
after 1898.

**WAVE CREST
WARE**

Box, Blown Out Purple Violets, Hinged Cover, 7 In. 460.00
Box, Blue Flowers, Medium Pink, Hinged Cover, 4 1/2 x 4 In. 403.00
Box, Bright Blue Daisies, On Pink, Hinged Cover, 4 1/4 x 4 3/4 In. 460.00
Box, Center Cartouche, Daisies, Scrolls, Satin Lining, Hinged Cover, 7 In. 632.00
Box, Cupid, Blue, Purple Flowers, Pale Pink, Hinged Cover, 4 1/2 x 3 3/4 In. 259.00
Box, Dresser, Flowers, White, Hinged Cover, 7 In. 560.00
Box, Dresser, Pink Flowers, Marked, 2 3/4 x 3 1/4 In. 450.00
Box, Egg Crate Shape, Pink Floral & Word Tobacco, Hinged Cover, Marked, 5 1/2 In. ... 1155.00
Box, Egg Crate Shape, Pink, Purple Wild Roses, Medium Green, 5 In. 1093.00
Box, Enameled Daisies, Hinged Cover, 7 In. 735.00
Box, Floral Sprays, Daisies, Pink, 1892, 5 1/2 In. 460.00
Box, Helmschmied Swirl, Flowers, Purple Scrolls, Hinged Cover, 7 In. 402.00
Box, Helmschmied Swirl, Gold, Yellow Apple Blossom, Pink, Hinged Cover, 6 In. 460.00
Box, Helmschmied Swirl, Pink Rose Design, Green Leaves, Hinged Cover, 7 x 4 1/2 In. ... 690.00
Box, Letter, Rococo, Flowers, 6 x 3 1/2 x 4 1/2 In. 355.00
Box, Scene Of Woman On Fence, Hinged Cover, 6 In. 500.00

Card Holder, Floral, Embossed Brass Rim, 6 In. 504.00
Clock, Rococo, Pink, White Flowers, Gilt Metal Frame, 1891, 7 x 7 In. 2703.00
Cracker Jar, Blue Flowers, Barrel Shape, 12 x 6 In. 316.00
Cracker Jar, Egg Crate Shape, Pink Mums, Metal Frame, 10 In. 287.00
Cracker Jar, Egg Crate Shape, Pink, White Clover, Green Leaves, 11 x 5 In. 374.00
Cracker Jar, Pink & Yellow Flowers, Silver Plated Lid & Bail 236.00
Fernery, Pink With Blue Flowers, Embossed Rope Border, Brass Feet, Rim, Signed, 8 In. .. 315.00
Fernery, Rococo, Pink Flowers, Signed, 5 In. 265.00
Humidor, Cigar, Blue Flowers, Word Cigars, Signed, 6 In. 735.00
Jardiniere, White & Blue Flowers, Signed, 7 In. 158.00
Lamp, Castle, Farm Scene, Cream, Pink Floral, Signed, 17 In. 420.00
Letter Holder, Egg Crate Shape, Floral, Brass Feet, Signed, 5 x 6 In. 340.00
Letter Holder, Egg Crate Shape, Pink, Blue Mums, 6 x 4 1/4 In. 375.00
Pin Box, Helmschmied Swirl, Ormolu Handles, 4 1/4 In. 112.00
Pin Tray, Scrolls & Flowers, Brass Trim, 3 1/4 In. 175.00
Plaque, Iris, Gilt Metal Frame, Paper Label, 7 1/2 In. 3780.00
Plate, Lake & Farm Scene, Gold Trim, Paper Label, 8 In. 130.00
Sugar & Creamer, Helmschmied Swirl, Daisies, Pink, White, 4 x 4 1/2 x 5 In. 635.00
Sugar & Creamer, Helmschmied Swirl, Pond Lilies, Pale Blue, 5 1/4 x 5 In., Pair 460.00
Sugar Shaker, Rococo, Pink Swags, Gray Blossoms, 3 x 3 1/4 In. 585.00
Tobacco Humidor, Pink, Medium Pink Roses, Green Leaves, 5 1/2 In. 750.00
Vase, Pink Wild Roses, Gold, 9 3/4 x 4 In. 1035.00
Vase, Rococo, Flowers, Gold Accents, Dolphin Feet, 17 In. 2760.00
Vase, Sailboat Scene, Brass Feet, 12 1/2 In. 2625.00
Vase, Spray Of Golden Flowers, Beaded Top, 6 1/2 In. 425.00
Vase, Stylized Apple Blossoms, 3 Medallions, 12 1/2 In. 1975.00
Vase, Wild Roses, Deep Blue, White, Marked, 12 x 9 In. 1955.00

WEAPONS listed here include instruments of combat other than guns, knives, rifles, or swords. Firearms are not listed in this book. Knives and swords are listed in their own categories.

Dagger, Clove Tempered Edge, Gold Case, Japan, 19th Century, 6 3/4 In. 1560.00
Gunpowder Measure, For Pistol, Brass, England, 18th Century 295.00
Handcuffs, Nickel Over Steel, Bean Prison Model, Key, Pat'd Nov. 28, 1882 .... 150.00
Handcuffs, Swing-Through, Key, Engraved, Peerless Handcuff Co. 150.00
Truncheon, Policeman's, c.1875, 11 1/2 In. 425.00
War Hammer, Ottoman, Iron Head, Silver Lattice, Cap, 18th Century, 24 3/4 In. 1250.00

WEATHER VANES were used in seventeenth-century Boston. The direction of the wind was an indication of coming weather, important to the seafaring and farming communities. By the mid-nineteenth century, commercial weather vanes were made of metal. Today's collectors often consider weather vanes to be examples of folk art, even though they may not have been handmade.

Arrow, Copper, Verdigris Patina, Gilt Traces, c.1890, 17 1/2 x 42 1/4 In. 2070.00
Arrow, Heart Shaped, Ball Finial, Copper, White Paint, Verdigris Finish, 16 x 23 In. 977.00
Arrow, Large Finial, Directionals, Copper, 19th Century, 58 In. 2420.00
Arrow, Spire & Ball Finial, Feathers, Copper, Gilt Finish, 25 1/2 x 43 1/2 In. 1725.00
Arrow, Swallowtail End, Old White Paint, Wood, 39 x 60 1/4 In. 1380.00
Arrow & Banner, Cutout Scalloped Banner, Gilt Zinc, Late 1880s, 13 x 68 In. 2070.00
Banner, Initials ECL, Directionals, Pole, Copper, 29 1/2 x 72 x 12 In. 575.00
Banner, Scrollwork, Smith, Copper, Verdigris Patina, 24 5/8 x 37 In. 1840.00
Banner, Sun Face, Painted, Orange, 9 1/2 x 22 In. 288.00
Bicycle, Iron, Painted, Green, Yellow, Late 19th Century, 24 x 43 In. 3960.00
Bicycle, Tandem, Man, Woman, Arrow, Cape Cod Weathervane Co., 1960s, 24 x 46 In. .. 255.00
Boy, Hoop & Dog, Boy Running With Hoop, Metal, Green Paint, 1930, 43 In. 7800.00
Bull, L.W. Cushing, 30 In. 11500.00
C-Scrolls, Riveted Strapwork, Bronze, 19th Century, 20 5/8 x 49 1/2 In. 750.00
Canada Goose, Applied Hind Feet, Glass Eyes, 52-In. Wingspan 140.00
Colonel Sanders, Kentucky Fried Chicken, With Cane, Painted, 58 In. ....250.00 to 450.00
Copper, Ocher Paint, 23 x 24 1/2 In. 13800.00
Cow, Full-Bodied, Copper, Bullet Holes, 18 1/2 x 26 1/2 In. 3190.00

Cow, Molded, Full-Bodied, Copper, Gilt, Weathered, 21 x 33 x 8 In. 13800.00
Cow, Pressed Tin, Black Paint, Wooden Stand, 9 1/2 x 14 1/2 x 1 In. 280.00
Deer & Hunter, Rifle Pointed, Buck, Sheet Iron, 15 x 33 3/4 In. 520.00
Eagle, Arrow, Hollow Body, Copper & Zinc, 16 In., 17-In. Wingspan 3880.00
Eagle, Full-Bodied Copper, 19th Century, 36-In. Wingspan 7200.00
Eagle, Hollow Body, Copper & Zinc, 18 1/2-In. Wingspan 385.00
Eagle, Sphere, Arrow, Copper, Full-Bodied, Gilt Surface, 1880s, 19 In. 1955.00
Eagle, Spread Wings, Cast Head, Feather Detail, 28 In. 2358.00
Eagle, Spread Wings, Full-Bodied, Ball Stand, Copper, 19th Century, 27 x 30 In. 825.00
Eagle, Spread Wings, Full-Bodied, Copper, Late 19th Century, 21 x 30 In. 3190.00
Eagle, Spread Wings, Full-Bodied, Copper, Perched On Spear, 25 1/4 In. 2415.00
Eagle, Spread Wings, Landing, Arrow On Separate Pole, Sheet Iron, 59 In. 600.00
Eagle, Spread Wings, Zinc Head, On Ball, Arrow Directional, 23 1/2 In. 605.00
Fish, Dark Green Paint, Wood & Iron Stand, 15 x 27 In. 4025.00
Fish, Flat Sheet Metal, Zinc, Green Glass Eyes, Gilt Finish, Painted, 13 3/4 x 16 In. 1035.00
Flag, Pierced Star, Fluted Center Ball, Star & Half Moon Finial, 31 3/4 In. 605.00
Fox, 4 Hounds, Directionals, Sheet Iron, Early 20th Century, 23 x 19 In. 1980.00
Horse, Directional Arrow, Tin, Pennsylvania, Late 19th Century, 20 1/2 In. 105.00
Horse, Prancing, Copper, Full-Bodied, Original Gold Leaf Patina, 17 x 31 In. 3575.00
Horse, Prancing, Gray Mane, Tail & Hooves, Sheet Iron, Bullet Holes, 26 1/2 In. 715.00
Horse, Prancing, Sheet Iron, Pa., Late 19th Century, 29 x 40 In. 2310.00
Horse, Running, Black Hawk, Old Patina, 25 x 31 In. 5225.00
Horse, Running, Copper, Full-Bodied, Black Hawk, 18 1/2 x 25 3/4 In. 4025.00
Horse, Running, Copper, Full-Bodied, Cast Iron Head, Verdigris, 22 1/2 In. 8625.00
Horse, Running, Copper, Gilding, Applied Zinc Ears, Steel Base, 31 1/4 x 17 In. 2530.00
Horse, Running, Full-Bodied, Flattened, Gilt Finish, 19th Century, 12 1/4 x 14 In. 2760.00
Horse, Running, Full-Bodied, Gilt Surface, Late 19th Century, 17 1/2 x 29 1/2 In. 2640.00
Horse, Running, Gilt Copper, Molded, Directionals, 15 1/4 x 24 1/2 In. 2530.00
Horse, Running, J. Harris & Son, Boston, 17 x 32 In. 6600.00
Horse, Running, Jockey, Cushing & White, Copper, Maker's Tag, 16 x 26 3/4 In. 13800.00
Horse, Running, Jockey, Full-Bodied, Gilt Copper, Cushing & White, 16 x 26 In. 8050.00
Horse, Running, Molded Copper, c.1870 . . . . 5170.00
Horse, Running, Mustard Yellow, J. Harris & Son, Boston, 30 x 20 In. 3165.00
Horse, Running, Sheet Copper, Gold Paint, 19 1/2 x 31 1/2 In. 1430.00
Horse, Running, Zinc, Hollow Body, Tin Rod, 22 x 31 In. 2420.00
Horse, Silhouette, Directionals, Red, Sheet Steel, 26 In. 275.00
Horse, Walking, Index, Zinc & Copper, J. Howard & Co., 1875 . . . . 19500.00
Horse, Wood, Painted, Full-Bodied, Sheet Iron Ears, Nail Head Eyes, 26 x 25 In. 11500.00
Horse & Rider, Running, Copper, Cast Zinc, Allover Verdigris, 18 1/2 In. 21450.00
Horse & Rider, Sheet Iron, 29 x 25 In. 5060.00
Indian With Bow & Arrow, Sheet Iron, Pa., 24 x 20 In. 495.00
Lightning Bolts, Copper, Hollow Body, Phillipsdale, R.I., 1879, 36 In. 15120.00
Man On High Wheel Bicycle, Sheet Metal, 22 x 31 In. 275.00
Pig, Sheet Metal, c.1900, 14 x 27 1/2 In. 630.00
Pig, Sheet Metal, White & Pink Paint, c.1900, 14 x 27 1/2 In. 560.00
Pig, Standing On Rod, Gold, L.W. Cushing, Mass., 19th Century, 23 x 36 In. 17250.00
Rooster, 32 In. 6380.00
Rooster, Cast & Sheet Iron, 36 In. 8050.00
Rooster, Copper, Green, Yellow Legs, 27 1/2 x 21 In. 9200.00
Rooster, Copper, Zinc, Ocher, Gilt, Howard & Co., Mass., c.1852, 29 1/2 x 26 In. 18400.00
Rooster, Rochester Iron Works, Cast Iron, 1880, 18 x 31 In. 4300.00
Rooster, Sheet Iron, Riveted Strapwork, American, 36 1/2 x 27 1/2 In. 980.00
Rooster, Sphere, Zinc, Copper Stand, Gilt Detail, Red, 16 3/4 x 10 1/2 In. 2070.00
Salmon, Light Gray, Green Verdigris, 30 In. 28000.00
Schooner, Old Repaint, Frank Adams, 32 In. 2500.00
Ship, 3 Masts, Billowing Sails, Red, Brown, Green Hull, Tin, 1900, 16 x 32 In. 2750.00
Ship, 3 Masts, Copper, Verdigris, Signed Felix, c.1950, 70 x 67 In. 1150.00
Ship, Sailing, Gilt Copper, Iron, Gloucester, Mass., 32 x 25 In. 2300.00
Ship, Sailing, Wood, Zinc, White, Black Paint, Frank Adams, 36 In. 1380.00
Ship, The Mayflower, Sheet Iron, 29 x 24 In. 200.00
Ship, Wood, Zinc, White, Black, 36 In. 1380.00
Stag, Leaping, Full-Bodied, Copper, Cast Zinc Antlers, Late 1800s, 26 1/2 x 35 In. 2530.00

Stag, Leaping, Hollow Body, Copper, L.W. Cushing, 24 x 29 In.	8250.00
Sulky, Rider, J. Nield, 20 x 32 In.	920.00
Swan, Spire, Sphere, Leafy Scroll, Arrow, Copper, Gilt Finish, 35 1/2 x 44 1/4 In.	4312.00
Trolley Car, On Arrow, 20th Century, 20 x 45 In.	7185.00
Whirligig, Cowboy On Horse, Wood & Tin, Herman Broxson, 26 x 51 In.	200.00
Wood, Arrow Indicator, S & B Hopkins, Red Glass Eyes, 31 In.	99.00

WEBB glass is made by Thomas Webb & Sons of Ambelcot, England. Many types of art and cameo glass were made by them during the Victorian era. Production ceased by 1991, and the factory was demolished in 1995. Webb Burmese and Webb Peachblow are special colored glasswares of the Victorian era. They are listed at the end of this section. Glassware that is not Burmese or Peachblow is included here.

Webb

Biscuit Barrel, Cherry Blossoms, Buds On Leafy Branches, Mint Green, Handle, 4 In.	632.00
Bride's Bowl, White Over Blue, Enameled Bird & Branch, Silver Plated Holder	420.00
Finger Bowl, Plate, Wood Bark, 5 x 2 In.	690.00
Pitcher, Amber, Rose, Blue, Applied Shaded Handle, 5 1/4 x 4 In.	1440.00
Pitcher, Flared Quatrefoil Neck, Applied Amber Handle, Late 19th Century, 5 1/4 In.	375.00
Pitcher, Red Floral On Ivory, Cream, Signed, 10 1/2 In.	131.00
Pitcher, Wide Body, Applied Amber Handle, Late 19th Century, 4 1/4 In.	495.00
Toothpick, Egg Shape, 3-Footed, Gold Leaf, 3 1/2 In.	315.00
Vase, Asian-Style, Flowers, White Over Blue, Satin, 4 1/4 In.	1095.00
Vase, Bronze Finish, Etched Deer Frieze, Trees, Hannah Barlow, 7 3/4 In.	230.00
Vase, Carved Leaves, Branches, Butterfly Scene, Blue, Signed, Thomas Webb, 8 1/4 In.	2100.00
Vase, Enameled Flowers, Satin, Pinched, Victorian, 7 In.	168.00
Vase, Flower Shape, Disc Foot, Cobalt Blue Rim, Signed, 4 In.	172.00
Vase, Flowering Vine, White Over, Blue Satin, Cameo, 4 In.	1035.00
Vase, Flowers & Leaves, Butterfly In Flight, White Over Cranberry, Cameo, 4 1/2 In.	632.00
Vase, Flowers & Vines In Gold, Gold Butterfly On Back, 4 In.	185.00
Vase, Gold Leaves, Butterfly, On White, Gem Cameo, 5 1/4 In.	245.00
Vase, Oak Branch, Leaves, White Over Citron, Satin, 6 1/2 In.	2415.00
Vase, Passion Flowers, White Over Deep Red, Satin, Cameo, 6 3/4 In.	2530.00
Vase, Stick, Applied Gold Prunts, Flowers, Green Base, Green Lining, 10 1/2 In.	525.00
Wine, Honeycomb, Optic, Blue Rim, 4 1/2 In.	975.00

WEBB BURMESE is a colored Victorian glass made by Thomas Webb & Sons of Stourbridge, England, from 1886.

Centerpiece, Fairy Lamp, 4-Light, Match Holder, Footed, 17 In. ....*Illus*	3450.00
Fairy Lamp, 5 1/2 x 5 3/4 In.	1285.00
Fairy Lamp, Clear Clarke Base, 3 In.	325.00
Rose Bowl, 3 In. ....172.00 to	360.00
Rose Bowl, Pale Purple Flowers, Ruffled Base, 4 x 2 1/2 In.	460.00
Vase, 5-Petal Flowers, Yellow Centers, 3 1/4 In.	325.00
Vase, 5-Petal Mouth, 3 1/2 In.	230.00
Vase, Acorns, Oak Leaves, 3 3/4 In.	375.00
Vase, Allover Enameled Flowers, 4 1/4 In.	425.00
Vase, Curior, White Fuchsias, Signed, Thomas Webb, 3 In.	402.00

Clean the plastic crystal of a vintage watch with silver polish.

Store cuff links or earrings in foam egg cartons.

Webb Burmese,
Centerpiece, Fairy Lamp,
4-Light, Match Holder,
Footed, 17 In.

WEBB PEACHBLOW is a colored Victorian glass made by Thomas Webb & Sons of Stourbridge, England, from 1885.

Bowl, Gold Prunus Blossoms & Branches, Gold Trim, Cream Lining, 2 1/2 In.	325.00
Vase, Applied Amber Grape & Leaves, Bulbous, 5 1/8 x 4 In.	230.00
Vase, Applied Pink, Off White Wild Roses, 2 Insects, Loop, 9 1/2 x 6 In.	750.00
Vase, Applied Satin Brown & Gold Design, 3 1/4 In., Pair	345.00
Vase, Bird In Flight, Gold Trim, White Lining, 10 In.	795.00
Vase, Gold Floral, White Lining, 9 3/4 In.	595.00
Vase, Mahogany Red, Silver Florals, Gold Stems & Leaves, 5 1/8 x 3 3/8 In.	275.00
Vase, Pine Needles, Butterflies In Flight, Jules Barbe, 11 1/4 In.	750.00
Vase, Wild Rose, Pinched, 10 1/2 In.	1450.00

WEDGWOOD, one of the world's most successful potteries, was founded by Josiah Wedgwood, who was considered a cripple by his brother and was forbidden to work at the family business. The pottery was established in England in 1759. A large variety of wares has been made, including the well-known jasper ware, basalt, cream ware, and even a limited amount of porcelain. There are two kinds of jasper ware. One is made from two colors of clay, the other is made from one color of clay with a color dip to create the contrast in design. The firm is still in business. Other Wedgwood pieces may be listed under Flow Blue, Majolica, Tea Leaf Ironstone or in other porcelain categories.

WEDGWOOD

Ashtray, Jasperware, Green & White, Leaf & Grape, 3 5/8 In.	35.00
Basket, Fruit, Basket Weave Center, Pierced Gallery, Oval, Stand, 1830s, 10 5/8 In.	316.00
Basket, Fruit, Caneware, Pierced Biscuit Body, Oval, Stand, 10 7/8 In.	1265.00
Basket, Pearlware, Reticulated Border, European Tall Ships In Harbor, 9 x 6 1/2 In.	352.00
Bidet, Pearlware, Botanical Flowers, Blue Transfer, 16 1/4 In.	805.00
Biscuit Jar, Cover, Jasperware, Green, Dancing Ladies, 7 1/2 In. ....*Illus*	865.00
Biscuit Jar, Cover, Majolica, Molded Flowers, Silver Plated Rim, Handle, 6 In.	750.00
Biscuit Jar, Grecian Men & Women, Cherubs, Signed, 7 In.	225.00
Biscuit Jar, Jasperware, Grecian Women, Silver Plated Rim, Lid & Handle, 6 1/2 In.	165.00
Biscuit Jar, Jasperware, Silver Plated Rims, Swing Handle, Cover, Figures, 10 1/2 In.	795.00
Biscuit Jar, Jasperware, White, Classical Figural Design, 8 In.	105.00
Bough Pot, Black Basalt, Scrolled Handles Ending At Ram's Head, Signed, 7 In.	1265.00
Bough Pot, Cover, Jasper Dip, Yellow, Applied Blue Relief, Cherubs, 5 In.	1610.00
Bough Pot, Cover, Pearlware, Buff, Gray Glaze, Pearl Ground, 10 3/4 In.	430.00
Bough Pot, Jasperware, Blue, White Trees, Roman Figures, 2 Handles, Eturia, 16 In.	1650.00
Bough Pot, Lid, Queen's Ware, 2 Figures Representing Seasons, 2 Urns, 1850s, 6 In.	460.00
Bough Pot, Pierced Cover, White Acanthus, Bellflowers, Foliage Borders, 7 In.	1610.00
Bowl, Basalt, Orange, Short & Flared Pedestal, Late 19th Century, 8 3/4 In.	1090.00
Bowl, Black & White Jasperware, Dancing Hours, 10 In.	560.00
Bowl, Black Basalt, Orange, Raised Floral Festoons, 9 In.	750.00
Bowl, Cover, Jasperware, Classical Children, 4 5/8 In. ....*Illus*	1495.00
Bowl, Cover, Queen's Ware, Orange, Leaves, Entwined Handles, 1971, 8 In.	345.00
Bowl, Domed Cover, Queen's Ware, Orange, Impressed Mark, 9 1/2 In.	635.00
Bowl, Dragon Luster, Oranges, 4 1/2 In.	265.00
Bowl, Fairyland Luster, Interior Lake Scene, Exterior Fairies In Trees, 10 1/2 In.	4400.00
Bowl, Jasper Dip, Dancers, Vine Top, Footed, Impressed Mark, 10 1/4 x 4 In.	245.00
Bowl, Jasper Dip, Dark Blue, White Classical Figures, Fruit, Handles, 5 1/2 In.	750.00
Bowl, Majolica, Argentaware, Basket Of Flowers In Relief, 1883, 9 1/2 In.	400.00
Bowl, Majolica, Women With Fishing Net, c.1871, 13 3/4 In.	7200.00
Bowl, Marbleized Purple Luster, Handles, 9 1/2 In.	45.00
Bowl, Queen's Ware, Black Transfer, Hunting Scenes Exterior, 11 1/2 In.	1265.00
Bowl, Queen's Ware, Center, Fruiting Festoons, Grapevine Borders, 1914, 12 In.	315.00
Bowl, Queen's Ware, Cover, Children In Landscape Scene, Emile Lessore, 1870	230.00
Bowl, Rooks, Nests, Tree, Farm Landscape, c.1914, 14 1/8 In.	2160.00
Bowl, Serving, Flow Blue, Floral, 15 1/2 In.	75.00
Box, Cover, Jasper Dip, Yellow, Applied Black Classical Relief, 3 5/8 In.	345.00
Box, Jasperware, Blue & White, Woman On Top, Cupids At Base, Cover, 1 3/4 x 3 In.	165.00
Box, Jasperware, Heart Shape, Blue & White, 5 1/8 x 3 3/4 In.	50.00
Box, Jasperware, Ivory, Hinged Cover, Light Blue, White Classical Figure, 2 In.	290.00
Box, Letter, Cover, Jasperware, Light Blue, Calamander Wooden Casket Form, 9 In.	230.00
Bread Plate, Blue Willow, 6 3/4 In.	25.00

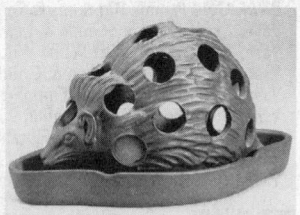

Wedgwood, Biscuit Jar, Cover, Jasperware, Green, Dancing Ladies, 7 1/2 In.

Wedgwood, Bowl, Cover, Jasperware, Classical Children, 4 5/8 In.

Wedgwood, Crocus Pot, Tray, Black Basalt, 9 5/8 In.

Bread Tray, Corn, Red Flowers, Turquoise Ground, Majolica, 13 In.	2200.00
Bulb Pot, Cover, Brown Glaze, Green Glaze, Scroll Border, Oval, 6 1/2 In.	575.00
Bust, Black Basalt, Ariadne, Waisted Circular Socle, 3 7/8 In.	230.00
Bust, Black Basalt, Byron, Waisted Circular Socle, 8 1/2 In.	575.00
Bust, Black Basalt, Locke, Waisted Circular Socle, 5 1/2 In.	315.00
Bust, Black Basalt, Minerva, Circular Socle, Title & Mark, 1850s, 17 1/2 In.	2415.00
Bust, Black Basalt, Minerva, Waisted Circular Socle, 4 1/2 In.	520.00
Bust, Black Basalt, Shakespeare, Circular Plinth, 19th Century, 6 In.	490.00
Bust, Black Basalt, Voltaire, Waisted Circular Socle, 5 3/4 In.	345.00
Bust, Black Basalt, Watt, Circular Socle, Impressed Title, c.1877, 14 In.	520.00
Bust, Mercury, Waisted Circular Socle, Late 19th Century, 18 1/4 In.	1035.00
Butter Tub, Cover, Argentaware, Ocean Tub Rim, Coral, 1880, 7 3/8 In.	980.00
Butter Tub, Cover, Stand, Sunflower, Twig Finial, 1861, 5 1/2 In.	750.00
Button, Religious Scene, Blue Ground	198.00
Calendar Plate, 1971, Cherubs, 9 7/8 In.	30.00
Candleholder, Jasperware, Blue & White, 3 3/4 In., Pair	80.00
Candlestick, Black Basalt, Dolphin Shape, Rectangular Base, 1972, 9 In., Pair	1090.00
Candlestick, Black Basalt, Holding Sconce, Title & Mark, 19th Century, 11 1/2 In.	1265.00
Candlestick, Black Basalt, Leaf Molded Body, Gilt Trim, 9 1/2 In.	1265.00
Candlestick, Jasper Dip, Lilac, White Classical Medallions, 6 In., Pair	1380.00
Candlestick, Jasper Dip, Lilac, White Relief, Leaf Borders, 7 In., Pair	980.00
Candlestick, Jasperware, Blue & White, Glass Prisms, 13 x 5 In., Pair	2040.00
Candlestick, Rosso Antico, Flowers, Enamel, Mid 19th Century, 7 In., Pair	690.00
Cann, Saucer, Jasper Dip, Dark Blue, White Classical Relief, 5 1/8 In.	1035.00
Cheese Dish, Dome, Underplate, Blue, White Oak Leaves & Acorns, 10 1/2 x 11 In.	410.00
Clock, Mantle, Jasperware, Green, Porcelain Dial, Brass Base, Stamped, 7 x 5 In.	170.00
Clock, Queen's Ware, Mantel, Architectural, Blue Glaze, 12 1/2 In.	575.00
Coffee Cup & Saucer, Black Basalt, 19th Century, 5 In., Pair	430.00
Coffeepot, Cover, Rosso Antico, Floral Sprays, Enameled, 1850, 7 1/2 In.	258.00
Compote, Horse Scene, Reticulated Border, 9 In.	385.00
Cream Jug, Cover, Jasper Dip, Dice Pattern, 3 Colors, Dark Blue Ground, 4 In.	4315.00
Creamer, 2 Classical Figures, Music & Drama, Leaf Borders, 4 1/2 In.	105.00
Creamer, Jasper Dip, Crimson, Applied White Classical Relief, 2 1/4 In.	750.00
Creamer, Jasperware, Blue & White, 5 x 3 1/2 In.	50.00
Crocus Pot, Black Basalt, Early 19th Century, 6 1/2 In.	520.00
Crocus Pot, Tray, Black Basalt, 9 5/8 In. ....*Illus*	978.00
Crocus Pot, Tray, Earthenware, Blue Glaze, 1860, 9 In.	1380.00
Crocus Pot, Tray, Earthenware, Drab Glaze, 12 1/4 In.	1035.00
Cup, Jasperware, Cobalt Blue, White Classical Scenes, Handleless, 2 5/8 In.	70.00
Cup & Saucer, Cover, Jasper Dip, Diceware, White Leaf Border, 3 In.	1495.00
Cup & Saucer, Drab Ware, Birds & Flowers, Enameled, 1830, 5 3/8 In., Pair	290.00
Cup & Saucer, Iris Kenlock Ware, Floral, c.1895, 5 3/4 In.	805.00
Dinner Set, Stoneware, Indiana, Imari Pallette Flowers, 47 Piece	1150.00
Dish, Argentaware, Majolica, Molded Flowers, Star Form Frame, 11 7/8 In.	400.00
Dish, Earthenware Hound, Blue Glaze, Handle, 1877, 11 1/2 In.	1495.00

Dish, Earthenware, Hound Handle, Trefoil, Blue Underglaze, c.1877, 11 In. 425.00
Dish, Jasper Dip, Crimson, Applied White Muse, Leaf Border, 1920, 6 In. 315.00
Dish, Queen's Ware, Cherubs In Landscape Scene, Emile Lessore, 1861, 7 1/2 In. 315.00
Dish, Queen's Ware, Nude Boys Supporting Tray Of Wine Glasses, 1870, 5 In. 1035.00
Dish, Stand, Queen's Ware, Strawberry, Floral, Foliage Borders, 1800, 10 1/2 In. 575.00
Ewer, Black Basalt, Classical Relief, Single Loop Handle, 6 3/8 In. 690.00
Figurine, Aphrodite, Molded As Female, Seated On Wave, c.1900, 10 5/8 In. 1150.00
Figurine, Boy, Sleeping, Black Basalt, Head On Basket Of Fruit, 4 7/8 In. 1090.00
Figurine, Boy, Sleeping, Black Basalt, Rectangular Base, 19th Century, 4 1/2 In. 575.00
Figurine, Boy, Sleeping, Black Basalt, Signed, 5 1/8 In. 145.00
Figurine, Bulldog, Black Basalt, Glass Eyes, c.1915, 2 3/4 In. 345.00
Figurine, Cat, Black Basalt, c.1915, 4 1/8 In. 258.00
Figurine, Cat, Black Basalt, Glass Eyes, c.1913, 4 1/2 In. 375.00
Figurine, Classical Female, Black Basalt, Feeding Large Bird, 5 In. 750.00
Figurine, Cleopatra, Black Basalt, Nude Female Figure Seated On Rock, 9 In. 980.00
Figurine, Crane, Black Basalt, Glass Eyes, Pierced Rocky Base, c.1915, 6 In. 460.00
Figurine, Faun & Flute, Black Basalt, Figure Standing By Tree Trunk, 17 In. 2185.00
Figurine, Faun & Goat, Black Basalt, Figure Supported By Tree Trunk, 21 In. 2185.00
Figurine, Faun, Black Basalt, Male Figure Standing, Partially Nude, 16 1/4 In. 1725.00
Figurine, Faun, Black Basalt, Stepped Circular Base, 15 3/4 In. 980.00
Figurine, Figure Of Winter, Black Basalt, Circular Base, 10 In. 1035.00
Figurine, Milton, Black Basalt, Figure Leaning On Pedestal, 1870, 16 1/4 In. 1090.00
Figurine, Nymph At Well, Black Basalt, Figure Holding Shell, 11 In. 2415.00
Figurine, Sphinx, Black Basalt, Female Figures With Lion Bodies, 11 In., Pair 1725.00
Figurine, Sphinx, Seated, Black Basalt, Stepped Rectangular Base, 9 1/4 In. 805.00
Figurine, Sphinx, Seated, Rectangular Base, 4 1/8 x 6 3/4 In. 490.00
Figurine, Venus On Rock, Black Basalt, Mid 19th Century, 18 3/4 In. 1955.00
Footbath, Pearlware, Pink, Green Panels, Early 19th Century, 17 1/2 In. 460.00
Fruit Cooler, Cover, Chinese Flowers, Yellow Honeycomb Ground, 1815, 7 In. 805.00
Hot Water Pot, Cover, Rosso Antico, Sybil Finial, 19th Century, 9 In. 920.00
Incense Burner, Pierced Cover, Dolphin Tripod Base, 1830, 5 7/8 In. 490.00
Ink Pot, Black Basalt, Sphinx Reclining, Circular Pot Set, 5 3/8 In. 375.00
Inkstand, Black Basalt, Enamel, Mid 19th Century, 8 In. 520.00
Inkstand, Black Basalt, Handles, Late 18th Century, 3 1/4 In. 575.00
Inkstand, Jasperware, Pale Blue, White Leaf Design, 1790, 2 In. 920.00
Inkwell, Black Basalt, Rosso Antico, Lantern Shape, Foliate, Beaded Border, 5 In. 490.00
Inkwell, Black Basalt, Rosso Antico, Leaf Relief, 7 1/4 In. 345.00
Inkwell, Queen's Ware, Black, Red Enamel Trim, Tripod Dolphin Feet, 1900, 6 In. 550.00
Jar, Cover, Black Basalt, Auro, Gold Leaf Design, c.1886, 12 In. 2530.00
Jar, Cover, Lahore, Figures & Animals, Swags Of Fabric, 1920s, 9 1/2 In. 5100.00
Jardiniere, Black Basalt, Vine, Grape Garlands, Classical Figures, 9 In., Pair 920.00
Jardiniere, Classical Figures, Swags, Lion's Heads, Light Green, 10 1/4 x 8 3/4 In. 220.00
Jardiniere, Jasper Dip, Lilac, Applied White Muses, Late 19th Century, 8 In. 690.00
Jardiniere, White On Light Blue, Classical Figures, Grapevine, Lion Head, 6 1/2 In. 280.00
Jug, Ale, Jasperware, Dark Blue, Marked, 7 1/2 In. 450.00
Jug, Argentaware, Majolica, Bird & Fan Design, 1870, 9 1/2 In. 860.00
Jug, Argentaware, Majolica, Sunflower, Hexagonal, 1882, 8 1/8 In. 575.00
Jug, Black Basalt, Central Bacchanalian Boys Frieze, 1800, 7 3/4 In. 1725.00
Jug, Black Basalt, Flowers, Rope Twist Handle, 6 1/8 In. 290.00
Jug, Black Basalt, Putti Between Bands Of Engine Turning, 7 1/4 In. 2875.00
Jug, Black Basalt, Scrolling Leaves, Motto, Harry Barnard, c.1898, 5 In. 340.00
Jug, Club, Black Basalt, Rosso Antico, Arabesque Floral Relief, 6 In. 1090.00
Jug, Club, Drab Ware, Hunt Subject, Grapevine Border, c.1830, 7 3/8 In. 490.00
Jug, Club, Flowers, 1870, 7 1/2 In. 490.00
Jug, Club, Hinged Lid, Black Basalt, Flowers, Enamel, 6 3/4 In. 460.00
Jug, Jasper Dip, Etruscan, Yellow, Applied Black Classical Relief, 1930, 6 In. 750.00
Jug, Jasper Dip, Yellow, Applied Black Classical Relief, 1930, 2 1/2 In. 260.00
Jug, Kenlock Ware, Black Basalt, Foliage Border, Rope Twist Handle, c.1900, 7 In. 5460.00
Jug, Liverpool Style, Black & White Transfer, Ulysses Ship, 10 3/4 In. 1150.00
Jug, Rosso Antico, Egyptian, Club Form, Black, White Sphinx On Side Of Bird, 7 In. 980.00
Ladle, Soup, Queen's Ware, Banded Foliage Vine, Signed, 19th Century, 11 1/4 In. 315.00
Lamp, Cover, Black Basalt, Vestal, Seated Female Figure Upon Oval Lamp, 9 In. 1495.00
Lamp, Oil, Basalt, 3 Dolphins On Tripod Base, 7 In. 250.00

Lamp, Oil, Black Basalt Classical Relief, Scrolled Handle, Leaves, 5 5/8 In. 575.00
Lamp, Oil, Queen's Ware, Cherub In Landscape Scene, Emile Lessore, 1869, 6 In. 630.00
Match Holder, Jasper Dip, Green, White, Classical & Floral Relief, 3 3/4 In. 75.00
Medallion, Bacchanalia Boys, Wedgwood & Bentley, 3 1/2 x 5 In. 1456.00
Mug, Caneware, Children In Landscape, Blue Enamel Trim, 3 3/8 In. 1265.00
Mug, Jasper Dip, Dark Blue, White Fruiting Grapevine Border, 1900, 5 In. 316.00
Mug, Jasper Dip, Dark Blue, White Slip Flowers, 5 1/2 In. 316.00
Mug, Pearlware, 2 Flowers, Gilt Handle, Latin Names Underside, 5 1/8 x 5 In. 220.00
Music Box, Cover, Jasperware, Light Blue, Casket Form, Medallions, 8 1/2 In. 575.00
Nappy, Blue Willow, 4 In. 35.00
Oyster Plate, 5 Wells, Majolica 1760.00
Pie Dish, Cover, Caneware, Dead Game, Fruiting Festoons, 1872, 7 In. 430.00
Pie Dish, Cover, Caneware, Dead Game, Fruiting Grapevine, 8 1/4 In. 430.00
Pie Dish, Cover, Caneware, Dead Game, Fruiting Grapevine, 9 In. 316.00
Pie Dish, Cover, Game, Caneware, Fruiting Grapevine Relief, 10 1/2 In. 345.00
Pie Dish, Raised Game, Terra-Cotta, Oval, 5 x 11 In. 460.00
Pitcher, Classical Figures Making Offerings, Grapevine Border, 6 1/2 In. 105.00
Pitcher, Hot Water, Jasperware, Grecian Women & Cupid, Plated Top, 6 1/2 In. 175.00
Pitcher, Hunt Scene, Hound Handle, 7 1/2 In. 130.00
Pitcher, Jasperware, Hinged Metal Lid, Grecian Figures, Dark Blue, 6 1/2 In. 185.00
Pitcher, Rosso Antico, Floral, Capri Design, 7 In. 110.00
Pitcher, Wheel & Coral, 5 In. 600.00
Plant Pot, Cover, Black Basalt, Scrolled Leaf Handles, 7 3/8 In. 750.00
Plant Pot, Stand, Black Basalt, Mid 19th Century, 4 1/2 In. 400.00
Planter, Jasper Dip, Dark Blue, White Classical Relief Of Muses, 6 1/4 In. 490.00
Planter, Jasper Dip, Muses, Garlands, Sage Green, Marked, 6 1/8 x 5 1/4 In. 135.00
Plaque, Black Basalt, Hercules Strangling The Nemean Lion, 7 1/2 In. 805.00
Plaque, Black Basalt, Lioness & Cupid, Oval, 10 7/8 In. 2300.00
Plaque, Black Basalt, The Judgment Of Hercules, Gilt Frame, 19th Century, 12 In. 1610.00
Plaque, Fairyland Luster, Picnic By River, Trees, Checkered Border, 1920s, 10 In. 6000.00
Plaque, Jasperware, Light Blue, Cupid, 5 3/4 In. 545.00
Plaque, Jasperware, Light Blue, Muses, 19th Century, 4 x 10 In. 490.00
Plaque, Venus & Cupid As Night, The Other Day, 19th Century, 11 In., Pair 575.00
Plate, Black Basalt, Rosso Antico, Fruiting Grapevine Border, 7 1/2 In., Pair 690.00
Plate, Blue Willow, 9 7/8 In. 65.00
Plate, Dog With Gun & Catch Of The Day, 9 In. 1045.00
Plate, Evangeline, Flow Blue, Down The Long Street She Passed, 10 In. 300.00
Plate, Jasperware, Light Blue, White, Mother's Day, 1987, 6 5/8 In. 50.00
Plate, Jasperware, Lilac, 9 1/2 In. 200.00
Plate, Monkey On Branch, Vine Border, 8 1/2 In. 605.00
Plate, Passion Flower, 8 1/2 In. 410.00
Plate, Queen's Ware, Black Transfer, Leaf Border, Central Sailing Ship, 10 In. 430.00
Plate, Queen's Ware, Enamel Center, Cupid & Psyche, Signed, c.1870, 8 3/4 In. 635.00
Plate, Shell & Seaweed, 8 3/4 In. 165.00
Plate, Strawberry & Grape, Turquoise, 8 1/2 In. 385.00
Plate, Trophy, Jasperware, Black, White Classical Relief, Festoons, 8 3/4 In. 1265.00
Platter, Argentaware Shell, 21 In. 1100.00
Platter, Baltimore, Floral Border, Transfer, Mark, 20 3/4 In. 290.00
Platter, Blue Willow, Rectangular, 12 1/4 In. 170.00
Platter, Boat, Wave Border, Brown Ground, 13 In. 495.00
Platter, Majolica, Salmon, Vegetation Scene, Light Blue Ground, 25 1/4 In. 4900.00
Platter, Majolica, Strawberry, Oval, 1880, 13 In. 920.00
Platter, Queen's Ware, Armorial, Green Oats Border, Gilt Berries, Enameled, 20 In. 575.00
Platter, Queen's Ware, Oval, 1774, 12 3/4 In. 476.00
Portrait Medallion, Black Basalt, Central Crown Supported By 2 Angels, 3 In. 315.00
Potpourri, Cover, Black Basalt Classical Frieze, Leaves, 6 In. 1265.00
Potpourri, Cover, Black Basalt Foliage Relief, 3 Dolphin Feet, 5 1/4 In. 1495.00
Potpourri, Cover, Jasper Dip, Light Blue, White Leaf Border, 5 In. 1150.00
Root Pot, Cover, Black Basalt, Cherubs Supporting Laurel Garland, 7 In. 2415.00
Sauce, Wicker, Ribbon & Bow, 6 1/2 In. 495.00
Sauceboat, Queen's Ware, Trellis & Scroll, Signed, 19th Century, 8 In. 460.00
Serving Dish, Stand, Biscuit Mold, Liner, 10 In. . . . . *Illus* 1035.00
Serving Dish, Strawberry, Majolica, Beige, Gray, Green, Leaf & Floral, 10 1/4 In. 420.00

Wedgwood, Serving Dish, Stand, Biscuit
Mold, Liner, 10 In.

Wedgwood, Vase, Auro,
Black Basalt, Leaves, 6 1/2 In.

Wedgwood, Vase,
Geometric, Keith
Murray, 1935, 10 3/4 In.

Sugar, Jasperware, Dark Blue, Marked, 3 1/4 In. 85.00
Sugar, Jasperware, Grecian Figures, White Leaves On Cover, 3 1/2 x 4 In. 110.00
Tankard, Black Basalt, Central Frieze With Children Hunting, 5 3/4 In. 1495.00
Tankard, Cover, Jasper Dip, Grapevines, Cobalt Blue, Branch Handle, 8 In. 110.00
Tea Canister, Cover, Children Scene, White Classical Relief, 5 3/8 In. 430.00
Tea Cup, Saucer, Caneware, Red Enamel Anthemion Banded Border, 5 In. 860.00
Teakettle, Cover, Black Basalt, c.1897, 6 1/4 In. 575.00
Teakettle, Cover, Black Basalt, Fruiting Grapevine Finial, 9 In. 400.00
Teapot, Cover, Arabesque Floral Body, Sunflower Finial, Early 19th Century, 3 3/4 In. 290.00
Teapot, Cover, Black Basalt, Bamboo Molded Body, Factory Mark, c.1897, 6 1/4 In. 575.00
Teapot, Cover, Black Basalt, Flowers, Enamel, Mid 19th Century, 8 1/4 In. 520.00
Teapot, Cover, Jasper Dip, Black, Applied White Classical Medallions, 4 In. 2070.00
Teapot, Cover, Rosso Antico, Spaniel Finial, Floral Body, 19th Century, 7 1/4 In. 575.00
Teapot, Cover, White Stoneware, Arabesque Floral Banding, Stippled Ground, 5 In. 200.00
Teapot, Strainer, Jasperware, Cobalt Blue, Classical, Ashburton Finial, 8 1/2 In. 770.00
Tobacco Jar, Cover, Jasper Dip, Dark Blue, Tavern Figures, White Relief, 7 In. 690.00
Tobacco Jar, Domed Lid, White Band At Top 185.00
Toothpick, Grape & Leaf, 2 1/4 In. 95.00
Tray, Earthenware, Landscape Scene, Birds Surrounding Fairy Figure, 16 3/4 In. 460.00
Tray, Fairyland Luster, Lily, Fairy Gondola, Birds, 1920s, 13 In. 4500.00
Urn, Cover, Black & White, Classical Figures, Turned Foot, Acorn Finial, 14 In., Pair ... 1680.00
Urn, Cover, Jasper Dip, Crimson, White Grapevine Swags, 16 In. 2970.00
Urn, Victoria Ware, White Classical Figures, Dark Teal Blue, Pedestal, 7 In. 495.00
Vase, Agate Ware, Black Basalt, Festoon Border, Handles, 10 1/2 In. 315.00
Vase, Agate Ware, Leaf Borders, Handles, Wedgwood & Bentley, 14 In. 1380.00
Vase, Auro, Black Basalt, Leaves, 6 1/2 In. ....*Illus* 1840.00
Vase, Bamboo, Black Basalt, Oval Base, 19th Century, 4 5/8 In. 980.00
Vase, Black Basalt, Central Arabesque Floral Band, 4 Paw Feet, Handles, 9 In. 800.00
Vase, Black Basalt, Child Seated, Flanked By 3 Cornucopia Spouts, 6 5/8 In. 1725.00
Vase, Black Basalt, Classical Figures, Red, Blue, White Lattice Border, 9 3/4 In. 4025.00
Vase, Black Basalt, Classical Medallions Between Laurel Festoon, 8 1/4 In. 520.00
Vase, Black Basalt, Cybele, Grapevine Handles, 9 3/4 In. 1380.00
Vase, Black Basalt, Flowers, Enamel, Late 19th Century, 6 1/4 In. 546.00
Vase, Black Basalt, Fruiting Grapevine Festoons, Wedgwood & Bentley, 5 In. 920.00
Vase, Black Basalt, Lion Mask Handles, Floral Body, Enamel, 5 In. 520.00
Vase, Black Basalt, Lion Mask Handles, Floral Sprays, Enamel, 4 In., Pair 1150.00
Vase, Black Basalt, Molded Leaves Relief, England, c.1900, 9 5/8 In., Pair 400.00
Vase, Black Basalt, Red, Black Classical Design, 1858, 5 7/8 In. 2300.00
Vase, Black Basalt, Red, Black Classical Figures, 1800, 13 In. 4900.00
Vase, Black Basalt, Red, Black, White, Spearhead, Dot Border, 7 1/4 In. 3220.00
Vase, Black Basalt, Rosso Antico, Florets, 7 1/2 In. 546.00
Vase, Black Basalt, Silver Overlay, c.1900, 6 In. 460.00
Vase, Butterfly Luster, Exotic Butterflies, Daisy Makeig-Jones, c.1920, 7 3/4 In. 3025.00
Vase, Cover, Applied White Dancing Hours Relief, Leaf Border, 1862, 9 In. 400.00
Vase, Cover, Bacchus Handles, Grapevine, Wedgwood & Bentley, c.1775, 10 1/4 In. 978.00
Vase, Cover, Black Basalt, Central Frieze Border, Wedgwood & Bentley, 9 In. 2070.00

Vase, Cover, Black Basalt, Classical Figures, Leaf Border, England, 9 In. 1035.00
Vase, Cover, Jasper Dip, Applied White Relief, England, 1930, 8 3/4 In. 860.00
Vase, Cover, Jasper Dip, Pale Lilac, Arabesque Flowers, 7 In. 1610.00
Vase, Cover, Jasper Dip, Tricolor, White Classical Medallions, 8 3/8 In. 1495.00
Vase, Dragon Luster, Pattern 4829, Blue Exterior, Mother-Of-Pearl Interior, 11 In. 1150.00
Vase, Earthenware, Brown Slip Banding, Field Of Dots, Mustard Yellow, 5 In. 490.00
Vase, Figural Scenes, Old Age & Infancy, Youth & Manhood, Handles, 7 In., Pair 1265.00
Vase, Foo Lion Handles, Ivory Vellum, Gilt Foliage, 10 In. 316.00
Vase, Geometric, Keith Murray, 1935, 10 3/4 In. ....*Illus* 250.00
Vase, Gilt Leaves, Ivory Vellum, Enameled, 9 3/4 In. 258.00
Vase, Gilt Leaves, Lilac Ground, Handles, 1885, 10 3/4 In. 140.00
Vase, Jasper Dip, Crimson, White Classical Relief, Portland, c.1920, 4 In. 2250.00
Vase, Jasper Dip, Disc Cover, Light Blue, Leaf Borders, 6 5/8 In. 430.00
Vase, Jasper Dip, Light Blue, Applied White Relief Of Cherubs, 7 3/4 In., Pair 400.00
Vase, Jasper Dip, Light Blue, White Relief Blind Man's Bluff, 6 1/2 In. 430.00
Vase, Jasper Dip, Lilac, White Classical Relief, Gadroon Border, 1871, 9 In. 545.00
Vase, Jasper Dip, Portland, Light Blue, White Classical Relief, 6 In. 290.00
Vase, Jasper Dip, Yellow, Applied Black Floral Borders, 1930, 5 In., Pair 805.00
Vase, Jasper Dip, Yellow, Applied Black Foliage Borders, 1930, 8 In. 546.00
Vase, Jasperware, Dark Blue, 3 Different Scenes, Marked, 5 x 3 In., Pair 185.00
Vase, Jasperware, Light Blue, White Classical Medallions Below Swags, 8 In. 290.00
Vase, Jasperware, Lilac Medallions, Grapes, Florets, Handles, 6 3/4 In. 630.00
Vase, Lady Templeton Design, Cream Ground, 6 1/2 In., Pair 630.00
Vase, Laurel Festoons, Goat Head, Handles, Wedgwood & Bentley, c.1775, 8 1/2 In. 920.00
Vase, Pearlware, Brown Slip, Green Glaze Basket Weave, Rope Handles, 5 In., Pair 520.00
Vase, Portland, Blue Glaze, White Classical Relief, Dark Blue Ground, 10 1/4 In. 1150.00
Vase, Portland, Jasper Dip, Dark Blue, White Classical Relief, 10 In. 1725.00
Vase, Portrait, Jasper Dip, Black, Applied White Relief, 6 1/2 In. 980.00
Vase, Potpourri, Cover, Caneware, Upturned Loop Handles, Classical, 1830, 8 In. 290.00
Vase, Queen's Ware, 2 Children In Landscape Scene, 1875, 12 1/2 In. 1840.00
Vase, Queen's Ware, Cherubs & Children In Landscape Scene, Handles, 8 In. 980.00
Vase, Queen's Ware, Cherubs On Either Side, Emile Lessore, 1862, 7 3/4 In. 7475.00
Vase, Queen's Ware, Vase, Putti On Either Side, Handles, 1866, 11 3/4 In. 690.00
Vase, Spill, Jasper Dip, Yellow, Applied Blue Leaves, 3 7/8 In. 980.00

WELLER pottery was first made in 1872 in Fultonham, Ohio. The firm
moved to Zanesville, Ohio, in 1882. Art wares were introduced in
1893. Hundreds of lines of pottery were produced, including
Louwelsa, Eocean, Dickens Ware, and Sicardo, before the pottery
closed in 1948.

LOUWELSA
WELLER

Appletree, Vase, Signed, 9 In. 350.00
Ardsley, Console, Kingfisher Flower Frog, 16 1/2 In. 735.00
Ardsley, Vase, Pillow, 7 1/2 x 8 In. 173.00
Aurelian, Ewer, Blackberry Design, Marked, 3 In. 316.00
Aurelian, Lamp Base, Oil, 2 Ivory Rose Medallions, Signed, C. Mitchell, 10 x 11 In. 633.00

Weller, Birdimal
Type, Vase, Incised
Birds In Trees,
Rhead, 14 In.

Weller, Coppertone, Sprinkler,
Garden, Frog, 14 x 18 In.

Weller, Louwelsa,
Vase, Owl On
Branch,
Ed Abel, 20 In.

Aurelian, Mug, Grape & Leaf Design, Left Handed, 4 1/2 In. 375.00
Baldin, Umbrella Stand, 22 1/2 In. 633.00
Baldin, Vase, 4 1/2 x 8 In. 173.00
Baldin, Vase, Blue, 10 1/4 In. 575.00
Bedford Matte, Umbrella Stand, Embossed Floral Rim, Green Matte Glaze, 20 x 11 In. .. 460.00
Birdimal Type, Vase, Incised Birds In Trees, Rhead, 14 In. ....*Illus* 2530.00
Blossom, Vase, 6 In. 225.00
Blue Drapery, Candlestick, Stamped, 7 1/2 In., Pair 150.00
Blue Drapery, Jardiniere, Blue Glaze, Pink Floral Highlights, 5 1/2 In. 115.00
Blue Ware, Jardiniere, Dancing Grecian Maidens, Rose Garland Band At Rim, 7 In. 125.00
Blue Ware, Jardiniere, Rosettes, Smudged Black Glaze, 6 1/4 x 8 In. 110.00
Blue Ware, Vase, Grecian Women, Dance Pose, Bunch Of Grapes Dangling, 9 In. 155.00
Blue Ware, Vase, Grecian Women, Rose Garland Bands Circling Rim, 10 1/2 In. 135.00
Bonito, Vase, Flowers, Marked, Half-Kiln Ink Stamp, 9 1/2 In. 85.00
Bonito, Vase, Flowers, Myrtle, 11 1/2 In. 295.00
Bonito, Vase, Flowers, Orange, Brown, Green Stripes On Base, Cream Ground, 9 In. 350.00
Breton, Bowl, 2 3/4 In. 150.00
Brighton, Figurine, Woodpecker, 5 In. 520.00
Bronze Ware, Lamp Vase, Rust, Gold Finish, 11 3/4 In. 470.00
Burntwood, Jardiniere, 11 1/2 In. 300.00
Burntwood, Vase, Unmarked, 5 3/4 In. 170.00
Camelot, Vase, White, Yellow, 4 3/8 In. 275.00
Cameo, Basket, Hanging, Blue, White Flowers, 7 1/2 In. ....72.00 to 105.00
Cameo, Basket, Hanging, Peach, White Flowers, 5 In. 65.00
Cameo, Basket, Peach, White Flowers, Marked, 7 1/2 In. ....65.00 to 90.00
Cameo, Ewer, Peach, Marked, 10 In. 100.00
Cameo, Vase, Blue, White Flowers, 6 1/2 In. 135.00
Coppertone, Console, 3 1/2 x 15 1/4 In. 690.00
Coppertone, Console, Flower Frog On Lily Pad, Incised, 4 1/4 x 4 In. 290.00
Coppertone, Flower Frog, Turtle Perched, Water Lilies, 6 x 17 In. 1955.00
Coppertone, Flower Frog, Water Lily Blossom, 4 3/4 x 5 In. 750.00
Coppertone, Pitcher, Fish Handle, 7 1/2 In. 1850.00
Coppertone, Sprinkler, Garden, Frog, 14 x 18 In. ....*Illus* 5500.00
Coppertone, Tile, 25 Separate Squares, Frame, 6 1/8 In. 355.00
Coppertone, Turtle, Signed, 5 1/2 In. 310.00
Coppertone, Vase, 2 Frog Handles, 8 In. 1600.00
Coppertone, Vase, 2 Handles, Green Patina, 7 In. 345.00
Coppertone, Vase, Bulbous, 6 1/2 x 5 1/4 In. 750.00
Coppertone, Vase, Frog Trying To Scale Group Of Reeds Swaying In Breeze, 9 In. 405.00
Coppertone, Vase, Green, Brown & Black Matte Glaze, Signed, 6 1/2 In. 300.00
Coppertone, Vase, Signed, 9 In. 475.00
Copra, Jardiniere & Pedestal, Tulip Design, 8 In. 1380.00
Delsa, Basket, Relief Flowers, Leaves, 7 In. 60.00
Dickens Ware I, Vase, Dark Blue, Signed, 11 In. 385.00
Dickens Ware I, Vase, Portrait Of Young Victorian Woman, Dark Green, 12 1/2 In. 605.00
Dickens Ware II, Mug, Stag Head Design, Handle, Sgraffito, 5 3/4 In. 375.00
Dickens Ware II, Vase, Kitten Group Cuddling, Green Eyes, Gray, White, 16 In. 2090.00
Dickens Ware II, Vase, Monk Pouring Draught From A Large Flagon Into A Mug, 10 In. . 660.00
Dickens Ware II, Vase, Narcissus, Flower Blossoms, Cream, White, Tan, 1897, 10 In. 290.00
Dickens Ware II, Vase, Old Woman & Old Man With Shovel Beside A Church, 13 In. ... 275.00
Dickens Ware II, Vase, Pilgrim On Tree-Lined Path, Marked, 9 In. 695.00
Dickens Ware II, Vase, Victorian Woman, Feathered Hat, R.G. Turner, c.1900, 12 1/2 In. . 615.00
Dickens Ware II, Vase, Woman & Moon, Lady Sitting On Moon, 9 In. 1450.00
Elberta, Jardiniere, Green & Brown, Signed, 5 1/2 In. 135.00
Eocean, Jardiniere, Iris & Leaves, Green & Cream Ground, c.1900, 12 3/4 In. 470.00
Eocean, Jardiniere, Jonquil Design, 3 Bun Feet, 7 In. 330.00
Eocean, Pitcher, Red Cherries, Green Leaf Design, 6 1/4 In. 575.00
Eocean, Vase, Berries & Leaves, Pastel, Black, Lavender Ground, 18 x 6 In. 1035.00
Eocean, Vase, Chrysanthemums, Albert Haubrich, 10 1/2 In. 785.00
Eocean, Vase, Ivory Wild Roses, Red, Gray Shaded Ground, 6 x 4 1/2 In. 375.00
Eocean, Vase, Leaves & Berries, Shaded Ground, Levi J. Burgeus, 1898, 8 1/4 In. 200.00
Eocean, Vase, Mauve, Yellow, Maroon Chrysanthemums, 10 1/2 In. 770.00
Eocean, Vase, Pink Cherry Blossoms, Brown, Gray Shaded Ground, 8 1/4 In. 345.00

Eocean, Vase, Pink Nasturtium, Gray Shaded Ground, 5 3/4 x 5 In. 315.00
Eocean, Vase, Pink Rose, Lavender Ground, 7 x 5 1/4 In. 374.00
Eocean, Vase, White, Gray Roses, Gray Shaded Ground, 14 In. 290.00
Etna, Jardiniere, Blue To Gray, Molded Grapes, 7 1/4 x 9 1/2 In. 170.00
Etna, Mug, Clown With Wide Brim Hat, Embossed, 5 1/8 In. 198.00
Etna, Vase, 3 Lavender Nasturtiums, 10 1/2 In. 195.00
Etna, Vase, Dragon Rim, Gray, Ivory, Pink Ground, 9 1/2 x 4 1/4 In. 520.00
Etna, Vase, Iris, Gray To White Ground, 11 In. 4450.00
Etna, Vase, Purple, Mauve Nasturtiums, 5 In. 175.00
Flemish, Pedestal, Exotic Flowers, Blue Parrot, Pink Cockatoo, 21 5/8 In. 340.00
Flemish, Umbrella Stand, 22 In. 1350.00
Flemish, Window Box, Designs Of Cows & Ducks, 12 In. 1400.00
Floretta, Vase, Embossed Pink Poppies, Gray Ground, 11 1/2 In. 360.00
Floretta, Vase, Pale Pink Flowers, Light Green Ground, 5 7/8 In. 175.00
Forest, Jardiniere, Forest Scene, Pedestal, 28 3/4 x 12 In. 575.00
Forest, Lamp Base, Forest Scene, 11 1/4 x 5 In. 460.00
Forest, Vase, Country, Woods, 7 In. 350.00
Garden Ware, Squirrel, On Bowl Edge, Brown & Green, 5 1/2 In. 65.00
Geode, Vase, Shooting Stars, White, Blue Ground, 5 1/2 In. 405.00
Glendale, Vase, Birds, Nesting, Marked, 6 1/2 In. 290.00
Glendale, Vase, Long Legged Plover Guarding Nest, Speckled Eggs, 12 In. 1610.00
Glendale, Vase, Wildlife & Flowers, Goldfinch Perched In Nest, 11 3/4 In. 1955.00
Gloria, Vase, Tan, Flowers, White & Cream, 5 1/2 In. 75.00
Greora, Vase, Band Of Ducks, Embossed, 5 In. 90.00
Greora, Vase, Green, Copper, 5 In. 115.00
Hobart, Flower Frog, Youth, Nude, Carrying A Goose, Marked, 9 In. 115.00
Hobart, Wall Pocket, Figural, Lady With Outstretched Arms, 8 1/8 In. 360.00
Hudson, Tile, Swimming Goose, Matte Glaze, Frame, Square, 4 In. 605.00
Hudson, Vase, Base, Blue, Floral Decoration, Hood, 15 In. 3190.00
Hudson, Vase, Blue & Yellow Iris, Yellow To Sage Green Ground, England, 3 x 8 1/4 In. .. 495.00
Hudson, Vase, Bud, Blue, Decorated, 10 In. 200.00
Hudson, Vase, Cylindrical, Seascape, McLaughlin, 9 1/4 x 3 3/4 In. 2415.00
Hudson, Vase, Fishing Boats, Flying Gulls, Hester Pillsbury, Signed, 9 In. 1344.00
Hudson, Vase, Horse Standing Among Flowering Bushes, 10 3/8 In. 2325.00
Hudson, Vase, Nasturtium, Green, Pink Shaded Ground, 10 1/2 In. 230.00
Hudson, Vase, White Roses, Sage Green To Blue Ground, McLaughlin, 12 In. 990.00
Hudson, Vase, Yellow Wild Rose Design, White Ground, Marked, 7 7/8 In. 460.00
Ivory, Jardiniere, Cream, Cupids, Stamped, 6 1/2 In. 85.00
Jap Birdimal, Vase, Cobalt Blue Trees, Incised Moon, Ocher Glaze, Blue, Gray, 8 1/2 In. .. 360.00
Jap Birdimal, Vase, Marked, 8 1/2 In. 450.00
Juneau, Vase, Pink & Rose, Dorothy England Initials, 6 In. 145.00
Juneau, Vase, Pink, Pastel Drip, Initialed Y, 6 1/4 x 5 In. 95.00
Kenova, Vase, Red Peony Flowers, Green Leaves, Rust Ground, 8 1/8 In. 605.00
Klyro, Vase, Ivory, Dogwood Blossoms, 7 1/8 In. 60.00
Lamar, Vase, Burgundy, Tapered, 8 1/2 In. 255.00
LaSa, Vase, Greens, Orange, Purple, Pine Trees, 13 5/8 In. 495.00
Lorbeek, Vase, Lavender, Modern Shape, Marked, 8 1/2 In. 140.00

Weller, Sicardo, Vase,
Chrysanthemums,
Iridescent, Signed,
1902, 26 1/2 In.

Weller, Silvertone, Console, Raised
Design, Flower Frog, 12 1/4 In.

Louwelsa, Clock, 5-Point Star Shape, Chrysanthemums, Enamel Face, Signed, 10 In. 860.00
Louwelsa, Clock, Mantel, Bright Yellow, Orange Chrysanthemums, 10 x 11 In. 925.00
Louwelsa, Clock, Mantel, Orange Nasturtiums, 10 1/2 x 12 1/2 In. 545.00
Louwelsa, Clock, Mantel, Roses, 11 x 11 In. 590.00
Louwelsa, Ewer, Berry Vines, Gold, Green, Brown Ground, 12 1/2 In. 525.00
Louwelsa, Ewer, Dark Brown, Blackberry Vine, 12 1/4 In. 775.00
Louwelsa, Ewer, Pansy Design, Dark Blue, Squat, 3 1/4 In. 495.00
Louwelsa, Jardiniere, Pedestal, Signed 2200.00
Louwelsa, Pedestal, Portrait Of St. Bernard, Dark Chocolate Ground, 21 5/8 In. 145.00
Louwelsa, Vase, Baby Chicks Looking For Grain, Straw Pile, C. Leffler, 15 In. .2970.00 to 3024.00
Louwelsa, Vase, Blackberry Leaves, Blooms, Stalks, Fruit, C. Minnie Terry, 17 1/8 In. . . . 990.00
Louwelsa, Vase, Blue Poppy Design, 11 5/8 In. 1320.00
Louwelsa, Vase, Brown, Flowers, Signed, 11 In. 275.00
Louwelsa, Vase, Orange Roses, Shaded Ground, 12 3/4 x 4 In. 290.00
Louwelsa, Vase, Owl On Branch, Ed Abel, 20 In. . . . .*Illus* 4950.00
Louwelsa, Vase, Painted Floral Sprig, Brown High Glaze, 1918, 8 In. 295.00
Louwelsa, Vase, Pansy Style Florals, White, Deep Azure Blue, 6 In. 990.00
Louwelsa, Vase, Pillow, Portrait, Dog, Brown, White Eyes, Red Tongue, 7 3/4 In. 850.00
Louwelsa, Vase, Portrait, Dog, Mouth Open, Dark Brown Ground, 11 In. 1320.00
Louwelsa, Vase, Squat, Handle, Orange Clover, Dark Ground, Signed, Stamped, 3 1/2 In. . 175.00
Louwelsa, Vase, Underglaze Of Palm Frond, 3 1/2 In. 34.00
Louwelsa, Vase, Underglaze Of Yellow Iris, 11 In. 112.00
Louwelsa, Vase, Wild Roses, Sarah Reid McLaughlin, Drilled For Lamp, 15 3/8 In. 1058.00
Louwelsa, Vase, Wild Roses, White Slip, c.1900, 15 3/8 In. 1060.00
Louwelsa, Vase, Yellow Nasturtiums, 9 1/4 x 5 3/4 In. 315.00
Louwelsa, Vase, Yellow, Ivory, Brown Buttercup, Green, Brown, 13 In. 495.00
Malvern, Vase, Brown, Yellow, Green, 8 In. 135.00
Malvern, Vase, Bulbous, 2 Handles, Initialed H, 7 x 6 1/2 In. 150.00
Malvern, Vase, Pillow, Yellow Buds, 8 1/4 x 7 1/2 In. 145.00
Marengo, Vase, Blue Ground, Dark Blue Base, 8 1/8 In. 190.00
Marvo, Bowl, Flower Frog, 8 1/2 In. 150.00
Marvo, Vase, Green, Cylindrical, 8 1/2 In. 145.00
Marvo, Vase, Palm Tree & Fern Design, 7 In. 150.00
Marvo, Window Box, Ferns, Leaves, 11 In. 105.00
Muskota, Figurine, Fishing Boy, 6 1/2 In. . . . . .210.00 to 245.00
Muskota, Figurine, Kingfisher, Flower Frog, Stamped, 8 x 6 1/2 In. 144.00
Muskota, Flower Frog, Light Green, Yellow, 2 5/8 In. 385.00
Novelty, Dog, Pop-Eye, Black & Brown, White Ground, Signed, 4 In. 410.00
Novelty, Figurine, Dachshund, 3 x 6 In. 85.00
Oak Leaf, Vase, Basket, Green, 9 1/2 In. 55.00
Oak Leaf, Vase, Raised Leaves & Acorns, 8 1/2 In. 175.00
Oak Leaf, Vase, Raised Leaves & Acorns, Green, 6 1/2 In. 125.00
Orris, Wall Pocket, Green & Brown, 8 In. 175.00
Panella, Pitcher, Gray, Green & Yellow, 6 1/2 In. 125.00
Panella, Vase, Pastel Blue, Cornucopia Shape, Marked, 5 3/4 In. 60.00
Panella, Vase, Yellow Pansy, Leaves, 3 Applied Feet, 5 3/4 x 17 1/2 In. 125.00
Raydance, Vase, Mint Green & Cream, Marked, 2 Handles, 9 In. 65.00
Roba, Vase, Rose Blossoms, Leaves, 2 Handles, Pale Orange Ground, 12 1/2 In. 115.00
Roma, Candelabrum, Garland Of Flowers, Marked, 8 In. 175.00
Roma, Flowerpot, Draped Garland, 3 3/4 x 5 In. 65.00
Roma, Wall Pocket, Cornucopia, Flowers, 10 1/4 In. . . . . .187.00 to 265.00
Sabrinian, Vase, Blue, Mauve, Sea Horse, Handles, Stamped, Initialed H, 10 1/2 In. 275.00
Sicardo, Candlestick, Luster Floral Glaze, Circular Drip Pan, 8 1/2 In. 365.00
Sicardo, Lamp Base, Embossed Gingko Leaves, Green Base, 13 7/8 In. . . . . . . .2420.00 to 2464.00
Sicardo, Vase, Blue & Green Iridescent, 5 In. 675.00
Sicardo, Vase, Celadon, Gold Poppies, Gold, Purple Iridescent Ground, 14 1/2 x 7 In. . . . 2925.00
Sicardo, Vase, Chrysanthemums, Iridescent, Signed, 1902, 26 1/2 In. . . . .*Illus* 11550.00
Sicardo, Vase, Flowers, Iridescent Glaze, Signed, 9 In. 2400.00
Sicardo, Vase, Leaf & Vine Design, Blue, Green Leaves, Iridescent, 6 In. 770.00
Sicardo, Vase, Shamrock Design, Iridescent, 5 In. 715.00
Sicardo, Vase, Stylized Chrysanthemums & Leaves, Iridescent, J. Sicard, c.1902, 26 In. . . 8730.00
Sicardo, Vase, Swirled Poppies, Gold, Blue, Green, Purple Iridescent, 8 x 5 In. 2925.00
Silvertone, Console, Raised Design, Flower Frog, 12 1/4 In. . . . .*Illus* 375.00

Silvertone, Vase, Grape Clusters, 2 Leaves, Handles, 6 3/8 In. 230.00
Silvertone, Vase, Green Matte Glaze, 7 3/4 In. 385.00
Silvertone, Vase, Green, Yellow, 2 Center Curved Handles, 5 5/8 In. 275.00
Silvertone, Vase, Tulip Poplar Leaves, 2 Handles, 8 In. 550.00
Souevo, Vase, Incised & Painted Native American Design, 2 Handles, 12 1/2 In. 410.00
Souevo, Vase, Native American Design, Signed, 5 1/2 In. 275.00
Souevo, Wall Pocket, Bands, Cone Form, Terra-Cotta, Cream, 6 In. 165.00
Sydonia, Vase, Double, Mottled Blue Glaze, Flared, 7 1/2 x 7 In. 65.00
Turada, Lamp Base, Gourd Shape, 10 x 10 1/2 In. 546.00
Turada, Lamp, Oil, 4 Bun Feet, 7 1/2 In. 125.00
Turkis, Vase, Lamp, Red Glaze, Closed Strap Handles, 7 1/2 In. 168.00
Turkis, Vase, Red Glaze, Medium Green Over Glaze, Ridged Swirl Handles, 4 3/4 In. ... 110.00
Turkis, Vase, Red Glaze, Ruffled Top, Footed, 8 In. 280.00
Turkis, Vase, Red Glaze, Spring Green, Yellow Dry Glaze, 4 3/4 In. 80.00
Tutone, Wall Pocket, Green, Raised Flowers, Rose, 10 1/2 In. .... 275.00 to 280.00
Velva, Jar, Cover, Brown, Handles, 11 1/8 In. 112.00
Velva, Vase, Brown, 7 x 5 1/2 In. 46.00
Warwick, Candlestick, Brown, Green, 7 1/8 In. 66.00
Warwick, Console, Brown, Green Leaves, 13 1/4 x 3 1/4 In. 132.00
Warwick, Planter, 2 Handles, Signed, 4 x 12 1/2 In. 168.00
Warwick, Planter, Dark Brown Branch Lying On Side, Green Leaves, 12 1/2 In. 77.00
Warwick, Vase, Brown, Green, 2 Tree Trunk Handles, 7 1/8 In. 99.00
Warwick, Vase, Dark Brown Tree, Green Leaves, 9 3/4 In. 165.00
Wild Rose, Basket, Pink, Roses, 5 1/2 In. 40.00
Wild Rose, Bowl, Pink, Roses, Marked, 3 In. 70.00
Wild Rose, Vase, Double, Pink, Roses, 6 In. 75.00
Woodcraft, Ashtray, 7 In. 53.00
Woodcraft, Bowl, Molded Squirrels, On Tree Limbs Eating Nuts, 6 In. 89.00
Woodcraft, Bowl, Squirrel, Black Slip Design, 3 1/2 x 6 1/2 In. 100.00
Woodcraft, Planter, Foxes In A Hole, 4 x 7 3/4 In. 345.00
Woodcraft, Planter, Hanging, Apple Laden Branches, 6 In. 89.00
Woodcraft, Wall Pocket, Branch Form, Flowers, 9 1/2 In. 175.00
Woodcraft, Window Box, Realistic Wood Pattern, 9 In. 32.00
Woodrose, Basket, Hanging, Oaken Bucket, 4 3/4 x 8 1/2 In. .... 143.00 to 180.00
Woodrose, Vase, Rose Floral, Incised, 6 3/4 In. 77.00
Woodrose, Wall Pocket, 6 In. 116.00
Woodrose, Wall Pocket, Oaken Bucket, Lavender, 5 1/2 In. 120.00
Woodrose, Window Box, Oaken Bucket, 9 In. 40.00
Zona, Umbrella Stand, Ladies Holding Flower Garlands, 20 x 10 In. 1610.00

WEMYSS ware was made by Robert Heron in Kirkaldy, Scotland, from 1850 to 1929. It is a colorful peasant-type pottery that is occasionally found in the United States.

Biscuit Jar, Cover, Cherries, Leaves & Branches, R. Heron & Son, 1920, 6 1/2 x 7 In. ... 230.00
Biscuit Jar, Plums, 1920s, 4 In. 200.00
Bowl, Porridge, Brown, Cream, 6 x 2 1/2 In. 220.00
Coffeepot, Purple Plums Amongst Branches, Foliage, 7 In. 700.00
Figurine, Cat, Bachelor Button, Dark Olive Green, Bright Blue, Rusty Brown, 10 In. 1135.00
Figurine, Pelican, Shamrock Design, Plichta, 9 In. 394.00
Figurine, Pig, Seated, Black Spots, Pink Nose, Ears, Tail, Scotland, c.1900, 2 1/4 In. 500.00
Figurine, Squirrel, Clover Design, Plichta, 5 1/2 In. 120.00
Honey Pot, Cover, Bees Around A Beehive, Yellow, Green, Brown, Black, Gray, 4 In. ... 105.00
Jug, Cherries & Leaves, Hand Painted, 10 x 15 3/4 In. 1005.00
Rose Plate, 5 1/2 In. 80.00
Soap Dish, Domed Cover, Roses, Rose Buds & Leaves, 5 1/4 x 4 In. 80.00
Vase, Cherry, Slight Brown Line, 1890, 8 In. 250.00

WESTMORELAND GLASS was made by the Westmoreland Glass Company of Grapeville, Pennsylvania, from 1890 to 1984. They made clear and colored glass of many varieties, such as milk glass, pressed glass, and slag glass.

Ashburton, Goblet, Pink, 5 1/2 Oz. 9.00

Beaded Edge, Bowl, Scalloped Rim, Milk Glass 9.00
Beaded Edge, Cup & Saucer, Enameled Fruit 23.00
Beaded Edge, Cup & Saucer, Enameled Peaches, Milk Glass 16.00
Beaded Edge, Plate, Enameled Cardinal, Milk Glass, 7 1/2 In. 40.00
Beaded Edge, Plate, Enameled Fruit, Milk Glass, 7 In. 15.00
Beaded Edge, Plate, Enameled Fruit, Milk Glass, 8 1/2 In. ....19.00 to 28.00
Beaded Edge, Plate, Enameled Strawberries, Milk Glass, 7 1/2 In. 12.00
Beaded Edge, Plate, Milk Glass, 6 In. ....9.00 to 11.00
Beaded Edge, Plate, Milk Glass, 7 1/2 In. 18.00
Beaded Edge, Plate, Milk Glass, 8 1/2 In. 8.00
Beaded Edge, Plate, Milk Glass, 10 1/2 In. 12.00
Beaded Edge, Sherbet, Milk Glass 18.00
Beaded Edge, Sugar, Footed, Milk Glass 18.00
Beaded Grape, Bowl, Cover, Milk Glass, 7 In. 55.00
Bunny On Picket Fence Cover, Dish, Milk Glass, 5 1/2 x 3 3/4 In. 95.00
Cherry, Sugar, Cover, Milk Glass, 8 1/4 In. 45.00
Colonial, Cruet Set, Green, Oval Tray, 3 Piece 80.00
Della Robbia, Candlestick, 2-Light, Stain, 4 In., Pair 350.00
Della Robbia, Nappy, Bell Shape, Handle, Stain 185.00
Della Robbia, Nappy, Heart Shape, Handle, Stain 200.00
Della Robbia, Plate, Dinner, 10 1/2 In. 145.00
Della Robbia, Plate, Stain, 9 In. 49.00
Della Robbia, Punch Bowl, 14 In. 250.00
Della Robbia, Punch Cup 15.00
Della Robbia, Salt & Pepper 50.00
Dolphin & Shell, Vase, Green Marble, 8 1/2 In. 95.00
English Hobnail, Ashtray, Milk Glass 13.00
English Hobnail, Bowl, Footed, Oval, 9 In. 55.00
English Hobnail, Cake Plate, Ruffled Edge, Pedestal, Milk Glass 42.00
English Hobnail, Claret, 4 1/2 In. ....11.00 to 13.00
English Hobnail, Cocktail, Footed, Square, 3 Oz. 12.00
English Hobnail, Cruet, Milk Glass, 5 In. 23.00
English Hobnail, Jam Jar, Cover, Pink 55.00
English Hobnail, Nappy, Pink, 6 In. 16.00
English Hobnail, Plate, 5 1/2 In. 5.00
English Hobnail, Plate, 8 In. 8.00
English Hobnail, Salt, Footed, Triangular 25.00
English Hobnail, Sherbet, Footed, Square ....10.00 to 12.00
English Hobnail, Sugar, Footed, Milk Glass 8.00
English Hobnail, Tumbler, Footed, 5 Oz. 18.00
English Hobnail, Tumbler, Footed, 12 Oz. 24.00
English Hobnail, Vase, Milk Glass, Ruffled Edge, 4 1/2 x 6 In. 18.00
Hen On Nest Cover, Dish, Milk Glass, 3 1/2 In. 19.00
Lilies Of The Valley, Vase, Green Marble, 7 1/2 In. 58.00
Lotus, Salt & Pepper, Light Blue 70.00
Lotus, Sugar & Creamer, Crystal Mist, Yellow Foot, Orchid Tips, 1921 ...... 50.00
Old Quilt, Pitcher, Milk Glass, 7 1/2 In. 48.00
Old Quilt, Rose Bowl, Milk Glass, 7 In. 35.00
Paneled Grape, Bowl, Bell, Footed, Milk Glass, 9 1/2 In. 100.00
Paneled Grape, Bowl, Crimped, Milk Glass, 6 In. 32.00
Paneled Grape, Bowl, Lipped, Footed, Milk Glass, 9 In. 120.00
Paneled Grape, Cake Stand, Milk Glass, 11 In. ....55.00 to 60.00
Paneled Grape, Candlestick, Milk Glass, 4 In., Pair 24.00
Paneled Grape, Candy Dish, Cover, Dark Blue, 5 1/2 In. 28.00
Paneled Grape, Cologne Bottle, Stopper, Milk Glass, Gold Trim 65.00
Paneled Grape, Creamer, Lacy Edge 22.00
Paneled Grape, Creamer, Tall 18.00
Paneled Grape, Cup & Saucer, Milk Glass ....18.00 to 24.00
Paneled Grape, Dresser Set, Milk Glass, 4 Piece 225.00
Paneled Grape, Pitcher, Milk Glass, 16 Oz. 50.00
Paneled Grape, Pitcher, Milk Glass, 32 Oz. ....25.00 to 45.00
Paneled Grape, Plate, Milk Glass, 8 1/2 In. 16.00

Paneled Grape, Puff Box, Milk Glass, Gold Trim 30.00
Paneled Grape, Sauceboat, Milk Glass 32.00
Paneled Grape, Tumbler, Milk Glass 17.00
Paneled Grape, Vase, Bell Shape, Milk Glass, 6 In. 22.00
Paneled Grape, Vase, Bud, Milk Glass, Pink & Blue Flowers, 9 In. 34.00
Paneled Grape, Vase, Milk Glass, 5 1/4 In. 23.00
Paneled Grape, Vase, Milk Glass, 8 1/2 In. 27.00
Paneled Grape, Vase, Milk Glass, 15 In. 85.00
Princess Feather, Basket, Center Handle, 6 1/2 In. 30.00
Princess Feather, Plate, 5 1/4 In. 25.00
Swirl & Ball, Candlestick, Amber, 3 In. 10.00
Swirl & Ball, Vase, Milk Glass, Foil Label, 9 In. 40.00
Thousand Eye, Decanter Set, Crystal, 6 2-Oz. Cordials, Tray, 8 Piece 165.00
Thousand Eye, Goblet, Crystal, 6 1/2 In. 11.00
Thousand Eye, Plate, Salad, Crystal, 8 1/4 In. 12.00
Three Kittens, Plate, 8 In. 50.00

WHEATLEY Pottery was established in 1880. Thomas J. Wheatley had worked in Cincinnati, Ohio, with the founders of the art pottery movement, including M. Louise McLaughlin of the Rookwood Pottery. Wheatley Pottery was purchased by the Cambridge Tile Manufacturing Company in 1927.

Bowl, Embossed, Broad Leaves, Green Matte Glaze, 3 x 11 1/4 In. 460.00
Chamberstick, Medium Green Matte Glaze, Loop Handle, 3 1/2 In. 330.00
Charger, Barbotine, Landscape, Castle By Lake, Incised, 1880, 14 1/2 In. 920.00
Charger, Barbotine, Mountain Landscape, c.1880, 14 1/2 In. 635.00
Jardiniere, 2 Rows Of Leaves, Green Glaze, Signed, 8 3/4 x 11 In. 1090.00
Jardiniere, Black Over Gray Matte Glaze, Dots, Marked, 29 3/4 In., Pair 1540.00
Jardiniere, Dark Green Matte Glaze, Tooled Flowers, Buds, 20 In. 3740.00
Lamp Base, Dark Green Matte Glaze, Peacock Feather Design, 21 In. 1320.00
Lamp Base, Gourd Shape, 4 Buttressed Handles, Green Matte Glaze, 11 x 10 In. .. 2810.00
Lamp Base, Tall Stems, Leaves, Green Matte Glaze, Embossed, 16 1/4 x 10 In. ... 1575.00
Pitcher, Figural Duckling, Incised Wings, Eyes Near Rim, 11 1/4 In. 600.00
Tile, Green, Gold, Black Ground, Square, 1928, 12 x 12 In. 220.00
Tile, Mythical Charging Knight, Lower Body Horse, 1928, Square, 12 In. 990.00
Urn, 4 Buttressed Handles, Matte Green Glaze, Signed, 10 1/4 In. 1035.00
Urn, Bright Yellow Matte, Marked WP, 18 1/2 In. 770.00
Vase, 2 Buttressed Wing Handles, Leaves & Buds, Oatmeal Glaze, 20 1/2 In. 3450.00
Vase, 3 Small Loop Handles, Buttress Feet, Dark Green Glaze, Paper Label, 10 7/8 In. 2100.00
Vase, 4 Buttresses, Green Matte Glaze, 7 1/4 x 9 In. 1800.00
Vase, Arrowhead Leaves, Medium Green Matte Glaze, 12 1/2 x 6 In. 1800.00
Vase, Bright Cranberry, Marked, 25 5/8 In. 605.00
Vase, Broad Leaves Alternating With Buds, Medium Green Matte Glaze, 12 x 7 In. 2700.00
Vase, Brown Matte Glaze, 12 1/2 x 9 In. 2450.00
Vase, Buds, Full-Length Leaves, Medium Matte Green Glaze, 9 1/4 x 7 1/4 In. ... 920.00
Vase, Carved Leaves, Olive Green, 8 1/2 In. 975.00
Vase, Dark Green Matte Glaze, 11 1/2 In. 605.00
Vase, Dark Green Matte Glaze, 3 Angular Handles, 4 1/2 In. 385.00
Vase, Dark Green Matte Glaze, 3 Loop Handles, 4 1/8 In. 440.00
Vase, Dark Green Matte Glaze, 3 Small Loop Handles, 10 7/8 In. 2310.00
Vase, Dark Green Matte Glaze, 3 Stylized Scarabs, 7 5/8 In. 1320.00
Vase, Dark Green Matte Glaze, 4 Elongated Handles, 17 3/8 In. 5000.00
Vase, Dark Green Matte Glaze, Buttresses, 8 1/8 In. 2000.00
Vase, Dark Green Matte Glaze, Deep Tooled Leaves, 8 1/8 In. 1200.00
Vase, Dark Green Matte Glaze, Doorway Arch Design, 13 1/4 In. 2420.00
Vase, Dark Green Matte Glaze, Fiddlehead Ferns, Handles, 11 1/2 In. 2500.00
Vase, Dark Green Matte Glaze, Tall Leaves & Buds, Embossed, 20 x 10 In. 4500.00
Vase, Dark Green Matte Glaze, Tooled Buds, Leaves, 7 3/4 In. 1200.00
Vase, Dark Green Matte Glaze, Tooled Leaf, Bud Design, 20 1/8 In. 5000.00
Vase, Dark Green Matte Glaze, Tooled Leaves, 4 1/8 In. 385.00
Vase, Dark Green Matte Glaze, Tooled Leaves, Marked, 5 3/8 In. 605.00
Vase, Dark Green Matte Glaze, Wild Goose Peering Through Foliage, 10 In. 1760.00

Stains on porcelains can be removed by soaking in a mixture of 2 tablespoons of Polident denture cleaner in 1 quart of tepid water

Set your sundial at noon, June 15. Place it so the shadow falls on the 12.

Wheatley, Vase, Green Matte Glaze, Arches Pattern, Cylindrical, 13 3/4 In.

Wheatley, Vase, Tooled Leaf & Bud Design, Green Matte Glaze, 20 1/8 In.

Vase, Embossed Arrowhead Leaves, Stalks, Green Matte Glaze, 6 x 5 In. 790.00
Vase, Embossed Broad Leaves, Green Matte Glaze, 13 x 9 In. 3940.00
Vase, Flowers, Brushed Brown, Ivory Glaze, 1880, 7 1/2 In. 193.00
Vase, Full Height Leaves, Leathery Matte Green Glaze, Signed, 14 1/4 x 6 1/2 In. 1175.00
Vase, Geometric Design, Green Matte Glaze, 11 1/2 In. 978.00
Vase, Gourd Shape, Dark Green Matte Glaze, 11 In. 1100.00
Vase, Gourd Shape, Dark Green Matte Glaze, 3 Buttressed Handles, 9 1/2 In. 2800.00
Vase, Green Matte Glaze, 4 Buttressed Handles, 14 1/4 x 8 In. 2875.00
Vase, Green Matte Glaze, 4 Cubes With Ridged Leaves, 14 1/4 x 9 1/4 In. 1610.00
Vase, Green Matte Glaze, 4 Rim Buttresses, Drainage Holes, Signed, 11 1/2 In. 2070.00
Vase, Green Matte Glaze, Arches Pattern, Cylindrical, 13 3/4 In. . . . . *Illus* 2420.00
Vase, Green Matte Glaze, Handles, Marked, 14 In. 4180.00
Vase, Lamp, Dark Green Matte Glaze, Dark Brown Wicker Shade, 7 1/4 In. 2750.00
Vase, Leaf & Bud, Dark Green Glaze, 20 1/8 In. 5600.00
Vase, Leaf Design, Dark Green Matte Glaze, 6 1/2 In. 1320.00
Vase, Lobed Rim, 4 Webbed Handles, Green Matte Glaze, 14 1/4 x 8 In. 3150.00
Vase, Ribbed Leaves, Green Matte Glaze, 6 3/4 x 5 In. 955.00
Vase, Ribbed Neck, Rows Of Leaves, Frothy Light Green, Amber Glaze, 7 x 7 In. 900.00
Vase, Stylized Buds, Tall Leaves, Green Matte Glaze, 26 1/2 x 10 1/2 In. 3940.00
Vase, Thick Green Matte Glaze, 8 In. 770.00
Vase, Tooled Leaf & Bud Design, Green Matte Glaze, 20 1/8 In. . . . . *Illus* 5000.00
Vase, Tooled Leaves Curl Away From Rim, Gloppy Glaze, Signed, 5 3/8 In. 616.00
Vase, Tooled Leaves To Body & Rim, Green Matte Glaze, 12 1/2 x 8 3/4 In. 3420.00
Vase, Tooled Leaves, Buds Exterior, Medium Green Matte Glaze, 13 In. 2640.00
Wall Pocket, Broad Leaves Alternating Buds, Medium Green Matte Glaze, 9 In. 675.00
Wall Pocket, Dark Green Matte Glaze, 8 1/8 In. 1430.00
Wall Pocket, Grapes & Leaves, Curdled Green Glaze, 7 x 7 In. 575.00

WHEELING Pottery Company of Wheeling, West Virginia, worked from 1879 to about 1923. The firm went through a number of mergers and name changes during that time. Pottery, semiporcelain, artware, and sanitary wares were made.

Bowl, Leaf Shaped, Flow Blue, Raised Design, Stem Handle, Gold Trim, 11 In. 51.00
Pitcher, Pink Tulip 31.00
Vase, Labelle, Flow Blue, Leaf Design, Cream Ground, Gold Trim, 6 1/8 In. 75.00

WHIELDON was an English potter who worked alone and with Josiah Wedgwood in eighteenth-century England. Whieldon made many pieces in natural shapes, like cauliflowers or cabbages.

Plate, Feather Edge, c.1740, 9 1/2 In. 795.00
Plate, Roses, Moth, Leaf Basket, Green, Mustard Mottled Glaze, Scalloped, 9 1/4 In. 520.00
Platter, Brown Tortoiseshell Glaze, Oval Well, Raised Rim, Octagonal, 12 x 16 3/8 In. . . 275.00

WILLETS Manufacturing Company of Trenton, New Jersey, began work in 1879. The company made Belleek in the late 1880s and 1890s in shapes similar to those used by the Irish Belleek factory. They stopped working about 1912. A variety of marks were used, all including the name Willets.

Bowl, Yellow Flowers, Green Leaves, Yellow Interior, Marked, 7 x 9 In.	300.00
Chalice, Pinecones, Berries & Leaves, Gilt Interior, Signed, 11 1/2 In.	286.00
Chalice, Raspberries & Leaves, Blue & Pink Ground, Signed, 11 In.	341.00
Jardiniere, Raised Gilt Web Design, Alternating Butterflies & Moths, 10 1/2 In.	662.00
Mug, Pinecones & Branches, Handle, Belleek, Brown Snake Mark, 5 1/2 In.	120.00
Pitcher, Yellow Lemon, Green Leaves, Green Ground, Belleek, 11 1/4 x 5 1/2 In.	375.00
Saltcellar, Heart Shape, Gold Trim, c.1905, 1 3/4 In.	73.00
Tankard, Monk, c.1879-1912, 14 3/4 In.	715.00
Teapot, Stylized Mountain Lake, Dark Green Ground, 9 x 5 1/2 In.	275.00
Vase, Blue Design Outlined In Black, Cream Ground, 1912, 10 In.	195.00
Vase, Ivory, 12 1/2 x 4 x 2 1/2 In.	68.00
Vase, Rose, Pink Roses, Soft Cream Ground, 17 x 4 3/4 In.	400.00
Vase, Round Trees All Around, 1909, 12 In.	550.00
Vase, Stylized Scene Of Trees & Clouds, Green, Orange, Brown Glaze, 1906, 5 In.	1904.00

WILLOW pattern has been made in England since 1780. The pattern has been copied by factories in many countries, including Germany, Japan, and the United States. It is still being made. Willow was named for a pattern that pictures a bridge, birds, willow trees, and a Chinese landscape. Most pieces are blue and white.

Bowl, 5 1/2 In.	14.00
Bowl, 7 1/2 In.	8.00
Bowl, Cereal, Footed, L. Strauss & Sons, New York & Brussels, England, 5 1/4 In.	85.00
Bowl, Cranberry, Homer Laughlin, 5 In.	27.00
Bowl, Japan, 5 3/4 In.	8.00
Bowl, Serving, Transfer, Border, Beaded Rim, 12 1/4 In.	50.00
Bowl, Vegetable, H.A. & Co., England, 8 1/2 x 7 3/4 In.	80.00
Bowl, Vegetable, Japan, 10 1/2 x 7 3/4 In.	50.00
Bowl, Vegetable, Oval, 10 1/2 In.	45.00
Bowl, Vegetable, Oval, Homer Laughlin, 9 5/8 In.	33.00 to 37.00
Bowl, Vegetable, Round, Homer Laughlin, 8 3/4 In.	25.00 to 30.00
Bowl, Vegetable, Round, Japan, 9 3/8 In.	22.00
Bread Plate, Homer Laughlin, 6 1/4 In.	10.00
Cake Plate, Dark Blue, Embossed Handles, Allerton, 10 In.	35.00
Casserole, Cover	50.00
Coffeepot, Cover	70.00
Compote, John Maddock & Sons, England, 3 In.	85.00
Creamer, 1 3/4 x 2 In.	18.00
Creamer, Japan	25.00 to 27.00
Cup, 2 Temples 2, Brown, Late 19th Century, 4 In.	35.00
Cup & Saucer, Japan, 2 1/4 In.	13.00
Cup & Saucer, Japan, After Dinner	20.00
Dinner Set, Oval, 50 Piece	345.00
Eggcup, Maddock Hotelware, England, 2 Piece	60.00
Grill Plate, Green, Royal China, 11 In.	30.00
Grill Plate, Moriyama Over Flower Basket Mark, Japan, 10 In.	25.00
Grill Plate, Shenango, 10 In.	25.00
Mug, 2 Temples, 2 Handles, Gold Trim, England, c.1890	200.00
Pepper Shaker, Japan	16.00
Plate, 3 1/2 In.	9.00
Plate, 4 1/4 In.	7.00
Plate, 6 1/4 In.	6.00
Plate, 9 In.	8.00 to 9.00
Plate, Homer Laughlin, 7 3/8 In.	7.00
Plate, Homer Laughlin, 8 1/4 In.	11.00
Plate, Homer Laughlin, 9 7/8 In.	10.00
Plate, Japan, 6 1/4 In.	7.00
Plate, Japan, 9 3/8 In.	12.00

Plate, Purple, Scotland, 9 In.	40.00
Plate, R. Hammersley, c.1891, 7 1/2 In.	12.00
Platter, Blue Band Reticulated Rim, Oval, Early 19th Century, 10 1/8 x 8 3/4 In.	230.00
Platter, Oval, 12 3/4 In.	37.00 to 47.00
Platter, Oval, Homer Laughlin, 11 3/4 In.	27.00
Platter, Oval, Homer Laughlin, 13 1/2 In.	34.00
Platter, Pell & Co, England, 11 In.	50.00
Saucer, Blue, 3 1/4 In.	8.00
Saucer, Homer Laughlin	3.00
Soup, Coupe, Homer Laughlin, 7 1/4 In.	13.00
Soup, Coupe, Japan, 7 1/2 In.	9.00
Soup, Dish, Homer Laughlin, 8 1/4 In.	12.00
Sugar, Cover	35.00
Sugar, Cover, Handle, Homer Laughlin	40.00
Sugar, Cover, Japan	11.00
Teapot, Cover, 4 In.	50.00
Tray, Aluminum, Chrome, Silver, Large	15.00
Tumbler, Juice, Japan, 3 1/8 In.	12.00
Tureen, Sauce, Cover, Underplate, 8 1/2 In.	160.00
Urn, Cover, 2 Handles, England, 8 3/8 In.	715.00
Warming Plate, Copper Bottom, Capped Spout, 2 Handles, Impressed England, 9 1/4 In.	150.00

WINDOW glass that was stained and beveled was popular for houses during the late nineteenth and early twentieth centuries. The old windows became popular with collectors in the 1970s; today, old and new examples are seen.

Beveled, Squares & Diamond Shaped Border, Pine Frame, 41 1/2 x 48 In.	295.00
Leaded, 7 Lavender Tulips, Arts & Crafts Style, Period Frame, 14 x 40 In.	345.00
Leaded, Allover Floral Design, 36 x 78 In.	3640.00
Leaded, Beveled, Clear Jewel Medallion, Frosted Diamonds, Jeweled, 30 In.	414.00
Leaded, Bow & Ribbon Design, 19 1/2 x 18 In., Pair	403.00
Leaded, Bow & Ribbon Design, 38 x 18 In.	374.00
Leaded, Bowfront, 3 Multicolored Bull's-Eyes In Center, 52 x 27 1/2 In.	517.00
Leaded, Center Flower, Leaves, Gothic Influence, 23 x 40 In.	115.00
Leaded, Central Chevron Above Checkerboard, Prairie School, 32 x 21 In.	1150.00
Leaded, Chevron Design, Prairie School, 76 x 26 In., Pair	5500.00
Leaded, Daffodil Design, Against Blue Sky, Period Frame, Arts & Crafts, 36 In.	4313.00
Leaded, Entryway, 2 Doors, Transom, Ponds, Cattails, Ducks, 114 x 26 In.	36400.00
Leaded, Floral Design, Mahogany Period Frame, Prairie School, 24 x 41 In., 4 Piece	1380.00
Leaded, Geometric & Floral, Frame, 23 x 75 In.	175.00
Leaded, Geometric Design, Caramel, Blue, Gold Glass, Prairie School, 26 x 24 In.	1840.00
Leaded, Geometric Design, Green, Red, Gold, Prairie School, 20 x 48 In.	1840.00
Leaded, Jesus In Center, Wearing Purple Robe, Surrounded By Sheep, 77 x 125 In.	9500.00
Leaded, Large Bull's-Eyes In Corners, Fruit Panel, Victorian, 54 x 35 1/2 In.	546.00
Leaded, Multicolored, Stylized Arts & Crafts Flower, Period Frame, 20 x 43 In.	345.00
Leaded, Opalescent Jewels, Yellow, Light Green, Chunk Glass, Drapery, 28 x 37 In.	9520.00
Leaded, Oval Medallion Inset, Beveled Glass, 4 Foliate Designs, Green Panels, 62 In.	483.00
Leaded, Panels, Grapevine, Green & Purple On Clear, 96 x 53 In., Pair	6325.00
Leaded, Prairie School, Green Stained Glass Jewels, Framed, 25 x 35 In.	1610.00
Leaded, Stylized Design, Ripple Glass, Jewels, Arts & Crafts Style, 19 x 18 In.	1495.00
Leaded, Sunrise Over Hillside, 12 x 34 In., Pair	345.00
Leaded, Vertical Design, Center Stem Leading To Tulips, Curved Foliage, 68 In., Pair	1063.00
Leaded, Yellow Tulip Design, Gold, Pink, Turquoise, 42 x 52 In.	1210.00
Post Office, Window Top, Top Sign, Envelope Box At Bottom, Oak, 1919, 48 In.	770.00
Stained Glass, Amber Center Medallion With Trees, Red, Blue, Frame, 22 In.	467.00
Stained Glass, Flying Swallows, Cobalt Blue, Orange With Trees, 32 x 29 1/2 In.	330.00
Stained Glass, Medallion At Center, Sailboat With Flowers, Light Amethyst Border, 34 In.	275.00
Stained Glass, Pillars & Flowers, Oak Frame, 65 x 24 3/4 In.	2860.00
Stained Glass, Semicircular, Leaded & Wooden Frame, Fired Floral, 33 3/4 In.	880.00
Stained Glass, Stylized Tree, 62 x 32 In.	1035.00
Stained Glass, Vintage Design, Amber, White Slag Ground, Green Vines, 42 1/2 x 30 In.	1320.00
Transom, Leaded, Floral, Crystal Jewels, Beveled Crystal Discs, 52 x 18 In.	1840.00
Transom, Leaded, Stained, Multicolored, Scrolling Leaves, 14 x 41 In.	518.00

Transom, Vase, Scrollwork, Scepter, Swag, Cabochon Red, 22 1/2 x 58 1/2 In. 196.00
Transom, Yellow, Green, Blue, Light Amber Beaded Border, 14 In. 852.00
Transparent & Slag Glass, 2 Fleur-De-Lis, Center Medallions, Frame, 31 3/4 In. 1610.00

WOOD CARVINGS and wooden pieces are listed separately in this book.
Many of the wood carvings are figurines or statues. There are also
wooden pieces found in other categories, such as Kitchen.

Abraham Lincoln, Strain Of War, Full-Length, Armand Lamontine, 65 In. 6250.00
American Eagle, 27 x 21 3/4 In. 2970.00
American Eagle, Holding Shield, Arrows, Painted, 45 x 13 In. 3335.00
Angel, Altar, Cloud Plinth, Painted, Germany, c.1700, 36 In., Pair 4480.00
Angel, Holding Torch, Italy, 63 x 9 x 4 1/2 In., Pair 2760.00
Angels, On Bases, Flowing Robes & Hair, 1 Turning To Right, 27 In., Pair 2070.00
Baltimore Orioles, Tree Root Base, Signed Stan Sparre, 7 x 11 1/2 In. 750.00
Bear, Carrying Tree Stump, 1910, 7 3/4 In. 385.00
Bear, Glass Eyes, 1920, 7 1/4 In. 1270.00
Bear, Holding Lance, Switzerland, c.1890, 14 3/4 In. 1450.00
Bear, Holding Shield With Swiss Flag, Glass Eyes, 1900, 8 1/2 In. 1155.00
Bear, Seated, Glass Eyes, 1900, 10 1/2 x 9 1/2 In. 2425.00
Bear, Smoking Pipe, Glass Eyes, 1900, 7 x 5 1/4 In. 695.00
Bear, Walking, Glass Eyes, 1910, 8 x 14 In. 1270.00
Bird, Wire Legs, Wooden Plinth, Pa., 1860, 5 x 5 In. 2090.00
Bishop, Polychrome, Gesso, Continental, Late 19th Century, 45 In. 230.00
Blackamoor, Turban, Floral Costume, Holding Rhyton, 29 In. 1495.00
Blue Jay, On Maple Leaves, A. Elmer Crowell, Mass., 5 1/2 x 7 1/2 In. 2645.00
Board, Smoothing, Butternut, Beveled Sides, Rosehead Nails, Hex Signs, 28 In. 440.00
Bookends, Lion Of Belfort, 7 1/2 In. 690.00
Buddha, Bronze & Red Painted, Relief Panels Base, 24 In. 220.00
Buddha, Gilt, Bronze Finish, Flower Petal Base, 14 x 12 x 30 In. 385.00
Bulto, San Antonio, Patron Of Fertility, Veracruz, 1800, 12 1/2 In. 120.00
Bulto, San Pascual, Patron Of Laborers, Veracruz, Mexico, 1800, 15 In. 175.00
Bust, Bishop, Bearded, Polychromed, Painted, Gilt Base, Paw Feet, 28 In. 2760.00
Bust, Reliquary, Saint, Crowned With A Wreath, Wearing A Tunic, 17 1/2 In. 2990.00
Bust, Saint, Gesso, Painted, Inset Eyes, Teeth, Mexico, c.1800, 8 1/2 In. 805.00
Bust, St. Bernardo, Bishop's Miter, Limewood, Gilt, Silverware, Italy, 38 In. 1380.00
Candlestick, Altar, Gesso, Painted, Monstrance, Apostle, Mexico, 1800s, 21 In. 431.00
Candlestick, Altar, Giltwood, Foliate Scrolled Standard, 3-Part Base, 28 In., Pair 1495.00
Car Model, Painted, Green, Gold Pinstripes, c.1930, 9 x 24 In. 360.00
Cherub, Painted, White, Giltwood, Leaf Circlet, 18th Century, 9 1/2 x 9 In. 1380.00
Christ, Ascendant, Painted, Gesso, Latin America, Early 1800s, 18 1/2 In. 374.00
Christ, Astride A Donkey, Polychrome, Gesso, Latin America, 18th Century, 21 In. 230.00
Christ, At The Pillar, Polychrome, Gesso, Continental, 17th Century, 19 1/4 In. 460.00
Christ, Flagellated, Gesso, Painted, Mexico, Inset Glass Eyes, c.1990, 13 1/2 In. 173.00
Christ Child, Holding Globe, Gesso, Painted, Latin America, 16 In. 316.00
Christ Child, Painted, Gesso, Inset Eyes, Velvet, Lace, Mexico, c.1790, 9 3/4 In. 288.00
Cow's Head, Painted, Stand, c.1840, 20 In. 288.00
Crucifix, Polychrome, South Germany, 19th Century, 50 In. 840.00
Deer, Standing On Rock Formation, 1880, 34 1/2 x 18 x 8 1/2 In. 4389.00
Deer Head, Glass Eyes, Antlers Attached With Screws, Mounted, c.1880, 52 x 27 In. 1065.00
Deity, 2 Smaller Figures, Standing, Animal, Floral Carving, 21 1/2 In. 862.00
Deity, Root, Oriental, 6 1/2 x 11 1/2 In. ....*Illus* 650.00
Dog, St. Bernard, Glass Eyes, Switzerland, c.1900, 10 In. 2414.00
Dog, St. Bernard, Tinted Tan, Black Collar, Flask, Switzerland, 6 1/2 x 4 In. 65.00
Eagle, Banner With Single Star, Polychromatic, Pine, 25 1/2 x 9 In. 2530.00
Eagle, Leaning Forward With Outspread Wings, Standing, Pine, 21 In. 3600.00
Eagle, Painted, Gold, Gilt Highlights, 19th Century, 12 1/2 x 19 1/4 In. 2300.00
Eagle, Pilothouse, 18 In. 8900.00
Eagle, Spread Wings, Glass Eyes, Red Paint, Gilt, 34 x 46 3/4 In. 3105.00
Eagle, Spread Wings, Gold Paint, 1940, 6 1/2 Ft. 2800.00
Eagle, Spread Wings, Painted, Gold, White, From Circus Wagon, c.1900, 20 x 20 In. 220.00
Eagle, Spread Wings, Perched On Rocks, Painted, 11 1/2 x 21 1/4 In. 1840.00
Eagle, Spread Wings, Talons Gripping Rock, American, c.1800, 30 x 47 In. 34100.00
Eagle, Spread Wings, Walnut, Painted, Pa., Stand, 10 1/2 x 15 1/2 In., Pair 2750.00

Use an old nylon stocking bunched into a ball to clean a rough-surfaced mirror frame, carved wooden piece, or other irregular surface.

Never leave a note outside explaining that you are not at home.

Wood Carving, Deity, Root,
Oriental, 6 1/2 x 11 1/2 In.

Eagle, Spread Wings, Walnut, Relief Feathers, 19th Century, 25 x 13 In.	1150.00
Eagle, Walnut, 19th Century, 32-In. Wingspan	3450.00
Eaglet, Painted, Attributed To Wilhelm Schimmel, 1890s, 5 1/2 In.	17600.00
Elephant Set, Teak, Graduated, Dark, Bone Trim, 3 3/4 To 14 In., 6 Piece	135.00
Female Ruffled Grouse, Red, Green Pedestal Base, Pa., 1900, 5 In., Pair	4125.00
Figurehead, Ship's, Young Woman, Blue Dress, New England, 1850, 24 In.	7200.00
Foo Dog, Red Lacquer, 6 3/8 In.	44.00
Foo Dog, Red, Green & Gray Repaint, Pierced, Oriental, 12 3/4 In.	55.00
Good Thief, Gesso, Painted, Inset Eyes, Mexico, 18th Century, 21 3/4 In.	150.00
Group, Creation, Eve, Adam, Serpent In Tree, Gesso, Painted, c.1900, 25 In.	489.00
Group, Madonna & Child, Germany, 1800, 17 1/2 x 6 In.	1955.00
Group, Sage With Acolyte & Recumbent Deer, On Stand, 8 In.	748.00
Group, Virgin, Child, Polychrome, Gesso, Leather, Mexico, 19th Century, 18 1/2 In.	115.00
Head Of Christ, Painted, Gesso, Glass Eyes, Eyelashes, Teeth, Mexico, 1790, 8 In.	575.00
Head Rest, Teak, Mortised, Step Carved, Scalloped Apron, Oriental, 9 3/4 x 5 In.	160.00
Heron, Bruce Barrett, Cumberland County, Pa., 18 In.	415.00
Hippocamp, Horse With Fishtail, Gilt, 13 x 7 1/2 In.	960.00
Hotei, Hands Above Head, 12 In.	135.00
Humidor, Wood Cover, Tree Trunk, Branches, Leaves, Climbing Bears, 1920, 10 In.	693.00
Humpty-Dumpty, Wilhelm Schimmel, 4 1/8 In.	9900.00
Hunter, Rifle, Rabbit, Switzerland, c.1880, 16 In.	4600.00
Indian, Standing In A Dance Position, Garland Of Flowers, Gessoed, 27 In.	230.00
Indian Maiden, Painted, Fringed Dress, Headband, 14 3/4 In.	2185.00
Isis, Sitting On Throne, Blue Paint, c.1850, 1 1/2 In.	8500.00
Jesus, Sermon In Garden, Soldiers, Painted, Verano Cardana, 21 x 17 In.	375.00
Juan Carlos Harriott, Polo Player, Horse, Walnut, E. Dombrowe, 23 x 29 In.	1595.00
Madonna & Child, Gesso, Painted, Glass Inset Eye, Gilt Crowns, 18 1/2 In.	184.00
Maiden, Giltwood, Painted, Ladder, 18th Century, 13 1/2 In.	460.00
Man, Bowler Hat, Painted, 10 In.	3335.00
Man, Flowing Robe, Gesso, Painted, 20 1/2 In.	345.00
Man, Holding Watermelon, Plinth Base, Pine, Polychrome, 14 x 6 1/2 In.	2310.00
Man, Training Bear, 1900, 10 x 7 3/4 In.	890.00
Martyr, Woman, Polychrome, Gesso, Continental, Late 18th Century, 20 In.	155.00
Mary Magdalene, Painted, Gesso, Glass Eyes, Hemp Robe, Spain, 1700s, 21 1/2 In.	1150.00
Mask, Folk, Daruma, Japan, 23 3/4 In.	316.00
Mask, Foo Dog, Plant Fiber Beard, Leather Ears, Paint, Qing Dynasty, 24 x 36 In.	8500.00
Mask, Horned Demon, Early 20th Century, 10 1/2 In.	60.00
Mask, Noh, Red Faced Man With Brass Eyes, Papier-Mache, 8 In.	345.00
Mask, Noh, Young Woman With White Face, Black Hair, Signed, 8 In.	230.00
Mask, Noh, Young Woman, Lacquer, 20th Century, 8 1/2 In.	170.00
Mask, Okame, Carved Signature, 19th Century, 7 1/2 In.	690.00
Mask, Red Faced Woman With Black Hair, Blackened Teeth, Signed, 8 In.	750.00
Matchbox, Ashtray, Bear, Backpack, Drawer, Switzerland, c.1910, 4 1/2 x 5 x 3 In.	245.00
Medallion, Stand, 5 Figures In Pagoda, Geometric Border, Oriental, 14 x 18 In.	55.00

Mirror, Eagle Holding Beveled Half Moon, Switzerland, c.1910, 12 x 12 In. 756.00
Monkey, Plate In Chained Hands, Standing On Rocky Base, 56 1/2 In. 7475.00
Monstrance, Virgin & Child, Saint, Cherubs, Gesso, Painted, 24 In. 403.00
Natives, Impressed Marks, Bronze, Patina, Art Deco, Hagenauer, 19 x 5 In. 1380.00
Nativity Group, Painted, Mary, Joseph, 2 Wise Men, 13 1/2 In. 81.00
Oriental Woman, Holding Child, Forest Niche, Red & Green, 11 1/2 In. 130.00
Panel, Beechwood, Mannerist Style, Galatea, Poseidon, 9 x 17 3/4 In., Pair 633.00
Panel, Dragons, Flowers, Black & Red Repaint, Gold, Chinese, 17 x 52 In., Pair 355.00
Panel, Floral, Red & Gold Design, Black Paint, Oriental, 22 x 46 In. 575.00
Panel, Geometric, Pierced & Carved Liner, Chinese, 36 5/8 x 13 In., 4 Piece 250.00
Panel, Gilt Figure & Woods Scene, Cinnabar Ground, Oriental, 5 x 17 In., Pair 55.00
Panel, Lotus Blossoms, Painted, Masonite Back, 7 3/4 x 71 In. 440.00
Panel, Pine, Mythical Flying Figure, Masonite Back, Oriental, 17 x 24 In., Pair 412.00
Panel, Poppies & Leaves, Masonite Back, Frame, Chinese, 10 x 40 In., Pair 440.00
Panel, Sculptured Flowers, Birds, Deer, Polychromed, Japanese, 64 x 12 In. 805.00
Parrot, Flat Cutout, Painted, Red, 17 x 11 In. 29.00
Parrot, Perched On Rockery Base, Ivory Wings, 6 5/8 In. 160.00
Plaque, Cross, Initials HIS, Clouds, 18th Century, 21 In. 308.00
Plaque, Flower Filled Urn, Bird, Gesso, Gilt Ground, Round, 12 In. 316.00
Plaque, Patriotic, Flag Shield, Our Country, Our Liberty, Stars, 16 x 40 1/2 In. 6325.00
Polar Bear, Looking At Crashing Wave, Switzerland, c.1910, 5 1/2 x 5 3/4 In. 363.00
Polo Player, Galloping Pony, Mahogany, BC On Saddle, 20 x 24 In. 385.00
Portal, Urn Issuing Suckling Flowering Branches, Boa Tiger, 83 In. 3450.00
Putti, Kneeling On Rectangular Base, 18th Century, 22 In., Pair 3450.00
Putti, Outstretched Wings, Giltwood, Gesso, Continental, 1700s, 30 In., Pair 2875.00
Reliquary, Casket, 4-Footed, Exposition Window, Italy, c.1700, 15 x 11 In. 1120.00
Reliquary, Forearm Delivering Blessing, Gilt, Silver Leaf, 18th Century, 15 In. 2912.00
Reliquary, Giltwood, Polychrome, Mary, Christ Child, Rococo, 17 1/2 x 11 x 6 In. 2990.00
Reliquary, Silver Gilt, Ebonized, Rococo Style, Scrolls, Cherubs, 26 1/2 x 11 In. 748.00
Reliquary Stand, Giltwood, Urn, Starburst, Tasseled Drapery, 35 x 18 x 6 In. 3450.00
Renaissance Noble Woman, Painted, Giltwood, Early 1800s, 15 x 8 x 10 In. 635.00
Rooster, Painted, Black, Red Comb, Wattle, Wire Legs, 19th Century, 5 1/2 In. 1035.00
Rooster, Plaque, Yellow Paint, Lancaster, Pa., Mid 1800s, 14 In. 1320.00
Sacrifice Of Isaac, Gilt, Frame, 14 x 24 In. 560.00
Saint, Gesso, Painted, Latin America, 11 1/2 In. 184.00
Saint, Polychrome, Gesso, Latin America, 19th Century, 23 3/4 In. 259.00
Saint, Polychrome, Holding Sword, Plinth Base, Latin America, c.1790, 18 1/2 In. 460.00
Salmon, Signed Paul Mailman, Montpelier, Vt., 20th Century, 33 In. 374.00
Santos, Polychrome, Gesso, Latin America, 8 In., 6 Piece 259.00
Santos, Polychrome, Latin America, 19th Century, 11 1/2 In., 4 Piece 115.00
Smoking Stand, Bear, Hinged Head, Edelweiss, Switzerland, c.1900, 29 In. 4130.00
Song Bird, On Stand, Red, Yellow, Black, Pa., 20th Century, 2 x 4 In. 250.00
Spoon, Norwegian, Fretted Handle, Incised Floral, c.1800, 15 In. 250.00
Spoon, Pierced Handle, Hook, American, 19th Century, 8 In. 546.00
St. Anthony, Polychromatic, 48 In. 2912.00
St. Anthony, Polychrome, Gesso, Mexico, Early 19th Century, 20 In. 430.00
St. Francis, Polychrome, Gesso, Inset Glass Eyes, Latin America, c.1800, 18 1/4 In. 518.00
St. James, Painted, Gesso, Red & Gold Cloth, Latin America, 18th Century, 18 In. 345.00
St. Jerome, Polychrome, Gesso, Inset Glass Eyes, Mexico, 19th Century, 23 1/2 In. 230.00
St. John The Baptist, Painted, Inset Eyes, Mexico, 18th Century, 15 1/2 In. 633.00
St. Joseph, Polychrome, Gesso, Glass Eyes, Linen, Silk, Mexico, c.1800, 19 In. 316.00
St. Wenceslas, Hold Shrine, Wearing Crown, 19th Century, 32 In. 1400.00
Stag, Reclining, Brown Glaze Finish, Lewis DeTurk, Pa., 14 In. 3850.00
Train Engine Model, Polychrome, A Borsig Berlin, Prussian, 19 x 24 1/2 In. 1100.00
Vase, Bird With Tall Leaves, Base Holder, Switzerland, c.1910, 9 In., Pair 1650.00
Vase Holder, Standing Bear, c.1910, 8 In. 270.00
Virgin, Painted, Inset Eyes, Articulated Body, Mexico, 18th Century, 26 1/2 In. 220.00
Virgin, Polychromatic, Mexico, 19th Century, 13 In. 115.00
Virgin & Child, Polychrome, Gesso, Carved Stand, Mexico, 19th Century, 22 1/2 In. 259.00
Virgin Mary, Polychrome, Gesso, Latin America, 13 1/2 In. 175.00
Virgin Of Guadeloupe, Painted, Mexico, 19th Century, 19 1/4 In. 207.00
Woman, Holding Basket Of Vegetables, 19th Century, 11 1/2 In. 250.00
Woodsman, Holding Salmon, Jim Bill, 1925, Life Size 3850.00

WOODEN wares were used in all parts of the home. Wood was used for many containers and tools. Small wooden pieces are called *treenware* in England, but the term woodenware is more common in the United States. Additional pieces may be found in the Advertising, Kitchen, and Tool categories.

Airplane Propeller, Hartzel, 20th Century, 73 In.	275.00
Bag Dispenser, Hand Painted, Label & Paint Traces, 19th Century	127.00
Barrel, Storage, Keyhole Fastened Bands, 18th Century	395.00
Bowl, Burl, Handle, 7 7/8 x 3 3/4 In.	185.00
Bowl, Chopping, Turned Lip, Raised Base, 25 1/2 In.	460.00
Bucket, Cover, Barrel, 3 Metal Bands, Porcelain Knob, Lehnware, 8 1/2 x 7 1/2 In.	3410.00
Bucket, Peat, Brass Handle, Leaf Carved Staves, Bun Feet, 1830s, 18 3/4 In.	3220.00
Bucket, Peat, Brassbound, Mahogany Staves, Brass Handle, 1830s, 13 1/2 In.	1095.00
Bucket, Peat, Mahogany, Regency, Brass Handle, Liner, Urn Shape Stem, 20 x 13 1/2 In.	546.00
Bucket, Peat, Mahogany, William IV, Scalloped Rim, Brass Handle, Liner, 16 1/2 x 15 In.	405.00
Bucket, Stave & Lapped Band, Swing Handle, Painted, 19th Century, 14 1/4 In.	1150.00
Bucket, Staved, Lapped Finger Wooden Bands, Iron Handle, Oval, 6 x 7 1/2 x 5 1/2 In.	315.00
Bucket, Sugar, Cover, Stave Sides, Iron Bands, Polychrome, Lehnware, 10 x 7 In.	6600.00
Bucket, Sugar, Metal Base Bands, Single Finger On Lid, Copper Tacks, Amish, 9 1/2 In.	110.00
Bucket, Sugar, Single Finger Bands, Copper Tacks, Wilder P. Clark, 9 3/4 In.	33.00
Bucket, Sugar, Stave Construction, So. Hingham, Mass., 10 x 9 1/4 In.	1265.00
Bucket, Sugar, Stave Construction, Swivel Handle, C. Wilson & Son, 15 x 14 In.	5775.00
Buggy Seat, Maple, Ash, Arched Slats, Turned Arms, Late 18th Century, 35 1/2 x 17 In.	1495.00
Canteen, Finger Joint Construction, Red Paint, New England, c.1800, 5 x 8 In.	440.00
Canteen, Iron Bands, Bail Handle, Embossed B.L., 8 1/2 In.	300.00
Canteen, Stave Vessel, Swing Handle, Black Paint, Early 19th Century, 9 3/4 In.	375.00
Canteen, Wagon Type, Twig Rims, Revolutionary War, 7 x 13 In.	345.00
Cask, Oak, William IV, Brass, King, Gold Bless Him, 21 1/2 In.	165.00
Cask, Painted, Red, Barrel Shape, Iron Bands, 16 1/4 x 10 1/2 In.	17.00
Casket, Damascus, Walnut, Domed Cover, Fall Front, Drawers, 11 x 8 x 6 In.	460.00
Casket, Group, Pyramidal Cover, Figural Design, 13 In.	86.00
Cheese Coaster, Mahogany, Boat Shape, Carved Roundels, Casters, 16 In., Pair	1150.00
Churn, Vermont Farm Machine Co., Davis No. 3 Swing, Patented 1870s	230.00
Flag Holder, Maple, Table Top, Round, 9 Flags, 8 In. Diam.	56.00
Glass Holder, Leaves, Eagle, Carved Stem, Holds 5, Switzerland, c.1900, 15 x 12 In.	730.00
Hat, Walnut Burl, Stars Around Band Top, Smoke, Painted, 1800s, 4 1/2 x 12 1/4 In.	920.00
Humidor, Burl, Silver Plate, Multisectioned, c.1900, 5 x 11 In.	275.00
Humidor, Cigar, Mahogany, Havana Harbor Fort Cover, Allover Carved, 10 x 8 In.	230.00
Humidor, Exotic Wood, Doughnut Box, Cedar Lined, W. Castle, 1989, 26 In.	6900.00
Jar, Cover, Flattened Ball Finial, Wire Bail, Wooden Handle, Pease, 4 3/4 In.	605.00
Jar, Cover, Red Vinegar Design, Rings At Base, Top & Lid, 12 1/4 In.	5280.00
Jar, Cover, Treenware, Teak, Red Stain, 1 Piece Handle & Lid, Oriental, 7 1/2 x 7 3/8 In.	55.00
Jar, Cover, Urn Finial, Pease, C. Ebendsole, 1863, 3 1/4 In.	275.00
Jar, Painted, Red Tulips, Green Leaves, Footed, Cover, Conical Finial, 4 5/8 x 5 In.	110.00
Keg, Continental, Walnut, Leaf, Bird Incised Decoration, c.1800, 9 1/2 x 9 In.	220.00
Keg, Water, Steel Rails, Stopper, Stave Constructed, 8 3/4 In.	275.00
Mold, Cigar, 22 In.	23.00
Pepper Castor, 18th Century, 3 1/2 In.	225.00
Pipe Rack, Pine, For Clay Pipes, Crest, 18th Century	650.00
Plate, Curly Maple, Incised Rings Around Top & Under Rim, 9 1/8 In.	470.00
Salt, Footed, Figured, Patina, 3 3/4 x 5 3/4 In.	58.00
Shelf, Candle, Square Nails, Shaped Sides, Holes In Sides For Missing Rod, 1850	450.00
Shooting Target, Man Wearing Red Cap, Military Inscription, R. Home, 1942, 20 In.	413.00
Spoon, Carved, Geometric Patterns, 19th Century, Pair	60.00
Strongbox, Iron Strap Hinges, Brass Nails, Fittings, Domed Cover, c.1730, 13 1/2 In.	2250.00
Tazza, Tiger Maple, Turned Baluster, Standard, American, 19th Century, 7 x 9 1/2 In.	1380.00
Tray, Faux Bamboo Stand, Black Lacquer, Flowers, 21 1/2 x 29 In.	805.00
Tray, Georgian Style, Burl, Brass Handles, Inlaid, Scallop Design, 23 1/2 x 16 In.	105.00
Tray, Mahogany, Central Shell, Striped Contrasting Wood, 1810s, 14 1/4 In.	546.00
Tray, Mahogany, Plain Oval Gallery Form, Open Brass Handles, 19th Century, 22 3/4 In.	46.00
Tray, Mahogany, Satinwood Banded Center Shell Patera, Glass Feet, 28 x 18 In.	750.00
Tray, Mahogany, William IV, Scalloped Edges, Scrolled Handles, 4 x 21 x 13 1/2 In.	920.00
Tray, Pine, 2 Handles, 36 x 25 In.	905.00

If you live in a damp
climate, keep a small
light bulb lit in each
closet to retard mildew.

World War II, Figure,
Hitler, Skunk, Pottery,
Painted, 5 x 5 1/2 In.

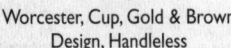

Worcester, Cup, Gold & Brown
Design, Handleless

Tray, Serving, Ceramic Trivet On One Side, Georges Briard, 12 x 7 In. 15.00
Tub, Cedar, Alternate Light & Dark, Cutout Handles, Andover, Mass., 5 1/4 x 6 1/4 In. 175.00
Tub, D Shape Cutout Handles, Metal, Lapped Bands, Round, 1800s, 8 3/4 x 12 In. 259.00
Wagon Seat, Maple, Splint, Mushroom Turnings, Arm Posts, 35 x 42 In. 1035.00
Wagon Seat, Painted, Square Crest, Tapering Spindles, Splint Seat, Red, 34 In. 460.00
Watch Hutch, Mahogany, Broken Arch Pediment, Floral & Scroll Base, 9 x 7 In. 5000.00
Windmill Tail, Dempster Mill Mfg. Co., 1916, Beatrice, Neb. 950.00

WORCESTER porcelains were made in Worcester, England, from 1751.
The firm went through many name changes and eventually, in 1862,
became The Royal Worcester Porcelain Company Ltd. Collectors
often refer to *Dr. Wall*, Barr, *Flight*, and other names that indicate time
periods or artists at the factory. It became part of Royal Worcester
Spode Ltd. in 1976. Related pieces may be found in the Royal
Worcester category.

Basket, Blue & White, Crescent Mark, Scalloped Open Work, 18th Century, 6 1/8 In. 863.00
Bowl, Blue & White, Chinoiserie Design, 9 In. 330.00
Bowl, Blue Floral Sprays, White Ground, Dr. Wall, 5 1/4 x 12 In. 1322.00
Bowl, Tea, Blue, White Flowers, Crescent Moon Mark, Dr. Wall, c.1780, 2 x 4 In. 138.00
Casolette, Vase, Cover, Exotic Shells, Seaweed, Puce Ground, Gilt Border, 1820, 5 In. 4370.00
Cup, Gold & Brown Design, Handleless . . . .*Illus*   15.00
Dish, Heraldic Lion, Gilt, Round, Stencil, Barr, Flight & Barr, c.1825, 1 1/4 x 7 7/8 In. 115.00
Dish, Junket, Basket Form, 3 Lobed Panes, Floral Border, 1765, 9 In. 1920.00
Dish, Squirrel Beneath Gray Banderole, Purple, Red Poppies, 1810, 9 In., Pair 7200.00
Dish, Sweetmeat, Leaf Form, Floral & Insect Interior, 18th Century, 3 In. 115.00
Honey Pot, Cover, Hive With 3 Bees Relief, Gold, Iron Red, 1800, 6 1/2 In. 3600.00
Mug, King Of Prussia 720.00
Mug, Thorny Rose, Butterflies, Bell Shape, 1770s 660.00
Pin Tray, Floral On White Ground, Gilt Borders 127.00
Plate, Oriental Floral, Gold, Blue Underglaze, 1815, 11 In., 12 Piece 6000.00
Plate, Overall Blue Flowers, Off-White Ground, Scalloped Border, Dr. Wall, 7 In., Pair . .   150.00
Plate, Pinecone, Blue Underglaze, Scalloped Rim, 6 1/4 In., Pair 316.00
Plate, Plumed Birds, Butterflies, Insects, Cobalt Blue Ground, 8 5/8 In. 165.00
Plate, Thumb & Finger, Oriental Floral, Blue, Green, Iron Red Glaze, 1810, 14 Piece 3302.00
Plate Set, Chamberlain, Apple Green Border, Flowers, 8 1/2 In., 18 Piece 1265.00
Sugar, Cover, Stand, Bird Perched On Branch Above Bridge, 1810, 6 1/2 In. 4500.00
Teacup, Saucer, Blue Floral Sprays, Puce, Blue Bellflowers, 1807, 5 1/2 In. 69.00
Teapot, Blue & White Flowers, Crescent Moon Mark, Dr. Wall, c.1780, 8 In. 1380.00
Tureen, Sauce, Cover, Panel Of Birds, Salmon Pink Ground, 1825, 6 7/8 In. 2400.00
Tureen, Tan Printed Chinoiserie, Elephant Handles, Ironstone, 1880s, 15 In. 373.00
Urn, Portraits Of Venus & Juno, Shell Pink Ground, Handles, 7 x 9 In., Pair 575.00
Vase, Baluster Shape, Mask Handles, Blue Flowers, Grainger & Co., 14 In., Pair 460.00
Vase, Floral Reserves, Enameled Beading, Sloping Handles, 7 In., Pair 920.00
Vase, Lotus Form, Marked, England, Late 19th Century, 9 3/8 In. 632.00

WORLD WAR I and World War II souvenirs are collected today. Be
careful not to store anything that includes live ammunition. Your local
police will tell you how to dispose of the explosives. See also Sword
and Trench Art.

WORLD WAR I, Album, Leather Cover, Postcards, Soldier Photographs, Letters, 1919 . . . . .   110.00

Album, Snap Cards, Of Dead Soldiers 200.00
Book, Why We Are At War, Woodrow Wilson, Harper & Bros., Dust Cover, 1917 .... 9.00
Box, Ammunition, Brass Hardware, 15 x 8 x 4 1/2 In. 110.00
Button, Pershing Photo, Salvation Army War Drive, Omaha, Sept. 13, 1918 .... 150.00
Button, Third Liberty Loan Volunteer, Flag Center, 1 In. 8.00
Button, Welcome Home Victory Boys, Pershing, Soldiers, Celluloid, 1 3/4 In. 45.00
Canteen, Leather Strap, Canvas Cover, Marked R.I.A., 1906 .... 144.00
Cap, Garrison, Olive Drab Worsted, Size 6 3/4 .... 15.00
Card, Soldier, This Card Will Buy Bullets If You Buy A War Stamp Here, Mercury Dime . 45.00
Compass, Zeppelin 4025.00
Hat, Biker, Black Leather 95.00
Helmet, German, Metal 430.00
Mess Fork, 7 1/2 In. 4.00
Mirror, General Pershing, Haig & Joffre, Flags Ground, Oval, 2 3/4 In. 105.00
Pin, Collar, R.O.T.C., Blackened Brass, Pinback, 1 5/8 x 3/8 In. 4.00
Pin, Collar, Signal Corps, Officer, Bronze, Pinback, 1 In. 7.00
Plate, Lauger Erfurt 1914-15, Kriegsgefangenen, Porcelain, Gold Trim, 8 1/2 In. 90.00
Poster, Broadside, President Wilson's Message To The People, Frame, 28 In. 46.00
Poster, Clear The Way!, Howard Chandler Christy, Linen, 28 x 22 In. 192.00
Poster, Daddy, What Did YOU Do In The Great War?, Linen, 28 x 22 In. 2310.00
Poster, For Every Fighter A Woman Worker, Adolph Treidler, YWCA, 41 x 27 In. 165.00
Poster, Forward!, Forward To Victory, Enlist Now, Kemp-Welsh, 59 1/2 x 39 In. 1045.00
Poster, Gee! I Wish I Were A Man, Howard Chandler Christy, 41 x 28 In. 1210.00
Poster, I Want You For The U.S. Army, Uncle Sam, James M. Flagg, 40 x 30 In. 2310.00
Poster, Irishmen Avenge The Lusitania, W.E.T., 30 x 20 In. 3850.00
Poster, It's Your Fight! Wrench Is The Rifle Here, Build Tanks, Ickes, 28 x 22 In. 550.00
Poster, Men Wanted For The Army, Michael Whelan, Linen, 40 x 30 In. 522.00
Poster, More Tanks, Lyford, American, Linen, 28 x 22 In. 550.00
Poster, On The Job For Victory, Shipyard Scene, Jonas Lie, 28 x 22 In. 880.00
Poster, Order Coal Now, Joseph C. Leyendecker, Fuel Administration, 28 x 22 In. 660.00
Poster, Order Your Coal Now, Copper Lithograph, Fred G., 1917, 28 x 20 In. 600.00
Poster, Skin Is Dark But Heart Is White, Canadian Patriotic Fund, 40 1/2 x 27 In. 550.00
Poster, Spirit Of Woman-Power, Woman Playing Snare Drum, 41 x 27 In. 467.00
Poster, Take Up The Sword Of Justice, B. Partridge, 41 x 27 In. 660.00
Poster, That Liberty Shall Not Perish From The Earth, Joseph Pennell, 41 x 27 In. 495.00
Poster, The New Spring, War Savings Stamps, Linen, 41 x 27 In. 385.00
Poster, The Ships Are Coming, James Daugherty, Linen, 28 x 22 In. 330.00
Poster, They Kept The Sea Lanes Open, L.A. Shafer, Linen, 41 x 27 In. 467.00
Poster, This May Be Your Boy, American Red Cross, Linen, 41 x 27 In. 412.00
Poster Set, Preserve, Housh, 41 x 27 In., 4 Piece 2970.00
Sheet Music, Break The News To Mother, C.K. Harris, 1917 .... 6.00
Sheet Music, Rose Of No Man's Land, J. Caddigan, J.A. Brennan, Leo Feist, Inc., 1918 .. 6.00
Sheet Music, Somewhere In France Is The Lily, J.E. Howard, P. Johnson, 1917 .... 6.00
Sheet Music, What Kind Of An American Are You?, 1917, 4 Page 20.00
WORLD WAR II, Bank, 1 Pounder Shell, Cast Iron, M 1416, 8 In. 85.00
Bank, English Grenade, Cast Iron, M 1427, 3 1/2 In. 130.00
Bank, Save For Victory, Cannon Shape, Dime, Tin, Wooden, Moore, 4 3/4 In. 165.00
Bank, Victory Ship, Chalkware, Moore, Box, 4 In. 100.00
Bank, War Bonds, Shell Shape, Chein, M 1403, 5 3/4 In. 255.00
Bayonet, Scabbard, Leather Sheath, Japan, 20 In. 75.00
Belt Buckle, Nazi 34.00
Button, B-J Day, 1 3/4 In. 25.00
Button, Dorie Miller, Pearl Harbor Hero, Celluloid, 1 1/4 In. 205.00
Button, Final V-J Day Victory, 1 1/4 In. 20.00
Button, Gasoline Rationing, World War II, Tab Type, Lithograph, 7/8 In. 8.00
Button, Navy Service Uniform, Eagle Facing Right, Gilt, 5/8 In. 3.00
Button, Oregon Emergency Corps, Flags, Red, White, Blue, Celluloid, 1 1/4 In. 11.00
Button, Our Hero, Brig. Gen. James Doolittle, Tokyo Raid, Photo, Celluloid, 1 1/2 In. ... 29.00
Button, Pack Up Hitler, The Yanks Are Coming, Brown, White, 1/1/4 In. 18.00
Button, Red Cross, Soldier, Woman, Celluloid, 1 1/2 In. 23.00
Button, U.S. Will Take The Nip Out Of Nipponese, Red, White, Blue, Celluloid, 1 1/2 In. 20.00
Button, Viva Italia, Benito Mussolini, Picture, Celluloid, 1920-1930, 1 1/4 In. 150.00
Button, With Ribbon, Welcome Home Celebrations, 1940, 1 1/4 In. 17.00

Cap, Garrison, Air Corps, Olive Drab Worsted, Size 7 .... 11.00
Cap, Garrison, Artillery, Olive Drab, Size 6 7/8 .... 12.00
Cap, Garrison, Medical Corps, Khaki, Size 7 1/4 .... 8.00
Figure, Hitler, Skunk, Pottery, Painted, 5 x 5 1/2 In. ....*Illus* 175.00
Handbill, Hitler, One Name, Hope For Millions, Hazi, Late 1920s 440.00
I.D. Card, U.S. Navy, Allied Naval Service 3.00
Menu, Camp Forrest, Station Hospital, Thanksgiving, 1942 .... 8.00
Newspaper, Delandings, Naval Air Station, Deland, Fla., Nov. 15, 1944 .... 8.00
Overcoat, USMC, Enlisted Man, 1942, Size 3L 55.00
Pencil, Mechanical, V For Victory, Specher's Diner, Lebanon, Pa. 35.00
Pin, Lapel, USO, Metal, Folding 2.00
Pin, Shoot The Pants Off The Japs, Red Ribbon, 1911, 3 x 9 1/2 In. 90.00
Postcard, Mein Kampf, Spoof On Coming Demise Of Adolf Hitler, Unused 20.00
Poster, Mein Kampf, Adolph Hitler, Advertising Book, 1930s, 13 x 20 In. 35.00
Poster, Navy, Sailors Manning Deck Gun, 19 1/2 x 29 1/2 In. 57.00
Poster, Tin Cans Going To War, U.S. War Productions Board, 36 In. 150.00
Poster, U.S. Forces Protecting Statue Of Liberty, Flags, 40 x 30 In. 1150.00
Questionnaire, Nuremberg Trial Wilhelm Frick, Who Drew Up Nuremberg Laws 1250.00
Ration Book, With Stamps, Certificate Of Ownership, Freihofer's VIM Bread, 1943 .... 10.00
Salt & Pepper, Chalkware, Patriot Eagles, USA, 2 1/2 In. 40.00
Sheet Music, Fellow On A Furlough, B. Worth, Martin Block Pub. Co., 1943 .... 6.00
Sheet Music, Hats Off To MacArthur And Our Boys Down There, 1942 .... 50.00
Sheet Music, There'll Be A Hot Time In The Town Of Berlin, Bushkin, De Vries, 1943 .. 3.00
Sheet Music, Vict'ry Polka, S. Cahn & J. Styne, Chappell & Co., N.Y., 1943 .... 7.00
Sign, Air Raid Shelter, Arrow, Cardboard, Black On Beige, 14 x 7 In. 12.00
Sign, Air Raid, 3 Languages, Frame 30.00
Soup, Dish, Nazi, Marked, Large 35.00
Trousers, USMC, Enlisted Man's, Green Wool, Zipper Fly, 36 x 30 .... 20.00
View-Master Reel, U.S. Naval Aviation Training Division 29.00

WORLD'S FAIR souvenirs from all of the fairs are collected. The first
fair was the Great Exhibition of 1851 in London. Some other impor-
tant exhibitions and fairs include Philadelphia, 1876 (Centennial);
Chicago, 1893 (World's Columbian); Buffalo, 1901 (Pan-American);
St. Louis, 1904 (Louisiana Purchase); San Francisco, 1915 (Panama-
Pacific); Philadelphia, 1926 (Sesquicentennial); Chicago, 1933
(Century of Progress); Cleveland, 1936 (Great Lakes); San Francisco,
1939 (Golden Gate International); New York, 1939 (World of
Tomorrow); Seattle, 1962 (Century 21); New York, 1964; Montreal,
1967; New Orleans, 1984; Tsukuba, Japan, 1985; Vancouver, B.C.,
1986; Brisbane, Australia, 1988; Seville, Spain, 1992; and Genoa,
Italy, 1992; Seoul, Korea, 1993; and Lisbon, Portugal, 1998. Memora-
bilia of fairs include directories, pictures, fabrics, ceramics, etc.
Memorabilia from other similar celebrations may be listed in the
Souvenir category.

Ashtray, 1964, New York, Milk Glass, Logo, Fair Montage, Anchor Hocking 12.00
Bandanna, 1876, Philadelphia, Centennial Exposition, 5 Buildings, 27 x 25 In. 86.00
Bank, 1893, Chicago, Indian Hunting Buffalo, Mayflower, Columbus, J&E Stevens 1000.00
Bank, 1893, Chicago, World's Columbian, Globe Shape, Salt Glaze, 4 1/2 In. 3740.00
Bank, 1939, New York, World Of Tomorrow, Tin, Chein, Moore, 12 In. 285.00
Banner, 1933, Chicago, Century If Progress, Electrical Building, Felt, 26 In. 18.00
Book, 1933, Chicago, A Century Of Progress 50.00
Book, 1939, New York, The Time Capsule, Westinghouse Electric Mfg. Co. 45.00
Book, 1964, New York, World's Fair, Pop-Up 20.00
Bookmark, 1893, Chicago, Star Spangled Banner Lyrics, Flag, Silk, 12 1/2 In. 155.00
Bookmark, 1901, Buffalo, Pan American, Pansy, Libby's Food Products, 5 1/4 In. 15.00
Bookmark, 1939, New York, Brass, Orange, Gold, Blue, Orange Tassels, 4 1/2 In. 33.00
Bookmark, Letter Opener, 1934, Chicago, Hall Of Science, On Linen Style Postcard 20.00
Bracelet, 1933, Chicago, Century Of Progress, Copper, Chicago Skyline Raised Relief ... 58.00
Bracelet, 1962, Seattle, Century 21, 9 Charms, 7 In. 25.00
Button, 1904, St. Louis, Louisiana Purchase, Ford Mfg. Co. 125.00
Button, 1909, Seattle, Alaska-Yukon, Dog Sled, Car, Celluloid, 1 3/4 In. 125.00
Cane, 1933, Chicago, Century Of Progress, Chrome Plated, Crook Handle, 35 In. 82.00

Cane, 1933, Chicago, Century Of Progress, Flashlight, Wooden Shaft, 35 In. 247.00
Cane, 1933, Chicago, Century Of Progress, Heywood Wakefield Co., 34 In. 82.00
Cane, 1933, Chicago, Century Of Progress, Wooden Shaft, 34 In. 467.00
Compact, 1933, Chicago, Century Of Progress 20.00
Creamer, 1964, New York, Amberina, Miniature, Crackle Glass, Mold Blown, 3 1/4 In. . . . 75.00
Cup, 1893, Chicago, World's Columbian, After Dinner 55.00
Cup & Saucer, 1893, Chicago, World's Columbian, After Dinner, Machinery Hall 54.00
Flask, 1904, St. Louis, Louisiana Purchase, Ground Lip, Shot Glass Screw Cap, 1/2 Pt. . . 235.00
Game, 1964, New York, World's Fair, Milton Bradley 20.00
Guide Book, 1939, New York, World Of Tomorrow, British Pavilion, Photos, 5 x 8 In. . . . 35.00
Handkerchief, 1933, Chicago, FDR Picture, Red, White, Blue, Brown, 8 1/2 In. 125.00
Key, 1933, Chicago, Century Of Progress, Key To The City, Box, 2 1/2 x 8 1/2 In. 25.00
Key Chain, 1962, Seattle, Century 21 . . . . 10.00
Magazine, 1939, New York, Life, March 13, 1939, American Beauties 15.00
Match Safe, 1904, St. Louis, Gardens, Terraces Of States, 3 x 1 In. 150.00
Mirror, 1904, St. Louis, Louisiana Purchase, Celluloid, Pocket 400.00
Mug, 1893, Chicago, World's Columbian, Salt Glaze, Handle, 4 3/4 In. 523.00
Mug, 1901, Pan American Exposition, Bristol Glass, Blue Accents, Buffalo, N.Y., 4 In. . . . 275.00
Mug, 1901, Pan American Exposition, Bristol Glass, Pewter Cover, Blue, 6 In. 358.00
Nodder, Montreal Expo, 1967s, 6 1/2 In. 95.00
Nut Set, 1939, New York, Trylon & Perisphere, Mr. Peanut, Metal 125.00
Padlock, 1904, St. Louis, Woman Holding Torch, World In Other Hand 382.00
Paperweight, 1893, Chicago, World's Columbian, Ferris Wheel, 3 In. 20.00
Pennant, 1933, Chicago, Century Of Progress 42.00
Pin, 1893, Chicago, World's Columbian, Connecticut, Flags, Inlaid Enamel 90.00
Pin, 1915, San Francisco, Panama-Pacific, Bear Holding Flags, Enamel 40.00
Pin, 1939, New York, Lucky Lindy, 10th Anniversary First Atlantic Flight, 2 In. 95.00
Pinball Machine, 1933, Chicago, Northwestern Mail Box Co., 12 x 20 In. 425.00
Plaque, 1915, San Francisco, Pan-American, Canal Opening, French Palace, Bronze 450.00
Plate, 1939, New York, American Potter, Turquoise, Homer Laughlin, 7 In. . . . . *Illus* 45.00
Playing Cards, 1933, Chicago, Century Of Progress, Avenue Of Flags Images 27.50
Postcard, 1904, St. Louis, Hold-To-Light, 1904 . . . . 130.00
Postcard, 1915, San Francisco, Remington-UMC Exhibit, Palace Of Manufacturing 150.00
Print, 1862, London, Universal, Majolica Fountain, 17 1/2 x 13 1/2 In. 59.00
Program, 1939, New York, World Of Tomorrow, 5 3/8 x 7 3/4 In. 25.00
Purse, 1964, New York, World's Fair, Child's 50.00
Record, 1964, New York, Walt Disney's It's A Small World . . . . *Illus* 35.00
Ribbon, 1893, Chicago, World's Columbian Exposition, Press, Dedication, Oct. 1892 . . . . 200.00
Ribbon, 1904, St. Louis, Louisiana Purchase, Teddy Roosevelt Picture 160.00
Ribbon, 1915, San Francisco, Panama-Pacific, Closing Day, Pin, Button, 2 1/4 In. 101.00
Ring Toss, 1939, New York, Trylon, Perisphere, 18 x 18 In. 1725.00
Salt & Pepper, 1933, Chicago, Quaker Shaker Set, Embossed Logo, Open Salt 85.00
Sheet Music, 1893, Ferris Wheel 38.00

World's Fair, Plate, 1939, New York,
American Potter, Turquoise,
Homer Laughlin, 7 In.

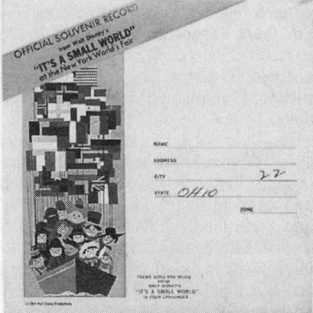

World's Fair, Record, 1964, New York,
Walt Disney's It's A Small World

Shell, 1893, Chicago, World's Columbian, Winged Figure, Wreath In Center 16.00
Spoon, 1904, St. Louis, Louisiana Purchase, Enamel On Gilt 75.00
Spoon, 1933, Chicago, Silver Plate, Hall Of Science & Science, Oneida, 6 In. 60.00
Spoon, 1964, New York, World's Fair 15.00
Sugar & Creamer, 1893, Chicago, World's Columbian, Peachblow 920.00
Tape Measure, 1901, Buffalo, Pan-American Exposition, Flag, Women As Continents . . . 100.00
Tapestry, 1933, Chicago, Century Of Progress, Velvet, Layout Of Buildings 37.00
Tapestry, 1939, New York, World Of Tomorrow, 40 x 21 1/2 In. 95.00
Toothpick, 1895, Chicago, Art Glass, Silver Plated Holder, Smith Bros. 395.00
Toy, 1939, New York, Train, Cars, Driver, Decals, Original Wheels, Canopies 1200.00
Tumbler, 1893, Chicago, World's Columbian, Germany, 3 1/4 In. 75.00
Tumbler, 1904, St. Louis, Louisiana Purchase, Milk Glass, Fair Scenes, 5 In. 35.00
Tumbler, 1964, New York, World's Fair Circus, Frosted Glass 8.00
View-Master Set, 1947, Montreal, National Pavilions 25.00
View-Master Set, 1954, New York, General Tour 28.00
View-Master Set, 1958, Brussels, Yesteryear, Booklet, 4 Reels . . . . .40.00 to 45.00
Viewer, 1933, Chicago, Tru-Vue, Bakelite, Rock Island Bridge, Iron Works, Box 150.00
Watch Fob, 1893, Chicago, Wild West, Cody On Horse, Beaded, Aluminum 375.00

WPA is the abbreviation for Works Progress Administration, a program
created by executive order in 1935 to provide jobs for millions of
unemployed Americans. Artists were hired to create murals, paintings,
drawings, and sculptures for public buildings. Pieces are marked WPA
and may have the artist's name on them.

Book, Guide To California, Soft Cover, 714 Pages, 5 1/2 x 8 1/2 In. 3.00
Button, U.S. Works Progress, Administrative Staff, 400, 1 1/4 In. 7.00
Doll, Juan Ponce De Leon, Composition, Painted Eyes, Velvet Outfit, On Stand, 18 In. . . . 300.00
Employment Record Postcard, 1939 . . . . 12.00
Figurine, Dickens' Tiny Tim, His Father, Sister, Pottery, Signed, E. Eckhardt, 9 1/2 x 5 In. 1125.00
Figurine, Mad Hatter & March Hare, Polychrome Glazes, Signed, E. Eckhardt, 4 3/4 In. . . . 1013.00
Figurine, Nude, Surfing, Bronze, 47 In. 7800.00
Game, WPA Action, Box, 1935 . . . . 175.00
Lithograph, 3 Children Sledding Under The El, New York, M. Macintyre, 15 x 23 In. . . . 103.00
Model, Russian House, Plaster, Wood-Colored Glaze, 12 1/2 x 9 x 9 In. 250.00
Poster, Cigarette Drive, A Smoke For Victory, John McCrady, Silkscreen, 23 x 17 In. 1035.00
Poster, Different Continental Army Uniform S, 1930s, 20 x 15 In., 6 Piece 81.00
Poster, He Gives 100%, You Can Give 10%, Buy War Stamps, John McCrady, 23 x 17 In. 748.00
Tile, Modern Art, For N.Y. City Subway Art, Arthur J. Anderlet, 1937, 36 In., 36 Piece . . . 1430.00

WRISTWATCHES came into use during World War I. Wristwatches are
listed here by manufacturer or as advertising or character watches.
Pocket watches are listed in the Watch category.

Altair, Woman's, 14K Gold Case, Teardrop Shape, Braided Band, Security Chain 495.00
Angelus, Chronograph, Triple Date, 18K Gold 2700.00
Baume & Mercier, 17 Jewel, White Roman Numerals, Case, 18K Yellow Gold 1725.00
Baume & Mercier, Double Time Zone, Gold Dial, Lizard Strap, 8 3/4 In. 1725.00
Black Onyx Baguettes, Black Cord Bracelet, 18K White Gold, Art Deco 2990.00
Blancpain, 23 Jewel, White, Gold Roman Numerals, Leather, 18K White Gold 6325.00
Blancpain, 37 Jewel, Black, Arabic Numerals, Leather Strap, Case 3680.00
Breitling, Chronograph, 18K Gold, Silver Matte Dial, 1950 . . . . 1560.00
Bulova, 17 Jewel, Gold Filled Bezel, Lift Top Case, Fifth Avenue, N.Y. 25.00
Cartier, Ivory Dial, Black Roman Numerals, 18K Yellow Gold 2300.00
Cartier, Woman's, White Dial, Black Roman Numerals, 18K Yellow Gold 6900.00
Character, Barbie, Goldtone, Blue Dial, Blue Patent Band, Bradley, c.1971, 1 In. 110.00
Character, Big Bad Wolf, Three Little Pigs, Ingersoll, 1934 . . . . 1600.00
Character, Blondie & Dagwood, King Features, 1949, ... 450.00
Concord, Saratoga, Goldtone Dial, Diamond Bezel, Switzland, 18K Yellow Gold 2990.00
Daniel Roth, 35 Jewel, Satin Silver Ring Dial, Roman Numerals, 18K Pink Gold 3680.00
Elgin, Black Split Cord Band, 14K Yellow Gold 70.00
Franck Muller, Silver Matte Dial, Roman Numerals, Case, 18K White Gold 4370.00
Geneva, 28 Full Cut Diamonds, 14K Yellow Gold Band 400.00
Geneve, Hours Of Love, 17 Jewel, Blue, Pink, Arabic Numerals, 18K Pink Gold 5980.00
Gerald Genta, Mother-Of-Pearl, Roman Numerals, Leather, 18K Yellow Gold 2990.00

Wristwatch, Vacheron &
Constantin, Leather Band

Gerald Genta, White Enamel, Auxiliary Dial, Baton Hands, 18K Yellow Gold 10925.00
Gerald Genta, Woman's, 18K White Gold, Diamond, Sapphire Numerals 7200.00
Groton, Silvertone Dial, Gold Bracelet, 14K Gold, 7 In. 170.00
Hamilton, Ivorytone Dial, 6 Diamond Lugs, Gray Cord Band 115.00
Hamilton, Savitar, Electric, Pearlized Dial, Sweep Second, 14K Yellow Gold 468.00
International Watch Co., Screw-Down Crown, White Hands, Self-Winding 2415.00
La Vallee, 17 Jewel, Champagne, Gold Indexes, Self-Winding, 1980 .... 1150.00
LeCoultre, 18K Gold, Gilt Lever Movement, Silver Matte Dial, 1950 .... 2640.00
LeCoultre, Gilt Dial, Yellow Gold Band, 18K Yellow Gold 1380.00
LeCoultre, Woman's, 14K Case, Wire Type Bangle Band, Round Dial 130.00
LeCoultre, Woman's, Black Baton Numerals, Braided Yellow Gold, 18K Gold 750.00
Lemania, 19 Jewel, Blue Enamel, Gold Breguet Numerals, 18K Yellow Gold 10925.00
Longines, 17 Jewel, Chronograph, Silver Matte Dial, Arabic Numerals, 1950 .... 7200.00
Marina B., Asymmetric Yellow, Gold Indexes, Leather, 18K Yellow Gold 2070.00
Movado, 8 Round Cut Diamonds, Mesh Bracelet, Steel Hands, 10K White Gold 230.00
Movado, Square Dial, Diamond Bezel, Mesh Strap, 14K Gold 520.00
Oliendorff, Gold Hinged Dial Over, Gold Mesh Band, 17 Jewel 165.00
Omega, Leather Band, 14K Yellow Gold 258.00
Patek Philippe, 18 Jewel, White Roman Numerals, Case, 18K Yellow Gold 5060.00
Patek Philippe, 18 Jewel, White Roman Numerals, Leather, 18K Pink Gold 4600.00
Patek Philippe, 18K White Gold, Gray Matte Dial, White Gold Bracelet, 1960 .... 7440.00
Patek Philippe, 29 Jewel, White With Stripes, 18K Yellow Gold 9200.00
Patek Philippe, Raised Numeral Dial, Platinum, 14K Yellow Gold, 1928 .... 8625.00
Patek Philippe, Square Silvertone Dial, Baton Numerals, 18K White Gold 1955.00
Patek Philippe, Woman's, Ivory Dial, Integral Mesh Band, 6 1/2 In. 1150.00
Piaget, 24 Full Cut Diamonds, 18K White Gold 1035.00
Piaget, Enamel Dial, Swiss Assay, Crocodile Strap, 18K Gold 1495.00
Pulsar, Digital Time, Month & Date, Gold, Time Computer, 1975 .... 115.00
Reverso, Woman's, Silvertone Dial, Black Arabic Numerals, Leather Strap 1380.00
Rolex, 18K Pink Gold, Black Matte Dial, Teardrop-Form Lugs, 1950 .... 2700.00
Rolex, Oyster Bracelet, 17 Jewel, Black, Baton Steel Hands, Case, 1970 .... 10925.00
Rolex, Oyster Perpetual, 25 Jewel, Pink Matte Dial, Self-Winding, 1946 .... 3600.00
Rolex, Oyster Perpetual, Ebonized Face, 18K Yellow Gold Case, 1960 .... 1955.00
Rolex, Oyster, 31 Jewel, Self-Winding, Baton Gold Hands, 18K Yellow Gold 10925.00
Rolex, Oyster, Woman's, Gold Dial, Gold Roman Numerals, Circular Case 2590.00
Rolex, Prince, 2-Tone Silver, Nickel Lever Movement, 2 Dials, 1935 .... 6600.00
Rolex, Woman's, Platinum & Diamond Bexel, Bracelet, 1920 .... 4800.00
Tapered Gold Band, Diamond, Rectangular Face, 24 Diamonds 220.00
Tissot, Porcelain Dial, Moon Phase Day Calendar, Crocodile Strap 750.00
Vacheron & Constantin, 17 Jewel, Silver Matte Dial, Baton Numerals, 1945 .... 2160.00
Vacheron & Constantin, Leather Band ....*Illus* 8250.00
Vacheron & Constantin, White Round Dial, 18K Gold 1495.00
Woman's, 18K Pink Gold, Diamonds, Rubies, Snake-Form Bracelet, 1945 .... 1800.00
Woman's, Diamond, Goldtone Dial, Rectangular Case, 18K Gold 805.00
Woman's, Diamond, Oval White Dial, Black Roman Numerals, 14K Gold 1150.00
Woman's, Platinum, 50 Bead Set Diamonds, Black Nylon Cord, 6 In. 920.00

YELLOWWARE is a heavy earthenware made of a yellowish clay. It
varies in color from light yellow to orange-yellow. Many nineteenth-
and twentieth-century kitchen bowls and jugs were made of yellowware. It was made in England and in the United States. Another
form of pottery that is sometimes classed as yellowware is listed in this
book in the Mocha category.

Bank, Pig, Pierced Eyes, Brown, Green Sponge Glaze, 3 1/2 x 6 In. 210.00
Beater Jar, Undecorated, 5 x 5 1/4 In. 45.00
Bottle, Toby, Man With Fiddle, 8 1/2 In. 715.00

Bowl, 1880, 4 x 9 1/2 In. 55.00
Bowl, 1890, 6 1/2 x 14 1/2 In. 66.00
Bowl, 4 Accent Bands, 4 3/4 x 10 1/2 In. 155.00
Bowl, Blue Stripe Design, 9 x 4 3/4 In., 4 Piece 109.00
Bowl, Blue Stripe Design, 14 x 7 In., 4 Piece 138.00
Bowl, Cover, Blue Bands & Stripes, 3 1/2 x 7 In. 220.00
Bowl, Large Brown Stripes & 2 Small Brown Stripes, 7 x 16 In. 100.00
Bowl, Mixing, 1 Light Blue, 2 White Accent Bands, 4 x 7 x 14 In. 44.00
Bowl, Mixing, Blue & White Bands, 10 1/2 In. 75.00
Bowl, Mixing, Brown Rimmed, White Band, 12 In. 95.00
Bowl, Petal Design, Dots, 1860, 4 1/4 x 10 1/2 In. 66.00
Bowl, Rockingham Glaze, 4 1/2 x 11 In. 33.00
Bowl, Rust & White Bands, 8 In. 145.00
Bowl, Slope Sides, Raised Ray Design On Bottom, 3 1/2 x 13 1/2 In. 170.00
Chamber Pot, Wild Water Sport, Pan-American, Brown Glaze, 1901, 2 In. 220.00
Colander 435.00
Creamer, Rockingham Glaze, 1860, 3 3/4 In. 66.00
Crock, Butter, Off White, Dark Brown Accent Bands, 4 3/4 In. 220.00
Custard Cup, Light Brown Glaze, 1870, 2 3/4 In. 11.00
Desk Set, Watering Can & Woven Baskets, Gilt, Silver Luster, 6 5/8 x 4 In. 220.00
Dish, 3 x 9 1/2 In. 55.00
Dish, Cover, 1910, 5 x 8 In. 66.00
Jar, Cover, Dog's Head Shape, Running Blue & Amber Glaze, Hoganas, 7 In. 50.00
Jar, Cover, Seaweed, Blue & White Band, East Liverpool, Ohio, 6 In. 605.00
Jug, Strap Handle, Blue Sponging, 10 1/2 In. 522.00
Lantern, Green, Red Glaze, 19th Century, 8 In. 110.00
Mold, Food, Lobster, Orange Glaze Interior, Footed, 12 3/4 In. 28.00
Mug, Cylindrical Shape, Green, Orange Splotch Decoration, 19th Century, 6 In. 517.00
Mug, Raised Pub Scene, 6 1/2 x 3 In. 42.00
Nappy, 1850, 3 1/2 x 14 In. 110.00
Pie Plate, 1850, 1 1/2 x 9 1/2 In. 44.00
Pie Plate, 1850, 1 3/4 x 12 In. 198.00
Pitcher, 1900, 7 In. 100.00
Pitcher, Barrel Design, 1900, 8 1/2 In. 78.00
Pitcher, Barrel Form, Ice Lip, 8 In. 45.00
Pitcher, Brown & Green Mottled Glaze, Ribbed, 5 3/8 In. 38.00
Pitcher, Brown Band, 5 1/4 In. 75.00
Pitcher, Chicken Wire, Brown, Green Sponge Glaze, 3 In. 220.00
Pitcher, Dark Blue & White Stripes, 7 3/4 In. 743.00
Pitcher, Double White Bands, 3 Double Sets Blue Bands, 8 1/2 In. 316.00
Pitcher, Hunting Dogs & Deer Design, Hound Handle, 1860, 9 3/4 In. 550.00
Pitcher, Lattice Design, Brown, Green Sponge Glaze, Handle, 9 1/4 In. 88.00
Pitcher, Man's, Smiling Face, Rockingham Glaze, 19th Century, 3 In. 55.00
Pitcher, Milk, Wide White Band, 2-Line Design, 6 In. 302.00
Pitcher, Mottled Rockingham Glaze, c.1880, 7 In. 66.00
Pitcher, Pewter Hinged Cover, Monkeys Playing At Being Indians, 9 In. 300.00
Pitcher, Pillar, Scroll Design, 7 1/4 In. 66.00
Pitcher, Tulip Design, Rockingham Glaze, 1890, 5 In. 120.00
Plaque, Dreaming Child, United States Fired Clay Co., c.1880, 8 x 9 1/2 In. 495.00
Plate, Rockingham Glaze, Scalloped Edge, Square, c.1880, 9 In. 90.00
Shaving Cup, Dark Albany Glaze, 1800s, 4 3/8 In. 170.00
Washboard, Brown Rockingham Glaze, East Liverpool, Oh, 1870, 22 In. 605.00

ZANE Pottery was founded in 1921 by Adam Reed and Harry McClelland in South Zanesville, Ohio, at the old Peters and Reed Building. Zane pottery is very similar to Peters and Reed pottery, but it is usually marked. The factory was sold in 1941 to Lawton Gonder.

Vase, Green Matte Glaze, Signed, 4 1/2 In. 132.00
Vase, Ivory Glaze, 8 In. 85.00
Vase, Light, Medium Blue, Green, Purple, Yellow, 6 In. 70.00
Vase, Shadow Blue, Gray Semimatte Glaze, 12 In. 105.00
Vase, Shadow Ware, Red, Blue, Brown Over Taupe Ground, Marked, 11 7/8 In. 140.00

ZANESVILLE Art Pottery was founded in 1900 by David Schmidt in Zanesville, Ohio. The firm made faience umbrella stands, jardinieres, and pedestals. The company closed in 1962. Many pieces are marked with just the words *La Moro*.

LA MORO

Jardiniere, Green Matte Finish, 7 1/4 x 8 3/8 x 9 1/2 In.	68.00
Jardiniere, Tulip Shape, Burgundy Semimatte Glaze, 6 1/2 x 7 3/4 In.	65.00
Vase, Brown Glossy Mottled Drip Glaze Over Tan, Angled Handles, 18 In.	258.00
Vase, Brown, Yellow Drip Glaze, 3 1/2 In.	28.00
Vase, Lavender, Stoneware, 5 In.	79.00

ZSOLNAY pottery was made in Hungary after 1862 and was characterized by Persian, Art Nouveau, or Hungarian motifs. A series of new Zsolnay figurines with green-gold luster finish is available in many shops today. Early Zsolnay was not marked, but by 1878 the tower trademark was used.

Box, Old Ivory Design, 3 x 4 x 4 In.	300.00
Chalice, Yellow, Ring Turned Pedestal, Gilt Trim, White Ground, 5 1/2 In.	165.00
Coffee Set, 6 Cups, 6 Saucers, Sugar & Creamer, Cake Plate, 8 1/2-In. Coffeepot	600.00
Figurine, Cat, 9 1/2 In.	109.00
Figurine, Deer, Green Iridescent Glaze, 1930, 9 In.	180.00
Figurine, Nude Woman, Colored Features, 1930, 9 In.	195.00
Figurine, Nude Woman, Iridescent, Art Deco, Stamped Zsolnay-Pecs, 9 In.	288.00
Figurine, Peasant Girl, Carrying Platter, Green & Yellow Glaze, 8 1/2 In.	110.00
Jar, Moorish Design, Dome Cover & Finial, Twisted Rope Handles, 10 3/4 In.	440.00
Jardiniere, Green & Gold Metallic Glaze, Flowers & Leaves, c.1915, 9 1/2 x 19 In.	3200.00
Jardiniere, Openwork On Outside, Reticulated Grill Work, Decal, 7 1/8 In.	336.00
Jardiniere, Reticulated Grill Work, White Ground, 4-Footed, 7 1/8 In.	330.00
Jug, Gold Gilt Band Of Design, c.1879, 16 In.	1750.00
Pitcher, Floral & Scroll Design On Base & Neck, Gold Ground, 11 1/2 In.	80.00
Vase, Lustrous Red Glaze, Fissured Surface, Signed, 1930s, 11 In.	1245.00
Vase, Secessionist Design, Metallic Blue, Green, Gold Glaze, Marked, 7 1/2 In.	4025.00
Vase, Tulip Form, 1900, 8 3/4 In.	6500.00

INDEX

This index is computer-generated, making it as complete as possible. References in uppercase type are category listings. There is also an internal cross-referencing system used in the main part of the book, so if you look for a Kewpie doll in the Doll category, you will be told it is in its own category. There is additional information at the end of many paragraphs about where to find prices of pieces similar to yours.

0-609-80757-9

0-609-80841-9

0-609-80312-3

0-517-57806-9

0-517-58840-4

0-517-88381-3

0-517-70137-5

0-517-55914-5

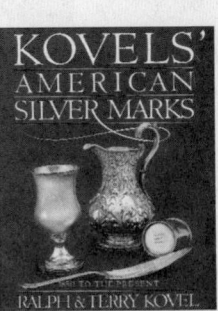

0-517-56882-9

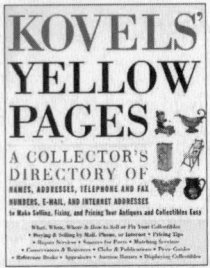

0-609-80417-0

0-609-60168-7

0-609-80640-8

K O V E L S

SEND ORDERS & INQUIRIES TO:
CROWN PUBLISHERS
C/O RANDOM HOUSE, 400 HAHN ROAD,
WESTMINSTER, MD 21157
ATTN: ORDER DEPARTMENT

SALES & TITLE INFORMATION:
1-800-733-3000

FOR ORDER ENTRY:
FAX# 1-800-659-2436

WEBSITE: WWW.RANDOMHOUSE.COM

NAME _____

ADDRESS _____

CITY & STATE_____ ZIP_____

Please send me the following books:

ITEM NO.	QTY.	TITLE	PRICE	TOTAL
0-609-80841-9	___	Kovels' Antiques & Collectibles Price List —34th Edition	PAPER $16.95	_____
0-517-70137-5	___	Dictionary of Marks—Pottery and Porcelain	HARDCOVER $17.00	_____
0-517-55914-5	___	Kovels' New Dictionary of Marks	HARDCOVER $19.00	_____
0-517-56882-9	___	Kovels' American Silver Marks	HARDCOVER $40.00	_____
0-609-80757-9	___	Kovels' Bid, Buy, and Sell Online	PAPER $14.00	_____
0-609-80312-3	___	Kovels' Bottles Price List—11th Edition	PAPER $16.00	_____
0-609-80640-8	___	Kovels' Depression Glass & Dinnerware Price List —7th Edition	PAPER $16.00	_____
0-517-57806-9	___	Kovels' Know Your Antiques, Revised and Updated	PAPER $17.00	_____
0-517-58840-4	___	Kovels' Know Your Collectibles Updated	PAPER $16.00	_____
0-517-88381-3	___	Kovels' Quick Tips: 799 Helpful Hints on How to Care for Your Collectibles	PAPER $12.00	_____
0-609-60168-7	___	The Label Made Me Buy It: From Aunt Jemima to Zonkers	HARDCOVER $40.00	_____
0-609-80417-0	___	Kovels' Yellow Pages: A Collector's Directory of Names, Addresses, Telephone and Fax Numbers, E-Mail, and Internet Addresses to Make Selling, Fixing, and Pricing Your Antiques and Collectibles Easy	PAPER $18.00	_____

____ TOTAL ITEMS   TOTAL RETAIL VALUE _____

CHECK OR MONEY ORDER ENCLOSED
MADE PAYABLE TO CROWN PUBLISHERS
or telephone 1-800-733-3000 (No cash or stamps, please)

CHARGE: ☐ Master Card ☐ Visa ☐ American Express
Account Number (include all digits) Expires: MO.___ YR.___

Shipping & Handling
Charge (per order) $5.50

Please add applicable
sales tax.   _____

TOTAL AMOUNT DUE   _____

PRICES SUBJECT TO CHANGE
WITHOUT NOTICE.

If a more recent edition of a price list
has been published at the same price,
it will be sent instead of the old edition.

....
Signature

Thank you for your order

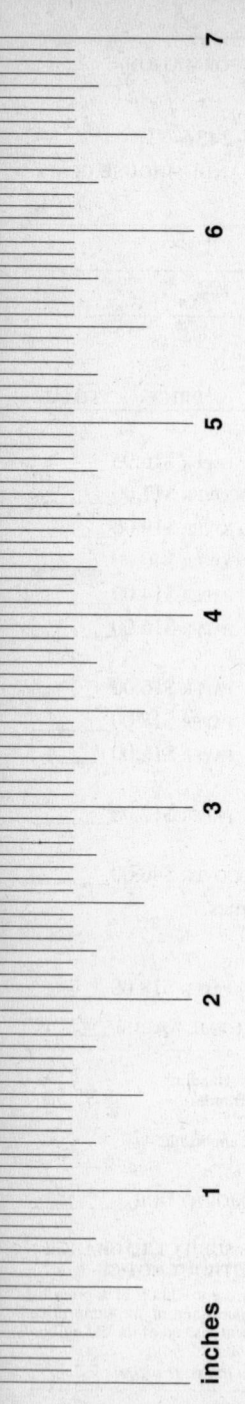

Make It a Rule to Use Kovels'

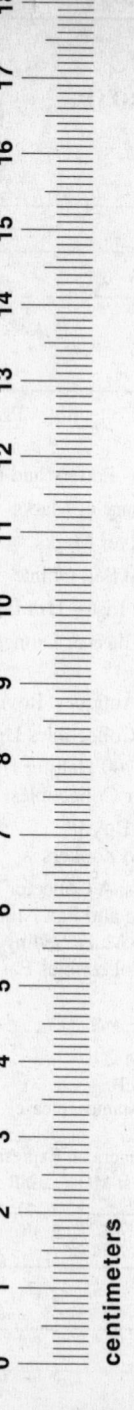

inches 0 1 2 3 4 5 6 7

centimeters 0 1 2 3 4 5 6 7 8 9 10 11 12 13 14 15 16 17 18